Encyclopedia of World Literature in the 20th Century

Encyclopedia of World Literature in the 20th Century

VOLUME 1: A–D

ST. JAMES PRESS

Steven R. Serafin, *General Editor*

Laura Standley Berger, *Project Coordinator*

Joann Cerrito, Dave Collins, Nicolet V. Elert,
Miranda Ferrara, Kristin Hart, Margaret Mazurkiewicz, Michael J. Tyrkus
St. James Press Staff

Peter M. Gareffa, *Managing Editor, St. James Press*

Mary Beth Trimper, *Production Director*
Deborah Milliken, *Production Assistant*

Cynthia Baldwin, *Product Design Manager*
Eric Johnson, *Art Director*
Pamela A. Reed, *Photography Coordinator*
Randy Bassett, *Image Database Supervisor*
Robert Duncan, Mike Logusz, *Imaging Specialists*

Susan Trosky, *Permissions Manager*
Kelly A. Quin, *Permissons Associate*

Copyright © 1999
St. James Press
27500 Drake Road
Farmington Hills, MI 48331

Encyclopedia of World Literature / Steven R. Serafin, general editor. — 3rd ed.
     p.   cm.
     Includes bibliographical references and index.
     Contents: v. 1. A-D — v. 2. E-K — v. 3. L-R — v. 4. S-Z and indexes
     ISBN 1-55862-373-6 (set). — ISBN 1-55862-374-4 (v. 1). — ISBN 1-55862-375-2 (v. 2). — ISBN 1-55862-376-0 (v. 3). — ISBN 1-55862-377-9 (v. 4).
     1. Literature, Modern—20th century—Bio-bibliography.
     2. Literature, Modern—20th century—Encyclopedias   I. Serafin, Steven.
     PN771.E5   1998
     803—dc21   98-40374
                                                        CIP

Printed in the United States of America
St. James Press is an imprint of Gale

10 9 8 7 6 5 4 3 2

BOARD OF ADVISORS

PERIODICALS USED

A&E	Anglistik & Englischunterricht	*AL*	American Literature
AAS	Asian and African Studies		Alaluz: Revista de Poesia, Narracion y Ensayo
AAW	Afro-Asian Writing	*AL&C*	African Languages & Cultures
ABnG	Amsterdamer Beiträe zur Neueren Germanistik	*ALEC*	Anales de la Literatura Española Contemporánea
ACLALSB	ACLALS Bulletin	*ALHis*	Anales de Literatura Hispanoamericana
	Actualidades: Consejo Nacional de la Cultura, Centro de Estudios Latinoamericanos "Romulo Gallegos"/Caracas, Venezuela	*ALR*	American Literary Realism, 1870-1910
		ALS	Australian Literary Studies
ADP	Arbeiten zur deutschen Philologie	*ALT*	African Literature Today
	Africa: Rivista Trimestrale di Studi e Documentazione	*AmerD*	American Drama
AfricaL	Africa: Journal of the International African Institute/Revue de l'Institut Africain International	*AmerP*	American Poetry
		AmerT	American Theatre
AfricaR	Africa Report	*AmLH*	American Literary History
AfrLJ	African Journal	*AmRev*	Americas Review
AfrLS	African Language Studies	*AN*	Acta Neophilologica
AfrSR	African Studies Review	*ANP*	Anales de la Narrative Española Contemporánea
AGald	Anales Galdosianos		
AGR	American-German Review	*AnUs*	Annual of Urdu Studies
AHR	Afro-Hispanic Review	*ANZSC*	Australian and New Zealand Studies in Canada
AICRJ	American Indian Culture and Research Journal	*APR*	American Poetry Review
AIPHOS	Annuaire de l'Institut de Philologie et d'Histoire Orientales et Slaves	*AQ*	American Quarterly
		AR	Antioch Review
AIQ	American Indian Quarterly		Arabica: Revue d'Études Arabes
AJFS	Australian Journal of French Studies	*ARD*	African Research and Documentation
AJPh	American Journal of Philology	*ArielE*	Ariel: A Review of International English Literature
AJS	American Journal of Semiotics		

ArielK	Ariel
ArO	Archív Orientální: Quarterly Journal of African, Asian, and Latin-American Studies
ArQ	Arizona Quarterly
ASch	American Scholar
ASEER	American Slavic and East European Review
	Asemka: A Literary Journal of the University of Cape Coast
ASPAC	Asian Pacific Quarterly of Cultural and Social Affairs Quarterly
ASQ	Arab Studies Quarterly
ASR	American Scandinavian Review
	Atenea: Revista de Ciencia, Arte y Literatura de la Universidad de Concepción
AUB-LLR	Analele Universității, București, Limbă și Litereră Română
AUC	Anales de la Universidad de Chile
AUMLA	AUMLA: Journal of the Australasian Universities Language and Literature Association—A Journal of Literary Criticism and Linguistics
AWR	Anglo-Welsh Review
BA	Books Abroad
BAALE	Bulletin of the Association for African Literature in English
BAC	Boletín de la Academia Colombiana
BALF	Black American Literature Forum
BalSt	Balkan Studies
BB	Bulletin of Bibliography
BeneN	Bete Noire

BEPIF	Bulletin des Etudes Portugaises et Brésiliennes
BF	Books from Finland
BHe	Baltische Hefte
BHS	Bulletin of Hispanic Studies
BlackI	Black Images: A Critical Quarterly on Black Arts and Culture
BMMLA	Bulletin of the Midwest Modern Language Association
BO	Black Orpheus
Boundary	Boundary 2: A Journal of Postmodern Literature and Culture
BRMMLA	Rocky Mountain Review of Language and Literature
BRP	Beiträge zur Romanischen Philologie
BR/RB	Bilingual Review/La Revista Bilingüe
BSIS	Bulletin of the Society for Italian Studies
BSS	Bulletin of Spanish Studies
BSUF	Ball State University Forum
BUJ	Boston University Journal
BuR	Bucknell Review
BW	Black World
CA	Cuadernos Americanos
CALC	Cahiers Algériens de Littérature Comparée
	Callaloo: A Black South Journal of Arts and Letters
CalSS	California Slavic Studies
CanL	Canadian Literature
CARHS	Canadian-American Review of Hungarian Studies
CarQ	Caribbean Quarterly

CasaA	Casa de las Américas
CAsJ	Central Asiatic Journal
CASS	Canadian-American Slavic Studies
CatR	Catalan Review
CBAA	Current Bibliography on African Affairs
CBC	Cesare Barbieri Courier
CCrit	Comparative Criticism
CCur	Cross Currents: A Yearbook of Central European Culture
CE	College English
CE&S	Commonwealth Essays and Studies
CEA	CEA Critic
CEAfr	Cahiers d'Études Africaines
CelfanR	Revue Celfan/Celfan Review
CentR	Centennial Review
CFM	Canadian Fiction Magazine
CFR	Canadian Fiction Review
CFrC	Contemporary French Civilization
CH	Crítica Hispánica
CHA	Cuadernos Hispanoamericanos
	Chasqui: Revista de Literatura Latinoamericana
ChicL	Chicano Literature
ChinL	Chinese Literature
ChiR	Chicago Review
CJAS	Canadian Journal of African Studies
CJLACS	Canadian Journal of Latin American and Caribbean Studies
CJIS	Canadian Journal of Irish Studies

CJItS	Canadian Journal of Italian Studies
CL	Comparative Literature
CLAJ	College Language Association Journal
CLAQ	Children's Literature Association Quarterly
CLC	Columbia Library Columns
CLEAR	Chinese Literature: Essays, Articles, Reviews
CLQ	Colby Library Quarterly
CLS	Comparative Literature Studies
CML	Classical and Modern Literature
CMo	Creative Moment
CMRS	Cashiers du Monde Russe et Soviétique
CNIE	Commonwealth Novel in English
CNLR	CNL/Quarterly World Report
CollG	Colloquia Germanica
Colóquio	Colóquio/Letras
ColQ	Colorado Quarterly
CompD	Comparative Drama
ComQ	Commonwealth Quarterly
	Confluencia: Revista Hispánica de Cultura y Literatura
ConL	Contemporary Literature
ContempR	Contemporary Review
CP	Concerning Poetry
CQ	Cambridge Quarterly
CR	Critical Review
CRCL	Canadian Review of Comparative Literature

CREL	Cahiers Roumains d'Études Littéraires: Revue Trimestrielle de Critique, d'Esthétique et d'Histoire Littéraires	*DSt*	Deutsche Studien
CRevAS	Canadian Review of American Studies	*DU*	Der Deutschunterricht: Beiträge zu Seiner Praxis und Wissenschaftlichen Grundlegung
Crit	Critique: Studies in Modern Fiction	*DUJ*	Durham University Journal
CritI	Critical Inquiry	*DUR*	Dublin University Review
	Critique: Revue Générale des Publications Françaises et Étrangères	*DutchS*	Dutch Studies
CritQ	Critical Quarterly	*DVLJ*	Deutsche Vierteljahrsschrift für Literaturwissenschaft und Geistesgeschichte
CS	Cahiers du Sud	*EA*	Études Anglaises
CSP	Canadian Slavonic Papers		Eco: Revista de la Cultura de Occidente
CSR	Christian Scholar's Review	*ECr*	L'Esprit Créateur
CSS	Canadian Slavic Studies	*ECW*	Essays on Canadian Writing
CTR	Canadian Theatre Review		Edebiyat: A Journal of Middle Eastern Literatures
CV II	Contemporary Verse II	*EF*	Études Françaises
Dada	Dada/Surrealism	*EG*	Études Germaniques
DASDJ	Deutsche Akademie für Sprache und Dichtung, Darmstadt, Jahrbuch	*EI*	Études Irlandaises
DeltaES	Delta: Revue du Centre d'Études et de Recherche sur les Écrivains du Sud aux États-Unis	*EinA*	English in Africa
	Diacritics: A Review of Contemporary Criticism	*Éire*	Éire-Ireland: A Journal of Irish Studies
	Dimension: Contemporary German Arts and Letters	*EJ*	English Journal
		ELH	English Literary History (formerly Journal of English Literary History)
DLB	Dictionary of Literary Biography	*ELit*	Études Littéraires
DLit	Discurso Literario: Revista de Temas Hispánicos	*ELT*	English Literature in Transition
DQ	Denver Quarterly	*ELWIU*	Essays in Literature
DQR	Dutch Quarterly Review of Anglo-American Letters		English: The Journal of the English Association
DR	Dalhousie Review	*Ensayistas*	Los Ensayistas: Georgia Series on Hispanic Thought

ES	English Studies	*GRM*	Germanisch-Romanische Monatsschrift
ESA	English Studies in Africa	*GSlav*	Germano-Slavica: A Canadian Journal of Germanic and Slavic Comparative Studies
ESC	English Studies in Canada		
	Escritura: Revista de Teoría y Crítica Literarias	*HAHR*	Hispanic American Historical Review
		HAR	Hebrew Annual Review
ETJ	Educational Theatre Journal	*HC*	Hollins Critic
ETR	East Turkic Review	*HisJ*	Hispanic Journal
Evergreen	Evergreen Review	*Hispam*	Hispamérica: Revista de Literatura
ExTL	Explicación de Textos Literarios		Hispania: A Journal Devoted to the Interests of the Teaching of Spanish and Portuguese
FE	France-Eurafrique		
FI	Forum Italicum	*Hispano*	Hispanófila
FLS	French Literature Series	*HJAS*	Harvard Journal of Asiatic Studies
FMLS	Forum for Modern Language Studies		Horizontes: Revista de la Universidad Católica de Puerto Rico
	Folio: Essays on Foreign Languages and Literatures		
		HR	Hispanic Review
FR	French Review	*HSL*	University of Hartford Studies in Literature
FS	French Studies		
Francofonia	Studi e Ricerche Sulle Letterature di Lingua Francese	*HSS*	Harvard Slavic Studies
		HudR	Hudson Review
FrF	French Forum	*HungQ*	Hungarian Quarterly
	Frontiers: A Journal of Women Studies	*I&FR*	Indian & Foreign Review
FSt	Feminist Studies	*I&L*	Ideologies and Literature
GaR	Georgia Review	*Ibero*	Iberoromania
GerSR	German Studies Review		IBLA: Revue de l'Institut des Belles Lettres Arabes
GettR	Gettysburg Review		
GL&L	German Life and Letters	*IBSB*	International P.E.N. Bulletin of Selected Books
GN	Germanic Notes	*IC*	Islamic Culture
GQ	German Quarterly	*IFR*	International Fiction Review
GR	Germanic Review	*IFRev*	International Folklore Review

IJMES	International Journal of Middle East Studies		*JARCE*	Journal of the American Research Center in Egypt
IJSLP	International Journal of Slavic Linguistics and Poetics		*JASO*	Journal of the Anthropological Society of Oxford
	Imagine: International Chicano Poetry Journal		*JASt*	Journal of Asian Studies
IndL	Indian Literature		*JATJ*	Journal of the Association of Teachers of Japanese
IndSch	Indian Scholar		*JBalS*	Journal of Baltic Studies
	Inti: Revista de Literatura Hispánica		*JBlS*	Journal of Black Studies
IonC	Index on Censorship		*JBRS*	Journal of the Burma Research Society
IowaR	Iowa Review		*JByelS*	Journal of Byelorussian Studies
IQ	Italian Quarterly		*JCF*	Journal of Canadian Fiction
IranS	Iranian Studies: Journal of the Society for Iranian Studies		*JCH*	Journal of Contemporary History
IRLI	Italianistica: Rivista di Letteratura Italiana		*JCL*	Journal of Commonwealth Literature
IS	Italian Studies		*JCLTA*	Journal of the Chinese Language Teachers Association
ItalAm	Italian Americana		*JCS*	Journal of Croatian Studies
Italianist	The Italianist: Journal of the Department of Italian Studies, University of Reading		*JCSR*	Journal of Canadian Studies/Revue d'Études Canadiennes
ItC	Italian Culture		*JCSt*	Journal of Caribbean Studies
IUR	Irish University Review: A Journal of Irish Studies		*JEGP*	Journal of English and Germanic Philology
IWT	Indian Writing Today		*JES*	Journal of European Studies
JAAC	Journal of Aesthetics and Art Criticism		*JEthS*	Journal of Ethnic Studies
JAC	Journal of American Culture		*JFCS*	Journal of Feminist Cultural Studies
JAOS	Journal of the American Oriental Society		*JGE*	Journal of General Education
JapQ	Japan Quarterly		*JHD*	Journal of the Hellenic Diaspora
JAPS	Journal of the American Portuguese Society		*JHI*	Journal of History of Ideas
			JIAS	Journal of Inter-American Studies
			JIL	Journal of Irish Literature
JArabL	Journal of Arabic Literature		*JIWE*	Journal of Indian Writing in English

JJS	Journal of Japanese Studies		*L&P*	Literature and Psychology
JLSTL	Journal of Literary Studies		*LAAW*	Lotus: Afro-Asian Writing
JMAF	Journal of Modern African Studies		*LALR*	Latin American Literary Review
JNALA	Journal of the New African Literature and the Arts			Landfall: A New Zealand Quarterly
JNT	Journal of Narrative Technique		*Lang&S*	Language and Style
JNZL	Journal of New Zealand Literature		*LangF*	Language Forum
JOL	Journal of Oriental Literature		*LangQ*	USF Language Quarterly
JPalS	Journal of Palestinian Studies		*LARR*	Latin America Research Review
JPC	Journal of Popular Culture		*LATR*	Latin American Theatre Review
JPrag	Journal of Pragmatics		*LBR*	Luso-Brazilian Review
JRS	Journal of Russian Studies		*LCUT*	Library Chronicle of the University of Texas
JSoAL	Journal of South Asian Literature		*LE&W*	Literature East and West
JSS	Journal of Semitic Studies		*LHY*	Literary Half-Yearly
JSSB	Journal of the Siam Society		*LitG*	Literary Griot
JSSE	Journal of the Short Story in English		*LitR*	Literary Review
JSSTC	Journal of Spanish Studies: Twentieth Century			Lituanus: Baltic States Quarterly of Arts & Sciences
JTamS	Journal of Tamil Studies		*LJ*	Library Journal
JUkGS	Journal of Ukrainian Graduate Studies		*LJGG*	Literaturwissenschaftliches Jahrbuch im Auftrage der Görres-Gesellschaft
JUkS	Journal of Ukrainian Studies		*LM*	London Magazine
JWIL	Journal of West Indian Literature		*LOS*	Literary Onomastics Studies
KanQ	Kansas Quarterly		*LPer*	Literature in Performance: A Journal of Literary and Performing Art
KFLQ	Kentucky Foreign Language Quarterly		*LQ*	Literary Quarterly
KFQ	Keystone Folklore		*LuK*	Literatur und Kritik
	Kiabàrà: Journal of the Humanities		*LWU*	Literatur in Wissenschaft und Unterricht
KR	Kenyon Review		*MAL*	Modern Austrian Literature
KRQ	Romance Quarterly (formerly Kentucky Romance Quarterly)			

MAPS	Memoirs of the American Philosophical Society	*MLS*	Modern Language Studies
MarkhamR	Markham Review	*MMisc*	Midwestern Miscellany
MAWAR	MAWA Review	*MN*	Monumenta Nipponica
MBL	Modern Black Literature	*ModA*	Modern Age
MCL	Modern Chinese Literature		Monatshefte: Für Deutschen Unterricht, Deutsche Sprache und Literatur
MD	Modern Drama		Mosaic: A Journal for the Interdisciplinary Study of Literature
MEF	Middle Eastern Forum	*MP*	Modern Philology: A Journal Devoted to Research in Medieval and Modern Literature
MEJ	Middle East Journal		
MelbSS	Melbourne Slavonic & East European Studies (formerly Melbourne Slavonic Studies)	*MPS*	Modern Poetry Studies
		MQ	Midwest Quarterly: A Journal of Contemporary Thought
	Merkur: Deutsche Zeitschrift für europäisches Denken	*MQR*	Michigan Quarterly Review
MES	Middle Eastern Studies	*MR*	Massachusetts Review: A Quarterly of Literature, the Arts and Public Affairs
MFS	Modern Fiction Studies		
MGS	Michigan Germanic Studies	*MRRM*	Monographic Review/Revista Monográfica
MHL	Modern Hebrew Literature	*MSFO*	Mémoires de la Société Finno-Ougrienne
MHRev	Malahat Review	*MSpr*	Moderna Språk
MichA	Michigan Academician: Papers of the Michigan Academy of Science, Arts, and Letters	*MuK*	Maske und Kothurn
		MV	Minority Voices: An Interdisciplinary Journal of Literature and the Arts
MinnR	Minnesota Review		
MissQ	Mississippi Quarterly	*MW*	Muslim World
ML	Modern Languages	*NAR*	North American Review
MLF	Modern Language Forum	*NConL*	Notes on Contemporary Literature
MLJ	Modern Language Journal	*NDEJ*	Notre Dame English Journal
MLN	Modern Language Notes	*NDH*	Neue Deutsche Hefte
MLQ	Modern Language Quarterly	*NDL*	Neue Deutsche Literatur
MLR	Modern Language Review		Neohelicon: Acta Comparationis Litterarum Universarum

Neophil	Neophilologus	*NTQ*	New Theatre Quarterly
NEQ	New England Quarterly	*NWR*	Northwest Review
NER	New England Review and Bread Loaf Quarterly	*NYHT*	New York Herald Tribune
NewA	New African	*NYHTBR*	New York Herald Tribune Books Review
NewC	New Criterion	*NYLF*	New York Literary Forum
NewL	New Letters: A Magazine of Fine Writing	*NYRB*	New York Review of Books
NewR	New Republic	*NYT*	New York Times
NewS	New Scholar	*NYTBR*	New York Times Book Review
NFS	Nottingham French Studies	*NYTMag*	New York Times Magazine
NGC	New German Critique: An Interdisciplinary Journal of German Studies	*NZSJ*	New Zealand Slavonic Journal
NGS	New German Studies	*O&C*	Œuvres & Critiques
NHQ	New Hungarian Quarterly		Obsidian II: Black Literature in Review
NL	Nouvelles Littéraires	*ÖGL*	Österreich in Geschichte und Literatur
NLH	New Literary History: A Journal of Theory and Interpretation	*OJES*	Osmania Journal of English Studies
NLitsR	New Literatures Review	*OL*	Orbis Litterarum
NMAL	Notes on Modern American Literature	*OLR*	Oxford Literary Review
NME	New Middle East	OnsE	One Erfdeel: Algemeen-Nederlands Tweemaandelijks Cultureel Tijdschrift
NMQ	New Mexico Quarterly	*OntarioR*	Ontario Review
NorS	Northern Studies	*OSP*	Oxford Slavonic Papers
NorthwestR	Northwest Review	*P&R*	Philosophy and Rhetoric
	Novel: A Forum on Fiction	*PA*	Présence Africaine
NR	New Republic	*PAJ*	Pan-African Journal
NRF	Nouvelle Revue Française	*PakR*	Pakistan Review
NRs	Neue Rundschau		Paragraph: The Journal of the Modern Critical Theory Group
			Parnassus: Poetry in Review
NS	New Statesman	*PCL*	Perspectives on Contemporary Literature

PCLS	Proceedings of the Comparative Literature Symposium		*PSMLAB*	Pennsylvania State Modern Language Association Bulletin
PCP	Pacific Coast Philology		*PStud*	Portuguese Studies
PEGS	Publications of the English Goethe Society		*QI*	Quaderni d'Italianistica
PFr	Présence Francophone: Revue internationale de langue et de littérature		*QIA*	Quaderni Ibero-Americani
	Plaza: Revista de Literatura		*QL*	La Quinzaine Littéraire
PLL	Papers on Language and Literature		*QQ*	Queen's Quarterly
	Ploughshares		*QRFS*	Quarterly Review of Film Studies
	Plural: Revista Cultural de Excelsior		*QRL*	Quarterly Review of Literature
	PMLA: Publications of the Modern Language Association of America			Quimera: Revista de Literatura
			RaJAH	Rackham Journal of the Arts and Humanities
PoetryR	Poetry Review		*RAL*	Research in Africa Literatures
PolP	Polish Perspectives		*RALS*	Resources for American Literary Study
PolR	Polish Review		*RCB*	Revista de Cultura Brasileña
POMPA	Publications of the Mississippi Philological Association		*RCEH*	Revista Canadiense de Estudios Hispánicos
PoT	Poetics Today		*RCF*	Review of Contemporary Fiction
PPNCFL	Proceedings of the Pacific Northwest Conference on Foreign Languages		*RChL*	Revista Chilena de Literatura
PQ	Philological Quarterly		*RCL*	Revue de Littérature Comparée
PQM	Pacific Quarterly (Moana)		*RCLL*	Revista de Crítica Literaria Latinoamericana
PR	Partisan Review		*RC-R*	Revista Chicano-Riqueña
PRev	Poetry Review		*RCSCSPL*	Russian, Croatian and Serbian, Czech and Slovak, Polish Literature
	Prismal/Cabral: Revista de Literatura Hispánica/Caderno Afro-Brasileiro Asiático Lusitano		*REH*	Revista de Estadios Hispánicos
PRL	Puerto Rican Literature		*RELC*	RELC Journal
PrS	Prairie Schooner			Renascence: Essays on Value in Literature
PSA	Papeles de Son Armandans			Renditions: A Chinese-English Translation Magazine
PSM	Philippine Studies		*RevB*	Revista Bilingüe

RevI	Revista/Review Interamericana
	Review: Latin American Literature and Arts
RG	Revue Générale
RH	Revue Hebdomaire
RHL	Revue d'Histoire Littéraire de la France
RHLQCF	Revue d'Histoire Littéraire du Québec et du Canada Français
RHM	Revista Hispánica Moderna
RI	Revista Iberoamericana
RIB	Revista Interamericana de Bibliografía/ Inter-American Review of Bibliography
RLA	Romance Language Annual
RLC	Revue de Littérature Comparée
RLJ	Russian Language Journal
RLI	Rassegna della Letteratura Italiana
RLMC	Rivista di Letterature Moderne e Comparate
RLT	Russian Literature Triquarterly
RLV	Revue des Langues Vivantes
RMS	Renaissance & Modern Studies
RNL	Review of National Literatures
RO	Revista de Occidente
ROMM	Revue de l'Occident Musulman et de la Méditerranée
RomN	Romance Notes
RoR	Romanian Review
RPh	Romance Philology
RR	Romanic Review

RRWC	Renaissance and Renascences in Western Literature
RS	Research Studies
RSI	Revista Storica Italiani
RUO	Revue de l'Université d'Ottawa
RUS	Rice University Studies
RusL	Russian Literature
RusR	Russian Review
SAB	South Atlantic Bulletin
SAD	Studies in American Drama
SAF	Studies in American Fiction
SAIL	Studies in American Indian Literature
SAJL	Studies in American Jewish Literature
SAQ	South Atlantic Quarterly
SatR	Saturday Review
SBL	Studies in Black Literature
SBR	Swedish Book Review
Scan	Scandinavica
ScanR	Scandinavian Review
SCB	South Central Bulletin
SchM	Schweizer Monatshefte
SCL	Studies in Canadian Literature
ScotIR	Scottish International Review
ScotR	Scottish Review
SCR	South Carolina Review
SDR	South Dakota Review
SEACS	South East Asian Cultural Studies
SEEA	Slavic and East European Arts

SEEJ	Slavic and East European Journal		*SSF*	Studies in Short Fiction
SEER	Slavonic and East European Review		*SSl*	Scando-Slavica
SFC	Science Fiction Chronicle		*SSL*	Studies in Scottish Literature
SFR	Stanford French Review		*SSLit*	Soviet Studies in Literature
SHEH	Stanford Honors Essays in the Humanities		*SSMLN*	Society for the Study of Midwestern Literature Newsletter
SHR	Southern Humanities Review		*SSR*	Scottish Slavonic Review
Siglo	Siglo XX/20th Century		*StBL*	Studies in Black Literature
	Signs: Journal of Women in Culture and Society		*StIsl*	Studia Islamica
SlavonicR	Slavonic Review		*StTCL*	Studies in Twentieth Century Literature
SlavR	Slavic Review			Studies: An Irish Quarterly Review
SLitI	Studies in the Literary Imagination			SubStance: A Review of Theory and Literary Criticism
SLJ	Southern Literary Journal		*SuF*	Sinn und Form
	Slovo: Časopis Staroslavenskog Zavoda u Zagrebu		*Sur*	Revista Sur
SlovLit	Slovenská Literatúra: Revue Pre Literárnu Vedu		*SUS*	Susquehanna University Studies
SlovS	Slovene Studies		*SWR*	Southwest Review
SNNTS	Studies in the Novel		*SXX*	Secolul XX
SoQ	Southern Quarterly			Symposium: A Quarterly Journal in Modern Foreign Literatures
SoR	Southern Review (Baton Rouge, LA)		*T&K*	Text & Kontext
SoRA	Southern Review (Adelaide, Australia)		*TA*	Theatre Annual
	Southerly: A Review of Australian Literature		*TAH*	The American Hispanist
SovL	Soviet Literature		*TamR*	Tamarack Review
SPFA	Bulletin de la Société des Professeurs Français en Amérique		*TC*	Twentieth Century
SPHQ	Swedish Pioneer Historical Quarterly		*TCL*	Twentieth Century Literature
SR	Sewanee Review		*TCrit*	Texto Crítico
			TDR	Tulane Drama Review/The Drama Review
SS	Scandinavian Studies		*TheatreQ*	Theatre Quarterly

	Theoria: A Journal of Studies in the Arts, Humanities and Social Sciences
TJ	Theatre Journal
TkR	Tamkang Review
TLS	[London] Times Literary Supplement
TM	Temps Modernes
TQ	Texas Quarterly
Transatlantic	Transatlantic Review
TRev	Translation Review
TriQ	TriQuarterly
TSAR	Toronto South Asian Review
TSLL	Texas Studies in Literature and Language
TSWL	Tulsa Studies in Women's Literature
TuK	Text + Kritik: Zeitschrift für Literatur
TWQ	Third World Quarterly
TxSE	Texas Studies in English
UDQ	Denver Quarterly
UDR	University of Dayton Review
UES	Unisa English Studies
UHSL	University of Hartford Studies in Literature
UkrR	Ukrainian Review: A Quarterly Magazine Devoted to the Study of the Ukraine
UQ	Ukrainian Quarterly: Journal of East European and Asian Affairs
UR	University Review
UTQ	University of Toronto Quarterly
UWR	University of Windsor Review (Windsor, Ontario)
V&I	Voix et Images: Littérature Québécoise

VLang	Visible Language
VQR	Virginia Quarterly Review
W&L	Women & Literature
WAJML	West African Journal of Modern Languages
WAL	Western American Literature
WascanaR	Wascana Review
WB	Weimarer Beiträge
WCR	West Coast Review
	Westerly: A Quarterly Review
WHR	Western Humanities Review
WI	Die Welt dea Islams
WIRS	Western Illinois Regional Studies
WLT	World Literature Today
WLWE	World Literature Written in English
WR	Western Review
WS	Women's Studies: An Interdisciplinary Journal
WSCL	Wisconsin Studies in Contemporary Literature
WSJ	Wiener Slavistisches Jahrbuch
WSl	Die Welt der Slaven
WSlA	Wiener Slawistischer Almanach
WVUPP	West Virginia University Philological Papers
WZ	Wort in de Zeit
WZUG	Wissenschaftliche Zeitschrift der Ernst Moritz Arndt-Universität Greifswald
YCC	Yearbook of Comparative Criticism

YCGL	Yearbook of Comparative and General Literature	*Y/T*	Yale/Thestre
YES	Yearbook of English Studies	*ZAA*	Zeitschrift für Anglistik und Amerikanistik
YFS	Yale French Studies	*ZS*	Zeitschrift für Slawistik
YItS	Yale Italian Studies	*ZSP*	Zeitschrift für Slavische Philologie
YR	Yale Review		

ACKNOWLEDGMENTS

For permission to reproduce the illustrations in this edition of the *Encyclopedia of World Literature in the 20th Century,* the publisher is indebted to the following:

Abe, Kōbō, photograph by Jerry Bauer. © Jerry Bauer. Reproduced by permission.—Achebe, Chinua, photograph. AP/Wide World Photos. Reproduced by permission.—Adams, Henry S., photograph. AP/Wide World Photos. Reproduced by permission.—Adorno, Theodore W., photograph. Archive Photos, Inc. Reproduced by permission.—Agee, James, photograph. The Library of Congress.—Akhmatova, Anna Andreevna, photograph. The Library of Congress.—Albee, Edward, photograph. The Library of Congress.—Alegría, Fernando, photograph. Arte Publico Press Archives, University of Houston. Reproduced by permission.—Aleixandre, Vicente, photograph. AP/Wide World Photos. Reproduced by permission.—Algren, Nelson, photograph. The Library of Congress.—Allende, Isabel, photograph. AP/Wide World Photos. Reproduced by permission.—Amado, Jorge, photograph. AP/Wide World Photos. Reproduced by permission.—Amichai, Yehuda, photograph by John Reeves. Reproduced by permission.—Amis, Kingsley, photograph. AP/Wide World Photos. Reproduced by permission.—Anderson, Sherwood, photograph. Archive Photos, Inc. Reproduced by permission.—Angelou, Maya, photograph. AP/Wide World Photos. Reproduced by permission.—Anouilh, Jean, photograph. AP/Wide World Photos. Reproduced by permission.—Aragon, Louis, photograph. The Library of Congress.—Ashbery, John, photograph. AP/Wide World Photos. Reproduced by permission.—Atwood, Margaret, photograph. The Library of Congress.—Auchincloss, Louis, photograph by Jerry Bauer. © Jerry Bauer. Reproduced by permission.—Auden, W. H., photograph. Corbis-Bettmann. Reproduced by permission.—Audiberti, Jacques, photograph. AP/Wide World Photos. Reproduced by permission.—Azuela, Mariano, photograph. The Library of Congress.—Baraka, Imamu Amiri (LeRoi Jones), photograph. Corbis-Bettmann. Reproduced by permission.—Barnes, Djuna, photograph. UPI/Corbis-Bettman. Reproduced by permission.—Baroja, Pìo, photograph. AP/Wide World Photos. Reproduced by permission.—Barrie, Sir James M., photograph. AP/Wide World Photos. Reproduced by permission.—Barth, John, photograph. AP/Wide World Photos. Reproduced by permission.—Barthelme, Donald, photograph by Jerry Bauer. © Jerry Bauer. Reproduced by permission.—Bates, H. E., photograph. Mark Gerson Photography. Reproduced by permission.—Beattie, Anne, photograph by Jerry Bauer. © Jerry Bauer. Reproduced by permission.—Beckett, Samuel, photograph. Archive Photos, Inc. Reproduced by permission.—Behan, Brendan, photograph. AP/Wide World Photos. Reproduced by permission.—Bellow, Saul, photograph. Archive Photos, Inc. Reproduced by permission.—Benét, Stephen Vincent, photograph by Pirie MacDonald. The Library of Congress.—Bergson, Henri, photograph. The Library of Congress.—Berryman, John, photograph. AP/Wide World Photos. Reproduced by permission.—Betjeman, Sir John, photograph. Archive Photos, Inc. Reproduced by permission.—Bialik, Hayyim N., photograph. The Library of Congress.—Bierce, Ambrose, photograph. Corbis-Bettmann. Reproduced by permission.—Bishop, Elizabeth, photograph. AP/Wide World Photos. Reproduced by permission.—Blaise, Marie Claire, photograph by John Reeves. Reproduced by permission.—Blasco Ibáñez, Vicente, photograph. AP/Wide World Photos. Reproduced by permission.—Bloom, Harold, photograph by Jerry Bauer. © Jerry Bauer. Reproduced by permission.—Böll, Heinrich, photograph. Archive Photos, Inc. Reproduced by permission.—Borges, Jorge Luis, photograph. The Library of Congress.—Bowen, Elizabeth, photograph. The Library of Congress.—Breton, André, photograph. Archive Photos, Inc./AFP. Reproduced by permission.—Brookner, Anita, photograph by Jerry Bauer. © Jerry Bauer. Reproduced by permission.—Brooks, Gwendolyn, photograph. The Library of Congress.—Brutus, Dennis, photograph. AP/Wide World Photos. Reproduced by permission.—Buber, Martin, photograph. The Library of Congress.—Bullins, Ed, photograph by Marva Rae. Helen Merrill Ltd. Reproduced by permission of the photographer.—Bunting, Basil, photograph by Thomas Victor. Copyright © 1986 by Thomas Victor. All rights reserved. Reproduced by permission of the Estate of Thomas Victor.—Burgess, Anthony, photograph. AP/Wide World Photos. Reproduced by permission.—Burke, Kenneth, photograph. The Library of Congress.—Burroughs, William S., photograph. AP/Wide World Photos. Reproduced by permission.—Caldwell, Erskine, photograph. The Library of Congress.—Čapek, Karel, photograph. AP/Wide World Photos. Reproduced by permission.—Capote, Truman, photograph. The Library of Congress.—Cardenal, Ernesto, photograph by Lou Dematteis. Reuters/Corbis-Bettmann. Reproduced by permission.—Carpentier, Alejo, photograph. Archive Photos, Inc. Reproduced by permission.—Carver, Raymond, photograph. Archive Photos, Inc. Reproduced by permission.—Cather, Willa, photograph by Carl Van Vechten. The Library of Congress.—Cela, Camilio José, photograph by Jerry Bauer. © Jerry Bauer. Reproduced by permission.—Celine, Louis F., photograph. Archive Photos, Inc. Reproduced by permission.—Chandler, Raymond, photograph. The Library of Congress.—Cheever, John, photograph. The Library of Congress.—Chekov, Anton, photograph. International Portrait

Gallery/Library of Congress.—Chesterton, G. K., photograph. Archive Photos, Inc. Reproduced by permission.—Claudel, Paul, photograph. The Library of Congress.—Cocteau, Jean, photograph. AP/Wide World Photos. Reproduced by permission.—Cortázar, Julio, photograph. AP/Wide World Photos. Reproduced by permission.—Coward, Sir Noel (Peirce), photograph. AP/Wide World Photos, Inc. Reproduced by permission.—Crane, Hart, photograph by Walker Evans. The Library of Congress.—cummings, e. e., photograph. The Library of Congress.—Day Lewis, Cecil, photograph. Archive Photos, Inc. Reproduced by permission.—de Beauvoir, Simone, photograph. AP/Wide World Photos. Reproduced by permission.—de la Mare, Walter, photograph. The Library of Congress.—Derrida, Jacques, photograph. Archive Photos, Inc. Reproduced by permission.—Dickey, James, photograph. AP/Wide World Photos. Reproduced by permission.—Didion, Joan, photograph by Jerry Bauer. © Jerry Bauer. Reproduced by permission.—Doctorow, E. L., photograph by Horst Tappe. Archive Photos, Inc. Reproduced by permission.—Doolittle, Hilda, photograph. The Library of Congress.—Dos Passos, John, photograph. The Library of Congress.—Drabble, Margaret, photograph. AP/Wide World Photos. Reproduced by permission.—Dreiser, Theodore, photograph by Pirie MacDonald. The Library of Congress.—DuBois, W. E. B., photograph. The Library of Congress.—Ehrenburg, Ilya Grigoryevich, photograph. The Library of Congress.—Eliot, T. S., photograph. The Library of Congress.—Ellison, Ralph, photograph. AP/Wide World Photos. Reproduced by permission.—Elytis, Odysseus, photograph. AP/Wide World Photos. Reproduced by permission.—Farrell, James T., photograph. The Library of Congress.—Faulkner, William, photograph by Carl Van Vechten. The Library of Congress.—Fitzgerald, F. Scott, photograph by Carl Van Vechten. The Library of Congress.—Fo, Dario, photograph. © Jerry Bauer. Reproduced by permission.—Forster, E. M., photograph. Archive Photos, Inc. Reproduced by permission.—France, Anatole, photograph. The Library of Congress.—Freire, Romulo Gallegos, photograph. The Library of Congress.—Freud, Sigmund, photograph. The Library of Congress.—Frost, Robert, photograph. The Library of Congress.—Fuentes, Carlos, photograph. AP/Wide World Photos. Reproduced by permission.—Furphy, Joseph, photograph. The Library of Congress.—Gaines, Ernest, photograph. AP/Wide World Photos. Reproduced with permission.—Gaitán Durán, Jorge, photograph. The Library of Congress.—García Lorca, Federico, photograph. Archive Photos/Popperfoto. Reproduced by permission.—García Márquez, Gabriel, 1982, photograph. AP/Wide World Photos. Reproduced by permission.—Gass, William, photograph by Miriam Berkley. © Miriam Berkley. Reproduced by permission.—Genet, Jean, photograph. Archive Photos, Inc. Reproduced by permission.—Gibran, Kahlil, photograph. UPI/Corbis-Bettman. Reproduced by permission.—Gide, André, photograph. UPI/Corbis-Bettman. Reproduced by permission.—Glissant, Edouard, photograph. AP/Wide World Photos. Reproduced by permission.—Golding, William, photograph by Caroline Forbes. The Library of Congress.—Gordimer, Nadine, photograph. AP/Wide World Photos. Reproduced by permission.—Gordon, Caroline, photograph. The Library of Congress.—Gorky, Maxim, photograph. The Library of Congress.—Grass, Günter, photograph by Fred Stein. The Library of Congress.—Graves, Robert, photograph. AP/Wide World Photos, Inc. Reproduced by permission.—Greene, Graham, photograph. AP/Wide World Photos, Inc. Reproduced by permission.—Hammett, Samuel D., photograph. The Library of Congress.—Hamsun, Knut, photograph. The Library of Congress.—Handke, Peter, photograph by Jerry Bauer. © Jerry Bauer. Reproduced by permission.—Hansberry, Lorraine V., photograph. The Library of Congress.—Hardy, Thomas, photograph. Archive Photos, Inc. Reproduced by permission.—Hauptmann, Gerhart, photograph. The Library of Congress.—Head, Bessie, photograph. Reproduced by the kind permission of the Estate of Bessie Head.—Hellman, Lillian, photograph. AP/Wide World Photos. Reproduced by permission.—Hemingway, Ernest, photograph. Archive Photos, Inc. Reproduced by permission.—Housman, A. E., photograph. Archive Photos, Inc. Reproduced by permission.—Hughes, James Langston, photograph by Carl Van Vechten. The Library of Congress.—Hughes, Ted, photograph by Mark Gerson. Mark Gerson Photography. Reproduced by permission.—Hurston, Zora Neale, photograph. AP/Wide World Photos. Reproduced by permission.—Inge, William R., photograph. The Library of Congress.—Ionesco, Eugéne, photograph. The Library of Congress.—Irving, John, photograph. AP/Wide World Photos. Reproduced by permission.—Isherwood, Christopher, photograph. Archive Photos, Inc. Reproduced by permission.—James, Henry, photograph. The Library of Congress.—Jarry, Alfred, drawing by F. A. Cazalz, 1897, photograph. Corbis-Bettmann. Reproduced by permission.—Jeffers, Robinson, photograph. The Library of Congress.—Jiménez, Juan Ramón, photograph. AP/Wide World Photos. Reproduced by permission.—Johonson, James Weldon, photograph. The Library of Congress.—Jones, James, photograph. Corbis-Bettmann. Reproduced by permission.—Joyce, James (Ulysses), photograph. The Library of Congress.—Jung, Carl, photograph. The Library of Congress.—Jünger, Ernst, photograph. Archive Photos/Camera Press. Reproduced by permission.—Kafka, Franz, photograph. AP/Wide World Photos. Reproduced by permission.—Kawabata Yasunari, photograph. AP/Wide World Photos. Reproduced by permission.—Kerouac, Jack, photograph. Archive Photos. Reproduced by permission.—Killens, John O., photograph by Carl Van Vechten. The Library of Congress.—Kristeva, Julia, photograph by Jerry Bauer. © Jerry Bauer. Reproduced by permission.—Kumin, Maxine, photograph. AP/Wide World Photos. Reproduced by permission.—Kundera, Milan, photograph. Archive Photos.

Reproduced by permission.—Lagerkvist, Pär F., photograph. The Library of Congress.—Lawrence, D(avid) H(erbert), photograph. AP/Wide World Photos. Reproduced by permission.—Lessing, Doris, photograph by Jerry Bauer. © Jerry Bauer. Reproduced by permission.—Levi, Carlos, photograph. Archive Photos, Inc. Reproduced by permission.—Levi, Primo, photograph. The Library of Congress.—Lewis, Sinclair, photograph. The Library of Congress.—Lindsay, Vachel, photograph. Corbis-Bettmann. Reproduced by permission.—London, Jack, photograph. The Library of Congress.—Lowell, Amy, photograph. UPI/Corbis-Bettman. Reproduced by permission.—Lowell, Robert, photograph. The Library of Congress.—Lukács, György, photograph. Hulton-Deutsch/Corbis-Bettmann. Reproduced by permission.—Macleish, Archibald, photograph. The Library of Congress.—MacLennan, Hugh, photograph. AP/Wide World Photos. Reproduced by permission.—Maeterlinck, Maurice, photograph. The Library of Congress.—Mailer, Norman, photograph by Carl Van Vechten. The Library of Congress.—Malamud, Bernard, photograph. The Library of Congress.—Mamet, David, photograph by Brigitte Lacombe. Grove/Atlantic, Inc. Reproduced by permission.—Mann, Luiz Heinrich, photograph. The Library of Congress.—Mann, Thomas, photograph. The Library of Congress.—Mansfield, Katherine, photograph. Corbis-Bettmann. Reproduced by permission.—Marcel, Gabriel, photograph. Archive Photos, Inc. Reproduced by permission.—Marquand, John, photograph. Archive Photos, Inc. Reproduced by permission.—Masefield, John, photograph. The Library of Congress.—Maugham, W. Somerset, photograph by Carl Van Vechten. The Library of Congress.—Mauriac, François, photograph. The Library of Congress.—McCarthy, Mary, photograph. The Library of Congress.—McCullers, Carson, photograph. AP/Wide World Photos. Reproduced by permission.—McKay, Claude, photograph. The Library of Congress.—Mencken, Henry Louis, photograph. The Library of Congress.—Merrill, James, photograph. AP/Wide World Photos. Reproduced by permission.—Millay, Edna St. Vincent, photograph. The Library of Congress.—Miller, Arthur, photograph. Archive Photos, Inc. Reproduced by permission.—Miller, Henry, photograph. The Library of Congress.—Milosz, Czeslaw, photograph by Jerry Bauer. © Jerry Bauer. Reproduced by permission.—Mishima, Yukio, photograph. AP/Wide World Photos. Reproduced by permission.—Mistral, Gabriela, photograph. The Library of Congress.—Momaday, N. Scott, photograph. AP/Wide World Photos. Reproduced by permission.—Moore, Marianne, photograph. The Library of Congress.—Moravia, Alberto, photograph. The Library of Congress.—Morrison, Toni, photograph. AP/Wide World Photos. Reproduced by permission.—Mukherjee, Bharati, photograph. AP/Wide World Photos. Reproduced by permission.—Nabokov, Vladimir, photograph. AP/Wide World Photos. Reproduced by permission.—Naipaul, V. S., photograph. AP/Wide World Photos. Reproduced by permission.—Narayan, R. K., photograph. The Library of Congress.—Nemerov, Howard, photograph by Margaret Nemerov. Reproduced with permission.—Neruda, Pablo, photograph by Jerry Bauer. © Jerry Bauer. Reproduced by permission.—Nin, Anaïs, photograph. The Library of Congress.—O'Casey, Sean, photograph. The Library of Congress.—O'Connor, Flannery, photograph. Corbis-Bettmann. Reproduced by permission.—O'Hara, Frank, photograph. AP/Wide World Photos. Reproduced by permission.—O'Hara, John, photograph. The Library of Congress.—O'Neill, Eugene G., photograph. The Library of Congress.—Oates, Joyce Carol, photograph. UPI/Corbis-Bettmann. Reproduced by permission.—Odets, Clifford, photograph. AP/Wide World Photos, Inc. Reproduced by permission.—Ōe Kenzaburō, photograph. Reuters/Kyodo/Archive Photos. Reproduced by permission.—Ortega y Gasset, José, photograph. AP/Wide World Photos. Reproduced by permission.—Orwell, George, photograph. AP/Wide World Photos. Reproduced by permission.—Osborne, John, photograph. AP/Wide World Photos. Reproduced by permission.—Ozick, Cynthia, photograph. Corbis-Bettmann. Reproduced by permission.—Parra, Nicanor, photograph by Miriam Berkley. © Miriam Berkley. Reproduced by permission.—Pasolini, Pier Paolo, photograph. AP/Wide World Photos, Inc. Reproduced by permission.—Paton, Alan, photograph. The Library of Congress.—Pavlović, Miodrag, photograph by John Reeves. Reproduced by permission.—Paz, Octavio, photograph. AP/Wide World Photos. Reproduced by permission.—Percy, Walker, photograph by Jerry Bauer. © Jerry Bauer. Reproduced by permission.—Pérez Galdós, Benito, photograph. The Library of Congress.—Perse, Saint John, photograph. AP/Wide World Photos. Reproduced by permission.—Pietri, Dr. Arturo Uslar, photograph. AP/Wide World Photos. Reproduced by permission.—Pinter, Harold, photograph. AP/Wide World Photos. Reproduced by permission.—Pirandello, Luigi, photograph. AP/Wide World Photos. Reproduced by permission.—Plath, Sylvia, photograph. Corbis-Bettmann. Reproduced by permission.—Porter, Katherine Anne, photograph. Archive Photos, Inc. Reproduced by permission.—Pound, Ezra, photograph. The Library of Congress.—Pritchett, V. S., photograph by Jerry Bauer. © Jerry Bauer. Reproduced by permission.—Proust, Marcel, photograph. The Library of Congress.—Puig, Manuel, photograph by Jerry Bauer. © Jerry Bauer. Reproduced by permission.—Purdy, James, photograph. The Library of Congress.—Pynchon, Thomas R., photograph. UPI/Corbis-Bettmann. Reproduced by permission.—Quasimodo, Salvatore, photograph. Corbis-Bettmann. Reproduced by permission.—Remarque, Erich M., photograph. The Library of Congress.—Renault, Mary, photograph. AP/Wide World Photos. Reproduced by permission.—Rexroth, Kenneth, photograph. AP/Wide World Photos. Reproduced by permission.—Rice, Elmer, photograph. AP/Wide World Photos.

Reproduced by permission.—Rich, Adrienne, photograph. AP/Wide World Photos. Reproduced by permission.—Richler, Mordecai, photograph by John Reeves. Reproduced by permission.—Robbe-Grillet, Alain, photograph by Jerry Bauer. © Jerry Bauer. Reproduced by permission.—Robinson, Edwin Arlington, photograph. AP/Wide World Photos. Reproduced by permission.—Roethke, Theodore, photograph by Imogen Cunningham. AP/Wide World Photos, Inc. Reproduced by permission.—Roth, Philip, photograph. Corbis-Bettmann. Reproduced by permission.—Rukeyser, Muriel, photograph. AP/Wide World Photos. Reproduced by permission.—Rulfo, Juan, photograph. AP/Wide World Photos. Reproduced by permission.—Rushdie, Salman, photograph. Archive Photos, Inc. Reproduced by permission.—Russell, George William, photograph. The Library of Congress.—Salinger, J. D., photograph. AP/Wide World Photos, Inc. Reproduced by permission.—Sandburg, Carl, photograph. The Library of Congress.—Santayana, George, photograph. The Library of Congress.—Saroyan, William, photograph. The Library of Congress.—Sarraute, Nathalie, photograph. AP/Wide World Photos. Reproduced by permission.—Sarton, May, photograph. UPI/Corbis-Bettmann. Reproduced by permission.—Sassoon, Siegfried, photograph. The Library of Congress.—Schnitzler, Arthur, photograph. Archive Photos, Inc. Reproduced by permission.—Sexton, Anne, photograph. AP/Wide World Photos. Reproduced by permission.—Shaw, George Bernard, photograph. The Library of Congress.—Shepard, Sam, photograph. Archive Photos, Inc. Reproduced by permission.—Simenon, Georges, photograph. AP/Wide World Photos, Inc. Reproduced by permission.—Sinclair, Upton, photograph. AP/Wide World Photos, Inc. Reproduced by permission.—Singer, Isaac Bashevis, photograph. UPI/Corbis-Bettmann. Reproduced by permission.—Sitwell, Edith, photograph. UPI/Corbis-Bettman. Reproduced by permission.—Škvorecký, Josef, photograph by John Reeves. Reproduced by permission.—Snow, Charles Percy, photograph. Corbis-Bettmann. Reproduced by permission.—Snyder, Gary, photograph. AP/Wide World Photos. Reproduced by permission.—Sontag, Susan, photograph. AP/Wide World Photos. Reproduced by permission.—Soto, Pedro Juan, photograph. Arte Publico Press Archives, University of Houston. Reproduced by permission.—Soyinka, Wole, photograph. Archive Photos/Trappe. Reproduced by permission.—Spark, Muriel, photograph. AP/Wide World Photos. Reproduced by permission.—Stein, Gertrude, photograph by Carl Van Vechten. The Library of Congress.—Steinbeck, John, photograph. Archive Photos, Inc. Reproduced by permission.—Stevens, Wallace, photograph. The Library of Congress.—Strachey, Lytton, photograph by E. O. Hoppe. Corbis-Bettmann. Reproduced by permission.—Strand, Mark, photograph. The Library of Congress.—Szymborska, Wislawa, photograph. AP/Wide World Photos. Reproduced by permission.—Tate, Allen, photograph. UPI/Corbis-Bettman. Reproduced by permission.—Thomas, Dylan, photograph. AP/Wide World Photos. Reproduced by permission.—Thurber, James, photograph. AP/Wide World Photos. Reproduced by permission.—Tolkien, J. R. R., photograph. AP/Wide World Photos. Reproduced by permission.—Tremblay, Michel, photograph by Yves Renaud. Agence Goodwin. Reproduced by permission of the photographer.—Trevor, William, photograph by Kristin Morrison. Mark Gerson Photography. Reproduced by permission.—Tyler, Anne, photograph. AP/Wide World Photos. Reproduced by permission.—Unamuno, Miguel de, photograph. Corbis-Bettmann. Reproduced by permission.—Undset, Sigrid, photograph. AP/Wide World Photos. Reproduced by permission.—Updike, John, photograph. AP/Wide World Photos. Reproduced by permission.—Valéry, Paul, photograph. Archive Photos, Inc. Reproduced by permission.—Vargas Llosa, Mario, photograph. AP/Wide World Photos. Reproduced by permission.—Vidal, Gore, photograph. AP/Wide World Photos. Reproduced by permission.—Villa, José Garcia, photograph. AP/Wide World Photos. Reproduced by permission.—Vonnegut, Kurt, Jr., photograph. Archive Photos/Saga 1991 Frank Capri. Reproduced by permission.—Walcott, Derek, photograph by Jerry Bauer. © Jerry Bauer. Reproduced by permission.—Walker, Alice, photograph. Archive Photos, Inc. Reproduced by permission.—Warren, Robert Penn, photograph. The Library of Congress.—Wassermann, Jakob, photograph. Archive Photos, Inc. Reproduced by permission.—Waugh, Evelyn, photograph. Mark Gerson Photography. Reproduced by permission.—Wedekind, Frank, photograph. Hulton-Deutsch Collection/Corbis-Bettmann. Reproduced by permission.—Weiss, Peter, photograph. AP/Wide World Photos. Reproduced by permission.—Weldon, Fay, photograph. AP/Wide World Photos. Reproduced by permission.—Wells, H. G., photograph. The Library of Congress.—Welty, Eudora, photograph. AP/Wide World Photos. Reproduced by permission.—Wesker, Arnold, photograph. UPI/Corbis-Bettman. Reproduced by permission.—Wharton, Edith, photograph. AP/Wide World Photos. Reproduced by permission.—White, E. B., photograph. AP/Wide World Photos. Reproduced by permission.—White, Patrick, photograph. AP/Wide World Photos. Reproduced by permission.—Wiesel, Elie, photograph by Nancy Rica Schiff. Archive Photos, Inc. Reproduced by permission.—Wilbur, Richard, photograph. AP/Wide World Photos. Reproduced by permission.—Wilder, Thornton, photograph by Carl Van Vechten. The Library of Congress.—Williams, Tennessee, photograph. AP/Wide World Photos. Reproduced by permission.—Wilson, August, photograph. AP/Wide World Photos. Reproduced by permission.—Wodehouse, P. G., photograph. AP/Wide World Photos. Reproduced by permission.—Wolfe, Thomas, photograph by Carl Van Vechten. The Library of Congress.—Wolfe, Tom, photograph. AP/Wide World Photos. Reproduced by permission.—Woolf, Virginia, photograph. AP/Wide World Photos. Reproduced by permission.—Wright, James, photograph by Ted Wright. Reproduced by permission of the Estate of James Wright.—Wright, Richard, photograph by Carl Van Vechten. The Library of Congress.—Yeats, William Butler, photograph. The Library of Congress.—Yourcenar, Marguerite, photograph. AP/Wide World Photos. Reproduced by permission.

INTRODUCTION

This four-volume third edition of the *Encyclopedia of World Literature in the 20th Century* is designed as a comprehensive survey of significant literary activity of international scope and proportion extending from the beginning of the century to the present. The breadth and complexity of this activity demands progressive study, analysis, and evaluation, and the *Encyclopedia* serves as an inclusive and authoritative guide for this purpose. Responsive to the needs of scholarly and general readers alike, the *Encyclopedia* provides in a reference work of singular importance the most extensive treatment of information necessary to the assessment and appreciation of the growth and development of modern world literature.

The twentieth century represents a period of extraordinary literary productivity and proliferation realized within the framework of unprecedented historical transformation and challenge. The decades preceding the publication of the *Encyclopedia* have produced global transition, dominated by the impact of social and political upheaval and the redefinition of national boundaries and identities. We have witnessed events that have altered the shape of the world in which we live and the terms by which we discuss literature. Although the sociopolitical as well as cultural ramifications of these alterations have yet to fully realize themselves and be understood, we have made every effort to incorporate these developments within the context of the *Encyclopedia,* thus enhancing the reader's perception of the relationship between literature and society.

This edition is a collaborative effort to cover, in more than 2,300 article entries in four volumes, the major aspects of world literature in the twentieth century. To this end, nearly all the literatures of the world with claim to a substantial productivity within the century are discussed in survey articles. Likewise, in their relationship to the literature of the century, literary movements of consequence (e.g., expressionism, futurism, surrealism) are covered in separate topical articles, as are movements in ideas (e.g., existentialism, historicism, postmodernism). The core of the *Encyclopedia* consists of separate articles on major and representative writers incorporating salient biographical information and critical analysis of the writer's major themes and works.

Bases of Selection: The selection of individual entries represents extensive assessment and evaluation of critical recognition earned from the international literary community as well as endorsement as figures of substantial literary importance from specialists of representative national literatures. In order to fulfill its purpose as a reference work, the *Encyclopedia* attempts to be as comprehensive as possible within the limitations imposed by the span of the edition. It is also important to maintain the international scope of the *Encyclopedia.* Thus, many authors—American, British, European—who are well known to English-speaking readers do not receive individual entries but are instead treated within the survey articles of national literatures. Many of the authors receiving individual entries are from less familiar literatures who have limited exposure to English-speaking readers, and a significant number to date have not been translated into English or have not generated criticism in English of scholarly merit. For these authors, the *Encyclopedia* serves as the primary source of reference to English-speaking readers.

Omissions: Despite the scope and magnitude of the *Encyclopedia,* it is inevitable that an appreciable number of writers have been omitted. In works of this kind, with claims of a wide coverage, the inclusion of some writers as against others is of course subject to debate. Regrettably, it was not always possible to identify a specialist of sufficient expertise to prepare individual author entries or to compile and research a national literature. As a result, there is unfortunately at times insufficient coverage of writers deserving of inclusion from relatively obscure or isolated literatures.

Entries: Organization and Data—Individual author entries have been arranged into four parts: a headnote containing vital statistics; a body that includes biographical information and a critical assessment of the author's achievement; a section titled *Further Works* containing publications not mentioned in the body of the article; and a final section titled *Bibliography* comprising selective bibliographical material concerning the author and his or her work. A list of periodicals and their abbreviations cited will be found at the front of Volume 1, and an index to the entries will be included at the end of Volume 4. In a very few of the headnotes the statistics are incomplete, owing to the difficulty of obtaining conclusive confirmation from accessible, reliable sources.

Works featured in the body of the article, as well as in the *Further Works* section, carry their full title and, wherever possible, their original year of publication. In the case of authors writing in languages other than English, titles of published English translations are cited in parentheses, along with their original publication dates. Where several translations of a non-English work have been made under the same title in English, only the publication date of the earliest translation is given. With those works that have been translated under more than one English title, we have tried to feature the titles of all such translations. For non-English works that have not been translated into English, original titles will appear followed by the year of publication and the title's literal translation in parentheses.

Cross References and Pseudonyms: Extensive cross-references to other authors, literatures, and movements appear wherever appropriate in the texts of articles. Where a writer with an individual entry is referred to in another entry, at the first mention his or her last name appears in small capital letters. Likewise, where a movement with a separate entry is referred to in another entry, at the first mention the topic appears in small capital letters. The survey articles on national literatures are cross-referenced by language so that the reader will be directed to the appropriate national literature or literatures (e.g., under Bengali Literature will be found "See Bangladeshi Literature and Indian Literature").

Authors known primarily by their *non de plume* will be listed under their pseudonym (e.g., Blixen under *Dinesen,* Gorenko under *Akhmatova,* Hadjiandreas under *Tsirkas*). For the convenience of readers certain of these names have been cross-referenced, but the abiding principle in this regard has been to avoid overelaboration.

Transliterated and Romanized Languages: As an international reference work, the *Encyclopedia* attempts to be as consistent as possible with the transliteration and romanization of non-English names, most notably those in Arabic, Chinese, Japanese, and Russian. In Arabic, prefixes that are part of the surname will be retained when the surname is used for alphabetizing (e.g., 'Abd al-Hamīd ibn Hadūga under *Ibn Hadūga*). In Chinese practice, the family name comes before the given name, which usually has two elements. The family name and the first element of the given name are capitalized, and the given name is hyphenated (e.g., Kao Hsiao-sheng). Chinese names wherever necessary are cross-referenced in the index by their updated romanization (e.g., Gao Xiaosheng. *See* Kao Hsiao-sheng). In Japanese practice, the family name also comes before the given name (e.g., Ōe Kenzaburō rather than Kenzaburō Ōe). While there are many systems for transliterating Russian names, the phonetic method adopted was considered the most appropriate for a general reader, and the most easily recognizable from the viewpoint of common usage (e.g., see *Gorky,* not Gorki, Gorkii, or Gor'kiy).

Quotations: To some entries, primarily authors of international repute, the *Encyclopedia* appends a selection of critical excerpts to further enhance the reader's understanding and perception of the author's productivity and contribution to world literature. The excerpts are cited by author, source, year of publication, and page number(s).

The Contributors: These have been drawn from a wide sphere of literary authorities, both from the United States and abroad, most often based on the recommendation of the advisers in national literatures. The name of the contributor appears at the end of each article in the *Encyclopedia.*

The general editor wishes to express his appreciation, first, to the hundreds of individuals whose contributions have helped to make the *Encyclopedia* a reference work of distinction. He is most indebted to those individuals listed in the board of advisers, whose generosity of time and expertise provided proportion, balance, and consistency in the preparation of the edition. He also expresses his appreciation to Peter M. Gareffa, managing editor of St. James Press, and Laura Berger, senior editor.

Assisting the general editor, Madeline D. Murray was the senior editor and production coordinator of the *Encyclopedia.* Production editors were Sonya Collins, Victoria Eng, and Matthew Miller. Technical assistance was provided by Enercida Guererro, Ana Angelillo, and Harlan Cayetano. Editorial assistance was provided by Carina Garcia, Bonnie MacSaveny, Denise Galang, Sean O'Hanlon, Chriscita Corbin, Rachel Shook, Michelle Gonzalez, Christine Cifra, Anna Degrezia, Francesca Fiore, Rebecca Lawson, Jill Bauer, Lisa Butler, Michelle Cutler, Julie Miele, Anna Gross, Karma Cloud, Nancy Moore, Joseph Weissman, Rose Sung, Jason Berner, and Greta Wagle.

STEVEN R. SERAFIN
HUNTER COLLEGE OF THE CITY UNIVERSITY OF NEW YORK

A

ABAZA LITERATURE
See North Caucasian Literatures

'ABD AL-SABŪR, Salāh

Egyptian poet, dramatist, and critic; b. 3 May 1931; d. Aug. 1981, Cairo

S. is the most prominent Egyptian poet since the mid-1950s. He obtained a degree from Cairo University in 1951 and worked mainly in cultural avenues all his life, first as teacher and journalist, then in several administrative positions, the last of which was as director of the General Organization of Egyptian Books. His premature death put an end to a most flourishing literary career.

He is the earliest Egyptian poet to achieve a modernist approach in the form and content of his poetry. As early as his first collection, *Al-nās fī bilādī* (1957; people in my country), he demonstrated a radical departure from the language, structure, and attitudinal characteristics of the inherited poetry. His sentence constructions were relaxed, and his vocabulary, intonations, and rhythms were greatly deelevated from the original eloquence and loud rhythms of Arabic verse, and his attitude and vision were markedly different. This is perhaps his greatest achievement, arrived at, in good measure, unwittingly. For although his experiment with language was as conscious as it was instinctive, his actual awareness, at that early period, of the other modernist dimensions of his work was perhaps not equal to the depth of the experiment itself. From the outset, S. was able to achieve modernity both in form and content. Early in his work, just as in the works of almost all Arab poets of the 1950s, the contemporary Arab predicament is fully recognized, yet he depicts it not in the loud, direct tones of protest and dissent typical of his contemporaries, but in the quiet tones and demure stance of the modernist poet. The problem of modernity in contemporary Arabic poetry has not mainly been a problem of language and form; these two elements had been more radically revolutionized than other equally important elements. The main problem has been one of tone and attitude, two elements that proved highly resistant to change, which stipulates first, a deelevated, declassed status for the poet who has traditionally viewed himself as prophet, leader, and liberator, and secondly, a vision that recognizes the helpless situation of the individual in an Arab world constantly subject to internal coercion and external aggression. S. instinctively realized all this, as well as the necessity to deelevate diction and approximate it to the living language of the people around him, without ever vulgarizing it. He is not an heir to self-assertiveness or demonstrative heroics, and his psychological and intellectual make-up—modest, gentle, urbane, and sophisticated—enabled him to achieve the necessary shift from the heroic stance and the aristocratic, old-world grandeur to the urban (sometimes even plebeian) contemporary expression. S.'s occasional employment of irony, as in his long poem "Hikāyat al-mughannī 'l-hazīn" (story of the sad minstrel), published in *Ta'ammulāt fī zaman jarīḥ* (1971; reflections on a wounded era), is subtle and highly effective and could have been achieved only because the poet's concept of himself and his role had changed dramatically. S. could see himself and everyone else as victims, not heroes, of the times. His protagonist uncovers a world of fraud, complicity, and false situations, but in his strife against this world he discovers that he is an integral part of it and that his life is controlled by its pernicious forces. His rebellion against his predicament is not a direct attempt to influence this world, but an expression of suffering reflecting the receptive stance of a victim who is acted upon by events. This suffering invariably helps transform the world of the reader through a recognition of his or her own similar situation. S.'s revolution in form, language, and syntax is supported by a genuine transformation of vision and depression of tone, all elements combining to reflect a precocious modernist spirit anticipating the works of such modernists as Sa'dī Yūsuf (b. 1943) and the younger poets of the 1980s.

S. has also rendered a major contribution to the verse drama in Arabic, writing highly experimental plays. In his first play, *Ma'sāt al-Hallāj* (1965; *Murder in Baghdad*, 1972), a tragedy, he incorporated the Greek principle of the fall of the manifestly doomed hero. Al-Hallāj, a famous mystic and staunch defender of the poor, was crucified for heresy in Baghdad in 922. Despite his precarious position as a spokesman for social justice, which made him undesirable to the authorities of his time, he was tempted, out of the joy and fulness of his heart, to divulge that he had achieved direct union with God, and the judges rose immediately to indict him, convincing the very people whom he had defended of his heresy. In other plays, S. diversified both his form and themes. *Musāfir layl* (1969; *Night Traveller*, 1980) is a symbolic black comedy, and *Al-Amāra tantazir* (1970; *The Princess Waits*, 1975) is a fairy tale-like story that celebrates the advent of hope and the rise to action after a long period of inertia and despair. Technically, S. manipulated dramatic poetry to convey the language and themes of daily life without loss to its poetic quality.

S.'s whole oeuvre is furthermore informed by cogent ideas and a definite stance toward both Arab life and the general universal condition, colored, where relevant, by deep empathy. His is one of the few poetic experiments to merge thought and art in a subtle mélange that sacrifices neither.

His many prose writings, though not of the same order as his poetic and dramatic works, still reflect an original mind; and such works as his book on classical Arabic poetry, *Qirā'a jadīda li shi'rinā 'l-qadīm* (1968; a new reading in our old poetry), are a departure from the usual way this poetry has been treated previously. Perhaps his most interesting prose work is his book on his own career as poet, *Hayātī fī 'l-shi'r* (1969; my life in poetry).

To sum up, S. is a notable experimenter and innovator, a poet with a sense of the tragic who reflects a vision of a broken world full of victims and failed endeavors. Yet he is sparse of emotion, devoted to questions, free of absolutes, completely stripped of heroics, and marvelously free of sentimentality. Addressing great universals and major national and human issues, he probes deeply into the meaning of life, combining the opposing poles of the tragic and the ironic, a truly tormented soul that finds no rest. As a true modernist, he has never accepted the conventional or catered to the expectations of the audience. Instead, his work is marked by an inversion of tradition and focuses on aspects of experience never before broached in poetry. His theme spans diverse aspects of experience ranging from a wide spectrum of communal preoccupations, to the cycle of life and death, to the joy of love and the desolation of its absence and to the diverse disappointments of life.

FURTHER WORKS: *Afkār qawmiyya* (1960); *Aswāt al-'asr* (1960); *Aqūlu lakum* (1961); *Ahlām al fāris al-qadīm* (1964); *Hattā naqhar al-mawt* (1966); *Wa tabqā 'l-kalima* (1970); *Shajar al-layl* (1970); *Rihla 'alā 'l-waraq* (1971); *Madīnat al-'ishq wa 'l-hikma* (1972); *Al-nisā' hīna yatahattamna* (1976); *Al-ibhār fi 'l-dhākira* (1979); *Kitāba 'alā wajh alrīh* (1980); *Mashārif al-khamsīn* (1981)

BIBLIOGRAPHY: Badawi, M. M., *A Critical Introduction to Modern Arabic Poetry* (1975): 209, 216–18, 260; Jayyusi, S. K., *Trends and Movements in Modern Arabic Poetry*, (1977) Vol. 2: passim; Ayyad, S. M., and Witherspoon, N., *Reflections and Deflections: A Study of the Contemporary Arab Mind through its Literary Creations* (1986): 200–11; Badawi, M. M., *Modern Arabic Drama in Egypt* (1987): 220–28; Jayyusi, S. K., "Modernist Poetry in Arabic," in *Cambridge History of Arabic Literature*, Vol. 4, forthcoming

—SALMA KHADRA JAYYUSI

ABE Kōbō

Japanese novelist, short-story writer, and dramatist, b. 7 March 1924, Tokyo; d. 22 January 1993, Tokyo

The son of a doctor practicing in Shenyang, Manchuria, A. attended school there and in Tokyo. He was exempted from military service during World War II because of a respiratory illness; he finished medical school in 1948, but decided against a medical practice in favor of a writing career. He allied himself with a literary group, led by Kiyoteru Hamada (b. 1909), that was committed to the goal of fusing the techniques of SURREALISM with Marxist ideology. Using an avant-garde, experimental style that quickly won the praise of the younger generation of readers, A. began to write stories, novels, and plays that expose the emptiness of life in modern society.

His short stories, published first in journals, established a special place for him in postwar Japanese literary life. He received coveted prizes in Japan for his three stories, "Akai mayu" (1950; "Red Cocoon," 1966), "Kabe" (1951; wall), and "S. Karuma-shi no hanzai" (1951; Mr. S. Karuma's crime). In the last mentioned, which is really a short novel, the style and subject matter are reminiscent of KAFKA. The narrator loses his name, and hence, access to normal relations with other human beings. As a result, however, he is mysteriously able to communicate with certain animals in the zoo and also with inanimate objects, such as store mannequins, which seem to come to life.

One of A.'s best-received short stories is "Chinnyūsha" (1951; intruders). An allegorical satire on democracy in postwar Japan, it tells how a group of people invades the narrator's one-room apartment and, by insisting on the democratic rule of the majority, enslave him.

A. is one of the most productive writers for the Japanese stage. His prize-winning play *Tomodachi* (1967; *Friends*, 1969) focuses on the members of one family, whose actions are predatory and

Abe Kōbō

cruelly destructive, although they claim to be devoting themselves to social good, to respect for life, and to the responsibilities of human brotherhood. The play *Omae nimo tsumi ga aru* (1978; *You, Too, Are Guilty*, 1979), set in a modern apartment, explores with sardonic humor the possible bond between the living and the dead. A. has also written film scripts and radio plays. His theater troupe has toured the U.S. and performed in New York City (1979).

A.'s international reputation rests largely on his novels and on the films based on them. In his masterpiece, *Suna no onna* (1962; *The Woman in the Dunes*, 1964), a conflict between two concepts of home emerges: the place where one is born as opposed to the place where one must actually live, the second being one's true home in an existential sense. The protagonist is a schoolteacher who, on a holiday expedition, happens on a village in danger of being buried by massive sand dunes that have accumulated around it. The schoolteacher accepts shelter from a woman who lives alone in one of the threatened houses. He is pressed to help her and the villagers in their constant struggle to keep the area free of sand. When a chance to escape comes, he refuses to take advantage of it. Seemingly, he has come to accept his strange life with the woman amid the constantly shifting, unpredictable sand, which at times seems to flow like water in slow motion. The woman represents the ability to adjust to life, while the sand is a symbol of reality, always changing in shape and inexorably demonstrating the power to move men and women, however reluctant they may be to respond.

In *Hako otoko* (1973; *The Box Man*, 1974) A. describes modern man's attempt to escape from himself. His protagonist does so by cutting a peephole in an empty cardboard carton, placing the box over his head, and walking away from his anxieties. The only danger to him lies in the possibility of meeting another "box man." A. has said of this novel, "Being no one means at the same time that one can be anyone." Aversion to bourgeois existence and the question of what is genuine and what is counterfeit here are expressed by means of a symbol—the box as a shield from the world—that represents disposability and concealment. For readers attuned to the traditions of Japan, the mask of the Nō actor, a thing of exquisite beauty to be treasured forever, has given way to a device that serves its utilitarian purpose and may then be abandoned.

In *Mikkai* (1978; *Secret Rendezvous*, 1979) A. has written a surrealistic detective story about an unidentified man searching for his wife at a hospital, to which she has been unaccountably taken in the middle of the night. The hospital seems like a bizarre laboratory, where the patients and staff alike are sexual cripples. The plot resonates with classical myths and Freudian symbolism.

A number of themes constantly recur in A.'s work: the individual's search for the "roots of existence," which may stabilize his identity; the difficulty people have in communicating with one another; and the discrepancy between inner and outer reality. By juxtaposing ordinary events and absurd ones A. compels his readers (or audience) to believe that his misshapen world is really Everyman's.

For three decades A. has detached himself to an unusual degree from the literary traditions of Japan. His writing, often stiff and formal, reveals his preoccupation with ideas rather than style. A. uses concepts and expressions drawn from science and philosophy for his criticisms of society. Allegory, irony, and satire all serve to delineate his principal theme—that of the outsider in modern society.

FURTHER WORKS: *Mumei shishū* (1947); *Owarishi michi no shirube ni* (1948); *Ueta hifu* (1952); *Kiga dōmei* (1954); *Kabe atsuki heya* (1954); *Āru rokujū-ni gō no hatsumei* (1956); *Mōken no kokoro ni keisanki no te o* (1957); *Kemono-tachi wa kokyō-o mesasu* (1957); *Tōō o yuku: Hangariya mondai no haikei* (1957); *Hakareru kiroku* (1958); *Daishi kampyōki* (1959; *Inter Ice Age 4*, 1970); *Yūrei wa koko ni iru* (1959); *Ishi no me* (1960); *Mukankei na shi* (1964); *Tanin no kao* (1964; *The Face of Another*, 1966); *Moetsukita chizu* (1967; *The Ruined Map*, 1969); *Bō ni natta otoko* (1969; *The Man Who Turned into a Stick*, 1975); *A. K.-shū* (1970; *A. K. gikyoku zenshū* (1970); *A. K. zen-sakuhin* (15 vols., 1972–1973); *Warau tsuki* (1978); *Kangaru noto* (1991; *Kangaroo Notebook*, 1996). FURTHER WORKS IN ENGLISH: *Four Stories by K. A.* (1973); *Beyond the Curve* (1991); *Three Plays* (1993)

BIBLIOGRAPHY: Ōta, S., and Fukuda, R., eds., *Studies on Japanese Culture*, 1 (1974): 401–5, 477–82; Kimball, A., *Crisis in Identity and Contemporary Japanese Novels* (1973): 115–39; Hardin, N. S., "An Interview with A. K.," *ConL*, 15 (1974): 438–56; Levy, A., "The Box Man Cometh," *NYTMag*, 17 Nov. 1974: 36ff.; Beasley, W. G., ed., *Modern Japan* (1975): 166–84; Tsuruta, K., and Swann, T. E., eds., *Approaches to the Modern Japanese Novel* (1976): 1–18; Rimer, J. T., *Modern Japanese Fiction and Its Traditions* (1978): 261–70; Yamanouchi, H., *The Search for Authenticity in Modern Japanese Literature* (1978): 153–74; Shields, N. K., *Fake Fish: The Theater of K. A.* (1996)

—LEON M. ZOLBROD

ABELL, Kjeld

Danish dramatist, b. 25 Aug. 1901, Ribe; d. 5 March 1961, Copenhagen

After taking a degree in political science at the University of Copenhagen in 1927, A. decided against a civil-service career and chose instead to follow his interest in the theater. Apart from a brief interval as an assistant to George Balanchine during the latter's guest stay at the Royal Theater in Copenhagen in 1930–31, A. worked as a stage and costume designer in London and Paris from 1927 to 1932. Between 1941 and 1949 he was manager of the Tivoli Gardens, the complex of theaters and restaurants in Copenhagen.

A.'s familiarity with dramatists such as STRINDBERG, GIRAUDOUX, and BRECHT and with directors such as Max Reinhardt (1873–1943), and his own experiences with theaters in other countries aided him in his efforts to change and revitalize the Danish stage and to break through the narrow confines of the naturalist tradition. Like Brecht, he wished to activate the audience politically and socially, and his point of view was decidedly Marxist. In his first comedies A. made use of all available theatrical devices, his own stage designs, dance, popular tunes, and impressionistically suggestive scenery and masks. He immediately won recognition, and his so-called experimental drama, *Melodien, der blev væk* (1935; *The Melody That Got Lost*, 1939), scored a great success. The play satirizes the stifling world of the petit bourgeois who lacks "melody" in his life, that is, true human values which, however, are found in a child and in the working class. The satire on the bourgeois family is continued in *Eva aftjener sin barnepligt* (1936; Eva does her duty as a child), where conventional, middle-class upbringing is seen as destructive to free development and individuality.

With the approaching threat of Nazism A.'s message of liberty gained a wider dimension. In *Anna Sophie Hedvig* (1939; *Anna Sophie Hedvig*, 1944), A.'s finest play, the title character is an insignificant, provincial schoolteacher who has the courage to liberate the school from a dictatorial principal. The analogy becomes clear when in the final act she stands side by side with a republican volunteer who fought in the Spanish Civil War. The drama is a sharp assault on passivity in the face of threatening totalitarianism. The occupation years 1940–45 confirmed A.'s belief in the necessity of taking firm action against evil. This view is expressed in two plays, *Judith* (1940; Judith) and *Dronningen går igen* (1955; *The Queen on Tour*, 1955), which were written during the war years, and in *Silkeborg* (1946; Silkeborg), a drama about the Danish Resistance in which indifference and isolation come under attack.

Following World War II A. continued to struggle with the problems of responsibility and social participation. For A., the main problem was the danger of intellectual isolation and withdrawal from the human community, and his dramas now dealt with the conflict between the death instinct and the will to live. In *Den blå pekingeser* (1954; the blue pekinese) a woman, Tordis Eck, has withdrawn into herself but is released from her suicidal impulses through the realization that she is part of the human fellowship. The play seems somewhat abstract, utilizing a technique that does away with the dimensions of time and space. Even more abstruse is A.'s last drama, *Skriget* (1961; the cry), which is set among tame and wild birds in a church tower and analyzes the possibility of recapturing original innocence and freedom. Because of its complicated network of motifs, the play lacks true dramatic force.

A. is the major innovator in 20th-c. Danish drama. Through his rich imagination and originality he regenerated the traditional theater. His experimental technique was inspired by both the ballet and the cinema, but he believed that the stage also could provide audiences with a necessary blend of fantasy and reality. A.'s weakness as a dramatist is, however, his inclination toward contrived structure and artificial dialogue that tend to lessen the dramatic force of his plays. Yet all of his works confirm A.'s belief in life and in man's responsibility to man.

FURTHER WORKS: *Paraplyernes oprør* (1937); *Børge Munch-Petersen* (1943); *Dage på en sky* (1947; *Days on a Cloud*, 1964); *Ejendommen matr. nr. 267 østre kvarter* (1948); *Teaterstrejf i påskevejr* (1948); *Miss Plinckbys kabale* (1949); *Vetsera blomstrer ikke for enhver* (1950); *Fodnoter i støvet* (1951); *Andersen; eller, Hans livs eventyr* (1955); *De tre fra Minikoi* (1957; *Three from Minikoi*, 1960); *Kameliadamen* (1959); *Synskhedens gave* (1962); *Dyveke* (1967)

BIBLIOGRAPHY: Gustafson, A., Introduction to *Scandinavian Plays of the 20th Century*, series 2 (1944): 17–20; Bredsdorff, E., Introduction to *Contemporary Danish Plays* (1955): 10–12; Madsen, B. G., "Leading Motifs in the Dramas of K. A.," *SS*, 33 (1963): 127–36; Marker, F. J., *K. A.* (1976)

—MARIANNE FORSSBLAD

ABKHAZ LITERATURE

See North Caucasian Literatures

ABRAHAMS, Peter

South African novelist (writing in English), b. 19 March 1919, Johannesburg

A. began his education at the age of eleven, attending Diocesan Training College in Grace Dieu and St. Peter's Secondary School in Rosettenville before leaving South Africa in 1939, when he was only nineteen years old. Today he lives in Jamaica, where he works as a broadcaster.

Nonetheless, the racial and political problems of his troubled native land have continued to dominate his imagination. All but two of his eight novels are set entirely or in part in South Africa, and the exception, *This Island Now* (1966), deals with race and politics in a Caribbean island which, like South Africa, has a poor, oppressed Black majority and an affluent white minority. A. has also written a volume of short stories, *Dark Testament* (1942), and two autobiographical books, *Return to Goli* (1953) and *Tell Freedom* (1954), both of which focus on his experiences as a mulatto in South Africa.

Influenced by Marxist ideas, A.'s early novels tend to be concerned more with race and economics than with politics. *Song of the City* (1945) and *Mine Boy* (1946) tell of the effects of urbanization and industrialization on the lives of young Black workers who move from the country to the city. *Song of the City* takes place at the time of World War II, *Mine Boy* against the backdrop of booming gold mines in Johannesburg. In both novels non-whites are mistreated and oppressed by whites.

In *The Path of Thunder* (1948) A. turned more fully to the theme of interracial love, exploring its impact on a young "Coloured" schoolteacher and an Afrikaner girl whose passionate affair ultimately ends in tragedy when the Afrikaner community discovers they are lovers.

Two years later A. moved in yet another direction, this time reconstructing the era of the Afrikaner migration, or "Great Trek," in *Wild Conquest* (1950), a historical novel in which he made an effort to be fair to all the major ethnic groups in South Africa—Bantu, Boer, and Briton.

After these early works A.'s fiction became more overtly political. *A Wreath for Udomo* (1956), published just before Ghana attained its independence, was an attempt to predict what might happen when independent Black African nations were confronted with the choice between the financial advantages of collaborating with the white regimes in southern Africa and the moral imperative of opposing them by actively supporting Black liberation movements. *A Night of Their Own* (1965) carried the revolutionary theme further by detailing the adventures of an African underground agent involved in smuggling funds to an Indian resistance organization in South Africa. And *This Island Now* told of racial tensions and internal power struggles in a small, Black-ruled Caribbean island-state.

In each successive novel A. has moved further away from a depiction of South African social realities to the construction of hypothetical situations which afforded greater creative liberties. Even *A Night of Their Own*, although set in South Africa, had elements of fantasy and wishful thinking in it. In his latest work, *The View from Cotaba* (1985), A. attempts a kaleidoscopic survey of 150 years of black history in the Caribbean, North America and tropical Africa, following the fortunes of successive generations in a single family who are exposed to archetypal as well as actual historical happenings in their quest for a better life. A.'s increased dependence on his imagination in these later novels may reflect how far out of touch he is with contemporary conditions in his native land.

A. has always written in a simple, direct prose style that wavers between superior reporting and maudlin romanticizing. He is at his best when transcribing newsworthy events having a basis in fact; his autobiographical and travel writings, for instance, are superb. But he has a regrettable tendency to sentimentalize personal relationships between men and women, especially if they are of different races, as they so often are in his novels. His accounts of miscegenation are nearly always marred by unconvincing melodrama.

FURTHER WORKS: *Jamaica: An Island Mosaic* (1957)

BIBLIOGRAPHY: Senghor, L. S., "P. A.; ou, le classique de la négritude" (1963), in *Liberté I: Négritude et humanisme* (1964): 425–30; Gérard, A., "P. A.," *Black Orpheus*, 2, 5–6 (1971): 15–19; Heywood, C., "The Novels of P. A.," in Heywood, C., ed., *Perspectives on African Literature* (1971): 157–72; Wade, M., *P. A.* (1972); Ogungbesan, K., *The Writings of P. A.* (1979); Muduka, C. T., "Limitation and Possibility: The Intellectual as Hero-Type in P. A.'s *A Wreath for Udomo*," *ZRL*, 24, 2 (1981); Koza, K. A., "Telling of Freedom: the Novels of P. A.," in Bock, H., and Wertheim, A., eds., *Essays on Contemporary Post-Colonial Fiction* (1986); Gray, S., "The Long Eye of History: Four Autobiographical Texts by P. A.," *Pretexts*, 2, 2 (1990): 99-115; Wade, J. P., "Song of the City and Mine Boy: The 'Marxist' Novels of P. A.," *RAL*, 21, 3 (1990): 89-101; Ensor, R., *The Novels of P. A. and the Rise of Nationalism in Africa* (1992)

—BERNTH LINDFORS

ABRAMOV, Fyodor

Russian novelist, short-story writer, and critic, b. 29 Feb. 1920, Verkola; d. 14 May 1983, Leningrad (now St. Petersburg)

A. is one of the most famous of the many Russian peasant writers who played an important role in post-Stalinist literature. Born in the Arkhangel region of northern Russia, A. studied at Leningrad University before volunteering for the front in World War II, where he is rumored to have worked for the Soviet counterintelligence unit SMERSH. After recovering from his war wounds, he joined the Communist Party in 1945, continued his studies, and received his graduate degree in 1951. In the early 1950s, he was a professor of Soviet literature in Leningrad and an influential critic; after the success of his first novel at the end of the 1950s, he devoted himself entirely to his writing.

A. began publishing literary criticism in 1949. His controverisal essay "Lyudi kolkhoznoy derevni v poslevoennoy proze" (1954; kolkhoz peasants in postwar prose) was one of several important attacks in the early Thaw years on Socialist Realist collective-farm novels. While undermining this type of hackneyed Soviet prose, A. praised the works of a number of writers, including Valentin Ovechkin (1904-1968) and Vladimir TENDRYAKOV. In many ways A.'s essay served as a blueprint for the evolution of collective-farm literature into "village prose," the largest and most coherent body of aesthetically and ideologically significant literature to be published in the U.S.S.R. in the decades between Stalin's death in 1953 and the advent of glasnost in the mid-1980s.

Unlike his fellow village-prose writers, who worked mostly in smaller forms or loosely constructed memoirs, A. began with the novel. He is best known for his four-volume series, set in the northern Russian village of Pekashino. *Bratya i syostry* (1958; brothers and sisters) began the chronicle of the Pryaslin family in the early years of World War II. While other Soviet writers focused on the battlefield itself or on the "hero cities" of the Soviet Union, A. was interested in how the war was experienced on the "second front" in the Russian village. *Dve zimi i tri leta* (1968; *Two Winters and Three Summers*, 1984) is the second and best-known part of this tetralogy, and covers the immediate postwar years when the task of rebuilding turns out to be as exhausting as the war effort. In his novels A. unites the reformist, nostalgic, and lyrical tendencies of village prose with elements of the epic and chronicle. He successfully captures the texture of Soviet life by reflecting the impact of major events on one small but ultimately representative area of the country. The third volume, *Puti-pereputya* (1973; at the crossroads), concentrates on the corrupt, unjust, and ineffective administration of collectivized agriculture, which so often undermined the hard work of the northern peasants. The final volume, *Dom* (1978; the house), takes the villagers into the early 1970s. While there is a tragic death in the Pryaslin family at the end of *Dom*, there is also a melancholy-luminous atmosphere that reassures the reader that not all traditional Russian peasant values have been lost. These novels were well received in the Soviet Union, and A. was awarded the State Prize for Literature in 1975.

While A. is primarily known for his Pekashino series, he wrote successfully in a number of other genres. The book-length essay *Vokrug da okolo* (1963; *The New Life*, 1963) contained his most frank and controversial appraisal of the kolkhoz system. He says here bluntly what had been introduced with greater subtlety in his fiction. This essay was seen in the West as an important example of Thaw literature, more critical but less artistic than Aleksandr SOLZHENITSYN's *Odin den v zhizni Ivana Denisovicha* (1962; *One Day in the Life of Ivan Denisovich*, 1963). A. was severely criticized at home for being too negative about the kolkhoz system, and he was able to publish very little between 1963 and 1968.

In his numerous short stories, A. chronicles the gradual fading of traditional rural ways in northern Russia. Sometimes he listens to the narratives of older villagers who recall the years before the Revolution and before collectivization; in other stories he focuses on the younger people who escape the countryside as soon as they can, and only return to boast about their wider knowledge of the modern world. A. also favored very short lyrical essays, which include such material as his own reminiscences about rural life, transcripts of conversations with villagers, and northern folklore. Some of these selections were published during his lifetime as *Trava-murava* (1982; the thick green grass), while further selections from his extensive notebooks were published posthumously as "Dom v Verkole" (1986; the house in Verkola). Among the many "delayed" works that appeared in the glasnost years, one of the most noteworthy is A.'s "Poezdka v proshloe" (1989; a journey into the past). This story, which A. worked on between 1963 and 1974, reveals some hard truths about the government's treatment of the kulaks during the process of collectivization in terms of one man's dramatic act of repentance.

A. was among the most talented and productive writers of Russian village prose, which makes him one of the most important literary figures of the post-Stalinist period. He championed the use of folk and regional speech in literature to reflect accurately the psychology of peasant characters and to preserve this rich linguistic heritage against the influence of an impoverished urban language. A.'s prose style stands in sharp contrast to the mostly homogeneous language of Socialist Realist novels. A. was in no way a dissident writer, but he always sought to write as honestly as possible about the contemporary peasant and life in the Russian countryside, and in this way to undo the damage that had been done to the rural theme in literature since 1917.

FURTHER WORKS: *Bezottsovshchina* (1962); *Derevyannye koni* (1972); *Poslednyaya okhota* (1973); *Izbrannoe* (1975); *Sobranie sochinenii* (1980); *Babiley* (1981); *Povesti i rasskazy* (1985); *Chemzhiven—kormimsya* (1986); *Pashnya zhivaya i mertyaya* (1987, with Antonin Chistyakov). FURTHER WORKS IN ENGLISH: *The Swans Flew By and Other Stories* (1986)

BIBLIOGRAPHY: Brown, D., *Soviet Russian Literature since Stalin* (1978): 233–37; Hosking, G., *Beyond Socialist Realism* (1980): 56–57; Brown, E. J., *Russian Literature since the Revolution* (rev. ed., 1982): 299–301; Marsh, R. J., *Soviet Fiction since Stalin* (1986): 173–76; Lowe, D. A., *Russian Writing since 1953* (1987): 85–86; Shneidman, N. N., *Soviet Literature in the 1980s* (1989): 97–101; Gillespie, D., "Ironies and Legacies: Village Prose and Glasnost," *FMLS*, 27, 1 (Jan. 1991): 70–84

—KATHLEEN PARTHÉ

ABŪ MĀDĪ, Īliyyā

Lebanese poet (writing in Arabic), b. 1889, Muhayditha; d. 1957, Brooklyn, N.Y., U.S.A.

A. M. is hailed by Arab critics as the foremost poet among *al-Mahjariyyūn*, a group of mainly Lebanese writers who emigrated to the U.S. and South America in the early 1900s and who are credited with innovations in the idiom, form, and content of Arabic poetry and prose. In 1900 A. M. left Lebanon for Egypt and lived there until 1911, the date of the publication of his first poetry collection, *Dīwān Tadhkār al-mādī* (remembering the past), which launched his career as a gifted young poet employing monometers and monorhymes in the classical traditional manner. That same year, he emigrated to the U.S., where he soon distinguished himself as poet and journalist and came into close contact with the members of the Society of the Pen, which he helped found in 1916. Three other collections, *Dīwān Īliyyā Abū Mādī* (1919; the divan of I. A. M.), *al-Jadāwil* (1927; streams), and *al-Khamā'il* (1940; gardens), appeared in New York. *Tibr wa Turāb* (1960; gold dust and earth) was published posthumously in Beirut, Lebanon, by his brother.

A. M. is a controversial poet. While *Dīwān Tadhkār al-mādī* brought him immediate recognition, critics of his poetry pointed to linguistic and stylistic weaknesses, which some blamed on his youth and lack of literary education. Others saw in those early stages little more than occasional poems in the overwhelming poetic tradition of the time. In the second collection, A. M. emerges as a strong imitator of his predecessors and contemporaries in the Arab world, but imitation, strong as it was in many of his poems, left him no room for poetic creation, and his personality remained submerged in a time and space not his own, in a poetic idiom foreign to his social reality. The reception of this collection by the members of the Society of the Pen was, to say the least, lukewarm, this in spite of the fact that the leader of *al-Mahjariyyūn*, Kahlil GIBRAN, wrote the short foreword to the volume.

A new stage in A. M.'s development as a poet coincides with his participation in the pioneering literary activities of his compatriots and the theoretical discussions they had on the nature of poetry, most prominently in A. M.'s literary journal *al-Sāmir* (1929-1957). Through their influence, especially in their own experimentation in the language of poetry, A. M. came to realize that only the inauguration of a new language can contribute to modern Arabic poetry.

The poems of *al-Jadāwil*, which earned him his distinction as a strong modern poet, were written between 1919 and 1927, the most important formative years of A. M.'s career. This was a new kind of poetry, contemplative, romantic, lyrical, and dramatic, a true revolution in both the content and the form of Arabic poetry. Some of the poems of this collection have become household items in the Arab world and have contributed to the romantic trend that ensued. The artificial abstract form of A. M.'s earlier collections gave way to a vital organic unity, a poetic distance that allowed the movements in the poems to grow without the poet's interference. Experimentation in meter and rhythmic variations characterize this collection, and the naive rationality of the poetry that preceded reverted here to a romanticism of dreams and visions, a poetry of color and music, unknown to the classical poetic tradition.

However, despite the enthusiastic praise of his friends and readers in the Americas and the Arab world, A. M. soon returned to his old imitative stage. His enthusiasm for the modern poetic manifesto of the Society of the Pen waned, perhaps because he was intensely aware of his larger public in the Arab world at that time, which often viewed the innovations of *al-Mahjariyyūn* with suspicion. Thus in *al-Khamā'il* and later on in *Tibr wa Turāb* A. M. exhibits an anxiety of influence that pulled him back and forth between his Arab heritage and his new Western sensibility.

In the development of modern Arabic poetry, A. M. remains one of the most important voices in the early decades of the 20th c. However, his innovations, strong as they were, lacked the philosophical conviction and the depth of Gibran, the most prominent member of the Society of the Pen.

BIBLIOGRAPHY: Badawi, M. M., *A Critical Introduction to Modern Arabic Poetry* (1975): 188–91; Jayyusi, S. K., *Trends and Movements in Modern Arabic Poetry* (1977), Vol. 1: 123–35, 326–28; Ostle, R. C., "I. A. M. and Arabic Poetry in the Inter-War Period," in Ostle, R. C., *Studies in Modern Arabic Literature* (1975): 34–45; Badawi, M. M., ed., *Modern Arabic Literature* (1992): 101-05

—ADNAN HAYDAR

ACCAD, Evelyne

Lebanese novelist and critic (writing in French), b. 6 Oct. 1943, Beirut

The daughter of a Swiss mother and an Egypto-Lebanese father, A. was reared in a strict Protestant household and attended French schools in the cosmopolitan Beirut of the 1950s and 1960s. She completed two years at the Beirut College for Women (now the Lebanese American University) before pursuing university studies in the U.S.A. obtained a B.A. in English literature from Anderson College (1967), an M.A. from Ball State University in French (1968), and a Ph.D. in comparative literature from Indiana (1973). She has been teaching at the University of Illinois, Champaign-Urbana since 1974, where she is professor of French, comparative literature, women's studies, African studies, and Middle East studies.

A. is the author of numerous scholarly works. These include *Veil of Shame: The Role of Women in the Contemporary Fiction of North Africa and the Arab World* (1978), which received the Delta Kappa Gamma Society International 1979 Educator's Award, and *Sexuality and War: Literary Masks of the Middle East* (1990), the French edition of which won the 1994 France-Lebanon Prize. This last work is a brilliant feminist analysis of Lebanese fiction that places the question of sexuality at the heart of war. A. contends that no real transformation of social relations will take place unless a sexual revolution is incorporated into a political one.

A.'s literary texts must be viewed in relation to those of other Arab women writers from the Maghreb (North Africa) and the Mashreq (Middle East) writing on war. Like Assia DJEBAR, Andrée CHEDID, Etel Adnan (dates n.a.), and Hanan AL-SHAYKH, A. demonstrates that sexuality and war are fundamentally related. Sexuality, like war, is used to conquer and possess, subordinate and control. This is demonstrated by looking at the violence of war in relation to how Arab women are treated in so-called times of peace. As the distinctions between war and peace, public and private, political and sexual become blurred, a new form of discourse on war becomes possible. It is one that is no longer fascinated by the epic arena of war, but rather preoccupied with "the body in pain."

The mutilated body of war and the oppressed, female body become one.

This image is central to A.'s first novel, *L'excisée* (1982; *The Excised*, 1989). The protagonist has no name. She is simply "elle," (she is French) or E., Eve (woman everywhere) or the excised woman. The eradication of female pleasure is intimately bound up with a Lebanon disfigured by the violence of war. The conflicting political and religious forces that dismember Beirut come together to oppress and mutilate women, be they Christian or Muslim.

For A., war is a magnifying glass that allows us to see certain things we would not have seen otherwise. A civil war brings home the violence that lies within one's nation, one's household, one's self. A. believes that resolution to war lies deep within ourselves.

A.'s second novel, *Coquelicot du massacre* (1988; *Poppy of the Massacre*), is accompanied by a cassette of songs whose music and lyrics she herself composed. Music and words are not only a means of overcoming grief; in this novel, a young woman's singing, as she crosses war-torn Beirut, momentarily halts the gunfire. It is a woman's poetic response to life in the war zone. By questioning the rhetoric of war as it pertains to women, A. seeks to demonstrate, both through her creative and scholarly writing, that relationships need not be oppressive and destructive, any more than the language that legitimates them.

In *Blessure des mots: Journal de Tunisie* (1993; *Wounding Words: A Woman's Journal in Tunisia*, 1996) A. deals with the problems of feminism and cultural identity in one of the few Arab countries where women's rights have received public recognition. In this poetic, autobiographical novel, the voice of a Lebanese woman living in Tunisia for a year unites with countless others for whom feminism is as much a personal as a political response to problems encountered in their daily lives. The collective voice evoked in this novel is one that builds on poetry and song, as a means of evoking an alternative vision that moves beyond linguistic and political boundaries. Freedom only comes from crossing over the demarcation line, be it political or writerly. That is why it is so important for A. to move beyond such distinctions as prose and poetry, theory and history, the public and the private, politics and sexuality.

A. is clearly a cosmopolitan and interdisciplinary writer, scholar, and teacher, for whom divisions, dichotomies, and compartmentalizations—be they geographic, ethnic, disciplinary, or political—merely hinder the flourishing and freedom of the individual. The act of crossing over the demarcation line is central to her work, reflecting at once her rooting—despite her exile—in the Lebanese civil war, and her passionate celebration of love and life amidst the debris and hatred of war. This ability to write differently on war and to move beyond political and generic distinctions is undoubtedly related to her relation to language and culture. Like the Egyptian writer Andrée Chedid, whom A. greatly admires, A. views her hybridity and cosmopolitanism as the departure point for enrichment, openness, and tolerance. These values are what the Lebanon of her childhood represented.

FURTHER WORKS: *Contemporary Arab Women Writers and Poets* (1986, with Rose Ghurayyeb)

BIBLIOGRAPHY: Cooke, M., *War's Other Voices: Women Writers on the Lebanese Civil War* (1988); Mudimbe-Boyi, E., "Enfermer et contrôler: lieu social et espace textuel dans *L'excisée* d'E. A.," *Francofonia*, 23 (1992): 3-19; Marx-Scouras, D., "Muffled Screams/Stifled Voices," *YFS*, 82, 1 (1993): 172-82; Hottell, R., "A Poetics of Pain: E. A.'s Critical and Fictional World," *WLT*, 71 (Summer 1997): 511-16

—DANIELLE MARX-SCOURAS

ACHDIAT Karta Mihardja

Indonesian novelist, short-story writer, and dramatist, b. 6 March 1911, near Garut, Java

The marked diversity of A.'s writing reflects his social and educational background. Brought up in a rural, strongly conservative Islamic environment, he studied a variant of the Nakshbandi stream of Islamic mysticism. His formal schooling led him through a Dutch-language high school to the study of Western philosophy at the University of Indonesia. He became attracted to socialism, traveled widely overseas, and in later life taught Indonesian literature for ten years (1961–71) at the Australian National University.

A.'s reputation was immediately and firmly established with the publication of his first novel, *Atheis* (1949; *Atheis*, 1972). It deals with the failure of the mystically tinged Islam of rural Java to react resiliently to the impact of values espoused by Indonesia's new, Western-influenced urban intelligentsia. The pious and naïve young protagonist of the novel finds his Islamic faith a painfully inadequate foil to the materialism, atheism, socialism, and license of his acquaintances in the city of Bandung.

The same theme is taken up, though less poignantly, in the short story "Sensasi di puncak nyiur" (1956; "Sensations at the Top of a Coconut Tree," 1961), which appeared in the collection of short stories and short plays *Keretakan dan ketegangan* (1956; fissures and tensions). Exasperated by poverty and domestic tensions, a destitute slum dweller seeks a solution to his troubles in the traditional religious practice of meditation and ascetic withdrawal from society. With farcical and sometimes sardonic humor, A. points to the ineffectualness and incongruity of this practice in the context of contemporary society.

Keretakan dan ketegangan offers critical, sharply drawn, and often witty portraits of Indonesia's politicians and nouveaux riches. Especially memorable is the portrait in "Kisah Martini" (Martini's story) of an immature and irresponsible politician who is better able to talk to animals than to people and who cultivates women for sexual consumption in the same way he fattens pets for merciless consumption at his table.

In several short stories A. shows how the innocent victims of violence and immorality have to live with the traumatic effects of what they have experienced long after the immediate cause of their suffering has disappeared. The long-term, polluting effect of immorality is depicted as a physical presence in the lives of its victims, a kind of stain ultimately demanding its own, often violent, excision. In the vivid and grimly violent story "Belitan nasib" (a twist of fate) a villager murders the man who rapes his wife, but only later exorcises the evil effect of the rape from within himself by murdering his wife and newborn baby.

In the collection of short stories and vignettes *Kesan dan kenangan* (1961; impressions and images) A. draws upon his experiences overseas to present a patchwork view of Western society seen through Indonesian eyes. This is also a prominent ingredient in his second novel, *Debu cinta bertebaran* (1973; the scattered dust of love), which portrays the lives of expatriate

Indonesians in the Australian city of Sydney on the eve of Indonesia's 1965 political upheaval.

A. has not been a prolific writer, yet the diversity of his small output makes it difficult to categorize his work. His writing is colored by fatalism and pessimism, but relieved by humor and a tentative faith in the power of love. His passionately felt novel *Atheis* deservedly stands as a major landmark in modern Indonesian literature, admired for its innovative structure, vivid characterization, and occasionally stiff but generally brilliant style. After *Keretakan dan ketegangan*, however, his work seems to suffer from a tendency to be more concerned with the perceived exotica of the West and with the unexpected twist to a story than with a satisfying exploration of themes. This later superficiality is exemplified in the revisions made in some short stories, including "Kisah Martini" and "Belitan nasib," which unquestionably diminish their power.

FURTHER WORKS: *Bentrokan dalam asmara* (1952); *Belitan nasib* (1975); *Pak Dullah in extremis* (1977); *Pembunuh dan anjing hitam* (1977); *Sensasi di puncak nyiur* (1978)

BIBLIOGRAPHY: Teeuw, A., *Modern Indonesian Literature* (1967): passim; Aveling, H., "Religion and Blasphemy in Modern Indonesian Literature," *Twentieth Century*, March 1970: 217–24; Johns, A. H., *Cultural Options and the Role of Tradition* (1979): 1–18, 30–64

—GEORGE QUINN

Chinua Achebe

ACHEBE, Chinua

Nigerian novelist, poet, and short-story writer (writing in English), b. 15 Nov. 1930, Ogidi

In 1953 A. became one of the first graduates of University College, Ibadan. He began working for the Nigerian Broadcasting Service the following year, and in 1961 became Director of External Broadcasting for Nigeria, a position he held until 1966, when he returned to his home in eastern Nigeria. During the Nigerian-Biafran conflict (1967–1970), A. worked for the Biafran government and afterward became a research fellow in the Institute of African Studies at the University of Nigeria in Nsukka. In 1972 he was appointed visiting professor in the English department at the University of Massachusetts at Amherst. Four years later he returned to the University of Nigeria in Nsukka, but he took early retirement in 1981 and later resumed teaching in the United States. Since 1990, he has occupied the Charles P. Stevenson Chair in Literature at Bard College.

Working within the conventions of the realistic novel, A. has succeeded in creating a very vivid picture of African society in the process of change. His first novel, *Things Fall Apart* (1958), deals with the human consequences of the collision of African and European cultures in Nigeria, a theme that has preoccupied Nigerian writers ever since. The story is set in a traditional Igbo community at the turn of the Century, when the first European missionaries and administrative officials were beginning to penetrate Inland. One of the strongest men in the community tries to arouse his people to oppose the white man, but some of them have been won over to the white man's faith, and the clan is no longer united. When his people refuse to follow the protagonist, he commits suicide in anger and despair; his death symbolizes the passing of the old order.

In his second novel, *No Longer at Ease* (1960), A. switched to a modern urban scene in order to focus on the life of an educated Nigerian in the late 1950s. The protagonist, an idealistic young man who returns from university education abroad with the ambition of reforming the Nigerian civil service, eventually succumbs to the temptation of accepting bribes. He also alienates his people by falling in love with a young woman they find unacceptable. Like his grandfather, the hero of *Things Fall Apart*, this headstrong young man can be seen as a victim of the conflict of cultures in Africa; westernization has made him confused, ill at ease in his own society, and vulnerable to corruption.

In *Arrow of God* (1964), A. moved back to an earlier era to tell the story of an old Igbo priest who tries to cope with the changing times by maintaining a flexible stance. He compromises with the new religion by sending his son to a mission school and cooperates with the British administration by testifying against his own people in a land dispute. But these actions subvert his authority in the community, and his people gradually turn away from him and his god and start worshiping at a mission church. Again Africa loses out to Europe; a traditional way of life is destroyed forever.

A Man of the People (1966) brought the historical record up to the early postcolonial era. The novel focuses on a corrupt politician who lives high for a while but finally is brought low by a military coup. The chaos in modern African society wrought by such politicians is seen to derive ultimately from an absence of stable values. The unprincipled politician is a product of the moral confusion created by the collision of African and European cultures. Even the relatively upright schoolteacher who functions as a foil to the corrupt politician in the novel cannot be said to be a model of virtue; he, too, has been twisted by the conflicting forces that swirl about him. Mere chaos is loosed upon the world.

In the fifth novel, *Anthills of the Savannah*, published twenty-one years later, A. tackles the period of military misrule in Africa that followed the collapse of democratically elected regimes. The new leader, a Sandhurst graduate who clearly relishes being called "Your Excellency," wishes to be proclaimed President-for-Life. When his ambitions are frustrated, he feels insecure and angry and seeks to punish those he perceives as his foes, including two of his closest school buddies. In the end all three men are killed, and their friends, associates and lovers are left to pick up the pieces. There is a suggestion that out of this new found unity among the long-suffering masses in Africa something positive will emerge, but one of the central questions raised in the course of the narrative— "What must a people do to appease an embittered history?"— remains unanswered. The future does not look particularly bright.

A. has articulated his views on writing in a number of cogent literary essays, recently collected in *Morning Yet on Creation Day: Essays* (1975). He believes that the African writer should be a teacher dedicated to explaining to his people how and why their world came to be the way it is today. To offset the psychological damage done during the colonial era, the writers of the 1950s and 1960s had a duty to create a dignified image of the African past, so that Africans could learn to take pride in their own culture and traditions. By the mid-1960s, however, Africa had changed so much that it became necessary for writers to expose injustice and corruption in their own societies. Any serious writer had to be politically committed, but in the transition from colonialism to independence the target of his protest had been transferred from Europe to Africa itself.

A.'s own commitment is evident not only in his novels but also in the shorter fiction and poetry he has published since the Nigerian-Biafran conflict. *Beware, Soul Brother and Other Poems* (1971) and *Christmas in Biafra and Other Poems* (1973) contain poignant and bitter reflections on wartime experiences. Several short stories in *Girls at War and Other Stories* (1972) also deal with the ironies and tragedies of war, as do the pieces he collected from other writers and edited in *The Insider: Stories of War and Peace from Nigeria* (1971). A.'s *How the Leopard Got His Claws* (1972), ostensibly a folktale written for children, has an allegorical dimension that made it possible for A. to comment both on the Biafran tragedy and on the international power struggles that lead to such situations in the Third World. As in his earlier works, A. constantly seeks to transcend the local and particular and point to matters of more universal significance.

A. has also been firmly committed to educating the young. He believes that the novelist in Africa today should deliberately attempt to regenerate his society by directing his message to impressionable young people, especially school children. A.'s novels have been widely read in high schools throughout Africa, and he has written several books expressly for use in African grade schools: *Chike and the River* (1966), *The Flute* (1977), and *The Drum* (1977). The emphasis that he places on sound moral education of the young is reflected in the high seriousness that permeates all his literary work.

A.'s writings not only chronicle a century of Nigerian history but also reflect the dominant African intellectual concerns of the postcolonial era. For this reason they are likely to be of enduring value. A.'s works seem destined to become classics of African literature.

FURTHER WORKS: *The Sacrificial Egg and Other Stories* (1962)

BIBLIOGRAPHY: Ravenscroft, A., *C. A.* (1969; rev. ed. 1977); Killiam, G. D., *The Novels of C. A.* (1969; rev. ed. entitled *The Writings of C. A.*, 1977); Carroll, D., *C. A.* (1970; 2nd ed., *C. A.: Novelist, Poet, Critic*, 1990); Melone, T., *C. A. et la tragédie de l'histoire* (1973); Böttcher, K. H., *Tradition und Modernität bei Amos Tutuola and C. A.: Grundzüge der westafrikanischen Erzählliteratur englischer Sprache* (1974); Peters, J. A., *A Dance of the Masks: Senghor, A., Soyinka* (1978): 93-158; Githae-Mugo, M., *Visions of Africa: The Fiction of C. A., Margaret Laurence, Elspeth Huxley and Ngugi wa Thiong'o* (1978), passim; Innes, C. L., and Lindfors, B., eds., *Critical Perspectives on C. A.* (1978); Wren, R. W., *A.'s World: The Historical and Cultural Context of the Novels of C. A.* (1980); Njoku, B. C., *The Four Novels of C. A.: A Critical Study* (1984); Coussy, D., *L'oeuvre de C. A.* (1985); Okoye, E. M., *The Traditional Religion and its Encounter with Christianity in A.'s Novels* (1987); Uwechie, C., et al., comps., *C. A.: A Bio-Bibliography* (1990); Ugah, A., *In the Beginning: C. A. at Work* (1990); Innes, C. L., *C. A.* (1990); Yankson, K. E., *C. A.'s Novels: A Sociolinguistic Perspective* (1990)

—BERNTH LINDFORS

ACHTERBERG, Gerrit

Dutch poet, b. 20 May 1905, Langbroek; d. 17 Jan. 1962, Oud-Leusden

By heritage an Evangelical Dissenter within the State Church in Langbroek, by training a teacher in The Hague and for a short while a bureaucrat in Utrecht, A. committed murder in 1937 and was sentenced to a psychiatric hospital. Released in 1943, he married, settled in Leusden, and intensified his earlier struggle to write.

A.'s experimental stance in theme, imagery, and religious psychology, incongruously combined with his traditional stance in formal metrics, compels attention. His chief theme was contact with the beloved dead. On 15 December 1937, a bachelor living in Utrecht, A. fired a revolver at his landlady and at her sixteen-year-old daughter. The daughter escaped; the landlady was killed. But even long before 1937 the union with an imaginary dead lover had been one of several themes in his poetry; after 1937 it became his only theme.

A.'s pronoun for the dead lover was *gij* ("you," an archaic pronoun reserved for the Deity in the piety of A.'s youth. In poem after poem forgiveness by God is necessary if the persona is to be forgiven by the murdered lover; forgiveness by the lover is necessary if the persona is to be forgiven by God. The effect is that God and the dead lover mingle, and the persona attempts to mingle with both of them. The imagery in these poems is borrowed from the physical sciences (osmosis, microbes), from technology (camera, telephone), and from psychology (autism, Rorschach tests, hallucinations).

A.'s religious sensibility was as typically modern as his imagery. Inheriting the dogmatic structures of Calvinism, A. transformed them into an idiosyncratic, existentialist, psychological mode of mysticism. A concept like "God's word," which would normally refer solely to a rigid interpretation of the Bible, became for Achterberg a dynamic three-way interaction involving his own poetic voice and his mystical awareness of the mingling of God with the dead lover as well as a persistent echo of the words of the Scriptures. The poems "Reiziger 'doet' Golgotha" (1939; "A Tourist Does Golgotha," 1972) and "En Jezus schreef in 't zand" (1947; "And Jesus Wrote in the Sand," 1972) are examples of this religious complexity.

A. chose more restricted forms than did his contemporaries. His favorite form was the sonnet. As A. took more control of his own life his poetry gradually turned more severely formal. *De ballade van de gasfitter* (1953; "The Ballad of the Gasfitter," 1972) has attracted more critical attention than any of A.'s writings. The whole work is a kind of macrocosmic sonnet: the first eight sonnets make up the "octave," with distinct elements handled in each quatrain; the last six sonnets make up a "sestet," the last two sonnets making a "couplet" with a shift in point of view. A gasfitter's job is to close holes, and a closer of holes is called a *dichter*, a pun on the Netherlandic word for "poet," as well as a pun on the word for "closer to." As the confused gasfitter walks down the street, he sees his lover in every house he passes, and he is tempted to stop to repair gas lines, whether the gas lines need it or not. By this device A. objectifies his quest for union with the dead woman and his own complicated task as poet in trying to fill the holes in his life, ironically suggesting that the idealized dead woman is no different from any woman in any house, and satirically suggesting that bourgeois life behind the facade of row houses is itself a state of death. The persona is a tentative, guilty, and self-mocking Orpheus, attempting against overwhelming odds to get closer to his Eurydice. Or, since the quest for the dead one is also the quest for God, the persona is a contemporary Dante, aspiring to union with Beatrice and God. "God is the hole" (Sonnet IX) that needs filling.

Spel van de wilde jacht (1957; play of the wild chase), a sequence of fifty-one poems, is undoubtedly A.'s masterwork. The narrative chase involves letting the deer escape, but the real chase is a verbal one, to catch life's complexity in words. The definitive interpretation has not yet appeared.

A. served Netherlandic poetry much as T. S. ELIOT served English poetry: both introduced psychological themes, scientific-industrial imagery, and a nondogmatic, existential religious awareness. A.'s penchant for traditional form is like W. H. AUDEN's. Every current school of Netherlandic poetry acknowledges its debt to A.

FURTHER WORKS: *De zangen van twee twintigers* (1925); *Afvaart* (1931); *Dead End* (1940); *Osmose* (1941); *Thebe* (1941); *Huis* (1943); *Sintels* (1944); *Morendo* (1944); *Limiet* (1945); *Eurydice* (1946); *Stof* (1946); *Radar* (1946); *Sphinx* (1946); *Energie* (1946); *Existentie* (1946); *Cryptogramen* (3 vols., 1946, 1951, 1961); *Doornroosje* (1947); *Hoontje* (1949); *Mascotte* (1950); *Voorbij de laatste stad* (1955); *Vergeetboek* (1961); *Verzamelde gedichten* (1963). FURTHER WORKS IN ENGLISH: *A Tourist Does Golgotha, and Other Poems* (1972); *Hidden Weddings: Selected Poems* (1987); *Selected Poems of G. A.: But This Land Has No End* (1989)

BIBLIOGRAPHY: Brockway, J., "The Trumpets of the Word: A Translator's Note on the Poetry of G. A.," *Odyssey*, 1 (1961):

240–45; Wiersma, S. M., "G. A., Gasfitter," *CSR*, 1 (1971): 306–17; Coetzee, J. M., "A.'s *Ballade van de gasfitter:* The Mystery of I and You," *PMLA*, 92 (1977): 285–96

—STANLEY M. WIERSMA

ADAMOV, Arthur

French dramatist and translator, b. 23 Aug. 1908, Kislovodsk, Russia; d. 15 March 1970, Paris

Although Russian by birth, A. received a French education, spent his youth in Germany, France, and Switzerland, and came to live in Paris at the age of sixteen. In addition to his career as a playwright, he translated many works into French from Russian and German, including some by CHEKHOV, GORKY, RILKE, and JUNG.

Somewhat influenced by Jung, A. wrote *L'aveu* (1943; the confession), an autobiographical essay with Dostoevskyan depths of neurotic self-revelation, in which he bares an all-encompassing, existentialist anguish.

While associating with Parisian SURREALIST poets, he was indelibly impressed by Antonin ARTAUD and by Artaud's aesthetic bases for a "theater of cruelty," which influenced A.'s own drama. His plays can be viewed as composing two cycles: (1) nightmarish, disjointed metaphysical visions of life's absurdity (from 1947 to 1955), and (2) sociopolitical "epic dramas" (from 1956 until the end of his life). *La parodie* (1950; parody), his first play, parodies life itself as a meaningless, inescapable whirl of pseudoactivity. Desensitized human relationships, incommunicability, and modern man's assault by invading objects—motifs A. shares with the midcentury's leading playwrights of the THEATER OF THE ABSURD, BECKETT and IONESCO—underline *L'invasion* (1950; *The Invasion*, 1968) and *La grande et la petite manœuvre* (1953; the large and the small maneuver). His almost incoherent dramatic forms, and his style—at first oblique, bare, and mysterious—become more comprehensible in *Le professeur Taranne* (1953; *Professor Taranne*, 1960) and *Tous contre tous* (1953; all against all). In these two plays we see the individual's annihilation by the ruthless mechanisms of society, by the government bureaucracy, and by esoteric probings of the ego.

In *Le ping-pong* (1955; *Ping Pong*, 1959) A. uses a pinball machine to symbolize organizational inhumanity and senselessness. It is a work of transition, foreshadowing A.'s "epic theater" influenced by BRECHT: *Paolo Paoli* (1957; *Paolo Paoli: The Years of the Butterfly*, 1959), *Les âmes mortes* (1960; dead souls), adapted from Gogol, and *Le printemps 71* (1961; Spring '71). Proletarian politics suffuse and too often deform these historical plays. One of the many paradoxes of A.'s life was that he was born of wealthy parents but adhered to communism. In *Paolo Paoli*, the only one of this trio of epic-theater pieces likely to survive, anticapitalism is a major motif. In its twelve scenes, commerce in butterflies, symbolic of beauty sacrificed for material gain, is shown as exploitative. *Le printemps 71* is an exhaustively researched play celebrating the heroes of the Paris Commune of 1871.

Political stridency marks A.'s dramaturgy after 1961. *La politique des restes* (1966; the politics of garbage) deals with the trial of a white South African who has killed a black man, and explores the nature of racism (A.'s actual target was the U.S.A.). He diversified his themes in his late plays: *Sainte Europe* (1966; holy Europe) is a grandiose vision of European unity. *Off Limits* (1969; original title in English), based on a trip to New York, is a nightmarish, perverse paean to an America haunted by drugs and Vietnam. Also in the realm of bad dreams is *Si l'été revenait* (1970; if summer returned).

A.'s terrifying dramas, especially those of his pre-1956 metaphysical mode, are significant in having paved the way for avantgarde Theater of the Absurd themes and techniques, which radically transformed European and American concepts of theater during the 1950s. In his later years, A. seems to have been a considerable talent gone astray.

FURTHER WORKS: *Poèmes* (1933); *Le désordre* (1951); *Le sens de la marche* (1955); *Comme nous avons été* (1953); *Théâtre I* (1953); *Les retrouvailles* (1955); *Théâtre II* (1955); *Auguste Strindberg* (1955); *Le pélican* (1956); *Intimité* (1958); *Je ne suis pas français* (1958); *La complainte du ridicule* (1958); *Les apolitiques* (1958); *Les petits bourgeois* (1959); *Anthologie de la Commune* (1959); *Rendezvous* (1961); *En fiacre* (1963); *Ici et maintenant* (1964); *Théâtre III* (1966); *M. le modéré* (1968); *Théqtre IV* (1968); *L'homme et l'enfant* (1968); *Je . . . ils* (1969)

BIBLIOGRAPHY: Lynes, C., "A. or *'le sens littéral'* in the Theatre," *YFS*, No. 14 (1954–1955): 48–56; Gelbard, P., "An Interview with A.," *Drama Survey*, 3 (1963): 253–56; Esslin, M., "A. A.: The Curable and the Incurable," *The Theatre of the Absurd*, rev. ed. (1969): 66–99; Gaudy, R., *A. A.* (1971); Mélèse, P., *A. A.* (1973); Reilly, J. H., *A. A.* (1974); McCann, J. J., *The Theater of A. A.* (1975); Jacquart, E., "Un célèbre inconnu: A. A.," *FR*, 51 (1977): 45–52

—KENNETH S. WHITE

ADAMS, Henry

American historian, biographer, essayist, and novelist, b. 16 Feb. 1838, Boston, Mass.; d. 27 March 1918, Washington, D.C.

As the direct descendant of two American presidents, and as the son of a congressman and diplomat, A. was acutely aware that his family had helped to shape American history. Yet he was content to remain, in his own words, a "stable-companion to statesmen," for his interests were more conceptual and literary than those of his ancestors. After graduation from Harvard College and further study at the University of Berlin, he went on to teach history at Harvard from 1870 to 1877 and to edit *The North American Review* during approximately the same period. Thereafter alternating his residence between Paris and Washington, he settled down to a varied career in letters, writing the biographies *Albert Gallatin* (1879) and *John Randolph* (1882), the anonymous novel *Democracy* (1880), the pseudonymous novel *Esther* (1884), the nine volumes of his much-admired *History of the United States during the Administration of Jefferson and Madison* (1884–91), the influential *A Letter to American Teachers of History* (1910), and, his major works, *Mont-Saint-Michel and Chartres* (1913, privately printed

1904) and *The Education of Henry Adams* (1918, privately printed 1907).

On its surface, *Mont-Saint-Michel and Chartres* is a graceful, guidebook appreciation of the art, literature, and cathedral architecture of medieval France. As such, it is flawed only by some factual inaccuracies and by an exaggerated picture of medieval unity; A. himself thought it his masterpiece. Yet the *Chartres* is more than a tourist's guidebook. Referred to in *The Education of Henry Adams* as "A Study in Medieval Unity," it is also a historian's awed meditation on the link between medieval man's prelogical belief in cosmic unity and his ability, in defiance of cosmic reality, to turn his belief into perceived fact. The book's central symbol for this medieval *Zeitgeist* is the Virgin Mary, a figure of love triumphing over logic in her medieval depictions, and reconciling political antagonisms and even irregularities of architecture with her overarching love.

The autobiographical *The Education of Henry Adams*, subtitled "A Study in Twentieth-Century Multiplicity," measures the distance man has come from the medieval synthesis. The charm of the book for many readers lies in its witty survey of the author's world and in its genial embrace of a dark mood, but A.'s more serious purpose was to present his intellectual growth as a symptom of 20th-c. discontinuity. Writing in the third person, and taking his cue from Carlyle's *Sartor Resartus*, A. describes his education as a series of discarded garments, all of its lessons patched or misfitting, and he offers the inhuman dynamo, celebrated in turn-of-the-century expositions, as the symbol and apotheosis of contemporary energy, balancing the symbol of the Virgin in the *Chartres*. The *Chartres* and *The Education of Henry Adams* are distinct works, assuredly, but the relationships between them are intricate and artful; indeed, their juxtaposition creates an effect akin to the sprawling and cunningly arbitrary works of Melville and Whitman, and with much the same effect of an experience too massive for telling.

Modern scholars are quick to point out that the experience of Western man is altogether too massive to be accommodated by A.'s dialectic of medieval instinct and modern logic, much less by his analogies to mechanical physics, but A.'s books remain important for the questions he asked about the relationship between history, art, and technology, and for the human relevance he required of his answers. His major works are preeminent of their kind in American letters, and, in their especial blend of intellectual vigor and romantic inwardness, of high theory and intimate detail, they have a kind of appeal unmatched in the national literature.

FURTHER WORKS: *Chapters of Erie and Other Essays* (1871, with C. F. Adams); *Historical Essays* (1891); *Memoirs of Marau Taaroa, Last Queen of Tahiti* (1893, rev. ed., 1901); *The Life of George Cabot Lodge* (1911)

BIBLIOGRAPHY: Samuels, E., *H. A.* (3 vols., 1948–1964); Hochfield, G., *H. A.: An Introduction and Interpretation* (1962); Spiller, R. E., "H. A.," in *Literary History of the United States* (1963): 1080–1103; Conder, J. J., *A Formula of His Own* (1970); Harbert, E. N., *The Force So Much Closer Home: H. A. and the Adams Family* (1977); Chalfant, E., *Both Sides of the Ocean: A Biography of H. A., His First Life 1838-1862* (1982); Chalfant, E., *Better in Darkness: A Biography of H. A., His Second Life 1862-1881* (1994)

—ROBERT F. KIERNAN

ADIVAR, Halide Edib

(often signed as Halide Edib) Turkish novelist (writing in Turkish and English), b. 1884, Istanbul; d. 9 Jan. 1964, Istanbul

A.'s father, a well-to-do high official of the Ottoman government, afforded her excellent schooling and private tutoring. She graduated from the American College for Girls in Istanbul, where she acquired an extensive knowledge of Anglo-American literature, which influenced her fiction. This explains the fact that some of her books were first written in English and published in Turkish later.

After many years of teaching, and following several trips to Egypt, Syria, and England, A. was appointed to the faculty at the University of Istanbul, where she taught European literature (1918–19). At the outset of the Turkish war of independence (1919–22) she and her husband, Dr. Adnan Adıvar, joined Mustafa Kemal Atatürk (1881–1938) in the nationalist cause. She chronicled the episodes of the war and its aftermath in *Memoirs* (1926) and *The Turkish Ordeal* (1928; *Türk'ün ateşle imtihanı*, 1962), both written in English. In 1923, the Adivars were forced to leave Turkey because of their disagreements with Atatürk, who was by then president of the new republic. In 1939 they were allowed to return, and in 1940 A. became a professor of English literature at the University of Istanbul. After her retirement in 1950, she served in the Turkish legislature until 1954.

In addition to the many romantic love stories she wrote, A. also distinguished herself in the patriotic and the sociopsychological novel. The Turkish war of independence inspired her to extol heroism and sacrifice for the national cause and for the emergence of a new state out of the ruins of the Ottoman empire. Her *Yeni Turan* (1912; the new Turan) became one of the most stimulating documents of Turkish nationalism.

Raik'in annesi (1910; Raik's mother) was a pioneering effort to expose the injustices perpetrated against women by men, and the male-dominated social system. With this poignant novel and many articles, A. advocated women's emancipation. Although highly praised for its incisive psychological portrayals of the female characters, this novel was criticized for its convoluted style.

A.'s most successful novel in Turkey and abroad remains *The Clown and His Daughter*, written in English and published in London. It is a masterful study of an Istanbul neighborhood—its inhabitants and its everyday life—during the reign of Sultan Abdul-Hamid II (1842–1918), at the same time offering glimpses of the life lived by a more wealthy group. *The Clown and His Daughter* is notable for its mastery of narration and dialogue, its evocation of life in Istanbul at the turn of the century, its depiction of clashing cultures, and its intriguing character analyses. The Turkish version, *Sinekli bakkal* (1936), has been an all-time bestseller, receiving, in 1942, Turkey's most prestigious fiction award.

A. also wrote short stories, prose poems, an operetta libretto (*Kenan çobanları*, 1918; the shepherds of Canaan), and a three-volume history of English literature, *İngiliz edebiyatt tarihi* (1940–49; history of English literature). Her only play, *Maske ve ruh* (1945), published in England in her own English version, *Masks or Souls* (1953), is a philosophical allegory that has among its principal characters the 13th-c. Turkish wit Nasreddin Hodja, Shakespeare, Ibn Haldun, and Tamerlane. In 1956, she published *Türkiye'de Şark, Garp ve American tesirleri*, a book about the influences of the Orient, the West, and the U.S. on Turkey. She also translated Shakespeare's *Coriolanus* and *As You Like It* into Turkish.

Henry Adams

FURTHER WORKS: *Seviye talip* (1910); *Harap mabetler* (1910); *Handan* (1912); *Mev'ut hüküm* (1918); *Son eseri* (1919); *Ateşten gölek* (1922; *The Shirt of Flame*, 1924); *Dağa çıtkan kurt* (1922); *Kalb ağrısı* (1924); *Vurun kahbeye* (1926); *Zeyno'nun oğlu* (1928); *Daughter of Smyrna: A Story of the Rise of Modern Turkey on the Ashes of the Ottoman Empire* (1928); *Turkey on Ashes of the Ottoman Empire* (1928); *Turkey Faces West* (1930); *Conflict of East and West in Turkey* (1935); *Inside India* (1937); *Yolpalas cinayeti* (1937); *Tatarcık* (1939); *Üniversite kafası ve tenkit* (1942); *Edebiyatta tercümenin rolü* (1944); *Sonsuz panayır* (1946); *Döner ayna* (1954); *Akile hanım sokağı* (1958); *Hayat parçaları* (1963); *Mor salkımlı ev* (1963); *Kubbede kalan hoş sada* (1974); *Kerim usta'nın oğlu; Heyula* (1974)

—TALAT SAIT HALMAN

ADORNO, Theodor W(iesengrund)

West German philosopher and essayist, b. 11 Sept. 1903, Frankfurt-am-Main; d. 6 Aug. 1969, Visp, Switzerland

The son of a German-French singer and a successful wine merchant, A. studied privately with Siegfried Kracauer (German historian and social critic, 1890–1966) while he was attending secondary school. From 1925 to 1928, he studied music with Alban

Theodor W. Adorno

Berg and Eduard Steuermann. In 1928 he returned to Frankfurt. Having written a qualifying paper on Kierkegaard's aesthetics, he became licensed in 1931 as a lecturer at the University of Frankfurt.

At this time A. began to work informally with the Institute für Sozialforschung (Institute of Social Research), and published numerous articles in its journal, *Zeitschrift für Sozial forschung*. The institute consisted of a group of radical scholars, Marxist in political affiliation, based at the University of Frankfurt, who undertook collectively to analyze modern society through an interdisciplinary approach, which included cultural studies, philosophical monographs, "studies in authority," and investigations of social prejudice. A. officially joined the institute on his arrival in New York City in 1938. (The institute had been transplanted to America soon after the advent of Hitler.)

Moving to Los Angeles in 1941, A. continued to write prolifically (although most of his manuscripts remained unpublished until after his return to Germany), renewed his acquaintance with the composer Arnold Schönberg, and assisted Thomas MANN with the musical portions of the latter's novel *Doktor Faustus*. He returned to Frankfurt in 1949, becoming assistant director of the Institute for Social Research in 1950, and codirector (with Max Horkheimer, 1895–1973) in 1955. He continued to teach and to publish numerous essays and books until his death.

A.'s earlier writings constitute what might best be described as a series of footnotes to his last book-length works: *Negative Dialektik* (1966; *Negative Dialectics*, 1973) and *Ästhetische Theorie*

(1970; *Aesthetic Theory*, 1983). These volumes establish a theoretical basis for the two principal modes of A.'s thought, the historical-dialectic and the aesthetic.

Ästhetische Theorie is concerned primarily with the interaction of works of art and their cultural context. In a culture such as that of the Western world in the 20th c., in which traditional art has been reduced by what A. calls the "culture industry" to a form of mere entertainment, the artist is obligated to create works which demand intellectual activity on the part of the audience. That is, any contemporary work of art, if it is to be an independent expression of the creative mind rather than a resignation to prevailing fashions, must be removed from those prevailing fashions. This removal implies the disappearance of common patterns of reaction on the part of the audience. Since the artist must establish an individual system of expression for each work which will effectively separate that work from the formalized patterns of the culture industry, the audience equally must be able to adjust to and eventually to comprehend many different modes of expression. Art is thus released from its traditional obligation to provide enjoyment, and becomes justified only insofar as it refuses to be assimilated as background but remains individually created in accord with the highest principles which the artist is able to establish.

But the artist's rejection of the culture industry, which is implied in this individuation of his work, is itself a realization of the social importance of art. It is in this moment that the "double character" of the modern art work appears: "Its social essence requires twofold reflection on its self-sufficiency and on its relationship to society. Its double character is manifest in all of its appearances; they change and contradict the work itself." The insistence of the artwork on its autonomy only serves to reflect its dependence on society for the possibility of its autonomous existence. Without the pressures imposed by society, and, in the particular case of the 20th c., by the culture industry, the artist would have no impetus for the creation of individually defined autonomous works.

Thus forms a "canon of the forbidden," in which are included any technical devices that fail to reflect the double character of art. In other words, devices are rejected that through their assimilation into the mechanized and superficial culture industry have become clichés. Also rejected are devices that through elevation into a cannon of jargon have become merely the appearance of substantive discourse.

Jargon der Eigentlichkeit (1964; *The Jargon of Authenticity*, 1973) serves as one connection between aesthetic theory and dialectic theory. A. deals here specifically with philosophical jargon as represented in German existentialism, but as befits the formal characteristics of a footnote (even though the "footnote" is some 200 pages long), there is throughout implicit reference to all situations in which language "overflows with the pretense of deep human emotion, [but] is just as standardized as the world that it officially negates." When raised to the level of a quasi-official set of symbols, jargon becomes translatable into more readily digested forms, since the symbols can be memorized and then replaced by another group of equivalent, but simpler, terms. Jargon, because it superficially denies conventional forms, is acceptable to the pseudointellectual who wishes to be thought above the use of commonly understood language, but who is incapable of anything more than a one-to-one replacement of that language with its equivalent jargon.

Philosophie der neuen Musik (1949; *Philosophy of Modern Music*, 1973) describes the other mediation between aesthetics and dialectics: the cliché. Again, a specific cultural situation (the music of Stravinsky) is established as a paradigm, and the theoretical superstructure remains implicit. The cliché, like jargon, evades the criteria imposed on art by an act of deception. Whereas jargon had deceived the audience with an empty pretense to meaning, the cliché is deceptive in that it attempts to avoid the historical situation by "regression." The cliché is the more obviously deceptive, since avoidance of the historical situation implies deliberate and noticeable anachronism. The cliche is neither more nor less than an anachronism, since its utility and originality—and thus its reason for existence—have evaporated. It is "as though the heedful recollection of the musician could cancel out history." In an attempt to dispose of history in this manner, technique becomes limited to operations rooted in and sanctioned by that history itself, thus involving the artist in a contradiction.

History must be accepted as such, for in that acceptance lies the foundation of the dialectical balance which is reflected in the double character of art. This is the thrust of *Negative Dialektik*. A. renounces all permanent and thus ultimate concepts, concluding that, "since the basic character of every general concept dissolves in the face of distinct entity, a total philosophy is no longer to be hoped for." History and process thus become the distinguishing characteristics of all philosophical thought, for thought depends on context both in its primary and secondary applications. That is, any historical situation demands particular qualities both in the thought of persons immediately involved in it and in thought about it.

Negative Dialektik is, therefore, self-contradictory. Its theory is that there can be no theory. The self-contradictoriness of the work is manifested even in its title, which ascribes negativity to the explicitly positive process of dialectic thought. A. demands that dialectics move outside itself so that genuine critical reflection can take place.

The *Noten zur Literature* (4 vols., 1958–74; *Notes on Literature*, 2 vols., 1991-92) show this distantiation in process. Societally determined aspects of literature (such as the physical appearance of books), historically determined aspects (genre theory), and individually determined aspects (the role of punctuation in establishing form) are all discussed in turn, and the tendency of the material to disintegration is displayed in the method of approach. Historical relativism becomes a determining criterion of the dialectical technique. The processual character of literary material is established by a technique that eschews continuity in favor of analyses of individual moments within the historical dialectic.

In its demands on the reader, A.'s philosophy is perhaps the most uncompromising of 20th-c. systems. Its continual self-reflection and distantiation, its rejection of continuity and coherence, and its determined removal from accepted and understandable patterns of thought, all constitute deliberate obstacles for the reader, which are designed by A. to dissociate his approach from systems that merely acquiesce uncritically to prevailing fashion. It requires that the reader re-create the dialectic process in his study, and thus regenerates itself on each new reading. Only such a philosophy, continually reshaping itself, can assimilate the events of modern social history. As such, it becomes incumbent on every 20th-c. reader to study this negative dialectic, this systematic antisystem, and to pursue it to its ultimate (though always unexpressed and inexpressible) end.

FURTHER WORKS: *Kierkegaard: Konstruktion des Ästhetischen* (1933; rev., 1962, 1966); *Dialektik der Aufklärung: Philosophische Fragmente* (1947, with M. Horkheimer; *Dialectic of Enlightenment*, 1972); *The Authoritarian Personality* (1950, with E. Frankel-Brunswik, D. Levinson, and R. N. Sanford); *Minima Moralia: Reflexionen aus dem beschädigten Leben* (1951; *Minima Moralia: Reflections from a Damaged Life*, 1978); *Versuch über Wagner* (1952); *Prismen* (1955; *Prisms*, 1967); *Dissonanzen: Musik in der verwalteten Welt* (1956); *Zur Metakritik der Erkenntnistheorie* (1956); *Klangfiguren* (1959); *Mahler* (1960; rev. ed., 1963); *Einleitung in die Musiksoziologie* (1962; *Introduction to the Sociology of Music*, 1976); *Sociologica II* (1962, with M. Horkheimer); *Eingriffe* (1963); *Drei Studien zu Hegel* (1963); *Der getreue Korrepetitor* (1963); *Quasi una Fantasia* (1963); *Moments musicaux* (1964); *Ohne Leitbild: Parva Aesthetica* (1967); *Impromptus* (1968); *Berg* (1968); *Stichworte* (1969); *Aufsätze zur Gesellschaftstheorie und Methodologie* (1970); *Erziehung zur Mündigkeit: Vorträge und Gespräche mit Hellmut Becker* (1970); *Über Walter Benjamin* (1970); *Gesammelte Schriften* (20 vols., 1970 ff.); *Kritik* (1971); *Philosophische Terminologie* (2 vols., 1973–1974). **FURTHER WORKS IN ENGLISH:** *The Positivist Dispute in German Sociology* (1976)

BIBLIOGRAPHY: Jameson, F., *Marxism and Form* (1971): 3–59; Lichtheim, G., *From Marx to Hegel* (1971): 125–42; Jay, M., *The Dialectical Imagination: A History of the Frankfurt School and the Institute of Social Research*, 1923–1950 (1973); Kellner, D. on, *The Jargon of Authenticity, Telos*, No. 19 (1974): 184–92; Mayo, B., "Introduction to A.'s 'Lyric Poetry and Society,'" *Telos*, No. 20 (1974): 52–55; Grenz, F., *A.'s Philosophie in Grundbegriffen* (1974); Buck-Morss, S., *The Origin of Negative Dialectics* (1977); Snow, B., "Introduction to A.'s 'The Actuality of Philosophy,'" *Telos*, No. 31 (1977): 113–19; Benjamin, J., "The End of Internalization: A.'s Social Psychology," *Telos*, No. 32 (1977): 42–46; Piccone, P., Arato, A., and Gebhardt, E., commentaries in *The Essential Frankfurt School Reader* (1978): xi–xxiii, 3–25, 371–406; Rose, G., *The Melancholy Science: An Introduction to the Thought of T. W. A.* (1978); Jay, M., "A. and Kracauer: Notes on a Troubled Friendship," *Salmagundi*, No. 40 (1978): 42–66; Jay, M., *A.* (1984); Jameson, F., *Late Marxism: A.; or, The Persistence of the Dialectic* (1990)

—GEOFFREY GREEN

ADŪNĪS

(pseud. of 'Alī Ahmad Sa'īd) Syrian-Lebanese poet, critic, and journal editor, b. 1930, Qassābīn, Syria

Born in Syria and graduated from the Syrian University in Damascus, A. left his native country in 1956 for political reasons and became a Lebanese citizen. In Lebanon, he and Yūsuf AL-KHĀL, another prominent poet, founded the pioneering poetry journal *Majallat shi'r*, devoted to the publication and discussion of poetry. In more recent years, he has been the editor of his own journal, *Mawāqif*, which, with its motto of "freedom, creativity, and change," has become one of the most influential literary magazines in the Middle East. In 1973, he earned a doctoral degree from the University of St. Joseph in Beirut with a study on the nature of classicism in Arabic literature. As part of his continuing interest in the reinterpretation of Arabic literature of the past he has published an anthology of classical Arabic poetry in three volumes under the title *Dīwān al-shiʻr al-ʻarabī* (1964–68; anthology of Arabic poetry).

Perhaps no other writer living in the Arab world today combines so effectively the roles of poet and critic (although the Lebanese poet Khalīl HĀWĪ might be considered as another example). While A.'s earlier poems, as contained in collections such as *Qālat alard* (1952; the earth said) and *Qasāid ūlā* (1957; first poems), may be considered fine contributions to the history of Arabic symbolist poetry, it is in the collection *Aghānī Mihyār al-Dimashqī* (1961; songs of Mihyar the Damascene) that A. begins to tread new paths in modern Arabic poetry. Mihyar, the medieval poet, comes to personify all of A.'s ideas and revolutionary notions, but his concern with the current and future state of Arab culture is also reflected in the identification of Mihyar with other mythical figures taken from the world of Greek literature and the Bible.

In *Kitāb al-tahawwulāt wa al-hijra fi aqālīm al-layl wa al-nahār* (1965; book of transformations and emigration in the regions of night and day) and *Al-Masrah wa al-marāyā* (1968; stage and mirrors), we detect an increasing use of prose poetry and also of experimentation in language. While A. can still address himself to some of the more pressing problems affecting the Middle East in general, his more typical statements tend to be expressed in poetry that many critics consider opaque and a few regard as obscure to the point of unintelligibility. Even so, in *Qabr min ajl New York* (1971; a tomb for New York) and *Mufrad fī sīghat al-jamʻ* (1975; singular in the form of the plural; excerpted in *Modern Arab Poets 1950–1975*, 1976), A. again gives forceful expression to his views on both his own and Western society in a unique and ever-developing language.

A. has not been reticent in writing about the principles which govern his writing and which, he believes, should govern the writings of others. In this regard, his work shows the influence of a number of French writers, especially Saint-John PERSE, whose poetry he has translated into Arabic. A representative statement of A.'s is *Zaman al-shiʻr* (1972; the time for poetry). In this and other works, A. declares that the major purpose of poetry is to use language in new ways; *tajdīd* (innovation) is a key word in his discussion of not only contemporary but also classical Arabic poetry. As a commentator on poetry's role in society through the ages, he has not only authored a number of studies, such as *Fatihah li-nihayat al-qarn* (1980; opening for the end of the century) and *Siyasat al-shir* (1992; politics of poetry), but has also contributed some of the most through and pioneering studies of the literary tradition of Arabs, including *Al-Thābit wa al-mutahawwil: Bahth fī al-ittibāʻ wa al-ibdāʻ ʻinda al-ʻArab* (1974ff.; stability and change: an investigation of classicism and creativity among the Arabs), *Al-Sufiyyah wa-al-suryaliyyah* (1992; sufism and surrealism), and *Al-Nass al-Qurʼani wa-afaq al-kitabah* (1993; the qurʼanic text and the dimensions of writing).

Poetry to A. is a vision (*ruʼyā*) and, to use his own words, it is a "leap outside of established concepts, a change in the order of things and in the way we look at them." This attitude not only affects A.'s view of his own role as a poet in contemporary Arab society, but also influences his views of classical Arabic poetry, which he has anthologized with such originality. Meanwhile, his views continue to be projected in his magazine, not only through his own poetry and writings, but also through the creative compositions, articles, and commentaries of a number of younger writers (including his wife, the prominent literary critic Khālida Saʻīd) who regard him as a major, if not *the* major, influence on the development of Arabic literature today.

The radical stance of A. toward language and its use in poetry makes him a controversial figure in the Middle East. It is certainly true that, to the uninitiated, his poetry may seem very obscure; A. has stated as much. However, even the most conservative critic has to acknowledge that his poetry often possesses a haunting beauty, while his critical and historical studies have led to a reexamination of the very bases of Arabic poetry and seem destined to bring about a revision of several received opinions on that subject.

FURTHER WORKS: *Dalīla* (1950); *Idhā qulta yā Suriyyā* (1958); *Awrāq fī al-rīh* (1958); *Waqt bayn al-ramad wa al-ward* (1970); *Muqaddimah li-al-shʻr al-ʻArabī* (1971); *Kitāb al-qasaʼid al-khams* (1980); *Shahwah tataqaddam di kharaʼit al-māddah* (1987); *Ihtifaʼ bi-al-ashyaʼ al-wadihah al-ghamidah* (1988); *Kalam al-bayidat* (1989); *Al-Nizām wa-al-kalām* (1993); *Hā anta, ayyuhā alwaqt* (1993); *Abjadiyyah thāniyyah* (1994). **FURTHER WORKS IN ENGLISH:** *The Blood of Adonis* (1971); *Mirrors* (1976); *Transformations of the Lover* (1983); *Victims of a Map* (1984); *If Only the Sea Could Sleep*; *The Pages of Day and Night* (1994)

BIBLIOGRAPHY: Badawi, M., *A Critical Introduction to Modern Arabic Poetry* (1975): 231–41; Boullata, I. J., "A.: Revolt in Modern Arabic Poetics," *Edebiyat*, 2 (1977): 1–13; al-Jayyusi, S., *Trends and Movements in Modern Arabic Poetry*, 2 (1977), passim; Amyuni, M. T., "Adonis's Time Poem: Translation and Analysis," *JArabL* 21, 2 (1990):172-82; Beard, M., and Haydar, A., "Making Mihyar; The Familiarization of Adunis's Knight of Strange Words," *Critical Pilgrimages; Studies in the Arabic Literary tradition, Literature East and West* (1989): 89-103; Deyoung, T., "Upon One Double String: The Metaphysical Element in Adunis's Poetry," *Al-ʻArabiyya*, 27 (1994):1-15; Snir, R., "A Study of Elegy for al-Hallaj by Adunis," *JArabL* 25, 3 (Nov. 1994): 245-56

—ROGER ALLEN

ADY, Endre

Hungarian poet, short-story writer, and journalist, b. 22 Nov. 1877, Ermindszent; d. 27 Jan. 1919, Budapest

A., descended from impoverished landed gentry and Calvinist ministers, was a born rebel. He dropped out of law school to pursue his search for social justice through journalism and to express his dreams and visions in poetry. He was still in his twenties when his efforts won the favor of intellectual circles in the progressive provincial city of Nagyvárad (now Oradea, Romania), where he joined the staff of a liberal daily. There he met and fell in love with a woman he called Leda, who was to inspire scores of his poems. When Leda returned to her residence in Paris, A. followed her, and from 1904 to 1912 spent much time in France while working as foreign correspondent for Budapest dailies, which also featured his poems.

The publication of his third collection of poems, *Uj versek* (new poems), in 1906 marked A.'s break with the romantic lyric poetry of the past era and initiated a revolution in Hungarian literature. In the prefatory poem of this collection A. called himself the son of biblical Gog and Magog and vowed ceaseless attacks against any force that shackles human progress. Another volume of poems, *Vér és arany* (1907; blood and gold), made A. the center of heated controversies. He openly declared that the "new songs of new times" are only the forerunners of Hungary's belated but unavoidable social transformation.

While conservative circles denounced A.'s prophecies and ridiculed his poetic forms, symbolic references, and cadences, a group of young Hungarian writers formed the Holnap literary society, with A. as its acknowledged leader. In the same year, 1908, the literary magazine *Nyugat* made its debut in Budapest, with A. as one of its editors. The prospect of closer association with the poet drew some of the best writers of the era to the journal, which gained wide respect for taking a major role in fostering the emergence of modern Hungarian literature.

After years of devotion to Leda, who introduced A. to French cultural life and awakened in him an awareness of the realm of his subconscious, the lovers quarreled and their relationship came to a bitter end. A. returned to his homeland to present new volumes of poems to his ever-growing following. In the spring of 1914 he became infatuated with a young girl just out of finishing school who, among a veritable army of women, besieged the poet with amorous letters. A. proposed marriage and wrote moving, colorful poems to his future bride. A year later they were married, but A. found only brief periods of happiness and respite from nervous tensions in the lovely, secluded Transylvanian home of his wife. The ravages of World War I weighed heavily on the poet's mind, and in the autumn of 1918, just before the collapse of the Austro-Hungarian monarchy, an event he had worked for and prophesied, he suffered a stroke and several weeks later died of pneumonia. A new government, formed in the wake of postwar revolution, arranged a state funeral for him.

A. wrote more than a thousand poems, scores of short stories, essays on literature, theater, and other arts, and hundreds of polemical articles on the political, social, and cultural scene. A great many of his poems reflect a messianic fervor, and some reveal an apocalyptic spirit, troubled by the mysteries of life and death. Although A. had been influenced by French SYMBOLISM, particularly by Baudelaire and Verlaine, he was too much of an individualist to commit himself wholly to any one literary school.

The power of A.'s imagination, his messianic fervor, his pride in his nation, and his poetic diction, reminiscent of old folk songs and the Hungarian-Calvinist version of the Bible, brought new color and depth to Hungarian lyric poetry. The American critic Edmund WILSON, who learned Hungarian to read the poems of A. and other poets in the original, pointed out in an essay entitled "My Fifty Years with Dictionaries and Grammars" (1963) that A.'s position in Hungary was comparable to that of YEATS in Ireland. Wilson says that A.'s stirring invocation of mythological figures, his wide range of moods, his repeatedly demonstrated patriotism, as well as his invention of a personal idiom, have been primarily responsible for the association of his name with his Irish contemporary.

The thematic variations of A.'s poetry reflect a complex, extremely sensitive personality struggling with profound contradictions. He yearned for salvation and feverishly appealed to and quarreled with God; he sought the mystical powers of faith and was committed to Calvinist simplicity; he was both nostalgic for and scornful of the past; he believed his nation was destined to be great, but saw it torn by social injustice and conflicting images. Even his poems written to and about women reveal a duality. In his "Léda asszony zsoltárai" (psalms for Leda), included in *Uj versek* of 1906, love became fused with the hedonist pleasures of life and the agonies of death. His superb poems written to his young wife, whom he called Csinszka, voiced his craving for her affection and his haunting fear of impending disaster.

Debates over A.'s place in Hungarian and world literature flared up time and again in his native land. One criticism has been reechoed by several literary historians, who claim that a part of A.'s poetry was essentially political journalism in verse form, requiring familiarity with the issues of the poet's time. No footnotes are needed, however, to understand the bold struggles waged by the poet. From his early youth on he fought for the betterment of the life of the common man and for a just place for his nation in the world order. When it seemed to him that the day of reckoning for past sins threatened the Hungarian state, A. turned vehemently to God, calling for His helpful intervention.

One of the greatest and most original of Hungarian poets, A. was almost a legendary figure in his lifetime. He opened new vistas to poets, writers, and critics and influenced the social thinking not only of his own contemporaries but also of subsequent generations.

FURTHER WORKS: *Versek* (1899); *Még egyszer* (1903); *Sápadt emberek és egyéb történetek* (1907); *Uj csapáson* (1909); *A tizmilliós Kleopátra és egyéb történetek* (1910); *Igy is történhetik* (1910); *Szeretném ha szeretnének* (1910); *A minden titkok verseiből* (1911); *Az Illés szekerén* (1911); *A menekiilő élet* (1912); *A magunk szerelme* (1913); *Muskétás tanár ur* (1913); *Ki látott engem?* (1914); *A halottak élén* (1918); *Az utolsó hajók* (1923); *Vallomások és tanulmányok* (1944); *Párizsban és napfényországban* (1949); *A nacionalizmus alkonya* (1959); *A. az irodalomról* (1961). FURTHER WORKS IN ENGLISH: *Poems of E. A.* (1969)

BIBLIOGRAPHY: Reményi, J., "E. A.: Apocalyptic Poet, 1877–1919" (1944), in Molnar, A. J., ed., *Hungarian Writers and Literature* (1964): 193–212; Klaniczay, T., Szauder, J., and Szabolcsi, M., *History of Hungarian Literature* (1964): 192–99 and passim

—PAUL NADANYI

ADYGHE LITERATURE

See North Caucasian Literatures

AFGHAN LITERATURE

The ideal personality type in Afghan culture is the warrior-poet. Poets abound in all strata of society and hold respected positions in every community, rural and urban. However, since about 90 percent of the population is non-literate, the literary circle is largely confined to the urban elite.

Dari (Afghan Persian) and Pashto, Indo-European languages written in the Arabic script, are the principal languages used by Afghan writers. Dari has traditionally predominated among the elite, but concerted efforts to revitalize Pashto have been made throughout the 20th c. Other regional and linguistic groups have rich oral traditions but occupy a minor place on the national literary scene.

Afghan literature may be characterized as eclectic. Persia, India, central Asia, Russia, Europe, and the U.S. have each contributed to its development. The synthesis, nevertheless, is uniquely Afghan. Furthermore, literature in the 20th c. has been inextricably involved with revolutionary attitudes. And, because of the absence of a mass literate audience and a paucity of publishing facilities, which are predominantly government-controlled, writers have been largely limited to journalistic outlets.

The first modern literary luminary was Mahmud Beg Tarzi (1865–1933). After more than twenty years of political exile in Syria and association with reform-minded Young Turks, Tarzi returned to Afghanistan to edit the Dari bimonthly nationalist newspaper *Seraj ul-akh-bar* (1911–19). In his essays he pleaded for Islamic unity, social justice, and internal reforms. His translations, including works by Jules Verne, not only introduced the elite to new ideas but recommended prose as a viable literary form.

A period of reform (1919–29) initiated by Tarzi's son-in-law, King Amanullah, ended in a rebellion led by conservative fundamentalists. In the following decade and a half of recovery, romantic escapism replaced calls for reform. Writing in a neoclassical style in the tradition of 11th-c. Persia, poets glorified nature and extolled optimism, Islamic idealism, and aesthetic values. Abdul Ali Mustaghni (1874–1934) wrote prolifically in a wide number of classic poetic forms, in Pashto as well as Dari. Sufi Abdul Haq Beitab (1888–1969), who became poet laureate in 1942, wrote eulogies to patriotism and mysticism in Dari, following the style of Mogul India's Abdul Qader Bedel (1644–1726).

When tentative moves toward democracy were initiated in the late 1940s, the poets responded with themes of sentimental socialism. They combined the mysticism of India's Rabindranath TAGORE with Maxim GORKY's revolutionary championing of the common people. Abdur Rauf Benawa (b. 1913) and Gul Pacha Ulfat (1909–1978), writing in Pashto, best represent the period from 1946 to 1953. Among various nationalistic and social topics, they addressed themselves to the restrictions on women in Afghan society. Khalil-ullah Khalili (b. 1908), who continued the neoclassical Persian tradition, published the first anthology of contemporary authors. *Muntakhabat-i-ashur* (1954; selections of poetry). Abdur Rahman Pazwak (b. 1919) employed the same style to explore contemporary problems, idealizing the past through his histories and retellings of folklore.

A burgeoning group of leftist writers gathered around Noor Mohammad Taraki (1917–1979), a journalist, novelist, and short-story writer who was influenced by the social-protest novels of Theodore DREISER, John STEINBECK, and Upton SINCLAIR. Suleiman Layeq (b. 1930) and Bareq Shafiyee (b. 1930?), poets in both Dari and Pashto, exemplify the development of these activists. Initially they wrote religious poems, but after 1953, when the Shah of Iran was reinstalled, Afghan poets were much influenced by the leftist literature produced underground or in exile by writers of the now-outlawed pro-Soviet Tudeh Party. This new wave of Afghan writing was heavily imbued with European socialist and EXISTEN-TIALIST forms, and the ideas of such writers as Jean-Paul SARTRE and Albert CAMUS were blended with Sufi Islam.

Other innovators include Mahmud Farani (b. 1930?), perhaps the major experimenter in rhyme and meter, and Mohammad Rahim El-Ham (b. 1932) and Saaduddin Shpoon (b. 1933), who have equal facility in both Dari and Pashto, in prose and poetry. Zia Qarizada (b. 1921) made major contributions with the poems in *Ashur-i-nau* (1957; new verse), written in Dari. The woman writer Kubra Mazhari (b. 1950?), Dari poet, novelist, and short-story writer, edited the literary magazine *Erfan* in the 1970s.

Prose as a mode of imaginative writing gained respectability in the 20th c., but the novel and the short story remain nascent. Young leaders in the field of short-story writting include Hassan Kaseem (b. 1944), Ghulam Ghaus Schodjaie (1940–1979), Sharifa Sharif (b. 1953), and Sposhmai Zaryab (b. 1949). Their works deal realistically with everyday contradictions inherent in a society in the process of modernization.

There is also a distinguished group of prose writers in history and philosophy, mainly in Dari. Among these are Ahmad Ali Kohzad (b. 1915), the nation's first archaeologist, who wrote *Afghanistan dar Shahnama* (1976; Afghanistan in the *Shahnama*); Said Qassim Rishtya (b. 1913), author of *Afghanistan dar nozdahi-quaran* (1958; Afghanistan in the nineteenth century); Mir Ghulam Mohammad Ghobar (1899–1978), leading socialist historian who wrote *Afghanistan dar masir-i-tarikh* (1968; Afghanistan's path through history); Hasan Kakar (b. 1932), whose *Government and Society in Afghanistan* (1979) was written in English; Abdul Hai Habibi (b. 1908), historian of Pashto Literature; and Bahauddin Majrooh (b. 1928) and the previously mentioned Ghulam Ghaus Schodjaie, essayists in social philosophy.

The theater, developing sporadically since the 1940s, enjoyed government support during the 1960s and 1970s, when a plethora of Dari adaptations of the plays of Anton CHEKHOV, Eugene O'NEILL, Tennessee WILLIAMS, and Neil Simon (b. 1927) appeared. The very small group of Afghan playwrights writing original material, led by Rashid Latifi, (1906–1972?), active since the 1940s, and the younger Sayyid Moqades Negah (b. 1925?), explored situations for social comment. Bureaucratic corruption and pseudosophisticated artificialities were favorite subjects of attack.

A free press flourished fitfully from 1965 to 1973. Newspapers carried poetry and short stories on themes ranging from Islamic conservatism to socialism to antimonarchy revolution clothed in the form of traditional love songs and Sufi lamentations.

But political stagnation denied political parties legality and writers open expression. The literary movement lacked dynamism and meaningful direction when the monarchy was overthrown in 1973. The free press was stifled and the political process lurched toward a second coup d'etat in 1978, which established the leftist Democratic Republic of Afghanistan with Noor Mohammad Taraki as prime minister. Numbers of Taraki's coterie from the 1950s and 1960s, including Suleiman Layeq and Bariq Shafiyee, occupied prominent positions in the government. All art forms are now geared toward Soviet-style SOCIALIST REALISM. Creativity has given place to polemical rhetoric. After the Russian invasion in 1979 many of the literary elite fled into exile, where they combine guerrilla activities with reappraisals of the ideals they once expressed.

BIBLIOGRAPHY: Dollot, R., *L'Afghanistan* (1937); Najibullah, M., *Islamic Literature* (1963), passim; Dianous, H.-J. de, "La littérature afghane de langue persane," *Orient/Paris*, 8, 31 (1964): 137–71; Dupree, N., "Archeology and the Arts in the Creation of a National Consciousness," in Dupree, L., ed., *Afghanistan in the 1970s* (1974): 203–38; Geerken, H., Introduction to Geerken, H., ed., *Afghanistan* (1977): 9–13; Schinasi, M., *Afghanistan at the Beginning of the Twentieth Century* (1979); Dupree, L., *Afghanistan* (1980)

—NANCY HATCH DUPREE

AFRIKAANS LITERATURE
See under South African Literature

AFRO-CUBANISM

Afro-Cubanism is a movement in Caribbean arts and letters which stemmed from a rediscovery of the region's African heritage during the 1920s and which to some extent paralleled the Harlem Renaissance in the United States. The initial stimulus for "Black" literature in the Antilles was the interest after World War I of European artists and intellectuals (Picasso, APOLLINAIRE, Stravinsky) in primitive African art and musical folk forms. A preexisting interest in African themes in the Caribbean, dating from the arrival of the slaves in the 16th c. and manifested in the 19th–c. antislavery novel, culminated in the publication by the Cuban ethnologist Fernando Ortiz (1881–1969) of *Los negros brujos* (1906; the black witch doctors).

The movement developed in two stages: an initial phase marked by the exclusive participation of white intellectuals—including the Puerto Rican Luis Palés Matos (1899–1959) and José Zacarías Tallet (b. 1893)—which produced a highly picturesque but external view of Black culture marked by a predominance of sensuous images and onomatopoetic rhythms, and a later phase characterized by a more serious depiction of the Black experience by writers such as Nicolás GUILLÉN and Reginio Pedroso (1896-1983). The trajectory of the entire Afro-Cuban vogue is reflected in Guillén's works, which begin with an emphasis on the comic and folkloric but evolve into a preoccupation with more universal themes and forms. The greatest period of activity for Afro-Cubanism was between 1926 and 1938; after 1940 it was gradually incorporated in the general current of Caribbean literature.

Although principally a poetry movement, Afro-Cubanism found expression as well in the essay and in fiction. The Cubans Emilio Ballagas (1910–1954), José Antonio Fernández de Castro (1897–1951), Ramón Guirao (1908–1949), and Juan Marinello (1898-1977) and the Uruguayan Ildefonso Pereda Valdés (b. 1899) produced important anthologies of and critical essays on Black poetry. In the field of fiction the two most important figures were Alejo CARPENTIER and Lydia CABRERA. Cabrera in particular bridged the gap between ethnology and literature in *Cuentos negros* (1940; black tales), which were adaptations of African stories.

Like the Spanish American movement of MODERNISM, Afro-Cubanism represented the creation of a uniquely New World art form resulting from the fusion of European and nativist aesthetic models.

BIBLIOGRAPHY: Fernández de castro, A., *Tema negro en la literature cubana* (1943); Coulthard, G. R., *Race and Colour in Caribbean Literature* (1962); Stimson, F. S., *The New Schools of Spanish American Poetry* (1970): 161–79; Ruiz del Vizo, *Black Poetry of the Americas* (1972): 9–17; King, L., "The Afro-Cuban Poetry of Nicolás Guillén," in King, B., and Ogunbesan, K., eds., *A Celebration of Black Writing* (1975): 30–45

—EDWARD MULLEN

AĞAOĞLU, Adalet

Turkish novelist and dramatist, b. 1929, Nallihan

A leading writer of fiction and drama, A. enjoys prestige as Turkey's premier woman novelist in the last quarter of the 20th c.

In 1950 she graduated from the University of Ankara with a degree in French language and literature. She had taken up writing in 1946 when she contributed reviews and essays on the theater to the Ankara daily *Ulus*. In 1948-1949 she published poetry in the literary journal *Kaynak*. In 1951 she joined the staff of Radio Ankara, where she worked successively as a librarian, dramaturge, and chief of literary programs and radio plays. From the mid-1960s to 1970 she served as consultant to the Turkish radio and television administration. In recent years she was a columnist for the Istanbul dailies *Milliyet* and *Cumhuriyet*.

A. first attracted attention as a dramatist: her 1964 play *Evcilik Oyunu* (1964; the marriage game) earned considerable praise from the critics. It is a well-made play that deals in ingenious ways with matrimonial crisis. *Çatıdaki Çatlak* (perf. 1965, pub. 1969; crack in the roof), *Tombala* (1969; lottery), and *Kendini yazan şarkı* (1976; the song that wrote itself) are remarkable for their explorations into the psychological motivations of the principal characters and for a Pinteresque flavor, especially in their dialogue. Her *Üç oyun* (1973; three plays), containing *Bir kahramanın ölümü* (death of a hero), *Çıkış* (exit), and *Kozalar* (cocoons), somewhat reminiscent of Samuel BECKETT, won the Drama Prize of the Turkish Language Society in 1974.

A.'s entry into the world of fiction in 1973 with *Ölmeye yatmak* (lying down to die) earned her a great deal of accolades and stimulated much debate about the innovations she introduced. This first novel, which interfuses incisive psychological portrayals, news items, and STREAM-OF-CONSCIOUSNESS techniques, is a masterwork dealing with political oppression, personal crisis, women's subjugation, and violations of human rights in modern Turkey. Although complete in itself, *Ölmeye yatmak* stands as the first part of a trilogy, together with *Bir düğün gecesi* (1979; a wedding night) and *Hayir* (1987; no). *Bir düğün gecesi*, perhaps the most lyrical of A.'s novels, was awarded Turkey's three major literary prizes. Her first collection of short stories, *Yüksek gerilim* (1974; high tension), which contains mostly conventional realistic stories, won the Sait Faik Prize in 1975.

Fikrimin ince gülü (1976; my mind's tender rose), a widely acclaimed novel of social injustice and private anguish, was banned by the military government of the early 1980s. Dealing mainly with the alienation of the Turkish guest workers in Germany, this book is A.'s most effective exposé of class differences, economic exploitation, and materialistic fetishism. Her second collection of short stories, *Sessizliğin ilk sesi* (1978; first sound of silence), broke new ground in introspective and surrealistic fiction. Some of the stories here can be seen as the quintessence of her best novels. *Yazsonu* (1980; summer's end), which the author herself identified as "a novelization of the creative act," represents a further foray into the realm of imaginative mysterium as do many of the masterful pieces in her third collection of short stories, *Hadi gidelim* (1982; come on, let's go).

In 1984 A. published *Üç beş kişi* (a few people), a novel of the social and personal dilemmas arising from the exodus from the countryside into the urban areas. In quick succession came *Göç temizliği* (1985; clean-up for moving), an avowedly autobiographical novel.

A. collected some of her essays and articles on literature in a volume entitled *Geçerken* (1986; in passing). A number of her radio and television plays produced in Turkey, France, and Germany remain unpublished, as do some of her stage works. In 1991 A. saw publication of her avant-garde play *Çok uzak—fazla yakın* (very far—too close).

Her novella *Ruh üşümesi* (1991; soul shivering), which is subtitled "a chamber novel," combines a powerful eroticism with flights of the imagination, making it one of the most compelling works of sexual enactments in the history of Turkish fiction.

A.'s experiments with form and substance of fiction, her explorations into the minds of her protagonists, her deft ways of evoking moods and atmosphere, and her singular style have secured a permanent place for her in the literature of Turkey in the 20th c.

BIBLIOGRAPHY: Ervin, E. W., "Narrative Technique in the Fiction of A. A.," *Edebiyat*, 1, 1 (1987): 128–46

—TALAT SAIT HALMAN

AGEE, James

American journalist, novelist, poet, film critic, and screenwriter, b. 27 Nov. 1909, Knoxville, Tenn.; d. 16 May 1955, New York, N.Y.

Although A. was educated at Exeter and Harvard and spent most of his subsequent literary career in New York working for *Fortune, Time,* and *The Nation*, his best work is firmly rooted in his Southern background and Episcopalian upbringing. The eclecticism of his literary forms reflects not only his fascination with multiple means of perceiving and recording experience but also his

James Agee

grave doubts about the capacity of art to treat the moral crises of the 20th c. with integrity.

A.'s first book was a collection of poems, *Permit Me Voyage* (1934), in which he handled traditional themes with facility and showed considerable finesse in a variety of metric forms. His next and best work, *Let Us Now Praise Famous Men* (1941), with photographs by Walker Evans, grew out of a *Fortune* magazine assignment to report on the lives of three Alabama tenant-farmer families. This book is a calculated defiant and chaotic mixture of prose styles—impressionistic and highly personal narrative, formal essays, meticulous catalogues and inventories—which returns to the squalid and miserable lives of the Southern poor some of the innate dignity, beauty, and holiness that A. felt they had been deprived of by the many well-intentioned writers who documented Great Depression suffering. A. deliberately created a perverse format in which he both insults and confuses his readers, challenging them to reject his unpalatable truths. He feared the ease with which American society canonized its most scourging artists; such acceptance only emasculated their dissent, and A. determined to make acceptance difficult.

During the 1940s A. became increasingly interested in film, writing reviews for *Time*, a regular column for *The Nation*, and later a number of movie scripts, including *The Blue Hotel, The African Queen,* and *The Night of the Hunter*. A.'s optimism about film as the most exciting and potentially truthful artistic medium led him to apply an unprecedented moral and aesthetic earnestness in his judgment of all the motley products of the movie industry; he created virtually single-handedly the first serious body of film criticism in English.

In his last two works of fiction, A. turned to his Knoxville childhood for the setting. *The Morning Watch* (1951), a novella, explores the consciousness of an adolescent boy as he attempts to realize the passion of Christ through his own Easter devotions. The prose is lyrical and symbolic, but A.'s sympathy for the boy's endeavors is touched with an ironic awareness of man's ability to disencumber himself of the burden of sin. The novel *A Death in the Family*, edited and published posthumously in 1957, is about the capacity of the members of a family to come to terms with bereavement through their diverse personal creeds and mutual love. The narrative, which is closely based on the death of A.'s father, is related from a variety of perspectives. The subjective point of view of each of the characters is presented without authorial intrusion, a method that demands maximum engagement and compassion from the reader.

A. died a relatively young man with only a small body of work completed and many ambitious schemes unfulfilled. Yet his single full-length novel, *A Death in the Family*, gained immediate and unanimous critical acclaim, his film criticism established the highest standards for that genre, and *Let Us Now Praise Famous Men* was described by Lionel TRILLING as "the most realistic and the most important moral effort of our American generation."

FURTHER WORKS: *A. on Film* (I., *Reviews and Comments*, 1958; II., *Five Film Scripts*, 1960); *Letters of J. A. to Father Flye* (1962); *Collected Poems* (1968); *Collected Short Prose* (1968)

BIBLIOGRAPHY: Holder, A., "Encounter in Alabama: A. and the Tenant Farmer," *VQR*, 42, 2 (1966): 189–206; Ohlin, P. H., *A.* (1966); Seib, K., *J. A.: Promise and Fulfillment* (1969); Barson, A. T., *A Way of Seeing: A Critical Study of J. A.* (1972); Kramer, V. A., *J. A.* (1975); Moreau, G., *The Restless Journey of J. A.*

(1977); Snyder, J. J., *J. A.: A Study of His Film Criticism* (1977); Bergreen, L., *J. A.* (1984); Lowe, J., *The Creative Process of J. A.* (1994)

—SYLVIA COOK

AGNON, S(hmuel) Y.

(born Czaczkes) Israeli novelist and short story writer, b. 17 July 1888, Buczacz, Austro-Hungarian Empire (now Ukraine); d. 17 Feb. 1970, Jerusalem

A. began to write poetry and prose in both Hebrew and Yiddish at the age of nine, and by the time he left his birthplace for Palestine in 1908, he was already known as a successful writer. He lived in Germany from 1913 to 1924, but resided in Jerusalem from 1924 to the end of his life. In his first work published in Palestine, the story "Agunot" (1908; "Agunot: A Tale," 1966), the special literary qualities that characterize many of his later works—such as multiple meanings, the use of ancient Jewish sources, and tragic and ironic overtones—are already apparent. On the basis of the title of this story (which literally means "deserted wives") he called himself Agnon, which he adopted as his legal surname in 1924. This change of name stands as a symbol of A.'s developing world view, and signifies both a cutting off and a new beginning. It meant a breaking away from his former name, Czaczkes, with all its implications of small-town Jewish life in eastern Europe. The new name, however, has two contradictory meanings, one deriving from the other: the first meaning is "anchored," the second "forsaken"—thus, continuity and cutoff.

A. created a virtuoso style by mining the hitherto neglected treasures of biblical, rabbinic, mystical, ethereal, homiletic, and folk writing, which he brought together into a balanced, organic whole.

A.'s protagonists undertake an arduous journey to reach a goal, which, upon attainment, turns out to be a failure. The stories are narrated in the ironic tone of one who pities the suffering of the naïve believer who has faith in his ability to reach the goal that has been revealed to him. The only way A.'s heroes can be saved from the mockery of fate is to submit to Divine Providence, wherever it shall lead. Such a character is the protagonist of the novel *Hachnasat kalah* (1931; *The Bridal Canopy*, 1937), whose survival is made possible by virtue of miraculous occurrences, which elicit astonishment and laughter. It tells of a poor Hasid, Reb Yudel, who goes on a journey in search of husbands and dowries for his three daughters. The attitude of the narrator to the naïve innocents in the tale vacillates between humor and irony, on the one hand, and forgiveness and restrained compassion, on the other.

The psychological novel *Sipur pashut* (1935; *A Simple Story*, 1985) presents a conflict between the desires of the individual and the demands of society. Hirshel Horowitz lacks the strength to struggle to attain his own goals (to marry the girl he loves rather than the one his parents have chosen) and withdraws into temporary insanity, which arouses compassion and mild mockery. He returns from the sanatorium an obedient, conforming member of a society that is involved in playing games called "Zionism" and "socialism" and whose members aspire to the ultimate goal of owning a little store that will earn a small profit. This society does not seek salvation, for it is not aware that it is in need of it.

In the novel *Oreach natah lalun* (1939; *A Guest for the Night*, 1968) the narrator returns to his native village after the ravages of World War I and finds it but a remnant of what it once was. Here, too, an ironic tone enters into his description of what once was, as well as of what he sees. All that is left for the narrator in his native town is to escape from it and to describe its grotesque death throes.

In *Temol shilshom* (1945; only yesterday), a novel set against the background of the wave of Jewish immigration to Palestine at the beginning of the 20th century, A. tells a psychological story with mystical implications. The hero travels from his shtetl to Palestine. His search for the union of old and new, his struggle and eventual failure to achieve it, and his tragic death from the bite of a rabid dog are described ironically and grotesquely from shifting points of view, including that of the dog.

The posthumously published novel *Shirah* (1971; *Shira*, 1989) is an epic chronicle of life in Palestine during the period of the British mandate. The protagonist is an intellectual torn between his dream to create a work of literary art and the reality of his life, which is an unending pursuit of scholarly footnotes. He destroys what could be a true love relationship with the nurse Shirah for the sake of preserving a conventional marriage. He vacillates continually, moving like a marionette in a world without roots in the past and without a foothold in the present.

A.'s literary creation is rich and varied, including psychological love stories in the manner of European realism, legends of saints, social satires, surrealistic stories, sagas, historical chronicles, and children's stories. In many of these works, as in the novel *Oreach natah lalun*, a hero seeks escape into the world of fantasy or into a mythical past because he dreads the world of reality. But these flights are attempts at reviving lost worlds that are beyond resurrection. The real world penetrates the worlds of fantasy and brings them tumbling down. Thus does the hero run from pillar to post in a bifurcated existence in which the dominant force is a confused commingling of past and future, dream and reality, myth and fear. The hero finally realizes that fate ultimately overpowers hope; despair nullifies the possibility of redemption.

Such themes are also familiar in the works of KAFKA, MANN, and JOYCE. A.'s genius was to crystallize a Hebrew style to fit the content and essence of such themes. In orchestrating language and image, mating richly associative materials from traditional sources with highly personal lyrical themes, he succeeds in integrating the archaic with the modern to form a unique aesthetic structure.

A. supported himself by his literary work for most of his creative life. He was awarded the Israel Prize (1954 and 1958) and was the first author writing in Hebrew to receive the Nobel Prize for literature (1966). Translations of his works have appeared in almost every European language, and more has been written about him and his works than about any other Hebrew writer of fiction.

FURTHER WORKS: *Vhaya heakov lemishor* (1912); *Meaz umeatah* (1931); *Sipure ahavim* (1931); *Bshuvah vanachat* (1935); *Bilvav yamim* (1935; *In the Heart of the Seas*, 1948); *Yamim noraim* (1938; *Days of Awe*, 1948); *Elu veelu* (1941); *Samuch vnireh* (1951); *Sefer hamaasim* (1951); *Ad hena* (1952); *Kol sipurav* (7 vols., 1953); *Al kapot hamanul* (1953); *Atem reitem* (1960); *Sifrehem shel tsadikim* (1961); *Haesh vhaetsim* (1962); *Ir umeloah* (1973); *Bachanuto shel Mar Lublin* (1974); *Lifnim min hachomah* (1975); *Meatsmi el atsmi* (1976); *Pitche dvarim* (1977); *Sefer, sofer vsipur* (1978); *Korot batenu* (1979). FURTHER WORKS IN ENGLISH: *Two Tales* (1966); *Twenty-one Stories* (1970)

BIBLIOGRAPHY: Wilson, E., "The Fiction of S. Y. A.," *Red, Black, Blond and Olive* (1956): 443–51; Stampfer, J., "S. Y. A.: Lyricist of

Modern Fiction," *Jewish Book Annual*, 25 (1967–1968): 17–26; Brandwein, N. C., "S. Y. A.: Alienation and Return," *Jewish Book Annual*, 25 (1967–1968): 27–38; Band, A. J., *Nostalgia and Nightmare: A Study in the Fiction of S. Y. A.* (1968); Rabinovich, I., "S. Y. A.'s Techniques of Characterization," *Major Trends in Modern Hebrew Fiction* (1968): 177–232; Hochman, B., *The Fiction of S. Y. A.* (1970); Fisch, H., *S. Y. A.* (1975); Hoffman, A. G., *Between Exile and Return: S. Y. A. and the Drama of Writing* (1991)

—N. C. BRANDWEIN

AGOLLI, Dritëro

Albanian poet and prose writer, b. 13 Oct. 1931, Menkulas

A. was born of a peasant family in the Devoll region near Korça and finished secondary school in Gjirokastra in 1952. He later continued his studies at the Faculty of Arts of the University of Leningrad and took up journalism upon his return to Albania, working for the daily newspaper *Zëri i Popullit* for fifteen years. A. was a deputy in the People's Assembly under the dictatorship and has continued to be active in politics as a member of parliament. From 1973 to 1992 he was also president of the Albanian Writers' Union.

A. established his reputation originally as a poet before turning to prose in later years. He is still widely admired in both genres. His first verse collections, *Në rrugë dolla* (1958; I Went Out on the Street), *Hapat e mija në asfalt* (1961; My Steps on the Pavement), and *Shtigje malesh dhe trotuare* (1965; Mountain Paths and Sidewalks), introduced him to the reading public as a sincere and gifted lyric poet of the soil and demonstrated masterful verse technique. In this early verse one senses the influence of his training in the Soviet Union, the spirit of Edvard BAGRITSKY and Dmitri Kedrin (1907-1945) in particular.

Pelegrini i vonuar (1993; The Belated Pilgrim) is A.'s first book printed without an eye to the invisible censor. It is an impressive collection of 217 previously unpublished poems in which we encounter a new chapter, not only in the life of the poet, but also in the struggle of his people for survival.

Like Ismail KADARE, A. turned increasingly to prose in the 1970s after attaining success as a poet of the soil. His strength in prose lies in the short story rather than in the novel. One early collection of tales, *Zhurma e ererave të dikurshme* (1964; The Noise of Winds of the Past), had the distinction of being banned and "turned into cardboard." Its author was accused of Soviet revisionism.

After two rather conformist novels of partisan heroism, the standard theme encouraged by the party, A. produced a far more interesting work of prose, his satirical *Shkëlqimi dhe rënja e shokut Zylo* (1973; The Splendor and Fall of Comrade Zylo), which has proved to be his claim to fame. Comrade Zylo is the epitome of the well-meaning but incompetent *apparatchik*, director of an obscure government cultural affairs department. His pathetic vanity, his quixotic fervor, his grotesque public behavior, in short his splendor and his fall, are all recorded in ironic detail by his hard-working and more astute subordinate and friend Demkë who serves as a neutral observer. Comrade Zylo is a universal figure, a character to be found in any society or age, and critics have been quick to draw parallels ranging from Daniel Defoe and Nikolay Gogol to Franz

KAFKA and Milan KUNDERA. It is doubtless the Eastern European reader who will best appreciate all the subtleties of the novel.

While it is true that A. made a name for himself while serving as a high political figure of the former regime, recent publications of poetry and prose have suggested that he can maintain his momentum as a writer without the trappings of public office.

FURTHER WORKS: *Devoll, Devoll* (1964); *Komisari Memo* (1970); *The Bronze Bust*, (1975); *Njeriu i mirë, tregime* (1973); *Nënë Shqipëri* (1974; *Mother Albania*, 1985); *Mosha e bardhë, dramë me tri akte* (1975); *Njeriu me top* (1975; *The Man with the Gun*, 1983); *Fjala gdhend gurin, vjersha dhe poema* (1977); *Poezi* (1979); *Trëndafili në gotë* (1979); *Të pagjumet* (1980); *Vepra letrare* (11 vols., 1980-87); *Udhëtoj i menduar* (1985); *Jeta në letërsi, artikuj dhe shënime* (1987); *Splendeur et décadence du camarade Zulo* (1990); *Dështaku, roman* (1991); *L'Homme au canon* (1994); *Çudira dhe marrëzi, fabula, epigrame* (1995); *Lypësi i kohës, poezi* (1995); *Njerëz të krisur: novela, tregime* (1995); *Kalorësi lakuriq, roman.* (1996); *Shpirti i gjyshërve, 101 këngë* (1996); *Vjen njeriu i çuditshëm, poezi* (1996); *Arka e djallit, roman* (1997); *Baladë për tim atë dhe për vete*(1997); *Teshtimat e lirisë: njeriu, politika dhe kultura* (1997). FURTHER WORKS IN ENGLISH: *Short Stories* (1985)

BIBLIOGRAPHY: Vinca, A., *Orët e poezisë* (1990): 135-63; Miracco, E., "A., dalle macerie una speranza nuova," *L'Altra Europa*, 2 (1992): 75-79; Elsie, R., *History of Albanian Literature* (1995): 570-72, 590-92

—ROBERT ELSIE

AGUILERA MALTA, Demetrio

Ecuadorean novelist, dramatist, and short-story writer, b. 24 May 1909, Guayaquil; d. 29 Dec. 1981, Mexico City, Mexico

A. M. started out as a teacher and later served his country as minister of culture. As his reputation as a writer grew, he took up residency in Mexico and in his later years was invited by universities in the U.S. as a writer in residence. In 1981 his native country honored him with the Eugenio Espejo Prize, the most distinguished literary prize awarded in Ecuador.

A. M. began his career with short stories in *Los que se van* (1930; those who leave), a volume that also included stories by Joaquín GALLEGOS LARA and Enrique Gil Gilbert (1912-1973). The book portrayed the violent, broken lives of the *cholos* or half-castes of Guayaquil and was both condemned and praised for the crude naturalism of its language and characterizations. In *Don Goyo* (1933; *Don Goyo*, 1980), A. M.'s first novel, the *cholo* is still his subject, but the regionalism of the mangrove swamps near Guayaquil is tinged with a magical quality, especially in the portrayal of the patriarchal tribal chief, Don Goyo Quimi, whom the *cholos* perceive as an almost mythical being at one with the surrounding natural world. *La isla virgen* (1942; the virgin island) similarly mixes reality and myth. The white man Nestor is the opposite of Don Goyo as he exploits the natural environment of San Pancracio. Nature, personified as woman, eventually takes its revenge on the one who would violate her. These two novels represent A. M.'s epic regionalist stage. In retrospect, they can be seen as precursors of the Latin American magic REALISM of the 1950s and 1960s.

A. M. spent the next decade writing mainly drama, although he composed journalistic fiction as well. For his farces, satires, and atmospheric theatrical pieces he is considered one of the outstanding dramatists of Latin America. In the mid-1960s A. M. returned to the novel with the publication of *La caballaresa del sol* (1964; *Manuela*, 1967), *El Quijote de El Dorado* (1965; the Quixote of El Dorado), and *Un nuevo mar para el rey* (1965; a new ocean for the king), three historico-biographical novels about Simón Bolívar, Francisco de Oreana, and Vasco Núñez de Balboa respectively. Well written but rather conventional and straightforward in form and style, they hardly anticipate his last and most imaginative period of magic-realist satire.

This last period saw the publication of *Siete lunas y siete serpientes* (1970; *Seven Serpents and Seven Moons*, 1976) and *El secuestro del general* (1973; *Babelandia*, 1984). The former is an expressionistic tour de force, a hallucinatory comedy set in the mythical island town of Santorontón and the surrounding coastal area of Ecuador. The regionalism of the earlier novels, however, is here subordinated to allegory as A. M. invents a self-contained microcosm for the unfolding of the archetypal story of the human fall from paradise in Latin America. On the one hand are the evil, satanical characters (representing the politician, the military, the exploitative upper class, and the institutional church), driven by lust and desire for power, who wreak their different kinds of destruction on Santorontón. Combating them are the forces for Good, the effigy of the burned Christ, the good Father Cándido, Doctor Balda, and the Earth Mother Clotilde, who represent authentic Christianity, scientific enlightenment, and nostalgia for a lost paradise respectively. Myth (Christian, Indian, African), legend, dream, and sheer fantasy permeate the novel; evil characters are transformed into crocodiles, serpents, and toads as they rape, murder, and pillage; the burned Christ carries on a dialogue with the good priest Cándido; and redemption occurs through the erotic rituals of the African shaman Bulu-Bulu. An often-incantatory prose style intensifies this radically defamiliarized reality. *El secuestro del general* is equally phantasmagorical but more grotesque in its use of BLACK HUMOR.

A. M. is a committed writer with a passion for social justice who has assimilated the vision and techniques of magic realism over the years. Rather than deepen our understanding of reality, however, the techniques are used to bring into focus a sociopolitical message. Because of this, it is unlikely that A. M. will ever have the wide international readership of a Gabriel GARCÍA MÁRQUEZ.

FURTHER WORKS: *Canal Zone* (1935); *¡Madrid!* (1936); *España leal* (1938); *Lázaro* (1941); *No bastan los átomos* (1955); *Dientes blancos* (1955); *El tigre* (1956); *Honorarios* (1957); *Trilogía Ecuatoriana* (1957); *Una cruz en la sierra maestra* (1960); *Infierno negro* (1967); *Fantoche* (1970); *Muerte, S.A.* (1970); *Teatro completo* (1970); *Jaguar* (1977)

BIBLIOGRAPHY: Davis, J., "The 'Episodios Americanos' of A. M.," *Foreign Language Quarterly*, 9 (1970): 43–47; Luzuriaga, G., "La evolución estilística del teatro de A. M.," *LATR*, 3, 2 (Spring 1970): 39–44; Davis, J., "The 'Episodios Americanos,' cont.," *Foreign Language Quarterly*, 9 (1971): 49–53; Monsanto, C., "Infierno negro: drama de protesta social," *Duquesne Hispanic Review*, 10 (1971): 11–22; Carter, B., "La novelística de A. M.: Enfoques y pareceres," *Chasqui*, 3 (1973): 66–70; Koldewyn, P., "Protesta

guerrillera y mitológica: Novela nueva de A. M.," *Nueva Narrativa Hispanoamericana*, 5 (1975): 199–205; Rabassa, C. C., *D. A. M. and Social Justice* (1980)

—ROBERT SCOTT

AGUSTÍN, José

Mexican novelist, short-story writer, dramatist, screenwriter, and essayist, b. 19 Aug. 1944, Acapulco

Although A. was born into a middle-class family, his work conveys a negative attitude toward this segment of society. In the early 1960s, while still a teenager, he traveled to Cuba to work for Fidel Castro's revolutionary government. After he returned to Mexico, his interest in the theater and the movies led to his studies at the National University and the Institute of Fine Arts. In recent years he has achieved prominence as a screenwriter and film director. He has also lectured at several American universities.

In the mid-1960s Mexican literary life was profoundly altered by a movement of young writers known as "The Wave," which was closely related to the worldwide student rebellion of this period and which reflected the nonconformity of youth and its rejection of bourgeois values. A.'s first novel *La tumba* (1964; the tomb), is generally regarded as the first manifestation of this movement. Its seventeen-year-old narrator belongs to a group of wealthy juveniles whose dissolute behavior derives at least in part from their debauched, hypocritical elders. The disrespectful tone and racy slang lend authenticity to the plot and, at the same time, slash at traditional syntax, an arm of the "establishment."

A.'s second novel, *De perfil* (1966; from the side), is also narrated by a teenager, but it is longer, more mature, and much funnier. Moreover, it makes use of a greater variety of structural devices to involve the reader more intimately with the narrator and to focus on his maturation process, the principal theme. *Seestá haciendo tarde (final en laguna)* (1973; it's getting late [ending in a lagoon]) indicates A.'s continued interest in the problems of young people, in this case a group caught up in the drug culture of Acapulco. The language remains typical of The Wave, but literary dimensions are expanded by allusions to *The Divine Comedy*, Acapulco representing an inferno the protagonist visits with his mentor, Virgilio.

A.'s best theatrical works are *Abolición de la propiedad* (1969; abolition of property) and *Círculo vicioso* (1974; vicious circle). The former is an experimental play consisting of a lively dialogue between two antithetical characters, a female nonconformist and a male traditionalist. Ingeniously integrated into the action are the audiovisual effects of a tape recorder, a film projector, and a live rock band, all of which suggests that in a society dominated by the mass media, values and ideals are reduced to clichés. *Círculo vicioso* exposes the corruption in Mexico City's infamous Lucumberri prison (where A. himself was once incarcerated for seven months). Written in crude, realistic language, this drama also implies a condemnation of Mexican society, the injustices of which are mirrored by life inside the prison.

Over the past thirty years A. has evolved into one of Mexico's most original and influential literary figures. His exceptional ability to convey contemporary Mexico's crisis-ridden atmosphere is best exemplified in his novels *Cerca del fuego* (1986; near the fire), written immediately after the earthquake of 1985, and *Dos horas de sol* (1994; two hours of sun), dramatizing U.S.-Mexican relations and a hurricane in Acapulco.

FURTHER WORKS: *Nuevos escritores mexicanos del siglo XX presentados por sí mismos: J. A.* (1966); *Inventando que sueño* (1968); *La nueva música clásica* (1968); *Los atardeceres privilegiados de la prepa seis* (1970); *De los tres ninguno* (1974, with Renéte Avilés Fabila and Gerardo de la Torre); *La mirada en el centro* (1977); *El rey se acerca a su templo* (1978)

BIBLIOGRAPHY: Carballo, E., "Prólogo" to *Nuevos escritores mexicanos del siglo XX presentados por sí mismos: J. A.* (1966): 5–13; McMurray, G. R., "Current Trends in the Mexican Novel," *Hispania*, 51 (1968): 532–37; Campo, X. Del, "La narrativa joven de México," *SSF*, 8, 1 (1971): 180–98; Langford, W. M., "J. A.," in *The Mexican Novel Comes of Age* (1971): 200–203; Bruce-Novoa, J. D., "*Abolición de la propiedad*: Mexican Experimental Theater," *LALR*, 8, 1 (1974): 5–9; Brushwood, J. S., *The Spanish American Novel: A Twentieth-Century Survey* (1975): 272–73: 319–20; Foster, D. W., and V. R. Foster, eds., "J. A.," *Modern Latin American Literature*, Vol. 1 (1975):10-15; Carter, J. C. D., and D. L. Schmidt, eds., *J. A.: "Onda" and Beyond* (1986)

—GEORGE R. MCMURRAY

AHLIN, Lars

Swedish novelist and short-story writer, b. 4 April 1915, Sundsvall

During A.'s childhood his family's fortunes worsened, and he had to leave school at thirteen to work. But aside from a few odd jobs he remained essentially unemployed. In his late adolescence he occasionally enrolled in courses in theology (especially Luther's), philosophy, and politics. In 1936 he moved to Stockholm and wrote without success for seven years before his first novel was published.

The psychological impact of A.'s hardship years is reflected in many of his novels, beginning with his first, *Tåbb med manifestet* (1943; Tåbb and the manifesto), about an unemployed worker and his struggle to find a sense of self-worth in a society that has rejected him.

A recurrent theme in A.'s work is the problem of preserving the belief in one's dignity in spite of feelings of inferiority created by confrontation with a hierarchical social structure and by awareness of unattainable ideals—ideals whose crushing burden A.'s protagonists survive only through the strength of love. Others die, like Aron in *Fromma mord* (1952; pious murders), who unsuccessfully strives to be everybody's ideal friend and ultimately satisfies nobody.

While Marx and Luther provided the philosophical basis for A.'s work, Dostoevsky was his major literary inspiration, a fact particularly apparent in his gallery of characters—grotesque, bizarre, miserable, and unsuccessful—who carry A.'s message of man's equality and the redeeming quality of love.

A. has a special talent for creating unforgettable female characters, like the girl in *Kanelbiten* (1953; *Cinnamoncandy*, 1990), who dies in despair when she is exposed to the irrationality of life, or like his old, often decrepit women, who preach his gospel of love. There is also a strong archetypal element in many of A.'s women,

for example the guiding anima figures in *Kvinna kvinna* (1955; woman woman), and *Bark och löv* (1961; bark and leaves), and the Great Mother figure in *Natt i marknadstältet* (1957; night in the market stall).

After World War II A. turned to a more experimental form of the novel in the tradition of the French and German novel of the 1920s, and now stands as one of the leading figures in the new aesthetics of Swedish literature. His most intricately written novel, *Om* (1946; if, about, *or* around) features a three-dimensional narrative perspective merged into one subject. The narrative flow in this novel and, for example, *Bark och löv* is fragmented by inserts of substories, discussions of aesthetics, and unexplained shifts in time and space. Even in his characterization, A. rejects demands for realism and conventional coherence. One of his major characters is Zackarias, an adolescent boy with far more wisdom than his age warrants, whom we meet in *Stora glömskan* (1954; the great amnesia) and in *Natt i marknadstältet*.

A.'s psychologically subtle short stories, with their rather tightly woven plots, have been more readily accepted by the public than his experimental novels.

A.'s aesthetics and his view that equality should be man's inalienable birthright have influenced many younger writers and contributed to the establishment of a philosophy suitable to the ideals of the contemporary Swedish welfare state.

FURTHER WORKS: *Inga ögon väntar mig* (1944); *Min död är min* (1945); *Jungfrun i det gröna* (1947); *Fångnas glädje* (1947); *Egen spis* (1948); *Huset har ingen filial* (1949); *Gilla gång* (1958); *Nattens ögonsten* (1958). FURTHER WORKS IN ENGLISH: *Selected Poems* (1982)

BIBLIOGRAPHY: Gustafson, A., *A History of Swedish Literature* (1961): 554–56; Palm, G., "L. A. and the New Swedish Novel," in Bäckström, L., and G. Palm, eds., *Sweden Writes* (1965): 86–95; Lundell, T., "L. A.'s Concept of the Writer as 'Identificator' and 'Förbedjare,'" *Scan*, 14 (May 1975): 27–35; Lundell, T., "L. A.'s Concept of Equality," *SS*, 47 (1975): 339–51; Lundell, T., *L. A.* (1977)

—TORBORG LUNDELL

AHMED, Faiz "Faiz"

See Faiz, Faiz Ahmed

AI Ch'ing

(pseud. of Chiang Hai-ch'eng) Chinese poet, b. 17 February, 1910, Iwu, Chin-hua County, Chekiang Province

Owing to his involvement with the League of Leftist Artists, A., a landlord's son from a southern province recently returned from Paris, where he had been introduced to the works of such European masters as Rimbaud and APOLLINAIRE, was arrested and detained in Shanghai's French Concession from 1932 to 1935. There he wrote his first poetry, later published as *Ta-yen-ho* (1936; great-dike river).

The title poem, dedicated to his beloved wet nurse, portrays the tragic existence of an illiterate woman who took the name of her native village. From that point on, A. turned his back on his own class, dedicating his life and art to China's dispossessed masses; proclaiming that "the poet must speak the truth," he was quickly caught up in patriotic-revolutionary activities, gathering material from the ordinary people and from his adopted home in northern China.

A.'s poems are among the most straightforward written in his time and display striking images and a bold use of color. A. was unwavering in his insistence that poetry must be a utilitarian art form, the "spiritual and educational instrument of the masses"; he exhorted his colleagues to "persist in the revolution brought into poetry by WHITMAN, VERHAEREN, and MAYAKOVSKY. We must make poetry into something that adequately meets the needs of a new era, without hesitating to use whatever poetic form is most suitable for this purpose."

The first of three periods in his career, which coincided with his incarceration, is marked by heavily autobiographical free and unrhymed verse, generally cast in sentimental hues. The second period, the early war years of 1935–41, witnessed the creation of his most important and influential works. The artistic self-assurance of the poet was complemented by a growing patriotic ardor and an even deeper involvement with the people and the land. The most noteworthy poem of this period is "T'a szu tsai ti-erh tz'u" (1939; he died a second time), a twelve-part narrative about the death of a soldier. The successful contrast of gruesome imagery with scenic beauty and of human glory with human indifference, the changing moods, and the simplicity of language make this poem a representation not only of a poet's sensitivities, but of an era.

The third period, which began after A.'s arrival in the Communist stronghold of Yenan in 1941, saw the complete politicization of his art. Having accepted the tenets and goals of Communism, he used folk forms to attack fascism and praise the party and Chairman Mao. This was not so much a change in philosophy as one of emphasis and degree. Although his poems from this period are generally undistinguished, his individualism occasionally surfaced, placing him in opposition to party policy. Mildly censured in 1942 and condemned as a rightist in the mid-1950s, he disappeared from public view for more than two decades, but has been rehabilitated following the fall of the "gang of four." In 1980 he participated in a writers' workshop at the University of Iowa.

FURTHER WORKS: *Hsiang t'ai-yang* (1938); *Liming te t'ung-chih* (1939); *Shih lun* (1940); *Huo-pa* (1940); *K'uang-yeh* (1940); *Hsüeh li tsuan* (1945); *Hsien-kei hsiang-ts'un te shih* (1945); *Wu Man-yu* (1946); *Shih hsin minchu chu-i te wen-hsüeh* (1947); *Tsou hsiang sheng-li* (1950); *Ai Ch'ing hsüan-chi* (1951); *Hsin wen-i lun-chi* (1952); *Pao-shih te hunghsing* (1953); *Ai Ch'ing shih-hsüan* (1955); *Hei man* (1955); *Ch'un-t'ien* (1956); *Haichia shang* (1957). FURTHER WORKS IN ENGLISH: *Selected Poems* (1982)

BIBLIOGRAPHY: Goldman, M., *Literary Dissent in Communist China* (1967): passim; Boorman, H. L., and Howard, R. C., *Biographical Dictionary of Republican China* (1971), Vol. I: 317–19; Lin, J. C., *Modern Chinese Poetry: An Introduction* (1972): 172–88 and passim; Průšek, J., ed., *Dictionary of Oriental Literatures* (1974), Vol. I: 1–2; Friend, R. C., "Return from Silence," *ChinL*, June 1979: 42–51

—HOWARD GOLDBLATT

AICHINGER, Ilse

Austrian novelist, dramatist, and short-story writer, b. 1 Nov. 1921, Vienna

A., a major representative of the generation of authors who first published immediately after World War II, grew up in Linz and Vienna. Because she was half-Jewish, she had to do forced service during the war and could not matriculate at the University of Vienna until after the end of the war. Thus she began medical studies rather late. After five semesters she discontinued her studies and became a reader for what would become her own publisher, S. Fischer Verlag. She soon became a member of Group 47 and received their prize for literature in 1952. Since 1953, when she married the German writer Günter EICH, she has lived and worked in Bavaria, in West Germany.

A.'s first publication was a contribution to *Plan*, a postwar Austrian literary periodical: "Aufruf zum Mißtrauen" (1946; call to mistrust) was a significant statement about the feelings of young Austrians after World War II. In it A. articulates the mood of Austrian literature in the postwar period: constant mistrust. Perhaps this mistrust is the reason she later chose to resurrect the dialogue, a genre that had been neglected in German literature until A. published *Zu keiner Stunde* (1957; not at any hour). In the various dialogues she has written, A. concentrates on one thought, one idea, or one theme through discussions between two or more individuals. Dialogues like "Belvedere" (1963; "Belvedere," 1969) and "Erstes Semester" (1963; "First Term," 1969) test a particular theme or point of view and thus become the literary applications of A.'s invocation to self-mistrust.

A. emerged as a presence in Austria with the publication of her only novel, *Die größere Hoffnung* (1948; *Herod's Children*, 1963), which established and exemplified what may be termed her style. Set against the background of World War II, the work stresses the conflict and interplay of fear and trust. There are always two levels at work—dream and reality—and it is through the dream that the truth of the reality is made clear.

A.'s use of the convergence of dream and reality in her novel and in many of her other works is one reason she has often been compared to KAFKA. But her works, especially her numerous short stories, are reminiscent of Kafka in other ways as well: A.'s style, which is relatively simple and without syntactical complications or difficulties, is like Kafka's in that its simplicity heightens the effect of the works. Like Kafka she uses the language and vocabulary of everyday experience, but arresting metaphors and unusual figures create a feeling of alienation from the experience. In the title story of *Der Gefesselte* (1953; *The Bound Man and Other Stories*, 1955), A. portrays a man who, upon awakening, finds himself bound with ropes and must learn to cope with his new limitations. With its theme of guilt and atonement, the story not only evokes a deeply felt religious sense, but, not surprisingly, also once again recalls Kafka's works. It is precisely A.'s religious sensibility, which is in part conveyed by the many biblical allusions and references in her work, that enables her to combine the mistrust she feels is necessary with a soaring belief in the human spirit. Despite the fear and uncertainty, elements A. sees as part of the human condition, a greater hope always remains.

Although A. has won many prizes for her work, including the City Prizes of Bremen and Düsseldorf (1955), the Immermann Prize (1957), the Literary Prize of the Bavarian Academy of Fine Arts (1961), the Nelly Sachs Prize of Dortmund (1971), the

Literary Prize of Vienna (1974), and the Georg Trakl Prize for Poetry (1979), her books never burst upon the literary scene in the sense that they cause great furor and discussion; they simply appear and are eventually read. Because of their universal themes of anxiety, hope, and compassion, her works continue to appeal to a wide audience.

FURTHER WORKS: *Rede unter dem Galgen* (1952; orig. Austrian ed. of *Der Gefesselte*); *Besuch im Pfarrhaus* (1961); *Wo ich wohne* (1963); *Eliza Eliza* (1965); *Auckland* (1969); *Nachricht vom Tag* (1970); *Dialoge, Erzählungen, Gedichte* (1971); *Schlechte Wörter* (1976); *Verschenkter Rat* (1978). FURTHER WORKS IN ENGLISH: *I. A.: Selected Poetry and Prose* (1983)

BIBLIOGRAPHY: Plant, R., on *The Bound Man, SatR*, 16 June 1956, 25; Magid, M., on *Herod's Children, Book Week*, 17 Nov. 1963, 6; Eggers, W., "I. A.," in Weber, D., ed., *Deutsche Literatur seit 1945* (1968): 221–38; Alldridge, J. C., *I. A.* (1969); Pickar, G., "'Das Feuermal'—Mark of Life and Death: Interpretive Comments to I. A.'s 'Das Plakat,'" *Xavier University Studies*, 10, 3 (1971): 20–27; Stanley, P. H., "I. A.'s Absurd 'I,'" *GerSR*, 6 2 (1979): 331–50

—RUTH V. GROSS

AIDOO, Ama Ata

(formerly Christina Ama Ata Aidoo) Ghanaian dramatist, poet, short-story writer, and novelist (writing in English), b. 23 Mar. 1942, Abeadzi Kyiakor

Educated at Wesley Girls School, Cape Coast, and the University of Ghana (in Legon), where she earned a B.A. with honors in 1964 and became a research fellow in African studies after graduation, A. participated in an international seminar at Harvard University in 1966 and studied creative writing at Stanford University. She has traveled extensively in Africa, the U.S., and Europe as a writer, teacher, and consultant. Beginning in 1970 she was based as a lecturer in English at the University of Cape Coast; but in January 1982, she accepted the appointment of secretary for education for Ghana and served until June 1983. Since September 1983, A. has lived in Harare, Zimbabwe.

While yet a student, A. won prizes for her short stories and witnessed the production of her first play. *The Dilemma of a Ghost* (perf. 1964, pub. 1965). Classified most often as a dramatist, A. has written in the major genres. All of her works, however, reflect the influence of the oral tradition, especially storytelling, which she states has power and pertinence for the contemporary writer and audience. While her creations are set primarily in Africa, particularly Ghana, and address the problems and situations of that continent, they are designed to engage her worldwide audience toward the recognition that the issues affect us all and, furthermore, that her readers too have a responsibility to help resolve these ills.

The Dilemma of a Ghost, her first play, adopts structural and thematic elements from the traditional dilemma tale as it dramatizes the conflicts that result when an African male who has been studying in the U.S. returns to Ghana with his African-American wife. *Anowa* (1969), the second dramatic piece, based on a legend

which A. says her mother told her, emphasizes the interlocking systems of gender, race, and class, especially as these structures impact on the lives of women. The beautiful, strong-minded, nonconforming Anowa, whose name provides the title, is the model for the other independent female figures who dominate the later works and who, along with their rebellious ideas, have earned for their creator the title of "feminist."

The short stories, many published in journals before being collected in *No Sweetness Here* (1970), illustrate, even more keenly, her ability to employ the techniques and performance skills of the oral artist and concurrently to serve as a voice for the African woman. These eleven tales explore themes of motherhood, womanhood, childhood, the family, marriage, and other issues confronting postindependent Africa.

A.'s poetry also first appeared in anthologies and journals. In addition, her plays, short stories, and longer pieces display her dynamic flair for combining narrative and poetry. *Someone Talking to Sometime* (1985), a volume of poems, takes one on a journey to experience the pain, hurt, and foolishness that African people have suffered on the continent, in the U.S., and throughout the world. Another subject, which emerged in the short stories, but receives prominence here and in *Our Sister Killjoy; or, the Reflections of a Black-Eyed Squint* (1977), is neocolonialism, the system of oppression and abuse by African leaders and the educated elites against their own struggling people. The collection appeals for an end to the suffering and strife.

Our Sister Killjoy; or, the Reflections of a Black-Eyed Squint and *Changes: A Love Story* (1991) represent A.'s contribution to the novel. Both works are similar in that they present the independent, educated, professional female protagonist in a book-length, poetic-prose form that defies conventional categories. *Changes*, subtitled "A Love Story," which is a surprise, since A. had vowed never to write on such a "frivolous" topic, moves closer in shape toward its Western counterpart. Nevertheless, this most recently published piece of fiction provides the provocative treatment and twist that characterize the writings of this author.

"Experimental," "innovative," "inimitable," "stimulating," "engaging," and "committed" describe this multitalented African female writer and her writings. Sometimes angry, sometimes witty, incisive yet sensitive, possessing remarkable insight into the human condition, A. blends the legacy of her African oral inheritance with the Western borrowings to produce eloquent and dazzling creations. For too long, neglected and underrepresented in critical circles, possibly because of publishing problems, availability of the books, and the originality in her performances, A. now appears to be gaining the recognition her powerful literature deserves.

FURTHER WORKS: *The Eagle and the Chickens and Other Stories for Children* (1986); *Birds and Other Poems for Children* (1987)

BIBLIOGRAPHY: Brown, L. W., "A. A. A.: The Art of the Short Story and Sexual Roles in Africa," *WLWE*, 13 (1974): 172–83; Adelugba, D., "Language and Drama: A. A. A.," in Jones, E. D., ed., *ALT*, 8 (1976): 72–84; Brown, L. W., "A. A. A.," *Women Writers in Black Africa* (1981): 84–121; Hill-Lubin, M., "The Relationship of African-Americans and Africans: A Recurring Theme in the Works of A. A. A.," *PA*, 124 (1982): 190–201; Elder, A., "A. A. A. and the Oral Tradition: A Paradox of Form and Substance," in Jones, E. M., et al., eds., *Women in African Literature Today* (1987): 109–18; Owusu, K., "Canons under

Siege: Blackness, Femaleness, and A. A. A.'s *Our Sister Killjoy*," *Callaloo*, 13, 2 (Spring 1990): 341–63

—MILDRED A. HILL-LUBIN

AIKEN, Conrad

American poet, critic, novelist, short-story writer, and memoirist, b. 5 Aug. 1889, Savannah, Ga.; d. 17 Aug. 1973, Savannah, Ga.

A.'s childhood in Savannah ended with the traumatic discovery one morning that his father had killed his mother and then committed suicide. After attending secondary schools in Massachusetts, A. studied at Harvard (where with T. S. ELIOT he edited the *Advocate*), married, and traveled in Italy, France, and England. His adult life was punctuated by trans-Atlantic journeys. In 1921 he moved from Massachusetts to England, settling in Rye, Sussex, as a professional writer. In 1927–28 he was tutor in English at Harvard. In 1930, having divorced and remarried, he returned to Rye. In 1933, after a brief stay in Spain, he sailed again for Boston. From 1934 to 1936 he was again in Rye, writing "London Letters" to *The New Yorker*. He then returned to New York and Boston, visited Savannah for the first time since 1901, and traveled to Mexico, where he married the artist Mary Hoover. A. and his third wife returned to Rye in 1937, moved to South Dennis, Mass., in 1939, returned to Rye in 1945, and after 1947 lived in Brewster, Mass. A. was consultant in poetry at the Library of Congress from 1950 to 1952. From 1962 on he wintered in a Savannah house adjacent to that of his childhood. He remained in Savannah throughout the last year of his life, so ending the "great circle" peregrinations (geographical, familial, and psychological) that inform his literary work.

A. was a prolific and mellifluous poet. Early influenced by Edgar Allan Poe, T. S. Eliot, and John Gould Fletcher (1886–1950), he sought to render the "resonances" of the quest for self-knowledge in musical forms that combine psychological strip-tease—the tantalizing semiexposure of the ego's most intimate secrets—and spiritual pilgrimage. Several "symphonies"—*The Charnel Rose* (1918), *The Jig of Forslin* (1916), *The House of Dust* (1920), *Senlin* (1918), and *The Pilgrimage of Festus* (1923)—were revised and supplied with a Freudian coda, "Changing Mind" of 1925, to make up *The Divine Pilgrim* (1949). A.'s major poetic works, however, are the restrained and clarified meditative sequences *Preludes to Memnon* (1931) and *Time in the Rock: Preludes to Definition* (1936), which explore the field of an irreducibly problematic consciousness and move toward disclosure of the religious dimensions of word and world. A.'s journey through Freudian psychology toward a revitalized Emersonian transcendentalism was completed in two strong later volumes, *A Letter from Li Po* (1955) and *Sheepfold Hill* (1958). Without slighting the modern burden of doubt and estrangement, his seasoned musicality there celebrates the eternal moment of consciousness and love that illuminates what he sees as a universal "Book of Change."

A.'s essays, collected in *Scepticisms* (1919) and *A Reviewer's ABC* (1958), comment acutely on modern poetry and fiction as they engage the questions provoked by his commitment to literature as a mode of self-understanding. A.'s fiction, too, engages such questions. The short stories may move from the mundane into hallucination, phobia, or dream ("Silent Snow, Secret Snow," "Mr.

Arcularis") or explore the writer's relation to his medium ("Life Isn't a Short Story"). The novels render the perilous edge of sanity, the ambiguous relations between love and death, the rediscovery of a childhood trauma, or the necessity of self-crucifixion through forms that combine lyrical description, virtuoso conversation, and post-Joycean interior monologue. Most central to A.'s own psychological journey are *Blue Voyage* (1927), which enacts a midlife turn in his career, and *Great Circle* (1933), which Freud considered a masterpiece of analytic introspection.

The climactic synthesis of A.'s work is *Ushant: An Essay* (1952), one of the most subtle and profound autobiographies in English. A multidimensional fiction, *Ushant* dramatizes the attempt of its protagonist, the author's persona, to read the palimpsest of hieroglyphs that constitutes the landscape of his soul. Evoking a vivid sense of many places and sketching witty vignettes of the literary generation between the wars, it traces the peregrinations of an author who seems fixated in narcissism by the murder-suicide of his parents but is nevertheless a medium for that creative evolution which must proceed through the spiraling expansion of language and consciousness. *Ushant* is a stunning performance in an eclectic tradition (Henry JAMES, Henry ADAMS, James JOYCE, and William FAULKNER are among those evoked by its prose), and it may be the work of A. to which future generations will most often return.

This versatile man of letters received the Pulitzer Prize for *Selected Poems* (1929), the National Book Award for *Collected Poems* (1953), the Bollingen Prize in 1956, and the Gold Medal in Poetry from the American Academy of Arts and Letters in 1958. But during his lifetime his range, his psychological penetration, and his verbal richness never received the wide recognition they deserve. Except for *Ushant*, A.'s works no doubt lack the concentrated power to be found in the best of Eliot, POUND, STEVENS, and Faulkner. But he stands with those figures, if somewhat to one side, an exemplar of another direction in modern American writing: liberal, ironic, and humane.

FURTHER WORKS: *Earth Triumphant* (1914); *Turns and Movies* (1916); *Nocturne of Remembered Spring* (1917); *Punch: The Immortal Liar* (1921); *Priapus and the Pool* (1922); *Bring! Bring!* (1925); *Costumes by Eros* (1928); *Prelude* (1929); *John Deth, a Metaphysical Legend* (1930); *The Coming Forth by Day of Osiris Jones* (1931); *Among the Lost People* (1934); *Landscape West of Eden* (1935); *Conversation* (1940); *And in the Human Heart* (1940); *Brownstone Eclogues* (1942); *The Soldier* (1944); *The Kid* (1947); *Skylight One* (1949); *The Short Stories of C. A.* (1950); *Mr. Arcularis: A Play* (1957); *Collected Short Stories* (1960); *Selected Poems* (1961); *The Morning Song of Lord Zero* (1963); *Collected Novels* (1964); *A Seizure of Limericks* (1964); *Cats and Bats and Things with Wings* (1965); *Tom, Sue and the Clock* (1966); *Thee* (1967); *Collected Poems 1916–1970* (1970); *The Clerk's Journal* (1971); *A Little Who's Zoo of Mild Animals* (1977); *Selected Letters* (1978)

BIBLIOGRAPHY: Peterson, H., *Melody of Chaos* (1931); Blackmur, R. P., "C. A.: The Poet," *Atlantic*, Dec. 1953: 77–82; Blanshard, R. A., "Pilgrim's Progress: C. A.'s Poetry," *TQ*, 1 (1958): 135–48; Martin, J., *C. A.: A Life of His Art* (1962); Hoffman, F. J., *C. A.* (1962); Denney, R., *C. A.* (1964); Whitaker, T. R., "Repeating Is What I Am Loving," *Parnassus* 1, 1 (1972): 59–68; Cowley, M., "C. A.: From Savannah to Emerson," *SoR*, 11 (1975): 245–59;

Martin, H., *The Art of Knowing: The Poetry and Prose of C. A.* (1988); Seigel, C. F., *The Fictive World of C. A.* (1993)

—THOMAS R. WHITAKER

AINI, Sadriddin

Tajik novelist, b. 27 Apr. 1878, Soktare, Uzbekistan; d. 15 July 1954, Dushanbe, Tajikistan

A. was the grandson of Sayyid Umar Khoja, a master carpenter, the imam of the village mosque, and heir to the legacy of the great poet Najm al-Din Kubra (d. 1221). As a follower of Kubra, A.'s father did not heed either the government or the nobility. Instead, he practiced free will and relied on his own rational capacity and abilities. The very titles of *khoja* (indicating nobility due to early submission to Islam) and *sayyid* (indicating descent from the Prophet) testify to the family's status. Emphasis on the Kubravi tradition is important for the strict rule under which the family lived and for the attention it paid to duty.

A.'s early education was informal. He studied the works of the major figures of Tajik culture, Firdowsi (935-1020 or 1026), Sa'di (1213-1292), Hafiz (1321-1389), Sa'ib (1603-1674), and Bedil (1644-1721) with his father, while observing the examples of the wisdom of those sages in the ordinary people of Bukhara. His career began as a cook in the Bukharan schools. Soon after, he was discovered by Sharifjan Makhdum Sadr-i Zia (1865-1931) who acquainted him with the Bukharan literary scene. Under the direction of Sadr-i Zia and helped by Ahmad Donish (1827-1897), A. became a poet, a reformist educator, and a revolutionary.

A.'s career was dedicated to education. Early in his career, he understood the importance of the reforms of the Tatar Ismail Bey Gaspirali (1854-1914) and moved to introduce new methodology in Tajikistan schools. He even cooperated with the *Jadids* to overcome the obstacles created by the Amir, Alim Khan, who ruled from 1910 to 1920, and the 'Ulema to stem the tide of modernization of Bukhara. His efforts, however, were unsuccessful. For his cooperation with the *Jadids* A. was imprisoned and tortured.

During the early years of socialism A. served in a number of capacities, including education director and literary editor and consultant. It was during this time (1918-21) that his poetic career changed and revolutionary slogans replaced his school-day themes. Dedicated to the socialist cause, he wrote fiery pieces like "Marsh-i Huriyyat" (1918; The Anthem of Freedom) "Basharaf-i Inqilob-i Oktiabr" (1918; In Honor of the October Revolution), "Inqilob" (1919; Revolution), and "Akhgar-i Inqilob" (1921; The Flames of Revolution). These pieces, written exclusively for the education of Muslim youths, played a major role in the construction of early Tajik curricula.

A.'s prolific career as a novelist began with *Jallodon-i Bukhara* (1920; The Bukhara Executioners), published first in installments in Uzbeki. It was later published in Tajiki translation in 1936 and, in full form in Uzbeki, in 1940. The setting is 1918 Bukhara, immediately after the Amir's receipt of F. I. Kalisov's (1891-1940) ultimatum for reform. To carry out the Amir's order for the elimination of the families and associates of the Young Bukharans, gallows had been set up in front of the Arg in the Registan with 200 people executed daily. Aini details the manner of the executions

and the atmosphere at the palace. After the day's work, the executioners wait for the carts that had taken the bodies to the dump. While waiting, they drink tea, take *nos* (a local drug substance), and talk about the atrocities of the *mullahs*, *mirshab*, *qushbegi*, and the Amir. A. reveals his own understanding of the identity of the *Jadids*, the role of the Young Bukharans, the events that led to the March 1918 executions, and the collusion of the Amir with the *mullahs* against the *Jadids*.

His next novel, *Sarguzasht-i Yak Tojik-i Kam Baghal yo ki Odinah* (1927; The Life Story of a Poor Tajik, or Odinah), is important in a different way. It details life in the Kuhistan region of Tajikistan, a region that even today is not well understood. *Ghulomon* (1934; The Slaves) is A.'s monumental work of fiction, rivaling his own historical research reflected in the *Ta'rikh-i Amiron-i Manghitiya-i Bukhoro* (1919; The History of the Manghit Amirs of Bukhara). It illustrates the role of the slave colonies in the class struggles that ousted Alim khan and established Soviet power.

Part of a trilogy, including *Dokhundah* and *Odina*, *Ghulomon* is a semihistorical novel covering events from the reign of Amir Haidar (1802-26) to the establishment of Soviet power and formation of the Kolkhozes. It was written in Uzbeki in 1934 and translated into Tajiki in 1935. The novel is divided into five parts. The most interesting part deals with the slave trade. Captured by the Turkmens, the victims are taught *shi'i* customs and rituals and sold in the markets of Bukhara, Shahrsabz, Qarshi, and Khiva. Life in slave colonies, as well as the lives of slave traders and caravaneers, is explored. The relationship between these low lives and the centers of power—the Amir, *rais*, *amlokdor*, and *mirshab*—is portrayed with care. Gradually, as slave colonies are transformed into labor camps and enter Bukhara's mainstream, the Amir takes control of all by denying access to new-method schools and to Islam, the hotbeds for reforms. Collaborating, the children of the slaves, intellectuals, administrators, and the landowners save Bukhara.

A. won the State Prize of the U.S.S.R. in 1950. Three of his works have received great attention among the Tajiks: *Namunaho-i Adabiyyot-i Tojik* (1925; Samples of Tajik Literature), *Marg-i Sudkhur* (1938; *The Death of the Money-Lender*, 1986) and *Yoddoshtho* (1949; Reminiscences). *Namunaho-i Adabiyyot-i Tojik* serves as the cornerstone of present-day Tajik literature, *Marg-i Sudkhur* depicts the demise of the old order in the person of a miser, while *Yoddoshtho* documents, with almost photographic precision, Bukhara's transition from a medieval sultanate into a modern state. Few individuals have experienced the events in which A. participated. Yet A. not only survived the atrocities of the Amirs of Bukhara, he documented them. His contribution to history is further enhanced by his poems and by novels that portray life in the most inaccessible regions of Eastern Bukhara.

FURTHER WORKS: *Kulliyot* (13 vols., 1958-77)

BIBLIOGRAPHY: Rajabov, Z. Sh., *A.—istorik Tadzhikskovo naroda* (1951); Tabarov, S., *S. A.: Asosguzor-i Adabiyyot-i Soveti-i Tojik* (1954); "S. A.," in *Ocherk-i Ta'rikhi-i Adabiyyot-i Soveti-i Tojik* (1959), Vol. 2: 3-84; Niazov, Kh. N., *Put' S. A.—Poeta* (1965); Saifullaev, A., *Roman-i Ustod S. A. "Dokhunda"* (1966); Qodiri, A., *Adibon-i Tojikiston* (1966): 5-13; Braginskii, I. S., *Hayot ve Ijodiyot-i S. A.* (1968); Braginskii, I. S., "A.," *Ensaiklopidio-i Soveti-i Tojik* (1978), Vol. 1: 86-90; Saifullaev, A. "A.," *Ensaiklopedio-i Adabiyyot ve San'at-i Tojik* (1988), Vol. 1: 116-25

—IRAJ BASHIRI

AISTIS, Jonas

(pseud. of Jonas Aleksandravičius) Lithuanian poet, essayist, and critic, b. 7 July 1904, Kampiškes; d. 13 June 1973, Hillcrest Heights, Md., U.S.A.

After initial studies at the University of Kaunas, A. went to France and took a degree in philology at the University of Grenoble. In 1946 he emigrated to the U.S., taught high school for six years, then joined the Free Europe Committee. From 1958 until his death he worked at the Library of Congress in Washington, D.C.

A.'s poetry spans twenty-five years and is characterized by thematic and stylistic continuities. His first volume of poetry, *Eilėraščiai* (poems), appeared in 1932 and concentrated on the poet's inner world of thought and feeling, thus breaking with the rhetorical tradition. A. drew inspiration from Lithuanian landscapes, from folklore, from the common fund of romantic motifs, from religious imagery, and also from the urban setting. He fused these disparate elements into intensely personal poems that reveal a highly individualistic consciousness, sometimes come out of deep, painful moments of the author's experience, and owe their power to subtle effects of rhyme, assonance, rhythm, and imagery. A. sought, through daring word assocations and the rich music of his delicate, lyric register, to capture half-remembered, half-perceived states, to endow simple happenings with fairy-tale magic, to give voice to feelings of love and longing, to lend reality to visions of beauty. A.'s natural mode of expression is gentle dreaming; his poems are brief, seemingly unstudied statements of mood that fuse emotion and sense perception in the manner of impressionist paintings.

Subsequent collections of poetry, notably *Imago mortis* (1933; the image of death), *Intymios giesmės* (1935; intimate hymns), *Užgesę chimeros akys* (1937; the burned-out eyes of the chimera), solidified A.'s reputation as a distinctive lyric poet. Taken together, these volumes show a drift toward the negative tonality, and they also illuminate A.'s view of poetry as an artificial construct, a theatrical gesture, a web of words spun around the wounds that open up in the poet's consciousness. A. associated the creative act with ecstasy and suffering; he experienced it as the mind's mysterious moving away from pain and also as the return to the original and necessarily painful point of conjunction between the world and the artist.

In the 1940s, reacting to World War II and the experience of exile, A. abandoned his exclusively personal manner and incorporated into his poetry meditations on Lithuania's destiny, as well as reminiscences of his native land framed in a language that leans on shared beliefs and aspirations. Sometimes he even assumed the voice of the community's spokesman. These thematic and stylistic innovations expanded A.'s range, but they did not signal a new departure. Subsequently, A. returned to the motifs and cadences of the earlier periods and concentrated on poems of intimate joys and sorrows that seemed little touched by history.

A. is one of the most significant Lithuanian poets of the generation between the two world wars. He shunned rhetorical statement, redefined poetry as the search for personal meaning, brought to perfection the lyric mode, demonstrated the value of artistic control, and expanded significantly the poetic possibilities of the Lithuanian language. In his poetry and essays he expressed a coherent view of art and of reality. Even though his poems did not provide an adequate model for the next generation, they exercised considerable influence and represent a significant phase in the evolution of modern Lithuanian poetry.

FURTHER WORKS: *Dievai ir smūtkeliai* (1935); *Poezija* (1940); *Be tėvynės brangios* (1942); *Nemuno ilgesys* (1947); *Pilnatis* (1948); *Sesuo būtis* (1951); *Apie laiką ir žmones* (1954); *Kristaliniam karste* (1957); *Poezija* (1961); *Milfordo gatvės elegijos* (1969)

BIBLIOGRAPHY: Šilbajoris, R., "Aspects of Poetic Imagery in the Work of J. A.," *Perfection of Exile: 14 Contemporary Lithuanian Writers* (1970): 77–93

—VIKTORIA SKRUPSKELIS

AITMATOV, Chinghiz
See Aytmatov, Chïngïz

ÅKESSON, Sonja

Swedish poet, b. 19 April 1926, Buttle; d. 5 May 1977, Stockholm

With only six years of schooling, Å. worked as a maid, waitress, and telephone operator before marrying at an early age. When her marriage broke up, she left her native island of Gotland with her two small children, moved to Stockholm, and remarried twice. Together with her latest husband, the poet Jarl Hammarberg-Åkesson (b. 1940), she published two collections of poetry—*Strålande dikter/nej så fan heller* (1967; splendid poems/certainly not) and *Kändis* (1969; well-known person)—and one play, *Hå! vi är på väg* (1972; ho! we're on our way).

Å.'s breakthrough as a poet came in 1963, with the collection *Husfrid* (1963; domestic peace), which portrays a housewife trapped at home, unhappy and frustrated. In a poetic style called the "new simplicity" in Sweden, Å. creates a sensualism that manifests itself in detailed descriptions of trivial, everyday objects and a concentration on the power of language to evoke sights and sounds. Her metaphors are as concrete as objects in a surrealistic painting. Her two most famous poems are included in this collection: "Vara vit mans slav" (be white man's slave), which became the fighting song of the radical feminist movement in Sweden during the 1960s, and "Självbiografi" (autobiography), a paraphrase of and reply to the American poet Lawrence Ferlinghetti's (b. 1919) "autobiography," *A Coney Island of the Mind* (1958). It is a deliberate attempt to show the other side, to create a dialogue between male and female points of view, to show the differences in the real-life situations of a man and a woman living in essentially the same kind of society during the same period of time.

In her later poetry, from the mid-1960s until her death, Å. continued to write in an even more openly confessional style, describing her own alcoholism, drug addiction, and nervous breakdowns.

Called the "national poet of the welfare state," Å. enjoyed great popularity during her lifetime. Because of her extraordinary ability to depict with humor and irony the life of a typical middle-class, middled-aged Swedish housewife, many women in Sweden easily see themselves in her poems. But her importance goes beyond that. Her theme is more than the housewife's alienation in modern society. It is the dilemma of both men and women coping with the contrasts between reality and an idyllic view of society.

FURTHER WORKS: *Situationer* (1957); *Glasveranda* (1959); *Skvallerspegel* (1960); *Leva livet* (1961); *Efter balen* (1962); *Ute skiner solen* (1965); *Jag bor i Sverige* (1966); *Man får vara glad och tacka Gud* (1967); *Pris* (1968); *Slagdängor* (1969); *Ljuva sextiotal* (1970); *Hjärtat hamrar, lungorna smälter* (1972); *Dödens ungar* (1973); *Sagan om Siv* (1974); *En värk att anpassa* (1975); *Ett liv att avverka* (1976); *Hästens öga* (1976); *En tid att avliva* (1978)

BIBLIOGRAPHY: Claréus, L., "S. Å.'s 'Autobiography': Reply to Ferlinghetti," *ScanR*, 67 (1979): 64–68; Graves, P., "S. Å. 1926–1977," *Swedish Books*, 1, 4 (1980): 36–37

—INGRID CLARÉUS

AKHMADULINA, Bella

Russian poet and translator, b. 20 April 1937, Moscow

A. was graduated in 1960 from the Gorky Institute, a literary school attended by many Soviet poets and writers. In 1962 a collection of her poems, *Struna* (the string), was published, bringing her a degree of popularity scarcely less than that of her first husband, the poet Yevgeny YEVTUSHENKO. A.'s second book of poems, *Uroki muzyki* (music lessons), appeared in 1969; in the view of most critics, it contains her best works: the allegorical "Skazka o dozhde" ("A Tale about Rain in Several Episodes," 1969) and "Moya rodoslovnaya" (my ancestry). She has also gained renown as a translator of poets from the former Soviet Union's smaller nationalities, such as the Georgians—especially the collection *Sny o Gruzii* (Georgian dreams), published in 1977.

A. is a lyric poet of exceptional power and expressivity. Her distinctive poetics encompass both traditional and innovative elements—the energy of sound and image, the excitement and truthfulness ("not a small word of a lie") of poetic self-expression. She is dedicated to creative freedom. In "Skazka o dozhde," in which the speaker visits a large but inhospitable house, the rain is a symbol of free poetic inspiration juxtaposed against philistine platitudes and official interdiction. "Moya rodoslovnaya," together with a genealogical excursus—on her mother's side A. has Italian ancestors and on her father's side Tatars—contains a subtle existential meditation on the formation of life.

A.'s poetry comprehensively divines the world and transcends the boundaries of ordinary measurement. This is the case both in her introspective works, "Oznob" (1963; "Fever," 1969), for example, and in her creative reconstructions of the past, as in "Priklyuchenie v antikvarnom magazine" (1967; "Adventure in the Antique Shop," 1969). The music of A.'s verse is very rich in rhyme and alliterations, and the rhythmic structure is often impeccable, as in "Starinny portret" (1962; the ancient portrait).

The works of Anna AKHMATOVA and Marina TSVETAEVA are sometimes echoed in A.'s poetry; and, with them, A. is among the greatest Russian woman poets of the century. She occupies a very high place in contemporary Soviet literature. The poetry readings she has given during foreign tours enhanced her fame in the West; she appeared in New York in the spring of 1977.

FURTHER WORKS: *Stikhi* (1975); *Metel* (1977). **FURTHER WORKS IN ENGLISH:** *Fever and Other New Poems* (1969); *The Garden: New and Selected Poetry and Prose* (1990)

BIBLIOGRAPHY: Reeve, F. D., "The Work of Russian Poetry Today," *KR*, 26 (1964): 533–53; Dunham, V. S., "Poems about Poems: Notes on Recent Poetry," *SlavR*, 24 (1965): 57–76; Yevtushenko, Y., Introduction to *Fever and Other New Poems* (1969): 1–8; Ketchian, S. I., *The Poetic Craft of B. A.* (1993)

—LEONID RZHEVSKY

AKHMATOVA, Anna

(pseud. of Anna Andreevna Gorenko) Russian poet, b. 11 June 1889, Odessa, Ukraine; d. 5 March 1966, Moscow

A., a major poet and one of the three great Acmeists (with Nikolay GUMILYOV and Osip MANDELSHTAM), was the daughter of a naval engineer who, when A. was sixteen, abandoned his family. During her childhood and adolescence she lived near St. Petersburg. In 1907 she began the study of law at the university in Kiev, but rapidly lost interest in it, preferring to devote her energies to literature, and she returned to St. Petersburg, the city that would remain her spiritual home. In 1910 she married the poet Gumilyov. In 1912 she gave birth to her only child. In the same year she published her first volume of verse, *Vecher* (evening), under her pseudonym, which was the Tatar name of her great-grandmother, and, together with Gumilyov and Mandelshtam, formed the Poets' Guild, another name by which the Acmeist movement was known. Her second volume of verse, *Chyotki* (1914; rosary), established her reputation and popularity. Although A. and Gumilyov had ended their less than idyllic marriage in 1918, Gumilyov's execution in 1921 for antirevolutionary activities forced A. into silence.

Because of repression and censorship, A. wrote very little and published no verse until 1940. In 1934 her son was arrested—the first of many times—on unspecified charges. These arrests appear to have been attempts to make A. conform or to keep her silent, and their effect on her poetry was deep. In 1940 she openly resumed writing and published—mostly verse treating the Russian people's indomitable will to survive—until 1946, when the Stalinist repression of literature regained its full force after the relative leniency of the war years. A. was vilified for "individualism," and her expulsion from the Soviet Writers' Union effectively kept her from publishing her poetry. A. turned to translation. From 1956 onward, with the post-Stalin thaw, she was able to resume publication of her verse and gradually became reaccepted on the literary scene. In 1964 she was permitted to travel to the West to receive the Etna-Taormina poetry prize in Italy and an honorary degree from Oxford. Two years before her death, A. was chosen president of the Soviet Writers' Union, the organization from which she had been expelled in disgrace some twenty years before.

A.'s poetry is characterized by precision, clarity, and economy. She does not discriminate against "nonpoetic" diction and subjects in her poetry, but rather chooses whatever serves her purposes. Unlike the SYMBOLISTS,, hers is not a poetic of connotation and transcendence through symbol into a distant world of "meaning," but is rather one of objects and feelings in themselves, of real-life experiences examined and transmuted into art.

A.'s literary career may be divided roughly into two periods: before and after World War I. In the first, her themes are love, parting, and loss. Her tone is often an intimate one of longing, delicacy of feelings, and sorrow, but sometimes, and importantly, one of quiet and tender joy. In her second period she did not so much change the themes (although new ones appear) as expand their scope and deepen their significance, moving into the public and social realm. A. was always a poet of exquisite skill, but in her later poetry her voice becomes "unshackled" from the beautifully crafted but somewhat limiting themes of her prerevolutionary life. The tone of sorrow is still there, but the delicate feelings are frequently replaced by the strong, clear-sighted, scrutinizing pain of a survivor, a survivor by force of will. World War I, and the revolution and its subsequent personal pain represent the crucible out of which A. emerged as a major modern poet.

The dominant pronoun in A.'s work is "I." Although this "I" may embody countless others—as in *Rekviem* (1963; *Requiem*, 1976), one of A.'s greatest achievements—it derives first and foremost from A.'s personal experience, thus giving her poems the immediacy of a particular, real feeling universalized rather than an abstracted or generalized feeling encapsulated. In A.'s poetry, we start with the "I" and move outward into the larger world. Thus, her wails of grief for her imprisoned son become, without losing any of their essential personal quality, a voice for many who suffered loss and degradation during the Stalinist repression. The relationship between biographical fact and literary expression is strong in A.

Place is especially important in A.'s poetry: the Black Sea coast where she spent her girlhood summers and where her resolve to be a poet emerged (see "U samogo morya" [1914; "By the Seashore," 1969]); the St. Petersburg/Leningrad—both of Pushkin and the Soviets—that she loved and whose past, present, and future she could hold within her sphere of vision (see "Poema bez geroya" [1960; "Poem without a Hero," 1973], one of her major works). She was not merely "backward-looking" with respect to Leningrad, as certain Soviet critics during the persecutions accused her of being. For her the city was the locus of a cultural tradition, and it was her responsibility to understand and savor its past, strengthen its present, and nurture its emerging future.

Her profound love of Russia, from the very soil upward, manifests itself in her poetry in the themes of cultural tradition, national heritage, and identity. During the 1920s and early 1930s many of her friends emigrated and implored her to follow them. At least in the beginning she had the opportunity, but she did not go, and in her poetry she calls her emigré friends' words "unclean" and the notion of abandoning her Russia "unworthy." She became instead part of the "inner emigration," refusing to be separated from "her people." During World War II her poem "Muzhestvo" (1942; "Courage," 1976) appeared, surrounded by war news and casualty lists, in the most prominent place on a front page of *Pravda*. The reason was not just that she spoke of the indomitable spirit of the Russian people, but that she was a shining representative of it. In A.'s poetry, courage and endurance are part of the national heritage, and we see how A. felt that her own identity and fate were intimately connected with those of Russia.

Anna Akhmatova

Pain and suffering were not what A. feared in her life and in her poetry; what she feared was forgetting what pain and suffering meant and thus betraying not only herself but all those countless others to whom she gave a voice. A. is a poet of strength, of love and tenderness retrieved from horror, and of unyielding integrity. In her exquisite and pure poetry, classic in its simplicity and among the best Russia has produced, there is a living link with the culture and tradition of Pushkin.

FURTHER WORKS: *Belaya Staya* (1917); *Podorozhnik* (1921); *Anno Domini MCMXXl* (1921); *Iz shesti knig* (1940); *Izbrannoe* (1943); *Izbrannye stikhi* (1946); *Stikhotvorenia* (1958); *Stikhotvorenia 1909–1960* (1961); *Beg vremeni* (1965); *Sochinenia* (2 vols., 1967–68); *A. A.: Stikhotvorenia i poemy* (1976). FURTHER WORKS IN ENGLISH: *Selected Poems* (1969); *Poems of A.* (1973); *Requiem and Poem without a Hero* (1976); *Poems* (1983); *Complete Poems of A. A.*, 2 Vols., (1990); *A Stranger to Heaven and Earth* (1993)

BIBLIOGRAPHY: Bickert, E., *A. A., silence à plusieurs voix* (1970); Verheul, K., *The Theme of Time in the Poetry of A. A.* (1971); Driver, S. N., *A. A.* (1972); Chukovsky, K., "A. and Mayakovsky," in Brown, E. J., ed., *Major Soviet Writers: Essays in Criticism* (1973): 33–53; Sinyavsky, A., "The Unshackled Voice: A. A.," in Brown, E. J., ed., *Major Soviet Writers: Essays in Criticism* (1973): 54–57; Verheul, K., "Public Themes in the Poetry of A. A.," in Van der Eng-Liedmeier, J., and Verheul, K., eds., *Tale without a Hero, and Twenty-two Poems by A. A.* (1973): 9–46; Van der Eng-Liedmeier, J., "Poema bez geroya" [essay in English], in Van der EngLiedmeier, J., and Verheul, K., eds., *Tale without a Hero, and Twenty-two Poems by A. A.* (1973): 66–114; Haight, A., *A. A.: A Poetic Pilgrimage* (1976); Polivanov, K., *A. A. and Her Circle* (1994); Reeder, R., *A. A.: Poet and Prophet* (1995)

—JOHN MALNICHUCK

AKSYONOV, Vasily Pavlovich

Russian novelist, short-story writer, and dramatist, b. 20 Aug. 1932, Kazan

Both of A.'s parents, prominent Kazan Communists, were arrested during the peak of Stalin's purges in 1937. His mother, Yevgenia Ginzburg (1906–1977), described the anguish of her eighteen-year ordeal in prisons and camps in the much-celebrated book *Krutoy marshrut* (2 vols., 1967, 1979; *Journey into the Whirlwind*, 1967, *Within the Whirlwind*, 1981). In the late 1950s, A. graduated from the Leningrad Medical Institute and practiced for a while as a physician until he became completely absorbed in literary work.

A. entered Soviet literature as a spokesman for young city intellectuals who after graduation found themselves exposed to the vicissitudes of "real" life. His first novels, *Kollegi* (1960; *Colleagues*, 1962) and *Zvyozdny bilet* (1961; *A Starry Ticket*, 1962), won immediate success owing to the author's romantic sentiments concerning the great potential of the young for overcoming the hateful legacy of Stalin's epoch and finding their own independent way in life. A.'s popularity also resulted from his significant contribution to enlivening literary form, which was emasculated by the thirty-year reign of compulsory SOCIALIST REALISM. He broadened the vocabulary, employing slang and various forms of colloquial speech. In order to achieve a greater narrative objectivity, A. used dialogue and monologue abundantly.

By the mid-1960s the bright outlook on life of his young characters, their energetic readiness to struggle against evil, and the ever-present touch of hope in the early books gave way to a bitter pessimism about the most probable end to the conflict between a decent man and an assured self-seeking rascal who is free from any moral scruples. This is perhaps the main conflict of most of A.'s short stories of this period.

A few short stories and the three plays written in the mid- and the late 1960s reflect A.'s intensive work on literary technique, which culminated in the novelette *Zatovarennaya bochkotara* (1968; the overstocked barrels) and in *Poiski zhanra* (1978; search of the genre). Here A. attempts to combine the social and philosophical possibilities of prose with the metaphorical richness of poetry in an attempt to emancipate prose narration from the fetters of logic. He freely uses dreams and fantastic, often surrealistic digressions of narration, alternates modes, and intersperses purely prosaic writing with rhythmical and rhymed prose.

A.'s quest for new forms and his sharp satire of the spiritless and pragmatic society that he occasionally exposes in his works have not been enthusiastically greeted by Soviet critics. Although he is one of the most interesting and promising Soviet writers, many of his works remain unpublished in the U.S.S.R. ("homeless," as he himself puts it), including novels written in the early 1970s, *Zolotaya nasha zhelezka* (our golden piece of iron) and *Ozhog* (the

burn), both subsequently published in Russian in the U.S. in 1980. In 1979 A. was among a group of writers who published in the U.S. a collection of banned works called *Metropol*; as a result of this unauthorized publication and subsequent conflict with the authorities, A. lost his membership in the Union of Soviet Writers. On 21 July 1980, he left the Soviet Union with his family to settle in the U.S.

FURTHER WORKS: *Apelsiny iz Marokko* (1963); *Katapulta* (1964); *Pora, moy drug, pora* (1965; *It's Time, My Love, It's Time*, 1974); *Na polputi k lune* (1966); *Zhal, chto vas ne bylo s nami* (1969); *Lyubov k electrichestvu* (1971); *Moy dedushka-pamyatnik* (1972); *Geografia lyubvi* (1975); *Vash ubytsa* (unpub. in Russian; *Your Murderer* (1977); *Chetyre temperamenta* (1979). FURTHER WORKS IN ENGLISH: *The Steel Bird* (1979)

BIBLIOGRAPHY: Hayward, M., and E. L. Crowley, eds., *Soviet Literature in the Sixties* (1964): passim; Johnson, P., *Khrushchev and the Arts: The Politics of Soviet Culture, 1962–1964* (1965): passim; Rogers, T. F., "Superfluous Men" and the Post-Stalin "Thaw" (1972): passim; Brown, E. J., *Russian Literature since the Revolution* (1973): 289; Segel, H. B., *Twentieth-Century Russian Drama* (1979): 407–10 and passim

—KONSTANTIN KUSTANOVICH

AKUTAGAWA Ryūnosuke

(born Niibara) Japanese short-story writer, b. 1 March 1892, Tokyo; d. 24 July 1927, Tokyo

"Heredity, environment, and chance—these three ultimately determine our fate," wrote A., obviously with his own case in mind. Because he was born when his parents were at ages considered ill-omened, he was made a foundling—an old ritual that would, it was believed, protect him from evil. Furthermore, shortly after his birth, his mother became insane; as a result, he was raised and eventually adopted by his maternal uncle Akutagawa, whose name he took. While still a student at the Tokyo Imperial University, A. became active in literary circles, and with "Hana" (1916; "The Nose," 1930), a comic story about a Buddhist monk's frustration with his oversize nose, he won the praise of Natsume SŌSEKI.

Although A.'s career was cut short by his suicide, it was an intensely creative one. Thoroughly grounded in literature, old and new, he rejected the native school of the pseudonaturalistic confessional novel in favor of modern European models. Always insistent on the primacy of critical intelligence, he fostered the intellectual tradition in modern Japanese literature. In thus helping to transform it into something richer—at once Oriental and Occidental—he followed closely in the footsteps of Natsume Sōseki.

A.'s short stories, some 150 in all, generally reflect the three phases of his development as a writer. His aesthetic phase began with "Rashomon" (1915; "Rashomon," 1920)—Kurosawa's celebrated film version combined it with "Yabu no naka" (1922; "In a Grove," 1952)—and culminated with "Jigokuhen" (1918; "The Hell Screen," 1936–37), depicting the madness of a painter who sacrifices his only daughter in order to complete his masterpiece;

the sight of her burning to death inspires him to paint the flames of hell on a screen. Many of his early stories are set in ancient Japan—historical tales with modern insights. During the ensuing phase, however, A. turned toward realism, in such stories as "Aki" (1920; "Autumn," 1928), registering the quiet resignation of a woman who yields her lover to her own younger sister; "Niwa" (1922; "The Garden," 1964), depicting the struggle of a once-wealthy family against the ravages of time; and "Ikkai no tsuchi" (1924; "A Clod of Soil," 1957), portraying the loneliness of an old peasant woman who survives her son and daugher-in-law.

During his last phase A., all the while wrestling with thoughts of suicide, managed to produce an astonishing variety of writings. His critical eye was at its best in "Bungeitekina amarini bungeitekina" (1927; literary, to literary)—knowledgeable, candid, and original. His realism found its final expression in "Genkaku sanbō" (1927; "The House of Genkaku," 1961), the pitiless portrait of a man facing a slow death. So did his satiric spirit, in "Kappa" (1927; "Kappa," 1947), a savage assault on human civilization. At the end of his life A. quite willingly laid his soul bare. In "Haguruma" (1927; "Cogwheels," 1965) he saw in himself the image of modern man wandering in his own private hell. And in both "Aru ahō no isshō" (1927; "The Life of a Fool," 1961), a series of vignettes recapitulating his own career, and "Seihō no hito" (1927; "Man of the West," 1961), another series, tracing the life of Jesus. A. sought to discover at last some definitive pattern that would justify his own existence as man and as artist.

Highly versatile and experimental, A. refused to repeat himself; relentlessly selfcritical, he aspired to perfection. He was a prose stylist with the soul of a poet. Always a favorite with the Japanese, he is considered one of the greatest national writers. With his increasing accessibility in translation. A, is finding his niche in world literature.

FURTHER WORKS: *A. R. Zenshū* (4 editions: 10 vols., 1934–35; 20 vols., 1954–55; 8 vols., 1964–65; 11 vols., 1967–69). FURTHER WORKS IN ENGLISH: *Tales Grotesque and Curious* (1930); *The Three Treasures and Other Stories for Children* (1944); *Hell Screen and Other Stories* (1948); *Rashomon and Other Stories* (1952); *Japanese Short Stories* (1961); *Exotic Japanese Stories* (1964); *A Fool's Life* (1970)

BIBLIOGRAPHY: Arima, T., "A. R.: The Literature of Defeatism," *The Failure of Freedom: A Portrait of Modern Japanese Intellectuals* (1969): 152–72; Hibbett, H. S., "A. R. and the Negative Ideal," in Craig, A. M., and D. H. Shively, eds., *Personality in Japanese History* (1970): 425-51; Tsuruta, K., "A. R. and I-Novelists," *Monumenta Nipponica*, 25 (1970): 13–27; Yu, B., *A: An Introduction* (1972); Ueda, M., *Modern Japanese Writers and the Nature of Literature* (1976): 111–44; Yamanouchi, H., *The Search for Authenticity in Modern Japanese Literature* (1978): 87–106

—BEONGCHEON YU

ALAIN

(pseud. of Émile-Auguste Chartier) French philosopher and essayist, b. 3 March 1868, Montagne; d. 2 June 1951, Le Vésinet

After completing his studies in 1892, A. taught philosophy at the secondary school in Pontivy for one year before being assigned

to a similar post in Lorient, where he remained until 1900. During the early years of his teaching career he published a number of articles in the *Revue de Métaphysique et de Morale*. Passionately interested in politics and incensed at the treatment accorded Dreyfus, he wrote several newspaper articles for *La Dépêche de Lorient* in which he exposed the hypocrisies of Dreyfus's accusers. From 1900 to 1902 he taught in Rouen in 1903 he was appointed to a school in Paris.

On February 16, 1906, he published in *La Dépêche de Rouen* the first of his short essays that were to appear daily under the title of "Propos d'un Normand." They were signed "Alain," the pseudonym having been derived from the name of the 15th-c. Norman poet. Eventually, he wrote more than five thousand such propos, which are brief aphoristic pieces on a wide range of subjects. The various collections of these *propos* remain A.'s most popular books. In 1909 he became a teacher of philosophy at another school in Paris, where he remained until his retirement in 1933. Except for the three years he spent in the French army (1914–17), he devoted his life to teaching and writing. A gifted teacher, A. exerted enormous influence on countless numbers of students, among them André MAUROIS and Simone WEIL, who adulated him, calling him simply "The Man." One month before he died he was awarded the National Grand Prize for Literature.

As a philosopher, A. belongs to the tradition of idealism that extends from Plato to Spinoza and Kant. Like the philosophers of ancient Greece, to whom he is perhaps closer in spirit than any other modern thinker of note, he does not distinguish between philosophy and ethics. Whereas most contemporary philosophers establish their reputations by elaborating an abstract system of thought, A. refuses to reduce philosophy to mere speculation and to divorce it from common sense.

At the heart of A.'s thought is his advocacy of liberty and his doctrine of the will. He opposed both political tyranny (*Le citoyen contre les pouvoirs*, 1926; the citizen against the powers [of the state]) and the dogmatism of the Church (*Propos sur le Christianisme*, 1924; remarks on Christianity). A. believed that the individual is in large part responsible for his own happiness, which is, he insisted, a state of mind that can be created by judicious use of the will. But before we can exercise our wills wisely, we must understand the mechanism of the passions, for, as A., a robust, passionate man, well knew, we are to a considerable degree creatures of passion. We must learn how our passions function so that we can channel them to ends that contribute to our happiness rather than unhappiness. In one of his most famous books. *Propos sur le bonheur* (1928; *Alain on Happiness*, 1973), he examines entertainingly the nature of our passions and proposes techniques by which we can become the artisans of our own destinies.

A.'s work is an act of faith in the human spirit. As pithy, succulent, and congenial as it is profound, it dispels fear and fosters hope. Among 20th-c. French writers, few are more likely to endure than he.

FURTHER WORKS: *Spinoza* (1901); *Cent un propos d'A.* (1908); *Vingt et im propos d'A. à l'usage des non-combattants* (1915); *Quatrevingt-un chapitres sur l'esprit et les passions* (1917); *Propos d'A.* (1920); *Systeme des Beaux-Arts* (1920); *Mars, ou ta guerre jugée* (1921; *Mars; or, The Truth about War*, 1930); *Propos sur l'esthétique* (1923); *Lettres au Docteur Henri Mondor, sur le sujet du cœur et de l'esprit* (1924); *Élémenis d'une doctrine radicale*

(1925); *Souvenirs concernant Jules Lagneau* (1925); *Sentiments, passions et signes* (1926); *Esquisses de l'homme* (1927); *Les sentiments familiaux* (1927); *Les idées et les âges* (1927); *Commentaires de "Charmes" de Paul Valéry* (1929); *Entretiens au bord de la mer* (1930); *Les Dieux* (1930; *The Gods*, 1974); *Vingt leçons sur les Beaux Arts* (1931); *Idées* (1932); *Propos sur l'éducation* (1932); *Propos de politique* (1934); *Propos de littérature* (1934); *Propos d'économie* (1935); *Stendhal* (1935); *Histoire de mes pensées* (1936); *Avec Balzac* (1937); *Souvenirs de guerre* (1937); *Entretiens chez te sculpteur* (1937); *Les saisons de l'esprit* (1937); *Propos sur la religion* (1938); *Minerve, ou de la sagesse* (1939); *Suite à Mars: Convulsions de la force* (1939); *Suite à Mars: Echec de la force* (1939); *Préliminaires à l'esthétique* (1939); *Éléments de philosophie* (1941); *Vigiles de l'esprit* (1942); *Humanités* (1943); *Abrégés pour les aveugles* (1943); *Les aventures du cœur* (1945); *En lisant Dickens* (1945); *Lettres à Sergio Soirni sur la philosophie de Kant* (1946); *Politique* (1951); *Définitions* (1953); *Lettres sur la philosophie première* (1955); *Vingt et une scènes de comédie* (1955)

BIBLIOGRAPHY: Maurois, A., *A.* (1950); Mondor, H., *A.* (1953); Pascal, G., *La pensée d'A.* (1957); Bridoux, A., *A: sa vie, son oeuvre* (1964); Sernin, A., *A: un sage dans la cité* (1985)

—ROBERT D. COTTRELL

ALAIN-FOURNIER

(pseud. of Henri-Alban Fournier) French novelist and poet, b. 3 Oct. 1886, La Chapelled'Angillon; d. 22 Sept. 1914 (killed in the Battle of the Marne)

A.-F.'s parents were both teachers, and he was raised in the atmosphere of their country school in the heartland of France near Bourges. His later education was completed in secondary schools in Paris and in Brittany. He nurtured a lifelong nostalgia, however, for the villages and the simple manners of his provincial childhood, calling himself a "peasant." At the same time sensitive and susceptible to the arts, A.-F. consciously struggled to rid himself of the effete literary characteristics of SYMBOLISM, which had contributed to his early tastes and writing style. A brief sojourn in England acquainted him with Dickens, Hardy, Stevenson, and practitioners of a more realistic aesthetic.

A.-F.'s first and only completed novel, *Le Grand Meaulnes* (*The Wanderer*, 1928) was published in 1913. Its hero, Augustin Meaulnes, is an adolescent country boy who, during his nocturnal wanderings, discovers a mysterious "domain" where costumed children are celebrating the wedding of Frantz de Galais. It is an enchanted universe in which the impossible becomes possible, and he is uncertain as to whether it is actual or a dream. Meaulnes falls in love with Frantz's sister Yvonne, but both young men are romantic idealists who elevate love and woman to too lofty a pedestal and cannot countenance reality. Each is fated to lose his beloved, yet destined to go on searching for unattainable happiness.

An early projected title for the novel was "Le pays sans nom" (the nameless land); the "land" or "domain" of which A.-F. wrote was that of childhood purity and innocence, lost to us as adults. Describing his creative technique as "encounters of dreams," A.-F.

sought to reveal the miraculous in everyday life, to interweave the imaginary and the real, to recapture the freshness and pristine wonder of the world as seen through the eyes of children. He wanted his novel to partake simultaneously of realism and the fairy tale. It can indeed be read as a tale of adventure and/or fantasy.

Le Grand Meaulnes is a reflection of A.-F.'s dogged if desperate idealism. While still a schoolboy, he had encountered a beautiful blonde girl named Yvonne who seemed the incarnation of all perfection. Long after her marriage, he continued to nurture memories of this romantic encounter and to brood on the loss of the unattainable, finally sublimating his melancholy by projecting it into a work of poetic fiction.

Miracles (1924) is a posthumous collection of early poems and prose fragments that show A.-F. seeking to define and refine his themes (childhood, idealistic love, the simple pleasures of rural life, the loss of innocence), and to formulate a quasi-poetic style appropriate to his vision.

A.-F.'s four-volume correspondence with his future brother-in-law Jacques RIVIÈRE—*Correspondence Rivière/A.-F. 1905–1914* (1926)—reveals the budding critical faculties of both writers: A.-F. takes pride in his subjectivism, his intuitive insights, shunning literary "schools" and critical methodology, while Rivière, later an editor of repute, champions a more reflective, analytical approach to literature. Their exchange of views on writers, styles, and artistic trends provides a precious document for the literary history of the early 20th c.

Although widely acclaimed as a classic and a masterpiece. *Le Grand Meaulnes* has also been variously criticized as formless, contrived, and overly sentimental, It came close to winning the Goncourt Prize of 1913, and has inspired successive generations of French youth by its idealistic integrity and subtle stylistic evocation of a purer world. In terms of both chronology and aesthetic conception, A.-F. bridges the gap between turn-of-the-c. symbolism and mid-1920s SURREALISM.

A year after the publication of *Le Grand Meaulnes*, A.-F. became a World War I casualty, just ten days before his twenty-eighth birthday. In 1936, the *lycée* at Bourges was renamed in his honor. GIRAUDOUX called A.-F. the "little brother of us all."

FURTHER WORKS: *Lettres au Petit B* (1930); *Lettres d'A.-F. à sa famille* (1930)

BIBLIOGRAPHY: Gibson, R., *The Quest of A.-F.* (1953); Champigny, R., *Portrait of a Symbolist Hero* (1954); Savage, C., "Nostalgia in A.-F. and Proust," *FR*, 38 (1964): 167–72; Levy, K., "A.-F. and the Surrealist Quest for Unity," *RomN*, 18 (1978): 301–10

—JAMES ROBERT HEWITT

ALAVI, Buzurg

Iranian novelist, short-story writer, essayist, and critic (writing in Persian, German, and English), b. 1907, Tehran; d. 16 Feb. 1997, Berlin, Germany

A. received his secondary and college education in Germany. He then taught in Tehran and joined a group of socialists. In 1937 he was arrested for his political activities and was imprisoned for four years. In 1941, after the Allied invasion of Iran, he was released and became one of the founders of the *Tudeh* (Communist) party. In 1953 A. left Iran for East Berlin, where he became a professer of Persian language and literature.

In 1934 A. had published six short stories under the title *Chamadan* (portmanteau), which show the influence of FREUD. These somber stories are outstanding in their descriptions and characterization.

While he was in prison he wrote *Panjah-o se nafar* (1942; fifty-three people), sketches of the other socialists who had been arrested with him. The horrible treatment they were subjected to in prison and at their trial is vividly portrayed. This book had a great impact upon the younger generation during the post-Reza Shah period. *Varaq pareha-ye zendan* (1941; scraps of paper from prison) was published directly after his release from prison. These descriptions of the suffering of the peasants, of political prisoners, and of opium addicts, and of the generally miserable conditions of life under Reza Shah carried a strong political message.

A.'s third collection of short stories. *Nameha, va dastanha-ye digar* (1952; letters, and other stories), for which he was awarded the Gold Medal of the World Peace Council in 1953, shows the culmination of his style. These are poignant vignettes of Persian life, described with consummate skill, which also strongly criticize corruption and injustice in Iran. These nine stories are considered by some critics as the best short stories ever written by a Persian author.

In the novel *Cheshmhayesh* (1952; her eyes) the protagonist is a socialist painter, a member of an illegal group working for the betterment of the downtrodden and against the tyrannical government. Another character, an upper-middle-class girl, is an example of extreme frivolity and self-seeking. For love of the painter, she makes an unsuccessful attempt to join his movement, but, unable to empathize with suffering people, she reverts to type. A great deal of political controversy surrounded this novel because of its sympathies to both sides.

From the mid-1950s to the early 1970s A.'s writing output was more academic than creative. In 1955 he wrote in German *Das kämpfende Iran* (embattled Iran), a history of the then recent times in Iran of which he was extremely critical. In a more serene mood he then wrote *Das Land der Rosen und der Nachtigallen* (1957; the country of the roses and nightingales) and a study on modern Persian literature, *Geschichte und Entwicklung der modernen persischen Literatur* (1964; history and development of modern Persian literature). A. is also a prolific translator of literary works from Persian into German and from German, English, and Russian into Persian.

In 1975, A. wrote another novel, *Salariha* (Salariha). His prose is simple and direct. He avoids the tendency toward ornamentation common in the writers of the past and also eschews the obscenities, vulgarisms, and slang expressions of many writers of today.

BIBLIOGRAPHY: Wickens, G. M., "B. A.'s Portmanteau," *UTQ*, 28 (1959): 116–33; Kamshad, H., *Modern Persian Prose Literature* (1966): 113–24; Kubičkova, V., in Rypka, J., et al, *History of Iranian Literature* (1968): 414–15; Alvi, S., "A.'s Writings from Prison," *MW*, 67 (1977): 205–22; Raffat, D., *The Prison Papers of B. A.* (1985)

—PETER J. CHELKOWSKI

ALBANIAN LITERATURE

Albanian Literature through World War II

The Albanian literary tradition, kept barely alive under Turkish rule (1468–1912), lingered on among the refugees in the regions of Calabria and Sicily in southern Italy, who had fled their country after the death of their leader Skanderbeg in 1467. Their language, archaic Southern Albanian, still survives, and it is largely due to its speakers that the Albanian literary revival took shape beginning in 1878. The freeing of Serbia, Bulgaria, and Romania, resulting from the Russian victory over the Turks in that year, sparked off an Albanian revolt that found expression in the formation, in the Kosovo city of Prizren, of the League of Prizren in the same year.

Paradoxically, the earliest efforts to create a national literature came from outside Albania. The Calabrian Albanian poet Jeronim De Rada (1814–1903) spent his long life in poverty collecting dimly remembered fragments of folk poetry, and edited a journal, *Fjámuri Arbërit*, which appeared from 1883 to 1887. Encouraged by two Sicilian Albanians, Dhimitër Camarda (1821–1882) and Zef Schirò (1865–1927)—the first a grammarian, the second a lyrical and epic poet of militant nationalism—he became the forerunner of the literary revival.

Three brothers, members of a pantheistic Bektash sect, Abdyl Frashëri (1839–1892), a political activist, Naim (1846–1900), a poet of Albanian nostalgia, and Sami (1850–1904), a political theorist and encyclopedist, were joined by Mehmet Vrioni (1842-1895) at Prizren, where they pledged themselves to free Albania from Turkey and to propagate Albanian books. Joined a year later by Jan Vreto (1822–1900) and Konstantin Kristoforidhi (1826–1895), a lexicographer and Bible translater, they formed a cultural society in Istanbul called *Drita* (The Light) under the very nose of Sultan Hamid II, who regarded the movement at first as a joke. The *Drita* society was composed of Christians and Moslems. Their first task was to devise an Albanian spelling, their second, to gain the adherence of a colony of recent exiles in Egypt, chief of whom were Thimi Mitko (1820–1890), a collector of folktales and folk-poems, Spiro Dine (1846–1922), author of a collection of tales and poems called *Valët e Detit* (1908; Waves of the Sea), and Anton Çako (pseud: "Çajupi"; 1866–1930), a nationalist poet.

The exiles in Egypt did not rally to the *Drita* movement, which eventually fell under the suspicion of the sultan. Sensing danger, Vreto fled to Romania, where the society continued to function, printing books in the phonetic alphabet devised in Istanbul, but which never gained popularity. Others fled to Sofia, Bulgaria. It was here that Mid'hat Frashëri (1880–1949), bibliophile and educator, a nephew of Naim, published between 1897 and 1927 a pocketsized journal called *Kalendari Kombiar* with the help of Kristo Luarasi (1875-1934). It was designed to distribute essays and poems, many of an exhortative character, sent in by patriots from far and near, and to report on literary movements inside and outside Albania. The journal proved unpopular with the northern Albanians, who spoke a different dialect, and who proposed alternative spellings.

The battle of the alphabets took place at a congress at Monastir (Bitola) in 1908. Ndre Mjedja (1866–1937), a poet from Shkodër, wanted Croat spelling; the southerners, chief architects of the League of Prizren, wanted to continue the spelling devised at Istanbul; and a modified style was proposed by Gjergj FISHTA, a monk from Shkodër, author of racy satirical ballads with patriotic overtones, of the national epic *Lahuta e Malcís* (1937; the highland lute), and editor of a long-running journal *Hylli i dritës* (1913–39). The last was decided upon, and the first Albanian books in the new spelling appeared in the following year, 1909.

After independence in 1912 a crop of poetry on patriotic themes appeared. Also important in this period were the novels of Mihal Grameno (1872–1931): *Oxhaku* (1909; the hearth); *Varri i pagzimit* (1909; the tomb of baptism), and *Rilindja e Shqipërisë* (ca. 1914; the rebirth of Albania). The first was set in the time of Ali Pasha of Tepelena (1741–1822), a local chieftain who defied the Turks; the second related an incident at Vithkuqi and told of the intrigues of the Greek clergy to gain frontier rectifications; the third retold the struggles that preceded independence. A fourth novel, *E púthura* (1909; the kiss), is a romantic tragedy of a wayward emigrant and a lovelorn girl who waits for him to return, but in vain. The crude plot, in which both lovers take their own lives, is interlarded with scraps of folklore.

Zef Harapi (1891-1946), a northerner, in *Pushka e Trathtarit* (1914; the traitor's gun) wrote in a similar vein. This loosely woven tale of intrigue and counterintrigue, blood feud, love and hate, fleshed out with descriptions of local customs, ends in violence and death.

Milto Sotir Gurra (1884-1972), an exile, is remembered for his short stories with a moral flavor, condemning Albanian lapses into foreign ways. His novel *Goca e malcisë* (1912; the highland girl) is a tale of local patriots at war with the Turks, and of betrayal, mass killings, and revenge.

Best remembered is Foqion Postoli (1889–1927), author of the novel *Për mbrojtjen e atdheut* (serially 1921; as a book 1926; in defense of the homeland), a tale of a mixed marriage, local fights against Turks and Greeks, liberation, hardship and death; and of *Lulja e kujtimit* (1924; the flower of remembrance), a naïve tale of rivalry and religious and nationalist conflict.

Mehdi Frashëri (1873–1963), a cousin of Mid'hat, wrote a novel, *Nevruzi* (1923; Nevruzi), set in the pre-1878 period. It is a wild tale of rivalry, blood feud, exile, intrigue, and a clash of local customs, ending in the death of the hero.

Short stories of this period reflect the themes of the novels and are represented by the moralizings of Mid'hat Frashëri in *Hi dhe shpuzë* (1915; ashes and embers), deploring blood feuds and the burning of villages.

The interwar period, identified mainly with the regime of King Zog, was one of literary stagnation, relieved by the work of Ernest Koliqi (1903–1975), whose collections of short stories *Hija e maleve* (1929; mountain shades) and *Tregtar flamujsh* (1935; flag merchant) are a blend of local events, simple plots, and didactic theories, all centered on his native Shkodër and its mountainous hinterland. An admirer and translator of the Italian poets, he collaborated with the Fascists but escaped after their defeat to continue his work in Rome, where he edited a journal. His prose is among the most imaginative in the Albanian language.

An important part in maintaining Albanian literacy was played by the Albanians of Boston. Exiles from various regimes, they include Kristo Floqi (1873-1951), who arrived in Boston in 1911, where he edited the journal *Dielli*. He was joined by two other exiles, Faik Konitsa (1875–1942), linguist, satirist, and journalist, and Bishop Fan Noli (1881–1965), founder of the Vatra (The Hearth) literary society, which published Postoli's play *Detyra e mëmës* (1925; a mother's duty). Returning to Albania for a time, Floqi held a number of ministerial appointments; still, his dramatic output is the largest of any Albanian writer. His plays are of two

kinds, nationalist-historical and political–satirical. Noli enriched the language from his exile home in Boston with brilliantly executed translations of Shakespeare, now in vogue at Albania's three national theaters.

Following the Communist takeover in 1946, Lasgush Poradeci (1899-1987) began writing some original, mystical poetry in the manner of William Blake. However, Marxist ideology dominated literature in the homeland, with the emphasis on past achievements, reconstruction, railways, power plants, the draining of marshes and the planting of fruit trees, and even the personal sufferings of a prewar consumptive writer of Shkodër, Millosh Gjergj Nikolla (pseud.: Migjeni; 1911–1938), poet of protest against poverty in villages, especially among children.

BIBLIOGRAPHY: Mann, S. E., *Albanian Literature* (1955); Skendi, S., *Albania* (1957): 304–19; Bihiku, K., *An Outline of Albanian Literature* (1964)

—STUART EDWARD MANN

Albanian Literature since World War II

After the Stalinist purges under Koçi Xoxe (1917-1949) and the elimination of the first postwar minister of cultural affairs, the liberal Marxist Sejfull Malëshova (pseud: Lame Kodra, 1901-1971), intellectual life in Albania had been virtually wiped out and literary production, as a consequence, had come to a standstill. The early writers of SOCIALIST REALISM in the 1950s, Dhimitër Shuterqi (b. 1915), Shevqet Musaraj (1914-1986), Jakov Xoxa (1923-1979), and Aleks Çaçi (1916-1989) could not demonstrate any particular talent under the unabating terror of the Hoxha regime.

From 1961, the year of Albania's break with the Soviet Union, a new generation of more talented writers arose, represented by Ismail KADARE, Dritëro AGOLLI, and Fatos Arapi (b. 1930). Kadare, in particular, did much to emancipate Albanian literature gradually from the shackles of the past and in the 1970s and 1980s came to dominate the literary scene. After the French-language publication of his first major novel, *Gjenerali i ushtrisë së vdekur* (1963; *The General of the Dead Army*, 1971), his international reputation grew, giving him confidence at home to continue his subtle attacks against the otherwise all-pervading doctrine of socialist realism. Among his pioneering novels to have appeared in English are *Kronikë në gur* (1971; *Chronicle in Stone*, 1987), *Prilli i thyer* (1978; *Broken April*, 1990), and *Nëpunësi i pallatit të ëndrrave* (1981; *The Palace of Dreams*, 1993). At the end of October 1990, a mere few months before the collapse of the dictatorship, Kadare sought political asylum in Paris, where he has been living and writing ever since. Other noted prose authors of the period include Petro Marko (1913-1991), Kasëm Treebeshin (b. 1926), Dhimitër Xhuvani (b. 1934), and Bilal Xhaferri (1935-1986). Of the poets of the 1980s and early 1990s, mention can be made of Xhevahir Spahiu (b. 1945), Natasha Lako (b. 1948), Barhyl Londo (b. 1948), Visar Zhiti (b. 1952) who survived seven years of prison and concentration camps, and Mimoza Ahmeti (b. 1963).

Albanian literature in Kosova was put into motion by poet Esad Mekuli (1916-1993) with the founding in 1949 of the literary periodical *Jeta e re*, but did not produce much of note until the 1960s. Exceptions must be made for the novelist Adem Demaçi (b. 1936) who was to spend the next twenty-eight years as a political prisoner of the Belgrade regime, and of the verse collections

Njifyell ndër male (1953; a flute in the mountains), and *Kânga e vërrinit* (1954; song of the lowland pastures) by Martin CAMAJ, later to become a leading scholar of Albanian studies in Rome and Munich. TheYugoslav constitution of 1974 gave Kosovo Albanians more freedom and a semblance of equality for the first time, and literature flourished on the Plain of the Blackbird in the decade to follow. Of leading prose writers, mention can be made of the experimental Anto Pashku (1937-1995), Rexhep Qosja (b. 1936), notably for his explosive political novel *Vdjeka më vjen prej syve të tillë* (1974; death comes from such eyes) the prolific Nazmi Rrahmani (b. 1941) and Teki Dervishi (b. 1943). The poetry of Kosovo has been far more experimental and creative than that of Albania. Among its leading proponents are Din Mehmeti (b. 1932), Besim Kokshi (b. 1932), Azem Shkreli (b. 1938), Rrahman Dedaj (b. 1939), Ali Podrimja (b. 1942), Eqrem Basha (b. 1948), Sabri Hamiti (b. 1950), and Asri Çapriqi (b. 1960). Since the military occupation of Kosovo and its forceful annexation by Serbia, the Albanians have returned to their status of second-class citizens. Economic, cultural, and literary life in Kosovo have been virtually destroyed in the process (suspension of Albanian-language secondary schooling, closing-down of the University of Prishtino for non-Serbs, takeover of the Rilindja publishing company, and the paramilitary occupation of the Institute of Albanian Studies in Prishtina). The future of Albanian literature in Kosovo is uncertain.

BIBLIOGRAPHY: Mann, S. E., *Albanian Literature* (1955); Bihiku, K., *History of Albanian Lierature* (1986); Elsie, R., *Anthology of Modern Albanian Poetry* (1993); Elsie, R., *Dictionary of Albanian Literature* (1995)

—ROBERT ELSIE

Edward Albee

ALBEE, Edward

American dramatist, b. 12 March 1928, Washington, D.C.

Adopted from a foundling home at the age of two weeks by Reed and Francis Albee, millionaire heirs to the vaudeville theater empire created by Edward F. Albee (1857–1930), A. was brought up with all the material benefits of a pampered only child. He chafed not only at family life but at the restrictions of the private schools to which he was sent. He was briefly and uncomfortably a student at Trinity College from 1946 to 1947. A. began to write at an early age—novel at fifteen, another at seventeen, and poetry between the ages of six and twenty-six-because, as he admits, he saw it as a means of becoming and staying independent. A legacy from his grandmother (later eulogized in *The Sandbox* and *The American Dream*) enabled him to leave home for good, at the age of twenty. He spent the next nine years living in New York City's Greenwich Village. In these years he worked at various jobs (office boy, salesman, Western Union messenger), continued to write poetry and fiction, and attended plays regularly. Then he wrote, in a matter of weeks, his first play, *The Zoo Story* (perf. 1959; pub. 1960), as a thirtieth birthday present to himself.

The Zoo Story opened in New York City in 1960, sharing the bill at the Provincetown Playhouse with BECKETT's *Krapp's Last Tape*. A.'s one-act play traces a confrontation between two strangers, Jerry and Peter, on a bench in Central Park, from its casual beginning to its shocking conclusion: Jerry's impalement on a

knife he baits Peter into holding. A. expressed the essential meaninglessness of life by fusing THEATER-OF-THE-ABSURD techniques (inconsequential activity, grotesque theatrical images, and the nonverbal language of cries, howls, gestures, speech rhythms, and breathing) with swift and realistic characterizations and dialogue.

It is Jerry's "Story of the Dog"—one of the great bravura monologues of modern theater—that not only defines structure and meaning in *The Zoo Story* but also anticipates many of the themes of A.'s later plays. Critics have suggested several possible interpretations for the monologue, pointing out the anagram of "dog," and generally conclude that Jerry's relationship with his landlady's dog alludes to the ills of modern society-alienation, loneliness, and the inability of human beings to communicate, whether with animals, with each other, or with their God.

A.'s two one-act plays—*The Sandbox* (1960) and *The American Dream* (1961)—are more obviously linked to the absurdist playwrights A. admired, specifically Beckett and IONESCO. In *The Sandbox*, Mommy and Daddy abandon a willing Grandma to a sandbox grave and the ministrations of a handsome "Angel of Death." The same Mommy and Daddy appear in *The American Dream*, this time forcing the irrepressible Grandma out of the house and accepting "The American Dream"—a handsome young man who admits to being "dead" inside—as a replacement for his twin brother, whom they had adopted as a baby and then killed by maiming him piece-meal in successively atrocious punishments. In both plays, domestic clichés, symbolic characters, and grotesquely exaggerated action provide bitter comment on American family life, particularly on cruelly dominating "Mommies," weaker but insidiously evil "Daddies," and their combined destruction of both the older and younger generations.

With *Who's Afraid of Virginia Woolf?* (1962), his first full-length play, A. was acknowledged as one of America's most promising young playwrights. Opening in New York City in 1962, the play was not only a box-office success, but a critical triumph as well. The film version, several years later, brought A. international distinction.

The success of *Who's Afraid of Virginia Woolf?* is attributable to A.'s adroit management of several levels of meaning. Structurally, the play is a night-long verbal fencing match between George and Martha, a middle-aged and childless couple. A second, younger couple, Nick and Honey, are offered as foils. A. turns the normal love-hate course of marital relationships into a sadomasochistic marathon of confrontations in which violence (George "kills" their imaginary child in retaliation for Martha's vicious goading) becomes the only means of communication.

On another level, the play is interesting as a series of ritualized games married people play, from the banal through the orgiastic to the cathartic. On yet a third level, *Who's Afraid of Virginia Woolf?* is an allegory (George and Martha's names recall George and Martha Washington, also childless) dramatizing what A. considers our great national flaw: the neglect and even rejection of reality in favor of illusion—"the American dream."

A.'s *Tiny Alice* produced considerable controversy during its five months on Broadway, and a score of conflicting interpretations since its publication in 1965. Although one can hear overtones of contemporary playwrights such as GENET, SARTRE, T. S. ELIOT, and Tennessee WILLIAMS, the basic concerns and techniques are A.'s. Here, again, the major theme is reality versus illusion—this time A. probes the elaborate structure of spiritual illusion, both personal and institutional. And, as in *The Zoo Story*, the protagonist's quest for meaning in an absurd world ends in his death.

Brother Julian, the Christ-like protagonist, is sent by the Cardinal to the castle-mansion of wealthy Miss Alice to handle a business transaction (Miss Alice's promised gift of millions to the church). There he is confronted with the central enigma of the play—a dollhouse-size model of the mansion in which every room and inhabitant is reproduced in miniature, even to a tinier model within the larger one. The metaphysical implications of this infinitely diminishing cosmos provide a perspective on the dramatic action of the play and a commentary on Brother Julian's spiritual and moral disintegration. Betrayed by the Cardinal, deceived by Alice's butler, seduced by Alice and married to her, Julian is shot on his wedding day by Alice's lawyer. He is abandoned by all of them and left to die in front of the dollhouse, in the consuming presence of the mysterious "Tiny Alice" they served.

A Delicate Balance (perf. 1966; pub. 1967) presents the most direct image of the absurd human condition that preoccupied A. in his previous plays: man's tortured vacillation between illusion and reality, between success and failure, between love and hate, between sanity and sickness, between life and death. The play concerns a seemingly ordinary suburban family whose domestic stability and individual equilibrium are upset by the invasion of old friends, a couple who have left their own home because of a nameless terror that overwhelms them. Interweaving fragmentary and shifting emotional tonalities to show his characters in search of the boundaries of their own painful existence, A. forces us to recognize the anxieties, insufficiencies, and guilt that create our own "delicate balance."

In *All Over* (1971), another powerful drama about man's fate, A. pursues his inquiry by using a single action as the catalyst for effecting personal revelations to seven characters. Throughout the play, a man, on the verge of death, is tended by a doctor and a nurse, while in the same room his wife, son, daughter, mistress, and best friend react to his dying, to each other, and to the network of circumstances and relationships that brought them together. The play ends with the doctor's announcement that it is "all over," but A.'s emotionally charged dialogue suggests that the anguish of our search, for answers to questions we only imperfectly understand, is not.

A.'s 1975 fantasy-comedy *Seascape* is a lighthearted (although somewhat pretentiously philosophical) look at four characters in search of life's meaning. An encounter on a deserted beach between a human husband and wife, Charlie and Nancy, and a lizard couple, Leslie and Sarah, is the means A. uses to explore the question of whether or not life is, essentially, worth living. Although the quartet make occasional attempts to plumb the depths of their existence beneath the surface of convention and habit, they are frequently distracted by quarrels and misunderstandings. The play cheerfully (if not profoundly) concludes that since there is no alternative to living, and no answers to life's mysteries, human and alien species alike should embark on a course of mutual help and encouragement.

Although A. courts ambiguity, and although his symbolism is occasionally obscure, he excels in the control of dramatic mood and situation, in his sure grasp of American idiomatic speech, and in the deft creation of some of the most memorable characters in modern theater. Unquestionably he deserves his place in the front rank of contemporary playwrights.

FURTHER WORKS: *The Death of Bessie Smith* (1960); *Fam and Yam* (1960); *The Ballad of the Sad Café* (adaptation of C. McCullers's novel; 1963); *Malcolm* (adaptation of J. Purdy's novel; 1966); *Everything in the Garden* (adaptation of G. Cooper's play; perf., 1967; pub., 1968); *Box; Quotations from Chairman Mao Tse-Tung* (1969); *The Lady from Dubuque* (1980); *Three Tall Women* (1995)

BIBLIOGRAPHY: Amacher, R. E., *E. A.* (1969); Cohn, R., *E. A.* (1969); Rutenberg, M., *E. A.: Playwright in Protest* (1969); Hayman, R., *E. A.* (1971); Paolucci, A., *From Tension to Tonic: The Plays of E. A.* (1972); Amacher, R. E., and M. Rule, eds., *E. A. at Home and Abroad* (1973); Bigsby, C. W. E., ed., *E. A.: A Collection of Critical Essays* (1975); Hirsch, F., *Who's Afraid of E. A.?* (1978)

—PENNY W. MORRIS

ALBERTI, Rafael

Spanish poet and dramatist, b. 16 Dec. 1902, Puerto de Santa María

A. studied at the Jesuit high school of his native town; in 1917 he moved with his family to Madrid, where he started out as an impressionist and cubist painter, a career he soon abandoned to dedicate himself to literature. His first book of poetry, *Marinero en tierra* (1925; sailor on land), for which he was awarded the coveted National Literature Prize, is a collection of short poems whose form and tone, while reminiscent of the old Spanish ballad and the *cancioneros* of the 15th and 16th cs., bear the distinct mark of his own style. Juan Ramón JIMÉNEZ praised this poetry, viewing it as very personal and traditional, yet fresh, new, and fully perfected.

The nostalgic undertones of *Marinero en tierra disappear in La amante* (1926; the mistress), a delightful poetic record composed by A. during his journey with his brother through Castille and the northern Spanish coast. The playful, delicate, and simple poetic diction of the former work still prevails. A more complicated linguistic pattern, however, starts to emerge in *El alba del alhelí* (1927; the dawn of the wallflower), another collection of songlike poems, this time based on his daily life in Andalusia.

A.'s stylistic complexity became intensified in the baroque *Cal y canto* (1929; quicklime and song), and reached its peak in his surrealist masterpiece *Sobre los ángeles* (1929; *Concerning the Angels*, 1967). *Cal y canto* is a highly metaphoric and intricate book, skillfully written to pay tribute to Don Luis de Góngora (1561–1627), the baroque Spanish poet whom he fervently admired. This is a crucial experimental step that led A. into the surrealist visions of *Sobre los ángeles* in order to portray the disquieting conflict between the forces of innocence and indifference, between nature and a dehumanized society; it is the recurrent conflict that thematically unifies all the works mentioned heretofore.

After *Sobre los ángeles*, A.'s poetry became political and social. At this time A. embraced communism, joined the forces of the republic during the Spanish Civil War, and later went into exile in Argentina and then in Rome. With the exception of *A la pintura* (1945; rev. ed., 1948; homage to painting) and *Retornos de lo vivo lejano* (1952; memories of the living past) the poetry of this period has neither the depth nor the breath of his early books.

A. did not limit himself to poetry. He also wrote ten interesting plays, which unfortunately have not been given the same critical attention as his verse. Like GARCÍA LORCA, he felt the need to inject new vitality into the contemporary Spanish theater that had been for so long—with the exception of VALLE-INCLÁN—in the hands of mediocre and pedestrian dramatists who repeated 19th-c. formulae and clichés. *El hombre deshabitado* (1930; the deserted man) is a modern allegory of a lost paradise, paralleling the themes, tone, and techniques of *Sobre los ángeles*. Also of high dramatic and poetic quality are *El trébol florido* (1940; the flourishing clover), a rural drama of lyrical songs echoing those of Gil Vicente (1470?–1536?) and Lope de Vega (1562–1635); and *El adefesio* (1944; nonsense), a drama of oppression in the line of García Lorca's *The House of Bernarda Alba* with the grotesque and detached perspective of Valle-Inclán's plays of the 1920s.

After Franco's death in 1977, A. returned to Spain, and is once again the leading and most respected literary figure of his country. His influence is being felt now more than ever before among the numerous literary groups in his native Andalusia, in Madrid, and in Barcelona.

FURTHER WORKS: *Consignas* (1933); *Poesía* (1934); *Verte y no verte* (1935); *Sermones y moradas* (1935); *Trece bandas y cuarenta y ocho estrellas* (1936); *De un momento a otro* (1937); *Entre el clavel y la espada* (1938); *Poesía* (1940); *Eh, los toros* (1942); *La arboleda perdida* (1942; *The Lost Grove*, 1976); *Pleamar* (1944); *Ora Marítima* (1953); *Baladas y canciones del Paraná* (1954); *Teatro* (1956); *Noche de guerra en el Museo del Prado* (1956); *Sonríe China* (1958); *Los viejos olivos* (1960); *Il trifoglio fiorito* (1961); *Abierto a todas horas, 1960–63* (1964). FURTHER WORKS IN ENGLISH: *A Spectre Is Haunting Europe* (1936); *Selected Poems* (1944); *Selected Poems* (1966); *The Owl's Insomnia* (1973); *The Other Shore* (1981); *90 Poems* (1992)

BIBLIOGRAPHY: Proll, E., "The Surrealist Element in R. A.," *BSS*, 18 (1941): 70–80; Proll, E., "'Popularismo' and 'Barroquismo' in the Poetry of R. A.," *BSS*, 19 (1944): 59–86; Alonso, D., *Poetas españoles contemporáneos* (1958): 179–87; Connell, G. W., "A Recurring Theme in the Poetry of R. A.," *RMS*, 3 (1959): 95–110; Connell, G. W., "The Autobiographical Element in the Poetry of R. A.," *BHS*, 40 (1963): 160–73; Monguió, L., "The Poetry of R. A.: An Introduction," in R. A., *Selected Poems* (1966): 1–34; Debicki, A. P., *Estudios sobre poesía española contemporánea* (1968): 224–61; Brown, G. G., *A Literary History of Spain: The Twentieth Century* (1972): 99–101; Jimenez-Fajardo, S., *Multiple Spaces: The Poetry of R. A.* (1985)

—VICENTE CABRERA

AL-E AHMAD, Jalal

Iranian novelist, short-story writer, essayist, critic, editor, and translator, b. 1923, Tehran; d. 1969, Khalif Abad Assalam

The major Persian writer of fiction and nonfiction of the 20th c., A. is regarded by some as the best prose writer in Persian since the middle of the 13th c. He was born to a religious Muslim family; his father and four other members of the family were Shi'ite clerics, and when he was twenty, A. was sent to the holy city of Najaf in Iraq to be trained as a cleric. At the age of twenty-one, A. broke off from his family and joined the Tudeh Communist Party. In 1946 A. became an editor of the Tudeh monthly magazines *Mardom* and *Rahbar*, as well as many other party publications. In the autumn of 1947, A. left the main core of the Tudeh party and was active in a splinter group that was not aligned with Moscow, and finally broke off with the communists. During the early 1950s, at the time of nationalization of oil by Mosaddeq, A. gravitated to the National Front Movement and was very active in the Third Force Party. From the mid-1950s until his death, A. was the main social critic and spokesman for the nonestablishment Iranian intelligentsia. In the last decade of his life, as he started to battle Western influences in Iran, he moved along the curve toward the point of his departure, to the Shi'ite Muslim environment. What he once criticized and even ridiculed, now he defended and considered the Twelver Shi'ism as the basic fabric of the Iranian civilization. During his lifetime he traveled almost a complete circle. As he propagated these views through his writing, he could be considered a precursor of the Islamic revolution that took place ten years after his death.

He received a high school education by attending classes in the evening, working during the day in the Tehran bazaar as an electrician, watch-maker, and leather merchant. A. graduated from Tehran Teachers' College in 1946. He worked as a teacher almost the rest of his life. In 1950 A. married Simin Daneshvar (b. 1921), a writer, translator, and art-history professor. On the literary scene he appeared in the spring of 1945 with a short story, "Ziarat" ("The Pilgrimage," 1949), published in the literary magazine *Sokhan*. This was followed by four collections of stories. *Did va bazdid* (1946; the exchange of visits), *Az ranji ke mibarim* (1947; our suffering), *Se tar* (1948; the sitar), and *Zan-e ziadi* (1952; the superfluous wife). A fifth collection appeared posthumously as *Panj dastan* (1974; five stories). The love and the compassion for the ordinary people of Iran led A. to become a self-taught ethnographer who traveled around the country doing field work.

This is reflected in his fiction writing, especially in his short stories, which are slices of everyday life. They are like blown-up frames of a movie reel, complete with sound track on which the colloquial speech patterns and characteristics of various social classes are recorded. The devotion of A. to the Iranian people is best underscored in the title of a collection of his stories translated into English and published in the U.S. as *Iranian Society: An Anthology of Writings by J. A. A.* (1982). In his long fictional narratives, A. is even more forceful in his social criticism. The first book, called *Sargozasht-e kandaha* (1955; the tale of the beehives), is an allegory of the exploitation of Iranian natural resources by foreign powers. Using the time-honored symbolism of the animal world, A. was able to deflect the pen of the censor. The most-acclaimed and most-read work of A. is *Modir-e madraseh* (1958; *The School Principal*, 1974). This masterpiece of narration and social criticism was reprinted many times, and a great number of copies, by Iranian standards, were sold. It is a first-person narrative of an elementary-school teacher who manages to become the principal of a school on the outskirts of Tehran. It is an indictment of the educational system of Iran and of Iranian society as a whole. Like many of his short stories, *Modir-e madraseh* is in great measure based on A.'s autobiographical material. The simple and direct prose makes the book very readable and credible. Another example of the first-person narrative is A.'s last novel, *Nafrin-e zamin* (1968; the cursing of the land). Again the main protagonist is a school teacher, but this time in a rural setting. In this book A. deals not only with education but with land reform, mechanized farms, and military conscription. The book also shows that the author, toward the end of his life, was more interested in cultural anthropology than in literature.

Nun wa'l qalam (1961; *By the Pen*, 1988) is regarded by the literary critics as his most mature work, and written in accordance with the modern standard of novel writing. It seems that the action of the book takes place in the capital of Safavid Esfahan, at the time of the growth of Shi'ism in Iran. The book, however, is not a historical novel since the city and the empire are in the realm of the imaginary. The title of the novel stems from chapter sixty-eight of the Koran, which is called "The Pen." That chapter starts with the letter "N," the meaning of which has not been determined by the scholars of the scriptures—it is therefore called a mystical letter.

Outside of Iran, A.'s most famous work belongs to nonfiction. It is a passionate attack on the Westernization of Iran under the Pahlavi monarchy, bearing the title of *Gharbzadegi* (1962; *Plagued by the West*, 1982). This work was also translated into English as *Gharbzadegi-Westruckness* (1982) and *Occidentosis: A Plague from the West* (1984). The plague is the Western encroachment in the East, infectious and sapping the vital strength of old countries like Iran. *Gharbzadegi* had a great impact on Iranian literary circles, on other intellectuals, and indirectly on the masses, as A. argued in it that the traditional Shi'ite Muslim values are the foundation of the Iranian masses.

To the nonfiction genre belong many works, especially his ethnographic studies. A. wrote travel accounts of his journeys to the Soviet Union, western Europe, and Iranian provinces. One of the most telling travelogues is his *Khasi dar miqat* (1964; *Lost in the Crowd*, 1985). In April of 1964, A. undertook a hajj, the pilgrimage to the most holy Muslim shrine in Mecca. *Khasi dar miqat* is an excellent description of the hajj and its rituals. Though A. at that time was moving toward the position of his origin in a strong religious framework, in the book he still comes through as a religious skeptic. Skeptic he was not, however, when he thought about the political application of the hajj as the great opportunity to mobilize Muslims against Western domination.

In Iran the role of the admired writer, especially an *engagé* one, can be compared only to that of eastern Europe: writers that are seen as mirrors of the conscience of the nation and its guiding beacons. There is no doubt that A. was such a writer.

BIBLIOGRAPHY: Kamshad, H., *Modern Persian Prose Literature* (1966): 125–27; Yarshater, E., "The Modern Literary Idiom," *Iran Faces the Seventies* (1971): 284–320; Hillmann, M. C., "The Mobilization of Iran," *LE&W*, 20: 1–4 (Jan.–Dec. 1976): 61–64; Chelkowski, P., "The Literary Genres in Modern Iran," in Lenczowski, G., ed., *Iran under the Pahlavis* 1978): 333–64; Yarshater, E., Foreword to *Plagued by the West* (1982): ix-x; Yarshater, E., ed., *Persian Literature* (1988): 301–2; Hillmann, M. C., *Iranian Culture: A Persianist View* (1990): 119–44; Clinton, J. W., "A. A. J.," in Yarshater, E., ed., *Encyclopaedia Iranica* (1982), Vol. 1: 745–47

—PETER J. CHELKOWSKI

ALEGRÍA, Ciro

Peruvian novelist and journalist, b. 4 Nov. 1909, Huamachuco region; d. 17 Feb. 1967, Trujillo

A. grew up on a family hacienda in the Andes of Northern Peru among Indians and mestizos. He attended high school in the coastal city of Trujillo, where he began work as a journalist and became identified with *indianismo*, the movement initiated by Manuel González PRADA to awaken the national conscience to the Indians. After joining APRA, a revolutionary party formed to free the Indians from bondage to white landlords, he was twice imprisoned, pardoned after serving fourteen months in the Lima penitentiary, then exiled to Chile in 1934, where he continued to produce journalism from a tuberculosis sanatorium.

His first novel, *La serpiente de oro* (1935; *The Golden Serpent*, 1943) grew out of a short story describing the perils of the river Marañón. To meet the deadline for a novel competition, he hurriedly enlarged the manuscript and won first prize. The title refers to the river, which is perceived by the Indians as the source of life and fruitfulness, death and renewal; more than any human character, the river is the protagonist. A minimal plot serves to portray the work, psychology, customs, and traditions of the Indian ferrymen and to record the legends and amusing tales with which they entertain each other. It marked a turning point in Latin American literature of social protest because of the humanity of the Indian characters, their sensibility, courage, and humor, more conducive to winning hearts to the cause of *indianismo* than the stark primitivism described in preceding novels on the topic.

A.'s second novel, *Los perros hambrientos* (1938; starving dogs) deals with Indian shepherds and their highly trained sheepdogs. Here A. introduces one of the white landowners who were, in his view, the cause of Peru's economic evils. This man shoots at the Indians who come begging for food during a famine.

A.'s third and most impressive novel, *El mundo es ancho y ajeno* (1941; *Broad and Alien Is the World*, 1941) was an immediate popular success and has been translated into ten languages.

Describing the simple, self-sufficient life of a communal village of Indian farmers high in the Andes, it deals with the futile efforts of the mayor to prevent the expropriation of the tribal lands by an avaricious rancher who hopes to compel the Indians to work for him. With its powerful depiction of anguish and cruelty, this moving document is most memorable for its rhapsodic perception of the Indians' harmonious relation to the land and for the philosophic lesson to be learned therefrom. The novel is designed to give a panoramic view of Peru as seen through the eyes of the displaced Indians; hence the title: the world may well be broad, but it is alien to them. It also corroborates the reformers' theory that if social revolution were to liquidate the large estates and return the land to the Indians, they would become valuable members of society.

Another book A. had planned and nearly finished was to tell of this revolution; it was to be a six-hundred-page semihistorical novel giving a comprehensive picture of Peru. After a twenty-five-year exile, he went home in order to finish it, but he was caught up in politics again, though not with APRA, and he died suddenly at the age of fifty-seven. So far only two hundred pages of the novel have been found; in the warm, flowing, and captivating narrative style that distinguishes A.'s works, *Lázaro* (1973; Lazarus) begins with an account of the heroic struggles of labor unionists and reformers that he himself had joined during the 1930s in Trujillo. Many short biographies, essays, tales, and legends that he wrote for newspapers are being collected and published by his widow.

A. was a gifted, old-fashioned storyteller, but either from a sense of duty or by compulsion he was first a man of action and only secondarily a novelist. Nonetheless, his books marked—according to Mario Vargas LLOSA, one of Peru's leading new writers—the beginning of the modern Peruvian novel.

FURTHER WORKS: *Duelo de caballeros* (1963); *La ofrenda de piedra* (1969); *Gabriela Mistral íntima* (1969); *La revolución cubana: un testimonio personal* (1971); *Mucha suerte con harto palo: memorias* (1976)

BIBLIOGRAPHY: Wade, G. E., Introduction to *El mundo es ancho y ajeno* (1945): ix–xxv; Aldrich, E. M., Jr., *The Modern Short Story in Peru* (1966): 114–27; Schwartz, K., *A New History of Spanish American Fiction*, Vol. 2 (1972):55-61; Bonneville, H., "Prólogo" to *Lázaro* (1973): 7–16; Rodríguez-Florido, J. J., "Bibliography of C. A.," *Chasqui*, 4, 3 (1975): 23–54

—RICHARD J. CALLAN

ALEGRÍA, Claribel

Salvadoran-Nicaraguan poet and novelist, b. 12 May 1924, Esteli, Nicaragua

A. is a prize-winning poet and novelist of renown who has also contributed to the growing body of testimonial literature from Central America. She was born in Nicaragua and moved with her family to El Salvador as a young child when her father, an anti-interventionist during the U.S. occupation of Nicaragua, was forced into exile. A. has subsequently lived in the U.S., Europe, and Mexico and other Latin American countries. She received her B.A. from George Washington University and is married to U.S.-born

journalist Darwin J. Flakoll, with whom she has collaborated on a number of projects including a novel as well as books of testimony and Central American history. In 1979, with the victory of the FSLN (Sandinista Front for National Liberation), A. returned to live in Nicaragua. She continues to travel extensively and to speak and write about the social and political situation in Central America, particularly in El Salvador and Nicaragua, the two countries she considers her homeland.

A.'s poetic expression has evolved thematically from the self-reflective meditations of the young poet in her first book, *Anillo de silencio* (1948; ring of silence), which evokes life and death, past and present, in her search for her identity, to the still self-reflective but more socially and politically committed voice of her later work. A constant self-questioning and looking inward, captured in metaphors of mirrors, islands, prisons, walls, caves, and grottoes, evolves toward a looking outward and an identification of the lyric voice with the voices of those who have struggled, resisted, disappeared, or otherwise suffered in the name of justice. A. finds the fullness of her lyric voice and personal identity within a tradition of socially committed poetry which she evokes in one of the central poems of *Sobrevivo* (1978; I survive), "Sorrow" (title in English), a powerful dream poem of searching for, mourning, and becoming one with Pablo NERUDA, Roque Dalton (1935–1975), and other poets whose lives and deaths were indictments of repression. Although her themes as well as the sophistication of her use of metaphor have evolved, her language has remained characteristically straightforward, at times colloquial and conversational.

The impulse to reclaim her Central American heritage and to participate actively in exposing the lies and injustices of history is first apparent in the novel *Cenizas de Izalco* (1966; *Ashes of Izalco*, 1988), written collaboratively by A. and Flakoll. Employing the technique of the found manuscript, in this case the diary of the narrator's mother's lover, the novel uncovers/unmasks, with the protagonist's reading of the diary, an infamous chapter of Salvadoran history: the massacre by government troops of over thirty thousand peasants in 1932. A. herself as a child in Santa Ana, El Salvador, witnessed this massacre, thus *Cenizas de Izalco* is a combination of personal testimony and fictional narrative, as well as a way for A. to bear witness to history while attempting to reinscribe herself in the life of the country where she locates her roots.

Carmen, the protagonist of *Cenizas de Izalco*, is a Salvadoran woman married to a middle-class North American and living in the U.S. In *Album familiar* (1984; *Family Album*, 1989) A. explores once again the dilemma of the middle-class Central American woman who lives elsewhere, in this case in Paris, and who struggles with distance, separation, and commitment, eventually finding her salvation and the key to her identity by deciding to work for the FSLN in Paris. A. takes the challenge of commitment a step further for the protagonist of *Despierta, mi bien despierta* (1986; wake up, my love, wake up), a Salvadoran woman married to a member of the country's ruling oligarchy. Through her relationship with a young revolutionary she becomes aware of the repressive situation in her country and her husband's complicity in a mass murder. She leaves her husband, thereby solving an identity crisis as well as her problems of boredom and political ignorance.

In 1983 A. and Flakoll published *No me agarran viva* (*They Won't Take Me Alive*, 1987), an account of the life and death of a young Salvadoran woman who is a member of the FMLN (Farabundo Marti Front for National Liberation). Based on interviews with friends and relatives of the protagonist, Eugenia, the text weaves together letters, personal testimonies, discussions of Salvadoran history, and dramatizations of scenes and conversations in which issues such as machismo within revolutionary organizations, the fate of the children of revolutionaries, and the evolving role of women in social struggles in Central America are illuminated. *No me agarran viva* represents what A. herself calls her *letras de emergencia* (emergency or crisis writing), texts that emerge from the writer's awareness and commitment and that respond to the brutal realities of contemporary Central American life. Death, whether the result of poverty or political repression, is a grim fact of life in Central America, and A. confronts this reality from a variety of perspectives, but always from a deeply personal and impassioned stance.

Whether in the form of poetry, prose, testimony, or a hybrid of these genres, such as *Luisa en el país de la realidad* (1987; *Luisa in Realityland*, 1987), A.'s texts are characterized by a female narrator's search for or declaration of her identity. Memory, the dead, imagination and imaginary interlocutors, love, and commitment aid the protagonists in their discovery of and subsequent battles against hypocrisy, machismo, and bourgeois complacency. Their hope or salvation is often found in their willingness to reidentify with their roots and with the disenfranchised in their political struggle.

A. is one of a small but growing number of women who are recognized by their male literary counterparts in Central America and whose production, quantitatively as well as qualitatively, is professional. To her credit, A. has managed to fuse the personal with the political to create texts important in their scope and powerful in their emotional content. Her attention to the concerns of women has contributed to the elevation of the female character in Central American literature to a higher level of autonomy and agency.

FURTHER WORKS: *Suite de amor, angustia y soledad* (1951); *Vigilias* (1953); *Acuario* (1955); *Tres cuentos* (1958); *Huésped de mi tiempo* (1961); *Víaúnica* (1965); *Aprendizaje* (1970); *Pagaré a cobrar y otros poemas* (1973); *El detén* (1977); *La encrucijada salvadoreña* (1980, with J. Flakoll Darwin); *Homenaje a El Salvador* (1981); *Suma y sigue* (1981); *Flores del volcán* (1982; *Flowers from the Volcano*, 1982); *Poesía viva* (1983); *Nicaragua: La revolución sandinista* (1983, with J. Darwin); *Para romper el silencio: Resistencia y lucha en las cárceles salvadoreñas* (1984, with J. Darwin); *Pueblo de Dios y Mandinga* (1985); *Y este poema río* (1988). FURTHER WORKS IN ENGLISH: *Woman of the River* (1988); *Fugues* (1993); *Death of Somoza* (1996); *Thresholds/Umbrales: Poems* (1996); *The Boy Who Searched for Yesterday/El niño que buscaba a ayer* (1997)

BIBLIOGRAPHY: Papastamatiu, B., "La sobrevida poética de C. A.," *CasaA* 110 (Sept.–Oct. 1978): 148–50; Peri Rossi, C., "Cuatro poetas latinoamericanas," *Hora de poesía* (Barcelona), 8 (Mar.–Apr. 1980); Arenal, E., "Two Poets of the Sandinista Struggle," *FSt*, 7, 1 (Spring 1981): 19–27; Benedetti, M., Introduction to *Suma y sigue. Antología* (1981): 9–16; Forché, C., "Interview with C. A.," *IonC*, 13, 2 (Apr. 1984): 11–13; Yúdice, G., "Letras de Emergencia: C. A.," *RI*, 51, 132–33 (July–Dec. 1985): 953–64; Saporta Sternbach, N., "C. A.," in Marting, D. M., ed., *Spanish American Women Writers* (1990): 9–19; Boschetto-Sandoval, S. M., and McGovern, M. P., eds., *L. A. And Central American Literature* (1994)

—JANET N. GOLD

ALEGRÍA, Fernando

Chilean critic, novelist, and poet, b. 26 Sept. 1918, Santiago

Currently the dean of Latin American critics, A. is a prolific writer of nearly fifty books and more than one hundred articles and is the Sadie Dernham Patek Professor in the Humanities, Emeritus, at Stanford University. A graduate of the University of Chile (1939), he earned a Ph.D. in Romance linguistics at the University of California, Berkeley, in 1947, and won a Guggenheim fellowship. For the next twenty years, he held full-time positions at both Berkeley and the University of Chile, spending roughly half the year in each post. Since 1967 he has taught at Stanford, where he also served as department chair. During his illustrious career A. has lectured at more than 100 universities.

In 1970 President Salvador Allende named him cultural attaché in Washington, D.C. But after the September 1973 coup that placed General Augusto Pinochet in power, A. was refused entrance to Chile and could not return for more than ten years. Because he personally identified with the exiles and their political plight, A. became one of the most vociferous of the Chilean exiles, founding and editing the *Revista de Literatura Chilena en el Exilio* (1974), now entitled *Literatura Chilena: Creación y Crítica*. He also edited an anthology, *Chilean Writers in Exile* (1982), which includes his *War Chorale*, an English translation of his *Coral de guerra* (1979); and with Jorge Rufinelli he edited *Paradise Lost or Gained?: The Literature of Hispanic Exile* (1990).

A. initiated his novelistic pursuits at age twenty with the publication of *Recabarren* (1938; Recabarren), a fictionalized biography of Luis Emilio Recabarren, revised as *Como un árbol rojo* (1968). A printer turned journalist, Recabarren founded Chile's Socialist Party in 1912, which in 1921 changed its name to the Communist Party when it joined the Third International.

But at age seventeen A. had also published his first critical article, "El paisaje y sus problemas" (1935; the landscape and its problems), in the leading Chilean journal *Atenea*. Thus for more than fifty years A. has been able to maintain an amazing equilibrium in both areas: fiction and criticism.

Following *Recabarren*, A. published *Lautaro, joven libertador del arauco* (1943; *Lautaro*, 1944), another fictionalized history, which won the Farrar & Rinehart Prize in New York (1943). A. feels that for a nation to be worthy of its heroes it must cause them to transcend history, recalling them to the public mind in terms of the present as well as projecting them into the future. As a young Araucanian Indian, Lautaro helped the fierce tribes of the Arauco region of Chile gain freedom from the imperialist Spanish. Thus A.'s Lautaro becomes a model for Chileans of the early 1940s to thrust off the yoke of foreign imperialism, Nazi influences, or threatening dictators. In a more recent work, *Allende, mi vecino el presidente* (1989; *Allende, My Neighbor the President*, 1990, pub. as *A.: A Novel*, 1993), A. turns again to a fictionalized biography or history.

In much of his later fiction A. varies his fictionalizing of history to create in his books two distinct views of humanity. The Hispanic immigrant in the U.S.A. is the subject of one group of novels, including *Caballo de copas* (1957; *My Horse Gonzalez*, 1964) and *Amerika, Amerikka, Amerikka, manifiestos de Vietnam* (1970; Amerika, Amerikka, Amerikkka, exposés about Vietnam, pub. in English as *The Funhouse*, 1986). A. pictures the plight of displaced Chileans and other migrant Hispanics in these works, and it is his exceptional view of the interfacing of the two cultures in his writings (the U.S. and the Hispanic) that will cause A. to be remembered and makes this fiction of the two cultures of major importance.

Testimonial literature, which replaced Socialist Realism (the proletarian novel) in leftist writing, is the second type of novel to which A. has recently turned. A. reproduces in his testimonial fiction paragraphs of magazine articles, swatches of voices in the wind, radio reports, oral anecdotes, letters, and a diary juxtaposed with a fictional account of a photographer's torture at the hands of the junta and his eventual death. A.'s attack on the despotic mentality of the Pinochet military régime and the cruelty predominant in Chile after the 1973 coup appear in *El paso de los gansos* (1975; goose-step march, pub. in English as *The Chilean Spring*, 1980). *Coral de guerra* is another testimonial novel, in the pattern of William FAULKNER's soliloquy novel, *As I Lay Dying* (1930).

A. returned again to a "fictionalized reality" in his autobiography, *Una especie de memoria* (1983; a kind of memoir), which, like *Mañana los guerreros* (1964; *The Maypole Warriors*, 1993), centers on the focal year 1938. It was a key year for his generation, known as the Generation of 1938, which was a group of novelists who through their literature helped established Marxist governments in Chile in 1938 and 1970. A. is one of the few of that large group who are still active in their writing. Their prose style is metaphorical and poetic.

As a poet, A. is not widely known in his own country because of his years of exile; yet, ironically, his poems are often recited by the masses or sung by international stars like Joan Baez, without the public realizing that A. is the author.

The winner of numerous national and international prizes for his writing, including the Medalla de Oro y Placa (1981), A.'s books have been widely disseminated through numerous editions and translated into eight languages. In his creative writing he inserts eroticism and humor, often championing the poor and making national heroes believably human in order to motivate the reader to participate in cultural change.

FURTHER WORKS: *Ideas estéticas de la poesía moderna* (1939); *Leyenda de la ciudad perdida* (1942); *Ensayo sobre cinco temas de Thomas Mann* (1949); *Camaleón* (1950); *Walt Whitman en Hispanoamérica* (1954); *La poesía chilena; orígenes y desarrollo del siglo XVI al XIX* (1954); *El poeta que se volvió gusano y otras historias verídicas* (1956); *Breve historia de la novela hispanoamericana* (1959); *El cataclismo* (1960); *Las noches del cazador* (1961); *Las fronteras del realismo; literatura chilena del siglo XX* (1962); *¡Viva Chile M . . . !* (1965); *Genio y figura de Gabriela Mistral* (1966); *La novela hispanoamericana del siglo XX* (1967); *Los días contados* (1968); *La maratón del Palomo* (1968); *Los mejores cuentos de F. A.* (1968); *La venganza del general* (1969); *La literatura chilena contemporánea* (1969); *Literatura y revolución* (1970); *La ciudad de arena* (1974); *Retratos contemporáneos* (1979); *Los trapecios* (1985); *Nueva historia de la novela hispanoamericana* (1986); *La rebelión de los placeres* (1990). FURTHER WORKS IN ENGLISH: *Ten Pastoral Psalms* (1968; bilingual ed.); *Instructions for Undressing the Human Race* (1969); *Changing Times/Cambio de Siglo* (1972; bilingual ed.); *Changing Centuries: Selected Poems of F. A* (1984; bilingual ed.)

BIBLIOGRAPHY: Giacomán, H. F., ed., *Homenaje a F. A.: Variaciones interpretativas en torno a suobra* (1972); Correas de Zapata, C., "Talking with A.," *Américas*, 24, 8 (1972): 9–12; Ruiz, R., *F. A.: vida y obra* (1979); Reeves, R. E., "Bibliografía de F. A.," *TCrit*, 7, 22–23 (1981): 31–58; Semprún de Donahue, M. de, *Figuras y contrafiguras en la poesía de F. A.* (1981); Valenzuela, V., *F. A.: el escritor y su época* (1985); Epple, J. A., ed., *Para una fundación imaginaria de Chile: La obra literaria de F. A.* (1987); Columbus, C. K., "'Affective' Strategies for Social Change: A.'s *The Chilean Spring*," *Mosaic*, 22, 1 (Winter 1989): 101–11; Oyarzún, K. and H. M. Cavallari, "F. A. Y la deconstrucción del facismo," *TCrit*, 7, 22-23 (July-Dec. 1981): 13-21; Opazo, V. C., "F. A.: Lauturo, joven liberator de Arauco," *ExTL*, 11, 1 (1982-1983): 59-73; Epple, J., *Nos reconoce el tiempo y silba su tonada* (1987); Epple, J. A., "Chilenos en California: Una trilogía narrativa de F. A.," *The Americas Review*, 23, 3-4 (1995): 217-25; Epple, J. A., "F. A.," *Diccionario Enciclopédico de las Letras de América Latina* I (1991): 107-111; Guerra Cunningham, L., "Historia y memoria en la narrativa de F. A.," *RChL*, 48 (April 1996): 23-38; Epple, J. A., ed., *F. A.: Obra narrative selecta* (1998)

—LON PEARSON

Fernando Alegría

ALEIXANDRE, Vicente

Spanish poet, b. 26 April 1898, Seville; d. 14 Dec. 1984, Madrid

A. spent the summers of his early years in Málaga, which provided some of his poetic subjects. He later moved to Madrid and

Vicente Aleixandre

taught mercantile law for a time. A long and grave illness, as well as his discovery of Freud's works in 1929, greatly influenced his poetry.

A. strives to convey feelings by the use of symbols and metaphors and does not concern himself with logical sequences. His familiarity with Freudianism makes him receptive to surrealistic imagery, though A. himself rejects the surrealist label. He has at various times been called an existentialist, a mystic pantheist, and a neoromantic. Eros and thanatos are dominant in his poems; the contrasting, yet equating, of these two forces is A.'s major leitmotif. He often achieves a kind of transfiguration through the evocation of his loves, human or cosmic. A. repeats negatives with affirmative force and also employs word clusters to create a vertiginous effect.

In *Ambito* (1928; ambit) the crystalline poems about the world of the senses project an elusive imagery of light and shadows, elements of nature, and A.'s youthful love. A.'s poems may be viewed as analogues of a psychological journey from repressed sexuality, annihilation, evasion, and despair to an affirmation of life, love, and light. In this first volume A. recognizes but rejects the limits imposed on his yearning for eternity. In later volumes the drive for love (and by implication, life) and the impulse toward destruction and darkness emerge more clearly.

The prose poems of *Pasión de la tierra* (passion of the earth), composed in 1928–29 but issued in a complete edition only in 1946, are, as indicated by the title, filled with earthbound elements. These poems, a series of irrationally ordered sequences and subconscious associations that lack coherence, reflecting a world in which real things disintegrate, are closer to SURREALISM and Freudianism than any other of A.'s works.

Espadas como labios (1932; swords like lips) seeks to freeze the reality of the moment in time as the poet likens erotic lips to deadly swords. Again, seeking to dissolve the limits imposed by existence and to obtain the warmth of love and life, A. exhibits an anxious possessiveness that resembles a shark's voracity.

A.'s poetic masterpiece, *La destrucción o el amor* (1935; destruction or love), explores erotic love in a universe of unchained telluric forces. The poet offers us a visionary transfiguration of the world in flux in which man's works remain peripheral to the instinctive life and in which love and death are synonymous. Against a cosmologic background where nature is both destroyed and engendered by the creative force, A. shows that eternal communion, a final total love, is possible only with death, transfigured into love itself.

Mundo a solas (world alone)—written in 1934 but not published until 1950—is filled with tormented love, and man is seen as but a vague shadow. In this volume A. introduces us to an uncorrupted virginal world of light and purity that is opposed to one of darkness and destruction; it served as a prelude to another of his great works, *Sombra del paraíso* (1944; shadow of paradise), wherein A. creates a poetic universe of serenity, innocence, love, and beauty, of which A., limited by recall and death, can perceive only a momentary shadowy outline; hence the title. A.'s ambivalence, his alternation between pleasure and pain, rises from his punitive expulsion from paradise into the real world, where he experiences the fear and foreboding of an impending death.

In *Nacimiento último* (1953; final birth) A. broadens and humanizes his perspectives on life and death. The title, conveying the thought of a birth into death, concerns human destiny. A. intensifies the contrast between light as illusion and life and darkness as eternal reality. *Historia del corazón* (1954; history of the heart) stresses the human element, as the poet, aware of the desperate solitary lives many people lead, sings nonetheless of social love and human solidarity in a world of fleeting time. A history of mankind generally and of the poet specifically, the collection concentrates on human life. *En un vasto dominio* (1962; in a vast dominion) unifies most of the previous themes, both the sorrowful, historical aspects of man and his fusion with the cosmos in a temporal framework. For A., man and nature become parts of a larger whole that integrates everything.

In his most recent two collections, *Poemas de la consumación* (1968; poems of consummation) and *Diálogos del conocimiento* (1974; dialogues of knowledge), A. reflects on the interrelationship of love, life, and death as old men wait for the end while they dream of life. In the first collection A. sees old age as a sterile recollection of what was once hope and a dream of innocence, for life is time, and man must succumb. In his *Diálogos del conocimiento*, two people confront one another; one speaker always talks of hope, liberty, and struggle, and the other of fatality, desolation, and renunciation.

In this final statement A. refines his total vision, juxtaposing stubborn existential awareness with a vague transcendental intuition. Inspired by the same enigmas that beset us all, A. recaptures an unconscious knowledge and creates a unity of perception. In his personal vision of experience and emotion, A. communicates moral and psychological imperatives with great originality and independence, as he tries to enrich the spiritual heritage of all mankind. His life's achievement was recognized with the award of the Nobel Prize for literature in 1977.

FURTHER WORKS: *Poemas paradisíacos* (1942); *Vida del poeta: el amor y la poesía* (1950); *Algunos caracteres de la nueva poesía española* (1955); *Mis poemas mejores* (1956); *Los encuentros* (1958); *Poemas amorosos* (1960); *Poesías completas* (1960); *Antigua casa madrileña* (1961); *Picasso* (1961; *Picasso*, 1964); *Retratos con nombre* (1965); *Presencias* (1965); *Obras completas* (1968); *Poesía surrealista* (1970); *Obras completas* (1977). FURTHER WORKS IN ENGLISH: *Poems* (1969); *Twenty Poems* (1973); *Poems-Poemas* (bilingual ed., 1978)

BIBLIOGRAPHY: Jiménez, J. O., "V. A. en dos tiempos," *RHM*, 29 (1963): 263–89; Schwartz, K., "The Sea, Love, and Death in the Poetry of V. A.," *Hispania*, 50 (1967): 219–28; Bousoño, C., *La poesía de V. A.* (1968); Ilie, P., *The Surrealist Mode in Spanish Literature* (1968): 40–56; Schwartz, K., *V. A.* (1970); Bourne, L. M., "The Spiritualization of Matter in the Poetry of V. A.," *Revista de Letras*, 22 (1974): 166–89; Bousoño, C., "The Greatness of A.'s Poetry," *Revista de Letras*, 22 (1974): 190–99; Schwartz, K., "The Isakower Phenomenon and the Dream Screen in the Early Poetry of V. A.," *Revista de Letras*, 22 (1974): 210–18; Cobb, C. W., "V. A. and the Solidarity of the Cosmos," *StTCL*, 2 (1977): 81–97; Durán, M., "V. A., Last of the Romantics: The 1977 Nobel Prize for Literature," *WLT*, 52 (1978): 203–8; Luis, L., de, *Vida y obra de V. A.* (1978)

—KESSEL SCHWARTZ

ALGERIAN LITERATURE

Algerian literature is now defined to include only the works of native Algerians in Arabic and French, and not those by French writers born in Algeria, such as Albert CAMUS. While a few literary schools, composed mainly of French writers who considered themselves Algerians, did flourish during the first half of the 20th c., a native literature in French did not begin to develop until around 1950.

In Arabic

But the Algerian literary renaissance manifested itself in Arabic from 1925, the date of the beginning of a national magazine, *Al-Shihab*, which in turn led to the founding of the Association of the Muslim 'Ulama of Algeria in 1931, whose activities revolved around the slogan "Algeria is my country, Islam is my religion, and Arabic is my mother tongue."

The Short Story

The most outstanding short-story writer of the pre-World War II period was Muhammad al-'Abīd al-Jilālī (1890?–1967). He criticized abuses of the French colonial system, as well as the evils of his own society. Al-Jilālī's attacks were at times so virulent that he used a pseudonym, "Rashīd." His didacticism, however, is relieved by his wit and irony.

Many short stories were written after World War II. The early postwar period was dominated by Ahmad Ridā Hūhū (1911–1956), who expressed indignation at injustices suffered by women, the corruption of the bourgeoisie, hypocrisy among intellectuals, and the unfavorable political conditions in Algeria. The tone of Algerian short fiction became gradually more revolutionary with changes in the political situation, particularly after the Sétif massacres in 1945.

Literary production came almost to a standstill during the period of armed revolution, beginning in 1954; but after independence came in 1962 it was resumed. The new writers wanted to give a complete picture of the war, although the choice of dramatic moments was almost impossible, since everything seemed crucial and moving. Many of the stories turned out to be mere documentaries. In the introductions to a number of collections the authors point with pride to the realism of their works: in *Nufūs thā'ira* (1962; rebellious souls), 'Abdallāh Ralkībī (b. 1932) declared that the reader could smell the gunpowder while reading his stories. Zuhūr WANĪSĪ adopted a similar attitude in her collection *Al-Rasīf alnā'im* (1967; the quiet sidewalk).

Long after independence the war of liberation continued to provide literary material. Yet some writers succeeded in shedding their emotional involvement and produced moving works on the war based mainly on human situations. "Nawwāh" (n.d.; Nawwāh), by al-Tāhir WATTĀR, is about a woman who runs away to hide during an air raid on her village, forgetting her child, who perishes. Other writers studied the large social changes wrought by the war, particularly in the life of the women who participated in the armed struggle, often astounding men by their courage and devotion.

Gradually, the story began showing greater interest in the present and the future of the country, and started dealing with personal themes. This change was headed by Wattār, who seems particularly concerned with the emotional life of young Arab men, stifled by old-fashioned norms and traditions, particularly in his collection *Dukhān min qalbi* (n.d.; smoke from my heart). Yet, he soon began concentrating his efforts on the presentation and defense of his socialist ideology, which after this volume infuses most of his works. Wattār, an idealist totally devoted to his cause, refuses to accept any halfway solutions, a position best portrayed in his collection *Al-Shu-hadā' ya'ūdūn hādhā al-usbū'* (1974; the martyrs are coming back this week).

Poetry

Although poetry continued almost uninterruptedly during the French occupation, its real renascence took place only in 1925, since the *Shihab* group included Muhammad al-'Īd Āl Khalifa (1904–1979). Yet despite the new life he infused in modern Algerian poetry, al-'Īd was at first a classical poet, guided by a rather traditional mentality much influenced by the style and spirit of the Koran. After independence, his attitude changed, together with that of society: he even wrote poems praising the role of women in the struggle for liberation. Other poets of al-'Īd's generation retained the forms of classical Arabic poetry while taking political themes and world affairs as their subject matter.

Many collections published after independence contain poems written during the war years by poets who were living outside Algeria during that period. These often reveal the poets' guilt about writing on love and other personal subjects while their country was suffering. Abū al-Qāsim Khammār (b. 1931), who was residing in Syria, in his collection *Awrāq* (1967; leaves), considers the very fact of indulging in the delicate art of poetry a dilettante's occupation, incompatible with the situation in Algeria.

A new, guilt-free treatment of personal themes is seen in the work of Sālih Kharfī (b. 1932), particularly in *Anti Laylāya* (1974;

you are my chosen one), which shows a mastery of expression and form, although the tone is somewhat too impassioned.

The younger poets of the 1970s look to the future, reject the emotional attachment to the past, and assess the present with a critical eye. They have adopted free, well symbolized by the title *Infijārāt* (1977; explosions), a collection by Ahmad Hamdī (b. 194?). With no embarrassment, Ahlām MOSTAGHĀNMĪ called her second collection *Al-Kitāba fī lahzat 'ārī* (1976; writing in a moment of nakedness); whether discussing her love life or political problems, her poems are totally frank.

The Novel

Unlike the short story, the novel in Arabic made a late appearance in Algeria; most critics consider 'Abd al-Hamīd IBN HADŪGA's *Rīh al-janūb* (1971; the southern wind) the first real Algerian novel. This and his second novel, *Nihāyat al-ams* (1975; the end of yesterday) plunge the reader into the unvarnished reality of postindependence Algeria. In his novels, as in his short stories, al-Tāhir Wattār, by contrast, offers positive solutions to Algeria's problems within the framework of his socialist ideology.

In French

Algerian literature written in French followed a path similar to that of the Arabic works in the years preceding and immediately following independence, in that writers appointed themselves defenders of their people's rights and their country's freedom. Their aim was to show the difference between the true Algerians and the *colons*, the French settlers who had usurped Algerian land and nationality.

The Novel

The first writings in this intellectual pilgrimage concentrated on contrasting the poverty of the Algerians with the scandalous wealth of the European community. Mouloud FERAOUN presents a poignant picture of the situation in his novel *Le fils du pauvre* (1950; the poor man's son); Mohammed DIB, too, paints a moving portrait of the poor in different sectors of Algerian society in his trilogy *Algérie* (Algeria): the city in *La grande maison* (1952; the big house), the country in *L'incendie* (1954; the fire), and the world of the workers in *Le métier à tisser* (1957; the loom). Rachid BOUDJEDRA presents an extreme case of alienation of the Algerian in France in his novel *Topographie idéale pour une aggression caractérisée* (1975; an ideal topography for a downright attack), where the hero knows only the dialect of his small isolated village. Culture shock, the contradictions between Muslim traditions and European customs, is the subject of Feraoun's *Les chemins qui montent* (1957; the climbing roads), in which the hero, Amer, oscillates between two worlds and is unable to adapt to any. A slightly different situation is described by Mouloud MAMMERI in *Le sommeil du juste* (1955; *The Sleep of the Just*, 1958), whose hero, Arezki, experiences discrimination and the clash between two civilizations while fighting in the ranks of the French army during World War II.

The importance of the Algerian cultural heritage, so different from the French, informs such works as Mammeri's *La colline oubliée* (1952; the forgotten hill), and Assia DJEBAR's *Les enfants du nouveau monde* (1962; children of the new world) and *Les impatients* (1958; the impatient ones).

Many novels centered on the political problems of the country. The most original of these was Kateb Yacine's *Nedjma* (1965; *Nedjma*, 1961). Nedjma is a woman the author loved, but she is also the symbol of the homeland.

In the first years of independence, a number of important novels about the war appeared. The most outstanding of these, because of its innovative approach, was Dib's *Qui se souvient de la mer* (1962; *Who Remembers the Sea*, 1985) in which the war is portrayed in apocalyptic terms. Mammeri used a different approach in *L'opium et le bâton* (1965; opium and the stick), which stresses the human angle, with the express intention of proving the brotherhood of men, in spite of religious, racial, and political differences.

But soon the mood changed, and writers began expressing their disappointments with the revolution, deploring its failure. The defenders turned critics, vehemently denouncing the abuses of the new leaders, the corruption of the bourgeoisie, the reactionaries, some religious traditions, and the exploiters. The most violent attacks came from Mourad Bourboune (b. 1938), and Rachid Boudjedra. Bourboune unleashed his anger in the novel *Le muezzin* (1968; the muezzin), in which the hero, a former imam, wants to start the real revolution. Boudjedra aimed his attacks in *La répudiation* (repudiation, 1995) at the Muslim religion, which he holds responsible for the injustices committed against women. Dib focused on the former fighters for liberation—those who feel cheated because they were forgotten in the race for positions and favors that took place after independence, and those who were unable to adapt to a life of peace, as in *La danse du roi* (1968; the dance of the king).

The 1970s saw a diminishing interest in social and political problems and a tendency to analyze the psychology of the individual in specific situations. Mohammed Dib, in *Habel* (1977; Habel), shows the disarray of the intellectuals in exile in France. Nabil Farès (b. 1941) in *Le champ des oliviers* (1972; the field of olive trees) and *Mémoire de l'absent* (1974; memory of the absent), tries to search for identity in the faraway past of his people.

Poetry

A similar search had been undertaken by the poet Jean Amrouche (1906–1962) in his collection *Étoile secrète* (1937; secret star); he hoped to find peace in the lost paradise of his ancestors. Little poetry in French was written in the preindependence period, although Ait Djafer (b. 1929) wrote a very moving poem *Complaintes des mendiants arabes de la Casbah et de la petite Yasmina tuée par son père* (1953; *Wail for the Arab Beggars of the Casbah*, 1973), showing the abysmal poverty and the injustices the Algerian people endured.

Poetry in French reached a high point during the years of the war of independence. Both Malek Haddad (1927–1978) and Jean Sénac (1926–1973) expressed support for the fighters. In *Le malheur en danger* (1956; wretchedness is in danger) Haddad feels ashamed at being alive while other Algerians have been killed and mourns his dead friends. Sénac, on the other hand, celebrates patriotic feelings in *Soleil sous les armes* (1957; sun under arms), as did other poets of the period, notably Bachir Hadj Ali (b. 1920), in his collection *Chants pour le onze décembre* (1961; songs for December 11), and Anna Gréki (1931–1966), much of whose poetry was written in prison.

Around the mid-1960s a new generation of poets appeared; their main preoccupation is "to be." They do not hesitate to use bold language to express a violently critical attitude toward society.

Drama

Plays are rather rare in Algerian literature, despite the enthusiasm of the public for theatrical performances. Kateb Yacine's drama can be described as revolutionary. A different spirit animates Mouloud Mammeri's *Le banquet* (1973; the banquet), in which, by dealing with the massacre of the Aztecs, the author subtly alludes to the situation of the Berber in Algeria.

The Short Story

The short story in French gained importance only after independence. The first postindependence stories revolved around the war of liberation and were more realistic than their Arabic counterparts. Kateb Yacine used the short story as a weapon for attacks against religious authority. Emigration was an important subject, as was psychological analysis, as in the work of Hacen Farouk Zehar (b. 1939). Yasmin Amar (pseud. of Leila Hacene, b. 194?) introduced a refreshing note in two stories that describe the experience of a young Algerian woman in Europe.

Algerian literature written distinctly Arab character: themes are derived from Algerian folklore and tradition, Arabic expressions abound, and a specifically Algerian spirit is pervasive.

BIBLIOGRAPHY: Von Grunebaum, D., *French African Literature: Some Cultural Implications* (1964); Memmi, A., Introduction to *Anthologie des écrivains maghrébins d'expression française* (1964): 11–19; Gordon, C. D., *The Passing of French Algeria* (1966); Lévi-Valensi, J., and Bencheikh, J.-E. *Diwan algérien* (1967); Mérad, A., *Le réformisme musulman en Algérie, de 1925 à 1940* (1967); Ortzen, I. ed., *North African Writing* (1970); Déjeux, J., *Littérature maghrébine de langue française* (1973)

—AIDA A. BAMYA

Algerian Literature since 1980

Born in the turmoil of the fight for the recovery of independence, Algerian literature was endowed with a vigor that did not abandon it in the post-independence period. A particularly profuse literary production characterized the 1980s, bringing new life and vitality onto the Algerian cultural scene. Among the various revolutions that shaped postindependence life in Algeria, the cultural revolution received special attention for more than one reason. There was the need to assert the national identity through the reinforcement of the national language, Arabic, as well as a great desire to open the gates of education to all the people, a process referred to as the democratization of education. It gave all children access to schools, particularly those who were once barred from the educational system. The concern with the rapid installation of the educational machine was almost feverish on the part of the responsible authorities. Many saw it as the means to join the world's advanced nations. A long period of search for the best educational system that would be uniquely Algerian was underway. An unexpressed desire for uniqueness and individuality seemed to guide these efforts. Regardless of the motivations and the outcome, however, the focus of attention was on the reinstitution of Arabic as the national language and the Arabization of the country. A natural overflow of Arabic writings was expected to follow, gradually displacing the literature written in French. But contrary to all expectations, literary production in French showed

an unabated growth. The debate on the use of French continued to funnel heated discussions and passionate arguments much similar to the ones heard twenty years earlier. Individual efforts at solving the dilemma were made by some writers. KATEB Yacine turned his attention to the theater, producing plays using spoken Algerian in the dialogue. Rachid BOUDJEDRA chose to publish his novels in Arabic first, followed by a French translation. All the predictions of the death of French literature proved wrong.

While the theme of the war of independence did not abandon the scene, it acquired a new character and served a different purpose. The anticolonial feeling found expression in a new reading of history as the writers traveled back to the precolonial period for a source of inspiration. Their national identity was achieved as they claimed their Arab-Islamic or Berber-Islamic heritage, leaning on the historical significance of the events of this far-away past to interpret and assess the present. It is a tendency that manifests itself equally in the literatures written in Arabic and in French. The writers using these two languages shared also the same concern for the failure of the revolution to fulfill its promises, particularly after the disintegration of the agrarian reform. Both groups devised ingenious ways to convey their message of disapproval, depending heavily on either a true or imagined return of a *maquisard* to cast a critical look on their society or using symbols from Algerian folklore.

The war of independence as a theme did not disappear, only its function changed as it became a tool to denounce hypocrites and parasites. Long after the war ended, the fighters and the martyrs continued to haunt Algerian literature. If al-Tāhir WATTĀR imagined only the return of the martyrs of the revolution, Rachid MIMOUNI portrayed the life of a fighter who returns to his village after he was presumed dead. Ironically, at a time and place where festivities were being held to celebrate the memory of the fighters and bury their remains in earmarked cemeteries, the hero of the novel spends his time and energy trying to prove that he is alive. His adventures are a real odyssey related in *Le fleuve detourné* (1982; the deviated river). The official position vis-à-vis the martyrs of the revolution is the subject of another novel by Taher DJAOUT entitled *Les chercheurs d'os* (1984; the bones seekers). The book portrays the painful awakening of a young man in search of his brother's bones. During his search he questions the real motives of the living in this hunt for the bones of the dead, which he sees in its essence as a means to confirm their death. Wasini AL-A'RAJ (b. 1954), on the other hand, depends purely on imagination in *Hal al-Dunya* (1987; the condition of the world) when he pushes a martyr out of the frame of a picture in a courtroom and gives him the opportunity to criticize the judge who was preaching morality while his past activities in the years of the war spoke to the contrary.

An added novelty in the literature written in French is the growing number of women novelists and essayists. While some maintained a continuity in their literary production, others changed vocation such as Aisha Lemsine (b. 1942), who after publishing two novels shifted to journalistic investigation with *L'ordalie des voix* (1983; the trial of the voices), a platform for Arab women's opinions. Some women writers simply fell into silence after a promising start, such as Yamina Mechakra (b. 1953), who earned praise for her novel *La grotte eclatèe* (1979; the shattered cave). Another feature of the last decade is the appearance of an unprecedented phenomenon among the young members of the new generation of Algerians born in France. For various reasons mainly related to the great difficulties in the acculturation process and the periodical resurgence of racism, many expressed a long suppressed rage over their conditions. Their voice is, in a special way, the silent cry of their parents who, handicapped by their illiteracy, failed to raise the vital issues that confronted them in the early years of emigration. The writings of the Maghribi youth, predominantly Algerian, is known as "Beur" literature.

As far as the various literary genres are concerned, all seem to be flourishing both in Arabic and in French. Drama, however, made little progress, and the rare published texts do not find their way to the stage. The opposite situation occurred when some plays were performed but their manuscripts were never published; an example is Yacine's *Mohammad prend ta valise* (1971; Mohammad, grab your suitcase).

The Arabic literary movement witnessed a certain change in its trend since the first quarter of the 20th c. with the gradual ascendancy of the novel and the continued abundant production of short stories and, to a lesser extent, poetry. While the established novelists continued to write at a somewhat slower pace, a number of younger writers, armed with a solid Arabic education, appeared on the literary scene. The literature of the 1980s is also characterized by the absence of inhibition in dealing with previously taboo subjects such as sexual relations and love. The reserve manifested by writers such as Mouloud FERAOUN or Mohammad DIB vanished almost totally with the writers of the new generation.

The growing political power of the Berber movement benefited its folk literature as it became the center of attention leading to the collection, translation, and interpretation of Berber poetry, as well as the appearance of periodicals in Amazigh language.

New names have made their appearance on the literary scene. Most prominent at least for historical reasons is Annissa Boumediene, wife of the late Algerian president Houwari Boumediene. Her first book *La fin d'un monde* (1991; the end of a world) is a historical novel which goes back to the early Islamic period.

While Algerians were still seeking a definition of their entity and looking back at the war of independence, a new event disturbed their uneasy life. The tragedy played on the stage of their everyday life is characterized not only by its violence and bloody nature but also by its incomprehensibility. The bewilderment is probably best expressed by Assia Djebar in *Le blanc d'Algérie* (1995; the whiteness of Algeria) as she refuses to acknowledge the death of her assassinated friends. She engages the dialogue with their memory to protect them from forgetfulness. The overwhelming nature of the events interrupted the work on her novel *Les Nuits de Strasbourg* (1997; the nights of Strasbourg) resumed later, in order to write her collection of short stories, *Oran, langue morte* (1997; oran, dead language).

Living in the shadow of the events, and writing about them without any perspective of time or space, Algerian writers seem unable to place them in any semifictitious setting. It seems almost indecent to relegate such violent reality to the realm of imagination. Djebar stayed close to reality, writing directly about the tragic events. Rachid Mimouni, on the other hand, conveyed the events in a novel, *La malédiction* (1993; the damnation), in which he failed to match the horror of reality through fiction. It can be sadly said that the main player in many of the writings since the early nineties, is death.

La'raj Wāsīnī is unable to detach himself from reality in spite of the love story in *Sayyitdatu'l-Maqām* (1995; the lady of the place). While some writers confront violence in their works, others like Rachid Boudjedra in *Timimoun* (1994; Timimoun) seek refuge in the remoteness of the desert and its purity. Nevertheless, the echoes of the acts of violence committed in the cities find their way to him. One also wonders whether Nabil Fares's *Le miroir de Cordoue*

(1994; the mirror of Cordova) in its evocation of religious tolerance during the Umayyad period, is not a message to his own people.

Leïla SEBBAR continues her prolific production with a variety of texts. Yet she never loses track of the theme of mother-son dialogue, begun in *Parle mon fils, parle à ta mère* (1984; talk my son, talk to your mother). Her novel *Le silence des rives* (1993; the silence of the banks) dramatizes the difficult communication between the generations. The war of independence as a theme in Algerian literary writings did not disappear from the scenes. It is either at the center of a narrative as in Ahlām Mostaghānmī's *Thākiratu'l-Jasad* (1993; the body's memory) or serves as a reference. It provided the writers in the nineties a means to establish parallels between the bloody events of their time and those of the war of independence. Djebar adopts this approach in *Le blanc d'Algérie* and so does Sebbar in her collection of short stories, *La jeune fille au balcon* (1996; the girl in the balcony). It is as if writers were striving to exorcize the dead by the dead.

Themselves victims of the violent events that shook their country since the early 1990s, writers viewed themselves as actors and observers, almost trapped in the whirlwind. Their writings reflect their distress but also their confusion, and their efforts to understand the incomprehensible.

In Arabic

The Novel

The scene of the novel continues to be dominated by the names of the two pioneers al-Tāhir Wattāar and 'Abd al-Hamīd IBN HADŪQA. The former walked the bridge of the war of independence between his first novel, *Al-Lāz* (1974; al-Laz), and one of his latest works, *Al-'ishq wa-al-mawt fī al-zaman al-Harāshī* (1978; passion and death in the Harrachi time). His hero, Al-Lāz, who loses his mind in the first novel, recovers his sanity in the latter book. *Tajriba fī al-'Ishq* (1990; an experience in passion), marks a turning point in his career stylistically and thematically, although he does not abandon his political revendication, which extends here beyond the borders of Algeria and tackles various Arab causes. Hadūqa continued the tendency manifested in his earlier novels to mix politics and love. In *Bāna al-subh* (1980; the morning appeared) he draws a picture of the complex and corrupt life in the city, whereas in *al-Jāziyah wa-al darāwīsh* (1983; the Jaziyah and the dervishes) Hadūqa returns to the country, which seems to exercise a special fascination on the author. He did not falter, however, on his feminist position portraying assertive women in his novels, in the rural and the urban environments. Although these two veteran novelists gradually moved away from the war themes, the younger writers revived the subject, as if the evocation of this major event in the history of their country was a national duty and a sign of patriotism. One such novelist, Mirzāq Biqtash (b. 1945) centers the action of his two books, *Tuyūr fī al-Zāhira* (1981; birds at noon) and *Al-Buzah* (1983; uniform wearers), on the war through the eyes of children. Wasini al-A'raj showed less involvement with the war of independence without ignoring it totally. With a tendency toward philosophical reflection he cast a critical eye on the postindependence period and its shortcomings, describing the disenchantment of the people and their efforts at maintaining a source of hope in an increasingly deteriorating situation. The hero of his novel *Waqā'i' rajul Ghamara Sawb al-Bahr* (1983; the adventures of a man who ventured toward the sea) goes in search of the missing elements in society. Al-A'raj brings to the Arabic novel in Algeria a poetic prose that added a great limpidity and fluidity to the language. He also broke the hard skin of certain social taboos by talking freely about love and sexual relations. In spite of his openness in dealing with this topic he succeeds in sublimating it. Although greatly concerned with the social realities and their handicapping effect on his people, al-A'raj probes deeply in his inner self for a variety of emotions and soul-searching that is unprecedented in the Arabic Algerian novel. The style in his latest novels copies the reality of the people's speech, incorporating colloquial expressions and French phrases and sentences in the Arabic text.

The Short Story

While the novel tried to infuse a sense of hope in the midst of a problematic reality, the short story was generally less optimistic in its approach. It revealed a world of fear, anxiety, failure, and shattered dreams. Emigration increased but failed to bring happiness in spite of the material prosperity it generally provided. Wives in particular resented their husbands' departures, fearful and apprehensive of their marriage to foreign women or their indulgence in the sins of the West. The health and security of the emigrant men was a constant worry. Many collections carry at least one story on the subject. In his collection *Al-Aswāt* (1985; the voices) Ammar Belhassan (b. 1953) entitles one of his short stories "Rahīl warā'a Khayt al-Damm" (setting out on the trace of blood drops). Al-A'raj devoted his collection *Alam al-Kitāba 'An Ahzān al-Manfā* (1980; the painful process of writing about the sorrows of exile) in its entirety to an evocation of his love for his country and returned to the theme in his collection *Asmāk al-Barr al-Mutawahhish* (1986; the fish of the savage shore). A greater maturity is apparent in the thinking of the characters of these writers as the decision to return to their homeland is dictated primarily by the desire to serve it.

Armed with little experience and much difficulty, the Algerians had to face a tough reality after the euphoria of freedom. As if overwhelmed by the magnitude of the responsibility and the accumulation of problems through the years, they found themselves in a "wasteland." Algeria suffered from the usual postindependence problems of the Third World countries such as exploitation, a growing number of parasites, a distorted sense of patriotism, a race for positions, and quick wealth. Added to these major problems were the daily vexations of life in the form of crowded and slow-running buses, traffic jams, housing crisis, the high cost of living, exacting social duties, and shortages of vital consumer goods. Seemingly insignificant, these material problems impacted profoundly on the psychology of the individuals. In "Humūm Saghīra," (1986; little worries) Ahmad Mannur's (b. 1945) hero echoes the other writers' concerns, lamenting the shortage of spare parts for his car, which forced him to use the overcrowded public transportation. This solution caused him unhappiness at work and at home and made him ponder on the policy of his government. The housing crisis, for example, which led to jamming more than one family in tiny apartments, caused not only continuous frictions between the inhabitants but also a loss of privacy impacting on marital relations, job performance, and productivity as a whole. A poignantly realistic account of such a painful experience is given in Mustaphā Natur's (b. 1950) "'Usr al-Wilāda" (difficult delivery) from his collection *Ahlām al-Jiyād al-mafjū'a* (1985; dreams of the frightened horses).

Voicing their frustration and anger on paper was for many writers the only escape from a reality that entrapped them. Frustrations exploded also in the popular and old form of singing known as *Al-Rai'*. Revived in the 1980s the *Rai* songs are profane and pernicious in their content and express an antiestablishment stand. They acted as a cry of freedom against the multiple restrictive laws of the government and were used by the "Beur" in France as an identity symbol.

Poetry

Algerian poetry took a few strides on the way to modernity in the 1970s and continued on this path in the 1980s. Yet the poetic production is weaker quantitatively as if more writers opted for prose. Some of the poets who achieved renown in the past, such as Ahlām Mostaghānmī, faded from the literary scene, while new names appeared. The themes in the more recent production revolve generally around the homeland and the memory of the martyrs of the revolution; there is also an interest in the Arab nation and the obstacles facing Arab unity. Sarcasm on the erosion of Arab wealth by the rulers is expressed in a manner reminiscent of the Syrian Nizār Qabbānī (b. 1923). Sarcasm is also present in Zeinab al-A'waj's (b. 1956) *Arfudu An Udajjan al-Atfāl* (1983; I refuse to see the children exploited), where a deep revendicative tone dominates the collection. The memory of the martyrs is usually evoked to stress their betrayal by the ruling power. But a note of hope pierces through her poems as well as those of the poets of her generation who believe in the rising sun. There is also a concern for the well-being of society and for justice as conceived from a socialist point of view, a predominant position among the poets of the 1980s. The Palestinian problem remained central to a number of poems, as it did in the short stories. In *Atfāl Port-Said Yuhājirūn Ilā Awwal May* (1983; the children of Port-Said emigrate to the first of May), 'Abd al-'Alī Razzāqī (b. 1949) expressed consternation at the state of Jerusalem and the war in Lebanon while the Arab rulers were indulging in their pleasures. A feeling of brotherhood for the Arabs motivated the poet to fight for the Arab cause, now that his country was free. Although full of anger, the language of the poems is subdued by the beauty of the imagery and a more flowing poetic style. Reading Razzāqī or Al-A'waj's poetry, one can't help but notice the impact of known Arab poets on their writings, in particular the Palestinian Mahmūd DARWĪSH. It is quite obvious that the true literary revival in the language of poetry took place in the 1980s with the growing number of Algerians studying in the *Mashriq*. Their interests and literary experience encompassed vaster spheres than those of their predecessors. These recent collections are written in free verse and reveal a tendency to experiment in form. Mustapha M. al-Ghamārī, with the publication of three consecutive collections of poetry, *Asrār al-Ghurba* (1977; the secrets of life in exile), *Naqs 'alā Dhākirati'l-Zaman* (1978; designs on time's memory) and *Ughniyāt al-Ward Wan-Nār* (1980; songs of roses and fire) contributes some important issues, one related to the need for objective literary criticism, in obvious shortage, and the materialization of an Islamic religious consciousness.

In French

It is possible to say without exaggeration that literature using the French language bloomed in Algeria in the last decade and a half contrary to all expectations. Works written in French were published both in France and Algeria, even by national publishing houses such as L'Édition Nationale du Livre, previously known as Société Nationale d'Édition et de Diffusion (SNED). The abundance of literary production and a tendency towards privatization at the end of president Chadhli Ben Jedid's administration led to the establishment of some private publishing houses, the best known of which is Laphomic. Some of the peculiarities of this literature are the versatility of its authors and their disregard for the adoption of a strict literary genre in a single book. Many mixed poetry and prose in the same work, while others contributed in separate works to poetry, the novel, the short story, and even drama. Acting as ethnologists, some writers collected folk literature. Mouloud MAMMERI's efforts centered on Mohand Si-Mohand (1840?–1906), a renowned Berber poet, while Rabah BELAMRI published popular tales.

The Novel

There is nevertheless a major difference between this literature and that of the colonial period and the early postindependence era. The new approach is that of a recovered entity and rediscovered roots. The young writers such as Taher Djaout and Habib Tangour (b. 1947) seem comfortably anchored in their history and at ease in their identity, neither embarrassed by the use of French nor apologetic. Acting as truly independent thinkers, they do not seem concerned by the danger of being claimed by another culture. They own the language that once owned them. Their appearance on the cultural scene is the anticlimax of the clash of civilizations that marked many of the works and lives of their predecessors. Taher Djaout journeyed back in history in *L'invention du désert* (1987; the invention of the desert) to trace the steps of the ancestors, the Almoravids. His contemporary Habib Tangour roamed history from the Jahiliyya to the Abbasid periods, contrasting past and present to assess and condemn conditions in Algeria. His novel *Le vieux de la montagne* (1983; the old man and the mountain) reveals the disillusionment of the people with their country's government. This return to precolonial history is neither an escape from reality nor an emotional consolation in past glories. It is rather a measuring rod for the present. A shift in outlook characterizes the works of established novelists such as Rachid Boudjedra and Assia DJEBAR. Boudjedra introduced a triumvirate of action in his most recent novels, moving from the past to the present to autobiographical information. This triple direction forms usually the woven text of his books. He embarked also on a triple-narrative and multiple-time sequences where the action moves freely, allowing him to give his own interpretation of the present by superimposing it on the past. Most events lead usually to incidents that marked deeply his personal life, such as his mother's death related in *La prise de Gibraltar* (1987; the conquest of Gibraltar). It is evoked parallel to the incident that led to the death of a large number of women killed by the French forces as they demonstrated in 1955 in Constantine. A more restricted narration of his autobiography appeared in *La macération* (1985; the maceration) through the rewriting of the *A Thousand and One Nights* for a film scenario. The novel is a new look at the more recent history of Algeria and the life of the novelist's father already evoked in *La répudiation* under a less flattering image.

Rachid Boudjedra's case raises a question of classification if we are to consider his novels written in French as simple translations of those he writes first in Arabic, a process he began with *Le démantèlement* (1982; the bringing down, in Arabic *Al-tafakkuk*; 1982). Two reasons dictate Boudjedra's inclusion in the section of the literature written in French. His readers are predominantly those of the French version of his novels, and his insistence on publishing the French and Arabic versions of his novels almost simultaneously reinforces the feeling among many critics that his Arabic novels are, contrary to his assertions, mere translations of the novels he writes first in French. A style heavily marked by French images and sentence constructions alien to Arabic strengthens this theory.

In this new phase of their production the novelists narrate their life through the windows of history with the comfort of a traditional storyteller like a purgation. There is clearly in Boudjedra's writings and in that of Assia Djebar's an abandonment of the self and the absence of the studentlike attitude desiring to impress the teacher-master characteristic of their early works. Djebar continued in her novels *L'amour, la fantasia* (1985; *Fantasia: An Algerian Cavalcade*, 1989) and *Ombre Sultane* (1987; *A Sister to Scheherazade*, 1987) to champion women's causes, but without the romantic spirit of her first few novels. Both in these new works and in the documentary films she produced, *La Zerda et les chants de l'oublie* (1982; the Zerda and the songs of forgetfulness) and *La Nouba des femmes du Mont Chenoua* (1978; the Nouba of the women of Mount Chenoua), she gave a historical perspective of women's importance in society, stressing their role in the history of their country. While relying heavily on autobiographical information in the *L'amour, la fantasia*, she enters the evocative and symbolic world of Shahrazad (Sherazade, Scheherazade) in *Ombre Sultane*. There she juxtaposes two lives, the traditional and the modern, considering the future with some apprehension at the possibility of seeing women failing to play a role in a world they helped create.

The reader should not be misled in thinking, however, that the novelists abandoned the task of political criticism. A veteran of the novel, Mouloud Mammeri, described the disillusionment of the intellectuals in their country's régime in *La traversée* (1982; the crossing). Equally critical of the political realities of his country is the young and promising novelist Rachid Mimouni. In *Le fleuve détourné* he denounced the government policy and its exploitation of socialism and the spirit of the revolution in order to dominate the people. In another novel, *Tombeza* (1984; Tombeza), he raised the question of traitors who benefited from the times of war and peace, a theme dear to Hadūqa. Another literary figure, Mohammad Dib, a veteran novelist, poet, and short-story writer, drew gradually away from his early concern with the sociopolitical problems of his country to pursue an old favorite topic, that of words and their fleeting meaning. Emanating from his short story "La dalle écrite" (1966; the inscribed stone), the pursuit of an ever-escaping significance of words continued to haunt him in his later work. Through Habel in the novel bearing the same name and Eid in *Les terrasses d'orsol* (1985; the roofs of Orsol) Dib chased death and love, playing what seemed like a hide-and-seek game with these major emotions in a person's life. Much of his reflection revolved around the thin line where reality and imagination are intertwined, where illusion often predominates over truth. One theme to which Dib remained faithful throughout his work is his high regard for women, who often play the role of the rescuer.

The character of Shahrazad was revived in more than one novel, possibly as part of this return trip to the roots. A new writer, Leïla Sebbar, gives the heroine of the *A Thousand and One Nights* a place of honor in her works. Three of her books carry her name as part of the title, the first one is *Sherazade, 17 ans, brune, frisée, les yeux verts* (1982; Sherazade, age 17, brunette, curly hair and green eyes), then *Les carnets de Sherazade* (1985; Sherazade's notes), and the most recent book, *Le fou de Sherazade* (1991; crazy about

Sherazade). Although belonging to two worlds, those of her French mother and her Algerian father, and living in France, Sebbar is attached to Algeria, where she found her identity. She followed in her predecessors' footsteps, particularly Kateb Yacine, for whom she has a special admiration, as she gives Jaffar in *J. H. cherche âme sœur* (1987; J. H. looking for a soul sister) the novel *Nedjma* (1956; Nedjma) to read while in prison. Like Yacine, she moves her characters from one novel to the other. Thus Jaffar, Sherazade, and Julien appear in *Les carnets de Sherazade*, and *J. H. cherche âme sœur*. The three reappear in *Le fou de Sherazade*, as Jaffar meets Sherazade in Beirut in the midst of a cross fire by invisible snipers. When they depart, Sherazade conveys Nedjma's protection on him. The significance of Sherazade's role is explained in the last novel through a commentary made by one of the characters, Pierrot; he interprets her endless talk as a means to protect herself against rape.

Sebbar centered her attention on the identity problems of the generation of emigrant children and their relation to their country of origin. After her own personal odyssey, she seemed to have reached a situation of comfort. At ease with her identity, she moved beyond the borders of France and Algeria, taking her characters to Beirut and Jerusalem with an effort to stress the brotherhood of the two peoples, Palestinians and Israelis. Sebbar stands at the demarcation line between the writers who live in self-imposed exile in France and the second generation of Algerians commonly known as the "Beur."

The "Beur," the new generation of Algerians born in France and citizens of their parents' country of exile, drew attention to themselves through a number of highly autobiographical novels published in the 1980s. Their works are cries of anger and calls for help. Projected into the midst of a Western society due to circumstances beyond their control, they found themselves oscillating between two cultures and at ease in neither. Children of a failed acculturation, they found in writing an outlet for their confusion and loss. Although most are so far the authors of a single book, some managed to achieve fame, such as Mehdi Charef (b. 1952), who wrote *Le thé au harem d'Archi Ahmed* (1983; *Tea in the Harem*, 1989). Another "Beur," Farida Belghoul (b. 1958?), wrote the best novel in this genre, *Georgette* (1986; Georgette). Each writer deals with a certain aspect of the life of the "Beur." While Charef described the despair and poverty of the emigrants' lives, transforming them into professional thieves at an early age, Belghoul concentrated on a life between two cultures and the lack of understanding between parents and children. This budding literature is still in the making; only the future will reveal whether it was an impetuous, one-time event or the first step on a serious literary movement. The activity of Beur groups extend beyond the literary texts. It found its expression in documentaries, radio stations, clubs and theater performances. Though the bulk of the movement is in France, two other European countries, Belgium and Holland are witnessing the springing of significant cultural Beur activities.

This new literature of the 1980s, whether "Beur" or that of the self-exiled writers such as Ali Boumadhi (b. 1934) or Rabah Belamri adopts a more descriptive style, faithful to reality and reminiscent of that of the early works of the 1950s—as if this new generation of Algerian writers is motivated by the desire to testify like its predecessors.

The Short Story

This literary genre continued to be widely used and published. It fulfilled the same role played by the Arabic short story and acted as a platform of dissatisfaction and frustration. The short story deals with seemingly unimportant incidents such as queuing for various kinds of purchases, or the race for stocking on merchandise, clearly a major preoccupation of the people always fearful of food or other shortages. Hamid Skif (b. 1951), however, dramatizes this banality in either a tragicomical art describing the rise and fall of a refrigerator or a pathetic glorification of tomato paste in *Les nouvelles de la maison du silence* (1986; news from the house of silence). For Assia Djebar, more versed in the novel, the few short stories she published, and also her collection carrying the title of Delacroix's painting, *Femmes d'Alger dans leur appartement* (1980; *Women of Algiers in Their Apartment*, 1992), there is not much new. The author continued her description of the women's world, their gestures and their dreams of the outside world as imagined from behind their closed doors. If there is an impressive number of published collections of short stories, there are more works that appeared separately in the national press. The message, however, remains the same.

Poetry

It seems difficult to talk about Algerian poetry without mentioning one of its champions, Mohammad Dib. Here more even than in the novel, Dib reveals his almost obsessive concern with the language, with words and their magical effects. Thematically, however, his poetry remains within the boundaries of his novels. *Omneros* (1975; Omnero) raised the usual reflection on love and death, whereas *O vive* (1987; Oh! long life) is a testimony of the author's deep affection and respect for women. Contrary to the younger generation of poets, Dib, Bashir Hadj-Ali (b. 1920), Malek Alloula (b. 1939), and Jamal-Eddine Bencheikh (b. 1930) deal with poetry as artists, whereas the others used it as a channel for their anger. Few among the poets of the 1980s produced significant numbers of poems to trace a certain continuity in their progression or to speak at all of any kind of evolution.

Some veteran poets, though, deserve more attention. Both Djamal Amrani (b. 1935) and Noureddine Aba (1921–1996) made a comeback in the last decade. The latter is endowed with a humanitarian outlook on the world's problems and manifested a particular concern for the Palestinian cause in collections such as *L'aube à Jerusalem* (1979; dawn in Jerusalem) and *Tel Zaatar s'est tu à la tombée de la nuit* (1981; Tel Zaatar was quiet at sunset). Amrani deals with national problems and is known as the chronicler of the war of independence. His latest collections, such as *Jours couleur de soleil* (1979; days with the color of the sun) and *Entre la dent et la mémoire* (1981; between tooth and memory), reveal an interest in the present while maintaining a link with the past.

This genre remains much alive and fed continuously by new contributions and experimentations, many written by unknown poets. For most members of this young generation poetry is perceived as an expression of freedom.

BIBLIOGRAPHY: Mortimer, M., *The Algerian Novel in French, 1954–1965* (1972); Dejeux, J., *Situation de la littérature maghrébine de langue française* (1982); Bouzar, W., *Lectures maghrebines: Essai* (1984); Djaout, T., *Les mots migrateurs* (1985); Bonn, C., *Le roman algérien de langue française* (1985); Mostaghanmi, A., *Algérie: Femmes et écritures* (1985); Yahiaoui, F., *Roman et société coloniale dans l'Algérié de l'entre-deux-guerres* (1985); Lacheraf, M., *Écrits didactiques sur la culture, l'histoire et la société en Algérié* (1988); Bonn, C., *Anthologie de la littérature* *algérienne* (1990); Achour, C., *Anthologie de la littérature algérienne de langue française* (1990); Mortimer, M., *Journeys through the French African Novel* (1990); Ibnlfassi, L., and N. Hitchcott, *African Francophone Writing* (1996); Mathieu, M., ed., *Littératures autobiographiques del la francophonie* (1996)

—AIDA A. BAMIA

ALGREN, Nelson

American noyelist and short-story writer, b. 28 March 1909, Detroit, Mich.; d. 9 May 1981, Sag Harbor, N.Y.

A. has lived most of his life in or near Chicago, the setting of much of his work. Unable to find newspaper work after receiving a degree in journalism from the University of Illinois in 1931, he hitchhiked and rode freight trains through much of the South, became a door-to-door salesman in New Orleans for a short time, then, briefly, a co-operator of a gasoline station in the Rio Grande Valley, an experience he fictionalized in his first short story. Published by *Story Magazine* in 1933, the effort led to a contract and a $100 advance for his first novel, *Somebody in Boots* (1935), written after his return to Chicago but based largely on his Depression-year wanderings. Disappointed by the book's meager sales (758 copies), A. worked as an editor on a WPA writer's project before publishing his second novel, *Never Come Morning*

Nelson Algren

(1942). After a three-year army stint during World War II, he returned once again to Chicago to resume his writing career.

Somebody in Boots is a chronicle of poverty and failure dedicated to "those innumerable thousands: the homeless boys of America." The novel contains the characters, the situations, and the locales that form the basis for A.'s future novels: his South populated by drunks, pimps, prostitutes, freaks, monsters, and perverts; and Chicago with an urban concentration of all of those plus cardsharps, prize-fighters, confidence men, hoodlums, and drug addicts. A.'s second novel, *Never Come Morning*, is a story of rape and murder with a Polish boxer as its hero. Heralded as a significant addition to the Chicago novelists' school of social protest, the story traces the youthful boxer's defeat as he struggles against the social and statutory laws that govern his world.

The Man with the Golden Arm (1949) received the first National Book Award. The story of a Chicago stud-poker dealer who becomes a morphine addict presents memorable characters in a style and language drawn directly from the world they inhabit. Blending naturalistic determinism with sympathy and compassion for his characters, A. insists that his readers recognize the personal worth and dignity of the socially disinherited.

A Walk on the Wild Side (1956) is the work A. himself and many of his critics consider his best. This book, which A. calls an "accidental novel," grew out of his attempts to revise *Somebody in Boots* for reissue after the success of *The Man with the Golden Arm*. A.'s changes were so extensive that reviewers failed to recognize its genesis and the new book became, A. claims, a kind never before written: "an American fantasy—a poem written to an American beat as truly as *Huckleberry Finn*." Although still the champion of the dispossessed, A. had by now polished and perfected his style and presented his story with a ribald, grotesque, and sometimes almost surrealistic sense of comedy.

In addition to his four novels, A. has published over fifty short stories, several travel books, criticism, prose poems, and poetry. A.'s books, with their rich veins of satire, irony, humor, and farce, are little catalogues of offbeat information. His dialogue is that of the gutter, the jungle—his neon wilderness—and his style, varying from staccato reporting to richly poetic passages, has earned him the title "poet of the Chicago slums." Two decades before drug addiction became a national dilemma, *The Man with the Golden Arm* portrayed the world of the drug addict with authority and impact as yet unsurpassed. As a spokesman for the world's derelicts, he belongs to a literary tradition of social protest to a degree unfashionable today. His popular appeal reached its height with *The Man with the Golden Arm* in 1949 and his last major work of fiction, *A Walk on the Wild Side*, was published in 1956. Nevertheless, his work is still acclaimed for its prophetic qualities and for its influence on other novelists and assures him a place in American literature.

FURTHER WORKS: *The Neon Wilderness* (1947); *Chicago: City on the Make* (1951); *N. A.'s Own Book of Lonesome Monsters* (1962); *Who Lost an American?* (1963); *Notes from a Sea Diary: Hemingway All the Way* (1965); *Conversations with N. A.* (1965, with H. E. F. Donohue); *The Last Carousel* (1973); *The Devil's Stocking* (1983); *America Eats* (1992); *He Swung and He Missed* (1993); *Nonconformity* (1994); *The Texas Stories of N. A.* (1995)

BIBLIOGRAPHY: Geismar, M., "N. A.: The Iron Sanctuary," *CE*, 14 (1953): 311–15; also *EJ*, 42 (1953): 121–25; Anderson, A., and

Southern, T. "N. A." (Interview), *Paris Review*, 11 (1955): 37–58; Bluestone, G., "N. A.," *WR*, 22 (1957): 27–44; Lipton, L., "A Voyeur's View of the Wild Side: N. A. and His Critics," *ChiR*, 10, 4 (1957): 4–14; Eisinger, C. E., "N. A.: Naturalism as the Beat of the Iron Heart," in *Fiction of the Forties* (1963): 73–85; Beauvoir, S., de, "An American Rendezvous: The Question of Fidelity," Part II, *Harper's*, Dec. 1964: 111–22; Cox, M. H., and W. Chatterton, *N. A.* (1975); Giles, J. R., *Confronting the Horror: The Novels of N. A.* (1989); Drew, B., *N. A.: A Life on the Wild Side* (1989)

—MARTHA HEASLEY COX

ALI, Ahmed

Pakistani novelist, short-story writer, poet, essayist, and translator (writing in Urdu and English), b. 1 July 1910, Delhi, India; d. 14 Jan. 1994, Karachi

A., Pakistan's best-known contemporary author, writes in both English (novels, poetry, essays) and Urdu (short stories). His numerous translations into English include poetry from Indonesian, Urdu, and Chinese, and the Koran from Arabic.

Educated in English-medium schools, A. received his B.A. and M.A. in English literature from Lucknow University. In addition to writing, he has had several other careers: a teacher of English in India, China, Pakistan, and the U.S.; a diplomat serving in the Pakistan foreign service in both China and Morocco; a public-relations advisor to several large Pakistani corporations; and a small businessman. He was awarded the Star of Distinction by the Government of Pakistan in 1980.

In 1932 A. and three friends published an anthology of ten short stories and a one-act play entitled *Angare* (burning coals). Attacking middle-class Muslim mores and attitudes, these works satirized religious hypocrisy, male chauvinism, and society's indifference to the poor. The book caused a major uproar, due primarily to the authors' cavalier treatment of Islam and the Koran. During this controversy the book was publicly burned, the authors denounced in the press and from the pulpit, and their lives threatened. Contests were even held to find the best way to punish them for their blasphemy. The volume was quickly proscribed, a ban that remains in force to this day.

Later, in 1936, A. played a key role in organizing the first meeting of the All-India Progressive Writers' Association, which, with encouragement from various European leftist writers, spread Marxist ideology and SOCIALIST REALISM to authors in India's dozen major languages. This organization remained a major force on the Indian literary scene for nearly two decades. As it grew increasingly doctrinaire in the late 1930s, A. broke with the group and assumed a literary stance more concerned with aesthetics and less encumbered by politics. At this time he also started writing in English.

A.'s first volume of short stories, *Shole* (1936; flames), contains about half of his corpus in this genre. These works show an acute social consciousness in which A. derides conservative Muslim social, political, and religious thinking. Several are highly symbolic and deftly use interior monologue and STREAM OF CONSCIOUSNESS. A second volume of short stories, *Hamari gali* (our lane), appeared in 1942, the title story from which is considered A.'s best. It was published in A.'s own English translation in *New Writing* (1937). Highly autobiographical and richly textured, it is set in A.'s

Kucha Pundit neighborhood of Old Delhi and depicts a variety of colorful, minutely etched characters who live out their hapless lives in superstition and fear.

A. traveled to England in 1939, where, assisted by E. M. FORSTER, he was able to place his first English language novel, *Twilight in Delhi*, with the prestigious Hogarth Press, which published it to considerable critical acclaim in the following year, one of only two works by Asian writers this press ever printed. A.'s masterpiece, this novel vividly and poignantly details the downward slide in the fortunes of several generations of a well-to-do Muslim family in Delhi at the start of this century. It is considered one of the most distinctive novels in Commonwealth literature.

A.'s poetry is deeply influenced by his stays in China, first in 1947-1948 as a British Council visiting professor of English in Nanking, when he started his study of Chinese, and later as a diplomat in 1951-1952. The themes of this poetry are similar to those found in the novels: the fading of youth and the evanescence of life, the loss of friends either through death or abandonment, the sadness of potential unrealized, and the emptiness of success achieved. Often modeled on classical Chinese lyrics, many of A.'s poems are collected in *Purple Gold Mountain* (1960).

As an essayist A. has published seven volumes of literary criticism, including *Mr. Eliot's Penny World of Dreams* (1942) and *Ghalib: Two Essays* (1969). An indefatigable translator, A. has published *The Flaming Earth: Poems from Indonesia* (1949), one of the earliest English-language collections of poetry from Southeast Asia, and four anthologies of classical Urdu poetry, the most important of which is *The Golden Tradition* (1973). In 1980 he completed his highly acclaimed translation of the Koran from Arabic, which he considers his magnum opus, currently in its ninth printing. He has translated and published in journals the works of a number of prerevolutionary Chinese poets, and has edited several English-language literary journals and books of creative writing from Asia and Africa.

A.'s prose style is a striking combination of opulent lyricism and stark realism, suffused with ellipses and purposely antiquated language that gives his fiction an epic, almost biblical, quality. Much of the diction of his early poetry is similarly textured, but later poems reflecting Chinese influences are remarkable in their simplicity of language. A man who moves with equal ease between West and East, A. has served as an important, though often unrecognized, intellectual and artistic link between these two polarities. Through his creative writings, scholarly publications, and translations, he has brought Asia and some of its choicest literary works to the often indifferent attention of the West.

FURTHER WORKS: *Break the Chains* (1932); *Poetry: A Problem* (1934); *The Land of Twilight* (1937); *Teaching of Poetry* (1940); *Qaid khana* (1944); *Maut se pahle* (1945); *Muslim China* (1949); *The Falcon and the Hunted Bird* (1950); *The Bulbul and the Rose* (1960); *Ocean of Night* (1964); *The Failure of an Intellect* (1968); *Ghalib: Selected Poems* (1969); *The Problem of Style and Technique in Ghalib* (1969); *The Shadow and the Substance: Principles of Reality, Art and Literature* (1977); *Al-Qur'ān: A Contemporary Translation* (1984); *Of Rats and Diplomats* (1985)

BIBLIOGRAPHY: Brander, L., "Two Novels of A. A.," *JCL* 3 (1967): 76–86; Anderson, D., "A. A. and *Twilight in Delhi*," *Mahfil, A Quarterly of South Asian Literature*, 7, 1–2 (1971): 81–86; Anderson, D., "A. A. and the Growth of the Pakistani Literary Tradition in English," *WLWE*, 16, 2 (1975): 436–49;

Kumar, A., "*Twilight in Delhi*: A Study in Lyricism," *IndL*, 19, 2 (1976): 25–38; Coppola, C., "The Short Stories of A. A.," *Studies in the Urdu Gazal and Prose Fiction* (1979): 214–42; Coppola, C., "The Poetry of A. A.," *JIWE*, 8, 1–2 (Jan.-July 1980): 63–76; Nevin, A., "Historical Imagination and the Novels of A. A.," *JIWE*, 8, 1–2 (Jan.-July 1980): 3–13; Coppola, C., "The *Angare* Group: The *Enfants Terribles* of Urdu Literature," *AnUS*, 1 (1981): 57–69; King, B., "From *Twilight* to *Midnight*: Muslim Novels of India and Pakistan," *The Worlds of Muslim Imagination* (1986): 243–59; Coppola, C., "The All-India Progressive Writers' Association: The European Phase," *Marxist Influences and South Asian Literature* (1988): 1–41; Askari, M., "A Novel by A. A.," *AnUS*, 9 (1994): 73-84; Coppola, C., "A. A. (1910-1994): Bridges and Links East and West," *AnUS*, 9 (1994): 97-101; Hashmi, A., "Professor A. A.," *AnUS*, 9 (1994): 91-95; Singh, K., "Face of a Friend: A. A. 1910-1994," *AnUS*, 9 (1994): 103-05; Zeno, "Professor A. A. and the Progressive Writers' Movement," *AnUS*, 9 (1994): 85-89

—CARLO COPPOLA

ALLENDE, Isabel

Chilean novelist and short-story writer, b. 2 Aug. 1942, Lima, Peru

A. was born to diplomat parents residing in Peru, but at the age of three her father abandoned the family, and she and her mother

Isabel Allende

returned to Chile. The focus of her early childhood was on her mother, and there was little contact with her father's side of the family except for a close relationship with an uncle, Salvador Allende Gossens, elected president of Chile in 1970. When A. was ten, her mother married another diplomat, Ramón Huidobro, who became a strong paternal figure in her childhood. A. traces her interest in storytelling to the tales she heard from her maternal grandparents and from the servants in the kitchen of the family estate. The fact that her mother gave her a notebook in which she could write her early impressions was another stimulus that ultimately led to a career in writing. Her early work in journalism and television was cut short by the 1973 coup d'état that resulted in the death of President Allende and the beginning of a sixteen-year military dictatorship under General Augusto Pinochet. Forced to leave Chile in 1975 as a result of the harsh treatment meted out to leftist supporters of the Allende government, her career as a writer of fiction began in Venezuela, where she and her family lived for over a decade as expatriates. Her first two novels show a growing nostalgia for Chile and for family members still there, but her third novel is set in her adopted country, Venezuela. A. now lives in the U.S.

A.'s first novel, *La casa de los espíritus* (1982; *The House of the Spirits*, 1985), was written as a long letter to her centenarian grandfather who was near death in Chile. Unable to publish the novel in Venezuela, A. sent the manuscript to the well-known literary agent Carmen Balcells, who facilitated its publication by Plaza & Janés in Spain. It is a panoramic view of Chile during the first seventy-five years of the 20th c. and of the vicissitudes of the Trueba family: the wrathful founder, Esteban Trueba; his hyper-sensitive wife; and the legitimate and illegitimate children sired by the founder. Its scope and purpose have often been compared to Gabriel GARCÍA MÁRQUEZ's *Cien años de soledad* (1967; *One Hundred Years of Solitude*, 1970). Dominant in the novel are the themes of Latin American politics, feminism, and the importance of writing. The novel contains many autobiographical details and integrates the plot with Chilean history.

In her second novel, *De amor y de sombra* (1984; *Of Love and Shadows*, 1987), A. explores the themes of repression and dictatorship as a photographer and his journalist girlfriend investigate a common crime that leads them to an unbelievable massacre ordered by the dictatorship. The two find love while they uncover a violent world of poverty, ignorance, misery, sickness, and torture. Whereas the action has a fictional setting, readers familiar with the Pinochet dictatorship would recognize the events as accurate and plausible. Although Chile is never mentioned in the novel, A. asserts that it is based on an event that took place there in 1978.

Eva Luna (1987; *Eva Luna*, 1988), although set in Venezuela, continues many of the themes seen in the first two novels. It recounts the life of the protagonist, born in the lower classes but blessed with a remarkable skill: storytelling. She uses this skill to get food, shelter, sex, and ultimately love, while she turns mundane events into extraordinary works of fiction and television scenarios. There are many autobiographical episodes that explore the themes of feminism, politics, journalism, and censorship against the back-drop of 20th-c. Venezuela. This novel contains a rich admixture of intertextuality in which A. probes the relationship between writing and reality, between herself the author and Eva Luna her creation, and between political reality and the television scripts Eva writes. A.'s next publication is a collection of twenty-three short stories, purportedly the ones Eva Luna wrote during the course of the third novel. *Cuentos de Eva Luna* (1990; *The Stories of Eva Luna*, 1991) is a collection of tales that have the common thread of love as their focus.

El plan infinito (1991; *The Infinite Plan*, 1993) is set in the 1970s in the western section of the U. S. It explores the period following the Second World War, the drug culture, and the Vietnam conflict and its trauma. *Paula* (1994; *Paula*, 1995) is a text A. wrote as a memorial to her dying daughter.

In less than a decade A.'s reputation in the field of contemporary fiction has risen meteorically. She continues to explore in particular the themes of feminism, politics, and the art of writing as seen in her five novels, all of which have been translated into twenty-one languages.

FURTHER WORKS: *Civilice a su troglodita* (1974); *La gorda de porcelana* (1983); *Afrodita: cuentos, recetas y otros afrodisiacos* (1997; *Aphrodite: A Memoir of the Senses* 1998)

BIBLIOGRAPHY: Agosín, M., "Entrevista a I. A./Interview with I. A.," *Imagine*, 1, 2 (1984): 42–56; Moody, M., "I. A. and the Testimonial Novel," *Confluencia*, 2, 1 (Fall 1986): 39–43; Gordon, A., "A. On Love and Shadow," *ConL*, 28, 4 (Winter 1987): 530–42; Earle, P. G., "Literarute as Survival: A.'s *The House of the Spirits*," *ConL*, 28 (1987): 543–54; Foster, D., "I. A. Unveiled," *Mother Jones*, 13, 10 (Dec. 1988): 42–46; Mitgang, H., "A. Explores Her Novels and Herself," *NYT*, 4, 16 (Feb. 1988); Meyer, D., "Exile and the Female Condition in I. A.'s *De amor y de sombra*," *IFR*, 15, 2 (Summer 1988): 151–57; Hart, P., *Narrative Magic in the Fiction of I. A.* (1989); Talmor, S., "The House of the Truebas," *DUJ*, 81, 2 (June 1989): 309–12; Hart, P., *Narrative Magic in the Fiction of I. A.* (1989); Levine, L. G., "I. A.," in Marting, D. E., ed., *Spanish American Women Writers* (1990): 20–30; Riquelme Rojas, S., ed., *Critical Approaches to I. A.'s Novels* (1991)

—HARLEY D. OBERHELMAN

"Living on" was a persistent tradition in I. A.'s family on her mother's side, and her late grandmother—the main model for Clara del Valle, "Clara la clarividente," in *The House of the Spirits*—had been practicing since premature death what Grandfather had always preached in life, with her periodic messages and visitations. The letter to Grandfather got longer, and longer. A year later (1982) it had grown to five-hundred pages. It was a diary in retrospect, a family chronicle, an autobiography, a political testimony, a group portrait and contemporary history, a series of experiments with magic. In other words, a novel. A. was a journalist in search of a complementary medium. Aesthetically, she would now participate in the basic ritual of Latin American literature: a celebration of reality. Ethically, she wanted to bear witness to social injustice, political violence, and repression—having been motivated by the betrayal and murder by right-wing conspirators of an uncle on her father's side, President Salvador Allende....

In what circumstances was the novel under consideration written? In [a] 1986 lecture... A. stressed the importance of the "moment of history the writer is born into," especially in Latin America, a world of great "struggles and defeats, brutality and magic."

Increasingly aware of the New World's five-hundred-year tradition of violence, she matured intellectually with her uncle's socialist movement and became a novelist at her reactionary grandfather's death. Thus, her book is the celebration of a momentous social struggle in which those two figures were principals. Only fictitious names are used in the story, for places as well as for people, but the implications are obvious: this was to be a composite testimony of many voices . . . written with a recent exile's sense of urgency, and a family member's intimacy.

Peter G. Earle, "Literature as Survival: A.'s *The House of the Spirits*," *ConL*, 28, 4 (Winter 1987), 543–45

While the first few sentences of *The House of the Spirits* seem to belong to [Gabriel] García Márquez and *One Hundred Years of Solitude*, the last few—which, ironically enough, are much the same—belong to I. A. "Rarely has a new novel from Latin America consciously or unconsciously owed more to its predecessors; equally rare is the original utterance coming out of what is now a collective literary tradition." That this is A.'s first novel does not excuse the presence of García Márquez (as the critics suggest), though it might explain it, perhaps in terms of a problem facing all post-Boom Latin American novelists, new and other-wise, who wish to follow in the tradition of magical realism: How does one get beyond *One Hundred Years of Solitude*, since all writing in the genre would seem, in the end, a rewriting of this novel? A. begins with this premise—consciously or unconsciously—and in the rewriting she discovers her own novel, one very different from *One Hundred Years of Solitude*.... *The House of the Spirits...* reads, initially, like a parody of García Márquez's novel, though not a *conscious* sort of parody.... But A. does not use García Márquez's language as an exposé to destroy it, speaking *through* it in her own language; rather, A. uses his language as a means to discover her own language, which she *substitutes* for García Márquez's. In other words, we would have trouble isolating a representing discourse which is simultaneously present, and at odds with the represented discourse: there is no obvious wink at the reader. We can, however, contrast an "initial" discourse with a "final" discourse, which *are* at odds with each other. A. begins speaking in a represented language—a language not her own, but García Márquez's, though perhaps she is not aware of it—and through this language she discovers her own representing language. It is as though A. "unconsciously" parodies García Márquez early in the novel, then stumbles happily onto her own language—her own story—in the end. But is there unconscious parody... or are we simply speaking here of inattentive writing? Are we simply comparing an established master with a first novelist?

Robert Antoni, "Parody or Piracy: The Relationship of *The House of the Spirits to One*

Hundred Years of Solitude," LALR, 16, 32 (July-Dec. 1988), 16

Chilean author I. A.'s second novel, published in Spain in 1984, confirms the impression made by *La casa de los espíritus. . .* of her skill as a storyteller. This time, however, instead of an epic portrayal of four generations of women, she has chosen a more limited historical perspective focusing on a transforming experience in the life of one young woman. Still, A. remains true to the moral imperative behind all her writing, which is to bear witness through literature to a time and place in Latin-American history: "All those of us who write and are fortunate enough to be published ought to assume the responsibility for serving the cause of freedom and justice. We have a mission to accomplish in the front lines. In the face of the obscurantism that oppresses various countries on our continent, we must offer words, reason and hope. Literature must be placed at the service of mankind. Ideas are the worst enemy of barbarism." Like *La casa de los espíritus, De amor y de sombra. . .* is a novel set in an unnamed country, which is unmistakably the author's homeland, under the dictatorship of an unnamed general, obviously Augusto Pinochet, in approximately 1978. As much as it is a tale of female self-discovery, it is equally, from beginning to end, a repudiation of military regimes and the mentality that sustains them.

Doris Meyer, "Exile and the Female Condition in
I. A.'s *De amor y de sombra,*" IFR, 15, 2
(Summer 1988), 151

Despite the incredibly painful and difficult material that A. writes about, neither she nor her novels are filled with a sense of pessimism or despair. A. has often said in her public lectures that such emotions are paralyzing. She believes profoundly in the ability of the human spirit to endure. It is perhaps for this reason that her novels are ultimately so uplifting as well as entertaining. A born storyteller, A. renders tribute to this gift in her most recent work, *Eva Luna. . .,* a modern picaresque novel about a 20th-c. Scheherazade who spins tales to survive in a politically unstable Latin American society.

It is difficult for one who has met I. A. not to immediately find pieces of her in all her female characters. They share her sharp intelligence, playful sense of humor, force of decision, love of words, romantic temperament, desire to live life as if it were a novel, and healthy sense of female identity. A. is a dynamic and exuberant public speaker who attracts packed audiences wherever she speaks. Her lectures are much like her novels themselves: a thoughtful blend of the personal and the political, a call for bearing witness, and a strong statement on the power of women and their ability to create a new morality in times of violence. A. has recently posed for herself in public forums the difficult questions: "For whom do I write? Why do I write?" If her answers are as complex as the questions themselves, they nonetheless can be synthesized in the following words: "I feel that writing is an act of hope, a sort of communion with our fellow men, a tiny bit of light. I certainly write for myself, but mainly for others. For those who have no voice and for those who are kept in silence. I write for you. I write so that people will love each other more."

Linda Gould Levine, "I. A.," in Diane E. Marting,
ed., *Spanish American Women Writers* (1990), 22

There are many elements in *Eva Luna* that will sound familiar to the reader of *La casa de los espíritus.* At the heart of the story is an independent female deeply attached to her mother's spirit, a child who drags around a stuffed animal, and who later evokes her mother's spirit while she is unjustly in jail. There is also a house filled with mummies and occasional spirits, a charming eccentric who believes in tarot cards and astrology, a mention here and there of auras, the occasional attempt at clairvoyance, and a prophetic dream or two. But for all of this, *Eva Luna* is a new and fresh novel, and if some of her characters are similar, they are in new situations and settings. After all, Faulkner's Compsons resurfaced again and again, and no one ever seemed too surprised to see the themes of incest, degeneracy, or suicide recur in Yoknapatawpha County. Besides, as was the case in *De amor y de sombra,* in *Eva Luna* the strictly "magical" occurrences in this new novel are few. The beautiful transsexual Mimí nurses a host of superstitions, and Eva seems to find this endearing, but she does not take them particularly seriously. Eva also "speaks" to her dead mother from time to time, and occasionally "sees" her, but on the literal narrative plane there is nothing more magical about this than the persistence of memory. Once again, there is a deliberate attempt to undercut the superstitions through which some of the characters (and readers?) view the world.

Patricia Hart, *Narrative Magic in the Fiction of
I. A.* (1989), 170–71

ALONI, Nissim

Israeli dramatist and short-story writer, b. 24 Aug. 1926, Tel Aviv

A. fought in Israel's war of independence (1947–49). Since then, after studying at the Hebrew University in Jerusalem (without taking a degree) and living a few years in Paris, he has been a professional writer, including a translator of plays from English and French into Hebrew. A. began his literary career with short stories based on his experiences as a soldier, on the Israeli state's early years, and on the life of the Sephardic neighborhood in south Tel Aviv where he grew up.

A.'s first play, *Achzar mikol hamelech* (1953; the cruelest of all—the king), is a biblical drama recounting the story of the revolt of Jeroboam, son of Nebat, against Rehoboam, son of Solomon, and the resulting division of the united Jewish kingdom into Israel and Judea. The play touches directly on issues pertaining to the new state of Israel: a small nation with rich religious and cultural traditions is torn between a belief in being a chosen people and a desire for a normal national life, between its self-definition as a divine messenger and its perception of itself as simply one among the family of nations. In the play Jeroboam's fate is to shape history, while he knows that revolutionary ideas and regimes are not necessarily better than the ones they wish to replace.

The theme of the discrepancy between the desired ideal and its realization recurs in many variations in A.'s work. While his first play was specifically about the Jewish nation and its historical fate, his second, *Bigdai hamelech* (1961; the king's clothes), based on Andersen's fairy tale, has a more clearly universal relevance. He presents modern man, living in a world in which tradition turns out to be a camouflage for crass pragmatists who know how to rule the masses by using all the communications media to sell them anything—other than freedom. Ironically—and typically—the young revolutionary who cries "The king is naked!" at the play's beginning, in the end marries the king's daughter and turns into the slyest, most cunning, most crooked tailor of them all. In such a world, A. implies, there is obviously no place for idealistic revolution, since revolutionaries inevitably embrace existing values.

A. does not invent stories for his dramas, but rather reshapes well-known biblical, mythological, and literary material. While mythological references can be found in most of his plays, they dominate *Eddy King* (1975; Eddy King), an Oedipus drama set in the New York underworld.

A.'s later work is less literary and more the-article than his early plays. While his first drama emphasized words, his later plays stress action, as evidenced by his use of the play-within-a-play and melodramatic and operatic devices. A. directs his own plays and has written a commedia dell'arte play, *Arlekino* (1963; Harlequin), as well as the best scripts for Israel's most popular satirical group.

A.'s fusion of verbal and nonverbal elements gives his theater the character of metatheater, or theater of theater, which A. considers the only way of describing and expressing what he sees as the gray reality of modern life. And it is precisely this grayness, which seems so antitheatrical, that A. wants to turn into theater, into what for him are the bright fireworks of kings and their courts.

FURTHER WORKS: *Hanesichah hamerikait* (1963; *The American Princess*, 1980); *Hamahapechah vehatarnegolet* (1964); *Hakalah vetsiad haparparim* (1967); *Hadodah Lisa* (1969); *Napoleon chai o met* (1970); *Hatsoanim shel Yafo* (1971); *Hayanshuf* (1975); *Haniftar mitparea* (1980)

BIBLIOGRAPHY: Porat, Z., "The Tragic-comedy of Fulfilment in N. A.'s Plays," *Ariel: A Quarterly Review of Arts and Letters in Israel*, No. 32 (1973): 177–87; Avigal, S., "N. A.'s Theatre of Mirrors and Reflections," *Theatron* (1975–76): 24–27; Shoham, C., "*The Owl* by N. A.," *MHL*, 2, 1 (1976): 45–49

—CHAIM SHOHAM

ALONSO, Dámaso

Spanish poet and critic, b. 22 Oct. 1898, Madrid; d. 25 Jan. 1990, Madrid

A. began his career as scholar-critic working under Ramón Menéndez Pidal (1869–1968), the philologist, in Madrid. He has taught in many famous universities, including Madrid, Oxford, Leipzig, Lima, and Harvard, and in recent years has received numerous honorary degrees. He has served as editor of the *Revista de filología española* and the series *Biblioteca románica hispánica*, and finally as president of the Spanish Academy.

As a poet, A. began in the postimpressionistic manner with *Poemas puros* (1921; pure poems), in which there is repeated contrast between the poetic ideal of heightened perception of beauty and stark everyday reality, especially that of the middle class. With his philological background, A. naturally emphasizes the extreme economy of expression and the elite metaphor of the "pure" poetry of the 1920s.

In 1944 A. published the two books that earned him his reputation as an influence on post-civil war poets: *Oscura noticia* (dark message) and *Hijos de la ira (Children of Wrath*, 1970). *Oscura noticia*, while still centered upon the conflict between the idealistic and the prosaic, emphasizes the problems of human life in their relation to time, death, and love. In "Manos" (hands), for example, these parts of the human body express both man's desperate need for touching and his desire (doomed to failure) to reach perfection, above all in art. *Hijos de la ira* has been very widely read in postwar Spain, especially the poem "Insomnio" (insomnia), which focuses upon Madrid as a city of "more than one million cadavers." In a modern version of the mystical journey the poet-protagonist reduces himself to a state of complete humiliation in order to begin his return to a viable existence. In *Hombre y Dios* (1955; man and God) he develops the God-man relationship with such poetic subtlety as to retain both existential freedom and Christian dependence.

As a critic, A. launched his career by writing on Góngora (1561–1627), whom he was to establish as a great Baroque poet. A.'s *Góngora y el "Polifemo"* (1960; Góngora and the "Polyphemus"), ultimately expanded to three volumes, is a model of great literary criticism. His *Poesía española: Ensayo de métodos y límites estilísticos* (1950; Spanish poetry: essay on methods and stylistic limits) is perhaps his fundamental work, the book that provides the basis for his criticism in general. In major studies of Garcilaso de la Vega (1539–1616), San Juan de la Cruz (1542–1591), Fray Luis de León (1527–1591), and Quevedo (1580–1645) he uses close textual analysis to increase understanding of the poem, without rejecting intuition in critical appreciation. In *Seis calas en la expresión literaria española* (1951; six soundings in Spanish literary expression), written with Carlos Bousoño (b. 1923), he approaches poetry through the study of parallelism and correlation. He has briefly treated the poets of his own era in *Poetas españoles contemporáneos* (1952; contemporary Spanish poets).

A. is considered one of the eight major poets of the Generation of 1927, that of García Lorca, Guillén, and Aleixandre. As a critic, he is without peer in 20th-c. Spain and enjoys an outstanding reputation in European literary criticism.

FURTHER WORKS: *Soledades de Góngora* (1927); *La lengua poética de Góngora* (1935); *La poesía de San Juan de la Cruz* (1942); *Ensayos sobre poesía española* (1944); *Estudios y ensayos gongorinos* (1955); *Menéndez Pelayo, crítico literario* (1956); *De los siglos oscuros al de Oro* (1958); *Primavera temprana de la literatura europea* (1961); *Del Siglo de Oro a este siglo de siglas* (1962); *Cuatro poetas españoles: Garcilaso, Góngora, Maragall, Antonio Machado* (1962); *Poemas escogidos* (1969); *Gozos de la vista* (1970)

BIBLIOGRAPHY: Cano, J. L., *Poesía del siglo XX* (1960): 240–60; Zardoya, C., *Poesía española contemporánea* (1961): 411–28; Torrente Ballester, G., *Panorama de la literatura española contemporánea* (1965): 375–79; Alvarado de Ricord, E., *La obra poética de D. A.* (1968); Debicki, A., *D. A.* (1970)

—CARL W. COBB

ALPAR, Murat

Turkish-Danish poet, b. 1943, Turkey

During the last third of the 20th c., Scandinavian literature received important impulses from foreign voices; the arrival of so-called guest workers and refugees from Turkey, Pakistan, Sri Lanka, Iran, and many other countries created milieus in Scandinavian cities that are distinctly ethnic and that stand in stark contrast to the preceding homogeneous culture. As new generations are born in the Scandinavian countries, an integration process is set in motion, and as emigrants turn into immigrants—and become fluent in their new "native" languages—accomplished artists come to the fore. A rich and varied literature by "new" Scandinavians is gradually developing, and that literature captures the often harrowing experience of being caught—even trapped—between two cultures, which in essence means that, no matter how successful the newcomers are economically, as new Scandinavians they find themselves living a marginalized existence. A. received a degree in physics from the University of Ankara and arrived in Denmark in 1967 on a grant, and he has remained there. He has worked as a translator and interpreter, and he has penned articles on the problems Turkish workers encounter in Denmark.

In 1974 A. published a collection of poems, *Memet en rejsende i arbejde* (a traveler selling his work), which reads as a narrative of the protagonist Memet's dire decision to leave Turkey in order to make money in Denmark. The poem that signals his departure touchingly records Memet's mother silently crying when he announces his decision to leave—a decision made for the sake of the economic welfare of the family—for she knows that she is losing him to another world. The power of A.'s poetry lies in its subtle and understated interpretation of her "silent tears."

Memet's decision is drastic in the sense that he leaves wife and children behind, but since his world rests in a "fatalistic sleep," it is imperative that he leave for an unknown, Western world that promises material gain. Memet arrives in Copenhagen; he is enthralled by the strangeness of the city, and he soon finds work in a factory, where he takes pride in handling his big machine to his boss's satisfaction. Memet, however, yearns back to his life as a farmer with its close contact to the animals and the land, and the fact that he barely knows Danish renders him lonely and sad in his everyday life.

A.'s concluding poems stake out a difference between narrator and protagonist, for the former's compassionate and sensitive portrayal of Memet nevertheless reveals that the average new arrival from Turkey, anyone like Memet, fails to understand that he brings along with him his native society's fatalism: he is here to sacrifice himself for his family, not to strike out for a different existence.

That first book—in a sense, a small epic poem—is in its understated way profoundly touching, for it captures a victim's unbearable loneliness, and it places no blame on the Danes around Memet—although it would not have been difficult to add some lines on the racism that had emerged in Scandinavia with the influx of migrant workers.

In 1978 A. continued his narrative of Memet with *Gæstearbejderen Memet* (the guest-worker memet). Apparently Memet has been able to pay for his wife and children to come to Denmark, and that is a sign of his economic success, but that, of course, creates its own problems. The second narrative perceptively points out that Memet's initial alienation was replaced by a sense of rootlessness: the immigrant lives two lives, that in his past, his true home, and that in his present one. Now that Memet has lived for a time in Europe, he knows that he has been fooled by a myth of prosperity; thus, the fatalist is waking up—but too late to go home again.

The narrative then records the trouble Memet has had in egalitarian Denmark in finding an apartment for his family; he finally finds one in a modern slum, but at least the family is together. In a sense that is true, but since their children attend Danish schools, a new sense of marginalization arises for Memet—and we assume for his wife, whose voice is not heard: the children learn Danish, learn Danish manners, want to be Danish, and are critical of their parents for not knowing Danish all that well, so a gulf between parents and children gradually widens.

A. perceptively then switches in his narrative to the second generation and reveals that it is not so easy to be a Turkish boy in a Danish school; Memet's son is teased about his accent and his looks, and when he comes home, he feels divided between his two cultures.

Insult is added to injury, for Memet, who has always striven to work hard, finds himself unemployed. Although he receives all the many Danish welfare benefits, they are not enough for him; he walks as if in a daze though the streets of Copenhagen, a city that still puzzles him and will never be a home to him; it is a place filled with his longing and homesickness.

In the concluding poem, A. widens the perspective to include Turks working everywhere in Western Europe. They return home in triumph, they have money, they are "Westerners," they bear gifts galore, but within themselves they know that the West has humiliated and ignored them, and yet no one must learn of that when they return to their villages.

—NIELS INGWERSEN

ALTERMAN, Natan

Israeli poet, dramatist, translator, and journalist, b. 10 March 1910, Warsaw, Poland; d. 11 March 1970, Tel Aviv

A. emigrated from Russia, where he had spent his boyhood, to Palestine in 1925 and later spent time in France to complete his higher education. Returning to Palestine in 1932, A. began publishing topical poetry in the major newspapers of the time. For twenty-two years, beginning in 1943, the local daily *Davar* featured his topical poetry in a column he called "Hatur hashvii" (the seventh column), reflecting the tribulations of the years before statehood.

A. translated many works from English into Hebrew, chief among them plays by Shakespeare. He also translated Scottish and

English ballads. Among his translations from French are Racine's *Phaedra* and several plays of Molière. A.'s own plays include *Kineret, Kineret* (1962; Galilee, Galilee), *Pundak haruchot* (1962; inn of the ghosts), *Mishpat Pitagoras* (1965; the Pythagorean law), and *Ester hamalkah* (1966; Queen Esther). A. received the Israel Prize for Literature in 1968.

The central theme in A.'s poetry is the lust for life. The lyrical-dramatic approach of the poems in *Kochavim bachuts* (1938; stars outside), his first collection, conveys the theme of the vagabond and his relationship with the road, woman, songs, the wind, lightning, autumn, and the woods. The vagabond's love for all of these is an obsessive love that lives on when life itself is over. The end of the road of life opens into a timeless, placeless space. Running in the "other world" represents the longing of the dead man for the land of the living, which is forbidden to him—a land imagined as a walled-in city.

The balladistic treatment of human existence runs through all of A.'s poetry. But his focus on love of woman, of song and poetry, and of the road of life in *Kochavim bachuts* gives way to the spirit of the living dead in A.'s second collection, *Simchat aniyim* (1941; joy of the poor), considered his most outstanding work. The intensely dramatic and fatalistic nature of these poems accords well with their ballad style. No line is drawn between the dead and the living other than the gap created by time and place. Just as the world of the living is filled with thoughts of death, so the world of the dead is pervaded by a wistful yearning for the life left behind. The soul of the dead man haunts his living love. The crucial meeting between them does not occur until after death. The image of the wayside inn, where the dead meet and sing the praises of the inn-keeper, that eternal *femme fatale* who lives on in spite of death, is a central one in A.'s work. The poems of *Simchat aniyim* follow a circular pattern based on the regularity of the wanderings after death. They are dominated by macabre effects, and there is no separating love from the inevitability of death.

In *Makot Mitsrayim* (1941; the plagues of Egypt), the Holocaust figures heavily in the background. The poems present a symbolic view of human suffering, which recurs through the ages, in a regular pattern of destruction and resurrection. Those who are tormented and destroyed at any given time are destined to be the persecutors and victors at some other time.

Ir hayonah (1957; the wailing city) presents A.'s historical-eschatological view of his time through both personal and topical poems. The cycle *Chagigat kayits* (1965; summer festival) consists of urban poems.

A.'s poetry is imagistic, highly decorated, and symbolic. Coquetry, beauty, and charm are always mingled with horror, violence, and shock. His poetry is remarkable for its affirmation of life. A.'s perception of the link between the living and the dead is without parallel in Hebrew literature. His portrayal of characters is extremely rich and multifaceted, and his handling of the metaphorical qualities of the language is among the most sensitive in modern Hebrew poetry.

FURTHER WORKS: *Hamasechah haacharonah* (1968); *Bamagal* (1971); *Hachut hamshulash* (1971); *Regaim* (1973); *Pizmonim vshire zemer* (1976). FURTHER WORKS IN ENGLISH: *Selected Poems* (1978)

—NILI SADAN-LOEBENSTEIN

ÁLVAREZ GARDEAZÁBAL, Gustavo

Colombian novelist, b. 31 Oct. 1945, Tuluá

A. G. is one of the most prominent Colombian novelists to emerge from the shadow of the Nobel Prize-winning novelist Gabriel GARCÍA MÁRQUEZ. Born in the small town of Tuluá, A. G. briefly studied engineering at Medellín, then attended the Universidad del Valle in Cali, from which he received his Licenciatura de Letras in 1970, writing a thesis titled "La novelística de la violencia en Colombia" (1970; the novel of violence in Colombia); he began writing fiction soon thereafter. He was a faculty member at the same university during much of the 1970s and in the early 1980s, when he also wrote a newspaper column. Although A. G. has generally lived in Colombia, finding in his home region a source of inspiration, he lived for a brief period in the U.S. in 1985. His novel *El divino* (1986; the divine) was written with a Guggenheim fellowship. A. G. has been involved in politics; he joined (and later left) the Movimiento Cívico in Colombia. He was their representative to the National Assembly. After his Guggenheim fellowship in the U.S. in 1985, he returned to Colombia and later became Alcalde (mayor) of Tuluá (1988–1990). A. G. has frequently been controversial, both as a professor and as an outspoken writer uninhibited about denouncing political chicanery by those in power.

A. G. began his novelistic career, after a self-admitted false start with *Piedra pintada* (1965; painted rock), with a trilogy concerning the epoch known unhappily to Colombians as "La Violencia," a period stretching from about 1948 to about 1960, during which political violence was endemic. This trilogy, consisting of *La tara del papa* (1971; the tare of the Papa), *Cóndores no entierran todos los días* (1972; condors don't bury every day), and *Dabeiba* (1973; Dabeiba), creates a complex portrait of the self-destructive and apocalyptic environment of violence and stresses the corrupting effects of the political struggle between liberals and conservatives. The hallmarks of the style of A. G. appear in these works. For instance, *Cóndores*, the story of León María Lozano, the cheese seller who becomes the leader of a powerful gang of killers for the conservatives, is told by means of innovative use of temporal reference, foreshadowings, and linguistic tags (such as the frequent use of *dizque*, "they say") that emphasize the oral quality of the narrative and establish the implied reader as having prior knowledge of the town and at least some of the events.

Much of the work of A. G. has been centered in the town of Tuluá, which acquires mythical and exaggerated qualities through his treatment of its inhabitants and social history. The mythifying tendency, which is nevertheless satirical and corrosive, is strongly present in *El bazar de los idiotas* (1974; *Bazaar of the Idiots*, 1991), which presents the story of two miracle-working idiots, using complex techniques of narrative organization and repetition to present a humorous and grotesque chronicle that attacks both religious superstition and faith in the efficacy of science.

El titiritero (1977; the puppet master) concerns violence arising from student demonstrations at the Universidad del Valle in Cali. The title refers to the manipulation of characters carried out by the novelist as well as to political manipulation and the distortion of truth by historians. The novel is an advance over the previous work of A. G., pointing toward his later novels, such as the complex *Los míos* (1981; my people) and *Pepe Botellas* (1984; Pepe Botellas) in its self-reflexive nature and collage of materials. His two subsequent novels, *El divino* and *El último gamonal* (1987; the last boss), while somewhat less "major," continue his critique of political and religious hypocrisy.

As Raymond L. Williams and others have noted, A. G. shares certain features with García Márquez, such as a cultivation of an "exotic" regional locale, a participation in innovative narrative strategies, an emphasis on orality, and a preoccupation with Colombian history. But A. G. has attained a strong and unmistakable style that is the mark of the truly individual artist. His work has gradually grown in complexity and richness, with its particular hallmarks being a complicated play on the nature of historical versus fictional "truth," typically carried out by means of a deceptively chatty narrative voice that draws the reader into a fascinating world of uncertainties and speculations about chronicled events, which nevertheless are meticulously and richly detailed. As have other Colombian novelists such as Eduardo Caballero CALDERÓN, hotlink, and García Márquez, A. G. has frequently concentrated on the period of "La Violencia." Recipient of numerous prizes for his work, he is one of the major writers now producing in Latin America.

FURTHER WORKS: *Cuentos del Parque Boyacá* (1978); *Manual de crítica literaria* (1980); *Cali* (1990); *Los sordos ya no hablan* (1991)

BIBLIOGRAPHY: Williams, R. L., ed., *Aproximaciones a G. A. G.* (1977); Gyurko, L. A., "The Phantasmagoric World of G.," *HisJ*, 2, 1 (Fall 1980): 27–40; Williams, R. L., "Structure and Transformation of Reality in A. G.: *El bazar de los idiotas*," *KRQ*, 27, 2 (1980): 244–61; Bell, S. M., "Hacia el apocalipsis: la violencia en los cuentos de A. G.," *CH*, 3, 1 (1981): 3–16; Luchting, W. A., "'Yo no fui': la poética de la no responsabilidad. *El titiritero*, de G. A. G.," *CA*, 236, 3 (1981): 208–21; Souza, R. D., "*Los míos* and the Burden of History," *Chasqui*, 11: 2–3 (Feb.-May 1982): 38–41; Williams, R. L., "El tiempo en la novela: observaciones en torno al tiempo en la novela colombiana contemporánea," *ExTL*, 11, 2 (1982–1983): 11–28; Souza, R. D., "Caos y orden en dos novelas de A. G.," *El café literario* (Bogotá), 6, 36 (1983): 9–12; Thompson, J., "The Creation of Myth with the Idiot as Hero in *El bazar de los idiotas*," *ArielK*, 1, 1 (Fall 1983): 2–8; Sklodowska, E., "*Pepe Botellas* de A. G.: ironías de un discurso histórico," *Revista de estudios colombianos*, 1 (1986): 17–22; Souza, R. D., *La historia en la novela hispanoamericana moderna* (1988): 129–48; Tittler, J., "*El último gamonal*: entrega final de la telenovela biográfica de A. G.," *Revista de estudios colombianos*, 9 (1990): 32–37; Williams, R. L., *The Colombian Novel, 1844–1987* (1991): 172–82

—KENNETH E. HALL

ÁLVAREZ QUINTERO, Serafín and Joaquín

Spanish dramatists, Serafín b. 26 March 1871, Utrera; d. 12 April 1938, Madrid; Joaquín b. 20 Jan. 1873, Utrera; d. 14 June 1944, Utrera

Despite personality differences, S. and J. Á. Q., better known professionally as the Quintero brothers, lived and worked closely and harmoniously throughout their lives. Outgoing, talkative Serafín

and quiet, introspective Joaquín collaborated not only on plays but on short stories, poetry, essays and newspaper articles as well. Of their 229 plays, approximately half were in such short forms as the *sainete* (one-act folk comedy), *zarzuela* (short operetta), *pasillo* (one-act farce), *juguete cómico* (comic sketch), and monologue.

In the final decade of the 19th c., the brothers found Spanish comic theater full of exaggerated stereotypes and outlandish rhetoric. They succeeded in establishing a simpler, more natural theater based on a faithful if somewhat sentimental observation of life, particularly as lived in southern Spain. While their plays lack profundity, they are thoroughly human and accomplish their authors' purpose: to entertain. The brothers occasionally broached serious themes, as in *Malvaloca* (1912; *Malvaloca*, 1916), but are best remembered for their light comedies set in Andalusia. Masters of characterization as well as of language, they are outstanding in the presentation of sprightly, older characters, particularly women, and created witty, humorous dialogue with the flavor of popular, southern Spanish. Although they did not propose to produce sociological or political theater, their plays document the manners, attitudes, and speech of the Andalusian bourgeoisie of the early 20th c. When criticized for failure to include the tragic aspects of their native region (i.e., the poor laborer bent from excessive toil), they replied that they had reflected their particular world and could hardly be expected to portray situations they had neither experienced nor witnessed. Essentially optimistic, conformist, and conservative, theirs was an attitude of good-natured approval rather than condemnation.

Their characters are basically good and have the ability to laugh at their own and at others' shortcomings. *Puebla de las mujeres* (1912; *The Women's Town*, 1919), the gently humorous portrayal of Andalusian life considered their masterpiece, contains representative characters: Don Julian, the kindly village priest; Concha, the local busybody-matchmaker; Doña Belen, the stickler for propriety. The title character of *Doña Clarines* (1909; *Doña Clarines*, 1932) is a perceptive gadfly who speaks her mind at all times; although not everyone's idea of the perfect neighbor, she is refreshing and portrayed as a necessary element in any society. In their one-act gem, *Mañana de sol* (1915; *One Sunny Morning*, 1916), an aging couple meets by chance in a dispute over a park bench. Subsequent conversation reveals that they had been in love in their early youth. The playwrights' alchemy elevates them to symbols of enduring youth and love.

The fact that the plays of the brothers Á. Q. have been translated into more than a dozen languages attests to their universal appeal.

FURTHER WORKS: *Los galeotes* (1900); *El patio* (1900); *La dicha ajena* (1902); *Pepita Reyes* (1903); *El amor que pasa* (1904; *Love Passes By*, 1932); *El genio alegre* (1906); *Las de Caín* (1908); *El centenario* (1909; *A Hundred Years Old*, 1926); *La flor de la vida* (1910); *Pipiola* (1918); *Don Juan, buena persona* (1918); *Doña Hormiga* (1930); *Lo que hablan las mujeres* (1932); *Obras completas* (7 vols., 1947–1969). FURTHER WORKS IN ENGLISH: *Four Plays* (1927); *Four Comedies* (1932)

BIBLIOGRAPHY: Losada de la Torre, J., *Perfil de los hermanos A. Q.* (1945); Brady, A. M, and Smith, H. L., Introduction to *El centenario; and, Doña Hormiga* (1950): xi–xiv; Valbuena Prat, A., *Historia del teatro español* (1956): 627–29; Parker, J. H., *Breve historia del teatro español* (1957): 153–54; Torrente Ballester, G., *Teatro español contemporáneo* (1957): 364–69; González Climent,

A., *Andalucía y los Q.* (1966); Ruiz Ramón, F., *Historia del teatro español: siglo XX* (1971): 49–53

—PATRICIA W. O'CONNOR

ALVARO, Corrado

Italian novelist, short-story writer, and essayist, b. 15 April 1895, San Luca; d. 11 June 1956, Rome

A. began his career as a journalist and literary critic in 1916 with the daily newspapers *Il resto di carlino* of Bologna and *Il corriere della sera* of Milan while studying for a degree in literature from the University of Milan, which he was awarded in 1921. In that same year, with the Fascist movement gathering strength, A. went to work for *Il mondo*, a very active anti-Fascist weekly whose publication was suppressed in 1926. In 1927, with ever-increasing threats and constant surveillance by the Fascists rendering his private and professional life virtually impossible, A. went to Berlin, where he lived for a time and continued his writing. During the 1930s A. traveled throughout western Europe, the Middle East and Russia. Vivid accounts of these journeys are found in his travel books. He returned to Italy, but because of his anti-Fascist convictions he had to spend the World War II years in hiding. Following the fall of Mussolini, he briefly edited the newspaper *Il popolo di Roma*. After the war A. intensified his literary activities, contributed articles to newspapers and literary journals, and continued writing essays, short stories, and novels. In 1947 A. was elected secretary of the Italian Association of Writers, a position he held until his death.

The recurrent theme throughout A.'s novels is the crisis of the individual in the 20th c. Acutely aware of the alienation of man and his search for identity within the social and historical context, A. pursues the portrayal of the reality of his times in all of his novels. This thematic preoccupation stems in large part from his background in southern Italy, where the sense of alienation is an endemic social and political condition. A. focuses on the plight of the individual, or of an entire class, in a certain society, under the strain of a stifling and oppressive environment, be it in an urban setting or the countryside of his native Calabria.

A.'s first novel, *L'uomo nel labirinto* (1926; man in the labyrinth) portrays the social crisis that became so acute in the years following World War I and immediately preceding the Fascist takeover in Italy. Set in a provincial city, it clearly indicates the author's grave concern with the moral implications of the human condition. Here, as in many of his subsequent novels, A. has as a protagonist a southern Italian who has migrated to the city, so that the main character's alienation is intensified. Yet this estrangement from society and the resultant confusion are not due merely to their geographical origins; rather, they are a depiction of the conditions affecting an entire society.

The publication of *Gente in Aspromonte* (1930; *Revolt in Aspromonte*, 1962) brought A. acclaim as a writer of national significance. In this novel he again treated the theme of the individual and society, but he now focused his attention on the trials of those southern Italians who are not prepared to move to the northern industrialized cities, with their enticement of good wages, but remain to endure the hardships of their native region. The book affords the reader a vivid portrayal of the life of these people and particularly of their struggle for survival. Except for the wealthy landowners, cruel poverty is everyone's lot—the mountain shepherds and the peasants of the town. To these people no misery is unknown and no resignation unbearable. But the story is also a drama of vengeance for wrongs suffered, and the novel is enriched by A.'s depiction of a legendary Calabria as well as the real one.

The theme of the individual and society took a new direction in *Vent'anni* (1930; twenty years), which is set against the background of World War I. Like D'ANNUNZIO, GADDA, Piero Jahier (1884–1966), Giuseppe Antonio Borgese (1882–1952), and other contemporaries, A. had first dealt with the world conflict in the form of personal impressions, in the short volume of poetry *Poesie grigioverdi* (1917; green-gray poems). But in *Vent'anni* he broadened his scope to include the war's impact on Italian society as a whole. He does not limit himself to the crisis of the small bourgeois world of *L'uomo nel labirinto* or the confined, static world of the Aspromonte shepherds. Rather, he is concerned with all levels of Italian society as it is affected by the world war.

A.'s visit to the Soviet Union in 1934 turned out to be a very compelling experience, engaging his total attention, and ultimately leading him on to his next novel, *L'uomo è forte* (1938; *Man Is Strong*, 1948); it is supposedly set in the Soviet Union, and some descriptions are suggestive of that country, but in effect it has no single identity. Rather, the fictitious country is representative of any country and any social system under a totalitarian regime. *L'uomo è forte* is one of the few political novels written in Italy during the twenty years of Fascism and is another manifestation of A.'s lifelong commitment to upholding the dignity and individuality of the human being during this age of crisis.

A. made a lasting and significant impact on 20th-c. Italian literature. The artistic success of novels such as *L'uomo nel labirinto*, *Gente in Aspromonte*, and *L'uomo è forte*, and the historical importance of *Vent'anni, Tutto è accaduto* (1961; all has happened), and other works assure him an important place in Italian literature.

FURTHER WORKS: *La siepe e l'orto* (1920); *L'amata alla finestra* (1929); *Misteri e avventure* (1930); *La signora dell'isola* (1930); *Calabria* (1931); *Viaggio in Turchia* (1932); *Itinerario italiano* (1933); *Il mare* (1934); *Cronaca (o fantasia)* (1934); *I maestri del diluvio: Viaggio nella Russia Sovietica* (1935); *Il diavolo curioso* (1935); *Caffè dei naviganti* (1939); *Incontri d'amore* (1940); *Il viaggio* (1942); *L'Italia rinunzia?* (1945); *L'età breve* (1946); *Lunga notte di Medea* (1949); *Quasi una vita: Giornale di uno scrittore* (1950); *Il nostro tempo e la speranza* (1952); *Settantacinque racconti* (1955); *Belmoro* (1957); *Roma vestita di nuovo* (1957); *Un treno nel Sud* (1958); *Ultimo diario* (1959); *Mastrangelina* (1960); *La moglie e i quaranta racconti* (1963); *Domani* (1969); *Come parlano i grandi* (1969)

BIBLIOGRAPHY: Prescott, O., on *Man Is Strong, NYT*, 18 Aug. 1948: 19; Rolo, C. S., on *Man Is Strong, Atlantic*, Oct. 1948: 106–7; Frank, N., "A. ou d'une conscience continentale," *Mercure de France*, 314 (1952): 351–53; Nouat, R., "Le méridionalisme dans la littérature italienne," *Critique*, 139 (1958): 1045–58; Heiney, D., *America in Modern Italian Literature* (1965): 138–40; Terrizzi, A. R., "Another Look at C. A.'s *L'uomo nel labirinto*," *FI*, 7 (1973): 23–29

—ANTHONY R. TERRIZZI

ALVER, Betti

Estonian poet, novelist, and translator, b. 23 Nov. 1906, Jõgeva; d. 19 June 1989, Tartu

The daughter of a railway-service supervisor, A. wrote a powerful, allegorical poem, "Jõgeva ja Pedja vahel" (between Jõgeva and Pedja), in 1970 suggesting that Estonia's fate is that of a "railroad flower," over which the trains of foreign oppression run. A. studied literature in Tartu, and in 1937 married the poet Heiti TALVIK. She was also interested in sports and in circus artists, which may account for the acrobatic virtuosity of her early verse. A. began her literary career with the novel *Tuulearmuke* (1927; wind's beloved), novellas, and prose poems. Her satirically spirited longer poem, *Lugu valgest varesest* (1931; tale of the white crow), characterized by painstaking care with form, and flexibility and lightness of language, brought her recognition as a master versemaker.

A.'s early poems are full of the decorative bohemian gestures of her mirthful being and express criticism of petit-bourgeois life. She first admired Heine and Poe, and later became a student of SYMBOLIST poetry and poetics, her principal teachers being Baudelaire and Talvik. A.'s first collection of poems, *Tolm ja tuli* (1936; dust and fire), written in harmonious meters and touched by cosmopolitanism, demonstrates her skill in closed but vibrant form, in originality of philosophical ideas, and in the convincing blending of fantastic and realistic settings. There is a stylistic purity in this early work that A. failed to achieve in later books, although throughout her life she probably has not written one single bad line.

With the Soviet Union's annexation of Estonia in 1940 and Talvik's death in a Soviet concentration camp, the tonality of A.'s verse darkened. She was not allowed to publish in any form from 1942 to 1964 and was partly rehabilitated only after producing an accomplished translation of Pushkin's *Eugene Onegin* (1964). Thematically, she became a surreal visionary, now with specifically Estonian subject matter. Structurally, A. began to experiment with open form, poetic prose, and free verse, mixing colloquial and refined wording. She has been successful in this new, vigorous manner, but, with the innate and distinct classical tendencies of a Hilda DOOLITTLE or a MANDELSHTAM, A. is strongest in poems of symmetrical verse schemes. Of these, a remarkable example is the late poem "Juveel" (jewel) from her book *Lendav linn* (1979; flying city), in which naturalistic images contrast with iconic symbols of precious stones.

In Estonian literature, A., who was a leading member of the Soothsayers group of the 1930s, may be taken as a representative of the poets of *formal art*, and Marie UNDER as a counterpart representative of the poets of *lyrical energy*. A.'s work, nonetheless, lacks neither color nor lyricism, and one may rank her among the finest poets of the 20th c.

FURTHER WORKS: *Ivaliidid* (1930); *Viletsuse komöödia* (1935); *Pirnipuu* (1936); *Mõrane pcegel* (1939); *Luuletused ja poeemid* (1956 [Stockholm]); *Tähetund* (1966); *Eluhelbed* (1971)

BIBLIOGRAPHY: Matthews, W. K., "Phases of Estonian Poetry," in Matthews, W. K., ed., *Anthology of Modern Estonian Poetry* (1953): xv–xxix; Ivask, I., "B. A.: Dust and Fire," in Kõressaar, V., and A. Rannit, eds., *Estonian Poetry and Language: Studies in Honor of A. Oras*, (1965): 287–92; Ivask, I., "Reflections on Estonia's Fate in the Poetry of B. A. and Jaan Kaplinski," *JBalS*, 4, 10 (1979): 352–60; Willmann, A., "B. A. and Her Poetic Lantern," in Leitch, V. B., ed., *The Poetry of Estonia: Essays in Comparative Analysis* (1981): 118–34

—ALEKSIS RANNIT

ALVES REDOL, António

See Redol, António Alves

AMADI, Elechi

Nigerian novelist and dramatist (writing in English), b. 12 May 1934, Aluu (near Port Harcourt)

A. belongs to a minority eastern riverine nation (tribe), the Ikwere. He studied at the Government College in Umuahia, and graduated in science from the University of Ibadan. He has been land surveyor, army officer, and teacher, serving as the only leading eastern Nigerian writer in the federal army during the Biafra War (1966–1970). Subsequently he joined the Rivers State government, heading the ministry of information and later its education ministry.

A.'s early novels, like Chinua ACHEBE's, are set in his traditional African world, but unlike Achebe's, which are shadowed by the colonial intrusion, treat exclusively that world's life of "tradition, propriety, and decorum." There is no alien disruption, no contrasting authorial perspective reflecting rational scepticism or modern change. Ihuoma, the "pure" heroine of A.'s first novel, *The Concubine* (1966), may be seen either in classical tragic terms, doomed by her link with the divine to be denied human life and love, or as a pathetic figure overshadowed by unlucky circumstances.

The Great Ponds (1969) more fully portrays than in Achebe a warrior society in action, showing in harsh measure the cost of intervillage and interclass violence. What again, as in *The Concubine*, has engaged us, is not how these events may be explained, but A.'s compassionate and thoughtful rendering of the tragedy's effects, in motive and behavior, upon those involved. This again distinguishes *The Slave* (1978), whose protagonist, Olumati, is denied an impossible happiness and takes refuge in slavery to a shrine, as in another society such a man might have become reclusive or suicidal.

A. describes *Sunset in Biafra: A Civil War Diary* (1973) as "an intimate personal story" of his experiences during the Nigerian Civil War. His narrative is dispassionate, understated, stoical; his experience of human folly and corruption, of human weakness and division, convinced him of the deep-rooted menace of tribalism, "the herd instinct." This account of the psychological effects of captivity is relatively measured and matter-of-fact next to Wole SOYINKA's *The Man Died* (1972), but more balanced overall, more credible even in its recognition that the tragedy and guilt alike were shared. A similarly sober viewpoint pervades the novel *Estrangement* (1986). Set in the war's aftermath, it portrays the struggle to regain normalcy, individual and communal.

A. has been overshadowed by Achebe, chiefly perhaps because he ignores the colonial encounter; furthermore, his English style is comparatively stilted, less idiomatic. He can, however, match Achebe in representing and interpreting the life and values of traditional village society, even surpassing him in his patient development of close relationships and familial attachments.

FURTHER WORKS: *Isiburu* (1973); *Pepper Soup* [and] *Ibadan* (1977); *Ethics in Nigerian Culture* (1982)

BIBLIOGRAPHY: Niven, A., "The Achievement of E. A.," in Rutherford, A., ed., *Commonwealth* (1971): 92–100; Palmer, E., *An Introduction to the African Novel* (1972): 117–28; Obiechina, E. N., *Culture, Tradition and Society in the West African Novel* (1975); Taiwo, O., *Culture and the Nigerian Novel* (1976): 197–209; Burness, D., ed., *Wanasema: Conversations with African Writers* (1985): 4–10; Eko, E., *E. A.: The Man and His Work* (1991)

—MICHAEL THORPE

AMADO, Jorge

Brazilian novelist, b. 10 Aug. 1912, Ilhéus

A. is a native of Brazil's Northeast, whose history, culture, and traditions constitute the heart of nearly everything he writes. During the late 1920s A. began to gain fame as a leader within the ranks of the Bahian (northeastern) modernist movement. In 1931 A. came to Rio de Janeiro to attend law school, but, encouraged by the publication of his first novel, *O país do carnaval* (1931; carnival land), he soon showed more enthusiasm for pursuing his literary inclinations. Three years later A. published *Suor* (1943; sweat), a propaganda novel that addressed itself to the sociopolitical questions of the day in Brazil. Although often harassed by the authorities during the 1930s and 1940s for the overtly leftist tone of his fiction, A.'s skill as a novelist grew rapidly, as did his reputation for being a champion of downtrodden people everywhere. A prolific writer, A. entered into a new phase of development with *Gabriela, cravo e canela* (1958; *Gabriela, Clove and Cinnamon*, 1962), a novel that, in English translation, enjoyed great commercial and critical success in the United States. A. was nominated for the 1961 Nobel Prize for literature (although he did not win) and was elected to the Brazilian Academy of Letters in that same year. At present, he continues to live and work in the city of Salvador.

During the first half of A.'s long career as a novelist, which Stretches from *O país do carnaval* to *Os subterráneos da liberdade* (1954; the subterraneans of liberty), he believed that the novel was the best vehicle to express his political convictions. This period, which encompasses work of uneven quality, is, however, highlighted by some excellent writing, three examples of which are *Jubiabá* (1935; *Jubiabá*, 1984), *Mar morto* (1936; *Sea of Death*, 1984), and *Terras do sem fim* (1943; *The Violent Land*, 1945). While *Mar morto* has many characteristics of the lyrical novel and *Terra do sem fim* is widely praised as one of the best regionalist novels of the decade in Latin America, *Jubiabá* was A.'s first attempt at capturing the spirit of Afro-Brazilianism in and around the city of Salvador, a concern that would later become a hallmark of his work. In subsequent novels, outstanding among which is *Tenda dos milagres* (1969; *Tent of Miracles*, 1971), in which A. addresses himself to the question of race relations in Brazil, this same interest in Brazil's African heritage is developed into a vital and broadly humanistic theme.

Initially famous as a social critic, A. has always shown himself to be most convincing when describing the lives of simple people rather than when espousing political ideology. Although A. enjoys

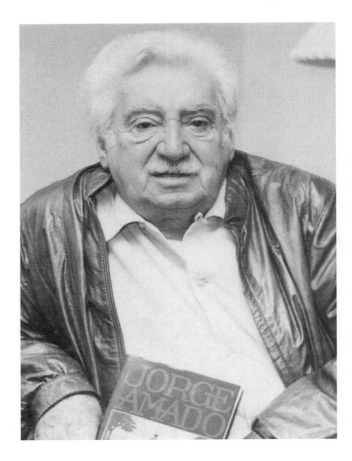

Jorge Amado

an international reputation because of his handling of the universal conflict between the exploited and the exploiter, his best novels center more on the daily existences of the lower-class inhabitants of Brazil's northeastern port cities.

A.'s masterpiece is *A morte e a morte de Quincas Berro Dágua* (1961; *The Two Deaths of Quincas Wateryell*, 1965), originally published together with *A completa verdade sôbre as discutidas aventuras do comandante Vasco Moscoso de Aragão, capitão de longe curso* (1961; *Home Is the Sailor*, 1964) under the collective title *Os velhos marinheiros* (the old sailors). *A morte e a morte de Quincas Berro Dágua* relates the comical yet poignant story of a man who rejects middle-class stability and respectability and embraces the life of a vagabond. While A. satirizes the shallowness and crass materialism of bourgeois life, he also extols the virtues of love, truth, and fidelity to one's friends. The "two deaths" referred to in the title highlight this short novel's utilization of one of the most colorful myths of Brazil's maritime Northeast, namely, that death at sea is sweeter than death on land. The conversion of Joaquin Soares da Cunha, the middle-aged public servant, is paralleled by two separate deaths, the first taking place on dry land, in which the deceased is once again victimized by the very people whose values he had categorically rejected in life, and the second, occurring at sea among his cronies. A.'s language, salty and piquant, is very much in tune with the colorful people he writes about. A.'s characterizations reflect both his unquenchable zest for life and his unflagging concern over class mores and social conflict in modern Brazil.

With *Gabriela, cravo e canela*, the "new" A., less polemical and more adept at handling irony, caricature, and humor, began to create a series of female protagonists who survive degrading circumstances early in their lives and grow into strong, independent women. This is a pattern which, by the time of *Tieta do agreste* (1977; *Tieta do Agreste*, 1979), has become somewhat formulaic. Nevertheless, A. continues to show himself a celebrant of life, a master of dialogue, and the creator of some of the most unforgettable characters in all of Brazilian literature.

A. is Brazil's most popular and widely read novelist. Having been translated into more than forty languages, he is also undoubtedly the Brazilian author best known abroad. A consummate storyteller, A. has learned to temper his social commentary with the subtlety of literary art. A. is not only an intensely Brazilian author, one steeped in all aspects of his multifaceted nation, but, through his love for both the passion and idealism of the human experience, is also an author of truly universal appeal.

FURTHER WORKS: *Cacau* (1933); *Capitães da areia* (1937; *Captains of the Sands*, 1988); *A estrada do mar* (1938); *ABC de Castro Alves* (1941); *São Jorge dos Ilhéus* (1944; *The Golden Harvest*, 1992); *Bahia de Todos os Santos* (1945); *Vida de Luís Carlos Prestes* (1942); *Seara vermelha* (1946); *O amor de Castro Alves* (1947); *O mundo da paz* (1950); *Os pastores da noite* (1964; *Shepherds of the Night*, 1967); *Dona Flor e seus dois maridos* (1966; *Dona Flor and Her Two Husbands*, 1969); *Tereza Batista cansada de guerra* (1973; *Tereza Batista, Home from the Wars*, 1975); *Farda fardão, camisola de dormir* (1979; *Pen, Sword, Camisole*, 1985); *Tocaia grande* (1985; *Showdown*, 1987); *O sumico da santa* (1989; *The War of the Saints*, 1993)

BIBLIOGRAPHY: Ellison, F. P., *Brazil's New Novel: Four Northeastern Masters* (1954): 83–108; Mazzara, R. A., "Poetry and Progress in J. A.'s *Gabriela, cravo e canela*," *Hispania*, 46 (1963): 551–56; Lowe, E., "The 'New' J. A.," *LBR*, 2 (1969): 73–82; Russo, D. T., "Bahia, Macumba and Afro-Brazilian Culture in J. A.'s *Jubiabá*," *WR*, 6 (1969): 53–58; Silverman, M. N., "Allegory in Two Works [*Jubiabá* and *Os pastores da noite*] of J. A.," *RomN*, 13 (1971): 67–70; Nunes, M. L., "The Preservation of African Culture in Brazilian Literature: The Novels of J. A.," *LBR*, 10 (1973): 86–101; Chamberlain, B. J., *J. A.* (1990)

—EARL E. FITZ

AMBRUS, Zoltán

Hungarian short-story writer, novelist, essayist, and translator, b. 22 Feb. 1861, Debrecen; d. 1 March 1932, Budapest

A., the son of a railroad official, lost his father just after finishing his secondary schooling. The family moved to Budapest, where A. supported his mother and a sister by giving lessons and working as a bank clerk. He also did journalistic work at night. In 1886 the then-obscure A. published his first short story, "Messziröl jött levelek" (letters from far away), a gripping tale about a conspiracy to conceal a young man's suicide from his mother. During the next quarter-century A. wrote another two hundred and fifty stories. Although he became a master of the terse narrative,

including the novella, his full-length novels fell short of the expectations of a generation nourished on the works of the great romantic Mór Jókai (1825–1904) and the realist Kálmán Mikszáth (1847–1910). From 1916 to 1922 A. was director of the National Theater.

A. was a poetic realist. In his stories he confined the realistic aspects of his work to the focusing on one short period in his characters' lives. The atmosphere thus created permits a seemingly unimportant incident to mark the turning point in a life. He regarded realism of detail as a mere scaffold that could quickly be discarded. Plotting was not his strength.

A.'s full-length novel *Midás kíraly* (1892; King Midas) begins with the romance of a poor young couple and the death of the lovely wife. Yet despite A.'s nearness to the characters (he himself had been twice widowed), his portrayal of their psychological states is unconvincing.

The depiction of concentrated moments of time was his forte, and A. generally avoided the descriptions of nature and settings common to broader canvases. It was the small symbolic object that caught his eye: a hat, ornate or cheap, or a piece of furniture often represents the essential feelings of its owner. Names in his works are also symbolic: by giving historical names to the simplest characters, he creates extraordinary comic effects.

The characters in A.'s short stories are widely varied—the young and the old, successes and failures. Among some of the more memorable are love-starved children of divorce and a senile mother who calls her visiting son by the name of an acquaintance, although her chatter reveals that her son is still real to her. A., a Roman Catholic, often criticized the agnosticism and materialism of his time in his essays. Yet he showed understanding for human frailties: gambling, drinking, petty pilfering. Social criticism is implicit in A.'s portrayal of the world of the gentry and high bureaucracy of his time. "Téli sport" (1908; winter sport) reveals the weaknesses of royalty, and "Estéban testvére" (1899; Esteban's brother) the fleeting glory of national heroes. When A. was elected to the Hungarian Academy of Learning in 1915, his inaugural lecture was an antiwar novella, *A kém* (the spy), about an old peasant woman who sacrifices her life for her young master, a lieutenant in the Franco-Prusian War. "Lullaby" (1909; original title in English) is a story *à clef* about a demoted general of the Italian-Abyssinian War in 1895, whose honor a journalist tries to restore—for the purpose of his own advancement.

The subject of suicide often figures in A.'s stories; it was rampant in Hungary during his time. The short novel *Őszi napsugár* (1893; autumn sunshine), about an amateur poet and unsuccessful lover, can be considered his masterpiece. In it the road to suicide is paved with inimitable irony. For once A. was able to manipulate an involved plot, which he embellished with humorous and symbolic details about the lives of penniless but ambitious members of the petit bourgeoisie: a host of odd characters spin a web that eventually catches and strangles the hapless hero. As can be seen in this book, A. had compassion for his characters, although he never mingled his tears with theirs. This objectivity indicates the influence of Flaubert; indeed, A.'s translation of *Madame Bovary* remains a classic.

FURTHER WORKS: *A. Z. munkái* (16 vols., 1906–1913); *A tóparti gyilkosság: Kisregények es válogatott elbeszélések* (1961)

—VALERIE KOREK

AMERICAN LITERATURE

American Literature through World War II

American literature achieved mature individuality and identity in the 20th c., after long imitation of European models. Its unmistakable independence became apparent in the 1920s, when American writers began to command worldwide respect. Before this time a number of Americans had been widely known, some had been praised, and a few had exerted limited influence; but American literature had remained subordinate, a branch of European letters on native subjects.

Very shortly after the Englishman Sydney Smith asked, "In the four corners of the globe, who reads an American book?" the English were enthusiastically reading the *Sketch Book* of Washington Irving, and the *Leatherstocking Tales* of James Fenimore Cooper enjoyed European popularity. Of the 19th-c. writers, the novels of Herman Melville, *Typee* and *Omoo*, were successful abroad; the essays of Ralph Waldo Emerson were generally considered to be of notable significance; Walt Whitman achieved considerable repute as a poet; while Edgar Allan Poe, whose special genius had passed almost unnoticed in America, came to influence the development of French symbolist poetry through translations of his work by Baudelaire. Later, Henry JAMES was held to have contributed to the development of the realistic novel in English.

Although there had been a lag of a generation or more in the development of American romanticism from its German and English predecessors, the time lapse between the development of realistic fiction on the Continent and its counterpart in America was of shorter duration. But, beginning about 1912 and continuing to the present, American writers have achieved remarkable developments in fiction, poetry, the drama, and criticism, all of which have established for American letters an important place in world literature and provided models for study and emulation in the work of such writers as John DOS PASSOS, Ernest HEMINGWAY, and William FAULKNER.

From the beginning, American literature was largely concerned with the quality of American experience and the portrayal of American character and conditions as shaped by independence and the influence of a frontier which once seemed limitless. The study of European models was combined with the search for a vernacular style free of the stiffness and formality of literary language. While the use of regional dialect was a step toward this goal, it was the work of Mark Twain that presaged creative writing of the future. Twain's *Huckleberry Finn* (1885) established a popular, colloquial style that broke with literary language and "fine writing," a style that has continued to exert influence. The work of this century developed organically from the earlier period. Twentieth-c. writers inherited from Henry James and Stephen Crane (1871–1900) an interest in technique that led to experiments and innovations in fiction and poetry. They were heirs to a critical realism in the fiction of James and William Dean Howells (1837–1920), as well as to naturalism in the work of Crane, Frank Norris (1870–1902), and Hamlin Garland (1860–1940). In poetry, Whitman had developed a type of free verse long before the technique was recognized or named, and Poe exerted a circuitous influence through the French symbolists toward choice of the exact emotive word in the short lyric. Emily Dickinson, unknown in her lifetime, has since been recognized as effectively modern in her ingeniously condensed verse.

During the 19th c. a persistent American strain in fiction turned from direct portrayal of reality to a more selective and romantic approach. Cooper presented the "beau-ideal" of character rather than the crudity of the Indians and frontiersmen he had known. Nathaniel Hawthorne gave his romances settings removed from the commonplace daylight of routine affairs so that, while holding fast to the truths of the heart, he could present them under circumstances of his choosing. This tendency persisted in the work of Melville and others, and it finds continuing support in contemporary disavowals of realism. But by the turn of the century, realism was the dominant literary mode, if not the mode of popular fiction. Naturalism was then beginning to affect the evolution of fictional techniques in the response of American writers to new descriptions of man's place and role in nature. The theories of Darwin, Marx, and FREUD powerfully affected the content as well as the form of America's 20th-c. literature. There were simultaneous trends toward objectivity in portrayal of the social milieu and toward detailed psychological analysis. The dominant realism-naturalism, consciously scientific in technique, tended, however, toward symbolic or mythic interpretations despite its surface style, while there was an opposing tendency, never quite a movement, toward impressionism, EXPRESSIONISM, and other nonrealistic techniques, particularly in the psychological novel.

Extreme diversity is apparent in 20th-c. American literature, and no single tendency typifies the age. Simultaneous efforts have been made to simplify and democratize the literature, while certain exclusive groups have attempted to make it an esoteric study. The tone of the century has been predominantly critical. Self-conscious concentration on American subjects, the exploitation of every aspect of American life, and the search both for a past and for a distinctive American mode of expression have not led to a spirit of nationalistic approval. The criticism has reflected wide variation in social views and response to the tumultuous events and changes attributable to two world wars and a crushing depression.

Initial objects of attack were the genteel tradition and puritanical standards as manifested both in the supposed simplicities and pieties of village and middle-class urban life, and in restrictions on subject matter and frankness of expression. After World War I swept away much Victorian restraint, the generation of the 1920s, disillusioned and cynical, either left for Europe or remained to attack the materialism of the boom period, though in nonpolitical fashion; or, as with the poets, developed forms and a language which alienated the larger public. The 1920s were a period of considerable experiment and innovation. With the onslaught of the Depression the political independence on which many writers prided themselves yielded to social concern and frequently militant leftist protest.

Fiction

The realism that James and Howells introduced to America was learned in part from such continental masters as Balzac, Flaubert, and Turgenev, but it was founded also on a rejection of romantic sentimentalism in favor of precise observation of manners, especially, at first, in contrasts between Americans and Europeans. Although Howells moved toward broad social criticism while James developed into a psychological novelist and a great stylist, both men influenced critics of middle-class manners, those who prided themselves on the artistic mastery of form and style that has been typical of the best realists.

Edith WHARTON satirized the New York society she both disdained and admired, and which she knew intimately. A master of detail, she was far more concerned with the moral dilemmas of her characters than with the fashionable world that created them. *The House of Mirth* (1905) and *The Age of Innocence* (1920), her best novels, are concerned with the price exacted of the sensitive by a materialistic society. *The Custom of the Country* (1913) is satire on the "New Woman," unmatched in vigor until Sinclair LEWIS appeared, but her later work expressed petulant dislike of a world from which she was progressively alienated.

Ellen Glasgow (1874–1945) was a Virginian whose approach to fiction was basically psychological and critical, and she observed the restraint and decorum of earlier realists while battling prudery and sentimentality. She wrote of the Old Dominion with ironic contempt of heroic myth and Victorian conventionality, and in her best-known novels, *Barren Ground* (1925) and *Vein of Iron* (1935), she was a convincing feminist. She also developed a gift for high comedy in such portrayals of Richmond society as *The Romantic Comedians* (1926) and *They Stooped to Folly* (1929).

Willa CATHER made the Great Plains and the Southwest the extensive region of her interest, but she was never merely a regionalist. In all her work she remained conscious of traditions brought by her immigrant protagonists, as in *O Pioneers!* (1913) and *My Ántonia* (1918), and she contrasted urban and rural ways in the psychological problems of her characters. Like Edith Wharton and, to some extent, Ellen Glasgow, she was increasingly alienated from modern life, and in *Death Comes for the Archbishop* (1927) and *Shadows on the Rock* (1931) she celebrated the faith and strength of the early builders of New World civilization.

With their precision, artistry, and control, the realists contrasted favorably with their naturalistic contemporaries, but their subjects often seemed pallid. Naturalism tended toward the sordid and shocking aspects of existence, and evinced greater interest in social forces than in character, in the basic human urges than in ideals. A prolific sociological naturalist, Upton SINCLAIR was more interested in social questions than in character or the art of fiction. His fervid attack on big business, monopoly, and disregard of human rights stemmed from a romantic idealism, and his straightforward, unliterary style gave him a wide audience for his unequivocally proletarian novel *The Jungle* (1906), whose milieu was the meatpacking industry of Chicago, and for his later novels *King Coal* (1917), *Oil!* (1927), and *Boston* (1928). In the 1940s, in a series of novels on the career of Lanny Budd, Sinclair dramatized the political crises of the century.

The early career of Theodore DREISER was thwarted by abuse from critics and self-appointed censors, yet he made possible the much franker work of later writers like Sinclair Lewis and James T. FARRELL. A complex and contradictory figure, he was a perennial seeker, compassionate and pessimistic, with sympathy for life's victims who, in their ignorance and blind submission to animal drives, are entrapped by forces they cannot control. Besides his preoccupation with mechanistic determinism, Dreiser exhibited a sense of the mystical relations of life and faith in human improvement and social amelioration. His style is frequently awkward and his characterization unimpressive. The sense of shock he aroused in many readers came not from lurid and sordid detail, but from his moral neutrality, offensive to the puritanical. Only his demonic energy and enthusiasm enabled his novels to triumph over their clumsiness of plot, character, dialogue, and style.

By modern standards, Dreiser's *Sister Carrie* (1900) is an innocent fable of the country girl in the city, but a publisher's attempt to withdraw it dissuaded its author from novel writing for several years. *The "Genius"* (1915) was even more vigorously attacked, and was withdrawn by the publisher until 1923. Even the triumph of *An American Tragedy* (1925) provoked new abuse and the banning of the novel in some cities. A trilogy on the career of an American finance capitalist, *The Financier* (1912), *The Titan* (1914), and *The Stoic* (posthumously, 1947), displays Dreiser's interest in the powerful as well as the humble, and reveals something of his own progress from fascination with the "chemisms" that he once believed control human conduct to the mystical religiosity of his novel *The Bulwark*, published posthumously in 1946.

The first American to win the Nobel Prize for literature, Sinclair Lewis was preeminently a satirist who directed his barbs at the life of the small town in *Main Street* (1920), the small businessman in *Babbitt* (1922), the medical profession in *Arrowsmith* (1925), organized religion in *Elmer Gantry* (1927), and, more sympathetically, the successful businessman in *Dodsworth* (1929). In about twenty further books he continued his documented caricature in other fields, but with less success. His characters reflect the mingled scorn and admiration Lewis felt for his subjects, and with one, George Babbitt, the personification of smug, middle-class ideals, he added a new epithet to the language.

Americans have been preeminent as writers of the short story, a form given its first definition by Poe, who emphasized concision and singleness of effect. Hawthorne provided an example of greater thematic depth, and Melville of the possibilities of the American character. The form became, and continues to be, an enormously popular literary medium. Mark Twain enlarged the possibilities of the Western "tall tale," and Ambrose Bierce (1842–1914?) sharpened the effects of shock he had learned from Poe. In his turning to subjective experience and emphasis on the shock of moments of illumination, rather than on plot, James too was a major contributor to the form.

Past the turn of the century the popular William Sidney Porter (1862–1910), under his pseudonym O. Henry, made of this genre a kind of literary trickery. A better writer, Edith Wharton, ordered her materials in such a way as to create a frequently satirical illumination for her readers, while local colorists like Mary E. Wilkins Freeman (1852–1930) and Sarah Orne Jewett (1849–1909) evoked the quality of life in New England. The documentary fullness typical of naturalism sometimes gave way in Dreiser to sympathetic concern with character; and with her "Paul's Case" (1905), in which the symbolic possibilities of detail are artistically realized, Willa Cather, not usually naturalist in technique, accomplished one of her best naturalistic stories.

The greatest literary achievements of the American 20th c. were effected by writers whose careers flourished in the years between the wars, especially the generation that developed in the twenties. It was this group, suffering in her opinion from disillusioned cynicism, that Gertrude STEIN dubbed a "lost generation." Expatriation had also been the lot of Miss Stein, along with Ezra POUND and T. S. ELIOT, and for years a chief current in the mainstream of American letters flowed by the Parisian Left Bank until altered rates of exchange drove the younger refugees home.

The spiritual godmother of the 1920s group was Gertrude Stein who, as an expatriate in France since 1903, had shared a similar experience to theirs. Her radical experimentation had shattered the conventional forms of grammar and syntax, and her rhythmical, repetitive prose influenced the styles of Hemingway and Dos Passos. It was her influence rather than her work itself that was important, yet in *Three Lives* (1909) she characterized accurately and convincingly, and wrote dialogue that instructed Hemingway and Sherwood ANDERSON. *Tender Buttons* (1914) was her most radically experimental work, little known until it was reprinted in 1928. In *The Autobiography of Alice B. Toklas* (1933), one of her "sensible" works, she wrote a popular memoir of her own life; *Wars I Have Seen* (1945) was more conventional autobiography.

Sherwood Anderson, who became a professional writer in his forties, influenced a generation of younger men who briefly held him in admiration for his sensitive honesty and scorn of middle-class hypocrisy. Like Edgar Lee MASTERS he castigated the life of the small town in the loosely grouped sketches of "grotesques" in *Winesburg, Ohio* (1919), his best-known work. In style he owed much of the lyrical impressionism of his novel *Dark Laughter* (1925) to Gertrude Stein, whose influence was already apparent in the lesser *Marching Men* (1917). Anderson was less successful as a novelist than as a writer of memoirs in such works as *A Story Teller's Story* (1924) and *Tar: A Midwest Childhood* (1926), and especially of stories depicting unheroic, grotesque victims of modern life, such as those in *The Triumph of the Egg* (1921) and *Death in the Woods* (1933).

Two other writers represented, more strikingly than Anderson, refusal to accept the dominant naturalism of the period. James Branch Cabell (1879–1958) enjoyed a great vogue after the publication of *Jurgen* (1919), a fanciful novel rich in irony and parody that departed from the contemporary world, as did the long series of volumes depicting Cabell's mythical region of Poictesme. Thornton WILDER was a consistent stylist of romantic tendency, an intellectual whose works are not primarily concerned with ideas, and a careful writer in a wider tradition of letters than contemporary naturalism. Subtlety and irony distinguish *The Cabala* (1926), while *The Bridge of San Luis Rey* (1927) is informed with Wilder's Christian humanism, which appears again in his satire on fundamentalist evangelism and American faith in salesmanship, *Heaven's My Destination* (1935).

The acknowledged historian of the Jazz Age, which collapsed after 1929, was F. Scott FITZGERALD, a Midwesterner who chronicled the period with a closer feeling for its characteristics than the documentary Sinclair Lewis. Romantic in temperament, intensely autobiographical, intelligent and extremely sensitive but without the power of abstract thought, Fitzgerald never achieved naturalistic objectivity nor attempted the shocking effects of naturalistic detail. Wealth and success fascinated him, but he was capable of satiric detachment and moral judgment. Tragedy in his private life accompanied the loss of his audience after a period of immediate, almost fantastic popularity that began with *This Side of Paradise* (1920) and reached its climax with the publication of his masterpiece, *The Great Gatsby* (1925), yet he continued valiantly with *Tender Is the Night* (1934), his weightiest novel. The unfinished *The Last Tycoon* (1941) and *The Crack-Up* (1945) were edited by Edmund WILSON after his death. Four volumes of short stories attest to his skill in that form, and a handful are among the best of their time. In one, "Babylon Revisited" (1930), Fitzgerald viewed the Jazz Age in longer perspective even than in his novels.

More intensely subjective than Fitzgerald, Hemingway rigidly limited himself to the many aspects of life he had encountered personally. So autobiographical is his work that with few exceptions his central characters are versions of Hemingway as he was or would like to have been, and their motivations were his; lacking Fitzgerald's intuitive understanding, he was less successful with portrayals of women. Publicity and an adventurous life sometimes obscured Hemingway's dedication to his artistic career and his achievement of the "powerful style-forming mastery of the art of modern narration" cited by the Nobel Prize committee in 1954. He was a rigorous craftsman from his earliest stories, and with an almost poetic economy of language and precision of imagery and a freshly individual colloquial style. His prose is terse, intense, and unliterary in tone, and he was a master of dialogue stripped to a pattern of responses and mannerisms characteristic of the speakers. By clear objectivity in the sequential recording of sensations and perceptions in typically short declarative sentences, he sought to fix "the way it was."

Hemingway's was a world of violence, from the collection of stories *In Our Time* (1925), in which Nick Adams suffers the psychic and physical wounds of the "Hemingway hero," as the type has since been called, to *The Old Man and the Sea* (1952), in which Santiago, representative of the recurrent "code hero," saves only his integrity in defeat. The Hemingway hero, whether Jake Barnes of *The Sun Also Rises* (1926) or Frederic Henry of *A Farewell to Arms* (1929), the two best novels, is no simple primitive. He is a sensitive, wounded man holding hysteria at bay in his attempt to learn the virtues of honor, courage, and endurance amid disorder and misery that he might, like the code hero who was variously soldier, bullfighter, or fisherman, exhibit "grace under pressure." Adams, Barnes, and Henry declared by withdrawal a separate peace, but in *To Have and Have Not* (1937) Hemingway showed his responsiveness to the times by making his hero discover that a man alone has no chance. He declared solidarity with mankind in *For Whom the Bell Tolls* (1940), a novel filled with more fully living secondary characters and richly evoked sensual life than his other work. *The Old Man and the Sea* completed the evolution from despair to a reverence for the decency and dignity of which a simple man is capable even in defeat.

Some of Hemingway's best work was accomplished with the short story, a definitive collection up to 1938 being *The Fifth Column and the First Forty-nine Stories* (1938). Typically, the stories portray moments of illumination, or define Hemingway's ideals of courage and self-control. A masterpiece, "The Snows of Kilimanjaro" (1936) is a stream-of-consciousness narrative which includes lyrical flashbacks reminiscent of the early influence of Gertrude Stein, and a symbolism which prepares for the multiple meanings of *The Old Man and the Sea*.

An artist of poetic temperament whose chief vehicle was the naturalistic *roman fleuve*, Dos Passos greatly influenced the technical development of the modern novel. *Three Soldiers* (1921) is a bitter antiwar novel in the tradition of the bildungsroman which Dos Passos continued to employ, but with *Manhattan Transfer* (1925) he turned to the pattern novel of the fragmented urban world. In his great trilogy, *U.S.A.*, consisting of *The 42nd Parallel* (1930), *1919* (1932), and *The Big Money* (1936), he attempted a panoramic view of American life from the turn of the century to the 1930s. Characters are subordinated to the collective life and the struggle of classes, and Dos Passos typifies the age through montages of newspaper headlines and biographies of eminent personalities. Devotion to Jeffersonian ideals of individual freedom explains Dos Passos's shift from Marxism in the 1930s to attacks on collectivists and liberals alike in a second trilogy (1939–49), and finally to a seemingly reactionary stand in *Midcentury* (1961).

Thomas WOLFE was a gigantic literary personality absorbed in his own experiences and sensations and incapable of control of his material, which invariably required editorial arrangement. Romantic in temperament, he was gifted with volcanic energy and creativity and portrayed himself as a genius living a self-created legend of loneliness and torment through four bulky novels, of which only *Look Homeward, Angel* (1929) and *Of Time and the River* (1935) were published in his lifetime. *The Web and the Rock* (1939) and *You Can't Go Home Again* (1940) are attempts at greater objectivity, but as with all Wolfe's novels their effectiveness lies in the vividness of characterization and the titanism of the gargantuan central figure's attempt to engorge the entire American experience.

The towering figure of the first half of the century was Faulkner, whose universal significance has everywhere been recognized, although the setting of his best work is the small, mythical Yoknapatawpha County, Mississippi, an area approximating Faulkner's own home region. Neglected during the years he was producing his best work, he was better appreciated at home after he won the 1949 Nobel Prize for literature; his acceptance speech taught Americans generally that he was no simple rural naturalist given to perverse complexity in his method of narration. Yoknapatawpha is one of the great imaginative creations of modern literature, and Faulkner was more daringly experimental in style and narrative technique than any of his American contemporaries, though Hemingway has been more widely imitated.

Most of Faulkner's seventeen novels and ninety short stories recreate Yoknapatawpha from Indian days to the present in a history related to actual events and Faulkner's family past, but seen dramatically through a kaleidoscope of varying viewpoints and periods of time rather than told as a chronicle. The effectiveness of single works is enhanced by others through complex interrelations and thematic reinforcements, and through the recurrence of characters and the recall of events outside the focus of a particular narrative frame. The South; the decay of old families; the life of city, town, and country; the heroic past and unworthy present; the role of the blacks; the cold viciousness of commercialism—these are all parts of Faulkner's subject, but the list merely suggests its rich variety and does not even hint at the timeless significance and mythic proportions he gives the inhabitants of Yoknapatawpha by concentration less on their history than on their morals and psychology.

"The problems of the human heart in conflict with itself" were to Faulkner the writer's true subject, and he portrayed them with subtlety and penetration accompanied by a moral Puritanism which, although compassionate, is as implacable in judgment as Hawthorne's. He used the techniques of the stream-of-consciousness, multiple points of view, a skillfully manipulated chronology reinforced by symbolic and mythic patterns, and a lyric auctorial voice reflecting his description of himself as a "failed poet." His preoccupation with passion and violence was not intended to shock so much as to reveal aberrations symbolic of the decline of the South. Faulkner was capable of the extremes of allegory and the wildly humorous "tall tale"; with equal skill he recorded objective action and the subjective torments of disordered minds. The depth of his best work is unmatched in contemporary American fiction, and he was one of the great humorists.

In a phenomenal creative period, his "time of genius," Faulkner published *The Sound and the Fury* (1929), *Light in August* (1932), and *Absalom, Absalom!* (1936), his three greatest works; *As I Lay Dying* (1930) and *Sanctuary* (1931), a popular success; and two other novels, two volumes of short stories, and a collection of

poems. His later trilogy on the Snopes clan, representative of all destructive modern tendencies, includes *The Hamlet* (1940), *The Town* (1957), and *The Mansion* (1959).

Faulkner's short stories range widely in subject and style, but the best are part of the Yoknapatawpha saga and share its depth of implication. A collection like *Go Down, Moses* (1942) forms a loosely articulated novel. So do the uncollected Nick Adams stories of Hemingway, but where Hemingway charted the stages of existential isolation, Faulkner related his figures to the timeless patterns of human experience. He did not mine his past for adolescent ecstasies and despairs, like Fitzgerald, nor did he content himself with the baffled limitations of Anderson's grotesques, or the satirical fixing of Ring Lardner's (1885–1933) mean-spirited character types. Yet in his work he comprehended something of the range of all these contemporaries, and he was a master of the short form.

Younger writers whose careers began in the 1930s faced a radically altered social climate in which literature and propaganda were widely confused. The best of them remained artists, however, and their varying responses to the times were not dictated by party programs. Farrell treated his great subject of the lower-class Catholic Irish of Chicago in thoroughly naturalistic fashion. His best work is his first trilogy, *Young Lonigan* (1932), *The Young Manhood of Studs Lonigan* (1934), and *Judgment Day* (1935), in which he recounts the defeat of a modern urban drifter in a hostile society. Farrell returned repeatedly to his familiar milieu in almost autobiographical accounts of his own escape through art, but never with equal success. Erskine CALDWELL was at another pole, and used the trappings of rural naturalism to shock, revolt, and frequently to titillate his large public through laconic, emotionless accounts of back-country rustics devoid of most human characteristics. *Tobacco Road* (1932) and *God's Little Acre* (1933) were enormously popular, the first also as a play, and Caldwell worked the Georgia vein with skillful calculation through numerous other titles. In the fascination which his Pennsylvania region exercised over him, John O'HARA resembles Wolfe, and in his use of it as a coherent world of the imagination, Faulkner. He differs from both in his sociological documentation, in which he resembles Lewis, though without Lewis's satiric bent in his attacks on middle-class hypocrisy. *Appointment in Samarra* (1934) has been considered as typical of the 1930s as Fitzgerald's *Gatby* was of the 1920s; *A Rage to Live* (1949) and *Ten North Frederick* (1955) also deal with O'Hara's fictional region. Interpreter to America of a whole people rather than a region, Pearl BUCK made China the subject of her very popular novels *The Good Earth* (1931), *Sons* (1932), and *A House Divided* (1935), a trilogy that earned her the Nobel Prize in 1938, a striking achievement in so short a time. Pearl Buck was an analytical realist rather than a naturalist in her concern with the individual, as was another popular writer, J. P. MARQUAND, who turned to serious fiction with *The Late George Apley* (1937). In such later work as *Wickford Point* (1939) and *H. M. Pulham, Esq.* (1941) Marquand continued as a novelist of manners, richly documenting the ways of well-to-do New Englanders trapped by convention.

A romantic regional naturalist of great vitality, John STEINBECK used Californian settings for the best of all but his last fiction, yet his artistic mastery of many modes gives his work variety and was recognized by the Nobel Prize in 1962. His first popularity was gained with *Tortilla Flat* (1935), an episodic mock-epic of Mexican-Americans in Monterey; *Cannery Row* (1945) and *Sweet*

Thursday (1954) continue the vein of whimsy with other ne'er-do-wells, sympathetically treated. *The Red Pony* (1945) is one of Steinbeck's great artistic successes, an adolescent *Bildungsroman* in four closely linked stories told in faultless style with unsentimental insight and sympathy. A folk tragedy, *Of Mice and Men* (1937), which also enjoyed great success as a play, is proof less of naturalistic fatalism in a defective society than of Steinbeck's respect for human hopes and aspirations, even in defeated outcasts. The typically American transcendental humanism that sustained Steinbeck's respect for individuals kept him from doctrinaire attitudes in his violent strike novel, *In Dubious Battle* (1936), and his most famous work, *The Grapes of Wrath* (1939), on the migration of displaced farmers to California. The style of the latter novel is objective and naturalistic, and in detail and language it was offensive to the squeamish; yet it is deeply moving and attains an epic significance unmatched in American naturalism. With *East of Eden* (1952) Steinbeck attempted to enlarge the scope of his fiction by relating his plot to the Cain-Abel myth ad its significance to the basic problem of evil.

In his short stories Steinbeck maintained the mingled objectivity and sympathy that typified the best of his work, qualities that distinguished them from the facile productions of Caldwell and O'Hara, both prolific in the form. Greater sensitivity and psychological penetration were apparent in the masterful short narratives of Katherine Anne PORTER, a very careful writer of limited scope but fine precision of style. Eudora WELTY is also a superb stylist in her regional Southern stories, in which she contrasts inner and outer worlds, while Caroline GORDON was a brilliant experimentalist in the form. Where Kay BOYLE interests herself in sophisticated and artistic metropolitan types, both American and European, William SAROYAN treats the simple with optimistic sympathy, in a tone of whimsy. At another pole, Richard WRIGHT wrote with scarifying bitterness of Negro life in the South in the collection *Uncle Tom's Children* (1938).

Robert Penn WARREN, also a distinguished poet and critic, published a first novel, *Night Rider* (1939), which reveals the combination of interests in politics, sociology, morality, and philosophy that mark his later work, particularly the impressive *All the King's Men* (1946). His naturalistic style is suited to the violence of his plots, but analysis of the moral dilemmas of his characters is a central concern, as is the problem of identity and the consideration of a number of philosophies. Warren goes far beyond the purely Southern regional identification, although he belonged initially to a self-conscious group determined to revivify Southern letters. Whatever their influence, an impressive number of excellent writers came from the American South, and, in addition to those already mentioned, the older generation included Elizabeth Madox Roberts (1886–1941), Hervey Allen (1889–1949), Marjorie Kinnan Rawlings (1896–1953), and others.

Poetry

American poetry attained such vitality by the 1920s that the period was termed a "Little Renaissance," but activity then declined until a conspicuous revival began in the 1950s. The early years of the century were inauspicious. Genteel poets aped the past, and the popular writers produced light or comic verse. William Vaughn Moody (1869–1910) died before he could mature his lyric gift and temper his critical, satiric powers, but his contemporary, Edwin Arlington ROBINSON, survived neglect and achieved recognition. Robinson was one of the great American poets in the scale

and versatility of his work, his perfection of structure and phrasing, and the depth of his thought and psychological penetration. With *The Town Down the River* (1910) he first won acclaim, and his long narrative poem *Tristram* (1927) was widely popular, the more so since Robinson, like Robert FROST, used the language and rhythms of common speech. Frost earned almost universal appeal through his simplicity and clarity, qualities that masked the poet's vision beyond his perennial New England subject. His work does not express a formal philosophy; like Robinson, Frost was a humanist concerned with character and responsibility, and made his own sturdy individualism a test of social movements. In sharp contrast to others of his time he addressed himself to the general reader. *The Poems of Robert Frost* (1969) is the comprehensive edition.

An opposing development, however, led to the adoption of symbolist techniques and the incorporation of mythic patterns and a sometimes burdensome weight of allusion, as in the poetry of Pound and Eliot. While Pound, the earlier expatriate, has affected most developments in modern poetry in English through his theorizing, criticism, and personal influence, he struck so many attitudes during a long career that he is considered the catalyst rather than the developer of movements. His own best work is *Hugh Selwyn Mauberly* (1920) and such of the *Cantos* (1917-68) as remained relatively free of his confusedly opinionated social theories, the product of a passion for literature that finally encapsulated him from reality. The early IMAGIST poets owed much to Pound, but leadership devolved on Amy LOWELL, whose first imagist anthology (1915) set forth requirements of precise use of common speech and unsentimental concentration on clear imagery, while demanding freedom of subject and form. Imagism only briefly affected the styles of a number of poets, but H. D. (Hilda DOOLITTLE), John Gould Fletcher (1886–1950), and Elinor Wylie (1885–1928) were more faithful to its canons. Amy Lowell herself contributed to the poetic renaissance by her lectures as by her example, while the founding of *Poetry, A Magazine of Verse* in 1912 gave imagists and others an outlet soon increased by the proliferous "little magazines." Pound was for a time editorially connected with *Poetry*, and among others whose careers he promoted with advice and opportunities for publication was Eliot, whose *The Waste Land* (1922) he cut to half its original length, with Eliot's approval Like Pound, Eliot reached beyond the simplicities of imagism; it is Eliot, however, whose development, as the Nobel committee noted in 1948, into a "trailblazing pioneer of modern poetry," has in contemporary times been accorded the highest plaudits.

Eliot's career was one of sustained development. The poems of *Prufrock and Other Observations* (1917) are comments on the deficiencies of the modern world indicative of the poet's persistent awareness of the past, his heavy indebtedness to literary predecessors, and his skill with free-verse rhythms and metaphysical conceits. *The Waste Land* was recognized as a distinctively modern poem of despair; it is shaped within a framework of mythic pattern and derives its emotional force from allusive passages that require source notes for their clarification. Unnoticed at the time, the religious implications of the final section point toward the development of the less mocking and despairing poem, *Ash Wednesday* (1930), and the deeply religious verse play, *Murder in the Cathedral* (1935). Eliot's supreme achievement is his *Four Quartets* (1943), a series of meditative poems parallel in structure, with recurrent themes reflecting Eliot's speculations on the problems of faith and existence through passages variously lyrical, meditative, or didactic, in a supple though conversational language.

Many poets followed Eliot's example and Pound's injunction to "make it [poetry] new," but in another development in the Middle West three poets of the Chicago School responded to other influences, notably the diversity of American life, the revolt against village pieties, and the bardic tradition of Whitman. Edgar Lee Masters produced one notable work, *Spoon River Anthology* (1915), a collection of supposed epitaphs spoken by the dead of a village graveyard in unremarkable free verse. It reflects the bitter naturalistic sense of frustration in individual lives which informed Sherwood Anderson's prose work, *Winesburg, Ohio*. Carl SANDBURG was of more optimistic temperament, and his humanitarian sympathies led him to a forceful interpretation of the commonplace in colloquial, unconventional free verse, notably in *Chicago Poems* (1916). Vachel LINDSAY made himself the romantic interpreter of an American past he largely misunderstood and was the originator of a jingling, rhythmic verse he termed "the higher vaudeville."

Among poets conspicuous in the 1920s was Conrad AIKEN, whose earlier narrative verse gave way to an individual lyric voice in his attempt to create the purely mystical effects of "absolute" poetry in such work as *Punch: The Immortal Liar* (1921). Edna St. Vincent MILLAY was a rebellious, romantic lyricist from the time of her then-sensational "Renascence" (1912) to her maturely disillusioned love sonnets. Marianne MOORE was recognized after her second volume, *Observations* (1924), as a meticulous craftswoman, a keen observer given to vivid imagery, and an inveterate commentator on her poetic subjects. Stephen Vincent BENÉT's *John Brown's Body* (1928) was one of the few American attempts at epic handling of a native theme, and Benét also made great use of folklore in his other work.

Among those of more considerable talent was Robinson JEFFERS, who, in his long narratives, beginning with *Tamar, and Other Poems* (1924), employed a rhythmic free verse of great flexibility and lyric beauty to detail violent family histories reminiscent of Greek tragic themes as understood in modern psychological terms. Wallace STEVENS was neglected by all save other poets and a few critics because the technical brilliance and erudition of his work make severe demands on the reader, and he seemed at variance with general trends in his concern with the nature of reality and the poet's imposition of order through the shaping powers of his imagination. Not until the publication of his *Collected Poems* (1954) was there anything approaching general appreciation of the "supreme fictions" of his art.

In contrast, William Carlos WILLIAMS pruned his work of all barriers to an immediate apprehension of the objective, often drab reality presented in his objectivist poetry, in which he shunned overt use of poetic devices and attempted to preserve the vigor and rhetoric of vernacular speech. While Williams seldom allowed intrusion into his poetry of ideas and considered convictions extraneous to verse, Archibald MACLEISH, after an initial period of subjective aestheticism, turned increasingly to the American heritage and was for a time a propagandist experimenting in many forms, though his later poetry is personal and lyrical.

Among the experimentalists, none was more overtly defiant than E. E. CUMMINGS who, with *Tulips and Chimneys* (1923), began his characteristic experiments with typography and punctuation, not in order to shatter syntax and pulverize the word but to force attention on the lyrical, associative movement of his verse, his masterful satire, or his bitter invective. Alone among the poetic generation of the 1920s, Hart CRANE in *The Bridge* (1930) attempted a symbolic epic that would oppose Eliot's obituary for Western

civilization in *The Waste Land* by celebrating American humanistic idealism, but the best poems of his brief and tragic life are his intense short lyrics, including passages within his major piece.

Of the group that published *The Fugitive* from 1922 to 1925 in Nashville, Tennessee, three produced distinguished poetry in addition to the criticism that established substantial reputations: John Crowe RANSOM's wit and irony were best represented in the late *Selected Poems* (1945); Allen TATE demanded for his antimodernist poetry the co-operation of all his readers' resources, as in "Ode to the Confederate Dead" (1926); Robert Penn Warren in *Brother to Dragons* (1953) experimented with the long narrative poem in a pageantlike form.

The poets of the 1930s who voiced social protest most vehemently included Kenneth Fearing (1902–1961) and Muriel RUKEYSER.

Drama

No plays of national originality or any dramatist of the stature of the great prose writers appeared in the 19th c., and escapist entertainment was the sole fare offered by the American theater until well into the 20th c. The commercial successes of popular actors and a public taste for melodramatic plays inhibited even partial response to continental developments in the theater until, in imitation of European groups that earlier demanded freedom from outworn modes, the Little Theatre Movement provided encouragement and production of the first American dramatist of stature, Eugene O'NEILL.

O'Neill's work was the outgrowth of his determination to present reality as he knew and felt it, and the urgent sincerity of his accomplishment was recognized by the Nobel Prize in 1936. His feeling changed considerably, however, during his creative lifetime, and he was a persistent experimentalist. His short plays before 1920 reveal a combination of concern for naturalistic environmental detail and a romantic sensitivity toward the longings and aspirations of his characters, an approach also evident in *Anna Christie* (1921). His first major production was *Beyond the Horizon* (1920), a drama of frustration and fatality that reflects his sense of tragic irony; and the same year brought *The Emperor Jones* (pub. 1921), an expressionistic play that shows both O'Neill's boldness in technical experimentation and his concern with the psychological depths of character. *The Hairy Ape* (1922) is a better expressionist play, and O'Neill's interest in nonnaturalistic drama is evident also in experimental modifications of realism in *All God's Chillun Got Wings* (1924), *The Great God Brown* (1926), *Lazarus Laughed* (1927), *Strange Interlude* (1928), and *Days without End* (1934). These experiments grew from O'Neill's persistent probing of the depths of character as understood by modern psychology, an interest that led him to domesticate the Phaedra myth in New England in *Desire under the Elms* (1924) and the *Oresteia* in *Mourning Becomes Electra* (1931). In his late work, O'Neill abandoned the masks, drums, asides, and split characters of his titanic effort to express the complexities of character, and adopted a morbidly pessimistic naturalism for such plays as *The Iceman Cometh* (1946) and his posthumous triumph, *Long Day's Journey into Night* (1956).

The example of O'Neill and the changed literary climate to which the theater also responded made possible the work of other dramatists whose careers began in the 1920s. To a lesser degree, all were experimentalists. Elmer RICE produced work in many styles, but his best-known plays belong to the decade of the 1920s. In *The Adding Machine* (1923), one of the first successful American expressionist plays, Rice satirized the anonymous clerks of the submerged urban mass, while *Street Scene* (1929) was a great popular success for its naturalistic portrayal of the New York slums. Maxwell Anderson (1888-1959)produced his best work when he turned to verse drama in the 1930s with *Elizabeth the Queen* (1930), *Mary of Scotland* (1933), and his masterpiece, *Winterset* (1935), in which the weakness of much of the verse is irrelevant beside the poetry inherent in the tragic mood of the play and the social indignation of its author. Robert E. Sherwood (1896–1955) used his gift for social criticism in attacks on the decay of Western civilization in *The Petrified Forest* (1934) and the growing war madness in *Idiot's Delight* (1936), but his *Abe Lincoln in Illinois* (1938) was founded upon faith in American humanitarian idealism.

The bitterly critical mood of the 1930s is most apparent, among the younger writers, in Clifford ODETS. Despite much other work, Odets is best known for his *Waiting for Lefty* (1935) and *Awake and Sing!* (1935). Lillian HELLMAN was no less a topical social critic of the modern realistic school in her antifascist *Watch on the Rhine* (1941) and *The Searching Wind* (1944); in her earlier work, *The Little Foxes* (1939), she criticized ruthless ambition and materialism. In contrast to Hellman's controlled artistry, the bittersweet, whimsical plays of William Saroyan, of which *The Time of Your Life* (1939) is typical, are almost formless but exert great charm of mood. Thornton Wilder was determinedly experimental with his two best works, *Our Town* (1938), in which the commonplaces of American village life are raised to significance, and *The Skin of Our Teeth* (1942), in which the troubles of the times are related to the perspective of human history.

Criticism and Other Prose

The self-conscious American attempt to define in national character and create an independent literature was reflected both in the writing of literary history and an unparalleled discussion of critical theory. The claiming of a distinctive American current in the main-stream of Western letters gradually yielded to a sense of mature American individuality that no longer had the need to insist on separateness but could relate to the world at large.

Van Wyck Brooks (1886–1963) began as a writer of cultural history with *The Wine of the Puritans* (1909), in which he attributed American materialism to the Puritan tradition, and *America's Coming of Age* (1915), in which he deplored the stifling effects of a "genteel tradition"; but he also turned to more conventional literary history in the five volumes of his *Makers and Finders* series (completed 1952), and discovered virtues overlooked before. Vernon Parrington (1871–1929) wrote a three-volume history, *Main Currents in American Thought* (1927–30), from a then-startling viewpoint—a refusal to consider American literature as a mere offshoot of English literature. It was followed by even more sociological and political interpretations, such as V. F. Calverton's (1900–1940) Marxist *Liberation of American Literature* (1932) and Granville Hicks's (b. 1901) *The Great Tradition* (1933). In the later *Literary History of the United States* (1948), edited by Robert Spiller and other scholars, more heed was paid to intellectual and aesthetic developments.

In criticism, the leading figures at the turn of the century were William Dean Howells and Henry James. Howells was powerfully influential in encouraging younger men even when he did not personally approve their experiments, and although conservative he deplored dictatorial tendencies in criticism, and its lack of

principles. James, in his essays and the prefaces to the New York edition of his work (1907), assembled an exhaustive discussion of the art of fiction, though appreciation of it was delayed for some decades. William Crary Brownell (1851–1928) was an admired critic, a foe of the impressionistic criticism practiced by James Gibbons Huneker (1860–1921), whose great service was to inform Americans of European developments in literature and music. By 1910, Joel Elias Spingarn (1875–1939) called for a criticism firmly based on principles that would turn attention from the reactions of the critic to the work itself, but for some time criticism remained nontechnical, as in the iconoclastic impressionism of H. L. MENCKEN, the socioliterary theorizing of Van Wyck Brooks and others, and the moralizing of the "New Humanism," as it was called. Paul Elmer More (1864–1937) and Irving Babbitt (1865–1933) were leaders in this movement, which violently opposed modern developments and produced such curiosities in the literature of denunciation as Babbitt's *Rousseau and Romanticism* (1919) and More's *The Demon of the Absolute* (1928). The general principles of the group, which stressed reason and restraint in ethics, art, and thought, were best summed up in a symposium, *Humanism and America* (1930), which provoked a notable rejoinder in George SANTAYANA's *The Genteel Tradition at Bay* (1931), and a counter-symposium, *The Critique of Humanism* (1930), the contributors to which eventually seized critical leadership as the New Humanism was superseded by the New Criticism.

The urgent concerns of the 1930s provoked much leftist comment—comment that was of no lasting interest except as it affected the attempted revisions of American literary history. At the same time, Edmund Wilson was practicing the eclecticism that made him an analyst of symbolism in *Axel's Castle* (1931) and allowed him to use Freudian and Marxist concepts as well as modern techniques of formal analysis without forgetting his role as literary critic or allying himself with any movement. T. S. Eliot was possibly even more influential as a critic than as a poet; his essays furnished many of the concepts of the New Criticism, which although primarily an American movement drew heavily on the semantic theories of the British I. A. RICHARDS and William EMPSON. As a movement, the New Criticism emerged in the 1930s and over the following decades made itself the dominant theoretical approach to the teaching of literature in the universities, insisting on painstaking formal analysis and denigrating traditional historical or biographical approaches. The method was brilliantly successful with poetry, but not generally applied to other forms, the decline of which was assumed. John Crowe Ransom was a leader as early as 1930 in *God without Thunder*, and Allen Tate's *Reactionary Essays on Poetry and Ideas* (1936) contributed to theory. Other partisans were Yvor WINTERS, R. P. BLACKMUR, Cleanth BROOKS, Kenneth BURKE, and Robert Penn Warren.

—DONALD EMERSON

American Literature from 1945 to 1980

American literature since World War II has harbored a considerable disaffection for the established culture. In reaction, first, against the gray-flanneled conformity of postwar America, and then in reaction against the olive-drab bloodletting of the Vietnam years, this disaffection has expressed itself in a tendency to reject the well-made play that was Broadway's staple, to discontinue the lyrical-realistic narrative given currency by F. Scott FITZGERALD and Ernest HEMINGWAY, and to disdain the formalist verse beloved by academia's New Critics, as if these eminently lucid expressions of the literary mind were inappropriate to the outer darkness of the period. The voices of the postwar years spring from places off the main line-from rural Georgia and from Off-Off-Broadway, from San Francisco communes and from industrial towns in New Jersey. Indeed, literature tends to be dominated in the postwar years by provincial solitaries and by members of groups who insist, more often than not, that there is no such thing as the mainstream culture, but only the individual and what he makes of his life, only his reality and how he shapes it. Postwar American writers have even tended, on occasion, to push to the brink their sense of the off-center human life, probing the geography of solipsism and the architecture of madness.

Fiction

In several important ways American fiction since World War II is still a continuation of the literature that preceded it. The tradition of realism survives, for instance, not only in the work of such prewar novelists as John Dos PASSOS, James T. FARRELL, and John STEINBECK, who continued writing into the late 1950s, but also in such estimable and diverse novels as James DICKEY's *Deliverance* (1970), Bernard MALAMUD's *The Natural* (1952), and Wright MORRIS's *Ceremony in Lone Tree* (1960). It survives also in an intermittent but nagging attempt in the period to compound journalism and fiction, most notably exemplified by Truman CAPOTE's *In Cold Blood* (1966), Norman MAILER's *The Armies of the Night* (1968), and Alex Haley's (b. 1921) *Roots* (1976). The more limited tradition of naturalism predictably survives in such war novels as Mailer's *The Naked and the Dead* (1948), James JONES's *From Here to Eternity* (1951), and Joseph HELLER's *Catch-22* (1961), and, less expectedly, in works as diverse as Joyce Carol OATES's *them* (1969), Ralph ELLISON's *Invisible Man* (1952), and John Rechy's (b. 1934) *City of Night* (1963). Commonly supposed a casualty of World War II, the novel of manners is also a survivor, not only in a popular book like James Gould COZZENS's *By Love Possessed* (1957), but with distinction in such deeply nuanced work as John CHEEVER's *Bullet Park* (1969), Louis AUCHINCLOSS's *Portrait in Brownstone* (1962), and John UPDIKE's *Couples* (1968).

But these three narrative traditions are ground swells, not epicenters. Postwar American fiction finds its primary expression in ethnic voices gestated in America's 19th-c. regional literature and born in the mid-1940s, when, in response to William FAULKNER's newly recognized achievement, it was abruptly realized that ethnicity is not parochialism. These voices have risen chorally since then from Malamud's Lower East Side storefronts, from Ellison's Harlem basements, from Cheever's Yankee backwaters, and from Updike's dreary exurbias, testifying to the drawbacks and privileges of ethnic perspective, especially the Southern, the Jewish, and the black.

The voice of the South in the period (as well as in the years between the world wars) is dominated inescapably by William Faulkner, whose second Yoknapatawpha cycle of novels was published between 1951 and 1962. Faulkner shares his prestige, however, with Robert Penn WARREN and Eudora WELTY. Warren's carefully crafted *All the King's Men* (1946) and magisterial essays have conferred on him the status of an *éminence grise*, and Welty's short fiction and novels have given her an almost equal distinction. The work of these three writers is typical of the modern South inasmuch as it is tradition-obsessed, hungry for continuity and connection, and anxious to discover the meaning of the self in

relation to history. Indeed, stormy passions run through Southern fiction, together with a deep antagonism for all things urban, abstract, and secular. This extravagance of temperament becomes gothic in Truman Capote's *Other Voices, Other Rooms* (1948) and William STYRON's *Set This House on Fire* (1960), becomes particularly violent in Flannery O'CONNOR's *The Complete Stories* (1971), and is no less so in Carson MCCULLERS's *The Heart Is a Lonely Hunter* (1940) and *The Ballad of the Sad Café* (1951). Walker PERCY's *The Moviegoer* (1961), John William Corrington's (1932-1988) *And Wait for the Night* (1964), and Peter TAYLOR's *Collected Stories* (1969) represent a later strain of Southern writing than McCullers's and O'Connor's, the gothicism attenuated and all but gone. And with this coming of a more dispassionate temper in Southern fiction, much of its vibrancy and direction seem to have gone, too, although interesting work is being produced by such writers as Marion Montgomery (b. 1925), Shelby Foote (b. 1916), Elizabeth SPENCER, Shirley Ann Grau (b. 1929), David Madden (b. 1933), Cormac MCCARTHY, Reynolds PRICE, and William GOYEN.

The Jewish novel in the postwar period is primarily urban, liberal, and Northern in its orientation, balancing the agrarian and conservative bias of the Southern novel. Saul BELLOW is its most accomplished practitioner. In his drawing on the combined resources of the realistic novel, the novel of manners, and the psychological novel, and in his acute awareness of ideologies and the sentiments to which they give rise, Bellow is especially representative of Jewish novelists, too. Indeed, such novels as *The Victim* (1947), *Seize the Day* (1956), *Herzog* (1964), and *Humboldt's Gift* (1975) have stereotyped a Jewish hero of considerable currency. Moody, intelligent, acutely aware, neither Old Worldly Jewish nor comfortably American, sometimes a *schlemiel*, this kind of protagonist also appears in Lionel TRILLING's *The Middle of the Journey* (1947), in Herbert Gold's (b. 1924) *The Man Who Was Not With It* (1956), in Edward Lewis WALLANT's *The Pawnbroker* (1961), in Daniel Stern's (b. 1928) *The Suicide Academy* (1968), and, with especial distinction, in the novels of Bernard Malamud, notably in *The Assistant* (1957), *The Fixer* (1966), and *The Tenants* (1971). With mock-heroical egotism, and relentlessly striking his pose of the enfant terrible, Norman Mailer has even dramatized himself as that hero in such amalgams of autobiography, journalism, and fiction as *Advertisements for Myself* (1959), *Miami and the Siege of Chicago* (1968), and *The Prisoner of Sex* (1971). There is much of the enfant terrible, too, in the wackily libidinous oeuvre of Philip ROTH, an oeuvre respected particularly for *Portnoy's Complaint* (1969), *My Life as a Man* (1974), and *The Professor of Desire* (1977). Bruce Jay Friedman's (b. 1930) *Stern* (1962) and *A Mother's Kisses* (1964) and Joseph Heller's *Good as Gold* (1979) are also superbly funny novels about Jewish suffering and misery, and the balance that such books strike with Malamud's poignant novels suggests the broad field, emotionally, psychologically, and intellectually, that Jewish ethnicity has taken as its province. That field embraces even the Yiddish writings of Isaac Bashevis SINGER, which evoke with singular imagination the *shtetl* life of east European Jews before the war. Stanley ELKIN, Irvin Faust (b. 1924), Mark Harris (b. 1922), Tillie OLSEN, Cynthia OZICK, and Grace PALEY (b. 1922) have also made significant contributions to a recognizably Jewish school of fiction in the postwar period.

Black fiction since the war is dominated by Ralph Ellison's *Invisible Man* (1952), a very considerable work of art, and probably the most profound novel about American identity written in the period. James BALDWIN approaches Ellison's stature as an artist, but he does so on the basis of his essays, collected in such volumes as *Notes of a Native Son* (1955), *Nobody Knows My Name* (1961), and *The Devil Finds Work* (1976), for his novels have failed to achieve the early promise of *Go Tell It on the Mountain* (1953). Indeed, the most powerful writing by blacks has generally been in the autobiographical, biographical, and essay modes, notably Richard WRIGHT's extraordinary *Black Boy* (1945), Eldridge Cleaver's (b. 1935) *Soul on Ice* (1968), Theodore Rosengarten's (b. 1944) compilation *All God's Dangers: The Life of Nate Shaw* (1974), and Alex Haley's *Roots*. The prolific Chester HIMES has moved gracefully from documentary realism to such "camp" detective thrillers as *Cotton Comes to Harlem* (1965), however, and Ishmael REED, Henry Van Dyke (b. 1928), Charles WRIGHT, and Clarence MAJOR have done significant work in the fabulistic vein. The majority of black novelists continue to work the realistic-naturalistic vein, however, with especially creditable work by John A. WILLIAMS, Ernest J. GAINES, and Toni MORRISON.

Other groups of writers have also made dispossession and alienation their subjects in a manner that parallels that of Southerners, Jews, and blacks. The neoromantic beat movement, for instance, fostered a mystique of sex, drugs, love, jazz, anarchy, and love of the road, and Jack KEROUAC's *On the Road* (1957) and *The Dharma Bums* (1958) were its holy writ. The hipster movement, more literate and somewhat more profound, discovered its high priest in William BURROUGHS, who, in such novels as *Junkie* (1953), *Naked Lunch* (1959), and *The Wild Boys* (1971), has written with autobiographical candor of those pressures that threaten man's individuality. With the publication of Henry MILLER's *Tropic of Cancer* (1934) and *Tropic of Capricorn* (1939) in the U.S. in the early 1960s, Miller became a movement unto himself—a virtual battlefield in the war over "pornographic" literature-and his seminal influence on both the beats and the hipsters made him something of an elder statesman among radically disaffected writers. In a more innocent, but equally controversial idiom, in the 1950s J. D. SALINGER was also a movement unto himself, filtering the national paranoia of the McCarthy/Eisenhower years through the eyes of alienated and escapist youth in his enormously popular novel *The Catcher in the Rye* (1951) and in the shorter works collected in *Nine Stories* (1953), *Franny and Zooey* (1961), and *Raise High the Roof Beam, Carpenters; and Seymour: An Introduction* (1963). Although unidentified with any of these movements, Nelson ALGREN's *The Man with the Golden Arm* (1949), Ken KESEY's *One Flew over the Cuckoo's Nest* (1962), Hubert Selby, Jr.'s (b. 1928) *Last Exit to Brooklyn* (1964), and Jerzy KOSINSKI's *The Painted Bird* (1965) are also important expressions of the disaffected sensibility, the books being very nearly as disturbing as Burroughs's in their depictions of violence and perversion.

Yet much of the best and most exciting writing in the postwar period has little to do with ethnic perspectives. It is surrealistic and fabulistic, growing out of international modernism, with some minor nourishment from the European absurdists, the Southern gothicists, and the New York and California hipsters. Stressing the *composed*, gamesmanship character of fiction, this body of work often puts both language and author in the foreground in an attempt not simply to undercut the illusions of realism but to discover new areas for narrative elaboration, becoming essentially fiction about the making of fictions. John HAWKES's *The Cannibal* (1949) was the first important manifestation of this new fiction. Written in a style at once menacing and darkly humorous, and evoking frightening correspondences between man's obsessions and their effect on external reality, it is in the mode of all of Hawkes's enormously poetic novels, including the very fine *The Lime Twig* (1961) and

The Blood Oranges (1971). Another early voice of this new fiction was William GADDIS, who in *The Recognitions* (1955) displayed greater volubility than Hawkes; this book, however, had only an underground success until the publication in 1975 of Gaddis's *J.R.* But it was the publication of Vladimir NABOKOV's dazzling sleights of hand *Lolita* (1955) and *Pale Fire* (1962), coupled with the publication in 1962 of Jorge Luis BORGES's *Ficciones* in English translation, that created the modern taste for intellectual gamesmanship in fiction. The sureness of Nabokov's style, the dexterity of his wit, and the intelligence of his narrative strategies made him the preeminent novelist in America in the postwar period-even, possibly, in the 20th c.

Although his ear for the rhythms of speech is deficient, his eye for the culturally telling detail has given Thomas PYNCHON considerable success in the surrealist mode of fiction in *V.* (1963), *The Crying of Lot 49* (1966), and *Gravity's Rainbow* (1973). John BARTH is wonderfully energetic in his major works, full of wry feints and loquacious asides, especially in *The Sot-Weed Factor* (1960), *Giles Goat-Boy* (1966), *Lost in the Funhouse* (1968), and *Chimera* (1972), less successfully so in the hypertrophied artifice of *Letters* (1979). Other works of distinction in the surrealistic and fabulistic modes include Thomas BERGER's *Little Big Man* (1964), James PURDY's *Cabot Wright Begins* (1964), William H. GASS's *Omensetter's Luck* (1966), Tom McHale's (b. 1941) *Farragan's Retreat* (1971), Paul West's (b. 1930) *Gala* (1976), Joan DIDION's *A Book of Common Prayer* (1977), John IRVING's *The World According to Garp* (1978), and the short stories and novels of Donald BARTHELME, Richard Brautigan (1935-1984), Robert COOVER, Ronald Sukenick (b. 1932), and Kurt VONNEGUT, JR. This mode of fiction is sometimes thought melancholic, but such amiable confections as Gore VIDAL's *Myra Breckinridge* (1968), E. L. DOCTOROW's *Ragtime* (1975), James McCourt's (b. 1941) *Mawrdew Czgowchwz* (1975), and Vance Bourjaily's (b. 1922) *Now Playing at Canterbury* (1976) prove the generalization false.

Poetry

American poetry since World War II has proliferated enormously, and its schools, creeds, and ideologies have been many and varied. Its tap roots, however, run straight to T. S. ELIOT and Ezra POUND, Eliot's stress on formality vying with Pound's emphasis on process and improvisation in the ageless dispute between the classic and the romantic, the Apollonian and the Dionysian. Both Eliot and Pound were concerned to revivify poetry, of course, and they are more properly understood as colleagues than as antagonists, but in a general way, much oversimplified, the 1940s and the 1950s belong to Eliot and his Apollonian notion that poetry is a refuge from personality, while the 1960s and the 1970s belong to Pound and his Dionysian indulgence of personality at every poetic turn. Consistent with this division of the decades, most of the prewar poets who closed out their careers in the first decades after 1945 were formalists rather than improvisationalists. Conrad AIKEN, E. E. CUMMINGS, Babette Deutsch (1895-1982), Robert FROST, Horace Gregory (1898-1982), Archibald MACLEISH, John Crowe RANSOM, Wallace STEVENS, Allen TATE, and John Hall Wheelock (1886–1978) are notable among them, and all have been acclaimed for the cool academicism that underlies even their most individual effects.

Indeed, a cool academicism is typical of most fine poetry in the formalist vein. Stanley Kunitz's (b. 1905) fine poems in *Passport to the War* (1944) and *Selected Poems 1928–1958* (1959) are marvels of quiet precision, for instance, and James MERRILL's works, from *First Poems* (1951) through *Scripts for the Pageant* (1980), always have an elegant, polished surface, and a deft, graceful movement. The poems of Elizabeth BISHOP, Marianne MOORE, and May Swenson (1919-1989) are characterized by elegance, grace, and precision, too, although they are sometimes trivialized by a recherche fastidiousness. Howard NEMEROV, in such collections as *The Salt Garden* (1955), *The Blue Swallows* (1967), and *The Western Approaches* (1975), has less technical facility than Bishop and Moore, but he has a more arresting sense of situation and tone than they, and he strikes a deeper, more resonant note. Richard WILBUR is probably the finest of these postwar poets of coolness and polish. In the patinaed lyricism of *The Beautiful Changes* (1947), *Ceremony* (1950), and *Things of This World* (1956), he illumines moments of being with grace and civility, and with etymological wit and agile imagination as well. Other poets who work with distinction in the formalist vein include John Fandel (b. 1925), Daniel Hoffman (b. 1923), John Hollander (b. 1929), Richard Howard (b. 1929), Randall JARRELL, Donald JUSTICE, Howard Moss (1922-1987), and Adrienne RICH (b. 1929).

In recent decades the so-called confessional poets have most directly contravened the formalist aesthetic. Inspired largely by the publication of Pound's *Cantos-Pisan Cantos* in 1948, *Rock Drill* in 1956, and *Thrones* in 1959—and touched deeply by Pound's incarceration in St. Elizabeth's Hospital from 1946 to 1958, they write poems in which they confess their humiliations and sufferings with extreme autobiographical candor. Improvised stanzaic forms, jagged syntax, and clotted metrics tend to be the appropriately Dionysian accompaniment of their frankness. Robert LOWELL is chief among them: beginning as a formalist in *Land of Unlikeness* (1944) and *Lord Weary's Castle* (1946), he moved gradually toward a freer, more indulgent, and more dramatic manner, until in 1959 *Life Studies* burst on the poetic scene with masterful pyrotechnics of style and statement, establishing the confessional almost overnight as a major poetic mode. In subsequent works, especially in *Notebook* (1970) and the triad *History* (1973), *For Lizzie and Harriet* (1973), and *The Dolphin* (1973), Lowell cemented his position as the greatest practitioner of the confessional idiom, and, indeed, as the greatest American poet of his generation. John BERRYMAN also helped establish this form with the intensely personal, somewhat desperate poetry of *Homage to Mistress Bradstreet* (1956), *The Dream Songs* (1969), and *Delusios, Etc.* (1972). Not always interesting, sometimes irritating and murky, Berryman takes great risks in his poetry, but he is powerful when he succeeds. Three poets who were once Lowell's writing students also did important work in the confessional mode: W. D. Snodgrass (b. 1926) in *Heart's Needle* (1959), Sylvia PLATH in the posthumously published *Ariel* (1965), and Anne SEXTON in *To Bedlam and Part Way Back* (1960), *All My Pretty Ones* (1962), *Live or Die* (1967), and *Love Poems* (1969).

Although the confessionalists have dominated the revolt against formalism, Black Mountain College in North Carolina and the cities of San Francisco and New York have been notable centers of revolt, and each locale has lent its name to a major school of poetry. These schools are loosely self-defined at best, and they are not entirely distinct from one another, inasmuch as they tend alike to reject strict meter, to ignore traditional structures of organization, to disdain paraphrasable content, and to spurn the use of masks and historical analogues. Yet the schools are useful groupings of poets and tend to fix lines of association and influence, if less satisfactorily to characterize style and technique.

The experimental Black Mountain College (now defunct) was a center for several of the avant-garde arts during the 1951–56 rectorship of Charles OLSON. The poets Robert CREELEY, Robert DUNCAN, Edward Dorn (b. 1929), Joel Oppenheimer (1930-1988), and Jonathan Williams (b. 1929), all associated at the time with the college, are acknowledged members of the Black Mountain movement in poetry, and Denise LEVERTOV, Paul Blackburn (1926–1971), and LeRoi Jones (later Imamu Amiri BARAKA, also share membership, although they were never formally associated with the college. The group's poetic manifesto is Olson's essay "Projective Verse" (1950), in which he advocates a prosody based on breathing, as well as other antiformalist principles of poetic discipline. Olson's heroically scaled *Maximus Poems* (1960, 1969) and Dorn's similarly scaled poems in *The North Atlantic Turbine* (1967) and *Gunslinger* (I, 1968; II, 1969) are interesting examples of the Black Mountain aesthetic, as are the minimalist poems of Robert Creeley, especially in *For Love: Poems, 1950–1960* (1962). But the most accomplished work of the movement is that of Denise Levertov. Her poems in such volumes as *O Taste and See* (1964) and *The Freeing of the Dust* (1975) are superbly realized artifacts-uncluttered, quietly mystifying, deeply spiritual, the work of a consummate poet. Her verse transcends the aesthetic of the Black Mountain movement at the same time that it is the movement's most illustrius product.

Less philosophical and more socially conscious than the Black Mountain school, the San Francisco school is made up of poets who turned in the 1950s to that city as the antithesis of the New York-dominated literary world, finding congenial the little magazines set on hand presses, the broadside publication of poems, and the poetry readings that were San Francisco's substitute for the commercial market. Little else distinguishes the San Francisco grouping of poets except a reverence for the poet Kenneth REXROTH, an important patron of young talent in the Bay Area. Indeed, Robert Duncan's erudite, mystical, and carefully worked poetry in *The Opening of the Field* (1960) and *Bending the Bow* (1968) is thought especially notable in the San Francisco oeuvre, yet it is claimed also by the Black Mountain school. And Duncan's poetry has little in common with the open lyrics of Lawrence Ferlinghetti (b. 1919), with the knotted verse of Brother Antoninus (William Everson, 1912-1994), or with the incantatory poems of Philip Lamantia (b. 1925), although all three poets belong to the San Francisco coterie.

The San Francisco school even subsumes the socially radical beat poets, who looked to Kenneth PATCHEN and, surprisingly, to Karl SHAPIRO as their patrons more directly than to Rexroth. Allen GINSBERG is the *Wunderkind* of the beats, almost entirely on the basis of *Howl* (1956), a poem of rage, denunciation, and a few beautifully lyric moments. Ginsberg, however, like many of the beats, is essentially a confessional poet, as *Kaddish* (1961), his best work, makes clear, and he is today a spokesman for countercultural youth worldwide, rather than a spokesman narrowly for the beats. Gary SNYDER and Gregory Corso (b. 1930) have retained their identification with the beats, and both have published impressive work, Snyder affecting romantic primitivism in such collections as *Riprap* (1959) and *The Back Country* (1968), and Corso affecting a savage naïveté in such collections as *Long Live Man* (1962) and *Elegiac Feelings American* (1970). Other notable poets linked in varying degrees to the beat school are Richard Brautigan, Ron Loewinsohn (b. 1937), Michael McClure (b. 1932), David Meltzer (b. 1937), and Philip Whalen (b. 1923).

The New York poets are the most radically antiformalist of these several schools. Influenced greatly by the Dadaists, by the

French surrealists, and by immediate involvement with New York and European painters, they reject the traditional coherencies of line, syntax, and stanza for an essentially spatial presentation. Clarity, logic, and explicability are disdained. Kenneth Koch (b. 1925), for instance, in volumes from *Ko; or, A Season on Earth* (1959) to *The Duplications* (1977), is aggressively madcap in his organization of disjunctive materials, utterly individual in his manner of disposing language on the page. Frank O'HARA's poems, not generally known until the posthumous publication of his *Collected Poems* (1971), are also insistently subjective and improvisational. At their best, however, O'Hara's poems catch admirably the essence of lighthearted spontaneity. And the prolific John ASHBERY, if witty and elegant in manner, is also uncompromisingly obscure, unconfiding, even impenetrable, especially in *Self-Portrait in a Convex Mirror* (1975). Ted Berrigan (1934-1983), Edward Field (b. 1924), Barbara Guest (b. 1920), James Schuyler (1923-1991), and David Shapiro (b. 1947), sharing the aversion of these poets to explicable statement, are also considered members of the New York school.

Black poets have generally gone their own way. Established black poets continued after the war to give voice to their ethnicity in more or less traditional modes, estimably so in Langston HUGHES's *Selected Poems* (1959), in Melvin B. TOLSON's *Libretto for the Republic of Liberia* (1953), and in Gwendolyn BROOKS's considerable oeuvre. The Black Power movement in the 1960s, however, engendered among younger writers a more ethnically intense poetry, often more vigorous and more militant than that of earlier writers, and often in a jazzily energetic black patois, as in Imamu Amiri Baraka's *Preface to a Twenty Volume Suicide Note* (1961), Nikki GIOVANNI's *Black Feeling, Black Talk, Black Judgment* (1970), and Sonia SANCHEZ's *We a Baddddddd People* (1970). Poetry of merit in a distinctively black idiom has also been published by Margaret Danner (b. 1915), Mari Evans (b. 1923), Robert HAYDEN, Etheridge Knight (1931-1991), Don L. Lee (later Haki R. MADHUBUTI), Dudley Randall (b. 1914), and Conrad Rivers (1933–1968).

Many other poets remain independent of the acknowledged schools, of course. William Carlos WILLIAMS's monumental *Paterson* sequence (1946–58) is an attempt to capsulize history in an epic of the self, and, as such, it has clear affinities with Pound's *Cantos*, Berryman's *Dream Songs*, Olson's *Maximus Poems*, and Lowell's *Life Studies*; yet Williams's very influential voice remains distinct from his colleagues,' its timbre fixed somewhere between the regionalists and the symbolists. W. S. MERWIN has so flexible a poetic voice that it can unstrainedly embrace formalism, surrealism, confessionalism, and even minimalism. Indeed, it does so with great élan in *The Moving Target* (1963), *The Carrier of Ladders* (1970), and *The Compass Flower* (1977). The voice of A. R. AMMONS is no less striking than Merwin's: in *The Collected Poems 1951–1971* (1972) Ammons deprives himself almost entirely of such amenities as adjectives and adverbs, and he achieves thereby an austere tone wonderfully suited to his transcendentalist sensibility, a tone that is his alone. James Dickey's voice, on the other hand, is rudely vigorous, and in a collection such as *Buckdancer's Choice* (1965) it arrests the reader's attention with a lurching rhythm that belongs, perhaps, to Theodore ROETHKE before Dickey, but assuredly to no poetic school. Robert BLY, Galway KINNELL, John Logan (1923-1987), William Stafford (1924-1993), and James WRIGHT are poets of considerable reputation who also remain generally independent of schools.

Drama

The variety, the excitement, and the social relevance that vitalized the American theater in the 1920s and 1930s did not survive World War II. Developments in America's postwar drama, in fact, are generally less interesting and less impressive than the simultaneous developments in fiction and verse. Of course, many playwrights who had established their reputations before the war continued to produce stageworthy drama: the years after 1945 saw new plays by Maxwell Anderson, S. N. Behrman (1893–1973), Marc Connelly (1890-1980), Russel Crouse (1893–1966), Moss Hart (1904–1961), Lillian HELLMAN, George S. Kaufman (1889–1961), Howard Lindsay (1889–1968), Eugene O'NEILL, Robert E. Sherwood, Elmer RICE, and Thornton WILDER. But their most important work predates the war. Of all the playwrights who survived from the 1920s and 1930s, only O'Neill had a major impact after the war, and that impact was based essentially on the successful posthumous production in 1956 of two works written before the war, *The Iceman Cometh* (first produced, less successfully, in 1946) and *Long Day's Journey into Night*.

The first major dramatists to emerge freshly after 1945 were Tennessee WILLIAMS and Arthur MILLER, the former absorbed in Krafft-Ebing aberrations, the latter in Oedipal psychology; both helped to commit the postwar stage to a gut-wrenching, raw, and emotional realism. Indeed, their more famous characters have a flesh-and-blood reality beyond that of any characters who walked the American stage before them, and even the authors' occasional use of expressionistic and symbolist devices has the effect, paradoxically, of emphasizing their commitment to realistic drama. The best work of each was written early in his career: Williams's *The Glass Menagerie* was produced in 1945, *A Streetcar Named Desire* in 1947, *Cat on a Hot Tin Roof* in 1955; and Miller's *Death of a Salesman* was produced in 1949, *The Crucible* in 1953. In failing to surpass these works both dramatists seem now to have failed their early promise—a phenomenon that haunts the modern American theater—and their considerable prestige in their time is thought today to have been somewhat inflated, a concomitant of the general impoverishment of the American stage in the postwar years.

If American drama from the end of the war through the 1950s is undistinguished except for the posthumous achievements of O'Neill and the early achievements of Williams and Miller, the lesser dramatist William INGE is probably the most representative playwright of the period. His career began promisingly with *Come Back, Little Sheba* (1950) and sustained its momentum through *The Dark at the Top of the Stairs* (1957), but his tone quickly became maudlin and his psychological realism unconvincing. The deficiencies of his plays tend also to be the deficiencies of such dramas of the period as Robert Anderson's (b. 1917) *Tea and Sympathy* (1953), Jane BOWLES's *In the Summer House* (1953), William Gibson's (b. 1914) *Two for the See-saw* (1958), Lorraine HANSBERRY's *A Raisin in the Sun* (1959), and Carson McCullers's *The Member of the Wedding* (1950). Love is an all-purpose anodyne in these plays, and, whatever their incidental excellences, they seem now to be naïvely conceived and glibly resolved, testament more to the temper of the Eisenhower era than to the possibilities of theatrical experience.

Off-Broadway theaters produced the most seminal and the most serious work of the 1950s, more in touch than Broadway with such European influences as Antonin ARTAUD's Theater of Cruelty and BECKETT's THEATER OF THE ABSURD, more interested than Broadway in mime and gesture, and more exploratory of silence and fantasy. Robert Hivnor's (b. 1916) *The Ticklish Acrobat* (1954) is a distinguished representative of what Off-Broadway was achieving at its best. Notably, O'Neill's *The Iceman Cometh*, Williams's *Summer and Smoke* (1948), and Miller's *The Crucible* received their first successful productions Off-Broadway during the 1950s, and as a result, Off-Broadway achieved a legitimacy in the 1950s that rivaled and finally surpassed Broadway's among serious theatergoers. But Off-Broadway was gradually infected with the ideal of commercial success, and by the end of the decade its productions were too often comparable to Broadway's in kind if not in scale. The most notable exception to this end-of-the-decade decline was the 1959 production of Jack Gelber's (b. 1932) *The Connection* by the aggressively independent Living Theatre group—a production now renowned for gaining acceptance for the use of antiillusionist technique on the American stage.

The first major dramatist to bring some of the vitality of the experimental theater to Broadway was Edward ALBEE. Even Off-Broadway theaters at first rejected his early, absurdist plays, and Albee had to look for his first productions to the avant-garde theaters of West Germany. But the Off-Broadway Provincetown Playhouse produced *The Zoo Story* in 1960, and Albee was soon established on Broadway as the most important American dramatist of the decade, especially admired for his realistic dramas *Who's Afraid of Virginia Woolf?* (1962) and *A Delicate Balance* (1966). Yet, like O'Neill, Williams, and Miller before him, Albee has gained a reputation that exceeds his achievement. His sense of theatricality is finely tuned, assuredly, but all of his work is quite derivative, and his later work has a moral and psychological sophistication not much greater than that of ordinary Broadway fare. A number of dramatists who never made Albee's move to Broadway also did serious and important work during the decade, although they have not earned Albee's reputation and do not have his sense of form. Jack Richardson's (b. 1935) *Xmas in Las Vegas* (1965) and Arthur Kopit's (b. 1937) *Indians* (1969) are dramaturgically impressive, for instance, and Arnold Weinstein's (b. 1927) *Red Eye of Love* (1961), Murry Schisgal's (b. 1926) *Luv* (1963), Amiri Baraka's *Dutchman* (1964), and William Hanley's (b. 1931) *Slow Dance on the Killing Ground* (1964) are worthy of note.

The lessening difference between Broadway and Off-Broadway productions gave rise during the 1960s to a new noncommercial alternative, variously labeled the new, the underground, and the Off-Off-Broadway theater, which established itself in New York City lofts, churches, and coffee houses. At the same time, regional theaters with resident companies in Washington, Dallas, New Haven, Minneapolis, Louisville, and other cities began to take on new significance and prestige as it became clear that Broadway was essentially a purveyor of conventional, pretested goods, and that the drama had to find its life elsewhere. Off-Off-Broadway dramatists such as Sam SHEPARD began to build substantial reputations on plays that found their way into print without the imprimatur of a Broadway production, and works such as Preston Jones's (1936–1979) *A Texas Trilogy* (1974) have survived negligible New York runs on the basis of regional productions.

The American theater in the 1970s, consequently, is less monolithic than ever before, with a broad range of techniques and a broad base of operation, and these factors make impossible, as yet, the discernment of its major character. There was a vogue at the turn of the decade for performances by theater collectives in which the writer's script was placed on a par with improvisations by the cast—an outgrowth of the "happenings" of the 1960s—and this vogue gave rise to such productions as Jean-Claude Van Itallie's

(b. 1936) *The Serpent* (1969), to the Performance Group's *Dionysus in 69* (1970), and to the Living Theatre's *Paradise Now* (1971). There has also been an allied, antirealism effort to transcend the limitations of sequential plots, coherent personae, and overt themes. Thus, discontinuous actions, cartoonlike characters, nondiscursive, sometimes incantatory language, and the selfconscious exposure of drama's inner workings have typified, to varying degrees, the work of Jules Feiffer (b. 1929), David MAMET, David RABE, Sam Shepard, Megan Terry (b. 1932), and Lanford WILSON. Sam Shepard has been particularly influential in his use of figures from popular culture to suggest a context that substitutes for illusionary settings, most impressively so in *Geography of a Horse Dreamer* (1974). Shepard, David Mamet (*American Buffalo*, 1975) and David Rabe (*Streamers*, 1976) stand out as the most consistently serious, productive, and successful American dramatists of the decade.

The antirealism of noncommercial drama in the 1970s affected the surface and not the substance of American plays, however: in the tradition that runs from *Long Day's Journey into Night* through *Death of a Salesman* to *Who's Afraid of Virginia Woolf?* most postwar drama continues to be situated in a kind of domestic courtroom, with attendant arraignments, investigations, condemnations, and punishments, and to play out the moral, generational, and essentially bourgeois obsessions of American life.

Criticism and Other Prose

From the end of World War II through the 1950s American literary theory was dominated by the New Criticism, a formalist movement that stressed the explication of literary texts and the detailed analysis of literature's language and structures while disdaining all interest in auctorial biography and readerly influence. Cleanth BROOKS's *The Well Wrought Urn* (1947) and W. K. Wimsatt's (1907–1975) *The Verbal Icon* (1954) are important texts of the movement, but its most impressive text is René WELLEK and Austin Warren's (1899-1986) *Theory of Literature* (1949), a judicious and learned construction of a total literary theory within the confines of a New Critical bias. In general, the New Criticism tended to harden rapidly into a set of narrow dogmas, but a group of scholars at the University of Chicago during the 1940s and the early 1950s broadened its scope considerably by incorporating into it their interest in neo-Aristotelianism. Led by R. S. Crane (1886–1967) and anthologized in his influential *Critics and Criticism, Ancient and Modern* (1952), they reintroduced notions of plot, action, and character into literary discussion, and they ultimately prepared the ground for Wayne C. Booth's (b. 1921) *The Rhetoric of Fiction* (1961), a work of incalculable influence in subsequent theorizing about narrative. The New Critical impulse lives on in the work of Susan SONTAG and others, who continue to argue the strict priority of form over content even while denigrating the value of explication.

A number of distinguished critics remained cool to the New Critical passions, of course, notably M. H. Abrams (b. 1912), Kenneth Burke, R. P. BLACKMUR, Leslie FIEDLER, Irving HOWE, and—probably the greatest American critics of the age—Lionel TRILLING and Edmund WILSON. But the most direct challenge to the New Criticism has come from a gathering of scholars at Yale University: Harold BLOOM, Geoffrey H. Hartman (b. 1929), and J. Hillis Miller (b. 1928); they do not really make up a school, but they share an esteem for European criticism, a proclivity for terminology, and a tendency to view the work of art in a tense relationship with other works of art rather than in New Critical isolation. Bloom's theory of poetic influence, elaborated in *The Anxiety of Influence* (1973) and *A Map of Misreading* (1975), is particularly insistent that the individual work of art is not the closed system it was thought to be by the New Critics, and his theory dominated literary discussion in the mid-1970s.

Literary biography has enjoyed something of a renaissance upon the decline of the New Criticism, Leon Edel's (1907–1997) five-volume *Henry James* (1953–72) being the most prestigious of many fine studies in the genre. General cultural studies have also been noteworthy, particularly Henry Nash Smith's (1906-1986) *Virgin Land* (1950), R. W. B. Lewis's (b. 1917) *The American Adam* (1955), Loren Baritz's (b. 1928) *City on a Hill* (1964), and Leo Marx's (b. 1919) *The Machine in the Garden* (1964)

BIBLIOGRAPHY: Quinn, A. H., *A History of the American Drama from the Civil War to the Present Day*, rev. ed. (1936); Matthiessen, F. O., *American Renaissance* (1941); Kazin, A., *On Native Grounds: An Interpretation of Modern American Prose Literature* (1942); Gregory, H., and Zaturenska, M., *A History of American Poetry: 1900–1940* (1946); Bogan, L., *Achievement in American Poetry: 1900–1950* (1951); Feidelson, C., *Symbolism and American Literature* (1953); Spiller, R. E., *The Cycle of American Literature: An Essay in Historical Criticism* (1955); West, R. B., *The Short Story in America* (1956); Chase, R., *The American Novel and Its Tradition* (1957); Hewitt, B. W., *Theatre, U.S.A., 1668–1957* (1959); Hoffman, D., *Form and Fable in American Fiction* (1961); Pearce, R. H., *The Continuity of American Poetry* (1961); Weales, G., *American Drama since World War II* (1962); Spiller, R. E., Thorp, W., Johnson, T, and Canby, H. S., *Literary History of the United States*, 3rd ed., rev. (1963); Straumann, H., *American Literature in the Twentieth Century*, 3rd ed. (1963); Donoghue, D., *Connoisseurs of Chaos: Ideas of Order in Modern American Poetry* (1965); Tanner, T., *The Reign of Wonder: Naivety and Reality in American Literature* (1965); Poirier, R., *A World Elsewhere* (1966); Gottfried, M., *A Theater Divided: The Postwar American Stage* (1967); Rosenthal, M. L., *The New Poets: American and British Poetry since World War II* (1967): 1–192; Waggoner, H. H., *American Poets from the Puritans to the Present* (1968); Klein, M., ed., *The American Novel since World War II* (1969); Tanner, T., *City of Words: American Fiction 1950–1970* (1971); Jones, H. M., and Ludwig, R. W., *Guide to American Literature and Its Background since 1890*, 4th ed. (1972); Tuttleton, J. W., *The Novel of Manners in America* (1972); Hassan, I., *Contemporary American Literature, 1945–1972: An Introduction* (1973); Kazin, A., *Bright Book of Life: American Novelists and Storytellers from Hemingway to Mailer* (1973); Hoffman, D., ed., *Harvard Guide to Contemporary American Writing* (1979); Vendler, H., *Part of Nature, Part of Us: Modern American Poets*(1980)

—ROBERT F. KIERNAN

American Literature since 1980

The period since 1980 has seen a general retreat in American literature from the surrealistic and confessional modes of expression that dominated new writing during the late 1960s and early 1970s. The retreat was due in part to a natural flux of taste, inasmuch as periods of extreme style tend to engender a reactionary taste for tradition. Probably the retreat was due also to a habitual

conservatism of Americans that reasserted itself as the disenchantments of the Vietnam period began to fade from consciousness. The 1970s esteem for arcane gamesmanship in fiction, for extraordinary doses of candor in poetry, and for confrontation in the theater came gradually to seem excessive, even manic. In their place came revivals of narrative realism, poetic formalism, and naturalistic dramaturgy. Postmodernism has not disappeared from the literary scene, assuredly, but its more obvious vaunts have suffered diminished prestige.

Fiction

Among the most notable writers of the period have been four novelists of long-standing reputation and established achievement: Saul Bellow, John Updike, Gore Vidal, and Philip Roth. A 1976 Nobel laureate, Bellow has continued to enjoy a reputation for intellectually formidable and densely textured novels, but by 1980 his best work was behind him. *The Dean's December* (1982) received a mixed reception, and the story collection *Him with His Foot in His Mouth* (1984), the novel *More Die of Heartbreak* (1987), and three novellas, *The Bellarosa Connection* (1989), *Theft* (1989), and *The Actual* (1997) failed to engender wide enthusiasm. In contrast, John Updike has continued to stimulate the literary scene with texts rich in seriocomic drama. He pleased his readers especially with *Rabbit Is Rich* (1981), *The Witches of Eastwick* (1984), and *Rabbit at Rest* (1990), the latter announced as the last in a series of four Harry "Rabbit" Angstrom novels. Less critically and commercially successful than these were the novels *Roger's Version* (1986), *Memories of the Ford Administration* (1992), *Brazil* (1994), and *In the Beauty of the Lilies* (1996). Gore Vidal has such divergent impulses as a novelist that the occasional clunker seems inevitable, but satiric misfires such as *Duluth* (1983) and *Live from Golgotha* (1992) are redeemed by novels such as *Lincoln* (1984), *Empire* (1987), and *Hollywood* (1990), three richly detailed and typically iconoclastic novels in Vidal's ongoing "American Chronicle" series. The generational Jewish conflict that is Philip Roth's distinctive subject is increasingly compounded with his negotiation of an elusive balance between life and art, notably in a sequence of novels linked by an autobiographical protagonist named Nathan Zuckerman: *The Ghost Writer* (1979), *Zuckerman Unbound* (1981), *The Anatomy Lesson* (1983), and *The Counterlife* (1986), the first three of these brought together in the omnibus *Zuckerman Bound* (1985). Roth has persevered with negotiating this balance in the novels *Deception* (1990), *Operation Shylock* (1993), *Sabbath's Theater* (1995), and *American Pastoral* (1997), in several of which characters named "Philip Roth" figure prominently.

This cluster of established novelists was augmented by a number of other writers whose achievements in the period brought to a kind of fulfillment the promise of earlier work, among them Reynolds Price, Peter Taylor, Don DELILLO, Anne TYLER, Ann BEATTIE, Larry MCMURTRY, and Toni Morrison. Price has climaxed a long and distinguished career of writing about the North Carolina up-country with a number of fine novels, among them the comically compelling *Kate Vaiden* (1986) and the tenderly bittersweet *The Tongues of Angels* (1990). Price is fond of the dynastic sweep and has several times resuscitated his characters. In *Good Hearts* (1988) he returned to the Mayfield-Hutchins clan of *The Surface of the Earth* (1975), concluding a "Great Circle" trilogy. Peter Taylor's achievement was similar as he crowned forty years of short stories with the collection *Oracle at Stoneleigh Court* (1993) and with two novels so technically adroit that they might be employed as textbooks of novelistic method: *A Summons to Memphis* (1986) and *In the Tennessee Country* (1994). Don DeLillo cemented a gathering reputation for hard-edged, rather chilling fictions with *White Noise* (1985), *Libra* (1988), and *Mao II* (1991). With equal force, Anne Tyler nailed down her reputation as a master of the crisply written comedy of manners in a series of novels, among them *Dinner at the Homesick Restaurant* (1982), *Saint Maybe* (1991), and *Ladder of Years* (1995). *The Accidental Tourist* (1985) remains her most engaging work. Ann Beattie is as interested as Tyler in the vagaries of human experience and her reputation for lyrical, deeply felt novels grows apace with Tyler's, notably in *Picturing Will* (1990) and *My Life, Starring Dara Falcon* (1997). In an uneven, sometimes ribald series of fictions about the American West, Larry McMurtry has been engaged in a revisionist mythologizing of that region, loosely akin to what Faulkner did for Mississippi. *Lonesome Dove* (1985), the epic tale of a Texas cattle drive, is his best work to date; *Streets of Laredo* (1993), a sequel, and *Dead Man's Walk* (1995), a prequel, fail its high standard. In *Beloved* (1987), which won her a Pulitzer Prize, Toni Morrison has written an assured masterpiece: an awesomely imagined and brutally powerful chronicle of slavery and its aftermath in rural Ohio several years after the Civil War. *Beloved* overshadows Morrison's *Tar Baby* (1981) and *Jazz* (1992), as it overshadows most novels of the period.

Several reputations declined somewhat in the period since 1980. Norman Mailer's attempts at genre fiction in novels like *Ancient Evenings* (1983), *Harlot's Ghost* (1991), and *The Gospel According to the Son* (1997) did little to buttress his once-substantial reputation. Similarly, Ishmael Reed's *The Terrible Threes* (1989) and *Japanese Spring* (1993) contributed to a consensus that the 1970s had overrated his screwball humor.

The postmodern impulse proved durable and especially successful in a number of novels that were based upon elegant, historical conceits. Among such novels are Carol De Chellis Hill's (b. 1942) *Henry James' Midnight Song* (1993), an intellectually complex work that compounds fiction and history in *fin de siècle* Europe; Lawrence Norfolk's (b. 1963) *Lemprière's Dictionary* (1993), set in the late 18th c.; and Cathleen Schine's (b. 1953) *Rameau's Niece* (1993), which manages to be at once an 18th-c. didactic tale and a parody of postmodern fiction. But postmodern fiction generally ceased in the 1980s to enjoy the critical deference that it received in the late 1960s and 1970s. John Hawkes's *Adventures in the Alaskan Skin Trade* (1985), Robert Coover's *Pinocchio in Venice* (1991) and *Briar Rose* (1997), Paul Auster's (b. 1947) New York trilogy, made up of *City of Glass* (1985), *Ghosts* (1986), and *The Locked Room* (1987), Gilbert Sorrentino's (b. 1929) *Rose Theatre* (1987), Ronald Sukenick's (b. 1932) *Blown Away* (1986), and James McCourt's (b. 1941) *Time Remaining* (1993) found critical respect but only limited audiences, not just because they are inherently difficult works of literature, but because their self-reflexive conceits and multidimensional nonlinear combination of fantasy, joke, and (sometimes) horror seemed to some readers a throwback to the intellectual temper of the early 1970s.

Indeed, any number of literary reputations declined in the period because novelists who had established themselves in the 1970s continued to write in an aggressively postmodern, self-consciously textual mode that had come to seem passé. The ponderous jocosity and outside scale of John Barth in *The Tidewater Tales* (1988) and *The Last Voyage of Somebody the Sailor* (1991) was generally found unreadable. Kurt Vonnegut, Jr.'s *Galapagos* (1985), *Bluebeard* (1987), and *Hocus Pocus* (1990) are

as funny as anything Vonnegut published between 1967 and 1976, but they proved ideationally and stylistically too much of that period to have found again the audience he once enjoyed. William Gaddis's trademark concern with authenticity and phoniness in *Carpenter's Gothic* (1985) and *A Frolic of His Own* (1994) came to seem an elephantine obsession, no longer relevant to the American experience as did Thomas Pynchon's concern with conspiracy-theory in *Vineland* (1990) and *Mason & Dixon* (1997). Other writers who seemed locked in the 1960s and 1970s mode of extravagance and whose reputations have declined markedly include Joseph Heller and John Irving. Heller's *God Knows* (1984), *Picture This* (1988), and *Closing Time* (1994) failed the standard of his blackly comic masterpiece, *Catch-22*. John Irving's *A Prayer for Owen Meany* (1989) recaptured some of the seductive extravagance of *The World According to Garp*, but *The Hotel New Hampshire* (1981), *The Cider House Rules* (1985), and *A Son of the Circus* (1994) proved comparatively leaden. Under the rubric of "Cyberpunk," science-fiction writers such as William Gibson (b. 1948) and Kathy Acker (1948-1997) continue to explore multiple technologies of reference and to imagine fertile relations between the text and all of the nondiscursive apparatuses that contextualize it.

Several novelists of the middle rank with distinctive but not distinctively postmodern signatures have enjoyed more stable reputations than the postmodern novelists, notably Louis Auchincloss, Joyce Carol Oates, E. L. Doctorow, and Cormac McCarthy. Among these novelists of the middle rank in America, no one has given that rank more distinction than Auchincloss. In novels like *Diary of a Yuppie* (1986) and *The Lady of Situations* (1990) and in the story collection *False Gods* (1992), his thirty-fourth work of fiction, he has continued to take the ethical pulse of WASP America with elegant, underappreciated art. Oates is less reliable than Auchincloss in her craft. In *You Must Remember This* (1987) she broke with the overwrought gothicism that had preoccupied her in such novels as *Bellefleur* (1980), *Foxfire* (1993), and *Zombie* (1995). Even when Oates's taste for gothicism is under narrative control, her fictions bear the impress of hasty, uncontrolled writing. E. L. Doctorow lays more successful claim than Oates to seriousness of craft, but his distinctive compound of historical and fictional characters in novels like *Billy Bathgate* (1989) and *The Waterworks* (1994) has come to seem a gimmick that limits him to mid-rank achievement. Cormac McCarthy, on the other hand, seems poised to break out of mid-rank achievement. In two volumes of a projected trilogy, *All the Pretty Horses* (1992) and *The Crossing* (1994), he has written darkly beautiful novels about a youthful hero who leaves Texas to work in Mexico.

A galaxy of relatively new writers has invigorated American fiction since 1980 by nudging it toward realism and away from the postmodern, surrealistic novels that dominated the late 1960s and 1970s. No writers led the way more clearly in this regard than those associated in the 1980s with what was then termed "hick chick": Louise ERDRICH, whose novels *Love Medicine* (1984) and *The Beet Queen* (1986) give life to the people of North Dakota; Carolyn Chute (b. 1947), whose extraordinary novels *The Beans of Egypt, Maine* (1985), *Letourneau's Used Auto Parts* (1988), and *Merry Men* (1994) deal with poverty, squalor, and sometimes hilarious violence in the tarpaper towns of the Northeast; Jayne Anne Phillips (b. 1952) whose novel *Machine Dreams* (1984) gives voice to assorted down-and-outers; Bobbie Ann MASON, whose *In Country* (1985) is a pitch-perfect novel of rural Kentucky; John Casey (b. 1939), whose toweringly beautiful *Spartina* (1989) plumbs unromantically the life of a Rhode Island fisherman.

Writers interested in the experience of marginality have come increasingly to the fore of literary consciousness since 1980, and they have tended to subsume the "hick chick" writers of the 1980s. With psychological, sometimes gritty realism, they explore ethnic, sexual, economic, and cultural aspects of the marginal experience. Such novels range widely in their focus—from Alice McDermott's (b. 1953) hauntingly eloquent novel *That Night* (1987), which is about adolescent confusions in 1960s suburbia, to Chang-Rae Lee's (b. 1946) sophisticated first novel, *Native Speaker* (1995), which deals with the Korean American experience of assimilation. No one built a major reputation more suddenly in that regard than William KENNEDY, the success of whose *Ironweed* (1983) was followed by the successful reprinting in 1983 of *Legs* (1975) and *Billy Phelan's Greatest Game* (1978). The three novels comprised briefly a so-called "Albany Trilogy," since expanded into an ongoing "Albany Cycle" with *Quinn's Book* (1988), *Very Old Bones* (1992), and *The Flaming Corsage* (1996).

Women writers were an especially impressive presence in this area of fiction, both statistically and qualitatively. Mary Gordon (b. 1949) wrote compellingly of Irish-American women's experience in *The Company of Women* (1980), *Men and Angels* (1985), and *The Rest of Life* (1993). Alice WALKER wrote of two black sisters facing terrible burdens of awareness in an epistolary novel entitled *The Color Purple* (1982), and Gloria NAYLOR wrote compellingly of the plight of black women in novels such as *The Women of Brewster Place* (1982) and *Bailey's Cafe* (1992). The American acculturation of Chinese immigrants was explored by Gish Jen (b. 1956), by Amy Tan (b. 1952), and by Fae Myenne Ng (b. 1957)—Jen, in *Typical American* (1991) and *Mona in the Promised Land* (1997); Tan, in *The Joy Luck Club* (1989) and *The Kitchen God's Wife* (1991); Ng, in a first novel about assimilation entitled *Bone* (1993). Leslie Marmon SILKO wrote about the deracination of Native American culture in *Almanac of the Dead* (1992); Harriet Doerr (b. 1910), about American expatriates in Mexico in *Consider This, Señora* (1993); and E. Annie Proulx (b. 1935), about unsophisticated Newfoundlanders in *The Shipping News* (1993). Among the most interesting expressions of gay and lesbian experience were Dale Peck's (b. 1967) nightmarish *Martin and John* (1993); Mark O'Donnell's (b. 1954) witty *Getting Over Homer* (1996); Blanche McCrary Boyd's (b. 1945) extraordinary *The Revolution of Little Girls* (1991); and Dorothy Allison's much-admired *Bastard Out of Carolina* (1993).

Fiction by Southern writers tends to be a part of this revival of realism, notably so in novels like James Wilcox's (b. 1949) *Sort of Rich* (1989), John Ed Bradley's (b. 1959) *Tupelo Nights* (1988), Padgett Powell's (b. 1952) *Edisto* (1984), and Allan Gurganus's (b. 1947) richly idiomatic, vastly ample *The Oldest Living Confederate Widow Tells All* (1989). Of particular distinction among such new-South works of realism are once again a number of works by women: Josephine Humphrey's (b. 1945) *Rich in Love* (1987) and *The Fireman's Fair* (1991); Gail Godwin's (b. 1937) *A Southern Family* (1987); Mary Lee Settle's (b. 1918) quintet about the West Virginia coal country, brought to completion with *The Killing Ground* (1982); Lee SMITH's *Oral History* (1983), *Fair and Tender Ladies* (1988), and *The Devil's Dream* (1992); Ellen GILCHRIST's *The Anna Papers* (1988); Jill McCorkle's (b. 1958) *Tending to Virginia* (1987) and *Ferris Beach* (1990); Robb Foreman Dew's (b. 1946) *Fortunate Lives* (1992); and Susan Straight's (b. 1960) extraordinarily powerful *I Been in Sorrow's Kitchen and I Licked Out All the Pots* (1992).

Since the mid-1980s, a group of mostly young writers has commandeered the reputation for insouciant up-to-datedness that the metafictionists once enjoyed. A number of these writers were voguishly identified as a "brat pack" in the 1980s, but they are not otherwise identifiable as a school. Among them are Madison Smart Bell (b. 1957), Jay McInerney (b. 1955), David Leavitt (b. 1961), Mary Gaitskill (b. 1954), Tama Janowitz (b. 1957), Bret Easton Ellis (b. 1964), Jill Eisenstadt (b. 1963), Richard FORD, T. Coraghessan BOYLE, Ron Hansen (b. 1947), and Rick Moody (b. 1961). The group's most accomplished publications to date are Bell's *A Soldier's Joy* (1989), Leavitt's *Family Dancing* (1984), *The Lost Language of Cranes* (1986), and *While England Slept* (1993; rev. ed. 1995), Boyle's *World's End* (1987) and *East Is East* (1990), Eisenstadt's *From Rockaway* (1987), McInerney's *Brightness Falls* (1992), and Moody's *Purple America* (1997).

A surprising development in American fiction since 1980 has been the proliferation of collections of short stories, a proliferation due in large part to a new interest in their publication by university and small presses. Story collections from the large, commercial presses tend still to favor the enigmatic minimalism endorsed by the influential *New Yorker* magazine, as in Mark STRAND's *Mr. and Mrs. Baby* (1985) and Frederick BARTHELME's *Natural Selection* (1990). Diversity and plurality are everywhere else the hallmarks of this short-story renaissance. Among the many well-remarked collections of the period are T. Coraghessan Boyle's *If the River Was Whiskey* (1989); Harold Brodkey's (1930-1996) *Stories in an Almost Classical Mode* (1988); Raymond CARVER's *What We Talk About When We Talk About Love* (1981), *Cathedral* (1983), and *Where I'm Calling From* (1988); Richard Ford's *Rock Springs* (1987); Ellen Gilchrist's *Victory Over Japan* (1984); Amy Hempel's (b. 1951) *Reasons to Live* (1985); Peter Matthiessen's (b. 1927) *Midnight Turning Gray* (1984); Lorrie Moore's (b. 1957) *Like Life* (1990); Mary Morris's (b. 1947) *The Bus of Dreams* (1985); John Edgar WIDERMAN's *Philadelphia Fire* (1990); and Tobias WOLFF's *In the Garden of the North American Martyrs* (1981) and *The Night in Question* (1996). Among the impressive *Collected Stories* were volumes by Grace Paley, Reynolds Price, Bruce Jay Friedman, and William Maxwell (b. 1908).

Poetry

There has been much talk since 1980 of a poetry renaissance in America, the talk inspired largely by an increase in the publication of poetry by small and university presses. Volumes of selected and collected poems from established writers have been especially plentiful. Anne Sexton was memorialized in a *Complete Poems* in 1981, and Robert Creeley amassed thirty years of verses for a *Collected Poems* in 1982. The years since then have seen volumes of selected or collected poems from such important figures as A. R. Ammons, John Asherby, Marvin Bell (b. 1937), Hayden Carruth (b. 1921), Donald Hall (b. 1928), Anthony HECHT, John Hollander, David IGNATOW, Carolyn KIZER, Stanley Kunitz, Gregory Orr (b. 1947), Robert Pinsky (b. 1940), Adrienne Rich, Charles Simic (b. 1938), W. D. Snodgrass (b. 1927), James TATE, Mona Van Duyn (b. 1921), and Richard Wilbur. Few of these collections proffered definitive overviews, however. Allen Ginsberg was enshrouded in 1984 in a massive *Collected Poems,* but that apparent summation of his oeuvre did not preclude a *New and Selected Poems* the very next year. In many ways the publication of selected or collected poems has become a *pro tempore* event; except in a few cases, it no longer signals the summation of a career.

Indeed, unexpected shifts of direction and startling achievements of poetic maturity have in many instances followed upon the publication of such collections. In *Sweet Will* (1985) Philip LEVINE moved beyond the scathing social pronouncements that typified his earlier *Selected Poems* (1984) to a poetry of resignation and pity; in *Axe Handles* (1983), Gary Snyder avoided the angry abstractions of his earlier poems and seemed, abruptly, a man who had discovered peace; and in feminist poems of *Yin* (1984) and *The Nearness of You* (1986) Carolyn Kizer markedly softened the rhetoric of her collected poems in *Mermaids in the Basement: Poems for Women* (1984). In a wholly unforeseen development, John Ashbery moved away from the clotted overpacked lines that were a Whitmanesque feature of his work to publish in collections like *A Wave* (1984), *April Galleons* (1987), and *Flow Chart* (1991), relatively straightforward poems that seem effortless in their growth. In a contrary drift A. R. Ammons brought to startling maturity a style that evokes not only Whitman's aesthetic of inclusion but Dickinson's sudden turns of abstraction and elliptical grammar. His *Sumerian Vistas* (1987) is especially distinguished in this regard—a collection as evocatively American as it is aesthetically bewitching.

Other established poets have written importantly without notably changing course. In the fine poems of *Mirrors* (1983) and *Memory Gardens* (1986) Robert Creeley continues to eschew symbolism, as he has for his whole career; in *A Few Days* (1985), James Schuyler manifests the taut, sharp-eyed inventiveness that one had come to expect from him; and in *The One Day* (1988), Donald Hall evokes landscapes with his distinctive particularity, grace, and melancholy. In the lovely *In Time and Place* (1986), John Hollander continues to be wholly high cultural—a resolute champion of the canonical modes of poetry; in *An Oregon Message* (1987), William Stafford creates once again his unlikely combinations of precise form and ineffable content; and in *The Continuous Life* (1990), Mark Strand pursues the elusive concord between words and wordlessness that has long preoccupied him.

No one has brought more distinction to American poetry in the period since 1980 than James Merrill and W. S. Merwin. Merrill's final collections *Late Settings* (1985), *The Inner Room* (1988), and *A Scattering of Salts* (1995) evidenced anew the exquisitely nuanced grace and technical dexterity of which he was a master, but the great achievement of his maturity was a quite different work, *The Changing Light at Sandover* (1982). Under that title he assembled the previously scattered parts of a 560-page poem that records his half-playful, half-serious experiments in communications with the spirit world. Although *Sandover* is in many ways a work of camp humor, the poem raises and attempts to resolve such important questions about visionary experience that it positions itself unmistakably in the tradition of Dante, Wordsworth, and Blake. It is arguably the most important long poem of recent decades. Of the many poets who turned inward in the 1960s, Merwin was the most successful in rendering images that floated freely in psychological space, and since the 1970s he has been equally successful in moving fluidly from the visionary to the phenomenal and partway back again. Indeed, the poems in magisterial collections like *Opening the Hand* (1983) and *The Rain in the Trees* (1988) seem to be located in fissures of consciousness, dream, and memory. A poet of prodigious competence, Merwin gives equal distinction to a series of sturdily written verse-tales in *Travels* (1993).

For several decades the preoccupation of American poetry has been the creation of a so-called "authentic" voice, which is to say, a voice that successfully conveys intimacy, sincerity, and a commitment to explorations of the self. More than any other poet, Robert Bly formulated that voice in his 1962 collection *Silence in the Snowy Fields,* and a legion of American poets continues to emulate the tasks Bly set himself. In their view, the inflated, rhetorical language of the modernists was an evasion of the self; thus, they tend to favor content rather than form, honest subjectivity rather than fictive personae, and simplicity of syntax rather than elegant interdynamics of texture and sound. Among the recent American poets who bring distinction to the authentic voice are C. K. Williams (b. 1936), Ellen Bryant Voigt (b. 1943), Tess Gallagher (b. 1943), Mary OLIVER, and Mary Jo SALTER. For some years now, and especially in *Flesh and Blood* (1987), Williams has been writing in long, capacious lines that suit his capaciousness of spirit; Voigt has manifested in *The Forces of Plenty* (1983) and in *The Lotus Flowers* a style that is successfully intimate and flexible; and Gallagher, in her *Amplitude: New and Selected Poems* (1987), has demonstrated a fine ability with anecdotal poems that are decorous only on their surface. Mary Oliver, who won a Pulitzer Prize in 1983 for *American Primitive* and a National Book Award in 1992 for her *New and Selected Poems*, is one of the purest lyricists writing today. And Mary Jo Salter is Oliver's equal. In two collections to date, *Henry Purcell in Japan* (1985) and *Unfinished Painting* (1989), she has proven herself an extraordinarily graceful and even exquisite lyricist.

But currents of discontent with the authentic voice have been discernible in the period since 1980. It is indicative of that discontent that one of the most talked-about texts in the period in Vikram SETH's *The Golden Gate* (1986), a novel-poem in intricate rhyme and meter that chronicles the lives and crises of a group of San Francisco Yuppies. Seth's poem is a striking instance of the so-called New Narrative, a school of poetry that rejects the free-verse spontaneity and prevailing lyricism of contemporary American poetry and finds relief in traditional modes of craftsmanship. The New Narrative poets have much in common with the so-called New Formalist poets. Amy Clampitt (1920-1994) was the acknowledged leader of the New Formalist, and she gowned her poems in academic learning and traditional craftsmanship in such collections as *What the Light Was Like* (1985), *Archaic Figure* (1987), and *A Silence Opens* (1994). Gjertrud Schnackenberg (b. 1953) is also interesting as New Formalist, although her poems in *The Lamplit Answer* (1985) are so carefully studied and insistently referential that they might have been excised from T. S. Eliot's *The Waste Land* (1922). The three poetic sequences of *A Gilded Lapse of Time* (1922) are darker and more visionary than her earlier work. A more interesting New Formalist than either Clampitt or Schnackenberg is Marilyn Hacker (b.1942), who seems to work exclusively in such traditional forms as sestinas, sonnets, and ballads, but with a lightness and irony of which Clampitt and Schnackenberg seem incapable.

"Expansive Poetry" became a loose, umbrella term in the 1980s for the output of the New Narrative and New Formalist poets, and, indeed, all poets who found common ground with those schools in their objections to the perceived narrowness of theme, range, and context in the authentic-voice poets. Those generally associated with Expansive Poetry include Brad Leithauser (b. 1953), Dana Gioia (b. 1950), Frederick Turner (b. 1943), Timothy Steele (b. 1948), Charles Martin (b. 1942), and sometimes Rita DOVE. Also opposed to the authentic voice poets is a group loosely termed by some the "Language-Centered Poets." These poets are troubled by a realization that all poetic stances are linguistic or social constructions, but, even so, they experience a need to mean and to speak. Ultimately, they tend to discover an ungrounded, electrically-charged space for poetry in the interstices and insufficiencies of language. Poets recently associated with this school include John Ashbery, Charles Bernstein (b. 1950), Robert Duncan, Jorie GRAHAM, Robert HASS, Lyn Hejinian (b. 1941), Ron Silliman (b. 1946), and C. K. Williams.

If the currents of discontent that have come together under the "Expansive" and "Language-Centered" banners agitate the poetic scene, they fail as yet to disrupt a flow of influence from the established American poets to their temporal successors. To that extent, the period since 1980 has lacked the discontinuities in tradition that are the hallmark of an authentic renaissance. Talented poets like Dana Gioia and Susan Ludvigson (b. 1942) seem in many ways to filter Robert Bly's influence through the immediate influence of Mark Strand; W. S. Merwin might claim a disciple in David St. John (b. 1949); James Merrill, in Pamela Alexander (b. 1948) and Alfred Corn (b. 1943). The influence of Wallace Stevens is everywhere evident, notably so in the work of J. D. McClatchy (b. 1945), Pattiann Rogers (b. 1940), and George Bradley (b. 1953). Indeed, in a volume entitled *Terms To Be Met* (1986) Bradley makes clear that he has learned a great deal not only from Stevens but from those whom Stevens taught. Thus, he mimics without apology John Ashbery's plangent tone, John Hollander's intellectual allusiveness, and Richard Howard's apostrophes. For better or worse, such respectful continuities define the present situation of American poetry.

Drama

The runaway economics of Broadway in recent decades has engendered a notable caution regarding the production of untested work—to the extent that the great majority of the plays that have reached Broadway since 1980 were revivals or pretested successes that had their origins either Off-Broadway, in London's West End, or in the American regional theaters. New musicals such as *Kiss of the Spider Woman* (1993) and *Bring in da Noise, Bring in da Funk* (1995) and revived musicals such as *Most Happy Fella* (1956) and *Chicago* (1975) were increasingly favored on Broadway as it became virtually impossible for nonmusical theater to return a profit to investors. In an attempt to counter such harsh economics, labor, management, and creative artists agreed to work at less than their usual salaries under the rubric of "The Broadway Alliance," an organization formed in 1990 to stage worthy, but fiscally unpromising plays in three underused Broadway theaters. Steve Tesich's (1943-1996) *The Speed of Darkness* (1989) was the first offering of the Alliance. The 1995 offering, Terrence MCNALLY's *Love! Valour! Compassion!* (1994), earned back its capitalization after only six weeks on Broadway.

Although less subject than Broadway to the economic risks of original presentation, theaters located elsewhere tended to share Broadway's conservatism and consequently to favor the presentation of realistic plays already established as stageworthy. Indeed, there was a clear preference everywhere for works sweet-tempered and nonthreatening. The confrontational dynamics and expressionistic staging of the preceding decades survived in scattered productions and in the work of militantly experimental companies like Richard Foreman's (b.1937) Ontological-Hysteric Theatre, but the general conservatism of the American Stage was conspicuous. No

manifestoes or movements dynamized the scene as they did in the 1960s and 1970s.

In such a climate, even *eminence grises* failed to command Broadway stages. Arthur Miller's *Danger: Memory!* (1987) and *The Ride Down Mt. Morgan* (1991) succeeded abroad, but not with American audiences, and *Broken Glass* (1994), Miller's first Broadway play in more than ten years, survived there for only ten weeks. Edward Albee's *The Man Who Had Three Arms* (1982), *Marriage Play* (1987), and *Fragments* (1993) were all produced elsewhere than Broadway, and even *Three Tall Women* (1991) failed to commandeer a Broadway stage, although it is arguably Albee's most impressive work since *Who's Afraid of Virginia Woolf?* (1962). Younger playwrights like Lanford Wilson and David Mamet tended to dominate Broadway in the stead of the old masters, but even they could not command Broadway houses as a matter of course. Wilson is widely thought to have emerged as Broadway's most satisfying dramatist, especially in a series of linked plays that includes *5th of July* (1978), *Talley's Folly* (1979) and *Talley & Son* (1985). Mamet's assured masterpiece is *American Buffalo* (1978), probably the most important American play of the 1970s, but a play like *Glengarry Glen Ross* (1983) is comparably energized, its rhythms of scatologic dialogue raised almost to the level of poetry. Mamet's *Speed-the-Plow* (1981) was trivialized on Broadway by the notoriety of its leading lady and became known as "The Madonna play"—a trivialization that seems to have provoked Arthur Kopit to write *Road to Nirvana* (1990), which is about a producer willing to sacrifice anything for film-rights to the biography of a Madonna-like performer. On the basis of his wisecracking comedies, Neil Simon (b. 1927) has not generally been considered a serious playwright, but in an autobiographical trilogy composed of *Brighton Beach Memoirs* (1982), *Biloxi Blues* (1984), and *Broadway Bound* (1986), and in the darker, more tonally ambitious *Lost in Yonkers* (1991), he created a stageworthy mix of nostalgia and cynicism that has gained him a new respect. In a further mining of autobiographical materials, Simon recreated his years of writing material for the comedian Sid Caesar in *Laughter on the 23rd Floor* (1993). David Rabe's and Terrence McNally's statuses on Broadway were somewhat complicated by the casting of their plays. Rabe's *Hurlyburly* (1985) is a minor work more esteemed than it would otherwise have been for having been cast with movie stars, and McNally's *The Rink* (1985) is a sturdy drama whose reception was probably less than it should have been because of excessively glamorous casting. His *Master Class* (1995) succeeded on Broadway both as theater and as a star-vehicle. Rabe and McNally tended to develop their most interesting work for non-Broadway theaters: Rabe with *Those with the River Keeps* (1993) and *A Question of Mercy* (1997), McNally in *Frankie and Johnny in the Clair de Lune* (1987), *The Libson Traviata* (1989), *Lips Together, Teeth Apart* (1991) and *A Perfect Ganesh* (1993).

Important newcomers, one or more of whose plays have received Broadway imprimatur, include A. R. GURNEY, Jr., Tina Howe (b. 1937), David Henry Hwang (b. 1957), Wendy WASSERSTEIN, and Beth Henley (b. 1952). Gurney is the author of an engaging stream of plays, many of which evoke affectionately the world of WASP America in the 1930s and 1940s, among them *The Dining Room* (1982), *The Cocktail Hour* (1988), and *The Old Boy* (1991). Howe came to attention with two delicately imaginative plays entitled *Painting Churches* (1983) and *Coastal Disturbances* (1986), in comparison with which her later plays *Approaching Zanibar* (1989) and *One Shoe Off* (1993) seem thin. Hwang is best known for the sturdy and elegantly implicational *M. Butterfly* (1988), which bears out the promise of his earlier, more evanescent dramas. After a considerable success Off-Broadway with *Uncommon Women and Others* (1977) and a modest success with *Isn't It Romantic?* (1983), Wasserstein came to Broadway in 1989 with *The Heidi Chronicles* (1984) and deservedly won almost every theatrical prize of the year. With subsequent productions of *The Sisters Rosensweig* (1992) and *An American Daughter* (1997), she has become something of a media celebrity. Henley had a substantial success on Broadway in 1981 with *Crimes of the Heart* (1979), a very funny play about three sisters living in Mississippi in 1974, and an equal success Off-Broadway with *The Miss Firecracker Contest* (1980), a delightful comedy about Southern oddballs. In *The Lucky Spot* (1986) she assembled an assortment of waifs, strays, and misfits for an uproarious celebration of Christmas 1934 in the first taxi-dance hall in Pigeon, Louisiana. A certain vogue for such Southern plays was discernible, although not always with characters of Henley's madcap sort. A more genial ambience was achieved by Robert Harling (b. 1951) in *Steel Magnolias* (1987) and by Alfred Uhry (b. 1936) in *Driving Miss Daisy* (1987) and *The Last Night at Ballyhoo* (1997).

No theatrical newcomer electrified the years since 1980 like Tony KUSHNER, whose extravagant *Angels in America,* subtitled "A Gay Fantasia on National Themes," arrived on Broadway in 1993 via earlier productions in London and Los Angeles. In two parts, staged independently as *Millenium Approaches* (1991) and *Perestroika* (1992), the work was widely perceived to suggest a rebirth of serious American theater—a rebirth, at least, of serious dramaturgy. Kushner is certainly a dramaturge adept at quick, flashing scenes, rapid-fire wit, and a reckless wisdom of the heart. *Angels in America* alternates three stories: one about AIDS-crossed gay lovers, another about a Mormon couple whose marriage is troubled by the husband's awakening homosexuality, and still another about Roy Cohn, dying of AIDS, while extravagantly denying his sexual orientation. The human fallout of the AIDS epidemic was a major theatrical subject of the period. Among the plays that took measure of the fallout were Cheryl L. West's (dates n.a.) *Before It Hits Home* (1989), Paul Vogel's (b. 1951) *The Baltimore Waltz* (1992), Scott McPherson's (1959-1992) *Marvin's Room* (1990), Paul Rudnick's (b. 1957) *Jeffrey* (1993), and Steven Dietz's (b. 1958) *Lonely Planet* (1995).

The major American playwright since 1980 and probably for a decade before that is Sam Shepard, who has resisted offering his work to Broadway theaters in his stated preference for the less-commercial theaters of Off-Broadway. Shepard's early plays were characterized by expressionistic staging and folkloric themes, but with *Curse of the Starving Class* (1978) and *Buried Child* (1978) he began to explore through a more naturalistic dramaturgy the subject of family relationships, especially the estrangements of fathers and sons. *True West* (1980), *Fool for Love* (1983), and *A Lie of the Mind* (1985) are further installments in that apparently autobiographical exploration, and they are works that clearly establish Shepard as the most prestigious and theatrically exciting American playwright of his generation. In *States of Shock* (1991), he takes his subject another step and renders the estrangement of fathers and sons in political terms, suggesting that war is an institution used to validate the compulsion of fathers to sacrifice their sons.

Like Shephard, a number of dramatists who build their reputations in the confrontational theater of the 1960s and 1970s have continued to write for the Off- and Off-Off-Broadway theater while participating in a perceptible drift of that theater back to the linear plots, coherent personae and explicable themes that it once spurned as Broadway pablum. Israel Horovitz (b. 1939) charmed audiences greatly with a trilogy of such plays based on Morley Ferlog's memoirs of a Jewish-Canadian youth, *Today I Am a Fountain Pen* (1986) being the best of them. And John GUARE charmed his audiences with the unabashed melodrama of three such installments in a projected tetralogy that proceeds backwards in time from the turn of the century: *Lydie Breeze* (1982), *Gardenia* (1982), and *Women and Water* (1985). More typical of Guare's work, however, is the antic *Six Degrees of Separation* (1990). Realism redivivus was especially influential in the work of August WILSON, who brings such integrity to the writing of his plays about the African-American experience that they are thought emblematic of what is best in the recent Off-Broadway theater. Especially esteemed among Wilson's plays are *Fences* (1985), *The Piano Lesson* (1987), and *Two Trains Running* (1990), which are installments in a projected ten-play cycle that is well on the way to completion.

Significant new dramatists on the Off- and Off-Off-Broadway scene include John Patrick Shanley (b. 1951), the author of what he calls an "emotionally connected" tetralogy that began with *Danny and the Deep Blue Sea* (1984) and concluded with *Italian American Reconciliation* (1989); Marsha Norman (b. 1947), the author of a nicely mordant play entitled *'night, Mother* (1983); Harvey Fierstein (b. 1954), the author of the vital and funny *Torch Song Trilogy* (1981); Richard Greenberg (b. 1959), whose *Eastern Standard* (1989) is as notable for its romantic sophistication as for its subversive punch; Jane Wagner (b. 1935), the author of a witty, one-woman play called *The Search for Signs of Intelligent Life in the Universe* (1986); and Nicky Silver (dates n.a.), whose considerable success Off-Broadway with *The Food Chain* (1996) revived interest in his earlier plays *Pterodactyls* (1993) and *Fat Men in Skirts* (1991).

It is arguable, however, that the most vital wellsprings of American drama since 1980 are no longer to be found Off- and Off-Off-Broadway, but in regional theaters. Companies in Louisville, San Francisco, Washington, Dallas, Chicago, Philadelphia, Minneapolis, and Los Angeles began to develop national prominence in the 1960s, and they have continued to flourish despite potentially ruinous cutbacks in funding. The number of such nonprofit, professional companies now exceeds four hundred nationwide, and only a small percentage of them are based in New York City. Concomitant with such growth, regional theaters have become a significant supplier of the Broadway and Off-Broadway theaters—a supplier, even, of intact productions. It was the American National Theater in Washington, for instance, that gave Broadway one of its most distinguished productions of the period, a 1985 revival of *The Iceman Cometh* (1946) that united the actor Jason Robards and the director Jose Quintero in a reprise of their legendary 1956 collaboration. Major Broadway successes of the period that originated in regional theaters include Mark Medoff's (b. 1940) *Children of a Lesser God* (1980) which had its genesis at the Mark Taper Forum in Los Angeles; John Pielmeier's (b. 1949) *Agnes of God* (1980), which traveled to New York from the Actor's Theater of Louisville, and August Wilson's *Ma Rainey's Black Bottom* (1984), which was first staged by Yale Repertory. Significantly, Robert Schenkkan's (dates n.a.) *The Kentucky Cycle* (1991) won the 1992 Pulitzer Prize in drama without the imprimatur of a New York production—the first play ever to do so.

BIBLIOGRAPHY: Klinkowitz J., *Literary Subversions: New American Fiction and the Practice of Criticism* (1985); Mernit, S., "The State of the Short Story," *VQR*, 62, 2 (1986): 302-11; McCaffrey, L., "The Fictions of the Present," in Elliott, E., et al., eds., *Columbia Literary History of the United States* (1988): 1161-77; Austin, A., "The Present State of Black Theater," *TDR*, 32, 3 (1988): 85-100; Feirstein, F., ed., *Expansive Poetry: Essays on the New Narrative and the New Formalism* (1989); McClatchy, J. D., *White Paper: On Contemporary American Poetry* (1989); Clarke, G., ed., *The New American Writing: Essays on American Literature since 1970* (1990); Pinsker, S., *Bearing the Bad News: Contemporary American Literature and Culture* (1990); Kostelanetz, R., ed., *American Writing Today* (1991); Vendler, H., *Soul Says: On Recent Poetry* (1991); Bigsby, C. W. E., *Modern American Drama: 1945-1990* (1992); Gardner, T., "American Poetry of the 1980s: An Introduction," *CL*, 33, 2 (1992): 712-35; Clayton, J., *The Pleasures of Babel: Contemporary American Literature and Theory* (1993); Kiernan, R., "The New Southern Novel: A Biographical Essay," *IdD*, 30, 2 (1993): 13-27; Saltzman, A., *The Novel in the Balance* (1993); Bellamy, D., *Literary Luxuries: American Writing on the End of the Millenium* (1995); Tabbi, J., *Postmodern Sublime: Technology and American Writing from Mailer to Cyberpunk* (1995)

—ROBERT F. KIERNAN

AMHARIC LITERATURE

See Ethiopian Literature

AMICHAI, Yehudah

Israeli poet, short-story writer, novelist, b. 3 May 1924, Würzburg, Germany

After emigrating to Palestine from Germany in 1936, A.'s parents settled in Jerusalem, where the poet received a religious education and later attended the Hebrew University. He fought in the Jewish Brigade of the British army during World War II and then served in the Palmach (the "striking division" of the Jewish defense forces) during the Israeli war of independence (1947–49). He now lives in Jerusalem, where he teaches secondary school and usually spends a few weeks a year lecturing and reading his poems abroad.

A. is primarily a love poet, concerned with examining the inner consciousness of a somewhat autobiographical persona whose love embraces women, family, city, nation, language, and mankind in general, with simultaneous gusto and ambivalence. His best lyrics individualize emotion with concrete objects, places, and ideas, which achieve symbolic significance through abstraction and general context. A.'s poems reflect his reading of RILKE and AUDEN and have been compared to the verse of 17th-c. metaphysical poets such as John Donne. His early volumes have been collected and expanded in *Shirim: 1948–1962* (1962; rev. ed., 1977; poems 1948–1962), which includes his "Haelegiah al hayeled sheavad" ("Elegy for a Lost Boy," 1969). This longer poem, and "Masot Binyamin haacharon miTudelah" ("Travels of a Latter-Day Benjamin of Tudelah," 1977), which appeared in *Achshav baraash: Shirim 1963–1968* (1968; now in the noise: poems 1963–1968)

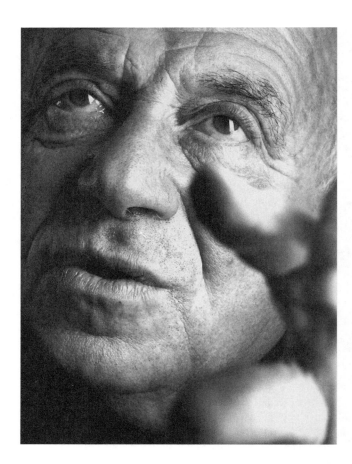

Yehudah Amichai

provide illustrations of his most characteristic techniques. Although explicit sexuality and decreasing interest in rhyme characterize A.'s work of the 1970s, his most recent collection, *Shalvah gdolah: Shelot utshuvot* (1980; *Great Tranquillity: Questions and Answers*, 1983), is less erotic and returns occasionally to ballads and rhymed couplets, albeit generally in an ironic manner.

A. has also written two novels, *Lo meachshav, lo mikan* (1963; *Not of This Time, Not of This Place*, 1969) and *Mi yitneni malon* (1971; hotel in the wilderness); a collection of short stories, *Baruach hanoraah hazot* (1961; in this terrible wind); and some radio plays, *Paamonim vrakavot* (1968; bells and trains). His prose extends the poetic techniques of lyric to longer, more fully detailed plots and structures. His short stories are built upon clusters of images which resound on a multitude of spiritual and emotional planes. His novels achieve similar effects with more traditional styles.

A. is generally recognized as one of the most important poets writing in Israel today. He often experiments with language and intertwines seemingly conflicting levels of meaning to strike a synthesis that celebrates an inner unity despite the despair that often emanates from his physical world. Although his control of Hebrew is both wide and deep, he prefers simple, colloquial language to a more pretentious literary vocabulary. This linguistic simplicity is combined with imagistic complexity that is more easily translated than A.'s many allusions to Jewish tradition.

FURTHER WORKS: *Vlo al mnat lizkor* (1971); *Meachore kol zeh mintater osher gadol* (1974; *Amen*, 1978); *Hazman* (1977; *Time*,

1979). **FURTHER WORKS IN ENGLISH:** *Selected Poems* (1971); *Love Poems* (bilingual ed., 1981); *The World Is a Room and Other Stories* (1984); *Songs of Jerusalem* (bilingual ed., 1987); *Selected Poetry* (1988)

BIBLIOGRAPHY: Friend, R., "Y. A.," in Burnshaw, S., ed., *The Modern Hebrew Poem Itself* (1965): 160–67; Sachs, A., "The Poetry of Y. A.," *Judaism*, 14 (1965): 407–13; Alter., R., *After the Tradition* (1969): 250–51; Hamburger, M., Introduction to Y. A., *Selected Poems* (1971): 7–11; Hughes, T., Introduction to Y. A., *Amen* (1977): 9–15; Flinker, N., "Jewish Tradition and the Individual Talent of Y. A.," *UDQ*, 12, 2 (1977): 69–76; Abramson, G., *The Writing of Y. A.* (1989)

—NOAM FLINKER

AMIS, Kingsley

English novelist, poet, and critic, b. 16 April 1922, London; d. 22 Oct. 1995, London

Son of an office worker, A. went to Oxford and, until he became a full-time writer in 1963, taught English at Swansea and Cambridge. His very successful first novel, *Lucky Jim* (1954), put him at the head of the "Angry Young Men." George ORWELL, not the great modernists like JOYCE and WOOLF, was a model of these writers, because he had rebelled against the Establishment, hated

Kingsley Amis

pretentiousness, and faced up to the world around him. Their world was as seedy as his, if less terrifying, and they wanted to describe it exactly.

"A new hero is risen among us," wrote the critic Walter Allen of *Lucky Jim*. An awkward misfit as a history lecturer at a provincial university, Jim Dixon is more comic butt than hero for most of the novel: he falls into one embarrassing and farcical situation after another. Scornful of all that is bogus in the academic racket, he has to mock in private, by means of a wide variety of comic faces and routines. But he is as lucky as his name implies; a hilarious lecture on "Merrie England," in which sherry loosens his tongue, puts an end to his university career, but fortune gives him a new girl friend and a new job in which he can drop pretense. He is no longer a spy in enemy territory.

A thoroughly professional writer, A. has published fifteen other novels since *Lucky Jim*; none of the others has had its humorous appeal. Many of them are variations on a theme, the relations between the sexes, as in *Take a Girl Like You* (1960), a sour comedy of seduction; *Girl, 20* (1971), which sets an aging philanderer, a classical musician, against the trendy, morally imbecilic young; and *Jake's Thing* (1978), whose title speaks for itself. At times, as in *I Want It Now* (1968), A. approaches but does not achieve the satiric force of Evelyn WAUGH. In this novel, whose central character wants "fame and money, with a giant's helping of sex thrown in," A. attacks the assumption of the rich that they should get what they want—and get it immediately. He has undoubtedly tried to broaden and deepen his art; for example, he deals seriously with germ warfare in *The Anti-Death League* (1966) and with the threat of old age and senility in *Ending Up* (1974).

Yet he continues to be accused of philistinism, superficiality, and evasion of the problems he raises. But some critics admire his social realism and moral honesty; they see him as reflecting the drab, pragmatic values of the world around him. A famous passage in *I Like It Here* (1958) shows him taking Henry Fielding for an ancestor—a writer who does not need to be apologized for because he presented the truth unflinchingly.

A. has also written poetry and criticism, including a book on science fiction, *New Maps of Hell* (1960), based on lectures given at Princeton. But he remains predominately a novelist—widely praised for the gusto, realism, and comic inventiveness of his first novel, but never going beyond it to write the comic masterpiece of which he was thought capable.

FURTHER WORKS: *Bright November* (1947); *A Frame of Mind* (1953); *That Uncertain Feeling* (1955); *A Case of Samples: Poems, 1945–1956* (1956); *Socialism and the Intellectuals* (1957); *My Enemy's Enemy* (1962); *The Evans Country* (1963); *One Fat Englishman* (1964); *The James Bond Dossier* (1965); *The Egyptologists* (1965, with Robert Conquest); *A Look Round the Estate: Poems, 1957–1967* (1967); *The Green Man* (1969); *What Became of Jane Austen* (1970); *The Riverside Villas Murder* (1973); *The Alteration* (1976); *Collected Poems, 1944–1979* (1979); *Russian Hide-and-Seek* (1980); *Collected Short Stories* (1980); *The Old Devils* (1987); *Difficulties with Girls* (1987); *The Folks That Live on the Hill* (1990); *Memoirs* (1991)

BIBLIOGRAPHY: Gindin, J., *Postwar British Fiction: New Accents and Attitudes* (1963): 1–13; 34–50; O'Connor, W. V., *The New University Wits and the End of Modernism* (1963): 75–102; Fiedler,

L. A., "British Writing," in Kostelanetz, R., ed., *On Contemporary Literature* (1964): 64–81; Lodge, D., *Language of Fiction* (1966): 243–67; Rabinovitz, R., *The Reaction against Experiment in the English Novel, 1950–1960* (1967): 1–63; Bergonzi, B., *The Situation of the Novel* (1970): 149–79 and passim; Morrison, B., *The Movement* (1980); Gardner, P., *K. A.* (1981); Salwak, D., ed., *K. A. in Life and Letters* (1990); Moseley, M., *Understanding K. A.* (1993); Jacobs, E., *K. A.: A Biography* (1995)

—D. J. DOOLEY

AMIS, Martin

English novelist and essayist, b. 25 Aug. 1949, Oxford

A. is the son of writer Kingsley AMIS, who was singled out by poet Philip LARKIN as one of Britain's "angry young men." Educated at Oxford, the younger A. received a double-first in English, then followed in his father's tradition of satirical writing. Early on he realized that the grotesque would be his specialty, especially that characterizing the London metropolitan scene. Attributing his fascination with transgression and viciousness not only to London itself but also to a stay in the U.S., which he visited for almost a year when he was twelve, in his novels A. treats lust and violence as they are exhibited in adolescent sex, drug use, communal living, bisexuality, and incest.

Many American readers first became aware of A. when he accused an American writer of plagiarizing whole scenes from his first novel, *The Rachel Papers* (1973), a work that details with brutal frankness the activities of a young man who seduces a faceless woman called Rachel, only to become almost immediately disillusioned with her. Treating Rachel merely in terms of how she appears to the protagonist, *The Rachel Papers* hints at the misogynous direction in which A. is to move in novels that depict women either as crudely anti-intellectual or sapping male strength with their vulnerability and sexual passivity.

A.'s novels also attack another aspect of British life, the British class system. In his 1978 novel, *Success*, for example, he describes the adventures of two mismatched stepbrothers, one a highrolling upper-class snob and the other a pitiable lower-class punk. Their social positions are reversed when the lower-class brother becomes successful by allying himself to union leaders while his upper-class counterpart vainly casts his fate with a failing art gallery. *Success* also records what reviewer Marla Levy calls "the breakdown in communication between people and their brutality toward each other." In fact, miscommunication and brutality seem the only options in the materialistic world that A. writes about, one in which his characters have no culture to draw on.

All of his works reveal A. as a highly self-conscious artist. For example, he is often present in his works as a narrator indulging in furious word-play, exploiting language as one of the few means of time-travel available in the claustrophobic environment that presses in on his characters. In some works, though, such as *Money: A Suicide Note* (1984) and *The Information* (1995), the narrator melts into other characters or disappears entirely in novels that offer a less satirical and more compassionate exploration. In *Money*, for example, although the hero is tellingly named John Self and is shown ruthlessly grappling his way to a lucrative position in

moviedom, for all the vulgarity of his need for money, sex, and success, audiences discern in Self an unaccountable charm.

At other times, like Harold PINTER in *Betrayal* and Vladimir NABOKOV in *Look at the Harlequins*, A. demonstrates his innovativeness by playing with the formal conventions of fiction, especially time. In *Time's Arrow* (1991), for example, A. starts with the hero's death and works back through his life to his birth. As Maya Slater comments, in a technique that forces readers to become proofreaders, in this backwards world, it is as though we had pressed the backwards button on a video recorder: flowers are reattached to plants, rain is sucked up into clouds and earthquake rubble forms back into perfect buildings. As already implied, A. is also fascinated by doubles and doubling. In *The Information* he seems to use doubling in the same way as Joseph CONRAD—to cater to two audiences. The larger audience is addicted to immediate information, wishful thinking and sensual gratification. It finds solace in the work of the protagonist, writer Gwyn Barry. The audience interested in struggle and exploration, on the other hand, enjoys the work of antagonist Richard Tull. In making their separate appeals, both authors alike, in their own ways, are doomed. A. seems to indicate that in order to be read an author must be like Conrad and cater to both types of audience in a single work.

Clearly, A. finds in the U.S. that the majority audience rules. In his book of essays, *The Moronic Inferno* (1986), he notes that America is ruled by sadists and that Americans are vulnerable to authoritarianism and escapism. These features he discovers in events like Sunny Von Bulow's alleged murder by her husband (the son of a convicted Nazi collaborator) as well as in the ascendancy of Jerry Falwell, the egomania of Elvis Presley, the utopianism of Gloria Steinem, and the general contempt of America for its poor. About the only thing he finds to admire about the U.S. is writer Saul BELLOW, whose long career he credits with reminding readers that "being human isn't the automatic condition of every human being" but "a gift, a talent, an accomplishment."

While he has been accused of anti-Americanism, A. claims that America is just a metaphor for what he finds wrong with the planet, asserting that England and America are anyway bound too closely by culture and language to be considered any longer as separate entities. As for the doomsday pessimism he has sometimes been charged with, his answer is that good novels (presumably his own included) through their carefully-balanced structure always offer a "complicated pessimism, or a qualified pessimism," rather than one that is "unadorned." That is, since he makes disturbing perceptions—what he calls "euphonious"—in book after book, A. is able to celebrate life with a forceful, crackling, savagely hilarious prose. Through this combination of heightened perception and controlled craft, then, the position of A. in literature seems assured.

FURTHER WORKS: *Dead Babies* (1975); *Other People* (1981); *Invasion of the Space Invaders* (1982); *Einstein's Monsters* (1987); *London Fields* (1989); *Visiting Mrs. Nabokov and Other Excursions* (1993); *Night Train* (1997)

BIBLIOGRAPHY: Bower, B., "M. A. on America," *NewC*, 5 Feb. 1987: 20-26; Diedrick, J., *Understanding M. A.* (1995); Miller, K., "M. A.," in *Doubles: Studies in Literary History* (1985): 105-98; Slater, M., "Problems When Time Moves Backward: M. A.'s *Time's Arrow,*" *English*, 42 (Summer 1993): 141-52

—SUSAN TETLOW HARRINGTON

AMMONS, A(rchibald) R(andolph)

American poet, b. 18 Feb. 1926, Whiteville, North Carolina

A. was reared on a farm in southeastern North Carolina. After serving in the navy during World War II, he studied biology and chemistry at Wake Forest College; much of his poetry reflects an interest in science. A. worked briefly as principal of a three-teacher school at Cape Hatteras, studied English for three semesters at the University of California at Berkeley, then worked twelve years for a New Jersey laboratory glass company. His first book, *Ommateum* (1955), named for the compound eye of an insect, was almost completely ignored. His second, *Expressions of Sea Level* (1964), won positive reviews, and that year he began a distinguished career teaching poetry writing at Cornell University.

A. is one of the most stylistically distinctive poets writing today. He writes free verse that, like that of William Carlos WILLIAMS, combines complex sentences with unexpected line breaks, thus adding an interesting tension to the poem's momentum down the page. What is most identifiable about A.'s style, however, is his use of colons, which he almost always substitutes for terminal punctuation marks. This unusual practice underscores his belief in the relatedness of all things, including ideas: one thought leads to another, which leads to another, and so on. Periods come only at the end of the poem, when they come at all.

A. sees a world forever in process. He is fascinated with the notion of economy, the interplay of many independent variables within a larger system. In his early work, gathered in his National Book Award-winning *Collected Poems* (1972), he often considers what he calls the "one:many problem," the need to find a balance between unity and diversity. A. celebrates the constituent parts that the idea of wholeness tends to obscure. "Corsons Inlet," one of his best-known poems, meditates on the balance of part and whole in terms of a shoreline ecology; he celebrates his inability to grasp this system totally, since that inability allows him the joy of perpetual discovery. Another poem, "One:Many," extends his interest in the dynamic between part and whole to politics and the money economy. In his Bollingen Prize-winning long poem *Sphere: The Form of a Motion* (1974), A. argues that an interest in the "one:many problem" is only natural for a poet whose country's motto is *E pluribus unum.*

Sphere is the third of A.'s five book-length poems. The first, *Tape for the Turn of the Year* (1965), is a verse diary he wrote on adding-machine tape, the width of which determined the poem's margins. *The Snow Poems* (1977), one long poem despite its plural title, exhibits a capriciousness that annoyed A.'s friendliest readers; he has nevertheless judged it his favorite among his long poems. *Garbage* (1993), inspired by a huge mound of refuse A. spotted from Interstate 95, repeated the tape-writing experiment of *Tape for the Turn of the Year* and won him his second National Book Award. In *Glare* (1997) A. tries to affirm the meaningfulness of human life, but he tends to be more convincing in his acknowledgment of evidence to the contrary. Both *Garbage* and *Glare* dwell much on the poet's struggles with old age. A. has also written a number of long but not book-length poems, five of which can be found in his *Selected Longer Poems* (1980).

In addition to long works, A. has written a number of very short poems; one of the briefest and best is the four-line, aptly titled "Small Song." He has even written monostiches (one-line poems), such as "Coward" and "The Story." Most of his minimalist efforts are collected in *The Really Short Poems of A. R. A.* (1990).

With over two dozen books to his name, A. is one of our most prolific poets. He has been criticized for that, and his poetry is indeed marked by a certain unevenness. On the other hand, his own claim to have written only a few extraordinary poems is far too modest. Despite his misgivings about poetry as a subject for academic study, his work has attracted considerable attention from academic critics. On the whole, A. is one of the best American poets of his generation, and probably the single most intellectually engaging.

FURTHER WORKS: *Corsons Inlet* (1965); *Northfield Poems* (1966); *Uplands* (1970); *Briefings* (1971); *Diversifications* (1975); *Highgate Road* (1977); *A Coast of Trees* (1981); *Worldly Hopes* (1982); *Lake Effect Country* (1983); *The Selected Poems: Expanded Edition* (1986); *Sumerian Vistas* (1987); *The North Carolina Poems* (1994); *Set in Motion: Essays, Interviews, and Dialogues* (1996); *Brink Road* (1996)

BIBLIOGRAPHY: Holder, A., *A. R. A.* (1978); Bloom, H., ed., *A. R. A.* (1986); Schneider, S., *A. R. A. and the Poetics of Widening Scope* (1994); Schneider, S., *Critical Essays on A. R. A.* (1997); Kirschten, R., *Approaching Prayer: Ritual and the Shape of Myth in A. R. A. and James Dickey* (1998)

—ROBERT WEST

AMORIM, Enrique

Uruguayan novelist, short-story writer, and poet, b. 25 July 1900, Salto; d. 28 July 1960, Salto

Although an Uruguayan by birth, A. was educated in Argentina, where most of his novels were published and where he was a regular contributor to the newspaper *La prensa*. He traveled extensively through Europe, the U.S., and Latin America, but he spent the later years of his life in his native Salto on the banks of the Uruguay River.

A. achieved early recognition with his creation of the figure of the *quitandera*, the itinerant harlot of his second novel, *La carreta* (1932; the wagon). In two other novels of his first cycle, *El paisano Aguilar* (1934; the farmer Aguilar) and *El caballo y su sombra* (1941; *The Horse and His Shadow*, 1943), A. developed his concept of the social, economic, and spiritual plight of the gaucho of the River Plate region. *El caballo y su sombra* is a violent social commentary on the conflict between the traditional landowners and a group of immigrants from Italy. In its theme and development it is not unlike the traditional 19th-c. realistic novel.

In later years A. wrote many novels with an urban setting. These demonstrated leftist political tendencies, which he espoused during the time of World War II, and also during the Perón dictatorship in Argentina. *Corral abierto* (1956; open corral) is a dismal picture of the decay of urban life in an industrial society. His posthumously published novel *Eva Burgos* (1960; Eva Burgos), is critical of the fate society has dealt the protagonist, a twenty-five-year-old convict who is about to leave prison for a bleak and uncertain future.

Toward the end of his life A. resumed his early interest in poetry, but his later novels never achieved the lucidity and perspicacity of the novels of the first cycle, which in their simplicity are eloquent statements about man and the boundless plains that surround him.

FURTHER WORKS: *Veinte años* (1920); *Amorim* (1923); *Tangarupá* (1925); *Horizontes y bocacalles* (1926); *Tráfico* (1927); *La trampa del pajonal* (1928); *Visitas al cielo* (1929); *Del 1 al 6* (1932); *Cinco poemas uruguayos* (1935); *Presentación de Buenos Aires* (1936); *La plaza de las carretas* (1937); *Historias de amor* (1938); *La edad despareja* (1938); *Dos poemas* (1940); *Cuaderno salteño* (1942); *La luna se hizo con agua* (1944); *El asesino desvelado* (1945); *Juan C. Castagnino* (1945); *Nueve lunas sobre Neuquén* (1946); *Primero de mayo* (1949); *La segunda sangre* (1950); *Feria de farsantes* (1952); *La victoria no viene sola* (1952); *Después del temporal* (1953); *Quiero* (1954); *Sonetos de amor en octubre* (1954); *Todo puede suceder* (1955); *Los montaraces* (1957); *Don Juan 38* (1958); *La desembocadura* (1958); *Mi patria* (1960); *Los pájaros y los hombres* (1960); *Temas de amor* (1960)

BIBLIOGRAPHY: Ortiz, A., *Las novelas de E. A.* (1949); Oberhelman, H. D., "Contemporary Uruguay as Seen in A.'s First Cycle," *Hispania*, 46 (1963): 312–18; Englekirk, J., and Ramos, M., *La narrativa uruguaya* (1967): 107–12; Benedetti, M., *Literatura uruguaya siglo XX* (1969): 77–82; López, B., *En torno a E. A.* (1970); Mose, K., *E. A.: The Passion of a Uruguayan* (1972); Brushwood, J., *The Spanish American Novel: A Twentieth-Century Survey* (1975): 114–15; 142–44; Mose, K. E. A. *E. A.: The Passion* (1973); Miranda Buranelli, A., ed., *E. A.* (1990)

—HARLEY D. OBERHELMAN

ANAND, Mulk Raj

Indian novelist, short-story writer, and art critic (writing in English), b. 12 Dec. 1905, Peshawar

Educated at the University of Punjab, Amritsar, and at University College, London, A. began his literary career in England in 1929 by writing short notes on books for T. S. ELIOT's *Criterion*. In 1930 he published *Persian Painting* (a study of Persian paintings from 200 A.D. to the present time), and followed it up with such diverse books as *Curries and Other Indian Dishes* (1932) and *The Hindu View of Art* (1933). But it was not until the publication of his first two novels, *Untouchable* (1935) and *Coolie* (1936), that he won recognition. He returned to India in 1945, and has since made Bombay his home and center of activity. He edits the fine-arts magazine *Marg* and takes a vital interest in India's literary and cultural life. Writing is still his main occupation, and he is working on *Seven Ages of Man*, a seven-volume autobiographical novel.

A prolific writer, A.'s novels show a passionate concern for the underdog in India. *Untouchable* deals with the fate of a sweeper lad, *Coolie* with a young boy reduced to work as a beast of burden, *Two Leaves and a Bud* (1937) with an uprooted field laborer, and the famous trilogy *The Village* (1939), *Across the Block Waters* (1940), and *The Sword and the Sickle* (1942) with a sturdy peasant lad fighting a losing battle against the dictates of a hidebound society. In his novels the enemies of the poor are clearly discernible: they are traditional Hinduism, capitalism, and foreign domination. A. has been accused of writing propaganda, but he is no facile propagandist; he is what George ORWELL was, an expositor, a political novelist, one who sees his characters and their actions in relation to the social, economic, and political upheavals of his time.

A.'s most impressive work is *Private Life of an Indian Prince* (1951). On the one hand the novel highlights the major social

concerns that characterize his earlier fiction; on the other, it goes beyond them to give us a rare insight into the human psyche. Here, for the first time in A.'s works, we have a character from the higher echelon of society who retains our sympathy, even though the order he represents is firmly condemned.

A. is one of the best known contemporary Indian novelists, and his reputation is secure. In technique, he was among the first writers to render Punjabi and Hindustani idioms into English; in subject matter, he was the first to give a realistic and sympathetic portrayal of India's struggling masses.

FURTHER WORKS: *The Golden Breath: Studies in Five Poets of the New India* (1933); *The Lost Child and Other Stories* (1934); *Lament on the Death of a Master of the Arts* (1938); *Marx and Engels on India* (1939); *Letters on India* (1942); *The Barber's Trade Union, and Other Stories* (1944); *The Big Heart* (1945); *Apology for Heroism* (1946); *Homage to Tagore* (1946); *Indian Fairy Tales* (retold by M.R.A.; 1946); *The Tractor and the Corn Goddess, and Other Stories* (1947); *The Bride's Book of Beauty* (1947); *On Education* (1947); *The King-Emperor's English* (1948); *The Story of India* (1948); *Lines Written to an Indian Air* (1949); *The Indian Theatre* (1950); *Seven Summers* (1951); *Reflections on the Golden Bed and Other Stories* (1954); *Selected Stories* (1954); *The Story of Man* (1954); *The Dancing Foot* (1957); *India in Colour* (1958); *Kama Kala* (1958); *The Power of Darkness, and Other Stories* (1959); *Aesop's Fables* (retold by M. R. A.; 1960); *The Old Woman and the Cow* (1960); *The Road* (1961); *More Indian Fairy Tales* (retold by M. R. A.; 1961); *Homage to Khajuraho* (1962); *Is There a Contemporary Indian Civilization?* (1963); *Death of a Hero* (1963); *The Story of Chacha Nehru* (1965); *Lajwanti and Other Stories* (1966); *The Volcano* (1967); *Morning Face* (1968); *Roots and Flowers* (1972); *Author to Critic: The Letters of Mulk Raj Anand to Saros Cowasjee* (1973); *Between Tears and Laughter* (1973); *Folk Tales of Punjab* (1974); *Confession of a Lover* (1976); *Seven Little Known Birds of the Inner Eye* (1978)

BIBLIOGRAPHY: Lindsay, J., *The Elephant and the Lotus: A Study of the Novels of M. R. A.* (1965); Naik, M. K., *M. R. A.* (1968); Berry, M., *M. R. A.: The Man and the Novelist* (1971); Gupta, G. S. Balarama, *M. R. A.: A Study of His Fiction in Human Perspective* (1974); Cowasjee, S., *Coolie: An Assessment* (1976); Cowasjee, S., *So Many Freedoms: A Study of the Major Fiction of M. R. A.* (1977); Niven, A., *The Yoke of Pity: A Study in the Fictional Writings of M. R. A.* (1978); Packham, G., *M. R. A.: A Check-list* (1979); Fisher, M., *The Wisdom of the Heart: A Study of the Works of M. R. A.* (1985); Rajan, P. K., *M. R. A.: A Reevaluation* (1994)

—SAROS COWASJEE

ANDAY, Melih Cevdet

Turkish poet, novelist, essayist, dramatist, and translator, b. 1915, Istanbul

A. briefly attended law school at the University of Ankara and took courses in sociology in Belgium (1937–38). He then worked as a consultant for the ministry of education, as an administrator of the library in Ankara, and as editor at the Istanbul daily *Akşam*.

From 1954 to 1978 he taught dramatic literature at the Istanbul City Conservatory. He also served for a time as a member of the executive board of the Turkish radio and television administration. In 1971 UNESCO honored A. by naming him "one of the prominent figures of world literature." From 1979 to 1980 he served as Turkey's education counselor in Paris.

In 1941 A. and two of his close friends—Orhan Veli Kanik (1914–1950) and Oktay Rifat (b. 1914)—burst on the literary scene with a book of poems entitled *Garip* (strange). Against the vehement criticism of the traditionalists, they vowed, in a manifesto included in *Garip*, to revolutionize Turkish poetry. Their objective was "to alter the whole structure from the foundation up. In order to rescue ourselves from the stifling effects of the writings that have dictated and shaped our tastes and judgments for too many years, we must throw overboard everything that those writings have taught us." They proceeded to eliminate traditional meters and verse forms, conventional diction, and stock epithets and metaphors. Their poetry aspired to become "an artless art," designed for the common people.

In his three collections of realistic poems that followed, *Rahatı kaçon ağaç* (1946; the restless tree), *Telgrafhane* (1952; telegraph office), and *Yanyana* (1956; side by side), A. championed the cause of social justice, focusing on the economic plight of the vast majority of the Turkish people. Characterized by angry indictments, scathing satire, and mordant wit, and written in a colloquial style, the poems of these years earned him recognition as "the poet of the little people."

From the late 1950s on, A.'s aesthetics underwent a gradual but extensive metamorphosis. Although he never abandoned his humanism, he evolved from a poet of social criticism to one of intellectual exploration and abstract formulation. His lucid diction remained, but the substance and orientation of his poetry changed radically. His finest achievement of this period is *Kolları bağlı Odiseus* (1962; Odysseus bound), a freely adapted version of the Odysseus myth, the protagonist of which is Everyman. This long poem, in which A. attempted to create a modern universal mythology depicting the mind of alienated man crushed by society, has been acclaimed as a landmark in the reflective poetry of Turkey. A. posits man's reason as the supreme repository of purpose and salvation. Nevertheless, his Odysseus as Everyman never reaches his homeland, but is condemned to live in a kind of suspension, surrounded by inner suffering and outer chaos.

A.'s first novel, *Aylaklar* (1965; the loafers), which spans the lives of four generations of a family, advocates a life style based on ethical responsibility while demonstrating the obsoleteness of the traditional hierarchial social structure. Leman Hanim, the grandmother and center of a family who enjoyed great social esteem during the Ottoman sultanate, believes herself to be the preserver of tradition and refuses to allow the members of her family to change their life style. In an eighteen-room villa in Erenköy, once a fashionable section of Istanbul, the family has long been living beyond their means, indulging the fantasies of past affluence, and closing their eyes to the reality of the present. Ever-increasing indebtedness finally leads to their inevitable downfall and eviction from the villa.

A.'s translations include works by Molière, Poe, and Gogol, as well as by Tarjei VESAAS, AUDEN, and Wallace STEVENS, among others. His own works have been translated into Russian, Romanian, German, Hungarian, French, and English.

A.'s collected poetry, *Sözcökler* (words) was published 1978 and received the Simavi Poetry Prize, one of the largest cash awards in Turkey, given annually by the leading daily newspaper *Hürriyet*.

FURTHER WORKS: *Doğu-batı* (1961); *Konuşarak* (1964); *İçerdekiler* (1965); *Gelişen komedya* (1965); *Gezi notları* (1965); *Mikado'nun, çöpleri* (1967); *Göçebe denizin üstünde* (1970); *Gizli emir* (1970); *Dört oyun* (1972); *Yeni tanrılar* (1974). **FURTHER WORKS IN ENGLISH:** *On the Nomad Sea: Selected Poems of M. C. A.* (1974); *Rain One Step Away: Selected Poems of M. C. A.* (1980)

BIBLIOGRAPHY: Halman, T. S., on *Kolları bağlı Odiseus, BA*, 39 (1965): 109–10; Halman, T. S., Introduction to *On the Nomad Sea: Selected Poems of M. C. A.* (1974):5-10

—TALAT SAIT HALMAN

ANDERSCH, Alfred

German novelist, essayist, poet, and radio dramatist, b. 4 Feb. 1914, Munich; d. 21 Feb. 1980, Berzona, Switzerland

A. came from a conservative officer's family but turned leftist under the stress of economic misery during his youth. His political detention after the Nazi takeover, military service during World War II, and ensuing captivity as a prisoner-of-war in the U.S. marked his formative years and sharpened his sense of individual responsibility in public affairs.

A.'s literary work grew out of the personal and political events of his life. With H. W. Richter (b. 1908), coeditor of the progressive postwar journal *Der Ruf* (1946–47), he acted as spokesman for Germany's young generation returning from the war in continuing the classical role of the German writer as a critic and teacher of public morals. He also helped to shape the early course of the literary Group 47, for which he tried to win an audience through his own programming for the German radio network. Critical of excessive conservatism in the reestablished political and social institutions of his country, he emphasized the need for freedom as the basis of social life. This attitude brought him into frequent opposition to established public opinion, and he decided to take up permanent residence in Switzerland in the early 1960s.

His first book, *Die Kirschen der Freiheit* (1952; freedom's cherries), is an account of his desertion from the German army in Italy as the war drew to a dose, reflecting his inner struggle and final assertion of selfhood. The novel *Sansibar; oder, Der letzte Grund* (1957; *Flight to Afar*, 1958), which relates the temptation felt by a young boy to follow the group of refugees from Nazi Germany he is ferrying to freedom across the Baltic in his fishing boat, has autobiographical elements. It launched A. on a literary career in which moral concern, formal experimentation, and poetic inspiration were in turn the motivating forces.

A.'s interest in formal experimentation is illustrated by an early collection of ten narrative sketches, *Geister und Leute* (1958; *In the Night of the Giraffe, and Other Stories*, 1964), which are concerned primarily with social or existential problems of individuals. His second novel, *Die Rote* (1960; *The Redhead*, 1961), an elaboration of the disengagement motif as a symbol of the moment of absolute freedom, of that "tiny fraction of a second preceding the second of decision," is a full-scale study of the individual human condition.

Efraim (1967; *Efraim's Book*, 1970) was A.'s next attempt to fuse recent history, social criticism, and literary experiment into a long novel. As the title figure—an uprooted Jewish emigrant from Germany—narrates his personal misfortunes of frustrated sexual relations and increasing disenchantment with his life as a journalist, he regains a precarious balance of mind through the act of telling his story, turning himself into a novelist.

Despite the novel-within-a-novel structure, *Efraim* is a diffuse and ambiguous mixture of realistic detail and an improbable series of characters and events. Some of these weaknesses are overcome in *Winterspelt* (1974; Winterspelt), which presents an imagined attempt of a major in the German army in 1944 to surrender his unit to the Allies. *Winterspelt* once again shows A.'s fascination with the implications of moral decisions. Since the plan of surrender is finally abandoned, the book is reduced to a collage of documents, reflections, and scenes of private encounter, with some of the ring of authenticity that had made *Sansibar* an immediate success.

Seldom noted but worthy of mention are A.'s experiments with poetry. His translations of modern American and Italian authors as well as his own terse yet highly sensitive lyrical texts—"slightly rhythmic prose" by his own definition—were collected in the volume *empört euch der himmel ist blau* (1977; rise up in revolt the sky is blue). Like his critical writings, they underscore A.'s fundamental humanist concern with an art that instructs while it delights.

FURTHER WORKS: *Piazza San Gaetano* (1957); *Von Ratten und Evangelisten* (1960); *Der Tod des James Dean: Eine Funkmontage* (1960); *Wanderungen im Norden* (1962); *Ein Liebhaber des Halbschattens* (1963); *Aus einem römischen Winter* (1966); *Hohe Breitengrade, oder Nachrichten von der Grenze* (1969); *Gesammelte Erzählungen* (1971); *Norden, Süden, rechts und links: Von Reisen und Büchern 1951–1971* (1972); *Hörspiele* (1973); *Mein Verschwinden in Providence: Neun neue Erzählungen* (1973); *Öffentlicher Brief an einen sowjetischen Schriftsteller, das Überholte betreffend: Reportagen und Aufsätze* (1977); *Die Blindheit des Kunstwerks: Literarische Essays und Aufsätze* (1979); *Neue Hörspiele* (1979); *Ein neuer Scheiterhaufen für alte Ketzer: Kritiken und Rezensionen* (1979); *Der Vater eines Mörders: Eine Schulgeschichte* (1980)

BIBLIOGRAPHY: Bienek, H., on *The Redhead, SatR*, 19 Aug. 1961: 19; Frankel, H., on *In the Night of the Giraffe, NYTBR*, 15 Nov. 1964: 62; Clements, R. J., on *Ephraim's Book, SatR*, 19 Dec. 1970: 33; Wittmann, L. Z., *A. A.* (1971); Bühlmann, A., *In der Faszination der Freiheit: Eine Untersuchung zur Struktur der Grundthematik im Werk von A. A.* (1973); George, E. F., "Paths of Escape in A, A.'s Works," *OL*, 29 (1974): 160–69

—KURT OPITZ

ANDERSEN, Benny

Danish poet, short-story writer, and dramatist, b. 7 Nov. 1929, Copenhagen

A. came to the fore in 1960 with his first collection of poems entitled *Den musikalske ål* (1960; the musical eel), which was inspired by his occupation as a jazz pianist. Although A.'s experiences as a musician traveling through Scandinavia and to New York are apparent in his work, it is primarily against the background of his native Copenhagen and its surroundings that he portrays his glimpses of the human condition.

In his poems he singles out everyday concerns for a closeup view: transitoriness, the generation gap, friends and enemies. By juxtaposing a character's positive attitudes with his counterproductive or even absurd actions, A. turns many aspects of our social existence into vehicles for unmasking consumer habits, self-righteousness, and prejudice as he shows—with wit and irony—the individual rotating in society's machinery.

A.'s concern with the quality of life is more extremely presented in his short stories, which center around the figure of the outsider. In numerous variations we perceive the individual caught in the circle of his or her inhibitions, clashing with society's norms, striving for personal happiness, sometimes in a nearpathological manner. The need for contact is portrayed in the story. "Passagen" ("The Passage," 1971), from the collection *Puderne* (1965; the pillows), where a clerk assumes the role of a pickpocket after his daily office routine. He finds substitutes for the lack of interpersonal relationships in the objects he steals, especially in a woman's glove, which he fills with warm pudding to obtain the illusion of holding a human hand. A. frequently depicts his characters' needs and desires for contact through their experimental actions to achieve this goal, but the actual state of chronic deprivation overshadows all attempts and hopes, in spite of deluding substitutes.

A.'s radio, television, and stage plays also project with fine psychological insight his characters' difficulties. They are harassed by trivia blown out of proportion by comic exaggeration, as in "Glassplinten" (the glass splinter) in the collection *Lejemorderen, og andre spil* (1970; the hired assassin, and other plays), where others insist on aiding the protagonist remove a splinter because they need to feel useful.

Throughout his work A. has maintained an affirmative attitude toward life coupled with a critical perspective on human weakness and on society's involvement in deviant behavior. There is a noticeable tendency to sympathize with the individual who is powerlessly confronted with the results of political schemes, as in *Orfeus i undergrunden* (1979; Orpheus in the underground). A.'s emphasis lies on life's bystanders who are not necessarily innocent; he tends to depict them misdirecting their efforts in order to increase the shock value and the number of questions raised by their actions.

A. occupies a prominent position among the writers commonly associated with the first phase of Danish modernism after World War II. Since his issues and comic strategy are not restricted to Danish culture, translations of A.'s poems and stories continue to appeal to an international audience.

FURTHER WORKS: *Kamera med køkkenadgang* (1962); *Den indre bowlerhat* (1964); *Portrætgalleri* (1966); *Tykke-Olsen m. fl.* (1968); *Det sidste øh* (1969); *Her i reservatet* (1971); *Man burde burde* (1971); *Man sku' være noget ved musikken* (1972, with Henning Carlsen); *Svantes viser* (1972); *Barnet der blev ældre og ældre* (1973); *Personlige papirer* (1974); *En lykkelig skilsmisse* (1975, with Henning Carlsen); *Nomader med noder* (1976); *Under begge øjne* (1978); *Himmelspræt eller kunsten at komme til verden* (1979); *Kolde fødder* (1979); *Danmark et lukket* (1980). FURTHER WORKS IN ENGLISH: *Selected Poems* (1975); *Selected Stories* (1983)

BIBLIOGRAPHY: Bredsdorff, E., Introduction to Holm, S., ed., *The Devil's Instrument* (1971): 9; Taylor, A., Introduction to *Selected Poems* (1975): vii–xi; Marx, L., "Exercises in Living: B. A.'s

Literary Perspectives," *WLT*, 52 (1978): 550–54; Marx, L., *B. A.: A Critical Study* (1983)

—LEONIE MARX

ANDERSON, Sherwood

American novelist and short-story writer, b. 13 Sept. 1876, Camden, Ohio; d. 8 March 1941, Colón, Panama

A.'s youth, which later frequently provided the material for his fiction, was spent in several small towns in Ohio. He attended school only intermittently, while helping to support his family by working as a newsboy, housepainter, stock handler, and stable groom. After serving in Cuba during the Spanish-American War, he returned for a final year of schooling at Wittenberg Academy, Springfield, Ohio. In 1900 he became an advertising writer in Chicago, and in 1907 a paint manufacturer in Elyria, Ohio. In 1913, dissatisfied with the life of a businessman, he returned to Chicago and a job in advertising, while attempting to establish himself as a writer of serious fiction. There he found encouragement among the writers associated with the "Chicago Renaissance"-DREISER, MASTERS, SANDBURG, and Floyd Dell (1887–1969). By 1921 he had published three novels, two books of short stories, and a volume of free-verse poems, and his achievement was recognized in that year when he received the first *Dial* Award for his contribution to

Sherwood Anderson

American literature. In that year he first visited Europe, meeting James JOYCE and Gertrude STEIN, whose work he much admired. After living for short periods in New Orleans, where he met the young William FAULKNER, he moved to Marion, Virginia, in 1925, where he built a country house that was his home for the rest of his life. In 1927 he bought both of Marion's weekly newspapers and edited them for two years. During the 1930s he studied the labor conditions in Southern mills and factories and published several books of articles on American industrial conditions. At the time of his death he was on an unofficial good-will tour of South America.

A.'s first novel, *Windy McPherson's Son* (1916; rev. ed., 1922), published shortly before his fortieth birthday, and his second, *Marching Men* (1917; rev. ed. 1972), contained the themes that he was to develop more skillfully in his later fiction: the psychological tensions in the inner lives of Midwestern villagers, the pursuit of success and power in the city by the small-town boy, and his eventual disillusionment with the values of the conventional businessman. A.'s concern with sexuality, fed by his early interest in Freudian psychology and deepened by his admiration for the fiction of D. H. LAWRENCE, was heightened into a mystique in his novels *Poor White* (1920), in which he details the invasion of the small town by a machine civilization; *Many Marriages* (1923), a sentimental celebration of sexual freedom; and *Dark Laughter* (1925), in which he contrasts the primitive wholeness of Negroes with the ineffectual sterility of neurotic whites. Marred by crude symbolism and a muddy subjectivity, but frequently containing vignettes of great acuteness and subtlety, these works indicate A.'s difficulty with the continuity and development required by the novel form.

In A.'s greatest book, *Winesburg, Ohio* (1919; rev. ed., 1960) he found a form hospitable to both his revelations of symbolic moments in the lives of small-town Americans and his interest in the effect of those revelations on the development of a young man who wants to become a writer. The "*Winesburg* form," as A. described it, was "half individual tales, half long novel form." It is half *Bildungsroman*: the two dozen sketches in the book are interrelated through common characters and setting and through the sustained appearance of George Willard, who acts as both register for and counterpoint to the other people of the town. It is also a collection of short stories that dramatize crucial episodes in the lives of the "grotesques," characters whose energy for growth and capacity for love are stifled in an isolation made all the more pathetic by its existence in a pastoral setting. In *Winesburg* A. found his unique style, a blend of muted lyricism and the deceptively simple rhythms of American colloquial speech, which was suited perfectly to his tender examination of the twisted lives of the "grotesques." The individual tales of *Winesburg, Ohio* and three books of short stories, *The Triumph of the Egg* (1921), *Horses and Men* (1932), and *Death in the Woods* (1933), strongly influenced the course of the American short story in a direction away from the neatly plotted tales of O. Henry (1862–1910) and his imitators. A.'s influence is to be found in the work of such later writers as FAULKNER, HEMINGWAY, and Thomas WOLFE. The stories are characterized by a casual, almost anecdotal development, complexity of motivation, and a compelling interest in psychological process. Some of the *Winesburg* stories ("Hands" and "The Untold Lie," for example) emerge from their context as especially brilliant in themselves. "I'm a Fool" and "I Want to Know Why," from the later volumes, which treat in the manner of Mark Twain the poignant perceptions of an adolescent being initiated into the adult world, have had an enduring popularity. "The Egg," "Unlighted

Lamps," "The Man Who Became a Woman," and "Death in the Woods" represent the height of A.'s achievement and must be considered masterpieces of the modern short story.

In the news stories, sketches, and articles that A. wrote for his two country newspapers he spoke in the familiar style of much of his fiction and sought to express the responses of a sensitive man to the minor events of Virginia small-town life, sometimes aided by the invention of a comic character like the mountain man Buck Fever. He collected some of his newspaper pieces in *Hello Towns* (1929), and others have been gathered in *Return to Winesburg* (1967) and *The Buck Fever Papers* (1971). Although they contain specimens of A.'s genius, they are chiefly interesting as the results of his efforts to combine his life as an imaginative writer with his role as a citizen in a rural community. At the time of his death he was at work on the book posthumously published as *Sherwood Anderson's Memoirs* (1942; rev. ed., 1969), an autobiography that contains some of his finest writing. Like the earlier autobiographical volumes, *A Story Teller's Story* (1924; rev. ed. 1968) and *Tar: A Midwest Childhood* (1926; rev. ed. 1969), the *Memoirs* have many of the elements of A.'s best fiction: an intimate knowledge of human behavior, a brooding pity for frustrated human aspirations, and a continual search for a style appropriate to his subjects.

In one sense almost all of A.'s writing was a fictional autobiography in which he created a myth of the American storyteller, continually struggling to overcome through the liberation of his imagination the repressive forces of materialism and Puritan moralism. The attractiveness of this personal stance, especially when it resulted in the creation of a personal voice exquisitely appropriate to the task of assisting the buried lives of his characters to emerge, accounts for the adulation of A. in the 1920s and the permanent mark he left on American fiction. This contribution came not only through the relatively small body of his own first-rate works, but also through the example he provided for almost every important American writer of the next generation. Although his limited intellectual range and his inability to sustain in a longer work the brilliance with which he could invest an episode led to a decline of his reputation in the decade immediately preceding his death, A.'s centennial year, 1976, found enduring interest in his work among scholars and critics, continued evidence of his influence on the directions taken by American fiction, and a steady gathering of new readers who delight in *Winesburg, Ohio* and the small parcel of his short stories that have become classics.

FURTHER WORKS: *Mid-American Chants* (1918); *The Modern Writer* (1925); S. A.'s *Notebook* (1926); *A New Testament* (1927); *Alice and the Lost Novel* (1929); *Nearer the Grass Roots* (1929); The *American County Fair* (1930); *Perhaps Women* (1931); *Beyond Desire* (1932); *No Swank* (1934); *Puzzled America* (1935); *Kit Brandon* (1936); *Plays, Winesburg and Others* (1937); *Five Poems* (1939); *A Writer's Conception of Realism* (1939); *Home Town* (1940); *The S. A. Reader* (1947); *The Portable S. A.* (1949); *Letters of S. A.* (1953); *S. A.: Short Stories* (1962); *S. A./Gertrude Stein* (1972); The *"Writer's Book"* (1975); *France and S. A.* (1976); *S. A.: Early Writings* (1989); *Certain Things Last: Selected Short Stories of S. A.* (1992)

BIBLIOGRAPHY: Howe, I., *S. A.* (1951); Schevill, J., *S. A.* (1951); Sheehy, E., and Lohf, K., *S. A.: A Bibliography* (1960); Burbank, R., *S. A.* (1964); Weber, B., *S. A.* (1964); White, R., ed., *The Achievement of S. A.* (1966); Anderson, D., *S. A.* (1967); Sutton, W., *The Road to Winesburg* (1972); Rideout, W., ed., *S. A.: Essays in Criticism* (1974); Anderson, D., ed., *S. A.: Dimensions of His Literary Art* (1976); Campbell, H., and Modlin, C., eds., *S. A.: Centennial Studies* (1976); Townsend, K., *S. A.* (1987); Papinchak, R. A., *S. A.: A Study of the Short Fiction* (1992)

—WILLIAM L. PHILLIPS

ANDRADE, Carlos Drummond de

Brazilian poet, b. 31 Oct. 1902, Itabira; d. 18 Aug. 1995, London

Although A. was born in a small mining town and reared on a backlands ranch, his literary career has led him to spend most of his creative life in Brazil's urban centers, especially Rio de Janeiro. Leaving for Rio first in 1923 to study pharmacy, a profession he has never practiced, A., giving vent to his literary inclinations, soon became involved in *A revista*, a progressive journal in his native state of Minas Gerais. In 1926 he took a job on the newspaper, *Diário de Minas*, eventually becoming its editor-in-chief and making the paper a staunch advocate of Brazil's then-burgeoning modernist revolt. In subsequent years, A. has continued to be both a prolific poet and a socially committed public servant, holding posts with various federal agencies. At present A. resides in Rio de Janeiro, having retired from his duties as archivist at the Ministry of Education in that same city.

A.'s first published book of poems, which appeared only after two earlier aborted efforts, was entitled *Alguma poesia* (1930; some poetry). In this work A, uses a straightforward style, one that allows him to observe coolly the tumultuous times in which he was living and to describe his world without feeling compelled to inject into it any personal commentary. A.'s poetry at this early stage also displays a certain tentativeness, hesitancy, and, on occasion, wry humor. In *Brejo das almas* (1934; wasteland of souls), however, his attitude changes from personal indecision and diffidence to commitment and resolve. The tone of this work is somber and introspective, even to the point of pessimism and nihilism. The poet comes to view his own existence, and that of others, as uncertain and anguished, but he takes solace, finally, in realizing that this is a condition common to all men, that his dilemma is shared, collectively, by everyone. The book ends on a determined note as the speaker resolves to resist the pain, solitude, and bitterness that threaten to engulf and truncate him.

Sentimento do mundo (1940; sentiment of the world), written during the horrors of World War II, begins in a similar vein but ends with the poet dedicating himself to the making of a better world, to the establishment of a meaningful brotherhood of man. Thus, we see A. struggling to link up emotionally and intellectually with other human beings, who, in his view, were everywhere striving to put an end to injustice, cruelty, and oppression. A. develops this same theme, that of a personal satisfaction wrought from a sense of human solidarity, in *Poesias* (1942; poems), a collection in which, by evoking scenes and memories of his youth, he attempts to tie together the past, present, and future of his existence and thereby gain a heightened sense of its direction and meaning.

Social reform, the baseness of modern life, and political morality are the themes overtly discussed in *A rosa do povo* (1945; the people's rose), a book of condemnation and of hope and one of the most important works of the decade, and *Poesia até agora* (1947;

poetry up to now), in which A. returns to a kind of hermetic self-assessment. By the time of *Claro enigma* (1951; clear enigma), however, which began the more purely aesthetic phase of A.'s development, and *Fazendeiro do ar* (1953; the planter of air), the dominant mood of his verse is more pacific and understanding, although no less rigorous in its constant demand for intellectual honesty and integrity, two hallmarks of all his work. Lição de coisas (1962; the lesson of things) sustains this more contemplative and ironic attitude on A.'s part, a tendency he develops even further in *Reunião 10 livros de poesia* (1969); reunion: 10 books of poetry) and in other more recent works.

Throughout his long and illustrious career A. has also written chronicles, essays, and short stories; his short fiction often contains a startling mixture of the quotidian and the bizarre. He has continually presented himself as both an idealistic humanitarian and as an original, powerfully affective poet. A. is the most influential and important poet of his generation, and his work in the 1930s and 1940s represents the very best that the crucial second or unifying phase of Brazilian modernism had to offer. One of A.'s most famous poems, "No meio do caminho" (1930; "In the Middle of the Road," 1965), which recalls William Carlos WILLIAMS's "A Red Wheelbarrow," served as a point of departure for the more avant-garde poets of the post-1945 generation in Brazil, eminent among whom is Joã Cabral de Melo Neto. In his blending of political consciousness with the highest standards of the poet's art, A. has shown himself, along with Pablo NERUDA and a few others, to be among the greatest of the modern Latin American poets.

FURTHER WORKS: *Confissões de Minas* (1944); *O gerente* (1945); *A mesa* (1951); *Contos de aprendiz* (1951); *Passeios na ilha: divagações sobre a vida literária e outras matérias* (1952); *Viola de bolso, novamente encordoada* (1955); *Soneto da buquinagem* (1955); 50 *poemas escolhidos pelo autor* (1956); *Ciclo* (1957); *Fala, amendoeira* (1957); *Poemas* (1959); *Antologia poética* (1962); *Quadrante* (1962); *A bolsa e a vida* (1963); *Vozes da cidade* (1965); *Cadeira de balanço* (1966); *Uma pedra no meio do caminho* (1967); *Versiprosa: crônica da vida cotidiana e de algumas miragens* (1967); *Os caminhos de João Brandão* (1970). **FURTHER WORKS IN ENGLISH:** *In the Middle of the Road* (1965); *Travelling in the Family: Selected Poems* (1986)

BIBLIOGRAPHY: Nist, J., "The Conscience of Brazil: C. D. de A.," *Am´ricas*, 15, 1 (1963): 32–35; Martins, W., ed., *The Modernist Idea* (1970): 282–84; Foster, D. and V. Foster, eds., *Modern Latin American Literature* (1975), Vol I: 53–62; Williams, F. G., and S. Pacha, eds., *C. D. de A. and His Generation* (1981)

—EARL E. FITZ

ANDRADE, Eugénio de

(pseud. of José Fontinhas) Portuguese poet, b. 19 Jan. 1923, Povoa da Atalaia

A. is Portugal's best-known living poet. Born in a village not far from the Spanish border, he was raised by a much beloved mother, whose death in 1956 deeply affected him. His feelings for his father may be deduced from the total absence of that figure in his work. After studies in Castelo Branco, Lisbon, and Coimbra, A. entered the civil service and worked in the department of public health and welfare until his retirement in 1983. From 1950 to the present, he has lived in the northern city of Porto.

Although he began to publish in his teens, A. has rejected his early work, preserving only ten poems from the period 1940–44 under the title *Primeiros Poemas*. He chooses to consider *As Mãos e os Frutos* (1948; Hands and Fruit) the book that began his career. That work has been followed to date by twenty-four more volumes of poetry, three prose works, two children's books, eight anthologies, and various translations into Portuguese of poets such as Federico GARCÍA LORCA and Yannis RITSOS. A.'s poetry has been translated into at least twenty languages, his complete works are currently being published in French, fourteen volumes have appeared in Spanish, five in Italian, and seven in English translation. He has won Portugal's three most prestigious literary awards: the Critics' Award in 1986 and the Grande Premio for Poetry and the D. Dinis Award in 1989.

A.'s poetry has always exhibited a carefully evoked simplicity. Through naked word and image, he strives to convey what he calls "the rough or sweet skin of things." Distrustful of abstractions, he focuses on the world of matter, proclaiming a love for "words smooth as pebbles, rough as rye bread. Words that smell of clover and dust, loam and lemon, resin and sun." His limpid and highly musical style engraves sharp images of the things of this earth, while evoking powerful fluctuations of desire, joy, loss, and regret. The four classical elements of earth, water, fire, and air are never absent from his work. Nor is the human body, which the poet sees as "a metaphor for the universe." The critic Luis Miguel Nava (1957–1995) draws together the three strands of A.'s poetic vision when he observes that "nature, the body, and the word meet on the same plane and in some way intermingle or merge."

A.'s pagan attachment to the body, its senses, and the world of things that surround it is accompanied, in his later works, by a deepening sense of impending death. Collections such as *Branco no branco* (1984; *White on White*, 1987) reveal an unresolved tension between nostalgia and resignation, with memory playing an important role as mixed blessing. "Shadow's weight," the cold sea, the threat of snow add poignancy and intensity to the characteristic life-affirmative lyricism of A.'s expression.

Marguerite YOURCENAR has referred to "the well-tempered clavier" of A.'s poems, Miguel Angel Flores (b. 1948) speaks of his "enduring language that becomes richer at every reading," and the Spanish writer Angel Crespo (1926–1996) proclaims that "his voice was born to baptize the world." Subtle musicality, deceptively simple imagery, and a richness of metaphor and symbolic suggestiveness combine to make A. the most popular contemporary poet in Portugal and, with the exception of Fernando PESSOA, the most widely translated Portuguese poet of the 20th century.

FURTHER WORKS: *Adolescente* (1942); *Pureza* (1945); *Os amantes sem dinheiro* (1950); *As palavras interditas* (1951); *Até amanhã* (1956); *Coração do dia* (1958); *Mar de setembro* (1961); *Ostinato rigore* (1964); *Obscuro domínio* (1971); *Véspera da água* (1973); *Escrita da terra e outros epitáfios* (1974); *Limiar dos pássaros* (1976); *Memória doutro rio* (1978; *Memory of Another River*, 1988); *Matéria solar* (1980; *Solar Matter*, 1995); *O peso da sombra* (1982; *The Shadow's Weight*, 1996); *Aquela nuvem e outras* (1986); *Contra a obscuridade* (1987); *Vertentes do olhar* (1987; *The Slopes of a Gaze*, 1992); *O outra nome da terra* (1988; *Another Name for Earth*, 1997); *Rente ao dizer* (1992); *Ofício de Paciência* (1994); *O Sal da Lingua* (1995); *Pequeno Formato*

(1997). FURTHER WORKS IN ENGLISH: *Inhabited Heart: The Selected Poems of E. de A.* (1985)

BIBLIOGRAPHY: Sayers, R. S., "E. de A.," in Bede, J. A., and Edgerton, W. B., eds., *Columbia Dictionary of Modern European Literature*, rev. 2nd ed. (1980): 21–22; Sayers, R. S., "Portuguese Poetry of Today and E. de A.," CP, 17, 2 (Fall 1984): 137–54; Bedate, P. G., Introduction to *Inhabited Heart* (1985): vii–x; Levitin, A., Afterword to *White on White* (1987): 57–60; Levitin, A., Introduction to *Memory of Another River* (1988): 1–6; Levitin, A., Introduction to *The Slopes of a Gaze* (1992): v–x; Levitin, A., Introduction to *Solar Matter* (1995): i–vii; Levitin, A., Introduction to *The Shadow's Weight* (1996): 19–20; Levitin, A., Introduction to *Another Name for Earth* (1997): i–vi.

—ALEXIS LEVITIN

ANDRADE, Mário de

Brazilian poet, novelist, short-story writer, critic, and essayist, b. 9 Oct. 1892, São Paulo; d. 25 Feb. 1945, São Paulo

Reared in São Paulo, A. studied at the Conservatory of Drama and Music, and at the age of twenty-two he was writing art criticism for several magazines and newspapers. In 1922 he became professor of musicology and aesthetics at the conservatory. In 1934 he helped in the organization of the São Paulo Department of Culture and became its first director, and in 1936 he collaborated in writing the important law that protects historical sites and buildings. He was the founder (in 1937) of the Brazilian Society of Ethnography and Folklore, of which he was the first president. He moved to Rio de Janeiro in 1938; there he was given the chair of art history and made director of the Art Institute at the newly established and short-lived University of the Federal District. He returned to São Paulo in 1940, and during the remaining years of his life he traveled extensively through Brazil, doing research in folklore and art history.

Although not the greatest of contemporary Brazilian authors, A. has been the most influential, for it is he who seems to express most completely the spirit of MODERNISM, the literary and artistic movement that has been the dominant force in Brazilian literature since the Week of Modern Art in 1922. In his poetry, his fiction, and his essays on art, literature, and music, he embodies the ideology of modernism, and in his letters and personal contacts, as well as in his classes and public lectures he constantly defended its dogmas: the necessity for the Brazilian writer to view reality through Brazilian eyes; the importance of writing about Brazil in its own brand of Portuguese; and the need for creative artists to develop media or forms that would be attuned to the spirit and the language of their country. His critical position is expressed in such books as *A escrava que não é Isaura* (1925; the slave who is not Isaura), an essay on aesthetics and criticism; *O empalhador de passarinho* (1944; the stuffer of birds) and *Aspectos da literatura brasileira* (1943; aspects of Brazilian literature); and his *Cartas* (1958; letters). In them we see both his originality of thought and his debt to foreign ideas, for he was an alert, sensitive man who understood not only Brazil and the Brazilians, but also the Europe of the 1920s and 1930s, and he was influenced by FREUD, SURREALISM, and, during the Depression, by Marxism.

The modern spirit, with its quirks and mannerisms, is apparent as early as 1922 in A.'s *Pauliceéia desvairada* (*Hallucinated City*,

1968), a hymn of love to his native city. His tendency toward sensationalism diminished over the years and, as his verse became simpler and more assured, more securely based on a language free of showy artifice, it seemed to express more deeply personal matters, as is evident in his finest poem, "A meditacão sober o Tietę" (meditation on the Tieté), published posthumously in *Lira paulistana* (1946; the São Paulo lyre).

Although A. was essentially a poet, his fiction reached a far wider public and created much more controversy than his poetry. *Macunaima* (1928; *Macunaima*, 1984) has a place in Brazilian literature equivalent to that of JOYCE's *Ulysses* in English literature. A novel or a "rhapsody" in prose, it has some of the characteristics of the epic poem in that its hero is a mythical figure who is supposed to symbolize the Brazilian spirit and to incorporate in his psyche the collective unconscious; the novel's style, which is permeated with linguistic innovations, is supposed to be based on the speech of all Brazil.

The rest of A.'s fiction is often satirical and humorous and very much concerned with urban São Paulo, with its old national groups and its first and second generations of immigrants. His only other novel, *Amar, verbo intransitivo* (1927; *Fräulein*, 1933), satirizes in a most original way the Brazilian's exaggerated respect for things European. His collections of short stories—*Primeiro andar* (1926; first floor), *Belazarte* (1934; Belazarte), and *Contos novos* (1947; new stories)—are among the best in the genre. Through his stylistic experiments, his critical theories, and his studies of Brazilian life he influenced both his own and the next generation of writers.

FURTHER WORKS: *Há uma gota de sangue em cada poema* (1917); *Losango cáqui* (1926); *Clã do jabuti* (1927); *Ensaio sobre a música brasileira* (1928); *Compêndio de história da música* (1929); *Remate de males* (1930); *Modinhas imperiais* (1930); *Música, doce música* (1933); *O Aleijadinho e Álvares de Azevedo* (1935); *Namoros com a medicina* (1939); *Música do Brasil* (1941); *Poesias* (1941); *O movimento modernista* (1942); *O baile das quatro artes* (1943); *Os filhos de Candinha* (1943); *Obras completas* (20 vols., 1944 ff.); *O padre Jesuíno do Monte Carmelo* (1946); *Poesias completas* (1955); *Danças dramáticas do Brasil* (1959); *Música de feitiçaria* (1963)

BIBLIOGRAPHY: Parker, D. W., "Some Formal Types in the Poetry of M. de A.," *LBR*, 2 (1965): 75–95; Nist, J., "The Creative Force of M. de A.," *Américas*, 17 (1965): 27–29; Rica, C. de la, "M. de A. en el modernismo brasileño," *RCB*, 5 (1966): 69–75; Nist, J., *The Modernist Movement in Brazil* (1967): 59–70; Martins, W., *The Modernist Idea* (1970): 244–50; Foster, D., and V. Foster, eds., *Modern Latin American Literature* (1975), Vol. 1: 53–62

—RAYMOND S. SAYERS

ANDRADE, Oswald de

Brazilian poet, novelist, dramatist, and critic, b. 11 Jan. 1890, São Paulo; d. 22 Oct. 1954, São Paulo

A. studied law but devoted most of his life to literary pursuits. As a young man he began to associate with writers and artists of São Paulo and adopted a bohemian life style. This rebellion against the traditional society of Brazil persisted throughout his lifetime and is a thread that runs throughout his work, in which he constantly called for social and cultural changes. In 1911 he made his first trip to Europe, where he came into contact with the avant-garde in literature and the arts.

Returning to Brazil, A. began to urge writers to break away from 19th-c. Parnassianism and realism, which were still being practiced, and to experiment with more modern forms and concepts. In 1920 he founded the literary periodical *Papel e tinta*. During that same year he discovered Mário de ANDRADE, who was to become one of Brazil's most important writers. With him A. worked to organize the Semana de Arte Moderna ("modern art week"), which, in 1922, marked the official beginning of Brazilian MODERNISM.

In 1925 A. published *Pau Brasil* (Brazil wood), in which he propounded a "primitive" poetry, free of foreign influences and of pedantry, with a disregard for established rules of meter and rhyme. In 1928 the premises of this publication were extended a good deal further by means of the establishment of *Revista de antropofagia*. In the first issue of the journal A. allegorically exalted the primitive custom of cannibalism to urge Brazilian writers to devour European culture and digest it into a Brazilian product.

Poesias reunidas (1945; collected poems) contains A.'s earlier poetry and some newer work. These inventive, short epigrammatic poems are made up of humorous, lyrical ideas and impressions of Brazilian life and customs. Many of the poems reveal A.'s sense of irony, which is sometimes sharpened into sarcasm.

A.'s prose reveals the same ideas and innovative spirit that characterize his poetry. He satirized established literary traditions and the bourgeois mentality of his countrymen. His prose style is marked by experiments with semantics and syntax, since he wanted to create an artistic language appropriate for the expression of 20th-c. Brazilian reality.

Memórias sentimentais de João Miramar (1924; the sentimental memoirs of João Miramar), because of its complete departure from traditional narrative techniques, is considered by many Brazilian critics to be one of the most important pieces of fiction written in Brazil in this century. Although not strictly autobiographical, this novel is a reconstruction of A.'s memories of his childhood, adolescence, and adult life, including his various trips to Europe. These memories, recounted in the first person by João Miramar (A. himself), are episodic, but lack a logical sequence within the narrative, giving it a surrealistic effect, as well as a cinematic quality. The preface is related by another character, Machado Penumbra, who represents the aesthetic conscience of both A. and the modernists. In the epilogue Penumbra appears again and interviews Miramar, who says that he will not finish his memoirs because they are inconclusive, as is life, and that the reader must supply his own ending if he wants one. The narrative technique, a mélange of narrative prose, dramatic dialogues, and poetry, and the ironic, humorous treatment are more interesting than the plot, which is minimal.

Only recently has A. been hailed as a dramatist of high caliber. His play *O rei da vela* (1937; the candle king), neglected for many years as a work to be read rather than performed, is now considered a vanguard work of Brazilian theater. In the drama A. employs the legend of Abélard and Héloïse and, through a process of demythification, turns these romantic characters into selfish, brutal individuals who marry only for economic reasons. While satirizing bourgeois thinking, A. also leveled criticism at the advance of industrialization, the exploitation of Brazil by foreigners, and the effect these were having on Brazilian society.

A. is now being studied and reevaluated by scholars who are finding in his work not only technical innovation but also great literary merit and social commitment.

FURTHER WORKS: *Trilogia do exilio* (I., *Os condenados*, 1922; II., *Estrêla de absinto*, 1927; III., *A escada vermelha*, 1934); *Primeiro caderno do aluno de poesia O. de A.* (1927); *Análise de dois tipos de ficção* (1933); *Serafim ponte grande* (1933); *O homen e o cavalo* (1934); *A morta* (1937); *Marco zero* (I., *A revolução melancólica*, 1943; II., *Chão*, 1946); *A arc´dia e a inconfidência* (1945); *Ponta de lança* (1945); *O rei Floquinhos* (1953); *Um homem sem profissão* (1954)

BIBLIOGRAPHY: Nist, J., *The Modernist Movement in Brazil* (1967): 179–83, 251–58; Martins, W., *The Modernist Idea* (1970): passim

—FRED M. CLARK

ANDREEV, Leonid

Russian short-story writer, novelist, dramatist, critic, and journalist, b. 21 Aug. 1871, Orel; d. 21 Sept. 1919, Neuvola, Finland

A. overcame the hardships and tragedies of his formative years (including an attempted suicide in 1892), and graduated from the Department of Law of Moscow University in 1897. Despite his handsomeness and his phenomenal literary success, most of A.'s life was fraught with unhappiness: he was afflicted with chronic ill health and periods of depression; he was arrested for political activities and had to leave Russia (1905); his wife Alexandra died in Berlin after giving birth to their second child (1906). Overcome by this tragedy and full of disdain and contempt for Germany, A. accepted Maxim GORKY's invitation to join him in Capri. The Capri sojourn alleviated A.'s depression, but at the same time alienated him from Gorky. He returned to Russia in 1907 and built a mansion for himself, across the gulf from St. Petersburg, that is, in Finnish territory. Following the proclamation of Finland's independence in 1917, the border between the two countries was closed (1918), and A. spent the last years of his life cut off from his native land, filled with a fierce hatred for Bolshevism and the new rulers of Russia.

A. began his literary career in 1895 by publishing short stories and feuilletons in the paper *Orlovsky vestnik*. Later, he served as a court reporter for two Moscow publications, *Moskovsky vestnik* and *Kurier*. Between 1898 and 1902 A. established his reputation as a writer by publishing court reports, satirical articles, and reviews, as well as twenty-eight stories in the *Kurier*. One of these, "Bargamot i Garaska" (1898; "Bargamot and Garaska," 1915), attracted the attention of Gorky, who furthered A.'s career by introducing him into various literary circles and by encouraging him to pursue a literary career. Around 1900 A.'s art began to evolve from the traditional story genre modeled on CHEKHOV and Gorky to a more modernist approach to such *fin-de-siècle* themes as isolation, loneliness, and death that reflected the influence of Schopenhauer and Nietzsche. This trend reached its culmination in the longer story *Zhizn Vasilya Fiveyskogo* (1903; *The Life of Vasili Fiveysky*, 1920), the tragedy of an Orthodox priest whose life is destroyed by hidden, incomprehensible forces. Although somewhat drawn out, the story is very powerful in its redolent despair. It forebodes, on the one hand, the imminent break between A. and Gorky and his *Znanie* group that was ultimately precipitated by the publication of A.'s story "Tma" (1907; darkness), and also reflects, at least partially, the prevailing *Zeitgeist* in Russia at the turn of the century. *Razskaz o semi poveshennykh* (1908; *The Seven That Were Hanged*, 1909) marks the zenith of A.'s career as a writer of fiction. It is a penetrating psychological study of condemned men and a powerful protest against the death penalty.

Drawing on his experience as a drama critic, A. wrote between 1915 and 1916 twenty-eight plays and established himself as the leading Russian playwright of his time. A.'s dramaturgy is, for the most part, thematically consonant with his fiction: a gloomy atmosphere, a pessimistic tone, a sense of the impotence of reason, and the insuperable power of irrational forces dominate his *dramatis personae*, whose initial dissatisfaction with life is usually replaced either by a quiet resignation or a nihilistic rebelliousness. A.'s first play, *K zvezdam* (1905; *To the Stars*, 1907), which was initially rejected by the Russian censors and had to be staged in Vienna, established A.'s reputation as a dramatist. Underlying the play, in addition to the Nietzschean problem of the incompatibility of love for one's "far ones" (those yet to be born) with the love for one's neighbors, is the theme of rebellion and revolution. *K zvezdam* was followed by *Savva* (1906; *Savva*, 1914), a play about a revolutionary who is destroyed by the violence he himself unleashes; the play conveys A.'s pessimistic conviction about man's intrinsic inability to become master of the reality surrounding him.

Zhizn cheloveka (1906; *The Life of Man*, 1914) contributed most to making A. famous in his lifetime. It is an allegorical abstraction based on a medieval representation of the stages in man's life. The play depicts the misery of life in a surrealistic atmosphere created chiefly by the stage settings under the direction of Vsevolod Meyerhold in St. Petersburg and Konstantin Stanislavsky in Moscow; it marked A.'s complete break with Russian dramatic realism. A. continued in this vein of allegorical abstraction with a sequel to *Zhizn cheloveka* entitled *Tsar golod* (1907; *King Hunger*, 1911), a protest against the stifling technocratic forces inherent in a capitalist society based on the idea that hunger is the prime motivating force in man; and *Chyornye maski* (1908; *The Black Maskers*, 1915), a Dantean search for authentic personality and truth, in which A. sought to extract some light from the gloom of external and internal realities that inform his plays. In that sense, *Chornye maski*, despite its obscurities, marks a turn toward a more optimistic representation of reality, which he developed further in *Anatema* (1909; *Anathema*, 1910), a play built on the Faust theme, with love as the final solution of man's existential dilemma. *Dni nashey zhizni* (1908; days of our life), *Anfisa* (1908; Anfisa), and *Gaudeamus* (1910; Lati: let us be merry) were written in an even more realistic vein, ostensibly to appease a public for whom his tragedies had become incomprehensible.

During the last years of his life (1912–19), A. elaborated on his earlier theses in a more mature and realistic manner. The most successful product of this period was the play *Tot, kto poluchaet poshchochinu* (1916; *He Who Gets Slapped*, 1921), a poignant and subtly autobiographical statement on man's intrinsic isolation and solitude. A. succeeded in harmonizing the surface realism of the play with the psychic tragedy of its hero and in making the entire work a symbol of man's futile struggle against destiny, both on the social and the metaphysical levels of existence.

Influenced primarily by Maurice MAETERLINCK's dramaturgy and Nietzsche's life and works, A. sought to remove all external action from the stage and to represent symbolically the inner life of man. He envisioned his theater of the "panpsyche" as the theater of the future. Unlike some of his works of fiction, which have stood the test of time, most of his plays have fallen into oblivion, and the hegemony of SOCIALIST REALISM in Russia precludes any immediate hope for their revival. However, his treatment of the themes of loneliness, alienation, and despair makes A. a precursor of EXISTENTIALISM and a spiritual father of the THEATER OF THE ABSURD.

FURTHER WORKS: *Novye razskazy* (1902); *Yuda Iskariot* (1907; *Judas Iscariot*, 1910); *Lyudov k blizhnemu* (1908; *Love of One's Neighbor*, 1914); *Sobranie sochineny* (1910); *Sashka Zhegulev* (1911; *Sashka Jigouleff*, 1920); *Okean* (1911); *Yekaterina Ivanovna* (1912; *Katerina*, 1923); *Prekrasnyya sabinyanki* (1912; *The Pretty Sabine Women*, 1914); *Professor Storitsyn* (1912; *Professor Storitsyn*, 1933); *Ne uby* (1913); *Korol, zakon i svoboda* (1914; *Sorrows of Belgium*, 1915); *Mysl* (1914); *Samson v okovakh* (1915; *Samson in Chains*, 1923); *Igo voyny* (1915; *War's Burden*, 1916); *Mladost* (1915); *Sobachy vals* (1916; *Waltz of the Dogs*, 1922); *Priznania malenkogo cheloveka o velikikh dnyakh* (1916; *The Confession of a Little Man During Great Days*, 1917); *Polet* (1916); *Ironicheskie razskazy* (1916); *Milye prizraki* (1916); *Rekviem* (1916; *Requiem*, 1917); *Zapiski Satany* (1921); *Dnevnik Satany* (1919; *Satan's Diary*, 1920); *Nochnoy razgavor* (1921); *Pisma* (1924); *Povesti i razskazy* (1957); *Piesy* (1959). FURTHER WORKS IN ENGLISH: *Silence and Other Stories* (1910); *The Little Angel and Other Stories* (1915); *Plays by L. A.* (1915); *The Crushed Flowers and Other Stories* (1916); *When the King Loses His Head and Other Stories* (1920); *Judas Iscariot; The Christians; The Phantoms* (1947); *Selected Stories* (1969); *Visions* (1987); *Three Plays* (1989)

BIBLIOGRAPHY: Brusyanin, V. V., Introduction to *Plays by L. A.* (1915): xi–xxvi; Kaun, A., *L. A.: A. Critical Study* (1924); Magarshack, D., *Stanislavsky: A Life* (1950): 289–93; Carlisle, O. A., *Voices in the Snow* (1962): 13–16; Woodward, J. B., *L. A.: A Study* (1969); Holthusen, J., *Twentieth Century Russian Literature* (1972): 48–49; Newcombe, J. M., *L. A.* (1972); Segel, H. B., *Twentieth-Century Russian Drama* (1979): 78–88, 118–23; Davies, R., ed., *Photographs by a Russian Writer: An Undiscovered Portrait of Pre-Revolutionary Russia* (1989); Hutchings. S. C., *A Semiotic Analysis of the Short Stories of L. A., 1900–1909* (1990); Gorky, M., *Reminiscences of Tolstoy, Chekhov, and A.* (1997)

—LEONID RUDNYTZKY

ANDRES, Stefan Paul

West German novelist, poet, and dramatist, b. 26 June 1906, Breitwies; d. 29 June 1970, Rome, Italy

Born into a rural Catholic family, A. was destined to take holy orders. He attended a monastery school (1917–26), entered the Capuchin order as a novice (1926–28), but then decided not to become a priest. Instead, he studied German literature, philosophy, and art history at the universities of Cologne, Jena, and Berlin (1928–32). Subsequent travels took him to Greece and Italy. His first novel was published in 1933 and awarded a prize from the Abraham Lincoln Foundation. Because of difficulties with the Reich's Chamber of Literature, he emigrated with his family to

Italy in 1937, staying in Positano until 1949, the year he received the Literature Prize of the Rhine. In 1950 he took up residence in Unkel am Rhein in West Germany and tried to contribute his share to the spiritual rebuilding of Germany, writing for newspapers and journals, giving lectures, and appearing on TV and radio. Between 1952 and 1957 he was awarded several more prestigious literary prizes. Yet, dissatisfied with life in the Federal Republic, he moved back to Italy in 1961, to live in Rome until his sudden death.

A., a highly original narrative talent, is a traditional rather than an iconoclast. He views the *theatrum mundi* ("theater of the World") from the vantage point of a Christian humanist who is neither a dogmatist nor a metaphysician. Because of his at times almost pagan enthusiasm for life and the joys and pleasures of this world, he has even been called a "Dionysian Christian." His writing shows a marked tendency to capture the essence of our times through myths and symbols of both pagan (Greco-Roman) and Christian origin. Thus, his trilogy *Die Sintflut* (the great flood)—*Das Tier aus der Tiefe* (1949; the beast from the depths), *Die Arche* (1951; the ark), and *Der graue Regenbogen* (1959; the gray rainbow)—depicts and interprets the diabolism of the totalitarian state in biblical terms as a timeless parable. Obvious as the references to the Third Reich and Nazism are, by establishing throughout parallels to the Old Testament and by relating the evils of our time to the apocalyptic vision of the rise to power of Saint John's "beast from the depths," A. transforms events of contemporary history, creating the model for any state that sets itself up as absolute, thus usurping the role of God. While dealing with the basic structure of dictatorship and the totalitarian state, A. also pointedly criticizes the attitude of individuals, as well as social groups and institutions, both before and after the deluge.

The *Sintflut* trilogy was by no means A.'s first comment on specific problems of his time, although his earlier works generally show a rather strong autobiographical bent or are pre-occupied with the religious themes of man's freedom and divine providence, individual guilt, grace, and redemption. The early novella *El Greco malt den Großinquisitor* (1936; El Greco paints the Grand Inquisitor) represents both a clarification of his own artistic task and an appeal to the artists of his time to remain faithful to their innermost convictions, maintaining the independence and incorruptibility of true art before the threatening demands of state and church. In *Wir sind Utopia* (1943; *We Are God's Utopia*, 1955)—dramatized in 1950 as *Gottes Utopia* (God's Utopia)—characterized by Graham Greene as "amongst the most shattering [works] of modern literature," an ex-monk who left his monastery to put his religiously inspired political idealism into practice finds himself caught up in the turbulent events of the Spanish Civil War. Confronted with the choice between death or murder in self-defense, he finally chooses to follow his religious convictions and to love his enemy, although the price for asserting his integrity will be certain death.

Although he also wrote dramas, radio plays, and poetry, A. was primarily a gifted storyteller, well versed in the craft of fiction, vigorous in his creation of plot and character, attentive to details of language and atmosphere. Skillful manipulation of point of view allows him to achieve a maximum of intensity and complexity. The strong realism with which he depicts the human drama is complemented by the mythical element which provides the framework for viewing the human enterprise in its universal form. Because of this fusion of mythical thinking and realistic representation, A. is counted, together with Elisabeth Langgässer (1899–1950) and Hermann Kasack (1896–1966), among the eminent writers of German MAGIC REALISM.

FURTHER WORKS: *Das Märchen im Liebfrauendom* (1928); *Bruder Luzifer* (1933); *Die Löwenkanzel* (1933); *Eberhard im Kontrapunkt* (1933); *Die unsichtbare Mauer* (1934); *Der ewige Strom* (1936); *Utz, der Nachfahr* (1936); *Vom heiligen Pfäfflein Domenico* (1936); *Moselländische Novellen* (1937); *Der Mann von Asteri* (1939); *Das Grab des Neides* (1940); *Der olympische Frieden* (1940); *Der gefrorene Dionysos* (1943; under the title *Die Liebesschaukel*, 1951); *Das goldene Gitter* (1943); *Wirtshaus zur weiten Welt* (1943); *Die Hochzeit der Feinde* (1947); *Ritter der Gerechtigkeit* (1948); *Requiem für ein Kind* (1948); *Tanz durchs Labyrinth* (1948); *Die Häuser auf der Wolke* (1950); *Der Granatapfel* (1950); *Das Antlitz* (1951); *Der Reporter Gottes* (1952); *Der Knabe im Brunnen* (1953); *Die Rache der Schmetterlinge* (1953); *Die Reise nach Portiuncula* (1954); *Wann Kommen die Götter* (1956/1957); *Positano* (1957); *Sperrzonen* (1957); *Das Abenteuer der Freude* (1962); *Der Mann im Fisch* (1963); *Der Taubenturm* (1966); *Gedichte* (1966); *Die Dumme* (1969); *Die Versuchung des Synesios* (1970)

BIBLIOGRAPHY: Travis, D. C., *Pattern of Reconciliation in the Works of S. A.* (1959); André, C., *Dichtung in Dritten Reich: S. A.s "Die Arche"* (1960); Hennecke, H., et al., *S. A.: Eine Einführung in sein Werk* (1962); Vandershaeghe, P., *S. A.* (1962); Cook, B. A., "Guilt in the Postwar German Novel," *Commonweal*, 28 Sept. 1962: 120–22; Nordstrand, K. O., *Hinter hundert Generationen: Monographisches zu S. A. in der Exil- und Nachkriegszeit* (1968); Piper, K., ed., *Utopia und Welterfahrung: S. A. und sein Werk im Gedächtnis seiner Freunde* (1972); Lorenzen, K., "S. A.," in Wiese, B. von, ed., *Deutsche Dichter der Gegenwart* (1973): 183–94; Wagener, H., *S. A.* (1974); Hadley, M., "Resistance in Exile: Publication, Context and Reception of S. A.'s *Wir sind Utopia* (1942)," *Seminar*, 19, 3 (1983): 157–76; Klapper, J., "S. A.: A Reassessment," *GL&L*, 43, 3 (1990): 234–45; Dyck, J. W., "On Questioning the Wisdom of Creation: Fyodor Dostoevsky and S. A.," in Dietrick, L., and D. G. John, eds., *Momentum Dramaticum: Festschrift for Eckehard Catholy* (1990): 337–49; Klapper, J., "The Search for Synthesis: Religion and Myth in the Works of S. A.," *GL&L*, 45, 2 (1992): 149–57

—FRIEDHELM RICKERT

ANDRESEN, Sophia de Mello Breyner

Portuguese poet, b. 6 Nov. 1919, Porto

A., the foremost woman figure in modern Portuguese poetry, was born to an aristocratic family in Porto, the country's second largest city, a commercial center on the banks of the Rio Douro, in the north. She was raised in a large house surrounded by extensive gardens, but her childhood summers were spent beside the sea, which left a happy, indelible mark on her life. At the age of twelve, when she discovered in Homer the same sea that she already loved, her lifelong attachment to Greece was assured. When she went to Lisbon to attend university, her field of study, quite naturally, was classics. And as she developed her poetic voice, the clean and limpid line from Greek antiquity was unmistakable.

A.'s first book, *Poesia* (1944; Poetry), already revealed her characteristic clarity of image and her attachment to "the splendor of the presence of things." For her, poetry always spoke of actual life, not of the ideal. Her joy at discovering the naked reality of things began with a certain known house, its garden and its breezes, and quickly expanded to include vaster miracles, such as the luminousness of sunlight and the transparency of the sea. The importance of the latter to her work is reflected in the titles of ensuing collections: *Dia do Mar* (1947; Day of the Sea), *Coral* (1950; Coral), and *Mar Novo* (1958; New Sea). One could argue that the poet even modeled her poetry after the sea, imitating its rolling waves and emulating its transparency and mystery with her sharp-etched images and mythological resonance.

In 1964 the Portuguese Writers Association awarded her its Grande Prémio for Poetry for her book *Livro Sexto* (1962; Sixth Book), a work that mixed courageous antifascist sentiments with her limpid recreation of the reality of things. In her acceptance speech, "Arte Poética III" (1964; "The Art of Poetry III"), A. made clear her belief that the conscientious quest for reality cannot be restricted to nature, for whoever "is motivated by the spirit of truth, whoever searches for the right relationship with a stone, a tree, or a river, must also search for the right relationship with man." She went on to argue that poetry is inherently moral and concerned with justice, "for justice is inseparable from the balance of things, the order of the world." And she concluded that art, no matter what its apparent subject matter, always reminds us that "we are heirs of freedom and the dignity of being." In the political sphere, A. was one of the founders of the Portuguese National Commission to Aid Political Prisoners, was an opposition representative for Porto in 1969, and was elected a deputy to the Portuguese Constitutional Assembly after the revolution of 1974.

A.'s poetry of things and of thought, of the physical and the metaphysical, of the sensory and the immanent, has won her other major awards, including the "Prémio Teixeira de Pascoaes" in 1977 for her collection *O Nome das Coisas* (1977; The Name of Things), the Literary Critics Award for Poetry for *Navagações* (1983; Navigations), and both the Portuguese PEN Club Prize for Poetry and the Grande Prémio of Inasset/Inapa for her book *Ilhas* (1989; Islands). A. has now published twenty-two volumes of poetry, including the three-volume *Obra Poética* (1990-1991; Poetical Works). Her poetry has been translated extensively into various languages, including Spanish, Italian, French, German, Russian, Chinese, and English.

In addition to her poetry, A. has also published a good deal of prose. She has written eight popular children's books, some of them already in a twentieth edition. There are also three volumes of criticism, including the important *O Nu Na Antiguidade Clássica* (1975; The Nude in Classical Antiquity), another work that manifests her great love for Greece. A. has also published two volumes of short stories, *Contos Exemplares* (1962; Exemplary Tales) and *Histórias da Terra e Do Mar* (1984; Tales of Land and Sea), which together have resulted in thirty-seven editions to date. Both of these books, along with *O Nu Na Antiguidade Clássica*, have appeared in translation in France. Besides her own poetry and prose, A. has translated Shakespeare's *Hamlet*, and *Much Ado about Nothing*, Euripedes' *Medea*, Paul Claudel's *The Tidings Brought to Mary*, and Dante's *Purgatory*, for which she received a medal of honor from the Italian government.

Although A. stands as Portugal's leading woman-of-letters, it is in the realm of poetry that she has had the greatest influence. Her work has been the object of much critical attention, and she has been compared to figures as diverse as Fernando PESSOA, Martin HEIDEGGER, and Rainer Maria RILKE. It is thanks largely to her

undisputed stature as a major poet that women have finally begun to gain equal consideration with men in the world of contemporary Portuguese poetry.

FURTHER WORKS: *No Tempo Dividido* (1954); *O Rapaz de Bronze* (1956); *A Menina do Mar* (1958); *A Fada Oriana* (1958); *Noite de Natal* (1960); *O Cristo Cigano* (1961); *O Cavaleiro da Dinamarca* (1964); *Geografia* (1967); *A Floresta* (1968); *Antologia* (1968); *Grades* (1970); *Dual* (1972); *A Árvore* (1985); *Musa* (1994); *Signo: Escolha de Poemas* (1994). FURTHER WORKS IN ENGLISH: *Marine Rose (Selected Poems)* (1988); *Islands: Selected Poems* (1995); *Selected Poems* (1995); *S. de M. B. Log Book: Selected Poems* (1997)

BIBLIOGRAPHY: Coelho, E. P., *A Palavra Sobre a Palavra* (1972); Rocha, C., "S. de M. B. A.: Poesia e Magia," *Coloquio-Letras*, 132-33 (April-September 1994): 165-82; Ceia, C., "Monologo Crítico-Nos 50 Anos de Vida Literária de S. de M. B. A.," *Coloquio-Letras*, 132-33 (April-September 1994): 183-87; Lobucka, A., "Sophia 'Escreve' Pessoa," *Coloquio-Letras*, 140-41 (April-September 1996): 157-76

—ALEXIS LEVITIN

ANDRIĆ, Ivo

Yugoslav novelist, short-story writer, essayist, and critic (writing in Serbian), b. 9 Oct. 1892, Dolac; d. 13 March 1975, Belgrade

Born into a petit-bourgeois family from a small Bosnian town near Travnik, A. completed his secondary education in Sarajevo and studied Slavic philology at the universities of Zagreb, Cracow, and Vienna. At the onset of World War I he was arrested by Austrian authorities for his involvement in the Young Bosnia revolutionary organization and imprisoned for three years. After the war he completed his studies at the University of Graz (Austria), receiving a doctorate in 1924 with a thesis on the cultural history of Bosnia. Between 1920 and 1941 he was engaged in the Yugoslav diplomatic service, holding posts in Rome, Bucharest, Graz, Paris, Madrid, Brussels, Geneva, and Berlin. After the Nazi invasion of Yugoslavia in 1941, he returned home and spent the war years writing in occupied Belgrade. During the postwar socialist period, although concentrating on writing, he combined his literary and political endeavors and served as president of the Association of Yugoslav Writers and as a parliamentary representative in the country's Federal Assembly.

A.'s earliest literary efforts were several poems in an anthology, translations of Walt Whitman and of August STRINDBERG, and two collections of somber, meditative; lyrical and deeply introspective prose poems, *Ex Ponto* 1918; Latin: from the sea) and *Nemiri* (1920; states of restlessness), which show some philosophical influence of Søren Kierkegaard. Beginning with the short story "Put Alije Djerzeleza" (1920; the journey of Alija Djerzelez) A. turned his attention to prose and during the subsequent two decades produced three collections of short stories (in 1924, 1931, and 1936) inspired by the life and traditions of his native Bosnia, in which the centuries of struggle among the Orthodox, Catholic, and Muslim forces and heritages created a milieu of rare complexity and striking contrasts. Many of these stories, and others that appeared after World War II in the collection *Nove pripovetke* (1948; new stories) and separately, are clustered in several large cycles built around particularly prominent characters such as the monks Fra Petar and Fra Marko, the peasant Vitomir Tasovac, the Višegradian jack-of-all-trades Ćorkan, and the brave but unlucky-in-love Muslim Alija. The protagonists in all of these cycles are usually shown in a number of temporally separate situations which, viewed chronologically, very successfully capture and depict those inner and outer changes of personality and milieu that are subtly achieved by the corrosive action of time.

A.'s tales of the Bosnian past both stylistically and thematically heralded his two great novel-chronicles, *Na Drini ćuprija* (1945; *The Bridge on the Drina*, 1959) and *Travnička hronika* (1945; *Bosnian Chronicle*, 1963), which he completed during World War II and published simultaneously shortly thereafter. *Na Drini ćuprija*, by far A.'s most famous work, is an elaborately constructed and superbly orchestrated chronicle of a Bosnian microcosm, represented by the town of Višegrad and its ancient bridge across the river Drina, over which ramble centuries of events and generations of townsfolk engaged in a ceaseless struggle against the ravages of natural forces and human malevolence. In addition to their tangible, real existence, both the bridge and the river depicted in this novel are endowed with symbolic significance. As a product of human toil, which resulted in a perfect blend of utility and beauty of form, the bridge epitomizes the permanence of man's artistic endeavor, while the river, as a perennially renewed, infinitely variable force of nature, symbolizes equally well the perpetuity of cosmic flow and change. The rest of the novel's broad canvas is filled with portraits of the townspeople and the recollection of events that account for the region's history from the building of the bridge in 1571 to its partial destruction at the outset of World War I. The novel's chronicle texture is felt through the leisurely unfolding of its plot, which as a whole is a huge mosaic of individual destinies revealed in measured succession to illustrate the steady one-directional voyage of all-conquering time.

The second novel, *Travnička hronika*, is an equally penetrating historical and psychological study of the same semi-Oriental Bosnian milieu, though conceived on a smaller scale. It depicts the town of Travnik, the seat of the Ottoman Vizier of Bosnia, and its diverse inhabitants of both native and foreign origin during the turbulent decade of the Napoleonic wars. Its most prominent characters are the newly appointed French consul and his young assistant, both heavily embroiled in competing with their Austrian counterparts for influence over the austere and Orientally aloof Turkish Vizier. The resultant local diplomatic maneuvers are complicated not only because they illustrate the clash of Occidental and Oriental ways and values but also because they reflect and echo the great political upheavals in Europe in which France and Austria are in different camps, and the distant rumblings of the Great Serbian Insurrection whose advent is deeply unsettling to the town's Orthodox and Muslim inhabitants alike.

Throughout A.'s long literary career these two novel-chronicles remained the apex of his creative output. Particularly notable for their subtle contrasts of East and West in the presentation of the Bosnian milieu and the superb portrayal of a constellation of characters belonging to the feuding but coexisting Christian, Muslim, and Jewish communities, these major works quickly achieved much popularity and recognition in both Yugoslavia and abroad, culminating, in 1961, with the world attention brought to their creator by the Nobel Prize for literature.

In the postwar, socialist era, A.'s output included several short stories on contemporary subjects and themes, some travel memoirs, a number of essays on writers and painters, and two shorter novels. The first of these novels, *Gospodjica* (1945; *The Woman from Sarajevo*, 1965), introduces a well-to-do old maid who is gradually destroyed by her feelings of insecurity, her miserliness, and her passion for hoarding. The second one, *Prokleta avlija* (1954; *The Devil's Yard*, 1962), harks back to the distant Ottoman past to depict the notorious Istanbul prison yard in which a motley crowd of both guilty and innocent inmates from all over the empire languishes in a morass of pain, degradation, and hopelessness.

Although A.'s work frequently reveals his utter sadness over the misery and waste inherent in an existence battered by the passing of time, it also contains some heartening messages of faith in the outcome of man's struggle against evil, and sympathy for his pains in either victory or defeat. A. is also an exemplary stylist with an impeccable sense for clear and measured expression. The vividness of his narrative, the depth of his psychological insight into the minutiae of human behavior, the wisdom of his frequent philosophical musings, and the universality of his symbolism remain unsurpassed in modern Serbian literature.

FURTHER WORKS: *Priča o vezirovom slonu* (1948; *The Vizier's Elephant*, 1962). FURTHER WORKS IN ENGLISH: *The Damned Yard and Other Stories* (1992); *The Days of the Consuls* (1992)

BIBLIOGRAPHY: Capouya, E., "I. A.: A World of Agony and Hope," *SatR*, 11 Nov. 1961: 25; Gaster, B., "Nobel Prizeman: I. A., the Bard of Bosnia," *BA*, 34 (1962): 25–26; Minde, R., *I. A.: Studien über seine Erzählkunst* (1962); Goy, E. D., "The Work of I. A.," *SEER*, 41 (1963): 301–26; Hitrec, J., "Tea with I. A.," *Reporter*, 23 May 1963: 47–49; Lord, A., "I. A. in English Translation," *SlavR*, 23 (1964): 563–73; Mihailovich, V., "The Basic World View in the Short Stories of I. A., " *SEEJ*, 10 (1966): 173–77; Simon, J., Afterword to *The Bridge on the Drina* (1967): 335–51; Moravčevich, N., "I. A. and the Quintessence of Time," *SEEJ*, 16 (1972): 313–18; McNeill, W., Introduction to *The Bridge on the Drina* (1977): 1–5; Eekman, T., *Thirty Years of Yugoslav Literature 1945–1975* (1978): 91–101; Hawkesworth, C., *I. A.: Bridge between East and West* (1984); Singh Mukerji, V., *I. A.: A Critical Biography* (1990)

—NICHOLAS MORAVČEVICH

ANDRZEJEWSKI, Jerzy

Polish novelist and short-story writer, b. 19 Aug. 1909, Warsaw; d. 19 April 1983, Warsaw

Born into a middle-class family, A. studied Polish literature at the University of Warsaw and worked at the literary weekly *Prosto z mostu*, in which he published his first novel, *Ład serca* (1938; mode of the heart). During World War II he was in Warsaw, and was active in the underground movement. After the war he joined the Writers' Union and in 1949 became its president. From 1952 to 1954 he was editor of a leading cultural weekly, *Przegląd kulturalny*; from 1952 to 1957 he was a member of the Polish parliament. During this period he published several volumes of journalism devoted to the defense of Communist rule in Poland. After the thaw of the mid–1950s, he returned to the writing of novels. Recently, he has become active in the Polish dissident movement.

Three names help situate A.'s position in the literary landscape: Georges BERNANOS, Joseph CONRAD, and Albert CAMUS. In the 1930s, he was hailed as a Catholic writer for *Ład serca*, a book reminiscent of the work of Bernanos and also François MAURIAC. It received the Polish Academy of Literature Award for Young Writers. From then on his writings reflected in turn the bitter experience of World War II; the writer's accommodation to Communist Poland, seen in *Popiół i diament* (1948; *Ashes and Diamonds*, 1962); his disillusionment with postwar optimism, expressed in *Ciemności kryją ziemię* (1957; *The Inquisitors*, 1960); and his increasing aloofness from mass movements and ideologies, evident in *Bramy raju* (1960; *The Gates of Paradise*, 1963) and in *Idzie skacząc po górach* (1963; *A Sitter for a Satyr*, 1965).

All these novels focus on moral problems and have a tendency to view them through the eyes of one man rather than of many. *Ład serca* examines the conscience of a priest. *Popiół i diament* shows how private decisions about politics are made.

Popiół i diament, A.'s most popular novel thanks to the 1958 motion picture made of it by Andrzej Wajda, succeeds in capturing the agony of people caught in a historical situation in which choices are limited. Set in postwar Communist Poland, it depicts several middle-class individuals who are seeking a place in life that would agree with their moral and political beliefs and would thus assure a continuation of their previous commitments and habits. Their choices include total submission to, and support of, the new rulers of Poland; activity in the underground movement that becomes more and more senseless as time goes on; an attempt to pretend to oneself that nothing has changed; or concentration on personal comfort and survival. Two of the characters are killed and others remain undecided or accommodate themselves to reality as best they can.

From the mid–1950s on, A.'s writings increasingly reflect two ideas: the crucial role of passion and desire in history, and the sinfulness of individual human conscience. Even though he long ago abandoned Catholic orthodoxy, A. has remained fascinated with sinfulness and responsibility, and their relation to the evils of the world. The complexity and ambiguity of man's guilt and innocence are investigated in *Bramy raju* and *Ciemności kryją ziemię* in a manner reminiscent of Albert Camus. Even in these two novels about large-scale historical events—the Children's Crusade of 1212 in *Bramy raju* and the Spanish Inquisition in *Ciemności kryję ziemię*—he uses small casts of characters. In that he resembles Joseph Conrad. Historical panoramas are not his specialty.

In *Bramy raju* A. portrays the youngsters in the Children's Crusade as being consumed with fleshly passion for one another. A.'s adolescents know no childish entertainment. They live and love with an intensity and singleness of purpose seldom attributed to children. This tale pursues the idea that childhood was invented in the 18th c. The biblical title of *Idzie skacząc po górach* is an ironic commentary upon the vagaries of love and desire in the modern world. The book contains a free interpretation of the life of Pablo Picasso.

A.'s style has kept changing with his themes. His early novels and stories use an omniscient narrator and contain few verbal experiments. In contrast, *Bramy raju* consists of only one sentence incorporating the internal monologues of several characters. It successfully avoids the trap of affectation and is characterized by a classical simplicity and conciseness. A complicated stream-of-consciousness style is used in *Idzie skacząc po górach*. Owing to

the objective narrator, the short story "Złoty lis" (1954; "The Gold Fox," 1962) is a model of laconism in spite of a heavy emotional charge. In addition, leitmotif phrases are employed in both *Bramy raju* and *Idzie skacząc po górach*.

A.'s writings are in many ways typical of the evolution that eastern European writers who stayed in their respective countries after World War II had to undergo if they wanted to be published without becoming forthright Party spokesmen. In austere times, they tried to be ambiguous, as A. was in *Popiół i diament*; in freer times, they spoke sincerely and profoundly, as in *Bramy raju*.

FURTHER WORKS: *Drogi nieuniknione* (1936); *Noc* (1946); *Święto Winkelrida: Widowisko* (1946, with Jerzy Zagórski); *Aby pokój zwyciężył Publicystyka* (1950); *O człowieku radzieckim: Eseje* (1951); *Partia i twóczość pisarza: Publicystyka* (1952); *Ludzie i zdarzenia: Publicystyka* (2 vols.,1952–1953); *Wojna skuteczna czyli opis bitew i potyczek z Zadufkami: Opowieści* (1953); *Książka dla Marcina: Opowiadania* (1954); *Złoty lis: Opowiadania* (1955); *Niby gaj: Opowiadania 1933–1958* (1959); *Apelacja* (1968; *The Appeal*, 1971)

BIBLIOGRAPHY: Miłosz, C., *The Captive Mind* (1953): 82–110; Shneiderman, S. L., "On the Evils of Fanatic Belief," *East Europe*, 9 (Oct. 1960): 51–53; Krynski, M. J., "The Metamorphoses of J. A.: The Road from Belief to Skepticism," *PolR* 6 (1961–62): 119–24; Krzyżanowski, J., "On the History of *Ashes and Diamonds*," *SEEJ*, 15 (1971): 324–31

—EWA M. THOMPSON

ANGELOU, Maya

American autobiographer and poet, b. 4 Apr. 1928, St. Louis, Mo.

A. has written poetry, plays for stage, screen, and television, and songs. A performer, she has appeared on three continents as a dancer, singer, and actress; her frequent American television appearances in these roles, as well as filling the functions of interviewer and panelist in discussions of race-related current issues, have made her one of the most widely known figures in African-American cultural life. But it is as the author of a multivolume memoir, still in progress, that she has made the deepest impression. Her life—as experience and as artifact—is the creation of hers that the reading public knows best.

A. spent part of her childhood in her birthplace with her mother, part with her grandmother in Stamps, Arkansas, in what she understood to be exile, and her adolescence in San Francisco. In California she spent many of her adult years, during which, as the successive installments of her autobiography outline, she has also lived and worked in New York, Africa, and Europe.

Although A.'s memoirs are her own story filtered through a number of narrative and even fictional conventions, many of the issues they raise consciously evoke generalizations about the content and meaning of black female life in the middle third of the 20th c. Thus her treatment of the sexual abuse that she suffered as a child is at once personal and archetypal. And the highly individual personalities of her mother and grandmother also point to broad conclusions about both the limitations and the power of black women in a racist society.

Maya Angelou

In her various autobiographical volumes, beginning with *I Know Why the Caged Bird Sings* (1970), A. discusses her experiences as a single mother, as San Francisco's first black female streetcar conductor, as a prostitute, as an artist, as a civil-rights worker, and as a black American expatriate living in Africa in the first heady years after independence. She worked with Martin Luther King, Jr., in New York, met with Malcolm X when he visited Ghana, was briefly married to a prominent African, and toured Europe in *Porgy and Bess*, and her memoirs connect all these experiences to her inner growth, what the title of one of the volumes calls *The Heart of a Woman* (1981).

Another theme that runs through the autobiography from the first volume on is what might be called the heart of a *writer*. More precisely, the autobiography is about the making of a writer under the particular social and cultural conditions of Southern black female life. In this by no means linear development, A. as narrator goes from the sexually molested child traumatized into aphonia, a literal not speaking, to a conscious subject who felt that Shakespeare, as she read him at age nine, spoke to and for her, to someone who could make use, for her own writing, of the canonical materials of white male Western culture and the languages of African-American folk life. In her collections of poetry, the influence of black American culture, especially musical and religious culture—spirituals and sorrow songs, gospel music, and popular sayings—is even more evident than in the autobiography, as A. translates her cultural heritage into the raw materials of a deliberate and sometimes overly self-conscious art.

FURTHER WORKS: *Just Give Me a Cool Drink of Water' fore I Diiie* (1971); *Gather Together in My Name* (1974); *Oh Pray My Wings Are Gonna Fit Me Well* (1975); *Singin' and Swingin' and Gettin' Merry Like Christmas* (1976); *And Still I Rise* (1978); *Poems* (1981); *Shaker, Why Don't You Sing?* (1983); *All God's Children Need Traveling Shoes* (1986); *Now Sheba Sings the Song* (1987); *I Shall Not Be Moved* (1990); *Wouldn't Take Nothing for My Journey Now* (1993); *Even the Stars Look Lonesome* (1997)

BIBLIOGRAPHY: Smith, S. A., "The Song of a Caged Bird: M. A.'s Quest after Self-Acceptance," *SHR*, 7 (Fall 1973): 365–75; Butterfield, S., *Black Autobiography in America* (1974): 203–9; Kent, G. E., "M. A.'s *I Know Why the Caged Bird Sings* and Black Autobiographical Tradition," *KanQ*, 7 (1975): 272–78; Neubauer, C. E., "Displacement and Autobiographical Style in M. A.'s *The Heart of a Woman*," *BALF*, 17, 3 (Fall 1983): 123–29; Evans, M., ed., *Black Women Writers (1950–1980): A Critical Evaluation* (1984): 6–24, 25–36; Ramsey, P. R., "Transcendence: The Poetry of M. A.," *CBAA*, 17, 2 (1984–85): 139–53; Froula, C., "The Daughter's Seduction: Sexual Violence and Literary History," *Signs*, 11, 4 (Summer 1986): 621–44; Gilbert, S., "M. A.'s *I Know Why the Caged Bird Sings*: Paths to Escape," *Mount Olive Review*, 1, 1 (Spring 1987): 39–50; Cudjoe, S. R., "M. A.: The Autobiographical Statement Updated," in Gates, H. L., Jr., ed., *Reading Black, Reading Feminist* (1990): 272–306; McPherson, D., *Order Out of Chaos: The Autobiographical Works of M. A.* (1990); Williams, M. E., ed., *Readings on M. A.* (1997)

—LILLIAN S. ROBINSON

Her genius as a writer is her ability to recapture the texture of the way of life in the texture of its idioms, its idiosyncratic vocabulary and especially in its process of image-making. The imagery holds the reality, giving it immediacy. That she chooses to recreate the past in its own sounds suggests to the reader that she accepts the past and recognizes its beauty and its ugliness, its assets and its liabilities, its strength and its weakness. Here we witness a return to and final acceptance of the past in the return to and full acceptance of its language, the language a symbolic construct of a way of life. Ultimately M. A.'s style testifies to her reaffirmation of self-acceptance, the self-acceptance she achieves within the pattern of the autobiography.

Sidonie Ann Smith, "The Song of a Caged Bird: M. A.'s Quest after Self-Acceptance," *Southern Humanities Review*, 7 (Fall 1973), 375

In many ways, *I Know Why the Caged Bird Sings* resembles Richard Wright's *Black Boy*. The setting is a small segregated town in the rural South; the parents have sent the children to live with relatives, one of whom owns a general store; Maya and her brother are forced to attend church, where they amuse themselves by making fun of the more zealous members of the congregation; the preacher comes to dinner and eats all the chicken; there is constant friction between the blacks and the poor whites; the fact of her oppression gradually intrudes on the writer's consciousness when she observes what happens around her—the hypocritical speeches of the white superintendent in their segregated school, the refusal of a white dentist to fix her teeth after her grandmother has salvaged his business; her brother helps fish a decomposed Negro body out of the pond while whites stand around and tell malicious jokes; the local sheriff gives them casual warnings whenever the Klan is about to go on a rampage; and finally, she migrates to a Northern city. M. A.'s complex sense of humor and compassion for other people's defects, however, endow her work with a different quality of radiance; she does not have Wright's mortal seriousness, or his estrangement, and does not take his risks. . . .

The distance in M. A.'s work is achieved by her sense of humor. She has the power of joking at herself, of re-creating the past in a comic spirit without belittling the other people involved and of capturing the pathetic and tragic overtones of the laughter without being overwhelmed by them. Frightened of a ghost story about the dead Mrs. Taylor, a woman who had always screamed her orders in the store because she was half deaf, A. remarks, "the thought of that voice coming out of the grave and all the way down the hill from the cemetery and hanging over my head was enough to straighten my hair." As in Langston Hughes, the humor is often a way of shattering racist images by using them. She knows that the "superstitious" dread Negroes are supposed to have for graveyards is the butt of racist jokes and has felt the perpetual torture of trying to make her hair conform to white standards of beauty; both experiences are subdued, and controlled, by the comic purpose. It is the fear, and the author's ability to laugh at her insecurities, that we remember most—the caged bird's mastery of her song.

Stephen Butterfield, Black Autobiography in
America (1974), 203–9

In *Heart of a Woman*, A. deliberately strives to capture the individual conversational styles of her relatives and friends. In a sense, her friends and acquaintances become "characters" in the story of her life, and like any good writer of fiction, she attempts to make their conversations realistic and convincing. With some of the people who figure in her autobiography, there is no objective measure for credibility other than the reader's critical appreciation for life itself. If the conversant in question is not well-known beyond the scope of the autobiography, A. need only ensure that the dialogue attributed to the individual be consistent with his character as delineated in the text itself. Yet many of her friends and associates were either highly successful celebrities or popular political figures, and the conversations recorded in her life story have points of reference beyond the autobiographical text. In other words, readers can test the degree of verisimilitude in the recorded dialogues with either firsthand knowledge or secondhand sources of information about the celebrities' lives.

It is highly probable, for example, that many of A.'s readers are already familiar with the rhetorical styles of Martin Luther King, Jr., and Malcolm X, and the popular lyrics of Billie Holiday. In fact the lives of these three people in such accounts as *Why We Can't Wait, The Autobiography of Malcolm X*, and *Lady Sings the Blues* have in many ways become part of our contemporary folk history. A. adds a personalized quality to her recollections of conversations with these individuals and many others. The record of their conversations in *Heart of a Woman* brings them to life again, because the autobiographer is sensitive to and even somewhat self-conscious about the accurate reconstruction of their individual styles.

Since memory is not infallible, fictionalization comes into play whenever the autobiographer reconstructs or, perhaps more correctly, recreates conversation. While the autobiographer relies on invention, he or she creates the illusion of an infallible memory that records exactly the feel of a place and the words spoken there.

Carol E. Neubauer, "Displacement and
Autobiographical Style in M. A.'s The Heart of a
Woman," BALF, 17, 3 (Fall 1983), 124–25

Unlike her poetry, which is a continuation of traditional oral expression in Afro-American literature, A.'s prose follows classic technique in nonpoetic Western forms. The material in each book while chronologically marking her life is nonetheless arranged in loosely structured plot sequences which are skillfully controlled. In *Caged Bird* the tenuous psyche of a gangly, sensitive, withdrawn child is traumatically jarred by rape, a treacherous act from which neither the reader nor the protagonist has recovered by the book's end. All else is cathartic: her uncles' justified revenge upon the rapist, her years of readjustment in a closed world of speechlessness despite the warm nurturing of her grandmother, her granduncle, her beloved brother Bailey, and the Stamps community; a second reunion with her vivacious mother; even her absurdly unlucky pregnancy at the end does not assuage the reader's anticipatory wonder: isn't the act of rape by a trusted adult so assaultive upon an eight-year-old's life that it leaves a wound which can never be healed? Such reader interest in a character's future is the craft from which quality fiction is made. Few autobiographers however have the verve to seize the drama of such a moment, using one specific incident to control the book but with an underlining implication that the incident will not control a life.

The denouement in *Gather Together in My Name* is again sexual: the older, crafty, experienced man lasciviously preying upon the young, vulnerable, and, for all her exposure by that time, naive woman. While foreshadowing apprehension guided the reader to the central action in the first work, Maya presses the evolvement in *Gather Together* through a limited first-person narrator who seems to know less of the villain's intention than is obvious to the reader. Thrice removed from the action, the reader sees that L. D. Tolbrook is nothing but a slick pimp, that his

seductive sexual refusals can only lead to a calamitous end; that his please-turn-these-few-tricks-for-
me-baby-so-I-can-get-out-of-an-urgent-jam line is an
ancient inducement for susceptible females, but Maya
the actor in the tragedy cannot. She is too much in
love. Maya, the author, through whose eyes we see a
younger, foolish "self," so painstakingly details the
girl's descent into the brothel that Black women, all
women, have enough vicarious example to avoid the
trap. Again, through using the "self", as role model,
not only is Maya able to instruct and inspire the reader
but the sacrifice of personal disclosure authenticates
the autobiography's integral depth.

Just as the title of *Gather Together* is taken from a
New Testament injunction for the travailing soul to
pray and commune while waiting patiently for deliverance and the *Caged Bird* title is taken from a poem
by the beloved Paul Laurence Dunbar, who gave call
to A.'s nascent creativity, the title of the third work.
*Singin' and Swingin' and Gettin' Merry Like Christ-
mas*, is a folkloric title symbolic of the author's long-
deserved ascent to success and fulfillment. This volume's plot and tone are lifted above adroit reenactments
of that native humor so effective in relieving constant
struggle in Black life which is holistically balanced in
the first two books. The buoyancy is constant because
Maya (who had theretofore been called Marguerite or
Ritie all her life) the singer, Maya the dancer, Maya
the actress, had shed the fearful image of "typical"
unwed Black mother with a dead-end destiny. She
knew she was more than that. But the racist and sexist
society—which had relegated her to dishwasher, short-
order cook, barmaid, chauffeur, and counter clerk;
which had denied her entrance into secure employment and higher education in the armed services; and
which programmed her into a familiar void when the
crush of changing modernity even eradicated the
avenues which partially liberated her foremothers—
seemed invincible. The culmination of her show
business climb is a dual invitation: either to replace
Eartha Kitt in the Broadway production of *New Faces*
or to join the star-studded cast of *Porgy and Bess*,
which began a world tour in 1954. From that climax
the settings shift to such faraway places as Rome,
Venice, Paris, Yugoslavia, Alexandria, Cairo, Athens, and Milan; and the narrator, character, and reader
view life from glorious vistas auspiciously removed
from the world of that dejected girl in Stamps, Arkansas.

Sondra O'Neale, "Reconstruction of the
Composite Self," in Mari Evans, ed., *Black
Women Writers* (1950–1980): *A Critical
Evaluation* (1984), 32–33

The public achievements have been many and yet
the private motivation out of which her writing generates extends beyond the mere search for words as
metaphors for purely private experience. Her poetry
becomes both political and confessional. Significantly, one sees in her autobiographies a role-modeling
process—one paradigmatic for other women—while

not allowing the didactic to become paramount in
either the poetry or the autobiographies.

Her autobiographies and poetry reveal a vital need
to transform the elements of a stultifying and destructive personal, social, political and historical milieu
into a sensual and physical refuge. Loneliness and
human distantiation pervade both her love and political poetry, but are counterposed by a glorification of
life and sensuality which produces a transcendence
over all which could otherwise destroy and create her
despair. This world of sensuality becomes a fortress
against potentially alienating forces, i.e., men, war,
oppression of any kind, in the real world.

Priscilla R. Ramsey, "Transcendence: The Poetry
of M. A.," *CBAA*, 17, 2 (1984–1985), 140

It was the culmination of a number of factors at the
end of the sixties that led to the outpouring of writings
by Afro-American women. First, the inherent shortcomings of the nationalism of the Black Power movement; second, the increased social and economic
pressures that led to the rapid deterioration of the
urban centers of America; third, the rise of the feminist movement that made Afro-American women
more conscious of their particularity; and, fourth, the
increasing tensions in black male-female relations. . . .
All of these factors led to a special kind of problematic to which the Afro-American woman had to address
herself, adding a new and dynamic dimension to
American literature. [Mel] Watkins's contention that
the white media exploited the rift between black men
and women that this literature examined, leading
subsequently to the popularity of black women writers, possesses some degree of truth.

It is out of these conditions and in response to these
specific concerns that M. A. offered her autobiographical statements: *I Know Why the Caged Bird
Sings* (1970), *Gather Together in My Name* (1974),
*Singin' and Swingin' and Gettin' Merry Like Christ-
mas* (1976), *The Heart of a Woman* (1981), and *All
God's Children Need Traveling Shoes* (1986). Although her last two works examine the manner in
which the events of the sixties impacted upon her life,
they were produced in a time when some of the social
and political fervor of the 1970s had abated and thus
allowed for a more sober assessment. Needless to say,
the political currents of the time are more prominent
in the last two segments of her statement. As a
statement, A. presents a powerful, authentic, and
profound signification of Afro-American life and the
changing concerns of the Afro-American woman in
her quest for personal autonomy, understanding, and
love. Such a statement, because of the simple, forthright, and honest manner in which it is presented, is
depicted against the larger struggle of Afro-American
and African peoples for their liberation and triumphs.
It is a celebration of the struggle, survival, and
existence of Afro-American people.

Selwyn R. Cudjoe, "M. A.: The Autobiographical
Statement Updated," in Henry Louis Gates, Jr.,

ed., *Reading Black, Reading Feminist* (1990), 284–85

ANGLO-WELSH LITERATURE

See Welsh Literature

ANGOLAN LITERATURE

In the latter half of the 19th c. the stirrings of protonationalist sentiment among black and mestiço (mixed-race) Angolans gave birth to a number of African-run newspapers in the capital, Luanda. A relatively small, but significant, educated elite expressed their social consciousness and reformist demands in editorials that echoed the strains of republican liberalism that drifted south from far-off Portugal. One of these early precursors of Angolan nationalism was Joaquim Dias Cordeiro da Matta (1857–1894), a journalist, poet, unpublished novelist, and collector of oral traditions in his native Kimbundu language, who first exhorted his fellow Angolans to devote their "leisure time to the founding of our literature."

Anything resembling a literary movement, however, had to wait until the second half of the 20th c. By the end of World War II the scene was set for a new militancy among educated Angolans. With the defeat of fascism in Europe and with the rising tide of national self-determination in Asia and elsewhere in Africa, social protest and cultural revindication contributed to the founding of a literary movement by a multiracial coalition that met on the common ground of anticolonialism and socialist ideology.

In 1950 a small nucleus of these mostly young intellectuals, belonging to the Association of Angola's Native Sons, founded the literary journal *Mensagem*. Although only two issues were published—one in 1951, another in 1952—this journal and a later one, *Cultura* (1957–61), challenged the colonial establishment and heralded the beginnings of a literature that would seek to reclaim Angola for its native sons and daughters. Ironically, but understandably, imaginative writing in the Portuguese language became the most accessible weapon against Western deculturation.

Contributors to *Mensagem* included António Agostinho Neto (1922–1979), of Kimbundu origin, Viriato da Cruz (1928–1973), a mestiço, and António Jacinto (1924-1991), of European descent. These poets, along with other militant writers, became political activists in the Movement of the Liberation of Angola (MPLA). Their literary activities, inseparable from a political consciousness that was strongly influenced by Marxist-Leninist thought, extended from Luanda to Lisbon and even to Paris, where Mário de Andrade (1928-1990), a poet, literary critic, and one of the founders of the MPLA, lived in exile.

In Lisbon the House of Students from the Empire became, from 1944 to 1965, a spawning ground for progressive political ideas and a center of literary activities. Paradoxically, the Salazar government that had sanctioned the organization's founding ordered its closing by the secret police. But in the 1950s and early 1960s the group succeeded in editing two anthologies of Angolan poetry and a number of works by individual authors.

When guerrilla warfare erupted in Angola in 1961 political repression, the mass arrests of dissident intellectuals and writers, and the heavy hand of the censor all but silenced the more militant voices. Nevertheless, Angolan literature had gotten its start, and

although the 1960s are often called the "decade of silence," writers did continue to produce in exile, at home for the desk drawer, or clandestinely in the quiet of a prison cell.

From their postindependence vantage point many Angolan writers like to claim that whereas NÉGRITUDE was conceived in defeat and born in resignation, Angolan writing was cast in struggle and forged in victory. In truth, during the 1950s, and even beyond, the attitudes and images of such black ideologies as pan-Africanism, racial singularity, and Négritude did find expression in some Angolan writing. On the other hand, class struggle did indeed undermine the cause of racial exclusivity. Intellectuals from the three racial communities joined forces in an ideological pact predicated on a militant concern for the plight of the dispossessed masses of Angola.

Thus the themes of identity, identification, and alienation dominate much of the poetry of the 1950s and early 1960s. And in many works the problem of alienation comes across more in terms of class than of race, as in António Agostinho Neto's "Mussunda amigo" (c. 1957; Mussunda friend). In this haunting poem of collective conscience the educated persona addresses a former companion who cannot read the poem that evokes his name.

Other poets who reached a level of artistic competence in the 1950s and 1960s are Mário António (1934-1989), António Cardoso (b. 1933), Aires de Almeida Santos (b. 1922), Fernando da Costa Andrade (b. 1936), and Arnaldo Santos (b. 1936). Their poems combined the intimate "I" with the collective "we" to convey these militant writers' sense of social and political commitment. Many of the best of these poems are lyrical narratives, written in colloquial style, depicting daily life in the African quarters that ringed the Europeanized central city of Luanda. Indeed, what developed in Angolan literature in general was a Creole and Kimbundu hegemony in which the poor neighborhoods and *musseques* (shanty towns) and their residents are the subjects of the poems and stories.

Love of Luanda also found expression in fiction, principally short stories. In the 1960s Arnaldo Santos was able to break the colonial cultural barrier with two collections of short stories: *Quinaxixe* (1965; Quinaxixe)—the title is the name of a Luanda neighborhood—deals mainly with the stresses of a racist environment on children, and *Tempo de munhungo* (1968; vertigo time) captures the social, cultural, and racial contradictions of preindependence Luanda.

But it was José Luandino VIEIRA who emerged as Angola's most prominent writer of fiction and chronicler of Luanda's Creole-Kimbundu hegemony. His *Luuanda* (1964—the archaic spelling of Luanda; *Luuanda: Short Stories of Angola*, 1980) marked a turning point in Angolan writing; for although ostensibly a Portuguese-language text, the three long tales simulate oral storytelling in form and language. Vieira invented a discourse that combines the creolized Portuguese of Luanda with the equally creolized Kimbundu of the *musseques*.

When independence came on 11 November 1975, Angola entered into what was almost a golden age of literary and editorial activities. Only one month after independence, and within earshot of a devastating civil war, the Angolan Writers' Union was proclaimed in Luanda; since its inception it has sponsored literature contests, organized colloquia, and launched an ambitious publishing program in conjunction with two Lisbon publishers.

As is the case with other emerging nations, Angolan writers have been called on to perform official functions that leave them little time to write. But until his untimely death in 1979, António Agostinho Neto, the poet-president of Angola and the president of the Writers' Union's General Assembly, led the way in stressing literature's role in the cultural revolution. Thus, with Neto's legacy and with the establishment of a literary and editorial base, Angola, despite its high illiteracy rate, is a country where imaginative writing is preeminent and writers are held in high esteem.

Not surprisingly, independence resulted in an outpouring of patriotism in the form of technically weak poems and stories. But out of this thicket emerged seasoned writers who applied their sense of craft to the production of literature at the service of the nationalist cause. Fernando da Costa Andrade returned from his years as a guerrilla in the bush to write the poems collected in his *Caderno dos herois* (1977; sketchbook of heroes). Arlindo Barbeitos (b. 1940) drew on the experiences in the eastern zone of combat to fashion the poems in his *Angola Angolé Angolema* (1977; Angola, hail Angola, Angola the word). Another professional poet, Manuel Rui (b. 1941), came home to celebrate independence with his *11 poemas em novembro* (11 poems in November), the title of four different books published since 1976. Rui also published *Sim camarada* (1977; *Yes, Comrade*, 1993), a book of stories that captures the essence of the events and the language generated by the civil war that engulfed Angola after the coup in Portugal. Ruy Duarte de Carvalho (b. 1941), a Portuguese-born writer raised in southern Angola, has published sensitive poems and stories about that region in *A decisão da idade* (1976; decisions of the times) and *Como se o mundo não tivesse leste* (1977; as if the world had no east). And PEPETELA (pseud. of Artur Pestana), another white writer from the south wrote *As aventuras de Ngunga* (1977; *Ngunga's Adventures*, 1980), a didactic and patriotic novella that has sold over 75,000 copies in Angola alone.

Although most of the works published after the coup and since independence revolve around the same overworked themes of anticolonialism and cultural revindication, new forms and styles of writing have begun to appear. Vieira's pioneering example has influenced other writers to experiment with language and technique. Foremost among this new crop of writers is Uanhenga Xitu (Kimbundu name of André Agostinho Mendes de Carvalho, b. 1924). Xitu only began to write after the age of forty, while a political prisoner. Prison mates, including Vieira and António Jacinto, encouraged him to produce stories about the people and customs of his Kimbunda homeland. Thus far, Xitu, writing in Portuguese, has published eight books, the most masterful being *Manana* (1974; Manana).

In the early 1980s economic crises, military aggression from the outside, and the demands of building a new nation have curtailed the even greater flourishing of Angolan literature. But despite all, Angolans seem to take for granted that imaginative writing is an integral part of their cultural revolution.

In spite of a bloody and socially disruptive civil war that raged off and on for nearly twenty years throughout Angola, writers continued to write and publish in the 1980s and 1990s. Since the mid-1980s, and in all genres, there have been several artistically and socially significant works by a both veteran and a growing number of writers who came of age after independence.

Angolan poets who published significant books in the 1980s and 1990s include Arlindo Barbeitos, Ruy Duarte de Carvalho, Puala Tavares (b. 1952), José Luís de Mendonça (b. 1955), Rui Augusto (b. 1958), Ana de Santana (b. 1960), and Lopito Feijó (b. 1963). This period also witnessed the appearance of several major prose works, including novels, by such seasoned writers as Pepetela, Manuel Rui, Arnaldo Santos, and Uanhenga Xitu. Playwrights Domingos Van-Dúnem (b. 1927) and José Mena Abrantes also

merit mentions. Finally, an Angolan literary criticism, by Angolans, began to develop in the 1980s. David Mestre (b. 1948), although best known as a poet, and Luís Kandjimbo (b. 1960) figure among these literary critics.

Angolan works translated into English during the last decade or so include Don Burness's *A Horse of White Clouds: Poems from Lusophone Africa* (1989), with a total of twenty-eight poems by fifteen Angolan poets. As for prose fiction, the English-language version of Pepetela's *Mayombe* (1980) was published, with the same title, in 1984.

Because of the unique circumstances of the author's life as well as those that inform his two novels, José Sousa Jamba (b. 1966) also deserves mention. Although born in Angola to Umbundu parents, at the age of nine Jamba went to study in Zambia, where he stayed for ten years before returning to his homeland. Then, in 1986 he won a scholarship to study in Great Britain. The trilingual Jamba wrote *Patriots* (1990), his first published novel, in English; in 1991 it was published in Portuguese. Both the Portuguese and English versions of Jamba's second novel, *A Lonely Devil* (*Confissão Tropical*), appeared in 1995.

BIBLIOGRAPHY: Moser, G. M., *Essays in Portuguese-African Literature* (1969); Hamilton, R. G., *Voices from an Empire: A History of Afro-Portuguese Literature* (1975): 25–159; Hamilton, R. G., "Black from White and White on Black: Contradictions of Language in the Angola Novel," *Ideologies & Literature*, 1 (1976–1977): 25–58; Burness, D., *Fire: Six Writers from Angola, Mozambique, and Cape Verde* (1977); Hamilton, R. G., "Portuguese-Language Literature," in Owomoyela, O., ed., *A History of Twentieth-Century African Literatures* (1993)

—RUSSELL G. HAMILTON

ANNENSKY, Innokenty

Russian poet, dramatist, translator, and critic, b. 20 Aug. 1856, Omsk; d. 30 Nov. 1909, St. Petersburg

A., one of the "elder symbolists" of modern Russian poetry, was also a classical scholar, translator, critic, and teacher. He led an uneventful life. Born in the western Siberian city of Omsk, where his father was a prominent school administrator, he came to the University of St. Petersburg, where he studied classics and received a degree in 1879, the year of his marriage. Then began his teaching career, first in private schools, then in Kiev, and finally at a prestigious secondary school in Tsarskoe Selo. From 1906 till his death he was a school inspector. He left one son, whose biographical sketch is the only good source of personal information about him.

By profession a teacher and scholar of classical literature—he translated all of Euripides and wrote numerous essays on Greek tragedy—A. wrote poetry mostly in the last fifteen years of his life. In his lifetime he published one collection, *Tikhie pesni* (1904; quiet songs). Two more, *Kiparisovy larets* (1910; *The Cypress Chest*, 1982) and *Posmertnye stikhi* (1923; posthumous verse), comprise the rest of his collected verse. One reading of these several hundred lyrics—A. wrote no long poems—is enough to show that calling him a SYMBOLIST is misleading.

It was, in any case, not the symbolists who prized him, but the Acmeists. He sat on the board of their legendary journal, *Apollon*, and his verse was considered a model of poetic technique and craftsmanship by AKHMATOVA, GUMILYOV and MANDELSHTAM. Like their poetry, A.'s has concrete detail, small focus, and precision. Unlike many of the symbolists, he was neither experimenter nor mystic. He was, however, like them much taken by Mallarmé, Verlaine, and Baudelaire.

He is a poet of anguish and melancholy, forever static and suffering. Poetic creation is for him pain and disease: in one of his lyrics he says he loves his anguished verse as only a mother can love her sick children. That A. feels physically helpless may be related to his frail health—he suffered from pleurisy and a bad heart—but it is at least as much a reflection of his outlook that life will forever be a road of onerous details. Like CHEKHOV, he looks at the small moments of existence and finds them of overpowering significance: an inkwell, a flickering candle, a white cup, a broken bottle all add up to a world that is gloomy and full of minutiae, not clearly seen or understood.

A. loves twilight and the interplay of reflections of a dying sun, for at twilight all fades from view. Dying is everywhere, in nature and man: it sends off reflections like so many shudders. A. loves the dying of autumn and regards the rebirth of spring as putrefaction. It is death that brings out the naturalistic and realistic in him: he sees and describes the suffering souls. In this graphic sense he comes very close to the Acmeist doctrine of focusing on the concrete and denying the metaphysical.

He does not speculate on death or make grandiose pronouncements. Rather, he focuses on those moments when decay is underway and not quite finished. He does not want to see it clearly, but always he is aware of it. He yearns for clarity, at the same time that he fears it. All is precarious and unintelligible. In his famous "Moya toska" (pub. 1923; my anguish) he calls this state *nedoumenie*, the inability to understand something fully, down to its last details.

Unlike so many of the symbolists he does not seek, for he cannot find, the final answers. His is a poetry curiously lacking in any strength, emotional or physical. It is all longing and no achieving. It is a poetry of inaction, where there are few active verbs, and much coloration—always in pale, never bright, shadings, such as dark purple and faded yellow or green. His vocabulary, like that of the Acmeists, is prosaic, even commonplace, and one even finds an occasional colloquialism.

He translated many of the French symbolists and also the plays of Euripides. His own dramatic output amounts to four tragedies, all based on classical myths. The most interesting is *Famira kifared* (1913; Thamiros the cithara player), which treats of the problem of creation: Thamiros is so sure of his poetic gifts that he challenges the muses and is thereby blinded. Poetry, A. is saying, is a challenge to natural forces which may, indeed probably will, result in pain.

His critical essays give good portraits of his contemporaries and excellent analyses and evaluations of the art of translating. His theoretical claims, however impressionistic, are important for an understanding of his own verse; they, too, tell us that at the base of all real creation lies terrible suffering.

A. is a unique figure in modern Russian verse. He combines the romantic sense of anguish with a symbolist search for meaning. In his concentration on the mundane details of life, he forms a bridge to the Acmeists, who were the first to appreciate his talents. His is a special blend of poetic craftsmanship and prosaic themes.

FURTHER WORKS: *Kniga otrazheny* (2 vols., 1906–1909); *Teatr Evripida* (1907); *Stikhotvorenia i tragedii* (1959)

BIBLIOGRAPHY: Poggioli, R., *The Poets of Russia, 1890–1930* (1960): passim; Setchkarev, V. M., *Studies in the Life and Works of I. A.* (1963); Borker, D., "A. and Mallarmé," *SEEJ*, 21, 1 (1977): 46–55; Borker, D., "A. and Pushkin's 'Osen,'" *SEEJ*, 22, 1 (1978): 34–38; Tucker, J. G., *I. A. And the Acmeist Doctrine* (1986)

—PHILIPPE RADLEY

ANOUILH, Jean

French dramatist, b. 23 June 1910, Cérisole; d. 3 Oct. 1987, Lousanne, Switzerland

At the age of twenty-five, after having studied law briefly and worked as a copywriter in an advertising agency, A. decided to devote himself exclusively to writing plays.

A.'s early work, influenced by realism and naturalism, presented somber studies of a sordid and corrupt world. Soon, however, following the examples of GIRAUDOUX, COCTEAU, and Roger Vitrac (1899–1952), A. broke with this style. Classical French theater—chiefly Molière—and the Italian dramatist PIRANDELLO also shaped his work. The result of so many influences on A. is a body of plays that is both typical of his age and distinctive. For A., theater must "create by every artifice possible something truer than truth." Accordingly, he invents devices and gimmicks to call attention to the artificiality of the presentation. Moreover, A. has been increasingly attracted to using the theater itself as the setting

Jean Anouilh

of his plays. For him the world of theater is not simply an artificial creation designed to reveal the truth; it is a representation of life as it is.

A. seeks a balance between farce and high seriousness, and in his best work he succeeds with breathtaking skill. He writes about the instability of social institutions, the absurdity of most human activity, and the emptiness of most lives—themes that are the common currency of 20th-c. literature. But unlike many of his contemporaries, A. bridges popular and serious theater, appealing to wide and diversified audiences. A.'s work is also infused with genuine compassion. His flawed and often ridiculous protagonists strive to preserve some vestige of integrity; their struggle, although doomed to failure, becomes profoundly touching. And the sharpness of A.'s sardonic vision makes his final compassionate conclusion the more effective.

A harsh world and a starkly naturalistic style characterize A.'s early *pièces noires* (black plays). In these, the conflict is between innocent youth and corrupt society, between the base present and the burden of the past. The dominant mood is bitter and cynical. In *Le voyageur sans bagage* (1937; *Traveler without Luggage*, 1959), dealing with a young amnesiac trying to rediscover his family and his past, A. introduced antinaturalistic elements to heighten the theatrical nature of the work. The result is an unlikely marriage—a philosophical meditation cast as a comedy.

The *pièces roses* (pink plays) and the *pièces noires* are opposite sides of the same coin, reflecting only differences of approach and technique. The earliest *pièces roses* are almost pure fantasies, balletlike in their artificiality. But A. is more in his element when he unites the comic and the serious, the fantastic and the real, as in *Le rendez-vous de Senlis* (1942; *Dinner with the Family*, 1958), whose protagonist hires a troupe of actors to act out his life as he wishes it to be.

In the *nouvelles pièces noires* (new black plays) A. uses myth to create an ironic refraction, a dual vision that is a hallmark of his theater. The simultaneous unwinding of the story in the realms of myth and of reality permits the heightened theatricality he had been cultivating. Since myth also presents values and ideals that exist only in a modified or diluted form in the real world, the story can comment ironically on the limitations of reality. *Antigone* (1944; *Antigone*, 1946) is the most successful of these adaptations of myth and is among the most popular of all A.'s plays. Antigone's confrontation with Creon is the ageless debate between youth and maturity, between the hero and the ordinary human, between the idealist and the pragmatist.

A.'s *pièces brillantes* (brilliant plays) are notable for their glittering language, their complex and multifaceted plotting, and their severe view of life. *Colombe* (1951; *Colombe*, 1952, also published as *Mademoiselle Colombe*, 1954), A.'s first play set entirely in a theater, uses this setting as a metaphor for life itself. Beneath the play's brilliant exterior it is somber and bitter: either one accepts the world as it is, participating in its corruption, like the young heroine, or one chooses uncompromising purity, like her husband, and is destroyed.

The *pièces grinçantes* (grating plays) are jarring plays in which A. experiments with ways of expressing his cynical and bitter view-point. In *La valse des toréadors* (1952; *Waltz of the Toreadors*, 1957) A. uses the comicromantic misadventures of a retired general to dramatize what happens to those who have said "yes" to life and who have made the compromises necessary to go on living. As A. himself said, nothing is believable in *La valse des toréadors*, and yet everything is true. The story is a caricature of reality,

simplified and distorted, but the grotesque and ridiculous are symbolic of the life A. sees around him.

A. uses historical material in the *pièces costumées* (costume plays) to create a critical distance between spectator and play, a distancing that is one of the bases of his theatrical method. *L'alouette* (1953; *The Lark*, 1956) is A.'s most experimental dramatization of history. The story of Joan of Arc is retold in a disarmingly simple tone, reinforced by images and attitudes from popular histories. In this interpretation, Joan's desire to fulfill her destiny places her, like her spiritual sister Antigone, in that special world reserved for the heroic. She is of that "insolent race" that resists the temptations of security and comfort to remain true to itself.

The themes of the *nouvelles pièces grinçantes* (new grating plays)—grating and irritating dramas that reveal A.'s cynicism—are familiar, but the style of the plays demonstrates a virtuosity and a daring unequaled in his theater. The nonlinear development of *Les poissons rouges* (1970; the goldfish), reminiscent of the stream-of-consciousness technique of many novels, allows A. to present a series of brief glimpses into the protagonist's life, free from the restrictions of any time sequence. Once again, the central theme is a man's struggle to retain his freedom and individuality. "Victory" here, as elsewhere in A.'s theater, is personal—it is the preservation of one's identity against all the pressures of family, friends, and society.

A. extended his metaphor of the theatrical performance as an image of the real world in his *pièces baroques* (baroque plays). *Cher Antoine* (1969; *Dear Antoine*, 1971) has as its protagonist an enormously successful playwright, but it is a play about failure: the failure of love, of friendship, of communication. Antoine is a man without the strength to endure the futility of existence or the heroism of those who say "no." Characteristically, A. presents an unrelievedly dark view of man, and, typically, although the message is unhappy, the vehicle is witty. A.'s talent is like the one the playwright in *Cher Antoine* sees in himself: the ability to take us to the edge of despair by a deceptively pleasant route.

In the *pièces secrètes* (secret plays), which A. only partly in jest calls his flops, he returns to themes and characters he has treated earlier and more convincingly. In spite of their appellation, these are not more personal or private plays, but are works in which he continues to struggle with situations and problems of technique he has obviously not completely resolved. *Tu étais si gentil quand tu étais petit* (1972; you used to be so nice when you were little), for example, is a retelling of the story of the house of Atreus performed by a troupe of second-rate actors, accompanied and criticized by an orchestra of third-rate musicians.

A.'s strength as a playwright, the reason for his eminence as a contemporary dramatist, is derived from his ability to present in a large body of work and to an extremely wide audience a rich statement of a personal vision, a lucid yet entertaining exploration of themes that involve the anxieties and preoccupations of his audience. Although not as intellectual as some other leading contemporary dramatists, A. is unquestionably a master playmaker, one of the most accomplished in modern French theater—indeed, in world theater. We respond emotionally to the humanity of A.'s writing as we are dazzled by the brilliance of its form, for his work is both a synthesis of and a contribution to the most creative elements in modern drama.

FURTHER WORKS: *Humulus le muet* (1929); *L'hermine* (1931); *Jézabel* (1932); *La mandarine* (1933); *Y avait un prisonnier*

(1935); *La sauvage* (1938; *Restless Heart*, 1957); *Le bal des voleurs* (1938; *Thieves' Carnival*, 1956); *Léocadia* (1940; *Time Remembered*, 1958); *Eurydice* (1942; *Legend of Lovers*, 1952); *Roméo et Jeannette* (1946; *Romeo and Jeannette*, 1958); *Médée* (1946; *Medea*, 1957); *L'invitation au château* (1947; *Ring Round the Moon*, 1950); *Ardèle; ou, La marguerite* (1948; *Ardèle*, 1959); *Épisode de la vie d'un auteur* (1948; *Episode in the Life of an Author*, 1967); *La répétition; ou, L'amour puni* (1950; *The Rehearsal*, 1958); *Cécile; ou, L'école des pères* (1954; *Cecile*, 1967); *Ornifle; ou, Le courant d'air* (1956; *Ornifle*, 1970); *Pauvre Bitos; ou, Le dîner de têtes* (1956; *Poor Bitos*, 1964); *Oreste* (1959); *L'hurluberlu; ou, Le réactionnaire amoureux* (1959; *The Fighting Cock*, 1960); *La petite Molière* (1959); *Becket; ou, L'honneur de Dieu* (1959; *Becket*, 1960); *Le songe du critique* (1960); *La grotte* (1961; *The Cavern*, 1966); *La foire d'empoigne* (1962; *Catch as Catch Can*, 1967); *L'orchestre* (1962; *The Orchestra*, 1967); *Le boulanger, la boulangère, et le petit mitron* (1968); *Ne réveillez pas Madame* (1970); *Le directeur de l'Opéra* (1972); *Monsieur Barnett* (1974); *L'arrestation* (1975); *Le scénario* (1976); *Chers zoiseaux* (1976); *Vive Henri IV* (1978); *La culotte* (1978). **FURTHER WORKS IN ENGLISH:** *J. A.: Five Plays* (1993)

BIBLIOGRAPHY: Didier, J., *À la rencontre de J. A.* (1946); Gignoux, H., *J. A.* (1946); Mury, G., *A. devant l'action* (1946); Marsh, E. O., *J. A.* (1953); Lasalle, J. -P., *J. A.* (1958); Luppé, R., *J. A.* (1959); Pronko, L. C., *The World of J. A.* (1961); Jolivet, P., *Le théâtre de J. A.* (1963); Harvey, J., *A.: A Study in Theatrics* (1964); Vandromme, P., *J. A.: Un auteur et ses personnages* (1965); Borgal, C., *A.: La peine de vivre* (1966); Thody, P., *A.* (1968); Fazia, A. Della, *J. A.* (1969); Ginistier, P., *A.* (1969); Falb, L. W., *J. A.* (1977); McIntyre, H. G., *The Theatre of J. A.* (1987); Smith, C. N., *J. A.: Life, Work and Criticism* (1985)

—LEWIS W. FALB

Hidden in the disturbing violence that has distressed so many people and turned them away from Anouilh's work is the expression of a deep and unremitting poetic anguish. He has grown more tolerant and more ready with pity, though still basically resentful—for the source of his pity is still a passionate feeling of disgust at the wretchedness of human destiny. He seems to have grown to an even more terrible understanding of the way in which petty defects and concessions, small meannesses and betrayals can turn life into a vile, festering sore. This genuine sense of pity and distress that is never lacking in Anouilh is a compensation for the harshness that his resentment against fate drives him to show.

Edward Owen Marsh, *J.A. Poet of Pierror and Pantaloon* (1953), p. 179

We must resist the temptation to impose any particular philosophical frame upon Anouilh's concepts, remembering that he is a dramatist first of all, or even exclusively, and any philosophy expressed through his plays must be considered an indication of the dramatist's sensitivity to and awareness of the tragic sense of life which is so much a part of our time. He has founded no school. But his ideas are significant

because, although sometimes contradictory, they reveal Anouilh as a writer who is bound to the cause of man's freedom, and an author whose work is valid first of all for his contemporaries. He shows us the difficulties and the anguish in store for the man who will accept his responsibilities, and the dignity of man true to himself.

Leonard Pronko, *The World of J. A.* (1961), p. 75

Anouilh once defined playwriting skill as the "ability to land on all fours." meaning the ability to maintain constant control over one's audience. As may be expected, Anouilh handles rhythm effortlessly, so effortlessly that in some of his plays . . . moments of tension and release succeed one another with truly predictable regularity. The characteristic pattern of Anouilh's theatre is of a different sort. There is a clear tendency to begin each piece in lightness and joy, to progress through a number of climaxes toward pessimism and truth, then to veer about abruptly and end in make-believe. This movement of penetration, this shifting of tonality or mood, is the only structure we find in his theatre. It is also a very logical one. . . . Novelty, exposure, alienation, identification—these are the elementary and banal laws of comedy that Anouilh naturally obeys as he makes his characters ludicrous on first appearance and profound or pathetic only when the audience has got to know them. Indeed, he has been so adept at this practice that he has been accused of sadism: he creates phantoms of pastel gaiety merely to impale them, several acts later, through their black souls.

John Harvey, *J. A.* (1964), pp. 24–25

To emphasize clearly the fatal degeneration of any ideal, Anouilh peoples his theatre with little boys and little girls, children who in fact are well past twenty. Over the years he has perhaps increasingly decided in favor of characters—from the old duchesses of his early plays to the politicians belonging to the race of Creon—who have viewed their childhoods from a necessary distance, repudiated them, and become true, realistic adults, not at all worried about dirtying their hands. But apart from this extratheatrical stand, he has constantly, from his very first plays to his most recent, created the ambiguous character in whom there is a mixture of an ideal that derived from ignorance and a corruption due to experience, the adult who never manages to repudiate completely his original purity.

Jacques Guicharnaud, *Modern French Theatre* (1967), p. 125

The unreal, grotesque, pathetically diverting characters and situations in Anouilh's plays link his fantasy with that of the *commedia dell'arte*. His modern French protagonists are similar to ancient zanies and Harlequins; they defend themselves against threatening "reason"; they answer with a grimace and a sneer the warnings and menaces of [the *commedia* character] Captain Spaventos under all of his guises; they avenge the poor with their instinctively plebian art. By his choice of melancholy stock characters combined with a technique of spontaneously complicating and unraveling extravagant plots, Anouilh has recaptured the spirit of the *commedia dell'arte's* kaleidoscopic inventiveness, its improvisation.

Alba della Fazia, *J. A.* (1969), p. 130

Anouilh is a romantic idealist whose idealism plagues him. He yearns for purity, nobility, moral courage, glory, but discerns little but pettiness, chicanery, deception, and vice. Life riles him because it isn't consistent: he abhors the bulk of humanity because it professes virtues it doesn't practice. There is something comic in this and a great measure of "fun," but though he is able to laugh at it, it upsets his vitals. He is a sentimentalist become bitter because everything he beholds, everything that has happened to him since he first conceived of the loveliness of experience—especially in matters of love—has proved false and vain.

Ah, if it were only not so, Anouilh's plays seem to wail—beauty not despoiled, grandeur not debased, purity not debauched. But since it is so, we must make the best of it in humankind's shabby fashion, bedecking ourselves in social courtesies, official pomp and at best in common-sense compromises. Once in a long while some splendid gesture or leap of the soul, like a lark in the sky, momentarily redeems us.

Harold Clurman, *Nation*, 8 Oct. 1973, p. 349

ANTHONY, Michael

Trinidadian novelist, short-story writer, and historian, b. 10 Feb. 1932, Mayaro

After his education in Mayaro and San Fernando, A. worked as a molder in an iron foundry; but he quit this job in 1954 and went to London, where he hoped to establish a writing career. He was, however, at odds with the social and racial climate in England, and he returned to Trinidad in 1970 after a two-year sojourn in Brazil, where he served in Trinidad's diplomatic corps. He has lived in Trinidad since then, and has had a long and rewarding career with the island's National Cultural Council.

Although he began his literary career as a poet, A. abandoned this after receiving discouraging comments from the editors of the BBC's "Caribbean Voices," a particularly important forum for aspiring West Indian writers in the 1950s, and turned his talents to fiction where he found his voice. Of his six novels, collected short stories, and various concise histories of Trinidad and Tobago, *The Games Were Coming* (1963), *The Year in San Fernando* (1965), *Green Days by the River* (1967), and *Cricket in the Road, and Other Stories* (1973) are outstanding achievements. Mayaro, a seaside community on Trinidad's southeastern coast, has exercised a tenacious hold on A.'s imagination, and its mystique pervades his fiction. *Green Days by the River*, one of his finest explorations of a youngster's developing consciousness, is set in Mayaro; and so too

are several of his short stories. But Mayaro is more than merely a lush setting for the action; its rustic charm and arcadian resonances suggest a timelessness and immutability that are congenial to A.'s artistic temperament. In *All That Glitters* (1981), A.'s most recently published novel, some of these symbolic resonances are set alongside the community's workers, individuals such as Clunis, a mere coconut picker, who, for all his rough exterior and disconcerting brashness, is as genuine and reliable as the Mayaro tides.

A.'s emphasis on the strong, dour character, especially the husbandless wife and mother, is one of his important contributions to West Indian fiction. Many of A.'s women are stoic persons who withstand the vicissitudes of life with admirable fortitude. For instance, the drunkard's wife in the short story "Drunkard of the River" (1960) perseveres despite her husband's frequent brutalities. The world is a place of much hardship for other characters such as the dogged protagonist of "The Girl and the River" (1955), A.'s first short story, and certainly one of his best efforts. For Leon Seal, the obsessed cyclist of *The Games Were Coming*, an austere regimen (which eventually alienates his otherwise pliable girlfriend) is the price he pays for winning the prestigious fifteen-mile race, which is a test of his physical and moral fiber.

A.'s characters, the growing youngster notably, are uncommonly sensitive and largely vulnerable. Many of them, consequently, come to grief. Several of these youngsters can be found in A.'s short stories, and some are early, but well-rounded, preparations for the more complex adolescents of the novels. In *The Year in San Fernando* and *Green Days by the River* A. uses the first-person narrator's shifting perceptions to explore with compelling sensitivity and effectiveness the maturing responses of two young heroes who must come to terms with the sober and sometimes sordid realities of the adult world. At the end of his sometimes harrowing sojourn in San Fernando, Francis, whose status in the Chandles's household is little more than a house slave, changes profoundly: he has acquired a deeper understanding of the driven Chandles family, and he has become less psychologically dependent upon others; and Shellie, the boy hero of *Green Days by the River*, after his symbolic baptism of fire and cleansing in the Edenic Cedar Grove, eventually understands that maturity is accepting the consequences of one's actions and decisions.

A.'s prose is another excellent feature of his best work. Although it can be emotionally charged, it is a prose of compelling sparseness—even of the tightness of poetry—and is often characterized by an effective blending of tone, rhythm, and figurative language. The clarity and simplicity of his prose remind one of Ernest HEMINGWAY's, and indeed A. has said that *A Farewell to Arms* (1929) was a fictional catalyst for him.

A.'s fiction is palpably West Indian, and it is tenaciously rooted in the physical reality of the West Indies. He examines the lives of men and women who are severely circumscribed by poverty and deprivation with candor and sympathy. His best work, moreover, shows a sensitive understanding of the West Indian personality, and this, together with his explorations of the physical and metaphysical contours of his society and his probing of the child psyche, assures him a permanent place in the history of West Indian literature.

FURTHER WORKS: *Sandra Street, and Other Stories* (1973); *Glimpses of Trinidad and Tobago* (1974); *King of the Masquerade* (1974); *Profile Trinidad: A Historical Survey from the Discovery to 1900* (1975); *Folk Tales and Fantasies* (1976); *Streets of Conflict* (1976); *The Making of Port of Spain* (1978); *Bright Road to El Dorado* (1982); *Port of Spain in a World at War 1939–1945*

(1983); *First in Trinidad* (1985); *Heroes of the People of Trinidad and Tobago* (1986); *A Better and Brighter Day* (1987); *Towns and Villages of Trinidad and Tobago* (1988)

BIBLIOGRAPHY: Edwards, P., and Ramchand, K., "The Art of Memory: M. A.'s *The Year in San Fernando*," *JCL*, 7 (July 1969): 59–72; Sander, R., "The Homesickness of M. A.," *LHY*, 16, 1 (1975): 95–125; Luengo, A., "Growing Up in San Fernando: Change and Growth in M. A.'s *The Year in San Fernando*," *ArielE*, 6, 2 (1975): 81–95; Niven, A., "My Sympathies Enlarged: The Novels of M. A.," *CE&S*, 2 (1976): 45–62; Ramchand, K., *An Introduction to the Study of West Indian Literature* (1976): 143–54; Noel, D., "The Muses Inhabit Mayaro: M. A.'s *Cricket in the Road*," *IFR*, 5 (1978): 61–62; Barratt, H., "M. A. and Earl Lovelace: The Search for Selfhood," *ACLALSB*, 5, 3 (1980): 62–73; Smyer, R. I., "Enchantment and Violence in the Fiction of M. A.," *WLWE*, 21, 1 (Spring 1982): 148–59; Barratt, H., "M. A.: A Critical Assessment," *Bim*: 66–67 (1983): 157–64; Carter, S., "M. A.'s *All That Glitters*: A Golden West Indian Experimental Mystery," *Journal of West Indian Literature*, 2 (1987): 41–54

—HAROLD BARRATT

ANWAR, Chairil

See Chairil Anwar

ANYIDOHO, Kofi

Ghanaian poet (writing in English), b. 25 July 1947, Wheta

Considered one of the most distinctive voices among African poets of English expression, A. was born in the Volta Region of Ghana to a family of composers and cantors of traditional poetry. He trained as a teacher and taught for several years before entering the University of Ghana in 1977 to study for an honors degree in English and linguistics. Since completing his Ph.D. in comparative literature at the University of Texas at Austin in 1983, A. has been based at the University of Ghana where he is professor of literature and director of the School of Performing Arts. Besides being a member of the board of directors of the W. E. B. du Bois Memorial Center for Pan-African Culture in Accra, he has, in addition, been an external examiner at several African universities, and a visiting scholar at a number of American universities including Cornell and Indiana.

The most outstanding quality of A.'s poetry has been the successful adaptation into English of elements that he has taken from the traditional verbal arts of the Ewe people of southeastern Ghana. Of these borrowings, perhaps the most significant is his adaptation of the traditional song of sorrow. It is from this source that A. derives some of the characteristic idioms and imagery of his poetry, such as the recurrent persona who is an orphan, a madman, or a hunchback, poverty-stricken, in torn clothes, and an object of scorn among his more fortunate kinsfolk. A.'s favorite persona is a man who sits at "the world's extreme corner," to borrow an image from Vinoko Akpalu, one of the most famous of the poet-cantors of Eweland. Also derived form this source is the proverbial quality of

A.'s poetry in the early stages, as well as the sorrowful chanting effect which he is able to achieve through repetition and measured pauses. His poem "Dance of the Hunchback," which appears in *Elegy for the Revolution* (1978), best exemplifies what A. has been able to accomplish with the traditional song of sorrow. The poems in this relatively early volume are not just an outpouring of private grief: the pervasive sorrow is a conventionalized response to the conditions prevailing in Ghana in the 1970s, particularly during the corrupt military government of General I. K. Acheampong. The situation in the poet's country, however, did not only provoke sorrow: sometimes it aroused anger and mockery. To express these sentiments the poet would draw his formal inspiration not from the song of sorrow, but from another traditional genre, the song of abuse or *halo*, in which the persona assumes a tone of moral indignation at the offensive and provocative behavior of the person(s) to whom the poem is addressed. A poem in this style is an unrestrained verbal attack full of hyperbole and not without invective. "Taflatse," which illustrates most strongly A.'s adaptation of this traditional genre, is not directly political in import, but "Oath of Destiny" is clearly an attack, couched in the combative rhetoric of *halo*, on some of Ghana's leaders.

Earthchild (1985), containing poems written mostly during the poet's years as a student in the U.S., brings out another of A.'s thematic concerns, namely, the antagonism between "Earthchildren" and "Moonmen." The former are the black peoples of the world, victims of colonial conquest, slavery, and exploitation. The Moonmen are the race whose technical wizardry has literally taken them to the moon and back, the self-proclaimed owners of the earth. What this collection emphasizes above all is A.'s growing Pan-African outlook, a view that he shares with another famous Ghanaian writer, Ayi Kwei ARMAH. A. sees himself in this collection as a mythmaker for his race; his task is to cry out against historical wrongs, to proclaim the achievement of a race that, in Aimé CÉSAIRE's phrase, "invented nothing," and ultimately to pronounce the healing words that will revitalize black people in the fight ahead for a more just world. The finest poem in the collection is the title poem, "Earthchild," in which A. preserves the traditional oral quality of the persona's voice but enriches it with elements taken from the African diaspora.

The Pan-African theme is further advanced in *Ancestral Logic and Caribbean Blues*, published in 1993, in which he expresses solidarity not only with peoples of African descent all over the world, but with others such as the Amerindians who, like blacks, have suffered from the so-called expansion of Europe and the genocidal arrival of "hurricane Columbus." The poems look forward optimistically to a future in which the barriers that divide black people would have been removed so that the African will be able to travel "with African Airways" on a "straight route from Ghana to Havana to Guyana / and on and on to Savannah in Georgia." The major stylistic quality of these later poems is the diminished reliance on the dirgelike tone derived from the Ewe songs of sorrow and a greater reliance on the power of the image and on a new more urgent voice.

A.'s importance as a poet rests firmly on his successful adaptation of the English language to express to a world audience a vision and experience that is distinctively African. Indeed some would urge, as Chinua ACHEBE does in "The African Writer and the English Language" (1964), that this adaptation is the first task which faces every African writer using a language inherited from Europe. Secondly, A. is important for the relevance of his message: his powerful appeal to the black race to reclaim their ancestral heritage and to break free of the psychic and economic shackles of colonialism.

FURTHER WORKS: *A Harvest of Our Dreams with Elegy for the Revolution* (1985); *Earthchild with Brain Surgery* (1985); *The Pan-African Ideal in Literatures of the Black World* (1989)

BIBLIOGRAPHY: Agovi, K., "*A Harvest of Our Dreams* and *Earthchild* by K. A.," *PA*, 133 (1985): 55-74; Awoonor, K., "The Poem, the Poet, and the Human Condition: Some Aspects of Recent West African Poetry," *Asemka*, 3 (1979): 1-23; Fraser, R., *West African Poetry: A Critical History* (1986): 333-40; Knipp, T., "Politics and Aesthetics: The Theory of Literature and Practice of Poetry in West Africa," in Harrow, K., et al., eds., *Criss-Crossing Boundaries in African Literatures* (1986): 171-90; Kubayanda, J. B., "Dream, Betrayal, and the Revolution: Independent Ghana in the Poetry of K. A.," *Legon*, 3 (1987): 62-78; Wilkinson, J., "K. A.: An Ewe Poet between Tradition and Change," *Africa*, 43 (1988): 543-73

—A. N. MENSAH

APOLLINAIRE, Guillaume

(pseud. of Wilhelm Albert Wladimir Alexandre Apollinaris de Kostrowitzky) French poet, short-story writer, and critic, b. 16 Aug. 1880, Rome, Italy; d. 9 Nov. 1918, Paris

An illegitimate child of a rebellious Polish girl and (probably) an Italian aristocrat, A. was raised by his gambling mother in Italy, in Monaco, on the French Riviera, and in Paris. The resulting cosmopolitanism of his outlook was to have a profound influence on the course of 20th-c. literature and art. Initially pious, he rebelled in his mid-teens against his orthodox Catholic upbringing and adopted the political anarchism and aesthetic messianism of fin-de-siècle SYMBOLISM. A year's sojourn in the Rhineland when he was twenty-one introduced him to German romantic poetry and to the torments of unrequited love, both of which played major roles in his seminal volume of poetry, *Alcools* (1913; *Alcohols*, 1964). Back in Paris (where he remained, except for a year of soldiering on the western front in 1915, until he died in 1918 of influenza and the effects of a war wound) he was a friend and inspiration of poets such as Max JACOB, André Salmon (1881–1969), and André Breton, and artists such as Picasso, Braque, Delaunay, and de Chirico. With them he helped to shape modernist art and letters into a number of forms following symbolism including CUBISM, FUTURISM, DADAISM, and SURREALISM and Orphism.

His first published work, *L'enchanteur pourrissant* (1909; the putrescent enchanter), illustrated by Derain, is a dramatic prose-poem about the entombment of Merlin the Enchanter by his love, Viviane. Written in an obscure symbolist style with a great deal of esoteric erudition, it was hardly appreciated by anyone except the surrealists before 1972, when a critical study by Jean Burgos brought out its deep originality and mythic power. Merlin is A. himself, buried alive by his unrequited love; but he creates from his suffering a new world of poetry and the marvelous. Artistic creation rises from the love-death of the artist, who thus becomes a kind of secular savior, imposing his vision on a hostile world. This is A.'s main theme, which runs through all his works; besides

Merlin, he portrays himself as Pan, Ixion, Orpheus, Christ, a holy clown, and a wandering god (cf. Picasso's Christlike harlequins and erotic bull-gods). Viviane, on the other hand, symbolizes the feminine ideal, part goddess and part siren, who is a force of nature like the night, the earth, and the sea. The phallic, solar poet dies in her embrace, to be reborn in a new godlike form—the work of art.

The thematic structure of *Alcools*, one of A.'s two major collections of poetry, follows this mythic pattern. It opens with the poem "Zone" ("Zone"), which, while heralding the aesthetic triumphs of the 20th c., chronicles the poet's torments as he wanders through a Paris made dark by the loss of his mistress, Marie Laurencin. He is a Christ figure, crucified by love; and the bitter final image of the poem is a beheaded (castrated) sun. Other well-known poems in *Alcools*, often relating to autumn and the passing of time, lament love's loss; most famous are the haunting and melodic "Le pont Mirabeau" ("Mirabeau Bridge") and that astonishing repertoire of ancient and modern legend, "La chanson du mal-aimé" ("Song of the Poorly Loved"). Yet the last poem, "Vendémiaire" (vintage month), is a Whitmanesque hymn to the poet-god in his New Jerusalem, Paris; and other poems sing poetic transcendence, notably "Cortège" ("Cortege"), "Le brasier" ("The Brazier"), and "Les fiançailles" ("The Betrothal"). In the last, for example, the poet passes from early Mariolatry to his crucifixion, in which he loses both his friends and his former poetic truths, to finally a solar-phallic resurrection on Easter day. He is reborn as the architect, as a Knight Templar, and as the Templar's god of a new temple of art.

Between the figures of the melancholy lover and the triumphant demiurge, one more persona is found in *Alcools*, that of the poetwanderer who observes and celebrates the picturesque in the modern. Three dominant symbols accompany his walks through Paris and other European cities: fire, shadow, and *alcools*. The three archetypes and the three symbols combine into an intoxicated Dionysian-Apollonian dance of life out of death, joy out of sorrow.

A.'s other major collection, *Calligrammes* (1918; *Calligrams*, 1980), published a few months before his death, is largely a poetic record of his war experiences, prefaced by poems of 1913—14 and concluded by a manifesto, "La jolie rousse" ("The Pretty Red-head"), addressed to literary traditionalists by a master of the avant-garde. The title of the collection comes from its inclusion of a number of concrete poems, an ancient literary form to which A. gives new life.

Calligrammes is more experimental than *Alcools* and was more influential on a younger generation of poets that included André BRETON, Tristan TZARA, Paul ÉLUARD, and Louis ARAGON. Their own explorations of the subconscious and the modern marvelous owe much to such poems as "Lundi rue Christine" ("Monday, Christine Street"), a collage of bits of conversation overheard in a cafe; and "Les collines" ("The Hills"), an apocalyptic call for investigation into new worlds of art by the poet-prophet. The war poems, on the other hand, were too chauvinistic to appeal to the young internationalists of the 1920s; yet read from our vantage point they constitute a unique record of life and love written literally under fire at the front. Journalistic and erotic, they celebrate the fantastic spectacle of war, with its priapic cannons, virile fireworks, and the labyrinth of fertile female trenches; and they call for a golden age of art to be born out of the savage love-death of nations.

Besides writing his two influential works of poetry, A. proved himself an innovator in the theater of the absurd with his antifeminist farce *Les mamelles de Tirésias* (1918; *The Breasts of Tiresias*,

1961). A. was also a facile writer of science fiction and anticlerical stories, the best of which are collected in *L'hérésiarque et cie* (1910; *The Heresiarch and Co.*, 1965); he was also a perspicacious if unprofessional art critic who oriented his articles in dozens of newspapers and magazines toward the defense of modern art and the paintings of his friends Picasso, Braque, Matisse, Picabia, Léger, Chagall, and Duchamp.

In his two main roles as prophetic innovator and elegiac lyricist, A. stands with Pablo Picasso at the beginning of the 20th c. as a model for subsequent generations of artists; his message of cultural and intellectual progress through art remains a primary goal for writers of our time.

FURTHER WORKS: *La grâce et le maintien français* (1902, with Molina da Silva); *Les onze mille verges* (1906; *The Debauched Hospodar*, 1953); *Le théâtre italien* (1910); *Le bestiaire ou cortège d'Orphée* (1911; *Bestiary*, 1978); *Les exploits d'un jeune Don Juan* (1911?; *The Amorous Exploits of a Young Rakehell*, 1953); *Chronique des grands siècles de la France* (1912); *L'enfer de la Bibliothèque nationale* (1913, with F. Fleuret and L. Perceau); *L'antitradition futuriste* (1913); *Les peintres cubistes* (1913; *The Cubist Painters*, 1944); *La fin de Babylone* (1914); *Les trois Don Juan* (1914); *Case d'armons* (1915); *Le poète assassiné* (1916; *The Poet Assassinated*, 1923); *Vitam impendere amori* (1917); *Le flâneur des deux rives* (1918); *L'esprit nouveau et les poètes* (1918); *La femme assise* (1920); *Contes choisis* (1922); *Il y a* (1925); *Anecdotiques* (1926); *Les épingles* (1928); *Contemporains pittoresques* (1929); *Ombre de mon amour* (1947); *Lettres à sa marraine 1915–1918* (1948); *Couleur du temps* (1949); *Que faire?* (1950); *Tendre comme le souvenir* (1952); *Casanova* (1952); *Le guetteur mélancolique* (1952); *Textes inédits* (1952); *Poèmes à Lou* (1955); *Œuvres poétiques* (1956); *Chroniques d'art* (1960; *Apollinaire on Art, Essays and Reviews 1902–1918*, 1960); *Les diables amoureux* (1964); *Les œuvres complètes* (1966); *Lettres à Lou* (1969); *La démocratie sociale* (1969); *La Bréhatine, cinéma-drame* (1971); *Œuvres en prose* (1977); *Correspondance avec André Level* (1978); *Poésies libres* (1978); *Apollinaire journaliste* (1979). FURTHER WORKS IN ENGLISH: *Selected Writings* (1950); *Selected Poems* (1965); *The Wandering Jew and Other Stories* (1967); *Poet Assasinated and Other Stories* (1984)

BIBLIOGRAPHY: Adéma, M., *A.* (1955); Steegmuller, F., *A., Poet among the Painters* (1963); Davies, M., *A.* (1964); Décaudin, M., *Le dossier d'Alcools* (1965); Bates, S., *G. A.* (1967); Breunig, L. C., *G. A.* (1969); Couffignal, R., *A.* (1975); Mathews, T., *Reading A.: Theories of Poetic Language* (1987); Grimm, J., *G. A.* (1993)

—SCOTT BATES

APPELFELD, Aharon

Israeli novelist and short-story writer, b. 16 Feb. 1932, Tschernovitz, Bukovina

A. reached Palestine in the wake of World War II in 1947, after surviving the period of the Holocaust by wandering the forests. Deprived of any primary or secondary education, he sidestepped these first stages, and studied Hebrew and Yiddish literature at the Hebrew University, Jerusalem. Hebrew has always been his sole literary language.

Although A.'s first literary foray was into poetry, he began publishing stories, of which his first collection, *Ashan* (smoke), appeared in 1962. This set the tone for his later work, as his stories are oblique reflections of the Jewish disaster in Europe. A.'s heroes and heroines have so absorbed the past that their current lives are often merely reflexes to what has gone before. They continue to exist in the shadow of a past experience that penetrated so deeply they could never shake it off or live a renewed, Israeli life.

A.'s sentences are short, the language deployed spare and only minimally rooted in Hebrew sources, although remote from the common Israeli argot. This helps to locate the text at some remove from contemporary Israel and toward the world of the deracinated Jew of central Europe. The action is usually situated in the prewar period, where the trapped individual is held in an enclosed space, speeding toward a future known by the reader, as in *Badenheim* (1980; *Badenheim 1939*, 1981). Or, it is placed in a postwar setting, as in *1946* (1980; 1946), with the intervening phase passed over. In the latter case, as in *Haor venakutonet* (1971; the skin and the coat), the protagonists are entirely locked into their past, scarcely alluding to the contemporary scene, stunted in a state of developmental paralysis. It is in such novels as *Badenheim* and *Tor haplaot* (1978; *The Age of Wonders*, 1981), where the action is dense and the narrative content forces the pace, that the author's strength is most manifest. In such stories, there is less tendency to luxuriate in repetition and poetic representation of paralysis. The old world is seen at its most confident, in its cultural and human value, and in its weakness, its self-deception and denial. As in the representation of the Holocaust in the media, the train serves as a powerful and culminating image of removal and dislocation, and both of these novellas conclude with its use. But then, too, other primary images are frozen in time and space in the record of the narrator.

Captured in A.'s prose is not the white heat of violence, the coals themselves, but rather the residue of the embers. The parallel concern is with the mental disposition among mid-European Jews that prevailed in the pre-Holocaust period. When Jews were separated from their Christian environment and compatriots, they could not understand why. Denial is uncomfortable, but where could anger and frustration be directed?

A.'s prose is oblique and the endings are open. However, an ironic dialogue is established with the reader, who, inevitably, in the light of history, knows more of the outcome than does the narrator. For all the narrative vagueness, the fiction is more or less located in time and place. When the factors are concretized as in *Badenheim* and *Tor haplaot*, the story is most effective. In such works, individual circumstance exemplifies national fate.

FURTHER WORKS: *Bagay haporeh* (1963); *Kfor al haaretz* (1965); *Beqomat haqarqa* (1968); *Adney hanahar* (1971); *Haor vehakutonet* (1971); *Keishon haayin* (1973); *Kemeah edim* (1975); *Masot beguf shlishiy* (1979); *Mikhvat haor* (1980); *Hakutonet vehapasim* (1985); *Be-et uveonah ahat* (1985; *The Healer*, 1990); *Ritspat esh* (1988); *Katerina* (1989; *Katerina*, 1995); *Mesilat barzel* (1991; *The Iron Tracks*, 1998); *Timyon* (1993); *Layish* (1994); *Ad sheyaaleh amud hashahar* (1995). FURTHER WORKS IN ENGLISH: *Tzili: The Story of a Life* (1983); *The Retreat* (1985); *To the Land of the Cattails* (1987); *The Immortal Bartfuss* (1988); *For Every Sin* (1989); *Unto the Soul* (1995)

BIBLIOGRAPHY: Yudkin, L. I., *Escape into Siege: A Survey of Israeli Literature Today* (1974): 118–23; Coffin, E. A., "A.'s Exceptional Universe; Harmony out of Chaos," *Hebrew Studies* (1983), Vol. 24: 85–98; Yudkin, L. I., *1948 and After: Aspects of Israeli Fiction* (1984): 31–32, 162–64; Nesvisky, M., "A. A.: A Profile," *Present Tense*, 12, 2 (Winter 1985): 58–60

—LEON I. YUDKIN

'AQL, Sa'īd

Lebanese poet, b. 4 July 1912, Zahla

A. is known as the most successful Arab interpreter of French 19th-c. symbolist theory. Born in the Christian town of Zahla, he studied, like the famous Khalīl Mutrān (1870–1949), at its well-known Oriental School, where he became acquainted with the classics of Arabic poetry and with 20th-c. neoclassic poets like Ahmad Shawqī (1868–1932) and Bishāra al-Khūrī (1885–1968). He was inspired by his readings of the Koran, the Bible, and Phoenician legends in his first works, but got his symbolist ideas from the works of French symbolists like Abbé Henri Brémond (1865–1933), Paul VALÉRY, and Stéphane Mallarmé (1842–1898). He wrote his most famous work, *al-Majdaliyya* (1937; the Magdalen), at the age of twenty-five. This long narrative poem is considered to be the best example in Arabic of symbolist poetry. A.'s symbolist experiment gave later poets a basis to build on. He also wrote a number of plays, and for many years he was the literary editor of the Beirut newspaper *Lisān al-Hāl*. He founded the weekly *Lubnān* and a publishing house, and has been considered as the architect of "Lebanonism."

A. started his literary career with a Bible-inspired poetic drama, *Bint Yaftāh* (1935; Jephtah's daughter). In this tragedy, with a theme chosen from the Book of Judges, he presented a mixture of romantic and classical poetry, but with a strong element of lyricism. It was followed by *al Majdaliyya*, characterized by Salmā Khadrā Jayyūsī as "one of the most charming poems in modern Arabic" and in it "A. proves himself a master of magic effects of sound and rhythm, manipulating the sounds of vowels and consonants with skill, and exploiting their latent musical power." The poem is a celebration of beauty but shows a lack of realism, and it overlooks the sexual implications of Mary Magdalene's story. This idealistic view of human love seems to be characteristic of A.'s love poetry in general. It is only a small step to the exaggerations that have been noted in A.'s work and which led some critics to call him more a romantic than a symbolist poet.

In 1944 A. published the verse drama *Qadmūs* (Qadmūs), which embodied his ideas on Lebanese nationalism. Here we find the influence of Phoenician mythology. Qadmūs, prince of Sidon, is in search of his sister Europe, who is in the power of Zeus. He has to fight a dragon before he can get his sister back. A. used the theme to defend his nationalistic ideas of Phoenicianism and to oppose Arab nationalism that prevailed at the time. *Qadmūs* is considered to be the first poetic drama in modern Arabic literature.

The poems he wrote between 1932 and 1949 were published in the volume *Rindalā* (1950; Rindalā). They are mostly love poems with little evidence of the poet's own experience with women. The beloved woman in this poetry assumes mythical dimensions, and the poet insists on a distance between him and his beloved. Not fulfillment but glorification seems to be the main objective of the poet. Here one finds again the romantic touch that is reminiscent also of old Udhrite poetry.

In 1960 there followed a collection of short poems in the same vein, written from 1932 onward, entitled *Ajmalu minki? Lā* (more beautiful than you? no!). A. also introduced the use of dialect elements in his poetry and caused a shock with his volume of experimental poetry in Lebanese dialect, *Yārā* (1961; Yara), written in Latin characters.

At that time, A. had already lost his leading position in the circle of Lebanese poets, after having fought "a losing battle with the avantgarde poets of the fifties," such as Yūsuf AL-KHĀL and ADŪNĪS. But they all owed to him to a greater or lesser extent their awareness of symbolist language. His poetry was the beginning of one of the most fertile symbolist trends as represented in the avant-garde poetry of the 1950s.

FURTHER WORKS: *Lubnān in hakā* (1960); *Ka's likhimr* (1961); *Ajrās al-yāsmīn* (1971); *Kitāb alward* (1972); *Qasā'id mīn daftarihā* (1973); *Kummā'l-a'mida* (1974); *Khummāsiyyāt* (1978)

BIBLIOGRAPHY: Durtal, J. S., *A.: un grand poète libanais* (1970); Jayyusi, S. K., *Trends and Movements in Modern Arabic Poetry* (1977), Vol. 2: 475–509; Nasr, N. S., *S. A. Faylasufan* (1980); Jayyusi, S. K., ed., *Modern Arabic Poetry: An Anthology* (1987): 57–60

—ED C. M. DE MOOR

AQUIN, Hubert

Canadian novelist and journalist (writing in French), b. 24 Oct. 1929, Montreal; d. 15 Mar. 1977, Montreal

A. received the traditional "classical" education at the Jean-Jacques-Olier, Sainte-Croix, and Sainte-Marie schools, following which he attended the University of Montreal where he received his M.A. in philosophy (1951). He completed his studies with a three-year stint at the Institute for Political Studies in Paris. Upon his return to Canada, he obtained employment at government institutions, first at Radio Canada as a writer, from 1954 to 1960, and then, until 1963, at the National Office for Film (Office national du film), where he was involved in the production of various films. From 1961 to 1971 he was director of the magazine *Liberté*.

Politically involved in the revolutionary changes taking place in the Province of Quebec, in the RIN (Rassemblement pour l'Indépendence Nationale), he was imprisoned for terrorist activity, and specifically for carrying weapons. It was during this incarceration that he wrote his first novel, *Prochain épisode* (1965; *Prochain épisode*, 1967). This was followed by others: *Trou de mémoire* (1968; *Blackout*, 1974), *L'antiphonaire* (1969; *The Antiphonary*, 1973), and *Neige noire* (1974; *Hamlet's Twin*, 1974). During these same years, he taught at the University of Quebec at Montreal, SUNY Buffalo, and Carleton University.

The noninitiated reader finds A.'s books difficult to access: The Quebec political scene and A.'s passionate involvement in it are important dimensions in his works; his exposure to and the influence by contemporary writers such as the French New Novelists have a direct bearing on his writing style, with its nontraditional approach to chronology and its unwillingness to adhere to stock techniques of characterization.

Prochain épisode exploded onto the literary scene in 1965, thoroughly disliked by a number of readers because of its mystifying style, but also greatly admired by many others who had the patience, training, and commitment necessary for understanding a work that does not make comprehension easy for the reader. On the one hand, it is the story of the author-narrator, imprisoned for political activity, telling his tale, who he is, what he has done; on the other hand, it is a detective story unfolding in Switzerland with flashbacks to Quebec in which the hero, madly in love with K.—a mystery woman with ties to his past in Quebec, and involved in his endeavor—pursues an enemy of his political group. But this enemy, who becomes one or two more characters, and who is all knowing, and has wealth and impeccable tastes, eludes the author. Intermingled are thus a passionate love story, taking place mainly in the past, in a Quebec lovingly evoked along with political commitments and attachments to it; a quest in Switzerland by the author for the enemy, who turns out to be his double; and the subsequent betrayal, capture, and imprisonment, which provide the author-narrator the time and place to recreate who he is, what he has done, and what will take place in the next episode.

Trou de mémoire continues the disrupted-disruptive process characteristic of the first novel by presenting a "story" told by different narrators who are free to add to the basic tale, change it, and explain or elaborate events that were presented only superficially. Here, too, in addition to A.'s reflections and preoccupations with the act of writing, we find involvement with politics and the revolution, love and violence (with rape evoking the British domination of Quebec), and intoxication and clear-headedness. The reader is kept in suspense, waiting for the pieces to fall into place.

These preoccupations are explored further in *L'antiphonaire*, a fragmented, disconnected story, part of it taking place in the 16th c., the other in the 20th, each replying to the other, as would the texts in an antiphonary, presenting oppositions and unions of the sexes, with accompanying violence and retribution in the form of rapes and murders and suicide (the latter also found in *Trou de mémoire*).

Neige noire transposes these interests to the film, evoking the pure lands of the north (northern Norway), where the filmmaker Nicolas plans to immolate his wife Sylvia, who will be segmented cinematographically, intermingling the female figure regenerated into other female figures who become a couple. The themes of death and rebirth, which form the basis of the work, present a new type of society and world order.

It is not so much for his stories that A. is interesting, but rather for his narrative techniques and his philosophical preoccupations, and for his grappling with the issues of politics, writing, activism, and life versus death. His political position led him to quarrel with many, among them René Lévesque. He refused to accept the Governor-General's Award in 1969. He received an award from the Province of Quebec (1970), as well as the David Prize (1972), the Press Prize (1974), and the Great Literary Prize of the city of Montreal (1975). His suicide in 1977 was a tragic event for the literature of Quebec and North America.

FURTHER WORKS: *Point de fuite (essai)* (1971); *Blocs erratiques* (1977)

BIBLIOGRAPHY: Smart, P., *H. A., Agent double* (1973); Martel, J., "Bibliographie analytique d'H. A. 1947–1982" *RHLQCF*, 7 (Winter-Spring 1984): 79–229; Martel, J., "Mise à jour (1983–1984) de la bibliographie analytique d'H. A.," *RHLQCF*, 10 (Summer-Autumn): 75–112; Mocquais, P.-Y., *H. A. ou La quête interrompue* (1985); Sheppard, G., and Yanacopoulo, A., *Signé H. A.: Enquête sur le suicide d'un écrivain* (1985); Lemire, M., et al., *Dictionnaire des œuvres littéraires du Québec* (1982), Vol. 3: passim; (1984), Vol. 4: passim; (1987), Vol. 5: passim; New, W. H., *A History of Canadian Literature* (1989): 284–86

—PAUL BARRETTE

ARAB-AMERICAN LITERATURE

See under Lebanese Literature

ARABIC LITERATURE

See articles on Algerian, Egyptian, Iraqi, Lebanese, Moroccan, Nigerian, Palestinian, Somali, Sudanese, Syrian, and Tunisian literatures

ARAGON, Louis

(Born Louis Andrieux) French poet and novelist, b. 3 Oct. 1897, Paris; d. 24 Dec. 1982, Paris

A.'s mother ran a boardinghouse that A. was later to depict in two of his novels. After completing his secondary studies in Paris in 1916, A. passed his baccalaureat examinations and enrolled in the preparatory year for medical studies. In 1917 he entered the army as a medical aide and met André BRETON and Philippe SOUPAULT, a meeting that was to prove of great significance in the history of SURREALISM. A. participated in the last operations of the war, for which he was awarded the Croix de Guerre, and then participated in the occupation of the Saar and the Rhineland. Upon his return to Paris, A. collaborated with Breton and Soupault on a review, *Littérature*, which was devoted to avant-garde poetry. These writers subsequently became affiliated with the DADAISTS led by Tristan TZARA.

A.'s work reflects the principal trends of thought of the 20th c. As the century has evolved, so has his work, which has been a mirror of his time, reflecting the growth of a writer of genius from the nihilistic responses of the youthful Dadaists to his acceptance of the role of a responsible, social citizen. There may be traced in A.'s novels, essays, and poems the transition from the narrowly individualistic to the vitally collective.

A.'s first published work, *Feu de joie* (1920; bonfire), a collection of 25 poems, echoes the proposal of the Dadaists to destroy all traditional institutions and values. A. and other Dadaists,

Louis Aragon

including Breton and Soupault, soon turned from the sterility of the Dadaists and moved toward SURREALISM. In a theoretical work, *Pour un réalisme socialiste* (1935; for socialist realism), A. wrote that surrealism was a desperate effort to go beyond the negation of DADAISM and to construct a new reality. The principal works of this period are a collection of poems, *Le movement perpétuel* (1926; perpetual motion), and the prose works *Anicet; ou, Le panorama: Roman* (1921; Anicet; or, the panorama: novel), *Les aventures de Télémaque* (1922; *The Adventures of Telemachus*, 1988), *Le libertinage* (1924; *The Libertine*, 1987), and *Le paysan de Paris* (1926; The peasant of Paris), considered to be one of the masterpieces of 20th-c. literature. In *Le paysan de Paris*, A. describes his adventures in quest of surreality. Using reality as his point of departure, A. creates an entirely new world through imagery, and demonstrates how the surrealist fusion of dream and reality into a super or sur-realism is brought about by imagination.

Surrealism had existed originally in a political vacuum. Gradually, the surrealists realized that a revolution in the field of ideas was impossible without a complete revamping of the social structure. Because A. and many of the surrealists found it necessary to ally themselves with a group that could give meaning to their revolt by working toward a practicable goal, they turned toward the Communists. In 1928 A. met the Russian-born Elsa Triolet (1896–1970), his future wife, whose sister was the mistress of the Russian Communist poet MAYAKOVSKY. The role played by Elsa in the life and work of A. has been incalculable, first as initiator to the Soviet revolution and Soviet literature, and then as a guide leading him to

a new concept of the social mission of the writer. A.'s collections of poetry, *Persécuté persécuteur* (1931; persecuted persecutor) and *Hourra l'Oural* (1934; hurrah the Urals), written after their meeting, express the revolutionary fervor of the new convert. In these works, which are political tracts rather than poetical works, A. seeks to demonstrate that poetry is not an end in itself, as he had formerly believed, but the expression of contemporary reality. It was not until the German invasion of France that A. was to reveal himself as a great French lyric poet.

After 1939, in the face of the German menace, a new nationalistic sentiment entered into A.'s poetry. Poetry was no longer the search for an absolute, or the invention of a super language, or a weapon to be used against the bourgeoisie, but an attempt to define transcendent values and to give a meaning to the French struggle against the Nazi invaders.

Le crève-coeur (1941; heartbreak), the first of A.'s wartime collections of poetry, is a chronicle of France under the stress of war and the Nazi occupation. This and five other collections of poetry run the gamut of wartime emotions, from the first bitterness and distress to the joy of liberation. A. attempted, by his poems, to keep alive the spirit of freedom among his countrymen. Because he wanted his message to reach the greatest possible number of Frenchmen, A. used simple versification. Many of his poems had the musical simplicity of the old ballads and could often be sung. He wanted to restore poetry to the important place it had occupied during the days of the troubadours of the 12th c. Unlike his early surrealist poetry, which had been directed toward a select few, A.'s wartime poetry was written for all of the French people.

A.'s fictional works following his conversion to Communism were to reveal the corruption and decadence of bourgeois society. *Les cloches de Bâle* (1934; *The Bells of Basel*, 1936) was the first in the series of novels "Le monde réel" (the real world), and was followed by *Les beaux quartiers* (1936; *Residential Quarter*, 1938), *Les voyageurs de l'impériale* (1942; *The Century Was Young*, 1941), and *Aurélien* (1944; *Aurélien*, 1947). The object of these novels was to present a history of the period from 1880 through the 1920s, characterized principally by the struggle of the bourgeoisie to maintain its money and privileges and to prevent the rise of the working class. They are written according to the doctrine of SOCIALIST REALISM, which, according to A., demanded of the artist a historically concrete and truthful presentation of reality in its revolutionary development. The six volumes of *Les Communistes* (1949–51; the Communists), which followed "Le monde réel," do not really constitute a novel, but rather a panoramic tract that gives the effect of a series of newspaper reports, editorials, and Communist Party speeches. It was only with *La semaine sainte* (1958; *Holy Week*, 1962) that A. was to surpass his earlier novels. *La semaine sainte* recounts the events that took place during Easter week of 1815, from the first news of Napoleon's escape from Elba to the breakup of the entourage of Louis XVIII on the Belgian border. The central view is that of the painter Théodore Géricault, who accompanies the royal retreat as a musketeer of the king. The basic theme of this vast work is the artist's discovery of the people of his nation and of the meaning of loyalty.

After A.'s meeting with Elsa Triolet, all of his work was dedicated to and inspired by her. The impersonal woman of his early poems became Elsa. While, in his surrealist period, love was an opening into the world of the marvelous, the love of Elsa provided an entry into the real world. Love was no longer a mystical participation, but the finding of another and, through the other, the discovery of the rest of humanity. A.'s communion with

Elsa led him to the concept of the couple as the embodiment of love in the 20th c. In a series of long, autobiographical poems beginning with *Les yeux et la mémoire* (1954; eyes and memory), and culminating in *Le fou d'Elsa* (1963; Elsa's madman), A. recounts in a variety of metric patterns and in verses ranging from lyric to epic, from satiric to elegiac, the story of his life both before and after his meeting with Elsa. It is because Elsa represents love, hope, and the future that A. dedicates a poetic cult to her which becomes a religion in *Le fou d'Elsa*.

In 1965 A. began a new series of novels in which his fictional material came from his own experiences. In *La mise à mort* (1965; the moment of truth), *Blanche; ou, L'oubli* (1967; Blanche; or, forgetfulness), and *Théâtre/Roman* (1974; theater/novel), A. attempts both to shed light on the mysteries of human existence and to formulate a new theory of the novel. He sees the novel as a great instrument for collective knowledge, a means for social vision. His thesis is that the novel is not a source of amusement or escape, but rather a means for acquiring knowledge. It is the novel that teaches the art of living and dying. At the end of all scientific analysis there remains a residue which cannot be analyzed, and that is man. What eludes science in this domain A. calls the novel, and man is the matter of which the novel is constituted. Anicet (in *Anicet; ou, Le panorama: Roman*) had dreamed of systematizing life, the "peasant of Paris" had dreamed of a new order, the Communist had believed that changing the methods of distribution would bring about this new order and that Socialist Realism would both reflect this order and contribute to it. In his last novels, A. expresses a hostile attitude toward Socialist Realism.

A.'s literary output, spanning a period of sixty years, has been prodigious, including every genre but drama. While much of his polemic work has already become dated, and while many of his ideas have changed with the continuing revelations of Soviet censorship and repression, A.'s influence on the theory of the novel and on poetic theory has been considerable. Many of his novels and poetic works are among the finest achievements in 20th-c. French literature.

FURTHER WORKS: *Les plaisirs de la capitale* (1923); *Une vague de rêves* (1924); *Le traité du style* (1928); *Le con d'Irène* (1928); *La grande gaïeté* (1929); *La peinture au défi* (1930); *Cantique à Elsa* (1941); *Les yeux d'Elsa* (1942); *Brocéliande* (1942); *En français dans le texte* (1943); *Le Musée Grévin* (1943); *La Diane française* (1945); *En étrange pays dans mon pays lui-même* (1945); *Servitude et grandeur des Français* (1945); *L'enseigne de Gersaint* (1946); *L'homme communiste, I* (1946); *Apologie du luxe* (1946); *La culture et les hommes* (1947); *Chroniques du bel canto* (1947); *Le nouveau crève-coeur* (1948); *La naissance de la paix* (1949); *L'exemple de Courbet* (1952); *Hugo, poète réaliste* (1952); *Avez-vous lu Victor Hugo?* (1952); *Le neveu de M. Duval* (1953) *L'homme communiste, II* (1953); *Journal d'une poésie nationale* (1954); *Mes caravanes et autres poèmes* (1954); *La lumière de Stendhal* (1954); *Littératures soviétiques* (1955); *Introduction aux littératures soviétiques* (1956); *Le roman inachevé* (1956); *J'abats mon jeu* (1959); *Elsa* (1959); *Entretiens sur le musée de Dresde* (1959, with Jean Cocteau); *Poésies* (1960); *Les poètes* (1960); *Histoire parallèle (U.R.S.S.-U.S.A.)* (1962, with André Maurois); *A History of the U.S.S.R. from Lenin to Khrushchev,* 1964); *Entretiens avec Francis Crémieux* (1964); *Il ne m'est Paris que d'Elsa* (1964); *Les collages* (1965); *Le voyage de Hollande* (1965); *Elégie à Pablo Neruda* (1966); *Aragon parle avec Dominique Arban* (1968); *Les chambres* (1969); *Je n'ai jamais appris à écrire,*

ou les Incipit (1969); *Henri Matisse, roman* (1971; *Henri Matisse: A Novel* 1972)

BIBLIOGRAPHY: Josephson, H., and Cowley, M., *A.: Poet of the French Resistance* (1945; repub. as *A.: Poet of Resurgent France,* 1946); Peyre, H., "The Resistance and the Literary Revival in France," *YR*, 35, 1 (1945): 85–92; Balakian, A., *Literary Origins of Surrealism* (1947); Breton, A., *Entretiens* (1952); Gavillet, A., *A. surréaliste: La littérature au défi* (1957); Juin, H., *A.* (1960); Lescure, P. de, *A. romancier* (1960); Garaudy, R., *L'itinéraire d'A.* (1961); Roy, A., *A.* (1962); Raillard, G., *A.* (1964); Labry, S., *A., poète d'Elsa* (1965); Nadeau, M., *History of Surrealism* (1965); Gindine, Y., *A., prosateur surréaliste* (1966); Haroche, C., *L'idée de l'amour dans "Le Fou d'Elsa" et l'œuvre d'A.* (1966); Sur, J., *A., le réalisme de l'amour* (1966); Aghereth, M., *Commitment in Modern French Literature* (1967); Becker, L., *L. A.* (1971); Lecherbonnier, B., *A.* (1971); Daix, P., *A.* (1975)

—LUCILLE FRACKMAN BECKER

[World War II] gave back to A. the world in which words have a real meaning, even the tritest of words that describe human experiences. He was like a traveler returning after years to his own countryside, in which everything is familiar and yet has a different value, being seen with different eyes. . . . There was no time for self-questioning, for writhing in the pains of composition; there was not much time to write at all, except for a man like A. who could do his work in barracks, in trains, in waiting rooms, or on the beach at Dunkerque. Unlike less naturally gifted poets, he was able to set down his impressions and emotions as they came, so that his six volumes of wartime poetry became a month-by-month record of the struggle: the boredom and loneliness of the "phony war"; the grotesque horror of the German invasion, like Breughel's conception of hell; the utter weight of defeat, under which A. was among the first to stand erect; then the impulse for reexamining French history, to find the real strength of the nation; and the growing power of the Resistance, which at first he merely suggested in his poems, but later mirrored frankly, so that his work was forbidden by the Vichy censors and he turned to writing ballads of combat to be printed in the underground newspapers or smuggled across the border and published in Switzerland; and at last the frantic joy of "Paris, Paris, of herself liberated"—all of it is there in A.'s verse.

Hannah Josephson and Malcolm Cowley, eds., *A.: Poet of the French Resistance* (1945), pp. 6–8

André Parinaud: [By the close of World War I] did A. already have the fascinating and original mind revealed later in *Le paysan de Paris*?

André Breton: Yes, he did. As for those tastes of his that could have put him in opposition to Soupault and to me as well, he very quickly put a damper on them. I can still remember him as an extraordinary walking companion. When one walked through parts of Paris with him—even the most colorless places—the experience was greatly enhanced by his magical-novelistic gift for stories, a gift that never failed and that came to him at any street corner or shop window. Even before *Le paysan de Paris*, a book like *Anicet* gave an idea of these riches. No one was more skilled than A. in detecting the unusual in all of its forms; no one else could have been led to such intoxicating reveries about the hidden life of the city. . . .

His memory was equal to any task, and long after reading them he could outline the plots of innumerable novels. The mobility of his mind was incomparable, but this mobility may have led to his rather considerable laxity in his opinions and also a certain susceptibility to impressions. Extremely warm, he devoted himself wholeheartedly to his friends. The only danger he risked came from his excessive desire to please. He *sparkled!*

> André Breton, *Entretiens* (1952), pp. 38–39

A.'s first novels are directed to the bourgeoisie—his readers—more than to the proletariat. In *The Communists* he is addressing the proletariat, to whose existing legend he is adding a new page. The fictional chronicle he writes is shamelessly partial and its fictional value almost nil. And yet, as is not very apparent in *The Communists*, A. is a born novelist. He knows how to tell an ample, living story, full of color and movement; he is able to sustain unusual and strongly differentiated characterizations; his satire is often pungent. In addition, a holdover perhaps from his surrealist years, he has a fertile imagination that often carries him into the realm of pure fantasy. One can detect in A. a poet whose senses are alive to form and color, in particular to the charm of feminine beauty and fashion. One can detect the romantic writer of melodrama—and melodrama can make exciting reading.

> Germaine Brée and Margaret Guiton, *An Age of Fiction: The French Novel from Gide to Camus* (1957), pp. 87–88

From this point of view [Socialist Realism], making himself the "secretary of society," the historian and novelist of the real world is, in each one of his works, to bring forth from behind the chaos of outer appearances the underlying law of development. It is not to accumulate events and facts indiscriminately, but to distinguish that which is decaying and dying from that which is being born and growing. It is to do the work of an explorer and a pioneer by destroying illusions and prejudices and by aiding men to become aware of the forces which bind them and hold them captive in an anarchistic and contradictory world. It is also to see the forces of the future on which their liberation depends: those of the proletariat in its deeprooted reality, that is to say, not only like a mass which suffers, but also like an army that fights.

Today's realism is identified with a new type of romanticism which is both active and revolutionary. It is no longer a question of dreaming in utopian fashion of an unreal life and of heroes who have only

the consistency of dreams, but on the contrary, to know how to peer into the future, into the real future which today's battle can build, which gives it its perspectives, its human warmth, its poetry.

> Roger Garaudy, *L'itineraire d'A.* (1961), p. 278

Throughout French poetry, from Tristan and Iseult and our medieval bards, the theme of love has been a major theme. It never seems to exhaust images or rhythms or make weary the inspiration which pursues its song throughout the centuries along a thousand roads of dreams and fantasy.

A. continues the tradition. . . . He has taken up in a princely manner the marvelous instrument of Chrétien de Troyes, Ronsard, Agrippa d'Aubigné and Victor Hugo. . . . Love, which he defines as a gift and a definitive choice, is the explanation of A.'s work and is, for him, the justification of his destiny. "They don't believe me when I say that I love. But look at me; I am perhaps a madman, perhaps a slave, perhaps a fool, but I say this to you, I have learned only one thing in this life, I have learned to love. And I can wish you nothing more than to know how to love."

Love is the sole and final revelation of man's destiny. It is the criterion for judging the purity and the depth of the soul. Its didactic virtue is undeniable in poetry and in novels.

> Charles Haroche, *L'idée de l'amour dans "Le fou d'Elsa" et l'ćuvre d'A.* (1966), pp. 105–6

The political autobiography [*Les yeux et la mémoire*] was followed in 1956 by a more personal one, *Le roman inachevé* [the unfinished novel]. The title deserves some explanation. On the back cover of his poem, A. points out that the word "roman" is used in two senses, in the medieval one, which describes long narrative poems, and in the modern sense, to indicate that out of his personal recollections, the author has created a work of fiction. The word "inachevé" also serves a double purpose; it is meant to remind us that aspects of A.'s life which he described elsewhere have been left out, and probably to stress that the story is by no means over since the central character is still alive. . . . It is not only because of its subject matter that *Le roman inachevé* represents a break from A.'s previous poems, but because it illustrates his skill in handling the widest variety of metres. These correspond to his various moods and they are a magnificent proof both of the deeply human content of commitment and of the fact that in "littérature engagée" technical achievement is far from despised.

> Maxwell Adereth, *Commitment in Modern French Literature* (1967), pp. 107–8

On November 6, 1928, A. met Elsa Triolet, who was to transform him completely as a man and as a writer.

The lyrical portion of his work ceaselessly revolves around this *extraordinary* event: A.'s being born to a second life at the age of thirty. From *Le* crève-coeur . . . to *Les chambres*, A.'s volumes of poetry from a constellation around the presence of Elsa, a presence that illuminates the poet's actions, thoughts, and words. And—an exceptional feature in the history of poets and their muses—it is not only the woman who inspires A. but the woman-novelist as well, each of whose works is a revelation to him. That is why A.'s fiction and poetry must be read side by side with the works of Elsa Triolet. . . .

To love mankind, one must have loved a woman and have been freed of one's egotism: therefore, the act of loving becomes the point of departure for all social faith, because only woman can give a meaning to life. To communicate this conviction, tested through the concrete experiences of life, A. tirelessly repeats that everything in him "can be summarized by the name of Elsa," who was the inspiration for his political action in the Resistance and the Party, and the inspiration for his works.

Bernard Lecherbonnier, A. (1971), pp. 143, 149

The multiplicity of [A.'s] definitions of the novel—just as, in the past, the multiplicity of definitions of surrealism—which accentuates the elusiveness of A.'s intentions, reveals the need in him—which is, finally, just as strong as the need for the novel or the search for lyrical intoxication—to theorize: to make people believe, to make himself believe that he maintains intellectual control. In other words, to weave there another novel . . . that of his own creation. But what changes in his third career is that, where surrealism was communication with that which was beyond the self, where "le monde réel" was the surrender of individualism in the hope of grasping hold of external reality, A.'s subject matter is henceforth his own life. . . . This whole effort to grasp hold of something, which seems to sum up his work since its inception, is henceforth turned toward biography, as if A. were recognizing his own elusiveness. Or rather, as if he accepted as the basic need underlying the act of writing the desire to finally be master of his own life, the privileged possessor of its meaning. Of his "novel."

Pierre Daix, A. (1975), p. 409

al-A'RAJ, Wāsīnī

Algerian novelist, short-story writer, and critic (writing in Arabic), b. 8 Aug. 1954, Sīdī Bū Jnān, near Tlemcen

The most prolific fiction writer of his generation, A. launched a new trend in the structure of the novel, abandoning the traditional linear form for the circular and the zigzag approach. Moving between present and past, he makes abundant use of flashbacks, borrowing fragments from his childhood and his county's history. He experimented with Arabic language, using a poetic, pure style in his early works, greatly influenced by Syrian writers as a result of his student years in Damascus. His latest novels, particularly

Sayyedatu'l-Maqām (1995, The Lady of the Place), reveal a different trend. Motivated, possibly by a desire to reinforce his Algerian identity, his style reflects the real pattern of speech in Algeria, mixing French and colloquial terms within the classical Arabic narrative.

A.'s innovative technique applied in his first novel, *Waqāe' min awjā' rajulin ghāmara sawba'l-bahr* (1983; Facts from the Sufferings of a Man Who Ventured Toward the Sea), attracted the attention of the critics to his writings. This trend continued in his subsequent novels beginning with *Masra' Ahlām Maryam al-wadī'a* (1984; The Death of Gentle Maryam's Dreams). The fluidity of the language and the limpidity of the style had characterized previous works such as *Jughrāfya al-ajsād al-muhtariqa* (1979; The Geography of the Burned Bodies) and *Nuwwār al-lawz* (1983; Almond Blossoms). A certain melancholy pervades his writings and becomes more tangible in his later novels—triggered possibly by the bloody events of the 1990s. This cloud of sadness that hovers over his writings appears to be due to nostalgia for the homeland in his early works such as in his collection of short stories, *'Alam al-kitāba 'an ahzān al-manfā* (1980; The Pain of Writing about the Sadness of Exile), and to an unfulfilled love that lingers throughout his fiction works. The woman called Maryam is central to his romantic evocations and symbolizes both the homeland and the beloved woman. While A. limited this evocation to a soliloquy, a narrative that conveys more an exercise in writing and a flow of emotions rather than storytelling, Maryam becomes very much alive in *Sayyidatu'l-Maqām*. The love story seems to bloom finally, but is soon crushed as Maryam falls victim to a stray bullet during the upheavals of the late 1980s. Elsewhere and even in love novels such as *Waq' al-Ahdhiya al-Khashina* (1981; The Sound of the Rough Shoes) the author gives precedence to style over action. Writing is clearly experimenting with words for A., but also a means of escape in moments of personal grief or national tragedies. It seems to be his refuge and weapon against the senseless and incomprehensible events that have been shaking his country since the late eighties.

A. did not spare the political power, criticizing its shortcomings and its failure to fulfill the promises made during the war of independence. One aspect of this failure is the continued state of poverty in postindependence times, the subject of his collection of short stories, *Asmāk al-barr al-mutawahhish* (1986; The Fish of the Wild Coast). Using the format of the "maqama," popular in Abbassid literature, A. denounces the killing of the French communists who fought with the Algerians during the war of independence and deplores the decadence of postindependence society in *Mā Tabaqqā min sīrat lakhdar hamrūshe* (1986; Whatever Remains of Lakhdar Hamruche's Biography).

Borrowing from a well-known Arabic classic, *Alf-Layla wa Layla*—known in the West as *The Arabian Nights*—A. wrote *Fāji'at al-layla as-sābi'a ba'da al-alf* (1993; The Tragedy of the Seventh Night after One Thousand) to portray life in postindependent Algeria. Major events of Arab-Islamic history are evoked to serve as an allusion to similar situations in the present time particularly the atrocities occurring in his own country. It is obvious that by recalling the story of the People of the Cave and the end of Arab rule in Andalusia, A. wants history to serve as a lesson for the Arab rulers. This camouflaged criticism of the political power is abandoned in *Sayyidatu'l-Maqām,* where a direct approach is adopted, with an open and unambiguous attack on the crime perpetrators, especially those who use Islam to justify their actions.

FURTHER WORKS: *Ahmad al-msīrdī at-tayyib* (1982); *Ash-Shāhid al-akhīr ʿalā ightiyāl mudun al-bahr* (1986); *An-nuzuʿ al-wāqiʿī al-intiqādī fiʾl-riwāya al-jazāʾiriyya* (1985); *Ittijāhāt al-riwāya al-ʿarabiyyah fiʾl-jazāʾir* (1986); *At-Tāher Wattār: tajribat al-kitābah al-wāqiʿeyyah, al-riwāyah namūdhajan* (1989)

BIBLIOGRAPHY: Bamia, A., "W. A.," in Simon, R. S., et al., eds., *Encyclopedia of the Modern Middle East* (1996), Vol. 1: 204-11; Bamia, A., "Literature, Arabic, North African," in Simon, R. S., et al., eds., *Encyclopedia of the Modern Middle East* (1996), Vol. 3: 1111-15; Khellas, D., "Littérature algérienne d'expression arabe: vers une deuxième génération de romanciers," *CelfanR*, 8 (1992): 13-18; Bamia, A., "Interview with W. A.," *CelfanR*, 7 (1989): 23-26

—AIDA A. BAMIA

ARALICA, Ivan

Croatian novelist, short-story writer, and essayist, b. 30 Sept. 1930, Promina

A. is one of the paradigmatic prose writers of Croatian POSTMODERNISM. After the debacle of the "Croatian Spring" in 1971, when Croatian communists, supported by a huge national movement, made an attempt to oppose the Yugoslav political and cultural unitarism, these writers found the way out of the political and cultural isolation in historical themes. As a secondary school teacher in Zadar, A. first wrote socially engaged prose—*Svemu ima vrijeme* (1967; Everything Has Its Time), *Filip* (1970; Filip), *A primjer se zvao Laudina* (1969; And the Example Was Called Laudina)—composed in the traditional regional manner, which is typical of Croatian literary modernism. The novel *Konjanik* (1970; Rider) and the collection of short stories *Opsjene paklenih crteža* (1977; Illusions of Infernal Drawings) reflect his interest in Croatian history. He corresponds with circumstances that did not permit any kind of free speech on contemporary topics. However, these circumstances allowed certain historical themes and the possibility to "decode" the contemporaneity in a fictional or semifictional story by means of a close net of gnomically disguised historical laws.

The beginning of A.'s most creative and most prolific phase, during which he definitely won literary critics' favor, is marked by his postmodern allegorical description of authorities—the epic novel-like triptich "from Turkish times" *Psi u trgovištu* (1979; Dogs in the Marketplace). His popularity continued with the "Morlac trilogy" consisting of the novels *Put bez sna* (1982; Sleepless Journey), *Duše robova* (1984; The Souls of Slaves), and *Graditelj svratišta* (1986; The Hostel-Builder). In this trilogy he depicts southern Croatia at the end of the 17th c. with its Venetian and Moslem Turkish components. This component dramatically influences not only individual fate but also the historical fate of the Croatian people in general. By restoring the traditional literary model, A. investigates new stylistic, linguistic, and technical possibilities of the historical novel. It is on the allegorical and parabolical levels that he combines a specific expression, epic narration, and gnomic metaphors as found in the ancient Franciscan chronicles, old travel-records, and the authentic vernacular spoken in Dalmatia's hinterland.

In the late 1980s A. resumed more contemporary socially engaged topics. In his novel *Okvir za mržnju* (1987; A Frame for Hate) he analyzes ethical deviations of the postwar socialist system and depicts the relationship between the creative individual and the collectivist authorities. In his more recent historical novels, notably *Asmodejev šal* (1988; Asmodej's Showl), *Propast Magnuma* (1988; Magnum's Destruction), and *Tajna sarmatskog orla* (1989; The Secret of the Sarmatian Eagle), he deepens and widens the context of the historical drama of the Croatian nation within a huge historical mosaic based on metaphoric relations.

During the agression war on Croatia (1991-95) he published the conspicously patriotic novel *Majka Marija* (1992; Mother Maria) and the collections of politically engaged essays *Zadah ocvalog imperija* (1991; Redolence of a Decayed Empire) and *Sokak triju ruža* (1989; Three Roses Lane). In the new social circumstances it was finally possible to write fiction on previously supressed topics from more recent Croatian history—the national tragedy at Bleiburg in 1945, which is the theme of A.'s novel *Četverored* (1997; File of Four). A.'s prose, and this is especially true of his historical fiction, is written in the tradition of Ivo ANDRIĆ's poetics, in which a wide and open narration interchanges with gnomically condensed digressions and images. However, the purposefulness of his novels comes not directly from the historical but from the trans-historical logic. Apart from this, the stress is not on the conceptual nature of history but on the performative level of the novel. This is why A. in his novels—free from patriotic pathos and historical documentarism—does not insist on a "message." Regardless of the fact whether his historical, and even contemporary themes, are written in the form of realistic or of symbolic and parabolic narration, his use of history is neither a mere (documentary) historicism, nor a "frame for hate," but a story on its own. A.'s protagonists are conditioned by circurmstances and by each other; they are caught within a story, which is caught within a huge historical fresco.

A. belongs to the generation of Croatian writers who—within a totalitarian framework—used to look for and find new stylistic means, forms, and topics: some of them resorted to fantasy fiction, and others to realistic or fictional documentarism. A.'s prose contains all these elements, but its predominant feature is history. It is the recognizable civilisational matrix, in which the authentic Croatian component becomes reality.

BIBLIOGRAPHY: Frangeš, I., *Povijest hrvatske književnosti* (1987): 409-13; Visković, V., *Pozicija kritičara* (1988); Milanja, C., *Hrvatski roman 1945-1990* (1996): 97-125; Jelčić, D., *Povijest hrvatske književnosti* (1997): 360, 401

—DUBRAVA SESAR

ARANHA, José da Graça

Brazilian novelist, essayist, and dramatist, b. 21 June 1868, São Luís, Maranhão; d. 27 Feb. 1931, Rio de Janeiro

A.'s background was in law, and when he was young he worked as a judge and public prosecutor. In 1899 he joined the Brazilian foreign service, taking part in border negotiations with neighboring countries. He served in Brazilian legations abroad off and on between 1900 and 1914, and returned permanently to Brazil only in 1920.

A. is remembered primarily for two reasons. The first is his novel *Canaã* (1902; Canaan, 1920), about German immigrants in Brazil and how they adjust to their new surroundings. Some of them want to make Canaan suit their particular needs. Others think, as does A., that the promised land will come from the unity of humanity and nature. In *Canaã* A. also implies that immigrants and native Brazilians together can build a better Brazil if all accept what Brazil has to offer them.

The second reason for A.'s survival in Brazilian literary history is his position after 1924 as a defender of the Brazilian modernists who had burst on the cultural scene in 1922. A.'s contributions to their defense may be found in *O espírito moderno* (1925; the modern spirit). This publication contains a speech made to the Brazilian Academy of Letters in 1924, a proposal to reform it, and A.'s letter of resignation. The speech was occasioned by the Academy's hostility to the vanguardists. A. accused it of inflexibility and closed-mindedness, and claimed it was not prepared to deal with a Brazilian spirit of creativity. But his views were rejected, and A., who had been a member since 1897, resigned.

A.'s works from the years between 1902 and 1924 follow lines of interest close to those expressed in *Canaã*. His play *Malazarte* (1911, Malazarte) also explores humanity's relationship with the cosmos. The title character, drawn from Brazilian folklore, is a free spirit whose strength comes from his oneness with the natural order. The essay *Estética da vida* (1921; aesthetics of life) is where A. explicitly states the premises on which he had based the novel and the play. According to A., the individual can avoid uncertainty and anxiety only by discovering a place in the cosmos, achieving identity with the land, establishing bonds with other human beings—and accepting the necessity of doing so.

After jousting with the Brazilian Academy over the modernists, A. published a second novel, *A viagem maravilhosa* (1929; the marvelous journey), in which he tried to use many avant-garde techniques but fell short of his aims. However, the novel's discussion of political and social questions soon taken up by the revolution of 1930 is interesting.

When all is said and done, A. remains a conventional figure whose best work, *Canaã*, draws from the literary currents of the years preceding World War I. His attempts to write as a vanguardist failed, but his pro-vanguardist postures helped bring the spirit of modernism to Brazilian culture and translate it into Brazilian terms.

FURTHER WORKS: *Obras completas* (8 vols., 1939–41)

BIBLIOGRAPHY: Goldberg, I., *Brazilian Literature* (1922): 234–47; Goldberg, I., "G. A. in Quest of the Promised Land," *NYTBR*, 15 July 1923: 18, 28; Martins, W., *The Modernist Idea* (1970): 209–11; Pacheco, A. C., *G. A.: La obra y el hombre* (1951); Veríssimo, E., *Brazilian Literature* (1947): 94

—GREGORY MCNAB

ARDEN, John

English dramatist, b. 26 Oct. 1930, Barnsley

Significant experiences from A.'s early life that have found expression in his work include his middle-class, post-Depression upbringing in the northern industrial town of his birth, in Yorkshire, the prototype for many small-town settings in his plays; prep school and public school education which helped him understand, though not align himself with, the Establishment social order; a year in the army as a lance corporal, which by his own admission

gave him a private's, rather than an officer's, mentality; and the study of art and architecture, which became a basis for his ongoing interest in details of staging and visual effects in his plays. A.'s marriage to the libertarian actress Margaretta D'Arcy (b. 1934) offered him both support for his political liberalism and a permanent collaborator in the production and sometimes the writing of his plays.

Although A. views himself as a political and sociological philosopher, his plays evidence no unequivocal factionalism or moral stance. Focus is on the psychological dichotomies inherent in human beings rather than on any didactic presentation of a sociopolitical world view. In his early play *The Waters of Babylon* (1957) the sympathetic protagonist is a Polish immigrant, now a pimp, who once served as a Nazi guard at Buchenwald. In *Live Like Pigs* (1958), a play on the welfare state, a family of outrageous gypsies seems more admirable than their conventional neighbors. Two plays with a measure of political import, the nativity play *The Business of Good Government* (1960) and *Left-Handed Liberty* (1965), written to commemorate the signing of Magna Carta, present their respective kings, Herod and John, as being trapped by political expediencies into making decisions that cast them in an unfavorable historical light. Thus, the situations and characters A. presents, regardless of any potential repulsiveness, appeal for mercy instead of judgment on the part of the audience.

A major theme in A.'s plays is that political, social, and even religious order is only a temporary control on the anarchy inherent in man's pursuit of personal autonomy, or conversely, that individual freedom will inevitably conflict with established order. In A.'s most renowned play, *Serjeant Musgrave's Dance* (1959), the title character sees the failure of both military discipline and religious fanaticism; he neglects to consider that those whose support he needs are primarily concerned with filling their bellies and staying warm in winter. In *Armstrong's Last Goodnight* (1964) the protagonist loses his life through overconfidence in his own power to maintain autonomy against the ruling monarch.

Although functioning as peripheral characters to his male protagonists, it is often A.'s women who strike a temporary balance between the exigencies of law and order and the chaotic needs of personal autonomy. By virtue of their secondary social role, women have historically been unable to control social or political outcomes except indirectly, but A.'s women (such as Annie and Mrs. Hitchcock in *Serjeant Musgrave's Dance* and Sir David Lindsay's Lady in *Armstrong's Last Goodnight*), who are willing to give of themselves sexually and hence simply to affirm life in the face of conflict, violence, and even death, maintain a sense of the proportional value of socio-political abstractions and personal ideologies.

Diverse artistic influences on A.'s plays include BRECHT for the combining of vernacular prose, verse, and song; William Dunbar (1460?–1520?) (specifically for the Scots dialect of *Armstrong's Last Goodnight*), Shakespeare, and the traditional English ballad for poetic language; Ben Jonson for grotesquerie in characterization; the mystery, morality, and mummers' plays of the Middle Ages for dramatic techniques and staging devices; and Aristophanes, the English music hall, and commedia dell'arte for comic visual effects (especially notable in *The Workhouse Donkey* [1963]).

A.'s plays are antinaturalistic, requiring the audience's direct response to actions onstage. In an attempt to make closer contact between performer and audience and to add vigor to his plays' performance, A. has often improvised with troupes of children and amateurs. Perhaps the most original of England's present crop of dramatists, A.'s contribution may well be revitalization of the theater through experimental dramatic techniques, orchestrated visual effects, and sheer poetic virtuosity.

FURTHER WORKS: *All Fall Down* (1955); *When Is a Door Not a Door?* (1958); *The Happy Haven* (1960, with Margaretta D'Arcy); *Soldier, Soldier,* (1960); *Wet Fish* (1961); *Ironhand* (1963); *Ars Longa, Vita Brevis* (1964, with M. D'A.); *Wozzeck* (1964); *Fidelio* (1965); *Play without Words* (1965); *Friday's Hiding* (1966, with M. D'A.); *The Royal Pardon; or, The Soldier Who Became an Actor* (1966, with M. D'A.); *The True History of Squire Jonathan and His Unfortunate Treasure* (1968); *The Hero Rises Up: A Romantic Melodrama* (1968, with M. D'A.); *The Soldier's Tale* (1968); *Harold Muggins Is a Martyr* (1968, with M. D'A. and Cartoon Archetypal Slogan Theatre); *The Bagman; or, The Impromptu of Muswell Hill* (1970); *Two Autobiographical Plays* (1971); *The Ballygombeen Bequest* (1972, with M. D'A.); *The Island of the Mighty* (1972, with M. D'A.); *The Non-Stop Connolly Show* (1975, with M. D'A.); *To Present the Pretence* (1977, with M. D'A.); *Pearl* (1978); *Vandaleur's Folly* (1978, with M. D'A.); *To Put It Frankly . . .* (1979); *The Little Gray Home in the West* (1980, with M. D'A.); *Don Quixote* (1980); *The Winking Goose* (1982); *Garland for a Hoar Head* (1982); *The Old Man Sleeps Alone* (1982); *Silence among the Weapons: Some Events at the Time of the Failure of a Republic* (1982; pub. in the U.S. as *Vox Pop: Last Days of the Roman Republic*, 1983); *The Mother* (1984; with M. D'A.); *The Making Of Muswell Hill* (1984, with M. D'A.); *The Manchester Enthusiasts* (1984, with M. D'A.; also pub. as *The Ralahine Experiment*, 1985); *Whose is the Kingdom?* (1988, with M. D'A.); *Books of Bale: A Fiction of History* (1988); *Awkward Corners: Essays, Papers, Fragments* (1988, with M. D'A.); *Cogs Tyrannic* (1991)

BIBLIOGRAPHY: Taylor, J. R., *Anger and After: A Guide to the New British Drama* (1962): 72–88; Hunt, A., "A.'s Stagecraft," *Encore*, 12, 5 (1965): 9–12; Wager, W., and Trussler, S., "Who's for a Revolution? Two Interviews with J. A.," *TDR*, 11, 2 (1966): 41–53; Gilman, R., "A.'s Unsteady Ground," *TDR*, 11, 2 (1966): 54–62; Blindheim, J. T., "J. A.'s Use of the Stage," *MD*, 11 (1968): 306–16; Wakeman, J., ed., *World Authors, 1950–1970* (1975): 66–69; Itzin, C., *Stages in the Revolution* (1980); Gray, F., *J. A.* (1982); Page, M., *J. A.* (1984); Page, M., ed., *J. A. on File* (1985); Wike, J., ed., *J. A. and Margaretta D'Arcy: A Casebook* (1995)

—HONORA M. LYNCH

ARENAS, Reinaldo

Cuban novelist and short-story writer, b. 16 July 1943, Perronales; d. 7 Dec. 1990, New York, N.Y., U.S.A.

Before his premature death, A. was one of the most talented Cuban and Latin American writers in recent memory. Although he is known mainly as a novelist and a short-story writer, he also wrote plays, poetry, and essays. Born and raised in Perronales, a town near Holguín in the former province of Oriente (now Holguín), A. was an only child raised by his mother, aunts, and grandparents. As a teenager A. participated in the rebel uprising against Batista. After the triumph of the Cuban revolution of 1959, he studied

agricultural accounting and worked on a poultry farm. In 1962 A. traveled to Havana where he abandoned his line of work; he became a researcher at the José Martí National Library, from 1963 to 1968, and wrote fiction. A. belongs to the second generation of writers of the Cuban revolution. Initially, he identified with the new government, but later, because of his writings and life-style, A. fell from grace and was arrested in 1973 and 1974, and sent to a rehabilitation camp until 1976. During the Mariel boatlift of 1980, A. fled the island and lived in New York; he contracted AIDS and subsequently committed suicide in his Manhattan apartment in 1990.

A.'s literature can be characterized by its attempt to free itself from the confines of any restriction, be it literary, historical, political, social, or sexual. His *Celestino antes del alba* (1967; Celestino before the dawn), a novel that invents its own reality, won a mention in the 1965 National Contest sponsored by the UNEAC (National Union of Cuban Writers and Artists). This was A.'s first and only novel published in Cuba. The others were either smuggled out of the country or written in exile.

With A.'s second novel, *El mundo alucinante* (1969; Hallucinations, 1971), he received international acclaim; although the novel had been awarded an honorable mention by the UNEAC in 1966, it was not published in Cuba. Instead, it was published in France in 1968 where it obtained *Le Monde's* First Prize for the best foreign novel of the year. *El mundo alucinante* is based on the life of friar Servando Teresa de Mier (1765–1827) and highlights his travels and persecutions for expressing his own ideas. The novel follows in theme and structure the friar's memoirs and recalls A.'s own life. It is written in the first, second, and third persons and suggests a continuous rewriting of events from different perspectives, but also a complete view of the events narrated.

In 1972 an unauthorized collection of stories, *Con los ojos cerrados* (with closed eyes), appeared in Uruguay. It was written after A. completed his first two novels; like them, it received an honorable mention by the UNEAC. *Con los ojos cerrados* contains two stories worth noting. "Comienza el desfile" (the parade begins) opens the volume and narrates the enthusiastic reception given to Castro's rebels as they entered the protagonist's home town; and "La vieja Rosa" (repub. 1980; *Old Rosa*, 1989) is a powerful novelette about an unyielding landowner in the revolution. After his exile, A. rewrote *Celestino antes del alba* and *Con los ojos cerrados*; the first was retitled *Cantando en el pozo* (1982; *Singing from the Well*, 1987) and the other *Termina el desfile* (1981; end of the parade). The story that gives title to the collection symbolically is placed at the end. It was written in exile and is a dramatic account of the takeover of the Peruvian Embassy, which preceded the Mariel boatlift. This story closes a chapter in the writer's life.

El palacio de las blanquísimas mofetas (1980; *Palace of the White Skunks*, 1990) was written in 1972 and was smuggled out of Cuba in 1973, appearing first in French in 1975. It narrates the economic, political, cultural, and psychological traumas of a family in the Cuban countryside. In 1976 A. began to rewrite *Otra vez el mar* (1982; *Farewell to the Sea*, 1986), which he wrote in 1969 and completed in New York. The original manuscript entrusted to a friend disappeared; the second version was confiscated by the authorities. The third version, smuggled out of Cuba, takes place after a six-day vacation and provides two viewpoints, that of Hector and of his wife, but in reality they are part of the protagonist's imagination. Both of these novels are a continuation of *Celestino antes del alba*.

After arriving in the U.S., A. founded Mariel in 1983, a periodical and publishing house, to give publicity to intellectuals who opposed the Castro government. In addition, he published four more novels. The first is *Arturo, la estrella más brillante* (1984; Arturo, the brightest star) which documents the life of a homosexual in a government rehabilitation camp in the late 1960s. In the end, his lover/executioner is transformed into his mother. The second one is *La loma del Angel* (1987; *Graveyard of the Angels*, 1987) and follows the pattern of the 19th-c. Cuban antislavery narrative as it rewrites Cirilo Villaverde's (1812–1894) *Cecilia Valdés* (1882; Cecilia Valdés), Cuba's national novel. A. describes the past from a contemporary perspective to suggest the continuity between slavery in the 19th c. and its manifestation under the present government. The two other works of fiction are *El portero* (1989; *The Doorman*, 1991), which takes place in New York and describes the protagonist's life in the city, and *Viaje a La Habana* (1990; journey to Havana), which gathers three novelettes about a Cuban exile who returns to the island.

A. was a versatile writer. His works include *El central* (1981; *El Central*, 1984), a long poem conceived while he was forced to work on a sugarcane plantation, *Persecución* (1985; persecution), an experimental play, and *Necesidad de libertad* (1986; need for liberty), a collection of essays. All of these works denounce the political, moral, social, and sexual oppressions of Cuban society by the Castro government. At the time of his death, A. left five unpublished manuscripts: the novels "El asalto" (the attack) and "El color del verano" (the color of summer), a collection of short stories, "Adios a mamá" (goodbye, mother), an autobiography, "Antes que a nochezza" (before the knight falls), and a collection of documents, "Un plebiscite de Fidel Castro" (plebiscite for Fidel Castro).

A. was a gifted writer with an extraordinary imagination. He was one of the few internationally renowned writers whose work is hardly known in his own country. But given the nature of his work and his stature in the world community, A.'s reputation will outlast the present administration and he will receive his overdue recognition in Cuba.

FURTHER WORKS: *Voluntad de vivir manifestán-dose* (1989); *Leprosorio* (1990); *Meditaciones de Saint-Nazaire* (1990)

BIBLIOGRAPHY: Borinsky, A., "Re-escribir y escribir: A., Menard, Borges, Cervantes, Fray Servando," *Rl*, 41, 92–93 (July–Dec. 1975): 605–16; Rodríguez Monegal, E., "The Labyrinthine World of R. A.," *LALR*, 8, 16 (1980): 126–31; Santí, E. M., "Entrevista con R. A.," *Vuelta* 4, 47 (1980): 18–25; Méndez Rodena, A., "*El palacio de las blanquísimas mofestas* Narración historiográfica o narración imaginaria?," *Revista de la Universidad de México*, 27 (1983): 14–21; Barreda, P., "Vestirse al desnudo, borrando escribirse: *El central* de R. A.," *Boletín de la Academia Puertorriqueña de la Lengua Española*, 12 (1984): 25–37; Olivares, J., "Carnival and the Novel: R. A.'s *El palacio de las blanquísimas mofetas*," *HR*, 53, 4 (Autumn 1985): 467–76; Volek, E., "La carnavalización y la alegoría en *El mundo alucinante* de R. A.," *Rl*, 51, 130–31 (Jan.–June 1985): 125–48; Rozencvaig, P., *R. A.: narrativa de la trangresión* (1986); Bejar, E. C., *La textualidad de R. A.* (1987); Bush, A., "The Riddled Text: Borges and A.," *MLN*, 103, 2 (March 1988): 374–97; Luis, W., "Present and Future Antislavery Narratives and R. A.'s *Graveyard of the Angels*," *Literary Bondage: Slavery in Cuban Narrative* (1990): 238–47; Soto, F., "*Celestino antes del alba: escritura subversiva/sexualidad*," *RI*, 57, 154 (Jan.–Mar. 1991): 345–54; Valero, R., *Otra vez el mar* de R. A.," *Rl*, 57, 154 (Jan.–Mar. 1991): 355–63; Solotorevsky, M., "*El relato literario como configurador de un referente histórico: Termina el desfile de R. A.*," *RI*, 57, 154 (Jan. Mar. 1991): 365–69

—WILLIAM LUIS

ARGENTINE LITERATURE

Although 19th-c. Argentine literature was dominated by European models, the romantic movement produced two remarkably original authors: Domingo Faustino Sarmiento (1811–1888), author of the essay *Facundo* (1845; *Facundo*, 1960), which described the struggle between civilization and barbarism in the sprawling, sparsely populated nation; and José Hernández (1834–1886), whose popular epic *Martín Fierro* (1872–79; *The Gaucho Martín Fierro*, 1936) defended the gaucho against the injustices of encroaching "civilization." Toward the end of the century naturalism and MODERNISM emerged as the two principal literary schools, the former inspired by the deterministic theories of Émile Zola, the latter by the aesthetic ideals of the French symbolists and Parnassians.

Poetry

The leading Argentine modernist, Leopoldo LUGONES, wrote verses characterized by fresh imagery and an intensity of expression that revitalized the cliché-ridden language of his predecessors. Two POSTMODERNISTS worthy of note are Enrique Banchs (1888–1968), a disciplined, classical stylist, and Alfonsina Storni (1892–1938), a forerunner of feminism, whose poems were molded by the themes of sensual love, solitude, and resentment of male domination.

In 1921 Jorge Luis BORGES brought ULTRAISM to Argentina from Spain, thus initiating the avant-garde reaction against modernism. Though short-lived, ultraism served to unite a group of fine poets who espoused art for art's sake and sought to universalize Argentine letters. This somewhat elitist group, which in addition to Borges included Macedonio Fernández (1874–1952), Ezequiel Martínez ESTRADA, and Ricardo GÜIRALDES, also founded the literary journal *Martín Fierro* (1924–27). They were challenged by proletarian writers who, influenced by the Russian Revolution, viewed literature as a vehicle for expressing social protest. Thus began the much-publicized clash between the Florida and Boedo circles, the former epithet designating the *martinfierristas* and the latter their leftist adversaries. (Florida and Boedo are the names of streets located, respectively, in upper- and lower-class sections of Buenos Aires.)

The 1930s saw a decline in the quality of Argentine poetry. Of vital importance, however, was the founding of *Sur* by Victoria Ocampo (1891–1979). One of the most prestigious Latin American literary journals of its time, *Sur* (1931–71) continued the literary tradition of *Martín Fierro*, publishing informative articles about both foreign and Argentine letters. The 1940s marked a subjective turn inward on the part of most poets, perhaps a reaction to the sordid political environment. Occasionally referred to as neoromantic, the poetry of this period was dominated by two movements: *invencionismo*, which is characterized by an antirhetorical style and rigorous linguistic discipline; and SURREALISM, which proposed to transform the world through the fusion of subjective and objective realities. Leading poets of the 1940s, all of whom continued to publish into the 1970s, were Ricardo E. Molinari (b. 1898), Alberto GIRRI, and César Fernández Moreno (b. 1919).

Although Argentine poetry has evolved in many directions since midcentury, it does reveal some basic tendencies. The so-called "parricide generation" of the 1950s (which also included prose writers) rejected the values of its predecessors, stressing freedom of the individual and advocating a simplified idiom more accessible to the common man. During the 1960s poets assumed a militant posture against political and social injustice, but more recently a kind of surrealist subjectivity has prevailed.

Borges inevitably first comes to mind when the subject of 20th-c. Argentine poetry is broached. Although he is considered an intellectual interested in literature and philosophy, Borges also poeticizes Buenos Aires and Argentina's colorful past. But his fascination with philosophical systems and aesthetics does indeed find expression in much of his poetry. Having become completely blind in the mid-1950s, he began to show a preference for classical meters because they were easier for him to memorize than blank verse. One detects in his subsequent poems a more intimate tone, underscoring his philosophical meditations on time, death, and solitude. In *La cifra* (1982; the figure), one of his last collections, he still longs for the ultimate poetic revelation.

Three other widely known poets are Alberto GIRRI, Olga Orozco (b. 1920), and Alejandra Pizarnik (1936–1972). Girri's work resembles Borges's in its philosophical content, but he is more obscure than his renowned colleague. He is also more pessimistic, viewing the world as a labyrinth of fear and hatred, and Western culture as degenerate and evil. His poems in *El ojo* (1964; the eye) and *Envíos* (1966; dispatches) underscore his somber world vision.

Orozco first became known as a member of the 1940 Generation, but during the 1960s she elicited greater interest. Difficult to comprehend, her work remains outside the range of many readers. She has obviously been influenced by SYMBOLISM and surrealism and seems obsessed with a desire to return to a vaguely described unity—perhaps her childhood—that existed before the Fall. She also obsessively searches for God, attempting to transcend the limitations imposed by him on humanity. *La oscuridad es otro sol* (1967; darkness is another sun) unfolds permutations of a single persona, that of the poet, and *Cantos de Berenice* (1977; songs to Berenice), tells of an enchantress reaching out to her alter ego in the realm of the dead.

Often compared to Sylvia PLATH, Pizarnik apparently committed suicide. The three major themes of her work are death, love, and poetry—death representing infinite peace, love inevitably turning into disenchantment, and poetry becoming an escape from loneliness. Pizarnik uses avantgarde techniques such as disjointed expression, illogical connections, and hermetic allusions, imbuing her poems with an oneiric quality. Her last collection, *El infierno musical* (1971; the musical hell), represents a desperate quest for self-identity and poetic perfection.

Argentine poetry of the 1960s is characterized by realistic, everyday language and an optimistic but revolutionary tone. Typical in this decade of worldwide turmoil are the works of Juan Gelman (b. 1930) and Noé Jitrik (b. 1928). Gelman denounces dictatorship and the bourgeois establishment in *Cólera buey* (1963; oxlike anger) and *Poemas* (1968; poems); Jitrik vents his fury against injustice in *Addio a la mama* (1965; farewell to mama).

Since the 1970s, because of adverse political and economic conditions, poets have fluctuated between frustration and resignation, but at the same time many have withdrawn to the subjective realm as a means of escape from reality. Thus surrealism is still alive, as indicated by the lasting influence of older poets such as Orozco, Juan L. Ortiz (1896–1978), Enrique Molina (b. 1910), César Fernández Moreno, Roberto Juarroz (b. 1925), and Raúl Gustavo Aguirre (b. 1927), the latter perhaps the nation's leading surrealist.

Fiction

The leading practitioner of Argentine fiction at the turn of the century was Roberto PAYRÓ, creator of realistic, and often picaresque, novels of everyday life. A few years later Manuel GÁLVEZ achieved considerable success with his naturalistic novels such as *Nacha Regules* (1919; Nacha Regules), a deterministic portrait of a prostitute. In contrast to Payró and Gálvez, Enrique Larreta (1875–1961) is remembered for his poetically conceived historical novel *La gloria de don Ramiro* (1908; Don Ramiro's glory), one of the finest examples of MODERNIST prose.

Regionalism in Argentina is best illustrated by the gaucho novel, the most prominent practitioners of the genre being Benito Lynch (1888–1951) and Ricardo Güiraldes. Lynch dramatizes country life more realistically than any of his contemporaries. In *El inglés de los huesos* (1924; the Englishman of the bones), for example, his characters gain verisimilitude not only through plot and setting, but also through the skillful manipulation of the rural Argentine dialect Lynch knew from firsthand experience. The masterpiece of 20th-c. gaucho fiction is *Don Segundo Sombra* (1926; *Don Segundo Sombra: Shadows on the Pampa*, 1935), a kind of *bildungsroman* by Ricardo Güiraldes. Having spent much of his life in France, Güiraldes was well acquainted with the avantgarde literary movements of the day. His gaucho protagonist emerges as a poetically idealized figure (*sombra* means "shadow") reflecting the author's nostalgia for his homeland's romantic past.

Another major literary figure of the 1920s was Horacio QUIROGA, who, although born in Uruguay, spent much of his life in the Argentine wilderness. Known principally for his short stories, Quiroga adopted stylistic devices of both modernism and naturalism to depict man locked in a titanic struggle against his overpowering environment. Quiroga's considerable success derives from his ability to capture the oppressive atmosphere of the jungle as well as the horror of falling victim to its superhuman forces. The tales collected in *Anaconda* (1921; anaconda) are excellent examples of his oeuvre.

Three major writers of fiction appeared on the literary scene during the decade prior to World War II: Roberto ARLT, Eduardo MALLEA, and Jorge Luis Borges. Arlt's complex novel *Los siete locos* (1929; *The Seven Madmen*, 1984) describes the frustrations engendered by urban life, the neurotic protagonist embodying man's anguished quest for knowledge and order in a world offering neither. The novel's expressionistic, Kafkaesque ambience perhaps explains Arlt's enthusiastic reception in recent years by young, disillusioned Argentines.

Mallea contrasts sharply with Arlt, his perception of the world being eminently intellectual and idealistic. Mallea's novels, which often border on the essay, abound in psychological and philosophical insights, as illustrated by *La bahía de silencio* (1940; *The Bay of Silence*, 1944). The protagonist of this EXISTENTIAL work is a thinly disguised persona of the author, a man in search of the purpose of life through self-awareness and commitment to humanity. Although Mallea has published prolifically over the years, he has had little influence on younger Argentine readers, perhaps because of his excessively intellectual approach to national problems.

Jorge Luis Borges has achieved an international reputation for his metaphysical short stories, the best of which have appeared in *Ficciones* (1944; *Ficciones*, 1962) and *El Aleph* (1949; *The Aleph and Other Stories*, 1970). This supreme writer's poetically condensed prose is fraught with hidden meanings that reveal not only his fascination with language, but also his wariness of all systems devised by human reason. Indeed, in Borges's works all fields of intellectual endeavor emerge as labyrinths created by man to explain the indecipherable universe in which he is compelled to live. These labyrinths of culture do not mirror reality, however, but only the minds of men, thus giving rise to the absurdity in Borges's tales.

The two most prominent novelists in post-World War II Argentina are Ernesto SÁBATO and Julio CORTÁZAR. Sábato's first novel, *El túnel* (1948; *The Outsider*, 1950, also published as *The Tunnel*, 1988), portrays a psychotic artist whose obsession with logic leads him into a metaphoric tunnel of isolation. *Sobre héroes y tumbas* (1961; *On Heroes and Tombs*, 1981) weaves several plots which, in their entirety, represent modern existential man's quest for meaning in a world dominated by incomprehensible, tragic events. The backdrop of Argentine history—the dictatorships of Juan Manuel de Rosas in the mid-19th c. and of Juan Perón in the mid-20th c.—helps to define the characters by relating their suffering to the nation's collective consciousness.

Julio Cortázar is famous for both his short and long fiction. A committed Marxist, he delights in lampooning the middle class, which he considers both stupid and dangerous. His best-known novel, *Rayuela* (1963; *Hopscotch*, 1966), constitutes an audacious experiment with language and structure; it also describes with mordant irony the absurd antics of a pseudo-intellectual searching for an ever-elusive identity. Cortázar's short stories often fuse reality with fantasy, suggesting that the orderly routine of everyday life can easily disintegrate into chaos.

The following writers indicate the broad spectrum of recent Argentine fiction. Leopoldo MARECHAL is known above all for his *Adán Buenosayres* (1948; Adam Buenosayres), a satirical, Rabelaisian roman à clef often described as an Argentine *Ulysses*. Bernardo Verbitsky (b. 1907) and David VIÑAS are the best exponents of Marxist-oriented SOCIALIST REALISM. Adolfo Bioy CASARES, well known as Borges's collaborator, has been labeled the "purest of the fantastic writers of Argentina." The historical novel *Bomarzo* (1962; *Bomarzo*, 1969) by Manuel Mujica LÁINEZ vividly re-creates the cultural atmosphere of the Italian Renaissance. Three outstanding women writers, all of whom expose the moral decay in Argentine society, are Silvina Bullrich (b. 1915), Beatriz GUIDO, and Marta LYNCH. Manuel PUIG, author of the widely acclaimed novel *La traición de Rita Hayworth* (1968; *Betrayed by Rita Hayworth*, 1971), utilizes pop-art and avant-garde techniques to describe the frustrations of provincial life.

Since the 1960s, Argentina has been governed mostly by military régimes, the principal exception being the period since 1983 when democracy was restored. Thus, much of the nation's recent literature reflects the conditions of life under heavy-handed dictators. During the past decade, however, the deteriorating economic situation has begun to occupy center stage, and, with the granting of freedom of the press, subjects previously considered taboo have been treated with increasing audacity.

Although they published their major works before 1980, the three most influential writers of fiction during the abovementioned period are Jorge Luis Borges, Ernesto Sábato, and Julio Cortázar. Borges, who died in 1986, is famous for his impeccably stylized,

metaphysical short stories based on philosophical themes; the novels of Sábato, who holds a Ph.D. in physics, reflect his turn to the humanities for solutions to present-day problems and his search for the elusive Argentine identity. Cortázar's death in 1984 ended his career as the author of novels and fantastic tales that still fascinate a wide reading public.

José Bianco (1908–1986) and Adolfo Bioy Casares are two of the leading representatives of the older generation. Both belong to an elite group of intellectuals that wrote for *Sur*, the prestigious literary journal that down played realism and advocated more sophisticated forms of writing. Bianco and Bioy Casares eschew politics, preferring to engage their readers in flights of fantasy, psychological speculations, and aesthetic reflections. Examples of their works are Bianco's *La pérdida del reino* (1972; the loss of the kingdom) and Bioy Casares's *La aventura de un fotógrafo en La Plata* (1985; the adventure of a photographer in La Plata), in which a photographer's grappling with his art parallels the author's creative process.

Of the novelists born during the 1920s and 1930s, Manuel PUIG is considered the most original. Puig writes in colloquial Argentine Spanish to depict the stultifying aspects of small-town life as well as the oppression and sexism in the national culture. He also reveals a fascination with the movies, which he views, as an escape for the average citizen trapped in a meaningless day-to-day existence. He is an innovator in his use of POSTMODERNIST techniques. His novels of the 1980s include *Sangre de amor correspondido* (1982; *Blood of Requited Love*, 1984), a sordid evocation of adolescent love with brutal insights into the human psyche, and *Cae la noche tropical* (1989; *Tropical Night Falling*, 1991), which depicts lonely Argentines living in exile.

Other important authors of Puig's generation are Humberto COSTANTINI, David Viñas, Tomás Eloy Martínez (b. 1934), Abel Posse (b. 1934), and Enrique Medina (b. 1937). Costantini's most successful novel is *De dioses, hombrecitos y policías* (1979; *The Gods, the Little Guys, and the Police*, 1984), a bitter allegory of the torture and disappearance of liberals under a ruthless military régime. An implacable Marxist critic of Argentine society, Viñas is best known for his attack on the military establishment in *Los hombres de a caballo* (1967; men on horseback). Eloy Martínez is the author of Argentina's finest nonfiction novel, *La novela de Perón* (1985; *The Perón Novel*, 1988), an engrossing account of the famed president's life, climaxing with his return from Spain in 1973. *Los perros del paraíso* (1983; *The Dogs of Paradise*, 1989), by Posse, recounts the Spanish conquest of the New World with leaps into the present and comic resonances of Gabriel García MÁRQUEZ's *Cien años de soledad* (1967; *One Hundred Years of Solitude*, 1970). One of Argentina's best-selling novelists, Medina has been criticized for his lurid, brutal sensationalism, but he is a gifted narrator whose frankness has softened attitudes toward many forbidden topics. His *Perros de la noche* (1977; night dogs), about the depraved behavior of an abandoned brother and sister, typifies his condemnatory portraits of his homeland.

Argentina has produced more exceptionally talented women novelists than any other Spanish American country. A few of the long list of names are Sylvina Bullrich, Beatriz Guido, Marta Lynch, Luisa VALENZUELA, and Marta Traba (1930–1983). An outspoken feminist, Bullrich writes in a realistic mode about political corruption, the suffering of the impoverished, and, in her satirical novel *La bicicleta* (1986; the bicycle), about the decline of Argentina's standing among nations. Guido also indicts Argentine society in her realistic novels such as *El incendio de las vísperas* (1964; the fire of vespers), a tale of the oligarchy's moral decay under Perón. A militant leftist and feminist, Lynch has left a legacy of intricately designed novels and stories, a fine example of which is *Los años de fuego* (1980; the years of fire). Critics also see Valenzuela as a feminist, but her nonrealistic approach to literature evokes Borges and Cortázar. Her *Cambio de armas* (1982; *Other Weapons*, 1985) is a grouping of sophisticated tales delineating male-female relationships. A prolific political and social critic, Marta Traba is best known for her *Conversación al sur* (1981; *Mothers and Shadows*, 1986), about the complex relationship between two leftist women brutalized by a tyrannical regime.

The younger generation of talented fiction writers (those born after 1940) includes, among others, Mario SZICHMAN, Ricardo PIGLIA, Osvaldo SORIANO, Cecilia Absatz (b. 1943), Jorge Asís (b. 1946), Mempo GIARDINELLI, and Reina Roffé (b. 1951).

The Essay

Of the many subjects treated by Argentine essayists, the quest for national identity (*argentinidad*) emerges as one of primary concern. This subject is particularly evident in the works of Ricardo Rojas (1882–1957), known for his dualistic theory of exoticism and "Indianism." Unlike Sarmiento, who contrasted European civilization with gaucho barbarism, Rojas viewed European culture as exotic and "Indianism" as a fundamental ingredient of the American ethos. He also believed that in his native land European culture had undergone a process of "nationalization," a transformation wrought by the telluric forces of the Argentine landscape. Although some of what Rojas wrote has been dismissed as imprecise mysticism, subsequent essayists have taken his work as a point of departure for the development of their ideas on *argentinidad*.

Carlos Alberto Erro (b. 1899) is primarily concerned with the meaning of *criollismo*, i.e., the identity of the *criollo*, or native Latin American. His investigations have led him to the conclusion that the essence of the *criollo* spirit is forever evolving and that it must continue to evolve free from the slavish imitation of European models. Though younger than Erro, Eduardo Mallea shares many of his existential concerns. His essay *Historia de una pasión argentina* (1937; history of an Argentine passion) sets forth the distinction between the "visible" and the "invisible" Argentine, the former characterized by egoism, insincerity, and mediocrity, the latter by introspection, communion with nature, and dedication to the good of humanity. Mallea optimistically concludes that the "invisible" Argentine will eventually prevail. His optimism is not shared by Ezequiel Martínez Estrada, a harsh critic of 20th-c. Argentine life. His fascinating *Radiografía de la pampa* (1933; *X-ray of the Pampa*, 1971) reflects a profound sense of futility, perhaps because of the nation's political and economic woes at the time of its publication. A leftist radical, he is vitriolic in his attacks against the bourgeoisie, but he is also repelled by violence and condemns any society, capitalist or Marxist, that relegates the individual to the position of a cog in a machine. Because of his uncanny insight into the ills of modern society, Martínez Estrada has been called the embodiment of the Latin American conscience.

Jorge Luis Borges's essays are unquestionably the most imaginative of those published by an Argentine. Although Borges writes principally about literature and philosophy, he is neither a conventional literary critic nor a true philosopher. Instead, he delights in playing with ideas such as the opaqueness of language, the paradoxes that confound human reason, and the mysterious ingredients of the aesthetic ideal. Many of Borges's best essays have been collected in *Otras inquisiciones* (1952; *Other Inquisitions*, 1964).

Argentina has produced many fine essayists, two of whom, Ezequiel Martínez Estrada and Eduardo Mallea, have brilliantly analyzed the Argentine character. Although Peter G. Earle laments the decline of the essay, there are signs that the genre is being revived.

The novelist Sábato not only condemns authoritarianism and the excessive mechanization in today's world but also, like Martínez Estrada and Mallea, analyzes the Argentine character, focusing on its national and European traits. Many of his essays have been collected in *La robotización del hombre y otras páginas de ficción y reflexión* (1981; the robotization of humans and other pages of fiction and reflection). Early in his career Borges wrote elegantly stylized essays on literary and philosophical topics and occasionally fused essay and fiction into his unique mode of expression. In a somewhat similar manner, Cortázar combined the essay and personal whims as, for example, in *Territories* (1978; territories), a series of amusing pieces on painting. In *Último round* (1969; last round) Cortázar predicts the eventual utopian fulfillment of the goals of Marxist economics and aesthetics.

In *Indios, ejércitos y fronteras* (1983; Indians, armies, and frontiers) Viñas condemns the slaughter of Indians during the 19th c. and also criticizes Domingo Faustino Sarmiento (1811–1888), the well-known politician who encouraged European immigration at the expense of the "uncivilized tribes" of the pampa. The injustice of the military regime of the 1970s is exposed in graphic detail in *Preso sin nombre, celda sin número* (1981; *Prisoner without a Name, Cell without a Number*, 1981), by Jacobo Timerman (b. 1923), a Jewish journalist imprisoned for thirty months.

Two prominent women essayists are Victoria Ocampo and Marta Traba, the abovementioned novelist. Founder of *Sur*, which she directed from 1931 until its demise in the early 1970s, Ocampo published ten volumes of essays entitled *Testimonios* (1935–1977; testimonies), dealing principally with Argentine and foreign literatures. Traba wrote extensively on painting, literature, and politics; the breadth of her knowledge is demonstrated in her *Siglo XX en las artes plásticas latinoamericanas: Un guía* (1982–1983; 20th c. in Latin American plastic arts: a guide).

Argentina's finest literary critics include Enrique Anderson Imbert (b. 1910) and the poet Jitrik. A fiction writer and longtime professor in the U.S., Anderson Imbert is the author of *Crítica interna* (1961; internal criticism) and many other texts. Jitrik has published several volumes on critical theory including *La vibración del presente: Trabajos críticos sobre textos y escritores latinoamericanos* (1987; the vibration of the present: critical studies of Latin American texts and writers).

Under the repressive military régime from 1976 until 1983, a program known as *El Proceso* (Process of National Restoration) was implemented to effect a return to the nation's traditional roots, with its commitment to the Catholic church and the patriarchal family. This program also suppressed liberal elements such as Peronists, Zionists, organized labor, and middle-class intellectuals. In *La cultura nacional: Examen crítico* (1987; the national culture: critical examination) essayist Eduardo S. Calamaro (b. 1940) rejects *El Proceso* and proclaims the need to reestablish pluralism to encourage the nation's dynamic cultural growth. Calamaro's study is an example of the diversity of ideas being fostered by the newly created democracy.

Drama

The modern Argentine theater is deeply indebted to Florencio SÁNCHEZ, who, although Uruguayan by birth, resided for many years in Buenos Aires, where his dramatizations of rural life were presented early in the 20th c. During the 1930s playwrights concentrated on the realistic depictions of social and political issues, often expressing their opposition to reactionary forces in Argentine society. The psychological drama *Pájaro de barro* (1940; mud bird) by Samuel Eichelbaum (1894–1967), the most prominent figure of this period, describes the confrontation between a wealthy youth and a proud young woman of humble origin.

The true flourishing of the Argentine theater is a post-World War II phenomenon, perhaps because of the influx of European intellectuals and the increasing awareness of the need for drastic social changes. The resultant politicization of the theater has been accompanied by two additional factors: the influence of foreign dramatists, notably BRECHT; and the use of techniques developed by the THEATER OF THE ABSURD. Osvaldo DRAGÚN, one of Argentina's most important playwrights, has successfully integrated Brechtian techniques into works such as *Y nos dijeron que éramos inmortales* (1962; *And They Told Us We Were Immortal*, 1971). A powerful example of the theater of the absurd is *Los siameses* (1967; the Siamese twins), by Griselda GAMBARO. The protagonists of this play represent the schizophrenic nature of the individual psyche, i.e., man as both hangman and victim. Read as a political allegory, *Los siameses* suggests the fratricidal persecution so rampant in Argentina today.

Argentina, along with Mexico, has been a leader on the Latin American literary scene since the mid-19th c. In addition to the major genres, the Argentine mystery story has achieved artistic heights unsurpassed elsewhere on the continent; street theater in Argentina is at times almost on a par with the legitimate stage; and Argentine children's books continue to lead the way in Spanish America. Argentine writers have demonstrated a remarkable ability to depict 20th-c. reality through a wide variety of literary styles and techniques. Their preoccupation with national issues and the innovative structures displayed in their works under-score their conviction that fundamental adjustments are essential in their strife-torn, economically troubled country. Their aesthetic perception constituted a bright spot on the bleak landscape of present-day Argentina.

Under the military dictatorship, dramatists were threatened with censorship or worse if they were too bold in their criticism of the authorities. In 1981, faced with a decline in the number of plays produced and the diminishing audiences, an association of dramatists, directors, and actors formed the *Teatro Abierto* (Open Theater), an experiment by which the three groups collaborated in the writing and producing of plays, their purposes being to revitalize the theater and achieve greater freedom of expression. Critics agree that the experiment has been at least moderately successful.

Argentine theater of the past two decades fluctuates between traditional realism and vanguardism. The principal practitioners of realism are Carlos Gorostiza (b. 1920), Roberto Cossa (b. 1934), and Ricardo Talesnik (b. 1935). Gorostiza develops the themes of human responsibility and the choices people are forced to make under stress; in *Los prójimos* (1967; *Neighbors*, 1970) witnesses to a woman's murder refuse to become involved in the judicial process. Cossa and Talesnik collaborated in *El avión* (1970; the airplane), an excellent example of political drama. An acerbic satire as well, it sketches the reactions on different social levels to the imminent arrival of an airplane carrying the long-awaited

general (Juan Perón), who did indeed return from exile three years later. The play's dramatic tension derives from the clash between the fanatical Peronists' ebullient mood of anticipation and the mounting apprehension on the part of the upper-middle-class citizens, who detest the populist leader.

The most important representatives of Argentina's vanguardist theater are Griselda Gambaro, Osvaldo Dragún, Eduardo Pavlovsky (b. 1933), and Ricardo Monti (b. 1945). Gambaro is linked to the existentialist Theater of the Absurd, but she is also a practitioner of the theater of cruelty. Her most successful plays include *El campo* (1965; *The Camp*, 1971), in which a Nazi concentration camp becomes a metaphor for Argentina, and *Las paredes* (1964; the walls), dramatizing the interrogation of a youth by government henchmen. The most important single influence on Dragún is Bertolt Brecht, whose techniques serve to denounce social injustice and assail hypocrisy. Although it was written early in his career, the most celebrated of his works is still a trilogy of one-act tragicomedies entitled *Historias para ser contadas* (1957; stories to be told). Pavlovsky, educated as a psychiatrist, is Argentina's leading creator of psychodrama. He, like Gambaro, has been influenced by the Theater of the Absurd, but he is best known for his theater of cruelty. His most widely presented work is *El señor Galíndez* (1976; Mr. Galíndez), a shocking exposé of torture and mutilation systematically practiced by the Argentine authorities. Monti has been lauded as one of Argentina's most innovative and serious voices in the contemporary theater. His works display a mélange of SURREALISM and the grotesque, which he utilizes to explore both national and universal concerns. His most overtly political work is *Historia tendenciosa de la clase media argentina* (1971; tendentious history of the Argentine middle class), whose central character is the Old Whore, a symbol of the nation.

Despite its numerous political and economic crises over the past half century, Argentina, a country of only thirty-two million citizens, has created an impressive volume of literary works. Mario Vargas LLOSA believes that if writers were satisfied with the status quo, there would be no need for literature. Argentine writers have had many reasons to express their dissatisfaction, which they have done with artistry and increasing openness. With the recent reestablishment of democracy, one can expect the large quantity and high quality of Argentine letters to continue unabated.

BIBLIOGRAPHY: Arrieta, R., *Historia de la literatura argentina* (6 vols., 1958–1960); Isaacson, J., and Urquía, C. E. *40 años de poesía argentina, 1920–1960* (3 vols., 1962–1964); Jones, W. K., *Behind Spanish American Footlights* (1966): 87–182; Stabb, M. S., *In Quest of Identity* (1967): 146–81; Castagnino, R. H., *Literatura dramática argentina, 1917–1967* (1968); Dellepiane, A., "La novela argentina desde 1950 a 1965," *RI*, 34 (1968): 237–82; Walsh, R., and et. al, "La literatura argentina del siglo XX," in *Panorama de la actual literatura latino americana* (1969): 193–210; Foster, D. W., and V. R. Foster, *Research Guide to Argentine Literature* (1970); Orgambide, P. G., and R. Yahni, *Enciclopedia de la literatura argentina* (1970); Viñas, D., *Literatura argentina y realidad política: De Sarmiento a Cortázar* (1971); Lagmanovich, D., "La narrativa argentina de 1960 a 1970," *Nueva narrativa hispanoamericana*, 2, 1 (1972): 99–117; Foster, D. W., *Currents in the Contemporary Argentine Novel* (1975); Zubatsky, D. S., "Annotated Bibliography of Latin American Author Bibliographies: Argentina & Uruguay," *Chasqui*, 8, 2 (Feb. 1979): 47–95; Foster, D. W., "The Demythification of Buenos Aires in Selected Argentine Novels of the Seventies," *Chasqui*, 10, 1 (Nov. 1980): 3–25;

Borello et al., R. A., *El ensayo argentino, 1930–1970* (1981); Zayas de Lima, P., *Diccionario de autores teatrales argentinos, 1950–1980* (1981); Himelblau, J., "The Argentine Avant-Garde Theater," *Symposium*, 39, 2 (Summer 1985): 104–12; Foster, D. W., "Narrativa testimonial argentina durante los años del 'Proceso,'" in Jara, R. and H. Vidal, eds., *Testimonio y literatura* (1986): 138–54; Running, T., "El lenguaje como tema en la poesía argentina actual," *Letras*, 15–16 (Apr.–Aug. 1986): 150–66; Balderston, D., et al., eds., *Ficción y política: La narrativa argentina durante el proceso militar* (1987); McMurray, G. R., *Spanish American Writing since 1941: A Critical Survey* (1987): 14–18, 23–27, 39–42, 52–58, 132–39, 191–95, 224–31, 310–18; Rizk, B. J., *El nuevo teatro latinoamericano: Una lectura histórica* (1987); Robino, A., "La poesía argentina de hoy," *Río de la Plata: Culturas*, 7 (1988): 121–32; Sosnowski, S., ed. *Represión y reconstrucción de una cultura: El caso argentino* (1988); Kohut, K., and A. Pagni eds., *Literatura argentina hoy: De la dictadura a la democracia* (1989); Lértora Mendoza, C. A., "Panorama del pensamiento argentina actual," *Ensayistas*, 26–27 (1989): 117–60; Rojo, G., *Crítica del exilio: Ensayos sobre literatura latinoamericana actual* (1989); Guerra Cunningham, L., ed. *Splintering Darkness: Latin American Women Writers in Search of Themselves* (1990)

—GEORGE R. MCMURRAY

ARGHEZI, Tudor

(pseud. of Ion N. Theodorescu) Romanian poet, novelist, and essayist, b. 21 May 1880, Bucharest; d. 14 July 1967, Bucharest

Rebelling against his parents' wishes that he become a priest in the Romanian Orthodox Church, A. left home at the age of eleven. Supporting himself, he studied at the Liceul Sf. Sava (1891–96). While there, he published his first poem in a review edited by Alexandru Macedonski (1854–1920).

In 1899 he took orders as an Orthodox monk but continued to write verse and read French poets, arousing the suspicions of fellow monks, so that he was sent away from the monastery to teach and then to receive further education at the Catholic University in Fribourg, Switzerland. Repelled by attempts to convert him to Roman Catholicism, he abandoned monasticism and began four years of wandering between Geneva and Paris, studying watchmaking and becoming skilled as a painter of miniature portraits. In 1910 he returned to Bucharest to become a journalist and illustrator and resume his publication of verses. With his former classmate, the writer Gala Galaction (1879–1961), he founded *Cronica* in 1915. In the meantime he began the cycle that came to be known as "Agate negre" (black agates), which shows the influence of Macedonski and Baudelaire, dwelling upon the macabre and deriving its musicality from rare words.

At the outbreak of World War I he declared his pacifism and opposition to Romania's joining the Allies. He indiscreetly worked on a newspaper whose staff collaborated with the Germans. In 1918, he was tried for treason, and served over a year in prison.

After the war his poetry shifted toward primitive speech patterns. "From their tongue used to call herds I've brought forth fitting words," A. announced in "Testament" (testament), the key poem in *Cuvinte potrivite* (1927; fitting words). Many poems in this first volume of verse showed consciousness of the Romanian ancestral mythos. Others, especially the *psalmi*, revealed a lonely soul dissatisfied with religious dogma, independently seeking contact with the Divine, and frightened by the prospect of a cosmos without certainty. He returned to this theme in the prose poems of *Ce-ai-cu-mine, vîintule?* (1937; what wilt thou of me, o wind?).

A different tone pervaded *Flori de mucigai* (1931; blossoms of mold), which, under the influence of Villon and Baudelaire, recalled A.'s experiences in prison and employed seamy images of violence and sexuality and under-world argot.

Cartea cu jucării (1931; toy book)—a collection of tales, games, and dramatic skits originally written for his own children—revealed A.'s love of family life and his gift for entering into the child's world—one inhabited not only by A.'s own children but by familiar folk creatures. And in the background always hovers the comforting mother-figure. This world reappeared in parts of *Ochii Maicii Domnului* (1934; the eyes of the Mother of God), and some poems of *Hore* (1939; round dances).

Most of A.'s novels have autobiographical elements. *Icoane de lemn* (1929; wooden icons) and *Poarta neagră* (1930; black gate), derived, respectively, from his monastic and prison experiences. His later fiction was distinguished by the overlay of fantasy upon the familiar world. *Tablete din Țara de Kuty* (1933; sketches of Kuty Land) is a Swiftian antiutopian novel. In *Ochii Maicii Domnului* A. superimposed the mythos of Jesus upon the story of a fatherless boy much like A. himself.

A.'s journalistic talents and wicked pamphleteering were exercised in his weekly *Bilete de papagal* (1929–43; fortunetelling tickets); his most famous lampoon attacked the German ambassador in Bucharest—*Baraone* (1943; hey, Mr. Baron)—and earned him internment at the Tîrgu-Jiu camp.

A.'s translations focused primarily on French writers like Baudelaire, Villon, La Fontaine, and Rimbaud, but he also translated Whitman into Romanian (1911).

Ill at ease with SOCIALIST REALISM, A. lapsed into silence between 1947 and 1954. His subsequent work, though prolific, consisted mostly of reminiscences and attempts to adapt to Marxist strictures: *Cîtare omului* (1956; song to man), a humanistic credo; poetic fables; gnomic verse; and "visions of mingled nightmares and carnival." None recaptured the lyrical felicity of his writing between the world wars.

In 1963, with the official lifting of the bans on previously proscribed poets and with the publication of his *Poeme noi* (new poems), A.'s fame reached its zenith, although based largely on his earlier work. However, he had been elected to the Romanian Academy in 1956 after the death of Stalin and Stalin and withdrawal of Russian troops from Romania. He was awarded the Vienna Academy Herder Prize in 1965.

Throughout his life A. was beset by a spiritual restlessness, from time to time expressed in a cry for spiritual reassurance, most evident in his Psalms. Later, dissatisfied with religious dogma, he independently sought contact with the Divine, a lonely soul frightened by the prospect of a cosmos without certainty. Although finally accepting a choatic, demiurgic universe, he periodically returned to his search, often preoccupied with questions about death.

A.'s verse and prose poems enlarged Romanian literary resources to include new use of peasant and underworld language, new syntactic and morphological patterns, and plastic images. At their best they voiced the universal cry for meaning, the warmth and joy of childhood, the Romanian's sense of his timeless past, and a sympathy for the underdog. His fiction reflected the Romanian awareness of the presence of the fantastic amid the ordinary and familiar.

FURTHER WORKS: *Cărticică de seară* (1935); *Cimitirul Buna-Vestire* (1936); *Povestirile boabei şi ale fărîmei* (1937); *Lina* (1942); *Seringa* (1943); *Manual de morală practică* (1946); *Una sută poeme* (1947); *Prisaca* (1954); *Pagini din trecut* (1955); *1907-Peisaje* (1955); *Stihuri noi* (1955); *Stihuri pestriţe* (1957); *Cartea mea frumoasă* (1958); *Lume veche, lume nouă* (1959); *Tablete de cronicar* (1960); *Cu bastonul prin Bucureşti* (1962); *Frunze* (1962); *Scrieri* (1962–1965); *Poeme noi* (1963); *Cadenţe* (1965); *Silabe* (1965); *Ritmuri* (1966); *Răzleţe* (1966); *Noaptea* (1967); *Litanii* (1967); *Crengi* (1970); *XC* (1970); *Călătorie în vis* (1973). FURTHER WORKS IN ENGLISH: *Selected Poems* (1976)

BIBLIOGRAPHY: Micu, D., *T. A.* (1965); Ivaşcu, G., "T. A.: Poet for Contemporary Man," *BA*, 43 (1969): 32–36; Impey, M., "The Struggle between Good and Evil in T. A.'s *Triumful*," *SXX*, 160–61 (1974): 45–51; Sorescu, R., "T. A. en français," *Synthesis*, 3 (1976): 241–43; Novaceanu, D., "T. A., un gran poeta rumano," *Plural*, 84 (1978): 4–9; Alexandrescu, S., "The Function of Symbol with T. A.," in *Romanian Essayists of Today* (1979): 331–46; Constantinescu, P., *T. A.* (1994)

—THOMAS AMHERST PERRY

ARGUEDAS, Alcides

Bolivian novelist, historian, and sociologist, b. 15 July 1879, La Paz; d. 6 May 1946, Chulumani

A lawyer by profession, A. later turned to writing, including journalism. During his long residence in Paris he held several diplomatic posts, and he also served in London and Bogotá, Colombia. The leader of the Bolivian Liberal Party, A. was once elected a senator.

As a writer, after a flirtation with romanticism, A. adopted realism and devoted his life to analyzing Bolivian society. In 1904 he published *Wata Wara* (Wata Wara), a short work that inaugurated in Latin America the *indigenista* novel, a social-protest literature in defense of the exploited Indians that has continued to this day. His next two works—the novel *Vida criolla* (1905, native life) and the essay *Pueblo enfermo* (1909; a sick people)—were such ferocious indictments that the term *arguedismo* was coined to describe attacks on the decadence and corruption in Bolivian society.

A. reworked *Wata Wara* into a far more ambitious novel, *Raza de bronce* (1919; race of bronze), the first Bolivian work to achieve international recognition. The characters of this novel are Aimara Indians living in the imposing but also hostile Andean highlands, who are pushed by their white oppressors to the extremes of open revolt. In it A. artistically blends lyricism with "nativism" (political and social protest, and local color). Coinciding with the advent of the Russian Revolution (1917), this novel effectively launched protest literature in South America. At the same time it encouraged Bolivian writers to concentrate on the novel as their best means of expression.

After *Raza de bronce* A. wrote sociohistorical works dissecting Bolivia's stormy past. His research was financed by the Bolivian tycoon Simón Patiño, a fact that alienated him from many Bolivian writers. In many respects A.'s sociohistorical works complement his fiction, since all his books have in common the goal of revealing the evils of Bolivian society and advocating reform.

The ugly epithets A. hurled at his countrymen in his writings made him unpopular, even hated. But he was acting as a true patriot, sorely grieved by the many evils that afflicted his country. And the last words he gasped before his death were "madre patria" (motherland).

FURTHER WORKS: *Pisagua* (1903); *Historia de Bolivia* (4 vols., 1920–1926); *Los caudillos bárbaros* (1929); *La danza de las sombras* (1934); *Obras completas* (1959); *Etapas en la vida de un escritor* (1963)

BIBLIOGRAPHY: Guzmán, A., *La novela en Bolivia* (1955): 59–62; Bellini, G., "A. A. en la novela moderna," *RHM*, 26: 3–4 (1960): 133–35; Echevarría, E., *La novela social en Bolivia* (1973): 37–124, 234–36; Alcázar, R., *Paisaje y novela en Bolivia* (1973): 41–71; Albarracín, J., *A.* (1979); Gumucio, M. B., *A. A.* (1979)

—EVELIO ECHEVARRÍA

ARGUEDAS, José María

Peruvian novelist and folklorist, b. 18 Jan. 1911, Andahuaylas; d. 28 Nov. 1969, Lima

The death of A.'s mother, a Quechuan Indian, when he was three years old had a profound effect on his life and writing. During his adolescence A. lived among the Utek Indians, and he entered their world through his knowledge of their language, Quechua. When A. went to Lima in 1929, he perfected his Spanish. At this time, he also began his study of Quechuan ethnology and folklore.

In 1932, while A. was studying at the University of San Marcos, the dictator Sánchez Cerro ordered the university closed. A. was arbitrarily imprisoned for one year in 1937, and his experiences in a Lima prison are bitterly recorded in *El sexto* (the sixth one), published in 1961.

Arduous application to teaching and studying brought on a physical collapse in 1943, from which A. claimed never to have recovered. (It may have contributed to his suicide in 1969.) In 1953 A. was named director of the Institute of Ethnological Studies of the National Museum of History. The following year, the University of San Marcos published A.'s dissertation, *Las communidades de España y del Perú* (1954; the communities of Spain and Peru), a comparative study of the Andean Indians of Puquio and the inhabitants of some isolated communities in Extremadura, Castille, and León in Spain.

Dismayed by the negative portrayal of the Indian in Peruvian literature, A. decided to give a positive, yet honest, picture of the Indians' way of life. His first short story, "Agua" (1935; water), relates how the Indians' courage and perseverance could free them from the white man's tyranny.

One of A.'s most highly acclaimed novels is *Yawar fiesta* (1941; Yawar fiesta). The title refers to the Indian version of the bullfight in which any brave young man fights the bull. Two particular themes dominate the novel: the Indians' courage and conviction will lead to their eventual freedom, and "civilized" or "Christian" men have their own forms of violence while condemning Indian traditions as "barbarian."

Of all of A.'s works, *Los ríos profundos* (1958; rev. ed., *Los ríos profundos y seleccion de cuentos*, 1978; *Deep Rivers*, 1978), has had the greatest impact on Latin American literature. In it A. succeeds in rendering Quechuan mentality by using Spanish in such a way as to suggest Quechuan turns of phrase, metaphors, and syntax. Conveyed in a poetic way are the Indian's mode of thinking, his religious beliefs, his animistic vision, and his total incomprehension of the white man's world. The protagonist, fourteen-year-old Ernesto, is A. himself. The young man realizes that Peruvian society is made up of masters and slaves—the white hacienda owners and the poor Indians. Many conflicts beset Ernesto; two races, two cultures, two languages with two ways of thinking, and urban versus country life. Unable to deal with such a diverse reality, Ernesto with draws into an inner world of dreams and past experiences. His life mirrors the tragedy of the Latin American Indian who seeks his own identity, not assimilation into the dominant Western culture.

Throughout his literary career, A. remained a serious student of Quechuan culture. His research resulted in anthologies of Quechuan songs and stories: *Canto Kechwa* (1938; Quechuan song), which begins with an essay defending Quechuan as a creative, poetic language; *Canciones y cuentos del pueblo quechua* (1948; *The Singing Mountaineers*, 1958); *Dioses y hombres de Huarochirí* (1966; gods and men of Huarochirí), a bilingual edition (Spanish and Quechuan) of a Quechuan text dating back to the 16th or 17th c.; *Poesía quechua* (1965; Quechua poetry); and *Temblar/Katatay* (1972; Temblar/Katatay).

A. distinguished himself by his precision, compassion, and subtlety in the treatment of the Quechuan Indians' reality. In so doing, he has illuminated the plight not only of the Indian but also of the peoples of newly emergent nations who must forge a third way—one that retains their indigenous culture while accepting modern technology and the postindustrial world.

FURTHER WORKS: *Diamantes y pedernales* (1954); *Todas las sangres* (1964); *Amor mundo y otros relatos* (1967); *El zorro de arriba y el zorro de abajo* (1971); *Páginas escogidas* (1972); *Cuentos olvidados* (1973)

BIBLIOGRAPHY: Sommers, J., "The Indian Oriented Novel in Latin America: New Spirit, New Forms, New Scope," *JIAS*, 6 (1964): 249–65; Aldrich, E. M., Jr., *The Modern Short Story in Peru* (1966): 127–40; Rodríguez-Peralta, P., "The Literary Progression of J. M. A.," *Hispania*, 55 (1972): 225–33; Marín, G. C., *La experiencia americana de J. M. A.* (1973); Cornejo Polar, A., *Los universos narrativos de J. M. A.* (1973); Urrello, A., J. M. A.: *El nuevo rostro del indio, una estructura mítico-poética* (1974); Columbus, C. K., *Mythological Consciousness and the Future: J. M. A.* (1986)

—KATHERINE J. HAMPARES

ARGUETA, Manlio

Salvadoran novelist and poet, b. 24 Nov. 1935, San Miguel

A. is considered El Salvador's most important living novelist and one of Central America's most prominent men of letters. In 1956, while studying at the National University in San Salvador, he joined a circle of young writers, the so-called Generation of 1956, who opposed the military dictatorship ruling the country at that

time. A. began his career as a poet, but he is much better known for his four novels, three of which have won literary prizes. Forced into exile in 1972, he lives in Costa Rica, where he founded and still directs the Salvadoran-Costa Rican Institute of Culture.

The settings of A.'s first novel, *El valle de las hamacas* (1970; the valley of the hammocks), are El Salvador and Nicaragua during the régime of the Salvadoran dictator José María Lemus (1956–1960). The political and social conflicts in both nations are dramatized through the lives of two lovers, Rosaura and Raúl, who become separated when Raúl leaves El Salvador for Nicaragua to command a group of Sandinistas. To explain the historical background of the strife, A. inserts into the text a lengthy chronicle of Pedro de Alvarado's conquest of Central America more than four centuries ago. A. also utilizes innovative techniques such as interior monologues, temporal and spatial dislocations, and shifting points of view to intensify individual sentiments and broaden the narrative focus.

Caperucita en la zona roja (1977; Red Ridinghood in the red zone) resembles A.'s first novel in several respects. The protagonists are, once again, two lovers (in this case Alfonso and Hormiga) who suffer long separations for political reasons; both novels juxtapose episodes set in different time frames and narrated from different points of view; and both depict clashes between government troops and protesters. The temporal dimensions of *Caperucita en la zona roja*, however, are restricted to the mid-1970s, and the relationship between the two lovers receives closer scrutiny, especially when Hormiga becomes involved in the "red zone" of forbidden political activities.

Un día en la vida (1980; *One Day of Life*, 1983), A.'s most highly acclaimed novel to date, is written in a more direct, coherent style, its principal narrator being a middle-aged peasant woman, Lupe Fuentes, whose growing awareness of social injustice provides the major theme as well as the unifying plot thread. The foreground action lasts only twelve hours, but in this short time frame Lupe's monologues evoke her childhood, her marriage to José at the age of fifteen, and, most important, the recent changes in their lives. Although the year of the foreground action is never revealed, it is probably in the late 1970s. The novel was published in 1980, the year El Salvador's civil war began and also the year of the assassination of Archbishop Salvador Oscar Arnulfo Romero, who is depicted as a harsh critic of the government. Furthermore, the chain of events underscores the tense environment that must have existed just prior to the wholesale violence.

Perhaps the strongest feature of the novel is its capacity to rivet the reader's attention on the tragic lives of its characters. Although illiterate, Lupe is obviously an intelligent woman whose devotion to her family and dedication to her religion reinforce her resolve to survive the violence swirling around her. The evolving role of the Catholic church also generates much of the action, reflecting the liberation theology that had spread throughout Latin America. And still another voice is that of an unidentified soldier whose fanatical hatred of "communists" results from his training by "gringo" army officers. Sprinkled with biblical symbols (Lupe's husband José ultimately emerges as a Christ figure), *Un día en la vida* is a fine example of the artistically conceived social-protest novel.

A.'s most recent work of fiction, *Cuzcatlán donde bate la Mar del Sur* (1986; *Cuzcatlán Where the Southern Sea Beats*, 1987), portrays several generations of a peasant family who, like the previous protagonists, suffer the atrocities of rightwing régimes determined to suppress all traces of opposition. But this novel is more complex, consisting of narrative fragments that compel the reader to realign events and uncover cause-and-effect relationships. Other passages allude to precolonial Cuzcatlán (the pre-Columbian name for El Salvador) and elements of Mayan mythology, which serve to elucidate the present-day situation.

In its entirety A.'s oeuvre offers a moving tribute to his compatriots' struggle for justice. His artistic treatment of the tragic political and social realities of El Salvador has attracted readers from many parts of the world.

FURTHER WORKS: *De aquí en adelante* (1967); *Poemas* (1967); *En el costado de la luz* (1968); *Las bellas armas reales* (1979)

BIBLIOGRAPHY: McMurray, G. R., "The Novels of El Salvador's M. A.," *Proceedings of the Rocky Mountain Council on Latin American Studies* (1984): 192–97; Martínez, Z. N., "M. A.," *Hispam*, 14, 42 (Dec. 1985): 41–54; Rodríguez Hernández, R., "La nueva novela histórica hispanoamericana: *La insurrección y Un día en la vida*," TCrit, 13, 36–37 (1987): 153–63; Santos, R., ed., *And We Sold the Rain: Contemporary Fiction from Central America* (1988): 201–2; Martin, G., *Journeys through the Labyrinth: Latin American Fiction in the Twentieth Century* (1989): 331; Beverley, J. and M. Zimmerman, *Literature and Politics in the Central American Revolutions* (1990): 192–94

—GEORGE R. MCMURRAY

ARIYOSHI Sawako

Japanese dramatist, short-story writer, novelist, and essayist; b. 21 Jan. 1931, Wakayama City; d. 30 Aug. 1984, Tokyo

When A. was born, in Wakayama City, her father was employed by the New York branch of the Yokohama Species Bank. Her mother came from the distinguished Kimoto family in Wakayama. Besides A., the couple had two sons. When A. was four years old, her family moved to Java (Jakarta, Indonesia); they lived a privileged life for the next few years, with natives serving as maids and houseboys. A precocious child, A. read avidly the works of Natsume SŌSEKI and Arishima Takeo (1878–1923).

Because of the tense international situation, the family soon returned to Tokyo. In fact, A. moved many times in the course of her childhood. Because she was extremely sensitive, her exposure to life abroad gave her an opportunity to see with new eyes Japan's rich cultural tradition, as well as Japanese society closed to outsiders. Her novel *Kinokawa* (1959; *The River Ki*, 1980) vividly describes details from the lives of her maternal grandmother, her mother, and the author herself as a child and a young adult.

During the bleak postwar years, her father, sensing her utter disenchantment with Japan, introduced A. to the Kabuki theater. This was the beginning of A.'s lifelong interest in the Japanese theater tradition. As the years went by, she became thoroughly familiar with Noō, Kabuki, and Bunraku plays. In later years she studied the modern theater of the West and grew to appreciate greatly the classical ballet and Western opera. Yet, she also appreciated the painting and decorative arts of Japan, enhanced by formal lessons in the Yabunouchi school of tea ceremony, and she amassed a fine collection of art and tea utensils.

Soon after graduating from Tokyo Women's College in 1952, A. joined the editorial staff of a publishing company. It was during

this phase in her career that she contributed to a literary coterie magazine, *Hakuchigun*. Between 1954 and 1956, she was employed by the Azuma Kabuki Association, performing secretarial duties and assisting in stage productions. A. began to be published in the 1950s. Active as both a dramatist and a writer of short stories, novels, and essays, A. would be classed together with such writers as Sono Ayako (b. 1931), Kurahashi Yumiko (b. 1935), Ōba MINAKO, and Kōno Taeko (b. 1926) for her intellect and literary talent.

A dance drama that A. wrote, based on a Noō play, was performed at the Shimbashi Embujō Theater in 1956. At this early stage in her career, it was already clear that A.'s two loves were literature and the theater. In subsequent years A., besides writing original plays or adaptations of other works, saw her novels and short stories adapted for the stage, the cinema, and television. Even after her death, her works continued to inspire stage productions and television films. Her novel *Hishoku* (1964; not because of color) is scheduled to be made into an American film; the screenplay is being written by Veline Hasu Houston (dates n.a.), an Amerasian poet and dramatist.

In November 1959 A. received a Rockefeller grant to study at Sarah Lawrence College in New York during the winter and spring terms. During her stay there, she studied the playwright Christopher Fry. In August 1960 she made her way to Europe and returned to Japan via the Middle East after spending nearly a year abroad. Her novels *Hishoku* and *Pueruto riko nikki* (1964; Puerto Rico diary) were written as a result of having lived on the American East Coast for a time.

In June 1961 A. was invited to Mainland China along with other Japanese writers. This was the first of her many trips to this country. Years later, in the summer of 1978, she was given an opportunity to view firsthand what life was like in a commune. At the same time she lectured on environmental pollution, a social problem in which she was deeply interested. A book about her impressions of China, *Ariyoshi Sawako no Chūgoku repotūto* (the China report of A. S.), was published in 1979.

In March 1962 A. married Jin Akira, the director of the Art Friend Association. A daughter, Tamao, was born to the couple in 1963, but the next year A. and Jin Akira were divorced. Throughout this crisis in her private life, A. continued to write.

She traveled widely from 1956 to 1970, going as far as New Guinea, where she stayed for about a month, working in the jungles with a Japanese woman anthropologist. In November 1970 she accepted an invitation to be a writer-in-residence at the University of Hawaii at Manoa and taught a graduate seminar on the Kabuki plays of Tsuruya Namboku IV. She returned to Japan via mainland U.S. and Europe, at the time deeply interested in the problem of caring for the elderly. *Koōkotsu no hito* (1972; *The Twilight Years*, 1984), recounts the moving story of Shigezō, a senile old man, and his caregivers.

A. received the Mainichi Cultural Prize for her historical novel *Kazunomiyasama otome* (1978; her highness princess Kazu). In retrospect it appears that the author had mentally exhausted herself in conducting research for the novel and imagined herself as one or the other of the characters in the novel who undergo great hardships in the 1860s when Japan was on the threshold of the modern period. Nevertheless A. continued to write and travel. During the last year of her life, she traveled to England and Wales.

One characteristic of A.'s writing is that, unlike other Japanese women writers, she is not known for her love stories. As a professional writer she believed that there were too many issues more important than love. Indeed, she wrote about a great many subjects: racial and other social prejudices, environmental pollution, caring for the elderly, the role of women in society, among other topics. Although her early short stories about artists and artisans dedicated to their craft are of interest, she will probably be best remembered for her social-problem novels. *Kiyu no shi* (1962; the death of Kiyu) describes a prostitute who commits suicide rather than becoming the mistress of an American merchant; A. attempts to trace the beginning of Japanese prejudice against Caucasians in this short story. In *Hishoku* A. has as her main character a Japanese war bride married to a black American. While living in Harlem, the heroine observes for herself the racial prejudice toward blacks and Hispanics in the U.S.

A. lived through a remarkable period in the modern history of Japan, and she thought deeply about the social problems that many industrial nations are facing. Her approach, however, was unique in that she focused on the victims of a social problem, be it radiation disease, caring for the elderly, or environmental pollution. She was deeply sympathetic to the less fortunate in the strictly stratified Japanese society—the pariahs and underprivileged, those who are not blessed with an impressive pedigree and fine upbringing, and she saw clearly the bigotry and prejudice of the Japanese toward these and other outsiders. Whether they are victims of the U.S. atomic-bomb blasts of August 1945 or victims of environmental pollution, they will be affected for generations.

As a divorced woman with a daughter to raise and educate, A. thought deeply about the position of women in Japanese society. She wrote about prostitutes and princesses, housewives and old women. Because, as a rule, women have had to struggle harder than men, they emerge as final victors in many of her stories. In A.'s works, none of them typical "love stories" or unrelentingly gloomy autobiographical works so characteristic of other Japanese woman writers, A. makes her characters come alive.

A. died of heart failure in her home in Tokyo in the summer of 1984. In January 1986 the media announced that an Ariyoshi Memorial museum would be established at the site of the Kimoto estate in Wakayama City. The plans include an adjacent branch of the Wakayama Municipal Library, and the museum will display A.'s personal possessions and original manuscripts. That she will be honored in the home of her maternal grandmother, the setting of *Kinokawa*, is most fitting, since a number of her works were set in Wakayama Prefecture.

A.'s works have a wide appeal to readers of all age groups. She often spent years planning and doing research for a particular work, whether it was a historical novel or a work treating a modern social problem. Her works have been translated into Chinese, English, and a number of European languages. A. will doubtless be remembered as a unique writer who admirably contributed to the great tradition of outstanding Japanese women writers in our time.

FURTHER WORKS: *Shojorento* (1957); *Dangen* (1957); *Masshiroke no ke* (1957); *Zuihitsu* (1958); *U-Tsui anjusan* (1958); *Hana no inochi* (1958); *Eguchi no sato* (1958); *Geisha warutsu Itariano* (1959); *Watashi wa wasurenai* (1960); *Shin onna daigaku* (1960); *Kitō* (1960); *Sanbaba* (1961); *Onna deshi* (1961); *Ariyoshi Sawako shū* (1961); *Hina no nikki* (1962); *Kōge* (1962); *Kyakko* (1962); *Sarashina fujin* (1962); *Heiten jikan* (1962); *Sukezaemon yondai ki* (1962); *Arita gawa* (1963); *Wakakusa no uta* (1963); *Renbu* (1963); *Karinui* (1963); *Kinokawa* (1964; *The River Ki*, 1980); *Onnayakata* (1965); *Ichi no ito* (1965); *Hidaka gawa* (1966); *Aka jishi: A gidayū* (1967); *Ranbu* (1967); *Hanaoka Seishū no tsuma* (1967; *The Doctor's Wife*, 1978); *Fushin no toki* (1968); *Midaremai*

(1968); *Umikura* (1968); *Onna futari no Nyūginia* (1969); *Watakushi wa wasurenai* (1969); *Izumo no Okuni* (1969); *Furu Amerika ni sode* (1970); *Shibazakura* (1970); *Kaminaga hime* (1970); *Yūhigaoka Sangōkan* (1971); *Shimmyo* (1971); *Keitonsbiru jiken no kunin* (1972); *Boke no hana* (1973); *Mō kyojo kō* (1973); *Sarasa fujin* (1973); *Nidai no ikeri* (1973); *Masagoya Omine* (1974); *Boshi Hen'yo* (1974); *Fukugō osen* (1975); *Kinugawa* (1975); *Yu-chi Tso-ho-tzu hsiao shuo hsuan* (1977); *Aoi tsubo* (1977); *Fukugō osen sono go* (1977); *Shojo rentō* (1978); *Akujo ni tsuite* (1978); *Kazunomiyasama otome* (1978) *Nihon no Shimajima, mukashi to ima* (1981)

BIBLIOGRAPHY: Heinrich, A. V., "'Startling Resonances': Some Comparative Feminist Issues," in Balakian, A., et al., eds., *Proceedings of the Xth Congress of the International Comparative Literature Association* (1985), Vol. 2: 608–13; Allen, L., "A Critique of A. S.: *Hanaoka Seishu no tsuma*," in Chapman, J., and Steeds, D., eds., *Proceedings of the British Association for Japanese Studies, 1984* (1985): 42–53

—MILDRED TAHARA

ARLT, Roberto

Argentine novelist, short-story writer, dramatist, and journalist, b. 2 April 1900, Buenos Aires; d. 26 July 1942, Buenos Aires

Born into a poor immigrant family, A. feared and detested his German father, who cruelly disciplined him for the slightest infraction. A.'s formal schooling ceased in the third grade, but he educated himself through voracious although indiscriminate reading, street experience, and numerous menial jobs. A. was identified with the leftist Boedo Group of writers. Although he also maintained close ties with the more cosmopolitan Florida Group, to which BORGES, GÜIRALDES, and others belonged, as a loyal Boedo author A. scorned refinement and elitism in literature.

A. came to literature by way of journalism. For many years he wrote a column in *El mundo*, vignettes depicting the passing urban scene. As a police reporter for *Crítica*, A. came into contact with the Buenos Aires underworld, and presentation of the seamy side of life in the great city became characteristic of his writing. In fact, he was one of the first Spanish American novelists to explore seriously the theme of the gigantic metropolis, its complex socioeconomic problems and the city's impact on the human spirit. He also wrote seven expressionistic plays, but his fame rests primarily on his contributions to fiction.

A. is best known for his first three novels. In the largely autobiographical *El juguete rabioso* (1926; the furious toy) a grim picture of slum poverty and juvenile delinquency is painted. Crime is, at first, the only avenue of escape from his hellish environment for Silvio Astier. Ironically, however, the only way he can ultimately "be" is by betraying an accomplice. Gratuitous betrayal soon became one of A.'s recurring themes.

The author's recognized masterpiece is *Los siete locos* (1929; *The Seven Madmen*, 1984) and its sequel, *Los lanzallamas* (1931; the flamethrowers). These two works are a caustic indictment of bourgeois values and morality and of capitalistic society in general. Erdosain, the protagonist, is the perfect antihero, the embodiment of alienated, contemporary man. Discovered in embezzlement and deceived by his wife, he is a financial and spiritual failure. In search of meaning and salvation, he joins a weird band of madmen determined to destroy urban society and save humanity by returning to a simpler, rural life. The bogus organization to bring down society is a parody of all totalitarian systems that promise people something better and then betray them. The novels have, however, also been interpreted as an allegory of Everyman, the dupe who never discovers the sham of our existence and persists in seeking some transcendental significance in life.

The nine short stories of *El jorobadito* (1933; the little hunchback) reflect the style, themes, and vision of his earlier novels. His second collection, *El criador de gorilas* (first published in Chile in 1937; the gorilla breeder), was the result of a trip to Spain and North Africa in 1935. Perhaps A.'s best work stylistically, these fifteen narratives deal with exotic African settings, themes, and characters. Like his play, *África* (1938; Africa), they demonstrate A.'s ability to intuit and express the essence of realities alien to him.

Popular among the masses in his own time, A. was either totally ignored or severely criticized by the elitist literary establishment for his proletarian leanings and his untutored approach to letters. Today, however, he is recognized as an important precursor of the "new Spanish American novel." His antiliterary style, laconic dialogues, interior monologues, cinematic sequences, frank treatment of previously taboo themes, open form, and use of ambiguous, unexplained incidents clearly anticipate the novels of such writers as Ernesto SÁBATO, Julio CORTÁZAR, and especially Juan Carlos ONETTI. A.'s value lies in his absolute sincerity and in his brilliant perception of modern man's loneliness and alienation.

FURTHER WORKS: *El diario de un morfinómano* (1920); *El humillado* (1930); *El amor brujo* (1931); *Prueba de fuego* (1932); *Trescientos millones* (1932); *Aguafuertes porteñas* (1933); *Aguafuertes españolas* (1936); *Saverio el cruel* (1936); *El fabricante de fantasmas* (1936); *La isla desierta* (1937); *La fiesta del hierro* (1940); *Un viaje terrible* (1941); *El desierto entra a la ciudad* (1953); *Nuevas aguafuertes porteñas* (1960)

BIBLIOGRAPHY: Núñez, A., *La obra narrativa de R. A.* (1968); Castagnino, R., *El teatro de R. A.* (1970); Onetti, J. C., "Semblanza de un genio rioplatense," in Lafforgue, J., ed., *Nueva novela latinoamericana* 2 (1972): 363–77; Guerrero, D., *R. A., el habitante solitario* (1974); Lindstrom, N., "Madness in A.'s Fiction," *Chasqui*, 4 (1975): 18–22; Foster, D. W., *Currents in the Contemporary Argentine Novel: A., Mallea, Sábato, and Cortázar* (1975); Gostautas, S., *Buenos Aires y A* (1977); Flint, J. M., *The Prose Works of R. A.* (1985)

—THOMAS C. MEEHAN

ARMAH, Ayi Kwei

Ghanaian novelist (writing in English), b.1939, Takoradi

In 1959 A. went to the U.S. to study at Groton School in Massachusetts, and later received a degree in sociology from Harvard. He worked as a translator for the periodical *Révolution Africaine* in Algiers and taught English at the Navarongo School in Ghana in 1966. He subsequently served on the staff of the magazine *Jeune Afrique* in Paris, and on the faculty of the University of Massachusetts. In 1972 he moved to Dar es Salaam, Tanzania.

A. published poems and short stories in the Ghanaian magazine *Okyeame*, and in *Harper's, The Atlantic Monthly*, and *New African* before his first novel, *The Beautyful Ones Are Not Yet Born*, appeared in 1969. Its simple, spare style evokes the smells and pain of living in the slums of Accra. Pitted in the daily struggle for survival against poverty on one side and high crime and the "high life" on the other is the major character, simply called The Man, and his family. The Man resists the temptations of bribery and corruption, but his virtues go largely unrewarded. His wife thinks him a fool, and his more sophisticated acquaintances mock him. Using images of excrement to symbolize the state of corruption in Ghana, A. nevertheless expressed hope in the faith of honest, simple men. At the end of the novel, The Man proves stronger than the once-powerful politician who has been deposed in a military coup. This novel is allegorical and poetic in its compressed style.

A.'s second novel, *Fragments* (1970), is realistic and possibly autobiographical. The protagonist is a "been-to," a man who has been to America and studied at one of the leading universities there. On his return to Ghana, he is welcomed as a hero, but he proves unable to live up to the expectations of the villagers. The irony in A.'s portrait is strong: the protagonist fails his villagers because they want him to shine, to flaunt his abilities, like a warrior chief. He prefers solitude and withdrawal. The young intellectual finally cracks under the strain of trying to live in and up to two worlds, and his mother has to commit him to an institution.

A.'s lyric tone becomes angry, and at times shrill, in his third novel, *Why Are We So Blest?* (1972). Its action is set largely in a famous American university. The protagonist, a student, feels he must abandon the humanistic principles that he believes are constraining his revolutionary plans of action. To establish his independence—and that of Africa—he believes he must reject Western values, even Western kindness. The protagonist also suffers because his passion for an American girl gives him the feeling of losing his individuality. These conflicts drive him to despair.

A.'s work shows throughout an emphasis on the conflict between integrity and expediency, responsibility and amorality, commitment and withdrawal. The simple man in *The Beautyful Ones Are Not Yet Born* survives his ordeal. But the sensitivity of the intellectually more gifted protagonists of A.'s next two novels makes them vulnerable to the painful awareness of the gap between the real and ideal, the ugly realities and the desired harmonies.

In *Two Thousand Seasons* (1973) A. finds a way out of his dilemma. His fourth novel spans a thousand years, or two thousand seasons–the wet and dry readings of African history. The narrator might be defined as the collective African consciousness. He indicts Arab and European exploiters, and denounces African imitators of Western ways. He describes the "predators," "destroyers," "parasites," and "zombies" who have raped Africa over the centuries. But he also prophesies a new age in which Africans will regain their identity and glory. Counselling against despair, he cries: "What suffering is there in our hearing only this season's noise, seeing only the confusion around us here. . . . That is not the nature of our seeing." This novel is mythic and close to the density of epic poetry. It shows less interest in characterization and more in allegorical tone. This wide shift from autobiographical and realistic detail to symbolist prose and generalized statements on human nature is a striking departure from his earlier style.

FURTHER WORKS: *The Healers* (1975)

BIBLIOGRAPHY: Aidoo, C. A. A., Introduction to *The Beautyful Ones Are Not Yet Born* (1969): viii—xii; Larson, C. R., *The Emergence of African Fiction* (1972): 113–19, 245–68; Palmer, E., *An Introduction to the African Novel* (1972): 129–42; Mphahlele, E., *The African Image* (rev. ed., 1974): 270–75; Owomoyela, O., *African Literatures: An Introduction* (1979): 104–11; Fraser, R., *The Novels of A. K. A.* (1980); Wright, D., *A. K. A.'s Africa: The Sources of His Fiction* (1989); Wright, D., ed., *Critical Perspectives on A. K. A.* (1992)

—MARTIN TUCKER

ARMENIAN LITERATURE

It may be telescopic to see the ancient Armenian epic *Sassountsi Tavituh* (*David of Sassoun*, 1964) as an antecedent for contemporary Soviet-Armenian novelist Hrant MATEVOSSIAN's protagonists, and to hear paganchant rhythms in the poetry of Barouyr SEVAG, but Armenia's treasury of folk, pagan, and early Christian literature nonetheless is one of two major factors that should be considered before reviewing modern writing. The second factor is the 1915 genocide. The course of the entire modern literature was changed and narrowed by the tragedy of two massacres, the first in 1896, and the second in 1915, which exterminated almost every writer.

For centuries after Armenians lost their independence and lands to the Ottoman Turks their flourishing literature declined and all but disappeared except in monasteries. But in the mid 1800s Turkish reforms allowed an artisan and merchant class to rise among the Armenians, and a new network of schools resulted. At the same time, Armenians began sending their children to study in Europe. The returning students, plus the migration of youth from the Anatolian interior toward Constantinople (Istanbul), resulted in the growth there of a cultural center for western Armenians. Newspapers, magazines, and literary groups developed. Meanwhile, the eastern provinces, under Russian tsarist rule, saw a similar convergence of Armenians in Tiflis. Because of this political division, the Armenian language, an Indo-European tongue, became divided into two dialects and two literatures, each comprehensible to the other. The Istanbul dialect drew on the structure of the classical Armenian, *Krapar,* and is the language of the Armenian diaspora; the eastern dialect is the language used in Soviet Armenia today. Classical and Middle Armenian survive in church rituals, old scholarly texts, and manuscripts.

The first poet to write subjective lyrics in modern Armenian was Bedros Tourian (1851–1872). Missak Medzarentz (1886–1908), who followed, has remained unsurpassed for the musicality of his poetry. His two volumes, *Dsiadsan* (1907; rainbow) and *Nor dagher* (1907; new verses) have been compared to Shelley's and Verlaine's work for structure and verbal splendor. In Tiflis, his contemporary, Vahan Derian (1885–1920), produced lyrics that were more sensual and more political.

Armenian poetry has always received greater critical attention than prose, not only because suppressed people need oblique ways of expression but because Armenians venerated their poets as political leaders, prophets, and illuminators of their time. None were honored in Istanbul more in the renascence years of 1908–15 than Siamanto (pseud, of Adom Yarjanian, 1878–1915) and Daniel VAROUJAN. Both were poets, teachers, and political leaders. Siamanto became famous for his declamatory poetry of protest: *Garmeer lourer pareqamess* (1909; the scarlet news from my friend), *Hokevarkee ev houysee chaher* (1907; lamps of hope and agony), and *Haiyrenee hraver* (1910; invitation of the fatherland). In these works the misery of the people and the poet's sympathy for the revolutionary movement are pictured symbolically. There are, however, some shorter poems, such as "Baruh" (1909; "The Dance," 1977), in which incidents of the massacres of 1909 in Adana are graphically depicted. Siamanto's incantational style was in the tradition of the great Armenian mystic poet, Gregory of Narek (951–1003).

Several groups formed among the Istanbul writers. Those who joined Varoujan as contributors to the *Mehian* magazine and who became known as the Mehian Group were the literary critic and novelist Hagop OSHAGAN, Aharon Dadourian (1877–1965), and Gosdan Zarian (1885–1969).

The gentle satire of short-story writer Arpiar Arpiarian (1852–1908) laid the foundations for the realist movement, whose leader, Krikor ZOHRAB, with his trenchant wit and sense of the absurd, focused on the pretensions and romantic illusions of city society. Eroukhan (pseud. of Ervand Srmakeshkhanlian, 1870–1915) and Hrand (pseud. of Melkon Giurjian, 1870–1915) concentrated on the wretchedness of the peasantry and the wandering exile *(bandoukht)* who traveled to the city in search of his fortune. Eroukhan's chief characters are fishermen; his stories blend parable with provocative realism. His most important novel, *Amirayeen aghchiguh* (1911; daughter of a prince) contrasts the spoiled rich society of Istanbul with the noble poor. Eroukhan was the first Armenian short-story writer to use psychological motivation in his character development.

The life of the peasants in the provinces was explored and preserved by Telkadintsi (pseud. of Hovaness Haroutiunian, 1860–1915) and his remarkable Student, Rouben Zartarian (1874–1915). Zartarian's country stories are layered with myths and legends, blending fantasy with realism. Zartarian's best-known short stories are "Sev havuh ganchets" (1910; the crowing of the black hen) and "Dan ser" (1910; love of home). He later wrote political pamphlets and essays.

Although Siamanto and other writers portrayed the Armenian revolutionary movement as a positive force, the satirist Ervand Odian (1869–1926) could not resist ridiculing those who had borrowed European socialist concepts without understanding that Armenian society did not fit the pattern of industrialized Europe. Odian's picaresque novel *Unger Panchouni* (1914; *Comrade Panchouni*, 1977) follows the adventures of a revolutionary zealot from village to village. Other Istanbul writers who should be singled out are Indra (pseud. of Diran Cherakian, 1875–1921), the mystic poet; Sybille (pseud. of Zabelle Asadour, 1863–1934); and Souren Bartevian (1876–1921).

During World War I, while world attention was focused on Europe, the Turkish government undertook the first genocidal program of the century and began by emptying Istanbul of its Armenian leadership. In 1915 more than two hundred writers and Armenian political leaders were rounded up and killed. Then the entire Armenian population of the country, close to two million, was uprooted; more than a million and a half were killed. Thus, the holocaust entered the psyche of each surviving writer, and to some degree the consciousness of each successive generation of writers.

The end of the war in 1918 saw the establishment of an independent Armenia in the former Russian Empire, which fell two years later to the advancing Red Army. At about the same time the Kemalist movement in Turkey took firm control of that nation, and the last stronghold of the Armenians who had survived the massacres in Cilicia also fell. Those Armenians also were deported to various countries of the Middle East.

The first cultural center of the diaspora became Paris, where the surviving writers gathered around the publications *Zvartnots, Menk,* and *Haratch.* Two separate trends developed here. The first, among the older writers, was an attempt to capture the past in fiction; a second, more nihilistic outlook was adopted by the younger artists.

In the 1930s the writers remaining in Paris became more and more pessimistic in their novels, as they saw a gradual assimilation of Armenian life into French culture. Notable writers of fiction were Vazken Shushanian (1902–1941), Hratch Zartarian (b. 1892), and Shahan Shahnour (1903–1977), whose novel *Nahanchuh arants erkee* (1929; retreat without a song) aroused a great deal of uneasy attention. Not only was it without hope for the future; it also minimized the past accomplishments of the Armenians.

This was the Paris of André Breton and the SURREALISTS; and no Armenian was so influenced by that movement as Nighohos Sarafian (1905–1973). Two other active poets of the time were Puzant Topalian (1902–1971) and Harout Gostandian (1909–1979).

Gosdan Zarian (1885–1969), poet and novelist, studied in Russia, Paris, and Brussels. He came into contact with the work of the surrealists and DADAISTS and experimented with their forms. His first book, *Antsortuh ev eer jampan* (1926; the traveler and his road), is a series of critical observations on the writer as a creator. His long narrative poem *Dadrakomi harsuh* (1930; the bride of Dadrakom) examines personal choice and honor. Zarian's most important work, *Navuh leran vra* (1943; the boat on the mountain), uses a Jungian approach to probe the peasant character and the myth of the motherland.

Zabel Yessayan (1878–1943) left the Paris group to live in Armenia, only to be exiled to Siberia in 1937. Her novels of unhappy marriages, set in Paris, were not so much the cause of her punishment as was her evocative *Silihdaree bardezneruh* (1934; the gardens of Silihdar), an autobiographical work that the Soviet authorities accused of fostering nostalgia. *Barba Khachi* (1936; Uncle Khachig) completed before her exile, although written with the mandatory social comments, did not save her.

In the U. S. and in Beirut, three writers continued the work of Telkadintsi and Rouben Zartarian in describing village life: Simon Simonian (b. 1915) in Beirut and Beniamin Nourigian (b. 1894) and Hamasdegh (pseud. of Hampartsoum Gelenian, 1895–1966) in the U.S. Hamasdegh's novel *Spidak tsiavoruh* (1931; the horseman in white) portrays a gentle national hero, a freedom fighter, who is a composite of all the leading figures of the revolutionary movement.

A major poet who escaped the massacre (because he happened to be away from Istanbul and in Jerusalem that April of 1915) was Vahan Tekeyan (1878–1945). He settled in Egypt and spent his business hours as an editor, his private life honing sonnets. Tekeyan has been called one of the great visionary and apocalyptic poets, a writer who expects God's righteousness to triumph, who waits for order to emerge from chaos. In some of his poems, however, he becomes impatient, and in one much quoted bitter sonnet, "Beedee esenk Asdedso" (1917; "We Shall Say to God," 1978), he says to

God, "Send us to hell again. You made us know it well. Keep your paradise for the Turk."

As assimilation continued in Europe, the Middle East, especially Beirut, became the center of Armenian culture for the diaspora, and schools, periodicals, and an Armenian theater evolved in the Lebanese capital. After the fall of the Armenian Republic, the critic Nigol Aghbalian (1873–1947) and the playwright Levont Shant (1869–1951) settled there. Shant's plays, influenced by Ibsen, were symbolic struggles between the individual and society, past and present, physical and spiritual needs. His best-known work, *Heen asdvadzner* (1912; the old gods) is still performed in Erevan, the capital of Soviet Armenia.

The role of the idealist in a time of suffering, poetry as consolation, and poetry as a forum for change were topics examined by the poets of *Ani, Nayiri,* and later *Spiurk,* three of the Beirut literary magazines. The leading voices belonged to Andranik Zaroukian, (b. 1912), Moushegh Ishkhan (b. 1913), Vahe-Vahian (b. 1902), and the Patriarch of Jerusalem Eghivart (pseud. of Eghishe Derderian, b. 1910). Their poems of love and transience, rooted in the holocaust, addressed the problems of retaining an Armenian identity in foreign lands. But the holocaust itself, although a constant, was never the subject of a successful Armenian novel. (*The Forty Days of Musa Dagh* by Franz WERFEL was in German.) The immensity of the losses and the horror of the experience were beyond Containment, Only Zaroukian's *Mangootioon choonetsogh marteek* (1954; men without a childhood), a story of orphans, succeeds. lshkhan's *Mnas parov mangootioon* (1972; goodbye to childhood) is a more recent attempt.

Younger poets—Vahé Oshagan (b. 1923), Zareh Melkonian (b. 1923), Jacques Hagopian (b. 1917)—and the novelist Kevork Ajemian (b. 1932) began experimenting with modern forms and postsurrealist techniques. But the recent civil strife in Lebanon has hindered the course of Armenian literature there. Many of the writers have moved to the U.S, or France, where the Armenian reading public is dispersed. In Turkey, and until recently in Iran, smaller literary communities exist with active journals. In Istanbul a group of modern poets is led by Zahrad (pseud. of Zareh Yaldizciyan; b. 1924), who began as an abstract writer but whose work is now more accessible and is marked by whimsical, sharp humor.

The eastern branch of Armenian literature flourishes in the Armenian S.S.R. In the early years of the Soviet regime literature's function was polemic. But there were established writers who could neither be molded into propagandists, nor ignored: Hovaness Toumanian (1860–1923) Shirvanzadeh (pseud. of Alexander Movsessian, 1858–1935), Terenig Demirjian (1877–1956), Stepan Zorian (1889–1967), and Avedik Issahakian (1875–1957). Toumanian and Issahakian are often linked together because of similarities m their style, their use of classical forms, and their adaptation of folklore and epics from early Christian and pagan times, Many of Issahakian's poems are wellloved songs; his masterpiece is a long visionary poem, *Abbou Lala Mahari* (1910; Abbou Lala Mahari), describing the wanderings of a disillusioned poet. Toumanian's narrative *Anoush* (1892; Anoush) has been made into a popular opera. Shirvanzadeh, who spent his youth in the oil city of Baku, drew on city life for his novels and plays, and was the first dramatist to stress both women's rights and women's failings.

After SOCIALIST REALISM was imposed by the Soviet regime, a great deal of mediocre writing was published. But there were some outstanding new writers, notably Eghishe CHARENTS, Kourken

Mahari (1903–1969), Mgrditch Armen (1906–1972), and Axel Bagounts (1899–1937). The last three wrote slice-of-life vignettes with undercurrents of irony and the flavor of myth. All three writers were exiled to Siberia during the Stalinist purges. (Charents was imprisoned in Erevan.) Mahari's novel of prison life, *Dsaghgads peshalarer* (1971; the blossoming barbed wires), has been compared favorably with SOLZHENITSYN's work.

Another outstanding writer who did not survive the purges was Vahan Totovents (1894–1938). He had graduated from the University of Wisconsin in 1912 and returned to Armenia in 1922. His luminous prose, with its simple style, is at its best in the autobiographical novel, *Kyankuh heen hromeakan janabarheen vra* (1930; *Scenes from an Armenian Childhood*, 1962), a poetic narrative filled with joy and pathos, about Totovents's native Kharpert.

In the early 1940s, at the onset of World War II, the Soviet government relaxed its ban on nationalistic themes, and two important historical novels were published: Tereng Demirjian's *Vartanank* (1943; of Vartan and his friends), and Stepan Zorian's *Bab Takavor* (1944; King Bab). Both novels were in the tradition of Raffi (1837–1888), who followed the lead of Katchadour Abovian (1805–1848), father of the Armenian novel (and called the founder of modern Armenian literature). Abovian's novel *Verk Hayasdanee* (1858; wounds of Armenia) put current problems and aspirations into ancient settings.

The Soviet-Armenian writers of fiction who gained prominence after the war were Hrachia Kochar (1910–1965), Viken Khechoumian (1916–1975), and Sero Khanzadian (b. 1915). Khanzadian gained acclaim in 1949 with *Mer kentee marteeg* (the people of our regiment). The writer attracting most critical analysis is Hrant Matevossian.

A freer, more vigorous style of poetry began to appear in the period following Stalin's death, written by a generation of poets that includes Hovaness Shiraz (b. 1915), the national troubadour and conscience, whose work is the most traditional; Hamo Sahian (b. 1914); Maro Markarian (b. 1915), Sylva Gaboodikian (b. 1919), Vahakn Tavtian (b. 1923), Gevorg Emin (b. 1919), and Barouyr Sevag. Sevag and Emin are the most widely known and translated abroad.

The new body of modern poetry, in spite of a preponderance of "Ararat," "stone" and "grape" images, and uniquely Armenian references, is universal in intent and experimentation. Gradually as it gets translated, Armenian writing will take its place in world literature, a place long deserved but made difficult because of its forbidding alphabet.

Meanwhile, a younger group of writers—including Razmig Davoyan (b. 1940), Vahakn Garents (1924–1980), Ardem Haroutiunian (b. 1944), Hovaness Krikorian (b. 1945), Arevshad Avakian (b. 1940), Tavit Hovaness (b. 1945), and Armen Mardirossian (b. 1943)—has taken up the task and responsibility of being Armenian poets, to recreate in their work lost kingdoms for lost generations.

BIBLIOGRAPHY: Thorossian, H., *Histoire de la littérature arménienne* (1951); Der Neressian, S., *The Armenians* (1970); Der Hovanessian, D. and M. Margossian, Introduction to *Anthology of Armenian Poetry* (1978): 1–10; Hamalian, L., and J. D. Yohannan, eds., *New Writing from the Middle East* (1978): 117–21; Lang, D. M., *Armenia, Cradle of Civilization*, 2nd ed. (1978); Chahinian, K., *Panorama de la littérature arménienne* (1980)

—MARZBED MARGOSSIAN

ARNÉR, Sivar

Swedish novelist, short-story writer, and dramatist, b. 13 March 1909, Arby

A. comes from a middle-class background. He acquired an academic degree and was a teacher for several years before his literary debut in 1943 with a collection of short stories and a novel.

A major theme in A.'s work is the conflict between conscience and will, justice and power, seen from a pacifistic, idealistic point of view. His protagonists are often passive types in subservient positions, yet they challenge men of power and establish their moral superiority even though they are attacked and beaten for their beliefs. In their striving to help the underdog, A.'s protagonists often nearly succumb, as for example in A.'s first novel, *Plånbok borttappad* (1943; lost wallet), or in the later *Fyra som var bröder* (1955; four who were brothers). According to A., interdependence is man's source of misery, yet A. thinks individualism requires too much of a sacrifice of unity and solidarity.

A.'s depiction of middleclass values versus human passions and evil is especially skillful in his domestic novels, where violence breaks through the surface of marital tranquillity. Sadomasochism rather than love marks the relationship between A.'s married couples, who usually consist of a weak intellectual man and a neurotic, power-hungry woman. The first of this type of novel is *Du själv* (1946; you yourself), followed by *Egil* (1948; Egil). But in several later novels there is a more positive view of male-female relationship, and the earlier irony is now softened by humor.

A. is a masterful writer of short stories. In the title story of his first collection, *Skon som krigaren bar* (1943; the shoe worn by the soldier), he presents the total dedication to pacifism in the shoemaker who commits suicide rather than make boots for an officer. The struggle between incompatible yet interdependent forces is portrayed in A.'s masterpiece, the story ''Luft och vatten'' (1954; air and water).

A. has also written plays, particularly for the radio. His general theme about the conflict between dominant and submissive people translates well into dramatic form. Notable is the play *Man lyder* (1953; one obeys), which deals with the erotic aspects of the political interaction between the weak and the strong.

A.'s style is a deceptively simple, low-keyed prose reflecting the spoken language. The structure of his work moves from the tightly knit plots in earlier works to a kaleidoscopic form in the 1960s. In his latest work, a series of autobiographical novels starting with *Där är han* (1975; there he is) he returns to a more conventional form.

Although A. has been criticized for slickness, he is undoubtedly one of Sweden's major contemporary writers. His portrayal of erotic relationships is superb, and his work also contains a powerful exposé of contemporary political dilemmas and conflicts where mysticism and Marxism are uniquely blended into a personal philosophy of life and man.

FURTHER WORKS: *Knekt och klerk* (1945); *Verandan* (1947); *Vackert väder* (1950); *Han-Hon-Ingen* (1951); *Man lyder, Den första människan, Uppifrån: Tre dramer* (1953); *Säkert till sommaren* (1954); *Som svalorna* (1956); *Fern hörspel* (1959); *Dag och natt. Hörspel* (1960); *Finnas till* (1961); *Nätet* (1962); *Tvärbalk* (1963); *ett ett eit* (1964); *Verkligen* (1965); *Solgata* (1967); *Vargkottletter* (1968); *Skon och god* (1969); *En satans person. Hon kommer ju. Två pjäser* (1970); *Det fanns en park. Sagopjäs* (1971);

Byta människa (1972); *Vattenvägar* (1973); *Vilken kämpe* (1976); *Öppna dörrar* (1978); *Aprilsol* (1980)

BIBLIOGRAPHY: Gustafson, A., *A History of Swedish Literature* (1961): 556–57

—TORBORG LUNDELL

ARNICHES, Carlos

Spanish dramatist, b. 11 Oct. 1866, Alicante; d. 16 Apr. 1943, Madrid

A. spent his early years in the provincial city of Alicante, where he staged short plays as a child while in school. During these years he had as a classmate Joaquín Dicenta (1863–1917), an important dramatist, novelist, and journalist years later. In 1880 A. and his family moved to Barcelona soon after his father was relieved of his post as paymaster at a factory as a result of local political intrigues. From this experience, A. developed a hatred for politics, an attitude that is reflected in his play *Los caciques* (1920; the bosses). In Barcelona, where he worked for its most important newspaper, *La Vanguardia*, he remained until 1885. Subsequently, he went to Madrid where, after serious financial difficulties, which led to his many contacts with the slum districts, he began to stage his plays and to publish them. He remained in Madrid for over fifty years. There he became a leading intellectual figure as reflected by his appointment as president of the Círculo de Bellas Artes in 1916, a cultural institution that has remained very important. In 1936, at the beginning of the Spanish Civil War, A. became an exile in Argentina, thus bringing his theater to the New World. Upon his return to Madrid in 1940, he resumed his activities as a dramatist.

A prolific author, A. was a master of the *sainete* (one-act farces) and the *zarzuela* (musical comedies), theatrical representations considered in Spain part of the *género chico* (petit genre), works that involve short, popular dramatic or dramatic-musical playlets, skits, or operettas, generally one act in length. These plays often depicted the plight of the lower classes in Madrid by capturing aspects of their language and customs. Over half of A.'s plays were written in collaboration with numerous other dramatists: among them, José Lopéz Silva (1861–1925), Joaquín Abati (1865–1936), and Enrique García Alvarez (1873–1931). It was specifically from García Alvarez that A. derived a keen understanding of the development of plots and the use of dialogue.

Without a doubt, A.'s fundamental contribution to drama stemmed from his ability to define the significance of the Madrilenian *sainete*. This paradigm became apparent with *El santo de la Isidra* (1898; Isidra's saint). Often the most important characters of the *sainete* were a rascal/pimp courageous in appearance but in fact a coward, and an honest blue-collar worker who was in love with a good and sophisticated girl who, in turn, was being seduced by the boastful rascal. Overall, the *sainete* confronts its readers/spectators with a clear conflict between good and evil, between a worker's respect for the prevailing social values as supported by the middle class and a rascal who attempts to intimidate those surrounding him as he violates the prevailing social codes. All this is portrayed by means of language that attempts, in an artificial and clever way, to capture a popular flavor appealing to the masses and conforming to the stereotypical views held by the middle class on the usual behavior of the masses. The language in much of A.'s works

depends heavily on comical effects that hide many of the technical deficiencies of his works. Among A.'s best *sainetes* are *Las estrellas* (1904; the stars) and *La flor del barrio* (1919; the flower of the district).

A. evolved from a *sainetero* to the writing of protest plays such as *Los caciques* and *La heroica villa* (1921; the heroic town) in which he criticized, respectively, political tyranny and provincial hypocrisy. From there he went to write "grotesque tragedies" in which, by means of caricature and exaggeration, he aimed to produce a tragicomic effect. Among A.'s grotesque plays are *Es mi hombre* (1921; that is my man), *La locura de Don Juan* (1923; Don Juan's madness), and *La diosa rie* (1931; the goddess smiles).

Overall, the theater of A. provides the current reader and spectator with an understanding of the Spanish stage during the early years of the 20th c. in both artistic and social terms. Furthermore, it constitutes the beginning of a break with a referential conception of dramatic art as it favors a more stylized view of the cosmos as evidenced by the use of carefully selected stereotypical situations and language.

FURTHER WORKS: *Casa editorial* (1888); *La verdad desnuda* (1888); *Sociedad secreta* (1889); *El reclamo* (1893); *Los bandidos* (1896); *La guardia amarilla* (1897); *El último chulo* (1899); *La cara de Dios* (1899); *La divisa* (1902); *Los guapos* (1905); *El Premio Nobel* (1911); *La casa de Quirós* (1915); *El mirar de sus ojos* (1922); *La dischosa honradez* (1923); *El señor Badanas* (1930); *El hombrecillo* (1941)

BIBLIOGRAPHY: Pérez de Ayala, R., *Las máscaras: ensayos de crítica teatral* (1919), Vol. 1: 117–98; Berenguer Carísomo, A., *El teatro de C. A.* (1937); Deleito y Piñuela, J., *Estampas del Madrid teatral de fin de siglo* (1946): 211–21, 363–69; Ramos, V., *Vida y teatro de C. A.* (1966); Monleón, J., ed., *C. A.: teatro* (1967); Seco, M., *A. y el habla de Madrid* (1970); McKay, D. R., *C. A.* (1972); Ruiz Ramón, F., *Historia del teatro Español: Siglo XX* (1986): 38–48

—LUIS T. GONZÁLEZ-DEL-VALLE

ARRABAL, Fernando

Spanish dramatist (residing in France and writing initially in Spanish, but publishing primarily in French), b. 11 Aug. 1932, Melilla, Spanish Morocco

The psychological and sociopolitical dimensions of A.'s prolific creations reflect a biography rich in bizarre experiences and traumatic events. On July 17, 1936, civil war broke out in Spain, and the young A.'s father was arrested by Franco's troops because of his liberal sympathies. A. was never to see him again. His family moved from Melilla to Ciudad Rodrigo that same year and then to Madrid in 1940. A. was raised by his devout, conservative mother in a repressive, warped ambience in which no reference to the boy's father was permitted. When he was seventeen. A. discovered some photos and letters of his father and began to comprehend the divisive impact of the civil war on his own family. He refused to speak to his mother for five years, seeking escape from the tensions at his home in American silent film comedies (Charlie Chaplin, Laurel and Hardy, and others) and the writings of Lewis Carroll,

KAFKA, and Dostoevsky. When the need for artistic and spiritual freedom became overwhelming, A. departed for Paris, where he has resided since 1955.

A.'s early theater represents, in part, a psychological exercise directed at the resolution of his feelings about his mother and the metaphorical search for his father. His first published plays were short works featuring amoral, childlike characters. The juvenile perspective of plays written in the 1950s like *Le tricycle* (1961; *The Tricycle*, 1967), *Cérémonie pour un noir assassiné* (1965; ceremony for an assassinated Black), and *Oraison* (1957; *Orison*, 1962) allowed the author to examine and exorcise the traumas of his youth. These early plays established A.'s personal style, which blends the absurd and the surreal into a nightmarish vision of the oppressive nature of existence. The uneasy clash between the tone and the content of these dramas gives rise to the grotesque, the central aesthetic of A.'s evolving work. *Le cimetière des voitures* (1959; *The Automobile Graveyard*, 1960) constitutes the culmination of A.'s early theater. Utilizing a parody of the Christ story, the drama further explores the concepts of good and evil examined in *Oraison*. The metaphor of the automobile graveyard constitutes A.'s most striking condemnation of the absence of morality and logic in a technological, repressive world.

The second period of A.'s theater coincides with his initiation of the "Panic" movement in 1962. "Panic" transcends the norms of a traditional literary movement; it is a life style governed by confusion, chance, and memory. A.'s panic theater of the 1960s, influenced by André BRETON and SURREALISM, developed further some of the tendencies of his earlier works, highlighting the role of ritual and ceremony in the conception and the staging of his dramas. His best-known play to date, *L'architecte et l'empereur d'Assyrie* (1967; *The Architect and the Emperor of Assyria*, 1969) was written in this mode. That play's two protagonists, who may ultimately represent components of man's psyche, utilize ceremony and role playing to explore their mutual fears and desires. *Grand Guignol,* humor, and blasphemy all coalesce in A.'s poetic exploration of the psychological and sociological forces confronting the human spirit.

In 1967, while vacationing in Spain, A. was arrested for writing a blasphemous dedication in a copy of one of his novels. He spent a month in prison before his acquittal. That experience heightened his empathy for the oppressed peoples of the world and strengthened his identification with his own father. His theater took on a new direction, becoming more overtly political. *Et ils passèrent des menottes aux fleurs* (1967; *And They Put Handcuffs on the Flowers*, 1969), directed by the author in both Paris and New York, utilized blasphemy and the grotesque to protest against political oppression in Spain. *Sur le fill; ou, La ballade du train fantôme* (1974; on the wire; or, the ballad of the phantom train), inspired by A.'s chance discovery of a ghost town in New Mexico named Madrid, combined the author's anguish over his exile with a striking central metaphor that illuminated the role of art in ameliorating conditions in Spain.

During the 1980s and 1990s A. has continued his prolific outpuuring of creative endeavors in a variety of genres. In addition to his primary focus, theater, he has received major prizes and accolades for his novels and essays. Especially noteworthy were the 1982 Nadal Prize for his novel *La torre herida por el rayo* (1983) and the 1994 Espasa Prize for his volume of essays *La dudosa luz del día*. Poetry, sometimes illustrated by major artists, films (*Adieu, Babylone!*, 1993), book-length letters to political leaders, and shorter essays on a wide range of subjects all attest to the diverse talents of A. who remains a controversial and provocative international figure capable of causing a scandal at one moment and embracing a social or political cause at another. Certainly, A.'s impact on contemporary drama and on the world of European arts and letters cannot be denied.

FURTHER WORKS: *Orchestration théâtrale* (1957); *Les deux bourreaux* (1958; *The Two Executioners*, 1962); *Fando et Lis* (1958; *Fando and Lis*, 1962); *Baal Babylone* (1959; *Baal Babylon*, 1961); *L'enterrement de la sardine* (1961; *The Burial of the Sardine*, 1965); *Guernica* (1961, *Guernica* 1967); *Le labyrinthe* (1961; *The Labyrinth*, 1967); *Pique-nique en campagne* (1961; *Picnic on the Battlefield*, 1967); *La bicyclette du condamné* (1961; *The Condemned Man's Bicycle*, 1967); *La communion solennelle* (1963: *The Solemn Communion*, 1970); *La pierre de la folie* (1963); *Striptease de la jalousie* (perf. 1967); *Le grand cérémonial* (1965: *The Grand Cerimonial*, 1970); *Le couronnement* (1965); *Les amours impossibles* (perf. 1965); *Une chèvre sur un nuage* (perf. 1966); *La jeunesse illustrée* (perf. 1967); *Fêtes et rites de la confusion* (1967); *Bestialité érotique* (1969); *Une tortue nommée Dostoievski* (1969); *L'aurore rouge et noire* (1969); *Le jardin des delices* (1969; *The Garden of Delights*, 1974); *Le lai de Barabbas* (1969); *Ars amandi* (1970); *Dieu tenté par les mathématiques* (1970); *Le ciel et la merde* (1972); *La grande revue du XXe siècle* (1972); *La guerre de mille ans* (1972); *Lettre au Générale Franco* (1972); *Le New York d'Arrabal* (1973); *Sur Fischer* (1974); *Jeunes barbares d'aujourd'hui* (1975); *La marcha real* (1975); *La tour de Babel* (1976); *Une orange sur le mont de Vénus* (1976); *La gloire en images* (1976); *Vole-moi un petit milliard* (1978); *Le pastaga des loufs* (1978); *Punk et Punk et Colégram* (1978); *Lettre aux militants communistes espagnols* (1978); *Inquisición* (1982); *La torre herida por el rayo* (1983); *Carta a Fidel Castro* (1983); *La virgen roja* (1987); *Como lirio entre espinas* (1992); *La dudosa luz del día* (1994); *Teatro completo* (2 vols., 1997)

BIBLIOGRAPHY: Esslin, M., *The Theater of the Absurd* (1961): 217–22; Diaz, J. W., "Theater and Theories of F. A.," *KRQ*, 16 (1969): 143–54; Killinger, J., "A. and Surrealism," *MD*, 14 (1971): 210–23; Kronik, J., "A. and the Myth of Guernica," *Estreno*, 2 (1975): 15–20; Orenstein, G., *The Theater of the Marvelous* (1975): 239–73; Podol, P., *F. A.* (1978); Donahue, T., *The Theater of F. A.* (1980); Tores Monreal, F., *Introducción al teatro de A.* (1981); Arata, L. O., *The Festive Play of F. A.* (1982); Glibota, A., *A. Espace* (1993); Torres Monreal, F., "Introduccion" to *Teatro completo* (1997)

—PETER PODOL

ARREOLA, Juan José

Mexican short-story writer, novelist, and dramatist, b. 21 Sept. 1918, Ciudad Guzmán (formerly Zapotlán)

Although A. received little formal education, he is a man of vast literary culture and a keen observer of human nature. After holding a variety of jobs in his native state of Jalisco, he moved to Mexico City, where he worked as a professional actor under the direction of Rodolfo USIGLI and Xavier VILLAURRUTIA, two of Mexico's best-known playwrights. In 1945 he received a scholarship to study theatrical arts in France and upon his return attended classes at the

College of Mexico. He has collaborated in the founding of literary journals and conducted workshops for aspiring writers. More recently he has become a prominent television personality.

A.'s first collection of short stories, *Varia invención* (1949; *Various Inventions*, 1964) was followed by his masterpiece, *Confabulario* (1952; *Confabulario, and Other Inventions*, 1964). The latter includes stories, parables, and vignettes displaying a broad range of themes, styles, and techniques. As its title suggests, *Bestiario* (1958; *Bestiary*, 1964) revives the art of mirroring human foibles in animal portraits. A.'s only novel, *La feria* (1963; *The Fair*, 1977), represents a poetically conceived, satirical mosaic of his hometown, Zapotlán. *Palindroma* (1971; palindrome) contains sundry short fiction as well as a one-act farce depicting the pitfalls of marriage.

A. has been called the Mexican BORGES. Both A. and Borges prefer universal to regional themes; both might be described as sophisticated eclectics, having read widely and utilized elements of their favorite books to create their own works; both have developed styles characterized by verbal precision and classical elegance; and both are masters at illuminating the absurdity of the human experience through irony, paradox, and fantasy. A. differs from Borges, however, in several respects. He is less intellectual and writes in a lighter, more satirical vein than his Argentine counterpart; unlike Borges, he has penned tales of social protest with moralizing overtones; and he is far more preoccupied with sexual relations, a theme almost entirely absent from Borges's fiction.

A.'s best story, "El guardagujas" (1952; "The Switchman," 1964), has been interpreted in a variety of ways: as a fantasy satirizing the inefficiency of the Mexican railroads, as an attack on political tyranny, and as a religious allegory. It can also be read as a masterful portrayal of existential absurdity, the switchman's tiny toy lantern symbolizing the dim light of human reason and the onrushing train the overwhelming vicissitudes of life the traveler ultimately comes to accept.

Additional existential pieces include "Autri" (1959; "Autri," 1964), a reworking of Jean-Paul SARTRE's *No Exit*, and "El silencio de Dios" (1952; "God's Silence," 1964), an imaginary dialogue between the narrator and God, who turns out to be the narrator's alter ego. Perhaps influenced by Sartre's psychology, A. is convinced that true love is an unattainable ideal. Thus, in tales such as "El rinoceronte" (1952; "The Rhinoceros," 1964) male domination and female deception destroy marital bliss.

A. expresses his preoccupation with aesthetics in "El discípulo" (1952; "The Disciple," 1964), which demonstrates that the ideal work of art should remain incomplete, activating the imagination. He strikes a moralizing note in "Un pacto con el diablo" (1952; "A Pact with the Devil," 1964), a popular tale patterned after Stephen Vincent BENÉT's "The Devil and Daniel Webster." "El fraude" (1949; "The Fraud," 1964) parodies the Prometheus myth by adapting it to an absurd, contemporary situation.

An outstanding craftsman, A. has left an indelible imprint on Mexican letters. He will undoubtedly be remembered for his linguistic virtuosity and his satirical presentations of human foibles tempered with literary allusions, flights of fantasy, and compassion.

FURTHER WORKS: *Gunther Stapenhorst* (1946); *La hora de todos* (1954); *Confabulario y varia invención* (1955); *Punta de plata* (1958, with Héctor Xavier); *Confabulario total* (1962); *Lectura en voz alta* (1968); *Antología de J. J. A.* (1969); *Cuentos* (1969); *La palabra educación* (1973); *Y ahora, la mujer . . .* (1975); *Inventario* (1976)

BIBLIOGRAPHY: Menton, S., "J. J. A. and the Twentieth-Century Short Story," *Hispania*, 42 (1959): 295–308; Carballo, E., *Diecinueve protagonistas de la literature mexicana del siglo XX* (1965): 359–407; Brushwood, J. S., *Mexico in Its Novel* (1966): 28–30; Washburn, Y. M., "An Ancient Mold for Contemporary Casting: The Beast Book of Juan," *Hispania*, 56 (1973): 295–300; Foster, D. W., and V. R. Foster, eds., *Modern Latin American Literature* (1975), Vol. I: 104–10; Herz, T. M., "Continuity in Evolution: J. J. A. as Dramatist," *LATR*, 8 (1975): 15–26; Larson, R., *Fantasy and Imagination in the Mexican Narrative* (1977): 79–82; McMurray, G. R., "Albert Camus' Concept of the Absurd and J. J. A.'s 'The Switchman,'" *LALR*, 6 (1977): 29–35; Washburn, Y. M., *J. J. A.* (1983)

—GEORGE R. MCMURRAY

ARSIENNIEVA, Natalla

Byelorussian poet, b. 20 Nov. 1903, Baku, Azerbaijan

Daughter of a tsarist official, A. grew up in several cities in the Russian Empire. She completed her secondary education at a Byelorussian school in Vilna, where her writing of poetry was encouraged by her teacher, Maksim Haretski (1893–1939), himself an eminent writer. Although she enrolled at Vilna University in 1921, her marriage in 1922 to Frantsishak Kushel, an officer in the Polish army and a Byelorussian political figure, took her to ethnic Poland. Deported by the Soviets to Kazakhstan in 1940, she was permitted to return because of the intercession of Byelorussian writers in 1941 and spent the years 1941–44 in German-occupied Minsk. After a period in displaced-persons camps in West Germany, A. came to the U.S., where she has lived since 1950.

A.'s poems began appearing in West Byelorussian periodicals in 1921; she was immediately acclaimed on both sides of the interwar border dividing Byelorussia between the U.S.S.R. and Poland. Until 1939 she was regularly featured in West Byelorussian periodicals. In 1927 her first book of poetry, *Pad sinim niebam* (under the blue skies) was published. This volume was followed by *Siahonnia* (1944; today) and *Mizh bierahami* (1979; between the shores). *Mizh bierahami*, published in New York, contains selected poems, 1920–70.

During the war years in Minsk A. translated several opera librettos from the Western repertory and wrote plays and songs. Many of her poems were set to music. The religious poem "Mahutny Bozha" (1943; o God Almighty), set to music by Mikola Ravienski, is now sung in Byelorussian churches in the West, both Orthodox and Catholic.

Although from her high school years A. identified with the Byelorussian national cause, her poetry before World War II was personal and lyrical, thus differing from that of most of her Byelorussian contemporaries, whose works were dominated by sociopolitical themes. A.'s verses from that period vibrate with the beauty of nature, especially the "yellow autumn," enchantment with the blue, starry sky, the mystery of the universe, and a wistful longing for the unknown. Through all of this pulsates an optimistic thirst for life. From this point of view, A. stands close to Maksim BAHDANOVICH.

The hardships of Soviet exile and the horrors of World War II brought forth new qualities in A.'s poetry: a pained concern for her country, spiritual fortitude, great courage, and calls for endurance as the only way to wring out from fate a share in life.

A.'s versification is traditional, rich in assonance and alliteration, with a majestic tone. Having spent but twenty years in Byelorussia, A. has produced a body of work remarkable for the richness of its language and folklore, for its imaginative texture and erudition.

—JAN ZAPRUDNIK

ARTAUD, Antonin

French poet and essayist, b. 4 Sept. 1895, Marseille; d. 4 March 1948, Paris

Born into a bourgeois Marseille family, A. had a severe case of meningitis as a child and suffered from ill health throughout his life, often resorting to drugs to kill pain. He came to Paris in 1920, and in 1923 published his first volume of poems, *Tric-trac du ciel (The Heavens at Backgammon*, 1968). In 1924, friendly with adherents of SURREALISM such as André BRETON and André Masson (b. 1896), he joined the surrealist group and became an important contributor to their review, *La révolution surréaliste.* Expelled from the group in 1926 for disagreeing with Breton on the need for political commitment, in "À la grande nuit; ou, le bluff surréaliste" (1927; "In the Dark; or, The Surrealist Bluff," 1968) A. expressed his belief that revolution was first and foremost metaphysical in nature. During the 1920s A. wrote poetry, film scenarios (only one of which, "La coquille et le clergyman" [1927; *The Seashell and the Clergyman*, 1972] was actually made into a film), acted in films (his most famous roles were in Abel Gance's *Napoléon* and Carl Dreyer's *Jeanne d'Arc*) and in the theater (under the direction of Lugné-Poë, Georges Pitoëff, and Charles Dullin). In 1927, with Roger Vitrac and Robert Aron, he founded the Alfred Jarry Theater and in 1932, by himself, the Theater of Cruelty, which staged *Les Cenci* (1964; *The Cenci*, 1969), A.'s adaptation of Shelley's poetic drama. In 1935, when the Theater of Cruelty collapsed, he left for Mexico, where he wrote *Au pays des Tarahumaras* (1945; *The Peyote Dance*, 1976). After returning from Mexico and undergoing several attempts at drug detoxification in France, he left for Ireland, where he had a tumultuous stay. His strange behavior on the boat returning to France was such that he was committed to a mental institution upon his return. Transferred to the asylum of Rodez in 1943, he began to write again, and his *Letters de Rodez* (1946; *Letters from Rodez*, 1960) express his rage against God, sex, and his own body. After his release in 1946 he was to write some of his greatest poems—"Artaud le Momo" (1947; "Artaud the Momo," 1976), "Ci-gît, précédé de la culture indienne" (1948; "Here Lies" and "Indian Culture," 1976)—as well as *Van Gogh, le suicidé de la société* (1947; *Van Gogh, the Man Suicided by Society*, 1949), a work in which he indicts a society that had "suicided" him, as it had the painter. He died, from cancer, in 1948—the last in a line of "poètes maudits."

Although A. had only one play of his own produced, his writings on the theater are well known. In various manifestos written between 1931 and 1933 for the Theater of Cruelty, and gathered together in *Le théâtre et son double* (1938; *The Theater and Its Double*, 1958), he demands a metaphysical, ritualistic theater which, like that of the Greeks or the medieval mysteries, or like the plague (to use his own metaphor), would exert a great

catharsis in the spectators, and allow them to rediscover cosmic, mythic forces. At one point he defined the Theater of Cruelty (a term that has given rise to many interpretations) as the sense of "appetite for life, cosmic rigor, implacable necessity." Influenced by Cambodian dancers seen in Marseille in 1922 and by a Balinese theater group that came to Paris in 1931, he rejected the psychological and verbal tradition of Western theater in favor of Oriental theater, in which sounds, music, gestures, costumes, and lights all play an important role and work upon the spectators' emotions. Although A. was never able to realize his ideal of a mythic, physical, liberating theater, many of his ideas concerning a "total" theater influenced directors, such as Jean-Louis Barrault and Roger Blin.

When A. left for Mexico in 1935, he intended to seek outside of France this magic combination of ritual and life: if theater played no part in life, then life itself, his life, would have to become theater. In Mexico he believed he had found the collective rituals he had sought to create on stage. In *Au pays des Tarahumaras* he describes the peyote rituals of the Tarahumaras Indians in terms that are very close to his description of the Theater of Cruelty. Similarly, *Héliogabale; ou, l'anarchiste couronné* (1934; partial tr.: "Heliogabalus; or, the Anarchist Crowned," 1976) shows an A. fascinated by the strange blend of Christian and pagan religion and ritual, violence and sexual perversion, that marked the end of the Roman Empire.

While A.'s influence on the theater was acknowledged even before his death, other aspects of his work—concerning the nature of artistic creation and language, the relationship between writing and corporeality, between writing and madness—had to await the 1960s before they were brought to the fore, particularly by critics such as Jacques Derrida (b. 1931) and Philippe SOLLERS, associated with the French review *Tel Quel.* In the early 1920s, after sending some poems to the *Nouvelle revue française*, A. entered into a correspondence with the review's editor Jacques Rivière (1886–1925). The resulting letters, first published under the title of *Correspondance* (1924), then *Correspondance avec Rivière* (1927; *Correspondence with Jacques Rivière*, 1968) have been called the first declaration of the "impossibility of literature" itself, one of the major issues in contemporary French literary thought. In these letters, A. complains that his thought escapes him, that he cannot make language coincide with thought and being, cannot "capture" himself through what he writes. A.'s life-long despair about the incapacity of language to capture life itself, his preoccupation with language and the body, characterize his theatrical writings and even more his late poems, which are full of bodily imagery and in which language itself—always a problem for A.—has been stressed to its utmost. Puns, invented words, sound games all attest to A.'s desperate attempts to make language exceed its limits to express what is beyond language.

Still another way in which A. attempted to go beyond "language" was through visual expression. Beginning in the 1980s, his own drawings—especially those done in the last decade of his life—gave rise to several collections, notably *A. A.: portraits et gris-gris* (1984), *A. A.: desseins et portraits*, (1986), and exhibits including those held at the Pompidou Center in Paris (1987), the Musée Cantini in Marseilles (1995), and the Museum of Modern Art in New York (1996).

FURTHER WORKS: *Le pèse-nerfs, suivi de Fragments d'un journal d'enfer* (1925; *Nerve Scales*, 1968); *L'ombilic des limbes* (1925; *Umbilical Limbo*, 1968); *L'art et la mort* (1929; *Art and Death*,

1968); *Les nouvelles révélations de l'être* (1937); *Lettre contre la Cabbale* (1949); *Letters à Jean-Louis Barrault* (1952); *Vie et mort de Satan le feu* (1953; *The Death of Satan*, 1974); *Œuvres complètes* (1956–1994). FURTHER WORKS IN ENGLISH: *A. A. Anthology* (1965); *Collected Works*, Vols. 1–4 (1968–1972); *The Death of Satan and Other Mystical Writings* (1974); *To Have Done with the Judgement of God* (1975); *Selected Writings* (1976); *Peyote Dance* (1976); *Indian Culture* (1987); *Selected Writings* (1988); *A. On Theater* (1989); *Watchfiends and Rack Screams* (1995)

BIBLIOGRAPHY: Sellin, E., *Dramatic Concepts of A. A.* (1968); Knapp, B., *A. A.: Man of Vision* (1969); Greene, N., *A. A.: Poet without Words* (1971); Hayman, R., *A. and After* (1972); Esslin, M., *A.*, (1976); Sontag, S., Introduction to *Selected Writings* (1976): xvii–lix; Bermel, A., *A.'s Theater of Cruelty* (1977); Virmaux, A., *A.: un bilan critique* (1979); Gavelli, J., *A. A. et la question du lieu* (1982); Levesque, J.-J., *A. A.* (1985); Virmaux, A., *A. A.: Qui êtes-vous* (1986); Borie, M., *A. A.: le théâtre et le retour aux sources* (1989); Barber, S., *A. A.: blows and bombs* (1993); Goodall, J., *A. and the Gnostic Drama* (1994); Plunka, G., ed., *A. A. and the Modern Theater* (1994); Stout, J. C., *A. A.'s Alternate Geneologies* (1996)

—NAOMI GREENE

ARTMANN, H(ans) C(arl)

Austrian poet and novelist, b. 12 June 1921, Vienna

The only child of a shoemaker in one of Vienna's working-class districts, A. attended only his compulsory eight years of school. As a self-taught bohemian, he has never really led a settled life, the thought of which he despises.

A. became famous in 1958 when *med ana schwoazzn dintn* (with black ink), his sensational book of Viennese dialect poetry, was published. Ever since, evaluations of this and subsequent works written in standard German have caused a controversy over the interpretation of his literary intentions. He is now well established as one of the forerunners of the entire German-language literary scene since the end of World War II, and he has led several movements. He has been compared to writers as diverse as Federico GARCÍA LORCA, Ezra POUND, and François Villon; however, each of the comparisons fails to pinpoint A.'s varied spectrum of style and mood. At the time of the appearance of his dialect literature A. also published baroque-style poetry and prose (*Von denen Husaren und anderen Seil-Tänzern*, 1959; on those hussars and other tightrope walkers) as well as translations from Irish prayers (*Der Schlüssel des Heiligen Patrick*, 1959; the key of Saint Patrick). His translations of many works from English, French, Italian, Yiddish, Russian, and particularly from Spanish all bear the touch of his superb literary sensibility.

A.'s work is generally quite apolitical; yet, art in any form is seen by A. as the existentialist pathway to a reasonable life style. His first poems after 1946 lean toward impressionism; later SURREALIST and manneristic elements predominate in his writings, as in his *greguerías* modeled after those of Ramón Gómez de la SERNA. He was exposed to concrete poetry through the experiments of Konrad Bayer (1932–1964) and Gerhard Rühm (b. 1930) in the early 1950s.

Indirectly influenced by the early ideas of the philosopher Ludwig Wittgenstein (1889–1951) and other neopositivists, A. entered a phase of skepticism toward language, and he and his friends experimented with various linguistic phenomena. He first used the phonetic patterns found in dialect and improvised on them, later writing ironic poems imitating different Viennese characters and incorporating fantastic types such as vampires, monsters, and demons into his poetry. He also adopted the notion of writing every word in lower case. By 1960 his dialect literature had made him into a folk hero, but as a fierce opponent of any kind of establishment he left this comfortable path of popularity and has since written only in standard German. After a brief pause, his fictional diary *das suchen nach dem gestrigen tag* (1964; in search of yesterday) demonstrated again his unimpaired capacity to create fascinating metaphors.

In 1969–70 several friends published collections of his works: his lyrical works in *Ein lilienweißer brief aus lincolnshire* (1969; a lilywhite letter from lincolnshire), his dramatic works in *die fahrt zur insel nantucket* (1969; the journey to the isle of nantucket), and a compendium of his most remarkable writings in *The Best of H. C. A.* (1970—the original title is in English).

In the 1970s his work began to reflect the new sensitivity apparent in Austrian literature, and his poetry returned to verse, rhyme, and meter, as in *Aus meiner Botanisiertrommel: Balladen und Naturgedichte* (1975; from my plant collection: ballads and nature poems), renewing his popular image, this time, according to the literary critic Hans Weigel, as "one of the greatest poets of the German tongue in the 20 c." When A. published his first novel in 1978, the literary world was once again overcome with surprise and bewilderment. In *nachrichten aus nord und süd* (news from north and south) there are neither capitalized words nor any punctuation or other grammatical divisions. The novel is a revelation of A.'s ideas and thoughts on the contemporary scene, mixed with his memories of yesteryear. He again manipulates traditional language by distorting idioms and proverbs and inventing new metaphors that obliquely refer to actual events and historical facts. The alogical approach to the material world seen here and in his other works is the hallmark of his basically poetic oeuvre.

FURTHER WORKS: *hosn rosn baa* (1959, with Gerhard Rühm and Friedrich Achleitner); *verbarium* (1966); *Dracula, Dracula* (1966); *Der Landgraf zu Camprodon* (1966); *Grünverschlossene Botschaft: 90 Träume* (1967); *tök ph'rong süleng* (1967); *allerleirausch: neue schöne kinderreime* (1968); *Frankenstein in Sussex. Fleiß und Industrie* (1968); *Die Anfangsbuchstaben der Flagge: Geschichten* (1969); *Mein Erbteil von Vater und Mutter* (1969); *Das im Walde verlorene Totem: Prosadichtungen 1949–1953* (1970); *how much, schatzi?* (1971); *Der aeronautische Sindtbart* (1972); *Von der Wiener Seite: Geschichten* (1972); *Gedichte über die Liebe und über die Lasterhaftigkeit* (1975); *Grammatik der Rosen: Gesammelte Prosa* (3 vols., 1979)

BIBLIOGRAPHY: Polakovics, F., Preface to *med ana schwoazzn dintn* (1958): 9–16; Chotjewitz, P. O., "16 Jahre A.," *LuK*, 3 (1966): 18–32; Rühm, G., *Die Wiener Gruppe* (1967); Schneider, H., "A.s frühe Werke," in *Das im Walde verlorene Totem* (1970): 103–10; Alldridge, J. C., "H. C. A. and the English Nonsense Tradition," in Last, R. W., ed., *Affinities: Essays in German and English Literature* (1971): 168–83; Bisinger, G., *Über H. C .A.* (1972); Pabisch, P., *H. C. A.: Ein Versuch über die literarische*

Alogik (1978); Pabisch, P., and A. Rodríguez, "H. C. A.'s Adaptation of Ramón Gómez de la Serna's Greguería," *WLT*, 53 (1979): 231–34

—PETER PABISCH

ASCH, Sholem

Yiddish novelist, dramatist, and short-story writer (also writing in Hebrew), b. 1 Jan. 1880, Kutno, Poland; d. 10 July 1957, London, England

A. attended Hebrew religious schools but did not fulfill his parents' hopes for a rabbinical career. Instead, like so many of his contemporaries, A. was caught up in the Jewish Enlightenment movement, began to read widely in Hebrew, Polish, German, and Russian literatures as well as in Yiddish, and soon embarked on a career as a writer, first in Hebrew, then in Yiddish. Born into an era that experienced the rapid breakup of the largely isolated traditional Jewish world, A. embodied his generation's restlessness both intellectually and physically. In his work as well as his personal life, he covered almost the entire geography of Jewish life, having at various times—and on more than one occasion—either visited or settled in Palestine, the countries of eastern and western Europe, and the U.S.

A. first came to public notice as a short-story writer whose fiction was suffused with a mood of sadness and romantic nostalgia for the disappearing isolated, small-town, religious Jewish world that was vanishing along with the 19th c. He soon turned to other themes, moods, and forms, however. His plays with historical themes gained him recognition on the Polish and Russian stages. But it was the naturalistic *Got fun nekome* (1907; *God of Vengeance* 1918, 1965), his third play, that not only gained him a broader European audience but a large measure of notoriety as well; it precipitated the first of his several conflicts with Jewish public opinion. It is set in a basement brothel whose owner lives on the floor above with his wife, a former prostitute, and a daughter, whom he is trying to insulate from the world below—ultimately without success—by installing a sacred Torah scroll in her room. A. again used a tough naturalism in *Motke ganev* (1916; *Mottke the Thief*, 1918), a novel about a pimp who is betrayed by the innocent girl he loves.

A series of novels about the American scene depicts the confrontation of different values experienced by the eastern-European Jewish immigrants and the resulting economic, social, and cultural conflicts: *Amerike* (1911; *America*, 1918); *Di muter* (1925; *The Mother*, 1930, 1937); *Onkl Mozes* (1918; *Uncle Moses*, 1920); *Khayim Lederers tsurikkumen* (1927; *Chaim Lederer's Return*, 1938); and *Toyt urteyl*—also titled *Elektrik tsheyr*—(1926; *Judge Not*, 1938); *Ist River* (1946; *East River*, 1946); and *Grosman un zun* (1954; *A Passage in the Night*, 1953).

A broader subject attracted A. in the trilogy *Farn mabl* (*Peterburg*, 1929, *Varshe*, 1930, *Moskve*, 1931; *Three Cities*, 1933), in which he attempted to encompass the totality of Jewish life in eastern Europe—especially its social range—during the second decade of the 20th c. Only *Varshe* received the unqualified praise of Yiddish critics, who felt that the central character of the trilogy was too weak a creation to hold the three volumes together.

A.'s interest in the Jewish past and its implications for contemporary Jewish life, evident almost from the beginning of his career,

received powerful treatment in a number of later works of fiction. The idealized *Kidush Hashem* (1919; *Kiddish Ha-Shem*, 1926), set in Poland in 1648–49, during the revolt of the Cossacks under Bogdan Chmielnicki against their Polish overlords, emphasizes A.'s oftrepeated affirmation of the efficacy of faith. The similarly idealized *Der tehilim Yid* (1934; *Salvation*, 1934, rev. ed., 1951), about the life of a Hasidic master who overcomes his own and his followers' doubts and trials with a like affirmation of faith, was his most widely acclaimed novel among Yiddish critics and readers.

Der man fun Netseres (1943; *The Nazarene*, 1939)—the English translation was published before the original Yiddish—embroiled him in a bitter controversy. His reliance primarily on New Testament sources coupled with his attempt to depict Jesus as a rabbi faithful to Jewish law and tradition was almost universally denounced in the Jewish press as essentially Christian in interpretation and sympathy, despite A.'s repeated assertions in *What I Believe* (1941), *One Destiny* (1945)—both written in Yiddish but published only in English—and in various interviews that his aim was to remind the Christian world of its roots in Judaism and its debt to it. *The Apostle* (1943), based on the life of Paul, and *Mary* (1949), the two additional "Christological" novels, were written in Yiddish but have not been published in that language. The alienation of A.'s Jewish readers was not diminished by his novels *Moses* (1951), and *The Prophet* (1955), which also have not as yet been published in Yiddish.

Although A.'s work suffers from a tendency to didacticism and to weakness in characterization, it covers a broader social and geographic range than that of any other Yiddish writer, and it recreates its world with great vitality, color, and intensity. If it seems to display a central contradiction in its fluctuation between a hard realism on the one hand and sentimentality on the other, between an admiration for the two-fisted, earthy primitives—even underworld roughnecks—and a reverence for the spiritual and the pious, the apparent contradictions find their union in a common core of romanticism: both his ascetic saints and his brawny sinners are redeemed by their hunger for faith and morality. It is also A.'s historic achievement to have been the first to bring modern Yiddish literature to the attention of Western culture.

FURTHER WORKS: *Sipurim* (1902; in Hebrew); *In a shlekhter tsayt* (1903); *Dos shtetl* (1905; *The Town*, included in *Tales of My People*, 1948); *Tsurikgekumen* (1904, in book form as *Mitn shtrom*, 1909); *Meshiakh's tsaytn: A kholem fun mayn folk* (1906); *Momentn* (1908); *Yugend* (1908); *Erd* (1910); *Erets Yisroel* (1911); *Der landsman* (1911); *Der bund fun di shvakhe* (1912); *Reb Shloyme Nogid* (1913); *Mayselekh fun khumesh* (1913; *In the Beginning*, 1935); *Di yorshim* (1913); *Yiftakhs tokhter* (1913); *Khurbn Yerushelayim* (1913); *Meri* (1913); *Der veg tsu zikh* (1916); *Far undzer gloybn* (1914); *Der yidisher soldat, un andere dertseylungen* (1918); *Khurbn Poyln* (1918); *Dos heylike meydl oder a shnirl perl* (1916); *Ver iz der foter* (1918); *Der toyter mentsh* (1920); *Maranen* (1922); *Yoysef* (1924); *Reverend dokter Silver* (1927); *Koyln* (1928); *Di kishefmakherin fun Kastilyen* (1926); *Mayn rayze iber Shpanye* (1926); *Gots gefangene* (1933); *Baym opgrunt* (1937; *The War Goes On*, 1936); *Dos gezang fun tol* (1938; *Song of the Valley*, 1939); *Der brenendiker dorn* (1946). FURTHER WORKS IN ENGLISH: *Children of Abraham* (1942); *Tales of My People* (1948); *From Many Countries: The Collected Stories of S. A.* (1958)

BIBLIOGRAPHY: Madison, C. A., *Yiddish Literature: Its Scope and Major Writers* (1968): 221–61; Landis, J. C., ed., *The Great Jewish*

Plays (1972): 69–72; Liptzin, S., *A History of Yiddish Literature* (1972): 145–55; Siegel, B., *The Controversial S. A.* (1976)

—JOSEPH C. LANDIS

ASHBERY, John

American poet and art critic, b. 28 July 1927, Rochester, N.Y.

A. was raised in upper New York State, and attended Harvard, where he wrote a long study of Wallace STEVENS for the famous critic F. O. Mathiessen (1902–1950). In 1955 he moved to Paris, where he was art editor for the international edition of the *Herald Tribune*. After returning to America in 1965, he resided in New York City, where he served on the editorial board of *Art News*. Often associated with Frank O'HARA, Kenneth Koch (b. 1925), and James SCHUYLER, A. became known as one of the "New York School" of poets. In the late 1960s, his reputation began to grow, and in 1975 he won the Pulitzer Prize, the National Book Award, and the National Book Critics Circle Award. From this point on he was increasingly recognized as the leading American Poet, and his influence was felt in the work of dozens of young poets. He has won virtually every literary award including the Bollingen Prize (1984) and a MacArthur Prize fellowship (1985).

A.'s first full-length book, *Some Trees* (1956), was chosen by W. H. AUDEN for the Yale Series of Younger Poets. The introduction by Auden linked A. to a Rimbaudian, protosurrealist tradition, but A. disliked the distant tone of the elder poet, and when the book was later reprinted he had the introduction dropped. However, the question of A.'s use of French models and tradition continues to be an important part of the criticism and controversy his extremely challenging poetry has instigated. A. read, among others, the French surrealist Raymond ROUSSEL, and learned from him the use of "specious simile," in which the reader is told rather less than would-be conveyed by simple description. This playful, alogical device combines with others—such as frequently shifting pronominal reference and sentence subordination, and paragraph-length associative structures—to create a virtual polymorphous perversity of syntax. With *The Tennis Court Oath* (1962) this alogicality reached even greater heights, and some of those who defended A., like Harold BLOOM, found this volume impenetrable.

However, with the next two volumes, *Rivers and Mountains* (1966) and *The Double Dream of Spring* (1970), A. was well on his way to achieving one of the most distinctive styles in American poetry. Though he has spoken of his reluctance to discuss his work, A. has said that he writes "mainly for escapist purposes" and that "we need all the escapism we can get and even that isn't going to be enough." But because he often escapes into the dream landscapes of his own emotional life, and because he can never escape from his own vast and deeply cultured learning, A. writes a poetry that is often obsessive in its anxiety. States of great lyrical pleasure vie with moments of terror and anticipated loss. Conversely, moments of great loss and pain are won through until an air of wisdom, extremely rare in contemporary poetry, begins to seem easy of achievement. A campy sense of humor is seldom absent for long, but there is also a philosophical meditativeness, and the combination of these two attitudes is distinctive. This distinctiveness accounts for the willingness of many critics, despite the density of texture at both the level of the line and the overall metaphoric

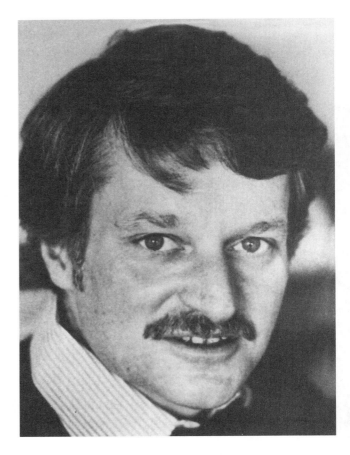

John Ashbery

structure of the lyric argument, to venture readings of an often subjective sort.

In 1975 A. published the prize-winning book that more than any other defined him: *Self-Portrait in a Convex Mirror*. The title poem, based on a painting by Parmigianino that A. says had haunted him for a long time, explores the instability of the self with a thoroughness that surpasses most of the modernist works, which use the same subject matter. Indeed, the poem is one of the central texts of POSTMODERNISM, and at the same time fully reveals how A. continues to rework many of the problems of ROMANTICISM. The key struggle in the book is perhaps the question of how to integrate transcendent or sublime insights and feelings into ordinary waking reality, and to achieve this integration while facing the self that is at once an empty container and an inescapable given. By pursuing his own reflective energies beyond any boundary of wit or irony or aesthetic decorum, A. was able to write his most emotionally resonant poem.

With *Three Poems* (1977) A. challenged even his most inventive critics, for this was a book-length meditation in prose. The sentences resembled his earlier verse, combining sinuous syntax and mundane vocabulary, flights of association and cold marches through his own emotional detritus. The "poem" eventually yields to a patient reader, and not surprisingly its themes and claims and concerns are those of the first five books. But especially notable is A.'s willingness, even his calculated commitment, to using clichéd constructions, phrases, and expressions, as if his first charge were to redeem the fallenness of existence in its most mundane language.

With *Houseboat Days* (1977) and *April Galleons* (1987) A. further perfected his lyric invention, being perhaps slightly less elliptical in his presentation. But *As We Know* (1979) and *Shadow Train* (1981) were felt by some to be of lesser intensity. *As We Know* contained the long "Litany," published in two columns, and *Shadow Train* was comprised exclusively of poems written in four quatrains. *A Wave* (1985) returned to the mix of long and medium-length lyrics that dominated most of the previous volumes. With *Flow Chart* (1991) A. again experimented with a book-length format, and produced a single work as long as *Three Poems*. This poem contains a double sestina, along with a welter of beautifully made sentences, moments of fine lyric control, and long passages of nearly indecipherable complexity. It shows how attached A. is to narrative, as moments and scenes rush by, clipped and elliptical, always suggesting some weighty revelation is at hand, yet always avoiding any firm sense of closure.

A.'s stature now seems nearly indisputable, and he has come to dominate the last third of the American century as Robert LOWELL dominated the middle and T. S. ELIOT the first third. Many of his critics have dampened, at least somewhat, the often polemic discussion that surrounded his work in the early 1970s, and have settled into the more difficult task of making discriminations inside what has grown into a large body of work. Most of the reviews of *Flow Chart* began with the assumption that it was high-quality poetry from an acknowledged master, and proceeded to praise it accordingly. However, almost no one offered a reading of the poem or even indicated how utterly baffling much of the book is. In "Litany" A. asked for critics who would be more responsive and yet probing. But having become a major poet, A. may have to settle for praise and respect.

FURTHER WORKS: *Turandot and Other Poems* (1953); *A Nest of Ninnies* (1969, with Schuyler James); *Three Plays* (1978); *Selected Poems* (1985); *Reported Sightings: Art Chronicles, 1957–1987* (1988); *Hotel Lautréamont* (1992); *And the Stars Were Shining* (1994); *Can You Hear, Birds* (1995); *The Mooring of Starting Out* (1997)

BIBLIOGRAPHY: Bloom, H., "J. A.: The Charity of the Hard Moments," *Salmagundi*, 22–23 (1973): 103–23; Packard, W., comp., *The Craft of Poetry* (1974): 111–32; Kalstone, D., *Five Temperaments* (1977): 170–99; Molesworth, C., *The Fierce Embrace* (1979): 163–83; Shapiro, D., *J. A.* (1979); Lehman, D., ed. *Beyond Amazement; New Essays on J. A.* (1980); Breslin, P., "Warpless and Woofless Subtleties," *Poetry*, 137 (1980): 42–50; Vendler, H., "Understanding A.," *New Yorker*, 16 Mar. 1981: 119–35; Altieri, C., *Self and Sensibility in Contemporary American Poetry* (1984): 132–64; Ross, A., *The Failure of Modernism* (1986): 159–208

—CHARLES MOLESWORTH

ASPENSTRÖM, Werner

Swedish poet, dramatist, short-story writer, and essayist, b. 13 Nov. 1918, Norrbärke

A.'s proletarian background and the necessity of making a living at menial occupations when young delayed his efforts to get an academic education. After receiving his B.A. degree at the age of twenty-six, he became closely associated with the influential literary journal *40-tal* as a critic and a poet.

With the collections of poetry *Skriket och tystnaden* (1946; the scream and the silence) and *Snölegend* (1949; snow legend), A., along with Karl Vennberg (b. 1910) and Erik LINDEGREN, assumed a position at the very forefront of the poetic renaissance in Sweden in the 1940s. In the intellectual climate created by KAFKA, T. S. ELIOT, and the French existentialists A.'s poetry expresses the pervading spirit of critical skepticism and deep despair. The frequent images of snow and wintry landscapes become metaphors of the paralyzing situation of a whole generation, its sense of alienation, its futile protests, and its longing for communication and human fellowship. This dark and anguished vision is in strange contrast with the luminous imagery and the melodious beauty of the form.

In subsequent collections of poetry A. has sought greater economy in style and a leaner diction, as opposed to the aestheticism and formality of his earlier poems. These efforts are paralleled by his attempts to find an antidote to immobilizing pessimism in a concentration on the positive forces in life and what he terms "exercises in reality." In *Litania* (1952; litany) and *Hundarna* (1954; the dogs) the apocalyptic visions of total destruction in the wake of Hiroshima are balanced by a tenuous optimism about the future of mankind. Although his poems are informed by an ever-present awareness of death and of life's irreconcilable contradictions, he turns increasingly to nature. With a sense of wonder he registers the incomprehensible manifestations of life around him, often in its most unglamorous aspects. These miniatures of animal life and seasonal transformations are prevented from becoming merely idyllic by unexpected touches of whimsical humor; at times they approach a mystical vision or open up vistas of cosmic dimensions.

A. re-creates his childhood world in the short-story collection *Bäcken* (1958; the brook). The volume of essays and articles, *Motsägelser* (1961; contradictions), testifies to his intellectualism and continuous participation in cultural debates.

A.'s considerable dramatic output consists mainly of one-act plays, often in the form of fairy tales or allegories; these dramatic miniatures, either lyrical or satirical, present human situations or contemporary problems in a symbolic stylization resembling that of the THEATER OF THE ABSURD.

A. has maintained his position as a major writer in contemporary Swedish literature and was the recipient of the Bellman Prize in 1959. His work, characterized by an intellectual honesty that refuses to resort to easy effects or simplistic solutions, displays concern for the great issues of our time and a humble reverence for life in all its forms.

FURTHER WORKS: *Förberedelse* (1943); *Oändligt är vårt äventyr* (1945); *Förebud* (1953); *Dikter under träden* (1956); *Teater I* (1959); *Om dagen om natten* (1961); *Teater II* (1963); *Trappan* (1964); *Teater III* (1966); *Sommar* (1968); *Inre* (1969); *Skäl* (1970); *Under tiden* (1972); *Blåvalen* (1975); *Ord bok* (1976); *Ögonvittnen* (1980); *Tidigt en morgon sent på jorden* (1980)

BIBLIOGRAPHY: Törnqvist, E., "Poet in the Space Age: A Theme in A.'s Plays," *SS*, 39 (1967): 1–15; Sjöberg, L., "W. A.: A Writer for All Seasons," *ASR*, 57 (1968): 385–92

—LARS G. WARME

ASSAMESE LITERATURE
See Indian Literature

ASTLEY, Thea

Australian novelist, b. 25 Aug. 1925, Brisbane

Brought up in a Roman Catholic family of journalists in the tropical state of Queensland, A. attended convent schools in Brisbane, then the University of Queensland. After leaving the university, she first taught in public schools; later, until her retirement, she lectured at Macquarie University in Sydney. Early on A. showed interest and ability in the arts, and is an accomplished pianist. The city of Brisbane and the vast state of Queensland, her Catholic background, her musical education, and her teaching career have all played a significant part in her writing.

A.'s first two novels, *Girl with a Monkey* (1958) and *A Descant for Gossips* (1960), draw from her teaching experience in country elementary schools. A city-bred teacher figures as the central character in both novels, which focus on the provinciality, the limitations, and the emotional harshness of life in the bush. Although autobiographical early novels, they display the sharp observation, irony, elaborate use of metaphor, and striking time shifts that characterize her later work. These works also introduce the satiric treatment of small towns and their inhabitants, which from the outset offended many Australian readers.

Moving away from the domestic concerns that dominate her first five books, A. takes up the role of the artist in a postcolonial society in *The Acolyte* (1972), which is her most complex novel to date and which stands as one of her finest works. Set first in country towns, then in the flamboyant Queensland beach resort, Surfer's Paradise, *The Acolyte* follows the career of Holberg, a blind Australian composer who gains international fame. The first-person narrator serves as the "acolyte" for Holberg, who is considered the blind "priest" of art—a typical use of Roman Catholic imagery throughout A.'s work. A. makes the imagery more complex by suggesting that Australia socially and politically has too long served as an "acolyte" for England; in turn, Australian artists have been content to be "acolytes" to the real artist "priests" from England, whether writers, painters, or composers.

A. addresses settler Australia's treatment of the Aborigines in her next novel, *A Kindness Cup* (1974), and in her 1996 novel, *The Multiple Effects of Rainshadow*. Both are based on historical events. *A Kindness Cup* recounts how a group of Queensland settlers drove a tribe of Aborigines to death off a cliff. Through a double time frame, A. combines the pioneers' cruelty twenty years earlier with the same group's celebration of their successful settlement in the region. One of A.'s misfits and would-be saints, who figure in several of her novels, tries to rouse the white townspeople's guilt. For his efforts, he is beaten by them and "accepts the fleshly damage of his enemies like some peculiar blessing." A. takes a more positive tone in the later novel, which retells the tragic events that took place during the 1930s on an island off the Queensland coast, where Aborigines lived in a kind of concentration camp. Covering several decades and ending in the present, the novel follows the fates of both the natives and their white keepers. In spite of all the injustice depicted, one of the Aborigines at the end says that times are changing and life will change for his people as well.

In her most outwardly religious novel, *An Item from the Late News* (1982), A. chooses an unstable narrator to reveal the events during one Christmas when a wanderer named Wafer (a Christ-figure) comes to a forlorn country town called Allbut. Known to have found a precious stone (the holy grail), Wafer is pursued by the greedy townspeople and finally dies at their hands in a mockery of crucifixion. This grim novel may well contain A.'s darkest view of the human condition.

Perhaps because of its complexity, its near poetic style, and its relentless portrayal of Australia, A.'s work was for a long time not widely received at home. In 1986 she began to gain a reputation overseas, and in the past few years has enjoyed a wider reception in Australia. Not long ago she was called "Australia's most important contemporary novelist."

FURTHER WORKS: *The Well Dressed Explorer* (1962); *The Slow Natives* (1965); *A Boat Load of Home Folk* (1968); *Hunting the Wild Pineapple* (1979); *Beachmasters* (1985); *It's Raining in Mango* (1987); *Reaching Tin River* (1990); *Vanishing Points* (1992); *Coda* (1994); *Collected Stories* (1997)

BIBLIOGRAPHY: Matthews, B., "Life in the Eye of the Hurricane," *SoRA*, 6 (1973): 148-73; Smith, G. K., "T. A.," *Kunapipi*, 4, 1 (1982): 20-37; Ross, R., ed., *International Literature in English* (1991): 593-602

—ROBERT ROSS

ASTURIAS, Miguel Ángel

Guatemalan novelist, short-story writer, poet, essayist, dramatist, b. 19 Oct. 1899, Guatemala City; d. 9 June 1974, Madrid, Spain

Raised under a dictatorship that he and fellow students helped to overthrow in 1920, A. left for Europe to evade the next strongman. For ten years he lived in Paris, where he wrote his first novel; he went back home in 1933, realizing that he must return to his roots, to the world that inspired his writing; by then the Ubico dictatorship had begun, and thirteen years passed before he could publish his novel, *El Señor Presidente* (1946; *El Señor Presidente*, 1963). It is a forceful and at the same time grotesque portrayal of social chaos fostered by a prototypical dictator in order to build his power. At first critics did not realize that this was not just another novel of protest but the innovative and expressionistic creation of a poet evoking a reality of terror as it existed in his youth. All the characters are presented as caricatures, grossly distorted puppets of no account. The novel presses relentlessly through scenes of explosive contrasts, sweeping from evil to beauty, from tenderness to barbarity, from blackest darkness to golden dawn, heightening all the natural contrasts of the tropics.

A. entered the diplomatic corps during a brief period of democracy (1944–54), then he was banished by the right-wing forces of Carlos Castillo Armas, never to live in Guatemala again. He settled in Argentina but did not remain after the military coup of J. M. Guido in 1962. After a sojourn in Italy, A. made his home in Paris. He died in Madrid on a lecture tour.

Although the social consequences of politics were to figure in his fiction, the central issue of his creative life was his feeling for

Indian culture, particularly since he was a mestizo. As a student in Paris, instead of taking economics as his father had intended him to do, he spent four years at the Sorbonne studying the mythology and culture of Maya and other American Indians. As A. pored over the myths of the sacred Maya writings *Popol Vuh* (the book of counsel), and other texts he helped to translate, he discovered the fundamental opposition between Maya and European mentalities and the limitations of Western thought stemming from its rationalism. Meanwhile in other Parisian circles, the SURREALISTS had launched their attack on logic and were engaged in dream analysis and other methods of tapping the subconscious to enrich their art. Myth is the collective dream of mankind, and A. recognized the Indians' nonrational perception of reality to be an expression of his Guatemalan subconscious; he felt a deep personal bond with this race so long repressed from national consciousness. The surrealist liberation also offered the means to express the mythic Indian mind independently of Western literary models. These realizations grew into a determination to preserve, interpret, and give new life to the Maya ethos as a basic component of his country's culture. Later he would call himself the spokesman of his people.

While *El Señor Presidente* utilizes surrealist techniques designed to blur the boundaries between nightmare and reality, his next novel, *Hombres de maíz* (1949; *Men of Maize*, 1975), plunges deep into the magic world view of Indians at different levels of culture and with varying degrees of faith in the ancestral myths and traditions preserved down the centuries by oral literature. Seen through the archaic mentality of the participants, it depicts a rebellion by a remote tribe of Indians against desecration of their mountains and their annihilation by the army. It tells the legends surrounding the rebellion—tales of magical revenge and of maledictions by spirits from primordial time—in the words of those who believe them. Because of its difficult style, which weaves in and out of reality with no concern for verisimilitude—a style of writing A. called magic REALISM—the novel was first ignored or dismissed by critics as being ill-conceived. Now it is considered to be A.'s masterpiece, perhaps greater than he himself realized, although it always was his favorite. Many later works, as yet unacclaimed, remain to be analyzed. A twenty-four-volume critical edition of his complete works is under way, sponsored by UNESCO and published simultaneously in Paris and Mexico.

First to appear in this critical edition was his literary testament, *Tres de cuatro soles* (1977; three out of four suns). One of his most abstract and difficult texts, it deals with the creative process of the poet and the gods, and presupposes a knowledge of his earlier works and of the Maya-Aztec creation myths to which the title refers. It continues in the vein of his longest and most important poem, *Clarivigilia primaveral* (1965; spring vigil), about the Maya predilection for poetry and the arts.

Mulata de tal (1963; *Mulata*, 1967) recounts in an ambience of sorcery and cataclysms the clash between native and Catholic priests, between Indian gods and Christian devil, a conflict that resolves itself in syncretism. *Maladrón* (1969; bad thief), subtitled *Epic of the Green Andes*, was especially dear to A.; it is his version of the conquest by the Spaniards; it tells of the encounter of five 16th-c. Spanish soldiers lost in the jungle with a group of Indians and of their mutual mistrust and wonderment, their interaction and transculturization. A. had strong emotional ties to both his lineages; he was proud of each strain and of the evolving American mestizo culture they produced, a fragmented culture affected by influences that range from the primitive to the latest technology.

In the social vein, A. wrote a trilogy about the ravages wrought by the United Fruit Company on his country's welfare. *Viento fuerte* (1949; *Strong Wind*, 1969) depicts the struggle of small growers against the gigantic corporation at the start of its operations. *El Papa verde* (1954; *The Green Pope*, 1971) portrays the consolidation of the company's power and its control over the government. *Los ojos de los enterrados* (1960; *The Eyes of the Interred*, 1973) concerns a general strike that topples the dictator and obliges the company to accept laws favorable to the workers. *Weekend en Guatemala* (1956) contains eight stories related to the 1954 invasion by Castillo Armas that overthrew the liberal government.

A.'s poetry generally addresses itself to the causes he espouses (such as the history, culture, and plight of Indians) or celebrates his loves (woman, family, homeland); his style is marked by the aestheticism of MODERNISM or by surrealism, but it always bears his individual stamp. He is also known for playful onomatopoeic nonsense verse. Of his five published plays, the most successful is *Soluna* (1955; a name meaning sun-moon), dealing with the subliminal conflict of modern Guatemalans with their Indian heritage.

Recent criticism of A. no longer judges him by established literary criteria, but in terms of his own objective: that of dealing with the coexistence in Guatemala (as elsewhere in the Third World) of all the different stages through which societies have passed. A. was the first writer to face the disorder and alienation of Guatemalan reality and to attempt a synthesis. His work marks the beginning of the mature phase of Latin American fiction.

FURTHER WORKS: *Sociología guatemalteca: el problema social del indio* (1923; *Guatemalan Sociology*, 1977); *Leyendas de Guatemala* (1930); *Sien de alondra* (1949); *El alhajadito* (1961; *The Bejeweled Boy*, 1971); *Rumania: su nueva imagen* (1964) *Teatro* (1964); *Espejo de Lida Sal* (1967); *Comiendo en Hungria* (1969, with Pablo Neruda); *América, fábula de fábulas* (1972); *Viernes de dolores* (1972)

BIBLIOGRAPHY: Harss, L., and B. Dohmann, *Into the Mainstream* (1967): 68–101; Callan, R., *M. A. A.* (1970); Martin, G., *"El Señor Presidente* and How to Read It," *BHS*, 47 (1970): 223–43; ; special A. issue, *PSA*, 62 (1971); Guibert, R., *Seven Voices* (1973): 121–79; special A. issue, *Europe* 53 (1975); Dorfman, A., "Myth as Time and Word," *Review*, No. 15 (1975), 12–22; Christ, R., "The Text as Translation," *Review*, No. 15 (1975): 28–33; Meneses, C., *M. A. A.* (1975); Brotherston, G., *The Emergence of the Latin American Novel* (1977): 25–44; *Publications du séminaire M. A. A.*, U. of Paris-Nanterre, Dec. 1977

—RICHARD J. CALLAN

ATENCIA, María Victoria

Spanish poet, b. 1931, Malaga

A lifelong resident of Malaga, A. contemplates its lighthouse and sea from her terrace. She travels abroad frequently and is also a licensed pilot. She studied music and painting, but after marrying the poet and editor Rafael León, she dedicated herself to writing. They have four children. Chronologically, not temperamentally or stylistically, she belongs to the second generation of poets to emerge after the Spanish Civil War (1936-39).

Her early books, *Arte y parte* (1961; Art and Part) and *Cañada de los ingleses* (1961; the english gully), were acclaimed. They foregrounded her concerns as a woman and her religious spirituality. There followed a fifteen year silence, broken with *Marta & María* (1976; Martha & Mary) and *Los sueños* (1976; dreams). The former, a complex dialogue between female self and other, is a psychologically profound book in which A. initiates her questioning of gender stereotyping. *Los sueños*, a captivating series of dreams of peaceful and spacious interiors, foregrounds A.'s children, her father, her mother, and Count Dracula (whom she revises and appropriates for female discourse).

A. next published *El mundo de M. V.* (1978; M. V.'s World) and *El coleccionista* (1979; the collector). The former is an exploration of memories of houses, family, close friends, ships, towns, and cities visited. It is remarkable for its numerous intertextual references to art and artists and for its revision of the Lady Godiva myth. In *El coleccionista*, with the genial sensibility and precision of an haiku poet, A. "collects" together her memories and impressions from art, literature, religion, and from the numerous European countries she has visited. Her reflections on life, love, death, and aging are laced with startling contrasts and profound enigmas as A. forges her particular gynocentric vision and style.

In the mid-1980s, in addition to two anthologies, A. published three new books: *Compás binario* (1984; binary compass, or two-four time), *Paulina o el libro de las aguas* (1984; Pauline; or, the book of waters), and *Trances de Nuestra Señora* (1986; moments in our lady's life). In *Compás binario* A. dives into the sea of her selves and cites Pierre de Ronsard's (1524-1585) advice to "Cueillez dès aujourd'hui les roses de la vie." In so doing, she elevates the quotidian—to be encountered in people, objects, memories, and impressions—to its essential perfection. *Paulina o el libro de las aguas,* a more philosophical volume, reflects on a visit she made alone to Venice. A. is questing here for perfection within the nagging disorder of life and time. She sees beauty as consuming itself to give light to the poem. At its conclusion, A. reaches a quasi-mystical state of emptiness. In *Trances de Nuestra Señora* she projects on to the Virgin Mary a mother's strong feelings for her conception, pregnancy, and child rearing. The Holy Mother wants to cloister her Son inside a bird cage to keep him safe from cats—A.'s favorite pet.

By the end of the 1980s, when three anthologies of her work were published, A. was recognized as an important poet. However, around that time A.'s tone, in four new books, became more somber and anguished: *De la llama en que arde* (1988; of the flame in which one burns), *La pared contigua* (1989; The Contiguous Wall), *La intrusa* (1992; the intrusive lady), and *El puente* (1992; the bridge). As the evening of her life burns in what A. calls the impassible flame of time, she writes more sensual and sensuous poems. In search of her soul, she plummets that sea of her selves, remembers the little girl she was, as well as the mother she is and has been; she also confronts the emptiness of the present and the frustrations of her desire. She continues to observe the quotidian and to transmute it into art. She figures the poetic artifice as a labyrinth made of mother-of-pearl that entraps rigid words and lets them flow on the sea of time. In *La pared contigua* A. reveals herself as a more self-conscious poet who explores the metapoetic dimensions of verse, although her fundamental concerns with the mysteries of inner selfhood remain. A.'s sense of mortality dominates this volume: death is that contiguous wall that separates the advancing years of her life from those who have died. As she wrestles to establish a haven of inner peace, her life is gushing out

of her, or it is a train heading toward a station in twilight beyond which her ticket is not valid. *La intrusa* is similar in tone and mood, yet A. recognizes that although she has not found fullness, she lacks nothing. Like T. S. ELIOT in "The Journey of the Magi," A.'s disturbing paradoxes set the beauty and perfection of what she has experienced against the painful yet certain sense of a diminished self and heart. *El puente* recalls a visit to Checkoslovakia, struggles with anguish over the loss of innocence, yet inscribes splendor and reinscribes female identity by its deployment of A.'s preferred symbols and metaphors: water, rivers, flowers, precious stones, statues, balconies, and fulfilling enclosures.

The publication in 1997 of *Las contemplaciones* took the Spanish literary world by storm and it awarded A. the highly prestigious National Critics' Prize. In *Las contemplaciones* A.'s imagination takes a quantum leap. Instead of diving into the wreck of the self, she sees her imagination as flying, and herself as swimming with decisive strokes through the sea of self and soul. In *Las contemplaciones* A. has wrought a vision of vibrant equilibrium between a despondent and a Promethean self. The vigor of this book hints that in future work A. will continue to harmonize all contrary impulses and stun with her mature poetic vision a larger circle of devoted readers.

In her fourteen volumes of poetry A. has refined the esthetic idealism and style of two major Spanish poets of the 20th c., Juan Ramón JIMÉNEZ and Jorge GUILLÉN and will continue to modify their mantle as she deepens her own, unique poetic vision.

FURTHER WORKS: *Tierra mojada* (1953); *Ex Libris* (1984); *La Glorieta de Guillén* (1986); *Nave de Piedra* (1990); *Antología poética* (1990); *La señal* (1990)

BIBLIOGRAPHY: Carnero, G., Epílogo to *Marta & María* (1984): 61-65; Ciplijauskaité, B., "La serena plenitud de A.," *Alaluz*, 22, 1 (1990): 7-12; García Martín, J. L., Introducción to *Antolojía poética* (1990): 7-38; Janés, C., Prólogo to *La señal* (1990): vii-xxxviii; Ugalde, S., "Conversación con A.," in *Conversaciones y poemas* (1991): 3-17; Ugalde, S., "A.," in Levine, L. G., et al., eds., *Spanish Women Writers: A Bio-Bibliographical Source Book*(1993): 54-65; Metzler, L. D., "Images of the Body in the Poetry of A.," *ALEC,* 18, 1 (1993): 173-81; Persin, M., "Yet Another Loose Can(n)on: the Place and Space of Women's Poetry in Twentieth-Century Spain," *Siglo,* 12, 1-2 (1994): 195-206; Kruger-Robbins, J., "(Not) Just a [(Wo)Man] Poet: The Dialectic of Identity and Difference in the Poetry of A.," *REH,* 29, 2 (1995): 231-44; Wilcox, J. C., "A.," in *Women Poets of Spain, 1860-1990: Toward a Gynocentric Vision* (1997): 247-56

—JOHN C. WILCOX

ATWOOD, Margaret

Canadian poet and novelist (writing in English), b. 18 Nov. 1939, Ottawa, Ont.

A. has lived in Ottawa, parts of the northeastern Canadian bush, and in several Canadian cities. She was educated at the University of Toronto and, briefly, at Harvard. She has taught, or served as writer-in-residence, at five Canadian universities, and now lives

Margaret Atwood

and writes on a farm near Alliston, Ontario, with writer Graeme Gibson and their daughter.

A. established herself as an award-winning poet in the middle and late 1960s, a decade in which a tremendous number of fine Canadian poets and novelists began publishing. In the fall of 1972 she achieved prominence with two works in one season: *Surfacing* (her second novel) and *Survival*, a thematic study of Canadian literature. The former became almost a cult novel with teachers of women's studies, while the latter rode the crest of a period of preoccupation with questions of nationalist identity and unity.

Survival is obviously influenced by A.'s own themes. It posits a national will to fail, a national sensibility concerned with suffering and death. A.'s poetry and fiction focus on the deceptiveness of human relations and the duality of human nature. Curiously, the ironic humor, which is a prominent feature of A.'s fiction, finds no place in her analysis. Her study, intended as a popular introduction to Canadian literature, greatly underestimates its affirmative qualities.

With her third novel, *Lady Oracle* (1976), A.'s fame as a novelist surpassed her reputation as a poet. This work represents a major advance on a form explored earlier in *The Edible Woman* (1969), that of the comic gothic novel. A.'s first four novels are all concerned with male/female relationships, social roles, and individual fantasies. But where *Surfacing* takes the gothic sensibility seriously, *Lady Oracle* turns the macabre into material for parody.

A.'s fiction is melodramatic and heavily symbolic. While her first and third novels are comic, the fourth (*Life Before Man*, 1979)

presents a bleak, harsh view of human life. This view is also found in some of her poetry and short fiction. The gothic genre becomes an analogue for human duplicity, and the necessity of inner freedom, self-reliance, and growth.

The publication of A.'s critically acclaimed *The Handmaid's Tale* (1986) was followed by a series of works that further enhanced A.'s status as a writer, notably *Cat's Eye* (1988), *Morning in the Burned House* (1995), and *Alias Grace* (1996).

Internationally, A. is one of the best-known Canadian writers. Her images can be comic and baroque, or keen, spare, and ironic. Her sensibility is highly complex. She moves easily between satire, celebration, and lament. But A. is already established as a humorist of considerable talent, and as a sensitive poet of intellectual and psychological depth.

FURTHER WORKS: *Double Persephone* (1961); *The Circle Game* (1966); *The Animals in That Country* (1968); *The Journals of Susanna Moodie* (1970); *Procedures for Underground* (1970); *Power Politics* (1973); *You Are Happy* (1975); *Selected Poems* (1976; repub. as *Selected Poems, 1965-1975*, 1987); *Dancing Girls* (1977); *Up in the Tree* (1978); *Two-Headed Poems* (1978); *Bodily Harm* (1982); *Bluebird's Egg and Other Stories* (1986); *Selected Poems II: Poems Selected and New, 1976-1986* (1987); *Wilderness Trips* (1991); *The Robber Bride* (1993); *Good Bones and Simple Murders* (1994); *Strange Things: The Malevolent North in Canadian Literature* (1995)

BIBLIOGRAPHY: Gibson, G., ed., *Eleven Canadian Novelists* (1973): 5–31; Morley, P., "Survival, Affirmation, and Joy," *Lakehead University Review*, 7, 2 (1974): 21–30; Morley, P., "The Gothic as Social Realism," *Can. Forum*, 56, 667 (1976): 49–50; Woodcock, G., "M. A.: Poet as Novelist," in Woodcock, G., ed. *The Canadian Novel in the Twentieth Century* (1975): 312–27; Klinck, C. F., ed., *Literary History of Canada: Canadian Literature in English*, 2nd ed. (1976), Vol. III: 172–73, 286–96; Rosenberg, J. H., *M. A.* (1984); McCombs, I., ed., *Critical Essays on M. A.* (1988); Howells, C. A., *M. A.* (1996)

—PATRICIA MORLEY

AUB, Max

Spanish novelist, dramatist, short-story writer, essayist, and poet, b. 2 June 1903, Paris, France; d. 23 July 1972, Mexico City, Mexico

A. lived in Paris until 1914. At the beginning of World War I his French-German family emigrated to Spain and settled in Valencia. Later, in Madrid, A. published his first writings in the prestigious *Revista de Occidente*. During the Republic he was cultural attaché in Paris and worked with André MALRAUX on the film *Sierra de Teruel*. At the end of the Spanish Civil War, A. fled from Spain to France, only to be imprisoned, along with thousands of other Spanish refugees, in concentration camps in southern France and Algeria. In 1942 he managed to escape and reach Mexico, where he wrote, taught, and lectured until his death.

The life and work of A. is clearly divided by the civil war (1936–39). His early publications show the style of the vanguardist writers of the time influenced by ORTEGA Y GASSET. These prose narratives are characterized by lyricism, vivid imagination, and a rich and sensuous language.

In *Discurso de la novela española contemporánea* (1945; a presentation of the contemporary Spanish novel) he strongly criticizes Ortega y Gasset and the dehumanization of art. He describes the novelist's mission as similar to that of the clerics of the Middle Ages: "to report historical events and compile legendary romances."

His major work, *El laberinto mágico* (1943–68; the magic labyrinth) is an epic chronicle of the Spanish Civil War, consisting of *Campo cerrado* (1943; enclosed range); *Campo de sangre* (1945; mortal range); *Campo abierto* (1951; open range); *Campo del moro* (1963; battlefield of the Moor); *Campo francés* (1965; French concentration camp); *Campo de los almendros* (1968; almond orchard). This gigantic tableau includes novels, short stories, sketches, and a movie script, covering events from the last years of the Republic to the end of the civil war and its aftermath. Both historical and fictional figures appear, disappear, and reappear, but the final impression is that of a collective character, a people engaged in a heroic struggle. A. sees the labyrinth as a definition of the novel, of our time, and of Spain: "Spain is the labyrinth. To keep on living they have to bring us a decent number of young people as sacrificial victims for our holocaust." The literary components of this work are as complex as its subject matter. It has detailed description, rapid action, flash-backs, monologues, letters, documents, long introspective passages, moral disquisitions, animated dialogues—all in an abundant and rich prose that combines cultural and popular elements with a mastery of the language in all its linguistic intricacies.

This mastery of the use of fantasy in a realistic, documented manner is shown in *Jusep Torres Campalans* (1958; *Josep Torres Campalans*, 1962), which brought him international renown. It is the story of an imaginary Catalan painter at the beginning of the century who lives in Paris during the highest moments of its artistic glory, and then, totally disillusioned, retires to a Mexican Indian village. The "novel" uses apocryphal documents, pictures, letters, and actual paintings and drawings. A. combines the techniques of a meticulous researcher and the seriousness and conscientiousness of a historian with a vigorous imagination and a superb sense of humor.

A.'s theater follows a trajectory similar to the one seen in his narratives: a few prewar plays that are ingenious experiments in the avant-garde style, and postwar works showing a more politicized and also humanized writer. These later plays deal with specific problems related to the civil war, ideological conflicts, treason, life in exile, World War II, the anti-Nazi struggle, Jewish refugees, and the Cold War.

A.'s work has been translated into many languages. His contribution to Spanish literature is a monumental account of his time in an original and provocative style.

FURTHER WORKS: *Geografía* (1929); *Fábula verde* (1932); *Luis Alvarez Petreña* (1934); *No son cuentos* (1944); *Diario de Djelfa* (1944); *Sala de espera* (1948–1951); *De algún tiempo a esta parte* (1949); *Yo vivo* (1953); *Las buenas intenciones* (1954); *Ciertos cuentos* (1955); *Cuentos ciertos* (1955); *Crímenes ejemplares* (1957); *Cuentos mexicanos (conpilón)* (1959); *La verdadera historia de la muerte de F. F., y otros cuentos* (1960); *La calle de Valverde* (1961); *Juego de cartas* (c. 1964); *El zopilote y otros cuentos mexicanos* (1964); *Manual de historia de la literatura española* (1966); *Pruebas* (1967); *Teatro completo* (1968); *Enero en Cuba* (1969); *Guía de narradores de la revolución Mexicana* (1969); *Ultimos cuentos de la guerra de España* (1969); *Subversiones* (1971); *La gallina ciega* (1971); *La uña y otras narraciones* (1972)

BIBLIOGRAPHY: Marra López, J. R., *Narrativa española fuera de España* (1963): 177–215; Borrás, A., "The Ideology of the Theatre of the Spanish Exile M. A.," *TA*, 25 (1969): 80–90; Nora, E. G. de, *La novela española contemporánea* Vol. III (1970): 18–30; Sobejano, G., *Novela española de nuestro tiempo* (1970): 54–62; Monleón, J., *El teatro de M. A.* (1971); Soldevila Durante, I., *La obra narrativa de M. A.* (1973); Borrás, A., "Time, the Fourth Dimension in M. A.'s Theater of Exile," *Mosaic*, 8 (1975): 207–21

—MARÍA-LUISA OSORIO

AUCHINCLOSS, Louis

American novelist, b. 27 Sept. 1917, Lawrence, Long Island, N.Y.

A.'s birth into a relatively old and prominent family in New York society has afforded him an insider's understanding of the dramas of wealth, arrogance, and infidelity that are his frequent themes as a novelist of manners. Indeed, he records in a memoir entitled *A Writer's Capital* (1974) that he began at an early age to see in terms of story both his family and the society in which he moved. But A.'s family chose to immerse him in a tribal world of

Louis Auchincloss

grandparents and cousins as much as in the haut monde, and from that immersion may have come a detachment from society that balances his insider's understanding. From his long career as a lawyer specializing in estates and trusts, A. seems to have derived an especially useful perspective as a novelist of manners: a sense that American society is a microcosm of the country's politics and power.

A.'s most impressive novel is generally thought to be *The Rector of Justin* (1964), which takes the form of a journal kept by a young teacher in an exclusive preparatory school modeled on the Groton School in Massachusetts, where A. was once a student. In a series of five memoirs incorporated into the teacher's journal, the founding headmaster of the school is seen from widely different view-points that keep open the question of his character and influence, whether good or bad. Some readers were unhappy to see in the headmaster a portrait of Endicott Peabody, who was Rector of Groton from 1884 to 1940, but *The Rector of Justin* is less a roman à clef than a novel of character enriched with a sense of the society that produced such a headmaster and finally brought his era to an end.

The grounding of characters like the Rector of Justin in social history, often in a dynastic overview, is a staple of A.'s fiction. *The House of Five Talents* (1960) and *Portrait in Brownstone* (1962) trace the lives of single families through several generations and illumine brightly the style of patrician life in New York and Newport from the last decades of the 19th c. to the mid–20th c. *The Winthrop Covenant* (1976) is a sequence of nine stories that trace between 1630 and 1975 the rise and fall of the Puritan ethic through the lives of still another New England-New York dynasty. *Watchfires* (1982) is a Civil War novel that covers three generations in the life of a family. Based in several respects upon the life of the journalist Walter Lippmann, *The House of the Prophet* (1980) invites comparison with *The Rector of Justin* inasmuch as its central narrative subsumes a number of other narratives spread over sixty years of American political history.

Indeed, almost all of A.'s fictions are historical in some mode. In dealing with European and British material, he relies less upon the illuminations of a dynastic or temporal sweep and more upon the recreation of contexts and personages. *The Cat and the King* (1981) is based on the memoirs of the second Duc de St. Simon and set at the court of Versailles. *Exit Lady Masham* (1983) is a fictive memoir of life at the court of Queen Anne that includes among its historical characters Sarah Churchill, the Duchess of Marlborough, Robert Harley, the Earl of Oxford, and Jonathan Swift, the pamphleteer and poet. In novels not overtly historical, A. tends to be historically allusive or literarily historical. *The Dark Lady* (1977), for instance, reprises the dark lady of Shakespeare's sonnets in a Hippolytus-Phaedra story about a failed actress who finds a career in politics after World War II. In *The Country Cousin* (1978) the title character tries energetically to understand her life in the 1930s in terms of a Victorian novel. In *The Lady of Situations* (1990) another title character fancies herself a Brontë sister invested with wit and ambition but divested of moors and genius.

It bears emphasis that A. is in none of his works simply a historian of manners. Indeed, because he is invariably concerned with issues of morality and psychology that transcend particular strata of society and time, A.'s fictions are part of a historical drift of the novel of manners into the realms of the psychological novel and the novel of character. If many of his protagonists feel trapped between an outmoded, rapidly vanishing past and a present that they can inhabit only with misgivings, other protagonists are troubled by atemporal feelings of inadequacy that set them on self-destructive courses, both personally and professionally.

Such protagonists are particularly evident in A.'s novels that deal with the world of law and finance: *The Great World and Timothy Colt* (1956), *Venus in Sparta* (1958), *Pursuit of the Prodigal* (1959), *The Embezzler* (1966), *A World of Profit* (1968), and *I Come As a Thief* (1972). With his usual care, A. details the social backgrounds of the attorneys, stockbrokers, and trust officers in these novels, and he details with equal precision the hierarchies and behavioral codes of the firms in which they work. But his focus is the beleaguered psyches of his characters, who play out in venal criminality their long-established insecurities and maladjustments. That Wall Street glides inexorably into rottenness while they do so does not explain adequately their malfeasances, any more than does the society into which they were born, or does time, with its changing conventions. Yet A.'s novels are typically at their best when such factors impinge upon the characters, shadowing their already dark psychological development with changing social prescriptions.

A. is justly famous for his novels of manners and particularly for his New York novels about bankers and lawyers, but the same straightforward style, psychological acuity, and command of period detail that characterize those works give distinction to his collections of short stories and his nonfiction. Each of his story collections is unified by a theme or a set of recurring characters that invites a reading almost like that of a novel—as, indeed, novels like *The Book Class* (1984) and *Fellow Passengers* (1989) seem reciprocally to invite the reading proper to a story sequence. Among the best of A.'s numerous story collections are *The Injustice Collectors* (1950), *Powers of Attorney* (1963), *Second Chance: Tales of Two Generations* (1970), *The Partners* (1974), and *Skinny Island* (1987). A.'s substantial body of nonfiction includes two collections of literary and historical essays, *Reflections of a Jacobite* (1961) and *Life, Law and Letters* (1979); a collection of essays on American women writers, *Pioneers and Caretakers* (1965); a book of Shakespearean criticism, *Motiveless Malignity* (1969); an edition of an 1890s diary, *Maverick in Mauve* (1983); a short study of Henry JAMES and longer studies of the court of Queen Victoria and of women in the age of Louis XIV; and popular biographies of Edith WHARTON and Cardinal Richelieu.

Critics have tended to label A. a novelist of manners writing in the tradition of John P. MARQUAND and John O'HARA, despite the fact that A.'s interests as a storyteller extend beyond the problems of social class that preoccupied the two older writers. A. himself consistently claims as his literary mentors Henry James and Edith Wharton, even referring to himself on occasion as a Jacobite. The difference between the two sets of antecedents measures the range of A.'s talent, for he is at once a popular novelist and a writer who is allusive, insightful, and literary in the best sense.

FURTHER WORKS: *The Indifferent Children* (1947); *Sybil* (1952); *A Law for the Lion* (1953); *The Romantic Egoists* (1954); *Edith Wharton* (1961); *Ellen Glasgow* (1964); *Tales of Manhattan* (1967); *On Sister Carrie* (1968); *Henry Adams* (1971); *Edith Wharton: A Woman in Her Time* (1971); *Richelieu* (1972); *Reading Henry James* (1975); *Persons of Consequence: Queen Victoria and Her Circle* (1979); *Unseen Versailles* (1981); *Three "Perfect" Novels and What They have in Common* (1981); *Narcissa and Other Fables* (1983); *False Dawn: Women in the Age of the Sun King*

(1984); *Honorable Men* (1985); *Diary of a Yuppie* (1986); *The Golden Calves* (1988); *The Vanderbilt Era: Profiles of a Gilded Age* (1989); *Love without Wings: Some Friendships in Literature and Politics* (1991); *The Collected Stories of L.A.* (1994)

BIBLIOGRAPHY: Kane, P., "Lawyers at the Top: The Fiction of L. A.," *Crit*, 7, 2 (1964–65): 36–46; Macaulay, R., "Let Me Tell You about the Rich . . ." *KR*, 27 (1965): 645–71; Tuttleton, J., "L. A.: The Image of Lost Elegance and Virtue," *AL*, 43 (1972): 616–32; Long, R., "The Image of Gatsby in the Fiction of L. A. and C. D. B. Bryan," *Fitzgerald/Hemingway Annual*, 4 (1972): 325–28; Tuttleton, J. W., *The Novel of Manners in America* (1972): 236–61; Westbrook, W., "L. A.'s Vision of Wall Street," *Crit*, 15, 2 (1973): 57–66; Tuttleton, J. W., "Capital Investment," *SR*, 82 (1974): 48–52; Bryer, J. R., *L.A. and His Critics: A Bibliographical Record* (1977); Milne, G., *The Sense of Society: A History of the American Novel of Manners* (1977): 236–53; Vidal, G., *Matters of Fact and of Fiction* (1977): 27–38; Dahl, C., *L. A.* (1986); Parsell, D. B., *L. A.* (1988); Piket, V., *L. A.: The Growth of a Novelist* (1991); Gelderman, C., *L. A.: A Writer's Life* (1993)

—ROBERT F. KIERNAN

AUDEN, W(ystan) H(ugh)

Anglo-American poet, b. 21 Feb. 1907, York, England; d. 29 Sept. 1973, Vienna, Austria

A. lived in England until he was thirty-two, when, on the eve of World War II, he emigrated to America. He had grown up in the Midlands of England, with early interests in science rather than literature. He published his first volume, *Poems* (1930), shortly after graduating from Oxford. Astonishing precocity brought early success. In America he continued to publish copiously, meanwhile gaining considerable influence through teaching (at various colleges and universities) and literary journalism, as well as through his poetry. He died in Vienna, and is buried in nearby Kirchstetten, where he had made his summer home since 1957.

A.'s early reputation was partly for political and intellectual boldness, for Marxism and Freudianism. In these matters he is very distinctly a modern poet. More remarkable was his sheer poetic skill. *Poems*, published when he was twenty-three, revealed "a Shakespearean gift," as one recent critic has put it, a dazzling inventiveness of language, meter, and image. The poems are short, untitled, often slightly cryptic, though rarely obscure beyond the surface. A. echoes such heterodox poets as Wilfred OWEN, T. S. ELIOT, and Gerard Manley Hopkins. The poems are unsentimental and impersonal, although distinctly identifiable as A.'s. One poem describes an anonymous traveler on an unidentified journey; "But ever that man goes/Through place-keepers, through forest trees,/A stranger to strangers over undried seas,/Houses for fishes, suffocating water." The language, phrasing, and rhythm imitate those of Anglo-Saxon verse, and the first line of the poem translates an Anglo-Saxon fragment. The echoes are sure-handed, and the poem captures more than the surface effects of the original. There is, in one sense, little self-expression in the poem; rather, another style and persona are adopted for the purpose of absorbing the poet's own personality: we sense a sharp reaction to romanticism, whether Yeatsian or Wordsworthian.

W. H. Auden

Like Stravinsky and Britten, composers who were friends and artistic collaborators, A.'s modernism was formal, somewhat cerebral, and yet at the same time lyrical. A. used slant rhymes and unusual rhythms to create dissonance and syncopation that echo a partly Lawrentian and partly Blakean message of liberation. For example: " 'O where are you going?' said reader to rider,/'That valley is fatal where furnaces burn,/Yonder's the midden whose odours will madden/That gap is the grave where the tall return.'" "Reader," a bookish person, warns "rider," a person of action, of the dangers of being adventurous. Echoing words like fatal and furnace and gap and grave epitomize the clash of types; and the jaunty rhythmical beat conveys a sense of excitement in a quest for new life. Such effects were contagious, and A.'s verse was heard by many first readers as a clarion revolutionary call.

A. seldom repeated successes. In *Look, Stranger!* (1936; pub. in the U. S. as, *On This Island*, 1937) and *Another Time* (1940) there appears a sensibility in tune with the age of Dryden and Pope. Compressed figures of speech, direct statement, formal scrupulosity, and excellent musical effects combine to create poems at once accessible, ethically precise, and musically fresh. Figures of speech are deceptively simple, as in "and the crack in the tea-cup opens/A lane to the land of the dead," where the purposely light idiom and rhythm of folk ballad carry a perfectly embodied insight that has considerable emotional force. Indeed throughout his career A. returned often to the song, limited in its means, decidedly unsublime in manner, yet often containing proverbial wisdom of an original and arresting sort.

In the late 1930s A.'s poems were perhaps less radical political- ly, but no less political, and more directly stated. In "Musée des Beaux Arts," the poet muses on Breughel's understanding of suffering's "human position; how it takes place/While someone else is eating or opening a window or just walking dully along." Suffering is part of ordinary life; artists who dramatize it as spectacular pull us away from the ethically real, such as the suffering occurring at the poem's moment outside the museum, in Europe in 1939.

Can the instruments of poetic enchantment be harnessed to the uses of disenchantment? That is the question A. grappled with during the late 1930s, a time of political collapse, some of which A. witnessed at first hand as an ambulance driver in Spain during the civil war and as a documentarist in China and Japan during their war. From the shambles of social and political decay there emerged a kind of contemporary quester-knight, the exiled artist intellectual who severed his commitments with class, nation, race, or party in the service of truth, a role A. himself adopted in his move to America and celebrated in *The Double Man* (1941). "New Year Letter," which occupies most of the volume, is an epistle in tetrameter couplets that displays A.'s gift for epigrammatic capsul- ing of ideas on a broad range of subjects, drawing from a very wide range of reading. A. had indeed uprooted himself, intentionally, in moving to America, had made his own life an example of the deracination he saw both as the social consequence of the war and as the position from which the most impressive modern writers were operating. From such a vantage point "New Year Letter" describes with exuberant compactness A.'s quest to understand and live in this deracinated state, while at the same time suggesting the steps by which A. reached the point of embracing the religion of his childhood, a step taken just about the time "New Year Letter" was being written. (A biographer suggests that A., having been "an extremely eccentric Marxist . . . now became an extremely eccen- tric Christian, one in whom the Audenish outweighed the Christian elements." Such a view, though partially accurate, misjudges the depths of A.'s religious commitments, as well as their fundamental orthodoxy.)

Other long poems followed, as well as *The Collected Poetry of W. H. A.* (1945), which gained popularity almost as great as contemporary collections of YEATS's, Eliot's, and FROST's poems. "The Sea and the Mirror" (1944, in *For the Time Being*), subtitled "A Commentary on Shakespeare's *The Tempest*," is perhaps the best and most important of the long works. It presents a Christian- allegorical reading of Shakespeare's work, couched in terms echo- ing Saint Augustine, Kierkegaard, the theologian Reinhold Niebuhr (1892–1971), and others. The clash between the ethical and the aesthetic so noticeable in the early poems is resolved or synthesized in a religious vision of man, seen as a creature fallen because of his pride and self-absorption. The poem works somewhat like a medieval allegorical drama, with Prospero representing the con- scious ego, Ariel the imagination, Caliban not only flesh but our awareness of ourselves as fallen creatures. Prospero, in A.'s version, comes to trust the imagination less, and to recognize himself as in part a Caliban. Appropriately, the virtuoso piece of the work is a long prose section, spoken by Caliban in imitation of the late manner of Henry JAMES; it is preceded by a dazzling display of poetic styles, each assigned to an appropriate character.

A. may be said to have reached his full poetic maturity at this point. For the rest of his career he continued to be extremely prolific, technically adept, intellectually alive, somewhat unpre- dictable. No single Everest dominates his career; rather, it is the unbroken range of peaks of some magnitude that most impresses a reader. He continued to find compatible a loose grouping of poems on a single subject displaying a range of different manners and styles, the different styles having to some extent an emblematic status, readable by a properly employed allegorical method and often embodying a critical or scholarly point of view. "Horae Canonicae" (written 1949–54; pub. in *The Shield of Achilles*, 1955) for example, consists of seven poems corresponding to the daily round of devotions sung particularly in religious communities, and containing some allusions to the events of Christ's passion and to the hours of Good Friday at which they occurred. A. uses these events and these offices partly liturgically and partly allegorically as a means of depicting aspects of human existence and conscious- ness. "Prime," the first office, is a meditation in the manner of VALERY on waking that attempts to convey an existentialist sense of "being in the world": "in complete obedience/To the light's laconic outcry, next/As a sheet, near as a wall,/Out there as a mountain's poise of stone,/The world is present, about,/And I know that I am . . ." Here A. seems to fulfill Martin Heidegger's (1889– 1976) conception of the poet as prototypical philosopher of exist- ence, using poetic tools to chart minutely the changing relations of man and world. Religious narratives and language are recognized as vehicles of the central truths of human existence: the Fall, for example, is a daily event, the crucifixion something in which we all take part, both as victim and as executioner.

Another good example of the mature manner is "Thanksgiving for a Habitat" (written 1958–64; pub. in *About the House*, 1965). Poems correspond to the rooms of A.'s Austrian house, and to the various human functions and actions performed in the house, once again with a profusion of forms and idioms. The complexity of the series mirrors the complexity of human life: humans are complex conglomerations, eating, sleeping, defecating, making love, speak- ing, worshiping, loving themselves, each other, and things beyond themselves. Critics have found the series the epitome of a kind of inconsequentiality, often seeing A. as someone who retreated from radically brave early commitments of mind and heart to a cheery, vaguely religious domesticity, full of sleepy homosexual good cheer and Christian platitude. Such works as "Thanksgiving for a Habitat" perhaps invite such misreadings, but careful reading reveals both a fullness of artistic conception and an intellectual sharpness easily as great as those of A.'s earlier works.

Shorter poems continued to appear simultaneously, and to show a similar profusion of method and, often, a carefully disciplined lightness. "The Willow-wren and the Stare" (1953) expresses the relationship of erotic, human, and divine loves with beautiful deftness and economy as an animal debate, as two birds watch a love scene between two humans and try to puzzle out its compo- nents and make sense of the terms of human language of commit- ment and affection: *Does he mean what he says*? said the willow- wren?/*Some of it*, said the stare." "Et in Arcadia Ego" (1964) is a modern pastoral written in a series of haikus: "I well might think myself/A humanist,/Could I manage not to see/How the autobahn/ Thwarts the landscape/In godless Roman arrogance." Such poems, and the great number of meditations in Horatian syllabic verse, show the commitment evident in Caliban's speech in "The Sea and the Mirror" to a poetry that embodies prose virtues on Christian grounds; strength comes from word choice and sentence structure, but subtly, and the music develops without reliance on the most lyrical techniques, which get their full play in the highly polished songs. With the publication of the *Collected Poems* (1976) after

A.'s death, it became clear how truly momentous his accomplishment had been.

A. talked of himself as a colonizer of modern verse, as distinct from the first generations, the explorers, people like Marianne MOORE, POUND, Wallace STEVENS, William Carlos WILLIAMS, Frost, Yeats, and Eliot. No poet of his stature has appeared since, however, and A. increasingly looks like the last of the great moderns: a prolific, technically audacious, and accomplished poet of considerable intellectual range whose impact was enormous. Among his greatest accomplishments was that of reconciling tradition and modernism. He deserves to be remembered in a way that would doubtless make him happiest, as a modern Horatian noted for formal scrupulosity, concern for the language, a keen eye, wariness of the powers that rule the world, a certain muted exuberance about both nature and art, and a measure of proverbial and epigrammatic wisdom.

FURTHER WORKS: *The Orators* (1932); *The Dance of Death* (1934); *The Dog Beneath the Skin* (1935, with Christopher Isherwood); *The Ascent of F6* (1936, with Isherwood); *Letters from Iceland* (1937, with Louis MacNeice); *On the Frontier* (1938, with Isherwood); *Journey to a War* (1939, with Isherwood); *The Age of Anxiety* (1947); *The Enchafèd Flood* (1950); *Nones* (1951); *Making, Knowing, and Judging* (1956); *Homage to Clio* (1960); *The Dyer's Hand and Other Essays* (1962); *The Dyer's Hand, and Other Essays* (1962); *Collected Shorter Poems 1927–1957* (1966); *Collected Longer Poems* (1968); *Secondary Worlds* (1968); *City without Walls* (1969); *A Certain World* (1970); *Academic Graffiti* (1971); *Epistle to a Godson* (1972); *Forewords and Afterwords* (1973); *Thank You, Fog: Last Poems* (1974); *The English A.* (1977); *Selected Poems* (rev. ed., 1979)

BIBLIOGRAPHY: Hoggart, R., *A: An Introductory Essay* (1951); Beach, J. W., *The Making of the A Cannon* (1957); Bayley, J., *The Romantic Survival* (1957); Spears, M., *The Poetry of W.H.A.* (1963); Spears, M., ed., *A.: Collection of Critical Essays* (1964); Blair, J. G., *The Poetic Art of W.H.A.* (1965); Ellman, R., *Eminent Domain* (1967); Greenberg, H., *Quest for the Necessary* (1968); Jarrell, R., *The Third Book of Criticism* (1969): 115–50; Bahlke, G., *The Later A.* (1970); Fuller, J., *A Reader's Guide to W.H.A.* (1970); Bloomfield, B.C., and Mendelson, E., *W.H.A.: A Bibliography 1927–1969* (1972); Duchene, F., *The Case of the Helmeted Airman* (1972); Johnson, R., *Man's Place* (1973); Buell, F., *W.H.A. as a Social Poet* (1973); Spender, S., ed., *W.H.A.: A Tribute* (1974); Hynes, S., *The A. Generation* (1976); Osborne, C., *W.H.A.: The Life of a Poet* (1979); Carpenter, H., *W. H. A.: A Biography* (1981); Callan, E., *A.: A Carnival of Intellect* (1983); Rowse, A. L., *The Poet A.: A Personal Memoir* (1987); Hecht, A., *The Hidden Law: The Poetry of W. H. A.* (1993); Davenport-Hines, R., *A.* (1995)

—RICHARD A. JOHNSON

A. has followed Yeats in showing how the intense private world of symbolism can be brought right out into the open, eclecticised, and pegged down to every point of contemporary interest and everyday life, while remaining none the less in a private and even a substitute world. A. is an emancipator of Romantic Symbolism, but it is in this tradition that his roots lie, and it is by the criteria applied to such poetry that he should ultimately be judged. Attacks on A. are invariably based on his irresponsibility, his unfounded pretensions to intellectual power and weight, and his enjoyment of the private joke or absurdity for its own sake, etc., and all these strictures lose their force if his poetry is read for what it is, and not for what his critics—misled by the poet's ambiguous attitude—have supposed it is attempting to be. . . .

What makes a poem of A. good or bad? The question, baldly put, can be as baldly answered: whether or not it is filled with vivid personal apprehensions of things—things and people, but above all things, for though A. never regards people wantonly or inhumanly he does depersonalize them and transform them into a bizarre extension of object or place. Their significance to the poet as emblems of some general condition may be large, but they are always seen against some appropriate background or linked to their unique and revealing properties of clothing, accent, or facial tic. A. is a Symbolist of the common fate, the humdrum situation. As soon as he generalises, steps out of the heightened world of the Symbolist's still life, his poetry sags and loses momentum. . . .

It is a very English vision, as English as that of Dickens. Though clinical, it is also extremely parochial. And the ideal A. reader should also have Dickensian tastes; he should be not unlike George Eliot's Mrs. Linnet. Mrs. Linnet was fond of reading the biographies of celebrated preachers, "and wherever there was a predominance of Zion and the River of Life, she turned to the next page; but any passage in which she saw such promising nouns as 'smallpox,' 'pony,' or 'boots and shoes,' at once arrested her."

John Bayley, *The Romantic Survival* (1957), pp. 155–57

In two studies published in 1951 I argued that A. was essentially a satirist. I have avoided using the term in this book; in fact I have refrained from propounding any single thesis, on the ground that it would be restrictive if not misleading. I should prefer now to emphasize most of all the variety of his poetry, its range and scope and capacity for surprise. A religious poet who is also a clown, a virtuoso who is incorrigibly didactic, a satirist who is also a musician and lyricist, is likely to perplex and annoy critics. But we have had enough critical condescension toward A.; instead of quibbling about whether he quite deserves the title of major poet or whether any of his poems is really quite satisfactory, we would do better to be grateful both for his skill and wisdom and for the fact that he is not yet classified or predictable. Let us hope that he will create more enchanted islands of opera, while continuing to cast his spells against magic and all forms of deception and intoxication. Light, candidly personal, ever more rigorously devoted to the naked truth, these are disenchantments that we deeply need.

Monroe K. Spears, *The Poetry of W.H.A.: The Disenchanted Island* (1963), p. 339

To categorize A.'s own aims, even "anti-Romantic" seems at the last too restrictive a term. While this study has shown how many of his poetic practices are most easily conceived as reactions against Romanticism, A. has accomplished more than simply negating the Romantic celebration of the poet's unique personality. In the perspective of a highly productive thirty-five years, A. emerges as a traditional poet in the most profound sense. He again and again demonstrates the relevance to the modern world of the artistic and moral wisdom of the past. Like Stravinsky in music, he has revivified in modern context and idiom nearly all the traditional forms and genres of his art, many of them previously in disuse if not disfavor. Auden reaches back through all of English poetry, even to its roots in Anglo-Saxon and Icelandic. If T. S. Eliot, largely through the use of quotation and explicit allusion, has made the modern poet and reader conscious of standing at the head of a tradition, A., the second-generation modern, has accomplished a similar end through poetic forms and implicit allusion. Though Auden's career may have begun in relatively simple anti-Romanticism, it has grown into an affirmation of the larger artistic and moral tradition of the western world.

John G. Blair, *The Poetic Art of W.H.A.* (1965), pp. 185–86

A. has put the matter cogently himself, in "The Dyer's Hand":

Any poetry which aims at being a clarification of life must be concerned with two questions about which all men, whether they read poetry or not, seek clarification.

1) *Who am I?* What is the difference between man and all other creatures? What relations are possible between them? What is man's status in the universe? What are the conditions of his existence which he must accept as his fate which no wishing can alter?

2) *Whom ought I to become?* What are the characteristics of the hero, the authentic man whom everybody should admire and try to become? Vice versa, what are the characteristics of the churl, the authentic man whom everybody should try to avoid becoming?

A. has been exploring, elucidating, and clarifying the first question—the nature of human nature—throughout his writing life. A great many of his most characteristic and successful poems carry out this analysis precisely along the lines of inquiry that he proposes above. . . . And there is everywhere a concern with the second question that he proposes, for all work is grounded in our obligation to evolve morally and spiritually. He has had the courage and the need, in an uncertain and skeptical age, to be an overt and tireless moralist. Clever as he is, he has been clever enough—it is the ultimate cleverness—to be morally and spiritually responsible. Much of this aspiration in his work has defined itself around the figures of a succession of heroes; about churls he has known quite enough to make the conflict between the authentic

and the unauthentic man, good and evil, a vivid focus of his meditations on human nature.

Robert Bloom, "W. H. A.'s Bestiary of the Human," *VQR*, 42 (1966), 209

A.'s problem has always been, then, the problem of our anxiety in connection with those factors shaping our relationship to ourselves. . . . Auden has considered the problem in terms bearing a close resemblance to these, for our anxiety arises from divided consciousness, a condition defined in his assertion that "Man's being is a copulative relation between a subject ego and a predicate self." As agent of mental awareness and volition, the "ego" is the unique consciousness seeming to each individual wholly free and coincident with his experience of personal being, while the "self" is that part of himself which seems separable from himself and, as object of the ego's attention, seems "given, already there in the world, finite, derived, along with, related and comparable to other beings" [*The Enchafèd Flood*]. This basic distinction may be regarded from endless perspectives: the ego is the "I" part of ourselves, the self the "me"; as the beholder of possibility and relationship, the ego may be identified with "imagination," but it is equally the agent of "reason"; the self, on the other hand, is the source of instinct, the emotions, and of unconscious needs; crudely conceived, the ego is mind, the self body. Furthermore, project this subjective division into the frame of reference of the objective multitudinous world, and it appears as that between "history" and "nature," realms in which we confront, respectively, those factors weaving a complex thematic pattern in the texture of A.'s work—freedom and necessity.

Herbert Greenberg, *Quest for the Necessary: W. H. A. and the Dilemma of the Divided Consciousness* (1968), pp. 5–6

. . . A.'s art is exemplary of an age in which metaphor is no longer man's link with the universe, but only an extension of himself; where the conceit is not a facet of external reality but a fancy of his own, a world not of Gods who offer a protective shell but of consciously supreme fictions which are too fictitious to offer supremacy. A.'s history is one long attempt to outgrow the tyranny of the analytical spirit over his own feelings and to evolve an outlook that will reconcile them with each other. By nature, this implies a highly intelectual art, and A. has many of the limitations of the brilliant intellectual, including a mobility of mind which outranges his emotional grasp. Yet the very force of his personal involvement in the culture's inner contradiction has enabled him to embrace its tensions more explicitly perhaps than any other poet and to find a form of clarity in the depths of his own entanglement. Struggling with the unresolved dilemmas which more or less affect us all, he has won through to a poetry which not only is always interesting but also spans a growth of thought and feeling as strongly founded and as broad as any in recent English literature.

François Duchene, *The Case of the Helmeted Airman* (1972), pp. 26–27

It was a Shakespearean gift, not just in magnitude but in its unsettling—and unsettling especially to its possessor—characteristic of making anything said sound truer than true. In all of English poetry it is difficult to think of any other poet who turned out permanent work so early—and whose work seemed so tense with the obligation to be permanent. In his distinguished essay on A., John Bayley penetratingly pointed out that it was not in A.'s creative stance ever to admit to being young. What has not yet sufficiently been noticed is that it was not in the nature of A.'s talent to win sympathy by fumbling towards an effect—to claim the privileges of the not yet weathered, or traffic in the pathos of an art in search of its object. Instant accomplishment denied him a creative adolescence.

As always in A., ethics and techniques were bound up together. Barely out of his teens, he was already trying to discipline, rather than exploit, the artistic equivalent of a Midas touch.

TLS, 12 Jan. 1973, 1

An emblem for A. would be an ambiguous profile looking from one side like a face and from the other like a map. His poems show a fondness for real faces and maps, but the purpose of the emblem would be to express his central and constant fusion of a private and a public world. The facelike map and the maplike face seem to be formed in the imaginative effort to look at private and public worlds at the same time, overlapping, blurred, mutually determining, or interlocked, their distinctiveness often diffused, dissolved, and dissipated.

The mutations of A.'s Eros have been sufficiently discussed, and I should like to take for granted both those special influences that impelled him, like other poets of England in the thirties, into the conscientious association of inner and outer experience, and those later forces that shifted him from psycho-political to a psycho-religious concept of Love. Though the impulse that relates love to Love in the thirties is shaped by Fascism and Communism, it is also a local and collectivised form of that artistic and moral conscience that more recently made a less rational poet, Sylvia Plath, insist that poetry should relate our private pains and madness to things like Dachau and Hiroshima. In the political and the not-quite-political poetry of the thirties, a relation is made not only between the private and social pain and madness, but also between the private and social feelings of joy, desire, love, indulgence, and indeed all or any aspects of relationship. One of the most original features of A.'s early poetry of love and politics is its exploration

of the details of passion and relationship, in which the lineaments of the face are constantly transferred to the map, the contours of the map to the face. We can only speculate about the sources of such an impulse to fusion; they lie in the contemporary political conscience, the compelling and terrible facts, and the Freudian interest in personal and social psychoanalysis.

Barbara Hardy, *The Adavantage of the Lyric* (1977), p.95

AUDIBERTI, Jacques

French dramatist, poet, and novelist, b. 25 March 1899, Antibes; d. 11 July 1965, Paris

A. claimed that his life had two poles: Antibes, his native city, and Paris, his adoptive one. Although at twenty-five he moved to Paris, in later years A. wrote that he never really left Antibes. And indeed, the influence of its Provençal climate, its language, mythology, and temperament are keys to his work. In Paris A. became a journalist, but by 1942 his literary output had become sufficiently established so that he could devote himself exclusively to literature.

One theme dominates all his work: the conflict between good and evil, between the soul and the flesh. "I always deal with the same insoluble problem, the same obsession—the incarnation."

Jacques Audiberti

For A., everything physical is tainted by sin, and the only way to escape this corruption is through the force of the imagination, through magic, dreams, and religion. And so metamorphoses, strange transfigurations, reappear as symbols of man's need to go beyond the limits of the world about him.

Although his language, imagery, and themes reveal his preoccupation with the marvelous and the fantastic, A.'s poetry, his first literary effort, was always conventional in form. In his early collection, *L'empire et la Trappe* (1930; the empire and the Trappist monastery), however, the poems are complicated and obscure. His later poems reveal a movement away from this hermetic style toward a simpler poetic language. In these, he uses contemporary speech, even slang, and his poetry approaches song.

A similar evolution can be traced in A.'s novels. *Abraxas* (1938; Abraxas), his first novel, is a complex and obscure metaphysical epic dealing with the occult in the 15th c. But in later books— *Urujac* (1941; Urujac), for example, about explorers looking for traces of primitive man—A.'s recurrent theme of the natural versus the "civilized" man is more simply and directly expressed.

A.'s first play, *Quoat-Quoat* (1946; Quoat-Quoat), like many of his later ones, is a blend of melodrama, farce, and Boulevard theater. Here an adventure story about a young man on board a ship turns into a metaphysical drama ending with the young man's death and the destruction of the ship, that is, the world. A.'s most popular play, *Le mal court* (1947; evil is in the air) is something of a conventional fairy tale presenting his vision of the evil at the heart of all existence: a young princess, discovering the world around her to be corrupt, determines not to be destroyed by this revelation but rather to become self-seeking and ruthless.

A.'s fame and international popularity rest on his plays. These philosophical farces and convoluted fantasies, suggesting the terrible reality behind human experience, are reminiscent of the universe of Antonin ARTAUD's Theater of Cruelty. A.'s extraordinarily rich and elaborate poetic language and his extravagant baroque imagination give his work an admirably distinctive tone and voice in contemporary experimental theater.

FURTHER WORKS: *Race des hommes* (1937); *Septième* (1939); *Paroles d'éclaircissement* (1940); *Des tonnes de semence* (1941); *Carnage* (1942); *La nouvelle origine* (1942); *Toujours* (1943); *La fin du monde* (1943); *Le retour du divin* (1943); *La nâ* (1944); *La bête noire* (1945); *Vive guitare* (1946); *L'opéra du monde* (1947); *Monorail* (1947); *Talent* (1947); *Les victorieux* (1947); *Les médecins ne sont pas des plombiers* (1948); *La fête noire* (1949); *Cent jours* (1950); *La globe dans la main* (1950); *Le maître de Milan* (1950); *La pluie sur les boulevards* (1950); *Pucelle* (1950); *Les naturels du Bordelais* (1952); *Marie Dubois* (1952); *Rempart* (1953); *Les jardins et les fleuves* (1954); *Molière dramaturge* (1954); *La logeuse* (1954); *Le retour du calife* (1954); *L'abhumanisme* (1955); *Le cavalier seul* (1955); *La beauté de l'Amour* (1955); *Les enfants naturels* (1956); *La poupée* (1956); *Opéra parlé* (1956); *Le ouallou* (1956); *Altanima* (1956); *Le sabbat ressuscité* (1957); *La mégère apprivoisée* (1957); *Infanticide préconcisé* (1958); *La hobereaute* (1958); *Lagune herissée* (1958); *Les carabiniers* (1958); *L'effet Glapion* (1959); *La fourmi dans le corps* (1961); *Cœur à cuir* (1961); *Le soldat Dioclès* (1961); *Les patients* (1961); *Pomme, pomme, pomme* (1962); *Bâton et ruban* (1962); *La Brigitta* (1962); *Boutique fermée* (1962); *Les tombeaux ferment mal* (1963); *Ange aux entrailles* (1964); *Dimanche m'attend* (1965); *Entretiens avec Georges Charbonnier* (1965)

BIBLIOGRAPHY: Deslandes, A., *A.* (1964); Wellwarth, G. E., *The Theater of Protest and Paradox* (1964; rev. ed., 1971):73-84; Giroud, M., *A.* (1967); Giroud, M., *A.* (1973); Guerin, J., *Le théâtre d'A. et le Baroque* (1976); Touloudis, C., *J. A.*, (1980)

—LEWIS W. FALB

AUERBACH, Erich

German philologist, critic, and historian, b. 9 Nov. 1892, Berlin; d. 13 Oct. 1957, Wallingford, Conn., U.S.A.

A. received a Doctor of Law degree from Heidelberg University in 1913. After serving in the German army during World War I, he changed disciplines and obtained his Ph.D. in Romance philology from the University of Greifswald in 1921. He was employed as a librarian on the staff of the Prussian State Library in Berlin from 1923 until 1929, when he was appointed to the chair of Romance philology at the University of Marburg. A.'s academic tenure in Germany ended after six years, when he was relieved of his position by the Nazi government. In 1936 A. resumed his career at the Istanbul State University in Turkey. With World War II at an end, A. moved to the U. S. in 1947, serving first at Pennsylvania State University and then as a member of the Institute for Advanced Study at Princeton. A. became Professor of Romance philology at Yale University in 1950 and was named as Yale Sterling Professor in 1956.

A. achieved his first recognition with his book *Dante als Dichter der iridischen Welt* (1929; *Dante, Poet of the Secular World*, 1961). In it, his background influences were evident: Hegel, German historicism, the historical speculations of Giambattista Vico (1668–1744), German Romance philology; the diverse aspects of his orientation were incorporated to consider Dante's *The Divine Comedy*. For A., Dante had broken with the practice of the ancients of separation of styles (the sublime for aristocratic subjects, the lowly for common materials) in order to initiate a "mixed style" (which utilized the lowly Italian vernacular to depict its lofty subject). Recalling Vico's "equation of the historical with the human," A. constructed a dialectic which contrasted the "changeless existence" of Dante's characters with the earthly-historical nature of their desires and stylistic depiction; A. argued for the primacy of history within *The Divine Comedy*.

"Figura" (1939; in *Scenes from the Drama of European Literature*, 1959) resolved A.'s difficulty with *The Divine Comedy* (namely, how could such earthy realism exist in a work evoking eternity?). Partly etymological and partly interpretative, the monograph presented scholarly evidence to demonstrate that *figura* is "something real and historical which announces something else that is also real and historical." Figural interpretation (which establishes a prediction-fulfillment relationship between two historical events) was offered as the principal view of reality during the European Middle Ages, in opposition to spiritualist and Neoplatonic positions. A. delineated a mode of interpretation in which lowly historical figures and events were able to remain historical, yet were invested with an exalted stature due to their connection with an all-encompassing grandiose conception.

During the years of World War II A. wrote his most important work, and one of the crucial works of literary history and criticism of the century, *Mimesis: Dargestellte Wirklichkeit in der abendländischen Literatur* (1946; *Mimesis: The Representation of Reality in Western Literature*, 1953). Drawing on his methodological roots in Romance philology, A. assembled a collection of passages from works from Homer to the contemporary period: the explication of each literary work would provide a key to the overall coherence of the historical era from which it dated; the accumulation of insights from different historical periods would suggest the evolution of the representation of reality in Western literature and cultural history. *Mimesis* is not only a series of extraordinarily perceptive textual explications from a variety of historical periods; it is also a comprehensive and original investigation of the evolution of our Western literature, undertaken at a time of crisis when our cultural heritage was being assaulted; A. distinguished between the "uniform illumination" of Homer's style and the more suggestive ambiguity of the Old Testament narrative. Employing the concepts of separation of styles and figural interpretation, A. affirmed the achievement of Dante, in whose work he could now demonstrate the unification of the elevated and lowly styles into one humanistic intermediate style. *Mimesis* praised depictions of the common man and approved when man's "general human quality" was made the "subject of serious, problematic, and even tragic representation"—this was, for A., the transformation of the lowly into the sublime. The culminating point of our literary tradition took place when humanistic and historicistic values supplanted the supreme position of Christianity, which had itself undermined the fixed hierarchical values of antique literary depiction. *Mimesis* was A.'s attempt to bolster our literary tradition: he ventured to "impose an order" upon our history and our values in a critical work of imagination and synthesis.

After the war A. resumed his earlier affinity for scholarly works of "extreme relativism." Emphasizing particulars instead of organizing principles, he produced a volume of medieval studies that he hoped would serve as a "supplement to *Mimesis*" but without the "loose but always perceptible unity of *Mimesis*." This "fragmented" work, *Literatursprache und Publikum in der lateinischen Spätantike und im Mittelalter* (1958; *Literary Language and Its Public in Late Latin Antiquity and in the Middle Ages*, 1965) was actually an accomplished whole based on the functional principle of selecting distinctive words or phrases and using them as points of origin for explications that resonate outward from the text into considerations of society.

A.'s later works possessed a spectral tonality, an intimation that the world would soon end (or, if not the world, then the historical process as he had known it). The stoic resignation of A.'s final works should not denigrate the overwhelming significance of his lifetime critical contribution. His influence has been pervasive: his work has helped expand the scope and purpose of our contemporary literary investigations; his realm of inquiry has stimulated a new attentiveness to literary genre; his notion that literary evolution was a coherent and fluid movement has influenced current conceptions of literary structure as a system. Throughout his literary career, A. struggled to unify essentially incompatible concepts of absolute morality and extreme relativism; if the result was less than totally successful, he is yet one of the few authors who conceived of his task as a resolve to renovate the priorities and institutions of Western civilization—and thus preserve them.

FURTHER WORKS: *Introduction aux études de philologie romane* (1949; *Introduction to Romance Languages and Literature*, 1961); *Vier Untersuchungen zur Geschichte der französischen Bildung* (1951; partially trans., together with selections from his *Neue*

Dantestudien [1944], in *Scenes from the Drama of European Literature*, 1959)

BIBLIOGRAPHY: Wellek, R., "A.'s Special Realism," *KR*, 16 (1954): 299–307; Fergusson, F., "Two Perspectives on European Literature," *HudR*, 7 (1954–55): 119–27; Muscatine, C., on *Mimesis, RPh*, 9 (1956), 448–57; Levin, H., "Two *Romanisten* in America: Spitzer and A.," in Fleming, D., and B. Bailyn, eds., *The Intellectual Migration* (1969): 463-84; Fleischmann, W. B., "A.'s Critical Theory and Practice: An Assessment," in Macksey, R. A., ed., *Velocities of Change: Critical Essays from MLN* (1974): 230–36; DePietro, T. M., "Literary Criticism as History: the Example of A.'s *Mimesis*," *Clio*, 8 (1979): 377–87; Green, G., *Literary Criticism and the Structures of History: E. A. and Leo Spitzer* (1982); Lerer, S., ed., *Literary History and the Challenge of Philology: The Legacy of E. A.* (1996)

—GEOFFREY GREEN

AUEZOV, Mukhtar Omarkhan-ulï

(Russianized form of Auez-uli) Kazakh novelist, dramatist, and academician, b. 28 Sept. 1897, Abai-aul; d. 27 June 1961, Alma-Ata

A. graduated from the Semipalatinsk Teachers' Seminary in 1919. After obtaining a degree in philology at Leningrad State University (1928), he did postgraduate work at the Central Asian State University in Tashkent, which he completed in 1930. In 1946 he was appointed to the Academy of Science of the Kazakh S.S.R., where he was involved in several scholarly projects, including the publication of Kazakh epical texts. He was a professor at the Kazakh Kirov State University.

A.'s creative output reflects both the rapidly changing political and social environment in which he lived and the related group of problems on which his mind focused with increasing intensity. While still a student at the Teachers' Seminary, he wrote the play *Änglik—Kebek* (1917; Änglik and Kebek) which achieved and maintained great popularity in Kazakhstan. During the following decade he wrote many plays and short stories, most of which dealt with the problems of common people living within the traditional Kazakh social structure or its "remnants" in the early Soviet period. Others, such as *Oqïghan azamat* (1923; an educated fellow), depict conflicts of good and evil that are relatively independent of social systems. In this story the treacherous main character marries the wife of a deceased friend whose family he abuses viciously.

During the mid 1920s A. began researching the subject that would become the major object of his creative life, namely, the career of Abai Qunanbaiev (1845–1904), the great poet of 19th-c. Kazakhstan. A.'s family had been strongly influenced by Abai's works, and A. came to feel a deep spiritual affinity for his literary predecessor, who symbolized for him the summit of intellectual creativity and idealism in the recent past of his people. A. recreated the life of Abai and his social environment in the two-volume historical novel *Abai* (1945 and 1947; *Abai: A Novel*, n.d.). Although two more volumes of this series (which A. called "Abai joli," the road of Abai) appeared in 1950 and 1952, A.'s international reputation as a novelist rests upon the earlier volumes. In them A. has created an arresting document of 19th-c. Kazakh life as well as a moving testimony to the ideals and sensibilities of his hero. Abai emerges as an epic champion whose weapon is the word, which he wields in the cause of social justice and intellectual awakening. A. tells this exciting tale in a fluent style that combines elements of Kazakh bardic poetry with classical Russian lyricism. This work deserves to be known as one of the greatest literary achievements of the Soviet period.

A. was as much a scholar as a writer, and through both of these means he sought to preserve and transmit what was of value in the traditional Kazakh way of life while helping to prepare his people for socialism and the modern world. It is surely significant that A. devoted almost all of his great creative energy during the last twenty years of his life to a figure who had lived when these ideals were still perceivable in all their freshness and purity.

FURTHER WORKS: *Äl aghasï* (1918); *Baybishe-Toqal* (1923); *Qaraköz* (1926); *Tartïs* (1934); *Tüngi sarïn* (1934); *Tas tülek* (1935); *Alma baghïnda* (1937); *Shekarada* (1937); *Ayman-Sholpan* (1937); *Abai* (1940); *Qara Qipshaq Qoblandï* (1943); *Alua* (1953); *Dos bedel dos* (1958); *Ösken örken* (1962); *Asïl näsilder* (1969)

BIBLIOGRAPHY: Winner, T. G., *The Oral Art and Literature of the Kazakhs of Russian Central Asia* (1958): 247–53 and passim; Allworth, E. A., ed., *Central Asia: A Century of Russian Rule* (1967; rev. ed., 1989); Allworth, E. A., "The Changing Intellectual and Literary Community," in Allworth, E. A., ed., *Central Asia: A Century of Russian Rule* (1967): 389, 420

—WALTER FELDMAN

AURELL, Tage

Swedish novelist and short-story writer, b. 2 March 1895, Christiania (now Oslo), Norway; d. 20 Feb. 1976, Mangskog

Although born in Norway, A. grew up in the Swedish provincial capital of Karlstad, in Värmland, a region that was to be important for most of his writing. After his schooling, he spent some years in Sweden as a journalist for a number of regional newspapers, followed by ten years in other European countries, mostly in France. In 1930 he returned permanently to Sweden.

A. made his literary debut with the short novel *Tybergs gård* (1932; Tyberg's place), whose terse form and language represented something new in Swedish fiction, a novelty not much appreciated by a public used to the rather long novels of the previous decades. Two more short novels, *Till och från Högåsen* (1934; to and from Högåsen) and *Martina* (1937; *Martina*), also failed to win much acclaim. With the publication of *Skillingtryck* (1943; pamphlets), however, a change in the reading public's attitude occurred, in part as the result of a perceptive essay by the influential critic Knut Jaensson (1893–1958). The action of the novel is simplicity itself: what is important is the power of the narrative to suggest emotion rather than to display it. It is typical of A.'s prose that he prevents sentimental feelings toward his characters from developing through as objective a narrative position as possible. In 1943 his first three novels were collected in one volume, called *Tre berättelser* (three stories), and this suggests the key to the next stage of his career.

It is as a storyteller that A. is best known today, although not in the tradition of the narrator as participant, as with DINESEN. He also stands outside the traditional technique of the continuous narration. He has thinned his language almost to the breaking point. Its syntax leaps as the mind leaps, merely shaping a framework for the reader

to hang his imagination on. By its very spareness, his language is highly charged and completely unsentimental. Pity is not in A.'s vocabulary.

His objective technique was even further refined in *Nya berättelser* (1949; new stories), where, in some cases, the narrator is completely missing and the story proceeds in snatches and brief, unrelated, scenes, what Professor Eric O. Johannesson calls "fragments of the public voice." This pointillistic effect demands the utmost attention of the reader.

In addition to his story-writing, A. was also active throughout his career as a translator, putting H. C. Andersen, Büchner, Stendhal, and KAFKA into Swedish.

In his stories A. never allows his technical virtuosity to obscure the point. His language only serves to resonate the inner lives of his characters.

FURTHER WORKS: *Smärre berättelser* (1946); *Serenad i Repslagargatan* (1948); *Bilderbok* (1950); *Liten fransk stad* (1954); *Viktor* (1955): *Vägar och möten* (1960); *Vi och vår värld* (1964); *Samtal önskas med sovvagnskonduktören* (1969). FURTHER WORKS IN ENGLISH: *Rose of Jericho and Other Stories* (1968)

BIBLIOGRAPHY: Gustafson, A., *A History of Swedish Literature* (1961): 536–37; Johannesson, E. O., Introduction to *Rose of Jericho and Other Stories* (1968):vii-xvi

—ALAN SWANSON

AUROBINDO GHOSE
See Ghose, Aurobindo

AUSTRALIAN LITERATURE

Like the literatures of most former British colonies, including the United States, Australian literature has gone through three principal phases: colonial, nationalist, and modern. Australia began as a British penal settlement in 1788; its first literary offerings were composed mainly by European settlers trying to recreate a European experience in a most un-European land. During the nationalist phase, Australian-born writers proclaimed their literary independence from Europe and asserted the distinctiveness and vitality of the Australian experience. With the issue of national identity settled, Australian literature has emerged in recent decades as a world literature whose universal vision of the human condition in the 20th c. is rooted in its particular view of the Australian experience.

At its best and most indigenous, the literature derives validity through its expression of Australian versions of world literary themes: frontier and nationalist utopianism; human victimization, as found in the treatment of convicts and aborigines; the impact of war; the transition from the values of an older, agrarian order to those of the technological-industrial present; and the search for individual identity.

The 1890s was perhaps the most significant decade in the development of Australian culture. Politically, the country was poised on the brink of independence; in social thought it was preoccupied with the problem of national identity. And, under the vigorous editorship of A. G. Stephens (1865–1933), Australia's first major literary critic, *The Bulletin* magazine provided a forum for the first serious discussion and dissemination of Australian literature. It played an important role, for example, in fostering the bush ballad, whose simple measures celebrated the adventurous, heroic life of the outback in delineating an Australian Adam who would sustain the nation-to-be, it was hoped, with his virtues of courage, compassion, and endurance. Chief among the bush balladists were Henry Lawson (1867–1922) and A. B. ("Banjo") Paterson (1864–1941), whose very popular *The Man from Snowy River, and Other Verses* (1895) was the first important example of Australian popular culture.

Influenced by European and American realism, the Australian short story also emerged and matured in the 1890s. Collections such as *Tales of the Convict System* (1892) by "Price Warung" (William Astley, 1855–1911), Edward Dyson's (1865–1931) stories of miners in *Below and on Top* (1898), "Louis" (George Lewis) Becke's (1855–1913) more exotic tales of the South Pacific in By *Reef and Palm* (1894), and Barbara Baynton's (1862–1929) *Bush Studies* (1902) demonstrate the variety of subject matter the new form quickly achieved. Towering above these, however, is the figure of Henry Lawson, whose volumes of short stories constitute one of the major achievements of Australian literature. In *While the Billy Boils* (1896) and *Joe Wilson and His Mates* (1901) Lawson's deft technique and sure insights enable him to capture definitively 19th-c. Australian outback occupations and character types.

Joseph FURPHY's *Such Is Life*, a book thought by many to be the Great Australian Novel, was written in the 1890s, although not published until 1903. In "temper democratic; bias, offensively Australian," to quote Furphy, *Such Is Life* is a comically deterministic, anecdotal medley of Australian attitudes and personality types. In its mockery of the style of the 19th-c. English novel it spawned a host of imitators and marked a new direction in Australian fiction.

As the currents of 19th-c. nationalism crested in political independence from Great Britain at the turn of the century, the signs that Australian literature was also coming of age were confirmed by the poetic genius of Christopher BRENNAN, the country's first writer-scholar of international stature. Brennan's *Poems* (1914) is a complex but unified record of the poet's emotional and intellectual growth from his days as a classics and philosophy major at the University of Sydney through a European year (1893–94), when he discovered the French symbolist poets. Although Brennan is the most Australian of poets, as Furphy is the most Australian of novelists, his poetry also represents the final flowering of the transplanted romanticism that permeated the poetry of much less impressive predecessors.

Besides Brennan, four quite diverse poets—Mary Gilmore (1865–1962), John Shaw Nelson (1872–1942), Hugh McCrae (1876–1958), and Bernard O'Dowd (1866–1953)—dominated early 20th-c. poetry. Gilmore published eleven volumes of poetry, from *Marri'd, and Other Verses* (1910) to *Fourteen Men* (1954), and was an influential voice in Australian poetry for more than half her ninety seven years. The most indigenous of Australian poets, her aim is always to tell the truths of feeling and the wisdom of the heart in poetry that is patriotic rather than jingoistic, lyrical rather than sentimental. A religious poet who is occasionally compared with William Blake, Neilson in volumes such as *Heart of Spring* (1919) combines delicacy of feeling with lyricism of poetic form in adumbrating a wisely innocent vision of the human condition.

Influenced by Nietzsche, Whitman, YEATS, and Blake, O'Dowd in central poems like *The Bush* (1912) is a passionate mystic attempting to create an Australian mythology of nationalism through a remarkably skillful use of symbolism, allegory, metaphor, direct statement, and prophetic innuendo. In the "vitalist" poetry of *Satyrs and Sunlight* (1909) McCrae also attempted to Australianize other cultures' ways of viewing experience, especially the Dionysian sensibility of ancient Greece. Despite his gusto, his vision now seems narrow.

Although more impressive both in variety and quality than the poetry of the period, early 20th-c. fiction was in fact dominated by one writer, "Henry Handel" RICHARDSON. Richardson lived abroad most of her life, and novels such as *Maurice Guest* (1908), a psychological study of the bohemian life of music students in Leipzig, and *The Young Cosima* (1939), based on the love affair of Richard Wagner and Cosima, the daughter of Franz Liszt, attest to the international dimension of her work. Richardson is best remembered, however, for *The Fortunes of Richard Mahony* (1917–29), a three-volume apotheosis of the Anglo-Australian genre of fiction. It is at once an examination of the destructive effects of cultural schizophrenia on the character of an immigrant Irish aristocrat and a richly detailed account of the late-colonial social and cultural scene in Victoria.

The paintings and novels of Norman Lindsay (1876–1969) were also influenced by European currents of thought, specifically Nietzschean philosophy. In novels like *Every Mother's Son* (1930) and *The Cautious Amorist* (1932) and in his essay *Creative Effort* (1920), Lindsay expounds the "vitalist" philosophy that idealizes impulse, youth, beauty, and physical strength. Originating as they did in a colorful and forceful personality, Lindsay's views proved a catalyst for younger avant garde writers eager to shock the Australian bourgeoisie and at the same time break away from Victorian restrictions of form and subject matter.

Perhaps the most representative novelists of the 1920s and 1930s, Katharine Susannah Prichard (1883–1969) and Vance Palmer (1885–1959) carried the new spirit of liberation into the political and social arena. Prichard's socialist thought and her interest in the regional occupations of her characters are found in novels like *The Black Opal* (1921) and *Working Bullocks* (1926), while Palmer's strong faith in the life of the small communities, especially rural ones, as seedbeds of egalitarianism in the new commonwealth is demonstrated in *The Passage* (1930), *The Swayne Family* (1934), and the trilogy consisting of *Golconda* (1948), *Seedtime* (1957), and *The Big Fellow* (1959).

With its emphasis on the rewards and hardships of life in the outback, pioneering fiction continued to hold the imagination of writers such as Miles Franklin (1879–1954) in *All That Swagger* (1936), but further confirmation of the newly expanded interests of Australian novelists can be found in the early work of two expatriate writers, Christina STEAD and Martin Boyd (1893–1972). Stead's *Seven Poor Men of Sydney* (1934) uses symbolic realism and a kaleidoscopic structure to convey what Virginia WOOLF called the "luminous halo of life." Once abroad, stead went on to international acclaim with *The Man Who Loved Children* (1940), *For Love Alone* (1944), *The Little Hotel* (1973), and a short story collection, *The Puzzle-Headed Girl* (1967). Boyd's *The Montforts* (1928) and *Lucinda Brayford* (1946), both novels of manners, juxtapose the English and Australian experiences of several generations of his ancestors. His most notable achievement is a later work, the "Langton" tetralogy—*The Cardboard Crown* (1952), *A Difficult Young Man* (1955), *Outbreak of Love* (1957), and *Where*

Blackbirds Sing (1962)—peopled with the aristocracy of Melbourne at the turn of the century. Novelists who stayed at home also opened up new veins of rich fictional ore. Xavier HERBERT's richly comic *Capricornia* (1938) is, among other things, the first considered novelistic indictment of white treatment of the Australian aborigine, while "Seaforth" (Kenneth) McKenzie (1913–1955) in *The Young Desire It* (1937) employs sensitivity and tact in dealing with homosexuality.

Although in the period between the two world wars Australian poetry achieved greater diversity, it fell somewhat short of the quality of fiction produced then. Kenneth Slessor (1901–1971) and Robert D. FitzGerald (1902–1987) were the only poets of exceptional merit. Slessor's *Thief of the Moon* (1924) marked him as Australia's first poet in the MODERNIST mold: ironic in sensibility, sophisticated in thought, subtle in technique. His best poetry is found in the long, meditative poem "Five Visions of Captain Cook" (1931). Australia's most intellectually stimulating poet since Brennan, FitzGerald shows a romantic metaphysicality in "The Greater Apollo" (1927), which continues through his "Essay on Memory." The latter and another long poem, "The Hidden Bole," make up his *Moonlight Acre* (1938). More broadly, the achievement of Slessor and FitzGerald consists in their expansion of both the quantity and variety of themes, vocabularies, and techniques available to Australian poets.

A somewhat moribund form since the 1890s, the short story quickened with new life in the 1940s and 1950s. Frank Dalby Davison (1893–1970), whose novels *Man-Shy* (1931) and *Dusty* (1946) were convincing attempts to render animal consciousness in fiction, published many stories in the *Bulletin* (collected in *The Road to Yesterday*, 1964) that combine looseness of structure with compactness of theme. Gavin Casey (1907–1964), in *It's Harder for Girls* (1942) and *Birds of a Feather* (1943), uses a similar method to deal with the lives of industrial workers and their families. Other short-story writers of note include Dal Stivens (b. 1911), Peter Cowan (b. 1914), John Morrison (b. 1904), "Brian James" (John Tierney, 1892–1972), and Margaret Trist (1914–1986).

The 1940s and 1950s also witnessed the finest flowering of Australian poetry, with a score of poets of world rank beginning their careers. Among the most outstanding is Judith WRIGHT. Her first volume, *The Moving Image* (1946), was the most successful attempt yet to wrest poetic significance from an alienating Australian environment. Her second volume, *Woman to Man* (1949), is a wide ranging treatment of love as a regenerative and creative principle. These and her many other books of poetry, criticism, biography, and history established Wright as a dominating presence in contemporary Australian literature. The poetic career of Douglas Stewart (1913–1985) may be said to have begun in 1946 with his *Dosser in Springtime*, although he had published earlier work. Stewart's achievement here was to capture the spirit of the Australian outdoors mentality—nonchalant, humorous, friendly—in poetry whose easy measures conceal an assured craftsmanship. Like Wright, Stewart has excelled in other genres, especially criticism and verse drama. His radio play, *The Fire on the Snow* (1941), and his stage plays, *Ned Kelly* (1943) and *Shipwreck* (1947), convey in mythic dimensions the author's preoccupation with history's visionaries—explorers, mystic lovers, bushrangers, opportunists—whose dreams inspire their followers to risk transcending obstinate reality.

James McAuley (1917–1976) became one of Australia's leading proponents and exponents of classicism in poetic form and, following his conversion to Catholicism, of traditionalism in poetic thought. McAuley's mark is found in *Quadrant*, a literary journal he founded in 1956, in his essay collection *The End of Modernity* (1959), and in *Captain Quiros* (1964) and *Surprises of the Sun* (1969).

While sharing McAuley's classicism and academic background, A. D. HOPE first gained a reputation, with *The Wandering Islands* (1955), as a poetic Pan satirizing his countrymen as creatures devoid of dignity and heroism. The later *Poems* (1960) and some of the *Collected Poems, 1930–1970* (1972) reveal Hope's versatility as an imitator of traditional poetic forms, often so as to make invidious comparisons with the present, as well as his new tolerance for modern society's Philistinism when viewed from the larger perspective of history and myth.

In post-World War II fiction the dominant figure has been Patrick WHITE Three early novels, *Happy Valley* (1939), *The Living and the Dead* (1941), and *The Aunt's Story* (1948), introduce many of White's and modern Australia's fictional themes: human isolation and the failure of communication, the individual's search for identity, the epiphany of the fleeting, visionary insight. However, *The Tree of Man* (1955), an assertion of the value that resides in inarticulate, mundane lives waiting for transcendent illumination, was his first book to attract international attention. White's style took on greater complexity with *Voss* (1957). The movement of White's fiction toward the mystical and away from the methods of realism accelerated with *Riders in the Chariot* (1961) and *The Solid Mandala* (1966), the latter a book that confirms White's growing skill as a social satirist. *The Vivisector* (1970) is a mordant paradigm of the artist's experience in 20th-c. Australia, while *The Eye of the Storm* (1973) and *A Fringe of Leaves* (1976), two rather airless, convoluted novels, are manifestations of White's increasing preoccupation with the nuances and idiosyncrasies of human character and situation.

White's blending of the methods of poetry and fiction is still the subject of critical debate, but his achievement in setting a new antirealist course for Australian fiction is beyond question. Of his many followers, Randolph Stow (b. 1935) is the most impressive. In novels like *A Haunted Land* (1956), *The Bystander* (1957), *To the Islands* (1958), *Tourmaline* (1963), and *The Visitants* (1979), Stow's darkly intense imagination produces an allegorical and symbolic vision of human motives and destiny. Unfortunately, this approach sometimes results in a certain incorporeality among his characters. Stow is also a poet of distinction.

Of the many writers of fiction who discarded an outworn naturalism yet remained independent of the baroque temptations of White, one of the most important is Hal Porter (1911–1984). His first novel was *A Handful of Pennies* (1958), a story of occupied Japan after World War II. He gained a reputation as a surpassing stylist with *The Tilted Cross* (1961), a Tasmanian tale of betrayal and vulnerability and of the ineffectuality and of the exploited. Porter's achievements extend to other genres as well: short stories, poetry, drama, and literary autobiography.

In the 1960s at least two new novelists made original contributions to Australian literature. Thomas KENEALLY, originally an aspirant to the Catholic priesthood, introduced religious themes into serious fiction, and Thea ASTLEY dissected social manners with a new urbanity and insight. Keneally's novels veer toward the gothic, as in *The Place at Whitton* (1964); recall Graham GREENE, as in *Three Cheers for the Paraclete* (1968); attempt satire and Freudian psychology, as in *The Survivor* (1969); and allegorize Australian history, as in *Bring Larks and Heroes* (1967). Gathering further stylistic assurance and broadening his subject matter in the 1970s, Keneally made a trenchant study of some broadens moral dilemmas in Australian history in *The Chant of Jimmy Blacksmith* (1972), based his next book, *Blood Red, Sister Rose* (1974), on the life of Joan of Arc, and wrote historical fictions about World War I in *Gossip from the Forest* (1975) and World War II in *Season in Purgatory* (1976). Astley, also a satirist, brings sharp wit to the often trivial concerns of her middle-class characters in such novels as *Girl with a Monkey* (1958), *A Descant for Gossips* (1960), *The Well-Dressed Explorer* (1962), and *The Slow Natives* (1965).

The richness and variety of the poetry of the 1960s and 1970s can be attributed to the work of poets (and critics) like Thomas Shapcott (b. 1935) and Rodney Hall (b. 1935). In tune with their poetic peers of the "me decade" abroad, Australian poets celebrated individual and alternative styles of living and being. Similar trends can be found in the fiction of the late 1960s and 1970s, especially in the ironic approaches to Australian history in the novels of Peter Mathers (b. 1931) and David Ireland (b. 1927).

Although currently flourishing, Australian drama has been slower to develop than fiction or poetry. In the 19th c. melodramas on such subjects as convicts, bushrangers, droughts, floods, and gold rushes were popular. In this century a number of developments have proved to be stimuli: the growth of amateur theater groups—for example, the Pioneer Players, which introduced Louis Esson (1879–1943), Australia's first playwright of distinction; playwriting competitions; radio and television drama; and the establishment of a national theater organization, the Elizabethan Theatre Trust. More critical treatments of urban life and of such revered myths as mateship and Anzac Day appeared in the 1950s, with Ray Lawler's (b. 1921) *Summer of the Seventeenth Doll* (1955), the most popular Australian play at home and abroad, Richard Beynon's (b. 1927) *The Shifting Heart* (1957), Alan Seymour's (b. 1927) *The One Day of the Year* (1960), and Patrick White's *The Season at Sarsaparilla* (1961). Other contemporary playwrights of achievement or potential include Barbara Vernon (1916–1978), Ric Throssell (b. 1922), Rodney Milgate (b. 1934), and David Williamson (b. 1942).

BIBLIOGRAPHY: Miller, E. M., and Macartney, F. *Australian Literature* (1956); Green, H. M., *A History of Australian Literature*, 2 vols. (1961); Wilkes, G. A., *Australian Literature: A Conspectus* (1969); Johnston, G., *Annals of Australian Literature* (1970); Rees, L., *The Making of Australian Drama* (1973); New, W. H., ed. *Critical Writings on Common-wealth Literature: A Selective Bibliography* (1974); Ferres, J. H., and Tucker, M. eds. *Modern Commonwealth Literature* (1977): 131–235

—JOHN H. FERRES

Australian Literature since 1970

The 1970s and 1980s have marked a growing sophistication and maturity in Australian literature: state patronage (on a small scale) of promising and established writers through the Arts Council of Australia; increasing confidence on the part of publishers that a national and international market exists for Australian literature; an increasing commitment to teaching it in schools and universities; a proliferation of literary prizes and festivals; the establishing of many journals and magazines that analyze the culture and its artifacts; the successful translation of many novels to the screen; and the development in 1978 of the Association for the Study of Australian Literature. In addition, many literary biographies and

autobiographies have been written; for example, Dorothy Green's (1915–1991) monumental study of Henry Handel Richardson, *Ulysses Bound* (1973), Brian Matthew's (b. 1936) postmodern *Louisa* (1987), and Dorothy Hewett's (b. 1923) left-wing *Wild Card: An Autobiography 1923–1958* (1990). All of these factors have resulted in an unprecedented production of literary works and an energetic discussion of them.

Accelerated immigration after World War II from countries other than the United Kingdom and Ireland (the traditional sources of migrants) has necessitated further redefinitions of Australian identity. The bush-based, male-dominated nationalism of the 1890s, fashionable again in the 1940s and 1950s, was seen as not true to the largely urbanized character of the Australian experience. The first postwar migrants from Italy, Greece, and central and eastern Europe experienced some pressure to assimilate. In the 1980s, with the government officially committed to a policy of multiculturalism and ethnic diversity, there has been a tendency for a literature by writers from a migrant background that celebrates ethnicity from within the ethnic culture. This represents a challenge in a substantially monolingual society to an historically monolithic nationalist ideology. The earlier generation of migrant writers, which included such writers as Judah Waten (1911–1985) and David Martin (b. 1915), has been augmented by the very considerable literary gifts of David MALOUF, poet, novelist, essayist, librettist, and literary critic, who lives partly in Australia and partly in Tuscany. He is perhaps most famous as a writer of poetic novels of great diversity; his *An Imaginary Life* (1978) chronicles the last years of Ovid in exile and charts subtly how language mediates experience. The newer groups of Asian migrants have yet to find powerful literary voices.

Aboriginal writing in English is a relatively new phenomenon in Australian literature, and it has been given considerable momentum, and practical financial assistance, by the Aboriginal Arts Board and the Aboriginal Publications Foundation. David Unaipon (1873–1967) produced the first book to be published by an Aboriginal writer in 1929, *Native Legends*. Chief among the next generation of writers are Kath Walker, who adopted her tribal name, Oodgeroo NOONUCCAL, in the late 1980s, and Kevin Gilbert (b. 1933), who have both been deeply influenced by the Black Power movement in the U.S. Oodgeroo Noonuccal's poetry, activist speeches, and stories for children constitute a defiant and proud assertion of her Aboriginal identity. Mudrooroo Narogin (formerly Colin Johnson, b. 1939), reared in a white orphanage, is the most substantial Aboriginal novelist to date. In *Wildcat Falling* (1965), the first Aboriginal novel in Australia, he writes of the plight of the dispossessed urban Aboriginal; in his best novel to date, *Doctor Wooreddy's Prescription for Enduring the Ending of the World* (1983), he deals with the genocidal history of the Tasmanian Aborigines, and tells it, significantly in an empoweringly ironic voice, from the point of view of the black man. The development of a national touring theater group has brought to white and black audiences a variety of Aboriginal plays, including the impressive trilogy of plays by Jack Davis (b. 1917), *The First Born* (published as *Kullark and The Dreamers*, 1982, and *No Sugar*, 1986). Since 1988, the bicentenary of white settlement in Australia, Aboriginal literature has been given a decided impetus, and white Australia is enjoying increased access to the works of this culture, both in its traditional and more modern manifestations.

In the late 1970s and 1980s, Patrick WHITE maintained his place as a major symbolic novelist concerned with exploring spirituality and the problematics of gender in prose that was always confrontationist, poetic, and experimental. The output and reputation of Christina STEAD continued to grow until her death in 1983, and Xavier HERBERT secured his place in Australian literary history with the publication of his epic *Poor Fellow My Country* (1975). Thomas KENEALLY, self-confessedly aiming at the serious but middlebrow and cosmopolitan reader, has won international acclaim for novels that delve into the ethics of particular historical events, notably *Confederates* (1979) and *Schindler's Ark* (1982; pub. in the U.S. as *Schindler's List*, 1982).

In the fertile literary environment of the late 1970s and 1980s, a new generation of writers has emerged. Most celebrated is Peter CAREY, whose blending of the surreal and the real in his 1988 Booker Prize-winning *Oscar and Lucinda* (1988) owes something to Gabriel GARCÍA MÁRQUEZ's MAGIC REALISM and his postcolonial stance, but it is indigenous and original in its satiric and self-consciously literary explorations of human failure. Several writers of the younger generation, notably Rodney Hall (b. 1935), Gerald Murnane (b. 1939), and Tim Winton (b. 1960), concern themselves with the mythology of their family, culture, or racial group, often doing so in visionary ways. A few, primarily Frank Moorhouse (b. 1938), David Ireland (b. 1927), and David Foster (b. 1944), are more boldly transgressive of their culture.

Many female novelists have emerged in these two decades, and with them new definitions of fiction and of national identity: Elizabeth JOLLEY, Jessica Anderson (b. 1916), and Olga Masters (1919–1986) are women who began to be published in their maturity; alongside these are a group of younger women whose consciousnesses have to some extent been constructed by feminism, notably Helen Garner (b. 1942), Beverly Farmer (b. 1941), Kate Grenville (b. 1950), and Barbara Hanrahan (b. 1939). Their fiction often demonstrates the gynocritical preference for realism, but sometimes they exploit and remake older genres like gothic and romance, or invent new ones in an attempt to explore *différence*. Two expatriate writers, Janet Turner Hospital (b. 1942) and Shirley Hazzard (b. 1931), write with a poignant consciousness of having been girls in Australia, and explore in very different ways what it means to be both Australian and cosmopolitan.

Although in the late 1970s and 1980s poetry has been to some extent eclipsed as a form, a substantial new talent has emerged in Les MURRAY. His laconic voice and his focus on the ordinary rural man are reminiscent of bush balladry, but he is profoundly religious in proclaiming the sacredness of the land and of the need to live in intimacy with it. Similarly, Judith WRIGHT continues her passionate attack on historical and contemporary abuses of the land and its original inhabitants in both poetry, biography, and political speeches. Much celebrated, A. D. Hope (b. 1907) continues to write measured, witty, formal, intertextual poetry that reflects his sense of respect for the poetry of the past, and poetry that at the same time incorporates his fascination with science and new ideas. Unlike the expatriate Peter Porter's (b. 1929) trenchant urbanity and sophistication, Bruce Dawe (b. 1930) satirizes, often ruefully, suburban Australia and its political institutions. Wit, irony, and precise observation, often of the predicament of women, mark the poetry of Gwen Harwood (1920–1995), Rosemary Dobson (b. 1920), and Fay Zwicky (b. 1933).

Since 1970 small independent theaters (La Mama, La Boîte, The Hole in the Wall, Jane Street, The Ensemble) and a wide range of community and alternative theaters have continued to play a seminal role in the development of new experimental theater works. Although some (like The Pram Factory and Nimrod) are defunct, many new theaters have taken over their functions. The National Playwrights' Conference is another venue in which new plays are workshopped before being produced commercially. Significantly, most of the prestigious, serious, professional theaters in the capital cities demonstrate substantial commitment to new Australian plays, and restage older ones, thus creating the sense of an Australian theatrical tradition, which did not exist twenty years ago. A new feature of Australian theater is its parochial nature, and while state companies regularly share production and actors, audiences tend to be less appreciative of imported productions. At the level of writing, such regionalism is coming to be seen as a strength rather than as a liability, as monolithic notions of national identity come under scrutiny.

While SOCIAL-REALIST theater and comedy of manners dominate the commercial venues and David Williamson (b. 1942) is the acknowledged master of these genres, there has been in the 1970s and 1980s a greater diversity in form and content, notably by Stephen Sewell (b. 1953), and nonnaturalistic exploratory forms are often successful, as is evident in the work of Dorothy Hewett, Louis Nowra (b. 1950), and Ron Elisha (b. 1951). While these writers' works are still concerned with issues of national identity, as are the novelists and the poets, the definitions are less narrow and less prescriptive than they were in the 1950s and 1960s and more self-consciously cosmopolitan, and there is a deepening and darkening of vision in terms of the issues debated.

BIBLIOGRAPHY: Fitzpatrick, P. H., *After "The Doll": Australian Drama since 1955* (1979); Docker, J., *In a Critical Condition: Reading Australian Literature* (1984); Green, H. M., *A History of Australian Literature: Pure and Applied*, rev. ed (2 vols., 1984–1985); Wilde, W. H., J. Hooton, and B. Andrews, *The Oxford Companion to Australian Literature* (1985); Holloway, p., ed., *Contemporary Australian Drama*, rev. 2nd. ed. (1987); Daniel, H., *Liars: Australian New Novelists* (1988); Hergenhan, L., ed., *The Penguin New Literary History of Australia* (1988); Gelder, K. and P. Salzman *The New Diversity: Australian Fiction, 1970–1988* (1989); McLaren, J. D., *Australian Literature: An Historical Introduction* (1989); Whitlock, G., ed., *Eight Voices of the Eighties* (1989); Davis, J., S. Muecke, M. Narogin, and M. Shoemaker, eds., *Paperbark: A Collection of Black Australian Writings* (1990); Radic, L., *The State of the Play: The Revolution in the Australian Theatre since the 1960s* (1991)

—FRANCES DEVLIN GLASS

AUSTRIAN LITERATURE

The witticism that Americans are separated from Englishmen by a common language is also applicable to Germans and Austrians. Austria's political, social, and economic history was so different from that of the principalities united under Prussian hegemony into a German nation in the 19th c. that separate national identities developed. Of even greater importance perhaps were the heterogeneous ethnic composition of the Austrian Empire and the impact of centuries of Hapsburg rule, both of which put their stamp on the cultural configuration of the country, an effect that remained even after the collapse of the monarchy in 1918.

Nevertheless, it is not easy to ascertain what is peculiarly Austrian about every poem, play, or novel written on Austrian soil.

Because of the fragmentation of experience, depending on place of birth, and on social, economic, and other conditions, it would be absurd to assert that all Austrian writers shared the same basic cultural and ideological concerns. But there can be no doubt that most literary works that originated in Austria are connected in some way with Austrian history. The following survey is divided into three parts, corresponding to the three most obvious divisions of Austrian history since 1900. Wherever possible the connection of authors and works with their sociohistorical matrix will be made.

The Last Years of the Empire

The literature of this period was influenced by two sociohistorical phenomena of dynamic impact: the belated modernization of the empire, and the migration of large numbers of Jews from the rural eastern parts of the empire to the western cities, particularly Vienna. The clash between the elements of a semifeudal order and the forces of capitalism had profound repercussions on broad segments of the population. Discontent, insecurity, uprootedness characterize the whole development. In the cultural realm this collision proved to be extremely stimulating. The explosion of productivity in all fields of intellectual endeavor was so violent that it has been compared to a supernova. Ever since then, Austrian literature has held a position of disproportionate importance in the larger sphere of German literature.

In contrast to other countries, such as France and Germany, in Austria great concentrations of Jews were part of this process of economic change and intellectual development, especially after the monarchy's union with Hungary and its annexation of Galicia. Because of these dynastic arrangements, Jews were drawn into the vortex of ever-expanding spheres of modern capitalism. In spite of extraordinarily difficult conditions, many Jews were able to succeed in the new setting, some even to play a major role. As a result, Jewish participation in the literary and overall cultural life of Vienna at the turn of the century became so all-pervading that it is almost easier to enumerate the prominent non-Jews than to name the Jews.

It has often been emphasized that Vienna's Jewish citizenry acted as an uncommonly receptive sounding board for cultural achievements and intellectual innovations. The important newspapers—the *Neue Freie Presse, Wiener Tagblatt,* and *Neues Wiener Journal*—were all in Jewish hands. These papers were voices of Austrian liberalism, the political creed of the upwardly mobile bourgeoisie, with the economic ideology of laissez-faire at its center.

The influx of masses of eastern Jews into a society that was conservatively Christian gave rise to an anti-Semitic countermovement of particular virulence, mixing traditional religious and economic theories with new sociobiological ones. The *Weltanschauung* arising from these various elements created the atmosphere in which the literature of the day had to exist and to which the vastly divergent individuals reacted.

At the turn of the century Marie von Ebner-Eschenbach (1830–1916) and Ferdinand von Saar (1833–1906) were still writing. Both returned repeatedly to the central theme of the impact of modernization and early capitalism on the social classes they knew best, the landed nobility and a prospering bourgeoisie bent on imitating the life style of the aristocracy. In Saar's novella *Schloß Kostenitz* (1883; Kostenitz castle) the delicately drawn triangle of characters imperceptibly takes on allegorical meaning: the hapless heroine, an image of indecisive Austria, is crushed by the struggle between two rival principles, the new ethos of the bourgeoisie and feudal arrogance. The true winners are the new inhabitants of Kostenitz, a different breed of people: they are interested in politics, the stock market, socialism, and the new works of the naturalist school of literature. Clearly, we have reached the age of Arthur SCHNITZLER.

The Jewish element does not always appear as conspicuously as it does in the works of Richard BEER-HOFMANN, who, in his biblical dramas *Jaakobs Traum* (1918; *Jacob's Dream,* 1946) and *Der junge David* (1933; young David) set out almost programmatically to restore the mythic sense of historic heroism and divine dignity of the Jewish people. Thoroughly secularized and assimilated as they were, nothing could have been more alien to most Viennese Jewish writers than the desire to flaunt their Jewishness. In most of them this profound but often unconscious experience of otherness manifested itself in very indirect, sometimes entirely sublimated and impalpable ways, in a subtle elitism or in an almost morbid sensitivity and vulnerability.

Like Leopold von Andrian-Werburg (1875–1951), a grandson of the composer Meyerbeer, who never fulfilled the hopes for a productive literary career aroused by his youthful novella *Der Garten der Erkenntnis* (1895; the garden of knowledge), Richard Beer-Hofmann was not a prolific writer. Rather, he inspired and promoted the work of other members of his circle. This group of highly gifted poets, essayists, writers of fiction, and playwrights is known as "Young Vienna," which, having introduced MODERNISM into a basically traditional literary scene, occupies a central position in the history of Austrian literature. It was a loose association of young writers who often had little more in common with one another than the Griensteidl, one of the ubiquitous Viennese cafés, where they liked to congregate. The habitués included Arthur Schnitzler and Hugo von HOFMANNSTHAL, as well as the theoretician Hermann BAHR, who brought literary incentives and intellectual impulses from his travels in foreign lands, notably France. His many novels and plays are largely forgotten today, but his chameleonlike changes—from naturalism to DECADENCE, from impressionism to EXPRESSIONISM, from German nationalism to Marxism and back to Austrian patriotism and the conservative Catholicism of his youth—tell the story of the intellectual currents and artistic fashions in the city where he lived.

Arthur Schnitzler was an uncommonly versatile artist. His training as a physician served him well in his literary endeavors: it made him the dispassionate diagnostician of his age. In his very first work, *Anatol* (1893; *Anatol: A Sequence of Dialogues,* 1911), Schnitzler succeeded in creating a symbol of the decadent bourgeoisie with its hypocrisies, frustrations, and pretensions. The title hero of this series of loosely knit episodes is a directionless playboy who tries in vain to capture the instant of fulfillment in a succession of love affairs with women of various social strata. Those who could see in Schnitzler's multifaceted portrayals only the glorification of the elegant sybaritic life in the imperial capital failed to sense the nihilistic despair underneath the glitter and the author's ethical disapproval of a purely aesthetic existence.

Schnitzler's seriousness of purpose is documented in a series of Ibsen-like thesis plays in which he rigorously reexamines the sexual and social prejudices of the Austrian bourgeoisie. In *Liebelei* (1896; *Light-o'-Love,* 1912) the two strands of Schnitzler's dramatic practice are brought together in a tragic confrontation. The "sweet girl" of the lower classes not only is a more profound human being than the elegant officers out for "a good time" but also possesses the secret that could transform this vacuum of values into a meaningful life: the capacity for love and commitment.

Schnitzler was also a powerful writer of narratives ranging from parables and fairy tales to novellas and full-length novels and dealing with the problems of sex, death, art, insanity, even the supernatural. Especially innovative is his stream-of-consciousness novella *Leutnant Gustl* (1901; *None But the Brave*, 1926), written at a time when this technique was practically unknown. The novel *Der Weg ins Freie* (1908; *The Road to the Open*, 1923) paints a broad as well as subtle sociopsychological panorama of fin-de-siècle Vienna with its declining aristocracy, alienated artists, socialists, anti-Semites, Zionists, and assimilated Jews. So profound were Schnitzler's psychological insights that Sigmund FREUD acknowledged his envy of an artist who attained his knowledge of the human soul intuitively.

Strongly influenced by Schnitzler, Raoul Auernheimer (1876–1948) wrote novels and entertaining social comedies of amiable irony about love and seduction. As feuilletonist, he was a sympathetic chronicler of Viennese society at the turn of the century.

Schnitzler's friend Hugo von Hofmannsthal was the "child prodigy" of Austrian literature. At the age of seventeen, still a schoolboy, he astonished the fastidious literary elite with his rich and mellifluous poetry. Because he depicted the "beautiful life" with great insight he was erroneously hailed as a proponent of Decadent ivory-tower art. Had his contemporaries paid closer attention to his essays (which accompanied his works of fiction throughout life), they would have recognized the critical passion present in him from the outset, his rejection of pure aestheticism and his yearning for an "involvement in life."

That Hofmannsthal was himself torn between the two orientations, the aesthetic and the ethical, is demonstrated by the outbreak of a crisis. Stunning his many admirers, he abruptly gave up lyrical poetry, which he described as the alluring but dangerous fruit of his "preexistence," and tried to enter "existence," a mature and socially responsible mode of art, by turning to the theater. From then on Hofmannsthal experimented with various forms. A novel remained fragmentary. A cycle of tragedies based on Sophocles reinterprets Greek culture in Nietzsche's Dionysian sense. The best known of Hofmannsthal's comedies, *Der Rosenkavalier* (1911; *The Rose-Bearer*, 1912) is the fruit of a collaboration of an accomplished poet and an equally notable composer, Richard Strauss, with whom he also wrote several other operas.

Together with the famous theater director Max Reinhardt (1873–1943), Hofmannsthal founded the Salzburg Festival, contributing two plays of his own to it. Inspired by the morality play of the Middle Ages and its undisputed 17th-c. master Calderón, he created his much acclaimed *Jedermann* (1911; *The Play of Everyman*, 1917) and *Das Salzburger große Welttheater* (1922; *The Salzburg Great Theater of the World*, 1963), in which he used the traditional Christian world view to criticize the effects of materialism, imperialism, and industrialization.

Both Schnitzler and Hofmannsthal had definite critical propensities that found expression in the aphorisms of the former and the numerous essays of the latter. But both were first and foremost creators of imaginative works. In contrast, the genius of Karl KRAUS ran much more in the direction of discursive prose. He did write nine volumes of poetry, but it was as the cultural critic of his time and as satirist that he achieved fame. In the influential periodical *Die Fackel*, which he founded in 1899, and which after 1911 was written by him alone, Kraus violently opposed the pervading debasement of the spirit in all segments of public life—politics, the administration of justice, literature, and art. But the target of his most scathing attacks was journalism, which he castigated not primarily for its sinister political influence but rather for its perversion of culture and its corruption of language. The official world of literature that Kraus had attacked for its lack of fiber and particularly for its disgraceful attitude during World War I surrounded him with a wall of silence, as the press had done before. It continued to envelop Kraus even after the end of the war, but following the collapse of the Third Reich in 1945 all his books were republished, including the thirty-seven volumes comprising all the issues of *Die Fackel*, and he is now one of the most frequently quoted writers in Austria and Germany.

Berthold Viertel (1885–1953)—EXPRESSIONIST poet, playwright, narrative writer, film director, and theater critic—was a friend of Karl Kraus, in whose *Die Fackel* Viertel's first poems were published. Otto STOESSEL's models for his novellas were the 19th-c. masters of poetic realism, Gottfried Keller (1819–1890), C. F. Meyer (1825–1898), and Adalbert Stifter (1805–1868). He carried on the traditions of Franz Grillparzer (1791–1872) and Ferdinand von Saar (1833–1906) in a truly noble way.

Peter Altenberg (1859–1919), who wrote delicate vignettes of Viennese city life, has been identified with impressionism, whereas it is often asserted that Austrian literature did not contribute much to expressionism. But one can postulate the existence of a "demonic" branch of this movement with the artists Alfred Kubin (1877–1959) and Oskar Kokoschka (1886–1980) as participants. Kubin wrote novels in which fantastic, dreamlike, and uncanny elements predominate, while Kokoschka's poems and plays have ecstatic, strongly antilogical traits. The ill-fated, drugaddicted Georg TRAKL wrote visionary poetry that ranks with the greatest of the century. Images of alienation and decadence intermingle with religious symbols in his difficult verse. He too, is normally classed with the expressionists. The Innsbruck-based liberal Catholic journal *Der Brenner*, where Trakl published his first poems, should be mentioned as an important reminder that Vienna did not have a cultural monopoly. Its editor, Ludwig von Ficker (1880–1967), maintained contacts with, among others, Karl Kraus, Rainer Maria RILKE, and the philosopher Ludwig Wittgenstein (1889–1951).

Anton Wildgans (1881–1932) was a widely performed dramatist of great social empathy. As a poet he developed from naturalism and impressionism toward expressionism. He was also an important essayist and director of the Vienna Burgtheater.

In addition to Vienna, Prague was also a center of German-language literature. Some of the Prague writers, such as Rilke and Franz KAFKA, surpassed their Viennese contemporaries in world renown. But it is questionable whether it is right to label them "Austrian writers." Rilke was always ambivalent about his Austrian background. There can be no doubt that many of his views were Austrian in origin, such as his skeptical attitude toward Germany and Prussia, his "anti-Christian," albeit miracle-loving mysticism tinged by Catholicism, and his peculiar weakness for the aristocracy. But he left his native Prague, which he disliked intensely, at the age of twenty. Soon he would speak of Russia as his true spiritual home. His first mature works, *Neue Gedichte* and *Der neuen Gedichte anderer Teil* (1907 and 1908; *New Poems*, 1964) and *Die Aufzeichnungen des Malte Laurids Brigge* (1910; *The Notebooks of Malte Laurids Brigge*, 1949), conceived in Paris and inspired by Rodin, Cézanne, and Baudelaire, are essentially French, if a national label has to be attached to them; whereas his crowning achievements, *Duineser Elegien* (1923; *Duinese Elegies*, 1930) and the *Sonette an Orpheus* (1923; *Sonnets to Orpheus*, 1936), are European in character, defying ethnic categories; and so are his late poems in French and his translations of Paul VALÉRY. Only his early works are typically Austrian, such as his *Zwei Prager Geschichten* (1899; two Prague stories), which center on the "Omladina," a failed Czech conspiracy against the Austrian ruling class, which Rilke depicted as both petrified and oppressive. Here the young author clearly sides with the Czechs against his own social and ethnic group.

Kafka's case is not dissimilar. It is true that he had been born and reached full maturity long before the dismemberment of the Danubian empire made him a citizen of the new Czechoslovak Republic, and there can be no doubt that his education and upbringing in the monarchy must have molded his personality to a considerable extent. The intricate and corrupt bureaucracies that play such an egregious role in his otherwise hermetic novels, *Der Prozeß* (1925; *The Trial*, 1937) and *Das Schloß* (1926; *The Castle*, 1930), have often been identified with their real-life Austrian equivalents and attributed to Kafka's service as an official in one of the state's insurance agencies. But Prague was an environment *sui generis*, and Kafka's identification with the Czechs and especially with the Jews residing in the city was infinitely stronger than with the abstraction "Austria." Attempts to shed light on his black parables and reverse fables by recourse to the Yiddish theater and Jewish lore have been more productive than many other approaches. And yet it cannot be denied that this "abstraction" too must have had its impact on the ethnic groups living their friction-plagued lives under Hapsburg rule. Nevertheless, what inspired or haunted generations of readers all over the globe as a paradigm of the confusions and absurdities of our age is not easily traceable to the tormented poet's historic milieu.

In connection with Kafka mention must be made of Max BROD, his contemporary and close associate, who wrote essays, autobiographical works, and novels, the best known of which are *Tycho Brahes Weg zu Gott* (1916; *The Redemption of Tycho Brahe*, 1928) and *Reubeni, Fürst der Juden* (1925; *Reubeni, Prince of the Jews*, 1928). Brod's most important literary contribution, however, lies in his refusing to destroy Kafka's literary remains, which comprise the bulk of his stories and novels, as Kafka wished him to do, and instead publishing them. It is fair to say that Brod, too, a passionate Zionist during most of his life, was more Jewish than Austrian in orientation.

The power of the milieu is well demonstrated by a predecessor of Kafka, Gustav MEYRINK, often mistaken for a Jew because of his novel *Der Golem* (1915; *The Golem*, 1928), about a robot created by a rabbi, in which the mystical atmosphere of Jewish occultism in the ghetto of Prague is masterfully evoked. In other works he depicted the narrow hypocrisies and petty bureaucracies of his time. In this respect he was "Austrian," even if he moved to Germany in later life and turned his satiric wit against civilian and militaristic excesses there.

Ernst Weiss (1884–1940) was a novelist with an intellectual kinship to Kafka. His professional experience as a physician, especially as an army doctor during World War I, was a determining factor throughout his work.

Like Rilke before him, Franz WERFEL remained in his native Prague only until he came of age and then migrated restlessly from one residence to another, from Leipzig to Munich, from Vienna to Italy, until he was driven to France and finally to the U.S. by the wave of Nazism that swept across Europe. Yet there is sufficient evidence that his beginnings as an ecstatic, expressionist lyricist, preaching social compassion and the universal brotherhood of men, were inspired by intellectual currents in the environment of his youth. Even more so than his poems, such prose works as *Nicht*

der Mörder, der Ermordete ist schuldig (1920; *Not the Murderer*, 1937) and *Der Abituriententag* (1928; *Class Reunion*, 1929) are recognizable as Prague experiences. Like the inhabitants of this multiethnic city, his characters reflect the social and metaphysical tensions between Judaism and Christianity that their creator himself never overcame.

The First Republic

The lost war and the Treaty of Saint Germain (1919) simplified the question as to what Austria was. It had now been reduced to a diminutive rump state with Vienna as its hydrocephalic capital, whose nearly two million inhabitants constituted almost one third of the total population. In its less than twenty years of existence the new republic was torn asunder by inflation, destitution, unemployment, social unrest, and political instability. During the last four years of its existence it was ruled by a church-oriented right-wing dictatorship. The "Anschluss" took place in 1938 when Hitler annexed the feeble commonwealth, obviously welcomed by millions of Austrians, driving into exile the majority of writers and reducing the country to artistic insignificance. Under these circumstances one of the dominant tendencies of Austrian literature during the interwar period was retrospection. Nostalgically or satirically, one writer after another devoted himself to the task of evoking prewar Austria and analyzing the reasons for its demise.

The earliest of these works was Karl Kraus's satiric tragedy *Die letzten Tage der Menschheit* (1922; *The Last Days of Mankind*, abridged version, 1974). Written during the war, the bitter accusations of the mammoth play (eight hundred pages, five hundred characters) had to wait several years before it could be published in book form. It strings together innumerable scenes over which the callousness of the rulers, the gullibility and fanaticism of the masses, the cruelty of the military leaders, the ruthlessness of the profiteers, and the agonies of the people cast a thickening pall as the war proceeds. Spread out over half of Europe, written in various dialects and shades of language, the drama captures the corruption of the semifeudal capitalism that was the system of the warring central Powers. But its most frightening aspect is its historical authenticity: a good part of the text is culled from official proclamations, public pronouncements, and the newspapers of the day. That these improbable conversations were actually held and these incredible misdeeds actually perpetrated makes Kraus's masterpiece a forerunner of the modern documentary theater.

Unlike Kraus, Hofmannsthal had been an ardent supporter of the Austrian war effort. The collapse of the Austro-Hungarian Empire caused him severe anguish. In a series of dramatic works he tried to come to grips with the new situation. The most successful of these and perhaps his theatrical masterpiece is the comedy *Der Schwierige* (1921; *The Difficult Man*, 1963), the swan song of the doomed aristocracy with whom he identified. In his next play, *Der Unbestechliche* (1923; the incorruptible man), he assessed the changed political climate more realistically. Here the new regime is allegorized in the figure of a rebellious servant who takes charge of an aristocratic household; but, incongruously, the playwright makes him use his newly won power to restore the old order. This solution foreshadows Hofmannsthal's drift toward the "Conservative Revolution," a loose association of right-wing intellectuals who were dangerously ambivalent about the rising flood of Fascism. In his last work, *Der Turm* (1925; *The Tower*, 1963), he conjures up once more the ghost of Austria-Hungary. In a 1927 revised version, the forces of modern totalitarianism triumph over the representative of aristocratic and humanistic values. Since Hofmannsthal died shortly after its publication, this prophetic tragedy can be regarded as his political testament.

Formidable contributions during the interwar period were made by Robert MUSIL, Joseph ROTH, and Hermann BROCH. Musil's *Der Mann ohne Eigenschaften* (3 vols., 1930–43; *The Man without Qualities*, 1953–54, 1965), almost totally unknown at the time of the author's death, is regarded today by many, in spite of the fact that it is unfinished, as the towering exemplar of the "Hapsburg necrology." Like many great works of fiction, it is rich in philosophical ideas and representative human types, full of psychological insight and penetrating social analysis; Musil's work nevertheless signals a departure from traditional narrative because of its ironic and reflective rather than synthetic character. Massive insertions of learned treatises and veritable essays make it an incomparable compound of fact and fiction. More than any other book it reflects the contradictions of the late Hapsburg empire and with them the problems of all of Europe at the turn of the century.

In spite of so much rationality and analytical fervor, Musil's writings, not only *Der Mann ohne Eigenschaften* but also his earlier *Die Verwirrungen des Zöglings Törleß* (1906; *Young Törless*, 1955) and several erotic novellas, exhibit unexpected mystical yearnings that are difficult to explain. But since similar experiments can be detected in many writers, they must be regarded as a generational tendency, perhaps as a phenomenon of secularization through which a measure of transcendence is retained even though religious beliefs have been weakened or lost. Not only Hofmannsthal, who coined the phrase, but almost all writers treated here, even Arthur Schnitzler, were such "mystics without mysticism."

Joseph Roth's *Radetzkymarsch* (1932; *Radetzky March*, 1933) depicts the waning Hapsburg realm as if it were a kind of Indian summer: a mild sun transfigures once more its seemingly unscathed scenery, but the coming frosts send their anticipatory shivers through the characters. Only a novelist of rare gifts like Roth could create such a scintillating portrait. In his hands the German language becomes, all prejudices to the contrary notwithstanding, a light and subtle instrument of communication. Born of Jewish parents in the easternmost recesses of the empire, he became literally homeless with its dissolution. After the negative early novels and essays in which he reconstructed life under the Austrian dynasty as experienced by the downtrodden Jewish ghetto dweller and the disaffected provincial Slav, Roth's retrospective assessment of the Hapsburg state became more and more affirmative until he glorified it in later works, such as *Die Kapuzinergruft* (1938; the crypt of the Capuchin monks), to the detriment of their artistic quality. His preoccupation with the past made him blind to the realities of the present and pushed him into the political proximity of reactionary monarchists around Otto von Hapsburg. A destroyed exile, he died in a Parisian hospital for the poor.

Hermann Broch was much less oriented toward history. Still, late in his life he also yielded to the quest for the past. In a brilliant essay, *Hofmannsthal und seine Zeit* (written 1947–48, pub. 1975; Hofmannsthal and his time), he analyzes the "gay apocalypse" of Vienna in the age of the dying monarchy. His entire development as a dramatist and novelist must be seen against the background of the crumbling bourgeois order from the turn of the century on. During World War I Broch began his search for a formal theory of values capable of resisting historical change. Politically, he tended

toward a neo-Kantian variant of socialism. In his trilogy *Die Schlafwandler* (1931–32; *The Sleepwalkers*, 1932) he combined his antibourgeois social criticism with the utopian hope for a new future, a mixture that also left its imprint on his later works, including the two novels completed in American exile, *Der Tod des Vergil* (1945; *The Death of Virgil*, 1945) and *Die Schuldlosen* (1950; *The Guiltless*, 1974).

According to one definition of Austrian literature, the Czech novelist Jaroslav HAŠEK's *Osudy dobrého vojáka švejka za světové války* (4 vols., 1921–23; *The Good Soldier švejk and His Fortunes in the World War*, 1973) qualifies as an eminently Austrian work. Translated into practically all European languages, including, of course, German, it is a picaresque novel about the absurdities of life during World War I from the point of view of the opposition to the Austrian army (from which the author was himself a defector): pretending to be mentally retarded, švejk outwits the military exponents of the monarchy, puncturing their inflated self-image and unmasking their spurious heroism. Erwin Piscator (1893–1966) and Bertolt BRECHT, working together, dramatized this immortal satire.

Stefan ZWEIG, a prolific author of widely admired historical biographies as well as a novelist, dramatist, essayist, and poet, was once the idol of an enthusiastic readership. In the context of postwar Hapsburg reminiscences his autobiography *Die Welt von gestern* (1944; *The World of Yesterday*, 1943) comes immediately to mind. Written shortly before his suicide, it transfigures the Danubian monarchy to the point of misrepresenting it as a rock of order, peace, and stability.

Alexander Lernet-Holenia (1897–1976), on the other hand, in a series of novels about the army, interpreted the events that sealed the doom of the Austro-Hungarian Empire. As a poet, he was a classicist in the tradition of Rilke and Hofmannsthal, as was Felix Braun (1885–1973).

In the rich interwar period there was an abundance of fine talent. In his plays Ödön von HORVÁTH stripped away the popular image of Vienna and showed a moribund society whose economic misery causes a breakdown in human solidarity and compassion. His novels *Jugend ohne Gott* (1938; *Youth without God*, 1939) and *Ein Kind unserer Zeit* (1938; *A Child of Our Time*, 1939) give a frightening vision of dictatorship. A master of irony and satire, he was a subtly perceptive portrayer of Austrian society between the wars.

Alfred POLGAR displayed rare wit and irony in deceptively simple short prose works. Although aware of the yawning abyss beneath man, he was a life-affirming moralist. Egon FRIEDELL, who wrote a number of successful skits and farces with Polgar, was also an essayist of an ironic, satirical bent. He won fame beyond Vienna with his three-volume *Kulturgeschichte der Neuzeit* (1927–31; *A Cultural History of the Modern Age*, 1930–32), in which his vivid, graphic language makes cultural, political, and economic facts come to life.

Robert Neumann (1897–1975) was a novelist of acid social criticism and an unsurpassed parodist; his most widely read book is *Mitfremden Federn* (1928; with the pen of other writers). Friedrich TORBERG, a realistic novelist, was an irrepressible but kindly social critic of his native land. Martina Wied (1882–1957) was a refined novelist and poet of romantic-impressionistic leanings. Her novels, rich in action, are multilayered and sometimes enigmatic. They always aspire to give meaning to human suffering in a chaotic time. Enrica von Handel-Mazzetti (1871–1955) wrote in the spirit of the

Austrian-Catholic Baroque, mainly in the time of the Counter-Reformation. Although maintaining a strict Catholic position, she advocated a purified Christian humanism. Felix Salten (1869–1947), novelist, playwright, essayist, and influential theater critic, is best remembered for his children's classic *Bambi* (1923; *Bambi*, 1928).

Leading interwar dramatists included Franz Theodor CSOKOR, Ferdinand BRUCKNER, and Richard Billinger (1893–1965). Csokor, who began as an expressionist, moved toward a more realistic theater of ideas, and in the three plays collected as *Europäische Trilogie* (1952; European trilogy) he analyzes the invidiousness of nationalism in the 20th c. Bruckner belongs to the disillusioned postexpressionist generation. His plays waver between extreme modernism and a return to the classical tradition. Strongly influenced by Freud, in plays like *Elisabeth von England* (1930; Elizabeth of England) he unmasks historical characters using psychoanalytical methods. Billinger, also a poet and novelist, was a dramatist in the tradition of the Baroque peasant play.

Among poets of the period, Theodor KRAMER, a representative of the "new faclualism," was influenced by Trakl and Brecht; his is a poetry of bitter social criticism. In supple, melodious language, Paula von PRERADOVIĆ sang longingly of Dalmatia, the homeland of her ancestors; all of her writing is characterized by deep religious feeling. Hans Leifhelm (1891–1947) was a melodious nature poet. Other fine poets were Alma Johanna Koenig (1889–1942) and Ludwig Goldscheider (1896–1976).

One way of understanding the interwar literary scene would be through the multiple tensions between the works of the cosmopolitan, avant-garde intellectuals, usually Vienna-based, and a traditionalist movement centered in the provinces. For another mode of escaping the oppressive present was through the espousal of antidemocratic "country" values. Most of the exponents of a "provincial art," such as Max Mell (1882–1971), Joseph Georg Oberkofler (1889–1962), Josef Friedrich Perkonig (1890–1959), Karl Heinrich Waggerl (1897–1973), and Guido Zernatto (1903–1943), were born in the Alpine regions and educated in the doctrines of traditional Catholicism. Many of them rejected Vienna as a "Balkanized" big city, with a democratic, un-Christian, and un-German ethnic mixture they detested. Instead they extolled the simple life and peasant virtues, sometimes succumbing to the clichés of anti-Semitic "blood-and-soil" literature. Not all of them went so far as the talented formalist poet Josef Weinheber (1892–1945), who joined the Nazis and let them further his career.

Such collective retreat from and misconception of mankind's real problems would have been unthinkable in a less tormented epoch, but these were far from serene times. The anomaly of the situation is borne out by the destinies of precisely the more forward-looking writers. Those who were not lucky enough to die before 1938 were swept abroad as refugees, from Italy to China, from France to South America and the U.S. In addition to many of the writers previously mentioned, the emigrés included Ernst WALDINGER, Hermann Grab (1903–1949), and Oskar Jellinek (1886–1940). Waldinger was a lyric poet of idealistic outlook, and a master of from. While living in the U.S., he retained a strong nostalgic bond to his homeland. Grab's love and emulation of Proust is seen in the way he conjures up the Prague of his childhood and adolescence. He left Czechoslovakia after the Nazi occupation in 1939, and only some of his early stories have been preserved. His later stories were published in the volume *Hochzeit in Brooklyn* (1945; wedding in Brooklyn). Grab has been compared not only

with Proust but with Virginia WOOLF and Katherine MANSFIELD as well. Yet this outstanding writer remains practically unknown even in his homeland.

Long before the Anschluss, however, sociopolitical conditions in Austria had ceased to be "normal" in any sense. As early as 1930 the Fascist Program was proclaimed in Korneuburg; it rejected parliamentary democracy and recognized as authorities only God, the leaders of the movement, and the adherents' own iron will. In 1933 Hitler took over in Germany, driving into Austria not only Austrian writers who had lived in the neighboring country, such as Franz Blei (1871–1942), Horváth, Musil, Polgar, Roth, and Werfel, but a whole host of Germans, among them GRAF, HERMLIN, MEHRING, WOLF, and ZUCKMAYER, who preferred a German-speaking country like Austria as their place of exile in spite of its own political situation, namely Dollfuss's right-wing dictatorship and the suppression of the Social Democratic Party after a bloody civil war. Thus once more the confusion was great and the desperate cry "What belongs to Austrian literature and what does not?" might have again been raised, had the Anschluss of 1938 and World War II not drowned out all voices of reason and peace.

The Second Republic

The Germans emerged from the nationalist paroxysms of World War II with a monumental hangover; nor were the Austrians exempt from it. Their flirtation with Hitler, for which they had paid so dearly, left many of them with a desire to build a future unencumbered by constant reminders of an incriminating past. But in the field of literature it proved impracticable, as the Germans attempted, to postulate an "hour zero," a beginning without antecedent in the period that had come to such a violent end. The reasons for this impossibility were simple: on the one hand, the writers who had made their debuts in the first republic were right on the scene or returned to it from their exiles; on the other hand, there was in many the equally strong desire to understand what exactly had gone wrong in the past.

Heimito von DODERER was one of those who represented continuity. His first works, both poetic and narrative, had appeared in the days of the first republic without causing much of a stir. But there is no question that his fiction dominated the postwar period. His two most important novels, *Die Strudlhofstiege* (1951; the Strudlhof stairs) and *Die Dämonen* (1956; *The Demons*, 1961) once more conjure up the Austrian tradition, albeit with emphasis on the time of the author's own youth, the 1920s. Weaving one gigantic tapestry of persons and events, they deal with the uncanny forces threatening man in modern mass society. His chance for becoming a genuine autonomous individual depends on his readiness to retain a universalist openness of perception. The loser in this battle is the person who encapsulates himself in the distorted world of his bureaucratic, sexual, or ideological illusions. Such abjuration of all ideology is typical of the restorative 1950s.

Fritz von Herzmanovsky-Orlando (1877–1954) and Albert Paris von GÜTERSLOH also span the epochs separated by World War II. Gütersloh's novel *Sonne und Mond* (1962; sun and moon) was both hailed as a treasury of Baroque riches and condemned as a labyrinthine monstrosity. Even more monstrous, but irresistibly funny, are Herzmanovsky-Orlando's fantastic grotesqueries in novel, story, and play form, for the most part posthumously published. The very titles are indicative of his scurrilous imagination: *Der Gaulschreck im Rosennetz* (1928; the nag's scare in the rose net), *Maskenspiel der Genien* (1928; genies' game of masks), *Cavaliere Huscher* (1963; cavalier scrambler).

Much more inclined toward social criticism was George Saiko (1892–1962). The most famous of his works is the psychoanalytical novel *Auf dem Floß* (1948; on the raft), he dichotomizes Austrian society in an "upstairsdownstairs"-like analysis of the prewar world.

Other writers whose work offered continuity in the early postwar years were Imma von Bodmershof (1895–1982), whose poems depict the land and peasant life of her native Lower Austrian Waldviertel; and Gertrud Fussenegger (pseud. of Gertrud Dietz, b. 1912), a traditional realistic novelist who deals profoundly with such basic problems as guilt and suffering.

With the work of two women, Austrian literature climbed to international heights almost immediately after the war. Herself persecuted by the Nazis, Ilse AICHINGER explored the plight of a young victim of the regime in a novel hovering between psychological realism and symbolic clairvoyance, *Die größere Hoffnung* (1948; *Herod's Children*, 1963), thereby setting high standards for her own future production as well as that of others. Like Aichinger, Ingeborg BACHMANN won acclaim as a writer of radio plays, a very respected literary genre after the war. But first and foremost, she was a lyrical poet. In her very first collection of poems, *Die gestundete Zeit* (1953; borrowed time), she excelled by uniting intellectual abstraction and symbolistic metaphors. Both writers belonged to the prestigious West German "Group 47," which ruled the literary scene for two decades, thus continuing the significant participation of Austrians in the larger sphere of German literature.

Two other Austrian women poets of high gifts in the years following World War II were Christine Busta (1915–1987) and Christine Lavant (1915–1973).

Possibly the most powerful poet in the German language after World War II was Paul CELAN, whose visionary verses became more and more cryptic. But with what justification this *poète maudit*, born of Jewish parents in a town in what was at the time part of Romania, who spent the war years in a labor camp and most of the rest of his ill-fated life in Paris, can be counted among the Austrians, as he often is, must remain a moot question. The same is true of the Sephardic Jew Elias CANETTI, an important novelist, essayist, and dramatist, who like Celan writes in German; he did study in Vienna for a few years, but he was born in Bulgaria and has lived mostly in England, as does the Vienna-born novelist Jakov LIND, who left Austria with his parents in 1938. Manès SPERBER, who was born in Poland and has spent most of his adult life in France, is a novelist of great power who has been deeply involved in Europe's anguished conflicts.

In the drama, as in poetry, there was an older group of playwrights who had started their careers before the war: Franz Theodor Csokor, Ferdinand Bruckner, Rudolf Henz (b. 1897), Arnolt Bronnen (1895–1959), and many others. In the middle generation of leading dramatists the most important is unquestionably Fritz HOCHWÄLDER, a dramatist of ideas whose plays are models of theatrical craftsmanship. Belonging to the tradition of the Vienna popular stage, they present historical situations in a colorful, theatrically effective way and deal with timeless conflicts. But Harald Zusanek (b. 1922), Raimund Berger (1917–1954), Rudolf Bayr (b. 1919), and Kurt Klinger (b. 1928) are not inconsiderable talents. They in turn are followed by ever younger writers, some of them dramatists, others without clear generic preference. They strongly rebel against an unregenerate society

which in their opinion is still neurotically dominated by too many undigested memories.

With these youngest literati, however, one enters a field of conflicting directions and confusing trends. It is therefore advisable to step back to the 1950s in order to gain critical perspective by comparing two representative authors, Hans Carl ARTMANN and Helmut Qualtinger (b. 1928), who in their polarity cover a broad spectrum of attitudes and become paradigmatic for the present phase of postwar Austrian literature.

Artmann's very first poems in *med ana schwoazzn dintn* (1958; with black ink), written in unadulterated dialect, were a great success. The innovative impact of this collection lies in its deviation from the chumminess and primitiveness of traditional dialect poetry. Instead of praising the "simple life" Artmann reveals the cruelty, sadism, and cynicism of the lower classes, which history records but which legend refuses to acknowledge. Not shrinking away from the themes of dread and latent violence, sexual perversion and nihilistic *Schadenfreude*, these poems express the neurotic streak and barely controlled resentments that slumber beneath the proverbial "golden heart" of the Viennese populace. This feature connects Artmann unmistakably with the postwar need for exposure and truth. Almost against his will, this "problematization" of a certain psychic backwardness had profound literary effects. But such timeliness enters Artmann's world only surreptitiously, since he is basically an experimentalist with an irrepressible imagination, forever exploring the formal possibilities of language.

Almost the opposite is true of Helmut Qualtinger, who is a writer of cabaret sketches and as such essentially a social critic. Everything he has written bears explicit reference to the social realities of the day. Whether his target is political corruption, collusion between press and police, the traffic chaos in Vienna, bureaucratic ineptitude, or Austria's unresolved relationship to the fascist past—the satirist trains his powerful gaze on the foibles and distortions of his social environment. His masterpiece is *Der Herr Karl* (1962, with Carl Merz; Mr. Karl), the culmination of the Austrian version of "coming-to-grips-with-the-past," a monologue of an antisocial, prejudice-ridden personality, portraying a special type. By rigorously localizing character and events, Qualtinger expands their significance far beyond their narrow boundaries. Her Karl has become the highly politicized image of the abysmally vacuous apolitical European. Moral indifference, exploitation of women, treachery, incipient pyromania, aestheticistic antihumanism, political prostitution, unprincipled opportunism: these are the counts of the verdict, an X-ray picture of modern mass man.

Despite their opposing stances as art-for-art's-sake and committed writers, Artmann and Qualtinger have more in common than meets the eye trained only in textual analysis. This common ground is provided by the Austrian social milieu.

A social critic like Qualtinger, Herbert Eisenreich (1925–1986) also represents continuity in Austrian literature because of his ties with Doderer and Gütersloh. His objective narratives display a highly original style.

The impulses emanating from the "Viennese Group," of which Artmann had once been a member, brought about a sharp caesura in Austrian letters. Writers like Friedrich Achleitner (b. 1930), Konrad Bayer (1932–1964), Gerhard Rühm (b. 1930), and Oswald Wiener (b. 1935) have been associated with this group; others, like Friederike MAYRÖCKER, Andreas Okopenko (b. 1930), and Ernst JANDL pursue comparable goals. By using folk literature, the regional dialect, and the props of the provinces, they attempt to break open the patterns of folk ideology. Seeking encouragement from Baroque, EXPRESSIONIST, and DADAIST sources, they engage in linguistic experiments whose aim it is to provoke and reorient their readerships. In the first, at least, they seem to succeed.

The novels by Thomas BERNHARD and Gert Friedrich Jonke (b. 1946) point in a similar direction. Those of Bernhard—for example *Das Kalkwerk* (1970; *The Limeworks*, 1973)—bombard the customary modes of thinking and feeling with a barrage of tragic motifs, such as disease, insanity, agony, and death. Jonke, in *Geometrischer Heimatroman* (1969; geometric village novel), disrupts the model of the traditional provincial story.

These tendencies spill over to the city of Graz, once a stronghold of reactionary forces, where another experimental center with Peter HANDKE, Barbara Frischmuth (b. 1941), Michael Scharang (b. 1941), and Wolfgang BAUER has begun its work of reorientation. Whether the public wishes to be thus reeducated is doubtful. Rather, it seems that a radical estrangement has taken place, since many of the young authors have left Austria because they were dissatisfied with what they regarded as the conservatism and the antiprogressive spirit of the Second Republic and its society. But as the enormous success of, say, H. C. Artmann, Thomas Bernhard, and Peter Handke in Germany demonstrates, Austria's loss is the gain of a pan-German literature. If some of these Austrian authors do not want to be *Austrian* authors, so be it. Whether they stay at home or prefer to live abroad, with their help German letters (excepting East German writing), long beleaguered by nationalistic, retrograde forces, seems to be entering an antiauthoritarian, antiparochial age of maturity.

BIBLIOGRAPHY: Schoolfield, G. C., "Exercises in Brotherhood: The Recent Austrian Novel," *GQ*, 26 (1953): 228–40; Torberg, F., "Austrian Literature since 1927," *BA*, 28 (1954): 15–20; Fischer, E., *Von Grillparzer zu Kafka: Sechs Essays* (1962); Magris, C., *Der habsburgische Mythos in der österreichischen Literatur* (1966); Trommler, F., *Roman und Wirklichkeit: Musil, Broch, Roth, Doderer* (1966) *MAL* (1968–); Johnston, W. M., *The Austrian Mind: An Intellectual and Social History* 1848–1938 (1972); Janik, A., and S. Toulmin, *Wittgenstein's Vienna* (1973); Ungar, F. ed., *Handbook of Austrian Literature* (1973); Williams, C. E., *The Broken Eagle: The Politics of Austrian Literature from Empire to Anschluss* (1974); Althaus, H., *Zwischen Monarchie und Republik: Schnitzler, Kafka, Hofmannsthal, Musil* (1976); Spiel, H. ed., *Die zeitgenössische Literatur Österreichs* (1976); Aspetsberger, F., ed., *Staat und Gesellschaft in der modernen österreichischen Literatur* (1977); Branscombe, P., ed., *Austrian Life and Literature, 1780–1938* (1978); Schorske, C., *Fin-de-siècle Vienna: Politics and Culture* (1980)

—EGON SCHWARZ

Austrian Literature since 1970

In the 1970s and 1980s the discussion about whether there was a distinct Austrian literature once again flared up at international scholarly conferences. By that time, Austria had established her national identity. With most of today's Austrians demonstrating an unsentimental and pragmatic attitude toward their country, they no longer need a "spiritual"—and often artifical—concept of what constitutes Austria or is "Austrian." Unlike the post-World War II

generation, today's Austrians do not find it necessary to use the literature that is being written in their country as a tool to help establish their individuality and set them apart from the Germans. They accept the fact that, with some exceptions, most new literary work to come out of their country after World War II has been published in Germany (until recently, in the Federal Republic of Germany). They also realize that, without readers in Germany, all talk about Austrian literature would be academic, and they are pleased to know that many of the most prominent "German" writers are actually from Austria. Peter HANDKE, Thomas BERNHARD, Ernst JANDL, Friederike MAYRÖCKER, Elfriede Jelinek (b. 1946), Peter Turrini (b. 1944), Christoph Ransmayr (b. 1954), and Barbara Frischmuth (b. 1941) are just a few examples.

While it is true that many literary works that originated in Austria are connected with the country's history, there is no consensus as to history's actual role in literature. According to Claudio Magris's (b. 1939) study *Der habsburgische Mythos in der österreichischen Literatur* (1966; the Habsburg myth in Austrian literature), escapism and attempts to portray the Habsburg era as a "harmonious blend of races and cultures" (Wolf-schütz) and to glorify the myth of the supranational Austro-Hungarian Empire are predominant in Austrian literature, even after the collapse of the monarchy. Magris sees evidence of this in authors as diverse as Franz Grillparzer (1791–1872), Adalbert Stifter (1805–1868), Arthur Schnitzler (1862–1931), and Joseph ROTH.

Following Magris, the German critic Ulrich Greiner (b. 1945) also emphasizes the retrospective aspect of Austrian literature. The title of his book, *Der Tod des Nachsommers* (1979; the death of the Indian Summer), is indicative of his view. It contains an allusion to Stifter's novel *Der Nachsommer* (1857; *Indian Summer*, 1985) with its atmosphere of passivity and "political calm." Having adopted Stifter as the "grandfather of Austrian literature," Greiner sees the majority of contemporary Austrian writers displaying apolitical, ahistoric, artificial, and narcissistic attitudes. They have, in his opinion, renounced politics out of a sense of frustration and a lack of vision for their country's future. Instead, they have subscribed to an ideology of "conflict avoidance," retreating into a world of radical subjectivism, into an ivory tower of aestheticism.

Greiner's perspectives have some validity, yet they do not show the complete picture. There are indeed a number of writers in the 1970s who have rejected reality out of their conviction that it is uncertain what reality is. Examples are Peter Handke, who in his novel *Die Stunde der wahren Empfindung* (1975; *A Moment of True Feeling*, 1977) raises the question whether there is objectivity beyond human sensations. Likewise, Gerhard Roth (b. 1942), in his novels *Der groß Horizont* (1974; the great horizon) and *Ein neuer Morgen* (1976; a new morning), introduces characters who frequently experience multilayered, dreamlike realities and are incapable of living their lives firsthand. Gert Jonke (b. 1946) also, particularly in his satirical novel about the art world, *Schule der Geläfigkeit* (1977; school of dexterity), manipulates his characters between dream and reality.

While these and other writers do not deny their emphasis on subjectivisim and nonideology, many of them reject the notion that they are apolitical and lack social consciousness. On the contrary, they see themselves carrying out a revolt—albeit in the aesthetic sphere. They insist on their individuality and do not want to be part of any group or school. In H. C. Artmann's (b. 1921) terms they are "unarmed individual anarchists with an Austrian character." Artmann, to this day one of Austria's most popular writers of poetry, stresses the freedom of the "poetic act." All art is to be value-free, spontaneous, and free of public criticism.

Writing in the vein of Magris and Greiner, the Viennese critic and novelist Robert Menasse (b. 1954), in his essay "Die sozialpartnerschaftliche Ästhetik" (1990; the aesthetics of social partnership), blames the Austrian system of cooperation between government, labor, and industry in virtually all fields of economic policy, affectionately known as "social partnership," for that subgenre of literature that can indeed be seen as apolitical and antirealistic. Social partnership has, as Menasse points out correctly, been a cornerstone of Austrian politics, it has had a deep effect on public consciousness. Not surprisingly, writers are not exempt from its appeal. Social partnership has a tendency to smooth over conflict and promotes compromise and consensus among the country's main group interests. While most Austrians cherish the system for having brought about political stability and economic success, Menasse—and others—reject it as antidemocratic, and they repudiate it for fostering a "naive ideology of harmony." Unlike their colleagues in the Federal Republic of Germany where authors such as Heinrich BÖLL and Günter GRASS actively participated, as artists and citizens, in the political life of their country, Austrian writers, Menasse laments, have succumbed to the "aesthetics of social partnership," resulting in a retrogressive attitude, in a renunciation of social and political involvement.

It is difficult to refute Magris, Greiner, and Menasse altogether. However, the idea that contemporary literature in Austria, much of which has been known under labels such as "new subjectivity" or "new sensitivity," is either obsessed with the past or totally apolitical and artificial has indeed become an "undesirable cliché." For example, it does not do justice to one important movement of Austrian prose writers known as *Anti-Heimatliteratur* (antiregional literature). A diverse group of writers, some of them using dialect, they introduced a brand of literary regionalism that was not only experienced as a novelty but also created a shock effect upon its readers. While traditional regional literature as exemplified by the popular Karl Heinrich Waggerl (1897–1973) extols the virtues of rural life and stresses harmony, tranquillity, and decency, antiregional writers destroy all romantic myths of sweet landscapes and strong peasants. On the country, they give the theme of rural life a savage and ironic twist that has no precedent.

On the basis of his first novel, *Schöne Tage* (1974; *Beautiful Days*, 1976), Franz Innerhofer (b. 1944) became the most prominent exponent of *Anti-Heimatliteratur*, but he is not the only one. Elfriede Jelinek's *Die Liebhaberinnen* (1975; *The Brassiere Factory*, 1987), Michael Scharang's (b. 1941) *Der Sohn des Landarbeiters* (1976; the son of a farm worker), and Gernot Wolfgruber's (b. 1944) *Herrenjahre* (1976; living like a lord) also stress the negative personal and social aspects of the region and take an aggressive attitude. Hans Lebert (b. 1919), Gerhard Fritsch (1924–1969), and George Saiko (1892–1962) are forerunners of this movement. Other writers who have portrayed their country in a critical fashion are Helmut Zenker (b. 1949), Josef Haslinger (b. 1955), and Brigitte Schwaiger (b. 1949), whose novel *Wie kommt das Salz ins Meer* (1977; *Why Is There Salt in the Sea?*, 1988) became an international best-seller.

In the 1980s no clear trends can be observed in Austrian literature. Many writers who, over the years, have become household words, are still productive: Jandl, Handke, Roth, Jelinek, Frischmuth, to name just a few. A number of new talents have emerged though. With his novel *Die letzte Welt* (1988; *The Last World*, 1990), which is based on Ovid's *Metamorphoses* and has been acclaimed as a modern masterpiece throughout Europe and the U.S., Christoph Ransmayr (b. 1954) created a huge best-seller. Alois Brandstetter (b. 1938), Peter ROSEI, Josef Winkler (b. 1953), Klaus Hoffer (b. 1942), and Julian Schutting (b. 1937) have gained increased prominence in the literary scene of their country.

In the world of theater, Thomas Bernhard together with Peter Turrini, Felix Mitterer (b. 1948), and Wolfgang BAUER are the dominant figures. Turrini and Mitterer are social critics who have outraged their audiences many times but whose plays have become important features on the contemporary stage and on television. Bauer, whose celebrity results from his early unconventional plays *Magic Afternoon* (1968; title in English) and *Change* (1969; title in English), has to this day remained faithful to his message: Desiring directness, immediacy, and naturalness, we all suffer from alienation in a characterless society. Bernhard's stormy relationship with his native country culminated in controversy over his will. Banning the sale of his books and prohibiting all performances of his plays in Austria, he sent a final signal of his animosity toward his native country, with which all of his writing was closely involved. With his final play, *Heldenplatz* (1988; heroes' square), which deals with the *Anschluß, Hitler's annexation of Austria in* 1938, and its repercussions on the life of an Austrian Jewish family, Bernhard created an unprecedented outcry. Focusing on Austrian complicity in the events of 1938, and dispelling the myth of Austrian innocence, the play touched the nation's sore spot.

Coming to terms with the past, something largely ignored in Austria, became a hot topic during the 1980s. Peter Henisch (b. 1943), Elisabeth Reichart (b. 1953), Gerald SZYSZKOWITZ, and Erich Hackl (b. 1954) are in the forefront of those writers who successfully attempted to address issues that had been suppressed until the time of the 1986 presidential elections that brought Kurt Waldheim to power. *Die kleine Figur meines Vaters* (1987; *Negatives of My Father*, 1990) by Henisch, *Puntigam oder Die Kunst des Vergessens* (1988; *Puntigam or The Art of Forgetting*, 1990) by Szyszkowitz, and *Abschied von Sidonie* (1989; *Farewell Sidonia*, 1991) by Hackl, candid accounts of the years in Austria between 1938 and 1945, have appeared in American editions.

Contemporary Austrian poetry, largely ignored by the reading public, is characterized by many lines of development. Traditional, experimental, and postexperimental writings have coexisted for many decades. In addition to Jandl, Mayröker, and Artmann, some of those who have maintained their reputation as the leading poets are Ilse Aichinger (b. 1921), Christine Busta (1915–1987), Erich Fried (1921–1988), Kurt Klinger (b. 1928), Alfred Kolleritsch (b. 1931), also the editor of Austria's leading literary journal, *manuskripte*, Doris Mühringer (b. 1920), and Gerhard Rüm (b. 1930).

Even though many of Austria's contemporary writers feel alienated from their native country, most of them want to be *Austrian writers*. Literature has traditionally taken a backseat in Austria compared to music and the performing arts. Nevertheless, the country's literary scene remains vibrant and vital. Having received much international acclaim, Austrian literature has also found increasing recognition as a unique entity.

BIBLIOGRAPHY: Greiner, U., *Der Tod des Nachsommers: Aufsätze, Porträts, Kritiken zur österreichischen Gegenwartsliteratur* (1979); Best, A. and H. Wolfschütz, eds., *Modern Austrian Writing: Literature and Society after 1945* (1980); Weber, N., *Das gesellschaftlich Vermittelte der Romane österreichischer Schriftsteller seit 1970* (1980); Polheim, K. K., ed. *Literature aus Österreich. Österreichische Literatur: Ein Bonner Symposion* (1981); Adel, K., *Aufbruch und Tradition: Einführung in die österreichische Literatur seit 1945* (1982); Bartsch, K., et. al., eds., *Für und wider eine österreichische Literatur* (1982); Zeman, H., ed., *Studien zur österreichischen Erzählliteratur der Gegenwart* (1982); Aspetsberger, F. and H. Lengauer, eds., *Zeit ohne Manifeste? Zur Literatur der siebziger Jahre in Österreich* (1987); Bormann, A. von, ed., *Sehnsuchtsangst: Zur österreichischen Literatur der Gegenwart* (1987); Daviau, D. G., ed. *Major Figures of Contemporary Austrian Literature* (1987); McVeigh, J., *Kontinuität und Vergangenheitsbewältigung in der österreichischen Literatur nach 1945* (1988); Hardin, J. and D. G. Daviau eds., *DLB:Austrian Fiction Writers after 1914* (1989); Zeman, H., ed., *Die österreichische Literatur: Ihr Profit von der Jahrhundertwende bis zur Gegenwart (1880–1980)* (2 vols., 1989); Menasse, R., *Die sozialpartnerschaftliche Ästhetik: Essays zum österreichischen Geist* (1990); "Special Issue: The Current Literary Scene in Austria," *MAL*, 23, 3–4 (1990)

—JÜRGEN KOPPENSTEINER

AVAR LITERATURE

See North Caucasian Literatures

AWOONOR, Kofi

(formerly George Awoonor-Williams) Ghanaian poet, novelist, dramatist, critic, and folklorist (writing in English), b. 13 March 1935, Wheta

A. attended the University of Ghana and upon graduation became a research fellow and lecturer in African literature at the school's Institute of African Studies. Later he served as managing director of the Ghana Film Corporation and as an editor of the Ghanaian literary review *Okyeame*. In 1967 he studied language and literature in England. From there he went to the U.S., where he continued his literary studies. A. returned to Ghana in 1975 and took up a position as chairman of the Department of English at Cape Coast Univeristy. He was arrested by the military government and detained for nine months in 1976 for allegedly aiding an officer who was planning a coup d'état.

During his student years in London, A. wrote several radio plays for the BBC. While only two of these plays have been published—*Ancestral Power* and *Lament*, in *Short African Plays* (ed. C. Pieterse, 1972)—they are important pieces in terms of the traditional imagery A. has consistently employed.

Despite his studies abroad, A.'s work has very strong links with his own Ewe culture. He writes mostly in English, but retains the rhythms and tonal quality of his native language as few other contemporary African writers have done.

Primarily through his poetry, A. has established himself as one of the most significant contemporary African writers. His first two books of poetry, *Rediscovery* (1964) and *Night of My Blood* (1971), show a powerful progression from a fascination with his roots, through an uncertain poetic and cultural synthesis with the West, to a voice that is confidently his own. More than any other western-African poet, with the possible exceptions of Christopher OKIGBO

and Wole SOYINKA, A. has succeeded in transcending the raw tensions of culture conflict. His poetry should be read as a series of attempts to find in the history and poetry of his people correlatives to his own personal anguish as a modern African. Poems that serve to accentuate the anguish and give definition to the progression may appear to be difficult, or simply uneven and rough, when removed from this context.

In both form and imagery A.'s poetry has been heavily influenced by the Ewe dirge. According to traditional Ewe beliefs, those who have just died and are entering another existence represent potential danger to those left behind, for the physical loss interrupts the continuity of society and threatens it with dissolution. Yet good may also come out of a death, for a successful transition ends with the dead individual becoming an ancestral being who can be a beneficial force in the community. The purpose of the Ewe dirge is to aid the individual in making this transition.

For A., the dirge becomes symbolic not only of an individual and societal process but also of the poet's passage from insufficiency to fulfillment, from chaos to order, from alienation to integration. Death and anguish pervade his poetry as mediating agents that force the continual restructuring, refocusing, and revitalizing of individual and communal order. In effect, A. explores the relationship between contemporary society and traditional myth and ritual.

A.'s novel, *This Earth, My Brother* (1971), is an allegorical exploration of the ideas he developed in his poetry. Influenced by James JOYCE no less than by the Ewe dirge, this highly lyrical novel is a re-creation of an Ewe funeral celebration. Alternating poetic and prose sections, A. writes of the anguish of a young African lawyer who ritually purifies his society, carrying the weight of its corruption with him into his own death.

In *Ride Me, Memory* (1973), a collection of poetry he published before returning to Ghana, A. looks at his sojourn in America. This examination is accomplished through a series of incisive images presented in the manner of traditional African praise and abuse poetry—the types of poetry through which the poet-priest could criticize the politically and socially powerful. Irony is present in many of his earlier works, but nowhere is it as pervasive or well controlled as in this collection.

Since his imprisonment A. has become more directly involved in the politics of Ghana, and this involvement is clearly reflected in his most recent collection of poetry, *The House by the Sea* (1978). The title is an ironic reference to the old slave castle (originally a fort, but still referred to as a "castle") in which he was imprisoned and a metaphysical reference to a place where he sees all his people held captive. In fact, the magic of these poems lies in the manner he has transfigured the "I" of the personal experience of imprisonment to the "we" of all humanity.

A. has shown a remarkable accomplishment in leading us into the world of the poet-priest and the African dirge, where the gaps between man and man, as well as those between man and his gods, must be continually confronted and bridged.

FURTHER WORKS: *Breast of the Earth: A Study of African Culture and Literature* (1973); *Ewe Poetry* (1973); *Until the Morning After: Selected Poems* (1987); *Ghana: A Political History From Pre-European to Modern Times* (1990); *Comes the Voyager at Last: A Tale of Return to Africa* (1992)

BIBLIOGRAPHY: Moore, G., "The Imagery of Death in African Poetry," *AfricaL*, 38 (1968): 57–70; Theroux, P., "Six Poets," in

Beier, U., ed., *Introduction to African Literature* (1970): 110–31; Priebe, R., "Escaping the Nightmare of History: The Development of a Mythic Consciousness in West African Literature," *ArielE*, 4, 2 (1973): 55–67; Moore, G., *Twelve African Poets* (1980); Priebe, R., *Myth, Realism and the West African Writer* (1988)

—RICHARD PRIEBE

'AWWĀD, Tawfīq Yūsuf

Lebanese novelist, poet, dramatist, and essayist, b. 28 Nov. 1911, Bhirsaf; d. 16 April 1989, Lebanon

A. was a well-known Lebanese literary figure and a diplomat. He got his primary education in Bhirsaf, a village in Mount Lebanon. In 1923 he moved to Beirut to study at St. Joseph's University, where his literary talents became apparent. A Catholic publishing house solicited him to translate two novels from French into Arabic. He accepted on a condition that he would sign only his initials on the translation, because he wanted the first published work signed with his full name to be of his own creation. A. worked as a journalist and contributed a great deal to the literary scene until 1946 when he was appointed as the consul of Lebanon to Argentina. He then worked in several diplomatic positions in Lebanon and abroad until he retired in 1975. A. died in 1989, a victim of the Lebanese civil war.

A.'s literary corpus, though meagre in number, is varied and rich in genre and subject matter. His first collection of short stories, *Al-sabī al-a'raj* (1936; the lame boy), was well received in the literary circles at that time. A.'s writing was immediately acclaimed as that of a social reformer, and his literary techniques as innovative in the methods of storytelling. A.'s subject matter is derived from his immediate surroundings depicting an exploitative upper class, the tyranny of a patriarchal society and corrupt clergy, the effects of modernization on traditional values, urban versus rural beliefs, and the oppressed condition of women. Although A.'s style suffers sometimes from authorial intrusion, he nevertheless experimented with new literary techniques, by using first-person narrative voice as opposed to the traditionally omniscient narrator; and by employing a story within a story, a technique that goes back to *A Thousand and One Nights*; also by manipulating time and flashbacks.

A.'s novel Al-raghīf (1939; a loaf of bread) shows his sensitivity and his internalization of the historical period he had witnessed as a child, mainly the Ottoman occupation and the famine that struck Lebanon during World War I. A. focuses in this novel on three major issues, the bread that every individual is entitled to have, the liberation from Ottoman rule, and an Arab identity for Lebanon. The novel is divided into five chapters, each of which represents a stage in Arab revolt against the Ottomans. These stages follow the development of a spike of grain: the soil, the seed, the rain, the spike of grain, and the harvest. A.'s artistic success in this novel lies in his ability to transform a purely Lebanese setting into an Arab revolt.

Tawāhīn Bayrūt (1972; Death in Beirut, 1976) is a prophetic novel, for it lays bare most of the issues contributing to the outbreak of the Lebanese civil war in 1975. It takes place in Beirut after the defeat of 1967, and its main characters are university students

demonstrating and demanding a better-equipped national institution, a firmer stand against Israel especially after its attack on the Lebanese international airport in 1968, and the elimination of sectarianism as a major element in Lebanon's political system. Tamima, the heroine of the novel, acts as a sounding board for the revolutionary ideas tested in the novel. Being a woman of a lower class and a Shi'ite from the south, Tamima's aspirations and actions for self-realization and freedom are doomed to failure. A.'s well-orchestrated novel with his clear vision for a better future for Lebanon, and his perception of the contradictory tendencies of human nature, heralded him to be a master in the novel's art form.

While working as a diplomat, A. stopped publishing but never stopped writing. After eighteen years of being away from the literary scene, A. published *Al-sā'ih wa-al-turjumān* (1962; the tourist and the interpreter), which won him the Lebanese prize of the Society's Book's Friends for best play. The philosophical dialogue in this play takes place in the Ba'alabak ruins in Lebanon between the tourist representing the search for knowledge and the interpreter representing the documentation of history. In 1973 A. published a collection of poems, Qawāfil al-zamān (caravans of time), two-line poems in which he followed the traditional patterns of Arabic rhyme and meter. A. also experimented with the prose poem in *Mansiyyāt* (1985; forgotten pieces).

A.'s contribution to the Lebanese intellectual atmosphere in particular and to Arabic literature in general is undeniable. While the Egyptian "New School" in the 1920s and 1930s was advocating new approaches to literature, A. was already experimenting with fresh narrative techniques in Lebanon. His critical articles on different genres and literary figures attest to his wide range of interest in the literary sphere. It was no surprise when UNESCO in 1974 chose him as one of the world's literary figures representing the spirit of his age. The organization also recommended that his entire oeuvre be translated into different languages.

FURTHER WORKS: *Qamīs al-sūf* (1937); *Al-'adhāra* (1944); *Fursān al-kalām* (1963); *Ghubār al-ayyām* (1963); *Matar al-saqī* (1982); *Hisād al-'umr* (1983)

BIBLIOGRAPHY: Allen, R., *The Arabic Novel* (1982): 52–55; Allen, R., ed., *Modern Arabic Literature* (1987): 61–65; Cooke, M., *War's Other Voices: Women Writers on the Lebanese Civil War* (1987), 89; Accad, E., *Sexuality and War: Literary Masks of the Middle East* (1990): 99–110

—SABAH GHANDOUR

AYALA, Francisco

Spanish novelist, short-story writer, essayist, and sociologist, b. 16 Mar. 1906, Granada

After receiving a law degree from the University of Madrid in 1929, A. spent the following year studying political philosophy and sociology in Germany. In 1931 he received a doctorate in law from the University of Madrid; from 1932 until the outbreak of the civil war he taught law there. In 1937 he served the Spanish Republic as a member of its diplomatic legation in Prague. Since the end of the Spanish Civil War he has lived in Buenos Aires (1939–50), in

Puerto Rico (1950–58), in New York (1958–66), in Chicago (1966–73), and since 1973 in both New York and Madrid.

In 1925 the young A. published his first novel, *Tragicomedia de un hombre sin espíritu* (tragicomedy of a man without a spirit), a creative reworking of the themes and style of Cervantes. Favorably received by Spanish critics, this book was followed by *Historia de un amanecer* (1926; tale of a dawn), a less successful novel. A.'s next narrative works, *El boxeador y un ángel* (1929; the boxer and an angel) and *Cazador en el alba* (1930; hunter at dawn), reflect the influence of the literary vanguard of the period. After *Cazador en el alba* A. abandoned fiction for fourteen years, feeling that imaginative literature, at least as he had practiced it, lacked seriousness and meaning.

With the publication of "El Hechizado" (1944; "The Bewitched," 1950), a short story that received high praise from BORGES and others, A. returned to fiction a much more mature, almost completely different writer. "El Hechizado"—a baroque work, labyrinthine in atmosphere and perspective—satirizes King Carlos II, the 17th-c. Spanish monarch, and thus, obliquely, state bureaucracies of the 20th c.

As a novelist A. is best known for *Muertes de perro* (1958; *Death as a Way of Life*, 1964) and *El fondo del vaso* (1962; the bottom of the glass), both set in the same imaginary Spanish American "republic"—in *Muertes de perro* under a dictatorship, in *El fondo del vaso* after the fall of the tyrant; significantly, nothing essential in the moral substance of the "republic" has changed.

A.'s narrative and essayistic works are marked by great diversity in both content and style. The author's profound reflections on man's moral nature as well as on his relation to society and to the cosmos distinguish his work and provide it with an underlying and continuing unity. In A., the artist and the concerned intellectual, the creative and the critical impulses, fuse in rare and brilliant equilibrium.

FURTHER WORKS: *Indagactión del cinema* (1929); *El derecho social en la constitución de la República española* (1932); *El pensamiento vivo de Saavedra Fajardo* (1941); *El problema del liberalismo* (1941); *Historia de la libertad* (1942); *Oppenheimer* (1942); *Razón del mundo* (1944); *Histrionismo y representación* (1944); *Los políticos* (1944); *Una doble experiencia: España e Italia* (1944); *Jovellanos* (1945); *Ensayo sobre la libertad* (1945); *Tratado de sociología* (1947); *La cabeza del cordero* (1949); *El cine, arte y espectáculo* (1949; enlarged ed. of *Indagación del cinema*); *Los usurpadores* (1949; *Usurpers*, 1987); *La invención del "Quljote"* (1950); *Introducción a las ciencias sociales* (1952); *Ensayos de sociología política* (1952); *Derechos de la persona individual para una sociedad de masas* (1953); *Historia de macacos* (1955); *El escritor en la sociedad de masas* (1956); *Breve teoría de la traducción* (1956); *La crisis actual de la enseñanza* (1958); *La integración social en América* (1958); *Tecnología y libertad* (1959); *De este mundo y el otro* (1963); *Realidad y ensueño* (1963); *El as de Bastos* (1963); *España, a la fecha* (1965); *De raptos, violaciones y otras inconveniencias* (1966); *Reflexiones sobre la estructura narrativa* (1970); *El "Lazarillo" reexaminado* (1971); *El jardín de las delicias* (1971); *El escritor y su imagen* (1975)

BIBLIOGRAPHY: Ellis, K., *El arte narrativo de F. A.* (1964); Ellis, K., "Cervantes and A.'s *El rapto*: The Art of Reworking a Story," *PMLA*, 84 (1969): 14–19; Irizarry, E., *Teoría y creación literaria en F. A.* (1971); Hiriart, R. H., *Los recursos técnicos en la novelística de F. A.* (1972); Amorós, A., *Bibliografía de F. A.* (1973); Irizarry, E., *F. A.* (1977); Richmond, C., Introduction to F. A., *Usurpers* (1987): vii-xiii

—CHARLES L. KING

AYBEK

(pseud. of Musa Tashmuhämmäd-oghli) Uzbek poet and novelist, b. 10 Jan. 1905, Tashkent; d. 1 July 1968, Tashkent

A. studied at the Institute of National Economy in Leningrad and at the economics department of the Central Asian State University in Tashkent (1925–30), where he subsequently taught political economy (1930–35). Later he taught at the Pushkin Institute of Language and Literature in Tashkent (1935–37). A. was president of the Uzbek Writers' Union from 1945 until 1950, when he lost this position as a result of criticism by the Communist Party. A. was the editor-in-chief of the academic journal *Ozbek tili vä ädäbiyati* from 1958 until his death.

A.'s earliest poems appeared in the volume *Tuyghulär* (1926; sentiments). In his poems A. uses images of the sun, the moon, stars, birds, and flowers, and he identifies his own moods with those of nature. In his lyrics, spring represents joy, happiness, love, creative aspirations, and freedom. Autumn, on the other hand, is a time of sadness, of slowly approaching gloom, of oppressive silence and captivity. Because it is not easy for a poet to talk about personal sadness openly in Soviet Uzbekistan, A. uses such symbols and images to describe his more melancholy moods. Another predominant group of images in A.'s lyric poetry is associated with women.

A.'s treatment of life, truth, and the universe reveals his intellectual side. At first, in the poems A. wrote in the 1920s, he tried to define life and his place in it. In his last lyric poems, however, he admits that he has not been able to decipher the meaning of life or solve the riddles of the universe. A. was the target of much Soviet criticism for writing personal and lyrical poems that were considered pessimistic and under the influence of symbolism.

During the early and mid-1930s, owing to political pressure, A. turned from writing lyric verse to translating classics of world literature—such as Goethe's *Faust*, Dante's *Divine Comedy*, Byron's *Cain*, and Pushkin's *Eugene Onegin*—into Uzbek (via Russian).

In his first novel, *Qutlugh qan* (1940; sacred blood), A. describes the heroic revolt of Central Asian peoples against tsarist rule in 1916. By naming the protagonist of this novel Yolchi (one on the way toward a specific goal) A. idealizes an unknown patriot who sacrifices his life for his country. In his second novel, *Nävaiy* (1944; Nävaiy), A. portrays the inner life of the Central Asian classical poet Mir Alisher Nävaiy (1441–1501) while drawing the attention of his readers to the glorious cultural heritage of Uzbeks in the 15th c.

Although A. also wrote ideological and didactic poems under political pressure between 1930 and 1959, his real contribution lies in his lyric poems, in which he creates a distinct poetic language and an individual world of his own ideals and artistic values. He will also be remembered for having developed the historical novel in Uzbek literature.

FURTHER WORKS: *Kongil näyläari* (1929); *Mäsh'älä* (1932); *Altin vädiydän shäbädälär* (1949); *Nur qidirib* (1957); *Quyash quaräymäs* (1959); *Balälik* (1963); *Ulugh yol* (1967); *Äsärlär* (10 vols., 1967–1975); *Tolä äsärlär toplämi* (19 vols., 1975f.)

BIBLIOGRAPHY: Allworth, E., *Uzbek Literary Politics* (1964): passim; Allworth, E., *Central Asia: A Century of Russian Rule* (1967), passim; Allworth, E., *Uzbek Literary Politics* (1964), passim; Allworth, E., ed., *Central Asia: A Century of Russian Rule* (1967, rev. ed., 1989), passim

—TIMUR KOCAOGLU

AYCKBOURN, Alan

English playwright, b. 12 Apr. 1939, London

Although A. never attended university, his volume of work with its ordinary characters has made him England's most successful modern playwright. He has been the artistic director of the Scarborough Theatre since 1970, produced radio drama for the BBC, directed for the Royal National Theatre, and been the Cameron Macintosh Professor of Contemporary Theatre at St. Catherine's College, Oxford. Yet it is for his comedies of the middle class that he is best known.

In spite of his massive output of popular work, the critics have not treated A. kindly, especially in his early years, declaring his work to be fluff with no serious intent. However, there is much in A.'s writing to commend. The struggles into which he places his characters are identifiable life situations, and many of his characters' concerns are ours. In *Absent Friends* (1974), for example, a group of longtime acquaintances gather to comfort Colin, who has lost his fiancée in a drowning accident. But this familiar scenario is transformed as it is not Colin who needs consoling, but the others. Each in his or her own way is grieving for a failed marriage, for lost chances, for shattered dreams. Colin is the catalyst who forces his friends to face their losses, though his efforts to help each confront truth and find peace are not appreciated.

Marriage in all its permutations is the recurring motif in A.'s work. *The Norman Conquests* (1975), a trilogy each in two acts, presents three couples, two of which are married and the third in a relationship of long-standing. In each play the women perform the dominating roles, manipulating their companions like puppets. Nevertheless, it is Norman who has set the action in motion with his amorous shenanigans. *Round and Round the Garden* is the best of the three, being the most innately funny and using the most verbal humor, in contrast to A.'s usual technique of emphasis on physical humor.

Another common technique in A.'s plays is the absent character. The concept is implied, of course, in the titles of *Absent Friends* and *Invisible Friends* (1991), but there are others who, though absent, still exert a presence. In *Absent Friends* Marge's husband Gordon has been kept home by illness, but his repeated pleas for help via telephone calls allows him to intrude into every scene. Similarly, in *The Norman Conquests* Mother, an invalid tucked away upstairs in her room, presides over the family dynamics being enacted below by being the reason the couples have gathered.

A.'s comedy often has a macabre twist to it, such as in *Absurd Person Singular* (1974). Placing the same three couples in each of their kitchens on three successive Christmases, he tricks the audience into laughing at potentially tragic situations. In act 2, Eva is trying to commit suicide, and the variety of her efforts, in spite of

four other people bustling about the kitchen ignoring her state of mind while intent on assisting with numerous household chores, is hilarious, until sudden realization of exactly what is taking place sets in. In getting his audience to laugh, A. has indicted thoughtlessness and insensitivity in both his characters and in us.

More recently A. has been able to move away from criticisms that his female characters in particular are mere stereotypes, as in his creation of *Woman in Mind* (1986). Susan steps on a garden rake, giving herself a nasty whack on the head which prompts illusions of an ideal family to replace her real life burdens. Eventually the fantasy overtakes the real, although whether this is caused by her injury or her dissatisfaction with her life is unclear. And to her consternation, the fantasy soon becomes tarnished as her fictional family begins to reveal very real flaws. This woman is certainly not to be admired, for she is rude and abrasive, yet the audience cannot dismiss her completely because her each of families match her unpleasant trait for unpleasant trait. Susan becomes the most defined of A.'s women, whose life circumstances dictate their means of coping.

A.'s work is not a political treatise but an exposure of modern society and the polite fictions which oil its wheels. He focuses on people with all their foibles facing situations which confound them. In doing so, he has documented our times.

FURTHER WORKS: *Relatively Speaking* (1968); *Ernie's Incredible Illucinations* (1969); *Mixed Doubles*(1970); *Countdown* (1970); *How the Other Half Loves* (1971); *Time and Time Again* (1973); *Absent Friends* (1975); *The Norman Conquests* (1975); *Absurd Person Singular* (1977); *Bedroom Farce* (1977); *Just between Ourselves* (1978); *Ten Times Table* (1978); *Joking Apart* (1979); *Sisterly Feelings* (1981); *Taking Steps* (1981); *Season's Greetings* (1982); *Suburban Strains* (1982); *Confusions* (1983); *Way Upstream* (1983); *A Chorus of Disapproval* (1985); *Intimate Exchanges* (1986); *Woman in Mind* (1986); *A Small Family Business* (1987); *Henceforward . . .* (1988); *Me, Myself, and I* (1989); *Mr. A.'s Amazing Maze Plays* (1989); *Man of the Moment* (1990); *The Revenger's Comedies* (1991); *A Cut in Rates* (1991); *Time of My Life* (1993); *Wildest Dreams* (1993); *Communicating Doors* (1995); *Dreams from a Summerhouse* (1997); *Things We Do for Love* (1998)

BIBLIOGRAPHY: Billington, M., *A. A.* (1983); Blistein, E. M., "A. A.: Few Jokes, Much Comedy," *MD*, 26 (1983): 26-35; Page, M., "The Serious Side of A. A.," *MD*, 26 (1983): 36-46; Dukore, B. F., *A. A.: A Casebook* (1991); Kalson, A. E., *Laughter in the Dark: The Plays of A. A.*(1993); Fisher, J., "A. A.," in Demastes, W. W., ed., *British Playwrights, 1956-1995* (1996): 15-27

—BEVERLY BRONSON SMITH

AYMÉ, Marcel

French novelist, dramatist, and short-story writer, b. 29 March 1902, Joigny; d. 14 Oct. 1967, Paris

A. was raised in rural Franche-Comté by relatives after his mother's death when he was two. He attended schools in Dôle and Besançon, completing studies in 1919. After military service with occupation forces in Germany, A. held such diversified jobs as bank clerk, insurance agent, movie extra, and bricklayer. In 1925 he turned to journalism; one of his specialties was crime reporting.

A six-month illness put an end to this vocation, but during his convalescence he turned to creative writing and, late in 1926, his first novel, *Brûlebois* (Brûlebois), was published. The novel, although not a great success, did bring him a minor literary award, and his writing career was launched. Thereafter he produced at least one volume per year, either a novel or a collection of short stories, until 1940. Perhaps his first substantial recognition came in 1929 with the novel *La table-aux-crevés* (*The Hollow Field*, 1933), for which he received the Théophraste Renaudot award. In 1933 *La jument verte* (*The Green Mare*, 1955) was reviewed very favorably. Each of the aforementioned novels portrays unadorned rural life and simple people struggling with misfortune, poverty, and drabness. A.'s early work was not, however, limited to regional settings. Several of his novels are set in Paris, but still with the focus on the common man, with his frailties and frequent victimization by an indeterminate fate. There are many touches of humor in these early novels, but this side of A. seems to have come forth more noticeably in his short stories, the first of which appeared in 1932 in the collection *Le puits aux images* (pictures in the well).

Although A. never totally abandoned regional settings there is a definite trend toward urban settings after the mid 1930s. Fantasy and mordant satire became greater during the years of the Nazi occupation—a twofold escape from possible censorship and from the bitterness and horror of that period. A.'s use of the miraculous, occasionally found also in earlier works, almost always follows the same pattern: he establishes a fantastic premise and then develops the plot in an otherwise completely logical manner. These initial premises may involve metamorphoses, miraculous powers, absurd sequences of time and place, multiplicity of a character, and other situations that defy logic. A.'s work, however, is never to be confused with that of the SURREALISTS or the absurdists.

Another side of A.'s writing is shown in his children's tales. They were written in the 1930s and published in 1939 in the collection *Les contes du chat perché* (*The Wonderful Farm*, 1951). They are delightfully fanciful accounts of two little girls and their experiences with various animals, all of whom, of course, talk to the girls in perfectly logical fashion.

Two more collections of short stories and three novels were published after the war, but A. mostly wrote for the theater during these years. Although he had earlier tried writing drama, it was not until 1944 that his first play was performed. Nine more plays were to follow in the last two decades of his life. *Clérambard* (1950; *Clérambard*, 1958) was a particularly popular success, both in Paris and in an off-Broadway run in New York during the 1957–58 season. In this play and in several others A. continues his satire and the use of the miraculous. He also collaborated on the adaptation for the movies of several of his own novels and short stories.

He died in 1967 where he had lived and created for so long, in his home in Montmartre.

FURTHER WORKS: *Aller retour* (1927); *Les jumeaux du diable* (1928); *La rue sans nom* (1930); *Le vaurien* (1931); *Le nain* (1934); *Maison basse* (1935); *Le moulin de la Sourdine* (1936; *The Secret Stream*, 1953); *Gustalin* (1937); *Derrière chez Martin* (1938); *Silhouette du scandale* (1938); *Le boeuf clandestin* (1939); *La belle image* (1941; *The Second Face*, 1951); *Travelingue* (1941; *The Miraculous Barber*, 1951); *Le passe-muraille* (1943); *La vouivre*

(1943); *Vogue la galère* (1944); *Le chemin des écoliers* (1946; *The Transient Hour*, 1948); *Lucienne et le boucher* (1947); *Le vin de Paris* (1947); *Uranus* (1948; *The Barkeep of Blémont*, 1950); *Le confort intellectuel* (1949); *En arrière* (1950); *Autres contes du chat perché* (1950; *More about the Wonderful Farm*, 1954); *La tête des autres* (1952); *Les quatre vérités* (1954); *Les oiseaux de lune* (1956; *Moonbirds*, 1959); *La mouche bleue* (1957); *Les tiroirs de l'inconnu* (1960; *The Conscience of Love*, 1962); *Louisiane* (1961); *Les maxibules* (1962); *La convention "Belzébir"* (1967). FURTHER WORKS IN ENGLISH: *Across Paris, and Other Stories* (1958); *The Proverb and Other Stories* (1961)

BIBLIOGRAPHY: Loy, J. R., "The Reality of M. A.'s World," *FR*, 28 (1954): 115–27; Voorhees, R. J., "M. A. and Moral Chaos," *The Personalist*, 39 (1958): 48–59; Temmer, M., "M. A., Fabulist and Moralist," *FR*, 35 (1962): 453–62; Brodin, D., *The Comic World of M. A.* (1964); Dumont, J. -L., *M. A. et le merveilleux* (1967); Lord, G., *The Short Stories of M. A.* (1980); Lord, G., *M. A.* (1987)

—FREDERIC M. MULLETT

AYTMATOV, Chïngïz

Kirgiz novelist, dramatist, and short-story writer (writing in Kirgiz and Russian), b. 12 Dec. 1928, Sheker

A. was a veterinarian by training and original profession, but his early stories in Kirgiz earned him a scholarship to take courses in creative writing in Moscow (1956–58). In 1959–60 he worked in Frunze as editor of *Literaturny Kirgizstan*, and in 1960–65 as correspondent of *Pravda* in Kirgizia; since 1965 he has earned a living through his writing.

A.'s works are mostly Kirgiz in theme and setting, but they deal with topics of universal human interest. He has a gift for psychological analysis and the ability to construct dramatic and believable plots. Most of A.'s works have both a Kirgiz and a Russian version (those cited here are the Russian), and in both languages he frequently evokes the color and rhythms of folk lyrics and epics of Kirgizia. His style is rich and flexible, moving from strongly visual evocations of natural beauty to careful, objective descriptions of human weaknesses.

In *Dzhamilya* (1958; Dzhamilya) A. describes how a young married woman defies society and the state to elope with her lover, the individualistic Daniar. The novel *Proshchay Gulsary!* (1966; *Farewell, Gulsary!*, 1970), whose title character is a horse, portrays the conflict of an old-guard Communist, Tanabay, who has raised Gulsary, with cynical party officials, who ultimately destroy both horse and man. *Bely parakhod* (1970; *The White Ship*, 1972, also pub. as *The White Steamship*, 1972) describes how the dreams and ideals of a boy and his grandfather are crushed by corrupt and sadistic government officials. A play, *Voskhozhdenie na Fudziamu* (1978; *The Ascent of Mount Fuji*, 1975), coauthored with the Kazakh writer Qaltay Mükhamedzhanov (b. 1928), was produced in Moscow in 1973 and in Washington, D.C. in 1975. Most of A.'s works have been made into movies in the Soviet Union.

A.'s integrity as writer and objective observer of society who follows his artistic and intellectual conscience is combined with allegiance to the Soviet state and faith in its political system concordant with his membership in the Communist Party. He has been awarded the Lenin Prize (1963), the State Prize of the U.S.S.R. (1968), and the title Hero of Socialist Work (1978), but he has not always escaped castigation for not abiding by the norms of SOCIALIST REALISM.

FURTHER WORKS: *Topolyok moi v krasnoy kosynke* (1961); *Verblyuzhy glaz* (1962); *Pervy uchitel* (1963); *Materinskoe pole* (1963); *Rannie zhuravli* (1975); *Pegy pyos, beguschy kraem morya* (1977)

BIBLIOGRAPHY: Aragon, L., "The Finest Love Story in the World," *Culture and Life*, No. 7 (1959): 39–43; Feifer, T. and G., Afterword, to C. A., *The White Steamship* (British trans., 1972): 165–88; Ginsburg, M., Introduction to C. A., *The White Ship* (1972): vii–xiii; Zhukov-Breschinsky, Z. A., *The Modern Encyclopedia of Russian and Soviet Literature*, 1 (1977): 56-64; Brown, D., *Soviet Russian Literature since Stalin* (1978): 282–84 and passim; Shneidman, N. N., "Soviet Literature at the Crossroads: The Controversial Prose of C. A.," *RLT*, 16 (1979): 244–68; Shneidman, N. N., "Bibliography of Works about C. A.," *RLT*, 16 (1979): 340–41

—SVAT SOUCEK

AZERBAIJANI LITERATURE

Azerbaijani literature in the 20th c. may be divided into two periods: the pre-1917 and the Soviet, with the 1920s serving as a transitional period.

Before the October Revolution two major literary currents dominated. One, centered around the journal *Füyüzat* (1906–7) continued the romantic and idealist traditions of the 19th c. and advocated the autonomy of art. Associated with it were the poets Abbas Sikhat (1874–1918) and Mukhamedi Khadi (1879–1920). Although romantic in spirit, Sikhat's poems contain realistic tableaux of peasant life. Khadi's moods were constantly in flux, as he went from Islamic piety to Darwinism and from nationalist exaltation to deep melancholy.

The other important literary current of the period was represented by *Molla Nasreddin* (1906–30), a weekly edited by Djalil MAMEDKULIZADE. Convinced that literature had important functions to fulfill, Mamedkulizade laid the foundations of realism in Azerbaijani fiction and poetry. His short stories are masterpieces of the satirist's art. In simple, concise language he directed pitiless scrutiny at those who perpetuated the absurdities and injustices of contemporary society. His plays, especially *Ölüler* (1909; the victims), the high point of pre-1917 Azerbaijani drama, are in the same spirit. Mamedkulizade's colleague, Mirza Alekper Sabir (1862–1911), cultivated realistic poetry. A consummate satirist, he abandoned love poetry for the stark portrayal of ordinary people and everyday problems, as in *Hophopname* (1912; hoopoe's book).

In the 1920s, after Azerbaijan had been incorporated into the new Soviet state, the Communist Party sponsored various organizations that were intended to mobilize writers behind its social and economic programs. But neither the Union of the Red Pens (1925) nor the Azerbaijani Association of Proletarian Writers (1927) was successful, and in 1932 the party established a Union of Writers for the whole country, and Azerbaijan had its branch. Under the formula of SOCIALIST REALISM, the Union tried to impose uniformity in literary values and forms, which has served as the official touchstone for successful writers down to the present.

Azerbaijani poetry in the 1920s ran the gamut from political lyrics to the avant-garde. One group advocated the autonomy of poetry and created a specific language for it. Phonetical and grammatical experiments and commitment to "pure poetry" brought these modernists close to the FUTURISTS and the constructivists. The other major movement, which eventually triumphed, stressed the social mission of literature and developed a poetic idiom close to the vernacular. Samed VURGUN, the outstanding Soviet Azerbaijani poet, extended the possibilities of traditional meter through free verse, which he considered the only means of expressing the new subject matter, created by vast social transformations. Debate over verse forms has continued, but the frame of reference has narrowed to fit the requirements of Socialist Realism.

The main themes of poetry since the 1920s reveal the extent to which literature has served social ends. Industrialization has received continuous attention, as in Vurgun's poems on the expansion of oil production at Baku. The heroes are simple laborers, who are guided by Marxist-Leninist teachings and the example of selfless Communists. Vurgun also glorified the collectivization of agriculture in such poems as "Raport" (1930; report), which described the profound changes in the patriarchal village wrought by "progressive" peasants, and "Basti" (1937; Basti), which traced the emergence of the new Soviet woman. In "Mugan" (1949; Mugan Valley) Vurgun studied the moral transformation of individuals engaged in socialist construction.

In the 1950s a kind of philosophical poetry emerged in the work of Rasul Rza (b. 1910). He investigated the inner world of his heroes. Despite its meditative nature, this poetry was rooted in the outer world and never lost sight of the fundamental aims of Communist society. Other poets wrote of romantic love and the family, but here, too, expression was often subordinated to ideology.

The 1920s were also a transitional period for Azerbaijani dramatists. The career of Husein Djavid (1882–1944) is instructive. Greatly influenced by 19th-c. Ottoman political reform, or Tanzimat, literature, he wrote romantic historical plays that glorified Islamic heroes and Azerbaijani nobles. Officially rebuked for creating "undesirable" models, he changed direction. Turning to the October Revolution for inspiration, in *Knyaz* (1929; the prince) he presented starkly contrasting social symbols in the figures of the cruel prince and the dedicated Bolshevik. A playwright whose work was more attuned to official aims was Djafar Djabarly (1899–1934). His plays provided the model of Socialist Realist drama and contained themes that became staples of the Azerbaijani theater. *Od gelini* (1928; bride of fire) tells of the struggles of the masses for freedom against the "dark forces" of Islam, and *Sevil* (1928; Sevil) deals with the emancipation of a young woman whose attitude toward herself is completely changed by revolution.

The national past has also received considerable attention. Vurgun's verse dramas dealt with traditional Azerbaijani heroes and recent ones—workers and Bolsheviks. All come from the common people, and all eventually triumph over injustice. Vurgun's finest artistic achievement was the historical drama *Vagif* (1938; Vagif), based upon the life of the 18th-c. Azerbaijani poet and statesman.

After World War II dramatists found inspiration in the building of socialism, as in *Bahar sulary* (1948; spring waters) by Ilyas Efendiev (b. 1914), in which conflict erupts between the old and the new in the village. Playwrights have also turned to psychological and domestic dramas. Efendiev, for example, has studied characters confronted by moral dilemmas. In *Atayevler ailesi* (1954; the Ataev family) he explores the reaction of the head of household, a dedicated party member, to the discovery that his home has become a base for blackmarketeers; and in *Sen hemishe menimlesen* (1965; you are always with me) he analyzes the crass egoism of his hero. In general, recent dramatists have excelled in realistic description and psychological insight, but have neglected comedy.

The most notable achievement of Soviet Azerbaijani fiction has been the creation of the novel. Broad social themes and realistic techniques have predominated. The first important novel was *Dumanly Tabriz* (4 vols., 1933–48; misty Tabriz) by Mamed Said Ordubady (1872–1950). Its subject—the struggles of the worker-revolutionary in pre-1917 Azerbaijan—became the substance of myriad novels. In *Shamo* (4 vols., 1931–68; Shamo) Suleiman Ragimov (b. 1900) described the awakening of the peasantry under the dynamic leadership of the proletariat; in *Dünya gopur* (1933; the world collapses) Alekperzade Abulhasan (b. 1906) traced the establishment of Bolshevik rule in a remote corner of Azerbaijan; and in *Apsheron* (1947; Apsheron) Mehti Gusein (1909–1965) extolled the humanity and self-sacrifice of the workers and engineers who developed the Baku oil fields. Here the image of the positive hero, the new man of Soviet society, assumed definite contours.

Many novels have dealt with fundamental ethical problems of Soviet society. In *Giulshen* (1949; Giulshen), by Ali Veliev (b. 1901), the heroine is the new Soviet woman who drives herself and her brigade to increase cotton production. In the process she converts an old peasant woman from her individualist ways to socialist competition. In *Büyük dayag* (1958; the great support) Mirza Ibrahimov (b. 1911) analyzes the relationship between the leader and the masses, and in *Körpüsalanlar* (1961; the bridge builders) Ilyas Efendiev allows his heroes to lead independent spiritual lives as a preparation for difficult moral choices.

Since the 1930s Azerbaijani literature has followed the general Soviet pattern in both subject matter and technique. Russian poets and novelists in particular have been extolled as examples worthy of emulation. The danger that Azerbaijani literature would become indistinguishable from officially approved stereotypes has, therefore, been ever present. To safeguard a literature that reflects the specific character of the Azerbaijani people, Azerbaijani writers must look beyond the Soviet Union and draw fully upon the experience of contemporary European letters.

In the 1970s and 1980s, Azerbaijani literature experienced significant changes. Writers, who since the 1930s and been obliged to adhere to general patterns of Soviet creativity, turned to Azerbaijani history and classical literature as primary sources of inspiration. Indicative of the revival of national consciousness were Sabir Rustemkhanli's poem, *Sagh ol, ana dilim* (1982; Thank you, mother language), which extolled the virtues of language in preserving national identity, and Aziza Jafarzade's novel, *Baku 1501* (1981), which explored Azerbaijan's historical individuality. The collapse of the Soviet Union in 1991 gave impetus to the national current in literature as writers linked Azerbaijan's cultural heritage to those of Turkey and Turkic Central Asia. Poetry maintained its primacy as the vehicle for expressing traditional values, as in Fikret Goja's (dates n.a.) *Azarbaijan* (1991), which spoke of struggle and hardship, but expressed confidence in the nation's future.

An Azerbaijani literature also exists in Iran, where poets and prose writers have used Persian and Turkish as well as Azerbaijani. Notable works have been produced, such as the novel *Gorkhulu*

Tehran (1927; sinister Tehran), a dissection of the mores of high society by Mushfik Kazimi (b. 1901), and the short poetic masterpieces of everyday life by Mehmed Husein Shehriyar, who turned colloquial Azerbaijani into a beautiful literary language. His long lyric poem, *Heydar Babaya salam* (2. vols., 1954-66; Greetings to Heydar Baba), has become famous throught the Turkic world. Azerbaijani literary activitiy in Iran was limited after World War II for political reasons, but since the Islamic revolution in 1979 a notable revival has occurred. Tabriz is the center of a vigorous literary life, where poetry predominates and varied influences from Azeraijan and Turkey shape social and cultural themes.

BIBLIOGRAPHY: Brands, H. W., "Aspekte der aserbaidschanischen Gegenwartsliteratur," *WI*, 8 (1963): 177–92; Bennigsen, A., and C. Lemercier-Quelquejay, *La presse et le mouvement national chez les Musulmans de Russie avant 1920* (1964): 104–33; Caferoglu, A., "Die aserbeidschanische Literatur," in *Philologiae Turcicae Fundamenta*, 2 (1964): 635–99; Hitchins, K., "Theme and Character in the Azerbaijani Novel, 1930–1957," *WLT*, 57 (1983):30-35; Altstadt, A., *The Azerbaijani Turks* (1992)

—KEITH HITCHINS

AZORÍN

(pseud. of José Martínez Ruiz) Spanish essayist, novelist, and dramatist, b. 8 June 1873, Monóvar; d. 2 March 1967, Madrid

Raised in a small town in Alicante, A. studied law in Valencia, where he began his career as a writer. His first books were either collections of articles in which he often satirically attacked the writers of his times, or theoretical pamphlets on literary criticism and sociology. A. was first recognized, however, for his radical social articles, influenced by anarchistic thought, published in the leftist newspapers and magazines of Madrid, where he lived from 1896 on. He once said that journalism and politics most interested him and indeed they occupied a large percentage of his work.

Toward the end of the 19th c., Spain was suffering from a confused sense of national identity, due to rapid industrialization, which resulted in shifting social classes and values, and to the loss of its last overseas colonies in 1898. Some writers called for the "Europeanization" of Spain, so it could participate in democratic capitalism; others turned to an examination of the distinguishing characteristics of Spanish culture or to pessimistic meditations on the human condition. The works of the writers of the Generation of 1898—of which A. was a key figure and which owed its definition in part to him—were pervaded by this tension between action and contemplation.

A.'s first novels—*Diario de un enfermo* (1901; diary of a sick person), *La voluntad* (1902; will), *Antonio Azorín* (1903; Antonio Azorín), and *Las confesiones de un pequeño filósofo* (1904; confessions of a little philosopher)—describe the ambivalent reactions of an autobiographical protagonist, Antonio Azorin (whose surname the author assumed as his pseudonym in 1905), toward his historical circumstances and his sensations and thoughts while contemplating the life, customs, and landscape of his country. His perspective on reality—a mixture of that of a social reformer and that of a skeptic—focuses on the destruction of time and the transcendence of art. These novels are in the form of episodes with little connective narrative structure, and they challenge the aesthetics of the traditional novel by reducing external reality to disconnected impressions that reveal the author's sensibility. They thus point to the chasm between life and the contemplation of life.

A. came to view the past and the countryside of Spain through other writers' works, and in the process he reevaluated almost the entire body of Spanish literature. Most of what A. wrote between 1905 and 1925 falls into the category of vignettes and essays published first in newspapers (mainly in *ABC*, the most widely circulated daily in Spain) and then collected in volumes: *La ruta de Don Quijote* (1905; Don Quixote's route), *Los pueblos* (1905; towns), *España* (1909; Spain), *Castilla* (1912; Castile), *Lecturas españolas* (1912; Spanish readings), and *Clásicos y modernos* (1913; classics and moderns). The novels of this period, such as *El licenciado Vidriera* (1915; graduate Vidriera; changed later to *Tomás Rueda*), *Don Juan* (1922; *Don Juan*, 1923), and *Doña Inés* (1925; Doña Inés) are also explorations of the Spanish heritage.

In these works, whose influence on how the contemporary Spaniard views his history and traditions is inestimable, A. defines Spanish sensibility as a painful awareness of time and change, but one tempered by the ability to transcend historical and material reality through a grasp of the eternal or mystical. His effort to find continuity and coherence in Spanish history was undoubtedly due to the influence of two of Spain's most notable conservative politicians, Antonio Maura (1853–1925) and Juan de La Cierva (1864–1938). Between 1907 and 1919 A. was elected five times as a deputy to the Spanish parliament from the Conservative Party and twice served as Undersecretary for Public Instruction.

A.'s novels *Félix Vargas* (1928; Félix Vargas; changed later to *El caballero inactual*; the nonpresent gentleman), *Superrealismo* (1929; surrealism; changed later to *El libro de Levante*; book of the Levant), and *Pueblo* (1930; the people) and his short stories in *Blanco en azul* (1929; *The Sirens, and Other Stories*, 1931) are experimental fiction written under the aegis of SURREALISM and EXPRESSIONISM. Here he seeks to describe, through attention to affective memory and evocative imagination, a strange form of existence beyond the ordinary bounds of time and space, with particular interest in the act of creation and the splitting of the personality into states of mind that radically change perspectives on reality.

During the 1920s and 1930s A. was also active as a drama critic, initiating Spaniards into the avant-garde theater of Europe, and as the author of several experimental plays, mostly farces and fantasies: *Old Spain!* (1926; the original title is in English), *Brandy, mucho brandy* (1927; brandy, a lot of brandy), *Comedia del arte* (1927; commedia dell'arte), *Lo invisible* (1927; the invisible), *Angelita* (1930; Angelita), and *Cervantes o la casa encantada* (1931; Cervantes; or, the enchanted house).

A. returned to social and political journalism, supporting liberal reform, during the Spanish Republic (1931–36); but he spent the entire civil war (1936–39) uncommitted in Paris, writing for *La Prensa* of Buenos Aires. Upon returning to Spain, A., considered a turncoat, was not allowed to write for the press until he justified collaboration with the "New Spain" under Franco in his novel *El escritor*. He then quietly wrote what were to be his last novels: *El escritor* (1942; the writer), *El enfermo* (1943; the sick person), *Capricho* (1943; caprice), *La isla sin aurora* (1943; island without

dawn), *María Fontán* (1944; María Fontán), and *Salvadora de Olbena* (1944; Salvadora de Olbena). The first two are largely autobiographical and reveal A.'s state of mind and some of his ideas on writing. The others are humorous, ironical fantasies in which the author attempts to remove all allusions to external reality as we normally conceive of it. After the failure of these last efforts at experimenting with the art of the novel, A. devoted the rest of his life to writing his memoirs and contributing to newspapers. The only edition of his complete works was published in 1953, but since then more than twenty volumes of articles not previously collected have followed. The reader must be aware of the fact that a number of the editions published in the 1940s and 1950s were modified for reasons of the censorship practiced by the Francist regime.

From 1905 on the works of A. are characterized in general by the vision of the artist as the "little philosopher," who tends to focus on the apparently unimportant or commonplace and to suggest its transcending qualities. A. wrote short, simple sentences in which he eschewed the potentialities of the verb, emphasized the noun, and changed the value of adjectives and adverbs. In fact, A.'s highly original use of language—impressionistic in style and CUBIST in overtone—is perhaps his most important contribution to Spanish letters.

FURTHER WORKS: *Anarquistas literarios* (1895); *Notas sociales* (1895); *Charivari* (1897); *La evolución de la crítica* (1899); *La sociología criminal* (1899); *El alma castellana* (1900), *El político* (1908); *Los valores literarios* (1913); *Al margen de los clásicos* (1915); *Un pueblecito (Ríofrío de Ávila)* (1916); *Parlamentarismo español* (1916); *El paisaje de España visto por los españoles* (1917); *Los dos Luises, y otros ensayos* (1921); *Una hora de España* (1924; *An Hour of Spain between 1560 and 1590*, 1930); *Españoles en París* (1939), *Pensando en España* (1940); *Madrid* (1941); *Tiempos y cosas* (1944); *Leyendo a los poetas* (1945); *Ante Baroja* (1946); *El artista y el estilo* (1946); *Con Cervantes* (1947); *Con permiso de los cervantistas* (1948); *El cine y el momento* (1953); *Sin perder los estribos* (1958); *Agenda* (1959); *La generación del 98* (1961); *Historia y vida* (1962); *Ultramarinos* (1966)

BIBLIOGRAPHY: Krause, A., *A., the Little Philosopher* (1948); Granjel, L. S., *Retrato de A.* (1958); Martínez Cachero, J. M., *Las novelas de A.* (1960); LaJohn, L. A., *A. and the Spanish Stage* (1961); Fox, E. I., *A. as a Literary Critic* (1962); Livingstone, L., "The Pursuit of Form in the Novels of A.," *PMLA*, 77 (1962): 116–33; Lott, R. E., *The Structure and Style of A.'s "El caballero inactual"* (1963); Lott, R. E., "A.'s Experimental Period and Surrealism," *PMLA*, 79 (1964): 305–20; Livingstone, L., *Tema y forma en las novelas de A.* (1970); Valverde, J. M., *A.* (1971); Glenn, K. M., *The Novelistic Technique of A.* (1973); Risco, A., *A. y la ruptura con la novela tradicional* (1980); Fox, E. I., *A.: guía de la obra completa* (1992)

—E. INMAN FOX

AZUELA, Arturo

Mexican novelist, b. 30 June 1938, Mexico City

The grandson of Mariano AZUELA, the most famous novelist of the Mexican Revolution, A. received his Ph.D. in mathematics from Mexico's National University, where he has served as both professor and administrator. He has lectured in universities throughout Latin America and the U.S. in the fields of mathematics, literature, and the history of science. A. has also served as president of the Confederation of Latin American Writers.

El tamaño del infierno (1973; the dimensions of hell), A.'s first novel, portrays four generations of a family, beginning in the late 19th c. and ending soon after the massacre of Tlatelolco in 1968. One of the principal characters is Uncle Jesús, who fled to Cuba after killing his fiancée's brother. Some seventy years later, having become a legendary figure among members of his family, he returns unexpectedly to die in his homeland. Two major aspects of *El tamaño del infierno* are its episodes depicting salient historical events in 20th-c. Mexico and its well-drawn characters, several of whom are taken from A.'s family. One of these is Mariano Azuela, whose real life is clearly reflected in the chain of events, especially during the Mexican Revolution and his subsequent years in Mexico City, where he practiced medicine and became the venerated family patriarch. Another interesting aspect of this work is its narrative techniques, including its multiple narrators and its frequent use of interior monologues.

Even more complex is *Un tal José Salomé* (1975; a certain José Salomé), the theme of which is the destruction of a town (Rosedal) when it is absorbed by an expanding metropolis, more than likely Mexico City. The life of the eponymous protagonist is the principal unifying thread of the novel, whose structure is characterized by a montage of episodes widely separated in both time and space. Thus voices of the past express the nostalgia of a world that has been all but severed from its roots. As the final lines suggest, however, the mythical soul of Rosedal endures in the memory of the town's oldest citizen and in the telluric image of an ancient elm that has survived the encroachment of voracious developers.

A.'s most successful novel to date, *Manifestación de los silencios* (1979; Shadows of Silence, 1985), portrays a group of intellectuals who become alienated from Mexican society because of the intolerable corruption and injustice around them. The foreground action begins in the mid-1960s when José Augusto Banderas, the leading character, kills a man and flees to Europe. During the subsequent decade (the novel ends in 1976, at the close of President Luis Echeverría's term of office) Banderas's friends evoke in desultory fashion details of his life, his broken love affair with Laura, his murder of her lover, his escape, and, at the end of the novel, his arrest in Edinburgh and return to Mexico where he is sentenced to twelve years in prison. The most important of the various narrators is Gabriel, a journalist and friend of José Augusto's who is imprisoned briefly after the massacre of Tlatelolco and who, in the final pages, leaves Mexico with a manuscript that turns out to be the novel itself. *Manifestación de los silencios* is replete with violence reflecting the turbulent years of its plot, both in and outside of Mexico. It is especially significant because of its adroit manipulation of narrative technique and its implicit condemnation of the flaws in Mexican society.

A.'s next novel, *La casa de las mil vírgenes* (1984; the house of the thousand virgins), records the history of the eponymous house of prostitution, which is located in Santa María de la Ribera, a section of Mexico City. Founded in 1892 and demolished during the 1960s, the brothel is remembered by numerous narrators, the most important of whom is Aliba, an employee of the brothel for many years. Aliba's recollections, along with those of other narrators, gradually transform "the house of the thousand virgins" into a mythical place from where many of the major events of recent Mexican history are scrutinized. Thus the Mexican Revolution, the Cristero rebellion of the 1920s, President Lázaro Cárdenas's expropriation of the oil industry in 1938, and the student demonstrations of the 1960s are interwoven with tales of violence and murder in the brothel, leading ultimately to its destruction. Although this novel is fraught with ironic ambiguity, due in part to the opinionated Aliba's unreliability, its blend of history and myth sheds light on Mexico's past.

The protagonist of *El don de la palabra* (1984; the gift of speech) is a successful middle-aged actress named Ana Maria who, while returning to her homeland (Spain), recalls her many years of residence in Mexico, her divorce from her womanizing husband Antonio, her rebellious daughter Adriana, and her wide circle of friends who have supported her in her career. Thus the novel dramatizes two journeys into the past, one evoked by Ana María and the other experienced by her in 1983, the year she returns to her former home in Spain. The least challenging of A.'s works, *El don de la palabra* demonstrates the author's skill not only in developing believable characters, but also in shifting smoothly between present and past tenses, thus creating a fluid, dynamic plot structure. The temporal transitions achieve greater credibility, moreover, because, through the frequent use of free indirect discourse, the omniscient narrator focuses on the character's field of vision to shorten the distance between the character and reader and, at the same time, to convey vital plot information.

A.'s novel *El matemático* (1988; the mathematician) is one of his most interesting from both a literary and a philosophical standpoint. The plot involves an English mathematician, Philip Cunningham, who, in the final hours of 1999, looks back on his life, along with the major events of the 20th c. His personal recollections include the death of his wife, the upbringing of his two children, one studying in Scotland and the other in Italy, and his fractured relations with his mistress, with whom he becomes reunited at the end of the novel. But the principal thrust of this work is Cunningham's professional career and his efforts as a mathematician to understand the world around him. Thus, although he has at times been optimistic about the capability of science to solve human problems, he has also experienced existential uncertainties caused by the gap between the sciences and the humanities. As both a humanist and a scientist, A. is quite possibly depicting his own personal efforts to come to grips with this dilemma. Like most of his other novels, *El matemático* expands literary and psychological dimensions through frequent shifts in the point of view and temporal fluctuations triggered by free association.

In their entirety A.'s writings dramatize numerous aspects of 20th-c. Mexican reality and, at the same time, convey their author's existential concerns for the fate of contemporary society. His narrative skill and sensitivity to the vagaries of human behavior have made him one of Mexico's leading men of letters.

BIBLIOGRAPHY: Tatum, C. M., on *Un tal José Salomé WLT*, 50, 2 (Spring 1976), 379; Anadón, J., "Entrevista con A. A.," *Hispam*, 11, 33 (1983): 61–78; Quinteros, I., "El mundo que parecía ser nuestro en *Un tal José Salomé*," CA, 259, 2 (1985): 205–18; Foxley, C., "*La casa de las mil vírgenes:* Convocación y parodia,"

RChL, 29 (June 1987): 39–56; Rodríguez Padrón, J., "La original narrativa de A. A.," *RI*, 55 (July-Dec. 1989): 148–49, 1033–46; McMurray, G. R., on *El matemático, Chasqui*, 18, 2 (Nov. 1989): 107–9;

—GEORGE R. MCMURRAY

AZUELA, Mariano

Mexican novelist, b. 1 Jan. 1873, Lagos de Moreno; d. 1 Mar. 1952, Mexico City

In 1899, shortly after receiving his medical degree in Guadalajara, A. returned to his hometown to practice medicine, a career he would pursue until his retirement in the mid-1940s. As an early supporter of the Francisco Madero revolutionary movement, he served briefly as political chief of Lagos de Moreno and later as director of Public Instruction for the state of Jalisco. In 1914 A. joined the forces of General Julián Medina as chief medical officer. With the defeat of Pancho Villa's armies in 1915, A. was forced to leave his wife and eight children as he followed the retreating troops northward, finally crossing the frontier to El Paso, Texas. Here he lived penniless but saw the publication of his novel *Los de abajo* (1916; *The Underdogs*, 1929) in serial form in a local newspaper in the fall of 1915. A few months later A. returned to Mexico, moving his family soon afterward to Mexico City, where for the next thirty years he worked as a doctor among the city's poor.

Mariano Azuela

A. read French authors of the time and owes to them the naturalist-determinist theories that are so clearly evident in his early works. *María Luisa* (Maria Luisa), his first novel (written in 1898, but not published until 1907), is based on an experience as a hospital intern. His best novel from these years is *Mala Yerba* (1909; *Marcela*, 1932), which focuses on the exploitation of the downtrodden classes by the large landholders. Its protagonist, the peasant girl Marcela, is seduced by upper-class men; she sometimes resists but at other times she exploits the situation for financial gain.

During the decade of the revolution (1910–20) A. wrote half a dozen novels and novelettes on the subject. He is usually credited with the creation of the "novel of the Mexican revolution," which is characterized by its ideological content, episodic structure, colloquial language, and use of the mass protagonist. In *Andrés Pérez, maderista* (1911; Andrés Pérez, supporter of Madero) we observe the opportunism of so-called revolutionaries. *Los de abajo* is unquestionably A.'s masterpiece; it is also one of the major novels of modern Latin America and has been translated into more than a dozen languages. Written during the low point in A.'s fortunes, it depicts the revolution in particularly pessimistic tones. Although by the time of its writing the federal government armies had been defeated by the revolutionaries, the fighting continued among the various revolutionary factions. Demetrio Macías, the chief character of the novel, has risen from pursued criminal to the rank of general but cannot explain why he is fighting; nor can he escape his tragic destiny—to be trapped in the revolution. The novelettes *Los caciques* (1917; *The Bosses*, 1956) and *Las moscas* (1918; *The Flies*, 1956) also focus on the revolution, the former picturing the rural conditions that produced the unrest. A.'s last work of this cycle, and one of his best, is *Las tribulaciones de una familia decente* (1918; *The Trials of a Respectable Family*, 1963), a study of a wealthy provincial family that loses everything in the revolution but in the end regains its dignity with its acceptance of the work ethic.

In the early 1920s A. still remained relatively unknown—*Los de abajo* would not be discovered by the critics and the public until 1925. For variety he briefly abandoned realism and in his next three novels turned to experimental techniques of structure and point of view. *La luciérnaga* (1932; *The Firefly*, 1979) is the best of this group. A. continued to write until shortly before his death, and several works appeared posthumously during the 1950s. Probably his best novel of the later years is *Nueva burguesía* (1941; new bourgeoisie).

A. also wrote biographies, plays, and a few short stories. In the essay, his most important and original contribution is his analysis of the Mexican novel from José Joaquín Fernández de Lizardi (1776—1827) to Heriberto Frías (1870–1925), *Cien años de novela mexicana* (1947; one hundred years of the Mexican novel).

A. is universally recognized as the founder and principal exponent of the subgenre, the "novel of the Mexican revolution," which continues in popularity with the writers of today and has probably produced close to a hundred works. A. remains the most important literary figure in Mexican fiction of the first half of the century and in Latin America is counted as one of the greats of the realist-regionalist school of writing.

FURTHER WORKS: *Los fracasados* (1908); *Sin amor* (1912); *Domitilo quiere ser diputado* (1918); *La Malhora* (1923); *El desquite* (1925); *Pedro Moreno el insurgente* (1933); *Precursores* (1935); *El camarada Pantoja* (1937); *San Gabriel de Valdivias*

(1938); *Los de abajo* (theater version, 1938); *El buho en la noche* (1938); *Del Llano Hermanos, S. en C.* (1938); *Regina Landa* (1939); *Avanzada* (1940); *El padre D. Agustín Rivera* (1942); *La marchante* (1944); *El jurado* (1945); *La mujer domada* (1946); *Sendas perdidas* (1949); *La maldición* (1955); *Esa sangre* (1956); *Obras completas* (3 vols., 1958–60)

BIBLIOGRAPHY: Englekirk, J. E., "The Discovery of *Los de abajo*," *Hispania*, 18 (1935): 53–62; Ocampo de Gómez, A. M., and Prado Velázquez, E. *Diccionario de escritores mexicanos* (1967): 29–31; Langford, W., "M. A.: A Break with the Past," *The Mexican Novel Comes of Age* (1971): 14–35; Leal, L., *M. A.* (1971); Monterde, F., ed., *M. A. y la crítica mexicana* (1973); Robe, S. L., *A. and the Mexican Underdogs* (1979)

—RICHARD M. REEVE

B

BABEL, Isaak Emanuilovich

Russian short-story writer, b. 13 July 1894, Odessa, Ukraine; d. 3 March 1941, place unknown, but apparently a Soviet concentration camp

B., the son of a Jewish warehouse owner and the grandson of a rabbi, was born in Odessa, and except for a few years in nearby Nikolaev, B.'s childhood and young manhood were spent in that seaport city, which was unique in the Russian Empire (east of Poland) for at least two reasons: its large number of Jews (139,000 out of a total of 403,000 inhabitants, according to the 1897 census) and its large number of foreigners (30,000 people out of a total of 630,000 in 1914, according to Baedeker). At a time when most Jews were forbidden to live in Moscow, St. Petersburg, Kiev, and other localities, Odessa had many times more Jews than any other city in the Russian part of the empire. And these were big city Jews, who often knew the Russian language well, not *shtetl* types who were mainly limited to Yiddish and Hebrew. All this left its imprint on B., who learned French in school from a Frenchman and came to love the works of Guy de Maupassant while still a schoolboy. B. first began publishing in 1913, three years before the misleading date he gives in his short *Avtobiografia* (1926; autobiography). He graduated from Kiev University (which had been evacuated to Saratov on the Volga because of the war) in 1915. In 1920, during the Russian civil war, B. became a correspondent with the Red forces of Semyon Budyonny for the Russian Telegraph Agency. Later that year, he returned to Odessa. His stories about his army experiences began to come out in 1923 and made him famous within a few months. His later life was lived mainly in Moscow, except for lengthy trips to the West, when possible. His wife had emigrated to Paris in 1925, and his mother and sister lived in Brussels from 1926 on. His daughter tells us that when he was arrested in 1937, he remarked, "they didn't give me time to finish."

B.'s fame is based on a very small body of work, mainly *Konarmia* (1926; *Red Cavalry*, 1929) and the Odessa tales. His subject matter generally deals with either of two themes: Jewish life in Odessa before the revolution of 1917, and life with the Red Cossacks fighting on the Polish front during the Russian civil war.

B.'s fame depends at least as much on his subjective manner as on his subject matter. One can easily believe the comment of his friend Konstantin Paustovsky that B. had literally twenty-two versions of just one story, "Lyubka kazak" (1924; "Lyubka the Cossack," 1935) before the final variant. B.'s imagery is highly individualized, and often startlingly effective, as in his famous description of Savitsky, the division commander under Budyonny: "His long legs were like girls clad to the shoulders in jack boots". So rhythmic can his prose be that Russians, upon hearing it read aloud for the first time, have been known to think it is poetry. These rhythms, like the deliberately substandard Russian of those whose speech B. quotes, which includes thieves' slang from Odessa and calques (loan translations) from Yiddish, are frequently lost (perhaps inevitably) in the English translations.

B.'s work seeks to create heroes: men who fight and win, both Cossacks in the Red Army and Jewish gangsters in Odessa. B.'s unique combination of empathy with the faith of his fathers and an intellectual rejection of it in the name of the revolution is felt best in what may be his masterpiece, the 700-word tale "Gedali" (1924; "Gedali", 1929) named for the old Jew who wishes to say "yes" to the revolution without saying "no" to his Sabbath, and whom B. calls "the founder of an unrealizable International."

As Nadezhda Mandelshtam has observed, B. possessed a childlike curiosity about others. His prose is filigreed and sensuous at the same time. In a letter of 12 May 1925 B. complains bitterly about the "prevailing conditions of our work in Moscow." But worse was to come. At his speech to the First Congress of the Union of Soviet Writers on 23 August 1934, B. even joked painfully at his own misfortune, saying, "If one talks about silence, one cannot fail to say that I am a great master of that genre."

Antonina Pirozhkova, with whom B. spent his last years in Moscow, states that B. was prolific during that period, and that he even produced a full-length novel. Who can say if this work and perhaps others will ever be recovered? The world has not even been informed about the false charge that resulted in B.'s being "illegally repressed" (to quote the Russian-language *Short Literary Encyclopedia* [Moscow, 1962–75]).

There were many Jewish writers who wrote about Jewish themes in the Russian language while this was still possible on Russian soil (mainly from 1890 or so to about 1930). But they had neither B.'s talents nor his mastery of Russian. B. was the only one whose compelling artistry, despite the enforced silence of almost two decades, is recognized to this day. His voice is distinctively individual and beautiful. His eventual fate reminds us of Franz Grillparzer's epitaph on the gravestone of Franz Schubert: "The art of music has here entombed a rich possession but even more beautiful hopes."

FURTHER WORKS: *Istoria moey golubyatney: rasskazy* (1927); *Odesskie rasskazy* (1931); *Izbrannoe* (1957 and 1966). FURTHER WORKS IN ENGLISH: *Benya Krik the Gangster and Other Stories* (1948); *Collected Stories of I.B.* (1955); *1920 Diary* (1995); *Lyubka the Cossack and Other Stories* (1963); *The Lonely Years: Unpublished Stories and Private Correspondence* (1964); *You Must Know Everything: Stories, 1915–1937* (1966); *Short Stories* (1969); *The Forgotten Prose* (1978); *1920 Diary* (1995)

BIBLIOGRAPHY: Carden, P., *The Art of I. B.* (1972); Hallett, R., *I.B.* (1973); Fallen, J. E., *I.B.:Russian Master of the Short Story* (1974); Friedberg, M., "Yiddish Folklore Motifs in I. B.'s *Konarmija*," in Terras, V., ed., *American Contributions to the Eighth International Congress of Slavists, Zagreb and Ljubljana, Sept. 3-9, 1978*, Vol. 2 (1978): 192-203; Bloom, H., *I. B.* (1987)

—EDGAR H. LEHRMAN

BABITS, Mihály

Hungarian poet, novelist, short-story writer, essayist, critic, and dramatist, b. 26 Nov. 1883, Szekszárd; d. 4 Aug. 1941, Budapest

B. was born into a family of Catholic intellectuals; his father was a judge. He received an excellent education in the classics and in Hungarian and world literature, and he taught school for many years. He made his chief contribution to Hungarian literary life as poet, critic, and especially editor of Hungary's most prestigious literary journal, *Nyugat*.

As an undergraduate at the University of Budapest he befriended fellow poets Gyula JUHÁSZ and Dezső KOSZTOLÁNYI; their correspondence illuminates the literary concerns and trends that preceded the formation of *Nyugat* in 1908. B. published in all the important journals, and his regularly appearing volumes made his name well known and respected. His courageous pacifist poems during World War, together with the fact that he accepted the chair of Hungarian and World Literature at the University of Budapest under the Communist regime of 1919, cost him his academic career and made his subsequent position precarious. In 1921 he married the poet Ilona Tanner (1895–1955; pseud.: Sophie Török), and they lived modestly on his earnings as a poet. From 1929 on, at first with Zsigmond MÓRICZ and then by himself, he devoted much of his energies to the difficult job of editing *Nyugat*. He also fulfilled the thankless tasks of an administrator of the Baumgarten Prize. These positions kept the shy, scholarly poet in a cross-fire of rivalry and antagonism, a trial he suffered patiently. One great triumph sweetened his last year: in 1940, his translation of the *Divine Comedy* received the Italian San Remo Prize as the best Dante translation in existence. At that time he was already dying of cancer of the throat; he revised his translation of Sophocles when he was on his deathbed.

His sobriquet *Poeta doctus*, "learned poet," was well earned. He learned from every great poet he read—and he read just about everyone. His greatest master was János Arany (1817–1882); among his contemporaries, his closest friend was Endre ADY, although B. was more philosophical and less passionate than Ady. His ambition was to penetrate the essence of every phenomenon, to absorb it into a deeply personal experience, and to project it in his poetry. His thirst for knowledge was insatiable, and the realization of man's inability to know and experience everything filled him with profound melancholy. Through love, he hoped to explore and assimilate the outside world: nature, mankind, God. His own poetic processes, his own personal sufferings—all these were dissected, observed, set down. He was a great experimenter, not only with new and different subject matter and ideas, but also with the possibilities of language, poetic form, and prosody. The variety of his poetic forms is astounding.

In his very first volume, *Levelek Irisz koszorújából* (1909; leaves from the wreath of Iris) he introduced themes and styles from western European poetry new to Hungarian literature. There followed nine more volumes of poetry, but his second volume, *Herceg, hátha megjön a tél is!* (1911; Prince, perchance winter shall come also!), was not surpassed and rarely equaled. He was immersed in ancient culture, fusing classical subject matter and true and tested values with the most modern achievements of the Parnassians and SYMBOLISTS. Among Hungarian poets, he was the foremost student of English and American poetry; some of his poems actually have English titles: "O lyric love" (1911), "Beloved, o beloved" (1911). Two of his World War I poems—"Fiatal katona" (young soldier) and "Husvét előtt" (before Easter) in *Versek* (1927; poems)—show his deep humanity in declaring his love of peace and abhorrence of war when the world around him erupted in madness. "Balázsolás" (1937; the rite of St. Blaise) is a testament of a deeply religious person confronting imminent death with a humble prayer to a saint supposed to help those suffering from diseases of the throat. His last volume of poetry, *Jónás könyve* (1939; Book of Jonah) is a masterful statement of the predicament of modern man trying to escape the will of God.

Although he is best remembered as a poet and editor, the totality of his work as a poet, novelist, short-story writer, poetic dramatist, essayist, critic, literary historian, translator of poetry—ancient, medieval, and modern—secure for him a very high place in Hungarian and world literature. He believed in literary workmanship when many authors stooped to writing commercially or politically viable works. His oeuvre shows the quality that can be reached when genius is shaped by tradition; that genius, in turn, creates a new tradition. It is unfortunate that, to date, only a handful of his poems appear in English translation.

His novels, short stories, and plays also demonstrate his brilliant insights into such diverse fields as history, sociology, psychology, linguistic reform, and classical studies. His prose style—whether in essays or creative works—delights with its versatility and charm. Well versed not only in philosophy and aesthetics but also in most areas of scholarship and of the natural sciences, with his catholic tastes and interests, his deep attachment to spiritual and moral values, his self-respect and faith in human dignity, B. is among those who represent the best, the noblest contributions of Hungarian letters to the literature of the world.

FURTHER WORKS: *Gólyakalifa* (1916); *Recitativ* (1916); *Shakespeare: A vihar* (1916); *Pávatollak* (1920); *Karácsonyi Madonna* (1920); *Goethe A Napló* (1920); *Nyugtalanság völgye* (1921); *Baudelaire A romlás virágai* (1921); *Laodameia* (1921); *Erato* (1921); *Timár Virgil fia* (1922); *Gondolat és írás* (1922); *Dante isteni színjátéka* (3 vols., 1913–1923); *Aranygaras* (1923); *Sziget és tenger* (1925); *Halálfiai* (1927); *Az istenek halnakaz ember él* (1929); *Élet és irodalom* (1929); *A torony árnyéka* (1931); *Oedipus király és egyéb műfordítások* (1931); *Elza pilóta vagy a tökéletes társadalom* (1933); *Amor Sanctus* (1933); *Versenyt az esztendőkkel* (1933); *Az európai irodalom története, 1760–1925* (2 vols., 1937–1938); *Összes versei* (1937); *Hatholdas rózsakert* (1937); *Összes művei* (10 vols., 1937 ff); *Összegyűjtött munkái* (10 vols., 1937 ff.); *Keresztül kasúl az életemen* (1939); *Írók két háború közt* (1941); *A második ének* (1942)

BIBLIOGRAPHY: Reményi, J., "The Passing of M. B.," *BA*, 16 (1942): 1–4; Reményi, J., "M. B., *Poeta Doctus*, 1883–1941," in Molnar, A. J., ed., *Hungarian Writers and Literature* (1964): 306–25; Hernadi, P., "Ungarische Dichtung im 20. Jahrhundert," *WZ*, 9, 12 (1963): 3–9

—DALMA H. BRUNAUER

BACCHELLI, Riccardo

Italian novelist, dramatist, poet, critic, and historian, b. 19 April 1891, Bologna; d. 8 October 1985, Monza

Since 1911, when he first contributed to *La voce*, a progressive cultural review, B. has been active as a critic, historian, poet, playwright, and novelist. Revealing of his character as a writer was his activity with *La ronda* (1919–24), a literary monthly that proposed Italian classical authors—from the Renaissance humanists through Leopardi and Manzoni in the 19th c.—as models for elegant style and for a concept of literature as a pursuit free of contemporary concerns.

In his prodigiously productive and versatile career as a novelist, B. has experimented with various themes and narrative forms. His talent for satire was revealed in *Lo sa il tonno* (1923; the tuna knows), a moral and political tale whose principal characters are a tuna and a swordfish, and was confirmed in *Città degli amanti* (1929; town for lovers), whose plot centers around a utopian, scientifically experimental colony for couples established by an American millionaire on the coast of the Gulf of Mexico. His most successful satirical allegory is *La cometa* (1949; the comet), which dramatizes man's political gullibility and wartime anxieties in the tale of a swindler who reaps rich profits by prophesying the end of the world among the naïve population of a fictitious provincial town. In *Rapporto segreto* (1967; secret report), purporting to investigate the moral and sociological consequence of a space flight, B. satirizes a variety of modern concerns in a manner both melancholy and comic.

Another persistent interest of B. is the analysis of love relationships in a range of manifestations, from tender feeling to aberrant attraction. His best novel in this manner is *Unapassione coniugal* (1939; a conjugal passion), the story of a morbid sexual attachment between a man and his dying wife, set against a background of northern Italian country life among the rich.

B.'s talents are best displayed in his historical novels. *Il diavolo al Pontelungo* (1927; *The Devil at the Long Bridge*, 1929) is a keen study of the minds, moods, and personal habits of a group of anarchists and a vivid description of the bourgeois and the proletarian classes of the Bologna region. Based on events of the 1870s, the plot is dominated by the figure of the Russian anarchist Mikhail Bakunin (1814–1876) as he settles down in the villa of a wealthy Italian backer on Lake Maggiore and then moves on to Bologna to give impetus to an ill-prepared local uprising.

B.'s outstanding work is the trilogy *Il mulino del po* (1938–40; *The mill on the Po*, 2 vols., 1950; *Nothing New under the Sun*, 1955), the story of a family of millers from the time of Napoleon's retreat from Russian to the end of World War I. The mill on the Po River is the symbol of man's struggle to survive and to defend his ideals and customs against the onslaught of time and events. In the Scacernis' small world are reflected all the political, economic, and social developments of their age: the awakening of the ideals of freedom, equality, and justice brought about by Napoleon's armies throughout Europe, the nationalistic uprisings during the post-Napoleonic period, the actions of anarchists and socialists in unified Italy. Here many of B.'s talents find a happy equilibrium: his psychological insight, his sweeping presentation of natural phenomena and of mass movements, his vast erudition, and his tendency to moralize in a sardonic vein. The result is a work of epic proportions, in which the fortunes of men are overwhelmed by the relentless progression of history.

Because of his aloof and basically nonreligious view of historical events, which he has elucidated in essays such as *Nel fiume della storia* (1955; in the river of history), B. was described by many critics as the poetic voice of Benedetto Croce's historicism. Both his concept and his practice of novel writing, which carry on the 19th-c. European tradition, set him apart from fashionable schools, and have contributed to an overall underestimation of his work. Its great value lies in the powerful re-creation of the past, in the perceptive analysis of historical events and of their moral and psychological components. Additionally, his style, which blends idiomatic and dialectical elements into a rich, harmonious prose, is inspired by the best Italian classical tradition.

FURTHER WORKS: *Il filo meraviglioso di Ludovico Clo* (1911); *Poemi lirici* (1914); *Amleto* (1919); *Spartaco e gli schiavi* (1920);

Presso i termini del testino (1922); *La famiglia di Figaro* (1926); *Bella Italia* (1928); *Bellamonte* (1928); *La ruota del tempo* (1928); *La notte di un nevrastenico* (1928); *Acque dolci e peccati* (1929); *Amore di poesia* (1930); *La smorfia* (1930); *La congiura di Don Giulio d'Este* (1931); *Oggi, domani e mai* (1932); *Confessioni letterarie* (1932); *Parole d'amore* (1935); *Mal d'Africa* (1935); *Il rabdomante* (1936); *Iride* (1937); *Gioacchino Rossini* (1941; *Seed of Steel*, 1963); *La fine d'Atlantide* (1942); *Il fiore della Mirabilis* (1942); *La notte dell'8 settembre* (1943); *Il pianto del figlio di Lais* (1945); *Lo sguardo di Gesù* (1948); *La bellissima fiaba di Rosa dei Venti* (1948); *La politica di un impolitico 1914–1945* (1948); *L'alba dell'ultima sera* (1949); *L'incendio di Milano* (1952; *The Fire of Milan*, 1958); *Italia per terra e per mare* (1953; *Il figlio di Stalin* (1953; *The Son of Stalin*, 1956); *Tutte le novelle* (1953); *Memorie del tempo presente* (1953); *Tre giorni di passione* (1955); *Passeggiate orobiche* (1956); *Il figlio di Ettore* (1957); *Nostos* (1957); *I tre schiavi di Giulio Cesare* (1958); *Non ti chiamerò più padre* (1959); *Viaggio in Grecia* (1959); *Ritorno sotto i portici* (1959); *Leopardi e Manzoni* (1960); *La notte di un nerausténico* (1960); *Garibaldi e i mille* (1960); *Saggi critici* (1962); *Secondo viaggio in Grecia* (1963); *Traduzioni* (1964); *Il brigante di Tacca del lupo* (1964); *Teatro* (1964); *Le bolognesi* (1964); *Manzoni* (1964); *Il coccio di terracotta* (1964; *A Potsherd of Clay* (1966); *L' "Afrodite" un romanzo d'amore* (1969); *La stella del mattino* (1971); *Bellezza e Umanità* (1973); *Confessioni letterarie* (1973); *Giorni di vita e tempo di poesia* (1973); *Il progresso è un razzo* (1975); *Il sommergibile* (1978)

BIBLIOGRAPHY: Bergin, T. G., "R. B.," *Italica*, 17 (1940): 64–68; Poggioli, R., "Italian Litterary Chronicles: II," *ltalica*, 25 (1948): 164–68; Hughes, S., on *The Mill on the Po*, *Commonweal*, Dec. 1950: 53; Bergin, T. G., on *La cometa*, *BA*, 27 (1953): 40–41; Allen, W., on *Nothing New under the Sun*, *New Statesman and Nation*, 15 Mar. 1955: 49; Bergin, T. G., on *Nothing New under the Sun*, *NYHTBR*, 11 Sept. 1955: 6

—RINALDINA RUSSELL

BACHMANN, Ingeborg

Austrian poet, dramatist, and novelist, b. 25 June 1926, Klagenfurt; d. 17 Oct. 1973, Rome, Italy

B. grew up in Carinthia. After World War II she studied philosophy at the universities of Innsbruck, Graz, and finally Vienna, where in 1950 she completed a doctoral dissertation on the philosopher Martin Heidegger (1889–1976). She worked for the Austrian radio until 1953, when she became a full-time writer, and later lived in several cities, including Rome, Munich, Zurich, and Berlin. In 1959–60 she lectured on poetry at the University of Frankfurt. Among the literary awards she received were the Group 47 Prize (1953), the City of Bremen Prize (1957), and the Georg Büchner Prize (1964).

B.'s verse is deeply indebted to a number of poetic traditions; similarities to many poets and literary movements, including Klopstock (1724–1903) and RILKE, classical antiquity and SURREALISM, have been noted. Nonetheless, her poetic voice is both modern and distinctive. A somber mood pervades most of her lyrics, and an intensely personal mode of expression is typically present. Unresolved existential dread can often be felt. The inevitability of guilt and human frailty, the difficulty of finding happiness in love, the inadequacy of language and the failure of communication, and, less frequently, the bleak political situation contribute to the dark vision of her poetry. Literary allusions, mythology, current events, and subjective exclamations are interwoven in a verse characterized by powerful and distinctive images, which often assume the quality of private ciphers. Snow and ice, suggesting the sterility of social relationships and the absence of love, are images of considerable importance.

With a single exception, the poems of *Die gestured Zeite* (1953; borrowed time) are written in free verse, and in general both the poems and the individual lines are rather long and possess a hymnic quality. The poetry of *Anrufung des Großen Bären* (1956; conjuration of the Great Bear) is in most respects similar. Rhyme, however, is used more frequently, and the pervasive elegiac tone is quite personnel. Semipolitical poems appear infrequently, but one exceptional is the famous little poem, in which the constellation Ursa Major is represented as a circus bear with the power to destroy the world at any time. In the the equally famous but more typical "Nebelland" (fogland), the monologue of a forsaken loverúa manúis pervaded by winter imagery. The concluding cycle of fifteen "Leader auk der Fluht" (songs in flight) develops the themes of the transience and painfulness of love. The beginning of the short final poem continues the elegiac tone, but in an unusual reversal B. ends the collection with an affirmation of the enduring nature of poetry. This conclusion, strongly reminiscent of Rilke, runs counter to the mood of the collection as a whole, and the transcendence suggested in it rarely appears in B.'s later works.

Malina (1971; *Malina*, 1989), one of B.'s last works, is a lyrical novel, an introspective love story with autobiographical elements. The title of the introductory section, "Vienna; Today," suggests a realistic setting, as do two characters sketched there: the nameless first-person narrator, a well-traveled woman writer who was born in Klagenfurt, and Ivan, her lover, a man in his thirties with two children and a job. As the love relationship deteriorates, the focus shifts from external reality to the troubled mind of the narrator. Haunted by nightmarish dreams, she loses contact with the world and establishes a relationship with Malina, a male alter ego, in which she loses her own identity. Her plans to write a book are abandoned, and at the end she is "murdered" by Malina. The murder is not to be taken literally, but as the representation of the change in the narrator's personality, the result of the traumatic end of her relationship with Ivan. The themes—the inadequency of languages, the problematic nature of love and of life itself—are familiar from B.'s lyrics. The style of the book is subjective and lyrical, and plot elements are more often suggested or intimated than actually narrated.

B.'s most successful radio play, *Der gute Gott von Manhattan* (1958; *The Good God of Manhattan*, sound recording, 1990), which like most of her other works is concerned with the tension between an ideal and reality, today seems naïve and dated. Her poetry and fiction, however, continue to receive high acclaim, and she is recognized as one of Austria's most accomplished postwar writers.

FURTHER WORKS: *Jugend in einer österreirchischen Stadt* (1961); *Das dreißigste Jahr* (1961; *The Thirtieth Year*, 1964); *Gedichte, Erzählungen, Hörspiele, Essays* (1964); *Ein Ort für Zufälle* (1965); *Simultan* (1972); *Gier* (1973); *Werke* (4 vols., 1978). FURTHER WORKS IN ENGLISH: *In the Storm of Roses: Selected Poems* (1986); *Paths to the Lake* (1989); *Songs in Flight: The Collected Poems of I. B.* (1994)

BIBLIOGRAPHY: Schlotthaus, W., "I. B.'s Poem 'Mein Vogel,'" *MLQ*, 22 (1961): 181–91; Lyon, J., "The Poetry of I. B.," *GL&L*, 17 (1964): 206–15; Benn, M., "Poetry and the Endangered World: Notes on a Poem by I. B.," *GL&L*, 19 (1965): 61–67; Schoolfield, G., "I. B.," in Keith-Smith, B., ed., *Essays on Contemporary German Literature* (1966): 187–212; Marsch, E., "I. B.," in Wiese, B. von, ed., *Deutsche Dichter der Gegenwart* (1973): 515–30

—JERRY GLENN

BACOVIA, George

(pseud. of George Vasiliu) Romanian poet, b. 17 Sept. 1881, Bacău: d. 22 May 1957, Bucharest

B. graduated from high school in Bacău (an important experience in his life) and studied law in Iasi, but never practiced it. Instead, he pursued an undistinguished administrative career and did some teaching—many of his positions in the cultural bureaucracy were mere sinecures meant to help an increasingly admired poet. He suffered from alcoholism, which either was caused by or led to several nervous breakdowns. After 1932 he lived in virtual seclusion on pensions and financial aid. He received many prizes, awards, and other honors. The vague socialist sympathies of his early youth led to the rehabilitation of his reputation late in his life by Marxist critics, after he had spent many years in isolation.

B. started writing rather early, largely under the influence of Romanian and French SYMBOLISM. He soon developed his own style and manner. B.'s first volume, *Plumb* (1916; lead), contains his best and most typical lyrical production. Later volumes, such as *Scîntei galbene* (1926; yellow sparks), *Comedii în fond* (1936; actually, just comedies), and *Stanţe burgheze* (1946; bourgeois verse), are not as important. B. also published short fragments of poetic prose, which were posthumously collected.

B. was fascinated by the symbolists' program and musicality, but he ended up by dismantling them and turning them inside out. His basic framework was that of radical solitude and alienation. Socially, the lyrical persona in *Plumb* is the lonely, hopeless intellectual lost in a little Moldavian town, stifled in dust and mud, and beset by the anxieties of time and space. He imagines himself descending in burial vaults, or surviving in a primitive lake home, while the universe is slowly drowning. The lyrical eroticism is always hopeless, fixing on pale, sick, or dying women. The friends are desperate drunkards, decaying intellectuals. Withering and rotting leaves, vast, empty plains in which the ghostly silhouettes of longdead warlords emerge for a second, the threat of slaughterhouses, the fleeting sound of ballrooms—all these images haunt them.

B.'s poetry is repetitive, monotonous, and gloomy. Ravens and deserted parks are favorite symbols; cancer, tuberculosis, and fainting spells beset the characters in the poems; echoes of learning and art ring nostalgically. Above all, B. is a poet of autumns and sunsets, with which he formulates a myth of universal decline, dull suffering, and agony completed. Winter scenes, on the other hand, signify in B.'s poetry the consummation of an unbearable life and a state of ugly peace. In B.'s poems there is more than a touch of self-parody, cynical and bitter. The lyrical persona reaches a point where the distinction between comic and tragic, joke and earnest becomes irrelevant. Puppets, barrel organs, oompah bands, mechanical figures, and amusement fairs are caricatures that ironically reveal the deadness of the world and the artificiality of society. Symbolist associations beget pain and disappointment with the world, not hope; but tragedy itself is seen degraded into vulgar whining, since existence is just boring and insipid, not conducive to dramatic gestures and decisive choices.

B. has an intriguing way of sliding from the concrete image to the allegorical abstract and back again. His style is direct and uncomplicated, his sentences concise, his poems short—he even experimented with poems reduced to one-word lines. His favorite colors are dark purple, white, and black, and many poems are monochromatic exercises around one simple suggestive color.

In spite of his meager output and his solitude, B. is a key figure in Romanian poetry, expressing the transition from symbolism and late romanticism to the dissonant tunes, the cruelties, and the mysteries of the modern era. He gave an entirely new poetic form to the traditional yearning for a lost paradise of 19th-c. Moldavian poets and to their expression of languid cosmic misery—one that is less personal, less plaintive. In his hard-edged, laconic, ironic statements, he relates not only to the French symbolist poets Albert Samain (1858–1900), Tristan Corbière (1845–1875), and Jules Laforgue (1860–1887), whom he admired, but also to Georg TRAKL and Gottfried BENN, to whose generation he belongs.

FURTHER WORKS: *Bucăţi de noapte* (1926); *Cu voi* (1930)

BIBLIOGRAPHY: Munteano, B., *Modern Romanian Literature* (1939): 259–61; Matta, S., *Existence poétique de B.* (1958); Petroveanu, M., B. *oder die Unmöglichkeit zu sein* (1968); Manolescu, N., *G. B., L'intraduisible* (1968): 11–32; Doinas, S. A., "G. B.s dichterische Welt," in *Bacovia Gedichte* (1972): 21–35

—VIRGIL NEMOIANU

BAGRITSKY, Edvard

(pseud. of E. Georgievich Dzyubin) Russian poet and translator, b. 4 Nov. 1895, Odessa, Ukraine; d. 16 Feb. 1934, Kuntsevo

B., son of a Jewish shopkeeper, was a sick and frail child. He finished his early schooling in Odessa, a major seaport, and a cultural center that afforded many nonacademic educational experiences for an aspiring young writer. In 1917 B. worked briefly for Odessa's police department and served on the Persian front in the Russian army. In 1918 B. returned to Odessa to devote himself more earnestly to his literary activities. Thus, as an artist, B. was a product of three distinct cultures: the Jewish heritage of his parents, the local Ukrainian culture of Odessa, and the Russian culture of the tsarist empire.

B.'s first poems (1915–16), modeled on the work of the FUTURISTS and the Acmeists, and especially on the exotic poetry of Nikolay GUMILYOV, celebrate the rugged, adventurous life and the heroic exploits of strong individuals.

B. supported the revolution both as a fighter and as a propagandist (he wrote political proclamations and pamphlets), and the revolution is a recurring image in his poetry written from 1919 to 1925, primarily under the influence of MAYAKOVSKY and BLOK. B.

exalted not only the Russian Revolution but also those that preceded it in other countries. In the poem "Kommunary" (1923; members of the commune) he glorifies the Paris Commune, and his "Pamyatnik Garibaldi" (1923; monument to Garibaldi) is a lasting tribute to the Italian freedom fighter.

Gradually, however, B.'s revolutionary fervor subsided, and the poet retreated to the romantic world of his earlier works. The result was his masterpiece, the narrative poem *Duma pro Opanasa* (1926; the lay of Opanas), written under the influence of the Ukrainian bard Taras Shevchenko (1814–1861). This *duma* (a genre of heroic Ukrainian folk song dating back to the 16th and 17th cs.) is the story of a Ukrainian peasant caught between the Reds and the Greens (Makhno's anarchist army), who is eventually executed by the former. Its hero, Opanas, in addition to being an actual character, is also a symbolic figure who represents the tragic plight of the Ukrainian people during the civil war following the revolution.

Ideological criticism leveled at the *Duma pro Opanasa* and disillusionment with Soviet reality drove B. into a severe depression and caused him to retreat even deeper into romanticism. The collection *Yugo-Zapad* (1928; southwest) is a quest for solace and comfort in the poetic affirmation of life. At that time too, he turned to nature and glorified simple biological life and its self-perpetuating force.

In the last years of his life. B. attempted to come to terms with the Soviet system. This shift is marked by the collections *Pobediteli* (1932; the victors) and *Poslednyaya noch* (1932; the last night)—both intensely ideological and filled with autobiographical material and psychological motifs.

B. was also a noted translator of poetry from English, French, Hebrew, Polish, Byelorussian, Tatar, and Ukrainian literature, as well as an illustrator of some of his own works.

Despite its stylistic eclecticism, B.'s poetry excels in richness and originality of imagery, intensity of feeling, and power of expression. While bemoaning the loss of spirituality in the world, B. affirms life and its natural grandeur.

FURTHER WORKS: *Til Ulenspigel* (1923); *Sobranie sochineny* (2 vols., 1938); *Izbrannoe* (1941); *Odnotomnik* (1941); *Stikhotvorenia i poemy* (1964); *Stikhi i poemy* (1972); *Zvezda Mordvina* (1972)

BIBLIOGRAPHY: Struve, G., *Russian Literature under Lenin and Stalin* (1971): 191–92; Moore, H. T., and A. Parry, *Twentieth-Century Russian Literature* (1974):88-89; Rosslyn, W., "The Path to Paradise: Recurrent Images in the Poetry of E. B.," *MLR*, 71 (1976): 97–105; Slonim, M., *Soviet Russian Literature: Writers and Problems 1917–1977* (1977): 132–33; Rosslyn, W., "B.'s *Duma pro Opanasa*: The Poem and Its Context," *CASS*, 11 (1977): 388–405; Cavaion, D., *Memoria e poesia: storia e letteratura degli Ebrei russi nell'eta moderna* (1988)

—LEONID RUDNYTZKY

BAGRYANA, Elisaveta

(pseud. of Elisaveta Belcheva) Bulgarian poet, b. 29 April 1893, Sliven

Born into a well-to-do family, B. received a solid education and showed an early interest in literature. Her first collection of poetry, *Vechnata i svyatata* (the eternal and holy woman), however, did not appear until 1927. The novelty of this volume consisted in its clear rejection of the hitherto dominating streams in Bulgarian literature and an embracing of the exceptionally rich traditions of Bulgarian oral folklore as a source of artistic inspiration. B. took from folklore a simplicity and directness of expression. Her poetic world is built on objects and phenomena around us. In its concreteness, B.'s early poetry was a reaction against SYMBOLISM; in its personal tone, it stood apart from the revolutionary rhetoric and old-fashioned patriotism of the 19th-c. poets.

Four major subjects—women, love, travel, and life as biological phenomenon—are clearly discernible in B.'s poetry, although they are constantly intertwined and constitute a homogeneous whole.

B. entered Bulgarian poetry as an advocate of women's emancipation. It would, however, be an oversimplification to see this stand as a revolt against existing social and moral conventions fostering the inequality of the sexes. The title of her first volume shows that B. was concerned with more fundamental issues. She refers to various archetypal images of women through the ages in classical, Christian, and pagan mythology. What B. values most are the primitive and primordial elements in human nature. The return to the origins of existence is combined with the biological joy of life. As far as woman is concerned, this vitality enables her to surmount prejudices and humiliation and break out of seclusion. The rebellious qualities within woman herself must burst through the ossified crust of prejudice.

The theme of woman is closely associated with that of love. From the time B. first began to write, to her poems of the 1970s, her work resounds with a cry for love, as in "Vik" (1923; cry) and "Zov" (1923; call). Without love-which the poet calls the "conscience of the earth" in "Kato sluntse" (1925; like the sunshine)—our world would be poor, sad, and gray; woman's liberation, her true equality with man, all hinge on love.

B.'s poems written immediately after World War II, in an atmosphere of increasing Stalinism and under the imposition of SOCIALIST REALISM, are more bombastic and politically motivated than her previous work. Fortunately, B. soon realized that this course was foreign to her artistic nature and aesthetic beliefs, and she returned to her original interests, although perhaps with more emphasis on the beauty of her country. The style of her poetry has become ever more simple and direct.

FURTHER WORKS: *Zvezda no moryaka* (1932); *Surtse choveshko* (1936); *Pet zvezdi* (1953); *Ot bryag to bryag* (1965); *Kontrapunkti* (1972)

BIBLIOGRAPHY: Moser, C. A., *A History of Bulgarian Literature* (1972): 239–42; Knudsen, E., "The Counter-Points of E. B.," *CSP*, 16 (1974): 353–70; Możejko, E., "The Private World of E. B." *WLT*, 51 (1977): 216–20

—EDWARD MOŻEJKO

BAHDANOVICH, Maksim

Byelorussian poet, short-story writer, essayist, critic, and literary historian, b. 10 Dec. 1891, Minsk; d. 25 May 1917, Yalta, Ukraine

B. is one of the three pillars, with Yanka Kupala (1882–1942) and Yakub Kolas (1882–1956) of modern Byelorussian literature. Because of his aestheticism and immersion in classicism, his

impact on Byelorussian literature has grown only gradually, as the slow liberalization in Soviet life has "rehabilitated" nonsocialist writers of the past.

B.'s father was a teacher and a Byelorussian ethnographer. From the age of six he lived with his parents in Russia, away from his native land, for which he developed an intense fascination. Byelorussia was the spring for his poetic inspiration and patriotic preoccupation. While in Russia, B. finished secondary school and the law school in Yaroslavl. In his spare time, with the help of his family, he studied Byelorussian language and folklore. He died young of tuberculosis.

When in 1906 the prohibition against publishing in Byelorussian in the Russian Empire was lifted and the weekly *Nasha niva* (1906–15), around which the young Byelorussian movement grew, began appearing in Vilna, B. established written contacts with the "Our Soilists" (from the title of the weekly) and published his first short story (1907) and first poem (1909) in the newspaper. When B. visited his native land in 1911, he was full of ardent, idealistic love and a desire for action. He was readily received by the publishers of *Nasha niva*, the brothers Ivan and Anton Lutskievich, who guided him in the Byelorussian national cause and were instrumental in the publication, in 1913, of B.'s book of poetry, *Vianok* (a garland). B. also contributed many essays and critical articles to Russian-and Ukrainian-language periodicals.

In B.'s poetry and prose, along with the themes of zest for life, beauty, and love, there are social and patriotic concerns, including a strong interest in Byelorussia's past and its mythology. B. especially emphasized his people's cultural achievements in the 16th c., when Byelorussian was the official language of the Grand Duchy of Lithuania and a vehicle of rich cultural and artistic expression.

B.'s erudition, and his knowledge of major Western languages, enabled him to introduce into Byelorussian literature translations from the masterpieces of world literature. Yet he exhorted Byelorussians not only to borrow but also to contribute original forms and subjects. He is among the most intellectual and philosophical poets in modern Byelorussian literature.

FURTHER WORKS: *Tvory* (2 vols., 1927–1928); *Vianok paetychnai spadchyny* (1960); *Zbor tvoraw* (2 vols., 1968); *Maladzik* (1968). FURTHER WORKS IN ENGLISH: *The Burning Candle* (1991)

BIBLIOGRAPHY: Rich, V., "M. B. in Byelorussian Literature," *JByelS*, 1, 1 (1965): 36–50; McMillin, A. B., *A History of Byelorussian Literature* (1977): 149–60, 351; McMillin, A. B., "Tradition and Innovation in the Poetry of B.," *SEER*, 56 (1978): 261–74

—JAN ZAPRUDNIK

BAHR, Hermann

Austrian novelist, dramatist, essayist, and critic, b. 19 July 1863, Linz; d. 15 Jan. 1934, Munich, Germany

B. was educated in Salzburg, Vienna, and Berlin (he studied political science and economics) but did not complete his dissertation on Karl Marx and thus never received his degree. While spending a year in Paris (1888–89) he decided upon a literary rather than a political career. One of the most versatile and talented authors of his generation, B. was a focal point of Austrian and

German literary and cultural history from his youth onward. In religion Bahr became an atheist but after 1914 fervently returned to the Catholicism of his birth. In politics he was a Schönerer pan-German radical as a student, advocating the overthrow of the Austrian government and annexation to Germany, became a socialist with Viktor Adler, and developed finally into a devoted Austrian patriot who believed that all of his works could best be grouped under the heading "alt Österreich" (old Austria).

B. helped to found the journal *Die Freie Bühne für modernes Leben* in 1889, and, following a trip to Russia, settled in Vienna in 1891, where he worked as a journalist and theater critic. His literary reputation, his amazing energy, and his charisma made him the catalyst of the Young Vienna group—Hugo von HOFMANNSTHAL, Arthur SCHNITZLER, Richard BEER-HOFMANN. Stimulated by the flourishing state of the arts in Vienna, B. embarked upon a grandiose cultural program, which he fostered primarily through his critical essays and through his own newspaper, *Die Zeit*. However, in 1906, disenchanted by the unreceptiveness of the Viennese to his cultural ambitions, and embittered by their hostile, unprogressive attitude, B. left for Berlin, where he worked for two years as a stage manager for Max Reinhardt, an experience that stood him in good stead when he became director of the Vienna Burgtheater briefly in 1918.

B. began as a naturalist with the dramas *Die neuen Menschen* (1887; the new people) and *Die groß Sünde* (1888; the big sin), written in the manner of Ibsen. Under the influence of the French novelists Paul Bourget (1852–1935), Maurice Barrès (1862–1923), and J. K. Huysmans (1848–1907), he wrote, in STREAM-OF-CONSCIOUSNESS style, his first novel, *Die gute Schule* (1890; the good school), which created a minor sensation in Berlin. Bahr was instrumental in introducing the concepts and techniques of the Decadents into Germany and Austria. As a critic he emulated Jules Lemaître (1853–1914) with a highly impressionistic approach that best suited his character and temperament. In his work on EXPRESSIONISM, *Expressionismus* (1916, *Expressionism*, 1916), he attempted to define this newest literary trend without personally subscribing to it.

As an idealist and socially responsible artist, B. acted as a seismograph for the intellectual movements of his time, transmitting the ideas of the leading intellectuals and writers to the public in an easily comprehensible manner. His self-imposed task, as mediator between the artists and the public, was in essence the central aim of his life and work. He aspired to an ideal society in which culture was not merely a veneer but was deeply rooted in each member of the social group. This central idea of culture makes understandable his apparent changeability and the variety of his activities, his heralding of new ideas, his discovery and personal assistance of young writers, and his sharp attacks on bureaucracy, which he felt inhibited progress.

Although B. published approximately 120 volumes, he failed to produce one work, except possibly his autobiography, *Selbstbildnis* (1923; self-portrait), that is truly representative of his multifaceted personality. His most lasting work, indeed, has been the light comedy *Das Konzert* (1909; *The Concert*, 1910). This fragmentation of his ideas and the lack of any complete edition of his writings have greatly impaired his reputation. However, critics are increasingly recognizing Bahr's major critical and theoretical contribution to the development of modernity in Austria, not only in literature, but also in art, music, theater, and criticism as well. His contribution to the Secessionist art movement, led by Gustav Klimt, is one of his major achievements. His valuable collections of essays, *Zur*

Kritik der Moderne (1890; on the criticism of modernity), *Die Überwindung des Naturalismus* (1891; the overthrow of naturalism), *Studien zur Kritik der Moderne* (1894; studies on the criticism of modernity), *Renaissance* (1897; renaissance), and *Secession* (1900; Secession) provide the main critical thrust toward a modern *Weltanschauung* and chart the course for Austria's transition into the 20th c. in all fields of artistic endeavor.

FURTHER WORKS: *Fin de Siècle* (1890); *Die Mutter* (1891); *Russische Reise* (1891); *Neben der Liebe* (1893); *Theater* (1897); *Das Tschapperl* (1898); *Josephine* (1899; *Josephine*, 1918); *Wiener Theater* (1899); *Der Star* (1899); *Bildung* (1900); *Der Athlet* (1900); *Der Franzl* (1900); *Der Krampus* (1902); *Premièren* (1902); *Rezensionen* (1903); *Der Meister* (1904; *The Master*, 1918); *Dialog vom Tragischen* (1904); *Dialog vom Marsyas* (1905); *Sanna* (1905); *Die Andere* (1906); *Der arme Narr* (1906); *Ringelspiel* (1907); *Glossen zum Wiener Theater* (1907); *Die Rahl* (1908); *Drut* (1909); *Tagebuch* (1909); *Wienerinnen* (1910); *O Mensch* (1910); *Die Kinder* (1911); *Austriaca* (1911); *Das Prinzip* (1912); *Inventur* (1912); *Das H. B. Buch* (1913); *Der Querulant* (1914; *The Mongrel*, 1924); *Himmelfahrt* (1916); *Die Stimme* (1916); *Tagebuch 1917–1919* (3 vols., 1918–1919); *Die Rotte Korahs* (1919); *Burgtheater* (1920); *Summula* (1921); *Liebe der Lebenden* (3 vols., 1921–23); *Kritik der Gegenwart* (1922); *Sendung des Künstlers* (1923); *Der Zauberstab* (1926); *Österreich in Ewigkeit* (1929); *Mensch, werde wesentlich* (1934); *Meister und Meisterbriefe um H. B.* (1947); *Essays von H. B.* (1962); *Kritiken von H. B.* (1963); *H. B. Zur Überwindung des Naturalismus* (1968)

BIBLIOGRAPHY: Macken, M., "H. B., His Personality and His Works," *Studies*, 15, 57 (1926): 34–46; Daviau, D., "The Misconception of H. B. as a Verwandlungskünstler," *GL&L*, 11 (1958): 182–92; Daviau, D., "H. B.'s Cultural Relations with America," in Hietsch, O., ed., *Österreich und die angelsächsische Welt*, 2 (1968): 482–522; Daviau, D., "H. B. and Decadence," *MAL*, 10, 2 (1977): 53–100; Kronegger, M. E., "L'écrivain dans une societé en mutation: Le cas de H. B. (1863–1934)," *LJGG*, 20 (1979): 173–82; Daviau, D., "H. B. and Gustav Klimt," *GerSR* 3 (1980): 27–49; Nimmervoll, H., "Materialien zu einer Bibliographie der Zeitschriftenartikel von H. B. (1881–1910)," *MAL*, 13, 2 (1980): 27–110

—DONALD G. DAVIAU

BAINBRIDGE, Beryl

English novelist, b. 21 Nov. 1933, Liverpool

B. grew up in Formby, outside Liverpool, was educated in London, and studied drama. She acted in repertory theaters for ten years, then gave up the stage to pursue a writing career. Before achieving recognition as a novelist she worked in a bottle factory and as a clerk for her English publishers.

B. has often said that the subject of her novels is the past as she has lived it—that had she owned a camera, she might never have written a word. Indeed, her shabby childhood home in Liverpool bears a close resemblance to the claustrophobic setting of *A Quiet Life* (1976), just as her creeper-covered house in Camden Town is very much like Binny's in *Injury Time* (1977). William in *Sweet William* (1975) was based on her second husband. The twenty-three-year-old Hitler in *Young Adolf* (1978) was drawn, she says, not only from the historical model but also from memories of her complex, ill-tempered father, a "minor dictator in his own way even if he never came to power."

Yet each of her novels is quite different from the others, and none is autobiographical in the usual sense of the word. B.'s point of view is that of the social satirist, the parodist, the black comic. Her prose is short and biting; her focus is on characters within groups as they struggle clumsily against a world gone wrong—usually tormenting one another in the process. The emphasis is always on social observation rather than on any one character's interior development.

In *The Dressmaker* (1973; pub. in U.S. as *The Secret Glass*, 1974), *The Bottle Factory Outing* (1974), and *A Quiet Life*, B. portrays the small, neglected existences of lower-middle- and working-class people whose buried impulses lead them to acts of great violence and rage. Looking for certainties in a world that cannot possibly provide them, the dressmakers, wine-factory workers, and disappointed mothers of these books all share the same bafflement at the bleak powerlessness of their lives. Colorful, eccentric, often gross and slatternly, these "ordinary" people have extraordinary passions and delusions, and an unerring knowledge of how to survive. Each book builds to a denouement that is at once absurd, hilarious, and horrifying.

In *Sweet William* and *Injury Time* B. casts her satiric eye upon romantic relationships. The title character of *Sweet William* is a Scottish playwright who, moments after meeting Ann, sends her a television set so that she can watch him on a talk show. Before long Ann is completely in thrall. B. captures the irresistibility of this irrational human attraction while unsparingly plotting its painful, unavoidable end. In the same way that handsome young William is an impossible yet inevitable object of love, middle-aged Edward of *Injury Time* is somehow—in spite of his hypocrisy, insensitivity, and general spinelessness—an engagingly right choice for his mistress Binny, who loves him although she knows he is a liar and a fool. B. moves her characters through a skillfully constructed plot, suggesting finally that in a dangerous and morally ambiguous world, those who survive live unsentimentally.

Young Adolf is an imaginative re-creation of Hitler's hypothetical visit to Liverpool in 1912. The subject is a departure for B., yet the novel contains some characteristic elements: blundering, small-minded but fascinating characters; funny, event-filled narrative; and a portrait of human life as an ominous mixture of burlesque comedy and inescapable horror.

The comedy of *Winter Garden* (1980), a short novel about an adulterous middle-aged man who flies to Moscow with his lover, a pretentious painter, comes out of a keenly satiric, sometimes cruel, apprehension of the discomfiting effects of most contemporary social arrangements.

Watson's Apology (1984), unlike most of B.'s works, is set in the past and depicts Watson, an elderly retired headmaster who pistol-whips his wife to death and who dies in prison a dozen years later, during which time he produces several dense scholarly works and an ambiguous Latin document about the killing. The novel includes courtship correspondence between Watson and his unstable wife and demonstrates his disciplined form of genius, a challenging scenario for satire, to be sure, but B. carries it off with such flair that the reader isn't sure whether to laugh or to cry.

The book is typical of B.'s recent novels in demonstrating brilliant wit and imagination that focuses on luckless misfits from post-World War II Liverpool. These are people she has encountered who are not quite tragic and certainly not intrinsically comic, but all, even the suicides and those doomed to live without hope, are depicted with an unsentimental eye and a highly original comic sense. B. has also written travel works such as *English Journey, or, The Road to Milton Keynes* (1984), based on J. B. PRIESTLEY's book with a similar title, and *Forever England North and South* (1987), both demonstrating the same acute observation.

B. is mistress of the unfashionable, the worn, the unspiritual. Her spare prose is highly original, and her ironic jabs leave a permanent mark.

FURTHER WORKS: *A Weekend with Claude* (1967); *Another Part of the Wood* (1968); *Harriet Said* (1972); *Mum and Mr. Armitage: Selected Stories of B. B.* (1987); *The Birthday Boys* (1991); *Something Happened Yesterday* (1993); *Collected Stories* (1994); *Every Man for Himself* (1996)

BIBLIOGRAPHY: Johnson, D., "The Sufferings of Young Hitler," *TLS*, 1 Dec. 1978: 1385; Milton, E., on *Injury Time, New Republic* 25 March 1978: 27–28; Wenno, E., *Ironic Formula in the Novels of B. B.* (1993)

—LUANN WALTHER

BAKHTIN, Mikhail Mikhailovich

Russian aesthetician, literary theorist, and philosopher, b. 16 Nov. 1895, Orel; d. 7 Mar. 1975, Moscow

B. spent much of his life in provincial cities and towns, in poorly paid intellectual and literary activities. Educated at Odessa and St. Petersburg universities, he lived mainly in Nevel, Vitebsk, Leningrad, and Saransk between 1918 and 1969. In Saransk he taught literature at the Mordovian State University. In Leningrad he was arrested for political reasons and sent into a six-year exile on a collective farm in Kazakhstan. He spent the years of World War II in Moscow, where he also lived from 1969 until his death in 1975. Wherever he lived, B. became the center of intellectual circles involving diverse humanistic interests and innovative thinking.

B.'s fields of interest included philosophy, psychology, folkloristics, linguistics, anthropology, and aesthetics. He is best known for his writings on literary theory and criticism, with special emphasis on the functions of language and on the novel as an art form. His most prominent and influential books are *Problemy tvorchestva Dostoevskogo* (1929, rev. ed., 1963; *Problems of Dostoevsky's Poetics*, 1973) and *Tvorchestvo Fransua Rable i narodnaja kul'tura srednevekov'ja* (1965; Rabelais and his World, 1968), and posthumously published collections of articles show him to have been a thinker of remarkable breadth and depth.

The basis of B.'s approach to aesthetics was his conception of language, which he perceived in terms of dialogue. The individual word, phrase, or sentence should not be considered as autonomous or self-contained, but rather as an utterance conditioned by the fact that it is exchanged between an individual speaker, with all his social and personal peculiarites, and a listener who also has his own peculiarities. Each speaker is more or less aware of the linguistic environment and values of his listener, and the speaker subsumes the listener's point of view. The listener is thus an active participant in the utterances of the speaker. Any dialogue, moreover, is governed by the particular time and place—the social, cultural, and historical situation in which it occurs. Properly apprehended, therefore, language is not a fixed phenomenon with a stable set of values and meanings, but a fluid, dynamic medium that expresses constantly changing psychological and social circumstances.

For B. the concept of dialogue involved not only speaking, but thought processes as well. When we think, we are aware of the voices and values of other people, which we in fact share and which live within us. Thought itself is therefore a form of unspoken dialogue between ourselves and others. Since society is made up of a multiplicity of voices, an accurate depiction of reality must involve a dialogic representation of these diverse and conflicting points of view. The literary form best suited for such a representation is the novel.

B. viewed the novel not as a fixed literary canon but as a tendency subverting established literary norms, a force observable even in classical Greece. The novel is an elastic and comprehensive literary entity, a developing, exploratory response to the popular and democratic urge for various kinds of individual and social expression. It embraces all levels, varieties, and possibilities of language. As exemplified in the works of Fyodor Dostoevsky (1821–1881), the novel achieves psychological and social profundity through "polyphony," a portrayal of the complex relationships between the individual voices of characters and the perspectives they represent. In Dostoevsky, the most striking example of polyphony is the use by one character, in interior monologue, of the speech of another character, to form a kind of subjective, unspoken dialogue.

B.'s book on Rabelais as well as his commentary on Dostoevsky and Nikolay Gogol (1809–1852) often emphasize the concept of medieval carnival, a folk celebration that mocks and defies established authority. Through laughter and parody, the spirit of carnival attacks the dogma and pomposity of official social ranks. By dwelling on the drollery of the world, carnival achieves a temporary liberation from the prevailing order. It is the element of carnival, according to B., that provides the novel with much of its social, psychological, and moral interest and depth.

Specialists in numerous fields—including linguistics, philosophy, sociology, and cultural history—find B.'s writings relevant to their interests, and partisans of particular tendencies, such as semiotics and STRUCTURALISM, claim at least part of B. for their own.

FURTHER WORKS: *Voprosy literatury i estetiki* (1975); *Estetika slovesnogo tvorcestva* (1979). [It is assumed that B. is also the author of works published under the name of others: Voloshinov, V. N., *Marksizm i filosofiya yazyka* (1930; *Marxism and the Philosophy of Language*, 1973); Voloshinov, V. N., *Freidizm: Kriticheskii Ocherk* (1927; *Freudianism: A Marxist Critique*, 1976); Medvedev, P. N., *Formal'nyi metod v literaturovedenii* (1928; *The Formal Method in Literary Scholarship*, 1978)]. FURTHER WORKS IN ENGLISH: *Speech Genres and Other Late Essays* (1979); *The Dialogic Imagination* (1981); *Art and Answerability: Early Philosophical Essays* (1990)

BIBLIOGRAPHY: Ivanov, V. V., "The Significance of M. M. B.'s Ideas on Sign, Utterance and Dialogue for Modern Semiotics," in Baran, H., ed., *Semiotics and Structuralism* (1976): 310–67; Tamarchenko, A., "M. M. B.," *Freidizm: Kriticheskii Ocherk* (1983): 225–80; Clark, K. and Holquist, M., *M. B.* (1984); Morson, G. S., and Emerson, C., eds., *Rethinking B.: Extensions and Challenges* (1989); Morson, G. S., and Emerson, C., *M. B.:Creation of a Prosaics* (1990)

—DEMING BROWN

BALDWIN, James

American novelist, essayist, and dramatist, b. 2 Aug. 1924, New York, N.Y.; d. 30 Nov. 1987, St. Paul de Vence, France

B. lived his first seventeen years in the ghetto of Harlem, eldest of a family of eight children. Release and protection from his poor and difficult surroundings came through a Pentecostal church, in which B. was converted at age fourteen and which he served as a minister until age seventeen; through school; through exhaustive reading and writing; and through movies. B. worked at many factory and service jobs after his high-school graduation in 1942, until his early book reviews and essays, together with the help of Richard WRIGHT, won him a Rosenwald Fellowship in 1948. He left for Europe, and there he finished his first novel and many essays. In 1957 he returned to the U.S. in order to become involved in the Southern school desegregation struggle. By 1963 his travels and writing had propelled him to a prominent position of spokesman for the civil-rights movement and for American blacks, an unwished-for position with which he was burdened from that point on. From the 1960s on, he traveled regularly between the U.S., Europe, and Africa, squeezing in writing between numerous speaking engagements, public debates, dialogues, and interviews.

Go Tell It on the Mountain (1953), B.'s first novel, is also his most powerful and artistically controlled. Heavily autobiographical, the story takes us through the religious conversion of fourteen-year-old John Grimes, at the same time giving the histories of his mother, his stepfather, and his aunt, which have an impact on unwitting protagonist. The dichotomies of religious escape or protection, of sexual guilt or release, of family love or destructiveness, of racial adjustment or rage, are all themes that appear here in the particularized histories of the Grimes family, against the backdrop of the historical and social realities of American race relations.

Similar themes appear in B.'s most recent and longest novel, *Just above My Head* (1979), with the American race struggle updated through the 1960s and 1970s. Music, a supportive motif in the first novel, moves to the fore in the latest, the story of a gospel singer, "Soul Emperor" Arthur Montana, as narrated by his older brother, Hall.

Between these two works, which seem to complete a circle in B.'s artistic and novelistic concerns, are *Giovanni's Room* (1956), a short novel about a tragic homosexual relationship in France between an American white man and a Frenchman; *Another Country* (1962), exploring creative but also destructive racial and sexual liaisons in New York and France; *Tell Me How Long the Train's Been Gone* (1968), the life seen in retrospect of a fictional black actor, Leo Proudhammer; and *If Beale Street Could Talk* (1974), the story of a black family's attempt to protect the unborn child of Tish Rivers and her unjustly jailed boyfriend. While each of these novels has its strengths, particularly in exposing the reader to American racial and sexual discrimination, each also has inhibiting stylistic difficulties.

B. wrote the play *The Amen Corner* (1965) out of his church background, skillfully using a two-level set of a church and the attached living quarters of the pastor, Margaret Alexander, to demonstrate his theme of the importance of living in full acceptance of life's pains and joys rather than escaping pain through religion. Inspired by the death of the young black man Emmett Till in Mississippi in 1955, B.'s *Blues for Mister Charlie* (1964) dramatizes the conflict in a Southern town before and after the death of a young black, a moderate minister's son, who is shot by a white store owner. Both plays are especially notable for and effective in the use of music-hymns, jazz, folk, union songs adopted for the civil-rights struggle.

B. is perhaps most widely read as a writer of essays, a form to which he has brought great honesty and skill. His best essays move outward from an autobiographical base to wideranging social comment and recommendation. The title essay in the collection *Notes of a Native Son* (1955), for example, uses the death of B.'s father, the birth of his youngest sister, and the Harlem riot of 1943 to develop the idea of the rage and hope of growing up black in America. With their parallelisms and deliberate repetitions, B.'s essays have electrified readers. *The Fire Next Time* (1963), containing two essays, became a manifesto for black liberation. Later publications of B. came in the form of "raps" or dialogues: one, *A Rap on Race* (1971), with anthropologist Margaret Mead (1901–1978; another, *A Dialogue* (1973), with the young black poet Nikki Giovanni (b. 1943).

Added to book publications are numerous published debates, interviews, and reviews that express B.'s views on art and society. B. is, indeed, a passionate, committed, versatile, honest, and courageous writer.

FURTHER WORKS: *Nobody Knows My Name* (1961); *Nothing Personal* (1964, with Richard Avedon); *No Name in the Street* (1972); *One Day, When I Was Lost* (1972); *The Devil Finds Work* (1976); *Little Man, Little Man* (1976); *The Price of the Ticket: Collected Nonfiction, 1948-1985* (1985); *The Evidence of Things Not Seen* (1985); *Jimmy's Blues: Selected Poems* (1985); *Conversations with J. B.* (1989); *Early Novels and Stories* (1998); *Collected Essays* (1998)

BIBLIOGRAPHY: Eckman, F., *The Furious Passage of J. B.* (1966); Kinnamon, K., ed., *J. B.: A Collection of Critical Essays* (1974); O'Daniel, T., *J. B.: A Critical Evaluation* (1977); Weatherby, W., *Squaring Off: Mailer vs. B.* (1977); Pratt, L., *J. B.* (1978); Standley, F., and N. Standley, *J. B.: A Reference Guide* (1980); Sylvander, C. W., *J. B.* (1980); Troupe, Q., ed., *J. B.: The Legacy* (1989); Campbell, J., *Talking at the Gates: A Life of J. B.* (1991); Leeming, D. A., *J.B.: A Biography* (1994)

—CAROLYN WEDIN SYLVANDER

BALINESE LITERATURE

See Indonesian Literature

BALLAGAS, Emilio

Cuban poet and translator, b. 7 Nov. 1908, Camaguey; d. 11 Sept. 1954, Havana

B. earned a Ph.D. in education in 1933 and a second Ph.D. in philosophy in 1945, both from the University of Havana, and was professor of literature at various institutions from 1933 until the year of his death. Besides his poetry B. was also an important translator from English and French into Spanish.

B. is considered one of Cuba's most original poetic voices. Although his work includes an important vein of poetry of the NÉGRITUDE, as in *Cuaderno de Poesía Negra* (1934; black poetry notebook), B. is today better known for the innocent, pure poetry of his first book, *Júbilo y Fuga* (1931; rejoicing and flight) and for the tortured intimism of his later books *Elegía sin nombre* (1936; nameless elegy), *Nocturno y elegía* (1938; nocturne and elegy), and *Sabor eterno* (1939; taste of the eternal). In these books B. expressed the existential anguish of the poet alienated from society with no recourse even to religious succor, which B. felt had been denied him because of the self-perceived sinfulness of his life. It is this counterpoint of the poet's guilt and the transparent innocence of much of his poetry that distinguishes B.'s production from that of other poets of his generation. B. traveled from the pure, virginal, jubilant production of his first book to the elegiac, self-absorbed, melancholy of *Nocturno y elegía, and Sabor eterno*.

Even though B. was at first better known for his poems of the black experience, the critical consensus now leans toward an enhanced appreciation of his later books, and a lessening of the interest in his Négritude poems, considering the latter largely as the picturesque product of an outsider. The initial interest in this poetry may have been rooted on B.'s publication of two ground-breaking anthologies of black poetry as well as on the central theme of his Ph.D. dissertation.

FURTHER WORKS: *Antología de poesía negra hispanoamericana* (1935); *Nuestra Señora del Mar* (1943); *Mapa de la poesía negra americana* (1946); *Décimas por el júbilo martiano en el Centenario del Apóstol José Martí* (1953)

BIBLIOGRAPHY: Vitier, C., Obra poética de E. B. (1955); Augier, A., *E. B.: Orbita de E. B.* (1965); Rice, A. P., *E. B.: Poeta o poesia* (1966); Pallas, R., *La poesia de E. B.* (1973)

—NICASIO SILVERIO

BALLARD, J(ames) G(raham)

English novelist and short-story writer, b. 15 Nov. 1930, Shanghai, China

B.'s earliest experiences encompassed both strange Eastern cultures, an apocalyptic war, and an early internment in a Japanese prison camp. Following this auspicious beginning, B. half-heartedly studied medicine, and eventually joined the Royal Air Force to become a pilot. While these early elements certainly influenced B.'s imaginative landscape, his own meditative connection to the New Wave of British science fiction is equally important. Responding keenly to the transformations in the postwar landscape, B.'s work not only navigated social space, but inner space as well.

B.'s first forays into speculative fiction were environmental and moral tales of man's inevitable decline, in the face of his constant tinkering. *The Wind from Nowhere* (1962) takes place in contemporary London, and gloomily narrates the disintegration of the city in the face of freak winds produced by scientific tampering. In the same vein, *The Drowned World* (1962) focuses on the delicate balances of nature, and the catastrophes which ensue after the accidental, and unforeseen, melting of the ice caps. *The Drought* (1965), the last of his early works, outlines the rise of a new economic system based on water, in a world shriveling up under its burden of radioactive waste. While these novels do tend to plod along in the familiar eco-disaster genre, they avoid either propagandizing or drawing facile conclusions about man's inherent evil. B.'s concerns range across deeper existential questions, in which man's accidental and precarious place in the universe becomes a puzzle in itself. These novels are less concerned with moralizing, as they are with the basic fact of life: one false move, and the entire species will become extinct.

Quickly exhausting the possibilities of the eco-drama, B.'s next phase shifted inwards. *The Crystal World* (1966), as the title suggests, is a place where life is frozen into place, where choices and questions of free will have no apparent baring on life. In such an environment, social and spatial relations tend to disintegrate, leaving nothing but the psychotic identity of the extreme individual. Questions of good and evil, correct behavior, and responsibility are rejected as irrelevant hindrances.

This move in B.'s work tended to characterize his next phase, though the questions of psychological identity were inescapably linked to technological development. The publication of *Crash* (1973) heralded a major change in B.'s work, marking a fascination for the encroachment of the technological into the human realm, and the ways in which human identity and psychology are mutated by technological surroundings. *Crash* explores the dehumanization of eroticism, and turns sexuality into an exploration of the mechanical and technological. By reducing sexual connection to the car crash, to the destruction of bought things, B. reduces the human to an extension of his own machines. Rampant consumerism overrides all other aspects of human identity, suggesting that his characters are literally the sum of what they own.

If B. is interested by the stuff of modern life, he is also fascinated with the shape of that life, with the places and escapes that life offers. *High Rise* (1975) outlines the life experiences of a group trapped within the disintegrating community of a high-rise complex. Their lives become so "programmed" by their living space, that it begins to produce new ways community thinking within the complex. The brutal environment that emerges sets class against class, in a war of control and an orgy of self destructive behavior. Left to their own devices, the inhabitants destroy themselves. For B. the modern architecture that was meant to liberate, perversely backfires, producing a new barbarism based on elitist attitudes, concretized class positions, and rampant consumption. B. shifts this concern into a surrealistic vein in *The Unlimited Dream Company* (1981). Blending plane crashes and encounters with the character's dead self, the novel explores a dreamscape that is entirely reliant on the projections of deep psychological needs. The new Messiah manages to unleash powerful erotic dreams in the people around him, and the community collapses into an orgy of perverse pleasures.

B.'s most recent phase has charted the relations between the autobiographical impulse, history, and the emergence of new televisual technologies. *Empire of the Sun* (1984) blends a boy's own adventure story with war-memoir, creating an adult fantasy about childhood. A wholly unsentimental novel, the supposedly innocent child struggles through a bleak landscape of loss and the human wreckage of World War II, only to come of age in the nuclear flash of the Nagasaki bomb. The novel unsettles traditional conventions because the boy imaginatively creates his world around him. Similarly, in *The Day of Creation* (1987) the protagonist creates a new river in Africa, and pursues it to its source, only to find it made up of video and television images that become more real than reality itself. Drifting in this landscape, for B., is akin to drifting in our own cultures.

B. remains a prolific and consistently disturbing writer, who crosses the lines of science fiction to produce novels of modern psychology, proving that inner space is boundless. His gradual switch from the fantastic world of the future to the even more fantastic, and horribly convincing, world of the present, only illustrates B.'s range and importance as a writer.

FURTHER WORKS: *The Voices of Time and Other Stories* (1962); *Billenium and Other Stories* (1962); *Passport to Eternity* (1963); *Terminal Beach* (1964); *The Impossible Man and Other Stories* (1966); *The Disaster Area* (1967); *The Day of Forever* (1967); *The Overloaded Man* (1967); *The Atrocity Exhibition* (1970); *Chronopolis and other Stories* (1971); *Vermillion Sands* (1971); *Concrete Island* (1974); *Low Flying Aircraft and Other Stories* (1976); *The Venus Hunters* (1980); *Hello America* (1981); *Myths of the Near Future* (1982); *Memories of the Space Age* (1988); *Running Wild* (1988); *War Fever* (1990); *The Kindness of Women* (1991)

BIBLIOGRAPHY: Goddard, J., *J. G. B.: The First Twenty Years* (1976); Pringle, D., *Earth is the Alien Planet* (1979); Brigg, P., *J. G. B.* (1985); Stephenson, G., *Out of the Night and into the Dream: A Thematic Study of the Fiction of J. G. B.* (1991)

—PAUL HANSOM

BALMONT, Konstantin Dmitrievich

Russian poet and essayist, b. 15 July 1867, Gumnishchi; d. 24 Dec. 1942, Nosy-le-Grand (near Paris), France

Born into an aristocratic family on a country estate, B. attended Moscow University. He suffered for his early revolutionary enthusiasms, both at home and in Moscow. Later, he lost interest in radical politics, devoting himself to writing poetry and excellent translations, as well as to extensive traveling. After the revolution of November 1917, he emigrated to France, where he remained the rest of his life.

Starting in 1890 with poetry devoted to country themes—*Sbornik stikhotvoreny* (a collection of verses)—he soon felt at home in the Russian city (Moscow), with its cult of individualism and brittle temperaments, as shown in the volumes *Pod severnym nebom* (1894; under the northern sky), *Tishina* (1898; stillness), and *Budem kak solntse* (1903; let us be like the sun). He also published a series of other collections.

He was one of the early major Russian poets who took their inspiration and creative cue from the European SYMBOLIST movement. Together with BRYUSOV and BELY, B. challenged the literary concepts and techniques of an earlier period, the Russian Golden Age. Glorying in the term "decadent," B. helped lead the way to a new, "Silver Age" in Russian literature and culture. He offended representatives of opposing groups grievously and deeply, a phenomenon most clearly shown by MAYAKOVSKY's often quoted proclamation that B. was a "perfumed whore."

While B.'s attraction to pornographic poetry and dandyish appearance no doubt provoked such extreme reactions, his unconventional and striking poetic forms unquestionably stimulated the passion and the anger, sometimes the bitter satire, directed at him in the first fifteen years of the 20th c. He had an uncanny ear for the sounds and rhythms of the Russian language and used them to produce the most striking and arresting music ever heard in Russian poetry, often twisting the medium in a way that seemed affected to many conservative readers. B. never shrank from extremes of assonance, dissonance, and immodest poetic claims. He merely stated that his poetry represented the exquisiteness of Russian sounds, and that all earlier poets were his precursors.

The only other 20th-c. poet to come near B.'s talent for the musical use of Russian words and sounds was Osip MANDELSHTAM. The reason for the latter's higher and wider reputation was his ability to infuse a high intelligence into the structure of his poetry. B. was never concerned about this; for him, the sound of the poetry was everything, including its meaning. Although he fell into repetition by 1910, and into oblivion in the later years, abandoned even by his early symbolist allies, he had made the language sing as few others managed to do. He mightily shaped the form of an entirely new style and mood in Russian poetry, which still affects the literary language. There has recently been a rekindling of interest in his work, both in the U.S.S.R. and abroad.

FURTHER WORKS: *V bezbrezhnosti* (1895); *Kniga razdumy* (1899); *Goryashchie zdania* (1900); *Tolko lyubov* (1903); *Gornye vershiny* (1904); *Feynye skazki* (1905); *Liturgia krasoty* (1905); *Zhar-ptitsa* (1906); *Polnoe sobranie stikhov* (10 vols., 1907–14); *Belye zarnitsy* (1908); *Zovy drevnosti* (1908); *Ptitsy v vozdukhe* (1908); *Moskoe svechenie* (1910); *Zmeinye tsvety* (1910); *Ispanskie narodnye pesni* (1912); *Zarevo zor* (1912); *Bely zodchy* (1914); *Kray Ozirisa* (1914); *Poezia kak volshebstvo* (1915); *Yasen* (1916); *Slovo o muzyke* (1917); *Svetozvuk v prirode i svetovaya simfonia Skryabina* (1917); *Re-volyutsioner ya ili net* (1918); *My* (1920); *Persten* (1920); *Sem poyom* (1920); *Dar zemle* (1921); *Pesnya rabochego molota* (1922); *Pod novym serpom* (1923); *Visions solaires* (1923); *Vozdushny put* (1923); *Gde moy dom?* (1924); *Moe-ey* (1924); *V razdvinutoy dali* (1930); *Stikhotvorenia* (1969); *Izbrannye stikhotvorenia i poemy* (1975)

BIBLIOGRAPHY: Poggioli, R., *The Poets of Russia* (1960): 89–96; Erenburg, I., *People and Life 1891–1921* (1962): 101–7; Althaus-Schönbucher, S., *K. D. B.* (1975)

—IRWIN WEIL

BALOCHI LITERATURE

See Pakistani Literature

BALTI LITERATURE

See Pakistani Literature

BANDEIRA, Manuel

Brazilian poet, critic, essayist, and translator, b. 19 April 1886, Recife; d. 13 Oct. 1968, Rio de Janeiro

B. went to Rio de Janeiro as a child; his secondary education in that city included study under two important critics, José Veríssimo (1857–1916) and João Ribeiro (1866–1934). Thereafter he went to the São Paulo Polytechnic School to specialize in architecture. But he contracted tuberculosis and was unable to finish his course. From 1913 to 1914 he stayed in a sanatorium in Switzerland, where he met the French poet Paul ELUARD. His poor health kept him from seeking regular employment, but in the 1920s he began to write music criticism and columns for the newspapers. In 1935, after his health had improved, he became an inspector of secondary education, and in 1938 he began teaching literature at the school in Rio where he had been a student. A little later the University of Brazil was founded in Rio, and he was appointed professor of Spanish American literature in 1943, a post from which he retired in 1956. In 1940 he was elected to the Brazilian Academy of Letters.

B.'s life story is told with humor and sensitivity in his autobiography *Itinerário de Pasárgada* (1954; the route to Passargada), and scenes from it are depicted in many poems, such as "evocação do Recife" (1930; evocation of Recife), "Na rua do Sabão" (1924; on Soap Street), and "Balõezinhos" (1924; little paper balloons). An excellent prose writer, B., in addition to art and music criticism, also wrote literary essays, letters, a biography of the romantic poet, *Gonçalves Dias* (1952), and a classic book about Ouro Preto, the museum city, *Guia de Ouro Preto* (1938; guide to Ouro Preto). He also did verse and prose translations from several languages, including Shakespeare's *Macbeth* (1956) and Schiller's *Mary Stuart* (1955). He is the author of *Noções de história das literaturas* (1940; elements of the history of literatures), among which is an excellent account of that of Brazil, published in English as *Brief History of Brazilian Literature* (1958). His edition of the fascinating letters that Mario de ANDRADE wrote him, *Cartas* (1958; letters,) shows the two men's close relationship.

Thus, as a prose writer, translator, and scholar B. has a distinguished reputation. His fame, however, rests chiefly on his poetry, which, although essentially lyrical, is astonishingly varied. He shows great mastery of transitional and experimental forms and styles, from the lyric of the medieval Galician-Portuguese poets to the Japanese haiku. He wondered about the genesis of poetry, tried SURREALISM, and concluded that at its best, poetry originates in the subconscious; one of his poems, he was surprised to discover, came to him in his sleep. In spite of his theorizing his poetry cannot be called intellectual. It is beautifully simple. Beneath the continual irony one senses a deep feeling of tenderness for others and a love for simple people, simple things, and simple experiences, as in "Irene no céu" (1930; Irene in heaven), a brief statement about a gentle Black woman.

His early lyrics—*A cinza das horas* (1917; the ashes of the hours); *Carnaval* (1919; carnival); and *Ritmo dissoluto* (rhythm in dissolution), first published in the collected edition *Poesias* (1924; poems)—reveal the influence of SYMBOLISM in theme and Parnassianism in form, but *Carnaval and Ritmo dissoluto* include some poems in genuine free verse, which were to serve as lessons in technique for other poets.

B. went to São Paulo in 1922 to participate in the Week of Modern Art. After his return to Rio he became the leader of the MODERNISM movement in that city. *Libertinagem* (1930; libertinage) shows how strongly he had been affected by São Paulo MODERN-ISM; the volume is modernist in manner and style; the language is colloquial, the form is free. The choice and treatment of subject matter are at times highly irreverent. In this volume one sees the breaking of the boundaries between prose and poetry in "Poema tirado de uma notícia de jornal" (a poem taken from a newspaper item) and "Pneumotórax" (pneumothorax), which is also an example of a favorite little modernist subgenre, the *poema piada* (joke poem), usually a very short affair with a surprising, ironic ending. In the next collections—*Estrela da manhã* (1936; the morning star), *Lira dos cinquent'anos* (poems at the age of fifty), both in the *Poesias completas* (complete poems) of 1944; and *Belo, belo* (beautiful, beautiful), in the 1948 *Poesias completas*—he was still elaborating on the early themes, but the former tone of disillusionment gradually made way for one of serenity and a stoical acceptance of his condition as a solitary human being. He bids farewell in "Preparação para a morte" (preparation for death) from *Estrela da tarde* (1963; evening star), which ends with "Blessed is death, the end of all miracles."

During his lifetime B. reached the point of being considered one of the two greatest poets of the modernist movement. Since his death he has been called a fine poet, but a minor one, perhaps because of the relatively small number of masterpieces he wrote and because of the rather limited thematic range of his work. In his corpus, however, there are two or three dozen poems of unquestioned greatness possessing an astounding technical virtuosity and a constantly surprising originality.

FURTHER WORKS: *Crônicas da província do Brasil* (1936); *Poemas traduzidos* (1945); *Mafuá do malungo* (1948); *Literatura hispano-americana* (1949); *Opus 10* (1952); *De poetas e de poesia* (1954); *Frauta de papel* (1957); *Poesia e prosa* (1958); *Estrela da vida inteira* (1966). FURTHER WORKS IN ENGLISH: *This Earth, That Story: Poems by M. B.* (1989)

BIBLIOGRAPHY: Pontiero, G., "The Expression of Irony in M. B.'s *Libertinagem*," *Hispania*, 48 (1965): 843–49; Nist, J., *The Modernist Movement in Brazil* (1967): 113–28; Martins, W., *The Modernist Idea* (1970): 217–22

—RAYMOND S. SAYERS

BANERJI, Bibhuti-Bhusan

Indian novelist and short-story writer (writing in Bengali), b. 12 Sept. 1894, Muratipur; d. 1 Nov. 1950, Ghatsila

B. studied at Ripon College, Calcutta, from which he received degrees in 1916 and 1918. He left law school to support his mother and younger brother. Before he became successful as a writer, he had held a variety of jobs, including that of schoolteacher, a profession that provided the background for his novel *Anubartan* (1952; movement in a circle).

Although B. had been publishing short stories since 1921, many in prestigious journals, it was *Pather panchali* (1929; *Pather Panchali: Song of the Road*, 1968), first serialized in the monthly *Bichitra*, that made his name a household word in Bengal. The publication of *Pather panchali* immediately made him a writer close to the Bengali reader's heart, an affection he was to retain. *Pather panchali* is not so much a novel as a sequence of episodes

from the life of the family of the poor Bengali Brahman Harihar. In many ways it is the story of B.'s own childhood. Although the narrative lacks a real plot, inner unity is nevertheless achieved by B.'s concentration on the main characters—Harihar's daughter, Durga, and her younger brother, Apu—and by his ingenious method of providing hints of events to come.

B. succeeded in conveying, from an Indian perspective, strong emotional experiences within the seeming pointlessness of human existence. Few other works in contemporary Indian literature reach the level of achievement of *Pather panchali*, now considered a world classic. The book and its sequel, *Aparajita* (1932; the unvanquished), were made into a widely acclaimed film trilogy by the Indian director Satyajit Ray. (A third novel, *Ashani samket* [1959; thunder signal], virtually his only novel that deals with an actual contemporary event, the Bengal famine of 1943, was also filmed by Ray.)

B.'s average reader found the author's world refreshingly different from the sordid, naturalistic worlds of his contemporaries, especially those writers associated with the progressive periodical *Kallol*. His writings reveal a love of nature unusual in Bengali fiction. In *Aranyak* (1934; the wild), the woodland is the protagonist, the force that controls the destinies of the human beings it shelters.

A second trait that characterizes B.'s writing, his faith in man's pristine innocence, has impaired his standing as a writer. Many of his protagonists, including Apu in *Pather panchali*, are somewhat Peter Pan-like in their mold; they never grow up beyond their guileless, bucolic, daydreaming childhood. For them, the complex life of cities, if they experience it at all, is like a bad dream, something to be endured. Like an unspoiled child himself, B. believed in the essential goodness of man and was always forgiving toward those who commit offense not out of design, but out of innocence. His tales convey a sense of compassion, never of tragedy.

The theme of the novel *Dristi pradip* (1935; the lamp of vision) is B.'s belief in a life beyond this one. But this belief in an afterlife, reincarnation, and the occult is sharply distinct from that of the Hindu faith, for it resembles the fancies, frequently found in children, that they have other personalities and lives. The borderline between the natural and the supernatural, as in a child's world, is not always clear.

FURTHER WORKS: *Meghamallar* (1931); *Mouriphul* (1931); *Jatrabadal* (1934); *Jamma o mrityu* (1937); *Chander pahar* (1937); *Bichitra jagat* (1937); *Kinnardal* (1938); *Maraner danka baje* (1940); *Adarsha Hindu hotel* (1940); *Abhinaba bangla byakaran* (1940); *Abhijatrik* (1941); *Smritir rekha* (1941); *Bipiner samsar* (1941); *Dui Bari* (1941); *Benigir Phulbari* (1941); *Mismider kabach* (1942); *Trinankur* (1943); *Nabagata* (1944); *Talnabami* (1944); *Urmimukhar* (1944); *Bane-pahare* (1945); *Upalkhanda* (1945); *Kedar raja* (1945); *Bidhumastar* (1945); *Ksana-bhangur* (1945); *Hira manik jvale* (1946); *Asadharan* (1946); *Utkarna* (1946); *Athai jal* (1947); *Mukhosh o mukhasree* (1947); *Acharya kripalni koloni* (1948); *He aranya katha kao* (1948); *Jyotiringan* (1949); *Ichamati* (1950); *Kushal pahari* (1950); *Chhotader srestha galpa* (1955); *Rupholud* (1957); *Anusandhan* (1960); *Chhayachhabi* (1960); *Amar lekha* (1961); *Sulochana* (1962); *Premer galpa* (1963); *Alaukik* (1963)

BIBLIOGRAPHY: Ray, A. and L. Ray, *Bengali Literature* (1942): 87–88; Bose, B., *An Acre of Green Grass: A Review of Modern Bengali Literature* (1948): 88–89; Chatterji, S. K., "*Aranyaka*,"

IndL, 2, 2 (1959): 32–37; Sen, S., *History of Bengali Literature* (1960): 363; Bagai, L. B., on *Pather Panchali: Song of the Road, BA*, 43 (1969), 646; Gerow, E., "The Persistence of Classical Esthetic Categories in Contemporary Indian Literature: Three Bengali Novels", in Dimock, E. C., Jr., et al, eds., *The Literatures of India: An Introduction* (1974): 212–38

—PABITRA SARKAR

BANGLADESHI LITERATURE

Although the country of Bangladesh was established as a political entity as recently as 1971, its literary heritage is both rich and long, and divides into three distinct phases. The first is the early modern period, dating from the latter part of the 19th c. to 1947; the second, the Pakistan interlude from 1947 to 1971; and the third, the independence era, starting in 1971.

Prior to 1947 Bengali-language literature existed as a single entity, although highly variegated and diverse in its themes, concerns, and genres. Traditional Hindu mysticism coexisted alongside Marxism; nationalist sentiments were expressed coevally with statements of romanticism and alienation; modernity and tradition clashed; and village and urban characters, the wealthy, the middle class, and the poor were all subjected to literary scrutiny.

In 1947 the Islamic Republic of Pakistan was created as a homeland for South Asian Muslims in the wake of the partition of the Indian subcontinent. Formed out of the eastern section of Bengal and parts of several states in northwestern India, the two parts, separated by a thousand miles of Indian territory, were held together by bonds of religion. Beyond sharing a common faith, the peoples of East and West Pakistan had little else in common.

From the outset West Pakistan asserted its domination over East Pakistan in nearly every sphere of life, including politics, industry, commerce, the civil service, and even language. Attempts were made to impose Urdu, the lingua franca of the elite of West Pakistan (where only three percent of the population spoke it as a first language), as the national language. Plans were also formulated to "Islamicize" Bengali by purging it of its Sanskritic-Indian identification and roots.

Resentment of such tampering built up rapidly among Bengalis. As a result of a strike called by Dacca University students to resist the imposition of Urdu as the national language, riots broke out on 21 February 1952, which left many dead. The single-language scheme was reluctantly abandoned, and Bengali, along with Urdu, was grudgingly recognized as a national language. Political and religious leaders, however, continued to give tacit approval to this process of Islamicization, and some writers acceded. The best of the East Pakistani writers, however, did not, even at the risk of censorship.

Between 1947 and 1971 a number of authors began to forge a Bengali literature independent of and distinct from that written in India. Poetry and fiction received the most attention. Among the poets to emerge during this period were Abdul Ghani Hazari (b. 1925) and Shamsur Rahman (b. 1929); among the fiction writers, Syed Waliullah (1922–1971).

Hazari's poetry possesses a highly modern, cosmopolitan flavor. His major collection, *Suryer strini* (1965; steps to the sun), contains a number of pieces that suggest the angst and disillusionment that pervaded the quality of life in post-1947 Pakistan. One of these poems, "Kotipoek amtar stri" ("Some Bureaucrats' Wives," 1967), is a bitter indictment of the vacuous, meaningless lives led by women whose nouveau-riche husbands shower them with things—gifts, spending money, expensive cosmetics, designer clothes—but little love or warmth.

Rahman's early poems, notably those in his second collection, *Roudra karotite* (1963; sunlight in the skull), are marked by a dynamic sense of experimentation. Many of these pieces are notable for their sense of irony, stunning visual images, and social consciousness. This last feature would later develop into an acute political awareness, an outstanding feature of his poetry written just before and since the Bangladesh war and freedom struggle of 1971.

Waliullah worked for many years as a press attaché and diplomat in the Pakistan foreign service. He published novels, plays, and several collections of short stories. His major work is the lyrical novel *Lal salu* (1948; *Tree without Roots*, 1967), the poignant story of the dedication, disillusionment, and tragic death of a young man who commits himself to the missionary work of the Tabighī movement, which sought to purge peasants and tribal peoples who had recently converted to Islam of their earlier Hindu customs and mores.

Because of West Pakistan's continued political and economic domination and oppression of East Pakistan, a short-lived but bloody civil war broke out in East Pakistan in 1971. The East Pakistanis, with the help of Indian troops, defeated the West Pakistanis, and the government of Bangladesh was established. Ironically, the new country took as its national anthem the famous song "Sonar bangla" (golden Bengal), written by the Hindu poet laureate of Bengal and Nobel Prize winner, Rabindranath TAGORE.

Understandably, the literature written during the latter part of the Pakistani "occupation" and immediately after Bangladesh's "liberation," terms now used to refer to these historical events, was overwhelmingly political. Poetry, fiction, and drama, as well as expository literature, dealt with the collapse of the ideal of Pakistan so cherished by Muslims of a generation earlier and with the problem of whether there was a genuine need for a single separate homeland for South Asian Muslims. The very asking of these questions brought about a profound identity crisis, and their answers have equally profound religious, philosophical, and historical ramifications.

Many writers who had established their reputations prior to 1971 were among those who contributed most passionately to the great mass of liberation literature. Shamsur Rahman's *Nija basbhume* (1971; one's own residence), *Duhsamaye mukhomukhi* (1973; confronting each other in bad times), and *Ek dharaner ahamkar* (1975; pride of one religion) are excellent examples of such writing. Alauddin Al-Azad (b. 1932) writes poetry as well as short stories and plays. His collection of short fiction *Amar rakta, svapna amar* (1975; my blood, my dream) and his play *Narake lalgolab* (1974; the red rose in hell) reflect the sense of disillusionment and rootlessness that pervades present-day Bangladesh, yet also suggest an undaunted spirit of renewal and rededication, which also constitutes the intellectual climate of the country.

Contact with the Bengali writers of India has been reestablished, and an enthusiastic intellectual and literary give-and-take, denied to both groups for over two decades, exists once again. The works of Bangladeshi writers regularly appear in print in India, and vice versa. While Bengal remains politically divided, its literature has been once again united.

Three distinct strains can be identified in Bangladeshi literature of the last two decades of the 20th c. The first of these is the discourse of political oppression, which chronicles the breakdown of societal values; another is feminist discourse, written mostly by women who challenge society's treatment of them; and third, fundamentalist discourse, a response, either positively or negatively, to the rise of fundamentalist religious thinking and action not only in South Asia but, it seems, throughout the world. Each of these, as well as others, mix and blend in various ways to underscore the political, religious, social, and economic foment that has been part of Bangladeshi national life since the country's founding in 1971.

The novel *The State Witness* (1985) by veteran Bangladeshi novelist and short-story writer Shaukat Osman (b. 1917) addresses the matter of political corruption, religious obscurantism, and the exploitation of women by powerful elites in Bangladeshi society in collusion with right-wing clerics and religious institutions. In the novel, Saburan, a village woman abandoned by her husband, moves to the city in hopes of finding work. There she eventually ends up running a brothel for Qazi Alamin (*qazi*, or kazi, ironically, is the title of a Muslim jurist or lawyer), who is also a low-level operative in a much larger international ring that ships women to Middle-Eastern countries as slaves. Saburan is arrested and held as a state witness against her employer. There are three separate points of view in the novel: Saburan narrating her story; Qazi Alamin relating his; and the proceedings against them both at the trial, at which the qazi's defense argues with some success that the Koran does not forbid slavery. Therefore, there is no case against him. The anguished fate of both the defendant and the state witness are predictable and inhumane, the outcome of a system whose laws are perverted to suit the interests and whims of the wealthy, or the biases of those who believe they possess a monopoly on truth. This novel caused a considerable reaction among various segments of Bangladeshi society not so much because of its depiction of political corruption or prostitution or the oppression of women, but rather because of its allegedly negative portrayal of Islamic law, or *shari'ah*, which, rather than British common law, is now applied in Bangladesh.

Similarly, Taslima Nasrin (b. 1962), a physician by training, author of eight volumes of poetry and a novel, *Lajja* (1993), and a prolific newspaper columnist on women's issues, was catapulted to international fame in November 1994 when religious fundamentalists rioted throughout Bangladesh calling for her imprisonment and death for having been quoted as saying, among other things, that the Koran, Islam's holy book, should be thoroughly revised. The novel, *Lajja*, chronicles the atrocities of Muslim fundamentalists in Bangladesh against their minority Hindu compatriots through the destruction of numerous Hindu temples, rape, and the confiscation of many Hindus' property. Across the border in India, the novel made Nasrin the unwitting darling of Hindu religious zealots who were carrying out their own brand of religious persecution of Indian Muslims, Nasrin's coreligionists. Nasrin claims she was misquoted regarding the Koran, but rioting crowds calling for her death forced her into hiding and her eventual departure to Sweden, where she was given sanctuary.

In *The Game in Reverse* (1995), a collection of select English translations of Nasrin's poetry, one encounters the author's liberal, feminist voice. The poem "Self-Portrait" contains the refrain, "I don't believe in God," but the narrator claims, instead, to see God in all things of Nature. She chides "the religion mongers" for dividing "us into castes" and excoriates politicians who "suppress all the terminology/of women's exploitation." In "Shame, 7 December 1992" the narrator relates how, on the day after Hindu fanatics in neighboring India destroyed the Babri Mosque in Ayodhya under the pretext that the mosque was built upon the very spot where the god Krishna was born (as it turned out, it wasn't), a gang of similarly pious Muslim men in Bangladesh stormed the home of a close Hindu neighbor and burned it down. When the poem's narrator later goes to offer sympathy and aid to the Hindu neighbor, (s)he finds him sitting amidst the charred ruins of his ancestral home, sympathy and help; "Out of shame," (s)he remarks, "I could not touch him." In "Lady Ayesha," the poet reinterprets the story of Ayesha, the Prophet Muhammed's favorite, youthful wife, who, while on an expedition with him, fell behind because she went to relieve herself. Discovered by a young soldier, she was returned to the group, but was later accused of adultery. Shortly thereafter, a revelation from God to the prophet asserted her innocence, and she was forgiven. Nasrin's poem, replete with ambiguity, suggests, first, that adultery did take place, but, more importantly, that such adultery is today viewed as "strength," which "give(s) life to women."

Taslima Nasrin was awarded the 1994 Sakharov Prize for Freedom of Thought; she continues to live in hiding and in exile.

BIBLIOGRAPHY: Amin, R., "Modern Poetry in East Pakistan: A Survey," *Mahfil*, 3, 4 (1967): 62–84; Chopra, P., *The Challenge of Bangla Desh* (1971); special Pakistan issue, *Mahfil* 7: 1–2 (1971); special Bengali poetry issue, *JSoAL*, 9, 4 (1974); Siddiqui, Z., *Literature of Bangladesh and Other Essays* (1984); Quader, O., *An Anthology of Modern Literature from Bangladesh* (1985); Huda, M., *Flaming Flowers: Poets' Response to the Emergence of Bangladesh* (1986); *Contemporary Literature from Bangladesh* (1990); Azim, F., *Infinite Variety: Women in [Bangladeshi] Society and Literature* (1994); Rustomji-Kerns, R., and M. Cooke, *Blood into Ink: South Asian and Middle Eastern Women Write War* (1994); Riaz, A., "Taslima Nasrin: Breaking the Structured Silence," *Bulletin of Concerned Asian Scholars*, 27, 1 (1995): 21ff; Murasida, K., *Contemporary Bengali Writing: Pre-Bangladesh Period* (1996); Murasida, K., *Contemporary Bengali Writing: Bangladesh Period* (1996); Nasrin, T., "A Disobedient Woman," *New Internationalist*, 289 (1997): 22

—CARLO COPPOLA

BANKS, Iain (Menzies)

Scottish novelist, b. 16 Feb. 1954, Dumferline

B.'s popularity among readers of fiction and science fiction began in 1984, fourteen years and six novels after he began to write seriously. In that year he published *The Wasp Factory*, a dark, disturbing novel with a truly disturbing yet effective twist that earned him instant success. Not one to be pinned down as a particular type of writer, B. moves easily between fiction and science fiction, equally competent and comfortable with both genres. He sees himself as a craftsman and, as such, takes both genres seriously and sees no distinction of worth between the two.

In 1987 B. published *Consider Phlebas*, a science-fiction novel. The title is taken from *The Waste Land* by T. S. ELIOT, B.'s favorite poem. This novel establishes "The Culture," sometimes called "extropian"—generally seen as an almost true utopia, which is the setting for several of his science-fiction books. The Culture is made up of a collection of many different organic species who are controlled by machine intelligences in a kind of benign dictatorship. A special feature is the possibility of immortality for the citizens of Culture, but it is not encouraged. B.'s novella entitled "The State Of The Art," published in 1989 in the U.S., examines how the Culture responds when it discovers the Earth. The juxtaposition of the two is a logical one for B. who constantly twists and turns his plots and characters. The novels that center on The Culture are parodies of "space operas." Not all of B.'s science-fiction novels feature The Culture but both he and his fans seem to prefer those that feature it. B. says that all writers of science fiction have their preferred worlds and this is his.

B.'s mainstream novels range from deeply disturbed and violent to almost cheerful, yet all can be satisfying to the reader. His favorite of his novels is *The Bridge* (1986), a Kafkaesque tale in which the protagonist finds himself in a world where fantasy and reality are fused together and he has little sense of what is happening to him. It is B. at his most provocative, tying in political and cultural references within the dreamlike reality/irreality. *Espedair Street* (1987) is a rare upbeat novel about a musician. B. recommends the novel as an introduction to his work. He likes to play with words and characters, trying out new ideas with each new book. In *Feersum Endjinn* (1994) B. actually constructed a phonetic language through which the character Bascule speaks. Using this language is provocative—forcing the reader to work to understand the text—and it works as a plot device, shifting the voice and tone of the novel to focus on particular elements of the story. The phonetics also works to ensure that Bascule's way of speaking, his pronunciation especially, is "heard" correctly by the reader.

B. is a writer who is often regarded as a cultish figure with unusual range and creativity. Recognized primarily as a science-fiction writer, B. is nonetheless a popular literary voice, and his dedication to his art is serious and determined.

FURTHER WORKS: *Walking on Glass* (1985); *The Player of Games* (1988); *Canal Dreams* (1989); *Use of Weapons* (1990); *The Crow Road* (1992); *Against a Dark Background* (1993); *Complicity* (1993); *Whit* (1995); *Excession* (1996); *A Song of Stone* (1997)

BIBLIOGRAPHY: Melia, S. A. "I. B.: 'Very likely impossible, but, oh, the elegance . . . ,'" *SFC*, 16 (1994): 7, 42-44

—MARCY TANTER

BANKS, Russell

American novelist, short-story writer, and poet, b. 28 Mar. 1940, Newton, Mass.

Born in Newton and reared in Barnstead, New Hampshire, B. was the oldest of four children abandoned by an alcoholic father when B. was twelve years old. After abortive attempts at college and at joining Castro's army in Cuba in 1958, B. eventually earned a graduate degree in 1967, the year his first book was published.

B.'s world—one with which he seems to have become familiar in his youth—is one in which people, mostly men, find themselves quietly desperate after years in their small working-class town, where they scrape to get by and lose themselves in drink and bitterness. They awake because either a sudden accident or a slow realization reveals to them the cold grayness of their lives. Their inevitable and inevitably doomed attempts to break out of these lives provide the driving force behind much of B.'s work; the deep determining connections between these towns and the larger forces of the world, and the psyches shaped by these environments, provide the texture, and the pathos.

B. first garnered a wider reputation, after years of collections of poetry and short fiction and largely unnoticed novels, with *Continental Drift* (1985), a novel some still consider his best work. In his portrayal of Bob Dubois's hopeful but ultimately hopeless attempt to realize the American Dream, by a scheme which entails uprooting his family from the cold North and leading them down to the sunny Florida Keys, B. creates both a full, deep picture of one man's inner struggle and at the same time a picture of the larger forces, material and cultural, that produce this struggle.

Success Stories (1986), a collection of short stories following *Continental Drift*, covers similar terrain, investigating the crippling discrepancy between American Dream and American reality, though perhaps more formulaically and so less successfully in the shorter form. In *Affliction* (1989), B. again returns to his cold North Country, here northern New Hampshire, and to men struggling with their world and with themselves. Wade Whitehouse is that powerless-feeling man here, but added to his position in the town (policeman and snow-plow operator) is his personal history: his place in a long, not-so-proud line of violent men. As told in the contrastingly reserved, educated voice of his younger brother, Wade's story is the story of his disappearance and of the tortured inner life that leads to his final, recounted days; it is this inner life, the psyche of the battered boy turned battering man, that most captures B.'s and his readers' attention.

Rule of the Bone (1995) might seem both a departure and a return for B.—a departure from his attention to the trapped men of his earlier novels and a return to the roots of American literature. But Chappie is, in some ways, less a departure from Bob Dubois and Wade Whitehouse, and more a younger, more extreme version of them. Growing up in an abusive world uninterested in providing much of a future for him, Chappie, as told in his Caulfieldesque voice, repeats this violence, turning to crime. In his relationship with his Jamaican Jim, B. revises *Huckleberry Finn* and repeats his connecting of Northern whites to Caribbean blacks and of both to the American Dream. Regardless of the possibly gratuitous and perhaps unflattering references to Mark Twain and J. D. SALINGER, *Rule of the Bone* continues B.'s relentless exposure of an increasingly shopworn American ideal.

Cloudsplitter (1998) represents his most radical departure of late. His not entirely successful portrait of abolitionist John Brown is given to us through the voice of Owen, the son who escaped after the massacre. Owen may be the wrong character for B. to use to tell this story; his inner conflicts receive too much attention, overwhelming what should have been a fascinating enough story in its own right. B.'s attention seems to have been drawn, perhaps to the detriment of this story, to the modern, alienated American man, unsure of his role in a hostile world, searching for meaning; it is his understanding of this man that has made for the success of so many of his novels.

FURTHER WORKS: *15 Poems* (1967); *Waiting to Freeze* (1967); *30/6* (1969); *Snow: Meditations of a Cautious Man in Winter*

(1974); *Searching for Survivors* (1975); *Family Life* (1975; rev. ed., 1988); *The New World* (1978); *Hamilton Stark* (1978); *The Book of Jamaica* (1980); *Trailerpark* (1981); *The Relation of My Imprisonment* (1983); *Brushes with Greatness* (1989)

BIBLIOGRAPHY: Reeves, T., "The Search for Clarity: An Interview with R. B.," *New Letters*, 53, 3 (1987): 44-59; Vandersee, C., "R. B. and the Great American Reader," *Cresset*, 53, 2 (1989): 13-17; Lee, D., "About R. B.," *Ploughshares*, 19 (1993-94): 209-13; Niemi, R., *R. B.* (1997)

—SAM COHEN

BARAKA, Amiri

(born LeRoi Jones) American poet, dramatist, essayist, novelist, and short-story writer, b. 7 Oct. 1934, Newark, N.J.

The son of a postal superintendent and a social worker, B. attended Howard University but left without a degree. After serving in the air force, he studied comparative literature at Columbia University. In the late 1950s and early 1960s B. was associated with the beat-poetry and avant-garde drama circles in New York's Greenwich Village.

Poems written between 1957 and 1961 were collected in B.'s first published book, *Preface to a Twenty Volume Suicide Note*

Amiri Baraka

(1961), a small paperback in an underground series that included work by Allen GINSBERG and Jack KEROUAC. While admiring Ginsberg and Kerouac, B. acknowledged the influence of William Carlos WILLIAMS on his early poetry and of Eugene O'NEILL on his early drama experiments.

From negativist preoccupation with death, suicide, and self-hatred in his early poetry, including *The Dead Lecturer* (1964), B. moved increasingly to positive exaltation of blackness and spiritualism, as in *Black Magic: Collected Poetry, 1961–1967* (1969). He began to use his writing talents for the proselytizing of black audiences, preaching separation of the races, self-discipline, self-love, and political activism.

In 1964 B. came into national prominence with the successful off-Broadway production of his play *Dutchman*, later presented in France, Germany, and Italy, and released as a film in 1967. The work is representative of his own middle-class background and of revolt against that background. A white woman is seen as a temptress to be avoided by a black man seeking roots. The same theme is found in a less successful short drama, *Madheart (A Morality Play)* (1967; first published in the anthology *Black Fire*, 1968). Here the level of violence is escalated, with ritualistic murder of a white woman. In 1969 B. collected this and three other short plays in *Four Black Revolutionary Plays*. As the title makes clear, B. considered literature a political weapon.

In 1965 B. divorced Hettie Cohen, his Jewish wife whom he had married in a Buddhist temple in New York in 1958. In 1966 he married a black woman, Sylvia Robinson (later to be called Amina Baraka). In 1967 he helped organize a National Black Power Conference. In 1968 he left behind his "slave name," Jones, for a new African identity, Imamu (Swahili, for spiritual leader) Amiri Baraka.

Black nationalism yielded in 1974 to a different political ideology for B., manifest first in articles for pamphlets and newspapers, then in plays such as *The Motion of History*, performed in New York 1977. The three-hour drama concludes with the transformation of white oppressors into Marxist co-workers. With his own conversion to Marxism, B. dropped "Imamu" from his name as having "bourgeois nationalist" implications.

B.'s better essays range from the formally structured English of the treatise *Blues People: Negro Music in White America* (1963) and *Home: Social Essays* (1966) to the consciously colloquial, choppy, vulgar, and invective style of *Raise Race Rays Raize: Essays since 1965* (1971), which is nevertheless eloquent in its own way. The later Marxist essays may contain some viable political alternatives but aesthetically suffer from the usual tired political jargon of the Marxist movements.

The System of Dante's Hell (1965), B.'s only novel, is written in the same choppy style as his essays and poems of the mid- and late 1960s. Loosely based on the themes of Dante's *Inferno*, it gives the effect of a prose poem—a series of impressionistic and expressionistic images, delivered with a rapid-fire, often disjointed technique, employing what B. himself calls "association complexes."

The short story "The Screamers," in *Tales* (1967), is especially successful in capturing the experience of being young and black in an urban environment—Newark in the late 1940s or early 1950s—and the emotional, galvanizing force of black music upon a black audience.

Much of B.'s work remains unpublished, and increasingly, what is printed appears in small, obscure pamphlets. B. is one of the most controversial contemporary authors. His chief importance may stem from his efforts to turn from a Western cultural background to a newly emerging black aesthetic flowing from the villages of Africa and the ghettoes of America. The strength and hard poetic beauty of his work are striking in originality. How his more recent immersion in Maoist-Marxist ideology will affect his work and what other paths he may take cannot with any certainty be predicted.

FURTHER WORKS: *The Slave* (1964); *The Baptism and The Toilet* (1964); *Slave Ship* (1967); *Arm Yourself or Harm Yourself* (1967); *Black Music* (1967); *In Our Terribleness: Some Elements and Meaning in Black Style* (1970); *Jello* (1970); *It's Nation Time* (1970); *Kawaida Studies: The New Nationalism* (1972); *Spirit Reach* (1972); *Crisis in Boston* (1974); *Hard Facts* (1975); *S-1* (published in *The Motion of History and Other Plays*, 1978); *Selected Poetry* (1979) *Sidney Poet Heroical* (1979); *Daggers and Javelins: Essays, 1974-1979* (1984); *The Music: Reflections on Jazz and Blues* (1987); *The LeRoi Jones/A. B. Reader* (1987); *Transbluesency: The Selected Poems of A. B./LeRoi Jones (1961-1995)* (1995); *The Autobiography of LeRoi Jones* (1997)

BIBLIOGRAPHY: Hudson, T., *From LeRoi Jones to A. B.* (1973); Benston, K. B., *The Renegade and the Mask* (1976); Sollors, W., *A. B./LeRoi Jones: The Quest for a "Populist Modernism"* (1978); Dace, L., "A. B. (Leroi Jones)", in Inge, M. T., J. R. Bryer, and M. Duke, eds., *Black American Writers*, 2 (1978), 121–78; Benston, K., ed., *Imamu A. B. (LeRoi Jones): A Collection of Critical Essays* (1978); Harris, W. J., *The Poetry and Politics of A. B.: The Jazz Aesthetic* (1985)

—DAVID BAKISH

BARAKAT, Hoda

Lebanese novelist, short-story writer, and journalist, b. ca. 1954, Lebanon

In 1974 B. graduated from the Lebanese University in Beirut with a degree in French literature. For two years she worked as a teacher in Lebanese villages, but left in 1975 to complete her education in Paris, France. However, after the outbreak of the Lebanese Civil War (1991-95), she returned to Lebanon where she earned her living as a teacher, journalist, and translator. In 1988 B. established a magazine for women, *Sherezade*. She currently resides in Paris, France.

B.'s most memorable novel to date is *Hajar al-Dohk* (1990; *Stone of Laughter* 1995). The novel won the presitigeous al-Naqid Award for a first novel, and received immediate critical attention. *Hajar al-Dohk* is a complex novel set during the Lebanese Civil War, and depicts the struggle of a gay man, Khalil, to define his identity within the confines of the war. The narrative fluctuates between a first person and third person narrative, with Khalil and an omniscient female narrator overlapping and at times merging. By interweaving the two voices, B. challenges the coersive nature of gender roles within society.

Although the novel focuses on Khalil's crisis, the novel has been hailed as one of the best novels written on the Lebanese Civil War, and has been recognized for its innovative treatment of the

psychological impact of war on everyday life. The novel is critical of many widely held beliefs. It confronts the nationalist preoccupation with death and self-sacrifice. It deconstructs the concept of martyrdom. In addition, it portrays the rigid overdetermining nature of war that locks human beings into clearly defined roles, both as victims and as perpetrators.

B.'s second novel, *Ahl al-Hawa* (1993; People of Love), returns to the impact of the Civil War on individuals but is simpler in approach and more conventional in content. The novel follows the delusions of an inmate in a mental institution, portraying his attempts to build an alternative reality to the war. The novel also explores gender issues, but without the harrowing details of *Hajar al-Dohk*.

While still at an early stage in her career as a writer, B. is already established as one of the foremost contemporary novelists in the Arab World. Within a short period of time her first novel has already been translated into French, Italian, and English. *Hajar al-Dohk* alone guarantees her a place in Arabic literature as one of the most original and technically innovative antiwar novelists in the 20th c.

FURTHER WORKS: *Za'irat* (1985)

BIBLIOGRAPHY: Sakhi, A., "Miqyas Majnun Li Harbin Majnuna," *al-Naqid*, 30 (1990): 69-70; Abdel Ilah, L., "Mi'mar Riwa'i Mudhish," *al-Naqid*, 32 (1991): 68-69; Binsa'oud, A., "Ta'riyat al-Harb," *al-Naqid*, 39 (1991): 70-71; Cooke, M., *Women and the War Story* (1996): 273-83

—MONA FAYAD

BARAŃCZAK, Stanislaw

Polish poet, literary critic, scholar, and translator, b. 13 Nov. 1946, Poznań

B., the most prolific representative of the New Wave in Polish literature and its main theoretician, graduated from Adam Mickiewicz University in Poznań (1969). During his student years, toward the end of the 1960s, he established with Ryszard KRYNICKI the poetic group "Attempts." Like Krynicki, he was considered an advocate of the so-called "linguistic poetry," and like other poets of the New Wave he expressed the social experience of the entire "Generation of '68" in his writing.

B.'s generational experience, the so-called March events of 1968, strongly influenced his first collection of programmatic articles, *Nieufni i zadufani. Romantyzm i klasycyzm w młodej poezji lat sześćdziesiatych* (1971; the distrustful and the overconfident: romanticism and classicism in the young poetry of the 1960s). Referring to the binary divisions into opposite and consecutive literary currents, the author distinguished two models of poetry, which in fact meant two different attitudes toward the world. The object of B.'s attack—classical tendencies of the 1960s—was characterized by poets' escaping from everyday life into the world of myth, avoiding the conversational idiom, and, as well, their inability of depicting social reality. In accepting the variant of a romanticism termed "dialectical," B. sought to unmask the antinomies of the social order. Consequently, his program turned into a vote of no-confidence in the political situation prevailing under real existing socialism.

B.'s early volumes of poetry, *Korekta twarzy* (1968; proofreading of a face), *Jednym tchem* (1970; in one breath), and *Dziennik poranny* (1971; morning diary), focused on a critique of the official language of the time. Irony and other devices adopted by B. usually liberated a series of associations that concealed derision of official press releases and slogans blazed onto banners and posters. They were meant to "teach how to think" and alert the reader to the danger of accepting in good faith everything that the indoctrinators served up.

The main characteristic of B.'s literary characters in the early and mid-1970s is vagueness. These characters are deprived of a sense of personal identity. They carry feretories in catholic processions as well as standards or banners in communist parades. They attend meetings condemning "rabblerousers" or "Zionists," and rely on the authority of others. They do not speak commonly used, colloquial Polish; they use a communist newspeak instead. All those features were most fully reflected in the volumes *Sztuczne oddychanie* (1974; Artificial Respiration) and *Ja wiem, że to niesłuszne* (1977; I Know It's Not Right). Neither of these books was officially published in Poland.

In 1975 B. became openly involved in protests against the restrictions of constitutional rights, and one year later he served as a cofounder of the Workers' Defense Committee (KOR). As a result of his political activity, he was fired from the post of assistant professor at the Adam Mickiewicz University, and his works were banned from official literary circulation by the censor. At the same time B., along with Krynicki, Adam ZAGAJEWSKI, and several others, started publishing the underground quarterly *Zapis*. In B.'s volume *Tryptyk z betonu, zmęczenia i śniegu* (1980; triptych of concrete, weariness, and snow), containing poems written in the late 1970s, a political reality constitutes the context within which the existential situation of an individual is described. New, metaphysical tones then appeared in the poet's works.

After "Solidarity" had come into existence, B. was allowed to leave Poland and to take up the duties as the Jurzykowski Professor of Polish Language and Literature at Harvard University. The imposition of martial law in Poland in December 1981 found him abroad. A series of B.'s poems, "Przywracanie porządku" ("The Restoration of Order," 1989), included in the volume *Atlantyda* (1986; Atlantis), remains a testimony to the poet's commitment to social questions, but political and moral problems are not isolated from the author's private life. Cross sections of these two commitments are also present in poems included in B.'s émigré volume *Widokówka z tego świata* (1988; postcard from this world). The scene and the very nature of the problems change, but the relationship between the world and the specific poetic ego remains as discordant and distrustful as it ever was. B.'s attitude toward language in general and the language of propaganda in particular is another characteristic of the author's faithfulness to his principle of distrust. B.'s playing with the conversational idiom and with the style of "bureaucratese" writing still produces splendid poetic effects. Yet the primary function of these games is not to expose the duplicity of this language, rather its mechanical and unreflective nature. In B.'s collections published in the 1990s, *Zwierzęca zajadłość* (1991; Animal Ferocity), *Zupełne zezwierzęcenie* (1993; Absolute Animals), and *Bóg, Trąba i Ojczyzna* (1995; God, Elephant's Trunk, and the Fatherland), a new distinctive quality appears: disinterested, nonsensical humor.

B.'s dualistic and internally split vision of the world has always been experienced in a dramatic way. The methods that reflect its semantic instability include paronomasia, ironically used homonyms, enjambment designed to play with the reader's expectations, and assonant rhyme. Rhyme in B.'s poetry is ostentatiously and purposefully casual, as if the author were suggesting that his world does not lend itself to rhymes.

B.'s literary criticism is strictly connected with his poetry through his system of the accepted literary values and through the author's passionate attitude toward the world. B. is interested in those writers whose works stimulate cognitive and moral questions as well as the techniques of persuasion themselves. He is also one of the most brilliant translators of English-language poetry into Polish and Polish poetry into English. His translations from English include a complete edition of sonnets by William Shakespeare, fifteen volumes of Shakespeare's plays, seventeen volumes of other English and American poets, and five anthologies of English poetry. B.'s translations from Polish to English include an anthology *Spoiling Cannibals' Fun: Polish Poetry of the Last Two Decades of Communist Rule* (1991, with Clare Cavanagh), Wisława Szymborska's *View with a Grain of Sand*, and Jan Kochanowski's *Laments* (1995, with Seamus Heaney).

During his literary career B. has been awarded several prestigious prizes—*Jurzykowski* (1980), Terrence Des Prés (1989), Culture Foundation Award (1997), and the Jan Parandowski Literary Award (1998).

FURTHER WORKS: *Ironia i harmonia* (1973); *Język poetycki Mirona Białoszewskiego* (1974); *Etyka i poetyka: Szkice* 1970–78 (1979); *Knebel i słowo* (1980); *Książki najgorsze* (1981); *"Bo tylko ten świat bólu"* (1981); *Wiersze prawie zebrane* (1981); *Czytelnik ubezwłasnowolniony. Perswazja w masowej kulturze literackiej PRL* (1983); *Uciekinier z Utopii. O poezji Zbigniewa Herberta* (1984; *The Fugitive from Utopia: The Poetry of Zbigniew Herbert*, 1987); *Przed i po. Szkice o poezji krajowej przełomu lat siedemdziesiątych i osiemdziesiątych* (1988); *Tablica z Macondo albo osiemnaście prób wytłumaczenia po co i dlaczego siępisze* (1990); *159 wierszy* (1990); *Ocalone w tłumaczeniu* (2 vols., 1992, 1994); *Podróż zimowa* (1994); *Poezja i duch uogólnienia: Wybór esejów* (1996); *Wybor wierszy i przekładów* (1997); *Chirurgiczna precyzja* (1998). FURTHER WORKS IN ENGLISH: *Where Did I Wake Up?* (1978); *Under My Own Roof* (1980); *Selected Poems: The Weight of the Body* (1989); *Breathing under Water and Other East European Essays* (1990)

BIBLIOGRAPHY: Witkowski, T., "The Poets of the New Wave in Exile," *SEEJ*, 33, 2 (Summer 1989): 204–16; Aaron, J., "Selected Poems: The Weight of the Body, S. B.," *Erato/Harvard Book Review*, 15–16 (Spring-Summer 1990): 10–11; Pettingell, P., "Exiled Poets," *The New Leader*, 53, 3 (1990): 19–20; Bernstein, R., "Breathing under Water in Poland," *NYT*, 30 Aug. 1990: C18; Cviić, C., "Communicating in Gurgles No More: Dissident's Insight," *Washington Times*, 24 Sept. 1990: F3; Crawford, R., "History As Curse," *PoetryR*, 18, 3 (1991): 35–36; Witkowski, T., "Politics for Art's Sake," *Periphery*, 3, 1-2 (1997): 62-68

—TADEUSZ WITKOWSKI

BARBADIAN LITERATURE

See English-Caribbean Literature

BARBU, Ion

(pseud. of Dan Barbilian) Romanian poet and critic, b. 19 March 1895, Cîmpulung Muscel; d. 11 Aug. 1961, Bucharest

Son of a magistrate, B.'s early education began in the provinces of Bacău and Argues and was completed in Bucharest. In 1914, he began his lifelong friendship with the critic Tudor Vianu (1897–1964) and enrolled at the University of Bucharest, concentrating on mathematics. Between 1921 and 1924 he went abroad to continue his studies at Göttingen, Tübingen (he returned there 1934–38), and Berlin. He taught mathematics at various secondary schools, and settled in Bucharest in 1925. In 1929 he received his doctorate in this field. A series of papers before international congresses in mathematics established his international reputation, and in 1942 he was appointed professor of algebra at the University of Bucharest.

In 1918 B. published his poem "Fiinta" (being) in Alexandru Macedonski's (1854–1920) symbolist *Literatorul*. Shortly afterward he took all his verses to Eugen LOVINESCU, editor of *Sburătorul*, who was so impressed that he published "Elan" (1919; elan), with a special article welcoming "this new poet." At this time B. took his pen name from his grandfather, a master mason from the slums on the outskirts of Bucharest. Other verses began to appear in various journals. In 1921 B. arranged for a private printing of *După melci* (looking for snails), the best poem of his early years. This poetry, Nietzschean in philosophy, with exotic landscapes and sensuous detail, written under the influence of the Parnassians and SYMBOLISTS, especially VALÉRY, eventually gave way to the "Isarlîk" cycle, set in Isarlîk, an imaginary city that evokes the colorful atmosphere of the Balkan region of Dobruja (with its Turkish heritage), somewhat in the manner of the tales by the popular folk writer Anton Pann (1796?–1854). These verses use detail from Romanian folk culture, often with a bizarre Oriental or Balkan coloration, a kind of strange poetic folk myth with such classic autochthonous characters as the gloomy jester Nastratin Hogea and the earthy, demonic Domnisoara (damsel) Hus.

Maturity came with the cycle "Joc second" (second game), the title deriving from the central metaphor: entrance as though through a mirror into a blue watery world where in the depths a second, "purer" game reproduces the surface game. This image embodies B.'s philosophy of reality and his concept of the function of poetry. In 1930 B. published his one book of verse, *Joc secund*, collecting together these poems from both cycles, which previously appeared only in periodicals.

A third cycle, "Uvedenrode" (a world beyond and beneath time and mode), published subsequently in various periodicals, was an attempt at "pure poetry," distinguished primarily by esotericism and folk symbols.

B.'s poetics link mathematics to poetry. In mathematics he had rejected narrow specialization for an enlightened eclecticism, an emphasis on metaphysical synthesis, and an insistence upon keeping in sight the homogeneity of the whole. Poetry, in like manner, he said, joins together separate elements by means of the metaphor. B.'s poetics are best expressed in two articles—"Poetica domnului Arghezi" (1927; the poetics of Mr. [Tudor] ARGHEZI) and "Cuvînt către poeti" (1941; advice to poets)—and his 1947 lectures on Rimbaud and the Greek-French SYMBOLIST writer Jean Moréas (1856–1910).

From 1947 to 1964 B.'s literary work was proscribed by the Romanian Communist Party authorities as "decadent," although he was permitted to contribute translations of Shakespeare.

B.'s articles and lectures on poetics, as well as comments left behind at his death, are included in the posthumously published *Pagini de proză* (1968; pages of prose). Also published posthumously were a collection of much of his verse, *Ochean* (1964; the spyglass), and then an all-inclusive edition using B.'s old title, *Joc secund* (1966), and including not only the original two cycles but also his early periodical verse, the "Uvedenrode" cycle, and two unpublished poems from his later years.

B. has been a major influence upon both the younger poets of the interwar years and more recent poets, for his craftsmanship and because of his poetics. He called attention to the multiple layers of meaning in ordinary Romanian words as well as in folk symbols and myths, available for poetic exploitation. He found in the poem a structure like that of the mathematical theorem, the axioms of poetry being the symbols from myth, from which a complex world is obtained. His own verse is distinguished by compact imagery, conceptual symbols, and language and metaphors with multiple meanings; an intellectualizing of the concrete; and transfiguration of everyday activities through "poetically descriptive incantations." His verse is multiplaned, reflecting what he called "the power of grasping a complex range of elements at one glance."

BIBLIOGRAPHY: Vianu, T., *I. B.* (1935; rev. ed., 1970)

—THOMAS AMHERST PERRY

BARBUSSE, Henri

French poet, novelist, and essayist, b. 17 May 1873, Asnières; d. 30 Aug. 1935, Moscow, U.S.S.R. (now Russia)

B. was born in a suburb of Paris. His father, a journalist and man of letters, had come from the south of France. His mother, a native of Yorkshire, England, died when the boy was still very young. As a student B. was influenced in turn by Zola, whom he eventually criticized for not going far enough in his social and political views, and by Catulle Mendès (1841–1909), whom he took for a poetic model.

Close for a time to the symbolist circles attached to José-Maria de Hérédia (1842–1905), B. as a young journalist contributed to daily and weekly periodicals and was awarded prizes for his early poetry, which also won the acclaim of Mendès. *L'enfer* (1908; *The Inferno*, 1918, also pub. as *Hell*, 1995), praised by Anatole FRANCE and Maurice MAETERLINCK, was his first major work. In this novel he sounded a note of visionary uneasiness and even despair, a discordant note in the complacent world of the early 1900s. B. asserts that in spite of his inadequacy, man continues to struggle to "reach beyond" himself.

B. also worked as literary editor in a large publishing house and became involved in pacifist activities during the years when hopes were high that war could be abolished. At the outbreak of World War I, although exempted from military service because he had had tuberculosis, he insisted on being drafted for front-line duty, believing this war would be the war to end all wars. As a private, he received several military citations.

His grueling war experiences resulted in the novel *Le feu: Journal d'une escouade* (1916; *Under Fire: The Story of a Squad*, 1917), which, although initially truncated by censorship, won him the 1917 Goncourt Prize. The book, translated into more than 50 languages, bears testimony to the sober humanism of reluctant soldiers and is a powerful indictment of War. B.'s eloquence lies in his fundamental simplicity. His characters speak naturally, often using soldiers' slang, and voice opinions vastly divergent from the then predominant glorification of patriotism. Evident, too, is his humane understanding of enemy soldiers.

After World War I, B. became a leader in French and international pacifist veterans' and writers' organizations and eventually joined the French Communist Party. *Clarté* (1919; *Light,* 1919) was an even more vigorous condemnation of war than *Le feu* and a rallying cry for intellectuals, who gathered for some years under the banner of the *Clarté* group. B., originally strongly influenced by naturalism, turned more and more toward history and became deeply committed to humanitarian and political causes. A number of his later books glorified Stalin, and he was on one of his trips to the Soviet Union when illness over-took him and he died.

FURTHER WORKS: *Le siècle* (1889); *Les pleureuses* (1895); *Les suppliants* (1903); *Meissonnier* (1912; written in French but pub. only in English); *Nous autres* (1914; *We Others,* 1918); *Paroles d'un combattant* (1920); *La lueur dans l'abîme* (1920); *Le couteau entre les dents* (1921); *Lettre aux intellectuals* (1921); *Quelques coins du cœur* (1921); *Les enchaînements* (1924; *Chains,* (1925); *Les bourreaux* (1926); *Élévation* (1926); *Force*; *L'au-delá Le crieur* (1926); *Les Judas de Jésus* (1927); *Jésus* (1928; *Jesus,* 1927); *Manifeste aux intellectuels* (1927); *Faits divers* (1928); *I Saw It Myself,* (1928); *Voici ce qu'on a fait de la Géorgie* (1929); *Russie* (1930; *One Looks at Russia,* 1931); *Ce qui fut sera* (1930); *J'accuse* (1932); *Zola* (1932; *Zola,* 1932); *Do You Know Thaelmann?* (written in French but pub. only in English, 1934); *Staline* (1935; *Stalin, a New World Seen through One Man,* 1935); *La Guerre en Ethiopie* (1936); *Lettres de H. B. à sa femme,* 1914–1917 (1937)

BIBLIOGRAPHY: Spitzer, L., *Studien Zu H. B.* (1920); Hertz, H., *H. B.* (1920); Cowley, M., *H. B.* (1922); Mancisodor, J., *H. B* (1945); Fréville, J., and J. Duclos, *H. B.* (1946); Vidal, A., *H. B., Soldat de la paix* (1955); Brett, V., *H. B.* (1963); Flower, J. E., *Literature and the Left in France* (1983): 29-49

—KONRAD BIEBER

BARGUM, Johan

Finnish novelist, short-story writer, and dramatist (writing in Swedish), b. 13 May 1943, Helsinki

B.'s maternal grandmother, with whom he spent much of his childhood, was the prolific novelist Margaret von Willebrand-Hollmerus (1894-1982); his mother, Viveca Hollmerus (b. 1920), made a brief but critically acclaimed sally into novella writing during the 1950s. His own career has been that of the disciplined professional author, without any ancillary calling and without advocating any particular economic or political cause—in contrast to some of his contemporaries in Finland's Swedish literature. Even in his early, radical years, he was never a polemicist; before all else, he has been interested in the psychological interplay of his characters. However, his works for various forms of theater—including cabaret, radio, and television—show a clear concern with society's ills, as do many of his narratives, with their harried, uprooted, and often vaguely seedy protagonists.

B. made his debut with the six novellas collected in *Svartvitt* (1965; black-white), of which "Kravbudet" ("The Demand Bid," 1974), about a young man estranged from, yet attached to, a religious father, has been translated into English. The entire collection bears what became one of B.'s hallmarks, his interjection of sudden violence into normal and even humdrum circumstances. *Femte advent* (1967; fifth advent) is ostensibly a novel but might better be called a collection of portraits, from the Christmas season, of lonely or unhappy people, among them a father snubbed by his son, a suicidal nymphomaniac, and a drunken Santa Claus. *Tre två ett* (1969; three two one) continues the exploration of violence, as it intrudes upon and is occasionally perpetrated by a television soundman, the prodigal son of a well-to-do Finland-Swedish family, who comes up against fascist perverts and admirable working men. The book is B.'s closest approach to the aggressive social criticism so often practiced by other writers from the minority during the revolutionary 1960s, notably Jörn DONNER, Christer KIHLMANN, and the poet Claes Andersson (b. 1937), with whom B. would collaborate on a number of short plays.

The urge to depict cruelty, debasement, and callousness was put under stricter artistic control during the next decade. *Finsk rulett* (1971; Finnish roulette) demonstrates how the weak are inevitably abused by the relatively stronger—a waitress, sexually harassed by the owner of the bar where she works, knocks him unconscious, steals a small sum from the till, and flees to a villa in the Finnish skerries, accompanied by her exploitative and unbalanced boyfriend, another of B.'s upper-class youths, who is eventually killed by the police. However, before the young woman is apprehended and sent to prison, she meets three decent men of a simpler stamp—refugees from a prosperous society that has no further use for them. Two are pensioners, the one shunted aside by an ambitious son, the other accompanied by his devoted but ineffectual offspring. The novel marked not so much a shift of themes as a refinement of B.'s favorite techniques: a cinematographic presentation of action scenes, and a careful construction of atmosphere—here some unusually warm September days, when summer homes (one of them taken over by the fugitives) are already closed.

In *Mörkrum* (1977; darkroom), B. began to cultivate a form that would be especially his own, the quasi-detective novel in which a puzzle is ostensibly solved while leaving the investigator still baffled. A free-lance photographer (somewhat come down in the world, but deeply devoted to his grandmother and his young daughter) interests himself in the cause of death of a retired farmer, relocated to Helsinki and neglected by his children. The fascination with familial relationships continues in *Den privata detektiven* (1980; the private detective), in which a former police inspector, a single parent, tries to discover what his daughter's guilty secret may be. In running down the sordid answer, the investigator frequents the streets and courtyards of the Helsinki section called Katajanokka, with its grand but often shabby apartment houses from the turn of the century. The strained web of the family returns in *Pappas flicka* (1982; daddy's girl). A woman in early middle age, with faint artistic ambitions, is able to cope neither with her beloved father's death nor with her practical-minded husband and daughter, nor with the young man who serves as her model: the last-named is revealed to be her illegitimate half-brother. *Sommarpojken* (1984; the summer boy) is comprised to an even greater extent of a main character's dipping into the past; at his mother's funeral, the narrator decides to locate his father, an effort that makes him relive the summers he spent as the poor-boy companion of rich children at a seaside cottage. Found at last, the father—a pop singer of the 1940s—turns out to be quite senile.

While in *Sommarpojken* the seeker is led down the paths of memory by his late mother's old dog, the short-story collection *Husdjur* (1986; pets) has the animal attachments of human beings at its very center: The seven stories are three pet stories in actual (and wry) fact, including "Bonnie" ("Bonnie," 1989), and four tales in which animals function as mirrors or role models or symbols. The quartet reveals a new aspect of B.'s talent, an ability to slide over into the credibly fantastic. The gift is developed further in "Arkitekten" (the architect), the first of the three novellas of *Resor* (1988; journeys); a daughter suspects that her father, in retirement at his summer place, has first been visited and then crushed by the giant elk of death. A masterpiece, it is accompanied by "Förläggaren" (the publisher), a painfully comic account of a lazy poet, a phrase maker who cuckolds his long-suffering protector, and by "Regissören" (the director), a flashback to a nasty childhood that has led to a severe disorder of personality. Most recently, in *Den svarta portföljen* (1991; the black briefcase), B. has taken up the mystery novel again (this time amidst the savageries of the international drug trade): A tired reporter—with a meddlesome mother and her dog—tries to unlock a dangerous riddle, racing through the Helsinki locales in which B. is so much at home.

All B.'s narratives are compact; in his deliberate craftsmanship and his deft suggestion of emotional nuances he may seem a descendant of the Finland-Swedish author Runar Schildt (1888-1925), whose novellas "Hemkomsten" (1919; the homecoming) and "Häxskogen" (1920; witchwood) B. rewrote for the stage in 1980 and 1984 respectively. His own dramas are less intricately wrought than his narratives, perhaps because they are often topical; extremely effective, they range from the impudent reviews of the 1960s and the plays of the early 1970s, about the trials of small businessmen, collected in *Tre skådespel* (1974; three plays), to *Finns det tigrar i Congo?* (1990; are there tigers in the Congo?), done in collaboration with the director Bengt Ahlfors (b. 1937), dealing with AIDS.

BIBLIOGRAPHY: Widén, G., "J. B.s Analyses," *BF*, 16 (1982): 66–76

—GEORGE C. SCHOOLFIELD

BARKER, George

English poet, b. 26 Feb. 1913, Loughton

Born of an English father and an Irish mother, B. spent his Catholic boyhood in London, where he attended Marlborough Road Elementary School and Regent Street Polytechnic. He worked at odd jobs until he met John Middletown Murry (1889–1957), who introduced him to Michael Roberts, editor of *New Signatures*; B. subsequently reviewed the new periodical and F. R. LEAVIS's *New Bearings in English Poetry* for *The Adelphi* (1932). From his Parton Street bookshop, David Archer published B.'s first poems in 1933. Thereafter B.'s life became the record of his travels, his loves, and his spiritual autobiography in poetry. In the 1930s he received grants from the Royal Society of Literature, the King's

Bounty, and Faber and Faber, which has published all of his major works. In 1939 he was visiting professor of English literature in Sendai, Japan. In 1940 he went to the U.S., where the poet and anthologist Oscar Williams (1899–1964) promoted his poetry. Subsequently he lived in England, Italy, and the U.S. as poet in residence at the University of Wisconsin and the University of Miami. Since 1967 his permanent residence, with his fourth wife and their five children, has been in East Anglia, England.

Often linked with Dylan THOMAS's verbal extravagance and the romanticism of the 1940s in England, B. intensifies 19th-c. romantic aesthetics and the tradition of poet as prophet-pariah, demonic and Byronic. An autodidact, he was at first especially sensitive to the literary mainstream as it flowed from YEATS, JOYCE, ELIOT, AUDEN, Thomas, and Gerard Manley Hopkins; later Tennyson's influence helped him to chasten his style. Still reflecting his response to the spirit of the times, his later verse is less experimental and less derivative, but no less energetically exposes his moral dilemmas.

His notable early works resemble SURREALIST poetry. The turning point in his early development is the tour de force, *Calamiterror* (1937), which records the traumatic death of the *poet-voyant* and the birth of the poet-*engagé*. With the driving rhetoric of *Elegy on Spain* (1939) and poems in *Lament and Triumph* (1940) he prophesies and protests against war and human suffering. In the elegies and love poems in *Eros in Dogma* (1944) he diagnoses the ills of modern civilization as deriving largely from man's alienation from God and the individual's betrayal by sex. After the pessimistic estrangement and hallucinatory internalizations of *News of the World* (1950), which is at its best in communicating the contradictions of love, the poems of the 1950s, such as the cynical *The True Confession of G. B.* (1950) and *A Vision of Beasts and Gods* (1954), are less obscure, more lucid and restrained, although self-irony, the coupling of sexual desire and guilt, and the desolating quest for tragic or religious affirmation continue to be central themes, even in the spare, compressed lyrics of the 1960s.

In the later poems, B.'s analogical imagination perceives in real settings and persons mythic archetypes and spiritual parallels. He is sometimes moved by landscapes (especially Italian), contemptuous of America, affected by the young, upon whose innocence existence will mount an assault, suspicious of his love of beauty in the women of his life, and tormented by his obsessive moral vision. The title of *The View from a Blind I* (1962) suggests the mood and that of *Poems of Places and People* (1971) the subject of his poems after 1960. The elegiac *In Memory of David Archer* (1973) reveals B.'s metaphysical anguish—a sense of failure and loss exacerbated by the painful necessity of religious faith, itself a confrontation with the absurd. *Dialogues* (1976) examines somewhat sardonically the conflict over the meaning of sex and death in a secular age in which the continuity of corrupted myth offers an uncertain remission of sin and suffering. *Villa Stellar* (1978) remembers occasions inspiring mordant meditations in which youth is threatened by age, natural beauty marred by technology, love assailed by lust, words seduced by silence, and the poet tantalized by his urgent and paradoxical need to profess belief in a spiritual reality confirmed by neither reason nor the senses. Although such poems offer luminous momentary solaces blurred by the fear that we cannot know anything for certain, they are balanced by three witty, fanciful volumes of children's verse—*Runes and Rhymes and Tunes and Chimes* (1969), *To Aylsham Fair* (1970), and *Alphabetical Zoo*

(1972)—which seek to capture the lost innocence that Barker's other poetry laments.

FURTHER WORKS: *Thirty Preliminary Poems* (1933); *Alanna Autumnal* (1933); *Poems* (1935); *Janus* (1935); *Selected Poems* (1941); *Sacred and Secular Elegies* (1943); *Love Poems* (1947); *The Dead Seagull* (1950); *Collected Poems* (1957); *Two Plays* (1958); *The True Confession of G. B.* (Book 2, 1964); *Dreams of a Summer Night* (1966); *The Golden Chains* (1968); *G. B.: Essays* (1970); *Collected Poems* (1987); *Street Ballads* (1992); *G. B.: Selected Poems* (1995)

BIBLIOGRAPHY: Scarfe, F., *Auden and After* (1942): 118–30; Daiches, D., "The Lyricism of G. B.," *Poetry*, 69 (1947): 336–46; Cronin, A., "Poetry and Ideas: G. B.," *London Magazine*, Sept. 1956: 44–52; Fodaski, M., *G. B.* (1969); Heath-Stubbs, J., and M. Green, eds., *Homage to G. B. on His Sixtieth Birthday* (1973)

—MARTHA FODASKI-BLACK

BARLACH, Ernst

German dramatist and novelist, b. 2 Jan. 1870, Wedel; d. 24 Oct. 1938, Rostock

B., who was a sculptor and graphic artist as well as a writer, drew material and inspiration for his work from personal experience and direct observation, which he refined and transformed through the expressive power of his style and vision into works of earthy realism and intense spirituality. He viewed the course of his own life as a sequence of phases and focused his autobiographical and artistic attention on the anguish of transition and on the breakthrough from one to the next. The first critical event was the death of his father in 1884.

B. quit school at eighteen, and for nearly two decades he moved from place to place and from one art school to another. Ultimately, his eye-opening journey through Russia and the birth of his illegitimate son, both in 1906, carried him safely through his midlife crisis and brought him overnight to artistic maturity. In 1910, after five years on the Berlin culture scene, he settled permanently in the town of Güstrow, Mecklenburg. By this time he had established himself as an artist and was at work on his first major play, *Der tote Tag* (1912; the dead day).

Recognized as Germany's leading expressionist sculptor and winner of the Kleist Prize for drama (1924), B. reached the pinnacle of his career in the middle and late 1920s. But by 1929 he was already under attack from benighted rightist fanatics for being allegedly unGerman and pacifist. In 1933 he was awarded the Prussian Order of Merit, the highest official recognition a German can attain. At the same time, with the Nazis' rise to power, theaters ceased to perform his plays, people were canceling commissions for sculptures, and the memorials he had created were being removed from public places. B. remained in Germany and carried on a fruitless battle against ideological persecution. He gave up the fight by the end of 1936. In 1937 he was declared a decadent artist. In 1938 he died in a Rostock hospital.

B. published seven dramas, of which five belong with the best of the theatrically busy 1910–1930 era. Their dramatic tension springs from the clash between the colorful, sometimes oppressively grotesque quality of the physical world and spiritual experiences of a mystical sort. *Der armed Vetter* (1918; the poor cousin) is a play full of rough and ready north German types celebrating Easter altogether irreverently at a country inn. In their midst are two persons determined to renounce this earthly life in favor of spiritual rebirth. The play's central figure, Siebenmark, finds himself caught between the two extremes. At the outset he belongs with the thoughtless sensualists. When he realizes at the play's climax with whom he has allied himself, he reacts with panic and disgust with himself. Though the end is left open, we know that he rejects suicide and finds his identity. This is, in brief, the characteristic B. plot: The self-satisfied bourgeois is shaken by a new perception of himself and the world; painfully and at great risk he moves to a higher phase of existence where, to be sure, the tensions are not fully resolved but where he can reaffirm his humanity and this life. B. assigned so much importance to secondary characters in *Der armed Vetter* that readers and audiences easily take the play as a sermon against worldliness, whereas in fact it situates humanity at the horizon point between heaven and earth.

In *Die echten Sedemunds* (1920; *The Genuine Sedemunds*, 1964), Sedemunds senior is brought to a frenzy by the perception of his personal guilt as husband and father. At the same time he is confronted with the ugliness of his animal nature and of the digestive process. Like Siebenmark, he emerges from the disgust cure a new man. The background for these religious experiences is the noise and color of a small-town carnival and circus.

The same combination of Breughelesque comedy, fear, and existential disgust occurs again in B.'s best drama, *Der blaue Boll* (1926; *The Blue Boll*, 1964). It works well because Squire Boll clearly dominates the action. His inner experience—a brush with suicide and then self-reaffirmation—is presented forcefully through concrete action, dialogue, lighting, and symbolism. The play also strikes the right balance between fantasy and realism, comedy and earnest religiosity.

The other strand of B.'s dramatic work is overtly mystical. In the best of these plays, *Die Sündflut* (1924; *The Flood*, 1964), the flesh-spirit conflict is resolved literally by letting the protagonist's eyes and body be eaten by rats. Freed from the tyranny of the senses, he is at the end granted the unmedicated perception of God as luminous presence.

Linguistically, *Die Sündflut* is the most radical of B.'s works, all of which are composed in idiosyncratic style. Through stress, repetition, and alliteration and through the striking formulaic use of everyday words, B. forces reader and audience to question traditional meanings and accepted ideas.

B. left two unpublished novel fragments, both of some consequence. The earlier one, *Seespeck* (1948; Seespeck), he wrote around 1913. It is an essentially autobiographical account of a midlife crisis and its ultimate resolution presented in a sequence of detailed visual experiences, through the last of which Seespeck learns to see and to be himself.

The second novel, *Der gestohlene Mond* (1948; the stolen moon), was composed near the end of B.'s life. It is an experimental antinovel in which the plot serves only as the barest excuse for reflections on guilt, joy, and good and evil, and for pyrotechnics displays of verbal virtuosity.

B.'s dramas are still produced on the German stage. He also continues to be the subject of scholarly studies. Yet there is no consensus on the interpretation of his work. His peculiar blending of seemingly incompatible elements—Protestant mysticism and grotesque realism, bursting vitality and weighty ideas—is both fascinating and elusive.

FURTHER WORKS: *Der Findling* (1922); *Ein selbsterzähltes Leben* (1928); *Die gute Zeit* (1929); *Der Graf von Ratzeburg* (1951); *Briefe: 1888–1938* (1968–1969)

BIBLIOGRAPHY: McFarlane, J., "Plasticity in Language," *MLR*, 49 (1954): 451—60; Keith-Smith, B., and A. Natan, eds., "E. B.," in Natan, A., ed. *German Men of Letters*, Vol. 3 (1964): 55—81; Just, K. G., ed. "E. B.," in Wiese, B. von, ed., *Deutsche Dichter der Moderne* (1965): 400—419; Chick, E., *E. B.* (1967); Graucob, K., *E. B.s Dramen* (1969); Hooper, K. W., *E. B.'s Literary and Visual Art* (1987)

—EDSON M. CHICK

BARNES, Djuna

American novelist and dramatist, b. 12 June 1892, Cornwall-on-Hudson, N.Y.; d. 19 June 1982, New York City

B. was raised by an unorthodox and creative father and a salon-hostess, suffragist grandmother; receiving her basic education at home, B. studied art at Pratt Institute and the Art Students' League before working as a feature writer and illustrator for the *Brooklyn Eagle* and other New York newspapers. Her first book, a collection of poetry and drawings called *The Book of Repulsive Women*, was published in 1915, and three of her one-act plays were produced in the 1919–20 season at the Provincetown Playhouse, where she worked with Eugene O'NEILL. Continuing to publish journalism in such magazines as *The Dial, Vanity Fair, Smart Set*, and *The Little Review* through the early 1930s, B. lived in Paris and London from 1928 until the outbreak of World War II, well acquainted there with avantgarde expatriates, including JOYCE and ELIOT, who strongly influenced her work. Subsequently she lived as a semi-recluse in Greenwich Village in New York City.

Selections from her early short fiction, poetry, and drama were published in *A Book* (1923), followed by two longer works of fiction in 1928. The privately printed *Ladies' Almanack* is a satirical "panegyric" to lesbian love in the form of a compendium of the wisdom and doings of a lesbian "saint," allegedly modeled on the notorious Natalie Barney, an American who had a lively literary salon in Paris, and written in a style imitating 16th-18th-c. comic and sentimental prose. More significant is *Ryder*, a picaresque novel about a family of independent spirits in some respects resembling B.'s own. Again, style rather than plot or character distinguishes the work: obviously influenced by Joyce's *Ulysses* and older picaresque narratives, it parodies the prose styles of an assortment of authors and historical periods.

The theme of all B.'s early work is the alienation and estrangement of people from nature, from other people, and from themselves. B.'s deracinated characters often admire the peaceful, sensuous existence of animals but cannot attain it. They are doll-like, less-than-human creatures, trying to come alive through

Djuna Barnes

causing or suffering pain. The experience of women as the sexual victims of men and the emotional victims of each other is a frequent subject.

These themes come to a climax in *Nightwood* (1936), B.'s only famous work. Written in an original style ranging from lucid and low-keyed to frenzied and eloquent, *Nightwood* begins with a conventional narrative line but soon launches into confession, meditation, and prophecy. It presents a series of lurid tableaux illuminating the damned state of the characters, held together by an elaborate pattern of cross-references among symbolic images and other verbal motifs—of descent, of night, sleep, and dreams, of animals and animalism. The characters strive for a stable relationship—marriage, motherly nurturing, lesbian pairing, friendship—but fail to achieve it. Their state is explicated in a long diatribe by the transvestite gynecologist (from *Ryder*) Matthew Mighty-Grain-of-Salt O'Connor, who with Robin Vote, the "beast turning to woman," are *Nightwood's* and B.'s most memorable characters. The book exemplifies the anxieties and techniques of modernist art *in extremis*.

B.'s next long work was a blank-verse play, *The Antiphon* (1958). An attempt to carry 20th-c. poetic drama beyond YEATS and Eliot, it uses a highly artificial style recalling the verse of Jacobean dramatists and the morphological manipulations and densely packed imagery of such modern poets as Dylan THOMAS. The subject is an alienated family—seemingly developed from the one in *Ryder*—in which a middle-aged daughter returns to the ancestral home to resolve a psychological conflict with her strong-willed but vacillating mother. A closet drama that attempts to tap the deep springs of conflict between the individual and the family in the manner of classical theater, *The Antiphon* seems to project B.'s personal experience into psychodrama.

While only *Nightwood* has remained consistently in print, most of B.'s other work has been reissued since 1962, in part because of *Nightwood's* continuing fascination and in part as a result of new interest in the feminist themes of her writing. Admired by T.S. ELIOT, Edwin MUIR, Graham GREENE, and Kenneth BURKE among her own generation, B. has influenced such later writers as Anaïs NIN, Lawrence DURRELL, and John HAWKES.

FURTHER WORKS: *A Night among the Horses* (1929; reprinted as *Spillway*, 1962); *Selected Works* (1962); *Vagaries Malicieux* (1974); *Creatures in an Alphabet* (1982); *Smoke and Other Early Stories* (1982); *New York* (1989)

BIBLIOGRAPHY: Messerli, D., *D. B.: A Bibliography* (1975); Frank, J., "Spatial Form in Modern Literature," (first pub. 1945), in *The Widening Gyre* (1963): 25-49; Williamson, A., "The Divided Image: The Quest for Identity in the Works of D.B.," *Crit*, 7 (1964): 58-74; Ferguson, S., "D. B.'s Short Stories: An Estrangement of the Heart," *SR*, 5 (1969): 26-41; Scott, J., *D. B.* (1976); Field, A., *D: The Formidable Miss B.* (1985); Plumb, C., *Fancy's Craft: Art and Identity in the Early Works of D. B.* (1986); Broe, M. L., ed., *Silence and Power: A Reevaluation of D. B.* (1991); Herring, P., *D: The Life and Work of D. B.* (1995)

—SUZANNE FERGUSON

BARNES, Julian

British novelist, b. 19 Jan. 1946, Leicester

Born in the north of England, B. moved to suburban London with his family. He graduated from Oxford and worked as a freelance writer. B. wrote as Edward Pygge during the 1970s, producing not only journalism but poetic parodies of figures such as American poet Richard WILBUR.

B.'s first two novels are realistic in tone and setting, but have a panache that displays B.'s unwillingness to be trammeled by referential narrative norms. In *Metroland* (1980) B. traces the growth of two friends, Christopher and Toni, who affect Gallic mannerisms in reaction against a stifling suburban upbringing. B. sets up a dichotomy between the bourgeois and the avant-garde, the latter represented by French culture and then by the idea of marital infidelity. B.'s protagonist seems to lapse back into bourgeois conformity, but this is only a thematic resolution. The conclusion hints that there is an artistic dimension beneath the most stolid exterior, and the tone of the book is antinaturalistic and flaunts its artistic style. What seems to be a resolution into conformity is really a statement of intent on the part of the author that his concerns are consciously highbrow. *Before She Met Me* (1982), a novel about a man obsessed with his second wife's past affairs, signals the central role sexual themes will come to play in B.'s vision, and, in its flair and erudition, exhibits his ability to entertain

at a high level. B. achieves an ingenious mixture of the thriller and the novel of manners.

Flaubert's Parrot (1984) was B.'s breakthrough novel, bringing him success and fame in England and abroad. Ostensibly concerning the efforts of Geoffrey Braithwaite, a British amateur researcher, to find out which actual parrot was the model for the bird used by Flaubert in "Un Coeur Simple," the novel is a sprightly meditation not only on Flaubert but on the nature and meaning of art, as well as roving over many other subjects including history, philosophy, and sex. "Flaubert's parrot" stands for the epistemological unknowability of any object of research, but also represents the material remains by which we have to make sense on an author's life and work.

The notoriety given to *Flaubert's Parrot* placed B. in the forefront of a group of British novelists such as Martin AMIS and Ian McEwan (b. 1948) who were avowedly postmodern in their literary perspective and, although overtly denunciatory of the Margaret Thatcher government, flourished in its free-market atmosphere. B. was acclaimed for liberating the British novel from coziness and stuffiness, and for making British fiction more sophisticated, more in line with developments in Eastern Europe and Latin America. Despite all this, however, B. remained an accessible author writing for a broad public.

Although *Staring at the Sun* (1986) was a disappointing follow-up in the eyes of many, it is perhaps B.'s most moving work. Chronicling the life of a lower-middle-class woman, Jean Serjeant, from the 1940s to a point well into a fictive 21st c., the book's key image comes from a passage where a World War II RAF pilot sees the sun rise twice in one day due to the speed of his flight. This serves as a pattern for the way that romance comes out of realism in the book while still remaining within realism in a manner circumventing POSTMODERNISM.

A History of the World in 10 ½ Chapters (1989) reestablished B.'s postmodern credentials. The book is whimsically centered around a few motifs in history, notably famous voyages (that of Noah's ark—seen from the perspective of a woodworm—and of the slave-ship *Medusa* as depicted by Géricault), culminating in the vision of the afterlife as a perpetual retirement home for historical figures. This novel is filled with facts, so much as to make it like a digest or almanac. The reader will probably be as interested in the facts B. presents as in the individual stories that make up the volume. Even though lacking a seamless narrative or organic form, *A History of the World* is fictively viable because it uses facts to intrigue the reader. This interest in conveying literal fact is juxtaposed against a postmodern awareness of history-as-narrative, a sense in which histories are fables rather than overarching patterns. Thus, B. stresses how love is the hidden prerequisite for stitching together historical meaning

Even though B. always has considered himself a man of the Left, some critics speculated that B.'s work sagged in the 1990s without the energy of Thatcherism to incite it. *Talking It Over* (1991), which drew much journalistic comment because of its rumored resemblance to real-life developments in B.'s marriage, concerns a love triangle in which a man finds out that his best friend is having an affair with his wife. B. salvages this not uncommon plot situation by having each character speak in his or her own voice. *The Porcupine* (1992) is a barely fictional account of the aftermath of Communism's fall in Bulgaria.

An instrumental figure in the development of the British novel from realism to postmodernism, B. is acknowledged as one of the leading practitioners of literate fiction in contemporary Britain.

FURTHER WORKS: *Duffy* (1980); *Fiddle City* (1981); *Put the Boot In* (1985); *Going to the Dogs* (1987); *Letters from London* (1995); *Cross Channel* (1995)

BIBLIOGRAPHY: Higdon, D., "'Unfocused Confessions': The Narrators of Graham Swift and J. B.," in Acheson, J., ed., *The British and Irish Novel since 1960* (1991): 174-91; Moseley, M., *Understanding J. B.* (1997)

—NICHOLAS BIRNS

BAROJA, Pío

Spanish novelist and essayist, b. 28 Dec. 1872, San Sebastián; d. 30 Oct. 1956, Madrid

Born of Basque parents in the Basque country, B. spent an unsettled childhood and adolescence living in San Sebastián, Madrid, Pamplona, and Valencia. He studied medicine (writing a thesis on pain), practiced briefly, and before beginning his career as a writer, tried his hand at running a bakery.

B. was to become not only one of the most prolific writers (he wrote more than sixty novels) of his generation, but one of the best Spanish novelists of modern times. His early novels, which most critics consider his most interesting, are characteristic of the Generation of 1898, of which B. was an important member. Like AZORÍN, UNAMUNO, and Ramiro de Maezlu (1874–1936), he was constantly preoccupied by Spain and was affected by the ambiguities and the crisis of identity brought on by the loss of the last overseas colonies in 1898 and by the changes in social structure due to rapid industrialization. A wavering between metaphysical inquiry and a desire for social action, supported by his readings of Kant, Schopenhauer, Nietzsche, and Dostoevsky on the one hand and of socialist and anarchistic thought on the other, is endemic to B.'s early work.

Aventuras, inventos y mixtificaciones de Silvestre Paradox (1901; adventures, inventions, and mystifications of Sylvestre Paradox) is a novel consisting of vignettes about bohemian intellectual life in Madrid, which, although charged with satire bordering on the grotesque, is the work of a careful observer of reality. *Camino de perfección* (1902; the road to perfection) and *El árbol de la ciencia* (1911; *The Tree of Knowledge*, 1928) are spiritual autobiographies. In fact, Fernando Ossorio and Andrés Hurtado, the respective protagonists, represent a composite of the concerns, frustrations, and ideological contradictions of most of the writers of B.'s generation. In both cases they are neurasthenic wanderers who become increasingly irritated by the absurdities of society and the immorality of people. Their reactions vacillate between a desire for iconoclastic destruction or radical reform and an almost mystical or metaphysical flight from reality. The solutions to this unsatisfactory existence are somewhat different, however: *Camino de perfección* ends in a romantic attempt at a return to nature; *El árbol de la ciencia*, more philosophical in nature and structured around Schopenhauer's ideas on suffering and knowledge, ends in suicide.

La busca (1904; *The Quest*, 1922), *Mala hierba* (1904; *Weeds*, 1923), and *Aurora roja* (1905; *Red Dawn*, 1924) form the trilogy *La lucha por la vida* (the struggle for life). These novels, which

Pío Baroja

constitute one of the most striking chronicles of city life in modern literature, are good examples of social realism. B. describes with sensitivity and marked ideological content the urban crisis in Madrid and the emerging class struggle resulting from the advances of capitalism and industrialization. The main character, Manuel, moves through the world of the working class, the delinquent, and the revolutionary in a way that shows B. to be conscious of the dialectics of the socio-economic realities of the society in which he lived. From the Spanish dictatorship of the 1920s through the dictatorship of Franco from 1940 until the 1960s, editions of B.'s first novels were often modified for reasons of censorship, as were other Spanish novels.

In *Zalacaín el aventurero* (1909; Zalacaín the adventurer), *César o nada* (1910; *Caesar or Nothing*, 1919), and *Las inquietudes de Shanti Andía* (1911; *The Restlessness of Shanti Andía*, 1959), among B.'s most popular novels, he exalts the man of action unfettered by intellectual preoccupations. The dialogues and digressions of his earlier novels give way to adventure, conflict, and suspense. In 1911 B. began a serious study of the life and times of a distant relative of his mother, Eugenio de Aviraneta, a liberal spy and agitator who participated in many of the plots and conspiracies centered around the struggle between the progressives and the traditionalists in Spain during the first half of the 19th c. This investigation led to a cycle of twenty-two novels, published between 1913 and 1935 and collectively known as *Memorias de un hombre de acción* (memoirs of a man of action). These historical novels depict Aviraneta as a man of consummate energy and a strong will, who becomes progressively disillusioned with what goes on around him but who remains content with the fact that he always acts in accordance with his conscience. B.'s final judgment on 19th-c. Spanish bourgeois liberalism is as hostile and cynical as it is on the Spain of his own day.

B.'s later novels are not representative of his true talent, according to most critics. Exceptions are *El cura de Monleón* (1936; the priest of Monleón) and *El cantor vagabundo* (1950; the wandering minstrel), in which B. creates convincing characters dominated by a neurotic anguish and a belief that it is best to live without hope or illusions.

Throughout his life B. published hundreds of articles and essays—ranging from literary criticism to social and political commentary—in the most important Spanish and Latin American newspapers and reviews of his time. Many of these writings were collected in volumes: *Tablado de Arlequín* (1904; Harlequin's stage), *Juventud, egolatría* (1917; *Youth and Egolatry*, 1920), *Momentum catastrophicum* (1919; title in intentionally incorrect Latin: catastrophic times) and *Divagaciones apasionadas* (1924; passionate digressions). His thought was characterized by pessimism, cynicism, and asceticism; very spontaneous in his reactions, B. also expressed anticlerical, antidemocratic, and anti-Semitic feelings. He wrote much about the novel, generally rejecting literary convention and technique and favoring intuitive creativity based on experience and observation of reality. B.'s seven volumes of memoirs, *Desde la última vuelta del camino* (1944–49; from the last turn in the road), provide a wealth of information for an understanding not only of his own personality and work but of those of a whole generation of Spanish writers and artists.

The typical novel of B. is related to the *Bildungsroman* and to the philosophical novel. Structure is normally simple, the plot being controlled by one character, who is served frequently by a counter figure; description, drawn mainly from observed reality, tends often to highlight B.'s subjective reaction to the experience at hand. B.'s prose eschews aesthetic effect: his language is direct, natural, and colloquial, and at times even incorrect. Considering the directness (one could almost say "violence") with which B. as a writer attacks physical reality and the irony and the acute sense of the absurd that dominate his perspective, it could be said that B.'s works fore-shadow mid-20th-c. existentialism.

FURTHER WORKS: *La casa de Aizgorri* (1900); *Idilios vascos* (1902); *El mayorazgo de Labraz* (1903); *La feria de los discretos* (1905); *Paradox, rey* (1906; *Paradox, King*, 1931); *Los últimos románticos* (1906); *Las tragedias grotescas* (1907); *La dama errante* (1908); *La ciudad de la niebla* (1909); *El mundo es ansí* (1912); *El aprendiz de conspirador* (1913); *El escuadrón del Brigante* (1913); *Los caudillos de 1830* (1918); *La sensualidad pervertida* (1920); *El laberinto de las sirenas* (1923); *La nave de los locos* (1925); *El gran torbellino del mundo* (1926); *Las veleidades de la fortuna* (1927); *Las noches del Buen Retiro* (1934); *Laura; o, La soledad sin remedio* (1939); *Canciones del suburbio* (1944); *Obras completas* (8 vols., 1946–1951)

BIBLIOGRAPHY: Granjel, L. S., *Retrato de P. B.* (1954); Shaw, D. L., "A Reply to *deshumanización*: B. on the Art of the Novel," *HR*, 25 (1957): 105–11; Eoff, S. H., *The Modern Spanish Novel* (1961): 148–85; Arbó, S. J., *P. B. y su tiempo* (1963); Patt, B., *P. B.*

(1971); González López, E., *El arte narrativo de P. B.: Las trilogías* (1971); Longhurst, C. A., "P. B. and Aviraneta," *BHS*, 48 (1971): 328–45; Ciplijauskaite, B., *B., un estilo* (1972); Martínez Palacio, J., ed., *P. B.: El escritor y la crítica* (1974); Shaw, D. L., *The Generation of 1898 in Spain* (1977); Fox, E. I., *Ideología y política en las letras de fin de siglo* (1988)

—E. INMAN FOX

BARRIE, James M.

Scottish dramatist, novelist, and journalist, b. 9 May 1860, Kirriemuir; d. 19 June 1937, London, England

Educated at Dumfries Academy and the University of Edinburgh (M. A., 1882), B. moved in 1885 to London where, as a Fleet Street journalist, he wrote idealized sketches of Scottish life. He soon turned to playwriting; his first play, *Richard Savage*, was produced unsuccessfully in 1891. In 1913 B. was created a baronet by King George V, and in 1919 he was elected Rector of St. Andrews University. He was appointed to the Order of Merit in 1922 and served as Chancellor of the University of Edinburgh from 1930 to his death.

B.'s early fiction is of the Kailyard ("cabbage-patch") school of "Ian Maclaren" (Rev. John Watson, 1850–1907), S. R. Crockett (1860–1914), Neil Munro (1864–1930), and others. The Kailyard writers drew idealized portraits of Scottish life, using sentiment and quaint dialect to depict a purely fictionalized Scotland. *Auld Licht Idylls* (1888) and *A Window in Thrums* (1889) are representative collections of B.'s early, Kailyard stories.

Margaret Ogilvy (1896), B.'s eulogy to his mother (d. 1895), reveals the deep-seated and unresolved Oedipal feelings that surface repeatedly in his novels and plays. Ambivalent attitudes toward parents and siblings underlie much of B.'s writing and account for his fondness for fantasy and his preoccupation with the childhood experience. Significantly enough, his best-known work is the children's classic *Peter Pan* (1904), a whimsical fantasy tale that he reworked in a variety of forms: story, play, novel, and sequel.

B.'s novels suffer from a journalistic approach, lack structural coherence, and are excessively sentimental. Only *The Little Minister* (1891), which B. dramatized successfully in 1897, and *Sentimental Tommy* (1896), his best nondramatic work, might engage a contemporary reader.

B.'s most notable achievements were in the theater. A master of one-act play form, he wrote some two dozen short plays, the best of which explore the fantasy themes that recur in his major plays: what-might-have-been, self-discovery, the contrast of youth and age, and so on. *The Twelve-Pound Look* (1910) and *The Old Lady Shows Her Medals* (1917) are the best of the one-acts.

Most of B.'s full-length plays are either whimsical social comedies or sentimental, psychological tragicomedies. The best of the latter type is *Dear Brutus* (1917), a drama rich in atmosphere and theatricality, in which the fantasy element is relegated to the dream-state and made entirely credible.

Among the best of the comic group are *Quality Street* (1901), *Alice Sit-by-the-Fire* (1905), and *What Every Woman Knows* (1908). The last is especially notable for its splendid characterization of Maggie Wylie, a "wily" Scot who advances her husband's

James Barrie

career through her innate canniness, illustrating B.'s thesis that behind every successful man there is a determined woman.

B.'s comic masterpiece and finest play is *The Admirable Crichton* (1902). Crichton is a self-effacing butler who, shipwrecked with his master's family, takes charge of their survival and demonstrates his natural superiority over the gentry. Once again in London, however, Crichton resumes the subservient role. The comedy is B.'s statement of the efficacy of a class-ordered society.

As an essayist and novelist B. is already largely forgotten, but as a dramatist his achievement is noteworthy. At worst, his plays display excessive sentiment and are limited by a vision too intensely personal and autobiographical for true universality. But his best plays are skillfully constructed, rich in characterization, and theatrically viable.

FURTHER WORKS: *Better Dead* (1887); *When a Man's Single* (1888); *An Edinburgh Eleven* (1889); *My Lady Nicotine* (1890); *Walker, London* (1892; pub. 1907); *A Holiday in Bed, and Other Sketches* (1892); *Jane Annie; or, The Good Conduct Prize* (1893); *A Tillyloss Scandal* (1893); *Two of Them* (1893); *An Auld Licht Manse* (1893); *The Professor's Love Story* (1892; pub. 1942); *Tommy and Grizel* (1900); *The Wedding Guest* (1900); *The Little White Bird; or, Adventures in Kensington Gardens* (1902); *Little Mary* (1903; pub. 1942); *Peter Pan in Kensington Gardens* (1906); *When Wendy Grew Up: An After-thought* (1908; pub. 1957); *Old Friends* (1910; pub. 1928); *Peter and Wendy* (1911); *Half an Hour*

(1913); *The Adored One* (1913; revised as *The Legend of Leonora*, 1914); *Half Hours* (1914; contains *Pantaloon* [1905], *The Twelve-Pound Look* [1910], *Rosalind* [1912], and *The Will* [1913]); *A Kiss for Cinderella* (1916; pub. 1920); *Seven Women* (1917; pub. 1928); *Echoes of the War* (1918; contains *The New Word* [1915], *The Old Lady Shows Her Medals* [1917], *Barbara's Wedding* [1918], and *A Well-Remembered Voice* [1918]); *Mary Rose* (1920; pub. 1924); *Shall We Join the Ladies?* (1921; pub. 1927); *Farewell, Miss Julie Logan: A Wintry Tale* (1931); *The Boy David* (1936; pub. 1938); *The Greenwood Hat* (1938); *Definitive Edition of Plays* (1942); *Letters* (1942)

BIBLIOGRAPHY: Phelps, W. L., "Plays of J. M. B.," *North American Review*, 212 (1920): 829–43; Roy, J. A., *J. M. B.* (1937); Mackail, D., *The Story of J. M. B.* (1941); Blake, G., *B. and the Kailyard School* (1951); Green, R. L., *J. M. B.* (1961); McGraw, W. R., "J. M. B.'s Concept of Dramatic Action," MD, 5 (1962): 133–41; Geduld, H. M., *Sir J. B.* (1971); Ormand, L., *J. M. B.* (1987)

—JACK A. VAUGHN

BARRIOS, Eduardo

Chilean novelist, short-story writer, and dramatist, b. 25 Oct. 1884, Valparaiso; d. 13 Sept. 1963, Santiago

When B. was five years old his father, an officer in the Chilean army, died, and the boy and his mother, a young woman of German, French, and Basque descent educated in Hamburg, went to live with her parents in Lima, Peru. Ten years later, B. and his mother moved back to Chile, to stay with B.'s paternal grandparents. In 1900 he was enrolled in military school which, despite the vigorous protests of his family, he abandoned after two years. These early experiences provided some of the subject matter for B.'s novel *Un perdido* (1917; a lost one). The ensuing break with his grandparents forced him to seek a series of odd jobs that carried him into many parts of South America. He was a salesman, searched for rubber in Peru, was a prospector, worked in an ice factory in Guayaquil, sold stoves in Buenos Aires and Montevideo, and lifted weights in a circus.

B.'s first book, *Del natural* (1907; concerning the natural), consisting of a novelette and several stories in the naturalist-Decadent fashion, was written while he worked as a book-keeper in a nitrate refinery. His experiences there served as material for a later novel, *Tamarugal* (1944; Tamarugo grove). The years from 1910 to 1916 saw the production of all his dramas—among which *Vivir* (1916; to live) is the most outstanding—and the publication of his famous novelette, *El niño que enloqueció de amor* (1915; the child who was maddened by love). This tale and *Un perdido* raised him to prominence in Spanish American letters.

El hermano asno (1922; *Brother Asno*, 1969) is considered by many to be his greatest work. The novel uses the atmosphere of a Franciscan monastery to sustain the examination of the sin of pride and the destructiveness of sublimated sexual energy. It is this work that established B.'s reputation as a great stylist.

A member of the famous literary group Los Diez, in 1925 he was made editor of the Chilean journal *Atenea*. In 1927 he was appointed director of the National Library and Minister of Education. His official civic responsibilities ended in 1931. From 1937 to 1943 he managed La Marquesa, a large ranch in the Central Valley. In 1946 B. was awarded the Chilean National Award for Literature.

B.'s stay at the La Marquesa ranch, combined with earlier experiences on his own rural estate, provided material for the novel *Gran señor y rajadiablos* (1948; great lord and hellion), a portrayal of a 19th-c. Chilean land baron with vivid depictions of the customs of that era. In 1950 *Los hombres del hombre* (the men in man), a novel containing some of B.'s finest writing, marked a return to the intimate first-person narration that had brought him fame in *El niño que enloqueció de amor* and *El hermano asno*. In this work, B. explores the agonies caused by doubt, jealousy, and uncertain paternity. The experience is examined by means of the device of a multiple personality—seven traits of man, each personified in dialogues, within the single being of the protagonist.

In 1953 B. became a member of the Chilean Academy. Having suffered from impaired vision from 1955 on, he was unable to continue his literary career.

B.'s work in general is subjective in tone, though he has produced fiction of great diversity. His styles reflect two distinct patterns: the highly introspective and lyrical on the one hand, and on the other, a psychological realism devoted to the portrayal of customs. The quest for identity, both personal and social, is the most powerful and constant motivation of his writing. His ultimate view of man is expressed in his major protagonists, who, to greater or lesser degrees manifest B.'s commitment to a belief in the duality of personality, in which the conflict of heart and reason, weakness and strength, introspection and action struggle for dominance. For B., life inevitably means defeat, although one must act as if victory were possible.

FURTHER WORKS: *Lo que niega la vida* (1913); *Páginas de un pobre diablo* (1923); *Y la vida sigue . . .* (1925); *Teatro escogido* (1947); *Obras completas* (2 vols., 1962)

BIBLIOGRAPHY: Orlandi, J., et al., *E. B.: Obras-Estilo-Técnica* (1960); Davison, N. J., *Sobre E. B. y otros: Estudios y crónicas* (1966); Davison, N. J., *E. B.* (1970); Hancock, J., "The Journalistic Writing of E. B.," *Hispania*, 59 (1976): 835–43; Walker, J., "Schopenhauer and Nietzsche in the Work of E. B.," *RCEH*, 2, 1 (1977): 39–53; Lozada, A., on *El hermano asno*, *Estudios críticos* (1978)

—NED J. DAVISON

BARTH, John

American novelist, b. 27 May 1930, Cambridge, Md.

B. received degrees from Johns Hopkins University in 1951 and in 1952, and returned there, in 1973, as a professor of English after teaching at other universities. The academy serves B. throughout his work as a symbolic landscape, most notably in the allegorical *Giles Goat-Boy* (1966), in which the hero's quest is dramatized entirely within a university setting. The reverence for variant texts that is nowhere as strong as it is in academia, polemical disputes,

and tutor-pupil relationships provide B. with situations and motifs for most of his narratives. Like many contemporary novelists, he is an active literary theoretician; in *Chimera* (1972) he speaks directly to the reader about literary technique as part of an interpolated "lecture" to the characters.

Though B. disclaims special knowledge of philosophy, the plots of his first two novels are deliberately organized around philosophical questions. In each, the protagonist discovers the limitations of reason by means of personal experience. Todd Andrews, in *The Floating Opera* (1956), narrates his own story, one that demonstrates how chance rules human affairs. In one scene he watches himself in a mirror during copulation and thereafter considers sexual activity (which he enjoys) an affront to human dignity. His murder of a German soldier in World War I adds to his ironic and loveless outlook on life. Throughout the novel, incidents involving sexual passion or death cause Todd to speculate on existentialist subjects: free choice, the nausea of bodily existence, and suicide. In a 1967 revision, B. restored an intended conclusion to the novel in which Todd chooses to murder the audience of a floating carnival show as a means of exposing the absurd quality of life. The attempt fails, proving his point.

The End of the Road (1958), written in the same year, contains few characters and a tightly knit plot with a violent climax. The two principal characters, Jake Horner and Joe Morgan, are imagined with a Swiftean contempt for the life alternatives they represent. Jake is too "weatherless" to prefer any goal above any other; indecision occasionally paralyzes his will and body. Joe compulsively makes decisions and accommodations in order to impose a coherent identity on himself. The struggle of these two philosophical agents, and the victimization of Rennie Morgan, caught between husband and lover, are rendered with convincing psychological realism. Though it has become a classic novel of the 1950s because of its nihilist philosophy and BLACK HUMOR, it is atypical of B. as a storyteller. It lacks the amplitude and complexity of narrative line that B. has made his specialty.

B.'s third novel—his masterpiece, in the opinion of many—is an exuberant pastiche of the Spanish and English picaresque tradition. *The Sot-Weed Factor* (1960) possesses a plot "fancier than *Tom Jones*" told in an 18th-c. English prose that is one of B.'s greatest feats of mimicry. B.'s choice of style deliberately calls attention to the artifice of the fiction, its contrived nature, as part of the entertainment. It is B.'s only novel in third-person voice. The plot follows Ebenezer Cooke, Poet Laureate of Maryland, through an epic's length of hilarious adventures in 17th-c. England and America. Ebenezer consistently learns from his resourceful tutor, Henry Burlingame III, that in worldly affairs action is more important than thought, experience superior to innocence. He also receives plentiful illustration from the lengthy tales of misfortune he hears from strangers, from a burlesque diary of colonist John Smith, and from his own errors in pressing claim to a family inheritance.

B. wrote *Giles Goat-Boy* after making a careful study of mythologies and legends that concern "that hero business." The novel is an attempt to employ all the conventions of heroic myth in a comic work of epic proportions. The center of this allegory is a university, which has separated into two opposing parts, East-Campus and West-Campus. One recognizes the cold-war world of the 1950s and 1960s in this divided academy; and contemporary personalities (e.g., the Kennedys, Khrushchev) are sometimes obvious models for the fictional characters. The plot concerns the efforts of a modern demigod, child of a human mother and a computer, to enter New Tammany College (West-Campus) and learn there the meaning of an enigmatic message—"Pass All Fail All"—left with him as a baby by the parents who abandoned him. As a student, Giles is persecuted by such demonic figures as Maurice Stoker (Dean O'Flunks) and Harold Bray, who attempt to corrupt Giles by sexual and spiritual temptations. Despite their efforts, Giles achieves Commencement by discovering the ambiguous meaning of the message. True to the motto on the Founder's Scroll—"Self-Knowledge Is Always Bad News"—Giles becomes an unhappy hero after his labors. The novel seems overburdened by the inclusion of all the conventions of heroic legends, but the dazzling succession of comic incidents, the immense number of well-defined characters, and B.'s command of a supple prose make it an impressive achievement.

B.'s fascination with mythology continues throughout two collections of short fiction, *Lost in the Funhouse* (1968) and *Chimera*. Both adhere to a principle he explains in *Chimera*: "Since myths themselves are among other things poetic distillations of our ordinary psychic experience, and therefore point always to daily reality, to write realistic fictions which point always to mythic archetypes is . . . to take the wrong end of the mythopoeic stick . . . Better to address the archetypes directly." B. is criticizing here the practice of updating the compelling narratives of antiquity. Rather than create a modern drama *based on* a classical Greek story, B. retells the story itself, using its original characters and time period. Works like the "Menelaiad," in *Lost in the Funhouse*, or the "Perseid" and "Bellerophoniad," in *Chimera*, are distinguished from historical fiction, however, by their modern idiom, and by an attention to the nuances of voice and persona that recalls JOYCE, BORGES, and NABOKOV. Increasingly, the aim of B.'s fiction is an investigation of the authorial imagination itself—its sources, devices, and metamorphoses.

B. has always found the myth of Proteus, the shape-shifter, a useful metaphor of the storyteller's craft. In *Lost in the Funhouse* he offers a variety of dramas (set in Cambridge, Md.) in a variety of voices—a sperm, a Siamese twin, a hero, a bard. Though the voices range in style from simple reportage to highly mannered rhetoric, they purport to chronicle the same "person," who is B. himself. In *Chimera* there is also a conscious attempt to unite the voices of classical Greek heroes, as well as Scheherazade, to the modern-day writer "John Barth" in order to merge the identities of hero and artist. The "Bellerophoniad" concludes, for example, with the heavenly descent of Bellerophon (hero) and a magical tutor into Maryland, there to be reborn as the text we have just finished reading. The ingenuity of such literary stratagems, and the obscurities of narrative form they necessitate, have led some critics, and even B. himself, to doubts about the viability of these fictions.

The novel, *Letters* (1979), is entirely in the epistolary mode. It comprises eighty-eight letters exchanged among seven correspondents, all of them related to the genealogy and history of the Cook/Burlingame line descended from the hero of *The Sot-Weed Factor*, Ebenezer Cooke. If the earlier novel had epic intentions, this work is more similar to a saga in which kinship and violent incident—here the War of 1812—are crucial elements. The odd refraction of distant historical events through the lens of modern sensibilities makes this an experimental work reminiscent of novels by JOYCE, GIDE, FAULKNER, and DURRELL. Language and story line are complicated by what B. calls "action historiography," a rhetorical

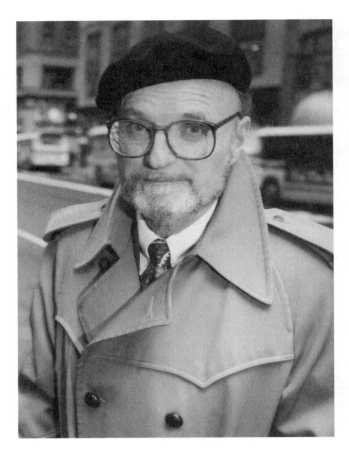

John Barth

game in which the historical past is treated as essentially a fictive subject akin to myth. The past is rife with evidence of its authentic existence (such as old letters), but lacking in sufficient order and meaning. B.'s correspondents, many of them writers or lovers of writers, persist in discovering, perhaps concocting, that meaning. It is their creative and procreative acts that shape the material. B.'s attempt to explore the "hazards and delights of Second Cycles in our lives and histories" is his most ambitious work since *Giles Goat-Boy*, and like that novel is a significant commentary on modern American culture.

B.'s ambitious experiments with narrative technique and subject matter aim at nothing less than a transformation of the American literary tradition. His influence on younger novelists can be perceived in the revival of myths as plot lines, and the erudite blend of erotic humor, dark thoughts, and exciting suspense that B. has mastered in his unique way.

FURTHER WORKS: *Sabbatical* (1981); *The Friday Book* (1984); *The Tidewater Tales* (1988); *The Last Voyage of Somebody the Sailor* (1991); *On with the Story* (1996)

BIBLIOGRAPHY: special B. issue, *Crit*, 6 (Fall 1963); Joseph, G., *J. B.* (1970); Tanner, T., *City of Words* (1971): 230–59; Dembo, L. S., and Pondrom, C. N., eds., *The Contemporary Writer* (1972): 18–29; Hassan, I., *Contemporary American Literature* 1945–1972 (1973): 56–60; Tharpe, J. L., *J. B.: The Comic Sublimity of*

Paradox (1974); Stark, J. D., *The Literature of Exhaustion: Borges, Nabokov, and B.* (1974); Morrell, D., *J. B.: An Introduction* (1976); Weixlmann, J., *J. B.: A Descriptive Primary and Annotated Secondary Bibliography* (1976); Walsh, T. P., and Northous, C., *J. B., Jerzy Kosinski, and Thomas Pynchon: A Reference Guide* (1978): 3–50; Scholes, R., *Fabulation and Metafiction* (1979): 75–102; Waldmeir, J. J., *Critical Essays on J. B.* (1980); Harris, C. B., *Passionate Virtuosity: The Fiction of J. B.* (1983); Fogel, S., and G. Slethaug, *Understanding J. B.* (1990); Green, D., "Metafiction and Romance," *SAF*, 19 (1991): 229-42; Tobin, P., *J. B. and the Anxiety of Continuance* (1992); Birns, N., "Beyond Metafiction: Placing J. B.," *ArO*, 49 (1993): 113-36; Bowen, Z., *A Reader's Guide to J. B.* (1994)

—LAURENCE GOLDSTEIN

BARTHELME, Donald

American short-story writer and novelist, b. 7 April 1931, Philadelphia, Pa.; d. 23 July 1989, Houston, Tx.

B.'s flair for the innovative and the madcap seems to have been endemic in his family. His architect father, a disciple of Mies van der Rohe, Le Corbusier, and Frank Lloyd Wright, designed for his family a home so startling on the Texas plain that passers-by would stop in front of it and stare, sometimes to have their surprise

Donald Barthelme

mocked when the family would form an impromptu chorus line. A brief stint as founding editor of the University of Texas *Forum* saw B. still confounding local sensibilities by his publication of such avant-gardists as William GASS and Alain ROBBE-GRILLET. An equally brief stint as editor of the journal *Location* brought B. to New York, and, in particular, into the sphere of the *New Yorker*, which has published almost all of B.'s fiction and through which his absurdist stories have found a more sophisticated audience than that which gathered before his Texas home.

The typical B. story is based on incongruities of reference and situation, and sometimes on incongruities of genre as well. The schoolmarmish Miss R. of "The Indian Uprising" (1968), for instance, insists that the only valid form of discourse is the litany; a mature man in "Me and Miss Mandible" (1966) finds himself suddenly a student in the sixth grade; and the title character in the novel *Snow White* (1968) is a Chinese-American who steps out of Disney and the Brothers Grimm to form a *ménage à huit* in Greenwich Village. For some readers, incongruities such as these seem to transform the banalities they subsume, freshening them with whimsy. It should be remarked, however, that the quality of the imaginative transformation is frequently banal itself. In the novel *The Dead Father* (1975), for instance, B. deals with a portentous Freudian theme—the need of children to eliminate father-figures. But when the Dead Father tells his children he would prefer not to be dismembered with a Skilsaw, the reference to the Skilsaw is typically shallow; it effectively cheapens the portentous situation and suggests that the imagination is unable to embrace both the world of Freud and the world of Skilsaws. And that is B.'s accustomed method: firstly, his stories play havoc with the syntax and the systematics through which we have made sense of our world by intermixing meaningless incidentals with them; secondly, the stories attempt to render this mélange whimsically, only to take on a manic tone that suggests imaginative incapacity and which can be deeply affecting.

Traditionalist critics dislike B.'s untraditional use of plot and character and his absurdist philosophy, but his stories have reached a far wider audience than the comparable writings of such innovators as Ronald Sukenick (b. 1932) and Ishmael REED, and he has been very influential on younger writers. Indeed, he is preeminent among those absurdist writers who attempt to simulate the disjunction of words and things in our environment and to relate that disjunction to the regenerative powers of the imagination.

FURTHER WORKS: *Come Back, Dr. Caligari* (1966); *Unspeakable Practices, Unnatural Acts* (1968); *City Life* (1971); *The Slightly Irregular Fire Engine* (1971); *Sadness* (1973); *Guilty Pleasures* (1974); *Amateurs* (1976); *Great Days* (1979); *Sixty Stories* (1981); *Overnight to Many Distant Cities* (1983); *Forty Stories* (1987); *Paradise* (1986); *The King* (1990); *The Teachings of D. B.* (1992)

BIBLIOGRAPHY: Gilman, R., *The Confusion of Realms* (1969): 42–50; Tanner, T., *City of Words* (1971): 400–406; special B. issue, *Crit*, 16, 3 (1975); Klinkowitz, J., *Literary Disruptions* (1975): 62–81, 212–17; Stott, W., "D. B. and the Death of Fiction," *Prospects*, 1 (1975): 369–86; Stevick, P., "Lies, Fictions, and Mock Facts," *WHR*, 30 (1976): 1–12; Molesworth, C., *D. B.'s Fiction: The Ironist Saved From Drowning* (1982); Trachtenberg, S., *Understanding D. B.* (1990); Patteson, R. F., ed., *Critical Essays on D. B.* (1992)

—ROBERT F. KIERNAN

BARTHELME, Frederick

American novelist and short-story writer, b. 10 Oct. 1943, Houston, Texas

B., after studying art in school, worked in a gallery, in an architectural firm as a draftsman, in an advertising firm as a writer, and as an artist. After finally turning full time to writing, B. in the late 1970s began to teach and edit the *Mississippi Review* and continues to do both.

B.'s sculptural materials were often not conventional raw materials but everyday found objects, brought together, recombined, and refashioned. His first two novels are filled with photographs and drawings as well as actual letters and autobiography, some actual, some not. The later works strain less against the boundaries of form, but retain this interest in bringing together the everyday in strange new ways.

In five novels written in the 1980s and 1990s, B. has covered similar ground in similar ways. His moderately plain syntax, suburban, regional settings, and attention to the everyday, B. has been associated with the minimalist writers who became prominent in the late 1970s and 1980s, such as Raymond CARVER and Ann BEATTIE. His attention to the ever-present media's impact on the American psyche, to popular culture as much more than mass entertainment, has led to comparisons to postmodern writers such as Thomas PYNCHON and Don DELILLO.

In these novels B.'s characters look for order and meaning in disordered circumstances, many of which appear in a number of place. An example of this repetition is the reappearance of Del Tribute and his girlfriend Jen in *The Brothers* (1993) and *Painted Desert* (1995). In both novels they are fascinated with communication, with the Internet, with the meaning hidden in roadside junk, with disaster, murder, and the bizarre as covered by a variety of media. In *Painted Desert*, they head off cross-country to see where the Los Angeles riots and the events surrounding O. J. Simpson occurred, and in their encounters with the everyday refuse on the side of the road earn some kind of release from their oversaturation with what is, on one level, unreal.

In *Bob the Gambler* (1997) B. turns from the Internet to the casino, from the disaster-saturated media to the escapism of playing for the Big Payoff. Ray and Jewel, another bored couple trapped in a not especially tragic but not especially interesting existence, respond to the opening of the not entirely ironically named new casino, Paradise, with what would seem disastrous consequences. The fact that the big Payoff never comes does not mean, for B., that the activity is any less useful than those undertaken by his earlier characters. Similar to the journeys made by other of B.'s characters, Ray and Jewel's descent into gambling addiction serves to free them from their old lives and old, not quite met dreams. Here, as elsewhere, B. goes beyond painting the familiar portrait of the decaying American dream to offer a novel, if curious, revision of it: lose everything you have and you don't have to feel bad about it not being enough. The idea of gambling as a kind of purposeful self-unsettling, pushing oneself out of one's rut, might seem perverse to those living out of shopping carts on the outskirts of Las Vegas and Atlantic City. B.'s presentation of this idea, nonetheless, is another example of his ability to take the latest American trend, like so much roadside junk, explore how it plays out in a certain kind of American psyche, and appreciate in the same way kitsch is appreciated—without judgment.

FURTHER WORKS: *Moon Deluxe* (1983); *Second Marriage* (1984); *Tracer* (1985); *Chroma* (1987); *Two Against One* (1988); *Natural Selection* (1990)

BIBLIOGRAPHY: Peters, T., "80s Pastoral: F. B.'s *Moon Deluxe* Ten Years On," *SSF*, 31 (Spring 1994): 175-85; Brinkmeyer, R. H., Jr., "Suburban Culture, Imaginative Wonder: The Fiction of F. B.," *SLitI*, 27 (Fall 1994): 105-14

—SAM COHEN

BARTHES, Roland

French essayist and critic, b. 12 Nov. 1915, Cherbourg; d. 26 March 1980, Paris

After his father's death in a naval battle in 1916 and a childhood in Bayonne, B. attended secondary school in Paris. Although suffering from recurring bouts with tuberculosis (most seriously in 1941), he received degrees in classical letters (1939) and grammar and philology (1943) from the University of Paris. B. taught French in Romania (1948-49) and Egypt (1949-50). In the early 1950s, he was the first critic to identify the goals and the risks of the writings of Alain ROBBE-GRILLET and Michel BUTOR. B. continued to rally support for avant-garde French writers such as Philippe SOLLERS and Pierre Guyotat (b. 1940). From 1960 to 1977, B. was director of the social sciences section of the École Pratique des Hautes Études in Paris. In January 1977 he was elected to the chair of literary semiology at the College of France, a position he held until his tragic death from injuries sustained in a traffic accident. In his lifetime B. published seventeen books and numerous articles, many of which were gathered to form books.

There are five thematic ties which overlap throughout his opus and which represent changes of interest in his literary consciousness. First, there is B.'s concept of *écriture* (writing that has an identity independent of that intended by the writer), announced with a collection of previously published essays united under the rubric of *Le degré zéro de l'écriture* (1953; *Writing Degree Zero*, 1967). This work, with its Marxist and phenomenological overtones, shows concerns similar to SARTRE's with the connections between a culture and its artifacts. There are four other thematic ties, overlapping with B.'s Sartrean heritage: (1) psychoanalytic themes dominated the essays that appeared in 1958; (2) B. embraced linguistic STRUCTURALISM (a concept that has been used, wrongly, to cover all of B.'s oeuvre); (3) B. adopted semiology in evaluating nonliterary cultural artifacts; (4) B. was concerned with the relationships governed by various types of "discourse" (language as a communicative medium).

Michelet par lui-même (1954; *Michelet by Himself*, 1987) and *Mythologies* (1957; *Mythologies*, 1972) represent diverse aspects of B.'s early affinity with Marxist analysis. His biography of Jules Michelet (1798-1874), a 19th-c. historian of the French Revolution, focuses on how Michelet's personal obsessions are part of his writing and, according to B., give existential reality to the historical moments related by Michelet's writing. *Mythologies* is a collection of fifty previously published short stories. The subjects are, for the most part, nonliterary: soap bubbles, wrestling matches, and television programs, for example. B. reveals these components of French culture that have been either ignored or mythologized by the dominant ideology.

Sur Racine (1963; *On Racine*, 1964) caused some controversy because of its nonscholarly appreciation of Racine. Although many of the mythical, phenomenological, and psychoanalytic studies in the book had been published elsewhere as early as 1958, B. collected them in one volume to herald a "new criticism," quite distinct from the historical scholarship previously done on Racine. Raymond Picard (b. 1917), a Sorbonne professor and Racine scholar, responded to B.'s essays with a sharp rebuttal of the nonsystematic, arbitrary, and subjective nature of this "new criticism," of which B. was taken as the leader. Picard's *Nouvelle critique ou nouvelle imposture?* (1965; *New Criticism or New Fraud?*, 1969) was answered by B. in *Critique et vérité* (1966; criticism and truth), which postulated a "science of criticism" to replace the "university criticism" perpetuated by Picard and his colleagues. The B.-Picard debates generated much interest both in France and abroad. In *Critique et vérité*; B. recommends that criticism become a science; this scientific approach led to his interest in structural linguistics.

B.'s most intensive application of structural linguistics can be found in *S/Z* (1970; *S/Z*, 1974), in which he attempts an exhaustive analysis of Balzac's short story "Sarrasine" with a line-by-line explication and an elaboration of the five "codes" that are interwoven into that narrative. This study has become the focal point and model for "structuralist" literary criticism because of its analytical concentration on the structural elements that constitute the literary whole. B. would have criticism be a creative endeavor that discovers the multiple "voices" implied in a literary work.

B.'s *Le plaisir du texte* (1973; *The Pleasure of the Text*, 1975) and his *Roland Barthes par Roland Barthes* (1975; *Roland Barthes by Roland Barthes*, 1977) bring together his thematics of phenomenology, psychoanalysis, semiology, and discourse into an awareness of his physical presence as a reader in history. *Le plaisir du texte* is a theoretical discussion of himself as a reader. His desire to read is analyzed along with his likes, dislikes, and motivations associated with that activity. Of course, reading entails learning and judgment of literary and nonliterary components of culture. For B., it also means writing, because reading was the catalyst for his writing. *Roland Barthes par Roland Barthes* is a sort of autobiography organized by topics which fascinate or obsess him and which link his life to his writings. The visual component is underscored by a scrapbook effect obtained by pictures of people and places crucial to his identity.

These books emphasizing B.'s personal presence are complemented by his *Fragments d'un discours amoureux* (1977; *A Lover's Discourse: Fragments*, 1978) and *La chambre claire: Note sur la photographie* (1980; *Camera Lucida: Reflections on Photography*, 1981), which discuss how memory and language interact to relate B. to other people. The first work is organized in dictionary-like fashion according to key words that would apply to a love relationship. In the second work photography is discussed as a communicating medium, and specific photographs are used to exemplify B.'s arguments.

B. was one of the most influential French literary critics of the past thirty years. Although his writing is allusive and tends to concentrate on French historical figures, his philosophical and intellectual challenges offer creative alternatives to the pragmatic and reductionist methods of traditional literary scholarship everywhere. B.'s writings have a considerable following among students and teachers in France, England, and the U.S., who are, as B. was himself, intent upon putting literature into an interdisciplinary focus.

FURTHER WORKS: *La tour Eiffel* (1964; *The Eiffel Tower and Other Mythologies*, 1979); *Essais critiques* (1964; *Critical Essays*, 1972); *Éléments de sémiologie* (1965; *Elements of Semiology*, 1977); *Système de la mode* (1967); *L'empire des signes* (1970); *Sade Fourier Loyola* (1971; *Sade Fourier Loyola*, 1976); *Erté* (1975); *Pourquoi la Chine?* (1976); *Nouveaux essais critiques* (1972; *New Critical Essays*, 1980); *Leçon* (1978); *Sollers écrivain* (1979). FURTHER WORKS IN ENGLISH: *Image Music Text* (1977); *A B. Reader* (1980); *New Critical Essays* (1981)

BIBLIOGRAPHY: Mallac, G. de, and Eberbach, M., *B.* (1971); special B. issue, *Tel Quel*, No. 47 (1971); Doubrovsky, S., *New Criticism in France* (Eng. tr., 1973); Calvet, L. S., *R. B.: Un regard politique sur le signe* (1973); Davidson, H. M., "Sign, Sense, and R. B.," in Chatman, S., ed., *Approaches to Poetics* (1973): 29–50; Heath, S., *Vertige du déplacement* (1974); Sturrock, J., "R. B.," *The New Review*, No. 1 (May 1974): 13–21; special B. issue, *L'arc*, No. 56 (1974); special B. issue *Magazine littéraire*, No. 97 (1975); Thody, P., *R. B.: A Conservative Estimate* (1977); special B. issue, *V Lang*, 11, 4 (1977); Sontag, S., "Remembering B.," *Under the Sign of Saturn* (1980): 169–77

—ROLAND A. CHAMPAGNE

BASHKIR LITERATURE

Authorities on the literature of Bashkiria (a region in the southern Urals populated by a Turkic people) disagree sharply over its age. Some assert that it originated no earlier than the mid-1920s, since writers previously used languages other than Bashkir. Others believe that a literature belongs to the culture that generates it, regardless of the language employed, and hence that Bashkir literature existed long before 1900. Whatever its age, it has been nourished by an extensive oral folk tradition.

Written Bashkir literature, which had previously also used the Turki (Chaghatay) language, expressed itself principally through the Tatar language of Kazan in the first decades of the 20th c. Nevertheless, poets like Mökhämmätsälim Ishemghol-ulï Omötbaev (1841-1907) had tried to sound a "Bashkir echo" in such verses as "Yomran ile" (1887; the Yomran tribe [of Bashkirs]). Another poet, Shäykhzada Mökhämmätzakir-ulï Babich (1895-1919), enthusiastically joined the Bashkir national independence drive in 1917. His poem "Khalqïm oson" (1914; for my people) is characteristically nationalistic; among his volumes of verse are *Yäsh Bashqortostan* (1918; young Bashkiria) and *Bashqort khalqïna köylö khïtap* (1919; a melodious book for the Bashkir people). Poetry has remained the most popular genre in Bashkir literature to this day.

Bashkir literary prose originated with poets experimenting with fiction shortly after the turn of the century, among them, Mäjit Nurghäniulï Ghafuri (1880-1934), who was to be named poet laureate of the Bashkir Autonomous Soviet Socialist Republic in 1923. His novelette *Fäqirdhär* (1907; poor people) depicts the misfortunes and disasters that befall a poverty-stricken family. Ghafuri's best prose work is his autobiographical short novel *Shaghirdheng altïïn priiskehendä* (1929-31; in a poet's gold fields). Narrated in the first person, it is based upon the author's experiences while on a summer holiday from school, when he labored in the gold mines of northern Kazakhstan and closely observed working families.

Ghafuri, who gained warm official acceptance for poetry and fiction that harmonized with the subjects and themes prescribed by Soviet ideology, died just as tightening regulation and censorship became firmly institutionalized under the Communist-Party-controlled Writers' Union and the state publishing monopoly. Bashkir writing continues to operate under these strictures. Farit Isyangul's (dates n.a.) fiction typifies writing guided by official motifs.

Bashkir drama was supplied early in the century by Fazïl Tuykin (1888-1938), whose religious seminary education did not deter him from publishing a patriotic play, *Vatan qahramanlarï* (1912; the homeland's heroes). In the 1920s theatrical literature continued to develop older Bashkir themes. Later many plays on Soviet subjects appeared, for example, Mostay Kärim's (dates n.a.) *Strana Aygul* (1968; Aygul's country), which premiered in Russian in Moscow. As with fiction and poetry, some dramatists have chosen to write in Russian, to strong approval from Moscow.

BIBLIOGRAPHY: "La littérature bašqort," *Philologiae Turcicae Fundamenta*, 2 (1964): 778–79; Ramazanov, G. Z., "Bashkir Literature," in *The Modern Encyclopedia of Russian and Soviet Literature* (1977), Vol. I: 113–18

—EDWARD ALLWORTH

BASQUE LITERATURE
See sections under French Literature and Spanish Literature

BASSANI, Giorgio
Italian novelist, short-story writer, and poet, b. 4 March 1916, Bologna

The son of Italian Jews, B. spent his youth in Ferrara and received a degree in literature from the University of Bologna in 1939. Active in the Italian resistance during World War II, he published his first book, *Una città di pianura* (1940; a city on the plains) under a pseudonym, Giacomo Marchi. After the war he took up residence in Florence and immersed himself in the writing of two volumes of poetry, *Storie di poveri amanti e altri versi* (1945; tales of poor lovers and other verses) and *Te lucis ante* (1947; opening of a Latin hymn: before the ending of the day, to Thee, o Lord). He earned a living as a journalist and as the editor of such well-known reviews as *Botteghe Oscure and Paragone*. In 1958, as editor of the publishing house Feltrinelli, he "discovered" and published the internationally successful novel of Giuseppe Tomasi di LAMPEDUSA, *The Leopard*. B. himself gained international literary renown with the publication of his major novel, *Il giardino dei Finzi-Contini* (1962; *The Garden of the Finzi-Contini*, 1965 and 1977), which won the coveted Viareggio Prize and was made into a successful film in 1970 by Vittorio De Sica. During his writing career B. has been active as a journalist, essayist, and literary critic. He has also published a number of volumes of poetry, including: *Epitaffio* (1974; Epitaph); *In gran segreto* (1978; With Great Secrecy); and *In rime e senza* (1982; In Rhyme and Not).

Although a poet of distinction and a perceptive essayist and critic, B. has gained fame both in Italy and abroad for his fiction. His early life in Ferrara as a member of the Jewish middle class, especially during the Fascist tyranny, were of fundamental importance to his creative urge and are reflected in his major writings. Almost emblematic of the significance of the plight of Italian Jews to B.'s fiction are *Le storie ferraresi* (1960; the stories of Ferrara)—by some critics considered to be his most important artistic achievement—and *Il romanzo di Ferrara* (1975; the novel of Ferrara), a collection of novels published earlier, in which the city of Ferrara and the finely drawn detail of life in the Jewish community serve as a backdrop for the basic isolation and loneliness of a people caught up in the flood of racial laws. In the novella *Gli occhiali d'oro* (1958; *The Gold-Rimmed Spectacles*, 1960; also pub. as *The Gold-Rimmed Eyeglasses*, 1975), the personal torment and ultimate suicide of a homosexual doctor is used as an allegory of the ostracized and defeated Jew. And the more recent *L'airone* (1968; *The Heron*, 1970), projecting human desolation beyond contemporary Jewish history, uses the image of a wounded bird as symbolic of the vain attempts of an individual to give meaning to a life that is constantly threatened.

B.'s major novel, *Il giardino dei Finzi-Contini*, is exemplary of the writer's style and the recurrent themes of his novels and shorter works of fiction. The prose is lyrical and precisely measured in its evocation of Ferrara and the cultural milieu of the city during the period of impending disaster, the Holocaust. For good reason, more than one critic has remarked that Jewish history and the ghetto environment become protagonists of B.'s world. The novel, rich in autobiographical elements, relates the gradual effects of racial laws upon a group of people unable to comprehend the enormity of what is happening around them: the Finzi-Continis, Jewish aristocrats living a cloistered life on the family estate, seem suspended in their daily activities as the realities of the world close in upon them. The novel's opening image of the burial grounds that contain the remains of the family's ancestors and therefore speak of culture and tradition is tragically balanced with its closing scenes of the family preparing to leave for the extermination camps.

Bassani is universally recognized as one of Italy's most accomplished writers, a superb stylist whose constant return to themes rooted in his own experiences as an Italian Jew and the traditions of his people has a transcendent quality whereby narrow historical events take on universal significance in the portrayal of loneliness and despair.

FURTHER WORKS: *Un'altra libertà* (1952); *La passeggiata prima di cena* (1953); *Gli ultimi anni di Clelia Trotti* (1955); *Cinque storie ferraresi* (1956; *Five Stories of Ferrara*, 1971); *Una notte del '43* (1960); *L'alba ai vetri* (1963); *Dietro la porta* (1964; *Behind the Door*, 1972); *Le parole preparate* (1966); *L'odore del fieno* (1972; *The Smell of Hay*, 1975); *Dentro le mura* (1973)

BIBLIOGRAPHY: Grillandi, M., *Invito alla lettura di G. B.* (1972); Shapiro, M., "The *Storie ferraresi* of G. B.," *Italica*, 49 (1972): 30–48; Eskin, S. G., "The Garden of the Finzi-Continis," *Literature/Film Quarterly*, 1 (1973): 171–75; Schneider, M., "Mythical Dimensions of Micòl Finzi-Contini," *Italica*, 51 (1974): 43–67; Radcliff-Umstead, D., "Transformation in B.'s Garden," *MFS*, 21 (1975): 521–33; Radcliff-Umstead, D., "G. B.: The Community of the Excluded," *PCL*, 3 (1977): 21–29; special B. issue *CJIS*, 1 (1977-78); Dolfi, A., *Le forme del sentimento: prosa e poesia di G. B.* (1981); Schneider, M. *Vengeance of the Victim: History and*

Symbol in G. B.'s Fiction (1986); Radcliff-Umstead, D., *The Exile into Eternity: A Study of the Narrative Writings of G.B.* (1987); Varanini, G., *B., narratore, poeta, saggista* (1991)

—ROBERT J. RODINI

BATAILLE, Georges

French novelist and essayist, b. 10 Sept. 1897, Billom; d. 9 July 1962, Paris

B. was a librarian by profession. Originally, however, he had wanted to become a monk, but his short stay in a Benedictine monastery resulted in a loss of faith; many of B.'s fictional works and essays deal with his close and problematic involvements with religion. B.'s work also demonstrates a profound preoccupation with his father's blindness, most notably in *Histoire de l'œil* (1928; *A Tale of Satisfied Desire*, 1953), where sightless eyes play an important role.

B. also founded many journals and groups that revealed his interests in sociology, religion, politics, and literature: *Documents* (1929–31); *La critique sociale* (1931–34); *Cahiers de Contre-Attaque* (1936), reflecting the positions of the group of revolutionary intellectuals called Contre-Attaque; *Acéphale* (1936–39); Collège de Sociologie (1939), founded with Michel LEIRIS and Roger Caillois (b. 1913) to explore the manifestations of the sacred in society; and *Critique* (1946–). Like most writers of his generation, B. was involved for a time in the SURREALIST adventure. He was deeply influenced by Sade, Hegel, and Nietzsche, publishing *Sur Nietzsche* (*On Nietzsche*, 1992) in 1944 and filling his works with aphorisms in a Nietzschean poetico-philosophical vein. He also reached intellectually beyond the confines of Western culture through ethnological studies that owed much to the French social anthropologist Marcel Mauss (1872–1950) in their examination of sacrifice and potlatch; through wide travels, particularly in Asia; and through the acquisition of considerable knowledge about Asian thought and literature.

B. was probably best known for the glorification of eroticism in many of his works, including *Histoire de l'œil, L'abbé C.* (1950; *The Abbot C.*, 1983), *Le bleu du ciel* (1945; *Blue at Noon*, 1978), *L'érotisme* (1957; *Eroticism*, 1962), *La littérature et le mal* (1957; *Literature and Evil*, 1973), and *La haine de la poésie* (1947; hatred of poetry; 2nd ed. pub. as *L'impossible* [1962; *The Impossible*, 1991]). His erotic works are not sadistic-scatological, anticlerical fantasies but rather a part of a larger theoretical framework that encompasses all his works and focuses on those areas of human experience that go beyond the realm of the possible and are outside the scope of any conventional systematization.

Laughter, religious ecstasy, sacrifice, the erotic, death, and poetry were considered by B. to be "impossible" or "sovereign" operations, since in their pure forms, unsubordinated to any useful goals, they violently transgress the limits of the livable and thinkable and approach states of pure "loss," including loss of self. Eroticism particularly fascinated B., since he felt that sexual union causes a momentary indistinguishability between otherwise distinct objects and that aberrant sexual activity in its extremely violent forms leads to death. Poetry, defined by B. as verbal art in general, also approaches the impossible when it succeeds in expressing an experience that escapes the confines of meaning. It dissolves the familiar "into the strange and ourselves with it."

On a formal level, the sacrifice of meaning is represented by the difficulty in assigning a definable or stable genre label to B.'s books. For example, *Le coupable* (1944; *The Guilty*, 1988) can be considered as a discursive work recording B.'s mystical experiences because it is one of three books—with *L'expérience intérieure* (1943; *The Inner Experience*, 1988) and *Méthode de méditation* (1947; method of meditation)—that have a philosophical subject, namely, "la somme athéologique" (the atheological total). However, the formal characteristics of *Le coupable* link it to *L'impossible*, which is usually classified as a fictional work. *L'impossible* itself is difficult to classify, since it is composed of three heterogenous works—*L'Orestie* (1945; the Oresteia), a collection of poems that in form and subject matter questions the traditional views of poetry; *Histoire des rats* (1947; story of rats), a diary of a dead man; and *Dianus* (1947; Dianus), the notes of a priest—all published originally as separate works and subsequently gathered together first under the title *La haine de la poésie*. Even the expository *La part maudite* (1949; *The Accursed Share*, 1988), a work that deals with economic theory and the phenonemon of waste (*dépense*) in nature and society, is ambiguous because it does not present its subject matter in an orderly and logical descriptive form.

Through his unceasing efforts to penetrate the unthinkable, to face the frightening and the grotesque, and to express the impossible, B. upset the categories of thought and writing that centuries of theological, philosophical, and poetic specialization had consolidated and took his place among those writers whose work immeasurably expands the horizons of thought and literature.

FURTHER WORKS: *L'anus solaire* (1931); *Sacrifices* (1936); *Madame Edwarda* (1937); *L'archangélique* (1944); *Dirty* (1945); *L'alleluiah* (1947); *Théorie de la religion* (1948); *Éponine* (1949); *Lascaux; ou, La naissance de l'art* (1955; *Lascaux: or, The Birth of Art: Prehistoric Painting*, 1955); *Manet* (1955; *Manet*, 1955); *Les larmes d'Éros* (1961); *Le petit* (1963); *Ma mère* (1966; *My Mother*, 1972); *La notion de dépense* (1967); *Le mort* (1967)

BIBLIOGRAPHY: Blanchot, M., *L'entretien infini* (1969): 70–83; special B. issue, *Critique*, 19 (1963): 677–832; special B. issue, *L'arc*, 32 (1967); special B. issue, *L'arc*, 44 (1971); *B.-colloque de Cerisy 1972* (1973); special B. issue, *Gramma*, 1 (1974); Libertson, J., "B. and Communication," *Substance*, 10 (1974): 47–65; Richman, M. H., *Reading G. B.: Beyond the Gift* (1982); Richardson, M., *G. B.* (1994); Gail, C. B., ed., *B.: Writing the Sacred* (1995)

—LARYSA MYKYTA

BATES, H(erbert) E(rnest)

English novelist and short-story writer, b. 16 May 1905, Rushden, Northamptonshire; d. 29 Jan. 1974, Canterbury, Kent

B., one of the most accomplished short-story writers of his generation, was born into an aspiring working-class family living in a small town in the English Midlands. By his own account, B. spent much of his childhood in happy exploration of the surrounding countryside; and, indeed, rural characters and locations appear frequently in his fiction.

Although B. was a good student, he chose not to pursue a university education. Instead, he began his working career as a reporter for the *Northampton Chronicle* and wrote fiction on the side. B.'s early work greatly impressed Edward Garnett (1868-1937), one of Britain's most influential literary editors. With Garnett's help, B.'s first novel, *The Two Sisters*, was published in 1926.

B., still in his early twenties, now also began publishing short fiction at a prodigious pace; much of this—collected in such volumes as *Day's End and Other Stories* (1928) and *Seven Tales and Alexander* (1929)—shows the influence, in structure and tone, of Anton CHEKHOV, whose stories the young B. particularly admired. By the mid-1930s, B. was frequently described as one of Britain's most industrious and promising younger writers, employing a lean but often richly descriptive and highly atmospheric style that would continue to characterize his finest fiction. *The Woman Who Had Imagination and Other Stories* (1934) shows B. reaching his artistic maturity; many critics, including Graham GREENE, praised the volume's deft depictions of country life and its often humorous treatment of highly memorable characters. Of these, the old but still spirited Uncle Silas—who appears in both "The Wedding" and "The Lily"—proved so popular that B. continued to feature him in a series of stories later published as *My Uncle Silas* (1939) and *Sugar for the Horse* (1957).

Another collection of stories, *Cut and Come Again* (1935), also brought B. wide acclaim. This volume contains several of his best-known stories, including "The Mill," a vivid but harsh portrayal of rural life that reveals something of the Thomas Hardy-like naturalism that occasionally surfaces in B.'s fiction and counterbalances the more gently romantic strain that undoubtedly played a large part in his wide appeal. Indeed, B. is a writer of considerable emotional range, capable of convincingly conveying the sadness and cruelty of life as well as its delights and pleasures.

During the 1930s, B. published several of his finest novels, including *The Fallow Land* (1932) and *The Poacher* (1935), both of which show the hard side of rural life while celebrating, in varying ways, the strength and ingenuity that survival in the country often requires.

In 1941 B. joined the air ministry, and spent World War II writing a series of stories designed to help build morale during the conflict's duration. These pieces, appearing under the pseudonym of "Flying Officer X," were collected in *The Greatest People in the World and Other Stories* (1942) and *How Sleep the Brave and Other Stories* (1943). They proved highly popular, and B.'s authorship of them soon became widely known.

In *Fair Stood the Wind for France* (1944), B. centers on a wounded English pilot trapped in occupied territory. With its precise prose and avoidance of both melodrama and propaganda, this is the best of the "Officer X" books, and remains one of the more enduring English novels about the war published during the 1940s. The lesser-known *Dear Life* (1950) also focuses on the war and its aftermath, but more darkly; it is now rightly considered to be one of B.'s most compelling novels.

After the war, B. continued to earn his living with his pen. Much of the work he came to produce—including such novels as *The Sleepless Moon* (1956) and *A Crown of Wild Myrtle* (1962)—cannot be ranked much higher than the general run of popular fiction published during the 1950s and 1960s. In such novels as *The Darling Buds of May* (1958) and *A Breath of French Air* (1959) B. portrays the comical and lusty Larkins, a family of junk dealers from Kent; doing so, he brings rather bluntly to the fore the same keen interest in sexuality that had more subtly informed much of his earlier fiction. B.'s Larkin novels were among the most profitable of his career. However, they are generally dismissed by

H. E. Bates

critics who see them as proof that, regrettably, B. came to abandon his artistic ambitions in favor of brisk and steady sales.

Undoubtedly, much of B.'s later fiction shows evidence of distraction and haste. But during his final phase he also produced *Love for Lydia* (1952), his most autobiographical novel, which features some of his strongest characterizations and an especially vivid depiction of life in the English Midlands during the 1920s. *The Triple Echo* (1970) is a superbly constructed novella that deals intriguingly with, among other things, questions of sexual identity. Such works demonstrate once more that B. is an unusually gifted writer whose achievement in both the novel and the short story is significant and deserves increasing recognition.

FURTHER WORKS: *Catherine Foster* (1929); *The Hessian Prisoner* (1930); *Charlotte's Row* (1931); *The Black Boxer* (1932); *Sally Go Round the Moon* (1932); *The Story without an End and The Country Doctor* (1932); *Thirty Tales* (1934); *The Duet* (1935); *Flowers and Faces* (1935); *A House of Women* (1936); *Down the River* (1937); *Something Short and Sweet* (1937); *Spella Ho* (1938); *The Flying Goat* (1939); *Country Tales* (1940); *The Beauty of the Dead and Other Stories* (1940); *The Seasons and the Gardener* (1940); *In the Heart of the Country* (1942); *The Bride Comes to Evensford* (1943); *Country Life* (1943); *There's Freedom in the Air: The Official Story of the Allied Air Forces from the Occupied Countries* (1944); *The Cruise of the Breadwinner* (1946); *The Tinkers of Elstow* (1946); *The Purple Plain* (1947); *Edward Garnett: A Memoir* (1950); *The Scarlet Sword* (1950); *Colonel*

Julian and Other Stories (1951); *The Country of White Clover* (1952); *The Face of England* (1952); *The Feast of July* (1954); *The Daffodil Sky* (1955); *The Watercress Girl and Other Stories* (1959); *An Aspidistra in Babylon: Four Novellas* (1960); *The Day of the Tortoise* (1961); *Now Sleeps the Crimson Petal and Other Stories* (1961); *The Golden Oriole: Five Novellas* (1962); *Achilles and Diana* (1963); *Oh! To Be in England* (1963); *The Fabulous Mrs. V.* (1964); *A Moment in Time* (1964); *The Wedding Party* (1965); *The Distant Horns of Summer* (1967); *The Four Beauties: Four Novellas* (1968); *The White Admiral* (1968); *The Wild Cherry Tree* (1968); *A Little of What You Fancy* (1970); *The Blossoming World* (1971); *The World in Ripeness* (1972); *A Fountain of Flowers* (1974); *The Vanished World: An Autobiography* (1979)

BIBLIOGRAPHY: Cavaliero, G., "The Enduring Land: H. E. B.," *The Rural Tradition in the English Novel, 1900–1939* (1977): 196–200; Vannatta, D. P., *H. E. B.* (1983); Baldwin, D. R., "Atmosphere in the Stories of H. E. B.," *SSF*, 21, 3 (Summer 1984): 215–22; Gindin, J., "A. E. Coppard and H. E. B.," in Flora, J. M., ed., *The English Short Story, 1880–1945* (1985): 113–41; Baldwin, D. R., *H. E. B.: A Literary Life* (1987)

—BRIAN MURRAY

BAUER, Walter

German poet, novelist, short-story writer, biographer, essayist, and dramatist, b. 4 Nov. 1904, Merseburg an der Saale; d. 23 Dec. 1976, Toronto, Canada

B. was the son of a workingman. After studies at a teachers college and at the University of Halle he served as a public-school teacher in central German towns and industrial areas for ten years. His writings were largely banned by the Nazi regime, and from 1940 to 1945 B. was an unwilling member of Hitler's army. Disappointed at the unregenerated, stifling postwar atmosphere in his native country, B. emigrated to Canada in 1952 with his "desperate love of Europe" in his baggage, and he found a new home in Toronto. Following years of hardship (he was employed as a dishwasher and factory laborer) B. resumed his education and his teaching career, receiving an M.A. in 1958 and rising to the rank of associate professor of German at the University of Toronto.

B. was one of the most versatile and most prolific writers of our time; his approximately sixty published volumes contain works in virtually every literary form. He began in the tradition of the *Arbeiterdichtung* (workingmen's literature) and the *Neue Sachlichkeit* (new factualism) of the 1920s. B. achieved early recognition with a volume of poetry entitled *Kameraden, zu euch spreche ich* (1929; comrades, it is to you I am talking) and another of verse and prose, *Stimme aus dem Leunawerk* (1930; voice from the Leuna factory). His first novel, *Ein Mann zog in die Stadt* (1931; a man moved to the city) deals with a farmer who relocates in search of happiness and finds only poverty and proletarianization. Like his mentor Stefan ZWEIG, B. was a master of the well-researched, fastpaced, stylistically attractive *vie romancée*, or biographical-historical novel. His life of Fridtjof Nansen, *Die langen Reisen*, (1956; the long journeys), won the Albert Schweitzer prize; other biographical works deal with Van Gogh (*Die Sonne von Arles*, 1951; the sun of Arles), Sieur de la Salle (*Folge dem Pfeil*, 1956; follow the arrow), and Pestalozzi (*Die Kinder und die Armen*, 1969; the

children and the poor). B.'s poetry is modern and even topical without being experimental or bitter; it is specific, highly personal, and eminently accessible. Collections like *Die Nachtwachen des Tellerwäschers* (1957; the vigils of the dishwasher) and *Mein blaues Oktavheft* (1962; my blue octavo journal) are largely autobiographical, as are a number of volumes of short stories, such as *Die Tränen eines Mannes* (1958; a man's tears) and *Fremd in Toronto* (1963; a stranger in Toronto).

Daumier's insight, "*Je suis de mon temps*," was B.'s lifelong watchword, and in his last decades his life and work were also decisively shaped by his almost obsessive awareness of being a "German of my generation," a man with a guilt to expiate, who felt it was his mission to counteract the dehumanizing tendencies of his time. In his new homeland B. continued his earlier championship of humanistic values, retaining his uncompromising truthfulness and marked social consciousness as well as his belief in the basic goodness and dignity of man. Born of a sense of solitude as well as a sense of community, B.'s writings reflect an affirmative outlook on life even as they mourn the miseries and tragedies of our age.

FURTHER WORKS: *Die notwendige Reise* (1932); *Das Herz der Erde* (1933); *Der Lichtstrahl* (1937); *Flamme und Asche* (1937); *Die zweite Mutter* (1937); *Tagebuchblätter aus Frankreich* (1941); *Die zweite Erschaffung der Welt* (1947); *Tagebuchblätter aus Rußland* (1947); *Das Lied der Freiheit* (1948); *Besser zu zweit als allein* (1949); *Die Erzählung des letzten Hirten* (1949); *Der Gesang vom Sturmvogel* (1949); *Michelangelo* (1949); *Blau und Rot im Regenbogen* (1950); *Erzählungen aus 1001 Nacht* (1951); *Griechische Sagen* (1954); *Die Stimme* (1961); *Klopfzeichen* (1962); *Der weiße Indianer* (1962); *Lorbeer für Hellas* (1964); *Der Weg zählt, nicht die Herberge* (1964); *Phönix stirbt nicht* (1965); *September 43* (1965); *Testament* (1965); *Verzicht auf einen Besuch* (1965); *Ein Deutscher meiner Generation* (1965); *Fragment vom Hahnenschrei* (1966); *Ein Jahr* (1967); *Lebenslauf* (1975); *Liebe zu Deutschland heisst leiden an Deutschland. Briefe aus Kanada 1962-1976* (1980); *Geburt des Poeten* (1980). FURTHER WORKS IN ENGLISH: *The Price of Morning* (1968); *A Different Sun* (1976); *A Slight Trace of Ash* (1976)

BIBLIOGRAPHY: Beissel, H., "A Few Words of Farewell to a Friend," *TamR*: Nos. 77–78 (1979): 5–13; Maurer, K. W., "A Particular Genius: Observations on B. and Translation," *CV II*, Fall 1979: 34–36; Watt, F. W., "A Different Son: W. B.'s Canadian Poetry," *Canadian Forum*, Sept. 1979: 20–24; Rieder, W. et al., eds., *Der Wanderer. Aufsätze zu Leben und Werk von W. B.* (1994)

—HARRY ZOHN

BAUER, Wolfgang

Austrian dramatist, poet, and novelist, b. 18 Mar. 1941, Graz

B. has been in the spotlight as one of Austria's most talked-about writers for over thirty years. Born in Graz and still residing in that city, he began to write while still young. Initially he attended law school; then, finding that too unimaginative, he took up French and geography. However, he decided against a teaching career and moved to Vienna to study drama. After a few semesters he returned to Graz to establish himself as a writer. With the exception of one novel, *Der Fieberkopf: Ein Roman in Briefen* (1967; the fever head: an epistolary novel), two volumes of poetry, *Das stille Schilf* (1969; the quiet reed) and *Das Herz* (1981; the heart), occasional short prose, and some journalism, B. has limited himself to drama.

B.'s early works are in the tradition of existentialist philosophy and the THEATER OF THE ABSURD. *Party for Six* (1967; title in English) forms a bridge between his absurd plays and the later realistic ones. Despite the play's ultrarealistic form and setting, the author's intentions to undermine conventional concepts of reality are obvious. By not presenting the party but only what is incidental to it, B. wants to demonstrate that everything that "really" happens either may or may not be presented on stage.

B.'s best-known play is *Magic Afternoon* (1968; title in English). In the 1969-1970 theater season it was among the six plays most frequently performed in German-speaking countries. Translated into many languages, it has been widely produced throughout the world. *Magic Afternoon* is the story of the boredom, the frustrations, and the violence of four young people. While the play's success has largely been attributed to B.'s having captured in it the spirit of the youth culture of the 1960s, it transcends time and place and can be seen as a study of cultural alienation and as a parable for human isolation and loneliness. Although *Magic Afternoon* has become a classic of sorts, it also established B.'s reputation as an author of chaos and perversion.

Change (1969; title in English), a provocative play about manipulation and countermanipulation, is in many ways similar to *Magic Afternoon*. Although frequently interpreted as a "mirror of the times," it too reflects B.'s existential anguish and illustrates his view that humans are no more than puppets—manipulated.

The artificial world of the culture industry, of film, pop music, and the theater, is the topic of *Film und Frau* (1971; *Shakespeare the Sadist*, 1972) and *Silvester oder Das Massaker im Hotel Sacher* (1971; New Year's Eve or the massacre in the Sacher Hotel). The characters in these plays all suffer from alienation and boredom and are without recognizable individuality.

Gespenster (1974; *Ghosts,* 1978), because of its earthy language and some obscenities, caused an uproar when shown on television and led to accusations of pornography and degenerate art. With a scanty and outright nonsensical plot, the play portrays individuals who, while aware of the emptiness and senselessness of their situation, mistakenly believe that they can live with substitute identities.

Magnetküsse (1976; magnetic kisses), a surrealistic crime thriller about a writer of detective stories, presents an almost identical message. Its hero's appeal for human freedom goes unheard, his quest for authenticity leads to insanity. Parallels between B.'s play and the portrayals of American culture by Jerzy KOSINSKI in literature and Roman Polanski in film are striking.

In *Memory Hotel* (1980; *Memory Hotel*, 1981), on the other hand, B., for the first time, expresses hope that the struggle for human liberation may not be futile after all. While the play, again, is a chaotic sequence of happenings, there are indications that a meaningful life and happiness are possible.

Despite the refusal of the public to go along with his philosophical plays, B. single-mindedly continued to write in this vein. With borderlines between dream and reality blurred and their logic limited only by the boundaries of imagination, his plays "*Woher kommen wir? Was sind wir? Wohin gehen wir?*" (1982; *Singapore Sling*, 1983), *Ein fröhlicher Morgen beim Friseur* (1983; a happy morning in the barber shop), and *Das kurze Leben der Schneewolken* (1983; The Short Life of the Snowclouds) read like a drama cycle

with a common theme. While *Ein fröhlicher Morgen* is a funfilled parable for the senselessness of the world, *Woher kommen wir?* reflects the author's conviction that the process of acculturation has destroyed the harmony that existed in prehistoric times. *Herr Faust spielt Roulette* (1987; Mr. Faust plays roulette), a play about a person's loss of identity, has philosophical implications too. B.'s Faust version has been praised as a bold interpretation of the world as a place of an infernal game of chance, but, with the stage once again becoming the scene of dreams, it has also strained viewers and critics alike to the point of total frustration. Nevertheless, his plays written in the 1990s are an indication that B. has remained faithful to himself. The heroes of *Ach, armer Orpheus!* (1991; Oh, Poor Orpheus) and *Insalata mista* constantly move between dream and reality. All rules of logic are suspended; only the logic of dreams carries weight. *Ach, armer Orpheus!* is a takeoff on the Orpheus myth, its hero being a writer reminiscent of those in previous plays. In *Insalata mista* (1992), a combination of absurdity and slapstick, ten people jabbering in a multitude of languages plan a bomb attack against a Japanese millionaire who wants to purchase Manhattan. Under the title *Tadpoletigermosquitos at Mulligan's*, this one-act play appropriately premiered in New York City in 1993.

B.'s seriousness as a dramatist, which has often been questioned, cannot be denied. Humor, situation comedy, witty dialogues, use of dialect and jargon, spontaneity and turbulence, combined with elements of American pop culture are some key ingredients of his plays. Whether the author presents his message realistically or in a surrealistic fashion, it is obvious that his plays contain a clearly recognizable continuity of ideas. They are all concerned with basic questions of human existence and a search for a meaningful life. The prestigious literary prizes B. has been awarded in Austria are an indication that he has finally been accepted in his native country as a major exponent of the contemporary theater with a growing international reputation.

FURTHER WORKS: *Mikrodramen* (1964); *Romeo und Julia: Mikrodrama* (1969); *Katharina Doppelkopf und andere Eisenbahnstücke* (1973); *Die Sumpftänzer: Dramen, Prosa, Lyrik aus zwei Jahrzehnten* (1978); *Pfnacht: Komödie in 3 Akten* (1980); *Batyscaphe 17–26 oder Die Hölle ist oben* (1980); *Woher kommen wir? Wohin gehen wir? Dramen und Prosa mit bisher unveröffentlichten und neuen Stücken* (1982); *In Zeiten wie diesen: Ein Drehbuch* (1984); *Werke in sieben Bänden*: Vol. 1. *Einakter und frühe Dramen* (1987), Vol. 2. *Schauspiele 1967-1973* (1986), Vol. 3. *Schauspiele 1975-1986* (1986), Vol. 4. *Der Fieberkopf: Ein Roman in Briefen* (1986), Vol. 6. *Kurzprosa, Essays und Kritiken* (1989); *Das Lächeln des Brian de Palma: Stück* (1988); "*Ach, armer Orpheus!*" in *manuskripte*, p. 106 (1989), 121–40; *Werke in sieben Bänden*: Vol. 1. *Einakter und frühe Dramen* (1987), Vol. 2. *Schauspiele 1967-1973* (1986), Vol. 3. *Schauspiele 1975-1986* (1986), Vol. 4. *Der Fieberkopf: Ein Roman in Briefen* (1986), Vol. 6. *Kurzprosa, Essays und Kritiken* (1989), Vol. 7. *Filme und Fernsehspiele* (1995), Vol. 8. *Schauspiele 1988-1995* (1996). FURTHER WORKS IN ENGLISH: *Change and Other Plays* (1976); "*All Change*" *and Other Plays: Magic Afternoon. Party for Six* (1973); *The Magic Afternoon* (1989); *Shakespeare the Sadist and Other Plays* (1977); *Memory Hotel* (1981); *The Feverhead: A Novel in Letters* (1993)

BIBLIOGRAPHY: Haberland, P. H., "Duality, the Artist, and W. B.," *MAL*, 11, 2 (1978): 73–86; special B. issue, *TuK*, 59 (1978);

Rorrison, H., "The 'Grazer Gruppe,' Peter Handke and W. B.," in Best, A., and H. Wolfschütz, eds., *Modern Austrian Writing: Literature and Society after 1945* (1980): 252–66; Carpenter, C. A., "The Plays of Bernhard, B., and Handke: A Checklist of Major Critical Studies," *MD*, 23, 4 (Jan. 1981): 484–91; Melzer, G., *W. B.: Eine Einführung in das Gesamtwerk* (1981); Stefanek, P., "Aus einem Gespräch mit W. B. (Graz) über Kritik, Stückeschreiben, Theater, Regie und Publikum," *MAL*, 18, 2 (1985): 79–89; Koppensteiner, J., "W. B.," in Daviau, D. G., ed., *Major Figures of Contemporary Austrian Literature* (1987): 67–88; "W. B. im Gespräch," in Friedl H., ed., *Die Tiefe der Tinte* (1990): 10–26; Grond, W., and G. Melzer, eds., *W. B.* (1994); Wenk, D., *Postmodernes Konverationstheater: W. B.* (1995); "Ich nehms als Faktum: Ein Gespräch mit W. B.," in Schödel, H., and G. M. Bauer, eds., *Paralyse: Beipackzettel zu Tausend Jahre Österreich* (1996): 39-48

—JÜRGEN KOPPENSTEINER

BAXTER, James K(eir)

New Zealand poet, dramatist, and critic, b. 29 June 1926, Dunedin; d. 23 Oct. 1972, Auckland

B.'s father was a Scots farmer, whose *We Will Not Cease* (1939) records his torture by the New Zealand army in Europe as a conscientious objector during World War I; his mother was an eminent local professor's daughter with a Cambridge degree. When he was eighteen B.'s first book, *Beyond the Palisade* (1944), was greeted with acclaim. In 1948 he married a Maori woman and converted to Anglicanism. At a 1951 Writers' Conference he said, "I believe our island is in fact an unjust, unhappy one," and the poet is to "remain a cell of good living in a corrupt society." Unsettled living led him to take on many unskilled jobs before doing governmental work in education. Severe drinking problems led him to Alcoholics Anonymous, which preceded his conversion to Roman Catholicism in 1958 and six months of UNESCO work in India. In 1969, shabby, bearded, sandaled, he left his family (with their consent) to work with young drug addicts and dropouts and finally to found a refuge in a remote Maori village, Jerusalem. When he died, his funeral was attended by hundreds; it included both a requiem mass and a Maori *tangi*.

B.'s earlier works, *Beyond the Palisade, Blow, Wind of Fruitfulness* (1948), *The Fallen House* (1953), and *In Fires of No Return* (1958), display late-Victorian melancholy, at times self-parodying eloquence, the presentation of landscapes, and the theme of isolation. Derivative British echoes abound, as in his second play, *Jack Winter's Dream* (1959), reminiscent of Dylan THOMAS. But the import of his 1951 address broke through in the 1958 volume's vernacular of "Lament for Barney Flanagan" and the social concern of "Crossing Cook Strait."

Howrah Bridge (1961), using his experiences in India, utilized a DURRELL-derived "carped, carved little two-lined stanza" and far less rhetoric. So also in the significantly titled *Pig Island Letters* (1966), in which he uses the South Island of New Zealand (Pig Island in the vernacular) to refer not only to the whole country but to the human condition in general. His last works reflect his experience in the Maori village of Jerusalem. *Jerusalem Sonnets* (1970), *Jerusalem Daybook* (1971), and the posthumously published *Autumn Testament* (1972) contain, with prose and some

other verse, over a hundred austerely "simple" unrhymed "sonnets" in his two-lined stanza—mundane, ironic, profane, profound records of spiritual striving.

B.'s late verse may represent a new plateau for New Zealand poetry. His life and works are one: both seem to reject false values for a life of simplicity; to protest against *pakeha* (white) materialism; and to advocate the precapitalist, rural, Maori, Catholic sanctities and the truths known to the underprivileged.

FURTHER WORKS: *Recent Trends in New Zealand Poetry* (1951); *Poems Unpleasant* (1952); *Two Plays: The Wide Open Cage, and Jack Winter's Dream* (1959); *Aspects of Poetry in New Zealand* (1967); *The Lion Skin* (1967); *The Rock Woman: Selected Poems* (1969); *The Devil and Mr. Mulcahy, and The Band Rotunda* (1971); *The Sore-footed Man, and The Temptation of Oedipus* (1971); *Ode to Auckland, and Other Poems* (1972); *Runes* (1973); *Two Obscene Poems by J. K. B.* (1973); *The Labyrinth: Some Uncollected Poems 1944–72* (1974); *The Bone Chanter: Unpublished Poems 1945–1972* (1976); *The Holy Life and Death of Concrete Grady* (1976); *Selected Criticism* (1976); *Collected Poems* (1981); *Collected Plays* (1982); *Horse* (1985)

BIBLIOGRAPHY: Stead, C. K., "Towards Jerusalem: The Later Poetry of J. K. B.," *Islands*, 2 (1973): 7–18; Weir, J. E., "An Interview with J. K. B.," *Landfall*, 28 (1974): 241–50; Broughton, W. S., "A Discursive Essay about Jerusalem," *WLWE*, 14 (1975): 69–90; Doyle, C., *J. K. B.* (1976); O'Sullivan, V., *J. K. B.* (1976); McKay, F., *The Life of J. K. B.* (1990)

—PETER C. M. ALCOCK

al-BAYYĀTĪ, 'Abd al-Wahhāb

Iraqi poet, b. 19 Dec. 1926, Baghdad

After graduating from the Teacher's Training College of Baghdad in 1950, B. taught in public schools. His leftist, antigovernment activities cost him his job and, to escape harassment, he left Iraq in 1954 for, in turn, Lebanon, Syria, and Egypt. After the overthrow of the royal regime in Iraq in 1958, the republican Iraqi government appointed him to a post in the Ministry of Education but in 1959 sent him to Moscow as cultural attaché at the Iraqi embassy. He resigned in 1961, taught at the Asian and African Peoples' Institute of the Soviet Academy of Sciences, then traveled widely in Europe, especially in socialist-bloc countries, before settling in Cairo in 1964. After the republican regime of Iraq came under the control of the pan-Arab, socialist Ba'th party in 1968, he returned home and is now cultural consultant at the Ministry of Information and Culture.

B.'s many years of separation from his homeland, his wife, and his four children are reflected in his poetry. But he has woven these nostalgic feelings into the main themes of his verse, which are inspired by an unswerving revolutionary commitment to proletarian struggle in order to improve the lot of man in the modern world. The romanticism of his first collection *Malā'ika wa shayāṭīn* (1950; angels and devils), gave way to SOCIALIST REALISM in his second *Abārīq muhashshama* (1954; broken pitchers) written mostly in free verse. His subsequent works established his leadership of the Socialist Realist movement in modern Arabic poetry.

B. made popular the economical use of language in poetry. Employing a succession of images joined together by conjunctions, he presents a montage of impressions, the result of which is a vivid picture of a situation as he sees it. Enlivened by conversational quotations and literary allusions, his poems are usually short and to the point.

In his later poetry he sheds the prosaic, strident style of some of his early poems but retains the commitment to fight injustice, exploitation, imperialism, and reactionary governments. His defense of the wretched of the earth becomes a mystical love, and B. couches it in symbols, allusions, and myths drawn from the rich literary legacy of the great Arab mystics, as in his collections *Sifr al-faqr wa al-thawra* (1965; the book of poverty and revolution), *Alladhī ya'tī wa lāya'tī* (1966; what will come and will not come), and *Qasāid hubb 'alā bawwābāt al-'ālam al-sab'* (1971; love poems on the seven gates of the world). Although his mysticism is almost impenetrable at times, B. remains a spokesman for radical change in Arab society.

FURTHER WORKS: *Risāla ilā Nazim Hikmet wa qas'āid ukhrā* (1956); *Al-Majd li al-atfāl wa al-zaytūn* (1956); *Ash'ār fī al-manfā* (1957); *'Ishrūn qasīda min Berlin* (1959); *Kalimāt lā tamūt* (1960); *Muhākama fī Nīsābūr* (1963); *Al-Nār wa al-kalimāt* (1964); *Al-Mawt fī alhayāh* (1968); *Tajribatī al-shi'riyya* (1968); *'Uyūn al-kilāb al-mayyita* (1969); *Bukā'iyya ilā shams hazirān wa al-murtaziqa* (1969); *Al-Kitāba 'alā al-tīn* (1970); *Yawmiyyāt siyāsī muhtarif* (1970); *Sīra dhātiyya li sāriq al-nār* (1974); *Kitāb al-bahr* (1974); *Qamar Shīrāz* (1976); *Mamlakat al-sunbula* (1979); *Sawt al-sanawāt al-daw'iyya* (1979). FURTHER WORKS IN ENGLISH: *Love, Death and Exile* (1990; bilingual ed.)

BIBLIOGRAPHY: Rossi, P., " 'A. al-W. al-B.," *Orient*, 9 (1959): 63–64; Stewart, D., "A. W. al-B.: Poet of Exile," *NME*, No. 5 (1972): 27–30; Badawi, M. M., *A Critical Introduction to Modern Arabic Poetry* (1975): 210–16; Jayyusi, S. K., *Trends and Movements in Modern Arabic Poetry* (1977), Vol. 2: 714–15 and passim

—ISSA J. BOULLATA

BEATTIE, Ann

American short-story writer and novelist, b. 8 Sept. 1947, Washington, D.C.

B. received her B.A. from American University in 1969 and her M.A. from the University of Connecticut in 1970. She has been visiting writer and lecturer at the University of Virginia at Charlottesville (1975-1977), Briggs-Copeland Lecturer in English at Harvard University (1977-1978), and was awarded a Guggenheim fellowship in 1978. B. received a Distinguished Alumnae Award from American University and an award of excellence from the American Academy and Institute of Arts and Letters.

B. began publishing short fiction in the *New Yorker* in 1974, and many of the stories that are later collected in book form were first published in that magazine. In 1976 her first such collection, *Distortions*, was published along with her first novel *Chilly Scenes of Winter*. The characters in her early works are aging hippies, alienated, helpless, and often hopeless. They drift lethargically through the apathy of the 1970s that followed the activism and idealism that was so much a part of the lives of many young Americans a decade earlier. Some are literally drifters, moving

Ann Beattie

from place to place almost randomly. Others are shallow, shiftless dropouts, wandering in and out of relationships, self-absorbed but lacking in self-knowledge. Most characters tend to be marking time, unwilling or unable to act, waiting, often in dread, to be acted upon.

In these early works B. focuses more on details of discrete moments rather than on the unfolding of events that constitutes traditional narrative. Her themes are underscored by the accumulation of mundane details and by the lack of action, structure, or resolution. The prose itself is direct, almost flat. Short, simple sentences work to establish mood rather than to build a carefully constructed plot. Most critics agree that her early style is most effective in her shorter works. The novels tend to suffer for the lack of plot and structure. However, *Chilly Scenes of Winter* was extremely popular, and B. was quickly acclaimed as chronicler of the lost souls of the 1960s. She herself strongly objects to such a label as being a reductive assessment of her work.

Secrets and Surprises (1978), *Jacklighting* (1981), and *The Burning House* (1982), all collections of short stories, show indications that B.'s style is beginning to evolve. Although many of the stories are still plotless and peopled by directionless, powerless, passionless men and women, there is evidence in others that B. is working more on character development. And in her second novel, *Falling in Place* (1980), it seems clear that she sets out to address some of the negative criticism *Chilly Scenes of Winter* received. The pace has picked up, the cast of characters has expanded, there are several centers of action, and there is even a climax.

In *Love Always* (1985) and *Picturing Will: A Novel* (1989), B.'s adult characters live somewhat denser lives, and the children are far more fully realized. The structure of these longer works is also somewhat stronger, yet it is still in the short-story form that B. continues to excel. Many of the pieces collected in *Where You'll Find Me* (1986) and most clearly those in *What Was Mine* (1991) show B.'s maturing vision and her marked tendency to move away from the cool, ironic stance in favor of a more sensitive and sympathetic view of the men, women, and children in these stories. In contrast to the earlier characters, most of whom were in their thirties, we now also meet people who are older and who must face tragedies more profound than loss of innocence and compromised idealism. There is a sadder, slightly more tender, note to their confusion and suffering. Many of the stories touch on issues concerning old age, illness, and death; others explore family relations, changing circumstances, and shifting affections. In the best of these stories, there is a recognition of the effects of time, a stronger and deeper focus, and a more profound sense of moral understanding that confirms B.'s continuing evolution as a major American writer.

FURTHER WORKS: *Spectacles* (1985); *Alex Katz* (1987); *Another You* (1995); *My Life, Starring Dara Falcon* (1997); *Park City: New and Selected Stories* (1998)

BIBLIOGRAPHY: Gelfant, B. H., "A. B.'s Magic Slate or The End of the Sixties," *NER*, 1 (1979): 374–84; Bell, P. K., "Marge Piercy and A. B.," *Commentary*, 70 (July 1980): 59–61; Gerlach, J., "Through 'The Octascope': A View of A. B.," SSF, 17, 4 (Fall 1980): 489–94; Murphy, C., *A. B.* (1986); Centola, S. R., "An Interview with A. B.," *ConL*, 31, 4 (Winter 1990): 405–22; Montresor, J. B., *The Critical Response to A. B.* (1993)

—MARGARET D. SULLIVAN

BEAUVOIR, Simone de

French memoirist, essayist, and novelist b. 9 Jan. 1908, Paris; d. 14 Apr. 1986, Paris

B. was born into an upper-middle-class family and raised in the Catholic faith. She began to write when she was eight years old. As an adolescent she rejected the religious and social values of her family, which she equated with those of the reigning bourgeoisie. She was a brilliant student, received her *agrégation de philosophie* in 1929, and taught philosophy in French lycées from 1931 to 1943.

B. was one of a group of outspoken, atheistic, left-wing writers who exerted a significant influence on the beliefs and opinions of readers both in France and abroad in the years following World War II. Throughout her life B. maintained an intimate and intellectual dialogue with Jean-Paul SARTRE, whose existentialist theorizing provided the philosophical categories for some of B.'s writings. Although the greater part of her publications appeared in the 1940s, 1950s, and 1960s, she has continued to write in an attempt to raise the consciousness of her readers about the intolerable status of old people—*La vieillesse* (1970; *The Coming of Age*, 1972)—and the oppression of women (in prefaces, interviews, manifestos).

The fundamental theme and obsession of B.'s writing is the growth and development, within a particular historical context, of herself. None of her works expresses and explores this central concern more completely than the four volumes of her memoirs: *Mémoires d'une jeune fille rangée* (1958; *Memoirs of a Dutiful Daughter*, 1959); *La force de l'âge* (1960; *The Prime of Life*, 1962); *La force des choses* (1963; *The Force of Circumstance*, 1965); *Tout compte fait* (1972; *All Said and Done*, 1975). They describe in an existentialist perspective the human adventure of a French female born into a Catholic bourgeois milieu who chose, within her given situation, to become specifically *this* intellectual and *this* writer; who deliberately planned her life and work, lived a great love, and revealed to thousands of readers what she considered to be her exemplary existence.

B. is always writing against the myth of the eternal feminine. The memoirs are an invaluable document for anyone interested in the formation and evolution of certain French intellectuals in the period between 1929 and 1970. They investigate the dilemmas that caused many writers, artists, and thinkers to shift from an ethics of individualism to an ethics of political commitment. More importantly, they relate the pilgrimage of a self moving constantly between the sense of the absurd and the need for commitment, between despair and hope. They contain enough specific references to people, places, and events to provide the outline for a psychological, sociological, anthropological study of her generation.

B.'s two major novels, *L'invitée* (1943; *She Came to Stay*, 1954) and *Les mandarins* (1954; *The Mandarins*, 1956), as well as her *récit* (narrative) on the death agony of her mother, *Une mort très douce* (1964; *A Very Easy Death*, 1966) are heavily autobiographical. Together with the memoirs they constitute one of the most important chronicles of the century.

Since the emergence of the women's liberation movement in the late 1960s, B.'s two volume treatise *Le deuxième sexe* (1949; *The Second Sex*, 1953) has become the most widely read and the most influential of her texts. It is clear, as it was not in 1949, that B. had provided a theoretical framework which made it necessary to raise the question of woman in any serious discussion of society and culture. B. occupies a central position within the feminist inquiry. Because she has fulfilled her desire to confront fundamental questions about life and death, good and evil, woman and man, and to present them to as wide an audience as possible, she is one of the best-known French writers of the century.

FURTHER WORKS: *Pyrrhus et Cinéas* (1944); *Les bouches inutiles* (1945); *Le sang des autres* (1945; *The Blood of Others*, 1948); *Tous les hommes sont mortels* (1946; *All Men Are Mortal*, 1955); *Pour une morale de l'ambiguité* (1947; *The Ethics of Ambiguity*, 1949); *L'Amérique au jour le jour* (1948; *America Day by Day*, 1952); *L'existentialisme et la sagesse des nations* (1948); *Privilèges* (1955); *La longue marche* (1957; *The Long March*, 1958); *Djamila Boupacha* (1962); *Les belles images* (1966); *La femme rompue* (1967; *The Woman Destroyed*, 1968); *Le ceremonie des adieux* (1981; *Adieux: A Farewell to Sartre*, 1984)

BIBLIOGRAPHY: Gennari, G., *S. de B.* (1958); Jeanson, F., *S. de B. ou l'entreprise de vivre* (1966); Marks, E., *S. de B.: Encounters with Death* (1973); Cottrell, R., *S. de B.* (1975); Leighton, J., *S. de B. on Woman* (1975); Bieber, K., *S. de B.* (1979); Bair, D., *S. de B.* (1990); Moi, T., *S. de B.: The Making of an Intellectual Woman* (1994)

—ELAINE MARKS

BECKER, Jurek

East German novelist, television dramatist, and screenwriter, b. 30 Sept. 1937, Łódź, Poland; d. 14 March 1997, Paris, France

B.'s early childhood, spent in the Jewish ghetto of Łódź and in Nazi concentration camps, determined a good deal of the subject matter of his writings. Following the war, B. and his father lived in Berlin, where he learned German (his native language was Polish) and completed his secondary education. From 1957 to 1960 he studied philosophy, after which he began his career as a Professional writer. In the early 1970s B. received several literary awards, among them the Heinrich Mann Prize and the Charles Veillon Prize in 1971, and the Bremen Literature Prize in 1974. During the academic year 1977–78 B. visited the U.S. as a guest professor at Oberlin College in Ohio. While he was in the U.S., *Schlaflose Tage* (1978; *Sleepless Days*, 1979) was published. The novel's subject met with disapproval by the government. B. did not return to East Germany but took up residence in the Federal Republic. He later accepted other guest appointments at universities and colleges in the United States, Essen, Augsburg, and Frankfurt am Main.

B.'s first creative writings consisted of television dramas and screenplays. However, not until publication of his first novel, *Jakob der Lügner* (1968; Jacob the Liar, 1975), was he recognized as a potentially important representative of the new generation of East German writers. His fresh, personal approach to the material of this work provided a welcome change from the typically programmatic creations of most of his East German contemporaries.

Jakob der Lügner has become a classic of antifascist literature. Its peculiarity lies not in its general theme—life in a Jewish ghetto during the war years—but rather derives from the intense humanity with which the specific situations of the novel are treated. Through successful psychological penetration of the unlikely hero Jakob Heym, B. created a work that contrasts sharply with more stereotyped presentations of ghetto conditions. B.'s theme is neither Nazi brutality nor the suffering of the Jews. Rather, he is concerned with the human characteristics that enabled some Jews to endure in the face of the dehumanizing ghetto experience. By focusing on the positive effects of Jakob's humane lies about the advancing Russians, B. emphasized strengths that make the human spirit unconquerable: the ability to lighten tragedy with humor; the ability to create effective psychological barriers against an inhuman situation; the power of the individual to feel and respond to community needs. To that extent, *Jakob der Lügner* makes a profound and timeless statement about the human condition.

B.'s second novel, *Irreführung der Behörden* (1973; deceiving the authorities), is the most directly autobiographical, of his works. In portraying Gregor Bienek, a young East German writer, B. documents his own problems in coming to grips with the East German literary and sociopolitical establishment. Although less compelling in presentation than *Jakob der Lügner, Irreführung der Behörden* is a successful variation on the central theme of the earlier novel. In order to cope successfully with East German reality, Gregor, like Jakob, must create a façade of lies as a defense against the outside world. Gregor's struggle is fascinating for its forceful, yet often subtle, commentary on conditions within the German Democratic Republic.

Der Boxer (1976; the boxer), B.'s treatment of the postwar existence of a Jewish father and son, is more pessimistic that the earlier novels. Aron, who copes with his situation in silent endurance, remains lonely and unfulfilled. His son seeks a more active

Simone de Beauvoir

solution in fleeing to Israel, but perishes in the 1967 war. The tragedy of their inability to communicate with each other becomes a powerful symbol for society's failure to penetrate the everpresent façade and satisfy the needs of the individual.

The air of bitter resignation that pervades *Der Boxer* is intensified in B.'s fourth novel, *Schlaflose Tage*. In his portrayal of the teacher Simrock's retreat and final surrender in the struggle for individuality and freedom of expression, B. utters his most forceful outcry against the repressiveness of a state in which "honesty is desired only when the honest man agrees with the majority of his superiors." The contrasting story of another character's abortive attempt to flee the country emerges then as a profound lament that for most, real escape is impossible.

Like *Der Boxer*, the later novel *Bronsteins Kinder* (1986; *Bronstein's Children*, 1988) focuses on the postwar Jewish experience. The work employs a dark perspective and bitter humor to underscore the impossibility of returning to normality because history, and particularly the experience of Auschwitz, remains ever present, even though the first-person narrator actively rejects being regarded as the son of a victim of fascism.

With the exception of *Bronsteins Kinder*, most of B.'s creative effort after 1985 was focused on literature as entertainment. There is a certain irony in the fact that although he decried the degeneration of literature into a form of commercial amusement in the lectures on poetics that were published in *Warnung vor dem Schriftseller* (1990; Warning against the writer), his most visible later accomplishments took the form of screen plays for two highly successful television series and his last major novel, *Amanda herzlos* (1992; Amanda heartless), a misunderstood work that actually treats the serious problem of individual isolation in the modern world, but which critics almost universally acclaimed primarily for its humor and entertainment value.

B.'s novels exhibit a degree of realism, an originality and maturity of conception, and a careful balance of composition that were quite rare in the literature of the German Democratic Republic. Yet the real strength of his serious literary efforts lies in a thoughtful humanism that sets him apart from other East German writers of his generation.

FURTHER WORKS: *Wenn ein Marquis schon Pläne macht* (1962); *Komm mit nach Montevideo* (1963, with K. Belicke); *Gäste im Haus* (1963); *Zu viele Kreuze* (1964); *Ohne Paß in fremden Betten* (1965, with K. Belicke); *Immer um den März herum* (1967); *Jungfer, Sie gefällt mir* (1968); *Meine Stunde Null* (1970); *Nach der ersten Zukunft* (1980); *Aller Welt Freund* (1982); *Erzählungen* (1986); *Das Märchen von der kranken Prinzessin* (1993); *Wir sind auch nur ein Volk* (3 vols., 1994-95); *Die beliebteste Familiengeschichte* (1995); *Ende des Größenwahns* (1996); *Jurek Beckers Neuigkeiten* (1997, with Manfred Krug). FURTHER WORKS IN ENGLISH: *Five Stories* (1993)

BIBLIOGRAPHY: Reich-Ranicki, M., "Die Liebe, die Literatur und der Alltag," in *Zur Literatur der DDR* (1974): 149-55; Hoffmann, M. R., on *Jacob the Liar*, LJ, 15 Oct. 1975: 1946; Korn, E., "Hope Proferred," *TLS* 6 Feb. 1976: 131; Price, J., "Matters of History: Some Recent Fiction," *Encounter*, 46 (May 1976): 74-75; Bremer, T., "Roman eines Störenfriedens: über J. B.s *Schlaflose Tage*," *NRs*, 89 (1978): 470–76; Johnson, S. M., *The Works of J. B.: A Thematic Analysis* (1988); Graf, K. and Konietzny, U., eds., *J. B.* (1991); Arnold, H. L., ed., *J. B.* (1992); Heidelberger-Leonard, I., ed., *J. B.* (1993)

—LOWELL A. BANGERTER

BECKETT, Samuel

Irish dramatist, novelist, and poet (writing in English and French), b. 13 April 1906, Dublin; d. 22 Dec. 1989, Paris

Of middle-class Protestant background, B. attended Portora Royal (Oscar Wilde's school) and Trinity College (Jonathan Swift's university), graduating in modern literature in 1927. Soon after, he left Ireland to take a two-year position as an English teacher in Paris. Although he returned for a brief period to teach French at Trinity, B. has spent almost all of his subsequent life in France, eventually changing his literary language from English to French (after World War II). In the late 1920s in Paris he became a member of the circle around James JOYCE—although he was not, as has been widely reported, Joyce's secretary.

During this early phase of his career B. wrote short stories, poetry, and literary criticism. In 1929 he published an essay on Joyce's *Work in Progress* ("Dante . . . Bruno. Vico .. Joyce"), as well as a story ("Assumption"). In 1930 his cryptic poem (with notes), *Whoroscope*, won first prize in a contest for poems written on the subject of time. In this dramatic monologue, the protagonist, Rene Descartes, waits for his morning omelette of well-aged eggs, while meditating on the obscurity of theological mysteries, the

passage of time, and the approach of death. Descartes, the best-known exponent of mind-body dualism, is an important thematic figure, along with the Cartesian A. Geulincx (1624–1669), in several of B.'s works. No Cartesian (or adherent of any philosophical theory) himself, B. has been fascinated by the way people perpetually attempt to solve insoluble puzzles; where Descartes and Geulincx developed theories of mind-body harmony, most of B.'s characters, including his own Descartes, are plagued by their disharmony. His critical monograph *Proust* (1931), originally written to advance his incipient academic career, continued B.'s reflections on the theme of time, as have many of his subsequent works. Its principle importance in B.'s development lay in its conception of man: Proust's picture of the individual as a multitude of selves in constant change defined by frequently irrational habits provided a more complex and adequate picture of human psychology than could a simple dualism like that of Descartes.

B.'s first major step in the direction of the novel was the collection of ten stories, *More Pricks than Kicks* (1934), all centering on a single protagonist, the indolent, solipsistic Belacqua Shuah, and set in and around Dublin, but B.'s career as a novelist really began in 1938 with *Murphy*. Murphy, consciously a Cartesian, is also implicitly something of a Manichean or Gnostic in his dualism; the dramatic action of *Murphy* has to do with the protagonist's inner struggle between his desires for his prostitute-mistress, Celia, and for total escape into the dark of the mind. The conflict is resolved when he is, possibly accidentally; atomized by a gas explosion. Celia, one of B.'s more sympathetic and appealing female characters, in the meantime converts to Murphy's way of thinking. The attitude toward Murphy is characteristically ironic: he sees through some illusions, especially the enticements the world has to offer, but not through those he generates himself.

In B.'s works it is of the essence of man that he is inevitably subject to illusions and to self-deception. *Murphy* and *More Pricks than Kicks* share an exuberant, if grim, sense of comedy and a playful use of language. His later writings became sparer, leaner, and more astringent. *Watt* (1953), written in the 1940s while Beckett was in hiding from the Germans in the Vaucluse (he had been active in the French Resistance), was the last of his novels written originally in English. Kafkaesque in atmosphere, it portrays the futile search of Watt (a play on "What"?) for understanding in the household of Mr. Knott ("Not"?), who continually changes shapes.

In the late 1940s B. changed his literary language to French, a change that brought much greater austerity to his style. His major contribution to the genre of the novel, a trilogy, was published first in French, then translated by B. (the first volume in collaboration with Patrick Bowles) into English: *Molloy* (1951; *Molloy* 1955), *Malone meurt* (1951; *Malone Dies*, 1956), and *L'innommable* (1953; *The Unnamable*, 1958). *Molloy* presents first Molloy's rambling account of his quest for his mother, then Moran's account of his quest for Molloy. Moran is an officious agent in the employ of a Kafkaesque organization with messengers who deliver orders from a distant "chief". He does not find Molloy, an old vagabond, but he does become like him as he gradually becomes dissociated both outwardly and inwardly from his earlier bourgeois existence. The trilogy as a whole seems to show its series of characters— Moran, Molloy, Malone, and the Unnamable, and those about whom the latter two tell stories—going through a progressive disillusionment that culminates ironically in the Unnamable's bitter realization that there is no escape from illusions and from the compulsion to think, to try to solve insoluble mysteries, and to tell stories. The Unnamable himself seems to be a figure who has survived death and finds his mind filled with stories, among them those of the earlier characters in the trilogy. At first he thinks he is telling stories to pass the time; then, as they become more patently boring, he finds he has no power to stop them; even that it is he who is telling them becomes questionable to him. B. was probably aware that the body-mind dualism of Descartes eventually led to David Hume's (1711–1776) radical criticism of the ideas both of causality and of the mind. B.'s trilogy seems an expression of Hume's picture of the mind as an assembly of fragments connected only by habitual associations, a picture of man that also finds echoes in Buddhist psychology, to which there may be occasional allusions in B.'s writings.

Although B. has written many short works of fiction, *Comment c'est* (1961; *How It Is*, 1964) was his last real novel. Its narrative line and atmosphere show similarities to *The Unnamable*, but it was a significant new departure in its musical structure and its highly poetic use of French prose. Unfortunately little of the effect survives in the translation.

Important as his novels are, it was his dramatic works that made B. famous. He first came to the attention of a large public with the production, first in Paris (1953), then in New York (1955), of *En attendant Godot* (1952; *Waiting for Godot*, 1954). This haunting play features two vagabonds, Vladimir and Estragon (Didi and Gogo), waiting in a desolate landscape for a supposed Mr. Godot, who does not come but sends a messenger saying he will come tomorrow. The two acts of the play represent two days sharing this same basic frame-work, but with important differences. The first day Didi and Gogo meet Pozzo, a swaggering landlord, and his slave Lucky; the second day Pozzo has suddenly lost his possessions (except for Lucky) and has become decrepit. Didi, the more intellectual of the pair, is driven by this change to reflections on time and reality, which seem to culminate in a realization of the absurdity of the universe. As the play ends, however, they intend to go on waiting.

B.'s next major work for the stage was *Fin de partie* (1957; *Endgame*, 1958). Again the setting is desolate, but this time the characters are isolated form the external world in a room owned by the paralytic Hamm, who tyrannizes his parents, Nagg and Nell, and his servant Clov. The exact relation between Hamm and Clov is unclear, as is almost everything else about the world of this play. The action seems to be a process of ending, as the name suggests. The effect, however, is static. The characters reminisce, tell stories, and speculate in an effort to find or create some sort of order in their existence. The one change in all this is that Clov seems to become more independent and to form the intention of leaving—whether he eventually does, however, is unclear, since he is still with Hamm at the end.

Of B.'s other plays, perhaps *La derière bande* (1959; *Krapp's Last Tape*, 1958) and *Oh les beaux jours* (1963; *Happy Days*, 1961) have been his most popular. The former depicts an old man sitting alone at night in his room listening to tape recordings from various periods of his past. B. said in *Proust* that life is a succession of habits, since the individual is a succession of individuals. Here the Krapp of young manhood, middle life, and old age are all alien to one another, though threaded together by certain memories and a constant self-preoccupation. Winnine, the protagonist of *Happy Days*, is more outward-looking perhaps, but this does not help her; she gradually becomes buried in the ground, for no apparent reason other than the absurdity of the universe, and is increasingly cut off from anything that could give her pleasure. She evokes affection and admiration, however, for her continuing struggle to keep alive

Samuel Beckett

her one-sided dialogue with her husband, Willie, and to believe that it is indeed a "happy day." Both plays offer virtuoso roles and have been performed to great effect.

B. also has written several plays for radio, generally somewhat more realistic in style, such as *Tous ceux qui tombent* (1957; *All That Fall*, 1957) and *Cendres* (1959; *Embers*, 1959); *Dis Joe* (1966; *Eh Joe*, 1966) was written for television. B. also wrote a screen-play, *Film* (1968), for a film starring Buster Keaton.

B.'s writings for the theater show the influence of a number of theatrical traditions not commonly drawn on by major dramatists, but used to great effect by him. These include burlesque, vaudeville, the music hall, *commedia dell'arte*, the silent-film style of such figures as Keaton and Chaplin. Generally speaking, the comic effects B. draws from such devices he uses to establish aesthetic distance and defend his frequently grim subject matter from descending to pathos. The ways in which B. achieves these effects as he begins with a version bordering on the pathetic and then rewrites it to establish distance and his characteristic blend of sympathy, bitterness, and playfulness can be seen from a study of successive drafts of his manuscripts, many of which are now available in the libraries of the University of Reading, Ohio State University, and the University of Texas.

In B.'s later writings there has been a general tendency toward reduction to bare essentials. This is true of his fiction as well as his drama. He has described his task as well as his drama. He has described his task as that of trying to create art out of minimal material, a task he sees as the inescapable lot of late 20th-c. artists.

When he has succeeded (which may not be always), the extreme compression this minimalism has given his works has made them uniquely evocative and technically brilliant. The mixture of irony and compassion in his attitude toward the human beings he portrays has also given his works a surprising warmth, despite the grotesquerie of both character and situation. B.'s importance has come to be widely recognized, and he was awarded the Nobel Prize in 1969.

FURTHER WORKS: *Nouvelles et textes pour rien* (1955; *Stories and Texts for Nothing*, 1967); *Bram van Velde* (1960); *Poems in English* (1961); *Comédie et actes divers* (1966); *No's Knife* (1967); *Têtes-Mortes* (1967); *Cascando, and Other Short Dramatic Pieces* (1968); *Sans* (1969; *Lessness*, 1970); *Premier amour* (1970); *First Love, and Other Shorts* (1974); *Ends and Odds* (1976); *Pour finir encore et autres foirades* (1976; *For to End Y et Again*, 1976); *Collected Poems in English and French* (1977); *Compagnie* (1980; *Company*, 1980); *Rockaby and Other Short Pieces* (1981); *Collected Shorter Plays* (1984); *Collected Poems, 1930-1978* (1984); *Dream of Fair to Middling Women* (1993); *S. B.: The Complete Short Prose, 1929-1989* (1995); *Nohow On: Three Novels* (1996)

BIBLIOGRAPHY: Kenner, H., *S. B.* (1961); Cohn, R., *S. B.: The Comic Gamut* (1962); Hoffman, F. J., *S. B.: The Language of Self* (1962); Fletcher, J., *The Novels of S. B.* (1964); Tindall, W. Y., *S. B.* (1964); Esslin, M., ed., *S. B.: A Collection of Critical Essays* (1965); Federman, R., *Journey to Chaos* (1965); Reid, A., *All I Can Manage, More than I Could* (1968); Robinson, M., *The Long Sonata of the Dead* (1969); Harvey, L., *S. B.: Poet and Critic* (1970); Webb, E., *S. B.: A Study of His Novels* (1970); Duckworth, C., *Angels of Darkness* (1972); Fletcher, J., and Spurling, J., *B.: A Study of His Plays* (1972); Webb, E., *The Plays of S. B.* (1972); Abbott, H. P., *The Fiction of S. B.: Form and Effect* (1973); Cohn, R., *Back to B.* (1973); Cohn, R., ed., *S. B.: A Collection of Criticism* (1975); Worth, K., ed., *B. the Shape Changer* (1975); Hamilton, K., and Hamilton, A., *Condemned to Life: The World of S. B.* (1976); Mercier, V., *B./B.* (1977); Bair, D., *S. B.: A Biography* (1978); Graver, L., and Federman R. *S. B.: The Critical Heritage* (1979); Trezise, T., *Into the Breach: S. B. and the Ends of Literature* (1990); Cronin, A., *S. B.: The Last Modernist* (1996); Knowlson, J. *Damned to Fame: The Life of S. B.* (1996); Acheson, J., *S. B.'s Artistic Theory and Practice* (1997)

—EUGENE WEBB

Ropewalker, though he keeps on, despairs, and for ample reasons. Clown mimes despair, transforming it into an exquisite ceremony. B., in various books, has played both roles, gradually working, by rigorous maneuvers, toward the clown's poise and amplitude. There are books—*Proust, More Pricks Than Kicks*, and various collections of poems—in which he is not clear whether he is a comic writer or simply a bitter one, and his first comic book, *Murphy*, achieves its daft freedom in a kind of air pocket, while simultaneously poems written in French precipitate into three or four hundred words his mounting nausea with the human state.

He has had a difficult development, for he has taken on himself the burden of one conscious that he is conscious, since the seventeenth century a peculiarly Western burden. That is the meaning of his

stories within stories, his plays within plays, his characters within characters. It is also, with its ecrie fidelity to the movements of a mind that has noted itself in motion, the point where his highly specialized, self-immolating art impinges on our sense of the familiar. When we find Molloy momentarily forgetting who he is and strutting before himself (his phrase) like a stranger, or reflecting on the exact sense of such an expression as "I said to my-self," we may be startled as by a violation of our own privacy: we recall not so much doing such things as catching ourselves doing them.

Hugh Kenner, *S. B.* (1961), p. 35

B. has achieved an ambiguously ironic confusion and communion of identity: B., his creation the "I" who creates, his creation, the "I" who sees. At this late stage of human history, when man cannot decipher his identity from the comic complexity of fictions and words, he nevertheless is compelled to seek that identity. Life and letters alike become a dianoetic joke of creations feeding upon their creators, with whom they are assimilable and irreconcilable. The artistic condition is no longer a pinnacle of privilege from which one may nod in neighborly fashion at God the Creator. Instead, creator and creature wallow together in dust or mud, whence they came. Or perhaps they never left it.

The modern man of letters who turns against letters was not fathered by B., but no other modern writer—not Proust or Gide or Joyce or Mann—has integrated the act of creation so consistently and ironically into his own creation. Joyce held that the greatest love of a man was for his own lies, and act the artist-liar is only one of his mythic prototypes. For B., all literature and all life reduce to his portrait of the artist-liar as old bum: "You either lie or hold your peace," says Molloy, and B.'s heroes do not hold their peace. Do we?

Ruby Cohn, *S. B.: The Comic Gamut* (1962), p. 296

The point is that, without the *necessity* of God, or of the metaphysical speculation consequent upon His discernible presence within a society of selves, the novel becomes, first, a novel of manners–that is of understood conventions and an understanding imagination; next, a novel of conscious selves maneuvering through spaces occupied by objects that are either testimonies of or challenges to them; and finally of selves almost exclusively, of the "interior selves" of interior monologue. This is a steady development away from metaphysics and toward self-definition *sub specie durationis*.

Frederick J. Hoffman, *S. B.: The Language of Self* (1962), pp. 67–68

We are, most of us, incorrigible symbolists, exceeding Watt, who reforms a little toward the end.

Our problem in reading B., like Watt's problem in Mr. Knott's house, is what to make of the bright and demanding objects that abound, all the bicycles, hats, pots, and all the circles. From B.'s obsessive particulars we feel compelled to extract ideas, as we should do in reading Joyce. What matter if Watt warns us not try? An author's intentions need not prevent our peace of mind. What if Molloy, as if speaking for B., says, "I like to record things that seem to signify nothing in particular"; and what if, elsewhere, he foresees a time when "there could be no things but nameless things, no names but thingless names"? This is for the future. Now we have to do with hats and circles, things with names and likely meanings. Example: Molloy's hat is on a string and so, he says, is his soul. His hat must be his soul; and, since one of his concerns is identity, his hat must assure him of this. Second example: the circle, which provides structure and incidental figure, surely this must have some meaning. Though not the old circle of perfection, B.'s circle must be like the temporal circles of Yeats and Joyce, though a little more hopeless perhaps. So our minds, convinced that nothing is more real than something, work eagerly on B.'s charged particulars. It is the charge in these things that obsesses us, as the things themselves obsess B. No matter. Our need for something more is harmless; for, whatever we say, his bicycle remains a bicycle and his pot a pot. Yet his Democritus is always saying, "Nothing is more real than nothing."

William York Tindall, *S. B.* (1964), p. 26

Perhaps what distinguishes B.'s poetic theory (as we can perceive it through the veil of his poetry) from similar theories and gives it real originality is this: the poetic death, which after all permits resurrection, since the poet as man can return to autonomously existing external reality and even resuscitate the prior life of the mind, is for him very closely and it may be almost necessarily associated with real death, or at least with the process of dying that is made up of aging, absence, suffering, diminutions of all kinds. Real suffering and death seem both to precede their poetic counterparts and to take precedence over them. Poetic metamorphosis is not a magician's facile trick, somehow fortuitously analogous to the disastrous changes that are part of human destiny (although on occasion it may momentarily masquerade as such); it is their ritual reenactment. In the life-art relationship, art is the servant, and B., ever aware of the servant's inclination to go her own independent way, suspiciously keeps her in menial and relatively unadorned subjection.

Lawrence E. Harvey, *S. B. Poet and Critic* (1970), p. 115

B.'s most recent work in the theatre has not yet gone beyond *Play*, except in paring down the content, in the same way his most recent fiction, the four short pieces, *Imagination Dead Imagine, Enough, Ping and Lessness* (French title: *Sans*), have been parings down of *How It Is*, but it is worth remarking that in these works the pictorial element and the prose-poetry in which it is conveyed are growing still more prominent and concentrated, that B. has always in the past used his fiction as the spear-head of changes in his work, and that every new technical impetus in his development has been brought about by the conflict between an apparently pulverized content and B.'s inexorable 'obligation' to invent a form capable of pulverizing it still further.

John Fletcher and John Spurling, *B.: A Study of His Plays* (1972), pp. 45–46

There are those who urge B.'s readers not to try to "understand" him but to surrender themselves to his words without attempting to interpret them logically. This is good advice, insofar as it indicates how B.'s works gain their meaning through the interplay of symbols, rather than through any direct statement. But symbols must be recognized to work as symbols, and this means that they must be interpreted. There is no way to read B. through one's pores, bypassing intellectual engagement. There is an illuminating anecdote which illustrates this point. When Patrick Magee was playing Hamm in *Endgame*, B. was at a rehearsal to advise the actors. John Gruen reports that "At the end of the day B. says: 'Don't look for symbols in my play.' Magee lights a cigarette and grins, *sotto voce*: 'He means don't *play* it like symbols. . . .'"

The plain fact is that it is impossible for us to read or hear any words without interpreting them in some fashion. We must choose between interpretation that is alert and intelligent and interpretation that is sluggish and unduly subjective. B.'s works are written so that they may be interpreted—they are not esoteric mysteries. But they are also written so that they may be interpreted easily and without engaging the reader's total powers of response.

Kenneth Hamilton and Alice Hamilton, *Condemned to Life*: *The World of S. B.* (1976), p. 195

BEĆKOVIĆ, Matija

Yugoslav poet (writing in Serbian), b. 29 Nov. 1939, Senta

Raised in an officer's family that lived in a number of locations during his childhood and adolescence, B. started writing poetry in 1957, while still in secondary school in Valjevo. From 1959 to 1963 he studied literature at the University of Belgrade, where he pursued his deep-rooted interest in poetry while supporting himself through journalistic writing. At first noted as a reader of his own verse in the style of YEVTUSHENKO and VOZNESENSKY, B. quickly matured into a poet of great verbal virtuosity and stylistic vibrancy.

While his long poem *Vera Pavlopolijka* (1961; the faith of Pavlopojie) and his first collection of verse, *Metak lutalica* (1963; the bullet wanderer) show that in his formative years he was under a notable influence of SURREALISM, his second book of verse, *Tako je govorio Matija* (1965; so spoke Matija), affirms that he soon found a far more potent source of inspiration in the content and form of the vast Serbian oral literary heritage, renowned for the majesty of its language and the epic strength of its thought and feeling. These facets are even more pronounced in B.'s subsequent creative output, in which he frequently outdistances even his best traditional models. His verse collections *Reče mi jedan čoek* (1970; said a man to me) and *Medja Vuka mahnitoga* (1976; Mad Vuk's boundary), written in the colorful dialect of the Montenegrin Rovci clan, recapture in a singularly powerful way the milieu, style, and ethos of a folk narrative, yet remain profoundly contemporary in their clinical recording of the final dissolution of a once noble but now useless heroic way of life. In both of these works B.'s linguistic virtuosity, his exalted, almost narcissistic preoccupation with poetically yet unrealized possibilities of the Serbo-Croatian language create a verbal tapestry of unusual beauty and suggestiveness.

Even more striking in the opulence of its language is his most recent book of verse, *Kuku-lele* (1978; woe and sorrow), which in the style of a folk lament bids an ultimate farewell to the long-standing tribal heroic tradition of Montenegro, already hopelessly sullied by the corrupting influence of the outside world overtaken by a petty love of self and a dreary preoccupation with everyday existence. And yet, viewed more closely, A. transmutes this sorrowful dirge to a proud mountaineer world of yesterday from a last farewell into a lasting monument, for in recording so vividly its passing, B. has given it a new home in his art and a new opportunity to impress posterity with its high-minded ideals.

FURTHER WORKS: *O medjuvremenu* (1969); *Če—tragedija koja traje* (1970)

BIBLIOGRAPHY: Eekman, T., *Thirty Years of Yugoslav Literature 1945-1975* (1978): 278–79

—NICHOLAS MORAVČEVICH

BEDNÁR, Alfonz

Slovak novelist and screenwriter, b. 13 Oct. 1914, Neporadza; d. 11 Nov. 1989, Bratislava

Born and educated in western Slovakia, B. studied at universities in both Prague and Bratislava before becoming a high school teacher until 1945. He was forty before his first book was published, but he had earlier worked as an editor, producer, and screenwriter. He was awarded the title of Worthy Artist in 1964.

B. is best known for his war novels about the Slovak Uprising that attempted to join with the advancing Russian army and help defeat German forces in late 1944. His first novel, *Sklený vrch* (1954; The Glass Peak), is credited with breaking the Stalinist schematism and reductionism of previous novels on the uprising or any aspect of wartime Slovakia. The critical polemic that followed condemned B.'s individualized and morally mixed partisans, both men and women. Similarly groundbreaking were his novellas in

Hodiny a minúty (1956; Hours and Minutes) and *Cudzí* (1960; Strangers), showing former partisans in the present being tested and failing the new demands for decency and self-sacrifice in building a socialist society. Besides the obvious political meanings, one feels that B. tentatively equates building with destruction of nature and egotism with violence against others. His next novel, *Hromový zub* (1964; Thunderclap), is a monumental historical epic of the changing patriarchal village even before socialism (1913-23), and he shows several extended families tested by the demand for new virtues in the crises of transformation, some failing but some rising in their humanity.

Radical change into the grotesque, allegory, and absurd became prominent when B. turned to contemporary life in his next novels. In the short novel, *Balkón bol privysoko* (1968: The Balcony Was Too High), the protagonist, a writer, is transformed into various kinds of animal (dog, frog, ant) and must live in those forms feeling the emptiness and alienation of a modern intellectual. In the long trilogy, *Za hrs drobných* (1970, 1974, 1981; For a Handful of Change), the chief narrator of this chronicle of a family is their dog speaking to his kennel mates. B. thus creates parallel commentary on human activities and attitudes with all the resources of satire, burlesque, and parody exposing a philistine society. The third volume pictures another planet as an upside-down world in which humane animals rule over wild humans.

Two of B.'s last novels show his increasing loss of hope in improving human society. The title of *Ako sme sušili bielizen* (1985; How We Used to Dry the Laundry) nostalgically refers to the old clean kinds of action, but ironically the hero is a blind painter and thus a self-parody representing artistic alienation. B.'s last major novel, *Ad revidendum, Gemini* (1988; title in Latin), uses language to create a metaphor of the linguistic violence perpetrated by political propaganda and secret police informers. Such misuse of communication is shown as part of the pollution destroying the social environment. B's earlier belief in the possibility of a just socialist society turned to sardonic pessimism.

B. also wrote screen and television plays reflecting the same concerns and literary strategies as his novels. His earliest screenplays were published as *Tri scenáre* (1966; Three Scenarios), followed by *Génius* (1969; Genius), *Ve ka noc, ve ky de* (1974; Great Night, Great Day), *Penelopa* (1978; Penelope), and *Kamerátky* (1979; Girl Friends). He turned to television for *Ráno pod mesiacom* (1980; Morning under the Moon) and the four-part *Moje kone vrané* (1981; My Black Horses).

B's novels have been called moralities for their contrast between the ideal and the amoral real, and for their good characters trying to prevail or even just persist surrounded by corruption. His most important historical effect is doubtless his pioneering break with Stalinist schematic reductionist novels.

FURTHER WORKS: *Grécke zátišie* (1958); *Novely* (1962); *Vybrané spisy* (3 vols., 1977-80)

BIBLIOGRAPHY: Tomiš, K., "Svetonázor a tvorba," *Slovenská literatúra*, 4 (1957): 436-58; Matuška, A., *lovek v slove* (1967): 177-81; Sivachenko, H., "Literary Tradition in the Satiric Prose of A. B.," in Pynsent, R. B., ed., *Modern Slovak Prose* (1990): 59-69; Štev ek, J., "Morality Novels: A. B., Rudolf Sloboda, Ivan Hudec," in Pynsent, R. B., ed. *Modern Slovak Prose* (1990): 134-42

—NORMA LEIGH RUDINSKY

BEER-HOFMANN, Richard

Austrian dramatist, poet, novelist, short-story writer, and essayist, b. 11 July 1866, Vienna; d. 26 Sept. 1945, New York

B.-H. was born into a Jewish family in Vienna, the son of an attorney, Hermann Beer. His mother died in childbirth, and B.-H. was raised in Brünn (Brno) by his maternal aunt and his uncle Alois Hofmann, who later adopted him. B.-H. took his law degree at the University of Vienna in 1890, but an inheritance made him financially independent and enabled him to devote himself to literature. He became a respected member of the "Young Vienna" circle of writers and established dose and cordial relations with Arthur SCHNITZLER, Hugo von HOFMANNSTHAL, and others, soon achieving success as a poet and dramatist. In the 1920s B.-H. collaborated with the great director Max Reinhardt (1873–1943) on various theatrical projects, adapting and staging Goethe's *Iphigenia in Tauris* in Reinhardt's theaters in Vienna and Berlin (1928, 1930). In 1932, the centennial year of Goethe's death, B.-H. abridged and arranged both parts of *Faust* in thirty-nine scenes for one evening's performance at the Burgtheater in Vienna. In 1936 B.-H. visited Palestine. Three years later he left Nazi Austria and reached the U.S. via Switzerland. From November 1939 to his death he lived in New York with his daughters Miriam and Naëmah, becoming a U.S. citizen in 1945. In his last year he gave lectures at Harvard, Yale, and Columbia, and in spring 1945 he received the Distinguished Achievement Award of the National Institute of Arts and Letters.

B.-H.'s literary output is relatively small but of high quality. He achieved early fame in 1897 with his "Schlaflied für Mirjam" ("Lullaby for Miriam," 1941), written at the cradle of his firstborn. This beautiful, widely admired poem is a philosophical lullaby intoned by a father. While it does express the *fin-de-siècle* feeling that life is mysterious and evanescent, that we cannot communicate our deepest experiences even to those nearest and dearest to us, and that each generation is doomed to recapitulate the past with its errors and sorrows, its also points out that there is a definite continuity of existence, with ancestral values and voices shaping us and guiding us to a purposeful existence.

While B.-H.'s early novellas still reflect the impressionistic, psychologizing tenor of the times, his novel *Der Tod Georgs* (1900, the death of Georg), notable for its interior-monolog technique, already points beyond aesthetic dalliance, dandyism, and decadence; Paul, the egocentric protagonist, is jolted out of his passivity and attains to a clear vision of his Jewishness and his responsibility toward life and his fellow men.

B.-H.'s first play, *Der Graf von Charolais* (1905, the count of Charolais) is based on the drama *The Fatal Dowry* (1632) by Philip Massinger and Nathaniel Field. B.-H.'s verse tragedy explores the father-son relationship, concluding that one cannot escape one's destiny and the moral obligations inherited from one's ancestors. A notable figure is the misanthropic Roter Itzig (red Itzig), who is reminiscent of the Wandering Jew and of Shylock.

B.-H.'s *magnum opus* is a grandly conceived cycle of poetic plays entitled *Die Historie von König David* (the history of King David), which was to have consisted of a prologue and three dramas. Of these, only *Jaakobs Traum* (1918; *Jacob's Dream*, 1946), *Der junge David* (1933; young David), and *Vorspiel auf dem Theater zu "König David"* (1936; stage prologue to King

David) were completed; only sketches exist for *König David* itself and for *Davids Tod* (David's death). In the biblical King David B.-H. saw the symbolic embodiment of the Jewish psyche in all its ambivalence, and through this figure he wished to explore the mystery of "chosenness" and divine grace as well as the age-old mission of the Jewish people. In *Jaakobs Traum* he gave shape to two biblical episodes: the conflict between Jacob and Edom (Esau), the sensitive dreamer and the earthbound realist, and Jacob's covenant with God at Beth-El and his assumption of the name Israel.

B.-H.'s writings in exile center largely about the beloved figure of his wife Paula, who had died in Switzerland in 1939 after a marriage of four decades. *Paula, ein Fragment* (1949; Paula, a fragment) consists of memoirs, sketches, fragments, confessions, and dreams relating to her. A collection of *Verse* (verses) issued in 1941 contains B.-H.'s lyrical output of a scant two dozen poems.

To Rainer Maria RILKE, the patriarchal figure of B.-H. represented the "greatness and dignity of Jewish fate," and shortly before B.-H.'s death the writer William Rose Benét (1886–1950) characterized him as "one of the finest examples of true European culture."

FURTHER WORKS: *Novellen* (1893); *Gedenkrede auf Wolfgang Amadé Mozart* (1906); *Herbstmorgen in Österreich* (1944); *Das goldene Pferd* (1955); *Gesammelte Werke* (1963); *Hugo von Hofmannsthal und R. B.-H. Briefwechsel* (1972); *Arthur Schnitzler und Richard B.-H. Briefwechsel 1891-1931* (1992)

BIBLIOGRAPHY: Reik, T., *Das Werk R. B.-H.s* (1919); Liptzin, S., *R. B.-H.* (1936); Oberholzer, O., *R. B.-H.* (1947); Werner, A., "R. B.-H.: Austrian and Jew," *Judaism*, 1 (1952): 227–37; Berman, T., "R. B.-H.," *Jewish Quarterly*, 14, 2 (1966): 37–39; Kleinewefers, A., *Das Problem der Erwählung bei R. B.-H.* (1972); Harris, K., et. al. "R. B.-H. A Bibliography," *MAL*, 15, 1 (1982): 1-60; Elstun, E. N., *R. B.-H. His Life and Work* (1983); Eke, N. O. et al., eds. *R. B.-H. Studien zu seinem Werk* (1993); Mayer, A., *R. B.-H. und das Wein des fin de Siècle* (1993); Scherer, S., *R. B.-H. und die Wiener Moderne* (1993); Fraiman, S., *God and Judaism in the Lives and Works of R. B.-H and Lion Feuchtwanger* (1998)

—HARRY ZOHN

BEGOVIĆ, Milan

(pseuds.: Tugomir Cetinski, Xerex de la Maraja, Stanko Dušić) Yugoslav poet, dramatist, novelist, essayist, and short-story writer (writing in Croatian), b. 19 Jan. 1876, Vrlika; d. 13 May 1948, Zagreb, Yugoslavia (now Croatia)

B. studied Romance and Slavic languages in Zagreb and Vienna and was a high-school teacher in Split (Spalato) until 1908. From 1908 to 1920 he worked as the artistic director of two theaters, the Deutsches Schauspielhaus in Hamburg and the Neue Wiener Bühne in Vienna, except for the years 1915–18, when he fought in World War I in the Austrian army. In 1920 B. returned to Zagreb, where he lived and worked until his death. From 1927 to 1932 he was the general manager of the Croatian National Theater.

B. was a very versatile author who left his mark on Croatian poetry, drama, and fiction. One of the first prominent rebellious poets of Croatian MODERNISM in the early 20th c., B. has been equally praised for his frank, erotic love poetry, as in *Knjiga boccadoro* (1900; the book of golden words), and for the humane liberalism and pacifism expressed in a long ballad of eighteen sonnets, *Život za cara* (1904; a life for the tsar), inspired by the horrors of the Russo-Japanese war.

As a dramatist B. gained international fame between the two world wars, when his plays were performed in the leading theatrical centers of Europe and the U.S. with an excellent feeling for the stage and a solid background in theatrical craft in general, B. created a series of lively and entertaining plays of universal appeal. In a nine-tableaux drama, *Pustolov pred vratima* (1926; the adventurer at the door), constructed as a play within a play, the young, dying heroine meets Death (tableau 1), who allows her to experience the life of her youthful dreams in one single delirious night (tableaux 2–8) before she dies (tableau 9). The presence of Death in the heroine's imaginary life is emphasized by his reappearance (in different disguises) in each of the seven central tableaux, which lends the play a chilling eeriness.

In fiction, B. is at his best in the short stories set in his native Dalmatian Zagora and in those which, like his important novel, *Giga Baricéva* (1940; Giga Barić), focus on the decadent life of the Croatian upper middle class between the two wars.

Although criticized in the early years of the Communist regime for his bourgeois attitudes and for his lack of concern for social ills and injustices in prewar Yugoslavia, B. remains an important figure in the Croatian literature of the first half of the 20th c. One of Croatia's most cosmopolitan literary figures, he was an excellent playwright, an amusing story-teller, and an important contributor to the modernization of Croatian literary expression.

FURTHER WORKS: *Gretchen* (1893); *Pjesme* (1896); *Hrvatska pjesma* (1901); *Myrrha* (1902); *Vojislav Ilić* (1904); *Menuet* (1904); *Gospodja Walewska* (1905); *Venus Victrix* (1905); *Biskupova sinovica* (1911); *Čičak* (1912); *Vrelo* (1912); *Fred ispitom zrelosti* (1913); *Dunja u kovčegu* (1921); *Male komedije* (1921); *Svadbeni let* (1922); *Nasmijana scra* (1923); *Božji čovjek* (1924); *Izabrane pjesme* (1925); *Hrvatski Diogenes* (1928); *Tri drame* (1934: *Božji čojek, Pustolov pred vratima* [first pub. 1926], *Bez trećeg*); *Kvartet* (1936); *Puste želje* (1942); *Put po Italiji* (1942); *Sablasti u dvorcu* (1952)

BIBLIOGRAPHY: Kadić, A., *Contemporary Croatian Literature* (1960): 22–24; Barac, A., *A History of Yugoslav Literature* (1973): 213–14, 242

—BILJANA ŠLJIVIĆ-ŠIMŠIĆ

BEHAN, Brendan

Irish dramatist and novelist (writing in English and Gaelic), b. 9 Feb. 1923, Dublin; d. 20 March 1964, Dublin

B. was a product of Dublin's far-from-opulent north side. But while of working-class origins and exposed to relatively little formal education, he was not the unlettered slum lad the media made him out to be. He was a widely read man with an alert and incisive mind. Brought up in a decidedly nationalistic family, B. joined the Irish Republican Army. Although active in this organization for only a brief time, he spent most of the years 1939–46 in English and Irish penal institutions on political charges. It was during this period that he decided to become a writer. Notoriety and critical attention came to B. in the mid-1950s and contributed to his downfall and death. His health broken by heavy drinking and careless living, he died at the age of forty-one.

B. wrote a few short stories, a crime novel, some poems in Gaelic, and a witty newspaper column, but he is best known for his two plays *The Quare Fellow* (1954) and *The Hostage* (1958) and the autobiographical novel *Borstal Boy* (1958). These works deal with serious themes but at the same time are informed with a humor that exposes the pretensions and prejudices of mankind, asserts the value of compassion and understanding, and in general celebrates humanity and life.

Borstal Boy, rooted in B.'s experiences as a teenager in English prisons and Hollesley Bay Borstal, is an interesting account of prison existence and youthful initiation. The young narrator moves from rebellious bravado to fear and shame, and finally to greater understanding of himself, his English prison mates and captors, and human nature in general. Well written, effectively crafted, and movingly narrated, this autobiographical novel reveals the source of the humor, sentiments, and emotions present in B.'s other literary works.

The Quare Fellow, set in an Irish prison during the twenty-four hours preceding an execution, is a realistic drama that not only attacks capital punishment but also exposes the sham and false piety behind public attitudes toward such matters as sex, politics, and religion. B. makes his points tellingly, using a variety of techniques. Among the effective devices are the scathingly ironic comments of Warder Regan and hilarious lines and situations that embody bitter and painful truths. Seeing the play is a bittersweet experience out of which emerges a strong affirmation of life.

In its original, Gaelic format, *The Hostage* was also realistic, but the English-language version, influenced by *avant-garde* producer Joan Littlewood, is a combination of music-hall comedy and THEATER OF THE ABSURD. Short on plot and filled with topical ad libs and non sequiturs, the play satirizes war and fanaticism and celebrates life.

B. was a talented writer whose personal problems and lack of self-discipline prevented him from realizing his full potential. A reading of his works reveals his skill with language, great wit, a vital sense of humor, and a moving and compassionate view of human nature. His best work is both lively and filled with insight.

FURTHER WORKS: *Brendan Behan's Island* (1962); *Hold Your Hour and Have Another* (1963); *Brendan Behan's New York* (1964); *The Scarperer* (1964); *Confessions of an Irish Rebel* (1965); *Moving Out and A Garden Party* (1967); *Richard's Cork Leg* (1973); *The Complete Plays* (1978); *The Letters of B. B* (1992)

BIBLIOGRAPHY: Simpson, A., *Beckett and B. and a Theatre in Dublin* (1962); McCann, S., ed., *The World of B. B.* (1965); Jeffs, R., *B. B.: Man and Showman* (1966); Boyle, T. E., *B. B.* (1969); O'Connor, U., *B. B.* (1970); Porter, R. J., *B. B.* (1973); Kearney, C., *The Writings of B.B.* (1977); Arthurs, P., *With B. B.* (1981)

—RAYMOND J. PORTER

BEHBUDIY, Mahmud Khoja

Uzbek dramatist, editor, and critic (writing in Uzbek and Tajik), b. 1874, Samarkand; d. 25 March 1919, Karshi

In the second decade of the 20th c. B. introduced the first modern genre into the traditional written literature then still prevailing everywhere in southern central Asia. He was a pioneer in that world dominated by lyric poetry, because he offered both a Western style of drama and a viable prose dialogue. He also established and trained the first modern central Asian theatrical troupe in his region. B.'s principal literary work, the play *Padarkush* (1911; *The Patricide*, 1979), which he called "a national tragedy," galvanized the small portion of Turkistan intellectual society devoted to reforming the arts and culture and modernizing society primarily through application of the *usul-i Jadid* ("new method") of educating the younger generation. B.'s short three-act play employs a family catastrophe allegorically to show that men kill the homeland by neglecting to bring up and educate their sons for future responsibilities to family and the Muslim community. *Padarkush* quickly became popular all over southern central Asia from the time it premiered in Samarkand, the same year it was published (1913). Performances continued until Soviet control was well established in Turkistan in spring 1918. One revival of a scene from *Padarkush* was staged at Tashkent in 1935, but this drama has never been reprinted in the Soviet Union. Like most *Jadid* literature from the pre-1917 period, the play fell into political disfavor under the rule of the Communist Party. A second play credited to Behbudiy was never published.

B. edited and published two influential periodicals, *Samarqand* (April 1913—September 1914) and *Ayinä* (August 1913—June 1915), in which he and others wrote frequently about the literature, including drama, of central Asia. In those essays, B. defined the theater for his countrymen as a sermon hall and critical mirror of life. B.'s broad liberal views toward women's emancipation, general education, and eradication of social evils had developed out of a traditional Muslim family background, seminary education, and extensive travels in the greater Middle East: to Arabia, Egypt, Syria, Turkey, Bashkiria, and Tatarstan in 1900 and 1914.

B.'s greatest contribution to Turkistan letters in the long run proved to be his creating a model for change and innovation, not in drama alone, but in central Asian literature generally.

BIBLIOGRAPHY: Allworth, E., "The Beginnings of the Modern Turkestanian Theater," *SlavR*, 23 (1964): 676–87; Allworth, E., "Murder as Metaphor in the First Central Asian Drama, *The Patricide,*" *Edebiyat*, 4, 1 (1979): 2–10

—EDWARD ALLWORTH

BEI DAO

(pseud. of Zhao Zhenkai) Chinese poet, b. 2 Aug. 1949, Peking (Beijing)

Bei Dao, which literally means North Island, is the best known of several pseudonyms B. adopted as an underground poet and fiction writer in the 1970s. As a child, B. attended one of the better schools in Peking, but his formal education was interrupted during his last year by the outbreak of the Cultural Revolution in 1966.

Brendan Behan

Briefly a Red Guard, and for a short time after that a building worker, he began writing as an alternative to political action and also to the official literature of his time. By the time the Cultural Revolution ended shortly after Mao Zedong's death in 1976, B. was already well known among literary youth as one of the originators of a new kind of poetry and prose. In the early 1980s he worked briefly at the Foreign Languages Press in Peking, but since 1985 he has supported himself primarily through writing and editing interspersed with teaching. At the time of the Tiananmen Massacre in 1989, B. was in Berlin, and since then he has not been permitted to return to China. After teaching in Sweden, Denmark, and Germany, B. moved to the U.S. in 1993 and is now resident at the University of Michigan. The literary magazine he coedited in 1978-79, *Jintian*, was reestablished in 1990 by B. and other former contributors.

Dubbed *menglong* (literally, shadowy or dim; obscure) by its critics, the new poetry created by B. and his fellow underground writers spoke of dreams and illusions rather than direct praise or criticism of the social reality of its time. But not to address political issues in China from the 1950s to the 1970s was itself a political statement, and B. and his colleagues were closely associated with the democratic movements in China of the late 1970s. To his readers at this time, B. was the voice of his generation, expressing a fierce but despairing desire for freedom, love, and autonomy of the self. His most famous poem of the 1970s, "Huida" (wr. 1976; pub. 1979; "The Answer," 1983), declared, "I don't believe the sky is blue," and nihilism permeates his early work.

B.'s younger readers had no trouble in working out the underlying meaning of lines like the one above, but when "obscure poetry" made the transition from "underground" to "unofficial" to "official" publications in the late 1970s and early 1980s, hostile critics representing the establishment complained that it was impossible to understand. B. and his fellow poets rejected the public voice of orthodox Chinese poetry since the 1950s, drawing on a sometimes private imagery usually expressed in brief, tightly constructed lines depicting natural phenomena and the urban furniture of their daily lives. In these early poems B. rarely resorted to literary allusions, though the structure and use of imagery in his poetry had clear precedents in classical Chinese and modernist Western verse. One favorite device, for instance, was to refer to what is not present, or what does not happen, by pointing out what is present or what does happen, as in the famous lines from "Taiyang cheng zhaji" (wr. early 1970s; pub. 1978; "Notes from the City of the Sun," 1983): "Life: The sun rises too," where the sun refers to Mao Zedong—known during the Cultural Revolution as "the red sun in our hearts"; B.'s lines imply that there is more to life than the sun alone.

Employing techniques from classical Chinese poetic grammar and Western free-verse patterns, B. also experimented with creating a new prosody in an attempt to resolve the age-old problem of Chinese poetry: the constantly renewed gulf between spoken and written Chinese due to the nature of the Chinese written script and its peculiar grammar. To some older readers, B.'s poetic syntax and vocabulary were irritatingly Westernized; to a younger generation of poets from the mid-1980s on, his style came to sound stiff and formal. Nevertheless, B.'s verse remains an outstanding achievement in the history of modern Chinese poetry.

B.'s fiction is less celebrated, although the novella "Bodong" (1978; "Waves," 1985), written and circulated underground during the Cultural Revolution, is no less innovatory than his poetry. Using the devices of multiple narrators and interior monologue, it successfully breaks away from the traditionally univocal and closed didacticism of both serious and entertainment fiction in China. "Bodong" was followed by five shorter pieces written between 1980 and 1985, on contemporary themes such as the distortion to family and marriage relationships caused by official campaigns and policies, the rigidly hierarchical nature of class distinctions in a so-called socialist China, corruption of various kinds in the official literary scene, and the sinister brutality of the Chinese police state.

During the 1980s B. was able to publish his work openly, but despite the notable relaxation of political controls during most of this period (with the equally notable exception of the campaigns against spiritual pollution in 1983-84 and against bourgeois liberalism in 1986-87), his poetry became more, not less, pessimistic. At the same time, his language became harsher, and his imagery featured illness, old age, madness, and the more obtrusive streetscapes of urban China. This culminated in the nightmarish "Bai ri meng" (1986; "Daydream," 1988), a long sequence of poems with a repeated motif of unfulfilled expectations.

To outward appearances, B.'s life may have seemed quite fulfilled during the second part of the 1980s. He married, fathered a child, was accepted into the offical Chinese Writers' Association, and frequently traveled abroad. Nevertheless, he remained stubbornly and unfashionably conscious of the underlying political tensions in China, and in 1988 expressed his forebodings in poems like "Zhong" ("The Bell," 1991). His petition in support for the imprisoned democratic activist Wei Jingshen in early 1989 was one of the events that sparked the student protests of the spring, and

lines written almost a decade earlier in "Xuangao" (1983; "Declaration," 1983): "I will not kneel on the ground, Allowing the executioners to look tall, The better to obstruct the wind of freedom" appeared on banners in Tiananmen Square.

B.'s poems from the early 1990s express grief, outrage, and personal anguish at his separation from family and home. Although written in his customary abstract and abbreviated style, they proved remarkably effective in poetry readings both in the original and in translation. B.'s genius as a poet lies primarily in his striking and universally comprehensible imagery, so that despite the usual caveat about the loss of effect in translation, translations of his poems into over a dozen languages have been warmly received. B. is thus one of the very few Chinese writers of the 20th c. to gain a truly international audience.

FURTHER WORKS: *B. D. shi xuan* (1985; rev. ed., 1987). FURTHER WORKS IN ENGLISH: *Notes from the City of the Sun* (1983); *The August Sleepwalker* (1988); *Old Snow* (1991); *Forms of Distance* (1994)

BIBLIOGRAPHY: McDougall, B. S., "Zhao Zhenkai's Fiction: A Study in Cultural Alienation," *MCL*, 1, 1 (1984): 103-30; McDougall, B. S., "B.'s Poetry: Revelation and Communication," *MCL*, 1, 2 (1985): 225-52; Owen, S., "What is World Poetry? The Anxiety of Global Influence," *NR*, 19 November 1990: 28-32; Li, D., "Ideology and Conflicts in B.'s Poetry," *MCL*, 9, 2 (1996): 369-85; Gleichmann, G., "An Interview with B.," *MCL*, 9, 2 (1996): 387-93; McDougall, B. S., and K. Louie, *The Literature of China in the Twentieth Century* (1997): 397-98, 428-31, passim

—BONNIE S. MCDOUGALL

BELAMRI, Rabah

Algerian novelist, short-story writer, and poet (writing in French), b. 11 Oct. 1946, Bougaa; d. 28 Sept. 1995, Paris, France

Born into a family of modest means in Bougaa, a small town in Lesser Kabylia, B. received a traditional Koranic education before being sent to a French school. His formative years were spent during the Algerian war of independence (1954-62), when as a boy he suffered from retinal detachment. In 1962, at the age of sixteen, he lost his sight completely. B.'s blindness did not deter him from continuing his education in Algeria before moving to France in 1972 for graduate studies. He settled in Paris where he wrote a doctoral dissertation on the work of the Algerian-domiciled French poet, Jean Sénac (1926-1973). After further graduate studies, he obtained a state doctorate (3rd cycle) for his thesis on Louis Bertrand (1866-1941), an important member of the Algiers-based Algérianistes school of French colonial writers. Fervently interested in the oral culture of his country, B. traveled frequently to Algeria where he collected popular fables, proverbs, and dictums, translating a number of them into French. He regularly gave talks on Algerian oral literature, addressing some of them to schoolchildren. An avid reader, he read works mostly in Braille, but relied also on the use of cassettes.

B. was one of the most prolific Algerian writers of his generation, publishing nineteen volumes in seventeen years. He made a forceful entry into the French literary scene in 1982 with three works, an autobiography, *Le soleil sous le tamis* (Sunshine through a Sieve), describing his early life and experiences in war-torn Algeria, and two collections of popular Algerian short stories, *Les graines de la douleur* (Seeds of Pain) and *La rose rouge* (The Red Rose). His last work, *Chroniques du temps de l'innocence* (1996; Chronicles of the Time of Innocence), an autobiographical novel, was published posthumously. B. wrote three other novels, *Regard blessé* (1987; Wounded Glance), *L'asile de pierre* (1989; The Stone Refuge), and *Femmes sans visage* (1992; Women without Faces). These works, which are considered to be important contributions to the Francophone novel genre, won French literary prizes. In *Regard blessé*, another autobiographical novel, B. describes, through his central character, Hassan, how he lost his sight. In his posthumous work, he relates his experiences at Koranic school. The central character, Badr, tries to escape from the much-hated school and the cruelty of the Koranic master which he has to endure out of obedience to his father. *Femmes sans visage* is an account of Algeria in the 1980s, introducing the reader to a number of Algerian women. B. maintained that the world of women, among whom he spent most of his life, was highly enriching for any writer. He was greatly influenced by his mother in early life, and as an adult depended on the help and support of his French wife.

Mémoire en archipel (1990; Memory in Archipelago), perhaps one of the most important of B.'s works, received the Hatier Prize. It is a collection of twenty-six independent stories, joined together by a main story, like islands in an archipelago, evoking the *Arabian Nights*. In each one the reader is introduced to a galaxy of characters drawn on people the author knew in childhood: his immediate family, close friends, and neighbors. The stories are also populated with demons, phantoms, and wild animals, based on characters in popular Algerian fairytales and legends. Mixing the real with the imaginary is at the root of nearly all B.'s fictional creation. He also blends literacy with oracy, introducing into all his literary works elements from Algerian oral folklore. Other contrasting features that characterize his works are a fusion of past and present, and darkness and light. Darkness, as a result of his total blindess, recurs in all his works, which consist of epithets like night, dark, black, gloom, and obscurity. B. maintained that the blind were privileged in memorizing and passing on the oral culture of their people to future generations.

B. also distinguished himself as a poet, publishing several poetry collections. The images drawn from the darkness of his subconscious give a poetic sensitivity to many of his prose works. He felt that he owed a special debt to certain poets. Apart from his dissertation on Sénac, later published as *Jean Sénac, entre désir et douleur* (1989; Jean Sénac, Amid Desire and Pain), he dedicated a poem to the Moroccan poet Abdellatif Laabi (b. 1942) in *Le galet et l'hirondelle* (1985; The Pebble and the Swallow). Another book of poetry, *Pour Hallaj* (1993; For Hallaj), is dedicated to the Persian Sufi poet, Husayn b. Mansūr al-Hallāj (d. 922), who composed verse in Arabic.

In spite of the fact that B. was a Francophone writer, the essence of the Arabic narrative tradition and popular sayings are in evidence in a number of his works, particularly in his two Arabic-French bilingual texts, *Proverbes et dictons algériens* (1986; Algerian Proverbs and Sayings) and *L' âne de Djeha* (1991; Djeha's Donkey).

In the interviews B. gave throughout his life he stated that a writer's first duty was to be the spokesperson of his generation and culture, explaining the era he lived in to future generations. B. was to prove true to his word. In a relatively short time he packed into

his works the social and political history of Algeria, as well as its rich oral heritage.

FURTHER WORKS: *Sept poèmes* (1983); *L'oiseau du grenadier* (1986); *L'olivier boit son ombre* (1989); *Les herbes de l'âne* (1992); *Pierres d'équilibre* (1993); *Dormants de l'oubli* (1994); *Soif* (1995)

BIBLIOGRAPHY: Déjeux, J., *Dictionnaire des auteurs maghrébins de langue française* (1984): 44-45; Bonn, C., *Anthologie de la littérature algérienne* (1990): 215-16; Achour, C., *Anthologie de la littérature algérienne de langue française* (1990): 226-28; 285; Déjeux, J., *La Littérature maghrébine de language française* (1992): 29-30; 32-33; Meisami, J. S., and P. Starkey, eds., *Encyclopedia of Arabic Literature* (1998)

—FARIDA ABU-HAIDAR

BELGIAN LITERATURE

In Flemish

After a prolonged period of economic, political, and cultural decline in the 18th and early 19th cs., there was a revival of Flemish literature in the second half of the 19th c., first with the stories and novels of Hendrik Conscience (1812–1883) and the poetry of Guido Gezelle (1830–1899), later on with the authors grouped around the periodical *Van nu en straks* (1893–1901), led by August VERMEYLEN. To a large extent, for these writers the revival of Flemish literature was closely linked to the emancipation of the Flemish language (when spoken a dialect variant of Dutch, but in writing indistinguishable from it) and of Flanders itself from the dominance of the numerically inferior but culturally and economically vastly superior French-speaking Walloons, and equally from the French-speaking Flemish bourgeoisie, who jointly monopolized the Belgian government through a unilingually Francophone administration.

Fiction

The turn of the c. was marked by the influence of naturalism and, in its wake, a proliferation of peasant novels and tales. The savagely realistic work of Cyriel Buysse (1859–1932) emphasized the economic and moral poverty of rural Flanders in "De biezenstekker" (1890; the rush cutter) and *Het recht van de sterkste* (1893; the right of the strongest). Stijn STREUVELS, strongly influenced by the great Russian and Scandinavian novelists, depicted peasant life in a prose of truly epic proportions. In *Langs de wegen* (1902; *Old Jan*, 1936), the life story of a farmhand, he sees man's existence as ruled by fate and by the forces of nature. His masterpiece, *De vlaschaard* (1907; the flax field), centers on the conflict between a stubborn farmer and his son, while the novella "Het leven en de dood in den ast" (1926; life and death in the kiln house) mingles the thoughts and memories of a group of farmhands.

Karel van de WOESTIJNE, although primarily a poet rather than a novelist, transformed the naturalistic peasant tale into a masterpiece of impressionistic and baroque sensualism in his novella "De boer die sterft" (1918; "The Peasant, Dying," 1964), in which a dying man reexperiences his entire life through associative memories brought on by the virtually autonomous functioning of his five senses, each of them intimately linked to a woman in his life.

The full-blooded naturalism of Buysse and Streuvels soon gave way to the folkloristic regionalism of Felix TIMMERMANS, enthusiastically wielding the luxurious dialect of his native Lier in vibrantly vitalistic novels such as *Pallieter* (1916; *Pallieter*, 1924) and *Boerenpsalm* (1935; psalm of the farmer); and of Ernest CLAES, mostly remembered for *De Witte* (1920; the fair-haired boy), a humorous tale of village life in the eastern Flemish region De Kempen.

Very rapidly the Flemish novel began paying attention to city life, with *Het ivoren aapje* (1909; the ivory monkey) by Herman TEIRLINCK. Teirlinck, an incredibly versatile writer, returned to vitalistic visions of country life in *Maria Speermalie* (1940; Maria Speermalie) and *Het gevecht met de engel* (1952; the fight with the angel), and ended his career with the aesthetically refined *Zelfportret of het galgemaal* (1955; *The Man in the Mirror*, 1963). Willem ELSSCHOT was almost exclusively concerned with provincial city life, mostly in his native Antwerp. His brief novels and novellas, the most representative of which are *Lijmen* (1924; *Soft Soap*, 1965), its sequel *Het been* (1938; *The Leg*, 1965), *Kaas* (1933, cheese), and *Het dwaallicht* (1946; *Will-o'-the-Wisp*, 1965), are unique in Flemish literature for their compassionately ironic view of everyday life.

Still rooted in rural Flanders is the work of Gerard WALSCHAP, but as a representative of the "new objectivity" movement in Flemish letters, Walschap preferred an abrupt, unadorned and direct prose to the baroque tortuousness of his predecessors'. His utopian novels *Houtekiet* (1940; Houtekiet) and its sequel *Nieuw Deps* (1961; New Deps) advocate a visionary and vitalistic humanism, sharply at odds with the militant Catholicism he defended in his earliest writings.

In his psychological novel *Komen en gaan* (1927; coming and going) and in the short story "De jazzspeler" (1928; "The Jazzplayer," 1947) Maurice ROELANTS expresses a profoundly humanist and compassionate philosophy of life. The work of both Raymond BRULEZ and Marnix GIJSEN testifies to their witty and skeptical stoicism. Brulez is at his best in *André Terval* (1930; André Terval) and *De verschijning te Kallista* (1953; the apparition at Kallista), both of them short episodic novels, and in his fictionalized autobiography *Mijn woningen* (1950–54; my homes). Gijsen, notable also for his mastery of style and for his ironic moralism, gives us a witty interpretation of the biblical story of Susannah and the elders as seen by her husband in *Het boek van Joachim van Babylon* (1947; *The Book of Joachim of Babylon*, 1951). Marked by a supreme concern with style, and by the musicality of its prose, is the work of Filip de PILLECIJN, who skillfully evokes a romantic atmosphere in *Monsieur Hawarden* (1935; Monsieur Hawarden) and in the historical *Hans van Malmédy* (1935; Hans of Malmédy); the same can be said of the work of Maurice Gilliams (1900–1982) whose *Elias; of, Het gevecht met de nachtegalen* (1936; Elias; or, the fight with the nightingales) is an artistic evocation of adolescence.

Since World War II, a number of "magic realists" have introduced a new note into Flemish fiction. Johan DAISNE experimented with techniques borrowed from the cinema, and boldly mixes dream, reality, and the exotic in *De trap van steen en wolken* (1942; the stairway of stones and clouds). Daisne's hypnotic prose, and the neurotic character of its protagonist, lend *De man die zijn haar kort liet knippen* (1947; *The Man Who Had His Hair Cut Short*, 1965) a

dreamlike quality. Hubert Lampo (b. 1920) relies on parapsychology and fantasy in *Terugkeer naar Atlantis* (1953; return to Atlantis) and *De komst van Joachim Stiller* (1960; *The Coming of Joachim Stiller*, 1974).

Clear links with the naturalist novel of the early 20th c. can be discerned in the work of Piet van Aken (1920–1984), whose *Klinkaart* (1954; Klinkaart) describes the first day at work of a girl who is raped by the foreman of the brickyard where she is employed. Louis Paul BOON was similarly concerned with the plight of the proletariat. His first great novels, *De kapellekensbaan* (1953; *Chapel Road*, 1972) and its sequel, *Zomer te Ter-Muren* (1956; summer in Ter-Muren), are multilevel narratives, intertwining a chronicle of the rise and demise of socialism in Boon's native Aalst as experienced by a proletarian woman, with various other narrative strands in which the author, his friends, and his neighbors discuss the main story and comment on contemporary affairs. In *De bende van Jan de Lichte* (1957; the gang of Jan de Lichte) and *De zoon van Jan de Lichte* (1961; the son of Jan de Lichte) Boon imitates a popular genre of books glorifying the feats of Robin Hood-like 18th-c. Flemish highwaymen, but by emphasizing social conditions and showing how greed and human weakness corrupt the gang's initial idealism, Boon easily transcends the limits of the genre. A concern with utopian and anarchic socialism had already expressed itself in his early *Vergeten straat* (1946; forgotten street), but manifests itself most clearly in Boon's later works, which show an increasing fascination with actual Flemish history. *Pieter Daens* (1971; Pieter Daens), a voluminous and detailed report of a short-lived, socialist-inclined, yet Catholic political party in Aalst around the turn of the c.; *De Zwarte Hand; of, Het anarchisme van de negentiende eeuw in het industriestadje Aalst* (1976; the Black Hand; or, nineteenth-c. anarchism in the industrial town of Aalst); and *Het geuzenboek* (1979; the beggars' book), a chronicle of 16th-c. Protestantism in the Netherlands and primarily in Flanders, are all based on extensive and meticulous historical research. Taken in its entirety, Boon's work is a scathing condemnation of all social injustice, and a moving testimony to Flemish and social emancipation.

Boon's concern with experiment in narrative technique, although not his strong concern with social issues, was shared by a number of younger novelists. Hugo CLAUS, a highly versatile and prolific author, uses Faulknerian techniques to evoke a backward and morally disintegrating peasant society in *De Metsiers* (1950; *The Duck Hunt*, 1955). In *De verwondering* (1962; the astonishment) he makes elaborate use of historical and literary allusion to revive the atmosphere of occupation and collaboration that haunted Flanders during and after World War II. Ivo Michiels (pseud. of Rik Ceuppens, b. 1923) experiments with stream-of-consciousness in *Het boek alfa* (1963; *Book Alpha*, 1979) and its sequel, *Orchis Militaris* (1968; *Orchis Militaris*, 1979). In *De vadsige koningen* (1961; the puppet kings) Hugo Raes (b. 1926) eavesdrops on one man's musings during a long and sleepless night. His *Het Smarán* (1973; the Smarán) is a chronicle of human violence, and his latest work moves toward science fiction. Gust Gils (b. 1924) writes extremely short stories, which he himself calls "paraprose," and which betray a strongly surrealistic bent.

More traditional, and strongly confessional, are the novels of Jef Geeraerts (b. 1930). In his earliest work, such as *Gangreen I: Black Venus* (1968; *Gangrene I: Black Venus*, 1973), Geeraerts, a one-time government administrator in the former Belgian Congo, uninhibitedly exposes the painful heritage of Belgian colonialism and the excesses to which it gave rise. In later works he savagely cauterizes the wounds a petit-bourgeois youth and a broken marriage have left him with. Also traditional are the numerous novels and stories of Ward Ruyslinck (pseud. of Raymond de Belser, b. 1929). In *Het dal van Hinnom* (1961; Hinnom's vale) and in *Het reservaat* (1964; reservation) Ruyslinck projects a pessimistic view of humanity, but in more recent works he has moved toward a more militant humanism.

Among the newest generation of novelists, Daniël Robberechts (b. 1937) occupies a special place with experimental novels that take the act of writing itself, even while it is taking place, as their subject.

In general, it seems safe to say that, whereas in most of the work of earlier generations of 20th-c. Flemish novelists there is a vivid awareness of a specific Flemish identity, undoubtedly as a correlative to the struggle for Flemish emancipation, later generations are more interested in questions of technique, and, rather than to any particularly nationalistic idea, they seek adherence to contemporary movements in the arts. The same can be said for Flemish poetry, and for the theater.

Poetry

Flemish poetry in the 20th c. first flowered with the SYMBOLIST verse of Karel van de Woestijne, the leading poet of the *Van nu en straks* group. Highly baroque and rhetorical, his poetry, which has a constant autobiographical ring to it, shows him to have been a tormented and sensual intellectual. Completely different is the poetry of Jan van Nijlen (1884–1965), Richard Minne (1891–1965), and Raymond Herreman (1896–1971). All three wrote short, simple, and conversational poems, with Minne excelling in bitter irony and often relying on folksy expressions.

By far the most original poet of the early 20th c. was Paul van OSTAIJEN. His poetry was influenced by CUBISM and EXPRESSIONISM, and his theoretical essays show him to have been keenly aware of European modernism. From being a follower of German expressionism and a writer of nihilistic verse, such as that contained in *De feesten van angst en pijn* (1921; *Feasts of Fear and Agony*, 1976), he developed into a strikingly original poet seeking inspiration in the "pure poetry" of Gezelle. His bitingly sarcastic short stories, which he called "grotesken" (grotesques), introduced a new genre in Flemish letters, and prefigure the work of Gust Gils. Wies Moens (1898–1982), whose poetry is visionary and nationalistically inclined, Gaston Burssens (1896–1965), and Victor J. Brunclair (1899–1944) were also expressionists. The poetry of Maurice Gilliams was influenced by expressionism, too, as well as by RILKE.

More traditional, and an explicit reaction against expressionism, is the poetry of Urbain van de Voorde (1893–1966). Likewise more classical in its approach is the work of Anton van Wilderode (pseud. of C. Coupe, b. 1918) and Hubert van Herreweghen (b. 1920).

Picking up where van Ostaijen left off, the generation of the "vijftigers" (the fifties poets) returned to a highly experimentalist mode of poetry. Hugo Claus, the leading genius among these poets, first wrote brashly innovative poetry marked by uninhibited eroticism and powerful metaphors, and culminating in *De Oostakkerse gedichten* (1955; poems from Oostakker). His later work shows a progressive integration of experiment, tradition, and history, as in *Het teken van de hamster* (1963; the sign of the hamster) and *Heer Everzwijn* (1970; Lord Board). All through his poetry, though, there sounds a shrill note of grotesque despair and of harsh criticism of his native country, as in the recent *De wangebeden*

(1978; evil prayers). The poetry of Albert Bontridder (b. 1921) is highly charged, at times almost chaotic in its use of spontaneous metaphor, and betrays a constant concern with all of suffering humanity, as in *Dood hout* (1955; dead wood) or in *Zelfverbranding* (1971; suicide by burning), a collection inspired by the suicide of the student Jan Palach after the Soviet invasion of Czechoslovakia in 1968.

Of the "vijfenvijftigers" (the 'fifty-five poets), Gils, in his poetry as in his prose, prefers an extremely down-to-earth vocabulary, and he often seeks refuge in BLACK HUMOR and wry cynicism. Paul Snoek (pseud. of Edmond Schietekat, 1933–1981) writes both experimental and more traditional, joyful poetry. The highly tormented, idiosyncratic poetry of Hugues C. Pernath (pseud. of H. Wouters, 1931–1975) is admired by a group of younger poets advocating a neoromantic revival. Their work is often overtly decadent as, for instance, in the poems of Nic van Bruggen (1938–1991) and Patrick Conrad (b. 1945).

Mark Insingel (pseud. of M. H. L. T. Donckers, b. 1935) experiments with concrete poetry, relying upon typographical and linguistic-structural variations, as does Paul de Vree (1909–1982) in his latest work, although his earlier collections were much more traditional. Willy Roggeman (b. 1934) has adopted a constructivist attitude, and in his highly fragmentary and cerebral poems he defends the view that art is the only worthwhile activity in an otherwise meaningless universe. Roggeman also published a number of prose works that, rather than being real novels, are mixtures of fictional, and very often autobiographical, fragments and essayistic reflections on 20th-c. European authors and on jazz music. A similar mixture of largely autobiographical fiction and essay is practiced by the novelist-critic Paul de Wispelaere (b. 1928).

Alongside the experimentalist and neoromantic schools, a rival school of neorealist poetry flourishes, with Roland Jooris (b. 1936), Herman de Coninck (b. 1944), and Patricia Lasoen (b. 1948) as its major exponents. These poets use a simple vocabulary and syntax, and they prefer throwing personal experience and everyday banality into sudden perspective by humorous twist endings or sudden generalizations critical of society.

Drama

The theater in Flanders has never been outstanding. Buysse wrote some naturalistic plays, the best-known of which is *Het gezin van Paemel* (1903; the Van Paemel family). An important contribution to Flemish emancipation was made by a number of theater companies such as the Theater at the Front and the Flemish Popular Theater, which, between the two wars, brought expressionist folk drama in open-air performances to mass audiences. Paul de Mont (1895–1950) provided plays for these companies, as did Herman Teirlinck, who also wrote a number of experimental plays such as *De vertraagde film* (1922; film in slow motion). Teirlinck also wrote a number of essays on the theater, and for a while he propagated a kind of "total drama" integrating various art forms.

The most important contemporary playwright is Hugo Claus. His earliest plays show the influence of Tennessee WILLIAMS, but later plays such as *Suiker* (1958; sugar) and *Vrijdag* (1969; *Friday*, 1972) are naturalistically rooted in Flemish life. Claus also adapted classical plays and a novel by H. Conscience for the modern stage. His oeuvre over the past decades closely follows international contemporary developments in the theater.

BIBLIOGRAPHY: Bithell, J., *Contemporary Belgian Literature* (1915); Bithell, J., *Contemporary Flemish Poetry* (1917); Backer, F., de,

Contemporary Flemish Literature (1939); Lilar, J., *The Belgian Theatre since 1890* (1950); Weevers, T., *Poetry of the Netherlands in European Context* (1960); Mallinson, V., *Modern Belgian Literature* (1968); Meijer, R. P., *Literature of the Low Countries* (1978)

—THEO D'HAEN

In French

In a country perpetually divided by linguistic disputes, writers of both the Flemish and Walloon communities have contributed to making Belgian literature in French one of the richest in that language outside France. At the same time, the Flemish-speaking majority of the country have refused to identify themselves with a literature in a language that was imposed upon them for too long by a centralized, monolingual government. Thus, the Flemish created a cultural identity much more rapidly than the French-speaking Walloons. Belgian writers in French are constantly torn between the need for an identity and the fear of staying outside of the great French and international movements.

Fiction

At the end of the 19th c. French realism and naturalism had given rise to a long line of regionalist novelists and short-story writers, who were Flemings from the north writing in French as well as Walloons from the south. They strove to become deeply rooted in the subject matter of their land, while each in his own way took his cue from the French masters. Camille Lemonnier (1844–1914) evolved with *Au cœur frais de la forêt* (1900; in the cool heart of the forest) and *Comme va le ruisseau* (1903; as the stream flows) toward a Franciscan pantheism. Attached to the region of Antwerp, Georges Eekhoud (1854–1927) expressed his personal anguish in *Escal-Vigor* (1899; *Strange Love*, 1933), a tragic story of homosexual love. The desolate and mystical De Kempen region attracted Georges Virrès (1869–1946). The province of Hesbaye inspired Hubert Krains (1862–1934), whose restrained but perhaps overly impersonal art culminated in *Le pain noir* (1904; black bread).

Gradually, regionalism, which encompassed social protest for writers such as Lemonnier and Eekhoud, became a mere source of subject matter for later writers. Although regionalism has undergone many transformations, it continues to be the distinctive characteristic of much of the fiction produced up to the present. It can be recognized in Jean Tousseul's (pseud. of Olivier Degée, 1890–1944) work; his five-volume epic novel, the Clarambaux cycle (1927–36; *Jean Clarambaux: A Novel*, 1939) blends Tolstoy's humanitarianism with Romain ROLLAND's pacifism in an appealing utopianism. In Marie Gevers's (1883–1975) writings, nature, the seasons, and the popular traditions of her Antwerp region are transformed into a secret key to wisdom and happiness, as is discovered by the young heroine of *Madama Orpha; ou, La sérénade de mai* (1933; Madama Orpha; or, the May serenade).

Gradually, psychological analysis took precedence over regionalism. The Fleming André Baillon (1875–1932), not a very prolific writer but a distinguished one for the quality and authenticity of his works, indulged in personal confessions in his diarylike novels. Charles Plisnier's (1896–1952) novels are social frescoes, with each work illustrating a particular conflict: difficulties between the sexes in *Mariages* (1936; *Nothing to Chance*, 1938), loneliness in

Meurtres (1939–41; murders), the feminine condition in *Mères* (1946–48; mothers).

In March 1937 about twenty writers, known as the Monday Group, published a manifesto denouncing the danger of reducing all literary activity to the airing of local problems. Regionalism, according to them, had done more harm than good, and it was time to get rid of it once and for all. This condemnation came late, and some writers had already begun to explore other paths. Franz Hellens (1881–1972) from Ghent recognized the potential of the territory beyond regionalism and realism in *Les réalités fantastiques* (1923; fantastic realities), and he combined his gifts as a visionary and as an observer in *Les mémoires d'Elseneur* (1954; memoirs of Elseneur). Jean de Boschère (1878–1953) recounted the childhood of a rebel in *Marthe et l'enragé* (1927; *Marthe and the Madman*, 1928) and in *Satan l'obscur* (1933; Satan the dark) created a fantastic universe, as did Robert Poulet (b. 1893) in *Handji* (1933; Handji). The Fleming Jean Ray (1887–1964) with *Malpertuis* (1955; Malpertuis) and Thomas Owen (b. 1910) from Ardenne with *La cave aux crapauds* (1945; the toad cellar) attest to the fact that the fantastic tradition, which dates back to the great Flemish painters of the 15th c., is still alive in Belgium.

Georges SIMENON, born in Liège but living abroad, invented his own literary dimension, becoming, after Maurice MAETERLINCK, the most famous Belgian writer. He began his career with popular novels and has written an impressive series of detective stories whose psychological penetration revitalized the genre (the Maigret series). Maud Frère's (1923–1979) *Les jumeaux millénaires* (1962; the millennial twins) is a masterpiece of psychological analysis written in a style stripped bare to the point of asceticism. Traditional realism is found in the work of Daniel Gillès (1917–1981), for example, *Les brouillards de Bruges* (1962; the fogs of Bruges). Pierre Mertens (b. 1939), on the other hand, uses all forms of narration to avoid the traps of the conventionally told story, as in *Les bons offices* (1974; services). Regionalism has worn away, but roots—or the nostalgia for roots—have, for all that, not disappeared: the roots of the Gaume region in *Les hameaux* (1978; the hamlets) by Hubert Juin (1926-1987); of Antwerp, in *Le rempart des béguines* (1951; *The Illusionist*, 1952), Françoise MALLET-JORIS's first novel; of Liège, in *Ludo* (1974; Ludo) by Conrad Detrez (1937-1984).

These writers were able to gain recognition only in Paris, as is also the case with Marcel Moreau (b. 1933), whose torrential prose in *Quintes* (1962; *The Selves of Quinte*, 1965) completely shattered all the boundaries of the novel. Nevertheless, the joy of having one's roots in a region and saying so is evident in *Vêpres buissonnières* (1974; vespers in the bush) by Jean Mergeai (b. 1927) and in *Julienne et la rivière* (1977; Julienne and the river) by Jean Pierre Otte (b. 1949).

The refusal to continue "to live under interposed Paris" and the desire to produce a specifically Belgian literature produced, at the end of the 1970's, a demand for a "belgitude," modeled on the "NÉGRITUDE" of Léopold Sédar SENGHOR and Aimé CÉSAIRE. This demand for the right to a cultural blending was the result of the marginal position occupied by Belgium with respect to France, and it permitted a greater porosity to other cultures. It is both interesting and significant that this will to affirm such a cultural specificity appeared at the very moment when Belgium's traditional structures were breaking down—the moment when Belgium became a federal country, divided between two linguistic communities.

The 1980s were decisive, characterized by this new cultural awareness and by the drum-beating, editorial politics of Marc

Quaghebeur (b. 1947), author of a revolutionary collection of French literature from Belgium entitled *Balises pour l'histoire de nos lettres* (1982; Beacons for the history of our literature). This work encouraged a healthy awareness which mobilized critics and writers alike, engaging a new debate on francophone Belgian cultural identity, and most importantly, provoking a new literary dynamism. The key figure in this new movement, Pierre Mertens, confirmed his mastery with *Les éblouissements* (1987; Dazzling lights), which received the Médicis Prize. A generation of new novelists—Francis Dannemark (b. 1955), Eugene Savitzkaya (b. 1955), Xavier Deutsch (b. 1965), Amélie Northomb (b. 1967)—provided proof that a new dynamism was in place and served as a reinforcement to the already established generation of writers, notably Gaston Compère (b. 1924), Guy Vaes (b. 1924), Henri Bauchau (b. 1913), and Jacqueline Harpman (b. 1929). In some cases, writers such as Bauchau and Harpman, who had already written several texts, were interrupted in their writing by a long period of silence followed by a return to writing which produced a remarkable collection of texts. In other cases, "expatriated" writers such as François Weyergens (b. 1941), Françoise Mallet-Joris, Dominique Rolin (b. 1913), Marcel Moreau, Patrick Roegiers (b. 1947), Jean-Claude Pirotte (b. 1939), and Jean-Philippe Toussaint (b. 1957), many of whom are naturalized French citizens, were already so solidly established in the Parisian literary system that they often "returned" to the French capital during these years.

Poetry

Because of their contribution to French SYMBOLISM, the French-speaking Belgians played a major role in European literature. The crisis in symbolist values had not, in any way, however, tarnished the glory of Maurice Maeterlinck, Emile VERHAEREN, Charles Van Lerberghe (1861–1907), or Max Elskamp (1862–1931). With *La multiple splendeur* (1906; multiple splendor) Verhaeren became the spearhead of a vitalist renewal that, at the beginning of the c., swept away the somewhat morbid dream climate of symbolism. In 1904 Van Lerberghe produced his masterpiece, *La chanson d'Ève* (Eve's song), and Max Elskamp, after more than twenty years of silence and before sinking into insanity, between 1921 and 1924 produced collections of poetry in which confessions, memoirs, and philosophical reflections are expressed in a poetic style unlike any other.

For Belgium, World War I was not only a tragedy that changed the intellectual climate; it also signaled the beginning of the split of the country. From then on, the divisive forces that continue even today to tear the kingdom apart ultimately relegated to the rank of an obsolete museum piece the myth of the "Belgian soul." A group of periodicals with an international outlook came into being after the war; even before the war, *Antée* had preceded and anticipated *La nouvelle revue française*, published in Paris. In the early 1920s, *Lumiére*, *Ça ira*, *Le disque vert*, *La renaissance d'Occident*, and in the early 1930s *Le journal des poètes* took their place at the head of the avant-garde battles.

Some of the major poets left the country for good: Jean de Boschère discovered in Ezra POUND and the English IMAGISTS that a new lyricism had risen out of the ashes of symbolism. His *The Closed Door* (1917; original title in English) and *Job le pauvre* (1922; Job the poor) were actually published in London in bilingual editions. Henri MICHAUX set out at first to wander about the world, then settled in Paris; his *Ecuador* (1929; *Ecuador*, 1970) is a travel diary, as are, in their own ways, *Mes propriétés* (1929; my

properties) and *L'espace du dedans* (1944; *The Space Within*, 1951), which explore the domain of the imaginary and the subconscious. The borders of hallucinatory perceptions—whether or not they are caused by drugs—opened the path for a "wild mysticism" whose fascinating evolution can be followed in *Misérable miracle* (1956; *Miserable Miracle*, 1963).

The few short books by Clément Pansaers (1885–1922) are directly linked to European DADAISM, but the Dadaist spirit, more pronounced in Belgium than in France, is still alive in the work of Paul Neuhuys (1897–1984) and Louis Scutenaire (1905–1987). Scutenaire was to be the faithful companion of the brilliant Belgian SURREALIST group that, in addition to painters like René Magritte (1898–1967) and musicians like André Souris (1899–1970), included writers like Marcel Lecomte (1900–1966), Paul Colinet (1898–1957), Camille Goemans (1900–1960), E. L. T. Mesens (1903–1970), and Paul Nougé (1895–1967). Paradoxically for a movement of an international scale, Belgian surrealism had a very marked provincial character. Moreover, it rapidly separated itself from the Paris group to establish itself as a community of independent and original thought, more sensitive to Jean PAULHAN's writings than to André BRETON's. The Hainault group, led by Achille Chavée (1906–1969), was also characterized by a spirit of independence.

More influenced by personalities like Max JACOB, Blaise CENDRARS, and Pierre REVERDY than by surrealism, Robert Guiette (1895–1976) followed a personal path, dedicated to a search for poetic concision and density. Flexibility and precision characterize the poems of Robert Vivier (1895–1989) and of Edmond Vandercammen (1901–1980), whose discovery of Spanish and Spanish American lyricism opened new horizons. From the wonderful adventures of his youth, Marcel Thiry (1897–1977), like Cendrars, drew the inspiration for his first poetry collections such as *Toi qui pâlis au nom de Vancouver* (1924; you who turn pale on account of Vancouver), written in a form reminiscent of symbolism. Another great traveler, Robert Goffin (1898–1990), continually wavers between a classical form and modern, cosmopolitan subject matter, as in *Le voleur de feu* (1950; the fire thief). Odilon-Jean Périer's (1901–1928) *Le citadin* (1924; the citizen) and *Le promeneur* (1927; the walker) contain probably the purest poems in Belgian French literature. Robert Mélot du Dy (1891–1956) combined a disillusioned irony with a traditional but flexible and varied versification. Géo Norge (1898–1990) and Maurice Carême (1899–1978) belong to the same generation, and both are characterized by the diversity of their rhythms and a verbal juggling.

In the rich poetic harvest of recent years, individual pursuits are more dominant than group concerns. The following poets all want to restore poetry to the realm of spiritual adventure, even at the risk of isolating themselves from the general reading public. Pierre della Faille (1906–1989), with *Requiem pour un ordinateur* (1970; requiem for a computer), presents his vision of the "retrained man," whose aim is to write a poetry of lucid revolt. For Fernand Verhesen (b. 1913), the poetic act is above all a striving beyond the self, as in *Franchir la nuit* (1970; to get through the night). In works like *Mémoire de rien* (1972; memory of nothing), in which she painstakingly strips the soul bare, Claire Lejeune (b. 1926) uses the power of negation to achieve a liberation from old shackles. André Miguel (b. 1920) aspires to a union of the external and internal worlds, yet he recognizes the distance between the two. The baroque poetry of Jacques Crickillon (b. 1940) is haunted by his vision of the void, whereas Jacques Izoard's (b. 1936) theme is the gulf between words and the things they stand for. Each collection of Christian Hubin (b. 1941) is like a ritual of waiting and hoping; the poet is on the threshold, watchful for what may bring release or illumination, as in *Coma des sourdes veillées* (1973; coma of the dull vigils).

In the country of "a hundred thousand poets," poetry could not remain idle. *Maîtres et maisons de thé* (1979; Masters and houses of tea) by Werner Lambersy (b. 1941) appeared immediately as an enormous poetic work of primary importance; Frans de Haes (b. 1945) and Marc Rombaut (b. 1939) remain attentive to the upheavals of language and the abysses of the subject. Guy Goffette (b. 1947) was rediscoverd with his work, *Éloge d'une cuisine de province* (1988; In praise of provincial cuisine), poetry with a human face; the attention to reality and the refusal of hermetic poetry also characterizes the works of Lucien Noullez (b. 1957) and Philippe Lekcuche (b. 1954). The presence of such indomitable writers as Philippe Jones (b. 1924), William Cliff (b. 1942), Jean-Pierre Vergeggen (b. 1942), and Marc Quaghebeur (b. 1947) must also be noted. These writers pursue, albeit sporadically, their unique, but important contributions to poetry.

Drama

Until World War I, drama was dominated by Maurice Maeterlinck, who gave up the static quality of his early plays for the movement of poetic fantasies like *L'oiseau bleu* (1909; *The Blue Bird*, 1909) or historical plays like *Le bourgmestre de Stilmonde* (1918; *The Burgomaster of Stilemonde*, 1918). Verhaeren attempted to write historical drama with *Philippe II* (1904; *Philip II*, 1916) and *Hélène de Sparte* (1909; *Helen of Sparta*, 1916), but the formal qualities of his plays greatly outweigh their theatrical effectiveness.

After World War II Belgian French drama held a place of honor on the Parisian stage because of the success of *Le cocu magnifique* (1921; *The Magnificent Cuckold*, 1966) by Fernand CROMMELYNCK. The plays of Henri Soumagne (1891–1951) were also performed at Lugné-Poë's Théâtre de l'Œuvre in Paris: *L'autre Messie* (1923; the other Messiah) is a lampoon attacking religious questions. Michel de GHELDERODE, like some of his predecessors, wrote tragic farce, but in his own distinctive style. His works were first performed by a troupe in Flanders, but he was not really recognized until the performance of *Hop Signor!* (1938; *Hop Signor!*, 1964) in 1947 in Paris revealed a work of extraordinary verbal force. Less violent but also inspired by history and legend, the work of Herman Closson (1901–1982) belongs to a renewal of the popular theater in Belgium, in which other playwrights participated in the 1950s: Georges Sion (b. 1913) with his *Voyageur de Forceloup* (1951; traveler from Forceloup); Charles Bertin (b. 1919); Suzanne Lilar (1901–1992); and especially Paul Willems (1912–1997), who with *La ville à voile* (1966; the sailing city) rediscovered the legacy of Maeterlinck by showing that theatrical effectiveness is not incompatible with a highly poetic and allusive style.

The disappearance of René Kalisky (1936–1981), author of *La Passion selon Pier Paolo Pasolini* (1977; Passion According to Pier Paolo Pasolini), and *Sur les ruines de Carthage* (1980; At the Carthage ruins), deprived Belgian theater of one of its most important figures. Paul Willems and Jean Sigrid (1920–1997) confirmed their dramatic talent for evoking worlds on the border of the real and the imaginary. Following in their footsteps, Jacques de Decker (b. 1945), Liliane Wouters (b. 1930), Philippe Blasband (b. 1964), Paul Emond (b. 1944) and Jean-Marie Piemme (b. 1944) assured, during the following two decades, an original theatrical repertoire brought to public attention by a group of talent young

producers. The activity of numerous young theatrical companies and the work of directors and producers such as Frédéric Baal (b. 1940) has put into place a theatrical process which transcends the Belgian theatrical scene, since these writers and producers are often called upon to perform their productions in France.

BIBLIOGRAPHY: Goris, J. A., *Belgian Letters: A Short Survey* (1946); Lilar, S., *The Belgian Theatre since 1890* (1950); Jonckheere, K., and R. Bodart, *Belgian Literature* (1958); Charlier, G., and J. Hanse, *Histoire illustrée des lettres françaises de Belgique* (1958); Seydell, M., *Poetry Profile in Belgium* (1963); Burniaux, C., "The French-Belgian Harvest," *BA*, 38 (1964): 122–23; Mallinson, V., *Modern Belgian Literature* (1968); Burniaux, R., and R. Frickx, *La littérature belge d'expression française* (1973); Jans, A., ed., *Lettres vivantes: Deux générations d'écrivains français de Belgique (1945–1975)* (1975); Sion, G., *150 ans de littérature* (1980); Trekker, A.-M., and J.-P. Vander Straeten, *Cent auteurs belges. Anthologie de littérature française de Belgique* (1982); Warmoes, J., *Cinquante ans d'avant-garde 1917-1967* (1983); Toussaint, F., *Le surréalisme belge* (1988); Paque, J., *Le symbolisme belge* (1989); Luc, A.-F., *Le naturalisme belge* (1990); Quaghebeur, M., *Lettres belges entre absence et magie* (1990); Trousson, R. and J. Cels, et. al., *1920-1995. Un espace-temps littéraire. 75 ans de littérature française en Belgique* (1995); Aron, P., ed., *La Belgique artistique et littéraire. Une anthologie de langue française (1848-1914)* (1997); Gorceix, P., ed., *La Belgique fin de siècle. Romans. Nouvelles. Théâtre* (1998)

—CHRISTIAN BERG
TRANSLATED BY DAYNA L. OSCHERWITZ

BELLI, Carlos Germán

Peruvian poet, b. 15 Sept. 1927, Lima

B. is one of the most expressive poetic voices of contemporary Peruvian and Latin American poetry. A descendant of Italian immigrants, B. began writing poetry at age thirty. His poems have gained recognition in all of Latin America, and a number of them have been translated into English and Italian.

In a country that enjoys a rich poetic tradition, B. has managed to establish a unique voice. His poetry manifests a deep preoccupation with a language based on the intricate verbal processes of Spanish Golden Age poetry displaced from its original context, coupled with a formalism that is both stringent and experimental. His language, confessional and symbolic, with its vocabulary of neologisms, is based on a variety of traditions and influences. On more than one occasion B. has discussed his affinity with SURREALISM, especially in the early stages of his career. After a brief encounter with "letrismo," or poetry that relies on the iconic power of the word for its impact, and on automatic writing, B. discovered the poetry of the modernists. Undertaking a systematic study of Rubén DARÍO, the leading poet of the movement, B. became intrigued by the formal beauty of modernist poetry and the refined eroticism he found in Darío's poems.

Although he relished the linguistic freedom provided by automatic writing, he soon turned toward the classical tradition with its closed, rigid forms. Influenced by Luis de Góngora y Argote (1562-1627), Fernando de Herrera (1534-1597), Francisco Medrano (1570?-1607), Francisco de Quevedo y Villegas (1580-1645), and other masters of Spanish Golden Age poetry, B. became obsessed by the formal aspects of this poetry as he copied the external forms, the meters and the rhymes, in the same manner that Renaissance painters imitated the masters. These intricate verbal processes, typical of Baroque poetry, with its disjointed syntax, stylistic formulae, and daring images, evoke a pastoral world of classical mythology, and form the basis of B.'s poetry. This is poetry that presents extreme difficulties for the reader. It is an intricate process elaborated with attention to detail and dominated by the tension produced by multiple points of focus, shocking contrasts, and subtle interplay of spatial and temporal forms. If it is easy to lose oneself in this labyrinth, there is also a reward for the attentive reader who is able to see a coherent architecture in B.'s work. This is poetry that is always expressed in a language that is charged with deep human feelings and a sense of humility.

In his first books of poems, *Poemas* (1958; poems) and *Dentro y fuera* (1960; inside and out), B. established the basic lines of his entire poetic production. Chief among them is the preoccupation with the theme of alienation that is caused by socioeconomic conditions. The poet feels excluded from a world dominated by those who have power. Another constant in his poetry is the theme of suffering, which is expressed in poems dedicated to his brother, Alfonso, who has been confined to a wheelchair since early childhood. His brother's suffering is equated to the suffering of humankind in general, and it symbolizes a sense of exclusion from the joys of life. The poet and his brother are viewed as imperfect beings destined to suffer the harshest physical and metaphysical privations.

The poet's fragmented voice, in a world that is beyond his control, seeks a sense of integration and liberation through the evocation of a utopic world based on the pastoral tradition. The poet, however, is frustrated in this attempt. His poetry captures the tension produced by two diametrically opposing forces, one that attempts to pull the poet apart, the other that seeks integration.

In *Oh hada cibernética* (1962; oh cybernetic fairy) B. expresses his faith in the power of science to deliver humans from the burden of labor. Technology will allow the poet to find the necessary free time to dedicate himself to his own poetic production. With the passing of time, this desire also becomes frustrated. In the same volume he expresses the desire to achieve a physical and metaphysical union with Filis, the ideal woman of the pastoral tradition. However, the poet soon discovers that this union is only possible through the poetic word itself. Each poem then becomes a small step in the long voyage of self-definition.

The poems of *El pie sobre el cuello* (1964; the foot on the neck) intensify the theme of the poet's suffering as a direct result of his metaphysical as well as his socioeconomic condition. This collection is followed by *Por el monte abajo* (1966; rushing down the mountain), with its predominant tone of exasperation, which is only assuaged by the appearance of a woman, an ideal even more generalized than Filis, as a positive force capable of alleviating the suffering of the poet. It is this idealized woman who restores the poet's humanity and faith in himself. B. experiments with larger poems in *Sextinas y otros poemas* (1970; sestinas and other poems), where the metric form of the Petrarchan canzone predominates. In this collection B.'s poetry becomes more sensual; it assumes an erotic posture that will become even more evident in subsequent works.

He achieves his highest level of complexity and intellectualization in the poems of *En alabanza del bolo alimenticio* (1979; in praise of undigested food), where the physical and natural processes are coupled with a complex process of regeneration. In *Canciones y otros poemas* (1982; songs and other poems) B. achieves a perfect sense of synthesis of his entire poetic production. The last poem of the collection, "Cuando el espíritu no habla por la boca" (when the spirit does not speak through the mouth) is the perfect symbiosis of the poetic word and the sexual act as a means toward transcendence. This same existential posture is also implicit in his latest books of poems: *Más que señora humana* (1986; more than a human lady), *El buen mudar* (1987; the big move), and *En el restante tiempo terrenal* (1988; what is left of this terrestrial time).

B.'s poetry may best be summed up in the words of his compatriot, the renowned writer Mario Vargas LLOSA, who says: "B.'s is a poetry for difficult times, like our own times, for societies in which the life of the spirit and culture seem to languish, without grandeur, in the midst of general indifference."

FURTHER WORKS: *Antología personal* (1988)

BIBLIOGRAPHY: Hill, W. N., "The Poetry of C. G. B.," *BHS*, 47 (1970): 327–39; Lasarte, F., "Pastoral and Counter-Pastoral: The Dynamics of B.'s Poetic Despair," *MLN*, 94, 4 (1979): 301–20; Garganigo, J. F., *C. G. B.: antología crítica* (1988)

—JOHN F. GARGANIGO

BELLI, Gioconda

Nicaraguan poet and novelist, b. 9 Dec. 1948, Managua

Born into an upper-class family, B. received her early education in Catholic schools, to which she credits her sense of social justice, and later in schools in England, Spain, and the U.S. B. joined the FSLN (Sandinista National Liberation Front) in 1970 to end decades of Somoza dynasty and dictatorship. As a cover for her political activism, B. worked in advertising. She was forced into exile because of her participation in support of the successful commando assault on a high official's home in 1974, an event that would later inspire her testimonial novel, *La mujer habitada* (1988; *The Inhabited Woman*, 1994). B. spent several years in Mexico and Costa Rica before returning home following the 1979 Revolution, which she served in various capacities: international press liaison for the FSLN; journalist for *Barricada*; official in the Ministry of Planning; member of the Nicaraguan Women's Association (AMNLAE); and other roles in advertising, publicity, and broadcasting for the new government. Although never a member of any literary circle, B. is known as one of "The Six"—with Michele Najlis (b. 1946), Yolanda Blanco (b. 1954), Vidaluz Meneses (b. 1944), Rosario Murillo (b. 1951), and Daisy Zamora (b. 1950)—bourgeois women writing political and feminist poetry, some of whom went on to hold government office as well. B. is the mother of four children who have often been the subject of her poetry. She currently lives and writes in California.

B. began publishing individual poems in local periodicals in the late 1960s and early 1970s. Her forthright and exuberant expressions of sensuality scandalized her family, friends, and polite society. In 1972 the National Autonomous University of Nicaragua (UNAN) awarded B. its Mariano Fiallos Gil Prize for poems she later published in her first collection, *Sobre la grama* (1974; On the Grass). Eroticism, themes of motherhood, and disdain of society's hypocritical treatment of women all mark her early work and set the tone of much of her later writing. In 1978 B. won the prestigious Casa de las Américas (Havana) Prize in poetry for *Línea de fuego* (1978; Line of Fire). What was once an intimate space is made public as B. joins the personal to the political, the sexual to the social. For B., revolution signifies freedom from sexual oppression as well as from economic injustice, dictatorship, and imperialism. She experiments with a blending of poetry and prose in a number of selections and incorporates surreal imagery with often conventional metaphors. While at times her poetic first person ("yo") submits to the desires of her lover in a traditional heterosexual relationship, she never loses sight of the strength of her own will and passion. *Línea de fuego* is a rite of passage which charts the transformation of the "new woman" much as leftist politics constructed the "new man." B's female subject is never passive.

Other important collections of poetry, for which she has received numerous prizes, include *Truenos y arcoiris* (1982; Thunder and Rainbows), *Amor insurrecto* (1984; Insurgent Love), and *De la costilla de Eva* (1987; From Eve's Rib, 1989). The tension continues between the private and the public, the suffering mother and the warrior-mother, woman as oasis and woman as revolutionary. B's imagery increasingly connects woman to natural life cycles. *Apogeo* (1997; Apogee) leaves the context of national politics to seek a more specifically feminist expression, exploring midlife, menopause, and mature sexual fulfillment. Many of B's poems have been translated into English, German, Dutch, and Italian.

B's novels develop the same themes in greater complexity. Her first, *La mujer habitada*, dramatizes the simultaneous struggle for national liberation and women's emancipation in her country at a time of increased Sandinista successes against the Somoza regime in the mid-1970s. B. never names Nicaragua, instead calling it the mythical Faguas, a name that reappears in later novels. A female "coming-of-age" novel, *La mujer habitada* examines the protagonist Lavinia's growing awareness of the injustice of "machismo" and, at the same time, links feminine consciousness with the earth, nature, and rebellious indigenous roots. The narrative voice alternates between a third person describing Lavinia's thoughts and activities and a first person representing the spirit of an Indian princess, who resisted the conquistadors 500 years earlier and now "inhabits" Lavinia. The text itself is a hybrid form combining elements of historical, sentimental, and testimonial novels with magical realism.

B. moves beyond a specific historical referent in her next novel, *Sofía de los presagios* (1990; Sophie of the Omens). B. has explained that this novel grew out of her disillusionment with the failures of Sandinismo on women's issues and that she distanced herself from the FSLN in the late 1980s. B's second novel is unabashedly feminist as it follows the exploits of its strong and independent protagonist. Ludic and carnivalesque, *Sofía* pursues themes of eroticism, motherhood, magic, illuminism, and necromancy, scorning social conventions and satirizing patriarchalism.

Waslala, o, Memorial del futuro (1996), B's third novel, revisits the mythical Faguas, this time far into the 21st c. Faguas is the first world's dumping ground for trash and toxic waste. The poets and dreamers have long since retreated to a utopian refuge, Waslala, somewhere deep in the jungle, while drug lords and arms dealers have sold the country out to the highest foreign bidder. The protagonist, the orphaned Melisandra, embarks on a search for her parents, for Waslala, and for lost dreams in a tale of love, adventure, politics, and environmental degradation. B's striking baroque

imagery recreates cities of rubbish and lost souls. She based her story on a 1988 radiation disaster in Brazil where scavengers, combing through a nuclear waste dump, happened upon a canister of bluish powder that glowed in the dark. Too late they discovered it contained deadly cesium chloride. The novel is also B's homage to her mentor, Nicaraguan vanguardist poet José Coronel Urtecho, who died before its completion.

B's is one of the most important female voices to emerge from Central America at a turbulent juncture in its recent history. Poet and storyteller, she explores the struggle for liberation on several fronts—gender, sexuality, and the national-popular—and lustily celebrates womanhood.

FURTHER WORKS: *Poesía reunida* (1989); *El ojo de la mujer* (1991); *Taller de las mariposas* (1994)

BIBLIOGRAPHY: Arenal, E., "Two Poets of the Sandinista Struggle," *FSt*, 7, 1 (1981): 19-37; March, K. M., "G. B.: The Erotic Politics of the Great Mother," *MRRM*, 6 (1990): 245-57; Richards, T. A. B., "Resistance and Liberation: The Mythic Voice and Textual Authority in B.'s *La mujer habitada*," in González-del-Valle, et al., eds., *Critical Essays on the Literatures of Spain and Spanish America* (1991): 209-14; Cohen, H., "'El amor . . . loca palabra': Eroticism in G. B.'s *De la costilla de Eva*," *Inti*, 39 (1994): 97-110; Hood, E. W., "Entrevista con G. B.," *Chasqui*, 23 (1994): 125-32; Arias, A., "G. B.: The Magic and/of Eroticism," in Ferman, C., ed., *The Postmodern in Latin and Latino American Cultural Narratives* (1996): 181-99; Craft, L. J., *Novels of Testimony and Resistance from Central America* (1997); Moyano, P., "The Transformation of Nation and Womanhood: Revisionist Mythmaking in the Poetry of Nicaragua's G. B.," in Ghosh-Bishnupriya, et al., eds., *Interventions: Feminist Dialogues on Third World Women's Literature and Film* (1997): 79-95

—LINDA J. CRAFT

BELLOC, Hilaire

English essayist, poet, social critic, novelist, and historian, b. 27 July 1870, Paris, France; d. 16 July 1953, Guildford

Son of a French barrister father and an English mother, B. inherited a legacy of radical liberalism and intellectual energy from both sides of the family. B.'s Catholicism, along with his antiaristocratic sentiments and his skill at disputation, made him a less than typical Oxford undergraduate. While at the university he began writing verses and soon after turned to a career as belletrist and polemicist. His social conscience led him to serve as a Liberal Member of Parliament from 1906 to 1910, but the inertia of the House of Commons enraged him, and he returned to the life of a man of letters.

B. is best understood through his loves and hatreds. Always the champion of wine, liberty, and his Catholic faith, he was disgusted by the blandness, conformity, and unbelief that he foresaw in England's future. In the spirit of Thomas Carlyle and John Ruskin, he tried to awaken his countrymen to the horrors and hypocrisies of capitalism. He was a romantic believer in the idea of community and looked to the Middle Ages for his paradigm of a just and sound society.

B.'s essays show an extraordinary range of subjects and styles. There are leisurely, digressive pieces on food and inns, whimsical treatments of "characters," biting satires and poignant recollections of people and places. He had an enormous capacity for pleasure as well as a keenly developed sense of the world's injustices and sorrows. For example, an "ideal" Belloc collection, *This and That and the Other* (1912), presents a luscious wish fulfillment in "The Pleasant Place" and also a savage attack on the cruelties of social class in "The Servants of the Rich."

B.'s more sustained prose works are often similarly varied in tone and theme. *The Path to Rome* (1902) and *The Cruise of the Nona* (1925) both allow B. to range over vast expanses of experience by using the framework of a journey. In *The Path to Rome* B. sets off with bread and wine, a strong will, and very little money; his struggles and disappointments along the way make the journey an allegory of modern spiritual progress.

As a social thinker and historian, B. is deeply personal and impressionistic. *The Servile State* (1912) draws together his views of European history and traces out an almost Marxian pattern of economic injustice, land seizure, and monopolism. B.'s villains are Henry VIII, the Whig aristocracy, the capitalists, and, in our time, the social planners. He argues that, in trying to prop up an unjust economic system, we have devised various kinds of tyrannical state controls that dwarf the individual. More often, however, B.'s approach to history is less abstract. *The French Revolution* (1911) uses portraiture as its method and delineates the passions and ideas of major figures. *Miniatures of French History* (1925) selects key conflicts and shows their significance as moments in the continuous drama of Europe.

The novels and poetry are thoroughly consonant with B.'s social philosophy. The novel *The Haunted House* (1927), a "Chesterbelloc" illustrated humorously by B.'s good friend G. K. CHESTERTON, is superficially a farcical romp, but is fundamentally charged by B.'s intense dislike of nouveau riche conspicuous consumption and by his love of tradition. The book pokes fun at overnight peers, phony genealogies, and vulgar middle-class types in a manner reminiscent of the early Thackeray. B.'s poetry has many moods. Some of his finest pieces, such as "The Ballade of Hell and Mrs. Roebeck" (1923) and "The Garden Party" (1932), have a sharp satirical edge as well as unsettling metaphysical undertones. B.'s most famous volume, *The Bad Child's Book of Beasts* (1896), is pure nonsense. He often succeeds in pure lyric—in the celebration of wine, friendship, and English country places—but his most enduring works are haunting social portraits, epigrammatic jabs, and denunciations.

B. is frequently blustery and almost always opinionated. He is altogether out of joint with literary modernism. Yet the cumulative impact of this author of some 150 volumes is considerable. As a social thinker, he is a beacon for radicals disillusioned with progress; as a historian, he is gripping and erudite; as an essayist he is a phenomenon of resourcefulness and emotional range.

FURTHER WORKS: *The Modern Traveller* (1898); *Danton* (1899); *Robespierre* (1901); *Avril* (1904); *Sussex* (1906); *Hills and the Sea* (1906); *On Nothing* (1908); *The Pyrenees* (1909); *Marie Antoinette* (1909); *On Anything* (1900); *On Something* (1910); *The Four Men* (1912); *The History of England* (1915); *Europe and the Faith* (1920); *On* (1923); *The Road* (1923); *Sonnets and Verse* (1923); *James the Second* (1928); *Belinda* (1928); *Richelieu* (1930); *A Conversation with a Cat* (1931); *Essays of a Catholic* (1931);

Ladies and Gentlemen (1932); *Milton* (1935); *Selected Essays* (1948); *Collected Verses* (1958); *Complete Verse* (1991)

BIBLIOGRAPHY: Wilhemsen, F., *H. B.: No Alienated Man* (1954); Speaight, R., *The Life of H. B.* (1957); Van Thal, H., ed., *B.: A Biographical Anthology* (1970); McCarthy, J. P., *H. B., Edwardian Radical* (1978); Markel, M. H., *H. B.* (1982); Wilson, A. N., *H. B.* (1984)

—DAVID CASTRONOVO

BELLOW, Saul

American novelist, b. 10 July 1915, Lachine, Que., Canada

The environmental influences upon B. might have been devised by one of the proletarian novelists of the 1930s. The child of Russian-Jewish immigrants, he was raised until the age of nine in an impoverished, polyglot section of Montreal, and he came to maturity in Chicago during the Depression, when that city was still in its colorful and gangster-ridden phase. Although B. himself was more inclined to sit in libraries than to stand on Chicago's street corners, the environment of his early life seems to have contributed to the emphasis on social realism and cultural relevance in his work and also, perhaps, to a strain of anti-intellectualism that runs deep in him, coexisting with his insistent intellectualism. B. is not in any

Saul Bellow

meaningful sense an autobiographical writer, but he assuredly writes from what he knows: his Canadian birth is handed over to the Dangling Man of his first novel; his scholarly interest in anthropology informs *Henderson the Rain King* (1959); his academic career is reflected in *Herzog* (1964); his writing career is echoed in *Humboldt's Gift* (1975); and his Jewish heritage and his several divorces are shared by many of his characters, most of whom live in Chicago or New York, the cities he knows. B. finds his literary antecedents in Flaubert and in DREISER, but he also admires the 19th-c. Russian writers, especially Dostoevsky, whose influence on B.'s work is considerable.

Indeed, *Dangling Man* (1944), B.'s first novel, is based loosely upon Dostoevsky's *Notes from the Underground* (1864). It affects to be the journal of a Chicagoan, identified simply as Joseph, who finds himself "dangling" between civilian and military status during World War II, his induction into the U.S. Army snarled with red tape because of his Canadian birth. Joseph is aware of dangling between intelligence and will, too, and between theory and experience, and between his customary mildness and his intermittent bursts of temper. He is B.'s typical protagonist—a man badly unnerved by his divergent impulses, and so deeply introspective that his contacts with external reality tend to be irrationally passionate. The novel is hermetically wrought and carefully styled, but it is generally thought to approach crabbedness: it has little or no plot; there is no lightness in its touch; and its ending is an unsatisfactory affair.

The Victim (1947) is also inspired, albeit unconsciously, by a Dostoevskian text—the short novel *The Eternal Husband* (1870). The Jewish protagonist, Asa Leventhal, discovers himself beleaguered by a Gentile named Kirby Allbee, who demands that Leventhal find him employment and provide him with money and housing. The validity of Allbee's claim on Leventhal is moot, and it is compounded by racial and religious prejudice, but Leventhal is paranoid and he discovers in Allbee a focus for his general insecurity and guilt. It is never clear that Allbee is not Leventhal's unconscious creation, a *Doppelgänger*, and, as Leventhal struggles ambivalently in Allbee's grasp, he is struggling ultimately with the same dialectics of human nature that afflict the protagonist of *Dangling Man*. The novel is artfully realistic, with New York City backgrounds of stifling heat and ominously pressing crowds, and it is elaborately plotted, in compensation, no doubt, for the plotlessness of *Dangling Man*. But once again B. delivers an unsatisfactory ending, unable to resolve the expressionistic treatment of Leventhal's psychology within the tightly realistic framework of his story.

With *The Adventures of Augie March* (1953), B. abandoned his overt Dostoevskian models and employed for the first time a picaresque form, tracing the journey of his title character from boyhood to adulthood, and from the Chicago slums to European capitals. The young Augie delights in the color, the vitality, and the considerable variety of his experiences, and his *joie de vivre* is beguiling. But as the novel progresses its mood inexplicably darkens: Augie becomes increasingly introspective and troubled, vaguely at war with himself, and his early exuberance comes to seem an evasion of life rather than its enlargement. Augie is a Jewish Huck Finn in this regard, as is often noted, and his story evokes not only Twain's masterpiece of realism but other masterworks of realism as well, compounding Augie's subtle failure with the entire tradition of literary realism. On the edge of breaking into his major style—at once picaresquely loose and expressionistically psychological—B. seems to have been saying goodbye to the narrowly realistic tradition that had confined his early work.

In his shorter fiction, however, B. has continued to employ hermetically rigid forms and an abundance of realistic detail. The most distinguished work in this mode is the novelette *Seize the Day* (1956). Tommy Wilhelm, its protagonist, is another Dangling Man, a failure both in business and in his family relationships, but, pivotally, he is the first of B.'s protagonists to be offered a saving glimpse into himself; paradoxically, he is also the first of B.'s protagonists to be broadly caricatured. Wilhelm is an obvious step to Eugene Henderson, the protagonist of *Henderson the Rain King*. At once sensitive and brutish, thoughtful and impulsive, Henderson is still another Dangling Man, but his marvelously demotic tongue and his endearing penchant for disaster make him more interesting than his realistic predecessors. He attempts to escape the chaos of his life by journeying to primitive Africa and living among the Arnewi and the Wariri tribes, only to find that those somewhat oddball tribes correspond to his inner duality, and that Africa is an expressionistic landscape of his essential self. Although Henderson survives the African duality, primarily through his energy and his extravagant temperament, he is affected deeply by the tutelage of the Wariri king Dahfu, for Dahfu's tutelage soothes Henderson's chaotic selfhood, enabling him to emerge from the dialectics of Africa with his soul intact, his extravagances somewhat tempered, and his heart open. Dahfu is a standard figure in a B. novel—a tutor in reality who is always something of a charlatan as well, for reality and salvation are not easily come by in B.'s fictional world. Indeed, *Henderson the Rain King* remains essentially a comic novel, and among its comic delights are parodies of the symbolic novel and of the nature mysticism of HEMINGWAY: Henderson's symbol-ridden and vaguely mystical salvation is, like Wilhelm's, very tentative.

Herzog incorporates successfully the two strains of B.'s fiction: like *Dangling Man* and *The Victim* it is a hermetic work, confining the reader rigidly to the mind of its title character, and like *The Adventures of Augie March* and *Henderson the Rain King* it is a picaresquely spacious and exuberant work, crammed with *ad hoc* meditations, highly colored characters, and dazzling turns of wit. These two strains define the complex mind of Moses Herzog, a university professor haunted by the utter disarray of his personal life, who compulsively writes letters of general social comment to persons living and dead. But there is a serious note of optimism in *Herzog*, for, *schlemiel* that he may be, Herzog comes to understand himself in homely little ways. He knows his tendency to see himself as a victim, for instance, and time and again he reevaluates his paranoid assumptions when he discovers reality to be simpler, more straight forward, and essentially fairer than he had thought it. He is the first of B.'s protagonists to transcend his divergent impulses seriously and convincingly.

Mr. Sammler's Planet (1970) is much like *Herzog* in its combination of a hermetic point of view and an intellectual spaciousness, but its overall effect is quieter and soberer. The most important reason for this is that the protagonist, a 74-year-old Polish Jew living on Manhattan's West Side, is neither a conspicuous bungler nor a wild *naïf* in the usual mode of B.'s later heroes. Rather he is an unabashed intellectual and merely the confidant of such types. More sententious than sardonic, he sees the vagaries of his confidants in a perspective split between Schopenhauerian pessimism and Jewish-inspired optimism, and he is generally dismayed by a New York filled with hippies, muggers, and miniskirts. His story involves a modest victory of his underdeveloped heart over his intelligence, in the mode of B.'s later novels, but there is a tendency, nonetheless, to read *Mr. Sammler's Planet* as a rather crotchety novel, and to dismiss its remarkable evocation of the 1960s as the intellectual contempt of an author whose liberal humanism found the decade distasteful.

Humboldt's Gift, B.'s most spacious novel since *The Adventures of Augie March*, has little of the hermetic about it, although it is narrated in the first person. Its protagonist, Charlie Citrine, is a successful writer who is maneuvered to the brink of financial and psychological disaster by those around him. The ivory tower and the marketplace battle for his soul, the former in the person of Von Humboldt Fleisher, a burned-out poet and an embodiment of received Western culture, the latter in the person of Rinaldo Canatabile, a blustering, would-be gangster and an embodiment of American materialism. Citrine is finally able to reject Cantabile and to accept the dead Humboldt's gift, but his state of exhaustion makes his rejection a bloodless affair, less interesting, narratively, than B.'s superb evocation of Chicago and his pungent mimicry of lawyers, businessmen, and hoodlums. Although *Humboldt's Gift* is not a roman à clef, and B. is not an autobiographical writer, the character of Humboldt is modeled on the poet Delmore SCHWARTZ, and the details of Citrine's life correspond to the details of B.'s life in many respects: some readers have suspected that Citrine's weariness with the intractable claims of high culture and felt experience is B.'s own weariness, and that, for all of its similarity to *Henderson the Rain King* and *Herzog*, *Humboldt's Gift* has an underlying affinity of mood with *Mr. Sammler's Planet*.

B. has come to be regarded as the dean of American novelists. As the recipient of two Guggenheim Fellowships (1948–49 and 1955–56), three National Book Awards (1953 for *The Adventures of Augie March*, 1964 for *Herzog*, and 1970 for *Mr. Sammler's Planet*), the Pulitzer Prize (1975 for *Humboldt's Gift*) and the Nobel Prize for Literature (1976), he is the most honored of living American novelists, and he towers over that school of furious Jewish humorists that has earned such a distinguished place in recent American fiction. The Nobel Prize citation spoke appropriately of the "human understanding and subtle analysis of contemporary culture that are combined in [B.'s] work" and praised the uplifting impact of the B. character—a man "who keeps trying to find a foothold during his wanderings in our tottering world, one who can never relinquish his faith that the value of life depends on its dignity, not its success." The Nobel citation did not speak of the darker side of experience in B.'s novels, but it is part of B.'s greatness that he has refused to be merely uplifting, and that in his continual effort to lure the facts about man's existence into equilibrium he has never denied their essential recalcitrance. Finally, no estimate of B.'s achievement can ignore the marvelous impasto of his language—that combination, often within the same paragraph, of gritty street slang and learned abstractions that expands with wit, flowers into epigram, and catches suddenly in the throat. It is a language, like the novels themselves, of enormous power great subtlety, and assured achievement.

FURTHER WORKS: *The Last Analysis* (1965); *Mosby's Memoirs and Other Stories* (1968); *To Jerusalem and Back: A Personal Account* (1976); *The Dean's December* (1982); *Him with His foot in His Mouth and Other Stories* (1984); *More Die of Heartbreak* (1987); *The Bellarosa Connection* (1989); *The Theft* (1989); *Something to Remember Me By* (1991); *The Actual* (1997)

BIBLIOGRAPHY: Fiedler, L., "S. B.," *PrS*, 31 (1957): 103–10; Hassan, I., "S. B.: The Quest and Affirmation of Reality," in *Radical Innocence* (1961): 290–324; special B. issue, *Crit*, 7 (1965): 4–45; Tanner, T., *S. B.*, (1965); special B. section, *Crit*, 9 (1967): 37–83; Harper, H. M., Jr., *Desperate Faith* (1967): 7–64; Malin, I., ed., *S. B. and the Critics* (1967); Opdahl, K. M., *The Novels of S. B.* (1967); Rovit, E., *S. B.* (1967); Clayton, J. J., *S. B.: In Defense of Man* (1968); Shulman, R., "The Style of B.'s Comedy," *PMLA*, 83 (1968): 109–17; Malin, I., *S. B.'s Fiction* (1969); Schulz, M. F., "S. B. and the Burden of Selfhood," in *Radical Sophistication* (1970): 110–53; Dutton, R. R., *S. B.*. (1971); Scheer-Schäzler, B., *S. B.* (1972); Kazin, A., *Bright Book of Life* (1973): 125–38; Cohen, S. B., *S. B.: A Enigmatic Laughier* (1974); Rovit, E., ed., *S. B.: A Collection of Critical Essays* (1975); Nault, M., *S. B., His Works and His Critics: And Annotated International Bibliography* (1977); Noreen, R. C., *S. B.: A Reference Guide* (1978); special B. issue, *NMAL*, 2, 4 (1978); Kiernan, R. F., *S. B.* (1989); Miller, R., *S. B.: A Biography of the Imagination* (1991)

—ROBERT F. KIERNAN

Bellow's personalist hero yelps, quite the gamecock of a new, urban wilderness, quite like his backwoodsman prototype impelled to brashness by dispossession and inadequacy and the feeling of threatening powers everywhere. He sings himself with quite the same nervy insolence with which Walt Whitman met the world, and like that witty comedian he makes a great gesture of including the whole world in himself, but then he adopts shifts and evasions and contrarieties to keep free of it. And like Whitman, he celebrates himself by the exercise of a free-wheeling, inclusive, cataloguing rhetoric, gripping great bunches of facts in sentences that just manage to balance, racing through various levels of diction, saying with every turn, "Look at me, going everywhere!" It is a gaudy fireworks of a style, in itself a brilliant affirmation of the self. At the same time it performs the ironic function, by its calculated in discriminateness (in Bellow and in Walt Whitman, too), of discarding everything it picks up. It is therefore the perfect expression of the dynamic, disengaging, mock hero.

> Marcus Klein, "A Discipline of Nobility: S. B.'s Fiction." *KR*, 24 (1962), 216–17

For Augie and Henderson the only way to see right side up is via primitivism, and Bellow seems to have realized or discovered that primitivism was for him more theoretically than actually valid. The answer in *Herzog* is quite different: a novel of ideas and a hero who feels his having come to the end of the line so well that the touters of the Void can be sneered at if only because they cannot reckon with Herzog's narcissism and buoyancy.

The result is the first or at least the largest step taken beyond Lawrence and the romanticism that is bought at the terrifying expense of fear and loathing of human kind. Dignity must go and without any accompanying comic reassurance—Herzog must scurry like a rat from his will and need to be kept in shelter, and he must end in silence. But the gains are great; a repeated and convincing insistence that the equation of reality with evil is sentimental and a demonstration that existentialism is only the most recent attempt of the romantic to be respectable and aristocratic.

Roger Sale, "Provincial champions and Grand Masters," *HudR*, 17 (1964–65), 617–18

. . . It was [in *Augie March*] that Bellow began to fashion a comic prose which could bear the simultaneous weight of cultural, historical, mythological evocations and also sustain the exposure of their irrelevance. His comedy always has in it the penultimate question before the final one, faced in *Seize the Day*, of life or death—the question of what can be taken seriously and how seriously it can possibly be taken. The result, however, is a kind of stalemate achieved simply by not looking beyond the play of humor into its constituents, at the person from whom it issues, at the psychological implications both of anyone's asking such questions and of the *way* in which he asks them. It seems to me that Bellow cannot break the stalemate with alienation implicit in his comedy without surrendering to the Waste Land outlook and forgoing the mostly unconvincing rhetoric which he offers as an alternative. That is why his comic style in *Herzog*, even more than in *Henderson or Augie*, is less like Nathanael West's than like that of West's brother-in-law, S. J. Perelman.

Richard Poirier, "Bellows to Herzog." *PR*, 32 (1965), 270–71

. . . Bellow might be said to apply the techniques of the novel of manners to the purposes of proletarian fiction. All of his characters exist in a carefully defined social context. He evokes not New York of Chicago, but neighborhoods within those cities. His characters play out their lives in coal yards, funeral parlors, police courts and aquariums. If his characters have no school tie they have telling occupations; if they find little tradition or class structure in America, they have the traditions of Judaism, the rigidity of colorful relatives, the nationalistic jealousies of a mixed community. Bellow substitutes the clash of ideologies for the intrigues of class, the pressures of money for the subtleties of social position. He is as conscious of "high quality" as James and as aware of the telling detail as Flaubert; he uses the rituals of ordering a meal, the protocol of the boarding house, the "picturesque gloom" of the Elevated to place his character firmly within society.

Keith Michael Opdahl, The Novels of S. B. (1967), p. 9

In [Bellow's] attempt to discover a way of resisting the "controls of this vast society" without falling into nihilism or empty rebellion, he concedes that he

may not have followed certain questions "to the necessary depth."

One can readily appreciate and be grateful for Bellow's desire to uphold some of the traditional sanities and balances, and one can accept his tentative affirmation that "There may be truths on the side of life." At the same time, I think this attempt to establish some middle ground between pessimism and optimism contributes to what Updike called "the soft focus of Bellow's endings." Bellow is not alone in disliking the sort of shock tactics exploited by a writer like Burroughs, yet there are times when extreme fictional strategies are necessary if certain questions are to be followed to the "necessary depth." For some writers there is something a little too easy, and even self-satisfied, in the way in which Herzog achieves the desired disburdenments and reconciliations in the pastoral moment of the last chapter.

Tony Tanner, *City of Words* (1971), p. 304

In Bellow's most recent novels, experiences are not so much being undergone as discussed in a probing approach that may well be called essayistic. More and more is being asked of the protagonists as characters. They are not merely reborn once as, for instance, Bummidge or Tommy Wilhelm were, but, through the circumstances of the contemporary world, are forced to lead three or four different lives the way Sammler was. Thus the demands made on their mental capacities to cope with this flood of events and perceptions increase proportionately. It leads to the near exclusion of action and real dialogue in favor of reflection and a steadily lessening desire for communication. The long stretches of almost audible quietness that pervades the room in which Sammler does most of his thinking may be indicative of Bellow's present inclination for the "nonfiction philosophical novel" as well as his modification of a literature courting silence.

Brigitte Scheer-Schäzler, *S. B.* (1972), pp. 127–28

I mention this limitation to suggest that Bellow's resources as a novelist, more impressive than ever, are not unlimited. But he is one of the important novelists because of the depth at which his options are made and his sense of the pressure they have to meet. This is what the novelist's integrity means, the measure of the scruple. If we think of *Herzog* as a severe examination of the modern orthodoxies in literature, the Wasteland myth and the arrogance of consciousness, we know at the same time that Bellow is not a smiling salesman selling toothpaste. His "positives" go no further than the propriety of silence, at this time; the illness is not miraculously cured. I would not ask him to go beyond this point. But *Herzog* is important because it reveals our whining orthodoxies for the shoddy things they are; and because it urges us to try again, and try harder. The book tells us that we are infatuated with our own illness, since we deem it the proof of our integrity. But health is better than illness, and *Herzog* points to at least one possibility.

Denis Donoghue, "Dangling Man," in Earl Rovit, ed., *S. B.: A Collection of Critical Essays* (1975), p. 26

BELS, Alberts

(pseud. of Jānis Cīrulis) Latvian novelist, short-story writer, and screenwriter, b. 6 Oct. 1938, County of Ropāži

As a child B. witnessed the radical changes brought about by World War II and his country's occupation by the Soviet Union. At the age of sixteen he moved to Moscow to begin training in the School of Circus Arts. The theme of circus life and its risks would become a recurrent motif in his short stories. His nickname at the school was "belka," or little squirrel—a term he would adopt as his pen name. An unfortunate fall in 1957 put an end to dreams of a circus career. B. then pursued a number of career possibilities before devoting himself exclusively to writing. Toward the end of the 1980s he became active in the political movement for independence, Latvijas Tautas Fronte, and from 1990 to 1993 he was a member of Latvijas Augstākā Padome (the National Council).

B.'s first collection of short stories, *Spēles ar nažiem* (1966; Games With Knives), contains eleven relatively short pieces, told in the first person, characterized by a free-flowing, light, and occasionally lyrical narrative. The best known of these works is "Karš bija jauks" (The War Was Lovely). Its tone marks a sharp contrast with conventions of the military genre in Soviet literature, which demanded monumental figures enthusiastically engaged in epic struggle and performing heroic deeds. The hero in B.'s story is a small boy who cannot accept that his father has been killed in war. This collection also inaugurated a thematic approach that would become a distinguishing trait of B.'s creativity: each story revolves around a particular theme and introduces a specific problem. In his novels, on the other hand, the moral, historical, or philosophical problems raised would acquire multiple layers and will branch out in unpredictable directions. B.'s first novel, *Izmeklētājs* (1967; The Investigator), has generally been appreciated for the impact its innovative treatment of form and character made on Latvian literature. According to Soviet literary standards of the 1940s and 1950s, it was deemed inappropriate to center a narrative on the human propensity for thinking about one's being. B. violates this principle by re-creating the interior monologue of a young sculptor who attempts to give shape to his dual role as sculptor and as investigator. B. also inaugurated another procedure that would become characteristic of his work—the conflation of time periods into one temporal dimension. The action of the novel spans a period of six hours within which are reviewed the events of the preceding days as well as the genealogy of the sculptor's family. These are retrospectives designed to deepen our understanding of the character's psychology; in later novels they become the most significant part of the novel's conceptual framework.

The subjective perspective of a consciousness is also at the center of B.'s next short-story collection *"Es pats" līdzenumā* (1968; "I Myself" on the Plain). The plain or open expanse of the title alludes to the human need for open space, for a place where one can be "oneself." Human existence is presented in terms of two

antithetical aspects: we see humans either as cogs of a bureaucratic or institutional mechanism or as independent entities able to assert their will. These are ideas that B. began to voice openly at this time, by raising the question of artistic freedom of expression. As a result, in 1969, having recently completed the novel, *Bezmiegs* (1987; Sleeplessness), he was accused of promoting anti-Soviet ideas. The novel had to wait almost twenty years to be published. The principal character of the novel is outwardly, apathetic—as are most of the heroes in B.'s novels of the 1960s and 1970s. The main action takes place in the thoughts and emotions of the characters. Critics have described the work as the "anatomy of an inert humanity" and as an essay on "the morality of the era of paralysis." It is an atmosphere that is re-created in *Melnā zīme* (1996; The Black Mark), a novel that evokes the author's frame of mind at the time he was writing *Bezmiegs*.

In *Saucēja balss* (1973; The Voice That Calls) B. turns to the past for his inspiration. The novel is based on a historical event taking place during the Revolution of 1905. Through metaphorical associations, B. interweaves the detailed descriptions of events with historical perspectives on Latvia and Russia at the beginning of the 20th c. and with meditations on such themes as freedom, betrayal, dishonor, and national identity. The narrative effectively combines a prosaic presentation of historical facts and statistical information with motifs taken from Latvian folklore and the Bible. The subject of *Cilvēki laivās* (1987; People in Boats) is once more the destiny of the Latvian people as it has unfolded over the centuries. Another related theme is the powerful relationship that binds an individual to his or her ethnic or national community. The story takes place in the 19th c., in a small village in Courland whose existence is threatened by the inexorable advance of a vast sand dune. In the course of the novel the dune becomes a multilayered symbol for all the principal themes that constitute the dramatic structure of the narrative: it stands for the flow of time, of history, for the might of nature, for state despotism, for the discord that tears communities apart, as well as for the self-destructive tendencies individuals harbor within themselves. Just as the dune swallows up the hamlet, history has devoured the once prosperous nation of the Courlanders. It is a work that made a significant contribution to the growing movement for independence in Latvia and opened the way for the author's subsequent political involvement.

The artistic quality and inspirational content of B.'s work have established him as one of Latvia's most prominent contemporary writers. His novels and short stories examine the fate of the Latvian people in the dual context of global transformations and of a temporal juncture marking the thematic intersection of historic retrospectives, present concerns, and future aspirations.

FURTHER WORKS: *Robeža* (1969); *Būris* (1972); *Uzbrukums slepenpolicijai. Mākslas filma* (1974); *Poligons* (1977); *Sainis* (1980); *Saknes* (1982); *Sāviens mežā. Mākslas filma* (1983); *Būris. Mākslas filma* (1993); *Slēptuve* (1986); *Sitiens ar teļādu* (1987); *Cilvēki pilsētās* (1988); *Cilvēki pārvērtībās* (1989); *Saulē mērktie* (1995)

BIBLIOGRAPHY: Lagzdiņš, V., "'Es pats' līdzenumā un citur," *Lauku Dzīve*, 7 (1974): 7-23; Priedītis, A., "A. B.," in Hausmanis, V., ed., *Mūsdienu latviešu padomju literatūra: 1960-1980* (1985): 187-98; Kronta, I., "Kā zemes lode griežas: A. B. prozas diviem gadu desmitiem cauri ejot," *Kritikas Gada Grāmata*, 16 (1988): 66-88; Treimane, I., "Cilvēki līdzenumos, būros, laivās . . . Parafrāze par A. Bela tēmu," *Grāmata*, 1 (1990): 47-51; Rožkalne, A., "A. B.," in Hausmanis, V., ed., *Latviešu rakstnieku portreti: 1970-1980* (1994): 7-20; Skujiņš, Z., *Jātnieks uz lodes* (1996): 153-66

—KARLIS RACEVSKIS

BELY, Andrey

(pseud. of Boris Nikolaevich Bugaev) Russian novelist, poet, and critic, b. 26 Oct. 1880, Moscow; d. 8 Jan. 1934, Moscow

B. was one of the foremost representatives of the "younger" generation of Russian symbolists, which included Alexandr BLOK and Vyacheslav IVANOV. Son of a prominent professor of mathematics, he received an excellent education in the natural sciences and was an avid student of the philosophy of Kant, Schopenhauer, and Nietzsche. As a youth he frequented the salon of his neighbor, M. S. Solovyov, where he absorbed the apocalyptic philosophy of Vladimir Solovyov (1853–1900). B. became the leader of the Moscow "Argonauts," a group of students interested in SYMBOLISM; after allying himself with Valery BRYUSOV he emerged as a major spokesman of symbolism and was actively engaged in the publication of the journal *Vesy* from 1903 to 1909. B. spent the years 1910–16 abroad, where he became an adept of anthroposophy under the personal tutelage of Rudolf Steiner (1861–1925). Recalled to Russia in 1916 because of World War I, he experienced terrible material deprivation and psychic suffering during the revolution and civil war. B. left for Berlin in 1921, only to return in 1923 to the Soviet Union, where he died in 1934.

B.'s early work is mostly in poetry and the "prose poem," the former represented by his three collections *Zoloto v lazuri* (1904; gold in azure), *Pepel* (1909; ashes) and *Urna* (1909; the urn), the latter by the four "symphonies" (1902, 1904, 1905, 1908). The first volume of poems is optimistic in tone, proclaiming, à la Solovyov, the imminent arrival of the "Divine Sophia"; the poems are couched in the imagery of the sunset, sustained by an elaborate symbolic network of colors, precious stones, and fabrics. The two later collections are darker in mood, voicing the painful awareness of the poet's failed dreams and the sufferings of Mother Russia. All three are innovative, utilizing fragmented lines and other typographical devices, sharp rhythmical and phonic effects, and daring metaphors. The "symphonies" are experiments in ornamental, lyrically oriented prose that exploit the techniques of musical structure, especially the repetition and counterpoint of leitmotifs that are characteristic of Wagnerian opera. They vary in content from symbolic fairy tales to contemporary mystical satire.

B.'s ultimate theme is the crisis of Western consciousness. The extreme conflict between the rational and irrational and the disruption of modern man's inner life, caused by the dominance of analytic thought, could be overcome, in B.'s view, only by an act of transcendence, whether on the cosmic or personal level. This theme emerges in astounding verbal embodiment in his three major works, the novels *Serebryany golub* (1909; *The Silver Dove*, 1974), *Peterburg* (first book ed., 1916; rev. ed., 1922; *Petersburg*, 1959, 1978) and *Kotik Letaev* (1917–18; first book ed., 1922; *Kotik Letaev*, 1971). All three exhibit a profound debt to the prose style of Gogol. Lyricism alternates with the grotesque, hyperbole and verbal punning abound, the narrative is sustained by rhythmic and intonational effects, and the author continually uses his narrator's eccentric slips in speech and logic to undermine the reader's sense

of reality. *Peterburg*, set in the imperial capital during the revolution of 1905, is B.'s masterpiece. It is the climax of the Petersburg theme in Russian literature (Pushkin, Gogol, Dostoevsky), which treats the city as the embodiment of the fantastic, of the duality between illusion and reality. *Kotik Letaev*, the autobiographical account of the growth of consciousness in a child, is the most anthroposophical of B.'s works.

B. the essayist was a prolific polemicist. His conception of symbolism was mystical and philosophical rather than aesthetic in emphasis, as is apparent in the collection *Simvolizm* (1910; symbolism). That volume also contains several studies of the Russian iambic tetrameter that blazed the trail for the scientific study of versification pursued later by the Russian FORMALISTS. The posthumously published *Masterstvo Gogolya* (1934; Gogol's craft) is a critical masterpiece, which remains to this day the best analysis of Gogol's style, composition, and symbolism. B.'s memoirs (1930–34) are essential documents for the history of Russian literature.

B.'s novels have entitled him to the label of the "Russian James Joyce." His reputation as one of the greatest Russian prose writers of the century is beyond challenge.

FURTHER WORKS: *Simfoniya, 2-ya, dramaticheskaya* (1902); *Severnaya simfoniya* (1904); *Vozvrat, 3-ya simfoniya* (1905); *Kubok meteley, 4-ya simfoniya* (1908); *Arabeski* (1911); *Pervoe svidanie* (1921; *The First Encounter*, 1979); *Posle razluki* (1922); *Vospominaniya ob A. A. B.* (2 vols., 1922); *Moskva* (2 vols., 1926); *Kreshchyony kitaets* (1927); *Ritm kak dialektika* (1929); *Na rubezhe dvukh stoletiy* (1930); *Mezhdu dvukh revolyutsiy* (1934); *Stikhotvoreniya i poemy* (1966). FURTHER WORKS IN ENGLISH: *Complete Short Stories* (1979); *Selected Essays of A. B.* (1985)

BIBLIOGRAPHY: Maslenikov, O., *The Frenzied Poets: A. B. and the Russian Symbolists* (1952); Honig, A., *A. B.s Romane* (1965); Elsworth, J., *A. B.* (1972); Cioran, S., *The Apocalyptic Symbolism of A. B.* (1973); special B.issue, *RusL*, new series 4, 4 (1976); Mochulsky, K., *A. B.* (1977); Janecek, G., ed., *A. B.: A Critical Review* (1978); Elsworth, J. D., *A. B.: A Critical Study of the Novels* (1983); Malmstad, J. E., ed., *A. B.: Spirit of Symbolism* (1987)

—STEPHEN RUDY

BEMBA, Sylvain

Congolese novelist, dramatist, and journalist (writing in French), b. 17 Feb. 1934, Sibiti; d. 8 July 1995, Paris

Columnist, broadcaster, and administrator, B. turned to fiction at least partly for political reasons. His country, Congo, is known both for its intense literary development and its active political life. The so-called "Les Trois Glorieuses"days of the 1963 revolution accelerated progressive activities and led to B. receiving a commission from the Movement of the Revolution to write one of his first plays, *Une eau dormante* (1973; dormant water). B.'s keen interest in political reform led to his arrest for his participation in the 1973 coup attempt, for which he received a three-year suspended sentence.

After first studying public administration, B. went to Strasbourg, France, to work on a degree in journalism before entering governmental service as an administrator. At about the same time, he began to write the articles and short stories for which he is known. In the 1950s he was one of the major contributors to the review *Liaison*, which played a major role in the flowering of Congolese and all of francophone African letters. From 1958 to 1961 he wrote a regular column for *Le Petit Journal de Brazzaville*. In 1963 his story "La chambre noire" (the dark room) won the Grand Prix de la Nouvelle Africaine. By the late 1960s B. had risen to director of the Agence Congolaise d'Information, from which he moved on to administer the radio and television stations of Brazzaville. In 1970 he became the director of information and in 1972 the director of cultural affairs of the Congo. In 1973 he had served one month as minister of information before his arrest.

Considered one of his country's most talented and hardworking writers, B. divided his time and energy between the theater and prose fiction. After publishing a number of plays in the 1970s and making a trip to the U.S. (a tour with other African writers sponsored by Crossroads Africa), which included participation in the 1979 African Literature Association meeting at Indiana University, he turned to the novel and produced four significant additions to African literature in the early 1980s, before turning back to the theater.

It was B.'s journalism and political interests that had propelled him into literature. Toward the end of his years as a newspaper columnist he strung together several columns into a dramatic narrative that led to experimentation with short didactic plays and the commission for *Une eau dormante*. These early short dramas, such as *L'enfer c'est Orféo* (1970; hell is Orpheus), *L'homme qui tua le crocodile* (1972; the man who killed the crocodile), and *Un foutu monde pour un blanchisseur trop honnête* (1977; a screwed-up world for a too-honest laundryman), were soon seen as "classics" of the new nation. B.'s early theater culminated in his most important drama to date, *Tarantelle noire et diable blanc* (1976; black tarantella and white devil), which analyzes Congolese history from 1890 to 1930 in three episodes and eleven scenes. *Tarantelle* is a Brechtian "morality play" that uses dramatic irony, distancing techniques, modern rhetorical figures, myth, the fantastic, and characters like the Sacred Tree/Men and Zombis to interpret the Congo's colonial heritage.

The central concern of *Rêves portatifs* (1979; portable dreams) is the relation of film to freedom. B. hangs all the diverse happenings on the story of a projectionist at the moment of independence, fictionalizing and interpreting the play of historical forces and figures in the first phases of national development. The projectionist, an African Every-man intoxicated with his power to project history and myth, is unable to comprehend the nefarious nature of Western mass culture imported into the Third World; he dreams his own film, or "cynical cinema," a "page from African history" (as seen through Hollywoodian lenses), a saga of cash, sex, and blood in the jungle. The forces of enlightenment sink under the weight of alienation, as native leaders equal the deserted colonizers in corruption. *Le soleil est parti à M'Pemba* (1982; the sun has left for M'Pemba), more unified and less baroque, uses a fantastic "phono-videograph" to tell the story of an extended family in a rapid rerun of recent African history, showing the transmutations from colonialism to independence in the transformations of psyches, identities, and family institutions.

Léopolis (1984; Leopolis), a short playful comic novel, B.'s most integrally structured, recounts the quest of a young black woman from Baltimore for the legendary African hero Febrice M'PFum. The detective romance, a fictionalized biography of Patrice Lumumba, seems to be an attempt to decode the inscrutable mask of the meteoric prime minister, using the means of the NEW NOVEL, scrambling realities and myths, reworking legends (Tarzan) and conventional interpretations to see Africa in a new light, or a new caricature, to take African culture out of the museum and into the political arena. Lumumba is humanized in the genial Fabrice, champion *joueur de dames*, who wins the African Trianon from the rich planter, only to see it dynamited in the ensuing revolution. But Fabrice/Lumumba emerges from the psychological hall of mirrors a new hero for our (African) times.

FURTHER WORKS: *Bio-bibliographie des écrivains congolais* (1979, with Leopold Mamonsono); *Les cargonautes* (1984); *Cinquante ans de musique du Congo-Zaire* (1984); *Profession avouée: sorcier de la famille* (1986); *Théâtre* (1989)

BIBLIOGRAPHY: Chemain, R., "Le théâtre militant: entretien avec S. B.," *Notre Librairie*, 38 (Sept. 1977): 87–93; Chemain, R., *Panorama critique de la littérature congolaise contemporaine* (1979); Ndzanga-Konga, A., "S. B.: Je suis un élève perpétuel, . . .," *Bingo*, 379 (1984): 25–27; Malanda, A., "L'œuvre de S. B.," *PA*, 130, 2 (1984): 93–117; Malanda, A., "Entretien avec S. B.," *Nouvelles du Sud*, 1 (1985): 127–35; Condé, M., "S. B.: Je suis un aventurier cérébral," *Africa*, 168 (1985): 59; Makhele, C., "S. B. ou le syndrôme du miroir brisé," *Notre Librairie*, 92–93 (Mar. 1988): 97–99; Wylie, H., "The Dancing Masks of S. B.," *WLT*, 64, 1 (Winter 1990): 20–24

—HAL WYLIE

BEMBA LITERATURE
See Zambian Literature

BENAVENTE, Jacinto
Spanish dramatist, b. 12 Aug. 1866, Madrid; d. 14 July 1954, Madrid

B., who wrote over 170 plays, had been interested in the theater since early childhood. His father was a famous pediatrician and a lover of Shakespeare, and B.'s interest in children's plays as well as his translations and adaptations of Shakespeare stem from this early influence. B. was also an actor. He became a member of the Royal Academy in 1912 and won the Nobel Prize for literature in 1922.

B. abandoned the moribund melodramatic tradition of *José Echegaray* (1832–1916) in his first successful drama, *El nido ajeno* (1894; another's nest), about a jealous husband. In the next dozen years he created over forty dramas in which he satirized the shortcomings of a series of character types, dissecting their hollow and hypocritical pretensions. He only occasionally portrayed characters whose virtue offsets the villainy of others. Among these studies of corrupt Spanish society are *La comida de las fieras* (1898; beasts' banquet), an attack on aristocrats, human vanity, and ingratitude; *Lo cursi* (1901; falsely elegant), an analysis of the traditional and the counterfeit modern; *La gobernadora* (1901) *The Governor's Wife*, 1918), a treatment of corrupt provincial politics; *La noche del sábado* (1903; *Saturday Night*, 1918), an allegory of good and evil and the meaning of reality; *El dragón del fuego* (1904; the fire dragon), a satire on imperialism; *Los malhechores del bien* (1905; *The Evil Doers of Good*, 1916), a study of religious hypocrisy and the meaning of true charity; and *La princesa Bebé* (1906; *Princess Bebé*, 1918), about the inhibiting force of a rigid traditionalism.

Twenty-five dramas written between 1907 and 1913 revealed B. as a versatile writer, more mature, confident, and compassionate than in his earlier work. In his masterpiece and most widely known play, *Los intereses creados* (1907; *The Bonds of Interest*, 1916), to which he wrote a sequel in 1916, *La ciudad alegre y confiada* (the merry, unsuspecting city), B. studies the selfish motives of humans. He portrays the heroes and antiheroes of society, the interrelationship of good and evil, and the possibility of overcoming this dualism of human nature through love. In *Señora ama* (1908; *A Lady*, 1924) B. attempted to analyze the Castilian soul. Like *Señora ama*, *La Malquerida* (1913; *The Passion Flower*, 1917) also has a rural setting. It is a psychological drama of hate and love between stepfather and stepdaughter. B. saw women not only as happy homemakers, symbols of spiritual regeneration and the redeeming power of love, but also as man's equal. These dramas display a pure and elegant style, intelligence, subtle philosophical touches, brilliant dialogue, and an assured theatrical sense and technique.

For the most part, his works after 1913 lacked the brilliance of his earlier plays; among the better ones of this later period are *La vestal de Occidente* (1919; the vestal virgin of the West), a study of Queen Elizabeth I and her love for Essex; *La noche iluminada* (1927; illuminated night), inspired by Shakespeare; *Pepa Doncel* (1928; Pepa Doncel), a psychological study of social climbers; *Para el cielo y los altares* (1928; for heaven and altars), expressing anticlerical sentiments; and *La infanzona* (1945; the noblewoman), about incest. While B. also experimented with writing allegorical, fantastic, SYMBOLIST, and even SURREALISTIC plays he never abandoned his fervent patriotism and continued to express his concern for social reform and the poor in his work.

Critics linked B. to Ibsen, a comparison he rejected, and to Molière. Introducing an ingenious drama into Spain, which shattered traditional molds, B. exposed society's defects but hoped for a better world, in which charity and justice might triumph and in which man might satisfy his idealistic yearnings and gain dominion over his own soul.

FURTHER WORKS: *Teatro fantástico* (1892); *Cartas de mujeres* (1893); *Versos* (1893); *Vilanos* (1893); *Gente conocida* (1896); *Figulinas* (1898); *Sacrificios* (1901); *El hombrecito* (1903); *No fumadores* (1904; *No Smoking*, 1917); *Rosas de otoño* (1905; *Autumnal Roses*, 1919); *La fuerza bruta* (1908; *Brute Force*, 1935); *El marido de su viuda* (1908; *His Widow's Husband*, 1917); *Ganarse la vida* (1909); *La escuela de las princesas* (1909; *The School of Princesses*, 1924); *El príncipe que todo lo aprendió en los libros* (1909; *The Prince Who Learned Everything out of Books*, 1918); *El criado de don Juan* (1911; *Don Juan's Servant*, 1957); *Teatro* (35 vols., 1922 ff.); *La verdad* (1915; *The Truth*, 1923); *Lecciones de amor* (1924); *La moral del divorcio* (1932); *La novia de nieve* (1934); *Cualquiera lo sabe* (1935); *La honradez de la cerradura* (1942; *The Secret of the Keyhole*, 1957); *Obras completas* (11 vols., 1942–46); *Nieve en mayo* (1945); *El alfiler en la boca* (1953). FURTHER WORKS IN ENGLISH: *Plays by J. B.* (4 vols., 1917–24)

BIBLIOGRAPHY: Starkie, W., *J. B.* (1924); Vila Selma, J., *El teatro de B., fin de siglo* (1952); Sánchez Estevan, I., *J. B. y su teatro* (1954); Schwartz, K., "Shakespeare's Influence on B.'s Plays,"

SCB, 20 (1960): 35–38; Lázaro, A., *Vida y obra de B.* (1964); Peñuelas, M. C., *J. B.* (1968); Dial, J. E., "B.: The Dramatist on Stage," *REH*, 8 (1974): 211–18; Sheehan, R. L., *B. and the Spanish Panorama*: 1894–1954 (1976)

—KESSEL SCHWARTZ

BENEDETTI, Mario

Uruguayan novelist, short-story writer, dramatist, and critic, b. 14 Sept. 1920, Paso de los Toros

Born of parents of Italian ancestry, B. was educated in Montevideo and at the age of twenty-five began an active career as a journalist, writer of fiction, and critic, sometimes using the pseudonyms Damocles and Orlando Fino. He is one of Uruguay's most popular writers and a frequent contributor to leftist journals published in Uruguay, Cuba, and other Latin American countries.

B. is best known for his fiction examining the workings of bureaucracy in Montevideo. His protagonists usually are middle-class office workers caught up in the routine pattern of their lives. *Esta mañana* (1949; this morning) and *Montevideanos* (1959; people of Montevideo) are his most important collections of short stories. Both reveal the authenticity of his characters' struggle aginst the faceless, lethargic government of a welfare state.

Quién de nosotros (1953; who among us), B.'s first novel, relates the same story from three different attitudes and points of view, leaving unanswered the three narrators' search for reality. *La tregua* (1960; *The Truce*, 1969) is concerned with the fleeting promise of fulfillment faced by an office worker as retirement approaches. Written in diary form, *La tregua* leaves the protagonist with a sense of void at the death of his young lover. *Gracias por el fuego* (1965; thanks for the light) is one of B.'s most complex and longest novels. Its theme, the gradual transformation of love into hatred between a father and his son, is to be viewed on a broader plane as a social and political conflict between generations. This novel is in many respects a representation of B.'s increasingly leftist opposition to the staid middle-class society so carefully studied in his earlier fiction.

While much of B.'s work as a critic is to be found in such journals as *Marcha, Número*, and *Casa de las Américas*, his *Literatura uruguaya siglo XX* (1963; twentieth-century Uruguayan literature) is widely recognized as one of the most serious studies of Uruguay's contemporary writers.

In 1973, when a period of dictatorship broke what had been a democratic tradition in Uruguayan politics, B. was forced into exile and lived successively in Argentina, Peru, Cuba, and Spain. Such works as *El escritor latinoamerican y la revolución posible* (1974; The Latin American writer and the possible revolution), *Con y sin nostalgia* (1977; With and without nostalgia), *Viento del exilio* (1981; Wind from exile), and *El olvido está lleno de memoria* (1995; Oblivion is full of memory) mark this oppressive period in Uruguay's history. Since 1985 he has spent part of each year in Montevideo and the rest in Madrid.

B.'s ability to take nondescript, urban protagonists and elevate their seemingly insignificant struggles to the level of serious literary concern, as well as his penetrating analysis of national political and literary trends, has made him one of his country's leading contemporary writers.

FURTHER WORKS: *La víspera indeleble* (1945); *Peripecia y novela* (1948); *Sólo mientras tanto* (1950); *Marcel Proust y otros ensayos* (1951); *Elúltimo viaje y otros cuentos* (1951); *Usted por ejemplo* (1953); *Poemas de la oficina* (1956); *El reportaje* (1958); *El país de la cola de paja* (1960); *Poemas del hoyporhoy* (1961); *Mejor es meneallo* (1961); *Ida y vuelta* (1963); *Inventario* (1963); *Narradores rumanos* (1965); *Genio y figura de José Enrique Rodó* (1966); *Contra los puentes levadizos* (1966); *Antología natural* (1967); *Esta mañana y otros cuentos* (1967); *Datos para el viudo* (1967); *Letras del continente mestizo* (1967); *A ras de sueño* (1967); *La muerte y otras sorpresas* (1968); *Sobre artes y oficios* (1968); *Dos comedias* (1968); *Cuaderno cubano* (1969); *Cuentos completos* (1970); *El cumpleaños de Juan Ángel* (1971); *Crítica cómplice* (1971); *Crónicas del 71* (1972); *Letras de emergencia* (1973); *Daniel Viglietti/M.B.* (1974); *El escritor latinoamericano y la revolución posible* (1974); *Hasta aquí* (1975); *Poemas de otros* (1975); *La casa y el ladrillo* (1976); *Con y sin nostalgia* (1977)

BIBLIOGRAPHY: Englekirk, J., and M. Romos, *La narrativa uruguaya* (1967): 121–23; Fernández Retamar, R., "La obra novelística de M. B.," *Universidad de la Habana*, 195 (1972): 111–21; Fernandez, O., *M. B.: Four Stories, Four Styles* (1974); Brushwood, J., *The Spanish American Novel: A Twentieth-Century Survey* (1975); Beberfall, F. P., *Thematic Continuity and Changing Emphases in the Work of M. B.* (1975); Castro, N., "La moral de los hechos aclara su palabra," *Casa de las Américas*, 15 (1975): 78–98; Bollo, S., *Literatura uruguaya* (1976): 308: 321–22, 327; Lewis, B., *The Political Act in M. B.'s "Con y sin nostalgia"* (1980); Tisnado, C., *Treatment of Silence and Discourse in M. B.'s Short Stories* (1994); Collins, D. A., *Four Themes in the Poetry of M. B.* (1994)

—HARLEY D. OBERHELMAN

BENET, Juan

Spanish novelist, short-story writer, and essayist, b. 7 Oct. 1927, Madrid; d. 5 Jan. 1993, Madrid

B. studied at the School of Engineering in Madrid and was a successful civil engineer long before he won recognition as a writer. However, his work building roads and dams is crucial to the formation of his fiction, since his long stays in isolated portions of northern Spain provided him with material for the physical and psychological backdrop of Región, the mythical area in which much of his fiction takes place. Apart from his focus on engineering, B. was also deeply immersed as a youth in the literary milieu of Madrid. He attended the literary *tertulia* of novelist Pío BAROJA in the 1940s and in 1953 participated in the important literary magazine *Revista Española*. Also during this period, B. read the complete works of William FAULKNER, the writer who would exert the most direct influence on his style, technique, and thematic concerns of time, war, and decay.

Volverás a Región (1967; *Return to Región*, 1975), the first of B.'s "Región" cycle of novels, is an important work in the development of postwar Spanish fiction. It represents a radical break with the norms of SOCIAL REALISM that characterize the major Spanish narrative of the 1950s and 1960s, and it has a marked influence on the young generation of novelists beginning to write near the end of the Franco regime. The novel explores the decay of the fictional Región (similar to Faulkner's Yoknapatawpha

County) during the 20th c. and is structured by the memories of its two principal characters, Dr. Sebastian and Marré Gamallo. Most importantly, *Volverás a Región* offers a compendium of traits that form the cornerstone of much of B.'s fiction: the themes of ruin and decay, a concern for history and the way in which it is narrated, the destructive flow of time, and a sense of the world as profoundly enigmatic and inexplicable. B.'s style and technique in the novel likewise reveal the principal characteristics of his future narrative. His sentences are frequently the length of full pages, and are replete with complex obtrusions, parentheses, ambiguous interpolations, and shifts in narrative perspective.

B.'s next two Región novels, *Una meditación* (1970; *A Meditation*, 1982) and *Un viaje de invierno* (1972; a winter's journey), won the author wide acclaim as one of Spain's most distinguished and complex novelists. Written in the first person, *Una meditación* is indeed a meditation by the narrator on the past. Using a Proustian memory and Faulknerian style, the narrator scrutinizes the period from 1920 to 1970 in an attempt to recover and understand the nature of his family, his friends, and the meaning of his life in the vicinity of Región. *Viaje* is more abstract than B.'s previous fiction (its characters are mere apparitions moving through a fatalistic winter's journey toward death), but the same labyrinthine style, accompanied by digressions placed in the margins of the text, make the novel one of B.'s most difficult to read.

B.'s fiction since *Un viaje de invierno* has both continued the author's exploration of Región and expanded into other areas. His best-selling *El aire de un crimen* (1980; the air of a crime), though set in Región, is a detective novel that appropriates and subverts traditional norms associated with the genre. In *En la penumbra* (1989; in the penumbra) B. moves outside Región to represent the meditations of two women on their lives as they await their mysterious destiny.

It remains in Región, however, where B.'s most important writing lies. *Saúl ante Samuel* (1980; Saul in the presence of Samuel) continues the author's saga of the civil war in Región. B. pursues fully in this novel the tragic consequences of the war. He urges that we understand the irredemptive destruction of the conflict and affirms that humankind's fall into despair cannot be prevented.

In his most recent trilogy of Región and the civil war, *Herrumbrosas lanzas* (1983—1986; rusty lances), B. probes the origin of the conflict in the 19th c. and lays out battle strategies in highly detailed fashion. Although the style and technique of the novels appear to shed much of their surface complexity, they assert a structural and ideological foundation similar to the most abstruse of B.'s earlier fiction: enigma as narrative determinant, the aporias of time as the core of ambiguity, and the essential contingency of all narration as the mediator of reality and truth.

As an essayist and literary theorist B. has written on a wide range of topics from a variety of perspectives. He is most frequently concerned with language and the epistemological questions raised by narrative discourse: how words mean; the grasping together of language to constitute narration; the uniqueness of a literary work outside of social and historical determinants. In *La inspiración y el estilo* (1965; inspiration and style) B. probes the way in which the use of language determines not only how writers write, but also what they write, and he explores as well the theoretical question of how language lends permanence to a literary work. In *El ángel del Señor abandona a Tobías* (1976; the angel of the Lord abandons Tobit) B. compares the narrative techniques of prose and painting and explores how they frame the reader's understanding of a text. In a lengthy segment in *Tobías* he attacks linguistic study and the obsession for developing a science of language in the face of the essential indeterminacy and ambiguity of how words mean.

B. has clearly emerged in the past two decades as one of Spain's most important novelists. His commingling of a complex prose style with a vision of despair and decay in modern Spain makes his fiction both sophisticated as literature and incisive as sociohistoric commentary. His novels have at times been criticized as too difficult and as resisting all modes of interpretive closure. In B.'s view, however, full coherence, the absence of enigma, and resolution of the problematic would make the world, as well as literature, a much impoverished place to explore.

FURTHER WORKS: *Nunca llegarás a nada* (1961); *Puerta de tierra* (1970); *Teatro* (1970); *Una tumba* (1971); *5 narraciones y 2 fábulas* (1972); *La otra casa de Mazón* (1973); *Sub rosa* (1973); *En ciernes* (1976); *¿Qué fue la guerra civil?* (1976); *Cuentos completos* (2 vols., 1977); *En el estado* (1977); *Del pozo y del Numa* (1978); *Trece fábulas y media* (1981); *Una tumba y otros relatos* (1981); *La moviola de Eurípides* (1982); *Otoño en Madrid hacia 1950* (1987); *Londres* (1989)

BIBLIOGRAPHY: Herzberger, D. K., *The Novelistic World of J. B.* (1976); Summerhill, S. J., "Prohibition and Transgression in Two Novels of J. B.,"*The American Hispanist*, 4, 36 (May 1979): 20–24; Cabrera, V., *J. B.* (1983); Compitello, M. A., *Ordering the Evidence: "Volverás a Región" and Civil War Fiction* (1983); Manteiga, R., et al., eds., *Critical Approaches to the Writings of J. B.* (1984); Herzberger, D. K., "Numa and the Nature of the Fantastic in the Fiction of J. B.," *StTCL*, 8, 2 (Spring 1984): 185–96; Vernon, K., ed., *J. B.* (1986); Margenot, J. B., "Cartography in the Fiction of *J. B.*," *Letras Peninsulares*, 1, 3 (Winter 1988): 331–43

—DAVID K. HERZBERGER

BENÉT, Stephen Vincent

American poet, short-story writer, novelist, and essayist, b. 22 July 1898, Bethlehem, Pa.; d. 13 March 1943, New York, N.Y.

Reared in a regular-army family, son of a colonel who served as commanding officer of ordnance posts in California and Georgia, B. grew up in an uncommonly humane, disciplined, and adaptable household in which literature was enjoyed and created. In 1915 B. followed his brother to Yale, and during the fall term B.'s first volume of verse, *Five Men and Pompey*, was published. Elected to the editorial board of *Yale Literary Magazine* in 1916, he assumed the chair of the board two years later. Yale bestowed an honorary degree on B. in 1937.

Five Men and Pompey, a series of dramatic monologues, shows the romantic influence of William Morris as well as the influence of modern realism. *Young Adventure* (1918), *Heavens and Earth* (1920), and *Tiger Joy* (1925), collections of ballads that acknowledge implicitly the influences of Keats and Shelley, reveal a technical versatility and a preoccupation with American matters of a realistic character that were to flourish and to sustain B. in later work.

During the 1920s B. wrote four novels, *The Beginning of Wisdom* (1921)—predictably autobiographical—followed by *Young People's Pride* (1922), *Jean Huguenot* (1923), and *Spanish Bayonet* (1926), a historical novel about the 18th-c. Florida of B.'s Minorcan ancestors, which is the most significant work of the group. The best of B.'s novels, however, is usually considered to be *James Shore's Daughter* (1934). Turning again with confidence in this novel to American historical subjects, B. wrote about wealth (James Shore is a western copper magnate) and the problems of mastering this wealth, of the power that came with the closing of the frontier, and of the weight of responsibility that comes with such wealth and freedom.

While on a Guggenheim fellowship in Paris, B. wrote *John Brown's Body* (1928), undoubtedly his most significant artistic achievement, which won him the Pulitzer Prize in poetry. It is an epic poem about the Civil War from the raid on Harper's Ferry to General Lee's surrender at Appomattox Court House. B. successfully interweaves the stories of historical and fictional figures to produce a richly textured account of the war, its causes and costs, and the range and depth of its impact on the country. In this poem B.'s characterizations are sure, and the metrical versatility of his early verse comes to maturity. B.'s epic is respected, moreover, by many historians for its sense of history, its accuracy, and its unusually perceptive insights into the personalities of the historical figures portrayed.

As a prolific author of formula short stories, which he wrote often under pressure to pay bills, B. is best known for "The Devil and Daniel Webster," which won the O. Henry Memorial Prize in 1936, and for "Freedom's a Hard-Bought Thing," which won the same prize in 1940. In 1939 the American Lyric Theatre produced an operetta, *The Devil and Daniel Webster*, with libretto by B. and music by Douglas Moore.

With the onset of World War II, B. enlisted his talents as essayist in the service of the Office of War Information, and, despite degenerating health, he wrote prodigiously until his death. Just before he died, B. wrote *America* (1944) for the OWI; it is a short history which attempts to define the "American idea," which was very widely translated and distributed by American agencies in Europe.

At his death, B. left the first part of *Western Star* (1943), a planned ten-part epic poem dealing with the history of America, which reflected Frederick Jackson Turner's thesis that the frontier was the dominant force in American history. Like *John Brown's Body*, *Western Star* was carefully researched, and the surviving fragment promises a poem that would certainly have rivaled the earlier epic. Published posthumously, *Western Star* won the 1944 Pulitzer Prize for poetry.

B.'s position in American literature is modest but secure. Unpretentiously dedicated to American themes and history, he was a national writer, who bears comparison to larger figures of the same stamp such as Emerson and Whitman. His versatility and humility as an artist made his work appealing to mass audiences and intellectuals alike. For *John Brown's Body*, for *James Shore's Daughter*, for a dozen exceptional short stories, for demanding service as a writer during World War II, and for what we have of *Western Star*, America stands indebted to B.

FURTHER WORKS: *The Drug Shop; or, Endymion in Edmonstown* (1971); *The Ballad of William Sycamore* (1923); *King David* (1923); *The Headless Horseman* (1927); *The Barefoot Saint* (1929);

The Litter of the Rose Leaves (1930); *Ballads and Poems, 1915–1930* (1931); *A Book of Americans* (1933, with R. C. Benét); *Burning City* (1936); *Thirteen O'Clock* (1937); *Johnny Pye and the Fool-Killer* (1938); *Ballad of the Duke's Mercy* (1939); *Nightmare at Noon* (1940); *A Child Is Born: A Modern Drama of the Nativity* (1942); *Dear Adolf* (1942); *Selected Works* (2 vols., 1942); *They Burned the Books* (1942); *Twenty-Five Short Stories* (1943); *We Stand United, and Other Radio Scripts* (1945); *The Last Circle* (1946); *Selected Letters of S. V. B.* (1960); *S. V. B. on Writing* (1964)

BIBLIOGRAPHY: Bacon, L., et al, "As We Remember Him," *SatR*, 27 March 1943: 7–11; Fenton, C. A., *S. V. B.: The Life and Times of an American Man of Letters, 1898–1943* (1958); Stroud, P., *S. V. B.* (1963)

—ARTHUR B. COFFIN

BENGALI LITERATURE
See Bangladeshi Literature and Indian Literature

BENGTSSON, Frans G(unnar)

Swedish essayist, novelist, and poet, b. 4 Oct. 1894, Rössjöholm; d. 19 Dec. 1954, Stockholm

The son of the manager of an estate in Skåne, B. matriculated at the University of Lund in 1912, receiving degrees much later. While living in Lund, he read extensively and developed skill as an extemporaneous speaker and chess player.

B. is a highly anachronistic figure in 20th-c. Swedish literature. A skeptical pessimist on guard against all forms of modernity, B. made his debut as a learned and accomplished poet, successfully reviving such time-worn verse forms as the canzone and the sonnet in *Tärningkast* (1923; throw of the dice) and *Legenden om Babel* (1925; the legend of Babel).

As a prose stylist, however, B. made a lasting mark on his nation's literature in a series of essay collections, among which *Litteratörer och militärer* (1929; literary and military men), *Silversköldarna* (1931; the silver shields), and *De långhåriga merovingerna* (1933; the longhaired Merovingians) contain his finest work. B.'s subject is typically men of action such as François Villon, Oliver Cromwell, or Napoleon; his tone is, by turn, objective and ironic.

B.'s obsession with the man of destiny can be clearly perceived in his monumental biography *Karl XII:s levnad* (2 vols., 1935–36; *The Sword Does Not Jest: The Heroic Life of King Charles XII of Sweden*, 1960). Eschewing all psychological speculation, B. creates an epic character who is admirable for his simplicity but who is, however, somewhat obscured by the mass of details that the author presents.

More readable—and far more popular—is B.'s two-volume novel *Röde Orm* (1941, 1945; *The Long Ships: A Saga of the Viking Age*, 1954). Using a narrative technique derived from the Icelandic sagas, B. depicts his characters largely on the basis of their actions and the words they speak rather than on their thoughts and feelings.

Stephen Vincent Benét

Flavored with B.'s burlesque humor and finely honed irony, it is an enormously entertaining work written with great spirit and an unerring instinct for the dramatic event. Stylistically, however, the novel's blending of "Icelandic" sobriety and B.'s own irrepressible zest is less than successful.

B.'s youthful skepticism in dealing with 20th-c. cultural and socioeconomic conditions hardened over the years into the predictable aversion of a weary reactionary, as too many pages in his volume of memoirs *Den lustgård som jag minns* (1953; the pleasure garden I remember) indicate. His essays on historical subjects remain the high-water mark of this brilliant prose stylist.

FURTHER WORKS: *Sällskap för en eremit* (1938); *För nöjes skull* (1947); *Samlade skrifter* (10 vols., 1950–55); *Folk som sjöng* (1955); *Inför kvinnan ställd* (1964). FURTHER WORKS IN ENGLISH: *A Walk to an Ant Hill, and Other Essays*, 1951

BIBLIOGRAPHY: Hunter, R. A., on *The Long Ships, ASR*, 43 (1955): 89–90; Gustafson, W. W., on *The Long Ships, SS*, 27 (1955): 115–17; Thompson, L. S., "*F. G. B., 1894–1954*," *KFLQ*, 2 (1955): 75–79; Sullivan, R. E., on *The Sword Does Not Jest, SPHQ*, 11, 4 (1960): 162–64; Lindahl, M., on *The Sword Does Not Jest, SatR*, 17 Dec. 1960: 25; Leach, H. G., on *The Sword Does Not Jest, ASR*, 49 (1961): 86; Gustafson, A., *A History of Swedish Literature* (1961): 529–32

—RAYMOND JARVI

BENINIAN LITERATURE

The written literature of the People's Republic of Benin (known as Dahomey until 1975) had its beginnings in the late 1920s. This small West African state became a French colony early in the 20th c., and writing by Beninians has been almost exclusively in the language of the colonizer. Over the years, Benin acquired the nickname of the "Latin Quarter" of French Africa, referring to its relatively large and active group of intellectuals, many of whom filled administrative positions throughout France's African colonial empire until independence in 1960; this may explain Benin's rather early start in the realm of creative literature in a non-African language.

Indeed, only four years after the publication in Senegal of the first French-African novel, Félix Couchoro (1900–1968), a Beninian writer later identified with Togo, published *L'esclave* (1929; the slave), the first of his many popular regional novels dealing with love, adventure, and the social problems of the coastal populations of Dahomey and Togo. Set in an earlier and more glorious time, the historical novel *Doguicimi* (1938; Doguicimi), by the teacher and scholar Paul Hazoumé (b. 1890), is one of the outstanding Francophone works of the pre-World War II era. Relating the tragic adventures of Doguicimi, a princess of the 19th-c. kingdom of Dahomey, this engrossing novel has the additional merit of being a storehouse of cultural information on one of the last of the great precolonial African kingdoms. Hazoumé is thus important as a pioneer in the revival of interest among African writers in their traditional cultures, a prominent feature of the NÉGRITUDE movement.

It was during this prewar period in the realm of drama, as well, that Beninians were involved in early literary activity, for the genesis of African theater in French may be traced back to the plays written and performed by students of the William Ponty School, a colonial training college in Senegal. The first of these plays, all of which deal with the African past or traditional life, was *La dernière entrevue de Behanzin et de Bayol* (first performance Gorée, Senegal, 1933; the last conversation between Benhanzin and Bayol). Beninian students of the college wrote and produced at least three more plays during this period, one of which was performed in Paris in 1937.

The postwar years, so fertile for the novel elsewhere in Africa, have thus far produced only one true novelist in Benin, Olympe Bhêly-Quénum (b. 1928). Eschewing the theme of culture conflict poetically treated in his *Le chant du lac* (1965; the song of the lake), he pessimistically explores the absurdity of existence in his best-known novel, *Un piège sans fin* (1960; Snares without End, 1981). *Liaison d'un été* (1968; a summer liaison) is a short-story collection of uneven quality.

Sharing recognition with Bhêly-Quénum beyond Benin's borders is Jean Pliya (b. 1931)—both have won literary prizes—who, in addition to an engaging collection of short stories, *L'arbre fétiche* (1974; the fetish tree), is known for two plays: *Kondo, le requin* (1969; Kondo the shark) deals with King Benhanzin's resistance to the French, while the satiric *La secrétaire particulière* (1973; the private secretary), echoing a new theme in African writing since independence, turns from history, traditional life, and confrontation with the West to criticism of the corruption of the new elite that has replaced the colonizer.

Among Benin's major poets, Paulin Joachim (b. 1931) and Richard Dogbeh (sometimes Dogbeh-David; b. 1932) have earned recognition, the latter for his collection *Cap Liberté* (1969; Cape Liberty), the former especially for his *Anti-grâce* (1967; anti-grace). Both are "humanists," singing compassionately of their people, eloquently evoking their anger and despair but also their fervent hope of future liberation. Eustache Prudencio (b. 1924) and Agbossahessou (dates n.a.) certainly deserve mention, as does Émile Ologoudou (b. 1935), an extremely promising poet whose work has appeared thus far only in periodicals or anthologies.

Note must finally be taken of two essayists whose books, although not classifiable as creative literature, have had wide circulation and influence, embodying as they do two principal currents of pre- and postindependence African thinking. (Many of the writers already mentioned have also published in such diverse fields as literary criticism, politics, education, religion, and ethnography.) The first, Albert Tevoedjre (b. 1929), roundly condemns Western colonialism in Africa in his much discussed *L'Afrique révoltée* (1958; Africa in revolt), while Stanislas Spéro Adotevi's (b. 1934) *Négritude et négrologues* (1972; Négritude and negrologists) is an impassioned and scathing attack on Négritude as a smoke screen for neocolonialism.

Written literary activity in African languages has been very slight until recently. Since 1975, however, an effort has been made in their promotion, and a few school texts of tales from the oral tradition in Fon and other national languages have appeared. If this trend continues, a parallel literature in these tongues could, with time, become a reality.

BIBLIOGRAPHY: Herskovits, M. J., *Dahomean Narrative* (1958); Anozie, S. O., *Sociologie du roman africain* (1970): 160–66; Jahn, J., and P. D. Dressler, *Bibliography of Creative African Writing* (1971), p. 397; Herdeck, D. E., *African Authors* (1973); Wauthier, C., *The Literature and Thought of Modern Africa*, 2nd ed. (1979); Baratte-Eno Belinga, T., et al., *Bibliographie des auteurs africains de langue française*, 4th ed. (1979): 21–29

—FREDRIC MICHELMAN

BENJÁMIN, László

Hungarian poet, b. 15 Dec. 1915, Budapest

The son of a petit-bourgeois family, B. was forced to drop out of secondary school at fifteen for financial reasons. Until the end of World War II he held jobs as textile worker, iron worker, printer, furrier, and factory clerk. After the war he became a journalist and later editor of various literary magazines. At present, he is librarian of the Budapest City Library. For his poetry, he was twice awarded the Kossuth Prize.

B. is the poet *engagé* par excellence, and thus is in the mainstream of Hungarian literary tradition, viewing himself, even in an early poem, as the descendant of the 19th-c. romantic-populists Mihály Vörösmarty (1800–1855) and Sándor Petőfi (1823–1849). B.'s identification with the working classes and their struggles is firmly anchored in his early experiences. His first poems, published in the Social Democratic daily *Népszava* and in the influential magazine of the intellectual left, *Szép Szó*, reveal his commitment to the working man. His first book of poems, *A csillag nem jött* (1939; the star did not come), further affirms B.'s dedication to the cause of the "oppressed." He is a humanist, a satirist, a moralist, with an excellent sense of humor and a mastery of form and language—characteristics that have remained the trademark of B.'s poetry ever since.

A leftist but never a radical, B. joined the Communist Party in 1948, only after a long period of hesitation and doubts. During the years of political and literary oppression, B.'s poetry remained largely free from dogma and slogans, displaying his sincerity and his commitment to dealing with the human aspects of the "socialist transformation of society." In books like *Örökké élni* (1949, to live forever) and *Tűzzel, késsel* (1951, with fire and knife) his optimistic belief in the progress of socialism is expressed in dithyrambic odes and epic narratives. With official recognition, however, came official displeasure. B. was criticized for having abandoned "socialist consciousness" and for having turned toward the problems of the "isolated individual."

B.'s poetry reached new heights during the years between Stalin's death and the outbreak of the Hungarian uprising in 1956. His fury and disillusionment is distilled in sparse, bitter, powerful poems attacking both the perpetrators of crimes against the people and his own gullibility and naïveté. He became one of the leaders of the intellectual revolt against the Stalinist bureaucracy. After the defeat of the uprising, he withdrew into virtual seclusion for years. He started writing and publishing again in the mid-1960s, reaffirming his commitment to the "community and the nation" but never forgetting the experiences of the Stalinist years.

The progressive content of B.'s poetry is cast in a conservative form. A brilliant master of the language, he is not an experimenter with form, and his originality and power lie in surprising turns, rhymes, and flashes of language, which reveal new meanings and relationships. Although not a very prolific poet, B. is nonetheless one of the most significant masters of contemporary socialist poetry in Hungary.

FURTHER WORKS: *Tollal és szerszámmal* (1941); *A betüöntők diadala* (1946); *A teremtés után* (1948); *Éveink mulása* (1954); *Egyetlen élet* (1956); *Ötödik évszak* (1962); *Világ füstje* (1964); *Sziklarajzok* (1972)

BIBLIOGRAPHY: Klaniczay, T., J. Szauder, and M. Szabolcsi, *History of Hungarian Literature* (1964): 325–27; Erdei, F., *Information Hungary* (1968): 798–801; Texla, A., *Hungarian Authors: A Bio-bibliographical Handbook* (1970): 689

—TAMAS ACZEL

BENJAMIN, Walter

(pseuds.: Detlev Holz, K. A. Stampflinger) German cultural critic and essayist, b. 15 July 1892, Berlin; d. 27 Sept. 1940, Port Bou, Spain

Son of upper-middle-class Jewish parents (his father was an art dealer, antiquarian, and investor), B. had an excellent, progressive education. He studied in Berlin, Freiburg, and Munich, and, avoiding service during World War I, completed his doctorate summa cum laude in Bern in 1919 with the dissertation *Der Begriff der Kunstkritik in der deutschen Romantik* (1920; the concept of art criticism in German romanticism). In 1915 B. met Gershom Scholem (b. 1897), who was to distinguish himself as a scholar of the Jewish mystical tradition; Scholem became B.'s closest friend

and later his biographer. Although Scholem left for Palestine in 1923, he continued to have an important impact on B.

In 1920 B. returned to Berlin because of financial difficulties caused by inflation in Germany, and during the 1920s he produced translations, critical works, and reviews. In 1924 B. met the Latvian actress Asja Lacis, who along with Bertolt BRECHT, to whom she introduced B., provided a substantial impetus to B.'s taking up Marxist thought. B. had earlier met two other important figures in the revitalization of Marxist discussion in the 20th c.: Ernst Bloch (1885–1977) and Georg LUKÁCS. Although he soon repudiated his own analysis found there, the early Lukács, in *History and Class Consciousness*, proved influential in B.'s ultimate incorporation of Jewish, Hegelian, and Marxist thinking into his own cultural analyses. During 1924 B. had been working on *Der Ursprung des deutschen Trauerspiels* (1928; *The Origin of German Tragic Drama*, 1977), which he submitted in 1925 as a required part of an application for a teaching position at the University of Frankfurt. The faculty, involved in intrigues and unable to recognize the profundity of the treatise, was intent on turning down his application, and B. withdrew his study from consideration. After accepting a fellowship arranged through Gershom Scholem to study Hebrew in preparation for a teaching position in Jerusalem, B. wrote Scholem in 1930 that he had decided to remain in Germany, outside academia, and to become Germany's foremost literary critic. As early as 1929 B. had begun a closer collaboration with Brecht, and he engaged with some success in a "consciousness-raising" of the German intelligentsia through newspaper essays and critiques.

With the rise of Hitler to power, B. went into exile in March 1933, first in Paris and with extended stays during the 1930s with Brecht in Denmark, on Ibiza, and elsewhere. During this period a few articles were published in Germany under the pseudonyms Detlev Holz and K. A. Stampflinger. In 1935 B. became officially associated in Paris with the Institute for Social Research (the earlier "Frankfurt School," whose headquarters had already been moved to New York), which paid him a regular stipend and published a number of his studies. He had developed a friendship with Theodor ADORNO of the Institute, whom he had first met in 1923. With the outbreak of the war in 1939, B. was interned for a time in a camp for foreign (German) refugees in Nièvre; he returned to Paris, obtained a visa to enter the U.S., picked it up in Marseille, and crossed the border into Port Bou, Spain, intending to go through Spain and embark from Lisbon to America. In Port Bou, threatened by a local functionary (in a blackmail attempt) with being returned to French authorities, who would turn him and his fellow exiles over to the Gestapo, B. took an immense dose of morphine, feigned natural sickness, refused full medical assistance, and died; his companions were permitted to proceed through Spain to Lisbon.

"The last of the Europeans" in his own estimation, "the last intellectual" in Susan SONTAG's, B. appeals in his analyses of culture to a wide range of sensibilities—to the more aesthetic or conservative approaches to the arts and literature as well as to the more modern, STRUCTURALIST, and the more radical materialist approaches. The earlier essentials of his critical analysis can be found in his later Marxist position, and the later development of his thought is anticipated in the "messianic" search for truth in his early work. If there is disagreement among his readers as to the extent and success of his eclectic efforts in combining Jewish mystical and traditional elements with Marxist, materialist, future-oriented aspirations, such debate is itself reflective of his methodological intentions to deal with social and cultural extremes in order to ascertain their validity, genuineness, and continuity.

In the three periods of B.'s cultural criticism, the methodological goal remains the same: the radical demolition (*Zertrümmerung*) of the world of appearances, in order to ascertain the underlying (socioeconomic) truth. The object of his critique in the first phase is the symbolical work of art, conceived as a myth of nature; in the second phase it is the faulty public consciousness of intellectuals (entailing a reflection upon his own development); in his later work his critique focuses upon consumerism, revealing the economic basis of bourgeois society.

In *Goethes "Wahlverwandtschaften"* (1924–25; Goethe's *Elective Affinities*), an early B. work, written in 1920–21, his esoteric critique attempted to destroy the aesthetic appearance of totality, that is, the appearance of nature in the symbolical work of art. The world of appearances is unmasked and demolished, allowing the "expressionless" (*das Ausdruckslose*) to be revealed. The "expressionless" truth is revealed through the essence of language itself, conceived in B.'s mystical language philosophy as going back to the Genesis creation story.

During the period 1926–33, B.'s second phase, he was almost entirely concerned with the role of the intellectual in society; he investigated the social meaning of the works he reviewed; these concerns mirrored his own awakening to political consciousness in, for instance, his discussion on the politicization of SURREAL-ISM. But the task of the intellectual is negative: to organize pessimism, making it comprehensible, and to carry out the dialectical destruction of false images. The object of B.'s criticism during this period was not the symbolical work of art, but rather public consciousness as evidenced by intellectuals as they fulfill a role (as in Lukács's *History and Class Consciousness*) of awakening themselves and then the masses to the contradictions of bourgeois society.

In his third phase, while publishing primarily in the *Zeitschrift für Sozialforschung*, B. completed only fragments of a book on Baudelaire, which was intended to show a connection between the economic organization of society and the expressive form used by society's poets. One section, "Über einige Motive bei Baudelaire" (1939–40; "On Some Motifs in Baudelaire," 1968), completed the year before his death and constituting one area in which he had the opportunity to demonstrate this connection in a historical context, treats the manner in which the cipher-character in allegory obscures the nature of things much as the exchange value of commodities shrouds their intrinsic or use value. With the loss of immediate personal experience in the standardization and denaturalization of life in the large metropolis, the individual can attain social truth only through "shock experiences." These shock experiences entail, on the traditional aesthetic and mythical level of experience, the demolition of "aura." The idea of an aura—difficult to delimit because it is more a complex literary image for B. than a precise concept—pertains to the art recipient's reverential attitude toward the artwork, evoked by the assumption of unique creativity found there; the work is perceived as if it were endowed with a nimbus. In "auratic appreciation" of art, one engages in intuitive contemplation of the artistic totality rather than in rational observation of a phenomenon. The intended "demolition of aura" in Baudelaire involves shocks achieved through language—the isolation and removal of words from their traditional contexts. Perceptions of the social world, of things and language, are demolished when appearances are unmasked by the shock experience of recognizing their aesthetic doubling, or perceiving their linguistic, allegorical thoght structure. The critic's role is to disclose what was latent in the social world and its aesthetic formulation, namely, the

correspondences discovered between the perceived structures of modernity, their aesthetic portrayal, and their socioeconomic organization. The critical process "reconstructs" the otherwise unperceived correspondences and, consequently, a "new synthetic aura"—no longer the mythical aura of symbolically portrayed nature, but a "synchronic" aura of "metahistorical" perspective. In their formal aspect the correspondences provide deeper insights, but what their perception opens up is the hellish modern world, absolute negativity. However, B.'s mystical faith looks forward with eschatological hope to a radical interruption of the contemporary hellish time continuum.

In the important early work *Der Ursprung des deutschen Trauerspiels*, written between 1923 and 1925, B. had also been concerned with the perception of truth behind linguistic and allegorical portrayal. There, too, especially in the "Epistemo-Critical Prologue," a certain demolition of images is undertaken: a critic's recognition of the primordial mode of apprehending words, in which ideas are separated from intentions, points out an idea's genuineness or validity, devoid of private interests. At the same time, the *Ursprung*, or origin, of phenomena is to be determined, but what is meant by *Ursprung* is not the coming into existence of a phenomenon, but rather what is essential in it throughout its historical becoming and fading away. The critic's role is here also vital in locating truth, by recognizing its genuine and essential characteristics through its interaction with historical reality in its early and later history. Cultural extremes, such as various aspects of the baroque tragic drama, lend themselves well to such investigations. The baroque use of allegory with manifold meanings is a particular example; like ruins, allegories allow a dialectical investigation by the observer or critic, leading to the demolition of literary images and the unveiling of the historical truth.

Two of B.'s most important essays written in the 1930s dealing in materialist perspectives are "Das Kunstwerk im Zeitalter seiner technischen Reproduzierbarkeit" (1936; "The Work of Art in the Age of Mechanical Reproduction," 1968) and "Der Autor als Produzent" (1966; "The Author as Producer," 1978). Here he treats the loss of aura in art of the modern era, when art has become a commodity of mass production. But the same technological innovations that have affected the reception of the work of art also make possible new progressive artistic forms that enhance shock experiences and the perception of socioeconomic truth. As exemplified in the work of Brecht, among whose important critics and advocates B. was one of the first, the progressive artist should alter the existing forces of artistic production and become a "producer" of a new art with new social relations between artist and audience. Through transformation of older modes of artistic production and the proper utilization of new media incorporating shock experiences, authors, readers, and spectators become active collaborators, perceiving truth and the necessity of a commitment to change.

B. was without a doubt the most important German critic of the first half of the 20th c. The categories and differentiations he developed provided for him the means for penetrating an insightful judgment of the works of many cultural figures. His analyses of KAFKA, Karl KRAUS, PROUST, and Baudelaire, among others, and of 20th-c. art forms (for example, media forms related to storytelling) have had great influence on recent discussions and evaluations.

FURTHER WORKS: *Über den Begriff der Geschichte* (1942; *Theses on the Philosophy of History*, 1968); *Zur Kritik der Gewalt* (1965; *Critique of Violence*, 1978); *Charles Baudelaire, Ein Lyriker im Zeitalter des Hochkapitalismus* (1969; *Charles Baudelaire, A*

Lyric Poet in the Era of High Capitalism, 1973); *Versuche über Brecht* (1966; *Understanding Brecht*, 1973); *Gesammelte Schriften* (1972–1977). FURTHER WORKS IN ENGLISH: *Illuminations: Essays and Reflections* (1968); *Reflections: Essays, Aphorisms, Autobiographical Writings* (1978); *One-Way Street and Other Writings* (1979); *Moscow Diary* (1986)

BIBLIOGRAPHY: Jameson, F., "W. B.; or, Nostalgia," *Marxism and Form* (1971): 60–83; Wellek, R., "The Early Literary Criticism of W. B.," *RUS*, 57 (1971): 123–34; Jay, M., *The Dialectical Imagination: A History of the Frankfurt School and the Institute of Social Research 1923–1950* (1973); Wellek, R., "W. B.'s Literary Criticism in His Marxist Phase," *YCC*, 6 (1973): 168–78; Witte, B., "B. and Lukács: Historical Notes on Their Political and Aesthetic Theories," *NGC*, No. 5 (1975): 3–26; Scholem, G., *On Jews and Judaism in Crisis* (1976): 172–243; Buck-Morss, S., *The Origins of Negative Dialectics: T. W. Adrono, W. B., and the Frankfurt Institute* (1977); Rosen, C., "The Ruins of W. B.," *NYRB*, 27 Oct. 1977, 317–40, and "The Origins of W. B.," *NYRB*, 10 Nov. 1977: 30–38; Jacobs, C. F., *The Dissimulating Harmony: The Image of Interpretation in Nietzsche, Rilke, Artaud, and B.* (1978); special B. issue, *NGC*, No. 17 (1979); special B. issue, "Perspectives on W. B.," *CollG*, 12, 3 (1979); Sontag, S., *Under the Sign of Saturn* (1980): 109–34; Eagleton, T., *W. B., or, Towards a Revolutionary Criticism* (1981); Witte, B., *W. B.: An Intellectual Biography* (1991); Steinberg, M. P., *W. B. and the Demands of History* (1996)

—JAY F. BODINE

The Hegelian concept of "second nature," as the reification of self-estranged human relations, and also the Marxian category of "commodity fetishism" occupy key positions in B.'s work. He is driven not merely to awaken congealed life in petrified objects—as in allegory—but also to scrutinize living things so that they present themselves as being ancient, "ur-historical" and abruptly release their significance. Philosophy appropriates the fetishization of commodities for itself: everything must metamorphose into a thing in order to break the catastrophic spell of things. B.'s thought is so saturated with culture as its natural object that it swears loyalty to reification instead of flatly rejecting it. . . .

The reconciliation of myth is the theme of B.'s philosophy. But, as in good musical variations, this theme rarely states itself openly; instead, it remains hidden and shifts the burden of its legitimation to Jewish mysticism. . . . He transposed the idea of the sacred text into the sphere of enlightenment, into which, according to Scholem, Jewish mysticism itself tends to culminate dialectically. . . . During his mature period, B. was able to give himself over fully to socially critical insights without there being the slightest mental residue, and still without having to ban even one of his impulses. Exegetical power became the ability to see through the manifestations and utterances of bourgeois culture as hieroglyphs of its darkest secret—as ideologies. He spoke occasionally of the "materialist toxins" that he had to add to his thought so that it might survive. Among the illusions

that he renounced in order not to concede the necessity of renunciation, was that of the monadological, self-contained character of his own reflection, which he measured tirelessly and without flinching at the pain of objectification against the overwhelming trend of the collective. But he so utterly assimilated the foreign element to his own experience that the latter improved as a result. [1955]

Theodor W. Adorno, *Prisms* (1967), pp. 233–35

B. was a philosopher. He was one through all the phases and in all the fields of his activity. On the face of it he wrote mostly about subjects of literature and art, sometimes also about topics on the borderline between literature and politics, but only rarely about matters conventionally considered and accepted as themes of pure philosophy. . . . His metaphysical genius . . . is manifested especially in two spheres that increasingly interpenetrate in his work: the philosophy of language and the philosophy of history. The one bent led to a growing preoccupation with literary critical analysis, the other similarly to social-critical analysis. . . .

In his best works the German language has achieved a perfection that takes the reader's breath away. It owes this perfection to the rare achievement of blending highest abstraction with sensuous richness and presentation in the round, and thus bears the hallmark of his notion of metaphysical knowledge. In a wonderful fashion his language, without abandoning depth of insight, closely and snugly fits the subject it covers and at the same time strives in competition with the subject's own language from which it keeps its precise distance. [1965]

Gershom Scholem, "W. B.," *On Jews and Judaism in Crisis* (1976), pp. 177–78, 180, 182–83

Metaphors are the means by which the oneness of the world is poetically brought about. What is so hard to understand about B. is that without being a poet he *thought poetically* and therefore was bound to regard the metaphor as the greatest gift of language. Linguistic "transference" enables us to give material form to the invisibile—"A mighty fortress is our God"—and thus to render it capable of being experienced. He had no trouble understanding the theory of the superstructure as the final doctrine of metaphorical thinking—precisely because without much ado and eschewing all "mediations" he directly related the superstructure to the so-called "material" substructure, which to him meant the totality of sensually experienced data. He evidently was fascinated by the very thing that the others branded as "vulgar-Marxist" or "undialectical" thinking. . . . With Brecht he could practice what Brecht himself called "crude thinking" (*das plumpe Denken*): "The main thing is to learn how to think crudely. Crude thinking, that is the thinking of the great," said Brecht, and B. added by way of elucidation: "There are many people whose idea of a dialectician is a lover of subtleties. . . . Crude thoughts, on the contrary, should be part and parcel of dialectical thinking, because they are nothing but the referral of theory to practice . . . a thought must be crude to come into its own in action." Well, what attracted B. to crude thinking was probably not so much a referral to practice as to reality, and to him this reality manifested itself most directly in the proverbs and idioms of everyday language. . . .

Hannah Arendt, Introduction to *Illuminations* (1968), pp. 14–15

. . . B.'s epistemological intention in his early writings is of a metaphysical nature. His method, however . . . can in no way be designated as philosophical in the traditional sense. It is according to B.'s own definition rather one of a historio-philosophical criticism. It found in literature its preferred medium of reflection. From the beginning accordingly B.'s unique approach can be designated: literary criticism as a method of historio-philosophical cognition. It's origin can be found particularly in his earliest writings, in which he takes a stance vis-à-vis Kant's epistemological theory, discusses the Romantic conception of history and develops out of the Jewish tradition his own language theory. Also his attempts to find solidarity in a group of like-minded thinkers within the Youth Movement and the experience of his isolation as an intellectual and opponent to the war left precipitations in his earliest works. Thus, all the elements of his thought appear manifest in them, elements which he later integrated into the indirect method of his criticism, removing them to a large extent from interpretive analysis. On the other hand, however, the esoteric, manifoldly authoritative language posture, with which B. sought to free words from their everyday communicative function, made the comprehension of his early texts more difficult. This contradiction characterizes the special hermeneutical problem facing the interpreter of his early writings. In order to resolve the problem the esoteric itself needs to be comprehended as a constitutive element of B.'s thought—a thought that seeks to relate in criticism the truth that is denied to the philosophical system.

Bernd Witte. *W. B.: Der Intellektuelle als Kritiker* (1976), p. 5

B. separates his own ideas from a "bourgeois" (i.e., commonplace) and a "mystical" philosophy of language; the bourgeois theory unfortunately holds that language consists of mere conventional signs that are not necessarily related to Being, and the mystical view falsely identifies words with the essence of things. In his own view, the being of a richly layered world, as divine creation, remains separate from language, yet cannot but commune "in" rather than "through" it. Language, far from being a mere instrument, lives as a glorious medium of being; all creation participates in an infinite process of communication (communion), and even the inarticulate plant speaks in the idiom of its fragrance. . . .

In articulating his vision of language, B. soon developed a strong interest in a theory of the sign and renewed semiotic tradition (which in Germany went back to the mid-eighteenth century). His romantic opposition to the idea that the meaning of the sign was mere convention pushed him on to courageous speculations about the sign and the mimetic urge of mankind, and his later interest in the technology of the new media forcefully widened his thinking about signs to include problems of book production, graphic experiments, and advertising. He has few equals in restoring semiotics to our attention.

Peter Demetz, Introduction to *Reflections* (1978), pp. xxii, xliii

Passionately, but also ironically, B. placed himself at the crossroads. It was important for him to keep his many "positions" open: the theological, the Surrealist/aesthetic, the communist. One position corrects another: he needed them all. Decisions, of course, tended to spoil the balance of these positions, vacillation kept everything in place. The reason he gave for his delay in leaving France, when he last saw Adorno in early 1938, was that "there are still positions here to defend."

B. thought the free-lance intellectual was a dying species anyway, made no less obsolete by capitalist society than by revolutionary communism; indeed, he felt that he was living in a time in which everything valuable was the last of its kind. He thought Surrealism was the last intelligent moment of the European intelligentsia, an appropriately destructive, nihilistic kind of intelligence. In his essay on Kraus, B. asks rhetorically: Does Kraus stand "at the threshold of a new age? Alas, by no means. He stands at the Last Judgment." B. is thinking of himself. At the Last Judgment, the Last Intellectual—that Saturnine hero of modern culture, with his ruins, his defiant visions, his reveries, his unquenchable gloom, his downcast eyes—will explain that he took many "positions" and defended the life of the mind to the end, as righteously and inhumanly as he could.

Susan Sontag, "The Last Intellectual," *NYRB*, 12 Oct. 1978, 82

B.'s intellectual existence has taken on so much of a surreal quality that one should not confront it with unreasonable demands of consistency and continuity. B. combined diverging motifs, yet without actually unifying them. And if they were unified, then it would have to be in as many individual unities as there are elements in which the interested gaze of succeeding generations of interpreters attempts to pierce the crust and penetrate to regions where there are veins of live ore. B. belongs to those authors who cannot be summarized and whose work is disposed to a history of disparate effects. We encounter these authors only with the sudden flash of contemporary immediacy in which a tnought takes power and holds sway for an historical instant. B. was accustomed to explicate contemporaneity (*Aktualität*) in terms of the Talmudic legend in which, "angels—innumerable host of new ones at every moment—(are) created in order to, once they have sung their hymn in God's presence, cease and disappear into the void."

Jürgen Habermas, "Consciousness-Raising or Redemptive Criticism: The Contemporaneity of W. B.," *NGC*, No. 17 (1979), 32

BEN JELLOUN, Tahar

Moroccan novelist, poet, and essayist (writing in French), b. 1 Dec. 1944, Fez

B. J., born in Fez, moved with his family to Tangier when he was eighteen. There he attended the French *lycée*. He went on to study philosophy at the university in Rabat, where he collaborated with the avant-garde group associated with the journal *Souffles* and published his first poems, *Hommes sous linceul de silence* (1971; men under a shroud of silence), and his first novel, *Harrouda* (1973; Harrouda). B. J. then went to France, where he earned a doctorate in psychiatric social work while counseling North African immigrant workers. His second novel, *La réclusion solitaire* (1976; *Solitaire*, 1988), fictionalized some of his case histories of sexual dysfunction among male immigrants, files that also formed the basis for his doctoral dissertation, subsequently published in a popular edition as *La plus haute des solitudes* (1977; the deepest solitude). Many of his works, such as *Moha le fou, Moha le sage* (1978; Moha the madman, Moha the wise man), *La prière de l'absent* (1981; prayer for the absent), *L'enfant de sable* (1985; *The Sand Child*, 1987), and *La nuit sacrée* (1987; *The Sacred Night*, 1989), invoke psychological data, psychosomatic effects, Freudian symbolism, androgyny and male-female ambivalence, and imagery pertinent to B. J.'s work with impotent immigrants.

B. J.'s early works attracted a small, devoted following but also elicited criticism from some who felt that he had distanced himself from his native Moroccan culture and should rather be considered a "European" stylist. This change appears to have been based on his urbane narrative techniques and his sometimes journalistic approach to his subjects, but it seems quite unfair since B. J.'s works contain many passages whose full appreciation requires recognition on the reader's part of the significant impact Arabic language, Koranic imagery, and other Maghrebian cultural givens have had on B. J.'s French discourse.

B. J.'s celebrity became international after the publication of *L'enfant de sable* and its sequel. *La nuit sacrée*, the latter having been awarded France's most prestigious literary prize, the Prix Goncourt, in 1987. This award seemed only to fan the debate concerning B. J.'s relative Frenchness. And yet B. J., like Abdelkebair KHATIBI, has repeatedly contended that he is able to use the French language without forfeiting his Moroccan soul. After the Goncourt, B. J. was reported in a syndicated press dispatch to have said that "Arabic is my wife, French is my mistress, and I have been unfaithful to both." The very debate and a need to clarify his position may have contributed in part to the thrust of B. J.'s *Les yeux baissés* (1991; *With Downcast Eyes*, 1993), the story of a young woman who travels from rural Morocco to France, learns the French language, and wishes to write in French. The protagonist is an allegory of the francophone experience, and the novel functions on two levels, as straight narrative and as a layer of symbolic references to biculturalism, and bilingualism.

Most of B. J.'s novels combine social and/or political questions with the disquieting psychological hurts, shortcomings, and yearnings of individuals. His finest novels are *Harrouda*, a haunting "psychospatial" tale of the quite different urban experiences of the two cities, Fez and Tangier, in which B. J. grew up, a tale reminiscent of Khatibi's *La mémoire tatouée* (1971; the tatooed memory), which inspired B. J.; *Moha le fou, Moha le sage*, whose story is told in the poetic, discontinuous ramblings of the confused and tortured mind of Moha, who nevertheless speaks eloquently on behalf of the downtrodden and disenfranchised; *La prière de l'absent*, a novel that recounts a somewhat obscure quest to the south of Morocco by a little band of strange bedfellows—two mentally troubled men, Body and Sindibad, an old woman, and an infant of destiny who has come under their care—during which we are afforded glimpses of the resistance to colonization by Krim in the north and Ma-al-Aynayn in the south as well as numerous allusions to, among other things, the Koran, as well as surrealism and the THEATER OF THE ABSURD, Moroccan policy on the Spanish Sahara (including the government—sponsored *Marche verte*. or Green March), classic Arabic-language poets, and a prime intertextual source in Maghrebian literature, *A Thousand and One Nights*; *L'écrivain public* (1983; the public scribe), a less well-known novel that brilliantly intertwines narratives in the letters, diaries, reminiscences, and dreams; and the diptych of *L'enfant de sable and La nuit sacrée*, which tells of the psychological malformation of a girl raised as a boy by her father and her subsequent retrieval of her female identity in a journey of inward questioning, self-realization through erotic manipulation, and, ultimately, violence.

Two works published since B. J. won the Prix Goncourt warrant special mention: *Jour de silence á Tanger* (1990; *Silent Day in Tangier*, 1991), which is the interior monologue of an old man whose waning days are articulated primarily in the listless introspection of reliving ancient, often erotic, memories; and the previously mentioned *Les yeux baissés*, in which B. J. once again has taken as his protagonist a woman, but in this instance one who incarnates many of the problems and preoccupations of the modern Maghrebian francophone writer. The message of *Les yeux baissés* is theorizing yet often playful, as when the young woman, who aspires to be a writer, seeks advice and encouragement from a "famous writer" who tells her the plot of one of his novels, which we recognize as that of B. J.'s own *La prière de l'absent*. Thus, even as we tend to identify the young woman's creative and cultural journey with that of B. J., the author lightly intervenes from without his alter ego.

B. J.'s poetry has been conceived in several styles, ranging from brief enigmatic texts to surrealistic prose poems, of which the best possess rich imagery and a compelling lyricism. Representative poems may be found in the 1983 edition of *Les amandiers sont morts de leurs blessures, suivi de á l'insu du souvenir* (the almond trees have died from their wounds, followed by beyond the ken of memory), which includes such earlier collections as *Cicatrices du soleil* (1972; sun scars) and *Le discours du chameau* (1974; the camel's speech).

FURTHER WORKS: *Grains de peau, Asilah* (1974); *La mémoire future* (1976); *La fiancée de l'eau, suivi de Entretiens avec M. Sai d'Hammadi, ouvrier algérien* (1984); *Hospitalité française: Racisme et immigration maghrébine* (1984)

BIBLIOGRAPHY: Gontard, M., *La Violence du texte* (1981): 64–79; Pallister, J. L., "T. B. J. and the Poetry of Refusal," *CelfanR*, 2, 3 (May 1983): 34–36; Tenkoul, A., *Littérature marocaine d'écriture française* (1985): 100–25; Déjeux, J., "T. B. J., romancier, poète et essayiste marocain," *Letters & Cultures de Langue Francaise*, 12 (1987): 1–5; Mouzouni, L., *Le roman marocain de langue française* (1987): 108–29; Déjeux, J., "Réception critique de *La nuit sacrée* de T. B. J. dans la presse europe´enne," *Sindbad* (Rabat), 67 (1988): 22–29; Silva, E. R. da, "T. B. J.: Identité arabe/expression française," *PFr*, 34 (1989): 63–71; Taleb-Khyar, M. B., "T. B. J. and *The Water's Bride* Introductory Notes," *Callaloo*, 13, 3 (Summer 1990): 396–425; Abdel-Jaouad, H., "Sacrilegious Discourse," *Middle East Report*, 163 (Mar.–Apr. 1990): 34–36; Rosen, M., "Interview—A Conversation with T. B. J.: Toward a World Literature?," *Middle East Report*, 163 (Mar.–Apr 1990): 30–33; Cazenave, O., "Gender, Age, and Narrative Transformations in *L'enfant de sable* by T. B. J.," *FR*, 64, 3 (Feb. 1991): 437–50; Erickson, J. D., "Writing Double: Politics and the African Narrative of French Expression," *StTCL*, 15, 1 (Winter 1991): 101–22; Revillon, N., "L'enfant endormi: Une lecture de *La prière de l' absent* de T. B. J.," *Itinéraires et Contacts de Culture*, 14 (1991): 90–98; Sellin, E., "Signes migrateurs: Approche transculturelle d'une lecture de la littérature maghrébine d'écriture française," *Itinéraires et Contacts de Culture*, 14 (1991): 42–50

—ERIC SELLIN

BENN, Gottfried

German poet, essayist, and novelist, b. 2 May 1886, Mansfeld; d. 7 July 1956, West Berlin

Like many prominent German writers, B. came from a pastor's family; his mother was French-Swiss, and in later life he made much of the contrasting traditions that shaped his childhood years. Similarly, he placed great emphasis on the social position of his family, which allowed him contact both with the nobility and the poor children of his village. Following his father's wishes, he studied theology and philosophy, at first in Marburg, then in Berlin; but he soon switched to medicine, for which he felt himself better suited. After abandoning his original plan of becoming a psychiatrist (he found that he was emotionally unable to cope with disturbed patients), he pursued his specialties, venereology and dermatology, as a medical doctor from 1911 until the end of World War II. He continued in private practice after the war. After a brief involvement with National Socialism in 1933–34, he experienced a change of attitude and was forbidden to publish after 1937; he termed his life in the German army during World War II as the "aristocratic form of emigration" and later saw it as a version of that withdrawal from political involvement known as "inner emigration." Not until after 1945 did he again begin a spate of publications.

During his early period, B. was best known for his lyric poetry. Although he had begun his poetic experiments in the laconic style of Detlev von Liliencron (1844–1909), he achieved his first success with a volume in the newly fashionable mode of EXPRESSIONISM, *Morgue* (1912; morgue). This collection of modernist poems takes up a theme characteristic of the period—the depersonalization of modern man in a society indifferent to individual life and death. Derived largely from B.'s experiences as a doctor, the poems

caused an outcry among bourgeois readers because of their provocative use of cynical descriptions of human putrefaction, their cold-blooded medical jargon, and their sophisticatedly ironic evocation of the Berlin atmosphere. This poetry is peopled by low-life characters—alcoholics, drug addicts, prostitutes, and the various frequenters of vulgar nightclubs and cafés. Often a stark and violent eroticism rises to the surface, an uncompromising physicality that jars against its sentimental undercurrent, a voluptuous longing for release. Transcendence is attained through drug-induced visions (cocaine is frequently apostrophized), and the mellower climate of southern Europe figures as a metaphor for the desired escape from modern civilization. *Söhne* (1913; sons) and *Fleisch* (1917; flesh) continued the style set by the *Morgue* volume.

The subtle shifts in tone, the clever use of montage, the undoubted modernity of this new voice, led to the rapid acceptance of B. in avant-garde circles. His poems appeared regularly in expressionist journals, and the important expressionist anthology *Die Menschheitsdämmerung* (ed. Kurt Pinthus, 1920; humanity's twilight) bears testimony to his central role in the development of the movement by including numerous of these early poems.

Quite apart from their connections with expressionism, however, B.'s early works already reflect a mode of thought that was to become B.'s hallmark: his complex blending of ecstatic (Dionysian) and rigidly formal (Apollonian) elements, his Nietzschean belief in art as the sole escape from nihilism, his fascination with ancient mythology, and his urge to return to the primal vision.

Nowhere does this paradoxical mixture become more apparent than in his strikingly innovative prose pieces, still today relatively underestimated. In a series of short stories, *Gehirne* (1916; brains)—B. rather misleadingly called them novellas—revolving around the semiautobiographical medical intern Rönne, B. begins his modernist exploration of the concept of self. In tune with many other works of the period, the stories recognize the fallacy of traditional literary psychology, with its assumption of a continuous individual psyche. Rönne perceives all too clearly the split in himself between thought and feeling, between the brain as an organ of thought and as a clump of matter in the cadavers he autopsies. Its bicameral nature is at once a profound symbol of the dualism of life itself and an insoluble, perennially tantalizing riddle. The Rönne stories contain the germ of what B. was later to see as his own type of "schizophrenia," as well as embodying the negative counterpoint to the release in mythic unity for which his poetry constantly gropes. Similar ideas are also developed in B.'s 1920 essay *Das moderne Ich* (the modern self). Taken together, the prose and poery of this early period illustrate B.'s unusual combination of modernist techniques and atavistic tendencies.

At first, his imaginary regression into the past seemed no more than a fascinating ingredient of his unorthodox new poetics; but with the advent of National Socialism and its dependence on primitivism, it took on a more disquieting dimension. B. greeted Hitler's rise to power with a series of enthusiastic articles, including the influential radio talk *Der neue Staat und die Intellektuellen* (1933; the new state and the intellectuals) and his essay on the relationship of art and power, entitled *Dorische Welt* (1934; Doric world). For about eighteen months, B. publicly supported the Nazi eugenics program and proclaimed the vital role he foresaw for modern art in the establishment of the new regime. In his essays of this period he used the example of ancient Greece to prove his thesis that art is inextricably linked with power and that great cultures have always been built "upon the bones of slaves." When several of his former expressionist confrères, now in Russian exile, reproached him for his failure to use the subversive edge of his earlier style to undermine support for the Nazi regime, B. poured scorn on them in an open letter of 1933, thus irrevocably cutting himself off from further contact with the emigrants. But contrary to his expectations, it soon became evident that the literary avant-garde was not to play the leading part he had envisaged for it; worse still, his own work was classified by the Nazis as an example of "degenerate" modernism. At the same time he became the butt of the "expressionism debate" of 1937 (conducted in the exile journal *Das Wort*), where the argument was put—in the first instance by Klaus Mann (1906–1948)—that B.'s mode of thought had always harbored Nazi tendencies and that his longing to return to man's preconscious beginnings as a "clump of cells in the primeval lime" was in essence no different from the Nazi ideology of "blood and soil." Although the emigrants' arguments were at times somewhat exaggerated, critics have since come to concur that B.'s involvement with Nazism was less the unfortunate "slip" he later made it out to be than a logical development of certain aspects of his earlier thinking.

B.'s dubious position during the war years made it doubly difficult for him to reestablish his reputation after 1945. But despite the concerted efforts of the official literary watchdogs of the East (Bertolt BRECHT) and the West (Alfred DÖBLIN), B. eventually succeeded in making a comeback. Here he was aided in part by the support of friends and literary critics, but more importantly through the publication of his long autobiographical essay *Doppelleben* (1950; double life), in which he explained the contradictions of his previous life in terms of an inexorable dualism. His rehabilitation culminated in the award of the Georg Büchner Prize for Poetry of 1951, following upon his Marburg lecture, *Probleme der Lyrik* (problems of poetry). Actually a melange of B.'s early ideas on the self and avant-garde poetic theory derived in the main from Anglo-American sources, the lecture was a sensation at the time and remained for most of the 1950s and early 1960s the most influential *ars poetica* of Germany's younger poets. Here B. exhorted his contemporaries to make a clean break with the "seraphic" tone of the still-dominant RILKE tradition, to eliminate subjectivity in the lyric, and to avoid outworn poetic devices like similes and adjectives. In this plea for a hard-edge style B. hardly progressed beyond his predecessors of the 1920s, POUND and ELIOT; more original was his highly metaphorical description of the modern poem as the "Ariadne thread" designed to lead us out of the labyrinth. The modern poet, he claimed, is a "monologic self," fragmented in his consciousness and imprisoned behind the bars of language; like primitive feelers, his senses grope through the darkness to create a discourse directed to no one and perennially destined to stop short of expressing the transcendent vision. By thus linking the concept of absolute art with a belief in the essential isolation of the modern individual, the lecture served as a guide for many young writers trying to find their way back into the mainstream of European modernism after the hiatus of the Third Reich.

B.'s postwar poetry, notably *Statische Gedichte* (1948; static poems), continued his earlier themes of the return to the mythic and visionary, while maintaining a strictly apolitical stance within a hermetic and formalist world of SYMBOLISM. His final volumes, *Destillationen* (1953; distillations) and *Aprèslude* (1955; afterlude), are marked by feelings of despair and disillusionment with modern life. Interwoven with poems of sheer virtuoso artistry typical of this later period are others in which B. again picks up his earlier open forms and more cynical language; but the emphasis is increasingly on the visionary escape from reality, the descent into darkness and

silence beyond the reach of rational consciousness. Overwhelmed by a pervasive sense of the hollowness of existence and the inadequacy of language, B. retreats more and more into an elegiac mood that poetry itself is helpless to counter. Futility and cosmic isolation are all that remain.

FURTHER WORKS: *Diesterweg* (1918); *Etappe* (1917); *Ithaka* (1919); *Der Vermessungsdirigent* (1919); *Die gesammelten Schriften* (1922); *Schutt* (1924); *Spaltung* (1925); *Gesammelte Gedichte* (1927); *Gesammelte Prosa* (1928); *Fazit der Perspektiven* (1930); *Das Unaufhörliche* (1931); *Nach dem Nihilismus* (1932); *Ausgewählte Gedichte* (1936); *Der Ptolemäer* (1947); *Ausdruckswelt* (1949); *Trunkene Flut* (1949); *Drei alte Männer* (1949); *Frühe Prosa und Reden* (1950); *Essays* (1951); *Fragmente* (1951); *Frühe Lyrik und Dramen* (1952); *Die Stimme hinter dem Vorhang* (1952); *Gesammelte Gedichte* (1956); *Ausgewählte Briefe* (1957); *Primäre Tage* (1958); *Gesammelte Werke* (4 vols., 1958–1961); *Briefe an F. W. Oelze 1932–1945* (1977). FURTHER WORKS IN ENGLISH: *Primal Vision: Selected Writings of G.B.* (1958); *G. B.: Selected Poems* (1970); *G. B.: The Unreconstructed Expressionist* (1972)

BIBLIOGRAPHY: Hamburger, M., *Reason and Energy* (1957): 275–312; Ashton, E. B., Introduction to *Primal Vision: Selected Writings of G. B.* (1958): vii–xxvi; Wellershoff, G., *G. B.: Phänotyp dieser Stunde* (1958); Lohner, E., *Passion und Intellekt: Die Lyrik G. B.S* (1961); Wodtke, F. W., *G. B.* (1962); Hannum, H, G., "George and B: The Autumnal Vision," *PMLA*, 78 (1963): 271–79; Hilton, I., "G. B.," in Natan, A., ed., *German Men of Letters*, Vol. 3 (1964): 129–50; Wodtke, F. W., Introduction to *G. B.: Selected Poems* (1970): 9–41; Ritchie, J. M., Introduction to *G. B.: The Unreconstructed Expressionist* (1972): 11–70; Schröder, J., *G. B.: Poesie und Sozialisation* (1978); Dierick, A. P., *G. B. and His Critics: Major Interpretations, 1912-1992* (1992)

—JUDITH RYAN

BENNETT, Arnold

English novelist, dramatist, essayist, and critic, b. 27 May 1867, Burslem; d. 27 March 1931, London

B. came from a middle-class family in the industrial Midlands. As a young man he went to London to work in a law office, and he was nearly thirty before he realized that he was a writer. His first novel, *A Man from the North*, was published in 1898; and from that time until his death he produced a novel a year, almost as many plays, well above a thousand short stories and essays, several opera libretti and film scenarios, an extensive journal, and a prodigious number of letters.

B.'s reputation rests upon his depiction of life in the "Five Towns" in the Midlands. He was not an innovator, but followed the lead of Balzac, Flaubert, Zola, and Dostoevsky in France and Russia, and George Moore and George Gissing in England. His finest novel, *The Old Wives' Tale* (1908), is usually regarded as the best example of English realism of its time. Of almost equal merit is the Clayhanger trilogy: *Clayhanger* (1910), *Hilda Lessways* (1911), and *These Twain* (1915). The last of these was also the last of the Five Towns novels, and by the time he wrote it, B.'s reputation had declined considerably. He reestablished himself briefly with *Riceyman Steps* (1923) and *Lord Raingo* (1926).

A considerable portion of B.'s writing has little to do with realism. He wrote nearly a dozen novels of intrigue, sensational incident, and spectacle, of which *Accident* (1928) is the best and *The Grand Babylon Hotel* (1902) the best known. He also wrote a few comic novels, such as *Buried Alive* (1908) and *The Card* (1911; pub. in U.S. as *Denry the Audacious*, 1911). One novel, *The Glimpse* (1909), is a fantasy about evolution and reincarnation. Among the plays, only *Cupid and Commonsense* (1909) approaches the realism of some of the novels. *The Honeymoon* (1911) is a comedy of sex, marriage, and nationalism; *Judith* (1919) is a biblical drama; *The Bright Island* (1924) is a political satire done along the lines of commedia dell'arte; *The Return Journey* (perf. 1928) is a modern version of the Faust legend.

As a journalist, B. was most famous for his "Books and Persons" articles, which appeared in *New Age* from 1908 to 1910 and in the *Evening Standard* from 1926 until his death. During these years he was the most forceful and influential literary critic writing in the popular press. His sociopolitical articles written during World War I were of almost equal importance. Over the years he also produced a half dozen "pocket philosophies," which found a wide audience for their common-sense, stoical wisdom.

In all its variety, B.'s writing exhibits detachment, compassion, and humor. Several phrases of his sum up his view of literature: "The foundation of good fiction is character creating, and nothing else"; "The single motive that should govern the choice of a principal figure is the motive of love for that figure"; "All literature is the expression of feeling, of passion, of emotion, caused by a sensation of the interestingness of life . . ."; "The book is nothing but the man trying to talk to you, trying to impart to you some of his feelings." Underlying these views, which are meant to be complementary rather than contradictory, is another: "To find beauty, which is always hidden—that is the aim." It is in his portraits of ordinary people living prosaic lives that B.'s views find their best expression.

FURTHER WORKS: *Polite Farces for the Drawing Room* (1899); *Fame and Fiction* (1901); *Anna of the Five Towns* (1902); *Leonora* (1903); *The Gates of Wrath* (1903); *The Truth about an Author* (1903); *A Great Man* (1904); *Teresa of Watling Street* (1904); *The Loot of Cities* (1905); *Tales of the Five Towns* (1905); *Sacred and Profane Love* (1905; rev ed., *The Book of Carlotta*, 1911); *Whom God Hath Joined* (1906); *Things That Have Interested Me* (1906); *The Sinews of War* (1906); *The Grim Smile of the Five Towns* (1907); *The City of Pleasure* (1907); *The Ghost* (1907); *The Reasonable Life, Being Hints for Men and Women* (1907); *How to Live on Twenty-four Hours a Day* (1908); *The Statue* (1908); *Literary Taste, How to Form It* (1909); *What the Public Wants* (1909); *Helen with the High Hand* (1910); *Milestones* (1912, with E. Knoblock); *The Matador of the Five Towns* (1912); *Those United States* (Am., *Your United States*, 1912); *Paris Nights* (1913); *The Great Adventure* (1913); *The Regent* (1913); *The Author's Craft* (1913); *The Price of Love* (1914); *The Lion's Share* (1916); *Books and Persons, 1908–1911* (1917); *The Pretty Lady* (1918); *The Roll-Call* (1918); *The Title* (1918); *Sacred and Profane Love* (play from the novel, 1919); *Body and Soul* (1921); *Lilian* (1922); *Mr. Prohack* (1922); *The Love Match* (1922); *Don Juan de Marana* (1923); *How to Make the Best of Life* (1923); *Elsie and the Child* (1924); *London Life* (1924); *The Woman Who Stole Everything* (1927); *Mr. Prohack* (play from the novel, 1927); *The Strange Vanguard* (1928); *The Savour of Life* (1928); *Mediterranean Scenes* (1928); *Journal* (1929; Am., *Journal of Things New and Old*, 1930); *Imperial Palace* (1930); *The Night Visitor* (1931); *Venus Rising from the Sea* (1931); *Dream of Destiny, an Unfinished Novel* and *Venus Rising from the Sea* (1932; Am., *Stroke of Luck and Dream of Destiny*, 1932); *The Journals of A. B.* (3 vols., 1932–1933); *A. B., A Portrait Done at Home* (1935); *A. B.'s Letters to His Nephew* (1936); *Letters of A. B.* (3 vols., 1966–1970); *Florentine Journal* (1967); *A. B. in Love* (1972); *A. B., The Evening Standard Years* (1974); *Sketches for Autobiography* (1979)

BIBLIOGRAPHY: Woolf, V., *Mr. B and Mrs. Brown* (1924); Smith, P., *A. B.* (1933); Lafourcade, G., *A. B.* (1939); Locherbie-Goff, M., *La jeunesse d'A. B.* (1939); Allen, W., *A. B.* (1948); Pound, R., *A. B.: A Biography* (1952); Hepburn, J., *Art of A. B.* (1963); Barker, D., *Writer by Trade* (1966); Drabble, M., *A. B.* (1974); Miller, A., *A. B.: An Annotated Bibliography* (1977); Swinnerton., F., *A.B.* (1978); Hepburn, J., ed., *A. B.: The Critical Heritage* (1981)

—JAMES HEPBURN

BENNETT, Louise (Simone)

Jamaican poet and folklorist, b. 7 Sept. 1919, Jamaica

B. began to write as a teenager and has performed her works since 1938. She attended Excelsior College in Jamaica. She began to publish her poetry in the *Jamaica Gleaner* in the 1930s, and developed a large following. She collected folklore from all over Jamaica, and at the age of twenty-six, she won a scholarship to the Royal Academy of Dramatic Art in London. In London she worked for the BBC and for repertory companies; in America she performed on stage and broadcast for radio. She has traveled widely to the U.S., Africa, and Europe. She returned to Jamaica in 1955, where she continued with a distinguished career as "Miss Lou," the persona of her poems and as a champion of the folk tradition.

Critic Selwyn Cudjoe believes that B. is responsible for establishing a unique Caribbean literature and a distinctive woman's voice within it—in that B.'s work challenged the privileged status accorded to the poetic tradition of colonial discourse in Caribbean letters. In the 1940s her popularity was as much a function of the new as it was the empowerment of voices and expressions of the Jamaican masses.

Many critics decry the lack of her representative poems in anthologies of Caribbean literature. Her poetry had not had the careful reading it deserves because of B.'s popular appeal with the persona of Miss Matt, as well as her work as an actress and entertainer. With the publication of Mervyn Morris's "On Reading L. B., Seriously," the literary world began to take notice. B. explores a particular type of Jamaican experience who distinguished herself as a comic poet. The comedy is not to be wondered at given the time of her rise to fame as well as the nature of the folk materials she collected and disseminated. Humor is very much a weapon of survival for those under siege—economically, culturally, socially. Yet, citing widely from B.'s *Jamaica Labrish* (1966), Morris explored her artistry in his essay.

B.'s greatest contributions to Jamaican poetry include the voice she gave to the masses of Jamaican people, the unearthing of characters heretofore hidden from public perusal. Her repertoire extends into subjects inclusive of traditional African practices, women's concerns, commerce, social issues, and mother wit. Her satire stings in the poem "Back to Africa" during which she questions the wisdom of the move. As emphasized by Cudjoe, B. initiated a tradition of popular verse to which the entire region is indebted.

FURTHER WORKS: *Dialect Verse* (1942); *Verses in Jamaican Dialect* (1942); *Jamaican Humour in Dialect* (1943); *Jamaican Dialect Poems* (1948); *M's' Lulu Sez: A Collection of Dialect Poems* (1949); *Lulu Says, Dialect Verses with Glossary* (1952); *Laugh with Louise, a Pot-pourrie of Jamaican Folk-lore, Stories, Songs and Verses* (1961); *Jamaican Labrish* (1966); *Anancy Stories and Dialect Verse* (1957); *Selected Poems* (1982)

BIBLIOGRAPHY: Burnett, P., *The Penguin Book of Caribbean Verse in English* (1986): xxxiii-xxxi, 378; Cudjoe, S. R., ed., *Caribbean Women Writers: Essays from the First International Conference* (1990); Herdeck, D. E., ed., *Caribbean Writers: A Bio-Bibliographical-Critical Encyclopedia* (1979); Morris, M., "On Reading L. B. Seriously," *Jamaica Journal*, 1 (1967): 69-74

—ADELE S. NEWSON

BERGE, H(ans) C(ornelius) Ten

Dutch poet, prose writer, and translator, b. 24 Dec. 1938, Alkmar

In the 1960s and 1970s T. B. lived in Amsterdam, where he studied Spanish; in 1979 he moved to Zutphen where he still lives as a lecturer at the Visual Arts Academy in nearby Arnhem. He has traveled extensively in Central Europe and in North and Central America. These journeys have stimulated his strong ethnological interests, which he developed largely through self-study.

T. B. made his debut as a poet in 1964. His first three collections, reprinted together in *Gedichten* (1969; poems), employ a bare, halting diction, a language full of discontinuities and pared down to essentials, so as to evoke powerful emotions while avoiding the risk of sentimentality. The poems, usually grouped into cycles, range widely in scope and theme and incorporate numerous literary and historical references, from Antarctic expeditions to medieval fairs and the Spanish invasion of Mexico seen through the eyes of the vanquished. Many of T. B.'s early poems use montage techniques to build multilayered narrative sequences in which different viewpoints and voices are juxtaposed; the technique derived from Ezra POUND, some of whose *Cantos* T. B. also translated into Dutch (1970).

Since the 1970s T. B.'s poetic diction has become more fluent and melodious, and more intent on combining innovative and traditional elements. *Va-banque* (1977; all or nothing) explores the notion of writing as a game of chance, involving play, risk, and high stakes. The volume *Nieuwe gedichten* (1981; new poems) counterpoints overtly political poems and autobiographical pieces in which the boundaries between fact and fiction are skillfully obscured. Impressive in their epic sombreness are the *Texaanse elegieën* (1983; Texan elegies), a symbolic descent into the underworld of the 20th c. The *Liederen van angst en vertwijfeling* (1988; songs of anguish and despair) revolve around meditations on art and on death, the latter mostly in a Mexican setting. *Overgangsriten* (1992; rites of passage), however, strikes a much more positive chord. T. B.'s collected poems 1963-93 appeared as *Materia prima* (1993). Since then he has published mainly critical prose.

The openness to the outside world which much of T. B.'s poetry has consistently displayed in its method and thematic range is confirmed in a long series of literary and ethnological translations. Several among these have visible traces in T. B.'s original poetry and prose. They include renderings of contemporary poets—Kenneth White (b. 1936), Christopher Middleton (b. 1926), Mark STRAND, and Gunnar EKELÖ of (qq.v)—but also versions of texts outside the Western tradition, such as Japanese Nō plays and Aztec sacral and secular hymans. His work in the ethnological field culminated in a three-volume annotated collection of myths and fables of North American Indians, Eskimo, and Siberian peoples.

T. B.'s early stories show the hand of the poet in their meticulous workings, visual imagery, and imaginative power. His protagonists are typically émigrés, travelers with an uncertain destination, rootless wanderers in some undefined border region who have at best a tenuous grip on reality and on themselves.

The novel *Een geval van verbeelding* (1970; a case of delusion), which was subsequently reissued in revised form as the two interlinked novellas *Zelfportret met witte muts* (1985; self-portrait with a white woolen hat) and *Matglas* (1982; frosted glass), is set among Polish émigrés in western Europe and contrasts the cautious, guarded life-style of Stefan K., a doctor, with the high risk existence of the girl Hannele. The book's elusive style, however, prevents a factual reconstruction of the denouement. T. B.'s most ambitious novel to date, *Het geheim van een opgewekt humeur* (1986; the secret of a cheerful mood), interweaves the modern story of a three-cornered relationship with a semihistorical account of a case of incest in 16th-c. Mexico and myths derived from Ovid's *Metamorphoses*. The various narrative strands, all embedded one into the other, contain subtle parallels and inversions, focusing on the notion of incest and hence on the opposition between nature and culture.

T. B.'s literary oeuvre has been described in terms of assemblage, the product of a sophisticated *bricoleur*, a "do-it-yourselfer," who combines lyrical with intellectual and critical impulses, a consciously international outlook, and an anthropological interest with an exceptionally fine sense of language. But the imaginative worlds that T. B. builds, whether in prose or in verse, consistently deal with discontinuities, ruptures, and uncertainties. In their radical questioning of our cultural and ideological assumptions they are profoundly unsetting.

FURTHER WORKS: *Poolsneeuw* (1964); *Swartkrans* (1966); *Personages* (1967); *Canaletto en andere verhalen* (1969); *De witte sjamaan* (1973); *Een schrijver als grenskozak* (1977); *Het meisje met de korte vlechten* (1977); *De beren van Churchill* (1978); *Levenstekens en doodssinjalen* (1980); *De mannenschrik* (1984); *Mythen en fabels van noordélijke volken* (3 vols., 1987); *De verdediging van de poëzie* (1988); *Een Italiaan in Zutphen* (1990); *De honkvaste reiziger* (1994); *Vrouwen, jaloezie en andere ongemakken* (1996). FURTHER WORKS IN ENGLISH: *The White Shaman, Selected Poems* (1991)

BIBLIOGRAPHY: De Moor, W., "Anonymous Restless Forms: The Dutch Writer, T. B.," *BA*, 47, 2 (Spring 1973): 266–72; *T. B. Informatie* (1987); special T. B. issue, *Yang*, (1988); Hermans, T., "T. B. Transmontanus: wat doen de feiten ertoe als er fiktie bestaat?," *OnsE*, 32, 4 (Sept.-Oct. 1989): 545–53; Hermans, T., "Translation and the Indirect Route: An Approximation to H. C. T. B.'s Disparate Worlds," in Westerweel, B., and D'haen, T., eds.,

Something Understood: Studies in Anglo-Dutch Literary Translation (1990): 305–17

—THEO HERMANS

BERGELSON, Dovid

Yiddish novelist, short-story writer, and dramatist, b. 12 Aug. 1884, Sarne, Ukraine; d. 12 Aug. 1952, Moscow?

B. is one of the leading writers of the second generation of modern Yiddish literature, following the "classical period" of Mendele Mocher Sforim (1835–1917), Sholem Aleichem (1859–1916), and I. L. Peretz (1851–1915). Born into the rapidly disintegrating traditional eastern European Jewish society, B. emphasized not the force of tradition, as his predecessors had done, but the atmosphere of palpable decline. His own childhood, begun in the wealthy household of a timber merchant but soon punctuated by the successive deaths of both parents, contributed to his personal experience of impoverishment. B.'s literary career, which spanned the unusually violent period 1906 to 1948, underwent several critical thematic and stylistic changes.

B.'s early stories and novellas interpret the torpor of Jewish small-town life in Russia at the beginning of this century. His typical characters—brooding grain merchants, restless students, wistful suitors—can neither escape their provincial confines nor grasp the reasons for their failure. The prose style, with its lengthy descriptive passages and indirect discourse, reinforces the mood of hopelessness.

This mood is fully developed in the novel *Nokh alemen* (1913; *When All Is Said and Done*, 1977), in which the first authentic heroine of Yiddish fiction flounders among her unsatisfying suitors and unrealized dreams. Here, and in *Opgang* 1921; departure), the young people are permanently estranged from their native Jewish culture, engaging, like CHEKHOV's characters, in endless ruminations about their futures but without practical hope of amelioration. The realistic descriptions of socioeconomic stagnation in prerevolutionary Russia are also effective vehicles for B.'s philosophical pessimism and psychological resignation.

During World War I and the revolutionary years B. defended artistic subtlety and attacked the rhetorical stridency of some new Yiddish writers. But after several years of expatriate residence in Berlin, he turned Communist politically as well as artistically. The novel *Midas hadin* (1925; full severity of the law) justifies the harshness of enforced collectivization. His subsequent fiction and journalism, written after his return to the Soviet Union in 1926, submitted to demands of SOCIALIST REALISM in the portrayals of revolutionary heroes and pioneering Jewish colonists in Birobidzhan.

B.'s two-volume fictional biography, *Baym Dnieper* (1932, 1940; along the Dnieper), is the ripest product of his socialist-determinist vision. It is alternately admirable as a panoramic study of a critical historical epoch, and lamentable as a tendentious work of self-justification. Structurally and thematically B.'s most ambitious novel, it interweaves the story of an unfolding artistic consciousness with the emerging drama of the successful revolution.

Roused by the Russian-German nonaggression pact (1939–41) and the Nazi war against the Jews, B. turned to Jewish themes during the 1940s. The historical drama *Prints Ruveyni* (1946;

Prince Reuveni) is a thinly veiled call for Jewish pride and resistance. B.'s stories of the period evoke the agony of forsaken fighters and survivors.

Along with the other major Soviet-Jewish writers, B. was arrested in 1949, imprisoned on a trumped-up charge, and executed. He was posthumously "rehabilitated" in 1961.

B.'s skill as an architect of narrative was important in the structural development of the Yiddish novel. Even more influential was the haunting beauty of his prose, which broke with the colloquial, mimetic tradition of Yiddish storytelling in favor of an impressionistic, personalized prose rhythm and style.

FURTHER WORKS: *Arum vokzal* (1909; *At the Depot*, 1973); *In a fargrebter shtot* (1914; *In a Backwoods Town*, 1953); *Tsugvintn* (1930); *Birobidzhaner* (1934); *Trot nokh trot* (1938); *Dertseylungen* (1941); *Geven iz nakht un gevorn iz tog* (1943); *Naye dertseylungen* (1947)

BIBLIOGRAPHY: Madison, C., *Yiddish Literature* (1968): 426–48; Shmeruk, C., "Yiddish Literature in the U.S.S.R.," in Kochan, L., ed., *The Jews in Soviet Russia since 1917* (1970): 232–68

—RUTH WISSE

BERGER, Thomas

American novelist, short-story writer, and dramatist, b. 20 July 1924, Cincinnati, Ohio

B. served in the U.S. Army for three years (1943–1946), after which he completed his B.A. with honors at the University of Cincinnati in 1948. He worked as a librarian at the Rand School of Social Science (1948–1951) and pursued graduate study at Columbia University from 1950 to 1951. B. was a staff member of the *New York Times* (1951–1952), served as associate editor of *Popular Science Monthly* (1952–1953), and wrote film criticism for *Esquire* (1972–1973). He has been distinguished visiting professor at Southampton College (now the Southampton Campus of Long Island University), New York (1975–1976), lecturer at Yale University (1981–1982), and Regents' lecturer at the University of California, Davis (1982). His awards and honors include a Dial fellowship (1962); the Western Heritage Award (1965) and the Richard and Hinda Rosenthal Award, National Institute of Arts and Letters (1965), both for *Little Big Man* (1964); the Ohioana Book Award (1982) for *Reinhart's Women* (1981); and a Pulitzer Prize nomination (1984) for *The Feud* (1983).

B. has published seventeen novels, two plays, and numerous short stories. The novels *Crazy in Berlin* (1958), *Reinhart's in Love* (1962), *Vital Parts* (1970), and *Reinhart's Women* follow the main character, Carlo Reinhart, from his days as a young G. I. during World War II through middle age in the 1970s. Two of B.'s novels, *Little Big Man*, set among the Cheyennes in the American Old West, and *Neighbors* (1981), a dark, Beckett-like tale, have been made into films, released in 1970 and 1981 respectively.

B.'s work is always carefully researched, but his methods, he claims, are not systematic in a scholarly sort of way—he reads extensively in the areas that interest him, taking very few notes, and then allows his imagination to take hold, transmuting "facts" into the truths of his fiction. B. is a master of satire and myth bashing, but that is perhaps the limit of generalizing possible in discussing his work. His range is enormous and each work must be judged on its own terms. Risky, too, is any attempt to categorize B.'s novels too strictly by genre, although B. has commented that his "conscious intention is always to write as conventional an example" of the genre within which he is working, "to celebrate it, to identify and applaud its glories." Thus *Regiment of Women* (1973) seems an experiment in science fiction, while *Who Is Teddy Villanova?* (1977) might be called a detective novel. And with his retelling of the legend of the Knights of the Round Table, B. enters the realms of fantasy/mythology in *Arthur Rex* (1978).

Many critics have described B.'s work as scathing social commentary, but B. says he is not so much interested in parodying social ills as he is in exploring the creative possibilities of language. Nor does B. think of himself as a writer of comedy, and he asserts that he is rarely if ever consciously trying to be funny. Instead he feels that "my way of looking at things, which is not humorless, no doubt tends to mislead the careless." And while B. does not suggest that he is "in the same league as the author of *Ein Hungerkünstler*," much of his work is comic in the sense that Franz KAFKA's work can be said to be comic. The nightmare is real, and there is nothing to do but laugh. And, indeed, it is Kafka's lesson—that the seemingly mundane can suddenly turn sinister—that much of B.'s prose reexamines and reshapes. Language can blur, can obscure reality, but it also presents and represents reality. B's rhetoric is the reality, and when the action, person, or concept being scrutinized is viewed from another angle, reality shifts just as quickly as perception does.

The breadth, depth, and variety of B.'s visions along with his exciting manipulation of the English language through which he presents them make him one of the most challenging writers working in the U.S.

FURTHER WORKS: *Killing Time* (1967); *Other People* (1970); *Sneaky People* (1975); *Granted Wishes* (1984); *Nowhere* (1985); *Being Invisible* (1987); *The Houseguest* (1988); *The Burglars* (1988); *Changing the Past* (1989); *Meeting Evil* (1992)

BIBLIOGRAPHY: Schickel, R., "Bitter Comedy," *Commentary* 50, 1 (July 1970): 76–80; Romano, J., "Camelot and All That," *NYTBR*, 12 Nov. 1978: 3, 62; Schickel, R., "Interviewing T. B.," *NYTBR*, 6 Apr. 1980: 1, 21–22; Landon, B., *T. B.* (1989); Landon, B., "The Measure of *Little Big Man*," *SAF*, 17, 2 (Autumn 1989): 131–42; Madden, D. W., ed., *Critical Essays on T. B.* (1995)

—MARGARET D. SULLIVAN

BERGMAN, Hjalmar

Swedish novelist, short-story writer, and dramatist, b. 19 July 1883, Örebro; d. 1 Jan. 1931, Berlin, Germany

B. came from a well-to-do, upper-middle-class family in Örebro. His father was a banker and entrepreneur who controlled extensive mercantile operations throughout the central Swedish mining district of Bergslagen; when he was still a child, B. was initiated into the complexities of these enterprises. His mother came from an established family with deep roots in Örebro and Närke. Oral traditions from this part of his background yielded a wealth of material for his works set in the mythical region of "Bergslag," with its abundance of sharply etched, eccentric figures.

B.'s early plays, novels, and stories groan under the weight of fin-de-siècle SYMBOLISM but are not lacking in psychological insight. A recurring theme is the conflict between the vulnerable ideals of youth and the cruel realities that survival dictates. This conflict also characterizes B.'s literary breakthrough, *Hans nåds testamente* (1910; his grace's last testament), a madly comic novel set at Rogershus Manor, "where a whim was a passion, passion a whim. Where whims alone ruled."

Hans nåds testamente established the ambience of B.'s mature works. A fictional town of Wadköping gradually emerges as the center of his imagined Bergslag, with its foundries and manor houses, the owners of which B. traces back many generations in novels and shorter narratives. Not unlike Balzac and FAULKNER, B. created his own richly detailed corner of the world; his Bergslag is both realistic and fantastic, teeming with closely observed characters and cumulatively developed families. Underneath his sharp wit, inventive style, and uncanny powers of imagination, he remains a fatalist. His artistry invariably leads him to the exposure and stripping away of the psychological armor and illusions of his characters. His own unmasking, his coming to terms with the complexities of his own tortured psyche, occurs by degrees throughout his works; B. reserves naked masklessness, however, for his last novel, *Clownen Jac* (1930; the clown Jac).

The novel *Mor i Sutre* (1917; mother in Sutre) exemplifies the balance of narrative brilliance and ethical intent characteristic of B.'s best works. Mother Boel is the nexus in a complex and highly, explosive skein of intrigues that B. compresses into a single day. Her manipulations and actions lie behind virtually everything that occurs; she is also the focal point of the erotic, social, and economic conflicts that arise. The theme—an egoist's attempt to force existence itself into the paradigm of her own will, and her inevitable failure to achieve this end—is the backbone of B.'s entire oeuvre.

In addition to novels, B. wrote numerous short stories and also made his mark as a dramatist. His deterministic view of life is strongly apparent in *Marionettspel* (1917; marionette plays) and the posthumously published *Sagan* (1942; the legend). His most popular play, however, has been *Swedenhielms* (1925; *The Swedenhielms*, 1951). This engaging presentation of an eccentric Nobel Prize candidate and his family of individualists may lack the multidimensional richness of B.'s fiction at its finest, but its intrigue is masterfully constructed, and its protagonist has been portrayed by leading Scandinavian actors.

B.'s vision is highly pessimistic and unrelieved by any notion of the relativity of ethical behavior. But compassion does mark his vision of the characters he created, and in telling their stories B. described moral struggles that demand great sacrifices.

FURTHER WORKS: *Maria, Jesu moder* (1905); *Solivro* (1906); *Savonarota* (1909); *Amourer* (1910); *Vi Bookar Krokar och Rothar* (1912); *Loewenhistorier* (1913); *Komedier i Bergslagen* (1914); *Knutmässo marknad* (1916); *En döds memoarer* (1918); *Markurells i Wadköping* (1920; *God's Orchid*, 1924 as play, 1930; *Markurells of Wadköping*, 1968); *Herr von Hancken* (1920); *Porten* (1921); *Farmor och Vår Herre* (1921; *Thy Rod and Thy Staff*, 1937); *Eros'*

Begravning (1922); *Jag, Ljung och Medardus* (1923); *Chefen fru Ingeborg* (1924; *The Head of the Firm*, 1936); *Flickan i frack* (1925); *Jonas och Helen* (1926); *Dollar* (1928); *Kerrmans i paradiset* (1927); *Patrasket* (1928); *Lotten Brenners ferier* (1928); *Kärlek genom ett fönster* (1929); *Hans nåds testamente* (as play, 1930; *The Baron's Will*, 1968); *Herr Markurells död* (1941); *Samlade skrifter* (30 vols., 1949–1958); *Hans nåds maitresse* (1964). FURTHER WORKS IN ENGLISH: *Four Plays* (1968)

BIBLIOGRAPHY: Gustafson, A., "H. B.'s 'Accounting' with the Swedish Middle-Classes," *Samlaren*, 36 (1955): 64–76; Vowels, R. B., "B., Branner, and Off-Stage Dying," *SS*, 33 (1961): 1–9; Gustafson, A., *A History of Swedish Literature* (1961): 383–92; Mishler, W., "A Reading of H. B.'s Story 'Konstapel William,'" *Scan*, 10 (1971): 33–41; Linder, E. H., "H. B. in Hollywood: A Sad Chapter," *American Swedish Historical Foundation Yearbook* (1972): 45–62; Linder, E. H., *H. B.* (1975)

—RAYMOND JARVI

BERGSON, Henri

French philosopher and essayist; b. 18 Oct. 1859, Paris; d. 4 Jan. 1941, Paris

B.'s father, a musician, was descended from a wealthy Polish-Jewish family; his mother came from an English-Jewish family;

Henri Bergson

but B.'s education, career, and interests were typically French. From 1878 to 1881 B. studied at the École Normale Superieure in Paris. Then he taught at various French secondary schools. In 1900 he became a professor of philosophy at the prestigious Collège de France, a post he held until 1921, when various health problems forced him to retire. He was granted many honors in his lifetime: he was elected to the French Academy in 1914, received the Nobel Prize for literature in 1928, and the Legion of Honor in 1930. Besides his academic career, B. also took an active part in international affairs and was sent on several missions outside France during World War I. From 1921 to 1926 he was president of the Commission for Intellectual Cooperation of the League of Nations.

B. developed his philosophy of life in opposition to the then-prevailing mechanistic view of nature. Although he fully appreciated the value of science, B. felt that man could not be studied solely as its subject matter, since science is not concerned with the meaning of existence beyond the physical world. For him, life is not the same as matter, and man's mode of existence as a spiritual being transcends the scientific construct of a universe determined by a purely mechanical process of fixed causal laws. Contrary to science, which operates with clearly defined, measurable segments of time (labeled past, present, and future), human experience does not perceive real life as simply a uniform progression along some imaginary line extended in space, but rather as a continuous flow, each moment unique and unrepeatable, forming an indivisible process of irreversible successive states that are fused into each other to generate the continuity of human consciousness.

The distinction between "real time" (*temps vécu*–literally, "lived time"), characterized by duration (*durée*), and scientific clock time, Newton's *Tempus quod aequaliter fluit* (time that flows evenly), is of central importance for B.'s philosophy, and had a profound influence on modern thought. B. frees time from its reduction to a function of space and reestablishes it as an altogether autonomous dimension. Whereas scientific time is a mathematical conception measured by instruments (clocks and chronometers), perceived and conceptualized by the intellect, it is only through "intuition," the immediacy of human experience, that the reality of consciousness in its pure duration can be grasped as a flow of qualitative transformations.

Intuition in turn is a manifestation of consciousness, which for B. is synonymous with what he calls "memory." As is the case with time, B. distinguishes between two radically different kinds of memory: "pure memory" possessed by man alone, and "habit memory." The latter, a system of fixed habits (such as walking or playing the piano), has been acquired by the repetition of the same effort or the proper mastery of a lesson or skill; stored in an organism's nervous system, those habits respond automatically to a given stimulus encountered in the physical world. "Pure memory," on the other hand, a wholly spiritual manifestation, represents the ever-present totality of one's past mental states and events. And whereas "habit memory" is but a physiological function and depends on the brain, "pure memory" is a spiritual phenomenon, not caused by the brain. The brain, however, does have the function of a screening device, selecting from the simultaneous presence of the totality of one's experiences those memories that are of practical relevance in a given situation. The brain thus acts not only as a filter, it also is the point of connection between habit memory and pure memory. The autonomy of the mind, the creative energy of consciousness, are for B. irrefutable arguments that man's freedom is real and not an illusion.

The psychic force which in the case of man shows the superiority of mind over matter is also, according to B., the driving force in the process of evolution. Rejecting the mechanical or materialistic tenets of evolution based on mechanisms of natural selection from among chance variations, B. ascribes what he terms the "creative evolution" toward greater and greater complexity of organisms to an original, though immaterial, impulse of life (*éelan vital*). This immaterial force, whose existence cannot be scientifically verified, provides the vital impulse that continuously shapes all life, developing, changing, and generating new forms. Man's intuition reveals this impetus to be at work in the genuine duration of constant becoming.

B.'s moral philosophy closely parallels his philosophy of life and again reflects his belief in the superiority of mind over matter, of intuition over intellect. According to him, the roots of religion and morality can also be traced to the polar opposition of static and dynamic principles.

B.'s distinctive philosophical outlook concerning the creative possibilities of life, his staunch defense of humanistic and spiritual values, though not giving rise to a Bergsonian school of philosophy as such, exerted a considerable influence on modern thought in France especially (among critics of scientism and pragmatism, and existential thinkers), but also in many other Western countries (for example, in the works of William James and Alfred North Whitehead), and as far as Japan.

His philosophy, stressing the open flow of time and insisting on the all-important role of intuition for a genuine knowledge of reality, also found a strong echo in artistic circles (Debussy's music, Monet's paintings). And although B.'s references to art and artistic creation do not constitute a fully worked-out theory of art, his view of art as nondiscursive communication and immediate revelation, his idea that the artist's mode of vision is essentially free of conceptual and utilitarian orientation and that the artist's power of expression resides in his faculty to grasp intuitively the pure essence of consciousness, left their mark both on literature (VALÉRY, PROUST, PÉGUY) and literary criticism (Albert Thibaudet [1874–1936] and Charles du Bos [1882–1939]). But most significant, B.'s approach to philosophy contributed much to the Roman Catholic revival that took place in the early part of the 20th c.

FURTHER WORKS: *Essai sur les données immédiates de la conscience* (1889; *Time and Free Will*, 1910); *Matière et meémoire* (1896; *Matter and Memory*, 1911); *Le Rire* (1900; *Laughter*, 1911); *Introduction à la métaphysique* (1903; *Introduction to Metaphysics*, 1913); *L'évolution créatrice* (1907; *Creative Evolution*, 1911); *L'énergie spirituelle* (1919; *Mind-Energy*, 1920); *Durée et simultanéité* (1922); *Les deux sources de la morale et de la religion* (1932; *The Two Sources of Morality and Religion*, 1935); *La pensée et le mouvant* (1934; *The Creative Mind*,1946); *Écrits et paroles* (3 vols., 1957–1959; partial trans., *The Philosophy of Poetry; The Genius of Lucretius*, 1959); *Œuvres* (1959)

BIBLIOGRAPHY: Russell, B., *The Philosophy of B.* (1914); Chevalier, J., *H. B.* (1928); Scharfstein, B. -A, *Roots of B.'s philosophy* (1943); Bonhomme, B., *Educational Implications of the philosophy of H. B.* (1944); Arbour, R., *H. B. et les lettres françaises* (1955); Alexander, I. W., *B.: Philosopher of reflection* (1957); Hanna, T., ed., *The Bergsonian Heritage* (1962); Kumar, S. K., *B. and the Stream of Consciousness novel* (1962); Pilkington, A. E.,

B. and His Influence (1976); Kolakowski, L., *B.* (1985); Lacey, A. R., *B.* (1989)

—BLANIDINE M. RICKERT

BERGSSON, Guðbergur

Icelandic novelist, short-story writer, and poet, b. 16 oct. 1932, Grindavík

Born in a fishing village near Keflavik B. attended teachers' training college in Reykjavik. He never took up the profession, however, and stayed abroad for many years (mainly in Spain) studying and writing. He has translated a number of works by Spanish and Latin-American authors.

B. is the most important author in a revolt begun in the 1960s against the realistic traditions that up to that time had dominated Icelandic fiction. Although his works have appeared as separate novels and short stories, they are most adequately described as one continuous work. B. creates his own world. Its center is a small fishing village and the same people come and go through the various stories.

Realism and fantasy are intermingled in the description of this world: people are seen in familiar situations at work and at leisure, but then the camera moves closer and we look through "unspeakable" regions of body and mind. The people we meet are almost exclusively of the working class. Overburdened with labor that has no meaning, they drift through life in a stupor, dominated by lazy desires and vague dreams. In their more awake moments they give expression to greed and aggression. These people are passive and have very limited understanding of the forces that govern their lives, although they are constantly quarreling about their own confused ideas.

B.'s greatest strength is his re-creation and caricature of daily speech. The conversations of his characters are often extremely funny; retaining a recognizable tone, they glide smoothly into the area of the absurd and back again, revealing the prejudices, illusions, and delusions of the speakers.

B. portrays the general deterioration of human relationships and also exposes the hollowness of such modern myths as the nation, the family, and so forth. Paradoxically, however, the fictional universe becomes increasingly mythological. This contradiction is most clearly expressed through his narrators. The reader is systematically confused about who is telling the story. A small group of central figures with unclear identities (two persons may fuse into one and then part again) appear both as character in the narrative and as its creators. Thus there is a fundamental uncertainty about who speaks the text, an uncertainty that finally makes the reader the one who determines its significance.

B.'s works depict passivity and lack of freedom, and they contain no hint about how such a state of affairs should be changed. But they demonstrate creativity and freedom of imagination and challenge the reader to see and create himself.

FURTHER WORKS: *Endurtekin orð* (1961); *Músin sem læðist* (1961); *Leikfög leiðans* (1964); *Tómas Jónsson metsölubók* (1966); *Ástir samlyndra hjóna: Tólf tengd atriði* (1967); *Anna* (1969); *Hvoð er eldi guðs?* (1970); *Það sefur í djúpinu* (1973); *Hermann og Di´diacute* (1974); *Það rís úr djúpinu* (1976); *Flateyjar-Freyr:*

Ljóðfórnir; (1978); *Saga af manni sem fékk flugu i höfuðið* (1979); *Sagan af Ara Fróðasyni og Hugborgu konu hans* (1980)

—VÉSTEINN ÓLASON

BERNANOS, Georges

French novelist and essayist, b. 20 Feb. 1888, Paris; d. 5 July 1948, Neuilly

B. is considered the creator of the modern theological novel and one of the last great representatives of the Catholic revival in French literature. A largely self-taught writer who kept apart from the literary establishment, he brought to 20th-c. French fiction the power and visionary realism of Balzac and Dostoevsky. In his polemical works, intermittent echoes of the vehement voice of Léon Bloy (1846–1917) can be heard, but the French writer to whom he seems closest in both his vision and lyricism is the poet Charles PÉGUY.

The seeming paradox of B.'s spiritual life, in which an unshakable and often exuberant faith in Christ and the Church was shadowed by a life-long fear of death, persistent attacks of anxiety, and an at times overpowering despair, was reflected in the outer circumstances of his existence. Deeply rooted in his native Artois, a royalist and for years active supporter of the rightist Action Française movement, he broke with its leader, Charles Maurras (1868–1953), in 1932. It was a move that marked one of the most bitter crises of his life. Subsequently, poverty, then rage and shame over his country's moral failings turned him into a nomad and expatriate. For ten years he lived abroad, first settling with his large family in Palma de Mallorca in 1935, then, having witnessed some of the atrocities of the Spanish Civil War, moving to Brazil in 1938. When he returned to France in 1945, he was deeply disappointed at the absence of any sign of spiritual renewal.

B. wrote most of his major fiction in a period of barely twelve years. In 1926, at the age of thrity-eight, he published his first and instantly acclaimed novel, *Sous le soleil de Satan* (*Under the Sun of Satan*, 1949); ten years later appeared his fictional masterpiece, *Journal d'un curé de campagne* (1936; *The Diary of a Country Priest*, 1937), and by the end of that same year he had completed *Nouvelle histoire de Mouchette* (1937; *Mouchette*, 1966) and all but the final chapter of his last novel, *Monsieur Ouine* (1943; *The Open Mind*, 1949). His art matured as he moved from the romantic, even melodramatic supernaturalism of the first novel to the flawless integration of the supernatural into the humble realities of everyday life in *Journal d'un curé de campagne*, and finally, to the starkly modern, labyrinthine narrative of *Monsieur Ouine*. Yet his novels constitute an essentially indivisible creation, evoking a world that is both contemporary and timeless. A supernatural drama unfolds throughout the texts, in which divine grace and Satanic nonbeing vie for possession of man's soul, steering his protagonists either toward self-transcendence and fulfillment or toward self-forfeiture. In its 20th-c. rural and Parisian settings, existence for B.'s children, priests, writers, impostors, and madmen is a perilous adventure as they struggle to realize a heroic vision of man and his world, first glimpsed in childhood, only to be arrested and diverted from their quest by the mirages held out to them by Satan, God's ape and rival. They find themselves tossed back and forth between two powers whose solicitations appear too ambiguous to be discerned clearly. On the one hand, divine grace denudes the soul, leaving it in darkness as if struck by a curse, and turning existence into a mysterious reenactment of Christ's agony in the Garden of Olives. On the other, Satan the usurper, having invaded the soul through the lesions caused by pride, fear, or simple weariness, lures it into a false paradise of freedom and immunity from pain, there to empty it of its substance.

In *Monsieur Ouine* (that is, oui-non—yes-no), B.'s vision of evil is transformed into a poetic myth. Absence, dislocation, and ambiguity govern the work's structure, sharply intensifying its themes of quest and betrayal, violence and death. However, even though Satan does indeed emerge as prince of the world in the writer's novels, and the bulk of his humanity as aborted "stumps of men" who have missed their vocation, B.'s universe is free from the Manichean dualism of a François MAURIAC. An abiding, childlike faith underlies the somber narratives and keeps them anchored in the pivotal theme of childhood to which all other themes are linked. Childhood, in the spiritual sense in which B. conceived it, is that state of integrity and trust in which man resists the Satanic mirror of life and its reversed images, and "faces up" to his true calling; namely, to become a saint in the total gift of his being to divine love. However deeply submerged it may be, the child in B.'s protagonists, with the sole exception of the mythical figure of Ouine, is never wholly lost. Hence its power to surge up at any of the novel's dramatic moments of crisis and to redeem a destiny subverted by delusion by reversing its course.

Except for the end of *Monsieur Ouine* and the film script, drawn from a novella by Gertrud von Le Fort, *Dialogues des Carmélites* (1949; *The Fearless Heart*, 1952)—first made famous by Poulenc's opera—which is generally recognized as B.'s spiritual and artistic testament, the writer devoted most of the last twelve years of his life to a succession of powerful polemical essays and articles. One after another, he denounced the Franco repressions in Catalonia, the appeasement at Munich, the shame of the armistice and collaboration, the West's mindless surrender to materialism and technology and, finally, the cruel aftermath of the Liberation of France, and pleaded for a new spiritual and moral integrity. Among the best-known of these works are *Les grands cimetieres sous la lune* (1938; *Diary of My Times*, (1938), *Lettre aux Anglais* (1942; *Plea for Liberty*, 1944); and *Les enfants humilie´* (1949; *Tradition of Freedom*, 1950), the last of which contains some of his most moving writing. Although occasioned by the contingencies of history, these works have lost little of their power to stir the conscience of the Western world. Together with the novels, they have secured for B. a reputation as one of the major writers of his generation.

FURTHER WORKS: *Français, si vous saviez* (1961); *Œuvres romanesques* (1966); *Essais et écrits de combat* (1972)

BIBLIOGRAPHY: Estang, L., *Présence de B.* (1947); Picon, G., *G. B.* (1948); Balthasar, H. U., *v., B.* (1954); Béguin, A., B. *par lui-même* (1954); Gillespie, J. L., *Le tragique dans l'œuvre de G. B.* (1960); Bush, W., *Soffrance et expiation dans la pensée de B.* (1961); Blumenthal, G., *The Poetic Imagination of G. B.* (1965); Hebblethwaite, P., *B.* (1965); Bush, W., *L'angoisse du mystère: Essai sur B. et "Monsieur Ouine"* (1966); Milner, M., *G. B.* (1967); Speaight, R., *G. B.* (1974); Rivard, Y., *L'imaginaire et le quotidien: Essai sur les romans de G. B.* (1978)

—GERDA R. BLUMENTHAL

BERNARI, Carlo

(pseud. of Carlo Bernard) Italian novelist, essayist, and poet, b. 13 Oct. 1909, Naples

After having been expelled from school for antitotalitarian ideology during the Fascist regime, B. became a self-educated man. While in Naples, he became associated with those who frequented Benedetto CROCE's circle. After a brief stay in Paris, B. moved to Milan and finally settled in Rome. His militant journalism has been published in various journals and newspapers since the 1930s.

B.'s first novel, *Tre operai* (1934; three workers), is one of the most important forerunners of NEOREALISM. Banned by the Fascist regime and criticized even by leftist writers, *Tre operai* laid bare the rather bleak socioeconomic and political realities of Italy by focusing on the lack of class consciousness in workers, on the poor leadership and the contradictions within socialist and communist parties, on the poverty in southern Italy, on high unemployment, and on the general disillusionment of many Italians. The work is set in what B. calls "the third Naples," the industrial area unknown to tourists and to most other Italians.

A clear historical perspective, the fusion of naturalistic and semi-impressionistic descriptions, and the confrontations of individuals with society are characteristics of B.'s fiction in general. The dialectical approach to investigating the multifaceted aspects of reality enables B. to search for what he calls the "reality of the reality" (that is, not a final truth, but a truth that is a step closer to the "truth"). Southern Italy has provided him with rich subject matter for his search.

Speranzella (1949; little hope) and *Domani e poi domani* (1957; tomorrow and tomorrow) are two of B.'s most accomplished works; while remaining within the neorealistic mode (the treatment of the masses, the theme of the Resistance, the contrast between north and south, and the fusion of dialect and standard Italian), they show B.'s masterful analysis of the relationship between individuals and an environment that dehumanizes, frustrates, and forces man to become an actor in order to survive. In both novels B. examines the contradictions, the theatricality, and above all the suffering of Neapolitans and other southerners.

Some critics have attacked B. for eclecticism and excessive experimentalism, as a way of trying to justify their failure to find a consistent profile in his works. The more recent *Era l'anno del sole quieto* (1964; it was the year that the sun was least active) and *Un foro nel parabrezza* (1971; a hole in the windshield) do, in fact, show the stylistic differences between B.'s early and later novels. But they also demonstrate that his fiction is too complex (rather than eclectic) to be limited to any specific trend, such as neorealism. *Era l'anno del sole quieto* both reminds one in many ways of the defeats and disillusionments of *Tre operai* and is an excellent representative of the short-lived movement of "literature and industry" (from 1959 to the mid-1960s). B. focuses on the numerous contradictions of Italian society in showing the ridiculous obstacles the protagonist must overcome in trying to start a modern industry in southern Italy during the so-called "economic boom" of the 1960s.

Un foro nel parabrezza, seemingly a romantic detective story, is B.'s most interesting application of metaliterary techniques that he had experimented with in previous novels. Of particular interest is the close identification between the author-narrator-protagonist and the text itself, and also of the effect of the act of writing on the narrator as he recognizes himself as a protagonist of the story that he is inventing.

B. is a true "critical realist" (in LUKÁCS's use of the term) in his attempt to present the "totality" of a given social and political reality. Although B. has never abandoned the perspective of the traditional 19th-c. novel, his works demonstrate that he has always kept an open mind to contemporary linguistic and narrative techniques. His fiction often verges on the "essay-novel" because, as B. suggests, his works are intended to present a truth and not simply a story or a fact. During the past decade B. has finally received long-overdue critical attention.

FURTHER WORKS: *Quasi un secolo* (1940); *Il pedaggio si paga all'altra sponda* (1943); *Napoli pace e guerra* (1946); *Tre casi sospetti* (1946); *Prologo alle tenebre* (1947); *Siamo tutti bambini* (1951); *Vesuvio e pane* (1952); *Il gigante Cina* (1957); *Amore amaro* (1958); *Bibbia napoletana* (1960); *Per cause imprecisate* (1965); *Le radiose giornate* (1969); *Alberone eroe, e altri racconti non esemplari* (1971); *Non gettate via la scala* (1973); *Tanto la rivoluzione non scoppierà* (1976); *26 cose in versi* (1977); *Napoli silenzio e grida* (1977); *Dall'Etna al Vesuvio* (1978); *Il giorno degli assassinii* (1980)

BIBLIOGRAPHY: Borelli, L., on *Un foro nel parabrezza*, *BA*, 47 (1973): 127; Ricciardelli, M., on *Non gettate via la scala*, *BA*, 48 (1974): 554; Capozzi, R., "The Narrator-Protagonist and the Creative Process in C. B.'s *Un foro nel parabrezza*," *RomN*, 17 (1976): 230–35; Capozzi, R., "*Napoli silenzio e grida*: Myth, Reality and Theatricality in C. B.," *FI*, 2 (1979): 231–48

—ROCCO CAPOZZI

BERNHARD, Thomas

Austrian novelist, dramatist, essayist, and poet, b. 10 Feb. 1931, Heerlen, Netherlands

B. was raised in Austria, essentially by his grandfather, the author Johannes Freumbichler (1881–1949), after whom the eccentric protagonists in many of B.'s writings are modeled. B. contracted a serious lung ailment in 1948, coming so close to death in 1949 that he was given last rites. After his recovery in 1952, he studied music and theater, supporting himself by working as a court reporter for a Salzburg newspaper. B. published short prose pieces in the mid–1950s and three volumes of poetry in 1957–58, but his literary breakthrough came in 1963 with his first novel, *Frost*. Since 1965 B. has lived alone in a farmhouse in Upper Austria and traveled widely in Europe, writing prolifically and gaining a reputation as the *enfant terrible* of Austrian literature.

The setting, characters, themes, and style of *Frost* were to become characteristic of his later writings. A cantankerous man, a flawed genius given to philosophical speculation and to cynical verbal attacks against most people and institutions he has known, has fled to a backward village in a mountain valley where both the people and weather are cold and brutal. In long, disjointed monologues, he relates his viewpoints and observations to a young medical student who has been sent to the village. The student records what he sees and hears in the form of a daily report.

B.'s next major work, the novel *Verstörung* (1967; *Gargoyles*, 1970), is narrated by a student who accompanies his country-doctor father on his calls to patients, most of whom are both physically and mentally defective. The first part consists of the son's descriptions of this journey through an isolated mountain landscape where the stories of depravity, brutality, and decay only increase as one moves farther up the valley. The second part is the son's recounting of the monologue delivered by the last patient visited, a prince living in the decaying remains of a once glorious castle. The prince and his situation emerge as clear allegories for Austria, a country whose diminished present cannot compare with its illustrious past.

In B.'s two other major novels, *Das Kalkwerk* (1970; *Limeworks*, 1973) and *Korrektur* (1975; *Corrections*, 1979), one also finds odd and obsessed geniuses, the anachronistic and rebellious heirs to aristocratic fortunes. In *Korrektur*, Roithamer, who had taught in Cambridge but had returned regularly to his beloved—and—despised Austria, most recently in order to dispose of his family's vast wealth by building for his sister an elaborate house which he had designed and redesigned numerous times, possesses many similarities to the philosopher Ludwig Wittgenstein (1889–1951), whose influence on B. has been enormous. But the novel is not simply a *roman á clef*. When the house is almost completed, the sister dies, and Roithamer hangs himself.

All of B.'s fictional works are constructed along the lines of musical compositions. The pervasive atonality and dissonance correspond to the emotional state of his characters and to the world he depicts. The themes that recur in his works in endless variations–death, insanity, cruelty, sickness, decay, obsession, artificiality–are, remarkably, all presented without pathos, and, one must conclude, as antidotes to the general unwillingness which B. observes around him to face the harsh realities of life (and death) and to move past the ubiquitous illusions, lies, and clichés.

Beginning with *Ein Fest für Boris* (1970; a party for Boris) B. has also written ten full-length plays. The protagonists are usually more artificial and machinelike than those in his novels, and people-turned-into-puppets become a central image. Several plays revolve around people in theater, who, through endless role playing, become artificial and inhuman, incapable of distinguishing between appearance and reality, afraid to remove the masks and confront the void beneath. The plots in B.'s dramas are sparse, and long monologues prevail, but there is irony, even humor, and, at times, as in *Macht der Gewohnheit* (1974; *The Force of Habit*, 1976) or in *Vor dem Ruhestand* (1979; before retirement), genuine black comedy.

Since 1975 B. has also published three installments of his autobiography, *Die Ursache* (1975; the cause), *Der Keller* (1976; the cellar), and *Der Atem* (1978; the breath), which indicate clearly how directly his pessimistic world view has resulted from personal experience and careful observation of the world around him.

B. has won virtually every literary prize available to a German-language author. He is ruthlessly consistent in shattering illusions and myths, forcing readers to face the dark and unpleasant sides of life.

FURTHER WORKS: *Auf der Erde und in der Hülle* (1957); *In hora mortis* (1958); *Unter dem Eisen des Mondes* (1958); *Die Rosen der Einöde* (1959); *Amras* (1964); *Prosa* (1967); *Ungenach* (1968); *An der Baumgrenze* (1969); *Ereignisse* (1969); *Watten* (1969); *Der Berg* (1970); *Midland in Stilfs* (1971); *Gehen* (1971); *Der Italiener* (1971); *Der Ignorant und der Wahnsinnige* (1972); *Die Jagdgesellschaft* (1974); *Der Kulterer* (1974); *Der Präsident* (1975); *Die Berühmten* (1976); *Minetti* (1976); *Immanuel Kant* (1978); *Ja* (1978); *Der Stimmenimitator* (1978); *Der Weltverbesserer* (1979); *Erzählungen* (1979); *Die Billigesser* (1980)

BIBLIOGRAPHY: Botond, A., ed., *Uber T. B.* (1970); Arnold, H. L., ed., special B. issue, *Tuk*, No. 43 (1974); Gamper, H., *T. B.* (1977); Sorg, B., *T. B.* (1977); Barthofer, A., "The Plays of T. B.: A Report," *MAL*, 11 (1978): 21-48; Dierick, A. P., "T. B.'s Austria: Neurosis, Symbol or Expedient?" *MAL*, 12 (1979): 73-93; Fetz, G. A., "T. B. und die österreichische Tradition," in Paulsen, W., ed., *Österreichische Gegenwart* (1980): 189-205

—GERALD A. FETZ

BERRADA, Mohamed

Moroccan novelist, short-story writer, and critic, b. 14 May 1938, near Rabat

Born in Rabat, B. spent most of his formative years in Fez where he went to school. After high school, he went to Egypt in 1955 to complete his education. He attended Cairo University where he was awarded a bachelor's degree in Arabic literature. He returned to Morocco in 1960 and enrolled at the Muhammad V University in Rabat for graduate studies in philosophy. After gaining his diploma of higher studies in 1962, he joined the Moroccan National Broadcasting Service, where he worked for about two years as head of the Arabic program. In 1964 he took up an assistant professorship in modern Arabic literature at Muhammad V University. In 1970 he took time off from his teaching duties to go to Paris for graduate studies. He gained a doctorate in 1973, having written his dissertation on the 20th-c. Egyptian literary critic, Muhammad Mandūr (1907-1965). Back in Morocco, he resumed his teaching post at Muhammad V University. B. is one of the cofounders of the Union of Moroccan Writers. He served one term as the Union's Secretary, and three as its president. During the 1980s he became the editor of the Union's periodical *Āfāq*.

B. is a highly respected writer and literary critic who has published extensively in the leading literary journals of the Arab world. His writings include short stories and studies on Arabic and Western literature. He translated into Arabic his dissertation written at the Sorbonne, giving it the title *Muhammad Mandūr wa Tanzīr al-Naqd al-'Arabī* (1979; Muhammad Mandūr and the Theory of Arabic Literary Criticism). In the same year he published a collection of short stories entitled *Salkh al-Jild* (1979; Stripping Off the Skin). The stories, which had appeared in various periodicals previously, deal with a variety of topics, focussing on contemporary Moroccan society. The two volumes, appearing in the same year, helped to establish B.'s literary reputation in the Arab world.

As a writer, intent on bridging the gap between Francophone and Arabic writing in Morocco, B.'s contribution to modern Moroccan literature has been considerable. He has translated into Arabic several Francophone works by fellow Moroccan authors. One of the first works he translated is Mohammed Aziz Lahbabi's (1922-1993) *Du clos à l'ouvert* (1961; To Close and Open), a collection of twenty essays on national and international culture and civilization. The title B. gave it in Arabic is *Min al-Munghaliq ilā al-Munfatih* (n.d.). He has also translated nonfictional works by Abelkébir KHATIBI, among them, *Le roman maghrébin* (1968; The Maghrebian Novel) and *L'art calligraphique arabe* (1976; The Art of Arabic Calligraphy), titling them *Al-Riwāya al-Maghribiyya* (1971) and *Dīwān al-Khatt al-'Arabī* (1981) respectively. B translated Tahar BEN JELLOUN's long poem *Le discours du chameau* (1974; The Camel's Speech) as *Hadīth al-Jamal* (1975). B. has also translated into Arabic the works of some Western writers. His highly acclaimed *Al-Daraja al-Sifr fi al-Kitāba* (1981) is a translation of *Le degré zéro de l'écriture* (1953; *Writing Degree Zero*, 1977) by the French critic Roland BARTHES, one of the practitioners of structuralist literary analysis. *Al-Rabi' wa Fusūl Ukhrā* (1993) is a translation of LE CLÉZIO's collection of short stories *Printemps et autres saisons* (Spring and Other Seasons).

B. continued to publish short stories, translations from French, and works of literary criticism until 1987 when his first novel *Lu'bat al-Nisyān* (1996; *The Game of Forgetting*, 1996) appeared. The novel was an immediate success. It was translated into French, Spanish, and later English, and reprinted in 1992. B.'s second novel, *Al-Daw' al-Hārib* (1993; The Fugitive Light), has not met with the same success as his first novel, which is now on the syllabus of Moroccan schools. On the title page B. defines *Lu'bat al-Nisyān* as "a novelistic text." Discarding chronological order, the novel, in seven chapters of episodic sequences, presents the story of the central character, Hadi, over a period of thirty years. Narrated by several voices, Hadi's biography is intertwined with that of Morocco's modern history. The opening and closing chapters "In the beginning was the mother" and "Who among you remembers my mother?" introduce the mother figure, an important theme in a number of Maghrebi Francophone and Arabic works. The first chapter has three beginnings, the first two appearing almost like false starts, before the author settles for the third beginning, which leads to the narrative. The first beginning consists of two short paragraphs, which are Hadi's thoughts at his mother's funeral, while in the second, made up of three lines, Hadi reflects on the role of the mother in one's life. The third beginning gives a detailed description of Hadi's home in Fez, and the members of his extended family, including his mother and maternal uncle.

Lu'bat al-Nisyān is a novel that can be read at different levels. On one level, it is a work based on the author's autobiographical reflections, which he recreates as his central character's story. On another level, it provides an eye witness report of Morocco's modern history and social customs. The novel consists of a variety of discourses where the different characters mingle and interact. The text is written mainly in literary Arabic, while some passages, including the dialogue and narratives of the women, are produced in Moroccan Arabic. There are also French words interspersed in the narrative, either in Latin characters or in Arabic transliteration. This diglossic and bilingual aspect of the text vividly symbolizes the multilingual nature of present-day Morocco. The main thesis of *Lu'bat al-Nisyān*, however, is the relationship between the individual and the external world, an essential aspect of B.'s creative works.

FURTHER WORKS: *Franz Fanon aw Ma'rakat al-Shu'ūb al-Mutakhallifa* (1963); *Lughat al-Tufūla wa al-Hilm* (1986); *Fī āl-Kitāba wa al-Tajruba* (1980); *Qasā'id tahta al-Kamāma* (1985); *Al-Khitāb al-Riwā'ī* (1987)

BIBLIOGRAPHY: Hallaq, B., and T. Gonzalez-Quijano, *Nouvelles arabes du Maghreb* (1991); al-Wazzani, H., *Dalil al-Kuttab al-Maghariba* (1993); Boullata, I., Introduction to *Lu'bat al-Nisyān* (1996): 1-12

—FARIDA ABU-HAIDAR

BERRYMAN, John

American poet, b. 25 Oct. 1914, McAlester, Okla.; d. 7 Jan. 1972, Minneapolis, Minn.

Born into a Roman Catholic family named Smith, B. was moved from Oklahoma to Florida at age ten. After two years of domestic strife, B.'s father shot himself. His mother moved north and remarried, and B. took his stepfather's name. He was educated at Columbia College, where he came under the influence of Mark Van Doren (1894–1972), and at Clare College, Cambridge University. Returning to the U. S. before the outbreak of World War II, B. taught at Wayne State, Harvard, and Princeton. He taught at the University of Minnesota from 1955 until 1972, when he killed himself by jumping from a bridge in Minneapolis onto the frozen bank of the Mississippi.

The complexities of B.'s poetry derive from his learning, gnarled syntax, and self-analysis. Attempting to understand himself, he sought parallels in literature with his own situation, major

John Berryman

examples being his biography of Stephen Crane (1950) and a long poem about the colonial Massachusetts poet Anne Bradstreet (1612?–1672). These are psychological probings and attempts to exorcise his personal demons of despair and alcoholism. A posthumously published autobiographical novel with the ironic title *Recovery* (1973) records the downhill course of his struggle.

The quite different influences of Stephen Crane, Gerard Manley Hopkins, W. H. AUDEN, and W. B. YEATS are apparent in his early work, *Poems* (1942). *The Dispossessed* (1948) exhibits only occasional signs of his mature style.

B.'s distinctive poetic voice is heard in *Homage to Mistress Bradstreet* (1956). This poem of fifty-seven largely eight-line stanzas, though ostensibly a biographical meditation on Anne Bradstreet, has the effect of a dramatic dialogue. It interplays the thoughts of a woman of the 17th c. and a man of the 20th, both poets, both "blasted" in childhood, one by smallpox, the other by the suicide of his father.

Thereafter, B.'s work became increasingly self-analytical, the grounds of his malaise sought out by an internalized cross-examination. This exchange occurs between the male components of his personality, dramatized as "Henry Pussycat" and "Mr. Bones."

Women in B.'s poems are treated as objects—of desire, wonder, irritation, rage—but despite the particularity of description, which is sometimes exotic in detail, women are observed as if at a distance, as if they belonged to another order of existence. This is true of the sonnet sequence written in the 1940s, *Berryman's Sonnets* (1967), about a passionate but unhappy liaison with a married woman lasting ten years. Even in poems addressing another, B. appears to be speaking to some part of himself.

B.'s major work, *The Dream Songs* (1969), presents Henry, "a white American in middle age sometimes in blackface," and "a friend who addresses him as Mr. Bones." B. denied that Henry was himself, but, as the Dream Songs developed over fourteen years after 1955, the points of contact with his own turbulent life became more overt: the memory of his father's suicide, the love affairs, the bouts with alcohol. "He is always fighting the thing out with himself," a remark in his biography of Crane, characterized the Dream Songs. Twelve of them (146–157) record B.'s anguish at the death of his friend Delmore SCHWARTZ, whose early great promise as a poet he had watched dwindle.

The unremitting struggle to put off his own poetic decline gives B.'s mature work a nervous power, in which wrenched syntax and ellipses register his disturbed condition. They are, as in Hopkins, the physical manifestations of a tortured spirit. But they are also the measure of his determination to forge a language that could "add to the stock of available reality," words of R. P. BLACKMUR's that he quotes in "Olympus."

Late in life B. returned to Catholicism. His last two volumes of poetry, *Love & Fame* (1970) and the posthumously published *Delusions, Etc.* (1972), are often concerned with matters of faith. But B.'s approach remained histrionic, only modified to create dramatic personae such as "Lord of happenings" and "Your Majesty" to stand alongside the still present "Henry" and "Mr. Bones."

At their weakest, these late poems are overstated and melodramatic; at their strongest, they convey a sense of divine presence. But the self-dramatizing quality persists. When he reads a history of the early church, as he describes in one of the poems, B. "identifies with everybody, even the heresiarchs." In "Eleven Addresses to the Lord" B. records his personal agony: "terrible, and full of refreshment," which might well stand as an epitaph for all his work.

FURTHER WORKS: *Poems* (1942); *His Thought Made Pockets & The Plane Buckt* (1958); *77 Dream Songs* (1964); *Short Poems* (1967); *His Toy, His Dream, His Rest* (1968); *The Freedom of the Poet* (1976)

BIBLIOGRAPHY: Weber, B., "Two American Men of Letters," *WR*, 16 (1952): 329–34; Meredith, W., "Henry Tasting All the Secret Bits of Life: B.'s 'Dream Songs,'" *WSCL*, 6 (1965): 27-33; Howard, J., "Whisky and Ink, Whisky and Ink," *Life* (21 July 1967): 67–76; Linebarger, J. M., *J. B.* (1974); Martz, W., *J. B.* (rev. ed., 1975); Conarroe, J., *J. B.: An Introduction to the Poetry* (1977); Arpin, G., *The Poetry of J. B.* (1978)

—MANLY JOHNSON

BERTO, Giuseppe

Italian novelist and dramatist, b. 27 Dec. 1912, Mogliano Veneto; d. 1 Nov. 1978, Rome

The son of an authoritarian policeman, B. received his early education in a Catholic school. In 1935, during the Abyssinian war, B. joined the army and remained in Africa for four years. In 1940 he received a degree in art history from the University of Padua. In 1942, during World War II, B. again saw service in Africa; he was captured and taken as a prisoner-of-war to Hereford, Texas, where he wrote his first novel. From the time of his return to Mogliano Veneto, in 1946, to the 1960s B. devoted himself to novels, journalism, and movie scripts. In the early 1950s the first symptoms of his obsessive neurosis appeared, and he sought psychoanalytical therapy. This illness clearly influenced his writings and was partly responsible for his secluded life. After nearly two decades of isolation B. died of cancer, the very disease he had feared for many years.

B.'s Catholic upbringing, his difficult relationship with his father, his military experiences, his contacts with fellow writers, his paranoia, and his psychoanalytic therapy often became part of his works.

Il cielo è rosso (1947; *The Sky Is Red,* 1948) epitomizes B.'s early works, which are NEOREALISTIC and allegorical. These early writings denounce violence, social injustices, the evils of war, and the legacy of Fascism. *Il cielo è rosso* focuses on four children who try to survive war, hunger, and disease after they have been abandoned by the adults, by resorting to thievery and prostitution; all four are typical of B.'s fictional characters, who are victims of a "universal evil" and a sense of "guilt" that afflicts everyone.

What distinguishes B.'s early novels from the majority of neorealistic works is the psychological realism in the descriptions, the dialogue, and even the silences of the protagonists. Moreover, during this so-called neorealistic phase one finds many of B.'s personal preoccupations, which became more explicit in later works: ontological and existential arguments about death, suicide, destiny, resignation, "universal evil," suffering, solitude; a sense of guilt; an inferiority complex; sexual frustrations; and a love-hate relationship with a father who represents tradition, authority, and censorship.

Il male oscuro (1964; *Incubus*, 1965), B.'s best-known and most-discussed novel, describes B.'s own "obscure disease"—neurosis—rooted in his guilt feelings about his relationship with his father, alternating between repulsion and attraction, and in desires, anxieties, and other complexes dating back to his adolescence. The narrator's self-explorations are recounted through the technique of free association—long paragraphs with little or no punctuation. B. derived this technique from his Freudian therapy sessions, which were intended to free him from the "male oscuro." Yet some critics have considered the juxtaposition of present and past and the rendering of the flow of memories as mere variants of stream of consciousness or interior monologue. B.'s excellent use of irony in *Il male oscuro* is also found in *La cosa buffa* (1965; *Antonio in Love*, 1968), a novel of similar themes.

The novel *La gloria* (1978; the glory) was published a few months before B.'s death. This highly controversial work, derived from his earlier play *La Passione secondo no stessi* (1972; the Passion according to ourselves), purports to analyze, from Judas' point of view, his role in Christ's death and consequent glory. The first-person narration, according to B., was intended to establish a personal identification between protagonist and author, who himself had numerous questions and doubts about his fate, his role, and the meaning of "glory" (in part, the recognition from fellow writers and critics). Jesus is portrayed as being motivated by a death wish, while Judas is a man who must bear the guilt for having done something that was preordained and necessary to carry out God's plan and to assure Christ's glory. Judas and Christ, B.'s last protagonists, are presented as extremely neurotic.

Unlike the work of many of the early neorealists, B.'s transcends all national barriers, revealing universal truths about contemporary man: his aberrations, anxieties, and neuroses.

FURTHER WORKS: *Le opere di Dio* (1948; *The Works of God*, 1950); *Il brigante* (1951; *The Brigand*, 1951); *Guerra in camicia nera* (1955); *Unpo' di successo* (1963); *L'uomo e la sua morte* (1964); *La fantarca* (1965); *Anomimo veneziano* (1971); *Modesta proposta per prevenire* (1972); *Oh, Serafina!* (1973); *È forse amore* (1975)

BIBLIOGRAPHY: Praz, M., "Hemingway in Italy," *PR*, 15 (1948): 1086–1110; Kazin, A., on *The Sky Is Red*, *NYTBR*, 10 Oct. 1948: 5; Heiney, D., *America in Modern Italian Literature* (1964): 152–67; Ricciardelli, M., "G. B.: From Liberation to Politics and an Interview," *IQ*, 49 (1969): 65–76; Heiney, D., "The Final Glory of G. B.", *WLT*, 54 (1980): 238–40

—ROCCO CAPOZZI

BESSETTE, Gerard

Canadian novelist and critic, b. 25 Feb. 1920, Sainte-Anne-de-Sabrevois

B. was reared in a traditional Quebec family of modest means, within the shadow of the village church. After classical studies at the Collège Saint-Ignace and Sainte-Croix, he received a B.A. in 1941. Further studies at the Université de Montréal earned him a *licence*, an M.A. (1946) and a Ph.D. (1950), with a dissertation on imagery in French-Canadian poetry. Early on he carried out different types of work in Montreal and New York among other places, in a bookstore and in a factory and elsewhere. His teaching

career began at the University of Saskatchewan and he continued in such institutions of higher learning as Duquesne University, Pittsburg, the Royal Military College, Kingston, Ontario, and, from 1960 to 1980 in Queen's University, in the same city, all, with the exception of a year's stint in the mid-1960s at the Université Laval, in English-speaking North America.

His literary career was launched with a collection of poems, *Poèmes temporels* (1954), but it is chiefly as a novelist and literary critic that he is known. His first novel, *La Bagarre* (1958; *The Brawl*, 1976) focused on the working-class milieu of Montreal. Its protagonist, Jules Lebeuf, works as a laborer at night while pursuing his studies in the daytime and experiences the worlds of the achievers as well as of those whose future is bleak. The varied cast of characters, each with his own brand of French, showed B.'s preoccupation with language, a fascination that was never to leave him. The story concerns Jules's involvement with his coworkers' problems and reveals a sensitivity to the position of the uneducated in an environment dominated by others—English-speakers at the workplace and representatives of the Church in traditional educational circles. Jules will not fulfill his dreams to complete his studies and to write a novel, and the gifted daughter of a coworker whose advancement he promotes will not achieve her full potential in the English-language school, but will continue in the French school with its limitations. In addition to language, B. is concerned with social tensions in Quebec in the late 1950s.

These social preoccupations are evident in his second novel, *Le libraire* (1960; *Not for Every Eye*, 1962), the work that was to bring considerable fame to B. It appeared on the scene at a time of great change in Quebec society. With the death of Maurice Duplessis in 1959, the leader of the conservative forces in the province, Quebec society was ripe for a dramatic change. B's novel showed why this might be so. Its protagonist, Hervé Jodoin, a failed academic, accepts a position in a bookstore, the *Librairie Léon*, in the village of Saint-Joachim, a place unencumbered by interests in progress. The proprietor, Léon Chicoine, keeps a secret room of forbidden books, and Hervé is entrusted with the sale of these items in addition to his other duties. A crisis occurs when a work by Voltaire falls into the wrong hands, those of a student at a religious school, and the wrath of Quebec's conservative tradition falls upon the proprietor, who saves himself by putting the blame on his employee. But Jodoin gets his revenge on his employer and through him on conservative society by selling the books in Montreal and keeping the profits all to himself.

The work is presented in the form of a diary, written on Sundays when there is nothing else to do, and focuses on the three parts of Jodoin's life—the bookstore, the bar in which Jodoin spends the rest of his time drinking beer, and his rented room and his concomitant involvement with his landlady. In all three Jodoin shows a supreme indifference to all activities and involvements. The story is written in a dry, simple yet refined style, with an appropriate amount of wry humor and irony.

B. was to continue describing the worlds he knew best, with a shift, however, from obvious social preoccupations to a more direct focus on the world he lived in, that is, the academic world and the interpersonal relations which can exist there. *Les pédagogues* (1961; The Academics) and *Le semestre* (1979; The Semester) best exemplify this type of work. The latter describes the last semester of teaching in a professor's academic career, the scrutiny and critical presentation given to works studied in the classroom, the involvements with colleagues and students, and with the women who have played a significant role in his life. Personal involvements are connected to literary ones: Omer Marin's ruminations on life and literature allow us to understand his relationships with women and what he values—and does not value—in a work of art; he takes the opportunity to cast stones at contemporary Quebec writers. Just as others of B's works explore different stylistic approaches, this one takes on that of STREAM-OF-CONSCIOUSNESS writing.

As a literary critic and promoter of Quebec literature, as seen with his *Histoire de la littérature canadienne-française* (with others, 1968), *Anthologie d'Albert Laberge* (1962) and *De Québec à saint-Boniface: récits et nouvelles du Canada français* (1968), B. has shown himself to be quite productive, beginning with the publication of his dissertation, one of the first in Quebec to focus on Quebec literature, with its special focus on one of Quebec's most famous and admired poets, Emile Nelligan, and continuing with evaluations of contemporary Quebec literature: *Une littérature en ébullition* (1968), *Trois romanciers québécois* (1973), *Mes romans et moi* (1979), the first two being studies of important Quebec writers, the last a semi-autobiographical literary-critical approach. B. indulges in this work, as he has in previous ones, in Freudian psycho-critical discourse, not destined to receive a warm welcome from his audience.

B. remains among the most committed promoters of his country's literature in French. He has been the recipient of many honors, among them, the Governor-General's Award, awards from the Province of Quebec, and the David Prize, and he was elected a member of the Royal Society of Canada.

FURTHER WORKS: *L'Incubation* (1965, *Incubation*), *Le Cycle* (1971), *La Commensale* (1975), *La Garden-Party de Christophine* (1980), *Les Dires d'Omer Marin, roman/journal* (1985), *Correspondance* (1994).

BIBLIOGRAPHY: Allard, J., "Le Libraire de G. B. ou Comment la parole vient au pays du silence," *Cahiers de Sainte-Marie* (April 1967): 51-63; Edwards, M. J., "G. B.: A Tribute," *CanL*, 8 (1981): 6-18; Shek, B.-Z, "G. B.," in New, W.H, ed., *DLB*, 53 (1986): 49-60; Robidoux, R., *La Création de G. B.* (1987); Sylvestre, G., "G. B. et son oeuvre," *Écrits du Canada français*, 65 (1989): 97-108; Hamelin, L., "Dans le ventre du récit: lecture de G. B.," *Voix et images*, 20 (1995): 440-50; Monette, G.," G. B. et Jacques Ferron: personnages réciproques," *Voix et images*, 22 (1996): 126-47

—PAUL BARRETTE

BETI, Mongo

(pseud. of Alexandre Biyidi) Cameroonian novelist and essayist (writing in French), b. 30 June 1932, Akometam

Born in a small village, B. attended Catholic mission schools and a French lycée in nearby Yaoundé before going to France to study literature. He has not returned to his own country, for political reasons, since 1959. He now teaches at a secondary school in Rouen.

B. was only twenty-one when his first short story appeared, and twenty-two when his first novel was published. Both were signed

Eza Boto, a pseudonym he has since abandoned. In his novels written before 1960 B. offers his vision of the interplay of the two worlds of colonial Africa: the African society, the only one in which the natives can survive with integrity, and the colonial society, whose imperialist tentacles reach everywhere. These opposing forces generate violence of all sorts, and the effects of that violence in both the city and in the most remote country areas are demonstrated in B.'s novels. Those of his characters who try to meet the demands of both worlds inevitably fail and are condemned to a form of exile, to an "endless life of wandering."

B. shares with many other writers of his generation this sense of tragedy created by colonialism. The originality of his early novels, however, lies in his viewpoint and in the tone he adopted. He looks at the colonial world through the enlarging and yet selective prism of irony, showing a marked talent for parody.

The laughter of blacks in B.'s work, and the increasing importance it assumes as his literary production develops, bear witness to B.'s inner liberation and that of the African characters he portrays. In his first novel, *Ville cruelle* (1954; cruel town), the tragic tension is almost constant, leaving little room for the comic. On the other hand, in *Mission terminée* (1957; *Mission to Kala*, 1958) and *Le roi miraculé* (1958; *King Lazarus*, 1960), there is an explosion of healthy laughter, expressing the African's solid resistance to the white world.

In *Le pauvre Christ de Bomba* (1956; *The Poor Christ of Bomba*, 1971), B.'s masterpiece, irony is at the base of the presentation of the missionary world. In this novel B. did more than castigate the practices of colonialism—he showed that even well-meant intentions can cause disaster if an understanding of the values and particularities of the indigenous culture is lacking.

In 1958 B. decided to abandon writing as an anticolonial weapon and to become an activist in the African struggle for self-determination. (Two years later, in 1960, Cameroon became an independent republic.)

Since then, B. has concentrated upon the political problems of his own country and of Africa as a whole, particularly decolonization, which is either not being carried out at all or being carried out in the wrong way. After a long period of silence and thought, he decided to speak out again, first in a book-length political essay, *Main basse sur le Cameroun* (1972; the plundering of Cameroon), which denounces the injustices of a regime that he considered to be subservient to the former French colonial powers.

For Beti, political thought and fictional works are now more closely linked than ever, as can be seen in three new novels and in the periodical he founded in 1978, *peuples noirs, peuples africains*. In the novel *Perpétue* (1974; *Perpétue*) the story of Essola and his sister Perpétue takes place against the backdrop of a supposedly independent society that yields to mediocrity and corruption, and in which the weak are oppressed by a police state. *Remember Ruben* (1974; title in pidgin English), is a recreation of the period of resistance that led to independence, dramatizing the agitation of labor unions, urban guerrilla warfare, and political action. His latest novel, *La ruine presque cocasse d'un polichinelle* (1979; the almost laughable downfall of a buffoon) is a sequel to *Remember Ruben* and presents a second stage of resistance, which keeps its raison d'être even after independence.

No other black African writer has followed so closely the political evolution of Africa. Yet B. avoids the trap of producing works simply about immediate circumstances because he has succeeded in constructing a coherent fictional universe in which oppressed man searches, with numerous defeats and some successes, for the way to his liberation.

BIBLIOGRAPHY: Brench, A. C., *The Novelists' Inheritance in French Africa* (1967): 63–74; Cartey, W., *Whispers from a Continent* (1969): 32, 56–77; Cook, M., and Henderson, S. E., *The Militant Black Writer in Africa and the United States* (1969): 23–31; Macaulay, J., "The Idea of Assimilation: M. B. and Camara Laye," in Pieterse, C., and Munro, D., eds., *Protest and Conflict in African Literature* (1969): 81–92; Cassirer, T., "The Dilemma of Leadership as Tragi-Comedy in the Novels of M. B.," *ECr*, 10 (1970): 223–33; Melone, T., *M. B., l'homme et le destin* (1971); Lambert, F., "Narrative Perspective in M. B.'s *Le pauvre Christ de Bomba,*" *YFS*, No. 53 (1976): 78–91

—FERNANDO LAMBERT

BETJEMAN, Sir John

British poet, b. 28 Aug. 1906, London; d. 19 May 1984, Trebetherick, Cornwall

B., perhaps the most popular of all 20th-c. British poets, is celebrated for his light, almost comic, and often satiric depictions of England's recent past. B.'s father was a prosperous London businessman, and the young B. grew up in an affluent London suburb. He was sent to a private preparatory school where T. S. ELIOT was one of his teachers. B. attended Magdalen College, Oxford, in 1925, where he was mentored by C. M. Bowram (1898–1971) and tutored by C. S. LEWIS. While at Magdalen, B. met Evelyn WAUGH who became his lifelong friend. Even with such a solid scholastic foundation, B. was not a serious student, and he left Oxford in 1928 with no degree after failing his divinity examination. While at the university, B. had developed his interest in English architecture into a considerable knowledge on the subject, and after a year of teaching he took a position as assistant editor of the *Architecture Review* in 1931.

Soon after taking this position, B. published his first collection of poetry, *Mount Zion* (1931). The volume met with moderate sales, and four more collections were published over the next seventeen years. But B.'s first major success was the publication of his *Collected Poems* (1958). This collection was a best-seller and drew enthusiastic response from readers and critics alike. The poems were performed on the radio in a regular BBC series of readings, serialized in the *London Daily Mail*, and enthusiastically endorsed by the royal family, Princess Margret in particular. In 1960 the poetic autobiography *Summoned by Bells* was published, followed by four more collections, *High and Low* (1966), *A Nip in the Air* (1974), *Church Poems* (1981), and *Uncollected Poems* (1982). All of these volumes met with considerable success, and B.'s fame as a poet continued to grow. In 1969 he was knighted, and in 1972 he succeeded Cecil DAY LEWIS as poet laureate of England.

Paralleling his career as a poet is B.'s career as an architectural historian of some note. He is both highly regarded and prolifically published in this field. B. was the editor of several of the *Collins Guides* of England, and the author of numerous articles and several

Sir John Betjeman

volumes of architectural history. His nonfiction publications include *Ghastly Good Taste* (1933), *First and Last Loves* (1952), and *English Churches* (1964, with Basil Clarke).

B.'s poetry is marked by his extremely vivid, solid depiction of the very real landscape of modern England. B.'s subjects are drawn from the everyday experience of British life. He writes in conventional forms and meters, and his language is very open and accessible. His tone is most often light though often nostalgic. His poetry examines the conjunction of the comic and the tragic that is symptomatic of the conservative individual in rapidly changing modern society. B. invokes images of churches, houses, and markets as they exist only in memory, and likewise depicts the structures of social class and Anglicanism as they once were or as they once seemed in childhood. It is through this template of the past that B. views the modern world, his active nostalgia creating a ritual of reassurance. That he has struck a familiar cord is evidenced by his poetry's tremendous popular success. This unprecedented popularity has remained B.'s singular accomplishment.

FURTHER WORKS: *Continual Dew* (1937); *An Oxford University Chest* (1938); *Antiquarian Prejudice* (1939); *Old Lights for New Chancels* (1940); *John Piper* (1944); *New Bats in Old Belfries* (1945); *Slick but Not Streamlined* (1947); *A Few Late Chrysanthemums* (1954); *Poems in the Porch* (1954); *A Ring of Bells* (1962); *The Best of B..* (1978); *Collected Poems* (4th ed., 1979); *Uncollected Poems* (1982)

BIBLIOGRAPHY: Stanford, D., *J. B.: A Study* (1961); Press, J., *B.* (1974); Stapleton, M., *B.: A Bibliography of Writings by and about Him* (1974); Taylor-Martin, P., *J. B.: His Life and Work* (1983); Hillier, B., *Young B.* (1988)

—ROBERT GREENUP

BETOCCHI, Carlo

Italian poet, b. 23 Jan. 1899, Turin

After traveling through Italy and abroad as a land surveyor and a construction engineer, B. settled in Florence in 1945, and turned to a full-time literary career. Earlier he had been one of the founders of the journal *Frontespizio* (1929–40), an organ for Catholic artists, and a contributor to several literary magazines. Later he became editor of the literary journal *Approdo letterario*.

His first volume of poetry, *Realtà vince il sogno* (1932; reality conquers the dream) reveals a gentle and serene vision of life. An unflinching religious faith pervades all B.'s descriptions: scenes of the countryside, the seasons, family affections, man's work. Ordinary objects and common situations are outlined with great purity of perception and with warm sympathy for people in both their joys and their sorrows. In his later volumes, such as *Notizie di prosa e poesia* (1947; news of prose and poetry) and *L'estate di San Martino* (1961; Indian summer), there is a slight change toward a more somber tone because of the catastrophic events of war. All experiences, however, are still felt as proofs of his love for God and his fellow men, and B. reaffirms his fundamental belief in the goodness of life. A growing anxiety, almost a despair of finding a solution to man's suffering and loneliness, pervades *Un passo, un altro passo* (1967; one step, another step), in which B.'s usually optimistic view of the world often gives way to a gloomy feeling of disquietude about the hopeless fragility of human existence. Here the insistent theme of old age and death becomes symbolic of man's existential unease.

B.'s lyrical poetry stands apart from all fashionable literary schools, although lately some critics have linked him with HERMETICISM because of his increased rhythmic freedom and elliptical phrasing and because of the frequent use of analogy and assonance. B.'s humane and generally sunny outlook has made him one of the most popular poets in Italy today.

FURTHER WORKS: *Altre poesie* (1939); *Un ponte nella pianura* (1953); *Festa d'amore* (1954); *Poesie* (1955); *Il vetturale di Cosenza, ovvero viaggio sentimentale* (1959); *Cuore di primavera* (1959); *Sparsi pel monte* (1965); *L'anno di Caporetto* (1965); *Vino di Ciociaria* (1965); *Lo stravedere* (1970); *Prime e ultimissime* (1974); *Di alcuni nonnulla* (1979). FURTHER WORKS IN ENGLISH: *C. B.: Poems* (1964)

BIBLIOGRAPHY: Petrucciani, M., on *L'estate di San Martino*, BA, 36 (1962), 321; Alexander, S., on *C. B.: Poems, NYTBR* (12 April 1964): 5; Solomon, I. L., Introduction to *C. B.: Poems* (1964): 13–19; Ricciardelli, M., on *Un passo, un altro passo*, BA, 42 (1968), 565; Bergin, T. G., on *Prime e ultimissime, BA*, 49 (1975): 300–301

—RINALDINA RUSSELL

BETTI, Ugo

Italian dramatist, poet, novelist, short-story writer, and essayist, b. 4 Feb. 1892, Camerino; d. 9 June 1953, Rome

The son of a physician, B. moved with his parents when he was nine years old from Camerino to Parma, where in 1915 he graduated in law. Within a few days of his taking his degree, Italy was at war, and B. promptly volunteered for army service, later becoming an artillery officer. Captured at Caporetto in 1917, B. spent the next two years as a prisoner-of-war in Germany, and on returning to Italy he specialized briefly in railroad law before being appointed as a magistrate in the province of Parma. In 1930 he moved to Rome, where for the next thirteen years he was a judge in the Italian supreme court. After the collapse of the Fascist regime in 1943, he was relegated in a purge of the judiciary to the less exalted calling of archivist in the Roman law courts. In later years he became legal consultant to the Society of Italian Authors and Publishers.

B.'s earliest significant published work was *Il re pensieroso* (1922; the pensive king), a volume of mainly escapist poems written almost entirely during the period of his confinement in Germany in 1917-18. His leaning toward the fable, seen both here and in the opening section of his second volume of verse, *Canzonette: La morte* (1932; canzonette: death), is also reflected in his first volume of short stories, *Caino* (1928; Cain) as well as in one of his earliest plays, *L'isola meravigliosa* (1930; the wonderful island). B. soon abandoned pure fantasy for a more concrete, realistic manner, but much of his later work, especially his plays (most of which may be read as allegories of the human condition), contains mythical overtones.

Being by profession a high-court magistrate, and having received a fairly strict Catholic upbringing, B. was keenly interested in the theme of justice, which occupies a dominant position in his drama. In the most successful of his prewar plays, *Frana allo Scalo Nord* (1935; *Landslide*, 1964), he underlines the collective responsibility of society as a whole for the dilemmas of its individual members, and prescribes compassion as the only relevant form of justice for a bewildered humanity. In *Corruzione al Palazzo di Giustizia* (1944; *Corruption in the Palace of Justice*, 1962) the members of the judiciary of an unspecified country are seen engaged in a ruthless, underhand struggle for personal power, thus emerging as more corrupt than the people they are called upon to judge. These two plays epitomize the inadequacy of human justice. Their chief characters ultimately evince an innate moral awareness, which B. regarded as inseparable from the state of being human, and it is the strength of this quality that he attempts to reveal in his heroes and heroines.

B.'s finest play is probably *L'aiuola bruciata* (1952; *The Burnt Flower-Bed*, 1956), which explores in fascinating detail the morality and motivations of those who are active in public life, at the same time probing into the possible causes of what was later to be termed the generation gap, or the sometimes tragic inability of parents and teenagers to bridge the chasm between their contrasting perceptions of life's purpose and meaning. The play's main character is a prematurely retired political leader, who for many years has lived with his wife near a remote mountain frontier, in the shadow of a deep personal tragedy involving the mysterious death of an adolescent son. His former political associates attempt to use him as a sacrificial victim in a conspiracy to precipitate war with a neighboring state. But their plot misfires, and the play concludes on a note of optimism.

B. wrote twenty-five full-length plays, four volumes of poetry, four of short stories, a novel, two important essays, and countless newspaper articles. The quality of his work is uneven, but his best plays have assured for him a position of preeminence among Italian dramatists of the period following the death of PIRANDELLO.

FURTHER WORKS: *La padrona* (1927); *La casa sull'acqua* (1929); *Un albergo sul porto* (1933); *Le case* (1933); *Una bella domenica di settembre* (1937); *Uomo e donna* (1937); *Il cacciatore d'anitre* (1940); *I nostri sogni* (1941); *Il pease delle vacanze* (1942; *Summertime*, 1956); *Notte in casa del ricco* (1942); *Il diluvio* (1943); *Il vento notturno* (1945); *Ispezione* (1947; *The Inquiry*, 1966); *Marito e moglie* (1947); *La Piera Alta* (1948); *Lotta fino all'alba* (1949; *Struggle till Dawn*, 1964); *Irene innocente* (1950); *Spiritismo nell'antica casa* (1950); *Delitto all'isola delle capre* (1950; *Crime on Goat Island*, 1961); *La regina e gli insorti* (1950; *The Queen and the Rebels*, 1956); *Il giocatore* (1951; *The Gambler*, 1956); *La fuggitiva* (1953; *The Fugitive*, 1964); *Favola di Natale* (1955); *Acque turbate* (1955); *Poesie* (1957); *Teatro completo* (1957); *Religione e teatro* (1957); *Scritti inediti* (1964)

BIBLIOGRAPHY: Ambros, C., *U. B.s Dramatisches Werk* (1959); Scott, J. A., "The Message of U. B.," *Italica*, 37 (1960): 44–57; McWilliam, G. H., "Interpreting B.," *TDR*, 5, 2 (1960): 15–23; McWilliam, G. H., Introduction to *Crime on Goat Island* (1961): vii-xiv; Rizzo, G., "Regression-Progression in U. B.'s Drama," *TDR*, 8, 1 (1963): 101-29; McWilliam, G. H., Introduction to *Three Plays on Justice* (1964): vii-xvi; McWilliam, G. H., Introduction to *Two Plays* (1965): ix-xxii; Curetti, E., *Zu den Dramen von U.B.* (1966)

—G. H. MCWILLIAM

BEYALA, Calixthe

Cameroonian novelist, b. 1961, Douala

B. was reared in New-Bell, a Cameroonian shanty-town where she was the sixth of twelve children. Her early exposure to devastating poverty haunts many of her novels. B. went to school in Douala and Bangui, and later moved to Europe, living in Malaga and Corsica before settling in Paris. Her novels have been translated into several languages, and more translations of her work can be expected, given B.'s popularity and the controversies she has raised among international scholars.

B.'s most well-known novel to date is *Les honneurs perdus* (1996; Lost Honors), which won her France's Grand Prix du Roman in 1996. The first African novel to be awarded the prize, *Les honneurs perdus* depicts the tumultuous lives of African immigrants in Paris. This theme also pervades her earlier novels, *Le petit prince de Belleville* (1992; *Loukoum: The Little Prince of Belleville*, 1995) and its sequel *Maman a un amant* (1993; Mother Has a Lover). As in all of her works, *Les honneurs perdus* focuses on African women's struggles for liberation from racism and sexism. The novel's narrator, Saida, is born in Cameroon and voyages to Paris with a "certificate of virginity" given to her by a local African pharmacist. The theme of the surveillance of woman's sexuality is also taken up in B.'s first novel, *C'est le soleil qui m'a brûlée* (1987; *The Sun Hath Looked upon Me*, 1996).

B.'s name made international headlines in the literary world when Pierre Assouline, editor of the French monthly literary magazine *Lire*, accused her of plagiarism. Assouline found similarities between passages in *Les honneurs perdus* and Nigerian author Ben OKRI's *The Famished Road* (1991). Okri did not press charges. However, B. was ordered to remove certain phrases from *Le petit price de Belleville* that resembled American author Howard Buten's (dates n.a.) novel *When I Was Five I Killed Myself* (n.d.). Assouline later accused B. of plagiarizing Alice WALKER's *The Color Purple* (1982). The incidents are known in France as "l'affaire B." B.'s defenders argue that her references to other texts were intentionally employed as literary devices, and that Assouline's attacks on B. were motivated by racism. The affair stirred up lively debates on poetic license, intertextuality, and literary originality.

All of B.'s novels strongly critique the exploitation of women and children. The Cameroonian narrator of *C'est le soleil qui ma' brûlée* tells of being physically prodded by her aunt who watches over her virginity in order to ensure a generous bride price. The plight of violated women is explored further in *Tu t'appelleras Tanga* (1988; *Your Name Shall Be Tanga*, 1996), where B.'s protagonist is prostituted by her mother as a young child. B. often focuses on the point of view of children who are silenced and dominated by adults. The settings for the narrations are usually the poor quarters of Paris or Cameroon, and the terrible conditions there are described in graphic detail. The need to escape from such oppressive environments permeates B's works.

All of B.'s works seem to invite controversy. The targets of her criticism are issues that have fueled much debate: prostitution, the treatment of illegal immigrants, polygamy, female excision, and hegemonic constructions of masculinity. While B's works explore painful experiences and serious political problems, her humor—often displayed through the active imagination of children—is a delight to read. Her novels are challenging, requiring that the reader participate fully in the process of interpretation. B's variant narrative styles, her humor, and her poignant interrogation of the exploitation of children, immigrants, and African women have made her not only a very popular writer, but also one of Cameroon's most important contemporary artists.

FURTHER WORKS: *Seul le diable savait* (1990); *Assèze l'Africaine* (1994); *La petite fille du révèrbere* (1998)

BIBLIOGRAPHY: Volet, J.-M., "C. B., or the Literary Success of a Cameroonian Woman Living in Paris," *WLT*, 67 (Spring 1993): 309-14; d'Almeida, I., *Francophone African Woman Writers* (1994): 72-87; Celerier, P., "'The Disorder of Order': Constructions of Masculinity in the Works of Mongo Beti and C. B.," *RomN*, 36 (Fall 1995): 83-92; Cazenave, O., *Femmes Rebelles: Naissance d'un nouveau roman africain au féminin* (1996): 80-92

—ELLIE HIGGINS

BEZRUČ, Petr

(pseud. of Vladimír Vašek) Czechoslovak poet (writing in Czech), b. 15 Sept. 1867, Opava; d. 17 Feb. 1958, Olomouc

The son of a nationalist grammar-school teacher, B. attended secondary school in Brno and studied classical and Czech philology as well as philosophy in Prague. Not completing his university studies, he became a postal employee, mainly in Brno, although his two-year stay in Místek, in Moravian Silesia near the coal-mining district (1891-93), had a profound influence on his literary work. Shy and modest, he used a number of pen names to avoid publicity, and remained unmarried and solitary. During World War I B. was imprisoned by the Austro-Hungarian authorities, since he was considered politically suspect because of his support of the Czechs' striving for national independence. Through his poetry he became an ardent spokesman for the social and political freedom of the Silesian people, the "first bard of the Beskyd mountains."

B.'s fame rests on one book. Compared with *Slezské písně* (1903, enlarged eds. 1909, 1937; *Silesian Songs*, 1966), a collection of truly great poems, his other publications are minor, marginal, or less inspired, although clever and witty. The first edition contained thirty-one poems, but B. always returned to his subject, enlarging the collection until the final version in 1937 listed eighty-two poems. B.'s inspiration was rooted in his childhood experiences and his love of his native Silesia: the suffering of poor coal miners and furnace workers, helpless against exploitation by the rich industrialists. Together with this social oppression went Germanization and Polonization of the area, and B. also saw that the poor people were exploited by shrewd businessmen, often Jewish, who encouraged them to spend their meager earnings on drink. The administration in the capital, Prague, too, was attacked by B. for its neglect and its rather casual attitude toward Silesian affairs. In *Slezské písně* B. identifies with the masses of nameless miners, expressing their frustration, anger, hopelessness, and hatred; his voice is often lamenting, even desperate, but sometimes strong and calling for action and revenge.

B. was influenced by a number of Czech as well as foreign poets; he learned the art of the ballad from Poe. In a number of poems, particularly the famous "Maryčka Magdónova" ("Maryčka Magdónova," 1966), B. applied Poe's theory that ballads should be short, have a refrain, and have as the main theme a death, especially of a young woman. "Maryčka Magdónova" and "Kantor Halfar" ("Schoolmaster Halfar," 1966) are perhaps the most powerful ballads in *Slezské písně*, since in these poems the social and national themes merge. A sad note, the result of erotic embitterment, can also be heard in B.'s fine intimate poems in the same collection.

B. frequently used words of local dialect, which gave his language a unique power and flavor without reducing him to the position of a mere regional poet. The clear symbolism of *Slezské písně* and the determined defense of the oppressed made B.'s poetry very popular, and he was awarded the title of National Artist in 1945.

FURTHER WORKS: *Studie z Café Lustig* (1889; *in book form*, 1928); *Moravská zem a moravská řeč: Republika před Svatým Petrem* (1923); *Stužkonoska modrá* (1930); *černá hodinka s. P. B.* (1931); *Jistebský či Jistebnický* (1936); *Paralipomena* (1937); *Lolo a druhové* (1938); *Křivý úsměv ještěrský* (1942); *Mláďátko* (1948); *Je nás šest* (1950); *Písně* (1953); *Verše starého ještěra* (1957); *Povídky ze života* (1957); *Přátelům i nepřátelům* (1958); *Labutinka* (1961)

BIBLIOGRAPHY: Harkins, W. E., ed., *Anthology of Czech Literature* (1953): 147–48; Korbel, P., "Writers in Czechoslovakia under Communism," *Thought Patterns*, 6 (1959): 91–126; French, A., ed., *Czech Poetry* (1973): 323; Novák, A., *Czech Literature* (1976): 236

—B. R. BRADBROOK

BHARATI, Subramania

(pseud. of C. Subramania Iyer) Indian poet, essayist, novelist, and short-story writer (writing in Tamil), b. 11 Dec. 1882, Ettayapuram; d. 12 Sept. 1921, Madras

B. grew up in the feudal surroundings of a petty south-Indian raja's court. Although he had little formal education, his natural gifts as a poet were recognized early on, and he soon became a companion and poet to the raja. As a court poet he took the name of Shelleydasan (servant of Shelley) and formed a literary club in Ettayapuram called the Shelley Club. The English romantic poets, especially Shelley and Byron, appealed to B. and other Indian writers of the period and influenced the styles of both their literature and politics.

In 1904 B. moved to Madras to become an editor of one of the numerous Tamil magazines that had sprung up in connection with the Indian nationalist movement. He soon became involved with activities of the Congress Party and because of that involvement was forced to flee to Pondicherry, then under French control, where he remained for the next ten years (1910-20) as a poet in exile. During this period B. became well known throughout the Madras region for his nationalist essays and poems. Only after his death, however, was he truly recognized as the father of modern Tamil poetry.

The fact that B. never left India had a profound influence on his work. Unlike many of his contemporaries, whose work now appears sadly derivative, B. used his Westernized education sparingly and borrowed much from the cadences and images of the two-thousand-year-old Tamil literary tradition. On this foundation, however, B. created a body of poetry that is radically modern; he is often called the "poet of revolution." More than three hundred lyric poems on patriotism and spiritual devotion and three longer poems are his best-known works. His poetry, however, represents only a fraction of his oeuvre. He also wrote hundreds of essays and was one of the first Tamil writers to experiment with both the short story and the novel.

B.'s three longer poems-*Kannan pattu* (1917; *The Krishna Songs*, 1977), *Pancali capatam* (1912; *Panchali's Vow*, 1977), and *Kuyil pattu* (1912; *Kuyil's Song*, 1977) represent his very best work. *Kannan pattu* and *Pancali capatam* both take their themes from Indian mythology. *Kannan pattu*, the shortest of these three works, glorifies the life of the god Krishna, while *Pancali capatam*, a longer work, retells one story from the Indian epic the *Mahabharata*. *Kuyil pattu* is a lyric fantasy recounting the daydreams of a poet who imagines himself entranced by the stories of a cuckoo bird. In all three poems he introduced the Tamil reader to a lyrical literary language, yet one almost everyone would find remarkably familiar.

FURTHER WORKS: *Mahakavi B. kavitaigal* (1957); *Mahakavi B. katturaigal* (1962); *Mahakavi B. kataigal* (1964). FURTHER WORKS IN ENGLISH: *Agni and Other Poems and Translations* (1937); *Essays and Other Prose Fragments* (1937); *B.'s Writings: Essays* (1940); *The Voice of a Poet: Renderings of B.'s Verses* (1951); *Poems* (1977)

BIBLIOGRAPHY: Ramaswami Sastri, S. K., *S. B.: His Mind and Art* (1951); Subramanian, K. N., ed., *B.* (1959); Nandakumar, P., *S. B.* (1968); Bharati, S. V., *C. S. B.* (1972)

—RICHARD S. KENNEDY

BIALIK, Chayim Nachman

Hebrew poet, short-story writer, and essayist (also writing in Yiddish), b. 9 Jan. 1873, Radi, in Volhynia, Russia; d. 4 July 1934, Vienna (buried in Tel Aviv)

Raised in rural Russia, B. lived with his strictly pious grandfather after his father's death in 1880, and received a thorough, traditional Hebrew education. In 1890 B. moved to Lithuania to study in an urban Talmudic seminary (yeshiva), where, in addition to the conventional curriculum, he read widely in Hebrew, Yiddish, and European literatures. In 1891 he left the yeshiva for Odessa, where he devoted himself to the study of Russian and German, in addition to his reading and writing in Hebrew. In Odessa, too, he met important writers of the Jewish enlightenment (*haskalah*) and wrote poems that reflected their themes and styles. After an unsuccessful business venture with his father-in-law (1893-97), B. became a Hebrew teacher in a small town near the Prussian border (1897-1900) and later (1900) found similar employment in Odessa, where he lived, aside from a stay in Warsaw (1903-5), until 1921. B. was active in Zionist and literary circles and, besides writing poetry and short stories in Hebrew and Yiddish, published criticism, compiled an anthology of rabbinic lore, prepared school versions of biblical stories for the press, edited the works of major medieval Hebrew poets, and translated various European works. In 1921, after considerable difficulty as a Zionist in Communist Russia, B. secured permission to emigrate, along with a small group of other Hebrew writers. He first went to Berlin and then to Tel Aviv (1924), where he spent most of the rest of his life. During his final years, B. accepted responsibility for a variety of cultural and civic projects including missions for the Zionist cause to Europe and America.

B.'s earlier poems confront the disintegration of the traditional Jewish world. The central conflict between religious faith and Western modernity provides thematic material for many of his poems, and the misery of Jewish exile is often juxtaposed, in tones that suggest biblical prophecy, with denunciation of his people's decay, dullness, and failure to act decisively. Numerous critics have pointed to the remarkable fusion of personal and national feeling in B.'s work, a quality that helped to win him the reputation of a national poet of the Jewish people. Nevertheless, his attitude toward official Zionism was somewhat ambivalent. Although he accepted the spiritual-cultural approach of the essayist and thinker Echad Haam (pseud. of Asher Hirsch Ginsberg, 1854-1927) to Jewish nationalism, its dryness of imagination often stifled him as a growing artist. B.'s early poems are more striking as descriptions of the bitterness of exile than as paeans of praise for the Zionist endeavor. They are characterized by images of weeping, a motif associated with both exilic misery and messianic redemption.

B. reached the peak of his poetic development while in Warsaw working as literary editor of *Hashiloach*, where his contact with SYMBOLISM had a broadening effect. He wrote passionate love poems that seem to have been conveniently ignored by the anthologizers who have "kidnapped" (R. Alter's term) B. for the

Chayim Nachman Bialik

schools. The national poet is usually represented in the classroom by his less erotic early poems with obvious overtones of public morality. The longer works written during or immediately after his stay in Warsaw teem with complexity, whether they treat nature or the traditional Jewish myths of exile and redemption. "Habrechah" (1904; "The Pool," 1932) infuses a naturalistic description of a pond in a forest with symbolist technique, so that the poem's vividly depicted scenes of calm and storm reflect a variety of emotional and spiritual worlds. Despite their symbolic resonance, however, B.'s forest and pond convey their spiritual significance only as a function of their physical presence. "Mgilat haesh" (1905; "The Scroll of Fire," 1924) combines all of the major themes of B.'s poetry in an amalgam of biblical language, mythic presentation of historical exile, and search for national and individual redemption that will remedy the almost mystical forces of destruction. A disturbing tension intrudes upon the public themes of national myth with the inexorable, sexual demands of love, which motivate much of even the most idealistic action of the poem. This epiclike prose-poem marks the height of B.'s poetic intensity and development. Soon after completing it he moved into a poetic world charged with silence and preoccupied with death. Thus, the end of this period also marks a decline in his productivity. After 1906 B. wrote more prose than poetry and devoted himself to scholarly and cultural pursuits.

B. is universally recognized as one of the most important Hebrew poets of the 20th c. His verse incorporates references to the same sources that served as models for his predecessors, but by forcing his allusions to do his own bidding, he achieved an originality in creative tension with his tradition that goes well beyond the slavish imitation of earlier Hebrew writing. Although in reading aloud, the contemporary Israeli pronounces B.'s poems very differently from the way the poet did (B. generally wrote in the Ashkenazic accent, as opposed to the Sephardic usage that has become normative in Israel), their influence on all aspects of Hebrew writing is still acutely felt. His works provide Israel with some of its only classics of the modern period, and critics have applied a wide range of analytical approaches to his texts.

FURTHER WORKS: *Kitve H. N. B. umivchar tirgumav* (4 vols., 1926); *Lider un poemen* (1935); *Igrot H. N. B.* (5 vols., 1937–1939). FURTHER WORKS IN ENGLISH: *Poems from the Hebrew* (1924); *Far over the Sea: Poems and Jingles for Children* (1939); *Complete Poetic Works of H. N. B.* (1948; only one vol. published)

BIBLIOGRAPHY: Spiegel, S., *Hebrew Reborn* (1930): 295–312, 457–58; Halkin, S., *Modern Hebrew Literature: Trends and Values* (1950), passim; Rubner, T., "H. N. B.," in Burnshaw, S., ed., *The Modern Hebrew Poem Itself* (1965): 18–34; Alter, R., *After the Tradition* (1969): 226–40; Silberschlag, E., *From Renaissance to Renaissance: Hebrew Literature* 1492–1970 (1973): 181–86, 382–83

—NOAM FLINKER

BIAŁOSZEWSKI, Miron

Polish poet, memoirist, essayist, short-story writer, and dramatist, b. 30 July 1922, Warsaw; d. 17 June 1983, Warsaw

Like every Polish writer of his generation, B. was deprived of an ordinary youth by the ravages of World War II. As a young man of twenty-two he lived through the horrors of the Warsaw Uprising—an event which he was later to label the most important experience of his life. His education was undertaken piecemeal in the underground Warsaw University, and his first strong opinions about literature and its social role were formed amidst the chaos of war. It is not surprising that he, like many of his peers, is leery of making any claims for the transcendency of artistic and aesthetic values.

B. is noted for his radical experimentation in each of the major areas of literature. His theatrical pieces, collected in *Teatr osobny 1955-63* (1971; private theater 1955-63), are idiosyncratic works based on absurd dialogues between bizarre figures in incongruous settings. In *Wiwisekcja* (vivisection), for example, the characters are ten fingers involved in pseudophilosophical discussions about infinity while a comb looming above them presents an imminent threat to their existence. The "private theater" for which these plays were written was directed and acted in by B., and was also housed, for a time, in his Warsaw apartment.

B. published his first book of poetry in 1956 after writing "for the drawer" during the worst years of Stalinist repression. *Obroty rzeczy* (1956; *Revolutions of Things*, 1974) displays an eccentric reverence for homely objects such as spoons and stoves, but is not strikingly experimental in form. In succeeding volumes of poetry B. has broken with almost every norm of poetic diction and structure. His poems depend to a great extent on linguistic playfulness, manifested in such obvious devices as punning and the use of neologisms, and also in the unexpected assimilation into poetic speech of features of urban slang and the language of young

children. The subject matter is idiosyncratic, and the later collections of poetry have the appearance and tone of fragmented excerpts from the diary of an urban neurotic who is blessed with a wry sense of humor.

B. apparently abandoned poetry for anecdotal prose miniatures by the early 1970s. The anecdotes of daily experience, brief occasional pieces, and fragmentary meditations which had previously appeared in poetic form (unrhymed and arhythmical, to be sure) took on the shape of prose pieces in *Donosy rzeczywistości* (1973; denunciations of reality). There is no clear borderline between poetry and prose in B.'s writings.

B.'s longest and perhaps most important work is *Pamietnik z Powstania Warszawskiego* (1970; *A memoir of the Warsaw Uprising*, 1977). Characteristically breaking with received tradition, B. effectively mixes the genres of diary, eyewitness account, memoir, and historical study in his effort to capture the essence of civilian life in besieged Warsaw during the sixty-three days of the 1944 uprising. His account is chaotic, clumsy, fragmentary, and, at the same time, lyrical. It is the most significant work of art to have come out of the tragic devastation of the city and population of Warsaw.

Although not a prolific writer, B. is an important figure in the "linguistic school" of Polish poetry. His formal experimentation has helped to enlarge the definition of poetic style, while his often prosaic subject matter demands a new definition of what is aesthetically acceptable. If in his lesser work he has only played the important role of the gadfly, in his memoirs and a number of his poems he has made a lasting contribution to the corpus of Polish literature.

FURTHER WORKS: *Rachunek zachciankowy* (1959); *Mylne wzruszenia* (1961); *Bylo i bylo* (1965); *Wiersze* (1976); *Szumy, zlepy, ciągi* (1976); *Zawal* (1977)

BIBLIOGRAPHY: Levine, M., "Fragments of Life: M. B.'s Poetic Vision," *SEEJ*, 20 (1976): 40–49; Levine, M., Introduction to *A Memoir of the Warsaw Uprising* (1977): 9–18

—MADELINE G. LEVINE

BICHSEL, Peter

Swiss short-story writer, novelist, essayist, and journalist (writing in German), b. 24 Mar. 1935, Luzern

B. is one of the best-known contemporary Swiss fiction writers and essayists. Born in Luzern, B. was raised in Olten, where he passed a quiet and introspective childhood. Following pedagogical studies in Solothurn, B. taught at an elementary school in Zuchwil (1957–1968). Increasingly involved in literary activity, B. participated in the Literary Colloquium in West Berlin (1963), and in 1965 soared to prominence after the publication of his *Frau Blum* collection of stories. Apart from his work as a writer of fiction, B. is an influential columnist whose numerous articles on literary and cultural topics have appeared in a variety of newspapers. B. has also taught and lectured extensively abroad. He is married and resides in Bellach.

B.'s rise to eminence was occasioned by the appearance of his first major work, *Eigentlich möchte Frau Blum den Milchmann*

Kennenlernen (1964; *And Really Frau Blum Would Very Much Like to Meet the Milkman*, 1968), a group of twenty-one miniatures focusing on the common-place activities of the ordinary middle-class characters. Unable to establish genuine human contact with others, and vaguely aware of a missing dimension in their lives, B.'s essentially passive figures seem ossified in the loneliness and isolation of daily routine.

Evident in a subsequent volume of stories, *Kindergeschichten* (1969; *Stories for Children*, 1971), is B.'s fascination with the individual's place in a world of "dead" knowledge that has lost its power to compel human belief and acceptance. Probably the best known of these stories is "Ein Tisch ist ein Tisch" ("A Table Is a Table"), in which an old man, hoping to create for himself a fresh world of sensory experience, gives new names to familiar objects only to end in the utter frustration of linguistic isolation.

B.'s stories reveal a narrative starkness approaching that of the fairy tale. Far from being traditional heroes, his sparsely drawn characters often resemble marionettes in their apparent simplicity. Notably absent in his work is an emphasis on the social, sexual, and philosophical problems frequently explored by other writers. B.'s approach to the story is essentially that of the unspoken. In contrast to earlier practitioners of short fiction, B. is reluctant to move into the clear light of day the problems affecting the average *petit bourgeois*. His is the art of the intimation, and of the narrative gap. Focusing on the concrete, his sentences are unfailingly simple in structure and diction, and without rhetorical flourish.

Apart from his contributions to the Swiss short story, B. is also known as a novelist, essayist, newspaper columnist, and sometime radio commentator. In the novel *Die Jahreszeiten* (1967; the seasons) B. reveals another of his auctorial preoccupations: the writer's relationship to the process of writing, and the unavoidable contrasts and contradictions implicit in that relationship. An account of a man's frustrating attempt at writing a novel, *Die Jahreszeiten* resembles an antinovel in its questioning of the traditional values and assumptions of fiction. B.'s essays embrace a broad range of literary, political, and cultural topics, and are marked by pithiness, economy, and a straightforward clarity of style. *Des Schweizers Schweiz* (1969; the Switzer's Switzerland), his earliest volume of essays, evoked widespread discussion and controversy with its unambiguous critique of contemporary Swiss culture. B. has also made a number of radio commentaries and addresses, and several of his works have been adapted for presentation on radio and television.

B.'s current reputation rests above all on his standing as a short-story writer of considerable talent. Early in his career the winner of the prestigious Prize of Group 47 (1965), B. is the holder of many additional literary awards and distinctions. Widely read both at home and abroad, B.'s best-known stories have been translated into numerous foreign languages. Although B.'s approach to fiction has often sparked critical controversy, there remains a strong consensus for his position as a leading writer of his generation.

FURTHER WORKS: *Versuche über Gino* (1960); *Das Gästehaus* (1965, with Walter Höllerer, et al.); *Geschichten zur falschen Zeit* (1979); *Der Leser, das Erzählen* (1982); *Schulmeistereien* (1985); *Der Busant; von Trinkern, Polizisten und der schönen Magelone* (1985); *Irgendwo anderswo; Kolumnen, 1980–1985* (1986); *Im Gegenteil; Kolumnen, 1986–1990* (1990)

BIBLIOGRAPHY: Bucher, W., and Ammann, G., *Schweizer Schriftsteller in Gespräch* (1970), Vol. 1: 13–47; Peukert, K., *Die Genese des Wissens in P. B.'s "Kindergeschichten"* (1973); Sherry, C., "Translating P. B.: Some Remarks," *Dimension*, 10 (1977): 66–73; Sell, R., "Stagnation und Aufbruch in B.s *Milchmann—und Kindergeschichten*" *ABnG*, 9 (1979): 255–73; Bänziger, H. P. B., *Weg und Werk* (1984); Hoven, H., ed., *Pi:Auskunft für Leser* (1984); Bohm, A., "Narratives for a Post-Heroic Age: P. B.'s Short Prose," *UDR*, 19, 2 (Summer 1988): 55–68; Ward, D., "A Swiss Author and His Languages: An Interview with P. B.," *Monatshefte*, 80, 1 (Spring 1988): 9–21

—MICHAEL V. WILLIAMS

BIERCE, Ambrose

American short-story writer, journalist, and poet, b. 24 June 1842, Horse Cave, Ohio; d. 11 Jan. 1914, Ojinaga, Mexico

The tenth of thirteen children, B. had a varied life and a controversial career as a writer. While a teenager, B. lived on a farm in northern Indiana and worked as a printer's assistant on *The Northern Indianan*, an antislavery paper. Beyond high school, his only formal education was a year (1859) at the Kentucky Military Institute. With the outbreak of the Civil War, B. enlisted in the Ninth Indiana Infantry. Subsequently commissioned, he served as topographical officer on General William B. Hazen's staff and fought in several battles including the one that later provided the setting for "Chickamauga" (1889), one of his best stories.

Ambrose Bierce

After the Civil War, General Hazen recruited B. as engineering attaché on an inspection tour of military posts in the Montana Territory, which eventually concluded in San Francisco, where B. found employment at the U.S. Sub-Treasury and continued to educate himself. In 1867 B. was first published in the *Californian* and in the following year in *The Golden Era* and the *News Letter*. When he became editor of the *News Letter* in 1868, he began to write "The Town Crier" column, which was soon recognized in New York and London for its acerbic wit and keen satire. In 1871 *The Overland Monthly* published "The Haunted Valley," his first story to appear in print. B. and his new wife moved to England in 1872, where he wrote and contributed to *Fun* and *Figaro*. Returning after three years to San Francisco, B. began, by 1887, to write for William Randolph Hearst's *San Francisco Examiner*. Although often resigning from Hearst's employ, B. worked more or less regularly for the publisher until 1909, when he resigned from *Cosmopolitan*. From 1900 to 1913, B. lived and worked mainly in Washington; late in 1913, at the age of seventy-one, B. departed Washington for a long-planned trip through Mexico to South America. Although the date and place of his death are uncertain, all available evidence indicates that he was killed on 11 January 1914, during the battle of Ojinaga in Mexico.

B. has always been a controversial figure, in person and in his works. During the 1890s, he was best known for his searing newspaper columns; many public figures and venerable institutions came under his severe scrutiny. It is difficult to locate B. in a period or movement, however, because he consistently put himself at odds with the views and values of his time. During the 20th c. he has been best known for his short stories, which have continued to hold a popular audience.

Even though he included the subconscious as a primary factor in many of his best stories, B. thought of himself as a "true realist": "The test of truth is Reason," he wrote, "not Faith." Presumably differentiating his own practice from that of others, he wrote elsewhere that "realism" is "the art of depicting nature as it is seen by toads." He frequently took exception to the work of William Dean Howells (1837–1920), whom he referred to as "Miss Nancy" Howells. In London B. acquired the sobriquet "Bitter Bierce"; while others wrote about utopias, he described dystopias. His satires are in the tradition of Rabelais, La Rochefoucauld, Swift, and Voltaire, all authors he studied. In addition to his challenging experiences in the Civil War, Stoicism was a major influence on his philosophical outlook, as one might expect of the son of Marcus Aurelius Bierce and of the nephew of Lucius Verus Bierce, who published a book on Stoicism in 1855. B. himself especially praised Epictetus.

The 1890s saw the publication of most of B.'s major volumes. His books published before this period bore various pseudonyms. A collection of stories, *Tales of Solidiers and Civilians* (pub. in England as *In the Midst of Life*, the title by which it is now known), appeared in 1892. In collaboration with Dr. Gustav A. Danziger, a dentist and sometime translator, B. published an adaptation of Richard Voss's *Der Mönch von Berchtesgaden* under the title *The Monk and the Hangman's Daughter*, which appeared first serially in the *Examiner* (1891), and in book form the next year. Also in 1892, B. published *Black Beetles in Amber*, a gathering of his satirical verse. Another collection of short stories, published in 1893, bore the title *Can Such Things Be?* In 1881 B. began including items in a weekly newspaper column that he gathered in *The Cynic's Word Book* (1906), which title was forced upon him, he claimed, by the times and his publisher. When he edited his

twelve-volume *Collected Works* (1909–1912), however, he changed the title of this work to *The Devil's Dictionary* (1911).

Although popularly known as "bitter" (as noted), "wicked," and "devilish," B. was, in fact, humane, generous, and compassionate. Clearly, B.'s work influenced Kate Chopin (1851–1904) and Stephen Crane (1871–1900). B. was profoundly interested in the ways faulty perception and communication troubled the lives of humans. Repeatedly his stories ask: Is a human being a rational creature? "Chickamauga" and "An Occurrence at Owl Creek Bridge" (1890), probably his best-known stories, turn on startling ironies about the ability of human beings to sort out reality, both physical and psychological. Because of these qualities in his fiction. B. has been "discovered" again, this time by reader-response theorists and semiologists. He has also attracted international interest among creative artists. Like Poe, he has been popular in France. Robert Enrico's *Au coeur de la vie* (1962) is a three-part film based on "Chickamauga," "An Occurrence at Owl Creek Bridge," and "The Mocking-Bird" (1891). In South America, toward which he was traveling when he disappeared at Ojinaga, B. has influenced Carlos FUENTES, Jorge Luis BORGES, and Julio CORTÁZAR. Japanese author AKUTAGAWA Ryūnosuke has also expressed indebtedness to B.

Until we have a comprehensive scholarly assessment of B.'s voluminous work (he included only about a third of his journalism in his *Collected Works*), it will be difficult to determine his rank and role in literature. In the interim, however, his fiction—in some ways surrealistic and anticipating modern science fiction—will continue to engage the common reader.

FURTHER WORKS: *The Fiend's Delight* (1873, pseud. Dod Grile); *Nuggets and Dust* (1873, pseud. Dod Grile); *Cobwebs from an Empty Skull* (1874, pseud. Dod Grile); *The Dance of Death* (1877, pseud. William Herman); *The Dance of Life: An answer to The Dance of Death* (1877, pseud. Mrs. J. Milton Bowers); *Fantastic Fables* (1899); *Shapes of Clay* (1903); *A Son of the Gods and a Horseman in the Sky* (1907); *The Shadow on the Dial and Other Essays* (1909); *The Letters of A. B.* (1922)

BIBLIOGRAPHY: McWilliams, C., *A. B.: A Biography* (1929); Fatout, P., *A. B.: The Devil's Lexicographer* (1951); Fatout, P., *A. B. and the Black Hills* (1956); Woodruff, S. C., *The Short Stories of A. B.: A Study in Polarity* (1964); Grenander, M. E., *A. B.* (1971); Davidson, C. N., ed., *Critical Essays on A. B.* (1982); Davidson, C. N., *The Experimental Fictions of A. B.* (1984); Saunders, R., *A. B.: The Making of a Misanthrope* (1984); Morris, R., Jr., *A. B.: Alone in Bad Company* (1995)

—ARTHUR B. COFFIN

BIERMANN, Wolf

German poet, b. 15 Nov. 1936, Hamburg

B., the son of a German Communist who was killed in Auschwitz, became convinced of the superiority of socialism as a youth and in 1952 immigrated to East Germany, where he studied philosophy and economics. He began to write in the early 1960s and, owing to his penchant for honestly confronting the weaknesses of the German Democratic Republic, immediately became the object of governmental harassment and censorship. From 1963 to

1965 he established a reputation as East Germany's enfant terrible, as he toured both German states, singing his songs of social and political protest. In 1965 a ban was imposed on the performance and publication of his works in the G.D.R. He continued to publish in the West and in 1976 was given permission to travel abroad. He was not allowed to reenter the G.D.R. and since then has resided in West Germany.

The verse of B.'s first two collections, *Die Drahtharfe* (1965; *The Wire Harp* [with some new poems], 1968) and *Mit Marx- und Engelszungen* (1968; with tongues of Marx and Engels [or: angels]) follows in the tradition of such writers as Villon and Heine, as well as BRECHT and Kurt TUCHOLSKY. A dedicated socialist in spite of his difficulties with the East German regime, he often writes on themes perfectly compatible with the Communist conception of Western decadence, including American racial problems, the Vietnam war, and reactionary elements in West Germany. Many of his works, however, deal with problems and conditions within the G.D.R. Some express sympathy with the goals of Communism, while others criticize the lack of freedom in the G.D.R. and, in effect, accuse the nation's leaders of having established a bureaucracy and ideology as ends in themselves, thereby losing sight of the needs of the people. *Preußischer Ikarus* (1978; Prussian Icarus) contains prose texts and poems written both before and after his expatriation. His scorn for both German states remains strong.

B.'s lyrical style is simple and effective. He typically uses colloquial language and a regular form, often with rhyme and a refrain. Narration alternates with subjective commentary. His popularity is to a large extent based on the music which complements his texts. Influenced by the composer Hanns Eisler, it forcefully underscores the message of the verse. Several recordings of B. performing his works are available. The frequent use of puns and the importance of rhyme make his verse difficult to translate effectively.

FURTHER WORKS: *Der Dra-Dra* (1970); *Deutschland-ein Wintermärchen* (1972); *Für meine Genossen* (1972); *Das Märchen vom kleinen Herrn Moritz, der eine Glatze kriegt* (1972); *Nachlaß 1* (1977); *Ich bin ein staatlich anerkannter Staatsfeind* (1977). FURTHER WORKS IN ENGLISH: *Poems and Ballads* (1977)

BIBLIOGRAPHY: Vallance, M., "W. B.: The Enfant Terrible as Scapegoat," *Survey*, No. 61 (1966): 177–85; Flores, J., in *Poetry in East Germany* (1971): 301–13; Arnold, H. L., ed., *W. B.* (1975); Morley, M., "The Songs of W. B.," *AUMLA*, No. 48 (1977): 222–33

—JERRY GLENN

BIGONGIARI, Piero

Italian critic, poet, and translator, b. 15 Oct. 1914, Navacchio

B. lived in Pistoia, the "ideal and real city" of his youth, from 1925 to 1938, although he commuted to Florence to study under renowned critics; Attilio Momigliano (1883–1952) directed his doctoral dissertation. There he met other famous critics, writers, and the young poets of HERMETICISM. In 1938 he decided to live in Florence, and since 1965 he has been a professor of modern literature at the university there.

In the Italian tradition of critic-poets, B. has become a spokesman for the third generation of hermeticists. As early as 1937, in *L'elaborazione della lirica leopardiana* (elaboration of Leopardian lyricism), B. wrote a book at once poetically inspired and empirically valid. In his own words, criticism "is an art in its departure and a science in its arrival." Moreover, his article "Il critico come scrittore" (1938; the critic as writer), published in *Bargello*, is the paradigm of his hermetic poetics. Compromised by history, B. aims "to historicize the work and penetrate the cultural situation in which it was born."

B.'s criticism, brilliant and engaging, is always poetically intuitive and scientifically grounded. He brings new dimensions to famous or obscure writers, handling a variety of modern critical tools: the study of variants, structure, the polyvalency (or multiple interpretation) of words, phonosymbolism (the connection of sound and meaning). He brings to bear on his subject history, psychology, sociology, and semiotics. A master of literary and artistic cross-reference, B. compares Dante and Cavalcanti (1255–1300), the poetics of PASCOLI's "Il fanciullino" (1897, 1903) with Clasio's (1754–1825); Leon Battista Alberti (1404–1472) and Mallarmé; Pascoli's *Poemi conviviali* (1904) and the paintings of Gauguin and Seurat.

B.'s first book of poems, *La figlia di Babilonia* (1942; the daughter of Babylon), is the expression of his faith in hermeticism. This book, together with *Rogo* (1952; pyre) and *Il corvo bianco* (1955; the white crow), were collected in *Stato di cose* (1968; state of things). B.'s poems are made of metaphysical elements and "seen things": they are a linguistic amalgam of physical things in their poetic transcendence. We are ushered into a kaleidoscopic world of colors and animals, bodies and crystals, in a cosmic intercommunion with the crisis of our time: "Poets are the men most involved with history because they interfere in it with their highest and most decisive tool: poetry."

A turning point in B.'s poetry is his latest book, *Moses* (1979; Moses). The poet explains: "The poem, the poem of love, almost a poetic 'novel' with all its ambiguities, not to say ubiquities, is the warning that the *I* is no longer mine, that it no longer belongs to me, it is the *other*; but that it is the *other* who has an *I* who can also, responding, refer to the subject, through the infinite series of objects." Briefly, the poems constitute an existential trip into history. Moses, saved from the waters, brings divine law to his people; the poet seeks hope and light for a life of "love".

FURTHER WORKS: *Studi* (1946); *Il senso della lirica italiana* (1952); *Le mura di Pistoia* (1958); *Poesia italiana del Novecento* (1960); *Il caso e il caos* (1961); *Il vento d'ottobre* (1961); *Leopardi* (1962); *Torre di Arnolfo* (1964); *Poesia francese del Novecento* (1968); *Capitoli di una storia della poesia italiana* (1968); *Prosa per il Novecento* (1970); *Antimateria* (1972); *La poesia come funzione simbolica del linguaggio* (1972); *Il Seicento fiorentino* (1975); *Poesia italiana del Novecento* (2 vols., 1978, 1980)

BIBLIOGRAPHY: Jaccottet, P., "La poésie italienne contemporaine," *NRF*, 9 (1961): 125–32; Burckhardt, G., *Italie poétique contemporaine* (1968): 474–81; Gardair, J. -M, "La poétique ininterrompue de P. B.," *Critique*, 25 (1969): 304–11

—M. RICCIARDELLI

BIOY CASARES, Adolfo

Argentine novelist and short-story writer, b. 15 Sept. 1914, Buenos Aires

Failing to complete law studies, B. C. turned to a career in editing and writing. His marriage in 1940 to the poet Silvina Ocampo (b. 1905), sister of Victoria Ocampo (1891–1969), the founder and director of *Sur*, brought him closer to the writers associated with that influential magazine. Among these were Jorge Luis Borges, whom he had met earlier, and who soon became a close friend and collaborator.

B. C. began writing stories in his teens, but publicly renounced all his work produced before 1937. Critics, however, have found in some of these books the promise of the master of imaginative fiction who would soon publish one of Spanish America's most unusual novels, *La invención de Morel* (1940; *The Invention of Morel*, 1964). Lying somewhere between science fiction and pure fantasy, *La invención de Morel* is set on a remote island and revolves about an experiment in the mechanical production of humans by means of a kind of motion-picture projector. The novel thus poses interesting questions regarding appearance and reality. Although science fiction is not widely cultivated in Spanish America, the book won the Buenos Aires municipal prize for literature in 1941.

B. C.'s stories of the late 1940s, especially the collection *La trama celeste* (1948; the skyblue plot), are generally considered to be among his best. In a second novel, *El sueño de los héroes* (1954; The heroes' dream) B. C. experimented with narrative time and leaves his readers with the option of deciding just when the action took place. B. C.'s more recent works—the novel *El diario de la guerra del cerdo* (1962; *Diary of the War of the Pig*, 1972), a number of works in collaboration with Borges, and several more short-story collections—although not completely abandoning the fantastic fiction of earlier years, show a greater emphasis on realism, human interest, and irony. Despite this turn to more traditional fiction, B. C. will probably be best remembered for his unusual, innovative works of the 1940s and 1950s—experiments in fiction that clearly foreshadow the Spanish American "new narrative" of recent decades.

FURTHER WORKS: *Prólogo* (1929); *17 disparos contra to porvenir* (under pseud. Martín Sacastrá, 1933); *Caos* (1934); *La neuva tormenta* (1935); *La estatua casera* (1936); *Luis Greve, muerto* (1937); *Plan de evasión* (1945); *El perjuro de la nieve* (1946); *Homenaje a Francisco Almeyra* (1954); *Historia prodigiosa* (1956); *Guirnalda con amores* (1959); *El lado de la sombra* (1962); *La tarde de un fauno* (1964); *El gran serafín* (1967); *La otra aventura* (1968); *Adversos milagros* (1969); *Memoria sobre la pampa y los gauchos* (1970); *Breve diccionario del argentino exquisito* (under pseud. Javier Miranda, 1971); *Historias de amor* (1972); *Historias fantásticas* (1972); *Dormir al sol* (1973); *El héroe de las mujeres* (1978). See also the Further Works section of the article on Jorge Luis Borges for works done in collaboration.

BIBLIOGRAPHY: Anderson Imbert, E., *Historia de la literatura hispanoamérica* (1957): 448; Kovacci, O., *A. B. C.: Antología, esbozo biográfico, y selección* (1963); Puig Zaldívar, R., "Bibliografía de y sobre A. B. C.," *RI*, 40 (1974): 173–78; Gallagher, D. P., "The Novels and Short Stories of A. B. C.," *BHS*, 52 (1975): 247–66; Carter, E. D., "A. B. C. y la distorsión del tiempo," *ExTL*, 5, 2 (1976): 159–64

—MARTIN S. STABB

BISAYAN LITERATURE
See Philippines Literature

BISHOP, Elizabeth

American poet, b. 8 Feb. 1911, Boston, Mass.; d. 6 Oct. 1979, Boston, Mass.

Eight months after B.'s birth, her father died. Her mother, suffering a nervous collapse, eventually became insane. As a consequence, B. lived until the age of six with her maternal grandparents in Nova Scotia, Canada. She then moved to Worcester, Massachusetts, to be with her paternal grandparents and begin school. Later, she lived with her father's sister in Boston. She finished Walnut Hill High School and in 1934 graduated from Vassar College. In 1933 she met the poet Marianne MOORE, who influenced B. in her own writing and became a lifelong friend.

After graduation she traveled extensively in Europe and North Africa and in 1939 she settled in Key West, Florida. Travel, in fact, became a central metaphor in her work. In 1951 B. set out to sail around South America. She fell ill in Brazil, and after her recovery she decided to settle in that country. During her fifteen-year residence there B. published two autobiographical stories in *The New Yorker*: "In the Village" (1953) and "Gwendolyn" (1953). Each is set in Nova Scotia; both concern a child's first experience of loss. "Gwendolyn" recalls the death of a childhood friend; "In the Village" concerns B.'s memory of her mother's final return to a mental institution. B. came to the U.S. in 1966 to teach, and returned permanently in 1969, where she was poet in residence at Harvard until her retirement in 1977.

B.'s first book of poetry, *North & South* (1946), contains many of her best-known poems, including "Florida," "The Map," "The Fish," "The Man-Moth," "The Unbeliever," and "A Miracle for Breakfast." The book received critical acclaim, with special praise for B.'s descriptive acumen, her reticence, and her ability to metamorphose encounters with simple objects or scenes into profound imaginary experiences. "The Map," for example, extends far beyond a more realistic description of a literal object. B. shows the way a work of art may embody an artist's subjective experience of an objective reality. The poem suggests that B.'s works are maps to and of her own sensibility.

Poems: North & South; A Cold Spring (1955), B.'s second book of poetry, won the Pulitzer Prize for poetry in 1956. Although not as widely acclaimed as her first volume, it contained several new poems that are masterpieces, including "At the Fishhouses," "Cape Breton," "Over 2000 Illustrations and a Complete Concordance," and "The Bight" The personal epistemology B. reveals in these poems is intriguing. For her, the nature of reality is always to be imagined; it can never be known fully. Nor would an encounter with whatever is "real," could we undergo it, be a desirable experience—for reality can be deadly as well as enlivening.

B.'s third book of poetry, *Questions of Travel* (1965), considered by many her best, contains several poems about Brazilian people and about B.'s experiences in Brazil, among them "Arrival at Santos," "Manuelzinho," "Brazil, January 1, 1502," "The Burglar of Babylon," and the volume's title poem, "Questions of Travel." In this last poem B. suggests that her initial experience with the interior of Brazil is so demanding that she begins to wonder if she should ever have come to this place, or if it would not have been better merely to stay at home where the scenery is familiar, comfortable, and safe. By the end of the poem, however, B. appears to discover her own resolution to her questions. She must witness all of the strangeness she can. Indeed, in all her work B. seems to imply that if one is to be a sensitive person, a perceptive tourist, or an imaginative artist, one must be constantly vulnerable to every new and strange horizon to which one is exposed.

The Complete Poems appeared in 1969 and won the National Book Award. *Geography III*, B.'s final volume of poetry, which contains ten of her last poems, was published in 1976 and was awarded the National Book Critics' Circle Award. In it, as in her earlier books, B. is preoccupied with place and with its appropriation. To B., the knowledge to which one may come either in life or in poetry occurs in specific places, which provide the grounding essential for any discovery. Knowledge comes about, as well, through the processes of specific times that provide both experience and memory, the two most important elements necessary for imaginative synthesis.

B. has been hailed for her virtuosity in descriptive poetry. Yet she differs from both nature poets and from the IMAGISTS. For B., phenomena are never merely "remarkable": representation is a process of artistic, subjective discovery. B. is mimetic in the sense of giving accurate perceptions of particular realities. Yet, in the manner of the English romantic poets before her, she combines observation with momentous imaginative leaps that make her work both distinctive and memorable within 20th-c. poetry.

FURTHER WORKS: *Brazil: Life World Library Series* (1962); *The Ballad of the Burglar of Babylon* (1968)

BIBLIOGRAPHY: Moore, M., "A Modest Expert," *Nation* (28 Sept. 1946): 354; Lowell, R., "Thomas, B., and Williams," *SR*, 55 (1947): 497–500; Jarrell, R., *Third Book of Criticism* (1965): 295–333; Stevenson, A., *E. B.* (1966); Kalstone, D., *Five Temperaments* (1977): 12–40; special B. issue, *WLT* 51, 1 (1977)

—SYBIL P. ESTESS

BJERKE, André

(pseud. for detective novels: Bernhard Borge) Norwegian poet, translator, novelist, and essayist, b. 21 Jan. 1918, Aker

Although he studied economics and natural sciences at the University of Oslo (1936–41), B. made his literary debut in 1940, leaving science permanently behind for the world of letters. Since then he has written numerous volumes of poetry, translated foreign writers into Norwegian, written four detective novels under his pseudonym, and figured centrally in the cultural life of Norway, particularly in its continuing debate on language. B. was the editor of *Ordet* (the world), the Journal of the conservative language society, Riksmalsforbundet, from 1950 to 1966, and foreman of the Authors' Union of 1952 from 1961 to 1966, when it merged with the Norwegian Authors' Union.

Elizabeth Bishop

With the publication of his first two volumes of poetry, *Syngende jord* (1940; singing earth) and *Fakkeltog* (1942; torchlight parade), B. was heralded as the heir of the great troubadours of Norwegian verse, in particular, Herman Wildenvey (1886–1959). To war-weary Norwegians his poetry offered spiritual nourishment, for his moods were light, his central theme the joy of life, and his style formal and elegant. Following the war B. published a third volume of poetry, *Regnbuen* (1946; the rainbow), in which he proved himself to be truly a master of traditional lyric forms, as well as a poet of more melancholic (for some, profounder) moods. But in 1951, with the publication of one of his most central volumes of poetry, *Den hemmelige sommer* (the secret summer), B. established himself once and for all as the poet of the glad heart, deliberately naïve, antirationalistic, trusting only those innocent enough to experience life's mysterious, spiritual dimension—B.'s "secret summer." B. has been a prolific poet, but he has not always lived up to the critics' early expectations; for although his poetry is graceful, witty, and remarkably musical, its content can be superficial and its tone, at times, annoyingly moralistic.

Perhaps as significant as his own poetry are his translations from the 1940s and 1950s of many foreign poets, including Goethe, Heine, RILKE, and Shelley, and of several plays by Shakespeare (*A Midsummer Night's Dream* and *Hamlet*) and Molière's *The Misanthrope*. B.'s translations are considered a triumph of the art.

Of B.'s own works, his detective novels are those most translated into other languages. *Nattmennesket* (1941; the night person) and *De dødes tjern* (1942; *Death in the Blue Lake*, 1961), as well as several written after the war, are among the finest examples of the detective novel in Norwegian literature.

Known for the formal elegance of his own style, B. emerged in the 1950s as an advocate of conservative colloquial as well as literary language and a major opponent of modernism. In collaboration with Carl Keilhau (b. 1919) he published a volume of mock modern verse, *Den bakvendte familieboken* (1949; the backward family book). His ideas on good literary style are more straightforwardly presented in *Hva er god stil?* (1955; what is good style?) and *Rim og rytme* (1956; rhyme and rhythm), and his ideas on correct colloquial language are pointedly conveyed in essays such as *Babels tårn* (1958; the tower of Babel) and *Sproget som ikke vil dø* (1964; the language that will not die).

A fine essayist, B. has also contributed to the broader cultural debate with several collections of essays, many written from the anthroposophical point of view of Rudolf Steiner (1861–1925).

FURTHER WORKS: *Fremmede toner* (1947); *Døde menn går i land* (1947); *Eskapader* (1948); *Fabelen om gry og gruble* (1948); *Dikt om vin og kjærlighet* (1950); *Skjult mønster* (1950); *Videnskap og lidenskap: To komedier* (1951, with O. Eidem); *Vers på vandring* (1952); *Prinsessen spinner i bjerget* (1953); *Norsk Decamerone* (1953, ed. with O. Eidem); *Slik frøet bærer skissen til et tre* (1954); *Norsk studenter* (1954); *Fuglen i fiksérbildet* (1955); *For moro skyld: barnerim* (1956); *Fra verdenslyrikken* (1957); *En jeger og hans hund* (1958); *Videnskapet og livet* (1958); *A. B.s ABC* (1959); *En kylling under stjernen* (1960); *Tryllestaven* (1961); *Hva er godt riksmål?* (1962); *Enhjørningen* (1963); *For anledningen* (1963); *Arnulf Øverland* (1965); *En skrift er rundt oss* (1966); *Dannet talesprog* (1966); *Før teppet går opp* (1973)

—MARY KAY NORSENG

BJÖRLING, Gunnar

Finnish poet (writing in Swedish), b. 31 May 1887, Helsinki; d. 11 July 1960, Helsinki

B. lived his entire life on the southern shore of Helsinki, most of it alone. As a youth, he was politically active against the Russian regime, then turned to the study of philosophy under Edvard Westermarck (1862–1939). During this period he arrived at a concept of the universe that was to influence his poetry significantly. He made his debut at thirty-five with *Vilande dag* (1922; resting day).

The collection *Solgrönt* (1933; sungreen), marks the appearance of the mature poet B. His previous production was heterogeneous and experimental, including the Scandinavian extreme in DADAIST poetry in *Kiri-ra* (1930; Kiri-ra [a made-up word]) and the contributions to the journal *Quosego* (1928–29). After *Solgrönt* B. sharpened his vision and diction along two central thematic axes, the so–called "you–"poetry and nature lyricism. The former consists of sensuous homilies addressed to an unidentified and shifting "you," the latter of ecstatic hymns to the ever expanding, never definable universe. His poetic development progressed through the collections *Fågel badar snart i vattnet* (1934; bird soon bathes in water), *Men blåser violer på havet* (1936; but blows violets on the sea), and *Att syndens blåa nagel* (1936; that the blue nail of sin), and culminated in *Där jag vet att du* (1939; where I know that you). Numerous aphorisms both about the nature of language and about a

unity at the intersection of incomplete events occur throughout B.'s work.

This unity is central to B.'s poetry, a reflection of his philosophical studies. The reality of the universe is revealed in a constant flux, which can at any time be sensed and indicated as the synthesis of partial experiences. B.'s poetry attempts to advance this concept in an idiom that directly mirrors the thesis. B.'s poetic diction, much maligned, is definable as an extremely developed mastery of metonymical relationships in language, such that any syntactic configuration may serve as the part for the whole. The text appears initially as the result of extensive syntactic elision, and has been so characterized by commentators. However, when the contrapuntal metonymies are understood, it is seen that B.'s syntax deviates only slightly from that of the ordinary language. This is particularly true of the abundantly occurring grammatical function words, such as "and, that, when."

B.'s collections are generally closed compositions with a discernible epic continuity. The works are divided into lengthy suites; the stanzas follow each other in undulating progress. Similarly, in the six selections edited by B. himself, utmost care has been taken to present the poems as suites, as in *Och leker med skuggorna i sanden* (1947; and playing with the shadows in the sand) and *Du jord du dag* (1957; you earth you day). Anthologists who select isolated stanzas by B. tend, therefore, to misrepresent him.

B. was for a long time vilified and ridiculed by the critical establishment, and shunned by the publishers. Nevertheless, his influence upon younger poets was enormous in Finland, and significant in Sweden, where his work was appreciated by a group of young writers. Bengt Holmqvist's (b. 1924) splendid essay in the journal *Prisma* (1949) carried B. across the threshold to wider acceptance. Opinions have been expressed to the effect that B. spreads his themes too thin, which might be true if his stanzas are removed from their contexts. But B.'s reputation is steadily gaining; today many regard him as the most important of the Finno-Swedish modernists; his very radical departure from previously accepted form continues to be a fresh source of inspiration.

FURTHER WORKS: *Korset och löftet* (1925); *Det oomvända anletet* (1939); *Angelängenhet* (1940); *Ohjälpligheten* (1943); *O finns en dag* (1944); *Ord och att ej annat* (1945); *Luft är och ljus* (1946); *Ohört blott* (1948); *Vårt kattliv timmar* (1949); *Ett blyertsstreck* (1951); *Som alla dar* (1953); *Att i sitt öga* (1954); *Du går de ord* (1955)

BIBLIOGRAPHY: Wrede, J., "The Birth of Finland-Swedish Modernism," *Scan*, 15 (1965): 73–103; Nilsson, K., "Semantic Devices in B.'s Poetry," *MGS*, 3 (1977): 54–73

—KIM NILSSON

BJØRNEBOE, Jens

Norwegian novelist, poet, and dramatist, b. 9 Oct. 1920, Kristiansand; d. 9 May 1976, Oslo

At an early age B. rebelled against his distinctly middle-class surroundings and went to sea. When he returned, he studied art in Stockholm and later in Oslo, where he lived as a teacher and writer. B.'s outstanding quality was a strong sense of compassion and justice that led him to understand and defend the underdog. Many of his works are highly provocative and caused great stirs in Norway.

B. began as a lyric poet, following classical themes and forms. His early poems are metaphysical and aesthetic. But later, in his satirical plays, which are social critiques in cabaretlike style in the manner of BRECHT, his songs became polemical and revolutionary.

B.'s novels about the moral, psychological, and social implications of evil aroused the greatest interest in the Norwegian public. *Før hanen galer* (1952; before the cock crows), deals with medical experiments on inmates in Nazi concentration camps. Science itself is questioned when its cold objectivity ignores moral values that apply to general human relationships. Divided moral values are exemplified in Dr. Heinrich Reynhardt, who, although seemingly an upright—even loving—family man, inflicts enormous suffering in the name of medical progress.

Jonas (1955; Jonas) shows the harm done by schools that are only conformist. The wordblind boy Jonas is mistreated by ignorant teachers, and finally saved by an undemanding, compassionate institution. B. attacks both school and prison systems in *Den onde hyrde* (1960; the bad shepherd), showing how society seems to play with juvenile delinquents as a large cat plays with a small, bloody mouse.

B.'s trilogy, *Frihetens øyeblikk* (1966; the moment of freedom), *Kruttårnet* (1969; powder keg), and *Stillheten* (1973; silence), is one of the principal works of postwar Norwegian literature. Mixing realism and allegory, satire and polemic, B. delineates the history of evil in Western civilization. Innumerable examples of bestiality make the world seem like a slaughterhouse. B. places the blame variously on the Germans, other Europeans, the Americans, or on human nature, but always on the authorities and men of power. Still, there is some hope. After one has recognized all the horror, one can come to the existential moment of freedom by realizing that one must bear all the responsibility oneself.

Haiene (1974; the sharks), B.'s last novel, is a shorter counterpart to the trilogy. It is a dramatic and suspenseful sea story, which may be taken as an allegory of the 20th c.: officers and crew struggle viciously against one another until a catastrophe brings about a reconciliation and thus hope for the future.

FURTHER WORKS: *Dikt* (1951); *Ariadne* (1953); *Under en hårdere himmel* (1957); *Vinter i Bellapalma* (1958); *Den store by* (1958); *Blåmann* (1959); *Drømmen og hjulet* (1964); *Til lykke med dagen* (1965); *Uten en tråd* (1966); *Fugleelskerne* (1966); *Norge, mitt Norge* (1968); *Aske, vind og jord* (1969); *Semmelweiss* (1967); *Amputasjonen* (1970); *Vi som elsket Amerika* (1970); *Politi og anarki* (1972); *Hertug Hans* (1972); *Samlede dikt* (1977)

BIBLIOGRAPHY: Mawby, J., "The Norwegian Novel Today," *Scan*, 14 (1975), 2

—WALTER D. MORRIS

BJØRNVIG, Thorkild

Danish poet, literary scholar, and essayist, b. 2 Feb. 1918, Århus

B. received his M.A. in comparative literary history at the University of Århus in 1947 and his Ph.D. in 1964, with a dissertation on Martin A. HANSEN. He studied in Paris (1950), Bonn (1951), Uppsala (1955), and Rome (1963–64), and toured

Iceland in 1977 and the U. S. in 1975 and 1978. B. was cofounder and coeditor of the literary journal *Heretica* (1948–50) and became a member of the Danish Academy in 1960.

Widely read, B. has been especially interested in T. S. ELIOT, RILKE, MANN, Poe, Keats, Nietzsche, Baudelaire, and Mallarmé. He won the gold medal of the University of Copenhagen for his paper on Rilke and the German tradition, and has published several translations of Rilke.

B.'s poetry is dense and complex; his subjective, carefully selected symbols are used in search of new insights and in pursuit of a new reality. To the modernist B., poetry not only serves an end; it also becomes an end in itself. B.'s modernism, however, is based on a humanistic attitude that involves an uncompromising and undaunted exploration of the human condition; the necessary confrontation with nihilism and chaos will eventually bring new meaning and content. B. is aware of the contradiction inherent in this existentialist modernism, and he recognizes the danger of the potential hubris on the part of a modernist poet wishing to improve the quality of human life. This problematic situation is dealt with in his first collection of poems, *Stjœrnen bag gavlen* (1947; the star behind the gable).

A fundamental thematic issue in B.'s poems is authenticity versus different kinds of alienation. The split between feeling and intellect is thus typical of modern man and manifests itself, for example, as a dichotomy between technocracy and sentimentality in contemporary society. The poet may play a crucial role in this context because his emotional experience and perceptive dissection of the malaise enables him to envision new meaningful patterns, as in *Figur og ild* (1959; figure and fire).

In close contact with other intellectuals and artists, B. was a friend of Karen Blixen (Isak DINESEN), described in his book *Pagten: Mit venskab med Karen Blixen* (1974; the pact: my friendship with Karen Blixen). Although deeply fascinated with Blixen, B.'s humanistic and moralistic outlook differs significantly from Blixen's more cosmic and heroic attitude. B. is perhaps the most representative and outstanding member of the group connected with the journal *Heretica*—highly intellectual and morally dedicated artists, all deeply affected by the post-World War II atmosphere of guilt and confusion, pessimism and anxiety.

FURTHER WORKS: *Anubis* (1955); *Rainer Maria Rilke og tysk tradition* (1959); *Begyndelsen* (1960); *Vibrationer* (1966); *Ravnen* (1968); *Udvalgte digte* (1970); *Oprør mod neonguden, et essay om beat* (1970); *Virkeligheden er til* (1973; *Det religiøse menneskes ansigter* (1975); *Stoffets krystalhav* (1975); *Delfinen: Miljødigte 1970–75* (1975); *Morgenmørke* (1977); *Også for naturens skyld* (1978)

—CHARLOTTE SCHIANDER GRAY

BLACK HUMOR

Black Humor describes a state of mind as much as a body of literature; and both are an expression of the historical anxieties of the 1960s, a decade filled with the din of the Vietnam conflict, television body counts of enemy dead, the assassinations of John and Robert Kennedy, and the cacophony of campus riots, the drug culture, and the drop-out generation. It is the decade when cumulative loss of faith in Western values, in a coherent world picture, and in the reliability of the human mind had a widespread impact on the form and theme chiefly of American fiction, and peripherally of European literatures.

The first published use of the term Black Humor occurred in 1964, in an article by Conrad Knickerbocker. Its popularization, however, is credited to Bruce Jay Friedman (b. 1930), who brought out an anthology of thirteen writers (himself included) in 1965 entitled *Black Humor*. Like the curious assemblage in Friedman's book, authors tagged as Black Humorists range from the comic realist Friedman to the SURREALISTIC symbolist John HAWKES, from the metaphysical fabulator Jorge Luis BORGES to the whimsical moralist Kurt VONNEGUT, JR. Even transitional novels like J. P. Donleavy's (b. 1926) *The Ginger Man* (1955; rev. ed. 1958), which derives as much from the British Angry Young Man novel of the 1950s as it presages the Black Humor fiction of the 1960s, and Joseph HELLER's *Catch-22* (1961), which partakes basically of an EXISTENTIALIST viewpoint and utilizes THEATER OF THE ABSURD techniques, have been characterized, probably too readily and facilely, as Black Humor. Similarly, Black Humor has at one time or another been linked tangentially with existentialist literature, SURREALISM,, absurd theater, happenings, gallows humor, sick humor, and Southern gothic fiction. In short, Black Humor alludes to so heterogeneous a range of material that its definition as a critical term and as a historical appellation becomes imperative if it is to have any meaningful literary use.

The superficial features of Black Humor fiction are quickly enumerated: comic and grotesque treatment of intrinsically tragic material, one-dimensional characters, wasteland settings, disjunctive and atemporal narrative structures, and mocking irreverent tone. More important to an understanding of this literature is its underlying philosophical agnosticism—its suspicion of all traditional, coherent systems of belief other than the all-embracing one (to quote Todd Andrews at the end of John BARTH's *The Floating Opera* [1956]) that "nothing has intrinsic value." From the Black Humorist's skepticism about the absoluteness or the adequacy of the metaphysical, theological, and scientific systems that have given solace and meaning to human existence derive the major aesthetic and thematic characteristics of Black Humor fiction: a pluralism of form and content, an ironic undercutting of theme and subject, a reliance on parody, and an apocalyptic view of society.

A favorite Black Humor metaphor for the world is a labyrinth—an indefinable space, boundaryless, without recognizable design, and incomprehensible as a whole. If one begins thus with the notion that there is no necessary coherence to the universe, no logic linking its parts, then one is led inexorably, given the options, to adopt, as when threading a maze, the operative plan of trying all possibilities. Whereas the existentialist sees being, his sense of self, as developing out of willed actions, hence exclusionary in effect, the Black Humorist pretends that the sense of being is realizable only through the embrace of multiplicity. Burlingame, in Barth's *The Sot-Weed Factor* (1960), expresses the appetite of Black Humor for "the entire parti-colored whole with all her poles and contradictories" when he exclaims: "I am Suitor of Totality . . . Husband to all Creation . . . I have known my great Bride part by splendrous part, and have made love to her *disjecta membra*, her sundry brilliant pieces; but I crave the Whole . . . I have no parentage to give me place and aim in Nature's order: very well—I am outside Her, and shall be Her lord and spouse!"

Intrinsic to a pluralistic universe is the absence of moral and logical guidelines, of concepts of right and wrong, and of cause and effect. Consequently, any action is potentially as good as the next until it is tested. Trial and error alone distinguishes the effective from the ineffectual. This factor influences the outcome of Black Humor fiction. At its most uncompromising, Black Humor fiction presents a plurality of conflicting stances without resolution, and the thematic statement is left unconfirmed by the narrative. Kurt Vonnegut, Jr., for example, has pursued a policy in such novels as *Mother Night* (1962), *Cat's Cradle* (1963), and *God Bless You, Mr. Rosewater* (1965) of posing ambiguously moral solutions to a problem.

Black Humorists are especially inventive in their parody (and hence demythification) of the historical, scientific, religious, metaphysical, and mythic models that have always sustained humans—parodies that pay tribute to the elegance of mind that can give the world meaning rather than extracting a meaning already there, while simultaneously acknowledging this meaning's limited human origin and its inadequacy *vis à vis* the limitless mystery of the universe. Literary parodies have abounded in the past. Usually, though, they never seriously question the form they imitate. Thus, even as Thomas Carlyle's *Sartor Resartus* parodies the spiritual autobiography reaching back to Saint Augustine's *Confessions*, it accepts the conventions of the genre. Similarly, Alexander Pope's parody of the heroic in *The Rape of the Lock*, and Byron's of the epic in *Don Juan*, never question the underlying assumptions of the form. No such respect for tradition moves the Black Humorist. An epistemological crisis about the nature of reality gnaws at his satisfaction in the categorization of things. He turns skeptically in the cosmic breeze between past and future, moved by the marvel of man's methodical mind but nonplussed by the absence of design. In such stories as "La Biblioteca de Babel" (1941; "The Library of Babel," 1962), "Tlön, Uqbar, Orbis Tertius" (1941; "Tlön, Uqbar, Orbis Tertius," 1962), and "Las ruinas circulares" (1941; "The Circular Ruins," 1962) Borges, as a leading strategist for Black Humor, chides—and memorializes—the human penchant to arrange the random and coincidental into interesting patterns. Many younger American writers have followed his lead, often realizing in parody their most fictionally liberating statements: Thomas PYNCHON in *V.* (1963) and *The Crying of Lot 39* (1966), Thomas Berger (b. 1924) in *Little Big Man* (1964), Robert Coover (b. 1932) in *The Universal Baseball Association, J. Henry Waugh, Prop.* (1968), and, among European writers, Günter GRASS in *Die Blechtrommel* (1959; *The Tin Drum*, 1962).

The impetus behind Black Humor is sociopsychological as well as metaphysical. Since the end of World War II America has transformed itself into a bureaucratized, technological society, so complex that a computer-skilled managerial class has been created to tend its day-to-day operation. From a land of rural individualists envisioned by the framers of the Constitution, it has become a mass society of anonymous dwellers in urban centers oppressively similar in appearance, a nation with strong conformist instincts (hence in part the rebellious contrary thrust of the under-thirty generations toward individualism, "doing one's thing," and the counter ideal of pluralism) as the best defense in preservation of private freedom. The demographic average has become a national index cherished by pollsters and an ideal aspired to by the citizenry. The abstractness and reductiveness of it all, not to mention the improbability of an individual embodying a hypothetical average, underscores the futile gestures of the homogenizing postwar period. This *reductio ad absurdum* receives its literary embodiment in the stock figure of the antihero as conformist, one-dimensional and manipulated by events. He is the title character of Friedman's *Stern* (1962), a man whose day is one long crisis of fantasied terrors; and he is Lester Jefferson in Charles Wright's (b. 1932) *The Wig* (1966), a black American seeking entry into President Johnson's Great Society by assuming a succession of identities and playing a succession of roles until the integral Lester exists for us as the sum of his disguises.

As for humor, the insistence on treating a terrifying situation as comic perhaps best characterizes Black Humor. It draws equally on post-World War II popular and underground humor, but unlike traditional humor, whose scapegoat is the aberrant, that which departs from the norm, it pessimistically finds the conventional, the universally acceptable, as the new target. Central to this desperate perspective on the nature of reality is a cosmic irony, which sees as pitifully inadequate man's attempt, ponderously inflated into systems and philosophies, to explain the "divine disorder" (so Borges alludes to it in "The Library of Babel") of the universe and the ultimate absurdity of history.

Practitioners of this comic-apocalyptic point of view include, besides the writers already mentioned, Stanley Elkin (b. 1930), Elliott Baker (b. 1922), James Herlihy (b. 1927), Thomas McGuane (b. 1939), Terry Southern (b. 1924), Leonard COHEN, Philip ROTH, Vladimir NABOKOV, Donald BARTHELME, William GASS, James PURDY, and Ishmael REED—although this by no means exhausts the list. Some of these writers continued into the 1970s to rely on a Black Humor perspective to justify their invention of endlessly varied pseudohistories as parodies of a labyrinthine world and as translations of their own states of mind. With the 1970s, however, the occasion for Black Humor's dissociated focus on reality and loveless manipulation of plot and characters seemed to have run its course. Verbal Black Humorists like Friedman, Southern, and Roth degenerated into shrill self-imitation; and those like Barth and Pynchon who rely on narrative structure for conveying their special anguished version of the moral enigma of events were driven to invent ever more baroque forms testifying to the paranoiac mood of the late 1960s. All this argues in favor of the judgment that underlying this antirealistic fiction are literary techniques intrinsically excessive and ultimately perhaps self-defeating.

BIBLIOGRAPHY: Knickerbocker, C., "Humor with a Mortal Sting," *NYTBR*, (27 September 1964), 3: 60–61; Schnickel, R., "The Old Critics and the New Novel," *Wisconsin Studies in Contemporary Literature*, 5 (1964): 26–36; Friedman, B. J., Foreword to *Black Humor* (1965): vii–xi; anon., "American Humor: Hardly a Laughing Matter," *Time*, (4 March 1966): 46–47; Miller, J. E., Jr., "The Quest Absurd: The New American Novel," *Quests Surd and Absurd* (1967): 3–30; D. M. Davis, ed., *The World of Black Humor* (1967); Feldman, B., "Anatomy of Black Humor," in M. Klein, ed., *The American Novel since World War II* (1969): 224–28; Olderman, R. M., *Beyond the Waste Land: A Study of the American Novel in the Nineteen-Sixties* (1972); Schulz, M. F., *Black Humor Fiction of the Sixties: A Pluralistic Definition of Man and His World* (1973); Trachtenberg, S., "Counter-humor: Comedy in Contemporary American Fiction," *GaR*, 27 (1973): 33–48; Hill, H., in H. Hill and W. Blair, *American Humor: From Poor Richard to Doonesbury* (1978): 498–506

—MAX F. SCHULZ

BLACKMUR, R(ichard) P(almer)

American poet and critic, b. 21 Jan. 1904, Springfield, Mass.; d. 2 Feb. 1965, Princeton, N.J.

B.'s formal education ended with his graduation from the Cambridge Latin School. In the years following, while he worked on and off as a reporter for the *Boston Evening Transcript* and as a free-lance critic, also getting some poems published, he audited many classroom lectures at Harvard College. He soon devoted himself to a lifetime study of humane letters that centered about his efforts to clarify his own intentions as a critic and interpreter of Western literature and Western thought. He became, like Henry ADAMS and George SANTAYANA, both of whom he greatly admired, eager to discern cultural contrasts between past and present, in terms of which we may assess the character of contemporary attitudes.

During the earlier years, B. was a frequent contributor to *Hound and Horn*, an important although short-lived avant-garde review. In 1940 he became affiliated with Princeton University, and thereafter, until his death, he taught at Princeton, with only occasional absences, as a member of the department of English literature. He soon became recognized as an important student of modern culture and a scholarly, even a philosophical, critic of catholic tastes. He turned his attention toward those writers whom he saw as the seminal authors of the modern period, especially Montaigne, Pascal, Stendhal, Dostoevsky, Tolstoy, Flaubert, Henry ADAMS, and Henry JAMES; James's prefaces, as well as his novels, profoundly influenced B.

B. is best known, however, as a close student of 20th-c. British and American poetry and as a thinker concerned to clarify the functions and the objectives of the literary critic. The critic of poetry should, he argues, call attention to the "parts" of the poem, such as vocabulary, tropes, formal structure, and conventional and general meanings, as well as to sources and influences, marshaling these in such a way that the reader is encouraged to accomplish their synthesis and to encounter the poem for himself as an imaginative concretion, finally realized as a *viva voce* rendering or performance of the poem. In this spirit B. has offered sympathetic interpretations of the work of many modern poets, especially FROST, YEATS, ELIOT, CUMMINGS, Wallace STEVENS, and Marianne MOORE. Many of these essays are collected in *Language as Gesture* (1952), which is perhaps B.'s most characteristic volume. As a theorist he has done much to justify the practice of the New Criticism and to determine the most fruitful relation between criticism and literary scholarship.

B. was far too sensitive a reader, too widely read, and too thoughtful a student of literature in its historical contexts to cherish the illusion that criticism may be reduced to a strict discipline or formal exercise. Thus he stood closer to CROCE than to Aristotle; but even here he moved with caution, hesitating to endorse Croce's insistence that the critic would do well to dismiss the concept of genre as irrelevant. The delicate consideration of this concept as it appears in B.'s essay "The Loose and Baggy Monsters of Henry James: Notes on the Underlying, Classic Form of the Novel" (1951) is characteristic of B.'s procedure. He felt that the critic has no right and no need to seek a finality of doctrine based on firm definitions and conclusive generalizations, both of which, he was sure, will always carry with them more than a suggestion of rigor mortis. On the other hand, critical thought relishes the tentative and is most alive in a moment of hesitation. It is Socratic and Jamesian in spirit and takes delight in uncharted horizons. This B. felt to be true both in criticism and in poetry itself. Thus the critic stands closer to the poet than to the scholar.

B.'s reputation as a poet has unfortunately been somewhat overshadowed by his distinction as a critic. His verse is both thoughtful and perceptive. It offers many happy glimpses of natural beauty, especially along the coast of Maine, where he was so much at home. Although he might well be called a philosophical poet, B. avoided in his verse as in his prose any too explicit statement of ideas. Rather he sought to capture those rhythms of feeling that reflect and make memorable a vitality latent in human consciousness, especially in moments of awareness through which the individual comes to a fresh encounter with his world. In this, B. reminds us of both Gerard Manley Hopkins and T. S. Eliot, although his skeptical caution withholds him from sharing their orthodox inclinations, and his irony is more persistent than Eliot's yet more restrained, in fact a more genuinely Yankee product.

FURTHER WORKS: *The Double Agent* (1935); *From Jordan's Delight* (1937); *The Expense of Greatness* (1940); *The Second World* (1942); *The Good European* (1947); *The Lion and the Honeycomb* (1955); *Anni Mirabiles, 1921–25* (1956); *Form and Value in Modern Poetry* (1957); *Eleven Essays in the European Novel* (1964); *A Primer of Ignorance* (1967); *Poems of R. P. B.* (1977)

BIBLIOGRAPHY: Hyman, S. E., *The Armed Vision* (1948): 239–72; Lewis, R. W. B., "Casellat as Critic: A Note on R. P. B.," *KR*, 13 (1951): 473–74; Ransom, J. C., "More Than Gesture" (1953), in *Poems and Essays* (1955): 102–9; Foster, R., *The New Romantics: A Reappraisal of the New Criticism* (1962): 82–107; Frank, J., *The Widening Gyre* (1963): 229–53; Donoghue, D., Introduction to *Poems of R. P. B.* (1977): ix–xxix

—NEWTON P. STALLKNECHT

BLAGA, Lucian

Romanian poet, philosopher, and dramatist, b. 9 May 1895, Lancrăm; d. 6 May 1961, Cluj

After receiving a doctorate in philosophy from the University of Vienna in 1920, B. pursued careers in journalism, diplomacy, and teaching. He was a founder of *Gîndirea*, one of the most innovative literary reviews of the interwar period. In the 1930s he became a member of the Romanian Academy, served as ambassador to Portugal, and was professor of the philosophy of culture at the University of Cluj from 1938 to 1948. After World War II he worked as a researcher in Cluj.

B. made major contributions to Romanian poetry, philosophy, and drama between the two world wars. His work was fundamentally innovative and cannot be compartmentalized; rather, it must be taken together as a single effort to penetrate the mysteries of existence and to understand man's role in the universe. Although he was a solitary figure who remained aloof from the political and social problems of the day and who belonged to no school, his impact upon contemporaries was profound.

In philosophy, B. was preoccupied with questions and used methods that were unfamiliar to the philosophical tradition of his country. He was greatly influenced by German romantic and irrationalist philosophy, by Henri BERGSON, and by FREUD and JUNG. He thus belongs to those currents of modern European thought that held that the ultimate sources of human activity, both individual and social, lay elsewhere than in logical thinking. B. accepted the absence of verifiable knowledge about the absolute and all the enigmas surrounding man's existence as permanent. He called the unknowable "mystery" and built his whole system around the attempt (and the failure) of man to "reveal" it. In *Trilogia cunoasterii* (1943; the trilogy of cognition), one of four trilogies in which he elaborated his philosophy, he concentrated on the methods of exploring ultimate reality. He recognized the absolute as essentially illogical and, hence, considered it accessible only to minds that were capable of going beyond the limitations imposed by reason.

B. was also concerned with the origins and significance of culture. In *Trilogia culturii* (1944; the trilogy of culture), in which he proposed a new theory of cultural style, he argued that all efforts at creativity were essentially directed by the "stylistic matrix," a series of categories in the unconscious. He also undertook to define the uniqueness of Romanian culture, which he associated with an idealized rural world. For him, culture had a metaphysical purpose. It was the product of man's efforts to reveal mystery, and, as such, the creative act became the supreme justification for man's existence.

B.'s philosophy cannot be separated from his poetry, for both reflect the same pursuit of first principles and the same cognitive strivings. Yet, his poetry is not simply a lyrical exposition of his philosophical ideas; it is a response to his own deep sensibility. B. was part of the modernist movement in European poetry and was influenced strongly by developments in Germany and Austria. The absence of a tangible universal order and of a divine intelligence that would give meaning to existence, the mechanization and standardization of modern life that deprived man of his soul and reduced him to utter insignificance in the world, and the extreme intellectualism that separated him from his natural, spontaneous being are major themes of B.'s poetry. They suggest a debt to Bergson's *élan vital*, Nietzsche's Dionysian vitalism, and expressionist metaphysical despair. B.'s obsession with the seeming emptiness of life, the yearning for nonbeing, and the urge for a reunion with elemental existence dominate the volumes *In marea trecere* (1924; the great passage) and *Lauda somnului* (1929; praise of sleep).

Like all modern poets, B. was dissatisfied with language as it was and experimented with new forms. His first volume, *Poemele luminii* (1919; poems of light) used free verse extensively and enriched Romanian poetry with new visions and techniques quite different from those of French symbolism, which had until then dominated Romanian modernism. B. also used myth on a scale not seen before in Romanian poetry.

In later volumes B.'s metaphysical anxiety was softened by more commonplace human feelings. A new serenity, a concern with the village as a place of "psychic refuge" from modern civilization, and a growing interest in folklore brought increased attention to classical meter and discipline of form. Yet, the longing for the absolute and the tragic sense of existence were never stilled.

B. pursued his search for answers to the riddle of existence in the drama, for which he devised new forms and new modes of expression. His ten plays are essentially dramas of ideas. The main characters are driven by powerful, obscure forces to achieve their creative destinies. They are rarely individualized, but rather embody fundamental ideas or states of being. The ontological element is dominant in the so-called expressionist plays like *Zamolxe* (1921; Zamolxe), in which B. explored the process of spiritual rebirth; in the Freudian dramas, like *Daria* (1925; Daria), where he tried to account for human behavior scientifically; in the dramas of national character, like *Avram Iancu* (1934; Avram Iancu); and in those that examined man's creative vocation, like *Meterul Manole* (1927; the master builder Manole).

For over a decade after World War II B.'s works were condemned by the representatives of the official (Communist) ideology or were simply ignored. But owing to a relaxation of controls on Romanian intellectual life in the 1960s and 1970s, a new generation of critics could examine his creative accomplishments with relative objectivity. Few would deny that B.'s works are turning points in the development of Romanian philosophy, poetry, and drama and that B. is one of the greatest poets of the Romanian language and the most original Romanian philosopher. Since the overthrow of the Communist regime in 1989 his work has been the subject of intense study and new critical evaluations.

FURTHER WORKS: *Pietre pentru templul meu* (1919); *Paşii profetului* (1921); *Cultură şi cunoşinţă* (1922); *Tulburarea apelor* (1923); *Filosofia stilului* (1924); *Feţele unui veac* (1925); *Fapta* (1925); *Învierea* (1925); *Ferestre colorate* (1926); *Daimonion* (1930); *Cruciada copiilor* (1930); *Eonul dogmatic* (1931); *Cunoaşterea luciferică* (1933); *La cumpăna apelor* (1933); *Cenzura transcendentă* (1934); *Orizont şi stil* (1936); *Spaţiul mioritic* (1936); *Geneza metaforei şi sensul culturii* (1937); *La curţile dorului* (1938); *Artă şi valoare* (1939); *Diferenţialele divine* (1940); *Despre gîndirea magică* (1941); *Poezii* (1942); *Opera dramatică* (1942); *Religie şi spirit* (1942); *Ştiinţă şi creaţie* (1942); *Nebănuitele trepte* (1943); *Arca lui Noe* (1944); *Discobolul* (1945); *Trilogia valorilor* (1946); *Hronicul şi cîntecul vîrstelor* (1965); *Gîndirea românească în Transilvania în secolul al XVIII-lea* (1966); *Poezii* (1967); *Experimentul şi spiritul matematic* (1969); *Ceasornicul de nisip* (1973); *Despre conştiinţă filosofică* (1974); *Opere*, 5 vols. (1974–1977); *Aspecte antropologice* (1976); *Fiinţa istorică* (1977). FURTHER WORKS IN ENGLISH: *Poems of Light* (1975)

BIBLIOGRAPHY: Gáldi, L., *Contributions à l'histoire de la versification roumaine: La prosodie de L. B.* (1972); Ciopraga, C., Preface to L. B. *Poems of Light* (1975): 37–58; Hitchins, K., "*Gîndirea*: Nationalism in a Spiritual Guise," in Jowitt, K., ed., *Social Change in Romania, 1860–1940* (1978): 140–73; Hitchins, K., *Romania 1866-1947* (1994):305-14

—KEITH HITCHINS

BLAIS, Marie-Claire

Canadian novelist, poet, and dramatist (writing in French), b. 5 Oct. 1939, Quebec, Que.

For so young a writer, B. has been prolific, having started in her teens. Born into a working-class family, she left a convent school without completing her education to work in a shoe factory, then an

Marie-Claire Blais

office. Although this background illuminates her work, it is not described in realistic detail, for B. is a poetic novelist depicting in powerful symbols the psychological states of troubled adolescence. Fellowships and prizes have enabled B. to live by her pen (as few Canadian writers do) in the rural seclusion of Cape Cod, Brittany, and recently Quebec.

B.'s first novel, *La belle bête* (1959; *Mad Shadows*, 1960), was published on the eve of the *révolution tranquille*—that laicization and urbanization of Quebec society in the early 1960s—and because it was read as a fable of a world struggling to be born, B. became identified with this social upheaval. Nevertheless, *La belle bête* is a psychological novel depicting Oedipal family situations. The novel reveals that B. is fascinated with human evil and obsessed with the mystery of damnation—thus showing an affinity with such French Catholic novelists as François MAURIAC. But the dramatic and sensual portrayal of the evil Isabelle—Marie creates a stylistic fluidity and visionary intensity in the line of Lautréamont and the SURREALISTS, whom B. admires.

Throughout the 1960s Blais continued to write novels of adolescence. *Une saison dans la vie d'Emmanuel* (1965; *A Season in the Life of Emmanuel*, 1966), B.'s masterpiece (awarded the prestigious French Médici Prize), is her most characteristic novel of this decade, combining an interiorized, hallucinatory intensity with a more objective viewpoint. An attack on the rural idyll, a staple of Quebec fiction, the novel depicts an infertile land, people without religion, a corrupt clergy, an unloving mother, and children who are mere ciphers—so many myths demolished. This inverted pastoral is conveyed through the feverish visions of the tubercular Jean-le-Maigre, a would-be writer; through the voice of Héloïse, who confuses convent and brothel; and through the eyes of Baby Emmanuel, looking up at the grotesque world from his cradle. The baby's "view from below" is the source of black comedy, a new element in B.'s work.

The fable of the artist, a secondary theme in many of her novels, is the central concern of the semiautobiographical trilogy written toward the end of the 1960s. In the first two volumes, *Manuscrits de Pauline Archange* (1968) and *Vivre! vivre!* (1969)—published together in English as *The Manuscripts of Pauline Archange* (1970)—B. charts the turbulent adolescence of Pauline Archange, aspiring artist, as she struggles against her environment to escape family, factory, and sanatorium. *Les apparences* (1970; *Dürer's Angel*, 1976) moves to the heart of Pauline's (and B.'s) aesthetic in the culminating vision based on Dürer's famous engraving, the "Melancholia." Angelic aspirations to create, seemingly dashed by the environment and its promise of damnation, may yet be realized if rooted in the reality of daily life.

In the 1970s a new realism came into B.'s writing, and she subjected the literary worlds of Montreal and Paris to an increasingly satiric pen. *Les nuits de l'Underground* (1978; *Nights in the Underground* 1979), however, focuses on the theme of homosexuality, which appears in all her writing, in a more personal and realistic mode. It tells the story of a painter who falls in love with a doctor she meets in a lesbian bar in Montreal. In what has become a characteristic structural feature, B. juxtaposes two paradoxical codes: the lesbian world is depicted in images drawn from conventional religion.

While B.'s career may yet take many new directions—as *Le sourd dans la ville* (1980, deaf man in the city) suggests—her powerful early novels are assured classics of Quebec modernism. Her efforts to mine the poetic vein in her writing, in the poems of *Pays voilés* (1963; veiled countries), have had surprisingly conventional results, given the power of her poetic prose, while her experiments with realism in drama, as in *L'exécution* (1968; *The Execution*, 1976) have proved awkward on stage. But her best novels do contain poetic and dramatic qualities, and they balance a piercing criticism of Quebec social ills with a haunting hallucinatory vision.

FURTHER WORKS: *Tête blanche* (1960; *Tête Blanche*, 1961); *Le jour est noir* (1962; *The Day Is Dark*, 1967); *Les voyageurs sacrés* (1962; *Three Travelers*, 1967); *Existences* (1964); *L'insoumise* (1966; *The Fugitive*, 1978); *David Sterne* (1967; *David Sterne*, 1973); *Le loup* (1972; *The Wolf*, 1974); *Un joualonais, sa joualonie* (1973; *St. Lawrence Blues*, 1974); *Une liaison parisienne* (1975; *A Literary Affair*, 1979); *Océan, suivi de Murmures* (1977)

BIBLIOGRAPHY: Davis, M., "La Belle Bête: Pilgrim unto Life," *TamR*, No. 16 (1960): 51–59; Wilson, E., "M.-C. B.," in *O Canada: An American's Notes on Canadian Culture* (1964): 147–57; Callaghan, B., "An Interview with M.-C. B.," *TamR*, No. 37 (1965): 29–34; Stratford, P., *M.-C. B.* (1971); Gordon, J. V., "An 'Incandescence of Suffering': The Fiction of M.-C. B.," *MFS*, 22 (1976): 467–84; Kertzer, J. M., "*Une saison dans la vie d'Emmanuel: A Season in Hell*," *SCL*, 2 (1977): 278–88

—BARBARA GODARD

BLAMAN, Anna

(pseud. of Johanna Petronelle Vrugt) Dutch novelist, b. 31 Jan. 1905, Rotterdam; d. 13 July 1960, Rotterdam

As a student of French literature, B. was familiar with progressive trends in fiction, as became evident when at age thirty-five the former schoolteacher published her first novel. Although in the remaining twenty years of her outwardly uneventful life she published only half a dozen other books, she soon gained considerable prominence, and was awarded several prestigious literary prizes, including, in 1957, the State Prize for Literature.

Her reputation was not universally acknowledged, however, because the relative emphasis on sexual and other bodily functions in her work shocked many readers and critics. *Eenzaam avontuur* (1948; lonely adventure), a novel that deals with a male writer's marital misadventures, was especially instrumental in establishing her image as a literary libertine, because it predated by more than a decade the general outbreak of erotomania in Dutch letters.

B.'s most important novel is probably *Op leven en dood* (1954; *A Matter of Life and Death*, 1974), in which many of her thematic preoccupations culminate in the account of a journalist's declining years. Beset by loneliness and illness, he is inexorably reduced to the most basic level of existence. Successively stripped of all confidence in his physical, mental, and emotional capabilities, he shows up the illusory and escapist nature of the values by which society operates. The novel is written in the traditional manner, and the setting and atmosphere, including the protagonist's heart-disease symptoms, are described quite realistically. But the realism is juxtaposed with a brief narrative in which another man expresses in dreamlike visions his ultimately unrequited love for the journalist. The conclusion of the novel echoes this interlude on a concrete level, transposed into a heterosexual relationship.

In its probing psychological orientation *Op leven en dood* is typical not only of B.'s oeuvre, but of a well-established trend in Dutch writing. Women writers have traditionally contributed to this genre, but B. differs from them in dealing predominantly with the male psyche. Because so much critical attention used to be focused on her fascination with unorthodox relations and her frankness in dealing with taboo subjects generally, her very considerable achievements in analyzing the male mind have not always been fully recognized. A more fundamental reason why her literary reputation has never quite overcome the sensationalist overtones of her original reception is probably the discrepancy between her ambitious intellectual aim to probe the fundamental truths about Man, and her technical literary skills. B.'s evocations of her characters are not substantial enough to stand up under the intellectual burden of the insights they have to convey. But although in this respect she fell short of greatness, she contributed significant impulses to the revival of Dutch letters in the postwar era and, for better or worse, pointed the way for the next generation of novelists.

FURTHER WORKS: *Vrouw en vriend* (1941); *Ontmoeting met Selma* (1943); *De kruisvaarder* (1950); *Rama Horna en andere verhalen* (1951); *Overdag en andere verhalen* (1957); *De verliezers* (1960); *A. B. over zichzelf en anderen* (1963); *Hotel Bonheur/ Singeldrama* (1975); *Fragmentarisch* (1978)

—EGBERT KRISPYN

BLANCHOT, Maurice

French novelist and critic, b. 22 Sept. 1907, Quain

B. began publishing fiction and literary criticism shortly after 1940. Earlier, from 1930 to 1940, he had pursued a career as a rightist journalist, serving as an editor of foreign affairs on the *Journal des débats*, contributing to *Réaction* and *Combat*, and working for a short time as one of the principal editors of *Aux écoutes* and as literary director of *Jeune France*. With the beginning of his literary career, however, he seemed to move away from politics, and since then the personal details of his life have remained a mystery. However, although B. rejects SARTRE's militant EXISTENTIALISM and its political commitment when he stresses that the exercise of real power should never be confused with writing, his position is not an apolitical restatement of "art for art's sake." After World War II. B. published in journals associated with a leftist position: *Les temps modernes* and *Critique*. His critical essays and rare political pronouncements subtly but explicitly express a leftist position that, in the collection of essays entitled *L'amitié* (1971; friendship), even include a place for Marxist analysis.

In his critical works B. writes on miscellaneous topics and deals with a vast number of novelists, poets, and philosophers. There is a constellation of writers who particularly inspire him and with whose work he has elective affinities: Kafka, Bataille, Rilke, Mallarmé, and Hölderlin, and the philosophers Heraclitus, Heidegger, Hegel, Nietzsche, and Emmanuel Levinas (b. 1905). B. is not generally interested in the content, form, or style of a writer's work but in the paradoxes and ironies of the practice of literature, in the dilemmas and agonies of modern literature that the writer faces. Rather than providing answers in his critical work, B. explores fundamental questions about the possibility and nothingness of literature by examining the process of writing in relation to language and the philosophically problematic experience of death/suicide. Three essays—"La littérature et le droit à la mort" (literature and the right to death) in *La part du feu* (1949; belonging to the fire); "Le regard d'Orphée" (the look of Orpheus) in *L'espace littéraire* (1955; the literary space); and "Le chant des Sirènes" (the song of the Sirens) in *Le livre à venir* (1959; the book to come)—most comprehensively and systematically present the complexities of B.'s meditations on the work of art and the act of writing.

B.'s largest collection of critical essays, *L'entretien infini* (1969; infinite conversation), differs from his previous theoretical works and introduces a new phase in his approach to criticism. Although B.'s interests remain the same, traditional critical discourse here begins to merge in form with his fictional works. Criticism in this work is presented as an interplay of philosophical and lyrical meditations interspersed with fragments of narrative dialogue. *Le pas au-delà* (1973; the step beyond), continuing this fragmentary style and blurring the boundaries between fiction and criticism and disrupting the very notion of genre, resembles a journal filled with philosophical aphorisms and snippets of narrative rather than a book of theoretical essays.

Among the first of B.'s published fictional works are the novels *Aminadab* (1942; Aminadab) and *Le très-haut* (1948; the most high). They are still fairly conventional in form but already highly complex experiments that owe much to the SURREALIST and fantastic short story; they are also very similar in their themes to Kafka's longer works. The protagonists move in a nightmarish bureaucratic world described as if it were ordinary and are destroyed by laws that function in bizarre and inexplicable ways. B.'s

originality in these works consists in defining writing as a revolutionary act that automatically transgresses the laws of society and in undermining the status of language as simply a device for communication.

A turning point in B.'s fictional production occurred when the began writing his *récits: L'arrêt de mort* (1948; *Death Sentence*, 1978), *Thomas l'obscur, nouvelle version* (1950; *Thomas the Obscure, New Version*, 1973), *Au moment voulu* (1951; at the willed moment), *Celui qui ne m'accompagnait pas* (1953; the one who did not accompany me), and *Le dernier homme* (1957, the last man). These are short fictions usually centered on a first-person narrator who is also a writer. They often focus on a mysterious "experience" related in some way to the problem of language or writing and mediated by a passionate encounter with another person. The person encountered is frequently a female who seems to die—that is, the nature of her death is ambiguous. Realistic description is minimal and fragmentary, while the action takes place in sparsely furnished apartments, in rooms and corridors that are separated from the everday life of the outside world. Little can be said about the content of these works because they drastically reduce the presence of elements such as chronological development and characterization.

B. reached another level in his series of narrative experiments with the publication of *L'attente, l'oubli* (1962; waiting, forgetting), which is neither a novel nor a *récit*. It is composed of a strange dialogue between "il" ("he") and "elle" ("she") interspersed with anonymous aphoristic passages that would later be repeated in *L'entretien infini*.

Historically, B.'s importance may well consist of carrying the self-reflexive tendency in fiction and criticism, begun by the German romantics, to its extreme and beyond.

FURTHER WORKS: *Thomas l'obscur* (1941); *Comment la littérature est—elle possible*? (1942); *Faux pas* (1943); *Le dernier mot* (1948); *Lautréamont et Sade* (1949); *Le ressassement éternel* (1951); *La bête de Lascaux* (1958); *La folie du jour* (1973); *L'écriture du désastre* (1980)

BIBLIOGRAPHY: Hartman, G. H., "M. B.: Philosopher Novelist," *ChiR*, 15, 2 (1961): 1–18; Oxenhandler, N., "Paradox and Negation in the Criticism of M. B.," *Symposium*, 16 (1962): 36–44; DeMan, P., *Blindness and Insight* (1971): 60–78; Lawall, S. N., *Critics of Consciousness* (1968): 221–65; special B. issue, *Substance*, 14 (1976); Derrida, J., *Deconstruction and Criticism* (1979): 75–176

—LARYSA MYKYTA

BLANDIANA, Ana

(pseud. of Otilia-Valeria Coman) Romanian poet, translator, and essayist, b. 25 Mar. 1942, Timişoara

Born in Timişoara, southwestern Romania, B. attended high school in Oradea and studied for a degree in philology at the University of Cluj. After graduation (1967), she served as poetry editor for *Viaţa Românească* and *Amfiteatru*. In 1975 she moved to a position as librarian at the Institute of Fine Arts in Bucharest, a job which she later gave up to work as a free-lance writer, publishing poetry and two regular columns in *Contemporanul* and

România literară. In the mid-1980s B. was banned from all Romanian publications because of her dissident poems. An active participant in the December 1989 uprising against Ceauşescu's dictatorial régime, B. was elected to the newly constituted Council of the National Salvation Front, but resigned from it as soon as its neocommunist leanings became apparent. B. is now a major rallying figure in the prodemocratic opposition.

Though her poems appeared in *Tribuna* from Cluj as early as 1959, B. could not publish her first volume until 1964, after the process of de-Stalinization had started. *Persoana întîia plural* (first person plural) surprised critics with its fresh, uninhibited treatment of subjective emotion and exuberant imagery. Her second volume, *Călcîiul vulnerabil* (1967; the vulnerable heel), toned down the youthful rhetoric, introducing a more reflexive, self-questioning style that was to become B.'s distinctive feature. By the end of the decade, B. was the acknowledged leader of a group of women poets who had made essential contributions to the "poetic revival of the 1960s." While B. has never allowed herself to be categorized as a "woman poet" ("poetry, like truth, like freedom, cannot be categorized into great and small, good and bad, male and female"), her poetry balanced from the start existential and sociocultural concerns, an imaginative exploration of individual experience with an emphasis on broader sociophilosophical issues such as women's lot and experience.

B.'s subsequent volumes of verse, *A treia taină* (1970; the third enigma), *Cincizeci de poeme* (1970; fifty poems), *Octombrie, noiembrie, decembrie* (1972; October, November, December), and *Poezii* (1974; poems), deepened and darkened this twofold concern. Very little of B.'s earlier expansive rhetoric survived in these poems: The reflection is internalized or impersonal—the motifs of sleep, silence, inner reflection predominate—the line is terse and nervous, devoid of "ornaments." Sentimentality is here refused in favor of an austere, detached mapping of essentials; poetry is no longer a transcription of emotional states, but an intense scrutiny of life, an act of skeptical cognition. Feminine themes are present—maternity, feminine sexuality, woman's spiritual needs—but they are broached from a transpersonal perspective that allows important moral and philosophical questions to be asked. The main emphasis is on cosmic "spending," on existential and poetic dissipation. And yet B.'s vision remains hopefully dialectic, highlighting alternatives, redefining the boundaries between nature and spirit, love and death, individual desire and norm. The competing terms are often described by striking oxymorons: Death is "Clear," despair is "happy" and "gentle," light is "ferocious," darkness is "clean" and "tender," "loneliness is a happy town." B.'s deliberately ambivalent, antipoetic style calls into question traditional literary discourse, its problematic claims to truth. Words become the poet's necessary "adversaries" in a lucid dialogue about the limitations of art.

B.'s recent poems continue to reevaluate critically the relation of literature to existential and social truth. *Somnul din somn* (1977; the sleep in sleep), *Ora de nisip* (1983; The Hour of Sand, 1990), and *Stea de pradă* (1985; predatory star) are underwritten by a sterner moral and metaphysical perspective, but also by a clearer understanding of a time of great personal and national crisis. B.'s sparse, thinly veiled imagery denounces collective compromises as in the famous lines that got an entire editorial board fired after their publication: "I believe we are vegetal people / How otherwise to account for this compliant / Shedding of our leaves. . ." By and large, B.'s poetic evolution parallels the broader course of contemporary Romanian poetry: expansive and lyrical in the early 1960s;

philosophically skeptical and self-ironic in the 1970s; politically engaged and questioning in the 1980s.

B.'s prose reflections published over the years in two short columns have been collected in *Calitatea de martor* (1970; rev. 2nd ed., 1972; the mark of a witness) and *Eu scriu, tu scrii, el, ea scrie* (1976; I write, you write, he, she writes). These pages of an ongoing "antidiary" gloss with aphoristic crispness Romania's recent cultural history, exposing its social and moral faults. B.'s gift for sharp observation and controversy is also reflected in *Convorbiri subjective* (1971; subjective dialogues) and *O discutie la masa tăcerii şi alte convorbiri subjective* (1976; a discussion around the silent table and other subjective colloquies)—two collections of spirited interviews coauthored with her husband, Romulus Rusan (b. 1935); and in a collection of short stories, *Proiecte de trecut* (1982; Projects for the Past). After the collapse of Ceauşescu's regime, B. published *Sertarul cu aplauze* (1992; The Applause Drawer), a satirical novel focusing on the last decade of a delirious personality cult. Alternating autobiography with fiction, this novel details the dramatic life of a politically persecuted writer.

FURTHER WORKS: *Cele patru anotimpuri* (1977); *Cea mai frumoasă dintre lumile possible* (1978); *Intîmplări din grădina mea* (1980); *Proiecte de trecut; Proze* (1982); *Imitaţie de coşmar* (1996). FURTHER WORKS IN ENGLISH: *Poeme/Poems* (1982); *Don't Be Afraid of Me: Collected Poems* (1985); *Silent Voices* (1986)

BIBLIOGRAPHY: Micu, D., Preface to *Poeme/Poems* (1982): 9–18; Buduca, I., "La qualité de poète: A. B.," *CREL*, 4 (1983): 87–91; Adcock, F., Introduction to *Silent Voices* (1986): 10–14; Jay, P., and A. Cristofovici, Preface to *The Hour of Sand* (1990): 6–9; Chamberlain, L., "*Mysteries and Visions,*" *TLS*, 19–25 Jan. 1990: 59

—MARCEL CORNIS-POPE

BLASCO IBÁÑEZ, Vicente

Spanish novelist and short-story writer, b. 29 Jan. 1867, Valencia; d. 28 Jan. 1928, Menton, France

B. I. was graduated from the University of Valencia with a degree in law. He founded the liberal newspaper *El pueblo*, which supported socialist policies and the establishment of a republic. B. I. was a political activist, and although he was elected to the Spanish parliament six times, he was imprisoned over thirty times and suffered exile at least twice because of his outspoken attacks against the government.

B. I. is the perfect example of a writer more greatly respected outside his country than in it. After Cervantes, he is the most widely translated Spanish novelist, but unfortunately, his popularity is based on novels that are sometimes little more than potboilers and do not measure up to the quality of his earlier novels, which colorfully and with utmost sincerity depict the lives of the people of Valencia. Most critics consider only this early group of regional novels of true literary worth. His later novels of social reform, those of psychological analysis, his war novels, and the so-called cosmopolitan novels, are all judged to be inferior to his earlier efforts.

La barraca (1898; The Cabin, 1919) and *Cañas y barro* (1902; Reeds and Mud, 1928) are B. I.'s undisputed masterpieces. Influenced by the naturalism of Zola, they both have tightly woven suspenseful plots, through which the misery and pain of the

Valencian peasants are portrayed with empathy and unfailing accuracy. The passages describing the area around Valencia—the fields, lakes, and swamps—which B. I. knew so well, contain some of his best writing.

La catedral (1903; *The Shadow of the Cathedral*, 1919), a novel of social reform, whose message is unabashedly anticlerical, has an ironic conclusion. It is a lyrical portrayal of Gabriel Luna, a world-weary radical who returns to his family home in the upper cloisters of Toledo's principal cathedral. He is wantonly killed by his friends and neighbors, whose social and political consciousness he thought he had properly raised, and is ultimately blamed for their crime of larceny. His assassins misconstrue Luna's ideas on social reform and prove to be as greedy and corrupt as the society that has oppressed them.

Sangre y arena (1908; *Blood and Sand*, 1919), a novel that has been categorized as psychological, and *Los cuatro jinetes del Apocalipsis* (1916; *The Four Horsemen of the Apocalypse*, 1918) are B. I.'s two most popular books, and were both made into successful films starring Rudolph Valentino. *Sangre y arena* is a saga of the bullring, bloody and crude. Its main interest is not the rather banal, lightweight plot centering around Juan Gallardo's rise and fall as a famous *torero*, or his shallow characterization, but rather the virile and trenchant descriptions of the pageantry, the traditions, and the presence of death always surrounding bullfighting. *Los cuatro jinetes del Apocalipsis* is another saga, this time of two branches of an Argentine family, one rerooted in France, the other in Germany, during the first months of World War I. It is a staunchly pro-ally tract, which prophesies with uncanny accuracy the horrors of Nazism and which is unrelenting in its vigorous descriptions of the death and the slaughter on the battlefields.

Perhaps B. I. wrote too many novels with a cosmopolitan background, like the posthumously published *El fantasma de las alas de oro* (1930; *The Phantom with Wings of Gold*, 1931). Set in the gambling casinos and aristocractic villas of Monte Carlo, it is illustrative of B. I.'s shortcomings. The novel is formulaic and peopled with characters who are unreal, and therefore uninteresting. It is as if B. I. himself were not really interested in what he was writing. The novel soon turns into pulp fiction, with a trendy plot of immoral love and cheap sentimentalism probably aimed at B. I.'s eager public.

Although B. I. was an uneven and at times careless writer, he produced enough well-crafted fiction to earn a solid reputation as *the* novelist of Valencia. Although frequently preachy, he was always on the side of justice, humanity, and peace. Like the painter Joaquín Sorolla (1863–1923), a fellow Valencian, he was a vivid colorist and exciting landscape artist who appealed to the senses. At his best, B. I. was a forceful and compelling writer.

FURTHER WORKS: *París, impresiones de un emigrado* (1893); *El juez* (1894); *Arroz y tartana* (1895; *The Three Roses*, 1932); *Cuentos valencianos* (1896); *En el país del arte* (1896; *In the Land of Art*, 1923); *Flor de mayo* (1896; *The Mayflower*, 1921); *Entre naranjos* (1900); *The Torrent*, 1921); *La condenada* (1900); *Sónnica la cortesana* (1901; *Sonnica the Courtesan*, 1912); *El intruso* (1904; *The Intruder*, 1928); *La voluntad de vivir* (1904); *La bodega* (1905; *The Fruit of the Vine*, 1919); *La horda* (1905; *The Mob*, 1929); *La maja desnuda* (1906; *Woman Triumphant*, (1920); *Oriente* (1907); *Los muertos mandan* (1909; *The Dead Command*, 1919); *Luna Benamor* (1909; *Luna Benamor*, 1919); *Argentina y sus grandezas* (1910); *Los argonautas* (1914); *Historia de la guerra europea de 1914* (13 vols., 1914–1919); *Mare Nostrum*

Vicente Blasco Ibáñez

(1918; *Our Sea*, 1919); *Los enemigos de la mujer* (1919); *The Enemies of Women*, 1920); *El militarismo mejicano* (1920; *Mexico in Revolution*, 1920); *El préstamo de la difunta* (1920); *La tierra de todos* (1921; *The Temptress*, 1923); *El paraíso de las mujeres* (1922); *La reina Calafia* (1923; *Queen Calafia*, 1924); *Novelas de la costa azul* (1924); *Una nación secuestrada: Alfonso XIII desenmascarado* (1924; *Alfonso XIII Unmasked: The Military Terror in Spain*, 1924); *La vuelta al mundo de un novelista* (3 vols., 1924–1925; *A Novelist's Tour of the World*, 1926); *El papa del mar* (1925; *The Pope of the Sea*, 1927); *Lo que será la república española: al país y al ejército* (1925); *A los pies de Venus* (1926; *The Borgias; or, At the Feet of Venusc*, (1927); *Novelas de amor y muerte* (1927); *El caballero de la Virgen* (1929; *Knight of the Virgin*, 1930); *En busca del Gran Kan: Cristóbal Colón* (1929; *Unknown Lands: The Story of Columbus*, 1929); *Historia de la revolución española, 1800–74* (3 vols., 1930); *Estudios literarios* (1933); *La novela de vivir, novela póstuma* (1953); *Discursos literarios* (1966); *Obras completas* (1967). FURTHER WORKS IN ENGLISH: *The Last Lion and Other Tales* (1919); *The Old Woman of the Movies and Other Stories* (1925); *The Mad Virgins and Other Stories* (1926)

BIBLIOGRAPHY: Dos Passos, J., *Rosinante to the Road Again* (1922): 120–32; Ellis, H., *Views and Reviews* (1932): 247–57; Eoff, S. H., *The Modern Spanish Novel* (1962): 115–19; Gascó Contell, E., *Genio y figura de B. I.* (1967); Grove, A., and E. C. Knowlton, Jr., *V. B. I.* (1972); Cardwell, R. A., *B. I.: "La barraca"*

(1975); Medina, J. T., "The Artistry of B. I.'s *Cañas y barro*", *Hispania*, 60 (1977): 275–84; Fox, A., "Estructuras totémicas en La barraca de B. I.," *Hispania*, 75 (1992): 275-84; Anderson, C., *Primitives, Patriarchy and the Pacaresque in B.'s Cañas y Barro* (1995)

—MARSHALL J. SCHNEIDER

BLATTER, Silvio

Swiss novelist and short-story writer (writing in German), b. 25 Jan. 1946, Bremgarten

B. studied to be an elementary-school teacher and taught for six years in Aarau. He then worked at various jobs in industry and studied at the University of Zurich. For a short time he directed radio plays for Swiss Radio. Since 1976 he has devoted himself entirely to his writing. He has won numerous literary awards, including the Conrad Ferdinand Meyer Prize (1974), and in 1984 was elected president of the German-Swiss P.E.N. Club. He lives in Zurich.

B.'s work portrays the everyday life of the Swiss in microscopic detail and examines the role that nature, alienation, and homeland play in the Swiss mentality. His works are often socially committed, and he frequently experiments with narrative techniques.

B.'s first major work, *Schaltfehler* (1971; switching error), examines the dehumanizing effect that piecework has on fourteen workers in a large factory. He also explores the world of work in his long story *Genormte tage, verschüttete zeit* (1976; conformist days, spilled time). Here he shows how demeaning, monotonous work has destroyed even the private life of the protagonist, Stöhr. In both cases B. uses nonconventional techniques to force his readers to disengage themselves from the story and reflect on its contents.

B. continues this duality of experimental narrative coupled with contemporary social problems in other works as well. *Mary Long* (1973; title in English) is a lengthy discourse on the possibilities of prose fiction combined with an exploration of Swiss identity; *Love Me Tender* (1980; title in English) examines the world of sports through a variety of perspectives; and *Die schneefalle* (1981; the snow trap) investigates the debilitating influence of the police apparatus and the mass media in contemporary society and is constructed in a mazelike fashion so that the reader must participate in deciphering the fragments.

B.'s magnum opus to date is a trilogy set in the Freiamt, a Catholic region in the predominantly Protestant canton of Aarau, which is located near Zurich: *Zunehmendes heimweh* (1978; increasing homesickness), *Kein schöner land* (1983; no more beautiful country), and *Das sanfte gesetz* (1988; the gentle law). These novels describe and examine the lives of a number of individuals in and around the fictive Villinger family, who live in B.'s hometown of Bremgarten. All of the characters' hopes, dreams, thoughts, and actions are interwoven with each other in montage fashion to form a gigantic pastiche of Swiss society. The present is often related to the past, and the characters seem to be constantly searching for their own identity within their regional and national frameworks. B. thus critically investigates the whole concept of what it means to be Swiss, incorporating a number of factors, including the influence of religion, nature, and tradition.

Most contemporary Swiss authors investigate in one way or another the phenomenon of Switzerland in their works, and B. is at the foreground of this movement. His piercing observations and his committed stance together with his intriguing stylistic innovations make him one of the leading young authors in the German-speaking world.

FURTHER WORKS: *Brände kommen unerwartet* (1968); *Eine wohnung im erdgeschoß* (1970); *Nur der könig trägt bart* (1973); *Flucht and tod des Daniel Zoff* (1974); *Wassermann* (1986); *Das blaue haus* (1990)

BIBLIOGRAPHY: Böll, H., "Aussichten eines Zwanzigjährigen," *Der Spiegel* (25 Sept. 1978): 220–21; Bernasconi, C., "Auf dem Weg zum Meistererzähler," *Börsenblatt*, 43, 7 (1987): 236–41; Ester, H., "Heimat und Identität im Werk S. Bs," in Acker, R., and Burkhard, M., eds., *Blick auf die Schweiz* (1987): 61–79

—ROBERT ACKER

BLECHER, M(arcel)

Romanian novelist and poet, b. 8 Sept. 1909, Botosani; d. 31 May 1938, Romania

In 1928, in Paris, where he had just started studying medicine, B. discovered that he was suffering from tuberculosis of the spine. He was encased in a plaster cast for the rest of his life, but his condition kept deteriorating in spite of the treatment he received in various sanatoriums in France, Switzerland, and Romania.

The spiritual family to which B. belongs is that of central and east European Jewish writers like KAFKA or Bruno SCHULZ. But unlike Kafka and Schulz, both of whom were born and raised in the old Austro-Hungarian Empire and who regarded Vienna as the natural cultural center of their world, B. was, like most Romanian intellectuals of his time, more familiar with what was going on in Paris, where he corresponded with, among others, André BRETON and contributed occasionally to surrealist periodicals.

B. was not a surrealist, however. His masterpiece, *Intîmplări în irealitatea imediată* (1936; adventures in the immediate unreality) is as unclassifiable, puzzling, and fascinating as Schulz's *Cinnamon Shops*. In a manner that is at the same time realistic and fantastic, the author recounts memories of childhood and adolescence, which are linked by the hidden theme of his agonizing search for identity in an alien, almost nightmarish universe. With a delicacy of perception, but also with a growing sense of anxiety, the narrator discovers behind the appearances of the most ordinary objects (described with a haunting precision that reminds one of Kafka) a lurking mischievousness, a core of malignant falsehood, a hallucinatory emptiness. Under his gaze, the contours of the most innocuous things turn invariably into menacing grimaces. The boy's only refuge from the aggressiveness of the "immediate unreality" of everyday life is the world of make-believe in its grossest, most obvious forms—the provincial waxworks museum, vulgar artificial flowers, dummies, cheap sideshow settings, silent movies seen in old, mildewy theaters. It is only in the midst of such shoddiness that the narrator feels more secure and is able to recover something of his lost sense of reality and authenticity.

B.'s second novel, *Inimi cicatrizate* (1937; scarred hearts) centers around the experiences of the author during his stay at a sanatorium in Berck, France. Externally, the novel resembles Thomas Mann's *The Magic Mountain*, but the conception of the two works is profoundly different. B.'s treatment of disease and suffering shuns the elaborate symbolism of Mann's approach, in an attempt to "demystify" them. Suffering, B. seems to imply, has no metaphysical meaning or redeeming value. Accordingly, the novel is written in a lucid, detached, subtly polemical style. The tragic banality of suffering, and particularly of physical pain, are suggested by countless detailed, cruelly accurate descriptions. *Inimi cicatrizate* is a powerful novel, but one cannot help regretting the absence from it of the paradoxical intricacies and rich ambiguities that make his earlier work unforgettable.

FURTHER WORKS: *Corp transparent* (1934); *Vizuina luminată* (1971)

BIBLIOGRAPHY: Crohmalniceano, O., Preface to M. B., *Aventures dans l'irréalité immédiate* (1973): 7–14; Bianciotti, H., "Des deux côtés de la vitre: M. B., *Aventures dans l'irréalité immédiate*," *QL*, 1–15 April 1973: 3–4

—MATEI CALINESCU

BLOK, Alexandr

Russian poet and dramatist, b. 28 Nov. 1880, St. Petersburg; d. 7 Aug. 1921, Petrograd (now St. Petersburg)

B. is the most important poet of the brief SYMBOLIST period of Russian literature (1890–1910) and one of the leading Russian poets of the 20th c. He was born into an aristocratic family of Russian and German descent. His father was a professor of law at Warsaw University; his mother, daughter of a distinguished biologist, was a writer and translator. After his parents were divorced, B. was brought up in the highly cultured milieu of his maternal home. Unsuccessful in his attempt at studying law, he entered the Philological Institute in St. Petersburg and was graduated in 1906. He began writing poetry at an early age, and his poetic gifts matured under the influence of the metaphysical poetry of Vladimir Solovyov (1853–1900). The small but vocal group of symbolist poets, Sergey Solovyov (1885–1941) and Andrey BELY among them, were the first to recognize his talent. B. married Lyubov Mendeleeva, the daughter of a famous scientist. She was the Beautiful Lady of his visionary poems. The marriage was interpreted by B.'s admirers as an event of prophetic significance: the poet's union with the embodiment of his vision. The marriage was far from idyllic, but neither B. nor Lyubov ever lost belief in its fateful character, and this conviction remained an enduring bond between them.

Stikhi o prekrasnoy dame (1904; poems about the beautiful lady) won B. widespread recognition. He was never again to write such exalted, idealistic verse. His subsequent poetry reflected his disillusionment with his former ideals, a growing depression, and moods that he later described as "attacks of despair and irony." No longer able to find fulfillment in the cold realm of metaphysics, B. turned for inspiration to real life. Into his poetry after 1905 entered people, things, the sights and sounds of city life. The new themes generated daring experiments in prosody. Yet, despite this newly found realism, a strong undercurrent of mysticism stirred beneath a deceivingly artless and seemingly straightforward narrative.

In 1906 B. added the drama to his artistic experiments, a genre toward which he had always felt drawn. His first play, *Balaganchik* (1906; the puppet show), a satire on symbolism, proved successful on the stage. Several trips abroad, to Italy in 1909 and to France in 1911, inspired the magnificent "Italyanskie stikhi" (1909–10; "Italian Poems," 1973) and *Roza i krest* (1912; *The Rose and the Cross*, 1936), his last and best play, based on a medieval French legend.

During World War I B. joined the army but remained behind the front lines. Having prophesied the necessity and inevitability of the revolution long before its coming, he greeted it joyously, seeing in its destruction and violence the death pangs of a corrupt culture and the dawn of a new, promising era. But his enthusiasm was short-lived. The struggle for existence and the humiliating pressures to write on command affected his mental and physical health. His poetic voice grew silent, and he died destroyed in body and spirit at the age of forty.

B. brought to art an almost religious dedication. In numerous articles he speaks of duty and service to humanity, of the poet as intermediary between this and "other worlds," and of "burning himself to ashes" in the process of creation. With his heightened mystical perceptivity, he reached for that symbolic entity he called the "spirit of music." To capture spiritually and poetically the harmony concealed beyond the chaos of life is to overcome the division between body and soul, to understand the purpose of man on earth, and thus to rise above the mediocrity of daily existence. B. viewed poetry and all great art as a freeing of the spirit as well as a dynamic force for progress.

The conception of the artist-poet as the carrier of the "spirit of music" (compare his essay "Krushenie gumanisma" [1919; the collapse of humanism]) is central to B.'s world view. He listened to the recondite music of other worlds: the rhythm and sounds of his verse reveal an extraordinary ear for melody, a unique music that is an echo of the harmony he sought to capture. In this search for symbolic purpose, which his verses reveal as a necessary aspiration and an unfulfillable longing, lie both the genius of his poetry and the tragedy of his life. The decline of B.'s lyrical powers is related in part to his realization of poetry's impotence and to his own inability to come to terms with the "amusical" reality of postrevolutionary Russia.

B.'s initiation into poetry and his search for the mystery of existence began with love. His first lyrics are addressed to the Beautiful Lady, the incarnation of Sophia—Vladimir Solovyov's concept of the Eternal Feminine, Divine Wisdom, the intermediary between God and man through whom man can hope to regain a lost unity and reconciliation with the divine. These early lyrics are hymns, prayers, and meditations addressed to a higher being whose spirit and earthly qualities B. saw in Lyubov Mendeleeva. At the same time as he is awed by the mystic promise of revelation, he is also tormented by anguish and fear that he is undeserving of divine grace and that his vision will vanish.

These poems are the first link in the long chain of B.'s love poetry. Although artistically they are not his best, he considered them his most important. In B.'s later love poetry, only the spirit of the poet's search remains: the yearning for infinite ecstasy, for contact with other realities, for oblivion. All his real and imagined women are only shadows of reality, transient and illusory embodiments of the One he sang of in his youth. Only one of the embodiments—Russia—emerges as an independent theme and one that runs through B.'s poetry and ends with his last important poem, "Skify" (1917; "The Scythians," 1955). In his lyrics on Russia, as in his love poems, symbol and reality mingle. Russia has many faces: the dark, uncouth, drunken Russia yet to awaken from the torpor of the Mongolian yoke; the despicable, spiritually dead Russia of civil servants and merchants and of the soulless bourgeoisie; and the "other," the Russia of huge awesome expanses, of "infinite anguish," a mystical Russia of "impenetrable silences" and wailing winds, the future leader of mankind. "O my Russia! My wife!" B. addresses her in his cycle "Na pole Kulikovom" (1908; "On the Field of Kulikovo," 1954), celebrating the victory of the Russians over the Mongols in 1380, a symbolic event according to B.—the first of Russia's victorious marches toward its prophetic destiny.

Between 1909 and 1914 black pessimism filled his pages, yet his somber moods produced some of his best poems. In the dark shadows of St. Petersburg lurk phantoms of the "terrible world," a world populated with drunkards, gypsies, prostitutes, demonic creatures, and death itself. They invade his poetry, leaving so powerful an impression as to make one forget that B. could also write light, graceful verses and passionately romantic love lyrics.

B. burned himself out early as a poet. After 1914 he wrote only three important pieces, the long poem "Vozmezdie" (1921; retribution), which he left unfinished; "Dvenadtsat" (1918; "The Twelve," 1920), and "Skify."

Best known among B.'s poems is "Dvenadtsat." It is symbolically divided into twelve chapters, and the poet's own individual voice blends with the colorful language and rhythms of the street. A band of twelve Red guardsmen is marching down blizzard-swept Petrograd streets, plundering and shooting. At the very end, their leader turns out to be none other than Christ himself, and the twelve villains are transformed into the twelve Apostles. This poem may differ in structure from anything else B. had written before, but it has one very basic feature in common with the rest of his art: "Dvenadtsat" is an ambivalent poem and it expresses the dichotomy that is a hallmark of B.'s personality and art. B. dwells somewhere between tradition and revolution, between his love of and contempt for the world, between the chaos of passions and the harmony of art. His poetry possesses a universal quality that goes beyond the narrow symbolist confines; his melodious, intense, and agonized verses express the dilemma of modern man and even in translation have the power of moving us emotionally and intellectually.

FURTHER WORKS: *Nechayannaya radost* (1907); *Zemlya v snegu* (1908); *Lirichiskie dramy* (1908); *Nochnye chasy* (1908–1910); *Stikhi o Rossii* (1915); *Teatr* (1916); *Sedoe utro* (1920); *Bozmezdie* (1922); *Sobranie sochineny* (8 vols., 1960–1963). **FURTHER WORKS IN ENGLISH:** *Poems of A. B.* (1968); *Selected Poems* (1972)

BIBLIOGRAPHY: Bowra, C. M., "A. B.," *The Heritage of Symbolism* (1943): 144–79; Bonneau, S., *L'univers poétique d'A. B.* (1946); Kisch, Sir C., *Prophet of Revolution* (1960); Poggioli, R., *The Poets of Russia: 1890–1930* (1960): 179–211; Muchnic, H., "A. B.," *From Gorky to Pasternak: Six Modern Writers* (1961): 104–84; Reeve, F. D., *A. B.: Between Image and Idea* (1962); Woodward, J. B., Introduction to *Selected Poems of A. B.* (1968): 1–32; Pyman, A., Introduction to *Selected Poems* (1972): 1–53; Vogel, L., *A. B.: The Journey to Italy* (1973); Pyman, A., *The Life of A. B.* (2 vols. 1978, 1980)

—LUCY VOGEL

BLOOM, Harold

American literary critic, b. 11 July 1930, Bronx, N.Y.

B. is one of the most influential critics of this century. Born in The Bronx, New York, to a working-class family, he attended Cornell University and received his Ph.D. from Yale University in 1955. He is the author of eighteen books ranging from studies of romantic poetry to an important redefinition of influence, and from American poetry to Sigmund FREUD, cabala and the Bible. As general editor for Chelsea House's Modern Critical Views and other series, he has written over five-hundred introductions that together constitute sharp and precise illuminations of a vast range of writers in the Western tradition. Among his many distinctions and awards are NEH and Guggenheim fellowships and a MacArthur grant. In 1987 he was the Charles Eliot Norton Professor of Poetry at Harvard. He is Sterling Professor of the Humanities at Yale and Berg Professor of English at New York University.

A prolific critic best known for his theoretical works on influence, B. began his career with an attack on New Critical methods of reading whose effect was to neglect romantic poetry. New Criticism's emphasis on form, irony, resolution, closure, and a poem frozen in space was inadequate to the specific energies of the romantic poem, which insisted on the breaking of form, on the poem as a fragment of a greater original vision, and on time as a disruption of space. Bloom's first three books—*Shelley's Mythmaking* (1959), *The Visionary Company* (1961), and *Blake's Apocalypse* (1963)—reopened the study of romantic poems as texts aware of their fragmentary status and of an imaginative vision that exceeded their rhetoric.

B.'s importance as a critic is due in large part to his tetralogy on influence: *The Anxiety of Influence* (1973), *A Map of Misreading* (1975), *Kabbalah and Criticism* (1975), and *Poetry and Repression* (1976). In these four books B. reverses the traditional notion of influence as a straightforward "handing over" and articulates a theory of tradition as a battleground in which each poet must confront and overcome the precursor poet in order to make a space for himself in the tradition. The poet's condition can be defined as "belated," and each successive poet, coming ever later upon the scene of poetry, must struggle to turn his belatedness into earliness. Earliness for B. constitutes originality, which stands in a peculiar alignment with difficulty. Each poet, in the process of overcoming the precursor, increases the difficulty of poetic tradition, so that there is an uneasy relationship between difficulty and strength.

The distinction between strong and weak poets is crucial to B.'s theory. Strong poets shape the tradition and in turn are the field of battle for those who come later; weak poets are forgettable, despite whatever political or cultural considerations might be brought to bear on their work, B. is uncompromising on the question of poetic strength, and rewrites the history of tradition as a history of influence-relations, of overturning and over-coming.

Because tradition is overcrowded and space difficult to achieve, influence in its traditional sense stands in opposition to originality. To be original is to break with the past in a moment of freedom. B. is careful to point out, however, that a poem is "an achieved anxiety." Freedom lies in the process of writing the poem, while the finished text is always a failure of that original vision. In this respect, his theory of influence recovers the high romantic notion of the fragment. The fragment is a fact of poetic life, and anxiety its most telling symptom and driving force.

Through this tetralogy and the seven books that follow, B. articulates and refines the "revisionary ratios" by which influence relations can be mapped. The peculiar effect of a poem whose power and originality turn belatedness into earliness is that it produces the illusion that the later poet has influenced the earlier one. The Greek name B. assigns to this phenomenon in *The Anxiety of Influence* is *apophrades*, the return of the dead, but under conditions in which the latecomer leaves the house open to the ghosts, without fear of silence or suppression. In *Wallace Stevens: The Poems of Our Climate* (1976) B. extends these ratios to construct a theory of "poetic crossings" by which the poet becomes and knows himself to be a poet. In a turn from British romantic poetry to American poetry, B. continues his studies of the high romantic tradition, canonizing STEVENS as the heir of a tradition haunted by its very strength.

A critic's canonization of a poet falls well within the purview of influence-relations that B. studies. Because the meaning of a poem wanders between poems, or as B. says, "the meaning of a poem is that there is, or rather was, another poem," criticism plays an important role in articulating that wandering. What B. calls for as essential to criticism is a "diachronic rhetoric," which he himself provides: a way of reading poems that will take into account the powerful effect of time and loss.

B.'s wide-ranging work on influence and on the Western canon draws writers into uncommon and original relations. Two such examples are Freud and cabala. Freud provides B. with the notion of a text as a living psyche, driven by desire toward an end it cannot possibly achieve and propelled into sublime moments by repression. Cabala provides him with the idea of creation as fall—the "catastrophe theory of creation." If in the beginning there is already a flaw, then the poet can offer us that "lost first chance," placing himself (and us) at an origin where freedom and self-creation are possible.

B.'s compelling intervention in literary criticism has had the effect of deidealizing literary relations. Contrary to traditional literary history, which traces influence-relations in chronological fashion, B. insists on the phenomenon of influence as a radical reversal that makes poetic freedom and poetic self-identification possible. His favored trope is *metalepsis*, a "trope-reversing trope" that turns late into early, and which signals the momentary and agonistic triumph of the belated poem. Equally compelling is B.'s argument against deconstruction's insistence on language as a final limit. *Metalepsis* allows a reversal that is also transcendence, a triumph over time and over the limits of language, B.'s theory of poetic influence, which he terms "antithetical criticism," has transformed criticism's view of literary tradition and of the poet's response to its extraordinary wealth.

Equally important is B.'s articulation of the role of the critic. Contrary to established practice, which demands a critic's objectivity in relation to the text, B. insists on the critic's uncompromising subjectivity—"There are no texts; there are only ourselves"—on a response to the text that is itself "a spark and an act," and inseparable from literature.

Though the closest term to define his work is literary criticism, in his most recent work B. has widened the meaning of the term by breaking down normative distinctions between sacred and secular literature. *Ruin the Sacred Truths: Poetry and Belief from the Bible to the Present* (1989), winner of the Christian Gauss Award for the best book of literary criticism, moves from Homer and the Bible to Samuel BECKETT as it studies the powerful discontinuities of the Western tradition. *The Book of J* (1990), a bestseller, argues that

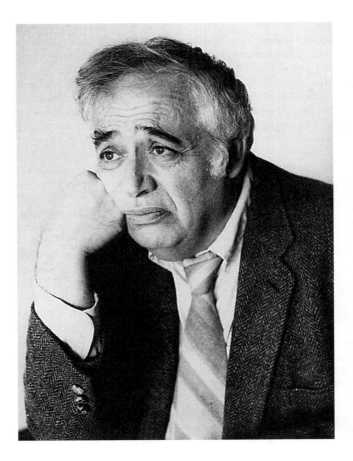

Harold Bloom

this text, which has given rise to so much biblical commentary, is the work of one writer, a woman, and that the God it depicts bears little resemblance to the God of normative religion.

An eminent critic who has stirred controversy again and again with his wholly original readings, B. has forged new paths for literary criticism and, in the tradition of Emerson and Longinus, brought it once again into kinship with great literature. *The Western Canon* (1994) is both a truly erudite book and a bestseller. Opening with an "elegy" on the canon, the book offers a powerful argument for aesthetic canonicity and a powerful critique of those who would demolish it. The book argues, as B. has been wont to do, for the centrality of Shakespeare, as he clusters major authors around and after him: Dante, Chaucer, Cervantes, all the way to Proust, Joyce, and Kafka. What is compelling about this book is not merely its breadth but that each chapter is a book in little, rich in erudition and insight about each writer. On Dickinson, possibly the strongest chapter in the book, B. comments that her greatness lies in the fact that she makes the visible a little harder to see. Such insights are rare yet indispensable currency in the tradition of high criticism to which B. belongs.

In a turn not quite completed, B. moves with *Omens of Millenium* (1996) into a mode that appears at first to be autobiographical, until one realizes that for B., who is a student of "self-reliance," the autobiographical *is* the prophetic. The link between autobiography and prophecy yet remains to be explored, as it moves in an arc encompassing Whitman and Wordsworth and also B. Few critics can lay claim to making the boundary between literature and criticism a little harder to see. B. is at work on a book on *Shakespeare: The Invention of the Human*, dealing as always with questions of how to read and why.

FURTHER WORKS: *Yeats* (1970); *The Ringers in the Tower: Studies in Romantic Tradition* (1971); *Figures of Capable Imagination* (1976); *The Flight to Lucifer* (1979); *Agon: Towards a Theory of Revisionism* (1982); *The Breaking of the Vessels* (1982); *Poetics of Influence* (1988)

BIBLIOGRAPHY: Burke, K., "Father and Son," *NewR*, 12 Apr. 1975: 23–24; Said, E. W., "The Poet As Oedipus: A Map of Misreading," *NYTBR*, 13 Apr. 1975: 23–25; Hollander, J., "Poetic Misprision," *Poetry*, 127 (1976): 222–34; Hartman, G. H., *Criticism in the Wilderness* (1980): 42–62; Riddel, J., "Juda Becomes New Haven," *Diacritics*, 10 (1980): 17–34; Smith, J. H., ed., *The Literary Freud* (1980): ix–xix; Wordsworth, A., "An Art That Will Not Abandon the Self to Language," in Young, R., ed., *Untying the Text* (1981): 207–22; Handleman, S. A., *The Slayers of Moses* (1982): 179–223; de Man, P., *Blindness and Insight*, rev. ed. (1983): 267–76; Axelrod, S. G., "H. B.'s Enterprise," *MP*, 81, 3 (Feb. 1984): 290–97; Fite, D., *H. B., The Rhetoric of Romantic Vision* (1985); Mileur, J. P., *Literary Revisionism and the Burden of Modernity* (1985); Moynihan, R., *A Recent Imagining* (1986): 3–47; Salusinszky, I., *Criticism in Society* (1987): 45–73; Weis, A., *Paris Review* (Spring 1991): 178–232; Elam, H. R., "H. B." in Jay, G. S., ed., *DLB: Modern American Critics since 1955* (1988): 32–48; Renza, L., "Influence," in Lentricchia, F., and T. McLaughlin, eds., *Critical Terms for Literary Study* (1990): 186–202

—HELEN REGUEIRO ELAM

BLY, Robert

American poet, translator, and editor, b. 23 Dec. 1926, Madison, Minn.

After graduation from Harvard, B. spent two years in New York City, years that reminded him how much he missed pastoral landscapes. In 1955 he traveled to Norway on a Fulbright grant and there began his activity as a translator. His editorship of the magazine *The Fifties* started in 1958 and continued for two decades, as the title changed to *The Sixties* and *The Seventies*. For the last twenty years he has spent much time on his isolated farm in Minnesota, occasionally traveling to give poetry readings, and, during the late 1960s, to organize resistance to the Vietnam War.

B.'s first volume of poetry, *Silence in the Snowy Fields* (1962), deals with pastoral subjects and is deeply imbued with a latter-day Protestant mysticism. Using an almost haikulike brevity, B. explores themes of solitude and inner purity. The poems are often loose in verse form, but they have a meditative strictness generated by concentration on what B. was to call the "deep image." Clearly influenced by JUNG and other antirationalists, this poetry has a strong polemical thrust (despite its often hushed tones of wonder and ecstasy), setting itself defiantly against the more accepted forms of academic poetry.

With the appearance of the National Book Award-winning *The Light around the Body* (1967), B. became known as a political poet; he even contributed his award money to a draft-resistance group. Many critics found the political poems tendentious and accused B. of self-promotion; others felt the work betrayed his natural

tendencies to a Midwestern quietism. But the political poetry shared common origins with the pastoral work: an emotional populism, with a strong thrust toward the salvational urgency of American evangelism.

Later works, such as the prose poems in *The Morning Glory* (1975), demonstrated B.'s life-long concern with intense observation of the natural world and a rather surreal longing to transform it into both an occasion and a guide for spiritual enlightenment.

B. has continued to use his polemical essays and his translations, in addition to his poems, to challenge what he sees as the parochial and over-rationalistic forces in American poetry and society. His work almost invariably invites partisan reaction, which is clearly one of B.'s intentions, since his vision is centered in his opposition to ordinary consciousness.

FURTHER WORKS: *Sleepers Joining Hands* (1973); *Old Man Rubbing His Eyes* (1975); *This Body Is Made of Camphor and Gopherwood* (1977); *This Tree Will Be Here for a Thousand Years* (1979); *Talking All Morning* (1980); *The Man in the Black Coat Turns* (1981); *Loving a Woman in Two Worlds* (1985); *Selected Poems* (1986); *Iron John: A Book about Men* (1990); *Angels of Pompeii* (1992); *The Rag and Bone Shop of the Heart* (1992); *Morning Poems* (1997)

BIBLIOGRAPHY: Carruth, H., "Critic of the Month," Poetry, 112 (1968): 418–27; special B. issue, *Tennessee Poetry Journal*, 2, 2 (1969); Howard, R., *Alone with America* (1969): 38–48; Molesworth, C., *The Fierce Embrace* (1979): 112–138; Altieri, C., *Enlarging the Temple* (1979): 82–93; Davis, W. V., *Understanding R. B.* (1988); Harris, V. F., *The Incorporative Consciousness of R. B.* (1992); Davis, W. V., *R. B.: The Poet and His Critics* (1997)

—CHARLES MOLESWORTH

BOAL, Augusto

Brazilian dramatist, director, and theoretician, b. 1931, Rio de Janeiro

B. is known as a major dramatist and director of Brazil's experimental group Arena Theater of São Paulo, and is recognized as Latin America's most significant theoretician of popular theater. Although his university training was in chemistry, B. became interested in the theater in 1950. After two years of study at Columbia University with John Gassner, he returned to Brazil schooled in playwriting and method acting. From 1956 to 1971 he was associated with Arena Theater, first as codirector and then as director. As a director, B. was instrumental in renovating Brazilian theater. His desire to define a dramatic format that was truly Brazilian led him to help develop new forms of dramatic interpretation for actors, encourage new methods of playwriting for dramatists, and eventually produce new theories of theater. He was jailed, tortured, and exiled by the military dictatorship in 1971. In 1979 he established a theater center in Paris. Since 1986 B. has based his activities in Rio de Janeiro, although he continues to direct plays and conduct workshops in Europe, North and South America, and Africa.

As a dramatist, B.'s interest in renovating the theater process led him to combine a consciousness-raising aesthetic focused on the problems of Brazil's working class with experiments in Bertolt

Brecht's distancing techniques. *Revolução na América do Sul* (1960; revolution in South America) is a lesson in the corruption, deception, and violence of politics as perceived through the experiences of one needy individual. The play's circuslike atmosphere, the short scenes, and the use of music as a thematic component became essential ingredients for B.'s later drama. Together with Gianfrancesco Guarnieri (b. 1934) B. authored two more plays while associated with Arena Theater, *Arena conta Zumbi* (1965; Arena tells the story of Zumbi) and *Arena conta Tiradentes* (1967; Arena tells the story of Tiradentes). Both plays rework historic fights for liberty as a means of commenting on the failed leftist reforms of the early 1960s and the ensuing imposition of a repressive military régime. Each play experiments with techniques that encourage the audience to emulate the past by becoming actors in their own history.

While at Arena Theater B. began developing his theories of popular theater, that is, theater that turns over part of the acting to the audience so that drama becomes a means of enacting change. After B.'s exile, he published several books explaining the theory and practice of popular theater. He gained international recognition for *Teatro do oprimido* (1975; *Theater of the Oppressed*, 1979), a treatise on how theater from Aristotle to Eugène IONESCO has usurped the transformative power of the audience. The final portion of the book outlines the Joker system, a method for simultaneously presenting and analyzing a performance. The key figure in the system is the Joker, a facilitator who participates in and questions the actions of the drama as it progresses. Newspaper Theater, an improvisation based on articles taken from the daily newspaper, and Invisible Theater, a prearranged kind of drama that takes place in public areas such as bus stations, parks, or grocery stores, encourage performers to engage the audience in making drama a vehicle for analysis and understanding of community problems. In *Stop: c'est magique!* (1980; stop: this is magic), B. shows how his European audiences, whose concerns are more psychological than social, were trained to stop the action on stage, take the place of a performer, and change the action in progress.

B. was an instrumental figure in revitalizing Brazilian theater during a critical time of its development. As Arena's director he contributed both organizational and creative foundations that have been widely adopted in Brazil. His plays brought new topics, treatments, and techniques to the stage and to Brazil's growing theater audience. As a theoretician B. is both original and revolutionary in his presentation of the political relationship between the action on stage and the potential for action among those in the audience. Recently, B. has adapted his theatrical method for psychotherapeutic aims, as described in his *Rainbow of Desire: The B. Method of Theatre and Therapy* (1995).

FURTHER WORKS: *Marido magro, mulher chata* (1957); *José, do parto a sepultura* (1962); *Tio Patinhas* (1968); *Torquemada* (1971); *200 exercícios e jogos para o ator* (1977); *Técnicas Latinoamericanas de teatro popular* (1977); *Crônicas de nuestra América* (1977); *A deliciosa e sangrenta aventura latina de Jane Spitfire* (1977); *Murro em ponta de faca* (1978); *A tempestade e As mulheres de Atenas* (1979); *Milagre no Brasil* (1979); *O corsário do Rei* (1985)

BIBLIOGRAPHY: Bisset, J. I., "Victims and Violators: The Structure of Violence in *Torquemada*," *LATR*, 15, 2 (Spring 1982): 27–34; Capo, K. E., "Performance of Literature As Social Dialectic," *LPer*, 4, 1 (Nov. 1983): 31–36; Carlson, M. A., *Theories of the Theatre* (1984): 475–76; Schechter, J., "The Jokers of A. B.," *Durov's Pig: Clowns, Politics, and Theater* (1985): 158–63; Albuquerque, S. J., "Conflicting Signs of Violence in A. B.'s *Torquemada*," *MD*, 29, 3 (Sept. 1986): 452–59; Enright, R., "To Dynamize the Audience: Interview with A. B.," CTR, 47 (1986): 41–49; Milleret, M., "Acting into Action: Teatro Arena's *Zumbi*," LATR, 21, 1 (Fall 1987): 19–27; special B. section, *TDR*, 34, 3 (1990): 24–87; George, D. S., "Theatre of the Oppressed and Teatro de Arena: In and Out of Context," *LATR*, 28, 2 (Spring 1995): 39-54

—MARGO MILLERET

BOBROWSKI, Johannes

German poet and novelist, b. 9 April 1917, Tilsit; d. 2 Sept. 1965, East Berlin

B. grew up in Tilsit, Rastenburg, and Königsberg, and briefly studied art history in Berlin prior to his induction into the German army. Throughout much of World War II he served on the eastern front; he was captured and spent four years as a prisoner-of-war in Russia. In 1949 he returned to East Berlin, where he worked as a reader for a publishing house. Among the many awards he received was the prestigious Group 47 Prize (1962).

Although B. published a few poems during the war, his reputation rests entirely upon his later works, which began to appear in the late 1950s. His first collection of poems, *Sarmatische Zeit* (1961; Sarmatian time), was followed closely by *Schattenland Ströme* (1962; shadow-land rivers). A third, *Wetterzeichen* (1966; storm signals) was prepared for publication by the author but appeared posthumously. The theme of much of B.'s work is the bitter history of the region in central and eastern Europe where he spent his earlier years. The entire history of national, religious, and racial prejudices, from the brutal persecution of the original Prussians in the Middle Ages to the atrocities of the Nazis in Poland, is often in the background, although seldom in the foreground of his works. His lyrics, by means of symbolic descriptions of landscapes and the people who inhabit them, capture the feeling of melancholy that is an integral part of the heritage of the regions they embrace. Poverty, unrest, and violence are the chief characteristics of B.'s landscapes, the components of which—rivers, stones, birds, and animals—are often personified. The poems are occasionally realistic but more often contain fanciful elements and unexpected juxtapositions, not unlike those seen in the paintings of Chagall. The tone, to some extent reminiscent of the verse of Klopstock (1724–1803), is consistently sublime. B. typically writes a melodious and rhythmical free verse. Short elliptical sentences alternate with longer units containing several parenthetical elements. Unusual word order is often used for emphasis, as is enjambment.

The problem of the relationship between Germany and her eastern neighbors is also central to B.'s principal work of fiction, the novel *Levins Mühle* (1964; *Levin's Mill*, 1970). It deals explicitly with an act of injustice committed against a Jew, but is set apart by its 19th-c. setting from the bulk of recent German fiction with similar themes. Narrated in the present by the grandson of the perpetrator of the injustice, the book is structurally complex. Dialogue and description alternate with comments directed to the reader that relate the issues of the book to contemporary society.

B., a Christian humanist who was sincerely dedicated to the advancement of human rights, had very few personal or political enemies. The total acceptance of his works in both German states is unique.

FURTHER WORKS: *Hans Clauert* (1956); *Mäusefest und andere Erzählungen* (1965); *Boehlendorff und Mäusefest* (1965); *Boehlendorff und andere* (1965); *Lithauische Claviere* (1966); *Der Mahner* (1967); *Im Windgesträuch* (1970); *Literarisches Klima* (1977). **FURTHER WORKS IN ENGLISH:** *Shadow Land* (1966); *I Taste Bitterness* (1970); *From the Rivers* (1975)

BIBLIOGRAPHY: Glenn, J., "An Introduction to the Poetry of J. B.," *GR*, 41 (1966): 45–56; Waidson, H. M., "B.'s *Levins Mühle*," in Prawer, S., et al., eds., *Essays in German Language, Culture and Society* (1969): 149–59; Keith-Smith, B., *J. B.* (1970); Flores, J., in *Poetry in East Germany* (1971): 205–72; Barnouw, D., "B. and Socialist Realism," *GR*, 48 (1973): 288–314; Rostin, G., ed., *J. B.: Selbstzeugnisse und neue Beiträge über sein Werk* (1975); Gajek, B., and E. Haufe, *J. B.: Chronik—Einführung—Bibliographie* (1977)

—JERRY GLENN

BODELSEN, Anders

Danish novelist and short-story writer, b. 11 Feb. 1937, Copenhagen

B. studied law, economics, and literature at the University of Copenhagen (1956–60) and became a journalist for the newspapers *Aktuelt, Ekstra Bladet,* and *Berlingske Aftenavis* (1959–64). He was editor of the literary journal *Perspektiv* (1963–65) and joined the staffs of the newspapers *Information* (1964–67) and *Politiken* (from 1967).

B.'s first novel, *De lyse nætters tid* (the time of the light nights), was published in 1959, but his best-known early work is the collection of short stories *Rama Sama* (1967; *Rama Sama*). With these stories, B. established himself as one of the leading Danish "neorealists." They deal with facets of contemporary middle-class life, such as work-related competition and stress, television viewing, group travel, and social get-togethers, and aspire toward an authentic portrayal of milieu through the use of "facts" and exact realistic details such as the often-cited example of the description of the Lyngby expressway out of Copenhagen during rush hour in "Succes" (success).

The suspense novels *Tænk på et tal* (1968; *Think of a Number,* 1969) and *Hændeligt uheld* (1968; chance accident) are about a bank robbery and drunken driving, respectively. They are typical of neorealism in their focus on the effect of certain social institutions and laws upon the human psyche. The novels *Frysepunktet* (1969; the freezing point) and *Bevisets stilling* (1973; the status of the evidence) also highlight the psychological problems caused by the inhumanity of technology and the administration of justice in society. However, this psychological orientation precludes a broader investigation of the social structures per se, and thus social criticism is undermined and diverted to the area of individual psychology. This is a limitation of a literary mode that professes adherence to authentic, detailed depiction of social life, and has, with some justification, also been labeled "surface empiricism" by certain Danish critics.

Because of his accessible form and topical subject matter, B. is widely read and plays a prominent role in contemporary Danish literature. Together with Christian KAMPMANN and Henrik Stangerup (b. 1937), B. is recognized as a leading (neo) realist writer in Denmark, and he is representative of an influential and vital literary movement.

FURTHER WORKS: *Villa Sunset* (1964); *Drivhuset* (1965); *En hård dags nat* (1966); *Til døden os skiller* (1967); *Ferie* (1970); *Hjælp* (1971); *Professor Mancinis hemmelighed* (1971); *Straus* (1971); *Pigerne på broen* (1972); *Skygger* (1972); *Lov & orden* (1973); *Alt hvad du ønsker dig* (1974); *Fjernsynet flimrer* (1974); *Uden for nummer* (1974); *Blæsten i Alleen* (1975); *Operation Cobra* (1975); *Pengene og livet* (1976); *De gode tider* (1977); *År for År* (1978)

—CHARLOTTE SCHIANDER GRAY

BOGAN, Louise

American poet, critic, and translator, b. 11 Aug. 1897, Livermore Falls, Maine; d. 4 Feb. 1970, New York, N.Y.

B. was educated at Mount St. Mary's Academy, Manchester, New Hampshire, the Boston Girls' Latin School, and for a year at Boston University. Her first husband, an army officer, died in 1920, shortly after the birth of their daughter, B.'s only child. Her second husband, Raymond Holden (1894–1972), was a poet and, from 1929 to 1932, managing editor of *The New Yorker;* the couple were divorced in 1937. For most of B.'s adult life her home was New York City. B. received many awards for her poetry. A Fellow in American Letters at the Library of Congress in 1944, she held the Chair in Poetry in 1945–46.

Reluctant to offer details about her personal life, B. valued privacy and close friendships. Published letters to Edmund WILSON, Theodore ROETHKE, May SARTON, the classicist Rolfe Humphries (1894–1969), the critic Morton Dauwen Zabel (1901–1964), and others reveal a warm, witty, spontaneous side of B., not often evident in her poetry. They also refer to recoveries from nervous breakdowns in 1931 and 1933, as well as to the severe financial difficulties she experienced in the mid-1930s.

Besides poetry, B. wrote some fiction and collaborated in translations from German and French. Two volumes of her criticism consist mainly of articles and reviews from *The Nation, Poetry, Scribner's, The Atlantic Monthly,* and *The New Yorker,* for which she was a regular reviewer of poetry from March 1931 to December 1968.

While B. advocated primarily formal poetry and, in ELIOT's words, "verse as speech" and "verse as song," her critical judgment was far from orthodox. She opposed women's attempts to imitate a "man's rougher conduct" in life and art, observing that there were no authentic women surrealists, since SURREALISM's "frequent harsh eroticism, its shock tactics, and its coarse way with language, comes hard to women writers, whose basic creative impulses usually involve tenderness and affection." The younger women poets she praised were, in following Marianne MOORE, "close but detached observers of the facts of nature," able to "display a woman's talent for dealing intensely and imaginatively with the concrete."

The qualities most frequently cited in B.'s poetry are those her friend Léonie Adams (1899-1988) noted in a 1954 review of *Collected Poems 1923–1952,* (1954): firmness of outline, prosodic accomplishment in traditional metrics, purity of diction and tone, concession of phrase, and concentrated singleness of effect. Allen TATE, Ford Madox FORD, and Theodore Roethke compared her lyrics to those of the metaphysical mode of the 17th c. Abjuring free verse and experimental forms, B. worked in consciously controlled lyric form with a restraint and precision that contained passionate feeling. "Minor art," she wrote, "needs to be hard, condensed and durable." A few critics of her work have found that control scrupulous to the point of limitation and perhaps the result of unwillingness to reveal herself entirely. There is a clear distancing of poet from subject in the early works of *Dark Summer* (1929); and in all but a few poems B. objectifies responses to experience and ideas through the use of third person or of a persona.

B.'s greatest skill lies in metric variation and in rendering descriptions in taut language whose sound values are brilliant yet seemingly effortless, as in "Night" (1962), "Song for the Last Act" (1949), "Animal, Vegetable, and Mineral" (1940), "Roman Fountain" (1935), and "After the Persian" (1951). The subject matter of B.'s poetry includes love, loss, grief, mutability, the struggle of the free mind, marriage, and dream. There is no mention of the city or society; settings and imagery are drawn from nature: the country or sea, seasons and storms. Landscape and weather are sometimes menacing, as in "The Flume" (1925); autumn is a positive, glowing season of endings. There is tension between passion of mind and flesh in early poems such as "The Alchemist" (1922) and "Men Loved Wholly beyond Wisdom" (1923), where the earth and love triumph over intellect.

There is also a recurrent interest in women: struggling to maintain a free mind and independent being ("Sonnet" [1929], "The Romance" [1923], "For a Marriage" [1929], "Betrothed" [1912]); failing to imagine and risk ("Women" [1922]); breaking into fury and madness ("The Sleeping Fury" [1936], "Evening in the Sanitarium" [1938]); experiencing love and surviving its endings ("Men Loved Wholly beyond Wisdom," "Fifteenth Farewell" [1923], "My Voice Not Being Proud" [1923], "Portrait" [1922]). Adrienne Rich (b. 1929) has justly called attention to the "sense of mask, of code, of body-mind division, of the 'sleeping fury' beneath the praised, severe, lyrical mode."

Although admired and praised by other writers, B.'s poetry did not receive wider attention until the publication of *Collected Poems*. Now recognized for their craft and independence from the prevailing styles of her generation, the best poems are anthologized. Like Roethke, young poets find in her work a felicity and subtlety nurtured by traditional forms. Her collected essays demonstrate a keen intelligence and catholic taste that helped to shape a more general acceptance of the range and variation of modern poetry.

FURTHER WORKS: *Body of This Death* (1923); *The Sleeping Fury* (1937); *Poems and New Poems* (1941); *Achievement in American Poetry*, 1900–1950 (1951); *Selected Criticism* (1955); *The Blue Estuaries: Poems*, 1923–1968 (1968); *A Poet's Alphabet: Reflections on the Literary Art and Vocation* (1970); *What the Woman Lived: Selected Letters of* L.B., *1920–1970* (1973); *Journey around My Room: The Autobiography of L. B.* (1980)

BIBLIOGRAPHY: Olson, E., "L. B. and Léonie Adams," *ChiR*, 8 (Fall 1954): 70–87; Roethke, T., "The Poetry of L. B.," *CritQ*, 3 (1961): 142–50; Ramsey, P., "L. B.," *IowaR*, 1 (1970): 116–24; Smith, W. J., *L. B.: A Woman's Words* (1971); Couchman, J., "L. B.: A Bibliography of Primary and Secondary Materials, 1915–1975: Parts I–II," *BB*, 33 (1976): 73–77, 104, 111–26, 178–81; Perlmutter, E. P., "Doll's Heart: The Girl in the Poetry of Edna St. Vincent Millay and L. B.," *TCL*, 23 (1977): 157–59

—THEODORA R. GRAHAM

BOJER, Johan

Norwegian novelist, b. 6 March 1872, Orkedalsören; d. 3 July 1959, Oppdal

Born out of wedlock to a businessman and a servant girl, B. was raised by foster parents who were tenant farmers at Rein. This historically significant estate by the Trondheimsfjord was part of the fishing-farming ambience that figures so prominently in many of B.'s novels. Life was hard but not unpleasant for young B., and he had early exposure to Norwegian tales and folklore. For the most part it was money from his natural father that enabled B. to receive a good education. This included business school, which led to his working at the export trade in the Lofoten islands, where he experienced vicariously the life of the Norwegian fisherman.

At that time, B. began writing poems and then plays and novels. When one of his plays was produced, and another play and novel published, he took off for Paris, determined to be a writer. Paris proved to be a heady, stimulating experience, but money that he had inherited from his father soon ran out, and he returned to Norway. Nevertheless, this was the start of a lifetime of extensive travel and writing. His wanderings took him for various periods to Italy, Denmark, the U.S., and especially to France, where his international reputation became established.

B. had a productive literary career that extended over more than six decades. His first major success was *Et folketog* (1896; a procession), a political satire of compromise and eventual betrayal by politicians of the poor fisher-folk they represented. The continuing theme in this and many other novels in this vein was B.'s respect for useful labor and for the people who toiled with their hands.

B. also wrote psychological morality studies, the most significant of which was *Troens magt* (1903; *The Power of a Lie*, 1908). This novel was honored by the French Academy, a rare distinction for a foreign writer. It is not coincidental that Zola and the Dreyfus affair were in the French conscience at the time, since the novel deals with a slanderer who believes his slandering justified and who emerges triumphant and vindicated by committing perjury in the legal case.

Another theme in B.'s writings was a celebration of the joy of living, emphasizing an amorality like that of Ibsen's Peer Gynt and a serene, nondenominational religion. The best of this group is probably *Fangen som sang* (1913; *The Prisoner Who Sang*, 1924), although *Den store hunger* (1916; *The Great Hunger*, 1918) was read more widely in Britain and the U.S. Both of these novels deal with the inevitability and irresistibility of the religious yearnings in man.

In the 1920s the full power of B.'s writing emerged, with three major folk epics: *Den siste viking* (1921; *The Last of the Vikings*, 1923), *Vor egen stamme* (1924; *The Emigrants*, 1925), and *Folk ved sjøen* (1929; *The Everlasting Struggle*, 1931). *Den siste viking* and *Folk ved sjøen* are graphic depictions of the lives of the poverty-stricken Norwegian farmers and fishermen. The stories are told with great narrative skill but without sentimentality or moralizing. These novels show B.'s intimate understanding of and great compassion for people and their problems. *Vor egen stamme* deals with Norwegian emigrant farmers struggling for survival on the cruel North Dakota prairie. B. reveals a sensitive understanding of the trauma of uprooting and readjustment, along with the inevitable problems of the second generation.

B. occupies a high seat in the Valhalla of Norwegian writers. He is not one of the gods, but he is surely one of the heroes. This assessment must be made despite the fact that B. is one of the few Norwegian writers whose works have been often more appreciated abroad than in Norway.

FURTHER WORKS: *En moder* (1894); *Helga* (1895); *Gravholmen* (1895); *På kirkevei* (1897); *Hellig Olaf* (1897); *Rørfløiterne* (1898); *Den evige krig* (1899); *Moder Lea* (1900); *Gamle historier* (1901); *En pilgrimsgang* (1902; *A Pilgrimage*, 1924); *Theodora* (1902); *Brutus* (1904); *Hvide Fugle* (1904); *Vort rige* (1908; *Treacherous Ground*, 1920); *Kjærlighetens øine* (1910); *Liv* (1911; *Life*, 1920); *Sigurd Braa* (1916); *Den franske fane* (1916); *Verdens ansigt* (1917; *The Face of the World*, 1919); *Dyrendal* (1919; *God and Woman*, 1921); *Stille veir* (1920); *Det nye tempel* (1927; *The New Temple*, 1928); *Mens årene gar* (1930); *Marie Walewska* (1932); *Huset og havet* (1933; *The House and the Sea*, 1934); *Dagen og natten* (1935; *By Day and by Night*, 1937); *Kongens karer* (1938; *The King's Men*, 1940); *Gård og grend* (1939); *Hustruen* (1941); *Læregutt* (1942); *Svenn* (1946); *Skyld* (1948); *Lov og liv* (1952); *Fjell og fjære* (1957); *Glimt og gleder* (1960)

BIBLIOGRAPHY: Gad, C., J. B.: *The Man and His Works* (1920); Lodrup, H. P., "J. B.," *ASR*, 14 (1926): 207–17; La Chesnais, P. G., *J. B.: Sa vie et ses œuvres* (1930); Jorgenson, T., *History of Norwegian Literature* (1932): 469–83; Vowles, R. B., Afterword to *The Last of the Vikings* (1964): 244–54; Downs, B. W., *Modern Norwegian Literature: 1860–1918* (1966): 193–96

—HAROLD P. HANSON

BOLIVIAN LITERATURE

The first decades of 20th-c Bolivian literature were dominated by the major 19th-c. currents of realism in fiction and romanticism in poetry. In 1904 Alcides ARGUEDAS published *Wata Wara* (Wata Wara), a short novel about the oppressed Indians of the country. He reworked his novel into the far more ambitious and influential *Raza de bronce* (1919; Race of Bronze), which for the first time brought international recognition to Bolivian literature. It encouraged national writers to choose the novel as the most effective means of expression and to channel their production along social and political lines. A contemporary and friend of Agruedas, the aristocratic poet Ricardo Jaimes Freyre (1868-1933) inaugurated MODERNISM in the country. Although a Parnassian at heart, he occasionally turned in his poetry and in his short fiction to social protest. The novelist Jaime Mendoza (1874-1939) also produced several works of "nativism" (political protest and local color).

From the publication of *Raza de bronce* to the present, the history of Bolivian literature is mainly the history of the novel. Novelists of this period produced a large number of works that concentrated heavily on the social protest. Reasons for this were many: the sad lot of oppressed Indian farmers and tin miners; the inept military rule, which had permitted repeated partitions of Bolivian territory; and the loss of genuine independence because of foreign mining companies that were taking control of the country's wealth. The majority of these novels were of low artistic quality; nevertheless, several fine works were also produced: Augusto Céspedes's (b. 1904) *El metal del diablo* (1946; The Devil's Metal), Oscar Cerruto's (b. 1912) *Aluvión de fuego* (1935; Flood of Fire), and Raúl Botelho's (b. 1917) *Altiplano* (1945; In the Highlands). Short fiction, the essay, and even poetry followed the path set by the novel. So important was this political literature that it became one of the best weapons of the movement that triumphed over the oligarchy and foreign monopolies in the revolution of 1952; its leaders instituted the reforms that writers had been demanding for almost half a century. Somewhat altered, political themes continued in Bolivian literature after 1952; however, in 1957 the dominance of SOCIALIST REALISM was challenged by a single novel that spoke a language hitherto not used by Bolivian nativists. Marcelo Quiroga's (b. 1931) *Los deshabitados* (The Empty Ones), which described the spiritual loneliness of man in the universe, introduced EXISTENTIALISM to Bolivia, and thus opened the door to further literary experimentation.

In the late 1950s and 1960s other genres began to make some gains. In 1967 Adolfo Cáceres (b. 1937) and Renato Prada (b. 1937) chose short fiction for their highly philosophical speculations in *Argal-Lagar* (1967; Argal-Lagar). The short story has since become a national favorite for themes other than those of social protest. Bolivian drama, as in most of Latin America, never produced a work that could transcend national borders. But in the thriving modern Bolivian essay three works stand out. Tristán Marof (pseud. of Gustavo A. Navarro, b. 1898) in *La justicia del Inca* (1926; The Justice of the Incas) treated a theme that has haunted Bolivians since then—a possible restoration of the Inca empire. Carlos Montenegro (1903-1953) wrote *Nacionalismo y coloniaje* (1943; Nationalism and Oligarchism), a methodical dissection of Bolivia's stormy past that asserts that patriotism can be found only in the oppressed classes of the country, not in the ruling class. *Mateo Montemayor* (1972; Mateo Montemayor), by the statesman Fernando Díez de Medina (b. 1908), is a treatise offering Latin Americans a highly spiritual code of ethics to cope with a brutally materialistic and technological world. In literary criticism, Augusto Gusmán (b. 1903) was the leading figure for much of the second half of the 20th c.

Besides the modernist Jaimes Freyre, another remarkable poet was Franz Tamayo (1879-1956). Like most Spanish American modernists, he was a Parnassian, whose work was characterized by musicality, nativism, sensuality and the use of exotic mythologies. But modernism in Bolivia gave way to the poetry of protest, which has lasted to this day. In 1972 Pedro Shimose (b. 1941) won the poetry prize of the (Cuban) House of the Americans with *Quiero escribir pero sólo me sale espuma* (1972; I Want to Write But I Can Only Foam at the Mouth). Two other Bolivians have also won the Cuban prize, but in the novel: Renato Prada, with *Los Fundadores del alba* (1961; *The Breach*, 1971) and Fernando Medina (b. 1941), with *Los muertos están cada día más indóciles* (1972; The Dead Are More and More Unruly).

In recent decades Bolivian writers have displayed a tendency to search for new themes and to gain a thorough knowledge of literary techniques. Within their ranks, however, few stand out. Some authors have produced a number of historical novels that delve into the rich social and mythological past of their country. And two have seen their novels gaining international recognition: José W. Montes's (b. 1965) *Jonás y la ballena* (1987; *Jonás and the Pink*

Whale, 1991) portrays a Kafkasque world that is dehumanized, hostile, and decadent; and Jesús Urzagasti's (b. 1941) *En el país del silencio* (1987; *In the Land of Silence*, 1991), is an existentialistic work questioning Western values of identity, love, life, and death.

Bolivian literature throughout the 20th c. has been defined by its persistent theme of conflict and struggle. New subjects and new techniques have entered the country's literature, but Bolivian writers continue to be as dedicated to the social crusade as they were at its onset.

BIBLIOGRAPHY: Finot, E., *Historia de la literatura boliviana* (1943); Díez de Medina, F., *La literatura boliviana* (1954); Echevarría, E., *La novela social de Bolivia* (1973); Echevarría, E., "The New Face of Bolivian Fiction," *LALR*, 1, 2 (1973): 105-10; Cáceres, A., and J. Ortega, *Diccionario de la literatura boliviana* (1977); Echevarría, E., "La novela histórica de Bolivia; temática y bibliografía, 1883-1994," *IRB*, 44, 1 (1994): 141-47

—EVELIO ECHEVARRÍA

BÖLL, Heinrich

German novelist, essayist, dramatist, and translator, b. 21 Dec. 1917, Cologne; d. 16 July 1985, Merten

Brought up in the Rhineland among lower-middle-class Catholics, B. attended secondary school, began an apprenticeship in a bookstore, and after brief university study of German literature was drafted at the outbreak of World War II. He served for six years in the German army in France, Russia, and elsewhere, was wounded several times, and eventually taken prisoner. After release from an Allied prisoner-of-war camp in 1945, he returned to his native Cologne, where he continues to live today, alternating work on his novels, short stories, radio plays, and essays with translations, done together with his wife Annemarie, of Irish and American authors (J. M. SYNGE, Brendan BEHAN, J. D. SALINGER and others).

B.'s sense of moral outrage at the political injustice and oppressive cruelties he witnessed during his youth and military service in Nazi Germany became the inspiration for most of his writings. While only his early works deal primarily with wartime miseries, he invariably assumes a strongly critical stance toward German society, present and past. From his commitment to an "aesthetic of the humane," elaborated in his *Frankfurter Vorlesungen* (1966; Frankfurt lectures), and his deep compassion for the oppressed and defenseless stem his major themes: attacks on the often arbitrary exertion of power by the establishments of state, church, military, and economy; exposure of the corruptive influence of the modern communications industries; and a profound concern about the alienation of the individual from the institutions controlling his life. B.'s regional orientation, his preoccupation with the problem of generations, and his tendency to endow seemingly insignificant details with symbolic import are reminiscent of FAULKNER and Thomas MANN; like Graham GREENE and Georges BERNANOS, he combines an unorthodox—though unshaken—Catholic belief with a sense for the absurd in human actions.

In his early fiction B. attempted to come to terms with the war and its aftermath by presenting its horrors in a sober, matter-of-fact manner. Works such as *Der Zug war pünktlich* (1949; *The Train*

Heinrich Böll

Was on Time, 1956), the short stories of *Wanderer, kommst du nach Spa* (1950; *Traveller, If You Come to Spa*, 1956), and *Wo warst du, Adam?* (1951; *Adam, Where Art Thou?*, 1955) make vividly tangible the brutalities of daily existence under the Nazis and the vacuity of army life. The style, reminiscent of HEMINGWAY, of understated, terse realism in these early works, an attempt to recover a "habitable" language after Nazi linguistic excesses, does not always combine well with overly sentimental passages of reported thought and interior monologue. Yet, in his most successful early novel, *Haus ohne Hüter* (1954; *Tomorrow and Yesterday*, 1957), which portrays initial postwar attempts to cope with the Nazi legacy of social and political chaos, B. achieves aesthetic coherence and emotional balance by introducing sharply satirical elements and employing five different narrative voices.

Biting satire, multiple narrative voices, and chronological complexity become characteristic for most of B.'s mature fiction. *Billard um halbzehn* (1959; *Billiards at Half Past Nine*, 1962) analyzes German history from the Wilhelminian empire of 1907 through Weimar and Hitler to the prosperous West Germany of 1958 by telling the story of three generations of Fähmels, a prominent family of Cologne architects. The crucial incidents in the past of the family, many of which concern father Heinrich Fähmel's major architectural achievement, the monastery of Saint Anthony, are not presented chronologically, but are gradually revealed in the course of one day (September 6, 1958), Heinrich's eightieth birthday. To capture the past events and the family's present response to them in the narrative framework of this decisive day, B. weaves an intricate network of present experiences, reminiscences, flashbacks, interior monologues, and passages of reported thought, which he interrelates through frequent shifts in narrative perspective. By introducing the symbolic categories of morally pure "lambs" and evil ones who "partake of the host of the beast," he comments satirically on the Fähmels' fortunes and on numerous problems of contemporary Germany, such as the continuing prevalence of ruthless power tactics learned from the Nazis. The novel ends with a gesture of forgiveness and reconciliation, for Heinrich has finally come to realize that people are more important than buildings.

B.'s satiric stance becomes almost morbid in *Ansichten eines Clowns* (1963; *The Clown*, 1965), a novel about a gentle, sensitive man who prefers the honest life of a clown to the hypocrisy required by any more socially acceptable existence and who is incapable of compromise, even for the woman he loves. In the course of a lonely March evening, the first-person narrator Hans Schnier re-creates his lost happiness with Marie in a series of monologues and desperate telephone calls. Longing for a settled life, Marie has left him to marry a prominent Catholic; Hans, hoping to win back his only shield against an absurd world, decides to appeal to strangers as a guitar-strumming beggar as he waits at the train station for Marie to return from her honeymoon. His attempt seems doomed to failure, and his position of complete alienation is surely extreme, yet B.'s impassioned fictional defense of the freedom of the individual is nevertheless profoundly moving.

In *Gruppenbild mit Dame* (1971; *Group Portrait with Lady*, 1973), his most successful novel to date and the work immediately preceding his award of the Nobel Prize for literature in 1972, B. moves beyond the ethical dualism and increasing pessimism characteristic of his earlier prose. While the protagonist Leni Pfeiffer, née Gruyten, is another outsider, the story of her life emphasizes not only protest, but also the search for new kinds of human relationships. Like a latter-day evangelist, an ostensibly neutral narrator tirelessly seeks documentation and interviews witnesses to reconstruct, from the vantage point of 1970, when Leni is in her late 40s, the "legend" of a woman he venerates, a lapsed Catholic who in most of her actions comes closer to genuine Christian charity than organized religion does. Leni has survived a difficult childhood, a bad marriage, a forbidden love affair with a Soviet prisoner-of-war, the bombing of Cologne, and a postwar series of losses psychologically intact and uncorrupted, and even retains the strength to be a model for others in her consistent refusal to adhere to the expectations of the established power structure. Her compassion and active altruism often have serious, if not outright catastrophic personal consequences, but the people she now so selflessly supports—foreign laborers, garbage collectors, and other social "discards"—demonstrate fierce loyalty to her in the end and organize a "Help Leni Committee" to bail her out of bankruptcy and prevent her eviction. Leni's creation of a kind of communal utopia represents a positive counterweight to her negative stance toward society, diagnosed by a psychologist in her son Lev as a case of "deliberate under achievement." The sense of balance maintained in this novel, the ironic distance ensured by the often parodistic language of the narrator, and the wide spectrum of characters who are rarely unequivocally good or evil make the work B.'s most subtle social satire.

In his latest works of fiction, the long story *Die verlorene Ehre der Katharina Blum; oder, Wie Gewalt entstehen und wohin sie führen kann* (1974; *The Lost Honor of Katharina Blum; or, How

Violence Develops and Where It Can Lead*, 1975) and the novel *Fürsorgliche Belagerung* (1979; precautionary siege), B. deals with more specific current problems in West Germany: yellow journalism and the excessive security precautions imposed in the mid-1970s in the wake of terrorist activities by the anarchistic Baader-Meinhof group. As the subtitle of the first work suggests, violence is done to Katharina Blum's honor by a sensation-seeking press; after enduring four days of false accusations and blatantly distortive newspaper coverage, she is finally driven to the desperate act of murdering the journalist responsible for ruining her reputation. A scrupulously objective and careful narrator, a counterpart to the journalist, relates the story by quoting documents and other evidence pertinent to all parties, including the *News* itself, and presents a devastating exposé of corrupt journalistic tactics. In the less convincing *Fürsorgliche Belagerung* B. attempts to convey the political necessity as well as the psychological destructiveness of security measures by portraying three days in the life of the newspaper magnate Fritz Tolm and the various members of his family. The Tolms have been closely guarded ever since they began to receive threats from a terrorist band joined by Fritz's ex-daughter-in-law. Returning to the techniques of *Billard um halbzehn*, B. shifts narrative perspective from one character to another to evoke the complex tangle of apprehension and claustrophobic restriction of movement felt by the security agents themselves as well as by the members of the besieged family. His satire of the siege mentality is perhaps somewhat too fraught with coincidence and sentimental touches, and the dénouement is certainly too pat. The novel is nevertheless important because of B.'s subtle portrait of Fritz, who is torn between understandable fear and the growing realization that security measures may in themselves criminalize innocent human beings, because of B.'s attack on the *Berufsverbot* (prohibition on choosing a specific profession or trade), because of his demonstration that security precautions tend to destroy all spontaneity and intimacy, and because of his plea for warmth, tolerance, and open communication in all human relationships.

From the outset B. has enjoyed enormous popularity among the general reading public, but critical assessment of his overall stature as a writer has varied widely. According to ideological persuasion, critics have lauded or ridiculed his Catholic orientation, his almost anarchistic attacks on political, economic, and social institutions of all kinds, his fierce defense of individual freedom and self-determination, his refusal (until recently) to align himself politically, and his emphasis on physical and emotional frankness. With some justification critics have called attention to artistic insufficiencies in individual works: the tendency to lapse into sentimentality, to make satire too entertaining and humor too broad or vulgar, to choose too energetic a tone of irony, and to overuse repetition as a stylistic device. It is indeed possible to detect isolated instances of implausible situations, melodramatic encounters, undifferentiated characterization of people and institutions, inconsistencies of logic, and forced symbolism in much of his prose, not to mention lesser works like his plays and occasional poems.

B.'s stature, however, should be defined by the totality of his oeuvre and the continuity of his creative vision, rather than by the success or failure of any single work. His writings give ever new poetic existence to a value system constantly undermined in the contemporary world, and he may legitimately be called the historical and moral conscience of West Germany. His passionate humanism and moral integrity, his ability to create believable characters, his infallible aim as a satirist, his sensitivity to both positive and

negative influences on the human psyche, the skillful craftsmanship of his complex narrative structures, which invariably call upon
the past to shed light on the present, and his verbal artistry,
particularly his parodistic attacks on contemporary jargon, remain
outstanding achievements and clearly establish his rank as a major
contemporary author.

FURTHER WORKS: *Die schwarzen Schafe* (1951); *Nicht nur zur
Weihnachtszeit* (1952); *Und sagte kein einziges Wort* (1953; *Acquainted with the Night*, 1954); *Das Brot der frühen Jahre* (1955;
The Bread of Our Early Years, 1957); *Irisches Tagebuch* (1957;
Irish Journal, 1967); *Doktor Murkes gesammeltes Schweigen*
(1958); *Erzählungen, Hörspiele, Aufsätze* (1961); *Als der Krieg
ausbrach. Als der Krieg zu Ende war* (1962; *When the War Ended*,
1964); *Ein Schluck Erde* (1962); *Entfernung von der Truppe* (1964;
Absent without Leave, 1965); *Ende einer Dienstfahrt* (1966; *End of
a Mission*, 1968); *Aufsätze, Kritiken, Reden* (1967); *Hausfriedensbruch.
Aufsatz* (1969); *Gedichte* (1972); *Neue politische und literarische
Schriften* (1973); *Berichte zur Gesinnungslage der Nation* (1975);
Drei Tage im März. Ein Gespräch (1975); *Gedichte* (1975);
Einmischung erwünscht (1977); *Eine deutsche Erinnerung* (1979);
Fürsorgliche Belagerung (1979; *The Safety Net*, 1986); *Was soll
aus dem Jungen bloß werden? Oder: Irgendwas mit Büchern*
(1981; *What's to become of the Boy? Or, Something to Do with
Books*, 1984); *Das Vermächtuis* (1982; *A Soldier's Legacy*, 1985);
Die Verwundung und andere Frühe Erzählungen (1983; *The
Casualty*, 1987); *Frauen vor Flußlandschaft* (1985; *Women in a
River Landscape*, 1988). FURTHER WORKS IN ENGLISH: *Eighteen
Stories* (1966); *Children Are Civilians Too* (1970); *Nobel Prize for
Literature 1972* (1973); *Missing Persons and Other Essays* (1977);
The Stories of H. B. (1986); *The Mad Dog: Stories* (1997)

BIBLIOGRAPHY: Ziolkowski, T., "H. B.: Conscience and Craft,"
BA, 34 (1960): 213–22; Sokel, W., "Perspective and Dualism in the
Novels of H. B.," in Heitner, R. H., ed., *The Contemporary Novel in
German* (1967): 9–35; Reich-Ranicki, M., ed., *In Sachen B.:
Ansichten und Aussichten* (1968); Thomas, R. H., and van der Will,
W., *The German Novel and the Affluent Society* (1968): 40–67;
Schwarz, W. J., *H. B., Teller of Tales* (1969); Demetz, P., *Postwar
German Literature* (1970): 185–99; Bernhard, H. J., *Die Romane
H. B.s* (1970); Duroche, L. L., "B.'s *Ansichten eines Clowns* in
Existentialist Perspective," *Symposium*, 25 (1971): 347–58; Ziolkowski,
T., "The Inner Veracity of Form. H. B.: Nobel Prize for Literature,"
BA, 47 (1973): 17–24; Reid, J. H., *H. B.: Withdrawal and Re-
Emergence* (1973); Durzak, M., *Der deutsche Roman der Gegenwart*,
2nd ed. (1973): 19–127; Jeziorkowski, K., "H. B.: Die Syntax des
Humanen," in Wagener, H., ed., *Zeitkritische Romane des 20.
Jahrhunderts* (1975): 301–17; Matthaei, R., ed., *Die subversive
Madonna: Ein Schlüssel zum Werk H. B.s* (1975); Nägele, R.,
H. B.: Einführung in das Werk und in die Forschung (1976);
Ghurye, C. W., *The Writer and Society: Studies in the Fiction of
Günter Grass and H. B.* (1976): 21–76; Reid, J. H., *H. B., A
German for His Time* (1988); Conrad, R. C., *Understanding H. B.*
(1992); Zachav, R. K., *H. B.: Forty Years of Criticism* (1994);
Butler, M., *The Narrative Fiction of H. B.* (1994)

—HELENE SCHER

B. is an artist of dignity, a writer who loves and
respects his craft and who, at the same time, is aware

of the full extent of its implications. B.'s concern
ranges from the artist's fond preoccupation with the
word as the smallest structural element in the edifice
of a novel, to the moral responsibility of social man
for the values expressed in his works. Conscience and
craft are the two poles that delimit B.'s scope as a
writer, and neither consideration is given short shrift
in his works.

. . .Two factors account, at least in part, for his
popular success. In the first place, B. is a master of the
art of storytelling. He does not regard his books
merely as vehicles to bear ponderous philosophical
speculations, but narrates interesting and poignant
stories that can be read by anyone. In the second
place, his main theme is one to elicit the sympathy—
or, more often perhaps, to arouse the antagonism—of
his countrymen: at any rate, it does not leave them
bored or indifferent. . . . This theme is essentially
Christianity or the Christian ideal. The basic trouble
with contemporary society, as B. sees it, is the anxiety
caused by the disparity between this ideal and the
actual state of affairs.

Theodore Ziolkowski, "H. B.: Conscience and
Craft," *BA*, 34 (1960), 213–14

B. cites the Protestant Kleist as his earliest and
most profound literary experience. There is indeed
something of Kleist's ideal of the marionette-figure,
an ultimately romantic and Rousseauistic ideal, in
B.'s heroes. . . . As in Kleist, the primary conflict in
B.'s work is that between innocence and worldly
crookedness, between the purity of the simple, natural soul and the envious arrogance of the twisted
careerist. But, whereas in Kleist innocence and justice win the battle in the end and force the world to
acknowledge them, the contemporary author makes a
distinction between the obvious physical victory that
goes to the wicked and false, and an intangible, ill-
definable, spiritual or moral victory that the just
obtain for themselves.

Even in *Ansichten eines Clowns* . . . a kind of
victory is wrested from bleak defeat. For the clown is
able to resist, and will continue to judge and to
accuse. . . . It is precisely as a beggar, however, that
the clown fulfills his role, which is to be the fool in the
traditional sense of the term—the jesting conscience
of his society, the living contradiction of its pretended
wisdom, the living refutation of its pretended happiness.

Walter Sokel, "Perspective and Dualism in the
Novels of H. B.," in Robert H. Heitner, ed., *The
Contemporary Novel in German* (1967), pp. 33–34

. . .His polemic against escapist cultural activities
stems partly from the recognition that German culture
was debased by the Nazis. . . . Not merely the content
of B.'s novels, however, but also their form is affected by the break with the past. The scene of the action
is always *aktuell*, present-day. They are all without
exception given a time-setting later than the collapse

of *Grossdeutschland.* . . . These settings are the more striking when one considers that from another angle B. is most vitally concerned with the past, with what took place before 1945. *Billard um halbzehn* (*Billiards at Half Past Nine*) might almost be described as a historical novel. The theme is the continuity of history between Wilhelm II and Adolf Hitler; the events described cover a period of over fifty years. But in fact the novel is set on a single day in 1958. All references to the past are made by means of flashback, interior monologue, or reminiscences. This montage technique is thus related to the content of the novel: the past is no longer *eine unmittelbar bewegende Wirklichkeit* (a directly moving reality) and can therefore be presented only indirectly.

James H. Reid, "Time in the Works of H. B.,"
MLR, 62 (1967), 477–78

Few contemporary German authors are more widely known than H. B. . . . In his own honest way B. fulfills many varied expectations: his revolutionary anger at the establishments of state, church, and army springs from conservative inclination; his bitter distrust of the modern communications industries from a strong moral sense; and his implacable hatred of power from boundless compassion for the wounded and defenseless. Catholics, Marxists, and belligerent intellectuals in Germany and elsewhere have legitimate reasons for admiring his moral force but often choose to overlook the more ambivalent challenges posed by his work.

Toward the end of the 'fifties B. was nearly everybody's "good German," but more recently he has annoyed his ideological friends: his serious moral commitment remains the unshakable foundation of his work, but he now demonstrates a new freedom of artistic choice, a thoughtful finesse, and a searching concern with the potential ironies of message and form. As Adenauer's gadfly B. contributed greatly to changing German literature, but his recent prose thrusts him in the direction of the bitter excellence of Georges Bernanos, Graham Greene, or Evelyn Waugh.

Peter Demetz, *Postwar German Literature* (1970),
pp. 185–86

Whoever ponders the significance of individual books by B. should not forget that he is far more than the sum of his literary works. . . . With differing degrees of success, but imperturbably, he serves the present by attempting to unify language and conscience, art and morality. The writer as the conscience of the nation? That is a formula that sounds quite old-fashioned, officious and melodramatic. But B. has succeeded in making it believable again. . . .

For he offers the world what it, consciously or not, continues to expect and demand from a German writer: morality and a sense of guilt. He refuses, however, to provide what is also thought typically German: thoroughness and solemnity. B. offers instead exactly what the world would least expect from

the descendants of the victors in the battle with the Romans in the Teutoburg Forest: charm and humor, an estimable sense of mischief and touching vulnerability.

Marcel Reich-Ranicki, in B. von Wiese, ed.
Deutsche Dichter der Gegenwart (1973),
pp. 338–39

The diversity of stylistic stances apparent from a survey of B.'s novels becomes the main theme, as it were, of the narrator of *Gruppenbild mit Dame*. As the narrator-arranger who does research and then organizes and integrates his various materials, the "Author" in this novel runs through the entire range of stylistic possibilities. This narrative eclecticism has a genuine function within this particular novel because it is essential to the "Author's" task. With this unusual artistic trick B. thus makes a virtue of necessity and lends artistic credibility to the discontinuous plurality of styles characteristic of his works.

It is nevertheless possible to detect another recurrent stylistic constant. I mean a stylistic intention which B. employed with great refinement and virtuosity, for example in the individual works in the volume *Doktor Murkes gesammeltes Schweigen und andere Satiren* [Dr. Murke's collected silences and other satires]: satirical unmasking by means of language. . . . In this satirical terseness, a quality of B.'s prose becomes manifest which may be found to a greater or lesser degree in all of his texts. Language satire is perhaps the most convincing artistic consequence of the moral impulse B. considers basic to the task of the writer. . . . This illumination of reality by means of language satire defines the particular achievement of B.'s prose in contemporary German fiction and makes credible the moral impetus of his writing.

Manfred Durzak, *Der deutsche Roman der Gegenwart* (1973), pp. 125–27

B.'s "involvement" entails moral commitment, which, however, does not automatically inform the act of writing. The strongest doubts about the social impact of literature during the postwar period had their source not so much in formalist ideologies, but rather in the experience that any sense of commitment seemed to remain totally ineffective in a pluralistic society. The writer as court jester, who may tell the truth because he is not taken seriously. . . . Criticism is similarly affected by this built-in disinterest. . . . The critic finds himself in the paradoxical position of stabilizing the criticized situation by means of his criticism—as long as he adheres to the unwritten rules, one must add.

B. attempts to avoid this dilemma by falling back on the medium with which he works, language. According to B. the troubles of society express themselves symptomatically in problems of language. Schiller had attributed the growing ambiguity of modern bourgeois art to society's new division of labor, which expressed itself in the divergence of private and public spheres. B. detects this divisiveness in contemporary language itself: " . . .it becomes apparent that there exists a public language and one spoken in private" (*Frankfurter Vorlesungen*). . . . He thus views the task of the writer as the attempt to reestablish trust in language by means of a new language . . . a "language of the humane."

Rainer Nägele, *H. B.: Einführung in das Werk und in die Forschung* (1976), pp. 32–33

BOLT, Robert

English dramatist, b. 15 Aug. 1924, Sale; d. 20 Feb. 1995, Petersfield

Originally a teacher, B. started writing plays for the BBC, then turned to writing for the stage. He achieved a reputation in England with *Flowering Cherry* (1958) and an international reputation with his best-known work, *A Man for All Seasons* (1960), a play about Sir Thomas More. He was also a highly successful writer of numerous screenplays and radio scripts. These well-regarded efforts included *A Man for All Seasons* as well as *Lawrence of Arabia* (1962), *Doctor Zhivago* (1963), *Ryan's Daughter* (1970), *The Bounty* (1984), and *The Mission* (1986). He also directed *Lady Caroline Lamb* (1973).

B.'s plays are traditional and realistic, with some symbolic elements; they have been compared with those of Terence Rattigan (1911–1977). B. has dealt with illusion and reality, the preservation of the self, political power, and nuclear disarmament. He has created solid rules that challenged master actors to give unforgettable portrayals.

In *Flowering Cherry*, Jim Cherry, an insurance salesman, is torn between the reality of working for money alone and his dream of owning a flowering orchard. When he has the opportunity to make his dream a reality, he abandons the dream—for a small insurance agency—and his wife abandons him. She has loved her immature, deceitful husband only for his dream.

B. has excelled in chronicle plays that draw historical portraits. In *A Man for All Seasons*, Sir Thomas More represents man's need to preserve his inner self and to act according to his conscience. More seeks a safe "causeway" in English law, but will face execution rather than swear to what he does not believe. Technically, the play gains from the device of the ubiquitous Common Man, narrator and commentator, who is both within and outside the action. This device seems derived from the epic theater of Bertolt BRECHT and from radio drama. *Vivat, Vivat Regina!* (1970) presents contrasting portraits of Elizabeth I and Mary Queen of Scots as the lives of the two queens intertwine and illustrate the pressure and penalties of political power. Mary is restless, passionate, impulsive; Elizabeth denies herself life and love to fulfill her duty and destiny as queen.

B.'s plays are not angry, controversial, or boldly innovative, but they offer some firm characterizations (especially More and Elizabeth), a thoughtfulness with contemporary relevance, and an affirmation of the significance of life. He was continually praised for his craftsmanship, his strong sense of theatre, and his acute, accurate sense of broad historical settings, though his reputation in his last years never regained the status it had after *A Man for All Seasons*.

FURTHER WORKS: *The Last of the Wine* (1956); *The Critic and the Heart* (1957); *The Tiger and the Horse* (1960); *Gentle Jack* (1963); *The Thwarting of Baron Bolligrew* (1965); *State of Revolution* (1977)

BIBLIOGRAPHY: Taylor, J. R., *Anger and After* (1962): 321–22; Trewin, J. C., "Two Morality Playwrights: R. B. and John Whiting," in Armstrong, W. A., ed., *Experimental Drama* (1963): 103–27; Tees, A. T., "The Place of the Common Man: R. B.: *A Man for All Seasons,*" UR, 36 (1969): 67–71; McElrath, J. R., "The Metaphoric Structure of *A Man for All Seasons,*" MD, 14 (1971): 84–92; Anderegg, M. A., "A Myth for All Seasons: Thomas More," *ColQ*, 23 (1975): 293–306; Free, W. J., "R. B. and the Marxist View of History," *Mosaic*, 14 (1981): 51-59; Paris, B. J., "Third Force Psychology and the Study of Literature," LitR, 24 (1981):181-221

—JOSEPH E. DUNCAN

BOMBAL, Maria Luisa

Chilean novelist and short-story writer, b. 8 July 1910, Viña del Mar; d. 6 May 1980, Santiago

After her father's death in 1922, B. was taken by her mother to Paris, where she lived until finishing her university degree in philosophy and literature at the Sorbonne. In 1931 she returned to Chile, living for two years on the family country estate in the south. In 1933 she accompanied her friend Pablo Neruda to Buenos Aires where she developed friendships with numerous writers, among them Federico GARCÍA LORCA and Jorge Luis BORGES. In this very creative environment, she wrote and published her two brief novels, *La última niebla* (1935; *The House of Mist*, 1947), which included the two stories "El árbol" ("The Tree," 1982) and "Las islas nuevas" ("The New Islands," 1982), and *La amortajada* (1938; *The Shrouded Woman*, 1948). After a thirty-year stay in Washington, D.C., where she lived with her second husband, B. once again returned to her native Chile, living out the remainder of her years in Santiago.

Despite B.'s limited production, two short novels and a handful of short stories, she is highly regarded today as an innovator. Her narratives are a radical departure from the picturesque regionalism and social protest of her Chilean contemporaries. Plot as action worked out in a process of cause and effect to a resolution or conclusion is not central to her work. Instead, in an evocative, poetic prose, reminiscent of French symbolism, and influenced by the later vanguardist movement, she elaborates in an almost musical fashion the inner emotional states of her alienated female protagonists. Secondary characters are viewed subjectively through the prism of an emotionally colored consciousness; atmospheric settings function as metaphorical projections of inner feelings; and the tone is pervasively one of melancholy.

La última niebla is a retrospective first-person narrative of no more than fifty pages in which an unnamed woman records over a period of some years, in a highly evocative and lyrical prose, her reflections on the reality or unreality of what most probably was an erotic dream. Denied her passionate desire for sensual love in her arid marriage, the woman weaves an elaborate fantasy around an imagined night of sexual union with a wraithlike male figure who has all the trappings of Carl Gustav Jung's *animus*. Gradually she becomes aware of the illusory nature of the experience, ultimately resigning herself to the sterility of her marriage and the utter conventionality of her mundane existence. In the first half of the novel, images of mist, water, and leaves—and in general of the erotic qualities of nature—create a dreamlike atmosphere in which reality and fantasy are ambiguously blended. By the end of the novel, images of death, old age, and suicide prevail.

La amortajada, a somewhat longer work, is also strongly retrospective in its narrative structure. Here, however, the protagonist, whose name is Ana María, lies dead in her casket at her wake, reflecting mentally on her past relationships with those who approach her one by one to pay their last respects—her young cousin (the passion of her life), her sister, her children, her father, her male confidant, her husband, and her priest. The narrative is for the most part third-person *style indirect libre* but slips from time to time into first person and occasionally into the perspective of one of the other characters. Despite these surface shifts, all voices are subsumed under the single voice or high-level stream-of-consciousness of Ana María. Again, the themes are failed relationships and erotic passion denied. In general, the novel illustrates the profound disparity between Ana María's naive Edenic expectations and the realities encountered in her relationships, between her wish-fulfillment concept of God as dispenser of sensual happiness and the God of her disillusionment who gave her anguish and suffering instead. In the end, she welcomes not only her "first death" but also her "second death" as she slips gradually into sweet oblivion.

The third work on which B.'s reputation rests is the short story "El árbol." Here Brigida, the child-woman protagonist, is carried by music through three distinct stages in her failed marriage to an older and indifferent man. Unlike the novels, however, the story contains a hint of optimism. In the epiphany of self-illumination, she seems to have matured, able perhaps to make an independent life for herself apart from her husband and beyond the protection of the "maternal" rubber tree outside the house where she had lived.

Although B.'s themes are limited, and although she never really received due recognition in her native Chile, she is universally considered a consummate stylist. In her Lyricism, in her psychological orientation, and in her ambiguous fusion of reality and fantasy, she is a precursor of what has been called the "new narrative" in Latin America.

FURTHER WORKS: "Mar, cielo y tierra" (1940); "Trenzas" (1940); "Washington, ciudad de las ardillas" (1943); "La historia de María Griselda" (1946); "La maja y el ruiseñor" (1976)

BIBLIOGRAPHY: Campbell, M., "The Vaporous World of M. L. B.," *Hispania*, 44, 3 (Sept. 1961): 415–19; Debicki, A., "Structure, Imagery, and Experience in M. L. B.'s 'El árbol,'" *SSF*, 8 (Winter 1971): 123–29; Levine, L., "M. L. B. from a Feminist Perspective." *RevI*, 4 (1974): 148–61; Adams, M. I., "M. L. B.: Alienation and the Poetic Image," *Three Authors of Alienation* (1975): 15–35; Nelson, E., "The Space of Longing: *La última niebla,*" *The American Hispanist*, 3 (1977): 7–11; Orlandi, C., "Mist, Light and Libido: *La última niebla,*" *KRQ*, 26, 2 (1979): 231–42; Rodríguez-Peralta, P., "M. L. B.'s Poetic Novels of Female Estrangement," *REH*, 14 (1980): 139–55; Kostopoulos-Cooperman, C., *The Lyrical Vision of M. L. B.* (1998)

—ROBERT SCOTT

BOND, Edward

English dramatist, b. 18 July 1934, London

B. says that his family was lower-working-class and that his background was typical of that of 75 percent of the English people. Seeing Donald Wolfit's performance in Shakespeare's *Macbeth* was the turning point in his life and gave him the incentive to write for the theater. During two years in the army he discovered the violence, dehumanization, and the class structure that are constant concerns in his plays.

B. is an important playwright in the "second wave" of modern English drama that includes Tom STOPPARD and David STOREY. He became a controversial figure when *Saved* (1966) and *Early Morning* (1968) were banned by the Lord Chamberlain. In fact, controversy about B.'s plays gave impetus to the abolition of stage censorship in England. In 1969, with censorship gone, the Royal Court Theatre, with which B. has been closely associated, presented three of B.'s works.

B.'s plays dramatize the effects of violence and a dehumanizing social structure on individuals, particularly the young. He depicts a society after the fall, but one for which there is still an almost irresponsible hope. B. believes that man has a natural need to love and create, that he can live without aggression and violence. But an unjust society forces humans to live in a way for which they were not designed. B. has gained scope by using Oedipal patterns and by setting plays in 17th-, 19th-, and 20th-c. England as well as in Japan and a primitive Asian land. He holds that the dramatist should be concerned with rationality, justice, and a classless society—all in conflict with conventional law and order.

Saved gained notoriety as the play in which a baby in a pram is stoned to death. Len lives with Pam, who dopes the baby with aspirin, and with her parents, who have not spoken for years; the hooligans who kill the baby are another part of his environment. Yet he maintains his goodness, though not easily. Therein lies the precarious optimism that is part of B.'s vision. The play is fundamentally naturalistic (in all B.'s English plays, lower-class characters consistently speak in dialect), but has many symbolic elements.

In *Early Morning* and *Lear* (1972) B. deals with upper-class oppressors and employs non-realistic, sometimes surrealistic, techniques. *Early Morning* is a phantasmagoric nightmare in which Queen Victoria, a lesbian, rapes Florence Nightingale, cannibalism is an accepted way of life, and all are killed in a mammoth tug-of-war. Yet Prince Arthur is able to survive his confrontation with reality and envision a better society. In *Lear*, B. implies that Shakespeare's Lear learns only in order to endure. B.'s Lear, on the other hand, learns to accept responsibility for all of his past, including the corruption of his daughters, acts to tear down the dehumanizing wall he had ordered built, and halts the trend of corruption from the older to the younger.

Several plays deal with the artist in society. In *Narrow Road to the Deep North* (1968), a sinewy parable, the Japanese poet Basho neither rescues nor kills the baby who grows up to be an oppressive dictator. *Bingo* (1974) shows Shakespeare betraying what B. believes should be the artist's commitment to justice. Shakespeare accepts payment from a wealthy landowner and in return does not oppose the expulsion of peasants from land that is to be enclosed for raising sheep. *The Fool* (1976) portrays the peasant-poet John Clare (1793–1864), who is true to his vision but ends his life in an asylum.

B.'s plays show memorable power and an intense commitment. They often depict opposing forces in terms of black and white but sometimes reveal more complexity. His characters are credible and consistent, but only Lear is developed in depth. The plays are often unified more by their ideas than by their dramatic action.

FURTHER WORKS: *Black Mass* (1970); *The Pope's Wedding* (1971); *Passion* (1971); *The Sea* (1973); *A-A-America* (1976); *We Come to the River* (1976); *The Bundle* (1978); *The Woman* (1978); *Theatre Poems and Songs* (1978); *The Worlds, and The Activists Papers* (1981)

BIBLIOGRAPHY: Arnold, A., "Lines of Development in B.'s Plays," *TheatreQ*, 2, 5 (1972): 15–19; Barth, A. K., "The Aggressive 'Theatrum Mundi' of E. B.: *Narrow Road to the Deep North*," *MD*, 18 (1975): 189–200; Durbach, E., "Herod in the Welfare State: *Kindermord* in the Plays of E. B.," *ETJ*, 27 (1975): 480–87; Scharine, R., *The Plays of E. B.* (1975); Duncan, J. E., "The Child and the Old Man in the Plays of E. B.," *MD*, 19 (1976): 1–10; Trussler, S., *E. B.* (1976); Coult, T., *The Plays of E. B.* (1978); Smith, L., "E. B.'s *Lear*," *CompD*, 13 (1979): 65–85

—JOSEPH E. DUNCAN

BÖNI, Franz

Swiss novelist and short-story writer (writing in German), b. 17 June 1952, Wintherthur

B. studied business and worked as a tradesman and itinerant salesman from 1973 to 1979. He then decided to give up this occupation and become a full-time writer. He has won several prizes in Switzerland and Germany, including the Conrad Ferdinand Meyer Prize (1980). He now resides in Zurich.

All of B.'s stories are set in the valleys and forests of the Lower Alps in Switzerland, but the country he portrays is one of disease, squalor, and extremely difficult work. His characters are obsessed with the struggle to survive and are haunted by poverty. They are devoid of love and compassion, and see little meaning in their bizarre and cruel existence, which they long to escape through death. B. has created here the epitome of an antihomeland literature, which itself is a metaphor for the alienation and despair rampant in contemporary capitalist societies.

Almost all of B.'s protagonists are on a journey in search of something they never find in a direct parallel to the meaningless quests of Franz KAFKA's characters. In *Die wanderarbeiter* (1981; the itinerant workers) the character A. leaves home for the hard physical labor of a factory, which allows him no time for other pursuits. Franz Zuber in *Schlatt* (1979; Schlatt) also leaves home to find work and returns six years later with a lung disease. In *Hospiz* (1980; hostel) an itinerant peddler endures daily hardships until a storm forces him to stay in a hostel, perhaps for the rest of his life. In *Ein wanderer in alpenregen* (1981; a wanderer in the alpine rain) young people travel into the Alps where they cannot enjoy the beauties of nature but instead encounter ignorant peasants, hard work, and death.

B.'s stories appear to have for the most part autobiographical traits, and this is particularly true of his three-part chronicle about the life of the laborer Nowak: *Wie die zeit vergeht* (1988; how time passes) covers the time 1955–1970, *Die alpen* (1983; the Alps) the

period 1970–1980, and *Alle züge fahren nach Salem* (1984; all trains travel to Salem) the period 1980–1984. Nowak grows up in a small Swiss town and tries to escape his dreary existence by delving into popular culture and by traveling to Italy, but he only finds himself surrounded by death and depression. He then decides to leave home for good to work in a small industrial town, but his series of demanding jobs make him more depressed than before. Suicides and death abound everywhere. The city is just as dehumanizing and cruel as the Alpine landscape.

Die residenz (1988; the city of residence) also portrays the negative elements of the city. Franz Kramer grows up in a farm milieu that he refuses to accept. He longs to flee to the capital city to work as a secretary in the castle there. His letters of application are in vain. Finally he travels to the city, Despina, and after many attempts manages to find a position. However, at the height of his career he decides to leave the city, because it has almost destroyed him. He meets Maya, his former love from the village, but their future together is uncertain. Kramer realizes that all his searching for fulfillment has been for naught.

B. is one of the most significant contemporary Swiss-German writers and his antihomeland, antiutopian philosophy shares many features with several other Swiss, Austrian, and German authors. Through distortion and hyperbole he wishes to underscore the bizarre and cruel components of contemporary existence and debunk the myths about Swiss society. Yet B. is prone to description instead of analysis, which produces a pessimistic worldview devoid of the possibility of change and progress.

FURTHER WORKS: *Der knochensammler* (1980); *Sagen aus dem schächental* (1982); *Alvier* (1982); *Der johanniterlauf* (1984); *Die fronfastenkinder: Aufsätze 1966–1985* (1985); *Das zentrum der welt* (1987); *Am ende aller tage* (1989)

BIBLIOGRAPHY: Moser, S., "Sprachzwerg und Sprachriese," *Schweizer Monatshefte*, 12 (1979): 1009–13; Nef, E., "Ausweglose Topologie," *Schweizer Monatshefte*, 3 (1983): 253–57; Hultberg, H., "Der Wanderer: über F. B.," *T & K*, 11, 2 (1983): 370–81; Michaelis, R., "Nachrichten von Archipel Gletscher oder Bild und Begriff der Heimat bei F. B.," *Manuskripte*, 28 (1988): 111–16

—ROBERT ACKER

BONI, Tanella S(usane)

Ivoirian poet and novelist (writing in French), b. 1954, Abidjan

B. was reared in Côte d'Ivoire, first with her parents, and later with her sister. Since the early 1980s she has lived in Abidjan with her own family. In contrast to many African women of her generation whose pursuit of intellectual recognition was foiled by innumerable difficulties, B. managed all the steps of academia. She attended primary school in the north of the country, then high school in Abidjan, followed by tertiary education in France where she studied philosophy in Toulouse and eventually earned her doctorate at the Sorbonne. Upon her return to Côte d'Ivoire, B. became a professor of philosophy at Cocody University, but it is rather as a writer and a patron of the arts that she has made a name for herself in Abidjan artistic and literary circles. B. was the chair of the Ivoirian Writers' Association from 1991 to 1997. In 1992 she was writer-in-residence at the Ninth Limousin Francophone International Festival in Limoges.

B.'s first attempts at poetry go back to her early teens. While her style has developed exceptional literary quality and power in later years, the reason behind her writing has remained the same: "to cheat death and to keep on living," as she says. The theme she is dealing with is both metaphysical and close to Africa's contemporary life. Myths of the origins are revisited and made to account for the thousand ways open to the living soul, for woman in particular but also for man. The author is keen to build bridges between genders and races. The narrator of *Labyrinthe* (1984; maze) defies the rules of conventional wisdom and she is happy to grope along, taking both the insignificant and the all encompassing as landmarks in her journey through life. Convinced that life is worth living, she also realizes that no one knows for sure what is really important and how to get around "the snare that lies at the intersection of the seven roads." A second collection of poems, *Grains de sable* (1993; Grains of Sand), builds upon the power of woman and the mystery of human love: the most unforeseeable reunion of two grains of sand scattered far and wide by circumstances and assembled in a whole consuming yet ephemeral and fragile encounter. *Il n'y a pas de parole heureuse* (1997; There Is No Happy Word) comes back to an uncompromising evaluation of both African society and poetic endeavor.

B. is a poet at heart and her two novels, *Une vie de crabe* (1990; A Crab's Life) and *Les baigneurs du lac roses* (1995; The Bathers of the Pink Lake), take liberties with conventional literary structures. Both novels are located in Africa and both tell the journey of liberation of a young and sensitive women confronted by a universe open to petty transgressions of the rules and conventions but ill prepared to tolerate a new evaluation of the fundamentals. Therefore, it is with great hope, courage, and persistence, punctuated by moments of apprehension, discouragement, and deception, that both narrators embark on discovering what they are, where they come from, and where they are going.

Côte d'Ivoire has produced some of the finest literary minds of Africa, and B.'s literary talent places her among the most important. Her decision to publish with small African publishers possibly accounts for her work being widely recognized in her country of origin but little known outside Africa and wider literary circles.

FURTHER WORKS: *De l'autre côté du soleil* (1991); *La Fugue d'Ozone* (1992)

BIBLIOGRAPHY: Borgomono, M., *Voix et visage de femmes* (1989): 70-74; Koulibaly, I. B., "T. B., Présidente des écrivains ivoiriens," *Amina*, 270 (1993): 26; Huannou, A., *Anthologie de la littérature féminine d'Afrique noire francophone* (1994): 79-86; Nkoumo, H., "Parole blessée," *Fraternité Matin*, 3 Feb. 1998: 11

—JEAN-MARIE VOLET

BONNEFOY, Yves

French poet, essayist, translator, and art historian, b. 24 June 1923, Tours

After studying mathematics and philosophy at the University of Poitiers, B. took a degree in philosophy at the University of Paris.

From 1945 to 1947 he was closely associated with the SURREALISTS. Since 1944 B. has lived in Paris. Widely traveled, he has made several trips to the U.S., where he taught literature at a number of universities. Together with André du Bouchet (b. 1924), Gaëtan Picon (b. 1915), and Louis-René des Forêts (b. 1918), he founded *L'éphémère*, a journal of art and literature, in 1967.

B.'s first important volume of poetry, *Du mouvement et de l'immobilité de Douve* (1953; *On the Motion and Immobility of Douve*, 1968), was received with considerable acclaim. It remains his most famous book. In subsequent collections of poetry, *Hier régnant désert* (1958; yesterday reigning desert), *Pierre écrite* (1959; *Words in Stone*, 1976), and *Dans le leurre du seuil* (1975; in the enticement of the threshold), B. has continued to develop themes implicit in the first book and to create a poetic world that is distinct from that of any of his contemporaries. He has also written numerous essays on aesthetics, poetry, and art, which have been collected in several volumes that are indispensable, *L'improbable* (1959; the improbable) and *Un rêve fait à Mantoue* (1967; a dream at Mantua), both of which are indispensable for a complete understanding of B.'s poetry.

The central theme in B.'s poetry is the dialectical relationship between life and death. *Du mouvement et de l'immobilité de Douve* (the title itself suggests a dialectical mode of thought) begins with an epigraph by Hegel asserting that the life of the mind is not frightened by death, but rather endures the presence of death within itself and preserves itself alive within death. The first poems in the volume evoke the anguished yet ecstatic death of Douve, who is simultaneously a woman, nature, and the mind. In a tone that is low, almost a whisper, and passionately intense, B. recounts the dismemberment of Douve, who descends into death without, however, losing an acute sense of life.

The poems themselves are fragments that momentarily burn against a dark, desolate landscape that is felt rather than clearly visualized. Key images reappear with hypnotic effect to suggest the reality that Douve now encounters: fire, wind, stone. Taut and condensed, B.'s poems are seldom more than twelve lines long; often they are reduced to four or even two lines; frequently they are untitled.

The subtle movement from one poem to the next is that of a circle slowly closing in on itself. B. has stated that he would like poetry to be first of all an incessant battle, a theater where being and essence, form and the non-formal, struggle fiercely against each other. Poetry of this kind is tinged with metaphysical speculation. It verges on the mystical. Indeed, B. has often been compared with the poet Maurice Scève (ca. 1503–1560) and to other Renaissance poets of the hermetic and gnostic traditions. The peculiar tension in B.'s work is the result of the poet's struggle to reconcile irreconcilables. Although he wishes to express "the present moment," "the immediate," "the here and now," he is also haunted by the Platonic vision of an ultimate reality beyond the ephemeral world of the present. The poet, as B. sees his role, "looks for the absolute on the threshold of the finite."

In the three volumes of poetry that follow *Du mouvement et de l'immobilité de Douve*, B. continues his quest for what he calls "the true place"—the place in which, to use a phrase by Coleridge that B. cites approvingly, "the many still seen as many becomes one." The final poem of the third volume, *Pierre écrite*, is a beautifully articulated "art de la poésie." Here, in seven lines, B. suggests that the demons that had inhabited his poetry have finally been exorcised and that a reconciliation of opposites has been effected. This resolution of tension is, however, a desideratum rather than fact, for in B.'s fourth volume of poetry, published sixteen years after the third, the demons are still very much present.

One of the most sensitive advocates of English literature in France today, B. has translated several of Shakespeare's plays. His translations are probably the best that have ever appeared in French.

Since 1965 B. has turned more and more to art history. Like his poetry, his art criticism reveals a preoccupation with death, time, and being. Taken as a whole, B.'s diverse and sometimes enigmatic works are richly complementary, each developing in a different register the restless thoughts of one of the most arresting minds in contemporary French literature.

FURTHER WORKS: *Traité du pianiste* (1946); *Peintures murales de la France gothique* (1954); *L'improbable* (1959); *La seconde simplicité* (1961); *Rimbaud par lui-même* (1961); *Anti-Platon* (1963); *Miró* (1964); *Un rêve fait à martoue* (1967); *Rome, 1630: L'horizon du premier baroque* (1970); *L'arrière-pays* (1972); *Le nuage rouge* (1977); *Rue traversière* (1977); *Tout l'œuvre peint de Mantegna* (1978); *Entretiens sur la poésie* (1981); *Dictionnaire des mythologies et des religions des sociétés traditionnelles et du monde antique* (1981); *Leçon inaugurée faite le 4 décembre* (1981); *Une autre époque de l'écriture* (1981); *Poèmes* (1982); *La présence et l'image* (1983); *Ce qui fut sans lumière* (1987; *In the Shadow's Light*, 1991); *Récits en rêve* (1987); *Sur un sculpteur et des peintres* (1989); *Vérité poétique et vérité scientifique* (1989); *Début et fin de la neige* (1991); *L'Arrière-pays* (1992); *Rimbaud: tradition et modernité* (1992); *Ramarques sur le dessin* (1993); *Delacroix et Hamlet* (1993); *Une vie errante* (1993); *La petite phrase et la longue phrase* (1994); *Palézieu* (1994); *La journée d'Alexandre Hollan* (1995); *La vérité de parole* (1995); *Dessin, couleur, lumière* (1995); *Alberto Giacometti: biographie d'une oeuvre* (1996). FURTHER WORKS IN ENGLISH: *Selected Poems* (1968); *Things Dying Things Reborn: Selected Poems* (1985); *The Act and the Place of Poetry: Selected Essays* (1989); *Early Poems, 1947-1959* (1991); *The Lure and the Truth of Painting: Selected Essays on Art* (1995); *New and Selected Poems* (1995)

BIBLIOGRAPHY: Richard, J. P., "Y. B.," in *Onze études sur la poésie moderne* (1964): 207–32; Albert, W., "Y. B. and the Architecture of Poetry," *MLN*, 82 (1967): 590–603; Gavronsky, S., *Poems & Texts* (1969): 125–41; Gordon, A., "Things Dying, Things New Born: The Poetry of Y. B.," *Mosaic*, 6 (1973): 55–70; Lawall, S., and Caws, M. A., "A Style of Silence: Two Readings of Y. B.'s Poetry," *ConL*, 16 (1975): 193–217; Dickson, A., "Movement and Immobility in a Poem by Y. B.," *MLR*, 72 (1977): 565–74; special B. issue, *WLT*, 53 (1979); Thélot, J., *Poétique d'Y. B.* (1983); Naughton, J., *The Poetics of Y. B.* (1984); Giguere, R., *Le concept de la réalité dans la poésie d'Y. B.* (1985); Gasarain, G., *Y. B.* (1986); Finck, M., *Y. B.: le simple et le sens* (1989)

—ROBERT D. COTTRELL

BONTEMPELLI, Massimo

Italian short-story writer, novelist, essayist, and poet, b. 12 May 1878, Como; d. 21 July 1960, Rome

B.'s father's position as railroad engineer caused his family to move frequently. Otherwise his early life and education were those of the average Italian bourgeois. B. began his career as a secondary-school teacher and journalist. With Curzio Malaparte (1898–1957) he founded the very important periodical *'900* (1926–29), whose editorial board included James JOYCE and Ilya EHRENBURG. Its aim was to modernize Italian culture and combat its provincialism. In addition to B.'s own brand of MAGIC REALISM, it welcomed experiments in SYMBOLISM, DADAISM, EXPRESSIONISM, and SURREALISM. B. was also known for his literary column in *Tempo* (1939–43). He was elected to the Italian Academy in 1930, and his collected works (*Opere*) began appearing in 1938. The communist Popular Front nominated him for a senatorship in 1948, but he was not elected because of alleged collaboration with the Fascist regime of Mussolini.

B.'s important work is all narrative. His early writing was influenced by Giosuè Carducci (1835–1907) and the typical "pathetic" and "intimate" style of much late-19th-c. writing. Traces of irony and grotesque elements typical of the later "surrealist" style may already be seen in the stories of *Socrate moderno* (1908; modern Socrates). Those of *La vita intensa* (1920; intense life) and *La vita operosa* (1921; hard-working life) reflect his brief honeymoon with FUTURISM. By 1922 he had begun to find his own style and published the magical and psychological tales of *La scacchiera devanti allow specchio* (the chessboard before the mirror), *Eva ultima* (1923; last Eve), and *La donna dei miei sogni, e altre adventure moderne* (1925; the lady of my dreams, and other modern adventures).

B. himself coined the term "magic realism." He used a technique of subtle and highly intellectual analysis to point out the adventurous and fantastic elements in everyday experience, investing them with an unreal, grotesque, or fabulous atmosphere that characterizes his work from *Vita e morte di Adria e dei suoi figli* (1930; life and death of Adria and her children) to *L'amante fidele* (1953; the faithful lover). B.'s best-known books are the novel *Gente net tempo* (1937; people in time), which combines a highly imaginative style with a profoundly human and very touching theme, and the three long stories in *Giro del sole* (1941; around the sun). He is best known today for his periodical *'900* and more generally as the inventor of "magic realism."

FURTHER WORKS: *Egloghe* (1904); *Verseggiando* (1905); *Costanza* (1905); *Odi siciliane* (1906); *Odi* (1910); *Amori* (1910); *Sette savi* (1912); *Dallo Stelvio al mare* (1915); *La piccola* (1916); *Meditazioni intorno alla guerra d'Italia e d'Europa* (1917); *Viaggi e scoperte* (1922); *La donna del Nadir* (1924); *L'Eden della tartaruga* (1926); *Donne nel sole e altri idilli* (1928); *Il figlio di due madri* (1929); *Novecentismo letterario* (1931); *Mia vita, morte e miracoli* (1931); *Stato di grazia* (1931); *Storia di una giornata* (1932); *Il purosangue-L'ubriaco* (1933); *Primi racconti* (1934); *Galleria degli schiavi* (1934); *Pezzi di mondo* (1935); *L'avventura novecentista* (1938); *Pirandello, Leopardi, D'Annunzio* (1938); *Arturo Martini* (1939); *Verga, l'Aretino, Scarlatti, Verdi* (1941); *Introduzione all'Apocalisse* (1942); *Sette discorsi* (1942); *Gian Francesco Malipiero* (1942); *Cenerentola* (1942); *Notti* (1945); *L'acqua* (1945); *Dignità dell'uomo 1843–1946* (1946); *Venezia salvata* (1947); *Appassionata incompiuta* (1950); *Passione incompiuta* (1958)

BIBLIOGRAPHY: Ragusa, O., "M. B. (1878–1960)," *BA*, 35 (1961): 131–32

—JOY M. POTTER

BOON, Louis Paul

Belgian novelist and critic (writing in Flemish), b. 15 March 1912, Aalst; d. 10 May 1979, Erembodegem

A lifelong resident of the town of Aalst, which also serves as the setting of most of his works, B. began his career as a painter, a profession he never completely relinquished. After World War II B. became the cultural editor of the Communist daily *De rode vaan*. An idealist rather than an activist, B. lost this position and began writing for a number of periodicals. From 1959 until his retirement in 1978 he wrote a popular column for the newspaper *Vooruit* under the pseudonym "Boontje." Equally popular were his satirical political cartoons in the same organ. The writer "Boon" used his pen as a social weapon, whereas the columnist "Boontje" was a benign commentator and a popular television personality as well. His appellation the "tender anarchist" reflects this duality.

Appearances notwithstanding, all B.'s works are renderings of actual events experienced in or near Aalst. In that sense his oeuvre constitutes a rather detailed biography. B.'s provincialism, including his adherence to the Flemish dialect rather than standard Netherlandic, runs contrapuntally to the universality of his themes. The most pervasive of these is the championing of the rights of the individual in society and his inevitable demise, no matter what kind of system he is subjected to.

B.'s first novel, *De voorstad groeit* (1942; the suburb is growing) began a long series of provocative social novels. This naturalistic work depicts life in the poverty-stricken suburb where B. lived. Similarly, in *Vergeten straat* (1946; forgotten street) B. writes about a utopian community consisting of the people living on his own street. But his dream of a utopian street (or state) founders, not only because of the usurpation of the individual by the masses, but also because of man's own selfish aims. In his poignant *Mijn kleine oorlog* (1946; my little war), an actual diary in which B. records events and anecdotes of the war years, the author declares war on war itself, which he sees as a mad, gamelike structure in which the individual is dissolved into a dehumanized body marching against mankind itself.

De kapellekensbaan (1953; *Chapel Road*, 1972) is B.'s most ambitious novel. His characteristic paradox is here expressed in a story about a peaceful revolution by Flemish workers against their exploitation by capitalism during the Industrial Revolution; the novel repeatedly touches upon the very root of the social evil of capitalism, which resides in the individual himself. This thematic duality is mirrored by the double structure of the novel. The sections in italic type tell the story of a young girl working in a factory in which she is exploited. The blocks of roman type, which alternate with those in italics, consist of B.'s personal reflections on man and society, art and life, and so forth, in different personae and from various points of view. The connection of these discussions and ideas to the parallel narrative only gradually becomes clear to the reader, but they serve to bring the story into a contemporary context. B. wrote a sequel, *Zomer te Ter-Muren* (1956; summer in Termuren), to this Brechtian antinovel.

B.'s writings are highly respected in both his native Flanders and the Netherlands. Even before he received the prestigious State Prize of Belgium in 1971, the Dutch had awarded him the coveted Constantijn Huygens Prize in 1966.

FURTHER WORKS: *Abel Gholaerts* (1944); *Twee spoken* (1952); *Menuet* (1955); *Wapenbroeders* (1955); *Niets gaat ten onder* (1956); *De kleine Eva uit de kromme bijlstraat* (1956); *De bende van Jan de Lichte* (1957); *Grimmige sprookjes voor verdorven kinderen* (1957); *De paradijsvogel* (1958); *Vaarwel krokodil of de prijslijst van het geluk* (1959); *Gustaaf Vermeersch* (1960); *De zoon van Jan de Lichte* (1961); *Het nieuwe onkruid* (1964); *Pieter Daens* (1971); *Mieke Maaike's obscene jeugd* (1972); *Als het onkruid bloeit* (1972); *Zomerdagdroom* (1973); *De meisjes van Jesses* (1973); *Verscheurd jeugdportret* (1975); *Memoires van de Heer Daegeman* (1975); *De Zwarte Hand* (1976); *Het jaar 1901* (1977); *Het geuzenboek* (1979); *Eros en de eenzame man* (1980)

BIBLIOGRAPHY: Meijer, R. P., *Literature of the Low Countries* (1971): 348–49; Snapper, J. P., *Post-War Dutch Literature: A Harp Full of Nails* (1971): 6–7

—JOHAN P. SNAPPER

BORCHERT, Wolfgang

German dramatist, short-story writer, and poet, b. 20 May 1921, Hamburg; d. 20 Nov. 1947, Basel, Switzerland

After leaving secondary school at the age of seventeen, B. was apprenticed to a bookseller, took acting classes in his spare time, and, in 1940, was awarded the State Diploma in acting. But his career as an actor lasted only three months. In the summer of 1941 he was called up and was soon sent to the Russian front, where he suffered his first attacks of jaundice, was wounded, and fell ill with diphtheria. Accused of having inflicted the wound himself, the convalescent was arrested in May 1942 and, pending his trial, held in solitary confinement for more than three months. Although acquitted of the charge by a Nuremberg military tribunal, B. remained imprisoned pending a second trial for seditious remarks against "State and Party." After serving six weeks of solitary confinement, he was sent back to Russia in December 1942, to serve "on probation under fire" as a courier without arms until his health failed again. He came down with jaundice and typhus, was shipped back to Germany in 1943, and eventually considered for a discharge as unfit for military service. But in 1944, just a day before he was to be discharged, B. was arrested again, accused of "demoralization of the troops," and sentenced to nine months in prison. On his release, in September 1944, he was again sent to fight, "on probation." He was taken prisoner by the French in the spring of 1945 but managed to escape. Recaptured by the Americans, B. was set free when his record as a political prisoner was discovered. Carefully following the northward-moving Allies, he then walked some six hundred kilometers back to Hamburg. There he tried to resume his career both on stage and as a writer. But in the winter of 1945–46 his health broke down completely. He spent several months in local hospitals, only to be discharged as incurable. Back home again, he soon found himself completely bedridden. When his friends finally succeeded in sending him to Switzerland, in 1947, he was in such a poor physical state that he barely made it to Basel, where he died two months after his arrival.

B. started writing poetry at age fifteen and had his first poem published in 1938. But his lyrical output shows, for the most part, too great a dependence upon the models imitated, especially RILKE, Friedrich Hölderlin (1770–1843), and the EXPRESSIONISTS. The fact that he later chose to suppress his unpublished poems written before 1940 would seem to indicate that B. himself was well aware of their shortcomings. The slim collection of poems from the years between 1940 and 1945, *Laterne, Nacht und Sterne* (1945; street lamp, night, and stars), limited to only fourteen poems, can be considered to be his lyrical swan song.

The work that made B. famous overnight was his drama *Draußen vor der Tür* (1947; *The Man Outside*, 1952), first presented as a radio play. It is a moving document of the bewildered agony and suffering of a truly lost generation disfigured by the war, with nothing left to believe in. Beckmann, the main figure of the play, comes back from the hell of war and prison camp only to discover that there simply is nobody and nothing to come home to. He feels expelled from the ranks of the living yet finds himself forced to live in a world that holds no meaning for him. The play ends with the desperate plea of a man overwhelmed by the chaos of physical and metaphysical ruin: "Will no one, nobody answer me?"

The senseless havoc, both physical and mental, wrought by war, the glaring contradiction between established values, once hallowed by tradition or authority, and the nightmarish reality of a world those values did not prevent from coming into existence—these are also the main themes of B.'s short stories. His sensitivity to human values enabled him to express the utter chaos and the poignant suffering of his time in artistic creations of powerful impact. An artfully perfected destruction of language—the reduction of language to the elementary level reminiscent of a first-grade primer and a fractured syntax—is complemented by the emotionally charged use of repetition and accumulation. Paradox and parody, together with the grotesque, are stylistic devices B. uses with devastating effectiveness.

B.'s implacable insight and the convincing style of his prose made him a most influential factor in the emotional climate of the immediate postwar years. An entire generation perceived in B. the authentic voice of their experience. He is, however, more than just a collective voice. His work can be considered the starting point of postwar West German literature, both formally and thematically. His artful technique, his original style, and his evocative poetic symbols exerted an intense influence on the younger generation of German writers. With B. the short story became the timely vehicle of creative expression in German fiction.

FURTHER WORKS: *Die Hundeblume* (1947); *An diesem Dienstag* (1947); *Das Gesamtwerk* (1949; *The Man Outside*, 1952 [except the verse]); *Die traurigen Geranien* (1962; *The Sad Geraniums*, 1972). FURTHER WORKS IN ENGLISH: *Selected Short Stories* (1964)

BIBLIOGRAPHY: Klarmann, A. D., "The Lost Voice of a New Germany," *GR*, 27 (1952): 108–23; Weimar, K. S., "No Entry, No Exit: A Study of B. with Some Notes on Sartre," *MLQ*, 17 (1956): 153–65; Mileck, J., "W. B.'s *Draußen vor der Tür*: A Young Poet's Struggle with Guilt and Despair," *Monatshefte*, 51 (1959): 328–36; Spaethling, R., "W. B.'s Quest for Human Freedom," *GL&L*, 14 (1960/1961): 188–94; Rühmkorf, P., *W. B.* (1961); Popper, H., "W. B.," in Natan, A., ed., *German Men of Letters* 3 (1964): 269–303; Wilson, A. L., "The Drowning Man: *Draußen vor der Tür*," *TSLL*, 10 (1968): 119–31; Nelson, D., "To Live or Not to Live: Notes on Archetypes and the Absurd in B.'s *Draußen vor der Tür*," *GQ* 48, 3 (1975): 343-54; Koepke, W., "German Writers after 1945: W. B.," *GSR* 2 (1979): 49-62; Padgett, J. O., "The Poet in War: Walt Whitman and W. B.," *Monatshefte* 72 (1980): 149-61; Keele, A. F., "'Through a (Dark) Glass Clearly': Magic Spectacles and the Motive of the Mimetic Mantic in Postwar German Literature from B. to Grass," *GR* 57, 2 (1982): 49-59; Stark, J. L., "W. B.'s 'Das Brot' and 'Die Küchenuhr': Love Among the Ruins," *JAISA* 1, 1 (1995): 93-101; Warkentin, E. J., *Unpublishable Works: W. B.'s Literary Production in Nazi Germany* (1997)

—FRIEDHELM RICKERT

BORDEWIJK, Ferdinand

Dutch novelist and short-story writer, b. 10 Oct. 1884, Amsterdam; d. 28 April 1965, The Hague

B. studied and practiced law, and also worked for a time as a teacher, but as his prolific literary output indicates, he devoted himself mainly to his writing. His novelistic career developed from a modernistic toward a more traditional style. His earliest publications of verse and prose aroused little interest, although the short stories blend such diverse influences as the New Factualism from Germany with Poe and with parapsychological traits.

B. did not hit his stride as a writer of fiction until the 1930s, when with his short novel *Blokken* (1931; blocs) he addressed the political mood of the day. The collectivism of an ideologically pure totalitarian state is shown to be inimical to the deepest human instincts. *Bint* (1934; Bint) uses the high school as the model of a fascistic state, run with ruthless severity by the title character who, as principal, uses a group of animal-like students to terrorize the rest. The portrayal of the characters is extremely hyperbolic, and the style is characterized by the use of short staccato sentences, eminently suited to the subject matter. In *Karakter* (1938; *Character*, 1966) the societal superego is personified by the protagonist's father, who tries to develop his son's personality by putting obstacles in his path, thereby triggering tragic conflicts between them. Here both the portrayal of the characters and the language are less extreme than in the earlier text, but the thematic preoccupation with the fate of the individual in the modern world is no less pronounced. B. also approached this topic from a cultural perspective in his novel *Apollyon* (1941; Apollyon), which deals with an encounter between a Dutchman and an American girl. Contrary to prevailing trends in European writing, she is portrayed as a paragon of moral strength and instinctual integrity, who ultimately rejects the haughty, rationalistic Dutchman.

In the following decades, B. continued to publish novels and short fiction in which the conflict between man and his world is explored in a variety of styles, settings, and situations. In 1954 his reputation was officially recognized with the award of the State Prize for Literature. In his later work, notably the novel *Tijding van ver* (1961; tidings from afar), the individual's existence is juxtaposed not only with society but also with the awareness of death.

B.'s artistic significance lies mainly in the linguistic creativity of the earlier works, but he continued to develop his cultural-critical theme to the very end of his literary career.

FURTHER WORKS: *Paddestoelen* (1910); *Fantastische vertellingen* (3 vols., 1919–24); *Knorrende beesten* (1933); *De laatste eer: grafreden* (1935); *Rood paleis* (1936); *De wingerdrank* (1937); *Sumbo n.v., spel van olie, dood en leven* (1938; with *Driehoek met den huisgenoot* and *De stier van Opland* in *Drie toneelstukken*, 1940); *De Korenharp* (2 vols., 1940, 1951); *Verbrande erven* (1944; under pseud. Émile Mandeau); *Eiken van Dodona* (1946);

Veuve Vesuvius (1946); *Bij gaslicht* (1947); *Noorderlicht* (1948); *Het Eiberschild* (1949); *Zwanenpolder* (1949); *Nachtelijk paardengetrappel* (1949); *Vertellingen van generzijds* (1950); *Studien in volksstructuur* (1951); *De doopvont* (1952); *Mevrouw en meneer Richebois* (1954); *Bloesemtak* (1955); *Onderweg naar de Beacons* (1955); *Halte Noordstad* (1956); *Tien verhalen* (1956); *Geachte confrère* (1956); *Idem* (1957); *De aktentas* (1958); *De zigeuners* (1959); *Centrum van stilte* (1960); *Lente* (1964); *Keizerrijk* (1965); *De Golbertons* (1965); *Paarlen avond* (1978)

BIBLIOGRAPHY: Meijer, R. P., *Literature of the Low Countries* (1978): 240–41 and passim

—EGBERT KRISPYN

BORGEN, Johan

Norwegian novelist, short-story writer, dramatist, journalist, and literary critic, b. 28 April 1902, Oslo; d. 16 Oct. 1979, Hvaler

Son of an attorney, B. was educated in private elementary and secondary schools. He began his writing career early as a reporter for *Dagbladet*, Oslo's leading newspaper, and in 1928 became a full-time columnist, a position he held for thirteen years. From 1925 to his death he published more than forty books, besides editing the literary magazine *Vinduet* for six years and working intermittently as a stage director and radio commentator. During the Nazi Occupation B. was confined in Grini Prison Camp near Oslo. On being released he joined the Resistance and was later forced to flee to neutral Sweden. B. traveled extensively in Europe and the Middle East, and lived for some months in London, Paris, Copenhagen, and California.

B. was sometimes a satirist and moralist, always a nonconformist and sensitive artist. Although he wrote in every genre, he excelled in the novel and short story. With all his versatility and experimentation in form and technique, he seldom abandoned his basic theme, first introduced in *Mot mørket* (1925; toward the darkness) and subsequently probed more deeply in *Mens vi venter* (1938; while we wait): Life is a persistent quest for self-identity and authenticity, a never-ending struggle for liberation from restraint and convention, both inward and outward. This theme reached its full development in B.'s major post-Occupation works. He was an archenemy of complacency, hypocrisy, repression, and every kind of pretense obstructing truth and freedom and keeping people from daring to be themselves.

Lillelord (1955; little lord), *De mørke kilder* (1956; the dark springs), and *Vi har ham nå* (1957; we have him now) comprise a masterful trilogy spanning the years 1912–45, with two world wars and Norway's Occupation. As settings shift among countries and events precipitate international tragedy, the novels offer a broad analysis of disintegration and disillusionment. This saga of Wilfred Sagen, a "little lord" of the bourgeoisie, traces the individual's efforts to come to terms with himself in circumstances uncongenial to his intellect and temperament.

In *Jeg* (1959; I), B.'s own favorite book, he again deals with the protagonist's psychological conflict as he wrestles with the problem of self-determination. The use of symbolism and somewhat formalized style lend concreteness and clarity to substance that in itself tends to be transitory. A highly introspective novel, *Den røde*

tåken (1967; the red mist), focuses on guilt and expiation. The theme is developed lyrically and allegorically.

B.'s subtle wit, intriguing plots, and empathic characterizations gained him a place among Norway's most important authors of the 20th c. He was honored by his government with several literary prizes.

FURTHER WORKS: *Betraktninger og anfektelser* (1932); *Når alt kommer til alt* (1934); *Kontorsjef Lie* (1936); *Seksti Mumle Gåsegg* (1936); *Barnesinn* (1937); *Høit var du elsket* (1937); *Andersene* (1940); *Ingen sommar* (1944); *Dager pa Grini* (1945); *Nordahl Grieg* (1945); *Kjærlighetsstien* (1946); *Akvariet* (1947); *Hvetebrødsdager* (1948); *Jenny og påfuglen* (1949); *Vikinger og eventyr* (1949); *Noveller om kjærlighet* (1952); *Natt og dag* (1954); *Innbilningens verden* (1960); *Noveller i utvalg 1936–1961* (1961); *Frigjøringsdag* (1963); *Blåtind* (1964); *Barndommens rike* (1965); *Nye noveller* (1965); *Ord gjennom år* (1966); *Bagateller* (1967); *Alltid på en søndag* (1968); *Traer alene i skogen* (1969); *Elsk meg bort* (1970); *Mitt hundeliv* (1971); *129 Mumle Gåsegg* (1971); *Min arm, min tarm* (1972); *Den store havfrue* (1973); *Eksempler* (1974); *Lykke til!* (1974); *I dette rom* (1975); *Notater fra hverdagen* (1975); *Noveller og annen kortprosa I–IV* (1977); *B. om bøker* (2 vols., 1977)

BIBLIOGRAPHY: Morris, W., on *Den røde tåken*, *BA*, 43 (1969), 121; Birn, R., "The Quest for Authenticity in Three Novels by J. B.," *Mosaic*, 4 (1970): 91–99; Brin, R., *J. B.* (1974); Brin, R., "Dream and Reality in J. B.'s Short Stories," *SS*, 46 (1974): 57–72

—AMANDA LANGEMO

BORGES, Jorge Luis

Argentine short-story writer, essayist, and poet, b. 24 Aug. 1899, Buenos Aires; d. 14 June 1986, Geneva, Switzerland

B. is one of the first Spanish-American writers of fiction to achieve an international reputation. His short stories, which are characterized by fantastic plots, metaphysical themes, and stylistic innovations, have influenced European, American, and other Spanish-American writers.

The fact that B.'s paternal grandmother was English explains his knowledge of the English language and his appreciation of literature in English. During World War I the Borges family lived in Geneva, where B. learned both French and German and read widely in the literatures of these languages. After the war the family spent approximately two years in Spain, where B. became associated with ULTRAISM, an avant-garde school of poetry inspired by EXPRESSIONISM and DADAISM. He returned to Buenos Aires in 1921 and, as the leader of Argentine ultraism, depicted life in the suburbs of his native city. A few years later he abandoned ultraism to concentrate on the essay and short fiction. The publication of his metaphysical fantasies in *Ficciones* (1944; *Ficciones*, 1962) and *El Aleph* (1949; *The Aleph, and Other Stories*, 1970) was to establish his reputation abroad. As a critic he wrote original interpretations of the Argentine classics and displayed a vast knowledge of European and American literature. And, at a time when most Argentine critics preferred realistic works treating national themes, B. extolled fantastic literature for its superior aesthetic qualities and stressed the need for greater universality. His interest in fantasy was shared by another well-known Argentine writer of fiction, Adolfo BIOY CASARES, with whom B. coauthored several collections of tales between 1942 and 1967.

In the mid-1950s B. was appointed Director of the National Library and Professor of English literature at the University of Buenos Aires. About this time he lost his sight due to a congenital defect that had afflicted several generations on his father's side of the family. During the 1960s, having achieved international fame, he was invited to the U.S. and Europe, and to other Latin American countries, where he was received by large, enthusiastic audiences.

El informe de Brodie (1970; *Dr. Brodie's Report*, 1972) is a collection of tales written in a direct, realistic vein reminiscent of the young Rudyard KIPLING, one of B.'s favorite authors. His most recent fictional endeavor, *El libro de arena* (1975; *The Book of Sand*, 1977), marks a return to fantastic themes, although the style of these pieces remains straightforward, like that of the previous collection. For the past two decades B. has also written poetry which, like his recent prose, reveals a simple, conversational vocabulary and syntax. Since the onset of his blindness he has shown a preference for classical meters because their rhythmic patterns are easier for him to commit to memory than blank verse. Some of his best poems from this period appear in *El hacedor* (1960; *Dreamtigers*, 1964) and *Elogio de la sombra* (1969; *In Praise of Darkness*, 1974).

B. is a sophisticated writer who views fiction not as an artistic representation of the real world, but rather as a poetic re-creation of the cultural labyrinths man has fabricated throughout history. He readily admits that his fictional universe stems from his varied and often esoteric readings in literature, philosophy, and theology, fields of human endeavor that, in his opinion, have analyzed and explained the world in fascinating but purely fictitious terms. His favorite authors, in addition to Kipling, include H. G. WELLS, G. K. CHESTERTON, Robert Louis Stevenson, Thomas De Quincey, and Walt Whitman; the philosophical theories of Berkeley and Schopenhauer have greatly influenced his writings; and the mysterious theological labyrinths of Gnosticism and the Cabala have reinforced many of his plots. As a result of these basic ingredients, his tales exude an aura of unreality that for him constitutes the very nature of art.

B. considers man's quest for truth utterly vain. Philosophy and theology represent "provisional" systems of thought destined to be discredited and replaced by others, history evolves as a product of the imagination tempered by time, and psychology is denigrated as fakery because individual behavior depends on phenomena far too complex to be understood. Thus, B. limits himself to the portrayal of faceless characters in archetypal situations that serve to conceptualize as well as to formalize his fictional world. His style reveals a brevity, compactness, and classical elegance seldom matched by his contemporaries.

Like many 20th-c. authors, B. depicts the absurdity of mortal man's search for meaning and transcendence in an infinite universe beyond his intellectual comprehension. The absurd is illustrated not only by the vain quest for truth but also by the artist's persistent, though futile, efforts to achieve aesthetic perfection. B. utilizes a symbolically evocative vocabulary and poetic devices such as the transferred epithet, oxymoron, and metonymy in order to disintegrate concrete reality and thrust his reader into an abstract, hallucinatory world fraught with irony and paradox. He frequently dons the mask of the bungling narrator, contradicting himself or frankly admitting that he does not know all the facts surrounding the events he is relating. Another of his techniques is to combine elements of

Jorge Luis Borges

fiction and the essay, often resorting to the use of the footnote in order to feign authenticity or to mock erudition. The result is the collapse of certainties and an ever-increasing awareness that beneath outward appearances there exists an uncharted realm of endless contradictions, the probing of which is a major facet of B.'s art.

B.'s principal themes include the metaphysical problems of time and human destiny; the fusion of reality and dream; the identity of the self; and the world as a labyrinth. Though universal, his tales are often firmly anchored in Argentine reality, as demonstrated by his poetic evocations of the Argentine setting and his fascination with the machismo cult. His frequent use of the mirror image serves to create a fictive, dreamlike reality and, on occasion, to dramatize the disunity of the personality. Other major elements of B.'s works are his reinterpretations of old myths to convey contemporary themes and his preoccupation with the creative process, which often results in a kind of self-mocking style.

Two of B.'s undisputed masterpieces that typify his celebrated fiction are "La muerte y la brújula" (1942; "Death and the Compass," 1962) and "El sur" (1953; "The South," 1962). A parody on reason, "La muerte y la brújula" portrays an excessively rational detective, Lönnrot, who finds himself trapped in a cerebral labyrinth of his own making while attempting to solve a series of crimes. Scharlach, the criminal, emerges not only as Lönnrot's antithetical double but also as a kind of diabolical deity who has been plotting Lönnrot's death from the beginning. "El sur" represents a masterful fusion of reality and dream. Juan Dahlmann, the protagonist, is a cultured librarian who subconsciously yearns for the primitive life of the mythical Argentine gaucho. He probably dies in a hospital during an operation, but moments before his demise he dreams of a journey to the South—a metaphor of the Argentine past—where he bravely faces death in a knife fight. The story's bipartite, reflecting-mirror structure derives from the parallels and contrasts between the drab reality of Dahlmann's life in Buenos Aires and the surreality of his romantic dream. And the idealized macho that Dahlmann ultimately becomes represents his alter ego or an inverted mirror image of his real self.

Other of B.'s masterpieces are "Tlön, Uqbar, Orbis Tertius" (1941; "Tlön, Uqbar, Orbis Tertius," 1962), which describes the intrusion on the real world of a fictional world founded on the principles of pantheistic idealism; "La Biblioteca de Babel" (1941; "The Library of Babel," 1962), in which a symmetrically structured library represents the universe as it is conceived by rational man and the library's illegible books man's basic ignorance; and "El Aleph" (1945; "The Aleph," 1967), which deals ingeniously with the aesthetic problem of creating an intuitive, simultaneous vision of the world in the lineal medium of language.

B.'s *Weltanschauung* has often been referred to as subversive because he mocks conventional modes of thinking, making his readers acutely aware that all doctrines are ephemeral creations of human reason and that concrete reality may consist only of mental perceptions. Although he depicts life as a labyrinth through which man wanders under the illusion of having organized and understood the chaotic, meaningless world, his unique oeuvre illustrates the triumph of art over the absurd human experience.

FURTHER WORKS: *Fervor de Buenos Aires* (1923); *Luna de enfrente* (1925); *El idioma de los argentinos* (1928); *Cuadernos de San Martín* (1929); *Evaristo Carriego* (1930); *Discusión* (1932); *Las Kenningar* (1933); *Historia universal de la infamia* (1935; *A Universal History of Infamy*, 1973); *Historia de la eternidad* (1936); *Seis problemas para don Isidro Parodi* (1942, with Adolfo Bioy Casares; *Six Problems for Don Isidro Parodi*, 1981); *Poemas* (1943); *Dos fantasías memorables* (1946, with A. B. C.); *Un modelo para la muerte* (1946, with A. B. C.); *Nueva refutación del tiempo* (1947); *Aspectos de la literatura gauchesca* (1950); *La muerte y la brújula* (1951); *Antiguas literaturas germánicas* (1951, with Delia Ingenieros); *Otras inquisiciones* (1952; *Other Inquisitions*, 1964); *Los orilleros: El paraíso de los creyentes* (1955, with A. B. C.); *Manual de zoología fantástica* (1957, with Margarita Guerrero); *Poemas (1923–1958)* (1958); *Libro del cielo y del infierno* (1960, with A. B. C.); *Macedonio Fernández* (1961); *Antología personal* (1961; *A Personal Anthology*, 1967); *Para las seis cuerdas* (1965); *Introducción a la literatura inglesa* (1965, with María Esther Vásquez); *Literaturas germánicas medievales* (1966, with M. E. V.); *Crónicas de Bustos Domecq* (1967, with A. B. C.;*Chronicles of Bustos Domecq*, 1976); *El libro de los seres imaginarios* (1967, with M. G.; *The Book of Imaginary Beings*, 1969); *Nueva antología personal* (1968); *El otro, el mismo* (1969); *El congreso* (1971; "The Congress," in *The Book of Sand*, 1977); *El oro de los tigres* (1972; *The Gold of the Tigers*, 1977); *B. on Writing* (1973); *Obras completas* (1974); *Prólogos* (1975); *La rosa profunda* (1975); *La moneda de hierro* (1976); *Androgué* (1977); *Asesinos de papel* (1977); *Historia de la noche* (1977); *La rosa de Paracelso* (1977); *Rosa y azul* (1977); *Tigres azules* (1977); *Obras completas en colaboración* (1979). FURTHER WORKS IN ENGLISH: *Labyrinths* (1962); *Selected Poems* (1973)

BIBLIOGRAPHY: Barrenechea, A. M., *La expresión de la irrealidad en la obra de J. L. B.* (1957); Jurado, A., *Genio y figura de J. L. B.* (1964); Barrenechea, A. M., *B. the Labyrinth Maker* (1965); Alazraki, J., *La prosa narrativa de J. L. B.* (1968; 2nd ed. with appendices, 1974); Murillo, L. A., *The Cyclical Night: Irony in James Joyce and J. L. B.* (1968); Sucre, G., *B. el poeta* (1968); Christ, R. J., *The Narrow Act: B.'s Art of Allusion* (1969); Wheelock, C., *The Mythmaker: A Study of Motif and Symbol in the Short Stories of J. L. B.* (1969); Stabb, M. S., *J. L. B.* (1970); Alazraki, J., *J. L. B.* (1971); Cohen, J. M., *J. L. B.* (1972); Garcilli, E., *Circles without Center* (1972); Gallagher, D. P., "J.L.B.," in *Modern Latin American Literature* (1973): 96–110; Stark, J. O., *The Literature of Exhaustion: B., Nabokov, and Barth* (1974); Shaw, D. L., *B.'s Ficciones* (1976); Sturrock, J., *Paper Tigers* (1977); Rodríguez Monegal, E., *J. L. B.: A Literary Biography* (1978); McMurray, G., *J. L. B.* (1980)

—GEORGE R. MCMURRAY

[B.'s] entire phantasmal world is expressed in highly original stories and essays which B. decorates with those themes and situations which universal philosophy, theology, and literature make available. And all three should be placed on the same level because all interest him for the imaginative possibilities they offer and their capacity for stirring the deepest feelings. His work does not contain the coherent evolution of metaphysical thought nor a doctrine which he adopts as the single and real key to the universe because B. is convinced that nothing in Man's destiny has any meaning. This incredulity incites him, nonetheless, to create a literature out of literature and philosophy in which the metaphysical discussion or the artistic problem constitutes the plot of the story. His literary creativity vitalizes what, a priori, would otherwise seem abstract, and he is capable of infusing drama and the throbbings of adventure into thoughts which in themselves lack narrative substance. [1957]

Ana María Barrenechea, *B. the Labyrinth Maker* (1965), p. 144

The work of J. L. B. is a species of international literary metaphor. He knowledgeably makes a transfer of inherited meanings from Spanish and English, French and German, and sums up a series of analogies, of confrontations, of appositions in other nations' literatures. His Argentinians act out Parisian dramas, his Central European Jews are wise in the ways of the Amazon, his Babylonians are fluent in the paradigms of Babel. Probably, withal, he is the most succinct writer of this century, and one of the most incisive as to conclusions, daring dryly to go beyond such a Mannerist master as James Joyce, who knew philology and felt legends, but eschewed meanings. Perhaps, though, his meaning is simply in the ritual tone of voice with which he suggests some eternal, unanswerable question.

Anthony Kerrigan, Introduction to *Ficciones* (1962), p. 9

The vision underlying B.'s works is that of a chaotic universe, formless and without natural laws, within which man wanders in search of his destiny. In this search, man imposes intellectual constructions designed to aid him in the search by ordering reality. But upon penetrating to the center of his own creation, man realizes the falsity of this construction, penetrates the meaning of existence, and is left with no recourse but to die, resigned to the implacable fact of the universe: its total pointlessness.

Frank Dauster, *HR*, 30 (1962), 148

Whether in prose or poetry, it is B.'s ultimate purpose to achieve not a mystical and irrational surrender to an inscrutable chaos, but, on the contrary, the clarity of perception that comes from reflection as well as the meticulous making of models. What B. offers us are poems and narratives that articulate the nature of our human situation. . . . He is a superb artist, who draws on life and books, on the sight of tigers and the moon, on the experience of poets and philosophers: "Few things have happened to me more worth remembering than Schopenhauer's thought or the music of England's words," he writes in the "Epilogue."

Victor Lange, Introduction to *Dreamtigers* (1964), pp. xxi–xxii

The Symbolists made their poetry self-symbolizing, but perhaps took the matter too seriously. This is not to say that they damaged their poetry; but their seriousness affected adversely some of those who followed, creating a number of diverging and short-lived "isms." They looked for God through poetry; they tried to be mythic in order to restructure the universe. But B., both as poet and as fiction-maker, knows that modern man cannot be mythic, not really, and that imagination only confirms idealism as the nearest substitute for a mythic view; for in order to be mythic, the mind must lack a structured rationality. Only man's reason can call into question the hierarchy of reality it has created. The conceptual fluidity of the mythmaker can exist only as a mentality that radically doubts the validity of its own constructs, or as one which consciously forays into fancy without expecting to transcend or fulminate the vast system of practical fictions that men live by. B. will not ride with Valéry on the seesaw of momentary subjective renewal followed by reentry into mundane reality; this smacks of psychedelic self-hypnosis, of religion, of escape. B. will not lose psychic control over the game; he will remain the chess player as well as the pawn.

Carter Wheelock, *The Mythmaker: A Study of Motif and Symbol in the Short Stories of J. L. B.* (1969), p. 17

André Maurois has written some terse pages on the greatness of the art of J. L. B., and he has said of his

vast erudition: "B. has read everything, and especially what nobody reads any more: the Cabalists, the Alexandrine Greeks, medieval philosophers." John Barth has referred to B. as one of "the old masters of twentieth-century fiction." The sophisticated reader has surely stumbled upon B.'s name in the most heterogeneous texts, in contexts that appear to have very little to do with his work. As with Joyce, Kafka, or Faulkner, the name of B. has become an accepted concept; his creations have generated a dimension that we designate "Borgesian." In the same way that much of contemporary Hispanic literature cannot be explained in its totality without keeping B. in mind, it is not an exaggeration to say that the map of twentieth-century fiction would be incomplete without his name.

Jaime Alazraki, *J. L. B.* (1971), p. 3

B. takes pains always to identify himself first as a reader, and the implication is that it is his reading which has caused his writing. I think this is true. But what B. means by being a reader is something we are losing fast. We no longer live in books. From the earliest incursions into books in his father's library, reading has been to B. an intense and separate life, a displacement in time, a shift to other dimensions, to a point where for him the borders between imagination and reality fuzz over and actually cease to exist.

I think that B., moving among languages, has always seen language itself as a separate plane of existence, on which words can manipulate everything, even the one who uses them; but at the same time, he is conscious always that language is paradox itself. Words like "forever" mock the one who utters them. The image that recurs in B.'s writings so often—that at certain points, one man is all men, that in reading Shakespeare we become Shakespeare—crops up because it has so often cropped up to B. in his reading. He takes in language in all forms—conversation and prayer, algebra and the tango, puzzles, maps, runes, the secret histories in objects, translation and mistranslation. He has even succeeded in making scholarship a device of the imagination.

Alastair Reid, *TriQuarterly*, No. 25 (1972), pp. 100–101

B.'s stories, in the end, are not only coolly lucid cerebral games but often highly affective, poetic expressions of the fragility of the world and of man. Again, that fragility is not a desperate one. It has a certain splendour. It is a measure of the odds against man and a measure therefore of his spirit. That spirit, which always reasserts itself in B.'s work, is perhaps best reflected in his poetry, particularly in those deeply personal, later poems such as the "Poema de los dones" or "Elogio de la sombra," where against all *personal* odds, in the face of ageing and of mounting blindness, in the face therefore of all that has dramatized the fragility of man for B. personally, a love of life, and a dogged, sensitive hope remain undestroyed.

They remain undestroyed in particular because they are relentlessly sustained by B.'s irrepressible sense of humour.

D. P. Gallagher, "J. L. B.," *Modern Latin American Literature* (1973), p. 121

Stories as rigorous and theoretically inclined as B.'s stand quite apart from the tradition of short-story writing in English. As exemplary narratives they are all plot and no psychology, and it is for the dissection of the psyche that most English readers suppose that the short story, with its strong unities of time and action, was invented. But B.'s fictions are "think-pieces," they are stories about ideas instead of people. He is, we shall see, absolutely a Classicist in literature, and he knows very well that his view of narrative is that of Aristotle, one of whose foremost precepts was that the poet should bring in character for the sake of the action, rather than the other way round. We are predisposed to the opposite view, that action is determined by character and what happens in a story by the sort of people involved in that story. This is essentialism: we conclude that what people do is the result of what they are. As a writer of fiction—and I say nothing of his opinions as a man—B. is existentialist: what his "characters" are is the result of what they do. They are no more and no less than the sum of their actions. There is no incentive to try and "understand" them because they are, patently, functions of the narrative in which they play a part. They are merely the actors without whose participation there could be no play.

John Sturrock, *Paper Tigers: The Ideal Fictions of J. L. B.* (1977), p. 3

BOROWSKI, Tadeusz

Polish short-story writer, poet, and essayist, b. 12 Nov. 1922, Zhitomir, U.S.S.R.; d. 3 July 1951, Warsaw

During his brief life B. experienced all the horrors of modern European history. As a young child he saw his parents disappear into the Soviet labor-camp system. The family was reunited in Poland in 1934; five years later Poland was invaded and B. soon moved into the literary-intellectual underground. His first literary efforts were distributed clandestinely at great risk. Arrested by the Germans in 1943, B. was interned first in Auschwitz, then in Dachau. He returned to Poland in 1946 as a fervent supporter of the Communist cause. He ended by taking his own life by gas, just a few years after receiving wide acclaim as a writer.

B.'s clandestine (and hence anonymous) debut was as the author of a volume of densely metaphoric poetry expressing, as was common at the time, an apocalyptic vision: *Gdziekolwiek ziemia* (1942; wherever the earth). He is best known, however, for his horrifying stories of the concentration-camp universe, collected in *Pożegnanie z Marią* (1948; farewell to Maria), and his portraits of the postwar world, *Kamienny świat* (1948; stone world). B.'s narrative strategy in the majority of his stories is to deny both himself and the reader the luxury of rhetorical condemnation of the

evils of Nazism. He expressed his outrage by concentrating upon the appalling specter of a moral degeneracy that engulfs both victims and torturers alike. He deliberately assumed the persona of a rather brazen, hardened inmate who had firmly adopted the code of a calculated self-interest geared to individual survival. In "Proszę państwa do gazu" (1948; "This Way for the Gas, Ladies and Gentlemen," 1967), for example, he describes the following scene, as it were, *en passant*: A terrified young woman, desperately hoping to be selected for slave labor rather than death, is running away from her frightened little child on the Auschwitz arrival platform. We might expect to see her stopped by the sadistic SS guards, but B.'s description challenges our eagerness to find relief in the automatic categorization of Nazis as the sole repository of evil. Reprisal comes swiftly to the woman, but it is dealt out by a Russian camp inmate who brutally hurls both the woman and child into a truck headed for the gas chambers. It is left for the SS guard merely to commend this way of handling "degenerate mothers."

B.'s later writings were marred aesthetically by a propagandistic harshness in defense of his new world view, but his concentration-camp stories mark him as one of the very few writers who have devised an ethically and aesthetically valid mode of speaking about the unspeakable.

FURTHER WORKS: *Imiona nurtu* (1945); *Byliśmy w Oświęcimiu* (1946, with K. Olszewski and J. Siedlecki); *Pewien żolnierz* (1947); *Czerwony maj* (1953); *Proza z lat 1948–1951* (1954). FURTHER WORKS IN ENGLISH: *This Way for the Gas, Ladies and Gentlemen* (1967)

BIBLIOGRAPHY: Kott, J., Introduction to *This Way for the Gas, Ladies and Gentlemen* (1976): 11–26; Milosz, C., "Beta, the Disappointed Lover," *The Captive Mind* (1953): 111–34; Olschowsky, H., "Reise an die Grenzen einer Moral: T. B.'s Auseinandersetzung mit Auschwitz als einem Modell des faschistischen Systems," *ZS*, 16 (1971): 615–21

—MADELINE G. LEVINE

BOTSWANA LITERATURE

The country formerly known as Bechuanaland Protectorate and bordered by South Africa to the south, Namibia on the west and Zimbabwe to the north is now the Republic of Botswana. It gained its independence from Britain in 1966 and has maintained an unbroken line of democratic governance since that time. Its first President was Sir Seretse Khama who passed away in 1980 and was succeeded by Sir Ketumile Masire who retired in 1998. Sir Ketumile Masire was succeeded by Mr Festus Gontebanye Mogae.

Besides good governance Botswana has earned the reputation of a sound economic management having emerged in 1997 as the fastest growing economy in the world. The motor industry has replaced beef export as the second biggest export after minerals. Starting from a poor base the economy picked up rapidly following the discovery of diamonds in 1967. The biggest problem facing the country is that of bringing the country's wealth to the vast majority of Botswana whose access to the main levers of economic empowerment remains problematic due to lack of suitable employment and relevant skills.

While the older generation of writers dwelt on themes common to most African writers such as the problems of identity, cultural conflicts, and the coming of independence, the younger generation of writers has tended to dwell on a literature with a social conscience. They write about the unemployed, the homeless, exploitation of one kind or another, and the usual "boy meets girl" story that is often informed by the marauding pandemic of AIDS. There is a strong awareness among writers that one of their moral obligations is to make their readers aware of AIDS and its tragic consequences. To the older generation of writers belong Raditladi, Seboni (Senior), Morulaganyi Kgasa (the lexicographer), Molema, and Molefe. Then come the younger writers who include Barolong Seboni, Albert Malikongwa, Kgomotso Mogapi, Manthsetsa Marope, M. Pheko, G. Baruti, Andrew Sesinyi, Cedric Thobega, G. Modise (dates n.a.). The expatriate element was brought in by Carolyn Slaughter, Norman Rush, Naomi Mitchison, and Isaac Schapera (dates n.a.). Bessie HEAD stands in a class of her own and would best be handled as a separate entry. She has become an icon in academe, and conference after conference is devoted to her.

Just as the economic skyline of Botswana has changed beyond recognition so has its literature. The devotion to literature is a joy to watch. Works are being tried in both English and the indigenous languages. The credit for this transformation goes to a number of organizations. The University of Botswana has built an impressive Travelling Theatre. The Department of English course in Drama has a group called UBE 423 whose improvisations have taken it to renowned theaters in South Africa. The Travelling Theatre has been all over Botswana and beyond into Namibia and Zimbabwe. Then there is Ngwao Botswa, which is the Setswana counterpart to the Travelling Theatre. Outside the University many theater groups have sprung up, of which Maitisong at Maru a Pula School is the best known. The University's Writers Workshop continues to flourish.

Above all, the writers of Botswana who now flock to readings of all kinds have gathered themselves into a lively body called the Writers' Association of Botswana (WABO). The future looks bright.

—FELIX MNTHALI

BOUDJEDRA, Rachid

Algerian novelist, screenwriter, and poet (writing in French and Arabic) b. 5 Sept. 1941, Aïn Beida

One of the few truly bilingual writers of the Maghreb, B. is the leading novelist of post-independence Algeria. B. is the author of thirteen novels and several volumes of poetry and plays. He has also written numerous screenplays for Algerian films as well as essays on Algerian and French culture and society. The recipient of many literary prizes, B.'s work has been translated into a dozen languages. B. is perhaps best known for his first novel, *La répudiation* (1969; *The Repudiation*, 1995), and for the screenplays to Mohamed Lakhdar-Hamina's *Chronique des années de braise* (chronicle of the years of embers), golden medal award winner of the 1975 Cannes Film Festival, and Ahmed Rachedi's *Ali au pays des mirages* (Ali in the country of mirages), winner of the Carthage and Moscow film festivals of 1980 and 1981. Although B.'s first six novels were written in French, he decided, in 1981, to write exclusively in Arabic. He has subsequently assisted Antoine Moussali (dates n.a.) in translating his works into French.

B. was one of the few Algerian writers of his generation to receive a bilingual education. Although he grew up near Constantine, Algeria, B. studied in Tunis, where Arabic continued to be a language of instruction. At the age of sixteen, he became a freedom fighter for the National Liberation Front during the Algerian revolution. After independence, B. studied philosophy in Paris and completed a thesis on the work of Louis-Ferdinand Céline, an author who has greatly influenced his own work. From 1966 to 1972 he taught philosophy in Algeria, France, and Morocco. He has since resided in Algeria, where he has been an adviser to the minister of information and culture, and taught at the Institute of Political Science in Algiers. B. is a militant atheist and Marxist.

B. published his first work, *Pour ne plus rêver* (1965; to no longer dream), in Algeria. Although dreams can liberate us, writes B., reality must be transformed. Marked by a revolutionary mystique and violence, these poems are clearly the work of a twenty-year-old who fought for the independence of his country. Nevertheless, for B., the liberation of a country does not necessarily imply the liberation of its people. Algerian women remain victims of traditional society. In "La mariée" (the bride) B. boldly depicts the wedding night of an Algerian bride as a sanctioned ritual of rape. This poem set the tone for B.'s successive works, all of which denounce the condition of traditional Algerian women.

Published in Paris, *La répudiation* established B. as the writer of a new literary generation. The first novel of postrevolutionary Algeria, *La répudiation* denounces a corrupt and lascivious society where sociopolitical and cultural abuses are legitimatized by religious practices and cultural traditions. Although B. focuses his attack on the feudal structure of the traditional family, he also faults the Algerian patriarchs for acquiescing to 130 years of colonialism and for aborting the revolution. Written in a brutal, visceral, and syncopated style, where the boundaries between the real, the delirious, and the oneiric are erased by a narrative voice seeking to exorcize the hold of the past through the subversion of sexual taboos, *La répudiation* is one of the most original texts of Maghrebian literature.

The historic past of Algeria, which is already present in *La répudiation*, becomes even more important in *L'insolation* (1972; insolation), where B. continues to examine the violence that underlies contemporary Algerian society. In *Topographie idéale pour une agression caractérisée* (1975; the ideal topography for a downright attack), the Paris metro becomes the ultimate site of racist aggression, whereas in *Le vainqueur de coupe* (1981; the winner of the cup) a French soccer stadium turns into the political arena of the Algerian War. Based on actual historical events, these novels examine acts of violence that are the direct result of the French-Algerian past.

In *Les 1001 années de la nostalgie* (1979; the 1001 years of nostalgia) and *Ma'rakat al-zuqāq* (1986; *La prise de Gibraltar*, 1987; the conquest of Gibraltar) B. juxtaposes episodes of the legendary Arab past with those of contemporary Algerian history. In rewriting history as a fictional narrative, B. seeks to release the hold of the past on the collective identity of a people. Writing becomes a form of liberation from both historical traumas and myths. In *Al-tafakkuk* (1981; *Le démantèlement*, 1982; the bringing down) a young woman born at the eve of the Algerian revolution deconstructs history as she engages in dialogue with a martyr of the revolution. (Beginning with *Le démantèlement*, B. published first in Arabic, then in French.)

The exorcism of the past is of a more personal vein in such novels as *Al marth* (1984; *La macération*, 1985; the maceration) and *Layliyyāt imra'a arik*—(1985; *La pluie*, 1987; the rain). In *La pluie* B. adopts the voice of an Algerian woman to write about the taboos of contemporary society. *Fawdāal-ashyā* (1990; *Le désordre des choses*, 1991; the disorder of things) centers on three main characters who represent different facets of Algerian society and history: a communist *pied noir* (French Algerian) guillotined during the Algerian War, an Algerian youth brutally torturned during the October 1988 uprisings, and the narrator's mother, falsely accused of adultery. As in *La répudiation*, the personal and the political converge in the mother figure, whose confinement and suffocation becomes the traumatic center of the novel.

B.'s most critical text is *FIS de la haine* (1992; FIS/Sons of Hatred), a vehement pamphlet against the Islamic Salvation Front (FIS), which has made him a prime target for fundamentalist death threats. The novel *Timimoun* (1994; *Timimoun*, 1994) is a love story set in the middle of the desert, with the terrorism of the early 1990s as the backdrop. The horrors of civil war are also at the heart of B.'s novel *La vie á l'endroit* (1997; Life on the Right Side). In *Lettres algériennes* (1995; Algerian Letters) B. writes about his relationship to France and Algeria in a lucid but critical manner.

B. brings a rich and original perspective to Maghrebian literature. He has always affirmed that writing must be rooted in the local and the particular, and that a writer can only address the problems of his society from within. Nevertheless, as an atheist and a Marxist, he maintains a dissident attitude with respect to the cultural traditions and political structures that paralyze his country. Perfectly bilingual, B. moves comfortably back and forth between the "Orient" and the West, between Islam, and psychoanalysis, between eroticism and mysticism, between literary modernity and the golden age of Arab literature.

FURTHER WORKS: *Naissance du cinéma algérien* (1971); *La vie quotidienne en Algérie* (1971); *Journal palestinien* (1972); *L'escargot entêté* (1977); *Likah* (1983; *Greffe*, 1984); *Mines de rien* (1995); *Peindre l'Orient* (1996)

BIBLIOGRAPHY: Bouraoui, H., "Politique et poétique dans l'univers de. B.," *PFr*, 14 (1977): 11–29; Déjeux, J., *Littérature maghrébine de langue française*, rev. ed. (1980): 381–404; Harrow, K., "Metaphors for Revolution: Blood and Schizophrenia in B.'s Early Novels," *PFr*, 20 (1980): 5–19; Bensmain, A., *Crise du sujet, crise de l'identité. Une lecture psychanalytique de R. B.* (1984); Bonn, C., *Le roman algérien de langue française* (1985): 237–79; Gafaïti, H., *B. ou la passion de la modernité* (1987); Gafaïti, H., "R. B.: The Bard of Modernity," *RAL*, 23, 2 (1992): 89–102

—DANIELLE MARX-SCOURAS

BOUTENS, Pieter Cornelis

Dutch poet, b. 20 Feb. 1870, Middelburg; d. 14 March 1943, The Hague

B. was sickly and studious as a child. Later, while in secondary school, he was exposed to inspired teaching of the classics, leading to a lifelong love affair with ancient Greek literature. As a university student in Utrecht he discovered the modern Dutch poetry of the "Movement of the Eighties." Its chief exponents—Herman Gorter (1864–1927), Willem Kloos (1859–1938), and Albert VERWEY—had launched a literary iconoclasm whose echoes reverberated for

generations. Their spokesman, Lodewijk van DEYSSEL, became B.'s friend and mentor and wrote a glowing preface to B.'s first volume of poetry, *Verzen* (1898; poems), comparing him to Verlaine and Heine. After a stint as a teacher in a preparatory school, B. settled down in The Hague as a private tutor, scholar-poet, and somewhat aloof sophisticate. During the next four decades of steady lyric production, his reputation grew among a Dutch public that was in awe of his virtuosity and, during much of the 1920s and 1930s, looked upon him as the poet laureate of the Netherlands. A champion of the supremacy of art, B. demanded a commensurate material security for the artist. He became an effective fund raiser for fellow poets and writers. In curious contrast, his poetry was not marked by a social consciousness, but rather was firmly rooted in the individualism of the 80 Movement.

The sensuous, impressionistic evocation of nature predominates in B.'s early work. Then, in *Praeludien* (1902; preludes) and the brilliant lyrics of *Stemmen* (1907; voices), he emerged as a SYMBOLIST with a mature voice of his own. Technically this verse is well-nigh perfect. B. is always in total control of his medium and a master of form. The length and rhythm of his lines vary freely, but he adheres strictly to a complex stanza pattern that serves his concise thought processes well. The effect is that of soaring feeling and contemplative thought. He delights in neologisms and the choice of uncommon or archaic-sounding vocabulary. *Stemmen* suggests affinities with Keats's sensuousness, but it is more closely akin to the poems of Shelley in its symbolic use of nature. In the lyric "Morgen nachtegaal" (1907; "Morning Nightingale," 1936), the poet listens to a nightingale whose song is splendidly conjured up in a deluge of intricate synesthetic images symbolic of joy and sorrow. Outstanding among the simpler nature lyrics is "Liefdes uur" (1907; "Love's Hour," 1936), beautifully translated by H. J. C. Grierson. *Carmina* (1912; Latin: songs) reflects an increasingly remote aestheticism. Prompted by Platonic metaphysics B. conceives of an earthbound existence as man's deepest joy, since its confinement makes him yearn for a return to divine perfection.

Attesting to his eclectic literary taste are his impressive translations from Homer, Aeschylus, Sophocles, Sappho, Plato, Goethe, Omar Khayyam, Novalis (1772–1801), and Dante Gabriel Rossetti (1828–1882). Drawn to themes of death and old age, B. moved increasingly from spontaneous to cerebral verse. Even though poems of gemlike beauty are numerous in later collections, B. often obscured his innermost feelings by enigmatic phrasing that perplexes the uninitiated and makes translation difficult. Among B.'s poems that have retained their popularity is "Beatrijs" (1908; Beatrijs), an exquisite modern adaptation in blank verse of the medieval poem of the same name.

FURTHER WORKS: *Vergeten liedjes* (1909); *Lentemaan* (1916); *Liederen van Isoude* (1919); *Sonnetten* (1920); *Zomerwolken* (1922); *Gedichten* (1930); *Bezonnen verzen* (1931); *100 hollandsche kwatrijnen* (1932); *Tusschenspelen* (1942); *Verzamelde werken* (7 vols., 1943–54)

BIBLIOGRAPHY: Grierson, H. J. C., *Two Dutch Poets* (1936): 29–46; Barnouw, A. J., *Coming After* (1948): 205–6; Weevers, T., *Poetry of the Netherlands in Its European Context, 1170–1930* (1960): 180–83; Meijer, R. P., *Literature of the Low Countries* (1971): 268–70

—PETER BRUNING

BOWEN, Elizabeth

Anglo-Irish novelist, short-story writer, essayist, and critic, b. 7 June 1899, Dublin; d. 27 Feb. 1973, London

Product of the Anglo-Irish landed gentry, orphaned at an early age, B. lived in Dublin and in Kildorrery, County Cork, during her girlhood, then in London, Italy, and France, returning alternately to "Bowen's Court," the family estate in Ireland, or to Regent's Park, London, where she was prominent in the post-Bloomsbury circle. B.'s first short stories were published in 1923, the same year she married Alan Cameron, British educator and broadcasting executive (d. 1952). Besides ten novels and seven volumes of short stories she wrote travel impressions, a family history, memoirs, and critical essays. B. served as an air raid warden in World War II and with the British Ministry of Information, while reviewing books for *The Tatler*. After the war she lectured at British, Continental, and American universities. A member of the Irish Academy of Letters (1937), B. was also on the Queen's Birthday Honors List as a Companion of the British Empire (1948). She received honorary doctorates from Trinity College, Dublin (1949), and Oxford University (1956). Her last novel, *Eva Trout* (1968), won the James Tait Black Prize.

Central to B.'s fiction is the Jamesian theme of innocence and experience–the dictates of the heart in conflict with the dictates of society. In examining deluded sensibility, B. balances between aloof irony and warm compassion. However precious the dream or poignant the awakening of the Bowenesque heroine, she must come to terms with life. "It is not only our fate," the novelist asserts, "but our business to lose innocence; and once we have lost that, it is futile to attempt a picnic in Eden." Prominent in this drama of lost illusions is B.'s "psychological landscape," in which natural settings and interiors, exquisitely delineated, become the hallucinatory counterpart of life's absurdities.

B. won almost instant recognition with short stories reminiscent of Henry JAMES, Anton CHEKHOV, and Katherine MANSFIELD. The urbane intellectuality of London's West End and the lyrical sensitivity of County Cork are joined in *Encounters* (1923). B.'s early novels, though impressionistic rather than developmental, reveal her efforts at complex characterization and symbolic form. *The Hotel* (1927) depicts emotional squalor at a resort on the Riviera with a British clientele at the moment that the heroine's romantic impulses are subtly checked by a worldly and selfish older woman. In *The Last September* (1929), B.'s second novel, the precarious mood of Ireland during "the Troubles" (the struggle for independence from England) pronounces its doom upon a premature love affair between a daughter of the Anglo-Irish gentry and a garrisoned English officer. *Friends and Relations* (1931), at once a tragicomedy and a social satire, confronts public values with private ones as two illicit lovers, habituated to conventional marriages, renounce each other with a distinct sense of relief. It was in 1932, however, that B. came of age as a novelist with *To the North*, in which symbolic complexity is enhanced by relentlessly paced scenes. Sensations of weather, light, speed, and temperature record the fall from innocence and the self-destruction of B.'s "angelic but astigmatic" heroine.

In *The House in Paris* (1935), the first of B.'s three major novels, the gloomy setting is used to intensify the mystery and dread surrounding a young wife's dilemma: she is urged by her knowing husband to adopt her illegitimate son by a former lover. *The Death of the Heart* (1938), a richly developed social satire and

Elizabeth Bowen

B.'s most memorable collection of worldly and unworldly portraits, apprentices a mercilessly frank and observant teenage heroine, Portia Quayne, to the world, the flesh, and the devil. Acknowledged widely as a superlative fictional achievement, *The Death of the Heart* is squarely in the Jamesian tradition and a link between Virginia WOOLF and Iris MURDOCH. *The Heart of the Day* (1949), an unconventional war novel, departs radically from B.'s usual themes and settings. Blitzkrieged London is transformed into a theater of deranged perceptions: mutely, the violence of war surfaces in a woman's forced choice between her lover, turned Nazi spy, and a sexually predatory British agent.

B.'s eighth novel, *A World of Love* (1955), belongs to her later phase. In a series of dreamlike episodes it mirrors the effect of resurrected love letters on the lives of three women on a decaying Irish farm during an unprecedented heat wave. Ardently nostalgic in tone, deliberately fragmented and impressionistic, this novel breaks with B.'s previous insistence on a "nonpoetic" technique spelled out in "Notes on Writing a Novel" (1946). Similarly oblique, *The Little Girls* (1964) is a wistful comedy of unearthed secrets in the lives of three former schoolmates, now adults, who attempt to reconcile the present with the past. *Eva Trout* (1968), B.'s last completed novel, is her most intricately symbolic embodiment of innocence lost and innocence redeemed. Money, her father's homosexuality, deadened feelings, the fantasy world of the mass media, and a general lack of communication—these all converge on the protagonist, who gropes through to self-understanding before she dies at the hands of her adopted son.

Astute, patrician, technically fastidious, B. unites rare critical gifts with a poetic sensitivity that resists labels. Her aloof ironies, laced with compassion, testify to the contemporary breakdown in faith. But they may also be read as the transposed autobiography of an orthodox Christian sensibility. If indeed the latter, B.'s social realism must be reinterpreted as essentially mythic and allegorical, her characters not so much the creatures of their own romantic wills as children of an Infinite Will. Criticism has just begun to reckon with B.'s pervasive duality.

FURTHER WORKS: *Ann Lee's and Other Stories* (1926); *Joining Charles* (1929); *The Cat Jumps* (1934); *Look at All Those Roses* (1941); *Seven Winters* (1942); *Bowen's Court* (1942); *English Novelists* (1942); *The Demon Lover* (1945; Amer., *Ivy Gripped the Steps*, 1948); *Anthony Trollope: A New Judgment* (1946); *Collected Impressions* (1950; Amer., *The Shelbourne Hotel*, 1951); *Stories by E. B.* (1959); *A Time in Rome* (1960); *After-thought* (1962; Amer., *Seven Winters: Memories of Childhood and Afterthoughts: Pieces on Writing*, 1962); *A Day in the Dark* (1965); *The Good Tiger* (1965); *Pictures and Conversations* (1975); *The Collected Stories* (1981)

BIBLIOGRAPHY: Brooke, J., *E. B.* (1952); O'Faolain, S., *The Vanishing Hero* (1956): 146–67; Heath, W. W., *E. B.: An Introduction to Her Novels* (1961); Austin, A. E., *E. B.* (1971); Coles, R., *Irony in the Mind's Life* (1974); Blodgett, H., *Patterns of Reality: E. B.'s Novels* (1975); Kenney, E. J., *E. B.* (1975); Glendinning, V., *E. B.* (1978)

—JOHN G. HANNA

BOWLES, Jane Auer

American dramatist and novelist, b. 22 Feb. 1917, New York City; d. 4 May 1993, Malaga, Spain

Born into a middle-class Jewish family with German-Hungarian ancestry, B. spent her childhood and youth in New York City and Woodmere, Long Island. From 1932 to 1934 she stayed at a sanatorium in Lysin, Switzerland, where she was treated for a tubercular ailment affecting her knee. There she read and perfected French, which she already had been studying. In 1938 B. married Paul BOWLES, known at the time primarily as a composer, and the two honeymooned in Latin America and Paris.

B.'s first novel, *Two Serious Ladies,* was completed in 1941 and published in 1943. Acknowledged as one of her major achievements, *Two Serious Ladies* is a kind of female picaresque or quest novel featuring Miss Goering and Mrs. Copperfield, both of whom probe their desires for men and women as they try to find spaces for themselves in a world marked by unpredictable, sometimes absurd twists and turns.

Of the handful of stories B. wrote during the 1940s, "Camp Cataract" stands out as one of the most intriguing. The story, which B. herself thought her best, explores the relationship between two sisters, Sadie and Harriet, who are separated when Harriet goes off to a nature camp. The narrative, which takes on a surreal character, chronicles Sadie's frustrated attempts to regain connection with her sister.

Relations between mothers and daughters are the central focus in B.'s one completed play, *In the Summer House* (1953). A town on the Pacific coast of Southern California, with a decidedly Mexican flavor, is the backdrop for a drama revealing the love-hate relationship between Gertrude Eastman Cuevas and her daughter Molly. Each painfully seeks to get what she needs from the other while at the same time pursuing attachments to men. What gives the play its vitality, as much as its thematic concerns, is its dazzling dialogue and outrageous action. B.'s play might be considered alongside plays of other women playwrights of the period, particularly those of Dorothy Parker (1893-1967) and Lillian HELLMAN. B's dramatic work also has much affinity with that of Tennessee WILLIAMS, who much admired and supported her work, calling *In the Summer House* "not only the most original play I have ever read, I think it is also the oddest and the funniest and one of the most touching."

By the time of the play's Broadway production in 1953-54, under the direction of Jose Quintero, B. had already been living for four or five years in Tangier, Morocco, with her husband, whose first novel *The Sheltering Sky* was widely acclaimed upon its publication in 1949. During the 1950s and up until the time of her death in Malaga, B. was able to write very little. No doubt the stroke she suffered in 1957 severely affected her ability to work. Morocco, it seems, while the site of her infatuation with the legendary Cherifa, did not provide literary nourishment as it did for her husband. She was to write only a couple of stories in Morocco.

B. poured considerable amounts of energy into her correspondence, which has been collected and edited by Millicent Dillon under the title *Out in the World* (1985). This correspondence should be considered as part of her achievement along with her unfinished work, particularly a novel she tentatively entitled *Out in the World*.

B. has always had her fervent fans. Though she did not write a great deal during her lifetime, what she wrote was highly original and distinctive. B.'s style is marked by a wild wit, zany imagination, unexpected narrative leaps, often bizarre dialogue, and quirky characters. Her work can be placed within the context of other American women writers of the 1940s, such as Jean Stafford (1915-1979) and Dawn Powell (dates n.a.). With her bold exploration of homosexual desire and her use of a style that might be characterized as postmodern, B. was certainly ahead of her times.

FURTHER WORKS: *Plain Pleasures* (1966); *Feminine Wiles* (1976); *My Sister's Hand in Mine: The Collected Works of J. B.* (1978); *The Portable J. and Paul Bowles* (1994)

BIBLIOGRAPHY: Dillon, M., *A Little Original Sin: The Life and Work of J. B.* (1981); Dillon, M., "J. B.: Experiment as Character," in Friedman, E. G., and M. Fuchs, eds., *Breaking the Sequence: Women's Experimental Fiction* (1989): 140-47; Lakritz, A. M., "J. B.'s Other World," in Doan, L., ed., *Old Maids to Radical Spinsters: Unmarried Women in the Twentieth-Century Novel* (1991): 213-34; Roditi, E., "The Fiction of J. B. as a Form of Self-Exorcism," *RCF*, 12, 2 (1992): 182-94; Gentile, K. J., "'The Dreaded Voyage into the World': J. B. and Her Serious Ladies," *SAF*, 22, 1 (1994): 47-60; Hibbard, A., "*Out in the World*: Reconstructing J. B.'s Unfinished Novel," *LCUT*, 15, 2 (1994): 121-69; Skerl, J., ed., *A Tawdry Place of Salvation: The Art of J. B.* (1997)

—ALLEN HIBBARD

BOWLES, Paul

American short-story writer, novelist, poet, translator, and essayist, b. 30 Dec. 1910, New York City

B. spent a typical childhood in the suburbs of New York City and after graduating from high school went to art school for a year and to the University of Virginia for a term (because Poe had been there). In 1929 he left abruptly for Paris, and ever since he has been wandering around the world. In his formative stage B. was steeped in MODERNISM, contributing poems to the journal *transition*, corresponding with Gertrude STEIN, and frequenting her home in Paris from 1931 on, while also keeping in touch with Christopher ISHERWOOD in Berlin. A dual talent, he then took up music, associating with Aaron Copland and Virgil Thomson, and proved his mettle as a composer before coming into his own as a writer of fiction in the late 1940s. Decisive for his development was his increasing immersion in primitive cultures and landscapes. Morocco, which became his headquarters after World War II, provides the symbolically enhanced background for the theme of quest and perdition pervading his major writing.

As early as his first novel, *The Sheltering Sky* (1949), a fatal clash between the civilized and the primitive is enacted in the story of the destruction of an American couple in the Sahara, where they had hoped to redefine their relationship; the end of the road is madness and death. The affinity with existential absurdism, particularly with CAMUS's *The Stranger*, is even clearer in B.'s second novel, *Let It Come Down* (1952). Its American protagonist, lured to Tangier in search of adventure and of a cohesive identity, ends up killing an Arab accidentally. In *The Spider's House* (1955) the American protagonists are not destroyed by the North African environment, but their betrayal of a sympathetically portrayed Arab reveals a self-defeating attitude; the author's vision is too complex, however, to be identified either with the East or with the West, let alone to afford a clear-cut political stand regarding the uprisings against the French.

While B.'s last novel, *Up above the World* (1966), is just an entertainment, his short stories continue to be as remarkable as the early ones. B.'s first collection, *The Delicate Prey* (1950), was dedicated to his mother, who introduced him to the stories of Poe. Even though the lasting impact of Poe's tales on the dreamlike brutality of B.'s imagination is evident, at his best B. succeeds in relating horror to a more significant range of values and experiences. His stature as one of the most fascinating storytellers of this century became clear when his *Collected Stories 1939–1976* (1979) made his work accessible as a whole. B.'s main weakness as a novelist, his inability to develop characters dramatically, is mitigated by the lyric compactness of his best stories. "Beside them most acclaimed fiction of our time . . . seems merely shallow," Joyce Carol OATES wrote in 1979.

B.'s self-imposed exile and his unwillingness to take part in literary life explain his status as a "neglected master."

FURTHER WORKS: *Two Poems* (1933); *Yallah* (1957); *The Hours after Noon* (1959); *A Hundred Camels in the Courtyard* (1962); *Their Heads Are Green and Their Hands Are Blue* (1963); *The Time of Friendship* (1967); *Scenes* (1968); *Pages from Cold Point, and Other Stories* (1968); *The Thicket of Spring* (1972); *Without Stopping* (1972); *Things Gone & Things Still Here* (1977); *Next to Nothing* (1977)

BIBLIOGRAPHY: Hassan, I., "The Pilgrim as Prey: A Note on P. B.," *WR*, 19 (1954): 23–36; Evans, O., "P. B. and the 'Natural' Man," in Waldmeir, J., ed., *Recent American Fiction* (1963): 139–52; Stewart, L. D., "P. B.: *Up above the World So High*," in *The Mystery and Detection Annual* (1973): 245–70; Stewart, L. D., *P. B.: The Illumination of North Africa* (1974); Bertens, J. W., *The Fiction of P. B.* (1979); Vidal, G., Introduction to P. B., *Collected Stories 1939–1976* (1979): 5–9; Oates, J. C., on *Collected Stories, NYTBR* (30 Sept. 1979): 9

—JORIS DUYTSCHAEVER

BOYE, Karin

Swedish poet, novelist, and critic, b. 26 Oct. 1900, Göteborg; d. 24 April 1941, near Alingsås

B. grew up in a middle-class family, first in Göteborg and later in Stockholm, where her father was a civil engineer. After receiving a diploma from a teacher's college in 1921, B. continued her studies at the universities of Uppsala and Stockholm, receiving an M.A. in 1928. As a student in Uppsala B. joined the left-wing organization "Clarté," founded in France by Henri BARBUSSE, and wrote for its magazine, which had MARX, FREUD, and psychoanalysis on its program. During the 1930s in Stockholm she cofounded the literary journal *Spectrum*, introducing T. S. ELIOT and the SURREALISTS to Swedish readers. Together with the critic Erik Mesterton (b. 1904), she translated Eliot's *The Waste Land*. She was a teacher at a secondary school from 1936 to 1938. B. was married for a short time to a fellow "clartéist" in a kind of friendship union. After several nervous breakdowns and crises in her life, B. committed suicide in 1941.

B. is probably most read as a poet. She was influenced by Buddhism in her early poems, later by Schopenhauer, and finally by Nietzsche. The strict classical style of her collections from the 1920s changed to a modernistic, expressionistic style in her later collections, of which *För trädets skull* (1935; for the sake of the tree) is considered her best. Her poetry deals mainly with the dualism in life, the outer and inner self, the split personality, the psychoanalyzed person who is both the strong person, the Amazon, ready to fight, "armed and erect" and the weak, vegetative, introverted person who cannot cope with the outside world.

Recently focus has been turned to B.'s importance as a feminist writer, especially in her novels and short stories, in which she deals with male and female role-playing, among them *Merit vaknar* (1933; Merit wakens) and *För lite* (1936; too little).

Influenced by her own experience of psychoanalytic therapy, both in Stockholm and Berlin, B. wrote the autobiographical novel *Kris* (1934; crisis), which reads like a psychoanalytic case history in which the superego is represented by the God of the established Lutheran church and by the principal of a teacher's college, both oppressive to the female protagonist, who, however, manages to overcome this power group and who leaves the school, enriched in the knowledge and acceptance of her own sexuality as deviating from the "normal."

Her best-known novel, *Kallocain* (1940; *Kallocain*, 1966), is also a kind of psychoanalytic description of people who through a truth serum come to understand and express their innermost selves.

The setting is a totalitarian, technocratic state in the year 2000, where everybody is oppressed and utterly afraid of showing any human feelings. It is a novel written in protest against an authoritarian, male-dominated society, where the individual is allowed to live and work only for the benefit of the state, and where marriage represents a kind of tyranny for both men and women. But through the drug Kallocain human feelings of love, trust, and creativity, symbolized by a woman in the green desert city in the midst of the World State, are revealed.

B. had a considerable impact on Scandinavian poets of her time, and as a prose writer both in Scandinavia and the English-speaking world through *Kallocain*, which in some respects can be seen as a link between HUXLEY's *Brave New World* and ORWELL's *1984*.

FURTHER WORKS: *Moln* (1922); *Gömda land* (1924); *Härdarna* (1927); *Astarte* (1931); *Uppgörelser* (1934); *Ur funktion* (1940); *Bebådelse* (1941); *De sju dödssynderna* (1941); *Dikter* (1942); *Samlade dikter* (1943); *Samlade skrifter* (11 vols., 1948–1950)

BIBLIOGRAPHY: Gustafson, A., *A History of Swedish Literature* (1961): 467–69, 636; Vowles, R. B., Introduction to *Kallocain* (1966): vii–xxi; Claréus, I., Translator's Note to "Poems by K. B.," *Swedish Books*, 2, 4 (1980): 11

—INGRID CLARÉUS

BOYLE, Kay

American novelist, short-story writer, and poet, b. 19 Feb. 1902, St. Paul, Minn.; d. 27 Dec. 1992, San Francisco, Cal.

B. studied violin and architecture before journeying in 1923 to Europe, where she lived with other American expatriates until the fall of France to the Germans. She was in occupied Germany as a correspondent for *The New Yorker* from 1946 to 1953, then taught at American universities. Since 1963 she has been professor of English at San Francisco State University. B. received Guggenheim Fellowships in 1934 and 1961, and the O. Henry prize for best short story in 1935 ("The White Horses of Vienna") and 1941 ("Defeat"). Always politically outspoken, she served thirty-one days in prison in 1968 for demonstrating against the Vietnam war.

B.'s settings are often European. Her first published novel, *Plagued by the Nightingale* (1931), comments bitterly on the struggle of a young Frenchman and his American bride against the fierce hypocrisy of his rigid, middle-class family. Her collection, *The Smoking Mountain: Stories of Germany during the Occupation* (1951), has been called (by the critic C. F. Madden) the "finest interpretation of that place and time . . . written in English." Although B. clearly does not sympathize with the Nazis and is careful to reveal the poison of anti-Semitism beneath the apparently honorable exterior, she nevertheless exhibits compassion for a proud and defeated people. Her international literary reputation was further strengthened by *Generation without Farewell* (1960), a novel of occupied Germany told from the viewpoint of a German journalist and former POW.

Frequently B. uses animals to embody the symbolic truth of a story. In "The White Horses of Vienna," set in the mountains of pre-Nazi Austria, a Jewish medical student wistfully recalls the Lippizaners, those famed white stallions emblematic of a lost nobility, in marked contrast to the half-wild little fox that foreshadows the savage future. In "The Crazy Hunter" (1940) a horse that is suddenly struck blind becomes the focus of inexpressible love and thwarted communication between a young girl and her spiritually blinded parents. And in "The Bridegroom's Body" (1940), one of B.'s most powerful novellas, the nesting swans (one is the "bridegroom" of the title) objectify the need for and destruction of human love, as two women stand chilled in the cold English rain, each hopelessly trapped in her own isolation.

Even though B. began her career as a poet, her poetry remains uneven, with her lyric poems perhaps the strongest. Her novels, always well crafted, often contain brilliant scenes; but her real strength lies in the short story, where she is able to create a single, shattering effect.

B. recognizes the complexity of life in its psychological, social, and political confusion. Her intense commitment to speaking out on issues that violate human dignity has resulted in a moral stance implicit in all her work, a celebration of the human spirit. She is recognized as a major American short-story writer.

FURTHER WORKS: *Wedding Day, and Other Stories* (1929); *Year before Last* (1932); *The First Lover, and Other Stories* (1933); *Gentlemen, I Address You Privately* (1933); *My Next Bride* (1934); *Death of a Man* (1936); *The White Horses of Vienna, and Other Stories* (1936); *Monday Night* (1938); *A Glad Day* (1938); *The Youngest Camel* (1939); *The Crazy Hunter* (1940); *Primer for Combat* (1942); *Avalanche* (1944); *American Citizen* (1944); *A Frenchman Must Die* (1946); *Thirty Stories* (1946); *1939* (1948); *His Human Majesty* (1949); *The Seagull on the Step* (1955); *Three Short Novels* (1958); *Breaking the Silence: Why a Mother Tells Her Son about the Nazi Era* (1962); *Collected Poems* (1962); *Nothing Ever Breaks except the Heart* (1966); *Pinky, the Cat Who Liked to Sleep* (1966); *The Autobiography of Emanuel Carnevali* (1967); *Being Geniuses Together: 1920–1930* (1968, with R. McAlmon); *Pinky in Persia* (1968); *The Long Walk at San Francisco State, and Other Essays* (1970); *Testament for My Students, and Other Poems* (1970); *The Underground Woman* (1975); *Fifty Stories* (1980)

BIBLIOGRAPHY: Carpenter, R. C., "K. B.," *CE*, 15 (Nov. 1953): 81–87; Moore, H. T., "K. B.'s Fiction" (1960), in *Age of the Modern, and Other Literary Essays* (1971): 32–36; Carpenter, R. C., "K. B.: The Figure in the Carpet," *Crit*, 7 (1965): 65–78; Geismar, M., on *Nothing Ever Breaks except the Heart*, *NYTBR*, 10 July 1966: 4, 16; Madden, C. F., ed., *Talks with Authors* (1968): 215–36; Tooker, D., and Hofheins, R., *Fiction: Interviews with Northern California Novelists* (1976): 15–35

—JOANNE MCCARTHY

BOYLE, T(homas) Coraghessan

American novelist and short-story writer, b. Dec. 2, 1948, Peekskill, New York

Born Thomas John Boyle, B. showed his flair for inventiveness early in life when he changed his middle name to Coraghessan at age seventeen. After earning his Ph.D. in literature, B. taught high school for a short time in the early 1970s, and then became an assistant professor at the University of Southern California, where he teaches in the creative writing program. B. has written about a wide range of subjects in a number of styles, but his critical reception has come in variations of only two forms. B. is sometimes appreciated for his ear for dialogue and for the unspoken turn of phrase, and for the sharp satirical sense he brings to his sprawling social canvases. When he is not praised as a kind of postmodern Dickens, he is panned as an adept but soulless craftsman, technically skilled but lacking engagement with characters, feeling for their failures, sympathy for their struggles.

B.'s short fiction was first collected in *Descent of Man and Other Stories* (1977) and since, most notably, in *Greasy Lake & Other Stories* (1985) and *If the River Was Whiskey* (1989). These stories are noted for their inventiveness of form and subject, and show, in addition to B.'s trademark biting comic take on the contemporary world, a sensitivity for the smaller stage of human emotions that many feel B. hasn't displayed in his novels.

B. first reached a wider audience with the PEN/Faulkner Award-winning *World's End* (1987), which tells the stories of three families in the lower Hudson Valley, over the course of four hundred years of its history, from their settling to their drug-addled present. He showed his versatility by traveling, over the course of subsequent novels, to Georgia, Michigan, and Southern California, and by telling the stories of an artists' colony, a sanitarium, entrepreneurs, yuppies, and illegal immigrants. The most successful of these, *The Road to Wellville* (1993), follows the story of the late 19th and early 20th-c. Battle Creek, Michigan, health-craze, which saw the birth of the corn flake and widespread application of the enema, and in which B. saw American folly reaching new heights.

B. returns to his use of history in *Riven Rock* (1998). The story of Stanley McCormick, the institutionalized son of the inventor of the reaper, provides B. with another opportunity to examine the modern American psyche in its formative moments. As in earlier works, this satire is felt by many readers to overwhelm any feeling for the characters; the long separation of Stanley and his wife, while a perfect situation for metaphorical consideration of gender relations and the tension between drives and decorum, doesn't offer much in the way of tangible emotion. What it does offer, aside from the sociological, is the comic—madness, while made quite real, is an opportunity for sport for B. And again, as in earlier works, the evaluations of *Riven Rock* fall in the same two-sides-of-the-same-coin pattern: the reaction to B. is largely to his obvious skill with words and his equally obvious fascination with the social. Whether these responses are positive or negative, seeing in B.'s work incisive satire or superficial mockery, they usually carry a tone of appreciation for fulfilled promise or of disappointment in his failure to fulfill that same promise. This tone itself shows the importance of the high bar B.'s fiction sets for itself.

FURTHER WORKS: *Water Music* (1981); *Budding Prospects: A Pastoral* (1982); *East Is East* (1990); *Without a Hero and Other Stories* (1994); *The Tortilla Curtain* (1995)

BIBLIOGRAPHY: Pope, D., "A Different Kind of Post-Modernism," *Gettysburg Review*, 3 (1990): 658-69; Walker, M., "B.'s Greasy Lake and the Moral Failure of Postmodernism," *SSF*, 31 (1994): 247-55; Schenker, D., "A Samurai in the South: Cross-Cultural Disaster in T. B.'s *East Is East*," *SoQ*, 34 (1995): 70-80; Vaid, K. B., "Franz Kafka Writes to T. B.," *MQR*, 35, 3 (1996): 43-57

—SAM COHEN

BRAAK, Menno ter

Dutch essayist, b. 21 Jan. 1902, Eibergen; d. 14 May 1940, The Hague

The social isolation in which B., the son of a rural physician, grew up, combined with the introspective traditions of his strictly Protestant origins to instill in him a contemplative outlook on the world. He considered studying theology, but ultimately obtained a doctoral degree in history. His religious and educational background largely determined his literary orientation when, as editor of a major daily newspaper and of the influential literary journal *Forum* he became a leading figure in the world of letters. B. subscribed to the view that the ethical substance of a work of literature is more important than its aesthetic aspects. Consequently, although he also tried his hand at the novel and drama, his own writing centered on book-length essays—a genre that has found very few practitioners in the Netherlandic language, and none more talented than B. His essays not only add a dimension to Dutch literature, but also document his own stylistic and philosophical evolution. Moreover, these texts reflect a change in B.'s attitude toward the emergence of fascism in the 1930s, which is typical for many European intellectuals.

Het carnaval der burgers (1930; carnival of the bourgeoisie) postulates the absolute duality of the more exalted realm of existence of the poets, and the world of the "fallen" bourgeois, in an appropriately dialectic style. His next essay, *Demasqué der schoonheid* (1932; aestheticism unmasked) still exhibits the same Hegelian conceptual structure in attacking the one-sided aestheticism that had for many decades characterized the mainstream of Netherlandic writing.

Both in form and substance *Politicus zonder partij* (1934; politician without a party) marked a new departure in B.'s essayistic work. The impact of Stendhal and Nietzsche, whose works B. had meanwhile come to admire, led to a less schematic approach and to a renunciation of historicism and strict intellectualism in favor of the intuitive intelligence inherent in human nature. This reorientation was obviously also connected with Hitler's rise to power in Germany in 1933. B. became deeply involved in the activities of the exiled German anti-Nazi writers, and first raised the controversial issue of the artistic inadequacy of many politically unimpeachable books. Although he incurred the hostility of many emigrants, others, including Thomas Mann, held him in high esteem. Political events in Germany and elsewhere deepened B.'s concern with the basic issue of human dignity, which was increasingly threatened by the prevailing totalitarian trends. The essay *Van oude en nieuwe christenen* (1937; of old and new Christians) addressed this topic in a manner more emotional than strictly rational.

B.'s last essay, *De nieuwe elite* (1939; the new elite), took his increasing awareness of nuances to the extremes of outright philosophical eclecticism, but fundamentally B. did not waver in his opposition to fascist totalitarianism. When German troops invaded the Netherlands, he committed suicide as the ultimate gesture of protest against the barbarity that was sweeping Europe.

FURTHER WORKS: *Cinema militans* (1929); *Hampton Court* (1931); *De absolute film* (1931); *Afscheid van domineesland* (1931); *Man tegen man* (1931); *Dr. Dumay verliest* (1933); *De pantserkrant* (1935); *Het tweede gezicht* (1935); *Douwes Dekker en Multatuli*

(1937); *In gesprek met de vorigen* (1938); *De duivelskunstenaar* (1943); *Reinaert opreis* (1944); *Het christendom* (1945, with A. van Duinkerken); *Over waardigheid en macht* (1945); *In gesprek met de onzen* (1946); *Briefwisseling 1930–1940* (1967; correspondence with Edgar du Perron); *De Propria Cures artikelen: 1923–1925* (1978)

BIBLIOGRAPHY: Vincent, P. F., "B.'s Anglo-Saxon Attitudes," *English Symposium Papers I* (1970): 362–85; Würzner, H., "B. als Kritiker der deutschen Emigrantenliteratur," *Zur deutschen Exilliteratur in den Niederlanden 1933–1940* (1977): 216–41

—EGBERT KRISPYN

BRADBURY, Malcolm

English novelist, critic, dramatist, poet, essayist, and screenwriter, b. 7 Sept. 1932, Sheffield

B. is a writer who has benefited greatly from the postwar expansion of the British university system, though at a remove from the prestige of Oxbridge. With degrees from Leicester, University College (London), and Manchester, he went on to teach at the University of Birmingham—where he became friends with David LODGE, the fellow comic novelist and literary critic with whom he is often linked and sometimes confused—before settling at the University of East Anglia, where he taught American studies and founded England's first university writing program. B.'s stints at American universities and as British Council lecturer have afforded him abundant materials for his satirical novels, stories, and plays. B. is no ordinary satirist however; his imaginative writing has benefited greatly from his work as an academic literary critic, enabling him to stretch the seemingly static, even provincial form of the campus novel into new, more postmodern shapes.

B.'s wittily titled first novel, *Eating People Is Wrong* (1959), bears the unmistakable imprint of Kingsley AMIS's famously irreverent *Lucky Jim* (1954). But B.'s satire, unlke Amis's, cuts two ways: as much into the novel's befuddled, feckless protagonist (hardly a version of Amis's antihero) as at the absurdly funny redbrick university, microcosm of postwar England. Campus fiction meets the Jamesian international novel (in reverse) in *Stepping Westward* (1966), the prototype for Lodge's even funnier *Changing Places* (1975). Here B.'s schlemiel is the aptly named James Walker, an erstwhile angry young man in England, just another English provincial in the brave new world and cultural wasteland of the modern American university with its aggressively new campus, abundant cash, and pervasive anti-intellectualism.

Although its style and setting are far removed from those of *Stepping Westward*, *The History Man* (1975) does not so much depart from the earlier books' essentially ethical concerns, as develop them closer to home but in a time quite different from the 1950s so brilliantly depicted in *Eating People Is Wrong*. Howard Kirk is a relentlessly trendy sociologist, the high priest (as his name ironically suggests) of the new religion of the behavioral sciences whose leftish politics mask an opportunism worthy of the Thatcherites soon to come to power. The novel's present-tense style mimics the depthless, schizoid quality of postmodern life and the postmodern

architecture of the newly built university where Kirk and all he represents prosper. Against the pervasive depthlessness and amorality of Kirk and his kind, B. posits the liberal humanist ideal and its literary embodiment, character: an ideal under threat, even erasure. B. provides a trenchant and by no means reactionary explanation of the fate of liberal humanism in a postmodern age in the essay "Putting in the Person" in *No, Not Bloomsbury* (1987). Kirk's ostensible triumph contrasts sharply with the defeats suffered by B.'s other, more comically passive, decidedly out-of-date protagonists—disturbingly so. For Kirk, eating people is by no means wrong.

It seems altogether appropriate that there should hang a certain, and certainly comic, end-of-empire air around the work of a writer who not only wrote a television play set against the backdrop of the 1956 Suez Crisis—"Love on a Gunboat," collected in *The After Dinner Game* (1982)—but who also chaired the committee that awarded the 1981 Booker Prize to Salman RUSHDIE for *Midnight's Children* (1980), the brilliant postcolonial novel that B. rightly saw ushering in a new era of British fiction. The future that seemed to be for better with Rushdie and for worse with Kirk is clearly not at all with British Council lecturer Petworth, a professor of linguistics adrift and out of his depth in a fictional as well as absurd East European country in *Rates of Exchange* (1983). B. can be wickedly funny (if politically incorrect) in satirizing "others," whether Americans in *Stepping Westward* or Slakans here and in the parodic guidebook, *Why Come to Slaka?* (1986). But any sense of lingering British superiority is offset by the sense that the Petworths, Walkers, and their England have been surpassed by the relentlessly and at times ruthlessly postmodern world of B.'s two *Gravy Train* television series on the European Community; of *Cuts* (1987), on the travails of a novelist turned television scriptwriter; and of *Doctor Criminale* (1992), on the fate of a young print-journalist, a decidedly verbal man, lost in an age of television and theory while on the trail of the elusive, enigmatic deconstructionist Bazlo Criminale, the ultimate floating signifier.

Neither as naive and nostalgic as his protagonists nor as trendy as his Kirks and Criminales, B. has successfully negotiated between two worldviews and increasingly between different media (adapting, for example, Tom Sharpe's fiction for television and Stella Gibbons's 1932 novel *Cold Comfort Farm* for film (1997). As a critic he has demonstrated a deep understanding of as well as tolerance for a wide range of critical approaches which as a fiction writer he has put to use to become one of the most intelligent and incisive comic novelists of the postwar period.

FURTHER WORKS: *All Dressed Up and Nowhere to Go* (1962); *Evelyn Waugh* (1964); *Who Do You Think You Are?: Stories and Parodies* (1976); *The Modern American Novel* (1983); *The Modern World: Ten Great Writers* (1988); *My Strange Quest for Mensonge* (1988); *Unsent Letters* (1988); *From Puritanism to Postmodernism* (1991, with Richard Ruland); *The Modern British Novel* (1992); *Dangerous Pilgrimages* (1995)

BIBLIOGRAPHY: Friedman, M. J., "M. B.'s 'Plot of History,'" in Bock, H., and A. Wertheim, eds., *Essays on the Contemporary British Novel* (1986): 213-26; Morace, R. A., *The Dialogic Novels of M. B. and David Lodge* (1989); Acheson, J., "The Small Worlds of M. B. and David Lodge," in Acheson, J., ed., *The British and Irish Novel since 1960* (1991): 78-92

—ROBERT A. MORACE

BRAHUI LITERATURE

See Pakistani Literature

BRAINE, John

English novelist, b. 13 April 1922, Bradford; d. 28 October 1987, London

B.'s life and fiction are both set primarily in the provincial Yorkshire town of Bradford, where the work is mostly industrial and the values puritanical. Born of lower-middle-class Anglo-Irish parents, B. attended the local grammar school, graduating by correspondence four years after he left. After a number of odd jobs, he settled into a career as a librarian. After the phenomenal success of his first novel, *Room at the Top* (1957), and of the film version, he devoted himself full-time to writing.

Room at the Top and its sequel, *Life at the Top* (1962), remain B.'s best fiction; most of his other novels read as variations on one or the other of them. Joe Lampton, young and ambitious, but with little ability or charm, is determined to make a material and social success of himself, and so escape his working-class background. His progress to the top is impeded only by a love affair with an older, married woman who dies conveniently, if horribly, in time for him to marry the boss's lovely, vacuous daughter. The death and marriage provide Lampton with everything he sought, but they signify the end of his moral existence, as the sequel (which is less successful because it is essentially static) demonstrates. In it, Lampton—no longer driven and now guilt-haunted by the death of his mistress—finds he has nowhere to go and that all he has attained tastes of ashes; yet in the end he wins a victory of sorts by affirming family, home, love—despite their fragility and his continuing doubts about them and himself.

Two subsequent novels parallel these early ones. In *The Crying Game* (1968) Frank Batcombe—also of working-class background, Catholic, right-wing (although claiming to be apolitical), and intensely ambitious—faces what Joe Lampton faced: a choice between life styles personified by two women. Frank, however, manages to get the best of both, for in the end he chooses against what is appealing yet hollow (decadence, excitement, risk) and finds love and material success while keeping his soul intact. Jim Seathwaite, in *Waiting for Sheila* (1976), sits up nights feeling sleazy and full of self-pity while awaiting his wife's return from a liaison. Interestingly, the entire novel—including extensive flashbacks of childhood loss of innocence and learning to fear and hate sex, recalled in imagery of warfare, violence, crime, and prison—occurs during one such night.

B. has long been linked with such other "Angry Young Men" who emerged in the 1950s as Kingsley AMIS, Alan SILLITOE, John OSBORNE, and John WAIN. The term, whether or not originally meaningful in connoting protest against a class-structured society, has lost currency, and the writers understandably asserted claims to be judged individually. B. himself is best at detailing the endless trivialities of daily life, the means by which people make choices about relationships (especially sexual ones), values, careers, and life styles, and the inevitable consequences they face. He is repelled yet fascinated by the obsession with success of most of his characters. Although technically unimaginative, most of B.'s novels are narrated retrospectively by their protagonists, who thereby imply the presence of a significant moral dimension and that lives as well or badly lived as theirs may serve as example for those who read with understanding.

FURTHER WORKS: *The Desert in the Mirror* (1951); *The Vodi* (1959); *The Jealous God* (1964); *Man at the Top* (1970); *Stay with Me till Morning* (1970); *The Queen of a Distant Country* (1972); *Writing a Novel* (1974); *The Pious Agent* (1975); *Finger of Fire* (1977); *J. B. Priestley* (1978); *One and Last Love* (1981); *The Two of Us* (1984); *These Golden Days* (1985)

BIBLIOGRAPHY: Weaver, R., "England's Angry Young Men," *QQ*, 65 (1958): 183–94; Hurrell, J. D., "Class and Conscience in J. B. and Kingsley Amis," *Crit*, 2 (1958): 39–53; Karl, F. R., *A Reader's Guide to the Contemporary English Novel* (1962): 220–37; Lee, J. W., *J. B.* (1968); Skovmand, M., and Skovmand, S., *The Angry Young Men* (1975): 104–32; Salwak, D., *J. B. and John Wain: A Reference Guide* (1980)

—ALAN WARREN FRIEDMAN

BRANCATI, Vitaliano

Italian novelist, dramatist, and critic, b. 24 July 1907, Pachino; d. 25 Sept. 1954, Turin

During his formative years in Sicily, B. was strongly attached to the language and customs of his region, to the illusions, hopes, and failures of his people. Although his native Sicily provided him with the major background for his novels and plays, B. cannot be labeled a regionalist, since his concern is not the locale, but political criticism and the psychological state of his characters. Indeed, with some exceptions in his early work, most of the characters and situations are Sicilian only in order to provide verisimilitude for a satire of the social and political systems.

The early plays *Fedor* (1928; Fedor), *Everest* (1930; Everest) and *Piave* (1932; Piave), as well as the early novel *L'amico del vincitore* (1932; the friend of the winner), written when B. was a fervent advocate of Fascism, exalt the myths of activity, virility, forceful domination of reality, and sentimental D'Annunzian mysticism.

Gli anni perduti (1935; the lost years), written as B. turned away from Fascism, represents the upsetting of those myths through a politically satirical narrative enacted by lethargic characters who manifest a lack of any direction in their search for happiness. An arid and immobile Sicilian ambience provides the background for their actions as they function in an interior world vitiated by boredom and anxiety while the external world encroaches upon them with its destructive force.

In his next novel, the very successful *Don Giovanni in Sicilia* (1942; Don Giovanni in Sicily), B. introduces *gallismo*—the boasting of sexual prowess—a concept that was to dominate his later works. Indeed, most of his later characters are sex-obsessed individuals who live through a series of erotic situations in a world totally preoccupied by sex. The author handles this excessive sexual preoccupation, however, with a touch of humor, achieved through a brilliant use of antitheses. *Gallismo*, really a veil for impotence and latent homosexuality, is metaphorically and ironically substituted for patriotism and for the forceful control of reality.

The metaphorical impotence of the main character, the central theme of *Il bell' Antonio* (1949; *Bell' Antonio*, 1978), is revealed in an atmosphere heavy with impending tragedy. Finally, B.'s gloomy obsession with sex explodes powerfully in his last novel (unfinished at the author's death), *Paolo il caldo* (1955; Paul the hot).

B. repeats with some nuances the themes and characters of his novels in his plays *Don Giovanni involontario* (1945; the unwilling Don Giovanni) and *Raffaele* (1948; Raphael). In these plays he proves his mastery of satire and mood. However, his popular success in the theater dates from the production of *La governante* (1952; the housekeeper), a social satire that explores the state of mind of a lesbian who struggles against her sexual orientation, which she wishes to vanquish, while the bourgeois judge views her conduct according to absurd conventions. The ethical motivation of the play, which is directed at first toward the contradictions prevailing between different sets of mores in a circumscribed milieu, broadens later to include an analysis of the conflicts between old customs and modern change, between society and nature, between province and metropolis.

Because of his treatment of the crucial problems and conflicts of our time, B. deserves a place of prominence among contemporary European novelists and playwrights.

FURTHER WORKS: *Il vecchio con gli stivali* (1945)

BIBLIOGRAPHY: Tavernier, R., "B.: Un Gogol italien," *Preuves*, No. 107 (1960): 23–26; De Tommaso, P., "V. B.," *RLI*, 64 (1962): 120–31; Dombroski, R., "B. and Fascism: A Profile," *IQ*, 13 (1969): 41–63; Huffman, C. L., "V. B.: A Reassessment," *FI*, 6 (1972): 356–77

—MARIO B. MIGNONE

BRANDÃO, Fiama Hasse Pais

Portuguese poet and dramatist, b. 15 August 1938, Lisbon

Known throughout Portugal as Fiama, B. grew up as an only child on a country estate in Carcavelos, close to where the Tagus flows into the Atlantic. This rural home played an essential part in nurturing her spiritual and intellectual attentiveness to nature, especially its smallest creatures such as locusts, cicadas, and bees. She attended the English School in Carcavelos for ten years, then continued her studies in German language and literature at the University of Lisbon, where she continues to this day as a researcher in linguistics, specializing in 16th-c. Portuguese literature. After raising two sons from her early marriage to the poet Gastão Cruz, she returned in 1992 to live at Vivenda Azul, the beloved home of her childhood.

B.'s literary career began with the publication of *Em Cada Pedra umVoo Imóvel* (1957; In Every Stone a Motionless Flight), a collection of poetry that earned her the Adolfo Casais Monteiro Award. This was followed by *Morfismos* (1961; Morphisms), which appeared in a student-dominated collective of chapbooks titled *Poesia 61* (Poetry 61), published in the Algarvian capital of Faro. The work of this experimental, postsurrealist group rejected traditional poetics and humanistic idealism and was critical of the sociopolitical status quo during the Salazar regime, with its prolonged colonial wars in Africa. However, the group's efforts toward change, influenced by psychoanalysis, Marxism, and newly established STRUCTURALISM, were principally directed at language itself, which they hoped to give renewed power through reliance on the image as the central element. Principal members of the group included Cruz, Maria Teresa Horta (b. 1937), Casimiro de Brito (b. 1938), and Luísa Neto Jorge (1939-1989).

Since then B. has published thirteen more collections of poetry, including the comprehensive *Obra Breve* (1991; Short Work). She has also published four prose works, two literary studies, translations of Novalis (1772-1801), CHEKHOV, ARTAUD, BRECHT, and John UPDIKE, and six volumes of plays. Her interest in theater developed during her student years and her first play, *Chapéus de Chuva* (1960; Rain Hats), actually preceded publication of *Morfismos*. As one of the founders of Theatre Hoje (Today's Theater), B. mounted an inaugural presentation of Garcia Lorca's *Marina Pineda* in 1975. She remained in active association with the company, for which she translated Chekhov's *The Sea Gull*, until its demise in 1995.

B.'s poetry has been translated into various languages, including French, Italian, Spanish, Polish, Romanian, Bulgarian, Slovenian, German, and English. A small selection called *F de Fiama* (1997; F for Fiama), was published for the 1997 Frankfurt Book Fair in Portuguese, with French, German, and English translations. In 1986, B. was awarded both the Grande Prémio of Poetry by the National Culture Center and the Portuguese PEN Club Poetry Prize. In 1992, she was one of three finalists competing for the European Literary Prize, established by the European Community. In 1996 she was awarded the D. Dinis Poetry Prize for her book, *Epístolas e Memorandos* (1996; Epistles and Memoranda). The same book won her the prestigious Grande Prémio of Poetry from the Portuguese Writers Association in 1997.

B.'s poetry is textually dense and philosophically challenging. In her work a swan or a bee from the real world may be closely observed, but the imagined creature or even the mythic creature is equally important, equally "real." She moves between light and shadow, shifts from present to past and back again, opposes mimetic description with imagined creation, and refuses ever to stake her claim on one realm against the other. She accepts the complexity of life, of the relationship between observed and observer, and seems to attack the distance we assume or construe betweed our receptive eye and mind. The critic Fernando Pinto do Amaral speaks of her "gaze that wants to fuse with the real, unite with Nature, breaking the distance between the one who contemplates and the contemplated object." And António Geurreiro says that for B. "art is not an end in itself, but a way of reading the text of Nature." Sprung equally from mind and heart, B.'s poetry offers us no answers, as it coils and uncoils, both rich and difficult, like a fabric of experience itself.

FURTHER WORKS: *Peças em 1 Acto* (1964); *Barcas Novas* (1966); *(Este) Rosto* (1969); *O Texto de Joan Zorro* (1974); *Novas Visões do Passado* (1975); *O Retratado* (1976); *Homenagem à literatura* (1976); *O Labirinto Camoniano e outros Labirintos* (1978); *Poe ou o Corvo* (1979); *Quem Move as Árvores* (1979); *Àrea Branca* (1979); *Sombras na Cara de Estefânea* (1980); *Âmago I* (1985); *F de Fiama*; *Três Rostos* (1989); *Sílvia de Lisardo* (1989); *Falar sobre o Falado* (1989); *Teatro-Teatro* (1990); *Movimento Perpétuo* (1990); *Cantos do Canto* (1995)

BIBLIOGRAPHY: Amaral, F. P., "L' 'Humble Métaphysiqué' de Fiama," *Europa/Europe*, 115 (1991): 199-202; Furtado, M. T., "Movimento Perpetuo," *Coloquio-Letras*, 123-24 (Jan.-June 1992): 383-84; special B. section, *Letras & Letras*, 5, 81 (21 October 1992): 7-16; Guerreiro, A., "F.H. P. B.—Obra Breve," *NE Europa*, 74-77 (1992-1993):156-58; Maldonado, F., "Portuguese Women Writers—F. H. P. B.," *Du-Die Zeltschrift der Kultur*, 9 (September 1996): 59

—ALEXIS LEVITIN

BRANDÃO, Raúl

Portuguese narrative writer and dramatist, b. 12 March 1867, Foz do Douro; d. 5 Dec. 1930, Lisbon

B.'s education prepared him for an army career, but by temperament he was given more to the life of an intellectual. He began writing in the 1890s for newspapers in Lisbon, where he also met many Portuguese fin-de-siècle personalities. His military career continued until 1912, when he retired with the rank of major.

B. was active during the first quarter of the 20th c. His works are marked by a fascination with the life of the poor and destitute, which B. portrays in terms both of tragedy and of grotesque farce. He probes the unconscious and subconscious of his characters, trying to make the reader understand their hopes, frustrations, violent passions, and, frequently, insanity. These people are misfits, dreamers and human wrecks who tenaciously struggle against the seemingly cosmic forces that beat back any attempts by them to overcome or make sense of their nightmarish existence.

B.'s major works are three narratives: *A farsa* (1903; the farce), *Os pobres* (1906; the poor), and *Humus* (1917; humus). These books should not be classified as novels; only *A farsa* comes close to achieving the internal cohesion of a novel. The true unifying principle in it and in the other two narratives is the mood of fright, grief, and pain that pervades them. This mood is as much an expression of B.'s reaction to concrete social realities as it is a metaphysical view of the world.

B.'s claim to an important place in contemporary Portuguese literature is also supported by his few but important plays. The three major ones—*O gebo e a sombra* (1923; the ragamuffin and the shadow), *O doido e a morte* (1923; the madman and death), and *O avejão* (1929; the specter)—have been staged in Portugal and in other European countries. All three express the same nightmarish vision of the human condition as do the narratives. *O gebo e a sombra*, in which figures from the narratives appear, and *O avejão* are tragic in tone, while *O doido e a morte* is comic.

B. was relatively unappreciated in his own time. By the 1960s, however, the realization that he posed existentialist questions and presented an absurd, grotesque vision of life before it was truly fashionable to do so led to greater interest in his works. Many of them have since been reissued.

FURTHER WORKS: *Impressões e paisagens* (1890); *História dum palhaço* (1896; reprinted 1926 as *A morte do palhaço e o mistério da árvore*); *El-rei Junot* (1912); *A conspiração de 1817* (1914; later titled *1817, A conspiração de Gomes Freire*); *Memórias* (3 vols.,

1919–1933); *O rei imaginário* (1923); *Eu sou um homem de bem* (1927); *Jesus Cristo em Lisboa* (1927, with Teixeira de Pascoaes); *O pobre de pedir* (1931)

BIBLIOGRAPHY: Ferro, T. R., "R. B. et le symbolisme portugais," *BEPIF*, 13 (1949): 210–28

—GREGORY MCNAB

BRANDT, Jørgen Gustava

Danish poet, novelist, essayist, and short-story writer, b. 13 March 1929, Copenhagen

B. has had a varied career. In 1946–47 he exhibited paintings in Copenhagen. During the 1960s he worked in various capacities for Radio Denmark. He has also been an editor, translator, and literary critic. B. is one of Denmark's most prolific authors, having published over fifty volumes of poetry, fiction, and critical writings. A natural lyricist, he has produced far more poetic than prose works.

B.'s poetic debut came in the masterful, stylistically complex *Korn i Pelegs mark* (1949; grain in Peleg's field). Filled with strikingly original, occasionally synesthetic imagery, this thin volume grapples, at times surrealistically and often ironically, with existential problems: birth, death, human isolation, love, man's place in the cosmos. Many of the poems are suffused with a spirit of mysticism. The poems of *Fragment of imorgen* (1960; fragment of tomorrow) similarly deal with these same motifs and problems. Despite the presence of numerous insoluble paradoxes, however, their tone is more positive than that of *Korn i Pelegs mark*. The poetic collection *Janushoved* (1962; Janus head) explores further such seemingly irreconcilable contradictions. Here again the poet's concerns reflect man's cosmic unease. From many of these poems there emanates a feeling of passivity and escape underscored by the recurrent motifs of sleeping, dreaming, blindness, memories of the past.

The poems of *Der er æg i mit skæg* (1966; there is egg in my beard) and *Ateliers* (1967; studios) represent a departure in both style and substance from B.'s earlier poetry. Still existential, they are, however, less angst-ridden and less surrealistic than previous collections. Written almost exclusively in the first person, these poems are more accessible than B.'s earlier verse. Here overwhelmingly cosmic considerations give way to everyday concerns and subjective reminiscences. Further indication of B.'s change of style and of his apparent desire to facilitate the reader's understanding is the presence of occasional prose pieces among the poems. The lyrical *I den høje evighed lød et bilhorn* (1970; in lofty eternity a car horn sounded) continues on the same course as that which B. charted in *Der er æg i mit skæg* and *Ateliers*.

In the volume of autobiographical poetry *Mit hjerte i København* (1975; my heart in Copenhagen), which forms a loose trilogy with *Jatháram* (1976; Jatháram) and *Regnansigt* (1976; face of rain), B. continues with a vividly personal, impressionistic poetry. Stylistically straightforward, *Mit hjerte i København* is both a panegyric to the "inner" Copenhagen and its inhabitants, with which B. clearly identifies himself, and a moving valedictory to the narrator's vanished childhood and his deceased family. This work stresses the evanescence of human contact and reveals an affection for the common man.

The poems of *Her kunne samtale føres* (1978; one could talk together here) retain this personal impressionism but add the new dimensions, already detectable in *Mit hjerte i København*, of a nascent romanticism and a tentative social criticism. The short "First Book" deals with human isolation, reality and illusion, the transitoriness of existence. The major "Second Book" records the narrator's perceptive, sometimes apprehensive observations of Jerusalem, Judaism, Jew and Arab, East versus West. These poems, as well as those of *Oh Israel* (1978; oh Israel) were in part inspired by B.'s visit to Israel in 1977.

Although more sensually oriented, B. the writer of fiction employs many of the same themes as B. the poet. In the short stories of *Stof* (1968; material) the problems of man's insularity, the nature of death, reality and illusion are intertwined with surreal description and reminiscence. The solitary narrator of the novel *Kvinden på Lüneburg hede* (1969; the woman on Lüneburg Heath) laboriously reconstructs two key past events—his chance sexual encounter with a young woman, and his brief friendship with an enigmatic stranger—in an attempt to establish some meaning for his own existence. In *Pink Champagne* (1973; the title is in English), B. lays bare the passivity, the superficiality, and the facile philosophizing of the aimless young in Copenhagen. In a broader sense, B. taps a vein of social and psychological malaise and lack of direction in the welfare state.

Throughout his career, B. has been the eloquent singer of his beloved Copenhagen. Characteristic of B.'s technique is his effective use of frequently recurring images, themes, and motifs as well as the appearance of the same persona in several works. Such devices emphasize the unity and continuity of B.'s art. Despite his vast productivity, B. is ever the careful craftsman and avoids the temptation of simply writing for writing's sake. The consistently high quality of his works places B. among contemporary Denmark's most prominent literary figures.

FURTHER WORKS: *Et essay om Karen Blixen* (1952); *Tjørne-Engen* (1953); *Dragespor* (1957); *Udflugter* (1961); *Digte i udvalg* (1963); *Præsentation: 40 danske digtere* (1964); *Etablissementet* (1965); *Digt på min fødselsdag* (1969); *Den geniale monotoni* (1969); *Vendinger* (1971); *Dudigte* (1971); *Detdigte* (1971); *Upraktiske digte* (1972); *De nødstedte djævle de er de værste* (1972); *Her omkring* (1974); *M. A. Goldschmidt: En tekstmosaik* (1974); *Lyset i stenene* (1974); *Almanak: Vendinger i 14 digte* (1977); *Ophold* (1977); *Tidens fylde: et udvalg digte fra 1970erne* (1979); *Ud af intet kommer du blødt gående* (1979); *Idiotes: med blade af livet i klotret 20. årh.* (1980); *Vente på et pindsvin: broget prosa, personlige essays* (1981); *Hvad poesi angår* (1982); *Hop: nye digte* (1982); *Harlekinade: digte* (1985); *Emanation: 23 besøg i billedhuggerens værksted: digte* (1985); *Scala-suite/lys: ateliers femte samling* (1986); *80 moderne danske digtere: præsentation & portræt: essays* (1988); *Et mørkes partitur* (1990); *Mit indre marked: erindringer, essays og andet* (1990); *Mens endnu sans og samling: digte* (1994); *Vise om vejen til Emmaus: et digt* (1994); *6 folkelige sange: for blanket kor* (1994); *Om dannelse* (1995); *Ansigt til ansigt* (1996); *Mine danske kilder: fem sange for blandet kor* (1997); *digte 1946-96: et udvalg* (1997). FURTHER WORKS IN ENGLISH: *Tête à Tête: Selected Poems* (1978); *And time shall be no more: four songs for mixed chorus* (1994)

BIBLIOGRAPHY: Glienke, B., "Anna, Balthazar und die Deutschen," *Skandinavistik*, 0 (1970): 19–35

—FRANK HUGUS

BRANDYS, Kazimierz

Polish novelist, short-story writer, dramatist, and essayist, b. 27 Oct. 1916, Lódź

B. began his literary career just before the outbreak of World War II, while studying law at the University of Warsaw. At that time he was already affiliated with the Polish leftist movement, and his first publications and subsequent critical, political, and fictional writings appeared in leftist periodicals. B. spent the war years in Warsaw and after the war ended decided to become a professional writer rather than a lawyer. He has been an editor for several journals since 1946 and resides in Warsaw.

B.'s first novel, *Drewniany koń* (1946; the wooden horse) is a bitterly satirical depiction of the moral and intellectual disintegration of a well-meaning member of the intelligentsia in the face of the Nazi occupation and the Resistance movement. His tetralogy, *Między wojnami* (1948–51; between the wars), gave evidence of his increasing acceptance of SOCIALIST REALISM. It too portrays members of the intelligentsia who are torn by doubts, political disillusionment, and paralysis of will. The "positive heroes" of the tetralogy, the Communist workers, suffer from neither doubts nor fears.

B.'s literary output in the post-Stalinist period (after the "thaw" of 1956) served the new Party line, that of exposing and condemning the "errors and mistakes" of Stalinism. In the novella *Obrona Grenady* (1956; the defense of Granada) B. attacks and criticizes political pressures put on the artists by Party officials. Another novella, *Matka Królów* (1957; *Sons and Comrades*, 1961), is a tragedy of a mother and her sons—true and idealistic Communists—who are defeated and victimized by a wrongly adopted official policy.

B. sincerely believed in the sacredness of the Communist cause. Yet he gradually came to the realization that some of the means used by the Communists were bad—and he was able to admit it. Probably as a result of this realization, after *Matka Królów* B. stopped writing longer fiction and concerning himself directly with political issues. Instead, B. wrote numerous short stories and narratives in epistolary form. The epistolary narratives have been collected into four different volumes with the title *Listy do pani Z.* (1957–60; letters to Madame Z.). The subsequent short stories, which have much in common with the "literature of the absurd" popular in post-Stalinist Poland, filled another four volumes published before 1966. In that year B. resigned from the Communist Party. Three more volumes of stories, similar to the earlier ones, appeared in 1968, 1970, and 1972.

After a five-year period of silence, the novel *Nierzeczywistość* (1977; *A Question of Reality*, 1980) was published clandestinely in Poland and then by a Polish emigré publisher in Paris. Told in the first person, B.'s favorite form of narrative, *Nierzeczywistość* is the story of an individual who refuses to accept Poland's present fate. The narrator looks back on his life, remembering Poland in the 1930s, the Nazi occupation and the Resistance, and his compromises and struggles within the Communist regime. The novel resounds with the narrator's final realization of the totalitarian distortions of Polish reality. With this book B. dared to cross the line: he no longer serves the Party but consciously and bravely follows his conscience regardless of the possible consequences, changing his status from that of a "writer in good standing," with all its benefits, to that of an "enemy of the people."

FURTHER WORKS: *Sprawiedliwi ludzie* (1954); *Hotel Rzymski* (1955); *Wyprawa do oflagu* (1955); *Czerwona czapeczka* (1956); *Romantyczność* (1960); *Sposób bycia* (1963); *Opowiadania* (1966); *Dżoker* (1966); *Rynek* (1968); *Mala księga* (1970); *Wariacje pocztowe* (1972)

BIBLIOGRAPHY: Kuncewicz, M., ed., *The Modern Polish Mind* (1962): 6, 239; Milosz, C., *The History of Polish Literature* (1969): 456, 498–99

—MALGORZATA PRUSKA-CARROLL

BRANNER, Hans Christian

Danish novelist, dramatist, short-story writer, and critic, b. 23 June 1903, Ordrup; d. 24 April 1966, Copenhagen

After an unsuccessful attempt at an acting career, in 1923 B. found employment with a Copenhagen publishing firm. In 1932 he resigned his position to devote his entire time to writing. He made his literary debut the same year with two short stories published in the weekly *Politikens magasin*.

B. can be characterized as a humanist who recognizes the need for charity in an impersonal, heartless world in which idealism is suspect and idealistic goals are almost unattainable. In his writings B. sets out to analyze exactly what it is in society and in the individual that prevents the harmonious development of the personality and creates loneliness and fear. While the early novels reveal B.'s strong penchant for Freudian psychoanalysis, his later works show that his interest has shifted to existential questions. According to B., life becomes real only when seen and understood in its intimate relationship with death. The path to true life leads through emptiness and isolation, which, however, can be overcome in the experience of love between man and woman. Existence itself thus becomes a drama about love and death.

B.'s first novel, *Legetøj* (1936; toys), shows the influence of the so-called collective novels of the period, with no central figure but rather many characters who are of equal importance in the narrative. The book provides penetrating analyses of people working in a toy company symbolic of society at large, with its struggles for power and prestige. Although an attack on capitalism, dictatorship, and Nazism, the novel is primarily psychological, with the behavior of the characters explained by inner conflicts that are traced back to childhood experiences. In *Barnet leger ved stranden* (1937; the child plays on the beach), written in diary form, the narrator, defeated as a husband and father, similarly blames his weaknesses and failures on childhood events. Following these purging confessions, his will to live is restored, and he is able to face reality. B.'s two collections of short stories, *Om lidt er vi borte* (1939; in a little while we shall be gone) and *To minutters stilhed* (1944; *Two Minutes of Silence*, 1966), are free of the somewhat mechanized Freudian psychology that characterizes the previous novels. They

include some of the finest stories in Scandinavian literature and deal with both the many irrational fears of childhood and the powerlessness of adults when death, persecution, or love shatters the security of everyday life. B.'s sympathetic insight into the minds of children is likewise demonstrated in *Historien om Børge* (1942; the story of Børge), a novel written to be read on the radio. It is a minute study of a child's painful process of liberation from dependence upon his mother.

During World War II B.'s writings began to reflect his new existential outlook. Set against the background of the outbreak of the war, *Drømmen om en kvinde* (1941; the dream about a woman), a boldly experimental novel utilizing the stream-of-consciousness technique, treats the questions of life and death. Through the use of interior monologue B. illuminates the isolation and fear of his four characters—one of them on the verge of death, another about to give birth—and the clash between their dreams and reality. The book ends on a somewhat optimistic note, however, with the birth of the child and the possibility of human fellowship.

B.'s best-known novel, *Rytteren* (1949; *The Riding Master*, 1951), originally written as a play, is a symbolic expression of the crisis of modern, rootless man and of his attempts to free himself from the past. Four characters, representing different modes of being, are described in their relation to the dead riding master, Hubert, who stands for primitive, nonreflective man and who still exercises his instinctive power even after his death. Liberation comes through Clemens, apparently weak and clownish, but strong in his warm humanity.

B. reached his highest artistic refinement in his masterpiece *Ingen kender natten* (1955; *No Man Knows the Night*, 1958), which depicts the dramatic events of one night during the German occupation. Through stream-of-consciousness narration, leaps in time and space provide background information on the two main characters, the Resistance fighter Simon, and Tomas, symbol of doubt and passivity. The two meet, are able to break out of their isolation, and experience a feeling of brotherly love. The novel is a work about spiritual death and rebirth; although a ray of hope shines at the end, the perspective is tragic in that Tomas, paradoxically, only gains life at the moment of death.

As a dramatist, B. won recognition with *Søskende* (1952; *The Judge*, 1955), which, like *Rytteren*, deals with various possibilities of being and proclaims a message of humanism. The destructive elements of fear and unlimited freedom are set against compassion and responsibility toward one's fellow man. The same topic is also discussed in *Thermopylæ* (1958; Thermopylae), where the main character, however, serves as a symbol of defeated humanism. While in his dramas of ideas B. makes use of the traditional naturalistic mode, he is far more experimental in his radio plays and television dramas, where his mastery is very impressive and his theatrical innovations daring and fruitful. The television drama *Matadoren* (1965; the matador) depicts the lonely death of a man of power whose life has been a total waste.

Religious overtones are noticeable in B.'s later writings, but his message is that of universal humanity rather than of Christianity. Characteristic of his entire work is the constant fight against the suppression of feelings and the defense of compassion and charity. B. is the major representative in Danish literature of humanistic ideals.

FURTHER WORKS: *Humanismens krise* (1950); *Bjergene* (1953); *Vandring langs floden* (1956); *Kunstens uafhængighed* (1957); *Et spil om kærligheden og døden* (1960); *Ariel* (1963); *Fem radiospil* (1965); *Gyldendals Julebog* (1966)

BIBLIOGRAPHY: Madsen, B. G., "H. C. B.: A Modern Humanist," *ASR,* 47 (1959): 39–45; Vowles, R. B., "Bergman, B., and Off-Stage Dying," *SS,* 33 (1961): 1–9; Markey, T. L., *H. C. B.* (1973)

—MARIANNE FORSSBLAD

BRATHWAITE, Edward Kamau

(born Lawson Edward Brathwaite) Barbadian poet and critic, b. 11 May 1930, Bridgetown

Educated at Harrison College in Barbados, B. went on to study history at Cambridge, graduating with honors in 1953. In 1950 B. began publishing poems and a few stories in Barbados and in England. After Cambridge, he worked for the ministry of education in what is now Ghana until 1962. While in Africa, B. published the first of his many essays on West Indian literature. When he returned to the Caribbean, he took a position teaching history at the University of the West Indies in Jamaica. Apart from studies at Sussex leading to his doctorate (1968) and numerous fellowships abroad, B. has remained in Jamaica, where in 1983 he was appointed professor of social and cultural history.

During the late 1960s, B. achieved international recognition with three books of poems, published in rapid succession and subsequently reissued in one volume as *The Arrivants* (1973). In *Rights of Passage* (1967) various black voices, from their different situations, all ask a version of the same question: What constitutes "home" for the descendants of Africans living in the diaspora? *Masks* (1968), in the course of a visionary pilgrimage to Ghana that reverts from the present to the golden age of the Ashanti empire, first offers and then rejects the predictable answer: "Africa." But this experience of Africa, by cleansing the poet's perceptions, makes it possible for B. in *Islands* (1969) to recognize a wealth of African survivals in the Caribbean and to bring to light the region's repressed culture, its gods and rituals, whether African or indigenous in origin. As a whole the trilogy celebrates the resourcefulness with which, even in adverse circumstances of slavery and colonialism, Caribbean peoples have taken possession of their world. In so doing, *The Arrivants* transcends its origins in the Black Power politics of the 1960s. Apart from the import of its themes and B.'s conclusions about them, it is also significant for its demonstration of the poetry inherent in the rhythms and resources of Caribbean English, and for the complex architecture of lyric forms that it achieves across the span of three volumes.

Like *The Arrivants,* B.'s earliest literary criticism is concerned with exile and diaspora. In response to the migration of so many Caribbean writers away from the region, B. insists on the social function of the contemporary writer, and emphasizes the nourishment that derives from the crucial relationship between writers and their local audience. Not surprisingly, B. was the first West Indian author of unquestionably "literary" verse to present himself widely as a performer of his work, going so far as to produce a commercial recording of his reading of *The Arrivants.*

The mid-1970s was a transitional period for B.; his title pages after 1976 identify the poet as Edward Kamau, and the change symbolizes his continuing attention as both poet and professional historian to the role played by African cultures in shaping contemporary Caribbean society. "The African Presence in Caribbean Literature" (1974) is the best known of several essays in which B.

documents what he calls "Africa-in-the-Caribbean." At the same time he has offered provocative analyses of the dynamics by which different cultures interact; he has pursued the study of "interculturation" most extensively in *The Development of Creole Society in Jamaica 1770–1820* (1971) and *Contradictory Omens: Cultural Diversity and Integration in the Caribbean* (1974). During this period, B. also completed important bibliographies of Caribbean culture and literary history.

Other Exiles (1975), a retrospective collection of thirty poems from the years 1950–1975, presents personal poetry, in contrast to the public poetry of *The Arrivants:* there are several unusually intimate poems, as well as portraits sketched from his travels as a student in Europe. A complementary volume, *Black+Blues* (1976), offers a more unified set of twenty-three poems preoccupied with imagery of relics, totems, fetishes, ruins, shards. There is a strong sense that these "fragments" are *survivals,* the past alive in the present, though damaged or broken, and that attention to them can bring them to life. While there are desperate, even incendiary voices in these poems, the characteristic movement of the book is a kind of metaphysical optimism familiar from *The Arrivants.*

B.'s second trilogy, which has no collective title, appeared over the course of a decade. *Mother Poem* (1977) depicts the experience of Caribbean women, ranging from the poet's own mother to the personified island of Barbados itself. *Sun Poem* (1982) focuses on fathers and male ancestors, while the central figures of *X/Self* (1987) are the various "children" of those parents, a gallery of personalities formed or deformed by the experience of colonialism throughout the world. This trilogy is at once autobiographically intimate and mythologically vast in its conception of the cycles of history and the dynamics of culture; its ambitious scale, and its radical experiments with language (based ultimately on Caribbean speech) make it less immediately accessible than *The Arrivants. X/Self* is B.'s most innovative work to date—though it is, paradoxically, also his most comic.

As a historian B. has situated African survivals within the dynamics of cultural contact. As a critic he may strive to define narrowly a "West Indian aesthetic," yet his *History of the Voice* (1984) is an essential study of the interactions between oral and scribal poetry. As a poet, B. acknowledges the early influence of T. S. Eliot, but his career has really been shaped in amiable contention with two West Indians; B.'s accomplishment is best measured in relation to the work of Derek WALCOTT, a confessional poet of consummate technique, and that of George LAMMING, who first gave voice to the life and landscape of Barbados. Of the three, it is B. who has most affected the art of a younger generation, both in the West Indies and in Britain.

FURTHER WORKS: *Four Plays for Primary Schools* (1964); *Odale's Choice* (1967); *Folk Culture of the Slaves in Jamaica* (1970); *Caribbean Man in Space and Time* (1974); *Days & Nights* (1975); *Our Ancestral Heritage: A Bibliography of the English-Speaking Caribbean* (1977); *Wars of Respect: Nanny, Sam Sharpe and the Struggle for People's Liberation* (1977); *Barbados Poetry: A Checklist/Slavery to the Present* (1979); *Jamaica Poetry: A Checklist/Slavery to the Present* (1979); *Third World Poems* (1983); *Colonial Encounter: Language* (1984); *Roots: Literary Criticism* (1986); *Jah Music* (1986); *Sappho Sakyi's Meditations: Savacou 16* (1989); *Shar* (1992); *Middle Passage* (1992)

BIBLIOGRAPHY: Ramchand, K., *An Introduction to the Study of West Indian Literature* (1976): 127–42; Lewis, M. W., *Notes to*

Masks (1977); Dash, M., "E. B.," in King, B., ed., *West Indian Literature* (1979): 210–27; Rohlehr, G., *Pathfinder: Black Awakening in The Arrivants of E. K. B.* (1981); Baugh, E., "E. B. As Critic: Some Preliminary Observations," *CarQ*, 28: 1–2 (May-June 1982): 66–75; Rohlehr, G., "Megalleons of Light," *Jamaica Journal*, 16, 2 (1983): 81–87; Brown, L. W., *West Indian Poetry* (1984): 146–68; Brathwaite, D. M., *EKB: His Published Prose & Poetry 1948–1986* (1986)

—LAURENCE A. BREINER

BRAUN, Volker

German poet, dramatist, and novelist, b. 7 May 1939, Dresden

Early employment experience in a printing shop, as a construction worker, and as a machinist provided important background for B.'s first literary creations. From 1960 to 1964 he studied philosophy at the Karl Marx University in Leipzig (now Leipzig University). Then he worked as a drama producer for the Berlin Ensemble. Between 1967 and 1971 he devoted himself exclusively to his writing, but since 1971 he has again produced plays in theaters in Leipzig and Berlin. Among the literary awards that he has received are the Heinrich Heine Prize (1971), the Heinrich Mann Prize (1980), and the Bremen Literature Prize (1986).

B.'s creative works reflect his perceptions of the constant tension that has existed between professed and actual reality in the society where he lives. His writings are noted for their intensive treatment of political and social problems, their focus on the harsh nature of the worker's world, and their visible highlighting of the establishment's failure to respond to individual needs. During the course of his early artistic development, B. repeatedly came into conflict with the official cultural policies of the German Democratic Republic. These confrontations ultimately led to his expulsion from the directorate of the East German Writers' Union in 1976, when he openly opposed the government's action in revoking the citizenship of the controversial poet Wolf BIERMANN.

The essential character of B.'s early lyric poetry is suggested in the title of his first book of verse, *Provokation für mich* (1965; provocation for me). Dissatisfaction is the formative principle for lines containing original images derived from the work-place and its conditions, city and rural landscapes, and human relationships of friendship and love. His poems express an inner longing for change and demand introspection and self-examination from the reader.

In later collections, including *Wir und nicht sie* (1970; we and not they), *Gegen die symmetrische Welt* (1974; against the symmetrical world), and *Training des aufrechten Gangs* (1979; training to walk upright), B. softened his tone somewhat. Rebelliousness and impatience are replaced by reflection and analysis, polemic by the dialectic of present and future, and tension by a more relaxed, even cheerful mood that accompanies concrete suggestions of strategies for overcoming problems. *Langsamer knirschender Morgen* (1987; slow crackling morning), however, contains satirical poems and epigrams that focus on uncomfortable questions concerning ethics and responsibility. They present a new demonstration of B.'s penchant for sharply pointed social criticism.

In more recent poems, such as those in the fourth section of *Lustgarten Preußen* (1996; Pleasure Garden Prussia), a collection

of poetry written between 1959 and 1995, B. gives voice to a pessimism that is characteristic of the writings of many authors and poets who have had difficulty in dealing with the realities of post-reunification Germany. Visions of a dark world of unemployment, closed factories, police with tear gas, and degenerating civilization in which the enemy eats fast food are dominant features of these lyric creations.

From the official cultural perspective of the German Democratic Republic, B.'s dramatic works, with their frank and inexorable exposure of social contradictions and conflicts, were even less comfortable than his poetry. In early plays, such as *Kipper Paul Bauch* (1966; tipper Paul Bauch), *Freunde* (1971; friends), and *Hinze and Kunze* (1973; Hinze and Kunze), by stressing the disparity between the ideal of socialist production and the real mechanical tedium of physical labor, and between the adulation of male productivity and the repression of female contributions to production, B. underscored the danger inherent in sacrificing fulfillment of personal needs on the altar of community demands. His dramas attempt to represent the life of the workers as part of a historical process, but they specifically illustrate his belief that the individual can and should constructively affect the flow of history and the development of society. Subsequent works, including *Guevara; oder, Der Sonnenstaat* (1975; Guevara; or, the sun state), *Der große Frieden* (1979; the great peace), *Simplex Deutsch* (1981; German simplex), and *Transit Europa* (1987; Europe in transit), show greater maturity in their dramatic tone and their portrayal of realistic characters. They are also particularly notable for their demonstration of B.'s special mastery of sexual metaphor.

Unfortunately, the dramatic power of B.'s plays declined after 1990, as his view of history became more gloomy. Although he had frequently mocked the German Democratic Republic during its last years, labeling it a permanently provisional entity without hope or future, after its demise he clung with melancholy defiance to the lost socialist utopia, a fact that is reflected most pointedly in the allegorical play *Iphigenie in Freiheit* (1992; Iphigenie in Freedom).

The central concerns and themes of B.'s poems and dramas also inform his prose fiction and essays. Social criticism takes on an especially personal note in the analytically autobiographical segments of *Das ungezwungene Leben Kasts* (1972; rev. ed., 1979; Kast's unconstrained life), where honest rejection of dictated conceptions of life under socialism is couched in language and descriptions that are filled with earthy vitality. In the controversial *Hinze-Kunze-Roman* (1985; Hinze-Kunze novel), however, with its open treatment of sexual themes, the artistic impact of B.'s attack on political hypocrisy and repression is reduced by tastelessness of presentation that is only partially offset by the uniqueness of the work.

In tone and attitude B.'s prose fiction of the 1990s reflects increasing despair caused by the necessity of facing the problems of transition into a capitalistic existence. *Der Wendehals* (1995; The Wryneck), which is actually a combination of prose and dialogue, is filled with pessimistic resignation toward a life of untenable conditions in which it is no longer necessary to think, to prove anything, or to work for the common good, while the bitterly humorous, didactic narrative *Die vier Werkzeugmacher* (1996; The Four Tool Makers) describes the cruel transformation of a socialist workers' brigade into a group of men who lose their identity with the loss of their property and jobs.

The strength of B.'s commitment to personal involvement in the processes of political and social change is perhaps most readily visible in some of his essays and occasional pieces. The collections

Es genügt nicht die einfache Wahrheit (1975; the simple truth is not enough) and *Verheerende Folgen mangelnden Anscheins innerbetrieblicher Demokratie* (1988; devastating consequences of the insufficient likelihood of internal democracy), besides being essays of high quality dealing with specific writers, works, and theoretical problems of art and literature, represent pointed treatments of environmental, social, and other issues, in which B. defends his right to assume a critical, revolutionary stance with respect to reality.

The nonconformity that made B. a controversial literary figure in the German Democratic Republic, his open, frank, and critical examination of contemporary problems, his gift for creating effective satire, and his open advocacy of cultural reform combine to make him one of the most significant and interesting writers to emerge in East Germany after 1960.

FURTHER WORKS: *Vorläufiges* (1966); *Kriegserklärung. Fotogramme* (1967); *Die Kipper* (1972); *Gedichte* (1972); *Stücke 1* (1976); *Unvollendete Geschichte* (1977); *Poesie Album 115* (1977); *Der Stoff zum Leben* (1977); *Tinka* (1977); *Im Querschnitt V. B.* (1978); *Gedichte* (1979); *Stücke 2* (1981); *Berichte von Hinze und Kunze* (1983); *Archaische Landschaft mit Loüsungen* (1983); *Stücke* (2 vols., 1983, 1989); *Rimbaud, ein Psalm der Aktualitatü* (1985; *Rimbaud, a Topical Psalm*, 1989); *Stücke 3* (1987); *Gesammelte Stücke* (1988); *Annatomie* (1989); *Bodenloser Satz* (1990); *Der Stoff zum Leben* (1990); *Die Tribüne. Training des aufrechten Gangs. Guevara oder der Sonnenstaat. Großer Frieden. Schriften* (1990); *Texte in zeitlicher Folge* (1990); *Böhmen am Meer* (1992); *Die Zickzackbrücke* (1992); *Das Nichtgelebte* (1995)

BIBLIOGRAPHY: Arnold, H., *V. B.* (1972); Subiotto, A., "The Lyric Poetry of V. B.," *GDR Monitor*, 4 (1980–81): 1–13; Wallace, I., *The GDR under Honecker 1971–1981* (1981): 43–62; Rosellini, J., *V. B.* (1983); Wallace, I., "V. B.'s Lyric Poetry: Problems of Reception," in Gerber, M., ed., *Studies in GDR Culture and Society*, Vol. 3 (1983): 179–93; Cosentino, C., "V. B.'s *Geschichten von Hinze und Kunze*: A New Look at an Old Problem," in Gerber, M., ed., *Studies in GDR Culture and Society* (1984), Vol. 4: 95–106; Profitlich, U., *V. B.* (1985); Hilton, J., "Back to the Future—V. B. and the German Theatrical Tradition," in Sebald, W. G., ed., *A Radical Stage: Theater in Germany in the 1970s and 1980s* (1988): 124–44; Dart, J., "The Death of a Provocateuse: Some Thoughts on V. B.'s *Tinka*," *GDR Monitor*, 20 (1988–89): 65–79; Jaquemoth, J., *Politik und Poesie* (1990); Jucker, R., ed., *V. B.* (1995); Costabile-Heming, C. A., *Intertextual Exile* (1997)

—LOWELL A. BANGERTER

BRAZILIAN LITERATURE

The end of the 19th c. in Brazil was marked by political and economic upheaval that gradually affected national attitudes and helped to open the way for great changes in the 20th c. At first, however, little change could be observed in literature.

Joaquim Maria Machado de Assis (1839–1908), the country's greatest novelist, continued to write fiction like *Dom Casmurro* (1900; *Dom Casmurro*, 1953) in his familiar detached, ironical style about what seemed a stable, self-centered society. The qualities of his work which are most appreciated by the modern

critic and which he had developed in the 1880s were not understood at the beginning of this century. His daring breaches of established canons of fiction—his experiments with style, structure, and even punctuation, the fragmentation of scenes, his personal intrusion as the author into the flow of the narrative—were considered defects by his critics.

Much less modern than Machado de Assis, although he was a full generation younger, was Brazil's most prolific writer, Henrique Coelho Neto (1864–1934), who alternated between two 19th-c. literary schools, SYMBOLISM and naturalism, in his most famous novel *Rei negro* (1916; the black king), the story of a slave of royal lineage. His cultivation of a highly literary, ornate style and a vast vocabulary for which he searched the classics of the Portuguese language, was the antithesis of the direction that Brazilian writers were to follow immediately after World War I.

The two dominant schools of poetry, Parnassianism and symbolism, which dated from the 1880s and 1890s respectively, ran their course with more attention to the international literary scene than to Brazilian reality, as may be seen in the Parnassian sonnets of Olavo Bilac (1865–1918) and the "medieval" and liturgical poetry of the symbolist Alphonsus de Guimaraens (1870–1921).

In contrast to the internationalism of the disciples of the French schools, by the early 1900s some other writers began to emphasize the need for a deeper understanding of Brazilian culture and an adequate preparation for future realization of the nation's possibilities. In 1902 Euclides da Cunha (1866–1909) published *Os sertões* (*Rebellion in the Backlands*, 1944), the greatest national literary achievement up to that time, an enormous work of nonfiction presenting an account of the primitive conditions of life of the millions of peasants who were completely forgotten by the dominant elite. In the same year José da Graça ARANHA published *Canaã* (*Canaan*, 1920), in which he argued that the future Brazil would be a multiracial mixed society; and Sílvio Romero (1851–1914), the first great Brazilian critic, brought out a revised edition of his *História da literatura brasileira* (history of Brazilian literature), which has been called the first great document to deal with the importance of nationalism as a criterion of literary greatness.

Afonso Henriques de Lima Barreto (1881–1922), like Machado de Assis a mulatto, was to become the first important writer of fiction dealing with social problems. In *O triste fim de Policarpo Quaresma* (1911; the sad destiny of Policarpo Quaresma) he tried to expose the basic intolerance of the government and the hypocrisy of society and its leaders. His great theme, however, was the unhappy lot of the blacks and mulattoes who found little opportunity for upward mobility in a society that considered itself European and Latin. This theme, which Machado de Assis scarcely touched, is developed in three of Barreto's other novels: *Recordações do escrivão Isaías Caminha* (1909; recollections of Isaías Caminha, notary public), *Vida e morte de M. Gonzaga de Sá* (1919; the life and death of M. Gonzaga de Sá), and *Clara dos Anjos* (serialized 1923–24; in book form, 1948; Clara dos Anjos). Barreto's friend and publisher, José Monteiro LOBATO, also questioned accepted values. He is at his best as a short-story writer, and his best stories are found in his collection *Urupês* (1918; Urupês), an unvarnished picture of rural and small-town life in the state of São Paulo. This work's importance cannot be underestimated in a study of Brazilian MODERNISM, a movement that was to dominate all the arts until after World War II and the influence of which is still felt on the cultural scene.

Though modernist tendencies were to be observed in the writers of the first two decades, the event that brought the movement to the public eye was A Semana de Arte Moderna (Modern Art Week) in February 1922, a series of sessions on the arts held in the Municipal Theater of São Paulo, in which the basic modernist tenets were set forth. Art was to look to native sources for inspiration, the writer was to write in the Brazilian vernacular, and the new artistic movements that had been sweeping Europe in the last decade were to be welcomed to Brazil. A second dramatic event was the session in 1924 of the Brazilian Academy of Letters in which José da Graça Aranha, a founding member, directed a strong attack at the literary conservatism of that body and resigned. Meanwhile, modernism, which had originally been identified with São Paulo, was spreading throughout the country, in part because of the activity of Mário de ANDRADE, its outstanding exponent and the author of what may be called its central work, *Macunaíma* (1928; Macunaíma). This has been variously called a novel, an epic, and a rhapsody. It is based on Indian legends and Brazilian history and written in a language incorporating vocabulary and idioms from different regions of the country. A second seminal influence was exercised by Oswald de ANDRADE, who best personifies the avant-garde character of modernism, with his irreverent attitudes, the telegraphic, staccato style of his colloquial verse, and the fragmentary structure of such fiction as *Memórias sentimentais de João Miramar* (1923; the sentimental memoirs of João Miramar). Another basic work is the poem about the Amazon region *Cobra Norato* (1931; Norato the snake) by Raul Bopp (b. 1898), which is associated with the irreverent, iconoclastic Antropofagia (cannibalism) group, as Oswald de Andrade's book of verse *Pau Brasil* (1925; brazil wood) is associated with the Pau Brasil group. A third modernist movement was intensely nationalistic, not only within its literary implications, but also because of its political philosophy. *Verde-amarelismo*, or "green-yellowness," got its patriotic name from the colors of the Brazilian flag. It found its intellectual basis but not its fascistic overtones in the writings of Euclides da Cunha, Alberto Torres (1865–1917), and other thinkers. Its leading literary representatives were the novelist and politician Plínio Salgado (1901–1975), who founded the ideologically fascist Integralista party, and Cassiano RICARDO, a poet who was later to abandon the movement and to stray as far as concrete poetry, but who at this stage wrote the epic poem of the modernist movement, *Martim Cererê* (1928; Martim Cererê).

Modernism in Portugal, despite its futurist leanings, was a very different movement from its Brazilian counterpart, for it came earlier and it had its roots in symbolism and not in nationalism, but the two movements are linked through the person of Ronald de Carvalho (1893–1935), a Brazilian poet, essayist, and critic. He was the coeditor of the first issue of the magazine *Orpheu* in 1915, which presented modernism to the Portuguese public, and seven years later he participated in the Semana de Arte Moderna. His book *Toda a América* (1926; all America) is a collection of poems in Whitmanesque cadences in which in a powerful expression of pan-Americanism he sings of the greatness, geographical, historical, and human, of the western hemisphere.

Manuel BANDEIRA, who also participated in the Semana de Arte Moderna, was the leader of the modernists of Rio de Janeiro. There the important modernist group was connected with the magazine *Festa* (founded 1927) which, because it felt the need to emphasize tradition and spiritual values, did not accept modernism completely. The leading *Festa* poet was Cecília MEIRELES, the greatest woman poet of the Portuguese language. Another *Festa* poet, Tasso da Silveira (1895–1968), returned to Catholicism, as did the poet Murilo Mendes (1901–1975), a kindred spirit although

not a member of the *Festa* group, who had been a contributor to the *Revista de Antropofagia* (founded 1928). Vinícius de Morais (1913–1980), like Cecília Meireles a native of Rio de Janeiro, was active in artistic fields not only as a poet who was faithful to the ironic, colloquial tradition of modernism, but also as a musician and composer of lyrics for popular music. He was the author of the play *Orfeu da Conceição* (1956; Orfeu da Conceição), on which the scenario of the film *Black Orpheus* is based.

In the state of Minas Gerais the great modernist poet was Carlos Drummond de ANDRADE who is now considered Brazil's greatest living poet. His poetry has progressed from the characteristic modernist irony of the 1920s through unsentimental family reminiscences to pessimistic social criticism, philosophical musings, and finally a serene contemplation of the world. The outstanding poet of the Northeast of the period, if we except Manuel Bandeira, who had left Recife as a child, was Jorge de Lima (1895–1951), who at his best wrote fine Negro poetry and profound religious poetry. Like Jorge de Lima in his *Poemas negros* (1947; negro poems), Ascenso Ferreira (1895–1965) in his *Catimbó* (1927; Catimbó) used the Blacks of the Northeast as a subject and incorporated African rhythms and vocabulary from African languages into his poetry.

The novel, however, was more important than lyric poetry in the literature of the Northeast. This region had developed its own variety of modernism, at the center of which was Gilberto FREYRE. In *Casa grande e senzala* (1933; *The Masters and the Slaves*, 1946) and later books he stresses the place in the culture of the region of traditions and the African legacy, themes that strongly affected the content of many other novels of the Northeast. Under Freyre's influence novelists became concerned primarily with economic and social problems: the collapse of old social structures, a bankrupt monocultural economy, and overwhelming poverty. Another common theme is that of the devastating droughts to which the region is periodically subject. The first of these novels, *A bagaceira* (1928; *Trash*, 1978) by José América de Almeida (b. 1887), is about traditional ways on a plantation and the changes brought by the arrival of a group of drought refugees. Almeida was followed by Rachel de QUEIROZ, the first woman to be elected to the Brazilian Academy of Letters; Graciliano RAMOS; José Lins do RÊGO; and Jorge AMADO.

After the 1930s and 1940s new forces began to revitalize this regional fiction. Adonias Filho's (b. 1915) *Memórias de Lázaro* (1952; memoirs of Lazarus) owes more to FAULKNER than to Freyre. João Guimarães ROSA, the great international figure of the second half of the century, wrote about a particular region in Minas Gerais that shares the culture and some of the problems of the Northeast, but he was more concerned with philosophical than social matters, and more interested in style, language, and structure than were the earlier novelists of the Northeast.

In the 1930s much fiction was written that was not especially sociological. Most of the novels of Érico VERÍSSIMO, such as *Olhai os lírios do campo* (1938; *Consider the Lilies of the Field*, 1947), were psychological in intent, although in the case of Veríssimo his best work is an epic trilogy of the history of his native Rio Grande do Sul, *O tempo e o vento* (1949–62; partial tr., *Time and the Wind*, 1951). Other psychological novels are *Salgueiro* (1934; Salgueiro) by Lúcio Cardoso (1913–1968), the chronicle of Rio's hilltop slums, and the thirteen volumes of *A tragédia burguesa* (1937–77; the bourgeois tragedy) by Octavio de Faria (b. 1908), a study of human beings in a world of crumbling social structures in which Catholicism is the only enduring force. Antônio Callado (b. 1917) also analyzes moral problems from the Catholic point of view, as in the excellent political novel *Quarup* (1967; *Quarup*, 1970), in which the action grows out of the relation of the devout Catholic to civil authorities and Marxist movements. The most highly praised political novel—partly because of the brilliant handling of regional language is *Vila dos confins* (1956; frontier town) by Mário Palmério (b. 1916), which is about political bossism and elections in a small town.

In addition to experimenting with language and style, many authors have experimented with narrative form and point of view. Some of the leading writers (among them several highly gifted women) write introspective fiction that shows the influence of Virginia WOOLF and the French NEW NOVEL. An example is the work of Lygia Fagundes Telles (b. 1919), whose novel *As meninas* (1973; the young girls) is composed of a series of excellent interior monologues. The most consistent writer of introspective fiction is Clarice LISPECTOR, in whose highly abstract narratives characterization and story line are completely subordinated to the presentation of mental states and emotional reactions. Her most famous novel, *A maçã no escuro* (1961; *The Apple in the Dark*, 1967), has been called an amazing search into the meanderings of the human soul. Nélida Piñón (b. 193?), a devoted student and practitioner of the most esoteric narrative techniques, has come under the influence of GARCÍA MÁRQUEZ in *Tebas do meu coração* (1974; beloved Thebes). Other Spanish American writers of fiction who have influenced the contemporary Brazilian novel are BORGES and CORTÁZAR. One very introspective novel in which Borges's circular form and Cortázar's aleatory method are adopted is *Avalovara* (1973; *Avalovara*, 1979) by Osman Lins (1924–1978), whose interest in exploring the possibilities of new techniques is seen in the geometrical, polyphonic narratives of *Nove, novena* (1966; nine, novena), which are variations on themes that recall the New Novel.

The tradition of the Brazilian short story goes back to Machado de Assis, the great master of the genre. Afonso Henriques de Lima Barreto wrote a few excellent short stories, and José Monteiro Lobato achieved lasting success only with his short fiction and children's tales. The genre flourished through the period of modernism, and in the work of Mário de Andrade it reached one of its heights of splendor. An equally fine artist was his contemporary, Antônio de Alcântara Machado (1901–1935), who is at his best in his tales of first and second-generation Italians in São Paulo. João Alphonsus (1901–1944), the son of the symbolist poet Alphonsus de Guimaraens, depicted with depth and sensitivity his native state of Minas Gerais. Recent noteworthy collections are João Guimarães Rosa's regional *Primeiras estórias* (1962; *The Third Bank of the River, and Other Stories*, 1968), Lygia Fagundes Telles's *Antes do baile verde* (1970; before the green dance), and *A imitação da rosa* (1973; the imitation of the rose), a volume of her short fiction selected by Clarice Lispector, whose own work in this genre is considered by many critics to be better than her novels because of its superior concentration of style and structure. The urban short story is of particular interest in the latter part of the 20th c. Frequently the theme is that of the individual faced by a complicated, impersonal, and violent civilization that he fears but cannot flee. The world of Dalton Trevisan (b. 1925) as it appears in *O vampiro de Curitiba* (1965; *The Vampire of Curitiba, and Other Stories*, 1972) is one in which abnormal personalities live and struggle violently with each other in a provincial city that has grown large too fast. Writing in a brilliant, ironic style, Rubem Fonseca (b. 1925?) uses cinematic techniques and surrealistic

settings to metaphorize the brutal irrationality of the modern city in his *Lúcia McCartney* (1969; Lúcia McCartney), and other fiction including *Feliz aniversário* (1975; happy birthday). Opening a new literary field, Samuel Rawet (b. 1929) writes about his personal experience as an alienated Polish-Jewish immigrant boy in Rio de Janeiro in his *Contos do imigrante* (1956; stories of an immigrant).

Postmodernist fiction did not abandon modernism. In poetry, on the other hand, in the 1940s there was a moment of nostalgia for traditional forms and "poetic" language that was marked by the appearance of a group called the Generation of '45. It consisted of several fine poets, including Domingos Carvalho da Silva (b. 1915), Mauro Mota (b. 1912), and Marcos Konder Reis (b. 1922), who resurrected the quest for pure poetry and the notion of the exalted nature of art. João Cabral de Melo Neto (b. 1920) was at first identified with this group, but his developing surrealism, his socially conscious verse, his mature style, which had become dry and conceptual, and his visual treatment of his subject matter separated him from it. Still, he was to become the poet most widely imitated by younger writers. Among those attracted by his visualism and his concentration on definition of his poetic object were the concrete poets, a São Paulo group emerging after 1954 and led by Haroldo de Campos (b. 1929), his brother Augusto (b. 1931), and Décio Pignatari (b. 1927). Their central theory, which they practiced as well as preached, was that the poem should have spatial dimension and visual form. Augusto Campos's *Equivocábulos* (1970; equivocables) is a collection of photo-poems—semantic visual texts. João Cabral de Melo Neto was an interested observer of this movement, and many older poets, including Cassiano Ricardo, wrote concrete poems. Ferreira Gullar (b. 1930) saw the limitations of concrete poetry that were caused by its sacrifice of communication to graphic effect, and he and others sought different solutions. Mário Chamie (b. 1933) demonstrated the necessity of research into the nature of poetry. Poetry, he felt, should communicate the message of Marxism, and he attacked the reification preached by the concrete poets.

The poet whose reputation has been climbing most steadily since the 1960s is Carlos Nejar (b. 1931), the author of *Silesis* (1960; Silesis) and other volumes of epics, lyrics, and narratives, including *O chapeu das estações* (1978; a hat for the seasons). He writes poems about nature, love, and death that express a feeling of the universal presence of God and the inevitability of suffering.

In the late 1920s, after a long barren period, the Brazilian theater began to stir to life with the emergence of theatrical groups in different parts of the country; however, except for *Deus the pague* (1932; may God reward you) by Juraci Camargo (1898–1973), which gained great notoriety because it seemed subversive in that prewar world, nothing of significance by a Brazilian dramatist was produced until *Vestido de noiva* (the wedding dress) was staged in 1943 by a Polish director named Ziembinski, who brought new life to the moribund theater. The author was Nelson RODRIGUES, whose psychological plays show the influence of EXPRESSIONISM and FREUD. Other groups and directors appeared, and by the 1950s the golden age of the Brazilian drama had begun with a series of fine social plays whose themes were developed through the subject matter of traditional folklore. Ariano Suassuna (b. 1927) became famous overnight with his sacramental drama *Auto da Compadecida* (1959; *The Rogue's Trial*, 1963), which showed the influence of the father of the Portuguese theater, Gil Vicente (1465?–1536?). It is a play of social criticism and popular Catholicism. Of similar nature is *O pagador de promessas* (1961; *Journey to Bahia*, 1964), which attacks ecclesiastical bureaucuracy and formalism and jour-nalistic venality but which, like *Auto da Compadecida*, owed its great popularity to its successful treatment of folk material. The most powerful contemporary dramatist is Jorge Andrade (b. 1922), who uses a variety of theatrical techniques to depict the decaying São Paulo aristocracy in *A moratória* (1959; the moratorium) and rural fanaticism, unrest, and violence in *A vereda da salvação* (1964; the road to salvation). He is the author of eight other first-rate dramas and comedies, but he seems now to have abandoned the theater for television drama and prose fiction. One of the leading figures of the recent Brazilian theater is Augusto Boal (dates n.a.), who has been experimenting with a theater of improvisation and participation, the purpose of which is Marxist indoctrination.

Brazilian literature may be considered a derivative literature in the sense that American literature is also derivative: both follow European literary movements and both look to cities in Europe as centers of intellectual inspiration. Yet, at the same time it is independent and preoccupied with a search for its own identity and for the meaning of the Brazilian experience. The Brazilian author is jealous of his indigenous material and of his own indigenous brand of Portuguese. He looks to the world around him for subject matter and finds strength in his local or regional background even when he has become an uprooted cosmopolitan. He has developed an excellent theater, a greatly varied corpus of fiction, and poetry of philosophical depth and intellectual power, and he has been guided during this century by disciplined and competent critics.

BIBLIOGRAPHY: Ellison, F. P., *Brazil's New Novel* (1954); Bandeira, M., *Brief History of Brazilian Literature* (1958); Martins, W., *The Modernist Idea* (1970); Bishop, E. and E. Brasil, Introduction to *An Anthology of Twentieth Century Brazilian Poetry* (1972): vii—xxi; Neistein, J., ed., M. Cardozo, trans., *Poesia Brasileira Moderna: A Bilingual Anthology* (1972); Martins, H., ed., Introduction to *The Brazilian Novel* (1976): iii—xii; special Brazil section, "The Three Worlds of Lusophone Literature," *WLT*, 53 (1979): 16–39

—RAYMOND S. SAYERS

Brazilian Literature since 1964

The military dictatorship that ruled Brazil from 1964 to 1985 and the struggling democracy following in its aftermath have so thoroughly conditioned the orientation of Brazilian literature over the last quarter century that they merit attention.

The military coup d'état in March 1964 was a result of the social upheaval under a democratically elected government. The sudden resignation of President Jânio Quadros, the assumption of power by his vice president (the supposedly left-leaning João "Jango" Goulart), continuing workers' protests in the cities, and the massive literary campaigns in the impoverished Northeast fueled hostility toward democracy among the military and its supporters in the traditional Brazilian elite.

While the initial military period (1964–1968) was seen as a brief detour in Brazil's democratic path, the regime confronted an internal guerrilla insurgency and continuing demands for improv-ing conditions of the majority of Brazil's then seventy million inhabitants living in dire circumstances. Five "Institutional Acts" were decreed, which gradually curtailed citizens' rights. "Institu-tional Act 5" of December 1968 established prior censorship and had disastrous effects on culture. It also signaled the beginning of a

despotic campaign of suppression, torture, and murder against "suspect" elements in the society.

By 1977 the international outcry against these human-rights abuses led the regime to foresee a gradual return to democracy: A general amnesty was decreed, opposition political parties formed, and some elections were allowed. The 1984 popular campaign for a direct vote for a civilian president failed. The military choice for president, Tancredo Neves, died on the night before assuming office in 1985. Vice-president-to-be Josée Sarney, a collaborationist politician associated with the traditional Brazilian brand of clientelist politics (and a literary figure), became the first nonmilitary presi-dent of Brazil since 1964.

The exit of the military led to a euphoria that soon turned to national depression. The military's much-heralded "economic mira-cle," financed by loans from international banks and governments, began to fade when the nation was unable to service these debts. The Sarney administration proved to be a debacle. In 1989 Fernando collor de Melo, a young, minor political figure was elected presi-dent. His promises to control wild inflation, bring a better life to all Brazilians, and protect the atmosphere—generally to remedy the conditions that had led the society of 155 million people into a total economic and social tailspin—have faltered.

During the initial period of dictatorship, the neorealist or social novelists of the 1930s and 1940s—Rachel de QUEIROZ, Érico VERÍSSIMO and Jorge AMADO—remained active, but powerful works of fiction by a newer group of writers (who are now established masters) appeared. Antônio CALLADO's *Quarup* (1967; *Quarup* 1970), as well as some of his later novels, raised the issue of Brazil's Indians to a philosophical level about the nation's future existence. Carlos Heitor Cony (b. 1926) published a semiauto-biographical novel, *Pessach, a travessia* (1967; "Passover, the Crossing," selection in *Jewish Spectator* [Winter 1984]), which narrates a middle-class Brazilian's political "awakening" and his participation in a guerrilla movement. Osman Lins's (1924–1978) collection of stories, *Nove, novena* (1966; *Nine, Novena*, 1995) reflected the world of social injustice surrounding him. More significantly, in these stories he engages in a debate about the artist's role in society. This last concern is preeminent in his novel *Avalovara* (1973; *Avalovara*, 1980), in which the author requires his reader's active participation in the writing process. Stylistic originality is also a concern of Autran Dourado's (b. 1926) work, notably *O risco do bordado* (1970; *Pattern for a Tapestry*, 1974).

Regionalism, a major tradition of Brazilian literature, had assumed an important reorientation under the influence of João GUIMARÃES ROSA. It continued to thrive in different reformulations in the works of Josué Montello (b. 1917) from Maranhão state, Herberto Sales (b. 1917) from Bahia state, and J. J. Veiga (b. 1915) from Goiãs state, among many others.

Poets of the stature of Drummond de Andrade, Mário Quintana (b. 1906), and João Cabral de MELO NETO were extremely active. The unity of the "concretists" poets, who had appeared in 1956 led by Haroldo de Campos (b. 1929), Augusto de Campos (b. 1931), and Décio Pignatari (b. 1927), began to dissipate in the early 1960s with a flood of tangential movements concerned with the use and image of the poetic word. Among the most important movements were Mário Chamie's (b. 1933) "praxis poetry"; "semiotic poetry," which offered code poems or collages lacking words; and the "process poem," whose poets declared the autonomy of the poem itself over its being written or read. Traditional approaches to poetry—Lyric, religious, philosophical—continued from a new angle. Lindolf Bell's (b. 1938) "poetic catechism movement" was preoccupied with social justice rather than religious issues. Moacyr Félix's (b. 1926) "street guitar movement" was aimed at mass participation in and comprehension of poetry as a path toward knowledge. Among the younger regionalist poets of note are Marcus Accioly (b. 1943) from Pernambuco state, Ruy Espinheira Filho (b. 1942), and the members of the "pocket lyre group" in Bahia state.

Brazilian theater was active in social causes throughout these years. The Popular Culture Centers were hotbeds of thematically leftist plays aimed at mobilization of the poor. The Opinião Theater Group under the direction of dramatist Oduvaldo Viana Filho (1936–1974) put on the *Show Opinião* in late 1964, which eloquently interwove song and individual testimony into a highly charged protest against the newly installed military regime. Viana Filho's greatest success—and perhaps the most important Brazilian drama of the last thirty years—was *Rasga coraçã* (1974; render heart). Using techniques of the Brechtian realist theater and the musical revue, Viana Filho debated the role of political existence in Brazil since the 1920s. The Arena Theater of São Paulo, under the direction of Augusto BOAL and Gianfrancesco Guarnieri (b. 1934), and the Oficina group, led by José Celso Martínez (dates n.a.), brought the debate over the national identity and direction to the forefront of discussion in highly successful allegorical musicals inspired by Brazil's past.

Literary criticism turned from superficial impressionism toward professionalism in the 1960s. Antônio Cândido (b. 1918) published *Literatura e sociedade* (1965; *On Literature and Society*, 1995), which led to a new emphasis on textual analysis; his disciples are among the leading literary critics of contemporary Brazil. Two other major figures of criticism of the last quarter century are Afrânio Coutinho (b. 1911) and Wilson Martins (b. 1921).

The "Institutional Act 5" of 1968 led to direct confrontations with the military censors, who attempted to prevent the publication or representation of any work even slightly critical of the political status quo. Writers began to be persecuted: Callado and poet Ferreira Gullar (b. 1930) were jailed; Boal was tortured; and drama came to an almost total halt owing to censorship or lack of resources.

Several works of fiction were banned outright. For example, Ignácio de Loyola Brandão's (b. 1936) novel *Zero* (1975; *Zero*, 1984) appeared first in Italian, but was prohibited in Brazil just after publication. *Zero* is a cinematic portrait of the squalor of urban life in a fictitious country resembling Brazil; the protagonist's only possible salvation is turning to revolution to attain his "freedom." Brandão has subsequently published major works at the heartbeat of Brazilian life: *Naão vera´s país nenhum* (1981; *And Still the Earth*, 1985), about the total atmospheric devastation of a future Brazil, and *O beijo nãao vem na boca* (1985; the kiss is not on the mouth). Rubem FONSECA, arguably Brazil's most popular novelist today, published a collection of stories, *Feliz ano novo* (1975; happy new year), that was banned by the regime for gross violence and pornography. Fonseca believes that the stories did no more than reflect the violence instilled in the society by military repression.

Writers sought new avenues for their expression of rage and resistance toward the regime through subtle or direct allegory, parody, testimonial literature, nonfiction fiction and (auto)biography. Oswaldo Franca Júnior's (1936–1989) allegory *Um dia no Rio* (1969; a day in rio) has two parallel plots: the beginning of the

students' protest against the regime and a small-time businessmen's schemes for rapid wealth during the "economic miracle"—both are doomed to failure. Ivan Ângelo (b. 1936) published *A festa* (1976; *The Celebration*, 1982), an allegory in which a historical event of the turn of the century represents the sociohistorical present of injustice in Brazil. It is notable for its unique puzzlelike structure and innovative use of language. Ângelo also published a collection of stories, *Casa de vidro* (1979; *Tower of Glass*, 1986), which further dramatized the nation's continuing dilemma.

Testimonial literature presented the marginalized elements of Brazilian society—those who live without the benefit of law and justice—particularly in urban centers. For example, João Antônio's (b. 1937) short fiction, such as *Leão de cha´cara* (1975; the bouncer), is set in the slums of São Paulo and Rio. Very unsubtle and nonfiction fiction appeared based on the real events: these novels were not only a form of protest, but also served as a means of documentation of events whose publication had been censored. Among these novels, Carlos Heitor Cony's *O caso Lou* (1975; the Lou file) and works by José Louzeiro (b. 1932) are of particular interest. Darcy RIBEIRO's *Maíra* (1976; *Maíra*, 1984) was yet another neo-Indianist appeal for justice for the indigenous Brazilians. In this novel, Indian civilization is portrayed as equal to that of other Brazilian races.

Outstanding women writers began to be noticed by the mid-1970s. Clarice LISPECTOR's reputation as Latin America's preeminent woman writer grew to international proportions by the early 1990s. Maria Alice Barroso (b. 1926), Lygia Fagundes TELLES, and Nélida PIÑON were outspoken about military repression and produced significant works of literature on the Brazilian woman's situation during the regime and afterward.

Contemporaneously with this protest fiction, a "poetry of suffocation" by younger poets expressed the mood of helplessness and alienation pervading the society. Unable to obtain mainstream publishing contracts, they turned to mimeographing their own poetry and handing it out for free. Many of the poets of the "mimeograph generation" became important figures of the 1980s: Ana Cristina César (1952–1983), Cacaso (pseud. of Antônio Carlos de Brito, 1944–1987), and Chico Alvim (dates n.a.). Chico BUARQUE, the master of protest song since the 1960s, was gradually recognized as a major poet and dramatist.

Overall, Brazilian theater was devastated by censorship. The social dramas of Leilah Assunção (b. 1943) and Consuelo de Castro (b. 1946) gained national attention and, consequently, were often censored. Many of the professional theatrical organizations went into bankruptcy and closed. Smaller alternative theater groups became common in the 1970s. José Vicente's (b. 1945) Ipanema Theater became the center of *tropicalismo*, the nationalistic, all-arts-inclusive movement, which had begun in 1967 and lasted through the early 1970s. *Tropicalismo* sought the reevaluation of Brazilian culture within the context of the modern technologies of cultural representation. Perhaps the culmination of this movement in the theater came in 1978 when director José Alves Antunes Filho's (b. 1929) adaptation of Mário de ANDRADE's 1928 nativist classic *Macunaíma* was staged and became an international hit.

The beginning of amnesty and the easing of censorship led to a flood of memoirs and testimonies about the 1960s and 1970s by the political and inner exiles, such as Fernando Gabeira (b. 1943), who had participated in the kidnapping of the American ambassador in 1969, and Pedro Nava (1903–1984). These memoirs sought to reclaim the recent past for all Brazilians.

New national literary concerns appeared in the early 1980s: the growth to dominance of urban Brazil; feminist concerns; the predominance of a young (under-thirty) population; ecological questions; the black Brazilian experience; and the role of the immigrant within the culture.

Some of the most successful works of recent fiction reflect the contradictions of a society hell-bent on industrialization and urbanization. In João Ubaldo RIBEIRO's *Vila Real* (1979; Vila Real) backlanders struggle for survival against an encroaching company. Márcio Souza (b. 1946) dealt mockingly with serious issues of internal and external neocolonialism in Brazil's Amazon in novels such as *O imperador do Acre* (1976; *The Emperor of the Amazon*, 1980) and *Mad Maria* (1980; *Mad Maria*, 1985). Rubem Fonseca's novels revitalized the 1930s detective-novel genre from a purely Brazilian angle. Ana Miranda (b. 1954) has garnered attention for her series of nationalistic historical fiction, most notably, *Boca do Inferno* (1989; *Bay of All Saints and Every Conceivable Sin*, 1991).

Several subcategories of fiction are of note in recent years. The gay life-style is dealt with in the works of writers such as João Silvério Trevisan (b. 1944), as in his *Em nome do desejo* (1983; in the name of desire), who also published a sociocultural history of homosexuality in Brazil: *Devassos no paraíso* (1986; *Perverts in Paradise*, 1986); and Herbert Daniel (b. 1944), who, in addition, has been an AIDS activist. Cassandra Rios (dates n.a.) has written numerous works of fiction about lesbian and bisexual activities; she is a best-selling author within her category. Afro-Brazilian writers have appeared in several urban centers. In São Paulo, the literary journal *Cuadernos Negros* publishes both fiction and poetry of these writers; the younger generation includes Adõ Ventura (b. 1946), José Carlos Limeira (b. 1951), Eli Semog (b. 1952), and Eustáquio Rodrigues (dates n.a.). Moacyr SCLIAR has distinguished himself as the most successful narrator of the Jewish-Brazilian immigrant experience.

The short story or ministory continues to be the most popularly read literary form. The newest generation of short-fiction writers focuses on the dilemmas of the young Brazilians who came to maturity during the regime. The widening generation conflict, the use of drugs, the flaunting of sex, the television and technological ages are repeated themes of stories by Luís Fernando Emediato (b. 1951), Domingos Pellegrini, Jr., (b. 1949), Joáo Gilberto Noll (b. 1947), and Caio Fernando Abreu (b. 1948).

Satire about the oftentimes surprising reality of Brazilian existence has become an important sub-category of short fiction and the Brazilian crônica. Luís Fernando Veríssimo's (b. 1936) *O analista de Bagé* (1983; the analyst from Bagé), a satirical view of Brazilian life, has become the all-time best-seller of Brazilian literature. Carlos Eduardo Novaes's (b. 1940) satires are of a similar nature, although his targets are the fleeting politicians of the moment.

Short fiction about the contemporary Brazilian woman's situation merits special note. Sônia Coutinho (b. 1939) has published both short fiction, such as *Uma certa felicidade* (1976; a certain happiness), and an important novel, *Atire em Sofia* (1989; shoot Sofia), in which women see themselves as outcasts in a macho society. Hilda Hilst's (b. 1930) and Mácia Dénser's (b. 1949) fiction uses blatant profanity to describe the life-style of newly liberated Brazilian women.

"Concert poetry" performed in restaurants, bars, on the beach, and during soccer games became popular in Rio of the mid-1980s among younger poets who express no particular attitude or approach of note. Some of the principal figures are Glória Horta (b. 1954), Suzana Vargas, Alex Polari, Régis Bonvicino, and Daisy

Damas (dates n.a.), who openly cultivate the "poema pornô" the pornographic poem.

Theater literally struggles for survival. Nonetheless, innovative works have been written and produced by Naum Alves de Souza, Maria Adelaide Amaral (dates n.a.), and Mauro Rasi (b. 1954). Gerald Thomas (b. 1955) has launched punk versions of classical dramas.

Solid literary criticism reflecting both nationalist and internationalist orientations flourishes with several preeminent figures, including Fábio Lucas (b. 1931), Silviano Santiago (b. 1936), Affonso Romano de Sant'Anna (b. 1937), Luís Costa Lima (b. 1937), Roberto Schwarz (b. 1938), Davi Arrigucci, Jr. (dates n.a.), José Guilherme Merquior (1941–1991), Walnice Galvão (dates n.a.), and Flora Sussekind (b. 1955), among many others.

Over this quarter century, the traditional social preoccupation of Brazilian literature has been reinforced and is now the predominant concern of literary activity. Without doubt, Brazilian writers view this approach as a form of participatory democracy, which the society as a whole has yet to fully enjoy.

BIBLIOGRAPHY: Lowe, E., *The City in Brazilian Literature* (1982); Haberly, D. T., *Three Sad Races: Racial Identity and National Consciousness in Brazilian Literature* (1983); Patai, D., *Myth and Ideology in Contemporary Brazilian Fiction* (1983); Brookshaw, D., *Race and Color in Brazilian Literature* (1986); Lobo, L., "Women Writers in Brazil Today," *WLT*, 61, 1 (Winter 1987): 49–54; Brookshaw, D., *Paradise Betrayed: Brazilian Literature of the Indian* (1988); Stern, I., ed., *Dictionary of Brazilian Literature* (1988); DiAntonio, R. E., *Brazilian Fiction: Aspects and Evolution of the Contemporary Narrative* (1989); Reis, R., ed., *Toward Socio-Criticism* (1991); Johnson, R., ed., *Tropical Paths: Essays on Modern Brazilian Literature* (1993); Schwarz, R., *Misplaced Ideas: Essays on Brazilian Culture* (1993); Vieira, N. H., *Jewish Voices in Brazilian Literature* (1996)

—IRWIN STERN

BRECHT, Bertolt

German dramatist, poet, and novelist, b. 10 Feb. 1898, Augsburg; d. 14 Aug. 1956, East Berlin (now Berlin)

B.'s father was the managing director of a paper company and a Catholic, his mother a Protestant, the daughter of a civil servant; he was raised in his mother's faith. He attended school in his hometown in Bavaria and in 1917 enrolled as a medical student at the University of Munich. In 1918 he was drafted as a medical orderly, but after the end of World War I he continued his studies while beginning to write and becoming involved with the theater in Munich; eventually he abandoned his medical studies. He married for the first time in 1922, and in 1924 moved to Berlin, where he became dramatic consultant at Max Reinhardt's (1873–1943) Deutsches Theater. In 1926 he read Marx's *Das Kapital*, and in 1927 his intensive studies of Marxism made him a convert to socialism. During the late 1920s he began his famous collaboration with the composer Kurt Weill (1900–1950) and also worked closely with the theater director Erwin Piscator (1893–1966). Divorced in 1927, in 1929 he married the actress Helene Weigel (1900–1971) by whom he had already had a son; a daughter was born in 1930.

With Hitler's rise to power in 1933 B. and his family fled Germany (the Nazis revoked his German citizenship in 1935) and settled in exile in Denmark, where he remained until 1939. With the outbreak of war imminent, he and his family went to Sweden (1939–40), then to Finland (1940–41), and finally to the U. S., where he lived in California (becoming part of the Hollywood refugee community) until 1947. On October 30, 1947, B. was summoned before the House Committee on Un-American Activities; on October 31 he left the country, taking up residence in Zurich, Switzerland. In 1948 he returned to Germany, moving permanently to East Berlin, although in 1950 he obtained an Austrian passport, thus assuring himself freedom of travel. In 1949 the Berliner Ensemble was established in East Berlin, with Helene Weigel as director and B. as artistic adviser and resident playwright. Although the Communist East German government gave its financial support to the Berliner Ensemble and B. was awarded many honors, and although politically B. supported the regime, his relations with the government were not without numerous wrangles and conflicts, and he took many opportunities to travel to the West. He died of a heart attack at the age of fifty-eight.

Critics have called B. "one of the most significant writers of this century" (Martin Esslin) as well as "the most ambiguous and perpetually fascinating figure of the twentieth-century European theatre" (Kenneth Tynan).

B. emerged as a literary and theatrical personality after World War I, in that Weimar Republic that was characterized by pacifism and radical idealism, concern for the economic and educational advancement of the masses, now living for the first time in a democracy, and by a vibrant intellectual atmosphere of artistic experimentation inspired by manifold historical epochs and regions of the world. B.'s work reflects this atmosphere in many ways. In form, mood, plot, and language it reveals the cultural impact of France, Russia, England, Finland, China, and the U.S., an impact that was to become even more pronounced during B.'s exile.

From the Russian and Chinese theaters B. derived some of his basic concepts of staging and theatrical stylization. His concept of the *Verfremdungseffekt*, or *V-Effekt* (sometimes translated as "alienation effect"), was probably inspired by the poetic theories of Russian FORMALISM, which centered on the idea of "making strange" and thereby making poetic. His early poetry, although abounding in German popular imagery, was at times adapted from German translations of Villon and Rimbaud. Shakespeare and John Gay (1685–1732) furnished him with plots and characters; China and the Scandinavian countries with legends; the U. S. with a wealth of names and situations from a largely fictitious gangster milieu. Even the Bible provided dramatically symbolic moments; and the work of classical German predecessors was drawn on for purposes of parody. B. freely acknowledged his indebtedness to these sources, for he considered it the writer's prerogative to take over whatever suited him and to place all the elements of life and literature in the service of a cause that transcended the individual: his aim was to reveal the truth through "making" reality appear "strange." He totally rejected the romantic notion of poetic inspiration. Yet, in spite of his deliberate borrowings, his own originality asserts itself strongly.

The early B.—balladeer and playwright—distinguished himself through poetic exuberance, popular rhythms, and an ability to combine malice and sensuousness with lyrical naïveté, brutality with melancholy tenderness. He said, in 1954, of his early writings: "I was mixing words together like strong drinks. I built whole scenes out of sensuous words of a certain consistency and color:

cherry pit, revolver, trouser pockets, paper god—a jumble of this sort. Of course, I worked at the same time on the story, the characters, and I tried to express my views with regard to human behavior and its effects, and perhaps I stressed form somewhat too much. But I wanted to get across how complex this business of writing is and how the one blends into the other: how form grows out of matter and then, in turn, affects matter. Now and then I used a different approach and worked along other lines so that the plays became more simple and more concerned with matter. But even as these gained shape, much that pertained to form became matter." At that time, B. voiced concern that his first play, *Baal* (1918; *Baal*, 1963), might appear to the uninitiated reader as a "glorification of individualism"—an individualism which B. had tried to abandon—and warned that the work was "lacking in wisdom."

With *Mann ist Mann* (1926; *A Man's a Man*, 1961) and *Die Dreigroschenoper* (1928; *The Threepenny Opera*, 1955) B. clearly tried to enter a phase of "engaged" literature. But even the protagonist of *Mann ist Mann* was later rejected by B. for having failed to make his point. B. considered man "a socially negative hero" and regretted having treated him "not without sympathy." B.'s attempts at parodying bourgeois smugness and hypocrisy in *Die Dreigroschenoper* did not fare much better. After the initial shock, a worldwide bourgeois audience was captivated by the play's colorful lyrics and unusual form and by Kurt Weill's music. It was only in his *Lehrstücke*—a series of musical dramas written in collaboration with either Weill, Paul Hindemith, or Hanns Eisler—that his didactic intentions became obvious and proved themselves in accord with the utilitarian movement in the music and art of the time: the trend toward *Neue Sachlichkeit* (new factualism). *Das Badener Lehrstück vom Einverständnis* (1929; *The Didactic Play of Baden: On Consent*, 1960), *Der Jasager/Der Neinsager* (1930; *He Who Says Yes/He Who Says No*, 1946), and *Die Maßnahme* (1930; *The Measures Taken*, 1960)—plays such as these were to teach social attitudes not only to the audience but also to the students who were acting in them. The plays were intended as *Schulopern* (school operas). Written with the utmost economy of language, they were inspired by totalitarian concepts of the individual's complete subjugation to the state, the Party, or the religious community. As a consequence, the protagonists are mere pawns in the hand of the playwright. But although B. wrote these plays under the impact of Communist ideology, they did not find favor in the eyes of Party leaders.

During his years of exile he returned to the robust lyricism of his youth, but with a deepening sense of human concerns, and although without any normal means of staging plays, he created his theatrical masterpieces: *Leben des Galileo* (1938; *Galileo*, 1957); *Mutter Courage und ihre Kinder* (1939; *Mother Courage and Her Children*, 1941); *Der gute Mensch von Sezuan* (1938–41; *The Good Woman of Setzuan*, 1948); *Herr Puntila und sein Knecht Matti* (1940–41; *Puntila and Matti, His Hired Man*, 1977); *Der kaukasische Kreidekreis* (1944–45; *The Caucasian Chalk Circle*, 1948).

The protagonists of these plays are no longer the anarchic heroes of B.'s earliest period or the stylized types of his intentionally didactic plays, but have become characters of universal validity and great depth in their pathetic struggle for survival in a society governed by neither justice nor intelligence. In the plays of this period human interest becomes predominant and life is seen in its baffling, absurd complexity rather than forced into intellectual stereotypes. The plays represent variations on the theme that it is difficult for man to be bad, but that he cannot be good in the face of the conditions prevailing in the world. With one exception, the protagonists are shown as defeated by the overwhelming powers of war, prejudice, and selfishness with which they must compromise in order to survive. They are not of heroic dimensions. They never set out to be idealists. What they want from life is a simple, sensuous happiness, the desire for which cannot be extinguished in man.

Broken in his clash with authoritarian prejudice, B.'s unscrupulous, sensualist Galileo recants and perishes, although preserving the truth he has found. Mother Courage is defeated in her struggle to protect her children and must suffer, in spite of her ruthless determination to extract the utmost of pleasure and profit from the miseries created by war. Sometimes the individual's innate goodness is so much at odds with the meanness forced upon him by a hostile and selfish world that the protagonist appears on the stage in two different guises. Thus the kindhearted prostitute of *Der gute Mensch von Sezuan* masks herself to play the part of a hardheaded businessman, supposedly her cousin, in order to secure a comfortable future for her unborn child. In *Herr Puntila und sein Knecht Matti*, the ruthless, wealthy landowner Puntila is good and unselfish when drunk. Kindness and meanness confront each other dramatically in the form of two mothers in *Der kaukasische Kreidekreis*: the servant girl who unselfishly rescues and cares for the child and thus considers him her own; and the actual mother who had abandoned him but who now, for reasons of social and financial advantage, seeks to regain control of him. In contrast to the other plays of this period, goodness actually wins out in this play: the unselfish adoptive mother is allowed to keep the child. But such justice comes about almost by default. Only an impostor such as Azdak, appointed to this high office by rebellious soldiers and disappearing quite as suddenly as he had emerged, could flout judicial tradition and create a "golden age of justice."

B. early concerned himself with theatrical theory and problems of stage direction. His articles on theory appeared as early as 1927, and he also wrote notes to accompany a number of his plays. But his most important observations concerning theatrical innovations and theory are in *Kleines Organon für das Theater* (1948; "Little Organon for the Theatre," 1951). They were put to the test while he was director of the Berliner Ensemble, from 1949 until his death.

Theoretical concepts mainly associated with B., although not necessarily original with him, are "epic theater," "alienation effect" or "distantiation," and "gestus." The concept of "epic theater" developed mainly as a reaction against the prevailing theater of Ibsen and of Gerhart HAUPTMANN, with its well-made plot in the Aristotelian sense and its concern for psychology and the emotional involvement of actors and audience alike. Belonging to the era of the film, "epic theater" was to be permitted to roam like a Russian film epic or an American Western, with little regard for time and space. It was appropriately implemented with film projections and posters. Its tendency to move away from all emotionalism made suspense unnecessary and this, in turn, permitted the commedia dell'arte tradition of song and clowning to intrude. It permitted theater to appear as theater rather than as imitation of reality. Hence the announcement, before each scene, of what is to be enacted. But the dispensing with psychology within the play required new stage techniques, such as the use of "gestus."

B.'s conception of "gestus" may be defined as the actor's externalization of feelings on the stage. Through "gestus" the actor establishes the basic attitude of his role in an objective, unemotional manner. It relieves both playwright and actor from the onus of detailed presentation of character, or slow evolution in character, in any Aristotelian or psychological sense. It makes it possible to neglect psychological motivation. Such externalization may be established through the use of masks, or it may be suggested by a concretization of feelings inherent in the play, for example in B.'s farce *Die Hochzeit* (*The Wedding*, 1970), written about 1919 (pub. in *Spiele in einem Akt*, 1961; one-act plays), where the furniture falling to pieces externalizes the decay within the family.

"Gestus" is an essential part of *Verfremdung* (alienation or distantiation), which must be thought of first of all in artistic terms. It represents the writer's attempt to show the world in a new light, that is, as something strange, and thereby to point out a new truth. In terms of the actor, it requires him to tell a story rather than to lose himself in it. In terms of the director, it means that the play must be presented as a play, and not as a slice of life. Thus he can dispense with stage effects, the magic of lighting, and even the curtain. B. regarded this de-emotionalized atmosphere as making an appeal to the audience's reason rather than to the emotions, and tried to exploit the effect of distantiation for didactic purposes. But in his later years he once more came to think of theater as theater: "Let us think of theater," he wrote, "as a place of amusement . . . and let us find out what sort of amusement we want."

The first production of *Die Dreigroschenoper* (1928) turned B. into a figure of national, then international repute. The play's staging in New York (1933) influenced American musicals. But during his years of exile his reputation as a playwright and innovator abated almost completely. His plays were banned from the German stage during the Nazi era. Only a few of his works were produced in the Scandinavian countries, Switzerland, and the U. S., where he was best known within the drama departments of universities. His greatest champion in this country has been Eric Bentley, who has translated and frequently produced his plays. But his influence increased again after 1948 when he returned from exile, and especially after the founding of the Berliner Ensemble (1949). In West as well as in East Germany B. soon became the most popular contemporary playwright, outdistanced only by such classics as Shakespeare, Schiller, and Goethe. Jean Vilar's production of *Mutter Courage* in 1951 secured B. a following in France, and the Berliner Ensemble's participation in the Paris International Theatre Festival (1954) further enhanced his reputation.

FURTHER WORKS: *Trommeln in der Nacht* (1918; *Drums in the Night*, 1961); *Im Dickicht der Städte* (1923; *In the Jungle of Cities*, 1961); *Leben Eduards des zweiten von England* (1924, with Lion Feuchtwanger; *Edward II*, 1966); *Das Elefantenkalb* (1924–1925; *The Elephant Calf*, 1964); *Hauspostille* (1927; *Manual of Piety*, 1966); *Happy End* (1929, with Elisabeth Hauptmann); *Der Flug der Lindberghs* (1929; title later changed to *Der Ozeangflug*; *The Flight of the Lindberghs*, 1930); *Aufstieg und Fall der Stadt Mahagonny* (1929; *The Rise and Fall of the City of Mahagonny*, 1976); *Die heilige Johanna der Schlachthöfe* (1929–1930; *Saint Joan of the Stockyards*, 1956); *Die Ausnahme und die Regel* (1930; *The Exception and the Rule*, 1954); *Die Mutter* (1932; *The Mother*, 1965); *Die Rundköpfe und die Spitzköpfe* (1932; *Roundheads and Peakheads*, 1937); *Das Sieben Todsünden der Kleinbürger* (1933; *The Seven Deadly Sins of the Lower Middle Class*, 1961); *Dreigroschenroman* (1934; *Threepenny Novel*, 1956); *Die Horatier und die Kuriatier* (1934; *The Horatians and the Curiatians*, 1947); *Furcht und Elend des Dritten Reiches* (1935–1936; *The Private Life of the Master Race*, 1944); *Die Gewehre der Frau Carrar* (1937; *Señora Carrar's Rifles*, 1938); *Das Verhör des Lukullus* (1939; *The Trial of Lucullus*, 1943); *Svendborger Gedichte* (1939); *Der Aufhaltsame Aufstieg des Arturo Ui* (1941; *The Resistible Rise of Arturo Ui*, 1976); *Die Gesichte der Simone Machard* (1943, with Lion Feuchtwanger; *The Visions of Simone Machard*, 1961); *Leben des Konfutse* (before 1944?; *The Ginger Jar*, 1958); *Schweyk im zweiten Weltkrieg* (1944; *Schweyk in the Second World War*, 1975); *Kalendergeschichten* (1948); *Die Antigone des Sophokles* (1948); *Die Tage der Kommune* (1949; *The Days of the Commune*, 1971); *Versuche* (15 vols., 1949–1957); *Der Hofmeister* (1950; *The Tutor*, 1973); *Hundert Gedichte* (1951; 5th amended ed., 1958); *Der Prozess der Jeanne d'Arc zu Rouen 1431* (1952; *The Trial of Joan of Arc at Rouen, 1431*, 1973); *Coriolan* (1953; *Coriolanus*, 1973); *Stücke* (14 vols., 1953–1967); *Pauken und Trompeten* (1956; *Trumpets and Drums*, 1973); *B. B.s Gedichte und Lieder* (1956); *Die Geschäfte des Herrn Julius Cäsar* (1957); *Schriften zum Theater* (1957); *Geschichten vom Herrn Keuner* (1958); *Gedichte* (9 vols., 1960–1969); *Prosa* (5 vols., 1965); *Schriften zur Literatur und Kunst* (3 vols., 1966–1967); *Gesammelte Werke* (20 vols., 1967); *Schriften zur Politik und Gesellschaft* (1968); *Texte für Filme* (2 vols., 1969); *Arbeitsjournal* (3 vols., 1973); *Tagebücher 1920–1922, Autobiographische Aufzeichnungen 1920–1954* (1975; *Diaries 1920–1922*, 1979). **FURTHER WORKS IN ENGLISH:** *Selected Poems* (1947); *Seven Plays* (1961); *B. on Theatre* (1964); *The Jewish Wife and Other Short Plays* (1965); *The Messingkauf Dialogues* (1965); *Collected Plays* (1970 ff.); *Poems 1913–1956* (1980)

BIBLIOGRAPHY: *Theaterarbeit: Sechs Aufführungen des Berliner Ensembles* (1952); Bentley, E., Introduction to B. B., *Seven Plays* (1961): xiii–li; special B. issue, *TDR*, 6, 1 (1961); Esslin, M., *B.: The Man and His Work* (1961); Demetz, P., ed., *B.: A Collection of Critical Essays* (1962); Brustein, R., *The Theater of Revolt* (1964): 231–78; Ewen, F., *B. B.* (1967); Spalter, M., *B.'s Tradition* (1967); Willett, J., *The Theatre of B. B.* (3rd rev. ed., 1967); Lyons, C. R., *B. B.: The Despair and the Polemic* (1968); Esslin, M., *B. B.* (1969); Haas, W., *B. B.* (1970); Grimm, R., *B. B.* (1971); *B. Heute/B. Today* (Vols. 1–3, 1971–73); Munk, E., ed., *B.: A Selection of Critical Pieces from The Drama Review* (1972); Benjamin, W., *Understanding B.* (1973); *B. Jahrbuch* (1974 ff.); Gilman, R., *The Making of Modern Drama* (1974): 190–233; Mews, S., and Knust, H., eds., *Essays on B.: Theater and Politics* (1974); Witt, H., ed., *B.: As They Knew Him* (1974); Hill, C., *B. B.* (1975); Gray, R., *B., the Dramatist* (1976); Schoeps, K. H., *B. B.* (1977); Volker, K., *B.: A Biography* (1978)

—RICHARD HAYES

The writer B. B. . . . is more interested in the work than the finished result; more in the problem than the solution; more in the road than the goal. It is his habit to rewrite his work interminably, twenty or thirty times, and then once again for each unimportant provincial production. He is not interested in a work being complete. Repeatedly, even if it has been published ten times, the final version turns out to be only the penultimate one; he is the despair of publishers and theatre directors. . . .

He shies away neither from crudity nor from extreme realism. He is an odd mixture of tenderness and ruthlessness; of clumsiness and elegance; of crankiness and logic; of wild cries and sensitive musicality. He repels many people, but anyone who has once understood his tones finds it hard to drop him. He is disagreeable and charming, a very bad writer and a great poet, and amongst the younger Germans undoubtedly the one showing the clearest signs of genius. [1928]

Lion Feuchtwanger, in Hubert Witt, ed., John Peet, tr. *B.—As They Knew Him* (1974), pp. 19–20

B. opposes his epic theatre to the theatre which is dramatic in the narrow sense and whose theory was formulated by Aristotle. This is why B. introduces the dramaturgy of this theatre as a "non-Aristotelian" one, just as Riemann introduced a non-Euclidean geometry. This analogy should make it clear that what we have here is not a competitive relationship between the forms of drama in question. Riemann refused the axiom of parallels; what B. refuses is Aristotelian catharsis, the purging of the emotions through identification with destiny which rules the hero's life.

The relaxed interest of the audience for which the productions of epic theatre are intended is due, precisely, to the fact that practically no appeal is made to the spectator's capacity for empathy. The art of epic theatre consists in arousing astonishment rather than empathy. To put it as formula, instead of identifying itself with the hero, the audience is called upon to learn to be astonished at the circumstances within which he has his being. [1939]

Walter Benjamin, "What Is Epic Theatre?" [second version], *Understanding B.* (1973), p. 18

I attribute B.'s enduring fascination chiefly to the fact that he offers us an example of a genuinely thought-directed life. . . . B. is engaged with the future; this always carries with it aggressiveness and the danger of freezing up at times and losing all receptivity. To be relaxed, tension-free—what an impossible demand to make upon a life such as B. led, a life governed by the design of a world still nonexistent anywhere in time, to be glimpsed only in his attitude, which is a living, inexorable contradiction, never weakened by those decades of travail as an outsider! Christians are engaged with the Hereafter, B. with the Here and Now. This is one of the differences between him and the priests, from whom he is not so very different, however much he—with his altogether different purpose—may deride them. . . .

Max Frisch, *Tagebuch 1946–1949* (1950), p. 286

For nothing must be taken for granted, in order that nothing may seem unalterable. Here is the theme of all B.'s later writing, and the key to his dramatic theories. "The same attitude as men once showed in face of unpredictable natural catastrophes," he wrote in the *Kleines Organon* nearly twenty years later, "they now adopt towards their own understandings." Or again: "One can describe the world today to the people of today only if one describes it as capable of alteration." And in a note to *Antigone* in 1951 he again warned against passive acceptance: "Man's fate is man himself."

John Willet, The Theatre of B. B.: A Study from Eight Aspects (1959), p. 77

At the end of *King Lear*, Kent sees the world as a rack on which human beings are stretched. That's Brechtian. People talk of the lack of emotion in his plays. Perhaps they mean in his theory of his plays, or perhaps they mean the lack of pleasant emotions. Being tortured is a violent emotional experience, and B.'s characters, from the earliest plays on, live (it is his own metaphor taken from Rimbaud) in an inferno. . . . What of the later plays written (we are told) in the spirit of rational positivism and permitting the audience to keep cool? . . , *The Good Woman [of Setzuan]* is the story of the rending asunder, all but literally, of a young woman. In *[Mother] Courage* we watch a mother lose all three children by the deliberate brutality of men. In *Galileo* (as not in actual history), everything hinges on the threat of physical torture. Though torture cannot very well (*pace* Shakespeare) be shown on stage, B. devised scenes which suggest great physical violence without showing it and push mental torment to the limits of the bearable.

Eric Bentley, Introduction to B. B., Seven Plays (1961), p. xx

B.'s readiness to sink his own personality in the work of his predecessors and contemporaries, to use the whole storehouse of past literature as so much material for his own handiwork, was in accordance with his views about the nature of poetry itself and the poet's function in society. Here, too, he rejected the mystical, romantic view of the poet as the vessel of divinely inspired intuitions, called upon to fulfill and express his unique personality. To him the poet was a craftsman serving the community and relying on his reason and acquired skill, a man among men, not a being set apart by virtue of some special quality or power. That is why B. was ready to accept the advice of numerous collaborators, whom he conscientiously named when his works were published. As he did not consider the work of art divinely inspired, he never hesitated to alter, and often debase, his own work, according to the circumstances of the moment. . . .

Within his own sphere of craftsmanship, however, B. never suffered from undue humility. . . . But his arrogance remained confined to the sphere in which he regarded himself as a craftsman, an expert. It never led him to regard the poet as a higher being.

Martin Esslin, B.: The Man and His Work (1961), pp. 117–18

On a formal level, *A Man's a Man* is an episodic illustration by parable in which B. is already utilizing much that will become staple in his later epic theater. Actors step out of character to underline the illustrative nature of the proceedings; moody lyrics make us

conscious of universal truths to which all the sound and fury of the moment will have to conform; commentary focuses on the illustration pattern's critical implications; and each scene, though it provides a building block to an interlocking pattern, contributes its share of self-explanatory tragicomic observations on such matters as military values, the importance of personality, the power of money, etc. As he will later on, B. loads his scenes with broad social satire, deflating left and right what he smells as fake. . . .

The B. who will mix comic and tragic effects in order to demonstrate that what seems comic is laden with tragic implications, is already present in *A Man's a Man*. So is the B. who will teach by grotesque example that man is his own worst enemy. *A Man's a Man* has all the ambivalence of the plays which we identify most fully with B.'s concept of epic theater, suggesting on the one hand a cynic who observes the human menagerie with a detached hopeless smile, on the other, a humanitarian who cannot shirk his emotional involvement. It even suggests that most glaring paradox about the later B.—his failure to confront the tragic implications of his deepest convictions.

Max Spalter, B.'s Tradition (1967). p. 174

Perhaps it was B. B.'s greatest intellectual achievement, the fulfillment of his belief in the dramatist as a species of philosopher, to have placed the problem of choice—or, rather, the fact that we have difficulty being conscious of it—at the center of his late plays. In one way or another, each of these dramaturgically spacious works takes up again the dilemma announced by Mr. Peachum: "Who would not be a good and kindly person, but circumstance won't have it so."

Yet not only goodness or kindliness in a circumscribed ethical sense is at stake. *Galileo* takes up the question of the truth of self, integrity in the face of social coercion, *The Caucasian Chalk Circle* that of justice in a world ruled by power. Moreover, all the plays are informed by a recognition of how concepts like goodness or justice are the enemies of ordinary corporeal life as long as they remain not simply "ideal" but without basis in an organized physical reality.

The Good Person of Setzuan and *Puntila* are the most schematic of the group, although in neither case does the schematism result in a narrow or "theoretical" drama. In *Puntila*, the slighter of the two, a man is shown to be kind and affectionate while drunk, and hard, cruel, *businesslike* when sober. His drunken state may be thought of as one of unconsciousness, closer connection to instinctual life, while his sobriety is the acceptance of the ruthlessness demanded by social actuality. The idea is eminently Brechtian that we are "better" and not more savage in the unconscious, and is an echo of his original dream in *Baal* of a freer, because less socially corrupted, life.

Richard Gilman, The Making of Modern Drama (1974), pp. 230–31

BRENNAN, Christopher John

Australian poet and scholar, b. 1 Nov. 1870, Sydney; d. 5 Oct. 1932, Sydney

A contemporary of W. B. Yeats, B. was the leading exponent of French SYMBOLISM in Australian verse, and one of the major scholars in classics and modern languages Australia has produced.

Brought up a Roman Catholic, B. became an agnostic in 1889 after reading Herbert Spencer's (1820–1902) *First Principles* (1862) while an undergraduate, and he spent the rest of his life trying to replace the absolute faith he had lost. Studying in Berlin (1892–94) on a traveling scholarship, he discovered the work of Stéphane Mallarmé and borrowed Mallarmé's concept of "Eden"— the perfect life which we can sense but which seems always unattainable. In Berlin B. also met his future wife, Anne Elisabeth Werth, who followed him to Sydney in 1897.

XXI Poems: Towards the Source (1897), published before his bride's arrival in Australia, is a sequence of poems recalling the happiness of the years in Germany and looking to its return: the work is an attempt to achieve "Eden" in human love. Its poetic method shows the influence of Mallarmé, to whom B. sent a copy, and who wrote back, "There is certainly a kinship of vision between us."

After *XXI Poems* B. developed a verse cycle on the pattern of the Symbolist *livre compose*, which he described (in referring to Baudelaire's *Les fleurs du mal*) as the "sublimation of a whole imaginative life and experience into a subtly ordered series of poems, where each piece has, of course, its individual value, and yet cannot be interpreted save in its relation to the whole." B.'s *Poems*, eventually published in 1914, was not so much a collection as a single poem in different movements, with part of its significance coming from the styles of typography used, the position of a poem on the page, and the use of "interludes" and epigraphs.

The lyricism of the cycle "Towards the Source" gives way to a dense mythical section, "The Forest of Night," in which the figure of Lilith represents the Edenic vision in its malign aspect, forever tormenting man yet never offering him fulfillment. Lilith is also the subconscious mind, reflecting Brennan's studies of mysticism and the occult. Release comes in "The Wanderer," in which the cycle resumes its dramatic mode, and the persona finds a resolution. This heroic stance is then qualified in the concluding sections, "Pauca Mea" and "Epilogues," and the cycle ends in a more sober mood. The conclusion may be interpreted in the light of B.'s philosophical response to pragmatism, in the work of F. C. S. Schiller (1864–1937) and William James (1842–1910), and of his reassessment of the subconscious as the latent full self.

B.'s prose and verse taken together provide a fine example of the late romantic. He took up the claim to total experience—the romantic belief that the self is immeasurable—and pursued it with full poetic and metaphysical rigor, eventually exhausting the possibilities of romanticism and leaving it behind.

FURTHER WORKS: *From Blake to Arnold* (1900); *A Chant of Doom* (1918); *XV Poems: The Burden of Tyre* (1953); *Verse* (1960); *Prose* (1962)

BIBLIOGRAPHY: Stephens, A. G., *C. B.* (1933); Hughes, R., *C. J. B.* (1934); Green, H. M., *C. B.* (1939); Chisholm, A. R., *C. B.* (1946); Wilkes, G. A., *New Perspectives on B.'s Poetry* (1953); McAuley, J., *C. B.* (1963); Chisholm, A. R., *A Study of C. B.'s "The Forest of Night"* (1970); Clark, A., *C. B.* (1980)

—G. A. WILKES

BRETON, André

French essayist and poet, b. 19 Feb. 1896, Tinchebray; d. 28 Sept. 1966, Paris

In his youth B. studied medicine and psychiatry and did his military service in the medical corps. Early on he met Paul VALÉRY and Guillaume APOLLINAIRE and from 1919 to 1922 was associated with DADAISM. He founded SURREALISM in 1924, and remained at the head of the movement until his death. He was temporarily associated with the Communist Party in the late 1920s and early 1930s, but his tendencies were closer to those of Trotsky; later in his life, he turned from his interests in politics to mysticism and occultism. He spent the years of World War II in New York in a broadcasting job, and gathered around him, as he had in Paris, a surrealist circle.

Although B. was also a poet, his importance lies as much in his definition of surrealism as a lyric comportment as in his actual poems, and above all in his essays, whose lofty and uncompromising tone combines all that is best in French rhetoric together with the genial perceptions of a man born to be a leader and a writer. His poetry resides in texts from all periods, from the early *Les Champs magnétiques* (1920; *The Magnetic Fields*, 1985), written "automatically," that is, without forethought, by B. in association with Philippe SOUPAULT, to the long later poems such as "Fata Morgana" (1941) and the *Ode à Charles Fourier* (1947; *Ode to Charles Fourier*, 1970).

His earliest Dada essays in *Les pas perdus* (1919; *The Lost Steps*, 1995), full of nostalgia and revolt, lead on one hand to the first and second manifestos of surrealism, and to the masterful autobiographical and poetic observations of *Nadja* (1928; *Nadja*, 1960), *Les vases communicants* (1932; *Communicating Vessels*, 1990), and *L'amour fou* (1937; *Mad Love*, 1987), and to the later and more occult *Arcane 17* (1945; *arcanum 17*, 1994); and, on the other hand, to the passionately critical and inflammatory essays gathered in *La clé des champs* (1953; the key to the fields), which revolve around the renewal of vision brought about by a contemplation of the unusually free and untraditional art of primitive people, madmen, and children, as well as of the nonwhite races.

It might seem odd to place the first *Manifeste du surréalisme* (1924; *Manifesto of Surrealism*, 1969) in the line of the poetic and the personal, but it is both. (The *Second manifeste du surréalisme* [1930; *Second Manifesto of Surrealism*, 1969] is more political.) The first manifesto is chiefly concerned with the excitement generated by the potential of automatic writing in unleashing what the restrictions of rationalist thought enchain and limit. Recounting of B.'s discoveries and his enthusiasms matches the interest of his theories.

Nadja, in spite of its title (the beginning of the Russian word for hope, and the name of a woman), is as much a portrait of B. as of the mad and inspired woman who loved him (a real one, in spite of theories to the contrary). This work, a masterpiece by any standard, is full of wonder and regret, and highlights the essential paradox of surrealist love. Although B. was loved by exactly the sort of person he eulogized in all his manifestos, essays and poems, he could not return the love, partly *because* of the madness attached to it and implicit in it. This book is concerned, like B.'s later ones, with the adaptation of the mind to society: the prelude of a self-referential question about discovery and self-discovery draws a distinction between facts that lead one gently to a discovery and facts that violently precipitate knowledge. B.'s encounter with Nadja was of the latter sort: incapable of adjusting to the world, as B. saw it, she would willingly have implicated him in the same predicament. The question, for the objective observer, remains: could he in fact ever have loved her? The question goes beyond the problems of bourgeois behavior in public and of individual comportment; it goes past the apparent insignificance of one doomed affair, to an implied investigation of the normal and mad worlds. Later, B.'s own defense of "mad love" in *L'amour fou* would in some sense be a statement upon the same subject, from a positive point of view.

Les vases communicants is a remarkable document of the often difficult relations between the surrealist temperament and the temperament of the collective. In it B. explores the question of how to justify the individual intellectual's place in the universe of the "productive" world. It is here that B., after his earlier optimism, recognizes and faces the problems that arise when the two ways of shaping the world for private and public life no longer seem quite so compatible. He questions especially the need for the "artistic" temperament. The consciousness of the surrealist group and B.'s own consciousness as its leader were never to imply an easy mixing with the multitude. These tensions, then, give to this volume its tone of anguish and final resolution, when a sort of meeting seems possible between interior and subjective mystery and exterior objective reality. Perhaps more than any other work, this volume provides the key to and the flavor of B.'s inquiry, surrealist inquiry at its best and its most troubled.

L'amour fou, the response, at a temporal distance, to Nadja's madness, is a defense of an "irrational" emotion. This time it is a joint emotion that transcends "normal" bounds, rather than an obsession of only one partner. The course of that "sublime" love, initiated by B., is described with a vibrancy that perhaps no other autobiography, essay, or novel of 20th-c. French literature captures. It is particularly moving when B. recounts the doubt and the self-doubt experienced by two lovers of such highly strung sensitivity.

After the outward-directed early works, in which B.'s response to political events was as important as his interior state, and after *Les vases communicants*, in which a balance between the states is established, *Arcane 17*, published just prior to his return to France after the war, shows B.'s profound turning toward the mystical. The encounter of contraries once again animates his work.

In his later years, B. wrote many of his essays on painters, by which a reader totally ignorant of surrealism could trace its basic tenets, especially the illumination of the world by a visionary gaze, which trusts to chance and is open to it. The surrealist has faith in the self and in the group as parallel forces, collective and private behavior being essentially interdependent, the true communicating vessels of the heart and mind and spirit with the world. This faith lies at the source of many of B.'s great poems, of the most poetic passages in his essays style, with its mix of emotion and irony, explosiveness and illumination. This faith is, finally, the source of the lasting strength of the surrealist movement to which B. gave his entire life and of which he was its most vibrant spirit. That he remains, even after his death.

FURTHER WORKS: *Mont de piété* (1919); *Les champs magnétiques* (1920, with Philippe Soupault); *Clair de terre* (1923); *Le surréalisme*

André Breton

et la peinture (1928; rev. ed. 1965); *Ralentir travaux* (1930, with René Char and Paul Éluard); *L'Immaculée Conception* (1930, with Paul Éluard); *L'union libre* (1931); *Misère de la poésie—"L'affaire Aragon" devant l'opinion publique* (1932); *Le revolver à cheveux blancs* (1932); *Qu'est-ce que le surréalisme?* (1934; *What Is Surrealism?*, 1974); *L'air de l'eau* (1934); *Point du jour* (1934); *Notes sur la poésie* (1936, with Paul Éluard); *Dictionnaire abrégé du surréalisme* (1938, with Paul Éluard); *Yves Tanguy* (1947); *Martinique, charmeuse de serpents* (1948); *Poèmes* (1948); *Entretiens 1913–52* (1952); *Farouche à quatre feuilles* (1954, with Lise Deharme, Julien Gracq, and Jean Tardieu); *L'art magique* (1957); *Manifestes du surréalisme* (1962; *Manifestoes of Surrealism*, 1969); *Perspective cavalière* (1970); *Les Pas perdus* (1924); *Légitime défense* (1926); *Position politique du surréalisme* (1935); *Anthologie de l'humour noir* (1940); *La Lampe dans l'horloge* (1948); *Constellations* (1959); *Le la* (1961). FURTHER WORKS IN ENGLISH: *Young Cherry Trees Secured against Hares/Jeunes cerisiers garantis contre les lièvres* (bilingual ed., 1946); *Selected Poems* (1969); *Poems* (1981); *Young Cherry Trees Secured Against Hares* (1946); *Selected Poems* (1969); *What Is Surrealism? Selected Poems* (1978); *Poems of A. B.* (1982)

BIBLIOGRAPHY: Gracq, J., *A. B.: Quelques aspects de l'écrivain* (1948); Soupault, P., *Le vrai A. B.* (1966); Caws, M. A., *Surrealism and the Literary Imagination: Bachelard and B.* (1966); Browder, C., *A. B.: Arbiter of Surrealism* (1967); Matthews, J. H., *A. B.* (1967); Audouin, P., *B.* (1970); Eigeldinger, M., *A. B.: Essais et témoignages* (1970); Balakian, A., *A. B.: Magus of Surrealism* (1971); Caws, M. A., *A. B.* (1971); Bonnet, M., *Les critiques de notre temps et B.* (1974); Carrouges, M., *A. B. and the Basic Concepts of Surrealism* (1974); Bonnet, M., *A. B.: Naissance de l'aventure surréaliste* (1975)

—MARY ANN CAWS

BRETON LITERATURE
See under French Literature

BREYTENBACH, Breyten

South African poet, novelist, and short-story writer (writing in Afrikaans and English), b. 16 Sept. 1939, Bonnievale

B. is the most important Afrikaans poet of his generation, and has also attained some fame as a painter. It is, however, through his political views and imprisonment by the South African government that he has become most prominent. In 1958 and 1959 he studied art and Afrikaans literature at the University of Cape Town. He left South Africa for Europe in 1960, settling in Paris where, in 1962, he married his Vietnamese wife, Hoang Lien. He became increasingly involved in antiapartheid activities and in 1975 was arrested in South Africa on charges of terrorism and imprisoned until 1982. Subsequent to his release he has lived in Paris and continues to be an important critic of the South African situation.

B.'s first published works are *Katastrofes* (1964; catastrophes), a collection of short stories, and *Die ysterkoei moet sweet* (1964; the iron cow must sweat), a volume of poetry. In the poem "Bedreiging van die siekes" (threat of the sick ones), B. introduces himself to his readers as a harmless poet whose task it is to acknowledge the imminence and inevitability of death; and in "Oopmaak" (opening up) from *Katastrofes* he presents himself as a spy setting out each day to build his case against life.

In these two early works, the twenty-five-year-old B.'s obsessional concern with degeneration and decay is countered, as in his later works, by the enduring possibilities of acts of creativity, and also by his love for his often-apostrophized wife. In *Die ysterkoei moet sweet* a number of poems relating to Zen Buddhism are included—an influence that critics have been much concerned with, often ascribing B.'s associative technique to this philosophy.

The most political of B.'s works, verging on invective, is *Skryt: om 'n sinkende skip blou te verf* (1972; shrite [a composite of shit, write, chalk, shrine, stride]: to paint a sinking ship blue), banned in South Africa until 1982. His visit to South Africa in 1973 is recounted in *'n Seisoen in die Paradys* (1976; *A Season in Paradise*, 1980), published under the name B. B. Lasarus. The title invokes Arthur Rimbaud's (1854–1891) *Une saison en enfer* (1873), with the implication that the return to his country of birth offered B. some respite; the nom de plume similarly invokes a resurrection.

After B.'s release from imprisonment, he published a number of works, collectively titled *Die ongedanste dans* (the undanced dance): *Eklips* (1983; eclipse), *'Yk'* (1983; gauge), *Buffalo Bill* (1984; Buffalo Bill), and *Lewendood* (1985; living death). This

cycle consists of long, somewhat formless poems, reminiscent of Ezra POUND. Some of these poems have been rendered into English by the poet in *Judas Eye and Self-Portrait/Death-watch* (1988). *The True Confessions of an Albino Terrorist* (1984) is an autobiographical text on his imprisonment (originally published in English and untranslated into Afrikaans); he recounts his interrogation and trial, and explores the condition of imprisonment.

B. has increasingly published in English, distancing himself publicly from the Afrikaans language and Afrikaner culture. *End Papers* (1986) contains reflections on South African society and culture written between 1967 and 1985. The novel *Memory of Snow and Dust* (1989) is, as is the case with much of B.'s work, a complex blend of autobiography and symbolism. It offers a reflection on exile by means of three characters living in Paris, one of them a white author who comes to South Africa and is arrested and sentenced to death for a murder he did not commit. In *All One Horse* (1989) twenty-seven short prose pieces and twenty-seven watercolors by the author are collected.

Breytenbach has been awarded the most prestigious Afrikaans language prize, the Hertzog Prize, which he declined for ideological reasons; he has also received the CNA award five times.

FURTHER WORKS: *Huis van die dowe* (1967); *Kouevuur* (1969); *Lotus* (1970); *Om te vlieg: 'n opstel in vyf ledemate en 'n ode* (1971); *Met ander woorde: vrugte van die droom van stilte* (1973); *De boom achter de maan* (1974); *Voetskrif* (1976); *Blomskryf* (1977); *Die miernes swel op* (1980); *Mouroir (bespieëlende notas van 'n roman)* (1983; *Mouroir: Mirrornotes of a Novel*, 1984); *Notes of Bird* (1984); *Boek (deel een): dryfpunt* (1987); *Soos die so* (1990). FURTHER WORKS IN ENGLISH: *And Death White As Words: An Anthology of the Poetry of B. B.* (1978); *In Africa Even the Flies Are Happy: Selected Poems, 1964–1977* (1978)

BIBLIOGRAPHY: Van der Merwe, P. P., "B. B. and the Poet Revolutionary," *Theoria*, 56 (May 1981): 51–72; Cope, J., *The Adversary Within: Dissident Writers in Afrikaans* (1982): 165–82; Dis, A. van, "I am not an Afrikaner any more," *IonC*, 12, 3 (June 1983): 3–6; Preés, T. Des, "Rimbaud's Nephew," *Parnassus*, 11, 2 (1983–1984): 83–102; David, C., "B. B.: Le point de non-retour est atteint," *Nouvel Observateur*, 2–8 August 1985: 32; Moore, G., "The Martian Descends: The Poetry of B. B.," *ArielE*, 16, 2 (April 1985): 3–12; Coetzee, J. M., "A Poet in Prison," *Social Dynamics*, 11, 2 (1985): 72–75; Roberts, S., "B. B.'s Prison Literature," *CentR*, 30, 2 (Spring 1986): 304–13; Jacobs, J. U., "B. B. and the South African Prison Book," *Theoria*, 68 (1986): 95–105; Egan, S., "B.'s *Mouroir* The Novel As Autobiography," *JNT*, 18, 2 (Spring 1988): 89–104; Coetzee, J. M., "B. and the Censor," *Raritan*, 10, 4 (Spring 1991): 58–84

—CARLI COETZEE

BŘEZINA, Otokar

(pseud. of Václav Ignác Jebavý) Czechoslovak poet and essayist (writing in Czech), b. 23 Sept. 1868, Počátky; d. 25 March 1929, Jaroměřice nad Rokytnou

B. was the only child of a poor cobbler in southern Bohemia. Both his parents died in 1890, and the death of his mother affected him particularly deeply. B. became a teacher; although not university-trained, his private study included ancient philosophers, medieval German and French mystics, and modern philosophers, especially Schopenhauer, Nietzsche, and BERGSON, as well as literature, particularly the French SYMBOLISTS. Diffident and solitary, he refused the professorship offered him by the University of Brno in 1921; in 1925 he was awarded an honorary Ph.D. by Prague University.

B.'s poetry is contained in five main volumes, each of them showing a distinct step forward in the author's spiritual and artistic development. In *Tajemné dálky* (1895; mysterious expanses) B. began his search for coherence amid the chaos of contemporary society and for a way to express it in artistic form. His poverty and loneliness tinge his work with deep pessimism; B., spiritually alienated from society, strives to find in poetry an escape from his predicament, as seen in "Mrtvé mládí" (dead youth), "Přátelství duší" (friendship of the souls), and "Vzpomínka" (reminiscence). But the poet also gives voice to his longing for his dead mother in the beautiful "Moje matka" (my mother), and to the feeling inspired by music and the visual arts in "Motiv z Beethovena" (a motif from Beethoven) and in "Umění" (art), which concludes the volume.

Although B.'s death wish and suffering still pervade *Svítání na západě* (1896; dawn in the west), the title suggests hope. His mysticism inspired the great poems of this collection, such as "Ranní modlitba" (morning prayer), "Žalm ke cti Nejvyššího" (psalm in honor of the Supreme Name), and "Tajemství bolesti" (the secret of pain); dawn for B. symbolizes his belief that all present mysteries will be solved in the life after death. In *Větry od pólů* (1897; winds from the poles) the poet's faith in spiritual values is reaffirmed. The poems appear more optimistic as B., detached from his own pain, sees the vision of all-embracing love in which everybody and everything participates. "Láska" (love), "Bratrstvo věřících" (the brotherhood of the believers), "Modlitba za nepřátele" (prayer for the enemies), and "Vládnoucí" (the ruler) are among the best of the poems. In *Stavitelé chrámů* (1899; builders of the temples) B. again expresses doubt and a sense of a mysterious hereditary guilt; he identifies himself with the suffering of the whole of mankind, but without losing his hope for redemption. In his last collection, *Ruce* (1901; hands), B.'s previously ecstatic mysticism is modified by the sense of reconciliation and equilibrium achieved by the wisdom of maturity; in the spirit of cosmic brotherhood, the poet optimistically glorifies all the visible and invisible "hands" that act according to the law of the universe. *Ruce* contains the famous "Dithyramb světů" (dithyramb of the worlds) and "Kolozpěv srdcí" (roundelay of the hearts) with the refrain "it is sweet to live"; the book culminates in "Čas" (time), appropriately expressing the poet's eternal striving after relief and redemption. This spiritual striving is also reflected in the constant revision and polishing of the form and style of the poetry.

B.'s sixth book of poems remained unfinished, but he published a collection of excellent essays, *Hudba pramenů* (1903, rev. ed. 1919; music of the springs), which illuminates his way of thinking and creating. At a time when the essay form was hardly known in Czech literature, B. effectively paved the way for it.

B.'s mysticism, his polished verse, and his belief that art can effectively serve God and mankind make him the greatest of Czech philosophical poets.

FURTHER WORKS: *Dopisy O. B.-F. Bauerovi* (1929); *Dopisy O. B.-A..Pammerové* (1930, 1933); *Dopisy O. B.-F. Bílkovi* (1932);

Dopisy O. B.-J. Demlovi (1932); *Sebrané spisy* (3 vols., 1933); *Korespondence O. B. s F. X. Šaldou* (1939); *Korespondence O. B. s O. Theerem* (1946); *Symfonie bratrských hlasů* (1970)

BIBLIOGRAPHY: Zweig, S., "O. B.," *Österreichische Rundschau*, 19 (1909): 444–50; Mágr, A. S., "O. B. in deutscher Sprache," *Prager Presse* (17 Apr. 1921): 12; Selver, P., *O. B.: A Study in Czech Literature* (1921); Jelínek, H., "Un poète de la fraternité des âmes: O. B.," *Revue de Genève*, 2 (1929): 223–36; Lesný, V., "Influence of Ancient Indian Philosophy on the Czech Poet O. B.," *India and the World*, 2, 4 (1933): 86–90; Harkins, W. E., ed., *Anthology of Czech Literature* (1953): 158–60; French, A., ed., *Czech Poetry* (1973): 339; Novák, A., *Czech Literature* (1976): 264–67

—B. R. BRADBROOK

BRIDIE, James

(pseud. of Osborne Henry Mavor) Scottish dramatist, b. 3 Jan. 1888, Glasgow; d. 29 Jan. 1951, Edinburgh

Only after B. had established a successful medical practice did he devote himself to the theater, writing over forty plays during the last twenty-three years of his life—a dramatic canon remarkable for its variety and range. He was also active in the founding of the Glasgow Citizens' Theatre and in the film section of UNESCO.

B.'s dramatic work was principally influenced by SHAW and Ibsen, although some of his plays, created specifically for the Scottish national theater, drew upon national themes and idioms. Religious questions provide the subjects for many of his best plays, such as *The Sunlight Sonata* (1928), *A Sleeping Clergyman* (1933), *Mr. Bolfry* (1943), *John Knox* (1947), and *The Baikie Charivari* (1951). And among his most popular works are biblical plays: *Tobias and the Angel* (1930), the *Jonah* plays (1932, 1942), and *Susannah and the Elders* (1937). The problem of moral responsibility is central to B.'s plays, in which he examines the relationships of man to man, man to God, man to evil. His favorite form was the sophisticated comedy, which he used to examine serious matters, never forgetting that disease and death were constant and basic facts of man's existence. B.'s control of popular theatrical modes made it possible for him to experiment with various forms; he sometimes introduced the fantastic in conjunction with the realistic to provide additional levels of dramatic comment, or mixed verse lines with realistic prose for special effects.

B.'s plays have received a mixed reception, often confusing critics who are made uneasy by a comedy which refuses to be single in purpose. B. is also not to be taken traditionally in his use of Christian materials. He is often compared to Shaw in his ironic use of characters and plots, and the plays purposely reinforce a statement of the irreducibility of experience to simple answers. For B., the only significant action is in man's capacity to strive to make sense out of a nonsensical world. It is the striving to be fully human that is a constant theme, from *The Switchback* (1929), his first published play, to *Meeting at Night* (1956), his last. B.'s own author's note on the main character in *The Black Eye* (1935) is a good description of his general intention: "'George' in *The Black Eye* was all the younger sons and Idle Jacks out of Grimm, and his story . . . is that of The Prodigal Son and of The Labourers in the

Vineyard of half the fairy tales in the world. It is that we are not justified by a catalogued series of sensible, social acts but by something very much more extraordinary."

FURTHER WORKS: *The Anatomist* (1930); *The Dancing Bear* (1931); *Marriage Is No Joke* (1934); *Colonel Wotherspoon* (1934); *Mary Reed* (1934); *Storm in a Teacup* (1936); *The King of Nowhere* (1938); *Babes in the Wood* (1938); *The Golden Legend of Shults* (1939); *One Way of Living* (1939); *Holy Isle* (1942); *The Forrigan Reel* (1944); *Lancelot* (1945); *Gog and Magog* (1948); *Daphne Laureola* (1949); *The Queen's Comedy* (1950)

BIBLIOGRAPHY: Bannister, W., *J. B. and His Theatre* (1955); Marcel, G., "Le théâtre de J. B.," *EA*, 10 (1957): 291–303; Wittig, K., *The Scottish Tradition in Literature* (1958): 318–22; Weales, G., *Religion in Modern English Drama* (1961): 79–90; Luyben, H. L., *J. B.: Clown and Philosopher* (1965); Michie, J. A., "Educating the Prophets," *MD*, 11 (1968): 63–74; Weales, G., "A Question of Success," *English*, 17 (1968): 48–52

—DONNA GERSTENBERGER

BRIGADERE, Anna

Latvian dramatist, poet, novelist, and memoirist, b. 1 Oct. 1861, Tērvete; d. 25 June 1933, Tērvete

Brought up in a family that did farm work and weaving, B. began to write poetry at fifteen, but did not make her literary debut until 1896. Although her work became known slowly, after 1897 she was able to devote herself entirely to literature. From 1908 to 1910 B. edited *Latvijas literāriskais pielikums* and from 1917 to 1933 the literary annual *Daugavas gada grāmata*, which she helped to shape into an impressive literary instrument. She was highly honored by the independent Latvian republic (1918–40).

After the staging of *Sprīdītis* (1903; Thumbkin), the first Latvian fairy-tale drama, B. became well known in Latvian literature. Folklore elements and motifs with a profoundly ethical point of view, reinforced by faith in poetic justice, were also utilized in the verse plays *Princese Gundega un Karalis Brusubārda* (1912; Princess Gundega and King Brusubārda), *Maija un Paija* (1921; *Maija and Paija*, 1979), and *Lolitas brīnumputns* (1927; Lolita's enchanted bird), as well as in the neoromantic folk tragedies *Pastari* (1931; the last ones) and *Karaliene Jāna* (1932; Queen Jāna). B.'s remaining eighteen dramatic works consist of satirical society comedies and psychological dramas in which the most important element is a woman's spiritual self-examination and self-discovery, often accompanied by religious search. Similarly, in many of her emotionally compelling and intellectually engaging short stories, such as those in the notable collection *Klusie varoni* (1933; silent heroes), B. is frequently concerned with the experiences and issues of womanhood and the desperate need for selfhood.

A literary event of the first order was B.'s autobiographical trilogy *Dievs, daba, darbs* (1926; God, nature, toil), *Skarbos vējos* (1930; in biting winds), and *Akmens sprostā* (1933; in a cage of stone)–an evocation of childhood with fine poetic observation of the local landscape and people, as well as an alert registration of the nuances of the spiritual growth and emotions of a young girl. In B.'s only full-length novel, *Kvēlošā lokā* (1928; within the blazing circle), the treatment of World War I and the Latvian war of liberation (1918–20), although nationalistically colored and socially militant, is open-minded and humane, with emphasis on what is basic in human nature.

B.'s aphoristic poetic opus, consisting of three small volumes—*Dzejas* (1913; poems), *Paisums* (1922; incoming tide), and *Kalngali* (1934; summits)—is permeated with quietly reassuring and austerely serene patriotism. The superb epic poem "Spēka dēls" (1916; mighty son), an allegory of Latvia during World War I, may well be one of B.'s strongest contributions to modern Latvian literature. B.'s patriotism presented problems to the Soviet authorities, who in 1948 banned all of her work except some fairy-tale dramas. B. has been partially rehabilitated since the mid-1950s.

What is most evident and most appealing in B.'s creative output are unusual wisdom, quiet optimism, warmth, and perspicacity, coupled with folkloric simplicity and directness of expression.

FURTHER WORKS: *Vecā Karlīne* (1897); *Aiz līdzcietības* (1897); *Izredzētais* (1901); *Ritenis* (1903); *Čaukstenes* (1904); *Cela jūtīs* (1906); *Vizbuli* (1906); *Ausmā* (1907); *Pazaudētais šnudauks* (1907); *Pie latviešu miljonāra* (1909); *Zvanīgs zvārgulītis* (1909); *Mazā māja* (1913); *Raudupiete* (1914); *Dzelzs dūre* (1920); *Ilga* (1920); *Sievu kari ar Belcebulu* (1925); *Lielais loms* (1926); *Dieviška seja* (1926); *Sniegputenis* (1927); *Kvēloša lokā* (1929); *Kad sievas spēkojas* (1929); *Šuvējas sapnis* (1930); *Kekatas nāk* (1932); *Raksti* (20 vols., 1912–39); *Pasaku lugas* (1956); *Stāsti* (1958); *Zem rīta zvaigznes* (2 vols., 1959); *Drāma un noveles* (1962); *Kristīnes stāsts* (1978); *Mūžība kā lāses krīt* (1978)

BIBLIOGRAPHY: Andrups, J. and V. Kalve, *Latvian Literature* (1954): 124–26; Ekmanis, R., *Latvian Literature under the Soviets 1940–75* (1978): 74–75, 172–74

—ROLFS EKMANIS

BRINK, André P(hilippus)

South African novelist, dramatist, and literary critic (writing in Afrikaans and English), b. 29 May 1935, Vrede, Free State

B. is one of the most popular South African novelists and an important critic of Afrikaans literature. He studied at Potchefstroom University, where he obtained an M.A. in English literature in 1958 and in Afrikaans literature in 1959. From 1959 to 1961 he studied at the Sorbonne in Paris. B. was a lecturer in the Afrikaans department at Rhodes University from 1961, and took up a position in the English department at the University of Cape Town in 1991. It is as spokesman for the Writers of the Sixties that he first gained prominence.

In a significant article, to some extent the manifesto of the group, "Oor religie en seks" (1964; on religion and sex), B. argued for a literature that was not limited by Calvinist morality. His own early works are formally experimental and attempt a treatment of sexuality, especially feminine sexuality. The first of these works is *Lobola vir die lewe* (1962; bride price for life), but his *Die ambassadeur* (1963; *The Ambassador*, 1964) marks his highest literary achievement. The novel, which has often been likened to Lawrence DURRELL's *The Alexandria Quartet* (4 vols., 1957–1960), is narrated from five different perspectives. The work is the account of a relationship between a South African ambassador and a woman he meets in Paris; she is one of the childlike sylphs B. is criticized for limiting female characters to. A later work, *Orgie* (1965; orgy), again dealing with a sexual ménage à trois involving such a woman, is formally the most experimental of B.'s works.

B.'s five novels of the 1970s are a return to a more conventional form, but were significantly new thematically in Afrikaans. The first of these, *Kennis van die aand* (1973; *Looking on Darkness* 1974), was the first book by an Afrikaans writer to be banned under the 1963 censorship legislation; it was unbanned in 1982. What distinguishes these novels is a concern with the South African actuality, characterized by state violence and injustice. The novels include *'n Oomblik in die wind* (1975; *An Instant in the Wind*, 1977); *Gerugte van reën* (1978; *Rumours of Rain*, 1978); *'n Droë wit seisoen* (1979; *A Dry White Season*, 1980); and *Houd-den-bek* (1982; *A Chain of Voices*, 1982). The last of these was written simultaneously in Afrikaans and English.

B.'s *States of Emergency* (1988) was published in English only. Explicitly utilizing postmodernist literary techniques, the novel explores the relationship between romantic love and the state of emergency declared in South Africa in 1986; B. has said in an interview that he regards the political situation as a starting point for attempts at exploring the loneliness of the human condition. In *An Act of Terror* (1991), a history of South Africa is presented, reconstructed by the main character, Thomas Landman, through the chronicle of thirteen generations of his family in the country, culminating in his own political resistance. B.'s *Imaginings of Sand* (1995), published one year after the election of the first democratic government, attempts to create an alternative history of the country through tracing events through the female line of a particular family.

B. has made a significant contribution to Afrikaans literature by his numerous translations of European literary works, as well as his literary criticism. He is a prolific author, and not all of his works are of equal quality. As one of the proponents of the "Sestigers," his formal experimention and exploration of new themes, especially sexuality and South African politics, have been significant.

FURTHER WORKS: *Die meul teen die hang* (1958); *Die gebondenes* (1958); *Die band om ons harte* (1959); *Eindelose weë* (1960); *Bakkies en sy maats—die bende* (1961); *Caesar* (1962); *Orde en chaos* (1962); *Platsak* (1962); *Pot-pourri* (1962); *Sempre diritto* (1963); *Olé* (1965); *Bagasie* (1965); *Elders mooiweer en warm* (1965); *Miskien nooit: 'n somerspel* (1967); *Aspekte van die nuwe prosa* (1967); *Midi* (1969); *Parys-Parys: retoer* (1969); *Fado* (1970); *Die verhoor* (1970); *Die rebelle* (1970); *Die poësie van Breyten Breytenbach* (1971); *Kinkels innie kabel* (1971); *Die bobaas van die boendoe* (1973); *Afrikaners is plesierig* (1973); *Die geskiedenis van Oom Kootjie Emmer van Witgatworteldraai* (1973); *Portret van die vrou as 'n meisie* (1973; *Portrait of the Woman as a Young Girl*, 1973); *Brandewyn in Suid-Afrika* (1973; *Brandy in South Africa*, 1973); *Dessertwyn in Suid-Afrika* (1974; *Dessert Wine in South Africa*, 1974); *Die klap van die meul* (1974); *Die wyn van bowe* (1974); *Pavane* (1974); *Aspekte van die nuwe drama* (1974); *Voorlopige rapport* (1976); *Die hamer van die hekse* (1976); *Jan Rabie se 21* (1977); *Toiings op die langpad* (1979); *Tweede voorlopige rapport* (1980); *'n Emmertjie wyn* (1981); *Heildronk* (1981); *Die fees van die malles* (1982); *Die muur van die pes* (1984; *The Wall of the Plague*, 1985); *Literatuur in die strydperk* (1985); *Waarom literatuur?* (1985); *Vertelkunde: 'n inleiding tot die lees van verhalende tekste* (1988); *Die eerste lewe van Adamastor* (1988); *Die kreef raak gewoond daaraan* (1991); *Intendeel* (1993); *SA 27 April 1994: A Writer's Diary* (1994); *Sandkastele* (1995); *27 April: One Year Later* (1995). FURTHER

WORKS IN ENGLISH: *Why Literature?* (1981); *Mapmakers: Writing in a State of Siege* (1983)

BIBLIOGRAPHY: Woods, D., "Brave Truths of a Rebel Author," *Observer*, 23 Sept. 1979: 11; Cope, J., *The Adversary Within: Dissident Writers in Afrikaans* (1982): 124–41; Herbert, H., "Courage in a Land of Darkness," *Guardian*, 6 May 1982: 10; Nkosi, L., "Escaping from the Laager," *TLS*, 16 Sept. 1983: 996; Viola, A., "A. B. and the Writer in State and Siege," *CE&S*, 7, 2 (Spring 1985): 64–71; MacDermott, D., "A Narrow Beam of Light: A Reading of Two Novels by A. B.," *WLWE*, 28, 2 (Autumn 1988): 178–88; Coetzee, J. M., *Giving Offense: Essays on Censorship* (1996); Jolly, R., *Colonization, Violence, and Narration in White South African Writing: A. B., Breyten Breytenbach, and J. M. Coetzee* (1996)

—CARLI COETZEE

BRINKMANN, Rolf Dieter

German poet, novelist, and short-story writer, b. 16 Apr. 1940, Vechta; d. 23 Apr. 1975, London

After high school B. held a variety of temporary jobs. In 1962 he moved to Cologne, where he studied at the Teachers College from 1963 to 1965. He gave this up to become a full-time writer. He was never financially successful but managed to keep his head above water with several small publications, with editorial tasks, and with scholarships, such as at the Villa Massimo in Rome (1972–1973) and at the University of Texas at Austin (1974). He was killed in an automobile accident while visiting London. He had almost ceased publishing after 1970, and many of his works appeared posthumously.

B. began publishing collections of his poems in 1962, but they received little critical attention, primarily because they appeared in limited editions of a few hundred copies or less. Only with the collections *Was fraglich is wofüur* (1967; what is questionable why) and *Die piloten* (1968; the pilots), and with the anthology *Standphotos: gedichte 1962–1970* (1980; still photos: poems 1962–1970) did he reach a wider public. B. began in a rather solipsistic, introverted vein but quickly emerged as the leading German-language pop poet. His poems have a snapshot quality by which he tries, through a series of very short lines, to capture a transitory occurrence of everyday reality, which is full of banality, brutality, and sex. The poems constitute a radical break thematically and stylistically with the German poetic tradition. B.'s last collection of poems, *Westwärts 1 & 2* (1975; westward 1 & 2), published shortly after his death and containing the poems written between 1970 and 1974, became a best-seller. It marks a return to a somewhat more standard verse form, although B. is still interested in experimentation. His thematics are also more traditional: criticism of society, praise of the simple life, and admiration for other authors.

B. was heavily influenced by the American pop movement and was largely responsible for introducing it to German readers. He edited three important and seminal works on this topic: *ACID: neue amerikanische szene* (1969; acid, new American scene, with Ralf-Rainer Rygulla), *Frank O'Hara: lunch poems und andere gedichte* (1969; Frank O'Hara: lunch poems and other poems), and *Silver screen: neue amerikanische lyrik* (1969; silver screen: new American poetry). B. believed that pop culture would help free German society from its inhibiting constraints.

B. also wrote a limited number of prose works, and most of them have an autobiographical flavor. The stories in his first collection, *Die umarmung* (1965; the embrace), are intensely personal, sexually graphic, and painfully exact in their descriptions. In his next collection, *Raupenbahn* (1966; caterpillar ride), he writes about youth and youth culture. In his novel *Keiner Weiß mehr* (1968; no one knows more) he describes a familial situation where consumerism inhibits any truly intimate relationships. In all these stories there is a sense of depression and suffering and an urge to rebel against all societal constraints. Most of the prose works written between 1965 and his death, together with other material, were published as *Der film in worten* (1982; the film in words).

B.'s stay at the Villa Massimo in Rome resulted in three diarylike posthumous publications: *Rom, blicke* (1979; Rome, views), *Erkundungen für die präzisierung des gefühls für einen aufstand* (1987; inquiries about making the feelings for a revolution more precise), and *Schnitte* (1988; cuts). They are large collages of photographs, found material, quotations, postcards, prose, and other material. They show an extremely lonely and tortured individual trying to find meaning in life and lashing out against everything and anything that infringes on his freedom.

Although partially ignored and then almost forgotten during his lifetime, B. has achieved in death what eluded him before, namely recognition as one of the most daring and innovative writers in postwar Germany.

FURTHER WORKS: *Ihr nennt es sprache* (1962); *Le chant du monde* (1964); *Ohne neger* (1966); *& gedichte* (1966); *Godzilla* (1968); *Gras* (1970); *Wold's end* (1973); *Burgruine hochburg* (1984); *Erzählungen* (1985); *Eiswasser an der guadelupe str.* (1985); *Der brand auf der festung hochburg 1684* (1985)

BIBLIOGRAPHY: special B. issue, *TuK*, 71 (July 1981); Lampe, G. W., *Ohne Subjektivität: Interpretationen zur Lyrik R. D. B.s vor dem Hintergrund der Studentenbewegung* (1983); Richter, H., *Ästhetik der Ambivalenz: Studien zur Struktur "postmoderner" Lyrik, exemplarisch dargestellt an R. D. Bs Poetik und der Gedichtband "West wärts 1 & 2"* (1983); Schulz, G., "Bandblasen der Seele: zur frühen Prosa und späten Lyrik R. D. Bs," *Merkur*, 39, 11 (Nov. 1985): 1015–20; Schenk, H., *Das Kunstverständnis in den späteren Texten R. D. Bs* (1986); Späth, S., "Rettungsversuche aus dem Todesterritorium": zur Aktualität der Lyrik R. D. B.s (1986)

—ROBERT ACKER

BROCH, Hermann

Austrian novelist, poet, and essayist, b. 1 Nov. 1886, Vienna; d. 30 May 1951, New Haven, Connecticut

B. was born into a well-to-do Jewish family that had made its fortune in the textile business. He directed the family business until 1927, when it was sold, but from his early years on he also pursued the study of philosophy and mathematics. From 1925 to 1929 he took courses at the University of Vienna. At the age of forty-five he published his first novel, *Die Schlafwandler* (1931–32; *The Sleepwalkers*, 1932). Among the great number of essays he published in the following years was one of the earliest appreciations of James JOYCE, "James Joyce und die Gegenwart" (1936; "James Joyce and

the Present Age," 1949). The spread of fascism across Europe convinced him that literature could not (as he had hoped it might) provide support and guidance in times of social and political upheaval. He abandoned his literary projects and in 1937–38 worked on the *Völkerbund-Resolution* (pub. 1973; resolution for the League of Nations), suggesting that the international recognition and enforcement of human rights might stem the tide of fascism. After the annexation of Austria by Germany in March of 1938, B. fled.

He arrived in New York City in the fall of the same year. During this early period of his exile he wrote his second major novel, *Der Tod des Vergil* (1945; *The Death of Virgil*, 1945). He also did research on mass psychology and mass hysteria. For seven years he lived in Princeton, N.J. He spent the last years of his life in New Haven, Conn., in close contact with Yale University. On the eve of a planned return to Europe he died of a heart attack.

Influenced by the prevalent philosophical moods of the turn of the century, B. was convinced that history progressed in cycles of disintegrating and reintegrating value systems. Perceiving his era to be one of disintegration, he sought to counteract the historical pessimism inherent in this view with the neo-Kantian hypothesis of "breakthroughs in knowledge," which allow man to influence the course of historical cycles. In B.'s philosophical system, as well as in his fiction, metaphysics, ethics, and politics are closely associated. Metaphysics provides the spiritual bond, attracting men to a common value center. B. suggests that the new value center be secular, and he finds it in the concept of an "ethical duty toward cognition." Striving for ever greater cognition leads to self-redemption. In the political context, demagogues and the masses try to avoid the arduous task of cognition and abandon themselves to the lure of false promises and easy solutions.

Die Schlafwandler amply demonstrates B.'s long involvement with the roots of the spiritual and cultural malaise of his era, and is an outstanding example of the philosophical novel. Each of its three parts focuses on a distinct historical period, for which a specific type of person and of style (which for B. includes a "style of thinking") are representative: "1888—Pasenow oder die Romantik" ("The Romantic [1888]"), "1903—Esch oder die Anarchie" ("The Anarchist [1903]"), and "1918—Huguenau oder die Sachlichkeit" ("The Realist [1918]"). According to B.'s view of history, the characters in the novel experience the social, political, and economic troubles as periods of personal difficulties and transitions. A compatriot of FREUD and well aware of the elaborate mechanisms of repression and sublimation, B. projects spiritual disorientation as psychological "sleepwalking."

Pasenow, a member of the Prussian landed gentry, senses in the "wild" Bohemian prostitute Ruzena a chance to break with the oppressive conventions inspired by the military code; yet he ends this period of extreme doubt and anguish by marrying Elisabeth, his neighbor and social equal. Esch belongs to the urban petite bourgeoisie. His world falls apart when he is fired from his job as a bookkeeper. B. shows how Esch uses and misuses his own sexuality in an ill-conceived attempt to bring order and stability back into the world. At the end of this period of wandering and turmoil, Esch marries a restaurant owner. Huguenau is the "value-free" person at the "nadir of the atomization of values." Consequently he can desert the army and swindle his way into prominence in a small Mosel town, where Esch owns the local newspaper and Pasenow is the town's military commander. At the end of the war Huguenau kills Esch, rapes Frau Esch, embezzles money, and settles, with impunity, into the comfortable existence of a respected businessman.

The form and style of the novel mimetically "enact" the process of disintegration. Bits of loosely connected plots, fragments of philosophical essays, pieces of journalism, surreal fantasies of great lyrical intensity, and long sections of dialogue follow each other. B. is able to show the mechanisms of disintegration at work, from the most personal experience to the most abstract philosophical statements. After the publication of *Die Schlafwandler*, which had great critical but little public success, B. was increasingly doubtful that the novel could fulfill the cognitive task he had conceived for it. His only play, *Die Entsühnung* (1933; the atonement) was performed in Zurich in 1934 under the title *Denn sie wissen nicht, was sie tun* (for they know not what they do). The fragmentary character of his literary work until his flight in 1938 testifies to his growing doubts and even despair over his ethical mission as an artist.

One of the fragments of these years, a novel completed only in a first draft in 1936, clearly continues to uphold B.'s triadic conception of metaphysics-ethics-politics and therefore ends in a forced and sentimentalized version of hope. Usually referred to as the *Bergroman* (mountain novel), it has a complicated publication history. One version, published under the title of *Der Versucher* (1953; the tempter), is a conflation of the three extant versions of the *Bergroman*. *Demeter; oder, Die Verzauberung* (1967; Demeter; or, the enchantment) is the unfinished third version. The edition published under the title *Bergroman* (1969) consists of four volumes, the first three being the three different versions and the fourth containing commentaries by the editors. *Der Versucher* presents, scarcely a few years after Hitler's rise to power, a miniature version of a totalitarian takeover. The anxiety and spiritual malaise of the farmers in a secluded mountain village are such that they fall for the promises of a demagogue and even participate in the ritual murder of a young girl. The book abounds in memorable descriptions of alpine scenes; by contrast, the passages in which B. attempts to provide metaphysical orientation through a "participation mystique" are heavy, even onerous. At the time of his death, B. was working on the third version of the text.

Inspired by the visions of impending death in the prison in Altaussee, where he had been confined briefly by the Nazis in 1938, B. had written a few elegies. They became the core of *Der Tod des Vergil*. The novel is a masterwork of the 20th c. and one of the great monuments of exile literature. Nevertheless, the extremely long sentences, the idiosyncrasies of B.'s language, and the heavy philosophical meanderings have given the novel the reputation of being excessively esoteric. The tendency of the language toward dissolution is counterbalanced by the precise structure and correspondences of the novel. Each of its four parts is ruled by one of the four elements (water, fire, earth, and ether), and associated with a deity from Greco-Roman mythology. While this scheme correctly intimates the historical Virgil's frame of references, it also allows B. to adopt the psychology of JUNG, with its emphasis on archetypes and a collective unconscious.

Within the framework of eighteen hours, the dying Virgil recapitulates the successive stages of ontogeny and of cognitive growth. During a night of feverish fantasies and hallucinations, he confronts his failures and delusions and comes to believe, from his radically ethical point of view, that the *Aeneid* must be destroyed, since it had failed in its cognitive mission. Returned at the breaking of daylight to the realm of worldly obligations, he engages in long philosophical conversations with his physician, with the emperor, and with his friends. The discussions reach their apogee in the struggle over the *Aeneid*, which Caesar Augustus wants preserved as a spiritual bond for his achievements. Virgil overcomes the narcissism of the artist and the rigorous position of the absolutist, and dedicates his work to the emperor.

During his years of exile, B. also continued with his multivolumed study of mass psychology and completed a number of essays, among them *Hofmannsthal und seine Zeit* (written 1947–48; pub. 1975; Hofmannsthal and his times), an astute analysis of fin-de-siècle Vienna and an enlightening appraisal of his own background from the perspective of old age. Out of financial necessity he completed another novel, *Die Schuldlosen* (1950; *The Guiltless*, 1974), composed of eleven loosely connected short stories, and divided, like *Die Schlafwandler*, into three historical periods. Through an exploration of the protagonists' psyches B. shows that Hitler's rise to power was long prepared for. Although remarkable for its structure and the use of Don Juan myth as leitmotif for yet another descent into "hell," the novel does not attain the intricate richness of either *Die Schlafwandler* or *Der Tod des Vergil*.

While it is true that B. is limited in his philosophy to an outlook that has recently been attacked as fatalistic or utopian beyond any hope of implementation, his contributions in the field of political theory nevertheless constitute some of the most serious thinking that has come out of neo-Kantianism in the first half of this century. B.'s achievement as a novelist, however, is unanimously acknowledged. *Die Schlafwandler* and *Der Tod des Vergil* are comparable to Joyce's *Ulysses* and *Finnegans Wake* in having contributed new definitions and dimensions to the modern novel. While B. focuses intensely on the perennial concern of the novel—the portrayal of the individual in society—his novels are also radically modern in that the self-consciousness of the modern novelist, the recognition of the near impossibility of creating a work of art, and the doubts about language have become integral parts of the works themselves.

FURTHER WORKS: *Die unbekannte Größe* (1933; *The Unknown Quantity*, 1935); *Dichten und Erkennen* (1955); *Zur Universitätsreform* (1969); *Gedanken zur Politik* (1970); *Barbara, und andere Novellen* (1973); *Kommentierte Werkausgabe* (13 vols., 1974–1981). FURTHER WORKS IN ENGLISH: *Short Stories* (1966)

BIBLIOGRAPHY: Cohn, D. C., *"The Sleepwalkers": Elucidations of H. B.'s Trilogy* (1966); Durzak, M., *H. B.* (1966); Ziolkowski, T., "H. B.: *The Sleepwalkers,*" *Dimensions of the Modern Novel* (1969): 138–80; Menges, K., *Kritische Studien zur Werttheorie H. B.s* (1970); Krapoth, H., *Dichtung und Philosophie: Ein Studie zum Werk H. B.s* (1971); Osterle, H. D., "H. B.'s *Die Schlafwandler* Revolution and Apocalypse," *PMLA*, 86 (1971): 946–57; Durzak, M., ed., *Perspektiven der B.-Forschung* (1972); Kahler, E., "The Epochal Innovations in H. B.'s Narrative," in Boyers, R., ed., *The Legacy of the German Refugee Intellectuals* (1972): 186–92; Lützeler, P. M., *H. B.: Ethik und Politik* (1973); Casey, T. J., "Questioning B.'s *Versucher,*" *DVLG*, 47 (1973): 467–507; Schlant, E., *H. B.* (1978); special B. issue, *MAL*, 13, 4 (1980)

—ERNESTINE SCHLANT

H. B. belongs in that tradition of great 20th-century novelists who have transformed, almost beyond recognition, one of the classic art-forms of the 19th century. The modern novel no longer serves as "entertainment and instruction" (B.) and its authors no longer relate the unusual, unheard-of "incident" (Goethe) or tell a story from which the reader will get "advice" (W. Benjamin). It rather confronts him with problems and perplexities in which the reader must be prepared to engage himself if he is to understand it all. The result of this transformation has been that the most accessible and popular art has become one of the most difficult and esoteric. . . .

Seen within the framework of literary history, *The Death of Virgil (Der Tod des Vergil)* solves the problem of the new form and content of the novel that *The Sleepwalkers (Die Schlafwandler)* raised. There the novel seemed to have reached an impasse between philosophy and lyricism, precisely because pure story-telling, entertainment and instruction, had been taken care of by extraordinary but second-rate talents. The historical significance of *The Death of Virgil* is the creation in both of a unity in which a new specifically modern element of suspense could materialize. It is as though only now those purely artistic elements which always gave the traditional novel its literary validity, the lyrical passion and the transfiguration of reality through the universal, have emancipated themselves from the merely informative and found a new and valid form.

Hannah Arendt, "The Achievement of H. B.," *KR*, 11 (1949), 476, 483

There are passages in *Die Schlafwandler, Der Versucher*, and even in *Die Schuldlosen*, in which H. B. could demonstrate with what sovereign virtuosity he made use of traditional prose styles, such as that of the "realistic" novel. . . . While we must . . . call B.'s books experiments—impressive experiments but not self-contained works of art in the usual sense—the fact is that B.'s creative work, precisely by its somewhat experimental character, is the most adequate representation of the plight of poetry in the present age, as B. saw that plight and as it concerned him. His books make no attempt to achieve that aesthetic self-sufficient completeness, which, B. believed, would make them insincere and turn them generally into *Kitsch*, in the worst sense. They give no more than they can give, no more than befits the consciousness of the age in its true sense. They are, in fact, an expression of that plight "between two ages," of that "still not and yet already," and just because they are passionate attempts that succeed in their "progress," they demonstrate the inadequacy of literary creation that B. had talked about repeatedly.

Richard Brinkmann, "Romanform und Werttheorie bei H. B.: Strukturprobleme moderner Dichtung," *DVLG*, 31 (1957), 197

Few novelists have developed a more exalted aesthetics for their genre. B. envisioned a novel that would be nothing less than a religious, a metaphysical, a cognitive search. . . . This conception of the novel grew out of a sense that science and philosophy

could no longer encompass the realities of life, out of a need to define a new realm of expression and communication.

Dorrit C. Cohn, *"The Sleepwalkers": Elucidations of H. B.'s Trilogy* (1966), pp. 13–14

Anyone who comes in contact with B.'s work immediately encounters one aspect so important that everything else seems dominated by it: this is the problem of creativity, especially the doubts about the justification of art. B. carries these doubts to their highest states of intensity in a work of art, *The Death of Virgil*, which could be called a work of art against art. . . . It is characteristic of B.'s life and work that his passionate dedication and his search for ways to exert an influence on his times led to vastly different modes of exploration.

Hermann Krapoth, *Dichtung und Philosophie: Eine Studie zum Werk H. B.s* (1971), p. 1

[B.'s] philosophy exhibits the basic pattern of integration in the past, disintegration in the present, and reintegration in the future of man and society. What appears behind it is the archetypal pattern of all religions: the triadic rhythm of life, death, and rebirth or innocence, fall, and innocence regained. It is a question of semantics whether this philosophy should be called apocalyptic or chiliastic.

Heinz D. Osterle, "H. B.'s *Die Schlafwandler*: Revolution and Apocalypse," *PMLA*, 86 (1971), 953

BROD, Max

Austrian novelist, biographer, essayist, poet, and dramatist, b. 27 May 1884, Prague, Czechoslovakia; d. 20 Dec. 1968, Tel Aviv, Israel

Although he is known in English-speaking countries mainly as the long-time friend, editor, and biographer of Franz KAFKA, B. was a versatile and prolific writer in his own right.

Member of a middle-class Jewish family that had been in Prague for generations, B. was graduated from the University of Prague in 1907 and became a postal official, continuing his government service as an art critic from 1924 to 1929. For the next ten years B. was employed by the *Prager Tagblatt* as a literary and art critic. In 1939 B. emigrated to Palestine and until the end of his life served as a dramatic adviser to the Habima company as well as continuing his activities as a music critic, composer, lecturer, and cultural mediator.

Having come under the influence of the Jewish and Zionist thought of Hugo Bergmann (1883–1975) and Martin BUBER from 1909 on, B. strove to come to terms with his heritage and his milieu—he was a German-speaking Jew in a Czech environment—and concluded that he was a *homo judaicus* with a *"Distanzliebe"* (a love characterized by detachment) for German culture and the

German people. From the "indifferentism" of his early fiction, notably the collection of novellas *Tod den Toten!* (1906; death to the dead!) and the novel *Schloß Nornepygge* (1908; Nornepygge Castle), B. increasingly turned to Jewish themes, in such works as *Jüdinnen* (1911, Jewesses); *Arnold Beer* (1912; *Arnold Beer*), subtitled "the fate of a Jew"; and *Eine Königin Esther* (1918; a Queen Esther). B.'s *magnum opus* as a fiction writer is a Renaissance trilogy collectively entitled "The Fight for Truth," consisting of *Tycho Brahes Weg zu Gott* (1916; *The Redemption of Tycho Brahe*, 1928), *Rëubeni, Fürst der Juden* (1925; *Rëubeni, Prince of the Jews*, 1928), and *Galilei in Gefangenschaft* (1948; Galileo in captivity).

The major work of B. the thinker is *Heidentum, Christentum, Judentum* (1921; *Paganism, Christianity, Judaism*, 1968), with its doctrine of "noble misfortune" (the inescapable limitations of the human condition) and "ignoble misfortune" (the kind that man has brought upon himself and must strive to alleviate). B.'s later works include books on Kafka, several novels, among them *Der Meister* (1951; *The Master*, 1951), centering on the public life of Jesus Christ; historical monographs such as *Johannes Reuchlin und sein Kampf* (1965; Johannes Reuchlin and his struggle); philosophical essays like *Das Unzerstörbare* (1968; the indestructible); and the autobiographical volumes *Streitbares Leben* (1960, 1969; a valiant life) and *Der Prager Kreis* (1966; the Prague Circle).

FURTHER WORKS: *Ein tschechisches Dienstmädchen* (1909); *Die Erziehung zur Hetäre* (1909); *Tagebuch in Versen* (1910); *Weiberwirtschaft* (1913); *Über die Schönheit häßlicher Bilder* (1913); *Das gelobte Land* (1917); *Adolf Schreiber* (1921); *Franzi; oder, Eine Liebe zweiten Ranges* (1922); *Klarissas halbes Herz* (1923); *Leben mit einer Göttin* (1923); *Die Frau, nach der man sich sehnt* (1927); *Das Zauberreich der Liebe* (1928; *Three Loves*, 1929); *Lord Byron kommt aus der Mode* (1929); *Die Frau, die nicht enttäuscht* (1933); *Heinrich Heine* (1934; *Heinrich Heine, The Artist in Revolt*, 1956); *Novellen aus Böhmen* (1936); *Annerl* (1937); *Franz Kafka* (1937; *Franz Kafka*, 1947); *Das Diesseitswunder* (1939); *Diesseits und Jenseits* (1947); *Franz Kafkas Glauben und Lehre* (1948); *Neue Gedichte* (1949); *Unambo: Roman aus dem jüdisch-arabischen Krieg* (1949; *Unambo: A Novel of the War in Israel*, 1952); *Franz Kafka als wegweisende Gestalt* (1951); *Die Musik Israels* (1951; *Israel's Music*, 1951); *Der Sommer, den man zurückwünscht* (1952); *Beinahe ein Vorzugsschüler* (1952); *Armer Cicero* (1955); *Leoš Janáček* (1956); *Rebellische Herzen* (1957; reissued as *Prager Tagblatt*, 1968); *Mira* (1958); *Jugend im Nebel* (1959); *Verzweiflung und Erlösung im Werk Franz Kafkas* (1959); *Die Rosenkoralle* (1961); *Gustav Mahler* (1961); *Die verkaufte Braut* (1962); *Durchbruch ins Wunder* (1962); *Prager Sternenhimmel* (1966); *Gesang einer Giftschlange* (1966); *Von der Unsterblichkeit der Seele* (1969)

BIBLIOGRAPHY: Weltmann, L., "Kafka's Friend M. B.," *GL&L*, 4 (1950–1951): 46–50; Kahn, L., "The Zionist Judaism of M. B.," *The Reconstructionist*, 7 Apr. 1961: 16–23; Zohn, H., "M. B. at Eighty," *Jewish Spectator*, 29 (May 1964): 7–9; Weltsch, F., "M. B.: A Study in Unity and Duality," *Judaism*, 14 (Winter 1965): 48–59; Gold, H., ed., *M. B.: Ein Gedenkbuch* (1969); Pazi, M., *M. B.: Werk und Persönlichkeit* (1970); Kayser, W. and Gronemeyer, H., *M. B.—Bibliographie* (1972); Schoeps, J. H., ed., *Im Streit um Kafka und das Judentum. Briefwechsel M. B. und H.-J. Schoeps* (1985); Pasi, M., ed., *M. B. 1884-1984* (1987); Pasley, M., ed., *B. -*

Kafka. Eine Freundschaft (1987); Pasley, M., ed., *B. - Kafka Briefwechsel* (1989); Bahr, E., "M. B.," in Hardin J., et al., eds., *Dicitonary of Literary Biography* 81 (1989): 61-70; Barsh, E.-E., *M. B. im Kampf um das Judentum* (1992); Bahr, E., "M. B. as a Novelist," in Gelber, M. H. et al., eds., *Von Franzos zu Canetti* (1996): 25-36

—HARRY ZOHN

BRODSKY, Joseph

Russian poet and essayist, b. 24 May 1940, Leningrad; d. 28 Jan. 1996, New York, N.Y.

B. dropped out of secondary school at the age of fifteen and had no further formal education. As a young man he worked at many occupations, including stoker and geologist-prospector.

B.'s poems became increasingly well known, first in Leningrad from 1960, then throughout the U.S.S.R. and abroad. The quantity of his poetry that appeared in *samizdat* (clandestine circulation) editions is matched only by that of Solzhenitsyn's prose. Few of B.'s poems were officially published in the Soviet Union.

B.'s reputation, which made him a spokesman for dissidents, also turned him into a target for the secret police. In February 1964 he was tried as a "social parasite" and was sentenced to five years of internal exile and compulsory work at a remote collective farm. The sentence provoked worldwide protest. At home such esteemed figures as the poets Akhmatova and Tvardovsky, the critic Korney Chukovsky (1882–1969), and the composer Dmitri Shostakovich petitioned on his behalf, and in 1965 he was released. In the same year a volume of collected poems, *Stikhotvorenia i poemy* (1965; poems and long poems), was issued in the U.S. Several later collections were also published abroad.

In June 1972 B. was forced to emigrate. He came to the U.S., where he has taught at various universities. He became an American citizen in 1977.

The genuine revolution in contemporary Russian poetry produced by B. can be fully understood only in the context of its development. The greatest achievements of such 20th-c. Russian poets as Akhmatova, Khodasevich, Mandelshtam, Pasternak, Tsvetaeva, and Alexandr Vvedensky (1904–1941) were in the elaboration of their individual poetic voices through the refinement of prosodic and figurative means. B. felicitously combined the best aspects of his predecessors' poetic techniques and applied them to profound philosophical themes that owe their inspiration to Dostoevsky, Vladimir Solovyov (1853–1900), and Lev Shestov (1866–1938). The English metaphysical poets, as well as Yeats and Eliot, also had an important influence on B.'s poetry.

Like most Russian poetry, B.'s is metrical and intended for recital rather than for silent reading. The variety of meters, rhymes, and stanzas B. created is extraordinarily rich. He also introduced into modern Russian poetry a great many English poetic forms and revived some forgotten Russian forms from the 18th and early 19th cs. Between 1960 and 1968 B. produced more than five hundred titles, plus numerous translations from modern Greek, Polish, English, and American poetry. From this prolific first period two long poems stand out in their profound expression of existential problems: "Isaak i Avraam" (1963; Isaac and Abraham) and

"Gorbunov i Gorchakov" (1965–68; "Gorbunov and Gorchakov," 1971). The first, based on the Old Testament story, is, in a way, a poetic interpretation of Kierkegaard's *School of Christianity*. The subject of the second is somewhat more closely tied to contemporary Soviet life, for the poem basically consists of a dialogue of two intellectuals confined to a mental institution, or perhaps by one suffering from a split personality. The illusoriness of the material world—or rather, the relativity of numerous "realities" discussed by two voices—reaches a climax in the section in which grammatical forms begin melting into one another: verbs act as nouns, as adjectives, as adverbs and so on.

Later poems reflect the poet's idea of the coming of a post-Christian era, when the traditional opposition of good and evil in Christianity would be replaced by moral relativism, which he sees as the confrontation of different levels of evil.

The most notable feature of B.'s poetry after 1968 is his use of realistic detail, to such a degree that some of his poems are in effect verse novellas. Outstanding examples of these are "Posvyashchaetsya Yalte" (1969; "Homage to Yalta," 1978) and "Post aetatem nostrum" (1971; title in Latin: after our age). Understandably, nostalgia became one of the leading themes in B.'s poetry after 1972. One manifestation of the theme is the series of poems set in the Belle Époque of the late 19th c. Another manifestation of nostalgia is the continuing cycle of short poems known as "Chast rechi" (a part of speech), characterized by the poet's fixed attention to the semantic and etymological nuances of Russian words and by intense lyricism.

At different periods of his life B. was personally close to two outstanding older poets: Akhmatova and W. H. Auden, the latter instrumental in bringing B. to the West. Both of them saw in B. an innovator who was at the same time a traditionalist. Herein lies the key to B.'s work. Like no one else since Pushkin, he has enriched the Russian poetry by developing its inner resources as well as by inoculating it with the artistic practices of the West.

FURTHER WORKS: *Ostanovka v pustyne* (1970); *Konets prekrasnoy epokhi* (1977); *V Anglii* (1977); *Chast rechi* (1977). FURTHER WORKS IN ENGLISH: *Debut* (1973); *Selected Poems* (1973); *A Part of Speech* (1980)

BIBLIOGRAPHY: Spender, S., "Bread of Affliction," *NS*, 14 Dec. 1973: 915; Erlich, V., "A Letter in a Bottle," *PR*, 41 (1974): 617–21; Sylvester, R. D., "The Poem as Scapegoat: An Introduction to J. B.'s *Halt in the Wilderness*," *TSLL*, 17 (1975): 303–25; Gifford, H., "The Language of Loneliness," *TLS*, 11 Aug. 1978: 902–3; Milosz, C., "A Struggle against Suffocation," *NYRB*, 14 Aug. 1980: 23–25; Brown, C., "The Best Russian Poetry Written Today," *NYTBR*, 7 Sept. 1980: 11, 16, 18

—LEV L. LOSEFF

BRÓDY, Sándor

Hungarian novelist and dramatist, b. 23 July 1863, Eger; d. 12 Aug. 1924, Budapest

One of the first important urban writers in Hungary, and in many ways the father of modern Hungarian prose literature, B. was nonetheless deeply influenced by the easygoing life style of 19th-c. provincial Hungary. He was born into a largely Magyarized Jewish merchant family and spent his childhood in Eger. His family moved in the 1870s to Budapest, where the young B. witnessed the growing pains of a city that was just then turning from a rather staid town into a bustling metropolis. B. was among the first in Hungarian literature to write about the urban proletariat, the first to introduce the coarse and pungent vernacular of the big city into literary works, although his often brutal naturalism was always tempered by the sentimentality of 19th-c. Hungarian literature. He himself became a celebrated, and often controversial, bohemian artist. His stormy love affairs and a well-publicized suicide attempt added to his notoriety.

B.'s literary output reflects his impulsive, unstable character. Almost all of his works contain carefully conceived and brilliantly executed passages, but many of the works themselves are verbose, unconvincing, at times dilettantish. He embarked on ambitious literary projects, which more often than not ended in partial or total failure. Between 1900 and 1902 he published a literary magazine, *Fehér könyv*, written entirely by himself, and in 1903 he founded another journal, *Jövendő*. In addition to offering poetry and prose influenced by new Western literary trends, the two periodicals became important forums for liberal political sentiments. Since B. the editor was as erratic as B. the writer, both ventures were short-lived. As he aged, B. grew more isolated, and his art became even more irregular. Although his approach to literature and his style influenced practically every member of the important group of early-20th-c. poets and novelists associated with the periodical *Nyugat*, B. at the time of his death was seen by many as a relic of a bygone era.

An enthusiastic follower of Zola's naturalism, B. in his early work exaggerated the importance of biological determinism. In his first collection of stories, *Nyomor* (1884; misery), the lives of his poverty-stricken workers, tradesmen, maids, and prostitutes are ruled entirely by passion. In his mature short prose, as well as in the novel *A nap lovagja* (1902; hero of the day), the bitter story of an upstart journalist, both his characterizations and his social criticism are considerably more subtle.

B. was also an important dramatist. His *A dada* (1902; the nanny), *A tanítóonő* (1908; the schoolmistress), and *A medikus* (1911; the medical student) are examples of Hungarian naturalist theater, which reveal the influence not only of the French school but of the great Russian realists as well. In them B. shows how people with a sense of honor become victims of a corrupt social order. *A tanítóonő*, which focuses on the conflict between a proud young teacher and her overbearing gentry employers, is an especially powerful work. Despite its rather stylized language, it does not seem as dated as some of B.'s other writings, and it is still performed in Hungary.

B. kept turning out plays and stories almost to the end of his life, but the only work that stands out from his late period is a cycle of narratives about Rembrandt, his longtime idol: *Rembrandt* (1925; *Rembrandt*, 1928). In these poignant sketches B. clearly identifies himself with Rembrandt's misfortunes, and tries to deal with the anguish of being an unappreciated artist.

FURTHER WORKS: *Ezüst kecske* (1898); *Erzsébet dajka és más cselédek* (1902); *Húsevők* (1913); *B. S. legszebb írásai* (1935); *Válogatott színművek* (1957)

—IVAN SANDERS

BRONIEWSKI, Władysław

Polish poet, b. 17 Dec. 1897, Plock; d. 10 Feb. 1962, Warsaw

In his early youth B. joined the Polish independence movement and fought against Russia in World War I as a soldier of the so-called *Legiony*, the Polish military force formed under the protectorate of Austro-Hungarian authorities, led by *Józef Pilsudski* (1867–1935). Later he enlisted as a volunteer to fight against the Soviets in the Polish-Soviet war of 1920. He left the army with the intention of becoming a writer. He went through an ideological crisis, however, as a result of which he felt that, as an individual and poet, he should devote his life to the struggle for social justice. Although he never formally joined the Communist Party, his cultural and social activities were closely affiliated with its philosophy and political stand for almost two decades.

This evolution from intransigent nationalist to ardent proponent of the revolutionary cause left a lasting imprint on B.'s poetry and determined its main characteristics. He was proclaimed the greatest exponent of proletarian poetry in Polish literature and, at the same time, was recognized as one of the best perpetuators of its romantic tradition.

In matters of poetic form B. was close to the Skamander group, which adhered to the principles of traditional poetics. Ideologically, however, he stood far to the left and never joined the group. B. formulated his artistic credo in the poem "Poezja" (1927; poetry): the goals of poetry are to serve the noble cause of social justice and to call for revolution. B. lived up to these canons in his early poetry, which described the misery of city life and the lot of the working class. Many poems are devoted to revolutionary events and personalities. He wrote about the Russian revolutionary Bakunin, the French poet Arthur Rimbaud, and the founder of the Polish Communist movement Ludwik Waryński (1856–1889).

In the late 1930s, when the political situation was heading toward military confrontation, B. showed increasing concern for the well-being of his country. Patriotic motifs occurred more often in his poetry and dominated it almost entirely during World War II, when he was in exile in the Soviet Union (1939–43) and in Palestine (1943–46). It should be stressed that both social and national themes in B.'s poetry are expressed through the prism of his very personal feelings, and therefore they never sound false or like political slogans.

Despite the fact that B. wrote a poem in praise of Stalin, these personal elements became an important factor in his poetry written after the war, most interestingly in the collection *Anka* (1956; Anka), dedicated to his beloved daughter, who died in 1954. Her death marked a definite change in his attitude as a poet. After *Anka* he stopped writing original poetry and limited himself to translating.

In B.'s poetry after World War II a new motif, the poet's enchantment with the nature of his native land, may attract the attention of readers. To be sure, this motif is present in a few prewar poems, and becomes increasingly evident in the lyrics written during the war. In postwar Poland it developed into an independent theme. B. describes the beauty of Polish landscape, its rivers, mountains, and fields. In these works B. does not just express his attachment to his country; these poems also give him an opportunity for reflection on life and art. His poems acquire an air of nostalgia. B. went through a long evolution from a position of a revolutionary bard to more moderate and introspective poet.

B. was also an active and excellent translator of Russian writers such as Pilnyak, Alexey TOLSTOY, Dostoevsky, and Gogol.

FURTHER WORKS: *Wiatraki* (1925); *Trzy salwy* (1925, with S. R. Stande and W. Wandurski); *Dymy nad miastem* (1927); *Komuna Paryska* (1929); *Troska i pieśń* (1932); *Krzyk ostateczny* (1938); *Bagnet na broń* (1943); *Drzewo rozpaczające* (1945); *Nadzieja* (1951); *Wiersze i poematy* (1962)

BIBLIOGRAPHY: Krejči, K., *Geschichte der polnischen Literatur* (1958): 482–88; Milosz, C., *The History of Polish Literature* (1969): 399–400; Kridl, M., *A Survey of Polish Literature and Culture* (1956): 490–91; Krzyżanowski, J., *A History of Polish Literature* (1978): 580–83

—EDWARD MOŻEJKO

BROOKE-ROSE, Christine

English novelist and critic, b. 16 Jan. 1923, Geneva, Switzerland

B., bilingual since childhood, knows several languages besides English and French. Educated at Oxford, she studied philology and, later, linguistics. She is currently Professor of Anglo-American Studies at the University of Paris, Vincennes. In the novel *Thru* (1975), B. creates English words that pun on French words and occasionally moves briefly into French and Italian. Like Samuel BECKETT, she works creatively with clichés and idioms, transferring them with wit and erudition from one context to another.

Structural linguistics occupies an important place in B.'s work. Her scholarly articles, characterized by clarity and formidable logic, have been appearing in such prestigious journals as *A Journal for Descriptive Poetics and Theory* and *New Literary History*.

The title story of the collection *Go When You See the Green Man Walking* (1970) is a clear example of B.'s mastery of the kind of descriptive method employed by practitioners of the NEW NOVEL. But the technique functions differently in her work, to force the interpretations that writers such as Alain Robbe-Grillet try to eliminate. The prostitute in the story, although described objectively, is not merely there; her presence is one of the elements that force the reader to recognize the relationship between two regulatory code systems, one for public motor traffic and one for private sex traffic.

B. disavows her earliest fiction. Beginning with *Out* (1964), her novels are increasingly nonreferential and linguistically complex. Literal apocalypse (volcanic explosion) in *The Middlemen: A Satire* (1961) becomes metaphorical disintegration of text in *Thru*. Binary reality (an imaginary love story in outer space reflecting the protagonist's real life and concerns) in *Such* (1966) reaches its most complex development in *Thru*, in which the mirror is explicitly and implicitly the controlling image and idea, starting with the image of the driver's rear-view mirror.

Thru, in describing its own activity, mirrors itself (although the mirroring occurs on many other levels also). *Thru*, which relies heavily on the concepts of Roland BARTHES and on Diderot's *Jacques the Fatalist*, which first explicitly expressed these concepts, incorporates citations from actual structuralist critics into the text and at the same time demonstrates their principles in practice. Gradually, we realize that the book has no plot, no characters, and no identifiable narrator. There is only text, implied author, and implied reader. In this novel, B. partially overcomes the limitation of textual linearity by embedding messages within other messages;

the simultaneity of given information requires that the reader continually learn new methods of deciphering. B.'s key method is repetition of phrases and passages, a method that teaches the reader, through changing informational contexts, to perceive the interrelatedness of systems of language, education, politics, sexual politics, and economics.

Although she resembles Beckett in some ways, B. does not emphasize the pain of inescapable consciousness. She treats specifically the idea of exchange in a coded system and consequently implies the idea of value. Most of her fiction deals with the war between the sexes and with the language in which it is carried on (seduction clichés, squabbling patterns). She also applies other language levels to the sex war: the language of molecular physics in the fiction of the 1960s, the language of structural linguistics in *Thru*. B.'s work as a whole may be considered a hermetic system of metaphor which seals us in and seals knowable reality out; but B.'s work, in laying bare the systems, reveals positive values that may form the basis for personal identity and for harmonious relations between one person and another.

FURTHER WORKS: *Gold* (1954); *The Languages of Love* (1957); *The Sycamore Tree* (1958); *A Grammar of Metaphor* (1958); *The Dear Deceit* (1960); *Between* (1968); *A ZBC of Ezra Pound* (1971); *A Structural Analysis of Pound's "Usura Canto": Jacobson's Method Extended and Applied to Free Verse* (1976)

BIBLIOGRAPHY: Hayman, D., and Cohen, K., "An Interview with C. B.," *ConL*, 17 (1976): 1–23

—JUDITH LEIBOWITZ

BROOKNER, Anita

British novelist and art historian, b. 16 July 1928, London

A Londoner by birth and residence, B. is the daughter of Polish Jews, her father born in Poland, her mother in England. Educated at James Allen's Girls' School, she read history at King's College, University of London, and received a Ph.D. in art history from the Courtauld Institute. During the next twenty years B. established a distinguished academic career and published widely recognized studies of 18th- and 19th-c. art. From 1959 to 1964 she was a visiting lecturer in the history of art at the University of Reading. In 1964 she was appointed lecturer at the Courtauld Institute and has continued there as a reader in the history of art since 1977. A Fellow of New Hall, Cambridge University, B. was the first woman to be named Slade Professor of Art at Cambridge (1967–1968). Her brief early studies of Ingres, David, and Watteau led to major critical works: *The Genius of the Future: Studies in French Art Criticism* (1971), *Greuze: The Rise and Fall of an Eighteenth-Century Phenomenon* (1972), and *Jacques-Louis David: A Personal Interpretation* (1980).

In 1980 B. began writing fiction and by 1985 had declared she would not return to art criticism. Since the appearance of *A Start in Life* (pub. in U. S. as *The Debut*) in 1981, she has published eleven novels to date, one each year through 1991.

From her early work to *Hotel du Lac* (1984), awarded the Booker Prize, and subsequently in fiction of enlarged scope and increasing complexity, B.'s writing has won critical acclaim for its nuance, subtlety, and wit. In some measure a satirist of contemporary relations between women and men, B. explores the inducements and rewards marriage held for earlier generations of women and captures the confusion and self-doubt of younger, independent women with careers but without love or the satisfactions of marriage. Discursive in the manner of Henry JAMES and Edith WHARTON, B.'s fiction reveals the pleasures and agonies, hopes and disillusions of her major characters through a stream of narrative commentary, frequently with little dialogue.

B.'s first four novels center on intelligent, educated career women—two are academics, one a librarian-turned-writer, another a novelist—plagued by loneliness and the prospect of the single life. In *A Start in Life* Ruth Weiss, like several B. characters the only child of disappointed, inept parents, finds her identity as a young woman through reading and eventually earns a Ph.D. as a Balzac specialist. While Ruth accepts a short-lived compromise marriage and continues her teaching career, the central characters in the next two novels must negotiate the expectations of egocentric men or rapacious couples parading as friends only to find themselves alone at the end. Kitty Maule of *Providence* (1982) and Frances Hinton of *Look at Me* (1983) both meet with rejection by men unworthy of them.

Like these novels, *Hotel du Lac* is a cautionary tale. Edith Hope, at thirty-nine a more urbane, self-accepting woman than earlier B. figures, manages to be objective about the hare and tortoise race of competitive females her novels depict and about her secret affair with a married man. On the brink of marriage to a conventional type who would have her relinquish her writing, she bolts and winds up—at her friends' urging—at a Swiss resort hotel in the midst of some of B.'s most colorful and amusing characters. Offered a marriage of convenience by a charming, intelligent but altogether unscrupulous man who promises her plenty of material for her fiction, Edith is tempted but decides the single state she has created for herself in London is preferable to this cynical arrangement.

B.'s work following *Hotel du Lac* has moved in new and unpredictable directions. Earlier criticism pointed out parallels in her portrayals of single women to Barbara PYM's "excellent women" who find no men to match them. However, the more recent novels demonstrate B.'s ability to work with a richer social fabric and to create characters with complex histories struggling to maintain a delicate balance in worlds foreign to them.

In *Family and Friends* (1985) and *Latecomers* (1988) B. introduces a number of European exiles who have established outwardly successful lives in England after World War II. The former, structured brilliantly around four photographs of wedding parties, suggests a play by Anton CHEKHOV. *Latecomers* is a study in contrasts: of business partners who had escaped to London from war-torn Germany as boys; of their close friendships and marriages; of their two unlikely children. In both works B. reveals—with impressive insight—the psychological dimensions of vastly different characters. With a light but devastating wit she anatomizes a society in transition.

In those writers she has identified as the touchstones of 19th–c. writing—Dickens, James, Trollope, Stendhal, Flaubert, and Zola—B. locates the close scrutiny, moral scruple, and indignation she values in fiction. The contemporary women novelists she admires, among them Rosamund Lehmann (b. 1901), Elizabeth Taylor (1912–1975), Edith Templeton (b. 1916), Mavis GALLANT, and

Fay WELDON, exemplify the restrained yet passionate storytelling and incisive social analysis of which she herself is master.

B.'s stylistic skill is evident in the painterly qualities of her descriptions and in the deft weaving of references to literary works, paintings, sculptures, and myth into details about her characters' careers and personalities. Sensuous renderings of objects, clothing, rooms, and landscapes create a rich atmosphere that offsets the more serious moral concerns of her writing.

FURTHER WORKS: *An Iconography of Cecil Rhodes* (1956); *J. A. Dominique Ingres* (1965); *Jacques Louis David* (1967); *Watteau* (1968); *A Misalliance* (1986); *A Friend from England* (1987); *Lewis Percy* (1989); *Brief Lives* (1990); *A Closed Eye* (1991); *Fraud* (1992); *A Family Romance* (1993); *A Private View* (1994); *Visitors* (1998)

BIBLIOGRAPHY: Jebb, J., "Unblinking," on *Hotel du Lac, Spectator*, 22 Sept. 1984: 26–27; Tyler, A., "A Solitary Life Is Still Worth Living," on *Hotel du Lac, NYTBR*, 3 Feb. 1985: 1, 31; Wilson, A. N., "Significant Silences," on *Family and Friends, TLS*, 6 Sept. 1985: 973; Haffenden, J., *Novelists in Interview* (1985): 57–85; Kakutani, M., on *The Misalliance, NYT*, 25 March 1987: C23; Guppy, S., "Interview: The Art of Fiction XCVII: A. B.," *Paris Review*, 109 (1987): 146–69; Hosmer, R. E., "A. B." in Brook, J. M. ed., *DLB: Yearbook 1987* (1988): 293–308; Bawer, B., "Doubles and More Doubles," on *Latecomers, NewC*, 7, 8 (April 1989): 67–74; Sadler, L. V., *A. B.* (1990); Lopate, P., on *Lewis Percy, NYTBR,* 11 March 1990: 10

—THEODORA RAPP GRAHAM

Anita Brookner

BROOKS, Cleanth

American literary critic, scholar, and educator, b. 16 Oct. 1906, Murray, Ky.; d. 10 May 1994, New Haven, Conn.

B. received his undergraduate education at Vanderbilt University, where he was a student of John Crowe RANSOM. B. took an M.A. at Tulane in 1928 and then, as a Rhodes Scholar, a B.A. (with honors) and a B. Litt. at Oxford in 1931 and 1932. From 1932 to 1947 he taught English at Louisiana State University, and in 1947 he moved to Yale, where he became Gray Professor of Rhetoric in 1960.

Influenced by the critical theories of T. S. ELIOT and I. A. RICHARDS, as well as by the work of the Southern Agrarians he met at Vanderbilt, B. became the leading spokesman for the revolution in literary study known as the New Criticism (*see* Literary Criticism). B.'s greatest influence probably stems from the work he did during his years at Louisiana State University. From 1935 to 1942, together with Robert Penn WARREN, B. edited *The Southern Review*, a journal that played a major role in the Southern literary renaissance and in the development of the New Criticism. Also in collaboration with Warren he wrote *Understanding Poetry* (1938) and *Understanding Fiction* (1943), two extraordinarily influential textbooks that taught a whole generation of American students (and many of their teachers) a new method for reading literature. During those years B. also published two important critical treatises,

Modern Poetry and the Tradition (1939) and *The Well Wrought Urn: Studies in the Structure of Poetry* (1947), in which he presented extended demonstrations of his critical method and powerful theoretical arguments for the New Critical methodology.

The main tenets of B.'s theory, as he developed it in the books cited above and in such essays as "Irony and 'Ironic' Poetry" (1948) and "Irony as a Principle of Structure" (1949), were based upon his belief that poetic form is organic and that irony is the distinguishing characteristic of poetic structure. For B., poetry is distinguished from other kinds of discourse, not by its vocabulary or by its subject matter, but rather by its use of ironic structure and paradoxical language, which allow the poet to "dramatize the oneness of the experience, even though paying tribute to its diversity." The meaning of a poem cannot be paraphrased, because in a successful poem form and meaning are inextricably united: a poem for B. is a complicated, unified verbal structure in which no word can be changed or rearranged without loss or alteration of meaning. Furthermore, a lyric poem should be read as a speech in a play is read—as the utterance of a particular character in a particular situation—and not as a direct statement by the poet.

B.'s critical method, which emphasized the close reading of individual literary works, and his theory, stressing the autonomy of each individual poem, tended to devalue the historical and biographical investigations that were the main stock in trade of literary scholars. As a result, the New Criticism in general and B. in particular, as its most articulate spokesman, were surrounded by controversy even during the 1940s and 1950s, when their method gained ascendancy in the American academic community.

B. has objected to the popular stereotype that cast him as a myopic New Critic with a fixation on close reading and a disdain for historical scholarship. During his years at Yale he collaborated with William K. Wimsatt (1907–1975) in *Literary Criticism: A Short History* (1957), produced numerous critical and scholarly works on a variety of topics, and turned his attention increasingly to the novels of his fellow-Southerner, William FAULKNER. B.'s concern in *The Hidden God* (1963) and in his two books on Faulkner (1963 and 1978) with religious, social, and ethical issues and his increasing attention to historical scholarship (he has served, for instance, as an editor of the multivolume *Correspondence of Thomas Percy*) indicate an impressive breadth of interests and expertise. Nonetheless, these later productions have not had the profound impact upon the study of literature that B. achieved with his controversial New Critical studies of the 1930s and 1940s.

FURTHER WORKS: *The Relation of the Alabama-Georgia Dialect to the Provincial Dialects of Great Britain* (1935); *An Approach to Literature: A Collection of Prose and Verse with Analyses and Discussions* (1936, with John Thibaut Purser and Robert Penn Warren); *Understanding Drama* (1945, with Robert B. Heilman); *Modern Rhetoric* (1950, with R. P. W.); *Poems of Mr. John Milton* (1951, with John E. Hardy); *American Literature: A Mirror, Lens, or Prism* (1967); *The Writer and His Community* (1968); *A Shaping Joy: Studies in the Writer's Craft* (1971); *The Poetry of Tension* (1971); *American Literature: The Makers and the Making* (1973, with R. W. B. Lewis and R. P. W.); *The Modern Writer and the Burden of History* (1976)

BIBLIOGRAPHY: Crane, R. S., "The Critical Monism of C. B." (1948), *Critics and Criticism: Ancient and Modern* (1952): 83–107; Krieger, M., *The New Apologists for Poetry* (1956): 205–20; Krieger, M., "Critical Dogma and the New Critical Historians" (1958), *The Play and Place of Criticism* (1967): 177–93; Foster, R., *The New Romantics: A Reappraisal of the New Criticism* (1962), passim; Handy, W. J., *Kant and the Southern New Critics* (1963), passim; Lemon, L. T., *The Partial Critics* (1965): 139–50; Simpson, L. P., ed., *The Possibilities of Order: C. B. and His Work* (1976)

—PHYLLIS RACKIN

BROOKS, Gwendolyn

American poet, b. 7 June 1917, Topeka, Kans.

When B. was barely one month old, her parents moved to Chicago, which would become an important and pervasive background for her artistic consciousness. She was educated in Chicago's public schools, graduating from Wilson Junior College in 1936. While young, B. worked briefly as a journalist, but poetry has dominated her existence, although not to the detriment of her role as wife and mother. *Mademoiselle* magazine named her one of its ten Women of the Year in 1945. She was a Guggenheim Fellow in 1946 and 1947, and the winner of a Pulitzer Prize for poetry in 1950 and of the Anisfield-Wolf Award for the best literary contribution

to interracial understanding in 1969. That same year she was appointed poet laureate of Illinois, succeeding Carl SANDBURG. In recent years she has taught poetry at colleges in the Chicago area.

A Street in Bronzeville (1945) introduced B. to an audience that has been steadily more and more appreciative of her poetic virtues. Bronzeville is the South Side of Chicago, second largest of America's black urban ghettos. Its nature and its concerns, with significant changes reflecting the Black ideology and strategies of post-Eisenhower America, have remained the center of her universe. Poetry's monopoly of her creative energy was interrupted by her one venture into the novel, *Maud Martha* (1953). She has also published an autobiography, *Report from Part One* (1972).

Essentially a lyric poet, B. is a virtuoso in her craft. Pithiness marks her style. She seems never to waste a word and often resorts to ellipsis with telling effect. And her diction is memorable. Spare though it is, and free from elevated terminology and rhetoric, it yet commands a wealth of apt expression. Moreover, its colloquialism, reflecting the speech patterns of B.'s environment, accords well with the conversational tone of B.'s verse. She is at ease both with rhyme and free verse, and often makes use of traditional verse forms, particularly the ballad and the sonnet. Nevertheless, she has experienced no difficulty in assimilating to her needs a notable measure of the revolutionary manners, as well as doctrines, of the poets of the following generation.

The subject matter of B.'s poetry has always tended to be the ordinary experience of the so-called average person. It happens that the average person she knows best has been Black. It also happens that she is a woman, so that whatever in our society is special about womanhood or the culture of womankind she has discovered at firsthand. Quite logically, then, she has derived the content of her poetry largely from images of characters, typically those of low social status, who are either Black or female, or both. She builds not on the grand, but on the intimate. Thus, she seeks, in her own words, "the concentration, the crush" through which to "vivify the universal fact."

The consensus is that her strategy has succeeded, at least for much of her career. Critics agree that, although her world is Black, the implications of her thoughts about that world are universal. Since *In the Mecca* (1968), however, some critics have detected in her work (and B. herself, in published statements, seems to agree with them) a break with her own past: the search for an intraracial identity and the affirmation of an ethnically oriented patriotism have superseded the integrationist predispositions of her earlier work.

FURTHER WORKS: *Annie Allen* (1949); *Bronzeville Boys and Girls* (1956); *The Bean Eaters* (1960); *Selected Poems* (1963); *Riot* (1969); *Aloneness* (1971); *Family Pictures* (1970); *Beckonings* (1975)

BIBLIOGRAPHY: Davis, A., "G. B.: Poet of the Unheroic," *CLAJ*, 7 (1963): 114–25; Kent, G., "The Poetry of G. B.: Part I," *Black World*, Sept. 1971: 30–43; Kent, G., "The Poetry of G. B.: Part II," *Black World*, Oct. 1971: 36–48; Lee, D., "The Achievement of G. B.," *Black Scholar*, 3 (1972): 32–41; Shands, A., "G. B. as Novelist," *Black World*, May 1973: 22–30; Jackson, B., and Rubin, L., *Black Poetry in America* (1974): 81–85; Hull, G., "A Note on the Poetic Technique of G. B.," *CLAJ*, 19 (1975): 280–85

—BLYDEN JACKSON

BROPHY, Brigid

Irish-English critic, novelist, and journalist, b. 12 June 1929, London; d. 8 Aug. 1995, Lincolnshire

Her father was an Irish writer working in England; B. started her literary career in childhood and developed a love of the classics as a result of her mother's teaching and her further training at St. Paul's Girls' School. After a year at Oxford, she (in her own words) "came down at nineteen without taking a degree and with a consequent sense of nudity. . . ." Thereafter she took a job as a stenographer before making her debut as a fiction writer in the early 1950s.

B.'s work should be seen in the context of Irish wit, imagination, and iconoclasm. In the tradition of Swift and JOYCE, she is outrageous in her flights of fancy and verbal gymnastics. She has a keen sense of the ridiculous and a hatred of cant, ignorance, and cruelty. Acknowledging SHAW as a mentor, she has worked to correct folly and clarify confusion in order to make a better life for all the world's creatures.

Despite her classical training, B.'s fiction is filled with strange excursions into language and experience. Her overarching theme is FREUD's "civilization and its discontents," the ways in which we suffer and inflict suffering as a result of our instinctual-rational nature. She embodies this idea in a variety of bizarre situations. *Hackenfeller's Ape* (1953) is the story of an ape who gradually becomes more human—and more of a burden to himself and his mate. *Flesh* (1962) is a novel with a slippery texture: on the surface a story of bourgeois newlyweds, it is also a mysterious, humorous, and troubling exploration of modern erotic life and its exactions. A young husband's transformation from a wallflower to a full-blown hedonist is the occasion for exploring the dark side of pleasure. Jamesian both in its emphasis on changing character and in its sinister, ironic approach to relationships, the novel succeeds as social and psychological portraiture. *In Transit* (1969) moves out into larger cultural and linguistic territories: stylistically very different from B.'s earlier work, it is a pun-riddled stream-of-consciousness narrative conducted by a person of uncertain sex and identity; this persona is waiting in the homogenized atmosphere of an airport terminal and musing on the absurdities of modern civilization as well as on man's contemporary discontents and uncertainties. B.'s own cultural unhousedness as an Irish woman in England, in addition to her obsession with the shapes and sounds of language, is evident throughout. Her latest fictional work, *Palace without Chairs* (1978), a fantasy about politics, is less successful in fusing her powers of social observation and her verbal gifts.

Critical writing is an integral part of her work and partakes of her best imaginative energies. As a whole, this work is relentlessly concerned with the ways that rationality has failed in Western life: it traces our follies and cruelties to a deficiency of imaginative response as well as to a variety of grand-scale cultural repressions. *Black Ship to Hell* (1962) is a mammoth study of violence and the death instinct. Equipped with a thorough knowledge of Freud and a prodigious number of cultural, literary, and social instances, B. attempts to prove several propositions about man's destructive impulses. Her most effectively presented argument involves the ways the Age of Reason suppressed instinct and imagination and therefore fostered a dangerous ignorance of man's psychological nature. *Mozart the Dramatist* (1964) continues to pursue this thesis: B. maintains that in his life and operatic works Mozart was a

Gwendolyn Brooks

pioneer psychologist struggling to represent human ambivalence and internal conflict in an inhospitable age. *Don't Never Forget* (1966) is a combative collection of essays that champions imagination and reason in what B. believes is our own world of literalminded and irrational people.

B.'s rational-humanistic principles, while sometimes leading her into irritating skirmishes, are at the center of her work: they are consistently embodied in her lucid and incisive arguments, her imaginative control of language, and her commanding view of culture and art.

FURTHER WORKS: *The Crown Prince* (1953); *The King of Rainy Country* (1957); *The Finishing Touch* (1963); *The Snow Ball* (1964, with Michael Levey and Charles Osborne); *Fifty Works of English and American Literature We Could Do Without* (1967); *The Burglar* (1968); *Black and White: A Portrait of Aubrey Beardsley* (1968); *Prancing Novelist: A Defense of Fiction in the Form of a Critical Biography in Praise of Ronald Firbank* (1973); *The Adventures of God in His Search for the Black Girl* (1974); *Beardsley and His World* (1976); *Baroque 'n' Roil and Other Essays* (1987)

BIBLIOGRAPHY: Krutch, J. W., on *Hackenfeller's Ape*, *SatR*, 12 June 1954: 36; Alvarez, A., on *In Transit*, *SatR*, 24 Jan. 1970: 25; Adams, P., on *In Transit*, *Atlantic*, Feb. 1970: 120; Borklund, E., *Contemporary Novelists* (1976): 188–90; Lawrence, K. R., *Penelope*

Voyages: Women and Travel in the British Literary Tradition (1994); Special B. issue, *RCF*, 15 (1995); Miller, M., "B. B.: A Memoir," *Raritan*, 15 (1996): 38-52

—DAVID CASTRONOVO

BROSSARD, Nicole

Canadian poet, novelist, and essayist (writing in French), b. 27 Nov. 1943, Montreal, Que.

B.'s preeminent role among the postmodern writers who transformed Quebec poetics between 1965 and 1970 to make language and gender central to an exploration of the production of meaning was recognized with the awarding of the Athanase-David Prize of Quebec (1991) for her life's work. Her international reputation as a feminist theorist has been fostered by translation of her work into English, German, Italian, and Spanish. This recognition is ironic, for B.'s writing has developed as critique of received practices and of the text as commodity. Educated at the Collège Marguerite Bourgeoys and the Université de Montréal, B. has been a leader in Quebec literary circles since she cofounded in 1965 the influential avant-garde literary periodical, *La barre du jour*. B. taught briefly at Queen's University, Kingston, Ontario, dedicating herself to her writing in Montreal. She traveled widely in North America, Europe, and Australasia to participate in international conferences and writers' symposia, winning the Harbourfront Festival Prize in Toronto (1991).

In the 1960s B. was influenced by SURREALISM to explore sexuality as a mode of consciousness in an associative flux of images with surprising juxtapositions. Her focus on women's desire challenged the dominant poetry that celebrated a Quebec national homeland through the metaphor of land-as-woman that rendered woman a silent object. *Aube à la saison* (1965; Dawn in Season)—which stayed within the boundaries of traditional syntax and semantics—shows traces of the influence of the preceding generation of Quebec poets; her metrical structures and use of metaphor are reminiscent of the work of Paul-Marie Lapointe (b. 1929) and Fernand Ouellette (b. 1930) in particular. But the irony and eroticism of her subsequent collections—*Mordre en sa chair* (1966; to bite the flesh), *L'écho bouge beau* (1968; the echo moves beautifully), *Suite logique* (1970; logical sequence), *Le centre blanc* (1970; the white center)—exhibit a determination to throw readers off balance by challenging normal expectations about punctuation, spacing, and typography. Transgression, B. advances, is the assertion of a subject whose desire realigns power relations, the rules of syntax, logic and narrative.

In the 1970s B. entered a formalist phase stimulated by the semiotic theory of Roland BARTHES for whom the text was a system of differential relations creating reality not a representation of a preexistent reality. Anything could be created in language, possibilities she explored in the paradox of white space/black marks and in the hypothesis-generating aspects of fiction and theory. She pursued her experiments in the novel with *Un livre* (1970; *A Book*, 1976), *Sold-out: étreinte/illustration* (1973; *Turn of a Pang*, 1976), and *French Kiss: étreinte/exploration* (1974; *French Kiss*, 1986), which extended the possibilities of the NEW NOVEL— delineated in France by Alain ROBBE-GRILLET, Nathalie SARRAUTE,

and Michel BUTOR—into self-reflexive meditations on language and identity. Writing became an act of subversion to overthrow logic and mimetic modes: this included playing with grammatical constructions, especially pronouns, the introduction of blanks, gaps, ruptures, and occasionally—as in *Sold-out*—the use of frames to confound the distinctions between text and comic strip, poem and film. B.'s rejection of convention extends to genre as evident in her preference for the term "text"—meaning process and production, a system of unfinalizable differences—over the closure of "poem" and "novel." A collection of her poetry, *Le centre blanc: poèmes 1965-1975* (1978; the white center: poems, 1965-1975) includes all her previous collections with *La partie pour le tout* (1975; part for whole) and some new poems. B. won a Governor-General's Award for a collection of new poetry, *Mécanique jongleuse suivi de masculin grammaticale* (1974; *Daydream Mechanics*, 1980), which critiques the dominance of masculinist language.

From 1974 feminism gave a new dimension to B.'s writing. In *French Kiss* an automobile moving through the city establishes an allegory of women's desire circulating in the public sphere in what has since become her major theme, urban radicals transforming the body politic. The lesbian kiss on which the novel concludes displaces the conventional fictional economy to constitute a "sapphic semantic chain" where the erotic body is no longer site of reproduction but of creative energies. Between 1976 and 1979 B. worked on the editorial collective of the feminist monthly *Les têtes de pioche* (Axeheads), made *Some American Feminists* (1976) about feminist theory for the National Film Board, and introduced feminist theory and writing into the renamed *La nouvelle barre du jour*. "L'écrivaine" ("The Writer"), her contribution to the collective play *La nef des sorcières* (1976; *A Clash of Symbols*, 1979), and the publication of *L'amèr ou le chapitre effrité* (1977; *These Our Mothers*, 1983) signaled both her realization of women's need to emerge from the silence imposed on them by the patriarchal society and her determination to voice their censored and repressed desire. In this latter hybrid text—novel and manifesto, fiction and theory—B. exposes the contradictions of the mother under patriarchy, when women are limited to the role of symbolic mother, and contrasts these with the different possibilities for relations between women figured in the embrace of three generations of women, a feminine plural inscribing women into the trajectory of history. The poems of *Amantes* (1980; *Lovhers*, 1986) and the fiction *Le sens apparent* (1980; *Surfaces of Sense*, 1989) continue this theoretical speculation into the "surfaces of sense," of textual surfaces as the skin of culture, and posit an association of the writing/reading process with sexual pleasure, meaning-making activities animated by desire. The production of meaning from a lesbian perspective ceased to hinge on a relation between a subject and an object, between a writer/reader and a text/interpretation, to become an interactive process between subjects.

Picture theory (1982; *Picture Theory*, 1991), B.'s major fiction to date, expands on these questions in a complex text that interweaves fiction (five women interact on a lesbian island utopia) with a theoretical investigation—problems of representation and language are analyzed in a vast conceptual apparatus that draws on the ideas of Wittgenstein, James JOYCE, Gertrude STEIN, Monique WITTIG, among others. In a "mathematics of the imaginary" influenced by contemporary science B. offers a model of the text as process of transformation to articulate a new inflection of the "real." These ideas are further elaborated in the collection of feminist theoretical essays *La lettre aérienne* (1985; *Aerial Letter*, 1988), which focuses on the problem of representation for women when the "real" has been constituted by masculine fictions, and in B.'s contribution to the collective *La théorie, un dimanche* (1988; theory, on sundays). Fiction is the way to fight these hegemonic patriarchal fictions constraining women. The possibilities for a different and lesbian economy of desire are also developed in essays included in *Double impression: poèmes et textes 1967-1984* (1984; double impression), winner of the Governor-General's Award, in the erotic prose poems *Sous la langue/Under Tongue* (1987), winner of the Therafields Chapbook Award, and *La nuit verte du parc labyrinthe* (1992; *The Green Night of the Labyrinth Park*, 1992). Questions of representation and narrative are also pursued in *Journal intime* (1984; diary), which refuses both the conventional temporal sequence and confessional form of the diary genre to expose how a life is constructed within sociolinguistic conventions. A life in writing is the focus of the text *Domaine d'écriture* (1985; field of writing). Concerns with the constitution of subjectivity are addressed in poetic texts such as *Installations (avec et sans pronoms)* (1989), awarded the Grand Prize of La Fondation les Forges, *A tout regard* (1989; to every gaze), *Langues obscures* (1992; obscure languages), which explores the adventures of the subjective pronoun "I," and *Vertige de l'avant-scène* (1997; vertigo of front stage), which meditates on "literature as a manner of translating I am."

B.'s work on language and social codes extends to translation as both a textual practice and a metaphor for transformation. English-French translation of texts by poet Daphne Marlatt (b. 1942) in *Mauve* and *Jeu de lettres/Character* (1985) was followed by homolinguistic translation in the book of poetry *L'Aviva* (1985) and, more extensively, in *Le désert mauve* (1987; *Mauve Desert*, 1990), a fiction about a translator's work. The most popular of B.'s works, this novel examines the interpretive processes a translator makes in transferring a text into a different cultural milieu and considers the ethics of such an encounter with alterity. Attracted by a woman character in the book-to-be-translated of the first section, the translator gives this beautiful corpse an afterlife in her own fiction, which includes both her reflection on translation and a third section which is an intralingual translation of the first section. Continuing her games with repetition and constraints, B.'s novel *Baroque d'aube* (1995; *Baroque at Dawn*, 1997) returns to her first title of thirty years previous revising the eroticism of her early poetry. "Dark Future," the middle section, where women serve as experimental subjects for the pornographic gaze within heterosexuality, is reframed critically by the "Dawn" of the lesbian lovemaking of the first section. The vertiginous perspectival play between the character "Brossard," an "English" novelist, and the author Brossard, a Québécois, stages B.'s continuing interest in the shifting boundary between "art" and "life" and in fiction as virtual reality offering manifold potentialities for transformation. B.'s interest in experiment is also reflected in her editing of *Les stratégies du réel/The Story so Far* (1979), an anthology of avant-garde Québécois writings published bilingually by Coach House Press, Toronto, and of feminist projects such as the *Anthologie de la poésie des femmes au Québec* (1991; anthology of women's poetry from Quebec) and those of her own publishing house, L'Intégrale éditrice, founded in 1982.

B.'s poetry has received many awards in Quebec and has an assured place in its poetic canon where she is a member of the Académie des Lettres du Québéc. However, it is her experiments with fictional form that have garnered international interest: her writing is highly esteemed in feminist literary circles as exemplary "écriture féminine" (writing in the feminine) and among the so-called Language poets in the U.S., postmodernist challengers to a referential use of language. In some feminist circles, the difficulty in grasping the meaning of her fictions which refuse anecdote and disrupt syntax is deemed elitist rejection of feminism's project of accessibility. With such a prolific and still active writer, no final assessment may be made at present.

FURTHER WORKS: *D'Arc de cycle la dérive* (1979); *Typhon dru* (1990)

BIBLIOGRAPHY: Godard, B., "N. B.," *Profiles in Canadian Writing*, 6 (1986); Forsyth, L., "N. B. and the Emergence of Feminist Literary Theory in Quebec since 1970," in Godard, B., ed., *Gynocritics/Gynocritiques* (1987): 211-22; Dupré, L., *Stratégies du vertige* (1989); Godard, B., "Producing Visibility for Lesbians: N. B.'s Quantum Poetics," *ESC*, 21, 2 (1995): 125-37; Parker, A., *Liminal Visions of N. B.* (1998)

—BARBARA GODARD

BROUWERS, Jeroen

Dutch novelist and short-story writer, b. 30 Apr. 1940, Batavia, Indonesia

When B. was born in Indonesia, it was a Dutch colony. From 1943 until the end of World War II, B. was imprisoned in Indonesia by the Japanese occupying forces with his mother, grandmother, and sister. In 1948 the family returned to the Netherlands. B. spent six years (1950–1956) at Catholic boarding schools. After working as a journalist for a year and a half, he moved to Belgium in 1964, where he started to work for a publishing company as an executive secretary and editor. He made his literary debut in 1964. After his Belgian period, which ended on a depressive note, B. moved back to the Netherlands in 1976, where he started to write novels, polemic essays, and literary contributions for newspapers and periodicals. In 1982 he was awarded the Flemish-Geuzen Prize for his complete oeuvre.

In B.'s works no book stands on its own; themes and constants are carried from one book to another, motifs repeat themselves, a new publication can cover an earlier one by improving it or by perfecting it. Writing like this is a necessity for B. In his work one meets him as a person who is in conflict with society and himself: He is pursued by an everlasting feeling of insignificance. His writing is centered around an "I" whose biographical data fit the life of B. His point of departure, especially after his Belgian period, is one of having lost the right track. This situation can be explained from earlier experiences, such as his childhood years before the Japanese concentration camp, his experiences in that camp, his years at boarding schools, a failed marriage, and a feeling of doom about his own future.

One can divide B.'s work into two phases. In Amsterdam and Brussels he started writing and slowly became a novelist. His debut, *Het mes op de keel* (1964; the knife at the throat), shows a preference for apocalyptic situations and mythological imagination. In the novel *Joris Ockeloen en het watchten* (1967; Joris Ockeloen and the waiting), for which he received the Vijverberg Prize (1967), B. uses magical realistic processes to attain his mirror effects. His stories reflect in one another; questions asked in one work are answered in another. B. considers this early work an exercise for his later work, which develops at the end of the Belgian period and brings us to his second phase.

In *Zonder trommels en trompetten* (1973; without drums and trumpets) B. deals with a number of themes: literature, death, the past, (impossible) love, materialized in events and thoughts that preoccupy him at that moment and which at the same moment make him the person he is. Each theme has its own voice. This process suggests that all events and the themes they represent illustrate one another and that they sometimes become one. This technique reaches its height in *Zonsopgangen boven zee* (1977; sunrises above the sea).

Bezonken rood (1981; *Sunken Red*, 1990) is perhaps his most important work. Important is the memory of bygone years, of the things that made him what he is. In this work B. describes his life in a Japanese concentration camp. At that time he still had a warm relationship with his mother, which lasted until the end of their stay there, when his mother was humiliated and abused by the Japanese. As of that moment he was lost: "My mother was the most beautiful mother, at that moment I stopped loving her." This experience has determined B.'s relations with other people, especially loved ones.

De zondvloed (1990; the deluge) completes the impressive and baroque "Indian trilogy"—the first part being *Het verzonkene* (1979; the submerged), and the second part, *Bezonken rood*. In addition, it synthesizes at the same time the complete works of B. It is considered a masterpiece, a phenomenon that one does not find easily in Dutch literature. In *De zondvloed* B. pursues his futile search for his lost love, the continuation of his search in "Orpheus," the first story of his debut, *Het mes op de keel*.

Until 1979 B. did not have a large audience. But his polemic activities and his work *Bezonken rood* caused quite a stir in the Netherlands, and his writings were discussed in public debates. B.'s works now attract a large public, which became apparent when his book *De laatste deur* (1983; the last door) was reprinted three times within one year. B. continues to cover all dramatic periods of his life. His work *Zomervlucht* (1990; summer escape) deals with a man's mid-life crisis. The work consists of a chain of associations that all fall into place. *Zomervlucht* is of course part of his biography: "I am the stories that I tell."

FURTHER WORKS: *De toteltuin* (1968); *Groetjes uit Brussel* (1969); *Zachtjes knettern de letteren* (1975); *Klein leed* (1977); *Mijn Vlaamse jaren* (1978); *De nieuwe revisor* (1979); *Kladboek* (1979); *De Bierkaai* (1980); *Zonder onderschriften* (1980); *Et in Arcadia ego* (1981); *De spoken van Godfried Bomans* (1982); *Alleen voor Vlamingen* (1982); *Esergo sum* (1982); *Zonder onderschriften* (1983); *Verhalen en levensberichten* (1983); *Winterlicht* (1984); *De levende stilte van Stig Dagerman* (1985); *De sprong* (1985); *Hij is reeds aan de overzijde* (1985); *Helene Swart* (1985); *De achterhoek* (1987); *De oude Faust* (1987); *Sire, er zijn geen Belgen* (1988); *De versierde dood* (1989); *Groetjes uit Brussel* (1989)

—LUDMILA M. KERMAN

BRUCKNER, Ferdinand

(pseud. of Theodor Tagger) Austrian dramatist and critic, b. 26 Aug. 1891, Sofia, Bulgaria; d. 5 Dec. 1958, West Berlin, West Germany (now Berlin, Germany)

The child of a wealthy Austrian businessman and a versatile artist, B. was born en route from Constantinople to Vienna. This unusual beginning seems to have foreshadowed the itinerant life that B. was to lead, with major stops in Vienna, Paris, Berlin, California, New York, and finally Berlin again. B. began his writing career as a music critic and essayist. In 1917 he started his own journal, *Marsyas*. He settled in Berlin in 1921 and after two years had established himself well enough in cultural circles to found his own theater, the Renaissance Theater.

In 1926, after having met with only limited success in his literary endeavors, B. decided to abandon his work as an essayist and comic playwright. To that end he circulated anonymously the manuscript of his sociocritical play, *Krankheit der Jugend* (1926; sickness of youth), among Berlin theater directors. When finally produced, the play became a success, and B. chose a name for the "new" dramatist based on his admiration for two fellow Austrians, the dramatist Ferdinand Raimund and the composer Anton Bruckner. *Krankheit der Jugend* is rooted in the lost-youth syndrome of the post-World War I period. The characters are young in age but old in their attitudes; they are successes in their studies but failures in their lives. The play depicts a total breakdown of social mores and an abandonment of positive life goals that leaves the characters with few other choices than either complete surrender to hedonism or suicide. The young people of the play suffer from the sickness that pervaded a wide segment of Weimar Germany.

B.'s next play, *Die Verbrecher* (1928; the criminals), was produced by Max Reinhardt in 1928. It, too, was a success and spread B.'s fame far beyond the German-speaking world. Using three parallel plots presented simultaneously on the stage, B. promulgates his view that society itself is to blame for the crimes committed by individuals.

General disillusionment with the contemporary world seems to have been the impetus for B. to turn to historical themes in the 1930s. *Elizabeth von England* (1930; Elizabeth of England) was the most successful of these plays and enjoyed long stage runs in Germany and in England.

When the Nazis came into power in 1933, B. left Germany because his mother was Jewish and also as an act of conscience, and settled in France, but not before he took a parting shot at the distorted racial theories of the new regime in his highly charged play *Rassen* (1933; *Races*, 1934). From France he moved to the U.S. in 1936, where he stayed until 1947.

After the war B. returned to West Berlin and played a major role in the rebirth of the German stage during the difficult postwar years. However, his influence was more in dramaturgical work than as a playwright. His plays of this era were presented on most West German stages, but he was not able to regain the stature he had in the early 1930s.

B. was an innovative stage practitioner who brought to the theater some of the techniques that had been developed by the cinema (for example, cross-cutting). His plays with contemporary settings provide excellent portrayals of the psychological phenomena that produced the excesses of Weimar Germany. The emigration forced upon him in 1933 came at a time when he was at the height of his productivity, and the hardships of constant resettlements and financial worries left their marks on his subsequent life and writings. B. is a playwright of considerable merit, and even in his tendentious plays he has his characters speak with a wisdom seldom found in other 20th-c. writers.

FURTHER WORKS: *1920; oder, Die Komödie vom Untergang der Welt* (1920); *Kapitän Christoph* (1921); *Te Deum* (1922); *Die Kreatur* (1929); *Timons Glück and Untergang* (1932); *Die Marquise von O* (1933); *Mussia* (1935); *Napoleon der Erste* (1936); *Denn seine Zeit ist kurz* (1945); *Die Befreiten* (1945); *Simon Bolivar I: Der Kampf mit dem Engel* (1945); *Simon Bolivar II: Der Kampf mit dem Drachen* (1945); *Die Namenlosen von Lexington* (1946); *Fährten* (1948); *Heroische Komödie* (1948); *Negerlieder* (1948); *Früchte des Nichts* (1952); *Pyrrhus and Andromache* (1956); *Der Kampf mit dem Engel*, also called *Clarisse; oder, Die Höllenangst* (1956); *Das irdene Wägelchen* (1957); *Vom Schmerz und von der Vernunft* (1960)

BIBLIOGRAPHY: Baukloh, F., "Ein Forscher der Wirklichkeit," *Wort in der Zeit*, No. 8 (1956): 1–7; Schwiefert, F., "F. B.," in *Maske und Kothurn* (1958): 358–70; Csokor, F. T., Introduction to *Vom Schmerz und von der Vernunft* (1960): 5–28; Mann, O., "Exkurs über F. B.," in *Deutsche Literatur im 20. Jahrhundert*, 4th ed. (1961): 152–78; Lehfeldt, C., *Der Dramatiker F. B.* (1975)

—DENNIS MUELLER

BRULEZ, Raymond

Belgian novelist, dramatist, and essayist (writing in Flemish), b. 18 Oct. 1895, Blankenberge; d. 17 Aug. 1972, Brussels

B. studied literature and philosophy at the University of Brussels and was a director of Flemish broadcasting of Radio Brussels from 1935 to 1960.

In his writing B. represents the pre-World War II philosophy that centered on the individual. In his very first novel, *André Terval* (1930; André Terval) B. showed a mildly skeptical view of life. The book also demonstrates a reaction against the elaborate descriptions of nature characteristic of Netherlandic literature. B.'s best-known work is a series of four novels under the collective title *Mijn woningen* (1950–54; my homes), in which he includes much autobiographical material. Thus, in the first volume, *Het huis te Borgen* (1950; the house in Borgen), B. recalls his childhood, spent at the Flemish beach resort where his parents ran a hotel.

B.'s satirical thrust is evident in a collection of short stories, *De laatste verzoeking van Antonius* (1932; the last temptation of Anthony), and even more so in *De verschijning to Kallista* (1953; the apparition at Kallista), in which the author pokes fun at those who believe in miracles. The anachronisms in the novel are intentional, and Alexander the Great becomes the prototype of fanatical warmongers.

B.'s first play, *De schoone slaapster* (1935; the sleeping beauty), has been staged with great success. It shows the fickleness both of hatred between nations and of so-called "eternal love." The

sleeping beauty, who had been the girlfriend of an officer of Napoleon before she fell asleep one day after the Battle of Waterloo (1815), is awakened a hundred years later by an officer of the German Kaiser, whom she soon takes as a lover. She wonders how those former enemies (the English and French) have now become friends. Finally she marries a Belgian pacifist. B.'s second play, *De beste der werelden* (1939; the best of worlds), is a reworking of Voltaire's *Candide*. In it he gives vent to his democratic convictions by ridiculing fascism and dictatorship.

B.'s place in Flemish literature is as an intellectual writer who speaks not to the masses but to a highly educated minority. He looks at life in every shape and form with skepticism, but never bitterness.

FURTHER WORKS: *Sheherazade; of, Literatuur als losprijs* (1931); *De Noord-Nederlandsche letterkunde sinds 1914* (1936); *Vertellen* (1937); *Het pakt der Triumviren* (1951); *De haven* (1952); *Het mirakel der rozen* (1954); *Diogeentjes* (1962); *De toren van Lynkeus* (1969)

BIBLIOGRAPHY: Hermanowski, G., *Die Stimme des schwarzen Löwen* (1961): 87–89

—JUDICA I. H. MENDELS

BRUSHUSKI LITERATURE
See Pakistani Literature

BRUTUS, Dennis

South African poet (writing in English), b. 28 Nov. 1924, Salisbury, Zimbabwe (then Southern Rhodesia)

B. was brought up in Port Elizabeth, South Africa, as a "coloured." He took his B.A. at the segregated Fort Hare University College and taught high school. In 1962 he entered Witwatersrand University to study law. Inevitably in South Africa, racial politics intruded and he became active against the regime. For his challenges to government racial policy he was first banned and then arrested and sentenced to serve on the notorious Robben Island prison. Concluding his sentence, he accepted enforced exile and has since lived in England and America, always involved with the anti-apartheid movement and particularly with SANROC (South African Non-Racial Olympic Committee). In 1971 he settled permanently in the U.S. and is now a professor of English at Northwestern University, but he continues to travel widely for political purposes. He is a teacher and a poet, yet his life remains dedicated to challenging the apartheid system.

Given his experiences, it is obvious that B.'s poetry is likely to derive from his own bitter encounter with racial prejudice. Yet the reader is impressed to discern how the activist never destroys the poet. His first collection, *Sirens, Knuckles and Boots* (1963), indicates much of the social context by its very title, yet rarely is B.'s work violent or hectoring, no matter the anger implicit in his

Dennis Brutus

lines. In all his writing there remains a palpable tenderness and humanity. His earlier poems have a rich diction employing an almost metaphysical complexity that he was later very consciously to simplify. Throughout this first collection there is the constant theme of love, both for his wife and, more unexpectedly, for his suffering country, for which he still holds the strongest affection. He asserts a tolerant love as a challenge to the insensate racial hatred that dominates South Africa.

Similarly, his poems from prison, designed as a series of epistles to his wife, *Letters to Martha* (1968), describe appalling and horrific abuse suffered at the hands of both guards and other inmates, but they are expressed with an unqualified honesty and acute compassion that never romanticizes or justifies the suffering, but rather regards it with a pained tenderness.

The titles of his later collections, written outside of South Africa, indicate the many countries in which they were written: *Poems from Algiers* (1970), *Thoughts from Abroad* (1970), *China Poems* (1975). His diction has become increasingly spartan and severe. In contrast with the occasional lushness of his earliest poems, his later ones are often almost haiku-brief in their precision and suggestiveness.

There is an obvious tension between the man's commitment to politics and the poet's commitment to his art. Yet B.'s protest verse provides continuing evidence of a poetic skill that is committed to social action and yet does not become aesthetically subservient to that obligation.

FURTHER WORKS: *A Simple Lust* (1973)

BIBLIOGRAPHY: Povey, J., "Simply to Stand," in Okpaku, J., ed., *New African Literatures and the Arts* (1970): 105–13; Egudu, R. N., "Pictures in Pain," in Heywood, C., ed., *Aspects of South African Literature* (1976): 131–45; Lindfors, B., "Dialectical Development in the Poetry of D. B.," in Niven, A., ed., *The Commonwealth Writer Overseas: Themes of Exile and Expatriation* (1976): 219–29

—JOHN POVEY

BRYCE ECHENIQUE, Alfredo (Marcelo)

Peruvian novelist, short-story writer, and journalist, b. 19 Feb. 1939, Lima

B. E. was born into a distinguished aristocratic family and seemed destined to become a writer: His mother, who admired French culture, had baptized him with the second name Marcelo in honor of Marcel PROUST. In 1964 B. E. graduated from law school, but he also received a degree in literature, writing a thesis on the function of dialogue in the works of Ernest HEMINGWAY. That same year he boarded a steamer for Europe to study and write there.

B. E. began his writing career after finishing law school and while continuing his doctoral studies at the Sorbonne. Beginning in 1968, he taught for twelve years at the Sorbonne and the Universities of Nanterre and Vincennes. Between 1980 and 1984, he taught Latin American literature and culture at the Paul Valéry University in Montpelier, France. More recently he has lectured at other European, Latin American, and North American universities. B. E. currently resides in Madrid, Spain.

B. E. is an accomplished fiction writer and journalist. To date, he has written two volumes of short stories and five novels. His works have been translated into fifteen languages (although English is not one of them). B. E. is an exciting feature story writer for popular journals and newspapers throughout the Hispanic world. He has written extensively about his travels in Europe and Latin America. In November 1988 he was commissioned by Spain's most important newspaper, *El Pais*, to visit Prague, Czechoslovakia, and write a series of articles analyzing the political scene in that country. Currently he writes a daily column for the opinion page of another newspaper, *Diario 16*. He has also been appointed to be a judge for the Premio Cervantes, the Hispanic world's most prestigious literary prize.

His short stories in *Huerto cerrado* (1968; closed orchard), which received a special mention at the Casa de las Américas literary competition in La Habana in 1967, and his first novel, *Un mundo para Julius* (1970; *A World for Julius*, 1992), gave him instant literary fame, not only in Peru, but also in literary circles from Mexico City, Caracas, and Buenos Aires to Europe. While B. E. has written four additional novels—his most recent was published in 1989—readers find themselves returning to his first novel. Like his other works, *Un mundo para Julius* is a novel based heavily on personal experience. Much of the novel is autobiographical, for references to Julius's childhood and schooling are

361

similar to the author's experiences at his grandfather's mansion or at the grade school run by North American nuns and priests in Lima. A charming, well-written piece of literature, it is about a youngster's first years of life until he reaches eleven. However, adult and child perspectives intermingle to create poignant irony, great humor, and penetrating social commentary about the relatively uncomplicated, rich, upper-class strata of Peruvian society in Lima in the 1950s. In Peru this novel has become an integral part of the nation's literary canon, and in other countries it has achieved prominence as well. The writing of the novel in 1969 and its publication in 1970 coincided with the 1969 coup d'état that took credit for expropriating vast land holdings belonging to Peru's oligarchy; not surprisingly, here literature and history fuse to symbolize the destruction of Peru's long-established ruling classes. Despite this first, political reading of the novel, making it very much a novel of its time, it won the Peruvian Premio Nacional de Literatura in 1972 and continues to generate lasting interest for contemporary readers. The novel is not only an engagingly corrosive portrayal of the pretentious, morally blind Peruvian oligarchy and its transition to the dominant nouveau riche class subsidized by an influx of North American capitalism in the 1950s; it is also an early postmodern urban novel in which the bildungsroman motif and its curious, questioning, sentimental protagonist Julius bring together elements of the drama of lost innocence, black comedy of manners, playful parody, and social satire. Translated into many foreign languages, it won first prize for the best foreign novel in translation in France in 1974. As we begin to review the importance of the so-called "boom" period of the 1960s—the fictional works of Carlos FUENTES, Mario VARGAS LLOSA, Julio CORTÁZAR, Gabriel GARCÍA MÁRQUEZ, and others—this novel ranks among the first works to emphasize the art of storytelling in which the notably oral tone of the novel handily juxtaposes invention and representation, hyperbole and reality, multiple points of view and the free indirect style, in addition to interior monologue. The incorporation of these elements into the novel does not place it among those in which the allusion to societal fragmentation is the goal, as in the narrative worlds of Vargas Llosa's and Fuentes's early novels; it creates instead an obvious hierarchy of class and ethnic differences in Peru.

FURTHER WORKS: *Muerte de Sevilla en Madrid* (1972); *La felicidad ja ja* (1974); *A vuelo de buen cubero; y otras crónicas* (1977); *Tantas veces Pedro* (1977); *Todos los cuentos* (1979); *La vida exagerada de Martín Romaña* (1981); *Magdalena y otros cuentos* (1986); *Crónicas personales* (1988); *La última mudanza de Felipe Carrillo* (1988); *El hombre que hablaba de Octavia de Cádiz* (1989); *Dos señoras conversan* (1990)

BIBLIOGRAPHY: Bensoussan, A., "A. B. E., le principe d'innocence," *Co-textes*, 9 (May 1985): 45–53; Eyzaguirre, L., "A. B. E. o la reconquista del tiempo," *RCLL*, 11, 21–22 (1985): 215–21; Mouat, R. Gutierrez, "Lector y narratario en dos relatos de B. E.," *Inti: Revista de Literatura Hispánica*: 24–25 (Fall–Spring 1986–1987): 107–26; Fajardo, G. Ruiz, "Entrevista epistolar a A. B. E.," *Plaza: Revista de Literatura*, 12 (Spring 1987): 7–12; Eyzaguirre, L., "La última mudanza de B. E.," *Hispam*, 18: 53–54 (Aug-Dec. 1989): 195–202; Rodriguez-Peralta, P., "The Subjective Narration of B. E.'s *La vida exagerada de Martín Romaña*," *HisJ*, 10, 2 (Spring 1989): 139–51; Fuentes, L. Padura, "Retrato y voz de A. B. E.," *Plural: Revista Cultural de Excelsior*, 224 (May 1990): 35–40

—DICK GERDES

BRYUSOV, Valery

Russian poet, novelist, and critic, b. 13 Dec. 1873, Moscow; d. 9 Oct. 1924, Moscow

B.'s paternal grandfather was an emancipated serf who established a profitable cork business in Moscow in the 1850s. His parents were typical radical intelligentsia of the 1860s, who gave their son free rein in his studies as well as in his personal life. Despite a standard secondary education and a degree from Moscow University, B. was largely an autodidact whose tremendous will power helped make him "the most intelligent man in Russia," in the words of Maxim GORKY.

B. was responsible for launching the symbolist movement in Russia, and during its hey-day, the first decade of the century, was generally acclaimed the greatest living Russian poet. His early collections—*Chefs d'œuvres* (1895; French: masterpieces), *Me eum esse* (1897; Latin: this is I), and *Tertia vigilia* (1900; Latin: third vigil)—all heavily indebted to French symbolism, flaunted the new aesthetics of "Decadence." His growing accomplishments as a versatile master of poetic technique, evidenced in his best collections—*Urbi et orbi* (1903; Latin: to the city and the world), *Stephanos* (1906; Stephanos), and *Zerkalo teney* (1912; mirror of the shades)—coupled with his prodigious labors as translator, polemicist, and editor (in particular, of the chief symbolist journal, *Vesy*, from 1904 to 1909), assured B. of fame. His later books show a marked decline in his poetic powers, and although he joined the Bolsheviks after the revolution and assumed various posts in the literary bureaucracy, B.'s real literary significance is limited to the "Silver Age."

B.'s major poetic theme was erotic love, whether treated in its exotic, decadent aspect or interpreted as a ritual of mystical communion. A man of immense learning and universal culture, B. used the form of powerful lryicoepic monologues or dialogues revolving around a central experience in the life of historical, mythical, or archetypal figures in various epochs to elaborate on this subject matter. Another major theme he addressed was that of the modern city (after Émile VERHAEREN, whom he translated) treated as an apocalyptic vision of spiritual crisis. Despite the mythic and anarchistic elements in his own poetry, B. the theoretician was adament in proclaiming symbolism an aesthetic rather than a religious or mystical philosophy.

B. experimented in every imaginable poetic form and meter. The most classically oriented symbolist after Vyacheslav IVANOV, he used a hieratic, elevated style, abstract and periphrastic in nature and embodied in an archaic, "poeticized" vocabulary. He stressed the "music of verse," attempting to create a tense emotive atmosphere through relentless rhythm, heightened rhymes, and suggestive phonic orchestration. In B.'s verse the word consistently avoids its logical meaning and material reference; it becomes a mere token of affect or a symbol of the ineffable. The limited range of his key poetic symbols and his constant use of repetition and stark thematic contrasts lend his verse at its best an effective, almost hypnotic stylistic unity and at its worst render it monotonous, strained, and highly mannered. B.'s style follows the "musical" or "melodic" tradition of Russian romanticism—Vasily Andreevich Zhukovsky (1783–1852), Fyodor Ivanovich Tyutchev (1803–1873), Afanasy Afanasievich Fet (1820–1892)—despite his self-identification with the classical restraint of Pushkin, whose unfinished *Egyptian Nights* he had the audacity to complete (1917).

Of B.'s three novels, *Ognenny angel* (1908; *The Fiery Angel*, 1930) is the most successful. One of the best historical novels of the period in Russian, it is set in 16th-c. Germany and is permeated by B.'s occult studies; stylistically it is a tour de force. B. the critic is best represented by his numerous contributions to Pushkin scholarship, although his earlier essays, written in the symbolist vein, are of great intrinsic merit.

Despite B.'s enormous fame in his time, present-day critics are unanimous in placing his poetic talent below that of other Russian symbolists like ANNENSKY, BELY, BLOK, HIPPIUS, SOLOGUB, and Ivanov.

FURTHER WORKS: *Russkie simvolisty* (3 vols., 1894–1895); *Polnoe sobranie sochineny i perevodov* (8 vols., 1913–1914); *Sobranie sochineny v semi tomakh* (7 vols., 1973–1975). FURTHER WORKS IN ENGLISH: *The Republic of the Southern Cross and Other Stories* (1919); *The Diary of V. B. (1893–1905)* (1980)

BIBLIOGRAPHY: Binyon, T. J., "Bibliography of the Works of V. B.," *Oxford Slavonic Papers*, 12 (1956): 117–40; Holthusen, J., *Studien zur Aesthetik und Poetik des russischen Symbolismus* (1957), passim; Poggioli, R., *The Poets of Russia: 1890–1930* (1960): 96–105; Erlich, V., *The Double Image: Concepts of the Poet in Slavic Literatures* (1964): 68-119; Stuk, D., "The Great Escape: Principal Themes in V. B.'s Poetry," *SEEJ*, 12 (1968): 407–23; Rice, M. P., *B. and the Rise of Russian Symbolism* (1975)

—STEPHEN RUDY

BUARQUE, Chico

(abbrev. of Francisco Buarque de Hollanda) Brazilian composer, poet, and dramatist, b. 19 June 1944, Rio de Janeiro

B., son of a renowned historian, grew up in São Paulo, in an environment enriched by his family's contracts with Brazil's artistic and intellectual elites. By the mid-1960s, he had already gained fame in his own right, fast becoming the country's leading contemporary bard, recording artist, and dramatist. B. soon came to embody the entire youth culture, especially in its persistent opposition to the excesses of the recently installed military dictatorship. Censorship, corruption, physical abuse, uncontrolled capitalism, foreign economic influence, and American cultural domination became recurrent themes as well as an increasingly cruel reality for B., as it was for many others of his generation; and, in fact, it even motivated him, at the end of the decade, to seek, for a time, voluntary exile abroad.

His early songs already demonstrated pronounced social overtones, a tendency later to incur repeated bouts with government censors. Such was the case, for example, of his "Pedro Pedreiro" (1965; Peter the stonemason), a troubling narrative whose musical poetics focus on the unenviable life-style of Rio's exploited working class. In the same year, B. also undertook his first theatrical project, creating the musical setting for *Morte e vida Severina* (1955; death and life of Severina), by famed poet João Cabral de MELO NETO. The trend was soon to be expanded upon considerably. Indeed, in the realm of theater, alive with intensified

protest of a sociohistorical nature, his controversial *Roda viva* (spinning wheel) came out in 1968; and three other pieces—all modern-day classics—followed, either authored or coauthored by B.: *Calabar—O elogio da traição* (1973; Calabar—the praise of treachery), *Gota d'água* (1975; a drop of water) and *Opera do malandro* (1978; hustler's opera). In addition, the 1970s also witnessed his hugely successful entry into cinematic song writing as well as the appearance of *Fazenda modelo* (1974; model farm), a novelette. Loosely inspired by George ORWELL's *Animal Farm* (1945), the allegorical narrative, too, became a best-seller by satirizing the regime through unmistakable hyperbole.

Roda viva, B.'s two-act *comédia musical*, is actually tragic, exhibiting musical instances, complete with versification and chorus, in no way detrimental to a prevalent dramatic venue. It is a structural mix that he adheres to, as well, in his remaining works. The play centers on the progressive makeover, by cynical promoters, of a humble singer, first into a pop-music idol in the Beatles mold, and then, when tastes change, into a Brazilianized, engagé version of country and western crooner. It is B.'s metaphor for the nation's perennial debate around the multiple binom of exploiter-exploited, rich-poor, foreign-autochthonous, city-countryside, even good-bad. The protagonist, overwhelmed by, as it were, the capitalist exigencies of show business—synthesized symbolically in the title—commits suicide, at which point his widow is already being groomed to succeed him. *Roda viva* proved to be a high point of 1960s theater, in terms of expression and innovative choreography, as well as of forceful protest in a Brazil fast knuckling under to military repression. Not surprisingly, the play was eventually banned.

Calabar—O elogio da traição, coauthored with film maker Ruy Guerra, was struck down early on by government censorship. In fact, it was not even allowed to be stated until 1980; and its immediate popularity was assured only through unobstructed publication in book form. The play deals, in a revisionist and, again, farcical light, with the real-life title figure and his role during Holland's protracted, 17th-c. occupation of northeastern Brazil. He is Calabar, who, in being hanged as a traitor to the Portuguese cause, has, much like Benedict Arnold, long since been turned into the embodiment of unpatriotic betrayal. However, doubts are raised as to his true motives, no longer detached from the convoluted, parallel web of intrigue and deception that so dominated both story line and character development. Indeed, Calabar's central role, achieved without his ever appearing in person, is extrapolated in light of the remaining and, for the most part, equally historical figures, all of whom also perform some or other rite of betrayal. This predominant motif, parodically alluded to in the subtitle, proves overwhelming, as well as a demythologizing reflection on all Brazilian institutions, past and, most significantly, present. Structurally, too, *Calabar* breaks with traditionalism through cinemalike shifts that reinforce the anarchic independence of each scene.

B.'s next play, coauthored with Paulo Pontes (1941?–1976), is decisively more tragic than comic. *Gota d'água*, a musical recreation of Euripides's *Medea*, is adapted to the sociolinguistic realities of the contemporary urban masses, and set, rather prototypically, in the working-class outskirts of Rio. The preface to the printed version, in fact, makes unambiguous reference to the ideological questions and collateral thematic baggage that the drama attempts to address: the dehumanizing consequences of a jungle capitalism where the elite co-opts promising have-nots; the need to stress popular culture over imported values; and the primacy of the spoken work vis-à-vis the dramatic art form.

The story line, like the Greek tragedy by which it is inspired, is fleshed out in verse, complete with a choral presence—made up, appropriately, of raucous wash women. Fortunately, neither compromises the pulsating spontaneity of the present day. Action centers on Jasão, who, after overnight fame with his title samba, abandons longtime companion Joana for another who is more socially advantageous. In desperation, Joana completes the trajectory of this *"carioca* tragedy," killing their children and then committing suicide. Myth and harsh reality join to provide for familiar themes around *Milagre* excesses, like corruption, real-estate speculation, and the manipulation of the masses. More than ever, it is B.'s songs that engender the desired feeling of popular perspective, especially his title composition, alive with rhythm and metaphor.

Ópera do malandro is considered B.'s most ambitious state production and, as implied in the title, the one where musical discourse is most significant. The composer-dramatist, working alone, based it on John Gay's *Beggar's Opera* (1798) as well as *The Three-Penny Opera* (1955) of Bertolt BRECHT and Kurt Weill (1900–1950). From the former comes a milieu imbibed with prostitutes and criminal elements designed to reflect vice on all levels of society; from the latter comes the basic cast of characters and melodramatic scheme, as well as many structural details. B.'s parodied hybrid proves itself as much a musical comedy as a sweeping satire, set not in contemporary Brazil but during the pre-1945 *Estado Novo* of dictator Getúlio Vargas. Once again, chronological dislocation serves as metaphor for more recent and familiar abuses, namely multinational penetration, import substitution, and runaway consumerism. Meanwhile, an especially caricatured cast personifies varied segments of the venal power structure. However, it is the demise of the popular, implicitly endearing title institution, in favor of the detached, upper-echelon chicanery so much a part of post-1964 Brazil, which overrides *Ópera do malandro*. The spectator's unavoidable nostalgia for a fascistoid state, in turn, derides, by its very appeal, the bitter realities of 1970s Brazil—a perception little diminished by the censorship to which the theatrical production was subjected.

The author's major piece of prose fiction, *Fazenda modelo*, also enjoyed wide success, although admittedly more for what it said (and when) than for any particular aesthetic qualities. In occupying the outer limits of zoomorphology, the satire allegorizes, with precision, Brazil's most frightening post-1964 period. The author subtitles this grotesque vision a "Novelette of Cattle-Raising," prefacing it with a mock-serious paean to his good intentions and concluding it with a technical bibliography. Such realist trappings, together with visual references like maps, diary entries, statistical data, and a newspaper article, serve well to "document" the surrealism of unfolding events. Over twenty short chapters, through various first-person narrator-witnesses, and in strict linear progression, *Fazenda modelo* traces the brief and tragic history of the modern, cost-effective bovine enterprise. April 1, the parodied date of the March 31 coup that in 1964 brought the military to power, is the explicit divider. Before, the microcosm was just a farm, somewhat chaotic, commercially stagnant, and refreshingly relaxed. Remembered throughout by a nostalgic populace, this Paradise Lost, fleetingly recounted in the first chapter, stands in sharp contrast to the remaining hundred odd pages of progressive, galloping misery.

Such is the touching humanoid nature, particularly of the half-dozen focused head of cattle, that its essentially caricatured presentation proves no impediment to evoking reader empathy. Indeed, the emotional vulnerability, palpable sexuality, and miserable fate of all the bovine characters, less the megalomaniacal Juvenal and his robotized, technocratic, and often sadistic subordinates, include, as well, the generic ingredients for Greek tragedy, modern totalitarianism, and 20th-c. genocide. (Repression, for instance, is delegated to a cadre whose names all begin with the non-Brazilian letter *K*, and, in their totality, sound unabashedly Germanic.) In such an atmosphere, the fact that docile cattle are bred for a profit, slaughtered and consumed (at one in-house barbecue for ranch administrators, in particular) assumes anthropophagous proportions. None dares to oppose an end to weaning, to dehorning, or to emasculation, while sperm harvesting and artificial insemination make comforting companionship and carnal knowledge near impossible.

This model farm utilizes tools for all too familiar, state-of-the-art repression and jungle capitalism: it manipulates the medium of television; it co-opts the most promising (or potentially rebellious) bulls; it erects electrified fences; and it encourages trigger-happy police. It also freezes minimum wage, outlaws strike action, exports its best production, becomes dependent on foreign capital, and is influenced by so-called "invisible interests." The need for the sacrifice of the majority, in the name of an economic "miracle" of benefit to few, is routinely harped upon by elitist Juvenal in his official pronouncements, and proves the antithesis of the folksy and resigned informality of the novel's narrator-witnesses. Furthermore, neighboring areas, hitherto untouched, are cleared for cattle raising, in the process eliminating the native, nondomesticated population. The reign of terror only ends when the bovine citizenry is "phased out" and, in its place, soy bean is anticlimactically planted. There is no justice, no happy ending, no hope, only an experiment gone wrong. The experiment in question, as is plain to see in the author's thinly veiled invective, is not the paradidatic, nonliterary style of his novella but rather the régime itself.

B. is, first and foremost, a poet and song writer—with well over two hundred musical pieces—whose active commitment to social justice has, unlike with less talented figures, enriched rather than prejudiced his creativity. His varying artistic endeavors—lyrical, musical, theatrical, and fictional—continue to distinguish him in terms of versatility, just as his sense of originality and willingness to experiment with combined art forms promises to keep him in the vanguard of the nation's 1968 Generation.

FURTHER WORKS: *Estorvo* (1991); *Tubulance* (1993); *Benjamin* (1995)

BIBLIOGRAPHY: Lowe, E., on *Gota d'água, BA,* 50, 4 (Fall 1976): 859; Woodyard, G., "The Dynamics of Tragedy in *Gota d'água," LBR,* 15 (Summer 1978): 151–60; Schoenbach, P. J., "Themes and Directions of the Brazilian Theatre: 1973–1978," *LATR,* 13, 2 (Summer 1980): 43–50; Rego, E. d. S., and Perrone, C. A., *MPB: Contemporary Brazilian Pop Music* (1985): 6–7; Perrone, C. A., "C. B.," in Stern, I., ed., *Dictionary of Brazilian Literature* (1988): 67–68; Perrone, C. A., *Masters of Contemporary Brazilian Song: MPB, 1965–1985* (1989): 1–44; Perrone, C. A., "Dissonance and Dissent: The Musical Dramatics of C. B.," *LATR,* 22, 2 (Spring 1989): 81–94

—MALCOLM SILVERMAN

Martin Buber

BUBER, Martin

Austrian religious and social philosopher, b. 8 Feb. 1878, Vienna;
d. 13 June 1965, Jerusalem, Israel

As a result of his parents' divorce, B. went at the age of three to
his grandfather, Salomon B., a man of great wealth and profound
Hebrew scholarship. There, in Lwow (then the capital of the
Austrian province Galicia; today Lviv, in the Ukraine), B. studied
in a Polish secondary school and also received a thorough education in Hebrew and Judaism. He spent the summers near Sadagora
and Czortkow, seats of famous dynasties of Hasidic leaders, and
thus established a first contact with Hasidism, whose interpreter he
later became.

In 1896 B. entered the University of Vienna and there, as well as
in Leipzig, Zurich, and Berlin, he studied philosophy and the
history of art. Of his teachers, Wilhelm Dilthey and Georg Simmel
impressed him most. The years 1898–1900 became in many ways
decisive for his development. He started reading the German
mystics of the Renaissance and Reformation periods; married a
Bavarian fellow student at the University of Zurich, Paula Winkler
(1877–1958), who later published several novels of great originality under the pen name of Georg Munk; and became an active
worker in the Zionist movement, founded in 1897 by Theodor
Herzl at the first Zionist Congress in Basel. B. took part in the third
Congress in Basel in 1899. He insisted there on the importance of
Jewish cultural life. Later he settled in Berlin-Zehlendorf.

At the fifth Zionist Congress (1901) B. broke with Herzl. He
was, together with Chaim Weizmann, a leading member of the
kulturelldemokratische (cultural democratic) opposition to Herzl's
political Zionism, and, on behalf of this group, he delivered a long
report on the importance of a Jewish cultural renaissance of art and
literature. The rejection of his proposals by the Congress led to his
withdrawal from active participation. He devoted the following
years to a close study of Hasidism. The result was several books,
which translated the Hasidic legends and sayings into the language
of the "new style," the *Jugendstil* of the early 20th c. In 1906
appeared his *Die Geschichten des Rabbi Nachman (Tales of Rabbi
Nachman*, 1956) and in 1908 his *Die Legende des Baal Schem (The
Legend of the Baal-Shem*, 1955), about Israel Ben Eliezer (1700–
1760), the founder of the Hasidic movement and Nachman's great-
grandfather. Later on, B.'s interpretations of Hasidism became less
poetic. They were collected in his *Die chassidischen Bücher* (1927;
the Hasidic books), and in *Die Erzählungen der Chassidim* (1949;
Tales of the Hasidim, 2 vols., 1947–48). In his early books B. saw
the Hasidic movement as part of the "subterranean," mystical
tradition of Judaism, opposed to the "official" rabbinic rationalistic
main current. During that period, which lasted until World War I,
B. also published editions of mystical writers of other religions,
the most important being *Ekstatische Konfessionen* (1909;
ecstatic confessions).

B.'s interpretation of Hasidism and of mysticism, his affirmation of life and life-enhancing values, was strongly influenced by
Nietzsche. B. emphasized man's responsibility, his creative response to God's challenge. His mysticism was characterized by his
Weltfrömmigkeit (worldly religiosity) and *Weltfreudigkeit* (joyful
affirmation of the world); he interpreted Jewish history as the ever-
present encounter of God and His people, of God's call ("Hear, O
Israel") and Israel's willing acceptance or obstinate refusal of the
difficult yoke of God's demands. At the same time the chief
responsibility was not on the people but on the individual personality. In his first "*Rede über das Judentum*" (speech on Judaism) B.
defined the Jewish problem not as a social, political, or economic one, but as an individual, personal one of an authentic existence: "The true Jewish problem is an inwardly individual
one, the attitude of each individual Jew to his inherited
substance [*Wesensbesonderheit*]."

This "*Rede über das Judentum*" opened a new period of B.'s
Zionist activity. It was delivered in January 1909 before the Jewish
student association, Bar Kochba, of Prague. The important *Drei
Reden über das Judentum* (1911; three speeches on Judaism) and
the more comprehensive *Reden über das Judentum* (1923; speeches on Judaism) elaborated B.'s new definition of Zionism. It was on
the one hand influenced by the then prevailing German neoromanticism,
which emphasized the fundamental importance of "blood" (biological descent) and the God-willed connection of a people with
"its" soil; and on the other, by the universalistic ethics of the
Hebrew prophets. B. never succeeded in fully accepting one of
these two contradictory tendencies. This ambivalence increased his
influence on Central European Jewish youth in the years between
1910 and 1930, two decades of great spiritual unrest and changes in
the intellectual climate of a disintergrating society. The Jew, B.
said in his "*Reden*," feels "in the immortality [of the chain] of
generations the community of the blood, and he feels it as . . . the
duration of his individual self. He discovers the blood as the deeply
rooted and nourishing power in the individual; he discovers that the
deepest layers of our existence are determined by the blood, that
our thought and our will are colored by it in their innermost substance."

At the same time, in large part under the influence of his friend Gustav Landauer (1870–1919), an idealistic, anti-Marxist anarchist whose posthumous works B. edited, B. praised the communal living and spirit of the workers' settlements in Palestine as the voluntary and nonviolent realization of socialism. World War I intensified in B., as in Landauer (and in the two Hebrew writers who were B.'s older contemporaries, Achad Haam [Asher Ginzberg, 1856–1927] and A. D. Gordon [1856–1922], both Russian Hebrew writers), his opposition to war and violence. In this sense B. spoke at the twelfth Zionist Congress in Karlsbad (Karlovy Vary, Czechoslovakia) in 1921 against a Jewish state in Palestine, for brotherly cooperation with the Arabs, who then formed the large majority of the country's population, and for a binational state which would safeguard the rights of both peoples on the basis of equality, irrespective of their numbers. His failure to influence the Congress and the Zionist movement brought about a second period of withdrawal from active participation in the movement. From 1916 to 1923 B. published an important monthly, *Der Jude*. A few years later, in 1926, he replaced it with a more general theological and philosophical quarterly, *Die Kreatur*, on which a Catholic German and a Protestant German were his coeditors.

In 1916 B. moved from Berlin to Heppenheim an der Bergstrasse, where he lived until 1938, when Hitlerism forced his emigration to Palestine. In that period he taught Jewish theology and ethics at the University of Frankfurt am Main, and later social philosophy at the Hebrew University of Jerusalem. B.'s years in Heppenheim were characterized by two decisive events. The first was the abandonment of mysticism in his book *Ich und Du* (1922; *I and Thou*, 1937; rev. ed., 1958). In this new interpretation of man's relationship to God there is no longer a question of their union (*unio mystica*). God is real, but man is real too; likewise the world. God and man can meet. In this encounter man enters into a true and demanding reality. This encounter always happens in a concrete situation; it is not part of theology, but of existence. God speaks to man; man realizes himself in his response. But an I-Thou relationship can also exist between human beings. Man lives a real life if he responds to his "Thou." There is no "I" except in the relationship to a "Thou." But the I-Thou is not the only relationship between human beings. There is also the I-it relationship, in which the "it" is no longer a true partner, but an object in daily experience. The I-it is also the world of science, of politics and economics.

The second decisive event in the Heppenheim period was B.'s encounter with the Bible, which took the place of his encounter with Hasidism twenty-five years before. As a result of this encounter B., with his friend Franz Rosenzweig (1889–1929), started a new translation of the Old Testament into a German which would faithfully render the meaning of the Hebrew text. The first volume appeared in 1925, the last one, following a revision of the former volumes, in 1962. Connected with his renewed study of the Bible, B. published *Königtum Gottes* (1932; 3rd ed., 1956; *The Kingship of God*, 1967), a study in the origins of messianism, and *Der Glaube der Propheten* (1950; *The Prophetic Faith*, 1949). In agreement with his general philosophy B. saw in the Bible a voice speaking to the reader; as in all true life, in the Bible, too, there is a life of dialogue; a life of confrontation of I and Thou. This "Thou" is everyone who hears the "Thou" and responds to it. In that way man participates in God's work.

True education is also a form of the life of dialogue. Hence B.'s growing interest in education, and in adult education. With the threat of Hitlerism growing, and later in Palestine and in Israel, B. devoted more and more of his time to "teaching." He was in depth and clarity an incomparable teacher. *Rede über das Erzieherische* (1926; discourse on the pedagogical), *Dialogisches Leben: Gesammelte philosophische und pädagogische Schriften* (1947; *Dialogues of Realization*, 1964), and *Reden über Erziehung* (1953; discourses on pedagogics) contain his main contributions in the field, which grew ever more important to him.

B.'s life in Jerusalem brought him into direct contact with the "Arab problem." Once more, and in a much more difficult situation, he demanded, together with a very small group of Palestinian Jews (among them the Chancellor of the Hebrew University, Dr. Judah L. Magnus), due consideration of the rights of the Arab Palestinians. Together they proposed, in 1946, a program of "Palestine: a Binational State." Their opinion did not prevail. Even after the new State of Israel had been created B. continued to plead for the civil and political rights of what had become an Arab minority in a Jewish state. As a unique gesture in the history of Israel, Arab students of the Hebrew University laid a wreath at the bier when Buber was lying in state after his death.

During the last years of his life B.'s influence, which remained very small in Israel, spread in the English-speaking world and was reestablished in Germany. He received the Goethe Prize from the City of Hamburg in 1953, and the Peace Prize of the German Book Trade in 1955. In each instance, a reason stated for awarding the prize was B.'s achievement as a writer of prose fiction in German. Solidly rooted in the stylistic traditions of romantic narrative prose, B. imposes formal elements in the 19th-c. German *Novelle* upon the traditions of Hasidic storytelling. The highly evocative, "magical" effect of this fusion upon readers of B.'s prose has been frequently noted. He visited the U.S. for the first time in 1951–52, when he lectured mainly at the Jewish Theological Seminary in New York and at the College of Jewish Studies in Los Angeles. During his following visits, in 1957 and 1958, he conducted seminars at Columbia University and at Princeton University. By then he was regarded among non-Jews as the representative Jewish thinker of the time. Many of his books were translated into English. One of the most important of them, with which he resumed and concluded his revelation of the Hasidic world, was his only novel, called *Gog und Magog* (pub. in Hebrew trans. 1943; pub. in German 1949; *For the Sake of Heaven*, 1945). It describes the crises and tensions in the Hasidic world during the Napoleonic war against Russia. One school believed that this great struggle inaugurated the coming of the messianic times, whereas another Hasidic school rejected this belief as heretical, because the coming of a Messiah does not depend on battlefields but on the inner life of man. B. manifestly sided with this second interpretation.

B.'s philosophic thought remained centered on the individual, but not in the same way as Kierkegaard or Heidegger, with whom B. was frequently compared as an "existentialist" thinker. For B. man is never man by himself, but man-with-man: "The fundamental fact of existence is not man, but man-with-man" (*Das Problem des Menschen*, 1948; the problem of man). Salvation cannot be found in individualism, which glorifies man's loneliness, nor in collectivism, which shifts responsibility from the individual to the group. Beyond subjectivism and objectivism, on the narrow ridge where "I" and "Thou" meet, is the realm of the dialogue ("*das Reich des Zwischen*"). B.'s philosophy had become in 1923 a philosophy of dialogue, of the authentic and immediate relationship of man to man, and so it remained throughout the rest of his life. In an open dialogue, not in the "unmasking" of the "adversary," B. saw the hope, the "*Hoffnung fürdiese Stunde*," the hope for our time and for all times.

FURTHER WORKS: *Lesser Ury* (1903); *Daniel* (1913; *Daniel*, 1964); *Vom Geist des Judentums* (1916); *Die jüdische Bewegung* (2 vols., 1916–1920); *Völker, Staaten und Zion* (1917); *Die Rede, die Lehre und das Lied* (1917); *Ereignisse und Begegnungen* (1917); *Mein Weg zum Chassidismus* (1918); *Der heilige Weg* (1919; *The Holy Way*, 1967); *Worte an die Zeit* (2 vols., 1919); *Cheruth* (1919; *Herut, on Youth and Religion*, 1967); *Der große Maggid* (1921); *Das verborgene Licht* (1924); *Hundert chassidische Geschichten* (1930); *Zwiesprache* (1930; *Between Man and Man*, 1947; rev. ed., 1965); *Kampf um Israel* (1933); *Erzählungen von Engeln, Geistern und Dämonen* (1934; *Tales of Angels, Spirits, and Demons*, 1958); *Deutung des Chassidismus* (1935; *Hasidism and Modern Man*, 1958, and *The Origin and Meaning of Hasidism*, 1960); *Die Schrift und ihre Verdeutschung* (1936, with F. Rosenzweig); *Die Stunde und die Erkenntnis* (1936); *Die Frage an den Einzelnen* (1936; *The Silent Question*, 1967); *Worte an die Jugend* (1938); *Chassidismus* (1945; *Hasidism*, 1948); *Moses* (1948; *Moses*, 1958); *Der Weg des Menschen* (1948; *The Way of Man*, 1950); *Pfade in Utopia* (1950; *Paths in Utopia*, 1950; repub. as *Der utopische Sozialismus* [1967; *The Utopian Socialism*, 1967]); *Zwei Glaubensweisen* (1950; *Two Types of Faith*, 1951); *Israel und Palästina: Zur Geschichte einer Idee* (1950; *Israel and Palestine: The History of an Idea*, 1952); *Urdistanz und Beziehung* (1951); *Zwischen Gesellschaft und Staat* (1952); *Gottesfinsternis* (1953; *Eclipse of God*, 1952); *Die chassidische Botschaft* (1952); *An der Wende* (1952; *At the Turning*, 1952); *Bilder von Gut und Böse* (1952; *Images of Good and Evil*, 1953); *Deutung einiger Psalmen* (1952); *Bücher und Menschen* (1952); *Recht und Unrecht* (1952; *Right and Wrong*, 1953); *Einsichten* (1953); *Hinweise* (1953; *Pointing the Way*, 1957); *Die Schriften über das dialogische Prinzip* (1954; "The History of the Dialogical Principle," in *Between Man and Man*, rev. ed., 1965); *Sehertum* (1955); *Der Mensch und sein Gebild* (1955; *The Knowledge of Man*, 1965); *Stationen des Glaubens* (1956; *To Hallow This Life*, 1958); *Schuld und Schuldgefühle* (1958); *Begegnungen* (1961; *Meetings*, 1973); *Die Juden in der UdSSR* (1961, with N. Goldmann); *Schriften zur Philosophie* (1962); *Werke* (3 vols., 1962); *Elija: Ein Mysterienspiel* (1963); *Schriften zum Chassidismus* (1963); *Pegishot* (1965); *Nachlese* (1965); *Das dialogische Prinzip* (1965); *Briefwechsel aus sieben Jahrzehnten* (3 vols., 1972–1975). FURTHER WORKS IN ENGLISH: *Mamre: Essays in Religion* (1946); *Israel and the World: Essays in a Time of Crisis* (1948); *Writings* (1956); *Ten Rungs: Hasidic Sayings* (1962); *The Way of Response: Selections from His Writings* (1966); *A Believing Humanism* (1967); *On Judaism* (1967); *On the Bible: Eighteen Studies* (1968)

BIBLIOGRAPHY: Friedman, M. S., *M. B.: The Life of Dialogue* (1955); Cohen, A. A., *M. B.* (1957); Diamond, M. L., *M. B., Jewish Existentialist* (1960); Balthasar, H. U. von, *M. B. and Christianity* (1961); Pfuetze, P. E., *Self, Society, Existence, Human Nature and Dialogue in the Thought of Herbert Mead and M. B.* (1961); Berkovits, E., *A Jewish Critique of the Philosophy of M. B.* (1962); BenChorin, S., *Zwiesprache mit M. B.* (1966); Smith, R. G., *M. B.* (1967); Oliver, R., *The Wanderer and the Way* (1968); Beek, M. A., and J. S. Weiland, *M. B.: Personalist and Prophet* (1968); Rollins, E. W., and H. Zohn, *Men of Dialogue: M. B. and Albrecht Goes* (1969); Friedman, M., *M. B. and the Theater* (1969); Hodes, A., *M. B.* (1971); Zink, W., ed., *M. B. 1878–1978* (1978); Horwitz, R., *B.'s Way to "I and Thou"* (1978)

—HANS KOHN, UPDATED BY HARRY ZOHN

BUCK, Pearl S(ydenstricker)

(pseud.: John Sedges) American novelist, short-story writer, and essayist, b. 26 June 1892, Hillsboro, West Virginia; d. 6 Mar. 1973, Danby, Vermont

B.'s best works are the products of her unique background. The daughter of missionaries to China, who believed in living among the Chinese people, B. became familiar at an early age with the life of the average Chinese peasant. Her life in China, however, was not always pleasant. When B. was only a child, she was forced to flee with her family from the rebel forces of the Boxer Rebellion. In 1909 B. returned to the U.S. and entered Randolph-Macon Women's College. In 1917 she married John Buck, and they returned to northern China where he served as an agriculture specialist. Her first novel *East Wind, West Wind* was published in 1930. It was followed in 1931 by *The Good Earth* and the critically acclaimed biographies of her mother, *The Exile* (1936), and her father, *Fighting Angel* (1938). In 1938 B. was awarded the Nobel Prize for these masterpieces of biography and for her description of Chinese peasant life. In 1934 B. permanently returned to the U.S. She continued to remain active as a writer up to the time of her death.

B.'s best-known book is her Pulitzer Prize-winning novel *The Good Earth*. The story chronicles the rise of a simple Chinese farmer, Wang Lung, from the day of his marriage to his founding of the wealthy House of Wang. The novel's style, a combination of biblical prose and the Chinese narrative saga, gives the seemingly unimportant lives of its characters a seriousness and dignity that is quite convincing. *The Good Earth* appeals to the reader in that it encompasses the full range of human experiences: marriage, birth, death, economic hardship, prosperity, and the conflict between the generations. Wang Lung also experiences the dangers of wealth with its accompany vices and finds that only in the earth can he purify himself and gain new strength. *The Good Earth* is naturalistic in many ways; the draughts controls Wang Lung's wealth, and the floods influence his morals. Wang Lung's determination, however, permits him to gain success despite the opposition.

The story of the House of Wang continues in its sequel, *Sons* (1932). The particular focus of this novel is the youngest son, Wang the Tiger. An idealist, Wang the Tiger is serving in the military at the novel's beginning. He has high hopes of becoming a powerful warlord and of uniting the nation in an effort to reform its political and social system. After some initial success, his plan stagnates, but he dreams of his goals being realized in the life of his son Yuan. *A House Divided* (1935) is Yuan's story. He revolts against his father's plan for his life and flees to the U.S. A number of years later he returns but finds himself in a state of transition unable to embrace either the wealth and power of his family or the soil that had given such strength to his grandfather. These sequels lack the dynamic characterization that makes *The Good Earth* so memorable. For example, in *Sons* each of the three boys seems to take on one of the predominate features of their father's personality, and thus become rather stereotypical.

Another important work with a Chinese setting, *The Patriot* (1939) records the emotional development of its central character, I-wan Wu, a university student in Shanghai with communist sympathies. When the revolt he is involved in is exposed, I-wan is forced to flee to Japan. While there, he finds happiness in marriage and comes to admire the Japanese for their discipline, a trait he finds so lacking in his own people. Once war breaks out between the countries, I-wan returns to China and fights as Chiang Kai-shek's representative to the communist Chinese forces. The book is noteworthy in the way it addresses the problems associated with interracial marriages. Also praiseworthy is the development in I-wan's character as he moves from being the communist idealist to rejecting that philosophy when he sees its brutality in war.

B. also wrote several novels with an American setting. *This Proud Heart* (1938) examines the issues of talent and commitment in achieving artistic achievement. *Command the Morning* (1959) concerns the efforts of the Manhattan Project to develop the atomic bomb and the ethics of dropping it on Japan. One of her best American novels is *The Townsman* (1945), written under the pen name of John Sedges. The protagonist Jonathon Goodliffe is a young English immigrant who settles in the fictional town of Median, Kansas. The novel is of the frontier variety; it is unique in that Jonathon is a teacher who has no dreams of great wealth but simply wants to build a good town where people can raise their families. The book is successful in its realistic development of settings and characters.

B. is not known for her short stories. Some of her best ones, however, include "The First Wife" and "The Woman Who Was Changed." B. wrote several works of nonfiction. Two of the most important—other than the biographies of her parents—include *The Chinese Novel* (1939), which is largely an explanation of her own writing style, and *The Child Who Never Grew* (1950), which concerns her mentally handicapped daughter.

Over the years B.'s work has not attracted extensive critical attention. She is largely criticized for her inability to experiment with stream-of-consciousness or to make use of elaborate symbolism. She has also been accused of focusing on plot at the expense of characterization and of using her novels to propagandize for various causes. B. has, however, captured the interest of a diverse and enthusiastic audience. Several of her novels have occupied high positions on the nation's best-seller lists, and her works have been translated into more languages than any other American author.

FURTHER WORKS: *East and West and the Novel: Sources of the Early Chinese Novel* (1932); *The First Wife and Other Stories* (1933); *The Mother* (1934); *Other Gods: An American Legend* (1940); *Today and Forever: Stories of China* (1941); *American Unity and Asia* (1942); *China Sky* (1942); *Dragon Seed* (1942); *The Promise* (1943); *The Spirit and the Flesh* (1944); *Portrait of a Marriage* (1945); *Talk about Russia* (1945); *Tell the People* (1945); *Pavilion of Women* (1946); *The Angry Wife* (1947, as John Sedges); *Far and Near: Stories of Japan, China, and America* (1947); *How It Happens* (1947); *Peony* (1948); *American Argument* (1949); *Kinfolk* (1949); *The Long Love* (1949, as John Sedges); *Of Men and Women* (1949); *God's Men* (1951); *Bright Procession* (1952, as John Sedges); *The Hidden Flower* (1952); *Voices in the House* (1953, as John Sedges); *Come My Beloved* (1953); *My Several Worlds* (1954); *Imperial Women* (1956); *Letter from Peking* (1957); *Fourteen Stories* (1961); *A Bridge for Passing* (1962); *Satan Never Sleeps* (1962); *Hearts Come Home and Other Stories* (1962); *The Living Reed* (1963); *Children for Adoption* (1964); *Stories of China* (1964); *Death in the Castle* (1965); *The Gifts They Bring: Our Debt to the Mentally Retarded* (1965); *Essay on Myself* (1966); *For Spacious Skies: Journey in Dialogue* (1966); *The People of Japan* (1966); *The Time Is Noon* (1967); *To My Daughters, with Love* (1967); *The New Year* (1968); *The Good Deed and Other Stories of Asia, Past and Present* (1969); *The Three Daughters of Madame Liang* (1969); *China as I See It*

(1970); *Mandala* (1970); *The Goddess Abides* (1972); *China Past and Present* (1972); *All Under Heaven* (1973); *The Rainbow* (1974); *East and West* (1975); *Secrets of the Heart* (1976); *The Lovers and Other Stories* (1977); *The Woman Who Was Changed and Other Stories* (1979)

BIBLIOGRAPHY: Doan, C., *The Image of the Chinese Family in P. B.'s Novels* (1964); Harris, T., *P. S. B.: A Biography* (1971); Doyle, P., *P. S. B.* (1980); Rizzon, B., *P. S. B.: The Final Chapter* (1989); Sherk, W., *P. S. B.: Good Earth Mother* (1992); Conn, P., *P. S. B.: A Cultural Biography* (1996); Liao, K., *P. S. B.: A Cultural Bridge Across the Pacific* (1997)

—MAX I. LOGES

BUENAVENTURA, Enrique

Colombian dramatist, theater director, and critic, b. 1925, Cali

B. studied in the Saint Librada of Cali School where after learning architecture, painting, and sculpture, he developed his lifelong love for art. As a journalist for the newspaper *El Pacifico*, he met an Argentinian theater director and traveled with him as his assistant through South America. When the group dissolved, B. began a wandering life in which he made a living performing the most various trades: journalist in Caracas and Trinidad, theater director in Argentina, sailor in the Caribbean, cook in Buenos Aires, actor and teacher of voodoo and Latin America's religious influence in Brazil and Bolivia, all experiences that he would later incorporate in his endeavors as a dramatist or theater director. In 1962 B. founded a theater company, Experimental Theater of Cali (TEC), with which he has produced about one-hundred plays; some of them have been presented in Europe and the U.S., including Puerto Rico. All TEC plays are a collective creation, although B. is the principal author and always the director. Some plays have had many variants throughout the years.

B.'s most important concern in his theater is to achieve a universalization of culture in Colombia, rejecting cultural colonialism and commercialization of the arts. In this pursuit, national traditions and folkloric roots are important. At the same time, he wishes to eradicate persistent social problems and to transform the social structure. Therefore, B.'s theater is didactic and ideological and has reached a political and philosophical tone. Based both in the past and in contemporary history, the reality he conveys is, however, stylized, poetic, and visionary since B. perceives his theater as an instrument of change. The public participates in all performances, making each event unique and changeable, popular, and collective. Therefore, B. believes that there is a dramatic literature but that theater is not a literary genre since it only exists when it confronts a public.

As a theatrical theoretician, B. has written many articles. His research has led him into acting methods and stage techniques that have influenced many groups in Latin America.

One of the most famous of B.'s plays is *En la diestra de Dios padre* (1958; on the right-hand side of our father) with five versions based on a tale of the Colombian writer Tomás CARRASQUILLA. The play shows medieval roots, presenting the influence of miracle plays and morality plays. B.'s sympathies in this play are with the poor, in spite of their being presented in a degrading and deformed way and with satiric humor.

Los papeles del infierno (1968; papers of hell) is a strong and poetic presentation of corruption, exploitation, suffering, injustice, and alienation. Farce and pantomine are some of the resources that make the characters seem grotesque. Enclosed in their suffocating spiritual reality, these characters are puppets of their passions, and the only liberating mechanism is violence.

In *La historia de una bala de plata* (1979; story of a silver bullet) the attack is on colonialism on a Caribbean island. Mythical-magic elements and the voodoo tradition add a cultural dimension to the theme and enrich it aesthetically. The 1980 Casa de las Américas Prize was bestowed on B. for this play.

B., considered by many the father of Colombian theater, has created an original oeuvre based on the Colombian reality and adapting contributions of the world theater and the great dramatists of the 20th c. With an irreverent and desacralized approach, he tries to restore dignity to the common person, advocating human rights. The New Theater in Latin America is greatly indebted to B. and looks toward him for guidance.

FURTHER WORKS: *El misterio de los Reyes Magos* (1957); *El Monumento* (1959); *Los inocentes* (1966); *La trampa* (1967); *Tirano Banderas* (1968); *El convertible rojo* (1969); *Un requien por el padre Las Casas* (1971); *La denuncia* (1973); *Se hizo justicia* (1977); *Seis horas en la vida de Frank Kulak* (1979); *Ópera bufa* (1982); *El encierro* (1987); *La estación* (1990)

BIBLIOGRAPHY: McIntyre, C., et al., "Charlando con E. B.," *Prismal/Cabral*: 9–10 (Spring 1983): 82–89; González-Cajiao, F., *Historia del teatro en Colombia* (1986), 307, 335: 380–81; Velasco, M., *El nuevo teatro colombiano y la colonizacion cultural* (1987): 89–143; Perales, E., *Teatro hispanoamericano contemporá 1967–87* (1989): 132–33, 141 "B.," *El tiempo* (6 April 1990): 2A

—INÉS DÖLZ-BLACKBURN

BUERO VALLEJO, Antonio

Spanish dramatist and critic, b. 29 Sept. 1916, Guadalajara

B. V. studied at the San Fernando School of Fine Arts in Madrid until the outbreak of the civil war in 1936, when he joined the Loyalist side as a medical aide. At the war's end he was arrested by the Franco government and imprisoned until 1946.

B. V.'s ideas about the nature of tragedy are basic to the understanding of his theater. Eschewing the "well-made," trite, and usually frivolous plots and comforting but banal sentimentality of the drama that prevailed at the time in Spain, B. V. wrote serious plays characterized by dignity and nobility, endeavoring to explore man's existential situation in the context of tragedy. In B. V.'s idiosyncratic view of tragedy, the essence is that there is always hope. In forcing man to confront his own reality without self-deception, tragedy in fact facilitates the quest for happiness—by raising questions, not by giving answers. Furthermore, B. V. feels that, by elevating emotions to a high ethical plane, tragedy will ultimately improve society.

Historia de una escalera (1950; story of a staircase), B. V.'s first play, for which he won the important Lope de Vega Prize,

presents three generations of four different families, living in a Madrid tenement, who are "stuck" on a staircase that leads nowhere. They are immobilized not so much by oppressive social conditions as by their reluctance to embark on the quest for selfhood. The play ends ambiguously, although perhaps on a note of hope: Fernando Jr. tells the younger Carmina of his plans for the future, including marrying her, although he uses the same words that his father did some thirty years before. There is a suggestion, however, in spite of this repetition, that Fernando Jr., unlike his father, will be true to his inner self.

En la ardiente oscuridad (1951; *In the Burning Darkness*, 1985) is set in a school for blind students. They are comfortable with their blindness until the arrival of Ignacio, blind since birth, who points out the limitations their handicap imposes on them. Blindness here is symbolic of man's inability, or perhaps lack of desire, to see reality or the obstacles to his self-realization. Blindness also suggests Spain's political situation at a time when there was little questioning of the Franco regime. At the end of the play Carlos, Ignacio's assassin, has already begun to "see" the truth and repeats Ignacio's very words denouncing the world of darkness and crying out for one filled with light.

Another drama, *El tragaluz* (1967; the basement window), uses the narrative device of having two investigators from the distant future present a hologram of a family suffering the consequences of defeat in the civil war. The family lives "underground" in a basement apartment, literally and symbolically trapped in darkness. Like the families in *Historia de una escalera*, these characters—except for the older son Vicente, who has left and succeeded in the outside world—have no social or economic mobility; they are broken people. At the end of the play Vicente is murdered by his father, who finally acknowledges what happened in the past and seeks to avenge the death of his daughter thirty years earlier, during the civil war. As the investigators tell us, because Vicente took all his family's provisions with him, his sister starved to death. In the father's brutal act we see his refusal to be further trapped by the past.

In *Las meninas* (1961; the ladies-in-waiting), whose protagonist is the artist Velázquez; in *El sueño de la razón* (1970; *The Sleep of Reason*, 1985), about Goya; and in *La detonación* (1978; *The Shot*, 1989), about Mariano José de Larra (1809–1837), a 19th-c. Spanish satirist, B. V., armed with a variety of dramatic techniques, uses historical figures to explore the individual's conflict with a repressive society. Borrowing from BRECHT's theories about distancing and more recent ideas about participatory theater, B. V. has created works that are personal and visionary.

B. V. is Spain's most important post-civil war dramatist. He rescued the sclerotic Spanish stage of the 1940s by showing a younger generation of playwrights, such as Alfonso SASTRE and Carlos Muñiz (b. 1927), how to challenge audiences by experimenting with form and seriously portraying the precariousness of human life. As critical as B. V. was of the Franco regime, so has he been of the post-Franco era. In *La detonación*, as well as in *Caimán: Relato escénico en dos partes* (1981; Cayman: a scenic tale in two parts) and *Música cercana* (1990; *The Music Window*, 1994), B. V. reveals the hypocritical pretensions of the new era by exposing its self-congratulatory myths of democracy and its insidious inauthenticity toward human relationships.

B. V. has also tried to protect man from his own blindness by giving him the courage to realize that the tragic sense of life does not imply defeat but rather a precondition for self-knowledge and thus for some kind of happiness.

FURTHER WORKS: *La señal que se espera: Comedia en tres actos* (1952); *La tejedora de sueños: Drama en tres actos* (1952; *The Dream Weaver*, 1967); *Las palabras en la arena: Tragedia en un acto* (1952); *Casi un cuento de hadas: Una glosa de Perrault en tres actos* (1953); *Aventura en lo gris: Dos actos y un sueño* (1954; rev. ed., 1964); *Madrugada: Episodio dramático en dos actos* (1954); *Irene o el tesoro: Fábula en tres actos* (1955); *Hoy es fiesta: Tragicomedia en tres actos* (1957); *Las cartas boca abajo: Tragedia española en dos partes y cuatro cuadros* (1957; *Today's a Holiday*, 1989); *Un soñador para un pueblo: Versión libre de un episodio histórico, en dos partes* (1959); *El concierto de San Ovidio: Parábola en tres actos* (1962; *The Concert at Saint Ovidio*, 1967); *La doble historia del doctor Valmy: Relato escénico en dos partes* (1967; *The Double Case History of Doctor Valmy*, 1967); *Mito: Libro para una ópera* (1968); *La llegada de los dioses: Fábula en dos partes* (1971); *García Lorca ante el esperpento* (1972); *Tres maestros ante el público* (1973); *La fundación: Fábula en dos partes* (1974; *The Foundation*, 1985); *Años difíciles* (1977); *Buenos días perdidos* (1977); *Jueces en la noche* (1979); *El terror inmóvil* (1979; Act II only, published with subtitle *Fragmentos de una tragedia irrepresentable*, 1954); *Jueces en la noche: Misterio profano en dos partes* (1980); *Diálogo secreto: fantasía en dos partes* (1985); *Lázaro en el laberinto* (1987); *Obras Completas* (1994); *Las trampas del azar* (1995). FURTHER WORKS IN ENGLISH: *Three Plays (The Sleep of Reason, The Foundation, In the Burning Darkness)* (1985)

BIBLIOGRAPHY: Lyon, J. E., Introduction to *Hoy es fiesta* (1964): 7–39; Anderson, F., "The Ironic Structure of *Historia de una escalera*," *KRQ*, 18 (1971): 223–36; Doménech, R., *El teatro de B. V.: Una meditación española* (1973); Halsey, M., *A. B. V.* (1973); Kronik, J., "A. B. V.'s *El tragaluz* and Man's Existence in History," *HR*, 41 (1973): 371–96; Anderson, R., "Tragic Conflict and Progressive Synthesis in *La ardiente oscuridad*," *Symposium*, 29 (1975): 1–12; Casa, F. P., "The Darkening Vision: The Later Plays of B. V.," *Estreno*, 5 (1979): 30–33; Herzberger, D. K., "The Painterly Vision of B. V.'s *El sueño de la razón*," *Symposium*, 39 (1985): 93-103; Halsey, M. T., *From Dictatorship to Democracy: The Recent Plays of B. V. from La fundación to Música Cercana* (1994)

—MARSHALL J. SCHNEIDER

BUGUL, Ken

(pseud. of Marietou M'baye) Senegalese novelist, b. 28 Nov. 1948, Gouye

B. was separated at an early age from her mother, and rarely saw her father, a Muslim marabout. Reared in the village of Gouye, she found comfort amid her loneliness in her studies at a French missionary school. She won a scholarship to study in Belgium, and recounted her experiences there in her first autobiography. Because the sexual content of her book was considered to be scandalous, she was advised to adopt a pseudonym. She chose "Ken Bugul," which literally means "nobody wants" in her native Wolof. The name Ken

Bugul is used in Senegal to protect young female children; if a family has a history of child mortality, they may name their newborn thus to dissuade evil spirits from taking her life.

B.'s first literary autobiography, *Le baobab fou* (1984; *The Abandoned Baobab*, 1991), tells of B.'s tragic experience of being abandoned by her mother. The young B. later dedicates herself to her studies at a French missionary school, where she is taught to recite the phrase, "my ancestors, the Gauls," despite her African ancestry. Believing that she shares a heritage with French-speaking Europe, she imagines that once there she will be welcomed as a daughter. When she does arrive in Belgium, she encounters racism, objectification, and disillusionment. Her story critiques the assimilation projects of French colonizers who denounced indigenous African cultures, encouraged Africans to emulate the French, and denied them equal rights as citizens. It is also a testimony to the alienation felt by many African scholars who studied abroad after being geographically and psychologically separated from their native communities.

Using poetic images and imaginative metaphors, B. weaves a psychological portrait of herself as she feels her identity fragment and her dreams of acceptance shatter. Her understanding of her own identity is plagued by colonization, racial discrimination, and sexual exploitation. The novel travels back and forth in time, emphasizing the importance of B.'s early experience of rejection on her desperate search for human affection. She tries to find solace in drugs and European lovers. When this fails, she turns to prostitution. Her description of her sexual encounters reveals the intricacies of Europe's exoticization and objectification of African women in the 1960s and 1970s.

B.'s second literary autobiography, *Cendres et Braises* (1994; *Ashes and Embers*), also delves into the traumas of her past, and emphasizes the importance of the mother-daughter bond in her development. A sequel to the first autobiography, B. divulges the details of her relationship with a French man who hurts her physically and emotionally. She finally leaves him and finds compassion in an African marabout, who for B., reconnects her to her roots. Here B.'s constant flight and experimentation with new identities seems to end as she settles more comfortably into traditional life with her husband and co-wives. For B., polygamy can be a positive experience for women. Her thoughts contribute to the debates on polygamous marriages that are found throughout Muslim women's literature.

B.'s fascinating story, her moving portrayal of alienation and abandonment, and her commentary on women's lives in Africa and Europe are enriched by her creative imagery. Some critics have expressed disappointment that such a strong woman would finally find solace in marriage. Yet B.'s stories do not merely narrate the quest for a husband, but rather explore the human need for love and acceptance, the fragmenting effects of psychological colonization, and the search for identity.

BIBLIOGRAPHY: Magnier, B., "K. B. ou l'écriture thérapeutique, *Notre Librarie*, 81 (1985): 151-53; Mudimbe, E., "The Poetics of Exile and Errancy in *Le baobab fou* by K. B. and *T. Jean l'Horizon* by Simone Schwarz-Bart," *YFS*, 83 (1993): 196-213; d'Almeida, I., *Francophone African Women Writers* (1994): 44-55; Cazenave, O., *Femmes Rebelles: Naissance d'un nouveau roman africain au féminin* (1996): 67-73

—ELLIE HIGGINS

BUKOWSKI, Charles

American novelist and poet, b. 16 Aug. 1920, Andernach, Germany; d. 9 Mar. 1994, Los Angeles, California

The only son of an American soldier and a German mother, B. immigrated with his family to Los Angeles in 1922. He grew up in working-class neighborhoods during the Great Depression. During World War II, instead of serving in the armed services, B. roamed from city to city, where he lived the life of a wondering hobo and skid row alcoholic. Returning to Los Angeles, he worked an endless series of menial jobs and drank heavily. His habitual drinking resulted in his hospitalization. B. was thirty-five when he began to write poetry. His international prominence was not meteoric; his wide-ranging popularity was gained slowly by great effort. B. was the product of the independent, small press publishers and literary magazines. During the social upheavals of the 1960s he was lionized as a rebel poet and the preeminent literary outsider. In 1970 publisher John Martin offered B. the opportunity to become a full-time author. As a result, the last two decades of B.'s life were marked by emotional peace and the regular publication of large collections of poetry, short stories, and novels. Until the end of his life he remained a resident of Los Angeles, where he died of leukemia in 1994.

B.'s first book, *Flower First and Bestial Wail* (1960), contained only fourteen poems. They were candid, intensely pondering, and introspective. In tone B.'s poems of this early period resemble those of Robinson JEFFERS. B., like Jeffers, admired strength and endurance. B. identified with base human emotions, and his poetry often featured violent confrontations between men and women and detailed the extreme pleasures of basic, primal human drives and compulsions such as defecation, intoxication, copulation, and creation. B.'s metaphors were sarcastic and jarring, and the poems were toughly worded. B's poems, however, were never as bleak and pessimistic as those of Jeffers. B. believed in luck, and there was always a strong vein of idealism, individualism, and romance in his poetry. With the advent of the 1960s demand for B.'s poems increased, and there was a shift from the introspective poems to the more expressionistic, spontaneous poems of *At Terror Street and Agony Way* (1968) and *The Days Run Away Like Wild Horses Over the Hills* (1969). Dominating the poems were the day-to-day experiences of the raucous B., the B. who was endeared by his many fans. The poetry is personal, even egotistical.

As his popularity increased, B.'s poems became more outrageous, sarcastic, and cynical. Transforming himself into a Dionysian, madman poet, B. wrote the poems of *Love is a Dog from Hell* (1977) and *Play the Piano Drunk like a Percussion Instrument until the Fingers Bleed* (1979). *Dangling in the Tournefortia* (1981) was the collection that began the final phase of B's poetic work. The poems no longer engaged the daily raucous adventures of a social outcast. They became reflective, meditative daybook entries that recorded simple occurrences, which B. enhanced with biting comment. He simply wrote poems about whatever occurred, trips to the race track or shaving. Nevertheless, his fierce philosophical outlook remained intact and more emphatic rather than metaphoric or ironic. *The Last Night of the Earth Poems* (1992) was the last book he published in his lifetime. Like his other collections, this book was rich in sarcasm, antiauthoritarian triads, Diogenistic cynicism, madness, satire, and death—death as the climax of life.

In this book B. revealed that he was involved in the great seasonal cycles of life. There was birth, death, and rebirth, and there was pain, sorrow, and love. B.'s principle desire was complete unity with the natural world uninhibited by civilization. It was this quest that caused the tension between the individual and humanity and culture in all his poetry.

B. also wrote short stories and novels. *Notes of a Dirty Old Man* (1969) was an early substantial collection that featured hastily written, harsh narrative fragments that bristled with crude vigor. B. was influenced by Ernest HEMINGWAY's style of quick, clear, unadorned reportage. Semiautobiographical, B's novels were formed by vignettes or short chapters enhanced and enriched by B's exaggerated, sarcastic, and cynical philosophy. His prose tells the life of Henry Chinaski, a hard-living, cantankerous, self-obsessed rogue, a character akin to Dostoyevsky's underground man, John Fante's (1909-1983) Arturo Bandini, or Louis-Ferdiand CÉLINE's protagonists. Chinaski was B.'s alter ego and his greatest literary creation and contribution. His adventures and misadventures were chronicled in B's novels *Post Office* (1971), *Factotum* (1975), *Women* (1978), and *Ham on Rye* (1982). In its impure simplicity B.'s prose became a profound and popular antiliterature. B.'s underground life, manifested as the life of Henry Chinaski, presented the life and times of an unconventional, antihero who was both victim and critic of post-World War II American culture.

B.'s reputation as a literary outlaw earned him a large and loyal nonacademic readership. He influenced scores of other writers and remains one of the most imitated of American poets. His European reputation and readership surpassed his American reception, and he is among the best selling of American poets. During his long career B. published more than sixty books of poetry and prose, including both short stories collections and six novels. He also authored a screenplay, *Barfly* (1987), which became a major motion picture in 1987. Three collections of letters have already been published. Many of his books have been translated into more than a dozen languages. A full-length biography is available, and two critical books have been published since his death. Outside the mainstream of American letters, B.'s place in the cannon of literary rebels is assured because of his wide readership and counterculture cult status.

FURTHER WORKS: *It Catches My Hart in Its Hands* (1963); *Crucifix in a Death-Hand* (1965); *Erections, Ejaculations, Exhibitions and Tales of Ordinary Madness* (1972); *Mocking Bird Wish Me Luck* (1972); *South of No North* (1973); *While the Music Played* (1973); *Burning in Water, Drowning in Flame* (1974); *Shakespeare Never Did This* (1979); *Hot Water Music* (1983); *War All the Time* (1984); *You Get So Alone at Times That It Just Makes Sense* (1986); *The Roominghouse Madrigals* (1988); *Hollywood* (1989); *Septuagenarian Stew* (1990); *Run with the Hunted: A C. B. Reader* (1993); *Screams from the Balcony: Selected Letters 1960-1970* (1993); *Pulp* (1993); *Living on Luck: Selected Letters 1960s-1970s* (1995); *Betting on the Muse* (1996); *Bone Palace Ballet* (1997)

BIBLIOGRAPHY: Cherkovski, N., *Hank: The Life of C. B.* (1991); Harrison, R., *Against the American Dream* (1994); Locklin, G., *A Sure Bet* (1995); Brewer, G., *C. B.* (1997)

—MICHAEL BASINSKI

BULATOVIĆ, Miodrag

Yugoslav short-story writer and novelist (writing in Serbian), b. 20 Feb. 1930, Bijelo Polje; d. 15 March 1991, Igalo

B. studied at the University of Belgrade and settled in Belgrade, working as a professional writer. His first works, the short-story collections *Djavoli dolaze* (1955; the devils are coming) and *Vuk i zvono* (1958; the wolf and the bell), received little recognition in Yugoslavia, despite their originality of content and form, largely because they failed to conform to the ideological and stylistic concepts considered "progressive" by postwar Yugoslav critics advocating SOCIALIST REALISM. It was his originality, however, that almost overnight made B. extremely popular in the West, particularly in West Germany, where he quickly acquired a reputation and visibility unmatched by any other contemporary Yugoslav writer.

B.'s first major work, the novel *Heroj na magarcu* (1967; *Hero on a Donkey*, 1966), appeared in German translation (in 1964) and in the U.S. in English before it was published in Yugoslavia. The German reviewers greeted it as one of the most provocative and imaginative experimental works of the decade. Its subject is the inferno of World War II as seen in the Italian-occupied territories of Montenegro. All the bizarre excesses in the struggle between the Montenegrins and the invaders are crowded into an apocalyptic portrait of a raving and unhappy world in which all things have gone awry.

One of the central characters of *Heroj na magarcu*, the Montenegrin Gruban Malić, reappears in B.'s even more phantasmagoric next novel, *Rat je bio bolji* (1969; *The War Was Better*, 1972). Dedicated to the Italian writer Curzio Malaparte (1898–1957), and in a number of ways very similar to Malaparte's own work, this novel both overwhelms with its sardonic intensity and exasperates with its concoction of superviolence, scatology, and horseplay. Constructed as a picaresque journey of Gruban Malić from Montenegro to the West, right after the collapse of the Axis powers, the novel introduces a band of absurd but energetic characters whose improbable wanderings and madcap orgies of sex, arson, self-debasement, and guilt feelings underline B.'s theme that war is the most degrading obscenity of all.

As Malić, an obstinate, sex-crazy communist buffoon, unfolds his megalomaniac crusade to conquer and fertilize moribund Europe, an assemblage of his friends, enemies, and hangers-on provides a grotesque background for this nightmares farce. During his advance on Rome the scene shifts to the postwar period in which he becomes a superstar in a grotesque war movie intended to capture, without script or direction, all the nuances of chaotic real-life happenings.

B.'s most recent novel, *Ljudi sa četiri prsta* (1975; the people with four fingers) depicts in a similar vein the murky underworld of foreign criminals, political émigrés, and guest workers found at the bottom of the booming industrial vortex of postwar Germany.

Structurally, B.'s novels are so diffuse and sprawling, so arbitrarily put together, that the reader must make a concentrated effort to follow their rambling plots. The monumental exhibitionism and garrulousness of his characters often descend to the level of sensationalism, while the satire frequently becomes overstrained and the eroticism approaches pornography. Nevertheless, B., at his best, is gripping and memorable. His delving into certain Boschian and Breughelesque dimensions of contemporary reality notably enriches the thematic span of modern Serbian literature and makes a poignant statement about the arbitrariness of human destiny in a world bereft of enduring values.

FURTHER WORKS: *Crveni petao leti prema nebu* (1959; *The Red Cock Flies to Heaven*, 1962)

BIBLIOGRAPHY: Kadić, A., *Contemporary Serbian Literature* (1964): 94–95; Lukić, S., *Contemporary Yugoslav Literature* (1972): 42–44; Eekman, T., *Thirty Years of Yugoslav Literature 1945–1975* (1978): 240–43

—NICHOLAS MORAVČEVICH

BULGAKOV, Mikhail Afanasievich

Russian novelist, short-story writer, and dramatist, b. 14 May 1891, Kiev, Ukraine; d. 10 March 1940, Moscow

B. was the son of a church historian and the nephew of a distinguished Orthodox theologian. His first profession was medicine, which he practiced briefly during World War I in the Smolensk district, an experience he described in "Zapiski yunogo vracha" (1925–26; notes of a young doctor). He witnessed the chaos of 1918 in Kiev—first the German occupation and then the occupation by the Red Army. From there, he went to the Caucasus, where he wrote his first plays for a local stage. In 1921 he moved to Moscow and worked for the literary department of the People's Commissariat of Education, writing for newspapers (an activity he disliked), in particular for *Gudok*, well known in the 1920s for its brilliant literary section.

B.'s outstanding work of the 1920s was his largely autobiographical novel *Belaya gvardia* (1925, full text 1966; *The White Guard*, 1971), an account of the turbulent years between 1914 and 1921 as reflected in the lives of a White Guardist's family in the Ukraine. The success of the novel understandably angered Soviet critics at the time, although the stage version—*Dni Turbinykh* (perf. 1926, pub. 1970; *The Days of the Turbins*, 1934)—has been frequently performed in Soviet theaters.

B. also wrote highly original and sophisticated satire, examples of which are the play *Zoykina Kvartira* (perf. 1926; *Zoya's Apartment*, 1972) and the story "Rokovye yaytsa" (1925; "The Fatal Eggs," 1972). The novella *Sobachie serdtse* (written 1925; *The Heart of a Dog*, 1968), published in Russian in 1969 in Paris, is an imaginative satire on Soviet life in the guise of science fiction. These and other stories, particularly the story "Diavoliada" (1925; "Diaboliad," 1972), suggest that the diabolic is at work in the ordinary world of men. In "Pokhozhdenia Chichikova" (1925; "The Adventures of Chichikov," 1972), B. revived the infamous protagonist of Gogol's *Dead Souls* to create havoc in Soviet Russia's New Economic Policy period (1921–27).

The world as projected by B. is strange; familiar landmarks acquire disturbing new dimensions and multiple meanings. There is an easy transition from the real world to the fantastic, from one time level to another, and experience readily escalates from the normal to the nightmarish, from the amusing to the terrifying. Forces beyond human control, but often in human guise, are at the center of existence.

The range of B.'s art is wide. His humor is a richly woven pattern of irony and parody; but there is also satire, Mephistophelean mockery, grotesque caricature, a strong sense of the incongruous, and sudden leaps into the fantastic. Philosophical and ethical implications emerge clearly from the background of circus-like charades and complicated farce. His incredible imagination is matched by his mastery of language, which is vivid and dynamic, flexible, superbly controlled, and capable of expressing the chaos of the world.

An unflinching nonconformist and (in some respects) ultraconservative, B. was an anomaly in the new U.S.S.R. According to Ilya ILF, he still found it hard to accept the 1861 emancipation of the serfs. He was also an observant and highly articulate critic of his environment, with a predilection for the occult and the supernatural. Not surprisingly, he came in for severe, misguided attacks from the official organization of proletarian writers and from other quarters. In 1930 the performance of B.'s plays was stopped, nothing he wrote was accepted for publication, and he was subjected to a number of stinging humiliations. He wrote to Stalin, asking for permission to leave the Soviet Union, but Stalin replied that he was to stay, promising his plays would be performed again.

For a while B. earned a living as assistant producer in the Moscow Art Theater, under Stanislavsky, during which time he wrote the satirical novel *Teatralny roman* (pub. 1965; *Black Snow*, 1967).

B.'s most important work is *Master i Margarita* (written 1928–40; *The Master and Margarita*, 1967), one of the great novels of the century. It takes place on two time levels—contemporary Moscow and Jerusalem at the time of Christ. A satirical work of great depth and complexity and of brilliant imagination, it offers a mystical vision of life. *Master i Margarita* was published in a censored edition, in 1966–67, in Moscow. The full text was not published until 1969, in West Germany. In 1973 *Romany*, a volume of three novels—*Belaya gvardia, Teatralny roman*, and the full text of *Master i Margarita*—was published in Moscow.

Only in recent years has the rediscovery of this fascinating and controversial writer begun. Plays such as *Bagrovy ostrov* (perf. 1928; *The Crimson Island*, 1972), *Beg* (perf. 1928, pub. 1970; *Flight*, 1972), and *Ivan Vasilievich* (1935; Ivan Vasilievich) are now produced, and more of his work is being unearthed.

B. is the most "un-Soviet" and probably the most original writer in modern Russian literature.

FURTHER WORKS: *Diavoliada* (1925); *Kabala svyatosh* (1934, pub. 1970); *Sbornik rasskazov* (1952); *Dramy i komedii M. B.* (1965); *Izbrannaya proza* (1966); *Poslednie dni* (1970); *Piesy* (1971); *Don Kikhot* (1971); *Rannyaya nesobrannaya proza* (1978). **FURTHER WORKS IN ENGLISH:** *Diaboliad, and Other Stories* (1972); *The Early Plays of M. B.* (1972)

BIBLIOGRAPHY: Lakshin, V., "M. A. B.'s Novel *The Master and Margarita,*" *Soviet Studies in Literature*, 5, 1 (1968): 3–65; Skorino, L., "Characters without Carnival Masks," *Soviet Studies in Literature*, 5, 2 (1968): 20–45; Vinogradov, V., "The Testament of the Master," *Soviet Studies in Literature*, 5, 2 (1968): 46–92; Proffer, E., "On B.'s *Master and Margarita,*" *RLT*, No. 6 (1973): 533–64; Milne, L., *The Master and Margarita—A Comedy of Victory* (1977); special B. issue, *RLT*, No. 15 (1977); Wright, A. C., *M.B.: Life and Interpretations* (1978)

—PETER HENRY

BULGARIAN LITERATURE

The climactic event in modern Bulgarian history was the country's liberation through the Russo-Turkish War of 1877–78 after nearly five centuries of Turkish oppression. The greatest Bulgarian novel, *Pod igoto* (1889–90; *Under the Yoke*, 1893) by Ivan Vazov (1850–1921), is set amid the April uprising of 1876 which preceded that war. At the end of the 19th c., Vazov, Bulgaria's most important writer, sought almost single-handedly to create a much-needed sense of nationhood among his people through literature.

By the turn of the century Bulgaria was well on the way toward overcoming the cultural backwardness that had been the result of the lack of political independence, and consequently new writers appeared who now argued that the time had come to internationalize Bulgarian art and literature. The most important of them were grouped about the literary journal *Misul* (1892–1907). Led by the critic and aesthetician Krustyo Krustev (1866–1919), the *Misul* circle included the poet Pencho SLAVEYKOV, who sought to introduce the treasures of Western civilization into Bulgarian culture and in effect to have his work supersede *Pod igoto* by writing a national epic poem on the liberation, the unfinished *Kurvava pesen* (1913; a song of blood); and Petko Todorov (1879–1916), the author of dreamy, otherwordly prose idylls incorporating native folklore motifs. The *Misul* circle also polemicized against Vazov and his supporters, whom they considered outmoded.

The early 20th c. saw the rise of MODERNIST and SYMBOLIST currents in Bulgarian culture. Although his writing varied in quality, perhaps the most important representative of Bulgarian modernism was Peyo YAVOROV, poet, essayist, journalist, and dramatist, whose themes included unrequited love and despairing cosmic loneliness, as well as a peculiarly Bulgarian philosophical nihilism. He ended by taking his own life, like the semiautobiographical hero of his finest play, *V polite na Vitosha* (1911; in the foothills of Mount Vitosha).

Although Yavorov's poetry shows traces of symbolism, along with social radicalism, symbolist motifs found larger expression in a small number of exquisitely nostalgic lyric poems written by Dimcho Debelyanov (1887–1916) before he was killed in World War I. He is the prime Bulgarian representative of the entire European generation destroyed by that conflict. But Bulgarian symbolism reached its apogee in such collections as *Regina mortua* (1908; Latin: the dead queen) by Teodor Trayanov (1882–1945), one of symbolism's chief theoreticians as well as practitioners. In fact Trayanov managed to keep Bulgarian symbolism artificially alive after World War I in the journal *Khiperion*, which he published throughout the 1920s. Another major prewar symbolist was Nikolay Liliev (pseud. of Nikolay Mikhaylov, 1885–1960), a poets' poet whose output was remarkably small.

When the smoke of World War I cleared, however, several writers who had earlier been symbolists or modernists because of intellectual fashion turned to Marxism. One such symbolist was Khristo Yasenov (1889–1925), who after the war first wrote humorous pieces for Communist magazines, then abandoned literature for politics until he disappeared during a government campaign against political radicals in 1925. A similar fate befell Geo Milev (1895–1925), a symbolist, modernist, and Decadent before and just after the war, who then committed himself to radical political doctrine in the early 1920s and wrote his famous narrative poem *Septemvri* (1924; *September*, 1961), in the manner of the

Russian MAYAKOVSKY, hailing an abortive popular uprising of September 1923 against the government. The early 1920s also witnessed the brief fame and untimely (natural) death of the idealistic Communist poet Khristo Smirnenski (1898–1923), a humorist and satirist who longed for the establishment of social justice on earth.

The political instability of the early 1920s, leading to the governmental repressions of 1923–25, however, led many authors to adopt an apolitical stance. Such an approach was promoted by the finest literary journal of the interwar period, *Zlatorog* (1920–43), edited by the perceptive literary critic Vladimir Vasilev (1883–1963); it published nearly all the best Bulgarian writers of its time except those with a strong philosophical orientation. The *Zlatorog* writers again dealt with native and national themes, especially the Bulgarian peasantry, for Bulgaria was, after all, an overwhelmingly agrarian country. The greatest master of modern Bulgarian prose, Yordan YOVKOV, delineated the outwardly simple but inwardly complex experiences and conflicts of ordinary peasants in such collections as *Staroplaninski legendi* (1927; Balkan legends) and *Vecheri v Antimovskiya Khan* (1928; evenings at the Antimovo inn). But even in his stories of World War I Yovkov sought to blunt the cruel edges of conflict through the reconciling power of beauty. Bulgarian literature sustained a great loss in his early death.

A subject of such large dimensions as the peasantry had to be dealt with in different ways by different writers. If Yovkov saw the peasantry primarily as the repository of moral good, there were others who pictured the village only as a sink of evil, depravity, and lust. Another of Bulgaria's leading prose writers, ELIN PELIN, took up an intermediate position. In *Geratsite* (1911; the Gerak family) he chronicled the decline and dissolution of an originally well-to-do peasant family, and in his novella *Zemya* (1922; land) he depicted the moral corruption arising from a man's unreasoning greed for land. In such works as these Elin Pelin may also be seen as continuing a Bulgarian tradition of what might be called cynical realism. Another adherent of this approach was the short-story writer Georgi Stamatov (1869–1942), who implicitly or explicitly maintained in his fiction that man's every action, no matter how idealistic it may appear superficially, is actually grounded in self-interest, usually of a rather crude variety. Yet another representative of this sterile nihilism and cynicism in Bulgarian literature was Georgi Raychev (1882–1947). It may be argued that this group of authors represented a certain trend in Bulgarian modernism.

Bulgarian writers have by and large done best in the briefer genres of the short story and the lyric poem. A lyric poet of quiet charm who spent his life in the provincial city of Pleven was Nikola Rakitin (1885–1934). In a series of small collections of poems he sang of the beauties of the changing seasons and of the fields with their ripening grain. But modernity also had its place in this corner of the Balkans; it found its highest expression in the work of Elisaveta BAGRYANA, perhaps the best poet of Bulgaria of this century. In such collections as *Zvezda na moryaka* (1932; the sailor's star) and *Surtse choveshko* (1936; the heart of man), she writes of asphalt and airplanes. She would liberate herself from the bonds of national and personal history: her ideal is the rootless wanderer over the featureless sea. In later life, however, she became more cognizant of the value of human ties and linkages.

The outbreak of World War II—when Bulgaria joined the Axis powers, but without declaring war upon the Soviet Union—disrupted the nation's cultural life relatively little. The watershed of 20th-c. Bulgarian history and culture was the coup of September 9, 1944, which swept away the old regime and led to the establishment of a Communist regime by 1947, as the Soviet Union consolidated its power over eastern Europe. For several years—until after Stalin's death—Bulgarian literature was forced into the mold of Soviet-style SOCIALIST REALISM: the great figures of the national past—even Ivan Vazov—were systematically denigrated.

Little literature worthy of remembrance appeared during the Stalinist years. In 1951 a leading novelist of the time, Dimitur Dimov (1909–1966), published *Tyutyun* (tobacco), which won a Dimitrov prize; subsequently, however, heavy ideological attacks compelled him to bring out a new version in 1953 along impeccably Socialist Realist lines, with the whitest of heroes and the blackest of villains. If one were an old-line Communist Party member like Georgi Karaslavov (b. 1904), one could publish novels like *Obiknoveni khora* (6 parts, 1952–1975; ordinary people), which described events of the relatively recent past, the 1920s. Other novelists, however, preferred to retreat into more distant history: Dimitur TALEV, for instance, went back to the early 19th c. to describe the struggle of that time for cultural and national independence in his famous trilogy consisting of *Zhelezniyat svetilnik* (1952; *The Iron Candlestick*, 1964), *Ilinden* (1953; *Ilinden*, 1966), and *Prespanskite kambani* (1954; *The Bells of Prespa*, 1966). Emiliyan Stanev (1907–1979), who in the 1940s acquired a substantial literary reputation as a keenly sympathetic observer of nature, had by the 1960s shifted to the historical novel with the publication of *Legenda za Sibin, preslavskiya knyaz* (1968; the legend of Sibin, prince of Preslav). Among younger historical novelists, Anton Donchev (b. 1930) merits special mention. His *Vreme razdelno* (1964; *Time of Parting*, 1968) describes the agonizing dilemma of 17th-c. Christian Bulgarians compelled by their Turkish conquerors to accept the Islamic religion on pain of death. In its psychological subtlety, beauty of language, and seriousness of purpose *Vreme razdelno* is one of the finest historical novels of the 20th c.

Stalin's death eventually brought about a temporary "thaw" in Bulgarian cultural life from 1955 to 1957. During those heady days writers could write something resembling the truth about their society; they could even describe Communist officials corrupted by the lust for power. Those same Bulgarian officials, following Soviet initiative, soon tightened the reins, but the situation remained significantly better than before, for Bulgarian writers no longer had to write of industrial construction or the corruption of the West, although many did anyway. Now poets in particular could write genuine lyric poems, and in so doing develop a considerable technical mastery. Their principal mentor in the 1960s was a very unprolific but excellent poet, Atanas Dalchev (b. 1904), much of whose mundane but curiously attractive poetry on everyday themes had appeared in the 1920s. During the worst Stalinist years he had been one of the few older writers who had refused to conform to the regime's political demands, and so earned his younger colleagues' admiration. Perhaps no one name stands out among the young poets who began publishing in the 1960s, but their ranks include such people as Vladimir Bashev (1935–1967), Damyan Damyanov (b. 1935), and Krustyo Stanishev (b. 1933). Among slightly older poets active in recent years are Blaga Dimitrova (b. 1922) and the satirists Valeri Petrov (b. 1920) and Radoy Ralin (b. 1923). Other prominent literary figures of today are Pavel Vezhinov (b. 1914), one of the finest storytellers in Bulgarian literature; and the short-story writer and playwright Nikolay Khaytov (b. 1919), who in one of his best-known works describes a bureaucrat who prevents a shoemaker from employing his spare time to construct paths so that his fellow citizens may enjoy the beauties of the forest.

Even in the 19th c., Bulgaria, for various reasons, had a very small emigration to the West. After 1944 a few writers of the second rank—for example, the poet and critic Khristo Ognyanov (b. 1911)—emigrated to or remained in the West, but no major writer did so. And the 1960s and 1970s, which witnessed the development of intellectual dissidence in most east European countries and in the Soviet Union itself, were comparatively quiet in Bulgaria, although a certain number of lesser-known Bulgarian intellectuals, writers, and artists have emigrated to the West in recent years. Perhaps the most prominent writer among them, Georgi Markov (1929–1978), was assassinated in London, apparently in retaliation for his political activities. Unlike those of other Eastern European countries, Bulgarian literature and culture have developed principally within the country itself in this century.

BIBLIOGRAPHY: Pinto, V., ed., Introduction to *Bulgarian Prose and Verse* (1957): xiiixli; Moser, C. A., "The Journal *Zlatorog* and Modern Bulgarian Letters," *SEEJ*, 7 (1963): 117–33; Kirk, F., Introduction to N. Kirilov and F. Kirk, eds., *Introduction to Modern Bulgarian Literature: An Anthology of Short Stories* (1969): 9–22; Brown, J. F., *Bulgaria under Communist Rule* (1970): 240–62; Moser, C. A., *A History of Bulgarian Literature 865–1944* (1972); Moser, C. A., ed., special Bulgaria issue, *LitR*, 16 (Winter 1972–1973); Djagarov, G., "On Contemporary Bulgarian Poetry," in R. J. Colombo and N. Rousanoff, trs., *Under the Eaves of a Forgotten Village: Sixty Poems from Contemporary Bulgaria* (1975): 62–64

—CHARLES A. MOSER

BULL, Olaf

Norwegian poet, b. 10 Nov. 1883, Oslo; d. 22 June 1933, Oslo

B. first worked as a journalist, but his only real profession was that of writer. Aside from short stays abroad, mostly in Paris and Italy, B. spent his life in Oslo, the city reflected in so much of his poetry.

He made his debut in 1909 with the volume of poetry entitled *Digte* (poems). His subsequent publication was relatively small but of the finest quality, and included *Nye digte* (1913; new poems), *Digte og noveller* (1916; poems and short stories), *Stjernene* (1924; the stars), *Metope* (1917; metope), and *Oinos og eros* (1930; Greek: wine and love). A thinker who believed that poetry and logic were inextricably intertwined, B. gave poetic form to the ideas of, in particular, Henri Bergson and Einstein in his last volume of poetry, *Ignis ardens* (1932; Latin: blazing fire).

B. is one of the finest Norwegian poets of the 20th c., continuing the line of the great, life-embracing lyricists of the 19 c., Henrik Wergeland (1808–1845) and Bjørnstjerne Bjørnson (1832–1910). But although there is a strong Norwegian tradition in his work, B. is an extremely individualistic poet whose fundamental inspiration is personal and from within.

His debut volume, *Digte*, received with unanimous critical acclaim, established the passionate tones and major themes of his work, particularly his love affair with spring. No poet since Wergeland had written so beautifully of the season. The later volumes of poetry are somewhat more reflective than the first, B.'s

vision growing less dependent on outer reality; but essentially it does not change.

At the heart of *Digte*, and of B.'s work in general, is the conflict between the transitory and the timeless, captured most poignantly for him in the image of early spring, the season of new growth that, nevertheless, must eventually give way to the snows of winter. For B., spring is youth, love, hope, and beauty, which he must rescue, through his poem, from time's passing. In all B.'s poetry, as in *Digte*, there is a relentless awareness of time moving ominously on, like a "stone forever falling." Images of chaos and death continually intrude on the most peaceful of poetic landscapes.

One of the finest expressions of the conflict between B.'s need for permanence and his realization of the necessity of transition is the poem "Metope" (metope) from the volume of the same name. The forces of life and death, immediate experience and memory, substance and spirit, are perfectly balanced, the poet desiring, paradoxically yet effectually, to carve a soft metope (the space between two triglyphs of a Doric frieze) of his lover's mind in memory's stubborn stone, thereby saving his lover and their love from the destruction of time. "Metope" is the epitome of B.'s art and one of the classic poems of Norwegian literature.

FURTHER WORKS: *Kjælighedens farce* (1919, with H. Korg); *Mit navn er Knoph* (1919); *De hundrede år* (1928); *Oslo-hus* (1931); *Samlede digte* (1934 and 1943)

BIBLIOGRAPHY: Beyer, H., *A History of Norwegian Literature* (1956): 299–303

—MARY KAY NORSENG

BULLINS, Ed

American dramatist and novelist, b. 2 July 1935, Philadelphia, Pa.

Educated at William Penn Institute (Philadelphia), Los Angeles City College, and San Francisco State, and recipient of a D. Litt. from Columbia College (Chicago), B. became known nationally during the politically active 1960s. A poet, an essayist, a filmmaker, a novelist (*The Reluctant Rapist*, 1973) and a teacher at several colleges, B. is best known for his achievements in theater. In addition to writing more plays than any other contemporary Black American, he has promoted Black Theater as cofounder and director of Black Arts/West, editor of *Black Theater* journal, author of numerous articles, and editor of anthologies emphasizing the "new" Black drama, and playwright-in-residence at the New Lafayette Theater in Harlem. His playwriting talents have earned him fellowships and grants, as well as awards.

Although he has experimented with a wide variety of dramaturgical techniques, B. is best known for his activity in the new Black drama that developed as part of the Black Liberation movement in the U.S. in the 1960s. Called Black Arts drama or Black revolutionary theater, the new drama sought to educate Afro-Americans through "message" plays calling for change, through plays describing the realities of Afro-American experience (especially in the inner-city world), and through ritual drama encouraging Afro-Americans to unite spiritually and intellectually to form a new nation.

Although some of his pronouncements and plays have led to his being identified as a proponent of "message" dramas of change, which use allegorical characters in didactic roles (in the manner of morality plays), B., in his most important work, has created complex characters whose lives in the inner city provoke questions rather than teach preconceived solutions. Frequently depicting the life style that must be altered before a healthy Black community can be created, he has focused on the importance of vision and on the manner in which love is betrayed, perverted, or poorly communicated. For example, *In the Wine Time* (1969), first of a projected series of twenty plays in a "Twentieth-Century Cycle," depicts Cliff Dawson, a young Afro-American who has exploited women and who communicates his love to his wife only through abuse, who glamorizes his dishonorable army record, but who struggles to acquire an education and ultimately sacrifices himself in order to make it possible for his nephew to have a chance to realize the vision of a world beyond the ghetto.

Other "Black reality" plays depict the betrayal of fraternal love, the jealous preservation of a lesbian relationship, and betrayal in friendship. In *In New England Winter* (1970), second in the Cycle, the planning of a robbery serves as background for the audience's discovery of the character traits and the interrelationships of Cliff Dawson and Steve Benson, half-brothers. Moving between the present of 1960 and a past five years earlier, the play reaches a climax when the audience learns that, despite Cliff's awareness that the younger Steve had an affair with Cliff's wife while Cliff was in jail, Cliff's love for his half-brother has caused him to conceal his knowledge even while Steve was accusing another man of responsibility for the wife's adultery. Similarly, *Goin' a Buffalo* (1969) is most remarkable for its emphasis on the theme of betrayal of friendship.

Characteristic of Bullins's "message" plays is *The Gentleman Caller* (1970). A silent young Black male calls upon the Manns, an affluent white couple, whose living room is decorated with the stuffed heads of a Black man, an American Indian, a Vietnamese, and a Chinese. In a virtual monologue broken only by laconic responses from the maid who has been her Mammy, Madame Mann reveals her bigotry and attempts to seduce the Gentleman Caller. The maid cuts the throat of Mr. Mann, kills Madame Mann with a shotgun, and, revealing herself as Queen Mother, calls on Black people to form a Black nation that will bring death to the enemies of Black people.

Although criticized occasionally for limiting his vision to the inner city, B. is generally acknowledged to be one of the most skillful and powerful contemporary playwrights.

FURTHER WORKS: *How Do You Do: A Nonsense Drama* (1965); *Five Plays* (1969); *The Duplex: A Black Love Fable* (1971); *The Hungered One* (1971); *Four Dynamite Plays* (1972); *The Theme Is Blackness: "The Corner," and Other Plays* (1973)

BIBLIOGRAPHY: X, Marvin, "Interview with E. B.," in Bullins, E., ed., *New Plays from the Black Theatre* (1969): vi–xv; Riley, C., Introduction to a *A Black Quartet* (1970): xx–xxi; Reilly, J., "E. B.," in Vinson, J., ed., *Contemporary Dramatists* (1973): 124–28; Smitherman, G., "E. B./Stage One: Everybody Wants to Know Why I Sing the Blues," *Black World* (April 1974): 4–13; Evans, D., "The Theatre of Confrontation: E. B., Up Against the Wall," *Black World* (April 1974): 14–18; Hay, S., "'What Shape Shapes Shapelessness?' Structural Elements in E. B.'s Plays," *Black World* (April 1974): 20–26; Page, J., *Selected Black American Authors* (1977): 32

—DARWIN T. TURNER

Ed Bullins

BULU LITERATURE
See Cameroonian Literature

BUNIN, Ivan

Russian short-story writer, novelist, memoirist, critic, and poet, b. 22 Oct. 1870, Voronezh; d. 8 Nov. 1953, Paris, France

In early childhood, B. witnessed the increasing impoverishment of his gentry family, who were ultimately completely ruined financially. In 1886 he left school, resuming his education at home under the guidance of his older brother. At age seventeen he made his debut as a poet and in 1893 published his first story. For a few years he was a follower of Tolstoy's moral and sociopolitical ideas, but in 1894, after meeting the writer in Moscow and realizing that he was not suited to living a simple, rural life, he abandoned his passion for Tolstoyism, which resolved itself in later years into merely respectful and unrestricted admiration for Tolstoy's art. For his translation of Longfellow's *The Song of Hiawatha* B. received the Pushkin Prize by the Russian Academy of Science in 1903. In 1909 the Russian Academy elected B. one of its twelve members. B. was an ardent traveler, and before World War I visited Ceylon, Palestine, Egypt, Turkey, and other countries; reminiscences of his numerous journeys are echoed in many of his poems and prose works. His hatred of the 1917 Bolshevik revolution, a leading motif in his diary *Okayannye dni* (1925–26; with additions, 1973, 1974, 1977; cursed days), led him, in 1920, to emigrate to France, where he remained in exile the rest of his life, becoming one of the foremost figures of Russian emigré literature. In 1933 he received the Nobel Prize for literature.

B. wrote poetry throughout his entire creative life. Yet as a poet he did not make an original contribution; his finely polished verse remained in the tradition of the 19th c., and he was not interested in new poetic techniques. Images of nature occupy a pivotal place in B.'s poetry. Words connoting "sadness" permeate his verse, and he gained a reputation as a poet of "twilight moods." B.'s well-known "autumnal poem" is "Listopad" (1900; leaves fall).

Peasants and small landowners are the protagonists of B.'s early short stories, such as "Sosny" (1901; the pines) and "Antonovskie yabloki" (1900; "Antonov Apples," n.d.). After the revolution of 1905 B. continued to write on peasant themes, but the stories of this period are gloomier than his previous work. In the novel *Derevnya* (1910; *The Village*, 1923) B.'s *muzhiks* (peasants) are brutal and primitive; their lives are painted in the darkest tones. A masterfully written novelette, *Sukhodol* (1912; *Dry Valley*, n.d.), which is a veiled biography of B.'s family, is a successful attempt to recapture the lost past of Russian rural life. Its realistic simplicity is imbued with spirituality and subtle symbolism.

Death and love are predominant themes in many of B.'s masterful works, such as "Grammatika lyubvi" (1915; "The Grammar of Love," 1933), the celebrated "Gospodin iz San Frantsisko" (1915; "The Gentleman from San Francisco," 1923), *Lyogkoe dykhanie* (1916; "Light Breathing," 1933), *Mitina lyubov* (1925; *Mitya's Love*, 1926), and *Delo korneta Yelagina* (1926; *The Elaghin Affair*, 1935). The longest and perhaps most important of all B.'s works is *Zhizn Arsieneva* (1927–33; *The Well of Days*, 1933). The classification of this book is a problem that led the Russian writer Konstantin PAUSTOVSKY to say that "*Zhizn Arsieneva* is neither a short novel, nor a novel, nor a long short story, but is of a genre yet unknown." Most critics state that the book is B.'s veiled autobiography. Countless numbers of people parade before the reader's eyes and dozens of events flash across the pages of the book.

The thirty-eight love stories in *Tyomnye allei* (1946; *Dark Avenues*, 1949) are, as B. put it himself, his best "in the sense of compactness, verve, and literary artistry in general." A certain measure of eroticism was always present in B.'s works, and is especially strong here. In all the narratives of this collection there is inexpressible sadness that everything in this world exists but a short while and that the fleeting moments of happiness are unrecapturable but unforgettable.

B. is often called a "magician of words." He possesses an extraordinary faculty, perhaps unique in Russian literature, to render in words the senses of sight, hearing, smell, taste, and touch. B.'s greatness lies in his concise style, his impeccable diction, his marvelous facility in creating atmosphere, his rendering of nature, and his lack of didacticism.

FURTHER WORKS: *Polnoe sobranie sochineny* (1915); *Sobranie sochineny* (11 vols., 1934–1936); *Osvobozhdenie Tolstogo* (1937); *Vospominania* (1950; *Memoirs and Portraits*, 1951); *Sobranie sochineny* (9 vols., 1965–1967); *Velga* (1970); *Izbrannoe* (1970); *Stikhotvorenia, rasskazy, povesti* (1973); *Pod serpom i molotom* (1977); *Poslednee svidanie* (1978). FURTHER WORKS IN ENGLISH: *The Dreams of Chang* (1923); *Shadowed Paths* (n.d., 195?);

The Gentlemen from San Francisco and Other Stories (1963); *The Gentleman from San Francisco and Other Stories* (1964)

BIBLIOGRAPHY: Stepun, F., "I. B.," *Hochland* (1933–1934): 548–63; Poggioli, R., "The Art of I. B.," *The Phoenix and the Spider* (1957): 131–57; Kirchner, B., *Die Lebensanschauung I. A. B.s nach seinem Prosawerk* (1968); Woodward, J. B., "Eros and Nirvana in the Art of B.," *MLR*, 65 (1970): 576–87; Kryzytski, S., *The Works of I. B.* (1971); Richards, D. J., "B.'s Conception of the Meaning of Life," *SEER*, 119 (1972): 153–72; Marullo, T. G., *B.'s Dry Valley*: The Russian Novel in Transition from Realism to Modernism," *FMLS*, 14 (1978): 193–207; Woodward, J. B., *I. B.: A Study of His Fiction* (1980)

—SERGE KRYZYTSKI

BUNTING, Basil

English poet, essayist, journalist, b. 1 March 1900, Scotswood on Tyne; d. 17 April 1985, Hexham

Educated in Quaker schools, B. spent some time in prison as a conscientious objector during World War I. He later attended the London School of Economics but left without taking a degree, traveling instead to Paris, where he became an assistant to Ford Madox FORD on the *Transatlantic Review*. During the 1930s he was associated with Louis ZUKOFSKY and Objectivism. Sent to Iran as a translator during World War II, B. stayed on after the war as an employee of the Foreign Office and then as a correspondent for the London *Times*. When he was expelled from Iran in 1951, he returned to his native Northumberland, which continued to be the focus of much of his verse.

Although his first book, *Redimiculum Matellarum*, was published in 1930, B.'s poetic output is relatively slim. Always an independent voice, B. nevertheless reflects his beginnings during the 1920s, when the international modernist style held sway. Like Ezra POUND and T. S. ELIOT, B. often used older literature, myth, and historical anecdote to create a poetic texture that could be highly allusive. "Attis: Or, Something Missing" (1931), for example, contains parodies of John Milton and T. S. Eliot, as well as requiring some knowledge of the myth of Attis, of Catullus's poem about that myth, and of Lucretius's attitude toward superstition. There is often little narrative structure to guide the reader through the longer poems, and "Villon" (1925), like *The Waste Land*, was in fact edited by Pound. In the absence of a more traditional discursive framework, the poems often depend on the statement, repetition, and variation of motifs, on the careful juxtaposition of allusions, and on the deliberate modulation of tone, diction, and point of view. According to B.'s own statements, however, the most important formal principle underlying his verse is a musical one. Deeply interested in music himself, B. attempted to see poetry in musical terms in at least two ways: the larger form of a poem might be conceived, like a sonata or a fugue, as the patterned repetition and development of a set of motifs; and on the more immediate level of language, sound could be given precedence over meaning. B. is quite explicit in condemning the search for any kind of "prose meaning" in poetry, insisting instead that it be read aloud, and that the listener need not even know the poet's language in order to enjoy the beauty of the poem.

In spite of his emphasis on musical sound at the expense of meaning, however, B. reveals a number of continuing concerns in his verse. In "Villon" he attacks the officious bureaucratic mind that reduces heroic beauty to a set of statistics, while "Aus Dem Zweiten Reich" (1931) portrays the sterile, decadent modernity of Berlin in the 1920s. Against the decadence of modern industrial culture, B. sets images drawn from the world of nature, and particularly the nature of his own rural Northumberland. He creates characters like the hermit-poet of "Chomei at Toyama" (1932), who rejects the comforts of urban life for a simple retreat to country poverty, although the country is never overly romanticized in B.'s verse. Most notably in some of the odes he wrote during the early 1930s, B. portrays the misery of small farmers who struggle against an economic system that is nearly as oppressive as the sandy soil and the cold weather of their northern farms.

After years of relative obscurity, when he was often regarded as a minor follower of Pound, B. began to be read again during the 1960s by a younger generation of poets tired of what they saw as the sterility of much British poetry written since World War II. Since the publication of his long autobiographical poem, *Briggflatts*, in 1966, and the *Collected Poems* (1968), B. has come to be regarded as a poet who successfully carried the modernist experiments of the 1920s to a new generation, in a voice uniquely his own.

FURTHER WORKS: *Poems 1950* (1950); *The Spoils* (1965); *First Book of Odes* (1965); *Loquitur* (1965); *Two Poems* (1967); *What The Chairman Told Tom* (1967); *Descant on Rawthey's Madrigal* (1968); *Collected Poems* (1978); *The Complete Poems* (1996)

BIBLIOGRAPHY: Special B. issue, *Agenda*, 4 (1966); Suter, A., "Time and the Literary Past in the Poetry of B.," *ConL*, 12 (1971): 510–26; Suter, A., "Art and Experience: An Approach to B.'s Ideal of Poetry and the Poet," *DUJ*, 35 (1974): 307–14; Muller, K., "B.'s Linguistic Poetics," *FMLS*, 13 (1977): 16–24; special B. issue, *Agenda*, 16 (1978); Terrell, C.-F., ed., *B. B.: Man and Poet* (1981); Makin, P., "The Post-War Poetry of B. B.," *YES*, 17 (1987): 1-15; Conniff, B., *The lyric and modern poetry: Olson, Creeley, B.* (1988); Alldritt, K., *Modernism in the Second World War: the later poetry of Ezra Pound, T. S. Eliot, B. B., and Hugh MacDiarmid* (1989); special B. issue, *SagetriebIO*, 9 (1990); Davie, D., "B. B. and His Masters," *PBA*, 76 (1990): 225-36; Tuma, K., "B. B.'s Briggflatts and Melancholy," *ConL*, 34 (1993): 266-92; Caddel, R., *B. B.: A Northern Life* (1997)

—JAMES F. KNAPP

BURGESS, Anthony

(pseud. of John Anthony Burgess Wilson) English novelist, critic, translator, b. 25 Feb. 1917, Manchester; d. 25 Nov. 1993, London

Born a Catholic to middle-class parents, B. graduated from Manchester University in 1940. After six years of military service on Gibraltar, he spent the next thirteen at assorted teaching posts throughout England and Malaya. B., who primarily had studied music composition, wrote comparatively little until 1959, when he was diagnosed as having a brain tumor and given less than a year to live. The diagnosis proved incorrect, but concern about leaving his

Basil Bunting

wife without means set off a rush of literary activity that has produced to date over thirty books and hundreds of journalistic pieces. His most notorious novel, *A Clockwork Orange* (1962), became an underground classic soon after publication, and its filming in 1971 rocketed B. to immediate fame.

B.'s first novel, *A Vision of Battlements* (completed, 1949; first published, 1965), which was written for the sake of purging the memory of his tour of duty on Gibraltar, foreshadows many of the themes of his later novels: the comedy and ambiguities of life; man's entrapment between myth and history, between his libidinous and puritanical natures, between freedom and necessity, and between the assertion of individualism and the pressures of society. It also introduces the seedy and victimized antihero who is often an artist, expatriate, rebel or lapsed Catholic—aspects of B.'s own character.

Loosely based on the *Aeneid, A Vision of Battlements* imitates JOYCE's method of underpinning *Ulysses* with the plot of the *Odyssey*. Both through language and structure, B. shows the influence of Joyce, just as his growing fascination with neologisms, word games, parodic pastiche, and blank-verse cadences in his prose show indebtedness to NABOKOV and Shakespeare.

Indeed, Shakespeare becomes the touchstone for the brilliant and eccentric *Nothing Like the Sun: A Story of Shakespeare's Love-Life* (1964). Incorporating—as dialogue, description, stream of consciousness—hundreds of quotations from Shakespeare's plays and sonnets, B. fabricates a biographical novel in which "WS" and the English language are the twin heroes. As a joyous wedding of

Anthony Burgess

language and structure, *Nothing Like the Sun* is excelled only by *Napoleon Symphony* (1974). Here, B. appropriates the score of Beethoven's colossal Third Symphony, the E-flat *Sinfonia Eroica*, to shape a musicoverbal comic epic on the last quarter-century of the life of another colossus, Napoleon Bonaparte.

Such stunning examples of literary play, however, were still years in the offing in the 1950s. B.'s second novel, *The Malayan Trilogy* (1956–59; Am., *The Long Day Wanes*, 1965), arose out of his tenure as an education officer in Malaya during the final throes of British rule. Throughout its three volumes (*Time for a Tiger*, 1956; *The Enemy in the Blanket*, 1958; *Beds in the East*, 1959), B. juxtaposes the progressive disintegration of a hapless civil servant, Victor Crabbe, against the birth of Malayan independence. Though the novel's pervasive note of futility owes much to ORWELL's *Burmese Days*, the grim comedy and linguistic riches are B.'s own. The trilogy remains one of the best accounts of Britain's decline as a power in the Far East.

In an incredible display of prolificness, B. wrote eleven novels between 1960 and 1964, three of supreme achievement. *The Right to an Answer* (1960) reflects B.'s feelings about the "mess" that has resulted from the birth of the welfare state, and despite its tragic denouement it is comic in a grotesque way. Conceived from the viewpoint of two expatriates—its narrator, an English businessman on leave from the East, and Mr. Raj, a Ceylonese student of "love"—the novel zeros in on the lust, adultery, xenophobia, racism, and materialism of a provincial town in order to symbolize the spiritual atrophy of England in general.

Such pessimism about contemporary society outweighs even that of *The Wanting Seed* (1962), where an overpopulated England of the future is caught up in the alternating cycles of libertarianism and totalitarianism. The former, B. calls the Pelphase. Based on the theology of Pelagius, who believed in free will, it allows man the freedom to populate himself almost out of existence. This phase of the cycle then yields to the Gusphase (based on Augustinian determinism), which stifles man's natural instincts and freedom in order to preserve the state.

The dominant ideas in these two novels are carried to their extreme in B.'s most shocking and inventive work, *A Clockwork Orange*, which is narrated in a philological conglomerate devised by B. called *nadsat*: a mixture of English and American slang, Russian, gypsy talk, and odd bits of Jacobean prose. Like Orwell's *1984* and ZAMYATIN's *We*, the book is a science-fiction fable of the not-too-distant future. It tells the story of a welfare state terrorized by roving bands of hardened delinquents who fight, steal, and rape in order to assert their freedom against the conformity and deadness of a clockwork society. One of these is the narrator, Alex, who, imprisoned for murder, is brainwashed to be "good" through a fiendish conditioning process, only to be turned into a passive and motiveless automaton. The central question of *A Clockwork Orange* is a metaphysical and social one: is an "evil" human being with free choice preferable to a "good" zombie without it?

The same question controls the theme of B.'s longest and funniest novel, *Enderby* (1968), in which a poet (who writes most of his poetry in the lavatory) executes hilarious maneuvers throughout England and the continent to avoid being squeezed into conformity and normality. It is B.'s most devastating satire on a society that fails to discriminate between acts of rebellion that are dangerous and destructive and those that are beneficial and creative.

The sequel to *Enderby—The Clockwork Testament; or, Enderby's End* (1975)—goes several steps further by asking if society is even intelligent enough to pursue the discrimination. Now living in New York as a visiting professor of creative writing, Enderby has become B.'s rather obvious alter ego, and his madcap experiences occasions for piling up splenetic glosses on American culture. *The Clockwork Testament* is by turns a farcical, comic, satiric, querulous, indignant, bitter, merciless assault on (particularly) American media and academia. Always iconoclastic, frequently inaccurate, generally reactionary, the novel is nevertheless a timely indictment of how these institutions—by creating, mass producing for, and catering to a new generation of functional illiterates—are systematically destroying the language and, consequently, turning us into mediocre components of a clockwork democracy.

In one way or another, all of B.'s novels reflect this anxiety: that the modern world has become more and more intent on depersonalizing and homogenizing the individual. Yet even so gloomy a theme has never constricted his genius for comedy, his varied range of subjects, his ability to tell a good story, his linguistic pyrotechnics, and his seemingly endless flow of wit and invention.

FURTHER WORKS: *English Literature: A Survey for Students* (as John Burgess Wilson; 1958); *The Doctor Is Sick* (1960); *The Worm and the Ring* (1961); *Devil of a State* (1961); *One Hand Clapping* (as Joseph Kell; 1961); *Honey for the Bears* (1963); *Inside Mr. Enderby* (as Joseph Kell; 1963); *The Novel Today* (1963); *The Eve of Saint Venus* (1964); *Language Made Plain* (1965); *Here Comes Everybody: An Introduction to James Joyce for the Ordinary Reader* (1965; Amer., *Re Joyce*, 1965); *Tremor of Intent* (1966); *The Novel Now: A Student's Guide to Contemporary Fiction*

(1967); *Enderby Outside* (1968); *Urgent Copy: Literary Studies* (1968); *Shakespeare* (1970; *MF* (1971) *Joysprick: An Introduction to the Language of James Joyce* (1972); *English Literature*, 2nd ed. (1974); *A Long Trip to Tea Time* (1976); *Beard's Roman Women* (1976); *Mose: A Narrative* (1976); *New York* (1977); *Abba Abba* (1978); *Ernest Hemingway and His World* (1978); *1985* (1978); *Earthly Powers* (1980)

BIBLIOGRAPHY: Aggelar, G., "The Comic Art A. B.," *Crit*, 12, 3 (1971): 77–94; Morris, R. K., *The Consolations of Ambiguity: An Essay on the Novels of A. B.* (1971); LeClair, T., "Essential Opposition: The Novels of A. B.," *Crit*, 12, 3 (1971): 77–94; Morris, R. K., "*The Malayan Trilogy*: The Futility of History," in *Continuance and Change: The Contemporary British Novel Sequence* (1972): 71–92; Dix, C., *A. B.* (1972); DeVitis, A. A., *A. B.* (1972); Stinson, J., "*Nothing Like the Sun*: The Faces in Bella Cohen's Mirror," *JML*, 5 (1976): 131–47; Boytinck, P., *A. B.: A Bibliography* (1977); Moyat, J., "Joyce's Contemporary: A Study of A. B.'s *Napoleon Symphony*," *ConL*, 19 (1978): 180–95; Petix, E., "Linguistics, Mechanics and Metaphysics in A. B.'s *A Clockwork Orange*," in *Old Lines, New Forces* (1978): 38–53

—ROBERT K. MORRIS

BURKE, Kenneth

American critic, poet, novelist, and short-story writer, b. 5 May 1897, Pittsburgh, Pa.; d. 19 Nov. 1993, Andover, N.J.

A college dropout (he attended both Ohio State and Columbia), B. has lectured at a number of American Colleges and universities; his longest affiliation, lasting from 1943 through 1962, was with Bennington College. B. has been the recipient of a number of honors, including a Guggenheim fellowship and a grant from the Rockefeller Foundation; in 1981 he was awarded the National Medal for Literature. His memberships include the National Institute of Arts and Letters and the American Academy of Arts and Sciences. And he has been for much of this century one of the most formidable and provocative mavericks on the American cultural scene.

B.'s fiction and poetry are of more than passing interest, but, most would agree, it is in a series of remarkable books of literary, social, and cultural criticism beginning with *Counter-Statement* (1931) that B. has produced his most impressive work. In this first book, some of whose contents were actually written as early as the mid-1920s, B.'s interests are more specifically, or narrowly, literary than they would be later. His discussions of literary form have achieved the status of classics within the tradition of literary FORMALISM. Even here, however, B.'s is a formalism with a difference. Rather than focusing on the work of literature as an autonomous object and defining form as essentially the system of relationships internal to that object, in the manner of the New Criticism that would by mid-century have established itself as the dominant version of American literary formalism, B. saw form in more open, dynamic, and human terms; in B.'s famous formulation, "the creation of an appetite in the mind of the auditor and the adequate satisfying of that appetite." Once one concedes that form is consummated in the mind of the auditor, the concept of the literary work as closed autonomous form gives way to the idea of the literary work in vital relation to its readers and their world.

Kenneth Burke

The introduction of the "auditor" into the equation suggests an opening to the sociology of literature, and indeed to still broader sociocultural considerations, that would characterize B.'s later work, although that work would never abandon the interest in the literary work as one of the most significant forms of human action. The difference is that the literary work becomes for B. most importantly one form of human action, specifically of what he comes to call "symbolic action"; B. moves beyond the formalist tendency to valorize what distinguishes literature from the rest of human behavior to an insistence that literature be seen as part of human behavior. The implication for critical method is that the barring from criticism of such "extrinsic" interests as the biographical, the historical, the ethical, the political—a negative strategy associated with critical formalism and especially, in the U.S., with the New Criticism—constitutes in B.'s view an unacceptable narrowing of the critical act, which, for B., has as its "main ideal. . . to use all that is there to use."

The exploration of symbolic action in all its implications that is a principal motif of B.'s work in the 1930s broadens in the 1940s and 1950s toward the development of a full-fledged system, the "dramatism" whose exposition is the burden of two of B.'s most impressive and important books, *A Grammar of Motives* (1945) and *A Rhetoric of Motives* (1950). These were originally intended to form the first and second volumes of a trilogy, but the third, B.'s "Symbolic of Motives," never appeared, even though B. apparently completed, and published in the form of articles, virtually all of the materials that would have made it up. Critics differ on the issue of whether dramatism, which aspires to nothing less than the study of the full range of human relations through the analogy of drama, is the fully achieved and coherent synthesis that B. was apparently aiming for, but at the very least the effort generated more insights, more revelations, and more intellectual provocations than most critics produce in a lifetime. In *A Grammar of Motives* the concept of the Pentad (Scene, Act, Agent, Agency, Purpose) as an instrument for the analysis of motives provides a point of departure for an intellectual display that is at once dazzling, playful, and deeply serious, as B. manages to bring the entire history of philosophy under the umbrella of his five terms. In *A Rhetoric of Motives*, the daring subsumption of poetry under the heading of rhetoric (in the context of the 1950s, a case of flagrant critical heresy), and the radical exploration of rhetoric and its workings that such an act entails, exhilarates as it disorients and, finally, illuminates by providing one of the "perspectives by incongruity" characteristic of B.'s contributions to modern social thought, contributions whose declared overriding aim is the "purification of war."

All the while that he was engaged in system building and in applying his system to interests that ranged far beyond the "literary" in the narrow sense, B. remained a perceptive and illuminating reader of texts. He differed from the New Critics, who were during the same period establishing an orthodox notion of "close reading," in that B.'s readings of individual texts were exercises in an evolving critical method and were offered in part as examples of that method in action. A consequence is that B. in his practical criticism is never concerned exclusively with the uniqueness of the work before him, although he certainly would not deny that uniqueness; a passion to classify is always involved as well.

Dramatism is deeply concerned with language and with the function of linguistic forms, including literary forms, within society at large. In the 1960s, B.'s work, while never abandoning any of its earlier attitudes, begins to place a greater emphasis on language as such, with a corresponding reduction of the interest in the tensions between verbal acts and the nonverbal scenes of those acts that mark the great works of dramatism. He begins to place increased stress on the ways in which "non-verbal" reality may be regarded as in fact determined by the verbal. B. gives this new emphasis the name of "logology," and in *The Rhetoric of Religion: Studies in Logology* (1961) B., whose work has more than once been described in terms of a secularized Christianity, explores the relations of logology and theology, considering such matters as the likeness between words about words (one way of defining "logology") and words about The Word (one way of defining "theology").

At his best, B. throughout his career, both by precept and by example, has suggested ways beyond the destructive dichotomies of criticism. He has shown us that a sensitivity to literary form can coexist with, indeed is essential to, an understanding of the social functions of literature. And he has shown us that an adequate understanding of society requires that we "read" society with the sensitivity a fine critic brings to a literary text. We are also beginning to appreciate the degree to which he anticipated the interests and insights of STRUCTURALISM and DECONSTRUCTION years before either of those terms had become current; indeed dramatism and logology may be regarded as rivals of those two intellectual movements. Much of B.'s placing of literature within its sociocultural context, including the relation of literature to the dynamics of power, seems to foreshadow the concerns of the new HISTORICISM as well. And recent commentators have noted further that the B. who so eloquently and ingeniously developed the

definition of form in terms of the appetites of the auditor quoted above, was a reader-response critic before we knew the name for it; it is not clear that we have had a better one. Given the scope of B.'s interests, and the intensity of thought and imagination he has brought to those interests, we classify B. as a critic simply for want of a better word.

FURTHER WORKS: *The White Oxen and Other Stories* (1924); *Towards a Better Life: Being a Series of Epistles or Declamations* (1932); *Permanence and Change: An Anatomy of Purpose* (1935); *Attitudes toward History* (1937); *The Philosophy of Literary Form: Studies in Symbolic Action* (1941); *Book of Moments: Poems 1915–1954* (1955); *Perspectives by Incongruity* (1964); *Terms for Order* (1964); *Language As Symbolic Action: Essays on Life, Literature, and Method* (1966); *Collected Poems 1915–1967;* (1968); *The Complete White Oxen: Collected Short Fiction of K. B.* (1968); *Dramatism and Development* (1972); *Selected Correspondence of K. B. and Malcolm Cowley* (1988)

BIBLIOGRAPHY: Parkes, H. B., *The Pragmatic Test: Essays on the History of Ideas* (1941): 202–20; Duffey, B., "Reality as Language: K. B.'s Theory of Poetry," *WR*, 12 (1948): 132–45; Hyman, S. E., *The Armed Vision: A Study in the Methods of Modern Literary Criticism* (1948): 347–94; Knox, G. A., *Critical Moments: K. B.'s Categories and Critiques* (1957); Frank, A. P., *K. B.* (1969); Rueckert, W. H., ed., *Critical Responses to K. B.* (1969); Booth, W. C., *Critical Understanding: The Powers and Limits of Pluralism* (1979): 99–137; Hartman, G. H., *Criticism in the Wilderness: The Study of Literature Today* (1980): 86–114; Kimberling, C. R., *K. B.'s Dramatism and Popular Arts* (1982); Rueckert, W. H., *K. B. and the Drama of Human Relations*, 2nd ed. (1982); White, H., and Brose, M., eds., *Representing K. B.* (1982); Lentricchia, F., *Criticism and Social Change* (1983); Heath, R. L., *Realism and Relativism: A Perspective on K. B.* (1986); Henderson, G. E., *K. B.: Literature and Language As Symbolic Action* (1988); Simons, H., and Melia, T., eds., *The Legacy of K. B.* (1989)

—W. P. KENNEY

BURKINABÈ LITERATURE

The rich and vibrant cultural scene in the West African nation of Burkina Faso presents a wide variety of literary forms and styles. Oral performance genres dominate this scene. Since over sixty languages are spoken within Burkina's borders, each with its own literary heritage, the concept of a single national literature has been a subject of debate in Burkina Faso, as elsewhere in Francophone Africa. Indeed, the current borders are relatively new, as this area was colonized in the 1890s by France. From 1904 to 1919 the area was part of the colony of Upper Senegal-Niger; in 1919 the area became part of French West Africa, only to be dissolved and partitioned between the colonies of Côte d'Ivoire, Niger, and French Soudan (now Mali) in 1932. The colony was reconstituted in 1947 as Upper Volta, and gained independence in 1960 as Upper Volta. It was renamed Burkina Faso in 1984 after one of a series of military coups. This history has clearly made it difficult to create a united national culture. However, the many multiethnic troupes now make it a point to offer a mosaic of performance genres and languages onstage, and a Burkinabè literature in French has emerged since the 1960s.

Although the first French schools were established in the 1920s, the colony produced intellectual figures who wrote in French quite early in its history; Dim Delobsom (dates n.a.), for instance, produced two studies of Mossi culture and history in the 1930s. However, the first truly literary production in French, Nazi Boni's (1912-1969) novel *Crépuscule des temps anciens* (Twilight of the Former Ages), was published in 1962 in Paris by Présence Africaine, the most important publishing house specializing in African literatures at the time. Focused on precolonial life in western Burkina Faso, the novel presents three centuries of Bwamu history. Rather than presenting the precolonial period as a static idyll, Boni details the conflicts and rivalries that weakened the community and facilitated the French conquest. Boni's passionate interest in tradition and the precolonial past has continued to influence Burkinabè letters.

This influence is most noticeable in contemporary poetry. Through his many volumes of poetry, as well as in his essays on oral traditions, Frédéric Pacéré Titinga (dates n.a.) has established the continuity between oral and written literatures, or "littérature culturelle d'Afrique" (cultural literature of Africa), in his terms. *Refrains sous le Sahel* (1976; Refrains of the Sahel), *Ça tire sous le Sahel* (1976; It's Over in the Sahel), *Quand s'envolent les grues couronnées* (1976; When the Crowned Cranes Fly Away), *Poèmes pour l'Angola* (1982; Poems for Angola), *La poésie des griots* (1982; The Poetry of the Griots), and *Du lait pour une tombe* (1984; Some Mild for a Tomb) have made Titinga the major Burkinabè poet writing in French. In his essays on "bendrology," he theorizes a specifically African esthetic based on the drum language that has its own literature, and extends this esthetic to written literatures. Titinga has also established the Titinga Foundation for the study of "cultural literatures" in Ouagadougou, the capital. Although his poetry constantly refers to oral tradition, this does not mean that Titinga ignores current problems; his poetry has a clear social and political vision.

Social commitment and engagement define the developments in postcolonial Burkinabè theater as well. The promotion of theater for development projects has made it possible for those involved in theater to build institutions such as the Théâtre de la Fraternité, the Atelier Théâtre Burkinabè, and other groups. UNESCO has funded some publications, while other nongovernmental organizations have also shown a strong interest in theater for development and adult education. In addition, television and radio programs frequently include plays, as do the programs of the various cultural festivals. Most towns and bigger cities can boast of several semi-professional theater troupes. Theater is extremely popular; moreover, it reaches a wider audience than novels or written poetry, for literacy rates in Burkina Faso do not exceed 10 percent of the population.

In spite of this factor, the novel has become the most popular written literary form in Burkina Faso. The two major novelists, Pierre Claver Ilboudo and Patrick Ilboudo (dates n.a.), have each produced several novels. Most Burkinabè novels focus on social problems. In *Dessein contraire* (1967; Contrary Purpose), Roger Nikiema (dates n.a.) describes the difficulties of rural youth who rebel against the older generation's tight control of their marital and professional choices, and choose to leave the village for the city. The themes of rural exodus and the difficulties of unemployed youth in the city are the major concerns of Augustin-Sondé Coulibaly (b. 1933) in *Les dieux délinquants* (1974; The Delinquent Gods), Ansomwin Ignace Hien (dates n.a.) in *L'enfer au*

paradis (1986; Hell in Heaven), Pierre Claver Ilboudo in *Adama, ou la force des choses* (1987; Adama, or the Strength of Circumstances) and several other novelists. Many novelists also write about the problems that migrant laborers face in Côte d'Ivoire, where Burkinabè youth dominate the lower end of the labor market. Kollin Noaga's (b. 1944) novel *Le retour au village* (1978; The Return to the Village) and several others have described the difficult labor conditions and the problems that such migrants face. Women's issues have also begun to catch the attention of Burkinabè writers. Patrick Ilboudo's 1988 novel, *Les carnets secrets d'une fille de joie* (1988; The Secret Notebooks of a Prostitute) presents a prostitute's fictional confessions. Mathias Kyelem's (dates n.a.) novel *L'épine de la rose* (1996; The Thorn of the Rose), which received the 1996 President's Grand Prize for Literature, deals with teenage pregnancy and unplanned pregnancies.

Although men clearly dominate the literary scene, several women writers have started to make an impact. Monique Ilboudo's (dates n.a.) novel *Le mal de peau* (1992; Skin Pain) was well received, and has already received international critical attention. Bernadette Dao's (dates n.a.) collection of poetry entitled *Parturition* (1986; Parturition) received that year's National Grand Prize for Arts and Letters, and Pierrette Sandra Kanzié (dates n.a.) published her collection of poems, *Des tombes qui pleurent* (Tombs that Weep), the following year. Several other women have been represented in the various anthologies published in conjunction with festivals such as the Semaine de la Culture (Cultural Week) that takes place in Bobo-Dioulasso on a biannual basis.

Oral artists—folktale raconteurs, epic singers, praisesingers, and other oral poets—in addition to the remarkable traditions of masquerade and mystery plays still play an important role in the religious and cultural life of many Burkinabè. In addition, the development of film and film studios continues to play an important role in Burkina Faso.

BIBLIOGRAPHY: Kom, A., ed., *Dictionnaire des oeuvres littéraires de langue française en Afrique au Sud du Sahara* (1996); Zimmer, W., *Répertoire du théâtre burkinabè* (1992); special Burkina Faso issue, *Notre Librairie*, 101 (1990)

—LISA MCNEE

BURMESE LITERATURE

In classical Burmese literature imaginative works, including drama, were written in verse, while prose was used for historical chronicles, didactic works and, by the late 18th c., for translations of the jataka, the richly varied stories of the previous lives of the Buddha that were the main source of inspiration for Burmese art and literature until the beginning of the 20th c. The natural development from a poetic court literature to popular prose fiction that would have followed soon after the establishment of Burmese-owned printing presses in the 1870s was delayed by the arrival of English as the language of government (and thus of social and educational advancement).

The earliest form of popular printed literature, from 1875 onward, was short verse plays, complete with songs; the first novel, *Maung Yin Maung Ma Me Ma* (Maung Yin Maung and Ma Me Ma), by James Hla Gyaw (1886–1920), a government translator, did not appear until 1904. The author was inspired by the memorable escape episode in *The Count of Monte Cristo* to write this totally nontraditional work—a love and adventure story—in Burmese. Other novels soon followed but, true to the tradition of prose writing, tended to contain much useful knowledge, ornate language, and short sermons, as well as poems and songs. The most famous early novel, *Shwei-pyi-zo* (1914; ruler of the golden land), by U Lat (1866–1921), has all these features together with the earliest portrayal of disillusion with the West caused by young men educated abroad returning home and rejecting traditional Burmese Buddhist values.

The development of the true modern novel, followed by the short story, is closely linked to the emergence of weekly literary magazines. Among their regular contributors were two writers who were largely responsible for abandoning traditional palace tales and introducing modern stories about contemporary people to the reading public: P. Mo-nin (1883–1940) and Shwei U-daung (1899–1973). The former, the father of simple modern Burmese prose, was a journalist and novelist who encouraged Burmans to think for themselves and to break with tradition; the latter, through a great number of masterly adaptations and translations, familiarized the Burmese reader with many of the favorite works of Western literature. Shwei U-daung's autobiography, *Bawa ta-thet-ta hmat-tan-hnin atwei-ahkaw-mya* (1962; notes and thoughts of a lifetime), is a major document in the history of Burmese literature.

During the 1920s, at the same time that short stories and novels, often inspired by Victorian fiction, were spreading new attitudes toward personal and family relationships, a new feeling of national consciousness, of pride in their traditional Buddhist culture, was awakening in the country. This feeling was strengthened by the first historical novels, about two great kings of Burma—*Nat-shin-naung* (1919; Nat-shin-naung) and *Tabin-Shwei-hti* (1925; Tabin-shwei-hti) by U Maung Gyi (1879—1949)—and more especially by the brilliant satirical verses of the great patriot and writer THAHKIN KO-DAW HMAING. No less a patriot in her own way was Burma's first important woman writer, Dagon Hkin Hkin Lei (b. 1904), granddaughter of a minister from the Mandalay court. During the 1920s and 1930s she wrote stories and novels; one in particular shows the hard life of the ordinary peasant: *Mein-ma bawa* (1931; a woman's life); this was followed by stirring historical novels such as *Shwei-sun-nyo* (1933; Shwei-sun-nyo) and *Sa-hso-daw* (1935; court poet).

The 1930s brought demands for independence from Britain, concern for the status of the Burmese language, and a new interest in the style and content of literature—especially evident in the works of the "Testing the Age" group. One member was U Sein Tin (1899–1942), who wrote of small-town and village life exactly as he experienced it working as a district officer in *Hkit-san pon-byin* (1934, 1938; experimental tales), a type of semi-fictional sketch copied by many writers then and after the war, notably Maung Htin (b. 1909), in *Ko Daung* (1946; Ko Daung) and *Myo-ok pon-byin* (1976; tales of a township officer); and Man Tin (b. 1915), in *Ko Hpolon* (1956; Ko Hpo-lon) and *Myo-baing Maung Pyon Cho* (1968; Township Officer Maung Pyon Cho). Zaw-gyi (pseud. of U Thein Han, b. 1908), a "Testing the Age" writer and Burma's leading literary historian and critic, experimented with translations of drama, short stories, and new freer verse forms; his cycle of poems *Bei-da lan* (1963; the hyacinth's way) is an outstanding work that traces a person's journey through life.

Major novels written between 1930 and 1945, reflecting the growing desire for independence, had a strong ideological content:

characters more often stood for causes, plots were allegories showing the oppressed rising against the oppressor. Representative are the works of Maha Hswei (1900–1953), such as *Do mei mei* (1934; our mother) and *Thabongyi* (1934; the rebel). Authors wrote of the particular Burmese condition, not of the larger human predicament.

Little could be published between 1942 and 1946, but as soon as the war was over writing and publishing burst forth in many forms, seeking new sources of inspiration in Soviet as well as English and American literature. Numerous literary magazines were started—vital channels for the country's literary lifeblood, since they carry all first printings of novels and short stories. The two most important have been *Shu-mawa* and *Mya-wadi* (the latter government-controlled since 1964).

Naturally, many authors wrote of their wartime experiences, such as Min Shin (b. 1929), in a collection of stories *Tahka-don-ga do yebaw* (1963; our comrade once). In addition, a dominant theme now became Burma's age-long struggle for independent nationhood: Min Kyaw's (b. 1933) *Pagan-tha* (1963; son of Pagan) is set at a critical moment in history when the Mongol hordes threatened the capital in the 13th c.; *Myan-ma-tha* (1966; son of Burma) by Yan-gon Ba Hswei (b. 1925) describes resistance to the British colonization. In contrast to earlier historical novels, the hero is a peasant, not a king.

An important development in serious fiction after the war was the increase in closely observed, realistic portrayals of all aspects of life and of all classes of people. A model of this genre was Maung Htin's *NgaBa* (1947; NgaBa), a moving account of the appalling sufferings of a simple peasant during the Japanese occupation. Aung Lin (b. 1928) often shows us the poor peasant struggling to make a living in the town, for example as a sidecar peddler in the company of bus drivers and prostitutes in *Pyit-daing htaung* (1958; never say die), while the independent-minded woman writer Hkin Hnin Yu (b. 1925) takes pagoda slaves—still social outcasts in Burma—as the subject of *Hmyaw-lin-lo-hpyin mahson-hnaing-de* (1958; hope never ends). Among many works describing the lives of prisoners, those of Lu-du U Hla (b. 1910) are memorable, especially *A-lon kaung-gya-ye-la* (1961; are you all all right).

Many writers felt that, having been at the forefront of the fight for independence, they should now lead the struggle to establish a new, equitable socialist society. Especially after the military regime enunciated the "Burmese Way to Socialism" policy in 1962, authors were under great pressure to produce works of SOCIALIST REALISM, preferably showing workers and peasants coping with and overcoming their hard lot. Maung Tha-ya (b. 1931), popular author of many sophisticated novels about the urban elite, showed that he was versatile enough to respond to this summons by working as, and then writing a very perceptive work about, a Rangoon taxi driver, *Mat-tat yat-lo lan-hma ngo* (1969; stood in the road and wept).

However, only when this detailed, often critical observation is combined with successful character drawing, as for example in the prize-winning novel *Mon-ywei mahu* (1955; not out of hate) by the leading woman writer, Gyane-gyaw Ma Ma Lei (b. 1917), do we see modern Burmese fiction at its best. This novel shows the suffering of an intelligent young woman of traditional upbringing who falls in love with and marries a Westernized Burman who has lost all sympathy and understanding for the things she cherishes. Perhaps the most influential writer and novelist of the last thirty years is THEIN HPEI MYINT, whose works, such as *Ashei-ga nei-wun htwet-thipama* (1958; as surely as the sun rises in the east), set against the background of the nationalist movement, successfully combine well-drawn characters, a strong plot, and love interest with immediate relevance to issues facing Burmese society.

Although theatrical shows are immensely popular, written drama does not flourish in Burma today. Poetry, on the other hand, is everyone's pastime and pleasure. Established favorites are the poets Nu Yin (b. 1916), Tin Mo (b. 1939), and Daung Nwe Hswei (b. 1931). But by far the most widely written and widely read genre is the short story (about a thousand are produced each year), and in this field it is the humorous, mocking, utterly honest Thaw-da HSWEI who more than any other speaks for and to his fellow citizens.

Uncertainty about what works will be approved for publication after compulsory review by the government's Press Scrutiny Committee has led, in the 1970s, to a decline in the quality of original works and a proliferation of adapted thrillers, romances, and comic books, a state of affairs deplored by serious writers.

BIBLIOGRAPHY: On Pe, "Modern Burmese Literture," in *Perspective of Burma, Atlantic Monthly Supplement* (1958): 56–60; Minn Latt, "Mainstreams in Burmese Literature," *New Orient-Bimonthly*, 2, 6 (1961): 172-75; 3, 6 (1962): 172–76; Bernot, D., "Quelques tendances actuelles de la littérature birmane," *Revue de l'École National des Langues Orientales*, 1 (1964): 159–78; Hla Pe, "The Rise of Popular Literature in Burma," *JBRS*, 51, 2 (1968): 125–44; Bernot, D., "Littérature birmane contemporaine," in Lafont, P. B. and D. Lombard, D., eds., *Littératures contemporaines de l'Asie du Sud-est* (1974): 9–17; Allott, A. J., "Prose Writing and Publishing in Burma," in Tham Seong Chee, ed., *Literature and Society in Southeast Asia* (1981): 1–35

—ANNA J. ALLOTT

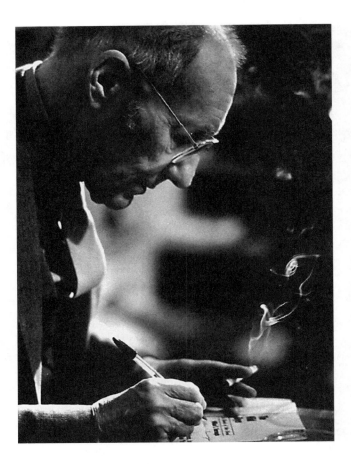

William S. Burroughs

BURROUGHS, William S.

American novelist, essayist, short-story writer, and poet, b. 2 Feb. 1914, St. Louis, Mo.; d. 2 Aug. 1997, Lawrence, Kans.

B.'s life and writings stand in refutation of his auspicious origins. His mother was a direct descendant of Robert E. Lee, his grandfather the inventor of the Burroughs adding machine. After his graduation from Harvard, a generous trust fund allowed B. to travel in Europe, where he studied medicine for a year in Venice. His decline from "respectability" began with a psychological discharge from the army and continued through activities involving homosexuality, drug addiction, and association with the criminal underworld. The final rupture from his elitist past occurred in 1951, when B. accidentally shot and killed the woman with whom he had lived since 1943. This event precipitated years of expatriation, in Tangier, where he lived for a time in a male brothel; in South America, where he went in search of the drug *yage*, the notorious "final fix"; in Paris, where he completed *Naked Lunch* (1959, also pub. as *Naked Lunch*, 1962); and in London, where he was cured of his drug addiction and where he finally settled.

B. first gained attention as a member of the so-called Beat Generation of writers that also included Allen GINSBERG and Jack KEROUAC. The self-consciously liberated life style of this group, which included unrestrained indulgence in sex and drugs, figures in much of B.'s fiction, a fact that accounts for its early notoriety. But it is the influential formal inventiveness of his fiction, not its sensational subject matter, on which rests B.'s reputation.

Full comprehension of B.'s difficult novels requires an understanding of what he has called a new mythology for the space age. This mythology is most clearly formulated in the tetralogy that includes *Naked Lunch, The Soft Machine* (1961), *The Ticket That Exploded* (1962), and *Nova Express* (1964). Cumulatively, these novels warn against the "Control Machine": those forces of homogeneity and conformity that would destroy the unique qualities of the individual. The exact nature of these forces varies from novel to novel. In *Naked Lunch* they include capitalism, the police, the Mob, and the military; in *Nova Express* and *The Ticket That Exploded* they are agents from other galaxies and a virus from Venus. Feeding on human need, these forces—like drugs—enter the human body through points B. calls "coordinates," dissolving all distinctively human characteristics and, like the insidious Liquifactionists of *Naked Lunch*, merging everyone into "One Man."

B.'s paranoid distrust of all control and pattern leads to the formal discontinuities of the tetralogy. Lacking linearity or consistent narrative presence, the books cut from incident to incident with no apparent centrality of purpose. Indeed, B. insists that *Naked Lunch* is composed in such a fashion that the reader may enter it arbitrarily at any point. B.'s aesthetic of randomness is most evident in the final three books of the tetralogy, as B. employs the "cut-up" and "fold-in" methods learned from the painter Brion Gysin. B. cuts passages from newspapers and literary works, then juxtaposes them on the page with his own words, or he takes an entire page of his own work and that of another writer, folds each down the middle, and arranges them side-by-side on the same page. The result is a narrative Babel of competing voices, not all of which are B.'s.

Such arbitrary techniques are not without rationale. B.'s architectonics attempt to expand the reader's consciousness beyond the constraints of normal perception. Words, B. believes, determine our perception of reality, and language is in the hands of the Control Machine. By "cutting the word-lines" in his works, thus disturbing conventional language patterns, B. attempts to reduce the conditioning influences of language. Like a Zen master, B. hopes to catapult his reader outside of world and word, literally outside of the body, into the mystical silence of space. His radical rearrangement of conventional verbal stratagems therefore aims at a radical restructuring of human consciousness.

B.'s more recent works continue the themes and images of the tetralogy, but in less radical forms. *The Wild Boys* (1971) involves the successful insurrection of a band of victims against their tormentors, and serves as an allegory for the revolution in consciousness B. seeks. *Exterminator!* (1973) is a series of sketches in which literal events, such as the 1968 Democratic convention in Chicago, are mixed with bizarre fantasies. In an attempt to gain a greater sense of immediacy, B. turns in later works such as *The Last Words of Dutch Schultz* (1975) and *Blade Runner (A Movie)* (1979) to the explicit use of cinematic form and techniques implicit in the earlier works.

Although B. remains a controversial figure, whose obsession with a violent, drug- and sex-infested world offends many, he has come increasingly to be viewed as an important innovator whose early works prefigure the experimentation of many important postmodernist writers.

FURTHER WORKS: *Junkie: Confessions of an Unredeemed Drug Addict* (under the pseudonym William Lee, 1953); *The Exterminator* (1960, with Brion Gysin); *Dead Fingers Talk* (1963); *Takis* (1963); *The Yage Letters* (1963, with Allen Ginsberg); *Time* (1965, with B. G.); *So Who Owns Death TV?* (1967, with C. Pelieu and C. Weissner); *The Dead Star* (1969); *The Book of Breething* (1975); *Cobble Stone Gardens* (1976); *The Third Mind* (1978, with B. G.); *Cities of the Red Night* (1981)

BIBLIOGRAPHY: Hassan, I., "The Subtracting Machine: The Work of W. B.," *Crit*, 6 (1963): 4–23; Knickerbocker, C., "W. B.," in *Writers at Work: The Paris Review Interviews*, 3rd series (1967): 143–73; McConnell, F. D., "W. B. and the Literature of Addiction," *MR*, 8 (1967): 665–80; Odier, D., *The Job*, interviews with B. (1969); DeLoach, A., ed., special B. issue, *Intrepid*, Nos. 14–15 (1969–70); Tanner, T., *City of Words* (1971): 109–40; Nelson, C., *The Incarnate Word* (1973): 208–29; Vernon, J., *The Garden and the Map* (1973): 85–109; Oxenhandler, N., "Listening to B.'s Voice," in Federman, R., ed., *Surfiction* (1975): 85–109; Tytell, J., *Naked Angles* (1976): 36–51, 111–39

—CHARLES B. HARRIS

BURYAT LITERATURE

As Russian explorers, traders, and clergy made their way eastward across Siberia in the early 1600s, they encountered the Buryats, a set of Mongolian tribes living on both sides of Lake Baikal north of Outer Mongolia, and closely related to the Kalkha-Mongols south of them in the present-day Mongolian People's Republic. As Russian cities in the Buryat country grew it became possible for young Buryats to receive an education. One leading Buryat intellectual was Tsyben Z. Zhamtsarano (1880–c. 1940), a translator, educator, folklorist, political leader, and publisher, active in the autonomous period of the newly independent Outer Mongolia.

Native literary tradition centered on tales, legends, and heroic epics, or *üligers*, all orally transmitted. The Buryats made use of literary Mongolian written in a vertical script common to all Mongols, but this literature dealt almost exclusively with Lamaist Buddhism deriving from Tibetan-Indian forebears, although some historical documents were also recorded. Some Russian scholars transcribed quantities of Buryat folklore and epics in the last decades of the 19th c., but even at that time they felt that the old culture was fast disappearing.

The acme of Buryat literary creativity is surely the medieval *Geser*, a long, versified, oral epic tale about the hero Geser's adventures with his stalwarts, his beautiful wives, fabulous palaces, his clever horse, and his battles against the *mangus*, or many-headed monster, of Mongolian folklore.

After the Russian Revolution and a long period of warfare between Whites and Reds that raged through Siberia, Mongolia, and the Buryat country, the government was stabilized and consolidated its power. Consequently, Buryat literature was put on the path of SOCIALIST REALISM when it began to employ new literary forms like the novel.

One of the first Buryat writers of this new age was Khotsa Namsaraev (1889–1959), who wrote of the struggle of the new revolutionary order with the remnants of the old order. In the 1930s a group of talented prose writers and poets emerged as the victories of socialism opened a new era, and themes grew wider and richer. During World War II Buryat writers called the people to tasks of labor and patriotism; in the postwar period Party decisions dictated both ideological and artistic development. Zhamso Tumunov's (1916–1955) *Noirhoo serheng tal* (1949; the valley that awakened from slumber) is a novel dealing with the struggle of Trans-Baikalian workers in the period of the civil war and foreign intervention. A novel by Namsaraev, *Uürei tolon* (1950; in the morning dawn), depicts the severe prerevolutionary life of the Buryats, their fight for freedom, the aid of the Russian proletariat, and the guiding direction of the Communist Party.

Today there is an active Union of Buryat Writers, whose literary journal publishes stories, poems, and plays. But the days, and long nights, when Buryat bards recited heroic epics under the sky, and chanted the lays of their traditional heroes, while not completely forgotten or unappreciated, belong to a lost past.

BIBLIOGRAPHY: Curtin, J., *A Journey in Southern Siberia* (1909): 92–310; Rudnev, A., "A Buriat Epic, Kha-Oshir, Son of Khan-Bugdur Khan," *MSFO*, 52 (1924): 238–49; Shoolbraid, H. G. H., *The Oral Epic of Siberia and Central Asia* (1975), passim; Poppe, N., *The Language and Collective Farm Poetry of the Buriat Mongols of the Selenga Region, Asiatische Forschungen*, Vol. 55 (1978)

—JOHN R. KRUEGER

BUTAZZONI, Fernando

Uruguayan novelist and journalist, b. 20 Mar. 1953, Montevideo

B. was reared in Montevideo where he completed his secondary education. After graduating from high school, he started working with independent theater groups, but his acting career ended quite abruptly when, in 1972, given the tense political situation, he decided to leave the country. Shortly after, the military staged a senseless coup, and ruled for twelve years. B. went first to Argentina and then to Chile. However, in light of the events that led to the death of President Salvador Allende and the brutal takeover by the forces lead by General Augusto Pinochet, B. sought exile in Cuba, where he stayed for quite some time. He started writing in 1978, and within a year had completed a collection of short stories that he decided to submit to the annual competition of *Casa de las Américas*. B. won the coveted prize with *Los días de nuestra sangre* (1979; Days of Our Blood), which was published by *Casa de las Américas*. Soon after, in April 1979, B. decided to become a freelance journalist and traveled to Nicaragua as a war correspondent, to report on the final stages of the Sandinista revolution that ended with the victory of the FSLN (Sandinista Front for National Liberation). His chronicles were eventually published in Sweden under the title *Con el ejército de Sandino* (1983; With Sandino's Army), and a few years after, also published in Montevideo with a different title: *Nicaragua; noticias de la guerra* (1986; Nicaragua; News of the War).

The Nicaraguan experience prompted B. to write poetry, and his text—still unpublished—*De la noche y la fiesta* (About the Night and the Celebration) obtained an honorable mention in the Rubén Darío poetry contest. In 1979 several of B.'s poems were published in the magazine *Nicarahuac*. Back to Cuba shortly after that, B. started working on his first novel. This text, *La noche abierta* (1982; The Open Night), was awarded the first prize for Latin-American narrative by the Costa Rican publishing house EDUCA. The jury indicated that "the author demonstrates an ample command of current narrative techniques, adding to that great creativity, an excellent command of his language and a vibrant sensitivity."

Through Mario BENEDETTI's mediation, B. started working at the Center for Literary Research of *Casa de las Américas*, and eventually became editor of their prestigious journal. In 1983, however, B. decided to leave Cuba and landed in Sweden where he worked as a freelance journalist. There, he wrote *El tigre y la nieve* (1986; The Tiger and the Snow), an intense novel about a young Uruguayan woman caught in Buenos Aires during the "Dirty War" period, when both the Uruguayan and Argentine military juntas worked in close cooperation. Based on a true story, *El tigre y la nieve* is a moving document that transcends its anecdote, and becomes a powerful allegation for human rights.

In 1985, when democracy was restored in his native land, B. promptly returned to Montevideo and started working for *Brecha*, a prestigious weekly publication, where he was in charge of the literary section. Later on, he was hired by the daily paper *La República* as senior editor, and in spite of a strenuous schedule he managed to finish another novel, *La danza de los perdidos* (1988; The Dance of the Lost Ones), a thriller that soon became a bestseller in Montevideo. Active as a freelance reporter for several international publications, B. did not publish any fiction for a while. He was hard at work, however, in the research for a veritable tour de force, that would not come out until 1993. A thoroughly documented historical novel about a hired killer who worked for such political giants as Mitre and Sarmiento, *El príncipe de la muerte* (The Prince of Death) shows B. at his very best. Now a writer at his creative peak, a superb craftsman with a commanding sense of style, he generates a dense text—long sentences, rare tense combinations, an abundance of adjectives, intense images—and seems to bask in the creation of what might be rather intricate prose for some readers. The result was perhaps B's most powerful text, and one with a rather unusual destiny. Although the original edition exhausted several reprintings, its small publishing house could not quite sustain the standard now set by both the text and its author. The edition was modest, and its distribution was somewhat inadequate, but the book was very much in demand. Eventually, B. took the unusual step of revising the text, clarifying certain particularly obscure passages, making some sections a bit more fluid, and published it once again, this time in Buenos Aires with Seix Barral and a slightly modified title, *Príncipe de la muerte* (1997; Prince of Death).

Perhaps due to his vast experience as a journalist, B. prefers to write fiction based upon real life and characters. Thus far, most of his works have been based upon well-documented materials. Yet, in most, if not all of them, the rigorous investigation of facts is not intended to construct a documentary text. No exception to that is his novel, *La noche en que Gardel lloró en mi alcoba* (1996; The Night Gardel Cried in My Room), a poetic text based upon the life of the greatest Tango singer of all times, yet quite effective in casting some doubts on the verity of certain common perceptions about such an incredibly popular figure—a true myth for many Latin Americans.

The epigraph to *El príncipe de la muerte* is a statement by José SARAMAGO: "Todo es ficción" (Everything Is Fiction), which seems to summarize quite aptly this writer's conception of his work. Sylvia Lago (b. 1932) has written about one of B.'s texts that "passionately searching for the truth [the novel] offers an original, profoundly poetic, version of contemporary reality and its violence," a statement that can likewise be made about all of B.'s works to date.

FURTHER WORKS: *Los ensayos del Orobón* (1997); *Mendoza miente* (1998)

BIBLIOGRAPHY: Lago, S., "Poesía y verdad de un texto violento," *Brecha*, 5 Sept. 1986: 30; Larre Borges, A., "De cuchillo y capote," *Brecha*, 8 Oct. 1993: 20-21; Achugar, H., "*El príncipe de la muerte* de F. B. y el esplendor de la escritura," *La República*, 8 Dec. 1993: 35; Xaubet, H., "Literatura en el exilio/exilio en la literatura: *La noche abierta* de F. B.," *Graffiti*, 7 (Dec. 1996): 52-56; Escanlar, G., "Instrucciones para construir a Gardel," *Tres*, 22 Mar. 1996: 32; Rocca, P., "La noche en que Gardel lloró en mi alcoba," *El País Cultural*, 20 June 1996: 14

—HORACIO XAUBET

BUTOR, Michel

French novelist, critic, poet, and dramatist, b. 14 Sept. 1926, Mons-en-Baroeul

Raised and educated in Paris, B. received advanced degrees in philosophy and literature. He has taught in Egypt, England, Greece,

Switzerland, and the U.S. and in France at the universities of Paris-Vincennes and Nice. Currently he is "professeur extraordinaire" at the University of Geneva.

B. came to the fore in the late 1950s, together with ROBBE-GRILLET, SARRAUTE, SIMON, and other writers who were published by the Éditions de Minuit and who were known collectively as the NEW NOVELISTS. As did the others in the group, at that time he refused to follow traditional concepts of plot and characterization and thus began his systematic exploration/description of the networks of relationships that make up our perception of the world, an exploration that has continued until this time and that has involved B. in collaborations with other artists, in experiments in structure and typography, and a total rejection of any concept of genre.

By tradition B. has been spoken of as novelist, poet, critic, dramatist, and experimental writer, but this is not satisfactory, for in his hands each of these categories spills over into the next. The distinctions they draw are not those that matter in his growing body of work. It would perhaps be better to think of B. as "notre Faust," defining Faust as an explorer of the universe and a famous teacher, for his work is voluntarily didactic and operates on all the planes of a good education; it requires the reader to attend to what he is being told, to make an active attempt to follow instructions in the manipulation of the material at hand, to utilize the resources of the outside world in his study, and finally to take what he has achieved out into his daily life.

If we take the above step by step, we find that *Passage de Milan* (1954; Milan passage, or, the passage of the kite [a play on words]), his first novel, offers a formalized description of society in its elemental context—history, time, and perpetual modification. In the second one, *L'emploi du temps* (1956; *Passing Time*, 1960), the protagonist realizes that he must understand his own past and the past of his environment in order to survive. We, the readers, watch him use books, buildings, and works of art to interpret his position and so get our first demonstration of the fact that art, architecture, literature can apply directly to modern life, and hence our first introduction to non-verbal language. The experience is developed in *La modification* (1957; also pub. as *Several Thoughts*, 1958, *A Change of Heart*, 1959) because this time existing sites, monuments, books, artworks, myths, and history are used and we can apply any knowledge we may have of them to our understanding of the hero—or, conversely, go out and discover Rome and Paris after reading B.'s novel. Either way, we are exploring further the realm of living symbols.

The next three books, which were published simultaneously, consolidate this attempt to adjust the reader's perception of his world: *Le génie du lieu* (1958; *The Spirit of Mediterranean Places*, 1986), *Degrés* (1960; *Degrees*, 1961), and *Répertoire I* (1960; *Inventory*, 1968—this is a selection from both *Répertoire I* and *II*). The essays in *Répertoire I*, although apparently diverse pieces of literary criticism, in fact are arranged in such a way as to provide a guide to the development of symbolic expression. Meanwhile, *Le génie du lieu* supplies a parallel key, this time to the external world, its language, and B.'s reading of it.

Degrés is a link between *Le génie du lieu* and *Répertoire I* because it is concerned with the level of experience of the author of each of them and also with that of the reader. Vernier (the first narrator) is a teacher of history and geography, Jouret (the final narrator) of literature; the central section of the book is supposedly written by Eller, their pupil. This demonstration of the learning process is, of course, important to the didactic element in the work

because we see both Eller and Jouret using the school texts to designate their attitude to the situation they are in. But more important still is the global approach to education. *Degrés* makes it clear that the school curriculum was once designed to teach a basic understanding of every aspect of the world. Physics and chemistry taught the makeup of the Earth and its mechanics; biology and geography, its surface; history, the collective development of its inhabitants; literature, the chronicle of individual experience and a possible means of personal expression; art, another means of communication. And through all the information run two major themes: that of personal relations and development, and that of exploration and the excitement of discovery.

Hence, by 1960 the skills B.'s readers must acquire have been shown to them; they are now fully conversant with the varieties of symbolic communication, and have been introduced to the different areas of interest. Since then readers have been invited to continue to exercise their awareness and increase their understanding by means of a series of texts pushing further into the previously established realms.

Encouragement is offered in two texts dealing specifically with the problem of increasing understanding. *Votre Faust* (1962; your Faust), an opera written in collaboration with the Belgian composer Henri Pousseur, stands as a monument to B.'s insatiable thirst for knowledge and also for our entrenchment within the same dilemma. The opera places the audience within the context of the legend by making them participate in the action, bombarding them with fragments of every version of the Faust story ever created, from the old German puppet play to the new version being played out by Henri (the composer) and the Director, and forces them to decide for Henri (Faust) what he must do next. Later, *Portrait de l'artiste en jeune singe* (1967; portrait of the artist as a young monkey), a "novel" that B. calls a "capriccio," forces the reader to follow the young B. through an initiation into learning and sharpened perception.

Other themes are also developed, and fall into five areas of exploration, which together cover most aspects of our life and world. These were laid out clearly in 1969 in the issue of the periodical *L'arc* that bears the title *Michel Butor*, which B. was invited to organize as he saw fit. It consists of short pieces, lists, diagrams, photographs, and so forth by B. and other contributors. He chose to divide the work into five sections called "Arts and Crafts, Sites, Museums, Spectacles," and "Books." Hence, everything rests on craftsmanship—a theme pursued in the series of critical essays called *Répertoire I, II* (1964), *III* (1968), *IV* (1974), in B.'s art and music criticism, and in his works on Montaigne, Baudelaire, and Rabelais. The next stage is the exploration of cultural sites illustrated by the *Génie du lieu* series—*Où: Le génie du lieu II* (1971; where/or: the spirit of the place II) and *Boomerang: Le génie du lieu III* (1978; boomerang)—by *Mobile* (1962; *Mobile*, 1963) and by *6,810,000 litres d'eau par seconde* (1966; *Niagara: A Stereophonic Novel*, 1969)—both descriptions of the U.S.A.—and by *Description de San Marco* (1963; description of St. Mark's). B. also set out to explore individual works of art and the resonances among them, a theme shown clearly by *Illustrations I* (1964; illustrations), *II* (1969), *III* (1973), *IV* (1976)—collections of poems growing out of B.'s reactions to the works of other people—as well as by the discussions of museums in works such as *L'emploi du temps* and *Portrait de l'artiste en jeune singe*. From these three elements of exploration grow the "Spectacles," which for B. are expressions of collective experience—the works in which he collaborates with artists or musicians—*Votre Faust, Dialogue avec 33 variations de Ludwig van Beethoven sur une valse de Diabelli* (1971; dialogue with 33 variations by Ludwig van Beethoven on a waltz by Diabelli); and "Books," which are personal ones, two examples of which indicate the extent of B.'s grasp on the world: *Réseau aérien* (1962; aerial network), a schematic description of the world, and *La rose des vents* (1970; the compass rose), an elaboration of Charles Fourier's (1772–1837) theory of the ages of the universe.

Thus, over the years B. has taught his readers how to organize the world around them so as to be aware of the immense creativity of the human race. His most recent venture is into the psychology of creativity in a series of ironic pseudo-dreams entitled *Matière de rêves: Matière de rêves I* (1975; dream material), *Second sous-sol: Matière de rêves II* (1976; second basement), *Troisième dessous: Matière de rêves III* (1977; third level down), and *Quadruple fond: Matière de rêves IV* (1980; fourth bottom).

In the breadth of his vision B. defies classification. SARTRE was quite right when in 1960 he said that he was the only contemporary writer capable of formulating the problem of totality.

FURTHER WORKS: *Historie extraordinaire* (1962); *Jacques Hérold* (1964); *Essais sur les essais* (1968); *La banlieu de l'aube à l'aurore*, suivi de *Mouvement brownien* (1968); *Les mots dans la peinture* (1969); *Travaux d'approche* (1972); *Les sept femmes de Gilbert le Mauvais* (1972); *Rabelais* (1972, with Denis Hollier); *Intervalle* (1973)

BIBLIOGRAPHY: Albérès, R.-M, *M. B.* (1964); Roudaut, J., *M. B.; ou, Le livre futur* (1964); Roudiez, L., *M. B.* (1965); Charbonnier, G., *Entretiens avec M. B.* (1967); Raillard, G., *M. B.* (1968); Sturrock, J., *The French New Novel* (1969): 104–69; van Rossum-Guyon, F., *Critique du roman* (1970); Spencer, M., *M. B.* (1974); Helbo, A., *M. B.: Vers une littérature du signe* (1975); Waelti-Walters, J., *M. B.* (1977); Special B. issue, *WLT*, 56 (Spring 1982)

—JENNIFER R. WAELTI-WALTERS

Butor's work represents extremely well a tendency which, having come into being slowly throughout the twentieth century, affirmed itself rather brutally in France in the last few years: the tendency to expect that a novel, instead of *describing* reality according to the method of description elaborated in the last three centuries of novel writing, devote itself to *calling into question* (as the poem does today) *our usual way of seeing* reality. At that moment, *the novel is no longer the analysis of the real but the analysis of our way of interpreting the real*, which is not so paradoxical, since modern physics has made the same shift. Nor very confusing either, since reading Butor's first novel, *Passage de Milan*, remains a comfortable, fascinating, and pleasant experience.

R.-M. *Albérès, M. B.* (1964), pp. 8–9

The sudden, total dislocation of the most banal of our perceptions, of the humblest of our attempts at representation (a night, a journey, an hour of class, simple and unified, show themselves to be infinitely complex), proves to us that we have an insufficient idea of the real. If this world seems worrying it is because we panic before the mass of information that is not integrated by our consciousness (*Degrés*), before the appearance of unforeseeable events (*Passages de Milan*), before the decay of our most clearly formulated and best founded intentions (*La modification*). We ourselves are implicated in this: the world and the idea we have of it, the false unity we accord to each. The fantastic is a sign of a deficiency in our understanding. Butor calls into question our ways of representing things, by showing that they are inadequate to take account of the real in its entirety and complexity: *the exploration of different novel forms shows the element of contingency in those we are used to* (*Répertoire I*: "the novel as research"). The novel sets off from a criticism of common knowledge; bringing together Butor's conception and that of the phenomenologists. . . . The world reveals itself to us in the effort that we make to understand it; reality is what we think. We have a variable and extensible knowledge of this fact; if this becomes closed, it is distorted radically.

Jean Roudaut, *M. B.; ou, Le livre futur* (1964), pp. 82–83

Generally speaking, one may view the works of Butor as the aesthetic expression of a deeply committed writer—*engagé*, not in the debased sense given that word by those who apparently confuse commitment with propaganda or journalism, but in the authentic Sartrian meaning. He is a writer committed to his time and to all its characteristics, not a proponent of this or that ideal. Of course, there is no denying his desire to influence his readers. When he emphasized the importance of surrealism to himself and to the contemporary writer, he fully endorsed Rimbaud's admonition: "We must transform life." André Breton had earlier bracketed that same statement with Marx's exhortation, "We must transform the world," adding that in his own mind the two were identical. Breton's view is shared by Butor, who has said that any literary work that does not in some way help us effect such a transformation is inevitably doomed.

Leon Roudiez, *M. B.* (1965), p. 45

"The novelist is beginning to know what he is doing, the novel to say what it is" affirms the author of *La modification*. To include a critique of itself by laying bare its methods is indeed one of the characteristics of the modern novel, and it is also characteristic of Michel Butor that he should "reflect" systematically in the structures what he is proposing as themes.

Françoise van Rossum-Guyon, *Critique du roman* (1970), p. 289

Butor's novels, like those of Robbe-Grillet, Nathalie Sarraute, or Claude Simon, are essentially a "mise en question" of a complicated and unstable world, owing a good deal to the descriptive philosophy of phenomenology. In the course of this questioning, most of the features of the traditional novel are discarded. Chronological narration of events is usually replaced by the protagonist's experience of time as something which is inevitably flexible and discontinuous, with past, present, and future alternating without any comforting pattern. The protagonist himself is no longer fixed, "rounded," or interesting in himself: it is not the anonymous photoelectric cell-narrator of Robbe-Grillet's *La Jalousie* who fascinates, but we are intrigued by the way in which "his" vision deforms certain objects "he" perceives. Nor does the protagonist hold very interesting conversations with his friends; instead, he usually reflects or reminisces mentally about his confusing experiences in a kind of interior monologue, the essence of which is the unavailability to him of a coherently organized body of knowledge. Sometimes the writer appears hardly less confused than his hero; at all events, the self-reflecting or narcissistic novel in which a fictional character is trying—usually unsuccessfully—to write the same novel as the author, has been a common phenomenon since the early 1950's. One very important consequence is that the reader tends to become involved in the creation of some kind of novel from the unassembled elements, "fictional" or "real," with which he is confronted.

> Michael Spencer, *M. B.* (1974), p. 159

The ideal "mobile polyphonic" book would be assimilated into that computer which, according to Butor, will allow us "to navigate through immense poetic territories, not only reading them but transforming them for ourselves or other readers as we need." Potentially, however, books can cover the opposite function: closure, possession of the tyrannical message. We maintain that this dichotomy is purely arbitrary and disappears as it is being developed. Indeed, Butor himself affirms: "Not only does every reader build a representation from the signs offered but also undertakes to rewrite what he reads."

Butor pulls this reader-writer into his works by means of:

—active implication or option within the quotations, parodies, juxtapositions, ideogrammes (*Illustrations, Où*)

—participation: the contrapuntal variations of *68,100,000 litres d'eau par seconde*

—control: the choice of scores in *Votre Faust* and their determination by vote.

If Butor thus reconciles the two degrees of openness defined by Eco and Stevenson, he keeps his place in a cultural continuity. The effort he makes to bring things together, effort which is proved constantly by his work plans, leaves no doubt about the humanistic *a priori* in Butor's activity: the author never preaches rupture; rather he demands that we should reutilize the past: "we play with 1957."

> André Helbo, *M. B.: Vers une littérature du signe* (1975), p. 25

BYATT, A(ntonia) S(usan)

English novelist, short-story writer, essayist, and poet, b. 24 Aug. 1936, Sheffield

B. belongs to an intellectual family, her father being a judge and writer, her mother an English teacher, and her sister the novelist and critic Margaret DRABBLE. B. achieved first-class honors at Newnham College, Cambridge, where she took the bachelor's degree; she pursued graduate study at Bryn Mawr College in Pennsylvania and at Somerville College, Oxford. She has taught literature at University College, London. Her life in intellectual and academic circles strongly influences her novels; indeed, at times the reader finds difficulty in separating autobiography from fiction, and B. deliberately emphasizes the confusion and overlapping. Her writing is a curious, self-conscious brand of metafiction, obviously directed not merely towards the intelligentsia, but in particular, towards postmodernist professors of literature.

Her novels have drawn critical attention from the first, and have become steadily more highly regarded. To date, her most important novels are *Possession: A Romance* (1990), which won for her the Booker Prize and the Irish Times/AER Prize; and a series of four, in progress, three of which are now completed: *The Virgin in the Garden* (1978); *Still Life* (1991); and *Babel Tower* (1996). *Possession* is most accessible to the nonscholarly intelligent reader. It makes full use of B.'s standard academic setting: Roland Mitchell, research assistant to the accepted expert on Victorian poet Randolph Henry Ash, comes across a heretofore undiscovered pair of letters by Ash to a mysterious lady, tucked inside a book in the London Library—a find that sets Roland off on a search for the rest of the story hinted at in the letters. However, in this novel, academe is the setting but not the only concern; the novel has much to recommend it to readers outside of academic circles. It is enjoyable for the mystery to be solved, the love story, the treasure hunt, the Gothic ending, the satisfying way that parts and pieces come together at denouement. All these are skillfully handled, with no annoying sense of deus ex machina. The literary setting, while adding a level of density and pleasure for literary readers, does not render the novel too arcane for a more widespread audience.

The three novels thus far published of the proposed "Powerhouse Four" are far less accessible. They recount the story, with leaps and starts and tremendous digressions, of the Potter family, Bill and Winifred and their son Marcus and daughters Stephanie and Frederica. *The Virgin in the Garden* is the most traditional in style, a more or less straightforward novel. The primary focus is on the children; Marcus and Frederica are teenagers and Stephanie is a young woman beginning her adult life. Marcus is vulnerable and terrified of his father; Stephanie is intelligent and kind; Frederica is difficult to like, being entirely self-serving and apparently without any virtues. Interestingly, it is Frederica who moves to center stage in the subsequent novels and begins to look more and more like an alter ego for the author; in *Still Life* Marcus virtually fades out of the story and Stephanie dies in an accident. The narrative takes on a more pronounced Byattesque flavor, as the author moves in and out of her own novel, making free use of the intrusive-narrator device, here pondering at length the significance of a metaphor she has just used; there expounding upon her knowledge of fields outside the story. This unfettered fascination with her own craft becomes increasingly characteristic of Frederica as well as her creator as the story moves into *Babel Tower* and Frederica becomes a professor of literature and writer of literary criticism. *Babel Tower* is built on parallelism; B. interweaves Frederica's story, in which she befriends Jude Mason, the author of an obscene novel, and segments of Mason's novel; a further parallel is drawn between two trials—Frederica's divorce trial and Mason's trial for obscenity. The story uses levels of irony throughout, as the author and her characters ponder the illusive quality of words. The final irony is that Mason's conviction on obscenity charges, after a lengthy trial, is overturned, not because any jury or judge has decided that his book is not obscene, but because of a technicality: the judge, in instructing the jury, was unable to give them an adequate definition of literature. Thus, the plot turns back to B.'s ever-present concern—her enthrallment with the power of words, of definitions, of writing. She seems to mean that naming is all, even though she holds back from definitely saying so.

B. writes primarily to a postmodern coterie of other litterateurs. Critics have noted that she fends off the dismantling and analyzing of her work by dismantling it herself as she goes along, stopping often to consider and criticize passages she has just written. She appears never to forebear one more learned allusion or one more ponderous analysis, not only of word-craft, but also of other subjects in which she has expertise, such as music and painting. It may be that her work will finally be judged at best pretentious and at worst coy, but she has established herself as an important writer in the 1990s, at least by her undeniable learnedness, and by the sheer volume of her writing. In 1989 she was honored with the title Commander of the Order of the British Empire.

FURTHER WORKS: *The Shadow of a Sun* (1964); *Degrees of Freedom: The Novels of Iris Murdoch* (1965); *The Game* (1968); *Wordsworth and Coleridge in Their Time* (1970); *Angels and Insects* (1992); *Passions of the Mind* (1992); *"Sugar" and Other Stories* (1992); *The Matisse Stories* (1993); *Imagining Characters: Six Conversations about Women Writers* (1995); *The Djinn in the Nightingale's Eye: Five Fairy Stories* (1997)

BIBLIOGRAPHY: Gitzen, J., "A. S. B.'s Self-Mirroring Art," *Crit*, 36 (Winter 1995): 83-95; Thurman, J., "A Reader's Companion," *New Yorker*, 19 Nov. 1990: 151; Kelly, K., *A. S. B.* (1996)

—CECELIA LAMPP LINTON

BYELORUSSIAN LITERATURE

The rulers of the Russian Empire did not encourage the development or growth of national consciousness among non-Russians, particularly among Byelorussians, the least numerous of the three East Slavic nationalities (after the Russians and the Ukrainians). So it is not surprising that the Byelorussians came to a mature self-awareness relatively late. When Byelorussia was incorporated into the Russian Empire by Catherine II in the last quarter of the 18th c., Russification of the Byelorussians became the official policy of the imperial government, and was continued by all of her successors. In 1840 even the name "Byelorussia" was banned from official use by the tsarist authorities. (Byelorussia was referred to simply by the geographic term Severo-Zapadny Krai, that is, Northwestern Region.)

For most of the last half of the 19th c., publishing in the Byelorussian language—with the exception of folkloric materials—was explicitly forbidden by order of the government. Frantsishak

Bahushevich (1840–1900), known as the "father of modern Byelorussian literature," had to publish his first book of poetry, *Dudka bielaruskaya* (1891; the Byelorussian flute) beyond the borders of the Russian Empire; it was then smuggled clandestinely into Byelorussia. Thus, modern Byelorussian literature had one of the least propitious beginnings of any in the Slavic world.

The 1905 revolution brought about momentous changes in the Russian Empire. One of its salutary results for Byelorussian literature was the lifting of the prohibition against the Byelorussian language. Religious and cultural activities among the empire's national minorities were also unfettered. Even earlier, the heady ideas of socialism had called attention to the lower social strata, which, in the case of Byelorussia, largely meant the peasantry. Following the appearance in 1903 of the first Byelorussian political party, the socialist Hramada, cultural activity expanded. In 1906 Hramada launched its newspaper, *Nasha dola*, which was supplanted in the same year by the more temperate *Nasha niva* (1906–15). This weekly, published in Vilna, a Byelorussian cultural center during those years, provided the vehicle and the forum for Bahushevich's successors to create a modern literature, which, while looking forward, also harked back to Old Byelorussian writing of the 12th through 15th cs., to homiletic, polemic, and satirical works of the 16th and 17th cs., and to the beginnings of modern prose, poetry, and drama in the 18th and 19th cs. The main concern of writers, however, was the downtrodden peasant in his bleak social world, deprived of education and redeeming cultural values. It was he, the peasant, who became the dominant subject of literary—predominantly poetic—works and the main object of exhortations. With the upper classes either Russified (those of the Orthodox faith) or Polonized (those of the Catholic faith), to elevate the awareness of the Byelorussians and to arouse the nation meant stimulating concern for human dignity and educating the peasant masses. The best way to achieve this goal was by depicting and reflecting on the hardships of daily life, as well as addressing wider social and political realities, the beauty and mystery of nature, and the ever-present hopes for a better future.

References to the historical past, especially to the period of the Principality of Polotsk (10th-12th cs.) as a source of pride and inspiration, became an important element in poems by Yanka Kupala (1882–1942), the most influential figure during the first two decades of the 20th c. Other writers who figured most prominently during this period and who have continued to be considered the major molders of the modern Byelorussian language, literature, and national consciousness are Yakub Kolas (1882–1956), Maksim BAHDANOVICH, Aleś Harun (1887–1920), Zmitrok Biadula (1886–1941), and Maksim Haretski (1893–1939). Their "Our Soil" literary group lasted until the political events of 1917–21, which witnessed the birth of Byelorussian statehood, first in the form of the Byelorussian Democratic Republic (established March 25, 1918), and then, as a reaction to it, the Byelorussian Soviet Socialist Republic (Jan. 1, 1919).

Between 1921 (the Riga Peace Treaty) and 1939, Byelorussian literature was forced to develop on both sides of the Soviet-Polish border and was shaped by political realities in the U.S.S.R. (the relatively liberal NEP period, succeeded by the harshness of Stalinism) and in Poland (with its policy of gradually suppressing Byelorussian expression).

On the Soviet side, "Our Soilism," with its plaintive tone and somber shades, gave way to a revolutionary élan and to nationalist (national Communist) tendencies. Established writers like Kupala and Kolas went through a phase of "inner emigration" as a result of their disillusionment with the Bolshevik policy toward national minority aspirations. The main literary group, "Saplings," whose ranks swelled to about five hundred members, cultivated proletarian themes as well as IMAGISM and FUTURISM, which were enjoying a great vogue in other eastern European literatures at that time. In 1926–27 it split up into several smaller groups, of which "Flame" and "Excelsior" became the principal ones; each of them published literary journals bearing its own name: *Polymya* and *Uzvyshsha*. Kupala and Kolas remained with "Flame." Among the leading members of "Excelsior" were Uladzimier Dubowka (1900–1975) and Yazep Pushcha (1902–1964), who emerged as the leaders in poetry, and Kuzma Chorny (1900–1944) and Michaś Zaretski (1901–1941) in fiction.

During the 1930s, with the rise of Stalinism, all literary organizations were disbanded and writers forced into one closely administered and regulated "union." Subsequently many of them lost their freedom; some, their lives. On the Polish side, in western Byelorussia, the most important literary activity was carried on by Natalla ARSIENNIEVA and Maksim Tank (b. 1912). Arsiennieva was purely lyrical and personal in her poetry of the interwar period, Tank largely concerned with social and political questions.

In 1939 the Soviet Union moved into eastern Poland and reunited western Byelorussia with the Byelorussian S.S.R. Hitler's army occupied Byelorussia from 1941 to 1944. From 1945 to 1992 Byelorussia was a constituent Soviet republic.

The cult of personality during the 1930s and the ravages of World War II not only left every fourth inhabitant of Byelorussia dead but caused a trauma in the psyches of Byelorussian writers that still reverberates in their literary works. During recent decades the writers' organization has grown from a few dozen persons to over three hundred members. Talented men and women have infused Byelorussian literature with the considerable riches of their regional language, higher artistic standards, and more variegated subject matter: the rural protagonists of earlier literary works have been joined by city dwellers, workers, and members of the intelligentsia. With growing urbanization—55 percent of Byelorussia's population is urban—and with cities being systematically Russified, Byelorussian literature is faced with the task of transferring its emphasis from the villages to the cities as a tactical move in resisting the campaign of Russification.

Maksim Tank, a prolific poet, has continued to write. Accomplished in traditional forms of poetry, he has immersed himself in Western literature, but also frequently turns to folklore and patriotic themes for inspiration. Nil Hilevich (b. 1931) finds the essence and power of poetry in expressing his sense of belonging to his people and in singing of the beauty of his country. Ryhor Baradulin (b. 1935), a virtuoso of the Byelorussian language, is a poet whose imagery and themes are strongly influenced by the experiences of World War II. Uladzimier Karatkevich (b. 1930) is best known for his historical novels; his *Kalasy pad siarpom tvaim* (1965; ears of corn under your sickle), about the 1863 Byelorussian uprising, aroused great interest in Byelorussia's pre-Soviet past. One older writer, Kandrat Krapiva (b. 1896), a major playwright, satirist, translator, and philologist, has gained wide recognition in present-day Byelorussia. His plays, written during the 1930s and 1940s, have become staples in the Byelorussian repertory. *Khto smiayetstsa aposhnim* (1939; he who laughs last), a satire on sycophancy and spinelessness in the bureaucratic and scholarly worlds, is especially popular. Other representative writers in Byelorussia are Vasil BYKAW, Andrei Makayonak (b. 1920), Anatol Vyartsinski (b. 1931), Larysa Hieniyush (b. 1910), Danuta Bichel-Zahnetava (b.

1938), Volha Ipatava (b. 1945), Piatrus Makal (b. 1932), and Yanka Bryl (b. 1917).

Byelorussian literature has also continued to develop outside the country. Driven from their homes by war or ideological incompatibility with the regime, emigré writers are still exponents of the Byelorussian national literary process in language, forms, imagery, and subject matter. Memories of their native country become catalysts for recalling war experiences, reacting to the Soviet persecutions of the 1930s, and expressing the yearning for a free and independent homeland.

Natalla Arsiennieva, in *Mizh bierahami* (1979; between the shores), maintains a spirit of fortitude and a hope of returning to a free Byelorussia. Aleś Salaviei (1922–1978) reflected the strength of the struggle for his people's liberation; he faithfully carried on the tradition and style of polished classical verse exemplified best by Maksim Bahdanovich. Ryhor Krushyna (1907–1979) expressed, often by erotic images, love of his native land accompanied by a fascination with international travel. Masiei Siadniou (b. 1915) in *Patushanyya zory* (1975; extinguished stars) ponders the lonely mission of the poet as herald of truth. Kastuś Akula (b. 1925), in the first two volumes of his trilogy *Haravatka* (the name of the mountainous locale in northern Byelorussia where the action is laid)—*Dziarlivaya ptushka* (1965; bird of prey) and *Zakryvaulenaye sontsa* (1974; blood-stained sun)—portrays the life and spirit of entrenched resistance of a Byelorussian family under three successive occupations: Polish, Soviet Russian, and Nazi German (the German invasion will be the subject of the third novel, as yet unfinished). His first English-language novel, *Tomorrow Is Yesterday* (1968), anticipates the themes of the last part of the trilogy. Uladzimier Hlybinny (pseud. of Vladimir Seduro, b. 1910) focuses on his fellow-countrymen abroad following World War II. His *Na bierahokh pad sontsam* (1964; on sunny shores) is a collection of short stories set in postwar U.S.

BIBLIOGRAPHY: Seduro, V., *The Byelorussian Theatre and Drama* (1955); Adamovich, A., *Opposition to Sovietization in Belorussian Literature* (1917–1957) (1958); special Byelorussia issue, *Soviet Literature*, No. 8 (1968); Rich, V., Introduction to *Like Water, Like Fire: An Anthology of Byelorussian Poetry from 1828 to the Present Day* (1971): 13–22; Akiner, S., "Contemporary Young Byelorussian Poets (1967–1975)," *JByelS*, 3 (1976): 342–63; Tank, M., "A Word with the Reader," in A. Vyartsinski, comp., *Fair Land of Byelorussia: An Anthology of Modern Byelorussian Poetry* (1976): 13–17; McMillin, A. B., *A History of Byelorussian Literature: From Its Origins to the Present Day* (1977); Bird, T. E., ed., *Modern Byelorussian Writing: Essays and Documents*, Queens Slavic Papers, Vol. III (1981)

—THOMAS E. BIRD

BYKAW, Vasil

Byelorussian novelist, b. 19 June 1924, Bychki

During a poverty-stricken childhood in rural Byelorussia B. became a voracious reader. His acquaintance with the works of such writers as Mayne Reid (1818–1883), Jules Verne, Lev Tolstoy, Jack LONDON, the Byelorussian Yanka Kupala (1882–1942), and Maxim GORKY shaped his own talent. When World War II broke out he volunteered for the Soviet armed forces and graduated from a military academy as a junior lieutenant.

His first work was published in 1949. The impetus for his writing sprang partly from his dissatisfaction with what had been written about World War II. For over twenty years, beginning in 1956, B. was on the staff of a local newspaper in Grodno. In 1980 B. was awarded the title of People's Writer of the Byelorussian S.S.R.

B.'s writings deal almost exclusively with conscience and morality in the strained and brutal circumstances of World War II. Within a confined group of soldiers on a battlefield, he explores the conflict between goals and the price to be paid in terms of human lives and suffering. He examines what is reasonable and what is not in the demands for exertion on behalf of victory. His system of values is governed by a profound humanism, which transcends national loyalties and ideological antagonisms even during war.

For B., a successful writer must combine talent with civic courage. His consistent opposition to evil brought him into conflict with Soviet officialdom, especially between 1965 and 1970. His novella *Miortvym nie balits'* (1965; the dead feel no pain) was severely criticized. In it B. condemns Stalinist secret police methods, attacks the cruelty and crimes of some Soviet war commanders, reveals the survival of old attitudes and the nonpunishment of war criminals in the post-World War II Soviet system, and clamors for justice. In *Sotnikaw* (1970; *The Ordeal*, 1972), a highly acclaimed novella about guerrilla warfare in Byelorussia, the writer contrasts the attitudes of a Byelorussian soldier and a Russian officer toward a complex war situation.

B.'s literary style is terse and laconic, with a touch of lyricism. His style, his penetrating analysis of the psychology of soldiers, and his mastery of physical detail produce an intensely realistic picture of war. By depicting the dense atmosphere of fiercely fought battles, B. condemns war as the worst scourge of humanity. His characters, stripped of outward convention, provide the reader with insights into courage and cowardice, loyalty and treason, and the sense of responsibility toward man and justice.

B. has also written short stories, screenplays, and stage plays, and has translated some of his own works into Russian. He is the foremost prose writer in modern Byelorussian literature and one of the best known throughout the Soviet Union. His novellas have been translated into the major languages of the U.S.S.R. and central Europe as well as into English, German, French, Italian, Arabic, Japanese, and others.

FURTHER WORKS: *Zhurawliny kryk* (1959); *Zdrada* (1960); *Tretsiaya rakieta* (1961; *The Third Flare*, 1964); *Alpiyskaya balada* (1962; *Alpine Ballad*, 1966); *Pastka* (1962); *Praklataya vyshynia* (1968); *Kruhlanski most* (1969); *Abelisk* (1971); *Dazhyts' da svitannia* (1972); *Vowchaya zhraya* (1975; *Wolf Pack*, 1975)

BIBLIOGRAPHY: Cathala, J., Introduction (in French) to *Sotnikov* (1974): 5–14; Hoppe, S., "Zu den neueren Erzählungen V. B.s," *ZS*, 5 (1974): 667–80; Orechwa, O., "B.'s Search for Moral Imperative," *Annals of the Byelorussian Institute of Arts and Sciences*, 14 (1976): 51–58; McMillin, A. B., *A History of Byelorussian Literature* (1977): 327–29

—JAN ZAPRUDNIK

C

CABALLERO CALDERÓN, Eduardo

Colombian novelist, essayist, and journalist, b. 6 Mar. 1910, Bogotá

A single novel published in 1952 made C. C. internationally known, but by then he had already acquired within his native country a reputation as a journalist, above all, and as an author of essays and a diplomat. *El Cristo de espaldas* (1952; Christ betrayed) was the work that placed him in the forefront of Spanish American fiction.

Born to an elitist family of highland landowners, C. C. began his career as a journalist for a prestigious conservative paper, Bogotá's *El Tiempo*. This activity gave him the necessary experience to enter the field of letters. He was also elected to the house of representatives, and then to the senate. From politics he transferred to diplomacy, representing his country in Latin American cities as well as in Paris. In 1967 he returned to Bogotá and dedicated himself fully to writing.

C. C. began with shorter novels, of which the first one of importance was *El arte de vivir sinsoñar* (1943; the art of living without dreaming), an ingenious tale starring two wise scholars from an Asian Salem of the past, where people knew how to dream; after much wandering the two men find themselves in Salem, Oregon, a typical city of the drab Western civilization, whose citizens no longer dream. It is a pessimistic view of modern Western life. C. C. abandoned then the novel for some ten years and built a reputation as an essayist. Main works in this genre were *Latino América un mundo por hacer* (1944; Latin America; a world to make come true), a sociological reflection of his travels, and *El nuevo príncipe: ensayo sobre las malas pasiones*, (1945; the new prince: an essay on bad passions), an almost apocalyptic preview of a society ruled by the despots of modern times—governments, supported by barbaric crowds. This latter book already indicated the path the author had begun to take and has kept to present: his treatment of the good and bad sides in the human being or, simply, Good versus Evil.

Beginning in 1948, Colombia was immersed into a state of civil war. Nationally known as *La Violencia*, this event lasted almost ten years. Famous Colombian authors, including Gabriel GARCÍA MÁRQUEZ and C. C. himself, based their most respected fiction on that genocide. In 1952, as noted, C. C. published *El Cristo de espaladas*. It is the story of a young priest whose high ideals and valiant efforts to bring peace and justice to a highland community beset by violence fail altogether, defeated by a feudalistic system and by human propensity to evil. The priest, himself a new Christ, submits to false accusations and to defeat with no other reward than that of his self-sacrifice. In the somber, but beautifully recounted story, C. C., like most Colombian writers, displayed the pure Castillian Spanish that astonishes Spanish academicians themselves.

Rural themes dominate a good part of C. C.'s fiction. *Siervo sin tierra* (1954; serf without land) is the typical novel of social protest save for the lack of a dogma or revolutionary appeal. It depicts the world of the destitute Colombian highlander who is simply born with his life and even his family already mortgaged to the feudal overlord. In *Manuel Pacho* (1962; Manuel Pacho) the novelist descends from the frigid moors into the torrid plains of eastern Colombia, to portray the unassimilable plainsman that for centuries has been bypassed by modern civilization. In *Caín* (1969; Cain) C. C. repeats a myth that recurs in his novels. Cain, the man unwanted by the gods, in this novel redeems himself through the love of a woman, his own unfaithful wife in this case.

Convinced that he should participate in the contest for the Premio Nadal, C. C. won in 1965 the prestigious prize with the manuscript of a novel that was published in Barcelona a year later. *El buen salvaje* (1966; the noble savage) takes place in Paris. It is the biography of an abulic, uprooted Latin American alienated by a semifossilized European society. In part this work voices the author's opinion that EXISTENTIALISM is more positive in Latin America than it can be in Europe, owing to the more optimistic outlook of life that exists on this side of the Atlantic.

Consistency has so far been the common denominator in the literature of C. C. In his fiction and in his essays he maintains a humanistic creed; he points to the redeeming sides of the individual, if not of the masses, while at the same time condemning that demoniac side of human nature that bases its values on greed and on privilege.

FURTHER WORKS: *Caminos subterráneos* (1936); *Tipacoque: estampas de provincia* (1941); *Suramérica, tierra del hombre* (1944); *Breviario del Quijote* (1947); *Cervantes en Colombia* (1948); *Cartas colombianas* (1949); *Ancha es Castilla* (1950); *Diario de Tipacoque* (1950); *Cuentos infantiles* (1953); *La penúltima hora* (1955); *Americanos y europeos* (1957); *Obras* (3 vols., 1963–1964); *Yo, el alcalde: soñar un pueblo para después gobernarlo* (1971); *Azote de sapo* (1976)

BIBLIOGRAPHY: Kirsner, R., "Four Colombian Novels of 'La Violencia,'" *Hispania*, 49, 1 (1966): 70–74; Menton, S., *La novela colombiana: planetas y satélites* (1978): 189–216; Arango, M. A., *Gabriel García Márquez y la novela de la violencia en Colombia* (1985): 91–110; Williams, R. L., "Colombia," in Foster, D. W. comp., *Handbook of Latin American Literature* (1987): 153–90

—EVELIO ECHEVARRÍA

CABRAL, Amílcar

Guinean poet and essayist (writing in Portuguese), b. 12 Sept. 1924, Bafatá; d. 20 Jan. 1973, Conakri

Born in Guinea, C. was educated in Cape Verde, where his family settled in 1931, and later attended university in Lisbon. He graduated with a degree in agronomy in 1950. Following the death of his father soon afterwards, C. returned to Cape Verde, where he now took up employment with the Provincial Department of Agricultural and Forestry Services of Portuguese Guinea. Mário de ANDRADE, in a biographical note in the 1980 edition of C.'s *Unidada e Luta* (1974; *Unity and Struggle*, 1980), posits that upon his return to Cape Verde C. was a changed man. The period spent as a student in Lisbon, in the company of many other Africans from

Mozambique and Angola, together with his association with Portuguese revolutionary groups, had awakened in him a determination to fight for the freedom of his fellow Guineans from Portuguese colonialism.

One of modern Africa's most sophisticated theorists of the postcolonial condition, C.'s truly impressive body of written work accounts for the continuing power C. as a political figure occupies in the pantheon of anticolonialist heroes. A number of central themes characterize his work: a concern with theories of colonialism and imperialism, the analysis of class struggles in the colonized world, the role and place of culture in a postcolonial society, pan-Africanism and solidarity with other revolutionary movements. A prolific writer, and a masterful player of the war of public relations intrinsic to any conflict, C. often produced work which lacked both the depth and refinement present in the majority of his writings. Like the Martinican Frantz Fanon (1925-1961), C. has been accused by commentators of presenting flawed and dogmatic arguments on many of the themes discussed in his works. Simultaneously, however, and like Fanon, he is seen by others as one of the most influential proponents of an effective anticolonial stance.

Yet for all his political instincts, and in spite of his determination to defeat Portuguese colonialism, C. was also a pragmatist. Time and again he stressed that the war fought by Guineans was not directed against the Portuguese people but rather against an oppressive and unjust colonial system. Unlike many other nationalist leaders he was keen to separate what he saw as the real oppressor, the Portuguese colonialist apparatus, from the Portuguese people, and indeed the Portuguese army, seeing them as fellow-oppressed peoples whom history had conspired to turn into enemies. As illustrated in *Revolution in Guinea: Selected Texts* (1969), translated from an unpublished text in Portuguese, class—not race or color—represented for C. the real enemy. What he saw as "the struggle of progress against misery and suffering, of freedom against oppression" was one which he believed to be also that of the Portuguese as a nation. Addressing a conference in Havana of Asian, African, and Latin American activists, C. alerted to the need to address "one's own weaknesses," referring thus to what he perceived as the dangers inherent in racism, tribalism and national chauvinism.

C. began writing at an early age, both essays and poetry. In a short story he wrote before his eighteenth birthday, entitled "Fidemar" (Creole: Son of the Sea), the protagonist, a revolutionary who claimed the right of all to "liberty and life," departs his island in the hope of returning "strengthened in order to liberate it." In yet another piece of juvenilia, written when C. was attending high school in the 1940s, C. wrote that "On earth there is a single people to which all peoples belong." In both passages the resonance with C.'s own pronouncement is uncanny to say the least, and in such adolescent humanist views might be found the root of C.'s later feelings towards the Portuguese people under Salazar's dictatorship.

As a poet C.'s contribution to Guinean writing was limited. Unlike his brother Vasco Cabral (b. 1926), who has since come to be seen as one of Guinea-Bissau's most important poets, in his poems C. wrote mostly about concerns common to much Cape Verdean poetry. In a soulful style he addressed the islands' isolation, the lack of employment, the need to emigrate in search of a better life. Although the brilliant revolutionary visionary was no *poète-manqué*, as a source of inspiration for poetry however his fate has been markedly different. Nevertheless, the verse constitutes an important archive in the development of C.: the idealistic adolescent, the young man filled with dreams who left for Lisbon in

1945, the committed leader who returned home in 1950, the politician who helped form the PAIGC in 1956 in Praia, the myth who remains forever shrouded by the mystery of a death that came too soon, and which much too prematurely deprived a nation of a leader of enormous and proven potential. C. was possessed of one of the finest minds among the nationalists of his day, and indeed among those who both preceded or followed him in the anticolonialist struggle. He alone seems to have been able to create the conditions which allowed for a smooth transition of power at the time of his death. Although Guinea-Bissau too would eventually experience some political turmoil, it was insignificant when compared to that faced by Mozambique and Angola. Although much of his work is available in a number of other languages, the vast majority of C.'s writings remain scattered among various publications in Portuguese, notably in *Nt Pintcha*, the offical organ of the PAIGC, and in *O Militante*, the newspaper of the Portuguese Communist Party. One of the most important archives of C.'s writings is the Centro de Informagao e Documentagao Amilcar Cabral (CIDAC) in Lisbon, Portugal.

FURTHER WORKS: *Estudos agrários de A. C.* (1988); *Obras Escolhidas de A. C.* (2 vols., 1976, 1977). FURTHER WORKS IN ENGLISH: *Return to the Source: Selected Speeches of A. C.* (1971)

BIBLIOGRAPHY: Chabal, P., *A. C.: Revolutionary Leadership and People's War* (1983); McCulloch, J., *In the Twilight of Revolution: The Political Theory of A. C.* (1983); Osório, O., *Emergência da Poesia em A. C.* (1984); Galli, R. E., and J. Jones, *Guinea-Bissau: Politics, Economics and Society* (1987); Chilcote, R. H., *A. C.'s Revolutionary Theory and Practice: A Critical Guide* (1991)

—TONY SIMOES DA SILVA

CABRERA, Lydia

Cuban short-story writer, folklorist, and ethnological essayist, b. 20 May 1900, Havana; d. 19 Sept. 1992, Miami, Florida

C. is a leading authority on AFRO-CUBAN cultures and folklore. Her contributions to Cuban literature include short stories based on African oral traditions taken to Cuba by slaves, as well as detailed investigations on the presence of those African traditions in Cuban society. Her work is a careful blend of childhood memories, research, and imagination: a mixture of documentation and poetry, the fantastic and the surreal, universal aspects of the human condition and regional characteristics of the Cuban Creole. C., the youngest daughter of a prominent Cuban family, was tutored at home among Afro-Cuban servants where she was free to explore her own imagination from an early age. In her youth, she accompanied her father to literary cafés, where only men gathered, and by age fourteen she published her first writings in *Cuba y América*, a prestigious political and literary magazine her father directed. In 1922, C. went to Paris to study at the École du Louvre and Beaux Arts. There she met Teresa de la Parra (1895–1936), Lucien Lévy-Bruhl (1857–1939), and Paul VALÉRY and became familiar with Leo Frobenius (1873–1938) and with vanguard movements in art, especially the techniques in CUBISM and SURREALISM, with which she later experimented in her short stories. During this time, C. also became interested in oriental civilizations whose religion and myths reminded her of the stories she had heard in her childhood from black Cuban servants. While vacationing in Havana, C. came in contact with Afro-Cuban believers, and in 1930, during another visit to the island, she established permanent contact with a poor community predominantly black, which would later become one of the main sources of information for her research.

In 1932 Teresa de la Parra contracted tuberculosis, and C. accompanied her to a sanatorium in Leysin. With the initial objective of entertaining the Chilean poet, C. wrote a series of short stories that humorously recaptured anecdotes she had heard from servants in her childhood. These were later collected, translated, and published in France (1936), where there was an increasing interest in African art. Four years later it was published in Cuba as *Cuentos negros de Cuba* (1940; Cuban black stories). In 1935, C. went with Teresa de la Parra to Madrid, where she established a friendship with the Chilean poet Gabriela MISTRAL, who, at this time and in later years, encouraged C. to continue writing. In 1936, when Teresa de La Parra died and the Spanish Civil War broke out, C. returned first to Paris and then, in 1939, permanently to Cuba. In 1942 she began a serious study of Afro-Cuban religion and folklore throughout the island. She also translated Aimé CÉSAIRE's *Cahier d' un retour au pays natal* (1939; *Memorandum on My Martinque*, 1947) which was published with illustrations by the Cuban painter Wilfredo Lam. It was C. who exerted a deep influence on Lam's shift to an Afro-Cuban imagery. In 1948 C. published her second collection of short stories, *¿Por qué? Cuentos negros de Cuba* (1948; why? Cuban black stories). Though a continuation in theme and style of her first book, these twenty-eight anecdotes show a more refined lyricism and philosophical humor than her earlier stories. However, it was C.'s monumental book *El monte: notas sobre las religiones, la magia,las supersticiones y el folklore de los negros criollos y del pueblo de Cub* (1954; the forest [bush/mount]: notes on the religion, magic, superstitions, and folklore of black Creoles and the Cuban people) that finally established C. as a major intellectual figure, as the author of a unique testimonial account of Afro-Cuban beliefs and lore. In 1957 C. published *Anagó Vocabulario lucumí* (Anagó Lucumí vocabulary), a dictionary of Spanish and Lucumí (the Yoruba-derived language spoken in Cuba). A year later, C. published another monumental work, *La sociedad secreta Abakuá* (1958; the Abakuá secret society), the first detailed and objective account of the rites, ceremonies, and beliefs of a secret society commonly known in Cuba as ñáñigos, related in their traditions to Carabalí nations in Africa.

In 1960 C.'s work came to a temporary halt. With the triumph of the Cuban revolution, C. resettled in Miami, Florida, and twelve years of silence went by before she initiated, if not the most important period of her work, definitely the most prolific, all of it from research material she had gathered in Cuba. Among the books of C.'s second period we find a third collection of short stories, *Ayapá Cunento de jicotea* (1971; ayapá tortoise stories), a group of nineteen anecdotes in which *hicotea*, a Caribbean land turtle, appears as the main character. Although cubanized as *jicotea*, C.'s stories of the Afro-Cuban turtle closely resemble the African fables of tortoise, a folkloric and mythological symbol of the Yorubas. C.'s carefully elaborated stories of *jicotea* play with the same philosophical humor and irony that character all of C.'s work, while, and at the same time, recapturing through imagination an ancestral African tradition present in Cuba. Three years later, returning again to the narrative form she used in *El monte*, C. published *Yemayá y Ochún* (1974; Yemonja and Oshun), a collection of various myths and legends about the Lucuní (Yoruba) deities Yemayá, the feminine force of the ocean waters, and Ochún,

the feminine force of the fresh waters, love, and fertility. C. also published two other important dictionaries: *Vocabulario congo* (1984; Congo [Backongo] vocabulary), a dictionary of the Bantu languages spoken in Cuba, and *La lengua sagrada de los ñáñigos* (1988; the sacred language of the ñáñigos), a dictionary of the Carabalí languages untilized in the ceremonies of the Abakuá society.

Most of C.'s research took place in the western provinces of the island, where Afro-Cuban lore was best preserved, but her findings and publications are applicable to the traditions of nearly all African descendants in Cuba. Next to the work of Fernando Ortiz (1881–1969), C.'s writing is considered to be the most vast, prolific, and detailed work done an Afro-Cuban cultures. While the importance of C.'s monumental research has at times caused critics to give scant attention to the aesthetic value of her work of fiction, C. is a master storyteller, and should rank among the best and most innovative short-story writers in Spanish America.

FURTHER WORKS: *Refranes de negros viejos* (1955); *Otán iyebiyéé: las piedras preciosas* (1970); *La laguna sagrada de San Joaquí* (1973); *Anaforuana; ritual y símbolos de la iniciació en la sociedad secreta Abakuá* (1975); *Francisco y Francisca: chascarrillos de negros viejos* (1976); *La regla kimbisa del Santo Cristo del Buen Viaje* (1977); *Itinerarios del insomnio: Trinidad de Cuba* (1977); *Reglas de congo, palomonte mayombe* (1979); *Koeko iyawó, aprende novicia: pequeño tratado de regla luchumí* (1980); *Cuentos para adultos, niños y retrasados mentales* (1983); *La medicina popular de Cuba: médicos de antaño, curanderos, santeros y paleros de hogaño* (1984); *Los animales an el folklore y la magia de Cuba* (1988)

BIBLIOGRAPHY: Ortiz, F. L. C., "(Una cubana afroamericana)," *Crónica*, 3 (Mar. 1949): 7–8; Zambrano, M., "L. C. poeta de la metamorfosis," *Orígenes*, 7, 25 (1950): 11–15; Saignes, M. Acosta, "*El monte de L. C.*," *Revista Bimestre Cubana*, 71 (1956): 153–87; Gonzalex, M. P., "Cuentos y recuentos de L. C.," *Revista Cubana*, 1, 2 (1959): 153–61; Calvo, L. Novás, "El monte," *Papeles de Son Armadans*, 150 (Sept. 1968): 298–304; Perera, H., *Idapo: El sincretismo de los cuentos negros de L.C.* (1971); Valdes Cruz, R., *Lo ancestral africano en la narrativa de L. C.* (1974); Sáchez, R., ed., *Homenaje a L. C.* (1978); Hiriart, R., *L.C., vida hecha arte* (1978); Hiriart, R., *Más cerca de Teresa de la Parra: diálogos con L. C.* (1980); Simo, A. M., *L.C.: An Intimate Portrait* (1984); Castellanos, I., and J. Inclan, eds., *En torno a L. C. cincuentenarios de Cuentos negros de Cuba 1936–1986* (1987); Soto, S., *Magia e historia en los Ei "Cuentos negros," "Por qué?" y "Ayapá" de L. C.* (1988)

—JULIA CUERVO HEWITT

CABRERA INFANTE, Guillermo

Cuban novelist, short-story writer, and essayist (writing in Spanish and English), b. 22 April 1929, Gibara

C. I.'s parents were involved in the establishment of the Communist Party in Cuba and he grew up in a world of insecurity, surrounded by those whose very mission in life was the overthrow of the existing order. Consequently, his literary works reflect a quest for order within the chaos about him. In his youth, during the Batista regime, he spent some time in prison for publishing a story containing "obscenities in English," and thereafter he was forced for some time to write under pseudonyms, notably "G. Caín." He held various positions in the Castro government, including that of director of the influential journal *Lunes de Revolución*. In 1962 he was sent to Belgium as cultural attaché at the Cuban embassy. But in 1965 he left that position, feeling that "Stalinist" elements were taking control of the government, and eventually became a citizen of Great Britain, making his home in London.

His first book, *Así en la paz como en la guerra* (1960; in peace as in war), consists of miscellaneous short stories interspersed with violent scenes of the Batista dictatorship. Of more significance is *Un oficio del siglo XX* (1963; *A Twentieth-Century Job*, 1991), essentially a collection of his film reviews, but also involving a treatment of G. Caín as a fictional character. C. I.'s use of humor in the work anticipated what was to come in his novels.

He was propelled to international recognition with the publication of *Tres tristes tigres* (1967; *Three Trapped Tigers*, 1971), which had actually been completed in a different form in 1964 as *Vista del amanecer en el trópico* (view of dawn in the tropics; not to be confused with the later book of the same title). It is a humorous work, and some critics have mistaken its humor for frivolity. With C. I. it is quite the contrary: he is committed to the principle that humor, because it involves the abolition of boundaries of what is thought possible or acceptable, can be highly creative. The work consists of an extended madcap romp through the world of Havana night life in 1958, and the humor is played off against an atmosphere of grim foreboding, searching as it does for new creative possibilities in wordplay, since creation is always by the word. The work is written not in literary Spanish but in "Cuban," the spoken language of the streets of Havana.

Tres tristes tigres, like the language that makes it up, lacks any traditional formal structure. Instead, C. I. speaks of its symmetry, in which certain processes set in motion in the first half of the book are completed or reversed in the second half. In addition, the characters and their acts are elevated by means of creative language to archetypal significance. The central character of the work is the huge Black bolero singer known as La Estrella, a negative image of the White Goddess. Also important is Bustrófedon, a character who desires to immerse himself so completely in language that he will become totally identified with it, as La Estrella has become identified with primordial sound.

La Habana para un infante difunto (1979; *Infante's Inferno*, 1984) consists of a series of amorous adventures ranging from the autoerotic through various combinations of premarital and extramarital experiences. It gradually departs from the autobiographical and realistic and culminates in a remarkable hallucinatory scene in which the Don Juan figure who is the protagonist descends into hell in the very act of achieving his goal of returning to the womb. It is all an initiation experience which may or may not result in new birth.

C. I. is recognized as one of the most imaginative writers of the period in which Latin American fiction rose to prominence in world literature. The technique of interweaving apocalyptic themes with humor and word play in *Tres tristes tigres* was his unique contribution to that period, and *La Habana para un infante difunto* also represents a new departure for the Spanish American novel in its handling of eroticism.

FURTHER WORKS: *Vista del amanecer en el trópico* (1974; *View of Dawn in the Tropics*, 1978); *O* (1975); *Exorcismos de esti(l)o* (1976); *Arcadia todas las noches* (1978)

BIBLIOGRAPHY: Rodríguez Monegal, E., "Estructura y significaciones de *Tres tristes tigres*," *Sur*, No. 320 (1969): 38–51; special C. I. section, *Review* 72, No. 4. (1971–1972): 5–32; Gallagher, D. P., *Modern Latin American Literature* (1973): 164–85; Guibert, R., ed., *Seven Voices* (1973): 339–436; Siemens, W. L., *Heilsgeschichte* and the Structure of *Tres tristes tigres, KRQ*, 22 (1975): 77–90; Souza, R. D., "C. I.: Creation in Progress," in *Major Cuban Novelists* (1976): 80–100; Siemens, W. L., "Mirrors and Metamorphosis: Lewis Carroll's Presence in *Tres tristes tigres*," *Hispania*, 62 (1979): 297–303; special C. I. issue, *WLT*, 61 (Autumn 1987)

—WILLIAM L. SIEMENS

CAIN, James M.

American novelist, journalist, short-story writer, and screenwriter, b. 1 July 1892, Annapolis, Md.; d. 7 Oct. 1977, Hyattsville, Md.

C., whose father was a college administrator and professor of English, graduated in 1910 from Washington College, of which his father was president at the time. After giving some thought to a career as an opera singer, an interest perhaps reflecting the musical training his mother had completed before her marriage, C. decided while in his early twenties that he would be some kind of writer. He first realized that ambition in journalism, working under Walter Lippmann (1889–1974) at the *New York World* from 1924 until the paper's demise in 1931, and writing articles for H. L. MENCKEN's *American Mercury* during the same period. Lippmann and Mencken were, of course, among the giants of the American cultural scene at this time, and C. enjoyed a cordial personal relationship with both men. Following the end of the *World*, C. worked at the *New Yorker* but he found the environment uncongenial, and after nine months moved to Hollywood to embark on what would prove to be an undistinguished career as a screenwriter.

As a writer of fiction, C. was a late starter. He was already in his forties when he produced the "native american masterpieces back to back," to borrow the language of Ross Macdonald (1915–1983), that continue to stand as the foundation of his critical reputation: *The Postman Always Rings Twice* (1934) and "Double Indemnity"(1936), serialized in *Liberty* magazine. These and two other novels of the prewar period—*Serenade* (1937) and *Mildred Pierce* (1941)—along with *The Butterfly* (1947) represent for many critics C. at his best. Complicating the picture, of course, is that all five of these novels have been adapted as films, at least one of which (*Double Indemnity*, 1944) is arguably superior to its source, while another (*Mildred Pierce*, 1945) won an Academy Award for Joan Crawford, who created one of the screen's great roles. It is difficult to know just at present how much of C.'s stature is derived from the cinematic afterlife of his fiction.

But to turn to that fiction today is to be convinced once again of its power, if not of its depth or complexity. C. is frequently classified as one of the American hard-boiled writers (although he denied the relevance of this term to his work) on the basis, at least in part, of the combination in his fiction of a vernacular style (C. generally prefers a first-person narrator), a frequently violent subject matter, and an absence of moralizing. In a typical C. novel, characters who are in themselves neither impressive nor heroic engage our fascinated attention, sympathy, and—at times at least—a kind of guilty indentification as they are compelled to destructive and often self-destructive acts by drives that they are pretty much incapable of understanding. They may stand for our frightened recognition of the presence within ourselves of similarly powerful and mysterious drives. The first-person narration encourages such an indentification, but it performs other functions as well. Because the story is a story told in the past tense—that is, the narration itself represents the narrator's confrontation of the consequences of his actions—the first-person narration has a kind of distancing effect; we are reminded, even as C.'s art works on our empathic imagination, where these compulsions and the actions based on them "must" lead. We can thus entertain these dark imaginings without surrendering to them; a kind of immunization occurs.

The first-person narration serves yet another function. If the characters don't understand the forces that compel them, the narrative as a whole is not necessarily any more illuminating on the question. One does not go to C. for psychological insight. Rather, we accept the psychological limitations of the novel as representing the narrator's limitations.

In only one of the five key texts, *Mildred Pierce*, does C. attempt third-person narration. This may contribute to the lack of concentration in the novel, a quality some critics have seen as shapelessness. And it may be that at this point in his career C. simply was not ready to take on the challenges involved in creating a woman narrator. Even here, though, the sense of the third-person narrator as a kind of "masculine" voice and presence creates an artful tension within a generally sympathetic portrait of a woman, while at least partly "motivating" the blind spots that may exist in that portrait.

Mildred herself, in her combination of drive and domesticity, is an interesting variation on the C. woman. Even the most homicidally driven of these women yearn for the stability of the domestic life; and even the most domestic, Mildred, is driven. A feminist critic might find sexism implicit in this image, and perhaps the only appropriate reply is that there is as little sociological as psychological insight in C.'s fiction, but that the unresolved paradoxes of his characters, including the "masculine" drive of his women and the "feminine" vulnerability of his men, are yet another source of their narrative power.

A sympathetic critic has argued that C.'s style and techinique function best when theme, character relationships, and milieu are kept simple. This suggests something of C.'s limitations and perhaps indicates why his successes come relatively early and constitute in all a rather small portion of his oeuvre. The narrative in his best work is as driven as the characters, and the characters, combinations of powerful psychological simplification and actions to which they are driven, but for which they ultimately accept responsibility (and perhaps that is the morality of the hard-boiled), assume the dimensions of archetype. One suspects, one hopes, that there will always be readers for whom C. is a discovery.

FURTHER WORKS: *Our Government* (1930); *Love's Lovely Counterfeit* (1942); *Three of a Kind* (1943); *Past All Dishonor* (1946); *Sinful Woman* (1947); *The Moth* (1948); *Jealous Woman* (1950); *The Root of His Evil* (1951); *Galatea* (1953); *Mignon* (1962); *The Magician's Wife* (1965); *Rainbow's End* (1975); *The Institute* (1976); *The Baby in the Icebox and Other Short Fiction* (1981); *Cloud Nine* (1984); *The Enchanted Isle* (1985); 60 *Years of Journalism* (1985); *Career in C Major and Other Fiction* (1986)

BIBLIOGRAPHY: Farrell, J. T, *Literature and Morality* (1947): 79–87; Van Nostrand, A. D., *The Denatured Novel* (1960): 126–32; Wilson, E., "The Boys in the Back Room: J. M. C. and John O'Hara," *NewR* (11 Nov. 1962): 665–66; Oates, J. C., "Man under Sentence of Death: The Novels of J. M. C." in Madden, D., ed., *Tough Guy Writers of the Thirties* (1968): 110–28; Madden, D., *J. M. C.* (1970); Hoopes, R., *C.* (1982); Root, R., "Hard-Boiled Tragedy: J. M. C.'s classical Design," *Clues: A Journal of Detection*, 5, 2 (Fall-Winter 1984): 48–57; Madden, D., *C.'s Craft* (1985); Skenazy, P., *J. M. C.* (1989); Hilfer, T., *The Crime Novel: A Deviant Genre* (1990): 55–62

—W. P. KENNEY

ČAKS, Aleksandrs

Latvian poet and short-story writer, b. 27 Oct. 1901, Riga; d. 8 Feb. 1950, Riga

Č., a tailor's son, reached Russia with other refugees of World War I, studied medicine in Moscow, and roamed all over Russia as a medical orderly attached to a contingent of Latvian riflemen during the civil war. He got to know MAYAKOVSKY and admired YESENIN's and AKHMATOVA's poetry. He returned to Latvia in 1922, resumed his medical studies, qualified as teacher, and then concentrated on literary work.

Č. infused Latvian poetry with fresh subject matter and a new style. In 1928 he published two small volumes of verse, *Es un šis laiks* (I and this era) and *Sirds uz trotuāra* (heart on the pavement), and in 1929, *Pasaules krogs* (the world's tavern) and *Apašs frakā* (Apache in a dresscoat), all of which portray the urban scene of Riga, its unattractive aspects often glossed over. Like Mayakovsky, he used highly original similes. Next, Č. turned to things destined for oblivion in the bustling city: the horse-drawn cab in *Poēma par ormani* (1930; poem about a cabby), a popular Riga game in *Umurkumurs* (1932; the contest of climbing a greased pole), and the outskirts—his paradise in his search for nature—in *Mana paradīze* (1931; my paradise). He presents a sensuously perceived flow of all life through the use of color, sound, and especially scent. His use of new imagery and his own kind of free verse was to play an important part in the further development of Latvian poetry, although followers of Č. emerged only after his death.

In story writing, Č. showed a delicate touch and finely drawn psychology in the volumes *Eņģelis aiz letes* (1935; angel behind the counter), *Aizslēgtās durvis* (1938; the locked door), and *Debesīs* (1938; in heaven).

His observation of the military exploits of Latvian riflemen resulted in the outstanding poetry of *Mūžības skartie* (2 vols., 1937, 1939; touched by eternity). During World War II Č. continued with lyrical-epic poetry, planning a trilogy on historical themes, of which only one part, *Matīss, kausu bajārs* (pub. 1973 in New York; Matīss, the noble drunkard), was completed; it is one of his most profound works, tending toward an idealistic philosophy of life. Soviet authorities delayed its publication in Latvia until 1972, as was also the case with some of his finest poetry written during World War II, the collection *Lakstīgala dzied basu* (the nightingale sings bass), published with omissions in *Raksti II* (1972; works, Vol. 2).

In his last years Č. was subjected to Soviet censorship and political pressures and his poetry suffered, as is apparent in *Patrioti* (1948; patriots), *Zem cēlās zvaigznes* (1948; under the lofty star), and *Cīnai un darbam* (1951; for struggle and toil). After his death, Č. was passed over in silence in Latvia. When *Sirds uz trotuāra* appeared in Russian translation in Moscow in 1966, he was "rediscovered" in Riga, and published there; his work inspired a new generation of poets.

Č. brought to Latvian poetry urban themes, but offset by a life-enhancing closeness to nature. He enlarged the scope of poetic expression by a variety of strikingly original metaphors and similes; he combined rhyme with assonance, basing his rhythms on natural accentuation.

FURTHER WORKS: *Izlase* (1961); *Raksti I–V* (1971–1976). FURTHER WORKS IN ENGLISH: *Let Us Get Acquainted* (1973); *Selected Poems* (1979)

BIBLIOGRAPHY: Andrups, J., and V. Kalve, *Latvian Literature* (1954): 155

—JĀNIS ANDRUPS

CALDERS, Pere

Catalan short-story writer and novelist (writing in Catalan and Castilian), b. 1912, Barcelona; d. July 1994, Barcelona

Son of the well-known dramatist Vicencs Calders i Arús, C. went to school in Barcelona. When he was only fifteen, he was accepted into the prestigious Barcelona School of Fine Arts, from which he graduated in 1929. After some years working in the field of commercial publicity, he became a journalist. He wrote in Catalan and Castilian for many Catalan publications of the 1920s and 1930s, such as *L'Esquella de la Torratxa, Avui,* and *El Diario Mercantil* and, during the Spanish Civil War, in *La Rambla* and the leftist *Treball.* He spent the war years as a topographer for the Republican army. In 1939 he had to leave Catalonia, fleeing to France where he was interned in a concentration camp. At the onset of World War II he exiled himself to Mexico where he lived for twenty-three years. In 1962 he returned to Barcelona and worked as a draftsman for a publisher until his retirement in the 1970s when he devoted himself full-time to writing until his death in 1994.

His first fictional work dates from 1936 when he published *El primer arlequíc* (The First Harlequin), a collection of short stories where one can find most of the themes and stylistic traits of all the subsequent works, including the absurdity of life, the unsuspected, and the uncertain. During the civil war, besides his work as a military topographer, he published the only true war novel of his career, *Unitats de XOC* (1938; Shock Troops), considered by many critics as one of the finest examples of Catalan writing on the Spanish Civil War. Unlike the vanguardist literature for which he is well known, this novel is written with a realistic and concise style, with a rather impressionistic view of the war's events. During his years of exile in Mexico, C. worked for a publisher and wrote stories and articles for such literary and Catalan political reviews as *La Nostra Revista, Pont Blau,* and *Revista de Catalunya.*

In 1954, still in Mexico, he was awarded the prestigious Víctor Català Prize from Barcelona for *Cròniques de la veritat oculta* (1955; Chronicles of Hidden Truth). In this collection of stories he represents a world torn between pure reason and the subconscious; a world in constant change, sometimes calm but more often frantic, apparently chaotic but never completely irrational. The same literary line appears in the following short-story collections: *Gent d'alta vall* (1957; People of the High Valley) and *Demà a les tres de la matinada* (1963; Tomorrow at Three in the Morning). The general consensus of many critics is that what characterizes C.'s works is the appearance of the unusual, the magical of the fantastic as something totally natural in the midst of everyday life. Reality could be seen or interpreted as a deep and unconscious desire to escape it whenever possible. In this sense C. belongs to the group of Catalan writers characteristic of the decade of the 1950s who tackled the need to re-create everyday reality through imagination and fantasy. With the benefit of hindsight we can now appreciate that C. belongs to the first generation of the so-called "magic realist" school of Catalan writers. This affinity with many Latin American prose writers who settled in Barcelona in the 1960s— when C. returned to his hometown—could explain the warm acceptance they all received by many Catalan publishers. C. was urged by many at that time to switch from Catalan, a minority language, to Spanish. Although he sacrificed international fame, he decided to remain true to his cultural heritage. From the 1960s on he produced his best works, not only as a short-story writer but as a polemical essayist for the most prestigious publications of the literary Catalan renaissance at the end of Franco's dictatorship: *Serra d'or* and the weekly *Tele-estel.*

FURTHER WORKS: *Josep Carner* (1964); *Ronda naval sota la boira* (1966); *Invasió subtil i altres contes* (1978); *Aquí descansa Nevares y altres narracions mexicanes* (1980); *Obres completes* (5 vols., 1985). FURTHER WORKS IN ENGLISH: *The Virgin of the Railway and Other Stories* (1991)

BIBLIOGRAPHY: Triadú, J., *Llegir com viure* (1963): 104-14; Roig, M., "P. C. I el seu món," *Serra d'or,* Sept. 1971: 29-31; Melción, J., Prologue to *Invasió subtil i altres contes* (1978): 5-16; Nadal, M., "P. C.," *Serra d'or,* April 1991: 6-9; Bath, A., Introduction to *The Virgin of the Railway and Other Stories* (1991): 3-14

—JOAN J. GILABERT

CALDWELL, Erskine

American novelist, short-story writer, essayist, and journalist, b. 17 Dec. 1903, Moreland, Ga.; d. 11 Apr. 1987, Paradise Valley, Az.

Son of well-educated parents, C. became interested in writing and in exploring regional folkways in his teens. Convinced that he wanted to be a professional writer after some newspaper experience, C. left the South and settled in Maine. In 1929, after several Spartan years, he had three stories accepted for publication. In 1930 C. celebrated the end of his apprenticeship with a July Fourth bonfire in which he destroyed all his unpublished work from previous years. His new stories quickly found publishers and were collected in *American Earth* (1931); Maxwell Perkins, the famous editor, decided to publish *Tobacco Road* (1932). During the remainder of the 1930s C. wrote prolifically.

Because his sexually explicit novel *God's Little Acre* (1933) and the long-running dramatic version of *Tobacco Road* (by Jack Kirkland) set off censorship battles across the country, and because of the anger and concern generated by the revelations of Southern poverty and racism in his fiction and nonfiction, C. was a well-known public figure by the end of the decade. In Moscow in 1941,

Erskine Caldwell

he covered the war in Russia for CBS radio and several periodicals. Although his output of short stories and nonfiction diminished for a period after the war, he continued to produce longer fiction at the rate of nearly a book a year.

C. has made significant literary contributions in three areas: the novel, the short story, and the essay. The decline in C.'s critical reputation during the 1940s was largely a result of a misunderstanding of his goals and methods, which are the direct result of his definition of "fiction": writing fiction is the process of discovering what a group of invented characters will do as a book or story is being composed. For C., the writing of fiction occurs only when the writer begins a narrative without knowing how it will end.

C.'s fiction is characterized by unpredictable plots and characters, presented in a simple, clear, direct style. The best of the novels are *Tobacco Road*, C.'s exposé of the effects of decades of poverty and starvation on a rural Georgia family; *God's Little Acre*, his exploration of sexual and social morality; and, perhaps, the most impressive demonstration of his method of writing: *Journeyman* (1935), a chronicle of the activities of a self-proclaimed minister who travels the South, providing orgasmic religious experiences for entertainment-starved rurals; and *Trouble in July* (1940), a fast-paced lynching novel.

C.'s early short-story collections—*American Earth*; *We Are the Living* (1933), *Kneel to the Rising Sun* (1935), *Southways* (1938), and *Jackpot* (1940)—may represent his most impressive achievement. While the stories portray a panorama of human vagaries, C.

was particularly interested in adolescent sexual awakening and the effects of racism and poverty.

Although C.'s essayistic work is no longer well known, much of it remains quite impressive. His earliest full-length nonfiction work was the inventive *Some American People* (1935), the long second section of which is made up of twenty-four sketches—some straight reportage, others more like short stories—in which C. documents his travels across Depression America. In 1936 C. met photographer Margaret Bourke-White; during the next six years they traveled together, married, divorced, and collaborated on four books. In *You Have Seen Their Faces* (1937) Bourke-White's memorable photographs of the rural Depression South and C.'s suggestive captions, his essays on the Southern agricultural system, and a series of first-person monologues based on the comments of Southerners fuse to create a powerful attack on economic and racial exploitation, and on those critics who had claimed that *Tobacco Road* and other C. works were exaggerated. Other notable nonfiction books include *North of the Danube* (1939, with Margaret Bourke-White), a beautifully written, powerfully anti-Nazi account of the Czechoslovak Republic's losing battle against German interference; *Moscow under Fire* (1942), a collection of C.'s reports during the Moscow blackout; *All-Out on the Road to Smolensk* (1942), a "nonfiction novel" based on C.'s experiences in war-torn Russia; and two more recent works: *Call It Experience* (1951), C.'s informal review of his career as a writer, and still the most valuable source of information about his life; and *Deep South* (1968), an informal investigation of varieties of Southern religion and an extended reminiscenc about C.'s father.

Working alone, consciously outside the academic literary tradition, C. was able to forge an original definition of fiction and compositional procedure. In addition to his specifically literary contributions, however, he should be remembered for the immense impact on American society of his attacks on poverty, racism, and the tenant farming system (he was discussed in Congress); and for his consistent challenge to censors, whose sensibilities have often been insulted by his willingness to write, so clearly and powerfully that anyone can understand, exactly what he has seen and believes possible.

FURTHER WORKS: *The Bastard* (1929); *Poor Fool* (1930); *Tenant Farmer* (1935); *The Sacrilege of Alan Kent* (1936); *Say! Is This the U.S.A.?* (1941, with Margaret Bourke-White); *Russia at War* (1942, with M. B-W.); *All Night Long* (1942); *Georgia Boy* (1943); *Tragic Ground* (1944); *A House in the Uplands* (1946); *The Caldwell Caravan* (1946); *The Sure Hand of God* (1947); *This Very Earth* (1948); *Place Called Estherville* (1949); *Episode in Palmetto* (1950); *The Humorous Side of Erskine Caldwell* (1951); *A Lamp for Nightfall* (1952); *The Courting of Susie Brown* (1952); *The Complete Stories of Erskine Caldwell* (1953); *Love and Money* (1954); *Gretta* (1955); *Gulf Coast Stories* (1956); *Certain Women* (1957); *Claudelle Inglish* (1958); *Molly Cottontail* (1958); *When You Think of Me* (1959); *Jenny by Nature* (1961); *Close to Home* (1962); *The Last Night of Summer* (1963); *Around About America* (1964); *In Search of Bisco* (1965); *The Deer at Our House* (1966); *Miss Mamma Aimee* (1967); *Writing in America* (1967); *Summertime Island* (1968); *The Weather Shelter* (1969); *The Earnshaw Neighborhood* (1971); *Annette* (1973); *Afternoons in Mid-America* (1976); *The Black and White Storie of E. C.* (1984); *With All My Might: An Autobiography* (1987); *Conversations with E. C.* (1988)

BIBLIOGRAPHY: Beach, J. W., "E. C.: The Comic Catharsis" and "Substitutes and Compensations," in *American Fiction: 1920–1940* (1941): 219–49; Cowley, M., "The Two E. C.s," *NR*, 7 Nov. 1944: 599–600; Benedict, S. H., "Gallic Light on E. C.," *SAQ*, 60 (1961): 390–97; Korges, J., *E. C.* (1969); Cowley, M., "Georgia Boy: A Retrospect of E. C.," in Bruccoli, M. J., and C. E. F. Clark, Jr., eds., *Pages* (1976): 62–78; MacDonald, S., "An Evaluative Check-List of E. C.'s Short Fiction," *SSF*, 15 (1978): 81–97; MacDonald, S., "Enough Good Reasons for Reading, Studying and Teaching E. C.," *Pembroke*, 11 (1979): 7–18; MacDonald, S., ed., *Critical Essays on E. C.* (1981); Devlin, J. E., *E. C.* (1984); Arnold, T. E., ed., *E. C. Reconsidered* (1990); Klevar, H. L., *E. C.: A Biography* (1993); Miller, D. B., *E. C.: The Journey from Tobacco Road* (1995); McDonald, R. L., *The Critical Response to E. C.* (1997)

—SCOTT MACDONALD

CĂLINESCU, George

Romanian critic, literary historian, novelist, poet, and dramatist, b. 19 June 1899, Bucharest; d. 12 March 1965, Bucharest

C. studied at the University of Bucharest and the Romanian School in Rome, where he trained to become a historian. He was, however, drawn to literature, to which he devoted the rest of his life. He taught aesthetics and modern Romanian literature at the universities of Iasi and Bucharest and pursued simultaneously a career in journalism as a newspaper editor and a regular contributor of literary criticism. He also wrote poetry of an erudite, classical turn and numerous short plays. After World War II he achieved preeminence as a critic and joined the literary establishment. He became a member of the Romanian Academy and the director of its Institute of Literary History and served in parliament and in other public capacities.

As a critic, C. advocated "complete criticism," and he drew upon all the disciplines in explicating a work. He also recommended a knowledge of history as indispensable to the critic, who needed a sense of perspective and of continuity in rendering sound aesthetic judgments. For the same reasons he urged a thorough grounding in other cultures, and he himself exhibited a keen appreciation of Italian and Spanish literatures. In the final analysis, however, he thought literary criticism was a creative act, which ultimately rested upon the sensibility and taste of the critic.

The work that secured C.'s place among the great creators of opinion in Romanian literary criticism was his monumental *Istoria literaturii române dela origini pînă în prezent* (1941; the history of Romanian literature from the beginnings to the present). A fundamental work of exegesis of the Romanian creative spirit, it was at the same time a sort of human comedy with its succession of characters and evocations of atmosphere, all described with an ample dose of subjectivity. In this remarkably original synthesis C. undertook to reevaluate all of Romanian literature on the basis of aesthetic rather than traditional cultural criteria.

C. combined critical rigor and artistic intuition in his two pioneering studies of Romania's greatest poet: *Viaţa lui Mihai Eminescu* (1932; the life of Mihai Eminescu) and *Opera lui Mihai Eminescu* (5 vols., 1934–36; the works of Mihai Eminescu). In the

first he re-created the life of the poet as if he were the hero of a novel. Yet, he did not fictionalize. Rather, he gave known facts a new, creative reading. *Opera lui Mihai Eminescu* is a fusion of interpretive curiosity and psychological analysis based upon the first exhaustive investigation of Eminescu's unpublished prose and poetry. C. treated this national hero with an unaccustomed objectivity, but in the process he revealed a far greater poet than even Eminescu's most uncritical admirers had suspected.

C.'s first great success as a novelist was *Enigma Otiliei* (1938; the enigma of Otilia). Its theme and narrative techniques recall the great novels of 19th-c. realism, especially Balzac's. There is the same careful attention to milieu and atmosphere and the same rich gallery of human types. C. was drawn particularly to enigmatic and unpredictable personalities. The portrait he draws of Otilia, one of the great complex heroines of the Romanian novel, is a masterpiece.

In *Bietul Ioanide* (1953; poor Ioanide) C. combined the realistic method of Balzac with the narrative techniques of PROUST. In a sense, the novel reproduces the world of Proust in a different cultural setting. This, too, is an urban novel, in which intellectuals appear as a distinct social class. They are treated as a mutilated humanity, sometimes with sympathy but more often with irony and satire. They do not derive satisfaction from their intellectual labors, but seek it rather from the desperate pursuit of political office and other extra-academic honors. The one notable exception is the architect Ioanide, a symbol of genius, who is driven to create without regard for personal gain. *Scrinul negru* (1960; the black chest of drawers) uses the same means and treats of the same subjects as C.'s earlier novels. It is an examination of upper-class society in disarray and a study of the complex personality, this time of Caty Zănoagă, a sort of Madame Bovary who is frustrated by the very fulfillment of all her aspirations. She is like C.'s Otilia, except that all myth has been stripped away. Once again C. showed himself thoroughly at home in the dissection of the upper classes and the intellectuals, but his attempt to portray the new, Communist man of the postwar era was a failure.

Although C.'s reputation rests primarily upon his works of criticism and novels, his influence touched every facet of literary life. Rather than for any single work he will perhaps be remembered longest as the embodiment of a particular "moment" in the history of Romanian culture.

FURTHER WORKS: *Alcuni missionari cattolici italiani nella Moldavia dei secoli XVII e XVIII* (1925); *Altre notizie sui missionari cattolici nei paesi romeni* (1930); *Cartea nunţii* (1933); *Poesii* (1937); *Viaţa lui Ion Creangă* (1938); *Principii de estetică* (1939); *Sun sau Calea neturburată* (1943); *Istoria literaturii române, compendiu* (1945); *Impresii asupra literaturii spaniole* (1946); *Trei nuvele* (1949); *Kiev, Moscova, Leningrad* (1949); *Am fost în China nouă.* (1955); *Nicolae Filimon* (1959); *Grigore M. Alexandrescu* (1962); *Lauda Incrurilor* (1963); *Cronicile optimistului* (1964); *Teatru* (1965); *Estetica basmului* (1965); *Opere,* (14 vols. 1965–1972); *Ion Eliade-Rădulescu ş şcoala sa* (1966). FURTHER WORKS IN ENGLISH: *Studies in Poetics* (1972)

BIBLIOGRAPHY: Piru, A., Introduction to G. C., *Studies in Poetics* (1972): v–xxi; Martin, M., "G. C. et Roland Barthes," *CREL* No. 4 (1978): 40–53

—KEITH HITCHINS

CALLADO, Antônio

Brazilian novelist, essayist, journalist, and dramatist, b. 26 Jan. 1917, Niterói

C. had a typical middle-class upbringing and spent most of his childhood in Niterói, Petrópolis, and Teresópolis. After his father's death, his family moved to Rio de Janeiro, where he studied law and worked as a journalist. In 1941 C. went to work at the BBC in England and from 1944 to 1947 at the French Radio in France. Although his "years of exile" in Europe were happy, C. felt a profound longing for Brazil and a deep desire to return and rediscover his own country. Back in Brazil, he worked for *Jornal do Brazil* and became known for the coverage of the most critical political, social, and economic issues in the 1950s and 1960s: the status of the Indians, the vast unexplored Amazons region, the burgeoning organization of the peasant leagues in the northeast, and the plight of the *favelados*.

However, it is in his literary works that all these issues are presented with a coherent vision of what the critic Ligia Chiappini Moraes Leite calls a "national and populist project of Brazilian culture." Although C. acknowledges that technically and stylistically he is influenced by his readings of James JOYCE, Marcel PROUST, and Alain ROBBE-GRILLET, C. as many other Brazilian intellectuals at the time was reevaluating the concept of Brazilian identity and was fully committed to creating a literature that is meant to be accessible to the masses.

His project—via landmark works such as *Os sertões* (1902; *Rebellion in the Backlands*, 1944) by Euclides da Cunha (1866–1909) and *Macunaíma* (1928; *Macunaíma*, 1984) by Mário de ANDRADE—is a continuation of the 19th-c. romanticism movement to build a national identity. Thus his novels are a kaleidoscopic voyage across Brazil, in an effort to portray what he found to be its multiple and genuine realities: the Indians in the Amazon forest, the peasants in Pernambuco and the backlands of Bahia, the colonial towns of Minas Gerais, the swamps of the Pantanal in the Midwest, and, back to the city, Rio de Janeiro.

His works can be roughly divided in two groups, religious and political, with his novel *Quarup* (1967; *Quarup*, 1970) serving as the divider. In the first phase there are two novels: *Assunção de Salviano* (1954; the assumption of Salviano) and *Madona de cedro* (1957; cedar Madonna). Although these novels present situations that are critical of the traditional church and the Communist Party in Brazil, their focus is the more universal theme of the struggle for grace and redemption. Frequently compared to the works of Graham GREENE, C.'s oeuvre is permeated by religious concerns, Catholicism being an important element in the daily lives of the people of his generation. This religious feeling, together with the messianic and martyrdom message, is present in his later books, shifting the focus from the individual sexual sin to the social sin perceived in society.

Quarup, a title taken from an Indian ritual of death and resurrection, is seen as one of the most influential books during the 1960s and 1970s in Brazil. The novel—considered realist by many critics—is a sweeping epic portrait of Brazil, of its people and institutions. C. presents a mosaic of the conflicting ideologies and problems that afflict the country through each one of his characters, such as the Europocentric point of view versus the indigenists; the urban (therefore peripheral: cities along the coast) versus the countryside (the Amazon, the mythical matriarchal center); the land-owning versus the dispossessed; the nationalist Left versus capitalist colonialism. All these themes are kept together by the story of Nando, a priest who wants to convert Indians to Christianity and eventually abandons the robe to become a revolutionary guerrilla hero. This is an optimistic novel, messianic and redemptive with both Christian and Marxist messages.

Bar D. Juan (1971; *Don Juan's Bar*, 1972) and *Reflexos do baile* (1978; reflections of the ball) are political urban novels that are more pessimistic. The first is about the disillusionment and paralysis surrounding the revolutionary cause, the second a fragmented testimonial of the chaotic period of terrorist acts and violent military persecution and repression.

Sempreviva (1981; *Sempreviva*, 1988), awarded the Goethe Institute Prize for fiction in 1982, is the story of an exile, a prodigal son, who returns to Brazil before the political amnesty to seek revenge for the death of his beloved woman. But Brazil, the Edenic mother country, is an illusion, and its nature, beneath its benevolent tropical lusciousness, has a dark, sinister, and rotten side. This novel, dense in literary and religious symbols, is a cathartic literary and mystical effort to capture the meaning of recent events in Brazilian history, in this case the underworld of torturers of the military régime and their victims, the tortured.

C.'s *Expedição Montaigne* (1982; Montaigne expedition) and *Concerto Carioca* (1985; carioca concert), like all his novels, unfold and expand themes central to the question of Brazilian identity, in particular the survival of the Indians. Furthermore, it exposes and satirizes the dilemma of the New World intellectual and his attempt to define what is unique about Brazilian identity without escaping his colonial attachment to European tradition.

FURTHER WORKS: *Cidade assassinada* (1954); *Retrato de Portinari* (1956); *Frankel* (1957); *O colar de coral* (1957); *Pedro Mico* (1957); *Os industriais da Seca e os Galileus* (1959); *Uma rede para Iemanjá* (1961); *Maria Chica* (1964); *Forró do Engenho Cananéia* (1964); *Tempo de Arraes* (1964); *Vietnã do norte* (1977); *A revoluta da Cachaça* (1983); *O homem cordial e outras histórias* (1993)

BIBLIOGRAPHY: Galagher, D., on *Quarup, NYTBR* (14 June 1970), 4; Aiex, N. C., "The Reality of Myth: A. C.'s *Assunção de Salviano,*" *PCL* (1979): 131–37; Aiex, N. C., "From Rhetoric to Revolution: A. C.'s *Bar D. Juan,*" *Seleta* (1980): 131–37; Moraes Leite, L. C., "Quando a Pátria Viaja: Uma leitura dos romances de A. C.," in Zilio, C., and Lafeta´, J. L. and Moraes Leite, L. C., eds., *O Nacional e o Popular* (1982): 120–234

—NAOMI HOKI MONIZ

CALLAGHAN, Morley

Canadian novelist and short-story writer (writing in English), b. 22 Feb. 1903, Toronto, Ont.; d. 25 Aug. 1990, Toronto

After an Irish-Catholic upbringing, C. received a degree from St. Michael's College at the University of Toronto in 1925, and a law degree from Toronto's Osgoode Hall Law School. While still a student, he worked as a reporter for the *Toronto Daily Star*. Encouraged by another *Daily Star* reporter, Ernest HEMINGWAY, he began to publish short stories in literary and popular magazines in England and the U.S. In 1928 C. was admitted to the Toronto bar.

In 1928 C. published his first novel, *Strange Fugitive*. In it he staked out a literary terrain previously unexplored in Canadian literature: the relationship between society and its moral outcasts. His spare, hard, reportorial style was also new in Canadian literature, although familiar enough to readers of Sherwood ANDERSON, whom C. acknowledged to be his "literary father," and Hemingway. In 1929, while a member of Paris literary expatriate society (a period recalled in *That Summer in Paris*, (1963), C. wrote *It's Never Over* (1930), a novel in which the reverberations of an execution are the focus of a psychological study of the never-ending effects of violence answered with more violence.

In the Great Depression decade that followed, C. wrote several novels concerning the human—specifically the spiritual—effects of social injustice. Influenced by the Christian-humanist thought of Jacques Maritain, C. advanced a liberalized, noninstitutional Christianity as a solution. *Such Is My Beloved* (1934) is a parable about a priest's attempt to rehabilitate prostitutes with conventional moral suasion that proves futile in the absence of charity from church or society. Yet, as C. sees it, Father Dowling's transcendent love is the only meaningful way by which lost souls can be redeemed. *They Shall Inherit the Earth* (1935) likewise posits a form of Christian humanism in solving an ingeniously contrived moral and social dilemma.

C. is more concerned, however, with the human predicament than with social criticism. Though the background for several of his books is the Great Depression, he does not directly attack the prevailing political, social, and economic conditions. Nevertheless, even his cloddish primitives attest the psychic scars of their bleak existence. They belong to the ranks of modern literary "heroes" for whom the mere fact of being alive is misery. Criminals, or blameless fugitives from life, or saints purified by worldly suffering, they are likely to be involved in an odyssey that takes them through crime and punishment to a newfound moral strength or into a situation that permits C. to examine the dialectical tensions between sacred and profane love.

C.'s books are in essence allegories about the necessity of striving to wrest religious meaning from the terrifying flux of modern life. Unlike the French and American naturalist writers with whom he has sometimes been compared, C. refuses to believe that man is deterministically trapped between biological and socioeconomic forces. Man can be remade, but first he must renounce the ego. C.'s later work emphasizes the individual's responsibility to himself and to his fellows in this regard. In *The Loved and the Lost* (1951), a man's renunciation of egoistic self-interest releases in him compassion and a genuine sense of responsibility. This occurs after his failure to impose his passion for order and security on the personality of the heroine, a free spirit with a large and indiscriminate capacity for love.

Though his ten novels make up by far the bulk of his work, C. is actually at his best in the short story, a form well suited to his straightforward, yet deft narrative style. Moreover, the restricted framework of the short story minimizes the melodramatic sensationalism and plodding realism that occasionally mar his novels. Typically, the stories of his first two collections, *A Native Argosy* (1929) and *Now That April's Here* (1936), depend on some seemingly trivial drama of human experience, which in fact symbolizes a deeper psychological or spiritual conflict. They end gently or sadly, their small ironies and awakenings suffused with tolerance and pity.

C. belongs to the group of realists and naturalists of the 1920s, mostly American, whose innovations in form determined the

course of mainstream fiction in English for decades to come. His own work combines unembittered irony and uncompromising honesty with a discriminating moral vision and an unsentimental compassion for life's misfits and rejects. C.'s best fiction to date was written between 1928 (*Strange Fugitive*) and 1937 (*More Joy in Heaven*). Though only one of his novels, *A Passion in Rome* (1961), takes place outside Canada, his concern with reaching an international readership has in turn deprived C.'s fiction of any searching speculation on Canadian life and experience. Critics have also contended that his sobriety precludes a comic—and also a genuinely tragic—sense of life. At the age of seventy-four, however, C. published *Close to the Sun Again* (1977), a novel resembling in its moral drama the best of his earlier fiction, and a triumphant refutation of the critical view that his best work was behind him.

FURTHER WORKS: *No Man's Land* (1931); *A Broken Journey* (1932); *Luke Baldwin's Vow* (1948); *The Varsity Story* (1948); *M. C.'s Stories* (1959); *The Many Colored Coat* (1960); *A Time for Judas* (1983); *Our Lady of the Snows* (1985)

BIBLIOGRAPHY: Lewis, W., "What Books for Total War," *Saturday Night*, Oct. 1942: 16; McPherson, H., "The Two Worlds of M. C.," *QQ*, 44 (1957): 350–65; Wilson, E., *O Canada* (1964): 9–31; Woodcock, G., *A Choice of Critics* (1966): 185–202; Conron, B., *M. C.* (1966); Hoar, V., *M. C.* (1969); Morley, P., *M. C.* (1978); Staines, D., ed., *The C. Symposium* (1981)

—JOHN H. FERRES

CALVINO, Italo

Italian novelist, short-story writer, and critic, b. 15 Oct. 1923, Santiago de las Vegas, Cuba; d. 19 Sept. 1985, Siena, Italy

C. was born in Cuba, a distant and exotic island, from the Italian viewpoint, where his father was on an agronomy mission. After the family's return to San Remo on the Italian Riviera, C. studied at the University of Turin and graduated in 1947 with a thesis on Joseph CONRAD. Soon afterward he became an editor for the Einaudi publishing house, a position through which he has influenced Italian cultural life in a manner comparable to that of Elio Vittorini and Cesare PAVESE. Between 1959 and 1966 he also coedited *Il Menabò* with Vittorini, a journal that encouraged discussions on the role of the intellectual in modern society. From 1967 to 1980 C. lived in Paris, the center of European cultural life at the time when structuralism and semiotics were revolutionizing contemporary thought, and became an active member of the OULIPO group. In 1980 he settled down in Rome and continued his writing, as well as his editorial and cultural role, until his death.

The anxious yet colorful years of the anti-Fascist Resistance and the aftermath of World War II are the background of C.'s beginnings as a narrative writer. His first novel, *Il sentiero dei nidi di ragno* (1947; *The Path to the Nest of Spiders*, 1957), immediately gained him critical praise by, among others, Pavese. C. chose to depict the Resistance through the eyes of Pin, a boy from the San Remo slums who is wise to the facts of the world and uses often obscene language, but maintains his innocence and astonishment in the face of life throughout his adventures with a ragged company of partisans. Using Pin as narrator, C. is able to give an accurate, but also irreverent and at the same time fantastic, portrayal of historical events he had witnessed. Pin lacks the NEOREALISTIC sadness to be found in the contemporary movies by Rossellini or De Sica, and is endowed instead with a gaiety and freshness that were to remain characteristic of C.'s writing, especially in his many short stories and novellas, even when the subject matter itself is serious or tragic.

C.'s tendency to transform reality into fable is perhaps best expressed in three "fantastic novels" he collected in a trilogy significantly entitled *I nostri antenati* (1960; our ancestors): *Il visconte dimezzato* (1952; *The Cloven Viscount*, 1962), *Il barone rampante* (1957; *The Baron in the Trees*, 1959), and *Il cavaliere inesistente* (1959; *The Nonexistent Knight*, 1962). The three protagonists of these novels are "our ancestors" because they precede us metaphorically as well as chronologically: they are the fantastic projections of ourselves, the fictional embodiments of our idiosyncrasies, fears, alienations, and discontents. Any reader can superimpose his or her own experience upon the beautiful tales of the good and evil halves of the viscount, the enlightened life of the baron in the trees, the force of will and the faith in a sacred cause by which the quixotic knight enables himself to live without a body inside his shining armor. Chivalric epics, *contest philosophiques*, adventure novels, and folktales are freely used and echoed by C. to construct these brilliant novels.

Another aspect of C.'s work appears very clearly in *Il cavaliere inesistente* (through the emphasis on and the final *coup de théâtre* by the narrator) and is greatly developed in his subsequent books, and that is his interest in and meditation on the act of narrating, the nature of writing itself. *Le cosmicomiche* (1965; *Cosmicomics*, 1968) and *Ti con zero* (1967; *t zero*, 1969) are short narrative pieces told by a "character" called Qfwfq and apparently dealing with such scientific topics as the distance of the moon from the earth, the origin of birds, of the disappearance of dinosaurs. Actually, each piece, while being a delightful exploration of distant millennia and galaxies, is also and above all the author's reflection on his written creation, a tale telling itself, a metafiction.

This reflection is carried on in harmony with contemporary literary theories; it is continued by C. in *Il castello dei destini incrociati* (1969; final ed. 1973; *The Castle of Crossed Destinies*, 1976) and *Le città invisibili* (1972; *Invisible Cities*, 1974), both based on the combinational units of which every narration is composed; and it is further developed in his latest novel, *Se una notte d'inverno un viaggiatore* (1979; *If on a Winter's Night a Traveler*, 1981). It is about a reader who cannot ever finish the novel(s) he had started reading, so that C.'s novel is made up of a frame (the story of the reader) encompassing ten different beginnings of unfinished novels-within-the-novel, each parodying a different way of writing a novel, and each presenting different problems of contemporary life, from ecology to censorship.

During his last years he published books that are important in different ways: *Una pietra sopra. Discorsi di letteratura e società* (1980; *The Uses of Literature*, 1986) is a collection of critical essays "on literature and society," as the Italian subtitle indicates; *Palomar* (1983; *Mr. Palomar*, 1985) is a meditation on the sense of sight, writing, and death; and *Collezione di sabbia* (1984; Sand collection) gathers descriptions of unusual objects and places. Among the works published posthumously are *Sotto il sole giaguaro* (1986; *Under the Jaguar Sun*, 1988), tales about the senses; *Lezioni americane. Seei proposte per il prossimo millennio* (1988; *Six Memos for the Next Millennium*, 1988), the Norton lectures he should have delivered at Harvard on the qualities or values of literature to be saved for the next millennium; and *La strada*

di San Giovanni (1990; *The Road to San Giovanni*, 1993), autobiographical pieces.

C. is a writer who, perhaps better than anyone else of his generation, has observed and captured the spirit of the times he lives in, and has transformed his philosophical, sociological, and moral observations into literary *inventions*—characters, images, and plots. His fundamental optimism is never superficial but is based on the unshakable faith in the power of reason and fantasy to understand, and therefore to overcome, the making of history. His way of writing is doubly "fabulous": he transforms everything into stories, into fables; and these fables, no matter how geometric or abstract they may appear, are graceful, powerful, and truly wondrous.

FURTHER WORKS: *Ultimo viene il corvo* (1949; *Adam, One Afternoon, and Other Stories*, 1957); *I giovani del Po* (1950); *La formica argentina* (1952); *L'entrata in guerra* (1954); *Fiabe italiane* (1956; *Italian Fables*, 1959; *Italian Folk tales: Selected and Retold by I. C.*, 1980); *La speculazione edilizia* (1957); *La nuvola di smog* (1958); *La giornata d'uno scrutatore* (1963); *Marcovaldo ovvero le stagioni in città* (1963); *Gli amori difficili* (1970); *Orlando furioso di Ludovico Ariosto raccontato da I. C.* (1970); *L'uccel belverde e altre fiabe italiane* (1972); *Il Principe Granchio, e altre fiabe italiane* (1974); *Cosmicomiche vecchie e nuove* (1984); *I libri degli altri. Lettere 1947-81* (1991); *Perché leggere i classici* (1991); *Romanzi e racconti* (1991–94); *Prima che tu dica "pronto"* (1993); *Eremita a Parigi* (1994); *Saggi* (1995)

BIBLIOGRAPHY: Woodhouse, J. R., *I. C.: A Reappraisal and an Appreciation of the Trilogy* (1968); Calligaris, C., *I. C.* (1973); Corti, M., "Le jeu comme génération du texte: Des tarots au récit," *Semiotica*, 7 (1973): 33–48; Vidal, G., "Fabulous C.," *NYRB*, 30 May 1974: 13–21; De Lauretis, T., "Narrative Discourse in C.: Praxis or Poiesis?," *PMLA*, 90 (1975): 415–25; Biasin, G. P., "4/3πr³: Literary vs. Scientific Space," *Versus*, 19/20 (1978): 173–88; Cannon, J. A., *Postmodern Italian Fiction. The Crisis of Reason in C., Eco, Sciascia, Malerba* (1989); Re, L., *C. and the Age of Neorealism: Fables of Estrangement* (1990); Hume, K., *C.'s Fictions: Cognito and Cosmos* (1992)

—GIAN-PAOLO BIASIN

CAMAJ, Martin

Albanian novelist, poet, and critic, b. 21 July 1925, Temali; d. 12 Mar. 1992, Lenggries, Germany

Born and reared in the Dukagjin region of the northern Albanian Alps, one of the wildest and most isolated reaches of Europe, C. was fortunate to receive a classical education at the Jesuit Saverian college in the town of Shkodër. In 1948, soon after the installation of the Hoxha dictatorship, he managed to escape from Stalinist Albania to neighboring Yugoslavia and studied at the University of Belgrade. From there he went on to do postgraduate research in Italy, where he taught Albanian and finished his studies in linguistics at the University of Rome in 1960. From 1970 to 1990 he was professor of Albanian studies at the University of Munich and lived in the mountain village of Lenggries in Upper Bavaria until his death.

C.'s literary activities over a period of forty-five years cover several phases of development. He began with poetry, a genre to which he remained faithful throughout his life, but in later years he also devoted himself increasingly to prose. His first volumes of classical verse, *Nji fyell ndër male* (1953; A Flute in the Mountains) and *Kânga e vërrinit* (1954; Song of the Lowland Pastures), were inspired by his native northern Albanian mountains to which he never lost his attachment, despite long years of exile and the impossibility of return. These were followed by *Djella* (1958; Djella), a novel interspersed with verse about the love of a teacher for a young girl of the lowlands. His verse collections, *Legjenda* (1964; Legends) and *Lirika mes dy moteve* (1967; Lyrics between Two Ages), which contained revised versions of a number of poems from *Kânga e vërrinit*, were reprinted in *Poezi 1953-1967* (1981; Poetry 1953-1967). C.'s mature verse shows the influence of the hermetic movement of Italian poet Giuseppe UNGARETTI. The metaphoric and symbolic character of his language increased with time as did the range of his poetic themes. A selection of his poetry has also been translated into Italian in the bilingual edition *M. C.: Poesie* (1985; Poetry), into English, *Selected Poetry* (1990), and into German, *Gedichte* (1991; Poems).

The novel *Rrathë* (1978; Circles) has been described as the first psychological novel ever to be written in Albanian. It is the author's most extensive prose work, one which he took fifteen years to write. Agron, a writer and agronomist in postrevolutionary "Arbenia," is sent to the village of Middle Ripa to report on the arrival of some new tractors. There he becomes enthralled with the haunted history of the mountains after saving the life of the wild and beautiful shepherdess Sose, a personification of the mountain nymphs. The "circles" of water, fire, and blood into which the novel is divided symbolize not only metaphysical and social constraints but also the writer's progress through the mythical heritage of Albania's past towards a new and personal future.

Among C.'s other literary publications are a volume of verse entitled *Njeriu më vete e me tjerë* (1978; Man by Himself and with Others), *Dranja* (1981; Dranja), a collection of self-styled madrigals, *Shkundullima* (1981; Quaking), a collection of five short stories and one play, and the novel *Karpa* (1987; Karpa), set on the banks of the River Drin in the year 2338, a long prose work that C. preferred to call a parable. General themes which occur in C.'s work are the loss of tradition, loneliness in a changing world, and the search for one's roots. His language is discreet, reserved, and trying at times, although the author regarded the term hermetic as coincidental. He relies on the traditional and colorful linguistic fountainhead of his native Geg dialect in order to convey a poetic vision of his pastoral mountain birthplace near the Drin with its sparkling streams and rocky headlands.

In Munich, where C. edited and printed most of his literary works, intellectual circles and his university colleagues in particular were often puzzled and bemused by the linguist who spent much of his time publishing obscure works of fiction in a language nobody in Central Europe could understand and for a public consisting of no more than a handful of other Albanian emigrants. C. was an author in exile in every sense of the word and was to remain so until the end of his days. His name remained a taboo in Albania throughout the long years of the communist dictatorship and was never mentioned in public. Indeed until 1991 virtually no one of the younger generation in Tirana had ever heard of him. Nonetheless, he established a considerable reputation abroad as a linguist and as professor of Albanian studies at the University of Munich, publishing numerous works on the history and dialects of the Albanian language and on Albanian folklore.

During the 1990s C. finally began to receive some of the praise and acclamation he was denied as a writer during his lifetime. Arshi Pipa's monograph on *Contemporary Albanian Literature* (1991), for instance, is devoted almost exclusively to two authors: Ismail KADARE and C. While many critics have been unbounded in their adulation and praise of C. as an author of national significance, initial reception of his works in fact proved very mixed. Many readers were confused and perplexed by the author's hermetic prose, his borderline genres, and a literary style quite new to them. Only time will tell if C.'s works can be appreciated by the Albanian public at large, above and beyond initial curiosity.

FURTHER WORKS: *Në hijen e gjarpnit* (1991); *Pishtarët e natë* (1991); *Kandili argjandit* (1993); *Vepra letrare* (1996)

BIBLIOGRAPHY: Pipa, A., *Contemporary Albanian Literature* (1991): 125-64; special C. issue, *Albanica*, 2 (1991); Elsie, R., *History of Albanian Literature* (1995): 680-82; Berisha, A., *Vepra letrare e M. C.* (1995); Berisha, A. "Das literarische Werk M. C.," *Dardania*, 4 (1995): 165-78

—ROBERT ELSIE

CAMARA Laye

Guinean novelist (writing in French), b. 1 Jan. 1928, Kouroussa; d. 4 Feb. 1980, Dakar, Senegal

C.'s formal French education began in local schools; he went on to a technical high school in Conakry and then left for France on a government scholarship. After earning a certificate of automotive technology at Argenteuil he moved to Paris, where, while continuing his studies toward a degree in automotive engineering, he held odd jobs and experienced great privation until he found employment in an automobile factory.

In 1956 C. returned to Guinea and worked there in a technical capacity for the French colonial regime. With the establishment of an independent Guinea, he was sent to several African countries on diplomatic missions and was named director of Sekou Touré's study and research center in the Ministry of Information in Conakry.

With other young intellectuals he had hoped that newly won independence would bring about greater personal freedom, but this was not to be. He fell out of grace with President Touré, partly because he attempted to withdraw from public service, partly because his writing became increasingly critical of the regime. In 1965 C. found it necessary to flee into exile in Senegal, where he lived until his death, working at the research institute commonly known as IFAN and trying to cope with failing health and the responsibility of raising his seven children by his first marriage and two by his second.

When still struggling in Paris, C., feeling alienated and overwhelmed by homesickness, began to write, which sustained him in those trying days. A series of nostalgic reminiscences from his earliest days in the family compound at Kouroussa to the time he left for Paris became his first book—*L'enfant noir* (1953; The Dark Child, 1954). The romantic, even rhapsodic, evocation of daily life in the village and the rituals of growing up, and especially the often quoted description of C.'s father, a goldsmith, who saw himself as working mystically with his raw materials, recognizing a snake as his protective spirit, caused *L'enfant noir* to be championed as a major prose example of the NÉGRITUDE movement. *L'enfant noir* is the most famous African novel in French.

C.'s finest work, *Le regard du roi* (1954; *The Radiance of the King*, 1956), is a surreal allegory whose most conspicuous attributes are (1) a reversal of the colonial racial roles in which the white protagonist must endure humiliation and loss of identity before he is accepted by the Africans; and (2) cinematographic effects, including repetitions, dissolves, flashbacks, shifts of place and time, and the like. The many layers of the novel admit of the most different interpretations: suggestions of Christian redemption and Islamic mysticism appear alongside reverberations of KAFKA's fictional concepts and African animism.

After a long silence broken only by the publication of a short story, "Les yeux de la statue" (1957; "The Eyes of the Statue," 1959), which is a pessimistic variation of *Le regard du roi*, C. brought out the hastily written novel *Dramouss* (1966; *A Dream of Africa*, 1968). *Dramouss* takes up where *L'enfant noir* ends, telling of C.'s trials and tribulations in Paris and his return after six years to newly independent Guinea. But nostalgia has turned to bitterness. He finds a ruthless political party in complete control, whose rulers have thrown overboard all African traditional values and those of France as well. Noteworthy is the description of a dream in which the totemic snake-woman Dramouss holds forth the hope of a liberated Guinea, whose people, secure in their autochthonous traditions, may once again enjoy the time-honored brotherhood of men. It is these traditions that C. felt had been destroyed by corruption and traded for power in the new Republic of Guinea. The book earned C. a death sentence *in absentia* from the Guinean authorities.

After another decade of silence, dictated in part by a lingering serious illness, C. published *Le maître de la parole* (1978; *The Guardian of the Word: Kouma Lafolo Kouma*, 1980). Although admittedly the retelling from existing chronicles of the story of the childhood and rise to power of the ancient emperor Sundiata Keita, the work is, in a sense, a broadening of the basic preoccupations that always haunted C., for the emphasis is on Sundiata's long and painful exile, and the two main themes running through C.'s overall literary work are those of exile and the quest for fulfillment.

BIBLIOGRAPHY: Brench, A. C., "C. L.: Idealist and Mystic," *ALT*, No. 2 (1969): 11–31; Sellin, E., "Alienation in the Novels of C. L.," *PAJ*, 4 (1971): 455–72; Larson, C. R., *The Emergence of African Fiction* (1972): 167–226; Palmer, E., *An Introduction to the African Novel* (1972): 85–116; King, A., "C. L.," in King, B., and Ogungbesan, K., eds., *A Celebration of Black and African Writers* (1975): 112–23; Bernard, P. R., "C. L.: A Bio-Bibliography," *AfrLJ*, 9 (1978): 307–21; Sellin, E., "Trial by Exile: C. L. and Sundiata Keita," *WLT*, 54 (1980): 392–95; King, A., *The writings of C. L.* (1981); Lee, S., *C. L.* (1984)

—ERIC SELLIN

CAMBODIAN LITERATURE

During the period of the French Protectorate (1863–1953), Cambodian writers tended to treat well-known themes, using the traditional medium of verse and the "high" language, although employing some postclassical meters (the "seven-syllabled" and the "eight-syllabled"). Thus, the greatly esteemed Acar In (1859–1924) wrote a long poem describing Angkor: *Nireas Angkor* (1926; a visit to Angkor). Madame Sit (1881–1963) retold an Indian tale in verse (*Pimpeapileap*, written 1920, pub. 1942; the lament of Pimpea). NuKan (1874–1950) rewrote a much-loved Cambodian story, *Teav ek* (1942; the one and only Teav).

Among prose works of the period were In's *Katilok* (1936; the way of the world), a collection of retold Buddhist moral tales; new versions of old folktales; translations of European novels; and articles, such as those by Bu-Po (dates n.a.) and Chhim-Sum (dates n.a.), on Buddhist or other cultural subjects.

A forerunner of the literature of the period after independence was the first modern Cambodian novel, a love story by Kim-Hak (b. 1905), *Tik Tonle Sap* (1939; the waters of the Tonle Sap). The significance of this work lay in the new style of writing (in plain and even colloquial prose) and in the subject matter (the present-day life of ordinary Cambodians instead of the exploits of gods and heroes).

After the gaining of independence in 1953, nationalist ideas soon penetrated the arts. Writers such as Leang Hap An (dates n.a.), director of the Buddhist Institute, wrote articles urging authors to help to raise the national literary standards. Ly Theam Teng (dates n.a.), in his *Aksarsastr Khmer* (1960; Cambodian literature), criticized some Cambodian authors for incorporating in their work undesirable Western ideas. However, the characters in the novels of the time—their background and their problems—were thoroughly Cambodian. Themes ranged from the arranged marriage in Im Chudet's (dates n.a.) *Bandol kon pa* (1956; Bandol, father's darling) to crime detection in Kang Bun Chhoeun's (dates n.a.) *Pecchakheat kramom* (1960; a young murderess). Adventure was provided by writers like Hel Sumphar (1921–1971) in *Chao bit muk* (1951; the masked bandit) or historical novelists such as R. Kovid (dates n.a.) in *Banteay Longvek* (1954; the citadel of Longvek). Social injustices were frequent themes. Suon Surin (dates n.a.) portrayed the struggle of a poor employee against his oppressive employers in *Preah atit thmey reah loe phen dey chas* (1961; the new sun rises over the old land), while Lang Peng Siek (dates n.a.) highlighted the corruption of officials in *Khyal Kambot tbong* (1972; the hurricane).

Politics became an important element in novels by, for example, Bun-Chan Mol (dates n.a.), the author of *Kuk neayobay* (1971; political imprisonment). Autobiography is represented by Madame Sothivongs (dates n.a.) with *Veasna khnhom* (1959; my fate). Characteristic of the mood of the times was a pessimistic novel by Sot-Polin (dates n.a.), *Chivit it ney* (1965; the futility of life). Other wellknown novels are *Sophat* (written 1938, pub. 1960; Sophat) by Rim-Kin (1911–1959), an artist, poet, and playwright; *Kolap Pailin* (written 1944, pub. 1959; the rose of Pailin) by Nhok-Them (b. 1903), who is also a successful translator of works from Pali, Thai and French; and *Phka srapon* (1965; the faded flower) by Nu Hach (b. 1916).

Much anonymous poetry, voicing new ideas about contemporary Cambodia, appeared in journals. Some poets' names are known, however. Makhali Phal (dates n.a.) wrote *Chamrieng santepheap* (c. 1953; song of peace) and Keng Vannsak (dates n.a.) published a collection of romantic poetry, *Chitt kramon* (c. 1955; a young girl's heart).

Two further genres emerged after 1953: the Western-style play (at first incorporating song, music, and dance) and the short story. Hang Thun Hak (dates n.a.) wrote many plays, among them one contrasting traditional and modern behavior entitled *Sambok it meba* (1965; nest without parents). Short stories, chiefly love stories, are to be found here and there in journals. Finally, postindependence publications have included many translations of Chinese novels.

The political upheavals of the 1970s seriously affected literary production. During the Pol Pot regime (1975-79), when cities were emptied and an estimated 2 million people died, literary activity was confined to revolutionary songs. After the ousting of the Khmer Rouge in 1979 there was a gradual revival in Cambodian literature with novelists taking the harshness and brutality of the Khmer Rouge period as their major theme. By the early 1990s the overtly political fiction promoted by the government was beginning to be replaced by romantic and crime fiction.

BIBLIOGRAPHY: Bitard, P., "La littérature cambodgienne moderne," *France-Asie*, 114–15 (1955): 467–82; Whitaker, D. P., et al., "Literature and Scholarship," *Area Handbook for Cambodia* (1973): 131–32; Lafont, P. B., "Introduction aux littératures comtemporaines de la Péninsule Indochinoise," in Lafont, L. P., and D. Lombard, eds., *Littératures contemporaines de l'Asie du Sud-Est* (1974): 3–7; Piat, M., "Contemporary Cambodian Literature," *Journal of the Siam Society*, 63, 2 (1975): 251–59; Nepote, J., and Khing Hoc Dy, "Literature and Society in Modern Cambodia," in *Literature and Society in Southeast Asia* (1981): 56-81; Khing Hoc Dy, *Contributions á l'histoire de la Littérature Khmère Vol. 1: L'époque classique XVe-XIXe siècle* (1990); Khing Hoc Dy, *Contributions à l'histoire de la Littérature Khmère Vol. 2: Ecrivains et expressions littéraires du Cambodge au Xxe siècle* (1993); Khing Hoc Dy, "Khmer Literature since 1975," in Ebihara, M. M. et al., eds., *Cambodian Culture since 1975: Homeland and Exile* (1994)

—JUDITH M. JACOB

CAMEROONIAN LITERATURE

Between 1884 and 1918 Cameroon was a German colony; after Germany's defeat in World War I, the country became a protectorate administered partly by France and partly by Britain. Cameroon became independent on January 1, 1960. On October 1, 1961 the reunification of East Cameroon, a mandated territory under French administration, and West Cameroon, previously a British colony took place.

Cameroon like many other African countries had an oral civilization before European colonization. In addition to French and English, the two official languages, linguists count more than 200 languages in Cameroon. Some of these languages are related to the Bantu group while others belong to the West African group. In northern Cameroon, Fufulde is the most common language, and in the far north, the influence of Arabic can be felt. In Bamoun land, sultan Ibrahim Njoya, who came to power in 1880, invented a form of writing comprising eighty-three signs and ten digits. Yet, apart from a few translations of the Bible, the extent of writing in local languages was rather limited. Although Jean-Louis Njemba Medou (1902-1966) wrote a chronicle in Bulu entitled *Nnanga Kon* (1932; Phantom Albino), it is thanks to oral genres like myths, legends, proverbs, the epic, tales, lullabies, fables, and songs that the cultural heritage of the people of Cameroon was handed down from one generation to another.

The first tendency in Cameroonian literature in French is eurocentric. The key figure in this tendency is Louis-Marie Pouka Mbague (1910-1991), whose poems—collected in *Rires et sanglots* (1947; Laughter and Tears) and *Paroles de sagesse* (1958; Words of Wisdom)—are representative of what Frantz Fanon calls in *The Wretched of the Earth* (1962) the period of assimilation, the period when "the colonized intellectual proves that he has assimilated the culture of the colonizer."

The abuses of colonialism soon opened the eyes of Cameroonian writers who chose to denounce it, including François Sengat Kuo (formerly Francesco Nditsouna, b. 1931), author of *Fleurs de latérite* (1954; Laterite Flowers), and most notably the novelists Mongo BETI and Ferdinand OYONE. Mongo Beti is a key figure in Cameroonian literature whose works cover the most important periods of the colonial and postcolonial history of Cameroon. In novels such as *Ville cruelle* (1954; Cruel Town), *Le pauvre Christ de Bomba* (1956; *The Poor Christ of Bomba*, 1971), *Mission terminé* (1957; *Mission to Kala*, 1958), and *Le roi miraculé* (1958; *King Lazarus*, 1960) B. castigates the actions of foreign invaders during the colonization of Cameroon. *Remember Ruben* (1974; *Remember Ruben*, 1980), *Perpétue et l'habitude du malheur* (1974; *Pertetua and the Habit of Unhappiness*, 1978), *La ruine presque cocasse d'un polichinelle* (1979; The Almost Laughable Downfall of a Buffoon), *Les deux mères de Guillaume Ismaël Dzewatama* (1983; The Two Mothers of Guillaume Ismaël Dzewatama), *La revanche de Guillaume Ismaël Dzewatama* (1984; The Revenge of Guillaume Ismaël Dzewatama), and *L'histoire du fou* (1994; The Mad Man's Story) criticize the neocolonial exploitation of Cameroon and the African continent at large.

Oyono, for his part, limits his vitriolic criticism to the colonial system in novels such as *Une vie de boy* (1956; *Boy!*, 1970, also translated as *Houseboy*, 1966), *Le vieux nègre et la médaille* (1956; *The Old Man and the Medal*, 1967), and *Chemin d'Europe* (1960; Road to Europe). After independence, Cameroonian literature made great strides with such writers as Rene Philombe (b. 1934), Benjamin Matip (b. 1932), Guillaume Oyone-Mbia (b. 1939), Paul Dakeyo (b. 1948), Patrice Kayo (b. 1942), and Francis Bebey (b. 1925), whose *Le fils d'Agatha Moudio* (1967; *Agatha Moudio's Son*, 1971) deals humorously with the problems of women. It was a successful maiden attempt that was edited several times. Since then, Bebey has also published *Embarras it cie* (1968; Embarrassment and Company), *La poupée ashanti* (1973; *The Ashanti Doll*, 1977), *Le roi Albert d'Effidi* (1976; *King Albert*, 1982), and *Le ministre et le griot* (1992; The Minister and the Griot).

Although Rene Philombe is often a victim of censorship, he follows in the footsteps of Mongo Beti. He has published works that strongly criticize the colonial order and postcolonial dictatorship, notably *Les blancs partis, les Nègres dansent* (1973; The Whites Are Gone, the Blacks Rejoice), *Choc, anti-choc* (1978; Clash, Anticlash), *Africapolis* (1979; Africapolis), and *L'ancien maquisard* (The Former Freedom Fighter), an unpublished text distributed secretly in manuscript form. Guillaume Oyone-Mbia is known primarily as a dramatist, whose plays *Trios prétendants, un mari* (1962; Three Suitors, One Husband) and *Notre fille ne se mariera pas* (1973; Our Daughter Will Not Get Married) are frequently performed in schools throughout Cameroon. Paul Dakeyo first made his mark as a revolutionary poet with *Les barbelés du matin* (1973; Morning Barbed Wire), *Chant d'accusation suivi de Espace carcéral* (1976; Song of Accusation and Prison Space), *Soweto, soleils fusillés* (1977; Soweta, Forgotten Dreams), and *J'appartiens au grand jour* (1979; I Belong to the Daylight). His later poetry, collected in *La femme où j'ai mal* (1989; The Woman Where I Hurt) and *Les ombres de la nuit* (1994; Night Shadows), is both autobiographical and self-absorbed.

Cameroon literature in English is identified primarily with dramatists, notably Bate Belong (b. 1954), author of *Beasts of No Nation* (1990) and *Requiem for the Last Kaiser* (1991), and Bole Betake (b. 1947), author of *The Rape of Michelle* (1984), *Lake God* (1986), *The Survivors* (1989), and *The Palm Wine Will Flow* (1990), whose confrontational and sarcastic plays are sometimes banned from the stage. Anglophone prose writers include Mbella Sonne Dipole (b. 1936), author of *A Few Nights and Days* (1966) and *Because of Women* (1968), and Kenjo Jumban (b. 1940), whose *The White Man of God* (1980) is reminiscent of Ferdinand Oyono's *Le vieux nègre et la médaille*.

Among the Cameroonian writers living in other African countries and France, Yoda Krone (b. 1954) gained critical attention with the publication of *Le bal des Caïmans* (1980; Crocodile Dance), a novel informed by the political trials that took place in Cameroon during the 1970s. He also published successively *A la recherche de cannibale amour* (1988; Looking for Cannibal Love) and *Les beaux gosses* (1988; The Beautiful Kids). Simon Njami (b. 1960), on the other hand, draws his inspiration from black underhand intrigues in Paris as well as from his African American counterparts, as illustrated in *Cercueil et cie* (1985; Coffin and Company) and *African Gigolo* (1989).

One of the most significant developments in contemporary Cameroon literature is the emergence of a dense, aggressive, sometimes controversial, but extremely popular body of works by women. Although there is an established tradition of female writing in Cameroon as demonstrated by Thérèse Kuoh Moukoury's (dates n.a.) *Rencontres essentielles* (1969; Essential Encounters), Lydie Dooh Bunya's (b. 1933) *La brise du jour* (1978; Bay Breeze), and Delphine Zanga Tsogo's (b. 1935) *Vies de femmes* (1982; Lives of Women) and *L'oiseau en cage* (1984; The Caged Bird). Yet, it is mostly through WEREWERE LIKING who settled in Abvidjan and Calixthe BEYALA who lives in Paris that female voices became truly self-assertive. Essayist, poet, and playwright, Werewere Liking is known particularly for her ritual drama that draws much from deeply rooted cultural traditions in Africa, but more specially from her native bassa land, notably in *La puissance de Um* (1979; The Power of Um, 1996), *Une nouvelle terre* (1980; A New Earth, 1996), and *La veuve dilemme* (1992; The Widow Dylemma, 1994). The most prominent Cameroonian female author is Beyala, the author of such novels as *C'est le soleil qui m'a brûlée* (1987; The Sun Hath Looked Upon Me, 1996), *Tu t'appelleras Tanga* (1988; Your Name Will be Tanga, 1996), *La petit prince de Belleville* (1992; The Little Prince of Belleville), *Asseze l'Africaine* (1994; Asseze, the African Girl), *Les honneures perdus* (1996; Lost Pride), and in the caustic essay "Lettre d'une Africaine à ses soeurs occidentales" (1995; Letter from an African Woman to Her Western Sisters), in which she endeavors to defend the honor of African women and to criticize the patriarchal system that subjugates them.

In spite of an economic environment that is not conducive to its prosperity, Cameroonian authors continue to assert themselves in a creative effort to advocate for change and recognition both in their own country and in the international community.

BIBLIOGRAPHY: Ortova, J., *Etude sur le roman au Cameroun* (1971); Rial, J., *Littérature Camerounaise de langue française* (1972); Umerzinwa, W., *La religion dans la littérature africaine: étude sur Mongo Beti, Benjamin Matip et Ferdinand Oyono* (1975); Kayo, P., *Panoramea de la littérature camerounaise* (1979); Konka R., *Histoire de la littérature camerounaise* (1983); Ackad, J., *Le roman camerounais et sa critique* (1985); Ndachi Tagne, D., *Roman et réalités camerounaises* (1986); Zimmer, W., *Répertoire du théâtre camerounais* (1986); Dehon, C., *Le roman camerounais d'expression française* (1989); Bjornson, R., *The African Quest for Freedom and Identity, Cameroonian Writing and the National Experience* (1991); Kandioura, D., *The Novel as Transformation Myth: A Study of the Novels of Mongo Beti and Ngugi wa Thiongo* (1991); Brietinger, E., and Butake, B., eds., *Anglophone Cameroon Writing* (1993); Kom, A., ed., *Dictionnaire des oeuvres littéraires de langue française en Afrique au sud du Sahara* (2 vols., 1983, 1996)

—AMBROISE KOM

CAMPANA, Dino

Italian poet, b. 20 Aug. 1885, Marradi; d. 1 March 1932, Florence

Akin in spirit to Mallarmé, Rimbaud, and other later-19th and early-20th c. poets who opened the way to a new poetic language through violent abandonment of traditional lyric forms, C. falls historically in a period of reaction in Italy against the decadence of D'ANNUNZIO and of the beginnings of HERMETICISM, whose major voices were to be UNGARETTI and MONTALE. C.'s tormented life was spent in a feverish attempt to escape the oppressiveness of European bourgeois life: periods of aimless wandering abroad, as far as South America, were punctuated by frequent confinement in psychiatric hospitals such as Castel Pulci near Florence, where he spent the last fourteen years of his life.

C.'s literary production was meager: some miscellaneous writings and a collection of verse and poetic prose, lost while in the possession of a prospective publisher and then recomposed from memory and called *Canti Orfici* (1914, rev. eds. through 1995; *Orphic Songs*, 1961, rev. ed., *Orphic Songs and Other Poems*, 1991), a title emblematic of poetry conceived as both a reflection of man's disintegration and his ultimate redemption. In writing these poems, the first versions of which were hastily completed in a frenzy of creative energy, the poet declared his intent to wed the memories of his past—a life of desperate loneliness, continually on the edge of madness—with a new sense of word coloring theretofore unknown in Italian verse. His style, on the threshold of a poetic avant-garde, rejects standard syntax and punctuation, classical imagery and metaphor, for the representation of an eternal struggle for purification and of immersion of the self into the silences of eternity by means of a poetic language that flies in the face of a traditional world of oppressive strictures. His poetic patrimony, quantitatively insignificant but of an incomparable imagistic force in its exploration of the darker confines of the tormented human soul, has left an indelible imprint on contemporary Italian verse.

FURTHER WORKS: *Inediti* (1942); *Taccuino* (1949); *Lettere* (correspondence with Sibilla Aleramo, 1958); *Fascicolo marradese inedito* (1972); *Opere e contributi* (1973); *Il più lungo giorno* (original version of *Canti Orfici*, discovered 1974); *Epistolario* (1985); *Taccuini* (1990)

BIBLIOGRAPHY: Chiappelli, F., *Langage traditionnel et langage personnel dans la poésie italienne contemporaine* (1951): 40–46;

Chiappelli, F., "An Introduction to D. C.," *IQ*, 2, 2 (1958): 3–15; Golino, C., *Contemporary Italian Poetry* (1962): xiii; Salomon, I., Introduction to *D. C., Orphic Songs* (1968): 13–22; Lind, L. R., *Twentieth-Century Italian Poetry* (1974): 381–82; Bondanella, P., and Bondanella, J. C., eds., *Dictionary of Italian Literature* (1979): 91–92; Cecchetti, G., "Sulla poesia associativa di C.," *Lettere italiane*, 32 (1980): 248-54; Corsaro, A., and M. Verenelli, *Bibliografia campaniana (1914-1985)* (1985); Wolfzettel, F., "'Il canto fu breve': Dino C. Im europaischen Kontext," *Italienisch Zeitschrift für Italienische Sprache und Literatur* (27 May 1992): 18-37; Salomon, I. L., Introduction to *D. C., Orphic Songs* (1998)

—ROBERT J. RODINI

CAMPBELL, Roy

South African poet and translator (writing in English), b. 2 Oct. 1901, Durban; d. 23 April 1957, near Setubal, Portugal

Memories of his happy childhood in an influential Durban family deeply affected C. throughout his life. Although he left his subtropical native city in 1919, to return only for short periods, C.'s love of his unfettered outdoor youth shaped many of his later attitudes. His adult life was spent in England, France, Spain, and Portugal. A perpetual outsider, he left English literary circles in disgust in 1928 to live an individualistic, sun-loving life along the Mediterranean coast and in Toledo, Spain, until the civil war forced him to return to the United Kingdom in 1936. A Catholic convert and a fervent right-winger, his support for Franco during the Spanish Civil War further alienated him from British literary coteries. During World War II, however, he served as a volunteer in the ranks of the British army. Following a postwar career in the B.B.C., he spent his last years in Portugal, his persona firmly established as a swashbuckling, down-to-earth man's man.

C.'s best poetry has a lyrical intensity unique among English-language poets of the 20th c. Neither his sensibility nor his models were British. His early enthusiasm for Elizabethan and Jacobean verse does inform his poetry, but the major influences on his work are French: Baudelaire, Rimbaud, and Valéry all served as models for his early and middle poems. A Spanish influence is more pronounced in his later work. The combination of these elements gives his best poems a distinctive, ringing certainty of tone, a vividness of imagery, and an insistent energy.

C. was acclaimed as a major new poetic talent when his first work was published. *The Flaming Terrapin* (1924) is a long poem, dealing with the mythical regeneration of man. In it C. encapsulated his rugged, southern rejection of postwar European demoralization. Strongly reminiscent of Rimbaud's *Bateau ivre*, the poem is a dazzling description of the towing of Noah's ark by the vital and exotic terrapin, which symbolizes masculine strength.

His next volume, *Adamastor* (1930), contains many of his best-known and justly celebrated short poems. They derive from an unhappy return visit to South Africa and C.'s later delight in his new-found Mediterranean home. In each case, natural scenes are evoked with verve and passion. Celebrations of natural beauty and vigor embody a distinctive moral tone in which C.'s own belief in heroic individualism is organic to his descriptions.

Flowering Reeds (1933), a volume of beautifully controlled Mediterranean lyrics, represents the culmination of C.'s early lyrical style. The French influence is at its strongest in these poems, and the control over a still-exotic imagery more marked.

A satirical and argumentative strain had been evident throughout C.'s early career. The *Wayzgoose* (1928) is a broad attack on Natal, his native South African province, and the provincialism C. had encountered there. *The Georgiad* (1931) is a biting personal attack on Harold Nicolson (1886–1968), Vita Sackville-West (1892–1962), and English literary coteries, again deriving from personal experience. This argumentative element became more pronounced in C.'s later work, particularly as he felt the need to defend his conservative views.

Mithraic Emblems (1936) contains many attacks on left-wingers and do-gooders as well as intricate, emblematic poems depicting the curiously ornate elements in C.'s brand of conservative, heroic Catholicism. His long, undisciplined defense of Franco, *Flowering Rifle* (1939), embodies the most extreme of his conservative attitudes and unyielding passions. C.'s last volume of original poems, *Talking Bronco* (1946), shows a return to some of the lyrical ease of his earlier work, but repetitive polemical attacks on left-wing groups and enemies spoil its total effect.

In his last years C. devoted much of his time to verse translations. In *Poems of St. John of the Cross* (1951) and *Baudelaire: Poems: A Translation of "Les fleurs du mal"* (1952) he produced vivid and controlled English versions, reflecting his own life-long sympathy with Continental styles and attitudes.

C.'s celebration of the heroic and the vital is distinctive, as is the rich texture of his poetry. He often lacked a sense of proportion, but his best work has an unequaled passion and vigor.

FURTHER WORKS: *Poems* (1930); *Taurine Provence* (1932); *Broken Record* (1934); *Sons of the Mistral* (1941); *Light on a Dark Horse* (1951); *Lorca* (1952); *The Mamba's Precipice* (1953); *Portugal* (1957); *Collected Poems I* (1949), *II* (1957), *III* (1960); *The Selected Poems of R. C.* (1982)

BIBLIOGRAPHY: Gardner, W. H., "Voltage of Delight," *The Month*, Jan. 1958: 5–17; Wright, D., *R. C.* (1961); Bergonzi, B., "R. C.: Outsider on the Right," *JCH*, 2 (1967): 133–47; Smith, R., *Lyric and Polemic: The Literary Personality of R. C.* (1972); Paton, A., "R. C.," in Heywood, C., ed., *Aspects of South African Literature* (1976): 3–23; Alexander, P. F., *R. C.: A Critical Biography* (1982)

—ROWLAND SMITH

CAMUS, Albert

French novelist, dramatist, essayist, and journalist, b. 7 Nov. 1913, Mondovi, Algeria; d. 4 Jan. 1960, near Paris

C. grew up poor but happy, enjoying the sun and sea of his native Algeria. He never knew his father, who died of wounds received at the Battle of the Marne when C. was less than a year old. C.'s mother, shocked by the news of her husband's death, suffered a stroke that permanently impaired her speech. C. bore a strong, unspoken love for this poor, hardworking, illiterate woman, and for Spain, where his maternal grandparents had been born. The two places where the young C. felt happiest were on the soccer field and in the theater. A case of tuberculosis quickly ended C.'s hopes of pursuing a sports career; but his love for the theater led to a lifelong career as actor, playwright, and director.

After being encouraged by Jean Grenier, his *lycée* teacher and faithful friend and mentor, C. studied at the University of Algiers and wrote a dissertation on Saint Augustine. C.'s travel impressions of North Africa, Spain, Italy, and Czechoslovakia are the subject of his first published work, the collection of essays *L'envers et l'endroit* (1937; *The Wrong Side and the Right Side*, 1968). C. first worked as a journalist in Algeria for *Alger républicain*, then during the Occupation for the French resistance newspaper *Combat*, and briefly for *L'express* at the outset of the Algerian crisis. When he was awarded the Nobel Prize for literature in 1956, he felt that the works of his maturity were yet to be written. He was planning to direct a theater company of his own and to write a major novel about growing up in Algeria. A fatal automobile accident on the road from Provence back to Paris put an end to these plans.

C.'s initial shock at the discovery of his tuberculosis, a chronic illness that was to plague him throughout his life, awakened him to a sense of the absurd, the divorce between reason and existence. Man desires absolute knowledge and is instead confronted with the irrational, capricious moves of destiny. Being ill and close to death, C. realized the basic incongruity of the fact that we rebel against death while knowing that we are all going to die. The problem of the absurd is reflected in three major works: the essay *Le mythe de Sisyphus* (1942; *The Myth of Sisyphus*, 1955), the novel *L'étranger* (1942; *The Stranger*, 1946), and the play *Caligula* (1944; *Caligula*, 1947), which C. wanted to publish as a one-volume triptych.

Le mythe de Sisyphe, a philosophical essay, begins with despair and ends in hope. Rejecting the false security of an afterlife, C. places his hope in *life*, telling the reader that he must cling to the absurd as the only certainty. We are to die unreconciled, since death comes against our will, but man's strength resides in his lucidity—his intense awareness of the absurd and of his resolve to be in constant combat with the absurd. C. concludes with the image of Sisyphus, whose penalty is to have to keep striving but to accomplish nothing. Yet because Sisyphus is conscious of his fate, he is superior to it. Totally involved in his activity, Sisyphus enjoys a kind of Promethean exultation.

The publication of *L'étranger* during the Occupation of France brought C. instant notoriety and fame. Jean-Paul SARTRE was the first to link the protagonist Meursault with the "absurd man" of *Le mythe de Sisyphe*. Meursault, an Algerian youth who lives for the immediate present, is indifferent to bourgeois morality. Until his imprisonment, Meursault was a "natural" man who followed his instincts, seeking pleasure in purely physical sensations. When Meursault, overpowered by the intensity of the sun, shoots and kills an Arab on the beach, it is because he has suddenly lost control of his actions. But Meursault gradually becomes conscious of the meaning of the absurd. Instinctively, he senses that in committing this unpremeditated murder, he has destroyed the harmony of nature and his own equilibrium. What is more important from the philosophical point of view is Meursault's growing awareness of the value of life as he sees himself tragically condemned to die. In his confrontation with the prison chaplain, M. grows in stature and reaches heroic dimensions by defending life as an end in itself. C.'s use of the first person, the conversational past tense, and short, terse sentences gives the reader the impression of listening to the narrator relate his story from his prison cell. But C.'s directness and simplicity, which have been compared to the style of HEMINGWAY, were actually the result of much calculated effort. Throughout his literary career, C. constantly strove to polish his style and trim away needless embellishments.

Caligula, the third panel of C.'s triptych on the absurd, dramatizes the transformation of a once-benevolent ruler after he experiences the shock of death's finality and inevitability. Caligula's own disillusionment is the source of his destructive, tyrannical behavior. Having himself come to realize the meaninglessness of life, Caligula inflicts death and punishment so as to make everyone else aware of the basic absurdity of the human condition. While *Caligula* raises interesting philosophical questions, it is less successful as drama. As is often the case with C.'s plays, the characters are abstract spokesmen for conflicting philosophical points of view rather than flesh-and-blood characters capable of emotionally involving an audience.

C.'s second triptych deals with the theme of revolt. The novel *La peste* (1947; *The Plague*, 1948), inspired in part by Daniel Defoe's *Journal of the Plague Year* (1721), is an allegorical novel that lends itself to interpretations on three different levels: on the literal level, the plague is a disease with specific physical symptoms; on the symbolic level, the plague represents the Nazi Occupation of France; on a broader symbolic level, the plague represents evil in general. For C., the plague does not have a purifying effect. Dr. Rieux's eventual victory over the disease is only a temporary one; evil is ready to strike again at any time.

In 1950 C. returned to the theater with *Les justes* (*The Just Assassins*, 1958), his best and most moving original drama. This play, the second work on the theme of revolt, was inspired by C.'s reading on the subject of Russian revolutionary terrorists. C. put much of himself into the hero Kaliayev: his sensitivity, his zest for life, his love of poetry, and his willingness to risk his life for his ideals. At the core of the drama is the debate between Kaliayev, the "just" revolutionary, and Stepan, the assassin. Kaliayev, having volunteered to throw the bomb that will kill the corrupt Archduke Serge, backs away from his task when he sees the archduke's niece and nephew riding with him in his carriage. Kaliayev's belief that killing the children would turn him into a murderer rather than a "just assassin" clashes with the beliefs of the hard-liner Stepan, who contends that the ends justify the means. The rest of the play is a series of confrontations illustrating Kaliayev's gradual ascent to martyrdom, culminating in his willing acceptance of his own death in order to insure the purity of his acts.

The third piece on revolt is the lengthy essay *L'homme révolté* (1951; *The Rebel*, 1953). This philosophical study is, first, an in-depth examination of the theories and forms of revolt throughout history that endeavors to discover why revolt does not shun murder; second, an attempt to establish the true paths to what C. believes is a necessary revolt against mankind's common fate. C. wanted to lay the foundations for a true, unblemished revolt not tarnished by crime or murder. Rejecting all rigid ideologies that stifle individual freedom, including the fascism of Franco's Spain and communism as practiced in the Soviet bloc, C. proposed a "Mediterranean humanism," which would restore man's sense of value and moderation.

The publication of *L'homme révolté* marks C.'s break with Sartre. C. was so offended when Sartre's periodical *Les temps modernes* published a severe critique of *L'homme révolté* that he wrote an angry reply, which, in turn, prompted Sartre to write a personal answer formally breaking off their friendship. Even before this open quarrel, however, C. and Sartre, who had been close friends, especially at the time of the Liberation of Paris, no longer had much in common. C. was an idealist, a moralist, and an anticommunist. Sartre was a convinced communist, an activist, who wanted to participate in the revolutions of his time.

After his break with Sartre, C. became increasingly isolated and tormented, especially by the worsening situation in Algeria. He did not favor independence for Algeria; nor did he want the French Algerian population, natives of the land for several generations, to be forced to flee to mainland France. C.'s moderate stand on Algeria incurred the wrath and hostility of both the political left and the right.

Following his withdrawal from the political scene, C. wrote a series of short stories published as *L'exil et le royaume* (1957; *Exile and the Kingdom*, 1958). These six stories, each of them a masterpiece of irony and concision, established C.'s reputation as one of the foremost contemporary writers of short fiction. The novella *La chute* (1956; *The Fall*, 1956), originally conceived of as part of this collection of stories, quickly outgrew its framework. A stylistic tour de force narrated in the first person, in the manner of *L'étranger*, *La chute* is a parable dealing with man's guilt and his attempts at repentance. The protagonist, Jean-Baptiste Clamence, was ironically referred to in an earlier title as "A Hero of Our Time." This once-successful lawyer, who failed to save a woman from drowning, becomes a judge-penitent, a voice crying out in the desert, who confesses his own sins in the hope of getting his listeners to confess their sins in turn. He becomes both his own prosecutor and the prosecutor of his peers. Unlike Meursault, who wins the reader's sympathy because of his sincerity and lack of pretension, Jean-Baptiste Clamence creates antagonism because of his slickness and hypocrisy. Herbert R. Lottman, in his 1979 biography of C., sees *La chute* as a "self-mocking self-portrait," and a key to an understanding of C.'s darkest years. C. himself intended the novel to be a portrait of the defects of his generation, our own feelings of guilt and our readiness to judge and condemn others.

The publication in 1971 of C.'s previously unpublished first novel, *La mort heureuse* (*A Happy Death*, 1972), revealed that much of what C. was later to write in *L'étranger* had already existed in his mind as early as 1936. Although C. matured stylistically, his themes remained constant throughout his career: intoxication with nature, revolt against injustice, and a genuine desire to improve the lot of suffering humanity.

FURTHER WORKS: *Révolte dans les Asturies* (1936, with others); *Noces* (1939; *Nuptials*, 1968); *Le malentendu* (1944; *Cross Purposes*, 1947); *Lettres à un ami allemand* (1945; *Letters to a German Friend*, 1961); *L'état de siège* (1948; *State of Siege*, 1958); *Actuelles I* (1950); *Actuelles II* (1953); *L'été* (1954; *Summer*, 1968); *Requiem pour une nonne* (1956); *Actuelles III, Chroniques algériennes* (1958); *Discours de Suède* (1958); *Les possédés* (1959; *The Possessed*, 1960); *Carnets, mai 1935-fevrier 1942* (1962; *Notebooks: 1935–1942*, 1963); *Carnets, janvier 1942—mars 1951* (1964; *Notebooks: 1942–51*; 1965). FURTHER WORKS IN ENGLISH: *Resistance, Rebellion, and Death* (1961); *Lyrical and Critical Essays* (1968)

BIBLIOGRAPHY: Frohock, W. M., "C.: Image, Influence and Sensibility," *YFS*, 2 (1949): 91–99; Simon, P. H., "A. C. . . . et l'homme," *Témoins de l'homme* (1951): 175–93; Peyre, H., "A. C.," *The Contemporary French Novel* (1955): 240–51; John, S. B., "Image and Symbol in the Work of A. C.," *FS*, 9 (1955): 42–53; Sartre, J.-P, "Camus' *The Outsider*," *Literary and Philosophical Essays* (1955): 24–41; Thody, P., *A. C.* (1957); Hanna, T., *The Thought and Art of A. C.* (1958); Maquet, A., *A.C.: The Invincible Summer* (1958); Brée, G., *C.* (1959; rev. ed., 1961); Cruickshank, J., *A. C.* (1959); Ullmann, S., "The Two Styles of A. C.," *The Image in the Modern French Novel* (1960): 239–99; Fitch, B., "Aesthetic Distance and Inner Space in the Novels of C.," *MFS*, 10 (1964): 279–92; Parker, E., *A. C., The Artist in the Arena* (1965); Grenier, J., *A. C. Souvenirs* (1968); Quillot, R., *The Sea and the Prison* (1970); Pollmann, L., *Sartre and C.: Literature of Existence* (1970); Freeman, E., *The Theater of A. C.: A Critical Study* (1971); Lottmann, H. R., *A. C.* (1979); McCarthy, P., *C.* (1982)

—DEBRA POPKIN

[Meursault, the protagonist of *The Stranger*] was neither good nor bad, neither moral nor immoral. These categories do not apply to him. He belongs to a very particular species for which the author reserves the word "absurd." But in C.'s work this word takes on two very different meanings. The absurd is both a state of fact and the lucid awareness which certain people acquire of this state of fact. The "absurd" man is the man who does not hesitate to draw the inevitable conclusions from a fundamental absurdity. . . .

What is meant by the absurd as a state of fact, as primary situation? It means nothing less than man's relation to the world. Primary absurdity manifests a cleavage, the cleavage between man's aspirations to unity and the insurmountable dualism of mind and nature, between man's drive toward the eternal and the *finite* character of his existence, between the "concern" which constitutes his very essence and the vanity of his efforts. Chance, death, the irreducible pluralism of life and of truth, the unintelligibility of the real-all these are extremes of the absurd. . . .

The stranger is man confronting the world. C. might as well have chosen the title of one of George Gissing's works, *Born in Exile*. The stranger is also man among men. . . . The stranger is, finally, myself in relation to myself, that is, natural man in relation to mind. . . . But that is not all; there is a *passion* of the absurd. The absurd man will not commit suicide; he wants to live, without relinquishing any of his certainty, without a future, without hope, without illusion, and without resignation either. He stares at death with passionate attention and this fascination liberates him. He experiences the "divine irresponsibility" of the condemned man. [Feb. 1943]

Jean-Paul Sartre, *Literary and Philosophical Essays* (1955), pp. 24–25, 27

With *The Plague*—which is close to a novel without ceasing to be a philosophical tale—C.'s classicism is no longer limited to his style: it has taken possession of his thought, which has become more moderate and humanized, and has gained in scope and depth what it has lost in paradox and set purpose. . . . The narrative is admirably constructed, with a crescendo of horror and panic followed by a decrescendo, a fall from the tragic grandeur of misfortune to the slightly drab wisdom of a daily happiness that has been rediscovered. . . .

The plague represents evil; it is the weight of fate on man; it is death. The character Tarrou says: "The plague is life," meaning life insofar as it is bad, absurd, gnawed at by suffering and destined for destruction. The city of Oran, isolated from the world, is like the Earth thrown into the immensity of space, dragging to some unknown destination the race of misery born in some unknown way into the torment of consciousness. As for the struggle that the citizens undertake against the scourge, each with his own kind of courage and in his own way, this struggle is morality itself, with its diversity of appearances and intensities; for what is morality, other than the choice man makes to attempt to overcome destiny? . . .

To save man through love and reason, to protect him against natural evil and the oppression of society, to have confidence in man's nature, which is good, while struggling against destiny, which is evil, and never to rely on any powers other than the human—that is C.'s humanism (augmented by the awareness of the "absurd" that has oddly narrowed the scope of this humanism). It is quite evidently a secular and positive humanism: ideas about divine mediation and grace have nothing to do with it.

Pierre-Henri Simon, *L'homme en procès* (1950), pp. 115–16, 122–23

The Stranger depicts a prewar private world of secure, apparently indestructible routine broken only by the sea and sun of successive Mediterranean weekends. The basic patterns of existence seem as tireless as the earth itself. *The Plague* installs the temporary but despotically dreary, petty, and deadly round of endless collective regimentation and privation in an atmosphere of weary horror—the atmosphere of the German occupation of France. In *The Plague* the rhythms of living of *The Stranger* are progressively displaced by the patterns imposed by the ever-increasing obsessive presence of the pestilence. Those patterns appear, blend like a musical theme with the rhythms of normal living, become all-embracing, and then, as the basic theme reasserts itself, they disappear. In general the evolution of the plague follows the modalities of feeling in the occupied countries during the war years.

The hero of *The Fall*, the "penitent judge," represents a certain aspect of postwar Europe, the postwar Europe of the erstwhile humanitarians, morally shaken, guilt-ridden, and in search of a dubious self-justification. Contemporaneous with the penitent judge, the renegade missionary [in the story "The Renegade"] voices the intellectual confusion and frustrated anguish of an idealistic, Christian "left" upon which Marxism exercises a perpetual fascination.

C.'s novels are thus rooted in the soil—a French soil essentially—of a specific period of time, but through the medium of fiction he frees them from too specific a context. Isolating one of the major ills of the time, as a doctor might isolate the virus of an epidemic, he embodies it in fictional characters who carry it to its ultimate limits, giving it a semisymbolical expression: the stranger, the penitent judge, the renegade, and, more abstract, the plague. C.'s novels

could, in a sense, be grouped together under one title, which well might read "Parables of the Mid-Twentieth Century" or, better still, "Cautionary Tales for Our Time and All Time."

Germaine Brée, *C.* (1959), pp. 89–90

The Fall is a more profoundly pessimistic novel than the two earlier ones [*The Stranger* and *The Plague*]. It appears to be the outcome of further brooding meditation on their subject-matter. And as its title suggests it questions that assumption of human innocence so noticeable in *The Stranger* and *The Plague*. No doubt it is not intended to be a Christian novel, but it is clearly not positively and confidently non-Christian in the way the earlier novels were. . . .

There are, admittedly, straightforward Christian parallels in *The Fall*. There are references to the Eden in which Clamence [the judge-penitent narrator] lived before his own fall. His very name, Jean-Baptiste Clamence, suggests John the Baptist, the *vox clamantis in deserto*. He refers to himself as a prophet preaching in the desert of stone, mist and stagnant water which is Amsterdam. But this biblical symbolism does not embody Christian convictions. The Christian doctrine of redemption, which goes hand in hand with the Christian doctrine of the fall, is explicitly rejected. There is a sense in which C. means by the fall human fallibility, but this fallibility is not original sin. It is, rather, human guilt experienced without reference to any law; human guilt rendered all the more acute because there is no available standard of innocence. Clamence says that the worst human torment is to be judged without reference to laws and that this is precisely our torment.

John Cruickshank, *A. C. and the Literature of Revolt* (1959), pp. 183, 187

We possess some qualities and acquire others. It can be said of A. C. that he possessed violence and acquired moderation. . . . C. could easily have gone from extreme violence to its opposite—absolute passivity. But there is no trace of passivity in his works, which are always governed by a heightened tension.

This inner tension is what makes C.'s works (*The Plague*, for example) seem to result from firmly held beliefs; this tension is what gives these works the power to persuade people to act. It might seem surprising that so many pages are needed in *The Plague* to provide a detailed description of an epidemic and its ravages, before reaching the conclusion given in the form of advice, or rather suggestion, that it is preferable not to abandon one's fellow men to a deadly fate, that evil must be fought, and that at the very least each man must declare himself the brother of those who suffer. But the *preparation* is precisely what makes the advice so urgent and so persuasive. If from the first page a call to solidarity had been hurled like a bomb, if that call had been a command, if man's destiny had been vehemently denounced, the reader would perhaps admire the writer's style but would not necessarily be convinced that the writer was correct. And the reader's energy would be all used up in this admiration; there would be no energy left for the subject matter. All the reader's work would have been done for him, and nothing useful would have resulted.

This principle of art, although universal and eternal, is usually misunderstood.

Jean Grenier, Preface to A. C., Théâtre, récits, nouvelles (1962), pp. xv-xvi

C. once jokingly proposed that he and Sartre should jointly state in a paid advertisement that they had nothing in common and declined to be responsible for each other's debts. This was an understandable reaction on C.'s part to inevitably being taken for an existentialist, even after he had written *The Myth of Sisyphus*, one object of which was to refute the so-called existentialists. Yet the amount of positive truth contained in such a statement would not have been very great, for despite all their differences Sartre and C. have much in common. They are children of the same century—Sartre was only four years older than C. They lived for many years in the same city, Paris. They were both close to the Communist Party. (C. was even formally a member of it for a time.) They were both writers and philosophers. But besides all this they are linked by something more profound which makes them brothers—though dissimilar ones—in spirit: a certain radical sense of what existence is for twentieth-century man, an endeavor not to dwell on fractional aspects such as society, religion, political action, nature, regionalism, family, and what not, but to go after the essence of existence itself and seek a fundamental solution for the problems it poses. . . .

Both writers successfully attempted four main genres: the philosophical treatise, the novel and short story, the drama, and the essay. Taken as a whole, their work is marked by persistent traits which give it the character of a journey. Yet these journeys take them in entirely different directions. . . . [C.'s work] is a journey in the human sense of the word, a journey on which we encounter both the one and the other, light and shade, death and life, sense and absurdity, in the kaleidoscopic shifts of what world and himself mean and can mean to man. This is not an abstract, formal journey but a *real* search which knows no formal philosophical either/or discipline but is always both *envers* (reverse) and *endroit* (obverse). [1967]

Leo Pollmann, Sartre and C.: Literature of Existence (1970), pp. 111–13

[C.'s] first attempt at extended fiction offers an instructive lesson in the strategies of the imagination. Though shot through with brilliant rays, *A Happy Death* is a chunky, labored work, cumbersome for all its brevity, so cluttered with false starts and halting intentions that it occludes its own themes. In C.'s published *Notebooks*, it first appears as some chapter titles listed in January of 1936, when he was twenty-two; the last relevant notation occurs in March of 1939, when work on *The Stranger* was well advanced. An entry of June of 1938—"Rewrite novel"—implies a finished draft of *A Happy Death* by that time, but a month earlier, in a sketch of a funeral in an old people's home, *The Stranger* had begun to germinate, and some months later the uncanny first sentences of the masterpiece were written out intact. During the interval when passages for both novels compete in the *Notebooks*, those relating to *A Happy Death* suffer by comparison, seeming febrile and flaccid amid the sharp glimpses of *The Stranger*.

Wisely, C. let the first novel be consumed by the second, reusing a number of descriptions, recasting the main theme (a happy death), and transforming the hero's name by the addition of a "u"—Mersault, the man of sea and sun, darkening to Meursault, with its shadow of *meurtre*, of murder. Technically, the third-person method of *A Happy Death*, frequently an awkward vehicle for alter egos (see, see the sensitive young man light his cigarette; now let's eavesdrop on his thoughts), becomes the hypnotic, unabashed first-person of *The Stranger*. Substantively, C. has located, outside of autobiography, the Archimedean point wherefrom he can acquire leverage upon his world.

John Updike, NY, 21 Oct. 1972, p. 157

When A. C. died in an automobile accident on the road back to Paris on January 4, 1960, he was carrying with him a bulging black leather briefcase, the expanding accordion type, with reinforced corners and a three-position lock he never used. Caked in mud, it was found on the road near the tree against which the car had smashed. Inside the briefcase, along with personal effects such as a journal, some letters, and a passport, was the manuscript of the novel he had been working on in his recently acquired Provençal retreat at Lourmarin. The book would have been called *Le premier homme* (The First Man). C. had written only part of the first draft—145 closely written manuscript pages, some eighty thousand words. According to the schedule he had mapped out for the project and for himself in the new year just beginning, he would not have completed the final version before 1961.

It would be difficult to overestimate the importance he attached to this work in progress. . . . He called the book his *éducation sentimentale*, its chief purpose being to reveal his Algeria to mainland France. The title of the book, his wife understood, signified that all men are the first man, but also that the French Algerian is without a past, the product of a melting pot. The unfinished manuscript left by C. takes his young hero to the age of fourteen; he was about to begin a chapter or section called "L'Adolescent." One reader noted a new element in C.'s writing: For the first time he was using a Faulknerian lyricism, with repetition of words (although of course there is no way to know how much of this would have been retained in the final draft). What is clear is that

C. was following the details of his own early life closely, while attempting to give epic form, some universality, to the Algerian saga.

Herbert R. Lottman, *A. C.* (1979), pp. 5, 658–59

CANADIAN LITERATURE

In English

As in other Commonwealth countries, English-Canadian literature began as a backwater of English literature. Because of the United Empire Loyalist influence, it early manifested a doughty conservatism that has survived the mutating effects of time and adaptation. In fact, survival of one kind or another has always been a dominant theme, subsuming the colonial preoccupation with the transplantation of European culture and the later search for national identity.

Poetry

Isabella Valancy Crawford (1850–1887) is perhaps the best of the pre-Confederation poets. Overlooked in its day, Crawford's *Old Spookses' Pass, Malcolm's Katie, and Other Poems* (1884) is now highly regarded as an intensely personal and mythopoeic view of the pioneer experience. Charles G. D. Roberts (1860–1943) is considered the father of English-Canadian poetry. His appealingly simple pictures of rural life in New Brunswick in the 1880s inspired the poetic careers of the Group of the Sixties—Bliss Carman (1861–1929), Archibald Lampman (1861–1899), Duncan Campbell Scott (1862–1947), and Wilfred Campbell (1858–1918). They were given to Victorian moralizing and passionate nationalism, but their significance for today's reader lies in their treatment of a quintessential colonial theme, the confrontation between European origins and raw beginnings in a new land.

But it was the poetry of the 1920s that argued a new maturity in English-Canadian literature. Modernist in technique and cosmopolitan in outlook, it rejected the cultural cringe of colonialism as well as the nationalism of the "Maple Leaf" school of poetry. Although strongly influenced by T. S. ELIOT and Ezra POUND, the Montreal Group—F. R. Scott (1899–1985), A. J. M. Smith (1902–1980), Leo Kennedy (b. 1907), and A. M. KLEIN—nevertheless abandoned aesthetic isolation to become satirical advocates of radical change in the Canadian society of the 1930s. In Toronto, Dorothy Livesay (1909–1996), a former social worker, moved in *Day and Night* (1944) from IMAGISM to a revolutionary poetry in the manner of AUDEN and SPENDER. Two other poets, Robert Finch (1900–1995) and E. J. PRATT, began their poetic careers in the Toronto of the 1920s. While Finch's *Poems* (1946), *Dover Beach Revisited* (1961), and *Silverthorn Beach, and Other Poems* (1966) represent a high level of poetic achievement, Pratt is often considered the most important modern Canadian poet. In long, epic poems he embodies enduring myths of the Canadian imagination.

Although contemporary poetry in Canada is as protean as elsewhere, it can be broadly classified as neotraditional or nontraditional. The neotraditionalists employ mythopoeia, symbolism, and the literary past. Prominent among them are Ann Wilkinson (1910–1961), whose *Collected Poems* (1968) employ delicate irony and wit to explore mortality and the affective life; and Jay McPherson (b. 1931), whose relatively small output

nevertheless reveals a consummate mastery of poetic form. The nontraditionalists are convinced that the naked encounter with experience is the only true source of poetry. They include Earle Birney (1904–1995), an influential poet who has moved from left-wing polemics to concrete poetry; Irving LAYTON, a charter member of the Canadian branch of the antiacademic school of Charles OLSON and Robert CREELEY; Alden Nowlan (b. 1933), the best of the Maritime poets of the 1960s and 1970s; Gwendolyn McEwen (b. 1941), whose poetry often traces the effects of ancient myth in daily experience; and Michael ONDAATJE, whose multiculturalism (he was born of Dutch parents in Ceylon and emigrated to Canada after a British education) allows him to reshape both history and present reality by subjective, symbolic means.

Fiction

Owing to the popularity of Sir Walter Scott in Canada, perhaps, the very early English-Canadian novelists favored the historical romance. Two pioneer sisters, Susannah Moodie (1803–1855) and Catherine Parr Traill (1802–1899), were the first to exploit the fictional possibilities of the confrontation between English culture and Canadian frontier.

Not until the 20th c., however, was the most important fiction on the pioneering experience written. Recalling the works of Thomas HARDY and Theodore DREISER, Frederick Philip Grove's (1871–1948) *Settlers of the Marsh* (1925), *Fruits of the Earth* (1933), and other novels are unsmiling accounts of the human costs incurred in the development of Canada's prairie farms. An equally somber, though more skillful, analysis of the Canadian spirit in a small-town context is Sinclair Ross's (1908–1996) highly regarded *As for Me and My House* (1941). In the comic spirit, a contemporary of Grove's, Stephen LEACOCK wrote *Sunshine Sketches of a Little Town* (1912) and *Arcadian Adventures with the Idle Rich* (1914), indulgent satires on the smug materialism of small-town and city life, respectively.

Apart from Grove and Leacock, only Morley CALLAGHAN and Mazo de la Roche (1879–1961) stand out from the ranks of fiction writers before World War II. Surviving the early influences of naturalism and Ernest HEMINGWAY, Callaghan went on, in *Such Is My Beloved* (1934), *The Loved and the Lost* (1951), and *The Many Colored Coat* (1960), to a philosophical position resembling the Christian personalism of the French philosopher Jacques Maritain (1882–1973). With her sixteen-volume Jalna saga, Mazo de la Roche, demonstrating an unswervingly romantic imagination, became Canada's best-selling author. In a similar vein, Thomas Raddall (1903–1994) revived the historical romance. Raddall is sometimes guilty of pouring old wine into old bottles, but in novels like *His Majesty's Yankees* (1942) and *The Governor's Lady* (1960) he tells consistently entertaining tales, evoking atmosphere and varying historical setting with much skill.

New directions in fiction at midcentury were promised by Henry Kreisel's (1922–1991) *The Rich Man* (1948), A. M. Klein's *The Second Scroll* (1951), Adele Wiseman's (1928–1993) *The Sacrifice* (1956), Sheila Watson's (b. 1909) *The Double Hook* (1959), and Leonard COHEN's *Beautiful Losers* (1966). Although the novels of Hugh MACLENNAN are scarcely innovative in technique, they represent the first sustained imaginative attempt to link the question of Canadian identity with Canada's emergence as a world power, a central concern of MacLennan's generation. Whether using the popular romance as a vehicle for social analysis of the World War I era in *Barometer Rising* (1941), dealing insightfully with the French-English schism in *Two Solitudes* (1945), or assessing the sociopsychological effects of World War II in *The Watch That Ends the Night* (1959), MacLennan is perhaps the most thoughtful, perceptive recorder and analyst of the Canadian experience the literature has produced. Considered by some the equal of MacLennan, however, Ethel Wilson (1890–1980) in *Hetty Dorval* (1947), *Swamp Angel* (1954), and *Mrs. Golightly, and Other Stories* (1961) combines technical virtuosity with explorations of love, human interdependence, and other unknown terrains of the human heart.

Five major talents carried English-Canadian fiction to new heights of distinction in the 1960s and 1970s. Robertson DAVIES's complex and richly comic probings of the sometimes mysterious determinants of human behavior find their fullest expression in his Deptford trilogy—*Fifth Business* (1970), *The Manticore* (1972), and *World of Wonders* (1975). In novels such as *The Stone Angel* (1964), *A Jest of God* (1966), *The Fire-Dwellers* (1969), and *The Diviners* (1974), Margaret LAURENCE involves her heroines in a struggle to achieve self-realization through liberation from their own and their culture's past. From the perspective of Jewish Montreal, Mordecai RICHLER's *Son of a Smaller Hero* (1955), *The Apprenticeship of Duddy Kravitz* (1959), and *St. Urbain's Horseman* (1971) are satires on the assumptions that sustain self and society in Canada and elsewhere. Margaret ATWOOD's fiction in *The Edible Woman* (1969), *Surfacing* (1972), *Lady Oracle* (1976), and *Dancing Girls* (1977) deals with the author's psychic survival in an unstable, treacherous, manipulative world. The best of Alice MUNRO's (b. 1931) short stories in *Dace of the Happy Shades* (1968), *Lives of Girls and Women* (1971), and *Something I've Been Meaning to Tell You* (1974) depict Canadian small-town life from the perspective of a precocious young girl who observes and judges its customs and prejudices.

Drama

Although there is now a coast-to-coast network of professional and semiprofessional theaters, English-Canadian drama developed slowly. Toronto's little-theater movement of the 1920s and 1930s helped develop playwrights such as Fred Jacob (1882–1926), Merrill Denison (1893–1975), and Gwen Pharis (b. 1910). Since 1945 the Canadian Broadcasting Commission has been an outlet for radio plays, notably those of Lister Sinclair (b. 1921). Once established in other genres, Robertson Davies and James Reaney (b. 1926) turned to drama. Davies's dramatic works include *Eros at Breakfast, and Other Plays* (1949), *Fortune My Foe* (1949), and *At My Heart's Core* (1950), a comedy involving the novelists Susannah Moodie and Catherine Parr Traill. Reaney's *The Red Heart* (1949) and *A Suit of Nettles* (1958) concern myth and archetype as keys to the inner world of self.

Several outstanding contemporary plays deal with the victims of racial and cultural prejudice. They include John Herbert's (b. 1924) *Fortune and Men's Eyes* (1967), which attacks the brutalization in prison of another minority group, homosexuals; and George Ryga's (b. 1932) *The Ecstasy of Rita Joe* (1967), a moving, if simplistic, study of the alienation of native people in Canada.

In French

Prior to the 20th c. French-Canadian literature suffered from virtual censorship, both religious and political. The theocratic establishment of Quebec effectively prevented any deviation in subject matter or form from what was acceptable to the *Ancien régime* of church and state. Social and political changes in the 20th c., however, combined gradually to weaken church-state influence in Quebec. Not only has French-Canadian literature served as a major catalyst and reflector of change, but it has flourished in the new atmosphere of artistic freedom.

Poetry

With the 20th c. came a change in European influences on French-Canadian poetry, the French SYMBOLISTS and Parnassians replacing the 19th-c. romantics. Émile NELLIGAN, at eighteen the leader of an innovative group, the Literary School of Montreal, was the first important poet to question the role of the Catholic Church in Quebec. Other significant poets of the period were Paul Morin (1889–1963), René Chopin (1885–1953), and Guy Delahaye (1888–1969).

Between the two world wars French-Canadian poets wavered between the romanticism and clericalism of the past and a new poetry of modernism and social protest. The progressive voices actually began with Alain Grandbois's (1900–1975) *Les îles de la nuit* (1944; islands of the night), Saint-Denys Garneau's (1912–1943) posthumously published *Poésies complètes* (1954; complete poems), and Anne HÉBERT's *Le tombeau des rois* (1953; the tomb of the kings), and reached revolutionary heights in Claude Gauvreau's (1925–1971) work. Gaston Miron (b. 1928) best exemplifies growing Québécois discontent with the literary and social status quo, serving as a catalyst for Marie-Claire BLAIS and others during the *révolution tranquille*, the urbanization and laicization of Quebec society in the 1960s.

The poetry of the 1960s completes the break with the past, although its celebration of the new Quebec is as fervently nationalistic as earlier commemorations of the *ancien régime*. Outstanding works are Paul Chamberland's (b. 1939) *Terre Québec* (1964; Quebec land), a landmark work in the imaginative reinvention of the province; Michel Garneau's (b. 1939) and André Major's (b. 1942) consciousness-raising *Ce pays, cette misère* (1963; this country, this misery); and Gilles Vigneault's (b. 1928) *Les gens de mon pays* (1967; my country's people), a collection of folk songs and poetry for a new Quebec.

Fiction

While 19th-c. French-Canadian fiction is often little more than pious propaganda for the Quebec theocracy, a more interesting psychological fiction dominated the early decades of the 20th c. Such works as Hector Bernier's (1886–1947) *Au large de l'éueil* (1912; beyond the reef) and Gaétane de Montreuil's (pseud. of Georgine Bélanger Gill, 1867–1951) *Fleur des ondes* (1912; flowers of the waves) prepared the way for a more accomplished generation of the 1930s, which included Harry Bernard (1898–1979) and Rex Desmarchais (b. 1908). In *L'homme tombé* (1924; fallen man) and *La maison vide* (1926; the empty house) the moralizing Bernard laments the American influence that is causing French-Canadian women to seek fulfillment outside home and family. Another would-be moralist, Desmarchais, in *L'initiatrice* (1932; the initiator) and *Le feu intérieur* (1933; the interior fire) analyzes love and the motives of the human heart. The influence of Louis Hémon's (1880–1913) novel of the soil, *Maria Chapdelaine* (1913; *Maria Chapdelaine*, 1921) is evident in other noteworthy novels of the pre-1945 period: Félix-Antoine Savard's (b. 1896) *Menaud, maître-draveur* (1937; *The Boss of the River*, 1947), RINGUET's *30 arpents* (1938; *Thirty Acres*, 1960), and Germaine Guèvremont's (1896–1968) *Le survenant* (1945; *The Outlander*, 1950). *Menaud, maîtredraveur* is a more stylistically satisfying treatment of the themes of *Maria Chapdelaine*, while *30 arpents* takes a grimmer view than Hémon's of the adverse effects of mechanization and communications technology on farm life in Quebec. *Le survenant surpasses* others of its genre in its use of popular speech to capture the flavor of the rural setting.

Together with the social novel, psychological fiction held its own in the 1940s, 1950s, and 1960s. Robert Charbonneau's (b. 1911) *Ils posséderont la terre* (1941; they will inherit the earth) preceded André Giroux's (b. 1916) *Au-delà des visages* (1948; beyond faces) and Robert Élie's (b. 1915) *La fin des songes* (1950; *Farewell My Dreams*, 1954), novels that dramatized interior conflicts of the self. European intellectual trends often afforded a prism through which the situation in Quebec could be analyzed. Gilbert Choquette (b. 1929) and Andreé LANGEVIN dealt with existential anguish, Réal Benoît (1916–1972) with the relation between the interior will and external fate, and Gilles Marcotte (b. 1925) and Eugène Cloutier (b. 1921) with the spiritual state of modern man. In social-realist fiction, Roger Lemelin's (b. 1919) *Au pied de la ponte douce* (1944; *The Town Below*, 1948) and *Les Plouffe* (1948; *The Plouffe Family*, 1950) and Gabrielle ROY's *Bonheur d'occasion* (1945; *The Tin Flute*, 1947) and *Alexandre Chenevert, caissier* (1954; *The Cashier*, 1955) were landmark studies of urban working-class life, while Yves THÉRIAULT explored the ethnic diversity of Canada's vertical mosaic in *Le dompteur d'ours* (1952; the bear tamer), *Aaron* (1954; Aaron), *Agaguk* (1958; *Agaguk*, 1963), and *Ashini* (1960; *Ashini*, 1972).

Using bitter humor to excoriate Anglo neocolonialism, authors such as Laurent Girourard (b. 1939), Marcel Godin (b. 1932), Claude Jasmin (b. 1930), André Major, and Jacques Renaud (b. 1943) sprang into a newly raised public consciousness. Anne Hébert turned from poetry to fiction in *Le torrent* (1950; *The Torrent*, 1972), *Les chambres des bois* (1958; *The Silent Rooms*, 1974) and *Kamouraska* (1970; *Kamouraska*, 1973). Marie-Claire Blais wrote of poverty, disease, evil priests, and the death of children in rural Quebec in *Une saison dans la vie d'Emmanuel* (1965; *A Season in the Life of Emmanuel*, 1969), and *David Sterne* (1967; *David Sterne*, 1973). Blais's *Un joualonais, sa joualonie* (1973; *St. Lawrence Blues*, 1974) is a boisterous, dazzling tour de force whose subject is the triumphant, if chaotic, liberation of the province from its past.

The novel of realism continues to be written by authors such as Gérard BESSETTE with *Les pédagogues* (1961; the pedagogues) and *L'incubation* (1965; *Incubation*, 1967), although other novels, exotic in form and subject, have attracted more attention. These include Hubert AQUIN's *Prochain episode* (1965; *Prochain Episode*, 1972) which deals with love, patriotism and revolution as thematic background for an examination of the relationship between the writer and his craft; Jacques GODBOUT's *Salut Galarneau!* (1967; *Hail Galarneau!*, 1970), a sympathetic farce about a suburban everyman who is also a scribbler obsessed with the therapeutic relationship between writing, memory, and a rebirth of the spirit; Jacques FERRON's *Contes du pays incertain* (1962; *Tales from the Uncertain Country*, 1972), which describes with satirical humor and fantasy the dilemmas of modern Quebec; Réjean Ducharme's (b. 1942) *L'avalée des avalés* (1966; *The Swallower Swallowed*,

1968), a stylistically brilliant indictment, in the manner of Marie-Claire Blais, of an adult world that cruelly exploits its children; and Roch Carrier's (b. 1937) *La Guerre, Yes Sir!* (1968; *La Guerre, Yes Sir!* 1970), the first part of a BLACK HUMOR trilogy that finds in the irrepressible Québécois spirit hope for survival, whatever the future brings. Clearly, all these works have allegorical implications for the continuing social and political upheaval in Quebec.

BIBLIOGRAPHY: Tougas, G., *History of French-Canadian Literature* (1966); Story, N., *Oxford Companion to Canadian History and Literature* (1967; supplement, 1973); Warwick, J., *The Long Journey: Literary Themes of French Canada* (1968); Frye, N., *The Bush Garden: Essays on the Canadian Imagination* (1971); Jones, D. G., *Butterfly on Rock* (1971); Sutherland, R., *Second Image* (1971); Atwood, M., *Survival* (1972); Klinck, C. F., et al., *Literary History of Canada* (1976)

—JOHN H. FERRES

Canadian Literature since 1980

In English

The diversity and abundance of English Canadian literature of a high quality continued undiminished through the 1980s and 1990s, with contributions by authors with established reputations as well as by new, younger members of the world of letters. The identity crisis, always close to the surface in many realms of Canadian matters—the constant challenge to maintain a distinctness in the face of a powerful neighbor sharing the same language and many spiritual values—continues to be a general concern, but is a special concern in French Canadian literature, manifesting itself recently (1988–1989) in uneasiness with or opposition to a Free Trade agreement with the U.S. Fears of being unable to maintain a viable existence on the one hand, especially with the menace of a separated Quebec, with its threat of creating a divided anglophone country, and, on the other hand, the continued immigration, with Asiatics establishing residence in British Columbia and elsewhere, with Indians and other commonwealth members and others settling in other anglophone provinces, have created tensions that are reflected in literature. The important continued activity of gifted women writers, both in English and in French, has added to the various dimensions explored in Canadian letters.

Literary quality is partly maintained through the support of the Canada Council, established in 1957, which has continued to give financial assistance to allow artists to pursue their art. This has resulted occasionally in creating the type of literature that is appealing to an elite, with a high level of literary sophistication; indeed, many Canadian authors have advanced degrees, including doctorates, from leading institutions of higher learning in Canada and the U.S.—such as Hugh MACLENNAN, Hugh Hood (b. 1928), Louis Dudek (b. 1918), Eli Mandel (b. 1922), James Reany (b. 1926), Robert Kroetsch (b. 1927), Elizabeth Brewster (b. 1922), and John Thompson (1938–1976)—and many others have played important roles in the world of higher education. This involvement with the academic world—many of the leading writers are teachers of English or creative writing—obviously leaves its mark on their works, with many authors being very conscious of the most recent literary theories and very aware of current aesthetic concerns.

Some of English Canada's most important literary figures died in the last two decades of the 20th c.: F. R. Scott (1899–1985), Milton Acorn (1923–1986), Al Purdy (1918–1986), Margaret LAURENCE in 1987, George Ryga (1932–1987), and, in 1990, Morley CALLAGHAN, Hugh MACLENNAN, and Northrop FRYE. Since most of these writers continued to be productive, their absence will be noticed. Significant among their latest works were Scott's *Collected Poems* (1981), Acorn's *Dig Up My Heart* (1983), Purdy's *The Stone Bird* (1981), *Piling Blood* (1984), and *The Collected Poems of Al Purdy* (1986), Laurence's *Dance on the Earth A Memoir* (1989), Callaghan's *A Time for Judas* (1983), *Lost and Found Stories* (1985), *A Wise Old Man on the Road* (1988), and Frye's *The Great Code* (1982), *Divisions on a Ground* (1982), *Myth and Metaphor: Selected Essays* 1974–1988 (1990), and *Words with Power: Being a Second Study of the Bible and Literature* (1990).

Although Marshall McLuhan (1911–1980) published his most important work during the 1950s and 1960s—*The Mechanical Bride* (1951), *The Gutenberg Galaxy* (1962), *Understanding Media* (1964), and, with Jerome Agel (b. 1930) of the U.S., *The Medium Is the Massage* (1967) and *War and Peace in the Global Village* [sic: *Massage*]—his contributions to the Canadian intellectual climate have not been forgotten. Indeed, recent works—*Letters of Marshall McLuhan* (1987) and *Marshall McLuhan: The Medium and the Messenger* (1989)—are reminders of his importance. He is among the most original thinkers Canada has produced.

Canadians who have recently made significant contributions to the world of literature include Robertson DAVIES, who completed his Simon Darcourt trilogy: *The Rebel Angels* (1981), *What's Bred in the Bone* (1985), and *The Lyre of Orpheus* (1988); Alice MUNRO with *The Moons of Jupiter* (1982), *The Progress of Love* (1986), and *Friend of My Youth* (1990); Timothy Findley (b. 1930) with *Famous Last Words* (1981), *Not Wanted on the Voyage* (1984), and *The Telling of Lies* (1986); Margaret ATWOOD, who continues to be one of Canada's most widely read authors, with *Bodily Harm* (1981), *Bluebeard's Egg* (1983), *The Handmaid's Tale* (1986), *The Cat's Eye* (1988), and *Morning in the Burning House*; Mavis GALLANT, particularly significant in the world of the short story, with *Home Truths* (1981), *What Is To Be Done?* (1983), *Overhead in a Balloon* (1985), *Paris Notebooks: Essays and Reviews* (1986), and *In Transit* (1988); and Mordecai RICHLER with *Home Sweet Home* (1984), *Solomon Gursky Was Here* (1989), and *Requiem for a Divided Country*. Among other writers who have been on the literary scene and continue to have an audience are the poets Irving LAYTON with *A Wild Peculiar Joy* (1982), *The Gucci Bag* (1983), and *Dance with Desire* (1986); Robert Kroetsch, with *Field Notes* (1981), *Alibi* (1983), *Advice to My Friends* (1985), and *The Lovely Treachery of Words: Essays Selected and New* (1989); Dorothy Livesy (b. 1909) with *The Phases of Love* (1983), *Feeling the Worlds* (1984), and *The Self-Completing Tree: Selected Poems* (1986); Ralph Gufstafson (b. 1909) with *Directives of Autumn* (1984), *Plummets and Other Partialities* (1987), and *Winter Prophecies* (1987); Carol Shields (b. 1935), who has written in various genres, with *Coming to Canada: Poems* (1992), *Thirteen Hands* (1993), and the Pulitzer Prize-winning *The Stone Diaries* (1993).

Michael ONDAATJE has continued to be active in the world of verse as well as in prose: *Running in the Family* (1982), *Secular Love* (1984), *In the Skin of a Lion* (1987), *The Cinnamon Peeler* (1991), and the Booker Prize-winning *The English Patient*. John Metcalf (b. 1938) has produced novels, short stories, and works of

criticism: *General Ladd* (1980), *Kicking against the Pricks* (1982), *The Bumper Book* (1986), and *Adult Entertainment: Short Fiction* (1986).

In the world of the theater, Timothy Findley and David French (b. 1939) have made important contributions, the latter with *Leaving Home* (1972), *Of the Fields, Lately* (1973), *Jitters* (1980), and *Salt Water Moon* (1984), works that have made him one of Canada's most important dramatists. Others successful writers for the stage are Sharon Pollock (b. 1936), with *Blood Relations* (1980), *Whiskey Six* (1983), and *Doc* (1984), and Ken Mitchell (b. 1940), with *Gone the Burning Sun* (1984) and *The Plainsman* (1985).

Particularly sensitive to the ethnic diversity of Canada are Rudy Wiebe (b. 1934), with *Peace Shall Destroy Many* (1964), *The Temptation of Big Bear* (1973), and *Where Is the Voice Coming From?* (1974); and many writers who focus on the Jewish experience, among them Norman Levine (b. 1923), C.J. Newman (b. 1935), and Mordecai Richler; as well as a writer who deals with the Japanese-Canadian experience, Joy Kogawa (b. 1935), with *Obason* (1981). Similar sensitivity is displayed by Bharati MUKHERJEE, with *Darkness* (1985), *The Middleman and Other Stories* (1988), and *Jasmine* (1989), and her husband, Clark Blaise (b. 1940), with *Lunar Attractions* (1979), *Lusts* (1983), and *Resident Alien* (1986).

In a tradition so rich in important women writers who do not avoid what could be called women's concerns, some occupy a special niche because of their specific focus, such as Jane Rule (b. 1931), with *The Desert of the Heart* (1964), *Lesbian Images* (1975), *Contract with the World* (1980), and *Inland Passage and Other Stories* (1985), and Mary Meigs (b. 1917), with *The Medusa Head* (1983).

In French

The ebullient literary scene in French continued unabated, fermented by the changing dramatic political environment, with votes on separatism, the instituting of language laws, and the state of suspense created by the Lake Meech Accords. Among the most eminent recent writers are Yves THERIAULT, Hubert AQUIN, Jacques FERRON, Jacques GODBOUT, and Michel TREMBLAY.

Other important and successful writers continued to publish in the 1980s: Gabrielle ROY revealed more of her personal life in her final works: *Ces enfants de ma vie* (1977; *Children of My Heart* 1979), *De quoi t'ennuies-tu, Eveline?* (1982; *What's bothering you, Eveline?*), her autobiography, *La détresse et l'enchantement* (1984; distress and enchantment), and some of her correspondence, *Ma chère petite soeur: Letters à Bernadette* 1943–1970 (1988; my dear little sister: letters to Bernadette 1943–1970). Anne HÉBERT, following on the success of her 1970 novel *Kamouraska* (*Kamouraska*, 1973), continued in this genre: *Héloise* (1980; *Heloise*, 1982), *Les fous de Bassan* (1982; *In the Shadow of the Wind*, 1983), and *Le premier jardin* (1988; the first garden). Hébert is above all a poet, and one always striking feature of her novels is the poetic dimension present in the imagery, style, and structure. Marie-Claire BLAIS has continued to produce novels characterized by a rich prose style and a rather pessimistic vision of the world, often with alienated individuals, among them homosexuals and lesbians: *Le loup. Roman* (1972; *The Wolf*, 1974), *Une liaison parisienne* (1975; *A Literary Affair*, 1979), *Les nuits de l'underground* (1978; *Nights in the Underground: An Exploration of Love*, 1979), *Le sourd dans la ville* (1979; *Deaf to the City*, 1981), *Visions d'Anna ou Le vertige* (1982; visions of Anna or vertigo), and *Pierre* (1984; Pierre).

Gérard BESSETTE (b. 1920) has been an outstanding figure in Quebec letters for his critical contributions—*Une littérature en ébullition* (1968; a literature in ebullition), *Histoire de la littérature canadienne-française par les textes* (1968; history of French-Canadian literature through texts)—in addition to his purely literary career. Some of his most important novels are *Le Libraire* (1960; *Not for Every Eye*, 1962), *L'incubation* (1965; *Incubation*, 1967), and *Le semestre* (1979; the semester). From one novel to another the style varies, going from realistic to imitative of the *nouveau roman*.

Claire Martin (b. 1914) in the space of approximately ten years created a body of novelistic works that brought her much acclaim. The theme of love and the traditional aspects of Quebec life are among those she develops in *Avec our sans amour* (1958; with or without love), *Doux-Amer* (1960; *Best-Man*, 1983), and *Dans un gant de fer* (1965; *In an Iron Glove*, 1968).

Antonine Maillet (b. 1929) received the Goncourt Prize, the prestigious French literary award, for her novel *Pélagie-la-charrette* (1979; *Pélagie*, 1982), a story about Acadians, which brought her international acclaim. In recent years she has written plays as well as novels.

Louise Maheux-Forcier (b. 1929), musician and novelist, won a certain fame for her first novel, *Amadou* (1963; tinder, or punk), which features a lesbian relationship amidst torn heterosexual rapports.

Claude Jasmin's (b. 1930) works have often been marked by the political climate, such as *Ethel et le terroriste* (1964; *Ethel and the Terrorist*, 1965), which evokes the confrontations of the early 1960s.

Louky Bersianik (b. 1930) is particularly concerned in her literary works with women and their role in civilization. *L'Euguélionne* (1976; *The Euguelionne*, 1981) and *Pique-nique sur l'Acropole* (1979; picnic on the Acropolis) established her as one of the leading feminist voices in Canada.

Roch Carrier (b. 1937), whose prose works have been well received throughout Canada, explores the Quebec mentality confronted with an all-enveloping English world in such works as *Les enfants du bonhomme dans la lune* (1979; *The Hockey Sweater and Other Stories*, 1979) and *Il n'y a pas de pays sans grand-père* (1977; *No Country without Grandfathers*, 1981). Recent works have taken him to other lands; *L'ours et le kangourou* (1986; the bear and the Kangaroo) and *Un chameau en Jordanie* (1988; a camel in Jordan).

Jacques Poulin (b. 1937) is a novelist whose works are reflective of the political scene in Quebec. However, his *Volkswagen Blues* (1984; title in English) finds his protagonists roaming through the U.S.

Susanne Paradis (b. 1936) has been one of Quebec's most productive writers, with books of poetry—*Un gout de sel* (1983; a taste of salt) and *Effets de l'œil* (1986; effects of the eye)—and novels: *Miss Charlie* (1979; title in English) and *La ligne bleu* (1985; the blue line)—as well as works of literary criticism.

André Major (b. 1942), with *Le cabochon* (1964; the headstrong kid) and *L'épouvantail* (1974; *The Scarecrows of Saint Emmanuel*, 1977), Yves Beauchemin (b. 1941), with *Le matou* (1981; *The Alley Cat*, 1986), and Louis Caron (b. 1942), with *L'emmitouflé* (1977; *The Draft Dodger*, 1980), all reflect involvement with contemporary issues in their novels.

Victor-Lévy Beaulieu (b. 1945) has displayed an uncommon energy in many areas—as an essayist, in *Pour saluer Victor Hugo* (1971; to salute Victor Hugo), *Jack Kérouac: Essai-poulet* (1972; *Jack Kerouac: A Chicken Essay*, 1975); as a dramatist, in *En attendant Trudot* (1974; waiting for Trudot); as a novelist, in *Les grands-pères* (1975; *The Grandfathers*, 1975) and *L'héritage* (1987; the inheritance); and finally as a publisher: as the founder and director of the series "Bibliothèque Québécoise."

In poetry, Gerald Godin (b. 1938), whose works have been based on *joual*, the language of the common people, is one of the most popular of Quebec poets; he has published many collections, among them *Ils ne demandaient qu'à brûler, poèmes 1960–1986* (1987; they asked only to burn, poems 1960–1986). Paul Chamberland (b. 1939) followed up on his *Terre Québec* (1964; Quebecland) with *L'enfant doré* (1980; the golden child), *Aléatoire instantané & Midsummer 82* (1983; instantaneous aleatoriness & midsummer 82), *Compagnons chercheurs* (1984; seeker companions), and *Phoenix intégral and Après Auschwitz, Poémes 1975–1987* (1988; integral phoenix and after Auschwitz, poems 1975–1987), in which the stress is on humankind, sexuality, and the simple life. Nicole BROSSARD has emerged as one of the important literary figures in contemporary Quebec, known both for her prose and poetic works, and appreciated especially by those who feel tyrannized by the masculine codes in the language; among her works are *Le centre blanc (poèmes 1965-1975)* (1978; the white center, poems 1965-1975), *Amantes* (1980; *Lovhers*, 1986), *Picture Theory* (1982; title in English), *double impression (poèmes et textes 1967-1984)* (1984; double impression, poems and texts 1967-1984), and *Domaines d'écriture* (1985; domains of writing); her efforts lead her to redirect communication by the abandonment of such imposed "patriarchal" features of the language as chronology and linearity. Madeleine Gagnon (b. 1938) accompanies her in this effort, in works such as *Les fleurs du Catalpa* (1986; the catalpa flowers).

Other poets, some from earlier generations, such as Rina Lasnier (b. 1915), Roland Giguère (b. 1929), and Jacques Brault (b. 1933), continue to have their admirers. Lasnier's poems have been collected in *Poèmes* (1972; poems) and *L'ombre jetée I et II* (2 Vols., 1988–1989; the shadow cast). Giguère, painter as well as poet, has produced *L'âge de la parole, poèmes 1949–1960)*, (1965; the age of speech, poems 1949-1960), *Forêt vierge folle* (1978; mad virgin forest), and *La main au feu* (1987; the hand in the fire). Brault's recent works include *Moments fragiles* (1984; fragile moments) and *Poèmes I, Mémoire, La Poésie ce matin. L'en dessous l'admirable* (1986; Poems I, memory, poetry this morning, the admirable underneath).

The world of the stage has flourished in the last decades, with many theaters enjoying success, with the production of many new plays, with great numbers of active theatergoers, and, most important, with the contributions of gifted creative artists. In addition to Michel Tremblay, others have played important roles in this success, among them Jean-Claude Germain (b. 1939), Réjean Ducharme (b. 1941), and Marie Laberge (b. 1940).

In contemporary Canadian literature we increasingly find authors in English as well as in French whose names no longer have the typical English or French ring, a state of affairs reflecting the many different cultures increasingly playing a role in the creation of Canadian culture and art, illustrated by Nino Ricci's *The Lives of the Saints* (1990) and *In a Glass House* (1993), Marco Micone's *Le figuier enchanté* (1992), Guillermo Verdecchia's *Fronteras Americanas (American Borders)* (1993), Yuan Li's *Daughters of the Red Land* (1995), Sergio Kokis's *Le pavillon des miroirs* (1994; the house of mirrors), and Yong Chung's (dates n.a.) *Le débit intérieur* (1995; the inner flow). And there are also those whose names do not immediately announce the language they will write in, illustrated by Clark Blaise's *A North American Education* (1973) and Nancy Huston's (dates n.a.) *Cantiques des plaines* (1993; plain hymns).

BIBLIOGRAPHY: Wilson, E., *O Canada, An American's Notes on Canadian Culture* (1965); Reid, M., *The Shouting Signpainters: A Literary and Political Account of Quebec Revolutionary Nationalism* (1972); Lemire, M., et al., *Dictionnaire des œuvres littéraires du Québec* (5 vols., 1980–1987); Weiss, J. M., "The Contemporary Theater and Its Public in Quebec," *Québec Studies*, 1, (1983): 166–77; Powe, B. W., *A Climate Charged* (1984); Keith, W. J., *Canadian Literature in English* (1985); Schwartzwald, R., "Literature and Intellectual Realignments in Quebec," *Québec Studies*, 3 (1985): 32–56; Cagnon, M., *The French Novel of Quebec* (1986); Weiss, J. M., *French-Canadian Theater* (1986); Mailhot, L., and P. Nepveu, *La poésie Québécoise des origines à nos jours* (1986); Andersen, M., "Subversive Texts: Québec Women Writers," *SCL*, 13, 2 (1988): 127–41; Hamel, R., et al., *Dictionnaire des auteurs de langue française en Amérique du nord* (1989); New, W. H., *A History of Canadian Literature* (1989); Royer, J., *Introduction à la poésie québécoise: les poètes et les œuvres des origines à nos jours* (1989); Benson, E., and L. Conolly, *The Oxford Companion to Canadian Theatre* (1989); Kandiuk, M., *French-Canadian Authors: A Bibliography of Their Works and of English-Language Criticism* (1990)

—PAUL BARRETTE

CANETTI, Elias

Austrian novelist, essayist, and dramatist, b. 25 July 1905, Rustschuk (Ruse), Bulgaria; d. 14 Aug. 1994, Zürich, Switzerland

A native of northern Bulgaria, C. had a polyglot and multicultural upbringing. As he details in *Die gerettete Zunge* (1977; *The Tongue Set Free*, 1979), his memoirs of childhood and youth, German was the fourth language he acquired—after Ladino (an archaic Spanish dialect spoken by Sephardic Jews), Bulgarian, and English. C. lost his father at age seven, and he was raised and educated in England, Switzerland, Germany, and Austria. After attending secondary school in Frankfurt, C. took a degree in chemistry at the University of Vienna in 1929 and became a free-lance writer and translator (Upton Sinclair). In 1938 he emigrated to England, and he has lived in London ever since, with periods of residence in Zurich.

C.'s *Die Blendung* (1935; *Auto-da-Fé*, 1946) is as impressive a first novel as has been written in our century. This widely acclaimed work is the complex and richly symbolic story of the ascetic Peter Kien, who describes himself as a "library owner." As reclusive as he is erudite, this renowned philologist and sinologist allows himself to get in the clutches of his scheming housekeeper Therese, whom he marries. Following his traumatic expulsion from the paradise of his enormous library, Kien descends to the lower depths of society, where Therese's work of degradation is continued and completed by the predatory chess-playing hunchback Fischerle and the philistine janitor Benedikt Pfaff. Their exploitative stratagems serve as a grotesque counterpoint to Kien's *idées*

fixes and the progressive unhinging of his mind, Kien's final act being an apocalyptic self-immolation amidst his books. The only oasis of sanity in this world gone insane is Kien's brother Georg, a psychiatrist. *Die Blendung* may be read as a subtle political and social satire, a chilling adumbration of the crushing of the vulnerable "pure" intellect by the brutish "practical" forces of our times.

The *magnum opus* of C. the thinker is *Masse und Macht* (1960; *Crowds and Power*, 1962), an unorthodox essay in social psychology in which C. presents a typology of the mass mind. Historical, political, psychological, anthropological, philosophical, sociological, and cultural elements and insights are enlisted in a search for the root causes of fascism and for the wellsprings of human behavior generally.

As a university student C. had come under the spell of Karl KRAUS, and his dramatic works exemplify his Krausian concept of "acoustical masks": he unsparingly sketches the linguistic (and, in a sense, moral) physiognomy of his characters on the basis of each person's individual, unmistakable speech pattern. *Hochzeit* (1932; *The Wedding*, 1986) presents a *danse macabre* of petit-bourgeois Viennese society motivated by cupidity and hypocrisy; the collapse of the house coveted by those attending a wedding party symbolizes the breakdown of this society. *Komödie der Eitelkeit* (1950; *Comedy of Vanity*, 1983) explores the genesis of a mass psychosis. A totalitarian government having proscribed vanity, all mirrors, photos, and films are burned. As vanity goes underground, distrust, dehumanization, and disaster ensue. *Die Befristeten* (1956, *Life-Terms*, 1983) is, as it were, a primer of death. People carry their predetermined dates of death in capsules around their necks. One man, Fünfzig ("Mr. Fifty"), finally rebels against this knowledge and breaks the taboo. The discovery that the capsules are empty replaces presumed security with fear of death.

After decades of relative obscurity, C. is now increasingly recognized as the sole surviving representative of a distinguished Austrian literary tradition and as one of the most original writers and thinkers of our time.

FURTHER WORKS: *Fritz Wotruba* (1953; *Fritz Wotruba*, 1955); *Welt im Kopf* (1962); *Derandere Prozess: Kafkas Briefe an Felice* (1969; *Kafka's Other Trial*, 1974); *Aufzeichnungen 1942–1948* (1965); *Die Stimmen von Marrakesch: Aufzeichungen nach einer Reise* (1967; *The Voices of Marrakesh: Record of a Visit*, 1978); *Alle vergeudete Verehrung: Aufzeichnungen 1949–1960* (1970); *Die gespaltene Zukunft* (1972); *Macht und Überleben* (1972); *Die Provinz des Menschen: Aufzeichnungen 1942–1972* (1973; *The Human Province*, 1979); *Der Ohrenzeuge: Fünfzig Charaktere* (1974; *Earwitness: Fifty Characters*, 1979); *Das Gewissen der Worte* (1975; *The Conscience of Words*, 1979); *Der Beruf des Dichters* (1976); *Die Fackel im Ohr* (1980); *Das Augenspiel* (1985); *Das Geheimherz der Uhr* (1987)

BIBLIOGRAPHY: Parry, I. F., "E. C.'s Novel *Die Blendung*," in Norman, F., ed., *Essays in German Literature* (1965): 145–66; Dissinger, D., *Vereinzelung und Massenwahn: E. C.'s Roman "Die Blendung"* (1971); Göpfert, H. G., ed., *C. lesen: Erfahrungen mit seinen Büchern* (1975); Roberts, D., *Kopf und Welt: E. C.'s Roman "Die Blendung"* (1975); Wiley, M. E., "E. C.'s Reflective Prose," *MAL*, 12, 1 (1979): 129–37; Barnouw, D., *E. C.* (1979); Sontag, S., "Mind as Passion," *Under the Sign of Saturn* (1980): 181–204; Feth, H., *E. C.'s Dramen* (1980); special C. issue of *MAL*, 16 (1983); Stieg, G., "Dommentierte Auswahlbibliographie," in Durzak, M., ed., *Zu E. C.* (1983): 171-180; Peil, E., *E. C.* (1984); Meili, B.,

Erinnerung und Vision (1985); Eigler, F., ed., *Essays in Honor of E. C.* (1987); Eigler, F., *Das autobiographische Werk von E. C.* (1988); Lawson, R. H., *Understanding E. C.* (1991); Falk, T. H., *E. C.* (1993); Elbaz, R., *E. C.: The Failing of the Novel* (1995); Barnouw, D., *E. C.* (1996)

—HARRY ZOHN

CANKAR, Ivan

Yugoslav prose writer, dramatist, poet, and critic (writing in Slovene) b. 10 May 1876, Vrhnika; d. 11 Dec. 1918, Ljubljana

C. was the kind of patriot who found it difficult to reside in his native land. During his most productive years, the decade from 1898 to 1909, he rented a room in Vienna, making only occasional trips to Ljubljana and other cities in Slovenia (then part of the Austro-Hungarian Empire) to see to the staging of his plays, deliver lectures or, once, to stand for election as a Slovene candidate of the Social Democratic Party (in 1907; he lost). When eventually he did take up residence again in Slovenia, he remained to some degree isolated, lonely, and unhappy. The memories of childhood poverty (he was the eighth of twelve children born to a tailor), the unremitting hostility of the clergy and most critics to his work, coupled with his own inclination to morbidity, conspired to keep him an alien even among his own people.

Although he wrote in most modern literary genres, C. is perhaps most justly renowned for his prose works. Among their characteristic features is an explicit autobiographical bent, especially in *Podobe iz sanj* (1917; *Dream Visions*, 1982), *Moje življenje* (1920; *My Life*, 1971), and *Grešnik Lenart* (1921; Lenart the sinner), as well as a readiness to polemicize openly and directly with his critics, as he did in *Bela krizantema* (1910; the white chrysanthemum). Early in his career C., like Émile Zola and Maxim GORKY, favored a naturalist and symbolist treatment of the ravages of poverty and illness, as, for instance, in *Na klancu* (1902; on the slope) and *Hiša Marije Pomočnice* (1904; *The Ward of Our Lady of Mercy*, 1976). His attention was particularly engaged by the sufferings of the creative mind—in *Tujci* (1901; foreigners) and *Martin Kačur* (1907)—as it struggled against provincialism and ignorance. But the plight of the simple, as in *Hlapec Jernej in njegova pravica* (1907; *The Bailiff Yerney and His Rights*, 1930), he could also depict with great sympathy. And in almost all of his works he explored the nature and workings of maternal love, particularly as it was experienced by a son. When C. moved from a naturalist bluntness to a symbolic, even at times romantic, treatment of his homeland's ills, as in *Križ na gori* (1904; cross on the mountain) and *Kurent* (1909; Kurent), he occasionally abandoned his somber tone. Although capable of managing the requirements of a lengthy narrative, C. was most at home with the anecdote and short sketch. Many of his "novels" are in fact little more than compilations of such sketches on related themes.

C. is today also famed as a dramatist, although in his own day he encountered many hindrances and delays in the staging of his plays as a result of his harshly critical attitude toward the hypocrisies of Slovene society. Reflective of the influence of Henrik Ibsen are C.'s early plays, *Za narodov blagor* (1901; for the good of the people) and *Kralj na Betajnovi* (1902; *King of Betajnova*, 1984), which, together with the somewhat later *Hlapci* (1910; the servants), staged only posthumously in Trieste in 1919, constitute a ringing indictment of the political machinations of the monied classes and the clergy. At issue in these works are not only power and the question of whose hands it should properly be in, but the responsibilities of sons and lovers to their women, of women to their men, and of all people to the truth. Less politically explicit but satirically devastating is *Pohujšanje v dolini šentflorjanski* (1908; scandal in St. Florian valley), a thinly veiled allegory of the Slovene artist's dubious position in the midst of the "patriotic" arrogance and narrow-mindedness of his fellow countrymen. And quite different from the others, in that it lacks dramatic action while focusing on love and longing, is the "dramatic poem" *Lepa Vida* (1911; Lovely Vida), which was based on a popular legend from Slovene literature. This last play has an elegiac quality that one can find usually only in the older C.

The least voluminous, but nonetheless enduring of C.'s works are his poems. *Erotika* (1899; eroticism), a combination of four of C.'s early poetic cycles, caused a stir among the clergy, who denounced its "immorality." Derivative in its decadence and neoromantic expression, C.'s poetry gives a clear idea of the lyric voice of this writer, who worked in so many 20th-c. genres.

C. remains the most versatile and widely read Slovene writer. His limpid and accessible prose style, his clear and virile dramas, his expressive poetry together yield the picture of a writer who served, consciously, as a prophet to his people: that is, he was unheeded and denied, but ultimately he proved to be the voice of the nation.

FURTHER WORKS: *Jakob Ruda* (1898); *Onkraj življenja* (1899); *Popotovanje Nikolaja Nikiča* (1900); *Knjiga za lahkomiselne ljudi* (1901); *Ob zori* (1903); *Gospa Judit* (1904); *Potepuh Marko in Kralj Matjaž* (1905); *Nina* (1906); *Krpanova kobila* (1906); *Aleš iz Razora* (1907); *Zgodbe iz doline šentflorjanske* (1908); *Milan in Milena* (1913); *Moja njiva* (1914); *Zbrano delo* (30 vols., 1967–76)

BIBLIOGRAPHY: Lavrin, J., *Aspects of Modernism* (1935): 197–207; Slodnjak, A., *Geschichte der slowenischen Literatur* (1958): passim; Barac, A., *A History of Yugoslav Literature* (1976): 227–32

—HENRY R. COOPER, JR.

CANSEVER, Edip

Turkish poet, b. 8 Aug. 1928, Istanbul; d. 27 May 1986, Istanbul

One of Turkey's leading modernist poets, C. had a relatively uneventful life. Having left his graduate studies at Istanbul's School of Business Administration, he worked as an antique dealer at the Covered Bazaar for nearly four decades. His earliest poems were published in literary magazines when he was only sixteen years old. In 1951 he published a small magazine called *Nokta*, which lasted through eight issues.

C.'s first two collections of poetry, *İkindi üstü* (1947; in the afternoon) and *Dirlik-düzenlik* (1954; living in harmony), exhibit the influence of his immediate predecessors, especially the group known as *Garip* (Strange), which had sought to liberate new poetry from strict stanzaic forms and jaded conventions and to make its style direct, idiomatic, humorous, and populist. At this stage, C. was writing as a young bourgeois-bohemian, but his promise as a powerful new voice was already apparent. It was with *Yerçekimli karanfil* (1957; the gravitational carnation) that he burst on the literary scene as a major innovator to contend with. Few collections have been as controversial, and even fewer have had as enduring an impact. In a sharp departure from all the earlier norms of the Turkish poetic tradition and renouncing the *Garip* movement, C. and some of his contemporaries, including Cemal SÜREYA, Turgut Uyar (1927–1985), and Ece Ayhan (b. 1931), launched a brave new poetry, which at first came to be known as "meaningless" or "absurd" and later took the more neutral name "The Second New." C. and his friends made a curious but scintillating mélange of SURREALISM and EXISTENTIALISM, casting it into unabashedly obscurantist but engagingly lyrical forms of verse. Their wild thrusts of imagination elicited such criticism as "gibberish," "word salad," and "distortion of language." "The Second New," however, succeeded in overcoming the vehement attacks and endured as a profoundly influential aesthetic ideology.

C.'s *Umutsuzlar parki* (1958; the park of the hopeless) and *Petrol* (1959; petroleum) continued to bring him harsh criticism for egregious innovation and much praise for opening new horizons. It would be realized in the next decade that C. and the movement had once and for all asserted the poet's creative autonomy by freeing him from political commitment, ready-made forms, jaded tradition, pat idiom, and the like. The result was essentially a dazzling narcissism.

In *Nerde Antigone* (1961; where is Antigone) C. moved into a restless alienation, exploring the predicaments of the modern human being in the realm of ancient mythology and new myths. This search led him in *Tragedyalar* (1964; tragedies) and *Çağrılmayan Yakup* (1969; Jacob uninvited) to a strong dramatic narrative style that conveys both dark despair and glimmers of hope. As the titles suggest, these books evoke the spirit of ancient tragedy and biblical lore. In these two books, C. achieved a grandeur of vision and a grand design.

From 1970 until his death, C.'s poetic art evolved as a new, more serene quest for happiness in the midst of a cruel, turbulent world. *Kirli ağustos* (1970; dirty August) and *Sonrasi Kalir* (1974; the rest shall remain) are stimulating yet tranquil statements about an immutably troubled life in which perhaps the only salvation may be found in simple pleasures and the rich realm of the imagination. *Ben Ruhi Bey Nasilim* (1976; I Ruhi Bey, how am I) and *Sevda ile sevgi* (1977; love and affection) contain many of C.'s most heart-warming poems about ordinary people and the joys and the tender sorrows of love. These are all, however, poems of intriguing subtlety, with a uniquely ingenious style. *şairin seyir defteri* (1980; poet's log book) is perhaps C.'s most openly personal, if not autobiographical, collection of poems.

In 1981 C.'s complete poems were published in a volume entitled *Yeniden* (anew), stimulating new critical assessments of his poetic career. Critics were unanimous in recognizing that C. had brought important dimensions to modern Turkish poetry. C. published two more collections, *Bezik oynayan kadinlar* (1982; women playing bezique) and *Ilkyaz şikayetçileri* (1984; complainers of spring), which contain some of his most impressive and consummate poems. Winner of the 1958 Yeditepe Poetry Prize for *Yerçekimli karanfil* and the Poetry Prize of the Turkish Language Society in 1977 for *Ben Ruhi Bey Nasilim*, C. was given the Literary Award of the Sedat Simavi Foundation in 1981 for his complete poems, *Yeniden*. C. will continue to enjoy high prestige as one of the towering figures of Turkish poetry in the second half of the 20th c.

—TALAT SAIT HALMAN

CAPE VERDEAN LITERATURE

Claridade, a cultural journal published sporadically from 1936 to 1960, and the so-called *Claridade* movement owe their existence to a unique set of historical circumstances at work in the Cape Verde islands since their discovery. The ten main islands, lying some 350 miles off the coast of Senegal, became inhabited only after the Portuguese happened on them in the 15th c. Slaves from the nearby Guinea coast, plantation owners, administrators, and not a few Portuguese convicts lived in a close if socially stratified proximity that over the centuries worked to bring about biological and cultural creolization. Thus, in the 1930s, two decades before anything similar would occur elsewhere in Portugal's then colonies, members of the largely mestiço (mixed race) bourgeoisie began to produce poems and stories that qualify as the beginnings of a characteristic, uniquely Cape Verdean literature.

Jorge Barbosa (1901–1971), one of the first major island poets, established a style and tone for Cape Verdean writers with the collection *Arquipélago* (1935; Archipelago); its nostalgia and tropical melancholy reflect the solitude of the forgotten archipelago, and the poems romanticize the common people as stoically resigned to their fate on the drought-stricken islands.

Under the pseudonym Oswaldo Alcântara, Baltasar Lopes da Silva (1907–1989) wrote poems in which he combined popular themes and the techniques of Portuguese "art" poetry. Under the shortened name Baltasar Lopes he produced *Chiquinho* (1947; Chiquinho); one of Portuguese Africa's earliest and most important novels. As a Romance philologist, he made an early contribution to the elevation of Cape Verde's Portuguese-based Creole language. Since the 19th c., Creole, while essentially the language of the common people, has been cultivated as a vernacular in all strata of society. By describing the language as merely an archaic dialect of Portuguese, intellectuals like Silva hoped to erase its pidgin stigma.

Manuel Lopes (b. 1907), although also a poet, is best known for his powerful social novels, *Chuva braba* (1956; wild rain) and *Os flagelados do vento leste* (1960; victims of the east wind).

In 1952, Amílcar CABRAL, founder of the African Party of the Independence of Guinea and Cape Verde, called for a new literature, one that did not merely accept the islands' problems with a faith in the people's capacity to survive while celebrating their Creole uniqueness, but a literature that identified with the Cape Verdean on the level of intervening to bring about change. Many young writers heeded Cabral's plea, and in 1962 Ovídio Martins's (b. 1928) "Anti-Evasā" (antievasion) raised a poetic call for the nonavoidance of Cape Verde's endemic social, economic, and political problems. Martins was joined by other militant poets like Gabriel Mariano (b. 1928) and Onésimo Silveira (b. 1937).

After independence, which came on 5 July 1975, dozens of patriotic poems were published by Cape Verdeans at home and in the immigrant communities of Europe and the Americas. Seasoned poets, like Oswaldo Osório (b. 1937), Arménio Vieira (b. 1941), and Tacalhe (pseud. of Al´rio Silva, b. 1943), produced verse in praise of the new nation. As a kind of cultural and national affirmation, some poets turned to the use of a virile, defiant Creole language that had been first used by Kaoberdiano Dambara (pseud. of Felisberto Vieira Lopes, b. 1937) in *Noti* (1964; night), a book of protest poems tinged with the images of NEGRITUDE.

In the late 1970s and early 1980s the literary scene in Cape Verde could best be described as at an impasse, and at worst as in crisis. Writers were struggling with the problem of little time to write as they join in the effort to build a new nation on top of the shambles of centuries of colonialism. Dr. Francisco Fragoso (b. 1940), under the defiant Creole pseudonym Kwame Kondé, made a gallant but not totally successful attempt to launch a national Cape Verdean theater based on popular themes and agit-prop productions. João Varela (b. 1937), who had published HERMETIC poems in the tradition of European metaphysics, adopted the Creole pseudonym Timóteo Tio Tiofe to produce his *O primeiro livro de Notcha* (1975; Notcha's first book), an epiclike poem that seeks to mediate between European values and an African Cape Verdean historicity. Corsino Fortes (b. 1933), even before independence, wrote *Pão & fonema* (1974; bread & phoneme), also an epiclike attempt to place Cape Verde into the course of African and world history.

Despite the impasse, there were other promising signs. With the founding in 1977 of *Raizes*, a cultural and literary journal, members of several generations of Cape Verdean intellectuals made a valiant attempt to lay the basis of a new literary movement. Henrique Teixeira de Sousa (b. 1919), published *Ilhéu de Contenda* (1978; Contested Islet), a novelistic saga that whetted the appetites of younger Cape Verdeans eager to retell the history of their islands. In 1993 a script based on *Ilhéu de contenda* became the first feature-length film by a native-born Cape Verdean. After his first novelistic success, Teixeira de Sousa published *Xaguate* (1988; The Xaguate Hotel) and *Djunga* (1989; Djunga), two more well-received novels set on his native island of Fogo. It was, however, Manuel Veiga (b. 1948) who made history with his *Oju d'agu* (1987; the wellspring), the first published novel written entirely in Cape Verdean creole.

In the 1990s, Germano Almeida (b. 1960) burst on the scene with his *O testamento do Sr. Mapumoceno da Silva Araújo* (1991; the last will and testament of Mr. Nupumoceno da Silva Araújo), which became a best-seller and on which a 1996 movie is based. Almeida went on to write *O meu poeta* (1990; my favorite poet), *A ilha fantástica* (1994; fantastic island), and *Os dois irmãos* (1995; two brothers).

Not suprisingly, the first two decades of Cape Verde's postcolonial period gave rise to a number of cultural movements and arts and letters journals, most of which have been short-lived. In the city of Praia, however, one of the more enduring initiatives has been the Movimento Pro-Cultura (pro-culture movement), spearheaded by José Luís Hopffer Almada (b. 1960). Almada, the author of two books of poetry, is also the director of *Fragmentos* (fragments), Pro-Cultura's journal of letters, art, and culture.

Vera Duarte (b. 1952) stands out among a number of craft-conscious Pro-Cultura writers. *Amanhã amadrugada* (1993; tomorrow's dawning), is Duarte's collection of sensitive poems and prose poems. Besides being Cape Verde's first female judge, Duarte is one of a very few women and feminist writers from the archipelago.

Mainly young and aspiring writers rallied around Pro-Cultura. Meanwhile, also in Praia, established poets, fiction writers, and playwrights, most being members of the Writers Union and associated with the National Book and Record Institute, continued to produce. Chief among those whose careers began before independence are the aforementioned poets Corsino Fortes, Oswaldo Osório, and Arménio Viera, all of whom have written and published new works since independence. Besides a book of poetry, Vieira also authored *O eleito do sol* (1989; The sun's chosen one), a novel set in ancient Egypt but meant to be read as a political allegory about present-day Cape Verde.

Although Praia is today firmly established as the literary capital of Cape Verde, the city of Mindelo maintains its vibrancy as a center of culture. Onésimo Silveira, the aforementioned militant writer of the pre-independence period, who spent the last two decades of the colonial period in self-imposed exile, returned to his native São Vincente and is currently serving his second term as mayor of Mindelo. Even while enmeshed in politics, Silveira was able to writer his first novel: *A saga das as-secas e das graças de Nossenhor* (1991; The saga of the droughts and the graces of the Lord).

Although the long-standing debate about creole and its use as a literary language has heated up during the second half of the 1990s, the issue seems not to have caused any major division among Cape Verdean writers and intellectuals. Whether in Mindelo, Praia, or elsewhere in the islands, in the 1990s Cape Verdean literary and other cultural activities reached a dynamic high, both quantitively and qualitatively.

BIBLIOGRAPHY: Araujo, N., *A Study of Cape Verdean Literature* (1966); Gérard, A. S., "The Literature of Cape Verde," *African Arts*, 1, 2 (1968): 66–70; Moser, G. M., "How African Is the African Literature Written in Portuguese?", *RNL*, 1, 2 (1971): 148–66; Hamilton, R. G., *Voices from an Empire: A History of Afro-Portuguese Literature* (1975): 231–357; Priebe, R. O., and T. A. Hale, "Cape Verdean Poetry and the PAIGC," in *Artist and Audience: African Literature as a Shared Experience* (1979): 103–25; Hamilton, R. G., "Amílcar Cabral and Cape Verdean Poetry," *WLT*, 53 (1979): 49–54; Ellen, M. M., ed., *Across the Atlantic: An Anthology of Cape Verdean literature* (1988); Hamilton, R. G., "Portuguese-Language Literature," in Ovomoyela, O., ed., *A History of Twentieth-Century African Literatures* (1993); Moser, G. M., *Changing Africa: The First Literary Generation of Independence Cape Verde* (1993)

—RUSSELL G. HAMILTON

CAPÉCIA, Mayotte

(pseud. of Josephe Combette) Martinican novelist, b. 1916, Carbet; d. 1955, Fort-de-France

C. was born in Carbet, a small town in Martinique, to a single, unwed mother. She was one of twin girls, and she grew up in Martinique, largely without a formal education. C. remained unmarried, but gave birth to three daughters. In 1946, following the death of her father, C. moved to Paris. She returned to Martinique in 1948 and died there from cancer in 1955.

While C.'s renown as a novelist is steadily growing, her reputation during her lifetime and for many years after was rooted in Frantz Fanon's (1925-1961) critique of her work in his book, *Peau noire, masques blancs* (1965; *Black Skin, White Masks*, 1967). Chapter 2 of Fanon's book is devoted to the examination of what he terms "lactification," by which he means the desire of the black race to "whiten" itself through sexual contact and reproduction with the white race. Fanon's chapter condemns C. for her own relationships with white men, and condemns her novels for promoting this type of behavior. In recent years Fanon's analysis of C.'s work has been seen to be faulty, both in its conflation of her personal history with her work and in its interpretation of her texts.

C. published only two novels, the first of which was *Je suis Martiniquaise* (1948; I Am a Woman from Martinique). This openly autobiographical novel, whose protagonist's name is Mayotte, is a first-person retrospective narrative that chronicles the experiences of a young, unmarried mulatto woman in postwar Martinique. The backdrop of the narrative is the stark race/caste system in place in Martinique at the time. This system, which divided the world into black and white, privileged white and denigrated black. Mayotte's status as mulatto places her in between the two poles around which the society in which she lives is constituted, and the novel explores and exploits this position of neither/nor to create an insight into the psychological effects of racism on those who are not included in the white elite.

The polarity of racial constitution is only one of two important binaries of identity in C.'s first novel. Equally important to her text is the question of gender. In an era long before the advent of feminism as such, C. portrays, in the character of Mayotte, a strong, self-supporting, and independent women who is on a journey of self-discovery. This self-discovery is, in many ways, inhibited by both her gender and the color of her skin, but this is not a failing on the part of Mayotte nor of C. herself; it is a failing on the part of the society in which C. is writing—a fact that *Je suis Martiniquaise* makes evident. At the end of the novel Mayotte departs for France, hoping to escape both Martinique and the rigidity of the racial and gender biases that characterize Martinican society of that time.

C.'s second novel, *La négresse blanche* (1950; The White Negresse), is a further development of the two themes established in *Je suis Martiniquaise*. Like the first novel, *La Négresse blanche* centers on the life of a strong, financially and sexually independent woman. While race is an issue in this novel, it is examined through a more complex and complicated lens than in *Je suis Martiniquaise*—the filter of interracial marriage.

Set against the emergence of the black identity movement in Martinique and the occupation of the island by the racist Vichy government, *La négresse blanche* presents the story of Isaure, a young mulatto, and her white fiancé/husband Pascal. The use of interracial marriage permits an exploration not only of the impact of white racism on people of color, but of the attitudes towards race and race mixing shared by persons of all races. Through the rejection of Isaure by Pascal's white family, and the lynching of Pascal by a black mob, C. foregrounds the hatred and violence of all racism, and the potential for black awareness to become an identical, if opposing, system of domination and discrimination to the racism of colonialism, which it seeks to subvert. Furthermore, like C.'s first novel, this novel suggests the impossibility of individual development in such a climate of racial polarity, as Isaure, like Mayotte, leaves for France at the novel's end.

Fanon's assertion that C.'s novels contain expressions of a desire by the protagonists to whiten themselves is true. Both Mayotte and Isaure overtly and subtly reveal the impact of the racist climate in which they live upon their own psyches. Both have absorbed, to some degree, the cultural valorization of white skin and the denigration of black skin, and in both cases, their internalization of this racism causes them a degree of self-rejection. However, where Fanon is mistaken is in his extension of the psyche's of C.'s characters to her own psyche. The existence of a desire to become white in C.'s characters is not necessarily evidence of the existence of such a desire in C. herself. In fact, it can be argued that the opposite is true—that C.'s inscribing of such attitudes in her text is her narrative attempt to lay bare the power of racist stereotypes, especially on those defined by them. Read this

way, C.'s texts are in no way an attempt to perpetuate the racist attitudes which they portray. Rather, her novels can be read as early attempts to undermine such racist attitudes. Furthermore, to read C.'s texts solely through the filter of race is to ignore a great deal of their power, since they are equally calls for a reexamination of the role of women in society, and as such, are early examples of textual feminism.

BIBLIOGRAPHY: Zimra, C., "Patterns of Liberation in Contemporary Women Writers," *L'Esprit Créateur*, 17 (1977): 103-15; Zimra, C., and L. Paravisini-Gebert, "Feminism, Race, and Difference in the Works of M. C., Michèle Lacrosil, and Jacqueline Manicom," *Callaloo*, 15 (1992): 6-74; Clark, B. "Who Was M. C.? An Update," *CLAJ*, 39 (June 1996): 454-57; Hurley, A. E. "Intersections of Female Identity or Writing the Woman in Two Novels by M. C. and Marie-Magdaleine Carbet," *FR*, 70 (1997): 575-86

—DAYNA L. OSCHERWITZ

ČAPEK, Karel

Czechoslovak dramatist, novelist, short-story writer, essayist, journalist, and poet (writing in Czech), b. 9 Jan. 1890, Malé Svatoňovice; d. 25 Dec. 1938, Prague

Č. was the youngest son of a highly cultured physician in a small east Bohemian town; his sister, Helena (1886–1969), wrote a

Karel Čapek

few novels, and his brother, Josef (1887–1945), was a painter, novelist, and dramatist who often collaborated with Karel. Č. studied at Charles University in Prague, where he got his doctorate in 1915, and in Berlin and Paris. During World War I Č. worked temporarily as a librarian and as a tutor to a count's son, but in 1917 he turned to journalism. His long association with the leading daily, *Lidové noviny*, made his name known to a wide readership. As a member of the press he was particularly aware of contemporary events, which became the inspiration for a number of his works.

On a small scale, Č. had already been writing and publishing in his teens and while a university student; during this period he became keenly interested in new trends in art abroad; SYMBOLISM, Decadence, and pragmatism later influenced his writings, as did CHESTERTON, WELLS, and SHAW. After 1918, when the first Czechoslovak Republic was established, Č. became an ardent spokesman for democracy; he took a very active part in the public life of the new state and became a close friend and biographer of its first president, T. G. Masaryk. Č.'s plays soon gained him fame both at home and abroad, as well as many friends in the West, whom Č. greatly valued; it is no wonder that the Munich agreement in 1938 broke his heart and spirit, and indirectly contributed to his premature death.

The first published collection of short stories, *Zářivé hlubiny* (1916, with Josef Č; luminous depths), already clearly indicates Č.'s lasting interest in the mysteries of human nature and existence. The rather gloomy stories in *Boží muka* (1917; wayside crosses) are clearly influenced by the war and by Č.'s latent, incurable illness, as well as by his spiritual pain, which originated in his vain search for an explanation of the human condition. But they also show Č.'s fine poetic gift and philosophical world view.

Delighted with the freedom that came after the war, Č. developed his art fully, particularly as a dramatist. In the famous satiric comedy *Ze života hmyzu* (1921; *The Life of the Insects*, 1923), written with his brother, human vices like lust, greed, pride, the striving after power, exploitation, and selfishness become the targets of the authors' wit; yet the play also expresses a plea for cooperation among people. In *R.U.R.* (1920; *R.U.R.* 1923), which gave the word "robot" to the English language, Č. introduced his artificial people as creations of human inventiveness; he had a strong belief in its potential, but doubted whether human nature could use the results of research wisely. In his view, modern discoveries may make life easier, but they are likely to be abused and to become destructive. Unlike the experimental, *commedia dell'arte*-type play, *Lásky hra osudná* (1922; the fatal game of love), which followed, the two earlier plays are, nevertheless, fully mature works, as is *Věc Makropulos* (1922; *The Macropoulos Secret*, 1925), in which Č. takes up another science-fiction theme—extreme longevity. Dramatically, this play surpasses Shaw's work on the same theme, *Back to Methuselah*, and it is no wonder that the composer Leoš Janáček was inspired to turn it into an opera. Č's treatment of the theme of longevity again reflects his awareness of the vanity of human wishes: however short, life becomes worthy if lived decently. Should man meddle with the world as it is, the situation could become even worse, as the brothers Č. reminded us in *Adam Stvořitel* (1927; *Adam the Creator*, 1929). The Alter Ego, created by the dissatisfied Adam, proves to be a much less satisfactory creature than the man-creator.

Although Č.'s philosophy of pragmatism permeates his work, in his last two plays, appalled by Hitler's threat to Europe, he advocates absolute values. *Bílá nemoc* (1937; *Power and Glory*, 1938), with its confrontation between the powerful military dictator and the pacifist doctor who has invented the only cure for the white plague (the meaning of the Czech title) not only offers some magnificently dramatic scenes, but also serves as a forum to express Č.'s antiwar ideas. The dictator finally consents to refrain from war and the doctor agrees to cure him, but on his way to the palace the doctor-savior, like Christ, is killed by an ignorant crowd. Similarly, political and moral convictions are weighed against each other in Č.'s last play, *Matka* (1938; *The Mother*, 1939), in which the heroine refuses to allow her youngest and last surviving son to go fight in the war for an idea, but gives him a rifle when atrocities specifically against her country as well as humanity in general are being committed.

It is among Č.'s novels that his finest works are to be found, although as a whole, they are not as well known as his plays. The future of humanity was very much in Č.'s mind in his science fiction novels *Továrna na absolutno* (1922; *The Absolute at Large*, 1927) and *Krakatit* (1924; *Krakatit*, 1925), both concerned with a powerful explosive that can serve mankind as well as kill, and *Válka s mloky* (1936; *War with the Newts*, 1937), which deals with the benevolent anthropoid newts who become destroyers as soon as they have acquired human traits. While in *Krakatit* the tone prompts the reader to think seriously, the other two novels combine the serious and the comic, with the latter prevailing.

In Č.'s masterpiece—the trilogy consisting of *Hordubal* (1933; *Hordubal*, 1934), *Povětroň* (1934; *Meteor*, 1935), and *Obyčejný život* (1934; *An Ordinary Life*, 1936)—his epistemological skepticism and pragmatic relativism are brought to bear on the plurality of a human personality and are analyzed within the framework of the systematic structure of the three novels. It is here, too, that Č. perfected his favorite technique of perspectivism, that is, viewing a character or problem from different angles, thus forming a whole. Those who think that they know the complete truth about the tragedy of the Carpathian peasant Hordubal find that they know only a fraction of it; in *Povětroň* it becomes clear that the same few facts lend themselves to a number of different interpretations of a situation because people's judgments necessarily spring from their individual experiences; the hero of *Obyčejný život*—ordinary as he is—shows that even he is a very complex combination of several different personalities. Č. also used the perspective technique in the creation of the pathetic protagonist of his last, unfinished, novel, *Život a dílo skladatele Foltýna* (1939; *The Cheat*, 1941): each person's view of the protagonist may be only partial and relative, but the standards of true art remain absolute, and Foltýn, with his pretenses, must fail.

Č.'s short stories are also very successful. They highlight his wit and humor, and show a wealth of subjects and ideas. Epistemology led Č. to explore human justice, crime, detection, and punishment, and this resulted in the brilliant stories in *Povídky z jedné kapsy* and *Povídky z druhé kapsy* (both 1929; *Tales from Two Pockets*, 1932), in which human weaknesses are gently ridiculed. These amusing and thoughtful tales show Č. at his best, just as do his serious stories in *Trapné povídky* (1921; *Money, and Other Stories*, 1929): pragmatic in their concept of truth, they present subtly painful, embarrassing situations that produce an effect of puzzlement and wonder. The wide-ranging subjects of the stories in *Kniha apokryfů* (1932; *Apocryphal Stories*, 1949) reveal Č.'s profound knowledge of human nature and deep sympathy with it.

As a journalist, Č. enriched Czech literature with "small" genres, such as travelogues, essays, feuilletons, causeries, and fairy tales; even trifles inspired him to write delightful books like *O nejbližších věcech* (1920; *Intimate Things*, 1935), *Marsyas* (1931; *In Praise of Newspapers*, 1951), *Zahradníkův rok* (1929; *The Gardener's Year*, 1931), and *Měl jsem psa a kočku* (1939; *I Had a Dog and a Cat*, 1940). He wrote little poetry, but his excellent translations from French, *Francouzská poesie nové doby* (1920; modern French poetry) strongly influenced young Czech poets.

Among Czech writers of this century, Č. was the most versatile, prolific, and best known abroad. Having tried successfully almost all literary genres, he gave Czech literature a new dimension and exerted a strong influence on younger writers. His deep understanding of human nature and his fertile imagination produced profound works that encourage people to think and to have respect for each other.

FURTHER WORKS: *Krakonošova zahrada* (1918); *Pragmatismus* (1918); *Loupežník* (1920); *Kritika slov* (1920); *Italské listy* (1923; *Letters from Italy*, 1929); *Anglické listy* (1924; *Letters from England*, 1925); *Skandální aféra Josefa Holouška* (1927); *Hovory s T. G. Masarykem* (3 vols., 1928–35; *Masaryk on Thought and Life*, 1938); *Minda; čili, O chovu psů* (1930; *Minda; or, On Breeding Dogs*, 1940); *Výlet do Španěl* (1930; *Letters from Spain*, 1931); *O věcech obecných; čili, Zóon politikon* (1932); *Obrázky z Holandska* (1932; *Letters from Holland*, 1933); *Devatero pohádek* (1932; *Fairy Tales*, 1933); *Dášeňka* (1933; *Dashenka*, 1940); *Legenda o člověku zahradníkovi* (1935); *Cesta na sever* (1936; *Travels in the North*, 1939); *První parta* (1937; *The First Rescue Party*, 1939); *Jak se co dělá* (1938; *How They Do It*, 1945); *Kalendář* (1940); *O lidech* (1940); *Vzrušené tance* (1946); *Bajky a podpovídky* (1946); *Sedm rozhláků K. Č.* (1946); *Ratolest a vavřín* (1947); *Obrázky z domova* (1953); *Sloupkový ambit* (1957); *Poznámky o tvorbě* (1959); *Viktor Dyk-S. K. Neumann-bratří Č.: Korespondence z let 1905–1918* (1962); *Nabřehu dnů* (1966); *Divadelníkem proti své vůli* (1968); *V zajetí slov* (1969); *Čtení o T. G. Masarykovi* (1969); *Místo pro Jonathana* (1970); *Listy Olze* (1971); *Drobty pod stolem doby* (1975); *Three Novels* (1990); *Toward the Radical Center* (1990); *Nine Fairy Tales* (1990); *Tales from the Two Pockets* (1994); *Talks with T. G. Masaryk* (1995)

BIBLIOGRAPHY: Chandler, F. W., *Modern Continental Writers* (1931): 453–63; Wellek, R., "K. Č." (1936–37), *Essays on Czech Literature* (1963): 46–62; Elton, O., "K. Č." *Essays and Addresses* (1939): 151–86; Harkins, W. E., *K. Č.* (1962); Matuška, A., *K. Č.: Man against Destruction* (1964); Bradbrook, B. R., "A Č. Revival," *SEER*, 99 (1964): 434–39; Dresler, J., "Č. and Communism," in Rechcigl, M., ed., *The Czechoslovak Contribution to World Culture* (1964): 68–76; Haman, A., and P. I. Trenský, "Man against the Absolute: The Art of K. Č.," *SEEJ*, 2 (1967): 168–84; Bradbrook, B. R., "K. Č.'s Contribution to Czech National Literature," in Rechcigl, M., ed., *Czechoslovakia Past and Present* (1968): 1002–12; Bradbrook, B. R., "Chesterton and K. Č: A Study in Personal and Literary Relationship," *Chesterton Review*, 4 (1977–78): 89–103; Kovtun, J., "Bibliography of K. Č.'s Works Translated into English and Published in the U.S.A.," *Library of Congress Information Bulletin*, Dec. 1978; Vočadlo, O., *Anglické listy Karla Čapka* (1975); Welchsler, R., "K. Č. in America," *Cross Currents*, 9 (1990): 173-86; Comrada, N., "K. Č. On Science, Progress and Responsibility," *Czechoslovak and Central European Journal* (summer 1991), Vol. 10.1: 64-72; Harkins, W. E., "The Structure of K. Č.'s Trilogy," *Czecholslovak and Central European Journal*, (summer 1991), Vol. 10.1: 60-64; Bradbrook, B. R., "K. Č., and the English Writers," in Hawkersworth, C., ed., *Literature and Politics*

in Eastern Europe: Selected Papers from the Fourth World Congress for Soviet and East European Studies, Harrogate, 1990 (1992): 149-65; Makin, M., and J. Toman, eds., *On K. Č.: A Michigan Slavic Colloquium* (1992); Toman, J., "'If I were a Linguist. . .' K. Č. and/vs. the Prague Linguistic Circle" in Mackie, A. W., T. McAuley, and C. Simmons, eds., *For Henry Kučera: Studies in Slavic Philogy and Computational Linguistics* (1992): 365-80; Thomas, A., "Humanism and Relativism in K. Č.,'s *Kniha apolryfů*," in Thomas, A., *The Labyrinth of the World* (1995): 116-31

—B. R. BRADBROOK

Č.'s essays and causeries are obviously very typical of him: their journalistic character, their colloquial coloring, and their typical attitude to reality substantially contribute to the complete outline of the writer's profile.... Č.'s prose is characterized by frequent accumulations of words in rich and varied enumerations.... Frequent examples from almost every page of the *Letters from England* or *The Gardener's Year* could be quoted. Essentially, the purpose is always the same: the accumulation of things or actions characterize the infinite many-sidedness, complexity, and fluctuation of reality.... One may sum up Č.'s causeries as follows: the usual style here is the parallelism of sentences and their parts; this kind of syntactical structure lends itself well to the alternations in meanings from one level to another. Even in other respects, such a sentence is flexible and fluctuating: it allows for quick changes of speed, alternating of intonation (indicative, interrogative, imperative, desiderative, and their variations), as well as the changes in the scale in which the subject is related.

Jan Mukařovský, *Výbor z prózy K. Č.* (1934), pp. 32–34

Through his great artistic skill Č diverts one's attention immediately after the scientific invention has been introduced, from its substance and causes to its effects. It would not occur to the reader or spectator to ask an explanation of the origin of the science-fiction element, because the latter immediately and abundantly produces effects entangling the plot. This is the case in two novels (*The Absolute at Large, Krakatit*) as well as in the plays: in the latter, Č. used a dramatic element most effectively, namely, the nonhuman taking on a human likeness. This may not be anything new; in the Don Juan plays there is the statute of the revived *commendatore* taking Don Juan to hell, but Č. freed this motif from its religious fancifulness, modernized it, and suitably altered it several times. A critic pointed out that human-size dolls, acting their lives, would have a terrific effect. Such is the case with the robots, the insects miming human life, even Emilia Marty when we begin to realize what she is, and, to a certain extent, even some characters in *Adam the Creator*. Č. appears here as an extraordinary technician of a dramatic effect.

Václav Černý, *K. Č.* (1936), pp. 157–16

Č.'s best work is the trilogy of novels: *Hordubal, The Meteor* and *An Ordinary Life*. Each of these novels tries to tell the same story from a different point of view in order to enhance the variety of its meaning and to suggest the utter mysteriousness of ultimate reality. *Hordubal* on the surface is a story of crime from the Carpathian mountains; *The Meteor* is made up of speculative reconstructions of the early history of a pilot who has come down in a crash; *An Ordinary Life* is a novel of a Czech bourgeois, the story of a railway clerk who discovers unexpected hidden selves in his own mind and past. But these books all centre round problems of truth and reality and constitute one of the most successful attempts at a philosophical novel, not only in Czech.

But Č. does not owe his success to his finest books: many readers will prefer his Utopian romances like the *Absolute at Large* or *Krakatit*, his many original crime stories and the charming sketches and travel books. Since my article [on him] appeared [in 1936], K. Č. has published another travel book, this time on Scandinavia, and a short novel, *The First Rescue Party* (1937), taken from the life of miners, which is full of Č.'s social feeling and his real understanding of the common man. Č. has been frequently called by Czech criticism too international, which is possibly true of some of his Utopian romances and plays. But a book like *An Ordinary Life* is a finely drawn picture of the Czech atmosphere, and there is something very representative and national in Č.'s love of the small man, in his genuine democratism and humanism. [1939]

René Wellek, *Essays on Czech Literature* (1963), p. 43

If ever art was didactic, it is here [in *Wayside Crosses*]. It instructs the reader systematically and effectively by allowing him to look into its purposefully directed train of thought, which develops in front of our eyes, step by step, point by point. It is the art of a scientifically exact and clear method that excludes everything that has not been logically prepared and deduced. There are no love coincidences, no ups and downs or decline of talent; everything is on the same methodically calculated and secured plane. How well one can now understand Č.'s longing for a miracle, for a direct act of God! His desire to burst out of the dreary vicious circle or chain! Such a passionate desire can only be expressed by slaves chained by rules, routine, formulae and habits. . . . Hence the gloomy, sometimes even oppressive effect emanating from this work. The merit and excellence of these stories lie in their method; impersonality in art has hardly ever been developed so far. This direct method is, in a sense, an aesthetic achievement of Č.

F. X. Šalda, *Kritické glosy k nové poesii české* (1939), pp. 159–60

Č. was a philosophical writer *par excellence*. Perhaps no one of his generation tried so systematically and consciously to express philosophical ideas through literature. Indeed, Č.'s attempt in the trilogy to embody epistemological ideas in literary form is well-nigh unique in fiction. He is also one of the few writers, even of our time, to deal with the problem of modern science and technology. . . .

Č.'s greatness as a writer often depends not on the success of his conscious intention, but on what has slipped in, almost in spite of the author. *In spite of* his experimentalism, his use of scientific or philosophic themes, traditional literary values abound in his works. In spite of his determined effort to come to grips with life, an unconscious terror of life returns again and again in his work. Though he tried not to admit it, Č. kept stumbling over the tragedy of life. All his work after *Wayside Crosses* is in a sense a defense against the metaphysical horror which he perceived in that book.

William E. Harkins, *K. Č.* (1962), pp. 168–69

An author remains tagged in our memory with a certain attribute, which appears to remain unchanged: Dickens as all "heart"; Tolstoy as "preaching nonresistance to evil." And, if we may make a comparison, the fate of K. Č. was similar in the eyes of his readers. He remained fixed in our subconscious as the inventor of the Robot, and, on the other hand, as the eulogizer of the little man, of little things. . . .

Č.'s passion for discovery, for cognition, was equally divided between theoretical literature and belles lettres. At the age of twenty-five, he was well versed in literature on the graphic arts. Evidence of this is found in his graduation thesis entitled "The Objective Method in Aesthetics, with Reference to Creative Art" (1915), which was extremely well received by his professors. He discovered the basic works of Czech literature as a boy, so that as he grew, his interest turned to the literature of Europe at large. In the cosmopolitan atmosphere of his beginnings, his acquaintance with European literature and art was made in a "natural" manner. Young Č. was convinced that "Bohemian art has always found it necessary to elaborate on European influence, throughout its entire history, for art was not invented in Bohemia." This point of view did not remain unchanged throughout Č.'s life.

Alexander Matuška, *K. Č.: Man Against Destruction* (1964), pp. 8, 15

In the long history of our literary links with England, Č. takes a prominent place. No Czech author since Comenius had been so wholeheartedly welcomed by leading English writers. In the period between the last two wars, no Czech literary work was more favored by English readers and praised by English critics than the work of Č. . . . As an artist, he felt instinctively that only the rich English literary tradition could offer him a choice of the greatest variety of genres, which eventually he himself successfully practiced: the drama of ideas, science-fiction prose, the entertaining essay, witty aphorism, detective story. . . . In the themes and problems of various English literary genres Č. found a special delight, satisfaction, and stimulation.

Otakar Vočadlo, *Anglické listy K. Č.* (1975), pp. 325, 332

CAPOTE, Truman

American novelist, short-story writer, and journalist, b. 30 Sept. 1924, New Orleans, La.; d. 26 Aug. 1984, Los Angeles, Cal.

Although categorized as a Southern writer, C. attended school in New York and spent the greater part of his life in that city. A much-traveled, gregarious man, C. had an international reputation, which extended beyond the work to his colorful personality. From his earliest days as a writer, he was a popular subject for interviewers and photographers.

C. has not produced an extensive body of fiction. Many of his books are collections of short stories, travel sketches, or occasional pieces that appeared originally in magazines.

The Louisiana-Mississippi-Alabama area is the setting for much of C.'s fiction; but even when he changes the locale, his characters often are displaced Southerners. Significantly, the single most typical element of the region, gothicism, pervades his best-known work.

Some of C.'s early stories are fictionalized autobiography. Generally, the protagonist is a child or teenager, orphaned and lonely. In some works he may be seeking love or understanding. In others he finds it briefly, only to have the beloved die or to be separated from her. C. has identified the lost child of various pieces as himself. After his parents' divorce and his mother's remarriage, the boy went to live with relatives, one of whom became the model for the loving, elderly spinster in several C. novels, stories, and plays.

Other Voices, Other Rooms (1948), C.'s first novel, tells of a boy's search for a father and a masculine identity. In the bizarre, surrealistic region to which he travels he hopes he will find someone to love him. Of the people he meets, each one is grotesque in some way. Although he struggles to achieve a heterosexual relationship, he does not succeed. When all else fails him, he finally accepts the world of the homosexual. In this heavily textured short novel C. introduced many of the poetic elements that were to become familiar in subsequent works.

In the novel *The Grass Harp* (1951) a young boy and his elderly cousin defy the conventions of a materialistic society that insists they conform to its rules. Joined by other individualists, they refuse to succumb to the pressures put on them. They discover, however, that some compromise is necessary if people are to live together in a community. All acknowledge finally that what matters most is love, not only for other people but also for the natural world. C.'s lyrical style and whimsical humor are tinged with a gentle melancholy and with a nostalgia that is characteristic of a number of his stories.

The elegiac note provides the counterpoint for the comedy in *A Christmas Memory* (1956), a story that became a perennially favorite television play. Once again the central figures are a little boy and his cousin, an eccentric old lady who is as much a child as he. For each of them the highlight of each year comes with the preparation for the holiday. Lonely and unhappy when he is sent

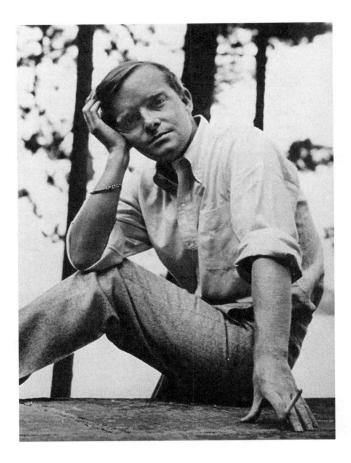

Truman Capote

away to school and parted forever from his cousin, the boy feels that something of himself is gone and can never be reclaimed.

In *Breakfast at Tiffany's* (1958), C. created a fun-loving, independent heroine who comes to New York seeking an elusive happiness. Orphaned and deprived as a child, she wants comfort and security as an adult. She longs for a place to belong to and a loving mate, but her code of honesty and morality permits only moments of pleasure and contentment. At last she must flee the city to keep her freedom.

Daylight and darkness are terms frequently used to describe two major moods in C.'s fiction. The collection of short stories *A Tree of Night* (1949) best exemplifies these. In several of the stories, inexplicable or supernatural events occur. Characters are confronted by their hidden, secret selves. Caught by inescapable nightmare, some characters become schizophrenic, while others live only on the edge of reality. The protagonists of the sunnier stories often are children or childlike. However, they, too, possess distinguishing characteristics that others long remember with awe and affection.

In Cold Blood (1966), C.'s best-known work, has been described by its author as a nonfiction novel. C. applied that label, a contradiction in terms, to explain that he had devised a new genre, combining the creative art of the novelist with the fact-finding methods of the journalist. Although some critics disagree with C.'s claim to have developed a unique form, unquestionably the work has had a significant influence on the development of documentary novels in both America and Europe. Using the techniques of suspense and detection, C. re-creates the murders of an exemplary

Midwestern family by two criminals, the investigation and trials that followed, and the execution of the murderers. Realism is mixed with novelistic imagination as C. discloses the facts, not as a straightforward newspaper reporter but as a creative artist selecting details, positioning and reiterating them for meaning or intensity. The influence of film technique on the structural pattern may be seen in the use of flashback and close-ups, carefully depicted settings, the building momentum behind the escape, pursuit, and capture of the criminals, the crowd scenes and the courtroom episodes. In his examination of the lives of the victims and the killers, C. explores societal as well as individual issues. The story carries universal appeal, no matter how the reader views its ultimate meaning: as symbol of violence in America; as the failure of the American Dream; or as a study of death-obsessed criminals. It is a contemporary American tragedy.

C.'s career began to falter in the late 1960s. Anxious, physically ill, and depressed, nevertheless, he declared his greatest novel was yet to come. For the remainder of his life he insisted he was working on his masterwork, a novel which would be the culmination of all he had learned as a writer. However, during the next two decades the novel did not appear, whereas he continued to publish in various magazines short pieces, stories, interviews, and conversations. These became the collection *Music for Chameleons* (1980); the segment that received the most critical attention is "Handcarved Coffins." It subtitle, "A Nonfiction Account of an American Crime," indicates C.'s intention of connecting the new story to *In Cold Blood*, thus renewing public and critical interest in his writing. Although C. proclaimed the story to be authentic, it actually was a hoax typical of his casual attitude toward truth.

C.'s long promised, much anticipated masterpiece never materialized. Instead, three years after his death, his editor put together a "novel" consisting of three gossipy destructive short stories that had been printed by *Esquire* in the 1970s. They were republished as *Answered Prayers: The Untitled Novel* (1986). The plotless, rambling stories narriated by a self-hating C. double are also salacious, angry, hostile, and ultimatiely sad, for instead of restoring C.'s languishing reputation they diminished it further. However, time has been good to C.; as memories of *Answered Prayers* have faded, the audience that responded to his best work from the beginning remains, still attuned to his poetic quality, his psychological perception, his humor—whimical or satirical—his journalist's instincts, and his photographer's eye.

FURTHER WORKS: *Local Color* (1950); *The House of Flowers* (1952); *The Muses Are Heard* (1956); *Observations* (1959, with Richard Avedon); *The Thanksgiving Visitor* (1967)

BIBLIOGRAPHY: Baldanza, F., "Plato in Dixie," *GaR*, 12 (1958): 151–67; Aldridge, J., *After the Lost Generation: A Critical Study of the Writers of Two Wars* (1958): 194–230; Hassan, I., *Radical Innocence: The Contemporary American Novel* (1961): 230–58; Kazin, A., *Contemporaries* (1962): 250–54; Schorer, M., "McCullers and C.: Basic Patterns," in Balakian, N., and Simmons, C., eds., *The Creative Present: Notes on Contemporary American Fiction* (1963): 83–107; Gossett, L., *Violence in Recent Southern Literature* (1965): 145–58; Malin, I., ed., *T. C.'s "In Cold Blood": A Critical Handbook* (1968); Nance, W., *The Worlds of T. C.* (1970); Fleming, A., "The Private World of T.C.," *NYTMag*, 9 July 1978: 22–25, and 16 July 1978: 12–15; Garson, H., *T. C.* (1980); Inge, M. T., ed., *T. C.: Conversations* (1987); Clarke, G., *T. C.: A Biography* (1988); Garson, H., *T. C.: A Study of the Short Fiction* (1992)

—HELEN S. GARSON

CARAGIALE, Mateiu

Romanian novelist, short-story writer, and poet, b. 25 March 1885, Bucharest; d. 17 Jan. 1936, Bucharest

C. was the illegitimate son of Romania's greatest comic playwright, Ion Luca Caragiale (1853–1912). He studied law at the universities of Berlin and Bucharest and held positions in the Departments of Internal Affairs and Public Works. His marriage (1923) to a wealthy older woman gave him financial independence, and he pursued research in heraldry and biography. In his lifetime he had already become a cult figure in aestheticist circles.

C. began his literary career by publishing sonnets and other short poems in the prestigious monthly *Viaţa românească*; they were later collected with other poems in *Pajere* (1936; emblems). These were Parnassian productions, enlivened by an occasional touch of irony and by a good deal of naturalist cruelty; they often presented typical figures of Romania's historical past. The poetic style was rich and sumptuous, with a careful dosage of archaic words and neologisms.

The short story "Remember" (1921; the title is in English) revealed the growing influence on C. of Western "Decadents" such as Jules Barbey d'Aurevilly (1808–1889), Villiers de L'Isle-Adam (1838–1889), Joris-Karl Huysmans (1848–1907), and ultimately Baudelaire and Poe. Its main character is an extravagant, aristocratic dandy who becomes the object of a mysterious, perhaps homosexually motivated, crime. Behind the ornate descriptions there is an allegorical purpose: the past, degenerate and bizarre as it may be, is still a living affront to a meaningless present.

This theme is expanded in C.'s masterpiece, the novel *Craii de Curtea-Veche* (1926–28; the knights of the Ruined Court). The action is placed in Bucharest before World War I and is organized as a series of "pilgrimages," some real, into the underworld and déclassé world of the city, others imaginary, into the past and in remote geographical areas. The innocent narrator, an intelligent and sympathetic by-stander, watches his friends, the main characters, in fascination. Pasadia, the descendant of ancient aristocracy and a former important politician, has become a bitter and disdainful cynic, who pursues vice and debauchery with gloomy ardor, but also with impeccably elegant distinction. Pantazi, his best friend, has aristocratic Italian-Greek ancestors; immensely rich, he is an adventurer and experimentalist, a technician of hedonism, aesthetically serene and gracious, indifferent to evil but not to baseness, to good but not to honor. They love to wander in memories of a crepuscular 18th c., watching sweet refinement feverishly quickened by impending doom; they love to fantasize about themselves roaming the South Seas and the isles of the West Indies. But in effect, they let themselves be guided by Pirgu, a gambler and procurer, a man of keen, infamous intelligence, without scruples and knowledgeable in the ways of vulgarity and sin. The novel ends in disaster. Pasadia dies, Pantazi leaves the country, Pirgu thrives— satirical tones are emphatic in a book that draws the savage picture of an unstable, unprincipled, unstructured society "at the gates of the Orient where everything is taken lightly," as the epigraph announces.

The redeeming feature is the stylistic splendor of C.'s prose. He is unsurpassed for his expansion of the Romanian language and for his glittering phonetic suggestiveness. Unquestionably, C. shares the belief that only out of decay can lasting, hard-edged beauty arise. The dangerous mixture of sublime and grotesque in his main work probably places him among the Romanian expressionists in spite of his singularity and dandyism.

FURTHER WORKS: *Sub pecetea tainei* (1930–1933)

BIBLIOGRAPHY: Munteano, B., *Modern Romanian Literature* (1939): 221

—VIRGIL NEMOIANU

CARAION, Ion

Romanian poet and essayist, b. 24 May 1923, Ruşavăţ, Buzău county; d. 21 July 1986, Bucharest

C. attended high school in Buzău and was graduated from college in Bucharest in 1945. Between 1942 and 1946 he was active as a journalist for democratic causes and briefly brought out *Agora*, a literary review published in five languages. He suffered political imprisonment (1949–63), but was later rehabilitated and became a literary editor. In the last years of his life he emigrated to Switzerland and pursued anti-Communist activities.

C. joined a Bucharest group of poets who were impatient with the style established during the interwar period and turned toward irony and insult as provocative devices. More than others, C. resorted to crass, earthy, and sexual imagery to attack the rosy pictures of prevailing pastoral writings, as well as the traditions of Romanian poetry in general. His linguistic naturalism, influenced by ARGHEZI and by SURREALISM, was furthered by the shocking experience of war, dictatorship, and prison. C. began to write cruel and gloomy poetry, which did not change much from *Cîntece negre* (1947; black songs) to *Dimineaţa nimănui* (1967; nobody's dawn) and *Cîrtiţa şi aproapele* (1970; the mole and the neighbor). C. feels the oppression of the world intensely, as a kind of material heaviness and grossness, but whereas his early poetry responds with insolence and defiance, hopelessness, anxiety, and bitterness prevail in his mature poetry. Hope itself takes a gloomy coloring in C.'s poems; it is based on a broad all-encompassing stream of vitality which indifferently carries downhill good and evil, lovely and ugly alike, and which seems destined to continue no matter what else happens. Meanwhile, the poet is one who wanders through ruined, desolate landscapes and sings sadly but exactly and intensely the requiem of an impossible world.

C. is a good translator of French, English, and American poets, among others, POUND, SANDBURG, MASTERS, Baudelaire, and Whitman. He has also published several volumes of essays, most of which are rather subjective and impressionistic reactions to Romanian writers; *Sfîrşitul continuu* (1976; a continuous ending), his study on BACOVIA, is notable insofar as it indicates one of his main poetic sources.

FURTHER WORKS: *Panopticum* (1943); *Omul profilat pe cer* (1946); *Eseu* (1966); *Necunoscutul ferestrelor* (1969); *Desupra deasuprelor* (1970); *Cimitirul din stele* (1971); *Selene şi Pan* (1971); *Duelul cu crinii* (1972); *Munţii de os* (1972); *Frunzele în*

Galaad (1973); *Enigmatica nobleţe* (1974); *O ureche de dulceaţă şi-o ureche de pelin* (1976); *Pălărierul silabelor* (1976); *Interogarea magilor* (1978); *Lacrimi perpendiculare* (1978)

BIBLIOGRAPHY: Catanoy, N., on *O ureche de dulceaţă şi-o ureche de pelin*, 50 (1976), 863; Catanoy, N., on *Interogarea magilor*, WLT, 54 (1980), 92

—VIRGIL NEMOIANU

CARBALLIDO, Emilio

Mexican dramatist, b. 25 May 1925, Córdoba, Veracruz

Although C. grew up and has spent most of his life in Mexico City, he has maintained specific ties to Veracruz for both professional and familial reasons. C. graduated from the National University of Mexico with an M. A. in drama and English literature. The author has traveled, lectured, and taught throughout the world; his knowledge of world theater is quite extensive. In addition to having written some one hundred dramatic works for stage, opera, and film, and having received numerous awards for his work, he has also been active as a director, drama professor, and editor of *Tramoya*, a drama journal.

Since the late 1940s, C., in association with a variety of collaborators, has worked tirelessly to change and upgrade the dramatic arts and drama in Mexico, both in terms of style and substance. In the 1970s, C. turned his attention to fostering young playwrights, ultimately collecting and publishing their works in anthologies, notably *Teatro Joven de México* (1973; young theater of Mexico), *Más teatro joven* (1979; more young theater), and *9 obras jovenes* (1985; 9 young works).

By 1949 C. had already written and produced or published several short dramatic pieces, and at the age of twenty-five he saw the debut of his first full-length play, *Rosalba y los Llaveros* (1950; Rosalba and the Llaveros). The work was directed by C.'s close friend Salvador NOVO, and it was an immediate critical success. Set in Veracruz, like many of C.'s works, it treats the clash of values and outlooks between a cosmopolite from Mexico City and her provincial relatives of Otalitlán, Veracruz.

C. followed *Rosalba y los Llaveros* with several other substantial works during the 1950s, including the comedy *La danza que sueña la tortuga* (1955; the dance of which the turtle dreams), a portrait of two middle-aged, single sisters seeking identity and liberation from an overprotective brother in the provincial setting of Veracruz. The following year, C. produced *La hebra de oro* (1956; the golden thread), in which, for the first time, he intertwines his already established theatrical realism with elements of fantasy. The result was a stunning and innovative production that relied on a wide array of experimental and pyrotechnical gimmicks. Various critics consider *La hebra de oro* C.'s most important dramatic work because of its great impact on the development of Mexican theater. Yet another highly successful play followed: *Felicidad* (1957; felicity). It was a semicomedic presentation of marital infidelity, egotism, and spousal oppression. C.'s stature was further elevated when *Felicidad* won the Ruíz de Alarcón Prize for Drama (1957).

During the 1960s C. produced numerous significant dramatic works, including *El relojero de Córdoba* (1960; the clockmaker from Córdoba), another of the author's clever mixes of reality and fantasy. Another success appeared with *El día que se soltaron los leones* (1963; the day they let the lions loose). In this work C. undertook, as a primary focus, social and political criticism of Mexico's repressive society and government. *El día que se soltaron los leones* won the Casa de las Américas Drama Prize in 1963. C. continued to explore new boundaries in his theater, being particularly drawn to the fantastic and magic, laced with realism. He wrote works based on Greek mythology, of which *Medusa* (1966; Medusa) is a fine example. At the same time, however, C. continued to produce traditional theater. Two better-known pieces are the comedies *Silencio, pollos pelones, ya les van a echar su mai`Z!* (1963; shut up, you damn chickens, you'll get your corn) and *Te juro, Juana, que tengo ganas* (1965; I swear to you, Juana, that I want you).

During the 1970s C. produced two works that deserve particular mention: *Un vals sin fin sobre el planeta* (1970; an endless waltz around the world) and *Las cartas de Mozart* (1975; the Mozart letters). In the latter, set in 19th-c. Mexico City, a mysterious young beggar-violinist, while interacting with a middle-class family, slowly metamorphosizes into a young Mozart.

The 1980s have seen yet more of C.'s dramatic works produced and published. *Orinoco* (1982; Orinoco), one of C.'s greatest theatrical successes, treats the plight of two erstwhile and broken-down show girls (prostitutes) who discover themselves floating down the Orinoco River in Venezuela on a boat abandoned by its crew. The pathetic, but comedic, interaction-argumentation between the two imperiled travelers informs the actions and plot. C. continues to enjoy great success in Mexican theater, producing a variety of dramatic works at regular intervals. His *Ceremonia en el templo del tigre* (1986; ceremony in the temple of the tiger) is dedicated to the dark side of Mexican agrarian reform and the intransigent feudalism in the countryside. Violence and despair, with a backdrop of oppression, pervade the book.

Aside from his drama, C. is also an accomplished narrative writer. His novellas *La veleta oxidada* and *El norte* (1956; *The oxidized weathervane* and *The Norther*, 1968) were well received, particularly the latter. *El norte* possessed, for its time, a clever alternating of temporal places (past and present) portraying both the birth and death of the sexual relationship between a young man and an older woman. C.'s fine collection of short stories, *La caja vacía* (1962; the empty box), also deserves mention.

Generally considered to be one of Latin America's most prolific dramatists, C. is unquestionably the principal personage in Mexico's rich world of theater. He has distinguished himself by producing an extremely varied body of dramatic work that is notable for both its quantity and quality. C.'s literary and dramatic legacy will be long-lasting and of immense significance.

FURTHER WORKS: *La zona intermedia* (1948); *La triple porfía* (1949); *Medalla al mérito* (1949); *El lugar y la hora* (1957); *D. F.* (1957, rev. ed., 1984); *Las estatuas de marfil* (1960); *Teatro* (1960); *Teseo* (1962); *14 obras en un acto* (1962); *Las vistactiones del diablo* (1965); *Las noticias del día* (1968); *El sol* (1970); *Yo también hablo de la rosa* (1970); *Almanaque de Juárez* (1972); *El arca de Noé* (1974); *Acapulco, los lunes* (1978); *Un pequeño díade ira* (1978); *Fotografía en la playa* (1979); *Tres comedias* (1981); *Tiempo de ladrones; La historia de Chucho el Roto* (1983); *A la epopeya, un gajo* (1983); *Los zapatos de fierro* (1983); *El tren que*

corría (1984); *Jardín con animales* (1985); *Teatro para adolescentes* (1985); *Teatro para obreros* (1985); *Avanzada: más teatro joven* (1985); *La rosa de dos aromasa* (1986); *El pizarrón encantado* (1988); *Teatro 2* (1988); *veces el D. F.* (1989). **FURTHER WORKS IN ENGLISH:** *The Golden Thread and Other Plays* (1970)

BIBLIOGRAPHY: Holzapfel, T., "A Mexican Medusa," *MD*, 12 (1970): 231–37; Oliver, W. I., *Voices in the Spanish American Theater* (1971), passim; Bravo-Elizondo, P., *El teatro hispano-americano de crítica social* (1975): 62–72; Dauster, F., *Ensayos sobre teatro hispanoamericano* (1975): 143–88; Lyday, L. F., and G. W. Woodyard, eds., *Dramatists in Revolt* (1976): 19–36; Peden, M. S., "E. C.: Curriculum operum," *TCrit*, 2, 3 (1976): 94–112; Peterson, K., "Existential Irony in Three C. Plays," *LATR*, 10, 2 (Spring 1977): 29–35; Peden, M. S., *E. C.* (1979); Bixler, J. E., "A Theater of Contradictions: The Recent Works of E. C.," *LATR*, 18, 2 (Spring 1985): 57–65; Cortés, E., "Las novelas cortas de E. C.: Temática y té nica," in Paolini, G., ed., *La Chispa 87: Selected Proceedings* (1987): 81–87; Taylor, D., "Mad World, Mad Hope: C.'s *El día que se soltaron los leones*," *LATR*, 20, 2 (Spring 1987): 67–76; Troiano, J. J., "Illusory Worlds in Three Stories by E. C.," *HisJ*, 10, 2 (Spring 1989): 63–79; Bixler, J. E., "E. C.," in Sole, C. A., ed., *Latin American Writers* (1989), Vol. 3: 1289–94; Taylor, D., *Theatre of Crisis: Drama and Politics in Latin America* (1991): 148–80

—SAM L. SLICK

Perhaps we can discover the existential moral of *Medusa* by comparing the proud and distant pose of Sartre's Orestes at the end of *The Files* with Perseus' final rigidity. Orestes, who in the course of the play changes from a mild and compromising youth into a man of resolute action, ultimately resists the gods' authority in the name of personal and responsible freedom. When Jupiter reminds Orestes that he will have to pay with suffering for the discovery that he is a free man, the Sartrean hero tells him proudly: "Men are free and human life begins on the other side of despair." From this viewpoint, Perseus' hardness of character, his incapacity for affection is the price he pays for his independence from the gods. For his recognition that men are not the toys of the gods or any other power, he must accept as a condition of his existence a state of anguish and estrangement.

In conclusion, *Medusa* is a play about man's quest for moral autonomy in life and politics. It offers a powerful message for the Latin American countries where the masses are oppressed by religion and unjust governments which, from the liberal point of view, are little more than puppet regimes of U. S. imperialism. A daring director could shape *Medusa* into an explosive drama of social revolution.

Tamara Holzapfel, "A Mexican Medusa," *MD*, 12 (1970), p. 237

E. C. is one of Mexico's leading authors, having written a large number of plays, novels, and short stories, as well as scenarios for various films. His playwrighting underwent a very real sea-change when he traveled abroad in the Mexican foreign service. His present work reflects an encounter with the techniques of modern European theater, such as the Berliner Ensemble. In 1966 C. enjoyed a great success with *I Too Speak of the Rose*. It is an epic drama with expressionist controls that explores human possibilities from political, psychological, moral, and metaphysical points of view. All of this seems ponderous, but quite the opposite is the case. More recently his play *Medusa*, a contemporary interpretation of the Perseus myth, was chosen as the main theatrical offering in Mexico City during the period of the Olympics.

> William I. Oliver, *Voices of Change in the Spanish American Theater* (1971), p. ix

E. C. has written many different kinds of plays: one-act vignettes, plays with historical settings, political commentary, and fantasies. The fantasy plays explore the psychological and archetypal delineations of human freedom. *Medusa, Teseo,* and *Las estatuas de marfil*, a trilogy, deal more singlemindedly with the characteristically existential notion of freedom as action, seeking to explore ''how far a free agent can escape from his particular situation in his choices.'' But these three plays include as many styles. *Medusa* is fantastic and heavily symbolic, and *Teseo*, the least complex of the three, is a one-act fantasy. *Las estatuas de marfil* is entirely realistic, but it is the most subtle and difficult. Together, the plays are three variations on a single theme, and C., through symbol and elegantly metaphorical plot, has incorporated the existential irony that is characteristic of Sartre's drama.

> Karen Peterson, "Existential Irony in Three C. Plays," *LALR*, 10, 2 (Spring 1977), p. 29

C. has changed the course of Mexican theater. In spite of his reservations about the term, C. contributed a number of works to the body of Mexican neorealistic costumbristic plays; more importantly, he has raised Mexican theater above the customarily limited level of that genre. C. introduced music, humor, poetry, formal innovation, and his own unique blend of realism and fantasy into the post-World War II Mexican theater. His activities as a teacher and administrator of several schools of theater (Instituto Poliécnico Nacional, Bellas Artes, and the cultural program of the University of Veracruz) have influenced the course of the careers of Mexico's current generation of young dramatists.

C. has a true sense of theater. He has created a concept of theater that is universal and enduring. His prose fiction is significant, but C. is at his best when he is his most theatrical, employing all the devices that enhance the direct communication that is theater's particular province. "Teseo," *Medusa*, and *El*

relojero de Córdoba, the trilogy *El lugar y la hora*, utilize the magic of myth. "El espejo," "Medalla al mérito," *La hebra de oro*, and "Yo tambiéen hablo de la rose" delve inventively into levels of individual consciousness. The basically theatrical values of music, dance, and ritual are used innovatively in "Silencio, pollos pelones," *Las cartas de Mozart*, and *El dacute;a que se soltaron los leones*. The cathartic power of humor permeates his plays. Serious Mexican theater was rocked out of its conventions by the affectionate warmth, the broad burlesque, the puckish fun of C.'s humor. . .

C.'s place in Latin American theater is well-established. He is among the half-dozen most important Latin dramatists of this century. His reputation as a prose writer is less secure, but he has made important contributions to fiction. C. loves to travel, and he has taught and lectured in many countries, spreading the warmth of his personality. His work has been performed throughout Latin America, on the Continent, and in many colleges and universities in the United States, exposing this major talent to ever wider audiences. C.'s mark on literature is assured.

> Margaret Sayers Peden, *E. C.* (1979), pp. 175–76

C. is undoubtedly the most prolific and versatile of contemporary Latin American dramatists. Since 1948, he has written over one hundred dramatic works, including operas, film scripts, librettos, adaptations, and children's theater. His works traverse the gamut of dramatic styles, from macabre fantasy to strict provincial realism, from allegorical farce to plays of explicit social protest. Despite the structural, technical, and topical diversity of his theater, there are certain C. trademarks: the compassionate portrayal of characters, particularly women, from either the capital or the Veracruz provinces; the gentle humor present in even his most socially committed pieces; the distinctly Mexican setting and language; and the fusion of diverse dramatic styles and levels of reality within individual works. . . .

Today, after forty years in the limelight of Mexican theater, C. shows no sign of slowing down. With a boundless energy, he continues to write one or two plays a year, travel widely, and foment the national theater in every way possible. By sharing his broad knowledge of the theater with the current generation of young playwrights, he is ensuring that the renaissance of Mexican theater will continue well into the future. His varied and limitless creative talents are apparent in the many works that he himself has contributed to this vital cultural movement. With each new play, he discovers a different way of transforming Mexican reality into art and thus of providing a meaningful yet artistic representation of modern man. While fully aware of the social and economic inequities present in his society, C. never allows his protest to dominate his art, but rather subtly voices his concerns through such vehicles as farcical exaggeration, historical perspectives, and parallels between fiction and reality. By successfully adapting form to content and incorporating imaginative elements into his portrayal of daily life and human relationships, C. has achieved a lasting theater of universal transcendence, meaning, and appeal.

> Jacqueline Eyring Bixler, "E. C.," in Charles A. Sole ed., *Latin American Writers* (1989), pp. 1290–92

Readers of Latin American theater may be surprised to find a chapter on E. C. . . . in a study of theater of crisis. C.'s plays, especially the two emphasized here—*El da que se soltaron los leones. . .*and *Yo también hablo de la rosa. . .*—are playful and expansive, calling for elaborate and complicated sets, large casts, bright colors, and music. These plays do not seem to belong to a violent, grotesque world of oppression and crisis. No one overtly torments or tortures anyone else; death comes only to those who deserve it. Compared with much Latin American drama in general and with all the other plays included here in particular, C.'s theater seems joyful, almost optimistic. This is no "poor" theater; there is no call to action associated with "revolutionary" theater. Nor are C.'s plays "committed," "popular," or didactic in any straightforward sense. But commentators will be deceived by C.'s playfulness if they do not recognize that these plays speak to revolution; they are profoundly "popular" . . . they offer a liberating vision of Mexican culture which evades the tugs of the West and yet resists the temptation to fall back onto some native traditionalism.

> Diana Taylor, *Theatre of Crisis: Drama and Politics in Latin America* (1991), p. 148

CARDARELLI, Vincenzo

(pseud. of Nazareno Caldarelli) Italian poet, essayist, literary theorist, and journalist, b. 1 May 1887, Corneto Tarquinia; d. 14 June 1959, Rome

Son of a railroad-station restaurant manager, C.'s difficult early years contributed to the development of a cantankerous nature that characterized him throughout his life. Primarily self-educated, interested in philosophy and, briefly, in anarchist movements, at nineteen he left home for Rome, where, between odd jobs and unemployment, he lived wretchedly until he turned to journalism. In 1911 he was in Florence, where for a few years he contributed articles to important literary journals. He was rejected for military service in World War I; in 1919 he was back in Rome, where he cofounded a major literary journal, *La ronda* (1919–23). From 1949 until his death, C. was editor of the well-known literary weekly *La fiera letteraria*.

In the pages of *La ronda* C. denounced contemporary experimental trends in literature: FUTURISM, the D'ANNUNZIO brand of

mythologizing, and psychological subjectivism. Insisting on the formal values of literature and on its independence from political and social causes, he nonetheless felt that stylistic purity and elegance had a humanistic and ethical function in keeping with the great Italian tradition of the past. Although he pointed to Leopardi (1798–1837) as the last great exemplar of that tradition and the model to be followed by modern writers both in prose and poetry, his view emphasized the idyllic and the formal aspects of the great 19th-c. poet while playing down his pessimism. While the principles espoused by C. and others of the *Ronda* group seemed to offer a way out for writers who were not favorable to fascism, the separation of literature from the life and problems of the nation proved to be at least a passive acceptance of the regime.

Yet C.'s was not an Arcadian entrenchment. Among the authors he cherished most, besides Leopardi, are Pascal, Baudelaire, and Nietzsche. That he found more than formal values in them is clear from the fact that it is the sense of an existential crisis that informs C.'s own creative writings. The most significant part of his prose production came in the decade between 1919 and 1929. The short narrative pieces collected in the volumes *Viaggi nel tempo* (1920; journeys into time), *Memorie della mia infanzia* (1925; memories of my childhood), and *Il sole a picco* (1929; the sun on high) are characterized by a nostalgic and elegiac lyricism tempered by a sobriety of tone. The sense of mystery in nature, and even the imitation of evil or imperfection in the heart of things are expressed by C. as he evokes the years and the land of his youth. But irony and aphoristic manner may go side by side here with idyllicism, as they do in the prose of *Favole della Genesi* (1925; fables of Genesis), in which the narrative is both parodistic and gnomic.

Awareness of an existential crisis also pervades C.'s poetry. The seasons (summer and autumn in particular), the charm and beauty of youth, the restlessness of the self, and love as experienced in the present or as called forth in memory and imagination appear in his verse in connection with the ever-present sense of the passage of time (the real subject of much of C.'s verse and prose) and with a longing for an absolute that is unattainable. From Leopardi he acquired the tendency to infuse these evocations with a meditative character. The result is verse that is admirable for its sustained yet unrhetorical tone and its formal composure.

FURTHER WORKS: *Prologhi* (1916); *Terra genitrice* (1924); *Il cielo sulle città* (1939); *Poesie* (1936; rev. eds. 1942, 1948, 1958); *Solitario in Arcadia* (1947); *Il viaggiatore insocievole* (1953); *Viaggio di un poeta in Russia* (1954); *Opera completa* (1962); *La Poltrona vuota* (1969)

BIBLIOGRAPHY: Perella, N. J., *Midday in Italian Literature* (1979): 195–99

—NICOLAS J. PERELLA

CARDENAL, Ernesto

Nicaraguan poet, b. 20 Jan. 1925, Granada

Poet, Marxist revolutionary, and Catholic priest, C. is one of Latin America's most important literary figures. After studying in

431

Mexico and in New York at Columbia University, C. returned to Nicaragua where he participated in the unsuccessful "April Conspiracy" (1954) to overthrow the dictator Somoza. In 1957 he entered the Trappist monastery in Gethsemani, Kentucky, where he was profoundly influenced by Thomas Merton's philosophy of nonviolence. Upon being ordained a Catholic priest in 1965, C. founded the religious community of Solentiname on an island in Lake Nicaragua. Increased government brutality in the 1970s, coupled with his study of Marxism and "liberation theology," inspired C. to become a member of the FSLN (Sandinista Front for National Liberation) and to espouse the doctrine of armed struggle.

One of the hallmarks of C.'s work, when viewed in its entirety, is a constant growth and renewal. His major themes—love (of women in his early poems, later of the Nicaraguan people, God, and the entire universe), history, Nicaragua, revolution—are expressed with great commitment and clarity and indicate the passionate evolution of a writer who has done much to popularize poetry and to stretch the limits of poetic expression.

C. began writing in the early 1940s, but it was not until he became familiar with the poetry of Ezra POUND, whose influence he openly acknowledges, that he began to adopt some of the technical devices that would become characteristic of his own poetic style, which he called *exteriorismo*, a term coined by C. and one of his early mentors, José Coronel Urtecho (b. 1906). This is a direct, unadorned poetry, composed of what C. calls the elements of real life. Through the use of a collage technique which often creates the effect of a cinematographic montage of images, C. retells history, narrates political events, gives lessons in economy and indigenous cultures, ponders the injustices of capitalism, and expresses his love of the people and his hatred of dictatorships. C. insists that nothing lies outside the realm of the poetic and freely incorporates proper names, statistical data, fragments of letters, information from newspapers, and passages quoted directly from historical chronicles. In accordance with his stated intention of clarity and intelligibility, his language is unpretentious, conversational, and often colloquial. Realizing that the history of the New World has been written largely by invaders and conquerors, C. has taken on the task of inserting history into poetry and in effect has rewritten significant portions of Latin American history. In poems such as "Raleigh" (1949; Raleigh) and "Con Walker en Nicaragua" (1950; "With Walker in Nicaragua," 1962), C. recreates the vision of the New World as seen through the eyes of foreigners. *La Hora O* (1966; *Zero Hour*, 1968), which has become a revolutionary classic in Latin America, begins with a portrayal of the Central American dictatorships of the 1930s. It examines the United Fruit Company's presence in the "Banana Republics" and tells of Nicaraguan patriot Augusto César Sandino's resistance to U.S. intervention in his country. It concludes with the "April Conspiracy" of 1954 against Somoza, thereby linking past and present in Nicaragua's continuing fight for self-determination. Like many of his poems, *La Hora O* is epic in scale and prophetic in tone. History is manifest through quotidian detail yet perceived with teleological vision. Explicit in C.'s vision is the kingdom of heaven on earth. Rather than an otherworldly or unattainable dream, he sees a classless society living in peace as a goal to be achieved in the present. His study of pre-Colombian Amerindian cultures convinced him that a model of a classless society was to be found in the indigenous communities of America. The poems in *Homenaje a los indios americanos* (1969; *Homage to the American Indians*, 1973)

Ernesto Cardenal

were inspired by this utopian vision of the past. "Economía de Tahuantinsuyu" ("Economy of Tahuantinsuyu"), for example, by juxtaposing images from a peaceful barter economy where there is no hunger or unemployment, with tourists snapping photos of indigent peasants and announcements of stockmarket prices, condemns capitalism and posits an indigenous socialism as a lost but recoverable possibility.

When C. visited Cuba for several months in 1970, he was impressed with the accomplishments of the revolution and Cuba's progress toward building a just society created by the "New Man." He began to question his strict adherence to the philosophy of nonviolence and came to accept the necessity of armed resistance in the struggle to create a society based on true Christian principles. He became increasingly supportive of the FSLN in the 1970s, working to encourage revolutionary activism in Nicaragua, as demonstrated by poems such as "Canto national" (1972; national song) and "Oráculo sobre Managua" (1973; *Oracle over Managua*, 1973). By 1977 the Solentiname commune, C.'s experiment in creating a small-scale ideal Christian society, had become a Sandinista cell and was subsequently destroyed by Somoza's National Guard. C. declared himself an active member of the FSLN and in 1979 assumed the position of minister of culture in the newly formed Sandinista government.

C.'s poetry during the approximately ten years after the Sandinista victory reflects his full-time involvement in the reconstruction of Nicaragua. Collected in the bilingual edition *Flights of Victory/ Vuelos de victoria* (1985), poems such as "Ocupados" ("Busy") and "Reflexiones de un ministro" ("Reflections of a Minister") speak of the visionary prophet and the practical man of action who have fused in the service of building a cultural democracy on a national level. In his enthusiasm for the revolution, his vision, as evidenced in "Waslala" ("Waslala"), is so insistently optimistic and supportive as to appear almost ingenuous. In the context of the difficulties facing the Sandinistas during the reconstruction, these poems may also be read as affirmations of a poet immersed in the historical moment, who sees his country's need for new myths and heroes and answers the call.

Since 1989 C. has removed himself from Nicaraguan political life. He is currently the director of the foundation House of Three Worlds and devotes his time to writing and to his work as a sculptor. In 1989 he published *Cántico cósmico* (*Cosmic Canticle*, 1989), a long poem on the evolution of the universe and of humanity, based on the power of divine love. He also published *Ovnis de oro* (1992; *Golden UFOs*, 1992), which includes poems from his earlier *Homage to the American Indians* as well as previously unpublished work. In this volume C. has gathered together poetry that, though diverse in style, is unified through the theme of the American Indian, both ancient and contemporary.

As minister of culture, C. was instrumental in establishing workshops where writing poetry based on the principles and techniques of *exteriorismo* was taught to farmers, workers, and soldiers, many of whom had only recently achieved literacy. C.'s themes and style have exercised profound influence among younger writers in Nicaragua and throughout Latin America. The poet-priest-revolutionary with the gray hair and beard, the unassuming style of dress, and the characteristic black beret, whose ability to write history into poetry and whose profound love for the individual, the collective, and the planet is manifest in his poetry along with his disdain of greed, consumerism, and injustice, is an example of the Latin American ideal of the socially committed writer.

FURTHER WORKS: *Gethsemani, KY* (1960); *Epigramas: poemas* (1961); *Oración por Marilyn Monroe y otros poemas* (1965); *El estrecho dudoso* (1966); *Salmos* (1967; *Psalms*, 1981); *Vida en el amor* (1970; *To Live Is To Love*, 1974); *Canto nacional* (1972); *En Cuba* (1972; *In Cuba*, 1974); *El evangelio en Solentiname* (1975; *The Gospel in Solentiname*, 1982); *La santidad de la revolución* (1976); *Tocar el cielo* (1981); *Quetzalcoatl* (1986); *Cántico cósmico* (1989). FURTHER WORKS IN ENGLISH: *The Psalms of Liberation and Struggle* (1971); *Marilyn Monroe, and Other Poems* (1975); "*Apocalypse,*" *and Other Poems* (1977); *Zero Hour, and Other Documentary Poems* (1980); *With Walker in Nicaragua, and Other Early Poems, 1949–1954* (1984); *From Nicaragua with Love* (1986)

BIBLIOGRAPHY: Oviedo, J., "E. C.: un místico comprometido," *CasaA*, 11, 53 (Nov.–Dec. 1969): 29–48; Benedetti, M., "E. C.: evangelio y revolución," *CasaA*, 63 (1970): 175–83; Arellano, J., "E. C.: de Granada a Gethsemani (1926–1957)," *CHA*: 289–90 (1974): 163–83; Brotherston, G., *Latin American Poetry: Origins and Presence* (1975): 173–77; García Cambeiro, F., *E. C., poeta de la liberación latinoamericana* (1975); Fraire, I., "Pound and C.," *Review*, 18 (1976): 36–42; Zimmerman, M., "E. C. after the Revolution," *Flights of Victory* (1985): 9–32:; Beverley, J., and Zimmerman, M., *Literature and Politics in the Central American Revolutions* (1990): 66–72

—JANET N. GOLD

CARDOSO PIRES, José

See Pires, José Cardoso

CAREW, Jan

Guyanese poet, novelist, and essayist, b. 24 Sept. 1925, Agricola, British Guiana (now Guyana)

Born in Agricola, C. has lived and worked all over the world, including a series of extended periods in Britain, Ghana, Jamaica, and Canada. He now lives in the U.S. and has taught at Northwestern University and at Princeton University, among other institutions. He continues to write nonfiction works about cultural and political issues while generating a small library of books for children. His novels reveal the eclectic nature of travels and his constant interest in exploring the condition of the black person in various geographical and cultural spaces. Indeed, C. would describe the instinct to travel among people of the Caribbean as a quest for an end to an exile imposed on them by the colonizers, who, like Propsero did to Caliban, made them exiles in their own home.

C.'s first novel, *Black Midas* (1958), is a "fictional biography" of the legendary Guyanese "prok-knockers" or gold miners. In this work C. tackles themes that will be repeated in his subsequent novels. His main character, Aaron, is an exile, but an exile in his own country. The novel becomes a quest by this West Indian Everyman to find a place of rooting and an emotional and psychological "home"; in the end the metaphorical quest for gold, "El Dorado," becomes a symbol for Aaron's own quest for a sense of self. However, it is a futile quest. C.'s second novel, *The Wild Coast* (1958), continues this quest. The central character, another young Guyanese man, Hector, is sent to his ancestral village, Tarlogie, to learn about himself and his identity. The resultant clash of cultures epitomizes C.'s own sense of the fundamental cultural divides that complicate West Indian life. C.'s characters in these early novels reveal little of psychological realism, but act in ways that are often puzzling and inexplicable. It is the landscape, however, that becomes the dominant character—a rich environment that speaks through the livid sounds of the Shango religion and the more earth-centered folk traditions of the community.

C.'s third novel, *The Last Barbarian* (1961), abandons Guyana as landscape and is set in the U.S. His characters are from all parts of the world, his themes of alienation and psychological instability in an alien environment. The male quest for self through sexuality and through the twisted machinations of philosophical reasoning is as poignant as in *The Wild Coast*, but here the landscape is different, if equally daunting. Stylistically C. moves away from the more conventional linear narrative form used in his first two novels and turns to a more jazz-oriented fragmentation that seeks to replicate the alienation felt by the character Tiberio. C.'s fourth novel, *Moscow Is Not My Mecca* (1964), appeared after C. himself visited the former Soviet Union and reflects his sense of disillusionment with the political and social realities of Moscow. The protagonist, Tojo Roberston, experiences harsh discrimination while a student in Moscow. The expectation that the U.S.S.R. would be a far more welcoming place to a black West Indian than would be England or the U.S. is shattered completely by C.

in this novel. Ultimately, in these works C. reveals that the hand of imperialism is essentially a racist one and remains that way regardless of the political ideologies that undergird the imperialist agenda.

C.'s view is always politically loaded and deeply pessimistic. His nonfiction works include *Ghosts, Our Blood: With Malcolm X in Africa, England and the Caribbean* (1994) and *The Rape of Paradise* (1997). C. has also published several books for children including *Third Gift* (1974) and *Children of the Sun* (1980).

C.'s position as one of the more important West Indian authors is unassailable. His storytelling gifts are matched by few West Indian writers, but it is his strong sense of the connectedness between the political transformation of the Caribbean and the role of art in achieving this that represents one of his unique contributions to Caribbean writing.

FURTHER WORKS: *Cry Black Power* (1970); *Sons of the Flying Wing* (1970); *Rape the Sun* (1973); *Save the Last Dance for Me* (1976); *The Twins of Llora* (1977); *Grenada: The Hour Will Strike Again* (1985); *Computer Killer* (1989); *No Entry* (1989); *Timeloop* (1989); *Death Comes to the Circus* (1990); *Footprints in the Sand* (1994); *Shadow in the Glen: A Short Adventure Play* (1996); *Lost Love and Other Stories* (1997); *Three Short Comedies* (1997)

BIBLIOGRAPHY: Cartey, W., "The Rhythm of Society and Landscape: Mittelholzer, C., Williams, Dathorne," *New World* (1966): 96–104; Maes-Jelinek, H., "The Myth of El Dorado in the Caribbean Novel," *JCL*, 6 (1971): 113–27; Warner, M. L., "J. C. Interviewed by Maureen Warner-Lewis, Prague, 1984," *JWIL*, 2 (1987): 37–40; Birbalsingh, F., "J. C. Interview," *JCST*, 6 (1988): 117–41; Birbalsingh, F., ed., *Frontiers of Caribbean Literatures in English* (1996)

—KWAME DAWES

CAREY, Peter

Australian novelist, b. 7 May 1943, Bacchus Marsh

Reared in post-World War II Australia, C. belongs to the first generation of Australians who seriously considered that they had a national identity apart from England. Educated at one of Australia's leading private secondary schools, patterned after the British model, C. attended Monash University for a year, then joined an advertising firm in Melbourne. Following a short stay in London, he settled in Sydney and again worked for an advertising agency. In the early 1990s, once he had established himself as a writer, he gave up advertising and Australia to settle in New York City, where he now lives and writes full time.

C. first drew attention with two collections of short stories, *The Fat Man in History* (1974) and *War Crimes* (1979). Both collections focus on the contemporary Australian experience as a postcolonial nation, which still clings to its British past while being influenced by the U.S. Departing from the social realism that long characterized Australian fiction, the stories—such as "American Dreams"—take a fantastic turn to examine his country's quest for a national identity.

This examination has continued in the novels, which display a tremendous range of subject matter, settings, periods, and characters. Although C.'s central thematic concerns may have remained consistent in his work so far, he has handled these concerns in a varied manner; above all, he is a master storyteller. In fact, the process of storytelling emerges as a subtext in several of the novels whose narrators question the value and form and source of the very stories they are relating.

In *Illywhacker* (1985) C. sets out to retell Australian history through the eyes of an "illywhacker"—an Australian slang term for con artist. An admitted liar, the narrator claims to be 139 years old, so he has lived through most of Australia's two-hundred-year history of white settlement. The narrative construction is reminiscent of the Latin American novelist Gabriel GARCÍA MÁRQUEZ. One bizarre adventure after another, half-believable and half-impossible, takes place as the "illywhacker," a part-time aviator and used car salesman, meets a host of colorful characters and incorporates the variegated strands of Australian history and mythology into his tale. The novel proposes indirectly that the country's official history as a British colony is the work of a con artist, full of lies and tricks.

Taking up the colonial period in *Oscar and Lucinda* (1988), which received the Booker Prize, C. expands on his theme of national identity and the inherited burden of colonialism. The unlikely pair in the book's title—one a Church of England priest, the other an Australian woman who owns a glass factory—meet on a ship bound for Sydney. Once there they carry on an unfulfilled romance and direct their energy into building a glass church. Their attempt to move the symbol of Christian civilization into the bush fails, and the shattered glass sinks into the river. The foolish project seems to reflect the absurdity and fragility of white settlement on the ancient continent.

C. creates an imaginary postcolonial nation called Efica (obviously Australia) in *The Unusual Life of Tristan Smith* (1994), which depends on and is dominated by a powerful country called Voorstand (obviously the U.S.). The central metaphor is popular culture, but like the glass church in the previous novel this metaphor again leads into Australia's precarious condition at the close of the 20th c.

In *Jack Maggs* (1997) C. attempts to fill out the story of the Australian convict Magwitch, who plays such a significant part in Charles Dickens's *Great Expectations*. Maggs, as the Dickens character is called in C.'s novel, goes home to Australia and accepts his new identity after a disastrous and brief return visit to England. Ironically, during his convict days in Australia, even when being whipped by fellow Englishmen, he had longed for what he considered his true home. Less inconclusive than the earlier novels, *Jack Maggs* suggests that C. may be coming to terms with Australia's national consciousness, seeing at last a shift in the country's allegiance.

If that is the case, perhaps C. will move away from his obsession with the postcolonial dilemma, which he has treated with such originality. He is a young writer, so he may well direct his considerable talents in new directions.

FURTHER WORKS: *Bliss* (1981); *The Tax Inspector* (1991); *The Big Bazoohley* (1995)

BIBLIOGRAPHY: Daniel, H., *Liars: Australian New Novelists* (1988): 145-84; Hassall, A., *Dancing on Hot Macadam: P. C.'s Fiction*

(1994); Bernard, A., "Unefican Activities," *NYRB*, 22 June 1995: 12-14; Willbanks, R., *Australian Voices* (1991): 43-57

—ROBERT ROSS

CARLING, Finn

Norwegian novelist, poet, dramatist, and essayist, b. 1 Oct. 1925, Oslo

C., who grew up in an upper-middle-class home, was born with cerebral palsy; consequently, in spite of financial and material well-being, his life has been a constant struggle to deal with his affliction. He studied psychology at the University of Oslo but never got his degree. He has essentially devoted his life to writing.

C. made his literary debut in 1949 with *Broen* (the bridge), a work that foreshadowed his subsequent work both in theme and form. *Broen* focuses on the difficulties adolescents experience in their struggle to form sexual relationships. Human isolation, and the conflicting desires both to hide within it and to break out of it, were then and have remained C.'s predominant concerns as a writer, concerns unquestionably rooted in the fact that his disability made it physically and psychologically problematic for him to function in the "normal" world. *Broen's* unusual form, consisting of two separate but related short stories and an incorporated play, signaled the experimental nature of C.'s work in general. One of the best of the literary innovators of the 1950s, he has written in various genres—prose fiction, poetry, drama, and documentary prose— often combining and/or juxtaposing them; and he has written in various modes, attempting to render and at times to merge concrete reality and the reality of the dreams of sleep, fantasy, illusion, and myth. Since 1949 C. has published a work, each consistently short and tightly structured, every year or two.

As a young writer C. had explored the relationship between reality and dream, fascinated by the dream, yet questioning ever more cynically its function. However, not until the novel *Desertøren* (1956; the deserter) and the autobiographical account *Kilden og muren* (1958; *And Yet We Are Human*, 1957), initially written in English, did C. reject dream as an inevitably destructive phenomenon engendering flight from reality. In both these works, more directly and personally in *Kilden og muren*, C. confronted without the comfort of fantasy of any kind the undeniable fact and permanence of his physical handicap. Together these works mark a turning point in his writing. He turned to documentary essays about others in society who were "set apart": *Vanskeligstilte barn i hjem og skole* (1958; disadvantaged children at home and in school), *Blind verden* (1962; blind world), and *Dehomofile* (1965; the homosexuals). In his fiction, too, he sought to render reality in a way more commensurate with daily life.

When, in the late 1960s, C. gradually turned away from such "realistic" forms back to his multigenre fiction with its various levels of reality, he did so with a much more positive attitude toward the function of dreams, suggesting that they can perhaps even be a common bond of experience. But C.'s predominant themes remain the isolation of individuals, even in the midst of the sophisticated Scandinavian welfare state, their haunting sense of failure to find permanent meaning in themselves and in their lives, and their subsequent need to assert themselves at the expense of

those they do not consider to be as legitimate citizens as themselves. C. remains the author of society's outsiders.

FURTHER WORKS: *Stemmene og nuet* (1950); *Arancæn* (1951); *Piken og fuglen* (1952); *Skyggen* (1954); *Fangen i det blå tårn* (1955); *Sensommerdøgn* (1960); *Kometene* (1964); *Gitrene* (1966); *Tilfluktsrummet* (1968); *Lys på et ansikt* (1969); *Slangen* (1969); *Skapende sinn* (1970); *Gjesten* (1970); *Skudd* (1971); *Skip av sten* (1971); *Resten er taushet* (1973); *Fiendene* (1974); *Skapt i vårt bilde* (1975); *I et rom i et hus i en have* (1976); *Hvite skygger på svart bunn* (1976); *Marginalene* (1977); *Mørke paralleller* (1978); *Tre lyriske pasteller* (1978)

BIBLIOGRAPHY: Muinzer, L., "F. C.: A Personal Introduction," *WLT*, 70 (Spring 1996): 277-82

—MARY KAY NORSENG

CAROSSA, Hans

German novelist, poet, and essayist, b. 15 Dec. 1878, Tölz; d. 12 Sept. 1956, Rittsteig

Son of a country doctor of Italian ancestry, C. grew up in various small Bavarian towns; hence, he had a chance to be close to nature and to observe his father's practice firsthand. Although he showed talent for poetry as an adolescent, C. studied medicine at the universities of Munich, Würzburg, and Leipzig and, in 1903, began practicing in Passau as a specialist in lung diseases. Later he moved his practice to Nuremberg and then to Munich. During World War I C. volunteered as a medical officer in the German army and served in Flanders, Romania, and France. He resumed his practice in Munich until his success as a writer allowed him to give up medicine in 1929 and to retire to a small family estate in Seestetten, and eventually, in 1941, to Rittsteig, near Passau.

C.'s literary achievements brought him prizes in Germany, Switzerland, and Italy, as well as honorary doctorates from the universities of Cologne (1938) and Munich (1948). Although not a very prolific writer, he was among the most highly regarded authors of the 1930s in Germany. Translations of his works made him known and respected abroad, especially in Italy, Japan, France, and England. C. tried to stay above politics and did not accept a membership in the once-illustrious Academy of Literature, since it was offered to him after Hitler came to power in 1933; but in 1941 the Nazis succeeded in tarnishing his reputation by persuading him to accept the presidency of a European writers union founded under their auspices. Still, he tried to use what little influence he may have gained to help friends and strangers oppressed by the authorities. As one of the few prominent writers who had passed through the Third Reich with some dignity, C. experienced a modest resurgence of popularity in the first decade after World War II.

C. was a conservative writer in the most positive sense. In an age of turmoil, destruction, and loss of values, he strove to preserve the true humanism. Just as he tried to support the restorative powers of the human organism as a physician, so as a writer he sought to rally the positive forces in the mind of the individual and to see even its dark and destructive urges as part of a larger organic life process. C. never lost faith in this life process, with its developmental stages, its cycles and metamorphoses, its beautiful and odd manifestations, which he observed with calm, scientific detachment and deep sympathy. Essential to C.'s writing were not only detailed observation and analysis of phenomena but, more importantly, imaginative synthesis and visions of an organic whole. Thus, in his ideas and attitudes, as well as in his style, C. closely resembles Adalbert Stifter (1805–1868) and Goethe.

C. had been attracted to Goethe's works even in his boyhood years, and he emulated him, consciously and unconsciously, throughout his life. In his first novel, *Doktor Bürgers Ende* (1913; Doctor Bürger's end; retitled *Die Schicksale Dr. Bürgers*, 1930; the fates of Dr. Bürger), C. writes about a young doctor who commits suicide after he fails to save his fiancée's life. Like Goethe in *The Sorrows of Young Werther*, C. seems to have released himself, with this rather emotional story, from a preoccupation with despair and death. Also like Goethe, C. wrote a series of autobiographical accounts describing the various developmental phases of his life from childhood to his early years as a doctor: *Eine Kindheit* (1922; *A Childhood*, 1930); *Verwandlungen einer Jugend* (1928; *Boyhood and Youth*, 1930); *Das Jahr der schönen Täuschungen* (1941; *Year of Sweet Illusions*, 1951), which tells of his student days in Munich; and *Der Tag des jungen Arztes* (1955; the day of the young doctor), with recollections of his studies in Leipzig and his early professional career. These volumes, later published together under the title *Geschichte einer Jugend* (1957; story of a youth), form the core of C.'s prose. In a style marked by classical balance, simplicity, accuracy, and free-flowing rhythm, he describes selected episodes from his life, dreams, landscapes, encounters, and thoughts, and records historical observations with special regard for those that transcend the merely personal and reveal the secret interconnections of human experience.

C.'s first widely successful publication was *Rumänisches Tagebuch* (1924; *A Roumanian Diary*, 1929), which, with visionary clarity and restrained compassion, describes man and nature as they suffer the ravages of war. Its unmilitaristic, humane approach was appreciated in countries that had been at war with Germany and established C.'s reputation abroad. C. attempts to deal with the problems of physical and moral reconstruction after the war in the novel *Der Arzt Gion* (1931; *Doctor Gion*, 1933). A circle of patients and friends around Dr. Gion grows into a small family as they help each other, thus forming one of the new cells of love and understanding from which a healing effect is to spread over the whole society. Ironically, the hope and optimism expressed in this book was in bitter contrast to the political realities of the period soon after its appearance. In *Geheimnisse des reifen Lebens* (1936; secrets of the mature life), the fictitious notes of an older man involved with three women seem to reflect in their symbolic allusions C.'s ambivalent feelings during the early years of the Third Reich. Of this whole difficult time he later gives a much clearer autobiographical account, tempered by hindsight, in *Ungleiche Welten* (1951; unequal worlds).

C. and many of his admirers considered his poetry his most important contribution. His first works were poems, and he frequently returned to the writing of poetry throughout his career. His *Gedichte* (1910; poems) was augmented several times, and he also published a few short volumes. Indebted to the great lyrical tradition from Goethe to RILKE, C.'s well-formed, sensitive, thoughtful poems describe nature, love, death, and the mysteries of life, but without adding any new note to that tradition.

C.'s lasting contribution to German literature is more likely to be his revival and refinement of autobiography as a means to provide insights into the universal condition of man and nature.

The equanimity with which C. can turn from a description of human suffering to look at a flower or up to the stars may be irritating at times, but the love of life and ultimate optimism his work exudes cannot but be appreciated.

FURTHER WORKS: *Stella mystica* (1907); *Die Flucht* (1916); *Ostern* (1920); *Führung und Geleit* (1933); *Wirkungen Goethes in der Gegenwart* (1938); *Abendländische Elegie* (1946); *Stern über der Lichtung (Gedichte 1940–1945)* (1946); *Aufzeichnungen aus Italien* (1948); *Gesammelte Werke* (2 vols., 1949–1950); *Die Frau vom guten Rat* (1956; new title: *Ein Tag im Spätsommer* 1947); *Der alte Taschenspieler* (1956); *Sämtliche Werke* (2 vols., 1962); *Briefe* (2 vols., 1978)

BIBLIOGRAPHY: Peacock, R., "C. a Moralist," *GL&L*, 2 (1937–1938): 217–25; Frey, J. R., "The Function of the Writer: A Study of the Literary Theory of C., Grimm and Kolbenheyer," *Monatshefte* 32 (1940): 226–78; Hofrichter, R. J., *Three Poets of Reality* (1942): 9–41; Bithell, J., "H. C.," *GL&L*, new series, 2 (1948–1949), 30–41; Herd, E. W., "The Dream Motif in the Work of H. C.," *GL&L*, new series, 4 (1950–1951): 171–75; Baier, C., "C. and Goethe," *Publications of the English Goethe Society*, 24 (1955): 33–52; Schlegel, H., *Die Lyrik C.s* (1963); Kahn, R. L., "C.'s *Ein Tag im Spätsommer 1947*: Healing the Wounds of War," *RUS*, 53, No. 4 (1967): 1–12; Alter, M. P., *The Concept of Physician in the Writings of H. C. and Arthur Schnitzler* (1971); Langen, A., *H. C., Weltbild und Stil* (1979)

—EBERHARD FREY

CARPELAN, Bo

Finnish poet, novelist, and dramatist (writing in Swedish), b. 25 Oct. 1926, Helsinki

After completing his preparatory education at Helsinki's oldest Swedish-language boys' school, C. continued his studies at Helsinki University and received his doctorate in 1960 with a dissertation on the modernist poet Gunnar BJÖRLING. Employed at the Helsinki City Library from 1946 on, he was promoted in 1964 to the post of associate director, which he still holds. He has also been active as a literary critic, as an author of scripts for both radio and television, and as a translator of contemporary Finnish literature into Swedish.

C.'s main contribution to Nordic letters, though, has been his own poetry. *Som en dunkel värme* (1946; like a somber warmth) showed him to be a disciple not of Björling, who had encouraged him to make his early debut, but of the "classicist" among the Finland-Swedish modernists, Rabbe ENCKELL. Young C.'s elegiac tone, his muted outcries, and his careful syntax are clearly reminiscent of Enckell's linguistic habits. In *Du mörka överlevande* (1947; you dark survivor) C. continued with themes of subdued sadness and experimented with short strophic poems, again in Enckell's style. But at the same time, he began to expand his range of images; as he has confessed, he learned from Wallace STEVENS and from the "image-laden" lyrics of the Swedish poets of the 1940s, particularly Erik LINDEGREN. However, C. never rivaled Lindegren in difficulty or obscurity; throughout *Variationer* (1950; variations) and *Objekt för ord* (1954; objects for words), a central attitude is readily discerned—the poet's affection for a world of beauty, principally to be found in nature. But this world's apparent serenity is troubled by intimations of pain or destruction. Recently, C. has severely censured his early work; yet every poem has been shaped by an exquisite taste, and the best lyrics demonstrate C.'s unusual ability to deal simply (but not simplistically) with complex emotional and aesthetic problems.

A new phase began with *Landskapets förvandlingar* (1957; the landscape's transformations); the opening poem assumes a community of experience between poet and reader. The collection can be considered a preparatory exercise for *Den svala dagen* (1961; the cool day), in which C. at last finds a tone completely his own; his aim is now to achieve a wholly direct mode of perception and expression. In *73 dikter* (1966; 73 poems), though, C.'s stringent laconicism leads to occasional incomprehensibility, a charge that C.—a discriminating critic—has himself subsequently leveled against the book.

Among the *73 dikter*, there is a suite devoted to dreams of a dead father; in *Gården* (1973; the courtyard), C. lets his fascination with childhood, and with his parents, have full rein, as he re-creates, from a child's viewpoint, the atmosphere of a Helsinki apartment house in the 1930s. Immediately accessible and often moving, *Gården* has become the most widely read of C.'s lyric volumes; of course, C. had already reached a broad audience by means of his television play, *En gammal mans dag* (1966; an old man's day), in which he captures the world of the aged as easily as he does that of the very young.

More recently, in *Källan* (1973; the source), *I de mörka rummen, i de ljusa* (1976; in the dark rooms, in the light), and *Jag minns att jag drömde* (1979; I remember that I dreamed), C. has continued to search for an absolute honesty in his depiction of what he perceives, while listening more and more to the voices of the dead. The familiar elegiac moods are still present, but are often overshadowed by fear of humanity's eradication.

C. has also published three novels: *Rösterna i den sena timmen* (1971; *Voices at the Late Hour*, 1988), an account of the outbreak of nuclear war, seen in the small framework of a Finnish summertime idyll; *Din gestalt bakom dörren* (1975; your form behind the door), about a young man pursued through Helsinki and London by a brutal double; and *Vandrande skugga: En småstadsberättelse* (1977; wandering shadow: a small-town tale), a detective story set in turn-of-the-century Finland. The first two grew out of radio plays C. wrote in the 1960s. The common denominator of these short novels is their concentrated atmosphere of anxiety, which stands in contrast to their easy style and their air of being mere entertainment.

In Scandinavia proper, the importance of C.'s lyrics has been recognized by the award, in 1977, of the Literary Prize of the Nordic Council. Outside the North, though, he is known principally by his books for juveniles.

FURTHER WORKS: *Minus sju* (1952); *Anders på ön* (1959); *Studier i Gunnar Björlings diktning 1922–1933* (1960); *Anders i stan* (1962); *Bågen* (1968; *Bow Island*, 1971); *Paradiset* (1973; *Dolphins in the City*, 1976)

BIBLIOGRAPHY: Schoolfield, G. C., "Canals on Mars: The Recent Scandinavian Lyric," *BA*, 36 (1962): 9–19; Laitinen, K., "B. C.: Introduction," *BF*, 11 (1977): 189–91

—GEORGE C. SCHOOLFIELD

CARPENTIER, Alejo

Cuban novelist, b. 26 Dec. 1904, Havana; d. 24 April 1980, Paris, France

Born of a French father and Russian mother, C., through his knowledge of French, easily assimilated the various European avant-garde movements during many sojourns in Paris. His professional knowledge of music helped him to incorporate aspects of AFRO-CUBAN culture into his works. Living away from Cuba (in Paris, Caracas, and other cities) for many years, C. searched in his novels for his roots and for the primitive element in the Cuba of his early years. He returned to Cuba in 1959, represented the Castro government on diplomatic and cultural missions, and became a member of the National Assembly. He was a member in good standing of the Cuban Communist Party (although some critics find the political messages of his novels at best ambiguous).

¡Eacute;cue-Yamba-Ó! (1933; a *lucumí* phrase: god be praised), a novel combining politics and primitive Afro-Cuban magical rites and religion that C. began as a political prisoner in Cuba in the early 1930s and finished in Europe, promotes, through the protagonist Menegildo Cué, the blacks' struggle against misery, corruption, and Yankee commercial exploitation.

El reino de este mundo (1949; *The Kingdom of This World*, (1957), based on a trip C. took to Haiti in 1943, deals with the revolt of Mackandal, an African slave, with French colonialism, and with the reign of Henri Christophe. A kind of collage of historical texts, the novel stresses the cyclic nature of history. C. here defines precisely, for the first time, his brand of magic REALISM, a reality permeated by mythology and magic. The exposure of Ti Noël, a friend of Mackandal's, to mistreatment by the French and the equal brutality of Henri Christophe's regime cannot kill his dreams, but Ti Noël finally realizes that salvation lies not in the kingdom of heaven proclaimed by Jesus but, through struggle, in the kingdom of this world.

Los pasos perdidos (1953; *The Lost Steps*, 1956), based again on a trip C. took in 1947 during part of his fourteen-year residence in Venezuela, contains many autobiographical elements. An anonymous musician, victimized by a daily, civilized routine and a meaningless marriage, searches for authenticity, purification, and honest creativity in a trip to the upper reaches of the Orinoco. In a sense he goes back in time, discovering among the Indians a kind of Eden and encountering a primitive love in this stone-age culture. He finally realizes that intellect is not superior to instinct. Unable, after a return to civilization, to rediscover his utopia, he can only have hope for the future. The natural beauty of an eternal America, where myths retain their power and time stands still, forms the magnificent backdrop for this journey.

The short novel *El acoso* (1956; the pursuit) relates, with a fragmentary, nonchronological structure, a bloody event involving a pursued young man accused of betraying the Communist Party. Against the ironic background of a performance of Beethoven's Eroica Symphony in a concert hall where the victim takes refuge, a performance whose duration corresponds to the last forty-six minutes of his life, C. creates an allegory of betrayal and vengeance at the end of Machado's dictatorship (1933).

Guerra del tiempo (1958; war of time) consists of three short stories plus the previously published *El acoso*. The three stories are pervaded by a preoccupation with both historical and personal time, and their existential themes involve will, morality, and action.

El siglo de las luces (1962; *Explosion in a Cathedral*, 1963) concerns the French Revolution and its representative in the New World, Victor Hugues, the governor of French Guiana. In addition to Hugues's ambivalent activities concerning the use of the guillotine, the freedom of the slaves, and the imposition of one tyranny for another, the novel deals with some young Cubans—Carlos, his frustrated sister Sofía, and their cousin Estebanall at least temporarily infected with Hugues's ideas of the Enlightenment. A panorama of the Caribbean world in the 18th c., this book examines the role of revolution in modern life. In spite of its brutality and bloodshed, it portrays a warm, sensual, magical world whose characters pursue liberty and personal goals in a world in transformation.

In *El recurso del método* (1974; *Reasons of State*, 1976), set in the period between 1913 and 1928, C. rather ambiguously mocks the concept of the "dictator," and even burlesques his own writing in the speeches of the dictator. This Frenchified First Magistrate enjoys good food, sex, and music even while allowing his compatriots to suffer and die. Cruelty to Indians, a general strike, corruption, and death are all treated with sardonic humor; only when he attacks the U.S. does C. seem deadly serious. After the fall of the First Magistrate his democratic successor finds it difficult to solve the problems of the people; his socialist rival sees little difference between the supposedly democratic new leader and the deposed dictator. C. seems to be denying the efficacy of revolution and stating that most governments are incompetent.

C. used geographical, political, and historical imagery to explore mythic, cyclical, and dialectical interpretations of history and its interrelationship with the individual. Frequently writing in an epic mode, he presented magical transformations of the environment and poetic evocations of Latin America whose citizens, he felt, are masters of their own destiny.

FURTHER WORKS: *La música en Cuba* (1946); *Tientos y diferencias* (1964); *La ciudad de las columnas* (1970); *Los convidados de plata* (1972); *El derecho del asilo* (1972); *Concierto barroco* (1973); *Novelas y relatos* (1974); *Crónicas* (1975); *Visión de América* (1976); *La consagración de la primavera* (1978). **FURTHER WORKS IN ENGLISH:** *War of Time* (1970; this collection does not correspond exactly to *Guerra del tiempo*)

BIBLIOGRAPHY: Weber, F. W., "*El acoso*: A. C.'s War on Time," *PMLA*, 68 (1963): 440–48; Giacoman, H., *Homenaje a C.* (1970); Rodríguez, A. Márquez, *La obra narrative de A.C.* (1970); Echeverría, R. González, "The Parting of the Waters," *Diacritics*, 4 (1974): 8–17; Cheuse, A., *Memories of the Future: A Critical Biography of A.C.* (1975); Echeverría, R. González, *A. C.: The Pilgrim at Home* (1977)

—KESSEL SCHWARTZ

CARRANZA, Eduardo

Colombian poet, literary critic, essayist, polemicist, journalist, and translator, b. 23 July 1913, Apiay; d. 13 Feb. 1985, Bogotá

C. was educated in Bogotá by the Brothers of the Christian Schools and as a young man studied to become a teacher. He taught Spanish and Colombian literature at universities and cultural centers in both countries. Since 1934 he has gained increasing

Alejo Carpentier

national recognition for the publication of his poetic works, for his collaboration in the cultural journal *Revista de Las Indias*, for editing literary pages in the newspaper *El Tiempo* of Bogotá, for his directorship of the National Library, and for his activities as a diplomat. C. was a member of the Colombian Spanish Academy. In 1939 C. founded the most important poetic group of Colombia, *Piedra y Cielo* (Stone and Sky), a name taken from a poetic notebook of the Spanish poet Juan Ramón JIMÉNEZ. C., along with Jorge Rojas (b. 1911), Arturo Camacho Ramírez (1910–1982), Carlos Martiacuten (b. 1914), Tomás Vargas Osorio (1908–1941), and Gerardo Valencia (b. 1911), worked intensively during the 1930s and 1940s to show, first, an ascensional impulse to transcend the traditionalism of Colombian poetry, followed by a countervailing terrestrial impulse to touch the stone of Latin America and her hard reality. This heterogeneous group worked to achieve a cohesion of style, vocabulary and syntax, meters and stanzas, metaphors and themes. Although each writer possessed in his work his own personality and characteristics, all departed from the same aesthetic position, which emphasized an eagerness for novelty and formal discipline, a predilection for illogical images, a disdain for the narrative, a respect for forms, an appreciation of classic and modern Hispanic writers, and a use of sentimentalism to create a world of fantasy and sensibility. In essence, the poets of *Piedra y Cielo* were more outspoken than genuinely revolutionary in their cultivation of a poetry of restraint, more artistic than vital as they tried to make the word more intense while firing the atmosphere of Colombian poetry with an enriched poetic sensibility.

Although C.'s favorite themes are universal nature, woman, childhood, memories, dreams, intimacy, sorrow, melancholy, death, and religious topics—his transcendental attitude and sensitive spirit, as well as the temporal and special perspectives of his poetry, with its picturesque vision and lyric strength, distinguish him from other poets of his time. His beautiful poems "La niña de los jardines" (1936; the girl of the gardens) and "Soneto insistente y soneto con una salvedad" (1944; insistent sonnet and sonnet with a salvation) are the best examples of his poetic sensibility and spirit.

Beyond his successful translations of Paul Verlaine (1844–1896), Paul ELUARD, and Guillaume APOLLINAIRE, C. has enjoyed a literary career brilliant in its own right; the critical success of his books has seldom been matched by that of other Colombian authors. C.'s work is characterized by graceful sensuality, refinement, and a vague melancholy. Critics have reproached C.'s works for their lack of human depth and concern for the most vital social problems of contemporary existence. Nevertheless, his treatments of love, nature, melancholy, and nostalgia have ensured his position among contemporary Hispanic writers. Although the Colombian poetic generation of today has criticized C.'s traditionalism and his rejection of the significant European and American literary currents, it is precisely his focus on uniquely Hispanic forms and themes that lends strength to his poetry.

FURTHER WORKS: *Canciones para iniciar una fiesta* (1936); *Seis elegías y un himno* (1939); *Ellas, los días y las nubes* (1941); *Sombra de las muchachas* (1941); *Azul de ti* (1944); *Los grandes poetas americanos* (1944); *Canto en voz alta* (1945); *Las santas del paraíso* (1945); *Éste era un rey* (1945); *Los días que ahora son sueñaos* (1946); *Diciembre azul* (1947); *Amor* (1948); *El olvidado y Alhambra* (1957); *El corazón escrito* (1967); *Los pasos contados* (1970); *El insomne* (1974); *Hablar soñando otras alucinaciones* (1974); *Epístola mortal y otras soledades* (1975); *Leyendas del corazón y otras páginas abandonadas* (1976); *Lección de poesía para los jóvenes de Cundinamarca* (1980); *20 poemas* (1982); *Carranza* (1985)

BIBLIOGRAPHY: Núñez Segura, J. A., *Literatura Colombiana* (1967): 448–54; De Francisco, G. S., *Gran reportaje a E. C.* (1978); García Maffla, J., "El movimiento poético de 'Piedra y Cielo,'" *RI*, 50: 128–329 (July-Dec.1984): 683–88; Charry Lara, F., *Poesía y poetas colombianos* (1985): 87–92, 105–15; Rozo de Moorhouse, T., "La palabra en la poesía de E. C.," *Thesaurus*, 40, 2 (1985): 415–22; Álvarez Restrepo, A., "E. C. y la poesía colombiana," *BAC*, 36, 153 (July-Sept. 1986): 163–81; Williams, R. L., *The Colombian Novel*, 1844–1987 (1991): 43

—VIRGINIA SHEN

CARRASQUILLA, Tomás

Colombian novelist, short-story writer, and essayist, b. 17 Jan. 1858, Santo Domingo; d. 19 Dec. 1940, Medellín

Early this century C. shone alone in the fiction of his native country. He might have risen to greater heights had not Colombia produced after the 1920s a brilliant corps of novelists. Today C. is read only within Colombia and especially within his native region of Antioquia.

C. led a rather uneventful life. Sustaining himself with clerical and bureaucratic posts, he devoted himself wholeheartedly to literature. Unmarried, stricken by blindness in old age, he was confined to a wheelchair for the last fifteen years of his life.

C. did not issue his first book until he was almost forty. He began with *Frutos de mi tierra* (1896; fruits of my native land), in which he began to set the pace he was to pursue throughout his literary life. It was the typical realist novel, describing bourgeois people with personal problems in ordinary circumstances. The title of this first novel also indicated the strong regionalistic bent he was to impress on his works. Other similar novels were *Grandeza* (1910; greatness), a biting satire of characters drawn from the Colombian upper and middle classes, their economic and social climbing; and *El padre Casafús* (1914; Father Casafús), written to expose the evils of religious intransigence. But the short novel was C.'s forte. In the mid-1920s he reached his peak. *El zarco* (1925; the blue-eyed boy) is a moving saga of human charity on behalf of a defenseless child. It was followed by *Ligia Cruz* (1926; Ligia Cruz), this being the name of a heroine terminally ill with tuberculosis, once again a powerful story of charity and of transformation through self-sacrifice. Then came *La marquesa de Yolombó* (1928; the marquise of Yolombó), considered C.'s foremost work. Basically a historical novel, it portrays an ambitious Creole woman whose loyalty to Mother Spain and her King is severely tested by the Independence upheaval. More important than the plot itself is the masterful recreation of the times and of peasants, miners, slaves, and Spanish noblemen, all adorned with a magnificent lore.

Several short stories by C. are found in anthologies. "En la diestra de Dios Padre" (1897; in the right hand of Our Lord) is a diverting tale of wit, wholly drawn from local lore. "A la plata!" (1901; money! money!), his best-known short story, definitely naturalistic, ridicules false parental honor that crumbles down when greed appears. But instead of the scientific structure of the literature of theses, C. reduced his naturalism to a simple description of bad passions and of sordid situations. In nearly all his fiction, both long and short, he put to use his autobiographical material, drawing a good many characters from the people he used to meet in his native Antioquia, as well as in Bogotá, the Colombian capital. Other recourses he employed were regionalism, psychology, and folklore. He did not use regionalism for static pictures but rather to give characters and situations a peculiarity all their own. His psychology was seldom deep; his characters lack internal development, but they are convincingly portrayed, like any live person found in the streets of Medellín or Bogotá. Folklore shows mainly in the speech of the farmers and hillmen that populate his fiction.

C. is not easy to classify. Having been active a good part of the 20th c., he is a modern realist. The lore and the local types he constantly employed placed him as a forerunner of the Spanish American nativistic school of the 1930s. However, he always refrained from entering into the realm of the literature of social protest, which was also a part of the nativistic movement of those years. Although a liberal who advocated freedom and tolerance, he did not allow any ideology to have a voice in his fiction.

With the several novels incorporated into the trilogy of *Memorias de Eloy Gamboa: hace tiempos* (1935–1936; memories of Eloy Gamboa: time ago) the creative power of C. came to an end. Blind, he had to dictate every line to a family member. This trilogy, the most psychological of his works, depicts the mental and spiritual evolution of a child guided by outside influences, both adequate and inadequate. Other works by this venerated Colombian were his essays called *Homilías* (1906; homilies), in which he set down his own literary principles: be sincere and free of affectation; endeavor to write "a national work with modern information"; maintain faithfulness to your native land and to "the hymn of life." And while stating that he had neither school nor favorite authors, his modern realism can be described as parallel to that of Spaniard Vicente BLASCO IBÁÑEZ.

Because of a defective technique, none of C.'s works can be called a masterpiece, but critics have always judged him as the uniformly good writer that prepared the ground for the vigorous Colombian and Spanish American novel of the midcentury. Labeled "a realist and an idealist," he exhibits the exemplary honesty of the artist that lived for literature alone.

FURTHER WORKS: *Salve, Regina* (1903); *Entrañas de niño* (1914); *Dominicales* (1934); *De tejas arriba* (1936); *Obras completas* (2 vols., 1958)

BIBLIOGRAPHY: Sanín Cano, B., *Letras colombianas* (1944): 199–201; Wade, G. E., "An Introduction to the Colombian novel," *Hispania*, 30, 4 (1947): 467–83; Curcio Altamar, A., *Evolución de la novela en Colombia* (1957): 139–48; Sylvester, N., *The "Homilías" and "Dominicales" of T. C.* (1970); Menton, S., *La novela colombiana: planetas y satélites* (1978): 109–44; Levy, K. L., *T. C.* (1980); Williams, R. L., "Colombia," in Foster, D. W., comp., *Handbook of Latin American Literature* (1987): 153–90; Levy, K. L., "T. C.," in Solé, C., ed., *Latin American Writers* (1989), Vol. 1: 343–50

—EVELIO ECHEVARRÍA

CARRERA ANDRADE, Jorge

Ecuadorian poet, b. 28 Sept. 1903, Quito; d. Dec. 1978, Quito

The son of a liberal jurist, C. A. soon became aware of the social injustices suffered by most of his countrymen who were Indians and descendants of the Incas. This concern for the underprivileged of his nation, which was a major theme of his early poetry, would eventually widen and become more universal as a result of C. A.'s world travels as a career diplomat and Ecuador's representative to UNESCO. Ultimately, he became a compassionate but serene witness of the ills afflicting 20th-c. man around the world, such as poverty, materialism, automation, alienation, and loneliness. C. A., a poetic spokesman from the Third World, denounced the dehumanizing effects of urbanization and modern technology, which threatened to destroy the earth's environment and humanity's original kinship with the rest of natural creation.

C. A. and other Latin American poets of his generation shed the POSTMODERNIST (see MODERNISM) trappings of Spanish American verse and sought new modes of lyrical expression through metaphor. Original metaphors have always been essential components of his poetry, whose visual imagery is especially striking. In contrast with the HERMETICISM and radical experimentation found in the works of his avant-grade contemporaries, C.A.'s poetry has been praised for its lucidity and logic in both organization and style, as well as for its universal themes grounded in the vicissitudes of modern life. The beauty of nature was a constant fascination in all his poetry: from the nostalgic and bucolic exaltation of the landscapes of his homeland and America, to a conscious

realization of their significance within the wider context of the natural wonders found throughout the world. In his most important work, *El hombre planetario* (1959; the planetary man), the mature poet discovers a fraternity with the rest of the human race as a creature of nature and in resisting modern society's emphasis on mechanization and efficiency at the expense of individual freedom and personal happiness.

In addition to his original employment of metaphors drawn from everyday life, C. A. combined recurring images (for example, an open window) and symbols with the emblems and archetypes commonly found in the Western poetic tradition in order to enhance his work's universal appeal. He must be considered one of Latin America's most important poets because of his mastery of metaphor and the international renown he has attained through translations into French, English, Italian, German, and Dutch.

FURTHER WORKS: *El estanque inefable* (1922); *La guirnalda del silencio* (1926); *Boletines de mar y tierra* (1930); *Rol de la manzana* (1935); *El tiempo manual* (1935); *Biografía para uso de los pájaros* (1937); *País secreto* (1940; *Secret Country*, 1946); *Microgramas* (1940); *Registro del mundo* (1940); *Canto al puente de Oakland/To the Bay Bridge* (Spanish/English text, 1941); *Poesías escogidas* (1945); *El visitante de niebla* (1947; *The Visitor of Mist*, 1950); *Aquí yace la espuma* (1950); *Lugar de origen* (1951); *Familia de la noche* (1953); *La tierra siempre verde* (1955); *Edades poéticas* (1958); *Moneda del forastero* (1958); *Mi vida en poemas* (1962); *Floresta de los guacamayos* (1964); *Crónica de las indias* (1965); *Poesía ultima* (1968); *Libro del destierro* (1970).
FURTHER WORKS IN ENGLISH: *Selected Poems* (1972); *Reflections on Spanish American Poetry* (1973)

BIBLIOGRAPHY: Lee, M., "An Ecuadorean Observes His World," *Poetry*, 59 (1942): 278–82; Bishop, J. P., "The Poetry of J. C. A.," in *Secret Country* (1946): v–xi; Heald, W. F., "*Soledad* in the Poetry of C. A.," *PMLA*, 76 (1961): 608–12; Ojeda, E., *J. C. A.: Introducción al estudio de su vida y de su obra* (1971); Hays, H. R., Introduction to *Selected Poems* (1972): ix–xxvi

—JAMES J. ALSTRUM

CARROLL, Paul Vincent

Irish dramatist and short-story writer, b. 10 July, 1900, near Dundalk; d. 20 Oct. 1968, Bromley, England

Son of a country schoolmaster, C. received a grounding in classics and literature before studying to be a teacher. His love of the theater was fed by frequent visits to the Abbey in Dublin during his student days, and his political and social consciousness was shaped by the Easter Rising of 1916 and the years of English occupation and violence. After graduation C. moved to Glasgow to escape the oppressive provinciality of his hometown; in Scotland he began to write short stories and reviews as well as his first plays. Later in life he also gave his talents to theater directing and screen and television writing.

C.'s vision is at once realistic and romantic. His works are rooted in the problems of Irish life—ideological conflict, bigotry, and violence—and at the same time infused with heroic idealism often derived from Celtic mythology. Deeply influenced by Ibsen's craftsmanship and indictment of bourgeois life, C. sought to expose the tyranny of puritanical clergymen and the cruelty and stupidity of "good citizens." Yet his search for passion and beauty led him to create symbolic characters, especially women, who suggest the possibilities for renewal.

His first major play, *The Watched Pot* (perf. 1930), a grisly slice of life set in his native County Louth, is concerned with an aged peasant and his all-too-anxious heirs. His next problem drama, *Things That Are Caesar's* (1934), skillfully presents the conflict between materialism and idealism in the characters of the grasping Julia Hardy and her gentle husband. The two fight over whether their daughter should be bartered in marriage or allowed to fulfill her higher aspirations. Father Duffy takes the mother's part and becomes the first worldly priest in C.'s clerical rogues' gallery.

Shadow and Substance (1937) again focuses on the sensitive individual in a hostile atmosphere. Canon Skerritt, a classicist and gentleman modeled on Jonathan Swift, feels isolated in a village of boobs and vulgarians. His pride—as well as the arrogance of the local radical, O'Flingsley—is nevertheless the cause of the play's complications. He fails to appreciate the devout nature of Brigid, a mystical servant girl, until it is too late. *The White Steed* (1939) also employs the image of a woman, the rebellious Nora, as the center of humane values. The play concerns Father Shaughnessy's Vigilance Committee and his attempts to bludgeon dissenters into submission. Nora struggles to turn the tide of intolerance and finally influences a young schoolmaster to stand up to the establishment and mount the White Steed of imagination and freedom.

C.'s later plays are increasingly romantic and even sentimental. *The Old Foolishness* (1944) represents the former tendency and has considerable beauty of language, despite its vague and sometimes high-flown use of the story of Queen Maeve. *The Strings, My Lord, Are False* (1940) and *Green Cars Go East* (1947) deal with the theme of self-sacrifice and are heavily dependent on paragons and on moral messages. C.'s stories are also strikingly uneven in quality. "Home Sweet Home," an early work of uncertain date, is filled with the sardonic, angry spirit of his best plays, but "The Stepmother" (1958) is as mawkish and predictable as a ladies' magazine piece.

Yet, despite such lapses, C.'s powers of characterization, his intensity, and his gift for embodying tense situations in idiomatic yet beautiful speech constitute a major contribution to the Irish theater.

FURTHER WORKS: *Plays for My Children* (1939); *Kindred* (1939); *Interlude* (1947); *Conspirators* (1947); *The Wise Have Not Spoken* (1947); *The Devil Came from Dublin* (1951); *The Wayward Saint* (1955); *Irish Stories and Plays* (1958); *Farewell to Greatness* (1966); *Goodbye to the Summer* (1970)

BIBLIOGRAPHY: Brown, J. M., "*Cathleen ni Houlihan* and *Shadow and Substance*," in *Two on the Aisle: Ten Years of the American Theatre in Performance* (1938): 130–32; MacLiammoir, M., "Problem Plays," in *The Irish Theatre* (1939): 200–227; Brown, J. M., "Ireland and *The White Steed*," in *Broadway in Review* (1940): 205–8; Pallette, D. B., "P. V. C.—Since *The White Steed*," *MD*, 7 (1965): 375–81; Hogan, R., "P. V. C.: The Rebel as Prodigal Son," in *After the Irish Renaissance* (1967): 52–63; Doyle, P. A., *P. V. C.* (1971)

—DAVID CASTRONOVO

CARTER, Martin

Guyanese poet and essayist, b. 7 June 1927, Georgetown; d. 17 Dec. 1997, Georgetown

C. was born, and lived almost his entire life, in Georgetown, and it is largely this cityscape that is woven throughout his work. After completing formal schooling at Queen's College, he held a number of jobs; as civil servant, as school teacher (1954-59), information officer for Bookers (1959-67), and as Minister of Information and Culture and member of Guyana's delegation at the UN General Assembly (1967-70), all of which crossed over into his writing and political activism and vice-versa. But perhaps the 1950s, when he was actively and passionately involved with the People's Progressive Party and its charismatic Marxist-Leninist leader, Dr. Cheddi Jagan (1918-1997) in the fight for independence from Britain, had the greatest impact on his work and the blossoming of his poetry. This was a period that also brought him in close contact with two other influential Guyanese writers, Wilson HARRIS and Jan CAREW.

In his first book of poetry, *The Hill of Fire Glows Red* (1951), with the exception of a bursting optimism, the traits that would become more evident at different stages of his writing were manifest: the very deep connection to the South American soil, its northeastern Atlantic coastline, the city, his dislike of oppression, the human condition, a deep engagement with the self, the quirks of life and above all, the meticulous articulation of the voice so that the oral and scribal were seamless in his poetry: as in "Looking at Your Hands," where the persona speaks not of sleeping to dream, but of dreaming to the change the world. This would become among the first of his many quotable lines.

The Hidden Man (1952) and *The Kind Eagle* (1952) deepened C.'s preoccupation with reaching for self, his ancestral pain in slavery, and the continuing manipulation of his people by European colonial powers and their ally—the U.S. Both books came out in a period when C. was actively involved with others from the People's Progressive Party in agitating for independence at various rallies where his poetry was read. C.'s poetry set crowds alight and people went away with lines from such poems as "Till I Collect" and "You are Involved" on their lips. It was a heady time preparing for the 1953 elections, the first in the colony under adult suffrage, which the PPP won with a landslide.

The PPP government lasted only 133 days before the British government suspended the constitution and sent in troops, citing a communist conspiracy. C., in Romania for a conference during the emergency, was jailed by the British for three months, along with other members of the PPP, on his return. In jail he would write many of the poems for his *Poems of Resistance* (1954), first published in London. It was this collection that brought him not only national but international fame and established him as a poet of the highest order. Large segments of several poems in this collection were to become powerful songs in the utterance of intellectual and ordinary people alike, notably poems such as "University of Hunger," "Weroon Weroon," "This is the Dark Time, My Love," and especially, "I Come from the Nigger Yard." This last became a battle cry for radicals and intellectuals across the British West Indies agitating for political independence.

C.'s next major work, *Poems of Succession* (1977), was more than twenty years in the making. Though some of the poetry included here dated back to the 1950s, this collection was less overtly political, dealing with a wider range of themes—including love—and seemingly less simple and more philosophical. Even the rhythm was slower. This was a poetry different from that of the 1950s but, as C. has pointed out, not a poetry that was better. The critics who had previously dismissed him merely as a left-wing, protest poet couldn't do so now. Some of the titles of the most famous poems in this book, "Rain Falls Upward," "On a Pavement," "In a Small City at Dusk," and "The Child Ran into the Sea," are good indicators why, and of his broader themes.

Poems of Affinity (1980), another major collection, is a return to politics, injustice and corruption, and as in *Poems of Succession* there seems to be a greater complexity and obliqueness in dealing with these issues. In "Playing Militia," "Inventor," "Bastille Day— Georgetown," and "Our Time" his disgust for the increasingly corrupt and racist postindependence regime, which he served as Minister of Information and Culture before resigning, is barely concealed.

His public presence contracted after 1970, and this resulted in little international attention, compounded by the fact that, with the exception of the 1975 academic year as Poet-in-Residence at Essex University, he lived all his life in Guyana. His left wing politics, the regime's attempt to silence him and disillusionment also contributed. That in the same period Derek WALCOTT and Edward Kamau BRATHWAITE were receiving widespread international attention had more to do with the politics of literature and their extraregional academic connections than to their being more accomplished poets.

The appearance of C.'s *Selected Poems* (1989), for which he won the Guyana Prize for Literature, the end of the cold war, the dissolution of the Soviet Union and the return of democracy to Guyana in 1992, have all contributed to renewed interest in C.'s work.

C. is unquestionably the finest Guyanese poet this century. Many consider him not only the finest poet from the English speaking West Indies, but also the finest poet in the English Language in the second half of the 20th c.—and the increasing critical attention his work is presently receiving is more that likely to bear this out.

FURTHER WORKS: *Jail Me Quickly* (1966); *The When Time* (1977); *A Martin Carter Prose Sampler* (1993)

BIBLIOGRAPHY: Brathwaite, E. K., "Resistance Poems: The Voice of M. C.," *CarQ*, 23 (1971): 7-20; Asein, S.O., "The Protest Tradition in West Indian Poetry from George Campbell to M.C.," *Jamaica Journal*, 6 (1972): 40-45; Brown, S., "M.C.: The Poet as Guerilla?," *New Voices*, 9 (1981): 50-61; McWatt, M. A., *West Indian Poetry: Proceedings of the Fifth Annual Conference on West Indian Literature*, (1985): 143-52; Robinson, J., "The Root and the Stone: The Rhetoric of M.C.'s *Poems of Resistance*," *JWIL*, 1 (1986): 1-12; McDonald, I., Introduction to *Selected Poems* (1989): xiii-xix

—SASENARINE PERSAUD

CARVER, Raymond

American short-story writer and poet, b. 25 May 1938, Clatskanie, Oreg.; d. 2 Aug. 1988, Port Angeles, Wash.

Like his literary hero Anton CHEKHOV, C. was a child of the working poor, born in a mill town on the Columbia River dividing

Raymond Carver

Oregon from Washington State. Married at nineteen and father of two before he turned twenty-one, C. experienced during his "first life" many of the vicissitudes he depicts in his writings: spirit-breaking ennui and underemployment, domestic " dis-ease" culminating in divorce, and life-threatening alcoholism. A comparatively tranquil and productive "second life" commenced in 1977, when C. stopped drinking, began his decade-long association with the writer Tess Gallagher (b. 1943), and steadily gained recognition as the foremost short-story writer of his generation. In 1983 the American Academy awarded C. one of its first Strauss "Livings," a fellowship bringing him five years of substantial income. C. and Gallagher married shortly before his death from lung cancer at age fifty.

The bulk of C.'s early fiction is contained in his first short-story collection, *Will You Please Be Quiet, Please?* (1976). In these twenty-two stories written over fifteen difficult years, C. fuses Chekhov's lyrical realism with the cryptic expressionism of Franz KAFKA. This deceptively simple mode of fabulation charges ordinary experience with uncanny significance, typically with an undertone of menace. For the most part, C.'s early characters are inarticulate working people whose sensibilities exceed their powers of expression. As the title story indicates, the mood of the book is anxious and interrogative. Stories such as "The Father," "Neighbors," and "Fat" end with antiheroes on the brink of crisis, their unvoiced conflicts unresolved. Critical recognition followed when *Will You Please Be Quiet, Please?* was nominated for a National Book Award.

A transitional middle period in C.'s fiction begins with the commencement of his postalcoholic "second life" in 1977. Over the course of five interlocking books, C. reinvents his art as his stories pass through a purgatorial dialectic of expansion, compression, and reexpansion in new forms. The opening phase of this process begins with *Furious Seasons, and Other Stories* (1977), an interim collection of eight stories, seven of which C. would revise for subsequent books. Next, following the "theory of omission" proposed by Ernest HEMINGWAY, C. cut his stories "to the marrow, not just to the bone" for his so-called "minimalist" masterpiece, *What We Talk About When We Talk about Love* (1981). As the lengthy title intimates, these seventeen tightly elliptical stories expose a painful gap between expression and feeling, talk and love, in the lives of men and women whose relationships have been fouled by alcoholism, infidelity, and the failure of youthful hopes. The arresting fusion of style and subject matter won C. acclaim as "a full-grown master," but it also left him at an artistic crisis point. As the stories in *What We Talk About When We Talk about Love* amply demonstrate, the outcome of failed communication is silence—for character and author alike. To avoid this impasse, C. executed a stylistic turnabout over the next two years, restoring and expanding previously pared-down stories and writing new ones in a richer, fuller, and more hopeful key. The first fruits of this widening phase are gathered in *Fires: Essays, Poems, Stories* (1983). The harvest follows in *Cathedral* (1983), a book of twelve new and expanded stories that won C. nominations for the Pulitzer Prize and National Book Critics Circle Award. In the title story and others such as "Feathers," "Fever," and "A Small, Good Thing" (the last story a revision/expansion of "The Bath" in *What We Talk About*), characters find their lives subtly transfigured as silence and isolation give way to compassion and community. A chapbook, *If It Please You* (1984), provides a concluding illustration of C.'s "more generous" mode of realism.

Although C. won fame as a fiction writer, his first and last calling was poetry. Writing in the vernacular lyric-narrative mode of William Carlos WILLIAMS and Charles Bukowski (b. 1920), C. published three small-press books of poems before his first short-story collection appeared: *Near Klamath* (1968), *Winter Insomnia* (1970), and *At Night the Salmon Move* (1976). Moreover, even as C. devoted himself to fiction in the late 1970s and early 1980s, he remained a poet. In 1984, after years away from the Pacific Northwest, C. returned to his homeland and his lifelong calling. The result was two poetry collections, *Where Water Comes Together with Other Water* (1985) and *Ultramarine* (1986), books that chart the changing course of C.'s life and art, including his deepening preoccupation with mortality. For these poems, C. shared the 1985 Levinson Prize.

C. returned to fiction in 1986–1987 with seven new stories eventually collected in *Where I'm Calling From* (1988), a burst of creativity that heralded further work to come. In retrospect, however, C.'s untimely death marks this efflorescence as his final phase. Stories of this period—among them "Boxes," "Blackbird Pie," and "Elephant"—are typically longer, looser, and more openly reflective than C.'s previous fiction. Their texture is novelistic and their tone autumnal, with C. freely exploring the interplay of character and incident. The capstone of the group is "Errand," C.'s last-written work of fiction. There, taking for his subject the final days of CHEKHOV, C. validates the life-transforming power of fiction over fact. Even as his own death approached, C. continued writing, completing a last book of poems, *A New Path to the Waterfall* (1989), in the closing weeks of his life.

Despite C.'s foreshortened career, his contributions to late-20th-c. literature are substantial. C. reinvented realism for postmoderns, set in motion the short-story renaissance of the 1980s, and gave voice to a formerly submerged population. By precept and example he served as mentor to an emerging generation of "post-postmodern" realists whose fiction is, like his, at once representational and self-interrogating. Following Chekhov, C. set himself a modest but enduring goal: "a bringing of the news from one world to another." At a deeper level, as one of his contemporaries observed, "The process of Mr. C.'s fiction is to transform our perception."

FURTHER WORKS: *Dostoevsky: A Screenplay* (1985, with Tess Gallagher); *Conversations with R. C.* (1990); *C. Country: The World of R. C.* (1990, with Bob Adelman); *No Heroics, Please: Uncollected Writings* (1991); *Carnations: A Play in One Act* (1992); *All of Us: The Collected Poems* (1996)

BIBLIOGRAPHY: Boxer, D., and Phillips, C., "*Will You Please Be Quiet, Please*? Voyeurism, Dissociation, and the Art of R. C.," *IowaR*, 10 (Summer 1979): 75–90; Chénetier, M., "Living On/Off the 'Reserve': Performance, Interrogation, and Negativity in the Works of R. C.," in Chénetier, M., ed., *Critical Angles* (1986): 164–90; special "Minimalist Fiction" section, *Mississippi Review*: 40–41, (1985): 7–94; Stull, W. L., "Beyond Hopelessville: Another Side of R. C.," *PQ*, 64, 1 (Winter 1985): 1–15; Saltzman, A. M., *Understanding R. C.* (1988); Meyer, A., "Now You See Him, Now You Don't, Now You Do Again: The Evolution of R. C.'s Minimalism," *Crit*, 30, 4 (Summer 1989): 239–51; Stull, W. L., "R. C.," in Brook, J. M., ed., *DLB Yearbook: 1988* (1989): 199–213; Halpert, S., ed., *. . .When We Talk About R. C.* (1991); Nesset, K., "'This Word Love': Sexual Politics and Silence in Early R. C.," *AL*, 63, 2 (June 1991): 292–313; Campbell, E., *R. C.: A Study of the Short Fiction* (1992); Runyon, R. P., *Reading R. C.* (1992); Stull, W., and M. P. Carroll, eds., *Remembering Ray: A Composite Biography of R. C.* (1993); Halpert, S., ed., *R. C.: An Oral Biography* (1995); Nesset, K., *The Stories of R. C.* (1995); Meyer, A., *R. C.* (1994)

—WILLIAM L. STULL

CARY, Joyce

Anglo-Irish novelist, poet, political essayist, b. 7 Dec. 1888, Londonderry, Northern Ireland; d. 29 March 1957, Oxford, England

Following preparatory years at Hurstleigh School and Clifton College, C. studied painting in Paris and Edinburgh between the ages of seventeen and twenty. Deciding against painting as a career, C. entered Oxford, from which he took a degree in 1912. He then served briefly with the British Red Cross during the Montenegrin-Turkish conflict. From 1913 to 1919 he was a colonial officer in the Nigerian Service and was slightly wounded during military service in the Cameroons campaign. Resigning early from the Nigerian Service, C. settled in Oxford and devoted the rest of his life to writing. Although by 1916 he had begun the first in a succession of uncompleted and abandoned novels, C. was not to publish for another decade and a half.

His first completed novels, *Aissa Saved* (1932), *An American Visitor* (1933), and *The African Witch* (1936), all drew upon his

Nigerian experiences and depicted the grotesque impact of divergent cultures on one another. Unsentimental and ironic, these books (however uneven aesthetically) were also sympathetic and free from racial stereotypes, although C. did not regard them as dealing with racial problems but as treating universal human concerns. In his last Nigerian novel, *Mister Johnson* (1939), C. demonstrated a masterly ability to create a vital and unforgettable character. Written in the present tense and paced so as to suggest the way in which "Johnson swims gaily on the surface of life," the novel records the career of an irrepressible native clerk, his triumphs, and his destruction, each of these the product of his imaginative vitality.

In *Castle Corner* (1938) and *A House of Children* (1941) C. drew successively upon the history of his distinguished County Donegal family and upon his early childhood in Donegal. *Castle Corner* is a chronicle intended as the first in a sequence that would trace the Corners, their relatives, retainers, and associates in Ireland, England, and Africa from the age of Victoria to the 1930s; it was given a critical reception that overlooked the rich social observations of the dominant Irish sections and dissuaded C. from completing the project. *A House of Children*, more a lyrical memoir of his childhood and family than a novel, subtly traces the development of its narrator's sensibility.

Two very uneven works also appeared in the 1940s. *Charley Is My Darling* (1940), which recounts the adventures of a slum boy evacuated from London during World War II, seems sometimes a case history, sometimes a discourse on juvenile delinquency. *A Fearful Joy* (1949), which traces the career of Tabitha Baskett from the 1890s to the post-World War II period and manifests again C.'s fondness for the chronicle, is improbable at points and often contrived; yet it offers striking vignettes of the trends and qualities of the decades and convincingly depicts Tabitha's power of survival.

The Moonlight (1946), with its vivid portraits of three Victorian sisters, Rose, Ella, and Bessie, as they respond to time and change and family, is an impressive work. Conceived as a reply to Tolstoy's *The Kreutzer Sonata*, the novel reveals C.'s view of the power of woman's sexuality and of society's restraints upon it; its ironic rendering of the forces that lead Ella to murder her sister is brilliant, and its portrait of Ella's daughter, Amanda, is well in advance of its time, anticipating a feminist type that would appear in fiction later in the century.

C.'s two trilogies, both influenced by the archetypal myths of William Blake, are generally regarded as his major achievements. *Herself Surprised* (1941), *To Be a Pilgrim* (1942), and *The Horse's Mouth* (1944) constitute the first trilogy; each of these novels is dominated by its first-person narrator so that, as C. saw the work, while the "three parts cover the same period of history, they are in different styles, about different people, and have a very casual relation in form." Sara Monday, narrator of the first novel, is mistress to the narrator of the second, Tom Wilcher, a Protestant sensibility trammeled by family and possessions, and also to the narrator of the third, Gulley Jimson, an anarchic artist whose essential commitment is to his moments of visionary creation; throughout the entire trilogy Sara represents the female principle and embodies the contraries of inhibition and freedom manifest in the two contrasting men. Although *The Horse's Mouth* is C.'s best-known single novel and Gulley Jimson has often been sentimentalized by interpreters, the thematic significance of the book and the human significance of Gulley are to be comprehended only in the context of the entire trilogy.

Believing that the parts of the first trilogy "were not sufficiently interlocked," in his second trilogy, *Prisoner of Grace* (1952), *Except the Lord* (1953), and *Not Honour More* (1955), C. concentrates on a central political theme and on the inextricable links binding the three narrators, Nina and her two husbands, Chester Nimmo and Jim Latter. He particularly focuses on the character of Nimmo, the Radical Liberal leader, as he is seen against the background of English politics from the turn of the century to the general strike of 1926. The form of the three narratives perfectly expresses the character of each narrator; revealing once again a Blakean sense of the opposition between contraries of freedom and inhibition, creation and destruction, C. produced a work that suggests the multiplicity of reality, the subjectivity of perception, and the ambiguity of character. As is the case with the first trilogy, the moral significance of the final one is not defined by any easy relativism but by the compelling irony of the parts in relation to the whole.

Often regarded as a conservative and traditional novelist outside of the mainstream of modernism and frequently compared to earlier novelists like Defoe and Dickens, C. identified as his masters "HARDY, CONRAD, JAMES and the great Russians"; the major effort of his career was to embody his complex vision of life in forms that would be at once realistic and symbolically suggestive. In *Mister Johnson, The Moonlight*, and the six novels that compose his trilogies, C. managed to imbue the amplitude of fictional detail he commanded, the three-dimensional characters he could create, and his persistent interest in religious and political forces with a tragicomic, highly personal, and intuitive existentialism. If not on the level of James JOYCE or D. H. LAWRENCE, at his best he was a boldly imaginative writer. His trilogies, particularly the second, rank high among multiple or sequential novels in English.

FURTHER WORKS: *Verse* (1908); *Power in Men* (1939); *The Case for African Freedom* (1941); *The Process of Real Freedom* (1943); *Marching Soldier* (1945); *Britain and West Africa* (1946); *The Drunken Sailor* (1947); *Art and Reality* (1958); *The Captive and the Free* (1959); *Memoir of the Bobotes* (1960); *Spring Song and Other Stories* (1960)

BIBLIOGRAPHY: Allen, W., *J. C.* (1953); Wright, A., *J. C.: A Preface to His Novels* (1958); Bloom, R., *The Indeterminate World: A Study of the Novels of J. C.* (1962); Adams, H., Introduction to *Power in Men* (1963): vii–xlvi; Hoffmann, C. G., *J. C.: The Comedy of Freedom* (1964); Mahood, M. M., *J. C.'s Africa* (1964); Foster, M., *J. C.: A Biography* (1968); Wolkenfeld, J., *J. C.: The Developing Style* (1968); Echeruo, M., *J. C. and the Novel of Africa* (1973); Hall, D., *J. C.: A Reappraisal* (1983); Bishop, A., *Gentleman Rider: A Life of J. C.* (1988)

—JAMES F. CARENS

CASONA, Alejandro

(pseud. of Alejandro Rodríguez Álvarez) Spanish dramatist and poet, b. 23 March 1903, Besullo; d. 17 Sept. 1965, Madrid

After attending the universities of Oviedo and Murcia, C. transferred to a teachers' college in Madrid, from which he was graduated in 1926. Following in the footsteps of his parents, who were both teachers, he went on to hold administrative positions in several education systems. C. combined his teaching career with work in the theater. He founded the children's theater, The Speckled Bird, and in 1931 he was made director of the People's Theater, a traveling troupe that brought culture to rural Spain. In the middle of a successful career as a poet and dramatist, C. left his homeland at the outbreak of the civil war and toured Latin America, where his plays were performed with great success. In 1939 he took up residence in Buenos Aires and lived there until his return to Spain in 1962.

C.'s return to Spain occasioned great celebration. From 1962 to 1965, theaters all over the country performed his plays. However, this so-called C. festival raised many questions about his theater. The general public and a number of critics received his plays with great enthusiasm, but the younger, more socially minded critics felt that C. sacrificed social and political realities and exigencies to theatrical illusionism, escapist poeticizing, and well-made plots. These critics were too harsh, for in C.'s plays there is always the strong assertion that truth and happiness can only be attained when one confronts reality, even if it is through fantasy and poetry. Fantasy and reality for C. are not oppositional but complementary.

This concept can be seen in C.'s first full-length play, *La sirena varada* (1934; the abandoned mermaid), for which he won the prestigious Lope de Vega Prize. Ricardo, like many of C.'s protagonists, is world-weary and tries to insulate himself from reality by creating a republic for lost souls. He falls in love with Sirena who, in her madness, believes that she is a mermaid. After she is cured and returns to being herself—María—she tenaciously clings to her newly found sanity. Ricardo realizes that he can love María just as much as he loved Sirena, if not more, and that true salvation can only be found when one confronts the real world.

That fantasy can be a learning and illuminating experience is also seen in *Prohibido suicidarse en primavera* (1943; *Suicide Prohibited in Springtime*, 1969) and in *Los árboles mueren de pie* (1951; the trees die standing), two key plays. In the first, Dr. Ariel has established a home for lost souls who are would-be suicides. The ostensible but ironic purpose of this institution is to make suicide palatable and pleasurable. In actuality, the purpose is to reconcile these unhappy people with reality and truth without eschewing the therapeutic nature of illusion. In *Los árboles mueren de pie* Dr. Ariel has established another kind of institution, whose main objective is to make the unhappy happy by allowing them to live in a world of illusions. This is precisely what happens to the grandmother in the play, who, although she knows the truth about her criminal grandson, chooses to conceal it. She comes to realize exactly how valuable the power of illusion can be.

La dama del alba (1945; *The Lady of the Dawn*, 1949) is C.'s personal favorite among his plays and an undisputed masterpiece. It is a hauntingly poetic parable about death and rebirth, punishment and redemption. With the help of Death, personified by the Lady of the Dawn, Martín is able to find true love and salvation in Adela, whom he saved from drowning after having been deceived by his wife Angélica on the third day of their marriage.

C. was an innovative playwright and along with GARCÍA LORCA helped to infuse the Spanish theater with poetry, imaginative flair, and originality. C.'s brand of fantasy, however, presupposed some sort of moral or pedagogical premise. His investigations into the relationship between reality and fantasy were not unlike those of PIRANDELLO.

That C.'s theater has been scorned as escapist by some critics ought not undercut its worth. While it may be true that C. was not a profound thinker, he was indeed a generous humanist and a dramatist who committed himself fully to the crafting of exciting plays.

FURTHER WORKS: *El peregrino de la barba florida* (1926); *La flauta del sapo* (1930); *Flor de leyendas* (1933); *El misterio del "María Celeste"* (1935, with Alfonso Hernández Catá); *Otra vez el diablo* (1935); *Nuestra Natacha* (1936); *Marie Curie* (1940, with Francisco Madrid); *Las tres perfectas casadas* (1943); *La molinera de Arcos* (1949); *Retablo jovial* (1949); *Sinfonía inacabada* (1949); *La barca sin pescador* (1950; *The Boat without a Fisherman*, 1970); *El crimen de Lord Arturo* (1951); *La tercera palabra* (1954); *Romance en tres noches* (1954); *Siete gritos en el mar* (1954); *Teatro infantil:* ¡ *A Belén, pastores!* (1954); *El lindo Don Gato* (1954); *La llave en el desván* (1959); *Carta de una desconocida* (1960); *Corona de amor y de muerte* (1960); *La casa de los siete balcones* (1960); *El caballero de las espuelas de oro* (1965); *Tres diamantes y una mujer* (1966); *Obras completas* (2 vols., 1974)

BIBLIOGRAPHY: Schwartz, K., "Reality in the Works of A. C.," *Hispania*, 40 (1957): 57–61; Leighton, C., "A. C.'s 'Pirandellism'," *Symposium*, 17 (1963): 202–7; Rodríguez Richart, J., *Vida y obra de A. C.* (1963); Gurza, E., *La realidad caleidoscópica de A. C.* (1968); Moon, H. K., *A. C., Playwright* (1985); García Alvares, M. T., "El homenaje a A. C. y La sirena varada 60 años después," *Boletín del Real Instituto de estudios asturianos*, 50 (1996): 49-60

—MARSHALL J. SCHNEIDER

CASSOLA, Carlo

Italian novelist and essayist, b. 17 March 1917, Rome; d. 24 Jan. 1987, Monte Carlo, Monaco

Although born and raised in Rome and graduated from the University of Rome, C. is considered a Tuscan. While growing up he spent his summer vacations in Tuscany, during World War II he fought there as a partisan, and since then has made his home there. Immediately after the war he earned his living as a journalist and then as a high-school teacher until 1961, after which he devoted himself exclusively to writing.

Because he used his own experiences as a partisan for material in many of the stories that he wrote during the 1950s, he was first categorized as a NEOREALIST. In retrospect it has been recognized that, regardless of material used, C.'s purpose in writing has always been to express the emotions aroused in him by the contemplation of the human condition, and by so doing to inspire in his readers an appreciation for and an attachment to life. In particular C.'s themes are the importance of the presence of a person of the opposite sex as a catalyst to active participation in life, the mysterious ways in which fate is determined, the irrevocable passing of time and the sense of loss that accompanies it, and the fundamental sadness caused by the inevitability of death.

C. usually represents a critical period of a person's life, most often the time when a character's youthful anticipation of life is overtaken by the realization that his or her destiny has been determined. More specifically, his most successfully portrayed protagonists are provincial girls presented first in their anticipation of love and then in their disillusionment. Narrative tension is supplied by two contrasting drives in the protagonist: an instinctive reaching out for participation in life and a more reflective resistance to such a participation because it implies emotional and social development, then decline, and eventually death. The end invariably finds the protagonist tranquilly resigned to his or her destiny and even happy in the simple acceptance of existence as an absolute value in itself.

Critics generally agree that C.'s masterpiece is the novella *Il taglio del bosco* (1950; *The Cutting of the Woods*, 1961), in which the grief of a man over the loss of his wife (C.'s wife had died in 1949) is expressed against a background of dreary solitude in which a small group of woodsmen live and work. *Fausto e Anna* (1952, rev. 1958; *Fausto and Anna*, 1960), C.'s most autobiographical novel, is the story of a middle-class intellectual from the time he finishes high school until several years later when his fate is apparently determined by a two-part failure: his unsuccessful love relationship with Anna and his equally unsuccessful attempt to resist a future of uneventful mediocrity by joining the partisans and trying to become a communist. *La ragazza di Bube* (1960; *Bèbo's Girl*, 1962), for which C. won the Strega Prize, Italy's most prestigious literary prize, is the story of Mara, a proletarian heroine whom fate links to Bube, an immature young partisan who is sentenced to fourteen years in prison for the murder of a police officer and his son while still caught up in the violent spirit of the partisan war. C. seems to admire his heroine for her ability to resign herself to what she considers an unjust destiny: knowing that society and fate have cheated her, she is nevertheless still able to hope for what little happiness life may have in store for her. Although set in much less eventful historical periods than *La ragazza di Bube*, *Un cuore arido* (1961; *An Arid Heart*, 1964) and *Paura e tristezza* (1970; fear and sadness) have female protagonists who are again the victims of a sad destiny to which they nevertheless are able to resign themselves.

Since 1975 C. has dedicated his talent to the preservation of life on our planet, which he believes is threatened by nuclear weapons and by the division of the world into armed sovereign states. He has published three essays on this subject—*Ultima frontiera* (1976; last frontier), *Il gigante cieco* (1976; the sleeping giant), and *La lezione della storia* (1978; the lesson of history)—and has made it the theme of three recent novels—*Il superstite* (1978; the survivor), *Il paradiso degli animali* (1979; animal paradise), *Ferragosto di morte* (1980; August of death)—and a volume of short stories, *La morale del branco* (1980; the moral of the herd).

Ultimately the most important characteristic of C.'s fiction is its deep earnestness, a quality that has often made the difference between success and a potential decline into banality. C. is among Italy's most widely read contemporary novelists and, with over twenty volumes of fiction published, he is certainly among its most prolific.

FURTHER WORKS: *Alla periferia* (1942); *La visita* (1942); *I vecchi compagni* (1953); *Viaggio in Cina* (1956); *I minatori della Maremma* (1956, with Luciano Bianciardi); *La casa di via Valadier* (1956); *Un matrimonio del dopoguerra* (1957); *Il soldato* (1958); *Il cacciatore* (1964); *Tempi memorabili* (1966); *Storia di Ada* (1967); *Ferrovia locale* (1968); *Una relazione* (1969); *Monte Mario* (1973; *Portrait of Elena*, 1975); *Poesia e romanzo* (1973, with Mario Luzi); *Gisella* (1974); *Fogli di diario* (1974); *Troppo tardi* (1975); *L'antagonista* (1976); *La disavventura* (1977); *L'uomo e il cane* (1977); *Un uomo solo* (1978); *Vita d'artista* (1980); *Il ribelle* (1980)

BIBLIOGRAPHY: Golino, C., "Strega 1960," *IQ* 4, (1960): 68–69; Tillona, Z., "Neo-realism Revisited: *La ragazza di Bube*," *FI*, 1 (1967): 2–10; O'Neill, T., Introduction and notes to *Il taglio del bosco* (1970); Klopp, C., "C.'s 'L'orfano': A Note on the Influence of Federigo Tozzi on the Young C.," *Italica*, 51, (1974): 454–64; Pedroni, P., "Neorealism or Existentialism in C.'s *Fausto e Anna?*," *La fusta*, 1 (1976): 73–89; Pedroni, P., "C.'s *La ragazza di Bube*," *FI*, 11 (1977): 47–65; Moss, H., "The Existentialism of C.," *Italica*, 54 (1977): 381–98; Pedroni, P. N., *Existence as Theme in C. C.'s Fiction* (1985)

—PETER N. PEDRONI

CASTELLANOS, Rosario

Mexican novelist, poet, short-story writer, and dramatist; b. 25 May 1925, Mexico City; d. 7 Aug. 1974, Tel Aviv, Israel

C. cultivated all literary genres but is best remembered for her poetry and novels. After graduation from the National University of Mexico with a master's degree in philosophy, C. was employed during the late 1950s in the Indian Institutes in Chiapas and Mexico City. She was later named Mexican consul to Israel and died there tragically as a result of an accident with an electrical appliance.

C. began writing in 1940 and published her first poetry in 1948 in a volume entitled *Trayectoria del polvo* (trajectory of dust). Her early verses avoid the autobiographical and in their abstractness demonstrate C.'s admiration for the metaphysical poetry of her compatriot José Gorostiza (1901–1973). *Poemas 1953–1955* (1957; poems 1953–1955) contains some of her finest writing, including two of her best known poems, "Misterios gozosos" (joyful mysteries) and "El resplandor del ser" (radiance of being). Her later poetry tends to be more personal and includes impressions of her travels abroad. Themes that predominate throughout her poetic work include love, destiny, loneliness, and death.

The novels *Balún-Canán* (1957; *The Nine Guardians*, 1960) and *Oficio de tinieblas* (1962; office of shadows) take place in the state of Chiapas, where C. lived as a child. The latter describes an imaginary Chamula Indian uprising in the 20th c. but is based on a real revolt that occurred in 1867. Both the old white families and the various Indian and mestizo groups are depicted. Characterization and structural techniques are traditional rather than experimental.

The short stories in *Ciudad real* (1960; royal city) and *Los convidados de agosto* (1964; the invited ones of August) focus on the lives of the declining landed aristocracy in Chiapas. Very different in tone and thrust are the stories in *Album de familia* (1971; family album), in which C. examines the role of the Mexican woman in modern society. Also feminist in content is the theatrical farce *El eterno femenino* (the eternal feminine), published posthumously in 1975.

C. is probably Mexico's most important woman poet of this c. In fiction her defense of the Indian continues an important Latin American literary tradition, while her feminist writings of her last years indicate a new development that unfortunately was cut short by her untimely death.

FURTHER WORKS: *Apuntes para una declaración de fe* (1948); *De la vigilia estéril* (1950); *Dos poemas* (1950); *Presentación en el* *templo* (1951); *El rescate del mundo* (1952); *Salomé y Judith* (1959); *Al pie de la letra* (1959); *Lívida luz* (1960); *Poesía no eres tú* (1972); *Selected Poems of R. C.* (1988); *Another Way to Be: Selected Works of R. C.* (1990)

BIBLIOGRAPHY: Leiva, R., "R. C.," *Imagen de la poesía mexicana contemporánea* (1959): 333–41; Sommers, J., "Changing Views of the Indian in Mexican Literature," *Hispania*, 47 (1964): 47–55; Carballo, E., "R. C.," *Diecinueve protagonistas de la literatura mexicana del siglo XX* (1965): 409–24; Ocampo de Gómez, A. M., and Prado, E., *Diccionario de escritores mexicanos* (1967): 18–20; Godoy, E., "R. C.," *Ábside* (1975): 350–54; Rodríguez-Peralta, P., "Images of Women in R. C.'s Prose," *LALR*, 11 (1977): 68–80; Ocampo de Gómez, A. M., and E. Prado Velázquez, *Diccionario de escritores mexicanos* (1967): 18-20

—RICHARD M. REEVE

CASTRO, José Maria Ferreira de

Portuguese novelist and essayist, b. 24 May 1898, Salgueiros; d. 29 June 1974, Oporto

The misfortunes of rural existence during the years of the First Portuguese Republic (1910–26) caused C., along with many of his compatriots, to emigrate to Brazil. There he worked on an Amazonian rubber plantation. His experiences during this period not only served as a source for his fiction but also conditioned his belief in socialism as the only possible solution to man's repression of his fellow man.

Upon his return to Portugal in 1919 C. began his career as a journalist. His first published volume *Mas . . .* (1921; but . . .) was socioliterary criticism. It was followed by the novel *Carne Faminta* (1922; starved flesh) about loneliness and sexual deprivation in the Amazon jungle, and by a series of other popular novels and stories.

C.'s first widely successful novel was the semiautobiographical *Emigrantes* (1928; *Emigrants*, 1962); *A selva* (1930; *The Jungle*, 1934) garnered him immediate international fame. Both novels share similar techniques, social concerns, and psychological detail. C.'s indignation about his characters' capricious desires for wealth and a better life, as well as about their resultant despair, points accusingly at the capitalist system. In addition, *A selva* vividly describes the Amazon jungle.

C.'s novels from the 1930s through the 1960s portrayed man's attempts at achieving a more just society. In *A lã e a neve* (1947; the wool and the snow) a shepherd justifies his impelling need to abandon an aimless rural existence. In *O intervalo* (written in 1936; the intermission), which C. kept unpublished until 1974, and in *A curva na estrada* (1950; the curve in the road), C. commented upon the tragedy of the fall of the Spanish Republic and the setback to proletarian revolutionary ideals. C.'s last novel is once again set in Brazil, where he has enjoyed great popularity and literary prestige. *O instinto supremo* (1968; the supreme instinct) insists upon man's dedication to his own salvation, reflected here through the humanitarian efforts of Colonel Rondon to pacify the Indians of Brazil's interior. C. also published narrations of his travels and histories of art.

C. consistently viewed brotherhood and moral unity as the basic keys to the resolution of human discord in the 20th c. He was more preoccupied with the validation of his beliefs than with matters of literary style; thus, he adopted a sometimes criticized journalistic approach to fiction. His works have been translated into seventeen languages and have won important awards. It was he who brought world attention to Portuguese fiction; C. is thus quite justly considered one of the major precursors of the NEOREALIST movement in Europe.

FURTHER WORKS: *O éxito fácil* (1923); *Sangue negro* (1923); *A boca do esfinge* (1924); *Metamorfose* (1924); *A morte redimida* (1925); *Sendas de lirismo e de amor* (1925); *O drama da sombra* (1926); *A peregrina do mundo novo* (1926); *A epopeia do trabalho* (1926); *O voo nas trevas* (1927); *A casa dos móveis dourados* (1927); *Eternidade* (1933); *Terra fria* (1934); *Pequenos mundos e velhas civilizações* (1937); *A tempestade* (1940); *A volta do mundo* (1944); *Terras do sonho* (1952); *A missão* (1954; *The Mission*, 1963); *As maravilhas artísticas do mundo* (1959–63); *Os fragmentos* (1974)

BIBLIOGRAPHY: Marsh, F. T., on *The Jungle*, *NYTBR* (3 Feb. 1935): 4; Brasil, J., "F. de C.," *BA*, 31 (1957): 117–21; Grossman, W. L., on *Emigrants*, *NYTBR* (18 Nov. 1962) 4, 64; Salema, A., Introduction to *The Mission* (1963): 5–28; Megenny, W. W., "F. de C.," *RomN*, 13 (1971): 61–66

—IRWIN STERN

CASTRO LITERATURE

See Soromenho, Fernando Castro

CATALAN LITERATURE

See under Spanish Literature

CATHER, Willa

American novelist and short-story writer, b. 7 Dec. 1873, Back Creek (now Gore), Va.; d. 24 April 1947, New York, N.Y.

When C. was nine years old her family migrated to the Nebraska frontier. The following year they moved to the nearby town of Red Cloud, where C. remained until she finished high school. She entered the University of Nebraska and while still an undergraduate began publishing short stories. She also wrote a weekly column and served as drama critic for the *Nebraska State Journal*. The year after her graduation she moved to Pittsburgh, where she spent several years working as a journalist and then taught for five years in Pittsburgh high schools. In 1906 she went to New York City to be on the staff of *McClure's Magazine*; she was managing editor from 1909 until she left the magazine in 1911 to devote herself full time to writing.

When C. left *McClure's* she had already published a book of verse (*April Twilights*, 1903) and a collection of Jamesian short stories (*The Troll Garden*, 1905), and had written a novel (*Alexander's Bridge*, 1912). But she did not develop the style and subject matter that were uniquely hers until she wrote *O Pioneers!*, a novel of the Nebraska frontier, which appeared in 1913. Lyrical, lucent, slowpaced in style, it evokes the land as an almost personal presence, and places the human stories of its characters in a setting that is realistic but also quietly resonant with mythic undertones. *My Ántonia* (1918), considered by some critics to be C.'s finest work, also celebrates the land and the immigrant pioneers, linking them to heroic adventurers like Coronado on a mythic quest and seeing in the enduring figure of Ántonia an image of the life-force itself.

The theme of the quest or journey also appears in *The Song of the Lark* (1915), where it takes the form of the singer Thea Kronberg's pursuit of artistic excellence. The desire for artistic achievement had been an important metaphor for C. since her college days; she continued to explore different aspects of it in the short stories about artists and would-be artists collected under the title *Youth and the Bright Medusa* (1920).

C. was gravely distressed by the spiritual aridity and loss of humane values that accompanied the growth of materialism and technology in the 20th c., particularly in the years following World War I. *A Lost Lady* (1923) and *The Professor's House* (1925) reflect C.'s judgment of contemporary society. The background of *A Lost Lady* provides the contrast between the heroic, generous, great-shouldered men who built the West in the pioneer period and the petty, cruel, and avaricious men of the present. Marian Forrester, the beautiful lost lady of the title, is caught in the decline of values and proves to have no resources of her own with which to cope with the new age. *The Professor's House* presents a world devoted to money, status, and acquisitiveness; its contrast is provided by the section called "Tom Outland's Story," which deals with the ancient Indian civilization of the cliff dwellers of the Southwest, who built a miniature city in stone that, in its organic relationship to its environment, was "worthy to be a home for man." The modern world, C. implies, offers no worthy home for man, but Professor St. Peter, the protagonist of the novel, is left at the end with at least a suggestion that there are fragments which, to paraphrase T. S. ELIOT, he can shore against his ruins.

A Lost Lady exemplifies what C. referred to as the "novel *démeublé*" (unfurnished), written with restraint, clarity, and absence of unnecessary detail. It has often been compared to *Madame Bovary* and has been called a "nearly perfect novel." Very similar to *A Lost Lady* in its narrative structure and *démeublé* style is *My Mortal Enemy* (1926), a short novel about a beautiful, dominating, and selfish woman who is at once attractive and repellent.

Death Comes for the Archbishop (1927) is based on the historical figures of Archbishop Jean Lamy, the first bishop of New Mexico, and his companion, Father Machebeauf. The novel is built out of a series of painting-like vignettes, some realistic, some legendary in subject, but all contributing to the evocation of a feeling of timelessness and serenity. *Shadows on the Rock* (1931), set in 17th-c. Quebec, is quite different in structure but is (thematically) similar in that it deals with the engrafting of the Catholic faith and traditions of Europe on a new land.

Obscure Destinies (1932), a collection of three short stories, marks the end of C.'s major work, though two more novels were published before her death and one collection of short stories appeared posthumously. The first two stories in *Obscure Destinies*, "Neighbour Rosicky" and "Old Mrs. Harris," are among C.'s finest.

Although a romantic in the importance she placed on the imagination and on the evocation of feeling, C. is a classicist in style and in her reverence for enduring values. The simplicity of the surfaces in many of her novels is handled with high artistry. There has been a tendency in C. criticism to fault her for a nostalgic

Willa Cather

celebration of the past and a rejection of the present, and some critics have interpreted her work as the expression of a person who failed to reach emotional maturity and was embittered in her old age. Nevertheless, interest in her as a writer is growing, and there is an increasing appreciation of the artistry and the thematic richness and subtlety of her work.

FURTHER WORKS: *One of Ours* (1922); *Lucy Gayheart* (1935); *Not under Forty* (1936); *Sapphira and the Slave Girl* (1940); *The Old Beauty and Others* (1948); *W. C. on Writing* (1949); *Writings from W. C.'s Campus Years* (1950); *Collected Short Fiction, 1892–1912* (1965); *The Kingdom of Art: W. C.'s First Principles and Critical Statements* (1967); *The World and the Parish: W. C.'s Article and Reviews, 1893–1902* (1970); *Uncle Valentine and Other Stories: W. C.'s Uncollected Short Fiction 1915-1929* (1973)

BIBLIOGRAPHY: Brown, E. K., *W. C.: A Critical Biography* (1953); Randall, J. H., *The Landscape and the Looking Glass: W. C.'s Search for Value* (1960); Bloom, E. A., *W. C.'s Gift of Sympathy* (1962); Van Ghent, D., *W. C.* (1964); Woodress, J., *W. C.: Her Life and Art* (1970); McFarland, D. T., *W. C.* (1972); Gerber, P., *W. C.* (1975); Stouck, D., *W. C.'s Imagination* (1975); Rosowski, S. J., *The Voyage Perilous: W. C.'s Romanticism* (1986); O'Brien, S., *W. C.: The Emerging Voice* (1987); Woodress, J., *W. C.: A Literary Life* (1987); Wagenknecht, E., *W. C.* (1994)

—DOROTHY TUCK MCFARLAND

CAVAFY, C(onstantine) P.

(Konstantinos Petrou Kavafis) Greek poet, b. 17 April 1863, Alexandria, Egypt; d. 29 April 1933, Alexandria, Egypt

The Cavafys, a wealthy family of the Greek diaspora, came originally from Constantinople, Turkey, where C. lived from 1880 to 1885, after his schooling in England. The family subsequently settled in Alexandria for good; the family's prosperity declined, and C. was compelled to work in the Irrigation Service, from which he retired in 1922. Enjoying his family's respectable position in the cosmopolitan society of Alexandria, C. led an uneventful life of routine, which was interrupted only by deaths of close relatives and short trips to Athens, France, England, and Italy for reasons of health or diversion.

C. started writing poetry in purist (*katharevousa*) Greek, in English, and in French in the 1880s, under the influence of late-Victorian and Decadent European models, as well as of Ancient Greek epigrams and lyrics and other literary, historical, classical, Hellenistic, Byzantine, and even demotic sources. Later, abandoning his unrealistic attempts to compose in foreign tongues, C. concentrated on the semiformal language spoken by educated Greeks in Alexandria, which he enriched with puristic, New Testament, and colloquial diction as the situations in his poems warranted.

C. wrote some two hundred fifty poems, fourteen of which appeared in a pamphlet in 1904 (enlarged private edition, 1910). Several dozen appeared in subsequent years in a number of privately printed booklets and broadsheets; these editions contained mostly the same poems, first arranged thematically, and then chronologically. He published no volume of poetry during his lifetime, and close to one third of his poems were never printed in any form while he lived. The first appearance of his work in book form came in *Piimata* (1935; *The Poems of C. P. C.*, 1951), posthumously published in Alexandria.

C. composed rhymed as well as free verse (mostly in later lyrics) but never loose, unstructured, or irregular poems. He used iambic, eleven-syllable lines and other measures, including the popular fifteen-syllable verse of the demotic tradition. His style is often dramatic, as in the famous "Perimenontas tous Varvarous" (1904; "Waiting for the Barbarians," 1924), and his subject matter is frequently historical. Many poems, such as "Ithaki" (1911; "Ithaca," 1924) are oracular and quasi-didactic, while others are narrative, psychological, contemplative, or even confessional, especially his candid although tactful homosexual poems like "O themenos omos" (1919; "The Bandaged Shoulder," 1971), an honest and powerful lyric much admired by Lawrence DURRELL.

The poet himself had arranged his pieces as historical, philosophical, and personal (erotic); in reality, however, all his poems present or examine man in various contexts and historical moments in specific localities, and they constitute sophisticated commentaries on man's adventure, be it of the mind, the soul, or the flesh. Despite the limited number of his compositions, C. succeeded in sketching a rich gallery of historical, semiobscure, or fictitious characters, whom he used as personae acting, or being discussed, in the episodes of his poems.

Varying tone and mood, although preferring a subtly ironic tone and an unadorned, dry, functional language (with a minimum of figures of speech), C. turned the centers of the Hellenistic world—especially Alexandria—into a legendary landscape of the mind where past and present, East and West, Greek and "barbarian,"

meet and become fused into a universal sensibility that comments aptly on the human condition of all times, notwithstanding the use of extremely specific details from his ethnic and personal experiences. Perhaps the best-known Greek poet of modern times, C. was never a chauvinist or a narrowly patriotic artist despite the pride he felt and expressed as a member of the Hellenic nation.

The poet and translator Robert Fitzgerald (1910–1985) called C. the "inventor of a modernity and an Alexandrianism of his own, so pungent and of such sad, dry elevation that his work transcends his language and century." The English novelist John FOWLES confessed that C. "is for me not only the great poet of the Levant, but of all culture in decline—which makes him universal in this century." George STEINER remarked that C.'s "secret music and learned sadness elips have influenced other currents in modern poetry." Indeed, W. H. AUDEN and Lawrence DURRELL often alluded to his influence on their artistic developments, as E. M. FORSTER had done when he persuaded T. S. ELIOT to publish several C. lyrics in *The Criterion* in 1924. Durrell based his famous tetralogy, *The Alexandria Quartet*, on the Alexandrian climate of decadence and even on some characters found in the poems of C. Few of Greece's recent poets have escaped his impact—the 1963 Nobel Laureate George SEFERIS was his ardent admirer—but no one was able even to approximate the personal tone, style, and quasi-existential angst of the epigrammatic, laconic pieces that were C.'s trademark. His poems have been translated into English, French, Italian, and German, and several other languages, and his position as a major 20th-c. poet is secure.

FURTHER WORKS: *Apanta, I, 1896–1918* (1963); *Peza* (1963); *Anekdhota piimata 1882–1923* (1968); *In Simple Clothes: Occcasional Works* (1992); *Collected Poems* (1992); *Greek Poems of C. C.* (1994); *Essential C.* (1995). FURTHER WORKS IN ENGLISH: *The Complete Poems of* C. P. C. (1961); *Passions and Ancient Days: New Poems* (1971); *Selected Poems* (1972); C.'s *Complete Poems* (1976); *Collected Poems* (1976); *The Greek Poems of C. P. C.* (2 vols., 1989)

BIBLIOGRAPHY: Forster, E. M., *Pharos and Pharillon* (1923): 91–97; Bowra, C. M., *The Creative Experiment* (1949): 29–60; Sherrard, P., *The Marble Threshing Floor* (1956): 83–123; Bien, P., *C. C.* (1964); Friar, K., *Modern Greek Poetry* (1973): 22–27; Liddell, R., *C.: A Critical Biography* (1974); Keeley, E., *C.'s Alexandria: Study of Myth in Progress* (1976); Pinchin, J. L., *Alexandria Still: Forster, Durrell*, and *C.* (1977); Jusdanis, G., *The Poetics of C.: Textuality, Eroticism, History* (1987); Robinson, C., *C. P. C.* (1988)

—M. BYRON RAIZIS

CAYROL, Jean

French novelist and poet, b. 6 June 1911, Bordeaux

After studies in law and philology, C. became a librarian. He published his first book of poems, *Le Hollandais volant* (the flying Dutchman), in 1936. He was arrested by the Germans in 1942 for Resistance activities and deported to Mauthausen concentration camp.

Although he continued to write poetry, after his return to France he began to publish novels. *Je vivrai l'amour des autres* (1947–50;

I will live the love of others), which won the Renaudot Prize, recounts the return from Hitler's camps of a man who appears as out of place as Lazarus back from the grave. His two other best-received works have been *Les corps étrangers* (1959; *Foreign Bodies*, 1960), whose title refers to ways in which both the world's objects and fictive memories inhabit the person of the narrator, and *Je l'entends encore* (1968; I still hear it), in which a son rewrites his father's life.

In retrospect, C.'s early postwar novels have been seen as precursors of the NEW NOVEL, although they lack the brilliance of some of its better-known exponents. Yet C. has always pursued his own path, one marked by his passage through the border posts between life and death, reality and nightmare, which Mauthausen literally came to signify. His work, despite a diversity attributable to an apparent desire to confront the modern world in all its tedium and danger (more recently, the oppressive technology of modern warfare, the life on an errant salesman, the hopeless itinerary of a fleeing wife), is unified by a consistently engaging search through memory in which the reader begins to lose his way, for the memories are invented, nothing is sure, and the narrating voice is plural.

C. has collaborated on films with Alain Resnais; best known among these are *Nuit et brouillard* (1956; night and fog), a haunting documentary of the concentration camps, and *Muriel* (1964; Muriel).

FURTHER WORKS: *Les poèmes du pasteur Grimm* (1936); *Le dernier homme* (1939); *Les phénomènes célestes* (1939); *Miroir de la rédemption* (1943); *Poèmes de la nuit et du brouillard* (1945); *Passe-temps de l'homme et des oiseaux* (1947); *La vie répond* (1948); *La noire* (1949); *Lazare parmi nous* (1950); *Le vent de la mémoire* (1952); *Les mots sont aussi des demeures* (1952); *L'espace d'une nuit* (1954; *All in a Night*, 1957); *Manessier* (1955); *Pour tous les temps* (1955); *Le déménagement* (1956); *La gaffe* (1957); *Le chantier natal* (1959); *Les plains et les déliés* (1959); *Le droit du regard* (1963); *Le froid du soleil* (1963); *Muriel* (1964); *Le coup de grâce* (1965); *Midi-minuit* (1966); *De l'espace humain* (1968); *Poésie-journal* (1969); *Histoire d'une prairie* (1969); *N'oubliez pas que nous nous aimons* (1971); *Histoire d'un désert* (1972); *Histoire de la mer* (1973); *Lectures* (1973); *Kakemono Hôtel* (1974); *Histoire de la forêt* (1975); *Histoire d'une maison* (1976); *Poésie-journal, tome II, 1975–1976* (1977); *Histoire du ciel* (1979); *Les enfants pillards* (1979); *Exposés au soleil* (1980)

BIBLIOGRAPHY: Lynes, C., "J. C.," *The Novelist as Philosopher* (1962): 183–205; Barthes, R., Afterword to *Les corps étrangers* (1964): 233–47; Oster, D., *J. C. et son œuvre* (1969); Carrol, D., "J. C. on the Fiction of the Writer," *MLN*, 88 (1973): 789–810; Edmond, P., *La mort dans le miroir: Écriture et représentation romanesque dans "La noire" de J. C.* (1974)

—RANDOLPH RUNYON

CELA, Camilo José

Spanish novelist and essayist, b. 11 May 1916, Iria-Flavia

C. belongs to the Generation of 1936, whose writers and intellectuals came of age during the Spanish Republic and the civil

Camilo José Cela

war. Born into a large middle-class family (his mother was of British origin), C. lived a varied and sometimes hazardous youth: he had a bout with tuberculosis, was wounded while fighting on the Nationalist side during the civil war, and was a traveler and the author of SURREALIST poems. In addition to pursuing a literary career, he became a serious student of regional Spanish history and local folkways and an erudite lexicographer of vulgar speech. C. was elected to the Spanish Academy of Letters in 1957. He is the editor of the literary review *Papeles de Son Armadans*; and during the 1960s the firm of Alfaguara, which he owned, published a number of young novelists as well as many scholarly books. Recently he has become interested in the theater; his modernized version of the early Renaissance classic *La Celestina* was staged in 1978.

C. is considered a master stylist and a bold innovator of prose genres. One of the outstanding novelists of the Franco era, C. offers a literary synthesis of Spain's national tragedy. Yet his political and ethical positions elude definition, and he has never espoused a literature of social commitment in the manner of some of his contemporaries.

C. burst on the literary scene in 1942 with *La familia de Pascual Duarte* (*The Family of Pascual Duarte*, 1964), a novel in which a primitive criminal awaiting execution for the murder of his mother tells in first-person naration of the cruel and senseless events of his life. This book inaugurated the so-called *tremendismo* movement, with its aesthetic of gratuitous violence and stark irrationality. It remains a modern classic that may be interpreted in many ways: on its psychological and structural terms; as the symbolic expression of a repressed people condemned to a dictatorial regime; or as the spiritual reflection of CAMUS's *The Stranger*.

C.'s subsequent novels are experimental in form and are marked by overtones of EXISTENTIALISM, brutal realism, and experiments with narrative time. The static, symmetrically constructed *Pabellón de reposo* (1944; *Rest Home*, 1961), which takes place in a sanatorium, records the process of dying as experienced by seven characters. In contrast, the picaresque *Nuevas andanzas y desventuras de Lazarillo de Tormes* (1944; new adventures and mishaps of Lazarillo of Tormes) presents a lively diversity of scenes and events, remodeling the traditional story of the social underdog by shuffling the conventional time sequence.

C.'s second major novel was *La colmena* (1951; *The Hive*, 1953), originally published in Latin America and banned in Spain for several years because of its pessimistic rendering of postwar Madrid and its people's moral bankruptcy. The very precision of its moods, its poignancy in depicting hunger and social callousness, indeed, the novel's fidelity to everyday urban speech, all contributed to its immediate success and to its being considered subversive by the Spanish governments censors. *La colmena* avoids direct moral judgments, yet such is the self-condemnatory nature of conditions as they are reported that the narrative opened new vistas for subsequent writers to pursue in cultivating the so-called "behaviorist" novel of the 1950s. In structure, *La colmena* resembles DOS PASSOS's *Manhattan Transfer*; it is a montage of cinematic fragments, temporally disjoined but able to interconnect the lives of several hundred personages. This radical form stimulated other Spanish writers to try innovative methods of narration, and it gave the rising generation a hitherto rare taste for technical experimentation.

Other novels by C. reflect aesthetic experimentation and technical virtuosity. *Mrs. Caldwell habla con su hijo* (1953; *Mrs. Caldwell Speaks to Her Son*, 1968) is a surrealist exploration into incestuous psychopathology, while *La catira* (1955; the blonde), set in Venezuela, is a tour de force of Latin American speech, less interesting for its echoes of Valle-Inclan's *Tirano Banderas* than for the controversial lexical mixtures that spice its tale of violent emotions.

Taken as a group, the six novels discussed above are heterogeneous and somewhat discontinuous. They are not steps in any discernible evolution that might logically lead to further creative development. After these novels C. turned to other literary genres for more than a decade, with the exception of *Tobogán de hambrientos* (1962; toboggan of the hungry), whose elusive, novel-like form offers an array of one hundred vignettes, organized into two "movements" in a circular way, the second movement being a reverse parallel to the first.

C. returned to the long narrative form with *San Camilo, 1936* (1969; *Saint Camilo, 1936*, 1991), his third novel of major import. The applause and consternation that followed its publication occurred this time not only because of the now familiar stylistic shock waves but also because of new factors arising from liberalized censorship regulations. Heretofore under Franco, literature was allowed only occasional and mildly allusive eroticism. In the regime's final phases, however, C. went beyond these limitations and used explicitly sexual language in this almost pornographic novel. Just as scandalous to all but the historical mythmakers is his depiction of Spain on the eve of civil war; he seemed to imply that Republican democracy could be equated with degraded sexuality and uncontrollable violence. Yet another source of titillation in this important work are the apparently autobiographical elements.

Readers are thus encouraged to raise the general question of C.'s ideological position during the Franco era. That his youthful protagonist, who is about to be drafted, is as indifferent to politics as he is preoccupied by sexual desire may or may not actually reflect C.'s own past; more certain is the silence on social and moral questions of C.'s novels and essays, with their obsession with language for the sake of its own pleasures.

The stylistically complicated monologue of *San Camilo, 1936*, using stream-of-consciousness techniques, was followed by intense syntactical turgidity in a later novel, *Oficio de tinieblas 5* (1973; ministry of darkness, 5). Consisting of over one thousand unpunctuated short paragraphs and prose fragments, the second-person narrative is, in C.'s own words, "not a novel but, naturally, a purging of my heart." Part sadistic and religio-erotic, and part defiantly obscure, it carries on the most controversial themes and language of *San Camilo 1936*.

C. has also achieved renown for having developed the genre of the "vagabondage" or book of travels. Most famous is the earliest and stylistically least self-conscious *Viaje a la Alcarria* (1948; *Journey to the Alcarria*, 1964). It presents on one level an escape from the complex and demoralized urban civilization to the unpretentiousness of rural culture. While country life is as economically impoverished as city life, and its antiquities and monuments fallen into decay, its vitality continues to be replenished through the perennial values and spirit of the common people. On a second level, the book is a quest for the deeper rhythms of Spanish history. By chronicling the day-to-day details of human subsistence, giving ample space to the physical environment and emotional life that shape basic experience, the detached traveler reconstructs the eternal attributes that sustain the continuities and resilience of the masses.

The historical element grows stronger in *Judíos, moros, y cristianos* (1956; Jews, Moors, and Christians), while the regions visited grow more numerous in later journeys, described in volumes such as *Del Miño al Bidasoa* (1952; from the Miño River to the Bidasoa), *Primer viaje andaluz* (1959; first Andalusian journey), and *Viaje al Pirineo de Lérida* (1965; journey to the Pyrenees of Lérida). In C.'s hands, the travel genre is a peripatetic cultural anatomy that defines Spain's national character. It has become a widely imitated literary form owing to yet a third level of significance. For sheer stylistic virtuosity, travel accounts provide endless opportunities to describe landscapes and picturesque individuals. C.'s enduring achievement is to have given an aesthetic dimension to reporting.

A final cluster of books attests to C.'s genius. His short stories, sketches, and vignettes constitute a genre in theselves, which he refers to as the "Carpeto-Vetonian etching," an allusion to the mountainous regions of central Iberia. These pieces are infused with pungent humor, sarcasm, pathos, bitterness, and love. They evoke the paintings and engravings of Goya and Gutiérrez Solana in their deformed vision of aspects of underdeveloped society—particularly in descriptions of beggars, blind men, and village idiots—although they also feature gentler, more colorful types. Stylistically they resemble Damon Runyon's (1880-1946) New Yorkese, but they have more authenticity.

The prolific, rich, and original literary production of C. assures him a place among the giants of Spanish literature. Some critics have reproached him for his political ambiguity and others for sensationalism. Yet his work will transcend any momentary judgments: his writing has taken root in the traditions of the Spanish language and has transformed its expressive capacities. The results have already stimulated countless interpretations of his work. In 1989, C. was awarded the Nobel Prize for Literature.

FURTHER WORKS: *Esas nubes que pasan* (1945); *Mesa revuelta* (1945); *Pisando la dudosa luz del día* (1945); *El gallego y su cuadrilla* (1949); *Baraja de invenciones* (1953); *El molino de viento* (1956); *Nuevo retablo de don Cristobita* (1957); *La rueda de los ocios* (1957); *Los cuatro ángeles de San Silvestre* (1957); *Cajón de sastre* (1957); *Historias de España. Los ciegos. Los tontos* (1958); *La obra literaria del pintor Solana* (1958); *La cucaña, memorias* (1959); *Cuaderno de Guadarrama* (1959); *Los viejos amigos* (2 vols., 1960, 1961); *Cuatro figuras del '98* (1961); *Obra completa* (10 vols., 1962–1978); *Gavilla de fábulas sin amor* (1962); *El solitario* (1963); *Once cuentos de futbol* (1963); *Toreo de salón* (1963); *Las compañías convenientes* (1963); *Garito de hospicianos* (1963); *Izas, rabizas, y colipoterras* (1964); *El ciudadano Iscariote Reclus* (1965); *Nuevas escenas matritenses* (2 vols., 1965, 1966); *Páginas de geografía errabunda* (1965); *La familia del héroe* (1965); *Madrid* (1966); *Viaje a U.S.A.* (1967); *María Sabina* (1967); *Diccionario secreto* (2 vols., 1968, 1971); *Al servicio de algo* (1969); *Bola del mundo* (1972); *Cristino Mallo* (1973); *A vueltas con España* (1973); *Balada del vagabundo sin suerte* (1973); *El tacatá oxidado* (1974); *El reto de los halcones* (1975); *Rol de cornudos* (1976); *Enciclopedia del erotismo* (1977); *Los sueños vanos, los ángeles curiosos* (1979)

BIBLIOGRAPHY: Kirsner, R., *The Novels of C. J. C.* (1963); Foster, D. W., *Forms of the Novel in the Work of C. J. C.* (1967); McPheeters, D. W., *C. J. C.* (1969); Suárex Solís, S., *El léxico de C. J. C.* (1969); Kronik, E., "Interview: C. J. C.," *Diacritics*, 2 (1972): 42–45; Seator, L. H., "The Antisocial Humanism of C. and Hemingway," *REH*, 9 (1975): 425–39; Wicks, U., "Onlyman," *Mosaic*, 8, 3 (1975): 21–47; Dougherty, D., "Form and Structure in *La colmena*: From Alienation to Community," *ANP*, 1 (1976): 7–23; Ilie, P., "The Politics of Obscenity in *San Camilo, 1936*," *ANP*, 1 (1976): 25–63; Fody, M., "*La familia de Pascual Duarte* and *L'étranger*: A Contrast," *WVUPP*, 24 (1977): 68–73; Thomas, M. D., "Narrative Tension and Structural Unity in C.'s *La familia de Pascual Duarte*," *Symposium*, 31 (1977): 165–78; Ilie, P., *La novelística de C. J. C.* (3rd ed., 1978)

—PAUL ILIE

CELAN, Paul

(pseud. of Paul Antschel) Austrian poet, translator, and essayist, b. 23 Nov. 1920, Cernăuti, Romania (earlier Czernowitz in the Austro-Hungarian Empire; now Chernovtsy, Ukrainian S.S.R.); d. 2 April 1970, Paris, France

C., the only child of German-speaking Jewish parents, studied medicine, as well as languages and literature. His parents were killed in the Holocaust, while C. escaped death by working in a Nazi labor camp. After the liberation of Romania by the Soviet army, he continued his language studies, but he left Romania for Vienna in 1947, only to move on to Paris in 1948, where he lived until his death, by suicide.

C.'s early poems, published in book form in the widely acclaimed collection *Mohn und Gedächtnis* (1952; poppy and memory), which also reprints previously published pieces, have many of the attributes of SURREALISM, among them a dreamlike association of diverse images. In C.'s work, however, unlike in surrealism, dream is not necessarily a positive force; it is multifunctional, as are all of C.'s poetic structures. Dream may be used to banish the horrors of the past, yet it recreates them in nightmarish images; it may lead to new creativity or a utopian perspective, but in the hands of a concentration camp guard it turns into a deadly weapon, as when he dreams—in "Todesfuge" (1945; "Death Fugue," 1959)—of his "master race": "Death is a master from Germany."

This multifunctionality constantly evokes traditional poetic conceptions only to undermine them in an ever-shifting relationship of the thing named and the name itself, thereby indicating that there is no ontological reality that determines the name (of that reality) once and for all. C., as well as other writers after 1945, were well aware of the fact that after Auschwitz and Hiroshima certain words had changed their connotations forever—the events altered the very meaning of words. And what will things be called after an even more horrifying repetition? Beginning with *Sprachgitter* (1959; *Speech-Grille*, 1971), the way in which he uses words like "breath," "breathing," "Strahlenwind" (radioactive wind), and "ashes" on at least one level refer to these horrifying questions.

Although the trend was first discernible in *Von Schwelle zu Schwelle* (1955; from threshold to threshold), with *Sprachgitter* C.'s poems became more and more condensed, with the vocabulary reflecting back on itself. Key words such as "stone," "ice," and "snow" are now taken out of their former poetic contexts with the intention of abolishing the prevalent misconception that there still was a poetically transformable world, a world that C's poetic method had been continually deconstructing. The poetic word "flower," for instance, won from the darkness of destruction, is now a word of and for the blind, that is, for those whose eyes had failed them when faced with the memories of the Holocaust again and again. Such *Blindenworte* indicate that the perception of reality, and hence the search for a better world, has been severely handicapped.

Die Niemandsrose (1963; the no-one's rose) marks a return to Jewish themes, although in an inverted manner. It is not the absence of God that is lamented, but rather the terrible meaninglessness of human suffering, and the urgent need to eliminate it. The words themselves, dismembered, become the wound that cannot be healed, because society is continually inflicting new wounds by not removing the causes of the old ones. The volume ends with the absurd and blasphemous image of the "clubfoot of the gods" stumbling over piled-up mountains of corpses.

C. continued fragmentation of words, in even more condensed verse lines, in his last four volumes: *Atemwende* (1967; breathturning), *Fadensonnen* (1968; thread-suns), *Lichtzwang* (1970; light-compulsion), and *Schneepart* (1971; snow-part), the last two posthumously published. Yet the increasingly abstract quality can be neither hailed nor criticized as a celebration of obscure postwar poetry, since the poems regard abstraction as a loss: Man himself has become an abstraction. All this is expressed in an ironic tone mixing many different idioms (technical, political, scientific), out of which results a certain type of BLACK HUMOR. Only in death, so it seems at times, can man become himself. But this, as C. has implied in "Der Meridian" (1960; "The Meridian," 1978)—his most important speech on modern poetry and poetics, given when he received the prestigious Georg Büchner Prize—is an extreme answer to an extremely dehumanizing situation, namely an allegorical gesture of veneration to Her Majesty the Absurd, who thus testifies to the presence of humanity.

The overall vision of C.'s poetry and poetics can be summarized as absurdity driven to its extreme limits, where man may set himself free so that he can liberate "the other," still-unknown truly human person.

C. has also masterfully translated and adapted the works of poets of at least six languages, among them MANDELSHTAM, BRETON, CHAR, APOLLINAIRE, UNGARETTI, PESSOA, Rimbaud, Emily Dickinson, and Shakespeare.

FURTHER WORKS: *Edgar Jené und der Traum vom Traume* (1948); *Der Sand aus den Urnen* (1948); *Gedichte* (2 vols., 1975); *Zeitgehöft* (1976). FURTHER WORKS IN ENGLISH: *Speech-Grille and Selected Poems* (1971); *Selected Poems* (1972); *Poems* (1980, bilingual); *Last Poems* (1986); *Collected Prose* (1986); *Poems of P. C.* (1989)

BIBLIOGRAPHY: Lyon, J. K., "The Poetry of P. C.: An Approach," *GR*, 39 (1964): 50-67; Stewart, C., "P.C.: Modes of Silence—Some Observations on *Sprachgitter*," *MLR*, 67 (1972): 127–42; Glenn, J., *P. C.* (1973); Meinecke, D., ed., *Über P. C.*, 2nd ed. (1973); Janz, M., *Vom Engagement absoluter Poesie: Zur Lyrik und Ästhetik P. C.s* (1976); Pretzer, L. A., *Geschichts- und sozialkritische Dimensionen in P. C.s. Werk* (1980); Menninghaus, W., *P. C.: Magie der Form* (1980); Chalfen, I., *P. C.: A Biography of His Youth* (1991)

—LIELO A. PRETZER

CELAYA, Gabriel

(pseud. of Rafael Múgica) Spanish poet and essayist, b. 18 March 1911, Hernani; d. 18 Apr. 1991, Madrid

C. attended elementary and high school in San Sebastián. In 1927 he moved to Madrid for preuniversity studies and for his subsequent enrollment in the school of engineering, while also devoting much of his time to writing and participating in the active literary life at the Students' Residence. In 1935 he published his first book of poetry, *Marea de silencio* (tide of silence), and finished a second, *La soledad cerrada* (1936; enclosed solitude), for which he was awarded the Bécquer Centennial Prize. During his career he has been awarded four major literary prizes, in Spain, Italy, and France. C.'s evolution as a poet shows several distinct phases. His SURREALIST poetry, written between 1934 and 1944, is characterized by an overwhelming conglomeration of irrational images within an uneven rhythmical pattern, which underscores the subconscious nature of his poetic visions. The moon, the sea, night, birds, colors, angels, and virgins are typical recurring symbols the poet employs to affirm his solidarity with the world and to delve into the instant of time, the here and now, which is a source of life and joy.

All this changed, however, between 1947 and 1954, when present reality (the here and now) became not a source of joy but of EXISTENTIALIST anguish. His poetic diction became less metaphorical; he was writing not for the specialist or an intellectual elite, but for the masses, a purpose typified in *Tranquilamente hablando* (1947; talking calmly). This change coincided with the mental and spiritual crises caused by family and personal problems. Between 1954 and 1962 C. became the leading writer of

"social poetry" in Spain. He regarded poetry as an instrument for transforming the world, an instrument not to conquer beauty or to seek aesthetic perfection or pleasure, but to fight against social injustices and class inequalities; *Cantos íberos* (1955; Iberian songs) is one of the important volumes of this phase. By this time his poems had acquired a more dramatic, anecdotal structure and language, a more prosaic texture.

During the 1960s and 1970s C. at first returned to his early style, as in *La linterna sorda* (1964; the deaf lantern) but later moved into the realm of the absurd to express his pessimistic view of a meaningless and nonsensical society, with, for example, *Función de Uno, Equis, Ene* (1973; the function of One, X, and N).

In addition to some fifty books of poetry, C. has also written extensively on poetic theory, social poetry, and the way social poetry was practiced in Spain in the years following the civil war. Of special importance are *El arte como lenguaje* (1951; art as language), *Exploración de la poesía* (1964; exploration of poetry), and *Inquisició de la poesía* (1972; inquisition of poetry).

FURTHER WORKS: *Movimientos elementales* (1947); *Objetos poéticos* (1948); *Se parece al amor* (1949); *Deriva* (1950); *Los espejos transparentes* (1968); *Cien poemas de un amor* (1971); *Buenos días, buenas noches* (1976)

BIBLIOGRAPHY: Cohen, J. M., "Since the Civil War: New Currents in Spanish Poetry," *Encounter*, 12, 2 (1959): 44–53; Luis, L. de, "Primera suma poética de G. C.," *RO*, No. 87 (1970): 319–27; Ugalde, K. S., *G. C.* (1978)

—VICENTE CABRERA

CÉLINE, Louis-Ferdinand

(pseud. of Louis-Ferdinand Destouches) French novelist, b. 27 May 1894, Courbevoie; d. 1 July 1961, Meudon

Dr. L.-F. Destouches became famous overnight under the pseudonym L.-F. Céline (one of his mother's given names) at thirty-eight, when his first novel *Voyage au bout de la nuit* (1932; *Journey to the End of Night*, 1934) was published and was a finalist in the Goncourt Prize competition. An immediate commercial success, it also shook the French literary world to its foundations, and was to be a major turning point in the author's life. This long novel draws upon C.'s biography up to 1932, although the actual events of his life are rearranged and re-created to fit in this epic tale of the journey of a modern antihero, Ferdinand Bardamu.

C. was born into a lower-middle-class family. His parents had planned a commercial career for him, and he was placed in apprenticeship, although he wanted to become a doctor. Having enlisted in the cavalry in 1912, he was sergeant when the war broke out. In October 1914 he was severely wounded and cited for extraordinary courage under fire. He was then assigned to the French passport office in London. In 1916 he went to Africa and spent a year as a commercial agent in the Cameroons. Back in France, he completed his secondary studies at the age of twenty-five and started medical studies. After receiving his degree in 1924, in the following year he left his practice, his wife, and his child to work for the League of Nations. Under its aegis he traveled to

Switzerland, England, the Cameroons, Cuba, Canada, and the U.S. In Detroit he studied working conditions in the Ford factory. In 1928 he set up private practice in the working-class Paris suburb of Clichy while writing *Voyage au bout de la nuit* in his spare time.

The extraordinary success of this book, which covered the main events of his life from 1913 to 1932, encouraged him to undertake the story of his first eighteen years. Completed four years later, *Mort à crédit* (1936; *Death on the Installment Plan*, 1938) confirmed C.'s reputation as one of France's major writers.

After two months spent in the U.S.S.R., C. wrote a pamphlet, *Mea culpa* (1936, *Mea Culpa*, 1937) denouncing the lies of Communist propaganda concerning the Soviet system. He started work on a third novel but interrupted it because he thought it was more urgent to try to prevent his country from entering a new war that he thought would be disastrous. In a short time he wrote two huge pamphlets, *Bagatelles pour un massacre* (1937; trifles for a massacre) and *École des cadavres* (1938; school for cadavers) in which he denounced a "Jewish international conspiracy" in France, England, and the U.S. to declare war on Hitler's Germany. His violent diatribes also express the fears of an anti-Semitic petit bourgeois who bitterly resented Léon Blum's Popular Front government (1936–38). After the collapse of France in 1940, C. wrote his last pamphlet on contemporary politics, *Les beaux draps* (1941; a nice mess). He continued to practice medicine and write novels. In July 1944 he fled to Germany to avoid a summary execution by the French Resistance for his alleged collaboration with the Germans. He did not reach Denmark, where he had deposited his savings, until March 1945. After six years of exile in Denmark, he was amnestied in 1951 and returned to France. Under contract with the publishing house of Gallimard, he practiced medicine in Meudon and wrote novels. Until his death he published seven books and managed to recapture an audience.

The story of his adventures and travels in the crumbling Reich at the end of World War II perfectly suited his apocalyptic vision and constitutes the material of a grandiose trilogy considered by many as his masterpiece: *D'un château l'autre* (1957; *Castle to Castle*, 1968), *Nord* (1960; *North*, 1971) and *Rigodon* (1969; *Rigadoon*, 1974). His first novel, however, would suffice to insure his claim on posterity. The impact of its innovative style on French writers was immediate and lasting: the French novel has not been the same since. It is a pessimistic view of a mad, mad world and of a "fallen" man. But its uncompromising attacks against war, colonialism, and the night-marish conditions of urban, industrial life in modern civilization have lost nothing of their freshness and punch. Contemporary American writers like Henry MILLER, Jack KEROUAC, Joseph HELLER, Kurt VONNEGUT, Jr., William BURROUGHS, and Ken KESEY are all in his debt.

FURTHER WORKS: *La vie et l'œuvre de Philippe-Ignace Semmelweis* (1924; *The Life and Work of Semmelweis*, 1937); *L'église* (1933); *Guignol's Band I* (1944; *Guignol's Band*, 1954); *Casse-pipe* (1949); *Féerie pour une autre fois I* (1952); *Normance: Féerie pour une autre fois II* (1954); *Entretiens avec le Professeur Y* (1955); *Ballets sans musique, sans personne, sans rien* (1959); *Le pont de Londres: Guignol's Band II* (1964)

BIBLIOGRAPHY: Hindus, M., *The Crippled Giant* (1950; rev. ed., 1986); Ostrovski, E., *C. and His Vision* (1967); Ostrovski, E., *Voyeur, Voyant: A Portrait of L.-F. C.* (1971); Thiher, A., *C.: The Novel as Delirium* (1972); Knapp, B., *C.: Man of Hate* (1974);

Louis-Ferdinand Céline

McCarthy, P., *C.* (1975); O'Connell, D., *L.-F. C.* (1976); Matthews, J. H., *The Inner Dream: C. as Novelist* (1978); Vitoux, F., *C.: A Biography* (1992)

—FREDERIC J. GROVER

CENDRARS, Blaise

(pseud. of Frédéric Louis Sauser) Swiss poet and novelist (writing in French), b. 1 Sept. 1887, La Chaux-de-Fonds; d. 21 Jan. 1961, Paris, France

The biographers of C. may never be able to unravel the truth of his life from his own mythologized narratives. It does seem now that he did not run away to Russia as a youth, but rather that after his family gave up on keeping him in school, C. had a job awaiting him there. But this circumstance was not without adventure too, in 1904. Did he take the Trans-Siberian railroad, or merely draw his accounts of landscapes and wounded troops from others? There is always truth at the core of the myth, but we often cannot tell where, or how much. No one ever saw the work he persisted in listing first in his bibliography, *La Légende de Novgorode* (1907; in Russia, 14 copies, white type on black paper), but a lone copy turned up in 1996, in Sophia, Bulgaria. Before and after World War I, C. was a foremost leader in the literary avant-garde in Paris; he was an important influence on APOLINAIRE, the DADAISTS, and the SUR-REALISTS, but after he lost his right arm on the battlefront he preferred to abandon the literary cliques and attempted to live a less artistic life.

C. published his most important works in groups of three or four at a time, each group a genre that he subverted to his purposes. *Du monde entire* (1919; from the whole world over) brought together his three epic poems, *Les Pâques à New York* (1912; *Easter in New York*, 1966), an Easter lament written in that city; *La prose du transsibérien et de la petite Jehanne de France* (1913; *Prose of the Transsiberian and of Little Jeanne of France*, 1966), a poem printed on two-meter-high sheets of paper with parallel abstract painting by Sonia Delaunay; *Le Panama*; ou, *Les aventures de mes sept oncles* (1918; *Panama; or, The Adventures of My Seven Uncles*, 1931), in the format of a pocket timetable for the Union Pacific with a map of Chicago-Los Angeles train routes inter-spersed among the lines of verse. These works established his reputation as a modernist poet, as well as that of the heroic voyager, a "Homer" of the modern world, as John DOS PASSOS saw him. And yet in these poems the speaker is a diminished man; his fragmented narrative is dominated by masses of people oppressed in cities, victimized by history, flung to the ends of the world, and the hero is only heroic to the degree that he appears to speak for all the others.

Modernity is oppressive, but it is our condition, and so a sort of mimesis dictates the disjointed narrative, the multiple focus, the incongruous or jarring imagery and juxtapositions. One of the first to write in this manner, C. went further than most who followed. More innovative yet were his short prewar poems collected as *Dix-neuf poèmes élastiques* (1919; nineteen elastic poems). Here C. embraced the so-called antipoetic, the repercussions of modernity in the most ordinary aspects of life. The poems depend largely on popular culture, often on pieces of newsprint, like cubist collage- "Dernièr heure" (1913; news flash) is probably the first "found poem."

Between 1925 and 1930 C. published four novels, three of which are important: *L'or* (1925; *Sutter's Gold*, 1926, rep. as *Gold*, 1970), a fictionalized story of John Sutter of California; *Moravagine* (1926; *Moravagine*, 1969), the worldwide adventures of a mad-man; and *Le Plan de l'Aiguille* (1928; *Antarctic Fugue*, 1948) and *Les confessions de Dan Yack* (1928; confessions of Dan Yack), a two-part novel published later in one volume, *Dan Yack* (1946). These are narratives of powerful men at grips with modern life and history in their most irrational and chaotic aspects.

Sutter's story, which C. brought to public attention, would seem too fantastic for a modern reader, but it is true: a lone man builds an empire consisting of a large section of northern California, and loses everything to the discovery of gold on his own land. C. relished the most unlikely aspects of reality, and we might call him a realist of the exceptional. *Moravagine*, C.'s most famous novel, follows a demented man across three continents as he instigates dissolution and destruction all around him. This time the character is fictional, but the narrative is always spilling over into a real events—the coming revolution in St. Petersburg, for example. A very real irrational world is itself only a plaything in the hands of Moravagine's more purely irrational, demonic imagination, which is totally without conscience. Dan Yack is a man of action in the first book about him, a man of contemplation in the second, where he dictates his "confessions" in an Alpine shack located at the Plan de l'Aiguille. *Dan Yack* is also a love story, about a man who alternately pursues and flees love. In an ending that anticipates renewed encounters with life and love, the novel seems to resolve the tension between Sutter the builder and Moravagine the destroyer.

The late 1940s saw C. at his most spectacular in works that recount, in a sort of epic, mythical autobiography, his life and imagination: living in Naples when he was a child, serving in the Foreign Legion, traveling in Brazilian jungles, making films, living with gypsies, and reading books about everything. Especially in *L'homme foudroyé* (1945; *The Astonished Man*, 1970), *Bourlinguer* (1948; *Planus*, 1972), and *Le lottissement du ciel* (1949; *Sky: Memoirs*, 1992) we discover the author as encyclopedia, whose powerful voice reorganizes all the incongruous material into the theme of his own identity.

FURTHER WORKS: *Novgorode* (1909); *Séquences* (1913); *La guerre au Luxembourg* (1916); *Profond aujourd'hui* (1917); *J'ai tué* (1918); *La fin du monde filmée par l'Ange Notre-Dame* (1919); *Anthologie nègre* (1921; *African Saga*, 1927); *Kodak (Documentaire)* (1924); *Feuilles de route* (1924); *L'eubage* (1926); *L'ABC du cinéma* (1926); *Éloge de la vie dangereuse* (1926); *Petits contes nègres pour les enfants des blancs* (1928; *Little Black Stories for Little White Children*, 1929); *Une nuit dans la forêt* (1929); *Rhum* (1930); *Comment les blancs sont d'anciens noirs* (1930); *Aujourd'hui* (1931); *Vol à voile* (1932); *Panorama de la pègre* (1935); *Holly-wood, la mecque du cinéma* (1936); *Histoires vraies* (1937); *La vie dangereuse* (1938); *D'outremer à indigo* (1940); *Chez l'armé anglaise* (1940); *Poésies complètes* (1944); *La main coupée* (1946; *Lice*, 1973); *La banlieue de Paris* (1949); *B. C. vous parlea . . .* (1952); *Le Brésil* (1952); *Emmène-moi au bout du mondel! . . .* (1956; *To the End of the World*, 1967); *Trop c'est trop* (1957); *Du monde entier au cœur du monde* (1957); *Films sans images* (1959); *Inédits secrets* (1969); *Dites-nous Monsieur B. C.* (1969); *Voyager avec B. C.* (1994); *La vie et la mort du soldat inconnu* (1995); *L'eubage* (1995). FURTHER WORKS IN ENGLISH: *Selected Writings* (1966); *Complete Postcards from the Americas* (1976); *Select-ed Poems* (1979); *A Night in the Forest* (1985); *Modernities* (1992); *Complete Poems* (1992); *Christmas at the Four Corners of the Earth* (1994); *Hollywood* (1995)

BIBLIOGRAPHY: Seldes, G., *The Seven Lively Arts* (1924): 384–90; Dos Passos, J., "Homer of the Transsiberian," *Orient Express* (1927): 155–67; Miller, H., *The Books in My Life* (1952): 59–83; Albert, W., Introduction to *Selected Writings* (1966): 1–44; Caws, M. A., *The Inner Theatre of Recent Poetry* (1972): 25–51; Bochner, J., *B. C.: Discovery and Re-creation* (1978); Chefdor, M., *B. C.* (1980); special C. issue, *StTCL*, 3, 2 (1980); Leamon, A., *Shades of Sexuality: Colors and Sexual Identity in the Novels of B. C.* (1997)

—JAY BOCHNER

CENTRAL AMERICAN LITERATURE

Although confederation has been a recurring aspiration of the isthmus, nationalism, complicated by the powerful presence of foreign economic and military interests, has kept the six Spanish-speaking republics politically separate yet culturally similar. Sec-tarian politics, repressive governments, national and regional rival-ries, and a social organization based on a ruling oligarchy that controls an impoverished rural agricultural sector form the context that has produced six national literatures with a distinct Central American flavor. Geographic and cultural isolation have encouraged the development of the dual phenomena of active literary groups dedicated to the cultivation and celebration of local figures, as well as the desire to transcend the local and produce a universal literary expression. Numerous literary journals of varying life spans have been vital to these efforts and continue to publish the works of new as well as established writers, although the recent appearance of publishing companies such as Guaymuras (Honduras), Editorial Nueva Nicaragua (Nicaragua), and EDUCA (Costa Rica) has created the opportunity for Central American authors to become known internationally. Whereas dictatorships, whether the strong-man régimes of the first half of the 20th c. or the military governments of the latter decades, typically have repressed any literature construed as oppositional, this censorship has in effect encouraged international communication and solidarity among writers, many of whom have lived in exile for significant periods of time. Central American literature has been influenced by and large by the same major currents as its Mexican and South American neighbors, although not all trends and genres have been developed with equal skill or enthusiasm in each of the six countries. Belize, the seventh Central American country, gained independence from Britain in 1981 and is beginning to produce a national literature, as evidenced by Zee Edgell's (b. 1950) novel *Beka Lamb* (1982), about daily life in the preindependence colony formerly known as British Honduras.

Guatemala. The seat of government for the entire isthmus during the colonial period, Guatemala was also the cultural center and continued to be for a number of years after independence. The University of San Carlos in Guatemala City was the region's first and most reputable institution of higher learning and was attended by students from all the Central American countries. This long and venerable cultural history and the rich traditions of the indigenous peoples of Guatemala are two important factors that have contributed to one of Central America's most developed literatures. The modernist trend that dominated much of Latin American literature, particularly poetry, at the turn of the century had its followers in Guatemala as well, but the best writers of this tendency are known primarily for their prose. Enrique Gómez Carrillo (1873–1927), immensely popular during his lifetime, wrote chronicles from Paris and Buenos Aires that were published in newspapers and periodicals throughout Latin America for over thirty years. His trilogy *Tres novelas inmorales* (1899; three immoral novels) is set in the aristocratic salons and bohemian cafés of turn-of-the-century Paris. They are refined, sensual, and antibourgeois, in the modernist style. Rafael Arévalo Martínez (1884–1975)—whose short story "El hombre que parecía un caballo" (1914; the man who looked like a horse) has frequently been anthologized for its unique approach to human psychology—was also an important novelist.

The Estrada Cabrera and Ubico dictatorships inspired the antiimperialist and *indigenista* works of writers of the 1920s and 1930s, notably Miguel Angel ASTURIAS, winner of the Nobel Prize in 1967, and Luis Cardoza y Aragón (1904–1992), whose prose work *Guatemala las líneas de su mano* (1955; Guatemala the lines of your hand) is a highly personalized and all-encompassing study of Guatemala. The period of social and political reform known as the October Revolution ran from 1944 to 1954. This decade saw a proliferation of cultural events and a significant growth in the number of books and journals published. A number of literary groups were formed, among them Saker-ti (Quiché for "dawn"), a

coalition of artists, writers, and intellectuals of various leftist ideologies whose stated goal was to creat a democratic, nationalist, and realist art. This renaissance of literary activity ended in 1954 when Arbenz was deposed in a military coup. Many writers were radicalized by the repression and censorship of the military régime and became known collectively as the "Committed Generation." Some were forced into exile, some joined the newly formed guerrilla groups and combined writing with active involvement, in the political struggle; many were killed or disappeared. Otto René Castillo (1936–1967) epitomized the romantic ideal of combining literary work with militancy. He founded the journal *Lanzas y letras* that published the work of the Committed Generation. His volume of poetry *Vámonos patria a caminar* (1965; Let's Go!, 1971) is a heroic call to action in direct, simple language. Its best-known poem, "Intelectuales apolíticos" ("Apolitical Intellectuals"), a condemnation of apathetic intellectuals and aesthetic snobs exemplifies the moralistic quality of his poetry. He was tortured and killed in 1967, thus solidifying his legendary status in Central American literary history.

Military governments and social and political problems continue to dominate the cultural consciousness of Guatemala, but since the late 1960s literature has expressed more complex and diverse responses to this national reality. The novel, whose practitioners have become increasingly engaged in formal experimentation, continues to hold a place of prominence in Guatemalan letters. Drawing on indigenous myth, irony, and wordplay, Arturo Arias (b. 1950) treats the theme of the erasure of historical memory and an individual's attempts to reconstruct his own and his country's past in *Después de las bombas* (1979; *After the Bombs*, 1990). Women writers are now more visible. Margarita Carrera (b. 1929), the first woman graduate in literature from the University of San Carlos, has an impressive output in poetry, essay, journalism, and literary criticism. Ana María Rodas (b. 1937) is representative of an increasingly popular feminist poetry, as evidenced in her *Poemas de la izquierda erótica* (1973; poems of the erotic Left), while Rigoberta Menchú (b. 1959), a Quiché Indian woman, exemplifies the recent appearance of indigenous voices. Her autobiography, *Me llamo Rigoberta Menchú* (1983; *I, Rigoberta Menchú*, 1985), as told to Venezuelan anthropologist Elisabeth Burgos-Debray, combines lyrical descriptions of the beliefs and customs of her community with eyewitness accounts of social injustice against the indigenous population of Guatemala. This kind of testimonial narrative has become one of the most vital literary forms in Guatemala today. Mario Payeras (dates n.a.), one of the founders of Guatemala's Guerrilla Army of the Poor, wrote *Días de la selva* (1980; *Days of the Jungle*, 1983) to describe the experiences of this group in the highlands, while Víctor Montejo (b. 1952), a school teacher working in a remote village, narrates the destruction of the village by the army in 1982 in *Testimony: Death of a Guatemalan Village* (1987), which to date has not been published in a Spanish edition.

El Salvador. In a region characterized by a pronounced division of classes and sectarian politics, El Salvador may well be the nation that has struggled the most with the dichotomies rural/urban, traditional/reformist, reformist/revolutionary. It is the smallest of the Central American countries as well as the most densely populated. A persistent interest in defining that which is truly Salvadoran has generated literary responses that range from highly romanticized and sentimental portraits of the national landscape and the humble country dweller, to harshly realistic depictions of social injustice, tyrannical dictators, and a violent military. With few exceptions, Salvadoran narrative shuns the magic REALISM so prevalent in other parts of Latin America. The massacre in 1932 by government troops of over 30,000 native Salvadorans and subsequent attempts by Indians to hide their identity by abandoning traditional dress and customs significantly erased the indigenous population, already greatly reduced since colonial times. Modern El Salvador is largely a mestizo nation, unlike neighboring Guatemala, where the indigenous influence persists in the national psyche.

Alberto Masferrer (1868–1932) is often considered the first genuinely national writer. He was a friend of Rubén DARÍO, but did not adopt the modernist aesthetic, using instead a clear, expository prose to develop essays that promoted his democratic humanism. Alfred Espino (1902–1928) continues to be one of El Salvador's most widely read poets. He cultivated a sentimental *costumbrism* of rural themes and idealized landscapes that extolled the virtues of family and tradition. His only book, *Jícaras tristes* (1936; sad water gourds), was published posthumously. Arturo Ambrogi (1876–1936) represented a departure from Espino's romantic vision. His chronicles and short stories project a vision more akin to NATURALISM. SALARRUÉ (pseud. of Salvador Salazar Arrué) was influential in popularizing the regionalist short story in Central America. In *Cuentos de barro* (1927; stories of clay) he portrays rural peasant and working-class life, recreating with great skill the rich Salvadoran vernacular.

Alice Lardé (b. 1896) introduced a sensual feminine eroticism to Salvadoran poetry with *Almaviril* (1925; virile soul), but it was Claudia Lars (pseud. of Carmen Brannon, 1899–1974) who first achieved a high level of professionalism among women writers. Both Lars and Salarrué correspond chronologically to the avant-garde generation, but neither participated in the formal experimentation of this school. Lars's poetry is lucid, distilled, and sincere. She skillfully blends the personal and the universal in poems of children, friends, and nature and in intimate philosophical meditations.

In the early 1950s a group of university-based writers was formed that, like their Guatemalan counterpart, came to be known as the Committed Generation. Members included Roque Dalton (1935–1975), Roberto Armijo (b. 1937), Mercedes Durand (b. 1933), Eugenio Martínez Orantes (b. 1932), and Manlio ARGUETA. Not part of the group, but of kindred spirit, is Claribel ALEGRÍA. Primarily poets, they were young, idealistic, highly socially and politically aware, iconoclastic, and antibourgeois. Dalton, who had been influenced by Guatemalan poet Otto René Castillo also became a legendary figure because of the circumstances of his death. His self-proclaimed poetry of "ugly words" is didactic, ironic, and self-mocking. His ambitious and original *Las historias prohibidas del pulgarcito* (1974; the forbidden stories of Tom Thumb) is a collage-poem of Salvadoran history. Many of the writers of this group live in exile. Argueta's novels are banned by the Salvadoran government, but have been widely translated. *Un día en la vida* (1980; *One Day of Life*, 1983) portrays Salvadoran peasants in their struggle against military repression. The writers of the Committed Generation who chose to stay in El Salvador, such as Martínez Orantes, have had to negotiate the perils of censorship. The most prolific and respected of the current generation of writers living in the El Salvador is David Escobar Galindo (b. 1943). He has served as director of the National Library, director of the ministry of culture's journal, *Cultura*, and has published over forty-two books of poetry, prose, and theatre.

Honduras. It is the most sparsely populated of the Central American republics, as well as the poorest. The capital city,

Tegucigalpa, located in the central highlands, was, until the second half of the 20th c., extremely isolated from other centers of population. The presence of the Standard and United Fruit Companies has largely determined the economy of much of the country. Although it has had its share of dictatorships and military governments, Hondurans often claim that the acute class distinctions that characterize other Central American countries exist in a more modified form in Honduras, since the oligarchy never amassed extreme wealth as did the ruling families of El Salvador and Guatemala, for example.

Isolation notwithstanding, Honduran writers at the turn of the century kept informed of international literary trends largely through the efforts of Froylán Turcios (1875–1943), who founded and/or directed numerous newspapers and literary journals, notably *Esfinge* and *Ariel*, which published the work of Honduran writers as well as excerpts of classics of world literature, and *Boletín de la defensa national*, an important political paper that denounced the occupation of Tegucigalpa by U. S. Marines in 1924. Turcios chronicled his most interesting life in *Memorias* (memories), published posthumously in 1980.

Romanticism, which swept the literary youth of Tegucigalpa at the end of the 19th c., remained popular well into the 20th. Lucila Gamero de Medina's (1873–1964) novel *Blanca Olmedo* (1903; Blanca Olmedo) employs the language and characterizations of romanticism in a scathing attack on the clergy. José Antonio Domínguez (1869–1903) is considered by critics to represent the transition from romanticism to modernism. His themes are often patriotic, but his concern for musicality in verse heralded this fundamental preoccupation of MODERNISM. His most important work, "Himno a la materia" (hymn to matter), is an ambitious long poem that addresses the philosophical question of humanity's spiritual and material nature and finds answers in a romantic scientism. A poet of modernist sensibilities who achieved international acclaim was Juan Ramón Molina (1875–1908). His lyric persona oscillates between the poles of an innocent lyricism and a worldly despair. His work was collected in *Tierras, mares y cielos* (1911; lands, seas, and skies).

One of the most creative and noteworthy periods of Honduran literature was that of the "Generation of '35." Their penchant for gathering in local cafés and the bohemian self-concept they shared contributed to their group identity, although they published no literary manifesto, as was common among avant-garde groups of the time. Of particular interest is the poetry of Claudio Barrera (pseud. of Vicente Alemán, 1912–1971), Jacobo Cárcamo (1916–1959), and Daniel Laínez (1914–1959). Influenced by the Spanish Civil War and personally affected by the dictatorship of Carías Andino, several writers of this generation turned to social and political themes after an initial period of experimentation with avant-grade techniques. Laínez is known for his skillful use of rural manners of speech. All experimented with the themes and rhythms of the then popular *negrista* poetry.

Clementine SUÁREZ, the grande dame of Honduran poetry, began her career with the romantic and formally traditional *Corazón sangrante* (1930; bleeding heart), but soon abandoned the sonnet in favor of the free verse with which she expressed her feminine sexuality and celebrated love, motherhood, freedom, and social commitment. Her work has been collected in *El poeta y sus señales* (1969; the poet and her signs).

The exploitation of national territory by foreign interests has been a major concern of Honduran prose writers. Coupled with a search to define and describe the national identity, these two elements inform the novels of Marcos Carías Reyes (1905–1949), Paca Navas (1900–1969), and Ramón Amaya Amador (1916–1966). Prolific novelist Argentina Díaz Lozano (b. 1912) won international acclaim for her autobiographical work *Peregrinaje* (1944; *Pilgrimage*, 1945). Contemporary fiction writers tend to be more experimental in technique and wide-ranging in theme, although the Honduran milieu prevails. Marcos Carías Zapata's (b. 1938) *Una functión con mobiles y tentetiesos* (1980; function with mobiles and roly-poly toys) is a linquistic and structural tour de force. Julio Escoto (b. 1944) has achieved an international reputation for his short stories and novels. Roberto Castillo's (b. 1950) short fiction is a rich blend of MAGIC REALISM, irony, and humor. Recent Honduran poetry is inspired largely by social concerns and a desire to create an awareness of the national reality. Roberto SOSA's finely crafted and deeply sensitive poetry has been widely translated; of note are *Los pobres* (1968; *The Poor*, 1983) and *Los días difíciles* (1971; *The Difficult Days*, 1983). The best of the young poets include José Luis Quesada (b. 1948), Rigoberto Paredes (b. 1948), and María Eugenia Ramos (b. 1959).

Nicaragua. Poetry is without a doubt the favored genre in what has been called a country of poets. It was the homeland of Rubén DARÍO, undisputed master of modernism. Regarded as a national hero, Darí exercised significant influence over Central American poetry in the first two decades of the 20th c. The group Vanguardia emerged in 1928 as a reaction to the aesthetic of Darío's modernism. Their mentor was José Coronel Urtecho (b. 1906). His famous "Oda a Rubén Darío" (1927; ode to Rubén Darío) signaled his generation's iconoclastic break with the past and its ambitious project to recreate Nicaraguan literature employing history, folklore, myth, and popular language. Pablo Antonio Cuadra (b. 1912) epitomized this effort in *Poemas nicaragüenses* (1933; Nicaraguan poems).

Cuadra has edited some of the most important literary journals of Nicaragua, including *El pez y la serpiente*, which introduced many poets of the "Generation of '40" whose members include Ernesto CARDENAL, Ernesto Mejía Sánchez (b. 1923), and Carlos Martínez Rivas (b. 1924). Unlike the Vanguardists, this group was united in its opposition to the Somoza dictatorship and formed a bridge between the more individualistic, disorganized iconoclasm of the preceding generation and the Sandinista poets of the 1960s and later. Cardenal is without doubt the major figure in contemporary Nicaraguan cultural life. He has profoundly influenced poetic production in Nicaragua through the poetry workshops he founded in 1979 as minister of culture.

Living up to its reputation as a country of poets, Nicaragua claimed the distinction, during the Sandinista government (1979–1989), of having several political leaders who are also writers, including President Daniel Ortega (b. 1945) and Vice President Sergio RAMÍREZ.

Several women have emerged since the 1960s whose poetry ensures the representation of a previously marginalized sector of society. The major figures, known as "The Six," are Gioconda BELLI, Vidaluz Meneses (b. 1944), Rosario Murillio (b. 1951), Michele Najlis (b. 1946), Yolanda Blanco (b. 1954), and Daisy Zamora (b. 1950). Collectively, their poetry attempts to define and celebrate femininity in the revolutionary context.

The narrative, while less developed than poetry, has existed in various forms, from a picturesque depiction of rural customs and speech in the work of Mariano Fiallos Gil (1907–1964), to the political novels of Hernán Robleto (1898–1969), such as his

Sangre en el trópico (1930; blood in the tropics), or *Trágame tierra* (1969; let the earth swallow me) by Lisandro Chávez Alfaro (b. 1929). More recently, Omar Cabezas (dates n.a.) has contributed to the testimonial narrative with *La montaña es algo más que una inmensa estepa verde* (1982; *Fire from the Mountain*, 1985), an autobiographical account of his participation in the Sandinista struggle against Somoza. Sergio Ramírez is widely considered the most accomplished short-story writer of Nicaragua today. Belli and Rosario Aguilar (dates n.a.) are the best and most prolific of the women novelists.

Costa Rica. Like the other republics of the isthmus, Costa Rican literature begins to acquire its unique national contours at the turn of the Century. Among those writers who comprised the Generation of 1900, *Costumbrism*—narrative sketches of manners and social customs, with an emphasis on the use of colloquial language—was the preferred mode. An early practitioner of *costumbrism* laced with naturalism was Joaquín García Monge (1881–1958), also the founder and director of *Repertorio Americano* (1919–1958) an influential and unusually long-lived journal of international circulation. In contrast to García Monge's critical attitude in displaying the ignorance and foibles of society, Manuel González Zeledón's (1864–1936) stories and essays portray a simpler and more idyllic national reality. Aquileo J. Echeverría's (1866–1909) highly popular *Concherías* (1905; peasant ways) humorously employs colorful rural speech. Carmen Lyra (pseud. of María Isabel Carvajal, 1888–1949) legitimized children's literature, which continues to be a respected genre in Costa Rican letters, with *Los cuentos de mi tía Panchita* (1920; my Aunt Panchita's stories), still read and loved by Costa Rican school children. Other writers of children's literature include Lilia Ramos (1903–1988), Carlos Luis Saenz (1899–1984), and Lara Ríos (pseud. of Marilín Echeverría, dates n.a.).

A wave of narrative fiction that denounced social injustice appeared in the 1940s, including *Mamita Yunai* (1941; Mommy United Fruit) by Carlos Luis Fallas (1909–1966), *El sitio de las abras* (1950; where the clearings are) by Fabián Dobles (b. 1918), and *Puerto Limón* (1950; Puerto Limón) by Joaquín Gutiérrez (b. 1918). While narratives of regionalism and social denunciation continue to be popular, cultivated by Julieta Pinto (b. 1922), Quince Duncan (b. 1940), and others, a number of Costa Rican writers have produced fiction more akin to the technical and thematic experiments of the modern period. A pioneer who openly rejected regionalism in favor of the urban psychological novel was Yolanda OREAMUNO, author of *La ruta de su evasión* (1948; the route of their escape). Other women have enriched the novel with their innovative contributions. Carmen NARANJO has written *Los perros no ladraron* (1966; the dogs did not bark), an existential novel, and *Diario de una multitud* (1974; diary of a crowd), a college of urban voices. Anacristina Rossi's (b. 1952) *María la noche* (1985; Maria the night) won a national novel award in 1985. Its exploration of feminine sensuality and its lyrical approach to reality is unusual in Costa Rican women's fiction, although recent women's poetry is often openly celebratory of female sexuality and questioning of gender roles. A precursor was Eunice ODIO, whose *Los elementos terrestres* (1948; terrestial elements) is a collection of eight long poems that project a mystical-erotic vision of gender relations. A noteworthy recent example is *La estación de fiebre* (1982; the season of fever) by Ana Istarú (b. 1960). Tatiana Lobo and Linda Berrón (dates n.a.) have emerged as outstanding prose writers at the end of the 20th c.

A number of poets and novelists, including Istarú and Samuel ROVINSKI have also written for the stage. Daniel Gallegos (b. 1930) is one of Costa Rica's outstanding dramatists.

Panama. This country, which separated from Colombia in 1903 to become an independent republic, has since then been identified primarily as the site of the Panama Canal, with the rights to the canal ceded to the U. S. Panama's relations with the U. S. have greatly influenced its history, politics, economy, and self-image; so it is not surprising that the canal should play a prominent role in Panamanian letters.

Modernism was in fashion when Panama became a nation. Darío Herrera (1870–1914), whose works remain uncollected, mastered the mellifluous prose and verse of this school. Ricardo Miró (1883–1940) founded the literary journal *Nuevosritos* (1907–1917), which published the works of Panamanian modernists. María Olimpia de Obaldía (b. 1891), considered Panama's national poet, wrote domestic and patriotic verse. Demetrio Korsi (1899–1957), author of *Cumbia* (1936; Cumbia), is Panama's best-known writer of the *negrista* poetry popular in the 1930s.

Rogelio Sinán (b. 1904) experimented with SURREALIST techniques in poetry as well as narrative. The most important Panamanian writer of this century, Sinán has influenced other avant-garde poets such as Ricardo J. Bermúdez (b. 1914). Novels that depict Canal themes have been popular throughout the century, particularly in the 1950s and 1960s. Sinán's *Plenilunio* (1947; full moon), which describes the destructive effects of the Canal on the city using innovative narrative techniques, is the best known of this genre. Another significant contribution is Joaquín Beleño's (b. 1922) trilogy *Luna verde* (1951; green moon), *Curundú* (1963; Curundo), and *Gamboa Road Gang* (1963; title in English).

Denunciation of imperialism and social injustice is prevalent in recent Panamanian literature. Esther María Osses (1914–1991), whose poetry is gentle and intimate, writes forceful essays and literary criticism celebrating popular liberation struggles. Bertalicia Peralta (b. 1939) and Pedro Rivera (b. 1939) are important voices of protest in poetry and short fiction, while novelists Carlos Francisco Changmarín (b. 1922) and Eustorgio Chong Ruiz (b. 1934) exemplify this tendency in the novel. A number of contemporary writers are experimenting with narrative techniques, such as the uninterrupted interior monologue of *El último juego* (1977; the last game) by Gloria Guardia de Alfaro (b. 1940). Enrique Jaramillo Levi and Rosa María Britton (dates n.a.) are widely considered to be two of Panama's outstanding late 20th-c. writers.

BIBLIOGRAPHY: Ramírez, S., *La narrativa centroamericana* (1969); García, I., *Historia de la literatura Panameña* (1977); Sandoval de Fonseca, V., *Resúmen de literatura costarricense* (1978); Gallegos Valdés, L., *Panorama de la literatura salvadoreña* (1981); Acevedo, R. L., *La novela centroaméricana* (1982); Albizúrez Palma, F., and C. Barrios, *Historia de la literatura guatemalteca* (1982); Arellano, J. E., *Panorama de la literatura nicaraguense*, 4th ed. (1982); Armijo, R., Introduction to *Poesía contemporanea de Centroamérica* (1983); Menton, S., *Historia crítica de la novela guatemalteca*, 2nd ed. (1985); Paredes, R., and M. Salinas Paguada, *Literatura hondureña* (1987); Engelbert, J., Introduction to *And We Sold the Rain: Contemporary Fiction from Central American Revolution* (1988); Beverley, J., and M. Zimmerman, *Literature and Politics in the Central American Revolutions* (1990)

—JANET N. GOLD

CEPEDA SAMUDIO, Alvaro

Colombian novelist, journalist, and short-story writer, b. 30 Mar. 1926, Ciénaga (or Barranquilla); d. 12 Oct. 1972, New York, N.Y.

C. S. was a member of the Group of Barranquilla, a set of Colombian "coastal" writers that included Alfonso Fuenmayor (b. 1917), Germán Vargas (b. 1919), and Gabriel GARCÍA MÁRQUEZ. He worked prolifically as a journalist from his days as a college student in the 1940s until the time of his death from cancer. From 1949 until 1951, he lived in the U. S., pursuing journalistic and literary studies at Columbia University. His short stories appeared sporadically in the early 1950s and were first collected in the volume *Todos estábamos a la espera* (1954; we were all waiting), whose title story is one of his most accomplished and shows strong influence by Ernest HEMINGWAY. As have many Colombian and Latin American writers of his generation, C. S. owed great debt to the work of North American authors such as HEMINGWAY, William FAULKNER, and William SAROYAN, as well as to Hollywood film noir. He wrote prolifically about film and founded the Cine Club of Barranquilla in 1957. He also directed several short subjects, including *La langosta azul* (1954; the blue lobster).

As critical literature has noted, C. S. fits well within the *Costeño* (coastal) tradition of Colombian literature, which Raymond L. Williams characterizes as ethnically mixed, with cosmopolitan and popular underpinnings. C. S.'s *La casa grande* (1962; *La Casa Grande*, 1991) employs Faulknerian strategies such as interior monologue as well as cinematic technique reminiscent of John DOS PASSOS to present a collective and symbolic yet highly intimate "history" of the 1928 massacre of banana workers during a strike in the Colombian town of Ciénaga. The perspectivism of the novel, seen in its accomplished presentation of similar events from different points of view and parts of a time sequence, evinces the long-standing interest of C. S. not only in cinema but also in painting. Williams stresses its combination of written and oral qualities, noting its importance as a precursor of García Márquez's *Cien años de soledad* (1967; *One Hundred Years of Solitude*, 1970). The concern of *La casa grande* with oral culture and the function of memory in recording and sifting historical events foreshadows not only the famous novel of García Márquez but also the work of Colombian novelist Gustavo ALVAREZ GARDEAZÁBAL.

The cosmopolitanism of the coastal tradition, that is, its relative openness because of its nature as a port, may in part explain the appeal for C. S. of foreign, especially North American, literary models as well as the varied nature of his career in journalism. C. S. dealt in his columns not only with subjects of local Colombian interest (soccer, local and national politics, and familiar locales) but also with problems of nuclear armament, with questions concerning the recently formed United Nations, with the influence of the U. S. on Latin America in general, and even with the opposition of French communists to the influence of Mickey Mouse on French culture, a position that he attacked. In general, as his editor and commentator Jacques Gilard notes, C. S. adopted a democratic socialist stance. His posture might be appropriately compared to that of George ORWELL, who though in sympathy with socialist ideals did not shrink in his journalism as in his fiction from opposing chicanery and hypocrisy from left or right.

C. S. also commented at length on cinema, generally favoring Italian NEOREALISM, British postwar cinema, and newer trends in European film over the productions of Hollywood. As Gilard points out when noting this tendency to glorify productions (such as some of the British ones) that have paled with the years in contrast with such phenomena as film noir from Hollywood, C. S. was perhaps sated with Hollywood movies, since these dominated the market during World War II, and thus considered the other films a relief of sorts. In any case, despite his frequent attacks on the Hollywood system, his fiction, especially *Todos estábamos a la espera*, shows probable influence not only from writers such as Hemingway but also from film noir.

C. S. is often cited as an important innovator in Colombian fiction shortly preceding the publication of *Cien años de soledad*. His untimely death left unanswered the question of his further development as a creative artist. He has at the very least contributed one masterpiece, *La casa grande*, and one important collection of stories, *Todos estábamos a la espera*. And he has served as an inspiration to other Latin American writers, including not only García Márquez but also, for example, Argentine Mario SZICHMAN, who was his journalistic colleague and who modeled his first novel, *Crónica falsa* (1969; false chronicle) after *La casa grande*. The recent translation into English of *La casa grande* will make available to a wider reading public the work of an interesting and energetically creative writer.

FURTHER WORKS: *Los cuentos de Juana* (1972); *Antología* (1977)

BIBLIOGRAPHY: Mena, L. I., "*La casa grande*: el fracaso de un orden social," *Hispam*, 1, 2 (Dec. 1972): 3–17; Gilard, J., Introduction to *Todos estábamos a la espera* (1980): 9–44; Gilard, J., "A. C. S., el experimentador tropical," *Quimera*, 26 (1982): 63–65; Ruffinelli, J., *Crítica en marcha: ensayos sobre literatura latinoamericana* (2nd ed., 1982): 146–47; Gilard, J., Introduction to *En el margen de la ruta (periodismo juvenil—1944–1955)* (1985): v-xc; special C. S. section in Williams, R. L., and A. Pineda Botero, comps., *Deficiones y realidades: perspectivas sobre literatura e historia colombianas. Memorias del Quinto Congreso de Colombianistas* (1989): 41–120; Menton, S., "La novelística de la costa colombiana: especulaciones históricas," in Neumeister S., ed., *Actas del IX Congreso de la Asociación Internacional de Hispanistas* (2 vols., 1989): 629–34

—KENNETH E. HALL

CERNUDA, Luis

Spanish poet and critic, b. 21 Sept. 1902, Seville; d. 5 Nov. 1963, Mexico City, Mexico

Like the Seville romantic poet Bécquer (1836–1870), C. discovered poetry in that particular Andalusia of Mediterranean light, white-washed walls, and multicolored flowers. Encouraged by his professor, the poet Pedro SALINAS, he published his first book of poetry in 1927, only to be deeply discouraged and hurt by negative reviews. He discovered no attractive profession, but life forced him into a permanent role as professor of Spanish literature, beginning in France. In 1938, escaping from war-torn Madrid, he wound up in Glasgow, Scotland, but later moved to London and learned to respect (even if he could not like) the English. After World War II he taught at Mount Holyoke College in Massachusetts; in 1952 he abandoned this position and took up residence in Mexico to be near the love of his middle age and to live in a Hispanic culture. He died there of a heart attack.

As early as 1936 C. formulated his philosophy of life and poetry under the title *La realidad y el deseo* (reality and desire), and ultimately all eleven collections of his poetry were published under this title. His first book, *Perfil del aire* (1927; profile of the air), contains postimpressionist lyrics in which the fledgling poet, between fervor and indolence, awakens to the world's promise, only to find it beyond his reach. The collection of poems *Egloga, elegía, oda* (written 1927–28, pub. 1936; eclogue, elegy, ode), suggests a return to the Renaissance manner of Garcilaso de la Vega (1539–1616); however, whereas in Garcilaso chaste nymphs decorate the pools, in C. a golden lad cavorts in the waters, entirely self-absorbed.

As C. matured, he gradually became aware of his homosexual nature, and for the rest of his life his ethical thrust became that of achieving "dignity" through his poetry. Now "reality" became the world, the "Establishment," naturally viewed negatively; his "desire" became the demand for total freedom in our time. Turning to SURREALISM in order to free himself emotionally and socially, the poet produced *Un río, un amor* (written 1929, pub. 1936; a river, a love), a book projecting the almost absolute alienation of the protagonist from society. In *Los placeres prohibidos* (written 1931, pub. 1936; forbidden pleasures), he further attempts to break out of the restrictions of society. After a disastrous love affair, he reached a nadir in *Donde habite el olvido* (written 1933, pub. 1936; where oblivion dwells).

From this point, influenced by Hölderlin (1770–1843), C. embraced his solitude as the essence of his being and concentrated on creating his poems. In *Las nubes* (1943; the clouds) he develops his reactions to the Spanish Civil War and to his own spiritual development. In "Lázaro" (1944; Lazarus) he projects his own painful rebirth in which he reaches the understanding that "beauty is patience." In the cycle *Como quien espera el alba* (1947; as one awaiting the dawn), after cutting himself off from his own family and rejecting any solace in supernatural belief, C. accepts the challenge of making poetry the vehicle for his self-affirmation.

In later years the poet pursued the theme of self-affirmation through the quest of beauty and the continuing expression of his alienation in *Vivir sin estar viviendo* (1949; living without being alive) and *Con las horas contadas* (1956; with time running out). His "Apologia pro vita sua" (1944; "Apologia pro Vita Sua," 1971) attempts to justify his life before both God and humankind; his "Los espinos" (1944; the hawthorns) reaffirms beauty as the only enduring value. At the end of the 1958 edition of *La realidad y el deseo* he placed a bitter poem "Birds in the Night" (the title is in English), in which he records his final disgust with humanity.

Despite his gentle and delicate nature, C. developed his personal and poetic existence in fierce conflict with Spanish culture. In his youth his "desire" created an Arcadian myth in which beautiful lads enjoyed a paradise of the senses in a realm of art; "reality" intruded in the form of a hostile world. Ultimately his homosexuality became a metaphor for his ontological solitude, and from this bleak position he consciously fashioned his poems of man-in-time. His collected poems, *La realidad y el deseo*, his spiritual autobiography, have earned him a respected position in the Generation of 1927, whose most outstanding members were GARCÍA LORCA, GUILLÉN, and ALEIXANDRE. His criticism serves mainly to help us understand the poet and his generation.

FURTHER WORKS: *Ocnos* (1942); *Estudios sobre poesía española contemporánea* (1957); *Poesía y literatura* (1960); *Desolación de la quimera* (1962); *Crítica, ensayos y evocaciones* (1970). FURTHER WORKS IN ENGLISH: *The Poetry of L. C.* (1971); *Selected Poems of L. C.* (1977)

BIBLIOGRAPHY: Silver, P., *"Et in Arcadia Ego": A Study of the Poetry of L.C.* (1965); Paz, O., "La palabra edificante," *Cuadrivio* (1965): 167–203; Coleman, A., *Other Voices: A Study of the Late Poetry of L. C.* (1969); Harris, D., *L. C.: A Study of the Poetry* (1973); Cobb, C., "L. C.," *Contemporary Spanish Poetry (1898–1963)* (1976): 133–38; Jiménez-Fajardo, S., ed., *The Word and the Mirror: Critical Essays on the Poetry of L. C.* (1989)

—CARL W. COBB

CÉSAIRE, Aimé

Martinican poet and dramatist, b. 26 June 1913, Basse Pointe

C. was born in the shadow of the volcano Mont Pelée on the northeast coast of Martinique. His father, a teacher and taxation officer, and his mother, a seamstress, had six children. After primary school in his hometown and secondary education in Fort-de-France and in Paris, C. studied literature and philosophy in Paris from 1935 to 1939, receiving a diploma for a dissertation on the theme of the South in Afro-American literature.

C. was the creator of the term NÉGRITUDE to signify his awareness of belonging to a black cultural heritage and his desire to enrich that inheritance. He, Léon DAMAS, and Léopold SENGHOR drew on many sources to develop their new sense of ethnic pride during the 1930s when they were students in Paris. After World War II C. manifested his concern for his race in poetry, theater, essays, and political activity. Since 1945 he has tried to improve socioeconomic conditions in Martinique by serving as mayor of Fort-de-France and as one of the island's three deputies in the French National Assembly.

Cahier d'un retour au pays natal (1939; *Memorandum on My Martinique*, 1947), a long poem which is his first and best-known work, went unnoticed when it appeared. But after the war, it attracted much attention, partly because of praise by André BRETON and Jean-Paul SARTRE. The narrator of the poem undergoes a metamorphosis from passive observer of a decaying island society to visionary messiah of black people, thanks to his discovery of his Négritude. The poem's complex inner dynamics, rich vocabulary and imagery, hammering rhythms, and often violent tone are some of the reasons why many readers consider it the most influential work for several generations of French-speaking blacks.

C. returned to Martinique in 1939 to teach and awaken Martinicans to their African roots. In 1941 he and his friends founded the cultural journal *Tropiques*, in which C. published the early SURREALIST poetry, which reflected his attempt to develop a highly personal aesthetic.

After the war C. published a series of collections that continue, in a slightly less hermetic mode, this surrealist period in his career: *Les armes miraculeuses* (1946; the miraculous weapons), *Soleil cou coupé* (1948; *Beheaded Sun*, 1973), and *Corps perdu* (1950; *Disembodied*, 1973, also pub. as *Lost Body*, 1986). All three volumes bear the common stamp of C.'s themes and images: slavery, freedom, paradise, earth, sun, volcanoes, islands, trees, and animals. Some critics did not appreciate what they termed the verbal excesses of C. (repetition, exotic imagery, and a vocabulary that sent readers to their dictionaries), while his comrades in the French Communist Party attacked him for the apparent obscurity of his poetry and his links with Breton.

During this period, C. worked assiduously in the French National Assembly for the transformation of Martinique from colony to overseas department, a change effected in 1946. But by the end of the 1940s, in spite of *de jure* changes in the colony's status, he saw the emptiness of government promises to offer total socioeconomic equality for the black French citizens of Martinique. After 1950 C. ceased to speak in parliament and did not publish poetry for several years.

In the mid-1950s, however, C.'s literary and political life underwent important changes. He began to publish more accessible poetry and rewrote for the stage *Et les chiens se taisaient* (1956; and the dogs were silent), a lyric oratorio about a rebellious slave (originally a part of *Les armes miraculeuses*). With *Ferrements* (1960; shackles), a collection that spans the entire decade of the 1950s, he addressed people and events in Africa, the Caribbean, and Afro-America, although he also continued to write poetry of a more personal, less open nature. He broke with the French Communist Party in 1956 and began to speak out in a series of international forums for the liberation of the Third World from Western imperialism. C. viewed culture as an important weapon in this struggle. In order to get his message across to a broader audience, he shifted from poetry to drama, a genre, he argued, that offered a multiplication of poetic force.

In *La tragédie du roi Christophe* (1963; *The Tragedy of King Christophe*, 1970) he portrays an early-19th-c. Haitian ruler whose heroic vision is warped by a cultural inferiority complex and insensitivity to the material needs of his people. Shakespearean in tone and structure, the play is a blend of verbal forms from several different cultures and constitutes C.'s message to the leaders of newly independent African states. The play was generally well received in Europe, Canada, the Near East, Africa, and the Caribbean.

Une saison au Congo (1966; *A Season in the Congo*, 1969), less successful than *La tragédie du roi Christophe*, was C.'s effort to demystify the story of Patrice Lumumba. C. depicts the late Congolese prime minister as a hero with ties to the masses and presents a sweeping pan-African vision in a format with Brechtian overtones.

His last play, *Une tempête* (1969, a tempest) is a black version of Shakespeare's *The Tempest*; it displeased European critics but drew praise in the Third World. C. attempted to show a servant's view of the Elizabethan play by providing a black cultural heritage for Caliban and portraying Prospero as a decadent colonizer.

The product of Caribbean experience, French education, and African studies, C. has had only limited contact with the continent of his ancestors, even though Africa dominates his writing. Critics are divided over the importance of these diverse cultural influences in his work, but many agree that he is the most widely read and studied black writer in the French-speaking world today.

FURTHER WORKS: *Discours sur le colonialisme* (1950; *Discourse on Colonialism*, 1972); *Lettre à Maurice Thorez* (1956; *Letter to Maurice Thorez*, 1957); *Cadastre* (1961 [rev. version of *Soleil cou coupé* and *Corps perdu*]; *Cadastre*, 1973); *Toussaint Louverture: La révolution française et le problème colonial* (1960); *Œuvres complètes* (1976). FURTHER WORKS IN ENGLISH: *A. C.: The Collected Poetry* (1983); *Now-Vicious Circle: Twenty Poems of A. C.* (1984)

BIBLIOGRAPHY: Harris, R., *L'humanisme dans le théâtre d' A.C.* (1973); Frutkin, S., *A. C.: Black between Worlds* (1973); Kesteloot, L., *Black Writers in French: A Literary History of Negritude* (1974); Ngal, M., *A. C.: Un homme à la recherche d'une patrie* (1975); Hale, T., *Les écrits d'A.C.: Bibliographie commentée* (1978); Warner, K., *La cohésion poétique de l'œuvre césairienne* (1979); Eshleman, C., and A. Smith, Introduction to *A. C.: The Collected Poetry* (1983): 1-28

—THOMAS A. HALE

CEWA LITERATURE

See Malawian Literature

CEYLONESE LITERATURE

See Sri Lankan Literature

CHACEL, Rosa

Spanish novelist, short-story writer, essayist, and poet, b. 3 June 1898, Valladolid; d. 27 July 1994, Madrid

C. studied painting and sculpture before becoming a writer. At age eight she began art classes in Valladolid. After moving to Madrid, she studied at the School of Arts and Professions and then at the Saint Ferdinand High School of Fine Arts. When bad health curtailed these studies, she joined the Atheneum of Madrid, thus beginning her formal association with the world of letters. There she met Ramón Gómez de la Serna and later the critic and philosopher José ORTEGA Y GASSET, who invited her collaboration in the leading intellectual journals of the period. She became Ortega's artistic follower and, thus, a member of the Generation of 1927. This group considered artistic expression and content equally important; therefore, psychological perceptions and interior monologue prevail over traditional novelistic plot in their works. C. manages to balance polished writing, intellectual exploration of personality, and genuine emotion.

At the Spanish Academy in Rome (1922–1929), C. wrote *Estación. Ida y vuelta* (1930; station, round trip), a *Künstlerroman* influenced by James JOYCE's *A Portrait of the Artist As a Young Man* (1916) and by Ortega and Marcel PROUST. The novel is an antecedent of the French NEW NOVEL. The word *estación* means both train station and season; thus, the title refers to the protagonist's round trip by train as well as to the cyclic nature of the work, a return of a season.

During this period C. published a book of vanguard sonnets, *A la orilla de un pozo* (1936; beside a well). She was preparing a biographical novel about Teresa Mancha—commissioned by Ortega for the series "Extraordinary Lives of the 19th Century"—when the Spanish Civil War began, delaying its publication indefinitely. During and after the war C. lived and traveled in Europe, finally emigrating with her family to Rio de Janeiro in 1940. She divided her time between Brazil and Buenos Aires. In the latter, she collaborated with the leading critics of her day, among them Victoria Ocampo (1891–1979), the editor of *Sur*.

Teresa (1941; Teresa) was finally published in Buenos Aires, when the Spanish political situation prevented its publication in Spain. The novel explores the themes of political exile and the ostracism and alienation experienced by a woman who defies 19th-c. mores. This fictional biography of the mistress of Spain's revolutionary romantic poet José Espronceda (1808–1842) portrays a bittersweet passion worthy of the romantic movement. The novel was C.'s second published in Spain, finally appearing in 1963, thirty-three years after *Estación*.

Her third novel, *Memorias de Leticia Valle* (1945; *Memoirs of Leticia Valle*, 1994), was planned in Italy before 1930. This novel in diary form presents the themes of jealousy, artistic education, and possible child molestation, from the perspective of a precocious adolescent female. One of C's best novels, *La sinrazón* (1960; beyond reason), is another confessional diary. The protagonist examines the existence and will of God as well as his own reason for being. His quest leads him beyond reason (*razón*) to *la sinrazón*, a term which literally means "without reason," while also connoting injury and injustice. The work, published in Spain in 1970, won the prestigious Critics' Prize in 1977.

C.'s *Barrio de Maravillas* (1976; *The Maravillas District*, 1992) had won the same prize the year before. This is the first volume in a trilogy that C. describes as a history of her literary generation. *Barrio de Maravillas* covers the period from the turn of the century until World War I. *Acrópolis* (1984; the Acropolis) follows the same female artists from 1914 to 1931. The trilogy concludes with *Ciencias naturales* (1988; natural science), tracing one protagonist's many years of exile in Buenos Aires until her return to Spain after Francisco Franco's death. C.'s prose reaches its zenith in this series, a female bildungsroman, combining interior monologue, omniscient narrative, Platonic dialogue, brilliant descriptions, and the narrator's philosophical-aesthetic discussion.

During her long exile C. also published short stories about life in Spain, Brazil, and Argentina, collecting them in *Icada, nevda, diada* (1971; nothingness). Its topics include double suicide, the exercise of one's will to overcome difficulties, self-created realities, a child's view of the world, and the artist's world view. C. visited Europe in 1961, researching *La confesión* (1971; confession), a comparative analysis of the confessional essays of Kierkegaard, Rousseau, and St. Augustine. With a Guggenheim fellowship, C. spent two years in New York City, writing a book-length essay, *Saturnal* (1972; saturnalia). In 1974 C. returned to Spain to live.

In Madrid C. continued to write in several genres. These include an autobiography of her early years, *Desde el amanecer* (1972; since dawn), and a two-volume diary under the general title *Alcancía* (1982; potpourri). Of special interest is a published collection of unfinished works, *Novelas antes de tiempo* (1981; novels before their time), in which she discussed the ideas and techniques used in each embryonic work presented, finally explaining how she would finish each, time permitting.

This author's basic style did not change during her more than sixty years of writing, though it matured and became increasingly concentrated. If the tragedy of the Spanish Civil War had been avoided, and C. had continued her craft uninterrupted in Spain, she probably would have been one of the most respected Spanish novelists of her day; had the financial exigencies of exile been avoided, she doubtless would have been more prolific. Late in her life C. received many honors, including the National Spanish Literature Prize (1988) and that of Castile and León (1991). King Juan Carlos I of Spain presented her with the Gold Medal of Fine

Arts (1994) during her last hospitalization. C. was one of the best novelists of the Generation of 1927.

FURTHER WORKS: *Sobre el piélago* (1952); *Ofrenda a una virgen loca* (1961); *Versos prohibidos* (1978); *Timoteo Pérez Rubio y sus retratos del jardín* (1980); *Los títulos* (1981); *Rebañaduras* (1986); *La lectura es secreto* (1989); *Balaam y otros cuentos* (1989); *Obras completas* (4 vols., 1989-93)

BIBLIOGRAPHY: Aguirre, F., "R. C., como en su playa propia," *CHA*, 296 (1975): 298–315; Myers, E. D., "Narcissism and the Quest for Identity in R. C.'s *La Sinrazón*," *PCL*, 8 (1982): 85–90; Myers, E. D., "*Estación. Ida y vuelta* R. C.'s Apprenticeship Novel," *Hisj*, 4, 2 (Spring 1983): 77–84; Porlán, A., *La sinrazón de R. C.* (1984); Johnson, R., "*Estación. Ida y vuelta*, de R. C.: Un nuevo tiempo para la novela," in Burgos, F., ed., *Prosa hispánica de vanguardia* (1986): 201–8; Myers, E. D., "*Teresa:* R. C.'s Novel of Exile and Alienation," *MRRM*, 2 (1986): 151–58; Mangini, S., "Women and Spanish Modernism: The Case of R. C.," *ALEC*, 12: 1–2 (1987): 17–28; Newberry, W., "R. C.'s *Barrio de Maravillas:* The Role of the Arts and the Problem of Spain," *Hisj*, 9, 2 (Spring 1988): 37–44; special C. issue, *Anthropos*, 85 (1988); Mangini, S., "Introdución:" *Estación: Ida y vuelta* (1989): 11–69; special C. homage, *Letras peninsulares* 3, 1 (Spring 1990): 11–82; *R. C.: Premio nacional de las letras españolas, 1987* (1990); Glenn, K., "Narration and Eroticism in C.'s *Memorias de Leticia Valle* and Nabokov's *Lolita*," *MRRM*, 7 (1991): 84-93; Six, A. L., "Perceiving the Family: R. C.'s *Desde el amanecer*," in Conde, L. P., and S. M. Hart, eds., *Feminist Readings on Spanish and Latin-American Literature* (1991); Maier, C., "Siting Leticia Valle; Questions of Gender and Generation," *MRRM*, 8 (1992): 79-98; Smith, P. J., "R. C.: The Repudiation of Femininity," *Laws of Desire: Questions of Homosexuality in Spanish Writing and Film, 1960-1990* (1992); Mateo, M. A., *Retrato de R. C.* (1993); Newton, C., Fenomenología, representación del sujeto y lenguaje en la poesía de R. C.," *RLA*, 7 (1995): 573-77

—EUNICE D. MYERS

CHAIRIL Anwar

Indonesian poet, b. 26 July 1922, Medan, Sumatra; d. 28 April 1949, Djakarta

C. began to write as an adolescent, before he came to Djakarta in 1940. He had had six years of elementary school and the first two years of a Dutch-language middle school; he had no other education and nothing is known about his parents; nor did he ever have any stable means of support, other than what he could get from his writing. He was married and had a daughter. None of his early poetry survives (he says he destroyed it himself, but C. is not too much to be trusted); even some of the later poetry seems to have been fairly casually lost, or destroyed, along with a collection of short stories. He published only in periodicals during his lifetime, although there are several posthumous books.

C. lived wildly, even carelessly, but he wrote with infinite care, and with a rare ability to absorb and transform a host of influences. His use of the Indonesian language was both magical and as close to totally new as is possible: many Indonesian writers confessed that, until his work appeared, they had had no idea what Indonesian

was capable of as a literary instrument. The sources of his poetry's tremendous power are his glowing, sometimes savage use of language, his divergence from traditional Indonesian themes and attitudes, his immensely fertile use of such Western writers as RILKE, T. S. ELIOT, Emily Dickinson, and, of course, Edgar du PERRON and other modern Dutch writers; all of Indonesian writing, poetry and prose alike, was in a sense pushed bodily into the 20th c. by C. It is more than justified that the "Generation of '45" is interchangeably referred to as the "Generation of C. A."

Some of his driving power, and also one of his main themes, an obsessive concern with sex, can be seen in "Lagu biasa" (1949; "An Ordinary Song," 1962), while his wry humor, his active involvement with political and patriotic issues, as well as his ability to work the Indonesian language to its limits can be seen especially in "Persetujuan dengan bung Karno" (1948; "Agreement with Friend Soekarno," 1962). And the soaring idealism of his affirmations is nowhere better displayed than in the final line of his most famous and most beloved poem, "Aku" (1943; "Me," 1970), a searing individualist challenge to Indonesia's communal ethic: "I want to live another thousand years."

Despite the slimness of his output—fewer than seventy poems, a handful of essays and radio addresses, and some fragmentary translations—C.'s position in Indonesian literature is and will forever be something like that of Pushkin in Russian letters. He may descend into shrillness now and then, he may posture and push drama to the point of melodrama, and he may (as he certainly did) occasionally plagiarize, but at his fierce best he is easily comparable to, say, Federico García LORCA and to Constantine CAVAFY. Even his weakest verse rings; his poetry echoes and reechoes in the minds of Indonesians, making him an important social force as well as an artistic icon.

FURTHER WORKS: *Deru tjampur debu* (1949); *Kerikil tadjam, dan Jang terampas dan Jang Putus* (1951); *Tiga menguak Takdir* (1950, with Rivai Apin and Asrul Sani); *C. A., Pelopor Angkatan 45* (1956). **FURTHER WORKS IN ENGLISH:** *The Complete Poetry and Prose of C. A.* (1970); *Voice of the Night: Complete Poetry and Prose of C. A.* (1993)

BIBLIOGRAPHY: Raffel, B., "C. A.—Indonesian Poet," *LitR*, 10 (1967): 133–57; Raffel, B., *The Development of Modern Indonesian Poetry* (1967): 80–110; Aveling, H., *A Thematic History of Indonesian Poetry: 1920–1974* (1974): 28–44; Johns, A. H., *Cultural Options and the Role of Tradition: A Collection of Essays on Modern Indonesian and Malaysian Literature* (1979): 65–81; Teeuw, A., *Modern Indonesian Literature*, 2nd ed. (1979), Vol. I: 145–59

—BURTON RAFFEL

CHAMOISEAU, Patrick

Martinican novelist, dramatist, and literary theoretician, b. 1953, Fort-de-France

Born and reared in Martinique, where he still resides, C. is one of the few writers to have spent the majority of his life in Fort-de-France, Martinique's departmental capital. These close ties with the capital and with Martinican culture have greatly influenced C.'s work as a writer, sociologist, political commentator, and activist.

With respect to C.'s fiction, the importance of Martinican culture can be seen in the continual exploration of what C. calls *créolité*— the blend of African and French language, custom and societal structure unique to the Antilles.

Although he has written plays, autobiographical works, theoretical texts, and a collection of folktales, C. is best known for his novels, the first of which was *Chronique des sept misères* (1986; The Chronicle of Seven Miseries). This novel interrogates Martinican cultural identity across the span of the island's history, and marks the beginning of C.'s ongoing exploration of the role of the storyteller in Martinican culture, particularly as mediator between *créolité* and the cultural, political, and linguistic domination of France.

C.'s examination of the role of the storyteller continues in his second novel, *Solibo magnifique* (1988; *Solibo Magnificent*, 1997), which foregrounds the disappearance of orality in Martinican life and its replacement with the written culture imported by France. The title character of the novel, Solibo, is a storyteller who dies while telling a story to a group of people, one of whom is a writer named Patrick Chamoiseau. The split between the oral tradition, personified by Solibo, and the written, represented by the character of Chamoiseau, becomes the focus of the novel, which examines the impact of this loss of orality on the integrity and specificity of Creole culture. The thrust of the novel is the questioning of whether *créolité* as a fundamentally oral culture can survive in the age of text, that is to say, whether the writer can replace the storyteller as guardian of Antillean history and identity.

To some extent the existence of such a novel is C.'s affirmation that, indeed, Creole culture can survive in written form—an affirmation concretized in the prose style that emerges in *Solibo magnifique*. This hybridized prose style, a blend of French and Creole, has become C.'s hallmark, and it demonstrates the two fold emphasis on orality in C.'s work, since language and *créolité* become both theme and substance in his texts.

While *Solibo magnifique* first assured critical interest in C.'s work, it was his third novel, *Texaco* (1992; *Texaco*, 1997), that assured his literary reputation. Winner of the prestigious Goncourt Prize, *Texaco* marks the maturation of C.'s hybridized writing style, and fuses the thematic concerns of C.'s first two novels into one text. As in *Solibo Magnifique*, C. incorporates himself into his text in the persona of a writer, whose name, Oiseau de Cham, is another presentation of C.'s own name. This writer, called the recorder of memories, is researching the history of the Martinican township of Texaco, so named because of its proximity to an oil refinery owned by the Texaco corporation. Texaco, as township, embodies the linguistic, historical, and cultural heritage of Martinique itself, which also developed under the shadow of European capitalism. For this reason the novel's presentation of an attempt by the French departmental authorities to demolish the township functions as a metaphoric representation of the threat to *créolité* posed by French political, linguistic and cultural presence, which aims to annihilate anything separate from itself.

What emerges from the pages of *Texaco* is not, however, a refusal of the French influence in Martinique. For just as the township manages to survive and coexist with French departmental rule, so too is *créolité* characterized by the simultaneous presence of French and African influences. In fact, C. understands the hybrid nature of Martinique all too well, and his novels are less a call for a return to some lost African past, than they are a call to revitalize the present—to maintain the diversity and dynamism of an identity that is unique to Martinique.

L'esclave vieil homme et le molosse (1997; *The Old Man Slave and the Mastiff*, 1997) expands C.'s investigation of Martinican identity, and openly invites interpretation through Edouard GLISSANT's theories of "marronage," which the novel openly incorporates. Through the figure of the slave, C. makes explicit Glissant's assertion that Antillean identity, unique from that of other African diasporic identities, is always constituted by the presence of the colonial oppressor, since the Antilles are still under French control. Like the runaway slave on an island , the Antillean can hide from the French, but he can not fully escape them. He must, therefore, find a way of maintaining his own autonomy while coexisting with the dominant power. This most recent novel is both an embracing of this dual Martinican identity, and an admission of its complexity.

C.'s insistence on the existence of a truly Martinican essence is revealed in his work through the hybridized prose in which he writes, through the focus on the reappropriation of Martinican history and tradition, and through the exploration of the importance of the writer in sustaining Martinican identity. What C.'s novels both illustrate and advocate is a reinscribing of that essence in order to preserve, energize, and develop it. This call to affirm and secure the linguistic, social, and historical hybridity of Antillean culture is the self-appointed mission of C.'s work, and it is this simultaneous call to self-affirmation and acceptance of hybridization that created and sustains the interest in C.'s works in Martinique, in France, and throughout the world. His concerns with language, with history, with tradition and identity are both specific to Martinique and universal, in the sense that questions of identity are central to readers everywhere.

FURTHER WORKS: *Manman Dlo contre la Fée Carabosse* (1981); *Au temps de l'antan* (1988); *Éloge de la créolité* (1989); *Martinique* (1989); *Antan d'enfance* (1990); *Lettres Créoles* (1991); *Écrire la parole de nuit: la nouvelle littérature Antillaise* (1994); *Chemin d'école* (1994); *Guyane, traces-mémoires du bagne* (1994); *Écrire en pays dominé* (1997)

BIBLIOGRAPHY: Burton, R., "Debrouya pa peche, or il y a toujours moyen de moyenner: Patterns of Opposition in the Fiction of P. C.," *Callaloo*, 16 (1993): 466-82; Hazael-Masseiux, M., "A propos de *Chronique de sept misères*: Une littérature en français regional pour les Antilles," *Antilla*, 11 (1989): 13-21; Ndiaye, C., "De la pratique des detours chez Semben, C. et Ben Jelloun," *Tangence*, 49 (1995): 63-77; Perret, D., "La Parole du conteur créole: *Solibo magnifique* de P. C.," *FR*, 67 (1994): 824-39; Sourieau, M., "P. C., *Solibo magnifique*: From the Escheat of Speech to the Emergence of Language," *Callaloo*, 15 (1992): 131-38

—DAYNA L. OSCHERWITZ

CHAMPOURCIN, Ernestina de

Spanish poet, b. 10 July 1905, Vitoria

Born in Spain's northeast Basque region, C. has never accented her surname since it is of Provençal origin. She was reared in Madrid, where she received a traditional Roman Catholic education, firmly rooted in literature and language studies, including Spanish, French, and English. Inspired and guided by poet Juan Ramón JIMÉNEZ, C. quickly achieved notoriety, being one of only two women named to the original Generation of 1927 in Gerardo Diego's influential anthology *Poesía española (Contemporáneos)*(1934; Contemporary Spanish Poetry). On November 7, 1936, she married another poet, Juan José Domenchina (1898-1959) on the day before Franco was to enter Madrid during the Spanish Civil War. Because of Domenchina's work as secretary to Manuel Azaña, leader of the Republican party, Domenchina and C. immediately fled into exile to Toulouse, France and then to Mexico. There, C. used her language training to form an association of technical translators, where she translated books and worked at international symposia. Domenchina died in Mexico in 1959; C. remained there until 1973, returning to Madrid where she continues to live and write. Her most recent book, *Del vacío y sus dones* (1993; Emptiness and Its Graces), addresses the frustrations of blindness and deafness that come with old age.

Even though she was a political exile, C. did not write political or social poetry. *Ahora* (1928; Now) plunges into the modernist and surrealist traditions with vibrant language, complex metaphors, and lush exoticism. Highly influenced by Juan Ramón Jiménez, *Ahora* and her next book *La voz en el viento* (1931; Voice in the Wind) insured her inclusion in the lively Madrid literary scene where she was granted exclusive book contracts and named among the Generation of 1927. A structurally complex and mature volume followed, *Cántico inútil* (1936; Useless Chant), which is arguably the finest in all her production and certainly the best of her early writing.

Because of her marriage and exile to Mexico, C. stopped writing poetry. When she resumed publishing in 1952, her approach had changed completely. No longer did she experiment with exuberant metaphors or focus on carefully crafted structure. All of her poetry from 1952 through 1974 adhered to the thematic credo that "God is in all poetry," a theme shared by her husband who believed that the poet's only life was to dialogue with God. Deeply felt and reliant on biblical themes, *El nombre que me diste* (1960; The Name You Gave Me) and *Cárcel de los sentidos* (1964; Prison of the Senses) convey her devotion to religious themes.

A noticeable shift in theme and structural acuity accompanies her return to Spain. Beginning with *Primer exilio* (1978; First Exile), C. abandons her religious orientation, now becoming more retrospective and pessimistic. Desperate for communication and increasingly frustrated by a lack of human contact and the loss of sight and hearing, C.'s poetry seeks transcendence through nature, awareness of the world around her and the consolation of poetic memory.

C.'s singular early successes, her forced exile, and her lifelong dedication to poetry even in the bleakest of circumstances distinguish her as one of Spain's most notable women poets of this century.

FURTHER WORKS: *En Silencio* (1926); *La casa de enfrente* (1936); *Presencia a oscuras* (1952); *Hai-Kais espirituales* (1967); *Cartas cerradas* (1968); *Poemas del Ser y del Estar* (1974); *La ardilla y la rosa: Juan Ramón en mi memoria* (1981); *La pared transparente* (1984); *Antología poética* (1988); *Huyeron todas las islas* (l988); *Poesía a través del tiempo* (1991); *La ola gratinada* (1991); *Los encuentros frustrados* (1991)

BIBLIOGRAPHY: Espejo-Saavedra, R., "Sentimiento amoroso y creación poética en E. de C.," *RevI,*12, 1 (1982): 133-39; Landeira, J. B., "E. de C. y Moran de Loredo," in Galerstein, C., ed., *Women Writers of Spain: An Annotated Bio-bibliographical Guide* (l986): 88-91; Villar, A., "Entrevista de E. C.," *Alaluz* 18, 2, (l986); Ascunce, J. A., Prologue to *Poesía a través del tiempo* (1991), ix-lxxv; Landeira, J. B., "E. C.," in Levine, L. G., et al., ed., *Spanish Women Writers: A Bibliographical Source Book* (1993): 141-47; Wilcox, J. C., "E. C. and Concha Méndez," *Women Poets of Spain, 1860-1990* (1997): 87-133

—JOY B. LANDEIRA

CHANDLER, Raymond

American novelist, short-story writer, and screen-writer, b. 23 July 1888, Chicago, Ill.; d. 26 Mar. 1959, La Jolla, Cal.

C. came late to a literary career. After the divorce of his parents, C. was taken at the age of eight by his mother to England, where he received a classical education at Dulwich College Preparatory School in London. Returning to the U.S. in 1912, he served in World War I as a soldier in the Canadian army, in which he enlisted while visiting British Columbia in 1917. After the war he entered the oil business in California, rising from the position of accountant to executive status before he was fired in 1932 for drinking and absenteeism. It was this turn in his life, occurring as it did in the middle of the Depression, that led C., who as a young man between 1908 and 1911 had published some poetry and translations, to consider whether he might be able to make a living as a writer.

By the time C. published his first short story in 1933, hard-boiled detective fiction had been an established literary subgenre, a mainstay of the "pulp" magazines of the period, for a full decade. "Knights of the Open Palm," by Carroll John Daly (1889–1958), widely regarded as the first hard-boiled detective story, had appeared in *Black Mask* in June 1923, and Dashiell HAMMETT's "Arson Plus," the debut of Hammett's "Continental Op," was published in October of the same year; by 1933, Hammett had published four novels as well. C., then, is hardly one of the founding fathers of the literary subgenre with which his name is so strongly associated, even though he was in fact older than both Daly and Hammett.

The pulps, printed on cheap paper, aimed at a largely male mass audience, paying writers by the word, held out to the unemployed C. the hope of earning money as a writer, however remote the world of pulp fiction was from C.'s earlier literary efforts. C. prepared himself for his first submission by carefully studying representative samples of pulp fiction, especially fiction published in the most respected of the pulps, *Black Mask*. He gave almost obsessively close attention to the work of Erle Stanley Gardner (1889–1970), who would later become one of the most prolific and prosperous of American writers of detective fiction. In all, C. spent five months writing his first story, "Blackmailers Don't Shoot," which appeared in *Black Mask* in December 1933, when C. was forty-five years old.

There is something comic, perhaps something pathetic, about C.'s painstaking approach to publication in the pulps. But the seriousness of C.'s apprenticeship is revealing and characteristic; no writer would be more devoted to the cause of establishing the artistic seriousness of the hardboiled crime and detective fiction, which, for him, represented the pulps' most significant contribution to American literary culture. And, for C., this contribution must not be assigned to a critical ghetto called "popular fiction."

C.'s most famous affirmation of the authentic literary value of the right sort of detective fiction (the sort, of course, he was himself engaged in writing) is the essay "The Simple Art of Murder," first published in the *Atlantic Monthly* in December 1944. In this frequently reprinted essay, C. dismisses as unworthy of serious critical attention the formal detective story, associated with writers like Agatha Christie (1891–1976) and Dorothy L. Sayers (1893–1957), that had flourished, especially in England, in the period between the two world wars, the so-called "Golden Age" of detective fiction. He championed instead the work of the "realist[s] in crime," his name for the writers of hard-boiled detective fiction, and especially the work of Hammett, whose best fiction, in C.'s view, had established the artistic value of detective fiction. And yet, C. goes on to say, what Hammett has achieved is not quite enough. Hammett's style lacks echoes, and his heroes (the Continental Op, Sam Spade in *The Maltese Falcon*) are not completely satisfying. In C.'s much quoted formulation, "Down these mean streets a man must go who is not himself mean. . . . He is the hero, he is everything." And this hero, it seems, is essential in providing the "quality of redemption" present in "everything that can be called art."

For C., "everything that can be called art" most emphatically includes his own fiction; and if Anglo-American critics are unable to see that, it is because in their fixation on subject matter and theme, they fail to appreciate writing as writing, by which C. seems to mean all that a writer adds to his subject matter. And it is C.'s goal to provide in his detective fiction those qualities missing, at least in C.'s judgment, even from Hammett at his best.

Above all in Philip Marlowe, the detective protagonist of his novels, C. provides his version of the hero, his "knight" as some critics would have it. Marlowe is beyond question C.'s most important creation and his most important contribution to hard-boiled detective fiction. At once cynical wisecracker and romantic idealist, he is a more complex figure than the code heroes of Hammett's fiction. Where Hammett emphasized surfaces, rarely offering more than a glimpse of the inner life of his protagonists, C. insists upon the psychological and, above all, the ethical richness of the inner life of Marlowe. In his role as narrator, Marlowe constantly comments on, judges, and tries against overwhelming odds to find hints of redemption in the mean streets that constitute his environment. The meanness is as much spiritual as socioeconomic. C. exploits the freedom of the detective hero, unlimited by a clearly defined class position, to move freely within the existing class structure. Marlowe in his investigations becomes the instrument by which C. brings us into confrontation with a fictional world of considerable range and complexity that is also a stylized but incisive portrait of Southern California as it sprawls toward midcentury. The tension between the romantic sensibility of the hero and the demands of survival in the threatening world C. depicts generates the celebrated C. style, an amalgam of tough talk, baroque simile, and that American vernacular which the American-born, but British-educated, C. always heard as a quasi-foreign tongue. It also generates the moral tension between the detective's need to know the world as it is and the idealist's desire to see the world as it might be that is yet another source of the power of C.'s best fiction.

C.'s most successful novels are his first two, *The Big Sleep* (1939) and *Farewell, My Lovely* (1940). The tensions that characterize and organize C.'s work are here most fully in play. The sixth novel in the series, *The Long Goodbye* (1953), is admired by many critics, but others find that the tensions of the best work have collapsed as Marlowe slides into a cynicism and self-pity from which the author does not succeed in distancing himself.

Raymond Chandler

Like many American writers of his generation, C. worked as a screenwriter. Although his experience working on Alfred Hitchcock's *Strangers on a Train* (1951) was not a happy one, his work as a collaborator on the script of Billy Wilder's *Double Indemnity* (1943), based on the novella by James M. CAIN, and his script for *The Blue Dahlia* (1945) have earned him an honored place among Hollywood scriptwriters.

C. ranks with Hammett as one of the two most influential writers of hard-boiled detective fiction. In fact, much of the fiction of this sort written since the 1950s is rather more in the spirit of C. than of Hammett. Although critics remain divided on the question of the relative merits of the two writers, there is little dissent from the proposition that they are the two finest writers of hard-boiled detective fiction.

FURTHER WORKS: *The High Window* (1942); *The Lady in the Lake* (1943); *Five Murderers* (1944); *Five Sinister Characters* (1945); *Finger Man and Other Stories* (1946); *The Little Sister* (1949); *The Simple Art of Murder* (1950); *Pickup on Noon Street* (1952); *Playback* (1958); *R. C. Speaking* (1962); *Killer in the Rain* (1964); *C. before Marlowe: R. C.'s Early Prose and Poetry* (1973); *The Notebooks of R. C.* (1976); *Selected Letters of R. C.* (1981)

BIBLIOGRAPHY: Elliott, G., "Country Full of Blondes," *The Nation* (23 April 1960): 354–60; Durham, P., *Down These Mean Streets a Man Must Go: R. C.'s Knight* (1963); Ruhm, H., "R. C.: From Bloomsbury to the Jungle—And Beyond," in Madden, D., ed.,

Tough Guy Writers of the Thirties (1968): 171–85; Lid, R., "Philip Marlowe Speaking," *KR*, 31 (1969): 153–78; Jameson, F., "On R. C.," *SoR*, 6 (Summer 1970): 624–50; MacShane, F., *The Life of R. C.* (1976); Gross, M., ed., *The World of R. C.* (1977); Knight, S. T., *Form and Ideology in Crime Fiction* (1980): 135–67; Speir, J., *R. C.* (1981); Arden, L., "A Knock at the Backdoor of Art: The Entrance of R. C.," in Benstock, B., ed., *Art in Crime Writing* (1983): 73–96; Newlin, K., *Hardboiled Burlesque: R. C.'s Comic Style* (1984); Wolfe, P., *Something More Than Night: The Case of R. C.* (1985); Marling, W., *R. C.* (1986); Lehman, D., *The Perfect Murder* (1989): 135–67

—W. P. KENNEY

CHANG Ai-ling

(Anglicized as Eileen Chang) Chinese novelist, short-story writer, and essayist, b. 1921, Shanghai?; d. 8 Sept. 1995, Los Angeles

Central to C.'s unusual childhood were the decline of her father's family, once prominent in the service of the last imperial dynasty, and traumatic episodes involving her father's separation from her Europeanized, cosmopolitan mother. After being tutored for a time, she received a grant to attend the University of Hong Kong, where her studies were ended by the Japanese attack and occupation of the British colony. Singlemindedly devoted to being a writer since childhood, C. returned to Shanghai to begin her career. In 1952 she went back to Hong Kong as a refugee from Communist China and then took up residence in the U. S. C. held positions at several universities in Great Britain and the U. S., most recently at the University of California at Berkeley.

C.'s earliest published stories were first collected as *Ch'uan-ch'i* (1944; romances) and later as *Chang Ai-ling tuan-p'ien hsiaoshuo chi* (1954; collected short stories of Chang Ai-ling). Fine, ironic studies of love and courtship set in Shanghai and Hong Kong, the stories offer skeptical portraits of Europeans, Eurasians and Chinese trapped by circumstance and self-delusion. Their sensuous imagery and their diction recall traditional Chinese literature, yet the style is controlled by symbolic technique and modern psychological vision. The most representative of these stories is "Chin-suo chi" ("The Golden Cangue," 1971).

The desolateness C. reveals at the core of her characters' experiences is accentuated in the first novel she wrote following her return to Hong Kong, *Yang-ko* (1954; *The Ricesprout Song*, 1955). As a depiction of peasants balking and rioting at excessive Communist demands to aid the Korean War effort, the novel is a dissident's work. The thematic continuity with her earlier stories is evident, however: time and circumstance are triumphant over the characters' attempts to transcend them through appeals to love or revolt, whether those characters be Communist cadres or peasants.

Similarly, in C.'s second major novel, *Ch'ih-ti chih lien* (1954; *Naked Earth*, 1956), Communism appears as the vehicle for more permanent themes in C.'s writing. Insofar as Maoist thought is fiction and simplification of reality, its actual implementation requires that party cadres perpetrate a callous charade in order to survive and to enjoy shallow rewards as the new elite of society. As prisoners of this system, two disillusioned cadres paradoxically face their first true freedom of choice as prisoners of war in Korea. In seeking to evoke the complexity of her characters and their

careers during the founding years of the People's Republic, the novel does not always maintain the degree of control over setting and imagery evident in C.'s best work.

C. has belonged to no school or major trend in modern Chinese literature, but she has had imitators. As a young writer she showed little of the concern for China's political fate that dominated the work of so many of her contemporaries, yet her treatment of love stands in marked contrast to that of other love literature of the time. Elements of the social protest in her later works correspond to the dissent of writers within China as well as outside, but her novels bear only superficial resemblance to the run of anti-Communist fiction in Chinese. To date, C.'s use of imagery, by turns compelling and subtle, remains unsurpassed.

FURTHER WORKS: *Liu-yen* (1944); *T'ai-t'ai wan sui* (1948); *Shih-pa ch'un* (under pseud. Liang Ching, 1950); *Yuan-nü* (1968); *Pansheng yuan* (1960); *Hung-lou yen-meng* (1976); *Chang k'an* (1976). FURTHER WORKS IN ENGLISH: *The Rouge of the North* (1967)

BIBLIOGRAPHY: Hsia, C. T., *A History of Modern Chinese Fiction*, 2nd ed. (1971): 389–431; Cheng, S., "Themes and Techniques in Eileen C.'s Stories," *TkR*, 8 (1977): 169–200; Gunn, E., *Unwelcome Muse: Chinese Literature in Shanghai and Peking, 1937–45* (1980): 200–231

—EDWARD M. GUNN

CHAO Shu-li

Chinese novelist and short-story writer, b. 1906, Ch'in-shui County, Shansi Province; d. 23 Sept. 1970

The son of peasants, C. had his secondary school education cut short by his imprisonment for activities against the provincial warlord. After his release he worked in theater and journalism until, following the call of Mao Tsetung in 1942 for a new literature to serve the population of northwest China, C. emerged as a writer of fiction. With the establishment of the People's Republic in 1949, C. chaired or served on various writers' organizations and edited several cultural periodicals, notably *Ch'ü-i*, devoted to folk-style oral and performing literature. In early 1967 he fell victim to the massive purges of writers and intellectuals during the Cultural Revolution and, according to later published accounts in the official press, died from maltreatment. In 1979 his reputation was restored, and some of his works were reissued.

With the stories "Hsiao Erh-hei chieh-hun" (1943; "Hsiao Erh-hei's Marriage," 1950) and "Li Yu-ts'ai pan-hua" (1943; "Rhymes of Li Yu-ts'ai," 1950) C. won recognition as being among the first and ablest interpreters of the new official prescriptions for literature. Breaking with the dominant trend to write fiction employing techniques learned from the West, C. addressed his peasant audience as one that largely needed to be read to, and consequently adopted the style common to popular storytellers, also making strong use of doggerel verse and colorful colloquialisms without resorting entirely to local dialect. These early stories of peasants overcoming superstitions, exploitive landlords, and corrupt authorities in matters of courtship and community affairs with the support of the Communist Party are also told with considerable humor.

A more serious tone dominates the novel *Li-chia-chuang ti pien-ch'ien* (1950; *Changes in Li Village*, 1953), which portrays developments in a village from the period of warlord control in 1928 to land reform in 1946. Generally valued for its superior depiction of Shansi and its suffering peasantry, the novel in its latter portion is unexceptional party propaganda.

C.'s major work, *San-li-wan* (1955; *San-liwan Village*, 1957) returns to a lighter vein in telling of village tensions over construction of irrigation canals and the creation of an agricultural cooperative. Yet, here again, C. was unable to make convincing characters of the "politically correct" party cadres or do more than provide a simplistic resolution to the complexities of the situation he introduced in which a significant number of the peasants are skeptical of and opposed to the cooperative movement.

After this work C. was overshadowed by other writers. His greatest supporter was always Chou Yang, vice-minister of propaganda, and C.'s fall from grace shortly followed Chou's. One of C.'s strongest points as a writer was his droll description of "backward" peasants uncommitted to Communist Party policies, and his not unsympathetic attention to them figured in charges of his inadequacy as a writer. C.'s importance as a writer lies primarily in the style he cultivated in most of his fiction in response to the policies inaugurated by Mao Tse-tung.

FURTHER WORKS: *Ling ch'üan tung* (1959); *Hsia-hsiang chi* (1963). FURTHER WORKS IN ENGLISH: *Rhymes of Li Yu-ts'ai and Other Stories* (1950)

BIBLIOGRAPHY: Chou Yang, "The Creative Works of C. S.," in C. S., *Rhymes of Li Yu-ts'ai and Other Stories* (1950): 7-30; Birch, C., ed., *Chinese Communist Literature* (1963): 77–82, 197–99; Hsia, C. T., *A History of Modern Chinese Fiction*, 2nd ed. (1971): 482–84: 491–94; Huang, J., *Heroes and Villains in Communist China* (1973): 238–42, 284

—EDWARD M. GUNN

CHAR, René

French poet, b. 14 June 1907, L'Isle-sur-Sorgue; d. 19 Feb. 1988, Paris

C. was born and grew up in a small village in the Vaucluse in the South of France, a region that was to provide him with much poetic material; he attended secondary school at Avignon. His works have been translated into many languages, an increasing number of critical works are devoted to him annually, and the two exhibitions devoted to him and the painters who are and were his friends (his "substantial allies," such as Braque, Giacometti, Miró, Picasso, Vieira da Silva, Nicolas de Staël), one at the Foundation Maeght in 1971 and one in 1980 at the Bibliothèque Nationale in Paris, drew many visitors. None of that, however, goes very far toward explaining what about him and his work is exceptional. One remark made by the poet James WRIGHT is relevant: that everything about him is mountainous—writing, stature, character, whether in generosity or in anger. C. represents, without any doubt, a rare case in French literature, by his history and by his presence, to which other poets, critics, and the reading and thinking public bear continuing witness.

Through his early work *Arsenal* (1929; arsenal), vivid and haunting, he was introduced to the SURREALIST group by Paul ÉLUARD, and the poems of *Le marteau sans maître* (1934; the hammer with no master), full of dream and alchemical imagery of a dark luminosity, can be characterized, to a certain extent, as surrealist in tone. But after 1933 little trace of surrealism remains: his attitude toward work and the world is fundamentally different from that of the surrealists, and it is only because of his brief association with that group that C. is still occasionally identified with them.

Many of his greatest poems, which were published only after World War II, in *Seuls demeurent* (1945; alone remaining) and *Le poème pulvérisé* (1947; the pulverized poem), date from the dark years of the Spanish Civil War and the coming of Nazism, although *Dehors la nuit est gouvernée* (outside the night is ruled) was published in 1938. Among the best are the long majestic love poem "Le visage nuptial" (1938; "The Nuptial Countenance," 1976) and some of his best-loved prose poems. During the war, C. was a leader of the Resistance in the Basses-Alpes; as Capitaine Alexandre, he wrote the notebook later published as *Feuillets d'Hypnos* (1946; *Leaves of Hypnos*, 1973), a series of aphorisms to whose brevity and ambivalence his powerful and concise style is admirably suited. They are simple in appearance—close to the land, to natural things, and profound. Yet they convey the atmosphere of violence, of unpitying examination of self and others, of impatience with the self-indulgent and self-interested with which his most typical writing is charged.

Although living apart from what the French refer to as "the world," he is nevertheless a part of it, sharing constantly in a *Commune présence* (1964; common presence). The mystery of poetry is never for him a disincarnated "magic," is never intended only for the few, is never oriented toward some mystical communion with what is above man. His gods are pagan, multiple, and found within man himself, sensed in everyday things, sensed in the moments of morning, as in *Les matinaux* (1950; *The Dawn Breakers*, 1992), as well as in the silent and watchful moments of night, where the hand is guided by the light of some candle, as in *La nuit talismanique* (1972; the talismanic night), and in the myths inhabiting his world and our sky: Orion the hunter, fallen in the world of man and rising perpetually skyward, to whom *Aromates chasseurs* (1975; hunting herbs) is dedicated.

Recherche de la base et du sommet (1955; search for the base and the summit) contains a wide range of essays, in time, and in spirit, including painters and writers and ordinary people as subjects, being thus directed toward the peak and the foot of the mountain. *Retour amont* (1966; return upland [or upstream]) is included, significantly, in the volume *Le nu perdu* (1971; nakedness lost); these are poems about bare upland, of a cosmic sensitivity, echoed recently by his *Chants de la Balandrane* (1977; songs of La Balandrane) and *Fenêtres dormantes et porte sur le toit* (1979; dormer windows and door on the roof); in well and water, in these doors open not just upon the sky but upon the other dwellings of man, as in the simplest walk up a mountain or the single stream traced toward its source, in the vital flow of the Sorgue as in the springtime swell of the Fontaine de Vaucluse, the spirit of poetry mixes in the song of the senses.

Contre une maison sèche (1972; against a dry house) urges us to lean on our past, as on timeless stone dwellings in the Vaucluse, so that we may move onward and upland. The path chosen by this poet himself, in its *unlikeness*, harsh and tender, leaves a trace difficult to follow and impossible to forget.

FURTHER WORKS: *Les cloches sur le cœur* (1928); *Artine* (1930); *Ralentir travaux* (1930, with André Breton and Paul Éluard); *Le tombeau des secrets* (1930); *L'action de la justice est éteinte* (1931); *Placard pour un chemin des écoliers* (1937); *Fureur et mystère* (1948); *Le soleil des eaux* (1949); *Art bref, suivi de Premières alluvions* (1950); *À une serenite crispee* (1951); *La paroi et la prairie* (1952); *Le rempart de brindilles* (1952); *À la sante du serpent* (1954); *Les compagnons dans le jardin* (1956); *Poèmes et proses choisis* (1957); *L'inclémence lointaine* (1961); *La parole en archipel* (1962); *Lettera amorosa* (1963); *Trois coups sous les arbres: Théâtre saisonnier* (1967); *Les transparents* (1967); *Dans la pluie giboyeuse* (1968); *L'effroi la joie* (1971); *Le monde de l'art n'est pas le monde du pardon* (1975). **FURTHER WORKS IN ENGLISH:** *Hypnos Waking* (1956); *Poems of R. C.* (1976)

BIBLIOGRAPHY: special C. issue, *L'arc*, No. 22 (1963); La Charité, V., *The Poetics and the Poetry of R. C.* (1968); Mounin, G., *La communication poétique; ou, Avez-vous lu C.?* (1969); special C. issue, *L'Herne*, No. 15 (1971); Caws, M. A., *The Presence of R. C.* (1976); special C. issue, *WLT*, 51 (1977); Lawler, M. A., *R. C.* (1977); Lawler, J., *R. C.: The Myth and the Poem* (1978); Piore, N. K., *Lightning: The Poetry of R. C.* (1981)

—MARY ANN CAWS

CHARENTS, Eghishe

(pseud. of Eghishe Soghomonian) Armenian poet, novelist, editor, and translator, b. 13 March 1897, Kars (now in Turkey); d. 29 Nov. 1937, Erevan

The most influential writer of his time in Soviet Armenia, C. continues to be the measure of Armenian literature since the 1930s. He began writing at fifteen, was famous as the "voice of the Great October Revolution" at twenty, and died at forty, in prison during Stalin's time, accused of "bourgeois nationalism."

During the Turkish massacres of the Armenians in 1915 he joined the volunteer army to fight the Turks. His experience resulted in *Danteakan araspel* (1916; Dantesque legend), in which he depicts the bestiality of the ruling government toward the defenseless citizenry, at the same time exploring will, choice, and responsibility. The same theme was expanded ten years later in the novel *Erkir Nayiri* (1926; land of Nayiri). Written in the mode of social realism, it re-creates C.'s native Kars. Outwardly a satire on Armenian life and types—shopkeepers, soldiers, priests—the book is an allegory of Armenia's past history and failures. The protagonist, Hamo, is drawn with love and irony.

In 1922, with two other poets, C. issued a manifesto calling for a literature using the language of the street, one with a healthy view of sex. While C. was studying in Moscow later that year, officials in Erevan found the work he wrote according to this manifesto, *Romance anser* (1922; romance without love) vulgar and dangerous; the book was not reprinted.

C.'s poetry, after an early period of imitation, broke with formalism, but kept the incantational, hypnotic style comparable to MAYAKOVSKY's and Whitman's, which can be traced back to the religious rapture of the 11th-c. Armenian mystic poet Gregory of

Nareg. C. used the rhapsodic style for political exhortation and satire. Influenced by Marx, FREUD, and the FUTURISTS, C. moved from ballads of external action and lyric personal poetry toward social comment and satire. Ironically, for the "great Red poet" his most quoted work is a love song to his country, "Yes eem anoush Hayasdanee" (1920–21; "I Love My Sweet Armenia," 1978).

By 1926 he himself was the moving spirit of the Writers' Union and the literary leader in Erevan, famous for his wit and erudite lectures as well as for his generosity in fostering literary talent as director of the state press. He was also the target of jealous attacks. When his disillusionment with Stalin's system began to show in his work, he was removed from his editorial post. His last work, *Keerk janabaree* (1934; book of the road), was not released for a year after its printing. There are four major poems in the work: "Sassountsi Tavituh" (David of Sassoun), a retelling of the epic as an allegory of the revolution showing how the people were deceived after all; "Badmoutian karoughinerov" (at the crossroads of history), a bitter view of Armenia's leadership; "Mahvan deseel" (vision of death), tracing the Armenian liberation movement; and a short poem, "Badkam" (the message), which has been blamed for his imprisonment because it suggests that C. was changing from proletarian internationalism to nationalism. The poem contains an acrostic spelling "O Armenian people, your salvation is in your collective power." The book was banned as slanderous, and C. was arrested on charges of nationalism. He had become a morphine addict after a kidney-stone operation, and it is said that he was denied the drug in prison and crushed his head against the walls of his cell. The actual circumstances are not known. But the poems he wrote in prison remain—intense, vigorous, many of them tributes to poets he had rebelled against in his youth.

FURTHER WORKS: *Erek erk dekhratalouk aghchekan* (1914); *Gaboudachea hairenik* (1915); *Dsiadsan* (1917); *Amenaboem* (1922); *Poezozourna* (1922); *Lenin* (1925); *Madjkal Sakoyee badmoutiounuh* (1924); *Rubaiyats* (1927); *Heeshoghoutiounner Erevanee Ougheech Dnitz* (1927); *Epikakan lousapatz* (1930)

BIBLIOGRAPHY: Saroyan, W., "Y. C.," in *Letters from 74 rue Taitbout* (1969): 117–22; Der Hovanessian, D., and M. Margossian, "E. C.: His Life, His Poetry and His Times," *Aratat*, 20, 1 (1979): 50-62; Allahverdian, H., "The Enigmatic Sensualist," *Ararat*, 20, 1 (1979): 63–67

—MARGOSSIAN MARZBED

CHART KORBJITTI

Thai novelist and short-story writer, b. 25 June 1954, Samut Sakhon

C. was born in Samut Sakhon in central Thailand, the second of nine children. His mother ran a grocery store and his father ferried salt from rented salt fields to Bangkok. After studying fine arts and printing at vocational college in Bangkok, C. set up in business manufacturing leather bags while writing poems, plays, and short stories in his spare time. His first published short story, "Phu phae" (1979; The Loser), was acclaimed by the Thai Writers Association as the best of the year. Major success followed quickly, with his first novel, *Kham phiphaksa* (1981; *The Judgement*, 1983), being awarded the 1982 SEA Write Award for the best novel among ASEAN countries. Social hypocrisy is the underlying theme of the novel, which chronicles the downfall of Fak, a lowly school janitor, who becomes an outcast in his own community after marrying his widowed stepmother.

C. won the SEA Write Award again with *Wela* (1984; Time), an evocative and stylistically sophisticated portrayal of life in a nursing home. C.'s novel, *Phan ma ba* (1988; Mad Dogs and Company), also deals with a marginalized group, the author using the amiable dropouts of this work to challenge Thai society's prevailing materialistic values. The novella *Chan trak* (1980; Dead End) offers an altogether darker vision of society in which the impoverished hero's efforts to improve his family's circumstances backfire with tragic consequences.

National and international literary prizes, and the frequent reprints of his works attest to C.'s appeal both to critics and the reading public. Among writers of serious fiction, he is said to be unique in being able to make a living entirely from his creative writing.

FURTHER WORKS: *Ru'ang thammada* (1983); *Ma nao loi nam* (1987); *Mit pracham tua* (1984); *Nakhon mai pen rai* (1989)

BIBLIOGRAPHY: Suvanna Kriengkraipetch, and L. E. Smith, *Value Conflicts in Thai Society: Agonies of Change Seen in Short Stories* (1992); Barang, M., *The Twenty Best Novels of Thailand* (1994); Smyth, D. A., and Manas Chitakasem, *The Sergeant's Garland and Other Stories* (1998)

—DAVID A. SMYTH

CHATTERJI, Saratchandra

Indian novelist (writing in Bengali), b. 15 Sept. 1876, Devanandapur; d. 16 Jan. 1938, Calcutta

Born into an impoverished Brahman family, C. had to abandon his education after his first year at college. He spent the subsequent years wandering about India dressed as a mendicant, a role he described more realistically in later life as that of a tramp. But then the burden of family support cast upon him by his father's death sent him in search of regular employment. He found a permanent position in Burma, where he worked for thirteen years as a clerk in the accountant general's office in Rangoon. The success of the literary career launched during this period permitted him to give up his job and return to India to devote the rest of his life to writing.

Much of C.'s own life experience is to be found in his largest and most ambitious work, *Srikanta*, which appeared in four volumes between 1917 and 1933 (Eng. tr. of Vol. 1, *Srikanta*, 1922). *Srikanta*, although more a narration of episodes than a novel, shares many of the distinctive qualities of C.'s other fiction. The enchantment that surrounds several of his characters in *Srikanta* in no way diminishes the particular realism he brought to character presentation in the Bengali novel. The various episodes of the story provide a potpourri of emotional experiences—adventure, pathos, and romance—yet throughout the work, a fine balance and harmony are sustained. C.'s style in this, as in other novels, is largely unadorned, yet vivid and compelling.

Social issues receive very prominent attention in C.'s works. One of his major themes is the oppression of women in Hindu society, particularly the negative attitude toward career women. Rajiakshmi, the dancing girl in *Srikanta*, exemplifies the life of social ostracism and automatic ill repute experienced by women following this profession. In *Dena paona* (1923; debts and dues) the tenuousness of a woman's position of respect and honor as custodian of the village temple is dramatically portrayed. His sympathetic treatment of women willfully deviating from accepted social rules, illustrated in his novels *Caritrahin* (1917; *Charitraheen*, 1962) and *Grhadaha* (1920; *The Fire*, 1964), is an eloquent indictment of the inhumane stand society took against them and had rarely, if ever, been seen before in Bengali literature. Woven through these and other stories is his persistent theme of the abusive influence of the dowry system on the lives of middle-class Bengali women.

C.'s literary career spanned the years of the rapidly growing independence movement in India. For a long period he was very active in the Congress Party, which was formed in the later 19th c. to express the Indian point of view to the British colonial government. Some of the disaffection that led to his withdrawal from the party—one reason for it was that Muslim members were treated with hostility by the Hindu majority—may be discerned in his powerful short story "Mahes" (1923; "Mahesh," 1967). Keenly sensitive to social injustices practiced by his community, C. turned his story into a piercing indictment of the appalling mistreatment of Muslims by Hindus. C.'s angry accusation of Hindu oppression is made tellingly yet without direct authorial comment. In this he differed markedly from his Bengali predecessors, whose fiction was often marred by long passages of commentary.

C.'s work consolidated the pioneering efforts of Bankimcandra Chatterji (1838–1894) and Rabindranath TAGORE. A much better novelist than either of those writers, he achieved a more highly developed plot structure and a far greater realism. His stories, often reduced to sentimental syrup by translators and scenario writers, are, in their original form, moving accounts of the varied changes in fortune, in human experience. Both with respect to form and theme, his fiction marked a turning point in the development of the Bengali novel and, insofar as Bengali literature provided a national model, of the novel in India.

FURTHER WORKS: *Bara didi* (1913); *Biraj bau* (1914); *Bindur chele o anyanya galpa* (1914); *Parinita* (1914); *Pandit masai* (1914); *Mejdidi* (1915); *Palli-samaj* (1916); *Candranath* (1916; *Queen's Gambit*, 1969); *Baikunther uil* (1916); *Araksaniya* (1916); *Debdas* (1917); *Niskrti* (1917; *The Deliverance*, 1944); *Kasinath* (1917); *Svami* (1918); *Datta* (1918; *The Betrothed*, 1964); *Saratcandrer granthabali* (7 vols., 1919–1935); *Chabi* (1920); *Bamuner meye* (1920); *Baroyari upanyas* (1921); *Narir mulya* (1923); *Nababidhan* (1924); *Harilaksmi* (1926); *Pather dabi* (1926); *Sorasi* (1927); *Rama* (1928); *Satyasrayi* (1929); *Taruner bidroha* (1929); *Ses prasna* (1931); *Svades o sahitya* (1932); *Anuradha-sati o pares* (1934); *Bijaya* (1934); *Bipradas* (1935); *Rascakra* (1936); *Saratcandra o chatrasamaj* (1937); *Chelebelar galpa* (1938); *Subhada* (1938); *Seser paricay* (1939). FURTHER WORKS IN ENGLISH: *The Eldest Sister and Other Stories* (1950)

BIBLIOGRAPHY: Thompson, E. J., Preface to *Srikanta* (1922): vii-xi; Basu, T., *La société bengalie du vingtième siècle dans l'œuvre de S. C. C.* (1940); Madan, I. N., *S. C.: His Mind and Art* (1944); Sen Gupta, S. C., *S.: Man and Artist* (1945, 1975); Van Meter

[Baumer], R. R., "Communal Attitudes in the Nineteenth and Twentieth Centuries," in Dimock, E. C., Jr., ed., *Bengal Literature and History* (1969): 93–104; Kabir, H., "S. C. and the Realistic Novel," *The Bengali Novel* (1968): 65–93; Naravane, V. S., *S.C.: An Introduction to His Life and Work* (1976); Mukhopadhyay, M., and S. Roy, eds., *The Golden Book of S.* (1977)

—RACHEL VAN M. BAUMER

CHATWIN, Bruce

English travel writer, novelist, essayist, and journalist, b. 13 May 1940, Sheffield, England; d. 18 Jan. 1989, Nice, France

Known primarily as a travel writer, C.'s stylishly written books revived the art of English and American travel writing in the latter half of the 20th c., and his work in that genre has been favorably compared to the best works of D. H. LAWRENCE and Graham GREENE. Like Lawrence, C.'s books document the negative impact of Western cultural imperialism on native cultures in South America and Australia; Western civilization and its legacy of technology and ownership devastated native spiritual traditions by separating the Indians of Chile and Patagonia and the aboriginals of Australia from connections to the source of their spiritual vitality, their natural habitat. Two of his most popular books, *In Patagonia* (1977) and *The Songlines* (1987), recorded his trips to those remote areas and became the kind of travel books he was most famous for.

C. decided that he would not pursue an academic career after graduating from the renowned British public school, Marlborough College, in 1958. Instead, he began working as a porter at Sotheby's, the prestigious London art dealers in the same year. He became the head of one of its departments when he uncovered some fake Picasso paintings that no one else had noticed. After eight frustrating years of the commercial art world, he decided that he wanted to travel to distant and exotic places and write about them. After a trip to the Sudan, he became fascinated with nomads and their seemingly free lifestyles. He also began to detect a consistent pattern of conflict between nomads and settlers that went back thousands of years. What emerged from his musings was his unique theory about the "fall of man" and found its clearest explanation not the story of Adam and Eve in the Garden of Eden but, rather, in the story of their sons, Cain and Abel. His Sudanese experience of a nomadic way of life—that is, traveling along ancient geographical paths within the cycles of the seasons—constituted the original innocent state of mankind. Abel was the first nomadic shepherd. Cain, on the other hand, was the first settler who, after he murdered his brother, traveled east of Eden and founded the first city, Enoch. For C., the history of the world became the conflict between pastoral nomadism and "the sins of settlement." All of his books from *In Patagonia* to his posthumously published *What Am I Doing Here* (1989) and *Anatomy of Restlessness* (1996) deal in some way with C.'s permanent theme of the origins of human restlessness.

C. continually sought out locations that might somehow have escaped the damage done to native peoples and environments by Western Europeans, and so he decided to take the ultimate journey south into the remote wilds of Patagonia. *In Patagonia*, his first book, he combines travel, history, literature, and adventure, but also documented the flight of Europeans from their so-called "fallen worlds" of Germany, Wales, and England. However, their attempt to regenerate their Edenic world in the new world destroyed the pristine innocence of the indigenous natives.

The Viceroy of Ouidah (1980) resulted from his research into a biography on one of the most notorious Brazilian slave traders of the 19th c., Francisco Felix de Souza. C. decided that the subject matter would be more appropriate for a novel, but a novel that would expose the cultural and human devastation to the natives of Dahomey, a West African country from which Brazil obtained many of its slaves due primarily to the sadistic efforts of the sociopathic De Souza.

His next novel, *On the Black Hill* (1980), completely reversed the direction in which his fiction had been moving for five years. Tired of being labeled a "travel writer," C. decided to write about twin brothers who rarely ever left their remote farm in eastern Wales. He also wanted to test his theory about the "sins of settlement" to see if these innocents could escape the corruptions of ownership and greed. It was C.'s highly imaginative version of the myth of Cain and Abel.

Though suffering from the early effects of AIDS, C. embarked on a lengthy journey to the Central Australian desert in 1984 and published his masterpiece, *The Songlines*, which recorded his remarkable experiences in one of the most remote areas of the world. The literary form of *The Songlines* is modeled on the 18th-c. French novelist Denis Diderot's *Jacques le Fatalist*, a dialogue novel. Not only is *The Songlines* a travelogue, but it is also a philosophical novel about the ominous fate of the helpless aboriginals. Much of the novel consists of lengthy meditations on the ruins of a primitive society forced to dwell in the fallen world of time and permanent location—that is, nomads coerced into settlement. C.'s major discovery was, however, the incredibly rich cosmology that informs the seemingly destitute lives of the native aboriginals: their "songlines" which geographically connect them and their ancestors to the "dreamtime." The "songlines" name in song all objects and features of the land and become an eternal and ever active method of redeeming a former paradisal condition even in the midst of their wasteland realities.

C.'s last novel, *Utz* (1988), was written as he lay dying of AIDS. Though much shorter than his earlier works, it possesses great humor and sophistication. It is a mystery in the tradition of Graham Greene or John LE CARRÉ and concerns the disappearance of Caspar Utz's million-dollar collection of rare Meissen figurines after his death. Though the narrator's interview with Utz lasts only nine hours, Utz humorously contrasts the bleak world of communist bureaucracies with the equally bleak world of capitalistic greed. But the novel also explores in great detail the pathology of the obsessive collector and contrasts the shortness of life with the permanence of art, a theme made more poignant by C.'s terminal illness.

Not only was C. a remarkable novelist and travel writer—each of his books was written in an entirely different form—but he was also a critically acclaimed journalist and essayist. His two collections of essays, stories, profiles, and travelogues covered André MALRAUX, Werner Herzog, Tibet, Chinese necromancy, and many other equally diverse subjects. However, the topic that runs throughout all of his works is his obsession with the nature of human restlessness and its relationship to pastoral nomadism.

BIBLIOGRAPHY: Murray, N., *B. C.* (1993); Meanor. P., *B. C.* (1997)

—PATRICK MEANOR

CHAUVET, Marie Vieux

Haitian novelist and playwright, b. 1919, Port-au-Prince; d. 19 June 1973, New York, N.Y.

C. was born into a bourgeois Haitian family to an Antillean mother and a Haitian father. C.'s father was a highly placed politician in the Haitian government, and C. spent her childhood in Port-au-Prince, in the midst of a privileged elite. C. went on, in 1933, to complete a degree in elementary education at the Haitian annex of the École normale for teachers. In 1948 C. married her second husband, Pierre Chauvet, having divorced her first husband the previous year. She and Pierre Chauvet had three children together, but eventually divorced as well. C. lived in Haiti, traveled frequently to Europe and the U.S., and worked as a writer and actress. In 1968 the publication of her trilogy of novels, *Amour, colère et folie* (1968; *Love, Anger, and Madness*, 1980), with its exploration and condemnation of the violence of the Duvalier regime, made it unsafe for her to remain in Haiti. She left her husband and fled to New York, where she remained until her death, from a brain tumor, in 1973.

Although C. is best remembered as a novelist, her first literary works were plays published under the name "Plume Colibri," in 1947. The first play entitled *La légende des fleurs* (1947; The Legend of Flowers) was a fanciful and optimistic piece dealing with flowers and nature. C., herself, played the role of mother nature in the play's inaugural performance in 1947. This play was followed by a second entitled *Samba* (1947; Samba), which was published the same year.

With the shift from theater to novel, C.'s work became less fantastic and more realistic. The consequence of the shift was a growing interrogation of Haitian history, identity, and politics. C.'s first novel, *Fille d'Haïti* (1954; Daughter of Haiti), was—like her plays—published pseudonymously. This novel, which was awarded the literary prize of the Alliance Française, signaled a change in style from the plays, and was shortly followed by a second novel, *La danse sur le volcan* (1957; *The Dance on the Volcano*, 1959), which was published under C.'s own name. The second novel is much more overtly sociopolitical than the first, and is the fictionalized account of two Haitian women's struggle for independence and for the independence of Haiti (then Sainte-Domingue). C.'s third novel, *Fond des nègres* (1960, The Business of Blacks), continues the historical and political exploration of Haiti and its past, and perpetuates the focus on the plight of women in Haitian history and society introduced in *La danse sur le volcan*.

Amour, colère et folie, C.'s fourth novel, is considered to be her masterpiece. Published amid the horrors of the Duvalier dictatorship, the novel examines the polarization of Haitian society along race, gender, and class lines, and foregrounds the violence and violation which were the mainstay of Duvalier's political power. The novel, which is actually three short novels assembled by C.'s publisher, revolves around the act of writing, and so inscribes, albeit indirectly, C.'s own subversive act of writing into the text. *Amour*, which is ostensibly the diary of Claire Dumont, a dark skinned mulatto Haitian bourgeoise, places in evidence the power and irony of racial divisions in Haiti. Claire, whose name means "light" envies her sisters for their light skin, while at the same time, as mulatto, she is seen by other Haitians as herself light-skinned and, therefore, as a symbol of bourgeois privilege and oppression. The novel depicts the brutalization of the Haitian people common

under Duvalier through its presentation of the abuses inflicted the brutalization by Calédu, a regional commandant whose name means "he who hits hard." This brutalization is also rendered symbolically in Claire's own violent fantasies, and through her eventual assassination of Calédu.

Colère, the second of the novels in the trilogy, is darker and more disturbing even than the first. This novel exposes the conflation of class and race under Duvalier, and the rape and assault of women as a political strategy for dominating the Haitian people as a whole, and for subverting the power of the bourgeoisie—a strategy actually used on the protagonist of the novel, a bourgeoise named Rose. As a means of protecting her family's land, Rose offers herself to a member of the Haitian army known only as "the Gorilla," a dark-skinned man who desires Rose because of her light skin, but desires to hurt and humiliate, rather than possess her. He repeatedly and brutally rapes Rose over the course of a thirty-day period, at the end of which she dies. *Colère*, therefore, more than any of the previous novels, focuses attention on the situation of the Haitian woman; Rose is regarded more as property than as a human being, and as such, she becomes a pawn in the war of one class against another.

Folie, the last of the novels, centers on the plight of the writer in a country under martial law. This novel, like the previous two, takes place in an enclosed, claustrophobic space, which serves as a correlative to the oppression of the Duvalier regime. In the novel, four writers who have criticized the government in their works are accused of being insane, then executed. *Folie* depicts the power of the governments, particularly dictatorships, to censure and silence their critics, and reveals the anxiety of all writers, C. included, who dare to challenge the authority of a brutal and oppressive regime.

C. is widely held to be one of Haiti's most important novelists, and her works have attained tremendous prestige among the members of the Haitian exile community. Dark, disturbing, and violent, C.'s novels embody the terror of existence in a world where murder and rape are commonplace, where skin color is used as a weapon by starkly opposing forces of identity, and where women are caught in between the clash of class and race. The terror of C.'s novels is not, however, the result of the graphic violence often depicted within them; it is, instead, the result of the psychological and emotional realism which C. uses to depict the situations in which her characters find themselves. C.'s novels do not simply represent, they re-present, implicating the reader in the sadism and brutality which are the darker side of political conflict and human reality.

BIBLIOGRAPHY: Zimra, C., "W/Righting History: Versions of Things Past in Contemporary Women Writers," in Ueda, M., ed., *Explorations: Essays in Comparative Literature* (1986): 227-52; Paravisini, L., and B. Webb, "On the Threshold of Becoming: Contemporary Women Writers," *Cimarron*, 1 (1988): 121-26; Gouraige, A., "Littérature Haïtienne: Le Rôle des femmes dans la société chez deux romancières," *Revue Francophone de Louisiane*, 4 (1989): 30-38; Mayes, J. A., "Mind-Body-Soul: Erzulie Embodied in M. C.'s *Amour, colère et folie*," *JCSt*, 7 (1989): 81-89; Dayan, J., "Reading Women in the Caribbean: M. C.'s *Love, Anger, and Madness*," in DeJean, J., and N. Miller, eds., *Displacements: Women, Tradition, Literatures in French* (1991): 228-53; Lavine, L., "The Feminizing of the Trojan Horse: M. C.'s *Amour* as War Machine," *WFS*, 2 (1994): 9-18; Scharfman, R., "Theorizing Terror: The Discourse of Violence in M. C.'s *Amour, colère et* *folie*," in Green, M. J., et al., eds., *Postcolonial Subjects: Francophone Women Writers* (1996): 229-45

—DAYNA L. OSCHERWITZ

CHECHEN LITERATURE
See North Caucasian Literatures

CHEDID, Andrée

Egypto-Lebanese-French novelist, poet, dramatist, and short-story writer (writing in French), b. 20 Mar. 1920, Cairo, Egypt

C. is one of the best-known and respected French writers, her works fusing ancient and modern ways, European and Middle-Eastern concepts embedded in a verbal and luminous canvas studded with images, symbols, premonitions, and mystery. Since C.'s parents were separated when she was very young, she was sent to boarding schools in Cairo and in Paris. She had little family life but always maintained a warm and loving relationship with both her father and mother. C. received a B.A. degree in journalism from the American University in her native city. In June 1988 she was awarded an honorary doctor's degree from the same university. Married at the age of twenty-one, she lived from 1942 to 1945 in Lebanon and moved to Paris in 1946.

C. has repeatedly said that she is the product of two civilizations, two ways of life, two psyches. Her childhood days and her early memories, particularly those associated with Egypt, played an important role in her formation as a writer, as evidenced in her novels: *Le sommeil délivré* (1952; *From Sleep Unbound*, 1983), *Jonathan* (1955), *Le Sixième jour* (1960; *The Sixth Day*, 1988), *Le Survivant* (1963; the survivor), *L'autre* (1969; the other), *La cité fertile* (1972; the fertile city), *Nefertiti et le rêve d'Akhnaton* (1974; Nefertiti and Akhnaton's dream), *Les marches de sable* (1981; steps into the sand).

In *Les saisons de passage* (1996; Passing Seasons) meditations on C.'s mother and herself as transmuted by the vicissitudes of the author's memory, the mother and daughter appear as concrete yet fleeting images; as gestures embedded in undefined haunting shadows; voices and their echoes. *Le jardin perdu* (1997; The Lost Garden) is a poetic narrative revolving around the expulsion of Adam and Eve from paradise, accompanied by Hassan Massoudy's stylized Arabic calligraphy. Her writings are a complex of endlessly shifting emotional climates, of disclosing and secreting shapes and hues—energy patterns—that are then transmuted into human beings or into landscapes.

Because C.'s writings for the most part are situated in Egypt, they all bear the veneer of the Middle East as well as the MODERNISM of her adopted land, France. C.'s characters are endowed with a sense of proximity and distance, rootedness and rootlessness. They are paradigms of a personal quest and a collective search: the need to communicate not only with one's own multileveled self but also with those organic and inorganic forces that surround each being. Her works, then, are stamped with universal feelings as well as with personal yearnings, each set apart or opposed to the other.

C.'s themes vary with her novels. The female protagonist of *Le sommeil délivré* is the product of a certain type of contemporary

Middle Eastern upbringing with its harsh and brutal customs, particularly in regard to women, whose earthly existence is wholly devoted to serving certain specific purposes: to service the male and to procreate. *Jonathan*, a rite of passage, deals with the choice that many young Christians make in the Middle East between religion and revolution. The classically constructed *Le sixième jour*, focusing on the cholera epidemic raging in Egypt in 1948, may be seen as a death-and-resurrection myth. *L'autre* is a canticle, a hymn, to life. It is also an exploration into the complex problem of human relationships in general. The archetypal mother figure, a practitioner of the ancient art of dance, reigns in *La cité fertile* as she sweeps into the story, arrests the reader's attention, then vanishes only to return moments later, energizing feeling, act, and word. A combination of history and fiction, *Nefertiti et le rêve d'Akhnaton* plunges the reader back into a remote period, 1388–1344 B.C. in Egypt, when the pharaoh Akhnaton rebelled against polytheism in favor of monotheism, favoring the concept of one God as manifested in the visible Sun. In *Les marches de sable* three women—people of all seasons—undertake the desert experience, withdrawing from the world, from life itself, in an attempt to discover an answer to their unfulfilled lives.

Poetry is humanity's common language. For C. poems are to a great extent plainchants in honor of life; hymns to the earth and the heavens, to the vastness of the cosmic experiences. C., the poet, belongs to no group, no school. Her poetry is her own, a unique distillation of what she has experienced and felt most deeply. Whether in *Textes pour une figure* (1949; texts for a face), *Textes pour un poème* (1950; texts for a poem), or *Textes pour le vivant* (1953; texts for the living), C.'s stanzas contain all sorts of aromatic flavors, collages of sensual arabesques, and disquieting abstractions. Hers is a poetry divested of all sentimentality and any taint of romanticism. Solidly structured, each word, line, verse is hewn from her inner being, anchored to her psyche, while its meanings, rhythms, and sensations impact through pleromatic spheres.

The philosophical and thematic import of C.'s theater, as dramatized in *Les nombres* (1968; numbers), *Bérénice d'Égypte* (1968; Bérénice of Egypt), *Le montreur* (1969; the puppeteer), and *Échec à la reine* (1984; queen's checkmate), is relevant to today's problems: issues such as large-scale war, pollution, questions of identity, and fulfillment are broached. Her protagonists are flesh-and-blood beings, but they also are atemporal, archetypal, arising from the deepest layers of the unconscious. They do not develop psychologically as in conventional theater. When they move about on stage weaving intricate patterns in space, each becomes an energy center, diffusing its own aura which either attracts of repels the others.

C.'s writings speak to audiences today. They are direct, unvitiated, divested of all preciosity and rococo elaboration. Unsparing in the authenticity of the feelings or sensations she seeks to convey, she innoculates her readers with pain and torment, if these are deemed necessary, to disclose the acute nature of the protagonist's struggle. Language for C. is *being*: a catalyst that acts and reacts on the reader visually, spiritually, and aesthetically.

FURTHER WORKS: *Textes pour la terre aimée* (1955); *Terre et poésie* (1956); *Terre regardée* (1960); *Double pays* (1965); *Contre-chant* (1969); *Visage premier* (1972); *Fêtes et lubies* (1973); *Prendre corps* (1973); *Fraternité de la parole* (1975); *Cérémonial de la violence* (1976); *Grandes oreilles, toutes oreilles* (1976); *Lubies* (1976); *Le cœur et le temps* (1977); *Cavernes et soleils* (1979); *Les corps et le temps suivi de l'Étroite Peau* (1979); *Le cœur suspendu* (1981); *L'étrange Mariée* (1983); *Épreuves du vivant* (1983); *Grammaire en fête* (1984); *La maison sans racines* (1985; *The Return to Beirut,* 1989); *Mondes Miroirs Magies* (1988); *L'enfant multiple* (1989); *Poémes pour un texte (1970–1991)* (1991); *A la mort, á la vie* (1992; *Theatre II,* 1993); *Par-delà des mots* (1995); *Le grain nu*; *Lucy. La femme verticale* (1998)

BIBLIOGRAPHY: Knapp, B. L., *French Novelists Speak Out* (1976): 57–64; Izoard, J., *A. C.* (1977); "Huit questions posées à l'auteur," in *À la rencontre d' A. C.* (1981); Knapp, B. L., *A. C.* (1984); Linkhorn, R., ed., *The Prose and Poetry of A. C.* (1990); special C. issue, *Sud:* 94–95 (1991)

—BETTINA L. KNAPP

CHEEVER, John

American short-story writer and novelist, b. 27 May 1912, Quincy, Mass.; d. 18 June 1982, Ossining, N.Y.

John Cheever

C.'s father lost his business in the 1929 crash and deserted the family. C. went to live with his brother in Boston after he was expelled from Thayer Academy for smoking and poor studies. His first story, "Expelled"—inspired by this experience—was published in *The New Republic* of October 1, 1930. C. spent the Depression writing in New York and attended the Yaddo writers' colony, for the first time in 1933. Except for four years' service in World War II, writing has since been his full-time occupation. He has been living in suburban Ossining, New York, since 1956. *The Stories of J. C.* won the 1978 Pulitzer Prize.

C. has often been described as a novelist of manners, because of his attention to suburbia in his fiction. He closely observed and often satirized the social rituals of the middle class in such mythical suburban towns as Proxmire Manor and Shady Hill. Early collections include *The Way Some People Live* (1943), *The Enormous Radio, and Other Stories* (1953), and *The Brigadier and the Golf Widow* (1964). Most of these stories were first published in the *New Yorker.*

In his short stories C. contrasts the affluent order of suburban decorum with the uncertain emotional states of his characters, who admire social decency, appear morally confused, suffer from strong nostalgic yearnings for their lost youth and a more innocent past, and often seek refuge in family love and the beauties of nature. In such famous stories as "The Swimmer" (1964), "The Death of Justina" (1961), and "The Country Husband" (1954) characters see through the suburban mirage and come face to face with their own shortcomings, intimations of death, and fear of ultimate chaos.

In C.'s four novels the forces of order and chaos confront one another. In three of these the opposing forces are symbolically represented by two brothers. One brother comes to represent a love of natural beauty, an appreciation of humanitarian values and social/religious ceremonies, an enlightened spirit, and a sense of decorum and grace. The other seems obsessed with the decay and ugliness of the world, embodied as they seem to be in a brutalizing materialism and a rootless self-concern. In both *The Wapshot Chronicle* (1957) and *The Wapshot Scandal* (1964) C. traces the decline of Coverly and Moses Wapshot from the traditional confines of St. Botolphs, an old New England town, to the wayward disintegration of suburban life in the modern world. In C.'s most

recent novel, *Falconer* (1977), about prison life, Ezekiel Farragut kills his brother, Eben, and becomes a heroin addict.

Falconer is perhaps the most overtly Christian of C.'s novels. Farragut's escape from prison symbolizes a kind of redemption, a release from a very unsuburban dark night of the soul. Moments of spiritual grace punctuate the text, as Farragut responds to natural beauty, the presence of light, and his own need for renewal. Some critics, while praising the novel's texture and its observation of the dependence within and despondency of prison life, have suggested that the Christian imagery often appears forced. Given the depth of Farragut's prison experience—the homosexuality, the despair, the violence—and his particular consciousness of these incidents, however, the Christian vision seems to emerge logically from the progression of events in the novel.

In C.'s most experimental and apocalyptic novel, *Bullet Park* (1969), Eliot Nailles, the perfect suburbanite, confronts Paul Hammer, the vengeful outcast (note the punning names). Hammer tries literally to crucify Nailles's son, Tony, as a sacrificial act to awaken the suburban world to its own smug pretensions and evasions. Nailles rescues Tony, but his victory is compromised by his own dependence on drugs and his inability to understand the depth of human suffering.

C. is essentially a writer of romance in the American tradition of Hawthorne. The episodic nature of his plots, the recurring psychological conflict between real and symbolic brothers, the manner in which he intrudes upon many of his stories to comment upon the action in the manner of a 19th-c. author, the often lyric intensity of his style—these characteristics, along with his constant use of allegorical, mythic, and Biblical images and references, transcend his suburban observations and attentions to middle-class manners. At the heart of his vision lies a moral consciousness within which no mere appreciation of comfort and affluence can ever hope to replace man's unending spiritual quest for self-knowledge and self-transcendence. He acknowledges the bitter aspects of modern life but celebrates those moments of beauty and spiritual illumination that can occur only within the sound moral framework of an ordered and disciplined way of life.

FURTHER WORKS: *The Housebreaker of Shady Hill, and Other Stories* (1958); *Some People, Places and Things That Will Not Appear in My Next Novel* (1961); *The World of Apples* (1973); *Oh, What a Paradise it Seems* (1982); *Thirteen Uncollected Stories of J. C.* (1994)

BIBLIOGRAPHY: Hassan, I., "Encounter with Possibility: Three Novels by Gold, C., and Donleavy," *Radical Innocence* (1961): 187–201; Bracher, F., "J. C. and Comedy," *Crit*, 6 (1963): 66–77; Garrett, G., "J. C. and the Charms of Innocence: The Craft of *The Wapshot Scandal*," *HC*, 1, 2 (1964): 1–12; Aldridge, J., "J. C. and the Soft Sell of Disaster," *Time to Murder and Create* (1966): 171–77; Rupp, R., "J. C.: The Upshot of Wapshot," *Celebration in Postwar American Fiction* (1970): 27–39; Greene, B., "Icarus at St. Botolphs: A Descent into 'Unwanted Otherness,'" *Style*, 5 (1971): 119–37; Coale, S., *J. C.* (1977); Cheever, S., *Home before Dark* (1984); Donaldson, S., *J. C.* (1988); O'Hara. J. E., *J. C.: A Study of the Short Fiction* (1989)

—SAMUEL C. COALE

CHEKHOV, Anton Pavlovich

Russian dramatist, short-story writer, and journalist, b. 17 Jan. 1860, Taganrog; d. 2 July 1904, Badenweiler, Germany

C. was one of six children born to a grocery store owner, Pavel Yegorovich C., son of a serf who had bought his freedom in 1841, and Yevgenia Morozov, the daughter of a cloth merchant in Taganrog.

C. remained in Taganrog until he completed his secondary education in 1879. The years 1876–79 were decisive in his early spiritual and intellectual development. The family was forced to move to Moscow following his father's bankruptcy, and C. remained alone in his native town, supporting himself through private tutoring. Calm, objective introspection coupled with voracious reading of both Russian and Western European writers and thinkers brought about an early metamorphosis in his *Weltanschauung*: the traditional peasant and merchant-class values, which had dominated his family life, yielded in C. to the intellectual and ethical standards of the liberal 19th-c. intelligentsia.

In 1879 C. joined his family in Moscow and enrolled at the medical school of Moscow University. While studying, he struggled to support his family by writing under numerous pseudonyms, such as Antosha C., Antosha, Antosha Chekhonte, Antonson, Makar Baldastov, *Prozaichesky poet* (a prosaic poet), and *Chelovek bez selezenki* (a man without a spleen), for various humor magazines and periodicals. After receiving his medical degree in 1884, C. began to practice medicine at the Zemstvo Hospital in

Voskressensk; later that year he suffered the first of a series of hemorrhages resulting from tuberculosis, which plagued him for the rest of his life.

In 1886 C. met H. S. Suvorin, the editor of the *Novoe vremya*, an influential St. Petersburg daily, who invited him to become a regular contributor. The subsequent friendship with Suvorin, which ended in 1898 because of C.'s objections to the anti-Dreyfus campaign conducted by the *Novoe vremya*, is reflected in his extensive correspondence with him. (C. was a prolific letter writer; the Russian edition of his letters comprises six volumes, and his archives contain over seven thousand letters written to him by many leading literary and artistic personalities of his time.) This friendship was largely instrumental in paving C.'s way to a literary career.

C. spent the next five years (1887–92) traveling. He visited the Ukraine, including the Crimea, and journeyed across Siberia to Sakhalin Island, where he conducted a census and studied convict settlements. This latter experience had a profound impact on him that culminated in his travelogue treatise *Ostrov Sakhalin* (1894; *The Island: A Journey to Sakhalin*, 1967), and his rejection of Tolstoy's doctrine of nonresistance to evil, which he heretofore had cherished. He returned to Russia via Singapore, India, Ceylon, and the Suez Canal. Following a journey to various cities in Western Europe, C. went to the Novgorod province to help the local peasant population, which was stricken by famine and disease.

In 1892 he moved his entire family from Moscow to a country estate. Here he continued to serve the peasants by treating the sick and by doing social and civic work, including building schools and organizing libraries. On the advice of his physicians, C. moved in 1899 to Yalta, Crimea, where he met Maxim GORKY, whom until then he had known only through correspondence. At that time, too, he committed what may well have been the greatest blunder of his life by selling the copyright of his past and future works to the St. Petersburg publisher A. F. Marx.

In 1901 he married Olga Knipat, an actress at the Moscow Art Theater, and in 1904, because of increasing ill health, left Russia with her to go to Badenweiler, Germany, where he succumbed to tuberculosis. He was buried in the cemetery of the Novodeviche Monastery in Moscow.

C. was awarded the Pushkin Prize in 1888, and was elected a member of the Society of Lovers of Russian Literature in 1889 and in 1903 its provisional president. In 1900 he became a member of the Academy of Sciences in St. Petersburg, but resigned his membership in 1902 as a protest against the cancellation by the authorities of Gorky's election to the Academy.

C.'s early prose encompassed a great variety of genres. In addition to short stories, sketches, and anecdotes, he also wrote theater reviews, critical essays, journalistic articles and reports, captions to cartoons and picture jokes, various other trifles and oddities, and two novels: *Drama na okhote* (1885; *The Shooting Party*, 1926), a full-fleged detective novel à la Dostoevsky; and *Nenuzhnaya pobeda* (1882; useless victory), a parody of the novels of the Hungarian writer Mór Jókai (1825–1904).

The bulk of what may be considered C.'s journalistic work was written between 1883 and 1893. Among the more significant contributions in this area are his column published between 1883 and 1885 in the St. Petersburg weekly *Oskolki* under the title "Oskolki moskovskoy zhizni" (splinters of Muscovite life); his work as a crime reporter for the St. Petersburg daily *Peterburgskaya gazeta* in 1884; and a series of nine travel articles published in *Novoe vremya* between June 24 and August 23, 1890.

C. made his literary debut in 1879 with a rather traditional piece of satire, "Pismo donskogo pomeshchika Stepana Vladimirovicha" ("Letter to a Learned Neighbor," 1919), published in *Strekoza*. Most of his early literary efforts published in this magazine as well as in *Budilnik, Zritel*, and other journals of humor and satire are unspectacular but entertaining. Among his best humorous stories of the time are "Smert chinovnika" (1883; "The Death of a Government Clerk," 1915), "Doch Albiona" (1883; "A Daughter of Albion," 1922), "Tolsty i Tonky" (1883; "Fat and Thin," 1922), "Orden" (1884; "The Decoration," 1914), and "Loshadinaya familia" (1885; "A Horsey Name," 1915). They are characterized by a touch of lyricism and wit and a terse style that C. developed at that time under the guidance of Nicholas Leykin, owner and editor of the *Oskolki*.

C.'s serious stories of this early period already foreshadow his later masterpieces in both theme and mood. "Tsvety zapozdalye" (1882; "Belated Blossom," 1946), for example, anticipates the clash between the aristocratic owners of the orchard and the self-made man who buys it from them in his last play, *Vishnevy sad* (1904; *The Cherry Orchard*, 1908), while "Barynya" (1882; "The Mistress," 1946), the story of an evil, lascivious female land owner who seduces her peasant coachman, contains seeds of the mood of and the social themes expressed in his later stories. Perhaps the best examples of his early nonhumorous stories are "Gore" (1885; "Woe," 1908), "Toska" (1886; "Sorrow," 1897), "Panikhida" (1886; "The Mass for the Dead," 1908), "Vanka" (1886; "Vanka," 1915), and "Eger" (1885; "The Huntsman," 1918).

C.'s career as a short-story writer may be divided into four periods. The first period (1880–86) was the time of the humor magazines, during which he wrote chiefly to make money. The second one (1886–89), during which he began publishing in serious periodicals, was marked by his flirtation with Tolstoy's doctrine of nonresistance to evil and his quest for new moral and ethical norms. C.'s preoccupation with Tolstoy's teachings can be seen in a number of stories, among them "Vstrecha" (1887; "An Encounter," 1947), a story of the conversion of a thief; "Khoroshie lyudi" (1886; "Excellent People," 1916), in which a typically Tolstoyan solution (that is, work among peasants) resolves a deep-rooted conflict between a brother and a sister; and "Nishchy" (1887; "The Beggar," 1914), in which love for one's fellow man transforms a tramp into a useful member of society. These and other didactic stories of that period are complemented by tales dealing with basic, everyday conflicts, including love affairs, which C. portrays without moralizing, such as "Zhiteyskaya meloch" (1886; "A Trifling Occurrence," 1915), "Volodya bolshoy i Volodya malenky," (1887; "The Two Volodyas," 1916), and "Neshchastye" (1886; "Misfortune," 1915).

The works of the third and most important period (1889–99) were written under the influence of the Sakhalin experience and the resultant rejection of Tolstoyism, which C. expressed most vehemently in his famous "Palata No. 6" (1892; "Ward No. 6," 1903), in the lengthy story "Moya zhizn" (1896; "My Life," 1917), and in "Muzhiki" (1897; "Muzhiks," 1908), a moving, realistic depiction of the material and spiritual poverty of Russian peasants. The Sakhalin experience is perhaps best captured in the long tale "Ubystvo" (1895; "The Murder," 1919), which offers grim, realistic insights into the horrors of life in the penal colony. The note of social protest that informs these works alternates with the melancholy pessimism expressed in other works of that period. Among the latter are "Skripka Rotshilda" (1894; "Rothschild's Fiddle," 1903); "Anna na shee" (1895; "Anna on the Neck," 1917); a series

Anton Pavlovich Chekhov

of three stories—"Chelovek v futlyare" (1896; "The Man in a Case," 1914), "Kryzhovnik" (1897; "The Gooseberry Bush," 1915), "O lyubvi" (1898; "About Love," 1918)—linked by the appearance of the same characters; and "Ionych" (1898; "Ionitch," 1915), a story about a country doctor (a typical C. hero) who begins his career as an idealist only to succumb eventually to the vulgarity of everyday life. In these and other stories of that period C. developed themes of existential loneliness, man's congenital inability to communicate, and the general despondency of the human condition.

The stories of the final period (1899–1903) are characterized by a cautious upswing in mood that began to develop in the mid-1890s with the story "Student" (1894; "The Student," 1918), which he considered his manifesto of optimism. The final period is dominated by his famous "Dama is sobachkoy" (1899; "The Lady with the Dog," 1917), a tale of adultery not unlike Tolstoy's *Anna Karenina*, written with great compassion and profound psychological insight; during this time he also wrote "Arkhierey" (1902; "The Bishop," 1915) and his last story, "Nevesta" (1903; "The Betrothed," 1921), which despite the theme of death common to both, manifest a more positive outlook through the protagonists' quest for inner freedom.

Endowing it with an almost classical stringency à la Maupassant, C. modernized the short story in Russian literature, and therefore he provided the Russians with a new and more subtle manner of depicting reality. But although C. wrote several hundred stories, his fame today rests primarily on his plays—seven full-length works and ten one-acters. The melancholy mood and the themes of despondency, disillusionment, and isolation found in his stories are also present in C.'s plays, thus linking his fiction and dramas; indeed, six of the ten one-acters are adaptations of earlier published stories.

C.'s first full-length drama, known as *Platonov* (1923; *Platonov*, 1964), was neither staged nor published in his lifetime. It is a romantic play, long-winded, filled with unsubtle theatrical effects and melodramatic action. Its hero, a curious mixture of Don Juan and Hamlet molded into a representative of the lost generation of the 1880s, is one of the numerous "superfluous men" who abound in modern Russian literature. The play is important because it contains all the principal themes of C.'s mature dramas and thus can be viewed as the embryo of his dramatic oeuvre. The hero of C.'s second play, *Ivanov* (1887; *Ivanoff*, 1912), although cast from the same mold, is a more complex character whose innate passivity and inability to make decisions leads to tragedy. Romantic elements together with moralizing infusions also abounded in C.'s next drama, *Leshy* (1889; *The Wood Demon*, 1924), before C. revised it as *Dyadya Vanya* (1897; *Uncle Vanya*, 1912).

While these plays were still steeped in the 19th-c. theater, C.'s next plays, *Chayka* (1896; *The Seagull*, 1912), *Dyadya Vanya, Tri sestry* (1901; *The Three Sisters*, 1916), and *Vishnevy sad* broke with established theatrical norms. Working closely with Konstantin Stanislavsky's (1863–1938) Moscow Art Theater, C. successfully fused naturalistic techniques with his impressionistic theater of mood and created a highly modern art form in which subtle symbolism and stark realism achieved a new stage presence. Thus, *Chayka* is made rather complex through its symbolism, its poetic imagery, and its rich fabric of interlaced stories, but its very basis is simple: the eternal triangle (two writers in love with a stage-struck girl), which eventually precipitates the tragic denouement of the drama. In contrast to this play, *Dyadya Vanya* ends on a note of cautious if resigned hope, but its main theme, the passing of beauty and life, generates the all-pervading mood of melancholy. Similarly, *Tri sestry* ends on a note of hope generated by the faith that remains, after all dreams and illusions have been shattered. *Vishnevy sad* focuses more distinctly on transience without holding out any promise of hope for the future. It is intrinsically bound to the here and now, but devoid of action, and based entirely on mood. In that sense, *Vishnevy sad* marks the zenith of C.'s dramaturgy.

Unlike his major plays, C.'s one-acters cannot be considered lasting contributions to the theater, although some of them have genuinely funny moments and were well received by the Russian audiences. Among the best of them are the farces *Medved* (1888; *A Bear*, 1908), *Predlozhenie* (1889; *A Marriage Proposal*, 1903), *Svadba* (1889; *The Wedding*, 1916), and *Yubiley* (1891; *The Jubilee*, 1916). For the most part, however, these farces are trivial slapstick comedies built on grotesque misunderstandings and absurd exaggerations.

C. was a modern artist in the best sense of the word. Both his stories and his plays reflect (perhaps better than many works of today) the spirit of our age by focusing on man's alienation. C. expressed poignantly the mystery of existence; in expressing it, he affirmed life in its totality.

FURTHER WORKS: *Khmurye lyudi: Razskazy* (1890); *Sochinenia* (11 vols., 1899–1906); *Polnoe sobranie sochineny* (23 vols., 1903–1918); *Polnoe sobranie sochineny* (12 vols., 1930–1933); *Rasskazy i dramy* (1934); *Vodevili* (1936); *Vodevili* (1944); *Rasskazy i povesti* (1944); *Polnoe sobranie sochineny i pisem* (20 vols., 1944–1951); *Rasskazy i povesti* (1947); *Rasskazy* (1947); *Rasskazy* (1948); *Rasskazy i povesti* (1949); *Rasskazy* (1951); *Rasskazy* (1952); *O literature* (1955); *Sobranie sochineny v dvenadtsati tomakh* (12 vols., 1960–1964); *Izbrannye proizvedenia* (1967); *Izbrannye proizvedenia* (3 vols., 1967); *Izbrannye Rasskazy* (1968); *Rasskazy* (1969); *Sobranie sochineny* (8 vols., 1969–1970); *Rasskazy* (1970); *Izbrannye proizvedenia* (3 vols., 1970–1971); *Rasskazy* (1972); *Izbrannoe* (1974); *Rasskazy* (1974); *Izbrannoe* (1975); *Polnoe sobranie sochineny i pisem* (30 vols., 1975 ff.); *Izbrannye proizvedenia* (1976); *Rasskazy* (1976); *Izbrannoe* (1977); *Izbrannye sochinenia* (2 vols., 1979). **FURTHER WORKS IN ENGLISH:** *The Black Monk and Other Stories* (1903); *The Kiss and Other Stories* (1908); *Stories of Russian Life* (1915); *Russian Silhouettes: More Stories of Russian Life* (1915); *The Steppe and Other Stories* (1915); *The Bet and Other Stories* (1915); *The Tales* (13 vols., 1916–1923); *Rothschild's Fiddle and Other Stories* (1917); *Nine Humorous Tales* (1918); *The House with the Mezzanine and Other Stories* (1920); *Letters of A. C. to His Family and Friends: With a Biographical Sketch* (1920); *Letters on the Short Story, the Drama, and Other Literary Topics* (1924); *The Grasshopper and Other Stories* (1926); *Literary and Theatrical Reminiscences* (1927); *The Works of A. C.* (1929; repr. as *The Best-Known Works of A.C.*, 1939); *Plays and Stories* (1937); *Five Famous Plays* (1939); *Nine Plays* (1946); *The Portable C.* (1947); *The Personal Papers of A. C.* (1948); *Six Famous Plays* (1949); *Four Short Plays* (1950); *Selected Short Stories* (1951); *The Woman in the Case and Other Stories* (1953); *The Unknown C.* (1954); *The Selected Letters* (1955); *Best Plays* (1956); *Peasants and Other Stories* (1956); *The Brute and Other Farces* (1958); *Four Great Plays* (1958); *Great Stories* (1959); *St. Peter's Day and Other Tales* (1959); *Plays* (1959); *Selected Stories* (1960); *Six Plays* (1962); *The Major Plays* (1964); *Lady with the Lapdog and Other Stories* (1964); *The Oxford C.* (9 vols., 1964–1980); *Ward No. 6 and Other Stories* (1965); *Ten Early Plays* (1965); *Seven Short Novels* (1971); *Letters of A. C.* (1973); *Chuckle with C.: A Selection of Comic Stories by A. C.* (1975); *Plays* (1979); *C.'s Great Plays: A Critical Anthology* (1981)

BIBLIOGRAPHY: Heifetz, A., *C. in English: A List of Works by and about Him* (1947); Yermilov, V., *A. P. C.* (1954); Bruford, W. H., *A. C.* (1957); Mann, T., "C.," *Last Essays* (1959): 178–203; Eekman, T., ed., *A. C.: 1860–1960: Some Essays* (1960); Magarshack, D., *C. the Dramatist* (1960); Yachniss, R., *C. in English: A Selected List of Works by and about Him* (1960); Corrigan, R. W., Introduction to *Six Plays of C.* (1962): xii–xlii; Simmons, E. J., *C.: A Biography* (1962); Valency, M., *The Breaking String: The Plays of A. C.* (1966); Winner, T., *C. and His Prose* (1966); Jackson, R. L., ed., *C.: A Collection of Critical Essays* (1967); Gillès, D., *C.: Observer without Illusion* (1968); Styan, J. L., *C. in Performance: A Commentary on the Major Plays* (1971); Smith, V. L., *A. C. and the Lady with the Dog* (1973); Pitcher, H., *The C. Play: A New Interpretation* (1973); Laffitte, S., *C.: 1860–1904* (1973); Gerhardie, W., *A. C.: A Critical Study* (1974); Rayfield, D., *C.: The Evolution of His Art* (1975); Hingley, R., *A New Life of A. C.* (1976); Brahms, C., *Reflections in a Lake: A Study of C.'s Four Greatest Plays* (1976); Hahn, B., *C.: A Study of the Major Stories and Plays* (1977); Johnson, R. L., *A. C.: A Study of the Short Fiction* (1988); Hingley, R., *A Life of A. C.* (1989); Rayfield, D., *A. C.: A Life* (1998)

—LEONID RUDNYTZKY

The vexed problem of the ultimate aim of art is of particular importance so far as C. the playwright is concerned. C.'s insistence on the absolute objectivity of the writer led him at first to assume a standpoint which is barely distinguishable from that of the art-for-art's-sake school. Indeed, it led him to write the only purely naturalistic play he ever wrote—*On the Highway*, a play that was forbidden by the censor on the ground that it was "sordid." The failure to differentiate between C.'s plays of direct action and his later plays of indirect action is to a certain extent due to the failure to realise that C.'s attitude towards the ultimate aim of art underwent a complete change during the seven years that separate his last play of the direct-action type from his first play of the indirect-action type. It is not only the purely structural form of the plays that underwent a change but also their inner content. If during his first period as a playwright C. seemed to assume that artistic objectivity was incompatible with the presence of a "message" in a work of art, it was due mainly to his own struggles to achieve personal freedom and eradicate all traces of slavishness which his upbringing by a bigoted and despotic father had left on his mind.

David Magarshack, *C. the Dramatist* (1960), p. 34

Among the "psychological" dramatists of any great merit, the most psychological are Ibsen and C. C. was from the first drawn to the standard type characters, and he put the farcical types to dazzling use in his one-act plays. Also from the first he worked at the creation of archetypal protagonists. His first full-length play was intended to present a Russian Don Juan; his second, a Russian Hamlet. Of the latter, *Ivanov*, he wrote: "No matter how bad the play is, I created a type that has literary value." As for his masterpieces, those who take them to be all mood and nuance have missed some of the more solid features, such as that each play contains a traditional Villain who serves the traditional purpose of villains in dramatic plots, namely, to drive the Action toward catastrophe. The Professor in *Uncle Vanya*, Natasha in *The Three Sisters*, and Madame Ranevsky in *The Cherry Orchard* do just that. In *The Seagull* the villainy is divided between Arkadina and Trigorin. . . .

An essential feature of the characters of Ibsen and C. is that each carries and gives off a sense of doom that is more than his own doom. Because what was doomed was a whole culture, they are both in the widest sense social dramatists. Their people typify a civilization and an epoch.

Eric Bentley, *The Life of the Drama* (1964), pp. 54–55, 58

. . . C. is not really a Naturalist at all. Despite his detachment—despite his extraordinary capacity for imitating reality—he cannot entirely suppress his personal attitudes or refrain from judging his characters. His plays reflect both his sympathy for human

suffering and his outrage at human absurdity, alternating between moods of wistful pathos and flashes of ironic humor which disqualify them from being mere slices of life. For if C. is a detached realist, permitting life to proceed according to its own rules, he is also an engaged moralist, arranging reality in a particular way in order to evoke some comment on it. . . . C. the moralist hovers in the depths of his plays, expressing himself through a hidden action which sometimes breaks into melodrama and a satiric attack which sometimes bursts into farce. But however subterranean he may be, the moralist is always dictating character, action, and theme, while the realist is reworking these so as to exclude whatever seems mannered, subjective, or unnaturally theatrical.

Robert Brustein, *The Theatre of Revolt* (1964), p. 139

C.'s art may be seen, finally, as representing implicitly an arbitration of the gigantic conflicts that split the Russian literary and cultural world into two entities—that of the radical democrats, the revolutionary activists, with their strongly rationalist, materialist, and fundamentally antiaesthetic program, and that of such writers as Turgenev, Tolstoy, Dostoevsky, Leskov, and others who (for all the intensity and diversity in their social and political viewpoints) remain faithful to the artistic vision; in the final analysis, these writers chose to give expression to the entire complex human, social, and historical dilemma imposed upon nineteenth-century Russian man. In C. the scientific and rationalist view is reasserted, but freed from that moral utopianism and "rational egoism" which Dostoevsky criticized so sharply in his *Notes from the Underground*.

Robert Louis Jackson, "Introduction: Perspectives on C.," in Robert Louis Jackson, ed., *C.: A Collection of Critical Essays* (1967), p. 6

With the exception of a few indurate egotists, the characters in all the plays are unhappy, defeated, and mostly futile, though restive, individuals, caught in situations that are pathetic and that skirt tragedy by suggesting what is irremediable in life. Aware of their failings, these people reach out for the meaning of their sufferings and on occasion dream of a glorious and distant future which would compensate for their wasted lives. For the rest, they are ordinary men and women, typical of the strata of society to which they belong, chiefly the intelligentsia and the rural gentry. The characters engage in much anguished talk about the shortcomings of Russian life and hold up work as the salvation of the country, but the heart of the plays lies not in action or in programs, but rather in states of mind, in the ebb and flow of feeling, in the nuances of inner experience. The frustration, the self-probing, the emotionalism, the starry-eyed aspiration—all this, with the enveloping mood of wistful musing, relieved by a saving touch of the grotesque, batches the plays in an atmosphere peculiarly their own, gives them a lyrical quality which to a large degree compensates for their lack of drama.

Avrahm Yarmolinsky, *The Russian Literary Imagination* (1969), pp. 104–5

. . . C. cannot be deduced from his plays the way, for example, Strindberg or more indirectly Ibsen can. To an astonishing degree the plays are without an authorial voice, which is to say . . . that they are untendentious and make no claim on any kind of personal territory, but more than this, that they appear to be natural objects, things come upon. These uncoerced dramas seem to issue from a distance in which a relinquishment has taken place: the characters have been placed on their own, there is no shaping and controlling creator arranging their movements and determining their fates. . . .

One of the demands the plays make is that we go beneath their surfaces, not in order to discover some "true" core, the secret heart of C.'s matter, but to perceive how these surfaces themselves contain the depths, how modesty in C.'s case is a question of a respect for truth and of a refusal to make experience more "dramatic" than it really is or . . . to construct his plays like mysteries. Which is to say that with perhaps greater clarity and resonance than any other playwright C. discovered the drama of the undramatic, the uninflected and commonplace. In this sense his plays are opposed to the reigning tradition of overt passion and significant culmination, the tradition of Greek and French classical tragedy, of Shakespeare and the Jacobeans and indeed of all drama rising out of an impulse to organize the world in systematic, hyperbolic fictions, to magnify it and convert it into legend.

Richard Gilman, *The Making of Modern Drama* (1974), pp. 119–21

Close examination of C.'s texts calls for the techniques of poetic analysis. Many of the typical features of prose narrative are often absent, such as intrigue and dénouement, even though there is a great deal of action; often the distinction between hero and narrator is blurred. Other elements dominate the structure: a recurrent, variable image, for instance of clear or contaminated water; or a senseless, half-conscious refrain uttered by one of the characters. C.'s sentences, especially in his landscapes or his interior monologues, have a rhythmic and international power just as important to the final effect as his handling of plot (or anti-plot).

Often as instructive as the definitive text are the deletions and alterations C. made when preparing his stories for book publication; sometimes he deleted a passage out of sheer delicacy, unwilling to impose an authorial interpretation on his reader; sometimes his own taste had altered. No other Russian writer made such extensive and such significant revisions of his

work, thus giving us valuable insights into his "creative laboratory."

Donald Rayfield, *C.: The Evolution of His Art* (1975), p. 4

To the humanist writer, for whom the most immediate personal value in life will probably be love and fulfilled relationships generally, there is a special pathos about lives which lack love or in which love is frustrated, and even about simple misunderstandings between people. Each instance of these is a lost opportunity for understanding or fulfilment which can never be regained. In some cases, as in "The Kiss," and "Verotchka," it is virtually a lost life. If, then, C.'s art is unusually preoccupied with the frustrations of loving purpose at the points where human lives intersect, it is because of the value that such relationships must bear in his view of things, and the waste of love that he must quietly deplore. The capacity for love in people who lack the opportunity for it, and the deprivation of love in those who have known it, are things of which he is unusually and painfully aware. It is in this context, and not one of morbid negativity, that C.'s presentation of "frustrated lives" should be viewed.

Beverly Hahn, *C.: A Study of the Major Stories and Plays* (1977), p. 68

CHENEY-COKER, Syl

(also spelled Cheyney-Coker) Sierra Leonean poet and novelist (writing in English), b. 28 June 1945, Freetown

C.-C. was born to Christian Creole parents in Freetown, Sierra Leone. Having received his early education in Sierra Leone, at the age of twenty-one he came to the U.S. to pursue postsecondary education at the Universities of Oregon and Wisconsin and also worked for a time as a journalist. He has taught at universities in the Philippines, Nigeria, and the U.S. and served as editor and publisher of a fortnightly newspaper, the *Vanguard*, in Freetown in the late 1980s and early 1990s.

C.-C.'s earliest uncollected poetry reflects a heavy debt to the ideas of the NÉGRITUDE movement. The poem "Ghetto Woman" (1970) is modeled after Léopold Sédar SENGHOR's ode to and objectification of African women, "Femme noire" (1945; "Black Woman," 1964). Although C.-C.'s subsequently collected verse shows less of Négritude's heavily romanticized and "Africanized" imagery, he continued to base much of his early critical evaluative works, through the 1970s, on the tenants of the Négritude ideology.

C.-C.'s first book-length poetry collection, *Concerto for an Exile* (1973), has as its driving force his wrestling with questions of identity and his personal and poetic place in the world. As a member of the Sierra Leonean Creole community, he is caught between the privilege that this afforded him in his youth and the instability of that identity, rooted as it is in the slave trade and the community of freed and returned slaves that settled in Freetown and came to dominate Sierra Leonean society. The poetry is passionate, almost masochistic, as C.-C. poetically figures himself as a Christlike figure, to be martyred for his community.

His next collection, *The Graveyard Also Has Teeth with Concerto for an Exile* (1980), reprints the first volume along with fifty-three new poems, poems "in conversation with" both Sierra Leone and death. These new poems also mark the beginning of C.-C.'s shift away from a focus on the tormented self and a turning of his poetic gaze ever outward. There is a much deeper sense of mission in these new poems together with a recognition of his needs and limitations as a poet. Whereas in the earlier verse the separation from his home is almost crippling, now "I want to return into exile to be your poet!" It is a collection of seeming paradoxes, the halfway point in his poetic development, torn between a sense of duty to his community—"I want only to plough your fields / to be the breakfast of the peasants who read"—and a recognition that this Creole history and consciousness he is so busy constructing necessitates that his poetry and his life is one that crosses "From continent to continent."

This development of C.-C.'s poetic persona is completed in his third volume of poetry, *The Blood in the Desert's Eyes* (1990). The Christlike persona of the earlier verses is replaced by the warnings and laments of the biblical prophet. This move away from martyr to trumpeter of injustice is reflected as well in his critical works and interviews starting in the early 1980s where C.-C. begins to view exile as the socially responsible alternative to sacrifice in the context of the repressive and often deadly state. The redemptive death of *Concerto for an Exile* is here reimagined as a brutal, chilling exercise of power and control.

Read in sequence, these three works illustrate quite clearly C.-C.'s development as an author and thinker. The actual poetic form varies little, however. His seeming aversion to the comma and almost unremitting presentation of often disturbing poetic conceits threatens at times to overwhelm the poetry itself and has triggered a certain wariness among critics of his work who are electrified by the passion and energy of C.-C.'s poetry and yet somewhat put off by the thematic bleakness and structural laxity of his verse.

His novel, *The Last Harmattan of Alusine Dunbar* (1990), won the 1991 Commonwealth Writers Prize, Africa Region and shows the influence of Latin American literary movements and authors, an influence notable from *The Graveyard Also Has Teeth* onward. It is a sprawling, massive work chronicling the history of Malagueta, an imaginary African country which neatly mirrors the actual—and C.-C.'s own poetically imagined—history of Sierra Leone. Framed by the execution of the contemporary "reformer," General Tamba Masimiara, the narrative traces the development of the community through slavery, resettlement, colonialism, and neocolonialism, the one constant being the figure of the prophetlike Alusine Dunbar/Sulaiman the Nubian. The novel and the figure of Alusine/Sulaiman are in many respects the novelistic embodiment of that "Creole consciousness" C.-C. is struggling after in his earliest poetic works.

Long characterized as one of the more exciting and strident voices among the younger African poets, C.-C. has put together a body of works that reflect a growing maturity of vision without losing any of its passion or righteous anger. His poetry is not noted for its use of more traditionally recognizably "African" imagery but rather for the ways in which he connects the themes born out of his own personal experience and upbringing to an ever widening poetic world. It is this thematic broadening as well as stylistic experimentation that makes C.-C. a poet of consequence both in Africa and beyond.

BIBLIOGRAPHY: Brown, S., "A Poet in Exile," *IonC*, 10, 6 (1981): 55-57; Fraser, R., *West African Poetry: A Critical History* (1986): 286-90; Nazareth, P., "Something New Is Happening in African Literature," *TSAR*, 9, 2 (1991): 78-84; Ojaide, T., "The Half Brother of the Black Jew: The Poet's Persona in the Poetry of S. C-C.," *CLAJ*, 35 (1991): 1-14; Cooper, B., "S.C-C.: *The Last Harmattan of Alusine Dunbar* and an Interview," *ALA Bulletin*, 20, 3 (1994): 3-17

—MARK L. LILLELEHT

CHESNUTT, Charles W.

American novelist and short-story writer, b. 20 June 1858, Cleveland, Ohio; d. 15 Nov. 1932, Cleveland, Ohio

Born in the North, from 1866 to 1883 C. lived in North Carolina, which provides both the geographical and the cultural setting for his work. Supplementing his few years of formal education by intensive study with private tutors, he became a teacher and a principal, then returned north to work as a stenographer and to study law. He published his first short story, "*The Goophered Grapevine*," in *The Atlantic* in 1887, the same year he passed the Ohio bar examinations. Although he published three novels, a biography, and two collections of stories between 1899 and 1905, after 1906, C. supported himself primarily as a court stenographer while continuing to participate actively in civil-rights causes and literary societies. In 1928 he received the Spingarn Achievement Award from the NAACP for his "pioneer work as a literary artist depicting the life and struggles of Americans of Negro descent."

C. considered fiction a medium through which he could subtly educate Americans to perceive the rights of contemporary Afro-Americans to equality and respect. His first book, however, reflects the cautiousness of publishers, who concealed his racial identity. *The Conjure Woman and Other Tales* (1899) is a collection of stories about slavery and magic ("conjuring") narrated from the perspective of a white Northerner who, after the Civil War, has become a plantation owner in North Carolina. In each story the narrator (identified only as John) recalls an experience in which he heard a tale of conjuring from Uncle Julius McAdoo, his coachman and a former slave. Writing from the perspective of the white John, C. criticizes slavery and refutes allegations of black American ignorance by revealing the shrewdness of Uncle Julius, who tells the tales only to profit from them, financially or otherwise. For example, when John plans to tear down an abandoned schoolhouse so that he can use the lumber, Julius warns him that the wood may be haunted. During slavery times, Julius says, a slave who resented separation from his wife persuaded a conjure woman to turn him into a tree as a first step toward escape. Before he could flee, however, the tree was cut down, and the wood later was used to build the schoolhouse. After John, persuaded by his wife, abandons his plans for the schoolhouse, he and the reader learn that Julius wants to use the building for meetings of a religious group he has organized.

In the collection *The Wife of His Youth, and Other Stories of the Color-Line* (1899) C. tried to win respect for Afro-Americans through interracial stories emphasizing their strengths. The title story of the volume refutes allegations of immorality and laziness by stressing the nobility of the protagonists. On the day he proposes to announce his engagement, Mr. Ryder, a prosperous and educated former slave, meets an old black woman who for twenty years has searched faithfully for the husband to whom she had been wed only by the slave ceremony of jumping over a broomstick. Although she does not recognize him, Ryder publicly identifies her as his wife and renounces all hope of marrying the younger, more attractive, better educated woman he loves.

Although C.'s novels continued to pursue his goal of winning respect for Afro-Americans, they reflect his increasing despair about their lack of opportunities and the oppression in the South. *The House behind the Cedars* (1900) shows the position of respect to which some Afro-Americans could rise if not restricted by white society. An octoroon, John Walden, becomes a successful lawyer after he passes for white, and his sister Rena becomes the belle of South Carolina society. When her racial secret is discovered, however, she is rejected by her fiancé. In *The Marrow of Tradition* (1901), written in reaction to a race riot in North Carolina, a highly trained Afro-American doctor, whose practice is restricted by bigotry, loses his son in a "riot" instigated by aristocratic whites as well as poor ones. *The Colonel's Dream* (1905) is the story of a Southerner who leaves the South after bigotry thwarts his efforts to unify the races into one society.

Recent critics sometimes judge C.'s novels to be inferior to his shorter works not only because of weaker structure but also because of the more obvious use of idealized characters, sentimentalized situations, and melodramatic coincidences. Because such qualities are characteristic of much popular English and American fiction of the 19th c., C. should be evaluated in comparison with writers of that time rather than with the realistic and naturalistic writers who followed.

One of the most talented short-story writers of his generation, C. gave artistic form to Afro-American folk tales and was the first distinguished black American writer of fiction.

FURTHER WORKS: *The Short Fiction of C.W.C.* (1974)

BIBLIOGRAPHY: Chesnutt, H., *C. W. C.: Pioneer of the Color Line* (1952); Keller, D., "C. W. C. (1858–1932)," *ALR*, 3 (1968): 1–4; Mason, J., Jr., "C. W. C. (1858–1932)," in Rubin, L., *A Bibliographical Guide to the Study of Southern Literature* (1969): 171–73; Ellison, C., and E. W. Metcalf, Jr., *C. W. C.: A Reference Guide* (1977); Render, S. L., *C. W. C.* (1980); Andrews, W. L., *The Literary Career of C. W. C.* (1980)

—DARWIN T. TURNER

CHESTERTON, G(ilbert) K(eith)

English essayist, journalist, novelist, biographer, and poet, b. 29 May 1874, London; d. 14 June 1936, London

C. was the eldest son of a liberal middle-class English family. As a day student at St. Paul's Preparatory School (1887–91) C. won the Milton Prize for poetry and founded the Junior Debating Club, thus exhibiting a precocious literary skill and simultaneously demonstrating and strengthening that passion for polemical argument and controversy that characterizes nearly all of his critical work. He entered the Slade Art School in 1892 (indeed, he remained something of a caricaturist until the end of his life) but left school for good in 1895 to work as an assistant editor on Fleet Street. Soon after, he began an extraordinarily prolific thirty-year writing career. In 1901 C. married Frances Blogg. The domestic

stability of their happy (though childless) marriage reinforced the sure movement in his thought away from skepticism and socialism and toward political conservatism and religious orthodoxy. This was publicly and symbolically confirmed by what was unquestionably the most important event of C.'s later life: his conversion to Roman Catholicism in 1922.

Between 1900 and 1936 C. published some one hundred books. Beyond these, hundreds of incidental essays and fugitive reviews were left uncollected at his death. He wrote journalistic articles, familiar and theological essays, literary criticism, travel books, social histories, book reviews, biographies of Victorian and Christian figures, poems, stories, and novels. He was a voracious reader and writer: indeed, the variety of genres in which he worked reflects his remarkable diversity and heterogeneity. Yet there are a few constants in C.'s multitudinous writings. There is first of all the characteristic Chestertonian voice: reasoning, paradoxical, witty, opinionated, conservative, impressionistic, moral. He was always highly subjective and personal, a recognizable voice sounding off from Fleet Street. He responded always to the moral content of other writers' work, and it was characteristic of him to say that "the most practical and important thing about a man is still his view of the universe" (*Heretics*, 1905). C.'s own view of the universe was unabashedly ruralist, antimodernist, Victorian. He was particularly sensitive to the insights and dilemmas of the Victorian writer, and one of his most perceptive little studies is *The Victorian Age in Literature* (1913). C.'s own political program was Distributism, a social policy offered as an alternative to the twin evils of capitalism and socialism, against both of which he often railed. In the 1930s his insightful, violent critique of the lawlessness and disabling uniformity of the modern world led him into an unfortunate flirtation with Italian Fascism. His particular brand of ethical Roman Catholicism sometimes manifested itself in strange ways. In some of his strident late work, such as *The Catholic Church and Conversion* (1927) and *The Well and the Shallows* (1935), his typical buoyant wit and lively innocence are replaced by a dogmatic anti-Protestantism and anti-Semitism. At its best, however, his Thomist ideals (see *St. Thomas Aquinas*, 1933) helped him create a philosophy of trenchant Christian humanism.

As a poet C. was a minor master of nonsense and light satirical verse (see *New Poems*, 1932). Many are anthologized, as are two of his long, somewhat prosaic romantic poems, *The Ballad of the White Horse* (1911) and "Lepanto" (1912). As a writer of fiction C. is well known for his series of detective stories centering on Father Brown. Although the five books of Father Brown stories (1910–35) are often didactic and formulaic, Father Brown himself remains a vividly drawn, paradoxical figure. The lively portrait of the priest as detective (outwardly innocent, inwardly wise and insightful) helps account for the widespread popularity and success of the stories.

C. is best remembered as a kind of lesser Dr. Johnson. He was a writer of prodigious energy and range, a master of the paradoxical style and the forceful critique. His best books continue to be read for the incisiveness of their arguments and the pleasures of their wit.

FURTHER WORKS: *Greybeards at Play* (1900); *The Wild Knight* (1900); *The Defendant* (1901); *Twelve Types* (1902); *Thomas Carlyle* (1902, with J. E. H. Williams); *Charles Dickens* (1903, with F. G. Kitton); *Leo Tolstoy* (1903, with others); *Tennyson* (1903, with R. Garnett); *Thackeray* (1903, with L. Melville); *G. F. Watts* (1904); *The Napoleon of Notting Hill* (1904); *The Club of Queer Trades* (1905); *All Things Considered* (1908); *Varied Types* (1908); *The Ball and the Cross* (1909); *Tremendous Trifles* (1909);

George Bernard Shaw (1909); *A Defence of Nonsense* (1909); *Alarms and Discussions* (1910); *William Blake* (1910); *Appreciations and Criticisms of the Works of Charles Dickens* (1911); *Manalive* (1912); *A Miscellany of Men* (1912); *Magic* (1913); *London* (1914); *The Wisdom of Father Brown* (1914); *The Appetite of Tyranny* (1915); *The Crimes of England* (1915); *Poems* (1915); *Wine, Water, and Song* (1915); *Divorce Versus Democracy* (1916); *A Shilling for My Thoughts* (1916); *Temperance and the Great Alliance* (1916); *A Short History of England* (1917); *Utopia of Usurers* (1917); *Lord Kitchener* (1917); *Irish Impressions* (1919); *The New Jerusalem* (1920); *The Superstition of Divorce* (1920); *The Uses of Diversity* (1920); *The Man Who Knew Too Much* (1922); *Eugenics and Other Evils* (1922); *What I Saw in America* (1922); *The Ballad of St. Barbara* (1922); *Fancies Versus Fads* (1923); *The End of the Roman Road* (1924); *The Exclusive Luxury of Enoch Oates and the Unthinkable Theory of Professor Green* (1925); *The Superstitions of the Sceptic* (1925); *William Cobbett* (1925); *Collected Works* (9 vols., 1926), *Collected Poems* (1926); *The Return of Don Quixote* (1926); *The Incredulity of Father Brown* (1926); *The Outline of Sanity* (1926); *The Queen of Seven Swords* (1926); *Culture and the Coming Peril* (1927); *Social Reform and Birth Control* (1927); *The Judgement of Dr. Johnson* (1927); *Gloria in Profundis* (1927); *Robert Louis Stevenson* (1927); *The Sword of Wood* (1928); *Do We Agree? A Debate Between G. K. C. and Bernard Shaw* (1928); *Generally Speaking* (1928); *The Moderate Murderer and the Honest Quack* (1929); *The Poet and the Lunatics* (1929); *The Thing* (1929); *G. K. C. as M. C.* (1929); *New and Collected Poems* (1929); *Ubi Ecclesia* (1929); *The Father Brown Stories* (collected ed., 1929); *Come to Think of It: Essays* (1930); *The Grave of Arthur* (1930); *The Turkey and the Turk* (1930); *The Ecstatic Thief* (1930); *Four Faultless Felons* (1930); *The Resurrection of Rome* (1930); *All Is Grist* (1931); *Chaucer* (1932); *Christendom in Dublin* (1932); *Sidelights on New London and New York* (1933); *All I Survey* (1933); *Collected Poems* (1933); *Avowals and Denials* (1934); *The Scandal of Father Brown* (1935); *As I Was Saying* (1936); *Autobiography* (1936); *The Paradoxes of Mr. Pond* (1936); *A. G. K. C. Omnibus* (1936); *The Coloured Lands* (1938); *End of the Armistice* (1940)

BIBLIOGRAPHY: Evans, M., *G. K. C.* (1939); Ward, M., *G. K. C.* (1943); Kenner, H., *Paradox in C.* (1947); Sullivan, J., *G. K. C.: A Bibliography* (1958); Clipper, L., *G. K. C.* (1974); Sullivan, J., ed., *G. K. C.: A Centenary* (1974)

—EDWARD HIRSCH

CHILEAN LITERATURE

Fiction

Alberto Blest Gana (1830–1920) initiated the Chilean novel with his Balzacian depictions of the society of his time. The literary scene of the late-19th and early-20th cs. was dominated by two antithetical schools: realism, which gradually assimilated NATURALISTIC elements, and MODERNISM, an aesthetic movement inspired by the French Parnassian and SYMBOLIST poets. Chile's leading realist of this period was Baldomero Lillo (1867–1923). Collected in *Sub terra* (1904; underground), his tales about the

G. K. Chesterton

miserable lives of miners reveal a marked influence of Émile Zola's famous novel, *Germinal*. Modernism is perhaps best represented by Pedro Prado (1886–1952), who owes his reputation to artistically conceived novels such as *Alsino* (1920; Alsino), a reworking of the Icarus myth.

The most important movement in Spanish American fiction during the first half of the 20th c. was regionalism or, as it is often called in Chile, *criollismo*. Having evolved from realism, this movement conveys a strong flavor of Spanish American life, with special emphasis on rural landscapes, provincial customs, and popular speech patterns. It also incorporates elements of modernism, and thus tends to poeticize the dramatic conflicts that pit man against his hostile natural or social environment. As the term "regionalism" suggests, these works usually focus on local rather than on universal issues.

Regionalist authors include Mariano Latorre (1886–1955), leader of the movement in Chile, Eduardo BARRIOS, Luis Durand (1895–1954), and Joaquín Edwards Bello (1887–1968). An excellent example of regionalist fiction is Barrios's *Gran señor y rajadiablos* (1948; great lord and hellion), which portrays a virile, self-reliant landowner typical of Chile's feudal oligarchy. Barrios is even better known, however, for his fine psychological novel *El hermano asno* (1922; *Brother Ass*, 1942).

During the 1930s young Chilean intellectuals became dissatisfied with regionalism because it no longer reflected the realities of a country in the throes of industrialization and urbanization. When the liberal Popular Front Party won the election of 1938, a group of left-wing writers took advantage of the political ferment to proclaim their literary ideals. This so-called Generation of 1938 shifted the focus of prose fiction from the countryside to the city and, inspired by Marx and Lenin, strove to achieve reforms by portraying the miserable lot of the downtrodden masses. Although the leader of this school was Juan Godoy (1911–1978), its best-known representative today is Carlos Droguett (b. 1915). Other prominent representatives are Nicomedes Guzmán (1914–1964), Guillermo Atías (b. 1917), and Fernando ALEGRÍA. (Alegría is also one of Chile's outstanding literary critics.)

Another literary trend of this period transcended the limits of regionalism and social protest by placing greater emphasis on the representation of dreams and ambiguous, multifaceted reality. Two important writers of this group are María Luisa BOMBAL, author of a lyrical novel entitled *La última niebla* (1935; *House of Mist*, 1947), and Manuel ROJAS, whose *Hijo de ladrón* (1951; *Born Guilty*, 1955) typifies the "new novel" that emerged during the 1950s.

The Generation of 1950 differs from that of 1938 by its skeptical indifference to political and social issues and its turn inward in search of new values. Better educated and more sophisticated than their predecessors, the members of this generation found inspiration abroad in the writings of JOYCE, WOOLF, FAULKNER, SARTRE, and CAMUS. And, through their alienated protagonists, they conveyed their existential anguish over the absurdity of life in a world without absolutes. The most widely acclaimed of these writers is José DONOSO, whose phantasmagoric masterpiece, *El obsceno pájaro de la noche* (1970; *The Obscene Bird of Night*, 1973), is perhaps the best novel ever published by a Chilean. Also included in this group are Enrique LAFOURCADE, Jaime Laso (b. 1926), Luis Alberto Heiremans (1928–1964), and Jorge EDWARDS.

Chilean literature of the past two decades reflects the conditions under the socialist regime of President Salvador Allende (1970–1973) and the military dictatorship headed by General Augusto Pinochet (1973–1989). Since the death of Pablo NERUDA in 1973, Donoso has been Chile's most widely acclaimed living man of letters, and although politics has seldom been a major theme in his works, his novels published since 1973 do indeed dramatize some of the salient issues treated by other Chilean writers of this period. After *El obsceno pájaro de la noche*, usually considered the last major accomplishment of the "boom," Donoso published *Casa de campo* (1978; *A House in the Country*, 1983), a self-conscious, fantasy-laced tale about a greedy bourgeois family (the Venturas) who browbeat their servants and ruthlessly subjugate the native population living in the vicinity of their sprawling estate (Marulanda). This sophisticated, entertaining novel can be read as a political allegory of Allende's rise and fall. Although Donoso had moved to Spain of his own free will long before the military coup in his homeland, he treats the problems of the exile in *El jardín de al lado* (1981; *The Garden Next Door*, 1992), a technically complex novel with two narrators (a husband and his wife) and feminist overtones. *La desesperanza* (1986; *Curfew*, 1988), Donoso's most overtly political work to date, focuses on the funeral of Matilde Urrutia, Neruda's widow, and the return to Chile of a popular singer who witnesses the harsh repression of the Pinochet government. Donoso's other recent fiction includes *La misteriosa desaparición de la marquesita de Loria* (1980; the mysterious disappearance of the Marquise de Loria), a psychological story of a young Nicaraguan widow consumed by animal instinct, and *Taratuta. Naturaleza muerta con cachimba* (1990; *Taratuta and Still Life with Pipe*, 1993), two novelettes, the first of which describes the process of inventing a story about a Russian terrorist, and the second, the

account of a bourgeois couple's liberation from a dull existence when they discover the world of art.

Chile's other major contemporary novelists include María Luisa Bombal, Jorge Edwards, Antonio Skármeta, Isabel Allende, Enrique Lafourcade, Ariel Dorfman, and Fernando Alegría. Although all of these authors except Bombal have based at least some of their works on the Chilean political experience of the past two decades, those who fled into exile (Skármeta, Allende, and Dorfman) quite naturally seem more preoccupied with the subject.

Among Chile's many other writers of fiction are Hernán Valdés (b. 1934), Poli Délano (b. 1936), Diamela Eltit (b. 1949), and Antonio Ostornol (b. 1954). Délano is best known for his novel *En este lugar sagrado* (1977; in this sacred place). The introspective protagonist finds himself in the men's restroom of a movie theater when the 1973 military coup occurs, and terrified of being arrested, he remains there for three days, evoking episodes of his past that provide insight into his, and Chile's, present situation. *Valdés's Tejas Verdes* (1974; *Diary of a Chilean Concentration Camp*, 1985) can be read as a novel, but in reality it is a compelling memoir the author wrote after he was released from Tejas Verdes, a concentration camp for enemies of the military government. Valdés composed his text in the form of a diary, using stylistic and structural devices to involve his readers in the horrors he experienced during the most hellish period of his life.

Representatives of a younger generation, Eltit and Ostornol have been classified as postmodernist writers whose experimental techniques require considerable concentration on the part of the reader. Eltit is also a strongly committed feminist, as demonstrated by her novel *Lumpérica* (1983; Lumpérica). In it she not only rebels against male domination and parodies such luminaries as Neruda, Gabriel GARCÍA MÁRQUEZ, and Julio CORTÁZAR, but denounces the repression of the military dictatorship as well. Eltit's more recent novels, in which she continues to express her political and feminist views, include *Los vigilantes* (1994; The Watchmen) and *El infarto del alma* (1994; The Infarct of the Soul). Also resonant with political overtones, Ostornol's *El obsesivo mundo de Benjamín* (1982; Benjamin's obsessive world) presents a forty-two-year-old paralytic confined to a wheelchair, who vents his frustrations with his family by murdering his domineering mother with a sword that formerly belonged to his English grandfather.

Poetry

Chilean poetry in the 20th c. has been dominated by four major figures: Gabriela MISTRAL, Vicente HUIDOBRO, Pablo Neruda, and Nicanor PARRA. Mistral and Neruda are both Nobel Prize winners, the former in 1948 and the latter in 1971. Mistral rejects the verbal virtuosity of MODERNISM and evolves a simpler, more direct style tinged with sadness and solitude. Her love for suffering humanity, especially children, and her yearning for communion with God and nature stand out as major themes in her intensely lyrical work.

Usually classified as *vanguardistas*, Huidobro, Neruda, and Parra have been influenced by 20th-c. avant-garde movements such as FUTURISM, EXPRESSIONISM, DADAISM, ULTRAISM, and SURREALISM. Huidobro began his career as a symbolist, but in 1916 he founded *creacionismo*, a highly subjective movement that likened the creation of a poem to nature's creation of a tree. Subsequently, like the *ultraístas*, he sought to renovate poetry by means of new and striking metaphors. Although his reputation waned toward the mid-1930s, interest in his works has revived in recent years.

The most powerful and universally acclaimed figure in Latin American poetry to date is Pablo Neruda. His vast production comprises the following phases: youthful love poems, surrealistic probings of the subconscious, militant paeans to communism, baroque evocations of the Latin American landscape, and, finally, sensitive descriptions of the everyday world in language readily understood by all readers.

Despite the censorship imposed by the Pinochet régime, Chilean poets refused to be stifled. Major currents in the genre include poetry of protest, existential poetry, and poetry influenced by surrealism. Since the death of Neruda, Nicanor Parra has been the nation's most widely read poet. Although he was strongly influenced by surrealism, Parra is known primarily for his antipoetry, which rejects traditional forms of verse and reexamines the purpose and nature of the genre. Thus his language tends to be unadorned, concrete, and often grotesquely humorous and bitterly satirical. An inveterate nonconformist, he rejects the bourgeois establishment, criticizes Allende's socialist government, and abhors Pinochet's military regime. Two of Parra's more recent collections of poems are *Prédicas y sermones del Cristo de Elqui* (1977) and *Nuevos sermones y prédicas del Cristo de Elqui* (1979), published together in translation as *Sermons and Homilies of the Christ of Elqui* (1985). In these hilarious verses, Parra dons the mask of a preacher taken from Chilean folklore in order to parody, with his solemn tone and absurd assertions, the Pinochet régime. In 1986, at the age of seventy-two, Parra became vitally concerned with environmental pollution and the danger of a nuclear holocaust. Thus, as Skármeta has observed, his career has come full circle: In 1954 he had written a poem entitled "Defensa del árbol" ("Defense of the Tree," 1960), and today he is publishing poems in defense of the environment.

Besides Parra, major contemporary Chilean poets include Enrique LIHN, Jorge TEILLIER, Oscar Hahn (b. 1938), and Raúl Zurita (b. 1951). A longtime resident of the U. S., Hahn writes in a range of styles that have been described as medieval, baroque, expressionist, surrealist, modernist, and vanguardist. He is known above all for his verses of erotic love, for his obsession with death, and for his apocalyptic visions of a nuclear holocaust. The title of his first collection, *Esta rosa negra* (1961; this black rose), becomes a metaphor for the dreaded nuclear cloud, which in turn is identified with copulation and death. Erotic love, with lovers imagined as both victims and killers, is a subject treated in *Arte de morir* (1979; *The Art of Dying*, 1988) and *Mal de amor* (1981; *Love Breaks*, 1991), the latter having been banned for several years by Chilean government censors. *Imágenes nucleares* (1983; nuclear images), which contains Hahn's famous poem "Visión de Hiroshima" (vision of Hiroshima), intensifies the author's apocalyptic visions, whereas *Flor de enamorados* (1987; flower of lovers) consists of a group of medieval love poems transformed by modern stylistic techniques.

Zurita is considered by some critics as Chile's most original poetic voice since Neruda. His style is characterized by a colloquial, everyday idiom, but, unlike Parra, Zurita sees language as sacred, a vehicle through which he neither mocks nor destroys but rather seeks an epiphany of the "poetic absolute" or of the "promised land" he would like Chile to become. As a result of his incarceration and torture after the military coup, Zurita created a Dantesque metaphor of his homeland in two of his most widely read collections: *Purgatorio* (1979; purgatory) and *Anteparaíso* (1982; on the border of paradise). More recently, in *El amor de Chile* (1987; the love of Chile), he has turned his gaze to the spectacular Chilean landscape for inspiration.

Essay

Some of Chile's best-known men of letters have followed the Latin American tradition of making personal involvement in affairs of state a basis for their aesthetic expression of ideas. Three fiction writers mentioned above fit into this category: Alegría, Edwards, and Dorfman. Fernando Alegría, is an excellent literary critic who has shown a vital interest in politics as well. His *Literatura y revolución* (1971; literature and revolution) contains essays on subjects ranging from Alejo CARPENTIER, Miguel Angel ASTURIAS, and Cortázar to Latin American society as reflected in the contemporary novel and the political implications of antiliterature. Alegría's *Nueva historia de la novela hispanoamericana* (1986; new history of the Spanish American novel) is one of the most perceptive and complete treatments of the subject. And his *Una especie de memoria* (1983; a kind of memory) is a fascinating recollection of his youth in Chile and of the ideological currents of that time.

Jorge Edwards is well known throughout the Hispanic world for his journalistic articles and essays, many of which combine politics and literature. Some of his finest pieces have been collected in *Desde la cola del dragón* (1977; from the tail of the dragon), which treats, among other subjects, the political polarization of Chile during Allende's term of office, the shadow of Arthur Rimbaud (1854–1891) in French politics during the 1970s, and, in the final essay, the policies of Felipe González of Spain for his moderate leftwing views (as opposed to those of Fidel Castro and his hardline supporters). Edward's *Adios poeta* (1990; good-bye, poet) is an engrossing memoir recalling his friendship and professional relationships with Neruda and other literary figures over a period of many years.

A brilliant analyst of both popular and high culture, Ariel Dorfman has collected in *Some Write to the Future* (1991) a group of articles he published in professional journals and had translated into English for American readers. The essays on García Márquez, Jorge Louis BORGES, and other renowned writers point out the coexistence in Spanish American fiction of metaphor, abstraction, the mundane, and the fantastic, all of which, Dorfman hopes, will eventually coalesce and bring about a better understanding of the vast region's richly textured reality—thus the title of the volume. Another long, provocative essay deals with recent examples of the testimonial genre in Chilean letters, that is, books that have been published by Pinochet's ex-prisoners. Here Dorfman demonstrates how the desire to remember, to accuse, and to inspire has enabled the authors of these texts to win the battle they once thought they had lost as human beings.

Drama

Although Chilean dramatists were active before World War II, the theater did not flourish until the 1950s. Since that time three basic tendencies have prevailed: dramatizations of the historical past, satirical exposés of social corruption, and presentations of the existential quest for personal values. Prominent social dramatists include Egon WOLFF, whose play *Los invasores* (1963; the invaders) uses Brechtian techniques, and Sergio Vodanovic (b. 1926), whose *Deja que los perros ladren* (1959; let the dogs bark) assails dishonesty in government. Chile's foremost contemporary playwright is Jorge Díaz (b. 1930), whose absurdist comedies such as *El cepillo de dientes* (1961; the toothbrush) suggest the influence of IONESCO and BECKETT.

During Salvador Allende's presidency (1970-73), Chilean intellectuals were optimistic about the prospects for their nation's cultural growth. With the coup of 1973 and the establishment of a military dictatorship, however, many intellectuals fled into exile. Representative of this group is Antonio SKÁRMETA, an excellent short-story writer and novelist who has also edited a book entitled *Joven narrativa chilena después del golpe* (1976; stories by young Chileans since the coup). This collection acquaints American readers of Spanish with promising writers in exile such as Ariel Dorfman, Poli Délano (b. 1936), and Hernán Valdés (b. 1934). Further examples of contemporary poetry and fiction by Chileans living outside their homeland have appeared in a recently founded journal, *Literatura chilena en el exilio*. These publications suggest that although the creative spirit has been all but stifled inside Chile, it is alive and thriving among Chileans scattered abroad.

Before 1973 the majority of contemporary Chilean plays were produced in the universities. After the military coup, many dramatists fled into exile as censorship and adverse economic conditions became major obstacles to the presentation of their works. By the mid-1980s, however, some of the exiled dramatists had returned, and the theater was gradually regaining its creative impulses. As censorship eased, the political themes of injustice, fear, and torture became increasingly prevalent, along with the use of nightmares, BLACK HUMOR, and elements of the absurd.

Leading dramatists of the older generation include Isadora Aguirre (b. 1919), Fernando Debesa (b. 1921), Jorge Díaz (b. 1930), Sergio Vodanovic (b. 1926), Louis Alberto Heiremans (1928–1964), Alejandro Sieveking (b. 1934), and Egon Wolff. Aguirre, known for her social criticism, her satire of the middle class, and her adroit manipulation of Brechtian techniques, demonstrates her sympathy for the exploited classes, whose lives are depicted in her highly acclaimed *Los papeleros* (1963; the trash collectors). Her *Lautaro* (1982; Lautaro), which draws some political parallels with modern Chile, dramatizes the epic struggle of the Mapuche Indians against the Spaniards during the 16th c. Another of her historical dramas, *Diálogo de fin de Siglo* (1989; end-of-century dialogue), is based on the suicide of Chilean President José Manuel Balmaceda in 1891. Aguirre uses an impressive array of avant-garde techniques in *El retablo de Yumbel* (1987; the altarpiece of Yumbel) to dramatize the disappearance of nineteen Allende officials soon after the military coup.

Debesa, who has also been influenced by Bertolt BRECHT, delves into history in what is still considered his best work, *Bernardo O'Higgins* (1961; Bernardo O'Higgins). This drama recreates the last days of Chile's national hero, who evokes a montage of episodes from his past, revealing his human reactions to crucial moments of history. Debesa's *Ca-ta-ion* (1979; ca-ta-ion), the title of which imitates the babble of a retarded child, is a psychological drama of solitude stemming from the lack of communication between a poverty-stricken divorcée and her son.

As Spanish America's leading dramatist of the absurdist tradition, Jorge Díaz utilizes irony, black humor, and physical violence to convey a grotesque, nonrealistic world vision reminiscent of Eugène Ionesco, Samuel Beckett, and Harold PINTER. Although his dramas develop the themes of alienation and lack of purpose in human existence, they tend to concentrate more heavily on political and social issues than does the French THEATER OF THE ABSURD. One of Díaz's early plays, *El cepillo de dientes* (1961; the toothbrush), remains his most widely performed and perhaps his best to

date. The overriding theme of lack of communication evolves through a series of ritualistic games enacted by a couple, He and She, who invent preposterous situations usually leading to a violent climax. *El lugar donde mueren los mamíferos* (1963; *The Place Where the Mammals Die*, 1971) continues the absurd tone of Díaz's worked. Here a charitable organization is in danger of disappearing for lack of welfare recipients. The disaster is prevented by the discovery of Rusty, a starving slum dweller who arrives at the organization headquarters in a crate and who eventually hangs himself because everything is offered him except the food he needs to stay alive. This play is obviously a satire on false charity, but it can also be read as a political allegory about the exploitation of the Third World by developed nations.

Sergio Vodanovic is best known for his satirical portraits of contemporary middle-class Chilean Society. In 1959 he achieved wide recognition for his prize-winning *Deja que los perros ladren* (let the dogs bark), an attack on political corruption. His masterwork, however, is *Viña: Tres comedias en trade de baño* (1964; *Viña: Three Beach Plays*, 1971), a trilogy of one-act plays limning Chile's rigid social stratification and the masks, role playing, and alienation characteristic of such a divided society. *El delantal blanco (The White Uniform)*, the most memorable of the three, presents a snobbish upper-class woman with her maid on the beach at Viña del Mar, Chile's most fashionable summer resort. When the two exchange clothing so that the woman can see the world through the eyes of her maid, the ensuing episodes are replete with both social and psychological implications. The political events of the 1970s provide the background for two of Vodanovic's more recent works: *Igual que antes* (1973; same as ever), telling of the breakup of a wealthy industrialist's family under Salvador Allende's régime; and *¿Cuántos años tiene un día?* (1970; how many years does a day have?), about four television journalists who, despite the repression on the heels of the 1973 military coup, remain in Chile, determined to assist in the nation's struggle for cultural survival.

Despite his short life, Louis Alberto Heiremans ranks as one of Chile's finest modern dramatists. *Moscas sobre el mármol* (1951; flies on the marble) represents a despairing view of life, its protagonist being a man named Julián who devises a plan to kill his friend Ernesto because he and Julián's wife are in love. When the plan backfires, causing Julián's death, his mother rejoices because she no longer has to share him with his wife. Heiremans weaves everyday reality, biblical myth, and the modern theme of solitude into the fabric of his most celebrated drama, *El Abanderado* (1962; the standard-bearer). The setting is a rural community where a religious festival is being prepared. El Abanderado, a bandit of local renown, is handed over to the police by a former friend, El Tordo, when he (El Abanderado) returns home to see his mother after many years of absence. Representations of a Christ figure and Judas Iscariot, El Abanderado and El Tordo are two of several biblical figures evoked in this play.

Well known for his penetrating psychological portraits and ingenious fusion of fantasy and reality, Alejandro Sieveking left Chile after the 1973 military coup but returned to his homeland in 1984. His *Animas de día claro* (1962; souls in the light of day) is based on the Chilean superstition that the spirits of those who die without having accomplished their lifetime goals remain on earth until their desires are satisfied. The setting is a dilapidated farmhouse where five deceased sisters, all spinsters, continue to dwell, each seeking some form of self-fulfillment. Though eighty years of age, Berta (the youngest of the sisters) is suddenly rejuvenated by the arrival of Eulolio, a handsome young man who, despite rumors that the house is haunted, wants to buy the property. The miracle of Berta's and Eulolio's relationship is celebrated by the sudden flowering of trees that have been barren for many years. *Pequeños animales abatidos* (1974; small abject animals) was inspired by the military coup of the previous year, its political subject being presented by the artful juxtaposition of living and dead characters swept up in rapidly changing time sequences. Also published in 1974, *La mantis religiosa* (*The Praying Mantis*, 1983), is a murder mystery freighted with powerful psychological, sexual, and mythical overtones.

Three other fine dramatists are Juan Radrigán (b. 1937), Jaime Miranda (b. 1956), and Carlos Cerda (b. 1956). Known for his strong political commitment, Radrigán portrays members of the proletariat, especially those living in the slums of Santiago, where his works are often performed. His sympathetic but realistic portrayal of the miserable lives of the dispossessed is underscored by the authenticity of their speech and by his incitement to resist the oppression to which they are subjected. Typical of his creations is *Hechos consumados* (1981; consummated deeds), a riveting dialogue between a penniless, ill-fated couple. More complex and elaborately staged, *El toro por las astas* (1982; the bull by the horns) takes place in a brothel (a metaphor of Chile under Pinochet), outside of which a war (the repression) rages. Miranda lived in exile in Venezuela, where he wrote his *Testimonio sobre la muerte de Sabrina* (1979; testimony about the death of Sabrina), a denunciation of the military régime, and upon his return to Chile he presented his highly praised, autobiographical *Regreso sin causa* (1984; return without cause). Cerda achieved prominence with his *Lo que está en el aire* (1986; what is in the air), a moving treatment of *los desaparecidos* (Chileans arrested and eliminated after the coup).

For a country with a population of just under thirteen million people, Chile has produced an astonishingly rich literature. Despite the censorship of the 1970s and 1980s, Chilean writers never ceased to depict and denounce the tragic reality they were witnessing. Thus shortly before his death, Enrique Lihn asserted before the Society of Chilean Writers that Chilean literature owed a great deal to General Pinochet. It is still too soon to assess the nation's creative production since the return to democracy, but it seems logical to assume that along with complete freedom of the press the floodgates have already been opened to an even greater surge of literary activity.

BIBLIOGRAPHY: Valenzuela, V. M., "A New Generation of Chilean Novelists and Short-Story Writers," *Hispania*, 37 (1954): 440–42; Jones, W. K., "Chile's Drama Renaissance," *Hispania*, 44 (1961): 89–94; Silva Castro, R., *Panorama literario de Chile* (1961); Alegría, F., *Las fronteras del realismo, literatura chilena del siglo XX* (1962); Goic, C., *La novela chilena, los mitos degradados* (1968); Durán-Cerda, J., *Teatro chileno contemporáneo* (1970); Concha, J., *Poesía chilena* (1973); Johnson, H. L., and P. B. Taylor, Jr., "Present-day Chilean Narrative," in *Contemporary Latin American Literature* (1973): 67–72; Ibáñez Langlois, J. M., *Poesía chilena e hispanoamericana actual* (1975); Villegas, J., *Interpretación de textos poéticos chilenos* (1977); Dorfman, A., "Literatura chilena y clandestinidad," *Escritura*, 4 (1977): 307–14; Ojeda, J. Promis, *La novela chilena actual* (1977); Villegas, J., *Interpretactión de textos poéticos chilenos* (1977); Foster, D. W., *Chilena Literature: A Working Bibliography of Secondary Sources* (1978); Foster, D. W., "Latin American Documentary Narrative," *Alternate Voices in the Contemporary Latin American Narrative* (1985): 1–44; Jara, R.,

Los límites de la representación: La novela chilena del golpe (1985); Rojo, G., *Muerte y resurrección del teatro chileno: 1973–1983* (1985); Alegría, F., *Nueva historia de la novela hispanioamericana* (1986): 329–436; Jofre, M. A., *Literatura chilena en el exilio* (1986); Cunningham, L. Guerra, "Polivalencias de la confesión en la novela chilena del exilio," *Texto e idealogía en la narrativa chilena* (1987): 227–49; McMurray, G. R., *Spanish American Writing since 1941: A Critical Survey* (1987): 58–63, 132–39, 195–97, 310–18; Pinedo, J., "La ensayística y el problema de la identidad, 1960–1988," *Ensayistas*: 22–25 (1987–1988): 231–64; Muñoz, I. Carrasco, "Poesía chilena de la última década (1977–1987)," *RChL*, 33 (Apr. 1989): 31–46; Rojo, G., *Crítica del exilio: Ensayos sobre literatura latinoamericana actual* (1989); Dorfman, A., "Political Code and Literary Code: The Testimonial Genre in Chile Today," *Some Write to the Future* (1991): 133–95

—GEORGE R. MCMURRAY

CHINESE LITERATURE

There are three periods in the development of 20th-c. Chinese literature which show a radical departure from the literature of the classical age. In the first period (1900–17), influenced by new-fangled Western ideas borrowed mainly from Japan, writers initiated a revolutionary movement that broke away from the past in thought and subject matter, although not in form and language. It paved the way for the rise in the second period (1917–49) of a nascent vernacular literature, which represented the mainstream of modern Chinese literature in opposition to traditional classical writings. This achievement would have been greater had it not been for the disruptions caused by the Sino-Japanese War (1937–45) and later the civil war between Nationalists and Communists. While literary activity continued unabated during these years, much of the war literature was ephemeral and mediocre. Meanwhile, in the guerrilla areas under Communist control, literary works for mass propaganda flourished. The Communist conquest of mainland China further extended this movement and produced during the third period (1949–present) a nationwide proletarian literature characterized by inflexible SOCIALIST REALISM and stereotyped ideological content. Simultaneously, there was a resurgence of literary activity in Taiwan, where a new generation of writers brought to the West an awareness of Taiwanese literature and a wave of anti-Communist fiction.

First Period: 1900–17

Chinese literature in the first years of the c. was noted for its innovativeness, versatility, and productivity. Its representative author was Liang Ch'i-ch'ao (1873–1929), whose polemic discourses in lucid and effective prose exerted a great influence. Turning from political activity to journalistic writing after the failure of the Reform Movement (1898), he led the campaign for new fiction and poetry, and advocated the emancipation of prose from its classical restraints, so as to better introduce new Western knowledge and ideas. Other noteworthy writers were Chang Ping-lin (1868–1936), who later became China's foremost classical scholar; Tsou Yung (1885–1905), author of the pamphlet, *Kê-ming chün* (1903; the revolutionary army), which led to his arrest and death in prison; and Ch'iu Chin (1878–1907), a woman revolutionary martyr, who left a slender volume of patriotic verses.

Three poets stood out for their multifarious accomplishments: Huang Tsun-hsien (1848–1905), SU Man-shu, LIU Ya-tzu. A widely traveled diplomat, Huang brought to Chinese poetry refreshingly new materials culled from experiences abroad; he also anticipated the movement in colloquial poetry in his dictum: "My hand writes words from my mouth." Cofounder of the Southern Society (Nan-shê), a large revolutionary literary organization, Liu Ya-tzu was a prolific poet who wrote on a wide variety of topics. As a revolutionist, he engaged in political activities that spanned the first half of the century and contributed significantly in his poems to the chronicling of contemporary historical events and figures. His friend Su Man-shu, a Sino-Japanese genius, gained fame for his poignantly emotional lyrics and sentimental love stories.

The bulk of Chinese fiction in this period, however, consisted of sociopolitical novels that served as powerful weapons for attack on the evils of Chinese society. Continuing an early tradition in satirical fiction, the novelists used their enormous creative energy to expose the bureaucratic corruptions of their time, while simultaneously advocating a new form of democratic government, revolution against the Manchu regime, and the emancipation of women. Among the hundreds of novels published in Shanghai, the newly prosperous treaty port, are *Kuan-ch'ang hsien-hsing chi* (1903; bureaucracy exposed) by Li Pao-chia (1876–1906); *Nieh-hai hua* (1905; a flower in an ocean of sins) by Tseng P'u (1872–1935); *Lao Ts'an yu-chi* (1907; *The Travels of Lao Ts'an*, 1952) by Liu E (1857–1909); and *Erh-shih nien mu-tu chih kuai hsien-chuang* (1906; *Bizarre Happenings Eyewitnessed over Two Decades*, 1975) by Wu Wo-yao (1866–1910). While different from each other in scope and treatment, these satirical novels presented realistic vignettes of decadent Chinese life and society at the turn of the century. By affirming the social functions of fiction, they raised its status as a form of serious literature. Unfortunately, satirical fiction soon gave way to erotic fiction of the so-called Mandarin Duck and Butterfly School, which featured the sensual life of the courtesans in Shanghai's red-light district. Much of this immense activity in fiction was shared by the translators, led by the classical scholar Lin Shu (1852–1924), who brought to China for the first time the wealth of Western fiction, totaling some 170 titles, including such English masters as Swift, Defoe, Scott, and particularly Dickens. Most of the translators wrote in the classical language and were quite free in their renditions.

One exception to the use of the classical language is the new drama, which had its origin abroad. Under the auspices of the Spring Willow Society (1907), Chinese students in Tokyo produced in a crude amateurish form stage plays performed in spoken vernacular Chinese, with naturalistic scenery and realistic social content. These plays were in sharp contrast to the traditional Peking opera, which stressed singing, dancing, and gesticulating. Later, these amateur actors returned to China and together with their followers initiated a new drama movement in Shanghai and other cities, but they met with little success. Their short-lived efforts served only as a prelude to the more sophisticated *hua-chü* (spoken drama) of the May Fourth (1919) era.

Second Period: 1917–49

The second and the major period of modern Chinese literature was heralded by the publication in 1917 of HU Shih's "Wenhsüeh

kai-liang ch'u-i" (a modest proposal for literary reform) in *Hsin ch'ing-nien*, a leading scholarly magazine. In this article, Hu Shih, sometimes called the "Father of the Chinese Renaissance," advocated the creation of a new national literature based upon the living language of the people. His call to arms was supported by Ch'en Tu-hsiu (1879–1942), editor of *Hsin ch'ing-nine*, who later became one of the founders of the Chinese Communist Party. Ever since its inception, the literary movement, reinforced by the May Fourth political movement, was revolutionary in nature and youthful in spirit; it served as a rallying point in the endeavor of Chinese intellectuals to free themselves from the shackles of a feudal past. It made a profound impact on modern Chinese thought and contributed to the current Chinese outlook toward life and society.

The leading writer of this period—and, in fact, the greatest name in 20th-c. Chinese literature—was LU HSÜN, whose short stories and essays have exerted a tremendous influence on the younger generation. In *Ah Q cheng-chuan* (1921; *The True Story of Ah Q*, 1926) and elsewhere, Lu Hsün presented tales and characters of a backward traditional society about to disintegrate and collapse on the eve of a far-reaching but still transitional revolution. A born fighter, he was noted for his caustic satire and fearless exposure of the dark aspects of the old society, thus initiating the modern trend toward social criticism. In his last years, Lu Hsün became increasingly resentful of the repressive nationalist literary policy. To combat it, he organized the League of Left-Wing Writers (1930) with alleged Communist support. Acrimonious controversy with the rightist and bitter dissension in the leftist camp pursued Lu Hsün to his grave.

Of the numerous narrative writers of this epoch, the most outstanding were MAO TUN, PA CHIN, and LAO SHE. A founder of the Literary Research Association (1920), Mao Tun exemplified its creed of "literature for life's sake" in his stories and novels by presenting a realistic analysis of contemporary Chinese society. The characters who live in the pages of his social chronicles range from peasants in bankrupt rural villages—"Ch'unts'an" (1932; "Spring Silkworms," 1956), "Ch'iu-shou" (1932; "Autumn Harvest," 1956), "Ts'an-tung" (1932; "Winter Ruin," 1956)—to industrial workers and capitalists caught in the financial maelstrom of metropolitan Shanghai—*Tzu-yeh* (1933; *Midnight*, 1957). Pa Chin, one of the most prodigious writers, started his career as an anarchist and romanticist, fascinating his readers with a series of novels featuring the romantic love and revolutionary activities of his youthful heroes and heroines. A typical theme of his novels—such as *Chia* (1931; *The Family*, 1958)—is the conflict between old and young in a large patriarchal family, where the children either submit passively to their elders' bigotry and dogmatism, or rebel against them in a vehement struggle. Conscientious and skillful in the art of fiction writing, Lao She excelled in architectural plot, vivid characterization, and racy dialogue. All these qualities characterize his best-selling *Lo-t'o hsiang-tzu* (1938; *Rickshaw Boy*, 1945). A good-natured sense of humor, running through a number of his novels, enlivens the otherwise somber and sometimes sordid atmosphere in modern Chinese fiction. Mention must also be made of TING LING, the only major Communist writer to have made a name in this period. Her socialist-inspired conscience dictated that she switch from her candid tales of women's uninhibited love, for which she became popular, to stories of peasant struggles against poverty, hunger, and natural calamities.

In poetry, Hu Shih's experiments in vernacular free verse, despite strong initial opposition, attracted a large following among contemporary writers. KUO Mo-jo, leader of the Creation Society

(1921), first earned his reputation as a poet with a volume of boldly original poems, *Nü-shen* (1921; *Selected Poems from the Goddesses*, 1958). Although opposite to Hu Shih in literary temperament and political view, Kuo Mo-jo, the spokesman of leftist writers, is as gifted and versatile as his rightist counterpart. In his later years he turned from poetry to autobiographical stories, historical plays, literary criticism, revolutionary polemics, and studies of ancient Chinese society based on bone and bronze inscriptions.

In the wake of these pioneers three important groups emerged: the Crescent Society (1928), the Contemporary Age (1932), and the Chinese Poetry Association (1932). Under the leadership of HSÜ Chih-mo and WEN I-to, the Crescent poets, who laid great stress on form and technique, attempted to introduce the beauty of music (rhyme and rhythm), painting (color), and architecture (form and structure) into poetry. Their efforts suffered a setback with the tragic deaths of their two leaders, Hsü Chih-mo in an airplane accident and Wen I-to by assassination. The poets of the Contemporary Age group attempted to express subtle emotions and delicate situations through the use of colors and images in the manner of French SYMBOLISM. This aesthetic delight in sheer lyricism was opposed by members of the Chinese Poetry Association, which was an arm of the League of Left-Wing Writers. In their view, poetry should sing realistically of the prevailing mood of the new era, "an era of the people's resistance against feudalism and imperialism." Their adoption of colloquial language, popular tunes, and folk forms led to a new mass-oriented poetry, to which the Communist poets eventually turned.

Some of the major poets of modern China, such as Feng Chih (b. 1906), Pien Chih-lin (b. 1910), Tsang K'o-chia (b. 1905), and HO Ch'i-fang, started their poetic careers under the shadow of the Crescent Society. While each had his individual traits—the contemplative mood and mythic experience of FENG's sonnets; the articulate, urbane poems of PIEN about the streets and people of Peking; the robust, rustic verses of TSANG, smelling of the soil of a wide-open country; the haunting romantic verses of HO in his youthful dreams of love and beauty—they were all devoted to their craft and fastidious in their search for "words that will startle the readers." This concern for poetic style and diction was still apparent in their later poems, even though there was a drastic change in theme and content. Unlike them, AI Ch'ing and T'ien Chien (b. 1916) broke away completely from lingering academic traditions and foreign influences to return to a colloquial style in their songs of peasants and soldiers. T'ien Chien especially quickened the pulses of the new age with his drumbeat poetry, which has only two to three words in each line.

Realistic social drama written in the vernacular, as mentioned earlier, was introduced from abroad even before the literary revolution; but it never secured a foothold on the popular stage until the advent in the early 1930s of a young playwright, TS'AO Yü, whose first play, *Lei-yü* (1934; *Thunder and Rain*, 1936), literally took the audience by storm. Previously, several notable attempts in staging vernacular plays had been made by Ou-yang Yü-ch'ien (1887–1962), a veteran of the Spring Willow Society; T'ien Han (1898–1968), leader of the South China Society; and Hung Shen (1894–1955), who had been a student in G. P. Baker's famous English 47 playwriting course at Harvard University. None of these efforts, however, had survived the competition of such popular entertainments as the Peking opera and American movies, with the result that the spoken drama was cultivated only by amateur groups and student dramatic organizations. Significantly, some of the better plays in their repertory were translations from the West, such as

Ibsen's *A Doll's House*, Wilde's *Lady Windermere's Fan*, and Dumas's *La dame aux camélias*. The situation changed with the appearance, in rapid succession, of Ts'ao Yü's *Lei-yü*, *Jih-ch'u* (1936; *The Sunrise*, 1940), and *Yüan-yeh* (1937; *The Wilderness*, 1979), each a brilliant play that won immediate popular and critical acclaim. Whether it is the tragedy of an ill-fated rich industrialist family smitten by the past sins of its members, or a realistic drama of a group of upper-class social parasites dragging out their useless existence, or a melodrama of rural revenge full of sound and fury, they haunt the reader's mind with their universal human appeal, emotional conflict, and dramatic tension. While still in his mid-twenties, Ts'ao Yü became overnight the major dramatist of modern China.

During the Sino-Japanese War, most writers mentioned above fled to the unoccupied hinterland, where they rallied under the banner of the All-China Anti-Aggression Federation of Writers and Artists and contributed to the war effort through literary works of a propagandist nature. The paths some of them trod, however, were quite different. While Ch'en Tu-hsiu pined away in a nationalist cell, Hu Shih became the Chinese ambassador to the United States, Kuo Mo-jo held a nominal government position in Chungking, and Lao She busied himself with patriotic work for the All-China Anti-Aggression Federation. Among them, Kuo Mo-jo and Lao She were the most productive; others like Mao Tun, Pa Chin, and Ts'ao Yü made similar important contributions. The young poets mellowed; faced with the harsh realities of life, they now sang of the living drama of war and blood enacted before them. Some visited the Communist stronghold in Yenan, and others, like Ai Ch'ing and T'ien Chien, stayed on to work for the Communist cause. As the war progressed, more and more intellectuals were disappointed with the Nationalist government in Chungking and turned to look northwestward to Yenan, where a new breed of proletarian writers began to emerge on the literary scene. The raging civil war that followed the Japanese surrender did not change the attitude of the writers. Most of them chose to remain in China, rather than flee to Taiwan, after the Communist victory (1949), which ushered in the third and present period of modern Chinese literature.

Third Period: 1949–80

Since 1949, Chinese literature on the mainland is as much a record of political campaigns and ideological battles as it is one of individual writers and their literary creations. The roots of this literature could be traced to guidelines promulgated by Mao Tse-tung in his "Tsai Yenan wen-i tso-t'an-hui shang it chiang-hua" (1942; "Talks at the Yenan Forum on Literature and Art," 1956), which laid down for Communist writers certain requirements concerning the role and form of literature in a socialist society and which initiated a series of rectifications campaigns that determined the future course of literary activities. The convening of the First National Conference of Writers and Artists (1949) in Peking resulted in the founding of the All-China Federation of Literary and Art Circles, with Kuo Mo-jo as chairman. The majority of older, established writers, however, soon ceased producing creative works, and over the ensuing three decades, their ranks were thinned by death and political purges; although many have resurfaced as a result of the recent anti-"gang of four" campaign, they are now well past their creative primes.

Mao's ideals in his Yenan talks were first realized by CHAO Shu-li, whose early short stories, such as "Li Yu-ts'ai pan-hua"

(1943; "The Rhymes of Li Yu-tsai," 1950), and his novel of land reform, *Li-chia-chuang it pien-ch'ien* (1950; *Changes in Li Village*, 1953), were models of proletarian literature embellished with folklore traditions. Land reform was central to two major works of this period, *Pao-feng tsou-yü* (1949; *The Hurricane*, 1955) by CHOU Li-po and *T'aiyang chao tsai Sang-kan-ho shang* (1949; *The Sun Shines over the Sangkan River*, 1954) by Ting Ling, which won a 1951 Stalin Prize for literature. Other novels written in this period sang the praises of the Party, the revolution, and the proletariat—the era of the exposé had passed. Among the most popular novels were *Pao-wei Yen-an* (1954; *Defend Yenan*, 1958) by Tu P'eng-ch'eng (b. 1921), *Hung-ch'i p'u* (1957; *Keep the Red Flag Flying*, 1961) by Liang Pin (b. 1914), *Ch'ing-ch'un chih ko* (1958; *The Song of Youth*, 1964) by the woman writer Yang Mo (b. 1915), and a novel of PLA (People's Liberation Army) heroism, *Lin-hai hsüeh-yüan* (1962; *Tracks in the Snowy Forest*, 1962) by Ch'ü Po (b. 1923). Special mention must be made of the novels of Hao Jan (b. 1932), which stood virtually alone during the Cultural Revolution. The older poets—prominent among them were Ai Ch'ing, Ho Ch'i-fang, T'ien Chien, and Tsang K'o-chia—fared well in the early years of the regime. They were most active in the revolutionary struggle, creating poems in praise of the heroism of soldiers during the Korean War, of peasants involved in land reform, and of workers who were building a new China in the cities. All continued to write up until the Cultural Revolution, when their voices were silenced.

Perhaps the greatest change took place in drama, which had a direct appeal to the less well-educated masses. Initially, the most note-worthy revolutionary plays came from the pens of Lao She—*Lung-hsü kou* (1951; *Dragon Beard Ditch*, 1956) and *Ch'a-kuan* (1957; teahouse)—and Ts'ao Yü—*Ming-lang ti t'ien* (1956; bright skies) and *Tan-chien p'ien* (1962; gall and sword). Immensely popular was *Pai-mao nü* (1945; *The White-haired Girl*, 1953) by Ho Ching-chih (b. 1924) and Ting Yi (d. 1954). During the Cultural Revolution, model revolutionary Peking operas such as *Sha-chia pang* (1964; *Shachiapang*, 1972) and *Hung-teng chi* (1964; *The Red Lantern*, 1965) gained preeminence. Since then, the spoken drama has made a resurgence and is showing signs of surprising vitality.

Mainland Chinese Literature since 1980

China had seventeen years from the founding of the People's Republic in 1949 to get its plans and institutions in place and working. They were not good years—some, in fact, were quite awful—but there was always activity, always a sense of movement; it wasn't long enough, however, and literature barely had a chance. For with the advent of the Cultural Revolution (1966–1976) the sterility of literary activities matched the general tenor of life, as Chinese society began to unravel. The death of Mao in 1976 and the fall of the Gang of Four began the emancipation process, but writers, usually the first to raise their voices on behalf of society and the individual, were understandably cautious about resuming this notoriously risky endeavor.

Toward the end of 1977, a literary phenomenon known as "scar literature" appeared, with courageous editors publishing thinly veiled fictional accounts of institutionalized cruelty and oppression during the chaotic decade. In a milieu characterized more by bewilderment than understanding of what had happened—and why—these writings, typified by the story "Pan chu-jen" (1977; the head teacher) by Liu Hsin-wu (Liu Xinwu, b. 1942), served to

unite the people in their common suffering. They also, more by design than coincidence, fixed the blame for China's contemporary ills on Lin Piao (Lin Biao) and the Gang of Four.

The years 1978 and 1979 have been grandiosely termed a golden era of modern Chinese history. Popular demands for reform, highlighted by the establishment of "Democracy Wall," for the righting of political wrongs, and for literary and artistic freedom spawned a liberalization movement that was manifested in a corpus of exposé literature often classified as NEOREALISM. The richest harvest was reaped in fiction, as writers turned a critical eye not to the Cultural Revolution, but to the crippled society left in its wake. Ranging from melodrama (though not nearly as maudlin as the somewhat sophomoric "scar" stories) to biting satire, these works revealed aspects of society and personal views that would have been heretical in the socialist-realist literature of the preceding period. One of the most successful writers was Kao Hsiao-sheng (Gao Xiaosheng), who wrote about the southern Chinese countryside with caustic humor, compassion, and outrage against bureaucratic excesses and mistakes. "Li Shun-ta tsowu" (1979; "Li Shunda Builds a House," 1983) relates the tale of a peasant whose goal of building a modest home is frustrated by three decades of political campaigns, only to be realized once he resigns himself to the ways of New China: "backdoorism," bribery, and other tricks. The sense of betrayal is palpable in this and other stories by Kao and his contemporaries.

Poetry also played a significant role in exposing social ills and official malfeasance. The long, prosaic poem "Chiang-chün pu-neng che-yang tso" (1979; "General, You Must Not Do This," 1983) by Yeh Wen-fu (Ye Wenfu, b. 1944) is a frontal attack on special privileges, easily the most galling of the many forms of social misconduct to the average Chinese citizen.

The screenplay *Chia-ju wo shih chen-te* (1979; *If I Were for Real*, 1983) by Sha Yeh-hsin (Sha Yexin, b. 1939) is yet another attack on the deeply entrenched practice of granting special privileges to people in power and those in their often extensive circles. Concerned with a young man who is mistaken for the son of a member of the Central Committee and thus treated as royalty, the screenplay was deemed so blatantly critical that it had to be filmed not in China but in Taiwan.

Ultimately it was a journalist, a former "rightist," who most powerfully captured the spirit of the writing community during that period of nearly unprecedented liberalization. "Jen-Yao Chih-chien" (1979; "People or Monsters?," 1983) by Liu Pinyen (Liu Binyan, b. 1925) is a long piece of reportage that exposes a web of corruption created by a powerful official in China's northeast, thereby setting the tone for a genre of writing that captured the fancy of Chinese readers for a number of years.

In November 1979 the Fourth Congress of Chinese Literary and Artistic Workers was convened in Beijing, with more than 3,200 delegates in attendance: The mood was upbeat and hopeful, as a call went out for support of the Four Modernizations, increased intellectual freedom, and a renewed commitment to socialist ideals. Unhappily, instead of prolonging the "literary spring," the congress proved to be the beginning of the end, for a scant two months later, Teng Hsiao-p'ing (Deng Xiaoping) demanded an end to a tolerance of dissent, the closing down of "democracy walls" once and for all, and the suspension of all unofficial journals. He also reaffirmed the wisdom of the purges of the 1950s, which had led inexorably to the horrors of the 1960s and 1970s. People like Liu Pin-yen, Yeh Wen-fu, and Sha Yeh-hsin were subjected to the very criticisms they had warned against with such eloquence and passion. Yet in the midst of this oppressive climate, a remarkable memoir of life during the Cultural Revolution was quietly published: *Kan-hsiao liu-chi* (1981; *Six Chapters from My Life "Downunder,"* 1983) by YANG Chiang (Yang Jiang) is at once a story of deep marital affection and institutional brutality set in the labor camps to which intellectuals were sent, some for nearly a decade, and is considered by some to be a parable on the effects of Maoism on contemporary Chinese society.

By 1981, as leftism made a rebound and NEOREALISM lost its official patronage, a minicampaign was launched against a film script entitled *K'u-lien* (1981; unrequited love) by Pai Hua (Bai Hua, b. 1930); it is the story of an overseas artist who returns to China in the wave of patriotism after 1949, only to suffer disillusionment and, ultimately, ignominious death. When his daughter asks him on his deathbed, "Father, you love this country, but does this country love you?" the reader is struck by the degree of cynicism created by three decades of political oppression. The criticism that followed pitted two generations of artists against one another, the older generally serving as mouthpieces for powerful bureaucrats. The campaign spread to include a new literary phenomenon pejoratively termed *meng-lung* ("obscure" or "misty") poetry. Actually a form of verse akin to Anglo-American IMAGISM, "misty" poetry was created by poets like PEI Tao (Bei Dao), Shu T'ing (Shu Ting, b. 1952), and Ku Ch'eng (Gu Cheng, 1956–1993), who gained an enthusiastic, if occasionally befuddled, audience for their difficult, innovative, fresh, and passionate verse. Pei Tao's line "I do not believe!" typifies the mood of alienation that gripped these young victims of the Cultural Revolution.

By 1983 those in charge of literary production were sufficiently concerned over attempts by writers to stretch the boundaries of acceptable literary forms and contents to launch yet another campaign, the short-lived, ill-conceived, and troubling attack against "spiritual pollution" (by which was meant humanism, modernism, and a view that alienation is historically compatible with Marxism). "Misty" poetry was still under the gun, as was the "modernist" fiction of the man slated to become minister of culture, Wang MENG, author of the novel *Pu-li* (1979; *Bolshevik Salute*, 1989), and of creators of new expressions of individuality, such as the "humanist" first novel *Ren a! ren* (1980; *Stones of the Wall*, 1985) by Tai Hou-ying (Dai Houying, 1938–1996). The architects of the campaign also kept a wary eye on the influx of literature from Taiwan, a phenomenon that had its beginnings at the turn of the decade; for while the earliest representatives of Taiwanese fiction and poetry were critical of Taiwan society, later offerings painted a more appealing picture of the island province. Particularly popular were the artistic stories of PAI Hsien-yung and the highly politicized nativist fiction of HUANG Ch'unming and Ch'en Ying-chen (b. 1936). Within a few years Taiwanese popular fiction would be the rage in China, particularly among the young.

By the middle of the decade an uneasy truce existed between literary bureaucrats and writers who lacked official patronage. In the novel *Nanjen te i-pan shih nü-jen* (1985; *Half of Man Is Woman*, 1986) Chang Hsien-liang (Zhang Xianliang, b. 1936) uses sexual impotence both as a metaphor for political incompetence and as an observable consequence of political oppression; in this and subsequent works he describes how the baleful legacy of the Cultural Revolution is firmly entrenched in contemporary society, embraced by hordes of bureaucrats whose "rice bowls" would be threatened by implementation of institutionalized political, economic, and cultural reforms. While it would be an overstatement to say that Chang's novels broke down literary barriers erected against descriptions of sexuality, they and similar works by female

writers such as WANG Anyi (Wang An-i), Chang Hsin-hsin (Zhang Xinxin, b. 1954), and Chang K'ang-K'ang (Zhang Kang-kang, b. 1950), as well as the feminist fiction of Chang Chieh (Zhang Jie, b. 1937), helped make Chinese fiction of the mid-1980s a bit less prudish and moralistic.

In 20th-c. Chinese poetry, generations sometimes span but a few years. It did not take long for "misty" poetry to spawn "postmisty" and other ephemeral schools of avant-garde poets interested in linguistic experimentation, the exultation of ancient cultural and literary traditions, and, in some cases, little more than sensationalism. The one-time "misty" poet Yang Lien (Yang Lian, b. 1955) used for his later inspiration China's ancient myths and legends, a move that linked him with a group of fiction writers known collectively as the *hsün-ken* (root-seeking) school, who captured a broad readership in China and the West by evoking cultural and historical roots in stories that blend heightened linguistic experimentation with a rural-based, nonideological approach to writing. China's past—ancient and recent—is at the core of the writing of novelists like MO Yen (Mo Yan), Han Shao-kung (Han Shaogong, b. 1953), the Tibetan Zhaxi Dawa (b. 1959), the Moslem Chang Ch'eng-chih (Zhang Chengzhi, b. 1948), and more. A series of "king" novellas by Ah Ch'eng (A Cheng, b. 1949), including the renowned "Ch'i-wang" (1984; "The Chess King," 1990), were held up as models of Chinese writing that succeeds by using a non-Westernized idiom while merging past and present.

The most resilient theme in 1980s literature was reform, including prescriptive, upbeat fiction like the factory stories of Chiang Tzu-lung (Jiang Zilong, b. 1941), as well as the more critical, even cynical, stories and novels that followed in the latter half of the decade. One does not emerge optimistic from a reading of *T'ien-t'ang suan-t' ai chih ko* (1988; *The Garlic Ballads*, 1995) by Mo Yen, *Fu-tsao* (1987; *Turbulence*, 1991) by Chia P'ing-wa (Jia Pingwa, b. 1954), or *Chen-nü* (1985; *Virgin Widows*, 1996) by Ku Hua (Gu Hua, b. 1942). Besides revealing the resistance to social reform in certain sectors, these works offer little hope for improvement, at least over the short haul. As though to underscore the pessimism, the government launched yet another political campaign in early 1987, this one targeted at "bourgeois liberalization" (once again an oblique swipe at such Western bugaboos as modernism); it culminated in the expulsion from the party of Liu Pinyen and others. An autumnal chill settled over the writing community during the next couple of years, when the best Chinese literature was published not on the mainland, but in Taiwan. World attention to Chinese culture was captured not by translations of novels, but by their cinematic adaptations, many of which won international prizes.

The decade of the 1980s in China closed with a general clampdown after the June Fourth violence at T'ien-an-men (Tiananmen), which effectively drove literature underground or into hibernation. Magazines were shut down, editors fired, and censorship reinstituted. Except for writers with official patronage, literary activities for the early post-T'ien-an-men years were limited to the stories and poems of a handful of youthful innovators and the occasional offering of an established author; more often than not, even this was published first outside of China, sometimes in translation. The work of Beijing's "bad boy," Wang Shuo (b. 1958), author of the irreverent novel *War-ti chiushih hsin-tiao* (1989; *Playing for Thrills*, 1997) Yü Hua (b. 1960), and Su T'ung (Su Tong, b. 1963), whose *Mi* (1991; *Rice*, 1995) paints an incomparably bleak picture of China in the first half of the 20th c. and is intended as a metaphor for a more recent time, among others, bears watching, owing to its tone of alienation and cynicism as well as its linguistic and technical innovations. Meanwhile, a burgeoning corpus of expatriate literature is emerging from the pens of writers whose residence in the West is taking on the appearance of permanent domicile; novels by Hung Ying (Hong Ying, b. 1962) and the poetry of Pei Tao and others continue to appear both in Chinese and in translation.

Taiwanese Literature: 1949-80

Across the Taiwan Strait, following upon the exodus of the Nationalist government to the island in 1949, a new beginning in literary production ensued, but with predictably poor results. Patriotic propaganda was the order of the day in a period that witnessed the creation of stereotyped anti-Communist fiction, and poetry and essays that were either benignly lyrical or dripping with sentimentality. The literary situation improved in the late 1950s, and anti-Communist fiction reached its high point with the publication of CHANG Ai-ling's *Yang-ko* (1954; *The Rice-Sprout Song*, 1955), and Chiang Kuei's (1908–1980) *Hsüan-feng* (1959; *The Whirlwind*, 1977). The founding of the journals *Wen-hsüeh chi-k'an* and *Hsien-tai wen-hsüeh* ushered in the modernist era. Heavily indebted to such Western masters as JOYCE, KAFKA, FITZGERALD, and others, a number of young authors, most notably Chu Hsi-ning (1927-1998), PAI Hsien-yung, and Wang Wen-hsing (b. 1939), exerted a strong influence. Modern vernacular poetry developed around three societies: the Modernist School, under the leadership of Chi Hsien (b. 1913); the Blue Stars Society, whose most prominent member was YÜ Kuang-chung; and the Epoch Society, where French SURREALISM was popular. The alien nature of much of the poetry produced by these poets did not gain wide acceptance for them, although they passed on a legacy of highly original imagery and a modern poetic idiom. Unlike prose fiction and poetry, the spoken drama never gained a foothold in Taiwan, although Peking opera has been exceedingly popular.

The mid-1960s witnessed a recrudescence of provincialism with the emergence of several native Taiwanese poets and novelists. For the first time in many decades the central subject in the works of a major segment of the writing community was the lives of the ordinary, predominantly rural Taiwanese. Under the leadership of HUANG Ch'un-ming, Wang Chen-ho (1940-1990), and others, this regional school has only recently begun to give way to a more organized and nationalistic literature, which reflects Taiwan's current political situation. Other Taiwan authors came to the U.S. to pursue professional careers. One of them, Ch'en Jo-hsi (b. 1938), went to the People's Republic for several years and described her firsthand impressions and experiences of Chinese life during the Cultural Revolution in a series of novels and story collections, notably *Yin hsien-chang* (1976; *The Execution of Mayor Yin*, 1978), an outstanding example of dissent literature from Communist China.

Taiwanese Literature since 1980

The past two decades in Taiwan, the other major venue of Chinese literature, have witnessed several significant swings in literary activities and output, not surprising given the startling changes in Taiwanese politics and society during that period. The most notable achievements of the 1960s, a decade of experimentation and growth, involved Westernized fiction and verse. By the mid-1970s, however, as the Cultural Revolution wound down

across the Taiwan Strait, Taiwan was the scene of a protracted debate over nativist writing, which can be viewed in part as a national affirmation movement while Taiwan was suffering a series of political reverses. Literary modernism, a hallmark of the previous decade, was attacked as a symptom of Western cultural imperialism, and replaced by a more politicized corpus that was extremely well received by the populace. Stories of rural Taiwan by Huang Ch'un-ming, Ch'en Ying-chen, and Wang Chen-he (1940–1990), using a mixture of standard Mandarin and local dialect, portrayed Taiwan in the grip of a wrenching social transition and increasing international isolation. Frequently prescriptive in its conception and generally mimetic in nature, this engagé literature reached a broad readership that was denied novelists like Wang Wen-hsing (b. 1939), whose experimental novels *Chia-pien* (1972; *Family Catastrophe*, 1995) and *Pei-hai te jen* (1981; *Backed Against the Sea*, 1993) confounded all but the most dedicated readers.

The 1980s saw the return of a more urban-based literature, as a younger group of novelists and poets, many of them women, drew closer to the mass media in their work and gained wide popularity. Novelists like Hsiao Sa (b. 1953), whose work has been characterized as journalistic realism, and LI Ang, the most daring novelist of her day, illuminated the lives, quotidian and spectacular, of contemporary women; occasionally they caused sensations in their own right, as did Li Ang's feminist novel *Sha Fu* (1983; *The Butcher's Wife*, 1986), with its graphic descriptions of sex and violence. Pai Hsien-yung created yet another controversy with the publication of *Nieh-tzu* (1983; *Crystal Boys*, 1990), the first modern novel on a gay theme. Both were reprinted on the mainland.

Taiwan's economic miracle of the late 1980s, coupled with profound political changes that would not have seemed possible only a few years earlier, had broad and immediate effects on literature. Many of the older generation of writers, such as the poet and essayist Yü Kuang-chung, were more involved with literary patronage than creative writing, while a few innovative writers like Chang Hsi-kuo (b. 1944) and Chang Ta-ch'un (b. 1957) continued to expand the boundaries of literature, experimenting in detective fiction, science fiction, MAGIC REALISM, and more. However, it was a "brat pack" of aggressively promoted young novelists who captured the lion's share of the market with a more "popular" brand of fiction, including romances, thrillers, and sexually explicit novels.

A trend toward more "consumer-oriented" literature is occurring wherever Chinese literature is written (including Hong Kong and overseas Chinese communities). While the issue of whether or not the 1990s or the 21st c. will witness Chinese political unification is open to debate, an astonishing measure of literary unification—owing to creative cross-fertilization and a Chinese readership that transcends political borders—is already a fait accompli.

See also Mongolian Literature, Tibetan Literature, and Uyghur Literature. For further writing in Chinese, see Malaysian Literature, Singapore Literature, and Vietnamese Literature.

BIBLIOGRAPHY: Hu Shih, *The Chinese Renaissance* (1934); Chow, Tse-tsung, *The May Fourth Movement* (1960); Hsia, C. T., *A History of Modern Chinese Fiction* (1961, 2nd ed. 1971); Birch, C., ed., *Chinese Communist Literature* (1963); Průšek, J., ed., *Studies in Modern Chinese Literature* (1964); Liu, Wu-chi, "The Modern Period, 1900–1950," supplement to Giles, H. A., *A History of Chinese Literature* (enlarged ed., 1967); Goldman, M., *Literary Dissent in Communist China* (1971); Lin, J., *Modern Chinese Poetry: An Introduction* (1972); Lee, L., *The Romantic Generation* of Modern Chinese Writers (1973); Huang, J., Heroes and Villains in Communist China: The Contemporary Chinese Novel as a Reflection of Life (1973); Hsu, K. Y., The Chinese Literary Scene (1975); Goldman, M., ed., Modern Chinese Literature in the May Fourth Era (1977); Faurot, J. L., Chinese Fiction from Taiwan: Critical Perspectives (1980); Gálik, M., The Genesis of Modern Chinese Literary Criticism (1980); Průšek, J., The Lyrical and the Epic: Studies of Modern Chinese Literature (1980); Hsu, K. J., ed., Literature of the People's Republic of China (1980); Yang, W. and N. Mao, eds., Modern Chinese Fiction: A Guide to Its Study and Appreciation (1981); Goldblatt, H., ed., Chinese Literature for the 1980s (1982); Lau, J. S. M., ed., The Unbroken Chain: An Anthology of Taiwan Fiction since 1926 (1983); Lee, Y., ed., The New Realism: Writings from China after the Cultural Revolution (1983); Siu, H., and Z. Stern, eds., Mao's Harvest: Voices from China's New Generation (1983); Link, P., ed., Roses and Thorns: The Second Blooming of the Hundred Flowers in Chinese Fiction, 1979–1980 (1984); McDougall, B. S., ed., Popular Chinese Literature and Performing Arts in the People's Republic of China, 1949–1979 (1984); Duke, M. S., Blooming and Contending: Chinese Literature in the Post-Mao Era (1985); Kinkley, J. C., After Mao: Chinese Literature and Society, 1978–1981 (1985); Lee, L., ed., The Legacy of Lu Xun (1986); Duke, M. S., ed., Modern Chinese Women Writers: Critical Appraisals (1989); Tai, J., comp., Spring Bamboo: A Collection of Contemporary Chinese Short Stories (1989); Carver, A. C., and S. Y. Chang, eds., Bamboo Shoots after the Rain: Contemporary Stories by Women Writers of Taiwan (1990); Goldblatt, H., ed., Worlds Apart: Recent Chinese Writing and its Audiences (1990); Siu, H. F., ed., Furrows, Peasants, Intellectuals, and the State (1990); Duke, M. S., ed., Worlds of Modern Chinese Fiction (1991); special Chinese literature issue, WLT, 65, 3 (Summer 1991); Lau, J., and H. Goldblatt, eds., The Columbis Anthology of Modern Chinese Literature (1995); Goldblatt, H., ed., Chairman Mao Would Not Be Amused (1995); McDougall, B. S., and K. Louie, eds., The Literature of China in the Twentieth Century (1997)

—GOLDBLATT HOWARD

CHINESE-INDONESIAN LITERATURE

See Indonesian Literature

CHINODYA, Shimmer

Zimbabwean poet, novelist, and writer of children's books (writing in English), b. 30 May 1957, Gweru, Rhodesia (now Zimbabwe)

C. became prominent in international circles relatively recently, with the winning of the Commonwealth Writers Prize, African Region, for his novel Harvest of Thorns (1989). That novel was preceded by several others, but as many of these have not yet been published for the international market, there is not yet a large body of critical discussion on C. All his novels concern issues of

personal development, of growing up, and of discovery of one's beliefs despite or because of constrained circumstances. Critics have noted a love of natural settings permeating C.'s work. His poems, not yet collected in a published volume, display this affection, as an example such as "African Grass" demonstrates. Dew in the Morning (1982) provides careful delineations of rural life, and the natural world provides a counterpoint for the experiences of the central protagonist, Benjamin Tichafa, in Harvest of Thorns. Caught in Rhodesia's death-throes, Tichafa struggles to grow up and live his life. Filled with the normal longings and concerns of young men, he is also a pawn in forces he only inchoately understands, which impose on him brutalities that he again does not fully assimilate. As a guerrilla, he moves through an awesome, foreboding forest that objectively represents his equally obscured path through human-made restrictions and expectations; these latter are as impenetrable as the undergrowth, and far more ominous.

C.'s treatment of military conflict subverts expected ways of treating such fights for independence. Battles and atrocities occur, but these are not the novel's central focus. Rather than glorifying young people swept up in a cause, the narrative voice becomes distanced, describing day-to-day concerns. The tedium of finding food, staying dry, and getting enough sleep interweaves with struggles against the group's leader and telling stories around fires to explain their mission to villagers.

Critics have referred to Harvest of Thorns as a "coming-of-age" story. Others emphasize its politics, reading it as an allegory of Zimbabwe's effort to gain independence. It is these, and more. C. demonstrates that unless people die—as some do in the novel—they must come of age, inescapably. What such maturation will bring with it, however, is shaped by idiosyncrasies of context marked by location and time, and emphasized through the strength of community, which alone can inject humanity into one's sense of maturity. Such communal values shape the novel's structure and content, imbuing it with a revolutionary vision belied by its straightforward and engaging style. Postmodern fireworks of language do not interrupt the story here; no narrator self-importantly trumpets about the difficulties of writing. Instead, we are caught up in the story of a young man—but one told in a way not imaginable in the traditional bildungsroman.

Harvest of Thorns blends private and public reality, setting the writer's perception of people and situations firmly in the context of social and political complexity. This writer's profound humanism, and his sharp awareness that the personal and specific make up the broad political picture, give this novel both its tragedy and its hope.

An interest in how young people mature and come to recognize their surroundings and contemporary issues, as well as how they then come to terms with the world they have found, also marks C.'s writing for children. Under the name Ben Chirasha, C. has produced a set of six traditional Zimbabwean folktales as well as plays and poems for classroom teaching. Clearly, his series of folktales helps shape children's appreciation of things Zimbabwean. Similarly, the plays and poems help make students aware of their heritage and its performative strengths.

C.'s voice represents the latest wave of African literature. Well aware of poststructuralist and other trends in contemporary writing, C. avoids the pitfalls both of self-indulgent reflexivity and of an unaware representation. He charts his own path to provide those strengths of enduring literature: an honest and powerful voice that explores human conditions in their local environments.

FURTHER WORKS: *Farai's Girls* (1984); *Child of War* (1985); *Classroom Plays for Primary Schools* (1986); *Traditional Tales of Zimbabwe* (6 vols., 1988-1992); *Young like Us: Poems for Primary Schools* (1990); *Everyone's Child* (1996)

BIBLIOGRAPHY: Matsidkidze, I., "C.: An Interview," *ALA Bulletin,*20, 2, (1994): 46-60; Gunner, L., "Power, Popular Consciousness and the Fictions of War: Hove's *Bones* and C.'s *Harvest of Thorns*," *AL&C*, 4, 1 (1991): 77-85

—VICTORIA CARCHIDI

CHKHEIDZE, Otar

Georgian novelist, playwright, essayist and literary critic, b. 1920, Kartli

After graduating with a degree in philology from Tbilisi State University, C. held teaching as well as administrative positions at various colleges in Georgia. From his early stories, published in 1940, until his latest novels and essays, the vocabulary, syntax, and general tone of C.'s narrative maintain the characteristic inflexions of the Kartli vernacular that sets him apart from other contemporary Georgian writers. The publication of the first collection of his stories, *Kheleuri* (1947; A Handful of Wheat), marked the beginning of his troubled literary career. In the 1950s, apart from short stories about the country life of his native Kartli, C. published a series of novels: *Tiniskhidi* (1950-55; A Stone Bridge), *Burusi* (1955; Haze), *Djebiri* (1956; A Dike), and *Mechechi* (1958; Shoal). The narrative style and scope of these works bring to mind the novels of William FAULKNER and James JOYCE. Loosely connected with each other by a general chronology of events and characters of different generations, these novels constitute an epic story recording deep social and psychological changes in contemporary Georgian society since the turn of the century. Almost every one of these novels was scathingly criticized or outrightly condemned by official censors for the "slanderous distortion" of Soviet reality.

The more liberal atmosphere of the 1960s allowed the relatively uneventful publication of the author's following works: *Kvernaki* (1965; Kvernaki), *Agmart-dagmarti* (1967; Hilly Road), and *Landebi* (1968; Shadows). His plays depicting the heroic past of Georgia, "*Visia visia*" (1964; Who Owns It, Who), *Tevdore* (1967; Tevdore), and *Ketevan* (1970; Ketevan), were staged by major theaters of the country. Apart from official ostracism C. has often suffered the almost total indifference of the reader, probably on account of his exceptionally and, in order to avoid sensorial wrath, often intentionally difficult style. In most of his stories and novels C. utilizes first-person narrative that unfolds like a stream of consciousness, an inner monologue half dreaming, half recollecting the events and experiences of the narrator's past. His complex sentences often stretch to an entire page and more. C.'s best novel, *Boriaqi* (1974; Hot Wind), is about the social turmoil in the early 1920s that lead to the abortive rebellion against Bolshevik power in 1924 and the consequent blood bath conducted by Sergo Ordjonikidze, then the head of Georgia's newly established Soviet government. The author used almost every available means to render the topic of his narrative as vague and evasive as possible. Subordinate clauses relentlessly following one upon the other turn his syntax into a verbal labyrinth that presents a real challenge for the reader, but those who persist in untangling its intricate web are rewarded by magnificent images of Apocalyptic magnitude and horror.

Works published during the 1980s and 1990s, such as *Tskhratsqaro* (1980; Nine Springs) and *Mtagrekhili* (1985; Mountain Range), established C. as a preeminent writer of contemporary Georgian literature. His novel, *Artistuli gadatrialeba* (1994; Artistic Coup d'état), is a scathing satire of the recent political turmoil in Georgia. In his play "*Mephe Ashot Didi Kuropalati*" (1996; King Ashot the Great, the Kuropalat) the author depicts the tragic events of the 9th c. when the country was ripped apart by internal strifes among feudal princes. His novel, *Chemi Savane* (1997; My Spiritual Retreat), sums up thematically and chronologically his previous works published in the 1950s and 1960s.

—DODONA KIZIRIA

CHOCANO, José Santos

Peruvian poet, b. 14 May 1875, Lima; d. 13 Dec. 1934, Santiago, Chile

C.'s tumultuous life was punctuated by political involvement in Peru, Guatemala, and Mexico. He was alternately a friend and poetic apologist for both ruthless dictators and revolutionary *caudillos*. Having killed another poet, he was subsequently granted amnesty but left his native Peru in disgrace in 1928 for a self-imposed exile in Chile, even though his homeland had crowned him as its poet laureate. He was assassinated there a few years later.

Undoubtedly, C. must be considered to be one of the most controversial figures in the history of Spanish American literature. Although he is usually identified with the MODERNIST movement, some critics disagree with this classification. In both tone and thematic content, most of C.'s poetry tends to be romantic and written in an epic and grandiloquent style, except for the lyrical quality of his last poetry, which was largely published posthumously. In *Alma América—Poemas indo-españoles* (1906; America soul—Indo-Spanish poems), with a preface written by UNAMUNO, C. came closest to realizing his ambition of being "the poet of America," similar in some ways to Walt Whitman in the U.S. This book helped turn Spanish American modernism away from exoticism and French influences and toward its Hispanic heritage and more American themes and settings. C.'s best-known poetry was marked by impressionistic visual imagery highlighted by the employment of bright colors, brilliant metaphors, and frequent allusions to American flora and fauna. He excelled at capturing the panoramic natural beauty of the American extending from Mexico to Tierra del Fuego. C. idealized the past grandeur of the Incan Empire and exalted the exploits of the Spanish conquerors from an aristocratic perspective. He also assigned a prophetic function to some of his poems.

With the passage of time, C. will probably be best remembered for the poignant lyrical poetry found in *Oro de indias* (1940, 1941; gold of Indies), where he depicts the tragic human condition and stoicism of the Peruvian Indian in the section called "Sangre Incaica" (Incan blood) and intimately reminisces about his family in "Nocturnos" (nocturnes). C.'s poetry will continue to interest literary historians as being representative of the epic and autochthonous tendencies within Spanish American modernism.

FURTHER WORKS: *Iras santas* (1898); *En la aldea* (1895); *Azahares* (1896); *Selva virgen* (1898); *El derrumbe* (1899); *El canto del siglo* (1901); *El fin de Satán* (1901); *Poesías completas* (1902); *Los cantos del pacífico* (1904); *Fiat Lux* (1908); *El Dorado* (1908); *Poemas escogidos* (1912); *Puerto Rico lírico* (1914); *Poesías selectas* (1920); *Idearium tropical* (1922); *La coronación de José Santos Chocano* (1924); *Ayacucho y los Andes* (1924); *El libro de mi proceso* (1927, 1931); *Primicias de oro* (1934); *Poemas del amor doliente* (1937); *Memorias* (1940). FURTHER WORKS IN ENGLISH: *Spirit of the Andes* (1935)

BIBLIOGRAPHY: Umphrey, G., "J. S. C., 'el Poeta de América,'" *Hispania*, 3 (1920): 304–15; Meza Fuentes, R., "La poesía de J. S. C.," *Nosotros*, 78 (1934): 286–311; Alegría, F., *Walt Whitman en Hispanoamerica* (1954): 276–81; Sánchez, L. A., *Aladino; o, Vida y obra de J. S. C.* (1960); Rodríguez-Peralta, P. W., *J. S. C.* (1970)

—JAMES J. ALSTRUM

CHORELL, Walentin

Finnish novelist and dramatist (writing in Swedish), b. 8 April 1912, Turku; d. 18 Nov. 1983, Helsinki

Because of C.'s productivity and his ability to write books that (in translation) interested the Finnish public as well as the Swedish-speaking minority, he found himself in the unusual situation of being a Swedo-Finnish writer able, more or less, to live by his pen. But C. also was active as an educator, teaching psychology at a Swedish language school in Helsinki, where he lived most of his adult life.

Although a rundown section of C.'s native Turku, a port and academic center in south-western Finland, has provided a major back-ground for his novels, Helsinki is the setting of much of his best narrative work. Yet his concern is not with the local milieus or with writing social criticism, but with the psychological states of his characters.

Throughout C.'s career, his novelistic world has either been dominated by unrelieved grimness or characterized by misery alleviated by optimism. His early novels of the 1940s consist almost entirely of dark psychological studies. The main characters of *Blindtrappan* (1949; blind stairs), for example, are a blind man, an ex-prostitute, and the sometime mistress—and student in sadism—of a Nazi officer.

In the novels of the 1950s the despair and the pettiness of C.'s world abated somewhat. But in the novels of the 1960s, from *Stölden* (1960; the theft) to *Agneta och lumpsamlaren* (1968; Agneta and the ragman), C. returned to the tormented world of marginal people, laying bare the conflicts that plague them. An alienated young boy, an alcoholic seaman, a disturbed veteran who accidentally kills his girlfriend, an orphan made bitter by a deformity: these are the objects of C.'s thoroughly realistic portrayals of humanity.

In his most recent novels, C. has again veered away from a negative view of life. In *Äggskalet* (1972; the eggshell), the love of a girl and a boy from different levels of Helsinki society seems to conquer all. Yet here, too, there are the seeds of future unhappiness—ingrained in her vitality and his passivity, and in the very

tightness of the little realm they have made for themselves. The sequels—*Knappen* (1974; the button) and *Livstrycket* (1976; the body garment, also, literally, the piece of life)—depict the relationship's painful collapse, after the birth of a child: the girl emerges from the affair with a new and mature sense of purpose. Similarly, the detective of *Pizzamordet* (1977; the pizza murder), accidentally blinded, manages to turn his handicap into a source of almost mystical power.

C. has also been a prolific writer for radio, the stage, and television. His radio plays, masterly mood creations, and his television plays are serious literary works containing probing psychological portraits. Several of them were collected in *Åtta radiopjäser: Haman* (1952; eight radio plays: Haman) and in the later *Femspel* (1967; five plays). The destinies lived out in these plays resemble those experienced by the characters in the blackest novels.

C. is one of the few Swedish-language dramatists of recent times of gain some recognition outside his own country. In his stage plays the twisted human beings of his other works reappear. They are either without hope or possess hopes whose fragility is all too apparent. The atmosphere of confinement that so often envelopes his plays is developed to horrifying advantage in *Kattorna* (1961; *The Cats*, 1978). The most successful of C.'s dramas, *Kattorna* was made into a movie.

C.'s work has a peculiarly Swedo-Finnish quality for the careful observer, particularly in its concern with narrow, throttling milieus. Yet, he makes little use of local coloring as such and lacks the desire (and perhaps the ability) of a Runar Schildt (1888–1925) or an Elmer DIKTONIUS to reproduce the nuances of Swedo-Finnish speech. Thus, the relative neutrality of his work has enhanced its translatability both into Finnish and into major languages. Although as a novelist, he has not fulfilled the promise of the careful craftmanship of his early works, notably *Blindtrappan*, his perceptive character portrayals are undeniably memorable.

FURTHER WORKS: *Vinet och lägeln* (1941); *Spegling* (1943); *Lektion för döden* (1947); *Jörgen Hemmelinks stora augusti* (1947); *Calibans dag* (1948); *Ensam sökan* (1948); *Fabian öppnar portarna* (1949); *Intim journal* (1951); *Madame* (1951); *Sträv gryning* (1952); *Vandringsman* (1954); *Miriam* (1954); *Systrarna* (1955; *The Sisters*, 1971); *Främlingen* (1956); *Tre skådespel* (1956); *Gräset* (1958); *Kvinnan* (1958); *De Barmhärtiga* (1962); *Saltkaret* (1964); *Grodan* (1966); *Sista leken* (1970)

BIBLIOGRAPHY: Schoolfield, G. C., "The Postwar Novel of Swedish Finland," *SS*, 34 (1962): 85–110; Salminen, J., "W. C.: An Appreciation," *ASR*, 56 (1968): 136–39; Warburton, T., "Literary Portrait: W. C.," *BF*, 3, 3, (1969): 11–12; Schoolfield, G. C., Introduction to *The Sisters*, in *Five Modern Scandinavian Plays* (1971): 103–17

—GEORGE C. SCHOOLFIELD

CHOU Li-po

Chinese novelist and short-story writer, b. 9 Aug. 1908, I-yang County, Hunan Province; d. 25 Sept. 1979

The son of a village schoolteacher, C. was early drawn to leftist activism in Shanghai, for which he was imprisoned. In 1934, following his release, he joined the League of Leftist Writers as an ardent supporter of the Communist vice-minister of propaganda, Chou Yang, a native of his home county. C. published short stories and translations of Russian literature. In 1937 he followed Chou Yang to the Communist base at Yenan, taught at the Lu Hsün Academy of Arts, and participated extensively in the land-reform campaigns of the 1940s. After 1949 he was an editor of *Jenmin wen-hsüeh* magazine and traveled among workers and peasants to do research for his novels. In 1966, in the general purge of intellectuals (which included Chou Yang), C. was disgraced. In 1977 he was rehabilitated and his works were republished.

C.'s reputation rests almost entirely on two long novels of socialist reconstruction: *Paofeng tsou-yü* (1949; *The Hurricane*, 1955) and *Shan-hsiang chü pien* (1958; *Great Changes in a Mountain Village*, 1961). Both novels are written in the Soviet-inspired style of SOCIALIST REALISM, using a realistic style to portray and idealize the implementation of Communist programs. *Pao-feng tsou-yü* was part of a crop of novels celebrating land reform and was awarded a third-place Stalin Prize for Literature in 1951. With scrupulous attention to the language and details of peasant life that he had observed closely, C.'s novel is perhaps the most dramatic portrayal of the tenacious work of party cadres in the late 1940s to involve the peasantry of a Hunan town in the trial and punishment of their landlords, to motivate them through land reform and property redistribution, and to instill in them socialist values and support for the Communist Party in its struggle with the Nationalists.

C.'s principal work, *Shan-hsiang chü pien*, is representative of the novels about the agricultural cooperative movement. The indebtedness of the novels to Soviet models is strong enough for aspects of it to be compared with Mikhail SHOLOKHOV's *The Quiet Don*. While C. gives individuality to his party cadre characters, they are unimpressive figures, and the focus of the novel is on peasant reluctance to give up their newly won private ownership of land to proposed cooperatives. While the peasants' resistance verges on defiance, the novel abruptly and anticlimactically concludes with an inadequate statement on the founding of the cooperatives.

When they were published, C.'s novels were recommended to inexperienced party cadres as illustrations of issues they had to face. In the West they attracted attention for C.'s sympathetic and sometimes poignant description of peasants' unhappiness with Communist programs and his revelation of the harsh treatment the party meted out to its enemies. While C.'s actual loyalty to the party at the time was never questioned, the implication in his novels that peasants commonly lacked enthusiasm for Mao's policies of collectivization had run afoul of party politics by 1966, and he was condemned for distorting the view of the people.

FURTHER WORKS: *Chin-ch'a-chi pien-ch'ü yin-hsiang chi* (1938); *Su-lien cha-chi* (1953); *Ts'an chün* (1953); *T'ieh-shui pen-liu* (1955); *T'ieh-men li* (1957); *Chou Li-po hsüan-chi* (1959); *Wen-hsüeh ch'ien-lun* (1959); *Shanhsiang chü pien hsü-p'ien Shou-huo* (1960); *Ho-ch'ang shang* (1960); *San-wen t'e-hsieh hsüan* (1963)

BIBLIOGRAPHY: Birch, C., ed., *Chinese Communist Literature* (1963): 116–19, 199–203; Hsia, C. T., *A History of Modern Chinese Fiction*, 2nd ed. (1971): 518–20; Huang, J., *Heroes and Villains in Communist China* (1973): 183–85, 195–210, 242–43, 284

—EDWARD M. GUNN

CHRAÏBI, Driss

French-Moroccan novelist (writing in French), b. 15 July 1926, El Jadida (fomerly Mazagan, French Morocco)

C. is the leading Moroccan writer of the so-called "Generation of '52." He is the author of twelve novels, which were published in Paris. The recipient of many literary prizes, C.'s works have been translated into English, Arabic, Italian, German, and Russian. C. was one of a token few native Moroccans to pursue secondary studies in a French *lycée*. At the age of nineteen, he left for Paris to study chemical engineering and neuropsychiatry. After becoming disillusioned with science, he abandoned his formal studies and traveled throughout Europe and to Israel. He has been a writer and producer for the National Radio and Television Broadcasting System in France, where he has resided for the past forty years.

C.'s first novel, *Le passé simple* (1954; *The Simple Past*, 1990) was published at the height of the French-Moroccan conflict. Still the object of critical controversy, this invective text was aimed as much at Moroccan patriarchal society as at French colonial rule. Attacked by his compatriots for having betrayed his country at a time when it was seeking independence from France, C. also became the pawn of French journalists who used *Le passé simple* to legitimate the need for French rule in Morocco. C. was so disturbed by the controversy surrounding his novel that he publicly disowned it in 1957, only to reget his action later. *Le passé simple* was banned in Morocco until 1977.

Unlike other Maghrebian writers of his generation, C. did not hesitate to denounce the autochthonous forces that precipitated and intensified colonialism. He was the first Maghrebian writer to portray the social injustice, corruption, hypocrisy, and opposition to change in his society. He was also the first Moroccan to write about the oppression of women and children in an Islamic, patriarchal society. *Le passé simple* remains the precursor text for the novels of decolonization that burst onto the literary scene in the 1960s and 1970s.

Hailed by critics as a classic tale of revolt against the father, *Le passé simple* is perhaps more a novel about love for a cloistered mother who also symbolizes the sequestered homeland. Although a number of Maghrebian francophone writers employ the mother figure as a symbol of loss and victimization, C. considers her as the basis for sociopolitical change in the Maghreb. She becomes a symbol of Third World liberation in *La civilisation, ma mère!* . . . (1972; *Mother Comes of Age*, 1984). For C., the future of the Maghreb depends on the social evolution of its women, the last colonized of the earth.

C. has never denied that he became a writer thanks to the aberrant historical context of colonialism. As a youth growing up in French Morocco, he was caught in the clash between two irreconcilable societies and cultures. His difficult youth might have conditioned him for a life of solitude and exile, but it has also made him an advocate for understanding among peoples in a world torn apart by national, ethnic, sexual, and religious differences.

C. has written on both the Arab world and the West. *Les boucs* (1955; *The Butts*, 1983) was the first novel to depict the abject conditions of North African immigrant workers in France. In *L'âne* (1956; the ass) C. took a hard look at Third World independence. In *Un ami viendra vous voir* (1967; a friend will come to see you) he depicted the alienation of women in postindustrial consumer society. In C.'s work, displaced peoples from the four corners of the globe come together in the common quest for freedom and happiness, peace with oneself and others.

In 1967 C. confessed that not only had it taken him ten years to exorcise his past and write *Le passé simple*, but it had also taken him eleven more years as well as five more novels to bridge the gap that separated him from his past. In writing about both the Arab world and the West, C. felt that Maghrebian francophone literature could play a fundamental role in bridging two very different worlds. Although he never denied the tremendous impact of French culture on his writing, he never renounced his Moroccan origins.

Succession ouverte (1962; *Heirs to the Past*, 1969) depicts the return to the native land. C.'s most recent novels, *Une enquête au pays* (1981; *Flutes of Death*, 1985), *La mère du printemps (l'Oum-er-Bia)* (1982; *Mother Spring*, 1989), and *Naissance à l'aube* (1986; *Birth at Dawn*, 1990) are dedicated to his people, the Moroccan Berbers. The last two novels explore the Arab-Islamic conquest of Morocco and Andalusia. In writing about the historic past of his people, C. adopts a sensuous and mystical style. An ancient people's survival over time takes the form of a hymn to life.

In *Une place au soleil* (1993; A place in the sun) C. casts a humorous but critical gaze on contemporary Morocco. In *L'homme du livre* (1995; *Muhammed*, 1998), a novel about the prophet Mohammed, C. distinguishes between Islam and Islamic fundamentalism.

C. has always insisted that we view him as nothing more than a writer of French expression. He believes that literature transcends national boundaries. Neither French nor Moroccan, C.'s cross-cultural writing shows how national, ethnic, and cultural differences can come together at the crossroads of tolerance for diversity.

FURTHER WORKS: *De tous les horizons* (1958); *La foule* (1961); *Mort au Canada* (1975); *L'inspecteur Ali* (1991; *Inspector Ali*, 1994); *Les aventures de l'âne Khal* (1992); *L'inspecteur Ali à Trinity College* (1996); *L'inspecteur Ali et la C.I.A.* (1998)

BIBLIOGRAPHY: Yetiv, I., *Le thème de l'aliénation dans le roman maghrébin d'expression française* (1972): 88–113; Déjeux, J., *Littérature maghrébine de langue française*, rev. ed. (1980): 276–300; Monego, J. P., *Maghrebian Literature in French* (1984): 108–25; Kadra-Hadjadji, H., *Contestation et révolte dans l'œuvre de D. C.* (1986); special C. issue, *CelfanR*, 5, 2 (Feb. 1986); Marx-Scouras, D., "A Literature of Departure: The Cross-Cultural Writing of D. C.," *RAL*, 23, 2 (1992): 131–44; Benchama, L., *L'oeuvre de D. C.: réception critique des littératures maghrébines au Maroc* (1994)

—DANIELLE MARX-SCOURAS

CHRISTENSEN, Inger

Danish poet and novelist, b. 16 Jan. 1935, Vejle

C. received her teacher's certificate in 1958 from Århus Teachers' College. Her first poems were published in the journal *Hvedekorn* between 1955 and 1959, a period in which she acquainted herself thoroughly with classic and modern poetry under expert guidance of the poet and critic Poul Borum (b. 1934), who was her husband at that time. A further source of inspiration was Noam Chomsky's (b. 1928) linguistic philosophy, which corresponded to her own thoughts on the power and purpose of language. C. has received numerous prizes and has been a member of the Danish Academy since 1978.

C.'s poetry and prose treat from various view-points the same principal theme: fearing the unknown, the individual escapes into established roles, which can be self-chosen but also imposed by society. These roles are seen as restrictive in our relationship to ourselves as well as to the external world and therefore not giving the desired security but, on the contrary, an increased sense of alienation. The language of poetry becomes the tool of imagination and liberation, which is able to penetrate and revive dead reality, creating new experiences reflected in language itself.

In a romantic fashion the *writing* self is placed in the center of all epistemological activity. In her first two poetry collections, *Lys* (1962; light) and *Græs* (1963; grass), C. focuses on the disquieting world of writing: on the gaining of self-knowledge but also on the fear of losing the self during the creative act. The brief, condensed prose poems are based on these themes: nearness versus distance and the tension between ordinary everyday life and the creative moments of inspiration seen in the context of nature, love, and death.

The two volumes anticipate C.'s principal work, and the greatest poetic achievement of Danish literature of the 1960s, the epic *Det* (1969; it). Structured strictly symmetrically, like a musical composition or a chemical experiment, the work stages its own creation, reaching back to the beginning of time, a modern cosmogony, and simultaneously it absorbs the political and social questions of the period. Shaped in a flowing verbal creativity with rhymed stanzas, prose, and song lyrics, *Det* concludes with a stirring exploration of the human being's existential conditions. Only the creative self is able to overcome the dominant split between language and experience and thus make possible a movement from initial chaos to an increasingly more refined differentiation within human life, a movement that is mirrored in the text itself. On the external, social level C. shows an obvious sympathy with the outsider, the rebel; on the textual level she defends openness and the determination to break up and venture into the unknown. Both levels meet in an overpowering tribute to the individual's integration into the fellowship of all human beings as well as into the cycle of nature, which is perhaps only Utopia: "I have attempted to tell about a world that does not exist in order to make it exist."

Linguistic experimentation as well as the analysis of creation and creativity was anticipated in C.'s two novels *Evighedsmaskinen* (1964; the eternity machine) and *Azorno* (1967; Azorno), but here it is seen in relation to the experience of love. The first is a Christ allegory about the incarnation of love in human beings and in society; the second is an epistolary and diary novel, in which various women try to explain their relationship with the man who has given the novel its title—a poet and Kierkegaardian seducer. Filled with jealousy, they all manipulate what they write down, whereby reality is turned into fiction. In her novel *Det malede værelse* (1976; the painted room), about the Italian Renaissance painter Mantegna, related to the fantastical story in the tradition of Isak DINESEN, C. attempts to maintain a synthesis of art and reality, image and life. Through three different narrators C. seeks to reach an understanding of the world as a creative process, of which art is a highly integrated part, but without ever reaching a final answer to the question of reality as being a form of art and art being a form of reality.

Det malede værelse concludes by letting one of the narrators, the ten-year-old son of the painter, walk into his father's painting as a symbol of the child's ability to transgress the borders by which the adult is confined. This unspoiled ability to experience life both in its mythic and basic form is illustrated in the poetry volume *Brev i april* (1979; letter in April). Externally C. describes a journey to southern Europe with a child, whose precise observations of the surrounding world open up new and unexpected perspectives for the first-person narrator, the writing self, which in its turn provokes creative wonder and change. A related awareness of death is found in the collection *Alfabet* (1981; alphabet), now directly connected with linguistic awareness. Formally C.'s use of the alphabet and sequences of numbers as the elements in the creative process links the volume to *Det*. New, however, is an ecological aspect, as C. attempts to reveal the demolishing forces of modern civilization, which is also evident in a disintegration of language. Her poems point to destruction and doom in a setting in which not even love is seen as a redeeming possibility.

C.'s entire oeuvre, which also includes a series of radio plays, published in *En vinteraften i Ufa* (1987; a winter's evening in Ufa), must be read as one single comprehensive linguistic and philosophical experiment to capture an elusive reality. C. is unquestionably the most prolific and distinguished Danish representative of the so-called "systemic" poetry, the theory that proposes that poetry is a linguistic construction guiding the author as a means of cognition by searching for reality in the words—between and outside the words—but always captured with the help of words. For a writer of less stature than C. such attempts could have approached a mathematical problem. However, C. is eminently successful in reaching far beyond such mechanical constructions through her visionary insights into the human mind and spirit, her enthralling mythic associations as well as an overwhelmingly fertile metaphoric imagination.

FURTHER WORKS: *Intriganterne* (1972); *Del af labyrinten* (1982); *Den store ukendte rejse* (1982)

BIBLIOGRAPHY: Nied, S., "Letting Things Be: I. C.'s 'Alphabet,'" *ScanR*, 70, 4 (Dec. 1982): 24–26; Wamberg, B., ed., *Out of Denmark* (1985): 135–48

—SVEN HAKON ROSSEL

CHRISTOV, Solveig

(pseud. of Solveig Fredriksen Grieg) Norwegian novelist, short-story writer, and dramatist, b. 29 Oct. 1918, Drammen

At an early age C. moved to Oslo. Her commercial studies and office work, as well as her knowledge of the publishing industry through her second husband, head of Gyldendal publishers, made her aware of the practical and intellectual problems facing Norwegian society.

C.'s works show a fine sense of stylistic concentration and a sharp eye for psychological complications; she has experimented in several directions and succinctly presents problems that often involve the reader in the search for a solution.

In two allegorical-symbolic novels, *Torso* (1952; torso) and *Demningen* (1957; the dam), C. offers visions of the world-political situation in which people are paralyzed by fear of war and their own helplessness, and exploited by speculators. The characters are successfully drawn, both as individuals and as representative types, as they try to find a course between principle and compromise, between pure ideals and what is politically possible.

Most of C.'s novels, however, deal with erotic themes and with the problems of guilt and responsibility. In the tradition of Norwegian women writers, C. is concerned with woman's unfree position in the family and in society. In the short, well-written erotic novel *Syv dager og syv netter* (1955; seven days and seven nights) a housewife with three children is caught between dreams of love and ecstasy on the one hand, and marriage and triviality on the other. She grows in self-knowledge and independence in a short affair that teaches her the importance of tenderness and experience, and also the price of trying to live in a dream. *Korsvei i jungelen* (1959; crossroads in the jungle) focuses on inauthentic feelings and relationships built on dishonesty and convention, while *Elskerens hjemkomst* (1961; the lover's return) provides a psychological study in which a man must confront his previous love affairs on his return home after almost twenty years abroad. *Skyldneren* (1965; the debtor) portrays the twisting and destroying of love by actual or imagined guilt.

In her short stories C. has shown humor and understanding in examining a variety of human predicaments. Her plays, in the tradition of Ibsen's *A Doll's House*, deal with marriage and sex roles. C.'s innovative style and accurate observations have earned her a prominent position in modern Norwegian literature.

FURTHER WORKS: *Det blomstrer langs blindveien* (1949); *På veiene til og fra* (1951); *Under vintermånen* (1954); *Det hemmelig regnskap* (1956); *På rødt pass* (1958); *Jegeren og viltet* (1962); *Tre paradis* (1966); *Befrielsen* (1966); *Tilfellet Martin* (1970)

—WALTER D. MORRIS

CHUBAK, Sadeq

Iranian short-story writer and novelist, b. 1916, Bushihr

C. was born on the Persian Gulf, the son of a cloth merchant. His early schooling was in Bushihr, later in Shiraz when the family moved to that city. After graduating from the Alborz American College in Tehran in 1937, he became a teacher in Khorramshahr and married. During World War II he returned to Tehran as an English translator to the Iranian General Staff. Subsequently, he also translated for the British Embassy. From 1949 to 1974 C. was the librarian for the National Iranian Oil Company.

With the publication of his first volumes of short stories, *Kheymeh shab-bazi* (1945; the puppet show) and *Antari ke lutiyesh murdeh bud* (1950; the baboon whose buffoon was dead), C. established a new tradition in short-story writing in Iran. His brief sentences paint pictures with the skill and perfection of detail of the Persian miniaturist. Every word is designed to bring about a unified effect. He presents a story from an angle that both limits and illuminates the action. His stories portray characters who act in a totally realized physical, social, and psychological setting; and although he stresses only those aspects of his characters that the situation requires, they still seem fully rounded. C. strips characters of their moral, religious, and social pretensions, exposing their instinctual lives by introducing speech patterns used by all classes throughout Iran.

C. brings his characters to life by what in modern terms might be called an accompanying sound track. Through this method he reproduces realistic pictures of Iranian locales and people. In his next volumes of short stories, *Ruz-e avval-e qabr* (1966; the first day in the grave) and *Cherakh-e akher* (1966; the last lantern) he goes even further in using the phonology and grammar of the common people and confronts the reader with the universality of the human struggle.

In addition to his short stories, which briefly present slices of life, C. has written two novels. In *Tangsir* (1963; Tangsir) a man from Tengestan is cheated by four prominent men from Bushihr. Unable to receive redress, he takes justice into his own hands and kills all four. He then tries to escape by ship. *Sang-e sabur* (1968; *The Patient Stone*, 1989) deals with the lives of several people in Shiraz during the late 1920s. This is a very disturbing but moving novel about prostitutes, religious fanatics, pimps, and an impoverished teacher.

In all his works, C. searches for new values. When traditional ones break down and crumble, C.'s trust and hope in the ultimate victory of good over evil helps the reader to face the vulgarity and ugliness in life.

BIBLIOGRAPHY: Kamshad, H., *Modern Persian Prose Literature* (1966): 127–30; Kubičkova, V., in Rypka, J., et al., *History of Iranian Literature* (1968): 415–16; Chelkowski, P., "The Literary Genres in Modern Iran," in Lenczowksi, G., ed., *Iran under the Pahlavis* (1978): 333–64

—PETER J. CHELKOWSKI

and *Iney na poroge* (1971; Russian version of title: rime on the threshold), which treat the decade preceding and following the revolution. His trilogy *Tite tylgyrkyn y'lyl* (Russian title: *Vremya tayania snegov*, 1958–67; when the snows melt) is autobiographical and plots the progression of his own life against Chukchi modernization. V. Yatyrgin's (b. 1919) *Sudba muzhchinu ne baluet* (1967; Russian version of title: fate does not pamper a man) is also autobiographical and deals with the education of a young person.

Chukchi poetry is best exemplified in the works of Viktor Keulkut (1929–1963) and Antonina Kymytval (b. 1938). The lives of trappers and reindeer breeders, as well as the familiar Chukchi landscape are common themes in the verse of Keulkut. Often called the "first" Chukchi poet, his literary output was small because of his early death but included three book-length collections. The musical and expressive poetry of Kymytval has been published in several collections. Vladimir Tymnetuvge (1935–1965), Mikhail Valgirin (b. 1939), and V. Tyneskin (b. 1945) have also contributed to Chukchi poetry.

BIBLIOGRAPHY: Kolarz, W., *The Peoples of the Soviet Far East*, (1954): 89–91; Holubnychy, L., "Cultural Changes among the Siberian Chukchi and Yakuts under the Soviet Regime," *East Turkic Review*, 2, 3 (1960): 82–101; SSSR, Akademiia nauk, *The Peoples of Siberia* (1964): 799–835; *Dictionary of Oriental Literatures* (1974), Vol. III: 162–63

—KENNETH NYIRADY

CHUKCHI LITERATURE

Before the 1930s there were no publications in Chukchi, one of the languages spoken in extreme eastern Siberia, except for a few scholarly transcriptions of folktales. Few Chukchi could read Russian, although some had attended school in Alaska and knew English.

After 1917 the Soviet government set about to eradicate illiteracy among the non-Russian peoples of the U.S.S.R. through the use and development of the languages of the various nationalities. A standardized Chukchi alphabet—based first on the Roman script and then on the Cyrillic—was devised in 1931 and a year later the first Chukchi book, the Russian Vladimir Bogoraz's (1865–1936) *Gelg' kalekal* (Russian title: *Krasnaya gramota*, 1932; red grammar) appeared. The first Chukchi writer is considered to be Tynetegyn (Feodor Tinetev, 1920–1940), whose *Skazki Chauchu* (1940; Russian title: tales of Chauchu) was written in both Chukchi and Russian.

Most notable among the group of writers who appeared in the 1950s and 1960s was Yury Rytkheu (b. 1930), whose works have even been published in non-Soviet languages. Reflecting the profound changes that the Chukchi have experienced in their way of life since the revolution, Rytkheu's novels combine Soviet elements—industrialization, education, the primacy of the party, and the need for selfless labor—with traditional aspects of Chukchi existence, such as the forbidding landscape, the harsh climate, and fishing and reindeer breeding as a livelihood. In *Proshchanie s bogami* (1961; Russian version of title: parting with the gods), Rytkheu deals with the conflict of old customs with a new life. Contrasts between old and new are also sharp in his *Son v nachale tumana* (1969; Russian version of title: a dream as the mist sets in),

CHURCHILL, Caryl

English playwright, b. 3 Sept. 1938, London

The only child of middle-class parents, C. was reared in London and Montreal. She attended Oxford University, where she began writing and produced her first plays. After college, however, she married and had three children, a process that changed the early years of her career considerably.

C. spent ten years writing more than a dozen radio plays while raising her children. In 1972 the Royal Court presented C.'s first professionally produced stage play, *Owners* (1973). Concerned with ownership and its corrupting influence, the black comedy presents no clear heroes or villains, and defies the audience's desire for an easy solution. Similar to her next play, *Objections to Sex and Violence* (perf. 1975), and the later *Traps* (perf. 1977, pub. 1978), it also experimented with theatrical form, using short scenes, quick changes of venue, chronological displacement, and occasional absurdity.

In 1976 C. began working with a new process. *Light Shining in Buckinghamshire* (perf. 1976, pub. 1978) and *Vinegar Tom* (perf. 1976, pub. 1978) are historical plays set in the 17th c.: the former explores the Civil War and the latter the persecution of women declared witches. Created with the collective Joint Stock, a company devoted to making political theater through collaboration and improvisation, they were the first of many plays C. would write in this way, with Joint Stock and a feminist collective, Monstrous Regiment.

Cloud Nine (1979), an exploration of gender roles and sexual mores created with Joint Stock, would become her most widely known work. Like her other collective work, the play intersperses short scenes with commentary in the form of musical numbers, sung by the actors outside their roles. Actors played multiple roles, often cast across race and gender lines, suggesting the performative nature of such categories. The first act is set in Victorian England, the second in the present, but the viewer is asked to believe that the characters have only aged twenty-five years, allowing C. to make historical connections.

Similar license is taken with history in the first act of *Top Girls* (1982), where an onstage dinner party includes famous women from throughout history as guests. The play goes on to explore the relationship between two sisters who have made very different choices in life, exploring ways of being of woman. The play's stunning portrait of the damage done by opposing motherhood and cultural achievement won it an Obie Award, Off-Broadway's top honor.

Experimenting with a completely new style, C. wrote *Serious Money* (1987), a play about the greed and corruption of the world of finance, entirely in rhymed verse. In spite of its stark indictment of corporate greed, the play was so strong that some critics felt it glorified the unethical, vicious characters it represented. Working with Joint Stock again, C. traveled to Romania to view firsthand the effects of the revolution. In the resulting play, *Mad Forest* (1990), the chaos and moral confusion resulting from the revolution counterbalance the repression of the regime it replaces, and the rhetoric of freedom quickly becomes a simple lust for money. The play's title refers to the folk history of the region: a similar mythical background is explored in *The Skriker* (1994), a frightening contemporized version of an old English folk tale.

C.'s work—like Bertolt BRECHT's—overturns theatrical convention as a way of questioning the status quo. At the same time, the dilemmas her characters face are heartfelt, and the characters themselves vivid and real. Recognized from her earliest plays as an important feminist voice, C. has become unquestionably one of the Britain's most important playwrights, without ever softening her message or moderating the strength and passion of her ideas.

FURTHER WORKS: *Fen* (1983); *Softcops* (1984); *C.: Plays One* (1985); *A Mouthful of Birds* (1987); *Ice Cream* (1989); *Shorts* (1990); *Plays 2* (1990); *Lives of the Great Poisoners* (1993, with Orlando Gough and Ian Spiak)

BIBLIOGRAPHY: Solomon, A., "Witches, Ranters and the Middle Class: The Plays of C. C.," *Theater,* 12, 2 (1981): 49-55; Keyssar, H., *Feminist Theatre* (1984): 77-101; Quigley, A., "Stereotype and Prototype: Character in the Plays of C. C.," in Brater, E., ed. *Feminine Focus: The New Women Playwrights* (1989): 25-52; Gray, F., "Mirrors of Utopia: C. C. and Joint Stock," in Acheson, J., ed., *British and Irish Drama since 1960* (1993): 47-59; Kritzer, A. H., "Madness and Political Change in the Plays of C. C.," in Redmond, J., ed., *Madness in Drama* (1993): 203-26; Reinelt, J., "Beyond Brecht: Britain's New Feminist Drama," in Keyssar, H., ed., *Feminist Theater and Theory* (1996): 35-48

—GINGER STRAND

CHUVASH LITERATURE

The Chuvash are a Turkic people inhabiting the central Volga region of the former U.S.S.R., about 375 miles due east of Moscow.

Their language has been influenced by neighboring Finnic languages and also has close ties to Kazan-Tatar and Bashkir. Since the Chuvash were not Muslims, there is little indication that Chuvash was ever written with Arabic script, although neighboring Turkic languages were. Their early conversion to Russian Orthodoxy resulted in the Chuvash using the Cyrillic alphabet to put their language into writing. During the 19th c. there was isolated Cyrillic printing in Chuvash, mostly for religious purposes, and in 1872 the educator Ivan Y. Yakovlev (1848–1930) created an improved alphabet for Chuvash by adding some letters.

In the late 19th c. some literary works based on folkloric themes, such as Mikhail R. Fyodorov's ballad *Arśuri* (1879; the wood-goblin), appeared. The most famous literary figure of the pre-Soviet period was the young Chuvash poet Konstantin Ivanov (1890–1915), a brilliant representative of the national ideology of the Chuvash peasant. His masterpiece is the epic romance *Narspi* (1908; Narspi), a long poem of fourteen cantos about a beautiful maiden heroine. Important themes for Ivanov were the autocratic power of father and husband and the lack of rights for Chuvash women.

Ivanov's contemporary, Nikolay V. Shubosinni (1893–1943), first reveled in Chuvash antiquity, depicting the countryside and dwelling on social inequality in the Chuvash village. An early socialist newspaper, *Khypar*, appeared in 1906–7, and contained works by the poets Nikolay I. Polorussov-Shelebi (1881–1945) and Timofey S. Semyonov (also known as Tair Timki) (1889–1916).

Early Soviet Chuvash literature treated the struggle for freedom from the centuries-old tsarist yoke. The Union of Chuvash Authors and Journalists was organized in 1923; its magazine, *Suntal* (1924–40), printed significant prose works of many young writers. Important works of this period are Mikhail F. Akimov-Arui's (1895–1972) *Bezvremennaya smert* (1918; Russian version of title: premature death), the first national play, and Fyodor P. Pavlov's (1892–1931) drama *Yalta* (1922; in the village). The Communist poet Mišši (Mikhail) Sespel (1899–1922) wrote revolutionary-patriotic lyrics.

In the 1930s, using techniques of SOCIALIST REALISM, Chuvash writers focused on industrialization and collectivization. The growth of the social consciousness of Soviet peoples is expressed in the lyrical songs of Ivan Ivnik (1914–1942) and the tales and stories of Ilya Tuktash (b. 1907). Semyon V. Elger's (1894–1966) historical poem "Pod gnyotom" (1931; Russian version of title: under the yoke) and Petr N. Osipov's (b. 1900) drama *Aydar* (1937; Aydar) are outstanding works of this time.

During World War II patriotic lyrics and accounts of the exploits of Soviet people in war and peace ranked high. A significant work of the war years was Petr Khusangay's (1907–1970) poem "Doch rodiny" (194?, Russian version of title: daughter of the motherland). The early postwar period (1946–60) produced some novels about tsarist times and the first Soviet years. The literary journal *Yalav* was begun in 1946; it is one of the main vehicles for contemporary Chuvash writing, along with the annually published almanac *Tăvan Atăl*.

BIBLIOGRAPHY: Krueger, J. R., *Chuvash Manual* (1961)

—JOHN R. KRUEGERS

CINEMA AND LITERATURE
See Film and Literature

CIORAN, E(mil) M.

Romanian philosopher and essayist (writing in Romanian and French), b. 8 Apr. 1911, Răşinari; d. 20 June 1995, Paris

Born in Romania, C. lived in Paris after 1937 and is recognized as one of France's most original existentialist philosophers. The son of a Greek Orthodox priest, he studied philosophy at the University of Bucharest, where he wrote a thesis on Henri BERGSON. Along with Eugène Ionesco, the absurdist DRAMATIST, and Mircea ELIADE, the philosopher of religions, he participated in Romania's cultural renaissance during the 1930s, the politically troubled interwar period. Though younger than either Ionesco or Eliade, C. was no less interesting. His first published book, *Pe culmile disperării* (1934; *On the Heights of Despair*, 1992), was awarded the King Carol II Foundation for Art and Literature Prize (1934). It expresses the nihilistic-apocalyptic sensibilities of the young generation of Romanian intellectuals and foreshadows the main themes of his later philosophical essays. It is thus highly significant as the original source spring of this modern philosopher's thought. By the time he left Romania for Paris on a fellowship from the French Institute in Bucharest, C. was the author of four published books. He lived modestly in Paris, doing part-time free-lance work as translator and manuscript reader and writing his books. His first book written in French, *Précis de décomposition* (1949; *A Short History of Decay*, 1975), was accepted by Gallimard in 1947, but C. retrieved it and rewrote it entirely four times. Writing in French was, according to him, "the most difficult task of my life," something akin to putting on a "straitjacket."

C.'s work consists mainly of collections of essays: *Syllogismes de l'amertume* (1952; syllogisms of bitterness), *La tentation d'exister* (1956; *The Temptation to Exist*, 1968), *La chute dans le temps* (1964; *The Fall into Time*, 1970), *De l'inconvénent d'être né* (1973; *The Trouble with Being Born*, 1976). The themes of his work are the themes of postmodern Western civilization: despair and decay, absurdity and alienation, futility and the irrationality of existence, the need for total self-awareness, and consciousness as agony. C.'s style is a unique combination of linguistic elegance and profound thought. Aphorism is his trademark; in turns lyrical and ironical, poetical and paradoxical, he rejects the technique of dry philosophical argument in favor of suggestive, graceful, and vivid formulations that reveal the intellectual and spiritual agony of the philosopher's mind in playful yet gripping ways. The Romanian C. of the 1930s is wilder and more passionate yet not totally unrelated to the French—and much better known—C. of the later decades. The French C. is a Nietzsche distilled through Chamfort, an elegant and ironic stylist who has curbed the fiery lyricism of his youth with moral aphorisms, because he knows, as he puts it in *Le mauvais demiurge* (1969; *The New Gods*, 1974), that "a moralist's first duty is to depoetize his prose."

Writing and philosophizing are for C. organically related to suffering. A running theme throughout his oeuvre is that sickness and suffering have "lyrical virtues" that alone lead to "metaphysical revelations." "To suffer is to generate knowledge," he writes, and he views his life and his work as the metamorphosis of tears turned into thoughts. The impulse to write to free himself of his obsessions motivates his entire work. As he put it in an interview with the Spanish philosopher Fernando Savater (b. 1938), "writing is for me a form of therapy."

C.'s work is characterized by a dramatic tension between the suffering, problematic man—the organic and lyrical thinker—and

his archenemy, the philosopher or the sage, the abstract man, a distinction reminiscent of Nietzsche's Dionysian and Socratic types. A connoisseur of despair, that state of heightened lucidity that is the "negative equivalent of ecstasy," the lyrical thinker rejects the intellectual optimism of the abstract human and those philosophical systems that only manage to reduce the profound to the expressible. For C. "a cry of despair is more revealing than the most subtle thought."

Savater calls C's philosophical discourse "antipedagogical." It tackles major philosophical themes but deliberately resists taking shape as an informative and constructive discourse. It does not aspire to produce anything new on the subject, thus renouncing false pretensions to originality. His destructive discourse, going against the grain of traditional philosophical practice, unremittingly seeks to expose the contradictions inherent in any philosophical system, and cultivates with relish all contraries, conferring upon them equally little significance.

C. may be a specialized taste, too sharp and bitter for many palates and, paradoxically, too lyrical and melodramatic for some others. Yet Jean-Paul SARTRE has always had a large following in English, and C. is a better pure writer than Sartre or any of the postwar French existentialists. His stylistic incisiveness has led some French critics to put him in the same class as Paul VALÉRY, an ultimate accolade of linguistic purity. But the shocking, bracing verve of his existential despair—and good humor—admits his philosophical prose to the great tradition of Nietzsche and Kierkegaard.

FURTHER WORKS: *Cartea amăgirilor* (1936); *Schimbarea la faţă a României* (1937); *Lacrimi şi sfinţi* (1937); *Histoire et utopie* (1960; *History and Utopia*, 1987); *Valéry face à ses idoles* (1970); *Joseph de Maistre: Essai sur la pensée réactionnaire* (1977); *Écartèlement* (1979; *Drawn and Quartered*, 1983); *Exercices d'admiration* (1986); *Aveux et anathèmes* (1987); *Cioran: Entretiens* (1995); *Oeuvres* (1996). FURTHER WORKS IN ENGLISH: *Anathemas and Admirations* (1991); *Tears and Saints* (1995)

BIBLIOGRAPHY: Mauriac, C., *La littérature contemporaine* (1958): 159–68; Sontag, S., Introduction to *The Temptation to Exist* (1968): 7–29; Said, E., "Amateur of the Insoluble," *HudR*, 21, 4 (1968–1969): 769–73; Savater, F., *Nihilismo y acción* (1970); Auden, W. H., "The Anomalous Creature," *NYTBR*, 28 Jan. 1971: 16, 20; Caws, P., "The Temptation To Exist," *NYTBR*, 14 March 1971: 5; Savater, F., *Ensayo sobre C.* (1974); Calinescu, M., "Reading C.," *Salmagundi*, 112 (1996): 192–216; Bollon, P., *C. l'hérétique* (1997); Kluback, W., *The Temptations of C.* (1997)

—ILINCA ZARIFOPOL-JOHNSTON

CISNEROS, Sandra

American short-story writer and poet, b. 20 Dec. 1954, Chicago, Illinois

Born in Chicago's South Side neighborhood to a working-class Mexican father and Mexican-American mother, C. moved frequently with her six brothers from one impoverished neighborhood to another. Her sense of displacement from these moves caused her to become introspective, reading extensively and writing by age ten. Additionally, to make herself heard in her large family, she recalled, "You had to be fast and you had to be funny—you had to be a *storyteller*." She attended Loyola University for her undergraduate degree and received her M.F.A. from the University of Iowa Writers' Workshop in 1978. C. has subsequently taught writing at all levels and has been a writer-in-residence and visiting lecturer at numerous universities, including the University of Michigan—Ann Arbor, the University of California—Irvine, and the University of New Mexico. Winner of numerous awards for writing, including two National Endowment for the Arts Fellowships, C. lives and writes in San Antonio, Texas.

C. developed her literary voice at the Iowa Workshop where she discovered that her notions of place, family, and community differed radically from her classmates. Rather than feeling a sense of reverie for her childhood home, she wrote about her memories of "third floor flats, and fear of rats, and drunk husbands sending rocks through windows." Her experiences of cultural division and the shame of poverty were incorporated in her book *The House on Mango Street* (1983), winner of the Before Columbus American Book Award. The forty-four narrative vignettes in this book merge the boundaries of short story, novel, and poetry, for each is compact and lyrical on its own but also contributes to the characterization and plot development of a serialized novel. In the bildungsroman tradition the young narrator Esperanza seeks her self-identity amidst the poverty and racism of a multiethnic Chicago barrio, confronting simultaneously the sexism within her own Latino culture. Esperanza is an aspiring writer who longs for a house of her own, and her reflections possess the sense of humor, spontaneity, and vitality of a storyteller in the oral tradition. But unlike conventional novels of initiation, Esperanza's self-determination is tied to the warmth and camaraderie of her community, especially its women. Writing is a way to re-create herself as a Chicana and a passage out of Mango Street, yet Esperanza knows she will return to her community for those who cannot leave on their own.

In her next short-story collection, *Woman Hollering Creek* (1991), C. uses a rich bilingual idiom to portray the cultural complexities of Mexican-American women living near San Antonio. Through interior monologues, these women reveal their complicity in American-inspired myths of love and femininity, but also display their strength and ingenuity—girls playing with charred fire-sale dolls in "Barbie-Q," for example, and a woman starting life anew when a soap opera-inspired marriage turns abusive in the title story. The characters also remain loyal to their Catholic heritage, but not without challenging its role in their lives. By noting the Virgin of Guadalupe's mythological heritage as a powerful Aztec goddess, C. even suggests a way to redefine and empower one of the predominant cultural stereotypes for Chicana women.

While C. is best known for her stories, her poetry is receiving increasing attention. Her poems, like her fiction, explore the often-conflicting desires for self-determination and loyalty to cultural ties. Her third volume, *My Wicked Wicked Ways* (1987), concerns her struggle with vestiges of guilt over leaving home, developing her sexuality, and even writing her own story without considering a male perspective. The collection *Loose Woman: Poems* (1994) plays on the various meanings of loose as not belonging—to men or to cultural ideals—as well as on its sexual connotations, again subverting and redefining Chicana cultural stereotypes. C.'s fiction and poetry revise the traditional mores of Latino culture from a feminist perspective. Iconoclastically, but always sympathetically, C. is bringing the diverse experiences of the Chicana community to a wider audience.

FURTHER WORKS: *Bad Boys* (1980); *The Rodrigo Poems* (1985); *Hairs: Pelitos* (1994)

BIBLIOGRAPHY: Olivares, J., "S. C.'s *The House on Mango Street* and the Poetics of Space," in Herrera-Sobek, M., and H. Viramontes, eds., *Chicana Creativity and Criticism: Charting New Frontiers in American Literature* (1988): 160-70; Yarbro-Bejarano, Y., "Chicana Literature from a Chicana Feminist Perspective," in Herrera-Sobek, M., and H. Viramontes, eds., *Chicana Creativity and Criticism: Charting New Frontiers in American Literature* (1988): 139-46; McCracken, E., "S. C.'s *The House on Mango Street*: Community-Oriented Introspection and the Demystification of Patriarchal Violence," in Delgado, A., ed., *Breaking Boundaries* (1989): 62-71; Saldivar, R., *Chicano Narrative: The Dialectics of Difference* (1990): 171-99; Tompkins, C., "S. C.," in Giles, J. R., and W. H. Giles, eds., *DLB*, vol. 152, *American Novelists since World War II* (1995): 35-41

—LINDA LEE COX

CIXOUS, Hélène

French fiction writer, essayist, and dramatist, b. 5 June 1937, Oran, Algeria

C., a major contemporary French writer, is known for her fictional texts, her poetic essays, and her plays. Born in Oran, Algeria, she became aware of social injustices—colonialism, anti-Semitism, antifeminism—at an early age and, in her words, learned to fight. She moved to Paris during her adolescence. C. studied English literature and became a professor of English. In Paris C. moved quickly to the forefront of the intellectual scene. She published her 800-page thesis *L'exile de Joyce ou l'art du remplacement* (1968; *The Exile of James Joyce*, 1972). She will always remain indebted to James JOYCE for his work on language and on the relation between living and writing. Marked by the intellectual climate of 1968, C. defines herself against EXISTENTIALISM and Socialist REALISM with their insistence on artistic realism. She writes experimental texts that claim to be more to the Left and subversive because they question the self and break the circuit between reader and writer. *Dedans* (1969; *Inside*, 1986), focusing on C.'s childhood and her coming to writing as a result of her father's death, was awarded the Médicis Prize in 1969. *Le troisième corps* (1970; the third body), *Les commencements* (1970; the beginnings), and *Neutre* (1972; neuter) are written at the intersection of biography and her readings of Freud, Joyce, Kleist, Shakespeare, and others. C. considers writing as an ongoing self-analysis and a path toward a freeing of the self.

At the same time, she militates for a transformation of the academy. In 1970 C. was appointed by the government to found the experimental University, Paris VIII-Vincennes, where she started the Center for Research in Feminine Studies in 1974. In 1970, with Tzvetan Todorov (b. 1939) and Gérard Genette (b. 1930), she founded the review *Poétique*, which proposed to study texts for their poetic merit rather than through chronological ordering.

Since for C. writing *is* life, her ongoing meditations lead to an abundant production. One of her major preoccupations is the undoing of what she calls the phallocentric, masculine, unified self. This critique makes her a champion of the woman's cause. Two polemical texts, "Le rire de la Méduse," (1975; "The Laugh of the

Medusa," 1976) and "Sorties" in *La jeune née* (1975; *The Newly Born Woman*, 1986), written in collaboration with Catherine Clément (b. 1939), urge women to break their silence and come to writing. As in all her other texts, C. affirms life against death. These "manifestos" were followed by numerous texts—militant texts to, from, and with woman—that appeared in a woman's publishing house, "des femmes," C. wrote a new feminine genesis, *Souffles* (1975; breathings), and a transformation of the feminine imaginary, *LA* (1976; she/there). She invented a new feminine myth of writing that would displace the masculine orphic myth based on the death of woman in *Illa* (1980; Illa).

C.'s encounters with Heidegger's writings about poetry or coming to language and with the writings of the Brazilian novelist Clarice LISPECTOR are decisive. Under the influence of Heidegger and Lispector, C. began to write texts that emphasize the *approach* of people, things or nature. She wrote about the paradox of riches through poverty and of the infinitely small. However, "L'approche de Clarice Lispector" (1979; the approach of Clarice Lispector) marks a new departure.

A renewed interest in history directed C. toward theater and the stage, to which her encounter with theater director Ariane Mnouchkine gave her access. Issues in cultural pluralism prompted her to write an essay on Nelson Mandela, "La séparation du gâteau" (1982; the separation of the wedding cake), for the collective volume *Pour Nelson Mandela*, and her historical plays about Southeast Asia, *L'histoire terrible mais inachevée de Norodom Sihanouk, roi du Cambodge* (1985; the terrible and unfinished story of Norodom Sihanouk, king of Cambodia) and *L'Indiade ou l'Inde de leurs rêves* (1988; the Indiad or the India of their dreams). Though historically accurate, C.'s epic theater wants to capture the essence of the human. Highly philosophical, it meditates on human destiny. It distinguishes between power struggles in contemporary politics and the love for humans exemplified by Norodom Sihanouk and especially by Gandhi.

A critique of totalitarianism in eastern Europe led C. to a reading of Russian poets. She read and wrote about how these poets responded positively or negatively to their historical situation in an unpublished play, *Anna Akhmatova*, and a piece of lyrical, theatrical fiction with multiple voices, *Manne* (1988; manna) that links Mandela with Anna AKHMATOVAand Osip MANDELSTAM. Her studies of Marina TSVETAEVA, carried out in her seminars, have been published in *Readings* (1991).

C. characterizes the shifts in her writing as going from the scene of the unconscious to that of history. Yet she never relinquishes the unconscious. She continues to publish fictional texts that resemble more and more meditations on writing and on the state of the author. Who is an author? With whom do I write? Who in me writes when "I" is always more than one? are some of the questions that make up texts like *Le livre de Promethea* (1983; *The Book of Promethea*, 1991), written in the quick of life and burning with positive passion; *Jours de l'an* (1989; days of the year), a collection of meditations on writing and on beginnings; *L'ange secret* (1991; the secret angel/the secret stake), on the secret of writing and on the problem of saying "I" in the writing scene. These texts hint at what truly motivates C., that is, writing itself as a self-reflective activity. If some of these recent texts tend to be ethereal, her new epic theater has been quite successful.

By the very nature of her enterprise, that is, of writing as living, C. keeps on producing texts. The underlying constants have been an undoing of the unified or narcissistic subject that wants to control the world or the other. C. affirms life against death, insists on undoing repression, be it personal or collective. Her lesson may be that political moves should never lead to simple power reversals but to the affirmation that "I" is always more than one.

FURTHER WORKS: *Le prénom de Dieu* (1967); *Un vrai jardin* (1971); *Tombe* (1973); *Prénoms de personne* (1974); *Portrait du soleil* (1974); *Révolutions pour plus d'un Faust* (1975); *Un K. incompréhensible: Pierre Goldman* (1975); *Partie* (1976); *Portrait de Dora* (1976; *Portrait of Dora*, 1977); *Angst* (1977); *La venue à l'écriture* (1977, with Annie Leclerc and Madeleine Gagnon); *Préparatifs de noces au-delà de l'abîme* (1978); *Vivre l'orange/To Live the Orange* (1979; bilingual ed.); *Anankè* (1979); *Ou l'art de l'innocence* (1981); *Limonade tout était si infini* (1982); *La prise de l'école de Madhubaï* (1984); *Entre l'écriture* (1986); *La bataille d'Arcachon* (1987); *L'heure de Clarice Lispector* (1989). FURTHER WORKS IN ENGLISH: *Reading with Clarice Lispector* (1990); *"Coming To Writing" and Other Essays* (1991)

BIBLIOGRAPHY: Andermatt-Conley, V., *H. C.: Writing the Feminine* (1984; rev. ed., 1991); Moi, T., "H. C.: an imaginary utopia," *Sexual/Textual Politics* (1985): 102–26; Willis, S., "Mistranslation: *Vivre l'orange*," *SubStance*, 16 (1987): 76–83; Guégan-Fisher, C., *La cosmogonie d'H. C.* (1988); Rossum-Guyon, F. van, and M. Diaz-Diocaretz, *H. C., chemins d'une écriture* (1990); Wilcox, H., et al, *The Body and the Text: H. C., Reading and Teaching* (1990); Motard-Noar, M., *Les fictions d'H. C.* (1991); Shiach, M., *H. C.* (1991)

—VERENA ANDERMATT-CONLEY

CLAES, Ernest

Belgian novelist and short-story writer (writing in Flemish), b. 24 Oct. 1885, Zichem; d. 2 Sept. 1968, Ukkel

Born into a large farm family in the eastern Flemish region of De Kempen, which was to be the setting of most of his short fiction, C. worked in a printing office as a young boy but was later allowed to study. He took his degree in Germanic philology at Louvain University in 1910. From 1913 until 1944 (except for a period during World War I) he held a post in one of the departments of the Belgian House of Representatives.

C. wrote innumerable short stories giving a realistic account of village life and depicting its various colorful characters. Although his realistic rural storytelling gradually developed into autobiographical stories and romanticized memoirs, most of his stories bring to life uncomplicated, simple people observed with loving humor. His experiences as a soldier and prisoner-of-war during World War I inspired his *Oorlogsnovellen* (1919; war stories), *Bei uns in Deutschland* (1919; original title in German: with us in Germany), and the bitter story *De vulgaire geschiedenis van Charelke Dop* (1923; the common story of Charelke Dop), a satirical description of a caddish and egotistical war profiteer. These themes were further elaborated after World War II, in the novel *Daar is een mens verdronken* (1950; a man was drowned there), in which C. juxtaposes sheer materialism and idealism, and in the autobiographical account of his brief imprisonment by the Allies after the liberation of Belgium in September 1944, *Cel 269* (1952; cell 269). (He was subsequently exempted from further prosecution.)

C.'s international fame was mainly established by *De Witte* (1920; the fair-haired boy), a partly autobiographical book about a country boy whose roguish adventures and inner conflicts are related with forgiving and ironical sympathy. It is not a tightly organized novel, but rather a sparkling and loose evocation of the author's youth and native region. A film (1934) and many translations made the work widely known.

C. excelled in shorter fiction. The long, partly autobiographical novel *Het leven van Herman Coene* (2 vols., 1925, 1930; the life of Herman Coene), containing an account of the protagonist's inner struggle and hence giving a greater depth to his subject, seems to fail because of its broader scope. More successful are C.'s psychological novel about a child, *Kiki* (1925; Kiki), and two animal stories, *De geschiedenis van Black* (1932; the story of Black) and *Floere, het fluwijn* (1951; Floere, the beech-marten).

With TIMMERMANS and STREUVELS C. is the most frequently translated Flemish author. Most of his works are available in German, although none has been translated into English as yet. For the most part his works are representative of the typically Flemish *Heimatkunst*, or regionalism, of his period.

FURTHER WORKS: *Uit mijn dorpken* (1906); *Namen 1914* (1919); *Sichemse novellen* (1921); *De fanfare ''De Sint-Jansvrienden''* (1924); *Wannes Raps* (1926); *Onze smid* (1928); *De Heiligen van Sichem* (1931); *De wondere tocht* (1933); *Kobeke* (1933); *Pastoor Campens zaliger* (1935); *Van den os en den ezel* (1937); *Reisverhaal* (1938); *De moeder en de drie soldaten* (1939); *Jeugd* (1940); *Clementine* (1940); *Herodes* (1942); *Kerstnacht in de gevangenis* (pseud. G. van Hasselt; 1946); *De oude moeder* (pseud. G. v. H.; 1946); *Gerechtelijke dwaling* (pseud. G. v. H.; 1947); *De oude klok* (1947); *Jeroom en Benzamine* (1947); *Sinter-Klaas in de hemel en op de aarde* (1947); *Die schone tijd* (1949); *Studentenkosthuis "Bij Fien Janssens"* (1950); *Het leven en de dood van Victalis van Gille* (1951); *Over reizen en reizigers* (1952); *Voor de open poort* (1952); *Het was een lente* (1953); *De nieuwe ambtenaar* (1953); *Ik en mijn lezers* (1955); *Dit is de sproke van Broederke Valentijn* (1956); *Twistgesprek tussen Demer en Schelde* (1957, with Filip de Pillecijn); *Ik was student* (1957); *Leuven: O dagen, schone dagen* (1958); *De mannen van toen* (1959); *Ik en de Witte* (1960)

BIBLIOGRAPHY: Lissens, R. F., *Flämische Literaturgeschichte des 19. und 20. Jahrhunderts* (1970): 150–51

—ANNE MARIE MUSSCHOOT

CLARK-BEKEDEREMO, J(ohn) P(epper)

(formerly John Pepper Clark) Nigerian dramatist and poet (writing in English), b. 6 April 1935, Kiagbodo

While a student at Ibadan University, where he studied English literature, C. founded and edited the student literary magazine, *The Horn*. After receiving his degree, he pursued graduate studies in the U. S. at Princeton University (he wrote about his American experiences in his caustic travel book *America, Their America* [1964]). Since his return to Nigeria C. has served on the staff of the *Daily Express* in Lagos and now lectures on African literature at the University of Lagos.

C.'s first play, *Song of a Goat* (1961), is loosely based on an Ijaw legend and is in the tradition of the village storyteller. A chief

sends his wife to a masseur for a cure for her supposed barrenness; in reality, it is the husband who is impotent. The masseur tells the wife that "another should take over the tilling of fertile soil." In this play, C. isolates two aspects of life—sex and heredity—and gives them a "popular treatment," as he does in the play's alleged sequel, *Masquerade* (1964), in which a father shoots his daughter for defying him and is in turn killed by her lover. Because both plays are melodramatic "love stories," where personal experience determines the activities of the group, a certain distortion of African life is evident.

On the other hand, *Ozidi* (1966), C.'s best play, returns to the prototype of traditional African drama—the myth. It is a contemporary political play based on an Ijaw saga, combining ritualistic elements of song, speech, and dance in a drama that is simultaneously concerned with ritual rebirth and the need for succession and moral growth and with a depiction of the corrupt politicians and the coups of a modern African state.

As a poet, C. is really a "versifier," because his concern with metrical technicalities frequently makes his work unspontaneous and artificial. Nevertheless, his purely descriptive poems sometimes succeed even though they are written in a fragmentary fashion, since he conveys accurate and personal observations and often imaginatively works folk beliefs into a significant whole. Many of his poems are about doom, the tragedy imposed by history. The way in which C. can be very close to his subject shows that he is not so much a reflective poet but rather one who observes what is near to him and reproduces it accurately. He is very much a poet of the active present, involved in what is near, and to him tradition is only real in a personal and contemporary situation.

FURTHER WORKS: *Poems* (1962); *Three Plays* (1964); *A Reed in the Tide* (1965); *Casualties: Poems 1966–1968* (1970); *The Example of Shakespeare* (1970); *A Decade of Tongues: Selected Poems, 1958-1968* (1981); *State of the Union* (1985)

BIBLIOGRAPHY: Beier, U., on *Poems, BO*, No. 12 (1963): 47–49; Esslin, M., "Two Nigerian Playwrights: Wole Soyinka, J. P. C.," in Beier, U., ed., *Introduction to African Literature: An Anthology of Critical Writing from "Black Orpheus"* (1967): 255–62; Banham, M., on *Ozidi, JCL*, No. 7 (1969): 132–134; Thumboo, E., "At Ibadan Dawn: The Poetry of J. P. C.," *BA*, 44 (1970): 387–92; Izevbaye, D., "The Poetry and Drama of J. P. C.," in King, B., ed., *Introduction to Nigerian Literature* (1971): 152–72; Roscoe, A. A., *Mother Is Gold: A Study in West African Literature* (1971): 36–39, 200–18; Dathorne, O. R., *The Black Mind* (1974): 285–91, 419–21, 427–28; Wren, R. M., *J. P. C.* (1984)

—O. R. DATHORNE

CLARKE, Austin

Irish poet, dramatist, and essayist, b. 9 May 1896, Dublin; d. 19 March 1974, Dublin

The son of Irish nationalists, C. was educated, like JOYCE, by Jesuits at Belvedere, then University College, Dublin. At U.C.D. his teachers included Douglas Hyde (1860–1949), founder of the Gaelic League, and Thomas MacDonagh (1878–1916), poet-martyr, who was executed in the Easter Uprising (1916). After the Uprising, C. took MacDonagh's place at U.C.D. Although his first book, *The Vengeance of Fionn* (1917) was acclaimed, he lost his university post after secretly marrying in a registry. The marriage lasted for barely two weeks and precipitated C.'s expatriation. He spent fifteen years in London reviewing books. After he returned to Dublin with a second wife, he founded the Dublin Verse Speaking Society (1938) and in the 1940s the Lyric Theatre to keep verse drama alive after the Abbey Theatre of YEATS was gone. After devoting himself to drama between 1938 and 1955, he emerged once again as a prolific, if uneven and parochial, poet.

The body of C.'s writing reflects his response to Ireland. Celtic landscapes permeate his poems. His early bardic poetry is part of the Irish Literary Revival. George RUSSELL was his mentor, and Yeats an influence that he struggled to escape. He knew Gaelic and repeatedly turned to medieval Irish legends as sources. After narrative poems such as *The Cattledrive in Connaught* (1925), he wrote prose romances such as *The Singing Men of Cashel* (1936).

Turning from the mythic past to self-revelation, he stresses in the idiosyncratic *Night and Morning* (1938) the turbulent conflict between individual conscience and Catholic authority. In angry protest against religious prohibitions, A. reveals in his poems the urgent need to overcome sexual guilt. *The Plot is Ready* (1943), perhaps C.'s best play, pits a nonconformist High King of Old Ireland against priestly orthodoxy.

C.'s poetry after 1955 persists in protest. *Later Poems* (1961) includes three "pamphlets": *Ancient Lights* (1955) exposes and satirizes "respectable" Irish society, attacking conservative Irish Catholic responses to current events and issues such as poverty, birth control, and divorce; compressed, elliptical, and increasingly ironic, *Too Great a Vine* (1957) reveals disillusion with church and state; in *The Horse Eaters* (1960) the new skeptic deplores killing horses to export their meat. *Flight to Africa* (1963), perhaps his best volume, reworks traditional Irish poems, satirizes clerics and corrupt social policy in a "Penal Age," pities the victims, and appreciates landscapes, lust, and love. *Mnemosyne Lay in Dust* (1966), a tour de force about the sojourn of Maurice Devane (a pseudonym of C.) in a mental hospital, reflects the paranoid alienation of the antihero in its nightmarish quality. Nostalgic and increasingly direct, *The Echo at Coole* (1968) includes some fine poems—variations on Gaelic poetry, Irish poets, places, and women, and the absurdities of religious censorship. A pacifist, C. scorned the aggressive capitalist spirit of modern industrialism almost as much as he scorned organized religion in Ireland.

C.'s two critical studies emphasize Irish concerns. *Poetry in Modern Ireland* (1967) insists that there is a continuous tradition of Irish national poetry distinct from English tradition. C. called for an Anglo-Irish poetry, written in English about Irish political and social subjects, intensified, yet useful and accessible. *The Celtic Twilight and the Nineties* (1969) claims Wilde's *fin de siècle* decadence as part of the Celtic Twilight, then acknowledges Yeats's hegemony and asserts that his drama, early and late, is an expression of this Irish national movement. Like other 20th-c. Irish writers, C. had two choices: exile, or involvement in Ireland. In midlife he chose the latter. He wrote to awaken the Irish to their rich Gaelic inheritance and to protest the complacent and curtailing orthodoxies of his country and its religion.

FURTHER WORKS: *The Sword of the West* (1921); *The Fires of Baal* (1921); *The Son of Learning* (1927); *Pilgrimage and Other Poems* (1929); *The Flame* (1930); *The Bright Temptation* (1932); *Collected Poems* (1936); *Sister Eucharea* (1938); *Black Fast* (1941); *The Straying Student* (1942); *The Kiss* (1942); *As the Crow Flies* (1943); *The Viscount of Blarney and Other Plays* (1944); *First Visit to England and Other Memories* (1945); *The Second Kiss* (1946); *The Plot Succeeds* (1950); *The Sun Dances at Easter* (1952); *The Moment Next to Nothing* (1953); *Forget Me Not* (1962); *Twice Round the Black Church* (1962); *Old-Fashioned Pilgrimage and Other Poems* (1967); *Two Interludes Adapted from Cervantes* (1968); *A Penny in the Clouds* (1968); *A Sermon on Swift and Other Poems* (1968); *Orphide* (1970); *Tiresias* (1971); *The Impuritans* (1973); *The Wooing of Becfola* (1974); *Collected Poems* (1974)

BIBLIOGRAPHY: Sealy, D., "A. C.: A Survey of His Work," *Dubliner*, Jan.–Feb. 1963: 7–34; Saul, G. B., "The Poetry of A. C.," in Browne, R. B., et al., eds., *The Celtic Cross*: 26–38; Harmon, M., "The Later Poetry of A. C.," in *The Celtic Cross* (1964): 39–55; Roscelli, W. J., "The Private Pilgrimage of A. C.," in *The Celtic Cross*: 56–72; Martin, A., "Rediscovery of A. C.," *Studies*, 54 (1965): 408–34; Montague, J., and Miller, L., eds., *A Tribute to A. C. on His 70th Birthday* (1966); Weber, R., "A. C.: The Arch Poet of Dublin," *MR*, 2 (1970): 295–308; Halpern, S., *A. C.: His Life and Works* (1974); Kinsella, T., Introduction to *A. C.: Selected Poems* (1976): ix–xvi; Schirmer, G. A., *The Poetry of A. C.* (1989); Ricigliano, L., *A. C.: A Reference Guide* (1993)

—MARTHA FODASKI-BLACK

CLAUDEL, Paul

French poet, dramatist, essayist, and theologian, b. 6 Aug. 1868, Villeneuve-sur-Fère-en-Tardenois; d. 23 Feb. 1955, Paris

C. was one of the three or four writers through whom French literature achieved its most enduring form during the first half of the 20th c. Except for the novel, he left his mark on every genre.

The Thinker. Although better known as a poet and dramatist, C. recorded his thought and apologetics as a practicing Catholic from 1886 on, when, during services on Christmas Day in Notre Dame Cathedral he was suddenly converted at the crest of a spiritual surge whose inspiration was in part the poetry of Rimbaud (see "Ma conversion" [my conversion] in *Contacts et circonstances* [1940; contacts and circumstances]). His native Aisne is cathedral country and symbolic of his roots that extend deep into the Gothic and Catholic soil of France; it also recalls the neighboring Ardennes, associated with the youth and reminiscences of Rimbaud. The literary cast of C.'s own youth was provided by SYMBOLISH and represents his only commitment to contemporary forms of literature (and even this influence he was eventually to shape according to his own mold). His isolation was abetted by an unlikely career: starting in 1893, and for over forty years, he was to live as a diplomat in intermittent exile, moving from Boston to Shanghai, from Peking to Hamburg, from Rome to Brussels—by way of Rio, Copenhagen, and, with the rank of ambassador, Tokyo and Washington.

Though respected by influential men of letters (see his *Correspondance*, with GIDE, 1899–1926, pub. 1949 [*Correspondence*, 1952]; with RIVIÈRE, 1907–1914, pub. 1926 [*Correspondence*, 1927]; with JAMMES, 1897–1938; and with André Suarès, 1904–1938), he was outside coteries and cliques. Meanwhile, despite his sense of exile, he enlarged his vision to a world scale, to

Paul Claudel

which several works bear witness: *Connaissance de l'Est* (1900; *The East I Know*, 1914); *Vers d'exil* (1912; verse of exile); *À travers les villes en flammes* (1924; through the burning cities); *L'oiseau noir dans le soleil levant* (1927; the black bird in the rising sun). At the same time he confirmed his sense of God as a supreme and purposeful architect Who blends together all things of His creation. In this view, man is indistinct from God's other materia (and thus in touch with all) except for his awareness, which makes him both a spectator and an actor within the immense drama of the world.

In the years following his conversion, the Bible became not only C.'s Word, but his book of images as well. These he placed within a framework derived from his readings of Thomas Aquinas, who took an optimistic view of man's powers and allowed that the source of natural knowledge is in the senses. In the Thomistic ladder of potencies that leads to the crowning actuality of God C. may also have found his sense that all created things are motion, as well as the reason for man's multiple contact, his erosion, and his temptation to deny the Divine constant.

In addition to his diplomatic duties and his literary production, C. remained a frequent commentator and translator of the Scriptures: after his retirement to Brangues in 1935, he devoted himself to such commentary almost exclusively: *Les aventures de Sophie* (1937; the adventures of Sophie); *Un poète regarde la Croix* (1938; *A Poet before the Cross*, 1952); *Le livre de Job* (1946; the Book of Job); *Paul Claudel interroge le Cantique des Cantiques* (1948; Paul Claudel looks at the Song of Songs); and *Emmaüs* (1949; Emmaus).

The Poet. In contrast with the SYMBOLISTS, whose spiritualization led them to a Platonic ideal of anti-forms, C.'s mysticism was affirmed in the multiplicity and the living evidence of Divine substance. His poetry is one of plenty—that of a Walt Whitman in whom rumble the Gothic Middle Ages of France. Although occasionally, in the years following his conversion, he still read Mallarmé, C. became drawn to more robust poets: those he studied especially were Virgil, Dante, and Shakespeare. Rejecting the inner contemplation of the modern poet, including even that of his master, Rimbaud, he turned instead to the Intelligence of all creation. He viewed his possession of the world as a spiritual act, rejecting in the poet the purveyor of mere objective truths ("animus"); but even though he accepted only the truth whose utterance is the poet's special gift ("anima"), he refused to be the "pure artist" envisaged by Mallarmé (see *La catastrophe d'Igitur* [1926; Igitur's catastrophe]). Rather, he assumed for the poet the godlike prerogative to "possess, his privilege being to give all things a name" (letter to Rivière, 1907); Mallarmé's need of the absolute became for C. the need of a total comprehension. It is this vision of a meaningful world, where all forces are complementary and where man has his own place and function, that is expressed in C.'s poetry. His metaphor is the coupling of these disparate and complementary parcels of creation. His imagery has the abundance of a healthy plant and finds in nature a medieval symbolism in which all forms signify a Divine essence.

C.'s exuberance could not be contained by the Alexandrine: his ample rhythm, not unlike that of the King James Bible, is a natural force similar to that which, in his poetry, is often symbolized by the great rivers. His vision seldom commits the mind: it is immediate and sensual. Even his theoretical writing, *Art poétique* (1907; *Poetic Art*, 1948), affords evidence that is tangible, brings as it were the gift of flesh to the principles of his poetic activity (see also *Positions et propositions* [1928, 1934; *Ways and Crossways*, 1933], especially the first volume).

Foremost among C.'s poetic works is his *Cinq grandes odes* (1910; *Five Great Odes*, 1967), a five-part poem whose initial inspiration is his reflection on a sarcophagus—"Les muses" ("The Muses")—relating the poet's inspiration and his gift of intelligible words by which it is made possible to grasp the essence of the universe. "Les muses" is followed by "L'esprit et l'eau" ("The Spirit and the Water"), symbols of freedom within the "immense octave of Creation." Next, the "Magnificat" ("Magnificat") expresses the thanks of the poet for having discovered God. The fourth part is a dialogue between flesh and spirit, "La muse qui est la grâce" ("The Muse Who Is Grace"). The last ode, "La maison fermée" ("Within the House") is C.'s poetic affirmation; he will not be alone, even in solitude, for he remains within the total harmony of the world. The work ends with a concluding hymn saluting the new century. C. sings again of a world vision in the *Cantate à trois voix* (1913; cantata for three voices); the voices of the three sisters, Fausta, Laeta, and Beata (the romantic, the pagan, and the Christian) blend with the voice of the Rhône ("Cantique du Rhône" [1910; "Canticle of the Rhône," 1950]), which lends its power, as did the sea in "L'esprit et l'eau," to the image of a Divine synthesis expressed in nature. Other noteworthy aspects of C.'s poetry are the symbolist elements in *Corona benignitatis anni Dei* (1915; *Coronal*, 1943), *Trois poèmes de guerre* (1915; *Three Poems of the War*, 1919), *La Messe là bas* (1919; the Mass down there), and in his short haikai poems, *Cent phrases pour éventails* (1927; one hundred phrases for a fan).

The Dramatist. Although his plays were not generally performed until after 1925, when their magnitude became less fearsome to directors, it is as a dramatist that C. is best known to the greatest number of people. His first collection of plays was called *L'arbre* (1901; the tree), an indication that his stage, like the rest of his work, draws its substance from nature and involves the world. C.'s dramatic nourishment was Aeschylus, several of whose plays he translated. Other major influences on him were Shakespeare and Lope de Vega. His first drama, *Tête d'Or* (1st version, 1890; 2nd, 1901; *Tête d'Or*, 1919), reflects his own religious struggle. In this drama of the "possession of the earth," Simon Agnel (later known as Tête d'Or)—man as strength and intelligence—strives to possess the earth but ends possessed by it. The attempt at possession ends in failure but provides the lustiness and the grandeur of the play. *La ville* (1st version, 1893; 2nd, 1901; *The City*, 1920) was a commentary on the meaning of man's social existence. The play's second version emphasizes Cœuvre, the Poet in his godlike function as the one who creates and represents reality. It is also noteworthy for Lâla, the first of a number of women in C.'s drama who bring into focus aspects of the aspirations and frustrations of man. In 1893, in Boston, C. exercised his own sense of frustration "by depicting [himself] as a young fellow who sells his wife to recover his freedom"; the play, *L'échange* (pub. 1901; *The Exchange*, 1973), is set upon what C. viewed as the American spiritual wasteland. In 1892 he had begun *La jeune fille Violaine* (the maiden Violaine), the second version of which was written in China (1899–1900). This became, after further changes, *L'annonce faite à Marie* (1912; *The Tidings Brought to Mary*, 1916). Perhaps the most successful of C.'s plays, it is the medieval evocation upon the soil of France of Pierre de Craon, the builder of cathedrals and the performer of an earthbound gesture, and Violaine, the performer of the celestial gesture, the girl who redeems the leper Craon and the stillborn child of her sister Mara ("bitter" in Hebrew). Violaine is one of the few women in this drama who mediates unambiguously between God and man.

In 1906 C. wrote a play that was not to be performed until 1948: *Partage de midi* (*Break of Noon*, 1960), a drama about a woman, Ysé, and adultery. As contrasted with Violaine, Ysé is a creature of the flesh. But the love that Mesa has for her eventually carries him beyond the frustrations of temporal desire and into a true spiritual union with Ysé. In 1908 C. began writing what was to be his dramatic trilogy, *L'otage*, 1911; *Le pain dur*, 1918; *Le père humilié*, 1920 (*Three Plays: The Hostage, Crusts, The Humiliation of the Father*, 1945), the triptych of postrevolutionary days depicting "the decadence . . . of noble families that were forced to capitulate to their former servants" (letter to P. Brisson, 1930). It traces the degeneration of the formerly noble Coûfontaines under Louis Philippe and ends in Rome, at the fountainhead of Christianity, expressing hope in a future spiritual regeneration.

At the climax of his dramatic career, between 1921 and 1925, C. wrote *Le soulier de satin* (pub. 1930; *The Satin Slipper*, 1931), an epic drama in the Spanish fashion, concerning the adventurer Rodrigue (spiritually related to Simon Agnel and Mesa) whose prey is the entire earth, and the woman he will never possess, Dona Prouhèze. She is a synthesis of all C.'s women, through whom Rodrigue ultimately spiritualizes his earthly mission.

The scope of C.'s dramas is as vast as the author's credo, and all his characters live out their lives within a teeming world—from those whose frailty precludes spiritual assertion and the protagonist's role, down to the simple monsters fit only for laughter, such as the many comic figures in C.'s satiric play, *Protée* (1914; *Proteus*, 1978), a necessarily pre-Christian adventure. Through them all C. conveys his great delight with the world in general. The stage that contains this vision is proportionately huge, and for years it was thought that no theater could accommodate it. *Le livre de Christophe Colomb* (1929; *The Book of Christopher Columbus*, 1930), for example, requires not only worlds and oceans, but also music and motion-picture projections. Over his drama, as over the rest of his work, C. has thrown the rich mantle of his poetry—although that mantle occasionally tears on the jagged and obdurate rock of doctrine.

FURTHER WORKS: *Le repos du septième jour* (1901); *Le chemin de la Croix* (1911); *La nuit de Noël 1914* (1915); *L'homme et son désir* (1917); *L'ours et la lune* (1919); *Introduction à quelques œuvres* (1920); *Ode jubilaire pour le six centième anniversaire de la mort de Dante* (1921); *Poèmes de guerre 1914–1916* (1922); *Feuilles de saints* (1925); *L'endormie* (1925); *Le vieillard sur le mont Omi* (1927); *Sous le rempart d'Athènes* (1928); *Fragment d'un drame* (1931); *Écoute, ma fille* (1934); *Conversations dans le Loir-et-Cher* (1935); *Introduction à la peinture hollandaise* (1935); *Figures et paraboles* (1936); *Toi, qui es-tu?* (1936); *Introduction au Livre de Ruth* (1938); *Jeanne d'Arc au bûcher* (1938); *L'épée et le miroir* (1939); *La sagesse; ou, La parabole du Festin* (1939); *L'histoire de Tobie et de Sara* (1939); *Présence et prophétie* (1941); *Seigneur, apprenez-nous à prier* (1942; *Lord, Teach Us to Pray*, 1948); *Dodoitzu* (French/Eng. text, 1945); *Poèmes et paroles durant la guerre de trente ans* (1945); *Les sept psaumes de la pénitence* (1945); *Introduction à l'Apocalypse* (1946); *Les révélations de la Salette* (1946); *La rose et le rosaire* (1946); *L'œil écoute* (1946; *The Eye Listens*, 1950); *Discours et remerciements* (1947); *Du côté de chez Ramuz* (1947); *Visages radieux* (1947); *Sous le signe du dragon* (1948); *Accompagnements* (1949); *La lune à la recherche d'elle-même* (1949); *Œuvres complètes* (20 vols., 1950–59); *Une voix sur Israël* (1951); *L'Evangile d'Isaïe* (1951); *Mémoires improvisés* (1954); *J'aime la Bible* (1955; *The Essence of the Bible*, 1957); *Théâtre* (2 vols., 1956); *Œuvre poétique* (1957); *Correspondance P. C.-Darius Milhaud 1912–1953* (1961)

BIBLIOGRAPHY: Rivière, J., *Études* (1911); Dieckmann, H., *Die Kunstanschauung P. C.s* (1931); Madaule, J., *Le génie de P. C.* (1933) and *Le drame de P. C.* (1936); Friche, E., *Études Claudéliennes* (1943); Chonez, C., *Introduction à P. C.* (1947); Samson, J., *P. C., poète musicien* (1948); Spitzer, L., *Linguistics and Literary History* (1948): 193–236; Angers, P., *Commentaire à l'Art Poétique de P. C.* (1949); Ryan, M., *Introduction to P. C.* (1951); Barjon, L., *P. C.* (1953); Chiari, J., *The Poetic Drama of P. C.* (1954); Mavrocordato, A., *L'ode de P. C.* (1955); Fowlie, W., *P. C.* (1957); Flumet, S., *P. C.* (1958); Mondoe, H., *C. plus intime* (1960); Matheson, W. H., *C. and Aeschylus* (1965); Maurois, A., *From Proust to Camus* (1966): 122–41; Watson, H., *C.'s Immortal Heroes: A Choice of Deaths* (1971); Lioure, M., *L'esthétique dramatique de P. C.* (1971); Blanc, A., *C.* (1973); Malicet, M., *Lecture psychanalytique de l'œuvre de C.* (1978); Knapp, B. L., *P. C.* (1982); Caranfa, A., *C.: Beauty and Grace* (1989)

—DAVID I. GROSSVOGEL

The inexhaustible outpouring of metaphors gives C.'s poetry a naïve, fresh sensuousness, which is perpetually effusive and dazzling and which summons the essences of things in all their reality and immediacy. C., moreover, thinks in images and thinks with his senses. His very thoughts, like all primitive and truly profound thoughts, are sensuous. His thoughts are not an extract of feelings, some kind of subtle but fleeting fragrance obtained by distilling thousands of flowers. His thoughts are weighty and real and still attached to things.

C.'s work is not a mechanical combination of abstract terms, but rather something analogous to the process of germination: painful, mysterious, slow, and groping. He also reaches a flowering, which, like the blooming of flowers, is completely imbued with colors, all exuding illumination and beauty. Thus, C.'s language does not proceed through the *application* of images to thoughts; instead, thought itself is developed through words, a chain of primary images arising just as they do in an uncorrupted mind. These images are not only visual; we perceive them through all our senses simultaneously. They rise, grow, envelop us, communicate their vibrations to us, and, while bathing our whole bodies with a sensuous tide, they leave their secret meaning in our souls. One has only to welcome them to understand them, for they enter us from all directions at the same time, uttering the same truth simultaneously in several ways. All of C.'s words, as well as having an appearance and a sound, have a texture, a smell and a taste. . . .

But to come under the influence of C.'s sensuousness, to feel his power, one has to have retained one's primitive spontaneity and simplicity, or to be able to recapture them. One must still possess the wonderful childlike gift of understanding through images, of grasping ideas through illustrations, of not separating an idea from its tangible forms.

Jacques Rivière, *L'Occident*, Oct. 1907,
pp. 162–63

Let us note again the abundance of beauties of a truly lyrical nature in the early works of C. and the abundance of beauties of a dramatic nature in his mature works. In *Tête d'Or,* in *The Seventh Day's Rest*, and in *The City*, one often has the impression of a struggle between the characters taking place at a distance. The dramatic conflict makes them grapple with one another, but the lyricism often isolates them. They speak for themselves, not too concerned about the replies they receive; they express their feelings at length, and much more through words than actions. In some scenes, they seem alienated from one another, although they are caught up in the same conflict and set loose in the same circus.

But with *The Exchange* and all the plays that have followed it, one can see the blossoming of the poet's more genuinely dramatic gifts. The dialogue is more tightly knit; the characters look at each other and attack one another face to face. The lyricism, arising from a source just as powerful as in C.'s earliest works, has become more closely related to the plot: it

serves the action better, it heightens the seriousness of the drama more often, and it more naturally draws its power from the dramatic movement.

Georges Duhamel, *P. C.* (1913), pp. 106–7

P. C. appears as the most demanding of contemporary poets. To be understood and followed, he requires from his reader a total spiritual submission and attention. It is not only the ornate and complex part of his work which tyrannizes the reader's intelligence, it is above all the harassing and well-nigh unbearable unity of his books. This unity provides his reader with no rest, no dream, no immobility. C. hammers in his truth without breathing between blows. Rightfully considered the most feared poet, he may also seem the most cruel. And yet, upon careful examination of his writings, it is impossible to discover precise examples of his cruelty. They give this general impression because they are unified in their criticism of the century's spirit. Paradoxically, C. is *par excellence* the poet of the world, the poet who has named the greatest number of objects in the world, the realist poet in his love for the humblest and most familiar objects; but he is also the most implacably hostile poet to the superficial world of our century. . . .

P. C. closes, recapitulates, and subsumes the modern movement in poetry. It has often been said that C.'s poetic power equals Victor Hugo's. This kind of remark reveals a basic misunderstanding of the two poets. Hugo's power is exclusively verbal. It bears no trace of the metaphysical struggle which is the glory and the distinction of modern poetry. And this is why Hugo's power is useless and impotent for men and poets today. . . .

After Baudelaire, who first stated the basic problem of modern poets; after Mallarmé, who was [the] master and theorist [of modern poetry] and whose brief work is a mine of secrets; after Rimbaud, who was its adolescent, that is, the one who underwent the experience in so personal and violent a way that we shall never be able to measure its profundity, comes P. C., whom we make bold to call the "poet." He is a poet in a more vital and more complete sense than these other artists. He is the poet of day who comes after a long line of poets obsessed with night.

Wallace Fowlie, *Clowns and Angels* (1943),
pp. 112, 114–15

Although the delectation of Grace triumphs in *The Satin Slipper* on the one hand, and adultery is consummated and a crime is pursued to its conclusion in *Break of Noon* on the other hand, these two great works both teach the same lesson, a lesson that we have never received with such clarity and persuasiveness since the *"etiam peccata"* of Saint Augustine: sins, too, sins perhaps above all, serve the purposes of Grace. . . .

In both dramas the two women, Ysé [in *Break of Noon*] and Prouhèze [in *The Satin Slipper*], remain closely linked to the spiritual destinies of their lovers. This is the other lesson that can be drawn from *Break of Noon* and even more from *The Satin Slipper*. On the level of Grace, any encounter, even a criminal encounter, has a significance; it creates bonds that we cannot break. You [C.] teach us that we shall not save ourselves alone, that the thread of our destinies is woven on a loom on which many other threads intertwine with our to form a final pattern that will not be revealed to us until after death. . . .

Those whom God has chosen cannot separate themselves from Him—this, too, is the meaning of these two dramas, which I prefer to all the others you have enchanted us with.

François Mauriac, *Réponse à P. C.* (1947), pp. 43, 45–46

He reminds me of a frozen cyclone. . . .One senses that his conversation, very animated and rich, never improvises. He propounds truths which he has patiently elaborated. And yet he can joke, and if he would only abandon himself a little more to the impulse of the moment, he would not be without a certain charm. I am trying to decide what is lacking in his manner of speaking . . .a little human kindness? . . .No, not even that; he has something far better. It is, I think, the most striking voice I have ever heard. No, he does not charm; he does not want to charm; he convinces—or inspires awe.

André Gide, *Journal 1889–1939* (1948), p. 189

I was excited the other night upon leaving the Théâtre de l'Atelier after a performance of *The Hard Bread*. This was not just excitement one may feel after hearing a great work admirably performed but also the excitement of receiving the shock of a revelation—a double revelation.

The first revelation is that C. is decidedly not only a poet of genius but a very great dramatist, something I had not been completely convinced of even after the dazzling production of *Break of Noon*. The second revelation is distressing, and I state it with great concern about even uttering it: the crushing impression of reality that comes from the play—an impression that perhaps no other theatrical work by C. imparts to the same degree—can be explained by the fact that in this play the viewer feels he is directly in the presence of a personality that has been violently stripped bare; can one even wonder whether this personality is not that of the author? A single word can characterize that personality—and the word is ferocity.

The Hard Bread offers us the terrifying sight of a C. who has shed before our eyes all his religious and mystical superstructures. We see what his inner world and life probably would have been without the miraculous event he celebrated in "Magnificat." Now that I think about it, even in *The Tidings Brought to Mary*, I had been struck by the force with which a

segment of humanity was presented, a segment, which seems to come out of the earth and which seems destined to return completely to the earth. I have always thought that the character of Mara merited a great deal of speculation and analysis. Still, Mara is only a dark spot in mystery of light. If there is a mystery in *The Hard Bread*, it is a mystery of darkness. One would hardly be exaggerating in saying that it is the drama of the liquidation of Christianity, of France as a Christian country, and perhaps of France itself.

Gabriel Marcel, *NL*, 24 March 1949, p. 8

P. C. was the last peasant: he drew his great strength from the earth. His earth was mystical. C. was a giant, a God of this earth. What can be called his comic side and his humor are the expression of the enormous spirit of mockery of the peasant. Through this mockery the characters seem more insignificant than ridiculous. Even when C. seems to shower his heroes with the most violent sarcasm, seems to hold them in the deepest contempt, there enters into this sarcasm and his contempt a kind of serenity, the feeling of an all-powerfulness on the author's part and of such an insignificance on the part of the characters he abuses that this very insignificance saves the characters from the worst. They are not (or not even) hateful; they become picturesque. In the end, evil does not seem to be dangerous, because it is clear that it only exists through God's will. C. may perhaps be the least charitable Christian poet, because the comic characters he puts on the stage are too insignificant for anyone to take pity on.

In C.'s works evil becomes almost funny; it is allowable—that is, C. is more than willing to present it—in order to emphasize the greatness, the sublimity, of the heroes: without evil, good would not have any meaning. The Devil is comic. Only saintliness is tragic. The ludicrous characters in C.'s works are the figures of the Devil, and that is why they are farcical. Evil is a farce; through evil God seems to tease men and their souls; as cruel as it may be, a farce is only a farce. The evil figures do not have souls; they are made up of appearances and illusions. Evil essentially *does not exist*. One does not have any attachment, any pity, any real hatred either, for something that does not exist. C.'s serenity derives from his certainty that evil in itself is impotent, and that evil is useful as a temporary, uncritical test, willed by God—and by P. C., who feels he is God's spokesman.

Eugène Ionesco, In *Cahiers P. C.* (1960), Vol. H, pp. 26–27

The wealth of counterpoint and minor characters, the interweaving and synthesis of all his themes, and especially the new variety of tones ranging from the most solemn to sheer burlesque, keep *The Satin Slipper* from seeming like a repetition or mere revision of *Break of Noon*, despite their similar structure and central theme. Technical innovations, especially the casual beginning (repeated for Act III in the stage version), perhaps derived from Pirandello's *Six Characters in Search of an Author* and/or Goethe's *Faust*, are likewise noteworthy. But the most important of all in this respect, as well as in the treatment of the theme of death, is the startling originality of the final act, the fourth day.

The last act, subtitled "To Windward of the Balearic Isles," with its ninety pages and thirty-three characters, is actually almost another play, though of course an integral sequal and indeed key and crown to the first three days. It was conceived and partly composed . . . before the rest of the drama, and its atmosphere of self-pacification and ironic detachment permeates the whole play. . . .Essentially, it is a shift from concern with this world to concern with the next. . . .

The most important difference between *The Satin Slipper* and the earlier plays may well be in the lighter, mocking tone, in the familiar, comic, even joyous view of death—and consequently of life. Assured of his immortality, man can have a more profound sense of humor. . . .

Harold Watson, *C.'s Immortal Heroes: A Choice of Deaths* (1971), pp. 143–44

CLAUS, Hugo

Belgian novelist, poet, dramatist, and critic (writing in Flemish), b. 5 April 1929, Bruges

After a very strict Catholic upbringing, C. left school at an early age in order to work on a farm while studying at the Academy of Ghent. Poverty-stricken, he became a seasonal worker in a sugar factory in Chevrières, France, the setting of several of his works. In Paris he met Antonin ARTAUD, whom C. considered his spiritual father. After returning to Belgium C. joined the Cobra movement of international painters and poets (named after the cities of Copenhagen, Brussels, and Amsterdam); this period marked the beginning of an artistic career of staggering versatility. His oeuvre includes poetry, novels, dramas, short stories, film scripts, essays, and translations, as well as an opera libretto. He is one of the very few Belgian writers to make a living entirely from his creative work.

Most of C.'s writing has an experimental quality, which aims at a constant renewal of form. Even in his early collection of poetry, *Registreren* (1948; registering), in which the influence of Artaud is clearly discernible, he rejects all traditional forms, and begins to view the role of the poet as that of an inventor, who is also, simultaneously, in search of his hidden self. His work is characterized by a playful style that combines oddly-matched images and sounds. The musical effect of his poetry is achieved through repetition and variations.

In his novels and short stories, and in his plays as well, C. likes to treat the family crisis as a major problem. *De Metsiers* (1950; *The Duck Hunt*, 1955), C.'s first great novel, is a naturalistic family chronicle in which the problems of puberty are sensitively treated. Reminiscent of FAULKNER's *As I Lay Dying*, this book shows how

youthful love, innocence, and longing for happiness and purity are crushed by an absurd fate. The novel *De hondsdagen* (1952; dog days) continues the theme of a youthful search for an exclusive truth amid falsehood, irony, and tragedy, between fantasy and oppressive reality. In *De verwondering* (1962; the astonishment) C. depicts this duality as a quasi-contest between reality and hallucination. A teacher in a rest home attempts to record recent events surrounding a mysterious girl he met during a masked ball. His quest to learn her identity brings him into her life and family, and eventually leads him into the perplexing and perverse life of organized fanaticism. Dominated by ex-warriors, this world of Flemish Nazis is ruled by the ghost of an SS leader. In this frightening world of slogans and symbols the teacher initially feels a stranger among strangers, but his role as observer turns into one of participant, and he ends by identifying with the ghost of the SS officer.

In C.'s works the emphasis is more on situation than on characters, for the latter are usually aberrant figures, whose mental abnormalities attest to the senselessness and hopelessness of life. In C.'s world the victim and the victimizer are often forced to stand as one against a common predator, which in the final analysis is the personification of life or nature itself.

C. is acknowledged as the foremost contemporary Belgian author writing in Flemish. He solidified an international reputation with the publication of *Het Verdriet van België* (1983; *The Sorrows of Religion*, 1990) and *De Zwaardvis* (1989; *The Swordfish*, 1996).

FURTHER WORKS: *Kleine reeks* (1944); *Zonder vorm van proces* (1950); *De blijde en onvoorziene week* (1950, with Karel Appel); *Over het werk van Corneille* (1951); *Tancredo infrasonic* (1952); *Een huis dat tussen nacht en morgen staat* (1953); *Natuurgetrouw* (1954); *Paal en Perk* (1955, with Corneille); *De Oostakkerse gedichten* (1955); *Een bruid in de morgen* (1955; *A Bride in the Morning*, 1960); *De koele minnaar* (1956); *Het lied van de moordenaar* (1957); *De zwarte keizer* (1958); *Suiker* (1958); *Mama, kijk, zonder handen!* (1959); *Een geverfde ruiter* (1961); *Acht toneelstukken* (1961); *De dans van de reiger* (1962); *Omtrent Deedee* (1963); *Love Song* (1963, with Karel Appel); *Oog om oog* (1964); *Het teken van de Hamster* (1964); *Karel Appel, Painter* (1963); *Louis Paul Boon* (1964); *Gedichten* (1965); *Het landschap* (1965); *De schilderijen van Roger Raveel* (1965); *Tijl Uilenspiegel* (1965); *Thyestes, toneelstuk naar Seneca* (1966); *Het goudland* (1966); *De vijanden* (1967); *De avonturen van Belgman* (1967); *Relikwie* (1968); *Masscheroen* (1968); *Morituri* (1968); *Wrraak!* (1968); *Vrijdag* (1969; *Friday* 1972); *Natuurgetrouwer* (1969); *Genesis* (1969); *Heer Everzwijn* (1970); *Van horen zeggen* (1970); *Het level en de werken van Leopold II* (1970); *Tand om tand* (1970); *Oedipus* (1971); *Interieur* (1971); *Dag jij* (1971); *Schola Nostra door Dorothea van Male* (1971); *Schaamte* (1972); *Het jaar van de kreeft* (1972); *De vossejacht, toneelstuk naar Ben Jonson* (1972); *Pas de deux* (1973); *Blauw blauw* (1973); *Gekke Gerrit* (1973); *De groene ridder* (1973); *Figuratief* (1973); *Wangebeden* (1973); *Thuis* (1975); *Het graf van Pernath* (1976); *Het huis van Labdakos* (1977); *Jessica!* (1977); *Het verlangen* (1978; *Desire*, 1997); *De wangebeden* (1978); *Gedichten 1969–1978* (1979). FURTHER WORKS IN ENGLISH: *H. C.: Selected Poems* (1986); *Four Works for the Theater* (1990)

BIBLIOGRAPHY: Meijer, R. P., *Literature of the Low Countries* (1971): 351–52, 357; Snapper, J. P., *Post-war Dutch Literature: A*

Harp Full of Nails (1971): 12–14 and passim; Snapper, J. P., "Teeth on Edge: The Child in the Modern Dutch Short Story," *RNL*, 8 (1977): 137–56; Hermans, T., Introduction to *H. C.: Selected Poems* (1986): 7–12; Willinger, D., Introduction to *Four Works for the Theater by H. C.* (1990): i–xix

—JOHAN P. SNAPPER

COCTEAU, Jean

French poet, novelist, dramatist, screenwriter, essayist, journalist, and critic, b. 5 July 1889, Maisons-Laffitte; d. 11 Oct. 1963, Milly-la-Fôret

C. was born into a wealthy Parisian family who spent every summer in the fashionable suburban home of his maternal grandparents. When C. was nine, his father committed suicide, a traumatic event which according to psychoanalytical critics was to profoundly influence C. and create his desire to put himself in the service of the mysterious forces in the universe that can communicate with the living only through poets. Of equal importance were C.'s first visits to the circus and then the theater, where he was struck by the conviction that all the performing arts, including the most popular ones, could serve equally well as vehicles for poetry. A mediocre student in secondary school who was unsuccessful after repeated attempts to pass the graduation examination, C. was at the same time a precocious poet whose works were presented in a public recital when he was only eighteen years old. His career as a young dandy was cut short when he was stunned by the Ballets-Russes's first performance in 1913 of Igor Stravinsky's *Le sacre du printemps* (rite of spring). At that point he decided to become an avant-garde artist, intent upon scandalizing the public and expanding the frontiers of art.

For the next twenty years, C. created a dazzling profusion of poems, novels, critical manifestos, plays, and ballet scenarios, while forming friendships with some of the foremost modern artists, including PROUST, APOLLINAIRE, Picasso, and the composer Erik Satie, with the last two of whom he collaborated on *Parade* (1919) in 1917 for the Ballets-Russes. The unremitting hostility of the SURREALISTS led C. to abandon the avant-garde for something closer to classicism after his experimental film *Le sang d'un poète* (script pub. 1948; *The Blood of a Poet*, 1949) had its première in 1932, and during the 1930s he met with great success as an author of wellmade plays. The 1940s saw an equally successful series of films, some of which C. wrote and some of which he both wrote and directed; all of them were primarily intended as vehicles for the actor Jean Marais. In his last decade C. worked in a wide variety of graphic arts. Throughout his entire career he wrote poetry, and it was always as a poet that he saw himself, no matter in which genre or art form he happened to be working.

The first book C. wrote after rejecting his three early collections of poetry was *Le Potomak* (1919; the Potomak), a shapeless novel centering around an equally shapeless creature who lives caged in an aquarium in the heart of Paris. The novel's style owes a great deal to *Paludes* by André GIDE but also shows what would be C.'s own characteristic mixture of self-absorption and wit. C.'s next three novels, which are much more traditional in form, present a closed space, which is opened outward only to be re-created again

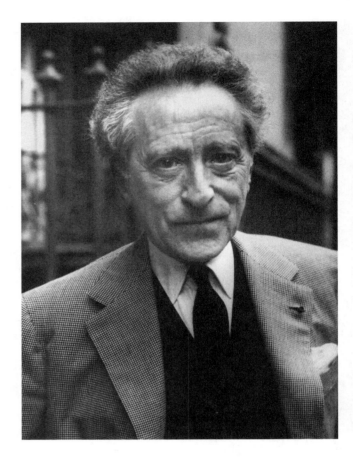

Jean Cocteau

elsewhere and from which there is no release except in death, either for the despondent adolescent in *Le grand écart* (1923; *The Grand Écart*, 1925) or for the inseparable brother and sister in *Les enfants terribles* (1929; *Enfants Terribles*, 1930). C.'s plays present a similarly claustrophobic situation, which has similar consequences. The link between C.'s novels and his plays can be seen in the conclusion to *Les enfants terribles*, when the walls tumble down and the secret room becomes a theater open to spectators. The difference between the novels and the plays is that in the plays the closed space remains open on one side so that the theater audience can observe—like the Poet in *Le sang d'un poète* at his keyholes—what happens in the bedchamber of Oedipus in *La machine infernale* (1934; *The Infernal Machine*, 1936) or in the "gypsy caravan" of *Les parents terribles* (1938; *Intimate Relations*, 1962). (A notable exception is *Parade*, in which the audience is denied the chance to penetrate the circus tent and remains confined to the open space outside.)

The films C. conceived directly for the screen share an entirely different structure, one in which the setting alternates between this world and another world, which stands sometimes for the underworld and sometimes for the inner world where poetry is made. In these films the closed space of the beginning is broken by a journey through the mirror into another world whose space is totally open, and when the central character returns from his journey, the closed space he returns to seems more constricted than ever. At the conclusions of the films, however, there is a second journey through the mirror—not into death (as in the novels and plays) but into the immortality that awaits poets. This basic structure is that of only one of C.'s plays—*Orphée* (1927; *Orpheus*, 1933), which C. used as the basis for his greatest film, *Orphée* (1950; screenplay pub. 1951; *Orphée*, 1972). C.'s other plays deal with such related oppositions as adulthood and childhood, illusion and reality, disorder and order. *Orphée*, however, is dominated by the idea characteristic of C.'s films and his poetry: that the poet's task is to create works of art that will explain the next world to the inhabitants of this one.

Even a prose poem as early as "Visite" (visit) from "Discours du grand sommeil" (discourse of the great sleep)—dated 1916–18, although first published in *Poésie, 1916–1923* (1924; poetry, 1916–1923)—has as its theme the poet's ability to see clearly into the world of the dead. In that poem the poet is visited by someone who has recently died and who validates the poet's claim to special insight. The poet's visitor, a soldier who fell in the war, is only the first of many such visitors from the next world; they find their most memorable representative in "L'ange Heurtebise" (1925; Angel Heurtebise), who reappears in the play and film of *Orphée*. Angels visit the poet because he already has one foot in their world; ironically he is misunderstood and even persecuted by his contemporaries, who do not appreciate him until after his death. The theme at the heart of C.'s poetry and criticism is the romantic myth of the *poète maudit*, the poet who is blessed with special powers but whose curse is lack of comprehension by others, and by invoking this myth C. was associating himself with Baudelaire, Rimbaud, and especially Apollinaire, whose star-shaped wound C. adopted as his own signature.

C. is often thought of as someone who specialized in modern versions of classical myth, and certainly such works as *La machine infernale*, which presents Oedipus as a plaything in the hands of the gods, are worthy of comparison with the best plays of GIRAUDOUX. But C. was less a modernizer of classical myth than a mythmaker, and the Orpheus myth is as central to his autobiographical writings, including his criticism, as to his films. C.'s first major work of criticism is *Le rappel à l'ordre* (1926; *A Call to Order*, 1926) which contains brilliant aphorisms about the nature of art mixed with reminiscences about C.'s own experience as an artist. In C.'s later volumes the criticism and autobiography become indistinguishable. In order to embody his own myth of the persecuted artist, C. kept retouching his self-portrait so that it would match his life and kept reinterpreting his life so that it would match his self-portrait. When the time finally came for C. to follow so many of his characters into the mirror, he had already created the mirror image he wished to rejoin. That double labor of self-creation culminates in the film *Le testament d'Orphée* (1961; *The Testament of Orpheus*, 1968), C.'s last major work, in which he plays himself on screen; the identity between artist and artifact is finally complete. The hero of C.'s novel *Thomas l'imposteur* (1923; *Thomas the Imposter*, 1925) is so successful at living an assumed role that at the end of the novel he and his assumed role have become inseparable. C. was not always successful—he is still not widely believed to have been a great poet—but he articulated one of the central myths of modern art more forcefully perhaps than any other writer.

The two reasons why a just evaluation of C.'s achievement is a difficult task are that C. was immensely celebrated and incredibly prolific. An omnipresent figure on the Parisian scene throughout his career, he worked in so many different art forms that, as W. H. AUDEN once wrote, "to enclose the collected works of C. one would need not a bookshelf, but a warehouse." Consequently, opinions about C. vary widely: he has been dismissed as a popularizer of other people's ideas and praised as one of the few modern artists in touch with the wellsprings of myth. The most enduring of his works will probably prove to be his films, which express most effectively C.'s chosen myth of the artist as Orpheus, journeying to the world beyond the mirror in order to return with a message for mankind.

FURTHER WORKS: *La lampe d'Aladin* (1909); *Le Prince frivole* (1910); *La danse de Sophocle* (1912); *Le coq et l'arlequin* (1918; *Cock and Harlequin*, 1921); *Le Cap de Bonne Espérance* (1919); *Carte blanche* (1920); *Escales* (1920); *Poésies (1917–1920)* (1920); *Le secret professionnel* (1922; *Professional Secrets*, 1926); *Vocabulaire* (1922); *Dessins* (1923); *Plain-chant* (1923); *Les mariés de la Tour Eiffel* (1923; *The Eiffel Tower Wedding Party*, 1963); *Le mystère de l'oiseleur* (1925); *Lettre à Jacques Maritain* (1926; *Letter to Jacques Maritain*, 1948); *Maison de santé* (1926); *Roméo et Juliette* (1926); *Opéra* (1927); *Antigone* (1927; *Antigone*, 1961); *Le mystère laïc* (1928); *Œdipe-roi* (1928); *Le livre blanc* (1928; *The White Paper*, 1957); *Une entrevue sur la critique avec Maurice Rouzaud* (1929); *25 dessins d'un dormeur* (1929); *Opium* (1930; *Opium*, 1932); *La voix humaine* (1930; *The Human Voice*, 1951); *Essai de critique indirecte* (1932); *Portraits-souvenir, 1900–1914* (1935; *Paris Album, 1900–1914*, 1956); *Soixante dessins pour Les enfants terribles* (1934); *Les chevaliers de la table ronde* (1937; *The Knights of the Round Table*, 1963); *Mon premier voyage* (1937; *Round the World Again in Eighty Days*, 1937); *La fin du Potomak* (1940); *Les monstres sacrés* (1940; *The Holy Terrors*, 1961); *Allégories* (1941); *Dessins en marge des Chevaliers de la table ronde* (1941); *La machine à écrire* (1941; *The Typewriter*, 1947); *Renaud et Armide* (1943); *Les poèmes allemands* (1944); *Léone* (1945); *La Belle et la Bête* (1946; *Diary of a Film*, 1950); *L'aigle à deux têtes* (1946; *The Eagle Has Two Heads*, 1948); *La difficulté d'être* (1947; *The Difficulty of Being*, 1966); *L'éternel retour* (1947; *The Eternal Return*, 1972); *Le foyer des artistes* (1947); *Ruy Blas* (1947); *Poèmes* (1948); *Reines de la France* (1948); *Lettre aux Américains* (1949); *Maalesh* (1949; *Maalesh*, 1956); *Théâtre de poche* (1949); *Jean Marais* (1951); *Entretiens autour du cinématographe* (1951; *Cocteau on the Film*, 1954); *Le chiffre sept* (1952); *La nappe de Catalan* (1952); *Journal d'un inconnu* (1952; *The Hand of a Stranger*, 1956); *Bacchus* (1952; *Bacchus*, 1963); *Appogiatures* (1953); *Clairobscur* (1954); *Colette* (1955); *Discours de réception de M. Jean Cocteau à l'Académie Française* (1955); *Le discours de Strasbourg* (1956); *Le discours d'Oxford* (1956); *La corrida du premier mai* (1957); *Entretiens sur le Musée de Dresde* (1957); *Paraprosodies* (1958); *Gondole des morts* (1959); *Le cordon ombilical* (1962); *Le requiem* (1962); *L'impromptu du Palais-Royal* (1962); *Entretien avec Roger Stéphane* (1964); *Entretiens avec André Fraigneau* (1965); *Faire-part* (1968); *Du cinématographe* (1973); *Poésie de journalisme* (1973); *Paul et Virginie* (1973). FURTHER WORKS IN ENGLISH: *A Call to Order* (1926); *The Journals of Jean Cocteau* (1956); *Five Plays* (1961); *The Infernal Machine and Other Plays* (1963); *My Contemporaries* (1967); *Two Screenplays* (1968); *Professional Secrets* (1970); *Cocteau's World* (1972); *Three Screenplays* (1972)

BIBLIOGRAPHY: Oxenhandler, N., *Scandal and Parade: The Theater of J. C.* (1957); Fraigneau, A., *C.* (1961); Sachs, M., *Witches' Sabbath* (1964); Bazin, A., *What Is Cinema?* (1967): 76–124; Brown, F., *An Impersonation of Angels: A Biography of J. C.* (1968); Sprigge, E., and J.-J. Kihm, *J. C.: The Man & the Mirror* (1968); Gilson, R., *J. C.* (1969); Brosse, J., *C.* (1970); Steegmuller,

F., *C.: A Biography* (1970); Evans, A. B., *J. C. and His Films of Orphic Identity* (1977); Crowson, L., *The Esthetic of J. C.* (1978)

—MICHAEL POPKIN

. . . C. thinks that the salvation of the Theatre lies in it returning to more primitive conditions. Get rid of apparatus, get rid, at least, of that air of elaborate preparation and pretension. Let everything about the theatre admit frankly to the barefaced make-believe that a stage entertainment really is. People will enjoy themselves much more if they go in the spirit of a visit to a circus or a fair. The theatre should reek of sawdust and orange-peel. Realism (this is a familiar cry) is played out; force the audience to collaborate in making ingenious makeshifts serve as hints to the imagination. Remember that apparent informality in stage design, in decoration, in technique, is also an opportunity for fantasy. . . .

The spectator must never press the symbolism too hard. He must enjoy himself at this show [*Orpheus*] first and foremost like a child; the symbols suggest ideas, but these should only produce a pleasant suspicion at the back of the sophisticated spectator's mind that there is more in the show than meets the eye and ear. [1928]

Desmond MacCarthy, *Humanities* (1954),
pp. 106–7

I used to go [to Offranville] often to stay, and the first time I went I met a young man of nineteen or twenty, who at that time vibrated with all the youth of the world. This was J. C., then a passionately imaginative youth to whom every great line of poetry was a sunrise, every sunset the foundations of the Heavenly City. Excepting Bay Lodge I have known no other young man who so recalled Wordsworth's "Bliss was it in that dawn to be alive." Every subject touched on—and in his company they were countless—was lit up by his young enthusiasm, and it is one of the regrets of later years to have watched the fading of that light. Life in general, and Parisian life in particular, is the cause of many such effacements—or defacements; but in C.'s case the pity is particularly great because his gifts were so many, and his fervours so genuine.

Edith Wharton. *A Backward Glance* (1934), p. 285

Now and then . . . an artist appears—J. C. is, in our time, the most striking example—who works in a number of media and whose productions in any one of them are so varied that it is very difficult to perceive any unity of pattern or development. To enclose the collected works of Cocteau one would need not a bookshelf, but a warehouse, and how then could one catalogue such a bewildering assortment of poems, plays in verse, plays in prose, mythologies, natural histories, travels, drawings, tins of film, phonograph records, etc.?

Both the public and the critics feel aggrieved. If they know about the drawing they resent the existence of the drama on which they are not experts, and vice versa, and are tempted to say "a dilettante" and pass on to someone from whom they know better what to expect. His fellow artists who know how difficult it is to succeed in one medium are equally suspicious and jealous of a man who works in several. I must confess that I found myself opening C.'s last volume of poems half hoping that they would be bad. They were not.

W. H. Auden, *Flair*, Feb. 1950, p. 101

That *The Infernal Machine* is frequently interesting cannot be denied. It may even be a success of the theatre—or of a "poetry of the theatre," to use C.'s own term. But it is surely a failure of drama as it is a failure of humanism, and it is a failure as drama *because* it is a failure as humanism, toward which it merely gestures. And the play, precisely because C. has skill, can sum up for us the failure of *theatricalism* as a reliable philosophy for high and serious dramatic art; the failure of the highly touted "histrionic sensibility" as a substitute for the less pretentious—in my opinion, far more difficult—business of playwrights and actors to bring characters to a full life on the stage when the subject to be presented is not simply a game to be played or an entertainment to be whipped up.

John Gassner, *The Theatre in Our Times* (1955),
p. 191

The contrast between Colette and J. C. could scarcely have been greater. What united them was that they were, both the one and the other, exceedingly curious; but they were not curious about the same things. Colette watched; Jean listened, sniffed the wind. He was a hunter, and hidden myths were his quarry; the extraordinary was his ordinary diet. The poetry of the one was in the grass roots; that of the other aimed at the stars. But Colette's probing in the earth reached the soil's heart, whereas C.'s flights sometimes went astray. It is not for me to pass judgment on his work; and besides, I still see its author too clearly through it. I believe that the magic wand so plainly visible at the end of his long poet's fingers did not prevent the magic from appearing when he summoned it, and that if Jean by no means stripped man's heart bare, he did at least expose its wilder beating.

Maurice Goudeket, *The Delights of Growing Old*
(1966), pp. 201–202

J. C. always thought of himself as an artisan, never as a philosopher. . . .As a creative artist he wanted to give form to Beauty, but he did not try to intellectualize it by writing about it, except to call it poetry. And poetry for C was an expression of beauty which could only be shared by those who spontaneously felt the beauty of the craftsmanship involved. To understand poetry as a craft was to participate in the experience of poetry as an expression of beauty. The craft and the mysterious beauty of the transcendent experience were in fact the two inseparable elements of the experience of poetry which C. spent his life trying to communicate to others by fusing them together into a single work of art. If he succeeded, it was undoubtedly with *Orpheus* (1949). . . .

In no other work did C. communicate so successfully the two processes which always accompany the act of creation; the labour pains, fatigue, hard work and drive necessary to give birth to the work of art, and the elimination of the normal concept of time and space which the expression and experience of poetry demands.

David Bancroft, *Meanjin*, March 1973, pp. 73–74

COETZEE, J(ohn) M.

South African novelist and translator (writing in English), b. 9 Feb. 1940, Cape Town

Born in South Africa, C. worked as an applications programer (1962–1963) and a systems programer (1964–1965) in England. He received his M. A. from the University of Cape Town in 1963. From 1968 to 1971 C. was an assistant professor of English at the State University of New York at Buffalo, and he received his Ph. D. from the University of Texas in 1969. In 1972 he became a lecturer in English at the University of Cape Town, where he is professor of literature.

From South Africa one anticipates realistic reportage disguised as fiction that spills forth political anger. Such expectation scarcely prepares the reader for C., with his bizarre imagination depicting psychotic cruelties, for his surrealistic world where violence is elevated into apocalypse. The first response is likely to be horrified revulsion, the motivations being so inhumane, the acts so irrational as to have gone beyond the remedy of pity. C. deliberately explores the inner neurosis that engenders brutality. His work is conceived as pure nightmare, yet there is an underlying alternative perception that the intolerable events are closely linked to the pathology of his country.

His first publication, *Dusklands* (1974), consists of two unrelated stories. The first, "The Vietnam Project," written while C. was in the U. S., is a kind of science fiction. A Pentagon psychologist attempts to give justification to the murderous incidents during the Vietnam War. His lunatic rationalizations infect his own morality, bringing him to a madness that can only be assuaged by an act of irrational violence. The theme, linking violence to a passionate but distorted commitment, presages C.'s later work, as does the structure. The explications are advanced, not by authorial intervention, but by monologue, the self-convicting commentary of the central character.

The second story of *Dusklands* is "The Narrative of Jacobus Coetzee," which is said to be a direct translation of a 1760 diary recording a disastrous exploration into the interior and a calamitous conflict with the natives who inflict harsh cruelties and then in turn are subjected to an even more vicious revenge. The highly detailed descriptions of the bodily sufferings and the passion with which they are inflicted become characteristic of C.'s later fiction.

In the Heart of the Country (1976; pub. in the U.S. as *From the Heart of the Country*, 1982) is set on a remote South African farm and displays C.'s reconstruction of the Boer world leavened by his extreme imagination. A daughter, reconciled to a spinster's role as the servant of her brutal father, is so incensed when he remarries that she murders him twice. One slaughter is a Freudian dream, but each is described in such exact detail that we are unsure which is intended as the reality. The contrivance of the structure makes all events questionable. Each paragraph of first-person narrative is numbered—a tiresome device presumably intended to increase the sense of disjointed experience. There is a question as to whether she is seduced by a servant or raped. The tensions between mistress and servant take on a fierce escalation toward murderous violence. So typical in C.'s work, there is an exactly depicted reality that exists alongside the fanciful neurotic degeneration. In 1976 *In the Heart of the Country* was awarded the CNA Prize, South Africa's highest literary award.

Waiting for the Barbarians (1980) takes C. into a deeper level of perception where violence and eroticism meet. The events take place on the barely defined border between "The Empire" and "The Barbarians." Under the command of an amiable magistrate, the fort survives comfortably until an inspection commanded by a sadist, Colonel Joll, demands an end to such tolerance. The harmless Barbarians are captured and treated with savage barbarity. Moralities are transposed. The magistrate's tentative protests are partly political, but also intimate and instinctive. He finds a strange salvation as he washes the tortured feet of a Barbarian girl. Before long the magistrate is in jail, along with the Barbarian captives. In turn, such are the twists of this metaphor, he becomes a Barbarian, starved and ill-treated until he seems only an animal. But within that experience he learns a deeper truth about survival and the necessities that human dignity requires in the face of "barbarity." C.'s terrible vision, when taken from that metaphoric frontier, is replicated in the present, where the barbarous battle between the confident torturers and the anxious humanitarians continues. *Waiting for the Barbarians* was awarded the Geoffrey Faber Memorial Prize (1980) and the James Tait Black Memorial Prize (1980).

Life and Times of Michael K. (1983) takes further the quest for human dignity in an atrocious society. Michael suffers from an ugly harelip birth deformity that condemns him to public scorn, yet he exposes a defiant resilience. After a violently destructive riot in Cape Town, he takes his dying mother back to the farm of her childhood memories, but she dies on the way. By now conditions have deteriorated and riots have become a full civil war. There are army posts, prison camps, work camps, and the constant oppression of authority. He falls into each trap, and yet in every case he escapes. His very innocence helps him to survive. All he seeks is the permission to cultivate a plot of land, which, in wartime, amounts to treason. After a series of torture and suffering, he ends up in a hospital camp where his determined passive resistance enrages the doctor, whose long, intimate monologue openly expresses C.'s theme. The doctor recognizes in Michael's unyielding stoicism the means of moral survival—the method of challenging a régime that has turned his noble role as healer into that of prison warder. *Life and Times of Michael K.* won the Booker Prize in 1983.

C.'s powerful work has attracted considerable attention. Many Western literary intellectuals adulate his unremitting search for the truths buried deeply in the human psyche. The more radical find his work elitist, in that its subtlety conceals the open denunciations they prefer.

FURTHER WORKS: *Foe* (1987); *A Land Apart: A Contemporary South African Reader* (1987, with André Brink); *White Writing* (1988); *Age of Iron* (1990)

BIBLIOGRAPHY: Penner, A. R., *Countries of the Mind: The Fiction of J. M. C.* (1989); Wright, D. N. T., "Fiction As Foe: The Novels of J. M. C.," *IFR*, 16, 2 (Summer 1989): 113–18; Attwell, D., "The Problem of History in the Fiction of J. M. C.," *PoT*, 11, 3 (Fall 1990): 579–615; Goddard, K., and J. Read, *J. M. C.: A Bibliography* (1990); Attwell, D., "On the Question of Autobiography: Interview with J. M. C.," *Current Writing: Text and Reception in Southern Africa*, 3, 1 (1991): 117–22; Gallagher, S. V., *A Story of South Africa: J. M. C.'s Fiction in Context* (1991); Stephenson, G., "Escaping the Camps: The Idea of Freedom in J. M. C.'s *Life and Times of Michael K.*," *CNIE*, 4, 1 (Spring 1991): 77–87; Attwell, D., ed., *Doubling the Point: J. M. C., Essays and Interviews* (1992)

—JOHN POVEY

COHEN, Leonard

Canadian poet and novelist (writing in English), b. 21 Sept. 1934, Montreal, Que.

C. grew up in the wealthy Westmount district of Montreal, a milieu he satirized in his first novel. He was educated at McGill University and, briefly, at Columbia, in New York. Since the early 1960s his places of residence have included a Zen monastery in California, a Greek island, and the native city to which he returns (in his words) to renew his "neurotic affiliations." His travels, his numerous romantic affairs, and his career as a popular entertainer (singer/guitarist) have helped to surround him with an aura of mystery and aloofness.

C.'s personal mythology has been influenced by Jewish and Eastern mysticism, and by rapid changes in social attitudes following World War II. These included the "angry young men" in Britain and the beat generation of GINSBERG, KEROUAC, *et al.* in the U.S. C.'s first collection, *Let Us Compare Mythologies* (1956), which helped to mark the end of the modernist era of Pound and Eliot, centered on similarities and differences in Hebrew, Greek, and Christian traditions. In poetry and fiction, C. protests against social conformity and urges a very personal and erotic metaphysic, seen as a paradoxical union of flesh and spirit.

Another persistent theme is the importance of art, and the contrast between its permanence and the impermanence of life. The latter is characterized by change, loss, and decay. Scarring becomes a central metaphor for life in C.'s first novel, *The Favorite Game* (1963), a *Kunstlerroman* in which the artist's spiritual odyssey brings him to the verge of an adult understanding of suffering, loss, and guilt.

Beautiful Losers (1966) is C.'s masterwork to date. The novel depicts time and life itself as one vast orgasm: the human body is the basis of human experience, the erotic is at the core of the spiritual. The novel presents a resounding yes to the question posed by its narrator: "Is matter holy?" Both novels attack the problems of a technological and manipulative society.

C.'s vision is expressed through a variety of traditional and experimental forms. His mood, typically, is Rabelaisian and lyric, grotesque and delicate. He has frequently been called a "black

romantic." C. urges self-abnegation while condoning self-indulgence; he deprecates and glorifies the artist-prophet. His latest book, *Death of a Lady's Man* (1978), combines fragments of poetry and philosophic commentary with reflections on the validity of these same fragments. The poet has become his own exegete, in what his narrator calls this "Final Revision of My Life in Art." The poet declines to judge whether his efforts represent genius or junk, but calls himself the only honest man in town.

This honesty, typically, is deceptive and multifaceted. Yet C.'s work embodies a creative iconoclasm that is essentially moral, and a vision of the human condition that holds all the paradoxes of our experience. His artist-seer is a modern Everyman, swinging the maelstrom.

FURTHER WORKS: *The Spice-Box of Earth* (1961); *Flowers for Hitler* (1964); *Parasites of Heaven* (1966); *Selected Poems, 1956–1968* (1968); *The Energy of Slaves* (1972)

BIBLIOGRAPHY: Ondaatje, M., *L. C.* (1970); Morley, P., *The Immoral Moralists: Hugh MacLennan and L. C.* (1972); Gnarowsky, M., ed., *L. C.: The Artist and His Critics* (1976); Scobie, S., *L. C.* (1978); Holden, S., "A Haunting by Spector," *Rolling Stone* (26 Jan. 1978): 17

—PATRICIA MORLEY

COLETTE, Sidonie-Gabrielle

French novelist and essayist, b. 28 Jan. 1873, Saint-Sauveur-en-Puisaye; d. 3 Aug. 1954, Paris

Reared in a small Burgundian village, C. spent her early years in a household that was dominated by the presence of plants, animals, and, above all, her mother, Sido. In 1893 she married Henry Gauthier-Villars, better known as Willy, who was a prominent figure in the Parisian publishing world and a habitué of the demimonde, to which he introduced his bride. Fifteen years her senior, Willy, for whom literature was essentially a commercial venture, published mildly risqué novels that were ghostwritten by his "stable" of hacks, usually young, impoverished writers who badly needed the pittance he offered them. Pressing his wife, too, into service, Willy locked C. in her room for four hours every day (later she said that she had not really objected) with instructions to write her girlhood memoirs. Further, he informed her that what his public liked best were piquant details and titillating situations. C. obliged and over the next several years wrote four "Claudine" novels, which were an immense commercial success, spreading Willy's fame far and wide (the books were published under his name) and filling his coffers handsomely.

Separated from Willy in 1906 (the divorce became final in 1910), C., who had no money of her own, supported herself for several years by performing as a mime and dancer in various Parisian music halls. She continued to write, however, and in 1910 published *La vagabonde* (*The Vagabond*, 1954), the story of a music-hall artist who, although she yearns for the comforting presence of a man, rejects with reluctance a suitable candidate and continues on her lonely but independent way. C. herself followed a somewhat different path, for in 1910 she married the aristocratic Henry de Jouvenel, newspaper editor and diplomat, from whom

Sidonie-Gabrielle Colette

she was divorced in 1925. Influenced no doubt by Jouvenel, C. turned to journalism during the war years but returned to fiction in 1920 with the publication of *Chéri* (*Chéri*, 1929), the novel that firmly established her reputation in France. Two years later she published *La maison de Claudine* (1922; *My Mother's House*, 1953), the first of several books that are highly stylized evocations of her childhood. In 1925 she began a liaison with Maurice Goudeket, who was seventeen years her junior. They were married in 1935, the year C. was elected to the Belgian Royal Academy. Lavishly praised by critics in the 1940s as the greatest woman writer France had ever possessed, C. was the recipient of numerous honors; she was elected to the Goncourt Academy in 1945 and named Grand Officer of the Legion of Honor in 1953. Despite the severe arthritis that made it difficult for her to move about during her final years, she supervised the publication of her *Œuvres complètes* (1949–50; complete works). At her death, she was accorded a state funeral.

The fifty-odd volumes that constitute C.'s work tend to fall into two general categories. First, there is her fiction, which nearly always deals with the subject of love, a harsh, fatalistic force that her protagonists—women, mostly—both desire and fear. Yearning for companionship, they wish to submit wholly to a beloved. At the same time, however, they dread the renunciation of independence that such submission implies. Deftly and variously, C. works out the consequences of this dilemma in novel after novel.

The men in C.'s fiction are generally feckless and shallow. Often they are nothing more than the objects of female desire.

Indeed, one of C.'s originalities is to portray the woman as subject and the man as object. Unable to cope with the complexity of life, several of her male characters commit suicide. Her women, on the other hand, are resilient and strong. They are survivors. Unlike their male counterparts, they "pick up the pieces" after a disappointment of one kind or another (frequently the breakup of a love affair) and adjust to a new situation. They display, to use C.'s phrase, "banal heroism," a characteristic of all her women who, although they may live on the fringe of society as music-hall dancers or courtesans, have an inflexible sense of propriety and morality, which of course has little to do with any official code of morals.

The novel that numerous readers have considered quintessential C. is *Chéri*. With consummate skill, C. here relates the story of Léa, a highly successful demimondaine who, nearing the age of fifty, accepts a rich, handsome, and self-centered young man some thirty years her junior (called Chéri, or darling) as her lover. In prose that is deft, restrained, and perfectly suited to the subject, C. traces the history of their liaison. Confronted one day with her own image in a mirror, Léa is shocked into recognizing the fact that she is growing old. At first she rebels. However, when she hears Chéri speak of their love in the past tense, she realizes that he too has sensed the distance that her age, which is becoming increasingly evident, has put between them. With sinking heart, she accepts her changed state and, renouncing love, gently dismisses Chéri. Penetration of insight and mastery of prose make *Chéri* one of C.'s most remarkable as well as most popular books.

In the 1920s and 1930s critics, nearly all of whom were male, tended to ignore or disparage the subject matter of C.'s novels while at the same time extolling her literary style. They agreed that C. was a superb stylist and often characterized her as a kind of literary Chanel with an infallible sense of the rhythms of the French language. More recent critics, many of whom are female, have sensed in this emphasis on C.'s style a certain patronizing attitude on the part of male critics. They appreciate C. less for her exquisitely mannered prose (rather too ornate for some tastes) than for her portrayal of women who seek to make their own way in a world in which the odds tend to be stacked against them.

Into the second broad category of C.'s work fall those books that may best be described as part memoir-narrative, part lyric essay. Female critics, focusing their attention on C.'s fiction, seldom discuss these books, which male critics consistently call C.'s greatest. If C.'s fiction is a reflection of the impure world to which Willy had introduced his bride, the books of reminiscences are dominated by the presence of Sido, whom C. called "the principal figure of my whole life." C.'s depiction of her childhood in such books as *La maison de Claudine, Sido* (1929; *Sido*, 1953), and *Mes apprentissages* (1936; *My Apprenticeship*, 1957) is no mere recollection of past days. Everything associated with her early life is bathed in the luminous light of a paradisiacal vision. Here C. fashions a world of purity, her version of the Garden of Eden. The lyricism that flows through her work reaches its finest expression in the pages that evoke her childhood and nature. To a remarkable degree the aging C. identified with Sido, finding in her mother an idealized image of herself. The quality that C. most admired in Sido was her constant delight in the natural world. The sense of discovery and wonderment is precisely the quality that illuminates two of C.'s last books, *L'étoile vesper* (1946; *The Evening Star*, 1973) and *Le fanal bleu* (1949; *The Blue Lantern*, 1963). Both are journals in which C. jots down thoughts, impressions, and reminiscences in a prose that is a model of elegance.

Viewed within the context of French literary history, C. belongs to the grandest of traditions. She is essentially a moralist whose view of love is as lucid and unsentimental as that of any of the famous 17th-c. writers of maxims. Throughout her fiction she elaborates an ethics based on self-knowledge and acceptance of one's limitations. And in her books of sketches and meditations she cultivates, as no French author had done before her, except perhaps the 16th-c. essayist Montaigne, the art of growing old and the art of finding beauty and joy in ordinary things.

FURTHER WORKS: *Claudine à l'école* (1900; *Claudine at School*, 1930); *Claudine à Paris* (1901; *Claudine in Paris*, 1958); *Claudine en ménage* (1902; *Claudine Married*, 1960); *Claudine s'en va* (1903; *The Innocent Wife*, 1934); *Minne* (1904); *Les égarements de Minne* (1905); *Sept dialogues de bêtes* (1904; *Barks and Purrs*, 1913); *La retraite sentimentale* (1907); *Les vrilles de la vigne* (1908); *L'ingénue libertine* (1909; *The Gentle Libertine*, 1931); *L'envers du music-hall* (1913; *Music-hall Sidelights*, 1958); *L'entrave* (1913; *Recaptured*, 1931); *La paix chez les bêtes* (1916; *Cats, Dogs, and I*, 1924); *Les heures longues* (1917); *Les enfants dans les ruines* (1917); *Dans la foule* (1918); *Mitsou* (1919; *Mitsou*, 1930); *Celle qui en revient* (1921); *Le voyage égoïste* (1922); *Le blé en herbe* (1923; *Ripening Seed*, 1955); *Rêverie du nouvel an* (1923); *Aventures quotidiennes* (1924); *La femme cachée* (1924); *L'enfant et les sortilèges* (1925; *The Boy and the Magic*, 1965); *La fin de Chéri* (1926; *The Last of Chéri*, 1932); *La naissance du jour* (1928; *A Lesson in Love*, 1932); *La seconde* (1929; *The Other One*, 1931); *Douze dialogues de bêtes* (1930; *Creatures Great and Small*, 1957); *Renée la vagabonde* (1931); *Prisons et paradis* (1932); *Paradis terrestres* (1932); *Ces plaisirs . . .* (1932; [after first ed., title changed to *Le pur et l'impur*, 1932]; *The Pure and the Impure*, 1967); *La chatte* (1933; *The Cat*, 1936); *Duo* (1934; *Duo*, 1935); *Splendeur des papillons* (1936); *Bella-Vista* (1937; "Bella-Vista," 1959); *Le toutounier* (1939); *Chambre d'hôtel* (1940; *Chance Acquaintances*, 1955); *Journal à rebours* (1941; *Looking Backwards*, 1975); *Mes cahiers* (1941); *Julie de Carneilhan* (1941; *Julie de Carneilhan*, 1952); *De ma fenêtre* (1942); *Le képi* (1943; "The Kepi," 1959); *Paris de ma fenêtre* (1944); *Gigi* (1944; *Gigi*, 1952); *Le tendron* (1944); *La dame du photographe* (1944); *Chats* (1945); *Correspondance de C. et de F. Jammes* (1945); *Trois . . . six . . . neuf* (1946); *Belles saisons* (1947); *Pour un herbier* (1948; *For a Flower Album*, 1959); *Trait pour trait* (1949); *Journal intermittent* (1949); *La fleur de l'âge* (1949); *Chats de C.* (1950); *En pays connu* (1950); *Lettres à Hélène Picard* (1958); *Lettres à M. Moreno* (1959); *Lettres de la vagabonde* (1961); *Lettres au Petit Corsaire* (1963); *Lettres à ses pairs* (1973). FURTHER WORKS IN ENGLISH: *Short Novels* (1951); *7 by C.* (1955); *The Tender Shoot and Other Stories* (1959); *Earthly Paradise* (1966); *Places* (1970); *The Thousand and One Mornings* (1973); *C. at the Movies: Criticism and Screenplays* (1980); *Letters from Colette* (1980)

BIBLIOGRAPHY: Crossland, M., *Madame C.: A Provincial in Paris* (1953); Goudeket, M., *Close to C.* (1957); Marks, E., *C.* (1960); Davies, M., *C.* (1961); Mudrick, M., "*C., Claudine and Willy*," *HudR*, 16 (1963): 559–72; Goudeket, M., *The Delights of Growing Old* (1966); Biolley-Godino, M., *L'homme object chez C.* (1972); Crossland, M., *C.—The Difficulty of Loving: A Biography* (1973); Cottrell, R., *C.* (1974); Mitchell, Y., *C.: A Taste for Life* (1975); Gass, W., "Three Photos of C.," *NYRB*, 14 April 1977: 11–19; Sarde, M., *C., libre et entravée* (1978); Ward, N., *C.* (1987); Fliger, J., *C. and the Fantom Subject of Autobiography* (1992); Huffer, C., *Another C.: The Question of Gendered Writing* (1992); Strand, D., *C.: A Study of the Short Fiction* (1995); Stewart, J., *C.* (1996)

—ROBERT D. COTTRELL

COLOMBIAN LITERATURE

The literature in Colombia of the 20th c. has been dominated by two writers: José Eustacio RIVERA and Gabriel GARCÍA MÁRQUEZ. Few other writers have established truly national and international reputations, although Colombia has a proud tradition in poetry, and a group of outstanding modern novelists that includes Héctor Rojas Herazo (b. 1922), Fanny Buitrago (b. 1945), Albalucía Angel (b. 1939), Rafael Humberto MORENO-DURÁN, Manuel MEJÍA VALLEJO, Manuel ZAPATA OLIVELLA, Gustavo ALVAREZ GARDEAZÁBAL, and Alvaro CEPEDA SAMUDIO.

The century was opened amidst a cultural identity crisis, as intellectuals debated whether Colombian literature should be "European" or "national" in its vision and sources. A group of writers identified as *modernistas*, located mostly in Santa Fe de Bogotá, argued in favor of a cosmopolitan aesthetic program that some intellectuals considered too European in conception to be considered authentically Colombian. The major *modernista* poets were José Asunción Silva (1865–1896), who wrote at the end of the 19th c., and Guillermo Valencia (1873–1943), who wrote at the beginning of the 20th c. The strongest opposition to this fin de siècle *modernismo* came from the region of Antioquia, from writers such as Tomás CARRASQUILLA, Francisco de Paula Rendón (1855–1917), and Alfonso Castro (1878–1943). Carrasquilla set forth an aesthetic program that included a sense of modernity and regional focus. According to Carrasquilla, such a literary program would constitute a literary independence for Colombia. In contrast with the cosmopolitan tastes of the *modernistas*, Carrasquilla defended a realist-naturalist type of fiction that carefully located characters in their regional environment. His major novels were *Frutos de mitierra* (1896; fruits of my native land), *Grandeza* (1910; greatness), and *La marquesa de Yolombó* (1926; the marquise of Yolombó). These works, as well as other novels and short fiction, were satirical critiques of contemporary Colombian society and nostalgic evocations of an idyllic, rural 19th-c. Colombia.

In addition to Carrasquilla, the most recognized turn-of-the-century novelists were Eustaquio Palacios (1830–1898), Soledad Acosta de Samper (1833–1913), José Manuel Marroquín (1827–1928), and José María Vargas Vila (1860–1933). Palacios, Acosta de Samper, and Marroquín were committed to the political ideas of a conservative political regime identified in Colombia as the Regeneration. Palacios and Marroquín wrote novels of local color and local customs; Acosta de Samper was more concerned with essays and bibliographies, although she did publish several historical novels that contained lengthy political and philosophical statements in the works. Vargas Vila was one of Colombia's most prolific novelists and, although he was one of Colombia's most fecund and widely read novelists ever, he never wrote a work considered "major." His novels contain scandalous plots, typically embellished with sexual practices considered taboo during the period, thus making them prohibited reading for generations of Colombian students. They also were viewed as literarily unacceptable for Regeneration Intellectuals and their Conservative heirs.

The major novelist of the 1920s was unquestionably José Eustasio Rivera. His writing responded to the nationalistic attitudes predominant in the 1920s and the attempts to establish a "national culture." This nationalistic project found its expression in the work of the pioneers of Colombian theater: Antonio Alvarez Lleras (1892–1956) and Luis Enrique Osorio (1896–1966). Rivera's now classic novel *La vorágine* (1924; *The Vortex*, 1935) was a timely response to this nationalistic period, and remained the model for several generations of Colombian novelists. It relates the story of the narrator-protagonist's flight to the jungle with his lover and his discovery of social injustice among the indigenous workers exploited there. Other novelists of the period, all traditionalists in theme and technique, were Arturo Suárez (1887–1977), Luis López de Mesa (1884–1967), Daniel Samper Ortega (1895–1943), and Gregorio Sánchez Gómez (1895–1942).

The 1930s and 1940s were dominated by the poets. The predominant literary activity of the 1930s was the founding of the *Piedra y Cielo* (Stone and Sky) group of poets in 1939 by the poet Jorge Rojas (b. 1911). The poets Rojas, Eduardo CARRANZA, Arturo Camacho Ramírez (b. 1910), Carlos Martín (b. 1914), Tomás Vargas Osorio (1908–1941), and Gerardo Valencia (b. 1911) are commonly placed in this generation of writers, who espoused inspiration from the poetry of the Spaniards Juan Ramón JIMÉNEZ, Rafael ALBERTI, and Gerardo Diego (1896–1987). Active novelists during the 1930s were César Uribe Piedrahita (1897–1951), Eduardo Zalamea Board (1907–1963), and Bernardo Arias Trujillo (1903–1938). These three writers sustained patterns established by Rivera. All three addressed issues of national identity and social conflict in a rural setting. Unlike Rivera, however, Uribe Piedrahita, Zalamea Borda, and Arias Trujillo exhibit a sharp awareness of oral culture and interest in assimilating it into their national novel projects. In 1944 the *Cántico* group (in obvious homage to the Spanish poet Jorge Guillén) was established by Jaime Ibáñez (b. 1919). The major novelists of the 1940s were Rafael Gómez Picón (b. 1900), Ernesto Camargo Martínez (b. 1910), Jaime Ardila Casamitjana (b. 1919), and Ibáñez. They addressed middle-class concerns to a middle-class readership, communicating a sense of the emotional and psychological experience of Colombia's middle class in this period. They were the pioneers of the modern novel in Colombia.

The first truly recognized modern novelistic production to have impact in Colombia, however, was constituted by three novels: *La hojarasca* (1955; *Leafstorm*, 1972) by García Márquez, *La casa grande* (1962; *La Casa Grande*, 1991), by Alvaro Cepeda Samudio, and *Respirando el Verano* (1962; breathing the summer) by Héctor Rojas Herazo. All three of these novelists, who rightfully consider themselves patently Faulknerian, brought the standard narrative strategies commonly associated with the modern novel to Colombia. Each of the three relates stories of Colombia's decadent aristocracy, adopting a plethora of Faulknerian narrative strategems. *La hojarasca* and *La casa grande* are related to the presence of the American Fruit Company on the Caribbean coast. The first deals with the effects of this foreign presence in a formerly traditional town; the latter dramatizes the massacre of striking banana workers by government soldiers, a historical event of 1928.

Significant contributions to the modern novel in Colombia during the 1960s were Manuel Mejía Vallejo's *El día señalado* (1964; the appointed day), García Márquez's *Cien años de soledad* (1967; *One Hundred Years of Solitude*, 1970), and Rojas Herazo's *En noviembre llega el arzobispo* (1967; the archbishop arrives in November). Each of these novels is considered the major work by

its respective author. Less known modern works that were highly experimental in narrative technique were *Después de la noche* (1964; after the night) by Eutiquio Leal (b. 1928), *El terremoto* (1966; the earthquake) by Germán Pinzón (b. 1934), and *Los días más felices del año* (1966; the happiest days of the year) by Humberto Navarro (b. 1932).

By the mid-1960s, modern and postmodern Colombian novelists were fully immersed in the writing of international fiction, rather than the traditional, regional, and oral cultures. Numerous factors had transformed Colombia and its novel. The irreverent *Nadaístas*, primarily poets, successfully scandalized the still predominantly conservative and conventional cultural establishment. Whether or not the poetry and proclamations of Gonzalo Arango (dates n.a.) and his *Nadaísta* cohorts will be judged of permanent value remains to be seen. Nevertheless, their rebellious textual and extratextual postures had a profound impact on literary tastes and paved the way for ongoing modern and postmodern literary activity in Colombia. The *Nadaísta* novel prize provided an outlet for the publication and distribution of the most experimental fiction of the time, even though the national concern for understanding and evaluating the civil war of the 1950s (La Violencia) was deemed much more important than novels of technical experimentation.

The novel of major impact during this period was García Márquez's *Cien años de soledad*, and the most resonant literary event of the 1960s was the international heralding of this novel. A second round of the García Márquez phenomenon took place in 1982, when he received the Nobel Prize. During the late 1960s and early 1970s, aspiring writers in Colombia often spoke of the "shadow" that García Márquez cast upon them. The general crisis of literary MODERNISM experienced in the West had a double edge in Colombia: On the one hand, García Márquez produced in 1967 one of the most celebrated texts of the supposedly exhausted modern tradition of the West; on the other hand, this modern product enjoyed such an enormous success that it made fiction writing afterward a formidable task in Colombia. By the mid-1970s the shadow of García Márquez's Macondo proved less burdensome as several writers, such as Moreno-Durán, Albalucía Angel, Gustavo Alvarez Gardeazábal, and Marco Tulio Aguilera Garramuño (b. 1949) found new, non-Macondian directions for the Colombian novel. Previously marginal and repressed discourses surfaced in the 1970s and 1980s as part of a new, postmodern attitude. They were discourses not necessarily related to the novel of La Violencia or Macondo.

García Márquez's may well be the most significant enterprise of modern fiction by a single author. Since the publication of *Cien años de soledad*, a pinnacle of the modern novel in Colombia and Latin America, García Márquez has written four novels: *El otoño del patriarca* (1975; *The Autumn of the Patriarch*, 1976), *Crónica de una muerte anunciada* (1981; *Chronicle of a Death Foretold*, 1981), *El amor en los tiempos del Cólera* (1985; *Love in the Time of Cholera*, 1988), and *El general en su laberinto* (1990; *The General in His Labyrinth*, 1990). In his total fiction, García Márquez appropriated some of the narrative techniques of modernism (such as fragmentation, collage, and multiple points of view) and used these techniques in what is an identifiable modernist project—the seeking of order and the expression of the ineffable in a world lacking order and waiting to be named. In many ways, all of García Márquez's novels published since 1975 represent a rupture from the fiction of Macondo. His recent novels are far less complex in structure than *El otoño del patriarca*, but nevertheless represent a continuation of his modern project.

Several writers have assimilated the strategems of modern fiction, among them Fanny Buitrago, Manuel Zapata Olivella, and Héctor Rojas Herazo. In addition to her short fiction, Buitrago has published the novels *El hostigante verano de los dioses* (1963; the harrassing summer of the gods), *Cola de zorro* (1970; fox tail), *Los pañamanes* (1979; *the pañamanes*), and *Los amores de Afrodita* (1983; Afrodite's loves). Much of her fiction emanates from the culture of the Caribbean coast. Several voices narrate *El hostigante verano de los dioses*, the totality of which communicates the state of boredom endured by a spiritually exhausted generation of young people. *Cola de zorro* is Buitrago's most complex work and shares some of the generational attitudes found in her first novel: The characters lack clear direction and their existence tends to be boring. It deals with human relations within the context of a large, extended family. *Los pañamanes*, set on a Caribbean island, portrays the conflicts between, on the one hand, the legends and traditions in a disappearing oral culture on the island and, on the other hand, modernization and its "beautiful people" that are taking over. *In Los amores de Afrodita* Buitrago recurs to popular culture in a manner reminiscent of Manuel PUIG.

Zapata Olivella has published six novels, including two works during the 1980s, *Changó, el gran putas* (1983; Changó, the big s.o.b.) and *El fusilamiento del diablo* (1986; the shooting of the devil). His most ambitious novel, the massive *Changó, el gran putas*, is broad in scope, spanning three continents and six centuries of African and African-American history. Zapata Olivella synthesizes a variety of voices and oral cultures in this saga of a people's striving for liberation. *El fusilamiento del diablo* is a historical novel about the death of an African-Colombian political leader.

Rojas Herazo has published a trilogy of novels consisting of the aforementioned *Respirando el verano* and *El noviembre llega el arzobispo*, and *Celia se pudre* (1986; Celia rots). These novels evoke the premodern, oral world of Celia, the central character of this trilogy, and her family. *Celia se pudre* is the summa of the world of Cedrón, the small town on the Caribbean coast where the three novels take place.

A group of younger writers has experimented with new directions for the Colombian novel in the 1970s and 1980s. Besides Moreno-Durán, Angel, and Aguilera Garramuño, Darío Jaramillo Agudelo (b. 1947), Rodrigo Parra Sandoval (b. 1937), and Alberto Duque López (b. 1943) have pursued an innovative and postmodern project during this period. Cosmopolitan in interests, most of them have preferred to write abroad. Moreno-Durán has published four novels and a volume of short stories; the roots of this work are not found in the empirical reality of Colombia but rather in modernist literature; they are all playful novels whose linguistic excesses make language their main subject. Angel's work has changed dramatically since the publication of her first work, *Los girasoles en invierno* (1970; sunflowers in the winter); her recent fiction, *Misiá Señora* (1982; the missus) and *Las andariegas* (1984; the travelers), is part of a feminist project that emanates directly from feminist theory and fiction. Aguilera Garramuño began his writing career with a self-conscious reaction against the work of García Márquez in his parodic *Breve historia de todas las cosas* (1975; brief history of everything); in *Paraísos hostiles* (1985; hostile paradises), a dialogue on fiction and philosophy, he moves away from the context of Colombia and García Márquez, but the continues in the metafictional mode. Jaramillo Agudelo's only novel, *La muerte de Alec* (1983; the death of Alec), is also a metafiction—in this case, a self-conscious metafiction on the function of literature.

Mateo el flautista (1968; Mateo the flutist) is an experimental novel that offers two versions of the life of Mateo, the protagonist.

Contemporary Colombian theater and poetry have also undergone a renovation. In theater, Enrique BUENAVENTURA and Santiago García (b. 1943) have been the main innovators. Buenaventura's *En la diestra de Dios Padre* (1958; on the righthand side of our father) and García's *Guadalupe, años sin cuenta* (1975; Guadalupe, uncounted years) are elaborate reworkings of previous texts. The new poets who have renovated poetic language in Colombia include Juan Gustavo Cobo Borda (b. 1948), María Mercedes Carranza (b. 1945), Giovanni Quessep (b. 1939), and Darío Jaramillo Agudelo (dates n.a.).

BIBLIOGRAPHY: Franco, J., *The Modern Culture of Latin America: Society and the Artist* (1967); Brushwood, J. S., *The Spanish American Novel: A Twentieth-Century Survey* (1975); Pope, R. D., "*La vorágine:* la autobiografía de un intelectual," in R. D. Pope, ed., *The Analysis of Literary Texts: Current Trends in Methodology* (1980): 256–67; Echevarría, R. González, "*Cien años de soledad* Novel As Myth and Archive," *MLN*, 99, 2 (March 1984): 358–80; Ortega, J., *Poetics of Change: The New Spanish-American Narrative* (1984); Magnarelli, S., *The Lost Rib: Female Characters in the Spanish-American Novel* (1985); Lewis, M. A., *Treading the Ebony Path: Ideology and Violence in Contemporary Afro-Colombian Prose Fiction* (1987); Gass, W. H., "The First Seven Pages of the Boom," *LALR*, 15, 29 (Jan.-June 1987): 33–56; McMurray, G. R., *Spanish American Writing since 1941: A Critical Survey* (1987); Alonso, C. J., *The Spanish American Regional Novel: Modernity and Autochthony* (1990)

—RAYMOND LESLIE WILLIAMS

COMPTON-BURNETT, Ivy

English novelist; b. 5 June 1884, Pinner; d. 27 Aug. 1969, London

C.-B. was the eldest daughter in the second marriage of Dr. James Compton-Burnett, a celebrated homeopathic physician, and grew up in a large family of brothers and sisters in the southern seacoast town of Hove. In 1902 she entered the Royal Holloway College, a branch of the University of London near Egham, where she studied classics (especially the Greek tragedies, whose influence can be seen in all her work) and from which she was graduated in 1907. In 1911 her first novel, *Dolores*, appeared, but it was not until the publication of *Pastors and Masters* in 1925 that she was fully committed to a writing career and began to bring out a novel regularly every two or three years. She had settled in London in 1915, and lived the rest of her life there, sharing a home in South Kensington for many years with Margaret Jourdain, an art and decoration expert, until Jourdain's death in 1951. Although never widely read, C.-B.'s critical fame continued to grow; in 1967 she was made Dame Commander of the British Empire, and in 1968, the year before her death, she was named one of the ten Companions of Literature by the Royal Society of Literature.

To describe one of her novels is to describe them all, as the similarity of the titles themselves indicates: from *Pastors and Masters* (1925), through *Brothers and Sisters* (1929), her work most imbued with the Greek tragic spirit, to the brilliant high comedy of *Manservant and Maidservant* (1947), and finally to the valedictory *A God and His Gifts* (1963) and the posthumously published *The Last and the First* (1971). They take place in a large, often penurious late-Victorian or Edwardian rural household, or, in two or three instances, in schools or colleges. Wherever they take place, their world is the same, a world in which the characters, whether masters or children or servants, constantly engage in sophisticated, witty dialogue, while the background events are, in complete contrast, dark and deep, and have to do with incest, illegitimacy, bigamy, dire secrets, and machinations. It is a strange combination of Sophocles and Jane Austen, though it is more for her comedy than for her ethics that she is read. Her cast of comic characters is huge: dolts, hypocrites, affected spinsters, and platitudinous parsons. Since her books are at least ninety percent dialogue, "something between a novel and a play," as she herself said, the arbitrary plots become relatively unimportant, and can be summed up in a phrase: There are secrets, and they are brought to light.

Curiosity is thus a dominant trait of her characters, particularly apparent in the chorus-like friends and neighbors, innocent and sometimes not-so-innocent bystanders, occasionally foolish but often alarmingly shrewd, who flock to the central household at each new catastrophe. The novels also concern power, and the catastrophes are usually precipitated by a tyrannical figure in the household, male or female, young or old, who is able to assert his will because he is stronger-willed than anyone else around, or because he controls the purse strings. Some of the tyrants are rather attractive figures, more are not; a few seem to learn a lesson, but most continue to pursue their vigorous egotistical path unscathed to the end. The tyrants themselves are without wit, while wit is the only weapon against them available to their dependents. It is ineffectual, but self-preservative, and the more desperate, the funnier.

A character in *Daughters and Sons* (1937) says, "Books are very like plants. They are better, the more they are weeded, and they come up out of each other and are all the same." To those who admire her sameness, C.-B. is one of the greatest of novelists; her very limitations of scene and subject account for her startling depth. To those who find her too circumscribed or obsessional, she is a novelist who must be ranked as minor or eccentric. Even among her admirers there are arguments over her essential outlook. Is she a cynic, in that she sees that goodness does not prevail, that power does; that intelligence and kindness do not protect one, in fact render one vulnerable; that human nature is not a pretty thing? Or is her outlook, after all, kinder, as in her compassion for the more pathetic victims of the tyrant, especially children and governesses and companions? Her austerity and objectivity make it hard to answer these questions. But of her greatest gift there can be no question: she is, in the line of Congreve, Thomas Love Peacock (1785–1866), Wilde, and Ronald FIRBANK (1886–1926), one of the masters of comedy, of paradox and epigram, of the ridiculous, preposterous, and absurd.

FURTHER WORKS: *Men and Wives* (1931); *More Women Than Men* (1933); *A House and Its Head* (1935); *A Family and a Fortune* (1939); *Parents and Children* (1941); *Elders and Betters* (1944); *Two Worlds and Their Ways* (1949); *Darkness and Day* (1951); *The Present and the Past* (1953); *Mother and Son* (1955); *A Father and His Fate* (1957); *A Heritage and its History* (1959); *The Mighty and Their Fall* (1961)

BIBLIOGRAPHY: Liddell, R., *The Novels of I. C.-B.* (1955); Baldanza, F., *I. C.-B.* (1964); Burkhart, C., *I. C.-B.* (1965); Burkhart, C., ed., *The Art of I. C.-B.* (1972); Sprigge, E., *The Life of I. C.-B.* (1973); Powell, V., *A C.-B. Compendium* (1973); Spurling, H., *Ivy When Young* (1974); Burkhart, C., *Herman and Nancy and Ivy* (1977); Burkhart, C., ed., special C.-B. issue, *TCL*, 25 (1979)

—CHARLES BURKHART

CONDE, Alfredo

Spanish novelist, short-story writer, journalist, and poet (writing in Galician and Spanish), b. 5 Jan. 1945, Allariz

Born and educated in Galicia, Spain's northwestern coastal region, C. studied naval operations in the College of Advanced Naval Studies in La Coruña and history and geography at the University of Santiago de Compostela. Work experiences include maritime posts with several Spanish companies, fifteen years of teaching in private schools, and Galician governmental service in its Cultural and Sports Department from 1987 to 1990. Politically active, C. helped form the Galeguista Independiente (Independent Galician) Socialist party, and serves as a deputy in the Galician Parliament. His journalistic writings appear in *El Correo Gallego* and other regional newspapers. C.'s novels have won multiple prizes in Spain, including the prestigious Nadal Literary Prize in 1991.

A dedicated Galician novelist, C.'s subjects and settings never stray far from his homeland, depicting the ocean, regional lore, and local history. Several of his books were first written in Galician, then later translated by the author himself into Spanish. The first such pairing was *Musica-Sacra: narracions e outros contos* (Sacred Music, Narrations and Other Stories) whose Galician version came out in 1989, followed a year later by his Spanish translation, *Música Sacra* (1990). Likewise, one of his most successful books began as the Galician *Xa vai o Griffon no vento* (1985; The Griffon Has Gone with the Wind), followed in Spanish as *El Griffon* (1987).

Reflecting C.'s wide knowledge of and fondness for naval adventure, Galician settings, and European history, *El Griffon* juxtaposes three narratives and time periods. All even-numbered chapters recount the travels of a 16th-c. "Visitador" (Inspector) of the Spanish Inquisition who is sent to Santiago de Compostela, one of Europe's oldest and most important pilgrimage sites. Although charged with eradicating hereticism and banning forbidden books, this Galician sailing knight cloaked in drab religious garb speaks half a dozen foreign languages and manages to rescue shiploads of contraband books and to free heretics. The odd-numbered chapters narrate misadventures of a Galician of another sort, a contemporary, fiftyish visiting ("Visitante," a counterpoint to the Inquisition's "Visitador") professor in Aix-en-Provence, who stumbles unprepared into class and into bed with his female students. He claims to be writing a novel about a Galician version of the mythological Griffon who has a lion's body and an eel's head, in contrast to the traditional eagle's head. This phantasmic and phallic Griffon never materializes, but it proves to be a useful device for kindling interest among the women professors and students.

Experimental narrative characterizes *Los otros días* (1991; Other Days). Completely distinct from *El Griffon's* multilayered, third-person, and epistolary narration, the first-person protagonist in *Los otros días* only concerns himself with his own world, memories and musings as he faces death from Parkinson's disease. Common features among all of C's novels include narrative and memory manipulations and the undeniable presence of Galician customs, heritage and identity. These tendencies distinguish him foremost as a Galician writer who is making strides in reaching the rest of Spain and overseas.

FURTHER WORKS: *Mencer de luas* (1968); *Mementos de vivos* (1974); *Come e bebe que o barco e do amo* (1978); *Contubernio Catro do Tome S.* (1978); *Breixo* (1981); *Memoria de Noa* (1982); *O contubernio* (1987); *Mementos de vivos*(1988); *O barco* (1995); *Siempre me matan* (1995); *A casa de Adara* (1996)

BIBLIOGRAPHY: Martinmaestro, A., "The Spanish Novel in 1984," *ALEC*, 10, 1 (1985): 123-41; Blanco Rodríguez, L., "Léxico de naútica na narrativa de A. C.," *Homenaxe o profesor Constantino García* (1991): 67-72; Platas Tasende, A. M., and L. Iglesias Feijoo, "A. C. y los laberintos de la memoria," *ALEC*, 18, 2 (1993): 345-53; Blanco Rodríguez, L., "La música en la narrativa de A. C.: Estudio léxico," *Scripta Philologica in Memoriam Manuel Taboada Cid* (1996): 805-12; Baujin, J. A., *Otro visitador del Griffon* (1996)

—JOY B. LANDEIRA

CONDE (ABELLÁN), Carmen

(pseud.: Florentina del Mar) Spanish poet, essayist, novelist, anthologist, writer of children's books, b. 15 Aug. 1907, Cartagena; d. 8 Jan. 1996, Madrid

In 1978 C. was the first woman ever elected as a member of the Spanish Royal Academy of the Language. Coming from a lower-middle-class family that had to spend six years in Melilla, the north African Spanish presidio, for economic reasons, the young C. began as an office worker at age fifteen. But her love of literature led first to a modest scholarship and finally in 1930 to a degree from normal school. In the meantime she began to be paid for her contributions to the literary sections of truly prestigious newspapers in Madrid such as *El Imparcial, El Sol, Informaciones*, and *El Heraldo de Madrid*. During this period, she met local poets and married one, Antonio Oliver Belmás (1903–1968), who had just published his first volume of poetry and was at the time earning his living as a telegrapher. She also continued to write, especially under the influence of Juan Ramón JIMÉNEZ and with the friendship of Miguel HERNÁNDEZ.

The advent of the Spanish Republic in conjunction with her and Oliver's history of work led them to become staunch supporters of the Republic's egalitarian programs. Most typical of this commitment is their work founding, directing, and teaching in the Popular University of Cartagena, their hometown. During the war years of 1936–1938, C. did work for her university degree in the Republican stronghold of Valencia, but it was not accepted in postwar Spain. Following some political difficulties during this time, she and Oliver settled in Madrid and came to attain and participate in the increasingly comfortable cultural life the capital offered to professor-writers such as themselves.

Although C. cultivates many fields of writing, it seems that her poetry is the most important. And in the wake of a problematic pregnancy in 1933 that left her childless and incapable of further conception, and of the Civil War and World War II, her best poetry demonstrates an extraordinary love for life and awareness of the

horror of anything that destroys it. In collections of her verse, such as *Mujer sin Edén* (1947; *Woman Without Eden*, 1986), *Sea la luz* (1947; let there be light), *Mientras los hombres mueren* (1953; while the men die), and *Derribado arcangel* (1960; overthrown archangel), C. as human being and woman registers powerfully the conditions and limits of human possibilities and the yearing for a more perfect world. Nonetheless, and perhaps as a consequence of the difficult socioeconomic conditions that she and her husband had to overcome, C.'s poetry, notably *Empezando la vida* (1955; beginning life), and personal philosophy take life on its own terms: Struggle is concomitant with our condition and must be accepted. In C. this attitude extends so far as to thanking her father for her childhood and early youth of privations and work because they prepared her for the wars and their aftermath that were in store for Spain and the whole world.

As a much-published author with a long career behind her, C. is well known but still not the object of much academic study. In the Spain of the last hundred years much has been made of literary generations or groupings by age and shared socioaesthetic interests. Age-wise C. could belong to either the Generation of 1927 or the Generation of 1936, but her production has been too varied and personal for easy insertion into one of the generations. As a result she presents a singular figure in contemporary Spanish poetry; since her name appears infrequently in discussions of poets belonging to given pre-or postwar generations, it normally appears by itself, or has until the pronounced flowering of interest in women writers during the 1980s by readers and critics with a feminist sensibility. In any case, C.'s poetry always will remain an eloquent and powerful expression of the mid-century crisis when humankind had to reassess its past and future in a way made new and urgent by the extent of wartime destruction and the numbers of people touched by it. Moreover, her *Mujer sin Edén* calls into question basic structures of human society when half of it is considered inferior from the moment of birth.

FURTHER WORKS: *Brocal* (1929); *Júbilos* (1934); *Don Juan de Austria* (1943); *Los enredos de Chismecita* (1943); *La amistad en la literatura española* (1944); *Dios en la poesía española* (1944); *Lapoesía de la eternidad* (1944); *Vidas contra su espejo* (1944); *Soplo que va y no vuelve* (1944); *Don Alvaro de Luna* (1945); *Aladino* (1945); *Ansia de la gracia* (1945); *Mi fin en el viento* (1947); *Cartas a Katherine Mansfield* (1948); *Mi libro de El Escorial* (1949); *En manos del silencio* (1950); *Iluminada tierra* (1951); *Cobre* (1953); *Las oscuras raices* (1953); *Vivientes de los siglos* (1954); *Poesía femenina viviente* (1955); *Los monólogos de la hija* (1959); *En un mundo de fugitivos* (1960); *Poemas del mar menor* (1962); *Jaguar puro inmarchito* (1963); *Viejo venís y florido* (1963); *Acompañando a Francisca Sánchez* (1964); *Once grandes poetisas américohispanas* (1967); *Obra poética (1929–66)* (1967); *Un pueblo que lucha y canta* (1967); *Menéndez Pidal* (1969); *Poesía amorosa contemporánea* (1969); *Gabriela Mistral* (1970); *A este lado de la eternidad* (1970); *Poesía femenina española* (2 vols., 1967, 1971); *Cancionero de la enamorada* (1971); *El caballito y la luna* (1974); *Corrosión* (1975); *Cita con la vida* (1976); *Días por tierra* (1977); *El Tiempo es un río lentísimo de fuego* (1978); *Al encuentro de Santa Teresa* (1979); *Poesía ante el tiempo y la inmortalidad* (1979); *La noche oscura del cuerpo* (1980); *Escritoras místicas españolas* (1981); *Desde nunca* (1982); *Cuentos para niños de buena fe* (1982); *Derramen su sangre las sombras* (1983); *Antología poética* (1985); *Juan Ramón Jiménez* (n.d.)

BIBLIOGRAPHY: Alonso, D., *Poetas españoles contemporáneos*, 3rd ed. (1965): 339–44; Fernández Barros, E., "Doña C. C., en la Academia," *REH*, 14 (1980): 41–49; Galerstein, C. L., ed., *Women Writers of Spain: An Annotated Bio-Bibliographical Guide* (1986): 77–81; Newton, C., "El discurso heroico de C. C.," *MRRM*, 6, (1990): 61–70; Richards, J. C., "The Word without End: Mythic and Linguistic Revision in C. C. A.'s *Mujer sin Edén*," *MRRM*, 6 (1990): 71–80

—STEPHEN MILLER

CONDÉ, Maryse

Guadeloupean novelist, short-story writer, dramatist, and critic, b. 11 Feb. 1937, Pointe-à-Pitre

C. is Guadeloupe's best-known writer. She was born into a middle-class family, and her early schooling took place on the island, but she earned a college degree and doctorate in comparative literature at the Sorbonne. During the 1960s she taught in Guinea, Ghana, and Senegal, and during the 1970s at various universities in Paris. She resides in Guadeloupe, where she continues her writing, but also teaches part of each year at the University of California, Berkeley, where she is a tenured professor of French. Her husband, Richard Philcox, translates many of her works.

Although C.'s first works were plays, she made her mark on the literary scene by writing novels. The first two—*Hérémakhonon* (1976; *Heremakhonon*, 1982) and *Une saison à Rihata* (1981; *A Season in Rihata*, 1988)—feature Guadeloupean women protagonists in search of their identity. They leave the island, spend time in France, and eventually settle in postcolonial West Africa, an Africa that has been devalorized by the French and romanticized by African writers. There they attempt to reconcile these two opposing images, but are unsuccessful. As a result of C.'s protagonists' failure and her depiction of newly independent countries dominated by dictators, C. has been accused by some critics of perpetuating negative views of Africa.

The two-volume historical novel *Ségou: les murailles de terre* (1984; *Segu*, 1987) and *Ségou: la terre en miettes* (1985; *The Children of Segu*, 1989) seems designed to answer her critics. While the first two novels are partly set in present-day imaginary African countries, the actual Bambara empire of 18th- and 19th-c. Mali with its rich cultural heritage provides the background of *Ségou*. The disruptions brought on by colonialism, slavery, and the influx of Islam and Christianity are seen affecting several generations of the Traouré family. So thoroughly researched and detailed, the work also includes historical and ethnographical notes, genealogies, and maps. In 1986 C.'s interest in history is again demonstrated with the publication of *Moi, Tituba sorcière . . . Noire de Salem* (1986; *I, Tituba, Black Witch of Salem*, 1992), which won the Grand Prize for Women's Literature. C. adds to what little is already known about Tituba, a woman from Barbados brought to Salem, where she was implicated and arrested in the witch trials. Marginalized in contemporary texts, C. allows her to narrate her own story.

C.'s latest novels—*La vie scélérate* (1987; *Tree of Life*, 1992), which received the bronze medal from the French Academy, *Traversée de la mangrove* (1989; *Crossing the Mangrove*, 1995), *Les derniers rois mages* (1992; *The Last of the African Kings*,

1998), *La colonie du nouveau monde* (1993; New World Colony), *La migration des coeurs* (1995; *Windward Heights*, 1998), and *Desirada* (1997; Desirada)—are set for the most part in the Caribbean and thus represent a third phase in her novel production.

C., innovative thematically and technically, is one of the French Caribbean's most prolific writers, having also published short stories, children's stories, plays, anthologies, and critical essays. When her characters cross national boundaries, she not only explores the relationships among people of the African diaspora, but she constructs bridges between the Caribbean, Africa, Europe, and the U. S. as well.

FURTHER WORKS: *Le morne de Massabielle* (1970); *Dieu nous l'a donné* (1972); *La mort d'Oluwemi Ajumako* (1973); *La civilisation du bossale* (1978); *Cahier d'un retour au pays natal; Césaire: analyse critique* (1978); *La parole des femmes* (1979); *Pays mêlé suivi de Nanna-ya* (1985); *Haïti chérie* (1987); *Pension les Alizés* (1988); *En attendant le bonheur* (1988); *Victor et les barricades* (1989); *An tan revolisyon* (1989); *Hugo le terrible* (1990); *L'héritage de Caliban* (1992); *Pensée la créolité*

BIBLIOGRAPHY: Ngate, J., "M.C. and Africa: The Making of a Recalcitrant Daughter," *CBAA*, 19, 1 (1986–1987): 5–20; Satineau, M., "Références politiques dans un roman antillais: *Une saison à Rihata* de M. C.," *Cahiers duCEDAF*, 4, 1–3 (1987): 362–76; Lionnet, F., "Happiness Deferred: M. C.'s *Hérémakhonon* and the Failure of Enunciation," *Autobiographical Voices: Race, Gender, Self-Portraiture* (1989): 167–90; Snutgen, J., "History, Identity, and the Constitution of the Female Subject: M. C.'s *Tituba*," *Matatu*, 6, 3 (1989): 55–73; Chamoiseau, P., "Considérations sur *Traversée de la mangrove*: une analyse du dernier roman de M. C.," *Antilla*, 364 (1990): 34–39; Clark, V. A., "Developing Diaspora Literacy: Allusion in M. C.'s *Hérémakhonon*," in Davies, C. B., and Fido, E. S., eds., *Out of the Kumbla: Caribbean Women and Literature* (1990): 303–19; Smith, A., "The Semiotics of Exile: M. C.'s Fictional Works," *Callaloo*, 14, 2 (Spring 1991): 381–88; Araujo, N., ed., *L'oeuvre de M. C.: à propos d'une écrivaine politiquement incorrecte* (1996); Pfaff, F., *Conversations with M. C.* (1998)

—RENÉE LARRIER

CONGOLESE LITERATURE

The Congo, bisected by the Equator and lying midway between the North and South Poles, is part of the ancient kingdom of "Kongo." There is an entire mythology associated with the name Congo, for it is the name of the ancient kingdom "Kongo" and the long, mighty River Congo, which forms the natural frontier between the Democratic Republic of Congo and Congo-Brazzaville. In European eyes there can even be confusion between "Africa" and/or the black inhabitants of Congo. But the literary map and history of Congo-Brazzaville are worthy of study because of their originality.

In spite of a modest geographic area and small population, Congolese literature is certainly among the finest that Africa has produced. It is rivaled only by writings from Cameroon, Senegal, and Algeria. In these countries, long before independence in 1960, there were such renowned writers as Ferdinand OYONO and Mongo BETI, Sembène OUSMANE and Léopold Sédar SENGHOR, Mouloud FERAOUN and Mohammed DIB, respectively.

As with all African literature produced in European languages, contemporary Congolese writings originate in part from oral or traditional literature. Upon this substrate of orality is superposed the recounting of historical events, as is clearly recognizable in Congolese writings. Such aspects of Congo history include Loango, a departure point for slave traders with their cargo, similar to that of Senegal's Goree Island. In 1910 Congo became part of French Equatorial Africa (AEF) with Brazzaville as the capital. Brazzaville thus was established as a nerve center of the federation of French colonies that included the Mid Congo, Gabon, Oubangui-Chari and Chad. The construction of the Congo-Ocean railway proved a disaster in terms of human lives expended; the figure of 20,000 deaths is reported as a consequence.

After independence in 1960, power struggles in the Congo were especially bloody, and in this way Congo symbolizes the drama that overtook much of black Africa at that time. Failed revolutions, political assassinations, coups d'état, an extreme socialist regime, civil wars, and other horrors followed each other in some sort of hellish succession. These lesions have all had their effect upon the literature of the Congo.

Democratic Republic of Congo

The region along the estuary of the Congo River was probably the first part of sub-Saharan Africa where there was writing in a European language. As early as the 16th c. the rulers of the Kongo kingdom exchanged written messages in Portuguese with royalty and officials in Lisbon. The whole area thereafter became a hunting ground for the slave trade and for the supply of cheap manpower to overseas plantations. When the Congo became the personal empire of Leopold II, King of the Belgians, in 1885, African muscle was used locally for feeding the ivory and rubber trades. Although these circumstances were not conducive to a high level of education, Protestant missionaries managed to establish a few stations and schools where the Kikongo language was used in writing for the propagation of Scripture. The need for reading material led to the translation of John Bunyan's *The Pilgrim's Progress* in 1912. Converts were encouraged to help in the translation and composition of the four hundred hymns that were printed in *Minkunga miayenge* (1887; Songs of Peace).

For several decades Kikongo literature consisted mostly of Protestant hymns. A new trend emerged after World War I when the disciples of the syncretic religious leader Simon Kimbangu (1889-1951) started composing hymns reflecting their own creed. During the 1930s a Swedish missionary, John Patterson (dates n.a), produced a didactic novel in the language, *Nsamu a Mpanzu* (3 vols., 1935-38; The Life of Mpanzu), and his example was followed by the first genuine Kongo novelists: Émile Disengomoka (1915-1965) with *Kwenkwenda* (ca. 1943; Kwenkwenda), and Jacques N. Bahele (b. 1911) with *Kinzonzi ye ntekelo andi Makundu* (1948; Kinzoni and His Grandson Makundu). These two main trends—hymn writing and edifying prose fiction—remained dominant in Kikongo literarure in the writing of André Massaki (b. 1923) and Noé Diawaky (b.1932), even though the Protestant clergyman Homere-Antoine Wantwadi's (b. 1921) novel *Niklisto mu Kongo dia kimpwanza* (1965; The Christian in Independent Congo) contained a belated indictment of colonial rule, and Fikiau

Kia Bunseki (b. 1934) devoted most of his attention to the traditional, pre-Christian Kongo worldview, especially in the poems collected in *Dingo-dingo* (1966; Life Cycle).

The other main vernaculars of the Democratic Republic of Congo have just started to be used for written art. In fact, it was not until World War II that writing in French began to emerge in the country. The tardiness was due to several factors: once Leopold II had bequeathed his empire to his country as its only African colony, the school system that was created was entrusted to Catholic missionaries. Its purpose was to spread a minimal degree of literacy so as to provide inexpensive but comparatively competent help to the colonizer: primary school teachers, junior clerks, medical assistants, and the like. Only by studying for the priesthood was it possible for a Congolese to acquire a modicum of higher education. No African in the Belgian Congo was in a position to enter a university.

It was only in the aftermath of World War II that a process of liberalization was initiated. *La voix du Congolais*, a magazine launched in 1945, offered educated Congolese an opportunity for airing some of their views under the colonial administration's sponsorship and paternalistic control; its editor, Antoine-Roger Bolamba (b. 1913), later gained some repute with *Esanzo: Chants pour mon pays* (1955; Esanzo [a musical instrument]: Songs for My Country), the first Congolese literary work to be printed in Paris.

Paul Lomami-Tshibamba (b. 1914) won a Belgian literary prize for his novel *Ngando* (1948; The Crocodile) and was subsequently published in Brussels. In the mid-1950s two universities were established, and scholarships became available for study abroad. At long last a favorable climate was created, which prepared for the growth of creative writing in French after independence in 1960.

During the chaotic years that followed independence a number of poetry clubs such as the Pléiade du Congo (1964-66) were formed by young intellectuals headed by Clémentine Nzuji (b. 1944), a well-known linguist and author of several poetry collections including *Murmures* (1968; Whispers), *Le temps des amants* (1969; Time for Lovers), *Kasala* (1969; Kasala), and *Lianes* (1971; Lianas). Their work was printed locally, as was *somme première* (1968; First Sum), a poetry collection by Philippe Masegabio (b. 1944). Other talented poets of this generation include the very prolific Elebe Lisembe (b. 1937), author of *Mélodie Africaine* (1970; African Melody) and *Rythmes* (1972; Rhythms); Sébastien Bontala (b. 1925), author of *L' amba des ancêtres* (1967; Ancestral Roots); Oscar Moningi (b. 1930), author of *Complainte Bantoue* (1970; Bantu Lamentation); Etienne Tshinday Lukumbi (b. 1940), author of *Marche pays des espoirs* (1967; March Onward Country of Hope); Adolphe Vianda (b. 1940), author of *Ombre sur l'équateur* (1968; Shadow on the Equator); Gaby Sumaili (b. 1941), author of *Testament* (1971; Testament); Lestin Tito Yisuku (b. 1941), author of *Coeur enflammé* (1973; Fired Heart) and *Tam-tams crépitants* (1974; Beating Tom-toms); V. Y. MUDIMBE, an eminent Congolese linguist, philosopher, and versatile creative writer whose numerous volumes include two collections of poetry titled *Déchirures* (1971; Shreds) and *Entretailles* (1973; Deep Etching); Matala Mukadi Tshiakatumba (b. 1942), author of *Réveil dans un nid de flammes* (1969; Awakening in a Nest of Flames); David-Césaire Tshiyombo (b. 1944), author of *Le brouillard* (1972; The Fog); Andre Boniface Nguwo (b. 1945), author of *Chants intérieurs* (1971; Interior Songs); Paul-Olivier Musangi (b. 1946), author of *Les reminiscences du soir* (1968; Evening Reminiscences) and *Ma terre perdue* (1968; My Lost Land); Mukala Kadima-Nzuji (b.

1947), who is also a critic and a historian of Congolese literature and the author of *Les resacs* (1969; Sacking) and *Préludes à la terre* (1971; Preludes to Earth); Gregoire-Roger Bokeme (b. 1948), author of *Douces rosées* (1969; Soft Dew) and *Prémices* (1974; First Fruits); Elisabeth-Francoise Mweya (b. 1948), author of *Remous des feuilles* (1072; Trembling Leaves); Pierre- Lambert Kabatantshi (b. 1949), author of *Flammèches* (1972; Sparks); Ivonne Marie-Claire Bolumbu (b.1951), author of *Feuilles d'Olive*(1972; Olive Leaves); and Francois-Medard Mayengo (b. 1952), author of *Mon coeur de saison* (1972; My Heart in Season).

Undoubtedly poetry dominated the literary scene of the Democratic Republic of Congo in the 1960s and early 1970s, and as can be seen through the titles of the collections mentioned in this essay, the poets of this generation were greatly influenced in their choices of subject matters—nature, love, celebration of African traditions and personal reminiscences—and styles by the French surrealist and NÉGRITUDE poetry. It was not until the publication of Mudimbe's novel *Entre les eaux* (1973; Between Waters) that Congolese writers started to heed the poet Tito Yisuku's appeal to them to comply with the demands of what he called "Zairean concretism" —to achieve in their writings a realistic, down-to-earth portrayal of the realities around them. Furthermore, the rapid deterioration of the standard of living of the Congolese people that followed the introduction of the ill-conceived and badly implemented nationalisation (zairianization) of foreign assets in the mid-1970s, the introduction of tough economic austerity measures dictated by the International Monetary Fund in the 1980s, and the continuation of murderous repression of political opponents and students by the Mobutu regime made it almost impossible for Congolese writers to continue to turn a blind eye on the deplorable realities of their society.

Among the themes that featured prominently in Congolese literature of the 1970s and 1980s were the misery of the Congolese masses, rampant bribery and corruption in public institutions, moral depravity, lack of accountability on the part of the ruling class, unemployment, nepotism, ethnic conflict and discrimination, the collapse of educational and health institutions, the two antigovernment armed rebellions in Shaba, government soldiers' brutality, alienation, and the flight of many Congolese into exile. Writers like V. Y. Mudimbe, Mbwil a Mpaang Ngal (b. 1933), Pius Nkashama Ngandu (b. 1946), and a host of others of this period also displayed a sense of literary maturity by introducing a variety of stylistic innovations, mainly from various traditional Congolese oral narratives and poetry, into their art. Thanks to these innovations they handled their themes effectively. Notable works of the period include V. Y. Mudimbe's novels *Le bel immonde* (1976; *Before the Birth of the Moon*, 1989), *L'écart* (1979; The Gap), and *Shaba ll: Les carnets de Mère Marie*-Gertrude (1989; Shaba II: The Diaries of Mother Mary-Gertrude); Mbala Ngombo's novel *Deux vies, un temps nouveau* (1973; Two Lives, a New Time); Mbwil a Mpaang Ngal's novels of ideas *Giambattista Viko; ou, Le viol du discours Africain* (1975; Giambattista Viko; or, the Rape of African Discourse) and *L'errance* (1979; Wandering); M. K. Mikanza's (b. 1944) play *La bataille de Kamanyola* (1975; The Battle of Kamanyola), one of the rare works that celebrated Mobutu's regime; Batukezanga Zamenga's novel *Carte postale* (1977; Postcard); Pius Nkashama Ngadu's play *La délivrance d'Ilunga* (1977; The Freeing of Ilunga) and his satirically biting novels *La malédiction* (1983; The Curse), *Le pacte de sang* (1984; The Blood Pact), *La mort faite homme* (1986; Death Made Man), *Vie et moeurs d'un primitif en Essonne quatre-vingt-onze* (1987; Life and Customs of a Primitive Man in Essonne 91), and *Les étoiles écrasées* (1988;

Crushed Stars); Tshibanda Wamuela Bujitu's (b. 1951) novel *Je ne suis pas un sorcier* (1981; I Am Not a Sorcerer); Bolya Baenga's novel *Cannibale* (1986; Cannibal); Charles Simba Djungu's novels *Cite 15: roman zaïrois* (1988; City 15: A Zairean Novel) and *On a échoué* (1989; We Have Failed); Emongo Lomomba's novel *L'instant d'un soupir* (1989; Moment of a Sigh); and Tshisungu wa Tshisungu's novel *Le croissant des larmes* (1989; The Crescent of Tears).

The political liberalization that followed the so-called "sovereign national conference for democracy" in 1990 brought with it free expression and multiparty politics. A young generation of Congolese writers, led by the prolific and versatile Pius Nkashama Ngandu and a number of old hands, also took advantage of the new political climate to explore and boldly expose in their writings— fiction, drama, and poetry—various facets of life under the repressive Mobutu regime characterised by greed, ethnic chauvenism, lawlessness, corruption, and other numerous vices. The most important works produced after the national conference, whose resolutions were subsequently subverted by the ever power hungry Mobutu and his cronies, include Pius Ngadu's satirical plays *L'empire des ombres vivantes* (1991; Empire of Living Shadows) and *May Britt de Santa Cruz* (1993; May Britt of Santa Cruz), and his novels *Le doyen mari* (1994; The Husband and Dean), *Yakouta* (1994; Yakouta), and *Citadelle d'espoir* (1995; Citadel of Hope); M. K. Mikabza Mobyera's novel *Notre sang* (1991; Our Blood); Batukezanga Zamenga's novel of exiled consciousness entitled *Un boy à Pretoria* (1991; A Boy in Pretoria); Mbuyu Mukalay's novella *L'empire du destin* (1991; Empire of Fate); Muyengo Mulombe's novel *Enfants du ciel, misères de la terre* (1991; Heaven's Children, Wretchedness of Earth); Mbwil a Mpaang Ngal's novella *Un prétendant valeureux* (1991; A Boasting Valuable) and his novel *Une saison de symphonie* (1994; A Season of Symphony); Kama Kamanda's collections of poetry entitled *L'exil des songes* (1992; Exile of Dreams), *Les myriades des temps vécus* (1992; Myriads of Lived Times), *Les vents de l'épreuve* (1994; Testing Winds), and *L 'étreinte des mots* (1995; Gripped by Words); Antoine M. Ruti's novel *Affamez-les, ils vous adoreront* (1992; Starve Them, They Will Worship You); Kabagema-Mirindi's novels *Mejo, la trahison d'un héros* (1992; Mejo, The Betrayal of a Hero) and *Le disciple* (1992; The Disciple); Fweley Diangitukwa's play *Quelle solution pour l'Afrique?* (1993; What Solution for Africa); Antoine Kabwasa's collection of short stories entitled *Les fleurs de Maskaram* (1993; Flowers of Maskaram); Achille Ngoye's novel *Kin la joie, Kin la joie* (1993; Kin Joy, Kin Joy); Clémentine Nzuji's novella *Frisson de la mémoire* (1993; Trembling Memories) and her collection of short stories entitled *Maia* (1995; Maia); J. B. Bilombo-Samba's poetry collection entitled *Hors la nuit* (1994; Out of the Night); M. T. Mayamba Nlandu's (b. 1954) play *Misère (*1994; Misery); Yvon Mbuyu's novel *Ceux à qui on a interdit l'amour* (1994; Those Forbidden to Love); Charles Simba Djungu's collection of short stories entitled *Sandruma: on demoncratise* (1994; Sandruma: We Demon-Cratise) and his novel *Des milliers de vies au taux du jour* (1996; Thousands of Lives at Today's Rate); Antoine Kongolo Tshitungu's novel *Fleurs dans la boue* (1995; Flowers in the Mud); Alain Mabanekou's poetry collection entitled *La légende de l'errance* (1995; The Wandering Legend); Kompany wa Kompany's novel *L'ogre-empereur* (1995; The Ogre-emperor); Tandundu Bisiki's plays *Quand les Afriques s'affrontent* (1995; When the Africas Clash) and *Les promesses de l'aube* (1997; Promises of Dawn); and Joseph Sivihwa Mumbere's novella entitled *Victime de mon nez* (1996; Victim of My Nose).

The overthrow of the oppressive Mobutu regime by the Kabila-led armed rebellion in 1997 has not brought about the democratic changes that the Congolese people had expected. On the contrary, the banning of political parties and intolerance of political activities have led many observers of the Congolese political scene to think that Kabila is not acting differently from Mobutu's dictatorship. In the circumstances, we are likely to see a wave of literary works focus on the themes of disillusionment and betrayal, as Tandundu Bisiki's play *Les promesses de l'aube* (1997; Promises of Dawn) has already shown the way.

The literary output of the Democratic Republic of Congo in the 20th c. is different from that of other French-speaking countries in notable ways. Since the Democratic Republic of Congo had never been under French rule, its writers did not benefit from the "French connection." Initially they seldom wrote with an eye on Paris publishers and the French audience. The country was practically compelled to self-reliance in publishing and can now boast a large number of local publishing houses. From the mid-1970s onward Congolese writers have displayed great "authenticity" in many ways. A prominent example is Mbwil a Mpaang Ngal: in the essayistic novels *Giambattista Viko; ou, Le viol du discours africain* (1975; Giambattista Vico; or, The Rape of the African Discourse) and *L'errance* (1979; Wandering) he condemns Westernized writers who degrade traditional belief and customs into exotic attractions for European readers, and he tries to devise some sort of adaptations of the novel as a genre to specific features of the oral narrative tradition.

BIBLIOGRAPHY: Jadot, J. M., *Les écrivains africains du Congo belge et du Ruanda-Urundi* (1959); Bujitto, K., *Pour mieux comprendre la littérature au Zaïre* (1975); Ntamunoza, M. M. "Quelques aspects de la poésie zaïroise moderne," *WAJML*, 2 (1976): 75-86; Kadima-Nzuji, M., "Approche de la littérature de langue française au Zaïre," *Afrique contemporaine*, 91 (1977): 13-18; Kadima-Nzuji, M., "Avant-propos pour une lecture plurielle de la poésie zaïroise," *PA*, 104 (1977): 86-93; Ngandu Nkashama, P., "Problématique de la littérature zaïroise," *PFr*, 17 (1978): 79-88; Gérard, A. S., *African Language Literatures* (1981): 291-93; special Zaire issue, *Notre librairie*, 63 (1982); Ngandu Nkashama, P., *Ecritures et discours littraires: Etudes sur le roman africain* (1989); "La littérature congolaise contemporaine (1980-1993), roman, récis et contes," *Matatu*, 13-14 (1995): 23-43; Losambe, L., ed., *An Introduction to the African Prose Narrative* (1996); Spleth, J., "Narrating ethnic conflict in Zairean literature," *RAL*, 29 (1998): 103-123

—ALBERT S. GÉRARD and LOKANGAKA LOSAMBE

People's Republic of Congo

Most critics agree that Congolese literature has its source in the literary revue *Liaison*, which appeared in seventy-five issues during the ten years of its publication (1950-60) and offered its support to aspirant writers. Although the literary journal served the whole AEF, it was dominated by Congolese contributors. These pioneering writers include Paul Lomani-Tschibamba (b. 1914), Dominique N'zalakanda, Jean Malonga (1907-1985), Sylvain BEMBA and others. In the second generation of such authors are Guy Menga and Théophile Obenga (dates n.a.), among many others.

Because of colonial censorship, *Liaison* was a rather timid publication, compared with *Présence Africaine*, produced by Alioune Diop in Paris. Jean-Baptiste Tati-Loutard (b. 1938) has described the general situation. "The contents had to be submitted to the established authorities, that is to say the colonial regime, which through its government both subsidized and censored the journal." At least the journal could offer a platform for any writer who aspired to a literary career, even though its editorial policy was under colonial control.

Although cramped and repressed by its experience of colonialism from the start, Congolese literature dissociated itself from the Négritude movement. This originality should be emphasized, in contrast to the then current vogue of producing pale imitations of the works of the founding fathers of Négritude. Congolese writers took quite another path and even showed their general disdain for an aping of Négritude. Generally acknowledged as the doyen of Congolese writers, Jean Malonga published *Coeur d'Aryenne* (1954; An Aryan's Heart) and *La Légende de M'Pfoumou ma Mazono* (1954; The Legend of M'Pfoumou ma Mazono) in the same issue of *Présence Africaine*. This number also contained *Ville cruelle* (1954; Cruel Town) by Mongo Beti and *Nini* by Abdoulaye Sadji (dates n.a.). With the appearance of *Mauvais sang* (1955; Bad Blood), TCHICAYA U TAM'SI displayed his poetic talent and became the inspiration of a number of Congolese writers. The pen name of Sony Labou TANSI is directly derived from Tchicaya U Tam'si, his senior role model. Impassioned and deeply personal, the poetry of Tchicaya U Tam'si has been widely acclaimed and has gained many literary prizes. *Feu de Brousse* (1957; Bush Fire) won the Grand Prize for Literature of the AEF and *A triche coeur* (1970; Cheating Heart) and *Epitomé* (1962; Epitomy) with a preface by Léopold Sédar Senghor, together with *Le Ventre* (1964; The Belly), *Arc musical* (1970; Musical Arc), *La veste d'intérieur* (1977; Indoor Jacket) and *Le Pain ou la cendre* (1978; Bread or Ashes) all won other awards. He was preeminent in establishing the fine reputation of Congolese literature. Tchicaya U Tam'si added the talent of a short story writer to his sensitivity as a poet and he displays the gifts of a novelist and dramatist.

With the deaths of Tchicaya U Tam'si in 1987 and of Sony Labou Tansi and Sylvain Bemba in 1995, Congolese literature seemed to be orphaned, with the loss of its most prominent exponents. But there are hopes that younger talents will begin to fill their places, with the advent of Caya Makhele, Marie-Léontine Tsibinda, Alphonse N'Dzanga-Konga, Philippe Makita, Tchicaya Unti B'kune, Jean-Blaise Bilombo Samba, and others (dates n.a.).

The *Anthologie de la litterature d'expression francaise* (1976; Anthology of Congolese Francophone Literature) of Jean-Baptiste Tati-Loutard covered about twenty years and demonstrated the great potential of literary creativity in the Congo at that time. Three years after the overview of Tati-Loutard, the *Panorama critique de la littérature congolaise contemporaine* (1979; A Critical Panorama of Contemporary Congolese Literature) of Roger and Arlette Chemain appeared, which confirmed there had been a creative outburst in Congolese literature. It should be noted that Tati-Loutard's anthology and the Chemains' panoramic work were the first publications of this nature in Africa. For the first time, Congolese literature is presented as a national literature. These works precipitated appearance of evaluations of other national literatures in Africa.

Here appears the difficulty of analyzing African literature as a whole, for the debate of African literature versus national literatures is far from concluded. The recognition and examination of a field of literary study using criteria of nationality certainly does not reduce the importance of any Pan-African quality it may have.

Congolese literature continues to claim more and more attention from literary critics. Roger Godard has published *Trois poètes congolais* (1985; Three Congolese Poets) and *Notre Librairie* has devoted three issues to Congolese literature (no. 38, 1977 and nos. 92-93, 1988). Henri LOPES is the Congolese writer whose work has probably attracted most attention of critics. Three resulting volumes are *Comprendre Tribaliques d'Henri Lopes* (1987; Understanding *Tribaliques* by Henri Lopes) by Guy Daninos, *Henri Lopes et l'impératif romanesque* (1987; Henri Lopes and the Compulsion of the Novel) by Ange-Severin Malanda and *Tribaliques d'Henri Lopes: étude critique* (1984; A Critical Study of *Tribaliques* by Henri Lopes) by Alain Rouch.

Sylvain Bemba: récits entre folie et pouvoir (1996; Sylvain Bemba: Narratives between Madness and Power) by André Djiffack opens up the work of one of the pioneers of Congolese literature to a general public, while *Littérature et politique en Afrique noire: socialisme et dictature comme thèmes du roman congolais d'expression francaise* (1990; Literature and Politics in Black Africa: Socialism and Dictatorship as themes in Congolese Francophone Novels) by Koffi Anyinefa is an ideological analysis of works by the renowned Congolese writers Emmanuel Dongala, Henri Lopes, Makouta-Mboukou, and Sony Labou Tansi.

Critical writings can take on the character of a tribute to certain Congolese writers. This has been so for *Sony Labou Tansi: écrivain de la honte et des rives magiques du Kongo* (1996; Soni Labou Tansi: Writer of the Shame and of the Magical Banks of the Congo) by Jean-Michel Devesa and especially in the special number of *Présence Francophone* (No. 52, 1998) edited by Fernando Lambert. *Jean Malonga: écrivain congolais* (1994; Jean Malonga: Congolese writer), edited by Kadina-Nzuji Mukala, is written in the same vein.

It is clear that critical analysis of Congolese literature complements the writing itself in testifying to the importance of this corpus of literature, for both in their own way stimulate its growth and appreciation. An example of the fruitful interaction between creativity and critical examination was the stay of the Chemains at the Marien Ngouabi University of Brazzaville and the important critical work that resulted.

Even more than this fruitful interaction, Sylvain Bemba explains this creative outpouring by "the fraternity of Congolese writers." This refers to the close bonds between these writers, quite independent of their individual prestige, productivity and age. These links can be recognized in the dedications of individual volumes, contributed prefaces, literary soirees, reading of manuscripts to each other, intertextuality in writings. All embody a general friendship, mutual respect and solidarity in a writers' world, where the usual currency is jealousy, rivalry and disputes over precedence. Such relations have even continued amongst writers who entered into politics and who, according to Bemba, "have acted in different ways with more success than is normally attributed, to attenuate the measures of reducing liberty for all, including writers." Henri Lopes and Tati-Loutard followed political careers in addition to their writing.

Sony Labou Tansi had always recognized his obligation to Sylvain Bemba, whom he acknowledged as having taught him the art of writing. Tchichelle Tchivela helped his co-writers to discover South American literature, a discovery that deeply influenced the Congolese novel in the 1980s, not least by its aspects of the fantastic and of magical realism.

Congolese literature seems to have experienced a gradual evolution from poetry to the novel, by way of the theater. Before the full flourishing in the 1980s of its inspired novelists, Congolese writers did their "basic training" in the fields of poetry and the theater. Several writers made their entry into literature through poetry, which ensured there was a solid lyrical underpinning for Congolese writing. Virtually all writers contributed poems to *Liaison*. Those who did not publish there, usually began their writing careers with poetry. Tchicaya U Tam'si, Jean-Baptiste Tati-Loutard, Maxime N'Debeka, Sylvain Bemba, Jean-Pierre Makouta Mbouta, Henri Lopes, Soni Labou Tansi, and many others made their literary debut as poets. This affinity with poetry has continued with some of the latest generation of writers, being manifested as an enduring lyricism in their writing.

Theater also flourishes in the Congo and inspires its culture, with a multiplicity of plays and many theatrical groups in evidence. Dramatists, producers and actors all contribute to a veritable massive team effort. Congolese theater has been a strong factor in the general recognition of Congolese literature. In *Notre Librarie* (nos 92-93, 1988, pp.174-177) Matondo Kubu Ture describes five stages in Congolese drama: "mbongi" or pre-colonial theater, theatrical activities of the years 1950-1960, school theater of the 1970s, other movements during the 1980s and finally the theater of resistance in the years since 1983.

Theatrical troupes were very varied. Between the "mbongi" of the Kingdom of Kongo and the Rocado Zulu Theater of Sony Labou Tansi, a whole horde of companies was active. Among them were the Association of Congolese Theater (ASTHECO), the Union of Congolese Theater (TUC), the National Congolese Theater (TNC), the Kamangos of Pointe-Noire, the Ngunga Artistic Company, the Lightning Theater, the Theater of the Brothers Tchang, the Three Francs Theater, and Auras Popularis, among others. Most of these troupes were inspired and directed by writers and so in effect they formed a school of literature. *La Marmite de Koka-M'Bala* (1969; Koka-M'Bala's Cooking Pot) by Guy Menga was received with enthusiasm. Sylvain Bemba wrote a dozen plays and has a reputation as a creator for the theater. Similarly the Rocado Zulu Theater of Sony Labou Tansi had critical acclaim within and outside Congo. Some of his most successful plays include *Conscience de Tracteur* (1979; The Conscience of a Tractor), *La Parenthèse de sang* (1981; The Parenthesis of Blood) and *Je soussigné cardiaque* (1981; I, the Undersigned, a Cardiac Patient), *Antoine m'a vendu son destin* (1986; Antoine Sold Me His Destiny) and *Moi, veuve de l'empire* (1987; I, the Widow of the Empire).

Initially in the Congo the novel was not a popular genre among writers, in contrast with poetry and theater, although *Coeur d'Aryenne* (1954; An Aryan's Heart) by Jean Malonga was one of the earliest African writings. *La Palabre Stérile* (1968; The Sterile Palaver) by Guy Menga was awarded the Grand Prize for Literature in Black Africa in 1969. Henri Lopes in 1972 was similarly honored for his novellas *Tribaliques* (1971; Tribalesque). Lopes rapidly evolved from producing novellas to concentrate upon novel writing and it is clear from his production of *La Nouvelle romance* (1976; The New Romance) until the appearance of *Chercheur d'Afriques* (1990; Searcher for Africas), that this transition met with much success. Critics warmly praised *Le pleurer-rire* (1982; Crying Laughter), which derided Life Presidents and other megalomaniacs of post colonial Africa and in one sense introduced to the continent a literature of derision and satire. The novels of Henri Lopes examined morals, society, the colonial past and errors committed by those exercising political power in post independence Africa. His realistic style is particularly effective in portraying human failings.

During the 1980s there was a fundamental change in Congolese literature, for the writers then determinedly took up the form of the novel. This period can be even described as a golden age of the Congolese novel. Tchicaya U Tam'si's trilogy *Les Cancrelats* (1980; The Cockroaches), *Les Méduses* (1982; The Jellyfish) and *Les Phalènes* (1984; The Moths) set in the Congo during colonial times, was published by Albin Michel in Paris. This trilogy was supplemented by *Ces fruits si doux de l'arbre à pain* (1987; These Sweet Fruits of the Breadfruit tree), published by Seghers, immediately before the author's death. In his final work Tchicaya U Tam'si examined the political and social situation of post colonial Congo, and beyond it, of the whole of Africa.

Sony Labou Tansi's series of novels appeared under the imprint of the publishing house, Seuil. These included *La Vie et demie* (1979; Life and a Half), *L'Etat honteux* (1981; The Shameful State), *L'Ante-peuple* (1983; The Ante People), *Les Sept solitudes de Lorza Lopez* (1985; The Seven Solitudes of Lorza Lopez) and *Les Yeux du volcan* (1988; The Eyes of the Volcano). His last work *Le commencement des douleurs* (1995; The Onset of Pains) appeared just after his decease. In order to ensure the publication of this final novel, Sony Labou Tansi who was dying, very reluctantly had to agree to revisions imposed by his editor, who believed that the manuscript was "anti-French." In all his works, Sony Labou Tansi derides and attacks head-on the crass stupidity of African tyrants. His writings, marked by the fantastic, the gross exaggeration and the farcical are influenced by the magic realism of Gabriel Garcia MARQUEZ. Tansi uses the grotesque and the carnivalesque to attack all dictatorships. His unbridled imagination and clockworklike publication schedule contributed significantly to the revival of African literature.

The acclaim that the novel achieved in the 1980s was such that Sylvain Bemba forsook the theater and Tati-Loutard his poetry and novella writing, in order to devote themselves to creating novels. This trend even included the chemist Emmanuel Dongola, whose novel *Le Feu des Origines* (The Flame of Origins) appeared in 1987.

Congolese writing has shown itself to be militant, committed and part of the avant-garde in formal innovative tendencies. It is a literature that has produced many novels of great merit and in it there can be clearly seen the influence of poetic forms and drama. All these writings have struggled to improve the Congolese socio-political situation and indeed to promote liberation throughout the continent. The mythical presence of Patrice Lumumba recurs often, as do André Gérard Matsoua, Simon Kibangu and indeed the River Congo, indicating that the ancient Kingdom of Kongo is present in the background canvas of a reality, damaged by the period of colonialism and subsequently ruined by the cruelty of neocolonialism. Such history and literary forms are tributaries contributing to the mighty flow of a Congolese river of writing, comparable to the River Congo itself.

BIBLIOGRAPHY: Tati-Loutard, J.-B., *Anthologie de la littérature congolaise d'expression française* (1978); Chemain, R., and A. Chemain, *Panorama critique de la littérature congolaise contemporaine* (1979); Rouch, A., *Tribaliques d'Henri Lopes: études critiques* (1984); Daninos, G., *Comprendre Tribaliques d'Henri Lopes* (1987); Malanda, A.-S., *Henri Lopes et l'impératif romanesque* (1987); Anyinefa, K., *Littérature et politique en Afrique noire: socialisme et dictature comme thèmes du roman congolais d'expression française* (1990); Kadima-Nzuji, M., *Jean Malonga: écrivain congolais (1907-1985)* (1994); Devasa, J.-M., *Sony Labou Tansi:*

écrivain de la honte et des rives magiques du Kongo(1996); Djiffack, A., *Syvain Bemba: récits entre folie et pouvoir* (1996)

—ANDRE DIFFACK and ANNY WYNCHANK

CONRAD, Joseph

(born Józef Teodor Konrad Korzeniowski) English novelist, short-story writer, and essayist, b. 3 Dec. 1857, near Berdyczów (Berdichev), Poland; d. 3 Aug. 1924, Bishopsbourne, England

C. is one of the principal writers of narrative fiction of the late 19th and early 20th es. Born into a Slavic-speaking world, early mastering French, he went on to develop one of the most distinguished styles in modern English literature. His complex novels and taies, always esteemed, have in recent decades become the subject of increasing critical appreciation. His works have been translated into more than a dozen languages, including Japanese.

C.'s innate sensitivity was shaped by a wretched and gloomy childhood. His father, Apollo Korzeniowski, a writer, and his mother, Evelina Bobrowska, belonged to families identified with Polish aspirations for freedom from Russian rule. Two of C.'s uncles died, a third was imprisoned, and a fourth was exiled to Siberia during Poland's futile struggle. In 1861 Apollo was arrested for revolutionary activities in Warsaw, and the next year he and Ewa, also charged with conspiracy, were deported into Russia. The four-year-old C. shared the horrors of exile and illness. Before the boy was twelve, both parents were dead.

C.'s enforced isolation and his father's example fostered a taste for letters, and from childhood on he read widely. He knew Shakespeare, Dickens, de Vigny, and Hugo in his father's translations. He early discovered Cooper and Marryat, as well as Cervantes and Polish writers of epic and romance. He reveled in books of geography and travel. He learned in later years from Stendhal, Balzac, Flaubert, Maupassant, Zola, Anatole FRANCE, and Turgenev; and he was influenced by writers as different as Dostoevsky and Melville, although he expressed his distaste for the American's "portentous mysticism"—he called *Moby-Dick* "a rather strained rhapsody"—and he rejected Dostoevsky as "too Russian for me." Chief mentor among his contemporaries was Henry JAMES; their affinity is suggested by the fact that C. called James the "historian of fine consciences." Scholars have identified multiple influences upon C.'s thought from European philosophers, notably Schopenhauer, and from Asian religions, especially Buddhism. Bertrand Russell (1872–1970) came to be a friend and an admirer of C.'s mind.

C.'s stern but affectionate guardian-uncle, Tadeusz Bobrowski, provided for the orphaned boy's only formal education, which culminated in vacation travels throughout Europe with his tutor, Adam Marek Pulman, from 1870 to 1874. During this time he began to press for permission to go to sea. In 1874, shortly before his seventeenth birthday, he went to Marseille, alone but with letters of introduction from his uncle, and soon he entered the French marine service. During the next four years, between voyages to the West Indies, he seems to have engaged in some gunrunning activities, possibly on behalf of Don Carlos, the Spanish pretender; C., in later years, also hinted at a romantic involvement with a young lady of Carlist sympathies. Apparently because of debts and other personal difficulties, he is presumed to have attempted to take his own life by shooting himself in the chest, an incident that was for many years disguised as a duel. The Marseille experiences are effectively obscured in C.'s autobiographical material as well as in a novel, *The Arrow of Gold* (1919), and an abortive fragment, *The Sisters* (1928).

Following his near disaster in Marseille, C. sailed on a British freighter, and in June 1878 landed at Lowestoft, England. He obtained his master's papers in 1886, the same year that he became a British subject. His connection with the Merchant Service lasted for sixteen years. He voyaged to many of the ports of Asia and the South Pacific, but appears to have gained relatively little satisfaction and suffered a great deal of frustration from his career as a seaman.

The transition from sea life to professional writing was casual and almost imperceptible, if we may believe C.'s own account in *A Personal Record* (1912; originally titled *Some Reminiscences*). As early as 1889 he had begun a novel; as late as 1898, five years after he gave up his last berth, he still was trying to obtain another sea assignment. By that time he had published three novels and a collection of tales, but writing was for him a slow and agonizing ordeal, intensified by a neurasthenic deficiency of energy and a continuing dread of inadequacy and failure. At that moment he was struggling with two manuscripts which he had already promised to publishers in desperate exchange for advances. "Jim, a Sketch" he expanded into *Lord Jim* (1900); but "The Rescuer" was to torment him for over twenty years before he completed and published it as *The Rescue* (1920). In 1896 C. married Jessie George. Borys, the first of two sons, was born in 1898; the second, John, in 1906.

With the failure of his last try at a sea berth, C. moved his family to Pent Farm, owned by Ford Madox FORD, and began a collaboration with the younger author. The product of their joint effort was ineffectual, but the experience confirmed C. as a professional writer. Powerful literary friends like Edward Garnett (1868–1937), and R. B. Cunninghame Graham (1852–1936), and some of his most distinguished contemporaries, including Henry JAMES, H. G. WELLS and Stephen CRANE, early recognized C.'s merit. Edmund Gosse (1849–1928), the painter William Rothenstein (1872–1945), and others secured for him grants from various royal funds, and John GALSWORTHY helped him to obtain a Civil List pension. But general recognition came slowly. Only with *Chance* (1913) did he achieve a best-seller. But by this time most of his important work was done. Nevertheless, he continued writing to the end; when he died he was working on *Suspense*, published unfinished in 1925. In 1924, the year of his death, he declined a knighthood; he steadfastly refused all offers of honorary degrees. He was buried in Canterbury.

C.'s natural talent was enhanced by a lifelong fidelity to moral and aesthetic ideals as he conceived them. But faithful as he was to these ideals, he produced work disappointingly uneven in quality. Alongside his austere masterpieces are tales that have the meretricious flavor of a potboiler. And even his finest artistic creations are sometimes flawed by unexpected sentimentality, as, for example, *The Nigger of the "Narcissus"* (1897). His usually effective irony occasionally degenerates into coyness or archness, as in *Chance*, a work that leaves the impression of trivial intricacy. Most often his trilingual genius found the "right word" and the "right accent"; but sometimes his studied rhythms and grandiloquent diction reduced his superb style to affectation and mannerism.

In the main, however, C. produced fiction of truly lasting merit. His first two books, *Almayer's Folly* (1895) and *An Outcast of the Islands* (1896), were a double earnest of his storytelling power. In these Malayan novels, as in many other works to come, he sets forth themes of self-deception and betrayal with psychological accuracy against a background of nature presented with atmospheric and visual detail that lifts his stories to the highest level of symbolic art.

His next novel, *The Nigger of the "Narcissus,"* is a master work of impressionism and symbolism in which ship, voyage, and violent storm are the means by which man is pitted against the treachery of external nature and the ambivalences of the human spirit. The real hero of this work is "unconscious" old Singleton, C.'s epitome of unthinking faithfulness to duty. ("He steered with care.") He might be related to Captain MacWhirr, of another descriptive tour de force, *Typhoon* (1902), who is heroic but "unaware," disdained by destiny if not at last by the sea.

"Youth," deriving from C.'s exhilarating experience with his "first command," in Asian waters, is an evocative sketch with overtones of disillusionment and death. Significantly, the piece introduces C.'s celebrated viewpoint device, Marlow.

In *Lord Jim*, his first long novel, Charlie Marlow is established as a character as well as a device. Through Marlow and other witnesses in the "case" of the title character, Conrad establishes a complex and tentative view of a complex and ambiguous world. The result is an achievement that Albert Guerard recognized as a new fictional form evolving midway between Melville's "Benito Cereno" and FAULKNER's *Absalom, Absalom!* This new form, the psychomoral novel, seeks to engage the reader's sensibilities "more strenuously and more uncomfortably than ever before." Two generations of critics have debated the fate of C.'s romantic hero who suffered an "acute consciousness of lost honour." That Jim is possibly the last protagonist in modern fiction who dies to redeem his honor may be a commentary on the evolution of tragic theory in the 20th c.

"Heart of Darkness" (published with "Youth" in 1902), based on C.'s own harrowing journey into the Congo in 1890, is presented as another of "Marlow's inconclusive experiences." Through C.'s narrative power and artistry, Marlow's physical journey up the Congo to find Kurtz modulates into a nightmarish itinerary of the human spirit, with the result that the tale becomes for the reader a pilgrimage to his own moral core. "All Europe contributed to the making of Kurtz," remarks Marlow to his listeners—and all of Western culture, it appears, contributed to C.'s accomplishment in "Heart of Darkness": Homer, Dante, Roman imperialism and Elizabethan buccaneering, the horrors of slavery and modern imperialism, as well as the ethics of the English philosopher Herbert Spencer (1820–1903) and insights similar to JUNG's into the world of dreams. Marlow's final "pose of a meditating Buddha" points to C.'s fascination with a dark illumination of illusion, emptiness, and silence.

Already in his early Malayan novels C. had demonstrated his control of the web of cross purposes and mutual deception that characterized the politics of Arabs, Malayans, and Europeans alike. Now, at the height of his powers, he worked two years to create *Nostromo* (1904), a prodigy of achievement which by reason of its scope of vision and its many textured substance invites comparison with *War and Peace*. C.'s ambitious design was "to render the spirit of an epoch in the history of South America." He succeeded in inventing the entire country of Costaguana—its landmarks, its people, its historical and social dynamics—and out of this imaginary time and place contrived a real world of men and women "short-sighted in good and evil." The tone of *Nostromo* moves from light irony to grim and bitter disillusionment. Individual conflicts and whole social movements are comprehended with equal ease. Uniquely for C., the center of tragic awareness is a woman—Mrs. Gould, one of his finest characters, a forerunner of the intelligent heroines of D. H. LAWRENCE, Virginia WOOLF, and E. M. FORSTER. Emilia Gould, her husband, Charles, Nostromo, Decoud, Dr. Monygham—all main characters of the novel—dramatize the tragic contradiction between private vision and public actions. Overshadowing the human activity are the mindless mountain range of Sulaco and the San Tomé silver mine, symbol of "materialistic interests" that drive the entire population of Costaguana through cycles of creativity and destructiveness.

The Secret Agent (1907), regarded by many as the first spy novel, is much more than the Graham GREENE "entertainments" it anticipates. It is a heavily ironic treatment of melodrama dealing simultaneously with international intrigue and domestic tragedy. C. devises a plot based on an actual terrorist conspiracy to blow up the Greenwich observatory, and then into a London setting reminiscent of Dickens he brings a shabby cast of mortals, including embassy officials, police officers, anarchists, and the secret agent, Adolph Verloc, and his wife and her slow-witted brother, Stevie. Winnie Verloc, who believed that "things do not stand much looking into," and the other characters are treated with scorn and pity as Conrad moves with a fiercely comic intention to prove that "perverse unreason has its own logical processes."

Under Western Eyes (1911), also dealing with the underworld of anarchists and *agents provocateurs*, contains the portrait of the student Razumov, a young Russian recalling the creations of Dostoevsky, which C. professed to despise, and anticipating the estranged antiheroes of GIDE and CAMUS. The book, which C. declared dealt "not so much with the political state as the psychology of Russia itself," as viewed through the "Western" mind of a professor of languages, is a study of human folly and of the absurd sequence of events "which no sagacity can foresee and no courage can break through."

Victory (1915) blends sympathy and irony as it deals symbolically with the consequences of a futile doctrine of detachment in a world that demands human action. Axel Heyst, the archetypal father-dominated son seen in Orestes, Hamlet, FREUD's essays, and KAFKA's Surrealist stories, has been taught by his philosopher-father to "look on—make no sound," a lesson he unlearns too late. This book, as well as other late works such as *Chance, The Arrow of Gold*, and *The Rover* (1923), contains a familiar motif: the rescuer of the damsel in distress.

But the chivalric aspect of C.'s temperament became evident very early in his career—in *The Rescue*. This novel cost him most in anguished expenditure of energy, exposed him to a long attrition of defeat and despair, and, in the end, turned out to be the book that has most disappointed critics. Nevertheless the "rescuer," Tom Lingard, is a pivotal figure, having first appeared in the early Malayan novels as a parody of innocent providence. Now, as a younger but maturer and more complex hero, Lingard strives vainly to fulfill his commitments to human solidarity and ends by failing his native friends, his fellow Europeans, and himself. From the splendid wreckage of this novel may be salvaged C.'s thematic achievement: a demonstration of the paralyzing force of distrust and the fatal consequences of faith misplaced and trust betrayed.

Throughout his career C. continued to produce minor pieces, including essays, autobiographical and critical sketches, and a few plays. Notable among short stories not already cited are "An Outpost of Progress," "The End of the Tether," "Amy Foster," "Falk," "Il Conde," and "The Secret Sharer"—the last a tale of initiation admired for its multilevel symbolism.

The Shadow-Line (1917), according to the author "not a story really but exact autobiography," is a tale of first command in which C. movingly restates his ideal of simple fidelity to a traditional code of conduct. This unusually direct statement of faith in the simple virtues, taken together with a misreading of the role of such characters as Singleton and MacWhirr, combined with C.'s frequent public affirmations to foster an "official" view of his philosophy. The golden text most frequently cited by critics comes from a preface written in 1912: "Those who read me know my conviction that the world, the temporal world, rests on a few very simple ideas; so simple that they must be as old as the hills. It rests notably on the idea of Fidelity."

But a statement written in 1895, and allowed by C. to stand in the preface to the definitive edition of *Almayer's Folly*, is much nearer to the skepticism and pessimism of his artistic vision, especially when taken in conjunction with the franker, grimmer tone of intimate correspondence during his early and middle period. After speaking of the bonds that unite mankind, he adds that all men's hearts "must endure the load of the gifts from Heaven: the curse of facts and the blessings of illusions, the bitterness of our wisdom and the deceptive consolation of our folly." This grimly paradoxical statement gives an extra dimension to C.'s celebrated preface to *The Nigger of the "Narcissus"* (written in 1897 but not published with the novel until 1914). In it he wrote: "My task which I am trying to achieve is, by the power of the written word to make you hear, to make you feel—it is, before all, to make you *see*. That—and no more, and it is everything." Often enough C. succeeded in his effort to make us see, so that (in his own words) "at last the presented vision of regret or pity, of terror or mirth, shall awaken in the hearts of the beholders that feeling of unavoidable solidarity; of the solidarity in mysterious origin, in toil, in joy, in hope, in uncertain fate, which binds men to each other and all mankind to the visible world."

C.'s position as an artist has become increasingly sure and clear. He ranks with his great 19th-c. forerunners: Balzac and Dickens, Flaubert and Maupassant, Turgenev and the Russian giants. He was respected by his great contemporaries: James and Forster, D. H. Lawrence and Thomas MANN, and Gide, who seems to have borrowed themes from C. and who painstakingly supervised the French translations of his works. C. recognized his own affinity with Marcel PROUST when he praised Proust's "power of analysis"; unquestionably, the two shared a great talent for creative uses of the memory. It is well known that T. S. ELIOT was dissuaded by Ezra POUND from attaching a Conrad quotation as an epigraph to *The Waste Land*, but Eliot in other ways acknowledged his debt to C.'s mind and method—there is evidence that C. anticipated, in practice and language, Eliot's famous definition of the objective correlative. Even Pound, Professor Frederick Karl notes, credits C. with helping to transform English prose as the poet hoped to transform English poetry.

F. Scott FITZGERALD took his cue for his Nick Carraway-Jay Gatsby formula from the Marlow-Kurtz relationship, as did Robert Penn WARREN for Jack Burden's quest for self-understanding during his discipleship under Willie Stark in *All the King's Men*. Ernest HEMINGWAY, who expressed special admiration for C., made a personal career out of one of C.'s themes—playing the futile game of life by the rules—while he created characters who moved to their doom with a Conradian freedom from delusion. C.'s impact is felt in the work of Arthur KOESTLER, André MALRAUX, Louis-Ferdinand CÉLINE, Jean-Paul SARTRE, and Graham Greene.

Faulkner's *Absalom, Absalom!* reflects the techniques of C., and his Nobel Prize acceptance speech owes much to the expressed idea and the rhetoric of passages in *Typhoon* and in C.'s essay on James. C's themes are to be seen in the plays of Eugene O'Neill and of Jean Genet, as well as in the ambitious cinematic efforts of Alfred Hitchcock, Carol Reed, and Francis Ford Coppola. The African novels of Chinua ACHEBE, NGUGI Wa Thiong'o, V. S. NAIPAUL, and Paul THEROUX incorporate various elements of C.'s literary vision, and critics are beginning to trace connections between C. and writers as varied as Malcolm LOWRY, Lawrence DURRELL, and Thomas PYNCHON.

This catalog of names is meant only to suggest the extent of C.'s wide-ranging influence upon 20th-c. literature. Critical intelligences in the modern world have received a deepened perception of the "visible world" and a dark enlightenment of the human spirit; and C. continues to inspire writers and readers alike who would probe the far reaches of imagination.

FURTHER WORKS: *Tales of Unrest* (1898); *The Inheritors* (1901, with Ford Madox Ford); *Youth and Two Other Stories* (1902); *Typhoon and Other Stories* (1903); *Romance* (1903, with Ford Madox Ford); *The Mirror of the Sea* (1906); *A Set of Six* (1908); *Twixt Land and Sea* (1912); *One Day More* (1913); *Within the Tides* (1915); *Notes of Life and Letters* (1921); *The Secret Agent: Drama in Four Acts* (1921); *Notes on My Books* (1921); *Laughing Anne* (1923); *The Nature of a Crime* (1924, with Ford Madox Ford); *Tales of Hearsay* (1925); *Five Letters by J. C. to Edward Noble in 1895* (1925); *Last Essays* (1926); *J. C.'s Letters to His Wife* (1927); *J. C.: Life and Letters* (1927); *C. to a Friend* (1928); *Letters from J. C., 1895–1924* (1928); *Lettres françaises* (1929); *Letters of J. C. to Marguerite Poradowska, 1890–1920* (1940); *Letters to William Blackwood and David S. Meldrum* (1958); *C.'s Polish Background: Letters to and from Polish Friends* (1964); *J. C. and Warrington Dawson: The Record of a Friendship* (1968); *J. C.'s Letters to Cunninghame Graham* (1969); *Congo Diary and Other Uncollected Pieces* [including *Up-RiverBook*, 1890] (1978); *The Collected Letters of J. C.* (5 vols., 1983–96)

BIBLIOGRAPHY: Crankshaw, E., *J. C.* (1936; 2nd ed. 1976); Gordan, J. D., *J. C.: The Making of a Novelist* (1941); Bradbrook, M. C., *J. C.: Poland's English Genius* (1941); Hewitt, D. J., *C.: A Reassessment* (1952; 2nd ed. 1968; 3rd ed. 1975); Guerard, A., *C. the Novelist* (1958); Baines, J., *J. C.: A Critical Biography* (1960); Stallman, R. W., ed., *The Art of J. C.: A Critical Symposium* (1960); Hay, E. K., *The Political Novels of J. C.* (1963); Sherry, N., *C's Eastern World* (1966); Fleishman, A., *C.'s Politics* (1967); Guetti, J., *The Limits of Metaphor: A Study of Melville, C., and Faulkner* (1967); Meyer, B., *J. C.: A Psychoanalytic Biography* (1967); Palmer, J. A., *J. C.'s Fiction: A Study in Literary Growth* (1968); Sherry, N., *C.'s Western World* (1971); Johnson, B., *C.'s Models of Mind* (1971); Teets, B. E., and H. E. Gerber, eds., *J. C.: An Annotated Bibliography of Writings about Him* (1971); Sherry, N., ed. *C.: The Critical Heritage* (1973); Thomas, C., ed., *Studies in J. C.* (1975); Sherry, N., ed., *C.: A Commemoration, 1974 International Conference* (1976); Morf, G., *The Polish Shades and Ghosts of J. C.* (1976); Nettels, E., *James & C.* (1977); Berthoud, J. A., *C.: The Major Phase* (1978); LaBossière, C. R., *J. C. and the Science of Unknowing* (1979); Conrad, J., *J. C.: Times Remembered* (1981); Meyers, J., *J. C.: A Biography* (1991); Bennett, C. D., *J. C.* (1991); Batchelor, J., *The Life of J. C.: A Critical Biography*

(1993); Jordan, E., *J. C.* (1996); Najder, Z., *C. in Perspective: Essays on Art and Fidelity* (1997)

—CARL D. BENNETT

What is so elusive about him is that he is always promising to make some general philosophic statement about the universe, and then refraining with a gruff disclaimer. . . . Is there not also a central obscurity, something noble, heroic, beautiful, inspiring half-a-dozen great books, but obscure, obscure? . . . These Essays *[Notes on Life and Letters]* do suggest that he is misty in the middle as well as at the edges, that the secret casket of his genius contains a vapour rather than a jewel; and that we needn't try to write him down philosophically, because there is, in this direction, nothing to write. No creed, in fact. Only opinions, and the right to throw them overboard when facts make them look absurd. Opinions held under the semblance of eternity, girt with the sea, crowned with stars, and therefore easily mistaken for a creed.

E. M. Forster, "J. C.: A Note," in *Abinger Harvest* (1940), pp. 159–160

The plight of the man on whom life closes down inexorably, divesting him of the supports and illusory protection of friendship, social privilege, or live, now emerged as the characteristic theme of his books. It is a subject that has become familiar to us in modern literature. . . . But it is doubtful if any . . . , possibly excepting Kafka, has achieved a more successful dramatic version of the problem than C. did—a more complete coincidence of the processes of psychic recognition and recovery with the dramatic necessities of the plot; and this for the reason which distinguishes C.'s contribution to modern fictional method: his imposition of the processes and structures of the moral experience (particularly the experience of recognition) on the form of the plot. Obviously this theme has a classic ancestry; it is the oldest mode of tragedy. C. was taxed with giving it its fullest possible analysis, for it virtually constitutes the whole and central matter of his work. . . .

The conditions that mark the plight of a C. character who is caught in the grip of circumstances that enforce self-discovery and its cognate, the discovery of reality or truth, are consistent throughout his books. The condition of moral isolation is the first of them. . . .

Morton D. Zabel, *The Portable C.* (1947), pp. 26–27

C. is never afraid of rhetoric or of a prose approaching the frontiers of poetry. His elaborately extended cadences, subtly gratifying the ear even while again and again cheating it of an expected pause, carry a large part of the burden of his constitutional melancholy. At the same time they form a kind of rhythmic correlative of that unintermitted striving to gain a longitude, to match the gale, which is his grand symbol for what we do best to address our lives to. It is recorded that he was fond of Jeremy Taylor—and from Taylor and other seventeenth-century writers he may have learned more directly than an Englishman would find it easy to do, simply because he was less aware of the dangers of archaism, fine writing, and pastiche. A larger and older eloquence than that of the Victorian age sounds often in his prose. . . .

J. I. M. Stewart, *Eight Modern Writers* (1963), p. 188

C. makes difficulties for his readers—often unconsciously, sometimes deliberately, . . . by concentrating on the self-deceptions that lead virtuous men astray in their pursuit of the good life, which must be a life of public as well as private good. Whether these deceptions are inherent in human nature or result from the pride of Western civilization, whether they are part of the plan of creation or only the effect of unscrupulously in man's thinking—these speculations crowd in upon the reader throwing a dense foliage across the path of the story. . . . The possibility that man is fundamentally good, potentially able to achieve the social harmony he mentally projects, stands against the possibility that man is basically corrupt and his utopian schemes "fairy tales" that create political miseries for the unimaginative, who wish only to be life alone. C.'s subtlety in contemplating these alternatives may be inferred from the wildly different conclusions critics reach on some of his works. . . .

Eloise Knapp Hay, *The Political Novels of J. C.* (1963), p. 16

The record of Conrad's political opinions is a record of growth. It shows no consistent application of first principles, nor systematic doctrine, nor even a sustained temperamental attitude. As in natural growth, there is an interplay of inner and outer forces which generates unlooked-for excrescences, and there is also an expanded comprehension—an ability to take in more of the world. Above all, this is the growth of an imagination: it is the mind of an artist with which we are concerned, not that of a philosopher or politician. The opinions are limited by naïveté, shaped by circumstance, charged with passion. They make up a set of ways of looking at the world, ways of seeing the impersonal forces of history to be instinct with human tragedy. With this somewhat vague but steadily growing imaginative comprehension, Conrad fashioned the personal dramas of his political novels as parables of man's life in history.

Avrom Fleishman, *C.'s Politics* (1967), p. 23

C.'s central moral concerns remain the same throughout his career—individual responsibility; self-knowledge; man's near inability to cope with (or even

discover) his own darkness, and yet the necessity of his doing so. . . . Many writers have seen that C. is deeply skeptical of all political idealism. But what is too rarely stressed is that this attitude is at bottom an ironic inversion of his more basic commitments: his scorn for political institutions is implicit in the value he places on the individual, and on the individual's paradox-ridden obligation to meet the darkness within himself; and his scorn for abstract doctrine is implicit in his intellectual skepticism. . . . In his final declaration for "life" despite the threats posed by human society and by an enigmatic universe, C. merely reaffirms his earliest values. And all his major works after *Lord Jim* may be seen as logical extensions of these commitments, exploring either their social implications or their broad philosophical assumptions.

John A. Palmer, *J. C.'s Fiction: A Study in Literary Growth* (1968), pp. xiv-xv

It is scarcely possible to imagine a more self-conscious writer than C., to imagine anyone more aware of his special relation to his material and to his audience. Yet he is, like any writer of adventure fiction, clearly descended from the "primitive storyteller." Indeed, in *Lord Jim* and elsewhere both C. and Marlow presume upon and subtly exploit their audience's patience. . . . In novel after novel C. tries to mingle the sophisticated and the primitive, tries to tell great old-fashioned stories complexly and fully. His subject matter is consistently that of the popular adventure story, his plots are nearly always potentially melodramatic, his rhetoric is always listing toward ornateness and excess. Yet his important work, far from succumbing to the simplification and banality inherent in these things, retrieves from them a rare and austere seriousness.

David Torburn, *C.'s Romanticism* (1974), pp. 162–63

C. never claims that "life" cannot be differentiated from "art." On the contrary, his entire aesthetic rest. . . . on the notion that the novelist's concern is not life merely, but life understood. If C.'s conviction of the primacy of vision or understanding in the creating of a novel is right, it follows that the novelist's values will be implicit rather than overt-that what he believes will not reside in what he sees, but in the kind of attention he give it; that it will be found not in the action he depicts, but in the way in which he depicts it. That C. devises narratives which turn on cases of suffering and defeat does not permit us to conclude with the modern realist that he is a moral nihilist, or even a moral sceptic. His positives are finally registered not in the mere sequence of represented events, but in the wealth and subtlety of the artistic context from which these events derive their significance.

Jacques A. Berthoud, *J. C.: The Major Phase* (1978), p. 190

COOVER, Robert

American novelist, b. 4 Feb. 1932, Charles City, Ia.

C. received his B.A. at Indiana University (1953) and his M.A. from the University of Chicago (1965). He served as fiction editor of the *Iowa Review* from 1974 to 1977. C. has taught at various colleges and universities and is currently at Brown University. He has received increasing critical acclaim and popular interest, as well as various awards, including the Faulkner Award (1966), a Rockefeller fellowship (1969), and Guggenheim fellowships in 1971 and 1974.

Although there is much that seems radically new in C.'s short stories and novels, they are demonstrably in the long line of American fiction whose origin is in Mark Twain's (1835–1910) *Adventures of Huckleberry Finn* (1884). We find in his work the same passion for the rhythms of an American spoken language, the same often critical concern with aspects of contemporary American culture, and the same immersion in American realities. In the wake of the great modernists and in response to an explosive new world, C., along with Thomas PYNCHON, John BARTH, Donald BARTHELME, E. L. DOCTOROW, and John HAWKES, has helped to forge a developing new American fiction that is very much in tune with the old. What they have added to Twain's example—this is especially true of C., Pynchon, Doctorow, and Barth—is an explicit involvement with American history and an endeavor to create from it a new mythopoesis. In the new process, a new reality emerges; C., like Hawkes, has at times been called a SURREALIST. Yet it is clear that, however unlimited his characters' actions may appear to be (by reason or convention), they consistently reflect a reality that is recognizably American.

The early stories collected in *Pricksongs and Descants* (1969) set the tone for all the longer fictions to follow: at their most effective, they display a wonderful inventiveness, a rare facility for language, and the ability to look at old models from new perspectives. At their weakest, they are self-indulgent and strain for effect. But, even then, they never fail to provoke. Illustrative is "The Brother," which views the Flood from the perspective of Noah's younger brother, a much better man than his sibling yet another of those who fail to survive. In C.'s revisionist version of the biblical myth, the moral imperative is reversed, and our modern heritage becomes more questionable and more understandable: Our universal ancestor is a man so self-absorbed that survival becomes his sole goal; he is easy enough for us to recognize in our own world.

There is a similar ambiguity in *The Origin of the Brunists* (1966), C.'s first novel, whose frame purports to be historical but which also borrows from myth; but history and myth alike are now C.'s creations. A mine disaster in a dying small town: ninety-seven miners die, and one survives. Around him, Giovanni Bruno, a cult forms, aided by a cynical local newspaperman. The town is divided; the cultists are driven from the town, and their icon is institutionalized; his sister dies a martyr; the mines close; the town stagnates further; the new religion, driven elsewhere, prospers. Echoes of mythopoesis, inverted, are everywhere: comic, irreverent, and also serious.

In *The Universal Baseball Association* (1968), a middle-aged accountant invents a game of baseball played with dice and accompanied by an elaborate set of statistics. But the child's game turns serious, and, gradually, it takes over the life of its creator; its characters supplant those from the world outside in his life. In the final chapter, only they appear; he too is absent in his own account of what is ostensibly his life. Again, the life-giving potential of myth is replaced with irony.

C.'s most ambitious novel is *The Public Burning* (1977), a powerful if sometimes excessive account of the Rosenberg spy case and trial of the early 1950s, a work based on close knowledge of the public record and an extraordinary imagination. Among the principal characters are Richard Nixon, ambitious and amoral vice president, and Uncle Sam, personification of the individualistic American tradition. C.'s Nixon is hateful, comic, and strangely sympathetic. Desperate for affection, he very nearly makes love with Ethel Rosenberg on the electric chair in Sing Sing prison. The scene is tasteless, in a sense, yet it is also very funny. And C. makes us believe that it is potentially true to the characters. It is exceeded only by the novel's conclusion, in which the national spirit is passed from Uncle Sam to Nixon by a graphically detailed act of sodomy, followed by the public execution of the Rosenbergs in Times Square, presided over by Betty Crocker for a national television audience. For an ahistorical people, C. suggests, only an exaggerated mythopoesis may serve; but it serves badly. In the midst of a nation marked everywhere by fertility archetypes, there is only sterility. (It is worth noting that the printed text of this novel is not quite what C. originally wrote but that the publishers evidently insisted on some changes because of a feared, but never actually threatened, libel suit by former President Nixon.)

Much of C.'s subsequent work seems almost consciously lesser: shorter works in a minor key, which investigate individual aspects of American culture but never coalesce completely as fictions. *A Political Fable* (1980) is a reprinting in book form, in an election year, of the early election-year novella "The Cat in the Hat for President" (1968). It is a comic-book vision turned brutally serious. Its somewhat surreal protagonist (he is able to lead out of a television set all the characters that it contains) satirizes and at the same time represents the failings of the American electoral system and sensibility. Published as a limited edition between hard covers, the short story *Charlie in the House of Rue* (1980) follows and subverts the ineffable Charlie Chaplin, who proves here limited, human, effable indeed. He starts through this house with all his familiar gestures and moves, troubled perhaps but surely in control. But then matters change and turn ominous and offensive. It is a very dark comedy that C. finds at the heart of the king of comedy. The roots of *Spanking the Maid* (1982) are in the domination fantasies of the Marquis de Sade (1740–1814), with all their pseudo-philosophical claptrap, in Victorian flagellation tales and in the fictions of Alain ROBBE-GRILLET. But it turns these sources on their tail; the master continues to discipline her because the manuals say that he must, and she accepts because she is learning so much from him about life. But in the end, their play is more wordplay than sexual or psychological, as if James JOYCE and not Sigmund FREUD or de Sade were his true master.

In *Whatever Happened to Gloomy Gus of the Chicago Bears?* C. returns, indirectly, to the Richard Nixon character of *The Public Burning*. But Gus (whose real name is Dick and who went to Whittier College) seems the fulfillment of the other Dick's wishes (as athlete and lover) but becomes, ironically, a political radical; he is killed by strike-breakers and police in a march on a steel plant. His tragicomic failure and futile death, allied to the references to Nixon and Jay Gatsby, make clear that this is another of C.'s readings of the American Dream, our central myth gone awry.

Pinocchio in Venice (1991) is C.'s first major work in more than a decade. It is, like so much of his work, ingenious, widly comic, marvelously inventive, and it builds on his long-term interests in language, myth, and national character (although here that character may be more Italian than American). But it, too, is ultimately not fully satisfying. From Collodi comes the idea of a puppet given life but remaining a puppet—not only Pinocchio but all his old puppet friends speak and act (as do various animals)—but C. adds to this idea a new, metaphoric dimension. Human potential, human foibles are thus revealed. But we cannot empathize with C.'s hero. The brilliance of the conception and of the writing is not transformed into emotion, may even detract from it at times. We note the ties to C.'s earlier work and his sustained mythic vision. But we remain less moved by Pinocchio's fate than by those of Noah's brother, or the Rosenbergs, or even Richard Nixon. C. remains one of our most vital and challenging novelists. Yet we may feel that he has never quite fulfilled all aspects of his potential.

FURTHER WORKS: *The Water Pourer* (1972); *A Theological Position* (1972); *Hair o' the Chine* (1979); *After Lazarus: A Filmscript* (1980); *The Convention* (1982); *In Bed One Night and Other Brief Encounters* (1983); *Gerald's Party* (1986); *John's Wife* (1996)

BIBLIOGRAPHY: Bacchilega, C., "Folktales, Fictions and Meta-Fictions: Their Interaction in R. C.'s *Pricksongs and Descants*," *New York Folklore*, 6, 3–4 (1980): 171–84; McCafferey, L., "R. C. on His Own and Other Fictions: An Interview," *Genre*, 14, 1 (1981): 45–63; LeClair, T., "The Garden in the Machine: Three Postmodern Pastorals," *MichA*, 13, 4 (1981): 405–20; Mazurek, R. A, "Metafiction, the Historical Novel, and C.'s *The Public Burning*," *Crit*, 23, 3 (Spring 1982): 29–42; Andersen, R., "The Artist in C.'s Uncollected Stories," *SHR*, 17, 4 (1983): 315–24; Gordon, L. G., R.C.: *The Universal Fiction-making Process* (1983); Lee, L. L., "R. C.'s Moral Vision: *Pricksongs and Descants*," *SSF*, 23, 1 (Winter 1986): 63–69; Caldwell, R. C., Jr., "Of Hobby-Horses, Baseball, and Narrative: C.'s *Universal Baseball Association*," *MFS*, 33, 1 (Spring 1987): 161–71; Mackey, L., "R. C.'s Dirty Stories: Allegories of Reading in 'Seven Exemplary Fictions,'" *IowaR*, 17, 2 (Spring-Summer 1987): 100–21; special C.issue, *DeltaES*, 28 (June 1989); Orlov, P. A., "A Fiction of Fantastic 'Facts': R. C.'s *The Public Burning*," in Sorkin, A. J., ed., *Politics and the Muse: Studies in the Politics of Recent American Literature* (1989)

—MORTON P. LEVITT

ĆOPIĆ, Branko

Yugoslav short-story writer, novelist, poet, dramatist, and writer of children's books (writing in Serbian), b. 1 Jan. 1915, Hašani; d. 24 March 1984, Belgrade

Ć. spent his "barefoot childhood" and early school years in his native Bosnia but moved to Belgrade in 1934 to attend the University of Belgrade School of Liberal Arts. By the time of his graduation in 1940 he had already published four collections of short stories, won two prestigious literary awards, and made a name for himself; Ć. became a member of the Serbian Academy of Sciences and Arts in 1967. In 1941 he joined the partisan forces lead by Tito.

The background for most of Ć.'s works is provided by his native region of Bosanska Krajina, with its rugged countryside, God-forsaken villages, and impoverished but high-spirited peasantry. In his pre-World War II stories, some of which are truly exquisite miniature character sketches, Ć. created a gallery of "dear faces" from his childhood memories. He constrasts their drab and color-less everyday life, devoid of even the simplest human necessities and pleasures, with their imaginative dreams into which they retreat when reality becomes too hard to bear.

During the war Ć. was able to witness the metamorphosis of his fellow countrymen from passive dreamers to courageous freedom fighters. His most memorable and by far most popular war hero is the legendary Nikoletina Bursać in the collection of related stories, "Doživljaji Nikoletine Bursaća" (1956; adventures of Nikoletina Bursać). Bursać is a huge, bearlike peasant youth and a brave machine gunner, with a great sense of humor and a gentle heart.

Of Ć.'s four novels, *Prolom* (1952; the eruption) and *Gluvi barut* (1957; the noiseless gunpowder) also deal with the theme of war. *Prolom* was meant to be a broad epic of the Bosnian uprising in 1941. Its many weaknesses (especially its excessive length and large number characters) forced Ć. to abandon the epic approach in *Gluvi barut* and to narrow down his focus to Vlado and Tigar, a political commissar and a partisan commander, who represent two different yet equally dehumanized types of overly zealous revolutionaries.

The humorous novel *Ne tuguj, bronzana stražo* (1958; do not grieve, bronze sentry), and the touching *Osma ofanziva* (1964; the eighth offensive), both set in the early postwar years, are much better than the first two. Former rugged peasants and recent war heroes now fight their last and perhaps most difficult battle for a successful adjustment to the new, unfamiliar conditions of their life after the war. Whether they are newly settled farmers in the fertile Banat Plains (*Ne tuguj, bronzana stražo*) or new urbanites on their way up in the Belgrade bureaucracy (*Osma ofanziva*), they all feel uprooted and out of place in their respective environments. Haunted by ghosts from the past, they are torn between the old and the new worlds, which clash in them and make their transplant difficult and painful.

Ć.'s children's books are as numerous as his works for adult readers. His popularity among young readers is enormous, and critics now compare him to his great predecessor, Jovan Jovanović Zmaj (1833–1904), the favorite author of Serbian children for the last hundred years.

Although Ć.'s early postwar works suffered a great deal from his allegiance to the strict Communist Party line, he eventually emerged from the turbulent period just after the war as a literary figure of impressive stature. Ć.'s witty and entertaining fiction, written in the rich and racy idiom of Bosnia and peopled with many likable, down-to-earth heroes, continues the best traditions of classic Serbian realism with a rural orientation.

FURTHER WORKS: *Pod Grmečom* (1938); *Borci (Bojovnici) i bjegunci* (1939); *Planinci* (1940); *Ognjeno radjanje domovine* (1944); *Nove žene* (1945); *Rosa na bajonetima* (1946); *Sveti magarac i druge priče* (1946); *Ratnikovo proljeće* (1947); *Živjeće ovaj narod* (1947); *Surova škola* (1948); *Ljudi s repom* (1949); *Major Bauk* (1949); *Srca u buri* (1952); *Dragi likovi* (1955); *Gorki med* (1959); *Vuk Bubalo* (1961); *Humorističke priče* (1962); *Izabrana dela* (6 vols., 1963); *Sabrana dela* (12 vols., 1964); *Bašta sljezove boje* (1970); *Sabrana dela*, (12 vols., 1975); *Seosko groblje* (1978). SELECTED WORKS FOR CHILDREN: *U Carstvu leptirova i medveda*

(1940); *Priče partizanke* (1944); *Udarnik ili Družina junaka* (1945); *Bojna lira pionira* (1945); *Vratolomne Priče* (1947); *Armija, odbrana tvoja* (1948); *Sunčana republika* (1948); *Rudar i mjesec* (1948); *Ježeva Kuća* (1949); *Priče ispod zmajevih krila* (1953); *Doživljaji mačka Toše* (1954); *Čarobna šuma* (1957); *Partizanske tužne bajke* (1958); *Orlovi rano lete* (1957); *Magareće godine* (1960); *Deda-Trišin mlin* (1960); *Sabrana dela za decu* (6 vols., 1960); *Slavno vojevanje* (1961); *Bitka u Zlatnoj dolini* (1963); *Sin brkate čete* (1965)

BIBLIOGRAPHY: , A. B., on *Prolom, IBSB*, 4 (1953): 59; Zorić, P., on *Osma oofanziva, IBSB*, 15 (1964): 273–74; Pribić, N., on *Osma ofanziva, BA*, 39 (1965): 104; Nikolić-Micki, D., "B. Ć.: The Tragic Lyre of Mirth," *Review* (Belgrade), No. 1 (1974): 38–39; Eekman, T., *Thirty Years of Yugoslav Literature (1945–1975)* (1978): 113–17

—BILJANA ŠLJIVIĆ-ŠIMŠIĆ

COPPARD, A(lfred) E(dgar)

English short-story writer and poet, b. 4 Jan. 1878, Folkstone; d. 13 Jan. 1957, London

On All Fool's Day 1919 C. abandoned the life of middle-class respectability that he had built from a background of poverty and ignorance to live in the woods and write stories. His life reads like one of his stories, and his readers and C. himself have confused the two. Forced to go to work at the age of ten, he eventually educated himself with books purchased from winnings as a professional runner. He read deeply in English literature with passion if not sophistication. He was always aware of his commonness, and his life and work paradoxically celebrate and abhor vulgarity, C. reveals his duality autobiographically in *It's Me, O Lord!* (1957) and fictionally in "My Hundredth Tale" (1931) and other Johnny Flynn stories.

C. also gained a reputation for poetry, especially with the publication of *The Collected Poems* (1928), but that writing is important only for its influence on his short fiction, the best of which is lyrical.

In his first collection, *Adam and Even and Pinch Me* (1921), the title story remains the best example of a whimsical supernaturalism that runs through his more popular, but weaker, fiction, while "Arabesque: the Mouse" shows that from the beginning C. consciously pursued complex artistry. "Dusky Ruth" is the first of his stories to investigate the secret sadness of women, and more, men's inability to understand them.

The theme of the fastidious man put off by the earthy woman appears notably in the title story of *The Black Dog* (1923), in which C. constructs an elaborate pattern of separation metaphors. In the title story of *Fishmonger's Fiddle* (1925) he employs affectionate comedy in reversing these roles. His best-known story, "The Higgler" (also in *Fishmonger's Fiddle*), explores the conflicts between men and women, freedom and necessity, vulgarity and sensitivity.

In his finest work, the title story of *The Field of Mustard* (1926), C. studies the psychology of women, the struggle against poverty, and the inevitability of loss in a subtly lyric construction. Two of three aging women collecting firewood on a cold afternoon have a conversation during which they discover that they have both loved the same man, and so lose all that remains of their youth and passion. In the course of the barely perceptible action the reader, like the characters, tastes the bitter flavor of life. As in many of his best tales, C. creates a faintly sinister natural setting.

Although C. has traditionally been thought of as a simple primitive, a romantic in the wrong century, more recent views consider him far more complex. The themes and techniques of his best work are distinctly modern and literary. C's influence and reputation have been restricted because his work was published in limited editions, because he was not part of a literary circle, and because he wrote far too much that was of poor quality. After 1931 the stories became mannered and artificial. He did, however, play a significant part in the creation of the modern short story, of which he produced a dozen of the finest examples.

FURTHER WORKS: *Clorinda Walks in Heaven* (1922); *Silver Circus* (1928); *Nixey's Harlequin* (1931); *Dunky Fitlow* (1933); *Polly Oliver* (1935); *Ninepenny Flute* (1937); *You Never Know, Do You?* (1939); *Ugly Anna* (1944); *The Dark-Eyed Lady* (1947); *Lucy in Her Pink Jacket* (1954)

BIBLIOGRAPHY: Schwartz, J., *The Writings of A. E. C.* (1931); Fabes, G., *The First Editions of A. E. C.* (1933); Bates, H. E., *The Modern Short Story* (1941): 133–40; O'Connor, F., *The Lonely Voice* (1965): 170–86; Beachcroft, T. O., *The English Short Story*, Vol. 2 (1967): 26–27

—FRANK EDMUND SMITH

CORTÁZAR, Julio

Argentine novelist, short-story writer, and poet, b. 26 Aug. 1914, Brussels, Belgium; d. 12 Feb. 1984, Paris, France

C. was born in Brussels of Argentine parents abroad on business, who returned to Buenos Aires when C. was four years old. As a young man he taught French literature at the University of Cuyo, where he joined a protest against Perón and was jailed for a short time. After his release he left his post at the university. In Buenos Aires C. became director of a publishing company. In 1952 he began his career as a freelance interpreter for UNESCO in Paris, where he lived until his death in 1984.

C. considered himself to be the only writer of his generation to be nourished by the two currents of Argentine literature that prevailed during his formative years: the sensual and realistic description of city life in the unkempt language of Roberto ARLT and the universality and rigorous prose of Jorge Luis BORGES. It was Borges, in fact, as editor of the journal *Los anales de Buenos Aires*, who published C.'s first short story, "Casa tomada" (house taken over) in 1946.

C. is a master of the fantastic short story. Many of his stories depict the everyday lives of common people whose tranquil existence is subtly and mysteriously subverted by unknown forces. By alluding to familiar places, commercial products, and routine activities, and by employing a straightforward, simple, and conversational prose, C. adeptly creates a recognizable atmosphere. After he has gained the reader's confidence, he injects the inexplicable, inexorable mystery into the story. In "Casa tomada" an unidentified noise takes over a house and forces an elderly man and his sister to abandon it. In another story, "La autopista del sur" (1966; "The Southern Thruway," 1973), a traffic jam lasts more than a year. In a third, "Axolotl" (1956; "Axolotl," 1963), a man visiting an aquarium becomes psychically imprisoned inside an axolotl, an amphibianlike creature. Even stranger than these mysterious occurrences is the attitude of most of the characters in the stories, for they seem to confront the unknown that alters their lives by either adapting to it or being vanquished by it.

Many of C.'s stories are based on his dreams, nightmares, and hallucinations brought on by illness or obsessions. As a vehicle for expressions of repressed, irrational instincts and phobias, his short stories often serve as exorcisms for him.

C. also writes realistic short stories, such as "La señorita Cora" (1966; "Nurse Cora," 1973) and "Los buenos servicios" (1958; "At Your Service," 1963), and his most famous, "El perseguidor" (1958; "The Pursuer," 1963), which reveal his talent for identifying with and expressing an adolescent's emotions, an ingenuous old woman's experiences, and the anguished life of a Black jazz musician.

C.'s short stories have been published in a number of collections, including: *Bestiario* (1951; bestiary), *Final del juego* (1956; end of the game), *Las armas secretas* (1959; the secret weapons), *Todos los fuegos el fuego* (1966; *All Fires the Fire*, 1973), *Octaedro* (1974; octahedron), and *Alguien que anda por ahí* (1977; someone's out there somewhere). Without signaling the disappearance of the "fantastic," this last volume marks a new departure in the style and themes of C.'s stories. In previous volumes the focus was usually unilateral: one protagonist bent upon an existential or ontological self-discovery, as in "Una flor amarilla" (1956; "A Yellow Flower," 1963), or an anguished self-contemplation, as in "Ahí pero dónde, cómo" (1974; "There but Where, How," 1980) or a collective adventure rendered from one perspective as in "El río" (1956; the river). In *Alguien que anda por ahí* various stories encompass a plight and relationship of complicity between two equally important protagonists by means of broadening the narrative perspective. In "Vientos alisios" ("Trade Winds," 1980) the author uses nonreferential verb forms, such as the reflexive, the gerund, and the infinitive, to relate the dilemmas of Vera and Mauricio. In "Usted se tendió a tu lado" (You lie down at your side), the narrator alternately addresses a mother and her son with the two Spanish forms for "you," respectively the formal "Ud." and the familiar "tú." In "Las caras de la medalla" ("The Faces of the Medal," 1980) a feigned first-person-plural stance results in certain distancing from Mireille and Javier while implying that either of them could be the narrator. Certainly, C. has undertaken experimentation with a "peripatetic" or "reflexive" narrative perspective in his short stories since "Las babas del diablo" (1958; "Blow-Up," 1963) and "La señorita Cora"; however, in these latest stories the purpose and the result of the technique are an authorial concern for protagonists of *equal* weight and the development of an atmosphere of *mutual* helplessness.

Alguien que anda por ahí deals with political situations more explicitly than his earlier fiction, although political themes were present in the short story "Reunión" (1966; "Meeting," 1973), in the novel *Libro de Manuel* (1973; *A Manual for Manuel*, 1978), and in the brief comic-strip narrative *Fantomas contra los vampires multinacionales* (1975; Fantomas takes on the multinational vampires). The political stories of *Alguien que anda por ahí* are more simple and direct in style than the earlier works, but powerful in their evocation of massacres—in "Apocalipsis en Solentiname" ("Apocalypse at Solentiname," 1980)—and of persecutions and torture—in "Segunda vez" ("Second Time Around," 1980).

Julio Cortázar

An earlier and rather unusual volume of fables and tales bordering on the short-story genre, *Historias de cronopios y de famas* (1962; *Cronopios and Famas*, 1969), clearly demonstrate several constant characteristics of C.'s writing: humor, imagination, and a playful approach to reality. Although these traits persist in his novels, they do not appear in such a gratuitous and cheerful manner as in this collection of anecdotes and fragments that create situations and characters that challenge the logic and routine of everyday life. One of C.'s many protests against the Western traditions of rationalism and pragmatism, this playful element, now tinged with melancholy, has surfaced again in anecdotes in the volume *Un tal Lucas* (1979; *A Certain Lucas*, 1984).

Much of C.'s fame rests on his second novel, *Rayuela* (1963; *Hopscotch*, 1966). The English version by Gregory Rabassa received the first National Book Award for translation. The protagonist, Oliveira, makes a variety of attempts to experience a world free from the constraining values of rational Occidental civilization. For his quest, a logical and pragmatic approach rooted in the very values of society is useless. Therefore, by means of happening like adventures, absurd endeavors, and humor that is at times tinged with tragedy, he leaps forward and falls back again, aiming for his "kibbutz of desire," as he calls it; to experience life as one desires it to be and not as one thinks it is. Though he never succeeds, in the course of the novel, he never loses hope.

Rayuela can be read as at least two books. In the "Table of Instructions" at the beginning, C. suggests that the reader who wants the narrative plot should read along from chapter one to chapter fifty-six. The story line, as in all C.'s novels, ends with an atmosphere of mystery, an open-ended plot that the reader must complete himself.

The second manner of reading *Rayuela*, as proposed by C., is to read the first fifty-six chapters—except for one—and ninety-eight shorter selections from a third section entitled "Expendable Chapters." For this reading, one is provided with directions for inserting the numbered selections among the numbered chapters. Thus the reader, led by the directions, jumps forward and backward through the book, as if he were playing hopscotch. He enters into the creation of another version of the novel and becomes what C. designates an "accomplice-reader." C. implicitly suggests that the reader can even arrange the chapters some other way, one to his own liking.

Rayuela is equally innovative in its use of language, for C. plays with works, sacrilegiously attacks the serious style of traditional fiction in Latin America and Spain, and invents languages.

C.'s novel *Libro de Manuel*, a mélange of fact and fiction, of humor and eroticism, focuses on his concern for the political condition of Latin America. C.'s intentions, in part, is to expose the organized torture of political prisoners in Latin American countries. In fact, the last portion of the novel is a purposefully shocking juxtaposition in parallel columns of published testimony by U.S. soldiers of their torture techniques in the Far East and testimony given in the U.N. by Latin American political prisoners who had undergone similar torture at the hands of their own countrymen. Upon its publication, C. ceded his future profits to two organizations that aid the families of political prisoners.

With his short stories C. has demonstrated to other Latin American writers that the fantastic is a part of everyday life. With his novels he has revolutionized the language and structure of the genre in Latin America. He has invited the Latin American novelist to abandon cultural taboos and to employ a naturalness, an inventiveness, a playful and erotic freedom in literature. Although he is a firm believer in the advent of socialism for Latin America and has expressed his support of Castro's Cuba and the fallen Allende regime in Chile, he defends his experimental fiction against accusations of hermeticism and asserts his right as an artist to explore and to enrich the notion of reality by subverting and revolutionizing Western tradition. He is widely translated, read, and admired throughout the Western world, as well as in Latin America.

FURTHER WORKS: *Presencia* (1938); *Los reyes* (1949); *Los premios* (1960; *The Winners*, 1965); *La vuelta al dí en ochenta mundos* (1967); *Buenos Aires, Buenos Aires* (1968); *62: Modelo para armar* (1968; *A Model Kit*, 1972); *Último round* (1969); *Viaje alrededor de una mesa* (1970); *Pameos y meopas* (1971); *Prosa del observatorio* (1972); *La casilla de los Morelli* (1973); *Territorios* (1978); *Deshoras* (1982; *Unreasonable Hours*, 1995). **FURTHER WORKS IN ENGLISH:** *End of the Game and Other Stories* (1967; repub. as *Blow-Up and Other Stories*, (1968); *A Change of Light* (1980)

BIBLIOGRAPHY: Harss, L., and Dohmann, B., *Into the Mainstream* (1966): 206–45; Sola, G., de, *J. C. y ei hombre nuevo* (1968); Giacoman, H., *Homenaje a J. C.* (1972); Guibert, R., *Seven Vioces* (1972): 277–302; special C. issue, *Review*, No. 7 (1972); Garfield, E. P., *Es J. C. un surrealista?* (1975); Garfield, E. P., *J. C.* (1975); Garfield, E. P., *J. C. por J. C.* (1978); Alazraki, J., and I. Ivask, eds., *The Final Island* (1978); Yovanovich, G., *J. C.'s Character Mosaic: Reading the Longer Fiction* (1991); Ramirez, S., *Hatful of Tigers: Reflections on Art, Culture, and Politics* (1995); Stavans, I., *J. C.: A Study of the Short Fiction* (1996)

—EVELYN PICON GARFIELD

In theory and practice [C.] seeks a total renovation, not out of an eagerness for originality but out of internal necessity. The renovations consists of the destruction of character, situation, literary style, forms ("of the formulas," he clarifies), and language. He speaks out against deceptive narrative easiness . . . Padded literature, verbal clichés; and he asks for a literature that is the "least literary possible," in short, and anti-literature, which dares to transgress the total literary deed, the book. He wants to open up the closed literary order, to establish an open order that offers multiple perspectives. Even more, he chiefly wants disorder, the breaking of logical and discursive expression into a disconnected and fragmented story, which he feels can best be compared to a kaleidoscope. . . .

C. does not adopt this narrative conduct only to shock the naïve reader or to be in the height of literary fashion. . . . Within the aesthetic cosmos that he wants "chaos" to be, the organization of the story and idiomatic invention have a function and are justified by the total context.

Ana María Barrenechea, *Sur*, No. 288 (1964), pp. 70–71

When C.'s most successful novel, *Hopscotch*, was published here last year, I read it with great pleasure . . . and boredom . . . and irritation! Here was a man whose writing flashed with wit, superb imagery and who obviously was possessed of—and by—a fantastic imagination. But what of the endless self-indulgences? The tricks and games played not with or for—but on the reader.

. . . Yet what magnificent tricks C. *does* play. . . . Still a bright texture of reality runs through these stories (in *The End of the Game, and Other Stories*). It is as if C. is showing us first that it is essential for us to reimagine the reality in which we live and which we can no longer take for granted; and second, he shows us how to do this by the use of infinite variety and possibilities. . . .

. . . The possibilities of the moral effects of art as action were totally obliterated in Antonioni's film [of *Blow-Up*]; but this implication is what makes the work a gem among contemporary stories.

Daniel Stern, *Nation*, 18 Sept. 1967, p. 248

Subtle, delicate, wavering, contradictory, the short stories, of C. make us marvel, but their meaning seems to slip through our hands like so much brilliant dust, like so much unstill and slippery water. The difficulties presented by his first stories turn out, nevertheless, to be almost insignificant if we compare them to the problems that arise in some of the particular "abstract" stories of the second period. I refer to the stories of C. which appeared first in literary reviews (some of the most interesting and significant ones in *Ciclón* of Havana) and which later were almost all grouped together to form the second part of the volume *Historias de Cronopios y de Famas*.

Manuel Duran, in La vuelta a C. en nueve ensayos
(1968), p. 33

Rayuela has been hailed by the *Times Literary Supplement* as the first great novel of Spanish America. I do not know if this is true; but it can indeed be stated that J. C. . . . has been writing . . . the most revolutionary narrative prose in the Spanish language. But to limit C. to what Philippe Sollers calls "Latin Americanism" would be a serious error. For the North American critic and novelist C. D. B. Bryan, writing in *The New Republic, Rayuela* is the most powerful encyclopedia of emotions and visions that the international generation of postwar writers has produced. The readers will be able to verify the validity of these statements soon after entering into one of the richest universes of contemporary fiction: the one containing the Pandora's box—play, death, and resurrection—that is *Rayuela*. . . .

J. C. has written a novel faithful to his deep convictions: Apart from our individual destinies, we are part of figures we do not know." Together with Octavio Paz and Luis Buñuel, J. C. today represents the vanguard of Spanish America.

Carlos Fuentes, La nueva novela
hispanoamericana (1969), pp. 67, 77

The narrative form is questioned at the start of [*Hopscotch*] itself, by the author's telling the reader how to read it. . . . C. goes a step further and proposes a classification of readers: the female reader, or hedonistic, one who reads only for pleasure; and the accomplice reader, the one willing to help in the actual creation of the novel. To this reader, C. offers a bonus, the possibility of following a sequence of chapters that will entrap him in an infinite circular reading: Chapter 58 refers to Chapter 131, which refers to Chapter 58, and so on and so forth, until kingdom come. The reader thus becomes another character in the book.

In *Hopscotch* the *form* of the novel—a labyrinth without a center, a trap that is always shutting the reader within it, a serpent biting its tail—is no more than another device to emphasize the deep, secret subject of the book: the exploration of a bridge between two existences (Oliveira, Traveler), a bridge between two muses (La Maga, Talita), a bridge between two worlds (Paris, Buenos Aires). The novel unfolds itself to question itself the better; indeed, the title indicates its symbolic form (a hopscotch is a labyrinth and a *mandata*, in the Jungian sense). Yet it is also a novel about the complexities of being an Argentine (a man between two worlds) and about the

double who menaces us in other dimensions of our lives. The *form* of the book has become what used to be called its *content*.

Emir Rodríguez-Monegal, in Ivar Ivask and Gero
von Wilpert, eds., World Literature since 1945
(1973), pp. 435–36

E.P.G.: Let's look at a third stage, that of *Cronopios and Famas* and *Hopscotch*, where you are thoroughly intent upon changing reality, upon looking for authenticity in life and in literature with a good dose of humor, play and optimism.

J.C.: . . . I am profoundly convinced, and every day more so, that we are embarked on a course, an erroneous road. That is, mankind has chosen the wrong path. I speak about Western man, above all, because I know little about the Orient. We have set off on an historically false course that is leading us to definite catastrophe, to annihilation for whatever reason—war, air pollution, boredom, universal suicide, whatever. In *Hopscotch*, especially, there is that continuous feeling of being in a world that should be otherwise because—here I'm going to make an important digression. There have been critics who have considered *Hopscotch* to be a profoundly pessimistic book since it seems to dwell on lamenting the state of things. I believe it to be deeply optimistic because despite Oliveira's wily character, as we Argentinians say, his tantrums, his intellectual mediocrity, his incapacity to go beyond certain limits, he is a man who throws himself headlong against the wall, the wall of love, the wall of daily routine, the wall of philosophical systems, the wall of politics. He knocks his head against all that because at heart he is an optimist, because he thinks that one day, not in his time but for others, some day, that wall will tumble down and on the other side is the "kibbutz" of desire, the "promised land," the true man, that human being that he imagines and that he has not been able to become up to this moment. . . . The general idea behind *Hopscotch*, you see, is the proof of a failure and the hope of a victory. But the book doesn't propose any solution; it simply limits itself to showing the possible paths one can take to knock down the wall, to see what's on the other side.

Interview from Evelyn Picon Garfield, Cortázar
por Cortázar (1978), pp. 63–64

Games and humor constitute techniques of withdrawal, cooling off, distancing, and distention; they intervene between the sentimental whirlwind and frenetic vanity as a desacralizing antidote. They restore language to the surface; they dismiss Apollonian rhetoric and bring to the surface the Dionysian language of the visceral depths. Against the possessive introduction of passion, erotic delirium and oneiric wandering, the unsubmissive, irreverent games and humor produce a lucid break, an ironic splitting, a liberating separation.

Games, humor and irony become possible when existential urgency abates. They diminish the pressure; they relax compulsion in order to restore independence. They entail a conscious practice of detachment, which Oliveira/Cortázar exercises to preserve his voluntary displacement as an outsider. Oliveira leaps into an alter ego with his ruptures, irruptions and surprising disruptions; with his confusion of hierarchies that makes the worthless transcendental and the supremely important almost worthless; with his black humor that suspends moral norms and emotional imperatives; with his exercises in profanation, his reductions to absurdity, his references to the ridiculous, his recourse to the outlandish, his absurd associations, his juxtapositions of the majestic with the popular or vulgar, his parodic mobility, his puns, his verbal irreverence, his word games, his burlesque language games, kicking himself with polyglot insults, his orthographic humor, his joking homophony and his street language inserted into passages of metaphysical inquiry or into decisive passages. His humor and irony impose a margin of absence; they entail indifference, leisure, intelligent aloofness from threatening demands, a detaching of himself from his identity, a willingness to pay the price of sacrilege and impiety.

Saúl Yurkievich, "*Eros ludens:* Games, Love and Humor in *Hopscotch,*" in J. Alazraki and I. Ivask, eds., *The Final Island* (1978), pp. 107–8

CORTEZ, Jayne

American poet, b. 10 May 1936, Arizona

C.'s background and experience as a poet has always been as much a public as a private activity. Reared in California, she was artistic director of the Watts Repertory Theater Company (1964-70) in Los Angeles and has performed her poetry at numerous poetry festivals. Moving to New York in 1967, C. was writer in residence at Livingston College of Rutgers from 1977 to 1983 and won (among other awards and honors) the Creative Artists Program Service Poetry Award in 1973 and 1981; she has collaborated with jazz and blues musicians since the 1960s. C.'s poetry is socially committed and, like the work of the best progressive jazz musicians, technically exploratory.

C. is known not only as a poet but a poet/performer who has presented her work internationally in solo performances and also with musical—primarily jazz—accompaniment. In addition to comprising seven books of poetry, her work has been widely anthologized and captured on sound and video recordings, notably in *Everywhere Drums*, a sound recording, and *Mandela Is Coming*, a music video, both of which appeared in 1991; she also contributed to *Poetry in Motion*, a 1983 video anthology of contemporary avant-garde American poets. Throughout her career C. has been able to merge a feel for language and the materiality of her medium (word sounds, rhythm, imagery) with overt sociopolitical concerns.

Although often polemical, C.'s work maintains its artistic integrity, as evidenced in the imagistic and phonemic edginess of the title of her first book, *Pissstained Stairs and the Monkey Man's*

Wares (1969). Symptomatic of the Black Arts movement, this book contains phonic portraits of the love/sex lives of jazz and blues artists such as Charlie Parker, Bessie Smith, Leadbelly, Billie Holiday, and John Coltrane; she sees these artists as, in their own ways, revolutionaries, whose mediums were their messages. C.'s second book, *Festivals and Funerals* (1971), explores similar themes, but is more self-consciously ideological, deliberating on topics such as colonialism, African nationalism/nationhood, and the artist as revolutionary; she also deals quite frontally, in language and imagery, with the harsh socioeconomic conditions of minorities and blue collar workers—the persona poem "I Am a Worker," for example, improvises on the voice of a haggard garment worker. Counterpointing its title, *Scarifications* (1973), C.'s third book salts social wounds, such as the Vietnam War and urban (specifically New York) strife, while at times offering as an alternative romanticized representations of life in Africa—where scarification is aesthetic/ritual practice. Like the ritual practice, C.'s poems are a praxis, a performed knowledge of the relationship among beauty, social status, and pain.

The linguistic improvisations of *Mouth on Paper* (1977) continue to explore many of the themes imaged in previous collections (jazz, Africa, sex, and revolution), in sometimes brutally direct detail; though the poems evolve as a series of poem/"scores" meant to be performed orally—a line like "aye ya ya ya ay yo Chocolate," for example, in "Chocolate," mimics the sound of a trumpet; another poem, "For the Poets," deploys a ritualistic call and response technique—the intent of the collection is not merely formal experimentation but social indictment. Moreover, C.'s surrealistic image juxtapositions/recombinations mark her debt to Beat poets like Bob Kaufman (b. 1925), Ted Joans (b. 1928), and Allen GINSBERG, while presenting a linguistically vital image of the materiality of a given sociocultural milieu—African and African American—and avoiding the exoticism of *Scarifications*.

Firespitter (1982) develops the surrealistic tendencies of C.'s poetry, evident in *Pissstained Stairs* but not gaining confidence as a voice until *Mouth on Paper*. As in her previous books, the style is a consequence of a sociopolitical—the revolution of thought/perception. Although *Coagulations: New and Selected Poems* (1984) offers little new in terms of theme or form, the collection underlines the rootedness of C.'s language and imagery in the psychosocial experience of blackness—especially of African Americanness—and in the aesthetic gestures common to Afro-oriented cultures, including orality, the performative, and musicality.

After almost a ten-year hiatus, C.'s seventh book, *Poetic Magnetic* (1991), arrived with a new twist on familiar themes. C. and artist Melvin Edwards have created a verbal-visual collage, perhaps the next logical move for a poetry whose line has run the linguistic gamut from phonic abstraction and surrealist experimentation to visceral, dialectic directness. The dialogue of illustration and poem is symptomatic of C.'s chronic need to get beyond the page (often leading to collaboration with others) to reach the largest possible audience and keep in touch with the increasingly audiovisual rhythms of African American culture, with the knowledge that "Africanness" has always been a "multimedia" experience.

FURTHER WORKS: *War on War* (1982); *Maintain Control* (1986)

BIBLIOGRAPHY: Lee, D. L., "Toward a Definition: Black Poetry of the Sixties," in Gayle, A., Jr., ed., *The Black Aesthetic* (1972); Redmond, E. B., *Drumvoices: The Mission of Afro-American*

Poetry, A Critical History (1976); Melhen, D. H., "A *MELUS* Profile and Interview: J. C.," *MELUS*, 21 (Spring 1996): 71–79

—TOM LAVAZZI

ĆOSIĆ, Dobrica

Yugoslav novelist and essayist (writing in Serbian), b. 29 Dec. 1921, Drenova

After studies at an agricultural school, Ć. was swept into World War II. Joining Tito's forces, he eventually became a political commissar in one of the regional armed detachments in central Serbia. After the Communists came to power in Yugoslavia (1945), he worked as a provincial party functionary and was later elected to the national assembly. From 1955 to 1963 he was a member of the editorial board of the Belgrade literary periodical *Delo*, and from 1961 to 1963 of the literary monthly *Danas* as well.

The subject of Ć.'s first novel, *Daleko je sunce* (1951; *Far Away Is the Sun*, 1963), is the struggle of the Communist-led resistance forces against the Nazis during World War II. It was the first successful literary attempt in Communist Yugoslavia to treat this subject without an *a priori* adherence to obligatory propagandistic falsities, black-and-white characterizations, and ideologically "correct" messages. The result was a powerful and moving study of the war-ravaged land, in which all the fighting factions are portrayed with psychological authenticity, no side is ideologically or morally spotless, and no individual entirely free from confusion, error, and the terrible guilt of wanton destruction.

In his second novel, *Koreni* (1954; the roots), Ć. turns his attention to the Serbian past in order to examine and discover those ethical, social, and psychological roots from which had sprung the bitter fruits of contemporary Serbian life. Cast in the last decade of the 19th c., this work depicts the sturdy peasant society just awakened from the centuries old slumber within the Turkish empire. In *Koreni* the drama of a country caught in a series of historical spasms trying to compensate for lost time, and simultaneously the drama of a family and clan that has the responsibility for transmitting the age-old vitality and vigor, are successfully intertwined to produce a vivid impression of patriarchal, rural Serbia poised on the brink of the modern age and yet utterly uncertain as to its proper place within the European family of nations.

In *Deobe* (1961; the divisions) Ć. returned to the subject of Yugoslavia in World War II. Here he focused on the civil-war years (1941–46), during which the battle for power raged between the Communist partisans led by Tito and the nationalist forces led by Draža Mihajlović. With rare poetic insight, Ć descends into the dark recesses of that irreparable discord to perceive and comprehend its historical, psychological, and moral causes. Out of this spiritual descent into the national subconscious emerges a vast poetic chronicle of the most turgid and destructive era in modern Serbian history, a thorough survey of all the moral and ideological crises of the era, and a moving reminder that man alone is the begetter of his most unbearable ordeals. Again, Ć. spreads the sin equally among the factions he presents. The political motivation that leads the characters to perform their actions recedes in the flood of blind malevolence and evil unleashed by man's diabolical instinct for destructiveness.

In his next novel, *Bajka* (1966; fairy tale), Ć. continues to ponder the concern so central to his writing—the defeat of human creativity by the forces of destruction. By synthesizing the most important contemporary problems and superimposing them on those of the historically relevant past, he attempts to conjure up the world of the future. The resulting vision is an unpleasant one, for the clues add up to the portrait of a world in which the flux of ideas will undermine the foundations of all beliefs and values.

By far, Ć.'s most ambitious literary endeavor is *Vreme smrti* (3 vols., 1972–75; *A Time of Death*, 1978; *Reach to Eternity*, 1980). Both a sequel to the psychological family chronicle of the Katić clan already introduced in *Koreni* and a vast historical panorama of the entire Serbian state struggling for its very survival against the Austro-Hungarian invasion during World War I, this novel was aptly labeled by the critics a Serbian *War and Peace*. While its enormous scope easily dwarfs anything else written on a war theme in Serbian literature so far, its artistic excellence, psychological subtlety, and stark, documentary truthfulness make it a major literary achievement comparable to the best endeavors of its kind in other literatures.

In *Vreme smrti*, as in all his other works, Ć.'s passionate involvement with the complexities of human behavior and survival is brilliantly highlighted by the exceptional color and richness of his verbal palette, which he uses to create unified works of art in which objective and poetic elements are not only coexistent but indivisible.

FURTHER WORKS: *Akcija* (1964); *Sabrana dela* (1965)

BIBLIOGRAPHY: A. B., on *Daleko je sunce, Bulletin of Selected Books* (International PEN), 5 (1964): 93; Drožić, M., on *Deobe BA*, 36 (1962), 26; Velmar-Janković, S., on *Deobe, Bulletin of Selected Books* (International P.E.N.), 15 (1964): 271–73; Mihailovich, V. D., on *Bajka, BA*, 42 (1968): 156–57; Lukić, S., *Contemporary Yugoslav Literature* (1972): 72–73; Timčenko, N., on *Vreme smrti, BA*, 47 (1973): 390–91

—NICHOLAS MORAVČEVICH

COSTA RICAN LITERATURE

See Central American Literature

COSTANTINI, Humberto

Argentine novelist, short-story writer, and dramatist, b. 1924, Buenos Aires; d. 7 June 1987 (or 31 May), Buenos Aires

C. contributed to Argentine narrative, novel and short story, and poetry. He garnered the Municipal Prize (Premio Municipal) for literature from the City of Buenos Aires for *Una vieja historia de caminantes* (1967; an old story about travelers) and for *Háblenme de Funes* (1970; talk to me about Funes). From 1977 until 1983, C. lived in Mexico in self-imposed exile after the disappearance of a friend during the time of the military dictatorship in Argentina. In 1979 he won the distinguished Casa de las Américas Prize for narrative with *De dioses, hombrecitos y policías* (1979; *The Gods, the Little Guys and the Police*, 1984).

Thematically C. follows the lines of a social realist, portraying the social and political realities of his native land and continent. He fuses this palpable reality with a knowledge of classic myths and legends. This fusion allows C. to recreate and to incorporate both elements into a contemporary daily setting using the urban environment of Buenos Aires to frame his works. Originally recognized for his efforts as a short-story writer, he was also an accomplished writer of novels, poetry, and theater. His collection of short stories *De por aquí nomás* (1958; just through here) is a first work. The individual stories are of unequal quality and originality. It is in this collection that C.'s style begins to shape itself. He continued to write short stories and to publish them in literary journals such as *Plural in Mexico*. Some of his short stories may clearly be classified as belonging to fantastic literature and are not in the same realistic vein as his novels.

C. imbues his novels with humor, satire, and commiseration for his fellow countryfolk, for it is often the common citizenry who unwittingly suffer the injustices of the system they do not understand and in which they find themselves trapped.

During his exile in Mexico, C. wrote *De dioses, hombrecitos y policías*. Banned in Argentina by the military, it was released there in 1984 after the free election of Alfonsín as president. The novel examines the Argentine national reality from which the author himself fled in the 1970s. In it C. denounces the random killing of innocent people at the hands of a paramilitary group. People are tortured and killed or "disappeared," which is the euphemism used to refer to this form of execution. There are no popular leaders or revolutionary figures as the target or focus of his novels. Their strength lies in the fact that they illustrate that the victims of repression are often unaware of the evil and untimely death that awaits them. The police, depicted as a paramilitary group, are not immune from their fate. They, too, are trapped by their providence to carry out orders they do not understand and fear to question.

Only two of C.'s novels have been translated into English, *De dioses, hombrecitos y policías* and *La larga noche de Francisco Sanctis* (1984; *The Long Night of Francisco Sanctis*, 1985). The latter characterizes the dilemma of helping one's associates by forewarning them of impending disaster and safeguarding oneself from personal harm. It is from these two novels, particularly the former, that C. is known to English-speaking readers.

Both novels thematically deal with the effect that the political turbulence in Argentina has on the average citizen. But Argentina may stand for numerous other countries where the exact same forms of repression thrive. Therefore, C.'s work takes on a universal tone embodying all unjust governments and the devastation wrought by them.

FURTHER WORKS: *Un Señor alto, rubio, de bigotes* (1963); *Tres monólogos* (1964); *Cuestiones con la vida* (1966); *Libro de Trelew* (1973); *Más cuestiones con la vida* (ca. 1974); *Bandeo* (1975); *En la noche* (1985)

BIBLIOGRAPHY: Mastrángelo, C., *El cuento argentino*, 2nd ed. (1975), 96; Cortés Gaviño, A., "Hombrecitos cotidianos," *Plural: revista cultural de Excelsior*, 9, 108 (Sept. 1980): 74–76; Hunt, L., *NYTBR* (29 April 1984): 34

—BETH POLLACK

COUPERUS, Louis

Dutch novelist, essayist, short-story writer, and journalist, b. 10 June 1863, The Hague; d. 16 July 1923, Rheden

C. was born into a prosperous upper-class family of eleven children, whose father had served as a judge in the Dutch East Indies. C. spent six years there as a child, returning to the Netherlands in 1878. He also lived in Italy for several years before he returned to the Indies in 1899 for one year. He made his last trip there in 1921 and at that time also visited other parts of Asia over a twelve-month period. Although he spent most of his adult life in Europe, his contact with the Indies was sustained by his acquaintance with Dutch civil servants of the Indies who returned to The Hague on leave or who retired there.

His first major work, and one of his most successful, was his prize-winning novel *Eline Vere* (1889; *Eline Vere*, 1892). Set in The Hague, as are many of his novels and stories, it is the first in a series of such works that rely heavily on fate, depict the aimlessness of life, portray the helplessness of individuals, and assert a strong belief in the importance of heredity.

Another highly successful novel was *De stille Kracht* (1900; *The Hidden Force*, 1921) which is set in the East Indies, where he had just spent a year. This novel reflects the influence of the Indies world in The Hague and C.'s keen observation of the life of a Dutch administrator and his gradual disintegration. Not overly long, unlike many of his works, it leaves the reader pondering the mystery of *goenagoena* (black magic) and its role in the disintegration of the main characters.

Certainly one of C.'s longest and most popular works is *De boeken der kleinen zielen* (4 vols., 1901–3; *The Book of the Small Souls*, 1914), which is occasionally referred to as the Dutch *Forsyte Saga*. The first three volumes describe the disintegration of a family that is brought on by the arrival of Constance, a sister from the Indies, who serves as a catalyst on the seemingly close-knit family. The fourth volume attempts, not very successfully, to depict the restoration of unity in the family.

The novel *Van oude menschen, de dingen die voorbijgaan* (1906; *Old People and the Things That Pass*, 1918) was C.'s last work to deal with upper-class society and an Indies background. It describes in great detail the last months in the lives of a ninety-four-year-old man and a ninety-seven-year-old woman, during which the long-kept secret of the murder of the woman's husband inexorably comes to light. The suspense is nicely maintained, but, as with other of C.'s works, the narrative continues beyond a logical conclusion, to the detriment of the story.

C. also wrote a number of novels that deal with ancient history, and later in life he devoted more time to essays, journalism, and travel accounts. One of the more popular travel books was *Oostwaarts* (1924; *Eastward*, 1924), a compilation of letters published in the *Haagsche Post* during his last trip to the East Indies.

Some critics place C. among the Decadents, and this "decadence" is well illustrated in his novel *De berg van licht* (3 vols., 1905–6; the mountain of light), which C. considered one of his best. Dealing with the rise and fall of the child-emperor Heliogabalus, it is, unfortunately, an example of C.'s tendency to overdo description with excessive use of adjectives and adverbs.

Although he spent much of his life abroad, C. typified the upper-class resident of The Hague. Not a moralist, he seems to have identified himself with his characters. He possessed a sense of humor and tended, in his autobiographical writings, to deprecate himself. C. is often called a naturalist and a follower of Zola, but he was more intuitive and less systematic in his approach than most adherents of naturalism, and depended more on the inspiration of the moment. One of the few internationally known Dutch writers of his time, many of his works were translated into English as well as into other European languages, and he must be regarded as a major Dutch author.

FURTHER WORKS: *Een lent van vaerzen* (1884); *De schoone slaapster in her bosch* (1885); *Orchideeën* (1886); *Noodlot* (1891; *Footsteps of Fate*, 1892); *Extaze* (1892; *Ecstasy: A Study of Happiness*, 1892); *Eene illuzie* (1892); *Majesteit* (1893; *Majesty*, 1894); *Reis-impressies* (1894); *Wereldvrede* (1895); *Williswinde* (1895); *Hooge troeven* (1896); *Metamorfoze* (1897); *Psyche* (1898; *Psyche*, 1908); *Fidessa* (1899); *Langs lijnen van geleidelijkheid* (1900); *Babel* (1901); *Over lichtende drempels* (1902); *God en goden* (1903); *Dionyzos* (1904); *Aan den weg der vreugde* (1908); *Van en over mijzelv en anderen* (4 vols., 1910–1917); *Korte arabesken* (1911); *De zwaluwen neêr gestreken* (1911); *Antiek toerisme* (1911; *The Tour: A Story of Ancient Egypt*, (1920); *Antieke verhalen* (1911); *Schimmen van schoonheid* (1912); *Uit blanke steden; Onder blauwe lucht* (1912); *Herakles* (1913); *De ongelukkige* (1914); *Van en over alles en iedereen* (5 vols., 1915); *De komedianten* (1917; *The Comedians: A Story of Ancient Rome*, 1926); *De verliefde ezel* (1918); *Legende mythe en fantave* (1918); *De ode* (1918); *Xerxes of de hoogmoed* (1919; *Arrogance: The Conquests of Xerxes*, 1930); *Iskander* (1920); *Met Louis Couperus in Afrika* (1921); *Het zwevende schaakbord* (1922); *Proza* (3 vols., 1923–1925); *Het snoer der ontferming en japansche legenden* (1924); *Nippon* (1925; *Nippon*, 1926); *Verzamelde werken* (11 vols., 1952–1957)

BIBLIOGRAPHY: Lovett, R. M., "L. C. and the Family Novel," *The Dial*, 66 (22 Feb. 1919): 184–85; Meijer, R. P., *Literature of the Low Countries*, 2nd ed. (1978): 250–55

—JOHN M. ECHOLS

COWARD, Noel

English dramatist, actor, songwriter, and short-story writer, b. 16 Dec. 1899, Teddington; d. 26 March 1973, Firefly Hill, Jamaica

Born into a highly musical family, C. displayed his musical and dramatic talents as a child, appearing at the age of twelve in his first professional London production, a children's fairy tale. He earned a reputation in the early 1920s as a spokesman for the disillusioned postwar generation by writing "degenerate" plays such as *The Young Idea* (1922) and *Fallen Angels* (1925). His first major success was *The Vortex* (1924), a fairly serious drama that dealt with narcotics addiction. He soon found his true métier, however, and in the 1920s and 1930s developed the style of witty social comedy for which he is best known today.

C., always a performer as well as a writer, appeared in most of his own plays and musical revues. During World War II he entertained the Allied troops, chronicling his experiences in *Middle East Diary* (1944). He wrote, directed, and acted in a number of

Noel Coward

films. In his final years C. earned great popularity throughout the world as a nightclub and cabaret entertainer. Although he remained a British subject and was knighted by Queen Elizabeth in 1970, he was truly a citizen of the world, making his home for varying periods of time in England, France, Switzerland, America, and the West Indies.

C.'s nondramatic works have not remained as popular as his plays, but they are entertaining and, characteristically, written with wit and style. His sole novel, *Pomp and Circumstance* (1960), recounts British life on a South Seas island and combines social satire with genuine sentiment. His two collections of short stories, *To Step Aside* (1939) and *Star Quality* (1951), give evidence of considerable narrative skill and a talent for character drawing. His two autobiographical accounts, *Present Indicative* (1937) and *Future Indefinite* (1954), reveal C. as a sensitive artist and a man of feeling, as well as providing anecdotes that must delight any fan of the theater.

C.'s fame rests mainly upon his career as a playwright and songwriter. He produced more than fifty plays and revues and composed nearly a hundred songs. His best musical is *Bitter-Sweet* (1929), the source of the well-known songs "I'll See You Again" and "If Love Were All." Perhaps his most famous song is the delightful "Mad Dogs and Englishmen" from *Words and Music* (1932).

Although he ventured occasionally into the serious dramatic vein with plays like *Post-Mortem* (1931), *Cavalcade* (1931), and *Point Valaine* (1934), C.'s forte was the comedy of manners, in which style he was the direct descendant of Congreve, Sheridan, and Wilde. Like those masters of social satire, C. was able to combine ridicule with romance, pointing up the superficiality of his folly-ridden characters while at the same time expressing an affection for them that bordered on the sentimental.

The ten one-act plays that make up *Tonight at 8:30* (1936) serve as a sampler of C.'s satiric style and craftsmanship; they are among the best one-acts in English. Of his full-length comedies, at least three remain popular on the professional and the amateur stages. *Private Lives* (1930) is perhaps the finest of modern manners comedies—more a brilliantly witty extended dialogue for its two central characters than a conventional drama of action. *Design for Living* (1933) is only slightly less appealing. Its portrayal of a sexual *ménage à trois*, somewhat shocking to its original audience, is tastefully handled and seems today utterly inoffensive and quite hilarious. *Blithe Spirit* (1941) is undoubtedly C.'s most popular play as well as his most skillfully crafted piece. Its plotting is nearly perfect, and its fantasy theme is made at once fully credible and delightfully entertaining. The comedy broke London records for the run of a nonmusical play, and it has been revived repeatedly with much success.

C. has frequently been criticized for glibness, superficiality, and weak characterization, but these qualities are not wholly inappropriate to the kind of comedy he chose to write. Moreover, he had a performer's sense of the theatrical, combined with craftsmanship and an extraordinary facility with language. The verbal dexterity of his dialogue is often dazzling, and his best characters—properly "caricatures"—are unforgettable. As a writer of manners comedy, C. achieved a certain timelessness through his detachment and observation of human folly—a reality in any age. Although his plays reflect the times in which they were written, they are no more dated than those of Sheridan or Wilde. C. was clever enough to minimize topicality and avoid preaching; politics, moral judgments, and messages have no place in his work. C.'s fame has not diminished since his death. He remains a major figure in 20th-c. theater.

FURTHER WORKS: *I'll Leave It to You* (1920); *A Withered Nosegay* (1922); *The Rat Trap* (1924); *Chelsea Buns* (1925); *Hay Fever* (1925); *Easy Virtue* (1925; pub. 1926); *On with the Dance* (1925; pub. 1929); *The Queen Was in the Parlour* (1926); *"This Was a Man"* (1926); *The Marquise* (1927); *Home Chat* (1927); *Sirocco* (1927); *This Year of Grace* (1928; pub. 1939); *Collected Sketches and Lyrics* (1931); *The Spangled Unicorn* (1932); *Play Parade* (6 vols., 1933–1962); *Conversation Piece* (1934); *Operette* (1938); *Australia Visited* (1941); *Present Laughter* (1942; pub. 1943); *This Happy Breed* (1942; pub. 1943); *Sigh No More* (1945); *Pacific 1860* (1946; pub. 1958); *Peace in Our Time* (1947); *Ace of Clubs* (1950; pub. 1962); *Relative Values* (1951; pub. 1952); *Quadrille* (1952); *The N. C. Song Book* (1953); *After the Ball* (1954); *South Sea Bubble* (1956); *Nude with Violin* (1956; pub. 1957); *Look After Lulu* (1959); *Waiting in the Wings* (1960); *Sail Away* (1961); *The Collected Short Stories* (1962); *Pretty Polly Barlow* (1964); *The Lyrics of N. C.* (1965); *Suite in Three Keys* (1966; contains *A Song at Twilight, Shadows of the Evening, and Come into the Garden, Maud*); *Bon Voyage* (1967); *Not Yet the Dodo* (1967)

BIBLIOGRAPHY: Braybrooke, P., *The Amazing Mr. N. C.* (1933); Greacen, R., *The Art of N. C.* (1953); Mander, R., and Mitchenson, J., *Theatrical Companion to C.* (1957); Morley, S., *A Talent to Amuse* (1969); Lesley, C., *Remembered Laughter* (1976); Briers,

R., *C. and Company* (1987); Fisher, C., *N. C.* (1992); Hoare, P., *N. C.: A Biography* (1995)

—JACK A. VAUGHN

COWLEY, Malcolm

American critic, editor, and poet; b. 24 Aug. 1898, near Belsano, Pa.; d. 24 March 1989, New Milford, NJ

Educated in the public schools and at Harvard University, C. lived the life he was to write about by joining the men of his generation as a military transport driver in France during World War I, as a struggling writer in postwar Greenwich Village, and as an expatriate in the 1920s. He studied literature at the University of Montpellier in France, wandered around the Continent, and contributed to several small magazines before returning to the U.S. in 1923. At the beginning of the Depression he took up a career as literary editor and essayist for the *New Republic*, but in 1941 he left his editorial post—along with its political conflicts.

C.'s sense of the writer's place in culture—the ways in which the writer reflects and shapes his age—is part of the general attitude of the 19th-c. French critics Hippolyte Taine, Sainte-Beuve, and Alexis de Tocqueville: C. surveys tendencies and looks for generational patterns. As a "natural historian" of writers, he generalizes about their backgrounds, working methods, and living conditions. His paradigmatic career has contributed to his special understanding of representative figures like HEMINGWAY and FAULKNER. Never provincial, C. measures American achievement against European, scores his contemporaries for their shortcomings, and speculates on the future of American literature.

C.'s poems in *Blue Juniata* (1929) capture the spirit of bohemian life in the 1920s and foreshadow his critical concerns. *Exile's Return* (1934) is an account of the lives of American expatriates: C. is persona and participant and uses his firsthand observations to narrate the story of the Lost Generation and describe its folkways and artistic attitudes. C.'s skeptical eye and his thorough understanding of European intellectual currents—DADAISM, SYMBOLISM—allow him to create a clear and balanced record of an era. Another book about a generation, *After the Genteel Tradition* (1937), proclaims the value of naturalistic writing and reveals C.'s profound respect for rebellion and experiment in art. *The Literary Situation* (1954) looks at the post-World War II period with less sympathy and finds it often tepid, narrow, and dangerously formalistic. C. maintains that many writers lack new mythic designs and are therefore intensely personal or derivative. Yet his prescience is evident in his close attention to BELLOW.

C.'s disdain for certain postwar enterprises—the symbol-hunting of critics and the confessional mode of novelists—is clear in *A Many-Windowed House* (1970): he is frank about his conviction that the novelist should deal with social values and quite sharp in summarizing criticism that is concerned with fallacies, explications, and doctrines rather than flesh-and-blood writers. He calls for a new "innocence" in an age when criticism has been overrun by ideologues.

And I Worked at the Writer's Trade (1978) is in part a history of his generation's achievements set against the larger perspective of what came after; in addition, the chronicle pauses to deal with C.'s own apprenticeship and his standards of judgment. "A Defense of

Storytelling," included in this book, holds up the model of the well-told story of development and is a kind of miniature manual of the art, complete with comparisons and shrewd advice.

Always the engaging and informal essayist, C. has scorned the exactitude and programmatic approaches of writers who think criticism is a science. His ability to see working writers in the context of time and place, along with the clarity of his prose, makes him an especially valuable critic for a broad range of readers.

FURTHER WORKS: *The Dry Season* (1941); *Black Cargoes* (1962, with Daniel P. Mannix); *The Faulkner—Cowley File* (1966); *Think Back on Us* (1967); *Lesson of the Masters* (1971, with Hugo Howard); *The Second Flowering* (1973); *The View from 80* (1980); *The Dream of the Golden Mountains* (1980)

BIBLIOGRAPHY: Kunitz, S., and H. Haycraft, eds., *Twentieth Century Authors* (1942): 320–21; Young, P., "For M. C.: Critic, Poet, 1898–," *SoR*, 9 (1973): 778–95; Wood, T., "M. C. Interview" *Lost Generation Journal*, 3 (1975): 4–6; Simpson, L., "M. C. and the American Writer," *SR*, 84 (1976): 221–47; Plimpton, G., ed., "M. C. Writing and Talking: Interview," *NYTBR*, 30 April 1978: 7

—DAVID CASTRONOVO

COZZENS, James Gould

American novelist, b. 19 Aug. 1903, Chicago, Ill.; d. 9 Aug. 1978, Stuart, Fla.

C. is one of the handful of major social novelists America has produced—and perhaps the best of that handful. "Social" is not to be confused with "society." Although C., like TOLSTOY and George Eliot, often did write about upper-class characters, like them his aim was to show the complex interaction of entire human groupings. In his two masterpieces, *Guard of Honor* (1948) and *By Love Possessed* (1957), he almost perfectly succeeds.

C.'s career began early. He published an article in the *Atlantic* while still a student at the Kent School. He wrote his first (highly romantic) novel when he was a Harvard sophomore, although it was not published until he was almost twenty-one.

For the next fifty-four years his life was entirely that of a professional writer—with one interlude of service as an officer in the U. S. Air Force during World War II. Besides a dozen more novels, he wrote thirty-one stories. He won the Pulitzer Prize in 1948 and the Howells Medal in 1960. Meanwhile, he led a totally private life—no TV appearances, no lectures, no interviews. At the time of his death he had just declined three honorary degrees offered in the same year by three Ivy League universities.

C. came to regret his early start. He felt that his first four novels expressed—in bad writing—a foolish romanticism, and he wished that they had not been published.

This judgment, although harsh, is valid. C.'s major career in fact began with his sixth novel, *The Last Adam* (1933), which examines the entire life of a small Connecticut town, from telephone operator to local squire, during a moment of extreme crisis. Successive novels did not always follow this pattern. *Cast-away* (1934), which has only one character, has been called the most powerful piece of surrealistic writing in America since Melville's "Bartleby," while *Ask Me Tomorrow* (1940) is a pure example of the *Bildungsroman*.

But the pattern C. established in 1933 developed through *Men and Brethren* (1936) and *The Just and the Unjust* (1942) to his two masterpieces. *Guard of Honor* presents the reader with the complete and complex life of a large American air force base during three dramatic days during World War II. *By Love Possessed* considers almost every possible permutation (*agape* as well as *eros*) of love among the inhabitants of a Pennsylvania town in the 1950s.

It is the combination of three skills that distinguishes C. from all other American novelists. To a minute realism he adds an unobtrusive but pervasive use of symbols, especially those connected with the myth of Eden, so that the normal experience of his major characters is a gradual expulsion from the false paradise of childhood into the chilling but real world of adult perception. And this experience he narrates in a style of exceptional brilliance and complexity.

C. has received relatively little critical attention, in part because of his self-chosen isolation, in part because his antiromanticism ran counter to the spirit of the age, but most of all because he seemed (and in part was) a frank elitist, an enemy of the common man. Whether he will eventually be recognized as the full equal of his three romantic contemporaries—FAULKNER, FITZGERALD, and HEMINGWAY—it is still too early to say.

FURTHER WORKS: *Confusion* (1924); *Michael Scarlett* (1925); *Cock Pit* (1928); *The Son of Perdition* (1929); *S.S. San Pedro* (1931); *Children and Others* (1964); *Morning Noon and Night* (1968)

BIBLIOGRAPHY: Bracher, F., *The Novels of J. G. C.* (1959); Maxwell, D. E. S., *C.* (1964); Michel, P., *J. G. C.* (1974); Perrin, N., "J. G. C.," *New Republic*, 17 Sept. 1977: 43–45; Bruccoli, M. J., ed., *A. J. G. C. Reader* (1978); Bruccoli, M. J., *J. G. C.* (1983)

—NOEL PERRIN

CRANE, Hart

American poet, b. 21 July 1899, Garretsville, Ohio; d. 27 April 1932, off the Florida coast

C. has generally been viewed as a bedeviled man, given to throwing typewriters out of windows, sailors into bed, and himself to a watery death. This reputation has led to his difficult poetry being understood as an overflow of his violent life, sharing in its excesses and dissipations. While C. did tend to find relief from his unhappy life in alcohol and waterfront sex, and while he assuredly had his devils, these proclivities have obscured the fact that C. was a thoroughly professional poet with a high sense of mission, at least through the summer of 1927. C. is better understood as a divided man—divided on what he called the "bloody battlefield" of his parents' marriage, divided by mixed feelings about his homosexuality, and divided by an insistent optimism that coexisted with a nagging sense of despair. Even his literary allegiances echo C.'s dividedness, encompassing William BLAKE and T. S. ELIOT, Herman Melville and Henry JAMES.

C.'s theme and poetic method seem to find their basis in the deep divisions of his life, for his theme is almost always the divided self in a divided world, and he typically forged his poems out of a hoard of verbal fragments that had personal meaning for him, as if to make his life coherent by the forging of those fragments into

Hart Crane

poetry. He liked to speak of metaphor, which he thought central to poetry, as just such a subliminal forging—as a combining and interplay of the subconscious connotations of words (see his essay "General Aims and Theories," published in 1937). Many of the twenty-eight poems of *White Buildings* (1926), his first collection of lyrics, are among the most difficult of modern verse precisely because they depend so heavily on connotative meaning. Indeed, the interplay of connotations is so intricate that *White Buildings* probably contains the most complexly emotive poems of C.'s generation, and possibly of any generation of poets since that of Wordsworth and Keats. Especially notable in this regard are the two poetic sequences "For the Marriage of Faustus and Helen" and "Voyages," the latter probably the greatest of C.'s works, and assuredly the only great poem about homosexual love in English.

C. thought of *The Bridge* (1930), a sequence of fifteen poems in seven sections, as his most important work. It was certainly his most ambitious. Seven years in the writing, it was intended to be an optimistic rebuttal to the pessimism of Eliot's *The Waste Land* and to be a mythic celebration of American history. But *The Bridge* is inevitably judged a failure (albeit a magnificent failure) by those who accept C.'s preconception uncritically, for *The Bridge* does not elaborate an American myth but rather a quest for a myth. As in much of C.'s poetry, the quest is given point by an unresolved conflict between reality and the visionary impulse. The subject is not America so much as the visionary temperament; the method is not so much expository as dramatic; and the theme is not anti-Eliot so much as the tragedy of the visionary impulse, how it is founded

in desperation, sustained by illusions, and climaxed by a question. Not all of the poems in the sequence are entirely successful, but their general quality is high, their metrical subtleties are especially impressive, and their effect in combination is powerful. A few poems, such as "The River" and "The Tunnel," are undisputed masterpieces, and the whole work must be numbered among the major poetic sequences of this century.

C. left the manuscript of "Key West: An Island Sheaf," a small collection of twenty-two poems, ready for publication at his death, but the poems were incorporated directly into *The Collected Poems* (1933) by his executors. With the exception of "The Broken Tower," C.'s last poems are thought to be less complex and less impressive than his earlier work, although some readers find them refreshingly accessible.

C. is not so much the mad poet of literary gossip, then, as a serious craftsman who transformed his personal demons into poetry of haunting intensity and affecting candor, at least until the demons overcame him. His technical proficiency was enormous, but he will be remembered for the romantic intersection of his art and his life. More, possibly, than any other modernist poet— Wallace STEVENS is the possible exception—he explored the demands of the creative vision: how it depletes the self, how it must do battle with uncertainty and doubt, and how it can, momentarily, triumph and exalt.

FURTHER WORKS: *The Letters of H. C.* (1952); *The Complete Poems of H. C.* (1958)

BIBLIOGRAPHY: Weber, B., *H. C.: A Biographical and Critical Study* (1948); Dembo, L. S., *H. C.'s "Sanskrit Charge": A Study of "The Bridge"* (1960); Quinn, V., *H. C.* (1963); Spears, M. K., *H. C.* (1965); Lewis, R. W. B., *The Poetry of H. C.: A Critical Study* (1967); Unterecker, J., *Voyager: A Life of H. C.* (1969); Uroff, M. D., *H. C.: The Patterns of His Poetry* (1974); Bennett, M. F., *Unfractured Idiom: H. C. and Modernism* (1987)

—ROBERT F. KIERNAN

CRAVEIRINHA, José

Mozambican poet and journalist (writing in Portuguese), b. 1922, Lourenço Marques

The son of a Portuguese father and a black Mozambican mother, C. trained as a journalist, and worked for many years for *O Notícias*, *A Tribuna* and *O Brado Africano*. Unlike many other Lusophone writers, C. continued to live in Mozambique after independence in 1975. He works at the library at the Eduardo Mondlane University.

Referring to his multiracial origins, C. once noted that he was "born twice"—first as a "white" child, later again as a Mulatto, when he was forced by the racialist structures of Portuguese colonialism, stronger in Mozambique than anywhere else in the Portuguese empire, to acknowledge his mixed blood descent. Such disarming honesty betrays already some of the multiple ironies through which C. disguises a complex and subtly subversive poetic vision. Most remarkably moreover his poetry has revealed little of the angst such a potentially traumatic "awakening" to race and color may have had on the young man as a poet. With the odd exception, as in the poem "Mulato" (Mulatto), suggestions of an internal conflict of identity are rare. Rather in his work C. has opted always for a celebration of his African heritage. In poems such as "Africa" (Africa), "Grito Negro" (African Cry), "Ode a um navio chamado Escravo" (Ode to a Lost Cargo in a Ship Called Slave), "Hino à minha terra" (Hymn to My Land), "Manifesto" (Manifest), "Quero ser tambor" (I Want to Be a Drum), and "Sangue de minha Mae" (The Blood of My Mother) the focus is very much on a black African identity, in a biological sense and in terms of a historical legacy of slavery and colonial oppression. Identity, in a national and in a personal sense, is crucial to C.'s writing. Indeed, in his poetry he offers what might be termed an archeology of the African black body within (Portuguese) colonialism.

In C. the personal and the political are always inextricably intertwined. Arrested in 1965 by the Portuguese authorities for his involvement with the nationalist movement, Frelimo (Frente de Libertaçao de Moçambique), his prison writings have been collected in *Cela, 1* (1980; Cell 1). C., however, was always much more a poet than a political activist. Thus, in "Inclandestinidade" (Inclandestinity), a word that in its original conveys a much more dense web of meanings than an English translation allows for, C. speaks of the subversive quality of his writing as the result not so much of direct political activity but rather of his being born a Mozambican, that is, an African. Moreover, in what is a common characteristic in other prison poems, such as "Aforismo" (Aphorism) and "Poemeto" (Little Poem), C. deploys to great effect the role of rumor in the destabilization of colonial structures of control. C. suggests thus the ways in which colonized peoples's resistance to colonial discourses often operated just as effectively at the level of a "whispered action" rather than active physical conflict. In C.'s masterful use of irony resides much of his writing's anticolonialist message.

Although much of his earlier poetry, particularly in *Chigubo* (1964; Chigubo or Xigubo) must be read within the context of a NÉGRITUDE model, not unlike that proposed by the Senegalese Léopold Sédar SENGHOR, there is also a more radical edge which at all times destabilized and disrupted the myth of Lusotropicalism endorsed by Portuguese colonialism. The focus on that which Portuguese colonial ideologies sought to suppress—the black body—speaks of a pride in being Other than that which Portuguese colonial parameters decreed as acceptable. The persona C. creates here is one willing to claim an identity whose reality is anchored on its very invisibility to the colonial master. It is no wonder then that C. should have found himself in jail by 1965, where he remained until 1969.

The issue of language, a common site of contention in any postcolonial context, is one also found in Mozambican writing. C. has long mastered the ability to "make language bear the mark of one's reality," in the sense identified by the Nigerian novelist Chinua ACHEBE, in his appraisal of the place of English in West African writing. In C.'s writing we find one of the most potently articulated tributes to *Moçambicanidade*, as slippery a notion of cultural identity as any in a postcolonial nation, but one to which his command of the Portuguese language is intrinsic. But *Moçambicanidade*, in the sense proposed by C., implies most of all the "re-Africanization" of one's mind that the Guinean intellectual and freedom fighter Amílcar CABRAL called for. C.'s appropriation, indeed his abrogation, of the Portuguese language rests on an ability to borrow at random from European and African cultural

and literary traditions. His use of the expression "Karingana ua Karingana," in the second of his collections of poetry and the one to which the expression serves as a title, *Karingana ua Karingana* (1974; Karingana ua Karingana), stresses this African(ized) dimension of his poetry. The ba-Ronga equivalent to "once upon a time," it signals C.'s commitment to a *Moçambicanidade* deeply rooted in the African world that surrounds him, and is reflective of an intentional homage to African oral traditions.

C. has evolved into one of Africa's most sophisticated poets, and by far the most important figure in the area of African verse in the Portuguese language. His long period of incarceration, combined with his decision to stay in colonial Mozambique afterwards in somewhat difficult conditions, help to explain the ten-year gap between his first two publications. Since its independence, Mozambique has been engulfed by a prolonged and horrendous civil war, and in *Babalaze das Hyenas* (1997; Babalaze of the Hyenas) C. bears witness to the suffering of the Mozambican people. Nevertheless, his elegant diction, combined with a sophisticated ironic style, at time leaves him very much an outsider to the political exigencies of the new nation. C. continues to be first and foremost a poet, and a political activist only through his being a Mozambican. Although his writing is often included in anthologies of African poetry, much of C.'s work remains dispersed throughout numerous publications in Mozambique, mostly in newspapers and magazines.

FURTHER WORKS: *Maria* (1988)

BIBLIOGRAPHY: Chabal, P., et al, *The Postcolonial Literature of Lusophone Africa* (1996); Chabal, P., *Vozes Mocambicanas* (1994); Cortez, M. de L., "The Edge of Discourse: Bodies and Rhythms in the Poetry of C.," *PStud*, 9 (1993): 189-99; Leite, A. M., *A Poética de J. C.* (1991); Baltazar, R, *Sobre a Poesia de J. C.* (1988)

—TONY SIMOES DA SILVA

CREELEY, Robert

American poet, b. 21 May 1926, Arlington, Mass.

After attending Harvard for a few years, C. left in 1945 to serve with the American Field Service in India and Burma. When he returned, he tried to start a magazine for contemporary poetry. Although unsuccessful, the venture introduced C. to others interested in free-verse experimentation. He lived in France in the early 1950s and later moved to Mallorca, where he founded the Divers Press. In 1954, back in the U.S., he went to Black Mountain College, where he took a B.A.; for the next two years he was a teacher and editor of the *Black Mountain Review*. He received an M.A. from the University of New Mexico in 1960 and has taught at a number of universities, most recently at the State University of New York at Buffalo.

C. is, with Charles OLSON, one of the most important of what Olson called the "Projectivists"; this group also includes Robert DUNCAN, Denise LEVERTOV, Louis ZUKOFSKY, Paul Blackburn (1926–1971), and Edward Dorn (b. 1929). Projectivism is rooted in the poetics of Ezra POUND and William Carlos WILLIAMS, both of whom C. corresponded with in the late 1940s. C. learned from

Pound the principles of constancy and variancy, that poetic rhythm is determined by some constant measure to which variations counterpoint, the variations creating as much meaning and effect as the words. Williams taught C. the concept of the variable foot and confirmed C.'s proclivity for the natural cadences of American colloquial speech, a movement in American poetry dating back to Whitman.

But the greatest influence on C. was Olson, C.'s mentor at Black Mountain, and many of C.'s early poems are tributes to Olson, who advocated the "breath line," a line of irregular meter whose length is determined not by arbitrary formal requirements (as iambic pentameter) but by the poet's inner voice.

C. manifests the breath line in his impulsive lineation. With his short, often truncated lines and eccentric punctuation, he creates jarring rhythms with frequent stops that force the reader's attention to the words themselves. He juxtaposes words and phrases, sometimes for ironic rhyme or alliteration, to produce an effect similar to the musical phrase. C.'s variable form reflects his often quoted remark that "form is never more than an extension of content."

Most of C.'s poems are epiphanies, simple, sometimes entirely domestic, observations on life's moments. He generally avoids conclusions, focusing instead on dilemmas that he considers constantly provocative. C. believes that the poet's energy is gathered and articulated through questions rather than resolutions. He "projects" those questions through emotionally charged perceptions of the present moment.

C.'s first major collection, *For Love: Poems 1950–1960* (1962), characterizes his introspective style. The poems center on human relationships, particularly between the poet and his "lady." In investigating these relationships, C. shows an almost obsessive regard for details, for the minute facts of daily life. Yet, unlike Pound and Williams, he does not focus on images for their own sake. For C., the images prompt a cognitive awareness of the self. Hence, his poems are acts of self-discovery.

Words (1965) continues C.'s poetry of longing and further expresses his sense of relentless isolation and loneliness. But the poems in *Words* reflect a fundamental change in C.'s attitude: in their disparity and frequent constriction, they represent poetry as process, a tracking of his perceptions rather than a record of distilled thought. At the end of *Words* are three "fragments," perceptions that C. has not extended into fuller poems. These fragments exhibit an austerity more and more characteristic of C.'s later poetry.

Pieces (1968) and *Thirty Things* (1974) are the result of C.'s movement toward reduction: these laconic poems are dissociated perceptions that do not follow the thematic development evident in his earlier work. Here is a poetry of the instant-quantum, high-energy perceptions that tend toward either metaphysical speculation or mundane domestic observation. These "pieces" are the inevitable result of C.'s poetics. They are more fully projective because their austerity expands the speculative possibilities and increases the perceptual associations that can follow from the little he does say.

Some critics find C.'s sparsity too obscure, too thoroughly personal, but most consider him an important contemporary poet. He is most respected for his precision with language, for his sensitivity to words—their meanings, their relation to other words, their placement on the page, their contributions to the rhythms of poetry. His intensely honest poems have had a major influence on many younger poets.

FURTHER WORKS: *Le Fou* (1952); *The Kind of Act of* (1953); *The Immoral Proposition* (1953); *The Gold Diggers* (1954); *All That Is Lovely in Men* (1955); *A Form of Women* (1959); *The Island* (1963); *Poems 1950–1965* (1966); *The Finger* (1968); *The Charm* (1968); *Numbers* (1968); *The Finger: Poems 1966–1969* (1970); *A Quick Graph* (1970); *St. Martin's* (1971); *1-2-3-4-5-6-7-8-9-0* (1971, with Arthur Okamura); *Listen* (1972); *A Day Book* (1972); *Contexts of Poetry: Interviews 1961–1971* (1973); *His Idea* (1973); *Presences* (1976, with Marisol); *Selected Poems* (1976); *Away* (1976); *Hello: A Journal, February 29-May 3, 1976* (1978); *Later* (1979); *Mabel, a Story and Other Prose* (1979); *Was That a Real Poem and Other Essays* (1979)

BIBLIOGRAPHY: Olson, C., "Introduction to R. C.," in Laughlin, J., ed., *New Directions Annual 13* (1951): 92–93; Stepanchev, S., "R. C.," *American Poetry since 1945: A Critical Survey* (1965): 151–57; Rosenthal, M. L., "The 'Projectivist' Movement: R. C.," *The New Poets: American and British Poetry since World War II* (1967): 148–59; Howard, R., "R. C.: 'I Begin Where I Can, and End When I See the Whole Thing Returning,'" *MinnR*, 8, 2 (1968): 143–50; Duberman, M., *Black Mountain: An Exploration in Community* (1973): 408–34; Stauffer, D. B., *A Short History of American Poetry* (1974): 415–19; Ford, A. L., *R. C.* (1978); Wilson, J., ed., *R. C.'s Life and Work: A Sense of Increment* (1987); Clark, T., *R. C. and the Genius of the American Common Place* (1993)

—TERRY R. BACON

CRIMEAN TATAR LITERATURE

See Tatar Literature

CRNJANSKI, Miloš

(also spelled Tsernaianski) Yugoslav poet, novelist, short-story writer, dramatist, and essayist (writing in Serbian), b. 26 Oct. 1893, Csongrád, Hungary; d. 30 Nov. 1977, Belgrade

C.'s study of art history at the University of Vienna was interrupted by service in the Austrian army during World War I. In 1922 he completed his humanistic studies at the University of Belgrade. He then worked as teacher and journalist. Entering the Yugoslav royal diplomatic service in 1928, he was attached to embassies in Berlin, Rome, Lisbon, and finally London. Here he decided to stay, as voluntary political exile, even after the end of World War II, but he returned to Yugoslavia in 1965.

C. started his literary career at the University of Belgrade, where he joined the circle of the young Serbian modernists of EXPRESSIONIST leanings. His first volume of poetry, *Lirika Itake* (1919; lyrics of Ithaca), was notable for the vividness of its protest against war and violence and its mellow lyricism. Throughout his poems run the yearnings and ecstasies of a narcissistic soul immersed in its dreams of love and human perfectibility.

C.'s first novel, *Dnevnik o Čarnojeviću* (1921; diary about Čarnojević), however, concentrated on the spiritual hollowness and uncertainties of postwar life as experienced by a veteran whose war experiences have robbed him of all hope.

The most significant of all of C.'s works is the monumental novel *Seobe* (Part I, 1929; Part II, 1962; *The Migrations*, 1994), which, with epic breadth and majestic sweep, unfolds a historical panorama of the 18th-c. Serbian exodus from the Ottoman-ruled Balkans into neighboring Vojvodina and other southern areas of the Austro-Hungarian empire. Its main theme, the futility of the quest for peace and tranquility by an uprooted person or a displaced national group, attains a universality that places this novel among the most notable works in Yugoslav literature.

Published after a lapse of thirty-three years, Part II differs substantially from Part I. Part I is richer in poetic exuberance and fullness of emotion. The more sedate, more chronicle-like Part II is characterized by greater breadth of perception and a firmer sense of history. It is also drier and less even in its narrative intensity.

Of C.'s numerous essays, the most accomplished is his study of Shakespeare's sonnets. Among his travel writings, which brought that genre to a new height in Serbian literature, the most memorable are *Ljubav u Toskani* (1930; love in Tuscany) and *Knjiga o Nemačkoj* (1931; book about Germany).

In his most recent novel, *Roman o Londonu* (1972; a novel about London), C. returned to the theme of the futility and emptiness of life in exile. The experiences of the two Russian protagonists of this work, a husband and wife displaced by the Russian Revolution and desperately struggling to retain their dignity in London after World War I, strongly echo those C. himself encountered there during the twenty years of his own exile. This weaving in of autobiographical material adds special poignancy to the story, although this work is not equal in scope and profundity to *Seobe*.

C.'s ability to portray the devastating effects of war and exile on the human spirit has made him one of the most influential postwar literary figures in Yugoslavia, particularly upon the youngest generation of writers greatly appreciative of his successful blending of traditional and modernist techniques in his poetry and prose.

FURTHER WORKS: *Maska* (1918); *Priče o muškom* (1920); *Sabrana Dela* (1930); *Odabrani stihovi* (1954); *Konak* (1958); *Itaka i komentari* (1959); *Lament and Beogradom* (1962); *Lirika-proza-eseji* (1965); *Sabrana dela* (1966)

BIBLIOGRAPHY: Kadić, A., *Contemporary Serbian Literature* (1964): 51–54; Moravčevich, N., On *Seobe, CSP*, 20 (1978): 369–79; Eekman, T., *Thirty Years of Yugoslav Literature 1945–1975* (1978): 17–20

—NICHOLAS MORAVČEVICH

CROATIAN LITERATURE

Croatian literature in the 20th c. is usually divided into three periods: the *moderna*, or modernist period, extending from 1895 to the end of World War I; the period between the two world wars; and postwar period to the present.

The modern period began with a student protest at the University of Zagreb in 1895. The young Croatian intellectuals dismissed from the University continued their studies in Prague, Vienna, and Munich—all centers of European MODERNISM. In this way the

Croatian literary milieu became familiar with the major European authors and literary schools of thought. Modernism pluralistically united various stylistic complexes: impressionism in poetry, natural realism in prose, and expressionism in drama.

Among the early proponents of Croatian modernism, Antun Gustav Matoš (1873-1914) provided a major contribution to the development of Croatian literature as a journalist, essayist, critic, poet, and prose writer. His long-term exile introduced him to European literary models while simultaneously creating a nostalgic love for Croatia. His novels, notably *Iverje* (1899; Shavings), *Novo Iverje* (1900, New Shavings), and *Umorne Priče* (1909; Tired Stories) are characterized by an original poetic intervention, which—depending on the topic—contains condensed symbolic, caricatural, and explicitly lyric expressions. Influenced by SYMBOLISM, Matoš's impressionistic oeuvre incorporated soliloquial and expressive elements.

In the early 20th c. Milan BEGOVIĆ produced erotic, hedonistic poetry, notably in *Knjiga Boccadoro* (1900; The Book of the Golden Mouth); however, in the interwar period he turned to drama and fiction, illustrated in his play entitled *Bez Trečega* (1933; Without the Third) and the novel *Giga Baričeva* (1940; Giga Baričeva). Vladimir Nazor (1876-1949), one of the most prominent and productive writers of the first half of the 20th c., produced collections of poetry, notably *Slavenske Legende* (1910; Slavic Legends), *Lirika* (1910; Lyrics), and *Hrvatski Kraljevi* (1912; Croatian Kings), as well as prose, illustrated by *Istarske Priče* (1913; Istrian Tales). Nazor's poetry is optimistic, rich in symbols, mythological motifs, and hymns to nature. Nazor's *Slavenske Legende* and Begovič's poetry are the bearers of the secessionist features in Croatian modernism. In his next phase Nazor wrote reflexive lyrics: *Intima* (1915; Intimacy) and *Priče iz Djetinjstva* (1924; Stories from Childhood). He later turned to social themes and wrote novels and short stories, and in the postwar period wrote heroic poems.

Vladimir Vidrič (1875-1909), a typical secessionist poet of the *fin de siècle*, first appeared on the literary scene with the publication of *Pjesme* (1907; Poems), followed by the publication of Dinko Šimunovič's (1873-1933) poetic stories *Alkar* (1908; Alkar) and *Rudica* (1909; Rudica). The modern Kajkavian dialectal poetry is represented by Dragutin Domjaniæ (1875-1933) and Fran Galoviæ (1887-1914). Ivo Vojnoviæ (1857-1929) first published a novel entitled *Geranium* (1880; Geranium), a number of prose texts, and the collection of sonnets, *Lapadski soneti* (1892; The Lapad Sonnets), before achieving popular and critical recognition as a dramatist with *Dubrovačka Trilogija* (1903; A Trilogy of Dubrovnik, 1921; later tr., 1951). The major theoretician of Croatian modernism was Milutin Cihlar Nehajev (1880-1931), who also wrote short stories and modernist novels, notably *Bijeg* (1909; Flight) and *Vuci* (1927; The Wolves). Josip Kosor (1879-1961), prose writer and dramatist, and short-story writer Ivan Kozarac (1885-1910) were also proponents of modernism. At the end of early modernist period Ivana Brlič Mažuranič (1874-1938), "the Croatian Andersen," published popular, mythologically inspired children's stories. At the same time the journalist Marija Jurič Zagorka (1873-1957) wrote popular adult fiction.

The second period of Croatian literature was announced by Janko Polič Kamov (1886-1910), an avant-garde critic, poet, dramatist, and prose writer who, through such works as *Psovka* (1907; A Swear Word) and *Isušena Kaljuža* (1957; Desiccated Puddle), introduced the literature of the absurd. The poet Ljubo Wiesner (1885-1951) published the anthology *Hrvatska Mlada*

Lirika (1914; Young Croatian Lyrics), which apart from modernists (the *Matošians*) included representatives of the new period (the *Kamovians*). Ulderiko Donadini (1894-1923) commenced the expressionistic tendencies in Croatian literature with his bizarre and fantastic *Lude Priče* (1915; Crazy Stories); the most prominent of the expressionists and one of the most important Croatian poets in general, Antun Branko Šimič (1898-1925), was original in combining simplicity and stylistic antirhetoricism with free verse in his collection of poems *Preobra Ženja* (1920; Metamorphoses).

The central author of the Croatian *novecento* Miroslav KRLEŽA began to publish poetry in 1916. In 1917 he published his first play, *Legende* (Legends), and in 1928 and 1931 the three plays making up the famous *Glembay* cycle. His *Hrvatski bog Mars* (1922; Mars, the Croatian God) is a collection of antiwar stories. His most original work is *Balade Petrice Kerempuha* (1936; Petrica Kerempuh's Ballads). The novels *Povratak Filipa Latinovicza* (1932; The Return of Filip Latinowitz), *Na Rubu Pameti* (1938; On the Edge of Reason), and *Banket u Blitvi* (1940, 1962; Banquet in Blitvia) make up an expansive, realistic yet fantastic mosaic of the political Europe. Krleža's essays are of a large scope, addressing literary and political themes; his best book is *Deset Kravih Godina* (1937; Ten Bloody Years). His opus was completed in the postwar period by the huge novel *Zastave* (1967; And Onwards—Flags).

To the interwar period also belongs one of the greatest Croatian poets, Tin Ujevič (1891-1955). In his collections *Lelek Sebra* (1920; A Serf's Lament), *Kolajna* (1926; Neck-Piece), *Ojađeno Zvono* (1933; Distressed Bell), and *Žedan Kamen na Studencu* (1955; Thirsty Stone at the Fountain) he synthesized the classical values of Croatian and European poetry.

Other poets include Gustav Krklec (1899-1977), an expressionist lyric poet who wrote the collections *Lirika* (1919; Lyric Poems), *Srebrna cesta* (1921; The Silver Road), and *Žubor Života* (1955; Purl of Life). Frano Alfirevič (1903-1956), a melancholic poet and author of journey descriptions, wrote *Pjesme* (1952; Poems). Poets of Christian inspiration are Nikola Šop (1904-1982) and Đuro Sudeta (dates n.a.). Dialectal Čakavian poetry was written by Mate Balota (1898-1962) and Drago Gervais (1904-1957).

Among the many interwar prose writers, the most important are Slavko Kolar (1891-1963), Vjekoslav Majer (1900-1975), Luka Perkovič (1900-1948), Ivo Kozarčanin (1911-1941), Hasan Kikič (1905-1943), and Novak Simič (1906-1981).

In the postwar period the most prominent poet is Dobriša Cesarič (1902-1980), a lyric poet in the impressionist tradition who became popular with his collections *Pjesme* (1951; Poems), *Osvijetljeni Put* (1953; Illuminated Road), and *Goli Časovi* (1956; Naked Moments). Dragutin Tadijanovič (b. 1905), a poet of autobiographic motivation and free verse, wrote *Sunce nad Oranicama* (1933; The Sun over the Ploughfield), *Srebrne Svirale* (1960; Silver Flutes), and *Prsten* (1965; Ring). Drago Ivaniševič (1907-1981), a poet of lapidary constructivist composition, wrote *Zemlja pod Nogama* (1940; The Earth Under One's Feet) and *Poezija* (1963; Poetry). Ivan Goran Kovačič (1913-1943), a poet of lyric tragedy and epic plasticism, wrote the shattering autobiographic poem *Jama* (1944; The Pit).

Other important poets of the new generation include Mak Dizdar (1917-1971), the author of the collection of poetry entitled *Kameni Spavač* (1965; Sleeper of Stone), who gave poetic expression to the archaic form of the medieval Bogumil gravestones. Jure Kaštelan (1919-1990) wrote one of the most expressive works on war, the shattering poem *Tifusari* (1950; Typhus Ill). Vesna Parun

(b. 1922), the greatest of Croatia's women writers, wrote the important collections *Zore I Vihori* (1947; Dawns and Whirlwinds), *Crne Masline* (1955; Black Olives), and *Vjetar Trakije* (1964; Wind of Trace). Nikola Miliæevič (b. 1922) is a poet of elegiac tunes whose important collections are *Obeæanje Žute Zore* (1956; Promises of Yellow Dawn) and *Snijeg I Crna Ptica* (1964; Snow and Black Bird). Zvonimir Golob (1927-1996), the most consistent representative of the surrealist concept of poetic creation, wrote *Okovane Oči* (1946; Chained Eyes), *Glas Koji Odjekuje Hodnicima* (1957; Voice Echoing in Corridors), and *Elegije* (1964; Elegies). Josip Pupačić (1928-1971), a poet of conspicuously lyric sensibility with a refined sense for Croatian poetic tradition, wrote *Kiše Pjevaju Na Jablanima* (1955; Rains Singing in Poplars), *Cvijet Izvan Sebe* (1958; Flower Outside Itself), and *Oporuka* (1965; Testament). Slavko Mihalič (b. 1928) is a poet of a modern, intellectualist sensibility whose collections are *Put U Nepostojanje* (1956; Journey into Nonexistence), *Poèetak Zaborava* (1957; Beginning of Oblivion), and *Godišnja Doba* (1961; The Seasons). Among notable Croatian exile poets is Viktor Vida (1913-1960) with his collections *Ceasing Vremena* (1956; Time's Slave) and *Otrovane Lokve* (1971; Poisoned Pools).

Ivan Raos (1921-1987) was one of the most fruitful prose writers of the postwar period, with a stylistic scope from the fantastic story to the naturalist chronicle to the grotesque play. Most famous are his short stories *Žalosni Gospin Vrt* (1962; Our Lady's Sorrowful Garden), the novel trilogy *Vječno Žalosni Smijeh* (1965; Eternally Sorrowful Laughter), and the novel *Prosjaci & Sinovi* (1971; Beggars and Sons).

Postwar Croatian prose has a number of other prominent representatives. Slobodan Novak (b. 1924) wrote the famous novel *Mirisi, Zlato I Tamjan* (1968; Scents, Gold and Incense). Vladan Desnica (1905-1967) wrote the novel *Proljeæa Ivana Galeba* (1957; The Springs of Ivan Galeb). Petar ŠEGEDIN wrote the novels *Djeca Borja* (1946; God's Children), *Osamljenici* (1947; Lonely People), and *Vjetar* (1986; The Wind). Ranko MARINKOVIČ wrote the short stories *Ruke* (1953; The Hands) and the novel *Kiklop* (1966; Cyclop).

The most important names of Croatian postmodernism, the period of the last quarter of the 20th c., are Ivan Slamnig (b. 1930), whose big opus of poetry and prose is represented in *Sabrane Pjesme* (1990; Collected Poems) and *Sabrana Kratka Proza* (1991; Collected Short Prose), and Antun Šoljan (1932-1993), the author of a large number of books of poetry, short stories, novels, including the famous *Luka* (1974; Haven), essays, and feuilletons. Also of note are the poets Danijel Dragojevič (b. 1934), Dubravko Horvatič (b. 1939), Nikica Petrak (b. 1939), Boris Maruna (b. 1940), and Luko Paljetak (b. 1943).

The most prominent prose writers of this generation wrote historical novels. Ivan Aralica's (b. 1930) works include *Psi u Trgovištu* (1979; Dogs in the Marketplace), *Put Bez Sna* (1982; Dreamless Road), *Duše Robova* (1984; The Souls of Slaves), and *Graditelj Svratišta* (1986; The Hostel-Builder); Nedjeljko Fabrio (b. 1937) wrote *Vježbanje Života* (1985; Training of Life), *Berenikina Kosa* (1989; Berenika's Hair), and *Smrt Vronskoga* (1944; Vronsky's Death). Feđa Šehovič (b. 1930) is a dramatist and the author of the famous cycle of six novels *Dubrovaèka Tralalogija* (1974-80; A Tralalalogy of Dubrovnik). Ivan Kušan (b. 1933) wrote ironical and sarcastic prose on contemporary themes. Pavao Pavličić (b. 1946) and Goran Tribuson (b. 1948) wrote novels of a modern European and American style.

547

Writing in Matoš's tradition, one of the greatest essayists, feuilletonists, and critics was Veselko Tenžera (1942-1985), the author of the books *En passant* (1978), *Zašto Valium Zagreb* (1987; Why Do I Love Zagreb) and *Preživljuje Dobro Pisanje* (1995; Only Good Penmanship Survives).

BIBLIOGRAPHY: Ujević, M., *Hrvatska književnost* (1932); Ježić, S., *Hrvatska književnost od početaka do danas, 1100-1941* (1944); Marjanović, M., *Hrvatska moderna I-II* (1951); Kadić, A., *Contemporary Croatian Literature* (1960); Pavletič, V., *Hrvatska moderna* (1961); Vaupotič, M., *Hrvatska suvremena književnost / Contemporary Croatian Literature* (1966); Batušič, N., *Povijest hrvatskog kazališta* (1978); Šicel, M., *Pregled novije hrvatske književnosti* (1979); Šicel, M., *Hrvatska književnost* (1982); Kadič, A., *The Tradition of Freedom in Croatian Literature: Essays* (1983); Frangeš, I., *Povijest hrvatske književnosti* (1987); Nemec, K., *Der kroatische Roman achtiziger Jahre* (1990); Milanja, C., *Hrvatski roman 1945-1990* (1996)

—DUBRAVKA SESAR

CROCE, Benedetto

Italian philosopher and literary critic, b. 25 Feb. 1866, Pescassèroli; d. 20 Nov. 1952, Naples

Benedetto Croce

C. was born into a moderately wealthy upper-middle-class family with homes in Naples and the Abruzzi. The tragic death of his parents and a sister in an earthquake during his eighteenth year left him ill-disposed to settle down to a university or professional career. Instead, he used his private means to travel and to amass an extensive library. As a leader of the conservative Liberal Party, C. actively sought political involvement. Particularly during the Fascist era, he stood out as a staunch supporter of democratic principles. By the end of his life C. had attained international eminence not only as a philosopher but as a public figure as well.

C.'s early schooling was typical of the later 19th-c. approach in its emphasis on positivistic methodology, which held that all knowledge must be based on empirically verifiable fact. To it may be traced the profound distrust of "facts" so characteristic of C.'s aesthetics. The first major elaboration of his aesthetic theory appeared in 1902 with the publication of the *Estetica* (aesthetics). In this work C. announced his theory of the autonomy of the poetic faculty. He was able to make this assertion by conceiving of the activity of the mind in terms of two broad categories: *cognition* and *volition*. To the cognitive belongs theoretical thought, speculation on the nature of the world. Volition, on the other hand, is the sphere of practice, of taking action to affect the nature of reality. Under the category of volition C. placed all economic, political, and utilitarian activity, whereas logical thought and intuition belonged to the cognitive realm. The cycle of human activity thus begins in the cognitive sphere with intuition and passes to logical thought and on into the economic and ethical sphere of violation in an unending and inseparable chain.

By placing the poetic act in the intuitive region of the cognitive realm C. affirmed the autonomy of the creative inspiration from other forms of mental activity. He was then able to argue that the work of art was *a priori* an aesthetic image, a unified mental picture of a particular thing. The image might be based upon sense data, might be drawn from inner experience, or both, but it was definitely an image of something specific, determined in space and time. Plot, setting, character, language—every detail of the work is itself a small image belonging to the larger, complex image, which is the entire work. The image is not built step by step, as a logical thesis might evolve, but exists from the moment of intuition in the mind of the artist. The ultimate work is totally present at the moment of intuition. In fact, the work *is* intuition. Clearly, C. does not use intuition in the Cartesian sense of a knowledge of self-evident truths, but rather in the sense of the German *Anschauung*, a cognition of the particular determined in space and time. Intuition, and thus art, is a concrete image of individual reality. This is important, for it means that each work of art is absolutely unique in that it, and only it, presents that particular reality.

Obviously, if the image is complete at the moment of intuition, it must also be *expressed* at the same time. Poetry must be realized verbally; it cannot exist abstractly, without verbal expression. C. argued that the language of a poem, being a part of the total image, is, like the other parts, given at the moment of intuition. Expression and intuition are, in fact, identical. It remains for the poet to realize the intuition through the physical process of writing. In terms of the division of human activity outlined above, the task of realizing the intuition that the poet has been given virtually falls into the sphere of volition—putting theory into practice. At that moment, poetic activity passes from the aesthetic to another domain of endeavor. If the poet fails to realize the intuition, he has been unable to subordinate his will to his intuition. He knows what he wants to say, but cannot say it. The proof that the total image is present before he undertakes the physical task of writing is that he can constantly compare what he has written to the mental image, correcting the former when it deviates from the latter.

The theory of the aesthetic image outlined in the *Estetica* of 1902 explained how poetry came into being, but did not say what it is. C. rectified the omission in 1908 with his theory of *lyrical intuition*. Briefly, this holds that poetry is emotion, the state of mind of the poet at the moment of intuition. As an expression of the soul of the writer at the moment of creation, poetry is lyrical, the nature of the lyricism depending on the kind of emotion expressed. For the poem to be successful, we must receive a definite impression of a single, integral personality. If no single personality—no unified image of the emotion—emerges, then the poem is a failure.

In saying that a poem succeeds or fails, one makes a critical judgment. C. believed a critical approach to be an essential part of the enjoyment of a work of art. For him, criticism was the exercise of judgment based upon the re-creation of the poetic art of expression. Recreation involves three steps: characterizing the image of the work, defining its emotion or lyrical aspect, and ultimately evaluating the reciprocal relationship between image and emotion. C. felt, for example, that romantic poetry was only partially successful because its emotion is far in excess of the image it offers.

The importance of C.'s aesthetic theory for modern criticism cannot be overemphasized. There is no question but that his theories laid the foundation for certain beliefs that are basic to critical schools today—notably the conviction that any critical study of art must begin by analyzing the work itself and that literary study must view the work in its own, entire context, evaluating any statement about a part of the work in light of the total image.

Since the early 1960s, C.'s work has increasingly been viewed as possessing historical, rather than contemporary, significance. Yet the importance of C.'s work on the evolution of literary and aesthetic theories in the first half of the 20th c. may be judged from the fact that his work continues to be cited. One due to C.'s enduring fame may be found in his revival of such protean 18th-and 19th-c. philosophers as Giambattista Vico and Hegel. In *Lafilosofia di Giambattista Vico* (1911; *The Philosophy of Giambattista Vico,*, 1913) C. perceived the importance of Vico for the concept of historicism, a historically grounded form of C.'s contextualist criticism successfully espoused, for example, by the influential critic Erich AUERBACH in such works as *Mimesis*. Auerbach always acknowledged his debt to him. C. remains then, a critic more cited than read, but whose historical importance cannot be contested.

FURTHER WORKS: *Materialismo storico* (1900; *Historical Materialism and the Economics of Karl Marx*, 1922); *Logica come scienza del concetto puro* (1909; *Logic as the Science of Pure Concept*, 1917); *Problemi di estetica* (1910); *Filosofia della pratica: Economica ed etica* (1913; *Philosophy of the Practical: Economics and Ethics*, 1923); *Goethe* (1917; *Goethe*, 1923); *Teoria e storia della storiografia* (1917; *History: Its Theory and Practice*, 1960); *Ariosto, Shakespeare e Corneille* (1920; *Ariosto, Shakespeare, and Corneille*, 1920); *Breviari di Estetica* (1920; *The Essence of Aesthetics*, 1921); *Nuovi saggi di estetica* (1920, 1926); *Poesia e non poesia* (1923; *European Literature in the 19th Century*, 1924); *Conversazioni critiche* (1924); *Etica e politica* (1931; *Politics and*

Morals, 1945); *Cultura e vita morale* (1936); *La storia come pensiero e come azione* (1938; *History as the Story of Liberty*, 1941); *Poesia antica e moderna* (1941); *Discorsi de varia filosofia* (1945); *Lettura di poeti e riflessioni sulla teoria e la critica della poesia* (1950); *La poesia* (1953). FURTHER WORKS IN ENGLISH: *The Conduct of Life* (1924); *My Philosophy, and Other Essays on the Moral and Political Problems of Our Time* (1949); *Essays on Marx and Russia* (1966)

BIBLIOGRAPHY: Wellek, R., "B. C.: Literary Critic and Historian," *CL*, 5 (1953): 75–82; Krieger, M., "B. C. and the Recent Poetics of Organicism," *CL*, 7 (1955): 252–58; Nahm, M. C., "The Philosophy of Artistic Expression: The Crocean Hypothesis," *JAAC*, 13 (1955): 300–13; Bertocci, A., "C.'s Aesthetics in Context," *The Personalist*, 38 (1957): 248–59; Scaglione, A., "C.'s Definition of Literary Criticism," *JAAC*, 17 (1959): 447–56; Wasiolek, E., "C. and Contextualist Criticism," *MP*, 57 (1959): 44–54; Orsini, G. N. G., *B. C.* (1961); Finocchiaro, M. A., "Towards a Crocean History of Science," *Rivista di Studi Crociani*, 11 (1974): 162–70; Jacobitti, E. E., "Labriola, C. and Italian Marxism (1885–1910)," *JHI*, 36 (1975): 297–318; Scaglione, A., "C. as a Cosmopolitan Critic," in *The Two Hesperias: Literary Studies in Honor of Joseph G. Fucilla* (1977): 339–47; Moss, N. E., *B. C. Reconsidered* (1987); Roberts, D. D., *B. C. and the Uses of Historicism* (1987)

—STEPHEN G. NICHOLS, JR.

CROMMELYNCK, Fernand

Belgian dramatist (writing in French), b. 19 Nov. 1886, Paris, France; d. 17 March 1970, Saint-Germain-en-Laye, France

C. was born to a Belgian father and French mother and spent his childhood in Paris. He left school at the age of twelve to work for a stockbroker; at fourteen he began appearing on the stage with his father and uncle, both actors. When C.'s father inherited some money, the family moved to Brussels, and C. started writing for the theater. *Nous n'irons plus au bois* (1906; we will not go to the woods any more) won the Thyrse Prize. *Le sculpteur des masques* (1906; the sculptor of masks), with its silences and hints of the unexpressed and inexpressible, leaves much to the imagination; characterization and plot are nuanced and subtle rather than clearly explained. C. founded a theatrical company, The Flying Theater, in 1916, but it was forced to close in 1918 because of financial difficulties.

After his marriage in 1908, C. settled in Ostend, where he met James Ensor, the Belgian painter. This artist's use of masks, of tortured and grotesque images, strongly influenced C.'s future creations. In fact, C. wrote a revised version of *Le sculpteur des masques* in 1911.

Le cocu magnifique (1921; *The Magnificent Cuckold*, 1966) brought fame to C. A farce about jealousy, full of bald characterizations and ribald situations, it uses caustic humor to caricature and satirize sordid personality traits. Throughout this comedy of sex the phallus is an instrument of both pleasure and destruction.

Les amants puérils (1921; the childish lovers) underscores the conflicts between illusion and reality. Powerful and simple, the play depicts life as a degrading experience. Beauty, happiness, and love are short-lived. The atmosphere of loneliness and solitude is reinforced by images of water, the moon, mirrors, and glass.

Tripes d'or (1925; golden guts), a farce centering around avarice, is perhaps C.'s best play. The main character is so obsessed—and possessed—by his sudden inheritance that he eats—and excretes—gold and is in a sense eaten by it. This lusty play uses slapstick techniques: vulgar insults, risqué repartee, violence, cruelty, broadly drawn characters.

In *Carine* (1929; Carine) C.'s innovative use of masks, ballet, and mime imbues the play with an atmosphere of mystery. Carine, a pure and beautiful young girl whose dream is to love and be loved and who believes in marriage and family, is crushed by those closest to her and destroyed by a cruel and perverted world.

Une femme qu'a le cœur trop petit (a woman whose heart is too small) and *Chaud et froid* (hot and cold), both performed in 1934, are EXPRESSIONIST in style. An excessively virtuous woman who becomes a tyrant in her own home is the subject of the first play, a powerful satire on middle-class women. The second drama features a woman who considers her husband such a bore that she takes on many lovers. Upon her husband's death she discovers that he loved, and was loved by, a young girl. She gives up her lovers and devotes her life to his memory. The play is crude, cruel, and ironic in its treatment of people's need for cults and shrines.

C.'s theater is filled with puppetlike characters: hard and brittle, they strike at each other in the most violent and vicious ways. C. points up, through expert use of caricature, the cruelty implicit in human nature. C.'s powerful humor depicts in broad and powerful brush strokes man's utter and eternal foolishness.

FURTHER WORKS: *Clematyde* (1906); *Chacun pour soi* (1907); *Le marchand de regrets* (1916); *Monsieur Larose est-il assassin?* (1950); *Théâtre complet* (1956)

BIBLIOGRAPHY: Lilar, S., *The Belgian Theater since 1890* (1950): 27–30; Grossvogel, D., *20th-Century French Drama* (1965): 220–53; Knapp, B., *F. C.* (1978)

—TAYITTA HADAR

CSOKOR, Franz Theodor

Austrian dramatist, poet, and essayist, b. 6 Sept. 1885, Vienna; d. 5 Jan. 1969, Vienna

C. became an important figure in Viennese literary circles after World War I, and by the late 1920s his reputation had spread throughout Austria and Germany. In 1933, when C. protested the Nazi book burnings and persecution of Jewish writers, his work was banned within the Third Reich. Following the Nazi annexation of Austria in 1938, C. fled Vienna and spent the next eight years in war-torn Poland, Romania, Yugoslavia, and Italy. When he returned to Vienna after World War II, C. actively participated in the revitalization of Austrian literature and served as president of the Austrian PEN Club for twenty-two years.

C.'s dramatic work consists primarily of historical social dramas and contemporary problem plays that examine the clash of traditional and revolutionary values, the nature of ideology, and the role of the individual in society. He embarked on his literary career by writing EXPRESSIONIST plays around the time of World War I. *Die rote Straße* (1918; the red street), an examination of crass

materialism and destructive relationships between the sexes, is C.'s best-known early work.

By the middle of the 1920s C. had abandoned expressionism and adopted a more realistic style of writing. He turned to historical events and figures to reflect the moral crises challenging contemporary man. C.'s most successful drama of the 1920s, *Gesellschaft der Menschenrechte* (1929; society for human rights), illustrates the German writer Georg Büchner's (1813–1837) struggle to reconcile his roles as an artist and social activist.

During the late 1920s and 1930s C.'s work criticized the fanaticism, brutality, and mass psychology that had begun to plague his world. Shortly after World War II C. linked together three historical dramas he had written over the preceding twenty-five years as the *Europäische Trilogie* (1952; European trilogy), which analyzes the development of ideology, particularly nationalism, in 20th-c. Europe, and investigates how ideology affects the individual and society. The first drama, *3. November 1918* (1936; November 3, 1918), one of the great dramas of modern Austrian literature, portrays the dissolution of the Austro-Hungarian Empire and the growth of nationalism after World War I. *Besetztes Gebiet* (1930; occupied territory), set during the French occupation of the German Ruhr in 1923, depicts the evolution of nationalism into a brutal, mindless force, while *Der verlorene Sohn* (1947; the prodigal son) uses the partisan resistance to the Fascist occupation in Yugoslavia to examine the transition from traditional beliefs to a new socialist society.

In his post-World War II work C. continued to draw upon contemporary and historical events to explore values, morality, and change in the individual and society. Although primarily a dramatist, C. also wrote poetry, essays, memoirs, and fiction. C.'s most noted prose work is a memoir of his wartime experiences in eastern Europe, *Auf fremden Straßen* (1955; on foreign streets), which had previously appeared in two separate parts as *Als Zivilist im polnischen Krieg* (1941; *A Civilian in the Polish War*, 1940), and *Als Zivilist im Balkankrieg* (1947; a civilian in the Balkan war).

C.'s life and work were influenced by the multinational structure of the Austro-Hungarian Empire and the rich literary tradition of *fin-de-siècle* Vienna. His early plays and poetry include some of the finest examples of expressionist writing in Austria. While some of his later historical dramas and contemporary problem plays are overly didactic, others are perceptive explorations into the nature of responsibility, freedom, individuality, and change in society. The focusing on contemporary history can be considered as foreshadowing the documentary drama that appeared in Germany in the 1960s.

FURTHER WORKS: *Thermidor* (1912); *Die Gewalten* (1912); *Der große Kampf* (1915 [play retracted by author]); *Die Sünde wider den Geist* (1918); *Der Dolch und die Wunde* (1918); *Der Baum der Erkenntnis* (1919); *Schuß ins Geschäft* (1924); *Ewiger Aufbruch* (1926); *Ballade von der Stadt* (1928); *Gewesene Menschen* (1932); *Die Weibermühle* (1932); *Das Thüringer Spiel von den zehn Jungfrauen* (1933); *Über die Schwelle* (1937); *Gottes General* (1939); *Das schwarze Schiff* (1944); *Kalypso* (1946); *Immer ist Anfang* (1952); *Olymp and Golgatha* (1954; contains *Kalypso, Caesars Witwe, Pilatus*), *Der Schlüssel Zum Abgrund* (1955); *Hebt den Stein ab!* (1957); *Der Zweite Hahnenschrei* (1959); *Du bist gemeint!* (1959); *Treibholz* (1959); *Die Erweckung des Zosimir* (1960); *Das Zeichen an der Wand* (1962); *Der Mensch und die Macht* (1963; contains *Jadwiga, Der tausendjährige Traum,*

Gesellschaft der Menschenrechte); *Zeuge einer Zeit* (1964); *Die Kaiser zwischen den Zeiten* (1965); *Ein paar Schaufeln Erde* (1965); *Alexander* (1969); *Zwischen den Zeiten* (1969; contains *Die Kaiser zwischen den Zeiten, Gottes General, 3. November 1918*)

BIBLIOGRAPHY: Bithell, J., "F. T. C.," *GL&L*, 8, 1 (1954): 37–44; Parker, L. J., "Two Drama Trilogies of F. T. C.," *SCB*, 21, 4 (1961): 37–43; Forst de Battaglia, O., "F. T. C.," in *Abgesang auf eine große Zeit* (1967): 70–80; Böhm, G., "F. T. C.: Visionen über die Zeiten hinweg," in Spiel, H., ed., *Kindlers Literaturgeschichte der Gegenwart: Die zeitgenössische Literatur Österreichs*, Teil IV (1976): 505–13; Zohn, H., "F. T. C.'s 3. *November 1918*," *MAL*, 11, 1 (1978): 95–102

—KATHERINE MCHUGH LICHLITER

CSOÓRI, Sándor

Hungarian poet and essayist, b. 3 Feb. 1930, Zámoly

The finest populist poet of his generation, C. was born in a small village in western Hungary to a poor Protestant peasant family. He attended local schools and reached early maturity during the war years. C. published his first volume of poems, *Felröppen a madár* (1954; the bird takes wing), while still in his twenties. The book was an instant success; it won him the József Attila Prize (1954) and a seat on the editorial board of the Budapest literary magazine *Szabad Ifjúság*. In the early 1950s C. represented the Communist Party-inspired poet of the people: the country boy singing in simple rhymes about the rural poor and the joy of building socialism. However, the 1956 revolt profoundly altered C.'s political views and his direct poetic diction. Showing the influence of such poets as Federico GARCÍA LORCA and Paul ÉLUARD, his verse gradually abandoned native imagism in favor of a more thorough treatment of a few basic themes: love, solitude, nature, and his native roots. This change became apparent in his next collection of poems, *Menekülés a magányból* (1962; escape from solitude).

In the 1960s, frustrated by the economic and psychological privations of his country, C. branched into prose. His essays in *Tudósítás a toronyból* (1963; report from the tower) are a blend of autobiography, sociography, folklore, and poetic social criticism in the manner of the poet Gyula ILLYÉS, his long-time mentor. In 1964, after a trip to Cuba, he wrote an exuberant travelogue, *Kubai napló* (1965; Cuban diary), praising Fidel Castro and Che Guevera. From the early 1970s C. has collaborated regularly on film scripts with directors Ferenc Kósa and Sándor Sára. Their first movie, *Tízezer nap* (1963; ten thousand days), won the Grand Prix at Cannes (1964). He also continued to publish poetry and prose. In a major volume of essays *Nomád napló* (1979; nomadic diary), C. advocated reliance on nonpolitical ethical values and an adherence to the folklore tradition, broadening his personal concerns into a yearning for universal social justice. He reached new heights in his new books of poetry *Tizedik este* (1980; the tenth evening), *Tenger és diólevél* (1982; sea and chestnut leaf), and *Kezemben a zöld ág* (1985; green twig in my hand). These volumes read like a romantic portrait of the artist himself, yet in them C. actually assumes varying poetic personae who speak movingly of the experience of death and past loves.

The heritage of romanticism blends in C.'s work with surrealist effects, which he claims to have learned from folk poetry. In each poem the hero is C. himself, an intellectual who has never ceased to be a peasant. In a world leveled by thoughtless modernization, he searches for ways to preserve uniqueness in the world. The poems illuminate his spiritual torment, unravel his deep feelings of isolation, while offering a taste, however slight, of that zestful natural condition from which he and his people were wrenched in the haphazardly transformed postwar world. In another prose volume, *Készülődés a számadásra* (1987; preparing for the reckoning), C. blamed himself and his generation for not speaking the whole truth about Hungary's ills: high suicide rates and low birth rates, diminished national consciousness, and general apathy. In a terse, poetic style he tried to instill a new moral awareness in his contemporaries.

More recently C. found himself at the center of a new political movement, being regarded as a kind of spiritual leader of the people. As editor of *Hitel*, a cultural journal identified with the Hungarian Democratic Forum, the leading political party, he has become an ardent spokesman for the new patriotism and a defender of the nation's populist tradition. He also has become internationally known in the past few years. Several of his works have been translated into English and German, and in 1981 he won Austria's prestigious Herder Prize. After the second liberation of Hungary in 1989, C. became a political leader. As president of the World Federation of Hungarians, he published hundreds of social and political articles. In fact, out of his seven books released to 1998, three are monumental essay collections.

C.'s style is a mixture of the traditional and the modern. His imagery is sensuous and natural, but his themes are those of a dislocated visionary. Behind his serene and delicate poetic lines there is always the wistful attempt to capture the unfathomable richness of fast-fading worlds as well as the sadness of universal transience. Nevertheless, C. is a highly respected national poet in Hungary today because his finest works transcend politics and also deal with survival, including national, cultural survival.

FURTHER WORKS: *Ördögpille* (1957); *A Költő és a majompofa* (1966); *Második születésem* (1967); *Faltól falig* (1969); *Párbeszéd a sötétben* (1973); *Utazás félálomban* (1974); *Sose harmadnapon* (1976); *A látogató emlékei* (1977); *Jóslás a te idődről* (1979); *Iszapeső* (1980); *A félig bevallott élet* (1982); *Elmaradt lázálom* (1982); *Várakozás a tavaszban* (1983); *Csoóri breviárium* (1988); *A világ emlékművei* (1989); *Nappali hold* (1991); *Senkid, barátod* (1992); *Tenger és diólevél* (2 vols., 1994); *Hattyúkkal, ágyútűzben* (1994); *Ha voltna életem* (1996); *Szálla alá a poklokra* (1997); *Válogatott versek* (1998). **FURTHER WORKS IN ENGLISH:** *Wings of Knives and Nails* (1981); *Memory of Snow* (1983); *Barbarian Prayer: Selected Poems* (1989)

BIBLIOGRAPHY: Vajda, M., ed., *Modern Hungarian Poetry* (1977): 233–38; Tezla, A., ed., *Ocean at the Window* (1980): 277–300; Czigány, L., *The Oxford History of Hungarian Literature* (1984): 460–62; Gömöri, G., on *Készülődés a számadásra*, *WLT*, 62, 3 (Summer 1988): 486; Gömöri, G., on *Barbarian Prayer: Selected Poems*, *WLT*, 64, 3 (Summer 1990): 500; Mottram, E., "Before the Revolution: Poetry by S. C.," *NHQ*, 118 (1990): 112–16; Szakolczay, L., "Egy kőltészet holdudvara: C. S. Dióhéjban," *Magyar Napló*, 12 (1997): 42-45

—CLARA GYORGYEY

CUBAN LITERATURE
See Spanish-Caribbean Literature

CUBISM

Cubism emerged in Paris around 1907, when painters under the influence of Picasso and Braque set out to discover a style that could penetrate beneath appearances and bring to light the inner substance of reality. This new pictorial mode was designated as cubist because it reduced objects to geometric forms. It attracted a number of writers who worked intimately with the painters and helped to elucidate cubist doctrines, extending some of them to literature. The poet Guillaume APOLLINAIRE was among the first to champion the cubist cause. His *Les peintres cubistes* (1913; *The Cubist Painters*, 1944) likened poets and painters to visionaries and described cubism as the art of painting new groupings out of elements imagined by the artist. He stressed the nonmimetic thrust of the new school, as did Max JACOB and André Salmon (1881–1969), who held that the cubist artist maintains a steady gaze on the world but through the process of conceptualization extracts from objects their essential characteristics, rearranging them after the pattern of his intuitive vision. In 1917 Pierre REVERDY, an articulate exponent of synthetic cubism, founded a literary review dedicated to cubism, *Nord-Sud*, and therein proposed a theory of the poetic image that mirrored the cubist technique of juxtaposing distant realities.

Transposed to literature, cubism went far in shaping modern sensibility in France and elsewhere. It nudged writers toward concreteness, precision, the study of themes from multiple perspectives and, in poetry, toward a more subtle statement of the relationship between the poet and reality. This initiated the post symbolist stance, which tends to blur the subject-object dichotomy and, in the manner of cubist painters who flattened planes and merged figure and background, disperses the poet's subjectivity among fragments of the exterior world.

On the level of language, cubism led to formal experimentation. In Russia the cubo-futurist poets Velimir KHLEBNIKOV and Vladimir MAYAKOVSKY advocated free verbal play and a complete overhauling of language. In France prose writers and especially poets created a forceful, iconoclastic style by suppressing sequential structures in favor of fragmented texts. They juxtaposed disjunct sequences and shifting perspectives, truncated syntax, fragmented the authorial voice, experimented with typography, arranging lines in blocks, eliminated punctuation. Apollinaire's *Alcools* (1913; *Alcools*, 1964) and *Calligrammes* (1918; *Calligrams*, 1980), Jacob's *Cornet à dés* (1917; the dice box), some poems by REVERDY, SALMON, and Blaise CENDRARS, and to a lesser degree André GIDE's experimental prose fit this new mode, as does the verse of the Chilean innovator Vicente HUIDOBRO. Among American writers, Gertrude STEIN utilized devices associated with cubism: repetition of homogeneous elements, the building up of images from recurrent statements, collagelike word portraits. William Carlos WILLIAMS, also indebted to visual art, transposed to poetry the cubists' fascination with objects and under their impact discarded narration and reflection to concentrate on the image defined not as metaphor but as the very subject of a poem.

In the 1920s cubism lost its force and unity of direction. It persisted, however, generalized into the doctrine of simultanism (which seeks to arrange all elements in a work of art in such a manner that they are perceived not successively but in a single instant of consciousness) or as a strand within SURREALISM.

BIBLIOGRAPHY: Lemaître, G., *From Cubism to Surrealism* (1941); Shattuck, R., *The Banquet Years* (1955); Sypher, W., *Rococo to Cubism in Art and Literature* (1960); Steegmuller, F., *Apollinaire: Poet among the Painters* (1963); Guiney, M., *Cubisme littéraire et plastique* (1966); Dijkstra, B., *Cubism, Stieglitz, and the Early Poetry of William Carlos Williams* (1969); Kamber, G., *Max Jacob and the Poetics of Cubism* (1971)

—VIKTORIA SKRUPSKELIS

CULLEN, Countee

(born Countee Porter) American poet, novelist, anthologist, and dramatist, b. 30 May 1903, either in Kentucky or Baltimore, Md.; d. 9 Jan. 1946, New York, N.Y.

At the age of eleven, C., an orphan, became the foster son of the prominent Harlem minister the Reverend Frederick Cullen and his wife. A brilliant student, C. was graduated from New York University Phi Beta Kappa. While studying for his master's degree at Harvard, he greatly impressed his teacher, the poet Robert Hillyer (1895–1961), with his virtuosity at versification and his lyric gift. He began his accumulation of literary prizes at an early age and served as assistant editor for *Opportunity*, where his column, "The Dark Tower," increased his reputation as a man of letters. He spent two consecutive years abroad, principally in Paris, on a Guggenheim Fellowship. From 1934 until his death he taught French and English in a New York City junior high school.

C. was a leading voice of the Harlem Renaissance, especially in poetry. *Color* (1925), a book of verse containing "Heritage," probably his most famous poem, firmly established his eminence as a New Negro, the appellation the artists and critics of the Renaissance assigned themselves. Commentators on *Copper Sun* (1927), C.'s second book of verse, tend to consider it inferior to *Color*. In *Caroling Dusk* (1927) C. anthologized Negro poetry, obviously as a partisan for his race. His only novel, *One Way to Heaven* (1932), combines, somewhat too loosely, a satire on the social elite of Harlem with a fable, more effective than the satire, of redemptive love, both romantic and religious. But except for his collaboration in the conversion of Arna Bontemps's novel *God Sends Sunday* (1931) into the musical comedy *St. Louis Woman*, which ran briefly on Broadway in 1946, C. rather avoided racial themes after the early 1930s. His last creative efforts produced only poems and stories about animals for children, albeit for children, as he not too facetiously proclaimed, of any age.

Whatever his origins, because of his upbringing in the Reverend Cullen's home C. lived at the heart of the black bourgeoisie, and by white American standards he was well-bred. By his own reckoning Keats was the poet with whom he had the greatest affinity, and he often wrote in the traditional sonnet form. His animadversions against a part of a system, namely, its institution of color caste, he expressed in forms intimately allied with that system. His poetry adheres to old, familiar orthodoxies of English prosody. Only once, as a matter of fact, did he resort even to free verse. Still, genuine artist that he was, his acquiescence to existing modes did not so much hamper as free him. His exposures of color caste are deft and comprehensive; his exceptional natural lyrical gift almost never deserted him. Nevertheless, the work that brought him recognition was soon done, without a sequel. And so he remains a poet conceivably of eternally arrested development.

FURTHER WORKS: *The Ballad of the Brown Girl* (1927); *The Black Christ and Other Poems* (1929); *The Medea, and Some Poems* (1935); *The Lost Zoo (A Rhyme for the Young, But Not Too Young)* (1940); *My Lives and How I Lost Them* (1942); *On These I Stand: An Anthology of the Best Poems of C. C.* (1947)

BIBLIOGRAPHY: Bone, R., *The Negro Novel in America* (rev. ed., 1965): 78–80; Fergusson, B., *C. and the Negro Renaissance* (1966); Perry, M., *A Bio-Bibliography of C. P. C. 1903–1946* (1971); Turner, D., "*C. C.: The Lost Ariel*," *In a Minor Chord* (1971): 60–88; Wagner, J., *Black Poets of the United States* (1973): 283–347; Davis, A., *From the Dark Tower* (1974): 73–87 and passim; Jackson, B., and L. Rubin, *Black Poetry in America* (1974): 46–51; Shucard, A. R., *C. C.* (1984)

—BLYDEN JACKSON

CUMALI, Necati

Turkish poet, dramatist, fiction writer, and essayist, b. 1921, Florina (now Greece)

One of Turkey's most versatile and prolific authors, C. graduated from the faculty of law at Ankara University at the age of twenty. He worked for brief periods for the ministry of public education, the office of the Turkish press attaché in Paris, and Radio Istanbul. From 1950 to 1957 he practiced law in Urla and Izmir, where he had spent much of his early life. In the 1960s he lived some time in Tel Aviv and Paris, where his wife was an attaché. During the second half of his adult life he has been an independent writer.

In the 1940s, C. attracted attention with his simple, straightforward poems which, like the work of his contemporaries Orhan Veli Kanik (1914–1950) and Melih Cevdet ANDAY among others, dealt with the life of an average person. C.'s poems often celebrated the beauty of nature and sometimes lamented the harsh realities of rural life. His youthful sentiments ranged from tenderness to open protest. His earliest collections, *Kızılçullu yolu* (1943; road to Kızılçullu), *Harbe gidenin şarkıları* (1945; songs of those gone to war), *Mayıs ayı notları* (1947; notes of May), and *Güzel aydınlık* (1951; lovely light), contain effortlessly accomplished poems of romantic involvements, life's simple pleasures, and the poignancy of poverty and war.

C.'s 1955 collection entitled *İmbatla gelen* (borne on the southern wind) features poems in the same vein, but also the striking narrative cycle "Karakolda" (in the precinct) about a blood feud in a rural village, composed like a folk elegy, which is perhaps his most powerful long poem. His *Güneş çizigisi* (1957; line of the sun), *Yağmurlu deniz* (1968; rainy sea), which combined the two previous books with a selection of new poems, *Başaklar gebe* (1970; pregnant are the grains), and *Ceylan ağıdı* (1974; antelope's elegy) chart the course of his transition to a compelling concern

about social and political upheaval in Turkey and abroad. In this period, C. visited and resided in several foreign cities, including Paris, New York, Sofia, and Leningrad, which inspired many fine poems. *Yağmurlu deniz* won the coveted poetry prize of the Trukish Language Society in 1969.

Bozkırda bir atlı (1981; a rider in the steppes) and *Yarasın beyler* (1982; to your health, gentlemen) are kaleidoscopic collections containing his lyric, satiric, political, and elegiac poems. In 1980 C. published his collected poems under the title *Aç güneş* (hungry sun) and in 1983 brought out an enlarged collection, *Tufandan önce* (before the deluge).

C.'s novels deal mainly with the dramas of rural life with which he became familiar during his formative years and later as a country lawyer. They are filled with action and memorable characters. The narrative style is remarkably lucid and crisp. His first novel, *Tütün zamanı* (1959; tobacco time), later reissued as *Zeliş* (1971; Zeliş) after the principal character, is a touching story of the life and love of an immigrant girl. *Yağmurlar ve topraklar* (1973; rains and the soil) is a stirring narrative of political turmoil, idealism gone awry, struggle against exploiters, and intellectual restlessness in Turkey in the early 1950s. *Acı tütün* (1974; bitter tobacco) and *Aşk da gezer* (1975; love too drifts) consolidated C.'s fame as a major novelist. Published in 1994, C.'s novel *Viran dağlar* (ruined mountains) won two of Turkey's most prestigious awards.

In the short-story genre C. has secured himself a place of high distinction. His collections *Yalnız Kadın* (1955; lonely woman), *Değişik gözle* (1956; with a fresh eye), *Ay büyürken uyuyamam* (1969; I cannot sleep while the moon grows larger), *Kente inen kaplanlar* (1976; tigers swooping on the city), *Dilâ Hanım* (1978; Lady Dilâ), *Revizyonist* (1979; revisionist), *Yakubun Koyunları* (1979; Jacob's sheep), and others contain a number of the most consummate short stories written in the Turkish language. *Değişik gözle* won the Sait Faik Prize in 1957. C. was awarded the prize once again in 1977 for his collection *Makedonya 1900* (1976; Macedonia 1900), stories based on the experiences and recollections of his parents.

C.'s novella *Susuz yaz* (1962; dry summer), which he had also written as a play by the same name, was made into a film and enjoyed success in Turkey and abroad, winning the Berlin International Film Festival Award in 1963. (The English translation of the play is included in T. S. Halman's *Modern Turkish Drama*, 1976.)

As a translator, C. has done two volumes of selected poems by Langston HUGHES and Guillaume APOLLINAIRE, in 1961 and 1965 respectively. His collections of essays *Niçin aşk* (1971; why love), *Senin için ey demokrasi* (1976; for you, o democracy), and *Etiler mektupları* (1982; letters from Etiler) contain some of his best critical pieces on literature and politics. His *Yeşil bir at sırtında* (1990; riding a green horse) is a collection of reminiscences and reflections.

C.'s plays have enjoyed successful runs at Turkish theaters and have been collected in many volumes. *Boş beşik* (1949; empty cradle), made into a film in 1955, won first prize at the Erlangen International Theater Festival (Germany) in 1955. *Nalınlar* (1962; *The Clogs*, 1982) was a huge success at Istanbul's Kent Players Theater. Most recently, *Derya gülü* (1963) was published in English as *Sea Rose* (1991). These three plays dramatize touching and sometimes humorous episodes of villagers and fishing people of Anatolia. C.'s other plays often deal with urban situations and universal themes. *Bir sabah gülerek uyan* (1990; wake up laughing one morning) is a bittersweet play, a wry comedy of errors, depicting the disquietude of some Turkish intellectuals. *Dün neredeydiniz* (1981; where were you yesterday) was awarded the Ministry of Culture Prize (1981). The range of imagination, the clever plots with surprising denouements, crisp dialogue, and fascinating characters have made C.'s plays highly interesting to watch and to read.

Few Turkish writers have achieved as impressive a success in so many genres—poetry, novel, short story, drama, essays, translations—as has C. His fame will probably endure as one of the most energetic creative forces in the literature of the Turkish republic.

—TALAT SAIT HALMAN

CUMMINGS, e(dward) e(stlin)

American poet and critic, b. 14 Oct. 1894, Cambridge, Mass.; d. 3 Sept. 1962, Joy Farm, N.H.

C. graduated magna cum laude from Harvard in 1915, with a major in classics. During World War I he served with a volunteer ambulance unit in France and was interned without trial by the French government for suspected pro-German sympathies. Throughout the 1920s, he contributed to *The Dial*, perhaps America's greatest literary journal. He received many awards, primarily toward the end of his career: *The Dial Award* (1925), Academy of American Poets fellow (1950), Guggenheim fellow (1951), Charles Eliot Norton Professor at Harvard (1952–53), and the Bollingen Prize in Poetry (1958).

C.'s work covers an impressive range of genres, subjects, settings, and forms: drama, essay, autobiography, travel book, ballet scenario, and over seven hundred poems. Much of his thought he inherited from Whitman and the New England transcendentalists—particularly Thoreau—a heritage evident in his celebration of the individual as against government and the masses, and of the vitality of cities and nature. C., however, reformed these influences into a highly original mix, so that while one may find echoes of Rimbaud and Blake, as well as the transcendentalists, C. himself remains difficult to classify as a follower of this one or that.

C.'s prose is less well-known than his poetry, although his two major prose works, *The Enormous Room* (1922) and *EIMI* (1933) are considered modern classics. In *The Enormous Room*, about his unjust internment in a French camp, C. praises the individual by opposing powerful, sympathetic, marvelously rich portraits of prisoners, jailed for no reason but bureaucratic whim, with sharp, acidly funny sketches of the jailers. *EIMI* tells of C.'s 1931 trip to the U.S.S.R., a "more enormous room." The obscure, small-time French camp has grown to enclose an entire country. C. could regard the camp almost as a haven from government regimentation because of the intensely alive prisoners within; he views a visit to Stalin's Russia however, as nothing less than a modern descent into Dante's hell. Death and fear of the secret police pervade the book, whose central image is the long line of Russians entering Lenin's tomb, inching slowly toward the grotesque corpse. C. describes the Russians themselves as the "undead." Yet even in this setting C. finds Russians as "alive" as possible, and his subdued tone makes them appear even more heroic than the French prisoners. *EIMI* ran counter to American intellectuals' infatuation with Russia at the time, but it has become a prophetic work, undeservedly neglected.

As a poet, C. continued the great formal and stylistic innovations of early modernism. After shedding initial influences of the

e. e. cummings

Pre-Raphaelites, Swinburne, and early POUND, he quickly found his own voice and began to experiment prodigiously with poetic construction and ways of meaning. Many of his poems are "once forms," that is, one-of-a-kind forms invented specifically for that poem. He also mastered free verse, song, ballad, and sonnet. He frequently used typography in a way that suggests Pound's view of the Chinese ideogram: the linguistic sign becomes a visual symbol of the thing signified. Thus, "mOOn Over tOwns mOOn" (1935) not only lengthens the vowels in the line but shows us the full moon. Considered by many the best sonneteer since Gerard Manley Hopkins (1844–1889), he wrote a large number in this form—mainly variations on the Petrarchan—inventive in diction, subject matter, stanzaic division, and arrangement on the page. C. also developed "exploded typography," his most famous device, although perhaps the least important to his poetry's quality. Punctuation is freed from syntax, often functioning as a kind of imagery or morpheme. He frequently breaks up words unetymologically, to discover "hidden" words within them. Other key elements of his style are the rhetorical device of tmesis; concurrent placement on the page of separate arguments and images to achieve the effect of simultaneity; concern for the singing line; and, in the early poetry especially, ingenious oxymorons.

Certain critics have argued that C.'s work shows no sign of growth, but they read him carelessly. Although he found his main themes and tone early, he refined both throughout his career. The early poetry is almost too rich in images, comparatively unconcerned with connecting disparate elements into cohesive statement.

C.'s later work is much leaner. A symbolic vocabulary, analogous to Blake's, replaces image, as his themes become more defined.

C.'s primary theme is mystical union of individual and universe. His is "positive" mysticism: man achieves this union through an ecstatic apprehension of things around him rather than through their rejection. The union is only momentarily possible, but because it meets the infinite, the moment becomes man's participation in eternity. In the early poetry, union is figured by sexual union; in the later, by a varied exploration of love and ecstatic "being."

C. wrote poetry in many ways divergent from the main course of modernism. He is characteristically affirmative and celebratory, and, unlike ELIOT, he does not win affirmation from an initial despair. Further, C.'s de-emphasis of the image in favor of symbolic vocabulary runs against a critical tradition that reveres "objective correlatives." For these reasons, academic critics, and New Critics in particular, have underrated him. Yet, C. had the regard of major contemporaries—Pound and Eliot, as well as Marianne MOORE and William Carlos WILLIAMS—and his books are still popular.

FURTHER WORKS: *Tulips and Chimneys* (1923); *& [AND]* (1925); *XLI Poems* (1925); *is 5* (1926); *Him* (1927); *[No title]* (1930); *CIOPW* (1931); *W [ViVa]* (1931); *No Thanks* (1933); *Tom* (1935); *Collected Poems* (1938); *50 Poems* (1940); *1 X 1* (1944); *Anthropos: The Future of Art* (1945); *Santa Claus* (1946); *XAIPE* (1950); *i: six nonlectures* (1953); *Poems: 1923–1954* (1954); *95 Poems* (1958); *Adventures in Value* (1962); *73 Poems* (1963); *Fairy Tales* (1965); *E. E. C., a Miscellany Revised* (1965); *Selected Letters* (1969); *Complete Poems: 1913–1962* (1972)

BIBLIOGRAPHY: Friedman, N., *E. E. C., the Art of His Poetry* (1960); Baum, S. V., ed., *EΣTI: e e c: E. E. C. and the Critics* (1962); Friedman, N., *E. E. C., the Growth of a Writer* (1964); Norman, C., *The Magic-Maker, E. E. C.* (rev. ed., 1964); Friedman, N., ed., *E. E. C: A Collection of Critical Essays* (1972); Dumas, B. K., *E. E. C., a Remembrance of Miracles* (1974); Kennedy, R. S., *Dreams in the Mirror: A Biography of E. E. C.* (1979); Rotella, G., ed., *Critical Essays on E. E. C.* (1984)

—STEVEN SCHWARTZ

CUNQUEIRO, Álvaro

Spanish novelist, poet, and dramatist (writing in Galician and Spanish), b. 22 Dec. 1911, Modoñedo

C. studied history at the University of Santiago de Compostela. He has been an active journalist as well as editor-in-chief of several newspapers and magazines, including the *Faro de Vigo*. C.'s literary world invokes his native Galicia. Through free association and fantasy, he integrates Galicia's Celtic and Roman heritages, its terrain reminiscent of the British Isles, and its medieval religious importance as a center of pilgrimages, and thus creates an eternal realm like that in the work of Jorge Luis BORGES, in which time and space are suspended. This attitude is also reflected in C.'s use of language; for instance, Hispano-Arabic archaisms appear alongside space-age neologisms.

C.'s first poems appeared just before the Spanish Civil War. *Mar ao norde* (1932; sea to the north) contains poems in Galician marked by maritime images and a SURREALIST bent. His later

collections are inspired by medieval Galician-Portuguese lyrics, as well as by voguish forms, like Japanese poetry.

Merlín e família (1955; Merlin and family) was C.'s first widely successful novel. Using characters from Arthurian legends, he reinvents their existence and activities according to popular Galician traditions, superstitions, and folktales. Other novels in Galician (which the author himself translated into Spanish) appeared in the early 1960s and re-created the legends of Ulysses and of Sinbad the Sailor.

C.'s direct invocation of his Galician heritage has been somewhat tempered recently. *Un hombre que se parecía a Orestes* (1969; a man who looked like Orestes) was written in Spanish and awarded the Nadal Prize. Here he narrated the tale of an Orestes grounded in a symbolic reality applicable to modern Spain. C.'s play *O incerto señor D. Hamlet* (1959; the uncertain Mr. Hamlet) is a Galician parody of Shakespeare's work.

C. is a rather anomalous figure today. Although his primary literary interests run counter to contemporary Spanish literature's preoccupation with social and ethical problems, and although he views himself as essentially a defender of the regional, minority Galician language and culture, he has nonetheless achieved a prestige that no other Galician writer of this century can claim.

FURTHER WORKS: *Poemas de si e non* (1933); *Cantiga nova que se chama Ribeira* (1933); *La historia del caballero Rafael* (1939); *Elegías y canciones* (1940); *Rogelia en Finisterre* (1941); *Balada de las damas del tiempo pasado* (1944); *San Gonzalo* (1945); *El caballero, la muerte y el diablo* (1947); *As crónicas do Sochantre* (1956); *Escola de meciñeiros* (1960); *Las mocedades de Ulises* (1960); *Se o vello Sinbad volviese ás ilhas . . .* (1962); *Tesouros novos e vellos* (1964); *Los siete cuentos de otoño* (1968); *Flores del año mil y pico de ave* (1968); *El descanso del camellero* (1970); *Laberinto y cía.* (1970); *La cocina cristiana de Occidente* (1970); *Xente de aquí e de acolá* (1971); *El año del cometa con la batalla de los cuatro reyes* (1974); *Os outros feirantes* (1979)

BIBLIOGRAPHY: García-Viñó, M., *Novela española actual* (1967): 113–28; Iglesias Laguna, A., *Treinta años de novela española* (1970): 313–19; Thomas, M. D., "Un hombre que parecía a Orestes," *Hispania*, 61 (1978): 35–45; Spires, R. C., *Beyond the Metafictional Mode: Directions in the Modern Spanish Novel* (1984)

—IRWIN STERN

CURNOW, Allen

New Zealand poet, dramatist, critic, and editor, b. 17 June 1911, Timaru

C. studied at the Universities of Canterbury and Auckland, receiving his B.A. in 1938, and at St. John's Theological College in Auckland (1931-33). After a career as a journalist in Christchurch and briefly in London, C. taught as a lecturer (1951-66) and as associate professor (1967-76) in English at the University of Auckland. For his poetry, published from the 1930s through the 1990s, C. has received numerous grants and awards, including a Library of Congress Whittall Fund Award (1966, 1974), the Katherine Mansfield Memorial Fellowship (1983), the Commonwealth Poetry Prize (1989), and the Queen's Gold Medal Award (1990).

It is not only C.'s poetry and dramatic works that have established him as one of the most enduring and influential figures in 20th-c. New Zealand literature. His criticism, in particular his introductions to the Caxton *Book of New Zealand Verse* (1945; rev. ed., 1951) and *The Penguin Anthology of New Zealand Verse* (1960), played a major part in establishing the terms for literary critical debate in New Zealand; moreover, his editorial decisions in these anthologies were crucial in establishing a mainstream postprovincial canon for New Zealand poetry. In recent decades this orthodoxy, along with C.'s status as the preeminent formative figure in New Zealand poetry, has come under attack. Postmodern critics, for example, identify in C.'s theoretical writing an insistence upon the poet's obligation to rigor and accuracy in the representation of an authentic local reality—a position that they find essentialist and naive in its conceptualization of the relation between the poetic signifier and the New Zealand referent.

C.'s poetry, although not immune from such accusations, has aged better than his criticism. His early works, including the important sequences *Not in Narrow Seas* (1939), *Island and Time* (1941), and *Sailing or Drowning* (1943), seek to map out a national identity and aesthetic that encompasses a mature attitude to New Zealand's peculiar colonial history, as well as a searching and skeptical confrontation between the human and the natural world. Recent commentators have alleged that this project, along with comparable efforts by C.'s contemporaries R. A. K. Mason (1905-1971), A. R. D. Fairburn (1904-1957), Charles Brasch (1909-1973), and Dennis Glover (1912-1980), partakes of the masculineness and elitism of high modernism, and that it moreover takes little or no account of the systematic repression of Maori culture by European political, social, and aesthetic paradigms. Nevertheless, in satirical poems such as "House and Land" (1941), and in his public pieces such as "The Unhistoric Story" (1941) and "Landfall in Unknown Seas" (1942), written for the tricentenary of Abel Tasman's visit to New Zealand and orchestrated by Douglas Lilburn, C. sustains a complex meditation on the relation between a provincial settler society and the violence and randomness of its foundation. In C.'s dramatic works—collected in *Four Plays* (1972)—these same concerns are staged by means of stylized, extended poetic dialogues in which language dominates any other dramaturgical element.

Following World War II, gradual changes in the tenor of New Zealand's cultural milieu produced a diversification of literary discourse. C.'s own publications at this time—the collections *At Dead Low Water* (1949), *Poems 1949-1957* (1957), and the selection *A Small Room with Large Windows* (1962)—construct a modulated and more personal voice than the grandiose tone characteristic of his earlier public poetry. The same territory—that of the poet-observer's relationship to nature, or to "the real"—is subjected to a sharper philosophical focus, accompanied by an increasing concern about the way language inevitably (mis)represents and (mis)shapes what it claims to describe. The speaker of these poems returns obsessively to the representation of a leaf, or a geranium against a muddy bank, or a bay at low tide, worrying over words, simultaneously stripping away and recovering with significance odd fragments of the local scene; as a result, C. revisits the various manifestations of his habitually postlapsarian sensibility: Christian and scriptural prototypes, the tropology of sacrifice, the original sin of colonialism, and the primal corruption of language.

Some critics have suggested that C. reinvented his poetic project during a period of nonpublication encompassing the ten years prior to the striking sequence *Trees, Effigies, Moving Objects*

(1972). But actually these poems, and those of subsequent volumes—*An Abominable Temper* (1973), *An Incorrigible Music* (1979), *You Will Know When You Get There* (1982), and *The Loop in Lone Kauri Road* (1986)—reveal the same phenomenological concern over the observer's encounter with a localized New Zealand referent, although modified by a more mannered and experimental deployment of C.'s typically modernist poses: the stalemate and agony between a recalcitrant nature and the poet's attempt to represent it; the juxtaposition of high philosophical rumination with moments of throwaway sexual vulgarity; the ironic tone and self-referential style.

C. continues to publish occasional poems, which return most often to the domain of personal memory and family history, rehearsing with increasing irony—bordering at times on pastiche—these characteristic gestures.

FURTHER WORKS: *Valley of Decision* (1933); *Three Poems* (1935); *Another Argo* (1935, with Dennis Glover and A. R. D. Fairburn); *Enemies: Poems 1934-1936* (1937); *A Present for Hitler and Other Verses* (1940, as Whim-Wham); *Recent Poems* (1941, with others); *Verses 1941-1942* (1942, as Whim-Wham); *Verses 1943* (1943, as Whim-Wham); *The Hucksters and the University* (1957); *Mr. Huckster of 1958* (1958); *The Best of Whim-Wham* (1959); *Collected Poems 1933-1973* (1974); *Selected Poems* (1982); *New Zealand Through the Arts: Past and Present* (1982, with T. Woollaston and Witi Ihimaera); *Look Back Harder: Critical Writings 1935-1984* (1987); *Continuum: New and Later Poems 1972-1988* (1988); *Selected Poems* (1990)

BIBLIOGRAPHY: Sturm, T., "Fictions and Realities: An Approach to A. C.'s *Trees, Effigies, Moving Objects*," *WLWE*, 14 (1976): 44-45; Roddick, A., *A. C.* (1980); Stead, C. K., "A. C.: Poet of the Real," in *In the Glass Case* (1981): 189-206; Davis, L., "Solo C.," *And/3* (1984): 49-62; Stead, C. K., "Second Wind: A. C.'s *Continuum*," in *Answering to the Language* (1989): 98-112; Calder, A., "Sacrifice and Signification in the Poetry of A. C.," in Williams, M., and M. Leggott, eds., *Opening the Book: Essays on New Zealand Writing* (1994): 83-104; special B. issue, *JNZL*, 15 (1998)

—PHILIP ARMSTRONG

CURTIUS, Ernst Robert

German philologist, literary critic, and essayist, b. 14 April 1886, Thann (Alsace); d. 19 April 1956, Rome, Italy

At the University of Strasbourg, C. studied with Gustav Gröber, whose positivistic and historicistic orientations helped establish the foundations of modern Romance philology. Other early influences were his peripheral association with the Stefan GEORGE literary circle in Berlin and his affiliation with the young literary figures in Paris. In 1914 C. became a university lecturer at the University of Bonn. He was appointed a professor at the University of Marburg in 1920 and served there for four years, until he accepted the chair of Romance languages and literature at the University of Heidelberg. C. returned to Bonn in 1929 as the successor to the noted Romance linguist W. Meyer-Lübke (1861–1936); C. remained at Bonn until his retirement in 1951.

With his roots in the Alsace region, with its French and German affinities, C. early conceived of his role as a mediator between the two literary cultures. His work *Die literarischen Wegbereiter des neuen Frankreich* (1919; the literary pioneers of the new France) had the purpose of familiarizing German literary audiences with recent modernist contributions in France. C. continued to emphasize these continuities in *Französischer Geist im neuen Europa* (1925; the French mind in the new Europe) and in *Einführung in die französische Kultur* (1930; *The Civilization of France*, 1932). In *Balzac* (1923; Balzac) C. described the "totality" and "unity" of Balzac's work in a manner designed to further the idea of the intrinsic unity of the work of art: inspired artists created literary works that were fired with the radiance of a heightened creative perception. C.'s work in modern literature was distinguished by its familiarity with the current French authors, his utilization of the new philosophical perspectives of Max Scheler (1874–1928) and Henri BERGSON, his ability to provide innovative explications of modernistic literary works, and his lively essayistic prose style. C.'s essays on PROUST, VALÉRY, T. S. ELIOT, JOYCE, and ORTEGA Y GASSET, as well as his personal relationships with many of the prominent modernist authors of the day, established him as a bastion of humanistic values in a Europe he found conceptually unified.

The political climate in Germany signaled an end to C.'s work in modern literature. He produced *Deutscher Geist in Gefahr* (1932; the German mind in peril), a work he conceived as a "polemic against the self-surrender of German culture, against the hatred of civilization and its sociological and political backgrounds." The establishment of the Nazi government prevented any subsequent works of protest. Instead, C. returned to his initial training in Romance philology and spent the World War II years researching Latin literature of the Middle Ages. The result, *Europäische Literatur und das lateinische Mittelalter* (1948; *European Literature and the Latin Middle Ages*, 1953), proved to be C.'s masterpiece and a monumental work of literary criticism and scholarship. The book proposes a theory of *topoi*: these are ideas and organizing patterns of classical antiquity; through the deterioration of the ancient societal institutions, they became rhetorical functions of the language and established themselves in literature as stock formulations. C. attempted to demonstrate that the study of these patterns, themes, and images in various literary periods affirmed the coherence of European literature along a humanistic basis from ancient to modern times. Although C.'s notion of *topoi* is inexact at times and does not seem to be as innovative as he claimed, the work is a tribute to C.'s enormous perseverance and mammoth talents.

After the war C.'s work was welcomed by a Europe eager to initiate a world of unity and universality. In his *Kritische Essays zur europäischen Literatur* (1950; *Essays on European Literature*, 1973) he assembled early and recent essays to demonstrate the fundamental continuities of his own critical investigations. C.'s critical career and interests reflect the essential movements of humanism in the 20th c. His attempts to confirm Europe's common literary culture were studies in history with the goal of establishing an inviolable and autonomous chain of literary evolution, staid and unalterable: his work reflects a movement away from volatile extrinsic historical formulations and charts a tendency toward faith in intrinsic conceptual organizations of spirit, myth, and the forces of eternal continuity.

FURTHER WORKS: *Maurice Barrès und die geistigen Grundlagen des französischen Nationalismus* (1921); *Der Syndikalismus der Geistesarbeiter in Frankreich* (1921); *Französischer Geist im zwanzigsten Jahrhundert* (1952); *Marcel Proust* (1952);

Büchertagebuch (1960); *Briefwechsel* (1963; correspondence with F. Gundolf)

BIBLIOGRAPHY: Spitzer, L., on *Europäische Literatur, AJPh*, 70 (1949): 425–31; Auerbach, E., on *Europäische Literatur, MLN*, 65 (1950): 348–51; Fergusson, F., "Two Perspectives on European Literature," *HudR*, 7 (1954–1955): 119–27; Spitzer, L., "E. R. C.," *HR*, 25 (1957): 24–25; Evans, A. R. in *On Four Modern Humanists* (1970): 85–145; Gelley, A., "C.: Topology and Critical Method," in Macksey, R. A., ed., *Velocities of Change: Critical Essays from MLN* (1974): 237–52

—GEOFFREY GREEN

CYPRIOT LITERATURE

Greek Cypriot Literature

Apart from a certain individuality, reflecting the island's own historical experience and circumstance, Cypriot literature in the Greek language can hardly be distinguished from Greek literature itself, of which it is part. Geographic proximity to three continents made Cyprus a meeting place of divergent cultures in a long history marked by successive invasions and considerable suffering. Only in 1960 was Cyprus finally proclaimed an independent republic. But its northern part was invaded and taken over by forces from Turkey as late as 1974.

The roots of the Greek population of Cyprus, which constitutes the large majority, go back to the settlement of the island by the Mycenaeans in ancient times; throughout history Greek Cypriots have had extremely close cultural ties to Greece proper. The foreign invasions strengthened rather than weakened the sense of identity of the Greek Cypriots; these constant challenges to survival resulted in a prevalently conservative culture and intellectual life, with a strong commitment to the Greek tradition—its mores, customs, ideas, and ideals—combined with a fierce love of life and the native soil and a deep appreciation of heroism and freedom as man's supreme good in life.

Modern Cypriot writers are proudly conscious of and indebted to their outstanding cultural and intellectual heritage. Cypriot poets and scholars made major contributions to Greek literature in ancient and medieval times, and the Cypriot poetic renaissance of the 16th c. preceded that of Crete in the 17th c. as the foundation of modern Greek literature itself. Strictly speaking, modern Cypriot literature began in 1878, when the island was ceded by the Ottoman Empire to the British, later to become a crown colony. This change in status allowed the island a freer contact with Greece, with whose intellectual orientations and literary trends Greek Cypriots have kept pace ever since. Despite the constantly troublesome political circumstances, the island's literary productivity in this century has been amazingly prolific, mostly in poetry, with the short story second. Several poets have, in fact, been short-story writers as well. Generally speaking, they progressed from lyrical, idyllic, and SYMBOLIST idealism to stark social realism, from conservatism to modernism, from regional localism and patriotism to universality in coping with modern man's social, political, psychological, and spiritual problems and anxieties. Local color found expression in tenderness, nostalgic meditation, rich description of natural beauty, and a mild didacticism, as well as in an unfailing concern for and sharing in the island's endless suffering and its battle for freedom and independence.

Vassilis Michaelides (1849–1917) is deemed the national poet of Greek Cyprus, particularly for his short epic poem "I ennati louliou 1821 en Lefkosia" (1911; "The Ninth of July 1821 in Nicosia, Cyprus," 1974), which describes the hanging of Archbishop Kyprianos by the Turks for his commitment to the Greek war of independence. On the whole his poetry ranges from the heroic and elegiac to the folkloric and satiric, written mostly in the Cypriot dialect, which he used with utmost skill, as did Dimitrios Lipertis (1866–1937) in his soft-toned, melodic, graceful, bucolic verse singing of the life of the simple rural people.

Glafkos Alithersis (pseud. of Michael Hadzidimitriou, 1897–1965), who lived many years in Alexandria, Egypt, where there was a significant Cypriot intellectual community during the first half of the 20th c., reflected in his powerful verse the greater visions that inspired the major poetry of Kostis PALAMAS, yet with a touch of a modern social awareness verging on the tragic.

With its emotional lyricism, the post symbolist poetry of Tefkros Anthias (b. 1903), Pavlos Krinaios (b. 1903), Nikos Kranidiotes (b. 1911), and Kypros Chrysanthis (b. 1915) gradually fostered modernist trends. It is, however, with Kostas Montis (b. 1912), Manos Kralis (b. 1914), and Nikos Vrahimis (1914–1963) that Greek Cypriot poetry achieved modernist originality. In *Stighmes* (1958; moments) and later collections, Montis, through economy, simplicity, and the use of metaphors and symbols drawn from everyday life, penetrates the deeper strata of modern man's awareness of the absurdity of the human condition. Equally original, Kralis, in the collections *Epitaphios tou pliromatos* (1946; epitaph for the crew) and *Yiefsi thanatou* (1974; taste of death), shows exquisite craftsmanship; influenced by Shakespeare and Rimbaud, as well as by CAVAFY, SEFERIS, and T. S. ELIOT, he sings of modern man's loneliness and alienation and the painful awareness of death's dark claims.

Of the prose writers, the most outstanding have been Nikos Nikolaides (1884–1956), Melis Nikolaides (b. 1898), Loukis Akritas (1909–1965), and Christakis Gheorghiou (b. 1928). In his short stories and more so in his novels *Per' ap' to kalo kai to kako* (1940; beyond good and evil) and *Ta tria karfia* (1948; the three nails), the well-traveled Nikos Nikolaides left regionalism behind in his sophisticated and profound analysis of characters involved in tragic experiences prior to, during, and after World War II. Akritas's novel *Armatomeni* (1947; armed men) is one of the most powerful and moving accounts of the Greek army's heroic struggle on the Albanian frontier in 1941.

The younger poets and prose writers, men and women, stand close to their colleagues in Greece in the existential anguish, the feminist upsurge, and the alienation brought about by the technological age that are their themes. The heroic uprising and fight against the British occupational forces from 1955 to 1959 and the deaths, sufferings, and cruel mass deracinations caused by the Turkish invasion in 1974 have inspired recent Greek Cypriot literature to some of its most powerful achievements.

BIBLIOGRAPHY: *Cyprus: A Handbook of the Island's Past and Present* (1964); Proussis, K., Introduction to A. Decavalles, B. Spanos, and K. Proussis, eds., *The Voice of Cyprus: An Anthology of Cypriot Literature* (1965): 9–14; Christophides, A., Introduction

to Montis, C., and Christophides, A., eds., *Anthology of Cypriot Poetry* (1974): i–v

—ANDONIS DECAVALLES

Turkish Cypriot Literature

The Turkish Cypriot community has a long tradition in poetry; in fact, it produced one of the best known poets laureate of the Ottoman Empire, Hilmi Efendi (1782–1847), the Mufti of Cyprus. But the era opened by the British occupation in 1878 was not bright. Pressures in the form of censorship and social insecurity were deeply felt. Even in these circumstances, Turkish Cypriot novelists and playwrights like Hikmet Afif Mapolar (b. 1920) and Nazif Süleyman Ebeoğlu (b. 1923) wrote novels and plays, in the 1940s and 1950s, drawing their materials principally from the Turkish war of liberation and the modern myths of Kemal Atatürk.

The years immediately after World War II saw a revival of poetry. A more liberal order established on the island following the appointment in 1946 of Lord Winster as the colonial governor offered fertile ground for this new flourishing. During this period Engin Gönül (b. 1926), Urkiye Mine (b. 1927), Pember Marmara (b. 1925), and Necla Salih Suphi (b. 1926) created a poetry of nostalgic feeling for the motherland, Turkey. The Istanbul magazine *Yedigün* published their simple but sincere poems.

Osman Türkay (b. 1927) created a much more sophisticated poetry and left Cyprus for London in search of new materials and techniques; five years later he returned to the island to edit a morning paper and two literary magazines. Quite distinct from his contemporaries, Türkay produced an ultramodernist poetry concerned mainly with the impact of space explorations upon the poetic sensibilities. When his long poem "Atomium" (atomium) appeared in his first book, 7 *telli* (1959; septet), he was hailed at home and abroad as the first truly space-age poet. In *Uyurgezer* (1969; *Sleepwalker*, 1972) he portrayed modern man as caught up in swift technological change and faced with possible nuclear annihilation; and *Beethoven' de aydınlığa uyanmak* (1970; *Beethoven, and Other Poems*, 1978) is written to prove Beethoven was and is the greatest astronaut of inner space. Türkay directs his poetic energies to the creation of a modern mythology of his own. His *Kıyamet günü gözlemcileri* (1975; doomsday observers) is a stirring epilogue to his magnum opus, *Evrenin düşünde gezgin* (1971; traveling the universal dream).

In the 1950s more new talents came to the fore: Özker Yaşin (b. 1932), Mustafa Adiloğlu (b. 1935), Taner Baybars (b. 1937), and Salahi Sonyel (b. 1932) were hailed as promising young poets. While still in their teens Adiloğlu and Baybars published collections of poems inspired by the yearning for their motherland. Sonyel, who later abandoned poetry for scholarship, wrote poems of social protest. Baybars left Cyprus in the mid-1950s, never to return and never to write in Turkish anymore. He adopted English as his literary language and published several novels and collections of poems in London. Yaşin stayed on in Cyprus and lived all through the violence and vicissitudes that Cyprus has undergone in the last quarter century; he has recorded the events in prose and in verse. In his lengthy novel *Kıbrıs'ta vuruşanlar* (1972; those who fought in Cyprus) he recounts the day-to-day life of Turkish Cypriot fighters from 1963 to 1967. In *Gırne'den yol bagladık* (1976; we opened up an avenue from Kyrenia) he describes how the population of a Turkish Cypriot village under Greek Cypriot control is resettled in a deserted Greek village following the Turkish military intervention of July 1974.

Neşe Yaşin (b. 1959) describes in her simple and humane poems the bewilderment of the young Turkish and Greek Cypriots now living on a firmly divided island.

—OSMAN MUSTAFA TÜRKAY

CZECH LITERATURE

In the last quarter of the 18th c., when the Czech lands were ruled from Vienna and exposed to Germanization, it seemed that Czech literature, despite its tradition of nearly a thousand years, had little chance of survival. Yet by the middle of the 19th c, it had achieved a resurgence in the National Revival, had reached in Karel Hynek Mácha's (1810–1836) poetry the peak of romanticism, and had made the first steps towards realism in the fiction of Božena Němcová (1820–1862). During the second half of the 19th c. it demonstrated its newly found vigor by producing a major literary school every decade. The 1890s were a time of great complexity. Earlier trends overlapped with new ones that were to reach well into the 20th c. Perhaps the most consistent writer was the Decadent poet Jiří Karásek ze Lvovic (1871–1951), while the more original work of another member of the small Decadent group, Karel Hlaváček (1874–1898) was cut short by his early death.

The Czech MODERNIST manifesto, published in 1895 and voicing the discontent of the younger generation, did not provide the basis for a stable grouping, since it stressed "individuality, brimming with life, creating life" as well as a rejection of old-fashioned patriotism. The author of a large part of the manifesto, František Xaver ŠALDA, achieved renown as a critic; his influence has survived into the present. On the other hand, the high esteem accorded the symbolist mystic Otokar BŘEZINA at home and abroad did not assure his work lasting interest. In the case of the skeptic realist poet Josef Svatopluk MACHAR, it is mostly his minor works that still attract the contemporary reader. The impressionist poet Antonín Sova (1864–1928) has fared better in the trial of time; but it was an unknown outsider from Silesia, Petr BEZRUČ, whose single book of poems appeared at the turn of the century, who achieved near immortality with his coarse-sounding, socially militant Slezské písně (1903, enlarged eds., 1909, 1937; Silesian songs).

Close to Bezruč's rebellious stance, but at the same time carrying a step further the ideas of the modernist manifesto, was a group of anarchists, most of whom later adopted more conventional left-wing ideas. An exception was Viktor Dyk (1877–1931), who chose right-wing nationalism and castigated Czech society for failing his high moral ideals. Luckier was the choice made by Stanislav Kostka Neumann (1875–1947), who having passed through various stages of Decadence, anarchism, and Satanism, found a vehicle for his hatred of the philistine and his love of "life and joy and beauty" in Communism. A steadfast supporter of the party and friend of the U.S.S.R., he still served in the 1950s as a model set up by Marxist ideologists for all Czech poets to follow. Anarchism was also the starting point for Fráňa Šrámek (1877–1952), but he soon transformed it into an erotic, sensualist impressionism and vitalism, as can be seen in his poetry and in his novels Stříbrný vítr (1910; silver wind) and Tělo (1919; the body), as well as in his plays, such as Měsíc nad řekou (1922; moon over the river), a sensitive evocation of young eroticism.

The experience of World War I left its mark on Šrámek;, who became a leftist pacifist, but except for subject matter it did not significantly affect the attitudes of most novelists of the first decades of the 20th c. There is little difference between the determinist philosophy of Kašpar Lén mstitel (1908; Kašpar Lén, avenger), Karel Matěj Čapek-Chod's (1860–1927) first major novel, and the determinism of his wartime or postwar work such as Antonín Vondrejc (1917–18; Antonín Vondrejc) and Jindrové (1921; the Jindras). The social upheaval of the war and its aftermath provided backgrounds for two women novelists. Anna Marie Tilschová (1873–1957) approached naturalism in her depiction of the decline of old families in Stará rodina (1916; old family) and Synové (1918; sons), but was also one of the first writers to turn attention to the modern working class in Haldy (1927; slag heaps). Tilschová's rudimentary psychological realism was surpassed in the short stories of Božena Benešová (1873–1936), who is, however, best remembered for her wartime trilogy Úder (1926; the blow), Podzemní plameny (1929; underground flames), and Tragická duha (1933; tragic rainbow).

World War I was indirectly responsible for the future fame of Jaroslav HAŠEK. When he began publishing Osudy dobrého vojáka Švejka za světové valky (1921–23; The Good Soldier Švejk, 1973), many saw in it just a crudely written, rambling story of an unprincipled scamp interested only in his own survival, while the author's vulgar ridiculing of the defunct Austro-Hungarian monarchy and its institutions was thought to be in poor taste. Since then, however, Švejk has been variously interpreted as an example of the adaptable Czech national character, a working-class rebel, the perennial little man at the mercy of anonymous powers, or a counterpart of KAFKA's Josef K.

Under Austro-Hungarian rule, however, particularly during the war, Czech patriotism had been nurtured on a very different fare. During his lifetime, the historical novelist Alois JIRÁSEK was held in a reverence that may seem somewhat exaggerated today, but in difficult times his numerous works helped to bolster national self-confidence.

With the end of World War I and the emergence of the Czechoslovak Republic, the vitalist trend flourished briefly. Soon, however, a pressing awareness of the social problems the new state had inherited and had to grapple with led many writers to adopt socialist ideas and to support the policies of the Communist Party (founded in 1921). A program for proletarian art was devised by the young poet Jiří WOLKER, who embraced revolutionary ideology with the naïveté of a boy scout. Believing that poetry should be easily comprehensible to the working class, he rejected the earlier influence of APOLLINAIRE in favor of a simplicity partly inspired by the quasi-folk ballads of Karel Jaromír Erben 1811–1870), and in his second collection, Těžká hodina (1922; difficult hour) he largely achieved his own ideal of proletarian poetry. His sentimentalism is outweighed by his sincerity, and the message is humane rather than overtly political.

Adherents of the proletarian movement were not numerous. Jindřich Hořejší (1886–1941) was a compassionate observer of seamy scenes of city life, as in his collection Hudba na náměstí (1921; music in the square). A sense of pity, sensitivity to social injustice, and a yearning for harmony brought Josef HORA to proletarian poetry for a time, and yielded three volumes, notably Pracující den (1920; the working day). Later he developed into a meditative lyricist, and in the face of the Nazi threat found, in Máchovské variace (1936; Mácha variations) and Jan houslista

(1939; Jan the violinist), an assurance in the immortality of his nation and its culture.

Jaroslav SEIFERT also was part of this movement for only a short time. The only real proletarian among its members, he combined in *Město v slzách* (1921; city in tears) and *Samá láska* (1923; all love) a youthful revolutionary message with a desire to enjoy the beauty of life, which signaled the advent of perhaps the most lastingly influential trend-poetism.

Its emergence reflected a split in Devětsil ("colt's foot," with pun on "nine powers"), a loose association of avant-garde artists and intellectuals, between those who, like Wolker, advocated traditional means to convey a revolutionary message, and those who claimed that the medium should be as revolutionary as the message. The main theoretician of poetism, Karel Teige (1900–1951), promoted the view that modern art for the masses should exploit all forms of popular culture.

Vítězslav NEZVAL, who was to become possibly the greatest and certainly the most prolific Czech poet of the 20th c., endowed with an exuberant, associative imagination, put the principles of poetism into practice almost before Teige could formulate its theory, particularly in his metaphoric autobiography *Podivuhodný kouzelník* (1922; marvelous magician) and *Pantomima* (1924; pantomime). The movement disintegrated before the end of the decade, but it left a mark on its many followers and on nearly all Czech culture.

Of the poets associated with poetism, most went their own way in the 1930s, when Czech poetry as a whole reached a peak. Nezval started experimenting with SURREALISM as early as *Edison* (1928; Edison); the best of his surrealist collections is *Absolutní hrobař* (1937; the absolute gravedigger). Poetism influenced the early poems of František HALAS, whose work shows an almost baroque obsession with death and only marginally his left-wing orientation. The tragic overtones in his jarring, unmelodious verse are particularly strong in his long poem *Staré ženy* (1935; *Old Women*, 1947). Halas deeply influenced the younger generation, and one could argue that he rather than Nezval was the greatest Czech poet of this century. A baroque cult of death also appeared in the work of the Catholic poet Jan Zahradníček (1905–1960), but it was soon replaced with a glorification of this world with God as the center of security.

Czech fiction between the wars also was affected by avant-garde theories, both artistic and political. Vladislav VANČURA probably would have become the most original writer of his time even without his initial association with poetism. Close to the proletarian ideal was his *Pekař Jan Marhoul* (1924; the baker Jan Marhoul), the story of a bakery worker whose goodness and honesty lead him to ruin in an evil world. *Pole orná a válečná* (1925; ploughed fields, battlefields), is an apocalyptic vision of the insanity of war. In the 1930s Vančura moderated his earlier fascination with language without losing his original style. *Markéta Lazarová* (1931; Markéta Lazarová) is a beautiful story of passionate love set in the Middle Ages. Later novels showed a tendency toward epic narrative, a development cut short when the Nazis executed him.

Although leftist, Vančura never really adopted SOCIALIST REALISM. An early attempt in this direction was made, with less than impressive results, by Ivan OLBRACHT in *Anna proletářka* (1928; Anna the proletarian). The novel remained the only one of its kind in Olbracht's work, most of which reflects the author's vacillation between realism and romanticism, which were successfully blended in *Nikola Šuhaj loupežník* (1933; *Nikola Šuhaj, Robber*, 1954),

about a modern Robin Hood. While Olbracht had begun his career with psychological novels, Marie MAJEROVÁ was from the outset involved with the working class. Her first books dealt mostly with the problems of women, but in *Náměstí republiky* (1914; Republic Square) she drew on her experience with anarchism in Paris. In *Siréna* (1935; *The Siren*, 1953) she chronicles a working-class family from the Kladno coal basin, a member of which is also the protagonist of *Havířská balada* (1936; *Ballad of a Miner*, 1960).

Marie Pujmanová (1893–1958) came from a patrician family and in her first books focused on her own class, however critically. But in *Lidé na křižovatce* (1937; people at the crossroads), the first part of a trilogy, she attempted a complex picture of Czech society from the first postwar years to the Depression, with her sympathies reserved for the left-wing intellectual and the worker. The second part, *Hra s ohněm* (1948; playing with fire) did not equal the first, and the third, *Život proti smrti* (1952; life against death), combining fiction and journalism, is little more than proof of the sterility of Stalinist dogma in literature.

Most popular in the interwar period was Karel ČAPEK, a liberal intellectual who achieved worldwide success with the play *R.U.R.* (1920; *R.U.R.*, 1923), which introduced the word *robot*. Čapek's faith in essential human decency was expressed in his short-story collections *Povídky z jedné kapsy* and *Povídky z druhé kapsy* (both 1929; *Tales from Two Pockets*, 1932) and in the trilogy of novels *Hordubal* (1933; *Hordubal*, 1934), *Povětroň* (1934; *Meteor*, 1935), and *Obyčejný život* (1934; *An Ordinary Life*, 1936). In the late 1930s he reacted to the threat of totalitarianism in the novel *Válka s mloky* (1936; *War with the Newts*, 1937) and in the play *Bílá nemoc* (1937; *Power and Glory*, 1938).

Besides the powerful poet and quarrelsome priest Jakub Deml (1878–1961), the outstanding Catholic writer was Jaroslav DURYCH, whose large fresco of the Thirty Years' War, *Bloudění* (1929; *The Descent of the Idol*, 1936), has been surpassed only by his variation on the same theme in *Rekviem* (1930; requiem). Of the ruralists, who continued the 19th-c. tradition of the Czech village novel and often shared with the Catholics a religious outlook, Josef Knap (1900–1973) remained close to the original conception, while František Křelina (1903–1976) and Jan Čep (1902–1974) paid more attention to the religious aspect.

The work of the ruralists and the Catholics was under a ban throughout the 1950s, and some of the writers spent long years in prison or in exile. A few new novels appeared in the short-lived period of liberalization in the late 1960s.

It was only in the 1960s, too, that the work of some emigré authors could be published again. The first to make a comeback was Egon HOSTOVSKÝ, in the interwar years a fine psychological novelist. This type of Czech fiction culminated during World War II in the novels of Václav Řezáč (1901–1956), among them *Rozhraní* (1944; *If the Mirror Break*, 1959). After the war, Řezáč adopted Socialist Realism, but only two volumes of an intended trilogy appeared: *Nástup* (1951; the start) and *Bitva* (1954; the battle), both of them documents of artistic failure. Another psychological novelist, Jarmila Glazarová (1901–1977) managed to avoid this pitfall by not publishing any fiction after her novels *Vlčí jáma* (1938; wolf trap) and *Advent* (1939; Advent), although she was a somewhat naïve supporter of official policies in the 1950s.

In the theater during the interwar period, besides Karel Čapek, the playwrights, actors, and producers Jiří VOSKOVEC and Jan WERICH were the most prominent figures. From a students' cabaret tinged with poetism they graduated to political satire. Another theater personality was Emil František Burian (1903–1959), artistic director of the D34 Theater.

With the German occupation of Czechoslovakia in 1939, some writers went into exile, while many others ended up in concentration camps. Those who escaped persecution turned to covertly patriotic themes. The younger poets promoted the concept of uprooted "naked man," outside society and turning inward to his fear and anxiety, which was close to the ideas of French EXISTENTIALISM. It found its most profound expression in the work of the Jewish poet Jiří Orten (1919–1941).

Immediately after the war the prevailing sense of relief and gratitude for the nation's survival manifested itself mainly in poetry. Even a poet so complex and esoteric as Vladimír Holan (1905–1980) gave vent to these feelings in tributes to the Soviet Union and the Red Army. The five-day Prague uprising in May 1945 inspired the short stories in *Němá barikáda* (1946; the silent barricade) by Jan Drda (1915–1970).

A renewed diversity was halted by the Communist takeover in February 1948. Literature became an instrument of propaganda, and writers unwilling to accept Socialist Realism were silenced. Most of what the leftist avant-garde had achieved between the wars was condemned and rejected. For the next few years, writers had to produce works written to formula. By the mid-1950s it was becoming obvious that an aesthetic based on the Soviet model was not going to produce great works of art. Among the first novels to introduce a less predictable plot and more than cardboard characters was *Ročník jedenadvacet* (1954; *Born 1921*, 1965) by Karel Ptáčník (b. 1921), about young men forcibly recruited for civil-defense work in Germany during the war. Political censorship made it difficult to deal similarly with the present, but some doubts and questions did find their way into *Občan Brych* (1955; citizen Brych) by Jan Otčenášek (1924–1979), a novel debating the dilemma of a non-Communist intellectual.

The relaxation that followed Khrushchev's denunciation of Stalin in 1956 was seized upon by writers and publishers as an opportunity for more variety. Besides the reappearance of names hitherto banned and the publication of new work by older writers, new writers emerged, most of them associated with the new literary magazine *Květen*. Against the failed idea of struggle and heroism in the construction of socialism, they advocated a more modest program: poetry of everyday life. Best known of them was the poet Miroslav Holub (b. 1923).

Having seen their elders burn their fingers while tackling contemporary subjects, even younger writers preferred to deal with controversial existential and ethical issues within the framework of wartime experience. In his two books of short stories, *Noc a naděje* (1958; *Night and Hope*, 1962) and *Démanty noci* (1958; *Diamonds in the Night*, 1962), Arnošt LUSTIG explored people in extreme circumstances, drawing on his own boyhood experience in a concentration camp. Serious political repercussions, however, followed the publication of *Zbabělci* (1958; *The Cowards*, 1970) by Josef ŠKVORECKÝ, in which events during the last days of the war were presented irreverently. The book was banned, and the authorities stemmed the tide of liberalism with a purge of all cultural institutions. One of many books and films that fell victim to it was the first collection of short stories by Bohumil HRABAL, which had to wait until 1963, when it appeared as *Perlička na dně* (the pearl at the bottom) and established its author as one of the most original talents in Czech literature.

The 1960s, however, had begun with a wave of young authors who ascribed great importance to individual sincerity in reaction to the collective, impersonal attitudes of the 1950s. Their novels aimed to convey the contemporary "feeling of life." Typical was *Zelené obzory* (1960; green horizons) by Jan Procházka (1929–1971).

As the norms prescribing subject and technique were being increasingly ignored, uniformity gave way to diversity, ranging from the linguistic experiments of Věra Linhartová (b. 1938) to the macabre fiction of Ladislav FUKS, whose best-known work is *Pan Theodor Mundstock* (1963; *Mr. Theodore Mundstock*, 1968), the story of a Jew preparing himself for the concentration camp. A scathing analysis of aspects of life hitherto associated with Western consumer societies was offered by Vladimír PÁRAL in his series of novels beginning with *Veletrh splněných přání* (1964; the fair of dreams fulfilled).

In many respects Czech literature in the 1960s was politicized. The injustices committed in the 1950s in the name of an ideal fascinated writers, and for some it was a matter of their own conscience. An early attempt at a political novel was *Hodina ticha* (1963; hour of silence) by Ivan Klíma (b. 1931), but the two major novels of disillusionment were *Žert* (1967; *The Joke*, 1970) by Milan KUNDERA and *Sekyra* (1967; *The Axe*, 1973) by Ludvík VACULÍK, while the ethical issues of conscience were examined by Jaroslav Putík (b. 1923) who successfully revived the psychological novel.

Poetry played a lesser role during this period. The main event was the reemergence, after fifteen years of enforced silence, of Vladimír Holan as an abstract metaphysical poet of the first order. František Hrubín (1910–1971), who in Holan's absence had been at the forefront of Czech poetry, had also turned to the theater, and his play *Srpnová neděle* (1958; a Sunday in August) was one of the first to break the role of the stereotype on the stage. Milan Kundera also turned to playwriting, but the most important dramatist of the period was Václav HAVEL, who brilliantly and grotesquely combined the philosophizing tendency of Czech art with the techniques of the Theater of the ABSURD. A late flowering of poetism could be detected in the songs and plays of Jiří Suchý (b. 1931) and Jiří Šlitr (1924–1969), whose *Semafor* followed in the footsteps of Voskovec and Werich. It was the most popular of many small theaters that sprang up in the 1960s.

The political involvement of writers brought severe reprisals when, following the Soviet invasion of Czechoslovakia in 1968, rigid party control over all public life was reimposed. Virtually all literary journals were closed down, and with only a few exceptions all leading authors either emigrated or were banned. Less than half a dozen recanted as required by the authorities. Of previously well-known writers, Páral has continued to publish work of good standard, Hrabal has become somewhat repetitious, and Fuks sharply declined, while the 1970s were dominated by the works of second and even third-rate writers.

Few first books of any significance appeared. Most young writers have not dared to move away from intimate experience, and their novels and short stories are characterized by extreme lyricism and a narrow range of mostly autobiographical subjects. Among the more talented are Jiří Navrátil (b. 1939) and Václav Dušek (b. 1944). A group of young writers from northern Bohemia, showing an influence of Páral's narrative technique and of the New NOVEL, most prominent among them Jiří Švejda (b. 1949), have occasionally ventured into slightly wider social territory.

A new feature of Czech literary life in the 1970s was the opening of several very active emigré publishing houses in the West. Besides bringing out new work by authors such as Jan Beneš (b. 1936), Pavel Kohout (b. 1928), Kundera, Lustig, and Škvorecký, who now live in exile, they have provided an outlet for the banned writers still living in Czechoslovakia. In addition, about two hundred titles of new work by banned writers have appeared in typescript *samizdat* editions. Of particular interest have been new plays by Václav Havel, dramatic miniatures examining moral dilemmas facing people under an oppressive system. They have enjoyed worldwide success, while the author, like his many colleagues, has been silenced and persecuted in his own country.

Czech Literature since 1970

Czechoslovakia was founded in 1918 primarily as a state of the Czechs and the Slovaks. The Czech and Slovak languages are closely related, but the Czechs and Slovaks regard themselves as separate nations, with their own independent identities.

After the fall of communism in 1989, the Czechs and the Slovaks assumed different political attitudes. This became especially obvious after the June 1992 general elections. In the Czech part of the Republic a right-wing coalition, led by Václaw Klaus and his Civic Democratic Party (ODS) gained power, while in Slovakia, the election was won by the post-communist Movement for Democratic Slovakia (HZDS), led by Vladimír Mečiar.

Even prior to the June 1992 elections, negotiations between the Czechs and the Slovaks on a number of important issues had resulted in serious difficulties. The election results led to a peaceful division of Czechoslovakia into the Czech Republic and Slovakia, which took effect 1 January 1993.

The division of Czech literature into three streams—"official," exile, and *samizdat*—caused by the repression of independent intellectual activities in the wake of the Soviet invasion in 1968, lasted until the fall of communism in November 1989. On the domestic scene, few imaginative developments of any significance were tolerated for twenty years by a neo-Stalinist régime whose main concern was the preservation of the status quo. Very few of the writers who fell into disfavor after 1968 could hope for a relaxation in the official attitude to themselves and their work. Even a revocation of their previously expressed views, which was a humiliating condition of return into public life, seldom achieved more than limited results.

Among those who after considerable harassment did issue a statement vaguely in support of the authorities was Bohumil HRABAL, but that part of his work that he was subsequently allowed to publish in Czechoslovakia was not the best and appeared only in emasculated versions. However, the unexpurgated originals as well as some unpublished manuscripts were either circulated in *samizdat* editions or printed abroad. Most noteworthy of them were *Příliš hluá samota* (1976; *Too Loud a Solitude*, 1986), which presented a grotesque view of the world from the perspective of a wastepaper warehouse, and *Obsluhoval jsem anglického krále* (1982; *I Served the King of England*, 1989), a bizarre story of a physically stunted and morally deficient careerist. Both were written in the early 1970s when there was little chance of ever seeing them in print. Some of the dilemmas and problems of conscience the author himself faced in the 1970s and 1980s while living in fear of the secret police were later hinted at in his autobiographical trilogy *Svatby v domě* (1987; weddings in the house), *Vita nuova* (1987; new life), and *Proluky* (1986; vacant lots), published in Canada.

The work of Vladimír Páral and Ladislav Fuks, who never were expelled from the ranks of "official" writers, also was affected by political pressures. As he tried to adjust to new circumstances,

Páral lost much of the creative drive and critical bite that he had shown in the 1960s, and his once innovative technique was getting worn out by overuse and repetition. This became especially apparent when he embraced the popular fashion of science fiction, which swept through Czechoslovakia in the 1980s. One novel that stood above several that Páral produced during that decade was *Válka s mnohozvířetem* (1986; war with the multibeast), an ecological variation on Karel ČAPEK's classic *Válka s mloky* (1936; *War with the Newts*, 1937). Fuks's writing suffered a sharp decline from which it had barely started to recover by the end of the 1980s.

Official literature produced little of genuine interest. The promising authors of the 1970s such as Jiří Navrátil (b. 1939), Václav Dušek (b. 1944), or Jiří Švejda (b. 1949) soon found themselves restricted by an invisible barrier of political taboos. Attempts to break the self-imposed bonds of private and intimate themes and to venture into a wider world inevitably led to failure. Although many writers treated in photographic detail the manifestations of moral decay rampant throughout the land, they could not, even if they had dared to, state the obvious, namely, that corruption was an attribute of a stagnant system. Social criticism, which had to bypass the pivotal role of the omnipotent Communist Party, lacked credibility. The picture it painted did not correspond with the reality familiar to readers from their everyday experience.

A number of young authors were granted the opportunity to enter literature during this period, although not the chance properly to deploy their talent. In a stifling environment where mediocrity and convention ruled, there was little scope for nonconformity or experiment. Compromise with the ruling ideology could rarely be avoided. One of the more noticeable of his generation, Zdeněk Zapletal (b. 1951), progressed from early autobiographical books, which followed the fortunes of a small group of young friends, to a broadly conceived novel, *Půlnoční běžci* (1986; midnight runners), in which he endeavored to present a cross section of Czech life in the mid-1980s. The general impression given by this ambitious undertaking, obviously influenced by contemporary American fiction, was that of all-pervading frustration and futility. Nonetheless, conspicuous lacunae in the setting demonstrated yet again that certain subjects remained unmentionable.

Writing of this kind was regarded as occupying a "gray zone" between officialdom and dissent. In the latter part of the 1980s, some gifted new authors, such as Alexandra Berková (b. 1949) and the dramatist Karel Steigerwald (b. 1945), managed to find a refuge in it and were able to publish as long as they could keep up the precarious balancing act.

Hardly any of the censored and self-censored books issued officially during the 1970s and 1980s had a hope of arousing interest in the West. One of the voices that continued to be listened to was that of the poet Miroslav HOLUB. Despite having publicly recanted in 1973, he did not publish in Czechoslovakia until 1982. Throughout that period, however, Holub's already substantial reputation abroad, particularly in the English-speaking countries, grew steadily as his new verse appeared there in translation. It overshadowed the rest of the rather excessive output of poetry in all three streams of Czech literature. Only the work of a handful, notably Karel Šiktanc (b. 1928) or Ivan Diviš (b. 1924), may prove to be lasting.

The books that were most frequently translated in the West were those written either by the banned authors living in Czechoslovakia or by those who had left the country after 1968. The road to recognition was paved for them by the remarkably vigorous Czech cultural and literary community in exile. Most efficient in this respect were two publishing houses, Sixty-Eight Publishers, Toronto, run by the writer Zdena Salivarová (b. 1933) and her husband Josef ŠKVORECKÝ, and Index, Cologne. Books of writers silenced at home could thus be printed in Czech abroad alongside those of writers living in exile. As they were subsequently smuggled back into the country, they helped to counteract to some extent the effects of the politically imposed divisions of Czech literature.

Of those who had settled in the West, Milan KUNDERA was soon after his emigration in 1975 acknowledged to be the most influential. His new, intricately structured novels, *Kniha smíchu a zapomnění* (1981; first pub. in English as *The Book of Laughter and Forgetting*, 1980), *Nesnesitelná lehkost bytí* (1985; first pub. in English as *The Unbearable Lightness of Being*, 1984), and *Nesmrtelnost* (1992; first pub. in English as *Immortality*, 1991), achieved spectacular success throughout the noncommunist world, but some of their aspects evoked mixed reactions in Czechoslovakia. It was felt that Kundera was taking too many liberties with the representation of his native country. No such criticism was leveled against Josef Škvorecký, who became a much honored Czech-Canadian author. However, Škvorecký's writings set in his Czech homeland are considerably more popular than his novels set in Czechoslovakia and in the West. Škvorecký located even some of his new work written in exile in the Czechoslovakia of his youth. That applies, for instance, to the account of his alter ego, Danny Smiřický's salad days, *Prima sezóna* (1975; *The Swell Season*, 1982). Danny appeared also in *Příběh inženýra lidských duší* (1977; *The Engineer of Human Souls*, 1984), a broadly conceived fresco of nearly half a century of life beset by tumultuous events in eastern Europe and the West. Elsewhere, Škvorecký turned to an unconventional rendering of events from the past. In *Scherzo capriccioso* (1984; *Dvořák in Love*, 1986) he dealt with the Czech composer's stay in the U.S.; in *Nevěsta z Texasu* (1992; a bride from Texas) he investigated the participation of Czech volunteers in the American Civil War.

Among the exiled Czech writers who gained recognition from Western readers and audiences during the two decades were Jiří Gruša (b. 1938), Pavel Kohout (b. 1928), and Arnošt LUSTIG. The works of dozens of others, including Jaroslav Vejvoda (b. 1940) and Vlastimil Třešňák (b. 1950), who did not really embark on their careers as authors until they had left Czechoslovakia, were translated less often.

The awarding of the Nobel Prize in 1984 to the poet Jaroslav SEIFERT was a great encouragement to the "dissident" or "alternative" culture maintained in Czechoslovakia by the community of banned artists and intellectuals of which he was a distinguished member. Unfortunately, it proved nearly impossible to adequately transpose into different environments the emotional intensity of Seifert's work so much cherished at home. This was not a problem encountered by the radio plays, short stories, and novels of Ivan KLÍMA; they were increasingly finding a positive response in the West, as were many other writers that appeared either on their own or in anthologies. Particularly well received were a collection of Ludvík VACULÍK's *feuilletons*, A Cup of Coffee with My Interrogator (1987), and his fictional, although not entirely fictitious, diary, Český snář (1983; Czech book of dreams.)

A large proportion of the outstanding books published over the past twenty years were written by women authors, those living in Czechoslovakia and abroad. The subtle, contemplative short stories of Eda Kriseová (b. 1940) are an example of the former, Zdena Salivarová's novel *Honzlová* (1972; *Summer in Prague*, 1975), written in Canada, but taking place in Czechoslovakia, of the latter.

New plays by Václav HAVEL, unperformed in Czechoslovakia, were being staged all over the world. After the three one-act plays *Audience* (1975; *Audience*, 1978), *Vernisáž* (1976; *Private View*, 1978), and *Protest* (1978; *Protest*, 1978), based on the personal experience of a dissident, the greatest success was achieved by Havel's contemporary adaptation of the Faustian legend, *Pokoušení* (1986; *Temptation*, 1986), particularly in the production of the Royal Shakespeare Company.

Since the late 1960s, Czech literature had become better known throughout the world than ever before in its history. It was a remarkable achievement, considering that most of the universally acclaimed authors were living in exile or were being persecuted while struggling against adverse political conditions at home.

In view of the role that a relatively few of these writers and intellectuals played in preserving essential human values under an oppressive régime and in a climate of social morass and moral decline, it could be regarded as a symbolic act of historical justice that after the "velvet revolution" of November 1989, which brought forty years of communist rule in Czechoslovakia to an end, Václav Havel was elected president of the Republic. As the country regained its freedom, the conditions were created for the separate streams of Czech literature to merge together. The transformation of a totalitarian system into democracy, however, proved to be more difficult than had been foreseen, and it soon became apparent that full integration could not be achieved overnight. It did not help that with the arrival of political pluralism and new economic circumstances Czech culture found itself occupying, perhaps temporarily, a less prominent place in public life than had been its tradition.

As old restrictions were lifted, hundreds of new private publishers mushroomed and a profusion of previously banned and half-forgotten books flooded the market. In addition, an uncontrolled outburst of hitherto unknown commercialism caused the near collapse of the well-established publishing houses with a forty-year reputation and of the distribution trade. The generation that had achieved prominence in the 1960s and in most cases suffered subsequent banning or exile enjoyed a comeback, with their books being sold in hundreds of thousands of copies. It was obvious, nonetheless, that the change had come too late for many of them and that the public, though acknowledging them as a worthy reminder of the past, had in the meantime become attuned to a slightly different taste. At the same time, dozens of new names were emerging of young authors who had never been involved either with the communist régime or in the dissident movement and were resolved to go their own way. Only the future would be able to tell whether their contribution to Czech literature was as significant as that of their predecessors.

The most promising authors on the Czech literary scene are probably Daniela Hodrová (b. 1945), author of experimental, dreamlike, fragmentary and intellectual fiction, including *Podobojí* (wr. 1977-84, pub. 1991), *Kukly* (wr. 1981-83, pub. 1991), and *Théta* (1992), Vladimír Macura (b. 1945), who wrote a complex, ironic, and playful novel *Občan Monte Christo* (Citizen Monte Christo), which was completed in 1981 and published in 1993, and Jiří Ktatochvil (b. 1940), whose first work *Medvědí román* (1990; A Bear's Novel) is a sophisticated dystopia with autobiographical features. Ktatochvil's second novel *Uprostřed nocí zpěv* (1992; Singing during the Nights) displays features of magical realism; its theme is a search for one's own identity and one's father in a world controlled by violence and lying. Michael Viewegh (b. 1962) produced an amusing, satirical account of life under communism entitled *Báječná léta pod psa* (1992; the marvelous years that were rubbish) and continued with a bravura parody of works by well-known Czech and international writers entitled *Nápady laskavého čtenáře* (1993; The Gentle Reader's Experiments).

BIBLIOGRAPHY: French, A., *The Poets of Prague* (1969); Mühlberger, J., *Tschechische Literaturgeschichte* (1970); Součková, M., *A Literary Satellite* (1970); Kunstmann, H., *Tschechische Erzählkunst im 20. Jahrhundert* (1974); Novák, A., *Czech Literature* (1976); Mihailovich, V. D., et al., eds., *Modern Slavic Literatures* (1976), Vol. 2: 38–230; Hájek, I., "The rule of the average," *IJSLP*, 33 (1978): 702–19; Pynsent, R., *Czech Prose and Verse* (1979); Trenský, P. I., *Czech Drama since World War II* (1978); Goetz-Stankiewicz, M., *The Silenced Theatre* (1979); Harkins, W. E., and Trenský, P. I., eds., *Czech Literature since 1956: A Symposium* (1980); French, A., *Czech Writers and Politics 1946–1969* (1982); Hájek, I., "Precarious Survival," *Formations*, 1, 1 (Spring 1984): 114–21; Pynsent, R. B., "Social Criticism in Czech Literature of 1970s and 1980s Czechoslovakia," *Bohemia*, 27 (1986): 1–36; Hájek, I., "Changing Attitudes in Recent Czech Fiction," in McMillin, A., ed., *Aspects of Modern Russian and Czech Literature* (1989): 214–23; Hájek, I., "Czech Culture in the Cauldron," *Europe-Asia Studies*, 46, 1 (1994): 127–42

—IGOR HÁJEK

CZECHOWICZ, Józef

Polish poet and critic, b. 15 March 1903, Lublin; d. 9 Sept. 1939, Lublin

Maddeningly little is known about C.'s childhood and early youth; he never helped to dispel this mystery. It is said that his father's mental illness (he died when C. was twelve years old) influenced the poet's visionary imagination. C. fought for Poland against the Soviets in 1920 but remained neutral in his political affiliations; on his return from the war, he chose a career as a teacher and was active in the Association of Polish Teachers. Professional activities prompted C.'s interest in children's literature, and he contributed poems for children to the magazine *Płomyczek*, of which he was editor for a time. As his fascination with literature grew, C. decided to devote himself entirely to writing. In 1933 he moved from Lublin to Warsaw to establish himself in his new profession. This career was cut short when he was killed in his home town in 1939 in one of the first bombardments by the German Luftwaffe.

In C.'s poetry the theme of death looms large—from the poems in his first collection, *Kamień* (1927; stone), to the ones published in the 1930s and those written at the end of his life. Death is presented by a variety of symbols and metaphors: as a butterfly

(indicating the poet's familiarity with this symbol in folklore), or as night, strong wind, black roses, autumn, dream, shadow, and time. In other words, death is present in almost every component of the world we live in. For C., death is the ultimate and transcendental value that leads beyond our earthly limitations. The juxtaposition of earth (life) and sky (death) often constitutes the core of his poems, particularly in the collection *dzień jak codzień* (1930; day as every day).

C.'s fascination with death presupposes a catastrophic world view. Catastrophe is a prevalent theme in Polish poetry of the 1930s, but C. gives it his own interpretation. His catastrophism is not tied to any specific historical situation; it has universal dimensions. But his anxiety grows out of concrete experience: World War I, the Depression, and the political uncertainty of the 1930s. The apocalyptic vision of doom is often expressed through images of fire and water, which at the same time have a purifying, mythic power; as such they do not necessarily have a pessimistic connotation.

The positive note in C.'s poetry is the dream of Arcadia—the unknown land of happiness. Indeed, the very essence of C.'s world view derives from the tension between the Arcadian vision and a sense of doom, sometimes raised to a cosmic struggle between the forces of good and evil.

Although C. abandoned punctuation and capital letters and shared to some extent the modernist admiration for urban civilization, he is hardly to be considered as representative of either the 1920s or the 1930s Polish avant-garde. His poetry is concerned with the ultimate questions about death, life, happiness, and the misery of mankind. He was an ardent adversary of realism and "committed literature." He believed that behind the appearance of our material world there are laws governing human destiny. The task of a poet is to discover these laws, an attitude that brings C. close to SYMBOLISM. In his critical works, especially those written in the late 1930s, he developed a theory of "pure poetry," a poetry that gives way to the play of powerful poetry that gives way to the play of powerful imagination and strives to "dematerialize" reality.

C. experimented with other genres as well and achieved some recognition as an author of one-act plays. One of his first published works was the short story "Opowieść o papierowej koronie" (1923; a tale about the paper crown). He had wanted to devote more attention to prose, but his intentions were thwarted by his early death.

FURTHER WORKS: *Ballada z tamtej strony* (1932); *Stare kamienie* (1934); *W błyskawicy* (1934); *Nic Więcej* (1936); *Arkusz poetycki* (1938); *Nuta człowiecza* (1939)

BIBLIOGRAPHY: Kridl, M., *A Survey of Polish Literature and Culture* (1956), p. 492; Miłosz, C., *The History of Polish Literature* (1969): 411–12; Krzyżanowski, J., *A History of Polish Literature* (1978): 580–83

—EDWARD MOŻEJKO

D

DABROWSKA, Maria

Polish novelist, short-story writer, essayist, and dramatist, b. 6 Oct. 1889, Russów (near Kalisz); d. 19 May 1965, Warsaw

Daughter of an estate manager, D. became interested in agrarian reform and peasant co-operatives during her university studies, and in 1909 she began to write on these subjects for Polish newspapers. In the 1920s, she published four collections of short stories. The family saga *Noce i dnie* (1932–34; nights and days) brought her several literary awards. She spent World War II in occupied Warsaw but never wrote about the horrors of war. In 1961 she began to publish her second long novel, *Przygody człowieka myślącego* (adventures of a thinking man), in serial form but died before it was finished (an edited version, using her drafts, was issued in book form in 1970). Throughout her life, and regardless of the political bias of the changing governments, D. was active in the civil-rights movement in Poland.

Apart from *Noce i dnie* D. published five volumes of short stories, two dramas, and many volumes of essays and translations. Her best short stories are contained in *Ludzie stamtąd* (1925; folks from over yonder) and *Gwiazda zaranna* (1955; the morning star). The first collection deals with the life of the poorest among Polish peasants in the early 20th c. The second contains the widely acclaimed "Nawsi wesele" ("A Village Wedding," 1957), a folksy description of a peasant wedding in Poland in the 1950s. Taken together, these stories document the rapid changes of setting and customs of central European peasantry in the 20th c.

The quality of D.'s masterpiece, *Noce i dnie*, is far above the rest of her literary oeuvre. Her short stories are quite good but the four-volume *Noce i dnie* is a work of rare power and insight. The only 20th-c. *roman-fleuve* written from a woman's perspective, *Noce i dnie* tells the story of a married couple, Bogumil and Barbara, both of whom come from a background of impoverished gentry, much like D.'s own family. The narrative begins with the courtship stage of their acquaintance and ends with the death of Bogumil and the destitution faced by Barbara (now a grandmother) as she hastily leaves her burning apartment at the outset of World War I. This rather uneventful plot provides a framework for D.'s major theme: how a person can develop and grow in a hopelessly mismatched marriage, while being burdened in addition with an assortment of personal and national neuroses, such as a sense of defeat and resentment. In her emphasis on the importance of roots for personal development and on the possibilities for growth in a seemingly stifling family atmosphere, D. is an atypical contemporary writer. Her most interesting characters never run away from anything in search of personal freedom. Uneasy as they are with the shortcomings of their families and friends, they nevertheless accept them in the name of the same principles which informed D.'s personal life and which can be described as ethical humanism. Ironically, *Noce i dnie* has been translated into Chinese but not into English.

D.'s presentation of continuity in human communities reflects her familiarity with the traditional female role of preserver and protector of the achievements of the community. Her feminine vision manifests itself also in her attention to the details that usually escape the eye of the male writer: preferences of various psychological types of people concerning food, clothing, housekeeping, and other apparent trivia of daily routine, as well as the acute awareness of weather and of the four seasons that certain characters display.

The style of *Noce i dnie* is "invisible," like that of Leo Tolstoy in *War and Peace*. The novel has been widely used as a source of examples of standard Polish by the authors of dictionaries and writing manuals. *Noce i dnie* follows the conventions of psychological realism; D.'s selectively omniscient narrator avoids total interpretation of characters, allowing them to remain slightly ambiguous and mysterious.

D. is one of the few contemporary writers who are not only respected and admired but who are also loved. *Noce i dnie* remains today the best single source of information on how contemporary Poles view themselves and how they use their language.

FURTHER WORKS: *Finlandia, wzorowy kraj kooperacji* (1913); *Kooperatywy na wsi belgijskiej* (1913); *Powstanie 1863: Powitanie wojny i swobody* (1916); *Dzieci ojczyzny* (1918); *Gałąź czereśni, i inne nowele* (1922); *Uśmiech dzieciństwa* (1923); *Rozdroże* (1937); *Znaki życia* (1938); *Geniusz sierocy* (1939); *Stanisław i Bogumił* (1945); *Myśli o sprawach i ludziach: Szkice literackie* (1956); *Szkice z podróży* (1956); *Szkice o Conradzie* (1959); *Pisma rozproszone* (1964). FURTHER WORKS IN ENGLISH: *A Village Wedding and Other Stories* (1957)

BIBLIOGRAPHY: Scherer-Virski, O., *The Modern Polish Short Story* (1955): 333–39; Folejewski, Z., *M.D.* (1967); Folejewski, Z., "M. D.'s Place in European Literature," *BA* 38 (1964): 11–13

—EWA M. THOMPSON

DADAISM

"The acts of life have neither beginning nor end. Everything happens in an idiotic fashion," said Tristan TZARA, the leading spirit of Dadaism, or again, "Dada is a state of mind. That's why it changes form according to its races and events. Dada applies to everything and is nevertheless nothing. . . ." True enough, and Tzara should know. Its birth, if not its beginning as a state of mind, occurred in 1916 at the Cabaret Voltaire in Zurich; its death was at the Soirée du *Cœur à barbe* (bearded heart) of 1923 in Paris, which ended in a free-for-all among various Dadas and future SURREALISTS. Dada was conceived in spectacle, and it ended in spectacle, noise, and violence, rather than some dull petering out characteristic of other movements: that should be, in fact, one of its definitions. The surrealist movement, to which Dada led, was a different animal altogether, although it took over such attitudes and theories as the sustained clash of contraries, and such techniques as collage (including Hans Arp's [1887–1966] sticking together of torn pieces of newspaper thrown on the floor) and automatic transcription; some of the Dadaists continued as surrealists, among them BRETON, ARAGON, and ÉLUARD, and even, upon occasion, Tzara.

Through its varied journals—*Dada* in Zurich, *Littérature* in Paris, *Mécano* in Holland (whose founder, I. K. Bonset, was the pseudonymous Dada representation of Theo van Doesburg [1883–1931], creator of De Stijl), *Merz*, run by Kurt Schwitters (1887–1948) in Hannover, *The Blind Man*, run by Marcel Duchamp (1887–1968) in New York, and *Die Schammade*, run by Johannes Baargeld (d. 1927) in Cologne—Dada lived a colorful existence before its extinction, which was more or less voluntary. In a sense, the quasi-simultaneous manifestation of these geographically distinct and spiritually similar organs corresponds to the multiple facets in simultaneous existence of such techniques as the Dada simultaneous poem, recited in several different languages at once. This technique links the movement to the Simultanism of CENDRARS and to the practice of Bruitism or Noisism, and to concrete poetry in some of its louder avatars. There is, of course, no resolution to the contraries, since these are to be retained intact. This is perhaps one of the major differences from surrealism, for Breton's "point sublime" was an ideal resolution of the two contrary states into a dialectic of a workable kind: Dada is against workability.

Many types of Dadaism flourished. There were, for instance, the mystical tendencies of Johannes Baader (1875–1955) (OberDada, or Superdada, who also considered himself the incarnation of Christ) and of Hugo Ball (1886–1927), equally if differently mystical, some more political Dadas, and so on. The word "Dada" is already multivalent, meaning all the following things, and also none of them: the child's first word "Da-Da," a hobby, and a rocking horse (or, in English, their convergence in a hobby-horse). One day, the story goes, according to Arp, it happened. "I declare hereby that Tzara invented the word Dada on the 6th of February 1916 at 6 in the evening. I was there. . . . It was at the Café de la Terrasse in Zurich and I was wearing a brioche in my left nostril . . ." Dada thus means nothing and refusal, or it means everything and anything and LIFE. Dada belongs to everyone and sweeps away all previous doctrines and national divisions, all human values (sentiment being the chocolate, according to Tzara, which stops up the veins of men and prevents the free flow of creation); Dada will clear away tears with its rapidity, will overcome moroseness in its salutary and violent rush down the volcanic slope, and will do away with prudence and morality, aestheticism and pride, in particular, national and artistic pride. Dada is funny and indifferent to its humor, serious and not serious, passionate and passionately indifferent.

Dada's theory was revolutionary, and Dada's techniques, visual and verbal, which were related to those of Italian and Russian FUTURISM and English vorticism (speed and turning about a central point) as well as to French simultanism, inspired masterpieces such as Schwitters's "sound sonatas," made up of nonsense words and single syllables and sounds, and recited with great seriousness and passion, and his collages of street litterings; and Raoul Hausmann's (1886–1971) *photomontages*, a juxta- and superposition of visual images corresponding to the collages of painting and the mixture of "real" objects and paint in the *tableau-objet*, all a challenge to the ordinary conceptions of real and false. They also correspond to Tzara's combination of elements in his *Vingt-cinq poèmes* (1918; twenty-five poems) and to the Dada Manifestos, all written at a high pitch of intensity and irony, and to Tzara's epic poem, *L'homme approximatif* (1931; *Approximate Man*, 1973), both disturbing and deeply moving, like the Dadaist movement itself.

BIBLIOGRAPHY: Motherwell, R., *The Dada Painters and Poets* (1951); Richter, H., *Art and Anti-Art* (1965); Sanouillet, M., *Dada* (1969); Rubin, W. S., *Dada and Surrealist Art* (1969); Caws, M. A., *The Poetry of Dada and Surrealism* (1970); Grossman, M. L., *Dada: Paradox, Mystification and Ambiguity in European Literature* (1971); Verkauf, W., *Dada: Monograph of a Movement* (1975); Kuenzli, R., and Foster, S., eds., *Dada Spectrum: Dialectics of Revolt* (1978)

—MARY ANN CAWS

DADIÉ, Bernard Binlin

Ivoiran novelist, short-story writer, poet, and dramatist (writing in French), b. 1916, Assinie

D.'s mother, a one-eyed woman who felt that her presence held a curse that had been responsible for the deaths of her first three children, decided to send away her fourth child, Bernard, to protect him from her evil spell. D. spent much of his childhood with his elderly uncle N'dabian, who told him many of the African folk tales that D. later adapted in his short-story collections. D. studied in Gorée, then served in the government administration for eleven years in Dakar, Senegal. A lover of the theater, D. set up an important center for dramatic arts. He served as director of line arts and research in the government of the Ivory Coast at Abidjan, and is currently Minister of Culture.

D. first gained prominence with the publication of his short-story collections *Légendes africaines* (1953; African legends) and *Le pagne noir* (1955; the black loincloth), the latter featuring the exploits of the legendary spider Kacou Ananzè, a clever, tricky, and conceited rogue similar to Renart the Fox of French medieval tales.

In 1956 the poems in *La ronde des jours* (the circle of days) were hailed by the Haitian poet René DÉPESTRE as an expression of "tender humor and joy in living." Because of the way they combine religion (Dadié is a Catholic) and humor, D.'s poems have been compared with those of Langston HUGHES.

D.'s first novel, the autobiographical *Climbié* (1956; *Climbié*, 1971), published in the same year as CAMARA's *L'enfant noir*, differs substantially from Camara's rosy picture of the joys of growing up in an innocent, unspoiled Africa. Unlike Guinea, D.'s homeland already had been corrupted by European rule. D. traces Climbié's development from passive acceptance of white rule to anger at white domination, an anger that emerges when he returns to the Ivory Coast from Senegal and is imprisoned for political reasons.

Un Nègre à Paris (1959; a Negro in Paris) and *Patron de New York* (1964; boss in New York), two novels of cultural contrasts, written in the light, bantering style of Montesquieu's *Persian Letters*, demonstrate how odd and foolish the customs and behavior of Parisians and New Yorkers appear to a West African. With irony and false naïveté, Tanhoé, the narrator of *Un nègre à Paris*, concludes that the Parisian, despite his ridiculous customs and attitudes, is really a human being in his own right, with his own history, traditions, and gods.

In the late 1960s D. found his true vocation when he returned to his first love, the theater. *Monsieur Thôgô-gnini* (1970; Mr. Thôgô-gnini), a farce in the tradition of Molière's *The Would-be Gentleman* and JARRY's *King Ubu*, was critically acclaimed at the 1969 Pan-African Festival in Algiers. Monsieur Thôgô-gnini takes advantage of the arrival of the white traders and exploits his own people in an attempt to gain fame and fortune. Like Molière's gullible Monsieur Jourdain, D.'s protagonist accepts anything the white traders give him, including a suit made from sacking, as the latest European fashion. D.'s next two plays, *Les voix dans le vent* (1970; voices in the wind) and *Béatrice du Congo* (1971; Beatrice of the Congo), treat the theme of the corruption and exploitation of Africa in a more serious vein, with multidimensional characters torn between conflicting desires.

Iles de tempête (1973; stormy islands), D.'s most ambitious drama, focuses on the moral dilemma of Toussaint L'Ouverture, whose excessive admiration for the French and especially for Napoleon made him reluctant to declare Haiti's independence. D. uses the techniques of the experimental theater in depicting simultaneous, parallel scenes, concluding with Toussaint's exile in Fort de Joux and Napoleon's exile on Saint Helena. Like Aimé CÉSAIRE's *The Tragedy of King Christophe*, *Iles de tempête* debunks the myth of a great Haitian revolutionary, but in D.'s drama the caricature of a legendary black hero is blended with warmth and compassion.

His simplicity and directness of style have made D. one of the best dramatists in French-speaking Africa. Without anger or hatred, D. demonstrates the evils of colonialism and gives hope for the Africa of the future through his message of peace, brotherhood, and love.

FURTHER WORKS: *Assé Déhylé* (1936); *Les villes* (1939); *Afrique debout* (1950); *Hommes de tous les continents* (1967); *La ville où nul ne meurt* (1968)

BIBLIOGRAPHY: Mercier, R., and M. Battestini and S. Battestini, *B. D.* (1964); Quillateau, C., *B. B. D.* (1967); Brench, A. C., *The Novelists' Inheritance in French Africa* (1967): 84–91; Wake, C., in Banham, M., ed., *African Theatre Today* (1976): 74–79

—DEBRA POPKIN

DAGERMAN, Stig

Swedish novelist, dramatist, essayist, and short-story writer, b. 5 Oct. 1923, Älvkarleby; d. 4 Nov. 1954, Stockholm

D. came from a working-class background. For a while he studied art and literature at the University of Stockholm, but he did not graduate. His marriage into a family active in the trade-union movement consolidated and inspired his political interest.

D. was one of the most talented among the writers of the 1940s, who captured the spirit of their time in works about agony and angst. No one could describe this feeling of dread as well as D., who envisioned it as a fundamental part of existence, impossible to eliminate, endurable only when made a conscious part of life. But for D. himself this may ultimately have become unbearable. While his early career was characterized by a great outburst of productivity, he committed suicide after five years of silence as a writer; many of his works were published long after they were written and some posthumously.

D.'s first novel, *Ormen* (1945; the snake), deals with angst as it affects the young men in a military camp. It was followed by *De dömdas ö* (1946; the island of the doomed ones), about seven people representing the seven deadly sins, on an island shaken by frightening natural events and filled with repulsive reptiles. Unable to create a sense of togetherness, they die, alone and horribly.

Although his novel *Bröllopsbesvär* (1949; wedding pains) displays a sense of the grotesque and the comic features of life, its final message is bleak: deceit, coincidences, and mistakes rule a chaotic world that offers no solace from the depressing realization that life is meaningless.

D. also wrote plays of great significance. *Den dödsdömde* (1947; *The Condemned*, 1951) deals with the limitations of justice and the sadistic instincts of the masses. *I skuggan av Mart* (1949; in Mart's shadow) describes the tragedy of a young man who lives in the shadow of his dead brother erroneously believed to have died as a martyr.

In his journalistic work, D. further confirmed his outstanding talent through sensitive descriptions of guilt and suffering in postwar Germany published in *Tysk höst* (1947; German autumn). He also wrote witty and satirical poetic commentaries on current events, collected in *Dagsedlar* (1954; notes on the day).

D. was an excellent stylist, his language ranging from poetic images to realistic dialogue. His collection of short stories, *Nattens lekar* (1947; night games), in which he uses a variety of narrators, displays his linguistic versatility. The autobiographical stories at the beginning of the collection had a greater appeal to the average reader than his angst-ridden novels. In these stories he describes people in working-class surroundings confronted with the ordinary problems of life. But the collection also contains expressionistic nightmares and horror stories.

D. never lost contact with his political roots in the trade-union movement, which he joined in his early youth, and he served as cultural editor for a syndicalist newspaper. An anarcho-syndicalist philosophy is also apparent in his fiction, notably his first two novels. Among other influences on D.'s work were HEMINGWAY, KAFKA, and KOESTLER. But he remains a leader of his generation by virtue of his powerful language and the strength of his vision of life, which enabled him to capture the despair of his time in works transcending time.

FURTHER WORKS: *Dramer om dömda* (1948); *Bränt barn* (1948; *A Burnt Child*, 1950); *Judasdramer* (1949); *Den yttersta dagen* (1952); *Tusen år hos Gud* (1954); *Vårt behov av tröst* (1955); *Samlade skrifter* (1955). FURTHER WORKS IN ENGLISH: *The Games of Night and Other Writings* (1959)

BIBLIOGRAPHY: Bergman, S. A., "Blinded by Darkness: A Study of the Novels and Plays of S. D.," *Delta,* No. 11 (1957): 16–31; Gustafson, A., *A History of Swedish Literature* (1961): 544–48; Howe, I., "The Games of Night," *New Republic,* 13 Nov. 1961: 22; Thompson, L., "S. D.'s 'Vår nattliga badort': An Interpretation," *Scan,* 13 (1974): 117–27; Thompson, L., "In Fear and Trembling: A Study of S. D.'s Imagery," in Siefken, H., and Thompson, A., eds., *Erfahrung und Überlieferung: Festschrift for C. P. Magrill* (1974): 206–22; Thompson, L., *S. D.: "Nattens lekar"* (1975)

—TORBORG LUNDELL

DAĞLARCA, Fazıl Hüsnü

Turkish poet, b. 1914, Istanbul

Often referred to as "Turkey's leading poet" since the 1960s, D. also has been one of his country's most prolific poets: by 1980 he had published more than sixty volumes of verse. On the day he graduated from the military academy and became a career officer in 1935, he published his first collection of poems, *Havaya çizilen dünya* (a world sketched on air), containing his conventional verse, which had been coming out in magazines since 1933. His reputation was established by his second book, *Çocuk ve Allah* (1940; child and God), which explores children's inner world and probes human and divine themes in partly rhymed free verse. Its inquiry into the mystery of life and the mystique of death, through innocent eyes and a quintessential language that combines simplicity and sophistication, expanded the philosophical frontiers of modern Turkish poetry more than any other work.

Spanning nearly five decades, D.'s huge output constitutes "total poetry" which embodies most of the movements and elements of Turkish modernism while avoiding participation in any group or specific school. D. pioneered, adumbrated, synthesized, influenced, reactivated, or broadened all of Turkey's poetic sensibilities and techniques. With moods ranging from tender infatuation to vehement denunciation of social injustice, he has produced verses in the lyric, epic, patriotic, metaphysical, mystic, and political genres.

Daha (1943; more), *Çakırın destanı* (1945; the epic of Çakır), and *Taş devri* (1945; the stone age) are explorations into the crises of man and his civilization. They contain many impressive poems, rich in their pagan imagery and evocations of mankind's timeless thoughts and passions.

D. has written a large body of epic poetry to celebrate Turkish victories and national heroes. His "patriotic" work includes cycles on the battle of Manzikert, the conquest of Istanbul, the Dardanelles, the Turkish war of independence, and modern Turkey's founding father Mustafa Kemal Atatürk. His books about international topics include *Cezayir türküsü* (1961; *Song of Algeria*, published with English, French, and Arabic translations), *Vietnam savaşımız* (1966; *Our Vietnam War*, 1967), *Hiroşima* (1970; Hiroshima), *Vietnam körü* (1970; blind in Vietnam)

In 1950 D. published *Toprak ana* (Mother Earth), a poignant cycle depicting the harsh realities of life in rural Anatolia that is generally considered as the best poetic work to come out of the huge corpus of so-called "village literature" since the late 1940s. D. produced hundreds of "current affairs" verses, mostly in the vein of SOCIALIST REALISM, protesting socioeconomic injustice and imperialism. He hung many of these verses on the window of his bookshop in Istanbul, which he operated from 1959 to 1972, after retiring from government service.

Mevlâna'da olmak—Gezi (1958; voyage-alive in Mevlana) is a cycle of neomystic poems in celebration of the great 13th-c. Anatolian Sufi thinker and poet Mawlana Djalal ud Din Rumi. *Hoo'lar* (1960; ho-os) comprises D.'s most complex philosophical poetic investigations; its abstruse style has caused this profound work to be virtually ignored by the public and the critics alike.

D.'s major collections—*Aç yazi* (1951; hungry writing), *Âsû* (1955), *Bati acısı* (1958; the agony of the West), *Aylam* (1962; moon life), and *Haydi* (1968; come on)—constitute a major achievement based on supreme craftsmanship in the use of the resources of the Turkish language, imaginative visions of the self and of external reality, pantheistic and humanistic themes, flawless lyricism, and engrossing metaphysical flights. From 1967 onward D. also produced a large number of verses for children, and some humorous and erotic verse as well.

FURTHER WORKS: *Üç şehitler destanı* (1949); *Bağımsızlık savaşı: Samsun'dan Ankara'ya* (1951); *Bağımsızlık savaşı: Inönüler* (1951); *Sıvaslı karınca* (1951); *Istanbul: Fetih distanı* (1951); *Anıtkabir* (1953); *Delice böcek* (1957); *Özgürlük alanı* (1960); *Karşı: Türk*

olmak (1963); *Yedi memetler* (1964); *Çanakkale destanı* (1965); *Karşı: Dişardan gazel* (1965); *Karşı: Kazmalama* (1965); *Karşı: Yeryağ* (1965); *Açıl susam açıl* (1967); *Kubilay destanı* (1968); *19 mayıs destanı*, (1969); *Dört kanatlı kuş* (1970); *Malazgirt ululamast* (1971); *Kuş ayak* (1971); *Kmali kuzu ağidi* (1972); *Haliç* (1972); *Bağımsızlık savaşı: Sakarya kıyıları* (1973); *Bağımsızlık savaşı: 30 ağustos* (1973); *Bagımsızlık savaşı: Izmir yollarinda* (1973); *Arkaüstü* (1974); *Yeryüzü çocuklari* (1974); *Yonık çocuklar koçaklaması* (1977); *Ağrı dağı bildirisi* (1977); *Alamanyalarda çöpçülerimiz* (1977); *Ikili anlaşma anıtı* (1977); *Pir Sultan Abdal günleri* (1977); *Horoz* (1977); *Balina ile mandalina* (1977); *Hollandalı dörtlükler/Quatrains of Holland* (1977; bilingual ed.); *Karşı duvar dergisi* (1977); *Yazıları seven ayı* (1978); *Göz masalı* (1979); *Yarmaz sözcükler* (1979). FURTHER WORKS IN ENGLISH: *Selected Poems* (1969); *The Bird and I* (1980)

BIBLIOGRAPHY: Nayir, Y. N., Introduction to *Selected Poems* (1969): xix–xxxvii; *D. Critical Approaches, Interviews, Selected Poems* (1974); Menemencioğlu, N., ed., Introduction to *The Penguin Book of Turkish Verse* (1978): 22, 53–54; Kraft, G., *F. H. D.: Weltschöpfund und Tiersymbolid* (1978)

—TALAT SAIT HALMAN

D'AGUIAR, Fred

Guyanese novelist, poet, and dramatist, b. 2 Feb. 1960, London, Engalnd

Born in London, D. was reared in Guyana, returning to Britain at age twelve. After training as a psychiatric nurse, he read English at the University of Kent and the University of Warwick. Following several stints as a writer-in-residence and as a literary fellow in England, he came to the U.S. in 1992, where he teaches at the University of Miami.

Despite—and perhaps partly because of—his early departure from Guyana, much of his work explores the enchantment and menace of island life. Other themes include an interrogation of the dynamics of slavery and examinations of social conditions and racism in Britain.

D.'s first book of poetry, *Mama Dot* (1985), won a Poetry Book Society Recommendation, while his second, *Airy Hall* (1989), received the Guyana Prize for Poetry. Both books concentrate on D.'s Guyanese upbringing. The title piece of the first volume, "Mama Dot," is a series of linked poems, some in dialect, around an almost mythical figure, a black Guyanese grandmother who seems able to persist over time. "Airy Hall" is a series of poems about life in the small Caribbean town where D. grew up with his grandparents. While there are poems in both volumes that address Britain, it is only with *British Subjects* (1993) that D. turns his focus decidedly toward the odd ambiguity of feeling both at home and not at home in Britain. Poems range from incisive social critique, as in "Ballad of the Throwaway People," to the more humorous parody of Wallace STEVENS: "Thirteen Views of a Penis."

It was not until 1994 that D. began publishing novels. His first, *The Longest Memory*, which won the Whitbread First Novel Award and the David Higham First Novel Award, was translated into eleven languages. In it, he turns away from Guyana as a locale, examining instead the interrelations of a slave plantation in the U.S. Taking place on a Virginia plantation in 1810, the novel chronicles the effect of a young slave's death on those who surround him, examining the event through several perspectives—from that of the slave's father to that of the master's daughter and the overseer. D.'s novel entitled *Feeding the Ghosts* (1997) examines slavery as well, chronicling massacre aboard an 18th-c. slave ship. It is the story of a slave who survives drowning to come back to haunt the ship's captain and crew. Both novels examine slavery from a unique and subtle perspective.

Dear Future (1996) is more experimental than *The Longest Memory*, piecing itself together from four varied but linked narratives. Central to several is Red Head, the youngest child of a variegated Caribbean family who later fall victim to politics. Accidentally struck on the head with an axe, Red Head acquires an ability to see the world from a torqued perspective. Written in an exuberant and lyric style, *Dear Future* recalls at times Ben OKRI's *The Famished Road* (1991).

D.'s strength comes from the choices he makes in content and for his innovative linguistic experimentation. His poems often have strong narrative impulses, the longer ones reading almost like short stories, while his novels possess a care for and attention to language and imagery that is rare for the form. Though still early in his career, D'Aguiar shows every sign of being in a position to become, alongside Wilson HARRIS, one of Guyana's strongest writers.

FURTHER WORKS: *A Jamaican Airman Forsees His Death* (1995); *Bill of Rights* (1998)

BIBLIOGRAPHY: Huggard, R., *D.'s "The Longest Memory"* (1997); Birbalsingh, F., "An Interview with D.," *Ariel*, 24, 1 (1993): 133-45; Bryson, R., *The NEAP Guide to "The Longest Memory"* (1997)

—BRIAN EVENSON

DAHOMEAN LITERATURE

See Beninian Literature

DAISNE, Johan

(pseud. of Herman Thiery) Belgian novelist, poet, dramatist, critic, and essayist (writing in Flemish), b. 2 Sept. 1912, Ghent; d. 9 Aug. 1978, Ghent.

D. studied economics in his native city and took his doctor's degree in 1936 with a thesis on philosophical values in political economy. He also studied Russian, Czech, Spanish, Bantu, and Swedish. He was a great traveler, and he worked at many different jobs, one of which was as a teacher of German. In 1945 he was appointed chief librarian of the Ghent Municipal Library, where he served until his retirement in 1977. Not only other writers but also film had a profound influence on his work. He played a major role in international film festivals and is the author of the much acclaimed quadrilingual *Filmographic Dictionary of World Literature* (3 vols., 1971–78).

D. made his literary debut as a poet. He was one of the founders of *Klaver(en)drie*, a poetry magazine, and was later on the editorial

board of the periodical *Nieuw Vlaams tijdschrift*. He was a prolific writer of poetry in a romantic vein, most of which is autobiographical and has a philosophical strain. He also wrote much occasional verse.

D. will mainly be remembered for introducing a unique blending of everyday reality and Platonic ideals to Netherlandic fiction. His interest in paraphysical and metaphysical reality became manifest from 1942 onward, with the publication of his first drama, *Charade van advent* ("The Advent Charade") and his first novel, *De trap van steen en wolken* (the stairway of stone and clouds). Representative of the genre he was later to call romantic magic realism was his masterpiece *De man die zijn haar kort liet knippen* (1948; *The Man Who Had His Hair Cut Short*, 1965). The unceasing and pitiless self-analysis of the hypersensitive main character, who is confronted with his own past in the person of a former student with whom he was in love, is accompanied by a starkly naturalistic description of an autopsy and romantic evocations of dreamlike memories and visions. It is one of the major novels of modern Netherlandic literature, brilliantly written, combining intellectual precision with imaginative power. The same technique of shifting from physical to metaphysical reality is applied in the surrealistic short story "De trein der traagheid" (1948; the train of slowness) in the collection *Met dertien aan tafel* (1950; with thirteen at table), in which hallucination plays an important part.

The intellectual originality and richness of D.'s major prose works put them in the first rank of modern European literature.

FURTHER WORKS: *Zes domino's voor vrouwen* (1944); *De liefde is een schepping van vergoding* (1946); *Schimmen om een schemerlamp* (1947); *Nitsjevo tot chorosjo: Tien eeuwen Russische literatuur* (1948); *De vier heilsgeliefden* (1955); *Filmatiek; of, De film als levenskunst* (1956); *Lago Maggiore* (1957); *Grüsz Gott* (1958); *De neusvleugel der muze* (1959); *Hoe schoon was mijn school* (1961); *Baratzeartea* (1963); *Als kantwerk aan de kim* (1965); *Reveillon-Reveillon* (1966); *Ontmoeting in zonnekeer* (1967); *Verzamelde gedichten* (1978); *Gepijnde honing* (1978)

BIBLIOGRAPHY: Closset, F., *J. D.: Poète, romancier, dramaturge, essayiste flamand* (1954); Mallinson, V., *Modern Belgian Literature 1830–1960* (1966): 98–99; Hermanowski, G., *Säulen der modernen flämischen Prosa* (1969): 29–45

—ANNE MARIE MUSSCHOOT

DALCHEV, Atanas

Bulgarian poet, translator, and essayist, b. 12 June 1904, Thessaloniki, Greece; d. 17 Jan. 1978, Sofia

A native of Greece, D. arrived in Bulgaria as a child and received most of his education there. Between 1927 and 1929 he lived in Italy and France, visiting London; in 1936–1937 he was in France again. In Bulgaria he worked at various times as a teacher, school inspector, and school principal, as well as a translator. After the communist seizure of power in 1944 he was with the ministry of information, and also edited a journal.

D. occupies a special place in the history of Bulgarian literature. Initially, in the 1920s, he had links with the symbolist poets, but soon moved away from them. The titles of his principal pre-1944 collections reflect the stages of his creative life at that period: *Prozorets* (1926; window), *Parizh* (1930; Paris), and *Angelut na Shartur* (1943; angel of Chartres). During the worst Stalinist years in Bulgaria, D. was among the very few who retreated into stubborn silence rather than acquiesce to political demands upon literature. He subsequently became a model for the younger generation of poets of the 1960s, a culturally more liberal time when D. himself returned to the scene with a thin but valuable volume of "Notes on Poetry, Literature, and Criticism" entitled *Fragmenti* (1967; fragments).

One of these "fragments" might serve as an epigraph to D.'s entire lifework: "Temperance is a virtue in literature as well." D.'s poems rarely run to more than a few stanzas, and his whole lifetime's original poetic output can easily be contained in one small volume. His vocabulary is deceptively simple, and at first glance seemingly easy to translate. D. was an intensely private man, who exposed no more of himself to his reader's view than necessary. Several of his earlier poems employ the image of the window, a delimited opening that enables him to watch others' lives from afar while he himself remains unobserved.

D. always kept his distance from the world. The theme of loneliness is a prominent one in 20th-c. Bulgarian literature, and D. contributed much to its elaboration. Thus in "Nosht" (1929; night) he surveys the night through his own reflection in the window, and concludes: "three times blacker, heavier becomes the gloom / and my own loneliness." In "Vecher" (1930; evening) the persona thinks of great cities he has known, such as Naples and Paris, and wishes he could somehow participate more fully in the life of society instead of consistently retreating from it.

The philosophical note sounded in "Vecher" attains even more concrete expression in a poem like "Kukuvitsa" (1964; cuckoo), where the poet recalls his Greek childhood and the popular belief that the cuckoo's call numbers the years of life remaining to the hearer. The poet stops his ears, refusing to listen, not because he is afraid, but because he is convinced it is wrong to seek to know the future. Whoever seeks knowledge of the future will discover not life, but death, although D. realizes full well that we cannot forever avoid death, "the eternal bandit."

D. adopts a classical approach to life and literature. His writing is usually extraordinarily clear, and he finds universal meaning, not in historic individuals or events, but in the everyday objects of our century that lie close at hand, in ordinary people like a man bearing an advertising board whom most of us scarcely notice. In his writing D. reflected in miniature the enduring traits of the Bulgarian character—thrown into relief through the experiences of a "Bulgarian abroad"—and the passing literary fashions in his native land, but he did so through the prism of his powerful individuality, which was simultaneously earthy and philosophical. His place among the small number of great Bulgarian Lyric poets of this century is secure.

FURTHER WORKS: *Stikhotvoreniya* (1928); *Stikhotvoreniya* (1965); *Balkon* (1972); *Stikhotvoreniya. Fragmenti* (1974); *Stikhotvoreniya. Fragmenti. Misli i vpechatleniya* (1978); *Suchineniya* (2 vols., 1984)

BIBLIOGRAPHY: Statkov, D., "A. D.'s poetische Welt," ZSP, 34, 2 (1969): 254–76; Mozejko, E., "The Poetry of A. D.," *Proceedings of the Second Bulgaro-Scandinavian Symposium*, Uppsala Slavic Papers, 13, 1 (1982): 85–95

—CHARLES A. MOSER

DAMAS, Léon-Gontran

French Guianese poet, journalist, and essayist, b. 28 March 1912, Cayenne; d. 22 Jan. 1978, Washington, D.C.

D. was born into a middle-class mulatto family and was brought up so that his entire way of thinking and behaving during his early years was subjected to patterns laid down by the white French bourgeoisie. He received his early education in French Guiana and in Martinique and later went to Paris, where he studied modern Oriental languages, literature, law, history, economics, and ethnology. In the 1930s he associated with the SURREALISTS, and as early as 1934 published poems in several prestigious French literary periodicals, including *Esprit*. During World War II he was active in the Resistance. Following the war he devoted himself to doing research in the culture of blacks of the New World. In 1948 he was elected to the French National Assembly from Guiana and served there for a number of years. The last period of his life was spent in the U.S., where he taught first at Federal City College and then at Howard University, both in Washington, D.C.

In Paris in the 1930s, together with Aimé CÉSAIRE and Léopold Sédar SENGHOR, D. was one of the founders of NÉGRITUDE, an important literary movement that attempted to present in artistic form the "sum total of the cultural values of the black world." Négritude, and the awakening of the black Caribbean consciousness, stimulated D.'s sense of outrage, and poetry and propaganda are neatly meshed in his work. The writers of Négritude were militant individuals, he said, who together posed a group threat as they went about their messianic mission.

D.'s early poems struck a note of mockery, muffled laughter, and irony. In *Pigments* (1937), for which his friend Robert DESNOS wrote the introduction, D. evokes the memory and history of an Africa that is, however, more a myth concocted by West Indians than a reality—an Africa of the mind. D. showed himself in this early verse to be an authentic poet, able to combine deeply felt emotions shared with his fellow blacks and a distinctly individual intellect.

In his later poetry, there is an intensity of violence, a definite rejection of the white world, and a turning more and more toward the African continent. D. is at his best when, as a participant in the culture, he can nevertheless strongly denounce it. This ritualistic denouncement of self can be found particularly in the poems in *Black-Label* (1956; Black label).

Today D. is read not because of his revolutionary fervor but rather because of the power of his poetry, which cuts across his attempts to proselytize. He was a poet who fiercely believed in a cause, but he did not allow that cause to blunt his vision. The small man's quick smile and ready handshake were a mask for the tiger, and a sober spirit underlay his passionate words. His poetry stresses not the collision of worlds but the manner in which humanity can triumph and overcome man-made obstacles.

FURTHER WORKS: *Retour de Guyane* (1938); *Poèmes nègres sur des airs africains* (1948; *African Songs of Love, War, Grief and Abuse*, 1961); *Graffiti* (1952); *Névralgies* (1966)

BIBLIOGRAPHY: Cook, M., "The Poetry of L. D.," *African Forum*, 3, 4 (1967): 127–32; Jones, E. A., *Voices of Négritude* (1971): 63–64; Dathorne, O. R., *The Black Mind* (1974): 314–19; Kesteloot, L., *Black Writers in French: A Literary History of Negritude* (1974): 123–58; Kennedy, E. C., ed., *The Negritude Poets* (1975):

39–44; Racine, D. L., "A Profile of L.-G. D.," *Negro History Bulletin*, 42 (1979): 61–63; Racine, D. L., ed., *L.-G. D., 1912–1978: Founder of Negritude* (1979)

—O. R. DATHORNE

DANISH LITERATURE

At the turn of the century three major trends were noticeable in Danish literature. In the early 1870s NATURALISM had been introduced by the critic Georg Brandes (1842–1927), who saw the task of literature as the consideration of political, social, religious, and sexual problems. During the 1880s radical naturalism was abandoned in favor of a more uncommitted realism. The 1890s saw a reaction against this factual and often pessimistic literature, and the young writers of the period turned inward, rediscovering the soul and the self. This third, neoromantic trend toward introspection and spirituality was strongly influenced by French SYMBOLISM and produced work mainly of a lyrical nature, as opposed to the prose that dominated the previous decade.

After 1900 these preoccupations are found in the works of Harald Kidde (1878–1918). In his major novel, *Helten* (1912; the hero), the evangelical main character is able to find happiness only in humiliation and renunciation of the self. The psychological is stressed by Knud Hjortø (1869–1931), who in several short stories and novels analyzes the inability of the daydreamer to cope with life. Karl Larsen (1860–1931) was the most consistent representative of nonideological realism. He revitalized Danish prose style through his stories about the inhabitants of the Copenhagen slums, accurately reproducing their slang. Gustav Wied (1858–1914) carried on in the vein of doctrinaire naturalism by employing its motifs of degeneration and of love as originating in pure instinct in a number of cynical and pessimistic, yet humorous novels and dramas.

As a consequence of the naturalism of the 1870s a regional fiction emerged around 1900, mainly based on a new materialistic and socialist point of view. The immense social changes and conflicts caused by industrialization, begun around 1870, became common topics of analysis and debate. Johan Skjoldborg (1861–1936) depicted the tenant farmers' struggle for economic justice, and Jeppe Aakjær (1866–1930) aimed his criticism at the well-to-do farmers and their exploitation of the farmhands. This indignation became more acute in Martin Andersen NEXØ's politically oriented works, which depict the defeat of the craftsman by the machine and portray the emerging urban proletariat.

Regional literature was also the point of departure for the poetry of Thøger Larsen (1875–1928), in *Jord* (1904; earth) and *Dagene* (1905; the days). Larsen's later poetry became permeated with his strong sense of life's cosmic dimensions and the interrelationship of everything, elevating it to one of the great pantheistic expressions in Scandivanian literature. Also rising above the period's social commitment and rooted in regional literature are two very different figures: Johannes V. JENSEN, whose stories, set in his home province, only form the point of departure for a poetic expansion in time and space; and Jakob Knudsen (1858–1917), the only one of the new generation of writers whose works are rooted in Christianity. Most of the neorealists after 1900 professed an enthusiastic belief in progress. In Jensen's case this belief is based on Darwin's theory of evolution and a faith in man's ability to improve society through the help of science. The big city and modern technology are major motifs in Jensen's early free verse. Knudsen remained skeptical about this optimism, and in his works the old peasant culture, as portrayed in the tragic story of crime and revenge *Sind* (1903; temper), is confronted with the modern, equalizing reform movements. In the novel *Fremskridt* (1907; progress) Knudsen expounds his belief that the basic weakness of modern times lies in the destruction of the spirit through mechanization.

World War I marked a definite turning point in Danish literature. Denmark's neutrality became the basis for an economic boom; among the artists, the threat of war intensified the feeling for life. A new generation of poets emerged, filled with ecstatic rejoicing in the splendor of existence. The two major representatives of this group, Tom KRISTENSEN and Emil Bønnelycke (1893–1953), published colorful, expressionistic poetry collections. Greatest attention was attracted by Bønnelycke's untraditional prose poems in *Asfaltens sange* (1918; songs of the asphalt), influenced by Johannes V. Jensen's and Walt Whitman's universal affirmation of life.

The euphoria of the war years was, however, soon over. The realization that the cultural and moral values of Western civilization had gone bankrupt resulted in skepticism, disillusionment, and nihilism, and culminated in a fierce debate on opposing world views. The poet Otto Gelsted (1888–1968) was the first to react against the materialism of the war years in *Jomfru Gloriant* (1923; Maiden Gloriant) and to criticize the ideological chaos. From a philosophical point of view based on Immanuel Kant's rationalism and Marxist dialectics, he called for a critical attitude, and from an artistic point of view, for a striving toward harmony and clarity, which found its most perfect expression in the collection *Rejsen til Astrid* (1927; the journey to Astrid).

More acutely than his contemporaries, Tom Kristensen had felt the clash between tradition and war experience within himself and had given it harrowing expression in his major novel, *Hærværk* (1930; *Havoc*, 1968). The novelist Jacob PALUDAN, next to Kristensen the foremost representative of this "lost generation," also was concerned with the crisis of the postwar period, but from the viewpoint of a satirical, conservative spectator. Paludan was the first to realize that the 1930s were not a period of peace but only an interval before another catastrophe. Criticism of the times was not, however, a concern of two major lyrical poets who made their debuts in the 1920s, Per Lange (1901–1991) and Jens August SCHADE. The poems in Lange's important collection *Forvandlinger* (1929; metamorphoses) express a stoic and pessimistic attitude based on the awareness that the world of the ideal cannot be reconciled with reality. Schade published numerous surrealistic poetry collections, novels, and dramas, all permeated by unrestrained fantasies.

More international in his outlook was Gustaf Munch-Petersen (1912–1938) whose concentrated, image-filled style is clearly influenced by French SURREALISM and the Finno-Swedish modernists Elmer DIKTONIUS and Edith SÖDERGRAN. To Munch-Petersen, art was an ideological tool to make life better. The volumes *det underste land* (1933; the land below) and *nitten digte* (1937; nineteen poems) sum up this dream of fellowship and happiness by laying bare the sources of the subconscious.

The optimism expressed by Schade and Munch-Petersen is counterbalanced by a great number of novels written in response to the worldwide depression precipitated by the Wall Street crash of 1929, which in Denmark resulted in an unemployment rate of previously unknown proportions. At the same time there was a growing awareness of the political threat of Nazism and Fascism. The poet Paul la Cour (1902–1956) began, in *Den galliske sommer* (1927; the Gallic summer), with a purely pantheistic attempt to identify with nature. His later collections, *Dette er vort liv* (1936; this is our life) and *Alt kræver jeg* (1938; I demand all), however, are based on the realization of the need to mobilize a stronger sense of humanitarianism against totalitarianism.

Greater disillusion infuses the psychological novel by Knud Sønderby (1909–1966), *Midt i en jazztid* (1931; in the middle of a jazz age), focusing on erotic and social conflicts and written in a hard-boiled style influenced by HEMINGWAY. Sønderby's basically tragic world view is also expressed in his second major work, *En kvinde er overflødig* (1936; dramatized 1942; *A Woman Too Many*, 1955), about the conflict of generations.

The period's anxiety and nihilism had their most desperate manifestation in the works of Nis PETERSEN, who completely rejected the concepts of guilt and fate. The result is a permanent state of irresolution that characterizes Petersen's confessional poetry and his fiction. In a striking contrast, Petersen's cousin, Kaj MUNK, strove to create a drama that primarily focused on man's relationship with God and that analyzes the problems of faith and doubt. Nevertheless, Munk lets man act as God's chosen tool in a concrete political situation, and he himself became a martyr to his convictions when he was murdered by the Gestapo in 1944.

The political situation before and during World War II likewise provided the motifs for the dramas of Kjeld ABELL, whose humanist views are represented by the individual's fight for freedom. An emphasis on social matters in Abell's early plays gives way in his later and more experimental works to general existential questions.

Direct social criticism was represented by Knuth Becker (1891–1974), whose autobiographical novel cycle about the character Kai Gøtsche was a fierce accusation against public institutions and the educational system, and by Harald Herdal (1900–1978), whose novels describe from firsthand experience the misery of the Copenhagen working class. The unrest of the 1930s in rural communities was dealt with from a consistently Marxist point of view by Hans KIRK. Whereas his earlier novels, such as *Fiskerne* (1928; *the fishermen*), contain credible human portraits, the psychology of Kirk's later works reveals more artificiality than depth. The same can be said of the characters in the novels by Hans Scherfig (1905–1979), next to Kirk the most markedly Marxist writer of the period; his fiction demonstrates how decadent capitalistic society, as depicted, for example, in *Idealister* (1945; *The Idealists*, 1949), inhibits and corrupts man's original goodness.

Pure psychological portrayal without any direct social or political comment is found in the works of Aage Dons (1903–1994) and Jørgen Nielsen (1902–1945). Dons depicts in such novels as *Soldaterbrønden* (1936; *The Soldier's Well*, 1940) the attempts of rootless human beings to overcome their isolation in cold, hostile surroundings. He prefers a cosmopolitan, aristocratic setting, whereas Nielsen, in his short-story collections *Lavt land* (1929; low country), *Vi umyndige* (1934; we the dependents) and *Figurer i et landskab* (1944; figures in a landscape), continued the regional-literature tradition of the turn of the century and combined it with a penetrating analysis of human beings troubled by spiritual conflicts.

The psychological drama in the interwar period is represented by Carl Erik Soya (1896–1983), both a stern moralist and an ironical humorist. His first play, *Parasitterne* (1929; the parasites), offered a precise, naturalistic depiction of human infamy and abuse. Inspired by Freudian psychoanalysis, his comedy *Hvem er*

jeg? (1932; who am I?) and the tetralogy *Brudstykker af et mønster* (1940; parts of a pattern), *To tråde* (1943; *Two Threads*, 1955), *30 års henstand* (1944; 30 years' reprieve), and *Frit valg* (1948; free choice) pose the question: Is life just and predestined? The plays do not answer the question but represent various options of human behavior in a world open to all possibilities. This psychoanalytical approach also characterizes the early writing of Hans Christian BRANNER. In the 1940s, however, he turned toward a purely existential analysis of the individual's contemporary situation.

The works of Isak DINESEN occupy a place apart from all political and social topics. Her main genre, the fantastic short story overlaid with mythical patterns, is deeply rooted in an aristocratic, romantic, and religious world. Martin A. Hansen began as a realistic social critic, but in his imaginative historical novels from the war years he, too, returned to the more harmonious culture of the Middle Ages. His subsequent works, which depict the present more realistically, represent an attempt to overcome evil and death through the Christian belief in the resurrection.

With the German occupation from 1940 to 1945 most of the writers—socialists, conservatives, nihilists—joined ranks to defend the culture of their country. Thus, one of the most characteristic poets of the war period, Halfdan Rasmussen (b. 1915), shifted from a somewhat romantic tone in his first volumes to a polemical one in *Digte under besættelsen* (1945; poems during the occupation), based upon the feeling of fellowship during the struggle. However, the last remnants of the belief in cultural progress had vanished, as expressed in the poetry of Morten Nielsen (1922–1944), whose collection *Krigere uden vaaben* (1943; warriors without weapons) shows him as a typical representative of a young generation, devoid of illusions, but still with the will to risk life for freedom.

The recognition of the cultural crisis, accompanied by a yearning for a rebirth of the unifying values of the Middle Ages, characterized the postwar poets who gathered around the journal *Heretica* (1948–53) as a reaction against the predominant rationalism and materialism of the 1930s. For Ole SARVIG, liberation from chaos is possible through the strong and mysterious forces of love and grace, while for Thorkild BJØRNVIG this liberation can only be achieved through the force of poetry. Erik Knudsen (b. 1922), too, acknowledges in his poems of the 1940s the rootlessness and anxiety of modern man. Typical in this regard is the volume *Blomsten og sværdet* (1949; the flower and the sword), which employs T. S. ELIOT's technique of allusions. In his later collections, *Sensation og stilhed* (1958; sensation and silence) and *Journal* (1963; journal), Knudsen demonstrates his socialist orientation. Increasingly he uses language as an agitational tool, as for instance in *Vietnam: Digte, taier og artikler* (1973; Vietnam: poems, speeches, and articles), directed against the American involvement in Vietnam, and in *Forsøg på at gå* (1978; attempts to walk), directed against capitalism in general.

The publisher of *Heretica*, Ole Wivel (b. 1921), gradually moved toward a similar political commitment. A strong messianic expectation in *Digte* (1943; poems), whose exquisite style is influenced by Rainer Maria RILKE and by Per Lange, was combined, in *I fiskens tegn* (1948; in the sign of the fish), with an elegiac longing for a new human community, whereas this expectation in *Nike* (1958; Nike) and *Gravskrifter* (1970; epitaphs) is set in contrast to a strong demand for action in a world threatened by war and nuclear catastrophe.

The youngest of the *Heretica* poets, Frank JÆGER, avoids any ideological engagement, as do two of the more traditional poets of the postwar years, Tove Ditlevsen (1918–1976) and Piet Hein (1905–1996). While Piet Hein strives for clarity and strictness and in his twenty volumes of *Gruk* (1940–63; *Grooks*, Vols. 1–6, 1966–68) demonstrates an exceptional feeling for the epigrammatic form, Tove Ditlevsen employs unpretentious, melancholy verse forms in her collections from *Pigesind* (1939; a girl's mind) through *Den hemmelige rude* (1961; the secret window). Her ruthlessly honest semiautobiographical novels, *Ansigterne* (1968; the faces) and *Vilhelms værelse* (1975; Vilhelm's room), are fascinating psychiatric studies.

It was undoubtedly the existentialist and internationally oriented poetry of the *Heretica* group that left the decisive marks on the literature of the 1940s. In the 1950s, however, prose dominated. In Hans Lyngby Jepsen (b. 1920), Poul Ørum (1919–1997), Tage Skou-Hansen (b. 1925), and Erik Aalbæk Jensen (b. 1923) the realistic and psychological tradition of the 1930s found four remarkable representatives. A more imaginative trend, incorporating elements of myth and fairy tale—characteristic was a renewed interest in Isak Dinesen—was typical of several prose writers of the 1950s. Dinesen's demand that man must accept his fate is a recurrent theme in the works of Albert Dam (1880–1972), who combined past, present, and visionary future in his collection of myths, *Morfars by* (1956; grandfather's town). In his first short stories, *Tyven i Tjørnsted* (1951; the thief in Tjørnsted), Leif E. Christensen (b. 1924) used a Dinesen-like, archaic style, and he and Willy-August Linnemann (b. 1914) share the conviction that man exists to realize God's plans. Linnemann's major work is the novel cycle *Europafortællinger* (1958–66; European stories), in which he mingled suspenseful narration with philosophical reflections. The framework is formed by the life stories of people hiding in a shelter during an air raid, attempting to find a pattern in their fate.

In addition to the fantastic and realistic trends during the 1950s, an experimental tone was also noticeable, and a conscious effort was made to bring Danish literature into step with European modernism, introduced in Denmark in the journal *Vindrosen* (1954–74). Danish modernism emerged in the first works of Villy Sørensen and Peter SEEBERG in 1953–54. Sørensen's three collections of short stories stylistically combine Hans Christian Andersen's seemingly naïve tone with an allegorical composition and irony reminiscent of Isak Dinesen. Yet they are completely modern and original in their symbolic depictions of the contradictions and conflicts in human life. Sørensen's mode of thought is patterned on German modernism, and above all on Herman BROCH, Franz KAFKA, and Thomas MANN. Seeberg's models are Samuel BECKETT and Eugene IONESCO; his point of departure is the absurdity of existence, but it is precisely this meaninglessness that demands of us that we give our lives meaning and continuity in solidarity with others.

Less exclusive and far more productive was Leif PANDURO, whose novels almost totally revolve around a certain type of human being, a person who is divided and inhibited because he is tied to his past—a theme closely related to that found in Max FRISCH's works. The themes of Panduro's novels recur in his dramas and television plays after 1960—among the best in Scandinavian theater. They are typical and successful examples of the growing interest in drama, which in the period 1965–75 became gradually more ideologically oriented. The greatest success on stage is enjoyed by Ernst Bruun Olsen (b. 1923), whose plays deal with current topics: *Teenagerlove* (1962; teenage love) satirizes the commercial cult of pop music, *Hvor gik Nora hen, da hun gik ud?* (1968; where did Nora go when she left?) discusses sex roles,

whereas the television play *Lille mand farvel* (1974; little man, goodbye) is a direct attack on the capitalist system.

The main artistic innovation of the 1960s, however, was a lyrical modernism, which, in contrast to the poetry of the previous decades, was not based on a general feeling of angst and destruction but challengingly embraced the external aspects of contemporary society. The new direction found its most successful expression in the breakthrough collection *Konfrontation* (1960; confrontation) by Klaus RIFBJERG, which conveys concrete experiences rendered through the associative power of the language. Rifbjerg has emerged as the most productive postwar Danish writer, with more than sixty publications. In addition to subsequent collections of poetry, he has published some less successful dramas and numerous highly praised novels, mainly written in a traditional, realistic form.

Whereas Rifbjerg in his poetry experiments with various styles, Jess Ørnsbo (b. 1932) adheres to classical modernism, with its confrontation between incompatible elements of reality and its sensory impressions reflected in a highly fragmented mode of expression. His first collection, *Digte* (1960; poems), however, adds a new dimension through its extraordinary social concern, focusing on a Copenhagen working-class milieu. In Ørnsbo's latest collection, *Mobiliseringer* (1978; mobilizations), his social criticism has turned into almost anarchistic protests against a society in the process of dissolution.

For Ivan MALINOVSKI, too, the aesthetics of confrontation is a basic principle, a formal expression of his experience of the senselessness of existence symbolized by the title of his debut collection, *Galgenfrist* (1958; respite from the gallows). His pessimistic viewpoint yields to an increasing socialist commitment during the 1960s and 1970s, while the two other significant poets of Malinovski's generation, Jørgen Gustava BRANDT and Jørgen Sonne (b. 1925) remain ideologically unengaged. Like Saint-John PERSE, Ezra POUND, and T. S. Eliot, Sonne moves in a comprehensive tradition and alludes in his texts to distant times and foreign cultures. A major motif in his poetry is the maturing process of man, most convincingly depicted in *Krese* (1963; cycles). The intellectual complexity of Sonne's poetry reaches its climax in *Huset* (1976; the house), which in its combination of observations, reflections, and visions is of strong emotional force and formal intricacy.

More accessible are the witty and ironical poetry and short stories of Benny ANDERSEN, who, moreover, perceives language not only as a means of creating poetic symbols but also as a means of cognition. This theory becomes increasingly predominant in Danish literature of the late 1960s. It found talented representatives in Poul Borum (1934–1996), Per HØJHOLT, and Hans-Jørgen Nielsen (1941–1991) and led to experiments with all levels of language and with typography. The high point of this philosophical and linguistic trend was Inger CHRISTENSEN's *Det* (1969; it), perhaps the most significant single poetic work of the 1960s.

The modernism in fiction of Villy Sørensen and Peter Seeberg, together with the influence of the French New Novel of Alain ROBBE-GRILLET and Nathalie SARRAUTE, led to a complete transformation of the structure of the novel and a destruction of the traditional plot. The boldest experimenter is Svend Åge MADSEN, whose *Otte gange orphan* (1965; eight times orphan) and *Tilføjelser* (1967; additions) are based on a relativistic view of the fictional world and frequent shifts in the narrative perspective. A new prose form was introduced with the semidocumentary novel *Tugt og utugt i mellemtiden* (1976; decency and indecency in the meantime), a political and social analysis of everyday life in Denmark of the 1970s, whereas in *Lad tiden gå* (1986; let time pass) the view is enlarged to include a more universal existential discussion.

In Sven Holm's (b. 1940) books a similar orientation gradually emerges. His first major work was a science-fiction novel, *Termush* (1967; *Termush*, 1969), which consists of diary entries by people who have sought refuge in an isolated hotel after World War III and live in a universe of sterility and powerlessness. In the novels *Det private liv* (1974; private life) and *Ægteskabsleg* (1977; marriage game) these themes are transposed to a contemporary setting.

The works of Madsen and Holm typify the increasing attention given to concrete reality that became significant in Danish literature after 1965. A forerunner of this trend is Thorkild HANSEN, who based his documentary accounts on historical material. Other models are to be found in contemporary Swedish literature and in the writings of Mary MCCARTHY. The most significant of these neorealists are Anders BODELSEN and Christian KAMPMANN. With great skill Bodelsen combines the realistic novel with the thriller or science-fiction genre in his sharp and critical accounts of today's welfare society. Kampmann's prose works are less satirical and more ironical in their acute psychological analyses of the Copenhagen bourgeoisie and their life style.

As a reaction to the linguistic experiments and the new matter-of-fact realism, a new romantic movement emerged on the threshold of the 1970s. In fiction its most convincing representative is Vagn Lundbye (b. 1933), whose revolutionary dreams of a new society of solidarity and beauty are expressed in such novels as *Tilbage til Anholt* (1978; back to Anholt) and *Hvalfisken* (1980; the whale). Mythology and ecological concern are intermigled in *Mythologisk rejse i et grønlandsk landskab* (1985; mythological journey in a greenland landscape) whereas pure mythology dominates Ib Michael's (b. 1943) best-selling novel *Kilroy kilroy* (1989). In poetry the sensitive and aestheticizing trend is carried further by Rolf Gjedsted (b. 1947), who combines it with psychedelic experiences and science fiction, and by Henrik NORDBRANDT, who adheres to an embellished and exotic surrealism with *Guds hus* (1977; god's house) he follows a metaphysical trend which becomes characteristic of many Danish writers of the 1980s such as Klaus Høeck (b. 1938) and Bo Green Jensen (b. 1955). Greater social interest is expressed by Kristen Bjørnkjær (b. 1943), who in 1976 published one of the most significant poetry collections of the decade, *Kærestesorg* (lover's grief), a deliberately trite re-creation of the joys and sorrows of love.

A direct continuation of the demand of the 1960s for political commitment is found in the so-called report genre, which entails studies of work environments done by students and the workers themselves, and, more particularly, in feminist writing. Of greater artistic value are, however, the novels by Henrik STANGERUP and Ole Hyltoft (b. 1940), which carry on the more diversified realism of the 1960s. Their strong satirical attacks on political opportunism and corruption are based on a humanistic concept of personal freedom and tolerance—key issues in older and modern Danish literature.

The documentary genre, combined with a political, although undogmatic awareness, has a representative in Ebbe REICH. In 1977 he published his version of the Cimbrian march against Rome around 100 B.C., *Fæ og frænde* (kith and kin). The author, clearly referring to the European Economic Community, which Denmark entered in 1973, makes Rome the prototype from which all evil emanates. Marianne LARSEN's writings deal with class struggle, political imperialism, and sex discrimination. Of greater intimacy are the two books by Vita Andersen (b. 1944), the poetry collection *Tryghedsnarkomaner* (1977; security addicts) and the short-story collection *Hold kæft og vær smuk* (1978; shut up and be beautiful), both revolving around experiences of childhood and places of work, as well as experiences of love and loneliness.

Søren Ulrik Thomsen (b. 1956) in his *City slang* (1982) focuses on the metropolis, whereas Pia Tafdrup (b. 1952) seeks to unite erotic experiences with impressions of nature. Characteristic is the title of her anthology, *Transformationer* (1985; Transformations), with which she presented her generation's poetry. Contemporary Danish literature is in a constant process of new departures and change. The writers do not form fixed schools. They are, on the contrary, prolific and productive individualists. They embody not only that undogmatic desire for experimentation but also for immersion in tradition, the most representative and most valuable elements in contemporary Danish literature.

Danish Literature since 1980

Most of the trends shaping Danish literature in the 1960s and 1970s continue in the following two decades. The neorealist novel retains its dominance. It was introduced by Anders BODELSEN and Christian KAMPMANN in the mid-1960s, analyzing the psychological impact of the modern welfare state. With his novel *Rolig flugt* (1974; quiet escape), the story of a middle-aged bureaucrat who tries to break with his previous life, the somewhat older Bent William Rasmussen (b. 1924) emerges as a gifted prose writer who develops the neorealist novel into a scathing account of a society in the process of rapid moral and political dissolution.

Already in the 1960s Thorkild HANSEN turned the neorealist novel into documentaries. Whereas Hansen employed historical material to elucidate contemporary existential problems, Ebbe REICH, since the 1970s, has continued his development of the documentary genre into a critique of contemporary politics. In the 1980s, a renewed interest in historical material focusing on personalities rather than periods becomes noticeable, with a series of biographical narratives, several of which have been translated into the major European languages. Particularly noteworthy is the three-volume series (1981–1991) by Henrik STANGERUP, structured on the philosophy of Søren Kierkegaard. Stangerup's sister, Helle Stangerup (b. 1939), a writer of detective novels, has been particularly successful with her portrayals from Danish national history, *Christine* (1985; *In the Courts of Power*, 1988), and *Spardame* (1989; queen of spades), whereas Dorrit Willumsen (b. 1940) chose an internationally known woman, Madame Tussaud, as the protagonist of her fascinating fictional account *Marie* (1983; *Marie*, 1986). The novel, like Willumsen's other works since her debut in 1965, is based on an experience of absurdity and loneliness, which makes us change roles to discover our own identity. Willumsen's interest in role problems received a masterful expression in a preceding novel, *Manden sompåskud* (1980; the man as pretext) which, incidentally, makes no distinction between the predicaments of modern man and woman, putting a distance between Willumsen and contemporary feminist writers, and, at the same time, indicates the change in direction in Danish women's literature since the 1960s and 1970s.

A particular subgenre within the documentary literature of the 1970s is the so-called confessional literature and the roman à clef. It was inspired by the focusing within the feminist movement on the more private aspects of human relations, and it was anticipated by the hidden autobiographical features in earlier works by Henrik Stangerup and Christian Kampmann. Indeed, a few years later they both contributed significantly to the confessional genre, as did the poet Tove Ditlevsen (1918–1976) with her novels *Gift* (1971; married/poison) and *Vilhelms værelse* (1975; Vilhelm's room), both merciless revelations of the destructive tendencies within marriage. Ditlevsen's novels were followed and partly imitated by a large number of less talented women writers, contributing—sometimes with a degree of sensationalism—to the breaking of taboos regarding alcoholism and sexuality.

Similar or related problems, but seen in a broader social context—often incorporating the motif of alienation in modern capitalist society—result in a partial return in the 1970s to the tradition of social realism of the 1930s and, like then, often accompanied by criticism of the establishment with distinct socialist undertones, focusing on the outsiders of the social mainstream. Whereas Ulrik Gräs (b. 1940) with his novel *Fatimas hånd* (1971; Fatima's hand) uses the milieu of the provinces as a backdrop for his attacks on the middle class, Kirsten Thorup (b. 1942) presented with epic breadth a much wider scope in her four-volume cross section of Danish society from the 1950s until today, which began with the novel *Lille Jonna* (little Jonna) in 1977. Thorup made her debut during the 1960s and was inspired by French absurdism and the psychiatry of R. D. Laing, which is reflected in her novel *Love from Trieste* (1969; *Love from Trieste*, 1980). Her first step toward describing a lower-class milieu was taken with the novel Baby (1973; Baby, 1980), but it is the books about Jonna that have made Thorup one of the most popular writers in today's Denmark. Like her great predecessor and model Martin Andersen NEXØ (1869–1954), Thorup manages—through an admirable myth-creating imagination—to raise her narrative above pure description, turning her characters and their dramatic fate into symbolic expressions of humankind's continuous striving toward a better and different life.

The realistic novel continues to find successful exponents during the 1980s. Jørgen Christian Hansen (1956–1989), in his trilogy *Guldsmeden* (1981; the goldsmith), *Hermelinen* (1982; the stoat), and *Knæleren* (1983; the praying mantis), offers fascinating insights into the world of childhood experience; Klaus Lynggaard (b. 1956), in his *Martin or Victoria* (1985; Martin and Victoria) and *Victorias år* (1986; Victoria's years), provides, in all likelihood, the most comprehensive portrayal of the 1970s. Whereas Lynggaard focuses on the experiences of youth, Arthur Krasilnikoff (b. 1941) uses the recollections of a woman suffering from cancer to render a picture of Denmark from the viewpoint of an older generation.

Due to relative political stability in the realm of foreign policy, Danish writers in the post-Vietnam War era are much less politically active—in connection with Denmark's entering the European Economic Community in 1972 political writing experienced a revival—but otherwise all political engagement takes the form of ecological debate. This development was furthered by the trend among a number of the Marxist-oriented writers of the 1960s, which Hans-Jørgen Nielsen (1941–1991) has labeled "attitudinal relativism." This forms the basis of his own works from the manifesto "*Nielsen*" og den hvide verden (1968; "Nielsen" and the white world) to the novel *Fodboldenglen* (1979; the soccer angel). This relativistic approach rejects the existence of set political norms in the same way as it denies the possibility of comprehending reality as something absolute.

The same turning-away from militant positions can be noticed in women's literature, which after 1968 launched provocative attacks—fictive and nonfictive—on a male dominated and oppressive society. Initially, a series of documentary reports were issued, such as *Kvinder på fabrik* (1971; women in factories) or *Kvindernes*

bog (1972; women's book), which were succeeded by more personal, subjective accounts, such as Suzanne Brøgger's (b. 1944) *Fri os fra kærligheden* (1974; *Deliver Us from Love*, 1976). Brøgger provides an excellent example of the development of Danish feminist literature, maturing into discussions of gender roles and moving from semidocumentary or autobiographical accounts, such as the kaleidoscopic *Crème fraîche* (1978; sour cream), toward pure fiction, such as the highly acclaimed epic poem *Tone* (1981; Tone). Brøgger's continued, unorthodox attempt at orienting herself in the contemporary world is also, mixed with religious elements, reflected in her latest work, *Den pebrede susen* (1986; the peppery soughing).

Whereas Brøgger's works are primarily public displays of her private life, other women writers choose a more general social—sometimes political—context. Charlotte Strandgaard (b. 1943) in her novel *Lille menneske* (1982; little human being) subscribed to a psychological approach; Inge Eriksen (b. 1935) displayed a more political orientation; Dea Trier Mørch (b. 1941) wrote a best-selling collective novel about a group of women in a Copenhagen maternity ward, *Vinterbørn* (1976; *Winter's Child*, 1986), abandoning her previous leftist orientation in a stirring account of solidarity and compassion.

Also within poetry there is a development away from programmatic feminism. The early 1970s were dominated by poetry collections that in many cases can only claim to be poetry by being printed in the form of shorter lines, which earned them the derogatory label of "broken prose." Granted, the poetry of Marianne LARSEN also deals with gender roles and sex discrimination. But it is removed from the intimate sphere of the majority of the works of "broken prose" in her advocacy of the liberation of the abandoned individual within the framework of political liberation, of a dream of community as expressed in the title of *Der er et håb i mit hoved* (1981; there is a hope in my head). Larsen's latest collections, *Hvor du er* (1987; where you are) and *I timerne og udenfor* (1987; in hours and outside), do mark a stronger orientation toward the personal realm in line with the general trend of the 1980s.

The linguistic experiments of the so-called systemic or concrete poets, like Inger CHRISTENSEN and Per HØJHOLT, and of a prose writer such as Svend Åge MADSEN, who established structures or "systems" of language material as sound, syntax, or image as means and origin of cognition, developed in the 1980s, under the influence of the linguistic theories of Ludwig Wittgenstein (1889–1951), into an even more scripturally oriented approach in the works of Jens Smærup Sørensen (b. 1946), Peter Laugesen (b. 1942), Henning Mortensen (b. 1939), and the younger Dan TURÈLL. To them *language* is identical with petrifaction and conformity, whereas *script* expresses rebellion, something that is alive and liberating. Klaus Høeck (b. 1938) recast language as a mirror of the problems of reality's unending mass of material by working with mathematical paradigms to structure his five-volume work *Rejse* (1971–1973; journey). His poetry collection of 608 pages, *Hjem* (1985; home), a grandiose attempt to encircle God, is a major work of the 1980s and can be seen as one avenue of "escaping" the linguistic system.

Generally, with all of the systemic writers an orientation toward the outer world took place. Inger Christensen and Svend Åge Madsen comment increasingly on contemporary events, Smærup Sørensen moved via exact realism toward the fantastic in his novel *Mit danske kød* (1980; my Danish flesh), and Højholt abandons his experiments in *Turbo* (1968; turbo), in which language has become

575

depersonalized to a degree that the poet lets a swirl of words spread more or less accidentally all over the pages, in favor of the realistic and humorous, and quite popular, *Gittes monologer* (1981–1983; Gitte's monologues). With his novel *Vangebilleder* (1975; pictures from Vangede) Turèll has replaced his previous systemic, computer-generated poetry with topographic realism, in his succeeding works incorporating beat and rock music as well as the detective genre in a flow of books of greatly fluctuating quality but always provocative and characterized by a skillful command of the smallest nuances of the language.

A central feature of women's literature since the 1960s has been the placement of alternative values against the norms of a rationalist and technological society. This feature is not only a question of focusing more strongly on feelings and emotional experiences, but is also expressed in grassroot movements to fight pollution and the destruction of the environment. Chief works in this ecologically oriented literature are the older Thorkild BJØRNVIG's poetry collections *Abeguder* (1981; monkey gods) and *Epimeteus* (1990; Epimeteus). Bjørnvig's ecological poems express an organic interdependence with animals, plants, and the earth's resources, an orientation that, during the 1970s, in the prose works of Ib Michael (b. 1943) and Vagn Lundbye (b. 1933) encompasses a sincere fascination with nature peoples who treat the natural world with greater sensitivity than our Western industrial society: Lapps, Eskimos, and Native Americans. A pronounced interest in their myths and religious beliefs is reflected in Lundbye's *Alvidende fortællinger* (1986; omniscient tales), whereas Michael's latest book, the best-selling *Kilroy Kilroy* (1989; Kilroy Kilroy) is a supenseful novel of identity.

The overall development of Danish literature within the last twenty years from an exclusive, modernistic, and experimenting attitude to a linguistic and stylistic openness and thematic accessibility stressing the aesthetic values of literature peaks in the 1980s, in particular among the poets of the decade. A work that both corresponds to this characteristic and, at the same time, also with supreme forcefulness eludes any categorization is the 537 prose-lyrical monologues entitled *Requiem* (1985; requiem) by Peer HULTBERG. In this monumental work Hultberg has laid open the complex concerns and questions of contemporary civilization, analyzing its emptiness and richness, its fragmentation and coherence.

In general, the poets of the 1980s are individualists not concerned with sociological or ideological analyses but rather with their own sensitive selves as they are exposed to impressions from the world of the media, pop culture, and breathtaking technology. Michael Strunge (1958–1986) came to be the almost cultist figurehead of this new generation, voicing disorientation and despair in a series of nine explosive and high-strung, often surrealist poetry collections. F. P. Jac (b. 1955), a brilliant linguistic equilibrist, protects himself in a poetic universe created around his self as the omniscient center, disrespectfully raiding Danish poetic tradition as well as contemporary slang.

Poetic tradition, in particular the sources of symbolism and early modernism, are rediscovered: Baudelaire, Mallarmá, and Rimbaud, as well as T. S. ELIOT and Ezra POUND, blending with texts often inspired by rock and punk musicians, such as Bob Dylan and David Bowie. This eclectic—or rather postmodernist—approach finds its most talented expression in Bo Green Jensen's (b. 1955) seven-volume cycle of poems, *Rosens veje* (the roads of the rose), completed in 1986. More subdued and reflective are the poems of Søren Ulrik Thomsen (b. 1956), notably in collections

from *City Slang* (1982; title in English) to *Nye digte* (1987; new poems), analyzing the creative process and the role of the poem as the point of departure for experiencing present life. The poetry of Pia TAFDRUP is characterized by the same lucidity and speculative sophistication. Since her debut in 1981 and reaching a highpoint with *Hvid feber* (1986; white fever), she has continuously attempted to merge her experiences of the erotic and of nature and her awareness of the necessity both to dream and to live this life, into images of rhythmic and sensual beauty.

Contemporary Danish literature is both dynamic and innovative. The topics seem endless: physical and spiritual love, euphoric experiences and Apocalypse, the stony wilderness of the metropolis, provincial idylls and distant exotic places and mythical utopias.

BIBLIOGRAPHY: Topsøe-Jensen, H., *Scandinavian Literature from Brandes to Our Day* (1929); Bredsdorff, E., *Danish Literature in English Translation: A Bibliography* (1950); Mitchell, P. M., *A Bibliographical Guide to Danish Literature* (1951); Claudi, J., *Contemporary Danish Authors* (1952); Mitchell, P. M., *A History of Danish Literature*, 2nd ed. (1971); Borum, P., *Danish Literature* (1979); Rossel, S. H., *A History of Scandinavian Literature, 1870–1980* (1981); Wamberg, B., ed., *Out of Denmark* (1985); Zuck, V., ed., *Dictionary of Scandinavian Literature* (1990); Rossel, S. H., ed., *A History of Danish Literature* (1993)

—SVEN H. ROSSEL

Faroese Literature

Few would deny that the medieval ballad is the most important Faroese contribution to world literature. Until the establishment of a Faroese orthography in the second half of the 19th c., it was the basis of Faroese culture, and it is still recited and danced to—and still serves as the inspiration for modern literature. With the advent of a Faroese orthography, a number of writers, such as Rasmus Effersøe (1857–1916), Jens Hendrik Oliver Djurhuus (1881–1948), and his brother Hans Andrias Djurhuus (1883–1951) gave the impetus to a modern literature both by way of translations (particularly on the part of Effersøe) and original prose, verse, and drama.

It was, however, the second generation of Faroese writers who really established their literature on a level with that of other European countries. Foremost is William Heinesen (b. 1900), who, ironically enough, writes exclusively in Danish, and whose works range from postsymbolist poetry through satirical and historical novels to short stories in a modernist, experimental style. His themes are social on the surface, but underneath he is concerned with man's place in the universe and with the conflict between life and death forces. This combination emerges clearly in *De fortabte spillemænd* (1950; *The Lost Musicians*, 1971), his best novel, and in *Moder Syvstjerne* (1952; *The Kingdom of the Earth*, 1974). Similar themes are found in Jørgen-Frantz Jacobsen's (1900–1938) *Barbara* (1939; *Barbara*, 1948), a historical novel based on a Faroese legend and also written in Danish.

Two outstanding Faroese-language writers belong to the same generation: Christian Matras (b. 1900), whose poetry reflects a profound consciousness of Faroese nature and history, the culture of the outlying settlements; and Heoðin Brú (b. 1901), whose novels combine the tensions inherent in a rapidly changing society with more general personal, family problems. *Feoðgar á ferð*

(1940; *The Old Man and His Sons*, 1970) is outstanding among them, humorously portraying the conflict of the old and the new cultures of the Faroe Islands as seen through the behavior of a simple family. In their descriptions of life in Faroese fishing villages, Martin Joensen's (1902–1966) novels are related to those of Heoðin Brú.

The mixture of particularly Faroese social themes and the wider concern with human relationships reappears in the work of younger writers. This is particularly so in the prose of Jens Pauli Heinesen (b. 1932), whose principal novel is the three-volume *Tú upphavsins heimur* (1962–66; oh world from which I come), dealing satirically with the power human beings exert on one another, and the poetry of Karsten Hoydal (b. 1912). Regin Dahl (b. 1918), who writes in both Faroese and Danish, is basically traditional in his poetry, while the younger poets like Steinbjørn Jacobsen (b. 1937) and Guoðrioð Helmsdal (b. 1941) are more experimental.

BIBLIOGRAPHY: Brønner, H., Introduction to *Faroese Short Stories* (1972): 1–10; R., West. J., *Faroe* (1972): 234–43; Jones, W. G., *Faroe and Cosmos* (1974); *Faroe Isles Review* (1976 ff.); Jones, W. G., "From Kingo to Matras," in H. Bekker-Nielsen, et al., eds., *Nordisk litteraturhistorie* (1978): 314–27

—W. GLYN JONES

D'ANNUNZIO, Gabriele

Italian poet, journalist, novelist, dramatist, and political writer, b. 12 March 1863, Francavilla; d. 1 March 1938, Gardone

D. is considered the best interpreter of European Decadence in post-Risorgimento Italy. In a late-romantic style he combined naturalism and SYMBOLISM, bringing to Italian prose and poetry the ferment of the new ideas that agitated European art at the turn of the century. He absorbed ideas and ideals that brought about a vigorous rejuvenation of forms and language. Based on transfiguring images, which reflect a sensitive inner self, his evocative style conveyed erotic nuances that greatly influenced his generation. The best of his poetry retains its value today.

D.'s first collection of poems, *Primo vere* (1879; in early spring), appeared when he was still in high school in Prato. Later he moved to Rome, where he attended the university and participated fully in the capital's social and cultural life while reporting about it for various newspapers and magazines. In 1882 D. published *Canto novo* (new song), which reflected the many facets of the sensual personality of the poet. In a world reduced artistically to images based on touch, smell, sight, and sound, he elevates the senses to a level of mystical bliss. *Terra vergine* (virgin land) appeared the same year, showing in prose the same elements that characterized his poetry. Even in apparently realistic descriptions it is always a sensitized self that responds to observed reality. This sensually heightened self is the center of his artistic interest. *Intermezzo di rime* (1883; interlude of poems) reflects a morbid languor, a sensual and sad tiredness, but not in response to actual psychological torment. The novel *Il piacere* (1889; *The Child of Pleasure*, 1898) was followed by the poems in *Chimera* (1890; chimera), the two psychological novels *Giovanni Episcopo* (1892; *Episcopo & Co.*, 1896), and *L'innocente* (1892; *The Intruder*, 1898), the

collections of poems *Elegie romane* (1892; Roman elegies), and *Poema paradisiaco* (1893; celestial poem), and the novel *Trionfo della morte* (1894; *The Triumph of Death*, 1896). In *Trionfo della morte*, Giorgio Aurispa, the hypersensitive protagonist, wavers between lucidity and madness.

By the turn of the century D.'s style was distinct and unmistakable. The erotic charge that characterizes his work is produced by rhetorical, evocative repetitions, esoteric neologisms, resurrected archaic terms, and an all-pervasive youthful exuberance tempered by anxiety that reflects an unquenched thirst. D.'s craving for a sensual, unachievable fullness led to the image of the artist as unsatisfied, super-sensitive creator. With his visionary, excited imagination, he opened the way to a concept of super-morality for super-beings, which after he became acquainted with Nietzsche's works was transformed into an aesthetic and philosophical system of art. His superman asserts his superior sensuousness and sets himself above common morality, creating his own rules and his own moral law. The same vision of life and art led this poet-politician to an exaggerated nationalism—and ultimately, in the 1920s and 1930s, to his support of Mussolini: D. saw the dictator's brand of nationalism and patriotism as rising above the masses and accompanied by the celebratory praise of heroes in a mythical representation of the spirit of the nation.

The heroic, evocative rhythms of *Maia* (1903; Maia), the glorifying epic of *Elettra* (1903; Electra), the Pan-like sensuousness of *Alcyone* (1904; *Alcyone*), and the patriotic songs of *Merope* (1913; Merope) show D.'s inexhaustible lyric imagery, which at times reaches moments of lasting artistic greatness, regardless of their content and meaning.

In 1909 D. went to Paris, ostensibly to join his new lover, but in reality to escape his creditors. While in France he wrote a number of works in French. He returned home in 1915 to advocate Italy's entry into the war on the side of France.

In the final phase of his prolific career D. revealed his feelings about various moments of his life and art—so intertwined that it was impossible to differentiate between the inspired aesthete and the histrionic demagogue, the lover and the artist, the hero and the actor.

D.'s love affairs, particularly his love relationship with the world-famous actress Eleonora Duse, his heroic and daring exploits during World War I as a pilot and as a sailor, and his occupation of Fiume in 1919 to claim the Dalmatian territory for Italy made him a legend in his own time. The amalgam of his life and his art, however, appeared to some critics as "sophomoric sensualism" compared to the more sedate period of his life, the meditative moments of the disillusioned lover-poet-hero, which produced works of lasting value.

FURTHER WORKS: *San Pantaleone* (1886); *Le vergini delle rocce* (1896; *The Maidens of the Rocks*, 1898); *La città morta* (1898; *The Dead City*, 1902); *La Gioconda* (1899; *La Gioconda*, 1902); *Sogno d'un mattino di primavera* (1899; *The Dream of a Spring Morning*, 1902; *The Dream of an Autumn Sunset*, 1904); *Il fuoco* (1900; *The Flame of Life*, 1900); *Francesca da Rimini* (1901; *Francesca da Rimini*, 1902); *La figlia di Jorio* (1903; *The Daughter of Jorio*, 1907); *La fiaccola sotto il moggio* (1905); *Più che l'amore* (1907); *La nave* (1908); *Fedra* (1909); *Le martyre de Saint Sebastien* (1911); *Contemplazione della morte* (1912); *La Pisanelle; ou, La mort parfumée* (1913); *Le chevrefeuille* (1914); *Notturno* (1921); *Il venturiero senza ventura* (1924); *Il compagno dagli occhi senza cigli* (1928); *Opera omnia* (1927–36); *Cento e cento e cento e cento pagine del libro segreto* (1935)

BIBLIOGRAPHY: James, H., "G. D." (1904), in *Notes on Novelists* (1914): 245–93; Winwar, F., *Wingless Victory: A Dual Biography of G. D. and Eleanora Duse* (1956); Rhodes, A., *D.: The Poet as Superman* (1960); Blissett, W., "D. H. Lawrence, D., Wagner," *WSCL*, 7 (1966): 21–46; Hastings, R., "D.'s Theatrical Experiment," *MLR*, 66 (1971): 85–93; Maixner, P., "James on D.: A High Example of Exclusive Estheticism," *Criticism*, 13 (1971): 291–311; Jullian, P., *D.* (1972); Mosse, G. L., "The Poet and the Exercise of Political Power: G. D.," *YCGL*, 22 (1973): 32–41

—GAETANO A. IANNACE

DARGIN LITERATURE

See North Caucasian Literatures

DARI LITERATURE

See Afghan Literature

DARÍO, Rubén

(pseud. of Félix Rubén García Sarmiento) Nicaraguan poet, short-story writer, essayist, critic, and journalist, b. 18 Jan. 1867, Metapa (now Ciudad Dario); d. 6 Feb. 1916, León

D.'s childhood and early youth lacked the security of customary parental concern but did have the guidance of solicitous relatives and friends who recognized his talent. Even so, an atmosphere of anguish, moral distress, and melancholy infiltrate his writings whenever he refers to the ambiguous circumstances and events of his early years. The loss of his young wife, Rafaela Contreras, and an infelicitous second marriage contributed to confirm his view of life as a state of uncertainty constantly at the mercy of capricious destiny, and of being itself as an enigma within multiple enigmas. His active sensuality was always in conflict with his religious and spiritual values, a conflict that resulted in periods of great remorse. But although he doubted and wondered, he never ceased to cling to his Catholic faith as a refuge from a life filled with intemperance and tribulation and plagued by lack of money.

D.'s literary career covered approximately sixteen years in both the 19th and 20th cs. His travels took him from his native Nicaragua to Chile (1888–1889); to various Central American countries, notably to Guatemala (1890); to Madrid (1892) as a member of Nicaragua's commission to the Quadricentennial Celebration of the New World's discovery; to New York and Paris (1893); to Argentina (1893–1898); and to Europe (Spain, France, 1898–1915).

Francisco Gavidia (1863–1955) of El Salvador introduced D. to French literature and especially to Victor Hugo, whose works influenced the style and tone of D.'s first writings. In Chile his literary mentors were Eduardo de la Barra (1893–1900), Pedro

Rubén Darío

Balmaceda (1868–1889, son of Chile's president), and writers for *La época, Revista de arte y letras*, and other publications on which D. collaborated. Through these friends and the resources of editorial offices he had easy access to current French books and reviews.

In 1888 appeared *Azul* (blue), which, after its review by Juan Valera (1824–1905) in *El imparcial* (Madrid), brought international recognition to D. and to MODERNISM, Spanish America's first widely recognized contribution to world literature. D. characterized *Azul*, which consists of stories and poetry, as a Parnassian book and therefore French in nature.

In 1893 D. was appointed Colombia's consul in Buenos Aires, through the good offices of that country's ex-president and eminent poet, Rafael Núñez (1825–1894). His five-year sojourn in that city was one of the most productive periods of his career. In 1894, in collaboration with Ricardo Jaimes Freyre (1872–1933), he founded the *Revista de América*, the Hispanic world's first review oriented toward SYMBOLISM. He published *Prosas profanas, y otros poemas* (1896; *Profane Hymns and Other Poems*, 1922), whose musicality, chromaticism, and thematic affinities reflect the influence of the Parnassians and especially of Paul Verlaine, whom he had met in Paris. *Los raros* (1896; mavericks) was a volume of essays on writers associated with symbolism.

Cantos de vida y esperanza (1905; songs of life and hope) is considered by some to be D.'s most significant work. In the initial stanzas of "Yo soy aquel que ayer no más decía" ("I am the man," 1943) D. recalls the images of nightingales, swans, doves, gondolas, lakes, and roses; 18th-c. reminiscences; and the admixture of the ancient and the modern and of the audacity and cosmopolitanism that were hallmarks of his previous work. This imagery of the Parnassians and of Verlaine is mostly absent from the rest of *Cantos de vida y esperanza*, the themes of which run the gamut from optimism to doubt to despair and to salvation through Christian faith. For example, the defeat of Spain strengthened his devotion to that nation and to Hispanism; the poems "Salutaciøn del optimista" ("The Optimist's Salutation," 1965), "Letanía de nuestro señor Don Quixote" ("Litany for Our Lord Don Quixote," 1928), "A Roosevelt" ("To Roosevelt," 1965), all attest to D.'s Hispanic nationalism and involved political awareness. On the other hand, the image of the swan's neck, formerly a symbol of purity, gracious harmony, and aristocratic dignity, now is seen as a question mark that denotes conjectures on the destiny of Hispanism and the meaning of life itself. Thus, apprehension about loss of youth's divine treasures is expressed in "Canción de otoño en primavera" ("An Autumn Song in Spring," 1943); the deploring of D.'s lack of direction in a bitter world in "Melancolía" ("Melancholy," 1965); how time has changed his muse in "De otoño" ("In Autumn," 1965); anguished evocations during sleepless nights in "Nocturno" ("You have heard the heart beat . . ." 1965); and corrosive reflections in "Lo fata" ("Fatality," 1965), a poem that contains the elements of existentialist thought. Counteracting such pessimism, however, is the optimism of faith expressed in "Canto de esperanza" ("Song of Hope," 1965) and in "Spes" ("Hope," 1965).

D.'s reputation as a poet has traditionally overshadowed his merits as a short-story writer, critic, thinker, aesthetician, and essayist, which are considerable. Since the worldwide observances of the centennial anniversary of D.'s birth in 1967, however, there has been a greater awareness of the comprehensive nature of D.'s literary achievements. The "Darío Week" (January 14–21) that Nicaragua officially sponsored in honor of its most illustrious citizen contributed much to fuller understanding of D.'s works.

The modernist tendency in Hispanic literature crested in D.'s writings. He made innovations in Spanish versification through experiments in unusual meters or combinations of meters, and added color, novel imagery, and musicality to the Spanish language; he enriched literary texts with mythological allusions and philosophical and metaphysical undertones; he went beyond the thematic limitations of romanticism and regionalism by drawing on the vast reservoirs of cosmopolitan culture, expression, and experience. But above all, his poetry (and some of his prose) has that rare originality of language that is numinous, unalterable, and mysterious, a quality necessarily present in the work of all great poets.

FURTHER WORKS: *Abrojos* (1887); *España contemporánea* (1901); *La caravana pasa* (1903); *El canto errante* (1907); *El viaje a Nicaragua* (1909); *Poema del otoño* (1910); *Autobiografía* (1912); *Semblanzas* (1912); *Impresiones y sensaciones* (1925); *Cuentos completos de R. D.* (1950); *Escritos dispersos de R. D.* (1968); *Poesías completas* (1967); *Obras completas* (5 vols., 1951–1955). FURTHER WORKS IN ENGLISH: *Selected Poems of R. D.* (1965)

BIBLIOGRAPHY: Mapes, E. K., *L'influence française dans l'œuvre de R. D.* (1925); Torres, E., *La dramática vida de R. D.* (1952); Oliver Belmás, A., *Este otro Rubén* (1960); Watland, C. D., *Poet-errant: A Biography of R. D.* (1965); Carter, B. G., *La "Revista de América" de R. D. y Ricardo Jaimes Freyre* (1967); Jirón Terán, J., *Bibliografía general de R. D., 1883–1967* (1967); Torres Bodet, J., *R. D.—abismo y cima* (1967); Mejía Sánchez, E., *Estudios sobre R. D.* (1968); Greco, A. A. del, *Repertorio bibliográfico del mundo de R. D.* (1969); Woodbridge, H. C., *R. D.: A Selective Classified and Annotated Bibliography* (1975)

—BOYD G. CARTER

DARWĪSH, Mahmūd

Palestinian poet, b. 13 Mar. 1941, Birwa, Palestine (now Israel)

D. is by far the best-known Palestinian poet alive. He was born in Birwa, a small village near Acre. During the war of 1948, his family, like so many others, fled the advancing Israeli army to Lebanon, where they lived as refugees for one year. When they "infiltrated" back into Israel, Birwa was no longer in existence. It had been razed by the Israeli army, and a new Jewish settlement stood on its ruins. The family relocated to another Arab village where D. grew up as an "internal" refugee. These traumatic childhood experiences of uprootedness and dislocation left an indelible mark on the poet's nascent consciousness.

By way of formal education, D. attended only elementary and secondary Arab schools in Galilee. After graduating from secondary school, he moved to Haifa to work in journalism. In 1961 he joined the Israeli Communist Party and remained active in its ranks until his permanent departure from Israel in 1971. Since then he has led a somewhat nomadic life, moving from one to another of the following capitals: Cairo, Beirut, London, Paris, and Tunis. He has been active in Palestinian national politics and has occupied several important positions in the cultural apparatus of the Palestine Liberation Organization. Currently, he is a member of the PLO's Executive Committee and chief editor of the Palestinian literary and cultural periodical *al-Karmel*, which is published in Nicosia. In 1969 D. was awarded the Lotus Prize by the Union of Afro-Asian Writers.

D. began writing poetry at an early age. His first collection, *'Asāfīr bilā ajniha* (1960; wingless birds), appeared when he was only nineteen. Mostly traditional, in form and style, the love lyrics of this collection have a modest artistic value. For this reason the poet disregarded this collection when compiling his collected works, which began to appear in 1973. It was his second collection, *Awrāq al-zaytūn* (1964; olive leaves), that established his reputation and gained him the epithet "poet of the Palestinian resistance," by which he is still widely known in much of the Arab world.

In general, it is possible to distinguish three distinct phases in D.'s poetry. The first phase spans the period before his departure from Israel in 1971, the second from 1971 to 1982, and the third from 1982 to the present. Thematically, D.'s poetry deals with little else besides the loss of Palestine. In fact, it is so steeped in Palestinian affairs that some knowledge of Palestinian history may be necessary for the proper appreciation of the poetry. But, while D.'s preoccupation with Palestinian concerns has remained constant, his treatment of these concerns has varied and evolved considerably through the years.

Like all the poems of the first phase, the poems of *Awrāq al-zaytūn* deal with two general topics: love and politics. The political poems stand out for their powerful polemics and fiercely defiant tone. Against Zionist claims on Palestine, they affirm the indissoluble historical bond between Palestinians and their land. A primary objective of these poems is precisely this: to strengthen the resolve of the Palestinian peasants in resisting Israeli attempts to dislodge them from their ancestral land. All artistic and aesthetic considerations are strictly subordinated here to this political imperative. Hence the simple form and direct style of these poems. D.'s poetic credo of this phase, contained in his poem "'An al-shi'r" (1964; "On Poetry," 1980), celebrates clarity as the highest virtue of poetry.

This combination of political and rhetorical qualities found a responsive chord in the Arab reading public. Some of D.'s best-known patriotic poems, such as "Bitāqat huwiyyah" (1964; "Identity Card," 1970) date from this early phase and are included in this collection. And although D. himself has long since outgrown the direct declamatory style of these poems and refuses to read them in public, most Arab readers know him for little else.

The image of an open wound is the dominant metaphor for Palestine in D.'s poetry. The pained awareness of loss and injury that pervades these poems, however, is largely alleviated by two positive factors that give D.'s poetry during this phase an optimistic outlook. The first factor is the moral rightness of the Palestinian cause. The second is the assumed solidarity of national liberation movements with the Palestinian people. Being a Marxist, D. assumed the inevitable success of the struggle for national liberation throughout the world, including Palestine. Incidentally, Palestine, in the poems of this phase, is exclusively identified with the peasantry and the working class.

The love poems of Awrāq al-zaytūn foreshadow the eventual transformation of the beloved female into the beloved homeland that is characteristic of D.'s subsequent poetry. The transformation appears complete in D.'s next collection, 'Āshiq min filastīn (1966; A Lover from Palestine, 1970). This intimate love relationship between poet and land grows steadily more intense until it reaches the fervor of mystical union in D.'s later poems.

D.'s encounter with the reality of the Arab world proved disillusioning and occasioned a withdrawal from certainty and an inward turn in his poetry. The common things of daily life in the homeland, such as the faces of family and friends and the topography of the landscape, become the object of poetic meditation in exile. A gripping note of nostalgia to Galilee, Haifa, Mount Carmel, and the coast of Palestine reverberates through the poems of the second phase. D.'s first collection in exile, Uhibbuki aw lā uhibbuki (1972; I love you, I love you not), suggests the direction and scope of the change in his poetry. Away from the homeland, it becomes a constant struggle to retain intact the details of its identifying characteristics. The words picture, memory, and dream join those of wound and death as key terms in D.'s poetic diction. In the working of dream and memory the body of the beloved female blends imperceptibly with that of the homeland until they become virtually indistinguishable.

While the introspective turn imparts to D.'s poetry a more personal, almost confessional quality, his progressively more frequent appeal to the prophetic tradition of the three great monotheistic religions imparts to it a universal dimension. The cross, crucifixion, and especially wounds and sacrificial death are permanent motifs (tropes) in D.'s poetry. D. also makes extensive use of the Old Testament prophets, notably Isaiah and Jeremiah on whom he frequently calls to condemn Israel's acts of injustice against the Palestinians. Uhibbuki aw lā uhibbuki begins with seventeen psalms to Palestine. In tone and style D.'s moving lamentations echo those of the Old Testament which D., being bilingual in Arabic and Hebrew, is able to read in the original.

D.'s poetic output has continued unabated during the third phase. Two important poems he wrote after the 1982 Israeli invasion of Lebanon, however, have already left a strong mark on this phase. Both Qasīdat Bayrūt (1982; ode to Beirut) and Madīh al-zill al-'ālī (1983; a eulogy for the tall shadow) are narrative poems of substantial length. The subject of both is the heroic Palestinian resistance to the Israeli siege of Beirut during the summer of 1982. Following the tradition of the classical Arab poets, D. abandons the subjective voice of the lyricist and sings the collective heroics of his people in the plural voice. Stanzaic in form, both poems mark a return to a simpler, more direct, and clearer style than the poems of the second phase. Of the two poems, the second is considerably longer and more accomplished artistically. It introduces into modern Arabic poetry the city (Beirut) and the sea (Mediterranean) as objects of sustained poetic interest. But it also continues D.'s cultivation of the prophetic voice. Here, D. assumes the voice of the Prophet of Islam, Muhammad, to chastise the Arab régimes for abandoning the Palestinians and the Lebanese to the Israeli onslaught. D.'s harshest invectives are reserved for the oil-rich Arab monarchies. No other modern Arab poet has used the language, style, and motifs of the Koran and the prophetic tradition as effectively as does D. in this poem.

FURTHER WORKS: Ākhir al-layl (1967); Yawmiyyāt jurh filastīnī (1969); al-'Asāfīr tamūt fī al-jalīl (1970); Muhāwalah raqm 7 (1974); Tilka sūratuhā wa-hādhā intihār al-'āshiq (1975); Ahmad al-za'tar (1976); A'rās (1977); Hiya ughniyah (1986); Dhākirah li-al-nisyān (1986); Fī wasf hālatinā (1987). FURTHER WORKS IN ENGLISH: Selected Poems (1973); The Music of Human Flesh (1980); Victims of a Map (1984, with Samīh al-Qāsim and Adonis); Sand and Other Poems (1986)

BIBLIOGRAPHY: Al-Messiri, A. W., and K. Boullata, Introduction to A Lover from Palestine (1970): 5–11; Johnson-Davies, D., Introduction to The Music of Human Flesh (1980): 7–19; Bennani, B., "Translating Arabic Poetry: An Interpretive, Intertextual Approach," in Rose, M. G., ed., Translation Spectrum: Essays in Theory and Practice (1981): 135–39; Backmann, P., "Pushkin's Eagle and M. D.'s Nest," in al-Qadi, W., ed., Studia Arabica et Islamica (1981): 27–37; "Three Poems," IonC, 13, 4 (Aug. 1984): 30–32; McBeath, N., "On the Translation of Poetry: Further Comments," The Linguist, 25, 2 (1986): 74–76

—MUHAMMAD SIDDIQ

DAS, Jibanananda

Indian poet (writing in Bengali), b. 18 Feb. 1899, Barisal, British India (now Bangladesh); d. 22 Oct. 1954, Calcutta

D. grew up in Barisal, a small town on the northeastern edge of the Sundarban jungle, some fifty miles inland from the Bay of Bengal. He received his education first at home from his parents, later in a local school and college, and then in Calcutta, earning his M. A. in English at Calcutta University. D. taught English literature at various colleges in Calcutta, Delhi, and Barisal. A shy person, he avoided politics and social interactions generally, acquiring early on the epithet of the "most alone of poets." In 1946, anticipating the independence of the subcontinent from Britain the following year with the concomitant partition of Bengal into East Pakistan and the province of West Bengal in India, D. left his beloved ancestral home for good and moved with his family to what was for him the inimical environment of big-city Calcutta.

D.'s initial book was of little consequence. His second volume, *Dūsara pāndulipi* (1936; gray manuscripts), contains the exotic West-Asian imagery typical of D.'s earlier writings, as well as two features that can be said to be his poetic signature: deep involvement in his natural surroundings and interaction with a fantasized, idealized woman who is at times solace incarnate and at other times the cause of his great psychological distress. "Kyāmpe" (1932; "In Camp," 1962) from this collection speaks with revulsion of a deer hunt using for decoy a doe in heat, which as a metaphor becomes "that woman" who allures her victim to emotional death.

Between the publication of his first and second books, D. composed—but never published—a series of sonnets posthumously titled *Rūpasī Bāmlā* (1957; *The Beauteous Bengal: Rupasi Bangla*, 1987) in which he luxuriated in the flora and fauna of his subtropical birthplace. Though a song by Rabindranath TAGORE became Bangladesh's national anthem, D.'s sonnets epitomized for the Bangladeshi freedom fighters during the independence struggle in 1971 the very essence of their homeland. D.'s third volume, *Banalatā Sena* (1942; Banalata Sena)—republished twice in his lifetime in expanded editions—was named for his most famous poem, "Banalatā Sena" (1935; "Banalata Sen," 1962) whose eponymous heroine succors the poet-narrator both in this lonely and exhausting life and for the thousands of years his spirit has wandered throughout the Indian subcontinent.

The advent of World War II and the pressure from politically committed fellow writers may have, during the late 1930s and 1940s, nudged D. into looking away from his personalized universe and toward the greater world. His fourth book, *Mahāprthibā* (1944; world at large), included all the poems from the *Banalatā Sena* volume plus a number of lyrics that reflect consternation and sometimes utter confusion about the plight at present, and the future of humanity—including the powerful "āta bachara āgera ekadina" (1938; "A Day Eight Years Ago," 1962) in which he tries to fathom the suicide of an acquaintance. D.'s fifth and last volume to contain all new poetry, *Sātati tārāra timira* (1948; darkness of seven stars), reveals a continuation of the befuddlement engendered in him by the war years. The "darkness" mentioned in the title pervades this collection. An expanded *Banalatā Sena*, replete with more poetry from the earlier prewar period, appeared in 1952 to considerable public acclaim. The anthology *Jābanānanda Dāśera śrestha kabitā* (1954; best poems of J. D.) garnered India's first-ever Sahitya Akademi Prize (1955) for Bengali, a national literary award.

Though known primarily as a poet, D. wrote novels and short stories, none of them published during his lifetime, however. The three seemingly complete novels date from the latter half of the 1940s, around the time or just after D. moved permanently to Calcutta, and have noticeable autobiographical elements.

As more and more of D.'s unpublished poetry and prose becomes available, there may be some re-evaluation of what are his finest contributions to Bengali literature, but his ranking as a poet is quite likely secure. The majority of critics consider him the second most important Bengali poet of the century, second only to Tagore. D.'s language could not be imitated by subsequent poets, for as Buddhadeva Bose (1908–1974)—D.'s first, initially most supportive, and, to date, most enduring critic—stated, D. created a language all his own, a mix of high style and colloquial, of indigenous and foreign words. D.'s example, while inimitable, emboldened others. His sensuous depiction of the Bengal countryside may never be surpassed. His poetry from the 1940s and 1950s, more obtuse than his earlier work, has yet to be comprehended

thoroughly and appreciated. It is D.'s poetry of the late 1920s and the 1930s upon which his reputation was made and still stands.

FURTHER WORKS: *Jharā pālaka* (1927); *Kabitāra kathā* (1956); *Belā abelā kālabelē* (1961); *Jībanānanda Dāśera śrestha Kabitā* (1970, Dhaka edition); *Jībanānanda Dāśera kābyagrantha* (2 vols., 1970–1971); *Jībanānanda Dāśera galpa* (1972); *Mālyabāna* (1973); *Sudarśanā* (1973); *Sutīrtha* (1977); *Manabihangama* (1979); *Āloprthibī* (1982); *Jābanānanda Dāśera kābya sambhāra* (1982); *Samālocanā samagra* (1983); *Jībanānanda samagra* (1985); *Jalāpaihāti* (1985); *Jībanānanda Dāśera premera kabitā* (n.d.). FURTHER WORKS IN ENGLISH: *Banalata Sen: Poems* (1962)

BIBLIOGRAPHY: Bose, B., *An Acre of Green Grass* (1948): 45–47, 56–57; Lago, M. M., and T. Gupta, "Pattern in the Imagery of J. D.," *JASt*, 24, 4 (1965): 637–44; Chakravarty, J., "The Spectrum of Modern Bengali Poetry," *Bengali Literature* (May 1967): 9–19; Cevet, D., "A Note on Bengali Poetry," *Bengali Literature* (Winter 1969): 34–45; Bose, A., "J. D.," in Ghose, N., ed., *Studies in Modern Bengali Poetry* (1968): 21–41; Dasgupta, C., J. D. (1972); Mukherjee, D., "J.—A World of New Sensibility," IndL, 20, 5 (1977): 97–100; Dimock, E. C., Jr. "Reflections on Two Poems by J. D.," *The Sound of Silent Guns and Other Essays* (1989): 33–51; Seely, C. B., *A Poet Apart: A Literary Biography of the Bengali Poet J. D.* (1899–1954) (1990)

—CLINTON B. SEELY

DAUMAL, René

French poet, novelist, and essayist, b. 16 March 1908, Boulzicourt; d. 21 May 1944, Paris

D.'s life and works were directed by the impulse of spiritual development and by the intensity of his vision as poet and mystic. At seventeen, D. embarked on a lifelong interest in sacred Hindu texts, which he translated from Sanskrit into French. In 1928 in Paris D. formed the group "The Great Game" and the journal named after it (*Le grand jeu*) together with such artists and poets as Roger Gilbert-Lecomte (1907–1943), Roger VAILLAND, André Rolland de Renéville (1903–1962), and Joseph Sima (1891–1971). In 1930 D. was introduced to the teachings of the Russian spiritual teacher Georges Gurdjieff (1872–1949), which he and his wife Vera embraced as a way to live the ancient secret knowledge. He died of tuberculosis at the age of thirty-six.

D.'s perception of poetry as leading to revelation is embodied in his posthumously published collection of poems *Poésie noire, poésie blanche* (1954; black poetry, white poetry); his poetry, dominated by the image of death, expresses his mission of a "poète blanc," a poet of purity and perfection. This concept is articulated in "La guerre sainte" (holy war), one of the poems in this volume, which is a call to wage a war for a true language.

The central themes of The Great Game and of D.'s contributions to its journal included "experimental metaphysics," permanent revolution, dreams, and a belief in transcendent reality and in the poet as prophet in the tradition of Rimbaud. The members of the group lived out these ideas: they took dreams seriously and experimented with extrasensory perception, drugs, and so forth. D.'s essays from this time are included in *L'évidence absurde* (1972; the absurd evidence)—which is a new edition of *Chaque fois que l'aube paraît* (1953; each time the dawn appears)—and *Les pouvoirs de la parole* (1972; powers of the word). Key among these are "Nerval le nyctalope" (1930; Nerval the night visionary), on clairvoyant poetry, and "Une expérience fondamentale" (1953; "A Fundamental Experience," 1959), where D. describes the transformation of consciousness through his use of drugs. The Great Game was viewed by the SURREALISTS as a deviating subgroup, while D. considered the surrealist projects as "petits jeux de société" (parlor games); consequently, in 1929, André BRETON put the group "on trial," and D. was "expelled" from the surrealist circle.

D.'s novel *La grande beuverie* (1938; *A Night of Serious Drinking*, 1979) is a scathing, satiric attack on Western intellectual society and values. An absurdist "pataphysical" humor in the manner of Alfred JARRY permeates it. *Le Mont Analogue* (1952; *Mount Analogue*, 1959) is the adventure story of the quest for and ascent of the symbolic mountain connecting humanity and the divine. This novel has been interpreted as an allegory of the Gurdjieffian experience.

The primordial mystery of life and the search for authentic wisdom find their true expression in D.'s writings.

FURTHER WORKS: *Le contre-ciel* (1936); *Petit théâtre de R. D. et Roger Gilbert-Lecomte* (1957); *Lettres à ses amis* (1958); *Bharata: L'origine du théâtre, la poésie et la musique en Inde* (1970); *Tu t'es toujours trompé* (1970)

BIBLIOGRAPHY: Rainoird et al., M., "Il y a dix ans, R. D.," *Cahiers du Sud*, No. 322 (1954): 345–404; Fouchet et al., M.-P, "Hommage à R. D.," *Fontaine*, 52 (1956): 778–805; Random, M., *Les puissances du dedans: Luc Dietrich, Lanza del Vasto, R. D., Gurdjieff* (1966); Biès, J., *R. D.* (1967); Dhotel et al., A., "R. D.," *La grive*: No. 135–136 (1967): 1–50; Masui, J., ed., special D. issue, *Les cahiers Hermès*, 5 (1967–1968); Random, M., *Le Grand Jeu* (1970)

—CLAIRE E. SCHUB

DAVIČO, Oskar

Yugoslav poet, novelist, and essayist (writing in Serbian), b. 18 Jan. 1909, Šabac

After finishing high school in 1926, D. lived for two years in Paris. In 1930 he graduated from the University of Belgrade (Romance languages department). His high school teaching career was cut short when he was sent to jail (1932–37) as a Communist Party organizer. From 1941 to 1943 he was held as a prisoner of war by the Italians; subsequently he joined the partisans. Since 1947, after a brief post-World War II journalistic career, he has lived in Belgrade.

D. began his literary career in the late 1920s as a member of the leftist-oriented Serbian SURREALIST movement, which became extinct in the early 1930s. In the years immediately preceding and following the war, D. wrote outstanding poetry inspired, in turn, by prewar social problems and by the heroes of the Communist revolution.

The turbulent 1950s found D. once again in the forefront of the poetic avant-garde. He championed freedom of literary expression and advocated the rejection of SOCIALIST REALISM, at the same time contributing to a revival of surrealism in Serbian literature.

D.'s entire poetic oeuvre is characterized by his rebellion against human limitations. In his own words, the collection *Višnja*

za zidom (1950; a cherry tree behind a wall) contains poems "snatched away from death"; *Čovekov čovek* (1953; a man's man) expresses rejection of the human need to pause and take a breath; *Flora* (1955; flora) expresses resistance to carnal desire, *Tropi* (1959; the tropics) to the boundaries of space, *Kairos* (1959; Greek: the right time) to time. Whatever the message of each individual collection, in all of them D. is primarily "the greatest magician of words" that Yugoslav literature ever had. His unsurpassed verbal imagination and an unquenchable thirst for experimenting with the language, however, often interfere with the clarity of his poetic message.

Of D.'s ten novels, the first one, *Pesma* (1952, revised version, 1953; *The Poem*, 1959) has so far remained his best, most influential, and most widely appreciated. Rejecting the black-and-white clichés of Socialist Realism, D. introduced here a new, more human type of literary hero and pondered over the potentially damaging effects of an unbending ideological puritanism in dealing with the complexities and imperfections of real life and real people. The novel is set in Axis-occupied Belgrade and deals with the underground activities of a group of Communist youths led by the protagonist Mića. Whether or not the prominent poet, Veković, who wants to join the partisans and among them write his best poem, is worthy of smuggling to the free territory is not decided until an eventful night when Mića (through a sexual experience) matures as a man and a revolutionary, and sheds his puritanical prejudices against the poet's sexual "prowess." The next day the group accomplishes its mission; Veković is on his way to the partisan territory, but Mića, in the process, dies a heroic death.

D. is one of the most prolific and important authors in today's Yugoslavia, but he is also one of the most eccentric and controversial. Besides his very important avant-garde role in the 1950s, D.'s major contribution to contemporary Serbian literature and his most beneficial influence lie in the realm of poetic expression. He freed it from all the chains, past and present, formal, grammatical, and even logical. A poet truly in love with the language, D. has tirelessly dissected it, even abused it, passionately searching for its new yet uncovered possibilities. His dazzling linguistic fireworks create fascinating, magical effects, and his daring images captivate the reader. At the same time, however, they tend to shock the reader and alienate him from the substance hidden beneath the dazzling surface.

As innovative as he has been with form, D. is surprisingly conservative in subject matter. In all his novels as well as in his poetic works he has remained faithful to his one and only favorite subject—communist man in his struggle for the victory of his ideology.

FURTHER WORKS: *Anatomija* (1930); *Pesme* (1938); *Medju Markosovim partizanima* (1947); *Do pobede* (1948); *Zrenjanin* (1949); *Hana* (1951); *Poezija i otpori* (1952); *Nastanjene oči* (1954); *Beton i svici* (1956); *Radni naslov beskraja* (1958); *Pesme* (1958); *Zrenjanin* (1958); *Pre podne* (1960); *Crno na belo* (1962); *Generalbas* (1962); *Sunovrati* (1963); *Gladi* (1963); *Snimci* (1963); *Ćutnje* (1963); *Tajne* (1964); *Za borce Trinaestog maja* (1964); *Bekstva* (1966); *Trg eM* (1968); *Sabrana dela* (20 vols., 1969); *Zavičaji* (1971); *Izabrana Srbija* (1972); *Pročitani jezik* (1972); *Telo telu* (1973); *Rituali umiranja jezika* (1974); *Veverice-leptiri ili nadopis obojenog žbuna* (1976); *Reči na delu* (1977); *Robije* (5 novels: *Gladi, Ćutnje, Tajne, Bekstva, and Zavičaji*, 1979); *Poezija O. D.* (8 vols., 1979); *Gospodar zaborava* (1980)

BIBLIOGRAPHY: A. B., on *Višnja za zidom*, *IBSB*, 2 (1951): 21–22; A. B. on *Pesma*, *IBSB*, 6 (1955): 71–72; Waterhouse, K., on *The*

Poem, NS (9 June 1960): 62–63; Gavrilović, Z., on *Ćutnje, Gladi,* and *Tajne, IBSB,* 15 (1964): 265–67; Mihailovich, V. D., on *Tajne, BA,* 39 (1965): 475–76; "The World of O. D." *Review* (Belgrade), No. 2 (1974): 38–39; Eekman, T., *Thirty Years of Yugoslav Literature (1945–1975)* (1978): 27–30

—BILJANA ŠLJIVIĆ-ŠIMŠIĆ

DAVIES, Robertson

Canadian dramatist, novelist, and critic. b. 28 August 1913, Thamesville, Ontario; d. 3 December 1995, Orangeville, Ontario

D. was one of Canada's most prominent and popular novelists, having enjoyed an international reputation since the late 1940s. His work wed an acute sense of Ontario as a point of origin with a striving to reach levels of culture and artistic recognition not possible within the narrow provincial and national confines that characterized the country well into the 1950s. Born in southwestern Ontario, he also lived in Renfrew and Kingston before attending Upper Canada College in Toronto. His movements followed the growing success of his father, Rupert Davies (later Sir Rupert), in the newspaper (also radio and television) business. D.'s education continued at Queen's University, then at Oxford, where he completed his B. LiH in 1938. Returning to Canada after working briefly with Tyrone Guthrie's Old Vic Company, D. then lived mostly in Toronto and Peterborough. In the latter city he edited his father's paper, the *Peterborough Examiner,* for nearly twenty years before being appointed the founding Master of Massey College at the University of Toronto in 1961. He retired in 1987.

D.'s first published work was his Oxford thesis *Shakespeare's Boy Actors* (1939). It reflects his deep interest in theater, nurtured by his parents and sought out at every opportunity during his youth. That interest has continued in collections celebrating Canada's Stratford Festival (1953–1955), his involvement in the *Revels History of Drama in English* (Vol. 6), and his *The Well-Tempered Critic* (1981). His great ambition was to be a dramatist, in particular by perpetuating the kind of rich theatrical experience he associated with Henry Irving and the English touring companies he saw in Canada. Those ambitions were further nurtured at Oxford and under Guthrie.

Married and back in Canada during the war, he threw himself into playwriting. The most ambitious of these works he sent back to England, without result. He also wrote one-act plays for amateur companies participating in the Dominion Drama Festival. While he wrote several three-act plays, including *At My Heart's Core* (1950) and *Fortune, My Foe* (1949), that explored the effects of Canada upon the tastes and aspirations of people of large vision, his most fertile relation was with the Crest Theatre (Toronto), which produced two full-length plays, *A Jig for the Gypsy* (1954) and *Hunting Stuart* (1972) in 1954 and 1955. Another, *Love and Libel,* made it briefly to Broadway in 1960. Despite ongoing frustrations with the theater, D. continued to write plays, mostly on request. His most notable later effort, *Question Time* (1975), uses the occasion of the arctic plane crash of a prime minister to construct a Jungian reading of the problems of the Canadian psyche.

The kind of writer D. became owed much to his early circumstances. First there was the problem of coming to grips with the powerful personalities of his parents and the alien rough-and-ready world of rural Ontario. Secondly he had to find room in the workaday world of journalism to develop his creative skills even as he had to struggle to find an audience for his plays in a country only marginally interested in theater. Not surprisingly, two other voices emerged in the 1940s: one, the urbane and knowledgeable voice of D. as professional book reviewer and cultural commentator; the other, the discursive gadfly voice of his comical alter ego Samuel Marchbanks, whose curmudgeonly observations on daily life became a staple of Saturday's *Examiner* and a syndicated column. The quality of D.'s reviews led Alfred Knopf to ask him to compile a collection, *A Voice from the Attic* (1960), while D. also collected and arranged the Marchbanks "diaries" into three volumes (1947–1967).

In the early 1950s D. began to explore the possibilities of fiction. His first novel, *Tempest-Tost* (1951), dealt with the problems besetting an amateur company that mounts an outdoor Shakespearean production. Brimful of D.'s knowledge of theater and dramaturgy, the book is simultaneously a satiric look at the pretensions and mixed motives of the townsfolk involved. It was followed by *Leaven of Malice* (1954) and *A Mixture of Frailties* (1958), the three together comprising "the Salterton trilogy," after the small university city in which they are mostly set.

The first phase of D.'s career as a novelist owes much to the realist tradition, particularly satirists like Evelyn Waugh and Sinclair Lewis, and his early fascination with Sigmund FREUD and oedipal relationships. Near the center of interest is Solly Bridgetower, a young Canadian with an Oxford degree and theatrical aspirations who lives under the pall of his socially prominent, formidable, and manipulative mother. In presenting the misadventures that follow from a false engagement announcement linking Solly to the daughter of his deceased father's academic enemy, *Leaven of Malice* studies the problems of a small-city newspaper and satirizes Salterton's social order and manners.

With *A Mixture of Frailties*, D. sought to investigate character more deeply. While the plot has a heavily satiric Salterton frame, its concern is the education of a young artist. Monica Gall, a singer of unpromising social background, receives a grant from the Bridgetower trust to study in Europe under the tutelage of a leading conductor, Sir Benedict Domdaniel. Education for Monica amounts to both professional and character training at the hands of several experts. In dramatizing the education of an artist as world-class singer, Davies plays with numerous distinctions between romance and reality, emphasizing the importance of tough-minded teachers and the difficult moral problems that follow from committing oneself above all to art. While flawed in several ways, this is D.'s first novel to focus upon the imperialism of art and to probe the relation of the artist to her roots.

The second of D.'s trilogies deservedly earned him a much larger audience. After a relatively fallow decade, he wrote *Fifth Business* (1970), *The Manticore* (1972), and *World of Wonders* (1975), a.k.a. "the Deptford trilogy," after the southwestern Ontario town where the action begins. *Fifth Business*, which is regarded by many as D.'s finest novel, is the private memoir of Dunstan Ramsay, a bachelor and retired school teacher whose deeper life has involved a career of writing about mythology, saints, and "psychological truth," and a lifelong friendship with one of Canada's most prominent public figures, Boy Staunton. The narrative traces Ramsay's life and interaction with Staunton, his "lifelong friend and enemy" over the six decades leading to Staunton's extraordinary death. At the heart of the book is the aging Ramsay's sense of his own worth, which the world and even those close to him easily overlook. Underpinned by D.'s increasing fascination with Jung, the novel is Ramsay's apologia for his life as "fifth business" in the lives of others and as hero of his own compelling adventure.

Constructed around the question of who killed Boy Staunton, the trilogy becomes explicitly Jungian in *The Manticore*. Seeking to recover from his father's death, David Staunton, a Toronto lawyer, seeks analysis in Switzerland. His treatment is abetted by a tougher form of self-recognition administered by a grotesque Swiss, Liesl Vitzlipützli, who has become Ramsay's close friend. *World of Wonders* recalls the life of a third Deptfordian, Paul Dempster (born prematurely as a result of an "accident" involving Staunton and Ramsay), who has gone on to world fame as the magician Magnus Eisengrim. Very much a celebration of theater, deception, and the links between psychology, religion, and art, the novel brings the relations among the three Deptfordians full circle and explicates Boy's death. At the same time it celebrates the individuated life of the wolfish artist and the hard-nosed wisdom of those who, having been truly tested by life, know themselves and what most matters in human experience.

D.'s third—or "Cornish"—trilogy uses Renfrew (Blairlogie), Massey College (Plowright College), and Toronto as its bases. It comprises a still more exhaustive look at the mixed motives of those Canadians driven by higher aspirations, be they scholars, artists, ministers, or students. By means of two narrative voices, *The Rebel Angels* (1981) investigates the world of academia both for its human interest and its serious scholarly purposes. *What's Bred in the Bone* (1985) uses a pair of narrating angels to reconstruct the life and death of Blairlogie-born Francis Cornish, an overlooked painter whose facility in creating works that seem to belong to the past raises significant questions about the nature of the creative act. *The Lyre of Orpheus* (1988) returns to the university setting dramatizing an attempt, sponsored by the Cornish Trust, to create and perform an opera begun by Hoffman but left only in note form. D.'s tenth novel, *Murther and Walking Spirits*, appeared in 1991.

Murther and Walking Spirits kills off its central character in the opening scene, but then allows him—as ghost—to trace lines of descent in his family and the problems that led to his cuckolding and murder. Complex in its study of family and often disjunctive, it received several negative reviews and was seen by many observers as a disappointing novel. However, *The Cunning Man* (1994), which traces the life, medical career, and enthusiasms of an Ontario doctor, Jonathan Hullak, assured readers that D. had not lost his capacity to entertain and fascinate. The novel sold 80,000 hardcover copies in the U.S. alone, despite its fond focus upon Toronto and Canadian experience.

As D. became more confident with the novel (he thought of his novels as romances), he became increasingly flamboyant in his use of technique, plot, and character. Always a storyteller and a keen dispenser of interesting information, he typically sought mystery rather than disruption in his techniques. Politically his outlook was conservative, sympathetic to the world of the wealthy and the unabashedly cosmopolitan. Still, his work celebrates distinction of character and personal achievement, whatever its roots. Consistently he remained a commentator on Canadian life and the uneasy attitude of Canadians to the arts, vigorously defending a life in art or in the pursuit of deeper kinds of understanding as the most worthwhile way to live. He won many awards and honors in Canada and was the first Canadian to be elected an honorary member (1980) of the American Academy and Institute of Arts and Letters.

FURTHER WORKS: *The Diary of Samuel Marchbanks* (1947); *Overlaid: A Comedy* (1948); *Eros at Breakfast and Other Plays* (1949); *The Table Talk of Samuel Marchbanks* (1949); *Fortune, My Foe* (1949); *At My Heart's Core* (1950); *A Jig for the Gypsy* (1954); *Marchbanks' Almanack* (1967); *Four Favourite Plays* (1968); *Stephen Leacock* (1970); *Hunting Stuart and Other Plays* (1972); *One Half of R. D.: Provocative Pronouncements on a Wide Range of Topics* (1977); *The Enthusiasms of R. D.* (1979); *Brothers in the Black Art* (1981); *The Well-Tempered Critic: One Man's View of Theatre and Letters in Canada* (1981); *High Spirits* (1982); *The Mirror of Nature* (1983); *The Papers of Samuel Marchbanks* (1985); *The Merry Heart: Selections 1980-1995* (1996); *Happy Alchemy: Writings on the Theatre and Other Lively Arts* (1997)

BIBLIOGRAPHY: McPherson, H., "The Mask of Satire: Character and Symbolic Pattern in R. D.'s Fiction," *CanL*, 4 (Spring 1960): 18–30; Roper, G., "R. D., *Fifth Business* and 'That Old Fantastical Duke of Dark Corners, C. G. Jung,'" *JCF*, 1 (Winter 1972): 33–39; special D. issue, *JCSR*, 12 (Feb. 1977); Grant, J. S., *R. D.* (1978); Lawrence, R. G., and Macey, S. L., eds., *Studies in R. D.'s Deptford Trilogy* (1980); special D. issue, *Canadian Drama*, 7, 2 (1981); Monk, P., *The Smaller Infinity: The Jungian Self in the Novels of R. D.* (1982); Stone-Blackburn, S., *R. D. Playwright: A Search for the Self on the Canadian Stage* (1985); Peterman, M. A., *R. D.* (1986); Cameron, E., ed., *R. D.: An Appreciation* (1991); Grant, J. S., *R. D.: Man of Myth*; Little, D., *Catching the Wind in a Net: The Religious Vision of R. D.*

—MICHAEL A. PETERMAN

The ore of his manufacture is mined from the rocky ground of his homeland; he merely works it his own way. He is pedestrian, meticulous, balanced—very much the Canadian, very much the teacher. He takes the raw materials of his existence, the quaint elements of Southern Ontario, and welds them into a mosaic that glows alive with digression, qualification and illumination. In this regard, the fictional Dunstan Ramsay and the factual R. D. are one. It goes beyond coincidence that they share the same initials, howbeit in reversed order; for reversed order is what *Fifth Business* is about. According to D., Canadians get themselves backwards because they cannot reconcile their reality with their image.

Wilfred Cude, "Miracle and Art in *Fifth Business* or Who the Devil is Liselotee Vitziputzli?" in Elspeth Cameron, ed., *R. D.: An Appreciation* (1981), 117

At the centre of each novel in the Deptford trilogy, then, is a character who strives for the integration of public and private selves that is D.'s ideal. D. takes David Staunton only part way along the journey towards self-knowledge, but Dunstan Ramsay and Magnus Eisengrim are presented as characters who have had considerable success in their pursuit of maturity. Neither character, though, is entirely convincing in that D. is unable to integrate all the complex elements at work in their personalities. Thus, rich ambiguity is replaced by a degree of confusion. This is not to deny, though, that the Deptford trilogy provides considerable insight into some central issues of human personality. D.'s analysis of the ways in which the Persona can overwhelm the rest of the personality is masterly, and through his sometimes certain and sometimes faltering analysis of the development of Dunstan Ramsay, David Staunton and Magnus Eisengrim he increases the reader's awareness of the proper relationship that should exist between public and private selves.

> David M. Monaghan, "People in Prominent Positions: A Study of the Public Figure in the Deptford Trilogy," *Studies in R. D.'s Deptford Trilogy* (1980), 55

The very language of his fiction is shaped by his aesthetic of ambivalence, of paradox. Decorum, though, weighs more heavily on language than on imagery, limiting the extent of formal dislocation in D.'s work. Under the highlighting eye of the dialogic imagination, which brings together within the same text the intersecting planes of the French Renaissance, of Marxist Russia, and of Calvinist Ontario, a carnivalesque element of D.'s writing emerges. The shifting horizon offered by such a multiplicity of perspectives illuminates the heterogeneity that is a characteristic of R. D.'s fictional world.

> Barbara Godard, "Writing Paradox, the Paradox of Writing: R. D.," in Elspeth Cameron, ed., *R. D.: An Appreciation* (1981), 253

The two views—one maintaining D. is a monologist with fixed hierarchical values and the other maintaining D. is a dialogist pitting one authority against others without reaching fixed conclusions—are radically opposed. And our understanding of D.'s ideology depends entirely on which of the two we endorse. If he is a monologist, it follows that his world view is elitist. But, if he is a sophisticated deconstructionist, deliberately using post-modern techniques in a Bakhtinian way, he displays an ideology that recognizes the relativity, and possibly the irrationality, of life.

> Elspeth Cameron, Introduction to *R. D.: An Appreciation* (1981), 6

What Carl Jung called the process of "individuation" provides a kind of general goal for many of D.'s characters, but it is individuation of a highly particularized stamp. D.'s later novels are increasingly preoccupied with the distinction between egotism and egoism, between selfishness and enlightened self-interest in men of special prominence, be they intellectuals, artists, or priests. The egoism of the hero figure—and D.'s novels and plays are seldom without heroes who are egoists—dominates his work. It is an egoism that he shows to be hard and harrowingly won. His characters typically have much to battle against. Domineering parents, threatening rivals, culturally imposed attitudes, and debilitating circumstances conspire to constrain native gusto and inhibit healthy selfhood in his sensitive protagonists. Battles rage around them on the social and psychological levels. Browbeating, advantage taking, jockeying for position, and playing upon the weaknesses of others come to seem to be a normal course of behavior. Inequity of power in a hostile world is everywhere apparent. The vulnerable ego must learn how to survive and to assert its own specialness in its own terms.

> Michael Peterman, *R. D.* (1986), Preface

D.'s critical output spans an astonishing range. He "was there" and responding to almost every Canadian literary work of significance in the forties, and he continued to tackle an amazing number (considering his other activities) in succeeding decades. Fiction drew the bulk of his attention, but he also reviewed poetry, criticism, biography, reference works, and humour. Usually he felt it a waste of time to discuss a book he did not like, so his response to those he did review was typically generous. He responded to felicitous style, to effective story-telling, to bright imagination, to strong characterization, and could admire any one of these even in the absence of the others. Although he was positive, however, he did not fail to make distinctions. His reviews are witty and enjoyable in themselves, but they also picked the winners. A list of the books he regarded as significant when they first appeared reads now like the syllabus for a course in Canadian literature.

> Judith Skelton Grant, ed., *The Well-Tempered Critic: One Man's View of the Arts and Letters in Canada* (1981), 14

DAVIES, W(illiam) H(enry)

Welsh poet, novelist, essayist (writing in English), b. 20 April 1871, Newport; d. 26 Sept. 1940, Nailsworth, England

D. grew up hearing seafaring tales from his grandfather, who kept an inn and raised the boy after his father's death. Something of a juvenile delinquent, D. finished school and was apprenticed to a framemaker. Upon receipt of a legacy at the age of twenty-two he booked passage for North America and began six years of wandering over that continent as a hobo, beggar, and casual laborer. After losing a leg while hopping a freight car in Canada, D. returned to England, where he lived in lodging houses and peddled his poems as broadsheets. He published his first collection of poetry, *The Soul's Destroyer and Other Poems* (1905) at his own expense.

Favorable reviews of this book by Edward THOMAS and George Bernard SHAW encouraged D. to write *Autobiography of a Super Tramp* (1907), which he completed in six weeks. This prose work assured his literary fame, and other books followed in rapid succession. During this Bohemian period in London, he hobnobbed with poets and artists, who found his expressive face and unfailing conversation good subject matter. At the age of fifty, D. married a young girl, Helen Matilda Payne. They moved out from town, first to Surrey, later to the village of Nailsworth, in Gloucestershire. There they lived happily, enjoying the simple pleasures of rural life and treasuring a fine collection of paintings.

D. continued to write prolifically until his death at the age of sixty-nine: poems, novels, and further autobiography. In 1919 he was awarded a Civil List Pension, and in 1926 an honorary Litt. D. degree from the University of Wales.

D.'s best works are in prose, particularly his autobiographical writings; his is a natural gift for the rhythms of the spoken language. His several accounts of the life of a tramp express irrepressible delight in encounters with eccentric personalities, both settled and unsettled, met in his travels. His matter-of-fact tone, absolutely without self-pity, subtly pulls the reader into the author's value system. D. is a born *raconteur*, who never fails to create an amusing incident from the most trivial experience.

His more numerous poems, however, a total of 749 innocuous lyrics, mostly express delight in nature. Sparrows, robins, a sense of warm sun and rain, form the bulk of his poetic matter, but occasionally his imagination takes a bizarre twist. There are poems of the sea, the tavern, and lovemaking on the green. A number of pastoral poems concern sheep, both in fields and on shipboard. Many contain dialogue and refrainlike repetition but never deviate from the discipline of rhyme and meter.

D. seemed unmoved by experiments in modern poetry going on about him, for his poetry did not really evolve in the course of his lifetime. The London poems are his most successful, for D. has a Blakeian sense of irony concerning the poor and idiosyncratic who people city streets. Echoes also of A. E. HOUSMAN are heard in his country poems and of Coleridge in his seafaring lyrics. D.'s works are hardly tortured testaments of the modern age, but rather the slight songs of a Georgian spirit in tune with his own small bit of the world.

FURTHER WORKS: *New Poems* (1907); *Nature Poems and Others* (1908); *Beggars* (1909); *Farewell to Poesy and Other Pieces* (1910); *A Weak Woman* (1911); *Songs of Joy and Others* (1911); *The True Traveller* (1912); *Foliage* (1913); *The Bird of Paradise and Other Poems* (1916); *Collected Poems* (1916); *A Poet's Pilgrimage* (1918); *Raptures* (1918); *The Song of Life and Other Poems* (1920); *The Captive Lion and Other Poems* (1921); *The Hour of Magic and Other Poems* (1922); *Collected Poems: Second Series* (1923); *True Travellers: A Tramps Opera in 3 Acts* (1923); *Secrets* (1924); *A Poet's Alphabet* (1925); *Later Days* (1925); *The Adventures of Johnny Walker, Tramp* (1926); *Autumn Leaves* (1926); *The Song of Love* (1926); *A Poet's Calendar* (1927); *Dancing Mad* (1927); *Forty-nine Poems* (1928); *Moss and Feather* (1928); *Ambition and Other Poems* (1929); *In Winter* (1931); *Poems 1930–31* (1932); *My Birds* (1933); *My Garden* (1933); *The Lovers' Song Book* (1933); *The Birth of Song, Poems 1935–36* (1937); *The Poems of W. H. D.* (1935); *The Loneliest Mountain and Other Poems* (1939); *Common Joys and Other Poems* (1941); *Collected Poems* (1943); *The Essential W. H. D.* (1951); *The Complete Poems of W. H. D.* (1963); *Young Emma* (1981)

BIBLIOGRAPHY: Moult, T., *W. H. D.* (1934); Sitwell, E., *Aspects of Modern Poetry* (1934): 90–98; Kernahan, C., *Five More Famous Living Poets* (1936): 17–48; Sitwell, O., Introduction to *The*

Complete Poems of W. H. D. (1963): xxvii–xxxiv; Stonesifer, R. J., *W. H. D.: A Critical Biography* (1965)

—JANET M. POWERS

DAY LEWIS, C(ecil)

English poet, novelist, critic, b. 27 April 1904, Ballintubber, Ireland; d. 22 May 1972, in Hertfordshire, England

Born into an Anglo-Irish family, D. L. was a descendant of Oliver Goldsmith and perhaps a distant relation of W. B. YEATS. When he was three years old, his mother died and the family moved to England, where he was educated at Sherborne School and Wadham College, Oxford.

D. L. is often associated with a number of writers who attained prominence during the 1930s, notably W. H. AUDEN, Stephen SPENDER, Louis MACNEICE, and Rex Warner (b. 1905). Although never constituting a movement in any sense, these writers did share with D. L. the conviction that they were a new generation that must distinguish itself from the high modernism dominated by T. S. ELIOT and Ezra POUND. D. L. and Auden first declared their intention to set poetry on a new course in the preface, which they coauthored, to *Oxford Poetry 1927*, (1927). The new direction D. L.'s verse took over the next decade was largely a result of the same historical developments that influenced many writers at the

C. Day Lewis

time: increasing awareness of social problems, including that of the artist's proper responsibility to society. Embracing Marxism, D. L. wrote verse that reflected his increasing social commitment until, in 1938, he abandoned political activism to return to a more private life and to greater concern with his poetry.

Although he had published two earlier volumes, *Transitional Poem* (1929) was the first book of verse that began to show D. L.'s maturity as a poet. A long sequence divided into four parts, this poem does not represent any radical departure from earlier 20th-c. verse, dwelling as it does on the familiar modern theme of the divided self searching for wholeness in a chaotic world. Organized around a series of rather abstract categories—metaphysical, ethical, psychological—the poem culminates in an exploration of the aesthetic as a means for synthesizing experience, a conclusion that ratified the modernist tendency to exalt language as the only principle of order in a world increasingly divided and unknowable.

In *From Feathers to Iron* (1931), another long sequence, D. L. recorded his personal experience during the nine months before his first child was born. The poem is filled with imagery of the passing of seasons, the coming to fruition of rich earth, and the movement over frontiers into promising (perhaps dangerous) new countries. But D. L. goes on to link his private experience of becoming a father with larger issues involving the frightening, difficult, and hopeful birth of new worlds. The portrayal of nature's processes was a continuing resource for D. L.'s verse, but here he used it to move beyond the concerns of self to larger social concerns, which were becoming more important to him. *The Magnetic Mountain* (1933), his next volume of poetry, is more direct in its critique of present society and its urging radical social change. D. L.'s language is more colloquial in this volume, more likely to employ "unpoetic" images drawn from mundane life, and more often used for satiric jibes at the status quo.

By the late 1930s D. L.'s verse began to concern itself less directly with social issues, turning once again to more personal, and traditional, lyric subjects: death, nature, the struggle of the self toward knowledge and wholeness. *Poems 1943–1947* (1948), for example, includes a number of poems that explore the experience of learning (or failing) to love. Although occasionally indulging in the sort of abstraction that had hindered some of his earlier verse, D. L.'s work during the 1950s and 1960s was an attempt to find a lyric form in which he could reconcile his search for psychic wholeness with a growing sense of history, both personal and cultural. The achievement of that lyric form might be represented by poems such as those in the first part of *The Whispering Roots* (1970), where D. L. explores memories of his youth in Ireland, combining personal recollection, a precise rendering of nature, and the clear consciousness of the political history that has shaped Irish life.

While primarily a poet, D. L., under the pseudonym of Nicholas Blake, wrote many detective novels, beginning with *A Question of Proof* (1935). During the 1930s he also wrote three "straight" novels—*The Friendly Tree* (1936), *Starting Point* (1937), and *Child of Misfortune* (1939)—but in his autobiography he concludes that his talents did not lie in the direction of serious fiction. D. L. also wrote a good deal of criticism, although his critical writings were never as influential as those of such contemporaries as Stephen Spender or William EMPSON. *A Hope for Poetry* (1934) was a characteristic expression of D. L.'s struggle to reconcile his search for a viable tradition with his commitment to a poetry of change, of social relevance. In *The Poetic Image* (1947) and *The Lyric Impulse* (1965) D. L. attempted to work out a poetics that

could support his gradual abandonment of the poetry of social engagement in favor of poetry that placed greater value on the personal and lyrical.

In 1951 D. L. became professor of poetry at Oxford, and in 1968 he was appointed Poet Laureate of England. An important minor poet, D. L. will be remembered among those writers of the 1930s who helped shape the relation of artist and society in the 20th c. But he also will be remembered because he carried forward the romantic tradition of a poetry of self-discovery set against a natural landscape touched by human history.

FURTHER WORKS: *Beechen Vigil* (1925); *Country Comets* (1928); *Revolution in Writing* (1935); *A Time to Dance, and Other Poems* (1935); *Collected Poems 1929–1933* (1935); *Noah and the Waters* (1936); *Overtures to Death* (1938); *Poems in Wartime* (1940); *Selected Poems* (1940); *The Georgics of Virgil* (trans., 1940); *Word Over All* (1943); *Short Is the Time: Poems 1936–1943* (1945); *The Colloquial Element in English Poetry* (1947); *Enjoying Poetry* (1947); *Collected Poems 1929–1936* (1948); *Selected Poems* (1951); *The Aeneid of Virgil* (trans., 1952); *An Italian Visit* (1953); *Christmas Eve* (1954); *Collected Poems* (1954); *Pegasus and Other Poems* (1957); *The Poet's Way of Knowledge* (1957); *The Buried Day* (1960); *The Gate and Other Poems* (1962); *The Eclogues of Virgil* (trans., 1963); *The Room and Other Poems* (1965); *Selected Poems* (1967); *The Whispering Roots* (1970); *The Mind in Chains; Socialism and the Cultural Revolution* (1972); *The Complete Poems of D. L.* (1992)

BIBLIOGRAPHY: Daiches, D., *Poetry and the Modern World* (1940): 190–213; Dyment, C., *C. D. L.* (1955); Replogle, J., "The Auden Group," *WSCL*, 5 (1964): 133–50; Riddel, J., *C. D. L.* (1971); Hynes, S., *The Auden Generation* (1977): 117–23, 199–204; Nash, W., The Lyrical Game: C. D. L.'s 'Last Words'," in Verdonk, P., ed., *Twentieth Century Poetry: From Text to Context* (1993): 46-56; Gelpi, A., *Living in Time: The Poetry of D. L.* (1997)

—JAMES F. KNAPP

DAZAI Osamu

(pseud. of Tsushima Shūji) Japanese novelist and short-story writer, b. 19 June 1909, Aomori; d. 13 June 1948, Tokyo

D. was the tenth of eleven children born into a wealthy land-owning family in northern Honshu. He enrolled in Tokyo University in 1930 to study French literature but did not complete his studies.

D. wrote in a simple and colloquial style. His best stories are based on his own experiences and thus fall into that category of Japanese fiction known as *shishōsetsu*, or autobiographical/confessional fiction. Given the facts of his life, the mood could have been lugubrious, but it is not. As D. studied himself from all angles in his stories he resorted to humor, irony, and subtle shifts in language to keep the tone light. In this respect, he learned much from Ibuse MASUJI, a writer famed for his humor and light touch.

D. first attracted attention in 1933 when his short stories began to appear in magazines. These were later collected in *Bannen* (1936; twilight years). The best-known stories in it are "Omoide" (recollections) and "Dōke no hana" (the essence of clowning), in which he dealt with an attempted suicide. D. was to turn to suicide as a theme in many of his stories, including "Tokyo hyakkei" (1941; one hundred views of Tokyo).

Two of D.'s best short stories before the end of World War II are "Fugaku hyakkei" (1943; one hundred views of Mount Fuji) and "Tsugaru" (1944; Tsugaru). The first, written in a lyrical style but melancholy in tone, has the writer-narrator settling down to work in a bucolic setting and observing a group of prostitutes out having a picnic in the foothills. In the second D. evokes the flavor and character of his native region, Tsugaru, as he made an attempt to go back home again.

For a brief period after the end of the war, D. came into his own when he published his most famous work, *Shayō* (1947; *The Setting Sun*, 1956), which deals with the fall of an aristocratic family. A mother and daughter are evacuated from Tokyo during the war and suffer privations, but they look hopefully to the return of the son from southeast Asia. He does return, but as a drug addict. He attempts to adjust to postwar conditions by joining the entourage of a dissolute writer but is unable to sever the ties with the life his mother represents, and when she dies, he commits suicide. The daughter gives herself to the writer and bears his child. She has made a complete break with the past and will survive the impending changes.

"Viyon no tsuma" (1947; "Villon's Wife," 1956) is probably D.'s best short story. The first-person narrator, a famed poet's wife, virtually abandoned by her husband, finds meaning in her existence by taking a job for a tavern keeper from whom her husband has stolen money. Nothing—retarded child, rape, or her husband's endless self-delusion—can crush her new-found determination to survive.

In *Ningen shikkaku* (1948; *No Longer Human*, 1958), a novel of profound pessimism, D. merged a number of earlier themes: distrust of self and of others, inability to compromise, the rape of an overly trusting wife, drug addiction, confinement in a mental institution.

Like all Japanese intellectuals since 1868, when Japan emerged from a self-imposed state of isolation that had lasted three centuries, D. tried to cope with the problem of discerning some sense of order in a society that had been torn from its moorings by enormous forces of change and that was becoming increasingly fragmented. This sense of dislocation continued for D. up to Pearl Harbor and the war in the Pacific, when national mobilization pressured writers into complying with state policy. After the war, D. lapsed into an even more virulent despair. His sardonic observation of those who had supported the militaristic regime before and during the war and who were now embracing democracy with equal fervor contributed to his sense of alienation. On 13 June 1948 D. killed himself.

FURTHER WORKS: *Nijusseiki kishu* (1937); *Kyokō no hōkō* (1937); *Ai to bi ni tsuite* (1939); *Joseito* (1939); *Onna no kettō* (1940); *Shin Hamuretto* (1941); *Seigi to bishō* (1942); *Udaijin Sanetomo* (1943); *Sekibetsu* (1945); *Otogizōshi* (1945); *Shin shokokubanashi* (1945); *Pandora no hako* (1946); *Fuyu no hanabi* (1946); *Kyōshin no kami* (1947); *Nyoze gabun* (1948); *Jinushi ichidai—Mihappyō sakuhin shū* (1949); *D. O. zenshū* (10 vols., 1952); *D. O. zenshū* (12 vols., 1955–1956)

BIBLIOGRAPHY: Keene, D., *Landscapes and Portraits: Apprecia-tions of Japanese Culture*, (1971): 186–203; Miyoshi, M., "Till Death Do Us Part: D. O.—*The Setting Sun*," *Accomplices of Silence* (1974): 122–40; Lyons, P., "Women in the Life and Art of D. O.," *LE&W*, 18 (1974): 44–57; O'Brien, J., *D. O.* (1975); Ueda, M., *Modern Japanese Writers and the Nature of Literature* (1976):

145–72; Wagatsuma, H., and DeVos, G., "A *Kōan* of Sincerity: O. D.," *HSL*, 10 (1978): 156–81

—FRANK T. MOTOFUJI

DEBELJAK, Aleš

Slovene poet, essayist, and translator, b. 25 Dec. 1961, Ljubljana

Educated in Ljubljana, D. received an M.A. from the University of Ljubljana. Afterwards, he was awarded a scholarship to study in the U.S., earning his Ph.D. from Syracuse University. He is a professor of sociology of culture and religion at the Faculty of Social Sciences in Ljubljana.

D. emerged at the beginning of the 1980s as a member of a generation of poets that succeeded a very strong avant-garde movement and soon imposed itself as the most interesting charac-teristic of contemporary Slovene literature. In the 1980s he pub-lished three outstanding books of poems: *Zamenjave, zamenjave* (1982; exchanges, exchanges), *Imena smrti* (1985; the names of death), and *Slovar tišine* (1987; dictionary of silence). The critics have seen them as each outlining one phase of his work. These phases are characterized primarily by a different encoding of the poetic discourse. From one collection to another, his poetry be-comes more refined, the hypertrophy of words from the first collection is later suppressed by a refined and precise expression. *Zamenjave, zamenjave* represents a consecration in the oracle of poetry, a joy of naming the world and its phenomena. *Imena smrti* crystallizes the poetics of the physical, the material. His expression becomes more condensed, heavier, and the rhythm of naming slower. The three collections are composed in a relatively strict form, with internal dynamic changes. The lyrical subject focuses on states characteristic for the 20th-c. intellectual: despair, isola-tion, fear, and the feeling of being cramped and confined.

His third and most important collection of poems, *Slovar tišine*, intensified his poetry with the states of melancholy, resignation and nostalgia. Such feelings of the lyrical subject result primarily from the experience of the world as a two-dimensional screen. The screen is a correlative of the consciousness, recording impressions. Images are interwoven with reflections on the hopelessness of life, and later become esoteric symbols. The author mixes styles, pathos with description, nostalgic moods with reflexivity, populist decora-tiveness with esoterism. All phenomena of his cosmology are present simultaneously in an everlasting present. Whereas the motives in *Imena smrti* are fragmented and relatively loosely connected, more cohesive lyrical passages are present in *Slovar tišine*, where fragments of motives follow each other according to the dictate of an intensive emotional flow, oscillating between a nostalgic reflection of the past and a melancholic resentment. Both of these emotional categories, present also in his previous collec-tions, represent a shift into a new, different poetic behavior. In all three collections an existential resignation of witnessing the uni-form pathology of everyday life and the meaningless racing is inscribed into the empty space.

The critics have labeled the poetics of *Slovar tišine* the poetics of the softened I. The paradigm of D's wandering is torn between the nostalgia for the primal, mythical paradise, which can no longer be entered, and the notion that "carbon monoxide is sufficient for death." In the space between, the subject surrenders to existential possibilities, closer to the other pole, longing for the agonized sinking into the abyss of silence and anonymity. The lyrical subject disappears into the text, as in the poem "Esej o melankoliji" (An Essay on Melancholy): "I've been trying for a couple of hours now, my whole life in fact, to disappear into the text. I do not talk to others, because I do not talk to myself."

In his essays collected in *Melankolične figure* (1988; melancholic figures) D. sheds light on his postmodern practice. In later texts some radical standpoints have been greatly moderated, even eliminated. In the collection of poetry *Grad i dijete* (1988; the city and a child) D. recapitulates his intensive experiences of life and art from the past decade, widening them into new metaphoric spaces, primarily the plant and animal world, into which he skillfully transfers the excess of meaning. He has enriched his poetic style with new rhetoric solutions promulgated in his essays.

FURTHER WORKS: *Američka metafikcija* (1988); *Postmoderna Sfinga* (1989); *Minute strahu—fotografije s poti* (1990). FURTHER WORKS IN ENGLISH: *Shifting Borders: East European Poetry in the Eighties* (1993); *Twilight of the Idols: Recollections of a Lost Yugoslavia* (1994); *Anxious Moments* (1994)

BIBLIOGRAPHY: Pantić, M., "Magična šifra A. D.," *Quorum*, 5 (1988): 43-46; Maković, Z., "Kada sam prvi put pročitao Slovar tišine," *Quorum*, 5 (1988): 47-48; Nikčević, Ž., "Opis teče že naprej," *Quorum*, 5 (1988): 49-54, Đurđević, M., "Tko su gospodari mijene?," *Vijenac*, 112 (1998): 15

—IRENA LUKSIC

DECONSTRUCTION

Deconstruction, or *la déconstruction*, is, in the first place, a word French philosopher Jacques DERRIDA has used to translate the German words *Destruktion* and *Abbau* in the writings of Martin Heidegger (1889–1976). His choice of the word demonstrates, among other things, the difficulty of translation in general, not because he holds that there is some untouchable original sense to be preserved, but rather because all meaning occurs as a result of a break in the origin—impulse, idea, word—that is supposed to give rise to it.

"Deconstruction" now has the general sense, in journalistic parlance especially, of "critiquing by dismantling," but in relation to Derrida's work it covers the set of ideas and strategies by means of which he seeks to analyze and displace what he finds to be the metaphysical underpinnings, or "logocentrism," of Western thought. In the terms of Derrida's analysis, Western philosophy, at least since Socrates and Plato, has reasoned and advanced its truth thanks to a series of oppositions—truth/error, man/woman, speech/writing, nature/culture, and so on—where the second term is perceived as a falling away from the first, which therefore assumes priority—anteriority and authority—over it. The now "classic" deconstruction is that of the opposition that, philosophers and common sense have consistently maintained, obtains between speech and writing. Derrida shows, by taking the theoreticians of language at their word, that speech in fact has all the negative characteristics attributed to writing, such as distance or absence, error or ambiguity. He finds the two to be structurally indistinguishable, for although writing functions in the absence of its

producer, speech similarly involves a "spacing" that prevents it from operating within any intact contextual confines.

Deconstruction thus aims to modify the model of reasoning that relies on such hierarchical thinking, according to whose logic thought can and should reduce to a single, simple unity—God, truth, the idea, the origin—for that has led to the repression of much in Western culture that has been deemed secondary, derivative, or peripheral. Derrida seeks to challenge the hierarchy by giving prominence to the second, repressed term, but he does so through what he calls "a double writing," developing forms of analysis and types of discourse that will avoid re-establishing the old hierarchy by simply reversing its terms. For in challenging that way of thinking, deconstruction wants to avoid imposing itself as a new single, simple truth. Indeed, for Derrida, tradition condemns us, generally speaking, to the logo centric framework, and in spite of the revolutionary impact of his ideas, he sees any process of change as being, from our perspective, interminable. His own effort of deconstruction involves reading the texts through which logocentrism expresses itself, from the writings of Plato. *La dissémination* (1972; *Dissemination*, 1982), to those of Sigmund FREUD and Jacques LACAN, *La carte postale* (1980; *The Post Card*, 1987), from Nietzsche's views on women, *Éperons* (1978; *Spurs*, 1979), to Speech Act Theory, *Limited Inc.* (1990; first pub. in English as *Limited Inc.*, 1988), from Kant's discourse on the status of the work of art, *La vérité en peinture* (1978; *The Truth in Painting*, 1987), to discussion of the nuclear deterrent, "No Apocalypse, Not Now" (1984) and the use of the word "apartheid," "Racism's Last Word" (1985). His contention is that Western thinking's will-to-singularity is of necessity impossible to sustain in practice, and he thus develops his analyses starting from the lapses, contradictions, and ambiguities that inevitably arise in a piece of writing. From this point of view deconstruction can be considered not so much a word or a set of strategies even, as a state of affairs; something that occurs, or is, and which thereby shows the paradoxes and difficulties of such central tenets of philosophy (and much else), as existence, the event, and being.

From the late 1960s and early 1970s, Derrida's work gained much exposure in the U.S., and it was taken up in particular by academics in literature departments at various institutions such as Yale, Johns Hopkins, and Cornell. Derrida's presence as a regular visiting faculty member, especially at Yale, led to the establishment of what became known as the Yale School, whose members included the scholars Paul de Man (1919–1983) and J. Hillis Miller (b. 1928). In spite of the often brilliant analyses of literary and philosophical texts that such authors, inspired by Derrida's ideas, produced, it was felt that his ideas had lost their edge in translation and, in their application as a form of literary analysis, amounted to little more than a search for the contradictions or impasses in a text or piece of reasoning.

Derrida's emphasis on reading as analysis and on a generalized notion of textuality has been interpreted by some as a retreat from the real world into the idealism of the text. That accusation came especially from humanists and social scientists who had been schooled in Marxism, and saw the possibility of its extension in the structuralist movement from which Derrida's work had to some extent developed. Central to their judgment was the appearance of *Glas* (1974; *Glas*, 1986), a book that was variously described as "vulgar," "diabolical," "corrupting," and "obscurantist," for its playing off of Jean GENET against Hegel and its radicalization of the practice of double writing. Later, various published pieces explicitly demonstrated Derrida's concern with political issues. But attacks on deconstruction, especially in the U.S., came as much from the right, which saw it as dangerous form of skepticism and as an important item on the radical agenda that the children of the 1960s, now tenured professors, were forcing down the throats of the student population. When it was revealed in the late 1980s that Derrida's most obvious precursor, Heidegger, was more active in Nazi politicking than had previously been thought, and that de Man had published anti-Semitic newspaper articles in Belgium in his youth, deconstruction's detractors of whatever ink cited such facts as more evidence of the moral and political bankruptcy of its ideas. "Deconstruction," a word that Derrida in fact used only sparingly for many years, has now become a common reference across the spectrum of academic knowledge and artistic endeavor. It remains the subject of continuing debate, yet is often the object of considerable misrepresentation.

One way of summing up the philosophical tradition that Derrida deconstructs would be in terms of the opposition between inside and outside. Where does the inside end and the outside begin? What is the status of the threshold or frame? These are questions that philosophy has never stopped asking, mostly by trying to avoid asking them or by presuming to be able to easily separate itself from the objects—art, literature, science—that it addresses. Literature often functions as the outside of philosophy, something the latter seeks not to be in claiming to represent truth and not fiction, but something that philosophical writing, from references to myth made by Socrates to Jean-Jacques Rousseau's *Confessions* (1782; *The Confessions of Jean-Jacques Rousseau*, 1904), seems both tempted and threatened by. This has led a philosopher like Richard Rorty (b. 1931) to collapse the difference between philosophy and other writing, but for Derrida the relation is more complicated, and many of his texts concentrate on it.

On the other hand, deconstruction is interested in borders and margins in general, contending that the points at which, and the means by which, a domain or discipline attempts to close itself off from what it is not in order to define itself, offer the most productive areas for analysis. Paradoxically, definition is made possible by the same means through which it proves its own impossibility, for the inside depends on the outside for its definition and is thus "infected" by it structurally rather than accidentally.

Relations between inside and outside form the basis of Derrida's work on the visual arts, and have led to the proliferation of deconstruction(s) in the fields of painting, film, architecture, and the law. For such fields, whose practice—works of art, buildings, cases—is held to be clearly distinguishable from its theory, the introduction of deconstruction's ideas has raised some fundamental questions concerning that separation, and, as is to be expected, deconstruction itself has undergone interesting developments and modifications.

Articles by Derrida on Kant's theory of aesthetic judgment and Heidegger's analysis of Van Gogh were published in book form in 1978 (*La vérité en peinture*) along with analyses of works by two contemporary artists, Valerio Adami (b. 1935) and Gérard Titus-Carmel (b. 1941), who have been inspired by his writings. Those essays provide incisive questioning about the status of the work of art and its relation to what *supports* it, in all senses of that word, as well as idiosyncratic readings that seriously challenge the norms of art criticism. Scholars have tried, in retrospect, to assign the label "deconstructionist" to any number of modern artists, but there is no identifiable school of painters or sculptors who call themselves

that. Nor are there such filmmakers, although traditional cross-fertilization between literary studies and film studies in the academy meant that deconstruction, drawing on Derrida's notion of writing and his work on painting, made a relatively early appearance in that field.

It is in architecture and law that deconstruction has made some of its most important inroads. Interest shown in Derrida's work by architects such as Bernard Tschumi (b. 1944) and Peter Eisenman (b. 1932) gave rise to articles by him on their work, and later a collaborative project by Derrida and Eisenman was commissioned by Tschumi. There has been intense debate by architects and others over the foundations of the discipline and the presuppositions, concerning form and function for instance, upon which it is based. For a number of architects, the questioning inherent in Derrida's work has been used in conjunction with a revived interest in the Russian Constructivist movement, such that the word "deconstruction" has been modified to "deconstructivism." Derrida has said that architecture may be regarded as a testing ground for deconstruction, examining the extent to which the foundations of thinking are tied up with thinking about foundations, that is to say about construction or building in general.

The importance of deconstruction for legal studies arises quite simply from the emphasis Derrida's ideas give to questions of interpretation. Deconstruction is but one form of a general revival of theoretical thinking that draws on a number of those known as poststructuralists (Derrida himself rejects the appellation), and that involves critique of the impartiality and freedom from political, social, or economic bias that is supposed to found the law in a democracy. But the matter comes into sharpest relief in the case of constitutional law, where proponents of the doctrine of "original intent" are challenged by those who advocate an activist judiciary. Since, for deconstruction, meaning only comes about as a result of a break in original intent, there would be no sense in attempting to retrieve an original meaning, such as that intended by the Founding Fathers, that is no longer accessible and cannot be second-guessed. Interpretation of the law, or of any text, necessarily becomes an active process, a form of writing that involves the production of new meanings.

Another important contribution in this context is the deconstruction of the question of decision. Derrida argues that any decision is structurally dependent upon a "moment" of undecidability, without which there could be no decision, everything reverting to a predetermined program. Undecidability, rather than being something that hinders decision-making, is essential to it and remains in force throughout the decision. That sort of logical impasse, or "aporia," has been the subject of much of Derrida's later work, and by means of analyses of such matter as the gift, *Donner le temps* (1991; *Given Time*, 1992), responsibility, "Donner la mort," (1992, *The Gift of Death*, 1995), hospitality, *Apories* (1996; *Aporias*, 1993), and witnessing, *Demeure* (1997), he has attempted to think through, if not beyond the aporia, in order to develop the fully ethical dimension of deconstruction.

The debate deconstruction has initiated over the operations of meaning, which touch on matters of communication and coding in general, carries over into fields seemingly as far apart as information and computing systems, and immunology and biotechnology. In fact, one way Derrida has suggested deconstruction be approached is in terms of a theory of the virus, a system with a life of its own yet imbedded within our own, difficult to prevent or track yet perhaps providing the basis for a rethinking of the origins of life. The effect of deconstruction is similarly to open language and sense-making processes in general to a whole range of possibilities, exciting yet often threatening, that do not submit to the control systems traditionally in force in Western thought.

BIBLIOGRAPHY: De Man, P., *Blindness and Insight: Essays in the Rhetoric of Contemporary Criticism* (1971); Miller, J. H., "Steven's Rock and Criticism as Cure," *GaR*, 30 (1976): 5–33, 330–48; Rorty, R., "Philosophy As a Kind of Writing: An Essay on Derrida," *NLH*, 10 (1978): 141–60; Bloom, H., et al., *Deconstruction and Criticism* (1979); Ropars-Wuilleumier, M.-C., *Le texte divisé* (1981); Culler, J., *On Deconstruction: Theory and Criticism after Structuralism* (1982); Norris, C., *Deconstruction: Theory and Practice* (1982); Ryan, M., *Marxism and Deconstruction* (1982); Arac, J., et al., eds., *The Yale Critics: Deconstruction in America* (1983); Krupnick, M., ed., *Displacement: Derrida and After* (1983); Harvey, I. E., *Derrida and the Economy of Difference* (1986); Llewelyn, J., *Derrida on the Threshold of Sense* (1986); Melville, S., *Philosophy beside Itself: On Deconstruction and Modernism* (1986); Sallis, J., ed., *Deconstruction and Philosophy: The Texts of Jacques Derrida* (1987); Weber, S., *Institution and Interpretation* (1987); Brunette, P., and D. Wills *Screen/Play: Derrida and Film Theory* (1989); Papadakis, A., C. Cooke, and A. Benjamin, eds., *Deconstruction: Omnibus Volume* (1989); Rapaport, H., *Heidegger and Derrida: Reflections on Time and Language* (1989); special Deconstruction issue, *Cardozo Law Review*, 11: 5–6 (1990)

—DAVID WILLS

DE FILIPPO, Eduardo

Italian dramatist and poet, b. 24 May 1900, Naples; d. 1 Nov. 1984, Rome

D. F. seemed destined to be a dramatist. Son of actors, he made his acting debut in the company of Eduardo Scarpetta in 1906. His writing career started around 1920, but he had his first success with *Sik-Sik, l'artefice magico* (1929; *Sik-Sik, the Masterful Magician*, 1967); a sketch whose qualities and themes announce the more nature artist.

D. F.'s interest in the theater went beyond acting and writing. In 1931, in Naples, he founded a theatrical group, the Teatro Umoristico, with his brother Peppino and his sister Titina, and directed a number of his own plays, which owe much both to the *commedia dell'arte* and the Neapolitan dialect theater. In addition to the very successful *Natale in casa Cupiello* (1931; Christmas with the Cupiellos), to this period belong the dramas written before World War II and collected under the title *Cantata dei giorni pari* (1959; song of the even days). A second group, *Cantata dei giorni dispari* (1951-58; song of the odd days), includes, in two volumes, plays written after 1945.

The difference between the two collections lies in the current of moral indignation and social concern beneath the farcical humor of his postwar comedies, which was lacking in the earlier plays. In 1945 D. F. set up a new company, the Teatro di Eduardo, and produced the works, from *Napoli milionaria* (1945; millionaire Naples) to *Le voci di dentro* (1948; the voices from within), that are generally considered his masterpieces.

The examination of the dilemma of modern man and his search for self-expression in an oppressive and dehumanizing society is continued in the plays written in the 1960s and 1970s. *Sabato, domenica a lunedì* (1959; *Saturday, Sunday, Monday*, 1974), *Il sindaco del Rione Carità* (1960; *The Local Authority*, 1976), *Il contratta* (1967; the contract) explore, at times with a rather abstract moralism, the tragicomic absurdity of life, the chasm of incomprehension between individuals, the hidden depravity of men. D. F.'s insistence of a few recurring themes has led critics to speak of a drift toward intellectuality and to judge the realistic phase of his work to be the most significant. D. F. defends himself in *L'arte della commedia* (1964; the art of comedy), an impassioned statement of his ideas on comedy and irony.

D. F. also has published two volumes of poetry: *Il paese di Pulcinella* (1951; the country of Pulcinella) and *'O canisto* (1971; the basket). He also has directed plays by other dramatists and written scripts for films and television.

D. F. the playwright is preeminent in his dramatization, through characterization rather than plot, of the light of common people under the pressures of poverty, disease, difficult family relations, the aftermath of war, and changing socioeconomic conditions. His characters are usually lower-class but sometimes middle-class, and dominant women have a special attraction for him. The typical D. F. character, which he has often played on the stage himself, is an introspective, ineffectual, unheroic hero struggling to survive in an indifferent world. This modern-day Pulcinella combines farce and tragedy, the pathetic and the grotesque. Clearly, D. F. is a deeply serious dramatist who views the human condition with disillusionment, if not with despair.

His art draws heavily from the life of his native city: his comedies are consistently set in Neapolitan locales and written mostly in dialect. Both in technique and style D. F. is traditional. Even though his work derives from regional realism, he uses the tools of realism to create a fablelike atmosphere suspended between reality and fantasy, placing the squalid facts of life in a comic, even burlesque frame. His chief virtues as a playwright are his ability to sustain dramatic energy through solid structure and his sense of timing in the dialogue and in the reversals of comedy into tragedy. While best known as a writer-producer, D. F. is also an actor with a subtle and restrained method of performance that has influenced generations of Italian actors.

Although D. F.'s reputation is solidly established in Italy and Europe, his undoubted originality and exceptional achievements have as yet not brought him much recognition in the U. S.

FURTHER WORKS: *Farmacia di turno* (1920); *Uomo e galantuomo* (1922); *Filosoficamente* (1928); *Chi è cchiù felice 'e me!* (1929); *Quei figuri di trent'anni fa* (1929); *Gennariella* (1932); *Il dono di Natale* (1932); *Quinto piano ti saluto!* (1934); *Uno coi capelli bianchi* (1935); *L'abito nouvo* (1936); *Pericolosamente* (1938); *La parte di Amleto* (1940); *Io, erede* (1942); *Questi fantasmi* (1946; *Oh, These Ghosts!*, 1964); *Filumena Marturana* (1946; *Filumena Marturana*, 1964); *Le bugie con le gambe lunghe* (1947); *La grande magia* (1948; *Grande Magic*, 1976); *Non ti pago* (1940); *Occhiali neri* (1945); *La paura numero uno* (1950); *I morti non fanno paura* (1952); *Amicizia* (1952); *Mia famiglia* (1955); *Bene mio e core mio* (1955); *De Pretore Vincenzo* (1957); *Il figlio di Pulcinella* (1960); *Tommaso d'Amalfi* (1963); *Peppino Girella* (1964); *Il cilindro* (1966); *Uomo e gentiluomo* (1966); *Il monumento* (1970); *Ogni anno punto e da capo* (1971); *I capolavori di Eduardo* (2 vols., 1973); *Gli esami non finiscono mai* (1974). FURTHER WORKS IN ENGLISH: *Three Plays* (1976)

BIBLIOGRAPHY: Bentley, E., "E. D. F. and the Neapolitan Theatre," *KR*, 13 (1951): 111–26; Codignola, L., "Reading D. F.," *TDR*, 8 (1964): 108–17; Bender, R. G., "A Critical Estimate of E. D. F.," *IQ*, 11 (1967): 3–18; Bender, R. G., "Pulcinella, Pirandello and Other Influences on D. F.'s Dramaturgy," *IQ*, 12 (1968): 39–71; Illiano, A., "A View of the Italian Absurd from Pirandello to E. D. F.," in Zyla, W. T., ed., *From Surrealism to the Absurd* (1970): 55–76; D'Aponte, M., "Encounters with E. D. F.," *MD* 16 (1972): 347–53

—ALBERT N. MANCINI

DE LA MARE, Walter

(pseud. until 1904: Walter Remal) English poet, short-story writer, novelist, essayist, and anthologist, b. 25 April 1873, Charlton; d. 22 June 1956, Twickenham

D., born of French Hugenot and Scottish parents, was educated at St. Paul's Cathedral Choir School in London, where he founded the school magazine. Unable to attend college, D. became a bookkeeper in the London offices of the Anglo-American Oil Company from 1890 until 1908. During these years his poetry was printed in various magazines, and a collection of poems, *Songs of Childhood*, was published in 1902. This was soon followed by D.'s. first long prose work, *Henry Brocken* (1904), a child's fantastic voyage through a world of his favorite literary characters. A Civil List pension allowed D. to retire from business and to devote himself entirely to writing. One of the most highly respected writers of his day, D. won many awards and was granted numerous honorary degrees.

Any brief summary of the more than one thousand poems contained in the definitive *The Complete Poems of Walter de la Mare* (1970) risks oversimplification. Still, there are some valid critical assessments to be made about this vast body of work. D.'s recurrent themes are death, the supernatural, nature, and children. He is not a topical poet or social critic; his themes are universal. His best poetry addresses the world with a highly imaginative, childlike sense of its wonder reminiscent of Blake and Emily Dickinson. While poems such as "Self to Self" (1928), "The Miracle" (1906), and "The Traveller" (1945) depict death as the ever-present shadow haunting our days, D. never assumes the morbid attitude of Poe. His characteristic tone is the hauntingly delightful one of "The Listeners" (1912), his most anthologized piece. Supernatural presences haunt his poems in the form of those listeners and watching eyes that fill the empty places once inhabited by men. Perhaps they are projections of the self, listening to what is beyond the "range of human speech," yearning to communicate the incommunicable.

Lord David Cecil (b. 1902) emphasizes D.'s "curious bias towards the miniature." The small creatures of the English countryside are frequent subjects for his poems. They share a community of nature with man, who has callously betrayed them by hunting and ecological destruction. This same bias is most clearly evident in D.'s many delightful poems for children. Such classics as "At the Keyhole" (1913) and "I Can't Abear" (1913) typically express his delight with and knowledge of the world of children which is neither sentimentalized nor patronizing.

For D., imagination is the saving grace, for without it there can be no human communication or compassion. This theme is vividly dramatized in his best short stories. The pitiable and delightful old

Walter De La Mare

woman in "Miss Duveen" (1923), separated by a stream from the garden of young Arthur, attempts to communicate with him. He completely fails to decipher a letter she tosses to him. Even across the distance of time, the boy, now the grown narrator freed from the haunting madness of Miss Duveen, merely feels great relief that the pathetic old woman was put away. The most frighteningly callous and unimaginative of all D.'s narrators is the little boy of "In the Forest" (1936). His matter-of-fact revelations of the death of his baby sister and of his father dying at the doorstep are appalling. The boy indeed inhabits a forest of his own crude isolation.

Memoirs of a Midget (1921), D.'s most successful novel, also emphasizes the liberating and humanizing power of the imagination. Sir Walter Dadus Pollacke, a trusted friend and adviser of the beautiful midget Miss Thomasina or Miss M, explains that he is presenting her private papers to the world so that her revelation of the truth about even the "least of things" might be the means of revealing the truth about everything. The reader is led to identify with the midget in the course of her sensitive account of her unique place in the world of the "common sized." Hence, we are given not so much a work of social criticism as a record of the progress of a little person of immense intuition and imagination in a misunderstanding and insensitive Brobdingnagian world. Miss M's deep and saving attention to the world allows her to perceive flashes of the ephemeral truth that remains hidden from those who care less. The final ambiguous disappearance of Miss M seems to be D.'s method of underscoring her role as special messenger of wonder to those suffering from 20th-c. malaise.

The strangeness of *Memoirs of a Midget* and of D.'s other novels is their strength. The critic Edward Wagenknecht argues that while D.'s interest in soul rather than in society places him outside the main tradition of the English novel, the very oblique-ness of his unique and inimitable novels charts the path of the future development of the novel.

FURTHER WORKS: *Poems* (1906); *The Return* (1910); *The Three Mulla-Mulgars* (1910, repr. *The Three Royal Monkeys*, 1919); *The Listeners, and Other Poems* (1912); *A Child's Day* (1912); *Peacock Pie* (1913); *The Sunken Garden* (1917); *Motley* (1918); *Rupert Brooke and the Intellectual Imagination* (1919); *Flora* (1919); *Poems, 1901–1918*, (2 vols., 1920); *Crossings: A Fairy Play* (1921); *The Veil* (1921); *Down-Adown-Derry* (1922); *Broomsticks, and Other Tales* (1925); *The Connoisseur, and Other Stories* (1926); *Stuff and Nonsense, and So On* (1927); *Told Again* (1927); *Poems for Children* (1930); *On the Edge* (1930); *Desert Islands and Robinson Crusoe* (1930); *The Fleeting, and Other Poems* (1933); *The Lord Fish* (1933); *Poems 1919–1934* (1935); *The Wind Blows Over* (1936); *Poetry in Prose* (1936); *This Year, Next Year* (1937); *Memory* (1938); *Pleasures and Speculations* (1940); *Bells and Grass* (1941); *Collected Poems* (1942); *The Old Lion* (1942; Am., *Mr. Bumps and His Monkey*); *The Magic Jacket* (1943); *Collected Rhymes and Verses* (1944); *The Scarecrow* (1945); *The Burning Glass* (1945); *The Dutch Cheese* (1946); *Collected Stories for Children* (1947; rev. ed., 1957); *Inward Companion* (1950); *Winged Chariot* (1951); *Private View* (1953); *O Lovely England, and Other Poems* (1953); *Selected Poems* (1954); *A Beginning, and Other Stories* (1955); *A Choice of D.'s Verse by W. H. Auden* (1963)

BIBLIOGRAPHY: Megroz, R. L., *W. D.: A Biographical and Critical Study* (1924); Reid, F., *W. D.: A Critical Study* (1929); Atkins, J., *W. D.: An Exploration* (1947); Bett, W. R., ed., *Tribute to W. D. on His Seventy-fifth Birthday* (1948); Hopkins, K., *W. D.* (1953); Wagenknecht, E., *Cavalcade of the English Novel* (1954): 533–46; McCrosson, D. R., *W. D.* (1966)

—MICHAEL W. MURPHY

DELBLANC, Sven

Swedish novelist and dramatist, b. 26 May 1931, Swan River, Man., Canada; d. 15 Dec. 1992, Uppsala, Sweden

D.'s father was a farmer in Canada, but when D. was young, the family went to live with relatives in a village in southern Sweden, which has lent many features to D.'s novels. He earned his doctorate in literature in 1965 and combined his writing career with university teaching up to the mid-1970s.

D.'s first novel, *Eremitkräftan* (1962; the hermit crab), deals with the problem of freedom, a recurrent theme in D.'s work. The protagonist tries to escape from the oppressive conditions of a military dictatorship into a hedonistic life, but eventually finds security in marriage and religion within the system.

In many of D.'s novels, the protagonist, usually the writer's thinly disguised alter ago, is pitted against an overpowering social structure. In *Homunculus* (1965; *Homunculus*, 1969) this conflict

leads to the destruction of a scientist's work, and in *Nattresa* (1967; night journey) to rebirth after a trial and escape from the clutches of a fraternal organization, which symbolizes the big-brother mentality of modern society.

Nattresa and D.'s next novel, *Asnebrygga* (1969; donkey's pier), were inspired by his visits to Berkeley, where he was a visiting professor at the University of California. He renders with satirical wit his impressions of student revolt and other aspects of American society, which he finds tainted by fascism.

Sweden, too, is the object of D.'s social criticism in several novels about the people of Hedeby, a small community, shortly before and during World War II. Neutral Sweden's not so neutral people are treated with humor and irony in the tetralogy beginning with *Aminne* (1970; remembrance) and followed by *Stenfågel* (1973; stone bird), *Vinteride* (1973; winter lair), the most important and also the best, and *Stadsporten* (1976; the city gate).

In *Grottmannen* (1977; the caveman) D. created a modern masterpiece about the passion, suffering, sense of responsibility, ecstasy, and depression brought on by love. Here, as in most of D.'s novels, the woman is little more than an object for the protagonist's feelings. She is the archetypal body versus man's soul, desperately needed but also much feared. In the great epic novel *Kära farmor* (1979; dear grandmother) woman rules the world as a matriarch of infinite power and strength.

Having done research in 18th-c. literature, D. also has written historical novels set in that period. *Prätkappan* (1963; the pastor's cloak), which uses the Hercules myth, deals with frustrated dreams of power, glory, and love. In *Kastrater* (1975; *The Castrati*, 1978) D. argues that only art can liberate mankind's longing from its physical circumstances. Both novels have been dramatized.

In a television play, *Morgonstjärnan* (1977; the morning star), D. re-evaluates a period in Swedish history, giving a not very flattering portrait of the ruling aristocracy in the mid-18th c. He has written several other plays, among them *Robotbas* (1963; robot base), about love and politics, and the poetic *Ariadne och påfågeln* (1964; Ariadne and the peacock). His stage play about Richard Strauss, *Den arme Richard* (poor Richard) had its premiere in 1978.

D. is noted for his use of the picaresque form, his epic perception of existence, his rich and diverse imagination, and his sense of burlesque. He mixes the common with the fantastic in a style marked by wordplay and many allusions to literary and historical events. D does not belong to any school of literature and sees no value in conforming to a literary program. He is generally regarded as Sweden's greatest modern storyteller.

FURTHER WORKS: *Zahak* (1971); *Trampa vatten* (1972); *Primavera* (1973); *Gunnar Emmannuel* (1978); *Speranza* (1980)

BIBLIOGRAPHY: Kejzlar, R., "D.'s Hedeby als Kritik der Zeit," *Scan*, 18 (1979): 35–47

—TORBORG LUNDELL

DELEDDA, Grazia

Italian novelist, b. 27 Sept. 1871, Nuoro; d. 15 Aug. 1936, Rome

Although she was born into a well-to-do Sardinian family, D.'s education was limited to grammer school and to a short period of private tutoring. She made her writing debut at the age of seventeen in a women's magazine. From the start, she had the support of editors and publishers. After her marriage she moved to Rome, where she wrote short stories and more than forty novels. In 1926 she was awarded the Nobel Prize.

Most of D.'s novels are set in the harshly beautiful Sardinian landscape, in the atmosphere of primitive rites and legends. Her characters are small landowners, servants, farmers, and shepherds; their conflicts, centering on struggles between good and evil, are dramatized in stories dealing with overpowering sexual attractions, precarious economic conditions, strong loves and hatreds, murders, and expiation. In *Elias Portolu* (1903; *Elias Portolu*, 1992) D. shows her great subtlety in creating psychologically troubled characters who are incapable of forthright decisions and who succumb to temptation and resort to violence. The shepherd Elias, in love with his sister-in-law, prepares to enter the priesthood in the hope of overcoming his passion, but yields to it and fathers a child. The novel describes his wavering between desire and guilt, his hesitation to marry the woman when she becomes a widow, his blind jealousy when her new husband proves an affectionate stepfather to the child. There is often here, as in D.'s other novels, a congruence between the psychological condition of the characters and the landscape in which they move: the resulting impression the reader receives is that evil and sorrow are intrinsic to life and nature and that no effort can enable men to escape them.

D.'s propensity to draw fiercely passionate women is exemplified in *Cenere* (1904; *Ashes*, 1908), the story of a young girl who has an illegitimate son, loses him to her luckier rival, and finally kills herself in order not to harm his prospects in life. D. describes psychological states of mind and an atmosphere of sin and tragic fatality with great artistry. From this novel was derived the only film made by the great Italian actress, Eleonora Duse. In *L'edera* (1906; the ivy) D. created what is perhaps her most powerful female character, a servant who commits murder in a futile attempt to save her weak and irresponsible master, whom she passionately loves, from economic disaster. Although he marries her in the end to repay her for her long-lasting loyalty, she embarks on a life of remorse and lonely toil.

Considerable attention has lately been paid to *Canne al vento* (1913; reeds in the wind): the theme of guilt and expiation is handled here with great delicacy in a complex, skillfully woven plot involving three sisters, their wayward nephew, and the dying servant Efix, who tries to save them from total financial ruin. D.'s view of the human condition comes to the fore in Efix's consideration that destiny is as unavoidable as the wind and that like reeds, men have to bend with it. In *La madre* (1920; *The Mother*, 1923), the novel best known to the English-speaking public, the protagonist is a woman who dies struggling to induce her son, a priest, to renounce his mistress. The sense of damnation and doom grows out of her exhausting attempt to save the young man from sin, and his weak efforts to resist sexual attraction.

A natural and highly original writer, D. escapes all literary classifications, although there have been attempts to liken her, in turn, to the realist Giovanni VERGA, to the Decadent poet and novelist Gabriele D'ANNUNZIO, to the great Russian novelists, and to writers such as George SAND, Emily BRONTË, and Thomas HARDY. D. is essentially a mythopoeic novelist, that is, one whose characters envisage all experiences through widely shared social traditions and unchallenged moral codes, who are so much in tune with the suggestive, changing landscape around them as to become themselves figures of forces animating the universe and the lives of men; hence the lyric, rather than the tragic, nature of her novels, in which feelings are delicately suggested, not precisely analyzed or dramatically juxtaposed.

FURTHER WORKS: *Amore regale* (1891); *Racconti sardi* (1894); *Anime oneste* (1895); *La via del male* (1896); *La giustizia* (1899); *Il vecchio della montagna* (1900); *Dopo il divorzio* (1902); *Il nonno* (1909); *Il nostro padrone* (1910); *Colombi e sparvieri* (1912); *Le colpe altrui* (1914); *Marianna Sirca* (1915); *L'incendio nell'uliveto* (1918); *Il segreto dell'uomo solitario* (1921); *Il Dio dei viventi* (1922); *Annalena Bilsini* (1927); *Il paese del vento* (1931); *La vigna sul mare* (1932); *Cosima* (1939)

BIBLIOGRAPHY: Lawrence, D. H., Introduction to *The Mother* (1928): 7–13; Collison-Morley, L., "The Novels of G. D.," *Edinburgh Review*, 247 (1928): 353–60; Meiklejohn, M. F. M., Introduction to *Canne al vento* (1964): i–xxii; McCormick, E. A., "G. D.'s *La madre* and the Problems of Tragedy," *Symposium*, 22 (1968): 562–71; Pacifici, S., *The Modern Italian Novel from Capuana to Tozzi* (1973): 86–97; Aste, M., *G. D.: Ethnic Novelist* (1990)

—RINALDINA RUSSELL

DELIBES, Miguel

Spanish novelist and short-story writer, b. 17 Oct. 1920, Valladolid

Born into an old Castilian family, D. has lived in his native city all his life. In 1945 he succeeded his father as professor of mercantile law in the Valladolid School of Commerce. The receipt of the Nadal Prize of 1947 for the manuscript of his first novel, *La sombra del ciprés es alargada* (1948; long is the cypress's shadow), encouraged him to pursue his writing career. By early 1979 he had published fourteen novels, two books of short narratives, and several volumes of travel and journalistic essays, in addition to treatises on hunting and fishing. While writing, D. continued teaching, and for a time also worked on the staff of the newspaper *El norte de Castilla*. In 1975 he was received into the Royal Spanish Academy.

D.'s most popular, although not his best novel, is his third, *El camino* (1950; *The Path*, 1961). Much shorter than its two predecessors, *El camino* portrays the special environment of a Castilian village through the memory flashbacks of its eleven-year-old narrator-protagonist (in dynamic interaction, at times, with the intervention of an author-narrator consciousness) on the night before his departure from the village to the city to begin the next phase of his education. Essentially plotless, the work marked a new stylistic direction for its author, and the country-city dichotomy, characteristic of most of D.'s subsequent fiction, assumed in it a central position. Structurally and thematically closely akin to *El camino* is *Las ratas* (1962; *Smoke on the Ground*, 1972), recipient of the Critics' Prize in Spain.

With *Cinco horas con Mario* (1966; *Five Hours with Mario*, 1988), a novel in which plot totally disappears, replaced by one long interior monologue, D. broke sharply but not entirely with his former, more conventional, patterns. Over Mario's corpse, his widow, D.'s first female protagonist, recalls, with free association of ideas, her life with her husband. The whole constitutes a remarkable probing of the mentality of a middle-aged, middle-class, Castilian woman while at the same time obliquely reflecting the society of which she and her husband are products.

D.'s enduring preoccupation with the fate of the individual in a technological age is most powerfully presented in *Parábola del náufrago* (1969; *The Hedge*, 1983) by means of stream-of-consciousness and interior monologue. Kafkaesque in its nightmarish atmosphere and vision, *Parábola del náufrago* depicts the dehumanization of man in an authoritarian, paternalistic, technological society through the progressive metamorphosis of the human protagonist, Jacinto, into a ram.

A masterful, inimitable use of language; a capacity for creation of vivid characters—with a preference for child protagonists—at the center of his narrations; a rich, personal portrayal of the life and landscape of old Castile; a profound sensitivity to the threats of contemporary society to the freedom and dignity of the individual; a respect, bordering on reverence, for nature; and a pervasive ethical concern characterize D.'s fiction and assure it a lasting place in Spanish literature.

FURTHER WORKS: *Aún es de día* (1949); *El Loco* (1953); *Mi idolatrado hijo Sisí* (1953); *La partida* (1954); *Diario de un cazador* (1955); *Un novelista descubre América* (1956); *Siestas con viento sur* (1957); *Diario de un emigrante* (1958); *La hoja roja* (1959); *Por esos mundos* (1961); *La caza de la perdiz roja* (1963); *Europa, parada y fonda* (1963); *El libro de la caza menor* (1964); *Castilla* (1964); *Viejas historias de Castilla la Vieja* (1964); *USA y yo* (1966); *Alegrías de la caza* (1968); *La primavera de Praga* (1968); *Vivir al día* (1968); *La mortaja* (1970); *Con la escopeta al hombro* (1970); *Un año de mi vida* (1972); *El príncipe destronado* (1973); *Las guerras de nuestros antepasados* (1975); *S.O.S.* (1976); *Aventuras, venturas y desventuras de un cazador a rabo* (1977); *Mis amigas las truchas* (1977); *El disputado voto del señor Cayo* (1978)

BIBLIOGRAPHY: Johnson, E. A., Jr., "M. D., *El camino*—A Way of Life," *Hispania*, 46 (1963): 748–52; Hickey, L., *Cinco horas con M. D.* (1968); Díaz, J. W., *M. D.* (1971); Kronik, J. W., "Language and Communication in D.'s *Parábola del náufrago*," *TAH*, 1 (1975): 7–10; Rey, A., *La originalidad novelística de D.* (1975); Spires, R. C., *La novela española de posguerra* (1978): 78–93

—CHARLES L. KING

DELILLO, Don

American novelist, b. 20 Nov. 1937, New York, N.Y.

D. is a novelist of considerable satiric power, but one who pictures personal identities and relationships within an encompassing vision of social power that is by turns paranoid, up-to-date, manic, rootless, and obsessive. Raised as a Roman Catholic, D. attended Fordham University in New York City, and now resides in Westchester County, N.Y. His critical reception has been slow to gather force, though he won the American Book Award in 1985, and his novel on the John F. Kennedy assassination, *Libra* (1988),

was a main selection of the Book-of-the-Month Club, and was for a few weeks on the best-seller lists. He is a novelist who bears some resemblance to Saul BELLOW and Norman MAILER in that he works in modes and genres that can appeal to both popular and academic audiences, and yet he generally spurns the spotlight of the media that often shines on (and shadows) successful novelists in America.

D. began as a novelist with a book called *Americana* (1971), but it was in his second novel, *End Zone* (1972), that his ability to conjoin popular subject matter with formal inventiveness was clearly displayed. Football becomes not only a game described with a phenomenological complexity, it is depicted as both national ritual and neurosis, even to the point that death and other cosmic questions seem natural extensions of the reflections that surround its power. The tour de force of the book is a description of a key game from the point of view of one of the players; here D. overturns the normal expectations of chronology and narrative pattern in a language that owes more to James JOYCE than to sports journalism.

D. continued his immersion in popular culture with *Great Jones Street* (1973), about a rock music star who has withdrawn from the pressures of publicity and contemporary mores. Turning to the genre of science fiction, D. created in *Ratner's Star* (1976) a truly paranoid vision of the social forms that have been variously labeled as the information society, the postindustrial age, and the totally administered society. Again the novel's main figure is both seer and victim, perceptive analyst and passive witness to the energies of an organized scheme that defies placement or full discovery.

Players (1977) and *Running Dog* (1978) are novels imbued with sinister plot elements, shadowy characters, and a thoroughly paranoid atmosphere. *The Names* (1982) centers on a cult and a serial murder plot, both of which are modeled on current events; D. clearly uses the newspaper and other information media for material even as he explores their corrosive effects on our sense of social stability and "normal" personality types. These three novels further established D. as a very flexible stylist. *Players*, for example, contained superb dialogue written with the surest of ears for how people really converse.

White Noise (1985) is perhaps D.'s most uninhibitedly satiric work, dealing as it does with an "airborne toxic event" (the widespread emission of a dangerous gas) and something called a program in Hitler studies. Few American novels have so thoroughly captured the hilarity and the terror of our cultural detritus. But with *Libra* D.'s fiction finally attracted the sort of widespread attention that is often the obsession and the bane of his characters. Many conservative reviewers and columnists, such as George Will, saw the novel as suggesting that America is a country dominated by, or at least represented by, conspiratorial psychopathic killers. Will said, for example, that D. has created "yet another exercise [that] blam[es] America for Oswald's act of derangement." With *Mao* (1991), D. continued to explore the values and conundrums of a mass society that is both fascinated and befuddled by the images and violence that it produces.

One of the central questions that bedevils readers of D.'s fiction is whether it critically questions the paranoia that dominated American society in the postwar era or whether it embodies (and even exults in) that paranoia. As a result of his skill at reworking popular genres, and his fascination with the apparently superficial aspects of modern life—and its semantic systems from brand names and media images to bureaucratic doublespeak—D. is a novelist of potentially wide appeal. But because of his acute intelligence and his awareness of complex thought, from systems theory to postmodern philosophy and cultural criticism, he can also be read as an art novelist in the tradition of high skepticism. In this case his predecessors are not only Joyce and Mailer, but also Flaubert and Franz KAFKA.

BIBLIOGRAPHY: Bryson, N., "City of Dis: The Fiction of D. D.," *Granta*, 2 (1980): 145–57; Nadeau, R., *Readings from the New Book on Nature: Physics and Metaphysics in the Modern Novel* (1981): 161–81; LeClair, T., *In the Loop: D. D. and the Systems Novel* (1987); DeCurtis, A., "Matters of Fact and Fiction," *Rolling Stone*, 17 Nov. 1988; Lentricchia, F., ed., *Introducing D. D.* (1991); Keesey, D., *D. D.*

—CHARLES MOLESWORTH

DENEVI, Marco

Argentine novelist, short-story writer, and dramatist, b. 12 May 1922, Sáenz Peña

D. was born in the Buenos Aires suburb of Sáenz Peña and there spent most of his adult years. Reflective by nature, he became an omnivorous reader and enjoyed the benefits of a tranquil, sheltered childhood and adolescence. He earned a degree in law but chose not to go into legal practice, accepting instead a position as legal consultant with the Argentine National Postal Savings Bank in Buenos Aires. This was the only job he ever held. It was in 1968, with his literary reputation then firmly established, that he decided to resign his post and undertake writing full time—a most uncommon determination for a Latin American writer. Indeed, in both commitment and dedication D.'s has been an exemplary literary career.

His maiden effort, a novel entitled *Rosaura a las diez* (1955; *Rosa at Ten O'Clock*, 1964), won the prestigious Kraft Prize for a new work by an Argentine author. The award probably surprised the contest judges as much as D., since until then he had never written a single word for publication. An extraordinarily suspenseful and engaging narrative, the novel relates from multiple perspectives the circumstances leading up to the murder of a young woman in a dingy Buenos Aires hotel room. It became an immediate bestseller and has proven to be one of the most popular works of Argentine fiction of this century.

Following the performance and publication of a play, *Los expedientes* (1957; the dossiers), dealing with the dehumanizing effects of a sprawling bureaucracy, D. entered another fiction competition. Chosen from over 3,000 manuscripts submitted from all over Spanish America, D.'s novelette, *Ceremonia secreta* (1960; *Secret Ceremony*, 1961) won first prize in the contest sponsored by the Spanish-language edition of *Life* magazine. Less colloquial, more poetic and intense in style than *Rosaura a las diez*, it nonetheless recounted once more a parable of haunting loneliness.

In the decade following the publication of *Rosaura a las diez*, D. wrote a number of short stories and began to accumulate scores of brief, humorous, and ironic sketches that dealt in a satirical way with the commonplaces of literature and history. These sketches were collected under the apt title *Falsificaciones* (1966; falsifications) and revealed a reserved, sophistic, and playful side to D.'s character that stood in contrast, for example, to the mood of his novelette of the same year, *Un pequeño café* (1966; a small café).

The latter, linked in theme and treatment to D.'s earlier spellbinding narratives, tells the story of a lonely, resentful government employee, smothered by the massive bureaucracy in which he toils, who is swept up into a heady adventure involving love, deception, and power. The longer stories of this period were collected in *El emperador de la China y otros cuentos* (1970; the emperor of China and other tales) and *Parque de diversiones* (1970; amusement park). Generally more realistic than the "falsificaciones," these stories demonstrate D.'s ability to observe and dramatize aspects of contemporary life in Buenos Aires and to communicate them in an elegant, entrancing prose style that still remains persuasively colloquial.

During the 1970s, D. produced a novel, *Los asesinos de los días de fiesta* (1972; the holiday murderers), and a total of six collections of short stories and sketches. For the last of these, *Parque de diversiones II* (1979; amusement park II), another abundant miscellany, he prepared this seemingly apologetic statement: "Incapable of articulating my critical ideas (concerning the world we live in) as an essayist might do, I fall back on the only resources at my disposal: the literary (or supposedly dramatic) confection, the minitale, the aphorism," *Los asesinos de los días de fiesta* came to represent for him a failure to deal effectively with his subject—a family of amoral brothers and sisters who invade and occupy a murky mansion in a suburb of Buenos Aires—and eighteen years later he would extensively revise and rewrite it under the title *Música de amor perdido* (1990; music of lost love).

In the 1980s D. changed his tone and his focus. In *Amarinta, o el poder* (1982; Amarinta, or the power) he offered his frankest and most personal work, a book that he dedicated to the memory of his mother and in which he included several sensitive autobiographical pieces. There is little impersonal artifice here, and an uncharacteristic sense of nostalgia invades each page.

Beginning in 1981, D. wrote a long series of moralistic and didactic essays for the Buenos Aires newspaper *La Nación* in which he took the Argentine people to task for the deplorable state in which the country found itself. For a writer who had always avoided the limelight, belonged to no writers organizations, and who zealously protected his personal life, these heatedly controversial columns constituted a huge step. The years of Perón's return to Argentina, his death, the presidency of his wife, Isabel, the "dirty war," the military coups, and the Faulkland Islands disaster encompassed a period when many prominent voices in Argentina remained silent. D. was not to be counted among them.

D.'s three novels of the 1980s, *Manuel de historia* (1985; Manuel of history), *Enciclopedia secreta de una familia argentina* (1987; secret encyclopedia of an Argentine family), and *La república de Trapalanda* (1989; the republic of Trapalanda), all deal directly with contemporary Argentine experience and can be seen as unmistakably admonitory in intent.

D. has come a long way from his family's peaceful garden in Sáenz Peña. Art and morality have eventually found in him an exemplary and eloquent spokesman. His contributions to both the literature and the civic perception of his country are unique and incalculable.

FURTHER WORKS: *Ceremonia secreta y otros cuentos* (1965); *Falsificaciones* (2nd ed., 1969); *Hierba del cielo* (1973); *Antología precoz* (1973); *Salón de lectura* (1974); *Los locos y los cuerdos* (1975); *Reunión de desaparecidos* (1977); *Robotobor* (1980); *Obras completas* (6 vols., 1980–1989); *Páginas de M. D., seleccionadas por el autor* (1983); *El jardín de las delicias* (1992);

El amor es un pájaro rebelde (1993); *Nuestra Señora de la noche*(1997); *Conversaciones con M. D.* (1995)

BIBLIOGRAPHY: Yates, D. A., "M. D.: An Argentine Anomaly, *Kentucky Foreign Language Quarterly*, 9, 3 (1962): 162–67; Yates, D. A., Introduction to *Ceremonia secreta y otros cuentos* (1965): 1–4; Gyurko, L., "Romantic illusion in D.'s *Rosaura a las diez*," *IBERO*, 3 (1971): 357–73; Yates, D. A., "Un acercamiento a M. D.," in Pupo-Walker, E., ed., *El cuento his panoamericano ante la crítica* (1973): 223–34; Grove, I. Revel, *La realidad calidoscópica de la obra de M. D.* (1974); Feeny, T., "The Influence of Wilkie Collins's *The Moonstone* on M. D.'s *Rosaura a las diez*," *RLMC*, 31 (1978): 225–29; Yates, D. A., "M. D.," in Solé, C. A., ed., *Latin American Writers* (1989), Vol. 3: 1265–69

—DONALD A. YATES

DENNIS, Nigel

English novelist, playwright, and critic, b. 16 Jan. 1912 in Surrey; d. 19 July 1989, London

Born in England, educated in Rhodesia and Germany, D. has worked for American and English publications—as a theater critic for *Encounter*, and a book reviewer for the *Sunday Telegraph* and *Time*. His literary reputation rests on a small but distinguished output. *Boys and Girls Come Out to Play* (1949; Amer., *A Sea Change*), a novel of education set chiefly in the Polish Corridor at the beginning of World War II, attracted some attention.

But it was his second novel, *Cards of Identity* (1955), that made his name. Three members of the Identity Club of London move into an abandoned country house, and quickly staff it by giving local residents new roles and new identities. An overworked doctor is turned into a gardener; his sister forgets her relationship with him, as she becomes a housekeeper mourning a deceased husband she never had; a man with a military moustache becomes a butler living down an imaginary disreputable past as a sailor. The satire implies that modern man's personality is defined by his social and cultural context; that he is so uncertain of himself, in fact, that he can be easily deprived of his own identity and given another; and that the pretended mind-healers are really mind-manipulators, quacks, and charlatans. When the Club as a whole meets, it is presented with three case histories concerning switches in identity. In one, the values of the past are turned into a marvelous comic charade, in which the principal characters see the fate of the nation as reposing in the paws of a stuffed badger. In another, a young man brought up as sexually liberated becomes unsure about what sex he belongs to; in fact, he is told that to be truly modern he must be ambivalent. The third is a parody account of a conversion from Communism, resembling that of Whitaker Chambers; in fact the convert, Father Golden Orfe, declares that the "only road to Rome nowadays is via Moscow." Some critics thought the novel too long and the joke too labored, but others called it one of the most brilliant books of the decade and referred to its author as the most accomplished satirist to appear since Wyndham LEWIS.

A dramatized version of *Cards of Identity* was performed at the Royal Court Theatre in London in 1956; the next year the same theater produced D.'s satire on religion, *The Making of Moo*. When these plays were published (*Two Plays and Preface*, 1958) D. wrote a preface that threw light on the objects of ridicule in *Cards of Identity* and the positive values that did not clearly emerge in that work. He made a startling comparison between the theologian and the satirist: both wear funny clothes, both think principally of what they wish to emphasize, both scorn truth and justice, both "eat" people. Rather than subscribing to the philosophy of Saint Augustine, who saw man as degraded and incapable of self-help, D. praised Pelagius, who insisted on man's fundamental goodness and capacity for self-improvement. He also emphasized the reality and importance of the visible world, criticizing at the same time any ideology—such as Christianity, Freudianism, or Marxism—that tries to curb man's free will and make him obey hidden laws. D. sees Freud, for example, as replacing the Trinity of Christianity with the ego and the id—the "two motors" of the psyche—and describing man as a broken vehicle.

In 1958 the critic Philip Toynbee called D. a genuine satirist, richly equipped for his enjoyable task, gleefully confronting a whole world of subject matter lying before him. However, D. did not really exploit the territory assigned him. Another play, *August for the People* (1961), showed the average man as a mean-spirited idiot and democracy as a "bloody disgusting thing," enforcing conformity to the "little dreams of little men." A volume of *Dramatic Essays* (1962) contained many vigorous thrusts and well-turned phrases. An essay on *Jonathan Swift* (1964) showed how well he could "place" and understand another satirist. A taut, terse parable, *A House in Order* (1966), dealing with a man trying to keep himself and some plants alive in a frigid hothouse during wartime, dealt ironically with the treatment of the man of independent mind in the modern world. D.'s total output, however, must be judged of high quality but not really substantial enough to fulfill an early prediction of him—that he would become the comic or satiric conscience of his generation.

FURTHER WORKS: *Exotics* (1970); *An Essay on Malta* (1972)

BIBLIOGRAPHY: Gindin, J., *Postwar British Fiction* (1962): 226–29; Karl, F. R., *A Reader's Guide to the Contemporary English Novel* (1963): 249–53; Fraser, G. S., *The Modern Writer and his World* (1964): 172–73; Wellwarth, G., *The Theatre of Protest and Paradox* (1964): 261–67; "In the Glasshouse," *TLS*, 11 Oct. 1966: 974; Bergonzi, B., *The Situation of the Novel* (1970): 71–77; Dooley, D. J., "The Satirist and the Contemporary Nonentity," *Satire Newsletter*, 10 (1972): 1–8

—D. J. DOOLEY

DEPESTRE, René

Haitian poet and novelist (writing in French), b. 29 Aug. 1926, Jacmel

Known for using literature as a tool of liberation, D. is considered a leader of the radical or Marxist critique of NÉGRITUDE. Coming of age during World War II, D. was influenced by Jacques ROUMAIN and the surrealist literary movement. As a student in Port-au-Prince, he published his first book, *Étincelles* (1945; sparks), which gave him national fame and the financial means to start a literary-political journal, *La Ruche*. Its subsequent banning set off a youth revolt that helped overthrow the dictatorial regime. D.'s militancy led to a short prison term, followed by a wandering life of exile, first in Paris and later in various Third World countries. During this time, he published a second collection of poems, *Gerbe de sang* (1946; spurt of blood). He was deported in 1950, but he continued his political writing, publishing *Végétations de clarté* (1951; vegetations of light) and *Traduit du grand large* (1952; translated from the high seas), which he subtitled "Poem of My Enchanted Land." He returned to Haiti in 1957, where his refusal to collaborate with the Duvalier régime forced him to leave for Cuba in 1959. D.'s reputation earned him an invitation from Che Guevara to play an important role in the development of the Cuban publishing house *Casa de las Américas*. While in Cuba, D. also participated in Creole radio programs broadcast to Haiti.

D.'s most important poetic works were written in Cuba, and they reflect the optimism of the early days of the revolution: *Journal d'un animal marin* (1964; journal of a marine animal), *Un arc-en-ciel pour l'occident chrétien* (1967; *A Rainbow for the Christian West*, 1972), and *Cantata de octubre a la vida y a muerte del Comandante Ernesto Che Guevara* (1968; October cantata on the life and death of comandante Ernesto Che Guevara). His theoretical work, *Por la revolución por la poesía* (1968; for revolution for poetry), consolidated a theory of Third World *littérature engagée*. In the 1970s he began to be more active in prose than poetry, publishing a volume of short stories, *Alléluia pour une femme-jardin* (1973; hallelujah for a woman-garden). His first novel, *El palo ensebado* (*Festival of the Greasy Pole*, 1990), was published in 1975. The poems of *Poète à Cuba* (1976; poet in Cuba) mark an explosive culmination of his revolutionary poetry and record his alienation from communist Cuba, which he left in 1978 for Paris and a job with UNESCO. Two works published in 1980 signify the end of D.'s militancy: *Bonjour et adieu à la négritude* (hello and good-bye to Négritude) and *En état de poésie* (in the state of poetry). In 1986 D. retired to a small town in the south of France. His *Hadriana dans tous mes rêves* (1988; Hadriana in all my dreams) won the Renaudot Prize (1988). In 1990 he reused the title *Journal d'un animal marin* for a volume of selected poems.

Un arc-en-ciel pour l'occident chrétien marshals the voodoo gods of Haiti and black heroes from around the world in a humorous literary assault on imperialist America. D. dramatizes the plight of the "Wretched of the Earth" in this mythic epic made up of a number of shorter poems, each devoted to a *loa* (god) or hero. D. admits that the agrarian gods are powerless against the nuclear "monsters" of the U.S., but uses the heroism of Patrice Lumumba, Malcolm X, and Charlemagne Peralte, the martyred Haitian leader, to rally resistance among the oppressed. *Por la revolución por la poesía* defines the responsibilities of the Third World writer in two essays, then explores particular case studies.

Poète à Cuba contrasts the healthy optimism of poets from the new countries of the world with the decadence of European writers, sketching a vision of innocence and wholeness rooted in community and harmony derived from the early days of the Cuban revolution. He sees Eros as an important factor in revolution and dramatizes autobiographical scenes, playing them against historical revolutionary panoramas. *Hadriana dans tous mes rêves* is a tongue-in-cheek use of realism to study the causes of the current stagnation in Haiti. D. presents the planned marriage of Hadriana as an allegory of a Utopian Haiti. This marriage would be the synthesis of Haitian national dichotomies: black versus mulatto,

Creole versus French, Catholic versus voodoo, peasant versus urban. But the reconciliation is dashed by the zombification of the bride, just as Duvalier's domination destroyed the unity achieved during the American occupation.

FURTHER WORKS: *Minerai noir* (1956); *Trente ans de pouvoir noir en Haiti* (1976); *Le mât de Cocagne* (French version of *El palo ensebado* with major changes, 1979); *Eros dans un train chinois* (1990)

BIBLIOGRAPHY: Warner, K., "R. D.: The Not So Terrible 'Enfant Terrible,'" *Blackl*, 3 (1974): 46–54; Dayan, J., Introduction to *A Rainbow for the Christian West* (1977); Wylie, H., "R. D. Speaks of Négritude, Cuba & Communist Eros," *The GAR*, 33 (Feb. 1979): 14–21; Cailler, B., "L'efficacité poétique du vaudou dans *Un arc-en-ciel pour l'occident chrétien* de R. D.," *FR*, 53 (Oct. 1979): 47–59; Jones, B., "Comrade Eros: Erotic Vein in the Writing of R. D.," *CarQ*, 27, 4 (Dec. 1981): 21–30; Wylie, H., "Creative Exile: Dennis Brutus and R. D.," in Parker, C. A., et al. eds., *When the Drumbeat Changes* (1981): 279–93; Wylie, H., "Négritude and Beyond," in Anyidoho, K., et al., eds., *Interdisciplinary Dimensions of African Literature* (1985): 43–51; Dayan, J., "Hallelujah for a Garden-Woman: The Caribbean Adam and His Pretext," *FR*, 59 (March 1986): 581–95; Couffon, C., *R. D.* (1986)

—HAL WYLIE

DERESSA, Solomon

Ethiopian poet, journalist, and translator (writing in Amharic, English, and French), b. 14 July 1937, western Wollega

Born in the heart of Oromo country in the rugged mountains of Wollega during the five-year Italian occupation of Ethiopia, D. attended school and university in Addis Ababa. At the university he studied English literature and philosophy. Heavily influenced by his grandfather, an oral historian, D., as a young boy, fell in love with Ethiopian folk poetry and the Azmari (minstrel) tradition. During a five-year sojourn in Europe he pursued a law degree and participated in the cultural life of the African diaspora in Paris. In 1965–1966 he worked as a translator and reporter for the United Nations Radio Service in New York.

Ethiopian poetry in Amharic is heavily dominated by the Qene (classical poetry). The literati of the Coptic Church who take pride in their pedigree by quoting from Ge'ez (an old Ethiopic language) are the saint guardians of classical poetry. D.'s early interest in the folk poetry made him realize the potential inherent in Ethiopian poetic tradition. Yet he could not agree with the prosodic rigidity of classical poetry. *Li'jnett* (1970; youth) is a challenge to classical poets. The subtitle is *Forty and a Half*, an allusion to the forty-four Tabots (covenant of infinite holiness). The poet seems to suggest that forty and a half could equally be as sacred, since the number is only a socially agreed-upon convention. Naturally, the Church was up in arms. It saw the poems as impudent, destructive, and iconoclastic. D. *was* certainly an iconoclast. In one of the poems, he exhorts a poet friend to stop being reverent of fathers so that "you yourself" will become a father.

The clergy was not the only institution that was offended. Traditional poets were also not pleased with the poems, not so much for their profanity as for their stylistic transgressions. In one poem, D. gives a new rendition to a popular song by truck drivers traveling the treacherous road between Mossawa and Addis Ababa. The traditionalists were offended by the poeticization of what they deemed doggerel. Across the border in Somalia, a new love poetry called Balwo gave the clergy and the classical poets a temporary respite from their war of words, so that they could jointly fight the new genre. To the priest, the new form smacked of profanity; to the classical poet, it was a degenerate form. Yet D. and his counterparts in Somalia continued to write poetry that defied the constraints of the traditional form.

D.'s Amharic poems, aside from their symbolic innocence, accomplish three purposes. First, by experimenting with language, the poet challenges the tradition by throwing the gauntlet. Secondly, he provides an alternative to the tradition by using free verse. Finally, he taunts the traditionalist to situate him and his poetry.

D. also writes poetry in English and French. These poems are scattered in many journals and anthologies, which span across time and continents. A short poem, "Prayers," harkens on a theme that is also found in the Amharic poems—the retrogressive dimension of tradition. The Ethiopian novelist Daniachew Worku (b. 1936) uses this poem as an epigram for his 1973 novel *The Thirteenth Sun*. Another collection of D.'s poetry is *Tone of Silence, A Mid-Century African Portrait*, for which the manuscript is, unfortunately, lost. D. is also featured in many anthologies including *Poems of Black Africa* (1975), edited by Wole SOYINKA.

D.'s Ethiopian poems tend to be bawdy, playful, and belligerent. His concern is that of cultural criticism. The impish defiance of the poetic voice and its unabashed "Do I care?" stance sometimes foster an attitude in which the play on words becomes an end in itself. In contrast, his poems in English and French are lyrical and self-reflexive and generally tend to be less critical. We can detect a tinge of surrealistic influence in the French poems. The same sensibilities, however, run through all his poems. One can legitimately state that D. is the precursor of modern Ethiopian poetry. His daring experimentations with Amharic have been inspirational for many young poets in Ethiopia.

—ALI JIMALE AHMED

DERRIDA, Jacques

French philosopher and literary theorist, b. 15 July 1930, El-Biar, Algeria

Born into a Jewish family in French Algeria, where he spent his childhood and adolescence, D. moved to Paris in 1949 to prepare for his university studies. He was associated with the literary group *Tel Quel* in the 1960s and began a major writing career in 1962 with his translation of Edmund Husserl's (1859–1938) *L'origine de la géométrie*. Since then he has continued to publish prolifically, diversifying his writing to cover fields from philosophy to literature, painting, architecture, law, and political issues. D. has lectured in many countries and since 1966 has been a regular visitor to the U.S. Previously at the École Normale Supérieure in Paris, in 1983 he was appointed professor of philosophy at the École des Hautes Études en Sciences Sociales. He lives outside of Paris.

From the time of his first publications, D.'s work has stirred controversy over the extent of its challenge to traditional ways of thinking and writing. Although calling himself a philosopher, D. questions the foundations of philosophy and the means by which it attempts to define and circumscribe other disciplines or domains. He has pursued this line of questioning through highly idiosyncratic analyses of both classical and modern philosophical works, testing the strategies by which those works seek, and fail, to control their own meaning. D. contends that it is logically impossible to suppose, as Western thinking traditionally does, that meaning emerges from an identifiable source or point of origin, such as a thought, or word, or author, and that that origin contains the first and final sense of whatever it produces. His ideas were most notably developed in terms of the treatment of the relation between speech and writing in the works of thinkers as far apart historically as Plato, Rousseau, and Ferdinand de SAUSSURE. In *De la grammatologie* (1967; *Of Grammatology*, 1972) D. analyzes the work of such writers to uncover their systematic denigration of writing as exterior, secondary, and derivative, a marker of absence and error, as opposed to the supposed interior and living presence represented by speech.

It is often in literature and in philosophy's reluctant but common recourse to literary effects, such as rhetoric in general, and metaphor and analogy in particular, that D. uncovers exemplars of the competing forces that threaten, of necessity, to derail logical discourse. The most striking example of this confrontation between the literary and the philosophical is *Glas* (1974; *Glas*, 1986), a 365-page book, beginning and ending in mid sentence, composed of two main columns that oppose the meditations on absolute knowledge of Hegel, and the celebrations of homosexuality and criminality of Jean GENET. There are no explicit connections between the two columns but an unlimited play of cross-fertilization occurs across the blank space separating them, suggesting the role of chance and excess, and the type of leap into the abyss of the unknown that underscores any discursive event and is necessary, according to D., for any meaning to emerge.

D.'s essays on the visual arts and architecture have grown out of an interest shown in his work by a variety of scholars and artists, but they also attest to the extent to which his writings challenge traditional disciplinary boundaries. In *La vérité en peinture* (1978; *The Truth in Painting*, 1987) he gives his earlier ideas "graphic" illustration by examining how our ideas about meaning in the plastic arts assume a clear delimitation of the work, by means of its frame, allowing the spectator or critic to go straight to the supposed center and seat of meaning. D. argues that no work can clearly delineate its inside from its outside, and that the frame, unsure of its status in this respect, demonstrates that quandary. His interest in relations between interior and exterior crosses over into architecture where he addresses the sense of "dwelling," both in physical terms and in terms of philosophy as a dwelling place for thinking. Recent work in these fields includes a collaboration and debate with Peter Eiserman, an exhibition of drawings at the Louvre, and essays on photography and the artwork of Antonin Artaud.

D. has been active in various political causes: resisting French government moves to reduce the teaching of philosophy in school while at the same time promoting a radical reworking of that discipline; speaking out against racism; working with dissident groups in the former Soviet bloc; writing on behalf of the anti-apartheid movement and the rights of the Palestinians; and calling for a renewed debate on the significance of Marxism, democracy and the role of Europe in the post-Cold War era. In recent years his work, which is now commonly described as DECONSTRUCTION, has come under attack, particularly in the U.S., from conservative groups that associate his ideas with challenges to the integrity of the literary canon and to an established and unchanging understanding of the values of Western civilization. Deconstruction is cited as a coercive orthodoxy in the humanities and has thus become embroiled in the debate over "political correctness." At the same time his ideas have found applications in many other fields of study, notably in law, where questions of interpretation and the possibility of linguistically demonstrable truth are fundamental to the operation of a legitimate modern society.

Some of the most important work by D. during the last decade has been subsumed by the question of the "gift," in terms of the anthropological, ethical and religious significance of exchange, economy, decision, sacrifice, and forgiveness, as practices which, while seeming to operate as automatic ritual, also raise the possibility of exceeding the limits of a program or fixed system. In fact these concerns have been explicit in D.'s work since the mid-seventies and each new publication—on friendship (*Politiques de l'amitié* [1994; *The Politics of Friendship*, 1997]), on language (*Le Monolinguisme de l'autre* [1996; *The Monolingualism of the Other*, 1998]), on religion ("Foi et savoir," [1996; "Faith and Knowledge," 1998]), or on the media (*Echographies* [1996])—confirms the breadth of a corpus that amounts to nothing so much as a minute reworking, each time from a different angle, of the productive questioning that comes into play wherever Western thinking encounters its own limits. In spite of the controversy and skepticism that his work often provokes, D.'s reputation as the world's most renowned living philospher now seems assured.

FURTHER WORKS: *La voix et le phénomène* (1967; *Speech and Phenomena*, 1973); *L'écriture et la différence* (1967; *Writing and Difference*, 1978); *La dissémination* (1972; *Dissemination*, 1982); *Marges de la philosophie* (1972; *Margins of Philosophy*, 1982); *Positions* (1972; *Positions*, 1981); *L'archéologie du frivole: Lire Condillac* (1976; *The Archeology of the Frivolous: Reading Condillac*, 1981); *Éperons: Les styles de Nietzsche* (1978; *Spurs: Nietzsche's Styles*, 1979); *La carte postale: De Socrate à Freud et au-delà* (1980; *The Post Card: From Socrates to Freud and Beyond*, 1987); *L'oreille de l'autre* (1982; *The Ear of the Other*, (1985); *D'un ton apocalyptique adopté naguère en philosophie* (1983; "Of an Apocalyptic Tone Recently Adopted in Philosophy," *OLR*, 6, 2 [1984], 3–37); *Signéponge/Signsponge* (1983); *Lecture de droit de regards* (1985; "Right of Inspection," *Art & Text*, 38 [1989]); *Parages* (1986); *Schibboleth—pour Paul Celan* (1986); *De l'esprit: Heidegger et la question* (1987; *Of Spirit: Heidegger and the Question*, 1989); *Feu la cendre* (1987; *Cinders*, 1992); *Psyché: Inventions de l'autre* (1987); *Ulysse gramophone: Deux mots pour Joyce* (1987); *Mémoires—pour Paul de Man* (1988; first pub. in English as *Mémoires—for Paul de Man*, 1986); *Limited Inc.* (1990; first pub. in English as *Limited Inc.*, 1988); *Le problème de la génèse dans la philosophie de Husserl* (1990)

BIBLIOGRAPHY: Said, E. W., "The Problem of Textuality: Two Exemplary Positions," *CritI*, 4, 4 (Summer 1978): 673–714; Rorty, R., "Philosophy As a Kind of Writing: An Essay on D.," *NLH*, 10, 1 (Autumn 1978): 141–60; Johnson, B., "The Frame of Reference: Poe, Lacan, D.," *The Critical Difference: Essays in the Contemporary Rhetoric of Reading* (1980): 110–46; Lacoue-Labarthe, P., and Nancy, J.-L., eds., *Les fins de l'homme: À partir du travail de J. D.* (1981); Hartman, G. H., *Saving the Text: Literature/D./Philosophy* (1981); Culler, J., *On Deconstruction: Theory and*

Jacques Derrida

Criticism after Structuralism (1982); Kofman, S., *Lectures de D.* (1984); Wood, D., and Bernasconi, R., eds., *D. and Différance* (1985); Ulmer, G. L., *Applied Grammatology: Post(e)-Pedagogy from J. D. to Joseph Beuys* (1985); Gasché, R., *The Tain of the Mirror: D. and the Philosophy of Reflection* (1986); Norris, C., *D.* (1987); Kamuf, P., ed., *A D. Reader: Between the Blinds* (1991); Bennington, G., "Derridabase," in Bennington, G., and Derrida, J., *J. D.* (1991)

—DAVID WILLS

Every one of D.'s extraordinarily brilliant readings since and including *De la grammatologie* . . . builds from and around that point in a text around which its own heterodox textuality, distinct from its message or meanings, is organized, the point also *toward* which the text's textuality moves in the shattering dissemination of its unorganizable energy. These points are words that are anticoncepts, bits of the text in which D. believes, and where he shows, the text's irreducible textuality to lie. These anticoncepts, antinames, counterideas escape definite or decidable classification. That is why they are only textual and why also they are heterodox. D.'s method of deconstruction functions then to release them, just as the climactic moment in each of *his* texts is a *performance* by these anticoncepts, these *mere* words. Thus what D.

points toward is "une scène d'écriture dans une scène d'écriture et ainsi sans fin, par necessité structurelle marquée dans le texte." Only words that are *syncatégorèmes*—words having, like the copula, a syntactic function but capable of serving semantic ones too—can reveal textuality in its element. These words are of an infinite, hence disseminative, pliability: they mean one thing *and* another (rather like Freud's antithetical primal words), but D.'s interest in them is that it is they, and not the big ideas, that *make* a text the uniquely written phenomenon that it is, a form of *supplementarity* to (or something necessarily in excess of) formulable meaning. And this supplementarity is that property of the text capable of repeating itself *(a)* without exhausting itself and *(b)* without keeping anything (for instance, a secret hoard of meaning) in reserve.

Edward W. Said, "The Problem of Textuality: Two Exemplary Positions," *CritI*, 4, 4 (Summer 1978), 694

Books tell the truth about things. Texts comment on other texts, and we should stop trying to test texts for accuracy of representation: "reading . . . cannot legitimately transgress the text toward something other than it, toward the referent (a reality that is metaphysical, historical, psychobiographical, etc.) or toward a signifier outside the text whose content could take place, could have taken place outside of language, that is to say, in the sense that we give here to that word, outside of writing in general. . . . There is nothing outside of the text." D. regards the need to overcome "the book"—the notion of a piece of writing as aimed at accurate treatment of a subject, conveying a message which (in more fortunate circumstances) might have been conveyed by ostensive definition or by injecting knowledge straight into the brain—as justifying his use of any text to interpret any other text. The most shocking thing about his work—even more shocking than, though not so funny as, his sexual interpretations of the history of philosophy—is his use of multilingual puns, joke etymologies, allusions from anywhere to anywhere, and phonic and typographical gimmicks. It is as if he really thought that the fact that, for example, the French pronunciation of "Hegel" sounds like the French word for "eagle" was supposed to be relevant for comprehending Hegel. But D. does not want to comprehend Hegel's books; he wants to play with Hegel. He doesn't want to write a book about the nature of language; he wants to play with the texts which other people have thought they were writing about language.

Richard Rorty, "Philosophy As a Kind of Writing: An Essay on D.," NLH, 10, 1 (Autumn 1978), 146–47

Surely the fact that words are powerful is as important as that *written* words are powerful in a way

that may be more basic still. There is a problem here, because *representation* (the realm of what is signified) and *rhetoric* (the signifying act that values oral performance) are seen as co-conspirators. The rhetoric that interests D. derives solely from the specific power of the *written*: from texts in which language discloses its groundlessness and injures the notion of substance too well for a "cure of the ground." Traditional rhetoric, however, as the art of persuasion, relies on a smooth consensual calculus of means and ends. Specific verbal devices are isolated as if they effectively corresponded to specific mental or affectional states. . . . As a highly sophisticated and teachable art this rhetoric has the same aim, if not the same lightness, as Nietzsche's *aesthetic*, which is said to keep us from a Dionysian stupor, from foundering absolutely (*zu Grunde gehen*).

For D., the rhetoric of representation, especially when insisted on as a science, is a sham; it is not a science but a pragmatic and consensual exercise; one that can distract from the true cogency of speech by interposing a mechanistic model of communication. Like Heidegger, he wants to liberate language from a doctrinal effectiveness that is honorific rather than authentic, accommodating rather than awe-inspiring. . . .

Since D. himself has stressed that the written sign is indefeasibly poison and cure, and that intertextuality also is radically ambivalent in that its mirror-play at once builds up the reality-effect and deconstructs it, this final chapter becomes, among other things, a counter statement to D. It is not a refutation but rather a different turn in how to state the matter. A restored theory of representation should acknowledge the deconstructionist challenge as necessary and timely, if somewhat self-involved—that is, only occasionally reflective of analogies to its own project in religious writing and especially in literary writing. A child acts, Wordsworth wrote, "As if his sole vocation / Were endless imitation"; and in D. there is the same strong "antitheatrical prejudice," an attempt in the name of maturity (and no longer of religion) to put away childish things, to overcome limitation. Yet the bonding involved in imitation may indeed be "endless" and therefore self-subverting.

Geoffrey H. Hartman, *Saving the Text: Literature/ D./Philosophy* (1981), 120–21

Those who champion a "historical approach" or chide deconstruction for refusing to appreciate the historical determination of meaning offer a dubious alternative. A "historical approach" appeals to historical narratives—stories of changes in thinking and of the thoughts or beliefs appropriate to distinguishable historical periods—in order to control the meaning of rich and complex works by ruling out possible meanings as historically inappropriate. These historical narratives are produced by interpreting the supposedly less complex and ambiguous texts of a period, and their authority to authorize or control meanings of the most complex texts is certainly questionable.

The history invoked as ultimate reality and source of truth manifests itself in narrative constructs, stories designed to yield meaning through narrative ordering. In *Positions* D. emphasizes his distrust of the concept of history, with its entire logocentric system of implications, but notes that he frequently uses the term *history* in a critical way, in order to reinscribe its force. . . . D. uses history against philosophy: when confronted with essentialist, idealizing theories and claims to ahistorical or transhistorical understanding, he asserts the historicity of these discourses and theoretical assumptions. But he also uses philosophy against history and the claims of historical narratives. Deconstruction couples a philosophical critique of history and historical understanding with the specification that discourse is historical and meaning historically determined, both in principle and in practice.

Jonathan Culler, *On Deconstruction: Theory and Criticism after Structuralism* (1982), 129

My contention is that D.'s marked interest in literature, an interest that began with his questioning the particular ideality of literature, has in his thinking never led to anything remotely resembling literary criticism or to a valorization of what literary critics agree to call literature. Paradoxically, D.'s initial inquiry into the ideality of the literary object had the effect of situating his work at the margins not only of philosophy but of literature as well.

Such an observation does not mean, however, that D.'s philosophy is without any relevance to literary criticism. Rather it implies that the importance of D.'s thinking for the discipline of literary criticism is not immediately evident, and that any statement of its relevance to that discipline requires certain mediating steps beforehand. So-called deconstructive criticism, which, however important, is but an offspring of New Criticism, has not, to my knowledge, undertaken these preparatory steps and has done little more than apply what it takes to be a method for reading literary texts to the unproblematized horizon of its discipline. As a result, the genuine impact that D.'s philosophy could have on literary criticism has not been, or at best has hardly been, noticed. The following remarks are not intended to offer a "true" version of deconstructive criticism but only to clarify some of the preliminaries which any deconstructive criticism would have to observe.

If it were possible to draw one major proposition from D.'s statements on literature, it would certainly not be that everything is literature, but on the contrary that "there is no—or hardly any, ever so little— literature". . . . How are we to understand this seemingly provocative claim? What this statement first of all suggests is that Aristotle's production of *the concept* of literature in the *Poetics* (in the aftermath of Plato's determination of poetry as *mimesis*) inaugurates the history of literature as a history in which the certification of literature's birth, the declaration of its name, coincides with its disappearance. Literature,

says D., was born of that history, which lasted until the 19th c., and died of that history. . . .

The interpretation of mimesis as subject to truth, as a mimetologism that proclaims the priority and precedence of the imitated over imitation, subjects literature to a status of metaphoric secondariness. Accordingly, literature possesses no specificity of its own and is reducible to its signified, its message, the truth it expresses. Yielding from the outset to the constraints of its philosophical conceptualization, literature, like philosophy, includes "the project of effacing itself in the face of the signified content which it transports and in general teaches." The specificity of philosophy and literature alike rests on this systematic curtailment of the signifier. Consequently, reading is in essence always a transcendental reading in search of the signified. D. writes of "the entire history of texts, and within it the history of literary forms in the West," that it "has almost always and almost everywhere, according to some fashions and across very diverse ages, lent itself to this *transcendental* reading, in that search for the signified."

Rodolphe Gasché, *The Tain of the Mirror: D. and the Philosophy of Reflection* (1986), 255–56

DÉRY, Tibor

Hungarian novelist, short-story writer, and memoirist, b. 18 Oct. 1894, Budapest; d. 18 Aug. 1977, Budapest

D.'s life story reads like the biography of the quintessential modern man: rebel, wanderer, antihero—he was all of these in his long career, although he came from an upper-middle-class Jewish background and grew up in affluence. But he soon rebelled against his bourgeois environment and by 1919 was a member of the Writers Board of the Hungarian Soviet Republic. After the defeat of the Republic D. fled but returned permanently in the 1930s. As a leftist writer he could not publish his own works in Hungary, so he took to translating Western best sellers into Hungarian. After World War II D. became—for a while—a successful and officially acclaimed writer. But during the period preceding the 1956 revolt, he was an outspoken critic of the Rákosi regime, and in 1957 the then sixty-three-year-old author was arrested and served three years in prison for his part in "laying the intellectual groundwork" for the 1956 uprising. After his release D. again became active in literature, and during the last and very prolific phase of his career produced some of his best work.

D. first made a name for himself as an experimental writer, but in the 1930s he switched to realistic fiction, producing *A befjezetlen mondat* (1947; the unfinished sentence), a long social novel about the diffident, rather undistinguished son of an industrialist who deserts his family and class and gravitates toward the proletariat. In the 1940s he started work on a tetralogy, *Felelet* (1950; answer), but after the first two volumes were published, they were denounced for their "bourgeois moralizing" and "rightist deviation," and D. abandoned the project.

D.'s finest works transcend politics. To be sure, stories like "Szerelem" (1955; "Love," 1958) and "Vidá temetés" (1955; "Gay

Funeral," 1966), or the short novel *Niki* (1956; *Niki*, 1958), accurately reflect the oppressive political climate of Hungary in the mid–1950s, but they also illuminate the author's humanism and compassion.

In the novels published in the 1960s and early 1970s, D. was preoccupied with the conflict between freedom and order. *G. A. úr X.ben* (1964; Mr. G. A. in X.), written in prison, is a Kafkaesque exposé of a coldly permissive society; and *A kiközösítő* (1966; the excommunicator), ostensibly a historical narrative about Saint Ambrose, is actually an ironic analysis of authoritarian rule. D. belongs to that important group of European intellectuals which at first enthusiastically embraced leftist ideals but later came to have painful second thoughts. In reading his works, one realizes that despite stated allegiances and proven loyalties, he always wavered between idealism and cynicism, between collectivism and individualism. With age he became even more of a skeptic and a relativist. He titled his remarkable memoirs *Itélet nincs* (1969; no verdict), in which recalling the dramas of his life, D. realizes that he is becoming more and more incapable of passing judgment, although an ineradicable ethical sensibility might still demand it.

D. was a Western-oriented modernist who, after his fling with the programmatic avantgarde, was alternately drawn to the complex, diffuse realism of PROUST, the dream-like surrealism of KAFKA, and the super-refined ironic realism of Thomas MANN.

FURTHER WORKS: *A két nővér* (1921); *Ló, búza, ember* (1922); *Az óriáscsecsemő* (1926); *Országúton* (1932); *Pesti felhőjáték* (1945); *Szemtől szembe* (1945); *Simon Menyhért születése* (1953); *Theokritosz Úipesten* (2 vols., 1967); *Az óriáscsecsemő* (1967); *Képzelt riport egy amerikai pop-festiválról* (1971); *A napok hordaléka* (1972); *Kedves bópeer . . .!* (1973); *A félfülű* (1975)

BIBLIOGRAPHY: Lukács, G., and T. Ungári, *T. D.* (1969); Szenessy, M., *T. D.* (1970); Sanders, I., "The Ironic Hungarian: T. D. at Eighty," *BA*, 49 (1975): 12–18

—IVAN SANDERS

DESAI, Anita

(formerly Anita Mazumdar) Indian novelist, short-story writer, and author of children's books (writing in English), b. 24 June 1937, Mussorie

Born of a Bengali father and a German mother, D. was educated in Delhi at Queen Mary's Higher Secondary School and Miranda House, Delhi University, where she received a B.A. in English literature in 1957. Married in 1958, D. became the mother of four children. Her first three novels, published in the 1960s and early 1970s, were not particularly successful in terms of plot or character. Her later writings, however, display a sensitivity to subtle emotions and family reverberations that some critics have referred to as Chekhovian, although this sort of intuitive awareness emanates from a distinctly feminine sensibility.

Voices of the City (1965) offers us a unique perception of Calcutta seen through the minds of three siblings who come from an aristocratic family in the northern reaches of India close to the Himalayas. The younger sister, Amla, is a young woman artist who

comes to Calcutta to work and is immediately struck by the way in which that city has transformed her brother and sister. Amla sees Calcutta as a monster born of the marsh, an ambivalent goddess preying upon people who live there. Thus, Nirode drifts from a job as editor of a literary magazine to writing a play, his physical body diminished by the coffeehouse life-style to which he is addicted. Monisha's diary shows her confined to an orthodox Hindu role as daughter-in-law in the household of a wealthy old Calcutta family; she cannot bear her stifling existence and commits suicide to protest the theft of her being.

Fire on the Mountain (1977), D.'s fourth novel, is also an exploration of place and its effect on the consciousness of three women, oppressed and crippled at various stages of their lives. The novel is set in Kasauli, a hill station with rocks, pines, and a sweeping view in every direction. Nanda Kaul, an older woman now widowed, comes to this place of light and air, freed finally from domestic responsibilities as hostess, wife, and mother. Her calm is disturbed by a visit from a great-grandchild, Paka, whose psychotic preoccupation with fire brings ruin to the hill community at a moment when the social fabric is being ripped apart by winds of change. Against this relationship, a third woman, Ila Das, struggles to earn a living as a social worker in a vain attempt to offset the genteel upbringing that has rendered her economically helpless.

Clear Light of Day (1980) is also the study of a city, Delhi, where urban history is interwoven with that of a middle-class Hindu family. Bim is a competent woman professor who still lives in the family home in Old Delhi, caring for Baba, the retarded younger brother, and assuming a role as keeper of the family. The relationship of Bim's house to the history of her family is that of Delhi to the history of India. The deepest selves of the family are rooted there, yet the past is multiple, not single, for conflicting memories of that place and the relationships it sheltered are held by all who lived there. Bim, as caretaker of both house and memories, resents the expense of spirit involved, yet realizes, paradoxically, that time the destroyer is also time the preserver. Bim's lifestyle as an independent thinking spirit raises questions, for her superhuman strength in giving without taking leads ultimately to a sterile existence.

The same sort of woman has turned up in several of D.'s recent novels: a newly heroic and thoroughly modern model of the saintly Indian woman. Those qualities that enabled the traditional woman to survive in an arranged marriage are those of D.'s independent woman, who is autonomous, yet bound up with caring for others. She has her own well of emotional strength with no need to draw on nourishment from others. No longer bound by traditional expectations, she is able to assert her need for independence, pursue a career, or decide not to marry or care for children. Although D. offers negative examples of women unable to realize their own needs because of oppression by traditional customs, she also presents the difficulties faced by newly liberated women in giving their lives purpose. The feminist message, that women are senselessly harmed by denial of opportunities for self-realization, comes through loud and clear; but so does the question of what an independent woman's identity might be.

In D.'s *In Custody* (1984) she explores the character of Nur, an Urdu poet fallen on hard times, appreciated only by Deven, a professor of Hindi who would rather be teaching Urdu. Both Deven and Nur verge on the comic, as D. gently mocks a fading literary tradition that persists despite absence of a cultural environment to nourish it. Though able to admire Urdu poetry to the extent of rendering Deven's love for it convincing, D. also comes at the tradition with a feminist perspective, which leads to satire. A venerated poet drinks literally the wine of which the *ghazals* speak (in Persian or Urdu literature, poems consisting of discrete couplets on love or philosophical themes), only to become an alcoholic. Devotee of women, Nur in old age is subject to the whims of two females who give him no peace. In Deven, D. creates a poetry-loving hero, so caught up in illusions that others take advantage of him. Yet Deven breaks free of his illusions by twice crossing over into the feminine: through the acceptance of a caretaker role, and by glimpsing the anguish of Nur's wife, who forces him to consider the viewpoint of woman, the other, the role to which Urdu tradition confines her.

Baumgardner's Bombay (1988) examines the life of a retired German businessman who had come to India in his youth to escape the Holocaust and stayed on in his old age. His needs are few, his companions a German woman expatriate and a menagerie of stray cats. Only when he reaches out in a rare moment of risk-taking to a drug-crazed German hippie is he punished for deviating from his reclusive existence. Nazi hatred surfaces in violence like that which had claimed his mother years before. In this novel, D. explores her own heritage, loading the text with untranslated passages in German (her first language), a source of frustration for the non-German speaking reader. *Baumgardner's Bombay* resembles Kamala MARKANDAYA's novel, *The Nowhere Man* (1972): both deal with elderly gentlemen living out their years in someone else's culture. Yet D. presents the European out of his element, victim not of Indian communalism but of German anti-Semitism, which has resurfaced and hunted him down in his place of exile.

D.'s novel, *Journey to Ithaca* (1996), traces the stories of two parallel generations of Westerners seeking the heart and soul of India: a young European couple of the 1970s, and Laila, whose relationship with an Indian dancer, Krishna, leads her, by way of a mystic vision, to become "the Mother." A nurturing guru figure for Matteo, she is an object of skepticism to Sophie coping with the reality of motherhood in a strenuous environment. With an international cast, D. again brings to life alienated figures, burdened by complex experiences, who struggle to invest with meaning the questionable choices they have made.

Read chronologically, D.'s novels demonstrate her constant experimentation and progressive maturation as a writer. In recent work, she has grappled with powerful themes: emotional poverty confronted by the liberated woman, the demise of a rich cultural tradition, and evil inherent in the German legacy of anti-Semitism. Her characters, although firmly rooted in reality, have become increasingly symbolic of particular philosophical stances in a multicultural universe. Her plots are steeped in irony while at the same time faithfully portraying life as lived in contemporary India. By scrutinizing small corners of India's diverse society, D. has created an astonishing mosaic of peoples and places within the subcontinent.

Place is always at the heart of her fiction, acting upon her characters, and casting the sort of spell that only a unique landscape can. One comes to understand that India is a country of many unique places, each caught in the struggle of a postcolonial identity crisis. In D.'s writing, place becomes a metaphor for individuals coming to grips with personal journeys into a world they never intended on. She accurately renders tumultuous changes in Indian society from the standpoint of an educated, Westernized sensibility. Although the underclass is not dealt with sympathetically in her writing, D. meets the Western reader on his or her own ground,

causing one to ponder a future in which social harmony becomes increasingly elusive.

FURTHER WORKS: *Cry, The Peacock* (1963); *Bye-Bye, Blackbird* (1971); *The Peacock Garden* (1974); *Where Shall We Go This Summer?* (1975); *Cat on a Houseboat* (1976); *Games at Twilight and Other Stories* (1978); *Village by the Sea: An Indian Family Story* (1982)

BIBLIOGRAPHY: Belliappa, M., *A. D.: A Study of Her Fiction* (1971); Ramachandra Rao, B., *The Novels of Mrs. A. D.* (1977); Prasad, M., *A. D. the Novelist* (1981); Sharma, R. S., *A. D.* (1981); Srivastava, R. K., *Perspectives on A. D.* (1984); Jain, J., *Stairs to the Attic: The Novels of A. D.* (1987); Bande, U., *The Novels of A. D.: A Study in Character and Conflict* (1988); Kanwar, A., *Virginia Woolf and A. D.: A Comparative Study* (1989); Jena, S., *Voice and Vision of A. D.* (1989); Sharma, K., *Symbolism in A. D.'s Novels* (1992); Solanki, M., *A. D.,'s Fiction: Patterns of Survival Strategies* (1993); Iyer, P., "Mystically Yours," *NYRB*, 43 (1996): 6–9; Mohan, R., "The Forked Tongue of Lyric in A. D.'s *Clear Light of Day*," *JCL*, 32 (1997): 47–66; Da Silva, T., "Whose Bombay Is It Anyway?: A. D.'s *Baumgartner's Bombay*," *Ariel*, 28 (1997): 63–77

—JANET M. POWERS

DESANI, G(ovindas) V(ishnoodas)

Indian novelist, poet, and short-story writer (writing in English), b. 8 July 1909, Nairobi, Kenya

Although D.'s mother tongue was Sindhi, he was educated in England and writes English with superb facility. From 1935 to 1939, he served as a correspondent for Reuters and the Associated Press. During World War II he was a lecturer for the British Ministry of Information and the Imperial Institute, and also worked as a BBC broadcaster. After the war he went to India, his family's homeland, to lecture on Buddhist and Indian philosophy. For the next nineteen years D. pursued a serious interest in Buddhism by living in monasteries in India, Burma, and Japan.

From 1960 to 1968, D. went back to journalism in Bombay as a special contributor to the *Illustrated Weekly of India*, for which he wrote a weekly column, "Very High and Very Low." He was a Fulbright-Hayes lecturer in the U. S. (1968–69) and since then has been teaching Buddhist philosophy at the University of Texas in Austin. D.'s literary output has been meager: a novel, a poetic drama, and a handful of short stories. Yet these works are of extremely high quality and have attracted a devoted circle of admirers.

All About H. Hatterr (1948) is a bumptious novel of the absurd concerning an Anglo-Malay who experiences seven life encounters in his simultaneous quest for money, women, and a guru. Like Don Quixote, this antihero emerges battered and bruised from each adventure, but returns, naïve and irrepressible, for the next round. Hatterr is himself a microcosm of well-known Indian types: the would-be holy man, the rogue, the *Sahib;* yet his pretensions are constantly thwarted by malevolent Britishers and cunning Indians.

D.'s verbal inventiveness is reminiscent of James JOYCE's *Finnegans Wake* or Laurence Sterne's *Tristram Shandy.* Hatterr speaks in a mixture of Cockney, South Asian bazaar English, American slang, criminal argot, medical and legal jargon, and literal translations from Hindi, all sprinkled with quotations from Shakespeare and other poets. Malapropism, sarcasm, vulgarity, and cynicism mark Hatterr's attempts to survive as a 20th-c. Everyman in a polyglot culture.

The language of *Hali*, (1950) is in a different vein: serene, exalted, prophetic. The work itself is a prose poem in dramatic form, which lacks dramatic quality but has been highly praised by E. M. FORSTER and T. S. ELIOT for its poetry. In contrast to Hatterr, Hali is Man Idealized, a young hero who surmounts fear, defeat, and sorrow in his attempt to achieve selfless compassion for all mankind. Through Hali D. examines a more serious face of man and reveals the Buddhist ethic at the core of his thinking.

D.'s short stories, not as yet collected, reflect both idealism and mock-comic strains, although never simultaneously. The encounter between Western and traditional aspects of Indian life is the most frequent theme in his short fiction, which often turns on misunderstandings inherent in attempts at cultural bridging. D.'s delight in language surfaces in his constant preoccupation with verbal irony.

The same sense of language is visible in his shorter poems, also uncollected, many in a comic vein. The footnoted "A Dirge" (1964), honoring a dead cockroach, and "No Reason, No Rhyme" (1965), an elaborate meditation on airline advertising, display his extraordinary wit. D.'s capacity for polar opposites of style is that of the philosopher who takes transcendental flight, then turns around to laugh at his own seriousness.

FURTHER WORKS: Uncollected poems and short stories

BIBLIOGRAPHY: Burgess, A., Introduction to *All About H. Hatterr* (1970): 7–10; Burjorjee, D. M., "The Dialogue in G. V. D.'s *All About H. Hatterr*," WLWE 13 (1974): 191–224; [Naim, C. M.], "A Note on *All About H. Hatterr*," *Mahfil*, 3 (1964): 1–3; Narasimhan, R., "The Strangeness of G. V. D.," in Mukherjee, M., ed., *Considerations* (1977): 102–10; Williams, H. M., *Indo-Anglican Literature, 1800–1970: A Survey* (1977): 7–9, 67–70

—JANET M. POWERS

DESHPANDE, Shashi

Indian novelist and short-story writer (writing in English), b. Aug. 1938, Dharwad, Karnataka

The daughter of a Kannada-speaking Sanskrit professor and a Marathi mother, D. was educated in English and Sanskrit. She read voraciously in English as a child, benefitting from her father's love of Western liberal ideas and his commitment to intellectual freedom. Because her father was a well-known Kannada writer, she grew up surrounded by books, literary figures, play-readings, and rehearsals. After earning a B.A. (Honors) in economics at Elphinstone College, Bombay University in 1956, D. went on to study law, earning her B.L. degree in 1959 at Mysore University, with a gold medal for standing first. In 1962 she married Dhirendrath Deshpande, a pathologist, with whom she had two sons. She also earned a Diploma in Journalism at Bharatiya Vidya Bhavan, Bombay (1970),

which garnered her three medals, including the Times of India gold medal. In 1984 she was awarded an M.A. in English literature from Mysore University.

Despite having grown up in a literary household, D. did not begin writing until she was nearly thirty, when, feeling stifled by her role as housewife and mother, she felt a strong urge toward self-expression and simply started to write. Surprised by the publication of her first three articles, she began writing short stories. Working in total isolation, without literary companions, she also suffered from poor health and low self-esteem. With time for writing at a minimum, she made use of the typewriter in her husband's office after hours. D. regards her story, "The Intrusion," as the turning point of her career, when she first experienced a sense of the unconscious collaborating with her. Women's magazines began publishing her stories, although her reputation was damaged by the assumption that because she wrote about women, she was not a serious writer.

D., however, persisted, and her first novel, *The Dark Holds No Terrors* (1980), attracted the attention of feminists and others struck by her courageous revelation of the anguish experienced by a middle-class professional woman struggling to live a normative life in an arranged marriage. Her own story is admittedly at the core of *That Long Silence* (1988), in which a woman, struggling against the silences that define her relationship with her husband, begins to write and spend hours alone with a man who is her kindred spirit. As Jaya becomes involved in the lives of servants and members of her extended family, abuse and silences at all levels of society are revealed. Yet in *The Binding Vine* (1993) she crosses class lines in a much more significant way, exploring the parallel stories of Mira, whose pain is decoded from her poetry, and Kalpana, who has been brutally raped and beaten. Writing the lives of multiple generations of Hindu women, D. asks why mothers could possibly want their daughters to repeat the very stories of which they themselves so despair.

A Matter of Time (1996), the first of her novels to be published in the U.S., deals with a husband's abandonment of his wife, but not for the usual reasons. Beset by a Gandhian sensibility, Gopal turns away from his family, inadvertently repeating a pattern that has occurred previously between his in-laws. Yet at the center of the story is neither Sumi, lonely as a single parent, or Gopal, but their daughter Aru, who discovers her won identity through an alternative role model: a woman lawyer who juggles marriage and a career with humane values. Although the genealogical connections in D.'s novels are often quite complex, readers who take the time to "map" family trees are richly rewarded with rare insights into the lives of middle-class Hindus. D.'s writing is wrought with memorable metaphors and similes, as well as charming allusions to Sanskirt literature. But most stunning are the nuggets of wisdom that her characters generate, as they think their way to endearing truths. Her woman-centered work offers new angles on traditional lives and raises significant questions about how Indian women might be able to construct new sorts of identities.

FURTHER WORKS: *The Legacy* (1978); *If I Die Today* (1982); *Come Up and Be Dead* (1982); *Roots and Shadows* (1983); *It Was Dark* (1986); *The Miracle* (1986); *It Was the Nightingale* (1986); *Dhrishti* (1991); *The Intrusion and Other Stories* (1994)

BIBLIOGRAPHY: Sandhu, S., *The Novels of S. D.: A Study in the Image of Woman* (1991); Aswasthi, A. K., "The Quest for Identity in the Novels of S. D.," *LangF*, 18 (Jan.-Dec. 1992): 95-111; D'Cruz, D., "Feminism in the Post-Colonial Context: S. D.'s Fiction," *SPAN*, 36 (1993): 452-70; Rajan, R. S., "The Feminist Plot and the Nationalist Allegory: Home and World in Two Indian Women's Novels in English," *MFS*, 39 (Spring 1993): 71-92; Dharkar, R. "Marriage as Purdah: Fictional Rendering of a Social Reality," in Jain, J., and A. Amin, eds., *Margins of Erasure: Purdah in the Subcontinental Novel in English* (1995): 49-59

—JANET M. POWERS

DESNICA, Vladan

Yugoslav novelist, short-story writer, essayist, and translator (writing in Croatian), b. 17 Sept. 1905, Zadar; d. 4 March 1967, Zagreb

D. came from an old Dalmatian family that gave his country a number of prominent political and cultural figures. After studying in Zagreb and Paris, he graduated from Zagreb University Law School in 1930. Before World War II, he practiced law in Split. Having given up his law practice soon after the war, he spent the rest of his life in Zagreb as a professional writer.

D.'s pre-war literary pursuits were limited to writing essays and doing translations. A "late bloomer," D. did not acquire prominence until the 1950s, his most important works being two novels and about thirty short stories. The smallness of his output is, however, more than compensated for by its exceptionally high literary quality.

As D. himself once suggested, most of his fiction falls into two general categories: works, like his first novel *Zimsko ljetovanje* (1950; summer vacation in winter), which are regionally oriented and in which realistic scenes and local Dalmatian characters prevail, and those of a universal character, in which the author dissects and analyzes the psychological makeup of his heroes and searches for solutions to the existential problems and dilemmas of the modern intellectual.

D.'s most important work, which can also be taken as an artistic manifesto and a key to understanding his work, is the novel *Proljeća Ivana Galeba* (1957, enlarged version 1960; the springs of Ivan Galeb). The hero is an aging violinist, a sensitive and complex man, confined to a hospital bed, hovering between life and death for about a year (1936–37). Having nothing else to do, Galeb reflects. In a mosaic-like fashion, he pieces his life together and reevaluates it in retrospect. Galeb's pessimistic philosophy, his bent toward merciless critical analysis of himself and the world around him, his subjectivity, his cynicism and bitterness, and especially his constant preoccupation with death—all these make him a perfect specimen of a disillusioned modern intellectual, a true "hero of our times." This static narrative, lacking overt action and almost entirely realized in the form of an interior monologue, represents a milestone in modern Yugoslav fiction: it is its first novel of ideas, addressing itself to the many needs of the "cerebralized" contemporary man.

The simple, clear, and highly functional syntax enhances the reading enjoyment of this talented and refined author, whose well-rounded and tightly knit body of work is one of the most impressive in modern Yugoslav literature.

FURTHER WORKS: *Olupine na suncu* (1952); *Koncert* (1954); *Proljeće u Badrovcu* (1955); *Slijepac na žalu* (1956); *Tu, odmah*

pored nas (1956); *Fratar sa zelenom bradom* (1959); *Izbor pripovjedaka* (1966)

BIBLIOGRAPHY: "V. D.,"*Yugopress Weekly Features (Belgrade)*, 2, 49 (1958): 8–10; Vaupotić, M., *Contemporary Croatian Literature*, (1966): 112–15; Banjanin, M. E., "The Short Stories of V. D.," *Florida State University Slavic Papers*, 2 (1967): 74–80; Eekman, T., *Thirty Years of Yugoslav Literature (1945–1975)* (1978): 63–65

—BILJANA ŠLJIVIĆ-ŠIMŠIĆ

DESNOS, Robert

French poet and novelist, b. 4 July 1900, Alençon; d. 8 June 1945, Theresienstadt concentration camp, Czechoslovakia

In his early years D. worked in publishing, advertising, and journalism. After military service in Morocco, he was connected for a time with the SURREALIST group. D. was praised by André BRETON as the "poet who has gone further than any of us into the unknown." This praise refers to D.'s remarkable powers of automatic transcriptions from dreams. Breton was eventually to turn against D. because of D.'s insistence on continuing the formal modes of poetry, and the equally contemptible (in the eyes of Breton) practice of journalism. D. was always engaged in political issues, played a large part in the Resistance, and was working on poetry in the classical mode at the end of his life when he died of typhoid fever in the hospital of liberated Theresienstadt concentration camp.

D. is to be remembered chiefly for his great early poetry, up until the 1930s, and his early novels; after 1930, the writing, both prose and poetry, is far more prosaic, concerned often with "daily" life, and by 1943, when the novel *Le vin est tiré* (the wine is drawn) was published, a certain moralizing, about the misuse of drugs and about the responsibilities of living in the real world, had set in.

Of the early love poems, *Les ténèbres* (1926; the shadows) and *À la mystérieuse* (1927; to the mysterious one) and of the longer poems following them—*Sirène-Anémone* (1921; siren-anemone), *Siramour* (1931; siren of love), and *The Night of Loveless Nights* (1930; original title in English)—it is necessary to know one historical detail: these were written in honor of Yvonne George, a popular singer of chanties: hence the multiple and connected references to sea and sailing, to mermaids and stars, to swimmers and unrequited love. The theme of unrequited love also finds its way into the early novels *Deuil pour Deuil* (1924; *Mourning for Mourning*, 1994) and *La liberté ou l'amour!* (1927; *Liberty or Love!*, 1993). In the surrealistic *La liberté ou l'amour!* wandering figures haunt the Paris sidewalks, lending enigma to the everyday world and adding to the intertwining of genres; for the mythology is the same as in the poetry, yet the figures are slightly different.

In the years after his break with surrealism D.'s writing seemed to acquire a willed fixity, after the profusion and flexibility of dream characteristic of his earlier work. Yet D. considered all the works he had written parts of one long work, and perhaps the reader should adopt that point of view. D., who was at once one of the great ironists and one of the great lyricists of the French language, represents French poetry at its most inventive.

FURTHER WORKS: *C'est les bottes de sept lieues cette phrase "Je me vois"* (1926); *Corps et biens* (1930); *Les sans cou* (1934); *Fortunes* (1942); *État de veille* (1943); *Le bain avec Andromède* (1944); *Contrée* (1944); *Trente chante-fables pour les enfants sages* (1944); *Félix Labisse* (1945); *La Place de l'étoile* (1945); *Choix de poèmes* (1946); *Nouvelles inédites: Rue de la Guité Voyage en Bourgogne; Précis de cuisine pour les jours heureux* (1947); *Les Trois Solitaires; Longtemps après hier; Poèmes pour Maire; À la Hollande; Mon tombeau* (1947); *Œuvres posthumes* (1947); *Chantefables et chantefleurs* (1952); *De l'érotisme considéré dans ses manifestations écrites et du point de vue de l'esprit moderne* (1953); *Domaine public* (1953); *Mines de rien* (1960); *Calixto, suivi de Contrée* (1962); *La Papesse du diable* (1966); *Cinéma* (1966); *Destinée arbitraire* (1975). FURTHER WORKS IN ENGLISH: *22 Poems* (1971); *The Voice* (1972); *Selected Poems of R. D.* (1991)

BIBLIOGRAPHY: Buchole, R., *L'évolution poétique de R. D.* (1956); Caws, M. A., *The Poetry of Dada and Surrealism* (1970): 170–203; special D. issue, *Europe*: Nos. 517–18 (1972); Grubenmann, H., *R. D.* (1972); Caws, M. A., *The Surrealist Voice of R. D.* (1977); Dumas, M. -C, *R. D., ou l'exploration des limites* (1980)

—MARY ANN CAWS

DEYSSEL, Lodewijk van

(pseud. of Karel Joan Lodewijk Alberdingk Thijm) Dutch belletrist, essayist, and critic, b. 22 Sept. 1864, Amsterdam; d. 26 Jan. 1952, Haarlem

Although his father was a professor, D. did not attend a university after his secondary-school education. After working in the book trade for some years, he devoted himself to his work as a writer and editor. The earlier part of his literary career was punctuated by controversies, which were partly due to his polemical style as a critic. When D. started to publish at the age of sixteen, he was a fervent admirer of the French naturalists, whose doctrines he upheld in his scathing reviews of the then-established Dutch writers. In doing so, he contributed materially to the renewal of the literature of the Netherlands in the last decades of the 19th c. D. also set out to incorporate the naturalist tenets in the first of his two novels, *Een liefde* (1888; a love), but in the five years it took to write, he shifted toward a more subjective and aesthetic approach to the depiction of reality. The resultant lack of stylistic unity did not prevent the book, with its detailed accounts of the heroine's sexual feelings, from causing a sensation. Eventually D. declared naturalism to be dead and embraced a mystical outlook on life and art, which he propagated in his reviews and prose poems. Close observation of reality was said to arouse specific sensations, which in turn lead to a state of ecstasy as the culmination of the aesthetic experience. In practice, this view resulted in an excessive preoccupation with the preciously evocative description of trifling objects.

Concurrent with his impressionistic work, D. employed a restrained style to write a biography of his father, *J. A. Alberdingk Thijm* (1892; J. A. Alberdingk Thijm) and a psychologically acute critical study of a Dutch novelist, *Multatuli* (1891; Multatuli). In the following years, as the impetus of the literary renewal weakened, D. also became less effective in his criticism and prose poems, whose substance was reduced to a mere vehicle for the display of his subtle style. More important are the psychological and philosophical observations collected in *Uit het Leven van Frank Rozelaar* (1911; from the life of Frank Rozelaar).

D. contributed more to Dutch writing as a critic and editor than as a creative artist. He came upon the literary scene at the right time, equipped with the right temperament, and helped bring down an artistic establishment that in its smug provincialism was ripe for being superseded. But the new movement, of which he was a prominent representative, itself soon became bogged down by controversy and aesthetic dogmatism, and so D.'s role as an innovator and gadfly had by the turn of the century come to a premature ending. He took no part in subsequent developments in Dutch writing, but lived the rest of his long life as a literary museum piece.

FURTHER WORKS: *De kleine Republiek* (1888); *De dood van het naturalisme* (1891); *In de zwemschool* (1891); *Menschen en bergen* (1891); *Jeugd* (1892); *Apocalyps* (1893); *Akedysséril* (1893); *Blank en geel* (1894); *Van Zola tot Maeterlinck* (1895); *Verzamelde opstellen* (11 vols., 1897–1912); *Kindleven* (1904); *Verbeeldingen* (1908); *Verzamelde werken* (10 vols., 1920–1924); *Werk der laatste jaren* (1923); *Gedenkschriften* (1924; expanded 2-vol. ed., 1962); *Nieuwe kritieken* (1929); *Aanteekeningen bij lectuur* (1950); *De briefwisseling tussen L. van D. en Arnold Ising Jr. 1883–1904* (2 vols., 1968); *De heer dr. Alberdingk Thijm laat vragen . . . : telefoonbriefjes* (1976); *Uit de schrijfcassette van L. van D.* (1978)

BIBLIOGRAPHY: Meijer, R. P., *Literature of the Low Countries* (1978), passim

—EGBERT KRISPYN

DIALLO, Nafissatou

Senegalese novelist, b. 1941, Dakar; d. 1982, Senegal

D. was part of a generation of Senegalese writers that in 1960 witnessed their country's transformation from a French colony to an independent nation. She was raised by her paternal grandmother after her mother died when she was not yet two years old. After attending Koranic school, she studied in French colonial schools in Dakar and later continued her education for two years in Toulouse, France. D. worked in Dakar as both a midwife and a pediatric nurse. She died under uncertain circumstances while she was only in her forties.

D.'s *De tilène au plateau, une enfance dakaroise* (1975; *A Dakar Childhood*, 1982) was the first autobiography published by a Senegalese woman, and marked the beginning of the stage in Francophone literary history when Sub-Saharan African women would write about their own experiences. The autobiography reveals D.'s love and respect for her family and traditions while it criticizes the restrictions on young girls' behavior imposed by paternal authority. It also represents African women's solidarity, especially between grandmothers and granddaughters as they work together to gain access to the public sphere and be heard. Her autobiography caused a stir in Senegal because of its depiction of the beatings that she received from her father after he witnessed her kissing a boy. D.'s courageous act of revealing what were considered women's private experiences was followed by other Senegalese women writers such as Ken BUGUL, Aminata Maiga Ka (b. 1940), Mariama Bâ (1929-1981), and Aminata SOW FALL.

D.'s protagonists are strong-willed women who refuse to remain in the background as their communities undergo drastic change. The heroine of *Le fort maudit* (1980; The Strongly Cursed), an historical novel set in the precolonial kingdoms of Cayor and Baol, fights against outside invasion of her village and later avenges the destruction of her family. Another powerful female protagonist, Awa of *Awa la petite marchande* (1981; Awa, the Little Merchant), works beside her mother in the fish market after her father becomes ill and loses his job. In addition to creating strong African female protagonists, D. critiques the Senegalese social systems that she finds unjust. Her depiction of the unfair treatment of the lower classes in the city of Dakar in *Awa la petite marchande* resembles her portrayal of the village caste system in *La princessse de Tiali* (1987; *Fary, Princess of Tiali*, 1987). Published posthumously, the latter novel chronicles a young woman's attempts to gain rights for "untouchable" griots. Like all of D.'s heroines, Fary charges to the forefront of resistance when her family and community suffers.

D.'s writing reveals the complexities of women's lives during both the precolonial and postindependence eras. Her works were some of the first literary portrayals from an African woman's point of view of polygamy, women's participation in class and caste struggles, the education of young girls, restrictions on women's sexuality, and women's solidarity. In each case her female characters seek harmonious resolutions between the conflicts of personal desire and the oppressive elements of traditional and modern life. She balances her critiques with beautiful accounts of the bonds between family members, most notably grandmothers, mothers, and daughters. Her novels also contribute to the counter-representation of images often evoked in colonial and postcolonial discourses of African women as submissive bystanders. She represents African women throughout history as possessing power, strength, and agency as they struggle against societal oppression and participate in the histories of their countries.

BIBLIOGRAPHY: Stringer, S., "N. D.—A Pioneer in Black African Writing," in Adamson, G., and E. Myers, eds., *Continental, Latin American, and Francophone Women Writers* (1987): 165-71; Bruner, C., "First Novels of Girlhood," *CLAJ*, 31, 3 (1988): 324-38; d'Almeida, I., *Francophone African Women Writers* (1994): 36-44; Hitchcott, H., "African 'Herstory':The Feminist Reader and the African Autobiographical Voice," *RAL*, 28, 2 (1997): 34-56; Watson, J., "Unruly Bodies: Autoethnography and Autorization in N. D.'s *De tilène au plateau*," *RAL*, 28, 2 (1997): 16-35

—ELLIE HIGGINS

DIB, Mohammed

Algerian novelist and poet (writing in French), b. 21 July 1920, Tlemcen

D. went to school in Tlemcen, and later in Oujda, Morocco. He never attended the traditional Koranic school, but he was raised as a Muslim. An introspective youth, he began to write poems and stories when he was about fifteen. From 1939 to 1959, D. held various jobs. In 1959 he settled in France, where he still resides.

D. was a member of the group of writers known as the "Generation of '54" (the year of the outbreak of the Algerian revolution), sometimes called the "Generation of '52" for the year of publication of D.'s *La grande maison* (the big house) and Mouloud MAMMERI's *La colline oubliée*, the first widely read novels in the modern wave of Algerian literature in French.

D.'s novels may be divided roughly into three categories: (1) the naturalism and social commentary of the early trilogy, *La grande maison, L'incendie* (1954; the fire), and *Le métier à tisser* (1957; the loom); (2) the deliberate experimentation with a variety of styles inspired by CUBISM, science fiction, the techniques familiar to readers of Virginia WOOLF, FAULKNER, and KAFKA, psychoanalysis, and SURREALISM, as well as the exploration of a Jungian world in which dichotomies of male-female impulses or good and evil compete for preeminence in the individual and in the couple, notably in *Qui se souvient de la mer* (1962; he who remembers the sea), *Cours sur la rive sauvage* (1964; run on the wild shore), *La danse du roi* (1968; the dance of the king), and *Habel* (1977; Habel); and (3) the candid scrutiny of clashes between life styles or sociopolitical convictions in war-torn and postbellum Algeria, as in *Un été africain* (1959; an African summer), *Dieu en Barbarie* (1970; God in Barbary), and *Le maître de chasse* (1973; the hunt master).

All of D.'s novels, as well as his short stories, possess many good qualities, but particularly successful are the narratives that fully convey D.'s keen insight into man's responses to the psychological pressures of human relationships and immediate external events, his sensitive use of discontinuity in time and space, and his vast poetic powers.

D.'s best novels to date are *Qui se souvient de la mer* and *Le maître de chasse*. The former is a tour de force in which a crumbling city, possibly representing colonial values, yields to a nether world where ancient values might once again take root. Frequent references to a mythic sea and variations on the theme of the concept of the soul reflect an imagination conversant with the writings of C. G. JUNG.

Le maître de chasse is a powerful ideological diptych contrasting the Algerian technocracy and the vision of a mystic who feels, as D. always has, that the *fellah* (peasant) is the rock of ages of Algerian society. The discussion between Waëd the technocrat and Madjar the mystic escalates to a confrontation over governmental priorities and the prospects of an irrigation project, and Madjar is killed when an army detachment tries to prevent him from leading the peasants in the quest for water. The novel, couched in a hard-edged idiom akin to Arabic, is nevertheless the vehicle for a highly lyrical evocation of the eternal earth, which, with Madjar's dust, will somehow outlive even the most tenacious injustice.

D.'s poetry, ever since his first collection, *Ombre gardienne* (1961; guardian shadow), has been consistently hermetic, characterized by haunting ambiguity, dense and truncated syntax, and subtle eroticism. In many of the poems, the compact imagery and intricate semantics, although hypermodern, bring to mind traditional Islamic polygonal and foliate designs. Some of his later poems are spontaneous flashes from the unconscious, while other texts were revised for years until reduced to their essentials.

The heart of D.'s creative vision lies at the intersection of the particular plane of modern Algerian history and the universal plane of Jungian psychological insight.

FURTHER WORKS: *Au café* (1955); *Le talisman* (1966); *Formulaires* (1970); *Omneros* (1975); *Feu beau feu* (1979); *Mille hourras pour une gueuse* (1980)

BIBLIOGRAPHY: Ortzen, L., *North African Writing* (1970): 20–43; Sellin, E., "Algerian Poetry: Poetic Values, M. D. and Kateb Yacine," *JNALA*, Nos. 9–10 (1971): 45–68; Déjeux, J., *Littérature maghrébine de langue française* (1973): 143–79; Kara, F. Sari-Mostefa, "L'ishrâq dans l'œuvre de M. D.," *ROMM*, No. 22 (1976): 109–18; Junkins, D., ed., *The Contemporary World Poets* (1976): 1–4; Salem, G., "The Algerian Writer: M. D. in the 'Algeria' Trilogy, the Life of a People in a Narrative Experiment," *LAAW*, 30, 4 (1976): 22–40; Déjeux, J., *M. D., écrivain algérien* (1977)

—ERIC SELLIN

DICKEY, James

American poet, novelist, and critic, b. Feb. 2, 1923, Atlanta, Ga.; d. 19 Jan. 1997, Columbia, S.C.

D.'s early life gave promise of an athletic career. In high school and at Clemson College he played football and developed an enduring interest in physical contests and the tension of competition. He interrupted his education in 1942 to join the air force and flew many bombing missions in the Pacific. During this period he

James Dickey

started reading poetry and trying his own skill at what he thought of as another contest. After the war he continued to study literature at Vanderbilt University, read the work of the Southern Agrarians, and began an academic career, but he soon became disillusioned with graduate school ideals and teaching freshman English. The Korean War brought him back into combat; when it was over he tried teaching again, but gave it up for a good living in advertising. Unlike Wallace STEVENS's serene reconciliation of business and poetry, D.'s career in the late 1950s was a tug-of-war. He gave up his job when his poetry began to gain recognition and reentered the academic world as a writer-in-residence at various colleges. In 1965 he won the National Book Award; thereafter, he served as Poetry Consultant for the Library of Congress.

D. is a romantic vitalist whose work is informed by instinct and passion. In this sense, he is estranged from the formalist, "locked-in" tradition of ELIOT and POUND. His writing is intense, adventurous, and unhampered by the inhibitions and preciosities of aesthetes. He maintains that poetry should be concerned with large, basic emotions, and he has "opened out" his own verse forms and rhythms to capture experience ranging from the excitement of hunting and the joyous communion with nature to the desperation of facing illness and death. D.'s obsession with mortality and his drive to struggle with life itself in sports and battle are reminiscent of HEMINGWAY's tragic striving. But his titanic enthusiasms, his belief in renewal and rebirth, and his "accessibility to experience" place him in the line of Whitman and the English romantics.

Into the Stone (1960) is a volume of tightly constructed and elusive poems that explore death and renewal. Thus, "Sleeping Out at Easter" dramatizes a ritual of spiritual rebirth through nature. The Hemingwayesque side of D. is prominent in *Drowning with Others* (1962): he commented that this volume is about the feeling of being "there . . . in that specific kind of life-or-death relationship." *Helmets* (1964) pursues this theme, most especially in "Drinking from a Helmet," in which a young soldier achieves intimacy with death by drinking from his fallen comrade's helmet.

D.'s best volume of verse, *Buckdancer's Choice* (1965), is remarkable for its compassion and self-knowledge. The poet's range is also on display: he moves from his mother's sickroom to the cockpit of a bomber; he registers again what it is to "be there"— and to be an ambivalent yet highly responsive witness to human suffering. The pilot of "The Firebombing" recollects his horrifying missions in suburban tranquility and cannot forget either the thrill of action or the anonymous Japanese "suburbanites" that he killed. D.'s famous "split line"—which involves gaps between words instead of punctuation—adds to the power and urgency of the poem.

Such technical changes in the service of "openness" make later works in *Poems 1957–1967* into "great shimmering walls of words": D. likens his poems of this period to the paintings of Mark Rothko. "Falling" has become an anthology piece not only because of this structural originality, but also because of its sheer audacity of conception: it records the sensations of an airline stewardess who falls to her death from a plane. "May Day Sermon" foreshadows the novel *Deliverance* (1970) in its wild obsession with violence and passion.

D.'s latest volume of poetry, *The Strength of Fields* (1979), is partly a reaffirmation of established themes: the cruelty and exhilaration of sports—machismo and its miseries—are dealt with in "For the Death of Lombardi"; other poems are haunting remembrances of flying.

Narrative is an important feature of D.'s poetry, and *Deliverance* is a sequel to many poems that tell the story of a man's confrontation with the otherness of nature. D. has said that "there is a part of me that is absolutely untouched by anything civilized." This is the part of the self that Ed Gentry, the novel's protagonist, encounters on a weekend trip down the remote Cahulawashee River in north Georgia. While often simplistic in its code of manhood and its arbitrary condemnation of the "unfit," *Deliverance* is a palpitating journey into self-awareness. The medium of recognition is the primitive, life-giving, and murderous river and its terrifying mountain inhabitants. Gentry—reluctant disciple of a back-to-nature fanatic—is delivered from suburban lethargy, from his own narrowness, and finally from the savagery of man and the implacable forces of nature. The plot of journey-return-repression is brilliantly symbolized by the inundation of the river valley by a dam project.

In the spirit of the poetry and *Deliverance*, D.'s criticism celebrates an aesthetic of "immediacy." *Self Interviews* (1970) is a tour of the poet's mind; the raw material of art is revealed as Dickey surveys his works and his feelings about them. *Sorties* (1971), a journal and essays, adopts a Wordsworthian stance—that of the poet trying to intensify common speech—and at the same time rejects the contemporary confessional mode of Sylvia PLATH and Anne SEXTON.

In an age that has vacillated between self-absorbed aestheticism and relevance, Dickey has taken his own direction: at once experiential and philosophical, he has won a large readership and considerable, though alloyed, critical praise.

FURTHER WORKS: *The Suspect in Poetry* (1964); *Two Poems of the Air* (1964); *Babel to Byzantium* (1968); *The Eye-Beaters, Blood, Victory, Buckhead and Mercy* (1970); *Jericho: The South Beheld* (1974); *The Zodiac* (1976); *God's Images* (1977); *Tucky the Hunter* (1978)

BIBLIOGRAPHY: Rosenthal, M. L., *The New Poets* (1967): 325–26; Howard, R., "J. D.: 'We Never Can Really Tell Whether Nature Condemns Us or Loves Us,'" in *Alone In America: Essays on the Art of Poetry in the United States Since 1950* (1969): 75–98; Paul Gray, P. E., on *Deliverance, YR*, 60 (1970), 101; Silverstein, N., "J. D.'s Muscular Eschatology," *Salmagundi*: 22–23 (1973): 258–68; Oates, J. C., "Out of the Stone, into the Flesh: The Imagination of J. D.," in *New Heaven, New Earth: The Visionary Experience in American Literature* (1974): 205–63

—DAVID CASTRONOVO

DIDION, Joan

American novelist and essayist, b. 5 Dec. 1934, Sacramento, Cal.

D. was graduated from the University of California at Berkeley with a B.A. in English in 1956, and in that same year became an associate feature editor with *Vogue* magazine in New York City. In 1964 she moved to Los Angeles, where (except for a brief stay in Trancas, on the Pacific coast) she has lived ever since. A disciplined writer who works daily at her craft, D. has published three novels, two collections of essays, and innumerable pieces for *Vogue, The National Review, Harper's, Holiday, Life*, and *The Saturday Evening Post*. She has collaborated with her husband, the

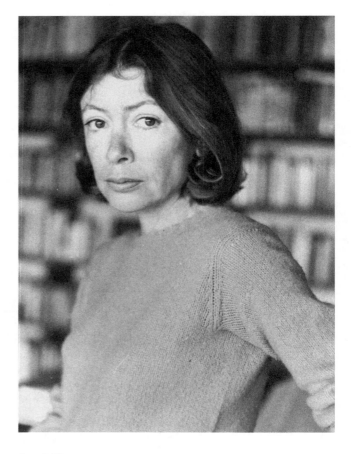

Joan Didion

writer John Gregory Dunne, on screenplays for several films, including *Panic in Needle Park* (1971), the 1972 movie of her novel *Play It as It Lays* (1970), and the 1976 version of *A Star Is Born*. Reclusive by temperament, D. forces herself to accept journalistic assignments, considering them a source of fictional material.

Unlike many other contemporary writers of fiction, D. retains many traditional features of the novel: real settings; plots that have a beginning, middle, and end; characters whose behavior is consistent. Her main characters, the majority of whom are women, attempt to live by the old American values of hard work, filial and parental devotion, and blind faith in the future, but fall victim to the dramatic social and economic changes of the 20th c.

The erosion of traditional values is a theme in the novel *Play It as It Lays*, a biting portrayal of the society of the Beverly Hills film world, in which people use each other to gain success, recognition or sensual pleasure. The novel chronicles the emotional breakdown of Maria Wyeth, an out-of-work actress who is tormented with longing for her dead mother and her institutionalized brain-damaged daughter. Toward all the men in her life—her estranged husband, former and current lovers—Maria feels intense ambivalence. She has an illegal abortion that becomes the central event in the novel, both literally, because she cannot recover from the guilt and loss that it produces, and figuratively, because all of her relationships are aborted—sometimes through her own fear, but more often through the cruelty or indifference of others.

D.'s latest novel, *A Book of Common Prayer* (1977), has a complex narrative structure and a rich cast of characters. The narrator, Grace Strasser-Mendana, is a former anthropologist of distinction who gave up her profession to marry a wealthy planter from Boca Grande, a fictitious Latin American country. Now widowed and dying of cancer, she is moved to tell the story of Charlotte Douglas, a California woman who, unable to accept the fact that her daughter has become a radical terrorist, wanders through the United States with her lover before settling alone in Boca Grande, where she finally dies in a revolution. Charlotte's traditional values failed to prepare her for the harsh political realities of contemporary society.

D.'s fictional style is tight and colloquial, stripped of any expansive descriptions or explanations. Much of the strength of her fiction resides in this dramatic style, which she uses to bring the reader close to the events and characters and to render complex, often ironic relationships through pure dialogue.

D.'s two published collections of essays, *Slouching towards Bethlehem* (1968) and *The White Album* (1979), make a powerful statement about American society in the 1960s and early 1970s, presenting also a candid and moving picture of D. as a reflection of that society. D. sees the society as fragmented and chaotic—she writes of the naïve "flower children" of Haight-Ashbury in San Francisco in 1967, of a Black militant arrested for murdering a policeman, of relatives of the Vietnam dead. She locates not only the tragedy of the era, but also its folly ("Marrying Absurd," a description of the three-minute-wedding industry in Las Vegas). In her more recent collection, D. discovers some hope in strong-minded individuals like Georgia O'Keeffe, the painter.

D. defines herself in the essays as an American, a Californian, and a scrupulously self-critical woman. Her essays reflect her conservative social and political philosophy, her deep belief that problems must be resolved by individual courage and responsibility.

D. is a peculiarly American novelist and essayist concerned with the particular dreams and experience of contemporary Americans. Her fiction portrays the moral dilemmas and human suffering resulting from the confrontation between illusions drawn from the nation's past and the harsh reality of its present. She is perhaps most distinguished as a nonfiction writer, however, for her essays are lucid and unsentimental, their style swift and crisp.

FURTHER WORKS: *Run River* (1963)

BIBLIOGRAPHY: Schorer, M., "Novels and Nothingness," *ASch*, 40 (1970–71): 168–74; Kazin, A., "J. D.: Portrait of a Professional," *Harper's* (Dec. 1971): 112–14; Stimpson, C., "The Case of Miss J. D.," *Ms.* (Jan. 1973): 36–41; Oates, J. C., on *A Book of Common Prayer, NYTBR* (3 April 1977): 1, 34–35; Winchell, M. R., *J. D.* (1980); Henderson, K. U., *J. D.* (1981)

—KATHERINE U. HENDERSON

DI GIACOMO, Salvatore

Italian poet, short-story writer, dramatist, and journalist, b. 12 March 1860, Naples; d. 4 April 1934, Naples

D. G.'s father was a pediatrician and his mother a teacher at a music conservatory in Naples. Following his father's wishes, D. G. entered medical school but soon abandoned it to become a newspaper correspondent and writer. In 1893 he became assistant librarian

at the conservatory, and in 1903 he was made director of the Lucchesi Palli Collection in the National Library in Naples, a position he held throughout his life.

D. G.'s short stories and plays, written in Neapolitan dialect, portray emotion-laden events in the lives of people caught in hopelessly miserable situations and living in the poorest districts of Naples, in its public dormitories, hospitals, and prisons. In his stories, characters and settings are described with masterly realistic touches and a lyrical fascination with detail that does not preclude an alert awareness of moral and social problems.

In his plays, the major dramatic issues and tragic tensions are deliberately diffused by the garrulous comings and going of secondary characters. In *'O mese mariano* (1900; month of Mary), for example, a poor widow goes to visit her son in a public orphanage and is turned away by indifferent and chattering clerks who lie about her child's death. *Assunta Spina* (1910; Assunta Spina) is about a woman who drives her lover to a crime of passion; here, too, the melodramatic events are distanced from the audience, since they are seen through the descriptions of police officers, bureaucrats, relatives, and friends. This work became a standard in the repertory of *verismo* (Italian naturalism).

D. G.'s early collection of poems, also in the dialect of Naples, have a unifying narrative structure. The sonnets of *'O funneco verde* (1886; the green alley) give touching and humorous insights into the life of a harbor slum; the poems of *'O munasterio* (1887; *The Monastery, and Other Poems*, 1914) tell the melodramatic story of a friar driven to suicide by his obsessive thoughts about a woman; in the crisply placed *A San Francisco* (1895; in San Francesco—"Francisco" is dialect spelling) a vengeful murder is perpetrated in a cell of the San Francesco prison in Naples. From the study of passion as a cause of tragedy, D. G. moved on, in his later poems, to capture a variety of human emotions abstracted from realistic situations and framed in exquisite visual and musical images. In *Ariette e sunette* (1898; arias and sonnets), *Vierze nuove* (1907; new verses), and *Ariette e canzone nove* (1916; new arias and songs) D. G. expresses the sorrows, the joys, and the dreams of common people. Throughout this poetry there lingers a sense of fleeting time and impending death, conveyed in tonalities ranging from the dramatic to the pathetic and the ironic. D. G.'s capacity to capture moments of exuberant participation in life while hinting at its underlying hopelessness makes him the most gifted interpreter of the Neapolitan character.

Among D. G.'s many successful contributions to Neapolitan song are the lyrics to "Nannì" (1882; Nannì), "Carulì" (1885; Carulì), "A Marechiare" (1886; at Marechiaro), "'E spingole frangese" (1888; safety pins), and "Palomma 'e note" (1907; night butterfly). D. G. was also an active journalist and wrote many books on Neapolitan life, its music, its theater, its social mores, and its celebrities.

FURTHER WORKS: *Minuetto settecentesco* (1883); *Nennella* (1884); *Sonetti* (1884); *Mattinate napoletane* (1886); *La fiera* (1887); *Rosa Bellavita* (1888); *Zi' munacella* (1888); *Mala vita* (1889); *Canzoni napoletane* (1891); *Pipa e boccale* (1893); *L'abate* (1898); *Fantasia* (1898); *La piccola ladra* (1899); *Perlina e Gobbetta* (1899); *Nella vita* (1903); *Rosanna rapita* (1904); *Novelle napoletane* (1914); *Garofani rossi* (1916); *L'ignoto* (1920)

BIBLIOGRAPHY: Vossler, K., *S. D. G., ein neapolitanischer Volksdichter in Wort, Bild und Musik* (1908); Bacaloglu, H.,

Naples et son plus grand poète (1911); Maurino, F. D., *S. D. G. and Neapolitan Dialectical Literature* (1951)

—RINALDINA RUSSELL

DIKTONIUS, Elmer

Finnish poet, novelist, and critic (writing in Finnish and Swedish), b. 20 Jan. 1896, Helsinki; Nikkilö

Born into a family of working people (his grandfather was a carpenter, his father a printer), D. was keenly aware that he came from humbler stock than did most of his contemporaries in Swedo-Finnish letters. The family spoke Swedish, but—for practical reasons—D. attended a Finnish-language school; he became bilingual to the extent that his Swedish is shot through with Finnish idioms. At sixteen D. left school and educated himself by voracious reading. For a time he studied violin and composition at the Helsinki Music Institute.

Despite his sympathies with the workers, D. did not participate in Finland's civil war (1918). After military service in the medical corps (1919–20), D. studied music in Paris, London, and Cornwall (1920–21). But, realizing that his talent lay in literature, he returned to Finland.

D.'s first book, *Min dikt* (1921; my poem), made up largely of aphorisms, was ignored in Finland, except for the favorable review by a young modernist critic, Hagar Olsson; in turn, she introduced D. to Edith SÖDERGRAN and other members of the modernist group. After a second book of aphorisms, *Brödet och elden* (1922; the bread and the flame), D. became a recognized member of Helsinki literary life, thanks in good part to the very personal note of the causeries and reviews he wrote for the socialist paper *Arbetarbladet*. A second sojourn in Paris (1925–27) ended in illness and personal and financial disaster, and D. settled in Finland for good; he participated in the establishment of the modernist journal *Quosego* (1928–29) and then developed his considerable talents as a music critic, contributing to the liberal journal *Nya Argus*. D.'s first marriage ended in divorce (and his wife's subsequent suicide); a second, stable union made the 1930s into a decade of busy and productive calm for D.

D. aged early, physically and artistically; the quality and quantity of his work decreased during the 1940s, his energy being devoted to an eccentric but brilliant Swedish translation (1948) of a Finnish classic, Aleksis Kivi's (1834–1872) *Seitsemän veljestä* (seven brothers). Most of the final decade of his life was spent in hospitals and sanatoriums.

D.'s poetry can be divided into three phases. First, there are the "radical" poems, political and otherwise, that characterize the collections of the 1920s. *Min dikt*, in addition to the aphorisms, contains verse salutes to two main formative forces in his life: the painter Vincent van Gogh and D.'s own grinding poverty. The debut book was followed by the collection *Hårda sånger* (1922; hard songs), in which is included perhaps the most famous of D.'s poems, "Jaguaren" (the jaguar). *Taggiga lågor* (1924; barbed flames) presents a set of portrait poems, influenced by Edgar Lee MASTERS, on D.'s great cultural heroes, among them Dostoevsky, Gustav Mahler, Masters himself, Nietzsche, and STRINDBERG.

Stenkol (1927; coke) is probably D.'s strongest verse collection. Here, his major revolutionary odes frightened his more conservative audience: "Hjältegravar" (heroes' graves), a lament for the

Red soldiers killed in the civil war; "Den stora flyttningsdagen" (the great moving day), with its vision of a bourgeois world turned upside down; and "Marseljäsen" (the Marseillaise). The same audience was assuaged, though, by D.'s continuation of his portrait poems, in which he turned to Bach, Blake, Balzac, Poe, Gogol, and Kivi.

The poems of D.'s second period (1930s, early 1940s), which reveal a mellower tone, are characterized by his bizarre humor and rambunctious love of the grotesque, by his new devotion to his country, and by his love of nature. *Jordisk ömhet* (1938; earthly tenderness) is an example of the poetry written in these years.

Varsel (1942; warning sign), which appeared during the second of Finland's wars with Russia, is the closest D. came to a patriotic book. Among the Finnish heroes he eulogized are the composer Jean Sibelius and Kyösti Kallio, the republic's president from 1937 to 1940. Interspersed among these tributes are attacks on an unnamed tyrant and pastoral poems written in D.'s country retreat, Tuomistonoja, a farm in northern Uusimaa.

Annorlunda (1948; otherwise) and *Novembervår* (1951; November spring), volumes published in his third phase, contain several of his finest poems. Among these are the memorial to his first wife, "Overkligt sant (Till Meri i skogen)" (unreally true: to Meri in the forest), in *Annorlunda*; the portrait in *Novembervår* of the Finnish poet Eino LEINO; and his epitaph for his mother. Yet both these collections also offer some of his most careless verse. Attempting to return to the radical ideas of his youth, he could not recapture the vitality of his earlier political and social statements. Thus, his emotionalism easily became lachrymose.

D.'s imaginative prose is as inventive as his poetry. His "Finnish idyll" *Onnela* (1925; Onnela) shocked many readers but pleased others by its affectionate familiarity with Finland's peasants. In the principal story, "Hang dej, pojkfan" (hang yourself, brat), in the collection *Ingenting* (1928; nothing), about a boy acrobat's almost suicidal efforts to please a mob of drunken lumberjacks, the narration becomes stronger, the portraiture darker.

In 1932 D. published the short novel *Janne Kubik* (Janne Kubik). It is the story of a longshoreman who, during the civil war, becomes a Red soldier, then in the 1930s, a bullyboy of the fascist movement; he dies while employed as a strikebreaker. Although clever (in a naively opportunistic way) and physically strong, Janne has neither the wits nor the strength to survive in a Finland racked by political and economic crises. The book's elliptic sentences, its quick shifts of time and place, and its use of a quasi-learned "commentary" on the narrative made it a pioneer work in the Scandinavian novel.

D. is a central figure in Scandinavian literature of the 20th c., and, thanks to his inimitable style and personality, helped enormously in the breakthrough of modernism. In his lifetime, however, he failed to achieve two cherished goals: recognition on the international scene, and acceptance in Finland as a poet read at all levels of society and in both linguistic camps. The enthusiasm for the radical D., recently demonstrated by leftist critics, has diverted attention from the originality and substantiality of his contribution to literature.

FURTHER WORKS: *Ungt hav: Ny dikt i översättning* (1923); *Stark men mörk* (1930); *Eino Leino: Lyriskt urval* (1931); *Carl Sandburg: Dikter i urval* (1932, with E. Blomberg and A. Lundkvist); *Opus 12* (1933); *Medborgare i republiken Finland* (1935, 1940); *Mull och moln* (1934); *Gräs och granit* (1936); *Höstlig bastu* (1943); *Ringar i stubben* (1954); *Kirjamia ja kirjavia* (1956); *Dikter* 1912–1942 (1956); *Prosa* 1925–1943 (1957); *Meningar* 1921–1941 (1957)

BIBLIOGRAPHY: Schoolfield, G. C., *"The Postwar Novel of Swedish Finland,"* *SS*, 34 (1962): 85–110; Schoolfield, G. C., "E. D. and Edgar Lee Masters," in Skard, S., and Naess, H., eds., *Studies in Scandinavian-American Relations: Dedicated to Einar Haugen* (1971): 307–27; Schoolfield, G. C., "E. D. as a Music Critic," *Scan*, 15 (1976): 29–44; Wrede, J., *"The Birth of Finland-Swedish Modernism,"* *Scan*, 15 (1976): 73–103; Schoolfield, G. C., *E. D.* (1985)

—GEORGE C. SCHOOLFIELD

DİLMEN, Gűngőr

(also known as Gűngőr Dilmen Kalyoncu), Turkish dramatist and translator (writing in Turkish and English), b. 1930, Tekirdağ

One of Turkey's prominent dramatists, D. was educated at Istanbul's British High School and did his graduate work at the Department of Classical Philology at the University of Istanbul, and he studied theater arts at Yale University and the University of Washington, Seattle (1961–1964). He served as a play editor for the Istanbul City Theaters (1964–1966) and at the theater department of Turkish Radio (1966–1968). He lectured at Durham University, England, from 1970 to 1972. Since the late 1980s he has been teaching at the Istanbul State Conservatory and Bosphorus University as well as working for the Istanbul Municipal Theaters.

Most of D.'s major plays deal with mythological themes and Anatolian, Ottoman, and modern Turkish history. His first play, *Midas'ın kulakları* (perf. 1959, pub. 1965; the ears of Midas), which earned him immediate fame, is the first part of "The Trilogy of Midas," of which the second part is *Midas'ın altınları* (1970; the gold of Midas), and the third part, *Midas'ın kőrdűğűmű* (1975; Midas's Gordian knot). This trilogy, written in a poetic style, dramatizes the three best-known legends relating to the Phrygian king.

D.'s second play is *Canlı maymun lokantası* (1965; live monkey restaurant). Originally written in English, it is a strong indictment of modern colonialism in Hong Kong. His *Ak tanrılar* (1975; white gods) unfurls the conquest of the Aztec Empire, pitting Cortez against Montezuma. *Kurban* (1967; sacrifice/victim) portrays, in a loose adaptation of the Medea theme, the victimization of an Anatolian peasant woman.

Akad'ın yayı (perf. 1967, pub. 1983; the bow of Akkad) is one of the most effective Turkish dramatizations of an ancient myth: Akkad's bow in the Canaanite land. The same book contains *Deli Dumrul* (1979; Dumrul the mad), drawn from the millennium-old Turkish national epic (*The Book of Dede Korkut*, twice translated into English). The play shows how the Angel of Death confronts the protagonist Deli Dumrul with arduous tests. Among D.'s plays based on early Turkish history are *Bağdat Hatun* (perf. 1972, pub. 1982; Lady Bağdat), about the Ilhanid princess demonically driven to become a queen who stopped at nothing (not even the death of her father and brothers and the loss of her unborn child), and *Hasan Sabbah* (1983; Hasan Sabbah), about the political visionary who created a terrorist organization of assassins hell-bent to destroy the Seljuk state in the 11th c.

D. has also written plays dealing with late Ottoman history. These include *İttihat ve Terakki* (1969; the party of union and progress), a docudrama about the misguided idealism and the corrupt regime of "The Young Turks"; *İnsan ve devlet* (perf. 1984, pub. 1990; man and the state), the tragic story of an eminent statesman who pits himself against the empire's powers that be; and *Aşkımız Aksaray'ın en bűyűk yangını* (1991; our love is the greatest fire of Aksaray), the heartrending tale of the unrequited love of an ex-odalisque for an Armenian musician, leading to her setting one of Istanbul's most destructive fires. D.'s 1992 play *Hakimiyet-i milliye aşevi* (national sovereignty diner) deals with the behind-the-scenes politics of the Turkish struggle for independence in the early 1920s.

Also a leading translator, D. has provided Turkish versions of *Antigone* and *King Oedipus* of Sophocles, *The Persians* and *The Oresteia* of Aeschylus, and August STRINDBERG's *The Ghost Sonata*.

Ben, Anadolu (1985; *I, Anatolia*, 1991) is perhaps D.'s most celebrated work. It portrays, in separate vignettes, women from Anatolian mythology and history in Act I and numerous Ottoman Turkish women in Act II. It is a one-actress play depicting poignant, sometimes funny or bittersweet, dramatic moments in the lives of Anatolian women. Turkey's most famous actress Yıldız Kenter presented *Ben, Anadolu* scores of times in Turkey and special English-language performances at London's Queen Elizabeth Hall, New York's Lincoln Center, Moscow's Art Theater, Washington's Kennedy Center, and also in Germany, Denmark, Canada, the Netherlands, and other places.

No Turkish dramatist has claimed an expanse of history larger than D.'s terra firma. Few have been as successful in creating vivid action and lyrical dialogue. Most of his plays have beautifully crafted poetic passages. His work, at its best, transposes myths, legends, and history into engrossing dramatic experiences and creates powerful tragic characters. He has received wide critical acclaim for having brought new dimensions to the modern Turkish theater. His dramas are remarkable for the universality of their themes, characters, and human concerns.

D. has won virtually all of the major drama prizes of Turkey, including the İbrahim Şinasi Efendi Award (1964), the İlhan İskender Prize (1966–1967), the Turkish Language Society Award (1977), the Muhsin Ertuğrul Prize (1979), the Ankara Sanat Kurumu Prize (1991), and the Ministry of Culture Prize (1993).

BIBLIOGRAPHY: Halman, T. S, ed., *Modern Turkish Drama* (1976): 237–84

—TALAT SAIT HALMAN

DIMITROVA, Blaga

Bulgarian poet, prose writer, and translator, b. 2 Jan. 1922, Byala Slatina

Brought up in the ancient capital of Turnovo, D. graduated in Slavic philology from Sofia University in 1945, shortly after the communist seizure of power in 1944. In 1946 she left to do graduate work in the Soviet Union, completing a dissertation on Vladimir MAYAKOVSKY in 1950. All during her career she has written consistently and prolifically, producing lyric poems, narrative poems, lyrical novels, plays, travel impressions, essays, journalism, and translations. By the mid-1980s D. had become a leading advocate of democratic reforms, and after the fall of the communist dictatorship she ran for parliament in the elections of 1990. In January 1992 she was elected vice president of Bulgaria.

D. began publishing shortly before World War II, and her early poems demonstrate both her lyric gift and her orientation toward the everyday; they are also traditional in form. Her attitude toward the terrible times of 1943 already demonstrated that she had a deep understanding of historical catastrophe but nevertheless affirmed that life was good.

Although never a party member, D. sympathized with certain communist objectives at the beginning. In 1950, after the death of the communist prime minister Georgi Dimitrov (no relation), D. brought out a small volume, *Stikhove za vozhda* (verses on the leader), a cluster of chronologically arranged biographical lyrics on Dimitrov, clearly influenced by Mayakovsky in their fabricated enthusiasm for the new political order. In recent years, however, D. has avoided mentioning this collection.

In 1952–1954 D. spent two years as a construction worker in the Rhodope mountains, an experience that found romanticized expression in the moderately modernist novel *Putuvane kum sebe si* (1965; journey to oneself), a story of a woman who wishes to do a man's work in this world without ceasing to be a woman.

Putuvane kum sebe si was the first of several novels, generally relatively short and as modernist in their approach as they could be under Bulgarian circumstances. They include *Otklonenie* (1967; deviation), *Lavina* (1971; avalanche), and *Litse* (1981;face), a book literally "imprisoned" by the authorities until the end of the decade. D. also traveled to Vietnam on at least five occasions during the course of the Vietnam War, describing her experiences in *Podzemno nebe: Vietnamski dnevnik* (1972; subterranean heaven: a Vietnam diary) and using them as material for lyric poems describing the admirable behavior of ordinary people confronting the adversities of war.

For years D. wrote in the shadow of Bulgaria's best-known 20th-c. woman poet, Elisaveta BAGRYANA. When the latter effectively withdrew from the literary scene, D. not only succeeded her as the country's leading woman poet and literary intellectual, but also became one of her chief interpreters through such volumes as *Mladostta na Bagryana* (1975; Bagryanan's youth), written in collaboration with her critic-husband Yordan Vasilev; it contains reminiscences, portraits, and detailed poetic analyses of which perhaps only another poet is capable.

Still, it is as a lyric poet that D. has made her mark in Bulgarian literature. For most of her career she has been a consistent modernist, though not an extreme one. She is very much aware of language as a medium, but also of language as an artifact created by an entire culture over many centuries. She has visited western Europe on several occasions, and values its cultural achievements, but her strongest commitment is to her own people's roots, both distant and more to hand. She pays explicit tribute to the older generation of Bulgarian poets—including Bagryana and Atanas DALCHEV—who helped create the more immediate culture in which she moved. And she honors her father and mother, whose declining days she has recorded in moving lyrics. She is sustained, not constricted, by her links with past generations. She incorporates the legacy of the past into her own personality, which she will transmit to others in its entirety only when she dies.

In recent years, as Bulgarian cultural constraints have loosened, D.'s writing has become progressively more complex and difficult, as it deals with some of the deepest issues of human existence. In 1968 she wrote: "The guilty feeling of a transit passenger—/this never deserts me." In 1990 she published a long poem, *Tranzit* (transit), an allegory of her country's contemporary difficulties cast in the form of reflections of an airline passenger delayed by bad weather. "But we shall certainly take off!" are her final words.

D. is now something of an elder "statesman" of Bulgarian culture. In the past she was not a hero, but neither did she commit any actions of which she need be deeply ashamed. She has publicly admitted her earlier shortcomings and, more important, paid eloquent tribute to those few who, unlike her, at critical points raised protesting voices. A bout with cancer in addition to recent political developments has made her resolve to write each of her poems "as if it were her last," and not to distort the truth as she perceives it. This moral determination, coupled with her linguistic mastery, has made her perhaps the foremost literary figure of contemporary Bulgaria.

FURTHER WORKS: *Pesni za Rodopite* (1954); *Na otkrito* (1956); *Do utre* (1959); *Liliana* (1959); *Svetut v shepa* (1962); *Ekspeditsiya kum idniya den* (1964); *Obratno vreme* (1966); *Osudeni na lyubov* (1967); *Migove* (1968); *Ime* (1971); *Impulsi* (1972); *Kak* (1974); *Zabraneno more* (1976); *Gong* (1976); *Prostranstva* (1980); *Glas* (1985); *Labirint* (1987); *Mezhdu* (1991). FURTHER WORKS IN ENGLISH: *Because the Sea Is Black* (1989)

BIBLIOGRAPHY: Phillipov, V., "Experimentation in Present-Day Bulgarian Drama (B. D.'s *Dr. Faustina*)," in Birnbaum, H., and Eekman, T., eds., *Fiction and Drama in Eastern and Southeastern Europe* (1980): 305–25; Zdanys, J., "Voices from the Other Europe," *YR*, 79, 3 (1990): 470–73

—CHARLES A. MOSER

DINESEN, Isak

(pseud. of Baroness Karen Blixen; other pseuds: Tania Blixen, Osceola, Pierre Andrézel, etc.) Danish novelist and short-story writer (also writing in English), b. 17 April 1885, Rungsted; d. 7 Sept. 1962, Rungsted

D. grew up in a well-to-do patrician family, the daughter of the writer and army officer Wilhelm Dinesen, whose adventuresome spirit and storytelling talents left indelible impressions on D. At an early age she showed an artistic inclination; she attended the Royal Academy of Art in Copenhagen and made her literary debut in 1907 with several short stories. A decisive turning point was her marriage and settlement on a coffee plantation in Kenya in 1914. Following a divorce, D. ran the plantation by herself until bankruptcy in 1931 forced her to return to her childhood home near Copenhagen, where she remained until her death.

D.'s first major work, the short-story collection *Seven Gothic Tales*, written in English and published in the U.S. and England in 1934, created a literary sensation and was proclaimed a masterpiece by critics in the English-speaking world. The reception in Denmark, where a Danish edition, *Syv fantastiske fortællinger*, appeared in 1935, was more mixed, and the author was criticized for her elitism and lack of a sense of social responsibility. The stories, most of them set in old aristocratic Europe of the 18th and 19th centuries, are lengthy, sophisticated, and complicated tales about destiny. Two main subjects, love and dreams, are linked by the element of fantasy. "The Roads around Pisa" and "The Poet" deal with the powerlessness of those who attempt to go against fate and the will of God; "The Supper at Elsinore" with the dream as a substitute for true life; "The Deluge at Norderney" and the highly fantastic "The Monkey" with masques and metamorphosis. Central to the seven stories is D.'s philosophy that only through a resigned understanding of one's true God-given role in life is one able to reach a lasting inner balance.

D. continued in this vein with *Vinter-eventyr* (1942; *Winter's Tales*, 1942), which derives its title from Shakespeare but also contains an allusion to the situation in a Denmark occupied by German troops. Although shorter in length, stricter in composition, and set in periods closer to modern times, the eleven stories are based on the same philosophical idea as *Seven Gothic Tales*. "Skibsdrengens historie" ("The Sailor-Boy's Tale"), the most fantastic of the stories, tells how an old woman in animal form is able to help the title character accept his destiny. "Sorg-agre" ("Sorrow Acre"), which is based on a legend from southern Jutland about a peasant woman who sacrifices her life for her son, illustrates D.'s belief in a strict world order where man is regarded as a marionette in the hands of God. After publishing a thriller, *Gengældelsens veje* (1944; *The Angelic Avengers*, 1946), D. returned to tales of fantasy with *Sidste fortællinger* (1957; *Last Tales*, 1957). The masterful "En herregårdshistorie" ("A Country Tale") is a companion piece to "Sorg-agre" and deals with the recognition of the laws of human tragedy. In *Skæbne-anekdoter* (1958; *Anecdotes of Destiny*, 1958) D. elaborates further on the theme that man must believe in God's plan for him.

D.'s two autobiographical works, *Den afrikanske farm* (1937; *Out of Africa*, 1937) and *Skygger på græsset* (1960; *Shadows on the Grass*, 1960), are related both in style and subject matter. They describe the author's years in Africa but must be read as artistic re-creations and free interpretations of reality, with events and things seen as symbols. Closely studied, they are an expression of the same view of life as is found in the fictional works.

When D. appeared on the literary scene in the 1930s she was regarded as a strange and exotic bird among the realists of the time. As a storyteller she drew her inspiration from the Bible, the *Arabian Nights*, the works of Homer, and the Icelandic sagas. Rejecting the materialistic view of life, she felt more akin to the romantics, and in style and point of view she recalls Heinrich von Kleist and E. T. A. Hoffmann. Only after World War II was the true value of D.'s literary production recognized, and although she remained above the main literary currents, her influence can be detected among authors both in Denmark and abroad. In America, writers such as Truman CAPOTE and Carson MCCULLERS have acknowledged their indebtedness to D.

FURTHER WORKS: *Daguerreotypier* (1951; *Daguerreotypes*, 1979); *Spøgelseshestene* (1955); *Sandhedens hævn* (1960); *Ehrengard* (1963); *Essays* (1965); *Efterladte fortællinger* (1975); *Breve fra Afrika* (2 vols., 1978 *Letters from Africa*, 1981). FURTHER WORKS IN ENGLISH: *Daguerreotypes and Other Essays* (1979)

BIBLIOGRAPHY: Johannesson, E. O., *The World of I. D.* (1961); Langbaum, R., *The Gaiety of Vision: A Study of I. D.'s Art* (1964); Migel, P., *Titania: The Biography of I. D.* (1968); Svendsen, C., and F. Lasson *The Life and Destiny of Karen Blixen* (1970); Hannah, D., *"I. D."* and *Karen Blixen: The Mask and the Reality*

(1971); Whissen, T. R., *I. D.'s Aesthetics* (1973); Thurman, J., *I. D.: The Life of a Storyteller* (1982)

—MARIANNE FORSSBLAD

DIOP, Birago

Senegalese short-story writer and poet (writing in French), b. 11 Dec. 1906, Dakar; d. 29 Nov. 1989, Dakar

D. grew up in a tradition-bound African family. In 1920 he left Dakar to study on a scholarship in Saint Louis, Senegal. After completing college and a year of military service, he left for France to study veterinary medicine at the University of Toulouse. D. then went to Paris to complete his studies.

It was in Paris that he met many African, Black American, and Caribbean students, including his compatriot Léopold Sédar SENGHOR and the Caribbean writers Léon-Gontran DAMAS and Aimé CÉSAIRE. The concept of NÉGRITUDE, a term coined by Césaire, was gaining importance, and these young students in Paris spoke and wrote about the need to affirm Black cultural values in a world in transition.

During this period of enthusiasm for African tradition, D. began to work with the African folktale. His aim was to make the oral tradition accessible to the French reading public, who had no previous contact with it, and to those Africans who, like himself, were living abroad. These tales are collected in *Les contes d'Amadou Koumba* (1947; tales of Amadou Koumba), *Les nouveaux contes d'Amadou Koumba* (1958; new tales of Amadou Koumba), and *Contes et lavanes* (1963; tales and commentaries).

D.'s tales are drawn from the Wolof tradition of Senegal, to which he is intimately bound, and from the traditions he learned about on his travels through Africa as a veterinarian. Men, animals, and supernatural beings are the protagonists. D. draws upon the cycle indigenous to one region of West Africa, that of Leuk, the hare, and Bouki, the hyena. Each animal is portrayed with a stereotyped personality. Leuk and Bouki are locked in eternal combat; the cunning Leuk usually outwits Bouki, who is voracious and dull-witted.

Within the African oral tradition, the *griot* (storyteller) recreates his tales of mystery and enchantment only during the eeriness of the night. D. adheres to the tradition of the *griot* by telling his readers that these tales come by way of Amadou Koumba, a *griot* well acquainted with D.'s family. D. recreates the *griot's* style, one of anecdotes, puns, repetitions, digressions, and the humorous use of daily expressions.

The charm of D.'s work is to be attributed to the poetry, which is interspersed throughout. By alternating prose with poetry and songs, D. introduces an authentic rhythmic element as well as a heightening of the poetic effect of the work. Within the framework of the written folktale, the songs allow the reader to share more fully in the poetic fantasy of the writer.

Although D. has made stylistic changes and innovations in the tales, his social and moral code and his philosophical commitment remain welded to tradition. In his works we find first a basic conservatism; one must submit to nature and live within its bounds. Second, the supernatural, which is present everywhere, must be respected. Finally, the individual is expected to subordinate himself to the community. Anyone who is at odds with the community is doomed to a tragic fate. The work of D. provides a perspective on African culture that is informative and sensitive.

FURTHER WORKS: *Leurres et lueurs* (1960); *La plume raboutée* (1978). FURTHER WORKS IN ENGLISH: *Tales of Amadou Koumba* (1966)

BIBLIOGRAPHY: Senghor, L. S., *Preface to Les nouveaux contes d'Amadou Koumba* (1958): 7–23; Maunick, E., "L'Afrique sans masque: B. D.," *NL*, 16 July 1964: 6; Mercier, R., and Battestini, M. and S., *B. D., écrivain sénégalais* (1964); Kennedy, E. C., Introduction to Kesteloot, L., *Négritude Is Born: Black Writers in French* (1974): 31–29; Kane, M., *"Les contes d'Amadou Koumba": Du conte traditionnel au conte moderne d'expression française* (1968); Mercier, R., M. Battestini, and S. Battestini, *B. D., écrivain sénégalais* (1964)

—MILDRED MORTIMER

DJAOUT, Tahar

Algerian poet, novelist, and journalist (writing in French) b. 11 Jan. 1954, Azeffoun (Greater Kabylia); d. 2 June 1993, Algiers

Born into a poor Berber family in Kabylia, D. studied mathematics at the University of Algiers and began writing poetry in his late teens. He published his first collection of poems, *Solstice Barbelé* (Barbed Wire Solstice), in 1975. In 1976 D. began his journalistic career writing articles on art and culture for the French language weekly *El Moudjahid* and then *Algérie-Actualité*. He also wrote for *L'Actualité de l'Immigration* in France and the *RevueCelfan/Celfan Review* in the U.S. under such pen names as Tayeb S. and Temim Dhofari. D. obtained a graduate degree in journalism and communications from the University of Paris II in 1985.

On May 26, 1993, D. was shot in the head as he was about to leave for work at the newspaper office of *Ruptures*, the independent weekly he had founded in January 1993. He went into a coma and, without ever regaining consciousness, died at the age of thirty-nine. D. was both the first journalist and the first writer after Jean SÉNAC—a French-Algerian poet brutally murdered in 1973 and a mentor to D.'s generation—to be assassinated in independent Algeria. He was at the peak of his journalistic and literary career. A hideous act of violence, D.'s assassination attacked the individual for whom language was an act of resistance: "If you keep quiet, you die. If you speak, you die. Then, speak and die!" wrote D. shortly before his death.

D. was the first Algerian intellectual to be assassinated by suspected fundamentalist terrorists (although it is still not clear who actually is responsible for his death) in a wave of unspeakable violence that has since cost the lives of thousands of Algerians. A Berber, writing in French, D. was condemned for being a "lay-communist." In a state advocating an Arabo-Muslim national identity, where Berber cultural claims were viewed as suspect, D., a spokesperson for ethnic, religious, linguistic and cultural pluralism, was definitely a persona non grata. He was as much against religious fanaticism as bureaucratic autocracy.

Although best known outside Algeria for his novels, D. always considered himself first and foremost a poet. He is the author of

five collections of poems that include *Solstice Barbelé, L'arche à vau-l'eau* (1978; The Ark Downstream), and *Perennes* (1993; Perennials). He also edited an anthology of young Algerian poets entitled *Les mots migrateurs* (1984; Migrating Words). Like birds (a prominent metaphor for childhood and freedom in D.'s writing), words must migrate, that is, be freed from their habitual usage and allowed to circulate freely, creatively.

Born at the eve of the Algerian war for independence, D. belongs to a literary generation that came into its own along with a new nation. It was a generation seeking to free itself from the paralyzing hold of an official historical discourse that could not account for the identity of a nation's youth marked by the thirst for independence and not the commemoration of war. If history, for D., is a discourse of usurpation, a site of dispossession, poetry is the means by which the habitual order of words and things is subverted, the place where freedom is learned.

Desire and revolt are at the heart of D.'s poetry. In one of his earliest poems, "Birthday," he notes that "There are cities where it is horrible to be twenty." Writing from the closed and guarded city of taboos and prohibitions, D. speaks for the alienated youth of his country, who comprise the majority of the population. Considering how prohibitions regarding freedom of the individual have led to a senseless civil war, it is clear that D.'s poetry is inherently political.

D. is especially known for his four novels, *L'exproprié* (1981; rev. ed., 1991; The Expropriated), *Les chercheurs d'os* (1984; The Bone-Seekers), *L'invention du désert* (1987; The Invention of the Desert), and *Les vigiles* (1991, The Vigils). *L'exproprié*, a poetic novel, alludes both to D.'s ancestors, Algerian Berbers whose lands were expropriated by the French and who rose up in arms in 1871, and to the plight of an uprooted and nomadic individual, who seeks to forge his language and identity in a postindependence Algeria torn between Arabo-Berber and French cultures. D. received the 1984 Duca Foundation prize for his second novel, *Les chercheurs d'os*, which deals with the Algerian war and its aftermath. A young adolescent must bring his brother's remains back to the village so that he can be assured of a proper burial. History takes the form of a cadaver: a new generation that has yet to experience life is forced to squabble over the remains of the dead, while the ruling elders gorge themselves with the spoils, like vultures feeding upon the sacrifices of others.

In *L'invention du désert* D. takes us back in time in order to reflect on the Arab conquest of the Maghreb. By focusing on Ibn Tumart, the founder of the Almohad dynasty, D. questions the notion of purity at the heart of religious fanaticism in Algeria today. *Les vigiles*, on the other hand, is a corrosive novel on the bureaucratic Algerian society of the late 1980s that has no use for the individual. Published posthumously, *Les vigiles* obtained the first Kateb Yacine Prize from the Noureddine-Aba Foundation, as well as the Mediterranean Prize. Despite their different historical settings and subjects, both novels allude to the rise of fundamentalism in the Maghreb.

Born at the eve of the Algerian revolution and killed in its aftermath—the bloody civil war of the early 1990s—it is no wonder that D.'s relationship with history has been so adversarial as he sought to give a voice to a new generation's quest for individual rights in an emergent nation. D.—whose first name, Tahar, means "the pure one"—will always be remembered as a symbol of resistance to fanaticism and totalitarianism.

FURTHER WORKS: *Insulaire et Cie* (1980); *L'oiseau minéral* (1982); *Les rets de l'oiseleur* (1984)

BIBLIOGRAPHY: Mammeri, M., *Entretiens avec T. D.* (1987); Lippert, A., "T. D.," *CelfanR*, 7, 3 (1988): 2-5; Fève, J., "Les écrivains algériens de la nouvelle génération," *Itinéraires et Contacts de Cultures* (1990), Vol. 2: 105-16; Naudin, M., "T. D.: Paysage métaphorique de l'Algérie," *FR*, 70, 1 (1996): 81-89; Geesey, P., "Exhumation and History: T. D.'s *Les chercheurs d'os*," *FR*, 70, 2 (1996): 271-79

—DANIELLE MARX-SCOURAS

DJAVAKHISHVILI, Mikheil

(pseudonym of Mikhail Adamashvili) Georgian writer, essayist, journalist, and translator, b. 1880, Kakheti; d. 1937, Georgia

The immediate success of D.'s first story "Chanchura" (1903; A Tramp) was particularly remarkable in view of the fact that he received a predominantly Russian education, first in Georgia, and then in Russia where he lived until 1901, and had all but forgot his native tongue. Soon, more of his short stories and several essays appeared in various Georgian periodicals. During this period he became closely associated with the group of Georgian intellectuals involved in the political movement for the national independence of Georgia. In the newspaper *Glekhi* (Peasant), of which he was an editor, D. published a series of articles strongly critical of Russia's colonial policy in Georgia.

After the defeat of the 1905-6 revolutionary movement that rocked the Russian empire, D. fled to Europe to avoid arrest and lived mostly in Paris, where he attended classes in classical philology at the Sorbonne. He returned to Georgia with a false passport in 1909, was twice arrested, and exiled to Russia. D. returned to Georgia after the October revolution of 1917. In February 1921 the country was forced to enter into an alliance with Soviet Russia and soon became one of the Soviet Socialist Republics of the U.S.S.R.

The year 1924 marks the beginning of the second period in D.'s literary career. Within a short period of time he published four novels: *Kvachi Kvachantiradze* (1924; Kvachi Kvachantiradze), *Djako's Khiznebi* (1925; Djako's Refugees), *Tetri saqelo* (1926; The White Collar), and *Givi Shaduri* (1928; Givi Shaduri). The first three are among the best works ever written in 20th-c. Georgian prose. His last two novels, *Arsena Marabdeli* (1933-36; Arsen from Marabda) and *Kalis tvirti* (1936; Woman's Bondage), were written at the request of Communist Party authorities, but they still maintain the technical brilliance of D.'s narrative style.

D. continued to write short stories and essays on Georgian and European literature, published his translations of Maupassant's stories and the novel *Cher Ami*. In 1936, for his literary work and public service, he was awarded Order of the Red Banner, the highest honor a Soviet writer could receive. However, the following year D. was arrested on charges of high treason and shot. In 1956 he was rehabilitated posthumously and his works, after being banned for twenty years, were published again.

D.'s early stories were, according to the writer's own admission, strongly influenced by Flaubert, Maupassant, and Maxim Gorky. In his novels of the 1920s, D. abandoned the extreme naturalism and detailed psychological analysis that dominated his early stories and shifted his attention to broader philosophical and

social problems pertaining to the historic events that redefined the future of his country. One can trace a certain influence of symbolist philosophy and esthetics in D.'s works. However, it is not the mystical and esoteric but the social and psychological aspects of human existence that constitute the major themes of his novels. His imagery often lends itself to allegorical rather than symbolic interpretations. Thus, in the novel *Djako's Khiznebi* the two main protagonists, Teimuraz, a sophisticated intellectual of aristocratic birth, and his former serf, Djako, an illiterate brute of a man, can be seen as allegorical figures representing two opposing social groups in Georgia just before and soon after the revolution of 1917. The characterization of these two men reveals D.'s attitude to and evaluation of the social and psychological phenomena that, in his opinion, made this revolution possible. Even Teimuraz's beautiful wife, Margarita, who is seduced by the cunning and ruthless Djako, the epitome of almost animalistic virility, can be seen as a possible allegory for Georgia.

The opposition between nature and civilization is the central theme of his novel *Tetri saqelo*. The title itself is an allegory with a dual meaning. On one hand, it stands for the starched white collar of a freshly laundered shirt for which the hero, an urban intellectual, longs while living in a small village high in the mountains where the patriarchal lifestyle and its values have remained unchanged since the 12th c. On the other hand, the title refers to the snow-covered mountain tops, the "white collar" of nature that protects the hero from the onslaught of modern civilization.

Kvachi Kvachantiradze is a picaresque novel with all the classic features of the genre. It chronicles the adventures of an unscrupulous rascal who benefits from every unexpected turn of his life. Realistic in manner and episodic in structure, the novel is a perfect vehicle for the author's satirical vision of life. Its temporal framework, which spans a little over three decades coincides with the lifetime of the main protagonist, Kvachi Kvachantiradze. He is a witness, and in his own peculiar way, a participant of the major historic events from the turn-of-the-century era to the mid-1920s. After the publication of the novel Kvachi became a common name for an insouciant rascal who can always find his way out of any difficult situation. The pessimistic implications of the novel are balanced with its comic plot and the exceptionally exuberant prodigality of the narrative style, which combines florid ornamentalism with colloquial jargon and dignified rhetoric with earthy humor. In the 1930s *Kvachi Kvachantiradze* was condemned by the critics as a "pulp novel," and only in the late 1950s was it recognized as a masterpiece of contemporary Georgian prose.

—DODONA KIZIRIA

DJEBAR, Assia

(pseud. of Fatima-Zohra Imalayen) Algerian novelist (writing in French), b. 4 Aug. 1936, Cherchell

D. is Algeria's most prominent woman writer. Known primarily as a novelist, she has also written poetry, plays, and short stories, and has produced two films. Born in Cherchell, a small coastal town near Algiers, D. completed secondary school studies in Algiers, did a preparatory year at the Lycée Fénélon in Paris in 1954, and the following year became the first Algerian woman admitted to the prestigious École Normale Supérieure de Sèvres in France. Joining in the Algerian student strike of 1956, in the early years of the Algerian independence struggle, she skipped final exams and wrote her first novel, *La soif* (1957; *The Mischief*, 1958).

D.'s earliest protagonist is a cultural hybrid. Half-French, half-Algerian, Nadia faces none of the constraints imposed upon traditional Arab women in colonial Algeria. She moves freely in public space and, when not sunbathing on the beach, drives around town in a flashy sports car. Below the surface of this portrait of a hedonist existence, the reader encounters a serious study of psychological development.

Dalila, the protagonist of *Les impatients* (1958; the impatient ones), typifies young women of the Algerian bourgeoisie just before the independence struggle. She expresses the impatience of a generation trying to free itself from an atrophied and hypocritical patriarchal society. D.'s first two novels complement each other: *La soif* depicts the breakup of a marriage viewed through the heroine's eyes; *Les impatients* centers upon the disintegration of a prospective marriage between the heroine and her fiancé. In D.'s early fiction, marriage and freedom seem incompatible.

At the end of the Algerian War (1954–1962), D. turned to the subject of women and war. With *Les enfants du nouveau monde* (1962; children of the new world) she focused on the collective experience of Algerian women awakening to new demands and using the war experience as a catalyst for personal growth. This novel also reworks a theme elaborated in *Les impatients*, the relationship between private and public space, the former reserved for women traditionally barred from public or male domain.

In historical terms, *Les alouettes naïves* (1967; the skylarks) is a sequel to *Les enfants du nouveau monde*, for it is set at the close of the war that had just begun in the previous novel. Introducing the multiplicity of scenes and characters, the emphasis upon daily life, and the lyrical prose of the earlier work, it is a text in which the combat provides a backdrop to the experiences of a young couple. D. now experiments with chronology and introduces an Arab woman assuming her sexuality within the couple. For the novelist, this work ends her first cycle in which female protagonists rebel against patriarchy, participate in the revolution, and expect a new order within which they may claim a public role in public space.

Beginning in the 1980s, D.'s quest for individual and collective identity led her to examine the legacy of the French conquest of 1830 via French Orientalist paintings and historical documents in French archives. *Femmes d'Alger dans leur appartement* (1980; *Women of Algiers in Their Apartment*, 1992), a collection of short stories that takes its title from Delacroix's painting, reveals D.'s new emphasis upon women bonding to struggle against an Algerian patriarchy that replaced the French colonial order. Women warriors discovered that with independence they had been excluded from the new order and were still denied access to public space and power.

L'amour, la fantasia (1985; *Fantasia: An Algerian Cavalcade*, 1993) alternates between an autobiographical journey and historical accounts of the French conquest of 1830 and the Algerian War. In search of women's contribution to Algerian history, D. uses documents and correspondence of the period as well as oral history of the Algerian revolution. She privileges the written and the spoken word as forms of liberation.

In Ombre sultane (1987; *A Sister to Scheherazade*, 1993) D. establishes bonds between traditional and emancipated women who share a common experience: patriarchy. The novel charts the process of liberation by which a cloistered and veiled woman

discovers the language and meaning of revolt. Finally, D.'s most recent work, *Loin de Medine* (1991; far from Medina), resuscitates the memory of seventeen historical women of the early years of Islam.

D.'s work has evolved in style from a linear first-person narrative wedded to realism to polyphonic postmodern texts. In the past three decades of her literary career, she has never departed from the commitment to explore the North African Muslim woman's world in all its contradictions and complexities.

FURTHER WORKS: *Poèmes pour l'Algérie heureuse* (1969); *Rouge l'aube* (1969); *La nouba des femmes du Mont Chenoua* (1969); *La Zerda ou les chants d'oubli* (1982)

BIBLIOGRAPHY: Zimra, C., " In Her Own Write: The Circular Structures of Linguistic Alienation in A. D.'s Early Novels," *RAL*, 1, 2 (1980): 206–23; Mortimer, M., "The Evolution of A. D.'s Feminist Conscience," in Wylie, H., et al., eds., *Contemporary African Literature* (1983): 7–14; Déjeux, J., *A. D.* (1984); Le Clézio, M., "A. D.: écrire dans la language adverse," *Contemporary French Civilization*, 9, 2 (1985): 230–44; Mortimer, M., "Language and Space in the Fiction of A. D. and Leila Sebbar," *RAL*, 19, 3 (1988): 301–11; Mortimer, M., *Journeys through the French African Novel* (1990): 147–64

—MILDRED MORTIMER

DÖBLIN, Alfred

German novelist, essayist, and dramatist, b. 10 Aug. 1878, Stettin (now Szczecin, Poland); d. 28 June 1957, Emmendingen

During his student years D. became deeply interested in the philosophy of Kant, Schopenhauer, and Nietzsche, and felt an early bent toward mysticism and religion; but he came to distrust these areas and decided to concentrate on the sciences. In 1905 he graduated from medical school in Freiburg (Breisgau), specializing in psychiatry and neurology.

For over twenty years D. practiced medicine in the east-side workers' district of Berlin, and also continued his earlier journalistic and essayistic endeavors. Writing became a passion with him. He developed into a prolific writer who used every available moment writing "in the streets and on the stairs," or while in attendance at hospitals and emergency stations. He became one of the founders of EXPRESSIONISM as well as of the literary magazine *Der Sturm* (1910). Soon, however, he discontinued his association with the group, and thereafter was an innovator unaffiliated with any literary program or organized movement.

For a time he believed in an economic and political solution to humanity's suffering, joined the Socialist Party, and developed a liberal, humanist socialism. After the burning of the Reichstag in 1933 he narrowly escaped arrest and emigrated to Zurich, Switzerland, and soon thereafter to Paris, acquiring French citizenship. When he had to flee the German occupying troops (he was Jewish) he had the good fortune to get to the U.S., where he settled in San Francisco.

In 1946 D. returned to Germany as a member of the French Ministry of Cultural Affairs. He worked toward a revival of German literary activity and published the magazine *Das goldene Tor* in Baden-Baden from 1946 to 1951. He was almost eighty at the time of his death, before which he had for several years been almost totally paralyzed.

A writer of vitality, originality, and visionary power, D. has often been described as one of the greatest narrative writers of 20th-c. Germany. His work is distinguished by an unusual multiplicity of forms and themes. Many critics have felt that he was deserving of the Nobel Prize. Still, of his many novels only one, *Berlin Alexanderplatz* (1929; *Alexanderplatz, Berlin*, 1931), achieved wide popularity.

From his early cynical view of a world operated blindly by mechanical law alone, D. advanced to that of a diabolically contrived world at the mercy of malevolent powers, thence to the theory of a petrified God. Now it was man's destiny to assert his faith in an invisible goodness and justice, thus calling to life the divine. In the course of his studies in natural history, D. gained the conviction that the world is composed of an all-pervading soul substance. Some parts of the primal substance, he thought, are always being pushed toward individuation and consciousness, while others sink back to "death," i.e., collectivity.

Basically, D. saw life as a battleground of the forces of good and evil. In the course of his work, he subordinated evil to an all-wise plan of Providence. Man is to become aware of his responsibility to seek out suffering in the spirit of sacrifice and atonement.

D.'s writing is dynamic and rebellious, but his baroque exuberance sometimes obscures central issues. His plots often lack a consistent plan, and details grow into confusing subsidiary themes.

D. presents amusing interludes, but their purpose is to instruct, not merely to entertain. Many of his comic effects are achieved by the use of the unadorned, often shocking language of the streets; even his poetic passages sometimes give way to Berlin slang. Newspaper articles, advertisements, and verbatim excerpts from reference works intermingle with surrealistic associations and fragments from the stream-of-consciousness of his characters, creating the compulsive sense of reality of a dream or hallucination. His use of realistically convincing and amusing material often serves only as a disguise for the real message. As D. stated, he did not wish to deteriorate into literary "artistry." For him writing was a quest for truth, not beauty, a serious matter of soul-searching and evangelism.

In spite of the seemingly varied selection of characters in D.'s novels, ranging from gods to beggars and criminals, he features only one basic person, an everyman elevated to cosmic proportions. This representative "man-in-the-street" is saved from haughty, complacent self-centeredness by a true avowal of poverty and humility. D.'s many geographic locations (India, South America, China, ancient Babylon, Greenland in the year 3000, or Berlin) are all the mythical land where man fights for his salvation amid demons and angels.

A true seeker, D. constantly abandoned earlier standpoints. He said that for him each of his books ended with a question mark.

D. received the Fontane Prize for his first epic masterpiece, the "Chinese" novel *Die drei Sprünge des Wang-lun* (1915; the three jumps of Wang-lun). In this work the author equates evil with "the fever" of the world, meaningless activity, sensual pleasure, complacent "happiness." The masses of the Truly Weak seek to escape from the bondage of carnal life by their creed of passivity, spiritual love, and self-sacrifice. The author used historically accurate data to obtain "the flavor of facts," but then progressed to magic and myth.

In his satirical-grotesque novel, *Wadzeks Kampf mit der Dampfturbine* (1918; Wadzek's fight with the steam turbine), D.

treats the dehumanizing aspects of technological progress. In the novel *Wallenstein* (2 vols., 1920; Wallenstein) the principles of activity and passivity are contrasted. Powerful mass scenes depict the chaotic, demoralizing features of war.

In a utopian novel of great visionary power, *Berge, Meere und Giganten* (1924; mountains, oceans and giants; rev. ed., *Giganten*, 1932), D. conjures up a frightening image of a monstrous, power-mad civilization. A thousand years hence he envisions experiments in the creation of artificial beings, global wars, subterranean cities, the volcanic de-icing of Greenland, and the reappearance of prehistoric monsters. The novel ends in a mood of hymnic return to nature, amid the veneration of spiritual, maternal powers.

Berlin Alexanderplatz seems at first glance merely a realistic novel about a teeming metropolis and the criminal activities of a transport worker, Franz Biberkopf. Soon, however, the baroquely cryptic chapter headings suggest deeper meanings, and parallels to Job and Jacob are inserted. Biberkopf, like Job, is subjected to a series of hardships to try his faith. After he submits willingly to death, everything is revealed to him, and he is reborn spiritually, becoming "seeing and feeling."

In the trilogy originally called *Amazonas* (the Amazon) D. once again examines the possibilities of escape from a spiritually corrupt civilization. In the novels of this trilogy, *Die Fahrt ins Land ohne Tod* (1937; the voyage to the land without death), *Der blaue Tiger* (1938; the blue tiger), and *Der neue Urwald* (1948; the new jungle), he describes the struggles of the Jesuit Fathers who attempted to found a religious state among the Indians of the South American jungles.

The trilogy *November 1918* (written in Paris and Los Angeles, 1937–41) consists of the following novels: *Verratenes Volk* (1948; betrayed people), *Heimkehr der Fronttruppen* (1949; return of the front-line troops), and *Karl und Rosa* (1950; Karl and Rosa). (A separate novel, *Bürger und Soldaten* [1939; citizens and soldiers] was originally planned as Volume I of the series). The chaos and political upheavals following World War I are the main topics of this work. Fantastic interludes are interspersed with factual data, and demons and phantoms communicate with historical figures such as Communist leader Rosa Luxemburg. A secondary theme is provided by the religious quest of a discharged army officer and teacher, Friedrich Becker.

Hamlet; oder, Die lange Nacht nimmt ein Ende (1956; written 1946; Hamlet; or, the long night is ended), the work of his old age, is the summation of a life that had probed the central problems of our time. It includes a relentless analysis of society during and after the war. In spite of many weaknesses it is a great novel, a worthy crowning of D.'s rich life's work.

FURTHER WORKS: *Lydia und Mäxchen* (1906); *Die Ermordung einer Butterblume* (1913); *Die Lobensteiner reisen nach Böhmen* (1917); *Der schwarze Vorhang* (1919); *Der deutsche Maskenball* (under pseud. Linke Poot;); *Die Nonnen von Kemnade* (1923); *Die beiden Freundinnen und ihr Giftmord* (1925); *Reise in Polen* (1926); *Das Ich über der Natur* (1927); *Manas* (1927); *A. D. im Buch—zu Hause—auf der Straße* (1928); *Die Ehe* (1930); *Wissen und Verändern! Offene Briefe an einen jungen Menschen* (1931); *Die deutsche Literatur im Ausland seit 1933* (1933); *Jüdische Erneuerung* (1933); *Unser Dasein* (1933); *Babylonische Wanderung* (1934); *Flucht und Sammlung des Judenvolkes* (1935); *Pardon wird nicht gegeben* (1935; *Men without Mercy*, 1937); *Nocturno* (1944); *Der Oberst und der Dichter; oder, Das menschliche Herz* (1946); *Der unsterbliche Mensch: ein Religionsgespräch* (1946);

Die literarische Situation (1947); *Heitere Magie: Zwei Erzälungen* (1948); *Unsere Sorge, der Mensch* (1948); *Schicksalsreise* (1949); *Ausgewählte Werke in Einzelbänden* (1960ff.); *Die Zeitlupe* (1962); *Gesammelte Erzählungen* (1971)

BIBLIOGRAPHY: Minder, R., "A. D.," in Friedmann, H., and O. Mann, eds., *Deutsche Literatur im 20. Jahrhundert: Gestalten und Strukturen* (1954): 283-303; Strelka, J., "Der Erzähler A. D.," *GQ*, 33 (1960): 197–210; Muschg, W., "Zwei Romane A. D.s," *Von Trakl zu Brecht* (1961): 198–243; Ziolkowski, T., *"A. D.: Berlin Alexanderplatz,"* *Dimensions of the Modern Novel* (1969): 99–137; Prangel, M., *A. D.* (1973); O'Neill, P., *A. D.'s "Babylonische Wanderung": A Study* (1974); Kort, W., *A. D.* (1974); Schoonover, H., *The Humorous and Grotesque Elements in D.'s "Berlin Alexanderplatz"* (1977); O'Neill, P., "The Anatomy of Crisis: A. D.'s Novel *Pardon wird nicht gegeben,"* *Seminar*, 14 (1978): 195–214; Fried, M., "The City as Metaphor for the Human Condition: A. D.'s *Berlin Alexanderplatz,"* *MFS*, 24 (1978): 41–64; Dollenmayer, D. B., *The Berlin Novels of A. D.* (1988)

—GLENN JERRY

DOCTOROW, E(dgar) L(awrence)

American novelist, b. 6 Jan. 1931, New York, N.Y.

E. L. Doctorow

D. is the grandson of Russian-Jewish immigrants and the son of parents he describes as "old-fashioned social democrats," a background that seems to account for his interest in leftist politics, Jewish experiences, and a wide range of Americana. He made a significant reputation as an editor during the 1960s, partially to the detriment of his own creative work, but his editor's knowledge of popular fiction has been useful to him as a writer.

Indeed, D.'s small body of writing exploits such stereotypical genres of popular fiction as the Western, the science-fiction story, the political and the historical novels. D.'s emphases are essentially social and psychological, however, and he does not turn to these popular genres either in loving tribute or in reaction against more literary genres. Rather, he thinks of them as crystallizations of popular culture into which he injects a serious level of social and psychological analysis.

In the bleakly poetic *Welcome to Hard Times* (1960), for instance, a man named Blue chronicles the rebuilding of his frontier town after its destruction by a desperado, only to witness later a compulsive self-destruction of the town, capped by the desperado's return. The Western genre interacts complexly with the sociology and psychology of the story, the naïve optimism of the Western playing against the sophisticated pessimism in a contrapuntal manner.

And this is much the effect, too, of *The Book of Daniel* (1971), a political novel in which Paul and Rochelle Issacson are fictional equivalents of the alleged spies Julius and Ethel Rosenberg. Daniel Isaacson, their son, narrates the story, interweaving his obsessive memories with his analytical insights in a desperate attempt to understand society's execution of his parents. But Daniel's analysis is turgid, inconclusive, and finally inadequate; political events defy understanding in this political novel, and the content again is in counterpoint to the genre.

D.'s most popular success has been the atypical *Ragtime* (1975), a loosely interwoven account of three families, one WASP, one Jewish immigrant, and one Black, all touched by the major social problems of the early 1900s, and all intermixing with such historical figures as Emma Goldman, J. P. Morgan, and Harry Houdini. The period elements give the book the semblance of a historical novel, but D. subordinates character, plot, and even social analysis to the period detail, and the net effect is a nostalgic celebration of the paraphernalia and personalities of the ragtime decade.

Critics have a way of disavowing an initially enthusiastic response to D.'s novels, particularly to the later novels, whose assemblage technique can seem undisciplined to some tastes. Few would deny D.'s technical facility, however, which extends even to a use of syncopated prose rhythms in *Ragtime*, nor would many refuse to grant that *Welcome to Hard Times*, with its taut elegance, is a very distinguished achievement.

FURTHER WORKS: *Big as Life* (1966); *Drinks before Dinner* (1979); *Loon Lake* (1980); *Lives of the Poets* (1984); *World's Fair* (1985); *Billy Bathgate* (1989); *Waterworks* (1994)

BIBLIOGRAPHY: Stark, J., "Alienation and Analysis in D.'s *The Book of Daniel,"* *Crit*, 16, 3 (1975): 101–10; Green, M., "Nostalgia Politics," *ASch*, 45 (1975–76): 841–45; Estrin, B. L., "Surviving McCarthyism: E. L. D.'s *The Book of Daniel,"* *MR*, 16 (1976): 577–87; Knorr, W. L., "D. and Kleist: 'Kohlhaas' in *Ragtime,"* *MFS*, 22 (1976): 224–27; Emblidge, D., "Marching Backward into the Future: Progress as Illusion in D.'s Novels," *SWR*, 62 (1977): 397–409; Neumeyer, P. F., "E. L. D., Kleist, and the Ascendancy of Things," *CEA*, 39, 4 (1977): 17–21; Parks, J. G., *E. L. D.* (1991); Fowler, D., *Understanding E. L. D.* (1992)

—ROBERT F. KIERNAN

DODERER, Heimito von

Austrian novelist, short-story writer, and poet, b. 5 Sept. 1896, Weidlingau; d. 23 Dec. 1966, Vienna

D., the son of an architect, grew up in Vienna. After graduating from secondary school in 1914, he saw combat in World War I as a lieutenant in the Dragoons, was captured by the Russians in 1916, and spent four years as a prisoner-of-war in Siberia. His war experiences form the background of his second novel, *Das Geheimnis des Reichs: Ein Roman aus dem russischen Bügerkrieg* (1930; the secret of the realm: a novel of the Russian civil war) and are taken up again in the unfinished second part of his last work, *Roman No. 7, Zweiter Teil: Der Grenzwald* (1967; novel no. 7, second part: the border forest). On his return to Vienna in 1920 he studied history and psychology at the university.

D.'s first book, the poetry collection *Gassen und Landschaft* (alleys and countryside), was published in 1923. This was followed in 1924 by the short novel *Die Bresche: Ein Vorgang in 24 Stunden* (the breakthrough: a proceeding in 24 hours). From 1927 to 1931 he contributed articles on literary and historical topics to newspapers. In 1929 he met Albert Paris GÜTERSLOH, whose first novel he had read in Siberia, and wrote the monograph *Der Fall Gütersloh: Ein Schicksal und seine Deutung* (1930; the Gütersloh case: a destiny and its interpretation). His friendship with Gütersloh influenced him profoundly as a writer. In World War II D. served as an officer in the German Air Force and was stationed mainly in France and Russia. He returned to Vienna in 1946, and in his later years was the recipient of many literary prizes.

D. published some poetry—*Ein Weg im Dunkeln* (1957; a way in the dark)—and essays, now collected in *Die Wiederkehr der Drachen* (1970; the return of the dragons), as well as two volumes of diaries, *Tangenten* (1964; tangents) and *Commentarii* (1976; Latin: commentaries), which span the crucial years 1940–56, and a collection of aphorisms entitled *Repertorium* (1969; Latin: repertory). But his main achievement undoubtedly lies in the short story and especially in the novel. *Die Erzählungen* (1976; the stories) contains all the short and "shortest" stories (*"Kürzestgeschichten"*) that D. wrote between 1920 and 1964. Among his outstanding works in shorter fiction are *Das letzte Abenteuer* (1953; the last adventure) and *Die Posaunen von Jericho* (1958; the trumpets of Jericho).

It was the publication of the novel *Die Strudlhofstiege; oder, Melzer und die Tiefe der Jahre* (written 1941–48, pub. 1951; the Strudlhof stairs; or, Melzer and the depth of the years) that brought D. his late fame at the age of fifty-five—a fame that continued to grow with the appearance of each subsequent novel, particularly with *Die Merowinger; oder, Die totale Familie* (1962; the Merovingians; or, the total family), and *Roman No. 7, Erster Teil: Die Wasserfälle von Slunj* (1963; *The Waterfalls of Slunj*, 1966). His fiction has earned him a secure place in the great tradition of the Austrian novel.

The central preoccupations of D.'s novels are (1) with the formative process, or rather the breakthrough, exemplified by *Die Bresche*, to the spiritually unique person latent in every human being, a process he calls *Menschwerdung* (humanization); and (2) with the varying degrees of apperception or the refusal of apperception of the given reality by his characters. The early novels of 1924–39—*Die Bresche, Ein Umweg* (written 1931–34, pub. 1940; a detour); *Ein Mord den jeder begeht* (1938; *Every Man a Murderer*, 1964); *Die erleuchteten Fenster; oder, Die Menschwerdung des Amtsrates Julius Zihal* (written 1938–39, pub. 1951; the illuminated windows; or, the humanization of Magistrate Julius Zihal)—confine themselves to a limited sector of reality and the "humanization" of one protagonist. No attempt is made to present a panoramic view of society.

The symphonically structured later novels deal with a broader range of subject matter and themes. *Die Dämonen* (1956; *The Demons*, 1961) was the more ambitious second effort (the first was *Das Geheimnis des Reichs*) to analyze the various revolutionary ideologies fermenting in the Austrian First Republic (which briefly infected D. himself). Over the years of the novel's various stages (he had begun work on it in 1931 after reading Dostoevsky's *The Devils*) the accent had shifted from the political events to a "symphonic" celebration of the depths and heights of Vienna. The novel is a panorama of Balzacian dimensions of all the strata of Viennese society. *Die Dämonen* is supplemented (or rather prefaced) by *Die Strudlhofstiege*, in which we meet many of the former novel's characters from the upper middle class at an earlier time (1910–25). Both novels exhibit D.'s sense of what Balzac termed the human comedy, and are enriched by his humor, which oscillates between irony and satire, his verbal wit, and his baroque imagination.

Until his death, D. was working on a novel cycle to which he had given the sparse overall title *Roman No. 7* (novel no. 7). This work was to consist of four self-contained novels or "symphonic movements," connected merely by formal design and thematic arrangement. It promised to be D.'s most systematically executed "total novel," a work with no main characters or dominant theme, in which D. the novelist-historian aimed to evoke the life "that happens in spite of history." Death silenced him in the middle of the second movement.

FURTHER WORKS: *Grundlagen und Funktionen des Romans* (1959); *Die Peinigung der Lederbeutelchen* (1959); *Unter schwarzen Sternen* (1966); *Meine neunzehn Lebensläufe, und neun andere Geschichten* (1966); *Frühe Prosa* (1968)

BIBLIOGRAPHY: Hatfield, H., "Vitality and Tradition," *Monatshefte*, 47 (1955): 19–25; Ivask, I., "H. v. D.'s *Die Dämonen, BA*, 31 (1957): 363–65; Jones, D. L., "Proust and D.: Themes and Techniques," *BA*, 37 (1963): 12–15; Weber, D., *H. von D.: Studien zu seinem Romanwerk* (1963); Hamburger, M., *From Prophecy to Exorcism* (1965): 131–39; "An International Symposium in Memory of H. v. D.," *BA* 42 (1968): 341–84; Schaffgotsch, X., ed., *Erinnerungen an D..* (1972); Larsen, M. D., "H. v. D.: The Elusive Realist," *ChiR*, 27, 2 (1974): 55–69; Pabisch, P. K., "The Uniqueness of Austrian Literature: An Introductory Contemplation on H. v. D.," *ChiR*, 27, 2 (1974): 86–96; Fischer, R., *Studien zur Entstehungsgeschichte der "Strudlhofstiege" H. v. D.s* (1975); Schmid, G., *D. lesen* (1978)

—IVAR IVASK

DOINAS, Stefan Augustin

(pseud. of Stefan Popa) Romanian poet and essayist, b. 26 April 1922, Caporal Alexa, Arad county

D., the son of a farmer, studied philosophy and literature at Sibiu and Cluj (under Lucian BLAGA), and was active in *Cercul Literar*, a group of young Transylvanian people committed to aesthetic and democratic ideas. After 1948 he could no longer publish and served a prison term for political reasons. Rehabilitated in 1962, he was on the editorial staff of several literary journals, won several prizes for poetry, and was for a few years a member of the leading body of the Romanian Writers' Union. After the 1989 revolution, D. joined one of the newly restored liberal parties, was for several years a senator, and honorary president of the Writers' Union. He was also elected a member of the Romanian Academy (1990).

D.'s early poetry, written in the 1940s, was intensely symbolic, fantastic and elegantly melodious, frequently resorting to ancient Greek and Roman, and medieval themes. The opulent, sometimes surrealistically luxuriant imagery was often integrated in a harmonious and hierarchical world image. The 1960s, and particularly the volume *Seminţia lui Laokoon* (1967; Laokoon's stock), brought decisive stylistic and thematic changes in D.'s poetry, which became pithy and often cruel and bitter; the delight in the wealth of creatures and objects gave way to suggestions of irony, absurdity, and despair. Poems after 1970, such as those included in *Papirus* (1974; papyrus) or *Anotimpul discret* (1975; prudent season), seem to strive for a synthesis—they are long poems, philosophical in matter and obscure in style, which nevertheless seem directed toward an approach to the inner mainsprings of reality. D.'s answer to his Platonic dilemmas is a fierce embracing of the palpably concrete. In many poems after 1960 one can recognize accents of social criticism or skepticism, even though these are firmly embedded in aesthetic imagery. The 1989 revolution gave D. a chance to write freely about political and social issues. The volumes *Interiorul unui poem* (1990; Inside a Poem), *Aventurile lui Proteu* (1995; Proteus' adventures) and others contain verse of great bitterness and vigor deploring the political and psychological state of the nation, both before and after 1989.

In his essays, collected in *Poezie şi modă poetică* (1972; poetry and poetic fashion) and *Măştile aderărului poetic* (1992; The masks of poetic truth), D. attacked mindless modernism as well as sloganeering poetasters. He is particularly concerned with joining modern linguistic and stylistic theories with the traditional search for value and beauty in poetry. Many essays seek to demonstrate a social need for the specifically aesthetic aims of poetic speech, or to show a compatibility between the rational and the irrational. D.'s translations of BENN, GUILLÉN, DARÍO, Goethe, Hölderlin, Dante, and Mallarmé have established him as the leading practitioner of this craft in postwar Romanian literature. His own works have been translated into English, Italian, German, and Hungarian.

FURTHER WORKS: *Cartea Mareelor* (1964); *Omul cu compasul* (1966); *Ipostaze* (1968); *Alter ego* (1970); *Lampa lui Diogene* (1970); *Versuri* (1973); *Orfeu si tentatiţia realului* (1974); *Alfabet poetic* (1978); *Hesperia* (1979); *Vînătoare cu şoim* (1985); *Lamentaţiile* (1993); *Psalmi* (1997)

BIBLIOGRAPHY: Aichelburg, W., *Pferde im Regen* (1974): 11–19; Nemoianu, V., on *Alter ego and Lampa lui Diogene, BA*, 45 (1971), 304; on *Anotimpul discret TLS*, 10 Sept. 1976: 1146; *Surîsul abundentei* (1994)

—VIRGIL NEMOIANU

DOKMAI Sot

(pseud. of M. L. Buppha Kunjara Nimmanhemin) Thai novelist and short-story writer, b. 17 Feb. 1905, Bangkok; d. 17 Jan. 1963, New Delhi, India

D., one of Thailand's first important novelists, was born into a noble family and educated in a French convent school in Bangkok. While a student there, she was introduced to Western literature and became particularly interested in the French woman writer M. Delly, author of didactic romantic novels for young women. They influenced her early works, *Sattru khong chaolon* (1929; her enemy) and *Nit* (1930; Nit), both of which were serialized in *Thai Khasem*, a leading magazine of the time.

D. believed it her responsibility to improve young people's conduct and morals, and a number of her novels, such as *Phu di* (1937; a well-bred person) and *Nung nai roi* (1934; one in a hundred), were written specifically for this purpose. But even the works that are not explicitly didactic reflect D.'s conservative and traditional moral and religious philosophy.

In most of D.'s works, the main characters are female, and their portrayal demonstrates the writer's genuine interest in and astute perception of women's nature. Additionally, the majority of D.'s fiction reflects the life she knew best—that of the Thai upper class from the last decades of the absolute monarchy up to World War II. Her novels are novels of manners, in which most of the characters are confined to the narrow world of their own class and interests. Nevertheless, the life style of the middle class did not escape her keen observation. "Ponlamung di" (1948; "The Good Citizen," 1958), a short story that realistically depicts that segment of Thai society, was awarded a prize by the Canberra Fellowship of Australian Writers.

D. reached the height of her fame when *Ni lae lok* (1935; This is life) won an international award. It was a marked departure from her earlier romantic fiction, since in this novel she endows her characters with much greater complexity and psychological realism. In fact, it is only in this book and in *Ubattihet* (1934; the accident) and in the posthumously published *Wannakrum chin sud thai* (1973; the last literary work) that her characters step out of their circumscribed world to display an interest in social problems and world affairs. Nevertheless, in spite of the generally limited scope of her writing, D. is recognized in Thailand as a novelist who truthfully depicted the life of the people of her time.

FURTHER WORKS: *Di fo* (1927); *Sam chai* (1932); *Karma kao* (1935); *Khwampit khrang raek* (1935); *Chai chana khong Luang Naruban* (1936); *Phu klin* (1937); *Nanthawan* (1942); *Busababan* (1948)

BIBLIOGRAPHY: Bhanthumchinda, S., *Jane Austen and Two Modern Thai Women Novelists: A Comparative Study* (1957); Senanan, W., *The Genesis of the Novel in Thailand* (1975): 91–98 and passim

—SAOWANEE INDRABHAKTI

DOMIN, Hilde

German poet, essayist, and novelist, b. 27 July 1912, Cologne

D., the daughter of a Jewish attorney, studied law, philosophy, and social science in Germany and, following her emigration in 1932, in Italy. She was awarded her doctorate by the University of Florence in 1935. She moved to England in 1939 and to the Dominican Republic the following year, where she taught German at the University of Santo Domingo. After spending a year in the U.S., she returned to Germany in 1954. Among her numerous literary awards are the Droste Prize (1971) and the Rilke Prize (1977).

D. began to write in 1951, when she was thirty-nine. An awareness of both the effects of the expatriate experience and the power of poetic expression were to remain important forces in her creative and critical writing. Her firsthand knowledge of the works of the great modern poets of Italy and the Spanish-speaking world proved to be a decisive factor in her own poetic development. In D.'s first volume of poetry, *Nur eine Rose als Stütze* (1959; only a rose for support), a lyrical record of her years in exile, the fragile nature of human existence is expressed in delicate, sensitive free verse. The image in the title reflects the mood of the collection; in an uncertain world the only support is found in a nonmaterial reality (especially of love and poetry), which, like a rose, is as fragile as it is beautiful. The title of her second collection, *Rückkehr der Schiffe* (1962; return of the ships), is misleading: these are not poems of homecoming. Poetry itself becomes an even more important theme, but otherwise these poems differ little from those of the previous collection. Exile remains a prominent motif. *Hier* (1964; here) marks a turning point in D.'s development. The poems become shorter, the images more concise, the mode of expression more laconic. The specific exile experience recedes into the background, and when reference to exile is made it seems to refer to an existential, and not a historical situation.

D.'s next collection, *Höhlenbilder* (1968; images from the caves), contains her very earliest poetry, written in 1951–52. The poems are extremely personal. Most deal with the problems of an isolated individual who attempts to overcome the effects of loneliness by means of a love relationship. A comparison of these early works with the poems of *Ich will dich* (1970; I want you) reveals the changes that took place during D.'s first twenty years of writing. The language of the latter collection is extremely terse, and the improvement of human relationships in a societal sense, rather than the narrowing of the distance between two lovers, is the major theme of the book. Although the words "Ich will dich" might suggest a love relationship, the text of the programmatic title poem reveals that the "you" addressed is not a lover, but freedom. Freedom has political implications in the collection; one poem, for example, refers to a television report on the effects of napalm. But the primary meaning of freedom is existential and is related to the poet's conception of the necessity of examining both subjective and objective reality with an honest and critical eye.

The novel *Das zweite Paradies* (1968; the second paradise) is the story of a couple forced into exile by Hitler's ascent to power. The relationship disintegrates as the man continues to look back to the lost idyll of the past while the woman anticipates a more realistic "second paradise." D. utilizes the stream-of-consciousness technique and flashbacks; quotations from the German press of the 1960s, set in the old German type face, ironically heighten the contrast between utopian dream and reality.

D. is no less significant as an editor and essayist than as a creative writer. In 1966 she edited *Doppelinterpretationen* (double interpretations), a collection of interpretations of contemporary German poems. In each case, the poet and a critic contribute independently written interpretations of the poem in question. Many of D.'s essays on poetry are collected in *Wozu Lyrik heute* (1968; what is the purpose of poetry today), a discussion of many aspects of the role of poetry in contemporary society, and, in some respects, an attempt to formulate a theory of modern poetry. The author consistently stresses the importance of viewing poetry in its social context, maintaining that art, and especially poetry, can be an effective means of communication and can contribute to the preservation of human dignity in a society that values technology and conformity so highly.

FURTHER WORKS: *Die andalusische Katze* (1971); *Von der Natur nicht vorgesehen* (1974); *Abel steh auf* (1979)

BIBLIOGRAPHY: Meller, H., "H. D.," in Wiese, B. von, ed., *Deutsche Dichter der Gegenwart* (1973): 354–68; Gadamer, H.-G., "H. D.," in *Poetica* (1977): 135–49; Krolow, K., "Drei Arten, Gedichte aufzuschreiben," in *Frankfurter Anthologie*, 2 (1977): 195–98

—JERRY GLENN

DOMINICAN LITERATURE
See English Caribbean Literature

DOMINICAN REPUBLIC LITERATURE
See Spanish-Caribbean Literature

DONNER, Jörn

Finnish novelist and journalist (writing in Swedish), b. 5 Feb. 1933, Helsinki

D. was born into an affluent family but, as a very young man, turned violently against his patrician background, coediting the radical journal *Arena* (1951–1954) with Christer KIHLMAN and writing several clumsy semiautobiographical novels, culminating with *Jag, Erik Anders* (1957; I Erik Anders). Further, in an effort to present his Marxist accusations to a variety of audiences, he frequently contributed to the Finnish-language communist-dominated *Vapaa Sana*, the tabloid *Nya Pressen*, and the liberal *Hufvudstadsbladet*, the last association continuing through the 1960s. In 1980, politically transformed and now famous, D. returned as a columnist to *Hufvudstadsbladet*, the country's largest Swedish paper; he also appears regularly in the Finnish *Aamulehti*, the second-largest member of Finland's Finnish-language press. His journalistic skills were also brought to bear in his pictures of postwar Europe, *Rapport från Berlin* (1958; *Report from Berlin*, 1968), *Rapport från Donau* (1962; report from the Danube), and

Världsboken (1968; the world book). His skill in the globetrotting genre was applied to a more tractable topic in *Sverigeboken* (1973; the Sweden book), an unflattering picture of the social paradise to which he had transferred his activities during the 1960s, when he became the leading film critic of the major Stockholm daily *Dagens Nyheter*. Simultaneously, under the aegis of Ingmar Bergman, to whom he devoted a book, *Djävulens ansikte* (1962; *The Films of Ingmar Bergman*, 1972), he became a director of some distinction, first in Sweden and then in Finland. Back on home ground, he began to observe his native land more objectively than before, in the large *Nya boken om vårt land* (1967; the new book about our country)—a title alluding to a school classic from the 19th c.—where D. presented his plans for an unabashedly capitalistic Finnish society. His own talents as an administrator and businessman were of great value to him as head of the Swedish Film Institute and then as chairman of the Finnish Film Foundation. In public life he also served as a Helsinki city commissioner from 1968 to 1972 and again from 1985 to the present, and, since 1987, as a representative of the Swedish People's Party in Finland's parliament.

It is hard to believe that D., in the midst of so much activity (frequently punctuated by trips around the world), could have time for literary creation; his manifold daily or weekly reflections on Finland's and Europe's public life—collected in *Sagt och gjort* (1976; seen and done), *Hemåt i höstregn* (1985; homeward in autumn rain), and *Motströms* (1988; against the current)—might well have absorbed all his authorial energy. However, during the last two decades, he has produced two series of books that guarantee him a place in Finland's literary history. A figure of national fame and notoriety, altogether willing to inform his fellow citizens of their opportunities and their shortcomings, his works have been widely translated into Finnish. The one set is concerned with D. himself, an ongoing record of his attitudes and shifts of opinion, illustrated by telling anecdotes and meaningful facts. The journal he kept of his alternate service as a pacifist in *På ett sjukhus* (1961; at a hospital) had been a preparatory step in this direction in *Sommar av kärlek och sorg* (1971; summer of love and grief) D. discussed, among much else, his rejection of his leftist phase; another such account, ostensibly more personal, was *Jag, J. J. D.* (1980; I, J. J. D.). Yet, even here, D. was less concerned with self-analysis than with giving his opinions on what he saw and, very often, questioned. In general, he is a keen detector of large political or social patterns but not a sensitive observer of individuals.

D.'s other major concern has been a suite of novels about the fate of a Finland-Swedish industrial dynasty from 1939 to the 1960s. The grand undertaking began with *Nu måste du* (1974; now you must, repub. as *Den sista sommaren*, 1989, the last summer), dealing with the great firm United Metals, and the persons surrounding it. The central figure at the start was Gabriel Berggren, a man of humble origins who married into the family twice, but as the cycle progressed, the spotlight was often moved to a woman, Angela, and her wartime affair with a German officer in *Angelas krig* (1976; Angela's war) and *Angela och kärleken* (1981; Angela and love), where it emerged that the German was homosexual. Other novels in this cycle include *Jakob och frighten* (1978; Jakob and freedom), *Gabriels dag* (1982; Gabriel's day), *Far och son* (1985; father and son), and *Frihetens fångar* (1988; prisoners of freedom). D. has a sovereign command of his settings, at home and abroad, and his narrative, particularly in the later volumes, is leavened by scenes of burlesque humor. But D.'s characterizations are often superficial, and his situations often reminiscent of John GALSWORTHY's Forsyte novels or the once popular Jalna series of

the Canadian Mazo De la Roche (1885–1961), or television's family epics.

In many respects, D. would remind Americans of William F. Buckley (b. 1925)—in his self-assurance, in his vast knowledge, and in his conservative nonconformism. His enormous industry, his attention to financial detail, and the range of his views have led a Finnish critic to compare him to Balzac. Certainly, he is a major figure in Finland's contemporary letters and public life; it is doubtful, though, that he is an author with a compelling vision or deep human insights.

FURTHER WORKS: *Välsignade liv!* (1951); *Slå dig into till ro* (1952); *Våra filmproblem—filmipulamme* (1953, with Martti Savo); *Brev* (1954); *Bordet* (1957); *Helsingfors—Finlands ansikte* (1961, with K. G. Roos); *Tapaus Naisenkuvia* (1970); *Marina Maria* (1972); *Ihmisen ääni* (1980); *Dagbok från filminstitutet 1978–1982* (1982); *Presidenten* (1986)

BIBLIOGRAPHY: Schoolfield, G. C., "The Postwar Novel of Swedish Finland," *SS*, 34 (1962): 85–110; Lehtola, E., "J. D.—Action Man," *BF*, 20 (1986): 10–13

—GEORGE C. SCHOOLFIELD

DONOSO, José

Chilean novelist and short-story writer, b. 5 Oct. 1924, Santiago; d. 7 Dec. 1996, Santiago

The son of a physician, D. was born into an upper-middle-class family of Spanish and Italian descent. He was educated in an English school in Santiago and at Princeton University, from which he received a B.A. in 1951. After returning to Chile he worked as a teacher, journalist, and literary critic, eventually becoming editor of the news magazine *Ercilla*. He lectured for two years (1965–67) in the Writers' Workshop at the University of Iowa and since then has resided in Spain.

During the 1960s, D. emerged as one of Latin America's most important writers of fiction, and with the death of Pablo NERUDA in 1973 he became, and remains today, Chile's most universally admired man of letters. Although he is known primarily as a novelist, he has also published seventeen short stories, all written between 1950 and 1962. These artistically drawn, psychologically penetrating studies of middle-class mores are present in embryonic form many of the themes developed in his novels. D.'s major themes include the decay of modern social institutions, the conflict between reason and instinct (or between order and chaos), the interplay of domination and dependence in human relations, the disunity of the personality (frequently illuminated by the display of masks), and the absurd futility of human existence.

Two of D.'s best stories are "Paseo" (1959; "The Walk," 1977), the portrait of a spinster whose rigidly structured existence is shattered by the entrance of a stray dog into her household; and "Santelices" (1962; "Santelices," 1977), in which a sadomasochist attempts to evade an unbearable reality by leaping from his office window into a garden teeming with imaginary tigers. D.'s first two novels, *Coronación* (1957; *Coronation*, 1965) and *Este domingo* (1966; *This Sunday*, 1967) have much in common, but at the same time, they reveal fundamental differences that demonstrate D.'s maturation as an artist. Both depict the sterile lives of upper-middle-class families whose deteriorating mansions symbolize the decline of bourgeois society. Both novels also capture the nightmarish forces of instinct and irrationality lurking beneath the placid surface of the social order. *Este domingo* is aesthetically superior, however, because it adroitly introduces avant-garde techniques that effect a more exacting scrutiny of human relationships and the explosive situations they engender.

El lugar sin límites (1966; *Hell Has No Limits*, 1972) is a grotesque depiction of the absurd human condition based on the Biblical myths of the Creation and the Fall. The action takes place in a stagnating community founded approximately twenty years earlier by a corrupt politician, Don Alejo, who emerges as an ironic god figure when he plots the death of the town. The homosexual protagonist, La Manuela, dances in a ramshackle bordello run by his frigid, unattractive daughter. His dreams of light and glory contrast strikingly with his sordid environment, creating a chiaroscuro ambience that reinforces the theme of absurdity and makes this novel D.'s most poetic creation.

With the publication of his masterpiece, *El obsceno pájaro de la noche* (1970; *The Obscene Bird of Night*, 1973), D. enhanced his growing international reputation. An antinovel combining many of his previous themes and obsessions, it also displays an impressive array of styles and techniques. The two settings are a luxurious estate, designed as a bastion of order against the forces of chaos, and a dilapidated home for retired servants, whose mental aberrations reflect the labyrinthine form of the structure. The grotesque fantasies and multiple identities of the schizophrenic protagonist, an aspiring writer named Humberto Peñaloza, alternate between these two diametrical opposites, creating tensions that reach a climax with the dissolution of Humberto's personality.

The numerous interpretations to which this masterfully executed novel lends itself attest to its ambiguity, an esthetic element D. holds in high esteem. On a superficial level it depicts the collapse of outmoded social and political institutions in today's world. Examined from a metaphysical point of view, it conveys an absurd, unstable reality in which man appears doomed to suffer terror, death, and nothingness. The rambling interior monologues, the dream sequences, and the juxtaposition of incongruous images suggest the SURREALISTS' probings of the uncharted psychic realm beyond the confines of rational consciousness. And the plot might be read as the nightmarish account of Humberto's ongoing creative endeavor, the end result of which is a novel that drives him mad and baffles his readers.

D.'s most recent novel, *Casa de campo* (1978; *The Country House*, 1984), is a fine piece of literary artifice replete with historical, philosophical, and aesthetic implications. The action begins when the adult members of the aristocratic Ventura family set out on a day's excursion, leaving their lively offspring unattended on their country estate, Marulanda. The magical elasticity of fictional time, however, stretches the day into a year, thus making possible the rise of a new social order that brings about the apocalyptic destruction of Marulanda and the Ventura dynasty. Although *Casa de campo* evokes the tragic Latin American experience, its fanciful plot and playful tone indicate the author's turn to a more deliberately contrived, fictive reality.

Most of D.'s more recent novels reflect his self-imposed exile in Spain and his return to Chile several years after the 1973 military coup. These include *El jardín de al lado* (1981; *The Garden Next Door*, 1992) and *La desesperanza* (1986; *Curfew*, 1988). *Donde van a morir los elefantes* (1995; where the elephants go to die)

satirizes academic life in the U. S. In its totality, D.'s work depicts a desperate play of masks donned by faceless men confronting a chaotic, indecipherable universe. Perhaps because of this timely world outlook he is attracting increasing interest in Latin America, Europe, and the U.S. His dark view of human nature and repeated insinuations of impending doom may seem overly pessimistic to some readers, but few will fail to appreciate his astonishing imagination, artistic sensitivity, and profound insight into the perils of life in the 20th c.

FURTHER WORKS: *Veraneo y otros cuentos* (1955); *Dos cuentos* (1956); *El charleston* (1960); *Los mejores cuentos de J. D.* (1965); *Cuentos* (1971); *Historia personal del "boom"* (1972; *The Boom in Spanish American Literature: A Personal History*, 1977); *Tres novelitas burguesas* (1973; *Sacred Families*, 1977); *La misteriosa desaparición de la marquesita de Loria* (1980). FURTHER WORKS IN ENGLISH: *Charleston and Other Stories* (1977)

BIBLIOGRAPHY: Rodríguez Monegal, E., "El mundo de J. D.," *Mundo nuevo*, 12 (1967): 77–85; Coleman, A., "Some Thoughts on D.'s Traditionalism," *SSF*, 8 (1971): 155–58; Vidal, H., *J. D.: Surrealismo y rebelión de los instintos* (1972); Tatum, C. M., "The Child Point of View in D.'s Fiction," *JSSTC*, 1, 3 (1973): 187–96; Foster, D. W., and Foster, V. R., eds., *Modern Latin American Literature* (1975), Vol. I: 305–17; Fraser, H. M., "Witchcraft in Three Stories of J. D.," *LALR*, 4, 7 (1975): 3–8; Martínez, Z. N., "J. D.: A Short Study of His Works," *BA*, 49 (1975): 249–55; Oberhelman, H. D., "J. D. and the 'Nueva Narrativa,'" *REH*, 9, 1 (1975): 107–17; Lipki, J. M., "D.'s Obscene Bird: Novel and Anti-Novel," *LALR*, 5, 9 (1976): 39–47; Stabb, M. S., "The Erotic Mask: Notes on D. and the New Novel," *Symposium*, 30, 3 (1976): 170–79; Magnarelli, S., "El obsceno pájaro de la noche: Fiction, Monsters, and Packages," *HR*, 45 (1977): 413–19; McMurray, G. R., *J.D.* (1979); Magnarelli, S., *Understanding J. D.* (1993); Gonzalez Mandri, F. M., *J. D.'s House of Fiction* (1995)

—GEORGE R. MCMURRAY

DOOLITTLE, Hilda

(pseud.: H. D.) American poet, b. 10 Sept. 1886, Bethlehem, Pa.; d. 29 Sept. 1961 Zurich, Switzerland

As a child D. participated in the rituals of the Moravian church, a sect that identified with the "mystery which lay at the center of the world." Profoundly affected by her early religion, in *Tribute to Angels* (1945) she described the enigmatic "mystery" as the "point in the spectrum where all light becomes one . . . as we were told as children." Educated chiefly in private schools, D. spent a year and a half at Bryn Mawr College. She began her writing career in New York in 1910, but soon after moved to London. After her marriage to the English poet and novelist Richard Aldington (1892–1962) she assumed editorship of *The Egoist* while pursuing her career as a poet. The period between 1915 and 1920 was filled with personal crises, including a miscarriage, the deaths of her father and older brother, and separation from Aldington (they were divorced in the 1930s). A severe breakdown caused D. to seek the help of Sigmund FREUD, the "blameless physician" of her brilliant psychobiography, *Tribute to Freud* (1956).

Currently identified as a modern, earlier D. was, regrettably, labeled the "perfect IMAGIST", the "Greek publicity girl." Tending on occasion to an obscurantism characteristic of modern poetry, her work, defying classification, nevertheless transcends the limitations of the imagist movement, although together with Ezra POUND and Aldington, she was a formulator of its principles.

Throughout her work D. was in search of what she dimly defined as "a myth, the one reality." This would become for her a "unifying pattern," one that would permit her to articulate myriad emotions, to create an "organizing structure" in which she could function as both woman and artist. Related to the search for structure was her acute awareness of the importance of identity to survival. Self-definition was imperative. The search for personal identity was contemporaneous with D.'s realization of her own creative talents, and eventually her poetry became, in a sense, a projection of herself. Fortunately for D. (unlike so many modern American poets), the experience was more productive than destructive.

D. ingeniously shaped the classical world to her own temperament, weaving the legends of the past into modern form, emulating myth to gain a sense of the spiritual, the timeless. Experiences became continuations of a simpler, more structured mythic past, which she found more manageable than the immediate, chaotic contemporary scene. As she developed her skills, however, D. was able to transfer mythic patterns from one culture to another, as reflected in her wide-ranging vision of woman in *Tribute to Angels*. More notably, in *The Walls Do Not Fall* (1944) she comfortably mingles classical allusions with observations of shell-shocked, bombed-out London.

As D. strove for self-fulfillment, tension developed—tension between physical love and artistic performance, between desire and creativity. Resolution, reconciliation, control could be achieved, she realized, by means of some "intermediate ground": an organizing structure, mythical patterns, legends, and symbols. These were elements of her "classical repertoire," and many techniques for making meaningful use of them had been reinforced during her experiences with Freud.

Ultimately, the search for "a myth, the one reality" was achieved by means of the legendary figure of Helen in D.'s last major work. In the earlier imagist poem "Helen" (1916) the heroine with "still eyes in [a] white face" is clouded with subtle ambiguities—the Helen Greece could love "only if she were laid white ash amid funereal cypresses." In *Helen in Egypt* (1961), however, the mature, intelligent, confident Helen struggles for and ultimately achieves self-definition following the cataclysmic Trojan War. With *Helen in Egypt*, D. finally brings to a close her search for an identity, the "one reality" for which she had been striving for more than fifty years.

FURTHER WORKS: *Sea Garden* (1916); *The Tribute and Circe* (1917); *Hymen* (1921); *Heliodora, and Other Poems* (1924); *Hippolytus Temporizes* (1927); *Red Roses for Bronze* (1931); *What Do I Love* (1944); *The Flowering of the Rod* (1946); *By Avon River* (1949); *Selected Poems* (1957); *Hermetic Definition* (1958); *Bid Me to Love* (1963); *End to Torment* (1978)

BIBLIOGRAPHY: Taupin, R., *L'influence du symbolisme français sur la póesie américaine* (1929): 100–105, 158–65; Hughes, G., "H. D.: The Perfect Imagist," *Imagism and the Imagists* (1931): 109–24; Monroe, H., "H. D.," *Poets and Their Art* (1932): 92–99, 319–20; Coffman, S. K., Jr., *Imagism: A Chapter for the History of Modern Poetry* (1951): 145–48; Swann, T. B., *The Classical World*

Hilda Doolittle

of H. D. (1962); Quinn, V., *H. D.* (1968); Waggoner, H. H., *American Poets: From the Puritans to the Present* (1968): 358–64, 683–84

—CLAIRE HEALEY

DORFMAN, Ariel

Chilean novelist, short-story writer, essayist, poet, and dramatist, b. 6 May 1942, Buenos Aires, Argentina

D. began his writing career as an essayist with a widely read book on the theme of violence in contemporary Spanish American fiction, *Imaginación y violencia en América* (1970; imagination and violence in America), and a second book that became an instant best-seller in Latin America entitled *Para leer al Pato Donald* (1971; *How To Read Donald Duck*, 1975), which casts a sardonic look at pop culture in the U.S. But in recent years it has been in the area of fiction that D. has attracted the greatest attention. Although born in Argentina, his family lived in the U.S. for ten years before settling in Chile in 1954. Between 1971 and 1973 he served on the board of directors of Quimantú, the government publishing house, and taught courses at the National University in Santiago on children's literature and mass media. As an ardent supporter of Salvador Allende's Popular Unity government he was forced into exile (France, Holland, and the U.S.) following the military coup of 11 September 1973, and it was only in 1983 that he was permitted to return to Chile by the Pinochet regime. Today he divides his time between Santiago and the U.S., where he is professor of literature and Latin American studies at Duke University. The years of exile, however, have left their mark on his literature. His are texts deeply imbued with a sense of loss and nostalgia for a world violently erased by political currents, and they reflect a spirit of relentless resistance to the forces of oblivion.

D.'s first novel, *Moros en la costa* (1973; *Hard Rain*, 1990), was written in 1972, and by the time it was published, the author had taken refuge in the Argentine embassy in Santiago in the hope of escaping the wave of violence unleashed by the Pinochet regime against its political enemies. The novel is a socio-literary chronicle whose twenty-seven narrative sequences contain book reviews, editorials, newspaper articles, letters, movie scripts, and interviews. D.'s first work of fiction written in exile is *Cría ojos* (1979: opening eyes), a highly political collection of short stories whose principal image is a society suffocated by dictatorship. The title of the collection is an inversion of a popular Spanish refrain that underscores the negative consequences of one's behavior. D.'s inversion, on the other hand, suggests a far more positive experience. To "open eyes" for the author implies a growing awareness of one's reality and a call to action against the forces of oppression.

In writing his next novel D. drastically changed his style in the hope that he could sufficiently disguise his authorship and elude the rejection of the official censor in Chile. *Viudas* (1981; *Widows*, 1983) is the story of a village beset by political terror. Absent are all direct and indirect references to Chile and the Pinochet government. Events take place at the end of World War II in a country whose identity is never stated explicitly. Characters' surnames and geographic details prompt the reader to identify it initially as Greece during the Nazi occupation, but Longa, the name of the fictional village, is really a metaphor for all communities throughout the world whose loved ones have disappeared at the hands of dictators. While *Viudas* is laconic and lean in its prose, *La última canción de Manuel Sendero* (1982; *The Last Song of Manuel Sendero*, 1987) is a complex novel whose labyrinthine structure and multiplicity of narrative voices taxes the abilities of even the most sophisticated readers. The text is composed of three apparently distinct narrative threads whose fusion produces a moving and often comic portrayal of the struggle against abusive power.

In *Máscaras* (1988; *Mascara*, 1988) D. moves beyond the question of exile and leads his reader into a chilling Orwellian world that explores the elusive identity of power and the infinite number of masks that it utilizes in presenting its face to the world. This elusiveness is reflected in the structure of the novel itself as the reader confronts a narrative world that continually slips from his grasp. Linguistic signs are unstable. Narrators become narratees, victimizers the victims, voyeurs the spied-upon, and the powerful the powerless, in an unrelenting process of transformation and disguise. More than anything else he has written, this is D.'s most compelling statement on power and the price paid by a society that makes it its principal goal.

D.'s fiction tends to be structurally open, pointing toward an alternative political reality that transcends an apparently frozen present. While his texts offer few specific details about what that future political culture might look like, it is obviously one based on notions of collective responsibility, the defense of human rights, and a just distribution of power. Each of his narrative texts closes with an implicit "to be continued," with a sense that the final

chapter in this long and arduous campaign has not yet been written. As his fiction evolves, D. tends to move farther away from any semblance of realism as a narrative strategy to one that is increasingly allegorical in nature.

FURTHER WORKS: *Superman y sus amigos del alma* (1974); *Ensayos quemados en Chile* (1974); *Culture et résistance au Chili* (1978); *La última aventura del llanero solitario* (1979); *Reader's nuestro que estás en la tierra: ensayos sobre el imperialismo cultural* (1980); *Pruebas al canto* (1980); *Hacia la liberación del lector latinoamericano* (1984); *Patos, elefantes y héroes: la infancia como subdesarrollo* (1985); *Dorando la píldora* (1985); *Los sueños nucleares de Ronald Reagan* (1986); *Cuentos para militares* (1986); *Sin ir más lejos* (1986). FURTHER WORKS IN ENGLISH: *The Empire's Old Clothes* (1983); *Death and the Maiden* (1990); *Some Write to the Future* (1991)

BIBLIOGRAPHY: Claro-Mayo, J., "D., cuentista comprometido," *RI*, 47: 114–15 (Jan.–June 1981): 339–45; Flora, C. B., "Roasting Donald Duck: Alternative Comics and Photonovels in Latin America," *JPC*, 18, 1 (Summer 1984): 163–83; Wisenberg, S. L., "A. D.: A Conversation," *Another Chicago Magazine*, 18 (1988): 196–210; Bennetts, L., "A. D., Agonized Exile, Writes To Fight," *NYT* (14 April 1988): C33; Atwan, R., on "Mascara," *NYTBR* (6 Nov. 1988): 14; Boyers, P., and Lértora, J. C., "Ideology, Exile, Language: An Interview with A. D.," *Salgamundi*: 82–83 (Summer 1989): 142–63; Incledon, J., "Liberating the Reader: A Conversation with A. D.," *Chasqui*, 2, 1 (May 1991): 95–107

—JOHN J. HASSETT

DOS PASSOS, John

American novelist, b. 14 Jan. 1896, Chicago, Ill.; d. 28 Sept. 1970, Baltimore, Md.

Although atypical in his origins and education, and as a young man passionately drawn to European culture, D. P. became the novelist who chronicled the 20th-c. American scene with the greatest originality and insight. Different as they are from each other, he, DREISER, HEMINGWAY, and FAULKNER are the four-square ark of American novelistic greatness in this century.

The illegitimate son of a wealthy man of Portuguese extraction, he was educated in private schools and at Harvard, but by his father's death he was cast almost penniless into the world of ordinary men and women at the same time that World War I cast him into situations for which no one of his generation was prepared. He was first a member of an ambulance corps and later an enlisted man (late enough to escape active service). This exposure enabled him to break away from Harvard aestheticism and sterile literary conventionality and to set down what he saw honestly and straightforwardly.

His first novel, *One Man's Initiation-1917*, which appeared in 1920, is little more than a series of impressions of war as seen by two ambulance drivers. *Three Soldiers* (1921) marks a striking advance. It is the first really authentic American war novel, important among other things for shifting the focus from men at war to the mechanism of war itself: an army is nothing but a machine that dehumanizes men, relentlessly seeking to destroy mind and feeling. Three fairly representative young men show how this process works. While two of them probably survive, they are all victims of the system, although not casualties of war on the field of battle.

Manhattan Transfer (1925) is a masterpiece in the vein of the cross-section novel. It re-creates the life patterns of New York City, and by implication, of the country at large, over the first quarter of the 20th c. We see a good many people—some of them anonymous, only two presented in depth—as they appear and disappear in some 130 scenes. As in most realistic novels, the lives shown go mostly downhill. Some are badly battered. Success, such as it is, entails conformity and thus dehumanization. The novel is full of images of treadmills, steamrollers, automatons. We are also aware of the world of dreams, visions of escape that get nowhere. New York as a physical entity is an intoxication of aspiration, but it is also a cruel trap. It looms on the horizon as great as Nineveh or Rome, but it, too, is ephemeral. It, too, will fall. This novel is little concerned with specific events. It seeks to examine changing mores and moral values and to record the gap between official morality and actual behavior. It is amazing for the range and credibility of proletarians and hangers-on who are presented, types outside the range of the author's intimate experience. The weakness of the work, if there is a weakness, is the detachment of the narrator and therefore of the reader, who rarely identifies with any of the characters, not even with the protagonist Jimmy Herf. It is an indifferent spectacle.

Fortunately, passion is present in D. P.'s greatest work, the trilogy of *The 42nd Parallel* (1930), *1919* (1932), and *The Big Money* (1936), brought out together as a single massive chronicle entitled *U.S.A.* (1937–38). In it is the device of the "Camera Eye" that permits the introduction of passion, as a poetic speaker, quite different from the impersonal narrator of the newsreels and short biographies, gives a subjective and often poetic insight into events. More than that, these fifty-one sections permit us to be one with a youth struggling to come to terms with the facts of adult life, salvaging a core of belief out of the apparent disintegration of value, becoming a radical in the sense that his loyalties are with the victims of psychosocial intolerance and the cynical aggression of wealth.

Unlike its predecessor, this work is acutely conscious of events in the first three decades of the 20th c., from the incipient imperialism of the Spanish-American War to the subsidence of social and economic equity in the years before the Depression. There are twelve major characters who appear in one or more of these novels. They do not constitute a true cross-section, since they lean heavily toward vacuity and failure. Whatever their level of achievement, they tend to drift into vocations rather than to be trained for them. Their incapacities are often underlined by the intercalation of the biography of a real-life character. What these novelistic elements provide in their ensemble is an anguished awareness of the havoc wrought by decades of misdirection and a quasi-religious determination to come to the rescue of the downtrodden.

There are two major emphases in this work. First there is the evidence of discrimination of all types, an automatic characterization of aliens and oddballs as less than human and therefore subject to denial of basic rights. Such characters as Mac, with whom the novel opens; Ben Compton, a nascent revolutionary; Joe Williams, a hapless working stiff; and Mary French, a selfless champion of the underdog, are central to this theme. Parallel with it is an even more emphatic demonstration of the aggressive and soulless power of wealth. This is given substance by the newsreels and short biographies of real people. But the narrative presents both minor figures who are the ubiquitous agents of wealth and major ones like

John Dos Passos

Charley Anderson, Dick Savage, and J. Ward Moorehouse, who are corrupted by the prevailing worship of wealth. The trilogy ends with an impersonal contrast of a hapless vagrant, victim of the Depression, making his way west on a dusty road, and the fat cats of the establishment streaking by in planes overhead.

D. P. came to maturity at the time of the Russian and other revolutions. His mind and heart were open to the possibility of improving the human condition. But he never identified with the doctrinaire left completely, and early in the 1930s he began to discern the capacity of Communism in particular for intolerance and victimization. Thus, his second trilogy, which appeared from 1939 to 1949, caused the rigid adherents of the left, who had once claimed him as their own, to assail him as a renegade, which was untrue, and to point out the decay of his literary talent, which was only partly true. These later novels cast doubt on the possibility of reform, of amelioration of the human condition, because of the ineluctable flaws in men both as individuals and as social bodies. In the first part of the trilogy, *Adventures of a Young Man* (1939), the chief character, Glenn Spotswood, exists to show the gap between a fundamental radical idealism and cynical Communist exploitation of that position, notably in the Spanish Civil War. It is a weak novel. On the other hand, *Number One* (1943) is a superb performance, largely ignoring broad social chronicle in favor of demonstrating the corruption of power, with Huey Long of Louisiana serving as model for the fictional Chuck Crawford. *The Grand Design* (1949) is the weakest of the three works because it lacks a focus. Basically it seeks to show the New Deal falling victim to a power drive in which individuals are subordinated to impersonal and unresponsive authority.

In his later years D. P. turned to more conventional fiction in *Chosen Country* (1951) and *Most Likely to Succeed* (1954). Fortunately, he regained critical esteem for a time with the appearance of *Midcentury* (1961). It makes modified use of the technical devices of *U.S.A.* for what amounts to a counterstatement. It attacks abuses of power by labor unions, a change of position more dramatic than his earlier repudiation of the Communist Party and the New Deal. The novel ends with a remarkable and telling contrast between two short biographies, that of General William F. Dean, held captive in Korea for three years but never in doubt about the moral matrix of the universe, and that of the movie actor James Dean, who had no moral center at all. The posthumously published novel *Century's Ebb* (1975) continues this chronicle of despair during the years from the death of Malcolm X to the launching of Apollo 10.

In addition to trying his hand at the drama, with little success, D. P. was a prolific writer of travel books and articles, such as *Rosinante to the Road Again* (1922), *Orient Express* (1927), *The Villages Are the Heart of Spain* (1937), and *Brazil on the Move* (1963). During World War II he traveled widely as a correspondent, seeking by his articles to strengthen the country's morale. In his later years his chief interest was American history and the political assumptions that underlie it. *The Men Who Made the Nation* (1957) and *The Shackles of Power* (1966) are benevolent studies of the emerging republic under the guidance of Jefferson. *Mr. Wilson's War* (1962) undertakes to show where in our history, basic principles were betrayed by foreign entanglement and concentration of governmental power. D. P.'s faith in an uncomplicated political philosophy is moving, but in time the reader has to recognize that his position is anachronistic because it is too simple. It makes insufficient allowance for the primacy of economic causality or the likelihood that passion will prevail over reason. Nonetheless these writings do, to a degree validate and make lucent the idealism of his greatest novels.

FURTHER WORKS: *A Pushcart at the Curb* (1922); *Streets of Night* (1923); *In All Countries* (1934); *Three Plays* (1934); *Journeys between Wars* (1938); *The Living Thoughts of Tom Paine* (1940); *The Ground We Stand On* (1941); *State of the Nation* (1944); *Tour of Duty* (1946); *The Prospect before Us* (1950); *The Head and Heart of Thomas Jefferson* (1954); *The Theme Is Freedom* (1956); *The Great Days* (1958); *Prospects of a Golden Age* (1959); *Occasions and Protests* (1964); *The Best Times: An Informal Memoir* (1966); *The Portugal Story* (1969); *Easter Island: Island of Enigmas* (1971); *The Fourteenth Chronicle: Letters and Diaries of J. D. P.* (1973)

BIBLIOGRAPHY: Astre, G. A., *Thèmes et structures dans l'œuvre de J. D. P.* (1958); Wrenn, J. H., *J. D. P.* (1961); Brantley, J. D., *The Fiction of J. D. P.* (1968); Landsberg, M., *D. P.'s Path to "U. S. A.": A Political Biography 1912–1936* (1972); Becker, G. J., *J. D. P.* (1974); Colley, I., *D. P. and the Fiction of Despair* (1978); Wagner, L. W., *D. P.: Artist as American* (1979); Ludington, T., *J. D. P.: A Twentieth Century Odyssey* (1980); Carr, V. S., *D. P.: A Life* (1984)

—GEORGE J. BECKER

It is more than a superficial analogy when [the author's] technique is likened to that of the film. . . .

That this method does not admit sufficiently of the presence of the artist's personal consciousness the device called 'The Camera Eye' seems to recognize—it at any rate seems to do little else. What this judgment amounts to is that the work does not express an adequate realization of the issues it offers to deal with.

How far the defect is due to method, and how far it lies in the consciousness behind the method, one cannot presume to determine. But Mr. D. P., though he exhibits so overwhelmingly the results of disintegration and decay, shows nothing like an adequate awareness of—or concern for—what has been lost. Perhaps we have here the disability corresponding to the advantage he enjoys as an American. In America the Western process has gone furthest, and what has been lost is virtually forgotten. . . . The memory of the old order, the old ways of life, must be the chief hint for, the directing incitement towards, a new, if ever there is to be a new. . . . And in *The Forty-Second Parallel* we read of "quiet men who wanted a house with a porch to putter around, and a fat wife to cook for them, a few drinks and cigars, and a garden to dig in." This is all that Mr. D. P. suggests (as yet) concerning the way in which meaning is to be restored to the agonized vacuity that it is his distinction to convey so potently.

F. R. Leavis, "A Serious Artist," *Scrutiny*, (May 1932), 173–79

D. P. is primarily concerned with morality, with personal morality. The national, collective, social elements of his trilogy should be seen not as a bid for completeness but rather as a great setting, brilliantly delineated, for his moral interest. In his novels, as in actual life, "conditions" supply the opportunity for personal moral action. But if D. P. is a social historian, as he is so frequently said to be, he is that in order to be a more complete moralist. It is of the greatest significance that for him the barometer of social breakdown is not suffering through economic deprivation but always moral degeneration through moral choice.

Lionel Trilling, "The America of J. D. P.," *PR*, 4 (April 1938), 26–42

A novel is a mirror. So everyone says. But what is meant by *reading* a novel? It means, I think, jumping into the mirror. . . . D. P. very consciously uses this absurd and insistent illusion to impel us to revolt. He has done everything possible to make his novel seem a mere reflection. . . . He wants to show us this world, our own—to *show* it only, without explanations or comment. . . . He arouses indignation in people who never get indignant, he frightens people who fear nothing. . . . D. P.'s hate, despair, and lofty contempt are real. But that is precisely why his world is not real; it is a created object. I know of none—not even Faulkner's or Kafka's—in which the art is greater or better hidden. . . . D. P.'s world—like those of

Faulkner, Kafka and Stendhal—is impossible because it is contradictory. But therein lies its beauty. Beauty is a veiled contradiction. I regard D. P. as the greatest writer of our time. [1938]

Jean-Paul Sartre, "J. D. P. and *1919*," *Situations I*
(1947), pp. 14–25

Technically *U.S.A.* is one of the great achievements of the modern novel, yet what that achievement is can easily be confused with its elaborate formal structure. For the success of D. P.'s method does not rest primarily on his schematization of the novel into four panels, four levels of American experience. . . . That arrangement, while original enough, is the most obvious thing in the book and soon becomes the most mechanical. The book lives by its narrative style, the wonderfully concrete yet elliptical prose which bears along and winds around the life stories in the book like a conveyor belt carrying Americans through some vast Ford plant of the human spirit. *U.S.A.* is a national epic, the first great national epic of its kind in the modern American novel; and its triumph is not the pyrotechnical display that the shuttling between various devices seems to suggest, but D. P's power to weave so many different lives together in narrative. . . . The great thing about *U.S.A.* is that though it sweeps up so many human lives together and intones their waste and illusion and defeat so steadily, we seem to be swept along with them and to see each life perfectly at the moment it passes by us.

Alfred Kazin, *On Native Grounds* (1942), p. 353

The U.S.A. which D. P. describes is thus more than simply a country or a way of life. It is a condition of death, a wasteland of futility and emptiness. In it, the best and the worst must be defeated; for defeat can be the only answer for the inhabitants of a world in which all goals are unattainable and the most powerful gods are corrupt. Yet, although the thing he describes is death, D. P. brings to his description a savage kind of power which saves it from becoming dead too. Through it all, he has consistently hated and condemned; and he has expressed his hatred with great strength and purpose. This has given meaning to the meaninglessness of his characters, value to their valuelessness. His style has been the perfect instrument of that meaning, protesting at every step in its development against the horror of the thing it was disclosing.

John W. Aldridge, *After the Lost Generation*
(1951), p. 76

If *U.S.A.* has within it a purpose, it is not to point readily or easily to solutions or to point up doctrinal strategies. The leftists are as dismally treated as the professional exploiters; the evidence, if anything, points to their being ridiculous and unhappy creatures. . . . To this massive document of corruption

and materialistic obsession D. P. brings the timid observation and the self-defeating despair of the Camera Eye's consciousness. It is both a way of underscoring the gross triumph of the world of *U.S.A.* and of pointing up the inadequacy of the Camera Eye's protesting insight. For *U.S.A.* is not a tragedy so much as it is a holocaust; and it is a holocaust because, however effective its narrative style is, its success leads mainly to a deadening automaton equality of motive and action. The manner is that of the surface reporter at his most brilliant. D. P. is unequalled in his talent for manipulating social and economic history in fictional forms; the details are selected with an almost uncannily acute perception of their pertinence. . . .

Frederick J. Hoffman, *The Modern Novel in
America 1900–1950* (1951) pp. 139–40

The homelessness of his people is, along with their individual and collective incapacity for self-criticism or detachment, the most obvious feature about them. And home is the positive though unstated and undefined dream of D. P. In wandering from the Jeffersonian ideal of a farmer-craftsman economy in the direction of Hamiltonian centralism, power and bigness, D. P. sees the main plight of his world. Hamilton set up the false beacon that brought shipwreck. But out of the shipwreck, which he depicts, for example, as the success of Henry Ford's enterprise, we can recover the dream and create a reality worthy of it.

Herbert Marshall McLuhan, "J. D. P.: Technique
vs. Sensibility," in H. C. Gardiner, ed., *Fifty Years
of The American Novel: A Christian Appraisal*
(1968), p. 164

DOUGLAS, Keith

English poet, b. 24 Jan. 1920, Tunbridge Wells; d. 9 June 1944, Normandy, France

D. began writing poetry as a schoolboy. By the time he entered Oxford in 1938 he had surpassed his first Arcadian imitations and was moving toward the modern idiomatic style that would characterize his later work. When war was declared in 1939 D. enlisted immediately, but was not called up for another year. His first Oxford war poems ("Soissons" [1940], "John Anderson" [1940]) mark the beginning of his mature work. Already the lyrical impulse in his writing was beginning to be tempered and informed by what he later called the "cynicism and the careful absence of expectation" with which he faced the war.

D. was assigned to the Middle East in 1941. He saw action a year later in the Battle of El Alamein and was wounded in combat early in 1943. During a six-week hospital stay he completed his first cycle of war poems and probably began his illustrated memoir of the desert fighting, *Alamein to Zem Zem*, published posthumously in 1946. Several months later he completed his second group of war poems. His regiment was sent back to England at the end of 1943 to prepare for the European campaign. D. commanded a tank troop in the Normandy invasion and on June 9, 1944, the twenty-four-year-old soldier-poet was killed by mortar fire near the village of St. Pierre.

World War II stands at the center of D.'s mature poems. In his work the poet is first and foremost a witness, an insider and an outsider, a participant but also a fiercely independent observer testifying to the truth of his own experience. D.'s poetry demonstrates a continual quest for an idiom equal to the harsh reality of that experience. In his early poems, as he said, "I wrote lyrically, as an innocent, because I was an innocent," but the war necessitated a fall "from that particular grace." It required a different style and stance, a tougher diction and a more restrained emotionalism. D. felt the danger of lyrical outpourings, sentimentality, and false generalizations; increasingly he rooted his poems in particular landscapes, using descriptions and actual experiences as points of departure. He wanted his poems to be read as "significant speech," cutting through the "curtain of rhetoric." Thus, his style progressed toward detached "reportage." In "Cairo Jag" (1943), for example, he describes a "new world" where "the vegetation is of iron/dead tanks" and "you can imagine/the dead themselves, their boots, clothes and possessions/clinging to the ground, a man with no head/has a packet of chocolate and a souvenir of Tripoli." D.'s war poems witness the terrible strangeness of "I in another place" discovering "how easy it is to make a ghost."

Throughout D.'s work there is the restrained but sure suggestion that he would not survive the war. His final poem speaks of the next month as a window through which he would crash. In "The Bete Noire Fragments" (1944) the Muse appears in inverted form as his "particular monster/a toad or a worm curled in the belly." It is the beast on his back, the death he carries within, the demon externalized in the destructiveness of war. Against the threat of annihilation D. posed the affirmative capability of love. The dialectic between death and love runs through his work like a powerful electric current. It is no less than the "arguments of heaven with hell."

It is a tragedy that D. did not survive the war he wrote so carefully about. We can be thankful, however, for the small but concentrated body of work he left behind. That work stands as a powerful testament to the transforming powers of the poetic imagination.

FURTHER WORKS: *Selected Poems* (1943); *Collected Poems* (1951); *Complete Poems* (1978)

BIBLIOGRAPHY: Waller, J., *"The Poetry of K. D.,"* *Accent* 8 (1948): 226–35; Ross, A., "The Poetry of K. D.," *TLS*, 6 Aug. 1954: xxii; Hughes, T., "The Poetry of K. D.," *CritQ* 5 (1963): 43–48; Hill, G., "'I in Another Place': Homage to K. D.," *Stand*, 4, 4 (1964–65): 6–13; Graham, D., *K. D. 1920–1944: A Biography* (1974)

—EDWARD HIRSCH

DOVE, Rita

American poet and novelist, b. 28 August 1952, Akron, Ohio

D. issues forth the richness of oral culture—in the tradition of African American writers such as Langston HUGHES, Zora Neale HURSTON, and Maya ANGELOU—transcribing the rhythms of the spoken word into a language so charged that each word is a condensation of its many emotional and descriptive possibilities. Whether she is telling her grandparents' story in *Thomas and Beulah* or narrating the murder of Haitian blacks in "Parsley," D.'s aim is to have poetry speak to people from all walks of life, as she says, "In writing a poem, if the reader on the other end can come up and say: 'I know what you meant, I mean I felt that too'—then we are a little less alone in the world."

As early as 1974, D.'s poetry gained prominence in literary publications, and her initial books, including *The Only Dark Spot in the Sky* (1980), *The Yellow House on the Corner* (1980), and *Museum* (1983), distinguished her as a leading American poet. D. is the second black woman to receive the Pulitzer Prize in poetry (for *Thomas and Beulah* [1987]), and in 1993 she became the first African American and the youngest poet to be appointed Poet Laureate. While being the recipient of many other honors for her writing, including several honorary doctorates, D. has remained committed to university teaching.

While *The Yellow House on the Corner* highlights family life and intimacy, enriching the commonplace with legendary elements, *Museum* explores histories of people around the world through such poems as "Parsley," which recounts the 1937 massacre of Haitian laborers by Dominican soldiers after the Creole-speaking Haitians failed to clearly annunciate the letter "r" in the Spanish word *perejil* (parsley). D also brings her gift of language to prose in *Fifth Sunday* (1985), a collection of eight concise short stories that dig deeply into the subjectivity of her characters, ranging from an adolescent girl awakening to her sexuality amidst the condemning eyes of fellow churchgoers to an old woman alienated from her family because grief and loneliness had once driven her into a brief incestuous relationship with her brother.

D.'s Pulitzer Prize-winning book of poetry, *Thomas and Beulah*, explores the impact white domination had on African Americans and how this greatly informed the life of a black man (Thomas) striving to define himself and to support his family, and a black woman (Beulah) enframed not only by racial bigotry but also by a domineering father. D's interest in her grandparents' history, spanning the years 1919 to 1968, sparked this epic work, which begins with her grandfather's journey from the farmlands of the South to the urban landscape of the North. These linked poems, parts of which began in *Mandolin* (1982), are separated into two segments and perspectives—"Mandolin" (twenty-three poems) is dedicated to Thomas, "Canary in Bloom" (twenty-one poems) to Beulah.

Thomas is greatly compromised as an African American, but as a man he is able to move freely, and his journey begins on a river boat leaving Tennessee for the North in the first poem, "The Event." As a woman Beulah does not have this same mobility; as a wife and mother she is kept within the boundaries of the home, and hers is an inward journey toward the wisdom and insight she realizes in her later years. Overall, *Thomas and Beulah* is an epic lyric of sustained love between two people and the sacrifices they make to keep their family together, and as D. noted, "It's the way one handles sacrifices that's crucial."

One of D.'s writerly preoccupations rests within the crevice between the singular identity of an individual and the needs of the family and surrounding community. In her collection of poems *Grace Notes* (1989) D. addresses this tension, and in her novel *Through the Ivory Gate* (1992) her vibrant descriptions impart the richness of life as she tells the story of Virginia, a talented cellist, puppeteer, and actress, who returns to her childhood home of

Akron to accept a teaching position in her old elementary school. The novel begins with a prelude that implicates how the identity of this black woman has been influenced by the social norming of white culture: a young Virginia is mourning the loss of her much loved white silky red-haired doll that has been supplanted by her family with a black doll, to whom she cannot relate.

D.'s literary accomplishment is measured by her lyrical and narrative expertise and the vivid portraits drawn within her poetry, as she illuminates the individual while signaling the milestones of black culture and American history. D.'s poetic vision unearths the duality of life's offering, finding strands of beauty in the hideous, possibilities of freedom in oppression, and fecundity in barren lands.

BIBLIOGRAPHY: Rampersad, A., "The Poems of R. D.," *Callaloo*, 9, 1 (Winter 1986): 52-60; Schneider, S., "R. D. and Steven Schneider in an Interview," *The Iowa Review*, 19, 3 (Fall 1989), 112-23; Vendler, H. H., *The Given and the Made: Strategies of Poetic Redefinition* (1995)

—LISA TOLHURST

DOVLATOV, Sergey (Donatovich)

Russian novelist, journalist, and short-story writer, b. 3 Sept. 1941, Ufa; d. 24 Aug. 1990, New York, N.Y., U.S.A.

Born of a Jewish father and an Armenian mother and bearing the Russian name of his stepfather, D. was a true representative of Soviet culture, though he wrote only in Russian. His birthplace was the Ural city of Ufa, where his family had been evacuated at the onset of the war, but D. grew up in Leningrad. He studied Finnish philology at Leningrad University, but tired of it and was dismissed from the institution. Drafted into the army, D. was assigned to a military unit in the far north guarding strict-regime labor camps, for habitual criminals. Discharged from the army in 1965, D. became a reporter and began to submit stories to magazines; few were published. Active in a circle of young writers, D. knew Iosif Brossky (b. 1940), and worked for a time as secretary to Vera PANOVA, who took him under her protection. From 1972 through 1975 D. worked for a leading daily newspaper in Talinn, chiefly writing human-interest stories. He was much in demand for his humor, but finally lost his position because of doubtful political company he kept. In addition, a book of stories scheduled for publication was canceled. On returning to Leningrad, D. began to circulate some of his writings in samizdat and to send others to the émigré press abroad. When the latter works appeared in print, D. was harassed by the authorities, jailed for nine days, but finally allowed to emigrate in 1978 to the U.S. He settled with his family in Queens, N.Y., where he found permanent work as a scriptwriter and announcer for Radio Liberty. D. found the time to write fourteen slender volumes during his American period, six of them translated into English. By the end of the 1980s, D. was not only well known in the U.S.—but he was beginning to be published in the U.S.S.R. But then D. died tragically of a massive heart attack at forty-nine.

Perhaps because of his journalistic background, D. was partial to short fiction. His novels, however, were brief, really novellas. In fact, none of his books was longer than 150 pages. Ten of his stories were published in the *New Yorker* between 1980 and 1989,

unprecedented for a Russian émigré and a remarkable testimony to D.'s implicit critical acceptance in the U.S.

Of D.'s four novels, the first is the weakest, but also the cause of some excitement owing to its having been published illegally abroad—appearing first in *Vremia i my*, the Israeli periodical, and then in book form as *Nevidimaia kniga* (1978; *The Invisible Book*, 1979). This work is somewhat fragmented, consisting chiefly of humorous and ironical quotations, anecdotes, observations, political jokes, gossip, and lamentations—all directed, though loosely, to the author's predicament as a samizdat writer who has reached the end of his rope. Because most of the names in it are changed, this text approximately qualifies as a novel.

Zona: Zapiski nadziratelia (1981; *The Zone: A Prison Camp Guard's Story*, 1986) is based in nearly every detail on biographical fact. It takes an existentialist view of guards and prisoners, perceiving them as in essence the same. D. implicitly challenges the rigid anticommunism of Alexander SOLZHENITSYN's *Gulag* fiction. Also, despite a number of horrible Dostoyevskian events, *Zona* offers considerable humor. For instance, a sergeant earns the nickname "Fidel," after he is asked in a political exam to name any Politburo member and replies, "Castro."

Though not as harrowing as *Zona, Inostranka* (1986; *A Foreign Woman*, 1991) is also remarkable for its setting: Queens, N. Y., in the 1980s. It is rate that an émigré writer like D., who hardly learned a word of English, would attempt to treat in a fictional work the myriad details of a foreign culture. The foreign girl of the title, Marusia, is the purely Russian daughter of well-to-do Communist Party members; she lives in the center of the Jewish-Russian émigré community in Forest Hills; and she falls in love with and marries a fifty-year-old Latin-American "ne'er-do-well" named Rafael Gonzáles. By providing a detailed biography of the heroine, D. is able to satirize upper-class Soviet life as well as middle-class émigré life and lower-class American life. It is a tour de force of Gogolian humor. In 1990 *Inostranka* was reprinted in the Soviet journal *Oktiabr'*.

D.'s final novel, *Filial* (1990; branch office), concerns the operation of a radio station similar to Radio Liberty (called "Radio Third Wave"), a Slavic conference in Los Angeles, and the sudden appearance at the latter of the author-narrator's first wife, Tasia, whom he has not seen in fifteen years. The scene shifts back and forth between the narrator's troublesome college days (D. himself had been married for two years, 1960–1962) and the hellish but very funny Slavic conference. The narrator continually assures his present wife by telephone that everything is fine. In truth, nothing "bad" happens, except that Tasia "borrows" virtually all of D.'s money. *Inostranka* is a more successful work, but the equally satirical *Filial* is of interest for its autobiographical depictions of mixed-up Soviet youth. The novel was reprinted in the Soviet journal *Zvezda* in 1989.

Of D.'s four collections of stories, three have been translated into English and are of special interest: *Kompromiss* (1981; *Compromise*, 1983), *Nashi* (1983; *Ours*, 1989), and *Chemodan* (1986; *Suitcase*, 1990). Each offers an artifice for assembling a collection. The first tells the "real" story behind eleven human-interest stories, most of them comic, published by D. for an Estonian newspaper in the 1970s; the second offers a dozen portraits of D.'s varied and eccentric family members: Jews, Armenians, and Russians, both communists and anticommunists, from Leningrad in the west, to farthest Siberia in the east: a true Soviet family; and the third reveals the autobiographical significance of each of eight items that had filled the single battered suitcase taken by D. to the new world.

The stories in all three collections, despite their satirical content, demonstrate a profound love and respect for humanity.

D.'s most important journalistic work, *Marsh odinokikh* (1983; march of the lonely), is a collection of editorial columns that D. had written for a weekly émigré newspaper, *Novyi amerikanets* (new American), he had founded in 1980. As D. makes clear, the popular publication was forced to close in 1982 by the established émigré press. (In other words, Russians in the U.S. turned out to be only a little better than those in the U.S.S.R.) D.'s main purpose in his editorial columns was to teach his fellow émigrés the way of democracy and the way of true liberalism—things he had managed to learn himself in the Soviet Union. The most basic feature of D.'s editorial philosophy—and it appears in all his writings—is the rejection of all ideology. For D. The only thing worse than a communist was an anticommunist. He had become an important figure of reconciliation between East and West when he died.

FURTHER WORKS: *Solo na Undervude: Zapisnye knizhki* (1980); *Zapovednik: Povest'* (1983); *Remeslo: Povest' v dvukh chastiakh* (1985); *Predstavlenie* (1987); *Ne tol'ko Brodskii* (1989); *Zapisnye knizhki* (1990)

BIBLIOGRAPHY: Loseff, L., "D., S. D.," in Weber, H. B., ed., *The Modern Encyclopedia of Russian and Soviet Literatures* (1981), Vol. 5: 239–41; Brown, E., *Russian Literature since the Revolution*, rev. ed. (1982): 385–86; Goodman, W., on *Compromise, NYT* (30 Aug. 1983); C14; Fiene, D. M., on *Compromise, SEEJ*, 28, 4 (Winter 1984): 552–53; Clark, K., on *The Zone, NYTBR* (27 Oct. 1985); 45; Grimes, W., on *The Zone, Christian Science Monitor* (21 Jan. 1986): 26; Fiene, D. M., on *Compromise* and *The Zone*, in Magill, F. N., ed., *Masterplots II: World Fiction Series* (1987), Vol. 1: 295–99, Vol. 4: 1808–13; Kasack, W., *Dictionary of Russian Literature since 1917* (1988): 87–88; Fiene, D. M., "S. D.," in Magill, F. N., ed., *Cyclopedia of World Authors II* (1989), Vol. 2: 452–54; Ruta, S., "Russia without Tears," *NYTBR* (30 April 1989): 1, 21–22; Fiene, D. M., on *Compromise* and *The Zone*, in Fiene, D. M., ed., *Cyclopedia of Literary Characters* (1990), Vol. 1: 317–18, Vol. 4: 1770–71; Gladysz, T., "A 'Suitcase' of Soviet Satire," *San Francisco Chronicle* (12 Aug. 1990): 6

—DONALD M. FIENE

DRABBLE, Margaret

English novelist, critic, biographer, b. 5 June 1939, Sheffield

D. grew up in the northern industrial city of Sheffield, was educated in York, and went on to earn a B.A. with honors at Cambridge. She married in 1960 and was a professional actress for a short time.

D.'s interest in 19th- and early-20th-c. British writers—as evidenced in her critical works on Thomas HARDY, Arnold BENNETT, Wordsworth, and Jane Austen—has strongly influenced and distinguished her fiction. Her own experiences figure prominently in her work, but the scope of her concerns has become larger and less "autobiographical" with each book; although she is well known for her strong female characters, the more recent novels feature complex and interesting male characters as well, and in *The Ice Age* (1977), the protagonist is a man.

There can be no doubt, however, that one of D.'s important contributions to literature has been the creation of women characters unlike any others previously found in fiction: witty, intelligent, independent, complete in themselves, yet decidedly maternal and devoted to their children. D.'s characteristic heroine is almost never supported by a husband; although the absence of a lover can open a void for her, she rarely chooses to live conventionally with a man.

The early novels focus on young women who are in the process of establishing, with some difficulty, their independence and worth. In *The Garrick Year* (1964), Emma Evans trails along to a provincial theater with her actor husband, who leaves her in a state of such boredom and lassitude that not even an affair with the producer of the play can rouse her. Her children, however—and a bizarre accident—bring her back to life and prove her sturdiness as a survivor. Similarly, in *The Millstone* (1965), an "idle, educated" young woman is brought to a greater awareness of herself and her place in the human community through an accidental pregnancy and the enlightening experience of motherhood. Particularly moving among the early novels is *Jerusalem the Golden* (1967), in which the main character, newly liberated by her education to a life of books and art in London, is forced to confront the dreary northern industrial background she has rejected; eventually, and not without pain, she comes to a new understanding of her sour, mean-spirited, puritanical mother, turning her former adolescent contempt into adult compassion.

D.'s first major novel was *The Needle's Eye* (1972), an achievement of almost Jamesian resonance, featuring fully adult characters living in the turmoil of contemporary Britain. At the center is the eccentric Rose Vassiliou, who, despite the corruption around her, seems determined to live a morally sensitive, even a spiritually meaningful, life. Deliberately giving up her financial advantages, she becomes an almost saintly presence. Yet, seen through the eyes of Simon Camish, her friend, lawyer, and potential lover, she represents only one aspect of the complex moral argument of the book, and her choices are not necessarily the right ones.

The Realms of Gold (1975), thematically the richest of all her books, joins one of D.'s major earlier concerns, the individual's search for personal origins, with a strong theme from her later work, the locating of contemporary Britain within some larger view of human history. The heroine, Frances Wingate, is an archaeologist, a mother, and a woman of indefatigable spirit and wit. Her views of life and death seem to hint at some ultimate meaning in history, although these are balanced against contrasting perceptions of history's senselessness and shame.

The Ice Age continues the themes of societal decay and moral incertitude begun in *The Needle's Eye*, but from the more dismal perspective of the England of the 1970s. When middle-aged and well-meaning Anthony Keating is senselessly imprisoned in a tiny Balkan country for "espionage," his plight is a horrifying but fitting conclusion to a story in which human freedom is threatened from all sides, political injustice is the common rule, and individuals are more or less innocently caught up in problems beyond their comprehension.

The Middle Ground (1980) is considerably less gloomy, although it too is concerned with the malaise of contemporary life in London. Its main character, a journalist and feminist, ponders what ought to come next in her now all-too-comfortable, middle-aged life. Whatever it is, she has not discovered it by the end of the novel. There is no doubt, however, that the protagonist will carry on with great courage and style. If there is one common denominator to

D.'s novels, it is that her characters are all survivors of one kind or another. Her people are heroes of the mundane: reasonable, decent, loving people, whose capacity for endurance redeems them from the fallen realms of everyday English life, giving them, and their threadbare nation, a genuine dignity.

FURTHER WORKS: *A Summer Bird Cage* (1963); *Laura* (1964); *Wordsworth* (1966); *Bird of Paradise* (1969); *The Waterfall* (1969); *Arnold Bennett: A Biography* (1974); *The Queen and Country* (1978); *A Writer's Britain: Landscape in Literature* (1979); *The Radiant Way* (1987); *A Natural Curiosity* (1989); *Safe as Houses* (1990); *The Gates of Ivory* (1991); *Angus Wilson: A Biography* (1995); *The Witch of Exmoor* (1996)

BIBLIOGRAPHY: Myer, V. G., *M. D.: Puritanism and Permissiveness* (1974); Schaefer, J. O., "The Novels of M. D.," *New Republic*, 26 Apr. 1975: 21–23; Libby, M. V., "Fate and Feminism in the Novels of M. D.," *ConL*, 16 (1975): 175–92; Poland, N., "M. D.: 'There Must Be a Lot of People Like Me,'" *MQ*, 16 (1975): 255–67; Manheimer, J., "M. D. and the Journey to the Self," *SLitI*, 11 (1978): 127–43; Fox-Genovese, E., "The Ambiguities of Female Identity: A Reading of the Novels of M. D.," *PR*, 46 (1979): 234–61; Cooper-Clark, D., "M. D.: Cautious Feminist," *Atlantic*, Nov. 1980: 69–75; Moran, M. H., *M. D.: Existing within Structures* (1983; Rose, E. C., ed., *Critical Essays on M. D.* (1985); Hannay, J., *The Intertextuality of Fate: A Study of M. D.* (1986)

—LUANN WALTHER

DRACH, Ivan

Ukrainian poet, translator, critic, and screenwriter, b. 17 Oct. 1936, Telizhentsi

D., the youngest of three sons born to a peasant family, was first exposed to literature through his father's collection of books, the largest in the village. Following his secondary education he taught literature in a village school and was active in the Komsomol (Young Communist League, established in 1918). After serving in the Red Army (1955–58), he enrolled at Kiev University and later studied film-scenario writing in Moscow. He became a Communist Party member in 1959.

D. belongs to the generation of Ukrainian writers known as *shestydesyatnyky*, that is, those who began publishing in the 1960s. He first attracted attention (and criticism) with his poem "Nizh u sontsi" (1961; "Knife in the Sun," 1978), which defied the conventions of SOCIALIST REALISM in both style and content. Unusual and at times obscure imagery (even by Western standards), an almost violent individualism, and the quest to come to terms with the past inform the poem without obscuring its basic theme: the poet's protest against war—against the use of nature and of man's scientific achievements for destructive purposes. D.'s first collection of poetry, *Sonyashnyk* (1962; sunflower) revealed its author's quest for an authenticity of expression and the unbridled power of his poetic imagination. "Balada pro sonyashnyk" (1961; "The Ballad of the Sunflower," 1978) and its accompanying piece, "Sonyashny etyud" (1961; etude of the sun), express D.'s early poetic credo, his attempt to intellectualize subjective images and metaphors drawn from his Ukrainian world and to establish "the

Margaret Drabble

one, ozone truth" of poetry and life without resorting to any existing philosophies and ideologies.

Among the best of D.'s works written in the early 1960s is the long poem "Smert Shevchenka" (1962; Shevchenko's death), by far the most stirring opus of the poetic tributes to the poet Taras Shevchenko (1814–1861), the father of Ukrainian literature, that were written under the Soviets. In addition to traditional Ukrainian motifs presented in a modern manner, the poem also contains an effective juxtaposition of tender lyrical passages with biting satirical verse directed at the petit-bourgeois aspect of the Ukrainian character. Its beauty and strength, however, lie in the poet's lyrical affirmation of the indestructability of the Ukraine.

One of the major themes of D.'s second collection of poetry, *Protuberantsi sertsya* (1965; protuberances of the heart), is his concern for man and the inviolability of human nature. "Balada DNK" ("The Ballad of DNA," 1969) attacks this problem in an ironic and shocking manner by presenting an apocalyptic vision of a nightmarish future brought about by genetic engineering. This collection is also characterized by a motif of doubt in oneself and in one's art, as expressed in "Kalynova balada" (the ballad of the snowball tree), where the problem is resolved by a return to the past; by the theme of isolation, as in "Samotnist" ("Loneliness," 1969), which seems to echo existentialist thought; and by an almost all-pervasive irony, which at times borders on the tragic.

Despite their exuberant originality, D.'s poems display traces of the philosophy of Hryhory Skovoroda (1722–1794), to whom he has dedicated an entire cycle of poems, "Skovorodiana" (1972;

Skovorodiana), and of creative impulses stemming from the poetry of Shevchenko. Among foreigners, Pablo NERUDA and Federico GARCÍA LORCA as well as Walt Whitman, have influenced him.

D. is also author of the film scripts *Idu do tebe* (1970; I am going to you) and *Krynytsya dlya sprahlykh* (1970; a well for the thirsty) and the translator of such poets as García Lorca, QUASIMODO, BACHMANN, and GINSBERG.

D. is without doubt a great original talent. His more recent verse, however, displays alarming symptoms of acquiescence and conformity to official guidelines.

FURTHER WORKS: *Poezii* (1967); *Balady budniv* (1967); *Do dzherel* (1972); *Korin i krona* (1974); *Kyivske nebo* (1976); *Sontse i slovo* (1978); *Lyst do kalyny* (1990). FURTHER WORKS IN ENGLISH: *Orchard Lamps* (1978)

BIBLIOGRAPHY: Pavlychko, D., "Getting to Know a Poet or Criticism," *Digest of the Soviet Ukrainian Press*, 14 (1970): 13–14; Browne, M., ed., *Ferment in the Ukraine* (1971): 177–78; Luckyj, G. S. N., "Ukrainian Literature," in Luckyj, G. S. N., *Discordant Voices* (1975): 129; Mihailovich, V. D., et al., eds., *Modern Slavic Literatures* 2 (1976): 459–62; Kolinko, V., "The World of I. D., Poet of the Ukraine," *Soviet Life*, Feb. 1977: 57–58; Kunitz, S., Introduction to *Orchard Lamps* (1978): 1–4; Galassi, J., "The Horses of Fantasy and Reality," *NYTBR*, 11 March 1979: 14, 25

—LEONID RUDNYTZKY

DRAGÚN, Osvaldo

Argentine dramatist, b. 7 May 1929, Paraná

In Argentina, where the theater has enjoyed popularity since the beginning of the 19th c. and where this genre has been cultivated in an unbroken line with varying degrees of success, D. is one of its most talented and innovative dramatists of the last four decades. His first years were spent in Paraná, but he soon moved to Buenos Aires, where at an early age he established contacts with various independent theater groups that purported to rebel against the tenets of commercial theater by offering an alternative to the predominant theater, which was aimed at middle-class values and tastes. These were groups that were established in the 1950s, fashioned after the North American Provincetown Players and Off-Broadway groups. These groups were united in a common effort. Their aim was to entertain and to make the public politically and socially aware.

D.'s indebtedness to Roberto Arlt (1900–1942), the Argentinean novelist and short-story writer who created a world populated by grotesque, alienated individuals has been thoroughly documented. Both underscore a deep-felt concern for human values. Both insist that human bonds must exist on a basis of reciprocity, in existential terms, and not on a basis of seriality.

In D.'s first successful play, *La peste viene de Melos* (1956; the plague comes from Melos), based on historical fact and depicting the struggle of the Greek isle of Melos against Athens in 416 B.C., the underlying theme is a social one. It emphasizes the negative effects of materialism on humans as it depicts the classic struggle of the business middle class against the peasant workers. On another plane, this play has been seen as an allegory that details the North

American invasion of Guatemala and the fall of the Arbenz government in 1954. It is an indictment of tyranny and oppression.

Tupac Amaru (1957; Tupac Amaru), is another historical play set between 1780 and 1781 treating the uprising of the Inca José Gabriel Condorcanqui against the repressive Spanish colonial regime in Peru. It is a play that points to the continuing battle of Third World countries in our own days as they seek to undo injustices that have reigned for hundreds of years.

D.'s unquestioned masterpiece is a series of one-act vignettes entitled *Historias para ser contadas* (1957; stories to be told). In these short pieces, which depict a "new realism," the scenery has been abolished and four actors assume interchangeable roles as they establish a direct bond with the public. The basic theme of human suffering in a society that has lost all values is presented in exaggerated situations that have been magnified to ridiculous proportions. D. employs Brechtian techniques to show the alienating effect of capitalism and the degradation of the individual trapped in his or her daily work. In *Historia de un flemón, una mujer y dos hombres* (1957; the story of an abscess, a woman, and two men), D. depicts the total disintegration of a family unit where each member is so concerned with financial gain that all levels of communication are severed. *Historia de como nuestro amigo Panchito Gonzales se sintió responsable de la epidemia de peste bubónica en Africa del Sur* (1957; the story of how our friend Panchito Gonzalez felt guilty for being responsible for the outbreak of bubonic plague in South Africa), in addition to showing the degrading effect of work, also treats the theme of racial discrimination and the failure of the intellectual to assume an active political role. On a more subtle plane the story indicts prevailing business practices of industrial nations in their relationship to Third World countries.

La historia del hombre que se convirtió en un perro (1957; the story of the man who turned into a dog) is so preposterous that the audience is forced to search for a deeper meaning on an allegorical level. A man loses all dignity when he is forced to turn into a dog in order to obtain a job. When the play was first produced, the audience empathized with the predicament of the character. In 1979 the same play in Buenos Aires produced entirely different results. The economic and political situation was so catastrophic that when the man turned into a dog he was actually happy and the audience cheered. As D. said, it was easier making a living as a dog than having to go out and work at the docks.

Historia de mi esquina (1957; story of my corner) and *Los de la mesa* 10 (1957; the couple at table 10) are plays that treat the theme of alienated youths separated from the values of their parents. It is during this period that D. begins to incorporate in his plays popular songs and a chorus effect to heighten the anguish of his characters.

From 1961 to 1963 D. lived in Cuba, where he organized a series of workshops and where he dedicated himself to the writing of *Y nos dijeron que eramos inmortales* (1963; and they told us we were immortal) and *Milagro en el mercado viejo* (1964; miracle in the old marketplace). The first is a strong indictment of war as well as a condemnation of the family and its failure with the youth of the day. The children are emotionally crippled and ill-equipped to face everyday life. The second play hinges on the theme of cruelty. The vagabonds that inhabit the marketplace are excluded from economic participation. The ending of the play with the killing of the powerful merchant points to the need for class change, by violent means if need be.

Heróica de Buenos Aires (1966; epic of Buenos Aires) is an extremely ambitious play that recreates Bertolt BRECHT's *Mother*

Courage. Written in a popular language, it portrays the epic of marginal beings who live with political ideologies that have not been totally assimilated. There is also the appearance of the intellectual, whose political position is well defined, and whose every word is correct, but who is cold and indifferent toward the sufferings of the masses.

Un maldito domingo (1968; a damned Sunday), produced in Spain and subsequently in Buenos Aires under the title of *El amasijo* (1968; mishmash), treats the theme of alienation in existential terms. It is the story of a middle-aged couple that leads a sterile existence. Each character takes turns hurting the other as they act out their fantasies in an effort to break their monotonous lives.

D. maintains the format of the *Historias* with his play *Historias con carcel* (1973; stories with a jail theme). At a time when Latin America was witnessing political persecutions in many of its countries, this play, which depicts the repression and loss of freedom that was so prevalent, was a finalist in the Casa de Las Américas Literary Prize for that year.

D.'s interest in the theater has never waned. In 1981, together with a group of dramatists, he founded the Teatro Abierto (Open Theater). Dramatist and artists worked together to create a new alternative theater that could be enjoyed and easily afforded by the masses. Many of the plays produced were political in nature, and their theater mysteriously burned down after the first week. They reopened at another location to great public acclaim.

One of D.'s latest plays is *Arriba corazón* (1987; take heart). It is the story of the main protagonist Corazón in different stages of his life. It closely parallels the history of contemporary Argentina with its social and political ills.

Since 1989 D. has been the director of the Escuela Internacional de Teatro de América Latina y del Caribe, in Havana, Cuba, which hosts seminars and workshops.

FURTHER WORKS: *Amoretta* (1957); *Hoy se comen al flaco* (1981); *Al violador* (1981); *Mi obelisco y yo* (1983); *Los hijos del terremoto* (1986)

BIBLIOGRAPHY: Reynolds, B. E., "The Theater of O. D.," in Lyday, L. F., Woodyard, G. W., eds., *Dramatists in Revolt* (1976): 77–94; Leonard, C. C., "D.'s Distancing Techniques in *Historias para ser contadas* and *El amasijo*," *LATR*, 16, 2 (Spring 1983): 37–42; Pross, E. E., "Open Theatre Revisited: An Argentine Experiment," *LATR*, 18, 1 (Fall 1984): 83–94; Garganigo, J. F., *O. D. Su Teatro* (1993)

—JOHN F. GARGANIGO

DREISER, Theodore

American novelist, b. 27 Aug. 1871, Terre Haute, Ind.; d. 28 Dec. 1945, Hollywood, Calif.

D. was born a year after the woolen mill his father had operated in Sullivan, Ind., was destroyed by fire. D.'s father was never able to reestablish himself, much less support his large family. D. was thus raised in an atmosphere of constant poverty, moving from one dismal lodging to another, scavenging for coal along the railroad tracks, often having nothing but mush to eat, and receiving only sporadic encouragement in a succession of schools. D.'s family

Theodore Dreiser

background, his own disposition, and the era in which he grew up sufficiently validated the dark outlook and brooding style inevitably associated with his writing. For D., this view of life was more than a matter of artistic method; to a large extent his behavior and his writing reflected the belief that life is a jungle, that man is an animal motivated and manipulated solely by desire and instinct.

At sixteen, much like the Sister Carrie of his first novel, D. set out for Chicago with six dollars in his pocket. He failed at a number of jobs, and then, ironically enough for a child of misfortune who was later to write so long and so grimly about the cruelties of fate, he was sent to Indiana University by Mildred Fleming, one of his former teachers. But D. did not like college and left after a year, eventually finding work as a newspaper reporter. D. knew nothing about writing; his natural style—long, cumbersome sentences—was unsuited even to the journalism of the 1890s. But he was willing to rewrite and rewrite the simplest of his assignments, and he had a powerful if morbid curiosity that made him a good observer of people and events. In a surprisingly short time he became an effective reporter. Until he was able to depend on his novels for financial support, D. remained a newspaperman and editor, working for the St. Louis *Globe-Democrat*, Cleveland *Leader*, Pittsburgh *Dispatch*, and the New York *World*, and later editing several magazines, including *Every Month, Broadway, The Bohemian*, and *The Delineator*.

D.'s personal life was certainly support for his belief that man's greatest appetite is sexual. D. went from one woman to the next, often carrying on several affairs at once. He apparently thought of himself in the same mechanistically biological way that he thought of the characters in his novels. D. considered himself driven by the biological and environmental factors he called "chemisms," a term he never defined exactly. But he did believe that chemisms led him into his marriage (1898) with Sallie White, a Missouri schoolteacher he had met while working in St. Louis. He separated permanently from her in 1909, but never earnestly sought a divorce. In 1919 he met his cousin Helen Richardson, with whom he lived thereafter, marrying her in 1944, two years after his first wife had died.

D.'s notion of chemisms, his attitudes toward women, and his eventual somewhat bizarre political involvements (he joined the Communist Party in 1945) all have a place in his peculiar scheme of things, a partly scientific, partly mystical collection of thoughts that come out of his emotions as much as his intellect. D.'s ideas have their roots in American transcendentalism, the tough line of Darwinism, the compassionate response of the Progressive era, and his own turn-of-the-century conglomeration of experience that found its first expression in *Sister Carrie* (1900), which D. began writing in the summer of 1899.

With *Sister Carrie*, it may be argued, American literature moved into the 20th c. *Sister Carrie* was accepted for publication by Doubleday, Page (at the insistence of Frank Norris [1870–1902], who was working for Doubleday as an editor), but it was not immediately successful in the United States because of a belated decision by the publisher to suppress it. The book was thought to be immoral because of D.'s apparent willingness to allow vice (as far as Carrie herself is concerned) to be rewarded instead of punished. But even though his publisher did little to promote the book, its rejection was not as complete as many have believed, nor was D. subject to as much vilification as he later claimed to have been. *Sister Carrie* actually received a number of favorable reviews and was particularly well received in England. The problem with the novel's first American publication was that few periodicals bothered to comment on it at all. But when *Sister Carrie* was reissued in 1907 it was given the attention that made it one of the most celebrated novels in literary history.

Present-day readers may find it difficult to understand what was so shocking and innovative about *Sister Carrie* (after all, there is no explicit sex in the book and no four-letter vulgarisms). D. was thought outrageous not because of his language, not even because of his subject matter, but because he presents Carrie without moral bias. In showing that her rise is a result of her fall, he turned Victorian melodrama upside down and created the first truly modern heroine in American fiction.

But another character in the novel, the Chicago saloon manager G. W. Hurstwood, whom Carrie eventually abandons in an ironic reversal of the old "ruined-maiden" plot, has been seen by many commentators as the most interesting character in the book. This is partly because Carrie's personality is not given much overt development; she says little that is memorable, although she possesses an unconscious calculating quality that makes her fascinatingly dangerous. Hurstwood, however, is presented with a different kind of complexity. He is at once a representative man and a unique creation whose decline and fall is strangely poignant.

There is in D. some of the same unconscious genius that is often attributed to Dickens, and this in itself goes a long way toward explaining his achievement in *Sister Carrie*. This unconscious genius is evident from the very first sentence of the novel in D.'s casual use of symbols that at once establish the elements of the story: "When Caroline Meeber boarded the afternoon train for Chicago, her total outfit consisted of a small trunk, a cheap imitation-alligator-skin satchel, a small lunch in a paper box, and a yellow snap purse, containing her ticket, a scrap of paper with her sister's address on Van Buren Street, and four dollars in money." As this first sentence indicates, Carrie is a fate unto herself, boarding the train (that simultaneous image of free will and determinism) with her cheap luggage (a sign of her poverty and an indication of an essential cheapness in Carrie herself that she *carries* with her wherever she goes), her purse the color of gold, her sister's address on a scrap of paper (an address that offers her only a scrap of hope), and only four dollars in cash (again and again what happens to Carrie is a function of certain sums of money). D. also mentions that Carrie is going to Chicago, and the city soon becomes a character in itself, powerfully evoking the beauty and terror of the American industrial state and its impact on the hopeful mind.

What the story builds toward is the point that in Carrie we see the impossibility of realizing one's hopes. From the start of the novel she is dreaming wildly implausible dreams of supremacy and success. And at the end she has that supremacy, her name in lights, her future assured. But in the final scene she sits in a rocking chair, perhaps having learned that she is still without happiness. The chair is another of D.'s powerful, almost unconscious symbols. We first see Carrie boarding a train; we last see her in a chair, rocking back and forth. She has traveled far, but the train has surrealistically turned into a rocking chair, which will take her nowhere. In Hurstwood we see an illustration of the opposite process—a life in which all dreams finally must be abandoned. Hurstwood, like Carrie, has his dreams; but unlike hers, his are not even superficially realized. And at the end of Hurstwood's story, D.'s subliminal symbolism enters again. Before turning on the gas, Hurstwood seals the crack at the bottom of his hotel-room door with his coat, and in reading about the act we are invited to think back to that moment when Hurstwood inadvertently closed the door of the safe in the back room of the saloon after removing the money. Such contrasting symbolism leading to sympathetic character portrayal makes D.'s deterministic philosophy seem oddly beside the point.

Explaining without moralizing—that is, in an essential way, the problem D. faced as a novelist; and his ability to handle that problem is what made *Sister Carrie* such a genuinely innovative work. The novels that followed, *Jennie Gerhardt* (1909), *The Financier* (1912), *The Titan* (1914), and *The "Genius"* (1915), succeed in lesser ways for the same reason, but it is in *An American Tragedy* (1925) that D. extends his abilities as a novelist and a thinker further than he was able to do before or after. His purpose in *An American Tragedy* is, on the face of it, both pretentious and ridiculous—to account for American politics, society, religion, business, and sex through a sensationalized narrative concerning the murder of a pregnant working girl and the subsequent trial of her lover, an ex-bellhop. But as D. worked the story out, threading his way through the tangle of melodrama, subconscious symbolism, and the private obsessions of the public mind, he comes up with a book that, whatever its faults (lengthiness, dated vocabulary, silly dialogue), is an explanation of how such murders happen and why they happen so often in the United States. It is also, in a darker way than any of his other novels, an explanation of D. himself. It is more than coincidence that F. Scott FITZGERALD's *The Great Gatsby*, a story about a big-time boot-legger, should have appeared in the same year as D.'s story about a small-time murderer. Though very different stylistically, both of these novels seek to deflate the American dream of success by showing how directly that dream is related to socially destructive acts.

Much of the deeply suggestive effect D. achieves in *An American Tragedy* derives from the same kind of subconscious symbolism found in *Sister Carrie*. Clyde is in a canoe when he first encounters Roberta outside out of the factory walls. Later, when he rows her out onto Big Bittern Lake, he falls into a trance like Thoreau on Walden Pond. And after the murder, he makes his escape through the woods. These symbols—the canoe, the lake, the woods—all so intricately involved in Clyde's tragedy, function to give the novel its dreamlike quality, as do certain other symbols. The hotels in which Clyde works become a metaphor of his life. He is doomed to be a transient, an American type forever on the move—until he is caught (and even then, like Daniel Boone, he is wishing he could disappear into the wilderness). Also noteworthy is D.'s use of doors, especially in the way that the death-chamber door awaiting Clyde contrasts with the "Door of Hope Mission" his religiously fanatical mother runs—a contrast inversely reminiscent of the safe door and the door of Hurstwood's suicide room in *Sister Carrie*. Again, one is hesitant to claim that the mythic implications or the symbolic structure of the novel were carefully planned by D. (the pieces fit together only roughly). Instead, D. seems to have been so attuned to the murmurings and cravings of the popular mind that these aspects of the book seem to be there by instinct.

D. certainly does not present a tragic story in the traditional sense. He reduces to the lowest common denominator the concept of the tragic hero, making not a king, but an ex-bellhop the protagonist. But it is an ironic reduction. Clyde turns out at times to be indecisive like Hamlet. Like Lear he is blind to his own personality. And like Othello he is uncertain of his own definition. Clyde goes to his death not knowing who he is, finding no home—even after wandering across half the continent. Like all tragic heroes, his fight ultimately must be seen as a struggle against the illusions D. attacks: wealth, power, love, and, most tragically, the self.

D.'s artistry in his greatest work is difficult to discuss because so much of it must be attributed to his natural tendency to let his dark symbols float through an extended narrative. But despite the many negative things that must be said about the way D. handles the form of most of his other novels, his technique, his style, and the power of his imagination work together to produce in *An American Tragedy*, a narrative that is at once a folk epic and an intricate work of something other than ordinary art—a psychology of reality.

An American Tragedy was banned in Boston in 1927, and it is significant that in his most ambitious work D. continued the battle against censorship that made him one of the foremost figures in the battle for freedom of expression in 20th-c. America. D.'s problems with censorship began with *Sister Carrie* and culminated in the uproar evoked by *The "Genius"* in 1916, when the New York Society for the Suppression of Vice, under the leadership of John S. Sumner, succeeded in frightening the publisher into withdrawing the novel. With the support of H. L. MENCKEN as well as the Author's League of America, D. brought suit against the publishers. D. lost the action and *The "Genius"* remained off the market until Liveright reissued it five years later, but the reality of the threat to freedom of expression was brought home to American writers, readers, and critics (previous legal suppressions had involved either foreign or long-deceased authors). In just a few years, much of what D. had battled for was to be achieved. In subsequent trials involving James JOYCE's *Ulysses* and D. H. LAWRENCE's *Lady Chatterley's Lover*, D.'s example remained an object lesson. Again and again throughout his career D. spoke out in defense of the artist's right to be heard.

In D. we have one of the most complex figures in American literature. He seems to have been born knowing things he did not have to learn. He knew little of literary history, yet his first novel became a turning point, a touchstone in American literature. Somehow, with nothing that can be seen as a sense of direction, he found himself at "the crossroads of the novel." He set up a permanent roadblock for the older writers of the genteel tradition and went on to lead the fight for freedom of expression that made possible the achievement of the whole generation of writers following him. As Mencken wrote in a letter sent to be read at D.'s funeral, "the fact remains that he was a great artist, and that no other American of his generation left so wide and handsome a mark upon the national letters. American writing, before and after his time, differed as much as biology before and after Darwin."

FURTHER WORKS: *A Traveler at Forty* (1913); *Plays of the Natural and Supernatural* (1916); *A Hoosier Holiday* (1916); *Free, and Other Stories* (1918); *The Hand of the Potter* (1918); *Twelve Men* (1919); *Hey Rub-a-Dub-Dub* (1920); *A Book about Myself* (1922); *The Color of a Great City* (1923); *Moods, Cadenced and Declaimed* (1926); *Chains* (1927); *D. Looks at Russia* (1928); *A Gallery of Women* (1929); *My City* (1929); *Epitaph: A Poem* (1929); *The Aspirant* (1929); *Fine Furniture* (1930); *Tragic America* (1931); *Dawn* (1931); *America is Worth Saving* (1941); *The Bulwark* (1946); *The Stoic* (1947); *The Best Short Stories of T. D.* (1947, 1956) *Letters to Louise* (1959); *Letters of T. D.* (1959); *Notes on Life* (1974)

BIBLIOGRAPHY: Rascoe, B., *T. D.* (1926); Dudley, D., *Forgotten Frontiers: D. and the Land of the Free* (1933); Elias, R. H., *T. D.: Apostle of Nature* (1949); Matthiessen, F. O., *T. D.* (1951); Kazin, A., and C. Shapiro, eds., *The Stature of T. D.* (1955); Shapiro, C., *T. D.: Our Bitter Patriot* (1962); Gerber, P. L., *T. D.* (1964); Swanberg, W. A., *D.* (1965); Thader, M., *T. D.: A New Dimension* (1965); McAleer, J. J., *T. D.: An Introduction and Interpretation* (1968); Moers, E., *Two D.s* (1969); Lehan, R., *T. D.: His World and His Novels* (1969); Warren, R. P., *Homage to T. D.* (1971); Lundquist, J., *T. D.* (1974); Pizer, D., *T. D.: A Primary and Secondary Bibliography* (1975); Pizer, D., *The Novels of T. D.: A Critical Study* (1977)

—JAMES LUNDQUIST

It must not be supposed, of course, as has now and then been done, that the writings of a man of his stature can be without artistic value. Far from it. He possesses the central artistic values, though he lacks the peripheral ones. . . . D. has the root of the matter in him, which is detachment and transcendence during the creative process. He can keep his eye on the object, only and solely and entirely on the object. . . . He can take the clay and mold men; he can create the relations between them. . . . What counts against him is . . . the heavy, amorphous verbiage, which will seem duller as time goes on, the unrestrained meticulousness in the delineation of the trivial, the increasing grittiness of his texture.

Ludwig Lewisohn. *Expression in America* (1932), pp. 481–82

It is because he has spoken for Americans with an emotion equivalent to their own emotion, in a speech as broken and blindingly searching as common speech, that we have responded to him with the dawning realization that he is stronger than all the others of his time, and at the same time more poignant; greater than the world he has described, but as significant as the people in it. To have accepted America as he has accepted it, to immerse oneself in something one can neither escape nor relinquish, to yield to what has been true and to yearn over what has seemed inexorable, has been D.'s fate and the secret of his victory.

Alfred Kazin, *On Native Grounds* (1942),
pp. 89–90

T. D. . . . suggested to me some large creature of the prime wandering on the marshy plains of a human foreworld. A prognathous man with an eye askew and a paleolithic face, he put me in mind of Polyphemus . . . a Rodinesque figure only half out from the block; and yet a remark that someone made caused him to blush even up to the roots of his thin grey hair. D. was hypersensitive, strangely as one might have thought—he was a living paradox in more than one way; but a lonelier man there never was.

Van Wyck Brooks, *Days of the Phoenix* (1957),
p. 20

D. was willing to risk being wrong; and he had great wrong-looking juts to his character. He was a stiff-armer, an elbower who never gave ground outside his novels or in them. And though outside the books he could be so obtuse and unjust, inside them his passion for justice rang true. At the height of his success, when he had settled old scores and could easily have become the smiling public man, he chose instead to rip the whole fabric of American civilization straight down the middle, from its economy to its morality. It was the country that had to give ground.

Nelson Algren, *Nation*, (16 May, 1959), 459

D.'s novels have an important aim, significant because he was a keen, if often naïve observer of the social and political realities of his day. He saw America as being at middle age, and he was concerned with a culture which, by creating and encouraging artificial goals, was perverting its worthwhile institutions and, more important, was robbing the individual of his chance to live up to a full, meaningful potential. Each of D.'s novels illustrates a different aspect of what he felt was a crucial misdirection of American energy. Often his insights were vague and muddied: in *The "Genius"* (1915), for example, D. attempts to explain the forces harmful to the creative artist, and by placing the blame on a curious mixture of capitalism and croticism his novel rests on a faulty base. Which is to say that D. is usually a bad writer at the point he leaps past his immediate feelings and his

own past. In his first two books, *Sister Carrie* (1900) and *Jennie Gerhardt* (1911), D. studies the failure of the American as an individual and of Americans as a family group, and his theme provides a valid and compassionate foundation for the novels. He was writing out of the misery and passion of his own experiences.

D.'s works, while exploring many sides to a problem, would adhere to a single point of view, and the focus, often shifting, from book to book, in various economic and philosophical directions, would originate in what he believed at the moment to be the deepest roots of American unhappiness.

Charles Shapiro, *T. D.* (1962), p. 4

The cosmos operating in his stories is uncaring, unfeeling; at bottom it is an unfair universe, controlled by gods who disdain involvement in their creation. We can nod in agreement with the writer or cavil at the darkness of his pessimism, but we are forced above all to stop, to consider, to think. . . . Probably because of his philosophy—we are all companions in the same sinking ship—D. feels keenly the plight of each individual human soul at the mercy of chance and of forces beyond his control. It is significant that, though failures abound in his novels, there are no villains, only human beings who are more or less fortunate than their neighbors. In the D. World, each life is necessarily a tragedy.

Philip L. Gerber, *T. D.* (1964), pp. 173–75

No newspaper could catch the prodigious drama of this strange life—the sensitive, shoeless Indiana boy with hurts that never healed, the anguish over the stillborn *Sister Carrie*, the interval of dress-pattern splendor, then the long, bitter struggle for freedom and acceptance that would be his greatest glory and that ended with *An American Tragedy* in 1925. That the work he had done in those years made a bridge between Howells and Hemingway that no one else could have built was achievement enough of itself. It was not the final achievement. Bridge or no bridge, the work was colossal in its own right.

W. A. Swanberg, *D.* (1965), pp. 523–24

Randolph Bourne once said that D. had the "artist's vision without the sureness of the artist's technique." This is true of much of D.'s work. . . . I have used the phrase "D.'s art" in full awareness that most critics, even critics as dangerous to deal with as Lionel Trilling, will find it absurd; and in full awareness that even those who admire D. will, with few exceptions, concede a point on "art," or apologetically explain that D.'s ineptitudes somehow have the value of stylistic decorum and can be taken as a manifestation of his grasping honesty, and will then push on to stake their case on his "power" and "compassion."

But ultimately how do we know the "power" or the "compassion"—know them differently, that is, from the power or compassion we may read into a news story—except by D.'s control? Except, in other words, by the rhythmic organization of his materials, the vibrance which is the life of fictional illusion, the tension among elements, and the mutual interpenetration in meaning of part and whole which gives us the sense of preternatural fulfillment? Except, in short, by art?

Robert Penn Warren, *Homage to T. D.* (1971), pp. 117–18

D.'s basic tendency as a novelist was to establish a clear central structure (Hurstwood's fall and Carrie's rise; Cowperwood's alternating business and love affairs; Clyde's parallel life in Kansas City and Lycurgus; Solon's double life as businessman and Quaker), to pursue this structure to its seeming conclusion (death or an emotional stasis), yet to suggest both by authorial commentary and by a powerful symbol within the narrative (a rocking chair, deep-sea fish, a street scene, a brook) that life is essentially circular, that it moves in endless repetitive patterns.... It is possible to visualize D.'s novels as a graphic irony—the characters believe they are pushing forward but they are really moving in a circle.

Donald Pizer, *The Novels of T. D.: A Critical Study* (1976), p. 25

DRIEU LA ROCHELLE, Pierre

French novelist and essayist, b. 3 Jan. 1893, Paris; d. 16 March 1945, Paris

D. was born into the bourgeoisie and had a protected childhood. He studied at the École des Sciences Politiques (1910–13) but failed the graduating examination and was drafted into the army. A corporal when World War I broke out, he participated in the battle of Charleroi (August 1914), the Dardanelles expedition (1915), and the battle of Verdun (1916). Wounded three times, he spent long periods in hospitals, where he wrote about his experiences. In 1917 he published his war poems, *Interrogation*. He soon became one of the promising authors of the Gallimard publishing house and a regular contributor to the *Nouvelle revue française*. A close friend of Louis ARAGON's, he took part in some of the surrealists' activities and contributed to their publications while writing autobiographical fiction and political essays. Between 1925 and 1934 he was tempted by communism and socialism, but he opted for fascism in 1934, wrote in the fascist press, and was one of the spokesmen for collaboration with Germany after the collapse of France in 1940. During the German occupation he became chief editor of the *Nouvelle revue française*, and held that post from December 1940 to June 1943. After two unsuccessful attempts, he committed suicide on March 15, 1945.

D. paid a heavy price for being, in D.'s own words, "one of those who, in a generation, make the liaison, at their own risk, between politics and literature." In his political essays he emphasized the changes that France, Europe, and the world were undergoing. In *Mesure de la France* (1922; France's measurements), he

made a realistic appraisal of a France dangerously misled by her victory in 1918 (won only with the help of a worldwide coalition) and actually weakened by the loss of a million and a half men. He showed that the emergence of two gigantic world powers, the U.S.A. and the U.S.S.R., with their immense territories and populations, had dwarfed the little nation of forty million Frenchmen, encamped in a balkanized Europe. In *Genève ou Moscou* (1927; Geneva or Moscow) and *L'Europe centre les patries* (1931; Europe against nationalism), he preached peaceful European unification as the only means for a weakened Europe to survive. After the defeat of 1940, he thought that Hitler would unify the continent. Soon disillusioned, he devoted most of his time to the study of Oriental thought and wrote his most ambitious novels during that period.

Although D. has long been neglected because of his politics, his importance as a writer of novels, short stories, and plays, and also as a critic, is now being recognized. He is a master of the novella. The short stories of *La comédie de Charleroi* (1934; the comedy of Charleroi) can stand comparison with the best that has been written about war in any language. The posthumous publication of *Histoires déplaisantes* (1963; cruel tales) has confirmed his reputation as one of the best French *nouvellistes*. His early novels expose the decadence of the modern world, and especially the decadence of sex, through two parallel means: pitiless introspection and social satire. *Le feu follet* (1931; *The Fire Within*, 1971) will survive as a compelling tragedy of a heroin addict. The autobiographical *Gilles* (1939) offers a sweeping portrait of the period 1917–37: the end of World War I, surrealism, the mad 1920s, between-the-wars French politics, and the Spanish Civil War. *Les chiens de paille* (1944; straw dogs) is a classic of the death agony of Europe. The posthumously published, unfinished *Mémoires de Dirk Raspe* (1966; memoirs of Dirk Raspe), based on the life of Van Gogh and on D.'s own evolution as an artist, would suffice to establish him as a major novelist. Even with his contradictions, his errors, and his failures, he is perhaps the most reliable witness of the *nouveau mal du siècle*, and his testimony is indispensable to any historian of contemporary European sensibility.

FURTHER WORKS: *Fond de Cantine* (1920); *État civil* (1921); *Plainte contre inconnu* (1924); *L'homme couvert de femmes* (1925); *La suite dans les idées* (1927); *Le jeune Européen* (1927); *Blèche* (1928); *Une femme à sa fenêtre* (1929); *L'eau fraîche* (1931); *Drôle de voyage* (1933); *Journal d'un homme trompé* (1934); *Socialisme fasciste* (1934); *Beloukia* (1936); *Rêveuse bourgeoisie* (1937); *Avec Doriot* (1937); *L'homme à cheval* (1943); *Charlotte Corday, le Chef* (1944); *Le Français d'Europe* (1944); *Récit secret* (1961); *Sur les écrivains* (1964)

BIBLIOGRAPHY: Andreu, P., *D. témoin et visionnaire* (1952); Grover, F., *D. and the Fiction of Testimony* (1958); Leal, R. B., *D.: Decadence in Love* (1973); Soucy, R., *Fascist Intellectual: P. D.* (1979); Andreu, P., and Grover F., *D.* (1979)

—FREDERIC J. GROVER

DRUMMOND DE ANDRADE, Carlos

See Andrade, Carlos Drummond de

W. E. Du Bois

DU BOIS, W(illiam) E(dward) B(urghardt)

American essayist, historian, novelist, sociologist, biographer, poet, and editor, b. 23 Feb. 1868, Great Barrington, Mass.; d. 27 Aug. 1963, Accra, Ghana

There is an almost too obvious symbolism in the fact that the death of D., in Africa, occurred on the eve of the March on Washington for Jobs and Freedom in 1963. Through a long life D., who held degrees from Fisk University and Harvard, had been one of those most influential in preparing the way for such a gathering, and, indeed, in establishing what would prove to be important guidelines for the Civil Rights Movement and for the Black Power movement that was soon to emerge as a significant force in American racial politics. D. was one of those present at the creation in 1909 of the NAACP (National Association for the Advancement of Colored People) and would be the hugely influential editor of that organization's publication, the *Crisis*, from its inception in 1910 until 1934. He had in his life played many roles, including those of scholar, propagandist, artist, activist, political candidate, and radical. In addition to the harassment that might be expected by any man of color who dared to challenge the racist structures of American society in the early part of the 20th c., D. was more than once the target of the nation's periodic red scares, to the point of being indicted in 1951 for failing to register as a foreign agent; the

judge directed a verdict of not guilty. D. was also involved in controversy within the black community, as an eloquent critic of what he regarded as the excessive accommodationism of Booker T. Washington, the demagoguery of Marcus Garvey, and the timidity of the NAACP. His joining the Communist Party in 1961 and his assumption of Ghanaian citizenship in 1962 may both be regarded as reflecting a late pessimism as to the possibility of significant reform within the structures of capitalist America. Whether his pessimism or the optimism of the demonstrators in Washington, who paused for a moment of mourning when his passing was announced, was the more appropriate response to the American reality is a question whose answer may still be debated.

The concerns of D. the man determine to a considerable extent the activities of D. the writer. It was as a historian that he was awarded the doctoral degree from Harvard University, and his dissertation, *The Suppression of the African Slave-Trade to the United States of America*, was published in 1896 as the inaugural volume of the Harvard Historical Studies series. The book demonstrates D.'s mastery of the principles of Germanic scholarship then in vogue, while at the same time reflecting D.'s commitment to the cause of arriving at a true understanding of the African-American past and its relation to American history at large. The same concern would later produce one of D.'s most important works, *Black Reconstruction*. By 1935, when this work was published, D. had become convinced that historical scholarship and advocacy, while not identical, could not be entirely separated. Thus *Black Reconstruction*, while a thoroughly responsible work of scholarship, is also a conscious attempt to undo the harm perpetrated by white racist historians, who had portrayed the era of Reconstruction as a mixture of scandal and farce, and to evoke a proper appreciation of the many substantial achievements of the black masses and of their political representatives in the years immediately following the end of the Civil War.

D. also turned his historian's attention to the subject of Africa and of those who trace their origins to that continent in a number of works, of which the foundation is *The Negro*, published in 1915. This text was expanded in 1939 to *Black Folk, Then and Now: An Essay in the History and Sociology of the Negro Race*. The later text reflects the growing influence of Karl Marx on D.'s thought. *The World and Africa: An Inquiry into the Part Which Africa Has Played in World History* (1947) is a further treatment of this subject.

As the subtitle of *Black Folk* suggests, D.'s scholarly interests included both history and sociology. His *The Philadelphia Negro: A Social Study* (1899), a pioneer work of ethnic and urban sociology, by examining with the objectivity of the social scientist the role of the environment in the shaping of character and conduct, also makes a subtle but compelling case against notions of innate racial inferiority. D.'s editorship from 1897 to 1910 of the annual publications of the Atlanta University conferences, substantial contributions to the sociology of black America, enhanced his reputation as a social scientist.

Scholarly writing, however, constitutes only a portion of D.'s total work. His five novels are perhaps not to today's critical taste, but none of them is without interest, especially when viewed as attempts to give imaginative form to the thought of one of the towering intellects of this century. Critics have tended to prefer *The Quest of the Silver Fleece* (1911), which combines social REALISM and romance in its symbolic depiction of the Southern cotton economy, its effect on black lives, and the transfiguration that follows when the black characters take control of their own lives. *Dark Princess: A Romance* (1928), which relates the struggles of black Americans to revolutionary unrest in what we have come to call the Third World, seems to have been D.'s favorite. The "Black Flame" trilogy, consisting of *The Ordeal of Mansart* (1957), *Mansart Builds a School* (1959), and *Worlds of Color* (1961), must be regarded as his most ambitious work of fiction, attempting to depict what it was like to be black in America in the last quarter of the 19th and the first half of the 20th cs. through the portrayal of four generations of a black family.

At least one critic has expressed regret that D. turned to the novel to deal with the materials of the trilogy, suggesting that a personal memoir might have been more powerful. And most critics would rate D.'s autobiographical *Dusk of Dawn: An Essay toward an Autobiography of a Race Concept* (1940) more highly than any of his novels. As the subtitle suggests, D. is not primarily concerned in this work to provide us with the intimate details of his personal life. Rather, we are to see that life in the light of the concept; it is the concept that gives significance to the life. One hardly knows whether to describe D.'s willingness to see himself as standing for the "race concept" as an instance of the arrogance of which he has sometimes been accused or as an indication of a humility that leads him to believe that his life is of moment only insofar as it may provide insight into such a concept. The posthumously published *The Autobiography of W. E. B. D.* (1968), while hardly confessional, is rather more personal.

If any one work by D. is to be singled out as his masterpiece, most critics agree it is *The Souls of Black Folk* (1903), a book of essays and sketches in which, by a combination of scholarship, personal reminiscence, reflection, and polemic, D. draws aside the veil of stereotype, condescension, and bigotry that had rendered black America invisible and affirms the full humanity, pathos, dignity, and promise of his people.

In his role as editor of the *Crisis*, D. was involved in publishing the work of a number of important black writers, including Langston HUGHES and other luminaries of the Harlem Renaissance of the 1920s. He was also engaged in the effort in that period to define the terms of a black literature and to spell out the criteria by which such a literature might be judged. Although Claude MCKAY and others regarded D. as incorrigibly genteel in his literary preferences, his practices as an editor and his pronouncements as a critic suggest that the truth was more complicated.

In fact, the truth about a man of such protean talents as D. must be complicated. That he lived a long and productive life in such eventful times adds to the complication, as does the fact that he was for much of his life a man in intellectual motion, constantly reexamining and moving beyond earlier formulations. Only in the last years of his life, and not entirely even then, does one have a sense of thought hardening into dogma.

FURTHER WORKS: *John Brown* (1909); *Darkwater: Voices from Within the Veil* (1920); *The Gift of Black Folk: The Negroes in the Making of America* (1924); *Africa—Its Place in Modern History* (1930); *Africa—Its Geography, People, and Politics* (1930); *Colour and Democracy: Colonies and Peace* (1945); *In Battle for Peace: The Story of My 83rd Birthday. With Comment by Shirley Graham* (1952); *An ABC of Color* (1963); *W. E. B. D. Speaks: Speeches and Addresses* (1970); *The Education of Black People* (1973); *The Correspondence of W. E. B. D.* (3 vols., 1973–1978); *Prayers for Dark People* (1980); *Writings by W. E. B. D. in Non-Periodical Literature Edited by Others* (1982); *Writings by W. E. B. D. in Periodicals Edited by Others* (1982); *Writings in Periodicals Edited by W. E. B. D.: Selections from the "Crisis"* (1983); *Writings in Periodicals Edited by W. E. B. D.: Selections from the "Horizon"* (1985); *Against Racism: Unpublished Essays, Papers, Addresses 1887–1961* (1985); *Creative Writings by W. E. B. D.: A Pageant, Poems, Short Stories, and Playlets* (1985)

BIBLIOGRAPHY: Broderick, F. L., *W. E. B. D.: Negro Leader in a Time of Crisis* (1959); Meier, A., "From 'Conservative' to 'Radical': The Ideological Development of W. E. B. D.," *Crisis*, 66 (1959): 527–36; Wesley, C., "W. E. B. D., Historian," *Freedomways*, 5 (Winter 1965): 59–72; Howe, I., "Remarkable Man, Ambiguous Legacy," *Harper's*, March 1968: 143–49; Clarke, J. H., et al., eds., *Black Titan: W. E. B. D.* (1970); Brodwin, S., "The Veil Transcended: Form and Meaning in W. E. B. D.'s *The Souls of Black Folk*", *JBIS*, 2 (1972): 303–21; Moon, H. L., ed., *The Emerging Thought of W. E. B. D.* (1972); Tuttle, W. M., Jr., ed., *W. E. B. D.* (1973); Moses, W., "The Poetics of Ethiopianism: W. E. B. D. and Literary Black Nationalism," *AL*, 47 (1975): 411–27; Rampersad, A., *The Art and Imagination of W. E. B. D.* (1976); Byerman, K., "Hearts of Darkness: Narrative Voices in *The Souls of Black Folk*," *ALR*, 14 (1981): 43–51; Stewart, J., "Psychic Duality of Afro-Americans in the Novels of W. E. B. D.," *Phylon*, 44, 2 (1983): 93–107; Andrews, W. L., ed., *Critical Essays on W. E. B. D.* (1985); Marable, M., *W. E. B. D.: Black Radical Democrat* (1986); McKay, N. Y., "The Souls of Black Women Folk in the Writings of W.E. B. D.", in Gates, H. L., Jr., ed., *Reading Black, Reading Feminist* (1990): 227–43; Byerman, K. E., *Seizing the Word: History, Art, and Self in the Work of W. E. B. D.* (1994)

—W. P. KENNEY

DUČIĆ, Jovan

Yugoslav poet and essayist (writing in Serbian), b. 17 Feb. 1871, Trebinje; d. 7 April 1943, Gary, Ind., U.S.A.

After a secondary-school education, D. first worked as a schoolteacher and a nationalist organizer among the Herzegvinian Serbs and later studied philology at the University of Geneva. From 1907 to 1918 he was in the Serbian diplomatic service in Istanbul, Sofia, and Athens, and, following World War I, in the service of the Yugoslav kingdom as its delegate to the League of Nations in Geneva and ambassador in Cairo, Rome, Bucharest, and Lisbon. When the Nazis overran Yugoslavia in 1941, he emigrated to the United States.

Though D. started writing poetry in 1886, his first collection of verse entitled *Pesme* (poems) appeared in 1901. Subsequently, study in Switzerland and visits to Paris brought him into close contact with the French Parnassians and SYMBOLISTS and their influence permeated all his later works. His next two collections of poems, *Pesme* (1908; poems) and *Plave legende* (1908; *Blue Legends*, 1983) already display an intense preoccupation with the formal perfection of the poetic line and a quest for organic unity in every detail of artistic composition. Exceptional facility for elegance and virtuosity of expression frequently give D.'s verses an aura of *bon mots*, maxims and concise philosophical or experiential truths, and this greatly enhanced his appeal to the poetry-reading public. As a confirmed partisan of "art for art's sake," D. consistently sacrificed concerns with narrowly Serbian subject matter and milieu in favor of the universal themes of love, death, faith, beauty, and the immortality of art. Through his fascination with classical antiquity and post-Renaissance Mediterranean culture, he greatly widened the traditional thematic and stylistic horizons of the native poetic tradition by universalizing its subject matter and refining its formal characteristics.

In stylistic elegance and charm D.'s prose writings rival his poetry. His essays on several Serbian authors are equally distinguished by their formal brilliance and their analytical perceptiveness. And his collection of memoirs, *Gradovi i himere* (1932; cities and chimeras) and his numerous letters from France, the Ionian Sea, Switzerland, and Spain rank among the best travel writing in all of modern Serbian literature.

FURTHER WORKS: *Sabrana dela* (7 vols., 1929–1932); *Grof Sava Vladislavć* (1942); *Lirika* (1942); *Staza pored puta; Moji saputanici; Jutra sa Leutara* (1951); *Stihovi i proza* (1951); *Izabrana dela* (1964)

BIBLIOGRAPHY: Kadić, A., *Contemporary Serbian Literature* (1964): 22–25

—NICHOLAS MORAVČEVICH

DUFF, Alan

New Zealand novelist, b. 1950, Rotorua

D.'s family background spans the extremes of New Zealand social life. As he puts it, "Maori mother, European father. Father educated, mother uneducated. Father rational, mother . . . volatile." On one side of his family D. encountered high culture and social respectability, on the other drunkenness, violence, and sentimentality. Both sides of his background figure in his writing, which is characterized by vertiginous disjunctions, both thematic and stylistic. Savage outbursts of domestic violence are juxtaposed with moments of beauty; the grim naturalism of the prose gives way to a thwarted aestheticism.

D.'s own experience of imprisonment as a young man is also worked into his fiction, both as a literal extension of the criminality of his characters and as a metaphor for the social, psychological, and spiritual condition of modern Maori people, as he sees it. Maori people, particularly youth, are imprisoned for acting out the confused instructions of their everyday lives. Maori adults are imprisoned by their overwhelming sense of injustice, grievance, and blame. D. insists that disadvantaged individuals and ethnic groups can change their worlds by positive thinking and concerted action; the key here is to change the mental outlook that determines the social one.

D.'s first novel, *Once Were Warriors* (1990), is organized around two counterposed movements: Jake Heke's career as the dominant male who falls from his position of power and declines into a state of abjection; his wife Beth's status as victim and suffering mother, which is reversed as Jake's dominance ends and she steps into the position of power he formerly occupied. The point of intersection between these two movements is the suicide of their daughter, Grace.

Grace's suicide is caused not only by the rape she suffers but also by her inability to imagine a means of escaping the world that brutalizes her. Staring through the window of the Hekes's neighbors, the rich white Tramberts, Grace glimpses a world of order, culture, and care that makes her own state all the more unbearable. This image concentrates the longing for transcendence—present in all D.'s fiction—that Grace, tragically, is unable to accomplish.

How to leap from one world to the other is the problem dramatized in D.'s next novel, *One Night Out Stealing* (1991). Here the protagonist, Sonny Mahia, discovers that both worlds—civilization and savagery—exist within the self. Sonny is a criminal who experiences epiphanies listening to music. One night out stealing, his aesthetic instincts overthrow the criminal and begin a process of change within his mental outlook.

Neither Grace nor Sonny is able to escape from their background except by death. In his third novel, *What Becomes of the Broken-Hearted* (1996), a sequel to *Once Were Warriors*, D. details the process of change and adaptation by Jake Heke as he moves from thuggery to assume a measure of control over his life. He even comes to consider the real, inner meaning of beauty.

D.'s work occupies a contentious position in the context of indigenous writing (a category in which he has no wish to be enlisted). Unusual among such writers, the considerable anger in his novels is directed not at Europeans or colonization but at the sense of grievance of the indigenous peoples themselves. He also declines to privilege the traditional past or cultural authenticity, and argues that Maori must address their own situation in modern terms.

Yet it is in a specifically New Zealand context that the contentions of his work need to be understood. D. is writing against a particular cultural consensus and a given body of writing. *Once Were Warriors* was published when biculturalism had become entrenched in New Zealand public life. The cultural wing of biculturalism was known as the Maori Renaissance. For D., Maori Renaissance writers such as Keri HULME, Patricia GRACE, and Witi Ihimaera (b. 1944) fail to engage with the reality of most contemporary Maori life. Maori people in the late 20th c., according to D., are predominantly an urban people who have allowed themselves to be captured by a false and irrelevant view of the past. The romanticization of the past leads to an inability to adapt to the modern world and to an addiction to violence.

In spite of the crudity of much his writing and the inassimilable character of much of his polemic, D.'s work deserves serious attention. D. carries us inside the incoherent minds of his characters by way of hectic, often chaotic, stream of consciousness. He is adept at cutting suddenly from vigorously dramatized scenes to passages of interior monologue. Above all, he has convincingly brought a particular demotic into literature: the Maori-inflected English of urban slums and prisons. His novels are saturated in this speech form, and if it is seen by the author as an inadequate and brutalizing language, it has nevertheless provided the medium of his fierce, complex, and occasionally self-transcendent prose.

FURTHER WORKS: *Maori: The Crisis and the Challenge* (1993); *State Ward* (1994)

BIBLIOGRAPHY: Harding, B., "Wrestling with Caliban: Patterns of Bi-Racial Encounter in *Colour Scheme* and *Once Were Warriors,*" *ANZSC*, 8 (Dec. 1992): 136-55; Thomas, N., "Gender and the Politics of Tradition: A. D.'s *Once Were Warriors,*" *Kunapipi*, 15 (1993): 57-67; Thompson, C. A., "In Whose Face?: An Essay on the Work of A. D.," *ConP*, 6 (1994): 398-412; Brown, D. "Pakeha, Maori and Alan: The Political and Literary Exclusion of A. D.,"

SPAN, 40 (1995): 72-80; Hereniko, V., "An Interview with A. D.," *ConP*, 7 (1995): 328-44

—MARK WILLIAMS

DUHAMEL, Georges

(pseud. of Denis Thévenin) French poet, novelist, dramatist, essayist, and critic, b. 30 June 1884, Paris; d. 13 April 1966, Valmondois

D. began studying medicine in 1903. In 1905, together with Charles Vildrac (1882–1971), Jules ROMAINS, and other young intellectuals, he established a communal colony for artists—the Abbaye de Créteil. It was there that he wrote his first poems, *Des légendes, des batailles* (1907; legends, battles). Créteil, a utopian venture, failed, and in 1908 each of the members went his separate way.

During World War I, D. served as an army surgeon. *La vie des martyrs* (1917; *The New Book of Martyrs*, 1918) focuses on the hideous scenes in makeshift hospitals behind the lines and on the courage shown by the soldiers in the face of suffering, excruciating pain, and death. *Civilization 1914–17* (1918; *Civilization 1914–17*, 1919), which won the Goncourt prize, chronicles his day-to-day existence as a physician in an army camp. He spares no details of the conditions under which he operated, describing the suffering of the soldiers and the incredible death rate, frequently caused by gangrene and unsanitary conditions.

Although D.'s plays were performed—*La lumière* (1911; *The Light*, 1914), for instance, at the Odéon and *La journé des aveux* (1923; the day of avowals) at the Comédie Française—the theater, D. felt, was not his medium.

D. excelled in the novel. From 1920 to 1932 he published his remarkable Salavin series, *Vie et aventures de Salavin* (*Salavin*, 5 vols., 1936). The cycle deals with the frustrations and perplexities of his soul-searching hero, Salavin, a mediocre man who tries to adjust to life but fails because he is too sensitive, too introspective, and too weak. Before he dies, he believes that if he were to start life anew, he would know what to do.

The ten-volume Pasquier family cycle, written between 1933 and 1944, *La chronique des Pasquiers* (*The Pasquier Chronicles*, 1938 [vols. 1–5]; *Cécile Pasquier*, 1940 [vols. 6–8]; *Two Novels from the Pasquier Chronicles: Suzanne, and Joseph Pasquier*, 1949 [vols. 9–10]), describes the life and struggles of a middle-class family from the 1880s to the 1920s. The central character, Laurent Pasquier, a scientist, devotes his efforts to better man's lot. Despite the difficulties he encounters, life remains for him a worthwhile experience.

D., who was elected to the French Academy in 1936, was a prolific essayist who often used irony and satire to attack society's evils. In 1930 he published *Scènes de la vie future* (*America: The Menace*, 1931), a forceful attack on American overindustrialization. In his essays and short stories D. expressed a fear of modern mechanized society and a longing for peace and harmony.

D.'s travel books also reflect this longing. Such volumes as *Géographie cordiale de l'Europe* (1931; cordial geography of Europe), *Le Japon entre la tradition et l'avenir* (1953; Japan between tradition and the future), and *La Turquie nouvelle* (1954; the new Turkey) are enhanced by abundant historical and cultural information and vivid descriptions of D.'s personal experiences.

At the end of his life, in spite of his dream for a better world, D. regretfully admitted man's inability to learn from past experience and mistakes.

FURTHER WORKS: *L'homme en tête* (1909); *Selon ma loi* (1910); *Compagnons* (1912); *Propos critiques* (1912); *Dans l'ombre des statutes* (1912; *In the Shadow of Statues*, 1914); *Paul Claudel* (1913); *Le combat* (1913; *Combat*, 1915); *Les Poètes et la poésie* (1915); *La possession du monde* (1919; *The Heart's Domain*, 1919); *Entretiens dans le tumulte* (1919); *Élégies* (1920); *L'œuvre des athlètes suivi de Lapointe et Ropiteau* (1920); *Guerre et littérature* (1920); *La musique libératrice* (1921); *Les hommes abandonnés* (1921); *Les plaisirs et les jeux* (1922; *Days of Delight*, 1939); *Le Prince de Jaffar* (1924); *Delibérations* (1925); *Essai sur le roman* (1925); *La pierre d'Horeb* (1926); *Ballades* (1926); *Les Erspaudants* (1926); *Lettre au patagon* (1926); *Le voyage de Moscou* (1927); *La nuit d'orage* (1928); *Pages de mon carnet* (1931); *Les jumeaux de Valangoujard* (1931); *Querelle de famille* (1932); *Mon royaume* (1932); *L'humaniste et l'automate* (1933); *Le notaire du Havre* (1933; *News from Havre*, 1934); *Le jardin des bêtes sauvages* (1934; *Caged Beasts*, 1935); *Vue de la terre promise* (1934; *In Sight of the Promised Land*, 1936); *Remarques sur les mémoires imaginaires* (1934); *La Nuit de la Saint-Jean* (1935; *St. John's Eve*, 1936); *Fables de mon jardin* (1936); *Le désert de Bièvres* (1937; *The House in the Desert*, 1937); *Défense des letters* (1937; *In Defence of Letters*, 1938); *Les Maîtres* (1937); *Auchevet de la civilisation* (1938); *Le dernier voyage de Candide* (1938); *Le combat contre les ombres* (1939); *Mémorial de la guerre blanche 1938* (1939; *The White War of 1938*, 1939); *Lieu d'asile* (1940); *Positions française* (1944); *The French Position*, 1940); *Les confessions sans peacutenitence* (1941); *Chronique des saisons amegraveres 1940–43* (1944); *La musique consolatrice* (1944); *Lumière sur ma vie* (5 vols., 1944–1953 *Light on My Days*, 2 of the 5 vols., 1948); *Souvenirs de la vie du paradis* (1946); *Paroles de médecin* (1946); *Tribulations de l'espérance* (1947); *Semailles au vent* (1947); *Consultations aux pays d'Islam* (1947); *Le voyage de Patrice Périot* (1950; *Patrice Périot*, 1952); *Cri des profondeurs* (1951; *Cry out of the Depths*, 1954); *Manuel du protestataire* (1952); *Les voyageurs de l'espérance* (1953); *Refuges de la lecture* (1954); *L'archange de l'aventure* (1956); *Les Compagnons de l'Apocalypse* (1956); *Israël, clef de l'Orient* (1957); *Le complexe de Théophile* (1958); *Travail, ô mon repos* (1959); *Nouvelles du sombre empire* (1960); *Problèmes de civilisation* (1963)

BIBLIOGRAPHY: Humbourg, P., *G. D. et son œuvre* (1930); Simon, P. H., *G. D.* (1946); Tereisse, A., *G. D.* (1951); Keating, L. C., *Critic of Civilization: G. D. and His Writings* (1965); Knapp, B. L., *G. D.* (1972)

—TAYITTA HADAR

DUMBRĂVEANU, Anghel

Romanian poet, novelist, essayist, and translator, b. 21 Nov. 1933, Dobroteasa, Oltenia

With a degree in philosophy at the University of Timisoara, D. was one of the "Labis generation" of young talented writers that emerged during the thaw of the 1960s in a kind of literary renaissance in a highly charged literary universe. The poets—that included Nichita STĂNESCU, Ana BLANDIANA, and Marin SORESCU, among others—produced a lyrical revival that reopened Romanian poetry to the influence of Western MODERNISM, abandoned the banalities of social realism, reestablished a connection with native, pre-Marxist Romanian traditions, and participated in rehabilitation of the important Romanian poets of the 1920s and 1930s. For D., it brought a renewed contact with SURREALISM, DADAISM, and absurdism—a current that was to have a pronounced effect on D.'s own poetry.

D. began his literary career in 1952 in the city of Timişoara in the Banat region with poems in literary reviews, which were collected in *Scrisul bănăţean* (Writing of the Banat Region). Eventually, he would author over thirty publications: fourteen single volumes and collections of poetry, five books of prose, and six works of translation. Most important were *Iluminările mării* (1967; Illuminations of the Sea), *Oase de corăbii* (1968; Bones of Ships), *Poeme de dragoste* (1971; Love Poems), *Faţa străină a nopţii* (1971; The Foreign Face of Night), *Singurătatea amiezii* (1973; Solitude at Noon), *Diligenţa de seară* (1978; The Evening Coach), *Intrarea în cetate* (1980; Entrance into the City), *Tematica umbrei* (1982; The Thematic Shadow), and *Curtea retorilor* (1989; The Court of Orators). A collected edition of two decades of his poems, *Poeme*, appeared in 1979, and a bilingual (Romanian-English) edition of selected poems, *Cuvinte magice* (Magical Words), in 1981. A second collection of his poems from the 1980s, *Iarna imperial* (Imperial Winter), was printed in 1986 by the new publishing house Biblioteca Pentru Toti.

During the Ceausescu regime, D. served as coeditor of the cultural journal *Orizont* and as a member of the national board of the Writer's Union until the upheavals of the Revolution of 1989. He was also one of the few writers permitted in the 1980s to visit the U.S. under the educational and cultural exchange program, under the sponsorship of the U.S. Information Agency. He was never one of the prominent dissidents, but neither was he one of the "palace apologists" servile to the Ceausescu regime. He won two Writers' Union Poetry Awards and in 1986 the grand prize of the Nichita Stănescu Poetry Festival. In the euphoria after the Revolution, in April 1990, he founded and edited one of the new private periodicals, a monthly magazine of literature and commentary, *Meridianul Timişoara*. In 1992 a bilingual (Romanian-English) edition of selected poems was published in the U.S., and in 1993 a collection of poems and, *Anghel Dumbrăveanu. Predica focului; Poeme,* appeared in Transylvanian Cluj.

D.'s earlier poems were marked by sensuous delights of a Balkan, neobaroque orientalism, in a kind of warm remedy and reaction to the angst of that moment in Romanian history. Then, under the influence of the avant-garde, they slowly became progressively cold and ironic, in a darker fantasy, a night reality. Finally, they became pilgrimages of erotic and spiritual disappointment with an actuality, a concomitant of the autocracy of the Ceausescu regime, expressed most vividly in *Iarna imperial*, which somehow escaped the attention of government censors.

D.'s usual poem is short and unrhymed, with an ironic detachment, in modes that range from the desolate and dramatic to the contemplative and visionary, from reminiscence to prayer, suggesting revelation and mystery. Often they resemble invented fairy tales with cold landscapes of the undesirable, a world suggestive of the primitive or the mythic. They may be centered in his own town or room, a space especially his own, within the space of his consciousness and his memory—a puzzling, yearning world. Love and the union of lovers evokes a larger, unifying world of fulfillment, and erotic union is a creative act. His world borders on the infinite sea, mocking the fragility and finiteness of human beings. The poems are full of paradoxes and strange juxtapositions, with beginnings in ends, ends in beginnings, death in growth, darkness in sunlight, hope in disappointment, discord in harmony, and memory in isolation. A sun-filled summer exists contrapunctually with wintry winds and frosts.

D.'s later works emphasize the mood of closure with life on a journey to departure into mortality. Existence is poised on the brink between life and nothingness, between dream and death, but there is also an idealistic search for perfection and for absolutes as a defense against the "imperial winter" of realities. In a way his poems of the 1980s were a kind of hidden, undeclared defiance of the Stalinist state, with its "winter" of physical and spiritual deprivations—a survival of the inward spirit, a sign that the world can be saved.

FURTHER WORKS: *Chemarea marilor* (1976); *Fonetica astrelor* (1986); *A. D. Predica focului*; *Poeme* (1993)

BIBLIOGRAPHY: Parvu, N. D., "A. D.: 'Poeme de dragoste,'" *Orizont*, 21, 8 (1971): 61-65; Sorkin, A. J., "A. D.," *CP*, 17, 2 (1984): 67-69; Mircea, I., "'Solemn ca leul si trist ca pasarea de prada,'" *Transylvania*, 18, 10 (1989): 34-36; Sorkin, A. J., Introduction to *Selected Poems of A. D.: Love and Winter* (1992): iii-xi

—THOMAS AMHERST PERRY

DUNCAN, Robert

American poet, essayist, dramatist, b. 7 Jan. 1919, Oakland, Cal.; d. 3 Feb. 1988, San Francisco, Cal.

As a child growing up in California, D. was exposed to Greek, Hebrew, and Germanic myths and to what he calls in *The Truth and Life of Myth* (1968) "Platonized theosophy." In the 1950s, D.'s association with Black Mountain College in North Carolina brought him in close contact with Charles Olson, Robert Creeley, and others in that circle. Later D. returned to California and became an instrumental figure in the San Francisco Renaissance. Usually associated with the Projectivists, D. has written extensively on his concepts of rhyme, open form, and field on the importance of myth.

D.'s major work is found in three volumes: *The Opening of the Field* (1960), *Roots and Branches* (1964), and *Bending the Bow* (1968). D.'s poetry, consistent with Ezra Pound's dictum that "poetry is difficult," can bewilder the reader and frustrate the literary critic. Thus, his work has been dismissed as esoteric, deliberately obscure, and unfocused; but D.'s verse, like Pound's, requires a grasp of cultural history and poetic tradition. D.'s comments on Hilda DOOLITTLE, published in various journals, reveal his intense and thorough understanding of the development of modern poetry.

D. has long been obsessed with writing the momumental poem—the grand collage, he terms it—similar to Pound's *Cantos*. His goal is a poem whose internal forces determine its final form. Two of these attempts, the ongoing series called "The Structure of Rime" and the one called "Passages," are unending, open poems.

The poems of "The Structure of Rime" were begun in the late 1950s while D. was still at Black Mountain. In them D. is a private, almost solipsistic, poet concerned primarily with his attempt to master poetry. This series presents the necessary stages through which the neophyte poet must pass on his journey toward mastery of the language; it is in a sense a modified epic, depicting the inspiration, problems, and growth of the poet as hero. In "Passages," begun in the 1960s, D. attempts to include a sense of expanded, communal consciousness. Through the deliberate assumption of a social and political voice, "Passages" extends what D. conceived as the role of the poet to parallel the tradition of Whitman, Pound, and William Carlos WILLIAMS.

A constant in D.'s work was his concern with myth. In poems such as "Nor Is the Past Pure" (1960), "Atlantis" (1960), "The Natural Doctrine" (1960), "A Poem Beginning with a Line from Pindar" (1960), "The Continent" (1964), and "Two Presentations" (1964) D. attempts to evoke a sense of mythic possibility—the "inner view," he terms it, in "Roots and Branches" (1964). His characteristic technique is to end the poem, as he does in "A Poem Beginning with a Line from Pindar," poised on the brink of the moment of transcendent reality.

FURTHER WORKS: *Heavenly City, Earthly City* (1947); *Poems 1948–1949* (1949); *Medieval Scenes* (1950); *Caesar's Gate: Poems 1949–1950* (1955); *Letters* (1958); *Faust Foutu* (1959); *Selected Poems* (1959); *As Testimony; The Poem & The Scene* (1964); *Writing Writing: A Composition Book Stein Imitations* (1964); *Medea at Kolchis: The Maidenhead* (1965); *The Sweetness and Greatness of Dante's Divine Comedy* (1965); *The Years as Catches: First Poems 1939–1946* (1966); *A Book of Resemblances; Poems* 1950–1953 (1966); *Fragments of a Disordered Devotion* (1966); *Epilogos* (1967); *Names of People* (1968); *The First Decade: Selected Poems 1940-1950* (1968); *Derivations: Selected Poems 1950–1956* (1968); *In Memoriam Wallace Stevens* (1972); *A Seventeenth Century Suite* (1973); *Dante* (1974); *Fictive Certainties: Five Essays in Essential Autobiography* (1979)

BIBLIOGRAPHY: Special D. issue, *MAPS*, 6 (1974); Weatherhead, A. K., "R. D. and the Lyric," *ConL*, 16 (1975): 163–74; Altieri, C., "The Book of the World: R. D.'s Poetics of Presence," *Sun & Moon*, 1 (1976): 66–94; Weber, R. C., "R. D. and the Poem of Resonance," *CP*, 11 (1978): 67–73; Rertolf, R., and Reid, I. *R. D.: Scales of the Marvelous* (1979); Johnson, M. *R. D.* (1988)

—ROBERT C. WEBER

DUNQUL, Amal

Egyptian poet, b. 23 June 1940, Al-Qal'a, governorate of Qina; d. 21 May 1983, Cairo

D. was the eldest son in a fairly comfortable, traditional, small family of Upper Egypt where he completed his secondary school. By age fifteen D. started writing his first poems in the traditional prosodic forms of Arabic verse primarily for school competitions and religious ceremonies. His introduction to the Arabic and Islamic literary heritage came very early during his childhood; his father had been a teacher, the first male in the village to obtain a degree from the foremost religious institution Al-Azhar, and owned a

library that was constituted mainly of religious, philogical, and literary texts. In 1958 D. moved to Cairo, thus becoming part of the young literary generation of the 1960s that included, among many other figures, D.'s close Upper Egyptian friends, the shortstory writer Yahyā al-Tāhir 'Abdallāh (1938–1981) and the poet 'Abd al-Rahmān al-Abnūdī (b. 1937). D.'s initial encounter with the capital was soon to be interrupted by long periods of residence and work in Alexandria, where he was enrolled for two years in the department of history at Alexandria University, and in Suez. D. finally returned to Cairo, where he settled until his untimely death in 1983 after a four-year struggle against cancer.

In Cairo D. lived in poverty, refusing to accept jobs that would compromise him as a poet. The only position that D. occupied was an honorary one in the Organization of Afro-Asiatic Unity, which guaranteed him a meagre but regular salary. In 1979, a few months before his illness was discovered, D. married the journalist 'Abla Al-Ruwaynī who, after his death, wrote the biographical text *Al-Janūbī* (1983; the southerner), titled after an autobiographical poem by D.

D.'s first published collection of poems, *Al-Bukā bayna yaday Zarqā al-Yamāmah* (lament before Zarqā' al-Yamāma), which appeared in Beirut in 1969, quickly established him as one of the Arab world's leading poets. The collection introduces the dialogical relationship between the poet, his present, and the historical past, whether that past be Roman, as in the poem "Kalimāt Spartakus al-akhīrah" (Spartacus's last words) or Christian as in "Al-'ashā' al-akhīr" (the last supper) or Arab as in the poem that gives the collection its title. Written during the later Nasser period in Egypt, when the régime was becoming increasingly sensitive and intolerant to criticism, the poems of this collection rely on the historical and the intertextual to parody the poet's present reality. D.'s rereading and rewriting of history continue to be of crucial importance throughout his poetic career as can be easily demonstrated in all other volumes of his poetry where he revives and reworks historical incidents and figures. Furthermore, the poems of the first collection announce the first instance of the prophetic and nationalist voice of the poet where D. foresees the 1967 Arab defeat in the war against Israel. D.'s subsequent collections are renewed instances of reading, interpretation, and critique of the Arab present.

D. believed that poetry derives its raison d'être from its audience. As such, it has an important sociopolitical function and is instrumental in the elaboration of a national identity. Hence his work foregrounded the political poem and fused it with elements of the classical Arabic tradition about which he was so knowledgeable. It is therefore no surprise that D.'s poetic language is characterized by the modernity of its lexicon and its ability to mediate between classical and spoken Arabic. Even though D.'s Cairo experience and encounters had led him to experiment with conventional forms and genres of classical Arabic poetry, he still continued to integrate traditional rhyme patterns as part of the musicality and orality of his work. It is for these reasons that some of D.'s poems became manifestos, memorized and recited both within Egypt and the Arab world at large. It is also for the same reasons that his poetry was eventually banned in Egypt and reimported to it through its publication elsewhere in the Arab World. Such was the fate of his 1972 poem "Safar al-khurūj: Ughniyat al-ka'kah al-hajariyyah" (exodus: chant of the stone cake), written for, and chanted by, the student movement in Egypt. In fact, the literary journal *Sanābil* was closed down by the Egyptian authorities because it published the poem. Similarly, D.'s

"Maqtal Kulayb" (Maqtal Kulayb), published in 1975, uses the historical war of Basūs, and the last words of the murdered Kulayb to his brother Al-Zīr Sālim, as a parody of Egypt's prospective peace with Israel: The poem opens with the line "Lā tusālih" (do not make peace).

If D.'s first five volumes of poems can be regarded as fulfilling predominantly his public role as an Arab nationalist poet, then certainly his last collection, *Awrāq al-ghurfa thamāniya* (papers of room eight), offers us his more private, contemplative, sometimes even hermetic self. Whereas the earlier work belonged to the period of struggle for freedom and for life, these poems belong to the four-year period of struggle against cancer and death. The title of the collection bears the room number that D. occupied in the cancer institute in Cairo. These poems provide not only reflections on life and death but, more importantly perhaps, an attempt at rereading the self, especially in D.'s much celebrated poem "Al-janūbī" (the southerner).

FURTHER WORKS: *Ta'līq 'alā mā hadath* (1971); *Maqtal al-qamar* (1974); *Ahādīth fi ghurfa mughlaqah* (1974); *Al 'ahd al-āti* (1975); *Awrāq alghurfa thamāniyah* (1983); *Al-A'māl al-shi'riyyah al-Kāmilah* (1983)

—SAMIA MEHREZ

DURANTI, Francesca

Italian novelist, b. 1935, Genoa

D. has slowly affirmed herself as one of the leading fiction writers in contemporary Italian literature. Her first novel *La Bambina* (1976; The Child) attracted the attention of both critics and the public. D.'s main ambition was to reach a wider readership without lowering the standards of her writings. Starting from the premises of autobiographical introspective fiction, *La Bambina* is a reconstruction of her childhood and of her difficult relationship with an imposing mother figure. After the poor reception of her second book D. moved on to experiment with a wider range of topics and narrative structures. A corollary of this change is D.'s subsequent abandonment (with rare exceptions) of the realm of the openly autobiographical, as she designs agile novels of pure fiction where the perfect use of language makes plots and character development easy to follow.

After years of research and meditation D. published a hugely successful postmodern novel, *La casa sul lago della luna* (1984; *The House on Moon Lake*, 1989), which gained her three literary prizes—Premio Bagutta, Premio Martina Franca, and the Città di Milano. Culture plays an important role in this novel inspired by the myth of Mitteleurope. The *topos* of the search for a disappeared manuscript to solve the mystery of life guides a love story at the margins of dystopia. The protagonist, Fabrizio Garrone, is a scholar of German literature traveling to Austria to inquire about the last days of a late author, Fritz Obersdorfer, whose personal life and loves then become inextricably enmeshed with those of the scholar. The novel combines suspense and enchantment within linear and skillful prose.

In *Lieto fine* (1987; *Happy Ending*, 1991) the author touches another topic crucial to Italian society: snobbery. Aldo Rugani, the narrator of the story, looks with his binoculars at the lives of three troubled Santini families. Being of poor background, Rugani has made a career for himself by literally "building" old art and selling it as an art dealer. After many years he still desires Lavinia, a member of the Santini family whom he has known since she was a child, but whose different social status makes her untouchable and unreachable. In the ending, as in the Sisyphus's myth, at the very moment that Rugani will finally have Lavinia his desire for her slowly disappears, having satisfied the most ancient desire of his life to be one of "them."

Although D. has always declared the necessity for a writer to aim toward a utopian, androgynous writing, the 1988 novel, *Effetti personali* (*Personal Effects*, 1993), winner of the Super Campiello and the Basilicata prizes should probably be considered as a feminist postmodern novel. Its main plot concerns the process of self-discovery experienced by the protagonist and first-person narrator, Valentina Barbieri, an educated Milanese in her mid-thirties, recently divorced and childless. The novel begins as she realizes that her psychological resistance to the feminist model imposed upon her by her mother's lifestyle—which favors an afro hairdo, hippy clothes, and a strange fixation on astrology—has managed to produce the apparent void in which she seems to be spending her existence. By rejecting her mother's stereotypical manifestations of the feminism of the 1960s and 1970s Valentina has basically moved backward in her life, accepting abuse and a very conservative role for herself, the only one her husband Riccardo allowed her to have in their failed marriage. Her husband is a university professor who completely exploited Valentina's education, culture, but above all, her docile disposition, and forced her to do all the scholarly research for and rewrite his books on the Church Fathers, thereby boosting his career. With her husband removing the brass name plate from their apartment door, Valentina realizes that her loss of identity has come full circle. It is time for a change. A book, just as for Fabrizio Garrone in *La casa sul lago della luna*, will provide the answer to her request for a change. Significantly titled *"The Answer,"* this book is written by a nondissident writer from behind the Iron Curtain. She departs Milan to interview him. The novel takes a postmodern bend, and its setting slowly changes from a chaotic and consumeristic Milan into the mysterious landscape of the Eastern country where Janco lives. After the discovery that Janco and Ante Radek, the poet with whom Valentina falls in love, are actually the same person, Valentina feels that she is finally able to leave her past behind. The novel is a bildungsroman, a journey, both physical and psychological, personal and political—personal because Valentina regains an identity through the journey, and political because she tries to bridge the ideological diversities of her occidental education and system of values with the ones perpetrated by the writer, a living metaphor of the Eastern European *intelligentsia*.

Progetto Burlamacchi (1994; The Burlamacchi Project) is an ambitious book in which D. voices through her characters all the anguish and anger she feels about the political situation in Italy. This book is a bittersweet novel dedicated to the post-1992 Italy modeled after the ideals of the business magnate Berlusconi and his media monopoly. In the novel Duranti proposes an ancient federalist utopia by Francesco Burlamacchi, who in 1548 organized a protestant conspiracy against the Medici family whose outcome would strictly depend on the eventual confederation of all Tuscan towns. All the characters rotate around a computer, Bonzo, in a professional school engaged in a project run by a young idealistic professor to try to recreate the Burlamacchi conspiracy, also linked to the mysterious disappearance of a Medieval wooden sculpture from the tower of a private house. The ethical and political considerations of the writer are voiced mainly by the idealistic professor. One notices especially Duranti's desire for the moral renaissance of her country, a "project" much felt by the writer throughout her career.

In 1984 D. moved to New York and started a "new" life there, trying again the art of the novel with *Sogni mancini* (Shifty Dreams). This is the story of an Italian professor of European Civilization at New York University, Martina Satriano, who lives in Manhattan. Like many other intellectuals, Martina did not want to cope with the suffocating academic Italian environment. She is a wonderful cook, she is modern by all means, and she has a dream that she shares only with a sophisticated machine—she has managed to invent a "macchina dei sogni" (machine of dreams), another computer like the one in *Progetto Burlamacchi* that is able to read dreams and thus do many other things such as warm up croissants in the morning, but especially to define Martina's other existence. One day the machine breaks down, and Martina must begin a new life without depending on virtual realities. But machinery and cyberspace are not the only topics of the novel: each day of this imaginary week in the life of Martina is a different chapter, titled by a different dish she prepares for her illustrious guest, "the professor" from Italy. Love for food, but also food for love, with the elaboration of food and recipes, are portrayed as an indiscernible element of Italianity with, furthermore, the love of her youth coming back into her life. The ending is ambiguous; whatever issues Martina was trying to solve are now up to the reader to find and solve.

According to D. such ambiguity must represent the essence of a novel. The open answer to the issues in the novel becomes then an integrating part of the magic of her narrative. The novel should provoke doubts rather than provide answers, leading each reader in the direction he/she wants to take after having read the book. D.'s place in feminist literature seems improbable; when she goes beyond the personal sphere of her female characters, she makes claims for humanity and social issues in general not limited to the feminine realm. It seems instead more beneficial to observe how important the actual writing experience is for her, the perennial search throughout European and American narrative to construct a perfect book, and her attempt to insert Italian literature into a much larger context. Whether her point of reference is Henry JAMES, for the precision by which she incorporates each tassel of the story into the "carpet," or whether she adopts Marcel PROUST's ability to portray the affluent class with all its tics and manias, D. always manages to create a narrative texture of undoubted originality and of high literary quality.

FURTHER WORKS: *Piazza, mia bella piazza* (1978); *Ultima stesura* (1991)

BIBLIOGRAPHY: Wilson, R., "Writing an Identity: The Case of F. D.," *SIAA*, 9, 2 (1996): 81-98; Wood, S., "From Feminism to Post-Modernism: D., Petrignani and Capriolo," *Italian Women's Writing 1860-1994*, (1995): 254-61; Wilson, R., "City and Landscapes: Theme and Variation in Calvino and D.'s Landscapes," *Literator*, 13, 2 (Aug. 1992): 85-95; Giobbi, G., "Know the Past: Know Thyself : Literary Pursuits and Quest for Identity in A. S. Byatt's *Possession* and in F. Duranti's *Effetti personali*," *JES*, 24

(March 1994): 41-54; Vinall, S., "F. D.: Reflections and Inventions," in Baranski, Z., and Pertile, L., eds., *The New Italian Novel* (1993): 99-120; Wood, S., "Seductions and Brazen Duplications: Two Recent Novels from Italy," *FMLS*, 28 (1992): 349-62; Wood, S., "Writers' Desktop: Writing in a Changing World: An Interview with F. D.," *Italianist*, 12 (1992): 186-95

—STEFANIA LUCAMANTE

DURAS, Marguerite

(pseud. of Marguerite Donnadieu) French novelist, dramatist, and screenwriter, b. 4 April 1914, near Saigon, Vietnam; d. 3 Mar. 1996, Paris

Born of French parents teaching in what was then French Indochina, D.'s youth in the Orient left a deep imprint on her sensitivity and on many of her works. At eighteen, she went to France to study law and political science. Her passionate opposition to social injustice and oppression induced her to join the Communist Party, but she later condemned its policies.

At least three periods are evident in her literary career. The first, lasting until 1953, includes four books of somewhat uneven quality, although they reveal most of the Durasian characteristics: intensity of feeling and desire reflected in the dramatic force of metaphors and in vocabulary; the impact of an event or an encounter as an emotional starting point; ambivalence of passion and of time's effects on love; expectation of the unknown as a hope for salvation; sleep as escape or symbol of inner void.

Les petits chevaux de Tarquinia (1953; *The Little Horses of Tarquinia*, 1960) was a preparation for the second period, one of aesthetic maturity, when she wrote her generally best-liked works, even though she later repudiated most of them. In this phase, D. eliminated earlier flaws in narrative technique and style and achieved greater conciseness and simplicity; she adopted a structure of two levels, each organized around a theme, a method that served her growing fondness for understatement and her preference for indirection and for avoiding the explicit.

After her sixth book, *Le square* (1955; *The Square*, 1959) D. was associated with the NEW NOVEL group because of certain elements in her work that challenged the traditional concept of the novel. She differs, however, from most New Novelists in her lack of interest in abstract theory. Moreover, an atmosphere of human warmth and the idea of the necessity of loving as well as the impossibility of loving forever lend thematic unity to her work. In *Moderato cantabile* (1958; *Moderato Cantabile*, 1960), the two-level structure is perfected to include a link between the imaginings of the main characters, while the duality of tempo suggested by the title is justified by a series of contrasting and contrapuntal effects. Fascinated by the need to understand how contrary feelings can coexist so that one may wish to be killed by one's lover, the heroine relives vicariously another woman's fatal obsession.

The screenplay *Hiroshima, mon amour* (1960; *Hiroshima, Mon Amour*, 1961), written for the film director Alain Resnais, made D.'s name internationally known. *Le vice-consul* (1966; *The Vice-Consul*, 1968), technically her most ambitious work, resembles a symphony with the themes of suffering and love introduced in a major and minor key through a series of parallel or antithetical motifs. Through the use of distancing devices such as a novel within a novel and impersonal phrases, D. conveys a pervasive atmosphere of suffering. Her firm control over form and mood succeeds in suggesting without sentimentality the mysterious ways of human destiny; incidents remain unexplained: the vice-consul's paradoxical shooting of lepers in the Shalimar gardens, the tears of the French ambassador's wife, the enigma behind the madness of the Indochinese beggar woman.

The May 1968 students' revolt had a profound impact on D.; she voluntarily rejected all the aesthetic and stylistic techniques she had developed during her middle period in favor of an increasing degree of abstraction under the sign of a recurring word, "destroy," which may imply the need for destruction before things can start anew. D.'s penchant for reworking novel into play or play into film or novel led her, in this third period of experimentation, to literary texts of perplexing ambiguity. In *L'amour* (1971; love), her last novel before she turned to movies, there is no story left; nothing is sure, while the rhythm of repetitive words, images, gestures, and situations functions as music and creates a compelling atmosphere reducible only to subjective interpretation. All D.'s late works, including her films, echo earlier ones and thus create a web of relationships and resonances.

Her cinematic production is based on the rejection of commercialism and any kind of realism, and is characterized by extreme slowness, by the prevalence of sounds overimages, and an aura of quasi-ritualistic mystery. In her best-received film, *India-Song* (1973: *India Song*, 1976), the sound track consists of a carefully orchestrated composition for voices, sounds, and music in various keys. *Le camion* (1977; the truck) has been strongly criticized for its extreme austerity and its radical departure from cinematic norms.

Despite the use of varying media and the transformation that took place in later years, D.'s novelistic and cinematic production gives the impression of continuing variations on a limited number of themes, all linked by polarities like love and death, remembering and forgetting, alienation and communion. All her works share a poetic quality; they rely on the evocative power of words and on their musical resonance to appeal to the emotions rather than the intellect. Over the years, D.'s increasing disregard for rules and conventions has made her work deeply personal and intensely original, and she has gone beyond the established limitations of any specific genre. D. is undoubtedly an extremely talented writer and ranks, with Simone de Beauvoir and Nathalie Sarraute, as one of the most important women writers in contemporary France.

FURTHER WORKS: *Les impudents* (1943); *La vie tranquille* (1944); *Un barrage contre le Pacifique* (1950; *The Sea Wall*, 1952); *Le marin de Gibraltar* (1952; *The Sailor from Gibraltar*, 1967); *Des journées entières dans les arbres* (1954; stage adaptation: *Days in the Trees*, 1965); *Dix heures et demie du soir en été* (1960; *Ten-Thirty on a Summer Night*, 1962); *Les viaducs de la Seine-et-Oise* (1960; stage adaptation: *The Viaducts*, 1967); *Une aussi longue absence* (1961; *Une Aussi Longue Absence*, 1966); *L'après-midi de Monsieur Andesmas* (1962; *The Afternoon of Monsieur Andesmas*, 1964); *Le ravissement de Lol V. Stein* (1964; *The Ravishing of Lol Stein*, 1966); *Théâtre I* (1965); *L'amante anglaise* (1967; *L'Amante Anglaise*, 1968); *Théâtre II* (1968); *Détruire, dit-elle* (1969; *Destroy, She Said*, 1970); *Abahn Sabana David* (1970); *Nathalie Granger, suivi de La femme du Gange* (1973); *Les parleuses* (1974); *L'Éden Cinema* (1977); *Le Navire Night* (1978). FURTHER WORKS IN ENGLISH: *Four Novels* (1965); *Three Plays* (1967); *Three Plays* (1975)

BIBLIOGRAPHY: Kneller, J. W., "Elective Empathies and Musical Affinities," *YFS*, No. 27 (1961): 114–19; Seylaz, J.-L., *Les romans de M. D.* (1963); Savage, C., "A Stylistic Analysis of *L'après-midi de Monsieur Andesmas*," *Lang&S*, 2 (1969): 51–63; Cismaru, A., *M. D.*, (1971); Guicharnaud, J., "The Terrorist Marivaudage of M. D.," *YFS*, No. 46 (1971): 113–24; Roudiez, L. S., *French Fiction Today* (1972): 104–31; Eisinger, E. M., "Crime and Detection in the Novels of M. D.," *ConL*, 15 (1973): 503–21; Cagnon, M., "M. D.: Willed Imagination as Release and Obstacle," *NFS*, 16 (1977): 55–64; Cohen, S. D., *Women and Discourse in the Fiction of M. D.* (1993); Vircondelet, A., *D.: A Biography* (1994)

—YVONNE GUERS-VILLATE

DURCAN, Paul

Irish poet, b. 16 Oct. 1944, Dublin

D. studied archaeology and medieval history at University College, Cork, and received the Patrick Kavanagh Award and Creative Writing Bursaries from the Irish Arts Council in 1976 and 1980. He has also represented Ireland at the Struga Poetry Festival in Yugoslavia and the Poetry International in Rotterdam. In 1983 he traveled in the Soviet Union by invitation of the Union of Soviet Writers.

He rose to prominence among a new wave of Irish poets to emerge in the 1970s and 1980s, but stands alone for his reputation as a biting satirist of political, social, and sexual conventions in Ireland. In book sales and reading attendances, he now rivals the "grand master" of Irish poetry, Seamus HEANEY, perhaps because, like no other Irish poet today, he is read widely by academicians and lay audiences alike.

While he may at first appear to be a mere iconoclast, out to shake the social foundations of an Ireland recalcitrant to change, D. stands out from his peers for his unprecedented penchant for the satirical and the surreal. The sacred institutions of family, marriage, and Catholicism are exposed to D.'s scrutiny, in the voice of a boy soprano.

D.'s like a priest celebrating the mass of the ordinary and the unpretentious. But the ordinary, in this case, is juxtaposed with the extraordinary in the form of the sacred. In "10:30 a.m. Mass, June 16, 1985," from *The Berlin Wall Café* (1985), the ordinariness of the scene depicted urges us to skip over the poem until we get to lines like "[the Priest] was a small stocky man in his forties / With a big mop of curly grey hair / And black, horn-rimmed, tinted spectacles. / I am sure that more than half the women in the church / Fell in love with him on the spot— / Not to mention the men. / Myself, I felt like a cuddle." This is a characteristic line of D.'s, for it shows his inability to resist a poke at elevated authority, but we also get the feeling that the speaker himself is on a sacred quest for spiritual elevation, even in the most satirical poetry.

In probably his greatest poem, "Six Nuns Die in a Convent Inferno," from *The Selected P. M.* (1982) and based on G. M. Hopkins's (1844–1889) "The Wreck of the Deutschland" (1875), D. mourns the deaths, but also celebrates the lives, of the six elderly nuns who died in the fire in 1986. While the title has D.'s characteristic journalistic ring, the persona is the devout, meek voice of one of the dying nuns who, at the moment of death, evaluates her life with the confidence of one whose destiny is being fulfilled, "Now tonight in the convent Christ is the fire in whose waves / We are doomed but delighted to drown." But D. can never resist the surreal touch: "Remember us for the frisky girls that we were, / Now more than ever—kittens in the sun."

D. confronts in his work the social and political turmoil in Northern Ireland. His poetry often admonishes what he perceives to be the inaction and apathy of the government of the Republic in response to the crisis in the north. In poems such as "The Anglo-Irish Agreement, 1986," from *Jesus and Angela* (1988), the political and social distance created by the border between Northern Ireland and the Republic is obliterated by D.'s surreal pen.

D. often seems determined to shock the Irish out of the nightmare of history and overdependence on the authority of politician and priest alike. In "Margaret Thatcher Joins the I.R.A.," also from *Jesus and Angela*, the speaker juxtaposes two polar opposites with the ironic wit of Swift. The reader is forced to look at a kind of unifying dialectic between the extremes of British imperialism and Irish separatism that explodes their differences and joins them in an absurd dance of death: "Margaret Thatcher joined the IRA / And the IRA joined Margaret Thatcher. / Black Dresses were worn by all for the occassion / In which a historical union was consummated."

D.'s established reputation in Ireland and Europe has now spread to the U.S., where in 1988 he was recognized by his appointment as poet in residence at The Frost Place, New Hampshire.

FURTHER WORKS: *Endsville* (1967); *O Westport in the Light of Asia Minor* (1975); *Teresa's Bar* (1976); *Sam's Cross* (1978); *Jesus, Break His Fall* (1980); *Ark of the North* (1982); *Jumping the Train Tracks with Angela* (1983); *Going Home to Russia* (1987); *Daddy, Daddy* (1990); *Crazy about Women* (1991)

BIBLIOGRAPHY: Dawe, G., "The Permanent City: The Younger Irish Poets," in Harmon, M., ed., *The Irish Writer and The City* (1984): 180–96; Mahon, D., "Orpheus Ascending: The Poetry of P. D.," *Irish Review*, 1 (1986): 15–19; Gahern, K., "Masks and Voices: Dramatic Personas in the Poetry of P.D.," *CJIS*, 13, 1 (June 1987): 107–20; Grennan, E., "A Different World: Reading P. D." in Brophy, J. D. and E. Grennan, eds., *New Irish Writing* (1989): 203–31; Longley, E., "Poetic Forms and Social Malformations" in Brown, T. and N. Grene, eds., *Tradition and Influence in Anglo-Irish Poetry* (1989): 159–80; Foden, G., "A Permanent Performance," *TLS* (23 Nov. 1990): 1273

—FERGAL O'DOHERTY

DURRELL, Lawrence

English novelist, poet, dramatist, travel and short-story writer, b. 27 Feb. 1912, Julundur, India; d. 7 Nov. 1990, Sommières, France

D., whose father was an English civil engineer and whose mother was Irish, attended school in Darjeeling until he was twelve, then in England at St. Edmund's in Canterbury. England, however, proved uncongenial: "That mean, shabby little island up there wrung my guts out of me and tried to destroy anything singular and unique in me. . . . The list of Schools I've been to would be a yard long. I failed every known Civil Service exam." D. also failed the Cambridge entrance examinations and never received a university degree. He worked as a jazz pianist and composer, automobile racer, real-estate agent, columnist, editor, correspondent, teacher, and diplomatic officer.

Prolific since writing his first novel, *Pied Piper of Lovers* (1935), D. suddenly achieved commercial and critical success with *The Alexandria Quartet: Justine* (1957), *Balthazar* (1958), *Mountolive* (1958), *Clea* (1960). Though protean and eclectic, D. displays consistent concerns and techniques: a lush, baroque style; a rich patterning of ideas and ideas about ideas; a multidimensional universe and vision built from juxtaposing multiple perspectives; an aesthetic dependent on personal mythos (often eroticism), on felt reality rather than "objective" fact, on the interplay of art, love, and death. A sense of deracination and a concomitant need to belong are central to D.'s writing (perhaps his most revealing book is a collection entitled *Spirit of Place*, 1969). Like most placeless men, D. worships place: his landscapes embody, parallel, even motivate and control the workings of his characters. Their individuality often seems suffused, subordinated to some *deus loci*—as, on the largest scale, Alexandria dominates the *Quartet*: "Only the city is real."

D.'s early fiction, poetry, verse plays, and island books all anticipate the *Quartet's* theme of isolation and the individual's attaining full potential in both art and life only through total commitment to the creative process: art for love's sake. Thus, Justine associates work with love; Mountolive's failures in love are correlatives of his hating his work; Darley and Clea become lovers and artists only after long struggle.

In both *The Black Book* (1938; published in the U.S. in 1960) and *The Revolt of Aphrodite* (originally published as *Tunc*, 1968, and *Nunquam*, 1970), demonically named protagonists seek freedom and creativity beyond constricting environments. *The Black Book's* Lawrence Lucifer struggles to escape the spiritual sterility of smug, dying England; he finally emerges into creative affirmation symbolized by Greece's warmth, color, and fertility. The book's style, like that of *Zero, and Asylum in the Snow* (1946), anticipates the *Quartet's*, for its rich interweaving of naturalistic and poetic narratives transforms language into something fluid, and free-form. In *Aphrodite*—a satire on science fiction and gothic, romantic, and business exposé novels—master inventor Felix Charlock becomes ensnared in the international cartel, Merlin. He sells—and sells out—his work; love consequently becomes horrific, for, in D., to negate one's work is to deny love. Charlock's ultimate task is to fashion an indistinguishable, "living" replica of the beautiful Io, deceased ex-prostitute and world-famous actress. But the wholly successful product (able even to copulate) cannot bear the world's reality and climactically "commits suicide."

Virtually all of D.'s protagonists ultimately flee inhospitable surroundings to seek meaning and selfhood in landscape and language. His verse plays (*Sappho*, 1950; *Acté*, 1961; *An Irish Faustus*, 1963), all of which have been successfully produced, dramatize attempts to transform life into works of art. The trilogy of island books most fully exploits D.'s love of place, of landscape corresponding and responding to human needs and proportions. The prewar Corfu of *Prospero's Cell* (1945), the postwar Rhodes of *Reflections on a Marine Venus* (1953), and the incipient civil-war Cyprus of *Bitter Lemons* (1957) are concomitants of failures in art and love. Yet the permanence and strength of D.'s Hellenism undergird and inspirit his island books, transforming them from travel reportage into what many consider his finest achievements.

The *Quartet's* mutually qualifying voices all speak with the force of privileged authenticity—especially on the subject of love. For love, without contradiction different for every participant and viewer, is endlessly various. The *Quartet*, does not harmonize all the dichotomies it depicts—that is impossible and undesirable—but brings them into organic interrelationship; although irreconcilable, they become mutually sustaining: interpenetrating, fusing, enriching one another. Inevitably, then, solutions only compound more mystery; even death is contingent and tentative.

All four parts of the *Quartet*, like most of D.'s other books, climax in death—which is almost always equivocal, other than what it seems. D., among the most death-haunted and self-reflexive of contemporary novelists, is obsessed with death's creative, vitalizing effects. In the *Quartet*, entitled "The Book of the Dead" during its genesis, death is incident, theme, motif, character, and setting. In Alexandria, city of death, virtually all its inhabitants, like those in *The Black Book*, are moribund from the first. They are "playing-card characters of the living," shades partaking of the city's "obsessive rhythms of death." When Darley, the main narrator and maturing writer and lover, returns, it is "like a summons back to the Underworld," for "the dead are everywhere," he says.

Numerous characters disappear, then reemerge in altered form. Chief among them is Pursewarden, D.'s spokesman for artistic vision and dedication *despite* his being a suicide of apparently minor significance in *Justine*. The death of Pursewarden is ambiguous because much of the *Quartet* attempts to explain its motivation; because large chunks of his posthumous papers are included and many characters quote him verbatim; and because he embodies (if somewhat sententiously) the central themes of art, love, and death, as well as the *Quartet's* ultimate focus on "resurrection from the dead" through all three. And so one character dies for another; a third apparently dies but returns after another is buried for him; one is resurrected as a saint, others as characters who seemed someone else; or they grow new parts to replace worn-out ones.

In D., character becomes, in effect, anticharacter, less imposing itself upon its surrounding than imposed upon, will-less, subordinated to such forces as Alexandria itself. Conventional distinctions—major/minor characters, main plots/subplots, protagonist/antagonist—are denied. Every character becomes the independent fountainhead of actions multiplying in consequence and impact. For D., certitude remains elusive; truth lacks validity unless and until someone responds and interprets it. Thus, the *Quartet* is simultaneously promise and fulfillment, culmination and prophecy, a finished work of art and one prematurely made public with scaffolding still lying about, a vast, complex genre bearing the signs of an enduring achievement.

Discussing the differences between Victorianism and modernism, D.'s *Key to Modern Poetry* (1952) provides a "key" to D. himself. D. maintains that human possibility, personality, values, validity, and time were transformed by Darwin, Einstein, and Freud, among others. Certainty's rock foundation has revealed itself as restive sand blown by winds of pluralism, relativity, quantum mechanics, subjectivity, indeterminacy. Like other impressionistic novels, the *Quartet* dramatizes a limited narrator who seeks to understand a sequence of events. Yet everything remains susceptible to, and receives, contradictory interpretations. In such novels, the more "facts" we learn, the less significant they become;

not although, but because *Mountolive* (1958) *tells* us most, depicts an "objective" reality, it says least about truth itself, the essence of reality captured, if anywhere, in the heart and mind of the interpreter. A 1946 poem, "Eight Aspects of Melissa," anticipates the *Quartet's* devices—mirrors, prisms, lake water—and expresses D.'s early concern with multifaceted personality, love, landscape, time. Both "Melissa" and the *Quartet* remain open-ended, implying that all aspects examined are equally valuable and that an indeterminate number of additional aspects await the seeker after truth. Neither pretends to exhaust the many questions it raises; each answer contains both new questions and a proliferating chain of "truths."

Durrell sought to replicate the success of *the Alexandria Quartet* with *The Avignon Quintet: Monsieur; or, The Prince of Darkness* (1974); *Livia; or, Buried Alive* (1978); *Constance; or, Solitary Practices* (1982); *Sebastian; or, Ruling Passions* (1983); *Quinx; or, The Ripper's Tale* (1985). But although the two works share many stylistic and substantive characteristics, the latter lacks the energy and flare of the great success. It is the *Quartet*—along with the island books and some of the poetry—that best expresses Durrell's love of language, verve, and risk-taking qualities.

FURTHER WORKS: *Panic Spring* (1937); *Esprit de Corps* (1957); *Stiff Upper Lip* (1958); *L. D. and Henry Miller: A Private Correspondence* (1963); *Monsieur; or, The Prince of Darkness* (1974); *Sicilian Carousel* (1977); *Livia; or, Buried Alive* (1978); *Collected Poems* 1931–1974 (1980)

BIBLIOGRAPHY: Perles, A., *My Friend L. D.* (1961); Moore, H. T., ed., *The World of L. D.* (1962); Unterecker, J., *L. D.* (1964); Weigel, J. A., *L. D.* (1965); Scholes, R., *The Fabulators* (1967): 17–31; Fraser, G. S., *L. D.: A Study* (1968); Friedman, A. W., *L. D. and "The Alexandria Quartet"* (1970); Creed, W. G., *The Muse of Science and "The Alexandria Quartet"* (1977)

—ALAN WARREN FRIEDMAN

DÜRRENMATT, Friedrich

Swiss dramatist, novelist, and short-story writer (writing in German), b. 5 Jan. 1921, Konolfingen; d. 14 Dec. 1990, Neuchâtel

D. grew up in an intellectually stimulating environment. His father was a Protestant minister, and his paternal grandfather was active in politics and known as a satirical writer. He attended secondary school in the village of Grosshöchstetten; in 1935 the family moved to Bern, when his father became chaplain at Salem Hospital. D. graduated from the Humboldtianum in Bern and registered as a student of literature and philosophy at the University of Zurich and later at the University of Bern; he also took courses in theology and the natural sciences. D. painted, made drawings, and read widely, becoming especially familiar with the classical Greek tragedies and the comedies of Aristophanes, and with the writings of Kierkegaard, of Georg Heym (1887–1912), and of Trakl, Kafka, and Ernst Jünger. After fragmentary and haphazard studies, he finally left the university and decided to make writing his profession. D. lived in Neuchâtel ever since he first moved there with his family in 1952.

D. once called himself an uprooted Protestant, who admires faith because he had lost it. An understanding of D.'s work begins with the recognition that his *Weltanschauung* rests in theology. Influences of both Kierkegaard and Kafka are especially striking in his early plays—*Es steht geschrieben* (1946; it is written), *Der Blinde* (1947; the blind man), *Die Ehe des Herrn Mississippi* (1952; *The Marriage of Mr. Mississippi*, 1965), *Ein Engel kommt nach Babylon* (1954; *An Angel Comes to Babylon*, 1962)—as well as in early works of fiction, such as *Die Stadt* (1952; the town) and *Pilatus* (1952; Pilate). In one of his short stories, "Der Tunnel" (1952; "The Tunnel," 1961), D. juxtaposes man's alienation from God with His irrefutable existence: God let man fall, and thus man is tumbling toward God. D.'s work as a whole, it might be argued, deals with the phase immediately preceding man's shattering collision with God. According to D., who conceives of God as the principle of love, the present condition of the world goes to prove that His love is not sufficient to save us; expressing no hope for salvation in this world, D.'s work is fundamentally eschatological in nature.

In sharp contradistinction to Bertolt BRECHT, who believed in man's reason and goodness and hence in the possibility of changing the sociopolitical structure for the better, D. maintains that our condition cannot be changed. The world, for D., is a monstrous, calamitous enigma which has to be accepted but to which there must be no surrender. D. sees mankind as God's failed experiment, describes the paradox of man's predicament, and registers in the play *Die Physiker* (1962; *The Physicists*, 1965), for instance, the "last dance" of the white race. Johann Wilhelm Möbius, the most gifted physicist of all time, pretends to be mad; and, playing the role of King Solomon, he has committed himself to an insane asylum because his scientific discoveries would annihilate the world were they ever to be put into practice. A Russian and an American physicist, the former claiming to be Einstein and the latter Newton, have tracked Möbius down and have joined him in the asylum in order to persuade him to work for their respective governments. Yet Möbius convinces his two colleagues that humanity in general and science in particular would be best served if they opted for total withdrawal, remained in the asylum, and continued to pretend to be mad. However, what once has been conceived in the mind cannot be revoked—and here D.'s view differs from Brecht's stance in *Galileo*, namely, that what once has been conceived must not be revoked. The director of the asylum, Dr. Mathilde von Zahnd, who is power-mad, has already copied Möbius's manuscripts before he destroyed them and now plans to seize control of the world by means of the technology derived from the physicist's discoveries. Then the three scientists are forced to remain in the asylum while their psychiatrist is about to begin her rein of terror and ultimate destruction.

Thus, as set forth in *Die Physiker* and other D. plays, the problems of the human community cannot be solved: Möbius's attempt to save the world, noble though it is, has failed, for the director has already acted where he did not! and D.'s Romulus, in *Romulus der Große* (1949; *Romulus the Great*, 1965), is condemned to watch history take its course entirely contrary to his wishes.

Individual redemption, however, can be achieved, either by a human being like Akki, the independent man in *Ein Engel kommt nach Babylon*, or through personal integrity regained, as is the case for Alfred Ill in *Der Besuch der alten Dame* (1956; *The Visit* 1962). Claire Zachanassian, who forty-five years earlier had lost her case

in a paternity suit against her former lover Alfred Ill, and who since then has become the richest woman on earth, is returning to her impoverished and run-down native town of Güllen (meaning "manure" in Swiss dialect). The bankrupt citizens have prepared a warm homecoming for her in the hope that she will pull them out of their financial distress. Claire Zachanassian, however, has returned to Güllen to buy justice: she will pay millions and millions to the town and to individual families if somebody will kill Alfred Ill. Despite the initial protest and moral outrage of the citizens, temptation proves hard to resist, and Alfred Ill is strangled at a community meeting. The official cause of death: a heart attack. While the townspeople are slowly but steadily corrupted by their greed, Ill achieves tragic dignity when he accepts his death in order to atone for the crime committed in his youth. Thus, the murder of Ill, motivated by the crudest form of materialism, becomes paradoxically an individually meaningful death.

On the one hand, D.'s eschatological perspective is reminiscent of medieval mystery plays and the Baroque tradition of "world theater," in which all men merely play the roles assigned to them by God on the stage of life; on the other hand, his recent plays, with their intentional near-complete inarticulateness, bear a strong resemblance to Samuel Beckett's works and their God-denying faith in man as an individual. D., however, sets himself apart from the THEATER OF THE ABSURD, which presents a world devoid of all meaning. His world is not absurd; it is paradoxical: it has meaning, yet its meaning is obscure and cannot be grasped by reason alone.

Although D.'s plays are concerned with existential and moral issues, their primary object is to tell a story in terms of the theater. For D., the theater is the domain for the creation of a totally contrived counter reality, and the stage thus becomes the medium for his vision of man's rapid and inevitable downfall. It assumes a function in full accordance with the formula set up in his appendix to *Die Physiker*, "21 Punkte zu den *Physikern*" ("21 Points Concerning the *Physicists*", 1982), namely, that a story or an idea has only been thought through when pursued to its worst possible consequences.

D.'s humor is exuberant and ribald, providing a counterbalance to his generally pessimistic view of man. The characters he draws are without individual personality; rather, they are types, psychologically two-dimensional play figures, created mainly for their effectiveness on stage, such as the crazed and hunch-backed Dr. Mathilde von Zahnd in *Die Physiker*, who believes she is acting in the name of King Solomon when she cheats her patients out of the "world formula." Equally so, in *Der Meteor* (1966; *The Meteor*, 1974), a play striking at the core of what is commonly called "faith"—its theme is nihilism—the central character overshadows the philosophical statement of the play: Nobel Prize-Winning author Wolfgang Schwitter, who was declared clinically dead, has arisen from the dead. Far from rejoicing, he wants to die again, yet he cannot; and like an absurd latter-day Lazarus he pulls everybody into the dynamics of his own death, to which he insists he has as much right as anyone. While backstage the Salvation Army celebrates the miracle of his resurrection, Schwitter—after having destroyed six people directly or indirectly—is left in the end to realize with horror that he alone must go on living forever.

Even in D.'s best play, *Der Besuch der alten Dame*, the broader theme of the play, namely, the corrupting power of money and the total subservience of an entire community to economic forces that are indifferent to ethical principles, is nearly overshadowed by the immense theatricality and grotesque appearance of Claire Zachanassian, the personification of love perverted into hatred, with her artificial limbs of pure ivory and her bizarre entourage comprising a judge turned butler, her seventh husband, a black panther, and a pair of eunuchs, as well as those gum-chewing monsters, her two servants, erstwhile gangsters from Manhattan.

With their grotesque qualities D.'s characters point back to Johann Nestroy's (1801–1862) and Ferdinand Raimund's (1790–1836) Viennese folk theater as well as to EXPRESSIONIST playwrights such as Wedekind and Kaiser. As with the expressionists, the grotesque style is a method of overcoming realistic and naturalistic modes by significantly overdrawing certain essential traits and aspects while allowing other, more trivial accompanying characteristics or circumstances to retain their realistic dimensions.

Like Brecht, D. has rewritten and directed the classics. Of his adaptations *Play Strindberg* (1969; *Play Strindberg*, 1973) is especially noteworthy: based upon Strindberg's *Dance of Death*, it is D.'s transmutation of a bourgeois marriage tragedy into a comedy about bourgeois marriage tragedies, wherein vicious domestic quarrels are represented as a boxing match in twelve rounds.

A striking characteristic of D.'s work is its unevenness: the theatrical ideas at the origin of all his plays as well as his stories (which often read like film scripts, and which indeed have been used as such) do not always come to maturity; instead they peter out like bad adolescent jokes, reflecting a trait of D., who enjoyed being seen as an *enfant terrible*. Thus, the platitudinous dialogue in *Porträt eines Planeten* (1970; portrait of a planet) or *Der Mitmacher* (1976; the collobarator), two thematically connected "endgame" versions, and the embarrassing tastelessness of *Die Frist* (1977; the reprieve), dealing with the ritualized death of a dictator resembling Franco, should hardly come as surprises.

On the other hand, D.'s early detective fiction, considered by the author as mere occasional pieces, has been praised for its inventiveness and impeccable structure, particularly *Der Richter und sein Henker* (1952; *The Judge and His Hangman*, 1955). Its protagonist, Bärlach, a fatally ill police inspector, persists in his pursuit of justice, knowing that the struggle against evil is his duty as a human being. Ultimately Bärlach can only be the judge: he comes to a point where he can pronounce sentence on evil; the execution of the sentence, however, is to be brought about by the transcendent order of the universe with its built-in tendency toward justice.

D.'s extensive writings on the theater are among the most important reflections on contemporary drama and are significant contributions to its theory. The time for writing tragedies has passed, D.—echoing Albert CAMUS—argues in *Theaterprobleme* (1955; *Problems of the Theatre*, 1958). Therefore, he terms his plays tragicomedies: their tragic element stems from man's inescapable predicament—the human condition; the comic arises from his hopeless attempts to escape it by ever new and futile plans and projects. He admits his indebtedness to Aristophanes, Nestroy, and Thornton WILDER, for only comedy can adequately portray a world "about to fold like ours."

In D.'s disintegrating world, with the principles of law and order lost and the standards of guilt and retribution abandoned, man becomes the victim of accidents and events bigger than himself precisely when he believes himself to be in full control of his destiny. Despite the similarity of D.'s plot development to that of Greek drama, his plays do not become genuine tragedies, since sacrifice is considered meaningless and catharsis does not occur. In modern societies, where, as D. writes in *Theaterprobleme*, "Creon's

secretaries close Antigone's case," tragedy as a dramatic form has become obsolete.

FURTHER WORKS: *Komödie* (1943); *Die Stadt: Prosa I–IV* (1952); *Der Verdacht* (1953; *The Quarry*, 1962); *Die Panne* (1956; *Traps*, 1960); *Grieche sucht Griechin* (1958; *Once a Greek*, 1965); *Das Versprechen* (1958; *The Pledge*, 1959); *Frank der Fünfte: Oper einer Privatbank* (1960); *Gesammelte Hörspiele* (1961); *Theater-Schriften und Reden* (1966); *Die Wiedertäufer* (1967); *König Johann: Nach Shakespeare* (1968); *Monstervortrag über Gerechtigkeit und Recht* (1969); *Titus Andronicus: Eine Komödie nach Shakespeare* (1970); *Urfaust* (1970); *Sätze aus Amerika* (1970); *Der Struz* (1971); *Dramatisches und Kritisches* (1972); *Zusammenhänge: Essay über Israel* (1976); *Stoffe I-II* (1981); *Achterloo* (1982); *Der Auftrag oder Vom Beobachten des Beobachters der Beobachter* (1986); *Turmbau: Stoffe IV-XI* (1990). FURTHER WORKS IN ENGLISH: *Writings on Theatre and Drama* (1976); *Friedrich Dürrenmatt: Essay and Plays* (1982); *The Assignment* (1988); *The Execution of Justice* (1989)

BIBLIOGRAPHY: Klarmann, A. D., "F. D. and the Tragic Sense of Comedy," *TDR* 4 (1960): 67–104; Daviau, D. G., "Justice in the Works of F. D.," *KFLQ*, 9 (1962): 181–93; Wellwarth, G. E., "The German-Speaking Drama: D.," *The Theater of Protest and Paradox* (1964): 134–61; Holzapfel, R. E., "The Divine Plan behind the Plays of F. D.," *MD*, 8 (1965): 237–46; Sheppard, V., "F. D. as Dramatic Theorist," *Drama Survey*, 4 (1965): 244–63; Helbling, R. E., "The Function of the Grotesque in D.," *Satire Newsletter*, 4 (1966): 11–19; Ashbrook, B., "D.'s Detective Stories," *Philosophical Journal*, 4 (1967): 17–29; Bänziger, H., *Frisch und D.*, 6th rev. ed. (1971); Peppard, M. B., *F. D.* (1969); Usmiani, R., "Masterpieces in Disguise: The Radio Plays of F. D.," *Seminar*, 7 (1971): 42–57; Morley, M., "D.'s Dialogue with Brecht: A Thematic Analysis of *Die Physiker*," *MD*, 14 (1971/72): 232–42; Arnold, A., *F. D.* (1972); Fickert, K. J., *To Heaven and Back: The New Morality in the Plays of F. D.* (1972); Spycher, P., *F. D.: Das erzählerische Werk* (1972); Profitlich, U., *F. D.: Komödienbegriff und Komödienstruktur* (1973); Knapp, G. P., ed., *F. D.: Studien zu seinem Werk* (1976); Brock-Sulzer, E., *D. in unserer Zeit* (1977); Mayer, H., *Über F. D. und Max Frisch* (1977); Tiusanen, T., *D: A Study in Plays, Prose, Theory* (1977); Jenny, U., *D.: A Study of His Plays* (1978); Federico, J., "Sopohsism and Spiel: D.'s Dramaturgy of the Self," *Germanic Review*, 54 (1979): 145-51; Whitton, K. S., *The Theatre of F. D.: A Study in the Possibilities of Freedom* (1980); Chich, E. M., *Dances of Death: Wedeking, Brecht and D. and the Satiric Tradition* (1984); Whitton, K. S., *D.: Reinterpretation in Retrospect* (1990); Lide, B., "D.'s Gastronomic Grotesqueries: Eating in a Disordered World," L. R. Fürst and P. R. Graham, eds., *Disorderly Eaters: Texts in Self-Empowerment* (1992)

—TAMARA S. EVANS

D. reprimands the world and mankind. He censures and accuses. The demoniac, the vital, playful, and parodistic elements of the grotesque . . . are repeatedly combined in his work with a strong satirical element. This satiric inclination received what is probably its most splendid literary realization in *Der Besuch der alten Dame (The Visit)*. But the satirist wants not only to censure but to improve as well. He is concerned with man—with "the freedom to act correctly and to do what is necessary," as is put in *Das Unternehmen der Wega* [the enterprise of the Wega]. Here a final, deeper principle of D.'s grotesque is revealed: "Dare to live now and to live here, in the middle of formless, desolate land." And: "Try to put sense into nonsense."

F.D., the great and cruel builder of grotesques, is a humanist in disguise.

Reinhold Grimm, "Parodie und Groteske im Werk F.D.s," *GRM*, new series, 11 (1961), 450

D. rests absolutely on the fundamental principle that man as a mortal and knowing creature is "condemned to death." But he takes up this ordinary, hackneyed expression in its fullest sense: "condemned" presupposes a judge and an executioner. This basic idea in D.—man under judgment—is reflected in the aesthetic sphere. When, after *Der Blinde* [the blind man], D. turned decisively to comedy, he did it on the basis that contemporary man no longer deserves tragedy. . . . It is obvious that such a moral, indeed metaphysical, justification of the comic must leave traditional comedy far behind. No single one of D.'s works ends cheerfully.

Elisabeth Brock-Sulzer, "F.D." *Monat* 15, 5 (1963), 57–58

D's plays may be characterized as fantasies from which lessons may be learned. The imputation of preaching frightens writers nowadays for some reason. Philosophy, D. insists, cannot be transmitted through drama. He feels that the theater exists solely as a medium for the creation of a special world—that the audience, in other words, comes to peep in at a new, wonderful, and strange world, a contrived set of circumstances in which fantastic things can happen quite as matter-of-factly as the spectators wistfully wish they might in real life. Beyond this D. refuses to go. He maintains that he does not care what lesson may be drawn from his plays, if any. . . . Like T. S. Eliot, he is often enlightened as to the inner meaning of his works by reading the critics. His own attitude is simply that each person will choose from these created worlds whatever appears desirable or useful in them to him.

George E. Wellwarth, *The Theater of Protest and Paradox* (1964), pp. 134–35

Theatrical means shape dramatic ends. Brecht appeals to the members of a social class, D. to individuals. Brecht's plays are intended to be challenges to change the world, D.'s are a summons to the individual to rethink the world in relation to himself. This is the crucial point of their difference. D's plays concretely demonstrate the impossibility of changing the world in the figures of revolutionaries who have failed. For him, there is no history in Brecht's sense.

The present situation for him is the result of a necessary and natural process. . . .

He believes this modern world, recognized by us as our destiny, should be resisted, not accepted.

Karl Pestalozzi, in Otto Mann and Wolfgang Rothe, eds., *Deutsche Literatur im 20. Jahrhundert* (1967), Vol. II, pp. 400–401

D. has sought to shock his contemporaries out of their smugness and stir their consciences. In presenting plays that deal with contemporary problems, he has not hesitated to use drastic means such as grotesque exaggeration, parody, slapstick satire, and cabaret tricks. He is rightly called "uncomfortable" by critics, a satisfying epithet for a playwright who wishes to arouse and excite and who has nothing but scorn for literature that soothes and comforts. Modern man is on trial in D.'s works; all his heroes—usually passive, "negative" heroes who endure rather than conquer—are tried, tested, and forced to make moral decisions in a confused world which they do not understand but must withstand.

Murray B. Peppard, *F. D.* (1969), p. 8

Everywhere in D. we meet contrasts: Between abundance and coherence, wild artistic inventions and artistic formulas, chance and consequence, practice and theory, relief and anxiety. Between chaos and order. The first halves in these pairs speak of freedom, of movement, of shapelessness; the latter, of an effort to find order. Whatever field of human thought we pick out, there are hidden and open conflicts and ambiguities in his works: religion, philosophy, science, sociology, politics, history, classical literature.

. . . He makes a persistent effort in his works to judge the various fictions man has kept creating for himself. Judging is for him a terrible and/or tragicomic event. Faithful to his polemical inclinations and to his extremism, he has given these conflicts a sharp form; he has heightened rather than mitigated. This has led him to both embarrassing errors and to valiant deeds, to powerful scenic images and plays with unreasonable conflicts.

Timo Tiusanen, *D.: A Study in Plays, Prose, Theory* (1977), p. 437.

The *feeling* about the world which comes across in D.'s works is an original, inexplicable intuition which takes precedence over any rational experience: man's feeling of smallness and impotence when faced with a chaotic, uncontrollable world which is "a monstrosity, a problem which we must learn to live with but to which we must on no account capitulate." In his theoretical pronouncements D. repeatedly connects this feeling with the state of the present-day world, with the terror implicit in mechanisms and organizations, with the intrusion of bureaucracy and technology into all forms of society, completely subjugating the powerless individual. Basically, however, these are only appearances in which an original sense of impotence finds itself confirmed, a helplessness which cannot be relieved by chancing society but only by believing in a universally just and divine world of order.

Just as fundamental as his "pessimism" is D.'s inclination for comedy.... The peculiar feature of D.'s style of drama resides in the vital pleasure he displays in things comical and grotesque set against the dark background of the world. [1965]

Urs Jenny, *D.: A Study of His Plays* (1978), p. 19.

DURYCH, Jaroslav

Czechoslovak novelist, poet, and dramatist (writing in Czech), b. 2 Dec. 1886, Hradec Králové; d. 7 April 1962, Prague

Orphaned at an early age, D. was entrusted to the care of relatives, who wanted him to become a priest. He was brought up in the strict discipline of a boardinghouse run by the Catholic Church, but having completed his secondary education, D. decided to study medicine. In World War I he served as a doctor in the Austrian army and later joined the army of the Czechoslovak Republic.

Between the wars D. was one of the few Czech writers to stand on the political right. Because of D.'s political past and his militant Catholicism, his work was under a ban in Czechoslovakia from the Communist takeover in 1948 until the partial liberalization in 1956, when some of it could be published again. Since the reimposition of strict controls in the early 1970s no new editions of his work have appeared.

Although D. produced several volumes of poetry, beginning in 1915, his contribution in this genre is of limited value. His poetic style, influenced by the folk song and very traiditionalist, is far removed from that of most of his contemporaries.

D's early prose work, published in the 1920s, consists mainly of novellas and short stories. The everyday world is depicted in naturalistic and often repulsive detail, but great compassion is shown for the suffering of the downtrodden. Through struggle and sacrifice the humble ultimately enter the world of absolute love that lies beyond the material world. Men, wandering and lost, attain grace with the help of women, who are strong in their faith and dedication. Characteristic of this early period of D.'s work are two collections, *Tři dukáty* (1919; three ducats) and *Tři troníčky* (1923; three farthings). His most popular work is the short novel *Sedmikráska* (1925; daisy of seven charms); although perhaps the sunniest and most conventional of all his books, it is not devoid of mystic symbolism. This story of an impoverished young man searching for a girl who appears to him in various disguises can also be read as the story of a quest for grace, ever so elusive yet ever so near.

While D.'s attempts at drama in the 1920s ended in failure, his novels at the close of the decade marked the peak of his artistic achievement. *Bloudění* (1929; *The Descent of the Idol*, 1936), is usually referred to as the "major Wallenstein trilogy." Although the rise and fall of Wallenstein, count of Friedland, the Bohemian general and politician of the Thirty Years' War, is a theme that is always present in the book, it is not at the center of the story. Nor is *Bloudění* a historical chronicle of a crucial period of Czech history.

Rather, the composition of the work suggests a spotlight moving along a huge mural, illuminating a succession of seemingly disjointed scenes of hatred, intrigue, and general savagery, whose real significance becomes obvious only at the end, when everything falls into place. Against this turbulent backdrop unfolds the story of the wandering of a Czech Protestant man and a Spanish Catholic woman, symbolizing respectively the Czech nation lost in its heresy and rebellion and the Roman Church, which alone can save it.

Both D.'s baroque style and his particular vision of the world were ideally suited to this subject. The identification of the author with the psychology and the religious outlook of the novel's characters is extraordinary: it is as if he lived in the mind of the 17th-c. man. Controversy has been aroused, however, by his sympathy for the cause of Counter-Reformation: most Czechs view this as a national disaster.

If *Bloudění* can be compared to a fresco, the "*minor* Wallenstein trilogy," *Rekviem* (1930; requiem) gives the impression of a delicate, masterly etching. The three short stories that make up this book—each of them a concise, vivid narrative—all take place after Wallenstein's death.

D. returned to the Thirty Years' War in *Masopust* (1938; carnival), but neither that novel nor any other work published during the 1930s matched the force of the Wallenstein books. In 1940 the first volume of a planned tetralogy, *Služebníi neužteční* (unprofitable servants) appeared; all four volumes were finally published in 1969, in Rome. The tetralogy is again a story of wandering, this time of Jesuit missionaries in search of martydom. Although parts are impression, particularly some drastic images of torture, the story is too stretched out to hold together, and the reader's attention tends to flag. The posthumously published novels *Boží duha* (1969; God's rainbow) and *Duše a hvězda* (1969; soul and star) are reminiscent of D.'s work of the 1930s.

Although D.'s work is not of consistently high quality, he made a rare contribution to Czech literature by the way in which he adapted literary style to his ideology and vision. The words in his prose writhe with suppressed sensuous passion, yet in true baroque manner the carnal is sublimated into a longing for the realm of light and love.

FURTHER WORKS: *Savtý Jiří* (1915); *Cikánčina smrt* (1916); *Jarmark života* (1916); *Na horách* (1919); *Cestou domů* (1919); *Nejvyšší naděje* (1921); *Svatý Vojtěch* (1921); *Obrazy* (1922); *Panenky* (1923); *Smích věrnosti: Legendac* (1924); *Hadí květy* (1924); *Savtý Václav* (1925); *Zebrácké písně* (1925); *Beskydy* (1926); *Štědrý večer* (1926); *Kouzelná lampa* (1926); *Eva* (1928); *Té nejkrás nějéí* (1929); *Paní Anežka Berková* (1931); *Píseň o růži* (1934)

BIBLIOGRAPHY: Kazin, A., on *The Descent of the Idol, NYTBR,* 18 Oct. 1936: 6–7; Mihailovich, V. D., et al., eds., *Modern Slavic Literatures,* 2 (1976): 67-71; Novák, A., *Czech Literature* (1976): 301–2

—IGOR HÁJEK

DUTCH LITERATURE

See Netherlands Literature; see also under Dutch-Caribbean and Indonesian literatures

DUTCH-CARIBBEAN LITERATURE

Surinam

It is seldom that something felicitous can be said about slavery. Yet the Dutch, by withholding their own culture from the Surinamese slaves, unwittingly did the inhabitants a favor. Slaves were encouraged to use their own language, believe in their own gods, and enjoy their own music; eventually a distinct Surinamese Creole culture and literature developed. Colonialism, however, affected the Surinamese in their attitudes toward their own language and culture. Dutch came to be looked on as the language of sophistication and Western civilization. Creole, derogatorily referred to as "Negro English" and "taki-taki" (prattle), stood for "negroization" and not civilization. The language is now known, however, as "Sranan tongo," that is the "Surinam tongue."

The first attempts by a Surinamese to instill pride in Creole were by a remarkable man called Papa Koenders (Julius Gustaaf Arnout Koenders, 1886–1957). He pointed out that the Surinamese language was capable of carrying the weight of the Creole experience in a series of articles in a publication called *Foetoeboi* in the mid-1940s. Together with Anton de Kom (1898–1945), who wrote *Wij slaven van Suriname* (1934; we slaves of Surinam), he laid the basis for Surinamese nationalism.

The first Surinamese writer of note, Trefossa (pseud. of Hennie De Ziel, 1916–1975), dispelled the notion that Creole was only for gossip and comic purposes. The importance of his poem "Bro" (repose), written in 1949, was that he employed with finesse the patois of Surinam.

In the early 1950s many Surinamese students went to the Netherlands, encountering prejudice because they were Black. They started their own organization, Our Own Things, and ironically found a ready response among the Frisians, who thought of themselves as an oppressed minority in the Netherlands. The early Surinamese poems were published in a Frisian magazine, *De tjerne*.

An early Surinamese novelist was Albert Helman (pseud. of Lou Lichtveld, b. 1903), author of *Zuid-Zuid West* (1926; south southwest), *Mijn aap schreit* (1928; my ape weeps), and *De Stille plantage* (1931; the silent plantation). Younger, more militant Surinamese writers hold it against Helman that he wrote for a Dutch public rather than for the Surinamese, and therefore considered him a Dutch writer.

Trefossa had paved the way for others, notably Johanna Schouten Elsenhout (b. 1910), one of the most important female poets in Sranan Tongo, who combines Christian belief and the deep-rooted African religion; and Michaël Slory (b. 1935), a socially involved and Marxist-oriented poet. Dobru (pseud. of Robin Ravales, b. 1935), in African praise-poem style, recites his poetry in public. In contrast to Dobru, Shrinivasi (pseud. of Martinus Harridat Lutchman, b. 1926), who is of Hindustani stock but grew up as a devout Roman Catholic, is more a poet of love and appeasement. Thea Doelwijt (b. 1938) has written novels, short stories, and cabaret texts. Lastly, there is the remarkable young Creole writer, Edgar Cairo (b. 1948), who has written about twenty books—novels, poetry, and drama—employing a social realism with a comic irony. *Temekoe* (1969; headache), written when he was eighteen, is an autobiographical account of his relationship with his father. This was the first novel in Sranan Tongo. His *Kollektieve schuld; oftewel, Famir'man-sani* (1976; collective guilt), in Surinamese

Dutch, made a tremendous impression in the Netherlands. Other writers of note are Eddy Bruma (b. 1925), one of the founding members of Our Own Things; Bea Vianen (b. 1934), short-story writer and novelist; and Rudi Kross (b. 1938), essayist and critic.

Netherlands Antilles

Dutch is the official language of all the islands, used by the government and schools. Yet there is, as in Surinam, a creolized language, papiamentu, the lingua franca. In addition, Aruba, Bonaire, and Curaçao are generally Dutch-speaking, while the inhabitants of Saint Eustatius, Saint Maarten, and Saba speak English or a variant of it.

Willem E. Kroon's (1886–1949) *Jambo bieew ta bolbe na wea* (1956; old love does not die) was written in Papiamentu. Nicolás Piña (1921–1967) wrote in Dutch, Spanish, and Papiamentu, preferring the last. He founded Papiamentu periodicals on Caraçao and Aruba. Cola Debroat (b. 1902), writing in Dutch, made his literary debut with *Mijn zuster de negerin* (1935; my sister the negress), a novel that is essentially about the search for roots and about racial and ethnic interrelationships.

Two novelists who gained recognition in the Netherlands are Tip Marugg (b. 1923), with *Weekendpelgrimage* (1957; weekend pilgrimage), and Boeli van Leeuwen (b. 1922), with *Derots der struikeling* (1959; rock of the fallen), *Een vreemdeling op aarde* (1962; stranger on earth), *De eerste Adam* (1966; the first Adam). The theme of death is essential to these books, which have existentialist undertones. Debrot, Leeuwen, and Marugg, who are white, emphasize the process of creolization as the solution to racial conflict.

The question of ethnic roots is again taken up in Guillermo Rosario's (b. 1917) *E rais ku no ke muri* (1969; the rot won't die out), a novel in Papiamentu, and Edward de Jongh's (b. 1923) *E día di mas histórico* (1969–70; the most historic day), a documentary in Papiamentu about riots that occurred in 1969. Diana Lebacs (b. 1947), in her novel *Sherry* (1971; Sherry) depicts characters suffering from ambivialent feelings about race. An important force in Antillean literature is Frank Martinus Arion (b. 1936), who writes from a decidedly Black and socialist perspective. His novel *Dubbelspel* (1973; double game), ostensibly about a game of dominoes played in Curaçao, gives a kaleidoscopic view of the society and the people. His *Afscheid van de koningin* (1975; farewell of the queen) is about Africa, while *De nobele wilde* (1979; the noble savage) deals with colonialism and neocolonialism.

An important dramatist was René de Rooji (1917–1974), of Surinamese origin; his comedy *Juancho Picaflor* (1954; Juancho Picaflor), written in Papiamentu, is a highlight of Antillean drama. Major figures in poetry include Pierre Lauffer (b. 1920) and Elis Juliana (b. 1927). Lauffer's poems are reminiscent of those by the Cuban Nicolás GUILLÉN. Juliana portrays typical Curaçoans.

Essential to the entire Antillean and Surinamese literary situation are the search for roots and the effort to find a modus vivendi that will accommodate all imperfections resulting from the protracted Dutch colonial presence.

BIBLIOGRAPHY: Debrot, C., *Literature of the Netherlands Antilles* (1964); Voorhoeve, J. and U. Lichtveldt, eds., *Creole Drum* (1975)

—VERNIE FEBRUARY

DUUN, Olav

Norwegian novelist and short-story writer, b. 21 Nov. 1876, Namdalen; d. 13 Sept. 1939, Botne

Born of peasant stock on the island of Jøa off the Trondheim coast, at an early age D. experienced the realities of hard work—he herded sheep, worked in the fields, and helped the fishermen—and observed the life and destiny of coastal people. He was an avid reader and at age twenty-five entered a teachers' training college. Subsequently he became an elementary-school teacher and followed this career in his native area and in southern Norway for more than twenty years. Most of his writing was accomplished on weekends and during school vacations.

Although perhaps less renowned internationally than his well-known contemporaries in fiction, Sigrid Undset and Johan Falkberget, or the famed poets of his day, Herman Wildenvey (1886–1959) and Olaf Bull, among many of his own countrymen D. ranks above them all. His stories are usually set against the background of the craggy island landscape, the characters are fishermen and farmers striving to make a living on stormy seas and barren soil, and the ongoing struggle between the forces of good and evil defines the thesis. While D.'s use of local color, regional dialect, and provincial scenes provides a true and lively picture of his native environment, thematically and psychologically the world is his site, mankind his protagonist, and human nature his topic.

The first decade of authorship, 1907 to 1917, is marked by great artistic growth and prolific production at the rate of a book each year. Successive volumes show steady refinement of style and composition and increasing sensitivity toward the human condition. By gradually breaking away from traditional narrative and experimenting with new modes of expression, D. developed his own epic skill, poetic intimacy, and genial humor. Among his best works of this early period are *På tvert* (1909; crosswise), a discerning analysis of feelings of inferiority; and *Det gode samvite* (1916; the good conscience), a story of change in ethical concern and responsibility through three generations.

Juvikfolke (1918–23; *The People of Juvik*, 1930–35), built on the same subject of social and civic evolution, still stands as one of Norway's masterful works of fiction. The first three of the six volumes record the history of several generations of an isolated rural family, going back to 1814. The following three in the series trace the lineage up to Duun's own era, when family ties began to loosen, community awareness broadened, and egoism yielded to altruism. Even in the first volume, *Juvikingar* (*The Trough of the Wave*), the reader sees a slight withdrawal from ancient pagan philosophy and an introduction of Christian morality, a change more clearly perceived in the character of Blind Anders in the second volume, *I blinda* (*The Blind Man*). In Volume III, *Storbrylloppe* (*The Big Wedding*), tradition and family no longer hold so firm a grip. The remaining volumes, *I eventyre (Odin in Fairyland)*, *I ungdommen (Odin Grows Up)*, and *I stormen (The Storm)*, tell of the protagonist's fight for change and of his supreme sacrifice in the determination to create a "new" man, willing to subdue evil by championing good.

The trilogy consisting of *Medmenneske* (1929; fellow-beings), *Ragnhild* (1931; Ragnhild), and *Siste leveåre* (1933; years of old age) again concentrates on the clash between good and evil within man's mind and soul. It asks, To what degree does the end justify the means in one's relationship to his fellow men?

Menneske og maktene (1938; *Floodtide of Fate*, 1960), a bold experiment both in style and substance, was published in the year preceding the outbreak of World War II and the subsequent occupation of Norway by the Nazis. When these catastrophes struck and annihilation threatened, old antagonisms vanished and men sought to overcome, not only for themselves but for others as well. *Menneske og maktene* proves how the will to live heightens courage and redoubles the capacity to endure.

Superb imagination, wisdom, insight, and wit combine to place D. in the top rank of Norwegian storytellers of all time.

FURTHER WORKS: *Storbåten* (1912); *Hilderøya* (1912); *Sommereventyr* (1913); *Tre venner* (1914); *Harald* (1915); *Paa lyngsøya* (1917); *Straumen og evja* (1926); *Osøygutane* (1927); *Carolus Magnus* (1928); *Ettermæle* (1932); *Gud smiler* (1935); *Samtid* (1936); *Skrifter* (12 vols., 1939)

BIBLIOGRAPHY: Jorgenson, T., *A History of Norwegian Literature* (1933): 457–69; Beyer, H., *A History of Norwegian Literature* (1956): 310–13; McFarlane, J. W., *Ibsen and the Temper of Norwegian Literature* (1960): 175–82

—AMANDA LANGEMO

DUWLAT-ŬLĬ, Mir Jaqib

Kazakh poet and novelist, b. 25 Nov. 1885, Turgay district; d. 1937–38?

Born in the northern part of central Asia, that is, Turkistan, under the tsarist Russian occupation, D. belonged to the Argyn nomadic tribe of the Kazakhs and was a member of its aristocracy. D. studied at the Russian-Kazakh school of Turgay and at the Galiyah madrassah of Ufa. He lectured for a short period at the Communist University of the Toilers of the East in Moscow. D. carried on the work begun by earlier activists of the Kazakh awakening into the 20th c., participating with other Kazakh and Kirghiz intellectuals in the formation of the Alash political party and then becoming one of the leading founders of the Alash Orda Autonomous Government (1917–20). Accused of "nationalism," D. is believed to have been liquidated during the Stalinist purges of 1937–38.

D. began his career as a writer with poetry. At first he wrote naturalistic verse in traditional folk meters. But after the Russo-Japanese war and subsequent antitsarist uprisings, he joined the ranks of the "nationalist," or patriotic, poets. D.'s first collection of poetry, *Oyan Qazaq* (1909; wake up, Kazakh!), quickly ran through two editions and was then banned in 1911 by the Russian Director of Press Affairs while D. was on the editorial staff of the monthly Kazakh-language magazine *Ay qap*. The main themes in D.'s poems vary from subjects such as the value of education, the virtue of diligence, and struggle with Russia, to subjects like love, the countryside, women, and the social problems of nomadic Kazakhs under the tsarist colonial administration. In his 94-page *Baqïtsïz Jamal* (1910; unlucky Jamal), the first Kazakh novel, D., draws attention to the tragic end of a young girl subject to the arbitrariness of existing marriage customs.

Although his poetry is generally weighted down with heavy didactic overtones, his simple style, his passionate tone, and his command of the Kazakh language made D. one of the most widely

657

read and the most commented upon writers of central Asia. Although D.'s contribution in developing Kazakh literature into a modern and independent national literature is very significant, he and his literary works have not as yet been rehabilitated in the U.S.S.R.

FURTHER WORKS: *Azamat* (1913)

BIBLIOGRAPHY: Allworth, E., *Central Asia: A Century of Russian Rule* (1967): passim; Bennigsen, A. A., and Wimbush, S. E., *Muslim National Communism in the Soviet Union* (1979): 110, 196

—TIMUR KOCAOGLU

DYGAT, Stanisław

Polish novelist and short-story writer, b. 5 Dec. 1914, Warsaw; d. 29 Jan. 1978, Warsaw

Born into a prominent Warsaw family, D. made his literary debut shortly before World War II, during which he was deported by the Nazis to a special detention camp in Germany. Upon his return to Warsaw after the defeat of the Germans, he used his war experiences for his first novel, *Jezioro Bodeńskie* (1946; Lake Constance), which mocks the overly patriotic tone of the traditional treatment of war themes that then prevailed in Polish literature.

D.'s next novel, *Pożegnania* (1948; farewells), written in a similar vein, addressed itself not only to the author's social background but took to task the whole concept of the bourgeois way of life, juxtaposing it to the image of simplicity, honesty, and an active approach to life he saw as typical of the new society emerging in postwar Poland, which at that time was becoming a socialist country ruled by a Communist regime. Although D., like the idol of his adolescence, Witold GOMBROWICZ, challenged petrifying traditions, his novels and his short stories of this period were much more lighthearted, humorous, and entertaining.

An intelligent observer of the changes taking place in Poland in the mid-1950s, D. welcomed the relaxation of controls over literature. In his novel *Podróż* (1958; a journey) he explored the reactions of a citizen of the allegedly socialist country to Western Europe during his long-dreamed-about journey to Italy. The theme of the confrontation of values—old versus new, conservative versus progressive, Polish versus Western European—reappears constantly in D.'s novels and short stories of the 1960s and many of them were satirical. His journalistic essays and feuilletons of that period disclosed his deep preoccupation with intellectual and social problems, although his seriousness was veiled by his jocular and often amusing tone.

In his next novel, *Disneyland* (1965; *Cloak of Illusion*, 1969), built around the problem of a young generation growing up in a world of confused values, D. once again demonstrated his interest in the basic issues of his time, although the structure and tone of the novel are farcical. More subdued and reflective was his last novel, *Dworzec w Monachium* (1973; the Munich railroad station), in which he returned again to his favorite theme—the contrast between his native country and the rapidly changing character of Western Europe.

D. continued to dominate Warsaw literary life during the 1970s, but his literary output noticeably diminished. Taken as a whole, his fiction typifies the attitudes of the Polish prewar intelligentsia, trying to adapt to the conditions of socialism and yet maintaining its rather skeptical posture, often disguised in humorous, satirical, and even grotesque forms.

FURTHER WORKS: *Pola Elizejskie* (1949); *Wiosna i niedźwidzie* (1953); *Słotne wieczory* (1957); *Różowy Kajecik* (1958); *Rozmyślania przy goleniu* (1959); *Na pięć minut przed zaśnięciem* (1960); *W cieniu Brooklynu* (1973); *Kołonotatnik* (1979)

BIBLIOGRAPHY: Miłosz, C., *The History of Polish Literature* (1969): 495–97

—JERZY R. KRZYŻANOWSKI